CONTENTS

INTRODUCTION

Being able to read, understand, and write good English are vital and fundamental skills that underpin success in exams and, ultimately, success in the world beyond school. Dictionaries and thesauruses are essential tools for all students who want to do well in exams, because if you know how to use them effectively you can improve your performance in all subjects, not just English. This is why literacy strategies all over the world set ambitious targets for students to acquire dictionary skills at every stage of their education.

Collins Easy Learning English Study Dictionary has been developed in association with teachers and takes a completely new approach to the dictionary. Entries are presented in the most clear and easy-to-use way possible, with fully integrated dictionary and thesaurus material.

With full sentence definitions, examples to show context for every thesaurus synonym, and special treatment for the most commonly-used words in English, **Collins Easy Learning English Study Dictionary** combines the best features from the critically-acclaimed **Collins School Dictionary** and **Collins School Thesaurus**, as well as a host of other features:

All the words and alternatives a student needs, with core vocabulary for all school subjects.

Thesaurus entries appear at their dictionary definition, so alternative words have never been easier to find.

A radical new design developed specifically for inexperienced users — with look-up words and matching alternatives in colour.

Word webs to give a clear picture of the most commonly-used words in English and help for getting to grips with how they work.

Essential information on what words mean, how they are used, spelling, grammar, and punctuation, so that students can use language well, communicate with others, and express their ideas more effectively.

IPA pronunciations given for all entries

Collins Easy Learning English Study Dictionary is exceptionally easy to use. It is relevant to school work in all subjects, accessible, and student friendly, and offers essential help on the route to success.

HOW TO USE THIS DICTIONARY

Collins Easy Learning English Study Dictionary is easy to use and understand. Below are some entries showing the dictionary's main features, along with an explanation of what they are.

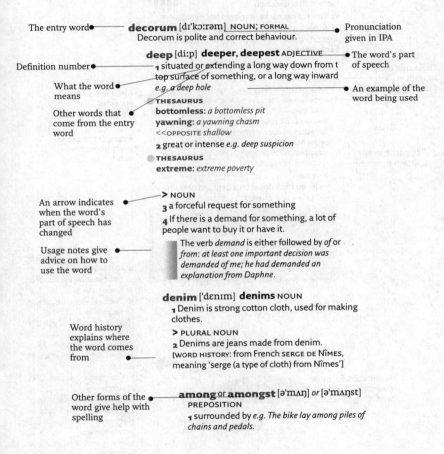

The entry word

decorum [dɪˈkɔːrəm] NOUN; FORMAL
Decorum is polite and correct behaviour.

Pronunciation given in IPA

deep [diːp] **deeper, deepest** ADJECTIVE

Definition number

The word's part of speech

What the word means

1 situated or extending a long way down from t top surface of something, or a long way inward *e.g. a deep hole*

An example of the word being used

THESAURUS
bottomless: *a bottomless pit*
yawning: *a yawning chasm*
<<OPPOSITE *shallow*

Other words that come from the entry word

2 great or intense *e.g. deep suspicion*

THESAURUS
extreme: *extreme poverty*

An arrow indicates when the word's part of speech has changed

> NOUN
3 a forceful request for something
4 If there is a demand for something, a lot of people want to buy it or have it.

Usage notes give advice on how to use the word

The verb **demand** is either followed by *of* or *from*: *at least one important decision was demanded of me; he had demanded an explanation from Daphne.*

denim [ˈdɛnɪm] **denims** NOUN
1 Denim is strong cotton cloth, used for making clothes.

Word history explains where the word comes from

> PLURAL NOUN
2 Denims are jeans made from denim.
[WORD HISTORY: from French SERGE DE NÎMES, meaning 'serge (a type of cloth) from Nîmes']

Other forms of the word give help with spelling

among or **amongst** [əˈmʌŋ] *or* [əˈmʌŋst]
PREPOSITION
1 surrounded by *e.g. The bike lay among piles of chains and pedals.*

> VERB

9 If a building backs onto something, its back faces in that direction.

10 When a car backs, it moves backwards.

11 To back a person or organization means to support or finance that person or organization.

back down

Thesaurus entry appears at dictionary definition ●

THESAURUS

advocate: *Mr Jones advocates longer school days.*
encourage: *The government is encouraging better child care.*
endorse: *Do you endorse his opinion?*
favour: *I favour a different approach.*
promote: *Ann is promoting Alan's ideas.*
support: *We supported his political campaign.*
<<OPPOSITE oppose

Alternative words are listed alphabetically

Examples of use for every alternative word

Opposite words shown ●

> VERB

12 If you back down on a demand or claim, you withdraw and give up.

harmful: *the harmful effects of radiation*
unhealthy: *illnesses caused by an unhealthy lifestyle*
unpleasant: *Some of the drug's side-effects are unpleasant.*
<< OPPOSITE good

Word webs for most commonly-used words ●

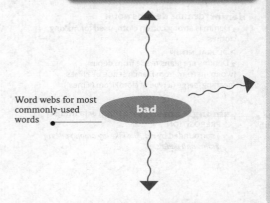

bad

2 ADJECTIVE
of poor quality *eg: bad road*
● **THESAURUS**
defective: *defective produc*
serious injury
deficient: *a lack of exercise*
diet
faulty: *customers who take*
imperfect: *Imperfect work*
accepted.
inadequate: *protests over i*
conditions
inferior: *the inferior quality*
pathetic: *a pathetic excuse*
poor: *an area with poor hou*
unemployment
sorry: *a sorry state of affairs*
unsatisfactory: *I complain*
unsatisfactory service I had r
<< OPPOSITE satisfactory

3 ADJECTIVE
evil in character *eg: a bad person*
● **THESAURUS**

Aa

a [eɪ] **an** ADJECTIVE
The indefinite article 'a', or 'an' if the next sound is a vowel, is used when you are talking about one of something. *e.g. an apple... There was a car parked behind the hedge.*

a- PREFIX **an-**
1 When 'a-' comes before an adjective it adds the meaning 'without' or 'opposite to'. 'An-' is the form used before a vowel. *e.g. amoral*
2 When 'a-' comes at the beginning of certain words it adds the meaning 'towards' or 'in the state of'. *e.g. aback... asleep*
[WORD HISTORY: sense 1 from Greek A- or AN- meaning 'not' or 'without']

aardvark [ˈɑːdˌvɑːk] **aardvarks** NOUN
an ant-eating African animal with a long snout

aback [əˈbæk] ADVERB
If you are taken aback, you are very surprised.

abacus [ˈæbəkəs] **abacuses** NOUN
a frame with beads that slide along rods, used for counting
[WORD HISTORY: from Greek ABAX meaning 'board covered with sand for doing sums on']

abalone [ˌæbəˈləʊnɪ] **abalones** NOUN
a shellfish which can be eaten

abandon [əˈbændən] **abandons, abandoning, abandoned** VERB
1 If you abandon someone or something, you leave them or give them up for good.
● THESAURUS
desert: *Medical staff have deserted the city's main hospital.*
jilt: *She was jilted by her first fiancé.*
leave: *My husband has left me.*
leave behind: *He walked out and left behind a wife and two young children.*

> NOUN
2 If you do something with abandon, you do it in an uncontrolled way. *e.g. He began to laugh with abandon.*
abandoned ADJECTIVE, **abandonment** NOUN
● THESAURUS
recklessness: *the headstrong recklessness of youth*
wildness: *Her wildness just needed to be channelled properly.*

<<OPPOSITE *control*

abate [əˈbeɪt] **abates, abating, abated** VERB
If something abates, it becomes less. *e.g. His anger abated.*
● THESAURUS
decrease: *The pain had decreased considerably.*
diminish: *The attacks on the village did not diminish.*
ebb: *Her strength was ebbing fast.*
lessen: *After a while, the cramps lessened.*
subside: *Their enthusiasm was beginning to subside.*
wane: *His popularity shows no sign of waning.*

abattoir [ˈæbəˌtwɑː] **abattoirs** NOUN
a place where animals are killed for meat

abbey [ˈæbɪ] **abbeys** NOUN
a church with buildings attached to it in which monks or nuns live

abbot [ˈæbət] **abbots** NOUN
the monk or priest in charge of all the monks in a monastery

abbreviate [əˈbriːvɪˌeɪt] **abbreviates, abbreviating, abbreviated** VERB
To abbreviate something is to make it shorter.

abbreviation [əˌbriːvɪˈeɪʃən] **abbreviations** NOUN
a short form of a word or phrase. An example is 'W', which is short for 'West'

abdicate [ˈæbdɪˌkeɪt] **abdicates, abdicating, abdicated** VERB
If a king or queen abdicates, he or she gives up being a king or queen.
abdication NOUN

abdomen [ˈæbdəmən] **abdomens** NOUN
the front part of your body below your chest, containing your stomach and intestines
abdominal ADJECTIVE

abduct [æbˈdʌkt] **abducts, abducting, abducted** VERB
To abduct someone is to take them away by force.
abduction NOUN

aberration [ˌæbəˈreɪʃən] **aberrations** NOUN
something that is not normal or usual

abet [əˈbɛt] **abets, abetting, abetted** VERB
If you abet someone, you help them to do something. *e.g. You've aided and abetted criminals to evade justice.*

abhor [əbˈhɔː] **abhors, abhorring, abhorred** VERB; FORMAL
If you abhor something, you hate it.
abhorrence NOUN, **abhorrent** ADJECTIVE

abide [əˈbaɪd] **abides, abiding, abided** VERB
1 If you can't abide something, you dislike it very much.
2 If you abide by a decision or law, you act in agreement with it.

abiding [əˈbaɪdɪŋ] ADJECTIVE
lasting for ever *e.g. an abiding interest in history*

ability [əˈbɪlɪtɪ] **abilities** NOUN
(PSHE) the intelligence or skill needed to do something *e.g. the ability to get on with others*
● THESAURUS
capability: *We have the capability of going out and winning.*
competence: *They have a high level of competence.*
expertise: *legal expertise*
skill: *the skill to play at a higher level*
talent: *a talent for music*
<<OPPOSITE *inability*

abject [ˈæbdʒɛkt] ADJECTIVE
very bad *e.g. abject failure*
abjectly ADVERB

ablaze [əˈbleɪz] ADJECTIVE
on fire

able [ˈeɪbəl] **abler, ablest** ADJECTIVE **(PSHE)**
1 If you are able to do something, you can do it.
2 Someone who is able is very clever or talented.
● THESAURUS
accomplished: *an accomplished pianist*
capable: *a very capable manager*
efficient: *a team of efficient workers*
expert: *My mother was an expert baker.*
first-rate: *This run is only suitable for first-rate skiers.*
skilled: *a skilled craftsman*
talented: *a talented actor*

-able SUFFIX
1 forming adjectives which have the meaning 'capable of' an action *e.g. enjoyable... breakable*
2 forming adjectives with the meaning 'able to' or 'causing' *e.g. comfortable... miserable*

> When you are writing, it is easy to confuse the -able suffix with its other form, -ible. It can be helpful to know that the -able spelling is much commoner than -ible, and that you cannot make new words using -ible. Occasionally, it is correct to use either ending

ably [ˈeɪblɪ] ADVERB
skilfully and successfully *e.g. He is ably supported by the cast.*

abnormal [æbˈnɔːməl] ADJECTIVE
not normal or usual
abnormally ADVERB

abnormality [ˌæbnɔːˈmælɪtɪ] **abnormalities** NOUN
something that is not normal or usual

aboard [əˈbɔːd] PREPOSITION OR ADVERB
on a ship or plane

abode [əˈbəʊd] **abodes** NOUN; OLD-FASHIONED, INFORMAL
Your abode is your home.

abolish [əˈbɒlɪʃ] **abolishes, abolishing, abolished** VERB
To abolish something is to do away with it. *e.g. the campaign to abolish hunting*
abolition NOUN
● THESAURUS
annul: *The marriage was annulled last month.*
do away with: *the proposal to do away with nuclear weapons*
overturn: *criminals seeking to overturn their convictions*
put an end to: *efforts to put an end to the traffic in drugs*

abominable [əˈbɒmɪnəbəl] ADJECTIVE
very unpleasant or shocking
abominably ADVERB

Aboriginal [ˌæbəˈrɪdʒɪnəl] **Aboriginals** NOUN
someone descended from the people who lived in Australia before Europeans arrived
Aboriginal ADJECTIVE
[WORD HISTORY: borrowed from ABORIGINES, the Latin word for the pre-Roman inhabitants of Italy]

abort [əˈbɔːt] **aborts, aborting, aborted** VERB
1 If a plan or activity is aborted, it is stopped before it is finished.
2 If a pregnant woman aborts, the pregnancy ends too soon and the baby dies.

abortion [əˈbɔːʃən] **abortions** NOUN
If a woman has an abortion, the pregnancy is ended deliberately and the baby dies.

abortive [əˈbɔːtɪv] ADJECTIVE
unsuccessful *e.g. an abortive bank raid*

abound [əˈbaʊnd] **abounds, abounding, abounded** VERB
If things abound, there are very large numbers of them.

about [əˈbaʊt] PREPOSITION OR ADVERB
1 of or concerning

THESAURUS
concerning: *documents concerning the estate*
on: *his book on Picasso*
regarding: *strict rules regarding the disposal of food*
relating to: *the rules relating to transfer fees*
2 approximately and not exactly

THESAURUS
almost: *Their wages have almost doubled.*
approximately: *It was approximately three times the size of a domestic cat.*
around: *The crowd here is around 12,000.*
nearly: *a tradition going back nearly 20 centuries*
roughly: *One unit is roughly equivalent to half a pint of beer.*

> **ADVERB**
3 in different directions *e.g. There were some bottles scattered about.*

> **ADJECTIVE**
4 present or in a place *e.g. Is Jane about?*

> **PHRASE**
5 If you are **about to** do something, you are just going to do it.

above [ə'bʌv] PREPOSITION OR ADVERB
1 directly over or higher than something *e.g. above the clouds*

THESAURUS
higher than: *There are no hotels higher than four storeys.*
over: *the picture over the fireplace*
<<OPPOSITE *below*

2 greater than a level or amount *e.g. The temperature didn't rise above freezing point.*

THESAURUS
beyond: *I expect to live way beyond 100.*
exceeding: *a floor area exceeding 50,000 square feet*

above board ADJECTIVE
completely open and legal *e.g. They assured me it was above board and properly licensed.*

abrasion [ə'breɪʒən] **abrasions** NOUN
an area where your skin has been broken

abrasive [ə'breɪsɪv] ADJECTIVE
1 An abrasive substance is rough and can be used to clean hard surfaces.
2 Someone who is abrasive is unpleasant and rude.

abreast [ə'brɛst] ADJECTIVE
1 side by side *e.g. youths riding their motorbikes four abreast*
2 If you keep abreast of a subject, you know all the most recent facts about it.

abroad [ə'brɔːd] ADVERB
(GEOGRAPHY) in a foreign country

abrupt [ə'brʌpt] ADJECTIVE
1 sudden and quick *e.g. His career came to an abrupt end.*

THESAURUS
sudden: *this week's sudden thaw*
unexpected: *His career came to an unexpected end.*
unforeseen: *unforeseen difficulties*
2 not friendly or polite
abruptly ADVERB, **abruptness** NOUN

THESAURUS
curt: *'The matter is closed,' was the curt reply.*
rude: *He was frequently rude to waiters and servants.*
short: *She seemed tense and was definitely short with me.*
terse: *He received a terse one-line rejection from the Ministry.*
<<OPPOSITE *polite*

abscess ['æbsɛs] **abscesses** NOUN
a painful swelling filled with pus

abseiling ['æbseɪlɪŋ] NOUN
Abseiling is the sport of going down a cliff or a tall building by sliding down ropes.

absent ['æbsənt] ADJECTIVE
Something that is absent is not present in a place or situation.
absence NOUN

THESAURUS
away: *She is away on a business trip.*
elsewhere: *Four witnesses can prove he was elsewhere at the time.*
gone: *I'll only be gone for ten minutes.*
missing: *Another 44 passengers are still missing.*
<<OPPOSITE *present*

absentee [,æbsən'tiː] **absentees** NOUN
someone who is not present when they should be

absent-minded [,æbsənt'maɪndɪd]
ADJECTIVE
forgetful

THESAURUS
distracted: *He seems distracted, giving the impression of being elsewhere.*
forgetful: *She's getting rather forgetful, and living mostly in the past.*
random: New Zealand *I'm sorry, I'm a bit random these days.*

absolute ['æbsə,luːt] ADJECTIVE
1 total and complete *e.g. absolute honesty*

THESAURUS
complete: *The operation was a complete success.*
total: *the total destruction of the city*
downright: *That's a downright lie!*
pure: *a work of pure genius*
sheer: *It would be sheer madness to carry on after this.*

thorough: *He has a thorough knowledge of the subject.*

utter: *He stared at me in utter disbelief.*

2 having total power *e.g. the absolute ruler*
absolutely ADVERB

● THESAURUS

dictatorial: *a dictatorial system of government*
supreme: *humble subjects of her supreme rule*
tyrannical: *popular uprisings against tyrannical rulers*

absolve [əbˈzɒlv] **absolves, absolving, absolved** VERB
To absolve someone of something is to state they are not to blame for it.

absorb [əbˈsɔːb] **absorbs, absorbing, absorbed** VERB
(SCIENCE) If something absorbs liquid or gas, it soaks it up.

● THESAURUS

digest: *Fats are hard to digest.*
soak up: *Stir until the wheat has soaked up all the water.*
take in: *A growing tree takes in light and processes it for food.*

absorbent [əbˈsɔːbənt] ADJECTIVE
Absorbent materials soak up liquid easily.

absorption [əbˈsɔːpʃən] NOUN
1 the soaking up of a liquid

2 great interest in something *e.g. my father's absorption in his business affairs*

abstain [əbˈsteɪn] **abstains, abstaining, abstained** VERB
1 If you abstain from something, you do not do it or have it. *e.g. The patients had to abstain from alcohol.*

● THESAURUS

avoid: *Heartburn sufferers should try to avoid fatty foods.*
deny oneself: *I won't deny myself some celebration tonight.*
forgo: *My wife and I have to forgo holidays now.*
give up: *She gave up smoking last year.*
refrain: *He appealed to all factions to refrain from violence.*

2 If you abstain in a vote, you do not vote.
abstention NOUN

abstinence [ˈæbstɪnəns] NOUN
Abstinence is deliberately not doing something you enjoy.

abstract [ˈæbstrækt] ADJECTIVE
1 An abstract idea is based on thoughts and ideas rather than physical objects or events, for example 'bravery'.

2 (ART) Abstract art is a style of art which uses shapes rather than images of people or objects.

3 Abstract nouns refer to qualities or ideas rather than to physical objects, for example 'happiness' or 'a question'.
abstraction NOUN

absurd [əbˈsɜːd] ADJECTIVE
ridiculous and stupid
absurdly ADVERB, **absurdity** NOUN

● THESAURUS

crazy: *informal It would be crazy to tinker with a winning team.*
illogical: *his completely illogical arguments*
ludicrous: *It was ludicrous to suggest that the visit could be kept secret.*
nonsensical: *He says many diets are harmful and nonsensical.*
ridiculous: *The programme is too ridiculous to take seriously.*

abundance [əˈbʌndəns] NOUN
Something that exists in abundance exists in large numbers. *e.g. an abundance of wildlife*

● THESAURUS

affluence: *Pockets of affluence coexist with poverty.*
bounty: *autumn's bounty of fruit, seeds, and berries*
plenty: *Allow plenty of time to get home.*
<<OPPOSITE shortage

abundant [əˈbʌndənt] ADJECTIVE
present in large quantities
abundantly ADVERB

● THESAURUS

ample: *ample space for a good-sized kitchen*
copious: *copious amounts of red wine*
full: *a full tank of petrol*
plentiful: *a plentiful supply of vegetables*
<<OPPOSITE scarce

abuse [əˈbjuːs] **abuses** NOUN
1 cruel treatment of someone *e.g. child abuse*

● THESAURUS

exploitation: *Most human life involves the exploitation of animals.*
harm: *the harm smokers willingly do to their own health*
hurt: *The victims suffer mental scars as well as physical hurt.*
ill-treatment: *the ill-treatment of political prisoners*
oppression: *the oppression of black people throughout history*

2 rude and unkind remarks directed towards someone

● THESAURUS

censure: *a controversial policy which has attracted international censure*
derision: *He was greeted with shouts of derision.*
insults: *They shouted insults at each other.*
invective: *A woman had hurled racist invective at the family.*

3 the wrong use of something *e.g. an abuse of power... alcohol abuse*

abuse [ə'bjuːz] **abuses, abusing, abused**
VERB

1 If you abuse someone, you speak insultingly to them.

2 To abuse someone also means to treat them cruelly.

3 If you abuse something, you use it wrongly or for a bad purpose.
abuser NOUN

abusive [ə'bjuːsɪv] ADJECTIVE
rude and unkind
abusively ADVERB, **abusiveness** NOUN

● THESAURUS
disparaging: *He made some disparaging remarks about the team.*
insulting: *She was charged with insulting behaviour to a police officer.*
offensive: *The book was seen by many Muslims as being deeply offensive to Islam.*
rude: *He is rude to her friends.*
scathing: *He made some particularly scathing comments about the design.*

abysmal [ə'bɪzməl] ADJECTIVE
very bad indeed *e.g. an abysmal performance*
abysmally ADVERB

abyss [ə'bɪs] **abysses** NOUN
a very deep hole
[WORD HISTORY: from Greek ABUSSOS meaning 'bottomless']

● THESAURUS
chasm: *The climbers strung a rope across the chasm and crawled along it.*
fissure: *The earthquake opened large fissures in the ground.*
gorge: *The valley narrowed to a gorge with cascading crags.*
pit: *Eric lost his footing and began to slide into the pit.*
void: *His feet dangled in the void.*

acacia [ə'keɪʃə] **acacias** NOUN
a type of thorny shrub with small yellow or white flowers

academic [ˌækə'dɛmɪk] **academics**
ADJECTIVE
1 Academic work is work done in a school, college, or university.

> NOUN
2 someone who teaches or does research in a college or university
academically ADVERB

academy [ə'kædəmɪ] **academies** NOUN
1 a school or college, usually one that specializes in one particular subject *e.g. the Royal Academy of Dramatic Art*

2 an organization of scientists, artists, writers, or musicians

accelerate [æk'sɛləˌreɪt] **accelerates, accelerating, accelerated** VERB
To accelerate is to go faster.

● THESAURUS
hurry: *He shouted at me to hurry.*
quicken: *Her pulse quickened in alarm.*
speed up: *It is designed to speed up credit-card transactions.*
<<OPPOSITE *decelerate*

acceleration [ækˌsɛlə'reɪʃən] NOUN
the rate at which the speed of something is increasing

accelerator [æk'sɛləˌreɪtə] **accelerators**
NOUN
the pedal in a vehicle which you press to make it go faster

accent ['æksənt] **accents** NOUN
1 a way of pronouncing a language *e.g. She had an Australian accent.*

2 a mark placed above or below a letter in some languages, which affects the way the letter is pronounced

3 an emphasis on something *e.g. The accent is on action and special effects.*

accentuate [æk'sɛntʃʊˌeɪt] **accentuates, accentuating, accentuated** VERB
To accentuate a feature of something is to make it more noticeable.

accept [ək'sɛpt] **accepts, accepting, accepted** VERB
1 If you accept something, you say yes to it or take it from someone.

● THESAURUS
acknowledge: *He was willing to acknowledge her as his child.*
agree to: *Hours before the deadline, the Chinese agreed to the conditions.*
concur with: *I concur with her opinion.*
consent to: *The Russians consented to the peace treaty.*
take: *He took the job.*
<<OPPOSITE *refuse*

2 If you accept a situation, you realize that it cannot be changed. *e.g. He accepts criticism as part of his job.*

3 If you accept a statement or story, you believe it is true. *e.g. The board accepted his explanation.*

4 If a group accepts you, they treat you as one of the group.
acceptance NOUN
[WORD HISTORY: from Latin AD meaning 'to' and CAPERE meaning 'to take']

acceptable [ək'sɛptəbəl] ADJECTIVE
good enough to be accepted
acceptably ADVERB

● THESAURUS
adequate: *a lack of adequate facilities*
all right: *The meal was all right for the price.*
fair: *He is a fair player, but not outstanding.*
good enough: *I'm afraid that excuse just isn't good enough.*
passable: *She can speak fluent Spanish and passable French.*
satisfactory: *The workmen have done a satisfactory job.*
tolerable: *a tolerable level of noise*

access ['æksɛs] **accesses, accessing, accessed** NOUN
1 the right or opportunity to enter a place or to use something
> VERB
2 If you access information from a computer, you get it.

accessible [ək'sɛsəbəl] ADJECTIVE
1 easily reached or seen *e.g. The village was accessible by foot only.*
2 easily understood or used *e.g. guidebooks which present information in a clear and accessible style*
accessibility NOUN

accession [ək'sɛʃən] NOUN
A ruler's accession is the time when he or she becomes the ruler of a country.

accessory [ək'sɛsərɪ] **accessories** NOUN
1 an extra part
2 someone who helps another person commit a crime

accident ['æksɪdənt] **accidents** NOUN
1 an unexpected event in which people are injured or killed
2 Something that happens by accident happens by chance.

accidental [ˌæksɪ'dɛntəl] ADJECTIVE
happening by chance
accidentally ADVERB

● THESAURUS
casual: *a casual remark*
chance: *a chance meeting*
inadvertent: *She giggled at the inadvertent pun.*
random: *the random nature of death in war*
<<OPPOSITE **deliberate**

acclaimed [ə'kleɪmd] ADJECTIVE
If someone or something is acclaimed, they are praised enthusiastically.

accolade ['ækə,leɪd] **accolades** NOUN;
FORMAL
great praise or an award given to someone

accommodate [ə'kɒmə,deɪt]
accommodates, accommodating, accommodated VERB
1 If you accommodate someone, you provide them with a place to sleep, live, or work.

● THESAURUS
house: *The building will house 12 boys.*
put up: *I wanted to know if she could put me up for a few days.*
shelter: *There were no facilities for sheltering the refugees.*

2 If a place can accommodate a number of things or people, it has enough room for them.

■ *Accommodate* has two *c*s and two *m*s

accommodating [ə'kɒmə,deɪtɪŋ] ADJECTIVE
willing to help and to adjust to new situations

● THESAURUS
considerate: *I try to be considerate to non-smokers.*
helpful: *The staff in the Newcastle office are very helpful.*
hospitable: *He was very hospitable to me when I came to New York.*
kind: *It was very kind of you to come.*
obliging: *an extremely pleasant and obliging man*

accommodation [əˌkɒmə'deɪʃən] NOUN
a place provided for someone to sleep, live, or work in

● THESAURUS
digs: British; informal *I was studying and living in digs all round the country.*
house: *He sold his house in London and moved to the country.*
housing: *a serious housing shortage*
lodgings: *At the moment the house provides lodgings for Oxford students.*
quarters: *the officers' quarters*

accompaniment [ə'kʌmpənɪmənt]
accompaniments NOUN
1 The accompaniment to a song is the music played to go with it.
2 An accompaniment to something is another thing that comes with it. *e.g. Melon is a good accompaniment to cold meats.*

accompany [ə'kʌmpənɪ] **accompanies, accompanying, accompanied** VERB
1 If you accompany someone, you go with them.
● THESAURUS
conduct: formal *He asked if he might conduct us to the ball.*
escort: *They were escorted by police to their plane.*
go with: *I haven't asked my friend to go with me yet.*
usher: *I ushered him into the office.*

2 If one thing accompanies another, the two things exist at the same time. *e.g. severe pain accompanied by fever*

THESAURUS
come with: *Stress comes with this job.*
go together with: *Poverty and illiteracy go together with high birth rates.*

3 If you accompany a singer or musician, you play an instrument while they sing or play the main tune.

accomplice [əˈkɒmplɪs] **accomplices**
NOUN
a person who helps someone else to commit a crime

accomplish [əˈkɒmplɪʃ] **accomplishes, accomplishing, accomplished** VERB
If you accomplish something, you succeed in doing it.

THESAURUS
achieve: *Achieving our aims makes us feel good.*
bring about: *the only way to bring about political change*
complete: *She has just completed her first novel.*
do: *Have you done it yet?*
fulfil: *All the necessary conditions were fulfilled.*
manage: *40% of children managed the required standard in reading.*

The *com* part of *accomplish* can sound like *kum* or *kom*

accomplished [əˈkɒmplɪʃt] ADJECTIVE
very talented at something *e.g. an accomplished cook*

accomplishment [əˈkɒmplɪʃmənt]
accomplishments NOUN
Someone's accomplishments are the skills they have gained.

accord [əˈkɔːd] **accords, according, accorded** VERB
1 If you accord someone or something a particular treatment, you treat them in that way. *e.g. He was accorded a proper respect for his status.*
> NOUN
2 agreement
> PHRASE
3 If you do something **of your own accord**, you do it willingly and not because you have been forced to do it.

accordance [əˈkɔːdəns] PHRASE
If you act **in accordance with** a rule or belief, you act in the way the rule or belief says you should.

according to [əˈkɔːdɪŋ] PREPOSITION
1 If something is true according to a particular person, that person says that it is true.
2 If something is done according to a principle or plan, that principle or plan is used as the basis for it.

accordion [əˈkɔːdɪən] **accordions** NOUN
a musical instrument like an expanding box. It is played by squeezing the two sides together while pressing the keys on it

accost [əˈkɒst] **accosts, accosting, accosted** VERB
If someone accosts you, especially someone you do not know, they come up and speak to you. *e.g. She says she is accosted when she goes shopping.*

account [əˈkaʊnt] **accounts, accounting, accounted** NOUN
1 a written or spoken report of something
2 If you have a bank account, you can leave money in the bank and take it out when you need it.
> PLURAL NOUN
3 Accounts are records of money spent and received by a person or business.
> PHRASE
4 If you **take something into account**, you include it in your planning.
5 On account of means because of
> VERB
6 To account for something is to explain it. *e.g. This might account for her strange behaviour.*
7 If something accounts for a particular amount of something, it is that amount. *e.g. The brain accounts for three per cent of body weight.*

accountable [əˈkaʊntəbəl] ADJECTIVE
If you are accountable for something, you are responsible for it and have to explain your actions. *e.g. The committee is accountable to Parliament.*
accountability NOUN

accountancy [əˈkaʊntənsi] NOUN
the job of keeping or inspecting financial accounts

accountant [əˈkaʊntənt] **accountants** NOUN
a person whose job is to keep or inspect financial accounts

accounting [əˈkaʊntɪŋ] NOUN
the keeping and checking of financial accounts

accrue [əˈkruː] **accrues, accruing, accrued** VERB
If money or interest accrues, it increases gradually.

accumulate [əˈkjuːmjʊˌleɪt] **accumulates, accumulating, accumulated** VERB
If you accumulate things or they accumulate, they collect over a period of time.

accurate [ˈækjərɪt] ADJECTIVE
completely correct or precise

accurately ADVERB, **accuracy** NOUN

THESAURUS

correct: *The correct answers can be found at the bottom of the page.*
exact: *an exact copy*
faithful: *a faithful translation*
precise: *precise sales figures*
right: *That clock never tells the right time.*
strict: *He has never been a playboy in the strict sense of the word.*
true: *a true account of what happened*
<<OPPOSITE *inaccurate*

accuse [ə'kjuːz] **accuses, accusing, accused** VERB
If you accuse someone of doing something wrong, you say they have done it.
accusation NOUN, **accuser** NOUN

THESAURUS

blame: *The police blamed the explosion on terrorists.*
censure: *The Stock Exchange took the unusual step of censuring him in public.*
charge: *Police have charged Mr Smith with murder.*
cite: *He was banned for 30 days after being cited for foul play.*
denounce: *He publicly denounced government nuclear policy.*

accustom [ə'kʌstəm] **accustoms, accustoming, accustomed** VERB
If you accustom yourself to something new or different, you get used to it.

accustomed [ə'kʌstəmd] ADJECTIVE
used to something

THESAURUS

adapted: *The camel's feet, well adapted for dry sand, are useless on mud.*
familiar: *He was very familiar with contemporary music.*
used: *I'm used to having my sleep interrupted.*
<<OPPOSITE *unaccustomed*

ace [eɪs] **aces** NOUN
1 In a pack of cards, a card with a single symbol on it.
> ADJECTIVE
2 INFORMAL
good or skilful *e.g. an ace squash player*

acerbic [ə'sɜːbɪk] ADJECTIVE; FORMAL
Acerbic remarks are harsh and bitter.

ache [eɪk] **aches, aching, ached** VERB
1 If you ache, you feel a continuous dull pain in a part of your body.
2 If you are aching for something, you want it very much.
> NOUN
3 a continuous dull pain

achieve [ə'tʃiːv] **achieves, achieving, achieved** VERB
(PSHE) If you achieve something, you successfully do it or cause it to happen.

THESAURUS

accomplish: *halfway towards accomplishing an important career goal*
carry out: *debate about how such reforms should be carried out*
complete: *The commission completed this task in March.*
do: *I have done what I came here to do.*
fulfil: *The army has fulfilled its objective.*
perform: *He has not performed his administrative duties properly.*

The *i* comes before the *e* in *achieve*

achievement [ə'tʃiːvmənt] **achievements** NOUN
(PSHE) something which you succeed in doing, especially after a lot of effort

THESAURUS

accomplishment: *The list of her accomplishments is staggering.*
deed: *His heroic deeds were celebrated in every corner of India.*
exploit: *His wartime exploits were later made into a TV series.*
feat: *A racing car is an extraordinary feat of engineering.*

acid ['æsɪd] **acids** NOUN **(SCIENCE)**
1 a chemical liquid with a pH value of less than 7 and which turns litmus paper red. Strong acids can damage skin, cloth, and metal
> ADJECTIVE
2 Acid tastes are sharp or sour.
acidic ADJECTIVE, **acidity** NOUN

acid rain NOUN
rain polluted by acid in the atmosphere which has come from factories

acknowledge [ək'nɒlɪdʒ] **acknowledges, acknowledging, acknowledged** VERB
1 If you acknowledge a fact or situation, you agree or admit it is true.
2 If you acknowledge someone, you show that you have seen and recognized them.
3 If you acknowledge a message, you tell the person who sent it that you have received it.
acknowledgment or **acknowledgement** NOUN

Acknowledgment and *acknowledgement* are both correct spellings

acne ['æknɪ] NOUN
lumpy spots that cover someone's face

acorn ['eɪkɔːn] **acorns** NOUN
the fruit of the oak tree, consisting of a pale oval

nut in a cup-shaped base

acoustic [əˈkuːstɪk] ADJECTIVE

1 relating to sound or hearing

2 An acoustic guitar is not made louder with an electric amplifier.

acoustics [əˈkuːstɪks] PLURAL NOUN
The acoustics of a room are its structural features which are responsible for how clearly you can hear sounds made in it.

acquaintance [əˈkweɪntəns]
acquaintances NOUN
someone you know slightly but not well

acquainted [əˈkweɪntɪd] ADJECTIVE
If you are acquainted with someone, you know them slightly but not well.

▨ You say that you are *acquainted with* someone

acquire [əˈkwaɪə] **acquires, acquiring, acquired** VERB
If you acquire something, you obtain it.

● THESAURUS
attain: *students who attain the required grades*
gain: *He gained valuable experience from the job.*
get: *My video's broken - I'll have to get a new one.*
obtain: *I couldn't obtain a ticket at any price.*
pick up: *You can pick up some real bargains at the January sales.*
procure: *It was still difficult to procure food and fuel.*
secure: *The team have secured a place in the semi-finals.*

acquisition [ˌækwɪˈzɪʃən] **acquisitions** NOUN
something you have obtained

acquit [əˈkwɪt] **acquits, acquitting, acquitted** VERB

1 If someone is acquitted of a crime, they have been tried in a court and found not guilty.

2 If you acquit yourself well on a particular occasion, you behave or perform well.
acquittal NOUN

acre [ˈeɪkə] **acres** NOUN
a unit for measuring areas of land. One acre is equal to 4840 square yards or about 4047 square metres
[WORD HISTORY: from Old English ÆCER meaning 'field']

acrid [ˈækrɪd] ADJECTIVE
sharp and bitter *e.g. the acrid smell of burning plastic*

acrimony [ˈækrɪmənɪ] NOUN; FORMAL
bitterness and anger
acrimonious ADJECTIVE

acrobat [ˈækrəˌbæt] **acrobats** NOUN
an entertainer who performs gymnastic tricks

acrobatic ADJECTIVE, **acrobatics** PLURAL NOUN
[WORD HISTORY: from Greek AKROBATES meaning 'someone who walks on tiptoe']

acronym [ˈækrənɪm] **acronyms** NOUN
a word made up of the initial letters of a phrase. An example of an acronym is 'BAFTA', which stands for 'British Academy of Film and Television Arts'

across [əˈkrɒs] PREPOSITION OR ADVERB

1 going from one side of something to the other

2 on the other side of a road or river

acrylic [əˈkrɪlɪk] NOUN

1 Acrylic is a type of man-made cloth.

2 (ART) Acrylics, or acrylic paints, are thick artists' paints which can be used like oil paints or thinned down with water.

act [ækt] **acts, acting, acted** VERB

1 If you act, you do something. *e.g. It would be irresponsible not to act swiftly.*

● THESAURUS
function: *All the computer systems functioned properly.*
operate: *In the first half he operated effectively in defence.*
perform: *He performed well in a World Cup match last summer.*
work: *All sides will work towards a political solution.*

2 If you act in a particular way, you behave in that way.

3 If a person or thing acts as something else, it has the function or does the job of that thing. *e.g. She was able to act as an interpreter.*

4 If you act in a play or film, you play a part.

● THESAURUS
act out: *It was made using real people to act out the scene.*
perform: *She performed the role on television twice more.*
play: *He plays agent Lillian Scully in a spoof of The X-Files.*
play the part of: *She agreed to play the part of Evita.*
portray: *His mean, moody looks are perfect for the cynical anti-hero he portrays.*

> NOUN

5 a single thing someone does *e.g. It was an act of disloyalty to the King.*

● THESAURUS
accomplishment: *Winning the tournament would be an incredible accomplishment.*
achievement: *She was honoured for her achievements as a film-maker.*
deed: *forgotten deeds of heroism*
feat: *an outstanding feat of athleticism*

undertaking: *Organizing the show has been a massive undertaking.*

6 An Act of Parliament is a law passed by the government.

7 In a play, ballet, or opera, an act is one of the main parts it is divided into.

acting ['æktɪŋ] NOUN
the profession of performing in plays or films

action ['ækʃən] **actions** NOUN
1 the process of doing something

● THESAURUS
activity: *the electrical activity of the brain*
operation: *It is quite a tricky operation.*
process: *the peace process*
2 something that is done

● THESAURUS
accomplishment: *sporting accomplishments*
achievement: *If we can win the league it will be a great achievement for me.*
deed: *daring and heroic deeds*
exploit: *the stories of his wartime exploits*
feat: *prodigious feats of engineering*
3 a physical movement

4 In law, an action is a legal proceeding. *e.g. a libel action*

activate ['æktɪˌveɪt] **activates, activating, activated** VERB
To activate something is to make it start working.

active ['æktɪv] ADJECTIVE
1 (PE) full of energy

● THESAURUS
energetic: *an energetic, happy young girl*
lively: *a lively and attractive teenager*
restless: *On Christmas Eve the kids are too restless to sleep.*
sprightly: *a small, sprightly 60-year-old*
vivacious: *He was very vivacious and great fun to work with.*
2 busy and hardworking

● THESAURUS
busy: *My husband lived a full and busy life.*
engaged: *The contenders are now fully engaged in their campaigns.*
enthusiastic: *As a student he was an enthusiastic member of the Communist party.*
hardworking: *a team of hardworking and dedicated volunteers*
industrious: *It is a happy and industrious community.*
involved: *She is heavily involved in local fundraising projects.*
occupied: *A busy social life will keep you fully occupied in February.*

3 In grammar, a verb in the active voice is one where the subject does the action, rather than having it done to them.
actively ADVERB

activist ['æktɪvɪst] **activists** NOUN
a person who tries to bring about political and social change

activity [æk'tɪvɪtɪ] **activities** NOUN
1 Activity is a situation in which a lot of things are happening at the same time.

● THESAURUS
action: *a film full of action and excitement*
bustle: *the hustle and bustle of a busy hospital*
energy: *I love the energy you find in big cities.*
liveliness: *a restaurant with a wonderful atmosphere of liveliness*
2 (PE) something you do for pleasure *e.g. sport and leisure activities*

● THESAURUS
hobby: *My hobby is birdwatching.*
interest: *Amongst his many interests are angling and painting.*
pastime: *You need a more active pastime than playing computer games.*
pursuit: *I like art, cooking and outdoor pursuits.*

actor ['æktə] **actors** NOUN
a man or woman whose profession is acting

actress ['æktrɪs] **actresses** NOUN
a woman whose profession is acting

actual ['æktʃʊəl] ADJECTIVE
real, rather than imaginary or guessed at *e.g. That is the official figure: the actual figure is much higher.*
actually ADVERB

● THESAURUS
authentic: *music played on authentic medieval instruments*
genuine: *a store selling genuine army clothing*
realistic: *a realistic picture of Dublin life*
true: *The film is based on a true story.*
verified: *verified reports of serious human rights violations*

> Don't use *actual* or *actually* when they don't add anything to the meaning of a sentence. Say *it's a fact* rather than *it's an actual fact*.

acumen ['ækjʊˌmɛn] NOUN
the ability to make good decisions quickly *e.g. business acumen*

acupuncture ['ækjʊˌpʌŋktʃə] NOUN
the treatment of illness or pain by sticking small needles into specific places in a person's body
[WORD HISTORY: from Latin ACUS meaning 'needle' added to 'puncture']

acute [ə'kjuːt] ADJECTIVE
1 severe or intense *e.g. an acute shortage of accommodation*

THESAURUS
critical: *suffering from a critical illness*
extreme: *a crippling disease which causes extreme pain*
grave: *His country faces grave problems.*
great: *He died in great agony.*
intense: *I felt an intense loneliness.*
serious: *It increases the risk of serious injuries.*
severe: *Nuts can trigger off a severe allergic reaction.*

2 very intelligent *e.g. an acute mind*

THESAURUS
alert: *He is old, but he has a very quick and alert mind.*
astute: *He has a remarkably astute brain.*
bright: *You don't need a bright mind to figure that one out.*
keen: *a competent economist with a keen intellect*
perceptive: *a perceptive analysis of the situation*
quick: *a child with an enquiring mind and a quick intelligence*
sharp: *His gentle manner disguised a sharp mind.*
shrewd: *He demonstrated a shrewd understanding of human nature.*

3 An acute angle is less than 90°.

4 In French and some other languages, an acute accent is a line sloping upwards from left to right placed over a vowel to indicate a change in pronunciation, as in the word *café*.

ad [æd] **ads** NOUN; INFORMAL
an advertisement

AD
You use 'AD' in dates to indicate the number of years after the birth of Jesus Christ.

ad- PREFIX
'Ad-' means 'near' or 'next to' *e.g. adjoining... adverb*
[WORD HISTORY: from Latin AD- meaning 'towards']

adage ['ædɪdʒ] **adages** NOUN
a saying that expresses some general truth about life

adamant ['ædəmənt] ADJECTIVE
If you are adamant, you are determined not to change your mind.
adamantly ADVERB

Adam's apple ['ædəmz] **Adam's apples** NOUN
the larynx, a lump at the front of the neck which is more obvious in men than in women and young boys
[WORD HISTORY: from the story that a piece of the forbidden apple got stuck in Adam's throat]

adapt [ə'dæpt] **adapts, adapting, adapted** VERB
1 If you adapt to a new situation, you change so you can deal with it successfully.

2 If you adapt something, you change it so it is suitable for a new purpose or situation.
adaptable ADJECTIVE, **adaptation** NOUN

THESAURUS
adjust: *He had to adjust the driver's seat.*
alter: *The government has altered the rules.*
change: *The law needs to be changed.*
convert: *a table that converts into an ironing board*
modify: *Our workshop is busy modifying the tanks for desert conditions.*

adaptor [ə'dæptə] **adaptors;** also spelt
adapter NOUN
a type of electric plug which can be used to connect two or more plugs to one socket

add [æd] **adds, adding, added** VERB
1 If you add something to a number of things, you put it with the things.

THESAURUS
attach: *Don't forget to attach the completed entry form.*
augment: *a way to augment the family income*
supplement: *I suggest supplementing your diet with vitamin A.*

2 If you add numbers together or add them up, you work out the total.

THESAURUS
add up: *adding up calories on a calculator*
count up: *They counted up all the hours the villagers worked.*
total: *They will compete for prizes totalling nearly £300.*
<<OPPOSITE *subtract*

adder ['ædə] **adders** NOUN
a small poisonous snake

addict ['ædɪkt] **addicts** NOUN
(PSHE) someone who cannot stop taking harmful drugs
addicted ADJECTIVE, **addiction** NOUN

addictive [ə'dɪktɪv] ADJECTIVE
If a drug is addictive, the people who take it cannot stop.

addition [ə'dɪʃən] **additions** NOUN
1 something that has been added to something else

THESAURUS
increase: *a substantial increase in workload*
supplement: *a supplement to their basic pension*

2 (MATHS) the process of adding numbers together

additional [ə'dɪʃənəl] ADJECTIVE
extra or more *e.g. They made the decision to take on additional staff.*
additionally ADVERB

additive ['ædɪtɪv] **additives** NOUN
something added to something else, usually in order to improve it

address [əˈdrɛs] **addresses, addressing, addressed** NOUN

1 the number of the house where you live, together with the name of the street and the town or village

2 a speech given to a group of people

> VERB

3 If a letter is addressed to you, it has your name and address written on it.

4 If you address a problem or task, you start to deal with it.

adept [əˈdɛpt] ADJECTIVE

very skilful at doing something *e.g. She is adept at motivating others.*

adequate [ˈædɪkwɪt] ADJECTIVE

enough in amount or good enough for a purpose *e.g. an adequate diet*

adequately ADVERB, **adequacy** NOUN

⬤ THESAURUS

acceptable: *a company which offers an acceptable benefits package*

ample: *You've had ample time to discuss this matter.*

enough: *enough money to live on*

satisfactory: *a satisfactory bid for the company*

sufficient: *One teaspoon of salt should be sufficient.*

<<OPPOSITE *insufficient*

adhere [ədˈhɪə] **adheres, adhering, adhered** VERB

1 If one thing adheres to another, it sticks firmly to it.

2 If you adhere to a rule or agreement, you do what it says.

3 If you adhere to an opinion or belief, you firmly hold that opinion or belief.

adherence NOUN

adherent [ədˈhɪərənt] **adherents** NOUN

An adherent of a belief is someone who holds that belief.

adhesive [ədˈhiːsɪv] **adhesives** NOUN

1 any substance used to stick two things together, for example glue

> ADJECTIVE

2 Adhesive substances are sticky and able to stick to things.

adjacent [əˈdʒeɪsᵊnt] ADJECTIVE; FORMAL

1 If two things are adjacent, they are next to each other. *e.g. a hotel adjacent to the beach*

2 (MATHS) Adjacent angles share one side and have the same point opposite to their bases.

adjective [ˈædʒɪktɪv] **adjectives** NOUN

a word that adds to the description given by a noun. For example, in 'They live in a large white Georgian house', 'large', 'white', and 'Georgian' are all adjectives

adjectival ADJECTIVE

adjoining [əˈdʒɔɪnɪŋ] ADJECTIVE

If two rooms are next to each other and are connected, they are adjoining.

adjourn [əˈdʒɜːn] **adjourns, adjourning, adjourned** VERB

1 If a meeting or trial is adjourned, it stops for a time. *e.g. The case was adjourned until September.*

2 If people adjourn to another place, they go there together after a meeting. *e.g. We adjourned to the lounge.*

adjournment NOUN

adjust [əˈdʒʌst] **adjusts, adjusting, adjusted** VERB

1 If you adjust something, you change its position or alter it in some other way.

2 If you adjust to a new situation, you get used to it.

adjustment NOUN, **adjustable** ADJECTIVE

ad-lib [ædˈlɪb] **ad-libs, ad-libbing, ad-libbed** VERB

1 If you ad-lib, you say something that has not been prepared beforehand. *e.g. I ad-lib on radio but use a script on TV.*

> NOUN

2 a comment that has not been prepared beforehand

[WORD HISTORY: short for Latin AD LIBITUM meaning 'according to desire']

administer [ədˈmɪnɪstə] **administers, administering, administered** VERB

1 To administer an organization is to be responsible for managing it.

⬤ THESAURUS

be in charge of: *Who is in charge of this division?*

command: *Who would command the troops in the event of war?*

control: *He controls the largest publishing house in the country.*

direct: *Christopher will direct day-to-day operations.*

manage: *Within two years he was managing the shop.*

run: *This is no way to run a business.*

supervise: *the men who supervised the project*

2 To administer the law or administer justice is to put it into practice and apply it.

⬤ THESAURUS

carry out: *You are not authorized to carry out disciplinary action.*

deal: *His attacker dealt him a severe blow to the face.*

dispense: *They have set up military courts to dispense swift justice.*

execute: *She leapt up and executed a spinning kick to his head.*

impose: *The judge had no choice but to impose a death sentence.*

inflict: *Inflicting punishment to stop crime is not the answer.*

perform: *He had to perform emergency surgery.*

3 If medicine is administered to someone, it is given to them.

dministration [əd͵mɪnɪ'streɪʃən] **administrations** NOUN

1 Administration is the work of organizing and supervising an organization.

2 Administration is also the process of administering something. *e.g. the administration of criminal justice*

3 The administration is the group of people that manages an organization or a country.
administrative ADJECTIVE, **administrator** NOUN

dmirable ['ædmərəbəl] ADJECTIVE
very good and deserving to be admired
admirably ADVERB

dmiral ['ædmərəl] **admirals** NOUN
the commander of a navy
[WORD HISTORY: from Arabic AMIR meaning 'commander']

dmiration [͵ædmə'reɪʃən] NOUN
a feeling of great liking and respect

● THESAURUS
appreciation: *gifts presented to them in appreciation of their work*
approval: *His son had an obsessive drive to gain his father's approval.*
esteem: *Their public esteem has never been lower.*
regard: *He has always been held in high regard.*
respect: *We all have so much respect for her.*

dmire [əd'maɪə] **admires, admiring, admired** VERB
If you admire someone or something, you respect and approve of them.
admirer NOUN, **admiring** ADJECTIVE, **admiringly** ADVERB

● THESAURUS
appreciate: *the need for children to appreciate their mother tongue*
look up to: *A lot of the younger girls look up to you.*
respect: *I want him to respect me as a career woman.*
value: *She genuinely values his opinion.*
<<OPPOSITE *scorn*

dmission [əd'mɪʃən] **admissions** NOUN
1 If you are allowed admission to a place, you are allowed to go in.
2 If you make an admission of something, you agree, often reluctantly, it is true. *e.g. It was an admission of guilt.*

admit [əd'mɪt] **admits, admitting, admitted** VERB
1 If you admit something, you agree, often reluctantly, it is true.

● THESAURUS
accept: *I accepted the truth of all that Nicola had told me.*
acknowledge: *Belatedly the government has acknowledged the problem.*
grant: *The magistrates granted that the RSPCA was justified in bringing the action.*
<<OPPOSITE *deny*

2 To admit someone or something to a place or organization is to allow them to enter it.

● THESAURUS
accept: *Stephen was accepted into the family.*
let in: *Turnstile operators were accused of letting in fans without tickets.*
receive: *He was received into the priesthood.*
take in: *The monastery has taken in 26 refugees.*
<<OPPOSITE *exclude*

3 If you are admitted to hospital, you are taken there to stay until you are better.

admittedly [əd'mɪtɪdlɪ] ADVERB
People use 'admittedly' to show that what they are saying contrasts with something they have already said or are about to say, and weakens their argument. *e.g. My studies, admittedly only from books, taught me much.*

adolescent [͵ædə'lɛsənt] **adolescents** NOUN
a young person who is no longer a child but who is not yet an adult
adolescence NOUN

adopt [ə'dɒpt] **adopts, adopting, adopted** VERB
1 If you adopt a child that is not your own, you take him or her into your family as your son or daughter.
2 FORMAL
If you adopt a particular attitude, you start to have it.
adoption NOUN

adorable [ə'dɔːrəbəl] ADJECTIVE
sweet and attractive

adore [ə'dɔː] **adores, adoring, adored** VERB
If you adore someone, you feel deep love and admiration for them.
adoration NOUN

adorn [ə'dɔːn] **adorns, adorning, adorned** VERB
To adorn something is to decorate it. *e.g. The cathedral is adorned with statues.*
adornment NOUN

adrenalin or **adrenaline** [ə'drɛnəlɪn] NOUN

a substance which is produced by your body when you are angry, scared, or excited and which makes your heart beat faster

adrift [əˈdrɪft] ADJECTIVE OR ADVERB
If a boat is adrift or goes adrift, it floats on the water without being controlled.

adulation [ˌædjʊˈleɪʃən] NOUN
great admiration and praise for someone
adulatory ADJECTIVE

adult [ˈædʌlt] **adults** NOUN
a mature and fully developed person or animal
● THESAURUS
grown-up: *Las Vegas is the ultimate playground for grown-ups.*
man: *He is now a man of 42.*
woman: *A woman of child-bearing age.*
<<OPPOSITE *child*

adultery [əˈdʌltərɪ] NOUN
sexual intercourse between a married person and someone he or she is not married to
adulterer NOUN, **adulterous** ADJECTIVE

adulthood [ˈædʌlthʊd] NOUN
the time during someone's life when they are an adult

advance [ədˈvɑːns] **advances, advancing, advanced** VERB
1 To advance is to move forward.
● THESAURUS
make inroads: *They have made impressive inroads in the movie business.*
press on: *Poland pressed on with economic reform.*
proceed: *He proceeded down the spiral stairway.*
progress: *the ability to progress from one step to the next*
2 To advance a cause or interest is to help it to be successful.
3 If you advance someone a sum of money, you lend it to them.
> NOUN
4 Advance in something is progress in it. *e.g. scientific advance*
● THESAURUS
breakthrough: *a breakthrough in cancer treatment*
development: *the development of the car*
gain: *a gain of nearly 10%*
progress: *signs of progress in his reading*
step: *the first step towards peace*
5 a sum of money lent to someone
> ADJECTIVE
6 happening before an event *e.g. The event received little advance publicity.*
> PHRASE
7 If you do something **in advance**, you do it before something else happens. *e.g. We booked up the room well in advance.*

advantage [ədˈvɑːntɪdʒ] **advantages** NOUN
1 a benefit or something that puts you in a better position
● THESAURUS
ascendancy: *The extremists are gaining ascendancy.*
benefit: *For maximum benefit use your treatment every day.*
dominance: *the battle for high-street dominance*
superiority: *military superiority*
<<OPPOSITE *disadvantage*
> PHRASE
2 If you **take advantage of** someone, you treat them unfairly for your own benefit.
3 If you **take advantage of** something, you make use of it.

advantageous [ˌædvənˈteɪdʒəs] ADJECTIVE
likely to benefit you in some way *e.g. an advantageous marriage*

advent [ˈædvent] NOUN
1 The advent of something is its start or its coming into existence. *e.g. The advent of the submarine changed naval warfare.*
2 Advent is the season just before Christmas in the Christian calendar.

adventure [ədˈventʃə] **adventures** NOUN
a series of events that are unusual and exciting

adventurer [ədˈventʃərə] **adventurers** NOUN
someone who enjoys doing dangerous and exciting things

adventurous [ədˈventʃərəs] ADJECTIVE
willing to take risks and do new and exciting things
adventurously ADVERB

adverb [ˈædˌvɜːb] **adverbs** NOUN
a word that adds information about a verb or a following adjective or other adverb, for example, 'slowly', 'now', and 'here' which say how, when, or where something is done
adverbial ADJECTIVE

adversary [ˈædvəsərɪ] **adversaries** NOUN
someone who is your enemy or who opposes what you are doing

adverse [ˈædvɜːs] ADJECTIVE
not helpful to you or opposite to what you want or need *e.g. adverse weather conditions*
adversely ADVERB

adversity [ədˈvɜːsɪtɪ] **adversities** NOUN
a time of danger or difficulty

advert [ˈædvɜːt] **adverts** NOUN; INFORMAL
an advertisement

advertise [ˈædvəˌtaɪz] **advertises, advertising, advertised** VERB **(ENGLISH)**

a

1 If you advertise something, you tell people about it in a newspaper or poster, or on TV.

● THESAURUS

plug: informal *If I hear another actor plugging his latest book I will scream.*

promote: *What are you doing to promote your new film?*

publicize: *He never publicized his plans.*

push: *a publisher who knows how to push a product*

2 To advertise is to make an announcement in a newspaper or poster, or on TV.

advertiser NOUN, **advertising** NOUN

advertisement [əd'vɜːtɪsmənt] **advertisements** NOUN

(ENGLISH) an announcement about something in a newspaper or poster, or on TV

● THESAURUS

ad: informal *an ad for a minicab company*

advert: British; informal *She appeared in a coffee advert.*

commercial: *She has turned down a small fortune to do TV commercials.*

notice: *The request is published in notices in today's national newspapers.*

plug: informal *a shameless plug for his new film*

advice [əd'vaɪs] NOUN

a suggestion from someone about what you should do

● THESAURUS

counsel: formal *He had always been able to count on her wise counsel.*

drum: Australian; informal *What's the drum on this?*

guidance: *The nation looks to them for guidance.*

opinion: *You should seek a medical opinion.*

suggestion: *She made suggestions as to how I could improve my diet.*

> The noun *advice* is spelt with a '*c*' and the verb *advise* is spelt with an '*s*'

advisable [əd'vaɪzəbəl] ADJECTIVE

sensible and likely to achieve the result you want *e.g. It is advisable to buy the visa before travelling.*

advisably ADVERB, **advisability** NOUN

advise [əd'vaɪz] **advises, advising, advised** VERB

1 If you advise someone to do something, you tell them you think they should do it.

● THESAURUS

caution: *The researchers caution against drawing general conclusions from this study.*

counsel: *My advisers counselled me to do nothing.*

recommend: *We strongly recommend reporting the incident to the police.*

suggest: *He suggested a visit to the Cézanne exhibition.*

urge: *We urge that vigorous action be taken immediately.*

2 FORMAL

If you advise someone of something, you inform them of it.

advisory ADJECTIVE

● THESAURUS

inform: *My daughter informed me that she was pregnant.*

make known: *The details will be made known by the end of August.*

notify: *The skipper notified the coastguard of the tragedy.*

> The verb *advise* is spelt with an '*s*' and the noun *advice* is spelt with a '*c*'

adviser [əd'vaɪzə] **advisers** NOUN

a person whose job is to give advice

● THESAURUS

aide: *a former aide to Ronald Reagan*

consultant: *a management consultant*

guru: *He became Britain's modern design guru after launching Habitat in 1964.*

mentor: *He is my friend and musical mentor.*

tutor: *my college tutor*

advocate **advocates, advocating, advocated** VERB ['ædvə,keɪt]

1 If you advocate a course of action or plan, you support it publicly.

● THESAURUS

back: *The newspaper is backing the residents' campaign.*

champion: *He passionately champions our cause.*

endorse: *We are reluctant to endorse such drastic measures.*

favour: *judges who favour the death penalty*

promote: *He promoted the idea of Scottish independence.*

recommend: *I can't recommend such a course of action.*

support: *people who supported his policies*

uphold: *We uphold the capitalist free economy.*

> NOUN ['ædvəkɪt]

2 An advocate of something is someone who supports it publicly.

3 FORMAL

a lawyer who represents clients in court

advocacy NOUN

aerial ['ɛərɪəl] **aerials** ADJECTIVE

1 Aerial means happening in the air. *e.g. aerial combat*

> NOUN

2 a piece of wire for receiving television or radio signals

aero- PREFIX

'Aero-' means involving the air, the atmosphere, or aircraft *e.g. aerobatics*

[WORD HISTORY: from Greek AĒR MEANING 'AIR']

aerobics [ɛəˈrəʊbɪks] NOUN
a type of fast physical exercise, which increases the oxygen in your blood and strengthens your heart and lungs
aerobic ADJECTIVE

aerodynamic [ˌɛərəʊdaɪˈnæmɪk] ADJECTIVE
having a streamlined shape that moves easily through the air

aeroplane [ˈɛərəˌpleɪn] **aeroplanes** NOUN
a vehicle with wings and engines that enable it to fly

aerosol [ˈɛərəˌsɒl] **aerosols** NOUN
a small metal container in which liquid is kept under pressure so that it can be forced out as a spray

▪ *Aerosol* starts with *aer* and not with *air*

aerospace [ˈɛərəˌspeɪs] ADJECTIVE
involved in making and designing aeroplanes and spacecraft

aesthetic or **esthetic** [iːsˈθɛtɪk] ADJECTIVE
(D & T) FORMAL
relating to the appreciation of beauty or art
aesthetically ADVERB, **aesthetics** NOUN

afar [əˈfɑː] NOUN; LITERARY
From afar means from a long way away.

affable [ˈæfəbəl] ADJECTIVE
pleasant and easy to talk to
affably ADVERB, **affability** NOUN

affair [əˈfɛə] **affairs** NOUN
1 an event or series of events *e.g. The funeral was a sad affair.*

◉ THESAURUS
business: *This business has really upset me.*
event: *A wedding should be a joyous event.*
issue: *a major political issue*
matter: *I never interfere in these business matters.*
question: *the difficult question of unemployment*
situation: *The whole situation is now under control.*
subject: *a subject which had worried him for some time*

2 To have an affair is to have a secret sexual or romantic relationship, especially when one of the people is married.

◉ THESAURUS
fling: *We had a brief fling, but it was nothing serious.*
liaison: *He denied that he had had a sexual liaison with his secretary.*
relationship: *She went public on her relationship with a Hollywood star.*
romance: *Our company discourages office romances.*

> PLURAL NOUN
3 Your affairs are your private and personal life.

e.g. Why had he meddled in her affairs?.

affect [əˈfɛkt] **affects, affecting, affected**
VERB
1 If something affects you, it influences you in some way.

◉ THESAURUS
act on: *This drug acts very fast on the central nervous system.*
alter: *The earth's climate appears to have been altered by pollution.*
change: *It was to change the course of my life.*
impinge on: *My private life does not impinge on my professional life.*

2 FORMAL
If you affect a particular way of behaving, you behave in that way. *e.g. He affected an Italian accent.*

▪ Do not confuse the spelling of the verb *affect* with the noun *effect*. Something that *affects* you has an *effect* on you

affectation [ˌæfɛkˈteɪʃən] **affectations**
NOUN
An affectation is behaviour that is not genuine but is put on to impress people.

affection [əˈfɛkʃən] **affections** NOUN
1 a feeling of love and fondness for someone
◉ THESAURUS
attachment: *Mother and child form a close attachment.*
fondness: *his fondness for cats*
liking: *a liking for flashy cars*
love: *My love for all my children is unconditional.*
warmth: *He greeted us both with warmth and affection.*
<<OPPOSITE *dislike*

> PLURAL NOUN
2 Your affections are feelings of love you have for someone.

affectionate [əˈfɛkʃənɪt] ADJECTIVE
full of fondness for someone *e.g. an affectionate embrace*
affectionately ADVERB
◉ THESAURUS
caring: *a loving, caring husband*
fond: *She gave him a fond smile.*
loving: *The children were very loving to me.*
tender: *a tender kiss*
<<OPPOSITE *cold*

affiliate [əˈfɪlɪˌeɪt] **affiliates, affiliating, affiliated** VERB
If a group affiliates itself to another, larger group, it forms a close association with it. *e.g. organizations affiliated to the ANC*
affiliation NOUN

affinity [əˈfɪnɪtɪ] **affinities** NOUN
a close similarity or understanding between two

things or people *e.g. There are affinities between the two poets.*

affirm [əˈfɜːm] **affirms, affirming, affirmed** VERB
If you affirm an idea or belief, you clearly indicate your support for it. *e.g. We affirm our commitment to broadcast quality programmes.*
affirmation NOUN

affirmative [əˈfɜːmətɪv] ADJECTIVE
An affirmative word or gesture is one that means yes.

afflict [əˈflɪkt] **afflicts, afflicting, afflicted** VERB
If illness or pain afflicts someone, they suffer from it. *e.g. She was afflicted by depression.*
affliction NOUN

affluent [ˈæfluənt] ADJECTIVE
having a lot of money and possessions
affluence NOUN

afford [əˈfɔːd] **affords, affording, afforded** VERB
1 If you can afford to do something, you have enough money or time to do it.
2 If you cannot afford something to happen, it would be harmful or embarrassing for you if it happened. *e.g. We cannot afford to be complacent.*

affordable [əˈfɔːdəbᵊl] ADJECTIVE
If something is affordable, most people have enough money to buy it. *e.g. the availability of affordable housing*

affray [əˈfreɪ] NOUN; FORMAL
a noisy and violent fight

affront [əˈfrʌnt] **affronts, affronting, affronted** VERB
1 If you are affronted by something, you are insulted and angered by it.
> NOUN
2 something that is an insult *e.g. Our prisons are an affront to civilized society.*

▪ Notice that *affront*, the noun, is followed by *to*

afield [əˈfiːld] ADVERB
Far afield means a long way away. *e.g. competitors from as far afield as Russia and China*

afloat [əˈfləʊt] ADVERB OR ADJECTIVE
1 floating on water
2 successful and making enough money *e.g. Companies are struggling hard to stay afloat.*

afoot [əˈfʊt] ADJECTIVE OR ADVERB
happening or being planned, especially secretly *e.g. Plans are afoot to build a new museum.*

afraid [əˈfreɪd] ADJECTIVE
1 If you are afraid, you are very frightened.

▶ THESAURUS
apprehensive: *People are still terribly apprehensive about the future.*
fearful: *Bankers were fearful of a world banking crisis.*
frightened: *She was frightened of flying.*
nervous: *Emotionally, he left me a wreck, nervous of everyone.*
scared: *I was too scared to move.*
<<OPPOSITE *unafraid*

2 If you are afraid something might happen, you are worried it might happen.

afresh [əˈfreʃ] ADVERB
again and in a new way *e.g. The couple moved abroad to start life afresh.*

Africa [ˈæfrɪkə] NOUN
Africa is the second largest continent. It is almost surrounded by sea, with the Atlantic on its west side, the Mediterranean to the north and the Indian Ocean and the Red Sea to the east.

African [ˈæfrɪkən] **Africans** ADJECTIVE
1 belonging or relating to Africa
> NOUN
2 someone, especially a Black person, who comes from Africa

African-American [ˈæfrɪkənəˈmɛrɪkən] **African-Americans** NOUN
an American whose ancestors came from Africa

Afrikaans [ˌæfrɪˈkɑːns] NOUN
a language spoken in South Africa, similar to Dutch

Afrikaner [afriˈkɑːnə] **Afrikaners** NOUN
a white South African with Dutch ancestors

aft [ɑːft] ADVERB OR ADJECTIVE
towards the back of a ship or boat

after [ˈɑːftə] PREPOSITION OR ADVERB
1 later than a particular time, date, or event

▶ THESAURUS
afterwards: *He was taken to hospital but died soon afterwards.*
following: *We shared so much, not only during the war, but in the many years following.*
later: *He resigned ten years later.*
subsequently: *She subsequently became honorary secretary.*
<<OPPOSITE *before*

2 behind and following someone or something *e.g. They ran after her.*

afterlife [ˈɑːftəˌlaɪf] NOUN
The afterlife is a life some people believe begins when you die.

aftermath [ˈɑːftəˌmɑːθ] NOUN
The aftermath of a disaster is the situation that comes after it.

afternoon [ˌɑːftəˈnuːn] **afternoons** NOUN
the part of the day between noon and about six o'clock

aftershave [ˈɑːftəʃeɪv] NOUN
a pleasant-smelling liquid men put on their faces after shaving

afterthought [ˈɑːftəˌθɔːt] **afterthoughts** NOUN
something you do or say as an addition to something else you have already done or said

afterwards [ˈɑːftəwədz] ADVERB
after an event or time

again [əˈgɛn] ADVERB
1 happening one more time e.g. He looked forward to becoming a father again.

● THESAURUS
afresh: The couple moved abroad to start life afresh.
anew: She's ready to start anew.
once more: Rage overcame him once more.

2 returning to the same state or place as before e.g. there and back again

against [əˈgɛnst] PREPOSITION
1 touching and leaning on e.g. He leaned against the wall.

2 in opposition to e.g. the Test match against England

● THESAURUS
averse to: He's not averse to a drink.
hostile to: countries that were once hostile to South Africa
in opposition to: radio stations set up in opposition to the BBC
versus: Portugal versus England.

3 in preparation for or in case of something e.g. precautions against fire

● THESAURUS
in anticipation of: His school was one of several which closed in anticipation of Arctic conditions.
in expectation of: The hotel was being renovated in expectation of a tourist boom.
in preparation for: The army massed troops and guns in preparation for a counter-attack.

4 in comparison with e.g. The pound is now at its lowest rate against the dollar.

age [eɪdʒ] **ages, ageing** or **aging, aged** NOUN
1 The age of something or someone is the number of years they have lived or existed.

2 Age is the quality of being old. e.g. a wine capable of improving with age

3 a particular period in history e.g. the Iron Age
> PLURAL NOUN
4 INFORMAL

Ages means a very long time. e.g. He's been talking for ages.
> VERB
5 To age is to grow old or to appear older.
▇ Ageing and aging are both correct spellings

aged [ˈeɪdʒd] ADJECTIVE
having a particular age e.g. people aged 16 to 24

aged [ˈeɪdʒɪd] ADJECTIVE
very old e.g. an aged invalid

agency [ˈeɪdʒənsɪ] **agencies** NOUN
an organization or business which provides certain services e.g. a detective agency

agenda [əˈdʒɛndə] **agendas** NOUN
a list of items to be discussed at a meeting

agent [ˈeɪdʒənt] **agents** NOUN
1 someone who arranges work or business for other people, especially actors or singers

2 someone who works for their country's secret service

aggravate [ˈægrəveɪt] **aggravates, aggravating, aggravated** VERB
1 To aggravate a bad situation is to make it worse.

2 INFORMAL
If someone or something aggravates you, they make you annoyed.
aggravating ADJECTIVE, **aggravation** NOUN
▇ Some people think that using aggravate to mean 'annoy' is wrong

aggregate [ˈægrɪgɪt] **aggregates** NOUN
a total that is made up of several smaller amounts

aggression [əˈgrɛʃən] NOUN
violent and hostile behaviour

aggressive [əˈgrɛsɪv] ADJECTIVE
full of hostility and violence
aggressively ADVERB, **aggressiveness** NOUN

● THESAURUS
hostile: The prisoner eyed him in a hostile silence.
quarrelsome: He had been a wild boy and a quarrelsome young man.
<<OPPOSITE peaceful

aggressor [əˈgrɛsə] **aggressors** NOUN
a person or country that starts a fight or a war

aggrieved [əˈgriːvd] ADJECTIVE
upset and angry about the way you have been treated

aghast [əˈgɑːst] ADJECTIVE
shocked and horrified

agile [ˈædʒaɪl] ADJECTIVE **(PE)**
able to move quickly and easily e.g. He is as agile as a cat.
agilely ADVERB, **agility** NOUN

THESAURUS
lithe: *a lithe young gymnast*
nimble: *He built his career around quick reflexes and nimble footwork.*
sprightly: *She is alert and sprightly despite her 85 years.*
supple: *She is as supple as a dancer.*
<<OPPOSITE *clumsy*

agitate [ˈædʒɪˌteɪt] **agitates, agitating, agitated** VERB
1 If you agitate for something, you campaign energetically to get it.

THESAURUS
campaign: *an organization which campaigns for better consumer rights*
demonstrate: *marchers demonstrating for political reform*
protest: *country dwellers who were protesting for the right to hunt*
push: *Some board members are pushing for the merger.*

2 If something agitates you, it worries you.
agitation NOUN, **agitator** NOUN

THESAURUS
bother: *It really bothers me when you talk like that.*
distress: *sudden noises which distressed the animals*
disturb: *These dreams disturb me for days afterwards.*
trouble: *Are you troubled by thoughts of the future?*
upset: *The whole incident upset me dreadfully.*
worry: *I didn't want to worry you with my own problems.*

agnostic [ægˈnɒstɪk] **agnostics** NOUN OR ADJECTIVE
Someone who believes we cannot know definitely whether God exists or not.
agnosticism NOUN
[WORD HISTORY: from Greek AGNŌSTOS meaning 'unknown']

ago [əˈgəʊ] ADVERB
in the past *e.g. She bought her flat three years ago.*

agog [əˈgɒg] ADJECTIVE
excited and eager to know more about an event or situation *e.g. She was agog to hear his news.*

agonizing or **agonising** [ˈægəˌnaɪzɪŋ] ADJECTIVE
extremely painful, either physically or mentally
e.g. an agonizing decision

agony [ˈægənɪ] NOUN
very great physical or mental pain

agoraphobia [ˌægərəˈfəʊbɪə] NOUN
the fear of open spaces
agoraphobic ADJECTIVE
[WORD HISTORY: from Greek AGORA meaning 'market place' + PHOBIA]

agrarian [əˈgrɛərɪən] ADJECTIVE; FORMAL
relating to farming and agriculture *e.g. agrarian economies*

agree [əˈgriː] **agrees, agreeing, agreed** VERB
1 If you agree with someone, you have the same opinion as them.

THESAURUS
assent: *I assented to the request of the publishers to write this book.*
be of the same opinion: *All the other players are of the same opinion.*
concur: *Four other judges concurred.*
see eye to eye: *He has not always seen eye to eye with his brother.*
<<OPPOSITE *disagree*

2 If you agree to do something, you say you will do it.

3 If two stories or totals agree, they are the same.

THESAURUS
accord: *I cannot support policies that no longer accord with my principles.*
conform: *It doesn't conform with current building regulations.*
match: *Attendances do not match the ticket sales.*
square: *Does that explanation square with the facts?*
tally: *The figures don't seem to tally.*

4 Food that doesn't agree with you makes you ill.

agreeable [əˈgriːəbᵊl] ADJECTIVE
1 pleasant or enjoyable

THESAURUS
delightful: *I've had a delightful time.*
enjoyable: *an enjoyable meal*
lovely: *I hope you have a lovely holiday.*
nice: *It would be very nice to get away from it all for a few days.*
pleasant: *This restaurant offers good food in pleasant surroundings.*
pleasurable: *the pleasurable task of deciding where to go on holiday*
<<OPPOSITE *disagreeable*

2 If you are agreeable to something, you are willing to allow it or to do it. *e.g. She was agreeable to the project.*
agreeably ADVERB

THESAURUS
game: *Are you game to try something a little bit different?*
happy: *I'm happy to go along with what everyone else thinks.*
prepared: *Would you be prepared to queue for hours for a ticket?*
ready: *I'm ready to take over if he resigns.*
willing: *Are you willing to take part in a survey?*

agreement [əˈgriːmənt] **agreements** NOUN

1 a decision that has been reached by two or more people

● THESAURUS
arrangement: *Eventually we came to an arrangement that suited us both.*
contract: *She has signed an exclusive solo-album contract.*
deal: informal *The company recently won a five-year deal to build runways.*
pact: *He ruled out any formal pact with the government.*
settlement: *She accepted an out-of-court settlement of £4000.*
treaty: *negotiations over a 1992 treaty on global warming*

2 Two people who are in agreement have the same opinion about something.

agriculture ['ægrɪ,kʌltʃə] NOUN
(HISTORY) Agriculture is farming.
agricultural ADJECTIVE

aground [ə'graʊnd] ADVERB
If a boat runs aground, it becomes stuck in a shallow stretch of water.

ahead [ə'hɛd] ADVERB
1 in front *e.g. He looked ahead.*
2 more advanced than someone or something else *e.g. We are five years ahead of the competition.*
3 in the future *e.g. I haven't had time to think far ahead.*

aid [eɪd] **aids, aiding, aided** NOUN
1 Aid is money, equipment, or services provided for people in need. *e.g. food and medical aid*
2 something that makes a task easier *e.g. teaching aids*
> VERB
3 FORMAL
If you aid a person or an organization, you help or support them.

aide [eɪd] **aides** NOUN
an assistant to an important person, especially in the government or the army *e.g. the Prime Minister's closest aides*

AIDS [eɪdz] NOUN
a disease which destroys the body's natural system of immunity to diseases. AIDS is an abbreviation for 'acquired immune deficiency syndrome'

ailing ['eɪlɪŋ] ADJECTIVE
1 sick or ill, and not getting better
2 getting into difficulties, especially with money *e.g. an ailing company*

ailment ['eɪlmənt] **ailments** NOUN
a minor illness

aim [eɪm] **aims, aiming, aimed** VERB
1 If you aim an object or weapon at someone or something, you point it at them.
2 If you aim to do something, you are planning or hoping to do it.

● THESAURUS
aspire: *people who aspire to public office*
attempt: *He will attempt to win the title for the second year running.*
intend: *I intend to remarry.*
plan: *Mr Beach was planning to sue over injuries he received.*
propose: *And where do you propose building such a huge thing?*
strive: *He strives hard to keep himself very fit.*
> NOUN
3 Your aim is what you intend to achieve.

● THESAURUS
ambition: *His ambition is to sail round the world.*
goal: *I have to keep setting goals for myself.*
intention: *It was always my intention to stay in Italy.*
objective: *His objective was to play golf and win.*
plan: *His plan was to acquire paintings by the best artists in Italy.*
target: *his target of 20 goals this season*

4 If you take aim, you point an object or weapon at someone or something.

aimless ['eɪmlɪs] ADJECTIVE
having no clear purpose or plan
aimlessly ADVERB, **aimlessness** NOUN

air [ɛə] **airs, airing, aired** NOUN
1 Air is the mixture of oxygen and other gases which we breathe and which forms the earth's atmosphere.
2 An air someone or something has is the impression they give. *e.g. an air of defiance*
3 'Air' is used to refer to travel in aircraft *e.g. I have to travel by air a great deal.*
> VERB
4 If you air your opinions, you talk about them to other people.

airborne ['ɛə,bɔːn] ADJECTIVE
in the air and flying

air-conditioning [,ɛəkən'dɪʃənɪŋ] NOUN
a system of providing cool, clean air in buildings
air-conditioned ADJECTIVE

aircraft ['ɛə,krɑːft] NOUN
any vehicle which can fly

airfield ['ɛə,fiːld] **airfields** NOUN
an open area of ground with runways where small aircraft take off and land

air force air forces NOUN
the part of a country's armed services that fights using aircraft

air gun **air guns** NOUN
a gun which uses air pressure to fire pellets

air hostess **air hostesses** NOUN
a woman whose job is to look after passengers
on an aircraft

airless ['ɛəlɪs] ADJECTIVE
having no wind or fresh air

airlift ['ɛə,lɪft] **airlifts** NOUN
an operation to move people or goods by air,
especially in an emergency

airline ['ɛə,laɪn] **airlines** NOUN
a company which provides air travel

airliner ['ɛə,laɪnə] **airliners** NOUN
a large passenger plane

airmail ['ɛə,meɪl] NOUN
the system of sending letters and parcels by air

airman ['ɛəmən] **airmen** NOUN
a man who serves in his country's air force

airport ['ɛə,pɔːt] **airports** NOUN
a place where people go to catch planes

air raid **air raids** NOUN
an attack by enemy aircraft, in which bombs are
dropped

airship ['ɛəʃɪp] **airships** NOUN
a large, light aircraft, consisting of a rigid balloon
filled with gas and powered by an engine, with a
passenger compartment underneath

airstrip ['ɛə,strɪp] **airstrips** NOUN
a stretch of land that has been cleared for aircraft
to take off and land

airtight ['ɛə,taɪt] ADJECTIVE
not letting air in or out

airy ['ɛərɪ] **airier, airiest** ADJECTIVE
full of fresh air and light
airily ADVERB

aisle [aɪl] **aisles** NOUN
a long narrow gap that people can walk along
between rows of seats or shelves

ajar [ə'dʒɑː] ADJECTIVE
A door or window that is ajar is slightly open.

akin [ə'kɪn] ADJECTIVE; FORMAL
similar e.g. The taste is akin to veal.

alabaster ['ælə,bɑːstə] NOUN
a type of smooth stone used for making
ornaments

alacrity [ə'lækrɪtɪ] NOUN; FORMAL
eager willingness e.g. He seized this offer with
alacrity.

alarm [ə'lɑːm] **alarms, alarming, alarmed**
NOUN
1 a feeling of fear and worry e.g. The cat sprang
back in alarm.

THESAURUS
anxiety: anxiety about crime
apprehension: I tensed every muscle in my body in
apprehension.
fright: The birds smashed into the top of their cages
in fright.
nervousness: I smiled warmly so he wouldn't see
my nervousness.
panic: There was panic in the streets of the capital.
scare: Despite the scare there are no plans to
withdraw the drug.
<<OPPOSITE calm

2 an automatic device used to warn people of
something e.g. a car alarm

THESAURUS
distress signal: The pilot was trying to send a
distress signal when the aircraft crashed.
siren: a police siren
warning: A second air raid warning sounded over
the capital.

> VERB
3 If something alarms you, it makes you worried
and anxious.
alarming ADJECTIVE

THESAURUS
distress: He is very distressed by what happened.
frighten: The future frightens me.
panic: He was panicked by his wife's behaviour.
scare: Horses scare me.
startle: startled by a gunshot
unnerve: Investors had been unnerved by the
country's ailing stockmarket.
<<OPPOSITE calm

alas [ə'læs] ADVERB
unfortunately or regrettably e.g. But, alas, it would
not be true.

Albanian [æl'beɪnɪən] **Albanians** ADJECTIVE
1 belonging or relating to Albania

> NOUN
2 someone who comes from Albania

3 Albanian is the main language spoken in
Albania.

albatross ['ælbə,trɒs] **albatrosses** NOUN
a large white sea bird

albeit [ɔːl'biːɪt] CONJUNCTION; FORMAL
although e.g. He was making progress, albeit slowly.

albino [æl'biːnəʊ] **albinos** NOUN
a person or animal with very white skin, white
hair, and pink eyes

album ['ælbəm] **albums** NOUN
1 a CD, cassette, or record with a number of
songs on it

2 a book in which you keep a collection of things
such as photographs or stamps

alchemy ['ælkəmɪ] NOUN
a medieval science that attempted to change ordinary metals into gold
alchemist NOUN

alcheringa [,æltʃə'rɪŋgə] NOUN
Alcheringa is the same as Dreamtime.

alcohol ['ælkə,hɒl] NOUN
Alcohol is any drink that can make people drunk; also the colourless flammable liquid found in these drinks, produced by fermenting sugar.

● THESAURUS
booze: informal *clutching a bottle of booze*
drink: *Too much drink is bad for you.*
grog: Australian and New Zealand; informal *They demanded a bottle of grog.*
liquor: *I could smell liquor on his breath.*
spirits: *a voluntary ban on advertising spirits on TV*

alcoholic [,ælkə'hɒlɪk] **alcoholics** ADJECTIVE
1 An alcoholic drink contains alcohol.
> NOUN
2 someone who is addicted to alcohol
alcoholism NOUN

alcopop ['ælkəʊ,pɒp] **alcopops** NOUN; INFORMAL
an alcoholic drink that tastes like a soft drink

alcove ['ælkəʊv] **alcoves** NOUN
an area of a room which is set back slightly from the main part
[WORD HISTORY: from Arabic AL-QUBBAH meaning 'arch']

ale [eɪl] NOUN
a type of beer

alert [ə'lɜːt] **alerts, alerting, alerted** ADJECTIVE
1 paying full attention to what is happening *e.g. The criminal was spotted by an alert member of the public.*

● THESAURUS
attentive: *an attentive audience*
observant: *an observant policeman*
on guard: *on guard against the threat of invasion*
vigilant: *letter bombs intercepted by vigilant post office staff*
wary: *He kept a wary eye on the dog as he passed the gate.*
<<OPPOSITE *unaware*
> NOUN
2 a situation in which people prepare themselves for danger *e.g. The troops were on a war alert.*
> VERB
3 If you alert someone to a problem or danger, you warn them of it.
alertness NOUN

● THESAURUS
forewarn: *The guide had forewarned me what to expect.*

inform: *The patient was not properly informed of the risks.*
notify: *The passengers were notified of the bomb threat.*
warn: *They warned him of the dangers of sailing alone.*

A level ['eɪ] **A levels** NOUN
an advanced exam taken by students in many British schools and colleges, usually following GCSEs

algae ['ældʒiː] PLURAL NOUN
plants that grow in water or on damp surfaces

algebra ['ældʒɪbrə] NOUN
a branch of mathematics in which symbols and letters are used instead of numbers to express relationships between quantities
algebraic ADJECTIVE
[WORD HISTORY: from Arabic AL-JABR meaning 'reunion']

Algerian [æl'dʒɪərɪən] **Algerians** ADJECTIVE
1 belonging or relating to Algeria
> NOUN
2 someone who comes from Algeria

alias ['eɪlɪəs] **aliases** NOUN
a false name *e.g. Leonard Nimoy, alias Mr Spock*

alibi ['ælɪ,baɪ] **alibis** NOUN
An alibi is evidence proving you were somewhere else when a crime was committed.

alien ['eɪljən] **aliens** ADJECTIVE
1 not normal to you *e.g. a totally alien culture*
> NOUN
2 someone who is not a citizen of the country in which he or she lives
3 In science fiction, an alien is a creature from outer space.

alienate ['eɪljə,neɪt] **alienates, alienating, alienated** VERB
If you alienate someone, you do something that makes them stop being sympathetic to you. *e.g. The Council's approach alienated many local residents.*
alienation NOUN

alight [ə'laɪt] **alights, alighting, alighted** ADJECTIVE
1 Something that is alight is burning.
> VERB
2 If a bird or insect alights somewhere, it lands there.
3 FORMAL
When passengers alight from a vehicle, they get out of it at the end of a journey.

align [ə'laɪn] **aligns, aligning, aligned** VERB
1 If you align yourself with a particular group, you support them.

2 If you align things, you place them in a straight line.

alignment NOUN

alike [ə'laɪk] ADJECTIVE

1 Things that are alike are similar in some way.

THESAURUS

analogous: *a ritual analogous to those of primitive cultures*

close: *a creature close in appearance to a panther*

identical: *Nearly all the houses were identical.*

similar: *These two wines are very similar in taste.*

the same: *products which are almost the same in every respect*

<<OPPOSITE *different*

> ADVERB

2 If people or things are treated alike, they are treated in a similar way.

THESAURUS

equally: *Democracy calls for all people to be treated equally.*

in the same way: *He speaks in the same way to his boss as to his own employees.*

similarly: *All the children were dressed similarly.*

uniformly: *The rules apply uniformly to everyone.*

alimony ['ælɪmənɪ] NOUN

money someone has to pay regularly to their wife or husband after they are divorced

alive [ə'laɪv] ADJECTIVE

1 living

THESAURUS

animate: *animate beings*

breathing: *Not only is he still breathing, but he lives right here in New York.*

living: *The blue whale is the largest living thing on the planet.*

<<OPPOSITE *dead*

2 lively and active

THESAURUS

active: *half an hour's physical activity, five times a week, will keep you active*

alert: *A brisk walk will make you feel more alert.*

animated: *He becomes animated when talking about his work.*

energetic: *a vital and energetic man*

full of life: *She was so chatty and full of life.*

lively: *Cheryl was a very lively and attractive girl.*

vivacious: *a vivacious personality*

<<OPPOSITE *dull*

alkali ['ælkə,laɪ] **alkalis** NOUN

(SCIENCE) a chemical substance that turns litmus paper blue

alkaline ADJECTIVE, **alkalinity** NOUN

all [ɔːl] ADJECTIVE, PRONOUN, OR ADVERB

1 used when referring to the whole of something *e.g. Why did he have to say all that? She managed to finish it all.*

THESAURUS

each: *Each of us received a free gift.*

every one: *Every one of you must take a share of the blame.*

everything: *Sit down and tell me everything.*

the whole amount: *Have you paid the whole amount of the fine?*

the (whole) lot: *The whole lot of you are under arrest.*

> ADVERB

2 'All' is also used when saying the two sides in a game or contest have the same score *e.g. The final score was six points all.*

Allah ['ælə] PROPER NOUN

the Muslim name for God

allay [ə'leɪ] **allays, allaying, allayed** VERB

To allay someone's fears or doubts is to stop them feeling afraid or doubtful.

allege [ə'lɛdʒ] **alleges, alleging, alleged** VERB

If you allege that something is true, you say it is true but do not provide any proof. *e.g. It is alleged that she died as a result of neglect.*

allegation NOUN, **alleged** ADJECTIVE

allegiance [ə'liːdʒəns] **allegiances** NOUN

loyal support for a person or organization

allegory ['ælɪgərɪ] **allegories** NOUN

a piece of writing or art in which the characters and events are symbols for something else. Allegories usually make some moral, religious, or political point. For example, George Orwell's novel 'Animal Farm' is an allegory in that the animals who revolt in the farmyard are symbols of the political leaders in the Russian Revolution

allergy ['ælədʒɪ] **allergies** NOUN

a sensitivity someone has to something, so that they become ill when they eat it or touch it *e.g. an allergy to cows' milk*

alleviate [ə'liːvɪ,eɪt] **alleviates, alleviating, alleviated** VERB

To alleviate pain or a problem is to make it less severe. *e.g. measures to alleviate poverty*

alleviation NOUN

alley ['ælɪ] **alleys** NOUN

a narrow passage between buildings

alliance [ə'laɪəns] **alliances** NOUN

a group of people, organizations, or countries working together for similar aims

alligator ['ælɪ,geɪtə] **alligators** NOUN

a large animal, similar to a crocodile

[WORD HISTORY: from Spanish EL LAGARTO meaning 'lizard']

alliteration [ə,lɪtə'reɪʃən] NOUN **(ENGLISH)** LITERARY

the use of several words together which all begin with the same sound, for example 'around the ragged rock the ragged rascal ran'
alliterative ADJECTIVE

allocate ['ælə,keɪt] **allocates, allocating, allocated** VERB
If you allocate something, you decide it should be given to a person or place, or used for a particular purpose. *e.g. funds allocated for nursery education*
allocation NOUN

allot [ə'lɒt] **allots, allotting, allotted** VERB
If something is allotted to you, it is given to you as your share. *e.g. Space was allotted for visitors' cars.*

allotment [ə'lɒtmənt] **allotments** NOUN
1 a piece of land which people can rent to grow vegetables on
2 a share of something

allow [ə'laʊ] **allows, allowing, allowed** VERB
1 If you allow something, you say it is all right or let it happen.

● **THESAURUS**
approve: *The Housing Minister approved the building of the flats.*
authorize: *authorized to carry weapons*
let: *They won't let her leave the country.*
permit: *Unauthorized personnel are not permitted to enter.*
stand for: *We won't stand for it any more.*
tolerate: *I won't tolerate sloppiness.*
<<OPPOSITE *forbid*

2 If you allow a period of time or an amount of something, you set it aside for a particular purpose. *e.g. Allow four hours for the paint to dry.*
allowable ADJECTIVE

● **THESAURUS**
allocate: *an efficient method of allocating resources*
allot: *We were allotted just 15 minutes.*
assign: *the full amount of economic aid assigned for the year*
grant: *Funding had been granted for the project.*
set aside: *money set aside for education*

Do not confuse the spellings of the past tense form *allowed* and the adverb *aloud*, which sound the same

allowance [ə'laʊəns] **allowances** NOUN
1 money given regularly to someone for a particular purpose *e.g. a petrol allowance*
> PHRASE
2 If you **make allowances** for something, you take it into account. *e.g. The school made allowances for Muslim cultural customs.*

alloy ['ælɔɪ] **alloys** NOUN
a mixture of two or more metals

all right or **alright** ADJECTIVE
1 If something is all right, it is acceptable.

● **THESAURUS**
acceptable: *We've made an acceptable start, but it could have been better.*
adequate: *Our accommodation was adequate.*
average: *I was only average academically.*
fair: *The overall standard of the entries was fair.*
okay or **OK:** informal *The prices here are okay.*

2 If someone is all right, they are safe and not harmed.
3 You say 'all right' to agree to something.

allude [ə'luːd] **alludes, alluding, alluded** VERB
If you allude to something, you refer to it in an indirect way.

You *allude to* something. Do not confuse *allude* with *elude*

allure [ə'ljʊə] NOUN
The allure of something is an exciting quality that makes it attractive. *e.g. the allure of foreign travel*
alluring ADJECTIVE

allusion [ə'luːʒən] **allusions** NOUN
an indirect reference to or comment about something *e.g. English literature is full of classical allusions.*

ally **allies, allying, allied** NOUN ['ælaɪ]
1 a person or country that helps and supports another
> VERB [ə'laɪ]
2 If you ally yourself with someone, you agree to help and support each other.

almanac ['ɔːlmə,næk] **almanacs** NOUN
a book published every year giving information about a particular subject

almighty [ɔːl'maɪtɪ] ADJECTIVE
1 very great or serious *e.g. I've just had an almighty row with the chairman.*
> PROPER NOUN
2 The Almighty is another name for God.

almond ['ɑːmənd] **almonds** NOUN
a pale brown oval nut

almost ['ɔːlməʊst] ADVERB
very nearly *e.g. Prices have almost doubled.*

● **THESAURUS**
about: *I was about nine at the time.*
approximately: *The family owns approximately 8% of the company.*
close to: *He spent close to 30 years in prison.*
nearly: *The beach was very nearly empty.*
not quite: *It's more than a hill but not quite a mountain.*

practically: *I've known him practically all my life.*

alms [ɑːmz] PLURAL NOUN; OLD-FASHIONED, INFORMAL
Alms are gifts of money, food, or clothing to poor people.

aloft [əˈlɒft] ADVERB
up in the air or in a high position *e.g. He held aloft the trophy.*

alone [əˈləʊn] ADJECTIVE OR ADVERB
not with other people or things *e.g. He just wanted to be alone.*

● THESAURUS
detached: *a 'counter-culture' detached from the rest of the world*
isolated: *Talking things over in a group meant none of us felt isolated.*
separate: *They were kept separate from the other prisoners.*
single: *I get depressed on Valentine's Day because I'm still single.*

along [əˈlɒŋ] PREPOSITION
1 moving, happening, or existing continuously from one end to the other of something, or at various points beside it *e.g. Put rivets along the top edge.*
> ADVERB
2 moving forward *e.g. We marched along, singing as we went.*
3 with someone *e.g. Why could she not take her along?*
> PHRASE
4 All along means from the beginning of a period of time right up to now *e.g. You've known that all along.*

alongside [əˈlɒŋˌsaɪd] PREPOSITION OR ADVERB
1 next to something *e.g. They had a house in the park alongside the river.*
> PREPOSITION
2 If you work alongside other people, you are working in the same place and cooperating with them. *e.g. He was thrilled to work alongside Robert De Niro.*

▓ Do not use *of* after *alongside*

aloof [əˈluːf] ADJECTIVE
distant from someone or something

aloud [əˈlaʊd] ADVERB
When you read or speak aloud, you speak loudly enough for other people to hear you.

● THESAURUS
audibly: *Hugh sighed audibly.*
out loud: *I tried not to laugh out loud.*

▓ Do not confuse the spellings of *aloud* and *allowed*, the past tense form of *allow.*

alphabet [ˈælfəˌbɛt] **alphabets** NOUN
(LIBRARY) a set of letters in a fixed order that is used in writing a language
alphabetical ADJECTIVE, **alphabetically** ADVERB

alpine [ˈælpaɪn] ADJECTIVE
existing in or relating to high mountains *e.g. alpine flowers*
[WORD HISTORY: from THE ALPS, a mountain range in central Europe]

already [ɔːlˈrɛdɪ] ADVERB
having happened before the present time or earlier than expected *e.g. She has already gone to bed.*

alright [ɔːlˈraɪt] another spelling of **all right**

▓ Some people think that *all right* is the only correct spelling and that *alright* is wrong

Alsatian [ælˈseɪʃən] **Alsatians** NOUN
a large wolflike dog

also [ˈɔːlsəʊ] ADVERB
in addition to something that has just been mentioned

● THESAURUS
as well: *She published historical novels as well.*
besides: *You get to sample lots of baked things and take home masses of cookies besides.*
furthermore: *Furthermore, they claim that any such interference is completely ineffective.*
into the bargain: *The machine can play ordinary cassettes into the bargain.*
moreover: *They have accused the government of corruption. Moreover, they have named names.*
too: *I was there too.*

altar [ˈɔːltə] **altars** NOUN
a holy table in a church or temple

alter [ˈɔːltə] **alters, altering, altered** VERB
If something alters or if you alter it, it changes.
alteration NOUN

▓ Do not confuse the spellings of *alter and altar*

altercation [ˌɔːltəˈkeɪʃən] **altercations** NOUN; FORMAL
a noisy disagreement

alternate alternates, alternating, alternated VERB [ˈɔːltəˌneɪt]
1 If one thing alternates with another, the two things regularly occur one after the other.
> ADJECTIVE [ɔːlˈtɜːnɪt]
2 If something happens on alternate days, it happens on the first day but not the second, and happens again on the third day but not the fourth, and so on.
3 (MATHS) Alternate angles are two angles on opposite sides of a line that crosses two other lines.

25

alternately ADVERB, **alternation** NOUN

alternating current [ˈɔːltəˌneɪtɪŋ]
alternating currents NOUN
a current that regularly changes its direction, so that the electrons flow first one way and then the other

alternative [ɔːlˈtɜːnətɪv] **alternatives**
NOUN
1 something you can do or have instead of something else e.g. alternatives to prison such as community service
> ADJECTIVE
2 Alternative plans or actions can happen or be done instead of what is already happening or being done.
alternatively ADVERB

> If there are more than two choices in a situation you should say there are three choices rather than there are three alternatives because the strict meaning of alternative is a choice between two things

although [ɔːlˈðəʊ] CONJUNCTION
in spite of the fact that e.g. He wasn't well-known in America, although he did make a film there.

altitude [ˈæltɪˌtjuːd] **altitudes** NOUN
The altitude of something is its height above sea level. e.g. The mountain range reaches an altitude of 1330 metres.

altogether [ˌɔːltəˈgɛðə] ADVERB
1 entirely e.g. She wasn't altogether sorry to be leaving.
2 in total; used of amounts e.g. I get paid 1000 pounds a month altogether.

aluminium [ˌæljʊˈmɪniəm] NOUN
a silvery-white lightweight metal

always [ˈɔːlweɪz] ADVERB
all the time or for ever e.g. She's always moaning.
● THESAURUS
continually: Malcolm was continually changing his mind.
every time: You can't get it right every time.
forever: He was forever attempting to arrange deals.
invariably: Their teamwork was invariably good.
perpetually: The two groups are perpetually at loggerheads.

am [æm] the first person singular, present tense of **be**

a.m.
used to specify times between 12 midnight and 12 noon, eg I get up at 6 a.m. It is an abbreviation for the Latin phrase 'ante meridiem', which means 'before noon'

amalgamate [əˈmælgəˌmeɪt]
amalgamates, amalgamating, amalgamated VERB

If two organizations amalgamate, they join together to form one new organization.
amalgamation NOUN

amandla [aˈmɑːndla] NOUN
In South Africa, amandla is a political slogan which calls for power for Black people.

amass [əˈmæs] **amasses, amassing, amassed** VERB
If you amass something such as money or information, you collect large quantities of it. e.g. He amassed a huge fortune.

amateur [ˈæmətə] **amateurs** NOUN
someone who does something as a hobby rather than as a job

amateurish [ˈæmətərɪʃ] ADJECTIVE
not skilfully made or done
amateurishly ADVERB

amaze [əˈmeɪz] **amazes, amazing, amazed** VERB
If something amazes you, it surprises you very much.
● THESAURUS
astonish: I was astonished by his stupidity.
astound: I am astounded at the comments made by the Chief Superintendent.
shock: She was shocked by the appalling news.
stagger: He was staggered by the sheer size of the crowd.
stun: Many cinema-goers were stunned by the film's tragic end.
surprise: We'll solve the case ourselves and surprise everyone.

amazement [əˈmeɪzmənt] NOUN
complete surprise
● THESAURUS
astonishment: They looked at each other in astonishment.
shock: I am still getting over the shock of winning.
surprise: To my surprise, I found I liked it.
wonder: Cross shook his head in wonder.

amazing [əˈmeɪzɪŋ] ADJECTIVE
very surprising or remarkable
amazingly ADVERB
● THESAURUS
astonishing: an astonishing display of physical strength
astounding: The results are quite astounding.
staggering: a staggering 17% leap in sales
startling: startling new evidence
stunning: a stunning piece of news
surprising: A surprising number of customers order the same sandwich every day.

ambassador [æmˈbæsədə] **ambassadors** NOUN
a person sent to a foreign country as the

representative of his or her own government

amber ['æmbə] NOUN

1 a hard, yellowish-brown substance used for making jewellery

> NOUN OR ADJECTIVE

2 orange-brown

ambi- PREFIX

'Ambi-' means 'both'. For example, something which is *ambiguous* can have either of two meanings.

[WORD HISTORY: from Latin AMBO meaning 'both']

ambidextrous [,æmbɪ'dɛkstrəs] ADJECTIVE

Someone who is ambidextrous is able to use both hands equally skilfully.

ambience ['æmbɪəns] NOUN; FORMAL

The ambience of a place is its atmosphere.

ambient ['æmbɪənt] ADJECTIVE

1 surrounding *e.g. low ambient temperatures*

2 creating a relaxing atmosphere *e.g. ambient music*

ambiguous [æm'bɪgjʊəs] ADJECTIVE

A word or phrase that is ambiguous has more than one meaning.

ambiguously ADVERB, **ambiguity** NOUN

ambition [æm'bɪʃən] **ambitions** NOUN

1 If you have an ambition to achieve something, you want very much to achieve it. *e.g. His ambition is to be an actor.*

2 a great desire for success, power, and wealth *e.g. He's talented and full of ambition.*

ambitious [æm'bɪʃəs] ADJECTIVE

1 Someone who is ambitious has a strong desire for success, power, and wealth.

2 An ambitious plan is a large one and requires a lot of work. *e.g. an ambitious rebuilding schedule*

ambivalent [æm'bɪvələnt] ADJECTIVE

having or showing two conflicting attitudes or emotions

ambivalence NOUN

amble ['æmbəl] **ambles, ambling, ambled** VERB

If you amble, you walk slowly and in a relaxed manner.

ambulance ['æmbjʊləns] **ambulances** NOUN

a vehicle for taking sick and injured people to hospital

ambush ['æmbʊʃ] **ambushes, ambushing, ambushed** VERB

1 To ambush someone is to attack them after hiding and lying in wait for them.

> NOUN

2 an attack on someone after hiding and lying in wait for them

amen [,eɪ'mɛn] INTERJECTION

Amen is said at the end of a Christian prayer. It means 'so be it'.

amenable [ə'miːnəbəl] ADJECTIVE

willing to listen to suggestions, or to cooperate with someone *e.g. Both brothers were amenable to the arrangement.*

amenably ADVERB, **amenability** NOUN

amend [ə'mɛnd] **amends, amending, amended** VERB

1 To amend something that has been written or said is to alter it slightly. *e.g. Our constitution had to be amended.*

> PLURAL NOUN

2 If you make amends for something bad you have done, you say you are sorry and try to make up for it.

amendment NOUN

amenity [ə'miːnɪtɪ] **amenities** NOUN

(GEOGRAPHY) Amenities are things that are available for the public to use, such as sports facilities or shopping centres.

America [ə'mɛrɪkə] NOUN

America refers to the United States, or to the whole of North, South, and Central America.

American [ə'mɛrɪkən] **Americans** ADJECTIVE

1 belonging or relating to the United States, or to the whole of North, South, and Central America

> NOUN

2 someone who comes from the United States

amethyst ['æmɪθɪst] **amethysts** NOUN

a type of purple semiprecious stone

[WORD HISTORY: from Greek AMETHUSTOS meaning 'not drunk'. It was thought to prevent intoxication]

amiable ['eɪmɪəbəl] ADJECTIVE

pleasant and friendly *e.g. The hotel staff were very amiable.*

amiably ADVERB, **amiability** NOUN

amicable ['æmɪkəbəl] ADJECTIVE

fairly friendly *e.g. an amicable divorce*

amicably ADVERB

amid or **amidst** [ə'mɪd] or [ə'mɪdst] PREPOSITION; FORMAL

surrounded by *e.g. She enjoys cooking amid her friends.*

The form *amidst* is a bit old-fashioned and *amid* is more often used

amiss [ə'mɪs] ADJECTIVE

If something is amiss, there is something wrong.

ammonia [ə'məʊnɪə] NOUN

Ammonia is a colourless, strong-smelling gas or liquid.

ammunition [ˌæmjʊˈnɪʃən] NOUN
anything that can be fired from a gun or other weapon, for example bullets and shells

amnesia [æmˈniːzjə] NOUN
loss of memory

amnesty [ˈæmnɪstɪ] **amnesties** NOUN
an official pardon for political or other prisoners

amoeba [əˈmiːbə] **amoebas** or **amoebae**
(*said* am-**mee**-ba); also spelt ameba NOUN
the smallest kind of living creature, consisting of one cell. Amoebas reproduce by dividing into two

amok [əˈmɒk] PHRASE
If a person or animal **runs amok**, they behave in a violent and uncontrolled way.
[WORD HISTORY: a Malay word]

among or **amongst** [əˈmʌŋ] or [əˈmʌŋst]
PREPOSITION
1 surrounded by *e.g. The bike lay among piles of chains and pedals.*

● THESAURUS
amid: *a tiny bungalow amid clusters of trees*
amidst: *His parents were found dead amidst the wreckage of the plane.*
in the middle of: *a tiny island in the middle of the Pacific*
in the thick of: *a restaurant built on stilts in the thick of a vast mangrove swamp*
surrounded by: *surrounded by bodyguards*
2 in the company of *e.g. He was among friends.*
3 between more than two *e.g. The money will be divided among seven charities.*

● THESAURUS
between: *Proceeds from the auction will be shared between the artists.*
to each of: *£2,000 to each of the five winners*

> If there are more than two things, you should use *among*. If there are only two things you should use *between*. The form *amongst* is a bit old-fashioned and *among* is more often used

amoral [eɪˈmɒrəl] ADJECTIVE
Someone who is amoral has no moral standards by which to live.

> Do not confuse *amoral* and *immoral*. You use *amoral* to talk about people with no moral standards, but *immoral* for people who are aware of moral standards but go against them.

amorous [ˈæmərəs] ADJECTIVE
passionately affectionate *e.g. an amorous relationship*
amorously ADVERB, **amorousness** NOUN

amount [əˈmaʊnt] **amounts, amounting, amounted** (MATHS) NOUN
1 An amount of something is how much there is of it.

● THESAURUS
expanse: *a vast expanse of grassland*
quantity: *vast quantities of food*
volume: *the sheer volume of traffic and accidents*

> VERB
2 If something amounts to a particular total, all the parts of it add up to that total. *e.g. Her vocabulary amounted to only 50 words.*

amp [æmp] **amps** NOUN
An amp is the same as an ampere.

ampere [ˈæmpɛə] **amperes** NOUN
a unit which is used for measuring electric current

ampersand [ˈæmpəˌsænd] **ampersands** NOUN
the character &, meaning 'and'

amphetamine [æmˈfɛtəˌmiːn] **amphetamines** NOUN
a drug that increases people's energy and makes them excited. It can have dangerous and unpleasant side effects

amphibian [æmˈfɪbɪən] **amphibians** NOUN
(SCIENCE) a creature that lives partly on land and partly in water, for example a frog or a newt

amphibious [æmˈfɪbɪəs] ADJECTIVE
An amphibious animal, such as a frog, lives partly on land and partly in the water.
[WORD HISTORY: from Greek AMPHIBIOS meaning 'having a double life']

amphitheatre [ˈæmfɪˌθɪətə] **amphitheatres** NOUN
a large, semicircular open area with sloping sides covered with rows of seats

ample [ˈæmpəl] ADJECTIVE
If there is an ample amount of something, there is more than enough of it.
amply ADVERB

● THESAURUS
abundant: *providing abundant food for local wildlife*
enough: *Do you have enough money for a taxi home?*
plenty of: *You've had plenty of time to make up your mind.*
sufficient: *The police have sufficient evidence to charge him.*

amplifier [ˈæmplɪˌfaɪə] **amplifiers** NOUN
a piece of equipment in a radio or stereo system which causes sounds or signals to become louder

amplify [ˈæmplɪˌfaɪ] **amplifies, amplifying, amplified** VERB
If you amplify a sound, you make it louder.
amplification NOUN

amplitude ['æmplɪ,tjuːd] NOUN
In physics, the amplitude of a wave is how far its curve moves away from its normal position.

amputate ['æmpjʊ,teɪt] **amputates, amputating, amputated** VERB
To amputate an arm or a leg is to cut it off as a surgical operation.
amputation NOUN

Amrit ['æmrɪt] NOUN
1 In the Sikh religion, Amrit is a special mixture of sugar and water used in rituals.
2 The Amrit or Amrit ceremony takes place when someone is accepted as a full member of the Sikh community, and drinks Amrit as part of the ceremony.

amuse [ə'mjuːz] **amuses, amusing, amused** VERB
1 If something amuses you, you think it is funny.
2 If you amuse yourself, you find things to do which stop you from being bored.
amused ADJECTIVE, **amusing** ADJECTIVE

amusement [ə'mjuːzmənt] **amusements** NOUN
1 Amusement is the state of thinking something is funny.
2 Amusement is also the pleasure you get from being entertained or from doing something interesting.
3 Amusements are ways of passing the time pleasantly.

an [æn] ADJECTIVE
'An' is used instead of 'a' in front of words that begin with a vowel sound

> You use *an* in front of abbreviations that start with a vowel sound when they are read out loud: *an MA; an OBE.*

-an SUFFIX
'-an' comes at the end of nouns and adjectives which show where or what someone or something comes from or belongs to *e.g. American... Victorian... Christian.*
[WORD HISTORY: from Latin -ĀNUS meaning 'of or belonging to']

anachronism [ə'nækrə,nɪzəm] **anachronisms** NOUN
something that belongs or seems to belong to another time
anachronistic ADJECTIVE
[WORD HISTORY: from Greek ANAKHRONISMOS meaning 'mistake in time']

anaemia [ə'niːmɪə] NOUN
a medical condition resulting from too few red cells in a person's blood. People with anaemia look pale and feel very tired
anaemic ADJECTIVE

anaesthetic [,ænɪs'θɛtɪk] **anaesthetics** NOUN
a substance that stops you feeling pain. A general anaesthetic stops you from feeling pain in the whole of your body by putting you to sleep, and a local anaesthetic makes just one part of your body go numb

anaesthetist [ə'niːsθətɪst] **anaesthetists** NOUN
a doctor who is specially trained to give anaesthetics

anaesthetize [ə'niːsθə,taɪz] **anaesthetizes, anaesthetizing, anaesthetized**; also spelt **anaesthetise** or **anaesthetise** VERB
To anaesthetize someone is to give them an anaesthetic to make them unconscious.

anagram ['ænə,græm] **anagrams** NOUN
a word or phrase formed by changing the order of the letters of another word or phrase. For example, 'triangle' is an anagram of 'integral'

anal ['eɪnᵊl] ADJECTIVE
relating to the anus

analgesic [,ænᵊl'dʒiːzɪk] **analgesics** NOUN
a substance that relieves pain

analogy [ə'nælədʒɪ] **analogies** NOUN
a comparison showing that two things are similar in some ways
analogous ADJECTIVE

analyse ['ænᵊ,laɪz] **analyses, analysing, analysed** VERB
(EXAM TERM) To analyse something is to break it down into parts, or investigate it carefully, so that you can describe its main aspects, or find out what it consists of.

analysis [ə'nælɪsɪs] **analyses** NOUN
the process of investigating something in order to understand it or find out what it consists of
e.g. a full analysis of the problem

analyst ['ænəlɪst] **analysts** NOUN
a person whose job is to analyse things to find out about them

analytic or **analytical** [,ænə'lɪtɪk] *or* [,ænə'lɪtɪkᵊl] ADJECTIVE
using logical reasoning *e.g. Planning in detail requires an acute analytical mind.*
analytically ADVERB

anarchy ['ænəkɪ] NOUN
a situation where nobody obeys laws or rules
[WORD HISTORY: from Greek ANARKHOS meaning 'without a ruler']

anatomy [ə'nætəmɪ] **anatomies** NOUN

1 the study of the structure of the human body or of the bodies of animals

2 An animal's anatomy is the structure of its body.

anatomical ADJECTIVE, **anatomically** ADVERB

ANC NOUN
one of the main political parties in South Africa. ANC is an abbreviation for 'African National Congress'

ancestor ['ænsɛstə] **ancestors** NOUN
Your ancestors are the members of your family who lived many years ago and from whom you are descended.
ancestral ADJECTIVE

THESAURUS
forebear: *our Victorian forebears*
forefather: *the land of their forefathers*

ancestry ['ænsɛstrɪ] **ancestries** NOUN
Your ancestry consists of the people from whom you are descended. *e.g. a French citizen of Greek ancestry*

anchor ['æŋkə] **anchors, anchoring, anchored** NOUN
1 a heavy, hooked object at the end of a chain, dropped from a boat into the water to keep the boat in one place
> VERB
2 To anchor a boat or another object is to stop it from moving by dropping an anchor or attaching it to something solid.

anchorage ['æŋkərɪdʒ] **anchorages** NOUN
a place where a boat can safely anchor

anchovy ['æntʃəvɪ] **anchovies** NOUN
a type of small edible fish with a very strong salty taste

ancient ['eɪnʃənt] ADJECTIVE
1 existing or happening in the distant past *e.g. ancient Greece*
2 very old or having a very long history *e.g. an ancient monastery*

ancillary [æn'sɪlərɪ] ADJECTIVE
The ancillary workers in an institution are the people such as cooks and cleaners, whose work supports the main work of the institution.
[WORD HISTORY: from Latin ANCILLA meaning 'maidservant']

and [ænd] CONJUNCTION
You use 'and' to link two or more words or phrases together.

androgynous [æn'drɒdʒɪnəs] ADJECTIVE; FORMAL
having both male and female characteristics

android ['ændrɔɪd] **androids** NOUN
in science fiction, a robot that looks like a human being

anecdote ['ænɪkˌdəʊt] **anecdotes** NOUN
a short, entertaining story about a person or event
anecdotal ADJECTIVE

anemone [ə'nɛmənɪ] **anemones** NOUN
a plant with red, purple, or white flowers

anew [ə'njuː] ADVERB
If you do something anew, you do it again. *e.g. They left their life in Britain to start anew in France.*

angel ['eɪndʒəl] **angels** NOUN
Angels are spiritual beings some people believe live in heaven and act as messengers for God.
angelic ADJECTIVE

anger ['æŋgə] **angers, angering, angered** NOUN
1 the strong feeling you get when you feel someone has behaved in an unfair or cruel way

THESAURUS
fury: *She screamed, her face distorted in fury.*
outrage: *The decisions provoked outrage from human rights groups.*
rage: *An intense rage was burning inside her.*
wrath: *He incurred the wrath of the referee.*

> VERB
2 If something angers you, it makes you feel angry.

THESAURUS
enrage: *He enraged the government by renouncing the agreement.*
infuriate: *Peter's presence had infuriated Gordon.*
outrage: *Customers are outraged by the bank's soaring profits.*
<<OPPOSITE calm

angina [æn'dʒaɪnə] NOUN
a brief but very severe heart pain, caused by lack of blood supply to the heart. It is also known as 'angina pectoris'

angle ['æŋgəl] **angles** NOUN
1 (**MATHS**) the distance between two lines at the point where they join together. Angles are measured in degrees
2 the direction from which you look at something *e.g. He had painted the vase from all angles.*
3 An angle on something is a particular way of considering it. *e.g. the same story from a German angle*

angler ['æŋglə] **anglers** NOUN
someone who fishes with a fishing rod as a hobby
angling NOUN
[WORD HISTORY: from Old English ANGUL meaning 'fish-hook']

Anglican ['æŋglɪkən] **Anglicans** NOUN OR ADJECTIVE

a member of one of the churches belonging to the Anglican Communion, a group of Protestant churches which includes the Church of England

Anglo-Saxon [ˈæŋɡləʊˈsæksən] **Anglo-Saxons** NOUN

1 The Anglo-Saxons were a race of people who settled in England from the fifth century AD and were the dominant people until the Norman invasion in 1066. They were composed of three West Germanic tribes, the Angles, Saxons, and Jutes.

2 Anglo-Saxon is another name for **Old English**

Angolan [ænˈɡəʊlən] **Angolans** ADJECTIVE

1 belonging or relating to Angola

> NOUN

2 someone who comes from Angola

angora [ænˈɡɔːrə] ADJECTIVE

1 An angora goat or rabbit is a breed with long silky hair.

> NOUN

2 Angora is this hair, usually mixed with other fibres to make clothing.

[WORD HISTORY: from ANGORA, the former name of Ankara in Turkey]

angry [ˈæŋɡrɪ] **angrier, angriest** ADJECTIVE
very cross or annoyed
angrily ADVERB

◉ THESAURUS

cross: *She was rather cross about having to trail across London.*

enraged: *The enraged crowd stoned the car, then set it on fire.*

furious: *He is furious at the way his wife has been treated.*

mad: informal *I'm pretty mad about it, I can tell you.*

angst [æŋst] NOUN
a feeling of anxiety and worry

anguish [ˈæŋɡwɪʃ] NOUN
extreme suffering
anguished ADJECTIVE

angular [ˈæŋɡjʊlə] ADJECTIVE
Angular things have straight lines and sharp points. *e.g. He has an angular face and pointed chin.*

animal [ˈænɪməl] **animals** NOUN
any living being except a plant, or any mammal except a human being
[WORD HISTORY: from Latin ANIMA meaning 'life' or 'soul']

◉ THESAURUS

beast: *the threat our ancestors faced from wild beasts*

creature: *sea creatures*

animate [ˈænɪmeɪt] **animates, animating, animated** VERB

To animate something is to make it lively and interesting.

animated [ˈænɪˌmeɪtɪd] ADJECTIVE
lively and interesting *e.g. an animated conversation*

animation [ˌænɪˈmeɪʃən] NOUN

1 a method of film-making in which a series of drawings are photographed. When the film is projected, the characters in the drawings appear to move

2 Someone who has animation shows liveliness in the way they speak and act. *e.g. The crowd showed no sign of animation.*
animator NOUN

animosity [ˌænɪˈmɒsɪtɪ] **animosities** NOUN
a feeling of strong dislike and anger towards someone

◉ THESAURUS

antagonism: *a history of antagonism between the two sides*

antipathy: *our growing antipathy towards our manager*

dislike: *She looked at him with dislike.*

hatred: *He didn't bother to conceal his hatred towards my mother.*

hostility: *unacceptable hostility toward minority groups*

ill will: *He didn't bear anyone any ill will.*

malice: *There was no malice in her voice.*

resentment: *There is growing resentment towards newcomers.*

aniseed [ˈænɪˌsiːd] NOUN
a substance made from the seeds of a Mediterranean plant and used as a flavouring in sweets, drinks, and medicine

ankle [ˈæŋkəl] **ankles** NOUN
the joint which connects your foot to your leg

annex **annexes, annexing, annexed;** also spelt **annexe** NOUN [ˈænɛks]

1 an extra building which is joined to a larger main building

2 an extra part added to a document

> VERB [æˈnɛks]

3 If one country annexes another, it seizes the other country and takes control of it.
annexation NOUN

annihilate [əˈnaɪəˌleɪt] **annihilates, annihilating, annihilated** VERB
If something is annihilated, it is completely destroyed.
annihilation NOUN

anniversary [ˌænɪˈvɜːsərɪ] **anniversaries** NOUN
a date which is remembered because something special happened on that date in a previous year

announce [ə'naʊns] **announces, announcing, announced** VERB
If you announce something, you tell people about it publicly or officially. *e.g. The team was announced on Friday morning.*

THESAURUS
advertise: *He did not want to advertise his presence in the town.*
make known: *Details will be made known tomorrow.*
proclaim: *He loudly proclaimed his innocence.*
reveal: *They were now free to reveal the truth.*
tell: *She was relieved that she'd finally told the full story.*

announcement [ə'naʊnsmənt] **announcements** NOUN
a statement giving information about something

THESAURUS
advertisement: *an advertisement placed in the local newspaper*
broadcast: *In a broadcast on state radio the government announced its plans.*
bulletin: *At 3.30pm a bulletin was released announcing the decision.*
declaration: *a public declaration of support*
report: *Local press reports estimate that at least sixteen people have died.*
statement: *a short statement by her solicitors*

announcer [ə'naʊnsə] **announcers** NOUN
someone who introduces programmes on radio and television

annoy [ə'nɔɪ] **annoys, annoying, annoyed** VERB
If someone or something annoys you, they irritate you and make you fairly angry.
annoyed ADJECTIVE

THESAURUS
bother: *I didn't think it would bother me so much to see Brian again.*
displease: *Not wishing to displease her, he avoided answering the question.*
get on someone's nerves: informal *That song gets on my nerves.*
hack off: British and New Zealand; slang *This will just hack people off more.*
hassle: informal *Then my husband started hassling me.*
irritate: *The flippancy in her voice seemed to irritate him.*
plague: *We were plagued by mosquitoes.*
vex: *Cassandra was vexed at not having noticed it herself.*

annoyance [ə'nɔɪəns] NOUN
1 a feeling of irritation

THESAURUS
displeasure: *She voiced her displeasure at her treatment.*

irritation: *He tried not to let his irritation show.*
2 something that causes irritation

THESAURUS
bore: *It's a bore to be off sick.*
drag: informal *A dry sandwich is a drag to eat.*
nuisance: *He could be a bit of a nuisance when he was drunk.*
pain: informal *The peacocks are a pain - beautiful but noisy.*
pain in the neck: informal *Traffic jams are a pain in the neck.*
pest: *He climbed on the table, pulled my hair, and was generally a pest.*

annual [ˈænjʊəl] **annuals** ADJECTIVE
1 happening or done once a year *e.g. their annual conference*
2 happening or calculated over a period of one year *e.g. the United States' annual budget for national defence*
> NOUN
3 a book or magazine published once a year
4 a plant that grows, flowers, and dies within one year
annually ADVERB

annuity [ə'njuːɪtɪ] **annuities** NOUN
a fixed sum of money paid to someone every year from an investment or insurance policy

annul [ə'nʌl] **annuls, annulling, annulled** VERB
If a marriage or contract is annulled, it is declared invalid, so that legally it is considered never to have existed.
annulment NOUN

anoint [ə'nɔɪnt] **anoints, anointing, anointed** VERB
To anoint someone is to put oil on them as part of a ceremony.
anointment NOUN

anomaly [ə'nɒməlɪ] **anomalies** NOUN
Something is an anomaly if it is unusual or different from normal.
anomalous ADJECTIVE

anon. an abbreviation for **anonymous**

anonymous [ə'nɒnɪməs] ADJECTIVE
If something is anonymous, nobody knows who is responsible for it. *e.g. The police received an anonymous phone call.*
anonymously ADVERB, **anonymity** NOUN

anorak [ˈænəˌræk] **anoraks** NOUN
a warm waterproof jacket, usually with a hood
[WORD HISTORY: an Inuit word]

anorexia [ˌænɒˈrɛksɪə] NOUN
a psychological illness in which the person refuses to eat because they are frightened of becoming fat

a

anorexic ADJECTIVE
[WORD HISTORY: from Greek AN- + OREXIS meaning 'no appetite']

another [ə'nʌðə] ADJECTIVE OR PRONOUN
Another thing or person is an additional thing or person.

answer ['ɑːnsə] **answers, answering, answered** VERB
1 If you answer someone, you reply to them using words or actions or in writing.
THESAURUS
reply: *He replied that this was absolutely impossible.*
respond: *'Mind your manners, lady!' I responded.*
retort: *Was he afraid, he was asked. 'Afraid of what?' he retorted.*
<<OPPOSITE ask
> NOUN
2 the reply you give when you answer someone
THESAURUS
reply: *I called out a challenge but there was no reply.*
response: *There has been no response to his remarks from the government.*
retort: *His sharp retort clearly made an impact.*
<<OPPOSITE question
3 a solution to a problem

answerable ['ɑːnsərəbᵊl] ADJECTIVE
If you are answerable to someone for something, you are responsible for it. *e.g. He must be made answerable for these terrible crimes.*

answering machine ['ɑːnsərɪŋ]
answering machines NOUN
a machine which records telephone calls while you are out

ant [ænt] **ants** NOUN
Ants are small insects that live in large groups.

-ant SUFFIX
'-ant' is used to form adjectives *e.g. important*

antagonism [æn'tægə,nɪzəm] NOUN
hatred or hostility

antagonist [æn'tægənɪst] **antagonists** NOUN
an enemy or opponent

antagonistic [æn,tægə'nɪstɪk] ADJECTIVE
Someone who is antagonistic towards you shows hate or hostility.
antagonistically ADVERB

antagonize [æn'tægə,naɪz] **antagonizes, antagonizing, antagonized**; also spelt
antagonise VERB
If someone is antagonized, they are made to feel anger and hostility.

Antarctic [ænt'ɑːktɪk] NOUN
The Antarctic is the region south of the Antarctic Circle.

Antarctic Circle NOUN
The Antarctic Circle is an imaginary circle around the southern part of the world.

ante- PREFIX
'Ante-' means 'before'. For example, *antenatal* means 'before birth'
[WORD HISTORY: from Latin ANTE, a preposition or adverb meaning 'before']

antecedent [,æntɪ'siːdᵊnt] **antecedents** NOUN
1 An antecedent of a thing or event is something which happened or existed before it and is related to it in some way. *e.g. the prehistoric antecedents of the horse*
2 Your antecedents are your ancestors, the relatives from whom you are descended.

antelope ['æntɪ,ləʊp] **antelopes** NOUN
an animal which looks like a deer

antenatal [,æntɪ'neɪtᵊl] ADJECTIVE
concerned with the care of pregnant women and their unborn children *e.g. an antenatal clinic*

antenna [æn'tɛnə] **antennae** or **antennas** NOUN
1 The antennae of insects and certain other animals are the two long, thin parts attached to their heads which they use to feel with. The plural is 'antennae'.
2 In Australian, New Zealand, and American English, an antenna is a radio or television aerial. The plural is 'antennas'.

anthem ['ænθəm] **anthems** NOUN
a hymn written for a special occasion

anther ['ænθə] **anthers** NOUN
in a flower, the part of the stamen that makes pollen grains
[WORD HISTORY: from Greek ANTHOS meaning 'flower']

anthology [æn'θɒlədʒɪ] **anthologies** NOUN
(LIBRARY) a collection of writings by various authors published in one book

anthropo- PREFIX
'Anthropo-' means involving or to do with human beings *e.g. anthropology*
[WORD HISTORY: from Greek ANTHRŌPOS meaning 'human being']

anthropology [,ænθrə'pɒlədʒɪ] NOUN
the study of human beings and their society and culture
anthropological ADJECTIVE, **anthropologist** NOUN

anti- PREFIX
'Anti-' means opposed to or opposite to something *e.g. antiwar marches*

[WORD HISTORY: from Greek ANTI- meaning 'opposite' or 'against']

antibiotic [ˌæntɪbaɪˈɒtɪk] **antibiotics** NOUN
a drug or chemical used in medicine to kill bacteria and cure infections

antibody [ˈæntɪˌbɒdɪ] **antibodies** NOUN
a substance produced in the blood which can kill the harmful bacteria that cause disease

anticipate [ænˈtɪsɪˌpeɪt] **anticipates, anticipating, anticipated** VERB
If you anticipate an event, you are expecting it and are prepared for it. *e.g. She had anticipated his visit.*
anticipation NOUN

anticlimax [ˌæntɪˈklaɪmæks] **anticlimaxes** NOUN
something that disappoints you because it is not as exciting as expected, or because it occurs after something that was very exciting

anticlockwise [ˌæntɪˈklɒkˌwaɪz] ADJECTIVE OR ADVERB
moving in the opposite direction to the hands of a clock

antics [ˈæntɪks] PLURAL NOUN
funny or silly ways of behaving

antidote [ˈæntɪˌdəʊt] **antidotes** NOUN
a chemical substance that acts against the effect of a poison

antihistamine [ˌæntɪˈhɪstəˌmiːn] **antihistamines** NOUN
a drug used to treat an allergy

antipathy [ænˈtɪpəθɪ] NOUN
a strong feeling of dislike or hostility towards something or someone

antiperspirant [ˌæntɪˈpɜːspərənt] **antiperspirants** NOUN
a substance which stops you sweating when you put it on your skin

antipodes [ænˈtɪpəˌdiːz] PLURAL NOUN
any two points on the earth's surface that are situated directly opposite each other. In Britain, Australia and New Zealand are sometimes called the Antipodes as they are opposite Britain on the globe
antipodean ADJECTIVE
[WORD HISTORY: from Greek ANTIPOUS meaning 'with the feet opposite']

antiquarian [ˌæntɪˈkwɛərɪən] ADJECTIVE
relating to or involving old and rare objects *e.g. antiquarian books*

antiquated [ˈæntɪˌkweɪtɪd] ADJECTIVE
very old-fashioned *e.g. an antiquated method of teaching*

antique [ænˈtiːk] **antiques** NOUN
1 an object from the past that is collected because of its value or beauty
> ADJECTIVE
2 from or concerning the past *e.g. antique furniture*

antiquity [ænˈtɪkwɪtɪ] **antiquities** NOUN
1 Antiquity is the distant past, especially the time of the ancient Egyptians, Greeks, and Romans.
2 Antiquities are interesting works of art and buildings from the distant past.

anti-Semitism [ˌæntɪˈsɛmɪˌtɪzəm] NOUN
hatred of Jewish people
anti-Semitic ADJECTIVE, **anti-Semite** NOUN

antiseptic [ˌæntɪˈsɛptɪk] ADJECTIVE
Something that is antiseptic kills germs.

antisocial [ˌæntɪˈsəʊʃəl] ADJECTIVE
1 An antisocial person is unwilling to meet and be friendly with other people.
2 Antisocial behaviour is annoying or upsetting to other people. *e.g. Smoking in public is antisocial.*

antithesis [ænˈtɪθɪsɪs] **antitheses** NOUN; FORMAL
The antithesis of something is its exact opposite. *e.g. Work is the antithesis of leisure.*

antivenene [ˌæntɪvɪˈniːn] **antivenenes** NOUN
a substance which reduces the effect of a venom, especially a snake venom

antler [ˈæntlə] **antlers** NOUN
A male deer's antlers are the branched horns on its head.

antonym [ˈæntənɪm] **antonyms** NOUN
a word which means the opposite of another word. For example, 'hot' is the antonym of 'cold'.

anus [ˈeɪnəs] **anuses** NOUN
the hole between the buttocks

anvil [ˈænvɪl] **anvils** NOUN
a heavy iron block on which hot metal is beaten into shape

anxiety [æŋˈzaɪɪtɪ] **anxieties** NOUN
nervousness or worry

● THESAURUS
apprehension: *a feeling of apprehension about the future*
concern: *growing concern about the environment*
fear: *His fears might be groundless.*
misgiving: *She had some misgivings about what she had been asked to do.*
nervousness: *I smiled, trying to hide my nervousness.*
unease: *a deep sense of unease about the coming interview*

worry: *a major source of worry to us all*

anxious ['æŋkʃəs] ADJECTIVE

1 If you are anxious, you are nervous or worried.

THESAURUS
apprehensive: *Their families are apprehensive about the trip.*
bothered: *I'm still bothered about what she's going to say.*
concerned: *a phone call from a concerned neighbour*
fearful: *We are all fearful for the security of our jobs.*
nervous: *I still get nervous before a visit to the dentist's.*
troubled: *He was troubled about his son's lifestyle.*
uneasy: *an uneasy feeling that something was wrong*
worried: *His parents are worried about his lack of progress.*

2 If you are anxious to do something or anxious that something should happen, you very much want to do it or want it to happen. *e.g. She was anxious to have children.*
anxiously ADVERB

any ['ɛnɪ] ADJECTIVE OR PRONOUN

1 one, some, or several *e.g. Do you have any paperclips I could borrow?.*

2 even the smallest amount or even one *e.g. He was unable to tolerate any dairy products.*

3 whatever or whichever, no matter what or which *e.g. Any type of cooking oil will do.*

anybody ['ɛnɪˌbɒdɪ] PRONOUN
any person

anyhow ['ɛnɪˌhaʊ] ADVERB
1 in any case
2 in a careless way *e.g. They were all shoved in anyhow.*

anyone ['ɛnɪˌwʌn] PRONOUN
any person

anything ['ɛnɪˌθɪŋ] PRONOUN
any object, event, situation, or action

anyway ['ɛnɪˌweɪ] ADVERB
in any case

anywhere ['ɛnɪˌwɛə] ADVERB
in, at, or to any place

Anzac ['ænzæk] **Anzacs** NOUN
1 In World War I, an Anzac was a soldier with the Australia and New Zealand Army Corps.
2 an Australian or New Zealand soldier

aorta [eɪˈɔːtə] NOUN
the main artery in the body, which carries blood away from the heart

apart [əˈpɑːt] ADVERB OR ADJECTIVE

1 When something is apart from something else, there is a space or a distance between them. *e.g. The couple separated and lived apart for four years... The gliders landed about seventy metres apart.*

> ADVERB
2 If you take something apart, you separate it into pieces.

apartheid [əˈpɑːthaɪt] NOUN
In South Africa apartheid was the government policy and laws which kept people of different races apart. It was abolished in 1994.
[WORD HISTORY: an Afrikaans word]

apartment [əˈpɑːtmənt] **apartments** NOUN
a set of rooms for living in, usually on one floor of a building

apathetic [ˌæpəˈθɛtɪk] ADJECTIVE
not interested in anything

THESAURUS
cool: *The idea met with a cool response.*
indifferent: *People have become indifferent to the sufferings of others.*
passive: *His passive attitude made things easier for me.*
uninterested: *unhelpful and uninterested shop staff*
<<OPPOSITE enthusiastic

apathy ['æpəθɪ] NOUN
a state of mind in which you do not care about anything

ape [eɪp] **apes, aping, aped** NOUN
1 Apes are animals with a very short tail or no tail. They are closely related to man. Apes include chimpanzees, gorillas, and gibbons.
> VERB
2 If you ape someone's speech or behaviour, you imitate it.

aphid ['eɪfɪd] **aphids** NOUN
a small insect that feeds by sucking the juices from plants

aphrodisiac [ˌæfrəˈdɪzɪæk] **aphrodisiacs** NOUN
a food, drink, or drug which makes people want to have sex

apiece [əˈpiːs] ADVERB
If people have a particular number of things apiece, they have that number each.

aplomb [əˈplɒm] NOUN
If you do something with aplomb, you do it with great confidence.

apocalypse [əˈpɒkəlɪps] NOUN
The Apocalypse is the end of the world.
apocalyptic ADJECTIVE
[WORD HISTORY: from Greek APOKALUPTEIN meaning 'to reveal'; the way the world will end is

considered to be revealed in the last book of the Bible, called 'Apocalypse' or 'Revelation']

apocryphal [ə'pɒkrɪfəl] ADJECTIVE
A story that is apocryphal is generally believed not to have really happened.

apolitical [ˌeɪpə'lɪtɪkəl] ADJECTIVE
not interested in politics

apologetic [əˌpɒlə'dʒɛtɪk] ADJECTIVE
showing or saying you are sorry
apologetically ADVERB

apologize [ə'pɒlədʒaɪz] **apologizes, apologizing, apologized**; also spelt **apologise** VERB
When you apologize to someone, you say you are sorry for something you have said or done.

THESAURUS
ask forgiveness: *He fell to his knees asking for forgiveness.*
beg someone's pardon: *I was impolite and I do beg your pardon.*
express regret: *Mr Galloway expressed regret that he had caused any offence.*
say sorry: *I wanted to say sorry to her.*

apology [ə'pɒlədʒɪ] **apologies** NOUN
something you say or write to tell someone you are sorry

apostle [ə'pɒsəl] **apostles** NOUN
The Apostles are the twelve followers who were chosen by Christ.

apostrophe [ə'pɒstrəfɪ] **apostrophes** NOUN
a punctuation mark used to show that one or more letters have been missed out of a word, for example "he's" for "he is". Apostrophes are also used with -s at the end of a noun to show that what follows belongs to or relates to the noun, for example *my brother's books*. If the noun already has an -s at the end, for example because it is plural, you just add the apostrophe, eg *my brothers' books*, referring to more than one brother.

appal [ə'pɔːl] **appals, appalling, appalled** VERB
If something appals you, it shocks you because it is very bad.

appalling [ə'pɔːlɪŋ] ADJECTIVE
so bad as to be shocking *e.g. She escaped with appalling injuries.*

apparatus [ˌæpə'reɪtəs] NOUN
(SCIENCE) The apparatus for a particular task is the equipment used for it.

apparent [ə'pærənt] ADJECTIVE
1 seeming real rather than actually being real *e.g. an apparent hit and run accident*

2 obvious *e.g. It was apparent that he had lost interest.*
apparently ADVERB

apparition [ˌæpə'rɪʃən] **apparitions** NOUN
something you think you see but that is not really there *e.g. a ghostly apparition on the windscreen*

appeal [ə'piːl] **appeals, appealing, appealed** VERB
1 If you appeal for something, you make an urgent request for it. *e.g. The police appealed for witnesses to come forward.*

THESAURUS
beg: *I begged him to leave me alone.*
call upon: *Frequently he was called upon to resolve conflicts.*
plead: *I pleaded to be allowed to go.*
request: *She had requested that the door to her room be left open.*

2 If you appeal to someone in authority against a decision, you formally ask them to change it.

3 If something appeals to you, you find it attractive or interesting.

THESAURUS
attract: *What attracted you to research work?*
fascinate: *Classical music had fascinated him since the age of three.*
interest: *It was the garden that really interested me.*
please: *It pleased him to talk to her.*

> NOUN
4 a formal or serious request *e.g. an appeal for peace*

THESAURUS
petition: *The court rejected their petition.*
plea: *his emotional plea for help in solving the killing*
request: *France had agreed to his request for political asylum.*

5 The appeal of something is the quality it has which people find attractive or interesting. *e.g. the rugged appeal of the Rockies*
appealing ADJECTIVE

appear [ə'pɪə] **appears, appearing, appeared** VERB
1 When something which you could not see appears, it moves (or you move) so that you can see it.

THESAURUS
come into view: *Nearly fifty gliders came into view to the south of the plateau.*
crop up: informal *Problems will crop up and hit you before you are ready.*
emerge: *The postman emerged from his van soaked to the skin.*
show up: informal *He failed to show up at the ceremony.*
surface: *The same old problems would surface again.*

turn up: *This is like waiting for a bus that never turns up.*

<<OPPOSITE *disappear*

2 When something new appears, it begins to exist.

● THESAURUS

become available: *In 1950, legal aid became available in Britain.*

be invented: *The lawn mower was invented in 1830.*

come into being: *Fireworks first came into being with the invention of gunpowder.*

come into existence: *before our solar system came into existence*

come out: *This book first came out in 1992.*

3 When an actor or actress appears in a film or show, they take part in it.

● THESAURUS

act: *She has also been acting in a sitcom.*

perform: *He is currently performing in the West End show "Grease".*

play: *He played Hamlet to packed houses.*

play a part: *His ambition is to play the part of Dracula.*

4 If something appears to be a certain way, it seems or looks that way. *e.g. He appeared to be searching for something.*

appearance [əˈpɪərəns] **appearances** NOUN

1 The appearance of someone in a place is their arrival there, especially when it is unexpected.

2 The appearance of something new is the time when it begins to exist. *e.g. the appearance of computer technology*

● THESAURUS

advent: *the advent of satellite and cable channels*

arrival: *the arrival of modern technologies*

coming: *the coming of the railways*

debut: *the debut of the new channel*

emergence: *the emergence of pay-per-view TV*

introduction: *the introduction of the minimum wage*

3 Someone's or something's appearance is the way they look to other people. *e.g. His gaunt appearance had sparked fears for his health.*

● THESAURUS

bearing: *a man of iron will and military bearing*

image: *He urged the rest of the band to update their image.*

look: *She is so much happier with her new look.*

looks: *a young woman with wholesome good looks*

appease [əˈpiːz] **appeases, appeasing, appeased** VERB

If you try to appease someone, you try to calm them down when they are angry, for example by giving them what they want.

appeasement NOUN

appendage [əˈpɛndɪdʒ] **appendages** NOUN

a less important part attached to a main part

appendicitis [əˌpɛndɪˈsaɪtɪs] NOUN

a painful illness in which a person's appendix becomes infected

appendix [əˈpɛndɪks] **appendices** or **appendixes** NOUN

1 a small closed tube forming part of your digestive system

2 An appendix to a book is extra information placed after the end of the main text.

> The plural of the part of the body is *appendixes*. The plural of the extra section in a book is *appendices*.

appetite [ˈæpɪˌtaɪt] **appetites** NOUN

1 Your appetite is your desire to eat.

2 If you have an appetite for something, you have a strong desire for it and enjoyment of it. *e.g. She had lost her appetite for air travel.*

appetizing or **appetising** [ˈæpɪˌtaɪzɪŋ] ADJECTIVE

Food that is appetizing looks and smells good, and makes you want to eat it.

applaud [əˈplɔːd] **applauds, applauding, applauded** VERB

1 When a group of people applaud, they clap their hands in approval or praise.

2 When an action or attitude is applauded, people praise it.

applause [əˈplɔːz] NOUN

(DRAMA) Applause is clapping by a group of people.

apple [ˈæpəl] **apples** NOUN

a round fruit with smooth skin and firm white flesh

appliance [əˈplaɪəns] **appliances** NOUN

any machine in your home you use to do a job like cleaning or cooking *e.g. kitchen appliances*

applicable [ˈæplɪkəbəl] ADJECTIVE

Something that is applicable to a situation is relevant to it. *e.g. The rules are applicable to everyone.*

applicant [ˈæplɪkənt] **applicants** NOUN

someone who is applying for something *e.g. We had problems recruiting applicants for the post.*

application [ˌæplɪˈkeɪʃən] **applications** NOUN

1 a formal request for something, usually in writing

2 The application of a rule, system, or skill is the use of it in a particular situation.

apply [ə'plaɪ] **applies, applying, applied**
VERB

1 If you apply for something, you formally ask for it, usually by writing a letter.

2 If you apply a rule or skill, you use it in a situation. *e.g. He applied his mind to the problem.*

3 If something applies to a person or a situation, it is relevant to that person or situation. *e.g. The legislation applies only to people living in England and Wales.*

4 If you apply something to a surface, you put it on. *e.g. She applied lipstick to her mouth.*

appoint [ə'pɔɪnt] **appoints, appointing, appointed** VERB

1 If you appoint someone to a job or position, you formally choose them for it.

2 If you appoint a time or place for something to happen, you decide when or where it will happen.

appointed ADJECTIVE

appointment [ə'pɔɪntmənt]
appointments NOUN

1 an arrangement you have with someone to meet them

● THESAURUS

date: *I have a date with Wendy.*
interview: *a job interview*
meeting: *Can we have a meeting to discuss that?*
rendezvous: *I had almost decided to keep my rendezvous with Tony.*

2 The appointment of a person to do a particular job is the choosing of that person to do it.

● THESAURUS

election: *the election of the government in 1997*
naming: *the naming of the new captain*
nomination: *They opposed the nomination of a junior officer to the position.*
selection: *his selection as a parliamentary candidate*

3 a job or a position of responsibility *e.g. He applied for an appointment in Russia.*

● THESAURUS

assignment: *my first assignment for The New York Times*
job: *He's trying for a job in the Civil Service.*
place: *All the candidates won places on the ruling council.*
position: *She took up a position at the Arts Council.*
post: *He has held several senior military posts.*

apposite ['æpəzɪt] ADJECTIVE
well suited for a particular purpose *e.g. He went before Cameron could think of anything apposite to say.*

appraise [ə'preɪz] **appraises, appraising, appraised** VERB

If you appraise something, you think about it carefully and form an opinion about it.
appraisal NOUN

appreciable [ə'priːʃəbəl] ADJECTIVE
large enough to be noticed *e.g. an appreciable difference*
appreciably ADVERB

appreciate [ə'priːʃɪˌeɪt] **appreciates, appreciating, appreciated** VERB

1 If you appreciate something, you like it because you recognize its good qualities. *e.g. He appreciates fine wines.*

● THESAURUS

admire: *All those who knew him will admire him for his work.*
prize: *Military figures made out of lead are prized by collectors.*
rate highly: *The four-year-old mare is rated highly by her trainer.*
respect: *I respect his talent as a pianist.*
treasure: *She treasures her memories of those joyous days.*
value: *I value the work he gives me.*
<<OPPOSITE *scorn*

2 If you appreciate a situation or problem, you understand it and know what it involves.

● THESAURUS

be aware of: *I am well aware of the arguments on the other side.*
perceive: *to get pupils to perceive for themselves the relationship between success and effort*
realize: *People don't realize how serious this is.*
recognize: *They have been slow to recognize it as a problem.*
understand: *They are too young to understand what is going on.*

3 If you appreciate something someone has done for you, you are grateful to them for it. *e.g. I really appreciate you coming to visit me.*

4 If something appreciates over a period of time, its value increases. *e.g. The property appreciated by 50% in two years.*
appreciation NOUN

appreciative [ə'priːʃɪətɪv] ADJECTIVE

1 understanding and enthusiastic *e.g. They were a very appreciative audience.*

2 thankful and grateful *e.g. I am particularly appreciative of the help my family and friends have given me.*
appreciatively ADVERB

apprehend [ˌæprɪ'hɛnd] **apprehends, apprehending, apprehended** VERB;
FORMAL

1 When the police apprehend someone, they arrest them and take them into custody.

2 If you apprehend something, you understand it fully. *e.g. They were unable to apprehend his hidden meaning.*

apprehensive [ˌæprɪˈhɛnsɪv] ADJECTIVE
afraid something bad may happen *e.g. I was very apprehensive about the birth.*
apprehensively ADVERB, **apprehension** NOUN

apprentice [əˈprɛntɪs] **apprentices** NOUN
a person who works for a period of time with a skilled craftsman in order to learn a skill or trade
apprenticeship NOUN
[WORD HISTORY: from Old French APRENDRE meaning 'to learn']

approach [əˈprəʊtʃ] **approaches, approaching, approached** VERB
1 To approach something is to come near or nearer to it.
2 When a future event approaches, it gradually gets nearer. *e.g. As winter approached, tents were set up to accommodate refugees.*
3 If you approach someone about something, you ask them about it.
4 If you approach a situation or problem in a particular way, you think about it or deal with it in that way.
> NOUN
5 The approach of something is the process of it coming closer. *e.g. the approach of spring*
6 An approach to a situation or problem is a way of thinking about it or dealing with it.
7 a road or path that leads to a place
approaching ADJECTIVE

appropriate appropriates, appropriating, appropriated ADJECTIVE
[əˈprəʊprɪɪt]
1 suitable or acceptable for a particular situation *e.g. He didn't think jeans were appropriate for a vice-president.*

THESAURUS
apt: *an apt title for his memoirs*
correct: *the importance of correct behaviour and social niceties*
fitting: *a fitting tribute to a great man*
proper: *the proper course for the court to take*
suitable: *a suitable location*
<<OPPOSITE *inappropriate*

> VERB [əˈprəʊprɪˌeɪt]
2 FORMAL
If you appropriate something which does not belong to you, you take it without permission.
appropriately ADVERB, **appropriation** NOUN

approval [əˈpruːvəl] NOUN **(PSHE)**
1 Approval is agreement given to a plan or request. *e.g. The plan will require approval from the local authority.*

THESAURUS
agreement: *The clubs are seeking agreement for a provisional deal.*
authorization: *We didn't have authorization to go.*
blessing: *Mr Ryabov appeared to give his blessing to Mr Yeltsin's plan.*
endorsement: *His endorsement has been fervently sought by all the main presidential candidates.*
permission: *They cannot leave the country without permission.*
sanction: *The King cannot enact laws without the sanction of Parliament.*

2 Approval is also admiration. *e.g. She looked at James with approval.*

THESAURUS
admiration: *a strategy that is winning admiration from around the world*
esteem: *Their public esteem has never been lower.*
favour: *He has won favour with a wide range of groups.*
praise: *She is full of praise for the range of excellent services available.*
respect: *We all have so much respect for her.*
<<OPPOSITE *disapproval*

approve [əˈpruːv] **approves, approving, approved** VERB **(PSHE)**
1 If you approve of something or someone, you think that thing or person is acceptable or good.

THESAURUS
admire: *I admire him for his work.*
favour: *The opposition parties favour constitutional reform.*
praise: *He praised the fans for their continued support.*
respect: *I want him to respect me as a career woman.*
think highly of: *He thought highly of his brother.*
<<OPPOSITE *disapprove*

2 If someone in a position of authority approves a plan or idea, they formally agree to it.
approved ADJECTIVE, **approving** ADJECTIVE

THESAURUS
authorize: *to authorize the use of military force*
consent to: *His parents consented to an autopsy.*
endorse: *I can endorse their opinion wholeheartedly.*
permit: *The doorman is not allowed to permit them entry to the film.*
sanction: *He may now be ready to sanction the use of force.*
<<OPPOSITE *veto*

approximate [əˈprɒksɪmɪt] ADJECTIVE **(MATHS)** almost exact *e.g. What was the approximate distance between the cars?*
approximately ADVERB

THESAURUS
estimated: *Our estimated time of arrival is 3.30.*

inexact: *Forecasting is an inexact science.*
loose: *a loose translation*
rough: *a rough estimate*
<<OPPOSITE *exact*

apricot ['eɪprɪˌkɒt] **apricots** NOUN
a small, soft, yellowish-orange fruit
[WORD HISTORY: from Latin PRAECOX meaning 'early ripening']

April ['eɪprəl] NOUN
the fourth month of the year. April has 30 days
[WORD HISTORY: from Latin APRĪLIS]

apron ['eɪprən] **aprons** NOUN
a piece of clothing worn over the front of normal clothing to protect it

apse [æps] **apses** NOUN
a domed recess in the east wall of a church

apt [æpt] ADJECTIVE
1 suitable or relevant *e.g. a very apt description*
2 having a particular tendency *e.g. They are apt to jump to the wrong conclusions.*

aptitude ['æptɪˌtjuːd] NOUN
Someone's aptitude for something is their ability to learn it quickly and to do it well. *e.g. I have a natural aptitude for painting.*

aqua- PREFIX
'Aqua-' means 'water'
[WORD HISTORY: from Latin AQUA meaning 'water']

aquarium [əˈkwɛərɪəm] **aquaria** or **aquariums** NOUN
a glass tank filled with water in which fish are kept

Aquarius [əˈkwɛərɪəs] NOUN
Aquarius is the eleventh sign of the zodiac, represented by a person carrying water. People born between January 20th and February 18th are born under this sign.

aquatic [əˈkwætɪk] ADJECTIVE
1 An aquatic animal or plant lives or grows in water.
2 involving water *e.g. aquatic sports*

aqueduct ['ækwɪˌdʌkt] **aqueducts** NOUN
a long bridge with many arches carrying a water supply over a valley

Arab ['ærəb] **Arabs** NOUN
a member of a group of people who used to live in Arabia but who now live throughout the Middle East and North Africa

Arabic ['ærəbɪk] NOUN
a language spoken by many people in the Middle East and North Africa

arable ['ærəbəl] ADJECTIVE
Arable land is used for growing crops.

arbiter ['ɑːbɪtə] **arbiters** NOUN
the person who decides about something

arbitrary ['ɑːbɪtrərɪ] ADJECTIVE
An arbitrary decision or action is one that is not based on a plan or system.
arbitrarily ADVERB

arbitrate ['ɑːbɪˌtreɪt] **arbitrates, arbitrating, arbitrated** VERB
When someone arbitrates between two people or groups who are in disagreement, they consider the facts and decide who is right.
arbitration NOUN, **arbitrator** NOUN

arc [ɑːk] **arcs** NOUN
1 a smoothly curving line
2 in geometry, a section of the circumference of a circle

Do not confuse the spellings of *arc* and *ark*.

arcade [ɑːˈkeɪd] **arcades** NOUN
a covered passage with shops or market stalls along one or both sides

arcane [ɑːˈkeɪn] ADJECTIVE
mysterious and difficult to understand

arch [ɑːtʃ] **arches, arching, arched** NOUN
1 a structure that has a curved top supported on either side by a pillar or wall
2 the curved part of bone at the top of the foot
> VERB
3 When something arches, it forms a curved line or shape.
> ADJECTIVE
4 most important *e.g. my arch enemy*

arch- PREFIX
'Arch-' means 'most important' or 'chief' *e.g. archangel*
[WORD HISTORY: from Greek ARKHEIN meaning 'to rule']

archaeology or **archeology** [ˌɑːkɪˈɒlədʒɪ] NOUN
the study of the past by digging up and examining the remains of buildings, tools, and other things
archaeological ADJECTIVE, **archaeologist** NOUN
[WORD HISTORY: from Greek ARKHAIOS meaning 'ancient']

archaic [ɑːˈkeɪɪk] ADJECTIVE
very old or old-fashioned

archangel ['ɑːkˌeɪndʒəl] **archangels** NOUN
an angel of the highest rank

archbishop ['ɑːtʃˈbɪʃəp] **archbishops** NOUN
a bishop of the highest rank in a Christian Church

archdeacon ['ɑːtʃˈdiːkən] **archdeacons** NOUN

an Anglican clergyman ranking just below a
bishop

archeology [ˌɑːkɪˈɒlədʒɪ] another spelling of
archaeology

archer [ˈɑːtʃə] **archers** NOUN
someone who shoots with a bow and arrow

archery [ˈɑːtʃərɪ] NOUN
a sport in which people shoot at a target with a
bow and arrow

archipelago [ˌɑːkɪˈpɛlɪˌɡəʊ] **archipelagos**
NOUN
a group of small islands
[WORD HISTORY: from Italian ARCIPELAGO meaning
'chief sea'; originally referring to the Aegean Sea]

architect [ˈɑːkɪˌtɛkt] **architects** NOUN
a person who designs buildings

architecture [ˈɑːkɪˌtɛktʃə] NOUN
the art or practice of designing buildings
architectural ADJECTIVE

archive [ˈɑːkaɪv] **archives** NOUN
Archives are collections of documents and
records about the history of a family or some
other group of people.

arctic [ˈɑːktɪk] NOUN
1 The Arctic is the region north of the Arctic
Circle.
> ADJECTIVE
2 Arctic means very cold indeed. *e.g. arctic
conditions*
[WORD HISTORY: from Greek ARKTOS meaning
'bear'; originally it referred to the northern
constellation of the Great Bear]

Arctic Circle [ˈɑːktɪk] NOUN
The Arctic Circle is an imaginary circle around the
northern part of the world.

ardent [ˈɑːdᵊnt] ADJECTIVE
full of enthusiasm and passion
ardently ADVERB
● THESAURUS
avid: *an avid follower of the team*
devoted: *surrounded by devoted fans*
enthusiastic: *enthusiastic collectors of Elvis
memorabilia*
fervent: *a fervent admirer of his*
intense: *his intense love of football*
keen: *a keen supporter of the cause*
passionate: *He developed a passionate interest in
motor racing.*
<<OPPOSITE *apathetic*

ardour [ˈɑːdə] NOUN
a strong and passionate feeling of love or
enthusiasm

arduous [ˈɑːdjʊəs] ADJECTIVE
tiring and needing a lot of effort *e.g. the arduous*

task of rebuilding the country

are [ɑː] the plural form of the present tense of **be**

area [ˈɛərɪə] **areas** NOUN
1 a particular part of a place, country, or the world
e.g. a built-up area of the city
● THESAURUS
district: *I drove around the business district.*
locality: *All other factories in the locality went on
strike in sympathy.*
neighbourhood: *She no longer takes evening strolls
around her neighbourhood.*
region: *a remote mountainous region of Afghanistan*
zone: *a war zone*
2 The area of a piece of ground or a surface is the
amount of space it covers, measured in square
metres or square feet.
● THESAURUS
expanse: *a huge expanse of blue-green sea*
extent: *the extent of the rain forest*
range: *a driver's range of vision*
size: *a country nearly three times the size of ours*

arena [əˈriːnə] **arenas** NOUN
1 a place where sports and other public events
take place
2 A particular arena is the centre of attention or
activity in a particular situation. *e.g. the political
arena*
[WORD HISTORY: from Latin HARENA meaning 'sand',
hence the sandy centre of an amphitheatre where
gladiators fought]

Argentinian [ˌɑːdʒənˈtɪnɪən] **Argentinians**
ADJECTIVE
1 belonging or relating to Argentina
> NOUN
2 someone who comes from Argentina

arguable [ˈɑːɡjʊəbᵊl] ADJECTIVE
An arguable idea or point is not necessarily true
or correct and should be questioned.
arguably ADVERB

argue [ˈɑːɡjuː] **argues, arguing, argued**
VERB
1 If you argue with someone about something,
you disagree with them about it, sometimes in
an angry way.
● THESAURUS
bicker: *They bickered endlessly about procedure.*
disagree: *They can communicate even when they
strongly disagree.*
fall out: informal *Mum and I used to fall out a lot.*
feud: *feuding neighbours*
fight: *We're always fighting about money.*
quarrel: *My brother quarrelled with my father.*
row: *We started rowing about whose turn it was
next.*

squabble: *The children were squabbling over the remote control.*
wrangle: *Delegates wrangled over the future of the organization.*

2 If you argue that something is the case, you give reasons why you think it is so. *e.g. She argued that her client had been wrongly accused.*

🔵 THESAURUS
assert: *The defendants continue to assert their innocence.*
claim: *Statisticians claim that the book contains inaccuracies.*
debate: *Parliament will debate the issue today.*
maintain: *He had always maintained his innocence.*
reason: *I reasoned that if he could do it, so could I.*

argument [ˈɑːgjʊmənt] **arguments** NOUN
1 a disagreement between two people which causes a quarrel

🔵 THESAURUS
barney: British, Australian and New Zealand; informal *We had such a barney that we nearly split up.*
blue: Australian; slang *He gets into more blues with authority than I do.*
clash: *clashes between police and demonstrators*
dispute: *a dispute over ticket allocation*
feud: *a two-year feud between neighbours*
fight: *We had another fight about money.*
row: *Maxine and I had a terrible row.*
squabble: *a family squabble over Sunday lunch*

2 a point or a set of reasons you use to try to convince people about something

🔵 THESAURUS
case: *the case for his dismissal*
grounds: *facts providing grounds for an unfair dismissal complaint*
logic: *The logic is that, without more growth, the deficit will rise.*
reasoning: *the reasoning behind the decision*

argumentative [ˌɑːgjʊˈmɛntətɪv] ADJECTIVE
An argumentative person is always disagreeing with other people.

aria [ˈɑːrɪə] **arias** NOUN
a song sung by one of the leading singers in an opera
[WORD HISTORY: an Italian word meaning 'tune']

arid [ˈærɪd] ADJECTIVE
Arid land is very dry because it has very little rain.

Aries [ˈɛəriːz] NOUN
Aries is the first sign of the zodiac, represented by a ram. People born between March 21st and April 19th are born under this sign.

arise [əˈraɪz] **arises, arising, arose, arisen** VERB
1 When something such as an opportunity or problem arises, it begins to exist.

2 FORMAL
To arise also means to stand up from a sitting, kneeling, or lying position.

aristocracy [ˌærɪˈstɒkrəsɪ] **aristocracies** NOUN
a class of people who have a high social rank and special titles

aristocrat [ˈærɪstəˌkræt] **aristocrats** NOUN
someone whose family has a high social rank, and who has a title
aristocratic ADJECTIVE

arithmetic [əˈrɪθmətɪk] NOUN
the part of mathematics which is to do with the addition, subtraction, multiplication, and division of numbers
arithmetical ADJECTIVE, **arithmetically** ADVERB

ark [ɑːk] NOUN
In the Bible, the ark was the boat built by Noah for his family and the animals during the Flood.

▬ Do not confuse the spellings of *arc* and *ark*

arm [ɑːm] **arms, arming, armed** NOUN
1 Your arms are the part of your body between your shoulder and your wrist.

2 The arms of a chair are the parts on which you rest your arms.

3 An arm of an organization is a section of it. *e.g. the political arm of the armed forces*

> PLURAL NOUN
4 Arms are weapons used in a war.

> VERB
5 To arm someone is to provide them with weapons.

armada [ɑːˈmɑːdə] **armadas** NOUN
a large fleet of warships

armadillo [ˌɑːməˈdɪləʊ] **armadillos** NOUN
a mammal from South America which is covered with strong bony plates like armour
[WORD HISTORY: a Spanish word meaning 'little armed man']

Armageddon [ˌɑːməˈgɛdᵊn] NOUN
In Christianity, Armageddon is the final battle between good and evil at the end of the world.
[WORD HISTORY: from Hebrew HAR MEGIDDO, the mountain district of Megiddo, the site of many battles]

armament [ˈɑːməmənt] **armaments** NOUN
Armaments are the weapons and military equipment that belong to a country.

armchair [ˈɑːmˌtʃɛə] **armchairs** NOUN
a comfortable chair with a support on each side for your arms

armed [ɑːmd] ADJECTIVE
A person who is armed is carrying a weapon or weapons.

armistice ['ɑːmɪstɪs] **armistices** NOUN
an agreement in a war to stop fighting in order to discuss peace

armour ['ɑːmə] NOUN
In the past, armour was metal clothing worn for protection in battle.

armoured ['ɑːməd] ADJECTIVE
covered with thick steel for protection from gunfire and other missiles *e.g. an armoured car*

armoury ['ɑːmərɪ] **armouries** NOUN
a place where weapons are stored

armpit ['ɑːm,pɪt] **armpits** NOUN
the area under your arm where your arm joins your shoulder

army ['ɑːmɪ] **armies** NOUN
a large group of soldiers organized into divisions for fighting on land

aroma [ə'rəʊmə] **aromas** NOUN
a strong, pleasant smell
aromatic ADJECTIVE
[WORD HISTORY: a Greek word meaning 'spice']

aromatherapy [ə,rəʊmə'θerəpɪ] NOUN
a type of therapy that involves massaging the body with special fragrant oils

around [ə'raʊnd] PREPOSITION
1 placed at various points in a place or area *e.g. There are many seats around the building.*
2 from place to place inside an area *e.g. We walked around the showroom.*
3 at approximately the time or place mentioned *e.g. The attacks began around noon.*
> ADVERB
4 here and there *e.g. His papers were scattered around.*

arouse [ə'raʊz] **arouses, arousing, aroused** VERB
If something arouses a feeling in you, it causes you to begin to have this feeling. *e.g. His death still arouses very painful feelings.*
arousal NOUN

arrange [ə'reɪndʒ] **arranges, arranging, arranged** VERB
1 If you arrange to do something, you make plans for it.
⦾ THESAURUS
fix up: *I fixed up an appointment to see her.*
organize: *She organized the trip to the museum.*
plan: *She planned to leave in August.*
schedule: *Our appointment is scheduled for Tuesday.*
2 If you arrange something for someone, you make it possible for them to have it or do it. *e.g. The bank has arranged a loan for her.*

3 If you arrange objects, you set them out in a particular position. *e.g. He started to arrange the books in piles.*
arrangement NOUN
⦾ THESAURUS
classify: *Weathermen classify clouds into several different groups.*
group: *The fact sheet is grouped into seven sections.*
order: *The French order things differently.*
organize: *He began to organize his materials.*
sort: *The students are sorted into three ability groups.*

array [ə'reɪ] **arrays** NOUN
An array of different things is a large number of them displayed together.

arrears [ə'rɪəz] PLURAL NOUN
1 Arrears are amounts of money you owe. *e.g. mortgage arrears*
> PHRASE
2 If you are paid **in arrears**, you are paid at the end of the period for which the payment is due.

arrest [ə'rest] **arrests, arresting, arrested** VERB
1 If the police arrest someone, they take them into custody to decide whether to charge them with an offence.
⦾ THESAURUS
apprehend: *Police have not apprehended her killer.*
capture: *Her accomplice was captured by Dutch police.*
nick: British; slang *Keep quiet or we'll all get nicked.*
seize: *Two military observers were seized by rebels yesterday.*
take prisoner: *He was taken prisoner in 1940 at the fall of Dunkirk.*
> NOUN
2 An arrest is the act of taking a person into custody.
⦾ THESAURUS
apprehension: *information leading to the apprehension of the killer*
capture: *He was trying to evade capture by security forces.*
seizure: *the mass seizure of terrorists*

arrival [ə'raɪvəl] **arrivals** NOUN
1 the act or time of arriving *e.g. The arrival of the train was delayed.*
2 something or someone that has arrived *e.g. The tourist authority reported record arrivals over Christmas.*

arrive [ə'raɪv] **arrives, arriving, arrived** VERB
1 When you arrive at a place, you reach it at the end of your journey.

2 When a letter or a piece of news arrives, it is brought to you. *e.g. A letter arrived at her lawyer's office.*

3 When you arrive at an idea or decision you reach it.

4 When a moment, event, or new thing arrives, it begins to happen. *e.g. The Easter holidays arrived.*

arrogant ['ærəgənt] ADJECTIVE
Someone who is arrogant behaves as if they are better than other people.
arrogantly ADVERB, **arrogance** NOUN

arrow ['ærəʊ] **arrows** NOUN
a long, thin weapon with a sharp point at one end, shot from a bow

arsenal ['ɑːsənəl] **arsenals** NOUN
a place where weapons and ammunition are stored or produced
[WORD HISTORY: from Italian ARSENALE meaning 'dockyard', originally in Venice]

arsenic ['ɑːsnɪk] NOUN
a very strong poison which can kill people

arson ['ɑːsən] NOUN
the crime of deliberately setting fire to something, especially a building

art [ɑːt] **arts** NOUN
1 Art is the creation of objects such as paintings and sculptures, which are thought to be beautiful or which express a particular idea; also used to refer to the objects themselves.

2 An activity is called an art when it requires special skill or ability. *e.g. the art of diplomacy*

> PLURAL NOUN
3 The arts are literature, music, painting, and sculpture, considered together.

artefact ['ɑːtɪˌfækt] **artefacts** NOUN
any object made by people

artery ['ɑːtərɪ] **arteries** NOUN
1 Your arteries are the tubes that carry blood from your heart to the rest of your body.

2 a main road or major section of any system of communication or transport

artful ['ɑːtfʊl] ADJECTIVE
clever and skilful, often in a cunning way
artfully ADVERB

arthritis [ɑːˈθraɪtɪs] NOUN
a condition in which the joints in someone's body become swollen and painful
arthritic ADJECTIVE

artichoke ['ɑːtɪˌtʃəʊk] **artichokes** NOUN
1 the round green partly edible flower head of a thistle-like plant; the flower head is made up of clusters of leaves that have a soft fleshy part that is eaten as a vegetable

2 A Jerusalem artichoke is a small yellowish-white vegetable that grows underground and looks like a potato.

article ['ɑːtɪkəl] **articles** NOUN
1 (LIBRARY) a piece of writing in a newspaper or magazine

● THESAURUS
feature: *a feature about Gulf War syndrome*
item: *I read an item about this only last week.*
piece: *I disagree with your recent piece about Australia.*
story: *Most newspapers had a story about the film's premiere.*

2 a particular item *e.g. an article of clothing*

● THESAURUS
item: *Various items have gone missing from my desk.*
object: *everyday objects such as wooden spoons*
thing: *I have a few things to buy for the trip.*

3 In English grammar, 'a' and 'the' are sometimes called articles: 'a' (or 'an') is the indefinite article; 'the' is the definite article.

articulate **articulates, articulating, articulated** ADJECTIVE [ɑːˈtɪkjʊlɪt]
1 If you are articulate, you are able to express yourself well in words.

> VERB [ɑːˈtɪkjʊˌleɪt]
2 When you articulate your ideas or feelings, you express in words what you think or feel. *e.g. She could not articulate her grief.*

3 When you articulate a sound or word, you speak it clearly.
articulation NOUN

artificial [ˌɑːtɪˈfɪʃəl] ADJECTIVE
1 created by people rather than occurring naturally *e.g. artificial colouring*

2 pretending to have attitudes and feelings which other people realize are not real *e.g. an artificial smile*
artificially ADVERB

artillery [ɑːˈtɪlərɪ] NOUN
1 Artillery consists of large, powerful guns such as cannons.

2 The artillery is the branch of an army which uses large, powerful guns.

artist ['ɑːtɪst] **artists** NOUN
1 a person who draws or paints or produces other works of art

2 a person who is very skilled at a particular activity

artiste [ɑːˈtiːst] **artistes** NOUN
a professional entertainer, for example a singer or a dancer

artistic [ɑːˈtɪstɪk] ADJECTIVE

a

1 able to create good paintings, sculpture, or other works of art

2 concerning or involving art or artists
artistically ADVERB

artistry ['ɑːtɪstrɪ] NOUN
Artistry is the creative skill of an artist, writer, actor, or musician. *e.g. a supreme demonstration of his artistry as a cellist*

arty ['ɑːtɪ] **artier, artiest** ADJECTIVE; INFORMAL
interested in painting, sculpture, and other works of art

as [æz] CONJUNCTION
1 at the same time that *e.g. She waved at fans as she arrived for the concert.*

2 in the way that *e.g. They had talked as only the best of friends can.*

3 because *e.g. As I won't be back tonight, don't bother to cook a meal.*

4 You use the structure **as ... as** when you are comparing things that are similar. *e.g. It was as big as four football pitches.*

> PREPOSITION

5 You use 'as' when you are saying what role someone or something has. *e.g. She worked as a waitress.*

6 You use **as if** or **as though** when you are giving a possible explanation for something. *e.g. He looked at me as if I were mad.*

asbestos [æs'bɛstɒs] NOUN
a grey heat-resistant material used in the past to make fireproof articles

ASBO ['æz,bəʊ] NOUN
an abbreviation for 'antisocial behaviour order': an order from a judge preventing people who have been persistently annoying or upsetting other people from continuing to do so

ascend [ə'sɛnd] **ascends, ascending, ascended** VERB; FORMAL
To ascend is to move or lead upwards. *e.g. We finally ascended to the brow of a steep hill.*

ascendancy [ə'sɛndənsɪ] NOUN; FORMAL
If one group has ascendancy over another, it has more power or influence than the other.

ascendant [ə'sɛndənt] ADJECTIVE
1 rising or moving upwards

> PHRASE

2 Someone or something **in the ascendant** is increasing in power or popularity.

ascent [ə'sɛnt] **ascents** NOUN
an upward journey, for example up a mountain

ascertain [,æsə'teɪn] **ascertains, ascertaining, ascertained** VERB; FORMAL
If you ascertain that something is the case, you

find out it is the case. *e.g. He had ascertained that she had given up smoking.*

ascribe [ə'skraɪb] **ascribes, ascribing, ascribed** VERB
1 If you ascribe an event or state of affairs to a particular cause, you think that it is the cause of it. *e.g. His stomach pains were ascribed to his intake of pork.*

2 If you ascribe a quality to someone, you think they have it.

ash [æʃ] **ashes** NOUN
1 the grey or black powdery remains of anything that has been burnt

2 a tree with grey bark and hard tough wood used for timber

ashamed [ə'ʃeɪmd] ADJECTIVE
1 feeling embarrassed or guilty

● THESAURUS

embarrassed: *I'm not embarrassed to admit I cried.*
guilty: *When she realized I was watching, she looked guilty.*
humiliated: *I felt humiliated at the scene he was causing.*
sheepish: *"I'm afraid it was my idea," he admitted, looking sheepish.*
sorry: *She's really sorry for all the trouble she's caused.*
<<OPPOSITE *proud*

2 If you are ashamed of someone, you feel embarrassed to be connected with them.

ashen ['æʃən] ADJECTIVE
grey or pale *e.g. Her face was ashen with fatigue.*

ashore [ə'ʃɔː] ADVERB
on land or onto the land

ashtray ['æʃ,treɪ] **ashtrays** NOUN
a small dish for ash from cigarettes and cigars

Asia ['eɪʃə] NOUN
Asia is the largest continent. It has Europe on its western side, with the Arctic to the north, the Pacific to the east, and the Indian Ocean to the south. Asia includes several island groups, including Japan, Indonesia, and the Philippines.

Asian ['eɪʃən] **Asians** ADJECTIVE
1 belonging or relating to Asia

> NOUN

2 someone who comes from India, Pakistan, Bangladesh, or from some other part of Asia

aside [ə'saɪd] **asides** ADVERB
1 If you move something aside, you move it to one side.

> NOUN

2 a comment made away from the main conversation or dialogue that all those talking are not meant to hear

ask see page 47 for Word Web

askew [ə'skjuː] ADJECTIVE
not straight

asleep [ə'sliːp] ADJECTIVE
sleeping

AS level ['eɪˌɛs] **AS levels** NOUN
an exam taken by students in many British schools and colleges, more advanced than GCSE but less advanced than A level

asparagus [ə'spærəgəs] NOUN
a vegetable that has long shoots which are cooked and eaten

aspect ['æspɛkt] **aspects** NOUN
1 An aspect of something is one of its features.
e.g. Exam results illustrate only one aspect of a school's success.

● THESAURUS
consideration: *The cost involved will be a chief consideration in our choice.*
element: *Fitness is now an important element in our lives.*
factor: *an important factor in a child's development*
feature: *the most significant feature of his childhood*
part: *Respect is an important part of any relationship.*
point: *There is another point to remember when making your decision.*
side: *He had a darker side to his character.*

2 The aspect of a building is the direction it faces.
e.g. The southern aspect of the cottage faces over fields.

asphalt ['æsfælt] NOUN
a black substance used to make road surfaces and playgrounds

aspiration [ˌæspɪ'reɪʃən] **aspirations** NOUN
Someone's aspirations are their desires and ambitions.

aspire [ə'spaɪə] **aspires, aspiring, aspired**
VERB
If you aspire to something, you have an ambition to achieve it. *e.g. He aspired to work in music journalism.*
aspiring ADJECTIVE

aspirin ['æsprɪn] **aspirins** NOUN
1 a white drug used to relieve pain, fever, and colds
2 a tablet of this drug

ass [æs] **asses** NOUN
a donkey

assailant [ə'seɪlənt] **assailants** NOUN
someone who attacks another person

assassin [ə'sæsɪn] **assassins** NOUN
someone who has murdered a political or religious leader

[WORD HISTORY: from Arabic HASHSHASHIN meaning 'people who eat hashish'; the name comes from a medieval Muslim sect who ate hashish and went about murdering Crusaders]

assassinate [ə'sæsɪˌneɪt] **assassinates, assassinating, assassinated** VERB
To assassinate a political or religious leader is to murder him or her.
assassination NOUN

assault [ə'sɔːlt] **assaults, assaulting, assaulted** NOUN
1 a violent attack on someone
> VERB
2 To assault someone is to attack them violently.

assegai ['æsəˌgaɪ] **assegais** (*said* **ass**-i-guy); also spelt **assagai** NOUN
In South African English, a sharp, light spear.

assemble [ə'sɛmbəl] **assembles, assembling, assembled** VERB
1 To assemble is to gather together.

● THESAURUS
collect: *We all collected round him to listen.*
come together: *a common room where we can come together and relax*
congregate: *Youngsters love to congregate here in the evenings.*
convene: *A grand jury has convened to gather evidence.*
gather: *We all gathered in the board room.*
mass: *Troops were massing on both sides of the border.*

2 If you assemble something, you fit the parts of it together.

● THESAURUS
build: *A carpenter built the shelves for us.*
construct: *He had constructed a crude explosive device.*
erect: *Stagehands are employed to erect the scenery.*
make: *I like making model aeroplanes.*
put together: *You can buy the parts and put it together yourself.*

assembly [ə'sɛmblɪ] **assemblies** NOUN
1 a group of people who have gathered together for a meeting
2 The assembly of an object is the fitting together of its parts. *e.g. DIY assembly of units.*

assent [ə'sɛnt] **assents, assenting, assented** NOUN
1 If you give your assent to something, you agree to it.
> VERB
2 If you assent to something, you agree to it.

assert [ə'sɜːt] **asserts, asserting, asserted** VERB

1 VERB
If you ask someone a question, you put a question to them for them to answer
● THESAURUS
inquire: *I rang up to inquire about train times.*
interrogate: *I interrogated everyone even slightly involved.*
query: *He queried whether sabotage could have been involved.*
question: *He was questioned by police.*
quiz: *He was quizzed about his eligibility for benefits.*
<< OPPOSITE *answer*

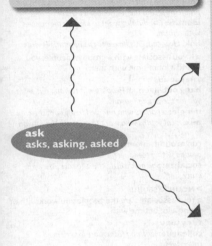

ask
asks, asking, asked

2 VERB
If you ask someone to do something or give you something, you tell them you want them to do it or to give it to you
● THESAURUS
appeal: *The police appealed for witnesses to come forward.*
beg: *I begged him to leave me alone.*
demand: *I demanded an explanation from him.*
implore: *I implored him not to give it up.*
plead: *She pleaded to be allowed to go.*
seek: *Always seek legal advice before entering into any agreement.*

3 VERB
If you ask someone's permission or forgiveness, you try to obtain it
● THESAURUS
bid (literary): *They all smiled at him and bade him eat.*
invite: *She invited him to her 26th birthday party.*

1 If you assert a fact or belief, you state it firmly and forcefully.

2 If you assert yourself, you speak and behave in a confident and direct way, so that people pay attention to you.

assertion [əˈsɜːʃən] **assertions** NOUN
a statement or claim

assertive [əˈsɜːtɪv] ADJECTIVE
If you are assertive, you speak and behave in a confident and direct way, so that people pay attention to you.
assertively ADVERB, **assertiveness** NOUN

assess [əˈsɛs] **assesses, assessing, assessed** VERB
(EXAM TERM) If you assess something, you consider it carefully and make a judgment about it.
assessment NOUN

assessor [əˈsɛsə] **assessors** NOUN
someone whose job is to assess the value of something

asset [ˈæsɛt] **assets** NOUN
1 a person or thing considered useful *e.g. He will be a great asset to the club.*
> PLURAL NOUN
2 The assets of a person or company are all the things they own that could be sold to raise money.

assign [əˈsaɪn] **assigns, assigning, assigned** VERB
1 To assign something to someone is to give it to them officially or to make them responsible for it.
2 If someone is assigned to do something, they are officially told to do it.

assignation [ˌæsɪɡˈneɪʃən] **assignations** NOUN; LITERARY
a secret meeting with someone, especially a lover

assignment [əˈsaɪnmənt] **assignments** NOUN
a job someone is given to do

assimilate [əˈsɪmɪˌleɪt] **assimilates, assimilating, assimilated** VERB
1 If you assimilate ideas or experiences, you learn and understand them.
2 When people are assimilated into a group, they become part of it.
assimilation NOUN

assist [əˈsɪst] **assists, assisting, assisted** VERB
To assist someone is to help them do something.
assistance NOUN

assistant [əˈsɪstənt] **assistants** NOUN
someone whose job is to help another person in their work

● THESAURUS
aide: *a presidential aide*
ally: *her political allies*
colleague: *a business colleague*
helper: *volunteer helpers*
right-hand man: *the resignation of the manager's right-hand man*

associate **associates, associating, associated** [əˈsəʊʃɪeɪt] VERB
1 If you associate one thing with another, you connect the two things in your mind.

● THESAURUS
connect: *a common problem directly connected with stress*
couple: *The papers coupled the Gulf crisis with the problems facing the former Soviet Union.*
identify: *Candidates want to identify themselves with reform.*
link: *Liver cancer is linked to the hepatitis B virus.*

2 If you associate with a group of people, you spend a lot of time with them.

● THESAURUS
hang out: informal *People want to hang out with you for the wrong reasons.*
mingle: *reporters who mingled freely with the crowd*
mix: *local youths who want to mix with the foreign tourists*
run around: informal *What's he doing running around with a teenager?*
socialize: *She made little effort to socialize with other staff.*

> NOUN [əˈsəʊʃɪɪt]
3 Your associates are the people you work with or spend a lot of time with.

● THESAURUS
colleague: *learning from more experienced colleagues*
co-worker: *Their Chinese co-workers often worked seven days a week.*
workmate: *employees who expose dishonest workmates*

association [əˌsəʊsɪˈeɪʃən] **associations** NOUN
1 an organization for people who have similar interests, jobs, or aims

● THESAURUS
body: *the chairman of the policemen's representative body*
club: *the local Young Conservatives' club*
company: *a major motor company*
confederation: *the Confederation of British Industry*
group: *an environmental group*
institution: *a member of various financial institutions*
league: *the World Muslim League*

a

society: *the Royal Society for the Protection of Birds*
syndicate: *a syndicate of international banks*

2 Your association with a person or group is the connection or involvement you have with them.

● THESAURUS
affiliation: *He has no affiliation with any political party.*
attachment: *Mother and child form a close attachment.*
bond: *There is a special bond between us.*
connection: *He has denied any connection with the organization.*
relationship: *Ours was strictly a professional relationship.*
tie: *I had very close ties with the family.*

3 An association between two things is a link you make in your mind between them. *e.g. The place contained associations for her.*

assonance ['æsənəns] NOUN
the use of similar vowel or consonant sounds in words near to each other or in the same word, for example 'a long storm'

assorted [ə'sɔːtɪd] ADJECTIVE
Assorted things are different in size and colour. *e.g. assorted swimsuits*

assortment [ə'sɔːtmənt] **assortments** NOUN
a group of similar things that are different sizes and colours *e.g. an amazing assortment of old toys*

assume [ə'sjuːm] **assumes, assuming, assumed** VERB
1 If you assume that something is true, you accept it is true even though you have not thought about it. *e.g. I assumed that he would turn up.*

● THESAURUS
believe: *I believe she'll be back next week.*
guess: *informal I guess she thought that was pretty smart.*
imagine: *You tend to imagine that you cannot put a foot wrong.*
suppose: *I see no reason to suppose that it isn't working.*
think: *They thought that they had the match won.*

2 To assume responsibility for something is to put yourself in charge of it.

● THESAURUS
accept: *He accepted the role of player-captain.*
shoulder: *He has had to shoulder the responsibility of his father's mistakes.*
take on: *Don't take on more responsibilities than you can handle.*
undertake: *He undertook to edit the text himself.*

assumption [ə'sʌmpʃən] **assumptions** NOUN

1 a belief that something is true, without thinking about it

2 Assumption of power or responsibility is the taking of it.

assurance [ə'ʃʊərəns] **assurances** NOUN
1 something said which is intended to make people less worried *e.g. She was emphatic in her assurances that she wanted to stay.*

2 Assurance is a feeling of confidence. *e.g. He handled the car with ease and assurance.*

3 Life assurance is a type of insurance that pays money to your dependants when you die.

assure [ə'ʃʊə] **assures, assuring, assured** VERB
If you assure someone that something is true, you tell them it is true.

asterisk ['æstərɪsk] **asterisks** NOUN
the symbol (*) used in printing and writing
[WORD HISTORY: from Greek ASTERIKOS meaning 'small star']

astern [ə'stɜːn] ADVERB OR ADJECTIVE; NAUTICAL
backwards or at the back

asteroid ['æstə,rɔɪd] **asteroids** NOUN
one of the large number of very small planets that move around the sun between the orbits of Jupiter and Mars

asthma ['æsmə] NOUN
a disease of the chest which causes wheezing and difficulty in breathing
asthmatic ADJECTIVE

astonish [ə'stɒnɪʃ] **astonishes, astonishing, astonished** VERB
If something astonishes you, it surprises you very much.
astonished ADJECTIVE, **astonishing** ADJECTIVE, **astonishingly** ADVERB, **astonishment** NOUN

astound [ə'staʊnd] **astounds, astounding, astounded** VERB
If something astounds you, it shocks and amazes you.
astounded ADJECTIVE, **astounding** ADJECTIVE

astray [ə'streɪ] ADVERB
1 To **lead someone astray** is to influence them to do something wrong.

2 If something **goes astray**, it gets lost. *e.g. The money had gone astray.*

astride [ə'straɪd] PREPOSITION
with one leg on either side of something *e.g. He is pictured astride his new motorbike.*

astringent [ə'strɪndʒənt] **astringents** NOUN
a liquid that makes skin less greasy and stops bleeding

astro- PREFIX
'Astro-' means involving the stars and planets. For example, *astrology* is predicting the future from the positions and movements of the stars and planets, and *astronomy* is the scientific study of the stars and planets

astrology [əˈstrɒlədʒɪ] NOUN
the study of the sun, moon, and stars in order to predict the future
astrological ADJECTIVE, **astrologer** NOUN

astronaut [ˈæstrəˌnɔːt] **astronauts** NOUN
a person who operates a spacecraft
[WORD HISTORY: from Greek ASTRON meaning 'star' and NAUTĒS meaning 'sailor']

astronomical [ˌæstrəˈnɒmɪkəl] ADJECTIVE
1 involved with or relating to astronomy
2 extremely large in amount *e.g. astronomical legal costs*
astronomically ADVERB

astronomy [əˈstrɒnəmɪ] NOUN
the scientific study of stars and planets
astronomer NOUN

astute [əˈstjuːt] ADJECTIVE
clever and quick at understanding situations and behaviour *e.g. an astute diplomat*

● THESAURUS
alert: *He is old, but he has a very quick and alert mind.*
clever: *a clever business move*
keen: *a keen understanding of politics*
perceptive: *his perceptive analysis of the situation*
quick: *He has an enquiring mind and a quick intelligence.*
sharp: *His gentle manner disguised a sharp mind.*
shrewd: *He demonstrated a shrewd understanding of human nature.*
smart: *a very smart move*

asunder [əˈsʌndə] ADVERB; LITERARY
If something is torn asunder, it is violently torn apart.

asylum [əˈsaɪləm] **asylums** NOUN
1 OLD-FASHIONED
a hospital for mental patients
2 Political asylum is protection given by a government to someone who has fled from their own country for political reasons.

asymmetrical or **asymmetric**
[ˌeɪsɪˈmɛtrɪkəl] *or* [ˌeɪsɪˈmɛtrɪk] ADJECTIVE
unbalanced or with one half not exactly the same as the other half
asymmetry NOUN

at [æt] PREPOSITION
1 used to say where someone or something is *e.g. Bert met us at the airport.*

2 used to mention the direction something is going in *e.g. He threw his plate at the wall.*
3 used to say when something happens *e.g. The game starts at 3 o'clock.*
4 used to mention the rate or price of something *e.g. The shares were priced at fifty pence.*

atheist [ˈeɪθɪˌɪst] **atheists** NOUN
someone who believes there is no God
atheistic ADJECTIVE, **atheism** NOUN

athlete [ˈæθliːt] **athletes** NOUN
(PE) someone who is good at sport and takes part in sporting events

athletic [æθˈlɛtɪk] ADJECTIVE **(PE)**
1 strong, healthy, and good at sports
2 involving athletes or athletics *e.g. I lost two years of my athletic career because of injury.*

athletics [æθˈlɛtɪks] NOUN
Sporting events such as running, jumping, and throwing are called athletics.

Atlantic [ətˈlæntɪk] NOUN
The Atlantic is the ocean separating North and South America from Europe and Africa.
[WORD HISTORY: from the ATLAS mountains in North Africa; the Atlantic lies to the west of these mountains]

atlas [ˈætləs] **atlases** NOUN
(GEOGRAPHY) a book of maps
[WORD HISTORY: from the giant ATLAS in Greek mythology, who supported the sky on his shoulders]

atmosphere [ˈætməsˌfɪə] **atmospheres** NOUN
1 the air and other gases that surround a planet; also the air in a particular place *e.g. a musty atmosphere*
2 the general mood of a place *e.g. a relaxed atmosphere*
3 **(ENGLISH)** the mood created by the writer of a novel or play
atmospheric ADJECTIVE

atom [ˈætəm] **atoms** NOUN
the smallest part of an element that can take part in a chemical reaction

atomic [əˈtɒmɪk] ADJECTIVE
relating to atoms or to the power released by splitting atoms *e.g. atomic energy*

atomic bomb atomic bombs NOUN
an extremely powerful bomb which explodes because of the energy that comes from splitting atoms

atone [əˈtəʊn] **atones, atoning, atoned** VERB; FORMAL
If you atone for something wrong you have done,

you say you are sorry and try to make up for it.

atrocious [əˈtrəʊʃəs] ADJECTIVE
extremely bad

atrocity [əˈtrɒsɪtɪ] **atrocities** NOUN
an extremely cruel and shocking act

attach [əˈtætʃ] **attaches, attaching, attached** VERB
If you attach something to something else, you join or fasten the two things together.

> THESAURUS
affix: *His name was affixed to the wall of his cubicle.*
connect: *Connect the pipe to the tap.*
couple: *The engine is coupled to a gearbox.*
fasten: *The shelves are fastened to the wall with screws.*
join: *two sticks joined together by a chain*
link: *tree houses linked by ropes*
tie: *He tied the dog to a post with its leash.*
<<OPPOSITE *separate*

attaché [əˈtæʃeɪ] **attachés** NOUN
a member of staff in an embassy *e.g. the Russian Cultural Attaché*

attached [əˈtætʃt] ADJECTIVE
If you are attached to someone, you are very fond of them.

attachment [əˈtætʃmənt] **attachments** NOUN
1 Attachment to someone is a feeling of love and affection for them.
2 Attachment to a cause or ideal is a strong belief in it and support for it.
3 a piece of equipment attached to a tool or machine to do a particular job
4
an extra document attached to or included with another document
5
a file that is attached to an e-mail

attack [əˈtæk] **attacks, attacking, attacked** VERB
1 To attack someone is to use violence against them so as to hurt or kill them.

> THESAURUS
assault: *The gang assaulted him with iron bars.*
charge: *He ordered us to charge.*
invade: *The allies invaded the Italian mainland at Anzio.*
raid: *He was found guilty of raiding a bank.*
set upon: *As the lorry drove east it was set upon by bandits.*
storm: *The refugees decided to storm the embassy.*
2 If you attack someone or their ideas, you criticize them strongly. *e.g. He attacked the government's economic policies.*

> THESAURUS
blast: *He blasted the referee for his inconsistency.*
censure: *The bank has been censured and fined by the authority.*
criticize: *The regime has been harshly criticized.*
have a go: British; informal *If they made a mistake the crowd would have a go at them.*
put down: informal *He was always putting me down.*
vilify: formal *He was vilified, hounded, and forced into exile.*

3 If a disease or chemical attacks something, it damages or destroys it. *e.g. fungal diseases that attack crops*
4 In a game such as football or hockey, to attack is to get the ball into a position from which a goal can be scored.
> NOUN
5 An attack is violent physical action against someone.

> THESAURUS
assault: *The rebels are poised for a new assault.*
charge: *a bayonet charge*
invasion: *the Roman invasion of Britain*
offensive: *the government's military offensive against the rebels*
onslaught: *civilians trying to flee from the military onslaught*
raid: *a raid on a house by armed police*

6 An attack on someone or on their ideas is strong criticism of them.
7 An attack of an illness is a short time in which you suffer badly with it.
attacker NOUN

attain [əˈteɪn] **attains, attaining, attained** VERB; FORMAL
If you attain something, you manage to achieve it. *e.g. He eventually attained the rank of major.*
attainable ADJECTIVE, **attainment** NOUN

attempt [əˈtempt] **attempts, attempting, attempted** VERB
1 If you attempt to do something, you try to do it or achieve it, but may not succeed. *e.g. They attempted to escape.*

> THESAURUS
endeavour: *I will endeavour to arrange it.*
seek: *We have never sought to impose our views.*
strive: *The school strives to treat pupils as individuals.*
try: *I tried hard to persuade him to stay.*
try your hand at: *He'd always wanted to try his hand at writing.*

> NOUN
2 an act of trying to do something *e.g. He made no attempt to go for the ball.*

THESAURUS
bid: *a bid to save the newspaper*
crack: informal *his third crack at the world heavyweight title*
go: informal *My mum suggested I should have a go at becoming a jockey.*
shot: informal *We'd like a shot at winning the league.*
stab: informal *Several tennis stars have had a stab at acting.*
try: *That makes the scheme worth a try.*

attend [ə'tɛnd] **attends, attending, attended** VERB
1 If you attend an event, you are present at it.
2 To attend school, church, or hospital is to go there regularly.
3 If you attend to something, you deal with it. *e.g. We have business to attend to first.*
attendance NOUN

attendant [ə'tɛndənt] **attendants** NOUN
someone whose job is to serve people in a place such as a garage or cloakroom

attention [ə'tɛnʃən] NOUN
Attention is the thought or care you give to something. *e.g. The woman needed medical attention.*

attentive [ə'tɛntɪv] ADJECTIVE
paying close attention to something *e.g. an attentive audience*
attentively ADVERB, **attentiveness** NOUN

attest [ə'tɛst] **attests, attesting, attested** VERB; FORMAL
To attest something is to show or declare it is true.
attestation NOUN

attic ['ætɪk] **attics** NOUN
a room at the top of a house immediately below the roof

attire [ə'taɪə] NOUN; FORMAL
Attire is clothing. *e.g. We will be wearing traditional wedding attire.*

attitude ['ætɪˌtjuːd] **attitudes** NOUN
Your attitude to someone or something is the way you think about them and behave towards them.

THESAURUS
outlook: *behaviour that seems contrary to his whole outlook*
perspective: *It gave me a new perspective on life.*
point of view: *Try to look at this from my point of view.*
position: *What's your position on this issue?*
stance: *the Church's stance on contraception*

attorney [ə'tɜːnɪ] **attorneys** NOUN; US
An attorney is the same as a lawyer.

attract [ə'trækt] **attracts, attracting, attracted** VERB
1 If something attracts people, it interests them and makes them want to go to it. *e.g. The trials have attracted many leading riders.*

THESAURUS
appeal to: *The idea appealed to him.*
draw: *The match drew a large crowd.*
entice: *She resisted attempts to entice her into politics.*
lure: *They were being lured into a trap.*
pull: informal *They have to employ performers to pull a crowd.*
tempt: *Can I tempt you with some wine?*
<<OPPOSITE *repel*

2 If someone attracts you, you like and admire them. *e.g. He was attracted to her outgoing personality.*
3 If something attracts support or publicity, it gets it.

attraction [ə'trækʃən] **attractions** NOUN
1 Attraction is a feeling of liking someone or something very much.
2 something people visit for interest or pleasure *e.g. The temple is a major tourist attraction.*
3 a quality that attracts someone or something *e.g. the attraction of moving to seaside resorts*

attractive [ə'træktɪv] ADJECTIVE
1 interesting and possibly advantageous *e.g. an attractive proposition*
2 pleasant to look at or be with *e.g. an attractive woman... an attractive personality*
attractively ADVERB, **attractiveness** NOUN

THESAURUS
appealing: *a sense of humour that I found very appealing*
charming: *a charming little village*
fetching: *a fetching outfit*
handsome: *a handsome man*
lovely: *a lovely island*
pretty: *a shy, pretty girl*
<<OPPOSITE *unattractive*

attribute attributes, attributing, attributed VERB [ə'trɪbjuːt]
1 If you attribute something to a person or thing, you believe it was caused or created by that person or thing. *e.g. Water pollution was attributed to the use of fertilizers... a painting attributed to Raphael*
> NOUN ['ætrɪˌbjuːt]
2 a quality or feature someone or something has
attribution NOUN, **attributable** ADJECTIVE

THESAURUS
characteristic: *their physical characteristics*
feature: *the most striking feature of his music*

property: *the magnetic properties of iron*
quality: *His humility is one of his most endearing qualities.*
trait: *personality traits*

attrition [əˈtrɪʃən] NOUN
Attrition is the constant wearing down of an enemy.

attuned [əˈtjuːnd] ADJECTIVE
accustomed or well adjusted to something *e.g. His eyes quickly became attuned to the dark.*

aubergine [ˈəʊbəˌʒiːn] **aubergines** NOUN
a dark purple, pear-shaped fruit that is eaten as a vegetable. It is also called an **eggplant**

auburn [ˈɔːbən] ADJECTIVE
Auburn hair is reddish brown.

auction [ˈɔːkʃən] **auctions, auctioning, auctioned** NOUN
1 a public sale in which goods are sold to the person who offers the highest price
> VERB
2 To auction something is to sell it in an auction.

auctioneer [ˌɔːkʃəˈnɪə] **auctioneers** NOUN
the person in charge of an auction

audacious [ɔːˈdeɪʃəs] ADJECTIVE
very daring *e.g. an audacious escape from jail*
audaciously ADVERB, **audacity** NOUN

audi- PREFIX
'Audi-' means involving hearing or sound *e.g. audible... auditorium*

audible [ˈɔːdɪbəl] ADJECTIVE
loud enough to be heard *e.g. She spoke in a barely audible whisper.*
audibly ADVERB, **audibility** NOUN

audience [ˈɔːdɪəns] **audiences** NOUN
1 the group of people who are watching or listening to a performance
2 a private or formal meeting with an important person *e.g. an audience with the Queen*

audio [ˈɔːdɪˌəʊ] ADJECTIVE
used in recording and reproducing sound *e.g. audio equipment*

audit [ˈɔːdɪt] **audits, auditing, audited** VERB
1 To audit a set of financial accounts is to examine them officially to check they are correct.
> NOUN
2 an official examination of an organization's accounts
auditor NOUN

audition [ɔːˈdɪʃən] **auditions** NOUN
a short performance given by an actor or musician, so that a director can decide whether they are suitable for a part in a play or film or for a place in an orchestra

auditorium [ˌɔːdɪˈtɔːrɪəm] **auditoriums** or **auditoria** NOUN
the part of a theatre where the audience sits

augment [ɔːgˈmɛnt] **augments, augmenting, augmented** VERB FORMAL
To augment something is to add something to it.

● THESAURUS
add to: *A fitted kitchen adds to the value of your house.*
boost: *people who boost their earnings by working part-time from home*
complement: *an in-work benefit that complements earnings*
increase: *He is eager to increase his income by any means.*
reinforce: *measures which will reinforce their current strengths*
supplement: *I suggest supplementing your diet with vitamin A.*
top up: *compulsory contributions to top up pension schemes*

August [ˈɔːgəst] NOUN
the eighth month of the year. August has 31 days

aunt [ɑːnt] **aunts** NOUN
Your aunt is the sister of your mother or father, or the wife of your uncle.

au pair [əʊ ˈpɛə] **au pairs** NOUN
a young foreign girl who lives with a family to help with the children and housework and sometimes to learn the language

aura [ˈɔːrə] **auras** NOUN
an atmosphere that surrounds a person or thing *e.g. She has a great aura of calmness.*

aural [ˈɔːrəl] ADJECTIVE
relating to or done through the sense of hearing *e.g. an aural comprehension test*

auspices [ˈɔːspɪˌsiːz] PLURAL NOUN; FORMAL
If you do something under the auspices of a person or organization, you do it with their support. *e.g. military intervention under the auspices of the United Nations*

auspicious [ɔːˈspɪʃəs] ADJECTIVE; FORMAL
favourable and seeming to promise success *e.g. It was an auspicious start to the month.*

austere [ɒˈstɪə] ADJECTIVE
plain and simple, and without luxury *e.g. an austere grey office block*
austerity NOUN

Australasia [ˌɒstrəˈleɪzɪə] NOUN
Australasia consists of Australia, New Zealand, and neighbouring islands in the Pacific.
Australasian ADJECTIVE

Australia [ɒˈstreɪliə] NOUN
Australia is the smallest continent and the largest island in the world, situated between the Indian Ocean and the Pacific.

Australian [ɒˈstreɪliən] **Australians**
ADJECTIVE
1 belonging or relating to Australia
> NOUN
2 someone who comes from Australia

Austrian [ˈɒstriən] **Austrians** ADJECTIVE
1 belonging or relating to Austria
> NOUN
2 someone who comes from Austria

authentic [ɔːˈθentɪk] ADJECTIVE
real and genuine
authenticity NOUN

● THESAURUS
bona fide: *We are happy to donate to bona fide charities.*
dinkum: *Australian and New Zealand; informal a place which serves dinkum Aussie tucker*
genuine: *Experts are convinced the manuscript is genuine.*
real: *It's a real Rembrandt.*
true: *Of course she's not a true blonde.*
<<OPPOSITE *fake*

author [ˈɔːθə] **authors** NOUN
(ENGLISH) The author of a book is the person who wrote it.

> Use *author* to talk about both men and women writers, as *authoress* is now felt to be insulting.

authoritarian [ɔːˌθɒrɪˈteəriən] ADJECTIVE
believing in strict obedience *e.g. thirty years of authoritarian government*
authoritarianism NOUN

authoritative [ɔːˈθɒrɪtətɪv] ADJECTIVE
1 having authority *e.g. his deep, authoritative voice*
2 accepted as being reliable and accurate *e.g. an authoritative biography of the President*
authoritatively ADVERB

authority [ɔːˈθɒrɪti] **authorities** NOUN
1 Authority is the power to control people. *e.g. the authority of the state*
2 (GEOGRAPHY) In Britain, an authority is a local government department. *e.g. local health authorities*
3 Someone who is an authority on something knows a lot about it. *e.g. the world's leading authority on fashion*
> PLURAL NOUN
4 The authorities are the people who have the power to make decisions.

authorize [ˈɔːθəˌraɪz] **authorizes, authorizing, authorized;** also spelt
authorise VERB
To authorize something is to give official permission for it to happen.
authorization NOUN

auto- PREFIX
'Auto-' means 'self'. For example, an automatic machine works by itself without needing to be operated by hand
[WORD HISTORY: from Greek AUTOS meaning 'self']

autobiography [ˌɔːtəʊbaɪˈɒɡrəfɪ]
autobiographies NOUN
Someone's autobiography is an account of their life which they have written themselves.
autobiographical ADJECTIVE

autograph [ˈɔːtəˌɡrɑːf] **autographs** NOUN
the signature of a famous person

automated [ˈɔːtəmeɪtɪd] ADJECTIVE
If a factory or way of making things is automated, it works using machinery rather than people.
automation NOUN

automatic [ˌɔːtəˈmætɪk] ADJECTIVE
1 An automatic machine is programmed to perform tasks without needing a person to operate it. *e.g. The plane was flying on automatic pilot.*

● THESAURUS
automated: *highly automated production lines*
mechanical: *the oldest working mechanical clock in the world*
robot: *a robot telescope*
self-propelled: *self-propelled artillery*

2 Automatic actions or reactions take place without involving conscious thought.

● THESAURUS
instinctive: *an instinctive reaction*
involuntary: *involuntary muscle movements*
natural: *the insect's natural instinct to feed*
reflex: *Blushing is a reflex action linked to the nervous system.*

3 A process or punishment that is automatic always happens as a direct result of something. *e.g. The penalty for murder is an automatic life sentence.*
automatically ADVERB

automobile [ˈɔːtəməˌbiːl] **automobiles**
NOUN US, FORMAL
a car

● THESAURUS
car: *My dad's promised me a car if I pass my finals.*
motor: *He's bought himself a flash new motor.*
vehicle: *A child ran straight out in front of the vehicle.*

autonomous [ɔːˈtɒnəməs] ADJECTIVE
An autonomous country governs itself rather

than being controlled by anyone else.
autonomy NOUN

autopsy [ˈɔːtəpsɪ] **autopsies** NOUN
a medical examination of a dead body to discover
the cause of death

autumn [ˈɔːtəm] **autumns** NOUN
the season between summer and winter
autumnal ADJECTIVE

auxiliary [ɔːɡˈzɪljərɪ] **auxiliaries** NOUN
1 a person employed to help other members of
staff *e.g. nursing auxiliaries*
> ADJECTIVE
2 Auxiliary equipment is used when necessary in
addition to the main equipment. *e.g. Auxiliary fuel
tanks were stored in the bomb bay.*

auxiliary verb **auxiliary verbs** NOUN
In grammar, an auxiliary verb is a verb which
forms tenses of other verbs or questions. For
example in 'He has gone', 'has' is the auxiliary
verb and in 'Do you understand?', 'do' is the
auxiliary verb.

avail [əˈveɪl] PHRASE
If something you do is **of no avail** or **to no avail**,
it is not successful or helpful.

available [əˈveɪləbəl] ADJECTIVE
1 Something that is available can be obtained.
e.g. Artichokes are available in supermarkets.
● **THESAURUS**
accessible: *This information is accessible on the
Internet.*
at hand: *Having the right equipment at hand will be
enormously useful.*
at someone's disposal: *Do you have all the facts
at your disposal?*
free: *There was only one seat free on the train.*
handy: *Keep your keys handy so you can get into your
car quickly.*
to hand: *Keep your insurance details to hand when
driving.*
<<OPPOSITE *unavailable*
2 Someone who is available is ready for work or
free for people to talk to. *e.g. She will no longer be
available at weekends.*
availability NOUN

avalanche [ˈævəˌlɑːntʃ] **avalanches** NOUN
a huge mass of snow and ice that falls down a
mountain side

avant-garde [ˌævɒnˈɡɑːd] ADJECTIVE
extremely modern or experimental, especially in
art, literature, or music

avarice [ˈævərɪs] NOUN; FORMAL
greed for money and possessions
avaricious ADJECTIVE

avenge [əˈvɛndʒ] **avenges, avenging,
avenged** VERB

If you avenge something harmful someone has
done to you or your family, you punish or harm
the other person in return. *e.g. He was prepared to
avenge the death of his friend.*
avenger NOUN

avenue [ˈævɪˌnjuː] **avenues** NOUN
a street, especially one with trees along it

average [ˈævərɪdʒ] **averages, averaging,
averaged** NOUN (MATHS)
1 a result obtained by adding several amounts
together and then dividing the total by the
number of different amounts *e.g. Six pupils were
examined in a total of 39 subjects, an average of 6.5
subjects per pupil.*
> ADJECTIVE
2 Average means standard or normal. *e.g. the
average American teenager*
● **THESAURUS**
normal: *I am now back to leading a perfectly normal
life.*
regular: *He's just a regular guy.*
standard: *the standard price of a CD*
typical: *A typical day begins at 8.30.*
usual: *This isn't the usual kind of mail-order
catalogue.*
> VERB
3 To average a number is to produce that number
as an average over a period of time. *e.g. Monthly
sales averaged more than 110,000.*
> PHRASE
4 You say **on average** when mentioning what
usually happens in a situation. *e.g. Men are, on
average, taller than women.*
● **THESAURUS**
as a rule: *As a rule, the fee is roughly equal to the
savings you have made.*
generally: *A glass of fine wine generally costs
about £4.*
normally: *Normally, the transport system carries
50,000 passengers a day.*
typically: *In America, estate agents typically charge
5-6% of the sale price.*
usually: *In good condition, these models usually
fetch up to 300 dollars at auction.*

averse [əˈvɜːs] ADJECTIVE
unwilling to do something *e.g. He was averse to
taking painkillers.*

aversion [əˈvɜːʃən] **aversions** NOUN
If you have an aversion to someone or
something, you dislike them very much.

avert [əˈvɜːt] **averts, averting, averted**
VERB
1 If you avert an unpleasant event, you prevent it
from happening.
2 If you avert your eyes from something, you turn
your eyes away from it.

aviary ['eɪvjərɪ] **aviaries** NOUN
a large cage or group of cages in which birds are kept

aviation [ˌeɪvɪ'eɪʃən] NOUN
the science of flying aircraft

aviator ['eɪvɪˌeɪtə] **aviators** NOUN; OLD-FASHIONED, INFORMAL
a pilot of an aircraft

avid ['ævɪd] ADJECTIVE
eager and enthusiastic for something
avidly ADVERB

avocado [ˌævə'kɑːdəʊ] **avocados** NOUN
a pear-shaped fruit, with dark green skin, soft greenish yellow flesh, and a large stone

avoid [ə'vɔɪd] **avoids, avoiding, avoided** VERB
1 If you avoid doing something, you make a deliberate effort not to do it.

⬤ THESAURUS
dodge: *dodging military service by feigning illness*
duck out of: *informal ducking out of the post-match press conference*
fight shy of: *She fought shy of confronting her critics.*
refrain from: *Mrs Hardie refrained from making any comment.*
shirk: *We won't shirk our responsibility.*

2 If you avoid someone, you keep away from them.
avoidable ADJECTIVE, **avoidance** NOUN

⬤ THESAURUS
dodge: *He refuses to dodge his critics.*
elude: *an attempt to elude photographers*
eschew: *formal He eschewed publicity.*
evade: *He managed to evade the police.*
shun: *Everybody shunned him.*
sidestep: *Rarely does he sidestep a question.*
steer clear of: *It would be best to steer clear of her.*

avowed [ə'vaʊd] ADJECTIVE
1 FORMAL
If you are an avowed supporter or opponent of something, you have declared that you support it or oppose it.
2 An avowed belief or aim is one you hold very strongly.

avuncular [ə'vʌŋkjʊlə] ADJECTIVE
friendly and helpful in manner towards younger people, rather like an uncle

await [ə'weɪt] **awaits, awaiting, awaited** VERB
1 If you await something, you expect it.
2 If something awaits you, it will happen to you in the future.

awake [ə'weɪk] **awakes, awaking, awoke, awoken** ADJECTIVE

1 Someone who is awake is not sleeping.
> VERB
2 When you awake, you wake up.
3 If you are awoken by something, it wakes you up.

awaken [ə'weɪkən] **awakens, awakening, awakened** VERB
If something awakens an emotion or interest in you, you start to feel this emotion or interest.

award [ə'wɔːd] **awards, awarding, awarded** NOUN
1 a prize or certificate for doing something well
2 a sum of money an organization gives to students for training or study
> VERB
3 If you award someone something, you give it to them formally or officially.

aware [ə'weə] ADJECTIVE
1 If you are aware of something, you realize it is there.

⬤ THESAURUS
acquainted with: *He was well acquainted with American literature.*
conscious of: *She was very conscious of Max studying her.*
familiar with: *I am not familiar with your work.*
mindful of: *Everyone should be mindful of the dangers.*
<<OPPOSITE *unaware*

2 If you are aware of something, you know about it.
awareness NOUN

⬤ THESAURUS
informed: *the importance of keeping the public properly informed*
in the picture: *He's always kept me in the picture.*
knowledgeable: *He's very knowledgeable about new technology.*

awash [ə'wɒʃ] ADJECTIVE OR ADVERB
covered with water *e.g. After the downpour the road was awash.*

away [ə'weɪ] ADVERB
1 moving from a place *e.g. I saw them walk away.*
2 at a distance from a place *e.g. Our nearest vet is 12 kilometres away.*
3 in its proper place *e.g. He put his chequebook away.*
4 not at home, school, or work *e.g. She had been away from home for years.*

awe [ɔː] NOUN; FORMAL
a feeling of great respect mixed with amazement and sometimes slight fear

awesome ['ɔːsəm] ADJECTIVE

1 Something that is awesome is very impressive and frightening.

2 INFORMAL

Awesome also means excellent or outstanding.

awful ['ɔːful] ADJECTIVE

1 very unpleasant or very bad

● THESAURUS

appalling: *living under the most appalling conditions*

dreadful: *They told us the dreadful news.*

frightful: *a frightful ordeal*

ghastly: *a mother accompanied by her ghastly unruly child*

horrendous: *The violence used was horrendous.*

terrible: *Her French is terrible.*

2 INFORMAL

very great *e.g. It took an awful lot of courage.*

awfully ADVERB

awkward ['ɔːkwəd] ADJECTIVE

1 clumsy and uncomfortable *e.g. an awkward gesture*

2 embarrassed or nervous *e.g. He was a shy, awkward young man.*

3 difficult to deal with *e.g. My lawyer is in an awkward situation.*

awning ['ɔːnɪŋ] **awnings** NOUN

a large roof of canvas or plastic attached to a building or vehicle

awry [ə'raɪ] ADVERB OR ADJECTIVE

wrong or not as planned *e.g. Why had their plans gone so badly awry?.*

axe [æks] **axes, axing, axed** NOUN

1 a tool with a handle and a sharp blade, used for chopping wood

> VERB

2 To axe something is to end it.

axiom ['æksɪəm] **axioms** NOUN

a statement or saying that is generally accepted to be true

axis ['æksɪs] **axes** NOUN (MATHS)

1 an imaginary line through the centre of something, around which it moves

2 one of the two sides of a graph

axle ['æksəl] **axles** NOUN

the long bar that connects a pair of wheels on a vehicle

ayatollah [ˌaɪə'tɒlə] **ayatollahs** NOUN

an Islamic religious leader in Iran

azure ['æʒə] ADJECTIVE; LITERARY

bright blue

Bb

babble ['bæbᵊl] **babbles, babbling, babbled** VERB
When someone babbles, they talk in a confused or excited way.

● THESAURUS
burble: *He burbles on about the goals he has scored.*
chatter: *Jane chattered about the children.*
gabble: *I started to gabble in the interview.*
prattle: *Alan is prattling on again.*

baboon [bə'buːn] **baboons** NOUN
an African monkey with a pointed face, large teeth, and a long tail
[WORD HISTORY: from Old French BABOUE meaning 'grimace']

baby ['beɪbɪ] **babies** NOUN
a child in the first year or two of its life
babyhood NOUN, **babyish** ADJECTIVE

● THESAURUS
ankle-biter: Australian and New Zealand; slang *I knew him when he was just an ankle-biter.*
bairn: Scottish *My wife's expecting a bairn.*
child: *They celebrated the birth of their first child.*
infant: *young mums with infants in prams*

baby-sit ['beɪbɪ,sɪt] **baby-sits, baby-sitting, baby-sat** VERB
To baby-sit for someone means to look after their children while that person is out.
baby-sitter NOUN, **baby-sitting** NOUN

baccalaureate [,bækə'lɔːrɪɪt] **baccalaureates** NOUN
an internationally recognized course of study made up of several different subjects, offered by some schools as an alternative to A levels

bach [bætʃ] **baches, baching, bached** NOUN
1 In New Zealand, a small holiday cottage.
> VERB
2 INFORMAL
In Australian and New Zealand English, to bach is to live and keep a house on your own, especially when you are not used to it.

bachelor ['bætʃələ] **bachelors** NOUN
a man who has never been married

back [bæk] **backs, backing, backed** ADVERB

1 When people or things move back, they move in the opposite direction from the one they are facing.

2 When people or things go back to a place or situation, they return to it. *e.g. She went back to sleep.*

3 If you get something back, it is returned to you.

4 If you do something back to someone, you do to them what they have done to you. *e.g. I smiled back at them.*

5 Back also means in the past. *e.g. It happened back in the early eighties.*

> NOUN
6 the rear part of your body

7 the part of something that is behind the front

● THESAURUS
end: *the end of the corridor*
rear: *the rear of the building*
reverse: *the reverse of the sheet*
stern: *the stern of a boat*
<<OPPOSITE *front*

> ADJECTIVE
8 The back parts of something are the ones near the rear. *e.g. an animal's back legs*

> VERB
9 If a building backs onto something, its back faces in that direction.

10 When a car backs, it moves backwards.

11 To back a person or organization means to support or finance that person or organization.
back down

● THESAURUS
advocate: *Mr Jones advocates longer school days.*
encourage: *The government is encouraging better child care.*
endorse: *Do you endorse his opinion?*
favour: *I favour a different approach.*
promote: *Ann is promoting Alan's ideas.*
support: *We supported his political campaign.*
<<OPPOSITE *oppose*

> VERB
12 If you back down on a demand or claim, you withdraw and give up.

back out VERB
13 If you back out of a promise or commitment,

you decide not to do what you had promised to do.

back up VERB

14 If you back up a claim or story, you produce evidence to show that it is true.

15 If you back someone up, you help and support them.

backbone ['bæk,bəʊn] **backbones** NOUN

1 the column of linked bones along the middle of a person's or animal's back

2 strength of character

backdate [,bæk'deɪt] **backdates, backdating, backdated** VERB

If an arrangement is backdated, it is valid from a date earlier than the one on which it is completed or signed.

backdrop ['bæk,drɒp] **backdrops** NOUN

the background to a situation or event *e.g. The visit occurred against the backdrop of the political crisis.*

backer ['bækə] **backers** NOUN

The backers of a project are the people who give it financial help.

backfire [,bæk'faɪə] **backfires, backfiring, backfired** VERB

1 If a plan backfires, it fails.

2 When a car backfires, there is a small but noisy explosion in its exhaust pipe.

background ['bæk,graʊnd] **backgrounds** NOUN

1 the circumstances which help to explain an event or caused it to happen

2 the kind of home you come from and your education and experience *e.g. a rich background*

● THESAURUS

culture: *people from different cultures*
environment: *the environment I grew up in*
history: *She has an interesting history.*
upbringing: *a strict upbringing*

3 If sounds are in the background, they are there but no one really pays any attention to them. *e.g. She could hear voices in the background.*

backing ['bækɪŋ] NOUN

support or help *e.g. The project got government backing.*

backlash ['bæk,læʃ] NOUN

a hostile reaction to a new development or a new policy

backlog ['bæk,lɒg] **backlogs** NOUN

a number of things which have not yet been done, but which need to be done

backpack ['bæk,pæk] **backpacks** NOUN

a large bag that hikers or campers carry on their backs

backside [,bæk'saɪd] **backsides** NOUN; INFORMAL

the part of your body that you sit on

backward ['bækwəd] ADJECTIVE

1 Backward means directed behind you. *e.g. without a backward glance*

2 A backward country or society is one that does not have modern industries or technology.

3 A backward child is one who is unable to learn as quickly as other children of the same age.

backwardness NOUN

backwards ['bækwədz] ADVERB

1 Backwards means behind you. *e.g. Lucille looked backwards.*

2 If you do something backwards, you do it the opposite of the usual way. *e.g. He instructed them to count backwards.*

bacon ['beɪkən] NOUN

meat from the back or sides of a pig, which has been salted or smoked

bacteria [bæk'tɪərɪə] PLURAL NOUN

Bacteria are very tiny organisms which can cause disease.

bacterial ADJECTIVE

The word *bacteria* is plural. The singular form is *bacterium*.

bad see page 60 for Word Web

bade [bæd] *or* [beɪd] a form of the past tense of **bid**

badge [bædʒ] **badges** NOUN

a piece of plastic or metal with a design or message on it that you can pin to your clothes

badger ['bædʒə] **badgers, badgering, badgered** NOUN

1 a wild animal that has a white head with two black stripes on it

> VERB

2 If you badger someone, you keep asking them questions or pestering them to do something.

badly ['bædlɪ] ADVERB

in an inferior or unimpressive way

● THESAURUS

inadequately: *He had been inadequately trained for the job.*
ineptly: *a department which is run ineptly*
poorly: *The event had been poorly organized.*
shoddily: *housing which is ugly and shoddily built an unsatisfactorily regulated system*
<<OPPOSITE *well*

Bafana bafana [ba'fɑːna ba'fɑːna] PLURAL NOUN

In South Africa, Bafana bafana is a name for the national soccer team.

1 ADJECTIVE
harmful, unpleasant, or upsetting *eg: I have some bad news.*
● **THESAURUS**
damaging: *Stress can be extremely damaging healthwise.*
destructive: *chemicals which have a destructive effect on the ozone layer*
detrimental: *This could have a detrimental impact on the environment.*
harmful: *the harmful effects of radiation*
unhealthy: *illnesses caused by an unhealthy lifestyle*
unpleasant: *Some of the drug's side-effects are unpleasant.*
<< OPPOSITE *good*

2 ADJECTIVE
of poor quality *eg: bad roads*
● **THESAURUS**
defective: *defective products which cause serious injury*
deficient: *a lack of exercise and a deficient diet*
faulty: *customers who take faulty goods back*
imperfect: *Imperfect work will not be accepted.*
inadequate: *protests over inadequate work conditions*
inferior: *the inferior quality of the recording*
pathetic: *a pathetic excuse*
poor: *an area with poor housing and high unemployment*
sorry: *a sorry state of affairs*
unsatisfactory: *I complained about the unsatisfactory service I had received.*
<< OPPOSITE *satisfactory*

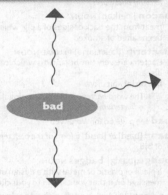

bad

3 ADJECTIVE
evil in character *eg: a bad person*
● **THESAURUS**
corrupt: *the morally corrupt court of Charles the Second*
criminal: *the criminal actions of a few sick individuals*
depraved: *depraved and hardened criminals*
evil: *the most evil man in history*
immoral: *people who believe gambling is immoral*
sinful: *behaviour considered sinful by society*
villainous: *Richard III, one of Shakespeare's most villainous characters*
wicked: *Snow White's wicked stepmother*
wrong: *If you do something wrong you must take the consequences.*
<< OPPOSITE *good*

baffle ['bæfᵊl] **baffles, baffling, baffled**
VERB
If something baffles you, you cannot understand or explain it. *e.g. The symptoms baffled the doctors.*
baffled ADJECTIVE, **baffling** ADJECTIVE

bag [bæg] **bags** NOUN
1 a container for carrying things in
> PLURAL NOUN
2 INFORMAL
Bags of something is a lot of it. *e.g. bags of fun*
[WORD HISTORY: from Old Norse BAGGI meaning 'bundle']

baggage ['bægɪdʒ] NOUN
the suitcases and bags that you take on a journey

baggy ['bægɪ] **baggier, baggiest** ADJECTIVE
Baggy clothing hangs loosely.

bagpipes ['bæg,paɪps] PLURAL NOUN
a musical instrument played by squeezing air out of a leather bag through pipes, on which a tune is played

bail [beɪl] **bails, bailing, bailed** NOUN
1 Bail is a sum of money paid to a court to allow an accused person to go free until the time of the trial. *e.g. He was released on bail.*
> VERB
2 If you bail water from a boat, you scoop it out.

bailiff ['beɪlɪf] **bailiffs** NOUN
1 a law officer who makes sure that the decisions of a court are obeyed
2 a person employed to look after land or property for the owner

Baisakhi [baɪ'sækiː] NOUN
a Sikh festival celebrated every April

bait [beɪt] **baits, baiting, baited** NOUN
1 a small amount of food placed on a hook or in a trap, to attract a fish or wild animal so that it gets caught
2 something used to tempt a person to do something
THESAURUS
bribe: *a politician who took bribes*
decoy: *He acted as a decoy to trap the murderer.*
inducement: *financial inducements to talk to the newspapers*
lure: *the lure of a huge salary*
temptation: *the temptation of easy money*
> VERB
3 If you bait a hook or trap, you put some food on it to catch a fish or wild animal.

baize [beɪz] NOUN
a smooth woollen material, usually green, used for covering snooker tables

bake [beɪk] **bakes, baking, baked** VERB

1 To bake food means to cook it in an oven without using liquid or fat.
2 To bake earth or clay means to heat it until it becomes hard.

baker ['beɪkə] **bakers** NOUN
a person who makes and sells bread and cakes

bakery ['beɪkərɪ] **bakeries** NOUN
a building where bread and cakes are baked and sold

bakkie ['bʌkiː] **bakkies** NOUN
In South African English, a bakkie is a small truck.

balaclava [,bælə'klɑːvə] **balaclavas** NOUN
a close-fitting woollen hood that covers every part of your head except your face

balance ['bæləns] **balances, balancing, balanced** VERB
1 When someone or something balances, they remain steady and do not fall over.
THESAURUS
level: *House prices have levelled.*
stabilize: *attempts to stabilize the economy*
steady: *He steadied himself and shot at goal.*
> NOUN
2 Balance is the state of being upright and steady.
3 Balance is also a situation in which all the parts involved have a stable relationship with each other. *e.g. the chemical balance of the brain*
THESAURUS
equilibrium: *the political equilibrium of Europe*
equity: *plans for greater equity of incomes*
equivalence: *the lack of equivalence between film and radio*
parity: *She won pay parity with male colleagues.*
4 The balance in someone's bank account is the amount of money in it.

balcony ['bælkənɪ] **balconies** NOUN
1 a platform on the outside of a building with a wall or railing round it
2 an area of upstairs seats in a theatre or cinema

bald [bɔːld] **balder, baldest** ADJECTIVE
1 A bald person has little or no hair on their head.
2 A bald statement or question is made in the simplest way without any attempt to be polite.
baldly ADVERB, **baldness** NOUN
[WORD HISTORY: from Middle English BALLEDE meaning 'having a white patch']

bale [beɪl] **bales, baling, baled** NOUN
1 a large bundle of something, such as paper or hay, tied tightly
> VERB
2 If you bale water from a boat, you remove it using a container; also spelt **bail**

balk [bɔːk] **balks, balking, balked;** also spelt **baulk** VERB
If you balk at something, you object to it and may refuse to do it. *e.g. He balked at the cost.*

ball [bɔːl] **balls** NOUN
1 a round object, especially one used in games such as cricket and soccer

● THESAURUS
drop: *a drop of blood*
globe: *the globe of the eyeball*
pellet: *an airgun pellet*
sphere: *a sphere the size of the Earth*

2 The ball of your foot or thumb is the rounded part where your toes join your foot or your thumb joins your hand.

3 a large formal social event at which people dance

ballad ['bæləd] **ballads** NOUN
1 a long song or poem which tells a story
2 a slow, romantic pop song
[WORD HISTORY: from Old French BALLADE meaning 'song for dancing to']

ballast ['bæləst] NOUN
any heavy material placed in a ship to make it more stable

ballerina [ˌbæləˈriːnə] **ballerinas** NOUN
a woman ballet dancer

ballet ['bæleɪ] NOUN
Ballet is a type of artistic dancing based on precise steps.

balloon [bəˈluːn] **balloons** NOUN
1 a small bag made of thin rubber that you blow into until it becomes larger and rounder
2 a large, strong bag filled with gas or hot air, which travels through the air carrying passengers in a compartment underneath
[WORD HISTORY: from Italian BALLONE meaning 'large round object']

ballot ['bælət] **ballots, balloting, balloted** NOUN
1 a secret vote in which people select a candidate in an election, or express their opinion about something

> VERB
2 When a group of people are balloted, they are asked questions to find out what they think about a particular problem or question.
[WORD HISTORY: from Italian BALLOTTA meaning 'little round object'; in medieval Venice votes were cast by dropping black or white pebbles or balls into a box]

ballpoint ['bɔːlˌpɔɪnt] **ballpoints** NOUN
a pen with a small metal ball at the end which transfers the ink onto the paper

ballroom ['bɔːlˌruːm] **ballrooms** NOUN
a very large room used for dancing or formal balls

balm [bɑːm] NOUN; OLD-FASHIONED, INFORMAL
a sweet-smelling soothing ointment

balmy ['bɑːmɪ] **balmier, balmiest** ADJECTIVE
mild and pleasant *e.g. balmy summer evenings*

balsa ['bɔːlsə] NOUN
Balsa is very lightweight wood.

balustrade ['bæləˌstreɪd] **balustrades** NOUN
a railing or wall on a balcony or staircase

bamboo [bæmˈbuː] NOUN
Bamboo is a tall tropical grass with hard, hollow stems used for making furniture.

ban [bæn] **bans, banning, banned** VERB
1 If something is banned, or if you are banned from doing it or using it, you are not allowed to do it or use it.

● THESAURUS
bar: *The press will be barred from the talks.*
disqualify: *He was disqualified from driving.*
exclude: *They were excluded from the maths class.*
forbid: *The rules forbid the use of force.*
outlaw: *regulations outlawing child labour*
prohibit: *a law that prohibits alcohol*
<<OPPOSITE *permit*

> NOUN
2 If there is a ban on something, it is not allowed.

● THESAURUS
disqualification: *a four-year disqualification from athletics*
embargo: *an embargo on trade with the country*
prohibition: *a prohibition on tobacco*
suppression: *the suppression of anti-government protests*
<<OPPOSITE *permit*

banal [bəˈnɑːl] ADJECTIVE
very ordinary and not at all interesting *e.g. He made some banal remark.*
banality NOUN
[WORD HISTORY: Old French BANAL referred to military service which all tenants had to do; hence the word came to mean 'common to everyone' or 'ordinary']

banana [bəˈnɑːnə] **bananas** NOUN
a long curved fruit with a yellow skin
[WORD HISTORY: from a West African language, via Portuguese]

band [bænd] **bands** NOUN
1 a group of musicians who play jazz or pop music together, or a group who play brass instruments together

THESAURUS
group: *They formed the group while they were still at school.*
orchestra: *she plays violin in the school orchestra*
2 a group of people who share a common purpose *e.g. a band of rebels*

THESAURUS
bunch: *A bunch of protesters were picketing the factory.*
company: *a company of actors*
crowd: *A small crowd of onlookers had gathered.*
gang: *a gang of criminals*
party: *a party of sightseers*
troupe: *She toured with a professional dance troupe.*
3 a narrow strip of something used to hold things together or worn as a decoration *e.g. an elastic band... a headband*

bandage ['bændɪdʒ] **bandages, bandaging, bandaged** NOUN
1 a strip of cloth wrapped round a wound to protect it
> VERB
2 If you bandage a wound, you tie a bandage round it.

bandicoot ['bændɪˌkuːt] **bandicoots** NOUN
a small Australian marsupial with a long pointed muzzle and a long tail

bandit ['bændɪt] **bandits** NOUN; OLD-FASHIONED, INFORMAL
a member of an armed gang who rob travellers
[WORD HISTORY: from Italian BANDITO meaning 'man who has been banished or outlawed']

bandstand ['bændˌstænd] **bandstands** NOUN
a platform, usually with a roof, where a band can play outdoors

bandwagon ['bændˌwægən] PHRASE
To **jump on the bandwagon** means to become involved in something because it is fashionable or likely to be successful.

bandy ['bændɪ] **bandies, bandying, bandied** VERB
If a name is bandied about, many people mention it.
[WORD HISTORY: from Old French BANDER meaning 'to hit a tennis ball back and forth']

bane [beɪn] NOUN; LITERARY
Someone or something that is the bane of a person or organization causes a lot of trouble for them. *e.g. the bane of my life*
[WORD HISTORY: from Old English BANA meaning 'murderer']

bang [bæŋ] **bangs, banging, banged** VERB
1 If you bang something, you hit it or put it somewhere violently, so that it makes a loud

noise. *e.g. He banged down the receiver.*

THESAURUS
beat: *They sat in a circle, beating small drums.*
hammer: *The supporters hammered on the windows of the bus.*
hit: *They were hitting the sides of the van with sticks.*
knock: *I knocked on the door for ages, but no-one answered.*
pound: *We pounded on the walls.*
slam: *I slammed down the receiver.*
thump: *The children cheered and thumped on their desks.*
2 If you bang a part of your body against something, you accidentally bump it.
> NOUN
3 a sudden, short, loud noise

THESAURUS
blast: *the ear-splitting blast of a cannon*
boom: *There was a boom and a cloud of smoke.*
crack: *the crack of a pistol shot*
detonation: *We heard several loud detonations coming from the building.*
explosion: *the deafening explosion of gunshots*
thump: *She dropped her case to the floor with a loud thump.*
4 a hard or painful bump against something

THESAURUS
blow: *a blow to the side of the head*
clout: *informal She gave him a swift clout on the ear.*
knock: *Knocks like this can cause damage to the spine.*
thump: *Ralph got a thump on the chest.*
whack: *She gave the horse a whack on the rump.*

Bangladeshi [ˌbɑːŋgləˈdɛʃɪ] **Bangladeshis** ADJECTIVE
1 belonging or relating to Bangladesh
> NOUN
2 someone who comes from Bangladesh

bangle ['bæŋgəl] **bangles** NOUN
an ornamental band worn round someone's wrist or ankle
[WORD HISTORY: from Hindi BANGRI meaning 'bracelet']

banish ['bænɪʃ] **banishes, banishing, banished** VERB
1 To banish someone means to send them into exile.

THESAURUS
deport: *Many fans are being deported from Italy.*
eject: *He was ejected from the club.*
evict: *Police evicted ten families from the building.*
exile: *He was exiled from Russia.*
expel: *patients expelled from hospitals*
transport: *He was transported to a prison camp.*
2 To banish something means to get rid of it. *e.g. It will be a long time before cancer is banished.*

banishment NOUN

THESAURUS
discard: *Read the instructions before discarding the box.*
dismiss: *I dismissed the idea from my mind.*
dispel: *The myths are being dispelled.*
eliminate: *They eliminated him from their enquiries.*
eradicate: *projects to eradicate certain diseases*
remove: *talks to remove the last obstacles to the deal*

banister ['bænɪstə] **banisters**; also spelt **bannister** NOUN
a rail supported by posts along the side of a staircase

banjo ['bændʒəʊ] **banjos** or **banjoes** NOUN
a musical instrument, like a small guitar with a round body

bank [bæŋk] **banks, banking, banked** NOUN
1 a business that looks after people's money
2 a bank of something is a store of it kept ready for use *e.g. a blood bank*

THESAURUS
fund: *a pension fund*
hoard: *a hoard of treasure*
reserve: *the world's oil reserves*
stock: *stocks of paper and ink*
store: *a secret store of sweets*

3 the raised ground along the edge of a river or lake

THESAURUS
brink: *orchards near the brink of the sea cliffs*
edge: *She stood too close to the edge and fell in.*
shore: *He swam towards the shore.*
side: *a picnic by the side of the river*

4 the sloping side of an area of raised ground
> VERB
5 When you bank money, you pay it into a bank.
6 If you bank on something happening, you expect it and rely on it.
banker NOUN, **banking** NOUN

bank holiday **bank holidays** NOUN
a public holiday, when banks are officially closed

banknote ['bæŋk,nəʊt] **banknotes** NOUN
a piece of paper money

bankrupt ['bæŋkrʌpt] **bankrupts, bankrupting, bankrupted** ADJECTIVE
1 People or organizations that go bankrupt do not have enough money to pay their debts.
> NOUN
2 someone who has been declared bankrupt
> VERB
3 To bankrupt someone means to make them bankrupt. *e.g. Restoring the house nearly bankrupted them.*

bankruptcy NOUN

banksia ['bæŋksɪə] **banksias** NOUN
an evergreen Australian tree or shrub with yellow flowers

banner ['bænə] **banners** NOUN
a long strip of cloth with a message or slogan on it

bannister ['bænɪstə] another spelling of **banister**

banquet ['bæŋkwɪt] **banquets** NOUN
a grand formal dinner, often followed by speeches

banter ['bæntə] NOUN
Banter is friendly joking and teasing.

baobab ['beɪəʊ,bæb] **baobabs** NOUN
a small fruit tree with a very thick trunk which grows in Africa and northern Australia

baptism ['bæp,tɪzəm] **baptisms** NOUN
(RE) a ceremony in which someone is baptized

Baptist ['bæptɪst] **Baptists** NOUN OR ADJECTIVE
a member of a Protestant church which believes that people should be baptized when they are adults rather than when they are babies

baptize [bæp'taɪz] **baptizes, baptizing, baptized**; also spelt **baptise** VERB
When someone is baptized water is sprinkled on them, or they are immersed in water, as a sign that they have become a Christian.
[WORD HISTORY: from Greek BAPTEIN meaning 'to dip in water']

bar [bɑː] **bars, barring, barred** NOUN
1 a counter or room where alcoholic drinks are served
2 a long, straight piece of metal

THESAURUS
pole: *He was tied to a pole.*
rail: *a curtain rail*
rod: *a fishing rod*
shaft: *the shaft of a spear*

3 a piece of something made in a rectangular shape *e.g. a bar of soap*
4 The bars in a piece of music are the many short parts of equal length that the piece is divided into.
> VERB
5 If you bar a door, you place something across it to stop it being opened.
6 If you bar someone's way, you stop them going somewhere by standing in front of them.

THESAURUS
obstruct: *Vehicles have obstructed the entrance.*
prevent: *A fence prevents people from entering.*

barb [bɑːb] **barbs** NOUN
a sharp curved point on the end of an arrow or fish-hook

barbarian [bɑːˈbɛəriən] **barbarians** NOUN
a member of a wild or uncivilized people
[WORD HISTORY: from Greek BARBAROS meaning 'foreigner', originally 'person saying BAR-BAR']

barbaric [bɑːˈbærɪk] ADJECTIVE
cruel or brutal *e.g. Ban the barbaric sport of fox hunting.*
barbarity NOUN

barbecue [ˈbɑːbɪˌkjuː] **barbecues, barbecuing, barbecued** NOUN
1 a grill with a charcoal fire on which you cook food, usually outdoors; also an outdoor party where you eat food cooked on a barbecue
> VERB
2 When food is barbecued, it is cooked over a charcoal grill.
[WORD HISTORY: from a Caribbean word meaning 'framework']

barbed [ˈbɑːbd] ADJECTIVE
A barbed remark is one that seems straightforward but is really unkind or spiteful.

barbed wire NOUN
Barbed wire is strong wire with sharp points sticking out of it, used to make fences.

barber [ˈbɑːbə] **barbers** NOUN
a man who cuts men's hair

barbiturate [bɑːˈbɪtjʊrɪt] **barbiturates** NOUN
a drug that people take to make them calm or to put them to sleep

bar code bar codes NOUN
a small pattern of numbers and lines on something you buy in a shop, which can be electronically scanned at a checkout to give the price

bard [bɑːd] **bards** NOUN; LITERARY
A bard is a poet. Some people call Shakespeare the Bard.

bare [bɛə] **bares, baring, bared** ADJECTIVE
1 If a part of your body is bare, it is not covered by any clothing.
● THESAURUS
exposed: *His whole back is exposed.*
naked: *a naked body*
nude: *a nude model*
stripped: *I got stripped to have a shower.*
uncovered: *His arms were uncovered.*
undressed: *She got undressed in the bathroom.*
<<OPPOSITE *covered*
2 If something is bare, it has nothing on top of it or inside it. *e.g. bare floorboards... a small bare office*

● THESAURUS
empty: *an empty room*
open: *open country*
spartan: *spartan accommodation*
vacant: *a vacant chair*
3 When trees are bare, they have no leaves on them.
4 The bare minimum or bare essentials means the very least that is needed. *e.g. They were fed the bare minimum.*
> VERB
5 If you bare something, you uncover or show it.

barefoot [ˈbɛəˌfʊt] ADJECTIVE OR ADVERB
not wearing anything on your feet

barely [ˈbɛəlɪ] ADVERB
only just *e.g. The girl was barely sixteen.*
● THESAURUS
almost: *I almost didn't make it.*
hardly: *I could hardly believe it.*
just: *They only just won.*
scarcely: *I can scarcely hear her.*

> Do not use *barely* with negative words like *not*: *she was barely sixteen* rather than *she was not barely sixteen*.

bargain [ˈbɑːgɪn] **bargains, bargaining, bargained** NOUN
1 an agreement in which two people or groups discuss and agree what each will do, pay, or receive in a matter which involves them both
2 something which is sold at a low price and which is good value
> VERB
3 When people bargain with each other, they discuss and agree terms about what each will do, pay, or receive in a matter which involves both.

barge [bɑːdʒ] **barges, barging, barged** NOUN
1 a boat with a flat bottom used for carrying heavy loads, especially on canals
> VERB
2 INFORMAL
If you barge into a place, you push into it in a rough or rude way.

baritone [ˈbærɪˌtəʊn] **baritones** NOUN
a man with a fairly deep singing voice

bark [bɑːk] **barks, barking, barked** VERB
1 When a dog barks, it makes a short, loud noise, once or several times.
> NOUN
2 the short, loud noise that a dog makes
3 the tough material that covers the outside of a tree

barley [ˈbɑːlɪ] NOUN
a cereal that is grown for food and is also used for making beer and whisky

bar mitzvah ['mɪtsvə] NOUN

A Jewish boy's bar mitzvah is a ceremony that takes place on his 13th birthday, after which he is regarded as an adult.

[WORD HISTORY: a Hebrew phrase meaning 'son of the law']

barmy ['bɑːmɪ] **barmier, barmiest**

ADJECTIVE; INFORMAL
mad or very foolish

barn [bɑːn] **barns** NOUN

a large farm building used for storing crops or animal food

barnacle ['bɑːnəkəl] **barnacles** NOUN

a small shellfish that fixes itself to rocks and to the bottom of boats

barometer [bə'rɒmɪtə] **barometers** NOUN

an instrument that measures air pressure and shows when the weather is changing

baron ['bærən] **barons** NOUN

a member of the lowest rank of the nobility
baronial ADJECTIVE

baroness ['bærənɪs] **baronesses** NOUN

a woman who has the rank of baron, or who is the wife of a baron

baronet ['bærənɪt] **baronets** NOUN

a man with a knighthood which has been passed to him from his father

barracks ['bærəks] NOUN

a building where soldiers live
[WORD HISTORY: from Spanish BARRACA meaning 'hut']

barracuda [ˌbærə'kjuːdə] **barracudas**
NOUN

a large, fierce tropical fish with sharp teeth

barrage ['bærɑːʒ] **barrages** NOUN

1 A barrage of questions or complaints is a lot of them all coming at the same time.

2 A barrage is continuous artillery fire over a wide area, to prevent the enemy from moving.

barrel ['bærəl] **barrels** NOUN

1 a wooden container with rounded sides and flat ends

2 The barrel of a gun is the long tube through which the bullet is fired.

barren ['bærən] ADJECTIVE

1 Barren land has soil of such poor quality that plants cannot grow on it.

◉ THESAURUS
arid: *the arid lands of Botswana*
desert: *desert regions*
desolate: *a desolate place*
dry: *poor, dry countries*
empty: *the empty desert*

waste: *waste land*
<<OPPOSITE *fertile*

2 A barren woman or female animal is not able to have babies.

◉ THESAURUS
childless: *childless couples*
infertile: *infertile women*
sterile: *sterile females*
<<OPPOSITE *fertile*

barricade [ˌbærɪ'keɪd] **barricades, barricading, barricaded** NOUN

1 a temporary barrier put up to stop people getting past

> VERB

2 If you barricade yourself inside a room or building, you put something heavy against the door to stop people getting in.

barrier ['bærɪə] **barriers** NOUN

1 a fence or wall that prevents people or animals getting from one area to another

◉ THESAURUS
barricade: *a barricade of vehicles*
fence: *a garden fence*
obstruction: *Check the exhaust pipe is clear of obstructions.*
wall: *the huge city walls*

2 If something is a barrier, it prevents two people or groups from agreeing or communicating, or prevents something from being achieved. *e.g. Cost is a major barrier to using the law.*

◉ THESAURUS
handicap: *It is a handicap not knowing a foreign language.*
hindrance: *a potential hindrance to the peace process*
hurdle: *the first hurdle in a job search*
impediment: *a serious impediment to free trade*
obstacle: *the main obstacle to the takeover*

barrister ['bærɪstə] **barristers** NOUN

a lawyer who is qualified to represent people in the higher courts

barrow ['bærəʊ] **barrows** NOUN

1 the same as a wheelbarrow

2 a large cart from which fruits or other goods are sold in the street

barter ['bɑːtə] **barters, bartering, bartered** VERB

1 If you barter goods, you exchange them for other goods, rather than selling them for money.

> NOUN

2 Barter is the activity of exchanging goods.

base [beɪs] **bases, basing, based** NOUN

1 the lowest part of something, which often supports the rest

● THESAURUS
bed: *the river bed*
bottom: *the bottom of the lake*
foot: *the foot of the mountain*
foundation: *They have laid the foundations for the new building.*
pedestal: *The statue is back on its pedestal.*
stand: *a microphone stand*
<<OPPOSITE *top*

2 A place which part of an army, navy, or air force works from.

● THESAURUS
camp: *refugee camps*
centre: *a health centre*
headquarters: *army headquarters in Colombo*
post: *a military post in the capital*
station: *the police station*

3 In chemistry, a base is any compound that reacts with an acid to form a salt.

> VERB

4 To base something on something else means to use the second thing as a foundation or starting point of the first. *e.g. The opera is based on a work by Pushkin.*

● THESAURUS
build: *a reputation built on lies*
derive: *The name is derived from a Greek word.*
found: *My hopes were founded on a mistake.*
ground: *I like a film to be grounded in reality.*
hinge: *The whole play hinges on one character.*

5 If you are based on somewhere, you live there or work from there.

baseball ['beɪsˌbɔːl] NOUN
Baseball is a team game played with a bat and a ball.

basement ['beɪsmənt] **basements** NOUN
a floor of a building built completely or partly below the ground

bases ['beɪsiːz] NOUN the plural of **basis**

bases ['beɪsɪz] NOUN the plural of **base**

bash [bæʃ] **bashes, bashing, bashed** VERB;
INFORMAL
If you bash someone or bash into them, you hit them hard.

bashful ['bæʃful] ADJECTIVE
shy and easily embarrassed

basic ['beɪsɪk] **basics** ADJECTIVE
1 The basic aspects of something are the most necessary ones. *e.g. the basic necessities of life*

● THESAURUS
elementary: *elementary computer training*
essential: *essential reading and writing skills*
fundamental: *fundamental rights*
key: *key skills such as communication and teamwork*

necessary: *They lack the necessary resources.*
vital: *vital supplies*

2 Something that is basic has only the necessary features without any extras or luxuries. *e.g. The accommodation is pretty basic.*

> PLURAL NOUN

3 The basics of something are the things you need to know or understand. *e.g. the basics of map-reading*
basically ADVERB

basilica [bə'zɪlɪkə] **basilicas** NOUN
an oblong church with a rounded end called an apse
[WORD HISTORY: from Greek BASILIKĒ meaning 'royal hall']

basin ['beɪsən] **basins** NOUN
1 a round wide container which is open at the top
2 The basin of a river is a bowl of land from which water runs into the river.

basis ['beɪsɪs] **bases** NOUN
1 The basis of something is the essential main principle from which it can be developed. *e.g. The same colour theme is used as the basis for several patterns.*

● THESAURUS
core: *the core of Asia's problems*
fundamental: *the fundamentals of road safety*
heart: *the heart of the matter*
premise: *the premise of his argument*
principle: *the principles of Buddhism*

2 The basis for a belief is the facts that support it. *e.g. There is no basis for this assumption.*

bask [bɑːsk] **basks, basking, basked** VERB
If you bask in the sun, you sit or lie in it, enjoying its warmth.

basket ['bɑːskɪt] **baskets** NOUN
a container made of thin strips of cane woven together

basketball ['bɑːskɪtˌbɔːl] NOUN
Basketball is a game in which two teams try to score goals by throwing a large ball through one of two circular nets suspended high up at each end of the court.

bass [beɪs] **basses** NOUN
1 a man with a very deep singing voice
2 a musical instrument that provides the rhythm and lowest part in the harmonies

bass [bæs] **basses** NOUN
a type of edible sea fish

basset hound ['bæsɪt] **basset hounds**
NOUN
a smooth-haired dog with a long body and ears, and short legs

bassoon [bə'su:n] **bassoons** NOUN
a large woodwind instrument

bastard ['bɑ:stəd] **bastards** NOUN

1 OFFENSIVE
People sometimes call someone a bastard when they dislike them or are very angry with them.

2 OLD-FASHIONED
A bastard is someone whose parents were not married when he or she was born.

baste [beɪst] **bastes, basting, basted** VERB
When you baste meat that is roasting, you pour hot fat over it so that it does not become dry while cooking.

bastion ['bæstɪən] **bastions** NOUN; LITERARY
something that protects a system or way of life
e.g. The country is the last bastion of communism.

bat [bæt] **bats, batting, batted** NOUN
1 a specially shaped piece of wood with a handle, used for hitting the ball in a game such as cricket or table tennis
2 a small flying animal, active at night, that looks like a mouse with wings
> VERB
3 In certain sports, when someone is batting, it is their turn to try to hit the ball and score runs.

batch [bætʃ] **batches** NOUN
a group of things of the same kind produced or dealt with together

bated ['beɪtɪd] PHRASE
With bated breath means very anxiously

bath [bɑ:θ] **baths** NOUN
a long container which you fill with water and sit in to wash yourself

bathe [beɪð] **bathes, bathing, bathed** VERB
1 When you bathe, you swim or play in open water.
2 When you bathe a wound, you wash it gently.
3 LITERARY
If a place is bathed in light, a lot of light reaches it. *e.g. The room was bathed in spring sunshine.*
bather NOUN, **bathing** NOUN

bathroom ['bɑ:θˌru:m] **bathrooms** NOUN
a room with a bath or shower, a washbasin, and often a toilet in it

baths [bɑ:θs] NOUN
The baths is a public swimming pool.

baton ['bætən] **batons** NOUN
1 a light, thin stick that a conductor uses to direct an orchestra or choir
2 In athletics, the baton is a short stick passed from one runner to another in a relay race.

batsman ['bætsmən] **batsmen** NOUN
In cricket, the batsman is the person who is batting.

battalion [bə'tæljən] **battalions** NOUN
an army unit consisting of three or more companies

batten ['bætᵊn] **battens, battening, battened** NOUN
1 a strip of wood that is fixed to something to strengthen it or hold it firm
batten down VERB
2 If you batten something down, you make it secure by fixing battens across it.

batter ['bætə] **batters, battering, battered** VERB
1 To batter someone or something means to hit them many times. *e.g. The waves kept battering the life raft.*
> NOUN
2 Batter is a mixture of flour, eggs, and milk, used to make pancakes, or to coat food before frying it.
battering NOUN

battery ['bætrɪ] **batteries** NOUN
1 a device, containing two or more cells, for storing and producing electricity, for example in a torch or a car
2 a large group of things or people
> ADJECTIVE
3 A battery hen is one of a large number of hens kept in small cages for the mass production of eggs.

battle ['bætᵊl] **battles** NOUN
1 a fight between armed forces or a struggle between two people or groups with conflicting aims *e.g. the battle between town and country*
2 A battle for something difficult is a determined attempt to obtain or achieve it. *e.g. the battle for equality*

battlefield ['bætᵊlˌfi:ld] **battlefields** NOUN
a place where a battle is or has been fought

battlements ['bætᵊlmənts] PLURAL NOUN
The battlements of a castle consist of a wall built round the top, with gaps through which guns or arrows could be fired.

battleship ['bætᵊlˌʃɪp] **battleships** NOUN
a large, heavily armoured warship

batty ['bætɪ] **battier, battiest** ADJECTIVE;
INFORMAL
crazy or eccentric

bauble ['bɔ:bᵊl] **baubles** NOUN
a pretty but cheap ornament or piece of jewellery

bawdy ['bɔ:dɪ] **bawdier, bawdiest**
ADJECTIVE
a bawdy joke or song contains humorous references to sex
[WORD HISTORY: from Middle English BAUDE

meaning 'brothel keeper']

bawl [bɔːl] **bawls, bawling, bawled** VERB

1 INFORMAL
To bawl at someone means to shout at them loudly and harshly.

2 When a child is bawling, it is crying very loudly and angrily.

bay [beɪ] **bays, baying, bayed,** NOUN

1 a part of a coastline where the land curves inwards

● THESAURUS
cove: *a sandy cove with white cliffs*
gulf: *the Gulf of Mexico*
inlet: *a deep inlet on the west coast*
sound: *streams that run into the sound*

2 a space or area used for a particular purpose *e.g. a loading bay*

3 Bay is a kind of tree similar to the laurel, with leaves used for flavouring in cooking.

> PHRASE
4 If you **keep something at bay**, you prevent it from reaching you. *e.g. Eating oranges keeps colds at bay.*

> VERB
5 When a hound or wolf bays, it makes a deep howling noise.

● THESAURUS
bark: *a small dog barking at a seagull*
cry: *I heard animals cry in the forest.*
howl: *distant coyotes howling in the night*
yelp: *A dog snapped and yelped at them.*

bayonet ['beɪənɪt] **bayonets** NOUN
a sharp blade that can be fixed to the end of a rifle and used for stabbing
[WORD HISTORY: named after BAYONNE in France, where it originated]

bazaar [bə'zɑː] **bazaars** NOUN

1 an area with many small shops and stalls, especially in Eastern countries

2 a sale to raise money for charity
[WORD HISTORY: from Persian BAZAR meaning 'market']

BC
BC means 'before Christ'. *e.g. in 49 BC*

be [biː] **am, is, are; being; was, were; been**
AUXILIARY VERB

1 'Be' is used with a present participle to form the continuous tense *e.g. Crimes of violence are increasing.*

2 'Be' is also used to say that something will happen *e.g. We are going to America next month.*

3 'Be' is used to form the passive voice *e.g. The walls were being repaired.*

> VERB
4 'Be' is used to give more information about the subject of a sentence *e.g. Her name is Melanie.*

be- PREFIX

1 'Be-' is used to form verbs from nouns and adds the meaning 'treat as'. For example, to *befriend* someone is to make friends with them.

2 'Be-' is also sometimes used to form verbs from verbs when it is used for emphasis or to mean 'covering completely'. For example, to *besmear* means to smear all over.

beach [biːtʃ] **beaches** NOUN
an area of sand or pebbles beside the sea

● THESAURUS
coast: *a day at the coast*
sands: *the long white sands of Goa*
seashore: *walks along the seashore*
seaside: *trips to the seaside*
shore: *He swam out from the shore.*
strand: *collecting shells on the strand*

beacon ['biːkən] **beacons** NOUN
In the past, a beacon was a light or fire on a hill, which acted as a signal or warning.

bead [biːd] **beads** NOUN

1 Beads are small pieces of coloured glass or wood with a hole through the middle, strung together to make necklaces.

2 Beads of liquid are drops of it.

beady ['biːdɪ] ADJECTIVE
Beady eyes are small and bright like beads.

beagle ['biːgəl] **beagles** NOUN
a short-haired dog with long ears and short legs

beak [biːk] **beaks** NOUN
A bird's beak is the hard part of its mouth that sticks out.

beaker ['biːkə] **beakers** NOUN

1 a cup for drinking out of, usually made of plastic and without a handle

2 a glass container with a lip which is used in laboratories

beam [biːm] **beams, beaming, beamed**
NOUN

1 a broad smile

2 A beam of light is a band of light that shines from something such as a torch.

3 a long, thick bar of wood or metal, especially one that supports a roof

> VERB
4 If you beam, you smile because you are happy.

bean [biːn] **beans** NOUN
Beans are the seeds or pods of a climbing plant, which are eaten as a vegetable; also used of

some other seeds, for example the seeds from which coffee is made.

bear [bɛə] **bears, bearing, bore, borne**
NOUN

1 a large, strong wild animal with thick fur and sharp claws

> VERB

2 FORMAL

To bear something means to carry it or support its weight. *e.g. The ice wasn't thick enough to bear their weight.*

● THESAURUS

carry: *He always carried a gun.*
convey: *The taxi conveyed us to the centre.*
shoulder: *He had to shoulder the blame for the mistake.*
support: *Thick wooden posts support the ceiling.*
take: *You'd better take an umbrella.*

3 If something bears a mark or typical feature, it has it. *e.g. The room bore all the signs of a violent struggle.*

● THESAURUS

exhibit: *He began to exhibit symptoms of the disease.*
harbour: *She still harbours feelings of resentment.*
have: *I have a grudge against her.*

4 If you bear something difficult, you accept it and are able to deal with it. *e.g. He bore his last illness with courage.*

● THESAURUS

abide: *I can't abide arrogant people.*
endure: *The pain was hard to endure.*
stomach: *He could not stomach violence.*
suffer: *I had to suffer his company all day.*
tolerate: *Women tolerate pain better than men.*

5 If you can't bear someone or something, you dislike them very much.

6 FORMAL

When a plant or tree bears flowers, fruit, or leaves, it produces them.
bearable ADJECTIVE

beard [bɪəd] **beards** NOUN
the hair that grows on the lower part of a man's face
bearded ADJECTIVE

bearer ['bɛərə] **bearers** NOUN
The bearer of something is the person who carries or presents it. *e.g. the bearer of bad news*

bearing ['bɛərɪŋ] NOUN

1 If something has a bearing on a situation, it is relevant to it.

2 the way in which a person moves or stands

beast [biːst] **beasts** NOUN

1 OLD-FASHIONED
a large wild animal

2 INFORMAL
If you call someone a beast, you mean that they are cruel or spiteful.

beastly ['biːstlɪ] **beastlier, beastliest**
ADJECTIVE; OLD-FASHIONED, INFORMAL
cruel or spiteful

beat [biːt] **beats, beating, beat, beaten**
VERB

1 To beat someone or something means to hit them hard and repeatedly. *e.g. He threatened to beat her.*

● THESAURUS

batter: *The waves kept battering the life raft.*
buffet: *Their plane was buffeted by storms.*
hit: *He hit me on the head.*
pound: *Someone was pounding on the door.*
strike: *She struck him across the mouth.*
thrash: *He was thrashed by his father.*

2 If you beat someone in a race or game, you defeat them or do better than them.

● THESAURUS

defeat: *The team hasn't been defeated all year.*
outdo: *One man was trying to outdo the other.*
outstrip: *The company is outstripping its rivals.*
overcome: *Molly had overcome her fear of flying.*
overwhelm: *One attack could overwhelm the enemy.*
vanquish: *the man who helped vanquish Napoleon*

3 When a bird or insect beats its wings, it moves them up and down.

4 When your heart is beating, it is pumping blood with a regular rhythm.

5 If you beat eggs, cream, or butter, you mix them vigorously using a fork or a whisk.

> NOUN

6 The beat of your heart is its regular pumping action.

7 The beat of a piece of music is its main rhythm.

● THESAURUS

cadence: *the pulsing cadences of his music*
metre: *the strict metre of the poem*
rhythm: *His foot tapped a rhythm on the floor.*
stress: *differences of stress in speech*
time: *a song written in waltz time*

8 A police officer's beat is the area which he or she patrols.

beat up VERB

9 To beat someone up means to hit or kick them repeatedly.
beater NOUN, **beating** NOUN

beaut [bjuːt] **beauts** NOUN; INFORMAL

1 In Australian and New Zealand English, a beaut is an outstanding person or thing.

> ADJECTIVE

2 In Australian and New Zealand English, beaut

means good or excellent. *e.g. a beaut house*

beautiful ['bju:tɪfʊl] ADJECTIVE
very attractive or pleasing *e.g. a beautiful girl...
beautiful music*
beautifully ADVERB

⬤ THESAURUS
attractive: *an attractive woman*
delightful: *The perfume is delightful.*
fine: *a fine summer's day*
gorgeous: *a gorgeous man*
lovely: *You look lovely.*
pleasing: *a pleasing appearance*
<<OPPOSITE *ugly*

beauty ['bju:tɪ] **beauties** NOUN
1 Beauty is the quality of being beautiful.

⬤ THESAURUS
attractiveness: *the attractiveness of the region*
charm: *a woman of great charm*
elegance: *the elegance of the overall design*
loveliness: *the loveliness of the scene*
<<OPPOSITE *ugliness*

2 OLD-FASHIONED
a very attractive woman

⬤ THESAURUS
stunner: informal *the 23-year-old stunner*

3 The beauty of an idea or plan is what makes it
attractive or worthwhile. *e.g. The beauty of the fund
is its simplicity.*

⬤ THESAURUS
advantage: *the advantages of the new system over
the old one*
asset: *The one asset the job provided was contacts.*
attraction: *The main attraction of the place is the
monument.*
benefit: *Every age has its benefits.*

beaver ['bi:və] **beavers** NOUN
an animal with a big, flat tail and webbed hind
feet. Beavers build dams

because [bɪ'kɒz] CONJUNCTION
1 'Because' is used with a clause that gives the
reason for something *e.g. I went home because I
was tired.*

⬤ THESAURUS
as: *Don't cook for me as I'll be home late.*
since: *Since you didn't listen, I'll repeat that.*

> PHRASE
2 Because of is used with a noun that gives the
reason for something *e.g. He quit playing because
of a knee injury.*

beck [bɛk] PHRASE
If you are at someone's **beck and call**, you are
always available to do what they ask.

beckon ['bɛkən] **beckons, beckoning,
beckoned** VERB

1 If you beckon to someone, you signal with your
hand that you want them to come to you.

2 If you say that something beckons, you mean
that you find it very attractive. *e.g. A career in
journalism beckons.*

become [bɪ'kʌm] **becomes, becoming,
became, become** VERB
To become something means to start feeling or
being that thing. *e.g. I became very angry... He
became an actor.*

bed [bɛd] **beds** NOUN
1 a piece of furniture that you lie on when you
sleep

2 A bed in a garden is an area of ground in which
plants are grown.

3 The bed of a sea or river is the ground at the
bottom of it.

bedclothes ['bɛd,kləʊðz] PLURAL NOUN
the sheets and covers that you put over you
when you get into bed

bedding ['bɛdɪŋ] NOUN
Bedding is sheets, blankets, and other covers
that are used on beds.

bedlam ['bɛdləm] NOUN
You can refer to a noisy and disorderly place or
situation as bedlam. *e.g. The delay caused bedlam
at the station.*
[WORD HISTORY: from BEDLAM, a shortened form of
the Hospital of St. Mary of Bethlehem in London,
which was an institution for the insane or mentally
ill]

bedpan ['bɛd,pæn] **bedpans** NOUN
a container used as a toilet by people who are too
ill to get out of bed

bedraggled [bɪ'dræg^əld] ADJECTIVE
A bedraggled person or animal is in a messy or
untidy state.

bedridden ['bɛd,rɪd^ən] ADJECTIVE
Someone who is bedridden is too ill or disabled
to get out of bed.

bedrock ['bɛd,rɒk] NOUN
1 Bedrock is the solid rock under the soil.

2 The bedrock of something is the foundation
and principles on which it is based. *e.g. His life
was built on the bedrock of integrity.*

bedroom ['bɛd,ru:m] **bedrooms** NOUN
a room used for sleeping in

bedspread ['bɛd,sprɛd] **bedspreads** NOUN
a cover put over a bed, on top of the sheets and
blankets

bedstead ['bɛd,stɛd] **bedsteads** NOUN
the metal or wooden frame of an old-
fashioned bed

bee [biː] **bees** NOUN
a winged insect that makes honey and lives in large groups

beech [biːtʃ] **beeches** NOUN
a tree with a smooth grey trunk and shiny leaves

beef [biːf] NOUN
Beef is the meat of a cow, bull, or ox.
[WORD HISTORY: from Old French BOEF meaning 'ox' or 'bull']

beefy ['biːfi] **beefier, beefiest** ADJECTIVE; INFORMAL
A beefy person is strong and muscular.

beehive ['biːˌhaɪv] **beehives** NOUN
a container in which bees live and make their honey

beeline ['biːˌlaɪn] PHRASE; INFORMAL
If you **make a beeline** for a place, you go there as quickly and directly as possible.

been [biːn] the past participle of **be**

beer [bɪə] **beers** NOUN
an alcoholic drink made from malt and flavoured with hops

beet [biːt] **beets** NOUN
a plant with an edible root and leaves, such as sugar beet or beetroot

beetle ['biːtəl] **beetles** NOUN
a flying insect with hard wings which cover its body when it is not flying

beetroot ['biːtˌruːt] **beetroots** NOUN
the round, dark red root of a type of beet, eaten as a vegetable

befall [bɪ'fɔːl] **befalls, befalling, befell, befallen** VERB; OLD-FASHIONED, INFORMAL
If something befalls you, it happens to you. *e.g. A similar fate befell my cousin.*

before [bɪ'fɔː] ADVERB, PREPOSITION, OR CONJUNCTION
1 'Before' is used to refer to a previous time *e.g. Apply the ointment before going to bed.*
⬤ THESAURUS
earlier: *Here is a cake I made earlier.*
formerly: *He had formerly been in the army.*
in advance: *We booked the room well in advance.*
previously: *Previously she had little time to work.*
sooner: *I wish I'd arrived sooner.*
<<OPPOSITE *after*

> ADVERB
2 If you have done something before, you have done it on a previous occasion. *e.g. Never before had he seen such poverty.*

> PREPOSITION
3 FORMAL
Before also means in front of. *e.g. They stopped before a large white villa.*

beforehand [bɪ'fɔːˌhænd] ADVERB
before *e.g. It had been agreed beforehand that they would spend the night there.*

befriend [bɪ'frend] **befriends, befriending, befriended** VERB
If you befriend someone, you act in a kind and helpful way and so become friends with them.

beg [beg] **begs, begging, begged** VERB
1 When people beg, they ask for food or money, because they are very poor.

2 If you beg someone to do something, you ask them very anxiously to do it.
⬤ THESAURUS
beseech: *Her eyes beseeched him to show mercy.*
implore: *I implore you not to say anything.*
petition: *He petitioned the Court to let him go free.*
plead: *She was pleading with me to stay.*

beggar ['begə] **beggars** NOUN
someone who lives by asking people for money or food

begin [bɪ'gɪn] **begins, beginning, began, begun** VERB
If you begin to do something, you start doing it. When something begins, it starts.
⬤ THESAURUS
commence: formal *He commenced his journey.*
inaugurate: *The committee was inaugurated ten days ago.*
initiate: *They wanted to initiate a discussion.*
originate: *Mankind may have originated in Africa.*
set about: *He set about tackling his problems.*
start: *The meeting starts at 10 o'clock.*
<<OPPOSITE *end*

beginner [bɪ'gɪnə] **beginners** NOUN
someone who has just started learning to do something and cannot do it very well yet
⬤ THESAURUS
apprentice: *an apprentice in a law firm*
learner: *young learners of French*
novice: *Many of us are novices on the computer.*
starter: *new starters at school*
trainee: *a trainee in a newspaper office*
<<OPPOSITE *expert*

beginning [bɪ'gɪnɪŋ] **beginnings** NOUN
The beginning of something is the first part of it or the time when it starts. *e.g. They had now reached the beginning of the city.*
⬤ THESAURUS
birth: *the birth of modern art*
commencement: formal *a date for the commencement of talks*
opening: *the opening of the trial*
origin: *the origins of civilization*
outset: *There were lots of problems from the outset.*
start: *the start of all the trouble*

<<OPPOSITE *end*

Remember that *beginning* has one *g* and two *ns*.

begonia [bɪ'gəʊnjə] **begonias** NOUN
a plant with brightly coloured flowers

begrudge [bɪ'grʌdʒ] **begrudges, begrudging, begrudged** VERB
If you begrudge someone something, you are angry or envious because they have it. *e.g. No one could begrudge him the glory.*

beguiling [bɪ'gaɪlɪŋ] ADJECTIVE
charming, but often in a deceptive way

behalf [bɪ'hɑ:f] PHRASE
To do something **on behalf of** someone or something means to do it for their benefit or as their representative.

behave [bɪ'heɪv] **behaves, behaving, behaved** VERB
1 If you behave in a particular way, you act in that way. *e.g. They were behaving like animals.*

● THESAURUS
act: *He is acting like a spoilt child.*
function: *They are functioning as a team.*
operate: *I know how Graham operates.*
work: *My mind is working well today.*

2 To behave yourself means to act correctly or properly.

behaviour [bɪ'heɪvjə] NOUN
Your behaviour is the way in which you behave.

behead [bɪ'hed] **beheads, beheading, beheaded** VERB
To behead someone means to cut their head off.

beheld [bɪ'held] the past tense of **behold**

behind [bɪ'haɪnd] PREPOSITION
1 at the back of *e.g. He was seated behind the desk.*
2 responsible for or causing *e.g. He was the driving force behind the move.*
3 supporting someone *e.g. The whole country was behind him.*

> ADVERB
4 If you stay behind, you remain after other people have gone.
5 If you leave something behind, you do not take it with you.

behold [bɪ'həʊld] INTERJECTION; LITERARY
You say 'behold' when you want someone to look at something.
beholder NOUN

beige [beɪʒ] NOUN OR ADJECTIVE
pale creamy-brown

being ['bi:ɪŋ] **beings**
1 Being is the present participle of **be**

> NOUN
2 Being is the state or fact of existing. *e.g. The party came into being in 1923.*
3 a living creature, either real or imaginary *e.g. alien beings from a distant galaxy*

belated [bɪ'leɪtɪd] ADJECTIVE; FORMAL
A belated action happens later than it should have done. *e.g. a belated birthday present*
belatedly ADVERB

belch [beltʃ] **belches, belching, belched** VERB
1 If you belch, you make a sudden noise in your throat because air has risen up from your stomach.
2 If something belches smoke or fire, it sends it out in large amounts. *e.g. Smoke belched from the steelworks.*

> NOUN
3 the noise you make when you belch

beleaguered [bɪ'li:gəd] ADJECTIVE
1 struggling against difficulties or criticism *e.g. the beleaguered meat industry*
2 besieged by an enemy *e.g. the beleaguered garrison*

belfry ['belfrɪ] **belfries** NOUN
the part of a church tower where the bells are
[WORD HISTORY: from Old French BERFREI meaning 'tower'; because towers often contained bells this word was later changed to BELFREY]

Belgian ['beldʒən] **Belgians** ADJECTIVE
1 belonging or relating to Belgium
> NOUN
2 someone who comes from Belgium

belief [bɪ'li:f] **beliefs** NOUN
1 a feeling of certainty that something exists or is true

● THESAURUS
confidence: *I have every confidence that you'll do well.*
conviction: *She speaks with conviction.*
judgment: *My judgment is that he should leave.*
opinion: *Robert has strong opinions.*
trust: *She has complete trust that you'll help her.*
view: *In my view, he is wrong.*

2 one of the principles of a religion or moral system

● THESAURUS
creed: *people of every race and creed*
doctrine: *Christian doctrine*
dogma: *religious dogma*
faith: *Do you practise any faith?*
ideology: *different political ideologies*
principle: *the principles of Jewish faith*
tenet: *the fundamental tenets of Islam*

believable [bɪˈliːvəbəl] ADJECTIVE
possible or likely to be the case

● THESAURUS
credible: *credible witnesses*
imaginable: *It is scarcely imaginable that it happened here.*
likely: *It's more likely that she forgot.*
plausible: *a plausible explanation*
possible: *It's quite possible that I'm wrong.*
probable: *the most probable outcome*
<<OPPOSITE *unbelievable*

believe [bɪˈliːv] **believes, believing, believed** VERB

1 If you believe that something is true, you accept that it is true.

● THESAURUS
accept: *He can't accept that he is wrong.*
assume: *I assume these eggs are fresh.*
presume: *The missing person is presumed to be dead.*
swallow: informal *I found their story hard to swallow.*
trust: *I trust that you will manage.*
<<OPPOSITE *doubt*

2 If you believe someone, you accept that they are telling the truth.

3 If you believe in things such as God and miracles, you accept that they exist or happen.

4 If you believe in something such as a plan or system, you are in favour of it. *e.g. They really believe in education.*
believer NOUN

belittle [bɪˈlɪtəl] **belittles, belittling, belittled** VERB
If you belittle someone or something, you make them seem unimportant. *e.g. He belittled my opinions.*

● THESAURUS
deride: *He is derided as weak and incompetent.*
detract from: *Her sour comments detracted from Meg's happiness.*
downgrade: *I fear failure, but I downgrade my successes.*
scorn: *Eleanor scorns the work of others.*
undervalue: *We must never undervalue freedom.*
<<OPPOSITE *praise*

bell [bɛl] **bells** NOUN

1 a cup-shaped metal object with a piece inside that swings and hits the sides, producing a ringing sound

2 an electrical device that rings or buzzes in order to attract attention

bellbird [ˈbɛlˌbɜːd] **bellbirds** NOUN
an Australian or New Zealand bird that makes a sound like a bell

belligerent [bɪˈlɪdʒərənt] ADJECTIVE
aggressive and keen to start a fight or an argument
belligerence NOUN

bellow [ˈbɛləʊ] **bellows, bellowing, bellowed** VERB

1 When an animal such as a bull bellows, it makes a loud, deep roaring noise.

2 If someone bellows, they shout in a loud, deep voice.

> PLURAL NOUN

3 Bellows are a piece of equipment used for blowing air into a fire to make it burn more fiercely.

belly [ˈbɛlɪ] **bellies** NOUN

1 Your belly is your stomach or the front of your body below your chest.

2 An animal's belly is the underneath part of its body.

belong [bɪˈlɒŋ] **belongs, belonging, belonged** VERB

1 If something belongs to you, it is yours and you own it.

2 To belong to a group means to be a member of it.

3 If something belongs in a particular place, that is where it should be. *e.g. It did not belong in the music room.*

belongings [bɪˈlɒŋɪŋz] PLURAL NOUN
Your belongings are the things that you own.

beloved [bɪˈlʌvɪd] ADJECTIVE
A beloved person or thing is one that you feel great affection for.

● THESAURUS
adored: *an adored father*
cherished: *his most cherished possession*
darling: *our darling child*
dearest: *my dearest Maria*
precious: *I love my precious cat.*
treasured: *treasured memories*
<<OPPOSITE *despised*

below [bɪˈləʊ] PREPOSITION OR ADVERB

1 If something is below a line or the surface of something else, it is lower down. *e.g. six inches below soil level*

● THESAURUS
beneath: *She hid the letter beneath her mattress.*
down: *I fell down to the bottom.*
lower: *The price will fall lower than this.*
under: *tunnels under the ground*
underneath: *He crawled underneath the table.*
<<OPPOSITE *above*

2 Below also means at or to a lower point, level, or rate. *e.g. The temperature fell below the legal minimum.*

belt [bɛlt] **belts, belting, belted** NOUN

1 a strip of leather or cloth that you fasten round your waist to hold your trousers or skirt up

2 In a machine, a belt is a circular strip of rubber that drives moving parts or carries objects along.

3 a specific area of a country *e.g. Poland's industrial belt*

> VERB

4 INFORMAL

To belt someone means to hit them very hard.

bemused [bɪ'mjuːzd] ADJECTIVE

If you are bemused, you are puzzled or confused.

bench [bɛntʃ] **benches** NOUN

1 a long seat that two or more people can sit on

2 a long, narrow table for working at, for example in a laboratory

bend [bɛnd] **bends, bending, bent** VERB

1 When you bend something, you use force to make it curved or angular.

● THESAURUS

buckle: *A wave buckled the ship's deck.*
curve: *The wall curves to the left.*
turn: *The road turns right at the end.*
twist: *glass twisted into elaborate patterns*
warp: *The wood had started to warp.*

2 When you bend, you move your head and shoulders forwards and downwards.

● THESAURUS

arch: *Don't arch your back!*
bow: *He turned and bowed to her.*
crouch: *We were crouching in the bushes.*
incline: *The woman inclined her head to one side.*
lean: *She leant out of the window.*
stoop: *Stooping down, he picked up a stone.*

> NOUN

3 a curved part of something

bent ADJECTIVE

● THESAURUS

arc: *the full arc of a rainbow*
corner: *He drove round the corner.*
curve: *the curve of the stream*
loop: *The river curves in a loop.*
turn: *a turn in the path*

bene- PREFIX

'Bene-' means 'good' or 'well'. For example, something *beneficial* makes you well or produces a good result, and a *benevolent* person is kind and good to others.

[WORD HISTORY: from Latin BENE meaning 'well']

beneath [bɪ'niːθ] PREPOSITION, ADJECTIVE OR ADVERB

1 an old-fashioned word for **underneath**

> PREPOSITION

2 If someone thinks something is beneath them,

they think that it is too unimportant for them to bother with it.

benefactor ['bɛnɪˌfæktə] **benefactors** NOUN

a person who helps to support a person or institution by giving money

beneficial [ˌbɛnɪ'fɪʃəl] ADJECTIVE

Something that is beneficial is good for people. *e.g. the beneficial effects of exercise*

beneficially ADVERB

● THESAURUS

advantageous: *an advantageous arrangement*
good for you: *Regular exercise is good for you.*
healthy: *trying to switch to a healthy lifestyle*
helpful: *This treatment is particularly helpful to hay fever sufferers.*
useful: *a useful addition to your first aid kit*
wholesome: *food made with good, wholesome ingredients*

beneficiary [ˌbɛnɪ'fɪʃərɪ] **beneficiaries** NOUN

A beneficiary of something is someone who receives money or other benefits from it.

benefit ['bɛnɪfɪt] **benefits, benefiting, benefited** NOUN

1 The benefits of something are the advantages that it brings to people. *e.g. the benefits of relaxation*

● THESAURUS

advantage: *The advantages of the new system far outweigh its disadvantages.*
asset: *A second language is an asset in this job.*
boon: *a great boon for busy housewives*
gain: *He used the knowledge for his personal gain.*
good: *Study for your own good!*
help: *It's no help to know I was right.*
profit: *the profits of working hard*
use: *His training was of no use to him.*
<<OPPOSITE *disadvantage*

2 Benefit is money given by the government to people who are unemployed or ill.

> VERB

3 If you benefit from something or something benefits you, it helps you.

● THESAURUS

aid: *measures to aid working mothers*
assist: *The extra money will assist you.*
enhance: *His injury does not enhance our chances.*
further: *His support will further our cause.*
help: *The new laws won't help the environment.*
profit: *It won't profit us to complain.*
<<OPPOSITE *harm*

■ *benefit* is spelt with two *e*s not two *i*s

benevolent [bɪ'nɛvələnt] ADJECTIVE

kind and helpful

benevolence NOUN, **benevolently** ADVERB

◉ THESAURUS
benign: *a benign and loveable man*
charitable: *charitable organizations*
compassionate: *my compassionate friends*
humane: *humane treatment of prisoners*
kind: *You have been kind and helpful to us.*

benign [bɪ'naɪn] ADJECTIVE
1 Someone who is benign is kind and gentle.
2 A benign tumour is one that will not cause death or serious illness.
benignly ADVERB

bent [bent]
1 Bent is the past participle and past tense of **bend**
> PHRASE
2 If you are **bent on** doing something, you are determined to do it.

bequeath [bɪ'kwiːð] **bequeaths, bequeathing, bequeathed** VERB; FORMAL
If someone bequeaths money or property to you, they give it to you in their will, so that it is yours after they have died.

bequest [bɪ'kwest] **bequests** NOUN; FORMAL
money or property that has been left to someone in a will

berate [bɪ'reɪt] **berates, berating, berated** VERB; FORMAL
If you berate someone, you scold them angrily. *e.g. He berated them for getting caught.*

bereaved [bɪ'riːvd] ADJECTIVE; FORMAL
You say that someone is bereaved when a close relative of theirs has recently died.
bereavement NOUN

bereft [bɪ'reft] ADJECTIVE; LITERARY
If you are bereft of something, you no longer have it. *e.g. The government seems bereft of ideas.*

beret ['bereɪ] **berets** NOUN
a circular flat hat with no brim

berm [bɜːm] **berms** NOUN
1 a narrow path at the edge of a slope, road, or canal
2 In New Zealand English, a strip of grass between the road and the footpath in areas where people live.

berry ['berɪ] **berries** NOUN
Berries are small, round fruits that grow on bushes or trees.

berserk [bə'zɜːk] PHRASE
If someone **goes berserk**, they lose control of themselves and become very violent.
[WORD HISTORY: from Icelandic BERSERKR, a kind of Viking who wore a shirt (SERKR) made from the skin of a bear (BJÖRN). They worked themselves into a frenzy before battle.]

berth [bɜːθ] **berths** NOUN
1 a space in a harbour where a ship stays when it is being loaded or unloaded
2 In a boat or caravan, a berth is a bed.

beseech [bɪ'siːtʃ] **beseeches, beseeching, beseeched** or **besought** VERB; LITERARY
If you beseech someone to do something, you ask them very earnestly to do it. *e.g. Her eyes beseeched him to show mercy.*
beseeching ADJECTIVE

beset [bɪ'set] ADJECTIVE; FORMAL
If you are beset by difficulties or doubts, you have a lot of them.

beside [bɪ'saɪd] PREPOSITION
If one thing is beside something else, they are next to each other.

◉ THESAURUS
adjacent to: *a hotel adjacent to the beach*
alongside: *a house alongside the river*
close to: *The restaurant is close to their home.*
near: *He stood very near the front door.*
next to: *She sat down next to him.*

besiege [bɪ'siːdʒ] **besieges, besieging, besieged** VERB
1 When soldiers besiege a place, they surround it and wait for the people inside to surrender.
2 If you are besieged by people, many people want something from you and continually bother you.

besought [bɪ'sɔːt] a past tense and past participle of **beseech**

best see page 77 for Word Web

best man NOUN
The best man at a wedding is the man who acts as the bridegroom's attendant.

bestow [bɪ'stəʊ] **bestows, bestowing, bestowed** VERB; FORMAL
If you bestow something on someone, you give it to them.

bet [bet] **bets, betting, bet** VERB
1 If you bet on the result of an event, you will win money if something happens and lose money if it does not.
> NOUN
2 the act of betting on something, or the amount of money that you agree to risk > PHRASE; INFORMAL
3 You say **I bet** to indicate that you are sure that something is or will be so. *e.g. I bet the answer is no.*
betting NOUN

betray [bɪ'treɪ] **betrays, betraying, betrayed** VERB

1 ADJECTIVE

of the highest standard *eg: the best film I have seen in a long time.*

● THESAURUS

finest: *the finest wines available*

first-rate: *a first-rate musical performance*

foremost: *the foremost painter of his generation*

greatest: *the greatest film ever made*

leading: *He has established himself as one of Britain's leading actors.*

outstanding: *one of England's outstanding tennis players*

pre-eminent: *her status as the pre-eminent pop act of her day*

principal: *London's principal publishing houses*

superlative (formal): *companies that offer superlative products*

supreme: *the supreme achievement of his career*

top: *one of the country's top athletes*

<< OPPOSITE *worst*

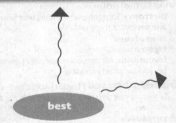

best

2 NOUN

the preferred thing *eg: Of all my presents, this is the best.*

● THESAURUS

cream: *a showcase for the cream of Scottish artists*

elite: *the elite of the sporting world*

finest: *Landlord, wine! And make it the finest!*

pick: *the pick of the crop*

<< OPPOSITE *worst*

1 If you betray someone who trusts you, you do something which harms them, such as helping their enemies.

THESAURUS

be unfaithful: *He's been unfaithful to his wife.*
break your promise: *I broke my promise to help her.*
double-cross: informal *I was angry that he double-crossed me.*
inform on: *people who inform on their colleagues*

2 If you betray your feelings or thoughts, you show them without intending to.
betrayal NOUN, **betrayer** NOUN

THESAURUS

expose: *She never exposed her hostile feelings.*
manifest: *Fear can manifest itself in many ways.*
reveal: *Her expression revealed nothing.*
show: *His eyes showed his unhappiness.*

betrothal [bɪ'trəʊðəl] **betrothals** NOUN;
OLD-FASHIONED, INFORMAL
an engagement to be married
betrothed ADJECTIVE OR NOUN

better see page 79 for Word Web

between [bɪ'twiːn] PREPOSITION OR ADVERB

1 If something is between two other things, it is situated or happens in the space or time that separates them. *e.g. flights between Europe and Asia*

2 A relationship or difference between two people or things involves only those two.

> If there are two things you should use *between*. If there are more than two things you should use *among*.

beverage ['bɛvərɪdʒ] **beverages** NOUN;
FORMAL
a drink

bevy ['bɛvɪ] **bevies** NOUN
a group of people *e.g. a bevy of lawyers*

beware [bɪ'wɛə] VERB
If you tell someone to beware of something, you are warning them that it might be dangerous or harmful.

THESAURUS

be careful: *Be careful what you say to him.*
be cautious: *Doctors are cautious about using the treatment.*
be wary: *Michelle is wary of marriage.*
guard against: *We have to guard against thieves.*
look out: *Look out, there's a train coming.*
watch out: *Watch out for fog and ice.*

bewilder [bɪ'wɪldə] **bewilders,
bewildering, bewildered** VERB
If something bewilders you, it is too confusing or difficult for you to understand.

bewildered ADJECTIVE, **bewildering** ADJECTIVE,
bewilderment NOUN

bewitch [bɪ'wɪtʃ] **bewitches, bewitching,
bewitched** VERB

1 To bewitch someone means to cast a spell on them.

2 If something bewitches you, you are so delighted by it that you cannot pay attention to anything else.
bewitched ADJECTIVE, **bewitching** ADJECTIVE

beyond [bɪ'jɒnd] PREPOSITION

1 If something is beyond a certain place, it is on the other side of it. *e.g. Beyond the hills was the Sahara.*

2 If something continues beyond a particular point, it continues further than that point. *e.g. an education beyond the age of 16*

3 If someone or something is beyond understanding or help, they cannot be understood or helped.

bi- PREFIX
'Bi-' means 'two' or 'twice' *e.g. bicycle... bigamy*
[WORD HISTORY: from Latin BIS meaning 'two']

bias ['baɪəs] NOUN
(HISTORY) Someone who shows bias favours one person or thing unfairly.

THESAURUS

bigotry: *religious bigotry*
favouritism: *His promotion was due to favouritism.*
prejudice: *racial prejudice*

biased or **biassed** ['baɪəst] ADJECTIVE
favouring one person or thing unfairly *e.g. biased attitudes*

THESAURUS

one-eyed: Australian and New Zealand *I may be a bit one-eyed because of the family connection.*
one-sided: *a one-sided argument*
partial: *a very partial view of the situation*
prejudiced: *Don't be prejudiced by what you read.*
slanted: *a slanted newspaper article*
weighted: *a scheme weighted towards those in need*
<<OPPOSITE *neutral*

bib [bɪb] **bibs** NOUN
a piece of cloth or plastic which is worn under the chin of very young children when they are eating, to keep their clothes clean

Bible ['baɪbᵊl] **Bibles** NOUN
(RE) The Bible is the sacred book of the Christian religion.
biblical ADJECTIVE
[WORD HISTORY: from Greek BIBLIA meaning 'the books']

bicentenary [ˌbaɪsɛn'tiːnərɪ]
bicentenaries NOUN

1 ADJECTIVE

of more worth than another *eg: Today was much better than yesterday.*

● **THESAURUS**

finer: *There is no finer place to live.*

grander: *moving to a much grander house*

greater: *Their eyes are now set on a greater prize.*

higher-quality: *We are trying to provide a higher-quality service.*

nicer: *This is a much nicer room than mine.*

preferable: *Owning property is preferable to renting.*

superior: *His work is far superior to yours.*

surpassing (formal): *a film of surpassing quality*

worthier: *You should save your energies for a worthier cause.*

better

2 ADJECTIVE

well after being ill *eg: I hope you feel better soon.*

● **THESAURUS**

cured: *I used to have insomnia but now I'm cured.*

fitter: *I'm a lot fitter now I've started jogging.*

fully recovered: *He had a back injury but now he's fully recovered.*

healthier: *I'm much healthier since I gave up smoking.*

improving: *His symptoms are not improving despite the treatment.*

on the mend (informal): *She's on the mend now.*

recovering: *She's recovering after an attack of appendicitis.*

stonger: *He's slowly getting stronger after his accident.*

well: *I hope you're feeling well again soon.*

<< OPPOSITE *worse*

The bicentenary of an event is its two-hundredth anniversary.

biceps ['baɪsɛps] NOUN
(PE) Your biceps are the large muscles on your upper arms.

bicker ['bɪkə] **bickers, bickering, bickered** VERB
When people bicker, they argue or quarrel about unimportant things.

bicycle ['baɪsɪkᵊl] **bicycles** NOUN
a two-wheeled vehicle which you ride by pushing two pedals with your feet

bid [bɪd] **bids, bidding, bade, bidden, bid**
NOUN
1 an attempt to obtain or do something e.g. He made a bid for freedom.
2 an offer to buy something for a certain sum of money
> VERB
3 If you bid for something, you offer to pay a certain sum of money for it.
4 OLD-FASHIONED
If you bid someone a greeting or a farewell, you say it to them.

> When bid means 'offer to pay a certain sum of money' (sense 3), the past tense and past participle is bid. When bid means 'say a greeting or farewell' (sense 4), the past tense is bade and the past participle is bidden

biddy-biddy ['bɪdɪ,bɪdɪ] **biddy-biddies**
NOUN
a prickly low-growing plant found in New Zealand

bide [baɪd] **bides, biding, bided** PHRASE
If you **bide your time**, you wait for a good opportunity before doing something.

bidet ['biːdeɪ] **bidets** NOUN
a low basin in a bathroom which is used for washing your bottom in
[WORD HISTORY: a French word meaning 'small horse']

big see page 81 for Word Web

bigamy ['bɪgəmɪ] NOUN
Bigamy is the crime of marrying someone when you are already married to someone else.
bigamist NOUN

bigot ['bɪgət] **bigots** NOUN
someone who has strong and unreasonable opinions which they refuse to change
bigoted ADJECTIVE, **bigotry** NOUN

bike [baɪk] **bikes** NOUN; INFORMAL
a bicycle or motorcycle

bikini [bɪ'kiːnɪ] **bikinis** NOUN
a small two-piece swimming costume worn by women

[WORD HISTORY: after BIKINI atoll, from a comparison between the devastating effect of the atom-bomb test there and the effect caused by women wearing bikinis]

bilateral [baɪ'lætərəl] ADJECTIVE
A bilateral agreement is one made between two groups or countries.

bile [baɪl] NOUN
Bile is a bitter yellow liquid produced by the liver which helps the digestion of fat.

bilge [bɪldʒ] NOUN
the lowest part of a ship, where dirty water collects

bilingual [baɪ'lɪŋgwəl] ADJECTIVE
involving or using two languages e.g. bilingual street signs

bill [bɪl] **bills** NOUN
1 a written statement of how much is owed for goods or services
● THESAURUS
account: Please charge it to my account.
charges: charges for eye tests
invoice: They sent an invoice for the damage.
statement: a credit card statement
2 a formal statement of a proposed new law that is discussed and then voted on in Parliament
3 a notice or a poster
4 A bird's bill is its beak.

billabong ['bɪlə,bɒŋ] **billabongs** NOUN
In Australia, a billabong is a lagoon or pool formed from part of a river.

billboard ['bɪl,bɔːd] **billboards** NOUN
a large board on which advertisements are displayed

billet ['bɪlɪt] **billets, billeting, billeted** VERB
When soldiers are billeted in a building, arrangements are made for them to stay there.

billiards ['bɪljədz] NOUN
Billiards is a game in which a long cue is used to move balls on a table.

billion ['bɪljən] **billions** NOUN
a thousand million. Formerly, a billion was a million million

> As the meaning of billion has changed from one million million to one thousand million, a writer may mean either of these things when using it, depending on when the book or article was written.

billow ['bɪləʊ] **billows, billowing, billowed**
VERB
1 When things made of cloth billow, they swell out and flap slowly in the wind.
2 When smoke or cloud billows, it spreads upwards and outwards.

1 ADJECTIVE
of a large size *eg: a big house*
● **THESAURUS**
colossal: *a colossal statue*
enormous: *an enormous building*
gigantic: *The brontosaurus was a gigantic creature.*
great: *Her arrival caused a great commotion.*
huge: *a huge birthday cake*
immense: *an immense task*
large: *a large map of the world*
massive: *a massive fireworks display*
significant: *a significant difference*
vast: *a vast football stadium*
<< OPPOSITE *small*

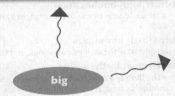

big

2 ADJECTIVE
of great importance *eg: a big name*
● **THESAURUS**
eminent: *an eminent politician*
important: *My teachers had an important influence on me.*
influential: *an influential figure in US foreign policy*
leading: *one of Britain's leading screenwriters*
major: *a major role in the company*
powerful: *a powerful businessman*
principal: *the principal guest at the reception*
prominent: *a prominent jazz musician*
significant: *the company in which he was a significant investor*
<< OPPOSITE *unimportant*

> NOUN

3 a large wave

billy or **billycan** ['bɪlɪ] or ['bɪlɪ,kæn] **billies** or **billycans** NOUN
In Australian and New Zealand English, a metal pot for boiling water over a camp fire.

bin [bɪn] **bins** NOUN
a container, especially one that you put rubbish in

binary ['baɪnərɪ] ADJECTIVE
(ICT) The binary system expresses numbers using only two digits, 0 and 1.

bind [baɪnd] **binds, binding, bound** VERB
1 If you bind something, you tie rope or string round it so that it is held firmly.
2 If something binds you to a course of action, it makes you act in that way. *e.g. He was bound by that decision.*

bindi-eye ['bɪndɪ,aɪ] **bindi-eyes** NOUN
a small Australian plant with prickly fruits

binding ['baɪndɪŋ] **bindings** ADJECTIVE
1 If a promise or agreement is binding, it must be obeyed.
> NOUN
2 The binding of a book is its cover.

binge [bɪndʒ] **binges** NOUN; INFORMAL
a wild bout of drinking or eating too much

bingo ['bɪŋgəʊ] NOUN
Bingo is a game in which players aim to match the numbers that someone calls out with the numbers on the card that they have been given.

binoculars [bɪ'nɒkjʊləz] PLURAL NOUN
Binoculars are an instrument with lenses for both eyes, which you look through in order to see objects far away.

bio- PREFIX
'Bio-' means 'life' or 'living things'. For example, a *biography* is the story of someone's life and *biology* is the study of living things
[WORD HISTORY: from Greek BIOS meaning 'life']

biochemistry [,baɪəʊ'kemɪstrɪ] NOUN
Biochemistry is the study of the chemistry of living things.
biochemical ADJECTIVE, **biochemist** NOUN

biodegradable [,baɪəʊdɪ'greɪdəbəl] ADJECTIVE
If something is biodegradable, it can be broken down into its natural elements by the action of bacteria. *e.g. biodegradable cleaning products*

biodiversity [,baɪəʊdaɪ'vɜːsɪtɪ] NOUN
the existence of a wide variety of plant and animal species in a particular area

biography [baɪ'ɒgrəfɪ] **biographies** NOUN
the history of someone's life, written by someone else

biographer NOUN, **biographical** ADJECTIVE

biology [baɪ'ɒlədʒɪ] NOUN
Biology is the study of living things.
biological ADJECTIVE, **biologically** ADVERB, **biologist** NOUN

biometric [,baɪəʊ'metrɪk] ADJECTIVE
relating to biometrics *e.g. a biometric passport*

biometrics [,baɪəʊ'metrɪks] NOUN
the use of mathematical measurements to analyse physical characteristics, especially to identify people

bionic [baɪ'ɒnɪk] ADJECTIVE
having a part of the body that works electronically

biopsy ['baɪɒpsɪ] **biopsies** NOUN
an examination under a microscope of tissue from a living body to find out the cause of a disease

birch [bɜːtʃ] **birches** NOUN
a tall deciduous tree with thin branches and thin bark

bird [bɜːd] **birds** NOUN
an animal with two legs, two wings, and feathers

birth [bɜːθ] **births** NOUN
1 The birth of a baby is when it comes out of its mother's womb at the beginning of its life.
2 The birth of something is its beginning. *e.g. the birth of modern art*

birthday ['bɜːθ,deɪ] **birthdays** NOUN
Your birthday is the anniversary of the date on which you were born.

birthmark ['bɜːθ,mɑːk] **birthmarks** NOUN
a mark on someone's skin that has been there since they were born

biscuit ['bɪskɪt] **biscuits** NOUN
a small flat cake made of baked dough
[WORD HISTORY: from Old French BES + CUIT meaning 'twice-cooked']

bisect [baɪ'sekt] **bisects, bisecting, bisected** VERB
To bisect a line or area means to divide it in half.

bisexual [baɪ'seksjʊəl] ADJECTIVE
sexually attracted to both men and women

bishop ['bɪʃəp] **bishops** NOUN
1 a high-ranking clergyman in some Christian Churches
2 In chess, a bishop is a piece that is moved diagonally across the board.

bison ['baɪsən] NOUN
a large hairy animal related to cattle

bistro ['biːstrəʊ] **bistros** NOUN
a small informal restaurant

b

bit [bɪt] **bits**

1 Bit is the past tense of **bite**

> NOUN

2 A bit of something is a small amount of it. *e.g. a bit of coal*

THESAURUS
crumb: *a crumb of comfort*
fragment: *glittering fragments of broken glass*
grain: *His story contains a grain of truth.*
part: *part of the problem*
piece: *The vase was smashed to pieces.*
scrap: *a scrap of evidence*

> PHRASE; INFORMAL

3 A bit means slightly or to a small extent *e.g. That's a bit tricky.*

bitch [bɪtʃ] **bitches** NOUN

1 a female dog

2 OFFENSIVE
If someone refers to a woman as a bitch, it means that they think she behaves in a spiteful way.
bitchy ADJECTIVE

bite [baɪt] **bites, biting, bit, bitten** VERB

1 To bite something or someone is to cut it or cut through it with the teeth.

THESAURUS
chew: *a video of a man having his leg chewed off by a bear*
gnaw: *The bones had been gnawed by wild animals.*
nibble: *She nibbled a biscuit.*
nip: *There were blotches where the mosquitoes had nipped him.*

> NOUN

2 a small amount that you bite off something with your teeth

3 the injury you get when an animal or insect bites you

bitter [ˈbɪtə] **bitterest** ADJECTIVE

1 If someone is bitter, they feel angry and resentful.

THESAURUS
acrimonious: *an acrimonious discussion*
begrudging: *He gave me begrudging thanks.*
embittered: *an embittered old lady*
rancorous: *the issue that has led to rancorous disputes*
resentful: *She is resentful of others' success.*
sour: *a sour expression*

2 A bitter disappointment or experience makes people feel angry or unhappy for a long time afterwards.

3 In a bitter argument or war, people argue or fight fiercely and angrily. *e.g. a bitter power struggle*

4 A bitter wind is an extremely cold wind.

5 Something that tastes bitter has a sharp, unpleasant taste.
bitterly ADVERB, **bitterness** NOUN

THESAURUS
acid: *the acid smell of sweat*
acrid: *clouds of acrid smoke*
astringent: *astringent disinfectant*
sharp: *a clean, sharp taste*
sour: *a rich, sour stew*
tart: *the tart qualities of citrus fruit*
<<OPPOSITE sweet

bivouac [ˈbɪvʊˌæk] **bivouacs** NOUN
a temporary camp in the open air

bizarre [bɪˈzɑː] ADJECTIVE
very strange or eccentric

THESAURUS
curious: *a curious mixture of ancient and modern*
eccentric: *Her eccentric behaviour was beginning to attract attention.*
extraordinary: *What an extraordinary character he is!*
odd: *a series of very odd coincidences*
outlandish: *her outlandish style of dressing*
peculiar: *a peculiar combination of flavours*
queer: *A very queer thing happened to me tonight.*
strange: *She's been behaving in a very strange way lately.*
weird: *his weird theories about UFOs*
<<OPPOSITE ordinary

blab [blæb] **blabs, blabbing, blabbed** VERB; INFORMAL
When someone blabs, they give away secrets by talking carelessly.

black [blæk] **blacker, blackest; blacks**
NOUN OR ADJECTIVE
Black is the darkest possible colour, like tar or soot.

1 Someone who is Black is a member of a dark-skinned race.

> ADJECTIVE

2 Black coffee or tea has no milk or cream added to it.

3 Black humour involves jokes about death or suffering.
blackness NOUN

> When you are writing about a person or people, *Black* should start with a capital letter.

blackberry [ˈblækbəri] **blackberries** NOUN
Blackberries are small black fruits that grow on prickly bushes called brambles.

blackbird [ˈblækˌbɜːd] **blackbirds** NOUN
a common European bird, the male of which has black feathers and a yellow beak

blackboard ['blæk,bɔːd] **blackboards**
NOUN
a dark-coloured board in a classroom, which teachers write on using chalk

black box **black boxes** NOUN
an electronic device in an aircraft which collects and stores information during flights

blackcurrant [,blæk'kʌrənt] **blackcurrants** NOUN
Blackcurrants are very small dark purple fruits that grow in bunches on bushes.

blacken ['blækən] **blackens, blackening, blackened** VERB
To blacken something means to make it black. *e.g. The smoke from the chimney blackened the roof.*

blackhead ['blæk,hɛd] **blackheads** NOUN
a very small black spot on the skin caused by a pore being blocked with dirt

blacklist ['blæk,lɪst] **blacklists, blacklisting, blacklisted** NOUN
1 a list of people or organizations who are thought to be untrustworthy or disloyal
> VERB
2 When someone is blacklisted, they are put on a blacklist.

blackmail ['blæk,meɪl] **blackmails, blackmailing, blackmailed** VERB
1 If someone blackmails another person, they threaten to reveal an unpleasant secret about them unless that person gives them money or does something for them.
> NOUN
2 Blackmail is the action of blackmailing people.
blackmailer NOUN

black market NOUN
If something is bought or sold on the black market, it is bought or sold illegally.

blackout ['blæk,aʊt] **blackouts** NOUN
If you have a blackout, you lose consciousness for a short time.

blacksmith ['blæk,smɪθ] **blacksmiths** NOUN
a person whose job is making things out of iron, such as horseshoes

bladder ['blædə] **bladders** NOUN
the part of your body where urine is held until it leaves your body

blade [bleɪd] **blades** NOUN
1 The blade of a weapon or cutting tool is the sharp part of it.
2 The blades of a propeller are the thin, flat parts that turn round.
3 A blade of grass is a single piece of it.

blame [bleɪm] **blames, blaming, blamed** VERB
1 If someone blames you for something bad that has happened, they believe you caused it.
● THESAURUS
accuse: *She accused him of causing the fire.*
charge: *He will be charged for murder.*
hold responsible: *I hold you responsible for this mess.*
> NOUN
2 The blame for something bad that happens is the responsibility for letting it happen.
● THESAURUS
accountability: *He escaped accountability for his crimes.*
fault: *The fault was all yours.*
guilt: *the sole guilt for the outbreak of war*
liability: *He admitted liability for the crash.*
rap: slang *A maid took the rap for stealing the letters.*
responsibility: *responsibility for the murder*

blameless ['bleɪmlɪs] ADJECTIVE
Someone who is blameless has not done anything wrong.

blanch [blɑːntʃ] **blanches, blanching, blanched** VERB
If you blanch, you suddenly become very pale.

bland [blænd] **blander, blandest** ADJECTIVE
tasteless, dull or boring *e.g. a bland diet... bland pop music*
blandly ADVERB

blank [blæŋk] **blanker, blankest** ADJECTIVE
1 Something that is blank has nothing on it. *e.g. a blank sheet of paper*
● THESAURUS
bare: *bare walls*
clean: *a clean sheet of paper*
clear: *a clear patch of floor*
empty: *an empty page*
plain: *a plain envelope*
unmarked: *an unmarked board*
2 If you look blank, your face shows no feeling or interest.
● THESAURUS
deadpan: *a deadpan expression*
dull: *a dull stare*
empty: *She saw the empty look in his eyes.*
impassive: *her impassive smile*
vacant: *the vacant expression on his face*
> NOUN
3 If your mind is a blank, you cannot think of anything or remember anything.

blanket ['blæŋkɪt] **blankets** NOUN
1 a large rectangle of thick cloth that is put on a bed to keep people warm
2 A blanket of something such as snow is a thick covering of it.

blare [blɛə] **blares, blaring, blared** VERB
To blare means to make a loud, unpleasant
noise. *e.g. The radio blared pop music.*

blaspheme [blæsˈfiːm] **blasphemes,
blaspheming, blasphemed** VERB
When people blaspheme, they are disrespectful
about God or religion.
[WORD HISTORY: from Greek BLAPSIS meaning 'evil'
and PHĒMEIN meaning 'to speak']

blasphemy [ˈblæsfɪmɪ] **blasphemies** NOUN
Blasphemy is speech or behaviour that shows
disrespect for God or religion.
blasphemous ADJECTIVE

blast [blɑːst] **blasts, blasting, blasted** VERB
1 When people blast a hole in something they
make a hole with an explosion.

> NOUN

2 a big explosion, especially one caused by a
bomb

3 a sudden strong rush of wind or air

blatant [ˈbleɪtᵊnt] ADJECTIVE
If you describe something you think is bad as
blatant, you mean that rather than hide it, those
responsible actually seem to be making it
obvious. *e.g. a blatant disregard for the law*

blaze [bleɪz] **blazes, blazing, blazed** NOUN
1 a large, hot fire

2 A blaze of light or colour is a great or strong
amount of it. *e.g. a blaze of red*

3 A blaze of publicity or attention is a lot of it.

> VERB

4 If something blazes it burns or shines brightly.

blazer [ˈbleɪzə] **blazers** NOUN
a kind of jacket, often in the colours of a school or
sports team

bleach [bliːtʃ] **bleaches, bleaching,
bleached** VERB
1 To bleach material or hair means to make it
white, usually by using a chemical.

> NOUN

2 Bleach is a chemical that is used to make
material white or to clean thoroughly and kill
germs.

bleak [bliːk] **bleaker, bleakest** ADJECTIVE
1 If a situation is bleak, it is bad and seems
unlikely to improve.

2 If a place is bleak, it is cold, bare, and exposed
to the wind.

bleary [ˈblɪərɪ] ADJECTIVE
If your eyes are bleary, they are red and watery,
usually because you are tired.

bleat [bliːt] **bleats, bleating, bleated** VERB

1 When sheep or goats bleat, they make a high-
pitched cry.

> NOUN

2 the high-pitched cry that a sheep or goat
makes

bleed [bliːd] **bleeds, bleeding, bled** VERB
When you bleed, you lose blood as a result of an
injury.

bleep [bliːp] **bleeps** NOUN
a short high-pitched sound made by an electrical
device such as an alarm

blemish [ˈblɛmɪʃ] **blemishes** NOUN
a mark that spoils the appearance of something

blend [blɛnd] **blends, blending, blended**
VERB
1 When you blend substances, you mix them
together to form a single substance.

● THESAURUS
combine: *Combine the ingredients in a large bowl.*
merge: *how to merge the graphics with the text*
mingle: *the mingled smells of flowers and cigar
smoke*
mix: *Mix the two liquids together with a whisk.*
<<OPPOSITE *separate*

2 When colours or sounds blend, they combine
in a pleasing way.

● THESAURUS
complement: *The flavours complement each other
perfectly.*
co-ordinate: *Choose accessories which co-ordinate
with your outfit.*
go well: *a wine which goes well with fish*
harmonize: *shades which harmonize with most skin
tones*
match: *Those shoes don't match that dress.*
suit: *glasses which suit the shape of your face*

> NOUN

3 A blend of things is a mixture of them,
especially one that is pleasing.

● THESAURUS
alloy: *an alloy of copper and tin*
amalgamation: *Bartók's rich amalgamation of
musical styles*
combination: *a fantastic combination of colours*
compound: *a compound of water, sugar and
enzymes*
fusion: *a fusion of cooking styles*
mix: *a delicious mix of exotic spices*
mixture: *a sticky mixture of flour and water*

4 a word formed by joining together the
beginning and the end of two other words; for
example, 'brunch' is a blend of 'breakfast' and
'lunch'

blender [ˈblɛndə] **blenders** NOUN
a machine used for mixing liquids and foods at
high speed

bless [blɛs] **blesses, blessing, blessed** or **blest** VERB
When a priest blesses people or things, he or she asks for God's protection for them.
[WORD HISTORY: from Old English BLÆDSIAN meaning 'to sprinkle with sacrificial blood']

THESAURUS
anoint: *The priest anointed the child with oil.*
consecrate: *ground that has been consecrated*
dedicate: *The well was dedicated to saints.*
hallow: *A building could be hallowed by prayer.*
<<OPPOSITE *curse*

blessed ['blɛsɪd] ADJECTIVE
If someone is blessed with a particular quality or skill, they have it. *e.g. He was blessed with a sense of humour.*
blessedly ADVERB

blessing ['blɛsɪŋ] **blessings** NOUN
1 something good that you are thankful for *e.g. Good health is the greatest blessing.*

THESAURUS
benefit: *the benefits of technology*
boon: *This service is a boon to the elderly.*
gift: *A cheerful nature is a gift.*
godsend: *The extra twenty dollars was a godsend.*
help: *My computer is a real help in my work.*
<<OPPOSITE *disadvantage*

> PHRASE
2 If something is done **with someone's blessing**, they approve of it and support it.

THESAURUS
approval: *Does this plan have your approval?*
backing: *We can't do anything without his backing.*
consent: *He gave his consent to the article.*
leave: *She gave us leave to start.*
permission: *You have my permission to go.*
support: *My manager has given his full support to my project.*
<<OPPOSITE *disapproval*

blew [bluː] the past tense of **blow**

blight [blaɪt] **blights, blighting, blighted** NOUN
1 something that damages or spoils other things *e.g. the blight of the recession*

> VERB
2 When something is blighted, it is seriously harmed. *e.g. His life had been blighted by sickness.*

blind [blaɪnd] **blinds, blinding, blinded** ADJECTIVE
1 Someone who is blind cannot see.
2 If someone is blind to a particular fact, they do not understand it.

> VERB
3 If something blinds you, you become unable to

see, either for a short time or permanently.

> NOUN
4 a roll of cloth or paper that you pull down over a window to keep out the light
blindly ADVERB, **blindness** NOUN

blindfold ['blaɪnd‚fəʊld] **blindfolds, blindfolding, blindfolded** NOUN
1 a strip of cloth tied over someone's eyes so that they cannot see

> VERB
2 To blindfold someone means to cover their eyes with a strip of cloth.

blinding ['blaɪndɪŋ] ADJECTIVE
A blinding light is so bright that it hurts your eyes. *e.g. There was a blinding flash.*

blindingly ['blaɪndɪŋli] ADVERB; INFORMAL
If something is blindingly obvious, it is very obvious indeed.

bling [blɪŋ] **blinger, blingest** INFORMAL
1 NOUN
jewellery that looks expensive in a vulgar way
2 ADJECTIVE
flashy; expensive-looking in a vulgar way

blink [blɪŋk] **blinks, blinking, blinked** VERB
When you blink, you close your eyes quickly for a moment.

blinkers ['blɪŋkəz] PLURAL NOUN
Blinkers are two pieces of leather placed at the side of a horse's eyes so that it can only see straight ahead.

bliss [blɪs] NOUN
Bliss is a state of complete happiness.
blissful ADJECTIVE, **blissfully** ADVERB

blister ['blɪstə] **blisters, blistering, blistered** NOUN
1 a small bubble on your skin containing watery liquid, caused by a burn or rubbing

> VERB
2 If someone's skin blisters, blisters appear on it as result of burning or rubbing.

blithe [blaɪð] ADJECTIVE
casual and done without serious thought *e.g. a blithe disregard for their safety*
blithely ADVERB

blitz [blɪts] **blitzes, blitzing, blitzed** NOUN
1 a bombing attack by enemy aircraft on a city

> VERB
2 When a city is blitzed, it is bombed by aircraft and is damaged or destroyed.
[WORD HISTORY: from German BLITZKRIEG meaning 'lightning war']

blizzard ['blɪzəd] **blizzards** NOUN
a heavy snowstorm with strong winds

b

bloated ['bləʊtɪd] ADJECTIVE
Something that is bloated is much larger than normal, often because there is a lot of liquid or gas inside it.

blob [blɒb] **blobs** NOUN
a small amount of a thick or sticky substance

● THESAURUS
bead: *Beads of blood spattered the counter.*
dab: *You've got a dab of glue on your nose.*
drop: *A few thick drops of fluid*
droplet: *droplets of congealed fat*

bloc [blɒk] **blocs** NOUN
A group of countries or political parties with similar aims acting together is often called a bloc. *e.g. the world's largest trading bloc*

block [blɒk] **blocks, blocking, blocked** NOUN
1 A block of flats or offices is a large building containing flats or offices.

2 In a town, a block is an area of land with streets on all its sides. *e.g. He lives a few blocks down.*

3 A block of something is a large rectangular piece of it.

● THESAURUS
bar: *a bar of soap*
brick: *concrete bricks*
chunk: *chunks of meat*
ingot: *a gold ingot*
lump: *lumps of metal*
piece: *a big piece of cake*

> VERB
4 To block a road or channel means to put something across it so that nothing can get through.

● THESAURUS
choke: *The town was choked with cars.*
clog: *Dishes clogged the sink.*
obstruct: *The crash obstructed the road.*
plug: *Have you plugged the leaks?*
<<OPPOSITE *unblock*

5 If something blocks your view, it is in the way and prevents you from seeing what you want to see.

6 If someone blocks something, they prevent it from happening. *e.g. The council blocked his plans.*

● THESAURUS
bar: *He was barred from entering.*
check: *a policy to check population growth*
halt: *attempts to halt the spread of disease*
obstruct: *Lack of funds obstructed our progress.*
stop: *measures to stop the rising crime rate*
thwart: *My plans were thwarted by Taylor.*

blockade [blɒ'keɪd] **blockades, blockading, blockaded** NOUN
1 an action that prevents goods from reaching a place

> VERB
2 When a place is blockaded, supplies are prevented from reaching it.

blockage ['blɒkɪdʒ] **blockages** NOUN
When there is a blockage in a pipe or tunnel, something is clogging it.

● THESAURUS
block: *a block in the blood vessel*
obstruction: *an obstruction on the track*
stoppage: *We have to clear the stoppage.*

blog [blɒg] **blogs** NOUN; INFORMAL
short for weblog: a person's online diary that he or she puts on the Internet so that other people can read it

blogger ['blɒgə] **bloggers** NOUN; INFORMAL
a person who keeps a blog

bloke [bləʊk] **blokes** NOUN; INFORMAL
a man

blonde [blɒnd] **blondes** or **blond blonds** ADJECTIVE
1 Blonde hair is pale yellow in colour. The spelling 'blond' is used when referring to men.

> NOUN
2 A blonde, or blond, is a person with light-coloured hair.

blood [blʌd] NOUN
1 Blood is the red liquid that is pumped by the heart round the bodies of human beings and other mammals.

> PHRASE
2 If something cruel is done **in cold blood**, it is done deliberately and without showing any emotion.

bloodhound ['blʌd,haʊnd] **bloodhounds** NOUN
a large dog with an excellent sense of smell

bloodless ['blʌdlɪs] ADJECTIVE
1 If someone's face or skin is bloodless, it is very pale.

2 In a bloodless coup or revolution, nobody is killed.

blood pressure NOUN
Your blood pressure is a measure of the force with which your blood is being pumped round your body.

bloodshed ['blʌd,ʃɛd] NOUN
When there is bloodshed, people are killed or wounded.

bloodshot ['blʌd,ʃɒt] ADJECTIVE
If a person's eyes are bloodshot, the white parts have become red.

blood sport blood sports NOUN
any sport that involves deliberately killing or injuring animals

bloodstained ['blʌd,steɪnd] ADJECTIVE
covered with blood

bloodstream ['blʌd,striːm] NOUN
the flow of blood through your body

bloodthirsty ['blʌd,θɜːstɪ] ADJECTIVE
Someone who is bloodthirsty enjoys using or
watching violence.

blood transfusion **blood transfusions**
NOUN
a process in which blood is injected into the body
of someone who has lost a lot of blood

blood vessel **blood vessels** NOUN
Blood vessels are the narrow tubes in your body
through which your blood flows.

bloody ['blʌdɪ] **bloodier, bloodiest**
ADJECTIVE OR ADVERB
1 Bloody is a common swearword, used to
express anger or annoyance.
> ADJECTIVE
2 A bloody event is one in which a lot of people
are killed. *e.g. a bloody revolution*
3 Bloody also means covered with blood. *e.g. a
bloody gash on his head*

bloom [bluːm] **blooms, blooming,
bloomed** NOUN
1 a flower on a plant
> VERB
2 When a plant blooms, it produces flowers.
3 When something like a feeling blooms, it
grows. *e.g. Romance can bloom where you least
expect it.*

blossom ['blɒsəm] **blossoms, blossoming,
blossomed** NOUN
1 Blossom is the growth of flowers that appears
on a tree before the fruit.
> VERB
2 When a tree blossoms, it produces blossom.

blot [blɒt] **blots, blotting, blotted** NOUN
1 a drop of ink that has been spilled on a surface
2 A blot on someone's reputation is a mistake or
piece of bad behaviour that spoils their
reputation. **blot out** VERB
3 To blot something out means to be in front of it
and prevent it from being seen. *e.g. The smoke
blotted out the sky.*

THESAURUS
eclipse: *The moon eclipsed the sun.*
obliterate: *Our view was obliterated by mist.*
obscure: *My way was obscured by fog.*
shadow: *Her veil shadowed her face.*

blotch [blɒtʃ] **blotches** NOUN
a stain or a patch of a different colour
blotchy ADJECTIVE

blouse [blaʊz] **blouses** NOUN
a light shirt, worn by a girl or a woman

blow [bləʊ] **blows, blowing, blew, blown**
VERB
1 When the wind blows, the air moves.
2 If something blows or is blown somewhere, the
wind moves it there.
THESAURUS
buffet: *The ship was buffeted by gales.*
drive: *The strong wind drove us forward.*
flutter: *The flags are fluttering.*
sweep: *A sudden blast swept away the cloth.*
waft: *His hair wafted in the breeze.*
whirl: *The fallen leaves whirled around.*
3 If you blow a whistle or horn, you make a sound
by blowing into it.
> NOUN
4 If you receive a blow, someone or something
hits you.
THESAURUS
bang: *He suffered some bangs and bumps.*
clout: informal *a clout on the head*
knock: *Knocks can cause damage to the spine.*
smack: *She gave the child a smack.*
thump: *Ralph got a thump on the chest.*
whack: *The horse got a whack from its rider.*
5 something that makes you very disappointed or
unhappy *e.g. Marc's death was a terrible blow.*
THESAURUS
bombshell: *His departure was a bombshell for the
team.*
disappointment: *My exam results were a real
disappointment.*
misfortune: *a series of misfortunes*
setback: *We faced many setbacks before we got the
house.*
shock: *The news came as a shock.*
upset: *The defeat caused an upset.*
> VERB **blow up**
6 To blow something up means to destroy it with
an explosion.
7 To blow up a balloon or a tyre means to fill it
with air.

blubber ['blʌbə] NOUN
The blubber of animals such as whales and seals
is the layer of fat that protects them from the
cold.

bludge [blʌdʒ] **bludges, bludging, bludged**
VERB; INFORMAL
1 In Australian and New Zealand English, to
bludge is to scrounge or cadge.
2 In Australian and New Zealand English, to
bludge is also to avoid work or responsibilities.

bludgeon ['blʌdʒən] **bludgeons,
bludgeoning, bludgeoned** VERB

To bludgeon someone means to hit them several times with a heavy object.

blue [bluː] **bluer, bluest** ADJECTIVE OR NOUN
Blue is the colour of the sky on a clear, sunny day.

> PHRASE
1 If something happens **out of the blue**, it happens suddenly and unexpectedly.

> ADJECTIVE
2 Blue films and jokes are about sex.
bluish or **blueish** ADJECTIVE

bluebell ['bluː,bɛl] **bluebells** NOUN
a woodland plant with blue, bell-shaped flowers

bluebottle ['bluː,bɒtˀl] **bluebottles** NOUN
1 a large fly with a shiny dark-blue body
2 In Australia and New Zealand, a bluebottle is also a small stinging jellyfish.

blue-collar ['bluː,kɒlə] ADJECTIVE
Blue-collar workers do physical work as opposed to office work.

blueprint ['bluː,prɪnt] **blueprints** NOUN
a plan of how something is expected to work *e.g. the blueprint for successful living*

blues [bluːz] NOUN
The blues is a type of music which is similar to jazz, but is always slow and sad.

bluff [blʌf] **bluffs, bluffing, bluffed;** NOUN
1 an attempt to make someone wrongly believe that you are in a strong position

> VERB
2 If you are bluffing, you are trying to make someone believe that you are in a position of strength.

blunder ['blʌndə] **blunders, blundering, blundered** VERB
1 If you blunder, you make a silly mistake.

> NOUN
2 a silly mistake

blunt [blʌnt] **blunter, bluntest** ADJECTIVE
1 A blunt object has a rounded point or edge, rather than a sharp one.

THESAURUS
dull: *a dull knife*
rounded: *rounded edges*
unsharpened: *an unsharpened pencil*
<<OPPOSITE *sharp*

2 If you are blunt, you say exactly what you think, without trying to be polite.

THESAURUS
bluff: *a bluff old man*
brusque: *His response was brusque.*
forthright: *a forthright reply*
frank: *I'll be frank with you.*
outspoken: *an outspoken critic*

straightforward: *She has a straightforward manner.*
<<OPPOSITE *tactful*

blur [blɜː] **blurs, blurring, blurred** NOUN
1 a shape or area which you cannot see clearly because it has no distinct outline or because it is moving very fast

> VERB
2 To blur the differences between things means to make them no longer clear. *e.g. The dreams blurred confusingly with her memories.*
blurred ADJECTIVE

blurt out [blɜːt] **blurts out, blurting out, blurted out** VERB
If you blurt something out, you say it suddenly, after trying to keep it a secret.

blush [blʌʃ] **blushes, blushing, blushed** VERB
1 If you blush, your face becomes red, because you are embarrassed or ashamed.

THESAURUS
colour: *I found myself colouring as I spoke.*
crimson: *He looked at her and she crimsoned.*
flush: *I saw her face flush.*
go red: *His face went red as a beetroot.*
turn red: *He turned red with embarrassment.*
turn scarlet: *She turned scarlet with humiliation.*

> NOUN
2 the red colour on someone's face when they are embarrassed or ashamed

THESAURUS
colour: *The walk will bring colour to your cheeks.*
flush: *A slow flush spread over the man's face.*
glow: *a healthy glow*

bluster ['blʌstə] **blusters, blustering, blustered** VERB
1 When someone blusters, they behave aggressively because they are angry or frightened.

> NOUN
2 Bluster is aggressive behaviour by someone who is angry or frightened.

blustery ['blʌstərɪ] ADJECTIVE
Blustery weather is rough and windy.

boa ['bəʊə] **boas** NOUN
1 A boa, or a boa constrictor, is a large snake that kills its prey by coiling round it and crushing it.
2 a woman's long thin scarf of feathers or fur

boar [bɔː] **boars** NOUN
a male wild pig, or a male domestic pig used for breeding

board [bɔːd] **boards, boarding, boarded** NOUN

1 a long, flat piece of wood

2 the group of people who control a company or organization

3 Board is the meals provided when you stay somewhere. *e.g. The price includes full board.*

> VERB

4 If you board a ship or aircraft, you get on it or in it.

> PHRASE

5 If you are **on board** a ship or aircraft, you are on it or in it.

boarder ['bɔːdə] **boarders** NOUN
a pupil who lives at school during term

boarding school ['bɔːdɪŋ] **boarding schools** NOUN
a school where the pupils live during the term

boardroom ['bɔːd,ruːm] **boardrooms** NOUN
a room where the board of a company meets

boast [bəʊst] **boasts, boasting, boasted** VERB

1 If you boast about your possessions or achievements, you talk about them proudly.

● THESAURUS
brag: *I don't mind bragging about my talents.*
crow: *Stop crowing about your success.*
skite: *Australian and New Zealand; informal That's nothing to skite about.*

> NOUN

2 something that you say which shows that you are proud of what you own or have done

boastful ['bəʊstfʊl] ADJECTIVE
tending to brag about things

● THESAURUS
bragging: *bragging stories about his time in the navy*
cocky: *The boxer is cocky and brash.*
conceited: *Young men tend to be conceited.*
crowing: *crowing remarks*
egotistical: *egotistical fibs*
swaggering: *He has a swaggering arrogance.*
<<OPPOSITE modest

boat [bəʊt] **boats** NOUN
a small vehicle for travelling across water

bob [bɒb] **bobs, bobbing, bobbed** VERB

1 When something bobs, it moves up and down.

> NOUN

2 a woman's hair style in which her hair is cut level with her chin

bobbin ['bɒbɪn] **bobbins** NOUN
a small round object on which thread or wool is wound

bobby ['bɒbɪ] **bobbies** NOUN; OLD-FASHIONED, INFORMAL

a policeman

bode [bəʊd] **bodes, boding, boded** PHRASE; LITERARY
If something **bodes ill**, or **bodes well**, it makes you think that something bad, or good, will happen.

bodice ['bɒdɪs] **bodices** NOUN
the upper part of a dress

bodily ['bɒdɪlɪ] ADJECTIVE

1 relating to the body *e.g. bodily contact*

> ADVERB

2 involving the whole of someone's body *e.g. He was carried bodily up the steps.*

body ['bɒdɪ] **bodies** NOUN

1 Your body is either all your physical parts, or just the main part not including your head, arms, and legs.

● THESAURUS
build: *He is of medium build.*
figure: *Janet has a nice figure.*
form: *clothes that flatter your form*
frame: *their bony frames*
physique: *a powerful physique*
shape: *his trim shape*

2 a person's dead body

● THESAURUS
carcass: *a sheep's carcass*
corpse: *the corpse of a young man*
dead body: *He'd never seen a dead body.*
remains: *human remains*

3 the main part of a car or aircraft, not including the engine

4 A body of people is an organized group.

● THESAURUS
association: *the Football Association*
band: *a band of rebels*
company: *the Royal Shakespeare Company*
confederation: *a confederation of workers*
organization: *student organizations*
society: *I joined the local opera society.*

bodyguard ['bɒdɪ,gɑːd] **bodyguards** NOUN
a person employed to protect someone

bodywork ['bɒdɪ,wɜːk] NOUN
the outer part of a motor vehicle

boer [bʊə] *or* ['bəʊə] *or* [bɔː] **boers** NOUN
In South Africa, a boer is a white farmer, especially one who is descended from the Dutch people who went to live in South Africa.

boerewors ['bʊərə,vɒs] NOUN
In South Africa, boerewors is a type of meat sausage.

bog [bɒg] **bogs** NOUN
an area of land which is always wet and spongy

[WORD HISTORY: from Gaelic BOGACH meaning 'swamp']

boggle ['bɒgᵊl] **boggles, boggling, boggled**
VERB
If your mind boggles at something, you find it difficult to imagine or understand.

bogus ['bəʊgəs] ADJECTIVE
not genuine e.g. a bogus doctor

bohemian [bəʊ'hiːmɪən] ADJECTIVE
Someone who is bohemian does not behave in the same way as most other people in society, and is usually involved in the arts.

boil [bɔɪl] **boils, boiling, boiled** VERB
1 When a hot liquid boils, bubbles appear in it and it starts to give off steam.

● THESAURUS
bubble: Potatoes bubbled in the pot.
fizz: The liquid fizzed and bubbled.
foam: When the butter foams, add the onions.
froth: The milk frothed over in the pan.

2 When you boil a kettle, you heat it until the water in it boils.

3 When you boil food, you cook it in boiling water.

> NOUN
4 a red swelling on your skin

● THESAURUS
blister: a blister on my index finger
swelling: a swelling under the eye
tumour: The tumours had all disappeared.

boiler ['bɔɪlə] **boilers** NOUN
a piece of equipment which burns fuel to provide hot water

boiling ['bɔɪlɪŋ] ADJECTIVE; INFORMAL
very hot

boisterous ['bɔɪstərəs] ADJECTIVE
Someone who is boisterous is noisy and lively.

bold [bəʊld] **bolder, boldest** ADJECTIVE
1 confident and not shy or embarrassed e.g. He was not bold enough to ask them.

● THESAURUS
brash: a brash young sergeant
brazen: a brazen young woman
cheeky: a cheeky grin
confident: I felt confident confronting him.
forward: It was forward of you to ask him.
impudent: an impudent child
<<OPPOSITE shy

2 not afraid of risk or danger

● THESAURUS
adventurous: an adventurous spirit
brave: a brave woman
courageous: courageous firefighters

daring: daring feats
fearless: a fearless warrior
intrepid: an intrepid explorer
<<OPPOSITE cowardly

3 clear and noticeable e.g. bold colours
boldly ADVERB, **boldness** NOUN

● THESAURUS
bright: bright light
flashy: flashy clothes
loud: a loud tie
striking: a striking tartan pattern
strong: dressed in strong reds and yellows
vivid: vivid green and purple
<<OPPOSITE dull

bollard ['bɒlɑːd] **bollards** NOUN
a short, thick post used to keep vehicles out of a road

bolster ['bəʊlstə] **bolsters, bolstering, bolstered** VERB
To bolster something means to support it or make it stronger. e.g. She relied on others to bolster her self-esteem.

bolt [bəʊlt] **bolts, bolting, bolted** NOUN
1 a metal bar that you slide across a door or window in order to fasten it
2 a metal object which screws into a nut and is used to fasten things together

> VERB
3 If you bolt a door or window, you fasten it using a bolt. If you bolt things together, you fasten them together using a bolt.
4 To bolt means to escape or run away.

● THESAURUS
dash: He dashed out of the room in a panic.
escape: They escaped across the frontier.
flee: We fled before the police arrived.
fly: She flew down the stairs with her attacker in hot pursuit.
run away: I called to him but he just ran away.
run off: The children ran off when they spotted me.
rush: They all rushed away as we approached.

5 To bolt food means to eat it very quickly.

bomb [bɒm] **bombs, bombing, bombed** NOUN
1 a container filled with material that explodes when it hits something or is set off by a timer

● THESAURUS
device: Experts defused the device.
explosive: a block of plastic explosive
missile: long-range missiles
rocket: a rocket launcher
shell: Shells began to fall.
torpedo: The torpedo struck the ship.

> VERB
2 When a place is bombed, it is attacked with bombs.

[WORD HISTORY: from Greek BOMBOS meaning 'a booming sound']

● THESAURUS
attack: *We are being attacked!*
blow up: *He attempted to blow up the building.*
bombard: *Warships began to bombard the coast.*
destroy: *Helicopters destroyed his village.*
shell: *They shelled the troops heavily.*
torpedo: *His ship was torpedoed in the Channel.*

bombard [bɒmˈbɑːd] **bombards, bombarding, bombarded** VERB

1 To bombard a place means to attack it with heavy gunfire or bombs.

2 If you are bombarded with something you are made to face a great deal of it. *e.g. I was bombarded with criticism.*
bombardment NOUN

bomber [ˈbɒmə] **bombers** NOUN
an aircraft that drops bombs

bombshell [ˈbɒmˌʃɛl] **bombshells** NOUN
a sudden piece of shocking or upsetting news

bona fide [ˈbəʊnə ˈfaɪdɪ] ADJECTIVE
genuine *e.g. We are happy to donate to bona fide charities.*
[WORD HISTORY: a Latin expression meaning 'in good faith']

bond [bɒnd] **bonds, bonding, bonded** NOUN

1 a close relationship between people

● THESAURUS
attachment: *Mother and child form a close attachment.*
connection: *a family connection*
link: *the links of friendship*
relation: *the relation between husband and wife*
tie: *the ties of blood*
union: *the union of father and son*

2 LITERARY
Bonds are chains or ropes used to tie a prisoner up.

3 a certificate which records that you have lent money to a business and that it will repay you the loan with interest

4 Bonds are also feelings or obligations that force you to behave in a particular way. *e.g. the social bonds of community*

● THESAURUS
agreement: *He has broken our agreement.*
contract: *He signed a two-year contract.*
obligation: *your obligation to your father*
pledge: *a pledge of support*
promise: *You must keep your promises.*
word: *I give you my word.*

> VERB
5 When two things bond or are bonded, they

become closely linked or attached.

● THESAURUS
bind: *Tape was used to bind the files.*
fasten: *I fastened the picture to the wall.*
fuse: *The pieces to be joined are melted and fused together.*
glue: *Glue the pieces together.*
paste: *He pasted posters to the wall.*

bondage [ˈbɒndɪdʒ] NOUN
Bondage is the condition of being someone's slave.

bone [bəʊn] **bones** NOUN
Bones are the hard parts that form the framework of a person's or animal's body.
boneless ADJECTIVE

bonfire [ˈbɒnˌfaɪə] **bonfires** NOUN
a large fire made outdoors, often to burn rubbish
[WORD HISTORY: from 'bone' + 'fire'; bones were used as fuel in the Middle Ages]

bonnet [ˈbɒnɪt] **bonnets** NOUN

1 the metal cover over a car's engine

2 a baby's or woman's hat tied under the chin

bonny [ˈbɒnɪ] **bonnier, bonniest** ADJECTIVE; SCOTTISH AND NORTHERN ENGLISH
nice to look at

bonus [ˈbəʊnəs] **bonuses** NOUN

1 an amount of money added to your usual pay

2 Something that is a bonus is a good thing that you get in addition to something else. *e.g. The view from the hotel was an added bonus.*

bony [ˈbəʊnɪ] **bonier, boniest** ADJECTIVE
Bony people or animals are thin, with very little flesh covering their bones.

boo [buː] **boos, booing, booed** NOUN

1 a shout of disapproval

> VERB
2 When people boo, they shout 'boo' to show their disapproval.

boobook [ˈbuːbʊk] **boobooks** NOUN
a small brown Australian owl with a spotted back and wings

book [bʊk] **books, booking, booked** NOUN

1 a number of pages held together inside a cover

● THESAURUS
publication: *publications about job hunting*
textbook: *He wrote a textbook on law.*
title: *We publish a range of titles.*
tome: *a heavy tome*
volume: *small volumes of poetry*
work: *my favourite work by this author*

> VERB
2 When you book something such as a room, you arrange to have it or use it at a particular time.

b

⬤ **THESAURUS**
charter: *A plane was chartered for them.*
engage: *We engaged the services of a plumber.*
organize: *I have organized our flights.*
reserve: *Hotel rooms have been reserved.*
schedule: *A meeting is scheduled for Monday.*

bookcase ['bʊkˌkeɪs] **bookcases** NOUN
a piece of furniture with shelves for books

bookie ['bʊkɪ] **bookies** NOUN; INFORMAL
a bookmaker

booking ['bʊkɪŋ] **bookings** NOUN
an arrangement to book something such as a
hotel room

book-keeping ['bʊkˌkiːpɪŋ] NOUN
Book-keeping is the keeping of a record of the
money spent and received by a business.

booklet ['bʊklɪt] **booklets** NOUN
a small book with a paper cover

bookmaker ['bʊkˌmeɪkə] **bookmakers**
NOUN
a person who makes a living by taking people's
bets and paying them when they win

bookmark ['bʊkˌmɑːk] **bookmarks** NOUN
a piece of card which you put between the pages
of a book to mark your place

boom [buːm] **booms, booming, boomed**
NOUN
1 a rapid increase in something *e.g. the baby boom*
2 a loud deep echoing sound
> VERB
3 When something booms, it increases rapidly.
e.g. Sales are booming.
4 To boom means to make a loud deep echoing
sound.

boomerang ['buːməˌræŋ] **boomerangs**
NOUN
a curved wooden missile that can be thrown so
that it returns to the thrower, originally used as a
weapon by Australian Aborigines

boon [buːn] **boons** NOUN
Something that is a boon makes life better or
easier. *e.g. Credit cards have been a boon to
shoppers.*

boost [buːst] **boosts, boosting, boosted**
VERB
1 To boost something means to cause it to
improve or increase. *e.g. The campaign had boosted
sales.*
> NOUN
2 an improvement or increase *e.g. a boost to the
economy*
booster NOUN

boot [buːt] **boots, booting, booted** NOUN

1 Boots are strong shoes that come up over your
ankle and sometimes your calf.
2 the covered space in a car, usually at the back,
for carrying things in
> VERB
3 INFORMAL
If you boot something, you kick it.
> PHRASE
4 To boot means also or in addition *e.g. The story
was compelling and well written to boot.*

booth [buːð] **booths** NOUN
1 a small partly enclosed area *e.g. a telephone
booth*
2 a stall where you can buy goods

booty ['buːtɪ] NOUN
Booty is valuable things taken from a place,
especially by soldiers after a battle.

booze [buːz] **boozes, boozing, boozed**
INFORMAL NOUN
1 Booze is alcoholic drink.
> VERB
2 When people booze, they drink alcohol.
boozer NOUN, **boozy** ADJECTIVE
[WORD HISTORY: from Old Dutch BUSEN meaning
'to drink to excess']

border ['bɔːdə] **borders, bordering,
bordered** NOUN
1 the dividing line between two places or things
⬤ **THESAURUS**
borderline: *the borderline between health and
sickness*
boundary: *national boundaries*
frontier: *the American frontier*
line: *the line between fact and fiction*
2 a strip or band round the edge of something
e.g. plain tiles with a bright border
⬤ **THESAURUS**
bounds: *the bounds of good taste*
edge: *the edge of town*
limits: *the city limits*
margin: *the western margins of the island*
rim: *the rim of the lake*
3 a long flower bed in a garden
> VERB
4 To border something means to form a
boundary along the side of it. *e.g. Tall poplar trees
bordered the fields.*
⬤ **THESAURUS**
edge: *the woods that edge the lake*
fringe: *Street lights fringe the bay.*
hem: *dresses hemmed with feathers*
rim: *the restaurants rimming the harbour*
trim: *coats trimmed with fur collars*

borderline ['bɔːdəˌlaɪn] ADJECTIVE
only just acceptable as a member of a class or

group *e.g. a borderline case*

bore [bɔː] **bores, boring, bored** VERB

1 If something bores you, you find it dull and not at all interesting.

2 If you bore a hole in something, you make it using a tool such as a drill.

> NOUN

3 someone or something that bores you

bored [bɔːd] ADJECTIVE

If you are bored, you are impatient because you do not find something interesting or because you have nothing to do.

● THESAURUS

fed up: *He is fed up with this country.*
tired: *I am tired of this music.*
uninterested: *He seems uninterested in politics.*
wearied: *He spoke in a wearied voice.*
<<OPPOSITE *interested*

> You can say that you are *bored with* or *bored by* someone or something, but you should not say *bored of*.

boredom ['bɔːdəm] NOUN
a lack of interest

● THESAURUS

apathy: *political apathy*
dullness: *a period of dullness*
flatness: *a feeling of flatness*
monotony: *the monotony of winter*
tedium: *the tedium of unemployment*
weariness: *a sense of weariness*
<<OPPOSITE *interest*

boring ['bɔːrɪŋ] ADJECTIVE
dull and lacking interest

● THESAURUS

dull: *dull tasks*
flat: *a flat performance*
humdrum: *humdrum lives*
monotonous: *the monotonous prison routine*
tedious: *The work is tedious.*
tiresome: *a tiresome old man*
<<OPPOSITE *interesting*

born [bɔːn] VERB

1 When a baby is born, it comes out of its mother's womb at the beginning of its life.

> ADJECTIVE

2 You use 'born' to mean that someone has a particular quality from birth. *e.g. He was a born pessimist.*

borne [bɔːn] the past participle of **bear**

borough ['bʌrə] **boroughs** NOUN
a town, or a district within a large town, that has its own council

borrow ['bɒrəʊ] **borrows, borrowing, borrowed** VERB

If you borrow something that belongs to someone else, they let you have it for a period of time.

borrower NOUN

> You *borrow* something *from* a person, not *off* them. Do not confuse *borrow* and *lend*. If you *borrow* something, you get it from another person for a while; if you *lend* something, someone gets it from you for a while.

Bosnian ['bɒznɪən] **Bosnians** ADJECTIVE

1 belonging to or relating to Bosnia

> NOUN

2 someone who comes from Bosnia

bosom ['bʊzəm] **bosoms** NOUN

1 A woman's bosom is her breasts.

> ADJECTIVE

2 A bosom friend is a very close friend.

boss [bɒs] **bosses, bossing, bossed** NOUN

1 Someone's boss is the person in charge of the place where they work.

● THESAURUS

chief: *the police chief*
director: *the directors of the bank*
employer: *He was sent to Rome by his employer.*
head: *Heads of government met in New York.*
leader: *The party's leader has resigned.*
manager: *the company's marketing manager*

> VERB

2 If someone bosses you around, they keep telling you what to do.

bossy ['bɒsɪ] **bossier, bossiest** ADJECTIVE
A bossy person enjoys telling other people what to do.

bossiness NOUN

● THESAURUS

arrogant: *arrogant behaviour*
authoritarian: *He has an authoritarian approach to parenthood.*
dictatorial: *a dictatorial management style*
domineering: *She is domineering and ruthless.*
imperious: *He has an imperious manner.*
overbearing: *an overbearing mother*

botany ['bɒtənɪ] NOUN
Botany is the scientific study of plants.

botanic or **botanical** ADJECTIVE, **botanist** NOUN

botch [bɒtʃ] **botches, botching, botched** VERB INFORMAL
If you botch something, you do it badly or clumsily.

● THESAURUS

bungle: *inefficient people who bungled the job*
mar: *She marred her exit by twisting her ankle.*
mess up: *He manages to mess up his life.*

both [bəʊθ] ADJECTIVE OR PRONOUN
'Both' is used when saying something about two things or people.

You can use *of* after *both*, but it is not essential. *Both the boys* means the same as *both of the boys*.

bother ['bɒðə] bothers, bothering, bothered VERB

1 If you do not bother to do something, you do not do it because it takes too much effort or it seems unnecessary.

2 If something bothers you, you are worried or concerned about it. If you do not bother about it, you are not concerned about it. *e.g. She is not bothered about money.*

● THESAURUS

annoy: *the things that annoy me*
concern: *The future concerns me.*
disturb: *It disturbs me to see you unhappy.*
get on someone's nerves: informal *This place gets on my nerves.*
trouble: *Are you troubled by nightmares?*
worry: *I'm worried by the amount he is drinking.*

3 If you bother someone, you interrupt them when they are busy.

> NOUN

4 Bother is trouble, fuss, or difficulty.
bothersome ADJECTIVE

● THESAURUS

annoyance: *Snoring can be an annoyance.*
difficulty: *The strikes are causing difficulties for commuters.*
inconvenience: *a minor inconvenience*
irritation: *Noise is an irritation.*
trouble: *You've caused me a lot of trouble.*
worry: *It was a time of worry for us.*

bottle ['bɒtəl] bottles, bottling, bottled NOUN

1 a glass or plastic container for keeping liquids in

> VERB

2 To bottle something means to store it in bottles.

bottleneck ['bɒtəl,nɛk] bottlenecks NOUN

a narrow section of road where traffic has to slow down or stop

bottle store bottle stores NOUN

In Australian, New Zealand, and South African English, a bottle store is a shop that sells sealed alcoholic drinks which can be drunk elsewhere.

bottom ['bɒtəm] bottoms NOUN

1 The bottom of something is its lowest part.

● THESAURUS

base: *the base of the spine*
bed: *the river bed*
depths: *the depths of the earth*
floor: *the ocean floor*
foot: *the foot of the bed*

<<OPPOSITE *top*

2 Your bottom is your buttocks.

● THESAURUS

backside: informal *the muscles in your backside*
behind: informal *He kicked me on the behind.*
buttocks: *exercises for your buttocks*
posterior: humorous *He fell on his posterior.*
rear: *I was thrown out on my rear.*

> ADJECTIVE

3 The bottom thing in a series of things is the lowest one.
bottomless ADJECTIVE

● THESAURUS

base: *the base edge of the curtain*
basement: *a basement flat*
ground: *ground level*
lowest: *the lowest part of the brain*
<<OPPOSITE *highest*

bough [baʊ] boughs NOUN

a large branch of a tree

bought [bɔːt] the past tense and past participle of buy

Do not confuse *bought* and *brought*. *Bought* comes from *buy* and *brought* comes from *bring*.

boulder ['bəʊldə] boulders NOUN

a large rounded rock

boulevard ['buːlvɑː] boulevards NOUN

a wide street in a city, usually with trees along each side

bounce [baʊns] bounces, bouncing, bounced VERB

1 When an object bounces, it springs back from something after hitting it.

● THESAURUS

bump: *My bicycle bumped along the rough ground.*
ricochet: *The bullets ricocheted off the jeep.*

2 To bounce also means to move up and down. *e.g. Her long black hair bounced as she walked.*

● THESAURUS

bob: *The raft bobbed along.*
bound: *He bounded up the stairway.*
jump: *They jumped up and down to keep warm.*

3 If a cheque bounces, the bank refuses to accept it because there is not enough money in the account.

bouncy ['baʊnsɪ] bouncier, bounciest ADJECTIVE

1 Someone who is bouncy is lively and enthusiastic.

2 Something that is bouncy is capable of bouncing or being bounced on. *e.g. a bouncy ball... a bouncy castle*

bound [baʊnd] bounds, bounding, bounded ADJECTIVE

1 If you say that something is **bound** to happen, you mean that it is certain to happen.

2 If a person or a vehicle is **bound** for a place, they are going there.

3 If someone is **bound** by an agreement or regulation, they must obey it.

> NOUN

4 a large leap

> PLURAL NOUN

5 Bounds are limits which restrict or control something. *e.g. Their enthusiasm knew no bounds.*

> PHRASE

6 If a place is **out of bounds**, you are forbidden to go there.

> VERB

7 When animals or people **bound**, they move quickly with large leaps. *e.g. He bounded up the stairway.*

8 Bound is also the past tense and past participle of **bind**.

boundary ['baʊndərɪ] **boundaries** NOUN
something that indicates the farthest limit of anything *e.g. the city boundary... the boundaries of taste*

boundless ['baʊndlɪs] ADJECTIVE
without end or limit *e.g. her boundless energy*

bountiful ['baʊntɪfʊl] ADJECTIVE; LITERARY
freely available in large amounts *e.g. a bountiful harvest*

bounty ['baʊntɪ] NOUN

1 LITERARY
Bounty is a generous supply. *e.g. autumn's bounty of fruits*

2 Someone's bounty is their generosity in giving a lot of something.

bouquet [bəʊ'keɪ] **bouquets** NOUN
an attractively arranged bunch of flowers

bourgeois ['bʊəʒwɑ:] ADJECTIVE
typical of fairly rich middle-class people

bourgeoisie [ˌbʊəʒwɑ:'zi:] NOUN
the fairly rich middle-class people in a society

bout [baʊt] **bouts** NOUN

1 If you have a bout of something such as an illness, you have it for a short time. *e.g. a bout of flu*

2 If you have a bout of doing something, you do it enthusiastically for a short time.

3 a boxing or wrestling match

boutique [bu:'ti:k] **boutiques** NOUN
a small shop that sells fashionable clothes

bovine ['bəʊvaɪn] ADJECTIVE; TECHNICAL
relating to cattle

bow [baʊ] **bows, bowing, bowed** VERB

1 When you bow, you bend your body or lower your head as a sign of respect or greeting.

2 If you bow to something, you give in to it. *e.g. He bowed to public pressure.*

> NOUN

3 the movement you make when you bow

4 the front part of a ship

bow [bəʊ] **bows** NOUN

1 a knot with two loops and two loose ends

2 a long thin piece of wood with horsehair stretched along it, which you use to play a violin

3 a long flexible piece of wood used for shooting arrows

bowel ['baʊəl] **bowels** NOUN
Your bowels are the tubes leading from your stomach, through which waste passes before it leaves your body.
[WORD HISTORY: from Latin BOTELLUS meaning 'little sausage']

bowerbird ['baʊə,bɜ:d] **bowerbirds** NOUN
a bird found in Australia, the male of which builds a shelter during courtship

bowl [bəʊl] **bowls, bowling, bowled** NOUN

1 a round container with a wide uncovered top, used for holding liquid or for serving food

2 the hollow, rounded part of something *e.g. a toilet bowl*

3 a large heavy ball used in the game of bowls or tenpin bowling

> VERB

4 In cricket, to bowl means to throw the ball towards the batsman.
bowler NOUN

bowling ['bəʊlɪŋ] NOUN
Bowling is a game in which you roll a heavy ball down a narrow track towards a group of wooden objects called pins and try to knock them down.

bowls [bəʊlz] NOUN
Bowls is a game in which the players try to roll large wooden balls as near as possible to a small ball.

bow tie [bəʊ] **bow ties** NOUN
a man's tie in the form of a bow, often worn at formal occasions

box [bɒks] **boxes, boxing, boxed** NOUN

1 a container with a firm base and sides and usually a lid

◉ THESAURUS
carton: *cartons full of books*
case: *It is still in its original case.*
chest: *She kept her heirlooms in a carved wooden chest.*

container: *substances kept in heavy metal containers*

trunk: *a trunk full of toys*

2 On a form, a box is a rectangular space which you have to fill in.

3 In a theatre, a box is a small separate area where a few people can watch the performance together.

> VERB

4 To box means to fight someone according to the rules of boxing.

boxer ['bɒksə] **boxers** NOUN

1 a person who boxes

2 a type of medium-sized, smooth-haired dog with a flat face

boxing ['bɒksɪŋ] NOUN
Boxing is a sport in which two people fight using their fists, wearing padded gloves.

box office **box offices** NOUN
the place where tickets are sold in a theatre or cinema

boy [bɔɪ] **boys** NOUN
a male child
boyhood NOUN, **boyish** ADJECTIVE

● THESAURUS
fellow: *a fine little fellow*
lad: *I remember being a lad his age.*
schoolboy: *a group of schoolboys*
youngster: *I was only a youngster in 1970.*
youth: *gangs of youths who cause trouble*

boycott ['bɔɪkɒt] **boycotts, boycotting, boycotted** VERB

1 If you boycott an organization or event, you refuse to have anything to do with it.

● THESAURUS
blacklist: *He has been blacklisted by various societies.*
embargo: *Imports of fruit were embargoed.*
exclude: *I exclude animal products from my diet.*
reject: *She rejected her parents' religion.*
spurn: *You spurned his last offer.*

> NOUN

2 the boycotting of an organization or event *e.g. a boycott of the elections*

[WORD HISTORY: from the name of Captain C.C. Boycott (1832–1897), an Irish land agent, who offended the tenants, so that they refused to pay their rents]

boyfriend ['bɔɪˌfrɛnd] **boyfriends** NOUN
Someone's boyfriend is the man or boy with whom they are having a romantic relationship.

bra [brɑː] **bras** NOUN
a piece of underwear worn by a woman to support her breasts

braaivleis or **braai** ['braɪˌfleɪs] *or* [braɪ] **braaivleises** or **braais** NOUN
In South African English, a braaivleis is a picnic where meat is cooked on an open fire.

brace [breɪs] **braces, bracing, braced** VERB

1 When you brace yourself, you stiffen your body to steady yourself. *e.g. The ship lurched and he braced himself.*

2 If you brace yourself for something unpleasant, you prepare yourself to deal with it. *e.g. The police are braced for violent reprisals.*

> NOUN

3 an object fastened to something to straighten or support it *e.g. a neck brace*

> PLURAL NOUN

4 Braces are a pair of straps worn over the shoulders and fastened to the trousers to hold them up.

bracelet ['breɪslɪt] **bracelets** NOUN
a chain or band worn around someone's wrist as an ornament

bracing ['breɪsɪŋ] ADJECTIVE
Something that is bracing makes you feel fit and full of energy. *e.g. the bracing sea air*

bracken ['brækən] NOUN
Bracken is a plant like a large fern that grows on hills and in woods.

bracket ['brækɪt] **brackets** NOUN

1 Brackets are a pair of written marks, ( ), [ ], placed round a word or sentence that is not part of the main text, or to show that the items inside the brackets belong together.

2 a range between two limits, for example of ages or prices *e.g. the four-figure price bracket*

3 a piece of metal or wood fastened to a wall to support something such as a shelf

brag [bræg] **brags, bragging, bragged** VERB
When someone brags, they boast about their achievements. *e.g. Both leaders bragged they could win by a landslide.*

● THESAURUS
boast: *She kept boasting about how many guys she'd been out with.*
crow: *Stop crowing about your victory.*
skite: Australian and New Zealand; informal *That's nothing to skite about.*

braggart ['brægət] **braggarts** NOUN
someone who brags

● THESAURUS
bigmouth: slang *He's nothing but a bigmouth.*
boaster: *an idle boaster looking for the main chance*
bragger: *He was quite a bragger.*
show-off: *I've always been a show-off.*

b

skite *or* **skiter:** Australian and New Zealand; informal *a bit of a skite*

Brahma ['brɑːmə] PROPER NOUN
Brahma is a Hindu god and is one of the Trimurti.
[WORD HISTORY: from a Sanskrit word meaning 'praise']

Brahman ['brɑːmən] NOUN
In the Hindu religion Brahman is the ultimate and impersonal divine reality of the universe.

brahmin ['brɑːmɪn] **brahmins** NOUN
a member of the highest or priestly caste in Hindu society

braid [breɪd] **braids, braiding, braided**
NOUN
1 Braid is a strip of decorated cloth used to decorate clothes or curtains.
2 a length of hair which has been plaited and tied
> VERB
3 To braid hair or thread means to plait it.

Braille [breɪl] NOUN
Braille is a system of printing for blind people in which letters are represented by raised dots that can be felt with the fingers.

brain [breɪn] **brains** NOUN
1 Your brain is the mass of nerve tissue inside your head that controls your body and enables you to think and feel; also used to refer to your mind and the way that you think. *e.g. I admired his legal brain.*
> PLURAL NOUN
2 If you say that someone has brains, you mean that they are very intelligent.

brainchild ['breɪn.tʃaɪld] NOUN; INFORMAL
Someone's brainchild is something that they have invented or created.

brainwash ['breɪn.wɒʃ] **brainwashes, brainwashing, brainwashed** VERB
If people are brainwashed into believing something, they accept it without question because they are told it repeatedly.
brainwashing NOUN

brainwave ['breɪn.weɪv] **brainwaves**
NOUN; INFORMAL
a clever idea you think of suddenly

brainy ['breɪnɪ] **brainier, brainiest**
ADJECTIVE; INFORMAL
clever

braise [breɪz] **braises, braising, braised**
VERB
To braise food means to fry it for a short time, then cook it slowly in a little liquid.

brake [breɪk] **brakes, braking, braked**
NOUN
1 a device for making a vehicle stop or slow down
> VERB
2 When a driver brakes, he or she makes a vehicle stop or slow down by using its brakes.

> Do not confuse the spellings of *brake* and *break*, or *braking* and *breaking*.

bramble ['bræmbᵊl] **brambles** NOUN
a wild, thorny bush that produces blackberries

bran [bræn] NOUN
Bran is the ground husks that are left over after flour has been made from wheat grains.

branch [brɑːntʃ] **branches, branching, branched** NOUN
1 The branches of a tree are the parts that grow out from its trunk.
2 A branch of an organization is one of a number of its offices or shops.
3 A branch of a subject is one of its areas of study or activity. *e.g. specialists in certain branches of medicine*
> VERB
4 A road that branches off from another road splits off from it to lead in a different direction.

brand [brænd] **brands, branding, branded**
NOUN
1 A brand of something is a particular kind or make of it. *e.g. a popular brand of chocolate*
> VERB
2 When an animal is branded, a mark is burned on its skin to show who owns it.

brandish ['brændɪʃ] **brandishes, brandishing, brandished** VERB; LITERARY
If you brandish something, you wave it vigorously. *e.g. He brandished his sword over his head.*

brand-new ['brænd'njuː] ADJECTIVE
completely new

brandy ['brændɪ] NOUN
a strong alcoholic drink, usually made from wine
[WORD HISTORY: from Dutch BRANDEWIJN meaning 'burnt wine']

brash [bræʃ] **brasher, brashest** ADJECTIVE
If someone is brash, they are overconfident or rather rude.

brass [brɑːs] NOUN OR ADJECTIVE
1 Brass is a yellow-coloured metal made from copper and zinc.
2 In an orchestra, the brass section consists of brass wind instruments such as trumpets and trombones.

brassière ['bræsɪə] *or* ['bræzɪə] **brassières**
NOUN; FORMAL

a bra

brat [bræt] **brats** NOUN; INFORMAL
A badly behaved child may be referred to as a brat.

bravado [brə'vɑ:dəʊ] NOUN
Bravado is a display of courage intended to impress other people.

brave [breɪv] **braver, bravest; braves, braving, braved** ADJECTIVE
1 A brave person is willing to do dangerous things and does not show any fear.

● THESAURUS
bold: *Amrita became a bold rebel.*
courageous: *a courageous decision*
fearless: *his fearless campaigning for justice*
heroic: *The heroic sergeant risked his life.*
plucky: *The plucky schoolgirl amazed the doctors.*
valiant: *a valiant attempt to keep going*
<<OPPOSITE *cowardly*

> VERB
2 If you brave an unpleasant or dangerous situation, you face up to it in order to do something. *e.g. His fans braved the rain to hear him sing.*
bravely ADVERB

● THESAURUS
face: *I can't face another three years of this.*
stand up to: *I have tried to stand up to the bullies.*

bravery ['breɪvərɪ] NOUN
the quality of being courageous

● THESAURUS
boldness: *an outward display of boldness*
courage: *They do not have the courage to apologize.*
fortitude: *He suffered with tremendous fortitude.*
heroism: *acts of heroism*
pluck: *He has pluck and presence of mind.*
valour: *He won a medal for valour.*
<<OPPOSITE *cowardice*

bravo [brɑ:'vəʊ] INTERJECTION
People shout 'Bravo!' to express appreciation when something has been done well.

brawl [brɔ:l] **brawls, brawling, brawled** NOUN
1 a rough fight
> VERB
2 When people brawl, they take part in a rough fight.

brawn [brɔ:n] NOUN
Brawn is physical strength.
brawny ADJECTIVE

bray [breɪ] **brays, braying, brayed** VERB
1 When a donkey brays, it makes a loud, harsh sound.
> NOUN
2 the sound a donkey makes

brazen ['breɪzᵊn] ADJECTIVE
When someone's behaviour is brazen, they do not care if other people think they are behaving wrongly.
brazenly ADVERB

brazier ['breɪzɪə] **braziers** NOUN
a metal container in which coal or charcoal is burned to keep people warm out of doors

Brazilian [brə'zɪljən] **Brazilians** ADJECTIVE
1 belonging or relating to Brazil
> NOUN
2 someone who comes from Brazil

breach [bri:tʃ] **breaches, breaching, breached** VERB
1 FORMAL
If you breach an agreement or law, you break it.
2 To breach a barrier means to make a gap in it. *e.g. The river breached its banks.*
> NOUN
3 A breach of an agreement or law is an action that breaks it. *e.g. a breach of contract*

● THESAURUS
infringement: *an infringement of the rules*
offence: *criminal offences*
trespass: *a campaign of trespasses and demonstrations*
violation: *a violation of the peace agreement*

4 a gap or break

● THESAURUS
crack: *a large crack in the ice*
gap: *a narrow gap in the curtains*
hole: *We cut holes in the fabric.*
opening: *an opening in the fence*
rift: *The earthquake caused a deep rift.*
split: *There's a split in my mattress.*

bread [brɛd] NOUN
a food made from flour and water, usually raised with yeast, and baked

breadth [brɛdθ] NOUN
The breadth of something is the distance between its two ends.

breadwinner ['brɛd,wɪnə] **breadwinners** NOUN
the person who earns the money in a family

break [breɪk] **breaks, breaking, broke, broken** VERB
1 When an object breaks, it is damaged and separates into pieces.

● THESAURUS
crack: *To get at the coconut flesh, crack the shell with a hammer.*
crumble: *Crumble the cheese into a bowl.*
disintegrate: *The car's windscreen disintegrated with the impact of the crash.*

b

demolish: *The hurricane demolished houses across the area.*
fracture: *You've fractured a rib.*
fragment: *The rock began to fragment and crumble.*
shatter: *safety glass that won't shatter if it's hit*
smash: *Two glasses fell off the table and smashed into pieces.*
snap: *She gripped the pipe in both hands, trying to snap it in half.*
split: *In the severe gale, the ship split in two.*
splinter: *The ruler splintered into pieces.*
wreck: *The bridge was wrecked by the storms.*

2 If you break a rule or promise you fail to keep it.

● THESAURUS

breach: *breaches of discipline*
contravene: *His behaviour contravenes our code of conduct.*
infringe: *The judge ruled that he had infringed no rules.*
violate: *They violated the peace agreement.*

3 When a boy's voice breaks, it becomes permanently deeper.
4 When a wave breaks, it falls and becomes foam.

> NOUN
5 a short period during which you rest or do something different **break down**

● THESAURUS

interlude: *a happy interlude in my life*
interval: *a long interval when no-one spoke*
pause: *After a pause Alex spoke.*
recess: *The court adjourned for a recess.*
respite: *They have had no respite from bombing.*
rest: *I'll start again after a rest.*

> VERB
6 When a machine or a vehicle breaks down, it stops working.
7 When a discussion or relationship breaks down, it ends because of problems or disagreements.

break up VERB
8 If something breaks up, it ends. *e.g. The marriage broke up after a year.* **breakable** ADJECTIVE

breakage ['breɪkɪdʒ] **breakages** NOUN
the act of breaking something or a thing that has been broken

breakaway ['breɪkəˌweɪ] ADJECTIVE
A breakaway group is one that has separated from a larger group.

breakdown ['breɪkˌdaʊn] **breakdowns** NOUN
1 The breakdown of something such as a system is its failure. *e.g. a breakdown in communications*
2 the same as a nervous breakdown

3 If a driver has a breakdown, their car stops working.

breaker ['breɪkə] **breakers** NOUN
Breakers are big sea waves.

breakfast ['brɛkfəst] **breakfasts** NOUN
the first meal of the day

break-in ['breɪkˌɪn] **break-ins** NOUN
the illegal entering of a building, especially by a burglar

breakneck ['breɪkˌnɛk] ADJECTIVE; INFORMAL
Someone or something that is travelling at breakneck speed is travelling dangerously fast.

breakthrough ['breɪkˌθruː] **breakthroughs** NOUN
a sudden important development *e.g. a medical breakthrough*

breakwater ['breɪkˌwɔːtə] **breakwaters** NOUN
a wall extending into the sea which protects a coast from the force of the waves

bream [briːm] **breams** NOUN
an edible fish

breast [brɛst] **breasts** NOUN
A woman's breasts are the two soft, fleshy parts on her chest, which produce milk after she has had a baby.

breath [brɛθ] **breaths** NOUN
1 Your breath is the air you take into your lungs and let out again when you breathe.

> PHRASE
2 If you are **out of breath**, you are breathing with difficulty after doing something energetic.
3 If you say something **under your breath**, you say it in a very quiet voice.

breathe [briːð] **breathes, breathing, breathed** VERB
When you breathe, you take air into your lungs and let it out again.

breathless ['brɛθlɪs] ADJECTIVE
If you are breathless, you are breathing fast or with difficulty.
breathlessly ADVERB, **breathlessness** NOUN

breathtaking ['brɛθˌteɪkɪŋ] ADJECTIVE
If you say that something is breathtaking, you mean that it is very beautiful or exciting.

bred [brɛd] the past tense and past participle of **breed**

breeches ['brɪtʃɪz] PLURAL NOUN
Breeches are trousers reaching to just below the knee, nowadays worn especially for riding.

breed [briːd] **breeds, breeding, bred** NOUN
1 A breed of a species of domestic animal is a particular type of it.

b

brick [brɪk] **bricks** NOUN
Bricks are rectangular blocks of baked clay used in building.

bricklayer ['brɪk,leɪə] **bricklayers** NOUN
a person whose job is to build with bricks

bride [braɪd] **brides** NOUN
a woman who is getting married or who has just got married
bridal ADJECTIVE

bridegroom ['braɪd,gru:m] **bridegrooms** NOUN
a man who is getting married or who has just got married

bridesmaid ['braɪdz,meɪd] **bridesmaids** NOUN
a woman who helps and accompanies a bride on her wedding day

bridge [brɪdʒ] **bridges** NOUN
1 a structure built over a river, road, or railway so that vehicles and people can cross
2 the platform from which a ship is steered and controlled
3 the hard ridge at the top of your nose
4 Bridge is a card game for four players based on whist.

bridle ['braɪdəl] **bridles** NOUN
a set of straps round a horse's head and mouth, which the rider uses to control the horse

brief [bri:f] **briefer, briefest; briefs, briefing, briefed** ADJECTIVE
1 Something that is brief lasts only a short time.

THESAURUS
fleeting: *a fleeting glimpse*
momentary: *There was a momentary silence.*
quick: *a quick look at the newspaper*
short: *a short holiday*
swift: *a swift glance at John's face*
<<OPPOSITE long

> VERB
2 (D & T) When you brief someone on a task, you give them all the necessary instructions and information about it.
briefly ADVERB

THESAURUS
advise: *I must advise you of my decision to retire.*
fill in: informal *Can you fill me in on Wilbur's visit?*
inform: *They would inform him of their progress.*
instruct: *He instructed us in first aid.*
prepare: *I will prepare you for this exam.*
prime: *Arnold primed him for his duties.*

briefcase ['bri:f,keɪs] **briefcases** NOUN
a small flat case for carrying papers

THESAURUS
kind: *What kind of horse is that?*
species: *Pandas are an endangered species.*
stock: *cattle of Highland stock*
strain: *a special strain of rat*
type: *What type of dog should we get?*
variety: *many varieties of birds*

> VERB
2 Someone who breeds animals or plants keeps them in order to produce more animals or plants with particular qualities.

THESAURUS
cultivate: *She cultivates fruit and vegetables.*
develop: *A new variety of potato is being developed.*
keep: *He keeps guinea pigs.*
nurture: *trimming and nurturing plants and saplings*
raise: *He raises birds of prey as a hobby.*
rear: *the difficulties of rearing children*

3 When animals breed, they mate and produce offspring.

THESAURUS
multiply: *Rats multiply quickly.*
produce: *She produced a son.*
propagate: *This plant is difficult to propagate.*
reproduce: *the natural desire to reproduce*

breeze [bri:z] **breezes** NOUN
a gentle wind

brevity ['brevɪtɪ] NOUN; FORMAL
Brevity means shortness. *e.g. the brevity of his report*

brew [bru:] **brews, brewing, brewed** VERB
1 If you brew tea or coffee, you make it in a pot by pouring hot water over it.
2 To brew beer means to make it, by boiling and fermenting malt.
3 If an unpleasant situation is brewing, it is about to happen. *e.g. Another scandal is brewing.*
brewer NOUN

brewery ['bruərɪ] **breweries** NOUN
a place where beer is made, or a company that makes it

briar ['braɪə] **briars** NOUN
a wild rose that grows on a dense prickly bush

bribe [braɪb] **bribes, bribing, bribed** NOUN
1 a gift or money given to an official to persuade them to make a favourable decision

> VERB
2 To bribe someone means to give them a bribe.
bribery NOUN

bric-a-brac ['brɪkə,bræk] NOUN
Bric-a-brac consists of small ornaments or pieces of furniture of no great value.
[WORD HISTORY: from an obsolete French phrase À

briefing ['briːfɪŋ] **briefings** NOUN
a meeting at which information and instructions are given

brier ['braɪə] another spelling of **briar**

brigade [brɪ'geɪd] **brigades** NOUN
an army unit consisting of three battalions [WORD HISTORY: from Italian BRIGARE meaning 'to fight']

brigadier [ˌbrɪgə'dɪə] **brigadiers** NOUN
an army officer of the rank immediately above colonel

brigalow ['brɪgələʊ] **brigalows** NOUN
a type of Australian acacia tree that grows in the bush

bright [braɪt] **brighter, brightest** ADJECTIVE
1 strong and startling *e.g. a bright light*
● THESAURUS
brilliant: *brilliant green eyes*
dazzling: *a dazzling white shirt*
glowing: *the glowing windows of the Cathedral*
luminous: *a luminous star*
radiant: *eyes as radiant as sapphires*
vivid: *strong, vivid colours*
<<OPPOSITE *dull*

2 clever *e.g. my brightest student*
● THESAURUS
brainy: *I don't consider myself brainy.*
brilliant: *She has a brilliant mind.*
clever: *a clever child*
ingenious: *an ingenious idea*
intelligent: *Dolphins are an intelligent species.*
smart: *He thinks he's as smart as Sarah.*
<<OPPOSITE *dim*

3 cheerful *e.g. a bright smile*
brightly ADVERB, **brightness** NOUN
● THESAURUS
cheerful: *Jack sounded quite cheerful about the idea.*
happy: *a confident, happy child*
jolly: *a jolly nature*
light-hearted: *They are light-hearted and enjoy life.*
lively: *He has a lively personality.*
merry: *bursts of merry laughter*

brighten ['braɪtᵊn] **brightens, brightening, brightened** VERB
1 If something brightens, it becomes brighter. *e.g. The weather had brightened.*
2 If someone brightens, they suddenly look happier. **brighten up** VERB
3 To brighten something up means to make it more attractive and cheerful.

brilliant ['brɪljənt] ADJECTIVE
1 A brilliant light or colour is extremely bright.
● THESAURUS
bright: *a bright star*

dazzling: *a dazzling white shirt*
gleaming: *gleaming headlights*
glowing: *glowing colours*
luminous: *luminous orange paint*
radiant: *a figure surrounded by a radiant glow*
sparkling: *a choker of sparkling jewels*
vivid: *the vivid hues of tropical flowers*
<<OPPOSITE *dull*

2 A brilliant person is extremely clever.
● THESAURUS
acute: *His relaxed exterior hides an acute mind.*
brainy: informal *You don't have to be too brainy to work that one out.*
bright: *an exceptionally bright child*
clever: *What a clever idea!*
intelligent: *a lively and extremely intelligent woman*
perceptive: *a perceptive analysis of the situation*
sharp: *a sharp intellect*
smart: *He's the smartest student we've ever had.*
<<OPPOSITE *stupid*

3 A brilliant career is extremely successful.
brilliantly ADVERB, **brilliance** NOUN
● THESAURUS
first-class: *a first-class violinist*
great: *one of the greatest novels of the century*
magnificent: *a magnificent display*
marvellous: *I've had a marvellous time.*
outstanding: *He's an outstanding actor.*
superb: *a superb artist*
tremendous: *a tremendous performance*
wonderful: *the most wonderful music I've ever heard*
<<OPPOSITE *terrible*

brim [brɪm] **brims** NOUN
1 the wide part of a hat that sticks outwards at the bottom
> PHRASE
2 If a container is filled **to the brim**, it is filled right to the top.

brine [braɪn] NOUN
Brine is salt water.

bring [brɪŋ] **brings, bringing, brought** VERB
1 If you bring something or someone with you when you go to a place, you take them with you. *e.g. You can bring a friend to the party.*
● THESAURUS
bear: *They bore the box into the kitchen.*
carry: *She carried her son to the car.*
convey: *Emergency supplies were conveyed by truck.*
lead: *She led him into the house.*
take: *He took cakes to the party.*
transport: *The troops were transported to Moscow.*

2 To bring something to a particular state means to cause it to be like that. *e.g. Bring the vegetables to the boil.*

b

THESAURUS
cause: *My mistake caused me some worry.*
create: *The new factory will create more jobs.*
inflict: *The attack inflicted heavy casualties.*
produce: *The drug produces side effects.*
result in: *Many accidents result in serious injuries.*
wreak: *Violent storms wreaked havoc.*

bring about VERB

3 To bring something about means to cause it to happen. *e.g. We must try to bring about a better world.*

THESAURUS
cause: *This may cause delays.*
create: *The new scheme will create even more confusion.*
generate: *the excitement generated by this film*
make happen: *If you want change, you have to make it happen yourself.*
produce: *His comments produced a furious response.*
provoke: *a move that has provoked a storm of protest*

bring up VERB

4 To bring up children means to look after them while they grow up.

5 If you bring up a subject, you introduce it into the conversation. *e.g. She brought up the subject at dinner.*

brinjal ['brɪndʒəl] **brinjals** NOUN
In Indian and South African English, an aubergine.

brink [brɪŋk] NOUN
If you are on the brink of something, you are just about to do it or experience it.

brisk [brɪsk] **brisker, briskest** ADJECTIVE
1 A brisk action is done quickly and energetically. *e.g. A brisk walk restores your energy.*
2 If someone's manner is brisk, it shows that they want to get things done quickly and efficiently.
briskly ADVERB, **briskness** NOUN

bristle ['brɪsəl] **bristles, bristling, bristled**
NOUN
1 Bristles are strong animal hairs used to make brushes.
> VERB
2 If the hairs on an animal's body bristle, they rise up, because it is frightened.
bristly ADJECTIVE

British ['brɪtɪʃ] ADJECTIVE
belonging or relating to the United Kingdom of Great Britain and Northern Ireland

Briton ['brɪtən] **Britons** NOUN
someone who comes from the United Kingdom

of Great Britain and Northern Ireland

brittle ['brɪtəl] ADJECTIVE
An object that is brittle is hard but breaks easily.

broach [brəʊtʃ] **broaches, broaching, broached** VERB
When you broach a subject, you introduce it into a discussion.

broad [brɔːd] **broader, broadest** ADJECTIVE
1 wide *e.g. a broad smile*

THESAURUS
expansive: *There also are several swing sets and an expansive grassy play area.*
extensive: *The palace grounds were more extensive than the town itself.*
large: *He was a large man with a thick square head.*
thick: *a finger as thick as a sausage*
vast: *rich families who own vast stretches of land*
wide: *a sunhat with a wide brim*
<<OPPOSITE *narrow*

2 having many different aspects or concerning many different people *e.g. A broad range of issues was discussed.*

THESAURUS
wide-ranging: *The aims of our campaign are wide-ranging but simple.*
comprehensive: *This book is a comprehensive guide to the region.*
extensive: *extensive research into public attitudes to science*
general: *The project should raise general awareness about bullying.*
sweeping: *sweeping economic reforms*
universal: *the universal problem of pollution*
wide: *a major event which brought together a wide range of interest groups*

3 general rather than detailed *e.g. the broad concerns of the movement*

THESAURUS
approximate: *They did not have even an approximate idea of what the word meant.*
general: *The figures represent a general decline in employment.*
rough: *I've got a rough idea of what he looks like.*
vague: *They have only a vague idea of the amount of water available.*
non-specific: *I intend to use these terms in a deliberately non-specific way.*
sweeping: *a sweeping statement about women drivers*

4 If someone has a broad accent, the way that they speak makes it very clear where they come from. *e.g. She spoke in a broad Irish accent.*

broadband ['brɔːd,bænd] NOUN
Broadband is a digital system used on the Internet and in other forms of

telecommunication which can process and transfer information input from various sources, such as from telephones, computers or televisions.

broad bean broad beans NOUN
Broad beans are light-green beans with thick flat edible seeds.

broadcast ['brɔːd‚kɑːst] **broadcasts, broadcasting, broadcast** NOUN
1 a programme or announcement on radio or television
> VERB
2 To broadcast something means to send it out by radio waves, so that it can be seen on television or heard on radio.
broadcaster NOUN, **broadcasting** NOUN

broaden ['brɔːdᵊn] **broadens, broadening, broadened** VERB
1 When something broadens, it becomes wider. *e.g. His smile broadened.*
2 To broaden something means to cause it to involve more things or concern more people. *e.g. We must broaden the scope of this job.*

broadly ['brɔːdli] ADVERB
true to a large extent or in most cases *e.g. There are broadly two schools of thought on this.*

broad-minded [‚brɔːd'maɪndɪd] ADJECTIVE
Someone who is broad-minded does not disapprove of behaviour or attitudes that many other people disapprove of.

broadsheet ['brɔːd‚ʃiːt] **broadsheets** NOUN
a newspaper with large pages and long news stories

brocade [brəʊ'keɪd] NOUN
Brocade is a heavy, expensive material, often made of silk, with a raised pattern.
[WORD HISTORY: from Spanish BROCADO meaning 'embossed fabric']

broccoli ['brɒkəli] NOUN
Broccoli is a green vegetable, similar to cauliflower.

brochure ['brəʊʃjʊə] **brochures** NOUN
a booklet which gives information about a product or service

brogue [brəʊg] **brogues** NOUN
1 a strong accent, especially an Irish one
2 Brogues are thick leather shoes.
[WORD HISTORY: from Irish Gaelic BRÓG meaning 'boot' or 'shoe']

broke [brəʊk] the past tense of **break** ADJECTIVE

broken ['brəʊkən]
1 in pieces
● THESAURUS
burst: *a burst pipe*

demolished: *a demolished house*
fractured: *He suffered a fractured skull.*
fragmented: *fragmented images*
shattered: *shattered glass*
smashed: *smashed windows*
2 not kept
● THESAURUS
infringed: *a case of infringed human rights*
violated: *a series of violated agreements*
3 INFORMAL
If you are broke, you have no money.

broker ['brəʊkə] **brokers** NOUN
a person whose job is to buy and sell shares for other people

brolga ['brɒlgə] **brolgas** NOUN
a large grey Australian crane with a red-and-green head

brolly ['brɒli] **brollies** NOUN; INFORMAL
an umbrella

bronchitis [brɒŋ'kaɪtɪs] NOUN
Bronchitis is an illness in which the two tubes which connect your windpipe to your lungs become infected, making you cough.

brontosaurus [‚brɒntə'sɔːrəs] **brontosauruses** NOUN
a type of very large, plant-eating dinosaur

bronze [brɒnz] NOUN
Bronze is a yellowish-brown metal which is a mixture of copper and tin; also the yellowish-brown colour of this metal.

brooch [brəʊtʃ] **brooches** NOUN
a piece of jewellery with a pin at the back for attaching to clothes

brood [bruːd] **broods, brooding, brooded** NOUN
1 a family of baby birds
> VERB
2 If you brood about something, you keep thinking about it in a serious or unhappy way.

brook [brʊk] **brooks** NOUN
a stream

broom [bruːm] **brooms** NOUN
1 a long-handled brush
2 Broom is a shrub with yellow flowers.

broth [brɒθ] NOUN
Broth is soup, usually with vegetables in it.

brothel ['brɒθəl] **brothels** NOUN
a house where men pay to have sex with prostitutes

brother ['brʌðə] **brothers** NOUN
Your brother is a boy or man who has the same parents as you.

brotherly ADJECTIVE

brotherhood ['brʌðəˌhʊd] **brotherhoods**
NOUN
1 Brotherhood is the affection and loyalty that
brothers or close male friends feel for each other.
2 a group of men with common interests or
beliefs

brother-in-law ['brʌðəɪnˌlɔː] **brothers-
in-law** NOUN
Someone's brother-in-law is the brother of their
husband or wife, or their sister's husband.

brought [brɔːt] the past tense and past participle
of **bring**

> Do not confuse *brought* and *bought*. *Brought*
> comes from *bring* and *bought* comes from
> *buy*.

brow [braʊ] **brows** NOUN
1 Your brow is your forehead.
2 Your brows are your eyebrows.
3 The brow of a hill is the top of it.

brown [braʊn] **browner, brownest**
ADJECTIVE OR NOUN
Brown is the colour of earth or wood.

brownie ['braʊnɪ] **brownies** NOUN
a junior member of the Guides

browse [braʊz] **browses, browsing,
browsed** VERB
1 If you browse through a book, you look through
it in a casual way.
2 If you browse in a shop, you look at the things
in it for interest rather than because you want to
buy something.

browser ['braʊzə] **browsers** NOUN
a piece of computer software that lets you look at
websites on the World Wide Web

bruise [bruːz] **bruises, bruising, bruised**
NOUN
1 a purple mark that appears on your skin after
something has hit it
> VERB
2 If something bruises you, it hits you so that a
bruise appears on your skin.

brumby ['brʌmbɪ] **brumbies** NOUN
In Australia and New Zealand, a wild horse.

brunette [bruːˈnɛt] **brunettes** NOUN
a girl or woman with dark brown hair

brunt [brʌnt] PHRASE
If you **bear the brunt** of something unpleasant,
you are the person who suffers most. *e.g. Women
bear the brunt of crime.*

brush [brʌʃ] **brushes, brushing, brushed**
NOUN

1 an object with bristles which you use for
cleaning things, painting, or tidying your hair
> VERB
2 If you brush something, you clean it or tidy it
with a brush.
3 To brush against something means to touch it
while passing it. *e.g. Her lips brushed his cheek.*

brusque [bruːsk] ADJECTIVE
Someone who is brusque deals with people
quickly and without considering their feelings.
brusquely ADVERB

brussels sprout [ˌbrʌsᵊlz ˈspraʊt] **brussels
sprouts** NOUN
Brussels sprouts are vegetables that look like tiny
cabbages.

brutal ['bruːtᵊl] ADJECTIVE
Brutal behaviour is cruel and violent. *e.g. the
victim of a brutal murder*
brutally ADVERB, **brutality** NOUN

brute [bruːt] **brutes** NOUN
1 a rough and insensitive man
> ADJECTIVE
2 Brute force is strength alone, without any skill.
e.g. You have to use brute force to open the gates.
brutish ADJECTIVE

bubble ['bʌbᵊl] **bubbles, bubbling,
bubbled** NOUN
1 a ball of air in a liquid
2 a hollow, delicate ball of soapy liquid
> VERB
3 When a liquid bubbles, bubbles form in it.
4 If you are bubbling with something like
excitement, you are full of it.
bubbly ADJECTIVE

buck [bʌk] **bucks, bucking, bucked** NOUN
1 the male of various animals, including the deer
and the rabbit
> VERB
2 If a horse bucks, it jumps into the air with its
feet off the ground.

bucket ['bʌkɪt] **buckets** NOUN
a deep round container with an open top and a
handle

buckle ['bʌkᵊl] **buckles, buckling, buckled**
NOUN
1 a fastening on the end of a belt or strap
> VERB
2 If you buckle a belt or strap, you fasten it.
3 If something buckles, it becomes bent because
of severe heat or pressure.

bud [bʌd] **buds, budding, budded** NOUN
1 a small, tight swelling on a tree or plant, which
develops into a flower or a cluster of leaves

> VERB

2 When a tree or plant buds, new buds appear on it.

Buddha ['bʊdə] PROPER NOUN
The Buddha is the title of Gautama Siddhartha, a religious teacher living in the 6th century BC in India and founder of Buddhism. Buddha means 'the enlightened one'.

Buddhism ['bʊdɪzəm] NOUN
(RE) Buddhism is a religion, founded by the Buddha, which teaches that the way to end suffering is by overcoming your desires.
Buddhist NOUN OR ADJECTIVE

budding ['bʌdɪŋ] ADJECTIVE
just beginning to develop e.g. a budding artist

budge [bʌdʒ] **budges, budging, budged** VERB
If something will not budge, you cannot move it.

budgerigar ['bʌdʒərɪ,gɑː] **budgerigars** NOUN
a small brightly coloured pet bird

budget ['bʌdʒɪt] **budgets, budgeting, budgeted** NOUN
1 a plan showing how much money will be available and how it will be spent
> VERB
2 If you budget for something, you plan your money carefully, so that you are able to afford it.
budgetary ADJECTIVE

budgie ['bʌdʒɪ] **budgies** NOUN; INFORMAL
a budgerigar

buff [bʌf] **buffs** ADJECTIVE
1 a pale brown colour
> NOUN
2 INFORMAL
someone who knows a lot about a subject e.g. a film buff

buffalo ['bʌfə,ləʊ] **buffaloes** NOUN
a wild animal like a large cow with long curved horns

buffer ['bʌfə] **buffers** NOUN
1 Buffers on a train or at the end of a railway line are metal discs on springs that reduce shock when they are hit.
2 something that prevents something else from being harmed e.g. keep savings as a buffer against unexpected cash needs

buffet ['bʌfɪt] or ['bʊfeɪ] **buffets** NOUN
1 a café at a station
2 a meal at which people serve themselves

buffet buffets, buffeting, buffeted VERB
If the wind or sea buffets a place or person, it

strikes them violently and repeatedly.

bug [bʌg] **bugs, bugging, bugged** NOUN
1 an insect, especially one that causes damage
2 a small error in a computer program which means that the program will not work properly
3 INFORMAL
a virus or minor infection e.g. a stomach bug
> VERB
4 If a place is bugged, tiny microphones are hidden there to pick up what people are saying.

bugle ['bjuːgəl] **bugles** NOUN
a brass instrument that looks like a small trumpet
bugler NOUN

build [bɪld] **builds, building, built** VERB
1 To build something such as a house means to make it from its parts.

⬤ THESAURUS
assemble: Workers were assembling planes.
construct: plans to construct a temple on the site
erect: The building was erected in 1900.
fabricate: All the tools are fabricated from steel.
form: hotels formed from cheap cement
make: a wall made of bricks
<<OPPOSITE dismantle

2 To build something such as an organization means to develop it gradually.

⬤ THESAURUS
develop: These battles could develop into war.
extend: Three new products extend the range.
increase: The population continues to increase.
intensify: The conflict is bound to intensify.
strengthen: Cycling strengthens the muscles.

> NOUN
3 Your build is the shape and size of your body.
builder NOUN

⬤ THESAURUS
body: a body of average size
figure: Janet has a nice figure.
form: clothes that flatter your form
frame: their bony frames
physique: a powerful physique
shape: his trim shape

building ['bɪldɪŋ] **buildings** NOUN
a structure with walls and a roof

⬤ THESAURUS
edifice: historic edifices in the area
structure: The museum is an impressive structure.

building society building societies NOUN
a business in which some people invest their money, while others borrow from it to buy a house

bulb [bʌlb] **bulbs** NOUN
1 the glass part of an electric lamp

2 an onion-shaped root that grows into a flower or plant

Bulgarian [bʌlˈgɛərɪən] **Bulgarians**
ADJECTIVE

1 belonging or relating to Bulgaria

> NOUN

2 someone who comes from Bulgaria

3 the main language spoken in Bulgaria

bulge [bʌldʒ] **bulges, bulging, bulged** VERB

1 If something bulges, it swells out from a surface.

● THESAURUS

expand: *The pipes expanded in the heat.*
protrude: *His blue eyes protruded from his head.*
stick out: *His stomach stuck out under his jacket.*
swell: *My ankles swelled.*

> NOUN

2 a lump on a normally flat surface

● THESAURUS

bump: *a bump in the road*
hump: *a camel's hump*
lump: *itchy red lumps on the skin*
protrusion: *a strange protrusion on his forehead*
swelling: *a swelling on my foot*

bulk [bʌlk] **bulks** NOUN

1 a large mass of something *e.g. The book is more impressive for its bulk than its content.*

2 The bulk of something is most of it. *e.g. the bulk of the world's great poetry*

> PHRASE

3 To buy something **in bulk** means to buy it in large quantities.

bulky [ˈbʌlkɪ] **bulkier, bulkiest** ADJECTIVE
large and heavy *e.g. a bulky package*

bull [bʊl] **bulls** NOUN
the male of some species of animals, including the cow family, elephants and whales

bulldog [ˈbʊlˌdɒg] **bulldogs** NOUN
a squat dog with a broad head and muscular body

bulldozer [ˈbʊlˌdəʊzə] **bulldozers** NOUN
a powerful tractor with a broad blade in front, which is used for moving earth or knocking things down

bullet [ˈbʊlɪt] **bullets** NOUN
a small piece of metal fired from a gun

bulletin [ˈbʊlɪtɪn] **bulletins** NOUN

1 a short news report on radio or television

2 a leaflet or small newspaper regularly produced by a group or organization
[WORD HISTORY: from Italian BULLETINO meaning 'small Papal edict']

bullion [ˈbʊljən] NOUN
Bullion is gold or silver in the form of bars.

bullock [ˈbʊlək] **bullocks** NOUN
a young castrated bull

bullroarer [ˈbʊlˌrɔːrə] **bullroarers** NOUN
a wooden slat attached to a string that is whirled round to make a roaring noise. Bullroarers are used especially by Australian Aborigines in religious ceremonies

bully [ˈbʊlɪ] **bullies, bullying, bullied** NOUN

1 someone who uses their strength or power to hurt or frighten other people

● THESAURUS

oppressor: *They were powerless against their oppressors.*
persecutor: *Eventually he stood up to his persecutors.*

> VERB

2 If you bully someone, you frighten or hurt them deliberately.

● THESAURUS

intimidate: *Jones had set out to intimidate and dominate Paul.*
oppress: *men who try to dominate and oppress women*
persecute: *Tom was persecuted by his sisters.*
pick on: *I don't like to see you pick on younger children.*
tease: *The boys in the village had set on him, teasing him.*
torment: *My older brother and sister used to torment me.*

3 If someone bullies you into doing something, they make you do it by using force or threats.
[WORD HISTORY: a 16th century word meaning 'fine fellow' or 'hired ruffian']

● THESAURUS

force: *I cannot force you in this. You must decide.*
intimidate: *attempts to intimidate people into voting for the governing party*
pressurize: *Do not be pressurized into making your decision immediately.*

bump [bʌmp] **bumps, bumping, bumped**
VERB

1 If you bump or bump into something, you knock it with a jolt.

● THESAURUS

bang: *I banged my shin on the edge of the table.*
collide: *The car collided with a tree.*
hit: *She hit the last barrier and fell.*
jolt: *We hit the wall with a jolt.*
knock: *He knocked on the door.*
strike: *His head struck the windscreen.*

> NOUN

2 a soft or dull noise made by something knocking into something else

● THESAURUS

bang: *I heard four or five loud bangs.*

knock: *They heard a knock at the door.*
thud: *She tripped and fell with a thud.*
thump: *There was a loud thump against the house.*

3 a raised, uneven part of a surface
bumpy ADJECTIVE

⬤ THESAURUS
bulge: *My purse made a bulge in my pocket.*
hump: *a camel's hump*
knob: *a door with a brass knob*
lump: *itchy red lumps on the skin*
swelling: *a swelling on my foot*

bumper ['bʌmpə] **bumpers** NOUN
1 Bumpers are bars on the front and back of a vehicle which protect it if there is a collision.
> ADJECTIVE
2 A bumper crop or harvest is larger than usual.

bun [bʌn] **buns** NOUN
a small, round cake

bunch [bʌntʃ] **bunches, bunching, bunched** NOUN
1 a group of people

⬤ THESAURUS
band: *Bands of criminals have been roaming some neighbourhoods.*
crowd: *All the old crowd have come out for this occasion.*
gaggle: *A gaggle of journalists sit in a hotel foyer waiting impatiently.*
gang: *Come on over - we've got lots of the old gang here.*
group: *The trouble involved a small group of football supporters.*
lot: *Future generations are going to think that we were a pretty boring lot.*
multitude: *surrounded by a noisy multitude*

2 a number of flowers held or tied together

⬤ THESAURUS
bouquet: *She laid a bouquet on his grave.*
posy: *a posy of wild flowers*
spray: *a small spray of freesias*

3 a group of things

⬤ THESAURUS
batch: *She brought a large batch of newspaper cuttings.*
bundle: *a bundle of sticks tied together with string*
cluster: *a cluster of shops, cabins and motels*
heap: *a heap of old boxes for the bonfire*
load: *His people came up with a load of embarrassing stories.*
pile: *I've got a pile of questions afterwards for you.*
set: *Only she and Mr Cohen had complete sets of keys to the shop.*

4 a group of bananas or grapes growing on the same stem
> VERB
5 When people bunch together or bunch up, they

stay very close to each other.

bundle ['bʌndəl] **bundles, bundling, bundled** NOUN
1 a number of things tied together or wrapped up in a cloth
> VERB
2 If you bundle someone or something somewhere, you push them there quickly and roughly.

bung [bʌŋ] **bungs, bunging, bunged** NOUN
1 a stopper used to close a hole in something such as a barrel
> VERB
2 INFORMAL
If you bung something somewhere, you put it there quickly and carelessly.

bungalow ['bʌŋgə,ləʊ] **bungalows** NOUN
a one-storey house
[WORD HISTORY: from Hindi BANGLA meaning 'of Bengal']

bungle ['bʌŋgəl] **bungles, bungling, bungled** VERB
To bungle something means to fail to do it properly.

bunion ['bʌnjən] **bunions** NOUN
a painful lump on the first joint of a person's big toe

bunk [bʌŋk] **bunks** NOUN
a bed fixed to a wall in a ship or caravan

bunker ['bʌŋkə] **bunkers** NOUN
1 On a golf course, a bunker is a large hole filled with sand.
2 A coal bunker is a storage place for coal.
3 an underground shelter with strong walls to protect it from bombing

bunting ['bʌntɪŋ] NOUN
Bunting is strips of small coloured flags displayed on streets and buildings on special occasions.

bunyip ['bʌnjɪp] **bunyips** NOUN
a legendary monster said to live in swamps and lakes in Australia

buoy [bɔɪ] **buoys** NOUN
a floating object anchored to the bottom of the sea, marking a channel or warning of danger

buoyant ['bɔɪənt] ADJECTIVE
1 able to float
2 lively and cheerful *e.g. She was in a buoyant mood.*
buoyancy NOUN

burble ['bɜːbəl] **burbles, burbling, burbled** VERB
To burble means to makes a soft bubbling sound.

e.g. The water burbled over the gravel.

burden ['bɜːdᵊn] **burdens** NOUN

1 a heavy load

● THESAURUS
load: *a big load of hay*
weight: *straining to lift heavy weights*

2 If something is a burden to you, it causes you a lot of worry or hard work.
burdensome ADJECTIVE

● THESAURUS
anxiety: *He expressed his anxieties to me.*
care: *Forget all the cares of the day.*
strain: *I find the travelling a strain.*
stress: *the stress of exams*
trouble: *The Sullivans have money troubles.*
worry: *My son is a worry to me.*

bureau ['bjʊərəʊ] **bureaux** NOUN

1 an office that provides a service *e.g. an employment bureau*

2 a writing desk with shelves and drawers

bureaucracy [bjʊəˈrɒkrəsɪ] NOUN
Bureaucracy is the complex system of rules and procedures which operates in government departments.
bureaucratic ADJECTIVE

● THESAURUS
administration: *high administration costs*
officialdom: *Officialdom is against us.*
red tape: *Our application was delayed by red tape.*
regulations: *absurd regulations about opening hours*

bureaucrat ['bjʊərəˌkræt] **bureaucrats** NOUN
a person who works in a government department, especially one who follows rules and procedures strictly

burgeoning ['bɜːdʒənɪŋ] ADJECTIVE
growing or developing rapidly *e.g. a burgeoning political crisis*

burglar ['bɜːglə] **burglars** NOUN
a thief who breaks into a building
burglary NOUN

burgle ['bɜːgᵊl] **burgles, burgling, burgled** VERB
If your house is burgled, someone breaks into it and steals things.

burial ['bɛrɪəl] **burials** NOUN
(RE) a ceremony held when a dead person is buried

burly ['bɜːlɪ] **burlier, burliest** ADJECTIVE
A burly man has a broad body and strong muscles.

burn [bɜːn] **burns, burning, burned** or **burnt** VERB

1 If something is burning, it is on fire.

● THESAURUS
be ablaze: *The houses were ablaze.*
be on fire: *The ship was on fire.*
blaze: *The wreckage blazed.*
flame: *We watched as the house flamed.*
flare: *The match flared in the dark.*
flicker: *The fire flickered and crackled.*

2 To burn something means to destroy it with fire.

● THESAURUS
char: *charred bodies*
incinerate: *Hospitals incinerate waste.*
scorch: *The bonfire scorched the grass.*
shrivel: *The papers shrivelled in the flames.*
singe: *Her hair was singed and her coat burnt.*

3 If you burn yourself or are burned, you are injured by fire or by something hot.

> NOUN

4 an injury caused by fire or by something hot

You can write either *burned* or *burnt* as the past form of *burn*.

burp [bɜːp] **burps, burping, burped** VERB

1 If you burp, you make a noise because air from your stomach has been forced up through your throat.

> NOUN

2 the noise that you make when you burp

burrow ['bʌrəʊ] **burrows, burrowing, burrowed** NOUN

1 a tunnel or hole in the ground dug by a small animal

> VERB

2 When an animal burrows, it digs a burrow.

bursary ['bɜːsərɪ] **bursaries** NOUN
a sum of money given to someone to help fund their education

burst [bɜːst] **bursts, bursting, burst** VERB

1 When something bursts, it splits open because of pressure from inside it.

● THESAURUS
break: *He broke the box open.*
crack: *A water pipe had cracked.*
explode: *The glass exploded.*
puncture: *The glass punctured the tyre.*
rupture: *His appendix ruptured.*
split: *The seam of my dress split.*

2 If you burst into a room, you enter it suddenly.

3 To burst means to happen or come suddenly and with force. *e.g. The aircraft burst into flames.*

● THESAURUS
barge: *He barged into the room.*
break: *Her face broke into a smile.*
erupt: *Violence could erupt soon.*

rush: *Water rushed out of the hole.*

4 INFORMAL
If you are bursting with something, you find it difficult to keep it to yourself. *e.g. We were bursting with joy.*

> NOUN
5 A burst of something is a short period of it. *e.g. He had a sudden burst of energy.*

THESAURUS
fit: *a fit of rage*
outbreak: *an outbreak of violence*
rush: *a sudden rush of excitement*
spate: *a spate of attacks on horses*
surge: *a surge of emotion*
torrent: *a torrent of words*

bury ['bɛrɪ] **buries, burying, buried** VERB
1 When a dead person is buried, their body is put into a grave and covered with earth.
2 To bury something means to put it in a hole in the ground and cover it up.
3 If something is buried under something, it is covered by it. *e.g. My bag was buried under a pile of old newspapers.*

bus [bʌs] **buses** NOUN
a large motor vehicle that carries passengers [WORD HISTORY: from Latin OMNIBUS meaning 'for all'; buses were originally called omnibuses]

bush [bʊʃ] **bushes** NOUN
1 a thick plant with many stems branching out from ground level
2 In Australia and South Africa, an area of land in its natural state outside of city areas is called the bush.
3 In New Zealand, the bush is land covered with rain forest.

bushman ['bʊʃmən] **bushmen** NOUN
1 In Australia and New Zealand, someone who lives or travels in the bush.
2 In New Zealand, a bushman is also someone whose job it is to clear the bush for farming.

Bushman ['bʊʃmən] **Bushmen,** NOUN
A Bushman is a member of a group of people in southern Africa who live by hunting and gathering food.

bushranger ['bʊʃˌreɪndʒə] **bushrangers** NOUN
In Australia and New Zealand in the past, an outlaw living in the bush.

bushy ['bʊʃɪ] **bushier, bushiest** ADJECTIVE
Bushy hair or fur grows very thickly. *e.g. bushy eyebrows*

business ['bɪznɪs] **businesses** NOUN
1 Business is work relating to the buying and selling of goods and services.

THESAURUS
commerce: *commerce between Europe and South America*
dealings: *All dealings with the company were suspended.*
industry: *the American car industry*
trade: *French trade with the West Indies.*
trading: *trading between the two countries*
transaction: *We settled the transaction over lunch.*

2 an organization which produces or sells goods or provides a service

THESAURUS
company: *the Ford Motor Company*
corporation: *international corporations*
enterprise: *small industrial enterprises*
establishment: *shops and other commercial establishments*
firm: *a firm of engineers*
organization: *a well-run organization*

3 You can refer to any event, situation, or activity as a business. *e.g. This whole business has upset me.*
businessman NOUN, **businesswoman** NOUN

THESAURUS
affair: *He handled the affair badly.*
issue: *What is your view on this issue?*
matter: *This is a matter for the police.*
problem: *solutions to the drug problem*
question: *the whole question of TV censorship*
subject: *He raised the subject of money.*

businesslike ['bɪznɪsˌlaɪk] ADJECTIVE
dealing with things in an efficient way

busker ['bʌskə] **buskers** NOUN
someone who plays music or sings for money in public places

bust [bʌst] **busts, busting, bust** or **busted** NOUN
1 a statue of someone's head and shoulders *a bust of Beethoven*
2 A woman's bust is her chest and her breasts.

> VERB
3 INFORMAL
If you bust something, you break it.

> ADJECTIVE
4 INFORMAL
If a business goes bust, it becomes bankrupt and closes down.

bustle ['bʌsəl] **bustles, bustling, bustled** VERB
1 When people bustle, they move in a busy, hurried way.

THESAURUS
dash: *We dashed about purposefully.*
fuss: *Waiters were fussing round the table.*
hurry: *Claire hurried along the road.*
rush: *I'm rushing to finish the cooking.*

scurry: *rats scurrying around*
scuttle: *Crabs scuttle along the bank.*

> NOUN

2 Bustle is busy, noisy activity.

THESAURUS
activity: *a burst of activity in the building*
commotion: *He heard a commotion outside.*
excitement: *The news created great excitement.*
flurry: *a flurry of activity*
fuss: *He works without any fuss.*
hurry: *the hurry and excitement of the city*
<<OPPOSITE *peace*

busy [ˈbɪzɪ] **busier, busiest; busies, busying, busied** ADJECTIVE

1 If you are busy, you are in the middle of doing something.

THESAURUS
active: *He is active in local politics.*
employed: *He was employed helping me.*
engaged: *He was engaged in conversation.*
engrossed: *She is engrossed in her work.*
occupied: *He is occupied with the packing.*
working: *I am working on a novel.*
<<OPPOSITE *idle*

2 A busy place is full of people doing things or moving about. *e.g. a busy seaside resort*

THESAURUS
active: *an active, independent country*
full: *a full life*
hectic: *my hectic work schedule*
lively: *a lively restaurant*
restless: *a restless mind*

> VERB

3 If you busy yourself with something, you occupy yourself by doing it.
busily ADVERB

THESAURUS
absorb: *Her career absorbed her completely.*
employ: *You'd be better employed helping me.*
engage: *He was engaged in a meeting when I called.*
immerse: *She immersed herself in her book.*
occupy: *Try to occupy yourself with something.*

but [bʌt] CONJUNCTION

1 used to introduce an idea that is opposite to what has gone before *e.g. I don't miss teaching but I miss the pupils.*

THESAURUS
although: *He was in love with her, although he had not yet admitted it to himself.*
though: *He's very attractive, though not exactly handsome.*
while: *The first two services are free, while the third costs £35.*
yet: *It is completely waterproof, yet light and comfortable.*

2 used when apologizing *e.g. I'm sorry, but I can't come tonight.*

3 except *e.g. We can't do anything but wait.*

THESAURUS
except: *I don't take any drugs except aspirin.*
except for: *No-one has complained except for you.*
save: *The people had no water at all save that brought up from bore holes.*
other than: *This route is not recommended to anyone other than the most experienced cyclist.*

butcher [ˈbʊtʃə] **butchers** NOUN
a shopkeeper who sells meat

butler [ˈbʌtlə] **butlers** NOUN
the chief male servant in a rich household
[WORD HISTORY: from Old French BOUTEILLIER meaning 'a dealer in bottles']

butt [bʌt] **butts, butting, butted** NOUN
1 The butt of a weapon is the thick end of its handle.
2 If you are the butt of teasing, you are the target of it.

> VERB

3 If you butt something, you ram it with your head.

butt in VERB
4 If you butt in, you join in a private conversation or activity without being asked to.

butter [ˈbʌtə] **butters, buttering, buttered** NOUN

1 Butter is a soft fatty food made from cream, which is spread on bread and used in cooking.

> VERB

2 To butter bread means to spread butter on it.

buttercup [ˈbʌtəˌkʌp] **buttercups** NOUN
a wild plant with bright yellow flowers

butterfly [ˈbʌtəˌflaɪ] **butterflies** NOUN
a type of insect with large colourful wings

buttocks [ˈbʌtəks] PLURAL NOUN
Your buttocks are the part of your body that you sit on.

button [ˈbʌtᵊn] **buttons, buttoning, buttoned** NOUN

1 Buttons are small, hard objects sewn on to clothing, and used to fasten two surfaces together.

2 a small object on a piece of equipment that you press to make it work

> VERB

3 If you button a piece of clothing, you fasten it using its buttons.

buttonhole [ˈbʌtᵊnˌhəʊl] **buttonholes** NOUN

1 a hole that you push a button through to fasten a piece of clothing

2 a flower worn in your lapel

b

buxom ['bʌksəm] ADJECTIVE
A buxom woman is large, healthy, and attractive.

buy [baɪ] **buys, buying, bought** VERB
If you buy something, you obtain it by paying money for it.
buyer NOUN

● THESAURUS
acquire: *I have acquired a new car.*
invest in: *I invested in a house.*
obtain: *She went to obtain a ticket.*
pay for: *He let me pay for his drink.*
procure: *attempts to procure more food*
purchase: *He purchased a sandwich for lunch.*
<<OPPOSITE sell

buzz [bʌz] **buzzes, buzzing, buzzed** VERB
1 If something buzzes, it makes a humming sound, like a bee.
> NOUN
2 the sound something makes when it buzzes

buzzard ['bʌzəd] **buzzards** NOUN
a large brown and white bird of prey

buzzer ['bʌzə] **buzzers** NOUN
a device that makes a buzzing sound, to attract attention

by [baɪ] PREPOSITION

1 used to indicate who or what has done something *e.g. The statement was issued by his solicitor.*
2 used to indicate how something is done *e.g. He frightened her by hiding behind the door.*
3 located next to *e.g. I sat by her bed.*
4 before a particular time *e.g. It should be ready by next spring.*
> PREPOSITION OR ADVERB
5 going past *e.g. We drove by his house.*

by-election ['baɪɪ'lekʃən] **by-elections** NOUN
an election held to choose a new member of parliament after the previous member has resigned or died

bygone ['baɪ,gɒn] ADJECTIVE; LITERARY
happening or existing a long time ago *e.g. the ceremonies of a bygone era*

bypass ['baɪ,pɑːs] **bypasses** NOUN
a main road which takes traffic round a town rather than through it

bystander ['baɪ,stændə] **bystanders** NOUN
someone who is not included or involved in something but is there to see it happen

byte [baɪt] **bytes** NOUN
(ICT) a unit of storage in a computer

Cc

cab [kæb] **cabs** NOUN
1 a taxi
2 In a lorry, bus, or train, the cab is where the driver sits.
[WORD HISTORY: from French CABRIOLET meaning 'light two-wheeled carriage'. Cabs were originally horse-drawn]

cabaret ['kæbə,reɪ] **cabarets** NOUN
a show consisting of dancing, singing, or comedy acts
[WORD HISTORY: from French CABARET meaning 'tavern']

cabbage ['kæbɪdʒ] **cabbages** NOUN
a large green or reddish purple leafy vegetable
[WORD HISTORY: from Norman French CABACHE meaning 'head']

cabbage tree cabbage trees NOUN
a palm-like tree found in New Zealand with a tall bare trunk and big bunches of spiky leaves; also a similar tree found in eastern Australia

cabin ['kæbɪn] **cabins** NOUN
1 a room in a ship where a passenger sleeps
2 a small house, usually in the country and often made of wood
3 the area where the passengers or the crew sit in a plane

cabinet ['kæbɪnɪt] **cabinets** NOUN
1 a small cupboard
2 The cabinet in a government is a group of ministers who advise the leader and decide policies.

cable ['keɪbᵊl] **cables** NOUN
1 a strong, thick rope or chain
2 a bundle of wires with a rubber covering, which carries electricity
3 a message sent abroad by using electricity

cable car cable cars NOUN
a vehicle pulled by a moving cable, for taking people up and down mountains

cable television NOUN
a television service people can receive from underground wires which carry the signals

cacao [kə'kɑːəʊ] NOUN
A cacao is a type of small tropical evergreen tree,
whose berries are used to produce chocolate and cocoa.

cache [kæʃ] **caches** NOUN
a store of things hidden away e.g. a cache of guns

cachet ['kæʃeɪ] NOUN; FORMAL
Cachet is the status and respect something has. e.g. the cachet of shopping at Harrods

cackle ['kækᵊl] **cackles, cackling, cackled** VERB
1 If you cackle, you laugh harshly.
> NOUN
2 a harsh laugh

cacophony [kə'kɒfənɪ] NOUN; FORMAL
a loud, unpleasant noise e.g. a cacophony of barking dogs
[WORD HISTORY: from Greek KAKOS + PHŌNĒ meaning 'bad sound']

cactus ['kæktəs] **cacti** or **cactuses** NOUN
a thick, fleshy plant that grows in deserts and is usually covered in spikes

cad [kæd] **cads** NOUN; OLD-FASHIONED, INFORMAL
a man who treats people unfairly

caddie ['kædɪ] **caddies;** also spelt **caddy** NOUN
1 a person who carries golf clubs for a golf player
2 A tea caddy is a box for keeping tea in.

cadence ['keɪdᵊns] **cadences** NOUN
The cadence of someone's voice is the way it goes up and down as they speak.

cadet [kə'dɛt] **cadets** NOUN
a young person being trained in the armed forces or police

cadge [kædʒ] **cadges, cadging, cadged** VERB
If you cadge something off someone, you get it from them and don't give them anything in return. e.g. I cadged a lift ashore.

caesarean [sɪ'zɛərɪən] **caesareans;** also spelt **caesarian** and **cesarean** NOUN
A caesarean or caesarean section is an operation in which a baby is lifted out of a woman's womb

through a cut in her abdomen.

café ['kæfeɪ] **cafés** NOUN

1 a place where you can buy light meals and drinks

2 In South African English, a café is a corner shop or grocer's shop.

cafeteria [ˌkæfɪ'tɪərɪə] **cafeterias** NOUN
a restaurant where you serve yourself

caffeine or **caffein** ['kæfiːn] NOUN
Caffeine is a chemical in coffee and tea which makes you more active.

cage [keɪdʒ] **cages** NOUN
a box made of wire or bars in which birds or animals are kept
caged ADJECTIVE

cagey ['keɪdʒɪ] **cagier, cagiest** ADJECTIVE; INFORMAL
cautious and not open e.g. They're very cagey when they talk to me.

cagoule [kə'guːl] **cagoules** NOUN
a lightweight waterproof jacket with a hood

cahoots [kə'huːts] PHRASE; INFORMAL
If you are **in cahoots** with someone, you are working closely with them on a secret plan.

cairn [keən] **cairns** NOUN
a pile of stones built as a memorial or a landmark [WORD HISTORY: from Gaelic CARN meaning 'heap of stones' or 'hill']

cajole [kə'dʒəʊl] **cajoles, cajoling, cajoled** VERB
If you cajole someone into doing something, you persuade them to do it by saying nice things to them.

cake [keɪk] **cakes, caking, caked** NOUN

1 a sweet food made by baking flour, eggs, fat, and sugar

2 a block of a hard substance such as soap

> VERB

3 If something cakes or is caked, it forms or becomes covered with a solid layer. e.g. caked with mud
[WORD HISTORY: from Old Norse KAKA meaning 'oatcake']

calamity [kə'læmɪtɪ] **calamities** NOUN
an event that causes disaster or distress
calamitous ADJECTIVE

calcium ['kælsɪəm] NOUN
a soft white substance found in bones and teeth

calculate ['kælkjʊˌleɪt] **calculates, calculating, calculated** VERB
(MATHS) If you calculate something, you work it out, usually by doing some arithmetic.

calculation NOUN
[WORD HISTORY: from Latin CALCULUS meaning 'stone' or 'pebble'. The Romans used pebbles to count with]

● THESAURUS
count: Shareholders are counting the cost of the slump.
determine: calculations to determine the rate of tax
reckon: an amount reckoned at 140 billion marks
work out: Work out the distance of the journey.

calculated ['kælkjʊˌleɪtɪd] ADJECTIVE
deliberately planned to have a particular effect

● THESAURUS
aimed: The restructuring is aimed at reducing costs.
designed: a scheme designed to help poorer families
intended: the intended effect of the revised guidelines
planned: a carefully planned campaign
<<OPPOSITE unplanned

calculating ['kælkjʊˌleɪtɪŋ] ADJECTIVE
carefully planning situations to get what you want e.g. Toby was always a calculating type.

calculator ['kælkjʊˌleɪtə] **calculators** NOUN
a small electronic machine used for doing mathematical calculations

calculus ['kælkjʊləs] NOUN
Calculus is a branch of mathematics concerned with amounts that can change and rates of change.

calendar ['kælɪndə] **calendars** NOUN

1 a chart showing the date of each day in a particular year

2 a system of dividing time into fixed periods of days, months, and years e.g. the Jewish calendar
[WORD HISTORY: from Latin KALENDAE the day of the month on which interest on debts was due]

calf [kɑːf] **calves** NOUN

1 a young cow, bull, elephant, whale, or seal

2 the thick part at the back of your leg below your knee

calibre ['kælɪbə] **calibres** NOUN

1 the ability or intelligence someone has e.g. a player of her calibre

2 The calibre of a gun is the width of the inside of the barrel of the gun.
[WORD HISTORY: from Arabic QALIB meaning 'cobbler's last']

call see page 115 for Word Web

call box call boxes NOUN
a telephone box

call centre call centres NOUN
an office in which most staff are employed to answer telephone calls on behalf of a particular

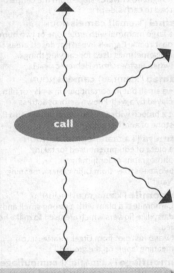

1 VERB
to give a name eg: *a man called Jeffrey*
● **THESAURUS**
christen: *He decided to christen his first-born son Arthur.*
designated: *The wood was designated an 'area of natural beauty'.*
dubbed: *the man dubbed 'the world's greatest living explorer'*
named: *They named their child Anthony.*

2 VERB
to telephone eg: *He called me at my office.*
● **THESAURUS**
contact: *Contact us immediately if you have any new information.*
phone: *Phone me as soon as you get home.*
ring: *I'll ring you tomorrow.*
telephone: *Please telephone to make an appointment.*

call

3 VERB
to say loudly eg: *I heard someone calling my name.*
● **THESAURUS**
announced: *"Dinner is served," he announced.*
cried: *"Run, Forrest!" she cried.*
cried out: *She cried out to us as she disappeared from view.*
shouted: *He shouted to me from across the room.*
yelled: *"Ahoy there!" the captain yelled over to us.*

4 NOUN
an instance of someone shouting out eg: *a call for help*
● **THESAURUS**
cry: *the cry of a seagull*
shout: *I heard a distant shout.*
yell: *He let out a yell.*

company or organization

calling ['kɔːlɪŋ] NOUN
1 a profession or career
2 If you have a calling to a particular job, you have a strong feeling that you should do it.

callous ['kæləs] ADJECTIVE
cruel and not concerned with other people's feelings
callously ADVERB, **callousness** NOUN

● THESAURUS
cold: *What a cold, unfeeling woman she was.*
heartless: *It was a heartless thing to do.*
indifferent: *indifferent to the suffering of others*
insensitive: *insensitive remarks*
<<OPPOSITE *caring*

calm [kɑːm] **calmer, calmest; calms, calming, calmed** ADJECTIVE
1 Someone who is calm is quiet and does not show any worry or excitement.

● THESAURUS
collected: *She was cool and collected during her interrogation.*
composed: *a very composed, business-like woman*
cool: *We have to keep a cool head in this situation.*
impassive: *He remained impassive as his sentence was passed.*
relaxed: *a relaxed manner*
<<OPPOSITE *worried*

2 If the weather or the sea is calm, it is still because there is no strong wind.

● THESAURUS
balmy: *balmy summer evenings*
mild: *a mild winter climate*
still: *The air was still.*
tranquil: *a tranquil lake*
<<OPPOSITE *rough*

> NOUN
3 Calm is a state of quietness and peacefulness. *e.g. He liked the calm of the evening.*

● THESAURUS
calmness: *an aura of calmness*
peace: *a wonderful feeling of peace*
peacefulness: *the peacefulness of the gardens*
quiet: *a quiet, relaxing holiday*
serenity: *the peace and serenity of a tropical sunset*
stillness: *the stillness of the summer night*

> VERB
4 To calm someone means to make them less upset or excited.
calmly ADVERB, **calmness** NOUN

● THESAURUS
quieten: *trying to quieten the restless horses*
relax: *This music is supposed to relax you.*
soothe: *I think a bath may soothe me.*

calorie ['kælərɪ] **calories** NOUN
a unit of measurement for the energy food gives

you *e.g. All alcohol is high in calories.*

calves [kɑːvz] the plural of **calf**

calypso [kə'lɪpsəʊ] **calypsos** NOUN
a type of song from the West Indies, accompanied by a rhythmic beat, about something happening at the time

calyx ['keɪlɪks] **calyxes** or **calyces** NOUN; TECHNICAL
In a flower, a calyx is the ring of petal-like sepals that protects the developing bud.

camaraderie [,kæmə'rɑːdərɪ] NOUN
Camaraderie is a feeling of trust and friendship between a group of people.

camber ['kæmbə] **cambers** NOUN
a slight downwards slope from the centre of a road to each side of it

camel ['kæməl] **camels** NOUN
a large mammal with either one or two humps on its back. Camels live in hot desert areas and are sometimes used for carrying things.
[WORD HISTORY: from Hebrew GAMAL]

cameo ['kæmɪ,əʊ] **cameos** NOUN
1 a small but important part in a play or film played by a well-known actor or actress
2 a brooch with a raised stone design on a flat stone of another colour

camera ['kæmərə] **cameras** NOUN
a piece of equipment used for taking photographs or for filming
[WORD HISTORY: from Latin CAMERA meaning 'vault']

camomile ['kæmə,maɪl] NOUN
Camomile is a plant with a strong smell and daisy-like flowers which are used to make herbal tea.
[WORD HISTORY: from Greek KHAMAIMĒLON meaning 'apple on the ground']

camouflage ['kæmə,flɑːʒ] **camouflages, camouflaging, camouflaged** NOUN
1 Camouflage is a way of avoiding being seen by having the same colour or appearance as the surroundings.

> VERB
2 To camouflage something is to hide it by giving it the same colour or appearance as its surroundings.

camp [kæmp] **camps, camping, camped** NOUN
1 a place where people live in tents or stay in tents on holiday
2 a collection of buildings for a particular group of people such as soldiers or prisoners
3 a group of people who support a particular idea or belief *e.g. the pro-government camp*

> VERB

4 If you camp, you stay in a tent.
camper NOUN, **camping** NOUN

campaign [kæm'peɪn] **campaigns,
campaigning, campaigned** NOUN
1 a set of actions aiming to achieve a particular
result e.g. *a campaign to educate people*

⬤ THESAURUS
crusade: *the crusade for human rights*
movement: *the human rights movement*
operation: *a full-scale military operation*
push: *an all-out push to promote the show*

> VERB

2 To campaign means to carry out a campaign.
e.g. *He has campaigned against smoking.*
campaigner NOUN

camp-drafting ['kæmp,drɑːftɪŋ] NOUN
In Australia, camp-drafting is a competition in
which men on horseback select cattle or sheep
from a herd or flock.

campus ['kæmpəs] **campuses** NOUN
the area of land and the buildings that make up a
university or college

can [kæn] **could** VERB
1 If you can do something, it is possible for you to
do it or you are allowed to do it. e.g. *You can go to
the cinema.*

2 If you can do something, you have the ability to
do it. e.g. *I can speak Italian.*

can [kæn] **cans, canning, canned** NOUN
1 a metal container, often a sealed one with food
or drink inside

> VERB

2 To can food or drink is to seal it in cans.

Canadian [kə'neɪdɪən] **Canadians**
ADJECTIVE
1 belonging or relating to Canada

> NOUN

2 someone who comes from Canada

canal [kə'næl] **canals** NOUN
a long, narrow man-made stretch of water

canary [kə'neərɪ] **canaries** NOUN
a small yellow bird

can-can ['kæn,kæn] **can-cans** NOUN
a lively dance in which women kick their legs
high in the air to fast music

cancel ['kæns³l] **cancels, cancelling,
cancelled** VERB
1 If you cancel something that has been
arranged, you stop it from happening.

⬤ THESAURUS
abandon: *He had to abandon his holiday plans.*
call off: *The union has called off the strike.*

2 If you cancel a cheque or an agreement, you
make sure that it is no longer valid.
cancellation NOUN

⬤ THESAURUS
annul: *The marriage was annulled.*
quash: *His jail sentence was quashed when new
evidence came to light.*
repeal: *The new law was repealed within the year.*
revoke: *His licence was immediately revoked.*

cancer ['kænsə] **cancers** NOUN
1 a serious disease in which abnormal cells in a
part of the body increase rapidly, causing
growths

2 Cancer is also the fourth sign of the zodiac,
represented by a crab. People born between June
21st and July 22nd are born under this sign.
cancerous ADJECTIVE
[WORD HISTORY: from Latin CANCER meaning 'crab']

candelabra or **candelabrum**
[,kændɪ'lɑːbrə] or [,kændɪ'lɑːbrəm]
candelabras NOUN
an ornamental holder for a number of candles

candid ['kændɪd] ADJECTIVE
honest and frank
candidly ADVERB, **candour** NOUN

⬤ THESAURUS
blunt: *She is blunt about his faults.*
frank: *They had a frank discussion about the issue.*
honest: *What is your honest opinion?*
open: *He had always been open with her and she
would know if he lied.*
truthful: *We've all learnt to be fairly truthful about
our personal lives.*
straightforward: *I was impressed by his
straightforward manner.*

candidate ['kændɪ,deɪt] **candidates** NOUN
1 a person who is being considered for a job

⬤ THESAURUS
applicant: *one of thirty applicants for the manager's
post*
competitor: *several competitors for the contract*
contender: *a strong contender for the
chairmanship*

2 a person taking an examination
candidacy NOUN
[WORD HISTORY: from Latin CANDIDATUS meaning
'white-robed'. In Rome, a candidate wore a white
toga]

candied ['kændɪd] ADJECTIVE
covered or cooked in sugar e.g. *candied fruit*

candle ['kænd³l] **candles** NOUN
a stick of hard wax with a wick through the
middle. The lighted wick gives a flame that
provides light

candlestick ['kænd³l,stɪk] **candlesticks**
NOUN

a holder for a candle

candy ['kændɪ] **candies** NOUN; USED ESPECIALLY IN AMERICAN ENGLISH
Candies are sweets.
[WORD HISTORY: from Arabic QAND meaning 'cane sugar']

cane [keɪn] **canes, caning, caned** NOUN
1 Cane is the long, hollow stems of a plant such as bamboo.
2 Cane is also strips of cane used for weaving things such as baskets.
3 a long narrow stick, often one used to beat people as a punishment
> VERB
4 To cane someone means to beat them with a cane as a punishment.

canine ['keɪnaɪn] ADJECTIVE
relating to dogs

canister ['kænɪstə] **canisters** NOUN
a container with a lid, used for storing foods such as sugar or tea

cannabis ['kænəbɪs] NOUN
Cannabis is a drug made from the hemp plant, which some people smoke.

canned [kænd] ADJECTIVE
1 Canned food is kept in cans.
2 Canned music or laughter on a television or radio show is recorded beforehand.

cannibal ['kænɪbəl] **cannibals** NOUN
a person who eats other human beings; also used of animals that eat animals of their own type
cannibalism NOUN

cannon ['kænən] **cannons** or **cannon** NOUN
a large gun, usually on wheels, used in battles to fire heavy metal balls

cannot ['kænɒt] VERB
Cannot is the same as can not. *e.g. She cannot come home yet.*

canny ['kænɪ] **cannier, canniest** ADJECTIVE
clever and cautious *e.g. canny business people*
cannily ADVERB

canoe [kə'nuː] **canoes** NOUN
a small, narrow boat that you row using a paddle
canoeing NOUN

canon ['kænən] **canons** NOUN
1 a member of the clergy in a cathedral
2 a basic rule or principle *e.g. the canons of political economy*

canopy ['kænəpɪ] **canopies** NOUN
a cover for something, used for shelter or decoration *e.g. a frilly canopy over the bed*

[WORD HISTORY: from Greek KŌNŌPEION meaning 'bed with a mosquito net']

cantankerous [kæn'tæŋkərəs] ADJECTIVE
Cantankerous people are quarrelsome and bad-tempered.

canteen [kæn'tiːn] **canteens** NOUN
1 the part of a workplace where the workers can go to eat
2 A canteen of cutlery is a set of cutlery in a box.

canter ['kæntə] **canters, cantering, cantered** VERB
When a horse canters, it moves at a speed between a gallop and a trot.

cantilever ['kæntɪˌliːvə] **cantilevers** NOUN
a long beam or bar fixed at only one end and supporting a bridge or other structure at the other end

canton ['kæntɒn] **cantons** NOUN
a political and administrative region of a country, especially in Switzerland

canvas ['kænvəs] **canvases** NOUN
1 Canvas is strong, heavy cloth used for making things such as sails and tents.
2 a piece of canvas on which an artist does a painting

canvass ['kænvəs] **canvasses, canvassing, canvassed** VERB
1 If you canvass people or a place, you go round trying to persuade people to vote for a particular candidate or party in an election.
2 If you canvass opinion, you find out what people think about a particular subject by asking them.

canyon ['kænjən] **canyons** NOUN
a narrow river valley with steep sides

cap [kæp] **caps, capping, capped** NOUN
1 a soft, flat hat, often with a peak at the front
2 the top of a bottle
3 Caps are small explosives used in toy guns.
> VERB
4 To cap something is to cover it with something.
5 If you cap a story or a joke that someone has just told, you tell a better one.

capable ['keɪpəbəl] ADJECTIVE
1 able to do something *e.g. a man capable of extreme violence*
2 skilful or talented *e.g. She was a very capable woman.*
capably ADVERB, **capability** NOUN

● THESAURUS
able: *a very able businessman*
accomplished: *an accomplished painter*

adept: *an adept diplomat*
competent: *a competent and careful driver*
efficient: *efficient administration*
proficient: *proficient with computers*
skilful: *the country's most skilful politician*
<<OPPOSITE *incompetent*

capacity [kə'pæsɪtɪ] **capacities** NOUN
1 the maximum amount that something can hold or produce *e.g. a seating capacity of eleven thousand*

● THESAURUS
dimensions: *a car of compact dimensions*
room: *There wasn't enough room in the baggage compartment for all the gear.*
size: *My bedroom is half the size of yours.*
space: *There is space in the back for two people.*
volume: *a container with a volume of two litres*
2 a person's power or ability to do something *e.g. his capacity for consuming hamburgers*

● THESAURUS
ability: *The public never had faith in his ability to handle the job.*
capability: *a country with the capability of launching a nuclear attack*
facility: *Humans have lost the facility to use their sense of smell properly.*
gift: *As a youth he discovered a gift for making people laugh.*
potential: *the economic potentials of Eastern and Western Europe*
power: *Human societies have the power to solve the problems confronting them.*

3 someone's position or role *e.g. in his capacity as councillor*

cape [keɪp] **capes** NOUN
1 a short cloak with no sleeves

2 a large piece of land sticking out into the sea *e.g. the Cape of Good Hope*

caper ['keɪpə] **capers** NOUN
1 Capers are the flower buds of a spiky Mediterranean shrub, which are pickled and used to flavour food.

2 a light-hearted practical joke *e.g. Jack would have nothing to do with such capers.*

capillary [kə'pɪlərɪ] **capillaries** NOUN
Capillaries are very thin blood vessels.

capital ['kæpɪt²l] **capitals** NOUN
1 The capital of a country is the city where the government meets.

2 Capital is the amount of money or property owned or used by a business.

3 Capital is also a sum of money that you save or invest in order to gain interest.

4 A capital or capital letter is a larger letter used at the beginning of a sentence or a name.

capitalism ['kæpɪtə,lɪzəm] NOUN
Capitalism is an economic and political system where businesses and industries are not owned and run by the government, but by individuals who can make a profit from them.
capitalist ADJECTIVE OR NOUN

capitalize ['kæpɪtə,laɪz] **capitalizes, capitalizing, capitalized;** also spelt **capitalise** VERB
If you capitalize on a situation, you use it to get an advantage.

capital punishment NOUN
Capital punishment is legally killing someone as a punishment for a crime they have committed.

capitulate [kə'pɪtjʊ,leɪt] **capitulates, capitulating, capitulated** VERB
To capitulate is to give in and stop fighting or resisting. *e.g. The Finns capitulated in March 1940.*
capitulation NOUN

cappuccino [,kæpʊ'tʃiːnəʊ] **cappuccinos** NOUN
coffee made with frothy milk

capricious [kə'prɪʃəs] ADJECTIVE
often changing unexpectedly *e.g. the capricious English weather*

Capricorn ['kæprɪ,kɔːn] NOUN
Capricorn is the tenth sign of the zodiac, represented by a goat. People born between December 22nd and January 19th are born under this sign.
[WORD HISTORY: from Latin CAPER meaning 'goat' and CORNU meaning 'horn']

capsize [kæp'saɪz] **capsizes, capsizing, capsized** VERB
If a boat capsizes, it turns upside down.

capsule ['kæpsjuːl] **capsules** NOUN
1 a small container with medicine inside which you swallow

2 the part of a spacecraft in which astronauts travel
[WORD HISTORY: from Latin CAPSULA meaning 'little box']

captain ['kæptɪn] **captains, captaining, captained** NOUN
1 the officer in charge of a ship or aeroplane

2 an army officer of the rank immediately above lieutenant

3 a navy officer of the rank immediately above commander

4 the leader of a sports team *e.g. captain of the cricket team*

> VERB
5 If you captain a group of people, you are their leader.

caption ['kæpʃən] **captions** NOUN
a title printed underneath a picture or photograph

captivate ['kæptɪˌveɪt] **captivates, captivating, captivated** VERB
To captivate someone is to fascinate or attract them so that they cannot take their attention away. *e.g. I was captivated by her.*
captivating ADJECTIVE

captive ['kæptɪv] **captives** NOUN
1 a person who has been captured and kept prisoner
> ADJECTIVE
2 imprisoned or enclosed *e.g. a captive bird*
captivity NOUN

captor ['kæptə] **captors** NOUN
someone who has captured a person or animal

capture ['kæptʃə] **captures, capturing, captured** VERB
1 To capture someone is to take them prisoner.
● THESAURUS
apprehend: *Police have not yet apprehended the killer.*
arrest: *Seven people were arrested.*
catch: *The thief was caught and the money was returned.*
seize: *seized by armed police*
take: *An army unit took the town.*
<<OPPOSITE *release*

2 To capture a quality or mood means to succeed in representing or describing it. *e.g. capturing the mood of the riots*
> NOUN
3 The capture of someone or something is the action of taking them prisoner. *e.g. the fifth anniversary of his capture*
● THESAURUS
arrest: *Police made two arrests.*
seizure: *the seizure of territory*
taking: *the taking of hostages*
trapping: *The trapping of these animals is illegal.*

car [kɑː] **cars** NOUN
1 a four-wheeled road vehicle with room for a small number of people
● THESAURUS
automobile: American; formal *the Japanese automobile manufacturer, Nissan*
motor: *Patricia's new motor*
vehicle: *She managed to scramble out of the vehicle.*
2 a railway carriage used for a particular purpose *e.g. the buffet car*

carafe [kəˈræf] **carafes** NOUN
a glass bottle for serving water or wine
[WORD HISTORY: from Arabic GHARRAFAH meaning 'vessel for liquid']

caramel ['kærəməl] **caramels** NOUN
1 a chewy sweet made from sugar, butter, and milk
2 Caramel is burnt sugar used for colouring or flavouring food.

carat ['kærət] **carats** NOUN
1 a unit for measuring the weight of diamonds and other precious stones
2 a unit for measuring the purity of gold

caravan ['kærəˌvæn] **caravans** NOUN
1 a vehicle pulled by a car in which people live or spend their holidays
2 a group of people and animals travelling together, usually across a desert
[WORD HISTORY: from Persian KARWAN]

carbohydrate [ˌkɑːbəʊˈhaɪdreɪt] **carbohydrates** NOUN
(D & T) Carbohydrate is a substance that gives you energy. It is found in foods like sugar and bread.

carbon ['kɑːbⁿn] NOUN
Carbon is a chemical element that is pure in diamonds and also found in coal. All living things contain carbon.

carbonated ['kɑːbəneɪtɪd] ADJECTIVE
Carbonated drinks contain bubbles of carbon dioxide that make them fizzy.

carbon dioxide [daɪˈɒksaɪd] NOUN
Carbon dioxide is a colourless, odourless gas that humans and animals breathe out. It is used in industry, for example in making fizzy drinks and in fire extinguishers.

carburettor [ˌkɑːbjʊˈrɛtə] **carburettors** NOUN
the part of the engine in a vehicle in which air and petrol are mixed together

carcass ['kɑːkəs] **carcasses;** also spelt **carcase** NOUN
the body of a dead animal

card [kɑːd] **cards** NOUN
1 a piece of stiff paper or plastic with information or a message on it *e.g. a birthday card*
2 Cards can mean playing cards. *e.g. a poor set of cards with which to play*
3 When you play cards, you play any game using playing cards.
4 Card is strong, stiff paper.
[WORD HISTORY: from Greek KHARTĒS meaning 'papyrus leaf']

cardboard ['kɑːdˌbɔːd] NOUN
Cardboard is thick, stiff paper.

cardiac ['kɑːdɪˌæk] ADJECTIVE; MEDICAL
relating to the heart *e.g. cardiac disease*

cardigan ['kɑːdɪgən] **cardigans** NOUN
a knitted jacket that fastens up the front

cardinal ['kɑːdɪnᵊl] **cardinals** NOUN
1 a high-ranking member of the Roman Catholic clergy who chooses and advises the Pope
> ADJECTIVE
2 extremely important *e.g. a cardinal principle of law*
[WORD HISTORY: from Latin CARDO meaning 'hinge'. When something is important, other things hinge on it]

care [kɛə] **cares, caring, cared** VERB
1 If you care about something, you are concerned about it and interested in it.
● THESAURUS
be bothered: *I am not bothered what others think about me.*
be concerned: *We are concerned about the problem.*
be interested: *He's not interested in what anyone else says.*
mind: *I do not mind who wins.*
2 If you care about someone, you feel affection towards them.
3 If you care for someone, you look after them.
> NOUN
4 Care is concern or worry.
● THESAURUS
anxiety: *anxieties about money*
concern: *Their main concern is unemployment.*
stress: *the stresses of modern life*
trouble: *She has had her share of troubles.*
woe: *They blame the government for all their woes.*
worry: *My biggest worry is how I will cope on my own.*
5 Care of someone or something is treatment for them or looking after them. *e.g. the care of the elderly*
6 If you do something with care, you do it with close attention.
● THESAURUS
attention: *medical attention*
caution: *Proceed with caution.*
pains: *She takes great pains with her appearance.*

career [kə'rɪə] **careers, careering, careered** NOUN
1 the series of jobs that someone has in life, usually in the same occupation *e.g. a career in insurance*
> VERB
2 To career somewhere is to move very quickly, often out of control. *e.g. His car careered off the road.*

carefree ['kɛə,friː] ADJECTIVE
having no worries or responsibilities

careful ['kɛəfʊl] ADJECTIVE
1 acting sensibly and with care *e.g. Be careful what you say to him.*
● THESAURUS
cautious: *a cautious approach*
prudent: *prudent management*
<<OPPOSITE careless
2 complete and well done *e.g. It needs very careful planning.*
carefully ADVERB
● THESAURUS
meticulous: *meticulous attention to detail*
painstaking: *a painstaking search*
precise: *precise instructions*
thorough: *a thorough examination*
<<OPPOSITE careless

careless ['kɛəlɪs] ADJECTIVE
1 done badly without enough attention *e.g. careless driving*
● THESAURUS
irresponsible: *an irresponsible attitude*
neglectful: *neglectful parents*
sloppy: *informal sloppy work*
<<OPPOSITE careful
2 relaxed and unconcerned *e.g. careless laughter*
carelessly ADVERB, **carelessness** NOUN
● THESAURUS
casual: *a casual remark*
nonchalant: *a nonchalant attitude*
offhand: *his usual offhand way*

caress [kə'rɛs] **caresses, caressing, caressed** VERB
1 If you caress someone, you stroke them gently and affectionately.
> NOUN
2 a gentle, affectionate stroke

caretaker ['kɛə,teɪkə] **caretakers** NOUN
1 a person who looks after a large building such as a school
> ADJECTIVE
2 having an important position for a short time until a new person is appointed *e.g. O'Leary was named caretaker manager.*

cargo ['kɑːgəʊ] **cargoes** NOUN
the goods carried on a ship or plane

Caribbean [,kærɪ'biːən] NOUN
The Caribbean consists of the Caribbean Sea east of Central America and the islands in it.

caricature ['kærɪkə,tjʊə] **caricatures, caricaturing, caricatured** NOUN
1 a drawing or description of someone that exaggerates striking parts of their appearance or personality
> VERB
2 To caricature someone is to give a caricature of them.

C

carjack ['kɑːˌdʒæk] **carjacks, carjacking, carjacked** VERB
If a car is carjacked, its driver is attacked and robbed, or the car is stolen.

carnage ['kɑːnɪdʒ] NOUN
Carnage is the violent killing of large numbers of people.

carnal ['kɑːnᵊl] ADJECTIVE; FORMAL
sexual and sensual rather than spiritual *e.g. carnal pleasure*

carnation [kɑːˈneɪʃən] **carnations** NOUN
a plant with a long stem and white, pink, or red flowers

carnival ['kɑːnɪvᵊl] **carnivals** NOUN
a public festival with music, processions, and dancing

carnivore ['kɑːnɪˌvɔː] **carnivores** NOUN
an animal that eats meat
carnivorous ADJECTIVE

carol ['kærəl] **carols** NOUN
a religious song sung at Christmas time

carousel [ˌkærəˈsɛl] **carousels** NOUN
a merry-go-round

carp [kɑːp] **carps, carping, carped** NOUN
1 a large edible freshwater fish

> VERB

2 To carp means to complain about unimportant things.

carpel ['kɑːpᵊl] **carpels** NOUN
the seed-bearing female part of a flower

carpenter ['kɑːpɪntə] **carpenters** NOUN
a person who makes and repairs wooden structures
carpentry NOUN
[WORD HISTORY: from Latin CARPENTARIUS meaning 'wagon-maker']

carpet ['kɑːpɪt] **carpets, carpeting, carpeted** NOUN
1 a thick covering for a floor, usually made of a material like wool

> VERB

2 To carpet a floor means to cover it with a carpet.

carriage ['kærɪdʒ] **carriages** NOUN
1 one of the separate sections of a passenger train

2 an old-fashioned vehicle for carrying passengers, usually pulled by horses

3 a machine part that moves and supports another part *e.g. a typewriter carriage*

4 Someone's carriage is the way they hold their head and body when they move.

carriageway ['kærɪdʒˌweɪ] **carriageways** NOUN
one of the sides of a road which traffic travels along in one direction only

carrier ['kærɪə] **carriers** NOUN
1 a vehicle that is used for carrying things *e.g. a troop carrier*

2 A carrier of a germ or disease is a person or animal that can pass it on to others.

carrier bag carrier bags NOUN
a bag made of plastic or paper, which is used for carrying shopping

carrion ['kærɪən] NOUN
Carrion is the decaying flesh of dead animals.

carrot ['kærət] **carrots** NOUN
a long, thin orange root vegetable

carry ['kærɪ] **carries, carrying, carried** VERB
1 To carry something is to hold it and take it somewhere.

● THESAURUS
bear: *He arrived bearing gifts.*
convey: formal *The minibus conveyed us to the station.*
lug: *lugging boxes of books around*
take: *Don't forget to take your camera.*
transport: *goods being transported abroad*

2 When a vehicle carries people, they travel in it.

3 A person or animal that carries a germ can pass it on to other people or animals. *e.g. I still carry the disease.*

4 If a sound carries, it can be heard far away. *e.g. Jake's voice carried over the cheering.*

5 In a meeting, if a proposal is carried, it is accepted by a majority of the people there. **carry away** VERB

6 If you are carried away, you are so excited by something that you do not behave sensibly.
carry on VERB

7 To carry on doing something means to continue doing it.
carry out VERB

8 To carry something out means to do it and complete it. *e.g. The conversion was carried out by a local builder.*

● THESAURUS
accomplish: *the desire to accomplish a task*
achieve: *We have achieved our objective.*
fulfil: *to fulfil a promise*
perform: *people who have performed acts of bravery*

cart [kɑːt] **carts** NOUN
a vehicle with wheels, used to carry goods and often pulled by horses or cattle

cartilage ['kɑːtɪlɪdʒ] NOUN
Cartilage is a strong, flexible substance found around the joints and in the nose and ears.

carton ['kɑːtᵊn] **cartons** NOUN
a cardboard or plastic container

cartoon [kɑːˈtuːn] **cartoons** NOUN
1 a drawing or a series of drawings which are funny or make a point
2 a film in which the characters and scenes are drawn
cartoonist NOUN
[WORD HISTORY: from Italian CARTONE meaning 'sketch on stiff paper']

cartridge ['kɑːtrɪdʒ] **cartridges** NOUN
1 a tube containing a bullet and an explosive substance, used in guns
2 a thin plastic tube containing ink that you put in a pen

cartwheel ['kɑːtˌwiːl] **cartwheels** NOUN
an acrobatic movement in which you throw yourself sideways onto one hand and move round in a circle with arms and legs stretched until you land on your feet again

carve [kɑːv] **carves, carving, carved** VERB
1 To carve an object means to cut it out of a substance such as stone or wood.
THESAURUS
chisel: *the mason chiselling his stone*
cut: *a figure cut from marble*
engrave: *an engraved crystal goblet*
inscribe: *the words inscribed on his monument*
sculpt: *a sculpted clay figure*
2 To carve meat means to cut slices from it.

carving ['kɑːvɪŋ] **carvings** NOUN
a carved object

cascade [kæsˈkeɪd] **cascades, cascading, cascaded** NOUN
1 a waterfall or group of waterfalls
> VERB
2 To cascade means to flow downwards quickly. *e.g. Gallons of water cascaded from the attic.*

case [keɪs] **cases** NOUN
1 a particular situation, event, or example *e.g. a clear case of mistaken identity*
THESAURUS
example: *an example of what can go wrong*
illustration: *a clear illustration of this point*
instance: *a serious instance of corruption*
occasion: *the last occasion on which he appeared*
occurrence: *a frequent occurrence*
2 a container for something, or a suitcase *e.g. a camera case*
THESAURUS
box: *a chocolate box*

container: *a huge plastic container*
3 Doctors sometimes refer to a patient as a case.
4 Police detectives refer to a crime they are investigating as a case.
5 In an argument, the case for an idea is the reasons used to support it.
6 In law, a case is a trial or other inquiry.
THESAURUS
action: *a civil action for damages*
lawsuit: *the rising cost of defending a lawsuit*
proceedings: *criminal proceedings against the former leader*
trial: *Police lied at the trial.*
7 In grammar, the case of a noun or pronoun is the form of it which shows its relationship with other words in a sentence. *e.g. the accusative case*
> PHRASE
8 You say in case to explain something that you do because a particular thing might happen. *e.g. I didn't want to shout in case I startled you.*
9 You say in that case to show that you are assuming something said before is true. *e.g. In that case we won't do it.*

casement ['keɪsmənt] **casements** NOUN
a window that opens on hinges at one side

cash [kæʃ] **cashes, cashing, cashed** NOUN
1 Cash is money in notes and coins rather than cheques.
> VERB
2 If you cash a cheque, you take it to a bank and exchange it for money.
[WORD HISTORY: from Italian CASSA meaning 'money-box']

cashew ['kæʃuː] **cashews** NOUN
a curved, edible nut

cash flow NOUN
Cash flow is the money that a business makes and spends.

cashier [kæˈʃɪə] **cashiers** NOUN
the person that customers pay in a shop or get money from in a bank

cashmere ['kæʃmɪə] NOUN
Cashmere is very soft, fine wool from goats.

cash register **cash registers** NOUN
a machine in a shop which records sales, and where the money is kept

casing ['keɪsɪŋ] **casings** NOUN
a protective covering for something

casino [kəˈsiːnəʊ] **casinos** NOUN
a place where people go to play gambling games

cask [kɑːsk] **casks** NOUN
a wooden barrel

[WORD HISTORY: from Spanish CASCO meaning 'helmet']

casket ['kɑːskɪt] **caskets** NOUN
a small box for jewellery or other valuables
[WORD HISTORY: from Old French CASSETTE meaning 'little box']

casserole ['kæsə,rəʊl] **casseroles** NOUN
a dish made by cooking a mixture of meat and vegetables slowly in an oven; also used to refer to the pot a casserole is cooked in
[WORD HISTORY: from Old French CASSE meaning 'ladle' or 'dripping pan']

cassette [kæ'sɛt] **cassettes** NOUN
a small flat container with magnetic tape inside, which is used for recording and playing back sounds

cassette recorder **cassette recorders** NOUN
a machine used for recording and playing cassettes

cassock ['kæsək] **cassocks** NOUN
a long robe that is worn by some members of the clergy

cassowary ['kæsə,wɛərɪ] **cassowaries** NOUN
a large bird found in Australia with black feathers and a brightly coloured neck. Cassowaries cannot fly.

cast [kɑːst] **casts, casting, cast** NOUN
1 all the people who act in a play or film
2 an object made by pouring liquid into a mould and leaving it to harden *e.g. the casts of classical sculptures*
3 a stiff plaster covering put on broken bones to keep them still so that they heal properly
> VERB
4 To cast actors is to choose them for roles in a play or film.
5 When people cast their votes in an election, they vote.
6 To cast something is to throw it.
7 If you cast your eyes somewhere, you look there. *e.g. I cast my eyes down briefly.*
8 To cast an object is to make it by pouring liquid into a mould and leaving it to harden. *e.g. An image of him has been cast in bronze.*

cast off VERB
9 If you cast off, you untie the rope fastening a boat to a harbour or shore.

castanets [,kæstə'nɛts] PLURAL NOUN
Castanets are a Spanish musical instrument consisting of two small round pieces of wood that are clicked together with the fingers.

[WORD HISTORY: from Spanish CASTAÑETAS meaning 'little chestnuts']

castaway ['kɑːstə,weɪ] **castaways** NOUN
a person who has been shipwrecked

caste [kɑːst] **castes** NOUN
1 one of the four classes into which Hindu society is divided
2 Caste is a system of social classes decided according to family, wealth, and position.
[WORD HISTORY: from Portuguese CASTO meaning 'pure']

caster sugar or **castor sugar** ['kɑːstə] NOUN
Caster sugar is very fine white sugar used in cooking.

castigate ['kæstɪ,geɪt] **castigates, castigating, castigated** VERB; FORMAL
To castigate someone is to criticize them severely.

cast iron NOUN
1 Cast iron is iron which is made into objects by casting.
> ADJECTIVE
2 A cast-iron excuse or guarantee is absolutely certain and firm.

castle ['kɑːsəl] **castles** NOUN
1 (HISTORY) a large building with walls or ditches round it to protect it from attack
2 In chess, a castle is the same as a rook.

cast-off ['kɑːst,ɒf] **cast-offs** NOUN
a piece of outgrown or discarded clothing that has been passed on to someone else

castor ['kɑːstə] **castors;** also spelt **caster** NOUN
a small wheel fitted to furniture so that it can be moved easily

castor oil NOUN
Castor oil is a thick oil that comes from the seeds of the castor oil plant. It is used as a laxative.

castrate [kæ'streɪt] **castrates, castrating, castrated** VERB
To castrate a male animal is to remove its testicles so that it can no longer produce sperm.
castration NOUN

casual ['kæʒjʊəl] ADJECTIVE
1 happening by chance without planning *e.g. a casual remark*
● THESAURUS
accidental: *a verdict of accidental death*
chance: *a chance meeting*
incidental: *an incidental effect*
<<OPPOSITE *deliberate*

2 careless or without interest *e.g. a casual glance over his shoulder*

C

THESAURUS

careless: *careless remarks*
cursory: *a cursory glance*
nonchalant: *his nonchalant attitude to life*
offhand: *a deceptively offhand style*
relaxed: *a relaxed manner*
<<OPPOSITE *concerned*

3 Casual clothes are suitable for informal occasions.

4 Casual work is not regular or permanent.
casually ADVERB, **casualness** NOUN

casualty [ˈkæʒjʊəltɪ] **casualties** NOUN
a person killed or injured in an accident or war
e.g. Many of the casualties were office workers.

casuarina [ˌkæsjʊəˈriːnə] **casuarinas** NOUN
an Australian tree with jointed green branches

cat [kæt] **cats** NOUN
1 a small furry animal with whiskers, a tail and sharp claws, often kept as a pet

THESAURUS

feline: *Even the most cuddly feline has claws.*
kitty: *a kitty stuck up a tree*
moggy or moggie: British and New Zealand; slang *a grey, long-haired moggy*
pussy, puss, or pussycat: informal *a fluffy little pussycat*

2 any of the family of mammals that includes lions and tigers
[WORD HISTORY: from Latin CATTUS]

catacomb [ˈkætəˌkəʊm] **catacombs** NOUN
Catacombs are underground passages where dead bodies are buried.
[WORD HISTORY: from Latin CATACUMBAS, an underground cemetery near Rome]

catalogue [ˈkætəˌlɒg] **catalogues, cataloguing, catalogued** NOUN
1 a book containing pictures and descriptions of goods that you can buy in a shop or through the post

2 (**LIBRARY**) a list of things such as the objects in a museum or the books in a library

> VERB

3 To catalogue a collection of things means to list them in a catalogue.

catalyst [ˈkætəlɪst] **catalysts** NOUN
1 something that causes a change to happen *e.g. the catalyst which provoked civil war*

2 a substance that speeds up a chemical reaction without changing itself

catamaran [ˌkætəməˈræn] **catamarans** NOUN
a sailing boat with two hulls connected to each other
[WORD HISTORY: from Tamil KATTUMARAM meaning 'tied logs']

catapult [ˈkætəˌpʌlt] **catapults, catapulting, catapulted** NOUN
1 a Y-shaped object with a piece of elastic tied between the two top ends used for shooting small stones

> VERB

2 To catapult something is to throw it violently through the air.

3 If someone is catapulted into a situation, they find themselves unexpectedly in that situation.
e.g. Tony has been catapulted into the limelight.

cataract [ˈkætəˌrækt] **cataracts** NOUN
1 an area of the lens of someone's eye that has become white instead of clear, so that they cannot see properly

2 a large waterfall

catarrh [kəˈtɑː] NOUN
Catarrh is a condition in which you get a lot of mucus in your nose and throat.

catastrophe [kəˈtæstrəfɪ] **catastrophes** NOUN
a terrible disaster
catastrophic ADJECTIVE

catch [kætʃ] **catches, catching, caught** VERB
1 If you catch a ball moving in the air, you grasp hold of it when it comes near you.

2 To catch an animal means to trap it. *e.g. I caught ten fish.*

THESAURUS

capture: *Poachers had captured a gorilla.*
snare: *He'd snared a rabbit.*
trap: *Their aim was to trap drug-dealers.*

3 When the police catch criminals, they find them and arrest them.

THESAURUS

apprehend: *the force necessary to apprehend a suspect*
arrest: *Police arrested the gunman.*

4 If you catch someone doing something they should not be doing, you discover them doing it.
e.g. He caught me playing the church organ.

5 If you catch a bus or train, you get on it and travel somewhere.

6 If you catch a cold or a disease, you become infected with it.

7 If something catches on an object, it sticks to it or gets trapped. *e.g. The white fibres caught on the mesh.*

> NOUN

8 a device that fastens something

THESAURUS

bolt: *the sound of a bolt being slid open*
clasp: *the clasp of her handbag*

clip: *She took the clip out of her hair.*
latch: *You left the latch off the gate.*

9 a problem or hidden complication in something

⬤ **THESAURUS**
disadvantage: *The disadvantage is that this plant needs frequent watering.*
drawback: *The flat's only drawback was its size.*
snag: *The snag is that you have to pay in advance.*

catch on VERB
10 If you catch on to something, you understand it.
11 If something catches on, it becomes popular. *e.g. This drink has never really caught on in New Zealand.*

catch out VERB
12 To catch someone out is to trick them or trap them.

catch up VERB
13 To catch up with someone in front of you is to reach the place where they are by moving slightly faster than them.
14 To catch up with someone is also to reach the same level or standard as them.

catching ['kætʃɪŋ] ADJECTIVE
tending to spread very quickly *e.g. Measles is catching.*

catchy ['kætʃɪ] **catchier, catchiest**
ADJECTIVE
attractive and easily remembered *e.g. a catchy little tune*

catechism ['kætɪ,kɪzəm] **catechisms**
NOUN
a set of questions and answers about the main beliefs of a religion

categorical [,kætɪ'gɒrɪkəl] ADJECTIVE
absolutely certain and direct *e.g. a categorical denial*
categorically ADVERB

categorize ['kætɪgə,raɪz] **categorizes, categorizing, categorized;** also spelt
categorise VERB
To categorize things is to arrange them in different categories.

category ['kætɪgərɪ] **categories** NOUN
a set of things with a particular characteristic in common *e.g. Occupations can be divided into four categories.*

⬤ **THESAURUS**
class: *dividing the stars into six classes of brightness*
classification: *There are various classifications of genres or types of book.*
group: *She is one of the most promising players in her age group.*

set: *Pupils are divided into sets according to ability.*
sort: *What sort of school did you go to?*
type: *The majority of complaints received are of this type.*

cater ['keɪtə] **caters, catering, catered**
VERB
To cater for people is to provide them with what they need, especially food.

caterer ['keɪtərə] **caterers** NOUN
a person or business that provides food for parties and groups

caterpillar ['kætə,pɪlə] **caterpillars** NOUN
the larva of a butterfly or moth. It looks like a small coloured worm and feeds on plants
[WORD HISTORY: from Old French CATEPELOSE meaning 'hairy cat']

catharsis [kə'θɑːsɪs] **catharses** NOUN;
FORMAL
Catharsis is the release of strong emotions and feelings by expressing them through drama or literature.
[WORD HISTORY: from Greek KATHAIREIN meaning 'to purge' or 'to purify']

cathedral [kə'θiːdrəl] **cathedrals** NOUN
(HISTORY) an important church with a bishop in charge of it

Catholic ['kæθəlɪk] **Catholics** NOUN
1 (HISTORY) a Roman Catholic
> ADJECTIVE
2 If a person has catholic interests, they have a wide range of interests.
Catholicism NOUN
[WORD HISTORY: from Greek KATHOLIKOS meaning 'universal']

▋ When *Catholic* begins with a capital letter, it refers to the religion. When it begins with a small letter, it means 'covering a wide range'

cattle ['kætəl] PLURAL NOUN
Cattle are cows and bulls kept by farmers.

catty ['kætɪ] **cattier, cattiest** ADJECTIVE
unpleasant and spiteful
cattiness NOUN

catwalk ['kæt,wɔːk] **catwalks** NOUN
a narrow pathway that people walk along, for example over a stage

Caucasian [kɔː'keɪzɪən] **Caucasians** NOUN
a person belonging to the race of people with fair or light-brown skin
[WORD HISTORY: from CAUCASIA, a region in the former USSR]

caught [kɔːt] the past tense and past participle of
catch

cauldron ['kɔːldrən] **cauldrons** NOUN
a large, round metal cooking pot, especially one that sits over a fire

cauliflower ['kɒlɪˌflaʊə] **cauliflowers**
NOUN
a large, round, white vegetable surrounded by
green leaves

cause see page 128 for Word Web

causeway ['kɔːzˌweɪ] **causeways** NOUN
a raised path or road across water or marshland
[WORD HISTORY: from Latin CALCIATUS meaning
'paved with limestone']

caustic ['kɔːstɪk] ADJECTIVE
1 A caustic chemical can destroy substances. *e.g.*
caustic liquids such as acids

2 bitter or sarcastic *e.g. your caustic sense of
humour*

caution ['kɔːʃən] **cautions, cautioning,
cautioned** NOUN
1 Caution is great care which you take to avoid
danger. *e.g. You will need to proceed with caution.*

● THESAURUS
care: *Scissors can be safe for young children if used
with care.*
prudence: *A lack of prudence may lead to
problems.*

2 a warning *e.g. Sutton was let off with a caution.*
> VERB
3 If someone cautions you, they warn you,
usually not to do something again. *e.g. A man has
been cautioned by police.*
cautionary ADJECTIVE

● THESAURUS
reprimand: *He was reprimanded by a teacher for
talking in the corridor.*
tick off: *informal Traffic police ticked off a pensioner
for jumping a red light.*
warn: *My mother warned me not to talk to strangers.*

cautious ['kɔːʃəs] ADJECTIVE
acting very carefully to avoid danger *e.g. a
cautious approach*
cautiously ADVERB

● THESAURUS
careful: *Be extremely careful when on holiday
abroad.*
guarded: *a guarded response*
tentative: *a tentative approach*
wary: *small firms remain wary of committing
themselves to debt*
<<OPPOSITE *daring*

cavalcade [ˌkævəl'keɪd] **cavalcades** NOUN
a procession of people on horses or in cars or
carriages

cavalier [ˌkævə'lɪə] ADJECTIVE
arrogant and behaving without sensitivity *e.g. a
cavalier attitude to women*

cavalry ['kævəlrɪ] **cavalries** NOUN
The cavalry is the part of an army that uses

armoured vehicles or horses.

cave [keɪv] **caves, caving, caved** NOUN
1 a large hole in rock, that is underground or in
the side of a cliff
> VERB
2 If a roof caves in, it collapses inwards.

caveman ['keɪvˌmæn] **cavemen** NOUN
Cavemen were people who lived in caves in
prehistoric times.

cavern ['kævən] **caverns** NOUN
a large cave

cavernous ['kævənəs] ADJECTIVE
large, deep, and hollow *e.g. a cavernous warehouse*

caviar or **caviare** ['kævɪˌɑː] NOUN
Caviar is the tiny salted eggs of a fish called the
sturgeon.

cavity ['kævɪtɪ] **cavities** NOUN
a small hole in something solid *e.g. There were
dark cavities in his back teeth.*

cavort [kə'vɔːt] **cavorts, cavorting,
cavorted** VERB
When people cavort, they jump around excitedly.

caw [kɔː] **caws, cawing, cawed** VERB
When a crow or rook caws, it makes a harsh
sound.

cc
an abbreviation for 'cubic centimetres'

CD
an abbreviation for 'compact disc'

CD-ROM
CD-ROM is a method of storing video, sound, or
text on a compact disc which can be played on a
computer using a laser. CD-ROM is an
abbreviation for 'Compact Disc Read-Only
Memory'.

cease [siːs] **ceases, ceasing, ceased** VERB
1 If something ceases, it stops happening.

● THESAURUS
be over: *The captured planes will be kept until the
war is over.*
come to an end: *The strike came to an end.*
die away: *The sound died away and silence reigned.*
end: *The college year ends in March.*
finish: *The teaching day finished at around four
o'clock.*
stop: *The rain had stopped.*
<<OPPOSITE *begin*

2 If you cease to do something, or cease doing it,
you stop doing it.

● THESAURUS
desist from: *His wife never desisted from trying to
change his mind.*
discontinue: *Do not discontinue the treatment*

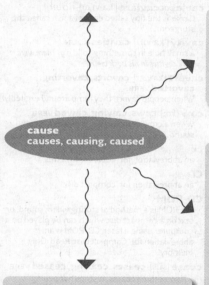

1 NOUN
The cause of something is the thing that makes it happen. *eg: the most common cause of back pain.*
● THESAURUS
origin: *the origin of the present war*
root: *We need to get to the root of the problem.*
source: *the source of the leak*

2 NOUN
an aim or principle which a group of people are working for *eg: dedication to the cause of peace.*
● THESAURUS
aim: *political aims*
ideal: *socialist ideals*
movement: *the women's movement*

cause
causes, causing, caused

3 NOUN
If you have cause for something, you have a reason for it *eg: They gave us no cause to believe that.*
● THESAURUS
basis: *There is no basis for this assumption.*
grounds: *discrimination on the grounds of race or religion*
justification: *There was no justification for what he was doing.*
motivation: *the motivation for his actions*
motive: *Police have ruled out robbery as a motive.*
reason: *You have every reason to be upset.*

4 VERB
To cause something is to make it happen *eg: This can cause delays.*
● THESAURUS
bring about: *We must try to bring about a better world.*
create: *The scheme may create even more confusion.*
generate: *the excitement generated by this film*
produce: *His comments produced a furious response.*
provoke: *a move that has provoked a storm of protest*

without consulting your doctor.
finish: As soon as he'd finished eating, he excused himself.
give up: smokers who give up before 30
stop: Stop throwing those stones!
suspend: The union suspended strike action this week.
<<OPPOSITE start

cease-fire ['si:s,faɪə] **cease-fires** NOUN
an agreement between groups that are fighting each other to stop for a period and discuss peace

ceaseless ['si:slɪs] ADJECTIVE
going on without stopping e.g. the ceaseless movement of the streets
ceaselessly ADVERB

cedar ['si:də] **cedars** NOUN
a large evergreen tree with wide branches and needle-shaped leaves

cede [si:d] **cedes, ceding, ceded** VERB
To cede something is to give it up to someone else. e.g. Haiti was ceded to France in 1697.

ceiling ['si:lɪŋ] **ceilings** NOUN
the top inside surface of a room

celebrate ['sɛlɪ,breɪt] **celebrates, celebrating, celebrated** VERB
1 If you celebrate or celebrate something, you do something special and enjoyable because of it. e.g. a party to celebrate the end of the exams

THESAURUS
commemorate: The anniversary of the composer's death was commemorated with a concert.
party: It's your birthday - let's party!
rejoice: My family rejoiced at the happy outcome to events.
<<OPPOSITE mourn

2 (RE) When a priest celebrates Mass, he performs the ceremonies of the Mass.

celebrated ['sɛlɪ,breɪtɪd] ADJECTIVE
famous e.g. the celebrated Italian mountaineer

celebration [,sɛlɪ'breɪʃən] **celebrations** NOUN
an event in honour of a special occasion
celebratory ADJECTIVE

THESAURUS
festival: a religious festival
festivity: the wedding festivities
gala: the Olympics' opening gala
party: a housewarming party

celebrity [sɪ'lɛbrɪtɪ] **celebrities** NOUN
a famous person

THESAURUS
big name: all the big names in rock and pop
name: some of the most famous names in modelling and show business

personality: a well-known radio and television personality
star: Not all football stars are ill-behaved louts.
superstar: a Hollywood superstar
VIP: such VIPs as Prince Charles and the former US President

celery ['sɛlərɪ] NOUN
Celery is a vegetable with long pale green stalks.

celestial [sɪ'lɛstɪəl] ADJECTIVE; FORMAL
concerning the sky or heaven e.g. The telescope is pointed at a celestial object.

celibate ['sɛlɪbɪt] ADJECTIVE
Someone who is celibate does not marry or have sex.
celibacy NOUN

cell [sɛl] **cells** NOUN
1 In biology, a cell is the smallest part of an animal or plant that can exist by itself. Each cell contains a nucleus.

2 a small room where a prisoner is kept in a prison or police station

3 a small group of people set up to work together as part of a larger organization

4 a device that converts chemical energy to electricity

cellar ['sɛlə] **cellars** NOUN
a room underneath a building, often used to store wine

cello ['tʃɛləʊ] **cellos** NOUN
a large musical stringed instrument which you play sitting down, holding the instrument upright with your knees
cellist NOUN

Cellophane ['sɛlə,feɪn] NOUN; TRADEMARK
Cellophane is thin, transparent plastic material used to wrap food or other things to protect them.

cellphone ['sɛl,fəʊn] **cellphones** NOUN
a small portable telephone

cellular ['sɛljʊlə] ADJECTIVE
Cellular means relating to the cells of animals or plants.

cellular phone cellular phones NOUN the same as **cellphone**

celluloid ['sɛljʊ,lɔɪd] NOUN
Celluloid is a type of plastic which was once used to make photographic film.

Celsius ['sɛlsɪəs] NOUN
Celsius is a scale for measuring temperature in which water freezes at 0 degrees (0°C) and boils at 100 degrees (100°C). Celsius is the same as 'Centigrade'.

Celtic ['kɛltɪk] ADJECTIVE
A Celtic language is one of a group of languages

that includes Gaelic and Welsh.

cement [sɪˈmɛnt] **cements, cementing, cemented** NOUN

1 Cement is a fine powder made from limestone and clay, which is mixed with sand and water to make concrete.

> VERB

2 To cement things is to stick them together with cement or cover them with cement.

3 Something that cements a relationship makes it stronger. *e.g. to cement relations between them*

cemetery [ˈsɛmɪtrɪ] **cemeteries** NOUN

an area of land where dead people are buried

cenotaph [ˈsɛnəˌtɑːf] **cenotaphs** NOUN

a monument built in memory of dead people, especially soldiers buried elsewhere

[WORD HISTORY: from Greek KENOS + TAPHOS meaning 'empty tomb']

censor [ˈsɛnsə] **censors, censoring, censored** NOUN

1 a person officially appointed to examine books or films and to ban parts that are considered unsuitable

> VERB

2 If someone censors a book or film, they cut or ban parts of it that are considered unsuitable for the public.

censorship NOUN

censure [ˈsɛnʃə] **censures, censuring, censured** NOUN

1 Censure is strong disapproval of something.

⬤ THESAURUS

blame: *I'm the one who'll get the blame if things go wrong.*

condemnation: *There was widespread condemnation of Saturday's killings.*

criticism: *This policy had repeatedly come under strong criticism.*

disapproval: *His action had been greeted with almost universal disapproval.*

reproach: *Those in public life should be beyond reproach.*

> VERB

2 To censure someone is to criticize them severely.

⬤ THESAURUS

condemn: *He condemned the players for lack of ability and application.*

criticize: *The regime has been harshly criticized for its human rights violations.*

denounce: *The letter called for civil rights, but did not openly denounce the regime.*

reproach: *She had not even reproached him for breaking his promise.*

census [ˈsɛnsəs] **censuses** NOUN

an official survey of the population of a country

cent [sɛnt] **cents** NOUN

a unit of currency. In the USA, a cent is worth one hundredth of a dollar; in Europe, it is worth one hundredth of a Euro

centaur [ˈsɛntɔː] **centaurs** NOUN

a creature in Greek mythology with the top half of a man and the lower body and legs of a horse

centenary [sɛnˈtiːnərɪ] **centenaries** NOUN

the 100th anniversary of something

centi- PREFIX

'Centi-' is used to form words that have 'hundred' as part of their meaning *e.g. centimetre*

Centigrade [ˈsɛntɪˌgreɪd] Centigrade is another name for **Celsius.**

▮ Scientists say and write *Celsius* rather than *Centigrade*

centilitre [ˈsɛntɪˌliːtə] **centilitres** NOUN

a unit of liquid volume equal to one hundredth of a litre

centime [ˈsɒnˌtiːm] **centimes** NOUN

a unit of currency used in Switzerland and some other countries, and formerly used in France and Belgium

centimetre [ˈsɛntɪˌmiːtə] **centimetres** NOUN

(MATHS) a unit of length equal to ten millimetres or one hundredth of a metre

centipede [ˈsɛntɪˌpiːd] **centipedes** NOUN

a long, thin insect-like creature with many pairs of legs

central [ˈsɛntrəl] ADJECTIVE

1 in or near the centre of an object or area *e.g. central ceiling lights*

2 main or most important *e.g. the central idea of this work*

centrally ADVERB, **centrality** NOUN

Central America NOUN

Central America is another name for the Isthmus of Panama, the area of land joining North America to South America.

central heating NOUN

Central heating is a system of heating a building in which water or air is heated in a tank and travels through pipes and radiators round the building.

centralize [ˈsɛntrəˌlaɪz] **centralizes, centralizing, centralized;** also spelt **centralise** VERB

To centralize a system is to bring the organization of it under the control of one central group.

centralization NOUN

centre [ˈsɛntə] **centres, centring, centred** NOUN

1 the middle of an object or area

● THESAURUS
core: *the earth's core*
focus: *Her children are the main focus of her life.*
heart: *the heart of the problem*
hub: *The kitchen is the hub of most households.*
middle: *in the middle of the back row*
<<OPPOSITE *edge*

2 a building where people go for activities, meetings, or help *e.g. a health centre*

3 Someone or something that is the centre of attention attracts a lot of attention.

> VERB
4 To centre something is to move it so that it is balanced or at the centre of something else.

5 If something centres on or around a particular thing, that thing is the main subject of attention. *e.g. The discussion centred on his request.*

● THESAURUS
concentrate: *Scientists are concentrating their efforts on finding a cure.*
focus: *Attention is likely to focus on sales growth.*
revolve: *Since childhood, her life has revolved around tennis.*

centrifugal [sɛnˈtrɪfjʊɡəl] ADJECTIVE
In physics, centrifugal force is the force that makes rotating objects move outwards.
[WORD HISTORY: from Latin CENTRUM + FUGERE meaning 'to flee from the centre']

centripetal [sɛnˈtrɪpɪtəl] ADJECTIVE
In physics, centripetal force is the force that makes rotating objects move inwards.
[WORD HISTORY: from Latin CENTRUM + PETERE meaning 'to seek the centre']

centurion [sɛnˈtjʊərɪən] **centurions** NOUN
a Roman officer in charge of a hundred soldiers

century [ˈsɛntʃərɪ] **centuries** NOUN
1 a period of one hundred years
2 In cricket, a century is one hundred runs scored by a batsman.

ceramic [sɪˈræmɪk] **ceramics** NOUN
1 Ceramic is a hard material made by baking clay to a very high temperature.
2 Ceramics is the art of making objects out of clay.

cereal [ˈsɪərɪəl] **cereals** NOUN
1 a food made from grain, often eaten with milk for breakfast
2 a plant that produces edible grain, such as wheat or oats
[WORD HISTORY: from Latin CEREALIS meaning 'concerning the growing of grain']

cerebral [ˈsɛrɪbrəl] ADJECTIVE; FORMAL
relating to the brain *e.g. a cerebral haemorrhage*

cerebral palsy [ˈpɔːlzɪ] NOUN
Cerebral palsy is an illness caused by damage to a baby's brain, which makes its muscles and limbs very weak.

ceremonial [ˌsɛrɪˈməʊnɪəl] ADJECTIVE
relating to a ceremony *e.g. ceremonial dress*
ceremonially ADVERB

ceremony [ˈsɛrɪmənɪ] **ceremonies** NOUN
1 a set of formal actions performed at a special occasion or important public event *e.g. his recent coronation ceremony*

● THESAURUS
observance: *a Memorial Day observance*
pomp: *His departure was celebrated with suitable pomp.*
rite: *a fertility rite*
ritual: *a Summer Solstice ritual*
service: *The President attended the morning service.*
2 Ceremony is very formal and polite behaviour. *e.g. He hung up without ceremony.*

● THESAURUS
decorum: *a responsibility to behave with decorum*
etiquette: *the rules of diplomatic etiquette*
formality: *his lack of stuffy formality*
niceties: *social niceties*
protocol: *minor breaches of protocol*

certain [ˈsɜːtən] ADJECTIVE
1 definite or reliable *e.g. He is certain to be in Italy.*
● THESAURUS
definite: *It's too soon to give a definite answer.*
established: *an established medical fact*
guaranteed: *Success is not guaranteed.*
inevitable: *If she wins her case, it is inevitable that other people will sue the company.*
known: *It is not known when the bomb was planted.*
sure: *Sharpe's leg began to ache, a sure sign of rain.*
undeniable: *undeniable proof of guilt*
<<OPPOSITE *uncertain*

2 having no doubt in your mind
● THESAURUS
clear: *It is important to be clear about what you are doing.*
confident: *I am confident that everything will come out right.*
convinced: *He was convinced that I was part of the problem.*
definite: *Mary is very definite about this fact.*
sure: *She was no longer sure how she felt about him.*
positive: *I'm as positive as I can be about it.*
satisfied: *People must be satisfied that the treatment is safe.*
<<OPPOSITE *uncertain*

3 You use 'certain' to refer to a specific person or thing. *e.g. certain aspects of the job*
4 You use 'certain' to suggest that a quality is noticeable but not obvious. *e.g. There's a certain resemblance to Joe.*

certainly ['sɜːt^ənlɪ] ADVERB

1 without doubt e.g. *My boss was certainly interested.*

● THESAURUS

definitely: *Something should definitely be done.*
undeniably: *Bringing up a baby is undeniably hard work.*
undoubtedly: *He is undoubtedly a great player.*
unquestionably: *He is unquestionably a star.*
without doubt: *The refugees are, without doubt, extremely vulnerable.*

2 of course e.g. *'Will you be there?'* — *'Certainly'.*

certainty ['sɜːt^əntɪ] **certainties** NOUN

1 Certainty is the state of being certain.

2 something that is known without doubt e.g. *There are no certainties and no guarantees.*

certificate [sə'tɪfɪkɪt] **certificates** NOUN
a document stating particular facts, for example of someone's birth or death e.g. *a marriage certificate*

certify ['sɜːtɪ,faɪ] **certifies, certifying, certified** VERB

1 To certify something means to declare formally that it is true. e.g. *certifying the cause of death*

2 To certify someone means to declare officially that they are insane.

cervix ['sɜːvɪks] **cervixes** or **cervices** NOUN; TECHNICAL
the entrance to the womb at the top of the vagina
cervical ADJECTIVE

cessation [sɛ'seɪʃən] NOUN; FORMAL
The cessation of something is the stopping of it. e.g. *a swift cessation of hostilities*

cf.
cf. means 'compare'. It is written after something in a text to mention something else which the reader should compare with what has just been written.

CFC CFCs NOUN
CFCs are manufactured chemicals that are used in aerosol sprays. They damage the ozone layer. CFC is an abbreviation for 'chlorofluorocarbon'.

chaff [tʃɑːf] NOUN
Chaff is the outer parts of grain separated from the seeds by beating.

chaffinch ['tʃæfɪntʃ] **chaffinches** NOUN
a small European bird with black and white wings

chagrin ['ʃægrɪn] NOUN; FORMAL
Chagrin is a feeling of annoyance or disappointment.

chain [tʃeɪn] **chains, chaining, chained** NOUN

1 a number of metal rings connected together in a line e.g. *a bicycle chain*

2 a number of things in a series or connected to each other e.g. *a chain of shops*

> VERB

3 If you chain one thing to another, you fasten them together with a chain. e.g. *They had chained themselves to railings.*

chain saw chain saws NOUN
a large saw with teeth fixed in a chain that is driven round by a motor

chain-smoke ['tʃeɪn,sməʊk] **chain-smokes, chain-smoking, chain-smoked** VERB
To chain-smoke is to smoke cigarettes continually.

chair [tʃɛə] **chairs, chairing, chaired** NOUN

1 a seat with a back and four legs for one person

2 the person in charge of a meeting who decides when each person may speak

> VERB

3 The person who chairs a meeting is in charge of it.

chair lift chair lifts NOUN
a line of chairs that hang from a moving cable and carry people up and down a mountain

chairman ['tʃɛəmən] **chairmen** NOUN

1 the person in charge of a meeting who decides when each person may speak

2 the head of a company or committee
chairperson NOUN, **chairwoman** NOUN, **chairmanship** NOUN

> Some people don't like to use *chairman* when talking about a woman. You can use *chair* or *chairperson* to talk about a man or a woman

chalet ['ʃæleɪ] **chalets** NOUN
a wooden house with a sloping roof, especially in a mountain area or a holiday camp

chalice ['tʃælɪs] **chalices** NOUN
a gold or silver cup used in churches to hold the Communion wine

chalk [tʃɔːk] **chalks, chalking, chalked** NOUN

1 Chalk is a soft white rock. Small sticks of chalk are used for writing or drawing on a blackboard.

> VERB

2 To chalk up a result is to achieve it. e.g. *He chalked up his first win.*
chalky ADJECTIVE

challenge ['tʃælɪndʒ] **challenges, challenging, challenged** NOUN

1 something that is new and exciting but requires a lot of effort e.g. *It's a new challenge at the right time in my career.*

2 a suggestion from someone to compete with them

THESAURUS
dare: *He'd do almost anything for a dare.*

3 A challenge to something is a questioning of whether it is correct or true. *e.g. a challenge to authority*

> VERB

4 If someone challenges you, they suggest that you compete with them in some way.

THESAURUS
dare: *I dare you to ask him.*
defy: *He looked at me as if he was defying me to argue.*

5 If you challenge something, you question whether it is correct or true.
challenger NOUN, **challenging** ADJECTIVE

THESAURUS
dispute: *He disputed the charge.*
question: *questioning the jury's verdict*

chamber ['tʃeɪmbə] **chambers** NOUN
1 a large room, especially one used for formal meetings *e.g. the Council Chamber*

2 a group of people chosen to decide laws or administrative matters

3 a hollow place or compartment inside something, especially inside an animal's body or inside a gun *e.g. the chambers of the heart*

chambermaid ['tʃeɪmbə,meɪd]
chambermaids NOUN
a woman who cleans and tidies rooms in a hotel

chameleon [kə'mi:lɪən] **chameleons**
NOUN
a lizard which is able to change the colour of its skin to match the colour of its surroundings
[WORD HISTORY: from Greek KHAMAI + LEŌN meaning 'ground lion']

chamois leather ['ʃæmɪ] **chamois**
leathers NOUN
a soft leather cloth used for polishing

champagne [ʃæm'peɪn] **champagnes**
NOUN
Champagne is a sparkling white wine made in France.

champion ['tʃæmpɪən] **champions,**
championing, championed NOUN
1 a person who wins a competition

THESAURUS
hero: *the goalscoring hero of the British hockey team*
title holder: *He became the youngest world title holder at the age of 22.*
victor: *the British Grand Prix victors*
winner: *The winner was a horse called Baby Face.*

2 someone who supports or defends a cause or principle *e.g. a champion of women's causes*

THESAURUS
advocate: *He was a strong advocate of free trade.*
defender: *a strong defender of human rights*
guardian: *The party wants to be seen as a guardian of traditional values.*
protector: *She sees him as a protector and provider.*

> VERB

3 Someone who champions a cause or principle supports or defends it.
[WORD HISTORY: from Latin CAMPUS meaning 'battlefield']

THESAURUS
defend: *his courage in defending religious and civil rights*
fight for: *Our Government should be fighting for an end to child poverty.*
promote: *You don't have to sacrifice the environment to promote economic growth.*
stick up for: *informal He has shown courage in sticking up for civil liberties.*
support: *The vice president has always supported the people of New York.*
uphold: *upholding the artist's right to creative freedom*

championship ['tʃæmpɪənʃɪp]
championships NOUN
a competition to find the champion of a sport

chance [tʃɑːns] **chances, chancing,**
chanced NOUN
1 The chance of something happening is how possible or likely it is. *e.g. There's a chance of rain later.*

THESAURUS
likelihood: *the likelihood of infection*
odds: *What are the odds of that happening?*
possibility: *the possibility of pay cuts*
probability: *a probability of victory*
prospect: *There is little prospect of peace.*

2 an opportunity to do something *e.g. your chance to be a TV star!*

THESAURUS
occasion: *I had no occasion to speak to her that day.*
opening: *an opening for finding a peaceful outcome to the conflict*
opportunity: *an opportunity to go abroad to study*
time: *There was no time to think.*

3 a possibility that something dangerous or unpleasant may happen *e.g. Don't take chances, he's armed.*

4 Chance is also the way things happen unexpectedly without being planned. *e.g. I only found out by chance.*

THESAURUS
accident: *a strange accident of fate*
coincidence: *It was no coincidence that she arrived just then.*

fortune: *a change of fortune*
luck: *His injury was just bad luck.*

> VERB

5 If you chance something, you try it although you are taking a risk.

chancellor [ˈtʃɑːnsələ] **chancellors** NOUN

1 the head of government in some European countries

2 In Britain, the Chancellor is the Chancellor of the Exchequer.

3 the honorary head of a university

Chancellor of the Exchequer NOUN
in Britain, the minister responsible for finance and taxes

chandelier [ʃændɪˈlɪə] **chandeliers** NOUN
an ornamental light fitting which hangs from the ceiling

change [tʃeɪndʒ] **changes, changing, changed** NOUN

1 a difference or alteration in something *e.g. Steven soon noticed a change in Penny's attitude.*

● THESAURUS

alteration: *some alterations in your diet*
difference: *a noticeable difference in his behaviour*
modification: *Some minor modifications were required.*
transformation: *the transformation of a wilderness into a garden*

2 a replacement of something by something else *e.g. a change of clothes*

3 Change is money you get back when you have paid more than the actual price of something.

> VERB

4 When something changes or when you change it, it becomes different. *e.g. It changed my life.*

● THESAURUS

alter: *There is no prospect of the decision being altered.*
convert: *a plan to convert his spare room into an office*
moderate: *They persuaded him to moderate his views.*
modify: *He refused to modify his behaviour.*
reform: *his plans to reform the economy*
transform: *The landscape has been transformed.*

5 If you change something, you exchange it for something else.

● THESAURUS

barter: *bartering wheat for cotton and timber*
exchange: *the chance to sell back or exchange goods*
interchange: *Meat can be interchanged with pulses as a source of protein.*
replace: *His smile was replaced by a frown.*
substitute: *You can substitute honey for the sugar.*

swap: *Let's swap places.*
trade: *They traded land for goods and money.*

6 When you change, you put on different clothes.

7 To change money means to exchange it for smaller coins of the same total value, or to exchange it for foreign currency.

changeable [ˈtʃeɪndʒəbəl] ADJECTIVE
likely to change all the time

● THESAURUS

erratic: *erratic driving*
fickle: *Fashion is a fickle business.*
irregular: *an irregular heartbeat*
unpredictable: *unpredictable behaviour*
unstable: *The political situation is unstable.*
variable: *a variable rate of interest*
volatile: *a volatile atmosphere*
<<OPPOSITE constant

changeover [ˈtʃeɪndʒˌəʊvə] **changeovers** NOUN
a change from one system or activity to another *e.g. the changeover between day and night*

channel [ˈtʃænəl] **channels, channelling, channelled** NOUN

1 a wavelength used to receive programmes broadcast by a television or radio station; also the station itself *e.g. I was watching the other channel.*

2 a passage along which water flows or along which something is carried

3 The Channel or the English Channel is the stretch of sea between England and France.

4 a method of achieving something *e.g. We have tried to do things through the right channels.*

> VERB

5 To channel something such as money or energy means to direct it in a particular way. *e.g. Their efforts are being channelled into worthy causes.*

chant [tʃɑːnt] **chants, chanting, chanted** NOUN

1 a group of words repeated over and over again *e.g. a rousing chant*

2 a religious song sung on only a few notes

> VERB

3 If people chant a group of words, they repeat them over and over again. *e.g. Crowds chanted his name.*

Chanukah [ˈhɑːnəkə] another spelling of **Hanukkah**

chaos [ˈkeɪɒs] NOUN
Chaos is a state of complete disorder and confusion.
chaotic ADJECTIVE

chap [tʃæp] **chaps, chapping, chapped** NOUN

1 INFORMAL a man
> VERB
2 If your skin chaps, it becomes dry and cracked, usually as a result of cold or wind.

chapel ['tʃæpᵊl] **chapels** NOUN
1 a section of a church or cathedral with its own altar
2 a type of small church
[WORD HISTORY: from Latin CAPELLA meaning 'small cloak'; originally used of the place where St Martin's cloak was kept as a relic]

chaperone ['ʃæpəˌrəʊn] **chaperones** (said **shap**-per-rone); also spelt **chaperon** NOUN
an older woman who accompanies a young unmarried woman on social occasions, or any person who accompanies a group of younger people

chaplain ['tʃæplɪn] **chaplains** NOUN
a member of the Christian clergy who regularly works in a hospital, school, or prison
chaplaincy NOUN

chapter ['tʃæptə] **chapters** NOUN
1 one of the parts into which a book is divided
2 a particular period in someone's life or in history

char [tʃɑː] **chars, charring, charred** VERB
If something chars, it gets partly burned and goes black.
charred ADJECTIVE

character ['kærɪktə] **characters** NOUN
1 all the qualities which combine to form the personality or atmosphere of a person or place

◉ THESAURUS
make-up: *Determination has always been a part of his make-up.*
nature: *a sunny nature*
personality: *an outgoing personality*
temperament: *his impulsive temperament*

2 A person or place that has character has an interesting, attractive, or admirable quality. *e.g. an inn of great character and simplicity*

◉ THESAURUS
honour: *He has acted with honour.*
integrity: *a man of integrity*
strength: *He had the strength to turn down the offer.*

3 (DRAMA) The characters in a film, play, or book are the people in it.
4 a person *e.g. an odd character*
5 a letter, number, or other written symbol

characteristic [ˌkærɪktəˈrɪstɪk] **characteristics** NOUN
1 a quality that is typical of a particular person or thing *e.g. Silence is the characteristic of the place.*

◉ THESAURUS
attribute: *a normal attribute of human behaviour*
feature: *a feature of the local culture*
property: *This liquid has many unique properties.*
quality: *leadership qualities*
trait: *personality traits*

> ADJECTIVE
2 Characteristic means typical of a particular person or thing. *e.g. Two things are very characteristic of his driving.*
characteristically ADVERB

◉ THESAURUS
distinctive: *a distinctive voice*
distinguishing: *no distinguishing marks*
typical: *his typical British modesty*
<<OPPOSITE *uncharacteristic*

characterize ['kærɪktəˌraɪz] **characterizes, characterizing, characterized**; also spelt **characterise** VERB
A quality that characterizes something is typical of it. *e.g. a condition characterized by muscle stiffness*

characterless ['kærɪktələs] ADJECTIVE
dull and uninteresting *e.g. a tiny characterless flat*

charade [ʃəˈrɑːd] **charades** NOUN
a ridiculous and unnecessary activity or pretence
[WORD HISTORY: from Provençal CHARRADO meaning 'chat']

charcoal ['tʃɑːˌkəʊl] NOUN
Charcoal is a black form of carbon made by burning wood without air, used as a fuel and also for drawing.

charge [tʃɑːdʒ] **charges, charging, charged** VERB
1 If someone charges you money, they ask you to pay it for something you have bought or received. *e.g. The company charged 150 pounds on each loan.*

◉ THESAURUS
ask (for): *The artist was asking £6,000 for each painting.*
bill: *Are you going to bill me for this?*
levy: *Taxes should not be levied without the authority of Parliament.*

2 To charge someone means to accuse them formally of having committed a crime.
3 To charge a battery means to pass an electrical current through it to make it store electricity.
4 To charge somewhere means to rush forward, often to attack someone. *e.g. The rhino charged at her.*

◉ THESAURUS
dash: *She dashed in from the garden.*
rush: *A schoolgirl rushed into the burning flat to help an old man.*
stampede: *The crowd stampeded.*
storm: *He stormed into the shop, demanding to see the manager.*

C

> NOUN

5 the price that you have to pay for something

⬤ THESAURUS
cost: *Badges are available at a cost of £2.50.*
fee: *Pay your solicitor's fees.*
payment: *I'll do it in return for a small payment.*
price: *We negotiated a price for the service.*

6 a formal accusation that a person is guilty of a crime and has to go to court

7 To have charge or be in charge of someone or something means to be responsible for them and be in control of them.

8 an explosive put in a gun or other weapon

9 An electrical charge is the amount of electricity that something carries.

charger ['tʃɑːdʒə] **chargers** NOUN
a device for charging or recharging batteries

chariot ['tʃærɪət] **chariots** NOUN
a two-wheeled open vehicle pulled by horses

charisma [kə'rɪzmə] NOUN
Charisma is a special ability to attract or influence people by your personality.
charismatic ADJECTIVE

charity ['tʃærɪtɪ] **charities** NOUN
1 an organization that raises money to help people who are ill, poor, or disabled
2 Charity is money or other help given to poor, disabled, or ill people. *e.g. to help raise money for charity*
3 Charity is also a kind, sympathetic attitude towards people.
charitable ADJECTIVE

charlatan ['ʃɑːlətᵊn] **charlatans** NOUN
someone who pretends to have skill or knowledge that they do not really have

charm [tʃɑːm] **charms, charming, charmed** NOUN
1 Charm is an attractive and pleasing quality that some people and things have. *e.g. a man of great personal charm*

⬤ THESAURUS
allure: *the allure of Egypt*
appeal: *confident of his appeal to women*
attraction: *the attractions of living by the sea*
fascination: *It is hard to explain the fascination of this place.*
magnetism: *a man of enormous magnetism*

2 a small ornament worn on a bracelet

3 a magical spell or an object that is supposed to bring good luck

> VERB
4 If you charm someone, you use your charm to please them.

⬤ THESAURUS
bewitch: *bewitched by her beauty*
captivate: *The crowd was captivated by her honesty.*
delight: *a style of music that has delighted audiences*
entrance: *entranced by her smile*

charmer ['tʃɑːmə] **charmers** NOUN
someone who uses their charm to influence people

charming ['tʃɑːmɪŋ] ADJECTIVE
very pleasant and attractive *e.g. a rather charming man*
charmingly ADVERB

chart [tʃɑːt] **charts, charting, charted** NOUN
1 a diagram or table showing information *e.g. He noted the score on his chart.*
2 a map of the sea or stars

> VERB
3 If you chart something, you observe and record it carefully.

charter ['tʃɑːtə] **charters, chartering, chartered** NOUN
1 a document stating the rights or aims of a group or organization, often written by the government *e.g. the new charter for commuters*

> VERB
2 To charter transport such as a plane or boat is to hire it for private use.
chartered ADJECTIVE

chase [tʃeɪs] **chases, chasing, chased** VERB
1 If you chase someone or something, you run after them in order to catch them.

⬤ THESAURUS
hunt: *He fled to Portugal after being hunted by police.*
pursue: *She pursued the man who had snatched her bag.*

2 If you chase someone, you force them to go somewhere else.

⬤ THESAURUS
drive: *The troops drove the rebels into the jungle.*
hound: *He was hounded out of his job.*

> NOUN
3 the activity of chasing or hunting someone or something *e.g. a high-speed car chase*

chasm ['kæzəm] **chasms** NOUN
1 a deep crack in the earth's surface
2 a very large difference between two ideas or groups of people *e.g. the chasm between rich and poor in America*

chassis ['ʃæsɪ] **chassis** NOUN
the frame on which a vehicle is built

■ The plural of *chassis* is also *chassis*

chaste [tʃeɪst] ADJECTIVE; OLD-FASHIONED
not having sex with anyone outside marriage
chastity NOUN

chastise [tʃæs'taɪz] **chastises, chastising,
chastised** VERB; FORMAL
If someone chastises you, they criticize you or
punish you for something that you have done.

chat [tʃæt] **chats, chatting, chatted** NOUN
1 a friendly talk with someone, usually about
things that are not very important

● THESAURUS
conversation: *a telephone conversation*
gossip: *Don't you enjoy a good gossip?*
natter: informal *Let's get together for a natter some
time.*
talk: *We will have a talk about it later.*

> VERB
2 When people chat, they talk to each other in a
friendly way.

● THESAURUS
gossip: *We gossiped into the night.*
natter: informal *His mother would natter to anyone.*
talk: *She's very easy to talk to.*

chat up VERB INFORMAL
3 If you chat up someone, you talk to them in a
friendly way, because you are attracted to them.

chateau [ˈʃætəʊ] **chateaux** NOUN
a large country house or castle in France

chatroom [ˈtʃæt,ruːm] **chatrooms** NOUN
an Internet site where users have group
discussions using e-mail

chatter [ˈtʃætə] **chatters, chattering,
chattered** VERB
1 When people chatter, they talk very fast.
2 If your teeth are chattering, they are knocking
together and making a clicking noise because
you are cold.

> NOUN
3 Chatter is a lot of fast unimportant talk.

chatty [ˈtʃætɪ] **chattier, chattiest** ADJECTIVE
talkative and friendly

chauffeur [ˈʃəʊfə] **chauffeurs** NOUN
a person whose job is to drive another
person's car

chauvinist [ˈʃəʊvɪ,nɪst] **chauvinists** NOUN
1 a person who thinks their country is always
right
2 A male chauvinist is a man who believes that
men are superior to women.
chauvinistic ADJECTIVE, **chauvinism** NOUN

cheap [tʃiːp] **cheaper, cheapest** ADJECTIVE
1 costing very little money

● THESAURUS
bargain: *selling at bargain prices*
economical: *These cars are very economical to run.*
inexpensive: *an inexpensive wine*
reasonable: *His fees were quite reasonable.*
<<OPPOSITE *expensive*

2 inexpensive but of poor quality

● THESAURUS
inferior: *an inferior imitation*
second-rate: *second-rate equipment*
tawdry: *tawdry souvenirs*

3 A cheap joke or cheap remark is unfair and
unkind.
cheaply ADVERB

cheat [tʃiːt] **cheats, cheating, cheated**
VERB
1 If someone cheats, they do wrong or unfair
things to win or get something that they want.

● THESAURUS
con: informal *He conned his way into a job.*
deceive: *Investors were deceived by a scam.*
defraud: *charges of conspiracy to defraud the
government*
dupe: *Stamp collectors were duped into buying
fakes.*
fleece: *He fleeced her out of thousands of pounds.*
rip off: slang *ticket touts ripping off soccer fans*
swindle: *two executives who swindled their
employer*

2 If you are cheated of or out of something, you
do not get what you are entitled to.

> NOUN
3 a person who cheats

check [tʃek] **checks, checking, checked**
VERB
1 To check something is to examine it in order to
make sure that everything is all right.

● THESAURUS
check out: informal *Check out the financial figures.*
examine: *He examined her passport and stamped it.*
inspect: *the right to inspect company files*
test: *The drug must be tested in clinical trials.*

2 To check the growth or spread of something is
to make it stop. *e.g. a policy to check fast population
growth*

● THESAURUS
control: *a measure to control illegal mining*
curb: *reforms which aim to curb spending*
halt: *an attempt to halt the spread of the disease*
inhibit: *factors which inhibit growth*
restrain: *the need to restrain wage rises*
stop: *measures to stop the trade in ivory*

> NOUN
3 an inspection to make sure that everything is
all right

● **THESAURUS**
examination: *a medical examination*
inspection: *a routine inspection of the premises*
test: *a test for cancer*

4 Checks are different coloured squares which form a pattern.

> **PHRASE**

5 If you keep something **in check**, you keep it under control. *e.g. She kept her emotions in check.*

> **ADJECTIVE**

6 Check or checked means marked with a pattern of squares. *e.g. check design*

check out VERB

7 If you check something out, you inspect it and find out whether everything about it is right.

checkmate ['tʃɛk,meɪt] NOUN
In chess, checkmate is a situation where one player cannot stop their king being captured and so loses the game.
[WORD HISTORY: from Arabic SHAH MAT meaning 'the King is dead']

checkout ['tʃɛk,aʊt] **checkouts** NOUN
a counter in a supermarket where the customers pay for their goods

checkpoint ['tʃɛk,pɔɪnt] **checkpoints** NOUN
a place where traffic has to stop in order to be checked

checkup ['tʃɛk,ʌp] **checkups** NOUN
an examination by a doctor to see if you are healthy

cheek [tʃiːk] **cheeks** NOUN
1 Your cheeks are the sides of your face below your eyes.
2 Cheek is speech or behaviour that is rude or disrespectful. *e.g. an expression of sheer cheek*

● **THESAURUS**
audacity: *I was shocked at the audacity of the gangsters.*
gall: *She had the gall to claim she had been victimized.*
impudence: *My sister had the impudence to go out wearing my clothes.*
insolence: *The pupil was excluded for insolence.*
nerve: *He had the nerve to ask me to prove who I was.*
rudeness: *Mother was cross at Tom's rudeness.*

cheeky ['tʃiːkɪ] **cheekier, cheekiest**
ADJECTIVE
rather rude and disrespectful

● **THESAURUS**
impertinent: *an impertinent question*
impudent: *his rude and impudent behaviour*
insolent: *a defiant, almost insolent look*

rude: *She was often rude to her mother.*
<<OPPOSITE *polite*

cheer [tʃɪə] **cheers, cheering, cheered**
VERB
1 When people cheer, they shout with approval or in order to show support for a person or team.

> **NOUN**

2 a shout of approval or support

cheer up VERB
3 When you cheer up, you feel more cheerful.

cheerful ['tʃɪəfʊl] ADJECTIVE
1 happy and in good spirits *e.g. I had never seen her so cheerful.*

● **THESAURUS**
bright: *"May I help you?" said a bright voice.*
buoyant: *in a buoyant mood*
cheery: *a cheery nature*
happy: *a confident, happy child*
jaunty: *a jaunty tune*
jolly: *a jolly, easy-going man*
light-hearted: *They were light-hearted and enjoyed life.*
merry: *a burst of merry laughter*
<<OPPOSITE *miserable*

2 bright and pleasant-looking *e.g. a cheerful and charming place*
cheerfully ADVERB, **cheerfulness** NOUN

cheerio [,tʃɪərɪ'əʊ] INTERJECTION
Cheerio is a friendly way of saying goodbye.

cheery ['tʃɪərɪ] **cheerier, cheeriest**
ADJECTIVE
happy and cheerful *e.g. He gave me a cheery nod.*

● **THESAURUS**
cheerful: *They are both very cheerful in spite of their circumstances.*
chirpy: *She sounded quite chirpy on the phone.*
good-humoured: *Charles was brave and remarkably good-humoured.*
happy: *Marina was a confident, happy child.*
jolly: *She was a jolly, kind-hearted woman.*
upbeat: *Neil's colleagues said he was in a joking, upbeat mood.*
sunny: *a nice lad with a sunny disposition*
<<OPPOSITE *gloomy*

cheese [tʃiːz] **cheeses** NOUN
a hard or creamy food made from milk

cheesecake ['tʃiːz,keɪk] **cheesecakes**
NOUN
a dessert made of biscuit covered with cream cheese

cheetah ['tʃiːtə] **cheetahs** NOUN
a wild animal like a large cat with black spots
[WORD HISTORY: from Sanskrit CITRA + KAYA meaning 'speckled body']

chef [ʃɛf] **chefs** NOUN
a head cook in a restaurant or hotel

chemical ['kɛmɪkəl] **chemicals** NOUN
(SCIENCE)
1 Chemicals are substances manufactured by chemistry.
> ADJECTIVE
2 involved in chemistry or using chemicals *e.g. chemical weapons*
chemically ADVERB

chemist ['kɛmɪst] **chemists** NOUN
1 a person who is qualified to make up drugs and medicines prescribed by a doctor
2 a shop where medicines and cosmetics are sold
3 a scientist who does research in chemistry

chemistry ['kɛmɪstri] NOUN
Chemistry is the scientific study of substances and the ways in which they change when they are combined with other substances.

chemotherapy [ˌkiːməʊˈθɛrəpi] NOUN
Chemotherapy is a way of treating diseases such as cancer by using chemicals.

cheque [tʃɛk] **cheques** NOUN
a printed form on which you write an amount of money that you have to pay. You sign the cheque and your bank pays the money from your account.

chequered ['tʃɛkəd] ADJECTIVE
1 covered with a pattern of squares
2 A chequered career is a varied career that has both good and bad parts.

cherish ['tʃɛrɪʃ] **cherishes, cherishing, cherished** VERB
1 If you cherish something, you care deeply about it and want to keep it or look after it lovingly.
2 If you cherish a memory or hope, you have it in your mind and care deeply about it. *e.g. I cherish the good memories I have of him.*

cherry ['tʃɛri] **cherries** NOUN
1 a small, juicy fruit with a red or black skin and a hard stone in the centre
2 a tree that produces cherries

cherub ['tʃɛrəb] **cherubs** or **cherubim** NOUN
an angel, shown in pictures as a plump, naked child with wings
cherubic ADJECTIVE

chess [tʃɛs] NOUN
Chess is a board game for two people in which each player has 16 pieces and tries to move his or her pieces so that the other player's king cannot escape.

chessboard ['tʃɛsˌbɔːd] **chessboards** NOUN
A chessboard is a board divided into 64 squares of two alternating colours on which chess is played.

chest [tʃɛst] **chests** NOUN
1 the front part of your body between your shoulders and your waist
2 a large wooden box with a hinged lid

chestnut ['tʃɛsˌnʌt] **chestnuts** NOUN
1 Chestnuts are reddish-brown nuts that grow inside a prickly green outer covering.
2 a tree that produces these nuts
> ADJECTIVE
3 Something that is chestnut is reddish-brown.

chest of drawers [drɔːz] **chests of drawers** NOUN
a piece of furniture with drawers in it, used for storing clothes

chew [tʃuː] **chews, chewing, chewed** VERB
When you chew something, you use your teeth to break it up in your mouth before swallowing it.
chewy ADJECTIVE
 THESAURUS
crunch: *She crunched the ice cube loudly.*
gnaw: *He sat and gnawed at an apple.*
munch: *Sheep were munching the leaves.*

chewing gum ['tʃuːɪŋ] NOUN
Chewing gum is a kind of sweet that you chew for a long time, but which you do not swallow.

chic [ʃiːk] ADJECTIVE
elegant and fashionable *e.g. a chic restaurant*

chick [tʃɪk] **chicks** NOUN
a young bird

chicken ['tʃɪkɪn] **chickens, chickening, chickened** NOUN
1 a bird kept on a farm for its eggs and meat; also the meat of this bird *e.g. roast chicken*
> VERB
2 INFORMAL If you chicken out of something, you do not do it because you are afraid.

chickenpox ['tʃɪkɪnˌpɒks] NOUN
Chickenpox is an illness which produces a fever and blister-like spots on the skin.

chicory ['tʃɪkəri] NOUN
Chicory is a plant with bitter leaves that are used in salads.

chide [tʃaɪd] **chides, chiding, chided** VERB;
OLD-FASHIONED, INFORMAL
To chide someone is to tell them off.

chief [tʃiːf] **chiefs** NOUN
1 the leader of a group or organization
 THESAURUS
boss: *He cannot stand his boss.*

chieftain: *the legendary British chieftain, King Arthur*
director: *the financial director of the company*
governor: *The incident was reported to the prison governor.*
head: *heads of government from 100 countries*
leader: *the leader of the Conservative Party*
manager: *a retired bank manager*

> **ADJECTIVE**

2 most important *e.g. the chief source of oil*
chiefly ADVERB

● THESAURUS

foremost: *one of the world's foremost scholars of ancient Indian culture*
key: *He is expected to be the key witness at the trial.*
main: *one of the main tourist areas of Amsterdam*
prevailing: *the prevailing attitude towards women in this society*
primary: *His language difficulties were the primary cause of his other problems.*
prime: *The police will see me as the prime suspect!*
principal: *The principal reason for my change of mind is this.*

chieftain ['tʃiːftən] **chieftains** NOUN
the leader of a tribe or clan

chiffon [ʃɪ'fɒn] NOUN
Chiffon is a very thin lightweight cloth made of silk or nylon.

chihuahua [tʃɪ'wɑːwɑː] **chihuahuas** NOUN
a breed of very small dog with short hair and pointed ears

chilblain ['tʃɪl,bleɪn] **chilblains** NOUN
a sore, itchy swelling on a finger or toe

child [tʃaɪld] **children** NOUN

1 a young person who is not yet an adult

● THESAURUS

ankle-biter: Australian and New Zealand; slang *I knew him when he was just an ankle-biter.*
baby: *She took care of me when I was a baby.*
bairn: Scottish *a two-year-old bairn*
infant: *young mums with infants in prams*
juvenile: *a prison for juveniles*
kid: informal *They've got three kids.*
minor: *charged with selling cigarettes to minors*
offspring: *parents choosing shoes for their offspring*
toddler: *a toddler in a pushchair*
tot: *The tot was too young to know what was happening.*
youngster: *I was only a youngster in 1965.*
<<OPPOSITE *adult*

2 Someone's child is their son or daughter.

childbirth ['tʃaɪld,bɜːθ] NOUN
Childbirth is the act of giving birth to a child.

childhood ['tʃaɪldhʊd] **childhoods** NOUN
Someone's childhood is the time when they are a child.

childish ['tʃaɪldɪʃ] ADJECTIVE
immature and foolish *e.g. I don't have time for childish arguments.*
childishly ADVERB, **childishness** NOUN

● THESAURUS

immature: *She is emotionally immature.*
infantile: *infantile jokes*
juvenile: *juvenile behaviour*
puerile: *a puerile sense of humour*
<<OPPOSITE *mature*

If you call someone *childish*, you think they are immature or foolish. If you call them *childlike*, you think they are innocent like a young child

childless ['tʃaɪld,ləs] ADJECTIVE
having no children

childlike ['tʃaɪld,laɪk] ADJECTIVE
like a child in appearance or behaviour *e.g. childlike enthusiasm*

childminder ['tʃaɪld,maɪndə]
childminders NOUN
a person who is qualified and paid to look after other people's children while they are at work

Chilean ['tʃɪlɪən] **Chileans** ADJECTIVE

1 belonging or relating to Chile

> **NOUN**

2 someone who comes from Chile

chill [tʃɪl] **chills, chilling, chilled** VERB

1 To chill something is to make it cold. *e.g. Chill the cheesecake.*

2 If something chills you, it makes you feel worried or frightened. *e.g. The thought chilled her.*

> **NOUN**

3 a feverish cold

4 a feeling of cold *e.g. the chill of the night air*

chilli ['tʃɪlɪ] **chillies** NOUN
the red or green seed pod of a type of pepper which has a very hot, spicy taste

chilly ['tʃɪlɪ] **chillier, chilliest** ADJECTIVE

1 rather cold *e.g. the chilly November breeze*

2 unfriendly and without enthusiasm *e.g. a chilly reception*

chilly-bin ['tʃɪlɪ,bɪn] **chilly-bins** NOUN;
INFORMAL
In New Zealand English, a container for keeping food and drink cool that can be carried.

chime [tʃaɪm] **chimes, chiming, chimed**
VERB
When a bell chimes, it makes a clear ringing sound.

chimney ['tʃɪmnɪ] **chimneys** NOUN
a vertical pipe or other hollow structure above a fireplace or furnace through which smoke from a fire escapes

[WORD HISTORY: from Greek KAMINOS meaning 'fireplace' or 'oven']

chimpanzee [ˌtʃɪmpæn'ziː] **chimpanzees** NOUN
a small ape with dark fur that lives in forests in Africa

chin [tʃɪn] **chins** NOUN
the part of your face below your mouth

china ['tʃaɪnə] **chinas** NOUN
1 China is items like cups, saucers, and plates made from very fine clay.
2 INFORMAL In South African English, a china is a friend.

● THESAURUS
buddy: informal *We've been buddies since we were kids.*
chum: informal *He went on holiday with his two best chums.*
crony: old-fashioned *She is always surrounded by her cronies.*
friend: *lifelong friends*
mate: British; informal *Come on mate, things aren't that bad.*
pal: informal *He'd never let a pal down.*

Chinese [tʃaɪ'niːz] ADJECTIVE
1 belonging or relating to China
> NOUN
2 someone who comes from China
3 Chinese refers to any of a group of related languages and dialects spoken by Chinese people.

chink [tʃɪŋk] **chinks** NOUN
1 a small, narrow opening *e.g. a chink in the roof*
2 a short, light, ringing sound, like one made by glasses touching each other

chintz [tʃɪnts] NOUN
Chintz is a type of brightly patterned cotton fabric.
[WORD HISTORY: from Hindi CHINT meaning 'brightly coloured']

chip [tʃɪp] **chips, chipping, chipped** NOUN
1 Chips are thin strips of fried potato.
2 In electronics, a chip is a tiny piece of silicon inside a computer which is used to form electronic circuits.
3 a small piece broken off an object, or the mark made when a piece breaks off
4 In some gambling games, chips are counters used to represent money.
> VERB
5 If you chip an object, you break a small piece off it.

chipboard ['tʃɪpˌbɔːd] NOUN
Chipboard is a material made from wood scraps pressed together into hard sheets.

chipmunk ['tʃɪpˌmʌŋk] **chipmunks** NOUN
a small rodent with a striped back

chiropodist [kɪ'rɒpədɪst] **chiropodists** NOUN
a person whose job is treating people's feet
chiropody NOUN

chirp [tʃɜːp] **chirps, chirping, chirped** VERB
When a bird chirps, it makes a short, high-pitched sound.

chisel ['tʃɪzəl] **chisels, chiselling, chiselled** NOUN
1 a tool with a long metal blade and a sharp edge at the end which is used for cutting and shaping wood, stone, or metal
> VERB
2 To chisel wood, stone, or metal is to cut or shape it using a chisel.

chivalry ['ʃɪvəlrɪ] NOUN
Chivalry is polite and helpful behaviour, especially by men towards women.
chivalrous ADJECTIVE
[WORD HISTORY: from Latin CABALLARIUS meaning 'horseman']

chive [tʃaɪv] **chives** NOUN
Chives are grasslike hollow leaves that have a mild onion flavour.

chlorine ['klɔːriːn] NOUN
Chlorine is a poisonous greenish-yellow gas with a strong, unpleasant smell. It is used as a disinfectant for water, and to make bleach.

chloroform ['klɔːrəˌfɔːm] NOUN
Chloroform is a colourless liquid with a strong, sweet smell used in cleaning products.

chlorophyll ['klɔːrəfɪl] NOUN
Chlorophyll is a green substance in plants which enables them to use the energy from sunlight in order to grow.

chock-a-block or **chock-full** ['tʃɒkəˌblɒk] or ['tʃɒkˌfʊl] ADJECTIVE
completely full

chocolate ['tʃɒkəlɪt] **chocolates** NOUN
1 Chocolate is a sweet food made from cacao seeds.
2 a sweet made of chocolate
> ADJECTIVE
3 dark brown
[WORD HISTORY: from Aztec XOCOC + ATL meaning 'bitter water']

choice [tʃɔɪs] **choices** NOUN
1 a range of different things that are available to choose from *e.g. a wider choice of treatments*

● THESAURUS
range: *a range of sun-care products*

selection: *an interesting selection of recipes*
variety: *a variety of candidates from which to choose*

2 something that you choose *e.g. You've made a good choice.*

3 Choice is the power or right to choose. *e.g. I had no choice.*

● THESAURUS

alternative: *He said he could not see any alternative.*
option: *He was given the option of going to jail or paying a fine.*
say: *We don't have a say in the company's decisions.*

choir [kwaɪə] **choirs** NOUN
(MUSIC) a group of singers, for example in a church

choke [tʃəʊk] **chokes, choking, choked** VERB
1 If you choke, you stop being able to breathe properly, usually because something is blocking your windpipe. *e.g. the diner who choked on a fish bone*

2 If things choke a place, they fill it so much that it is blocked or clogged up. *e.g. The canal was choked with old tyres.*

choko ['tʃəʊkəʊ] **chokos** NOUN
a fruit that is shaped like a pear and used as a vegetable in Australia and New Zealand

cholera ['kɒlərə] NOUN
Cholera is a serious disease causing severe diarrhoea and vomiting. It is caused by infected food or water.

cholesterol [kə'lɛstə,rɒl] NOUN
Cholesterol is a substance found in all animal fats, tissues, and blood.

chook [tʃʊk] **chooks** NOUN; INFORMAL
In Australian and New Zealand English, a chicken.

choose [tʃuːz] **chooses, choosing, chose, chosen** VERB
To choose something is to decide to have or do it. *e.g. He chose to live in Kenya.*

● THESAURUS

opt for: *He opted for early retirement.*
pick: *She was picked for the debating team.*
select: *She paused to select another cookie from the box.*
take: *She took the option he offered her.*

choosy ['tʃuːzɪ] **choosier, choosiest** ADJECTIVE
fussy and difficult to satisfy *e.g. You can't be too choosy about jobs.*

chop [tʃɒp] **chops, chopping, chopped** VERB
1 To chop something is to cut it with quick, heavy strokes using an axe or a knife.

● THESAURUS

cut: *Cut the vegetables up.*
fell: *43,000 square miles of tropical forest are felled each year.*
hack: *They hacked away at the undergrowth.*
lop: *Somebody had lopped the heads off our tulips.*

> NOUN

2 a small piece of lamb or pork containing a bone, usually cut from the ribs

chopper ['tʃɒpə] **choppers** NOUN; INFORMAL
a helicopter

choppy ['tʃɒpɪ] **choppier, choppiest** ADJECTIVE
Choppy water has a lot of waves because it is windy.

chopstick ['tʃɒpstɪk] **chopsticks** NOUN
Chopsticks are a pair of thin sticks used by people in the Far East for eating food.

choral ['kɔːrəl] ADJECTIVE
relating to singing by a choir *e.g. choral music*

chord [kɔːd] **chords** NOUN
(MUSIC) a group of three or more musical notes played together

chore [tʃɔː] **chores** NOUN
an uninteresting job that has to be done *e.g. the chore of cleaning*

choreography [,kɒrɪ'ɒgrəfɪ] NOUN
Choreography is the art of composing dance steps and movements.
choreographer NOUN

chortle ['tʃɔːtəl] **chortles, chortling, chortled** VERB
To chortle is to laugh with amusement.

chorus ['kɔːrəs] **choruses, chorusing, chorused** NOUN
1 a large group of singers; also a piece of music for a large group of singers

2 a part of a song which is repeated after each verse

> VERB

3 If people chorus something, they all say or sing it at the same time.
[WORD HISTORY: from Greek KHOROS, the group of actors who gave the commentary in Classical plays]

Christ [kraɪst] PROPER NOUN
Christ is the name for Jesus. Christians believe that Jesus is the son of God.

christen ['krɪsᵊn] **christens, christening, christened** VERB
When a baby is christened, it is named by a member of the clergy in a religious ceremony.

Christian ['krɪstʃən] **Christians** NOUN (RE)

1 a person who believes in Jesus Christ and his teachings

> ADJECTIVE

2 relating to Christ and his teachings *e.g. the Christian faith*

3 good, kind, and considerate
Christianity NOUN

Christian name Christian names NOUN
the name given to someone when they were born or christened

Christmas ['krɪsməs] **Christmases** NOUN
the Christian festival celebrating the birth of Christ, falling on December 25th

chromatic [krə'mætɪk] ADJECTIVE
(MUSIC) A chromatic scale is one which is based on an octave of 12 semitones.

chrome [krəʊm] NOUN
Chrome is metal plated with chromium, a hard grey metal.

chromosome ['krəʊmə,səʊm]
chromosomes NOUN
In biology, a chromosome is a part of a cell which contains genes that determine the characteristics of an animal or plant.

chronic ['krɒnɪk] ADJECTIVE
lasting a very long time or never stopping *e.g. a chronic illness*
chronically ADVERB

chronicle ['krɒnɪkəl] **chronicles, chronicling, chronicled** NOUN
1 a record of a series of events described in the order in which they happened

> VERB

2 To chronicle a series of events is to record or describe them in the order in which they happened.

chronological [,krɒnə'lɒdʒɪkəl] ADJECTIVE
(HISTORY) arranged in the order in which things happened *e.g. Tell me the whole story in chronological order.*
chronologically ADVERB

chronology [krə'nɒlədʒɪ] NOUN
(HISTORY) The chronology of events is the order in which they happened.
[WORD HISTORY: from Greek KHRONOS meaning 'time' and LEGEIN meaning 'to say']

chrysalis ['krɪsəlɪs] **chrysalises** NOUN
a butterfly or moth when it is developing from being a caterpillar to being a fully grown adult

chrysanthemum [krɪ'sænθəməm]
chrysanthemums NOUN
a plant with large, brightly coloured flowers

chubby ['tʃʌbɪ] **chubbier, chubbiest**
ADJECTIVE
plump and round *e.g. his chubby cheeks*

chuck [tʃʌk] **chucks, chucking, chucked**
VERB; INFORMAL
To chuck something is to throw it casually.

chuckle ['tʃʌkəl] **chuckles, chuckling, chuckled** VERB
When you chuckle, you laugh quietly.

chug [tʃʌg] **chugs, chugging, chugged** VERB
When a machine or engine chugs, it makes a continuous dull thudding sound.

chum [tʃʌm] **chums** NOUN; INFORMAL
a friend

chunk [tʃʌŋk] **chunks** NOUN
a thick piece of something

chunky ['tʃʌŋkɪ] **chunkier, chunkiest**
ADJECTIVE
Someone who is chunky is broad and heavy but usually short.

church [tʃɜːtʃ] **churches** NOUN
1 a building where Christians go for religious services and worship

2 In the Christian religion, a church is one of the groups with their own particular beliefs, customs, and clergy. *e.g. the Catholic Church*
[WORD HISTORY: from Greek KURIAKON meaning 'master's house']

Church of England ['ɪŋglənd] NOUN
The Church of England is the Anglican church in England, where it is the state church, with the King or Queen as its head.

churchyard ['tʃɜːtʃ,jɑːd] **churchyards** NOUN
an area of land around a church, often used as a graveyard

churn [tʃɜːn] **churns** NOUN
a container used for making milk or cream into butter

chute [ʃuːt] **chutes** NOUN
a steep slope or channel used to slide things down *e.g. a rubbish chute*

chutney ['tʃʌtnɪ] NOUN
Chutney is a strong-tasting thick sauce made from fruit, vinegar, and spices.

cider ['saɪdə] NOUN
Cider is an alcoholic drink made from apples.

cigar [sɪ'gɑː] **cigars** NOUN
a roll of dried tobacco leaves which people smoke
[WORD HISTORY: from Mayan SICAR meaning 'to smoke']

cigarette [,sɪgə'rɛt] **cigarettes** NOUN
a thin roll of tobacco covered in thin paper which people smoke

cinder ['sɪndə] **cinders** NOUN
Cinders are small pieces of burnt material left

C

after something such as wood or coal has burned.

cinema ['sɪnɪmə] **cinemas** NOUN

1 a place where people go to watch films

2 Cinema is the business of making films.

cinnamon ['sɪnəmən] NOUN
Cinnamon is a sweet spice which comes from the bark of an Asian tree.

cipher ['saɪfə] **ciphers**; also spelt **cypher** NOUN
a secret code or system of writing used to send secret messages

circa ['sɜːkə] PREPOSITION; FORMAL
about or approximately; used especially before dates *e.g. portrait of a lady, circa 1840*

circle ['sɜːkᵊl] **circles, circling, circled** NOUN

1 a completely regular round shape. Every point on its edge is the same distance from the centre.

2 a group of people with the same interest or profession *e.g. a character well known in yachting circles*

3 an area of seats on an upper floor of a theatre

> VERB

4 To circle is to move round and round as though going round the edge of a circle. *e.g. A police helicopter circled above.*

circuit ['sɜːkɪt] **circuits** NOUN

1 any closed line or path, often circular, for example a racing track; also the distance round this path *e.g. three circuits of the 26-lap race remaining*

2 An electrical circuit is a complete route around which an electric current can flow.

circular ['sɜːkjʊlə] **circulars** ADJECTIVE

1 in the shape of a circle

2 A circular argument or theory is not valid because it uses a statement to prove a conclusion and the conclusion to prove the statement.

> NOUN

3 a letter or advert sent to a lot of people at the same time
circularity NOUN

circulate ['sɜːkjʊˌleɪt] **circulates, circulating, circulated** VERB

1 (SCIENCE) When something circulates or when you circulate it, it moves easily around an area. *e.g. an open position where the air can circulate freely*

2 When you circulate something among people, you pass it round or tell it to all the people. *e.g. We circulate a regular newsletter.*

● THESAURUS
distribute: *distributing leaflets*
propagate: *They propagated their political ideas.*
spread: *spreading malicious gossip*

circulation [ˌsɜːkjʊˈleɪʃən] **circulations** NOUN

1 The circulation of something is the act of circulating it or the action of its circulating. *e.g. traffic circulation*

2 The circulation of a newspaper or magazine is the number of copies that are sold of each issue.

3 (SCIENCE) Your circulation is the movement of blood through your body.

circumcise ['sɜːkəmˌsaɪz] **circumcises, circumcising, circumcised** VERB
If a boy or man is circumcised, the foreskin at the end of his penis is removed. This is carried out mainly as part of a Muslim or Jewish religious ceremony.
circumcision NOUN

circumferences [səˈkʌmfərəns] NOUN
(MATHS) The circumference of a circle is its outer line or edge; also the length of this line.

circumstance ['sɜːkəmstəns] **circumstances** NOUN

1 The circumstances of a situation or event are the conditions that affect what happens. *e.g. He did well in the circumstances.*

2 Someone's circumstances are their position and conditions in life. *e.g. Her circumstances had changed.*

circus ['sɜːkəs] **circuses** NOUN
a show given by a travelling group of entertainers such as clowns, acrobats, and specially trained animals

cistern ['sɪstən] **cisterns** NOUN
a tank in which water is stored, for example one in the roof of a house or above a toilet

citadel ['sɪtədᵊl] **citadels** NOUN
a fortress in or near a city

cite [saɪt] **cites, citing, cited** VERB

1 FORMAL If you cite something, you quote it or refer to it. *e.g. He cited a letter written by Newall.*

2 If someone is cited in a legal action, they are officially called to appear in court.

citizen ['sɪtɪzᵊn] **citizens** NOUN
(HISTORY) The citizens of a country or city are the people who live in it or belong to it. *e.g. American citizens.*

citizenship ['sɪtɪzənˌʃɪp] NOUN
the status of being a citizen, with all the rights and duties that go with it *e.g. I'm applying for Australian citizenship.*

citrus fruit ['sɪtrəs] **citrus fruits** NOUN
Citrus fruits are juicy, sharp-tasting fruits such as oranges, lemons, and grapefruit.

city ['sɪtɪ] **cities** NOUN
a large town where many people live and work

⊜ **THESAURUS**
metropolis: *a busy metropolis*
town: *the oldest town in Europe*

civic ['sɪvɪk] ADJECTIVE
relating to a city or citizens *e.g. the Civic Centre*

civil ['sɪvəl] ADJECTIVE
1 relating to the citizens of a country *e.g. civil rights*

2 relating to people or things that are not connected with the armed forces *e.g. the history of civil aviation*

3 polite
civilly ADVERB, **civility** NOUN

civil engineering NOUN
Civil engineering is the design and construction of roads, bridges, and public buildings.

civilian [sɪ'vɪljən] **civilians** NOUN
a person who is not in the armed forces

civilization [ˌsɪvɪlaɪ'zeɪʃən] **civilizations;**
also spelt **civilisation** NOUN **(HISTORY)**
1 a society which has a highly developed organization and culture *e.g. the tale of a lost civilization*

2 Civilization is an advanced state of social organization and culture.

civilized ['sɪvɪˌlaɪzd] ADJECTIVE
1 A civilized society is one with a developed social organization and way of life.

⊜ **THESAURUS**
cultured: *a mature and cultured nation*
enlightened: *this enlightened century*

2 A civilized person is polite and reasonable.

civil servant civil servants NOUN
a person who works in the civil service

civil service NOUN
The civil service is the government departments responsible for the administration of a country.

civil war civil wars NOUN
a war between groups of people who live in the same country

cl
an abbreviation for 'centilitres'

clad [klæd] ADJECTIVE; LITERARY
Someone who is clad in particular clothes is wearing them.

claim [kleɪm] **claims, claiming, claimed**
VERB

1 If you claim that something is the case, you say that it is the case. *e.g. He claims to have lived in the same house all his life.*

⊜ **THESAURUS**
allege: *He is alleged to have killed a man.*
assert: *The defendants continued to assert their innocence.*
hold: *She holds that these measures are unnecessary.*
insist: *They insisted that they had no money.*
maintain: *I still maintain that I am not guilty.*
profess: *She professed to hate her nickname.*

2 If you claim something, you ask for it because it belongs to you or you have a right to it. *e.g. Cartier claimed the land for the King of France.*

> NOUN
3 a statement that something is the case, or that you have a right to something *e.g. She will make a claim for damages.*

⊜ **THESAURUS**
allegation: *allegations of theft*
assertion: *his assertion that he did not plan to remarry*

claimant ['kleɪmənt] **claimants** NOUN
someone who is making a claim, especially for money

clairvoyant [klɛə'vɔɪənt] **clairvoyants**
ADJECTIVE
1 able to know about things that will happen in the future

> NOUN
2 a person who is, or claims to be, clairvoyant
[WORD HISTORY: from French CLAIR + VOYANT meaning 'clear-seeing']

clam [klæm] **clams** NOUN
a kind of shellfish

clamber ['klæmbə] **clambers, clambering, clambered** VERB
If you clamber somewhere, you climb there with difficulty.

clammy ['klæmɪ] **clammier, clammiest**
ADJECTIVE
unpleasantly damp and sticky *e.g. clammy hands*

clamour ['klæmə] **clamours, clamouring, clamoured** VERB
1 If people clamour for something, they demand it noisily or angrily. *e.g. We clamoured for an explanation.*

> NOUN
2 Clamour is noisy or angry shouts or demands by a lot of people.

clamp [klæmp] **clamps, clamping, clamped** NOUN
1 an object with movable parts that are used to hold two things firmly together

> VERB

2 To clamp things together is to fasten them or hold them firmly with a clamp.

clamp down on VERB

3 To clamp down on something is to become stricter in controlling it. *e.g. The Queen has clamped down on all expenditure.*

clan [klæn] **clans** NOUN
a group of families related to each other by being descended from the same ancestor

clandestine [klæn'dɛstɪn] ADJECTIVE
secret and hidden *e.g. a clandestine meeting with friends*

clang [klæŋ] **clangs, clanging, clanged**
VERB
When something metal clangs or when you clang it, it makes a loud, deep sound.

clank [klæŋk] **clanks, clanking, clanked**
VERB
If something metal clanks, it makes a loud noise.

clap [klæp] **claps, clapping, clapped** VERB
1 When you clap, you hit your hands together loudly to show your appreciation.
2 If you clap someone on the back or shoulder, you hit them in a friendly way.
3 If you clap something somewhere, you put it there quickly and firmly. *e.g. I clapped a hand over her mouth.*

> NOUN

4 a sound made by clapping your hands
5 A clap of thunder is a sudden loud noise of thunder.

clapper ['klæpə] **clappers** NOUN
A clapper is a small piece of metal that hangs inside a bell and strikes the side to make the bell sound.

claret ['klærət] **clarets** NOUN
a type of red wine, especially one from the Bordeaux region of France

clarify ['klærɪˌfaɪ] **clarifies, clarifying, clarified** VERB
(EXAM TERM) To clarify something is to make it clear and easier to understand. *e.g. Discussion will clarify your thoughts.*
clarification NOUN

clarinet [ˌklærɪ'nɛt] **clarinets** NOUN
a woodwind instrument with a straight tube and a single reed in its mouthpiece

clarity ['klærɪtɪ] NOUN
The clarity of something is its clearness.

clash [klæʃ] **clashes, clashing, clashed**
VERB
1 If people clash with each other, they fight or argue.

● THESAURUS
battle: *In one town thousands of people battled with police officers.*
fight: *two rival gangs fighting in the streets*
quarrel: *My brother quarrelled with my father.*
wrangle: *Delegates wrangled over the future of the organization.*

2 Ideas or styles that clash are so different that they do not go together.

● THESAURUS
conflict: *He held opinions which sometimes conflicted with my own.*
contradict: *Cut-backs like these surely contradict the Government's commitment to education.*
differ: *The two leaders differed on several issues.*
disagree: *Our managers disagreed on several policy issues.*
go against: *Changes are being made which go against my principles.*
jar: *They had always been good together and their temperaments seldom jarred.*

3 If two events clash, they happen at the same time so you cannot go to both.
4 When metal objects clash, they hit each other with a loud noise.

> NOUN

5 a fight or argument

● THESAURUS
battle: *a gun battle between police and drug traffickers*
conflict: *attempts to prevent a conflict between workers and management*
confrontation: *This issue could lead to a military confrontation.*
fight: *He had had a fight with Smith and bloodied his nose.*
struggle: *a struggle between competing political factions*
skirmish: informal *Border skirmishes between the two countries were common.*
squabble: *There have been minor squabbles about phone bills.*

6 A clash of ideas, styles, or events is a situation in which they do not go together.
7 a loud noise made by metal objects when they hit each other

clasp [klɑːsp] **clasps, clasping, clasped**
VERB
1 To clasp something means to hold it tightly or fasten it. *e.g. He clasped his hands.*

● THESAURUS
clutch: *She was clutching a photograph.*
embrace: *People were crying for joy and embracing each other.*
grip: *She gripped the rope.*
hold: *He held the pistol in his right hand.*

hug: *She hugged her legs tight to her chest.*
press: *I pressed the child closer to my heart and prayed.*
squeeze: *He longed to just scoop her up and squeeze her.*

> NOUN

2 a fastening such as a hook or catch

● THESAURUS

buckle: *He wore a belt with a large brass buckle.*
catch: *She fiddled with the catch of her bag.*
clip: *She took the clip out of her hair.*
fastener: *a product range which includes nails, woodscrews, and fasteners*
fastening: *The sundress has a neat back zip fastening.*

class [klɑːs] classes, classing, classed
NOUN

1 A class of people or things is a group of them of a particular type or quality. *e.g. the old class of politicians*

● THESAURUS

category: *different categories of taxpayer*
genre: *films of the horror genre*
grade: *the lowest grade of staff*
group: *a plan to help people in this group*
kind: *the biggest prize of its kind in the world*
set: *The fashionable set all go to this club.*
sort: *several articles of this sort*
type: *various types of vegetable*

2 a group of pupils or students taught together, or a lesson that they have together

3 Someone who has class is elegant in appearance or behaviour.

> VERB

4 To class something means to arrange it in a particular group or to consider it as belonging to a particular group. *e.g. They are officially classed as visitors.*

● THESAURUS

categorize: *His films are hard to categorize.*
classify: *Carrots are also classified as a fruit.*
designate: *The house is designated as a national monument.*
grade: *This ski-run is graded as easy.*
rank: *She is ranked in the world's top 50 players.*
rate: *He rates the film highly.*

classic ['klæsɪk] classics ADJECTIVE

1 typical and therefore a good model or example of something *e.g. a classic case of misuse*

2 of very high quality *e.g. one of the classic films of all time*

3 simple in style and form *e.g. the classic dinner suit*

> NOUN

4 something of the highest quality *e.g. one of the*

great classics of rock music

5 Classics is the study of Latin and Greek, and the literature of ancient Greece and Rome.

classical ['klæsɪkᵊl] ADJECTIVE

1 traditional in style, form, and content *e.g. classical ballet*

2 Classical music is serious music considered to be of lasting value.

3 characteristic of the style of ancient Greece and Rome *e.g. Classical friezes decorate the walls.*
classically ADVERB

classified ['klæsɪˌfaɪd] ADJECTIVE
officially declared secret by the government *e.g. access to classified information*

classify ['klæsɪˌfaɪ] classifies, classifying, classified VERB
(LIBRARY) To classify things is to arrange them into groups with similar characteristics. *e.g. We can classify the differences into three groups.*
classification NOUN

● THESAURUS

arrange: *Arrange the books in neat piles.*
categorize: *This film is hard to categorize.*
grade: *musical pieces graded according to difficulty*
rank: *He was ranked among Britain's best-known millionaires.*
sort: *sorting the material into folders*

classroom ['klɑːsˌruːm] classrooms NOUN
a room in a school where pupils have lessons

classy ['klɑːsɪ] classier, classiest ADJECTIVE;
INFORMAL
stylish and elegant

clatter ['klætə] clatters, clattering, clattered VERB

1 When things clatter, they hit each other with a loud rattling noise.

> NOUN

2 a loud rattling noise made by hard things hitting each other

clause [klɔːz] clauses NOUN

1 a section of a legal document

2 **(ENGLISH)** In grammar, a clause is a group of words with a subject and a verb, which may be a complete sentence or one of the parts of a sentence.

claustrophobia [ˌklɔːstrəˈfəʊbɪə] NOUN
Claustrophobia is a fear of being in enclosed spaces.
claustrophobic ADJECTIVE

claw [klɔː] claws, clawing, clawed NOUN

1 An animal's claws are hard, curved nails at the end of its feet.

2 The claws of a crab or lobster are the two jointed parts, used for grasping things.

> VERB

3 If an animal claws something, it digs its claws into it.

clay [kleɪ] NOUN
Clay is a type of earth that is soft and sticky when wet and hard when baked dry. It is used to make pottery and bricks.

clean [kliːn] **cleaner, cleanest; cleans, cleaning, cleaned** ADJECTIVE
1 free from dirt or marks

● THESAURUS
immaculate: *immaculate white flannels*
impeccable: *dressed in an impeccable trouser suit*
laundered: *freshly laundered shirts*
spotless: *The kitchen was spotless.*
washed: *newly washed hair*
<<OPPOSITE *dirty*

2 free from germs or infection

● THESAURUS
antiseptic: *an antiseptic hospital room*
hygienic: *a hygienic kitchen*
purified: *Only purified water is used.*
sterilized: *sterilized milk*
uncontaminated: *uncontaminated air*
unpolluted: *unpolluted beaches*
<<OPPOSITE *contaminated*

3 If humour is clean it is not rude and does not involve bad language.

4 A clean movement is skilful and accurate.

5 Clean also means free from fault or error. *e.g. a clean driving licence*

> VERB

6 To clean something is to remove dirt from it.
cleanly ADVERB, **cleaner** NOUN

● THESAURUS
cleanse: *a lotion to cleanse the skin*
dust: *I vacuumed, dusted and polished the living room.*
scour: *He scoured the sink.*
scrub: *I started to scrub off the dirt.*
sponge: *Sponge your face and body.*
swab: *an old man swabbing the floor*
wash: *He got a job washing dishes in a restaurant.*
wipe: *He wiped the sweat from his face.*
<<OPPOSITE *soil*

cleanliness [ˈklɛnlɪnɪs] NOUN
Cleanliness is the practice of keeping yourself and your surroundings clean.

cleanse [klɛnz] **cleanses, cleansing, cleansed** VERB
To cleanse something is to make it completely free from dirt.

clear [klɪə] **clearer, clearest; clears, clearing, cleared** ADJECTIVE

1 easy to understand, see, or hear *e.g. He made it clear he did not want to talk.*

● THESAURUS
apparent: *There is no apparent reason for the crime.*
blatant: *a blatant piece of cheating*
conspicuous: *one conspicuous difference*
definite: *a definite advantage*
evident: *He ate with evident enjoyment.*
explicit: *He was very explicit about his intentions.*
obvious: *There are obvious dangers.*
plain: *The results are plain to see.*

2 easy to see through *e.g. a clear liquid*

● THESAURUS
crystalline: *crystalline green waters*
glassy: *The water was a deep glassy blue.*
translucent: *translucent stones*
transparent: *transparent glass walls*
<<OPPOSITE *cloudy*

3 free from obstructions or unwanted things *e.g. clear of snow*

> VERB

4 To clear an area is to remove unwanted things from it.

5 If you clear a fence or other obstacle, you jump over it without touching it.

6 When fog or mist clears, it disappears.

7 If someone is cleared of a crime, they are proved to be not guilty.
clearly ADVERB

● THESAURUS
absolve: *He was absolved of all charges.*
acquit: *acquitted of disorderly conduct*
<<OPPOSITE *convict*
clear up: VERB

8 If you clear up, you tidy a place and put things away.

9 When a problem or misunderstanding is cleared up, it is solved or settled.

clearance [ˈklɪərəns] NOUN
1 Clearance is the removal of old buildings in an area.

2 If someone is given clearance to do something, they get official permission to do it.

clearing [ˈklɪərɪŋ] **clearings** NOUN
an area of bare ground in a forest

cleavage [ˈkliːvɪdʒ] **cleavages** NOUN
the space between a woman's breasts

cleaver [ˈkliːvə] **cleavers** NOUN
a knife with a large square blade, used especially by butchers

cleft [klɛft] **clefts** NOUN
a narrow opening in a rock

clementine [ˈklɛmənˌtiːn] **clementines** NOUN

a type of small citrus fruit that is a cross between an orange and a tangerine

clench [klɛntʃ] **clenches, clenching, clenched** VERB

1 When you clench your fist, you curl your fingers up tightly.

2 When you clench your teeth, you squeeze them together tightly.

clergy ['klɜːdʒɪ] PLURAL NOUN
The clergy are the ministers of the Christian Church.

clergyman ['klɜːdʒɪmən] **clergymen** NOUN
a male member of the clergy

clerical ['klɛrɪkəl] ADJECTIVE

1 relating to work done in an office e.g. clerical jobs with the City Council

2 relating to the clergy

clerk [klɑːk] **clerks** NOUN
a person who keeps records or accounts in an office, bank, or law court

clever ['klɛvə] **cleverer, cleverest** ADJECTIVE

1 intelligent and quick to understand things

● THESAURUS
brainy: informal I don't consider myself to be especially brainy.
bright: an exceptionally bright child
intelligent: a lively and intelligent woman
shrewd: a shrewd businessman
smart: a very smart move
<<OPPOSITE stupid

2 very effective or skilful e.g. a clever plan
cleverly ADVERB, **cleverness** NOUN

clianthus [klɪˈænθəs] NOUN
A clianthus is a plant found in Australia and New Zealand which has clusters of scarlet flowers.

cliché ['kliːʃeɪ] **clichés** NOUN
(ENGLISH) an idea or phrase which is no longer effective because it has been used so much

click [klɪk] **clicks, clicking, clicked** VERB

1 When something clicks or when you click it, it makes a short snapping sound.

2 When you click on an area of a computer screen, you point the cursor at it and press one of the buttons on the mouse in order to make something happen.

> NOUN

3 a sound of something clicking e.g. I heard the click of a bolt.

client ['klaɪənt] **clients** NOUN
someone who pays a professional person or company to receive a service

clientele [ˌkliːɒnˈtɛl] PLURAL NOUN
The clientele of a place are its customers.

cliff [klɪf] **cliffs** NOUN
a steep high rock face by the sea

climate ['klaɪmɪt] **climates** NOUN

1 (GEOGRAPHY) The climate of a place is the typical weather conditions there. e.g. The climate was dry in the summer.

2 the general attitude and opinion of people at a particular time e.g. the American political climate
climatic ADJECTIVE

climax ['klaɪmæks] **climaxes** NOUN
The climax of a process, story, or piece of music is the most exciting moment in it, usually near the end.

[WORD HISTORY: from Greek KLIMAX meaning 'ladder']

climb [klaɪm] **climbs, climbing, climbed** VERB

1 To climb is to move upwards.

● THESAURUS
ascend: He ascended the ladder into the loft.
clamber: They clambered up the stone walls.
mount: He mounted the steps.
scale: the first British woman to scale Everest

2 If you climb somewhere, you move there with difficulty. e.g. She climbed out of the driving seat.

> NOUN

3 a movement upwards e.g. this long climb up the slope... the rapid climb in murders
climber NOUN

clinch [klɪntʃ] **clinches, clinching, clinched** VERB
If you clinch an agreement or an argument, you settle it in a definite way. e.g. Peter clinched a deal.

cling [klɪŋ] **clings, clinging, clung** VERB
To cling to something is to hold onto it or stay closely attached to it. e.g. still clinging to old-fashioned values

clingfilm ['klɪŋˌfɪlm] NOUN; TRADEMARK
a clear thin plastic used for wrapping food

clinic ['klɪnɪk] **clinics** NOUN
a building where people go for medical treatment

clinical ['klɪnɪkəl] ADJECTIVE

1 relating to the medical treatment of patients e.g. clinical tests

2 Clinical behaviour or thought is logical and unemotional. e.g. the cold, clinical attitudes of his colleagues
clinically ADVERB

clip [klɪp] **clips, clipping, clipped** NOUN

1 a small metal or plastic object used for holding things together

2 a short piece of a film shown by itself

> VERB

3 If you clip things together, you fasten them with clips.

4 If you clip something, you cut bits from it to shape it. *e.g. clipped hedges*

clippers ['klɪpəz] PLURAL NOUN
Clippers are tools used for cutting.

clipping ['klɪpɪŋ] **clippings** NOUN
an article cut from a newspaper or magazine

clique [kliːk] **cliques** NOUN
a small group of people who stick together and do not mix with other people

clitoris ['klɪtərɪs] **clitorises** NOUN
a small highly sensitive piece of flesh near the opening of a woman's vagina

cloak [kləʊk] **cloaks, cloaking, cloaked** NOUN

1 a wide, loose coat without sleeves

> VERB

2 To cloak something is to cover or hide it. *e.g. a land permanently cloaked in mist*

cloakroom ['kləʊkˌruːm] **cloakrooms** NOUN
a room for coats or a room with toilets and washbasins in a public building

clock [klɒk] **clocks** NOUN

1 a device that measures and shows the time

> PHRASE

2 If you work **round the clock**, you work all day and night.

clockwise ['klɒkˌwaɪz] ADJECTIVE OR ADVERB
in the same direction as the hands on a clock

clockwork ['klɒkˌwɜːk] NOUN

1 Toys that work by clockwork move when they are wound up with a key.

> PHRASE

2 If something happens **like clockwork**, it happens with no problems or delays.

clog [klɒg] **clogs, clogging, clogged** VERB

1 To clog something is to block it. *e.g. pavements clogged up with people*

> NOUN

2 Clogs are heavy wooden shoes.

cloister ['klɔɪstə] **cloisters** NOUN
a covered area in a monastery or a cathedral for walking around a square

clone [kləʊn] **clones, cloning, cloned** NOUN

1 In biology, a clone is an animal or plant that has been produced artificially from the cells of another animal or plant and is therefore identical to it.

> VERB

2 To clone an animal or plant is to produce it as a clone.

close see page 151 for Word Web

closed shop [kləʊzd] **closed shops** NOUN
a factory or other business whose employees have to be members of a trade union

closet ['klɒzɪt] **closets, closeting, closeted** NOUN

1 a cupboard

> VERB

2 If you are closeted somewhere, you shut yourself away alone or in private with another person.

> ADJECTIVE

3 Closet beliefs or habits are kept private and secret. *e.g. a closet romantic*

close-up ['kləʊsˌʌp] **close-ups** NOUN
a detailed close view of something, especially a photograph taken close to the subject

closure ['kləʊʒə] **closures** NOUN

1 The closure of a business is the permanent shutting of it.

2 The closure of a road is the blocking of it so it cannot be used.

clot [klɒt] **clots, clotting, clotted** NOUN

1 a lump, especially one that forms when blood thickens

> VERB

2 When a substance such as blood clots, it thickens and forms a lump.

cloth [klɒθ] **cloths** NOUN

1 Cloth is fabric made by a process such as weaving.

● THESAURUS

fabric: *waterproof fabric*
material: *This material shrinks badly.*
textiles: *a trader in clothes and textiles*

2 a piece of material used for wiping or protecting things

clothe [kləʊð] **clothes, clothing, clothed** VERB
To clothe someone is to give them clothes to wear.

clothes [kləʊðz] PLURAL NOUN
the things people wear on their bodies

● THESAURUS

attire: *formal attire*
clothing: *men's clothing*
costume: *national costume*
dress: *traditional dress*
garments: *winter garments*
gear: *informal trendy gear*

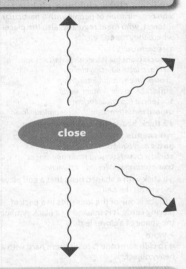

close

1 VERB
to shut something *eg: Close the gate behind you.*
● THESAURUS
secure: *The shed was secured by a padlock.*
shut: *Someone had forgotten to shut the door.*
<< OPPOSITE *open*

2 VERB
to block so that nothing can pass *eg: All the roads out are closed.*
● THESAURUS
bar: *Protesters barred the way to his car.*
block: *The road was blocked by debris.*
obstruct: *buskers obstructing the pavement*
seal: *Soldiers had sealed the border.*

3 ADJECTIVE
near to something *eg: a restaurant close to their home*
● THESAURUS
at hand: *Don't worry, help is at hand.*
adjacent (formal): *The fire spread to adjacent buildings.*
adjoining: *the smell of hamburgers from the adjoining stall*
handy: *Keep a pencil and paper handy.*
near: *The station is quite near.*
nearby: *I dashed into a nearby shop.*
neighbouring: *a man sitting at a neighbouring table*
<< OPPOSITE *distant*

4 ADJECTIVE
friendly and loving *eg: We became close friends.*
● THESAURUS
attached: *We've got very attached to one another over the years.*
dear: *a dear and valued companion*
devoted: *My parents were a deeply devoted couple.*
familiar: *I don't like men who try to get too familiar.*
friendly: *We gradually became very friendly.*
intimate: *one of my most intimate friends*
loving: *They forged a loving relationship.*
<< OPPOSITE *distant*

151

outfit: *a stunning scarlet outfit*
wardrobe: *next summer's wardrobe*
wear: *evening wear*

clothing ['kləʊðɪŋ] NOUN
the clothes people wear

cloud [klaʊd] **clouds, clouding, clouded**
NOUN
1 a mass of water vapour, smoke, or dust that forms in the air and is seen floating in the sky

● THESAURUS
billow: *Smoke billowed from the engine.*
fog: *a fog of cigar smoke*
haze: *a haze of exhaust fumes*
mist: *The valley was wrapped in thick mist.*
vapour: *warm vapour rising from the ground*

> VERB
2 If something clouds or is clouded, it becomes cloudy or difficult to see through. *e.g. The sky clouded over.*
3 Something that clouds an issue makes it more confusing.
[WORD HISTORY: from Old English CLUD meaning 'hill']

cloudy ['klaʊdɪ] **cloudier, cloudiest**
ADJECTIVE
1 full of clouds *e.g. the cloudy sky*

● THESAURUS
dull: *It's always dull and wet here.*
gloomy: *gloomy weather*
leaden: *leaden skies*
overcast: *a damp, overcast morning*
<<OPPOSITE clear

2 difficult to see through *e.g. a glass of cloudy liquid*

● THESAURUS
muddy: *a muddy duck pond*
murky: *murky waters*
opaque: *an opaque glass jar*
<<OPPOSITE clear

clout [klaʊt] NOUN; INFORMAL
Someone who has clout has influence.

clove [kləʊv] **cloves** NOUN
1 Cloves are small, strong-smelling dried flower buds from a tropical tree, used as a spice in cooking.
2 A clove of garlic is one of the separate sections of the bulb.

clover ['kləʊvə] NOUN
Clover is a small plant with leaves made up of three similar parts.

clown [klaʊn] **clowns, clowning, clowned**
NOUN
1 a circus performer who wears funny clothes and make-up and does silly things to make people laugh

> VERB
2 If you clown, you do silly things to make people laugh.

cloying ['klɔɪɪŋ] ADJECTIVE
unpleasantly sickly, sweet, or sentimental *e.g. something less cloying than whipped cream*

club [klʌb] **clubs, clubbing, clubbed** NOUN
1 an organization of people with a particular interest, who meet regularly; also the place where they meet

● THESAURUS
association: *the Women's Tennis Association*
circle: *a local painting circle*
group: *an environmental group*
guild: *the Screen Writers' Guild*
society: *a historical society*
union: *the International Astronomical Union*

2 a thick, heavy stick used as a weapon

● THESAURUS
bat: *a baseball bat*
stick: *a crowd carrying sticks and stones*
truncheon: *a policeman's truncheon*

3 a stick with a shaped head that a golf player uses to hit the ball
4 Clubs is one of the four suits in a pack of playing cards. It is marked by a black symbol in the shape of a clover leaf.

> VERB
5 To club someone is to hit them hard with a heavy object.

● THESAURUS
bash: *They bashed his head with a spade.*
batter: *battered to death*
beat: *beaten with rifle butts*
bludgeon: *bludgeoning his wife with a hammer*

club together VERB
6 If people club together, they all join together to give money to buy something.

cluck [klʌk] **clucks, clucking, clucked**
VERB
When a hen clucks, it makes a short, repeated, high-pitched sound.

clue [kluː] **clues** NOUN
something that helps to solve a problem or mystery

clump [klʌmp] **clumps, clumping, clumped** NOUN
1 a small group of things close together

> VERB
2 If you clump about, you walk with heavy footsteps.

clumsiness [ˈklʌmzɪnɪs] NOUN
awkwardness in the way someone or something moves

● THESAURUS
awkwardness: *They moved with the awkwardness of mechanical dolls.*
ungainliness: *his physical ungainliness*

clumsy [ˈklʌmzɪ] **clumsier, clumsiest**
ADJECTIVE
1 moving awkwardly and carelessly

● THESAURUS
awkward: *an awkward gesture*
gauche: *He makes me feel stupid and gauche.*
lumbering: *a big, lumbering man*
uncoordinated: *an uncoordinated dancer*
ungainly: *As a youth he was lanky and ungainly.*
<<OPPOSITE *graceful*

2 said or done without thought or tact *e.g. his clumsy attempts to catch her out*
clumsily ADVERB

cluster [ˈklʌstə] **clusters, clustering, clustered** NOUN
1 A cluster of things is a group of them together. *e.g. a cluster of huts at the foot of the mountains*

> VERB
2 If people cluster together, they stay together in a close group.

clutch [klʌtʃ] **clutches, clutching, clutched** VERB
1 If you clutch something, you hold it tightly or seize it.

> PLURAL NOUN
2 If you are in someone's clutches, they have power or control over you.

clutter [ˈklʌtə] **clutters, cluttering, cluttered** NOUN
1 Clutter is an untidy mess.

> VERB
2 Things that clutter a place fill it and make it untidy.

cm
an abbreviation for 'centimetres'

co- PREFIX
Co- means together. *e.g. Paula is now co-writing a book with Pierre.*

coach [kəʊtʃ] **coaches, coaching, coached** NOUN
1 a long motor vehicle used for taking passengers on long journeys

2 a section of a train that carries passengers

3 a four-wheeled vehicle with a roof pulled by horses, which people used to travel in

4 a person who coaches a sport or a subject

> VERB
5 If someone coaches you, they teach you and help you to get better at a sport or a subject.

coal [kəʊl] **coals** NOUN
1 Coal is a hard black rock obtained from under the earth and burned as a fuel.

2 Coals are burning pieces of coal.

coalition [ˌkəʊəˈlɪʃən] **coalitions** NOUN
a temporary alliance, especially between different political parties forming a government

coarse [kɔːs] **coarser, coarsest** ADJECTIVE
1 Something that is coarse is rough in texture, often consisting of large particles. *e.g. a coarse blanket*

2 Someone who is coarse talks or behaves in a rude or rather offensive way.
coarsely ADVERB, **coarseness** NOUN

coast [kəʊst] **coasts, coasting, coasted** NOUN
1 the edge of the land where it meets the sea

● THESAURUS
beach: *a beautiful sandy beach*
border: *the border of the Black Sea*
coastline: *the stunning Caribbean coastline*
seaside: *a day at the seaside*
shore: *a bleak and rocky shore*
strand: *boats fishing from the strand*

> VERB
2 A vehicle that is coasting is moving without engine power.
coastal ADJECTIVE

coastguard [ˈkəʊstˌɡɑːd] **coastguards** NOUN
an official who watches the sea near a coast to get help for sailors when they need it, and to prevent smuggling

coastline [ˈkəʊstˌlaɪn] **coastlines** NOUN
the outline of a coast, especially its appearance as seen from the sea or air

coat [kəʊt] **coats, coating, coated** NOUN
1 a piece of clothing with sleeves which you wear outside over your other clothes

2 An animal's coat is the fur or hair on its body.

● THESAURUS
fleece: *a blanket of lamb's fleece*
fur: *a kitten with black fur*
hair: *He's allergic to cat hair.*
hide: *rhino hide*
pelt: *a wolf pelt*
skin: *convicted of attempting to sell the skin of a Siberian tiger*
wool: *Lanolin comes from sheep's wool.*

3 A coat of paint or varnish is a layer of it.

> VERB
4 To coat something means to cover it with a

C

thin layer of something. *e.g. walnuts coated with chocolate*

coat hanger coat hangers NOUN
a curved piece of wood, metal, or plastic that you hang clothes on

coating ['kəʊtɪŋ] **coatings** NOUN
a layer of something

● THESAURUS
coat: *a coat of paint*
covering: *a covering of dust*
layer: *a layer of dead leaves*

coax [kəʊks] **coaxes, coaxing, coaxed** VERB
If you coax someone to do something, you gently persuade them to do it.

● THESAURUS
cajole: *Her sister cajoled her into playing.*
persuade: *My husband persuaded me to come.*
talk into: *They've talked him into getting a new car.*

cobalt ['kəʊbɔːlt] NOUN
Cobalt is a hard silvery-white metal which is used for producing a blue dye.

cobble ['kɒbəl] **cobbles** NOUN
Cobbles or cobblestones are stones with a rounded surface that were used in the past for making roads.

cobbler ['kɒblə] **cobblers** NOUN
a person who makes or mends shoes

cobra ['kəʊbrə] **cobras** NOUN
a type of large poisonous snake from Africa and Asia

cobweb ['kɒb‚wɛb] **cobwebs** NOUN
the very thin net that a spider spins for catching insects

cocaine [kə'keɪn] NOUN
Cocaine is an addictive drug.
[WORD HISTORY: from Spanish COCA meaning 'preparation of cocoa leaves']

cock [kɒk] **cocks** NOUN
an adult male chicken; also used of any male bird

cockatoo [‚kɒkə'tuː] **cockatoos** NOUN
a type of parrot with a crest, found in Australia and New Guinea

cockerel ['kɒkərəl] **cockerels** NOUN
a young cock

Cockney ['kɒknɪ] **Cockneys** NOUN
a person born in the East End of London

cockpit ['kɒk‚pɪt] **cockpits** NOUN
The place in a small plane where the pilot sits.

cockroach ['kɒk‚rəʊtʃ] **cockroaches** NOUN
a large dark-coloured insect often found in dirty rooms

cocktail ['kɒk‚teɪl] **cocktails** NOUN
an alcoholic drink made from several ingredients

cocky ['kɒkɪ] **cockier, cockiest; cockies**
INFORMAL ➤ ADJECTIVE
1 cheeky or too self-confident

● THESAURUS
arrogant: *an air of arrogant indifference*
brash: *On stage she seems hard and brash.*
conceited: *I thought him conceited.*
overconfident: *She couldn't cope with this new generation of noisy, overconfident teenage girls.*

➤ NOUN
2 in Australian English, a cockatoo
3 in Australian and New Zealand English, a farmer, especially one whose farm is small
cockiness NOUN

● THESAURUS
crofter: Scottish *the financial plight of crofters in the islands*
farmer: *He was a simple farmer scratching a living from the soil.*

cocoa ['kəʊkəʊ] NOUN
Cocoa is a brown powder made from the seeds of a tropical tree and used for making chocolate; also a hot drink made from this powder.

coconut ['kəʊkə‚nʌt] **coconuts** NOUN
a very large nut with white flesh, milky juice, and a hard hairy shell

cocoon [kə'kuːn] **cocoons** NOUN
a silky covering over the larvae of moths and some other insects
[WORD HISTORY: from Provençal COUCOUN meaning 'eggshell']

cod [kɒd] NOUN
a large edible fish

▬ The plural of *cod* is also *cod*

code [kəʊd] **codes** NOUN
1 a system of replacing the letters or words in a message with other letters or words, so that nobody can understand the message unless they know the system
2 a group of numbers and letters which is used to identify something *e.g. the telephone code for Melbourne*
coded ADJECTIVE

coffee ['kɒfɪ] NOUN
Coffee is a substance made by roasting and grinding the beans of a tropical shrub; also a hot drink made from this substance.
[WORD HISTORY: from Arabic QAHWAH meaning 'wine' or 'coffee']

coffin ['kɒfɪn] **coffins** NOUN
a box in which a dead body is buried or cremated

cog [kɒg] **cogs** NOUN
a wheel with teeth which turns another wheel or part of a machine

cognac ['kɒnjæk] NOUN
Cognac is a kind of brandy.

coherent [kəʊ'hɪərənt] ADJECTIVE
1 If something such as a theory is coherent, its parts fit together well and do not contradict each other.
2 If someone is coherent, what they are saying makes sense and is not jumbled or confused.
coherence NOUN

cohesive [kəʊ'hiːsɪv] ADJECTIVE
If something is cohesive, its parts fit together well. *e.g. The team must work as a cohesive unit.*
cohesion NOUN

coil [kɔɪl] **coils, coiling, coiled** NOUN
1 a length of rope or wire wound into a series of loops; also one of the loops
> VERB
2 If something coils, it turns into a series of loops.
● THESAURUS
curl: *dark, curling hair*
loop: *A rope was looped between his hands.*
spiral: *vines spiralling up towards the roof*
twine: *This lily produces twining stems.*
twist: *She twisted her hair into a bun.*
wind: *a rope wound round her waist*

coin [kɔɪn] **coins, coining, coined** NOUN
1 a small metal disc which is used as money
> VERB
2 If you coin a word or a phrase, you invent it.

coinage ['kɔɪnɪdʒ] NOUN
The coinage of a country is the coins that are used there.

coincide [ˌkəʊɪn'saɪd] **coincides, coinciding, coincided** VERB
1 If two events coincide, they happen at about the same time.
2 When two people's ideas or opinions coincide, they agree. *e.g. What she said coincided exactly with his own thinking.*

coincidence [kəʊ'ɪnsɪdəns] **coincidences** NOUN
1 what happens when two similar things occur at the same time by chance *e.g. I had moved to London, and by coincidence, Helen had too.*
2 the fact that two things are surprisingly the same
coincidental ADJECTIVE, **coincidentally** ADVERB

coke [kəʊk] NOUN
Coke is a grey fuel produced from coal.

colander ['kɒləndə] **colanders** NOUN
a bowl-shaped container with holes in it, used for washing or draining food

cold [kəʊld] **colder, coldest; colds** ADJECTIVE

1 having a low temperature
● THESAURUS
arctic: *arctic conditions*
biting: *a biting wind*
bitter: *driven inside by the bitter cold*
bleak: *The weather can be bleak on the coast.*
chilly: *It's chilly for June.*
freezing: *This house is freezing.*
icy: *the icy north wind*
raw: *a raw December morning*
wintry: *wintry showers*
<<OPPOSITE *hot*
2 Someone who is cold does not show much affection.
● THESAURUS
aloof: *He seemed aloof and detached.*
distant: *She was polite but distant.*
frigid: *a frigid smile*
lukewarm: *a lukewarm response*
reserved: *emotionally reserved*
stony: *He gave me a stony look.*
<<OPPOSITE *warm*
> NOUN
3 You can refer to cold weather as the cold. *e.g. She was complaining about the cold.*
4 a minor illness in which you sneeze and may have a sore throat
coldly ADVERB, **coldness** NOUN

cold-blooded [ˌkəʊld'blʌdɪd] ADJECTIVE
1 Someone who is cold-blooded does not show any pity. *e.g. two cold-blooded killers*
2 A cold-blooded animal has a body temperature that changes according to the surrounding temperature.

cold war NOUN
Cold war is a state of extreme unfriendliness between countries not actually at war.

coleslaw ['kəʊlˌslɔː] NOUN
Coleslaw is a salad of chopped cabbage and other vegetables in mayonnaise.
[WORD HISTORY: from Dutch KOOLSLA meaning 'cabbage salad']

colic ['kɒlɪk] NOUN
Colic is pain in a baby's stomach.

collaborate [kə'læbəˌreɪt] **collaborates, collaborating, collaborated** VERB
When people collaborate, they work together to produce something. *e.g. The two bands have collaborated in the past.*
collaboration NOUN, **collaborator** NOUN

collage [kə'lɑːʒ] **collages** NOUN
(ART) a picture made by sticking pieces of paper or cloth onto a surface

collapse [kə'læps] **collapses, collapsing, collapsed** VERB

155

1 If something such as a building collapses, it falls down suddenly. If a person collapses, they fall down suddenly because they are ill.

THESAURUS
fall down: *The ceiling fell down.*
give way: *The bridge gave way beneath him.*

2 If something such as a system or a business collapses, it suddenly stops working. *e.g. 50,000 small firms collapsed last year.*

THESAURUS
fail: *His hotel business has failed.*
fold: *We were laid off when the company folded.*
founder: *a foundering radio station*

> NOUN

3 The collapse of something is what happens when it stops working. *e.g. the collapse of his marriage*

THESAURUS
downfall: *the downfall of the government*
failure: *the failure of his business empire*

collapsible [kə'læpsəbəl] ADJECTIVE
A collapsible object can be folded flat when it is not in use. *e.g. a collapsible ironing board*

collar ['kɒlə] **collars** NOUN
1 The collar of a shirt or coat is the part round the neck which is usually folded over.
2 a leather band round the neck of a dog or cat

collateral [kɒ'lætərəl] NOUN
Collateral is money or property which is used as a guarantee that someone will repay a loan, and which the lender can take if the loan is not repaid.

colleague ['kɒliːg] **colleagues** NOUN
A person's colleagues are the people he or she works with.

THESAURUS
associate: *business associates*
fellow worker: *She started going out with a fellow worker.*
partner: *her business partner*
workmate: *the nickname his workmates gave him*

collect [kə'lɛkt] **collects, collecting, collected** VERB
1 To collect things is to gather them together for a special purpose or as a hobby. *e.g. collecting money for charity*

THESAURUS
accumulate: *Most children enjoy accumulating knowledge.*
assemble: *trying to assemble a team*
gather: *gathering information*
raise: *They've raised over £100 for charity.*
<<OPPOSITE *scatter*

2 If you collect someone or something from a place, you call there and take them away. *e.g. We*

had to collect her from school.

3 When things collect in a place, they gather there over a period of time. *e.g. Food collects in holes in the teeth.*
collector NOUN

collected [kə'lɛktɪd] ADJECTIVE
calm and self-controlled

collection [kə'lɛkʃən] **collections** NOUN
1 (ART) a group of things acquired over a period of time *e.g. a collection of paintings*

THESAURUS
assortment: *an assortment of pets*
group: *a group of songs*
store: *a vast store of knowledge*

2 Collection is the collecting of something. *e.g. tax collection*

3 the organized collecting of money, for example for charity, or the sum of money collected

collective [kə'lɛktɪv] **collectives** ADJECTIVE
1 involving every member of a group of people *e.g. The wine growers took a collective decision.*

> NOUN

2 a group of people who share the responsibility both for running something and for doing the work
collectively ADVERB

collective noun collective nouns NOUN
a noun that refers to a single unit made up of a number of things, for example 'flock' and 'swarm'

college ['kɒlɪdʒ] **colleges** NOUN
1 a place where students study after they have left school
2 a name given to some secondary schools
3 one of the institutions into which some universities are divided
4 In New Zealand English, a college can also refer to a teacher training college.

collide [kə'laɪd] **collides, colliding, collided** VERB
If a moving object collides with something, it hits it.

collie ['kɒlɪ] **collies** NOUN
a dog that is used for rounding up sheep

colliery ['kɒljərɪ] **collieries** NOUN
a coal mine

collision [kə'lɪʒən] **collisions** NOUN
A collision occurs when a moving object hits something.

colloquial [kə'ləʊkwɪəl] ADJECTIVE
Colloquial words and phrases are informal and used especially in conversation.

colloquially ADVERB, **colloquialism** NOUN
● THESAURUS
conversational: *a conversational style*
everyday: *He used plain, everyday English.*
informal: *an informal expression*

cologne [kə'ləʊn] NOUN
Cologne is a kind of weak perfume.

colon ['kəʊlən] **colons** NOUN
1 the punctuation mark (:)
2 part of your intestine

colonel ['kɜːnəl] **colonels** NOUN
an army officer with a fairly high rank

colonial [kə'ləʊnɪəl] ADJECTIVE
1 relating to a colony
2 In Australia, colonial is used to relate to the period of Australian history before the Federation in 1901.

colonize ['kɒlə,naɪz] **colonizes, colonizing, colonized**; also spelt **colonise** VERB
(**HISTORY**) When people colonize a place, they go to live there and take control of it. *e.g. the Europeans who colonized North America*
When a lot of animals colonize a place, they go there and make it their home. *e.g. Toads are colonizing the whole place.*
colonization NOUN, **colonist** NOUN

colony ['kɒlənɪ] **colonies** NOUN (**HISTORY**)
1 a country controlled by a more powerful country
● THESAURUS
dependency: *the tiny British dependency of Montserrat*
dominion: *The Republic is a dominion of Brazil.*
territory: *territories under Israeli control*
2 a group of people who settle in a country controlled by their homeland
● THESAURUS
community: *the Sikh community in Britain*
outpost: *a remote outpost*
settlement: *a Muslim settlement*

colossal [kə'lɒsəl] ADJECTIVE
very large indeed
● THESAURUS
enormous: *The main bedroom is enormous.*
gigantic: *a gigantic task*
huge: *They are making huge profits.*
immense: *an immense cloud of smoke*
mammoth: *This mammoth undertaking was completed in 18 months.*
massive: *a massive steam boat*
vast: *farmers who own vast stretches of land*
<<OPPOSITE *tiny*

colour see page 158 for Word Web
colour blind ADJECTIVE
Someone who is colour blind cannot distinguish between colours.

colourful ['kʌləfʊl] ADJECTIVE
1 full of colour
● THESAURUS
bright: *a bright green dress*
brilliant: *The garden has burst into brilliant flower.*
intense: *an intense shade of blue*
jazzy: informal *a jazzy tie*
rich: *a rich blue glass bowl*
vibrant: *vibrant orange shades*
vivid: *vivid hues*
<<OPPOSITE *dull*
2 interesting or exciting
colourfully ADVERB
● THESAURUS
graphic: *a graphic account of his career*
interesting: *He has had an interesting life.*
lively: *a lively imagination*
rich: *the rich history of the island*
vivid: *a vivid description*
<<OPPOSITE *dull*

colt [kəʊlt] **colts** NOUN
a young male horse

column ['kɒləm] **columns** NOUN
1 a tall solid upright cylinder, especially one supporting a part of a building
2 a group of people moving in a long line

columnist ['kɒləmɪst] **columnists** NOUN
a journalist who writes a regular article in a newspaper or magazine

coma ['kəʊmə] **comas** NOUN
Someone who is in a coma is in a state of deep unconsciousness.

comb [kəʊm] **combs, combing, combed** NOUN
1 a flat object with pointed teeth used for tidying your hair
> VERB
2 When you comb your hair, you tidy it with a comb.
3 If you comb a place, you search it thoroughly to try to find someone or something.

combat combats, combating, combated NOUN ['kɒmbæt]
1 Combat is fighting. *e.g. his first experience of combat*
> VERB [kəm'bæt]
2 To combat something means to try to stop it happening or developing. *e.g. a way to combat crime*

combination [,kɒmbɪ'neɪʃən] **combinations** NOUN
1 a mixture of things *e.g. a combination of charm and skill*

1 NOUN
the appearance something has as a result of reflecting light
● THESAURUS
hue: *delicate pastel hues*
pigmentation: *skin pigmentation*
shade: *walls painted in two shades of green*
tint: *a distinct orange tint*

2 NOUN
a substance used to give colour
● THESAURUS
dye: *hair dye*
paint: *a pot of red paint*
pigment: *a layer of blue pigment*

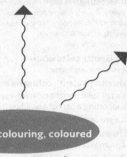

colour
colours, colouring, coloured

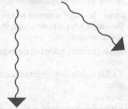

3 VERB
If you colour something, you give it a colour
● THESAURUS
dye: *Only dye clean garments.*
paint: *She paints her toenails red.*
stain: *Some foods can stain the teeth.*
tint: *tinted glass*

4 VERB
If something colours your opinion, it affects the way you think about something
● THESAURUS
bias: *a biased opinion*
distort: *The shock of the accident distorted my judgement.*
prejudice: *Criticism will prejudice the Government's decision.*
slant: *deliberately slanted news coverage*

● THESAURUS
amalgamation: *an amalgamation of two organizations*
blend: *a blend of wine and spring water*
mix: *a mix of fantasy and reality*
mixture: *a mixture of horror, envy and awe*

2 a series of letters or numbers used to open a special lock

combine [kəm'baɪn] **combines, combining, combined** VERB
1 To combine things is to cause them to exist together. *e.g. to combine a career with being a mother*

2 To combine things also means to join them together to make a single thing. *e.g. Combine all the ingredients.*

● THESAURUS
amalgamate: *a plan to amalgamate the two parties*
blend: *The band blends jazz and folk music.*
fuse: *a performer who fuses magic and dance*
integrate: *integrating various styles of art*
merge: *The two countries have merged into one.*
mix: *mixing business with pleasure*
unite: *people uniting to fight racism*
<<OPPOSITE *separate*

3 If something combines two qualities or features, it has them both. *e.g. a film that combines great charm and scintillating performances*

combustion [kəm'bʌstʃən] NOUN
(SCIENCE) Combustion is the act of burning something or the process of burning.

come [kʌm] **comes, coming, came, come** VERB
1 To come to a place is to move there or arrive there.

● THESAURUS
appear: *He appeared at about 9 o'clock.*
arrive: *My brother has just arrived.*
enter: *The class fell silent as the teacher entered.*
materialize: *The car just materialized from nowhere.*
show up: *informal He showed up over an hour late.*
turn up: *informal I'll call you when she turns up.*

2 To come to a place also means to reach as far as that place. *e.g. The sea water came up to his waist.*

3 'Come' is used to say that someone or something reaches a particular state *e.g. They came to power in 1997... We had come to a decision.*

4 When a particular time or event comes, it happens. *e.g. The peak of his career came early in 1990.*

● THESAURUS
happen: *Nothing ever happens on a Sunday.*

occur: *How did the accident occur?*
take place: *The meeting never took place.*

5 If you come from a place, you were born there or it is your home.

> PHRASE
6 A time or event **to come** is a future time or event. *e.g. The public will thank them in years to come.*

come about VERB
7 The way something comes about is the way it happens. *e.g. The discussion came about because of the proposed changes.*

come across VERB
8 If you come across something, you find it by chance.

come off VERB
9 If something comes off, it succeeds. *e.g. His rescue plan had come off.*

come on VERB
10 If something is coming on, it is making progress. *e.g. Let's go and see how the grapes are coming on.*

come up VERB
11 If something comes up in a conversation or meeting, it is mentioned or discussed.

come up with VERB
12 If you come up with a plan or idea, you suggest it.

comeback ['kʌm,bæk] **comebacks** NOUN
To make a comeback is to be popular or successful again.

comedian [kə'miːdɪən] **comedians** NOUN
an entertainer whose job is to make people laugh

comedienne [kə,miːdɪ'ɛn] **comediennes** NOUN
a female comedian

comedy ['kɒmɪdi] **comedies** NOUN
a light-hearted play or film with a happy ending
[WORD HISTORY: from Greek *kōmos* meaning 'village festival' and *aeidein* meaning 'to sing']

comet ['kɒmɪt] **comets** NOUN
an object that travels around the sun leaving a bright trail behind it

comfort ['kʌmfət] **comforts, comforting, comforted** NOUN
1 Comfort is the state of being physically relaxed. *e.g. He settled back in comfort.*

● THESAURUS
ease: *a life of ease*
luxury: *brought up in an atmosphere of luxury*
wellbeing: *a wonderful sense of wellbeing*

2 Comfort is also a feeling of relief from worries or unhappiness. *e.g. The thought is a great comfort to me.*

> THESAURUS
consolation: *He knew he was right, but it was no consolation.*
help: *Just talking to you has been a great help.*
relief: *temporary relief from the pain*
satisfaction: *At least I have the satisfaction of knowing I tried.*
support: *His family were a great support to him.*

> PLURAL NOUN
3 Comforts are things which make your life easier and more pleasant. *e.g. all the comforts of home*

> VERB
4 To comfort someone is to make them less worried or unhappy.

> THESAURUS
cheer: *The thought did nothing to cheer him.*
console: *"Never mind," he consoled me.*
reassure: *He did his best to reassure her.*
soothe: *She took him in his arms and soothed him.*

comfortable ['kʌmftəbəl] ADJECTIVE
1 If you are comfortable, you are physically relaxed.
2 Something that is comfortable makes you feel relaxed. *e.g. a comfortable bed*

> THESAURUS
cosy: *a cosy living room*
easy: *You've had an easy time of it.*
homely: *a homely atmosphere*
relaxing: *a relaxing holiday*
restful: *a restful scene*
<<OPPOSITE *uncomfortable*

3 If you feel comfortable in a particular situation, you are not afraid or embarrassed.
comfortably ADVERB

> THESAURUS
at ease: *He is not at ease in female company.*
at home: *We soon felt quite at home.*
contented: *a contented life*
happy: *I'm not very happy with that idea.*
relaxed: *a relaxed attitude*
<<OPPOSITE *uneasy*

comic ['kɒmɪk] **comics** ADJECTIVE
1 funny *e.g. a comic monologue*
> NOUN
2 someone who tells jokes
3 a magazine that contains stories told in pictures

comical ['kɒmɪkəl] ADJECTIVE
funny *e.g. a comical sight*

comma ['kɒmə] **commas** NOUN
(ENGLISH) the punctuation mark (,)

command [kə'mɑːnd] **commands, commanding, commanded** VERB
1 To command someone to do something is to order them to do it.

> THESAURUS
bid: *The soldiers bade us turn and go back.*
demand: *They demanded that he leave.*
direct: *His doctor has directed him to rest.*
order: *He ordered his men to cease fire.*

2 If you command something such as respect, you receive it because of your personal qualities.
3 An officer who commands part of an army or navy is in charge of it.

> THESAURUS
control: *He now controls the whole company.*
head: *Who heads the firm?*
lead: *He led the country between 1949 and 1984.*
manage: *I manage a small team of workers.*
supervise: *He supervised more than 400 volunteers.*

> NOUN
4 an order to do something

> THESAURUS
bidding: *They refused to leave at his bidding.*
decree: *a presidential decree*
directive: *a government directive*
injunction: *He left her with the injunction to go to sleep.*
instruction: *They were just following instructions.*
order: *I don't take orders from you.*

5 Your command of something is your knowledge of it and your ability to use this knowledge. *e.g. a good command of English*

> THESAURUS
grasp: *a good grasp of foreign languages*
knowledge: *He has no knowledge of law.*
mastery: *a mastery of grammar*

commandant ['kɒmən,dænt] **commandants** NOUN
an army officer in charge of a place or group of people

commander [kə'mɑːndə] **commanders** NOUN
an officer in charge of a military operation or organization

commandment [kə'mɑːndmənt] **commandments** NOUN
(RE) The commandments are ten rules of behaviour that, according to the Old Testament, people should obey.

commando [kə'mɑːndəʊ] **commandos** NOUN
Commandos are soldiers who have been specially trained to carry out raids.

commemorate [kə'mɛmə,reɪt] **commemorates, commemorating, commemorated** VERB
1 An object that commemorates a person or an event is intended to remind people of that person or event.

2 If you commemorate an event, you do something special to show that you remember it.
commemorative ADJECTIVE, **commemoration** NOUN

● THESAURUS
celebrate: *celebrating their golden wedding*
honour: *celebrations to honour his memory*

commence [kə'mɛns] **commences, commencing, commenced** VERB; FORMAL
To commence is to begin.
commencement NOUN

commend [kə'mɛnd] **commends, commending, commended** VERB
To commend someone or something is to praise them. *e.g. He has been commended for his work.*
commendation NOUN, **commendable** ADJECTIVE

comment ['kɒmɛnt] **comments, commenting, commented** VERB
1 If you comment on something, you make a remark about it.

● THESAURUS
mention: *I mentioned that I didn't like jazz.*
note: *He noted that some issues remained to be settled.*
observe: *"You're very pale," he observed.*
point out: *I should point out that these figures are approximate.*
remark: *Everyone had remarked on her new hairstyle.*
say: *"Well done," he said.*

> NOUN
2 a remark about something *e.g. She received many comments about her appearance.*

● THESAURUS
observation: *a few general observations*
remark: *snide remarks*
statement: *That statement puzzled me.*

commentary ['kɒməntərɪ] **commentaries** NOUN
a description of an event which is broadcast on radio or television while the event is happening

commentator ['kɒmən,teɪtə] **commentators** NOUN
someone who gives a radio or television commentary

commerce ['kɒmɜːs] NOUN
Commerce is the buying and selling of goods.

commercial [kə'mɜːʃəl] **commercials** ADJECTIVE
1 relating to commerce
2 Commercial activities involve producing goods on a large scale in order to make money. *e.g. the commercial fishing world*

> NOUN
3 an advertisement on television or radio

commercially ADVERB

commission [kə'mɪʃən] **commissions, commissioning, commissioned** VERB
1 If someone commissions a piece of work, they formally ask someone to do it. *e.g. a study commissioned by the government*

> NOUN
2 a piece of work that has been commissioned
3 Commission is money paid to a salesman each time a sale is made.
4 an official body appointed to investigate or control something

commit [kə'mɪt] **commits, committing, committed** VERB
1 To commit a crime or sin is to do it.

● THESAURUS
carry out: *attacks carried out by terrorists*
do: *They have done a lot of damage.*
perform: *people who have performed acts of bravery*
perpetrate: *A fraud has been perpetrated.*

2 If you commit yourself, you state an opinion or state that you will do something.
3 If someone is committed to hospital or prison, they are officially sent there.
committal NOUN

commitment [kə'mɪtmənt] **commitments** NOUN
1 (RE) Commitment is a strong belief in an idea or system.
2 something that regularly takes up some of your time *e.g. business commitments*

committed [kə'mɪtɪd] ADJECTIVE
A committed person has strong beliefs. *e.g. a committed feminist*

committee [kə'mɪtɪ] **committees** NOUN
a group of people who make decisions on behalf of a larger group

commodity [kə'mɒdɪtɪ] **commodities** NOUN; FORMAL
Commodities are things that are sold.

common ['kɒmən] **commoner, commonest; commons** ADJECTIVE
1 Something that is common exists in large numbers or happens often. *e.g. a common complaint*

● THESAURUS
general: *the general opinion*
popular: *a popular belief*
prevailing: *the prevailing atmosphere*
prevalent: *Smoking is becoming more prevalent among girls.*
universal: *The desire to look attractive is universal.*
widespread: *widespread support*

<<OPPOSITE *rare*

2 If something is common to two or more people, they all have it or use it. *e.g. I realized we had a common interest.*

3 'Common' is used to indicate that something is of the ordinary kind and not special

● THESAURUS
average: *the average teenager*
commonplace: *a commonplace observation*
everyday: *your everyday routine*
ordinary: *an ordinary day*
plain: *My parents were just plain ordinary folks.*
standard: *standard practice*
usual: *In a usual week I watch about 15 hours of television.*
<<OPPOSITE *special*

4 If you describe someone as common, you mean they do not have good taste or good manners.

● THESAURUS
coarse: *coarse humour*
rude: *It's rude to stare.*
vulgar: *vulgar remarks*
<<OPPOSITE *refined*

> NOUN
5 an area of grassy land where everyone can go
> PHRASE
6 If two things or people have something **in common**, they both have it.
commonly ADVERB

commoner ['kɒmənə] **commoners** NOUN
someone who is not a member of the nobility

commonplace ['kɒmən,pleɪs] ADJECTIVE
Something that is commonplace happens often. *e.g. Foreign holidays have become commonplace.*

common sense NOUN
Your common sense is your natural ability to behave sensibly and make good judgments.

● THESAURUS
good sense: *He had the good sense to call me at once.*
judgment: *I respect your judgment.*
level-headedness: *He prides himself on his level-headedness.*
prudence: *His lack of prudence led to financial problems.*
wit: *They don't have the wit to realize what's happening.*

Commonwealth ['kɒmən,wɛlθ] NOUN
1 The Commonwealth is an association of countries around the world that are or used to be ruled by Britain.
2 a country made up of a number of states *e.g. the Commonwealth of Australia*

commotion [kə'məʊʃən] NOUN
A commotion is a lot of noise and excitement.

communal ['kɒmjʊnəl] ADJECTIVE
shared by a group of people *e.g. a communal canteen*

commune ['kɒmju:n] **communes** NOUN
a group of people who live together and share everything

communicate [kə'mju:nɪ,keɪt] **communicates, communicating, communicated** VERB
1 If you communicate with someone, you keep in touch with them.

● THESAURUS
be in contact: *I'll be in contact with him next week.*
be in touch: *He hasn't been in touch with me yet.*
correspond: *We correspond regularly.*

2 If you communicate information or a feeling to someone, you make them aware of it.

● THESAURUS
convey: *They have conveyed their views to the government.*
impart: *the ability to impart knowledge*
inform: *Will you inform me of any changes?*
pass on: *I'll pass on your good wishes.*
spread: *She has spread the news to everyone.*
transmit: *He transmitted his enjoyment to the audience.*

communication [kə,mju:nɪ'keɪʃən] **communications** NOUN
1 (PSHE) Communication is the process by which people or animals exchange information.
> PLURAL NOUN
2 Communications are the systems by which people communicate or broadcast information, especially using electricity or radio waves.
> NOUN
3 FORMAL a letter or telephone call

communicative [kə'mju:nɪkətɪv] ADJECTIVE
Someone who is communicative is willing to talk to people.

communion [kə'mju:njən] NOUN
1 Communion is the sharing of thoughts and feelings.
2 In Christianity, Communion is a religious service in which people share bread and wine in remembrance of the death and resurrection of Jesus Christ.

communism ['kɒmjʊ,nɪzəm] NOUN
Communism is the doctrine that the state should own the means of production and that there should be no private property.
communist ADJECTIVE OR NOUN

community [kə'mju:nɪtɪ] **communities** NOUN
all the people living in a particular area; also used

to refer to particular groups within a society *e.g. the heart of the local community... the Asian community*

commute [kə'mjuːt] **commutes, commuting, commuted** VERB
People who commute travel a long distance to work every day.
commuter NOUN

compact [kəm'pækt] *or* ['kɒmpækt]
ADJECTIVE
taking up very little space *e.g. a compact microwave*

compact disc ['kɒmpækt] **compact discs**
NOUN
a music or video recording in the form of a plastic disc which is played using a laser on a special machine, and gives good quality sound or pictures

companion [kəm'pænjən] **companions**
NOUN
someone you travel or spend time with
companionship NOUN
[WORD HISTORY: from Latin com- meaning 'together' and PANIS meaning 'bread'. A companion was originally someone you shared a meal with]

⬤ THESAURUS
comrade: *Unlike so many of his comrades he survived the war.*
crony: old-fashioned *a round of golf with his business cronies*
friend: *Sara's old friend, Charles.*
mate: *A mate of mine used to play soccer for Liverpool.*
pal: informal *We've been pals for years.*
partner: *a partner in crime*

company ['kʌmpəni] **companies** NOUN
1 a business that sells goods or provides a service *e.g. the record company*

⬤ THESAURUS
business: *a family business*
corporation: *multi-national corporations*
establishment: *a commercial establishment*
firm: *a firm of engineers*
house: *the world's top fashion houses*

2 a group of actors, opera singers, or dancers *e.g. the Royal Shakespeare Company*

⬤ THESAURUS
assembly: *an assembly of citizens*
band: *bands of rebels*
circle: *a large circle of friends*
community: *a community of believers*
crowd: *I don't go around with that crowd.*
ensemble: *an ensemble of young musicians*
group: *an environmental group*

party: *a party of sightseers*
troupe: *a troupe of actors*

3 If you have company, you have a friend or visitor with you. *e.g. I enjoyed her company.*

⬤ THESAURUS
companionship: *He keeps a dog for companionship.*
presence: *Your presence is not welcome here.*

comparable ['kɒmpərəbəl] ADJECTIVE
If two things are comparable, they are similar in size or quality. *e.g. The skill is comparable to playing the violin.*
comparably ADVERB

comparative [kəm'pærətɪv] **comparatives**
ADJECTIVE
1 You add 'comparative' to indicate that something is true only when compared with what is normal. *e.g. eight years of comparative calm*

> NOUN
2 In grammar, the comparative is the form of an adjective which indicates that the person or thing described has more of a particular quality than someone or something else. For example, 'quicker', 'better', and 'easier' are all comparatives.
comparatively ADVERB

compare [kəm'pɛə] **compares, comparing, compared** VERB
1 (EXAM TERM) When you compare things, you look at them together and see in what ways they are different or similar. *e.g.*

⬤ THESAURUS
contrast: *In this section we contrast four possible approaches.*
juxtapose: *art juxtaposed with reality*
weigh: *She weighed her options.*

2 If you compare one thing to another, you say it is like the other thing. *e.g. His voice is often compared to Michael Stipe's.*

comparison [kəm'pærɪsən] **comparisons**
NOUN
(ENGLISH) When you make a comparison, you consider two things together and see in what ways they are different or similar.

compartment [kəm'pɑːtmənt]
compartments NOUN
1 a section of a railway carriage

⬤ THESAURUS
carriage: *Our carriage was full of drunken football fans.*

2 one of the separate parts of an object *e.g. a special compartment inside your vehicle*

⬤ THESAURUS
bay: *the cargo bays of the aircraft*

chamber: *the chambers of the heart*
division: *Each was further split into several divisions.*
section: *a toolbox with sections for various items*

compass ['kʌmpəs] compasses NOUN

1 an instrument with a magnetic needle for finding directions

> PLURAL NOUN

2 Compasses are a hinged instrument for drawing circles.

The proper name for the drawing instrument is *a pair of compasses*

compassion [kəm'pæʃən] NOUN

pity and sympathy for someone who is suffering [WORD HISTORY: from Latin COMPATI meaning 'to suffer with']

compassionate [kəm'pæʃənət] ADJECTIVE

feeling or showing sympathy and pity for others
compassionately ADVERB

THESAURUS

caring: *He is a lovely boy, very gentle and caring.*
humane: *She began to campaign for humane treatment of prisoners and their families.*
kind: *I must thank you for being so kind to me.*
kind-hearted: *He was a warm, generous and kind-hearted man.*
merciful: *a merciful God*
sympathetic: *She was very sympathetic to their problems.*
tender: *Her voice was tender, full of pity.*

compatible [kəm'pætəbᵊl] ADJECTIVE

If people or things are compatible, they can live or work together successfully.
compatibility NOUN

THESAURUS

congenial: *congenial company*
consistent: *injuries consistent with a car crash*
harmonious: *a harmonious partnership*
in keeping: *This behaviour was in keeping with his character.*
<<OPPOSITE incompatible

compatriot [kəm'pætrɪət] compatriots NOUN

Your compatriots are people from your own country.

compel [kəm'pɛl] compels, compelling, compelled VERB

To compel someone to do something is to force them to do it.

compelling [kəm'pɛlɪŋ] ADJECTIVE

1 If a story or event is compelling, it is extremely interesting. *e.g. a compelling novel*

2 A compelling argument or reason makes you believe that something is true or should be done. *e.g. compelling new evidence*

compensate ['kɒmpɛnˌseɪt] compensates, compensating, compensated VERB

1 To compensate someone is to give them money to replace something lost or damaged.

THESAURUS

atone: *He felt he had atoned for what he had done.*
refund: *The company will refund the full cost.*
repay: *collateral with which to repay swindled investors*
reward: *Their patience was finally rewarded.*

2 If one thing compensates for another, it cancels out its bad effects. *e.g. The trip more than compensated for the hardship.*
compensatory ADJECTIVE

THESAURUS

balance: *The pros balance the cons.*
cancel out: *The two influences cancel each other out.*
counteract: *pills to counteract high blood pressure*
make up for: *I'll make up for what I've done.*
offset: *The loss is being offset by a new tax.*

compensation [ˌkɒmpɛn'seɪʃən] compensations NOUN

something that makes up for loss or damage

THESAURUS

amends: *an attempt to make amends for his crime*
atonement: *an act of atonement for our sins*
damages: *damages for libel*
payment: *a redundancy payment*

compere ['kɒmpɛə] comperes, compering, compered NOUN

1 the person who introduces the guests or performers in a show

> VERB

2 To compere a show is to introduce the guests or performers.

compete [kəm'piːt] competes, competing, competed VERB

1 When people or firms compete, each tries to prove that they or their products are the best.

THESAURUS

contend: *two groups contending for power*
contest: *the candidates contesting in the election*
fight: *rivals fighting for supremacy*
vie: *The contestants vied to finish first.*

2 If you compete in a contest or game, you take part in it.

competent ['kɒmpɪtənt] ADJECTIVE

Someone who is competent at something can do it satisfactorily. *e.g. a very competent engineer*
competently ADVERB, **competence** NOUN

competition [ˌkɒmpɪ'tɪʃən] competitions NOUN

1 When there is competition between people or groups, they are all trying to get something that not everyone can have. *e.g. There's a lot of competition for places.*

● THESAURUS
contention: *contention for the gold medal*
contest: *the contest between capitalism and socialism*
opposition: *They are in direct opposition for the job.*
rivalry: *the rivalry between the two leaders*
struggle: *a power struggle*

2 an event in which people take part to find who is best at something

● THESAURUS
championship: *a swimming championship*
contest: *a beauty contest*
event: *major sporting events*
tournament: *a judo tournament*

3 When there is competition between firms, each firm is trying to get people to buy its own goods.

competitive [kəmˈpɛtɪtɪv] ADJECTIVE

1 A competitive situation is one in which people or firms are competing with each other. *e.g. a crowded and competitive market*

2 A competitive person is eager to be more successful than others.

3 Goods sold at competitive prices are cheaper than other goods of the same kind.
competitively ADVERB

competitor [kəmˈpɛtɪtə] **competitors** NOUN
a person or firm that is competing to become the most successful

● THESAURUS
adversary: *his political adversaries*
challenger: *20 seconds faster than the nearest challenger*
competition: *staying ahead of the competition*
contestant: *contestants in the Miss World pageant*
opponent: *the best opponent I've played all season*
opposition: *They can outplay the opposition.*
rival: *a business rival*

compilation [ˌkɒmpɪˈleɪʃən] **compilations** NOUN
A compilation is a book, record, or programme consisting of several items that were originally produced separately. *e.g. this compilation of his solo work*

compile [kəmˈpaɪl] **compiles, compiling, compiled** VERB
When someone compiles a book or report, they make it by putting together several items.

complacent [kəmˈpleɪsᵊnt] ADJECTIVE
If someone is complacent, they are unconcerned about a serious situation and do nothing about it.
complacency NOUN

complain [kəmˈpleɪn] **complains, complaining, complained** VERB

1 If you complain, you say that you are not satisfied with something.

● THESAURUS
carp: *She is constantly carping at him.*
find fault: *He's always finding fault with my work.*
grouse: *You're always grousing about something.*
grumble: *It's not in her nature to grumble.*
kick up a fuss: informal *He kicks up a fuss whenever she goes out.*
moan: *moaning about the weather*
whine: *whining children*
whinge: informal *Stop whingeing and get on with it.*

2 If you complain of pain or illness, you say that you have it.

complaint [kəmˈpleɪnt] **complaints** NOUN
If you make a complaint, you complain about something.

● THESAURUS
criticism: *The criticism that we do not try hard enough to learn other languages was voiced.*
grievance: *They had a legitimate grievance against the company.*
grumble: *Her main grumble is over the long hours she has to work.*
objection: *I have no objections about the way I have been treated.*
protest: *Despite our protests, they went ahead anyway.*

complement complements, complementing, complemented VERB
[ˈkɒmplɪˌmɛnt]

1 If one thing complements another, the two things go well together. *e.g. The tiled floor complements the pine furniture.*

> NOUN [ˈkɒmplɪmənt]
2 If one thing is a complement to another, it goes well with it.

3 In grammar, a complement is a word or phrase that gives information about the subject or object of a sentence. For example, in the sentence 'Rover is a dog', 'is a dog' is a complement.
complementary ADJECTIVE

complete [kəmˈpliːt] **completes, completing, completed** ADJECTIVE

1 to the greatest degree possible *e.g. a complete mess*

● THESAURUS
absolute: *absolute nonsense*
consummate: *a consummate professional*
outright: *an outright victory*
perfect: *a perfect stranger*

thorough: *a thorough snob*
total: *a total failure*
utter: *an utter shambles*

2 If something is complete, none of it is missing. *e.g. a complete set of tools*

● **THESAURUS**
entire: *the entire plot*
full: *a full report*
intact: *the few buildings which have survived intact*
undivided: *I want your undivided attention.*
whole: *I told him the whole story.*
<<OPPOSITE *incomplete*

3 When a task is complete, it is finished. *e.g. The planning stage is now complete.*

> **VERB**
4 If you complete something, you finish it.

● **THESAURUS**
conclude: *The judge concluded his summing-up.*
end: *The crowd was in tears as he ended his speech.*
finish: *I'll finish my report this week.*

5 If you complete a form, you fill it in.
completely ADVERB, **completion** NOUN

complex ['kɒmplɛks] **complexes** ADJECTIVE
1 Something that is complex has many different parts. *e.g. a very complex problem*

● **THESAURUS**
complicated: *a very complicated voting system*
difficult: *the laborious and difficult process of adopting a child*
intricate: *intricate patterns*
involved: *a long, involved explanation*
tangled: *His personal life has become more tangled than ever.*
<<OPPOSITE *simple*

> **NOUN**
2 A complex is a group of buildings, roads, or other things connected with each other in some way. *e.g. a hotel and restaurant complex*

3 If someone has a complex, they have an emotional problem because of a past experience. *e.g. an inferiority complex*
complexity NOUN

● **THESAURUS**
fixation: *She has a fixation about men with beards.*
obsession: *95% of patients know their obsessions are irrational.*
phobia: *The man had a phobia about flying.*
preoccupation: *his total preoccupation with neatness*
problem: *an eating problem*
thing: *He's got this thing about women's shoes.*

complexion [kəm'plɛkʃən] **complexions** NOUN
the quality of the skin on your face *e.g. a healthy glowing complexion*

complicate ['kɒmplɪ,keɪt] **complicates, complicating, complicated** VERB
To complicate something is to make it more difficult to understand or deal with.

complicated ['kɒmplɪ,keɪtɪd] ADJECTIVE
Something that is complicated has so many parts or aspects that it is difficult to understand or deal with.

● **THESAURUS**
complex: *a complex issue*
convoluted: *a convoluted plot*
elaborate: *an elaborate theory*
intricate: *an intricate process*
involved: *a long, involved explanation*
<<OPPOSITE *simple*

complication [,kɒmplɪ'keɪʃən] **complications** NOUN
something that makes a situation more difficult to deal with *e.g. One possible complication was that it was late in the year.*

compliment compliments, complimenting, complimented NOUN ['kɒmplɪmənt]
1 If you pay someone a compliment, you tell them you admire something about them.

> **VERB** ['kɒmplɪ,mɛnt]
2 If you compliment someone, you pay them a compliment.
[WORD HISTORY: from Spanish CUMPLIR meaning 'to do what is fitting']

complimentary [,kɒmplɪ'mɛntərɪ] ADJECTIVE
1 If you are complimentary about something, you express admiration for it.

2 A complimentary seat, ticket, or publication is given to you free.

comply [kəm'plaɪ] **complies, complying, complied** VERB
If you comply with an order or rule, you obey it.
compliance NOUN

component [kəm'pəʊnənt] **components** NOUN
The components of something are the parts it is made of.

compose [kəm'pəʊz] **composes, composing, composed** VERB
1 If something is composed of particular things or people, it is made up of them.

2 To compose a piece of music, letter, or speech means to write it.

● **THESAURUS**
create: *He has created a new ballet.*
devise: *a play devised by the drama company*
invent: *the man who invented gangsta rap*

produce: *He has produced a book about the city.*
write: *I've never been able to write poetry.*

3 If you compose yourself, you become calm after being excited or upset.

composed [kəm'pəʊzd] ADJECTIVE
calm and in control of your feelings

composer [kəm'pəʊzə] **composers** NOUN
someone who writes music

composition [ˌkɒmpə'zɪʃən] **compositions** NOUN
1 The composition of something is the things it consists of. *e.g. the composition of the ozone layer*
2 (MUSIC) The composition of a poem or piece of music is the writing of it.
3 (MUSIC) a piece of music or writing

compost ['kɒmpɒst] NOUN
Compost is a mixture of decaying plants and manure added to soil to help plants grow.

composure [kəm'pəʊʒə] NOUN
Someone's composure is their ability to stay calm. *e.g. Jarvis was able to recover his composure.*

compound compounds, compounding, compounded NOUN ['kɒmpaʊnd]
1 an enclosed area of land with buildings used for a particular purpose *e.g. the prison compound*
2 In chemistry, a compound is a substance consisting of two or more different substances or chemical elements.
> VERB [kəm'paʊnd]
3 To compound something is to put together different parts to make a whole.
4 To compound a problem is to make it worse by adding to it. *e.g. Water shortages were compounded by taps left running.*

comprehend [ˌkɒmprɪ'hend] **comprehends, comprehending, comprehended** VERB FORMAL
To comprehend something is to understand or appreciate it. *e.g. He did not fully comprehend what was puzzling me.*
comprehension NOUN

● THESAURUS
appreciate: *She has never really appreciated the scale of the problem.*
fathom: *I really couldn't fathom what Steiner was talking about.*
grasp: *The Government has not yet grasped the seriousness of the crisis.*
see: *I don't see why you're complaining.*
take in: *I try to explain, but you can tell she's not taking it in.*
understand: *They are too young to understand what's going on.*
work out: *It took me some time to work out what was causing the problem.*

comprehensible [ˌkɒmprɪ'hensəbəl] ADJECTIVE
able to be understood

comprehensive [ˌkɒmprɪ'hensɪv] **comprehensives** ADJECTIVE
1 Something that is comprehensive includes everything necessary or relevant. *e.g. a comprehensive guide*
> NOUN
2 a school where children of all abilities are taught together
comprehensively ADVERB

compress [kəm'pres] **compresses, compressing, compressed** VERB
To compress something is to squeeze it or shorten it so that it takes up less space. *e.g. compressed air*
compression NOUN

comprise [kəm'praɪz] **comprises, comprising, comprised** VERB; FORMAL
What something comprises is what it consists of. *e.g. The district then comprised 66 villages.*

> You do not need *of* after *comprise*. For example, you say *the library comprises 500,000 books*

compromise ['kɒmprə,maɪz] **compromises, compromising, compromised** NOUN
1 an agreement in which people accept less than they originally wanted *e.g. In the end they reached a compromise.*
> VERB
2 When people compromise, they agree to accept less than they originally wanted.
compromising ADJECTIVE

compulsion [kəm'pʌlʃən] **compulsions** NOUN
a very strong desire to do something

compulsive [kəm'pʌlsɪv] ADJECTIVE
1 You use 'compulsive' to describe someone who cannot stop doing something. *e.g. a compulsive letter writer*
2 If you find something such as a book or television programme compulsive, you cannot stop reading or watching it.

compulsory [kəm'pʌlsərɪ] ADJECTIVE
If something is compulsory, you have to do it. *e.g. School attendance is compulsory.*

● THESAURUS
mandatory: *the mandatory retirement age*
obligatory: *an obligatory medical examination*
required: *the required reading for this course*
requisite: *the requisite documents*
<<OPPOSITE *voluntary*

computer [kəm'pju:tə] **computers** NOUN
an electronic machine that can quickly make
calculations or store and find information

computer-aided design
[kəm'pju:tə,eɪdəd,dɪ'saɪn] NOUN
Computer-aided design is the use of computers
and computer graphics to help design things.

computerize [kəm'pju:tə,raɪz]
**computerizes, computerizing,
computerized**; also spelt **computerise** VERB
When a system or process is computerized, the
work is done by computers.

computing [kəm'pju:tɪŋ] NOUN
Computing is the use of computers and the
writing of programs for them.

comrade ['kɒmreɪd] **comrades** NOUN
A soldier's comrades are his fellow soldiers,
especially in battle.
comradeship NOUN

con [kɒn] **cons, conning, conned** INFORMAL
VERB
1 If someone cons you, they trick you into doing
or believing something.

● THESAURUS
cheat: *a deliberate attempt to cheat employees out
of their pensions*
deceive: *She deceived us into giving her a job.*
mislead: *Ministers must not knowingly mislead the
public.*
swindle: *A City businessman swindled investors out
of millions of pounds.*
trick: *They tricked him into parting with his life
savings.*

> NOUN
2 a trick in which someone deceives you into
doing or believing something

● THESAURUS
bluff: *The letter was a bluff.*
deception: *You've been the victim of a rather cruel
deception.*
fraud: *an investigation into frauds in the world of
horseracing*
swindle: *a tax swindle*
trick: *a cheap trick to encourage people to switch
energy suppliers*

concave ['kɒnkeɪv] ADJECTIVE
A concave surface curves inwards, rather than
being level or bulging outwards.

conceal [kən'si:l] **conceals, concealing,
concealed** VERB
To conceal something is to hide it. *e.g. He had
concealed his gun.*
concealment NOUN

concede [kən'si:d] **concedes, conceding,
conceded** VERB

1 If you concede something, you admit that it is
true. *e.g. I conceded that he was entitled to his views.*
2 When someone concedes defeat, they accept
that they have lost something such as a contest
or an election.

conceit [kən'si:t] NOUN
Conceit is someone's excessive pride in their
appearance or abilities.

● THESAURUS
egotism: *typical showbiz egotism*
pride: *a blow to his pride*
self-importance: *his bad manners and self-
importance*
vanity: *her vanity about her long hair*

conceited [kən'si:tɪd] ADJECTIVE
Someone who is conceited is too proud of their
appearance or abilities.

● THESAURUS
bigheaded: informal *an arrogant, bigheaded man*
cocky: *I was very cocky as a youngster.*
egotistical: *an egotistical show-off*
self-important: *self-important pop stars*
vain: *a shallow, vain woman*
<<OPPOSITE *modest*

conceivable [kən'si:vəbəl] ADJECTIVE
If something is conceivable, you can believe that
it could exist or be true. *e.g. It's conceivable that
you also met her.*
conceivably ADVERB

conceive [kən'si:v] **conceives, conceiving,
conceived** VERB
1 If you can conceive of something, you can
imagine it or believe it. *e.g. Could you conceive of
doing such a thing yourself?*
2 If you conceive something such as a plan, you
think of it and work out how it could be done.
3 When a woman conceives, she becomes
pregnant.

concentrate ['kɒnsən,treɪt] **concentrates,
concentrating, concentrated** VERB
1 If you concentrate on something, you give it all
your attention.

● THESAURUS
be engrossed in: *He was engrossed in his work.*
focus your attention on: *focusing his attention on
the race*
give your attention to: *I gave my attention to the
question.*
put your mind to: *You could do it if you put your
mind to it.*

2 When something is concentrated in one place,
it is all there rather than in several places. *e.g.
They are mostly concentrated in the urban areas.*
concentration NOUN

● THESAURUS
accumulate: *Cholesterol accumulates in the
arteries.*

collect: *dust collecting in the corners*
gather: *residents gathered in huddles*

concentrated ['kɒnsən,treɪtɪd] ADJECTIVE
A concentrated liquid has been made stronger by having water removed from it. *e.g. concentrated apple juice*

concentration camp [,kɒnsən'treɪʃən]
concentration camps NOUN
a prison camp, especially one set up by the Nazis during World War Two

concept ['kɒnsɛpt] **concepts** NOUN
an abstract or general idea *e.g. the concept of tolerance*
conceptual ADJECTIVE, **conceptually** ADVERB

conception [kən'sɛpʃən] **conceptions**
NOUN
1 Your conception of something is the idea you have of it.
2 Conception is the process by which a woman becomes pregnant.

concern [kən'sɜːn] **concerns, concerning, concerned** NOUN
1 Concern is a feeling of worry about something or someone. *e.g. public concern about violence*

⬤ THESAURUS
anxiety: *anxiety about the economy*
apprehension: *apprehension about the future*
disquiet: *a growing sense of disquiet*
worry: *She has no worries about his health.*

2 If something is your concern, it is your responsibility.

⬤ THESAURUS
affair: *If you want to go, that's your affair.*
business: *This is none of my business.*
responsibility: *He's not my responsibility.*

3 a business *e.g. a large manufacturing concern*

> VERB
4 If something concerns you or if you are concerned about it, it worries you.

⬤ THESAURUS
bother: *Nothing bothers me.*
distress: *They are distressed by the accusations.*
disturb: *disturbed by the news*
trouble: *Is anything troubling you?*
worry: *an issue that had worried him for some time*

5 You say that something concerns you if it affects or involves you. *e.g. It concerns you and me.*

⬤ THESAURUS
affect: *the ways in which computers affect our lives*
apply to: *This rule does not apply to us.*
be relevant to: *These documents are relevant to the case.*
involve: *meetings which involve most of the staff*

> PHRASE
6 If something is **of concern** to you, it is important to you.

concerned ADJECTIVE

concerning [kən'sɜːnɪŋ] PREPOSITION
You use 'concerning' to show what something is about. *e.g. documents concerning arm sales to Iraq*

concert ['kɒnsɜːt] **concerts** NOUN
a public performance by musicians

concerted [kən'sɜːtɪd] ADJECTIVE
A concerted action is done by several people together. *e.g. concerted action to cut interest rates*

concerto [kən'tʃɛətəʊ] **concertos** or
concerti NOUN
a piece of music for a solo instrument and an orchestra

concession [kən'sɛʃən] **concessions** NOUN
If you make a concession, you agree to let someone have or do something. *e.g. Her one concession was to let me come into the building.*

conch [kɒntʃ] **conches** NOUN
a shellfish with a large, brightly coloured shell; also the shell itself

concise [kən'saɪs] ADJECTIVE
giving all the necessary information using as few words as possible *e.g. a concise guide*

⬤ THESAURUS
brief: *a brief description*
short: *a short speech*
succinct: *a succinct explanation*
terse: *a terse statement*
<<OPPOSITE long

conclude [kən'kluːd] **concludes, concluding, concluded** VERB
1 If you conclude something, you decide that it is so because of the other things that you know. *e.g. An inquiry concluded that this was untrue.*

⬤ THESAURUS
decide: *I decided he must be ill.*
deduce: *She deduced that I had written the letter.*
infer: *His feelings were easily inferred from his reply.*
judge: *The doctor judged that he was not fit enough to play.*
reckon: *informal I reckon we should wait a while.*
suppose: *There's no reason to suppose he'll be there.*
surmise: *It is surmised that he must have known.*

2 When you conclude something, you finish it. *e.g. At that point I intend to conclude the interview.*
concluding ADJECTIVE

⬤ THESAURUS
close: *They closed the show with a song.*
end: *His speech ended with a prayer for peace.*
finish: *We finished the evening with a walk on the beach.*
round off: *This rounded the afternoon off perfectly.*
wind up: *She quickly wound up her conversation.*
<<OPPOSITE begin

conclusion [kən'kluːʒən] **conclusions**
NOUN

1 a decision made after thinking carefully about something

● THESAURUS

deduction: *a shrewd deduction about what was going on*
inference: *There were two inferences to be drawn from her letter.*
judgment: *My judgment is that things are going to get worse.*
verdict: *The doctor's verdict was that he was fine.*

2 the finish or ending of something

● THESAURUS

close: *bringing the talks to a close*
end: *The war is coming to an end.*
ending: *a dramatic ending*
finish: *the finish of the race*
termination: *the termination of their marriage*
<<OPPOSITE *beginning*

conclusive [kən'kluːsɪv] ADJECTIVE
Facts that are conclusive show that something is certainly true.
conclusively ADVERB

concoct [kən'kɒkt] **concocts, concocting, concocted** VERB

1 If you concoct an excuse or explanation, you invent one.

2 If you concoct something, you make it by mixing several things together.
concoction NOUN

concourse ['kɒnkɔːs] **concourses** NOUN
a wide hall in a building where people walk about or gather together

concrete ['kɒnkriːt] NOUN

1 Concrete is a solid building material made by mixing cement, sand, and water.

> ADJECTIVE

2 definite, rather than general or vague *e.g. I don't really have any concrete plans.*

3 real and physical, rather than abstract *e.g. concrete evidence*

concubine ['kɒŋkjʊˌbaɪn] **concubines**
NOUN; OLD-FASHIONED, INFORMAL
A man's concubine is his mistress.

concur [kən'kɜː] **concurs, concurring, concurred** VERB; FORMAL
To concur is to agree. *e.g. She concurred with me.*

concurrent [kən'kʌrənt] ADJECTIVE
If things are concurrent, they happen at the same time.
concurrently ADVERB

concussed [kən'kʌst] ADJECTIVE
confused or unconscious because of a blow to the head

concussion NOUN

condemn [kən'dɛm] **condemns, condemning, condemned** VERB

1 If you condemn something, you say it is bad and unacceptable. *e.g. Teachers condemned the new plans.*

● THESAURUS

blame: *I blame television for the rise in violence.*
censure: *a motion censuring the government*
criticize: *He was criticized for his failure to act.*
damn: *The report damns the government's handling of the affair.*
denounce: *He was denounced as a traitor.*

2 If someone is condemned to a punishment, they are given it. *e.g. She was condemned to death.*

● THESAURUS

damn: *sinners damned to eternal torment*
doom: *doomed to die for his crime*
sentence: *sentenced to ten years in prison*

3 If you are condemned to something unpleasant, you must suffer it. *e.g. Many women are condemned to poverty.*

4 When a building is condemned, it is going to be pulled down because it is unsafe.
condemnation NOUN

condensation [ˌkɒndɛn'seɪʃən] NOUN
(SCIENCE) Condensation is a coating of tiny drops formed on a surface by steam or vapour.

condense [kən'dɛns] **condenses, condensing, condensed** VERB

1 If you condense a piece of writing or a speech, you shorten it.

2 When a gas or vapour condenses, it changes into a liquid.

condescending [ˌkɒndɪ'sɛndɪŋ] ADJECTIVE
If you are condescending, you behave in a way that shows you think you are superior to other people.

condition [kən'dɪʃən] **conditions, conditioning, conditioned** NOUN

1 the state someone or something is in

● THESAURUS

form: *The team are not in good form this season.*
shape: *He's in great shape for his age.*
state: *Look at the state of my car!*

> PLURAL NOUN

2 The conditions in which something is done are the location and other factors likely to affect it. *e.g. The very difficult conditions continued to affect our performance.*

3 a requirement that must be met for something else to be possible *e.g. He had been banned from drinking alcohol as a condition of bail.*

● THESAURUS

prerequisite: *A science background is a prerequisite for the job.*

provision: *a provision in his will forbidding the sale of the house*
proviso: *The answer is yes, with one proviso.*
qualification: *He agreed, but with some qualifications.*
requirement: *The product meets all legal requirements.*
requisite: *the main requisite for membership*
stipulation: *The only dress stipulation was 'no jeans'.*
terms: *the terms of the agreement*

4 You can refer to an illness or other medical problem as a condition. *e.g. a heart condition*

> PHRASE

5 If you are **out of condition**, you are unfit.

> VERB

6 If someone is conditioned to behave or think in a certain way, they do it as a result of their upbringing or training.

conditional [kənˈdɪʃənᵊl] ADJECTIVE
If one thing is conditional on another, it can only happen if the other thing happens. *e.g. You feel his love is conditional on you pleasing him.*

condolence [kənˈdəʊləns] **condolences**
NOUN
Condolence is sympathy expressed for a bereaved person.

condom [ˈkɒndɒm] **condoms** NOUN
a rubber sheath worn by a man on his penis or by a woman inside her vagina as a contraceptive

condominium [ˌkɒndəˈmɪnɪəm]
condominiums NOUN
In Canadian, Australian, and New Zealand English, an apartment block in which each apartment is owned by the person who lives in it.

condone [kənˈdəʊn] **condones,
condoning, condoned** VERB
If you condone someone's bad behaviour, you accept it and do not try to stop it. *e.g. We cannot condone violence.*

conducive [kənˈdjuːsɪv] ADJECTIVE
If something is conducive to something else, it makes it likely to happen. *e.g. a situation that is conducive to relaxation*

**conduct conducts, conducting,
conducted** VERB [kənˈdʌkt]
1 To conduct an activity or task is to carry it out. *e.g. He seemed to be conducting a conversation.*

● THESAURUS
carry out: *carry out a survey*
direct: *Christopher will direct day-to-day operations.*
do: *I'm doing a piece of important research right now.*

manage: *his ability to manage the business*
organize: *The initial mobilization was well organized.*
perform: *Several grafts were performed during the operation.*
run: *Each teacher will run a different workshop.*

2 FORMAL The way you conduct yourself is the way you behave.

● THESAURUS
act: *a gang of youths who were acting suspiciously*
behave: *He'd behaved badly.*

3 When someone conducts an orchestra or choir, they stand in front of it and direct it.

4 If something conducts heat or electricity, heat or electricity can pass through it.

> NOUN [ˈkɒndʌkt]

5 If you take part in the conduct of an activity or task, you help to carry it out.

6 Your conduct is your behaviour.

● THESAURUS
attitude: *His attitude made me angry.*
behaviour: *Make sure that good behaviour is rewarded.*
manners: *He dressed well and had impeccable manners.*
ways: *urged him to alter his ways*

conductor [kənˈdʌktə] **conductors** NOUN
1 (MUSIC) someone who conducts an orchestra or choir

2 someone who moves round a bus or train selling tickets

3 a substance that conducts heat or electricity

cone [kəʊn] **cones** NOUN
1 a regular three-dimensional shape with a circular base and a point at the top

2 A fir cone or pine cone is the fruit of a fir or pine tree.

confectionery [kənˈfɛkʃənərɪ] NOUN
Confectionery is sweets.

confederation [kənˌfɛdəˈreɪʃən]
confederations NOUN
an organization formed for business or political purposes

confer [kənˈfɜː] **confers, conferring,
conferred** VERB
When people confer, they discuss something in order to make a decision.

conference [ˈkɒnfərəns] **conferences**
NOUN
a meeting at which formal discussions take place

● THESAURUS
congress: *a congress of coal miners*
convention: *the Geneva convention*

discussion: *a round of formal discussions*
forum: *a forum for trade negotiations*
meeting: *a meeting of shareholders*

confess [kən'fɛs] confesses, confessing, confessed VERB

If you confess to something, you admit it. *e.g. Your son has confessed to his crimes.*

● THESAURUS
acknowledge: *He acknowledged that he was a drug addict.*
admit: *I admit to feeling jealous.*
own up: *The headmaster is waiting for someone to own up.*
<<OPPOSITE *deny*

confession [kən'fɛʃən] confessions NOUN

1 If you make a confession, you admit you have done something wrong.

2 Confession is the act of confessing something, especially a religious act in which people confess their sins to a priest.

● THESAURUS
acknowledgment: *an acknowledgment of his mistakes*
admission: *an admission of guilt*

confessional [kən'fɛʃənəl] confessionals NOUN

a small room in some churches where people confess their sins to a priest

confetti [kən'fɛtɪ] NOUN

Confetti is small pieces of coloured paper thrown over the bride and groom at a wedding.
[WORD HISTORY: from Italian CONFETTO meaning 'a sweet']

confidant [ˌkɒnfɪ'dænt] confidants NOUN; FORMAL

a person you discuss your private problems with

> When the person you discuss your private problems with is a girl or a woman, the word is spelt *confidante*

confide [kən'faɪd] confides, confiding, confided VERB

If you confide in or to someone, you tell them a secret. *e.g. Marian confided in me that she was very worried.*

confidence ['kɒnfɪdəns] confidences NOUN

1 If you have confidence in someone, you feel you can trust them.

● THESAURUS
belief: *his belief in his partner*
faith: *He has great faith in her judgment.*
reliance: *I don't put much reliance on that idea.*
trust: *He destroyed my trust in people.*
<<OPPOSITE *distrust*

2 Someone who has confidence is sure of their own abilities or qualities.

● THESAURUS
aplomb: *She handled the interview with aplomb.*
assurance: *He led the orchestra with great assurance.*
self-assurance: *his supreme self-assurance*
self-possession: *an air of self-possession*
<<OPPOSITE *shyness*

3 a secret you tell someone

confident ['kɒnfɪdənt] ADJECTIVE

1 If you are confident about something, you are sure it will happen the way you want it to.

● THESAURUS
certain: *certain of getting a place on the team*
convinced: *He is convinced it's your fault.*
positive: *I'm positive it will happen.*
satisfied: *We must be satisfied that the treatment is safe.*
secure: *secure about his job prospects*
sure: *I'm not sure I understand.*
<<OPPOSITE *uncertain*

2 People who are confident are sure of their own abilities or qualities.
confidently ADVERB

● THESAURUS
assured: *His playing became more assured.*
self-assured: *a self-assured young man*
self-possessed: *a self-possessed career woman*
<<OPPOSITE *shy*

confidential [ˌkɒnfɪ'dɛnʃəl] ADJECTIVE

Confidential information is meant to be kept secret.
confidentially ADVERB, confidentiality NOUN

confine confines, confining, confined VERB [kən'faɪn]

1 If something is confined to one place, person, or thing, it exists only in that place or affects only that person or thing.

2 If you confine yourself to doing or saying something, it is the only thing you do or say. *e.g. They confined themselves to discussing the weather.*

● THESAURUS
limit: *Limit yourself to six units of alcohol a week.*
restrict: *The patient was restricted to a meagre diet.*

3 If you are confined to a place, you cannot leave it. *e.g. She was confined to bed for two days.*

● THESAURUS
hem in: *hemmed in by spectators*
imprison: *imprisoned in a tiny cell*
restrict: *We were restricted to the building.*
shut up: *He can't stand being shut up in the house.*

> PLURAL NOUN ['kɒnfaɪnz]
4 The confines of a place are its boundaries. *e.g. outside the confines of the prison*

confinement NOUN

confined [kən'faɪnd] ADJECTIVE
A confined space is small and enclosed by walls.

confirm [kən'fɜːm] **confirms, confirming, confirmed** VERB
1 To confirm something is to say or show that it is true. *e.g. Police confirmed that they had received a call.*

THESAURUS
bear out: *The figures bear out his words.*
endorse: *This theory has been endorsed by research.*
prove: *The results prove his point.*
substantiate: *no evidence to substantiate the claims*
validate: *It is difficult to validate this belief.*
verify: *I was asked to verify this statement.*

2 If you confirm an arrangement or appointment, you say it is definite.

THESAURUS
fix: *The date for the election was fixed.*
settle: *I've settled a time to see him.*

3 When someone is confirmed, they are formally accepted as a member of a Christian church.
confirmation NOUN

confirmed [kən'fɜːmd] ADJECTIVE
You use 'confirmed' to describe someone who has a belief or way of life that is unlikely to change. *e.g. a confirmed bachelor*

confiscate ['kɒnfɪˌskeɪt] **confiscates, confiscating, confiscated** VERB
To confiscate something is to take it away from someone as a punishment.

conflict conflicts, conflicting, conflicted
NOUN ['kɒnflɪkt]
1 Conflict is disagreement and argument. *e.g. conflict between workers and management*

THESAURUS
antagonism: *antagonism within the team*
disagreement: *The meeting ended in disagreement.*
discord: *public discord*
friction: *friction between him and his father*
hostility: *hostility between parents and teachers*
opposition: *a wave of opposition*
strife: *a cause of strife in many marriages*

2 (**HISTORY**) a war or battle

THESAURUS
battle: *a battle between two gangs*
combat: *men who died in combat*
fighting: *Villagers have left their homes to avoid the fighting.*
strife: *civil strife*
war: *the war between Israel and Egypt*

3 When there is a conflict of ideas or interests, people have different ideas or interests which cannot all be satisfied.

> VERB [kən'flɪkt]
4 When ideas or interests conflict, they are different and cannot all be satisfied.

THESAURUS
be at variance: *His statements are at variance with the facts.*
be incompatible: *These two principles are incompatible.*
clash: *a decision which clashes with official policy*
differ: *The two leaders differ on several issues.*
disagree: *Governments disagree over the need for action.*

conform [kən'fɔːm] **conforms, conforming, conformed** VERB
1 If you conform, you behave the way people expect you to.
2 If something conforms to a law or to someone's wishes, it is what is required or wanted.
conformist NOUN OR ADJECTIVE

confront [kən'frʌnt] **confronts, confronting, confronted** VERB
1 If you are confronted with a problem or task, you have to deal with it.
2 If you confront someone, you meet them face to face like an enemy.
3 If you confront someone with evidence or a fact, you present it to them in order to accuse them of something.

confrontation [ˌkɒnfrʌn'teɪʃən] **confrontations** NOUN
a serious dispute or fight *e.g. a confrontation between police and fans*

confuse [kən'fjuːz] **confuses, confusing, confused** VERB
1 If you confuse two things, you mix them up and think one of them is the other. *e.g. You are confusing facts with opinion.*

THESAURUS
mistake: *I mistook you for someone else.*
mix up: *He sometimes mixes up his words.*
muddle up: *I keep muddling him up with his brother.*

2 To confuse someone means to make them uncertain about what is happening or what to do.

THESAURUS
baffle: *Police are baffled by the murder.*
bewilder: *His silence bewildered her.*
mystify: *I was mystified by his attitude.*
puzzle: *One thing still puzzles me.*

3 To confuse a situation means to make it more complicated.

confused [kən'fjuːzd] ADJECTIVE
1 uncertain about what is happening or what to do

● THESAURUS
baffled: *He stared in baffled amazement.*
bewildered: *bewildered holidaymakers*
muddled: *She was muddled about the date.*
perplexed: *perplexed by recent events*
puzzled: *a puzzled expression*

2 in an untidy mess
● THESAURUS
chaotic: *the chaotic mess on his desk*
disordered: *a disordered pile of papers*
disorganized: *a disorganized lifestyle*
untidy: *an untidy room*
<<OPPOSITE *tidy*

confusing [kən'fju:zɪŋ] ADJECTIVE
puzzling or bewildering
● THESAURUS
baffling: *a baffling statement*
bewildering: *a bewildering choice of products*
complicated: *a complicated voting system*
puzzling: *a puzzling problem*

confusion [kən'fju:ʒən] NOUN
a bewildering state or untidy mess
● THESAURUS
chaos: *economic chaos*
disarray: *The nation is in disarray.*
disorder: *The emergency room was in disorder.*
disorganization: *scenes of chaos and disorganization*
mess: *He always leaves the bathroom in a mess.*
<<OPPOSITE *order*

congeal [kən'dʒi:l] **congeals, congealing, congealed** VERB
When a liquid congeals, it becomes very thick and sticky.

congenial [kən'dʒi:njəl] ADJECTIVE
If something is congenial, it is pleasant and suits you. *e.g. We wanted to talk in congenial surroundings.*

congenital [kən'dʒɛnɪtəl] ADJECTIVE; MEDICAL
If someone has a congenital disease or handicap, they have had it from birth but did not inherit it.

congested [kən'dʒɛstɪd] ADJECTIVE
1 When a road is congested, it is so full of traffic that normal movement is impossible.

2 If your nose is congested, it is blocked and you cannot breathe properly.
congestion NOUN

conglomerate [kən'glɒmərɪt] **conglomerates** NOUN
a large business organization consisting of several companies

congratulate [kən'grætjʊˌleɪt] **congratulates, congratulating, congratulated** VERB

If you congratulate someone, you express pleasure at something good that has happened to them, or praise them for something they have achieved.
congratulation NOUN, **congratulatory** ADJECTIVE

congregate ['kɒŋgrɪˌgeɪt] **congregates, congregating, congregated** VERB
When people congregate, they gather together somewhere.

congregation [ˌkɒŋgrɪ'geɪʃən] **congregations** NOUN
The congregation are the people attending a service in a church.

congress ['kɒŋgrɛs] **congresses** NOUN
a large meeting held to discuss ideas or policies
e.g. a medical congress

conical ['kɒnɪkəl] ADJECTIVE
shaped like a cone

conifer ['kəʊnɪfə] **conifers** NOUN
any type of evergreen tree that produces cones
coniferous ADJECTIVE

conjecture [kən'dʒɛktʃə] NOUN
Conjecture is guesswork about something. *e.g. There was no evidence, only conjecture.*

conjugate ['kɒndʒʊˌgeɪt] **conjugates, conjugating, conjugated** VERB
When you conjugate a verb, you list the different forms of it you use with the pronouns 'I' 'you' (singular) 'he' 'she' 'it' 'you' (plural) and 'they'.

conjunction [kən'dʒʌŋkʃən] **conjunctions** NOUN

1 (ENGLISH) In grammar, a conjunction is a word that links two other words or two clauses, for example 'and', 'but', 'while', and 'that'.

> PHRASE
2 If two or more things are done **in conjunction**, they are done together.

conjurer ['kʌndʒərə] **conjurers** NOUN
someone who entertains people by doing magic tricks

conker ['kɒŋkə] **conkers** NOUN
Conkers are hard brown nuts from a horse chestnut tree.

connect [kə'nɛkt] **connects, connecting, connected** VERB

1 To connect two things is to join them together.
● THESAURUS
affix: *His name was affixed to his cubicle.*
attach: *Attach the curtains to the rods with hooks.*
couple: *The engine is coupled to a gearbox.*
fasten: *A hatchet was fastened to his belt.*
join: *two springs joined together*
link: *the Channel Tunnel linking Britain with France*

C

<<OPPOSITE *separate*

2 If you connect something with something else, you think of them as being linked. *e.g. High blood pressure is closely connected to heart disease.*

● THESAURUS
ally: *The new government is allied with the military.*
associate: *symptoms associated with migraine headaches*
link: *research which links smoking with cancer*
relate: *the denial that unemployment is related to crime*

connection [kə'nɛkʃən] **connections;** also spelt **connexion** NOUN
1 a link or relationship between things

● THESAURUS
affiliation: *He has no affiliation with any political party.*
association: *the association between the two companies*
bond: *the bond between a mother and child*
correlation: *the correlation between unemployment and crime*
correspondence: *the correspondence between Eastern and Western religions*
link: *a link between smoking and lung cancer*
relation: *This theory bears no relation to reality.*
relationship: *the relationship between humans and their environment*

2 the point where two wires or pipes are joined together *e.g. a loose connection*

● THESAURUS
coupling: *The coupling between the railway carriages snapped.*
fastening: *a zip fastening*
junction: *the junction between nerve and muscle*
link: *a link between the city and the motorway*

> PLURAL NOUN
3 Someone's connections are the people they know. *e.g. He had powerful connections in the army.*

connective [kə'nɛktɪv] **connectives** NOUN
a word or short phrase that connects clauses, phrases or words

connoisseur [ˌkɒnɪ'sɜː] **connoisseurs** NOUN
someone who knows a lot about the arts, or about food or drink *e.g. a great connoisseur of champagne*
[WORD HISTORY: from Old French CONNOISTRE meaning 'to know']

connotation [ˌkɒnə'teɪʃən] **connotations** NOUN
The connotations of a word or name are what it makes you think of. *e.g. a grey man for whom grey has no connotation of dullness*

conquer ['kɒŋkə] **conquers, conquering, conquered** VERB

1 To conquer people is to take control of their country by force.

2 If you conquer something difficult or dangerous, you succeed in controlling it. *e.g. Conquer your fear!*
conqueror NOUN

conquest ['kɒnkwɛst] **conquests** NOUN
1 Conquest is the conquering of a country or group of people.

2 Conquests are lands captured by conquest.

conscience ['kɒnʃəns] **consciences** NOUN
the part of your mind that tells you what is right and wrong

● THESAURUS
principles: *It's against my principles to eat meat.*
scruples: *a man with no moral scruples*
sense of right and wrong: *children with no sense of right and wrong*

conscientious [ˌkɒnʃɪ'ɛnʃəs] ADJECTIVE
Someone who is conscientious is very careful to do their work properly.
conscientiously ADVERB

conscious ['kɒnʃəs] ADJECTIVE
1 If you are conscious of something, you are aware of it. *e.g. She was not conscious of the time.*

2 A conscious action or effort is done deliberately. *e.g. I made a conscious decision not to hide.*

3 Someone who is conscious is awake, rather than asleep or unconscious. *e.g. Still conscious, she was taken to hospital.*
consciously ADVERB, **consciousness** NOUN

consecrated ['kɒnsɪˌkreɪtɪd] ADJECTIVE
A consecrated building or place is one that has been officially declared to be holy.

consecutive [kən'sɛkjʊtɪv] ADJECTIVE
Consecutive events or periods of time happen one after the other. *e.g. eight consecutive games*

consensus [kən'sɛnsəs] NOUN
Consensus is general agreement among a group of people. *e.g. The consensus was that it could be done.*

> There are three ss in *consensus*, do not confuse the spelling with *census*. You should not say *consensus of opinion*, as *consensus* already has *of opinion* in its meaning

consent [kən'sɛnt] **consents, consenting, consented** NOUN

1 Consent is permission to do something. *e.g. Thomas reluctantly gave his consent to my writing this book.*

2 Consent is also agreement between two or more people. *e.g. By common consent it was the*

best game of these championships.

> VERB

3 If you consent to something, you agree to it or allow it.

consequence ['kɒnsɪkwəns]
consequences NOUN

1 The consequences of something are its results or effects. *e.g. the dire consequences of major war*

2 FORMAL If something is of consequence, it is important.

consequent ['kɒnsɪkwənt] ADJECTIVE
Consequent describes something as being the result of something else. *e.g. an earthquake in 1980 and its consequent damage*
consequently ADVERB

conservation [ˌkɒnsə'veɪʃən] NOUN
Conservation is the preservation of the environment.
conservationist NOUN OR ADJECTIVE

conservative [kən'sɜːvətɪv] **conservatives**
NOUN

1 In Britain, a member or supporter of the Conservative Party, a political party that believes that the government should interfere as little as possible in the running of the economy.

> ADJECTIVE

2 In Britain, Conservative views and policies are those of the Conservative Party.

3 Someone who is conservative is not willing to accept changes or new ideas.

● THESAURUS
conventional: *conventional tastes*
traditional: *a traditional school*
<<OPPOSITE *radical*

4 A conservative estimate or guess is a cautious or moderate one.
conservatively ADVERB, **conservatism** NOUN

conservatory [kən'sɜːvətrɪ]
conservatories NOUN
a room with glass walls and a glass roof in which plants are kept

conserve [kən'sɜːv] **conserves,**
conserving, conserved VERB
If you conserve a supply of something, you make it last. *e.g. the only way to conserve energy*

consider [kən'sɪdə] **considers,**
considering, considered VERB

1 If you consider something to be the case, you think or judge it to be so. *e.g. The manager does not consider him an ideal team member.*

● THESAURUS
believe: *I believe him to be innocent.*
judge: *His work was judged unsatisfactory.*
rate: *The film was rated excellent.*

regard as: *They regard the tax as unfair.*
think: *Many people think him arrogant.*

2 (EXAM TERM) To consider something is to think about it carefully. *e.g. If an offer were made, we would consider it.*

● THESAURUS
contemplate: *He contemplated his fate.*
deliberate: *The jury deliberated for three days.*
meditate: *He meditated on the problem.*
muse: *She sat musing on how unfair life was.*
ponder: *pondering how to improve the team*
reflect: *I reflected on the child's future.*
think about: *I've been thinking about what you said.*

3 If you consider someone's needs or feelings, you take account of them.

● THESAURUS
bear in mind: *There are a few points to bear in mind.*
make allowances for: *Remember to make allowances for delays.*
respect: *We will respect your wishes.*
take into account: *another factor to be taken into account*
think about: *more important things to think about*

considerable [kən'sɪdərəbəl] ADJECTIVE
A considerable amount of something is a lot of it. *e.g. a considerable sum of money*
considerably ADVERB

considerate [kən'sɪdərɪt] ADJECTIVE
Someone who is considerate pays attention to other people's needs and feelings.

consideration [kənˌsɪdə'reɪʃən]
considerations NOUN

1 Consideration is careful thought about something. *e.g. a decision demanding careful consideration*

● THESAURUS
attention: *I gave the question all my attention.*
contemplation: *The problem deserves serious contemplation.*
deliberation: *After much deliberation, he called the police.*
study: *The proposals need careful study.*
thought: *I've given the matter a great deal of thought.*

2 If you show consideration for someone, you take account of their needs and feelings.

● THESAURUS
concern: *concern for the homeless*
kindness: *We have been treated with great kindness.*
respect: *no respect for wildlife*
tact: *a master of tact and diplomacy*

3 something that has to be taken into account *e.g. Money was also a consideration.*

● THESAURUS

factor: *an important factor in buying a house*
issue: *Price is not the only issue.*
point: *There is another point to remember.*

considered [kən'sɪdəd] ADJECTIVE
A considered opinion or judgment is arrived at by careful thought.

considering [kən'sɪdərɪŋ] CONJUNCTION OR PREPOSITION
You say considering to indicate that you are taking something into account. *e.g. I know that must sound callous, considering that I was married to the man for seventeen years.*

consign [kən'saɪn] **consigns, consigning, consigned** VERB; FORMAL
To consign something to a particular place is to send or put it there.

consignment [kən'saɪnmənt] **consignments** NOUN
A consignment of goods is a load of them being delivered somewhere.

consist [kən'sɪst] **consists, consisting, consisted** VERB
What something consists of is its different parts or members. *e.g. The brain consists of millions of nerve cells.*

● THESAURUS

be composed of: *The committee is composed of ten people.*
be made up of: *The bouquet was made up of roses and carnations.*
comprise: *The show comprises 50 paintings and sketches.*

consistency [kən'sɪstənsi] **consistencies** NOUN
1 Consistency is the quality of being consistent.
2 The consistency of a substance is how thick or smooth it is. *e.g. the consistency of single cream*

consistent [kən'sɪstənt] ADJECTIVE
1 If you are consistent, you keep doing something the same way. *e.g. one of our most consistent performers*
2 If something such as a statement or argument is consistent, there are no contradictions in it.
consistently ADVERB

console **consoles, consoling, consoled** VERB [kən'səʊl]
1 To console someone who is unhappy is to make them more cheerful.
> NOUN ['kɒnsəʊl]
2 a panel with switches or knobs for operating a machine
consolation NOUN

consolidate [kən'sɒlɪˌdeɪt] **consolidates, consolidating, consolidated** VERB

To consolidate something you have gained or achieved is to make it more secure.
consolidation NOUN

consonant ['kɒnsənənt] **consonants** NOUN
(ENGLISH) a sound such as 'p' or 'm' which you make by stopping the air flowing freely through your mouth
[WORD HISTORY: from Latin CONSONARE meaning 'to sound at the same time']

consort **consorts, consorting, consorted** VERB [kən'sɔːt]
1 FORMAL If you consort with someone, you spend a lot of time with them.
> NOUN ['kɒnsɔːt]
2 the wife or husband of the king or queen

consortium [kən'sɔːtɪəm] **consortia** or **consortiums** NOUN
a group of businesses working together

conspicuous [kən'spɪkjʊəs] ADJECTIVE
If something is conspicuous, people can see or notice it very easily.
conspicuously ADVERB

● THESAURUS

apparent: *It has been apparent that someone has been stealing.*
blatant: *a blatant disregard for rules*
evident: *He spoke with evident emotion about his ordeal.*
noticeable: *the most noticeable effect of these changes*
obvious: *an obvious injustice*
perceptible: *a perceptible air of neglect*

conspiracy [kən'spɪrəsi] **conspiracies** NOUN
When there is a conspiracy, a group of people plan something illegal, often for a political purpose.

conspirator [kən'spɪrətə] **conspirators** NOUN
someone involved in a conspiracy

conspire [kən'spaɪə] **conspires, conspiring, conspired** VERB
1 When people conspire, they plan together to do something illegal, often for a political purpose.
2 LITERARY When events conspire towards a particular result, they seem to work together to cause it. *e.g. Circumstances conspired to doom the business.*

constable ['kʌnstəbəl] **constables** NOUN
a police officer of the lowest rank
[WORD HISTORY: from Latin COMES STABULI meaning 'officer of the stable']

constabulary [kən'stæbjʊlərɪ] **constabularies** NOUN

C

a police force

constant ['kɒnstənt] ADJECTIVE

1 Something that is constant happens all the time or is always there. *e.g. a city under constant attack*

◗ **THESAURUS**
continual: *continual pain*
continuous: *continuous gunfire*
eternal: *an eternal hum in the background*
nonstop: *nonstop music*
perpetual: *her perpetual complaints*
relentless: *relentless pressure*
<<OPPOSITE *periodic*

2 If an amount or level is constant, it stays the same.

◗ **THESAURUS**
even: *an even level of sound*
fixed: *a fixed salary*
regular: *a regular beat*
stable: *a stable condition*
steady: *travelling at a steady 50 miles per hour*
uniform: *a uniform thickness*
<<OPPOSITE *changeable*

3 People who are constant stay loyal to a person or idea.
constantly ADVERB, **constancy** NOUN

constellation [ˌkɒnstɪˈleɪʃən] **constellations** NOUN
a group of stars

consternation [ˌkɒnstəˈneɪʃən] NOUN
Consternation is anxiety or dismay. *e.g. There was some consternation when it began raining.*

constipated ['kɒnstɪˌpeɪtɪd] ADJECTIVE
Someone who is constipated is unable to pass solid waste from their bowels.
constipation NOUN

constituency [kənˈstɪtjʊənsɪ] **constituencies** NOUN
a town or area represented by an MP

constituent [kənˈstɪtjʊənt] **constituents** NOUN

1 An MP's constituents are the voters who live in his or her constituency.

2 The constituents of something are its parts. *e.g. the major constituents of bone*

constitute ['kɒnstɪˌtjuːt] **constitutes, constituting, constituted** VERB
If a group of things constitute something, they are what it consists of. *e.g. Jewellery constitutes 80 per cent of the stock.*

constitution [ˌkɒnstɪˈtjuːʃən] **constitutions** NOUN

1 (HISTORY) The constitution of a country is the system of laws which formally states people's rights and duties.

2 Your constitution is your health. *e.g. a very strong constitution*
constitutional ADJECTIVE, **constitutionally** ADVERB

constrained [kənˈstreɪnd] ADJECTIVE
If a person feels constrained to do something, they feel that they should do it.

constraint [kənˈstreɪnt] **constraints** NOUN
something that limits someone's freedom of action *e.g. constraints on trade union power*

constrict [kənˈstrɪkt] **constricts, constricting, constricted** VERB
To constrict something is to squeeze it tightly.
constriction NOUN

construct [kənˈstrʌkt] **constructs, constructing, constructed** VERB
To construct something is to build or make it.

◗ **THESAURUS**
assemble: *She had been trying to assemble the bomb when it went off.*
build: *Workers at the plant build the F-16 jet fighter.*
create: *We created a makeshift platform for him to stand on.*
erect: *The building was erected in 1900.*
make: *The company now makes cars at two plants in Europe.*
put together: *the mechanic whose job was to put together looms within the plant*
put up: *He was putting up a new fence.*

construction [kənˈstrʌkʃən] **constructions** NOUN

1 The construction of something is the building or making of it. *e.g. the construction of the harbour*

2 something built or made *e.g. a shoddy modern construction built of concrete*

constructive [kənˈstrʌktɪv] ADJECTIVE
Constructive criticisms and comments are helpful.
constructively ADVERB

consul ['kɒnsəl] **consuls** NOUN
an official who lives in a foreign city and who looks after people there who are citizens of his or her own country
consular ADJECTIVE

consulate ['kɒnsjʊlɪt] **consulates** NOUN
the place where a consul works

consult [kənˈsʌlt] **consults, consulting, consulted** VERB

1 If you consult someone, you ask for their opinion or advice.

◗ **THESAURUS**
ask for advice: *Ask your bank manager for advice on mortgages.*
confer with: *He is conferring with his lawyers.*

C

refer to: *I had to refer to the manual.*

2 When people consult each other, they exchange ideas and opinions.

3 If you consult a book or map, you look at it for information.

consultancy [kən'sʌltᵊnsɪ] **consultancies**
NOUN
an organization whose members give expert advice on a subject

consultant [kən'sʌltᵊnt] **consultants**
NOUN
1 an experienced doctor who specializes in one type of medicine
2 someone who gives expert advice *e.g. a management consultant*

consultation [ˌkɒnsᵊl'teɪʃən]
consultations NOUN
1 a meeting held to discuss something
2 Consultation is discussion or the seeking of advice. *e.g. There has to be much better consultation with the public.*
consultative ADJECTIVE

consume [kən'sjuːm] **consumes, consuming, consumed** VERB
1 FORMAL If you consume something, you eat or drink it.
2 To consume fuel or energy is to use it up.

consumer [kən'sjuːmə] **consumers** NOUN
someone who buys things or uses services *e.g. two new magazines for teenage consumers*

consumerism [kən'sjuːməˌrɪzəm] NOUN
Consumerism is the belief that a country will have a strong economy if its people buy a lot of goods and spend a lot of money.

consuming [kən'sjuːmɪŋ] ADJECTIVE
A consuming passion or interest is more important to you than anything else.

consummate consummates, consummating, consummated VERB
['kɒnsəˌmeɪt]
1 To consummate something is to make it complete.
2 FORMAL If two people consummate a marriage or relationship, they make it complete by having sex.
> ADJECTIVE [kən'sʌmɪt] or ['kɒnsəmɪt]
3 You use 'consummate' to describe someone who is very good at something. *e.g. a consummate politician*
consummation NOUN

consumption [kən'sʌmpʃən] NOUN
The consumption of fuel or food is the using of it, or the amount used.

contact ['kɒntækt] **contacts, contacting, contacted** NOUN
1 If you are in contact with someone, you regularly talk to them or write to them.
◉ THESAURUS
communication: *The leaders were in constant communication.*
touch: *I've lost touch with her over the years.*
2 When things are in contact, they are touching each other.
3 someone you know in a place or organization from whom you can get help or information
◉ THESAURUS
acquaintance: *We met through a mutual acquaintance.*
connection: *She had a connection in England.*
> VERB
4 If you contact someone, you telephone them or write to them.
◉ THESAURUS
approach: *A journalist has approached me for a story.*
communicate with: *We communicate mostly by email.*
get hold of: *I've been trying to get hold of you all week.*
get in touch with: *I will get in touch with my solicitors.*
reach: *Where can I reach you in an emergency?*

contact lens contact lenses NOUN
Contact lenses are small plastic lenses that you put in your eyes instead of wearing glasses, to help you see better.

contagious [kən'teɪdʒəs] ADJECTIVE
A contagious disease can be caught by touching people or things infected with it.

contain [kən'teɪn] **contains, containing, contained** VERB
1 If a substance contains something, that thing is a part of it. *e.g. Alcohol contains sugar.*
◉ THESAURUS
comprise: *The band comprises two singers and two guitarists.*
include: *The price includes VAT.*
2 The things a box or room contains are the things inside it.
3 FORMAL To contain something also means to stop it increasing or spreading. *e.g. efforts to contain the disease*
containment NOUN
◉ THESAURUS
control: *He could hardly control his rage.*
curb: *measures to curb inflation*
repress: *people who repress their emotions*
restrain: *unable to restrain her anger*

stifle: *stifling the urge to scream*

container [kənˈteɪnə] **containers** NOUN

1 something such as a box or a bottle that you keep things in

● THESAURUS
holder: *a cigarette holder*
vessel: *storage vessels*

2 a large sealed metal box for transporting things

contaminate [kənˈtæmɪˌneɪt]
**contaminates, contaminating,
contaminated** VERB

If something is contaminated by dirt, chemicals, or radiation, it is made impure and harmful. *e.g. foods contaminated with lead*
contamination NOUN

contemplate [ˈkɒntɛmˌpleɪt]
**contemplates, contemplating,
contemplated** VERB

1 To contemplate is to think carefully about something for a long time.

● THESAURUS
consider: *She paused to consider her options.*
examine: *I have examined all alternatives.*
muse on: *Many of the papers muse on the fate of the President.*
ponder: *He didn't waste time pondering the question.*
reflect on: *I reflected on the child's future.*
think about: *Think about how you can improve the situation.*

2 If you contemplate doing something, you consider doing it. *e.g. I never contemplated marrying Charles.*

● THESAURUS
consider: *Watersports enthusiasts should consider hiring a wetsuit.*
envisage: *He had never envisaged spending the whole of his life in that job.*
plan: *I had been planning a trip to the West Coast.*
think of: *Martin was thinking of taking legal action against his employers.*

3 If you contemplate something, you look at it for a long time. *e.g. He contemplated his drawings.*
contemplation NOUN, **contemplative** ADJECTIVE

contemporary [kənˈtɛmprərɪ]
contemporaries ADJECTIVE

1 produced or happening now *e.g. contemporary literature*

2 produced or happening at the time you are talking about *e.g. contemporary descriptions of Lizzie Borden*

> NOUN

3 Someone's contemporaries are other people living or active at the same time as them. *e.g. Shakespeare and his contemporaries.*

contempt [kənˈtɛmpt] NOUN

If you treat someone or something with contempt, you show no respect for them at all.

● THESAURUS
derision: *He was greeted with shouts of derision.*
disdain: *Janet looked at him with disdain.*
disregard: *total disregard for the safety of the public*
disrespect: *complete disrespect for authority*
scorn: *They greeted the proposal with scorn.*
<<OPPOSITE respect

contemptible [kənˈtɛmptəbəl] ADJECTIVE
not worthy of any respect *e.g. this contemptible piece of nonsense*

contemptuous [kənˈtɛmptjʊəs] ADJECTIVE
showing contempt
contemptuously ADVERB

contend [kənˈtɛnd] **contends,
contending, contended** VERB

1 To contend with a difficulty is to deal with it. *e.g. They had to contend with injuries.*

2 FORMAL If you contend that something is true, you say firmly that it is true.

3 When people contend for something, they compete for it.
contender NOUN

**content contents, contenting,
contented**

PLURAL NOUN [ˈkɒntɛnts]

1 The contents of something are the things inside it.

> NOUN [ˈkɒntɛnt]

2 (LIBRARY) The content of an article or speech is what is expressed in it.

3 Content is the proportion of something that a substance contains. *e.g. White bread is inferior in vitamin content.*

> ADJECTIVE [kənˈtɛnt]

4 happy and satisfied with your life

5 willing to do or have something *e.g. He would be content to telephone her.*

> VERB [kənˈtɛnt]

6 If you content yourself with doing something, you do it and do not try to do anything else. *e.g. He contented himself with an early morning lecture.*

contented [kənˈtɛntɪd] ADJECTIVE
happy and satisfied with your life
contentedly ADVERB, **contentment** NOUN

contention [kənˈtɛnʃən] **contentions**
NOUN; FORMAL
Someone's contention is the idea or opinion they are expressing. *e.g. It is our contention that the 1980s mark a turning point in planning.*

contest contests, contesting, contested
NOUN [ˈkɒntɛst]

1 a competition or game *e.g. a boxing contest*

THESAURUS
competition: *a surfing competition*
game: *the first game of the season*
match: *He was watching a football match.*
tournament: *Here is a player capable of winning a world tournament.*

2 a struggle for power *e.g. a presidential contest*

THESAURUS
battle: *the eternal battle between good and evil*
fight: *the fight for the US Presidency*
struggle: *locked in a power struggle with his Prime Minister*

> VERB [kən'tɛst]

3 If you contest a statement or decision, you object to it formally.

THESAURUS
challenge: *The move was immediately challenged.*
dispute: *He disputed the allegations.*
oppose: *Many parents oppose bilingual education in schools.*
question: *It never occurs to them to question the doctor's decisions.*
<<OPPOSITE *accept*

contestant [kən'tɛstənt] **contestants**
NOUN
someone taking part in a competition

context ['kɒntɛkst] **contexts** NOUN
1 The context of something consists of matters related to it which help to explain it. *e.g. English history is treated in a European context.*
2 The context of a word or sentence consists of the words or sentences before and after it.

continent ['kɒntɪnənt] **continents** NOUN
1 a very large area of land, such as Africa or Asia
2 The Continent is the mainland of Europe.
continental ADJECTIVE

contingency [kən'tɪndʒənsɪ]
contingencies NOUN
something that might happen in the future *e.g. I need to examine all possible contingencies.*

contingent [kən'tɪndʒənt] **contingents**
NOUN
1 a group of people representing a country or organization *e.g. a strong South African contingent*
2 a group of police or soldiers

continual [kən'tɪnjʊəl] ADJECTIVE
1 happening all the time without stopping *e.g. continual headaches*

THESAURUS
constant: *She suggests that women are under constant pressure to be abnormally thin.*
continuous: *a continuous stream of phone calls*
endless: *her endless demands for attention*

eternal: *In the background was that eternal hum.*
nagging: *a nagging pain between his shoulder blades*
perpetual: *the perpetual thump of music from the flat downstairs*
uninterrupted: *five years of uninterrupted growth*

2 happening again and again *e.g. the continual snide remarks*
continually ADVERB

THESAURUS
frequent: *He is prone to frequent bouts of depression.*
recurrent: *buildings in which staff suffer recurrent illness*
regular: *He is a regular visitor to our house.*
repeated: *Mr Smith did not return the money, despite repeated reminders.*
<<OPPOSITE *occasional*

continuation [kən,tɪnjʊ'eɪʃən]
continuations NOUN
1 The continuation of something is the continuing of it. *e.g. the continuation of the human race*
2 Something that is a continuation of an event follows it and seems like a part of it. *e.g. a meeting which was a continuation of a conference*

continue [kən'tɪnjuː] **continues,**
continuing, continued VERB
1 If you continue to do something, you keep doing it.

THESAURUS
carry on: *The assistant carried on talking.*
go on: *Unemployment is likely to go on rising.*
keep on: *He kept on trying.*
persist: *She persists in using his nickname.*

2 If something continues, it does not stop.

THESAURUS
carry on: *My work will carry on after I'm gone.*
endure: *Their friendship has endured for 30 years.*
last: *Nothing lasts forever.*
persist: *The problem persists.*
remain: *The building remains to this day.*
survive: *companies which survived after the recession*

3 You also say something continues when it starts again after stopping. *e.g. She continued after a pause.*

THESAURUS
carry on: *He took a deep breath, then carried on.*
recommence: *He recommenced work on his novel.*
resume: *Police will resume the search today.*

continuous [kən'tɪnjʊəs] ADJECTIVE
1 Continuous means happening or existing without stopping.

THESAURUS
constant: *under constant pressure*

continued: *a continued improvement*
extended: *conflict over an extended period*
prolonged: *a prolonged drought*
uninterrupted: *uninterrupted rule*
<<OPPOSITE *periodic*

2 A continuous line or surface has no gaps or holes in it.
continuously ADVERB, **continuity** NOUN

contorted [kən'tɔːtɪd] ADJECTIVE
twisted into an unnatural, unattractive shape

contour ['kɒntʊə] **contours** NOUN
1 The contours of something are its general shape.

2 (GEOGRAPHY) On a map, a contour is a line joining points of equal height.

contra- PREFIX
Contra- means against or opposite to. *e.g. contraflow... contraindication*

contraception [ˌkɒntrə'sɛpʃən] NOUN
Contraception is methods of preventing pregnancy.

contraceptive [ˌkɒntrə'sɛptɪv] **contraceptives** NOUN
a device or pill for preventing pregnancy

contract **contracts, contracting, contracted** NOUN ['kɒntrækt]
1 a written legal agreement about the sale of something or work done for money
> VERB [kən'trækt]
2 When something contracts, it gets smaller or shorter.
3 FORMAL If you contract an illness, you get it. *e.g. Her husband contracted a virus.*
contractual ADJECTIVE, **contraction** NOUN

contractor ['kɒntræktə] **contractors** NOUN
a person or company who does work for other people or companies *e.g. a building contractor*

contradict [ˌkɒntrə'dɪkt] **contradicts, contradicting, contradicted** VERB
If you contradict someone, you say that what they have just said is not true, and that something else is.
contradiction NOUN, **contradictory** ADJECTIVE

contraption [kən'træpʃən] **contraptions** NOUN
a strange-looking machine or piece of equipment

contrary ['kɒntrərɪ] ADJECTIVE
1 Contrary ideas or opinions are opposed to each other and cannot be held by the same person.
> PHRASE
2 You say **on the contrary** when you are contradicting what someone has just said.

contrast ['kɒntrɑːst] **contrasts** NOUN
1 a great difference between things *e.g. the real contrast between the two poems*

2 If one thing is a contrast to another, it is very different from it. *e.g. I couldn't imagine a greater contrast to Maxwell.*

contrast [kən'trɑːst] **contrasts, contrasting, contrasted** VERB
1 (EXAM TERM) If you contrast things, you describe or emphasize the differences between them.

2 If one thing contrasts with another, it is very different from it. *e.g. The interview contrasted completely with the one she gave after Tokyo.*

contravene [ˌkɒntrə'viːn] **contravenes, contravening, contravened** VERB; FORMAL
If you contravene a law or rule, you do something that it forbids.

contribute [kən'trɪbjuːt] **contributes, contributing, contributed** VERB
1 If you contribute to something, you do things to help it succeed. *e.g. The elderly have much to contribute to the community.*

2 If you contribute money, you give it to help to pay for something.

3 If something contributes to an event or situation, it is one of its causes. *e.g. The dry summer has contributed to perfect conditions.*
contribution NOUN, **contributor** NOUN, **contributory** ADJECTIVE

contrive [kən'traɪv] **contrives, contriving, contrived** VERB; FORMAL
If you contrive to do something difficult, you succeed in doing it. *e.g. Anthony contrived to escape with a few companions.*

contrived [kən'traɪvd] ADJECTIVE
Something that is contrived is unnatural. *e.g. a contrived compliment*

control [kən'trəʊl] **controls, controlling, controlled** NOUN
1 Control of a country or organization is the power to make the important decisions about how it is run.

● THESAURUS
authority: *You have no authority here.*
command: *He was in command of the ceremony.*
direction: *The team worked well under his direction.*
government: *The entire country is under the government of one man.*
management: *the day-to-day management of the business*
power: *a position of great power*
rule: *15 years of Communist rule*

supremacy: *The party has re-established its supremacy.*

2 Your control over something is your ability to make it work the way you want it to.

3 The controls on a machine are knobs or other devices used to work it.

> VERB

4 To control a country or organization means to have the power to make decisions about how it is run.

THESAURUS

administer: *the authorities who administer the island*

be in charge of: *She is in charge of the project.*

command: *the general who commanded the troops*

direct: *He will direct day-to-day operations.*

govern: *his ability to govern France*

have power over: *Her husband has total power over her.*

manage: *the government's ability to manage the economy*

rule: *the dynasty which ruled China*

5 To control something such as a machine or system means to make it work the way you want it to.

6 (PSHE) If you control yourself, you make yourself behave calmly when you are angry or upset.

> PHRASE

7 If something is **out of control**, nobody has any power over it.

controller NOUN

controversial [ˌkɒntrəˈvɜːʃəl] ADJECTIVE
Something that is controversial causes a lot of discussion and argument, because many people disapprove of it.

controversy [ˈkɒntrəˌvɜːsɪ] *or* [kənˈtrɒvəsɪ]
controversies NOUN
discussion and argument because many people disapprove of something
[WORD HISTORY: from Latin CONTROVERSUS meaning 'turned in an opposite direction']

Notice that there are two ways to say *controversy*. The first way is older, and the second is becoming more common.

conundrum [kəˈnʌndrəm] **conundrums**
NOUN; FORMAL
a puzzling problem

convalesce [ˌkɒnvəˈlɛs] **convalesces,
convalescing, convalesced** VERB
When people convalesce, they rest and regain their health after an illness or operation.

convection [kənˈvɛkʃən] NOUN
Convection is the process by which heat travels

through gases and liquids.

convene [kənˈviːn] **convenes, convening,
convened** VERB
1 FORMAL To convene a meeting is to arrange for it to take place.

2 When people convene, they come together for a meeting.

convenience [kənˈviːnɪəns] **conveniences**
NOUN
1 The convenience of something is the fact that it is easy to use or that it makes something easy to do.

2 something useful

convenient [kənˈviːnɪənt] ADJECTIVE
If something is convenient, it is easy to use or it makes something easy to do.
conveniently ADVERB

THESAURUS

handy: *Credit cards can be handy.*

helpful: *a helpful fact sheet*

useful: *a useful invention*

<<OPPOSITE *inconvenient*

convent [ˈkɒnvənt] **convents** NOUN
a building where nuns live, or a school run by nuns

convention [kənˈvɛnʃən] **conventions**
NOUN
1 an accepted way of behaving or doing something

THESAURUS

code: *the code of the Shaolin monks*

custom: *The custom of lighting the Olympic flame goes back centuries.*

etiquette: *the rules of diplomatic etiquette*

practice: *It is normal practice not to reveal the sex of the baby.*

tradition: *different cultural traditions from ours*

2 a large meeting of an organization or political group *e.g. the Democratic Convention*

THESAURUS

assembly: *an assembly of women Olympic gold-medal winners*

conference: *a conference attended by 450 delegates*

congress: *A lot changed after the party congress.*

meeting: *the annual meeting of company shareholders*

conventional [kənˈvɛnʃənʳl] ADJECTIVE
1 You say that people are conventional when there is nothing unusual about their way of life.

THESAURUS

conformist: *He may have to become more conformist if he is to prosper.*

conservative: *The girl was well dressed in a rather conservative style.*

unadventurous: *He was a strong player, but rather unadventurous.*

2 Conventional methods are the ones that are usually used.
conventionally ADVERB

● THESAURUS
customary: *the customary one minute's silence*
ordinary: *It has 25 per cent less fat than ordinary ice cream.*
orthodox: *Many of these ideas are being incorporated into orthodox medical treatment.*
regular: *This product looks and tastes like regular margarine.*
standard: *It was standard practice for untrained clerks to deal with serious cases.*
traditional: *traditional teaching methods*

converge [kən'vɜːdʒ] **converges, converging, converged** VERB
To converge is to meet or join at a particular place.

conversation [ˌkɒnvə'seɪʃən] **conversations** NOUN
If you have a conversation with someone, you spend time talking to them.
conversational ADJECTIVE, **conversationalist** NOUN

converse converses, conversing, conversed VERB [kən'vɜːs]
1 FORMAL When people converse, they talk to each other.
> NOUN ['kɒnvɜːs]
2 The converse of something is its opposite. *e.g. Don't you think that the converse might also be possible?*
conversely ADVERB

convert converts, converting, converted VERB [kən'vɜːt]
1 To convert one thing into another is to change it so that it becomes the other thing.
2 If someone converts you, they persuade you to change your religious or political beliefs.
> NOUN ['kɒnvɜːt]
3 someone who has changed their religious or political beliefs
conversion NOUN, **convertible** ADJECTIVE

convex ['kɒnvɛks] ADJECTIVE
A convex surface bulges outwards, rather than being level or curving inwards.

convey [kən'veɪ] **conveys, conveying, conveyed** VERB
1 To convey information or ideas is to cause them to be known or understood.

● THESAURUS
communicate: *They successfully communicate their knowledge to others.*

express: *She did her best to express wordless disapproval by scowling.*
get across: *I wanted to get my message across.*
impart: *the ability to impart knowledge*

2 FORMAL To convey someone or something to a place is to transport them there.

conveyor belt [kən'veɪə] **conveyor belts** NOUN
a moving strip used in factories for moving objects along

convict convicts, convicting, convicted VERB [kən'vɪkt]
1 To convict someone of a crime is to find them guilty.
> NOUN ['kɒnvɪkt]
2 someone serving a prison sentence

conviction [kən'vɪkʃən] **convictions** NOUN
1 a strong belief or opinion
2 The conviction of someone is what happens when they are found guilty in a court of law.

convince [kən'vɪns] **convinces, convincing, convinced** VERB
To convince someone of something is to persuade them that it is true.

● THESAURUS
assure: *She assured me that there was nothing wrong.*
persuade: *I had to persuade him of the advantages.*
satisfy: *He had to satisfy the doctors that he was fit to play.*

convincing [kən'vɪnsɪŋ] ADJECTIVE
'Convincing' is used to describe things or people that can make you believe something is true. *e.g. a convincing argument*
convincingly ADVERB

● THESAURUS
conclusive: *conclusive proof*
effective: *an effective speaker*
persuasive: *persuasive reasons*
plausible: *a plausible explanation*
powerful: *a powerful speech*
telling: *a telling criticism*
<<OPPOSITE *unconvincing*

convoluted ['kɒnvə,luːtɪd] ADJECTIVE
Something that is convoluted has many twists and bends. *e.g. the convoluted patterns of these designs*

convoy ['kɒnvɔɪ] **convoys** NOUN
a group of vehicles or ships travelling together

convulsion [kən'vʌlʃən] **convulsions** NOUN
If someone has convulsions, their muscles move violently and uncontrollably.

coo [kuː] **coos, cooing, cooed** VERB
When pigeons and doves coo, they make a soft flutelike sound.

cook [kʊk] **cooks, cooking, cooked** VERB

1 To cook food is to prepare it for eating by heating it.

⬤ THESAURUS

bake: *a machine for baking bread*
barbecue: *a Korean method of barbecuing meat*
boil: *Boil the fruit and syrup together for half an hour.*
fry: *Garnish the rice with thinly sliced fried onion.*
grill: *Grill the fish for five minutes.*
microwave: *Microwaved vegetables have a fresher flavour.*
poach: *I had ordered poached eggs on toast for breakfast.*
roast: *Roast the aubergine in the oven for about one hour until soft.*
steam: *mussels on a bed of steamed cabbage*
stew: *You can stew the vegetables in oil.*
toast: *This currant loaf is delicious either fresh or toasted.*

> NOUN

2 someone who prepares and cooks food, often as their job

cooker [ˈkʊkə] **cookers** NOUN
a device for cooking food

cookery [ˈkʊkərɪ] NOUN
Cookery is the activity of preparing and cooking food.

cookie [ˈkʊkɪ] **cookies** NOUN

1 a sweet biscuit

2 a small file placed on a user's computer by a website, containing information about the user's preferences that will be used on any future visits he or she may make to the site

cool [kuːl] **cooler, coolest; cools, cooling, cooled** ADJECTIVE

1 Something cool has a low temperature but is not cold.

⬤ THESAURUS

chilled: *a chilled bottle of wine*
chilly: *a chilly afternoon*
cold: *Your dinner's getting cold.*
refreshing: *a refreshing breeze*
<<OPPOSITE *warm*

2 If you are cool in a difficult situation, you stay calm and unemotional.

⬤ THESAURUS

calm: *Try to stay calm.*
collected: *She was cool and collected throughout the interview.*
composed: *a composed player*
level-headed: *Simon is level-headed and practical.*
relaxed: *a relaxed manner*
serene: *a serene smile*
<<OPPOSITE *nervous*

> VERB

3 When something cools or when you cool it, it becomes less warm.

coolly ADVERB, **coolness** NOUN

⬤ THESAURUS

chill: *a glass of chilled champagne*
cool off: *Dip the carrots in water to cool them off.*
freeze: *Make double the quantity and freeze half for later.*
refrigerate: *Refrigerate the dough overnight.*
<<OPPOSITE *heat*

coolabah [ˈkuːləˌbɑː] **coolabahs;** also spelt **coolibar** NOUN
an Australian eucalypt that grows along rivers

coop [kuːp] **coops** NOUN
a cage for chickens or rabbits

cooperate [kəʊˈɒpəˌreɪt] **cooperates, cooperating, cooperated** VERB

1 When people cooperate, they work or act together.

⬤ THESAURUS

collaborate: *They collaborated on an album.*
join forces: *The two political parties are joining forces.*
pull together: *The staff and management pull together.*
work together: *industry and government working together*

2 To cooperate also means to do what someone asks.

cooperation NOUN

cooperative [kəʊˈɒpərətɪv] **cooperatives** NOUN

1 a business or organization run by the people who work for it, and who share its benefits or profits

> ADJECTIVE

2 A cooperative activity is done by people working together.

3 Someone who is cooperative does what you ask them to.

coordinate coordinates, coordinating, coordinated VERB [kəʊˈɔːdɪˌneɪt]

1 To coordinate an activity is to organize the people or things involved in it. *e.g. to coordinate the campaign*

> PLURAL NOUN [kəʊˈɔːdɪnɪts]

2 (MATHS) Coordinates are a pair of numbers or letters which tell you how far along and up or down a point is on a grid.

coordination NOUN, **coordinator** NOUN

cop [kɒp] **cops** NOUN; INFORMAL
a policeman

cope [kəʊp] **copes, coping, coped** VERB
If you cope with a problem or task, you deal with it successfully.

copious ['kəʊpiəs] ADJECTIVE; FORMAL
existing or produced in large quantities *e.g. I wrote copious notes for the solicitor.*

copper ['kɒpə] **coppers** NOUN
1 Copper is a soft reddish-brown metal.
2 Coppers are brown metal coins of low value.
3 INFORMAL a policeman

copse [kɒps] **copses** NOUN
a small group of trees growing close together

copulate ['kɒpjʊˌleɪt] **copulates, copulating, copulated** VERB; FORMAL
To copulate is to have sex.
copulation NOUN

copy ['kɒpɪ] **copies, copying, copied** NOUN
1 something made to look like something else

⬤ THESAURUS
counterfeit: *This credit card is a counterfeit.*
duplicate: *I lost my key and had to get a duplicate made.*
fake: *How do I know this painting isn't a fake?*
forgery: *The letter was a forgery.*
imitation: *Beware of cheap imitations.*
replica: *a replica of the Statue of Liberty*
reproduction: *a reproduction of a famous painting*

2 A copy of a book, newspaper, or record is one of many identical ones produced at the same time.
> VERB
3 If you copy what someone does, you do the same thing.

⬤ THESAURUS
ape: *Generations of women have aped her style and looks.*
emulate: *Sons are expected to emulate their fathers.*
follow: *Where America goes, Britain will surely follow.*
imitate: *Children imitate what they see on TV.*
mimic: *He mimicked her accent.*

4 If you copy something, you make a copy of it.
copier NOUN

⬤ THESAURUS
counterfeit: *These banknotes are very easy to counterfeit.*
duplicate: *Videos are being illicitly duplicated all over the country.*
reproduce: *a new method of reproducing oil paintings*

copyright ['kɒpɪˌraɪt] **copyrights** NOUN
(**LIBRARY**) If someone has the copyright on a piece of writing or music, it cannot be copied or performed without their permission.

coral ['kɒrəl] **corals** NOUN
Coral is a hard substance that forms in the sea from the skeletons of tiny animals called corals.

cord [kɔːd] **cords** NOUN
1 Cord is strong, thick string.
2 Electrical wire covered in rubber or plastic is also called cord.

cordial ['kɔːdɪəl] **cordials** ADJECTIVE
1 warm and friendly *e.g. the cordial greeting*
> NOUN
2 a sweet drink made from fruit juice

cordon ['kɔːdən] **cordons, cordoning, cordoned** NOUN
1 a line or ring of police or soldiers preventing people entering or leaving a place
> VERB
2 If police or soldiers cordon off an area, they stop people entering or leaving by forming themselves into a line or ring.

corduroy ['kɔːdəˌrɔɪ] NOUN
Corduroy is a thick cloth with parallel raised lines on the outside.

core [kɔː] **cores** NOUN
1 the hard central part of a fruit such as an apple
2 the most central part of an object or place *e.g. the earth's core*
3 the most important part of something *e.g. the core of Asia's problems*

cork [kɔːk] **corks** NOUN
1 Cork is the very light, spongelike bark of a Mediterranean tree.
2 a piece of cork pushed into the end of a bottle to close it

corkscrew ['kɔːkˌskruː] **corkscrews** NOUN
a device for pulling corks out of bottles

cormorant ['kɔːmərənt] **cormorants** NOUN
a dark-coloured bird with a long neck

corn [kɔːn] **corns** NOUN
1 Corn refers to crops such as wheat and barley and to their seeds.
2 a small painful area of hard skin on your foot

cornea ['kɔːnɪə] **corneas** NOUN
the transparent skin that covers the outside of your eyeball
[WORD HISTORY: from Latin CORNEA TELA meaning 'horny web']

corner ['kɔːnə] **corners, cornering, cornered** NOUN
1 a place where two sides or edges of something meet *e.g. a small corner of one shelf... a street corner*
> VERB
2 To corner a person or animal is to get them into a place they cannot escape from.

cornet ['kɔːnɪt] **cornets** NOUN
a small brass instrument used in brass and military bands

C

cornflour ['kɔːnˌflaʊə] NOUN
Cornflour is a fine white flour made from maize and used in cooking to thicken sauces.

cornflower ['kɔːnˌflaʊə] **cornflowers** NOUN
a small plant with bright flowers, usually blue

cornice ['kɔːnɪs] **cornices** NOUN
a decorative strip of plaster, wood, or stone along the top edge of a wall

corny ['kɔːnɪ] **cornier, corniest** ADJECTIVE
very obvious or sentimental and not at all original
e.g. corny old love songs

⬤ THESAURUS
banal: *banal dialogue*
hackneyed: *a hackneyed plot*
maudlin: *a maudlin film*
sentimental: *a sentimental ballad*
stale: *stale ideas*
stereotyped: *a stereotyped image of Britain*
trite: *a trite ending*

coronary ['kɒrənərɪ] **coronaries** NOUN
If someone has a coronary, blood cannot reach their heart because of a blood clot.

coronation [ˌkɒrəˈneɪʃən] **coronations** NOUN
the ceremony at which a king or queen is crowned

coroner ['kɒrənə] **coroners** NOUN
an official who investigates the deaths of people who have died in a violent or unusual way

coronet ['kɒrənɪt] **coronets** NOUN
a small crown

corporal ['kɔːpərəl] **corporals** NOUN
an officer of low rank in the army or air force

corporal punishment NOUN
Corporal punishment is the punishing of people by beating them.

corporate ['kɔːpərɪt] ADJECTIVE; FORMAL
belonging to or done by all members of a group together *e.g. a corporate decision*

corporation [ˌkɔːpəˈreɪʃən] **corporations** NOUN
1 a large business
2 a group of people responsible for running a city

corps [kɔː] NOUN
1 a part of an army with special duties *e.g. the engineering Corps*
2 a small group of people who do a special job *e.g. the world press corps*

⬛ The plural of *corps* is also *corps*

corpse [kɔːps] **corpses** NOUN
a dead body

corpuscle ['kɔːpʌsˀl] **corpuscles** NOUN
a red or white blood cell

correa ['kɒrɪə] **correas** NOUN
an Australian shrub with large green and white flowers

correct [kəˈrɛkt] **corrects, correcting, corrected** ADJECTIVE
1 If something is correct, there are no mistakes in it.

⬤ THESAURUS
accurate: *an accurate description*
exact: *an exact copy*
faultless: *Hans's English was faultless.*
flawless: *a flawless performance*
precise: *precise calculations*
right: *That clock never shows the right time.*
true: *a true account*

2 The correct thing in a particular situation is the right one. *e.g. Each has the correct number of coins.*
3 Correct behaviour is considered to be socially acceptable.

⬤ THESAURUS
acceptable: *It is becoming more acceptable for women to drink.*
appropriate: *appropriate dress*
fitting: *behaving in a manner not fitting for a lady*
okay or **OK:** informal *Is it okay if I bring a friend with me?*
proper: *In those days it was not proper for women to go on the stage.*
seemly: *It is not seemly to joke about such things.*
<<OPPOSITE *wrong*

> VERB
4 If you correct something which is wrong, you make it right.
correctly ADVERB, **corrective** ADJECTIVE OR NOUN

⬤ THESAURUS
amend: *They want to amend the current system.*
cure: *an operation to cure his limp*
improve: *We must improve the situation.*
rectify: *attempts to rectify the problem*
reform: *He promised to reform his wicked ways.*
remedy: *What is needed to remedy these deficiencies?*
right: *I intend to right these wrongs.*

correction [kəˈrɛkʃən] **corrections** NOUN
the act of making something right

⬤ THESAURUS
adjustment: *My car needs a brake adjustment.*
amendment: *He has made lots of amendments to the script.*
righting: *the righting of the country's domestic troubles*

correlate ['kɒrɪˌleɪt] **correlates, correlating, correlated** VERB
If two things correlate or are correlated, they are closely connected or strongly influence each other. *e.g. Obesity correlates with increased risk of stroke and diabetes.*

correlation NOUN

correspond [ˌkɒrɪ'spɒnd] **corresponds, corresponding, corresponded** VERB

1 If one thing corresponds to another, it has a similar purpose, function, or status.

⬤ THESAURUS
agree: *His statement agrees with those of other witnesses.*
be related: *These philosophical problems are closely related.*
coincide: *He was delighted to find that her feelings coincided with his own.*
correlate: *Obesity correlates with increased risk for diabetes.*
fit: *The punishment must always fit the crime.*
match: *Our value system does not match with theirs.*
tally: *This description did not tally with what we saw.*

2 (MATHS) If numbers or amounts correspond, they are the same.

3 When people correspond, they write to each other.

correspondence [ˌkɒrɪ'spɒndəns] NOUN

1 Correspondence is the writing of letters; also the letters written.

2 If there is a correspondence between two things, they are closely related or very similar.

correspondent [ˌkɒrɪ'spɒndənt] **correspondents** NOUN
a newspaper, television, or radio reporter

corresponding [ˌkɒrɪ'spɒndɪŋ] ADJECTIVE

1 You use 'corresponding' to describe a change that results from a change in something else. *e.g. the rise in interest rates and corresponding fall in house values*

2 You also use 'corresponding' to describe something which has a similar purpose or status to something else. *e.g. Alfard is the corresponding Western name for the star.*
correspondingly ADVERB

corridor ['kɒrɪˌdɔː] **corridors** NOUN
a passage in a building or train

corroboree [kə'rɒbəri] **corroborees** NOUN
an Australian Aboriginal gathering or dance that is festive or warlike

corrode [kə'rəʊd] **corrodes, corroding, corroded** VERB
When metal corrodes, it is gradually destroyed by a chemical or rust.
corrosion NOUN, **corrosive** ADJECTIVE

corrugated ['kɒrʊˌɡeɪtɪd] ADJECTIVE
Corrugated metal or cardboard is made in parallel folds to make it stronger.
[WORD HISTORY: from Latin CORRUGARE meaning 'to wrinkle up']

corrupt [kə'rʌpt] **corrupts, corrupting, corrupted** ADJECTIVE

1 Corrupt people act dishonestly or illegally in return for money or power. *e.g. corrupt ministers*

⬤ THESAURUS
crooked: *a crooked cop*
dishonest: *a dishonest scheme*
fraudulent: *fraudulent trading*
shady: informal *shady deals*
unscrupulous: *unscrupulous landlords*
<<OPPOSITE *honest*

> VERB

2 To corrupt someone means to make them dishonest.

⬤ THESAURUS
bribe: *accused of bribing officials*
buy off: *Police were bought off by drugs dealers.*
fix: informal *He fixed the match by bribing the players.*

3 To corrupt someone also means to make them immoral.
corruptible ADJECTIVE

⬤ THESAURUS
deprave: *material likely to deprave those who watch it*
pervert: *perverted by their contact with criminals*

corruption [kə'rʌpʃən] NOUN
Corruption is dishonesty and illegal behaviour by people in positions of power.

⬤ THESAURUS
bribery: *on trial for bribery*
dishonesty: *She accused the government of dishonesty and incompetence.*
fraud: *jailed for fraud*

corset ['kɔːsɪt] **corsets** NOUN
Corsets are stiff underwear worn by some women round their hips and waist to make them look slimmer.

cosmetic [kɒz'mɛtɪk] **cosmetics** NOUN

1 Cosmetics are substances such as lipstick and face powder which improve a person's appearance.

> ADJECTIVE

2 Cosmetic changes improve the appearance of something without changing its basic nature.

cosmic ['kɒzmɪk] ADJECTIVE
belonging or relating to the universe

cosmopolitan [ˌkɒzmə'pɒlɪt³n] ADJECTIVE
A cosmopolitan place is full of people from many countries.
[WORD HISTORY: from Greek KOSMOS meaning 'universe' and POLITĒS meaning 'citizen']

cosmos ['kɒzmɒs] NOUN
The cosmos is the universe.

cosset ['kɒsɪt] **cossets, cosseting, cosseted** VERB
If you cosset someone, you spoil them and protect them too much.

cost [kɒst] **costs, costing, cost** NOUN
1 The cost of something is the amount of money needed to buy it, do it, or make it.

THESAURUS
charge: *We can arrange this for a small charge.*
expense: *household expenses*
outlay: *Buying wine in bulk is well worth the outlay.*
payment: *an initial payment of just $100*
price: *House prices are expected to rise.*
rate: *specially reduced rates*

2 The cost of achieving something is the loss or injury in achieving it. *e.g. the total cost in human misery*

THESAURUS
detriment: *These changes are to the detriment of staff morale.*
expense: *I supported my husband's career at the expense of my own.*
penalty: *paying the penalty for someone else's mistakes*

> VERB
3 You use 'cost' to talk about the amount of money you have to pay for things. *e.g. The air fares were going to cost a lot.*

THESAURUS
come to: *Lunch came to nearly £15.*
sell at: *The books are selling at £1 per copy.*
set someone back: informal *This wedding will set us back thousands of pounds.*

4 If a mistake costs you something, you lose that thing because of the mistake. *e.g. a reckless gamble that could cost him his job*

costly ['kɒstlɪ] **costlier, costliest** ADJECTIVE
expensive *e.g. the most costly piece of furniture*

costume ['kɒstjuːm] **costumes** NOUN
1 (DRAMA) a set of clothes worn by an actor
2 Costume is the clothing worn in a particular place or during a particular period. *e.g. eighteenth-century costume*

cosy ['kəʊzɪ] **cosier, cosiest; cosies** ADJECTIVE
1 warm and comfortable *e.g. her cosy new flat*

THESAURUS
comfortable: *a comfortable fireside chair*
snug: *a snug log cabin*
warm: *warm blankets*

2 Cosy activities are pleasant and friendly. *e.g. a cosy chat*

THESAURUS
friendly: *a friendly little get-together*

informal: *The house has an informal atmosphere.*
intimate: *an intimate candlelit dinner for two*
relaxed: *a relaxed evening in*

> NOUN
3 a soft cover put over a teapot to keep the tea warm
cosily ADVERB, **cosiness** NOUN

cot [kɒt] **cots** NOUN
a small bed for a baby, with bars or panels round it to stop the baby falling out
[WORD HISTORY: from Hindi KHAT meaning 'bedstead']

cottage ['kɒtɪdʒ] **cottages** NOUN
a small house in the country

cottage cheese NOUN
Cottage cheese is a type of soft white lumpy cheese.

cotton ['kɒtᵊn] **cottons** NOUN
1 Cotton is cloth made from the soft fibres of the cotton plant.
2 Cotton is also thread used for sewing.
[WORD HISTORY: from Arabic QUTN]

cotton wool NOUN
Cotton wool is soft fluffy cotton, often used for dressing wounds.

couch [kaʊtʃ] **couches, couching, couched** NOUN
1 a long, soft piece of furniture which more than one person can sit on
> VERB
2 If a statement is couched in a particular type of language, it is expressed in that language. *e.g. a comment couched in impertinent terms*

cough [kɒf] **coughs, coughing, coughed** VERB
1 When you cough, you force air out of your throat with a sudden harsh noise.
> NOUN
2 an illness that makes you cough a lot; also the noise you make when you cough

could [kʊd] VERB
1 You use 'could' to say that you were able or allowed to do something. *e.g. He could hear voices... She could come and go as she wanted.*
2 You also use 'could' to say that something might happen or might be the case. *e.g. It could rain.*
3 You use 'could' when you are asking for something politely. *e.g. Could you tell me the name of that film?*

coulomb ['kuːlɒm] **coulombs** NOUN
a unit used to measure electric charge

council ['kaʊnsəl] **councils** NOUN

189

1 a group of people elected to look after the affairs of a town, district, or county

● THESAURUS

assembly: *the National Assembly*
board: *the Pakistan Cricket Board*
committee: *the management committee*
panel: *a panel of judges*

2 Some other groups have Council as part of their name. *e.g. the World Gold Council*

councillor [ˈkaʊnsələ] **councillors** NOUN
an elected member of a local council

counsel [ˈkaʊnsəl] **counsels, counselling, counselled** NOUN

1 FORMAL To give someone counsel is to give them advice.

> VERB

2 To counsel people is to give them advice about their problems.
counselling NOUN, **counsellor** NOUN

count [kaʊnt] **counts, counting, counted** VERB

1 To count is to say all the numbers in order up to a particular number.

2 If you count all the things in a group, you add them up to see how many there are.

● THESAURUS

add up: *Add up the sales figures.*
calculate: *First, calculate your monthly living expenses.*
tally: *Computers now tally the votes.*

3 What counts in a situation is whatever is most important.

● THESAURUS

carry weight: *a politician whose words carry weight*
matter: *It doesn't matter what she thinks.*
rate: *This does not rate as one of my main concerns.*
signify: *His absence does not signify much.*
weigh: *This evidence did not weigh with the jury.*

4 To count as something means to be regarded as that thing. *e.g. I'm not sure whether this counts as harassment.*

5 If you can count on someone or something, you can rely on them.

> NOUN

6 a number reached by counting

● THESAURUS

calculation: *I did a quick calculation in my head.*
reckoning: *By my reckoning we were about two miles from camp.*
sum: *I've never been good at sums.*
tally: *They keep a tally of visitors to the castle.*

7 FORMAL If something is wrong on a particular count, it is wrong in that respect.

8 a European nobleman

countdown [ˈkaʊntˌdaʊn] **countdowns** NOUN
the counting aloud of numbers in reverse order before something happens, especially before a spacecraft is launched

countenance [ˈkaʊntɪnəns] **countenances** NOUN; FORMAL
Someone's countenance is their face.

counter [ˈkaʊntə] **counters, countering, countered** NOUN

1 a long, flat surface over which goods are sold in a shop

2 a small, flat, round object used in board games

> VERB

3 If you counter something that is being done, you take action to make it less effective. *e.g. I countered that argument with a reference to our sales report.*

counteract [ˌkaʊntərˈækt] **counteracts, counteracting, counteracted** VERB
To counteract something is to reduce its effect by producing an opposite effect.

● THESAURUS

act against: *The immune system acts against infection.*
offset: *The slump was offset by a surge in exports.*

counterfeit [ˈkaʊntəfɪt] **counterfeits, counterfeiting, counterfeited** ADJECTIVE

1 Something counterfeit is not genuine but has been made to look genuine to deceive people. *e.g. counterfeit money*

> VERB

2 To counterfeit something is to make a counterfeit version of it.

counterpart [ˈkaʊntəˌpɑːt] **counterparts** NOUN
The counterpart of a person or thing is another person or thing with a similar function in a different place. *e.g. Unlike his British counterpart, the French mayor is an important personality.*

countess [ˈkaʊntɪs] **countesses** NOUN
the wife of a count or earl, or a woman with the same rank as a count or earl

counting [ˈkaʊntɪŋ] PREPOSITION
You say 'counting' when including something in a calculation. *e.g. nearly 4000 of us, not counting women and children*

countless [ˈkaʊntlɪs] ADJECTIVE
too many to count *e.g. There had been countless demonstrations.*

● THESAURUS

infinite: *an infinite number of atoms*
innumerable: *innumerable problems*
myriad: *pop music in all its myriad forms*

C

untold: *untold wealth*

country ['kʌntrɪ] countries NOUN

(GEOGRAPHY)

1 one of the political areas the world is divided into

● **THESAURUS**
kingdom: *The kingdom's power declined.*
land: *America, land of opportunity*
state: *a communist state*

2 The country is land away from towns and cities.

● **THESAURUS**
bush: New Zealand and South African *a trip out to the bush*
countryside: *surrounded by beautiful countryside*
outback: Australian and New Zealand *nostalgic paintings of the outback*
outdoors: *He loves the great outdoors.*

3 'Country' is used to refer to an area with particular features or associations *e.g. the heart of wine country*

countryman ['kʌntrɪmən] countrymen NOUN

Your countrymen are people from your own country.

countryside ['kʌntrɪˌsaɪd] NOUN

The countryside is land away from towns and cities.

county ['kaʊntɪ] counties NOUN

(GEOGRAPHY) a region with its own local government
[WORD HISTORY: from Old French CONTÉ meaning 'land belonging to a count']

coup [kuː] coups NOUN

When there is a coup, a group of people seize power in a country.
[WORD HISTORY: from French COUP meaning 'a blow']

couple ['kʌpəl] couples, coupling, coupled NOUN

1 two people who are married or having a sexual or romantic relationship

2 A couple of things or people means two of them. *e.g. a couple of weeks ago*

> VERB

3 If one thing is coupled with another, the two things are done or dealt with together. *e.g. Its stores offer high quality coupled with low prices.*

couplet ['kʌplɪt] couplets NOUN

two lines of poetry together, especially two that rhyme

coupon ['kuːpɒn] coupons NOUN

1 a piece of printed paper which, when you hand it in, entitles you to pay less than usual for something

2 a form you fill in to ask for information or to enter a competition

courage ['kʌrɪdʒ] NOUN

Courage is the quality shown by people who do things knowing they are dangerous or difficult.
courageous ADJECTIVE, **courageously** ADVERB

● **THESAURUS**
bravery: *an act of bravery*
daring: *tales of daring and adventure*
guts: informal *He didn't have the guts to admit he was wrong.*
heroism: *the young soldier's heroism*
nerve: *I didn't have the nerve to complain.*
pluck: *You have to admire her pluck.*
valour: *He was decorated for valour in the war.*
<<OPPOSITE *fear*

courgette [kʊəˈʒɛt] courgettes NOUN

a type of small marrow with dark green skin. Courgettes are also called **zucchini**.
[WORD HISTORY: from French COURGETTE meaning 'little marrow']

courier ['kʊərɪə] couriers NOUN

1 someone employed by a travel company to look after people on holiday

2 someone employed to deliver special letters quickly

course [kɔːs] courses NOUN

1 a series of lessons or lectures

● **THESAURUS**
classes: *I go to dance classes.*
curriculum: *the history curriculum*

2 a series of medical treatments *e.g. a course of injections*

3 one of the parts of a meal

4 A course or a course of action is one of the things you can do in a situation.

● **THESAURUS**
plan: *Your best plan is to see your doctor.*
policy: *She decided the best policy was to wait.*
procedure: *He did not follow the correct procedure.*

5 a piece of land where a sport such as golf is played

6 the route a ship or aircraft takes

● **THESAURUS**
direction: *He went off in the opposite direction.*
line: *the birds' line of flight*
path: *the path of an oncoming car*
route: *the most direct route*
trajectory: *the trajectory of the missile*
way: *What way do you go home?*

7 If something happens in the course of a period of time, it happens during that period. *e.g. Ten people died in the course of the day.*

> PHRASE

8 If you say **of course**, you are showing that

something is totally expected or that you are sure about something. *e.g. Of course she wouldn't do that.*

court [kɔːt] **courts, courting, courted**
NOUN

1 a place where legal matters are decided by a judge and jury or a magistrate. The judge and jury or magistrate can also be referred to as the court.

● THESAURUS
bench: *He was brought before the bench.*
law court: *prisoners tried by a law court*
tribunal: *The claim was thrown out by a European tribunal.*

2 a place where a game such as tennis or badminton is played

3 the place where a king or queen lives and carries out ceremonial duties

> VERB

4 OLD-FASHIONED If a man and woman are courting, they are spending a lot of time together because they intend to get married.

● THESAURUS
go steady: *They've been going steady for six months now.*
woo: *He wooed and married his first love.*

courteous [ˈkɜːtɪəs] ADJECTIVE
Courteous behaviour is polite and considerate.
[WORD HISTORY: from Old French CORTEIS meaning 'courtly-mannered']

courtesy [ˈkɜːtɪsɪ] NOUN
Courtesy is polite, considerate behaviour.

● THESAURUS
civility: *Handle customers with tact and civility.*
courteousness: *his courteousness and kindness*
gallantry: *He treated me with old-fashioned gallantry.*
good manners: *the rules of good manners*
grace: *He didn't even have the grace to apologize.*
graciousness: *The team displayed graciousness in defeat.*
politeness: *basic standards of politeness*

courtier [ˈkɔːtɪə] **courtiers** NOUN
Courtiers were noblemen and noblewomen at the court of a king or queen.

court-martial [ˌkɔːtˈmaːʃəl] **court-martials, court-martialling, court-martialled** NOUN

1 a military trial

> VERB

2 If a member of the armed forces is court-martialled, he or she is tried by a court martial.

courtship [ˈkɔːtʃɪp] NOUN; FORMAL
Courtship is the activity of courting or the period of time during which a man and a woman are courting.

courtyard [ˈkɔːtˌjɑːd] **courtyards** NOUN
a flat area of ground surrounded by buildings or walls

cousin [ˈkʌzᵊn] **cousins** NOUN
Your cousin is the child of your uncle or aunt.

cove [kəʊv] **coves** NOUN
a small bay

covenant [ˈkʌvənənt] **covenants** NOUN
a formal written agreement or promise

cover [ˈkʌvə] **covers, covering, covered**
VERB

1 If you cover something, you put something else over it to protect it or hide it.

● THESAURUS
cloak: *a land cloaked in mist*
conceal: *The hat concealed her hair.*
cover up: *I covered him up with a blanket.*
hide: *His sunglasses hid his eyes.*
mask: *A cloud masked the sun.*
obscure: *One wall was obscured by a huge banner.*
screen: *The road was screened by a block of flats.*
shade: *shading his eyes from the glare*
<<OPPOSITE *reveal*

2 If something covers something else, it forms a layer over it. *e.g. Tears covered his face.*

● THESAURUS
coat: *Coat the fish with batter.*
overlay: *The floor was overlaid with rugs.*

3 If you cover a particular distance, you travel that distance. *e.g. He covered 52 kilometres in 210 laps.*

> NOUN

4 something put over an object to protect it or keep it warm

● THESAURUS
case: *a spectacle case*
coating: *steel covered with a coating of zinc*
covering: *a plastic covering*
jacket: *the jacket of a book*
mask: *a surgical mask*
screen: *They put a screen round me.*
wrapper: *Take the product from its sealed wrapper.*

5 The cover of a book or magazine is its outside.

6 Insurance cover is a guarantee that money will be paid if something is lost or harmed.

7 In the open, cover consists of trees, rocks, or other places where you can shelter or hide.

cover up VERB

8 If you cover up something you do not want people to know about, you hide it from them. *e.g. He lied to cover up his crime.*
cover-up NOUN

coverage [ˈkʌvərɪdʒ] NOUN
The coverage of something in the news is the reporting of it.

covering [ˈkʌvərɪŋ] **coverings** NOUN
1 a layer of something which protects or conceals something else *e.g. A morning blizzard left a covering of snow.*

covert [ˈkʌvət] ADJECTIVE FORMAL
Covert activities are secret, rather than open.
covertly ADVERB

covet [ˈkʌvɪt] **covets, coveting, coveted**
VERB; FORMAL
If you covet something, you want it very much.

cow [kaʊ] **cows** NOUN
a large animal kept on farms for its milk

🟤THESAURUS
bovine: *a herd of deranged bovines*
cattle: *fields where cattle graze*

coward [ˈkaʊəd] **cowards** NOUN
someone who is easily frightened and who avoids dangerous or difficult situations
cowardice NOUN

🟤THESAURUS
chicken: slang *We called him a chicken.*
wimp: informal *He seems like a wimp to me.*

cowardly [ˈkaʊədlɪ] ADJECTIVE
easily scared

🟤THESAURUS
chicken: slang *I was too chicken to complain.*
faint-hearted: *This is no time to be faint-hearted.*
gutless: informal *a gutless coward*
sookie: New Zealand *a sookie thing to do*
<<OPPOSITE *brave*

cowboy [ˈkaʊˌbɔɪ] **cowboys** NOUN
a man employed to look after cattle in America

cower [ˈkaʊə] **cowers, cowering, cowered**
VERB
When someone cowers, they crouch or move backwards because they are afraid.

🟤THESAURUS
cringe: *I cringed in horror.*
quail: *She quailed at the sight.*
shrink: *He shrank back in terror.*

cox [kɒks] **coxes** NOUN
a person who steers a boat

coy [kɔɪ] **coyer, coyest** ADJECTIVE
If someone is coy, they pretend to be shy and modest.
coyly ADVERB

coyote [ˈkɔɪəʊt] **coyotes** NOUN
a North American animal like a small wolf

crab [kræb] **crabs** NOUN
a sea creature with four pairs of legs, two pincers, and a flat, round body covered by a shell

crack [kræk] **cracks, cracking, cracked**
VERB

1 If something cracks, it becomes damaged, with lines appearing on its surface.

🟤THESAURUS
break: *She broke her leg playing rounders.*
fracture: *You've fractured a rib.*
snap: *The mast snapped like a dry twig.*

2 If you crack a joke, you tell it.

3 If you crack a problem or code, you solve it.

🟤THESAURUS
decipher: *trying to decipher the code*
solve: *attempts to solve the mystery*
work out: *I've worked out where I'm going wrong.*

> NOUN

4 one of the lines appearing on something when it cracks

🟤THESAURUS
break: *a train crash caused by a break in the rails*
cleft: *a cleft in the rocks*
crevice: *a crevice in the cliff-face*
fracture: *a hip fracture*

5 a narrow gap

> ADJECTIVE
6 A crack soldier or sportsman is highly trained and skilful.

cracker [ˈkrækə] **crackers** NOUN
1 a thin, crisp biscuit that is often eaten with cheese

2 a paper-covered tube that pulls apart with a bang and usually has a toy and paper hat inside

crackle [ˈkrækəl] **crackles, crackling, crackled** VERB
1 If something crackles, it makes a rapid series of short, harsh noises.

> NOUN
2 a short, harsh noise

cradle [ˈkreɪdəl] **cradles, cradling, cradled**
NOUN

1 a box-shaped bed for a baby

> VERB
2 If you cradle something in your arms or hands, you hold it there carefully.

craft [krɑːft] **crafts** NOUN
1 an activity such as weaving, carving, or pottery

2 a skilful occupation *e.g. the writer's craft*

3 a boat, plane, or spacecraft

▎ When *craft* means 'a boat, plane, or spacecraft' (sense 3), the plural is *craft*

craftsman [ˈkrɑːftsmən] **craftsmen** NOUN
a man who makes things skilfully with his hands
craftsmanship NOUN, **craftswoman** NOUN

crafty [ˈkrɑːftɪ] **craftier, craftiest** ADJECTIVE
Someone who is crafty gets what they want by

C

tricking people in a clever way.

● THESAURUS
artful: *the smiles and schemes of an artful woman*
cunning: *I have a cunning plan to get us out of this mess.*
devious: *By devious means she obtained the address.*
scheming: *You're a scheming little devil, aren't you?*
slippery: *a slippery customer*
sly: *He is a sly old beggar if ever there was one.*
wily: *the wily manoeuvring of the President*

crag [kræg] **crags** NOUN
a steep rugged rock or peak

craggy ['krægɪ] **craggier, craggiest**
ADJECTIVE
A craggy mountain or cliff is steep and rocky.

cram [kræm] **crams, cramming, crammed**
VERB
If you cram people or things into a place, you put more in than there is room for.

● THESAURUS
jam: *The place was jammed with people.*
pack: *The drawers were packed with clothes.*
squeeze: *The two of us were squeezed into one seat.*
stuff: *wallets stuffed with dollars*

cramp [kræmp] **cramps** NOUN
Cramp or cramps is a pain caused by a muscle contracting.

cramped [kræmpt] ADJECTIVE
If a room or building is cramped, it is not big enough for the people or things in it.

cranberry ['krænbərɪ] **cranberries** NOUN
Cranberries are sour-tasting red berries, often made into a sauce.

crane [kreɪn] **cranes, craning, craned**
NOUN
1 a machine that moves heavy things by lifting them in the air
2 a large bird with a long neck and long legs
> VERB
3 If you crane your neck, you extend your head in a particular direction to see or hear something better.

crank [kræŋk] **cranks, cranking, cranked**
NOUN
1 INFORMAL someone with strange ideas who behaves in an odd way
2 a device you turn to make something move *e.g. The adjustment is made by turning the crank.*
> VERB
3 If you crank something, you make it move by turning a handle.
cranky ADJECTIVE

cranny ['krænɪ] **crannies** NOUN
a very narrow opening in a wall or rock *e.g. nooks and crannies*

crash [kræʃ] **crashes, crashing, crashed**
NOUN
1 an accident in which a moving vehicle hits something violently

● THESAURUS
accident: *a serious car accident*
bump: *I had a bump in the car park.*
collision: *a head-on collision*
pile-up: informal *a 54-car pile-up*
smash: *He nearly died in a car smash.*

2 a sudden loud noise *e.g. the crash of the waves on the rocks*

● THESAURUS
bang: *The door slammed with a bang.*
clash: *the clash of cymbals*
din: *the din of battle*
smash: *the smash of falling crockery*

3 the sudden failure of a business or financial institution

● THESAURUS
bankruptcy: *Many firms are now facing bankruptcy.*
collapse: *The economy is on the edge of collapse.*
depression: *the Great Depression of the 1930s*
failure: *a major cause of business failure*
ruin: *Inflation has driven them to the brink of ruin.*
> VERB
4 When a vehicle crashes, it hits something and is badly damaged.

● THESAURUS
bump: *I've just bumped my car.*
collide: *Two trains collided in London today.*
drive into: *He drove his car into a tree.*
have an accident: *My brother's had an accident on his moped.*
hurtle into: *The racing car hurtled into the spectator enclosure.*
plough into: *The plane had ploughed into the mountainside.*
wreck: *He's wrecked his van.*

crash helmet **crash helmets** NOUN
a helmet worn by motor cyclists for protection when they are riding

crate [kreɪt] **crates** NOUN
a large box used for transporting or storing things

crater ['kreɪtə] **craters** NOUN
a wide hole in the ground caused by something hitting it or by an explosion

cravat [krə'væt] **cravats** NOUN
a piece of cloth a man can wear round his neck tucked into his shirt collar
[WORD HISTORY: from Serbo-Croat HRVAT meaning 'Croat'. Croat soldiers wore cravats during the Thirty Years' War]

crave [kreɪv] **craves, craving, craved** VERB
If you crave something, you want it very much. *e.g. I crave her approval.*

craving NOUN

crawl [krɔːl] **crawls, crawling, crawled**
VERB

1 When you crawl, you move forward on your hands and knees.

2 When a vehicle crawls, it moves very slowly.

3 INFORMAL If a place is crawling with people or things, it is full of them. *e.g. The place is crawling with drunks.*

crawler NOUN

⬤ THESAURUS
be alive with: *The river was alive with frogs.*
be full of: *The place was full of insects.*
be overrun: *slang The area is overrun with tourists.*
swarm: *The wood was swarming with police officers.*
teem: *ponds teeming with fish*

crayfish [ˈkreɪˌfɪʃ] **crayfishes** or **crayfish**
NOUN

a small shellfish like a lobster
[WORD HISTORY: from Old French CREVICE meaning 'crab']

crayon [ˈkreɪən] **crayons** NOUN

a coloured pencil or a stick of coloured wax

craze [kreɪz] **crazes** NOUN

something that is very popular for a short time

⬤ THESAURUS
fad: *a new-age fad*
fashion: *the fashion for Seventies toys*
trend: *the latest trend among film stars*
vogue: *a vogue for so-called health drinks*

crazy [ˈkreɪzi] **crazier, craziest** ADJECTIVE;
INFORMAL

1 very strange or foolish *e.g. The guy is crazy... a crazy idea*

⬤ THESAURUS
foolish: *It is foolish to risk skin cancer for the sake of a tan.*
insane: *If you want my opinion, I think your idea is completely insane.*
mad: *You'd be mad to work with him again.*
ridiculous: *It was an absolutely ridiculous decision.*
wild: *all sorts of wild ideas*
zany: *zany humour*
<<OPPOSITE *sensible*

2 If you are crazy about something, you are very keen on it. *e.g. I was crazy about dancing.*
crazily ADVERB, **craziness** NOUN

⬤ THESAURUS
fanatical: *fanatical about computer games*
mad: *She's not as mad about sport as I am.*
obsessed: *He was obsessed with American gangster movies.*
passionate: *He is passionate about the project.*
smitten: *They were totally smitten with each other.*
wild: *I'm just wild about Peter.*

creak [kriːk] **creaks, creaking, creaked**
VERB

1 If something creaks, it makes a harsh sound when it moves or when you stand on it.

> NOUN

2 a harsh squeaking noise
creaky ADJECTIVE

cream [kriːm] **creams** NOUN

1 Cream is a thick, yellowish-white liquid taken from the top of milk.

2 Cream is also a substance people can rub on their skin to make it soft.

> ADJECTIVE

3 yellowish-white
creamy ADJECTIVE

crease [kriːs] **creases, creasing, creased**
NOUN

1 an irregular line that appears on cloth or paper when it is crumpled

2 a straight line on something that has been pressed or folded neatly

> VERB

3 To crease something is to make lines appear on it.

creased ADJECTIVE

create [kriːˈeɪt] **creates, creating, created**
VERB

1 To create something is to cause it to happen or exist. *e.g. This is absolutely vital but creates a problem.*

⬤ THESAURUS
bring about: *helping to bring about peace*
cause: *Sugar causes dental decay.*
lead to: *The takeover led to widespread redundancies.*
occasion: *the distress occasioned by her dismissal*

2 When someone creates a new product or process, they invent it.
creator NOUN, **creation** NOUN

⬤ THESAURUS
coin: *the man who coined the term 'virtual reality'*
compose: *Vivaldi composed many concertos.*
devise: *We devised a scheme to help him.*
formulate: *He formulated his plan for escape.*
invent: *He invented the first electric clock.*
originate: *the designer who originated platform shoes*

creative [kriːˈeɪtɪv] ADJECTIVE

1 Creative people are able to invent and develop original ideas.

⬤ THESAURUS
fertile: *a fertile imagination*
imaginative: *an imaginative writer*
inspired: *his inspired use of colour*

inventive: *an inventive storyline*

2 Creative activities involve the inventing and developing of original ideas. *e.g. creative writing* **creatively** ADVERB, **creativity** NOUN

creature ['kriːtʃə] **creatures** NOUN
any living thing that moves about

crèche [krɛʃ] **crèches** NOUN
a place where small children are looked after while their parents are working
[WORD HISTORY: from Old French CRÈCHE meaning 'crib' or 'manger']

credence ['kriːdəns] NOUN; FORMAL
If something gives credence to a theory or story, it makes it easier to believe.

credentials [krɪ'dɛnʃəls] PLURAL NOUN
Your credentials are your past achievements or other things in your background that make you qualified for something.

credible ['krɛdɪbəl] ADJECTIVE
If someone or something is credible, you can believe or trust them.
credibility NOUN

credit ['krɛdɪt] **credits, crediting, credited** NOUN
1 If you are allowed credit, you can take something and pay for it later. *e.g. to buy goods on credit*

2 If you get the credit for something, people praise you for it.

● THESAURUS
commendation: *Both teams deserve commendation.*
glory: *basking in reflected glory*
praise: *Praise is due to all concerned.*
recognition: *She got no recognition for her work.*
thanks: *He received no thanks for his efforts.*
<<OPPOSITE *disgrace*

3 If you say someone is a credit to their family or school, you mean that their family or school should be proud of them.
> PLURAL NOUN
4 The list of people who helped make a film, record, or television programme is called the credits.
> PHRASE
5 If someone or their bank account is **in credit**, their account has money in it.
> VERB
6 If you are credited with an achievement, people believe that you were responsible for it.

creditable ['krɛdɪtəbəl] ADJECTIVE
satisfactory or fairly good *e.g. a creditable performance*

credit card **credit cards** NOUN
a plastic card that allows someone to buy goods on credit

creditor ['krɛdɪtə] **creditors** NOUN
Your creditors are the people you owe money to.

creed [kriːd] **creeds** NOUN
1 a religion
2 any set of beliefs *e.g. the feminist creed*

creek [kriːk] **creeks** NOUN
a narrow inlet where the sea comes a long way into the land
[WORD HISTORY: from Old Norse KRIKI meaning 'nook']

creep [kriːp] **creeps, creeping, crept** VERB
To creep is to move quietly and slowly.

creepy ['kriːpɪ] **creepier, creepiest** ADJECTIVE INFORMAL
strange and frightening *e.g. a creepy feeling*

● THESAURUS
disturbing: *There was something about him she found disturbing.*
eerie: *I walked down the eerie dark path.*
macabre: *macabre stories*
scary: *informal We watched scary movies.*
sinister: *There was something sinister about him.*
spooky: *The whole place has a slightly spooky atmosphere.*
unnatural: *The altered landscape looks unnatural and weird.*

cremate [krɪ'meɪt] **cremates, cremating, cremated** VERB
When someone is cremated, their dead body is burned during a funeral service.
cremation NOUN

crematorium [,krɛmə'tɔːrɪəm] **crematoriums** or **crematoria** NOUN
a building in which the bodies of dead people are burned

crepe [kreɪp] NOUN
1 Crepe is a thin ridged material made from cotton, silk, or wool.
2 Crepe is also a type of rubber with a rough surface.

crescendo [krɪ'ʃɛndəʊ] **crescendos** NOUN
When there is a crescendo in a piece of music, the music gets louder.

crescent ['krɛsənt] **crescents** NOUN
a curved shape that is wider in its middle than at the ends, which are pointed

cress [krɛs] NOUN
Cress is a plant with small, strong-tasting leaves. It is used in salads.

crest [krɛst] **crests** NOUN
1 The crest of a hill or wave is its highest part.
2 a tuft of feathers on top of a bird's head
3 a small picture or design that is the emblem of a noble family, a town, or an organization

crested ADJECTIVE

crevice ['krɛvɪs] **crevices** NOUN
a narrow crack or gap in rock

crew [kru:] **crews** NOUN
1 The crew of a ship, aeroplane, or spacecraft are the people who operate it.

2 people with special technical skills who work together *e.g. the camera crew*

crib [krɪb] **cribs, cribbing, cribbed** VERB
1 INFORMAL If you crib, you copy what someone else has written and pretend it is your own work.
> NOUN
2 OLD-FASHIONED a baby's cot

crib-wall ['krɪb,wɔːl] **crib-walls** NOUN
In New Zealand English, a wooden wall built against a bank of earth to support it.

crick [krɪk] **cricks** NOUN
a pain in your neck or back caused by muscles becoming stiff

cricket ['krɪkɪt] **crickets** NOUN
1 Cricket is an outdoor game played by two teams who take turns at scoring runs by hitting a ball with a bat.

2 a small jumping insect that produces sounds by rubbing its wings together
cricketer NOUN

crime [kraɪm] **crimes** NOUN
an action for which you can be punished by law *e.g. a serious crime*

● THESAURUS
misdemeanour: *a financial misdemeanour*
offence: *a serious offence*
violation: *tax law violations*
wrong: *I intend to right that wrong.*

criminal ['krɪmɪnᵊl] **criminals** NOUN
1 someone who has committed a crime

● THESAURUS
crook: informal *The man is a crook and a liar.*
culprit: *the true culprit's identity*
delinquent: *juvenile delinquents*
offender: *a first-time offender*
skelm: South African *a skelm from the city*
villain: *He tackled an armed villain single-handed.*

> ADJECTIVE
2 involving or related to crime *e.g. criminal activities*
criminally ADVERB

● THESAURUS
corrupt: *corrupt practices*
crooked: *crooked business deals*
illegal: *an illegal action*
illicit: *illicit dealings*
unlawful: *unlawful entry*

<<OPPOSITE *legal*

criminology [ˌkrɪmɪˈnɒlədʒɪ] NOUN
the scientific study of crime and criminals
criminologist NOUN

crimson ['krɪmzən] NOUN OR ADJECTIVE
dark purplish-red

cringe [krɪndʒ] **cringes, cringing, cringed** VERB
If you cringe, you back away from someone or something because you are afraid or embarrassed.
[WORD HISTORY: from Old English CRINGAN meaning 'to yield in battle']

crinkle ['krɪŋkᵊl] **crinkles, crinkling, crinkled** VERB
1 If something crinkles, it becomes slightly creased or folded.
> NOUN
2 Crinkles are small creases or folds.

cripple ['krɪpᵊl] **cripples, crippling, crippled** VERB
1 To cripple someone is to injure them severely.

● THESAURUS
disable: *disabled by polio*
lame: *He was lamed for life.*
maim: *mines maiming and killing civilians*
paralyse: *paralysed in a riding accident*

2 To cripple a company or country is to prevent it from working.
crippled ADJECTIVE, **crippling** ADJECTIVE

● THESAURUS
bring to a standstill: *The strike brought France to a standstill.*
impair: *Their actions will impair France's national interests.*
put out of action: *The port has been put out of action.*

crisis ['kraɪsɪs] **crises** NOUN
a serious or dangerous situation

crisp [krɪsp] **crisper, crispest; crisps** ADJECTIVE
1 Something that is crisp is pleasantly fresh and firm. *e.g. crisp lettuce leaves*

2 If the air or the weather is crisp, it is pleasantly fresh, cold, and dry. *e.g. crisp wintry days*
> NOUN
3 Crisps are thin slices of potato fried until they are hard and crunchy.

crispy ['krɪspɪ] **crispier, crispiest** ADJECTIVE
Crispy food is pleasantly hard and crunchy. *e.g. a crispy salad*

criterion [kraɪˈtɪərɪən] **criteria** NOUN
a standard by which you judge or decide something

Criteria is the plural of *criterion*, and needs to be used with a plural verb

critic ['krɪtɪk] **critics** NOUN

1 someone who writes reviews of books, films, plays, or musical performances

2 A critic of a person or system is someone who criticizes them publicly. *e.g. the government's critics*

critical ['krɪtɪkəl] ADJECTIVE

1 A critical time is one which is very important in determining what happens in the future. *e.g. critical months in the history of the world*

● THESAURUS
crucial: *a crucial election campaign*
deciding: *Price was a deciding factor.*
decisive: *a decisive moment in my life*
momentous: *a momentous decision*
pivotal: *He played a pivotal role in the match.*
vital: *vital information*
<<OPPOSITE *unimportant*

2 A critical situation is a very serious one. *e.g. Rock music is in a critical state.*

● THESAURUS
grave: *grave danger*
precarious: *a precarious financial situation*
serious: *His condition is said to be serious.*

3 If an ill or injured person is critical, they are in danger of dying.

4 If you are critical of something or someone, you express severe judgments or opinions about them.

● THESAURUS
carping: *carping comments*
derogatory: *derogatory references to women*
disapproving: *a disapproving look*
disparaging: *He spoke in disparaging tones.*
scathing: *a scathing attack*
<<OPPOSITE *complimentary*

5 If you are critical, you examine and judge something carefully. *e.g. a critical look at the way he led his life*
critically ADVERB

criticism ['krɪtɪsɪzəm] **criticisms** NOUN

1 When there is criticism of someone or something, people express disapproval of them.

● THESAURUS
censure: *They deserve praise rather than censure.*
disapproval: *a chorus of disapproval*
disparagement: *their disparagement of this book*
fault-finding: *her husband's constant fault-finding*
flak: informal *I got a lot of flak for that idea.*
panning: informal *a panning from the critics*
<<OPPOSITE *praise*

2 If you make a criticism, you point out a fault you think someone or something has.

criticize ['krɪtɪ‚saɪz] **criticizes, criticizing, criticized;** also spelt **criticise** VERB

If you criticize someone or something, you say what you think is wrong with them.

● THESAURUS
censure: *a decision for which she was censured*
condemn: *He refused to condemn their behaviour.*
find fault with: *She keeps finding fault with my work.*
knock: informal *Don't knock it till you've tried it.*
pan: informal *Critics panned the show.*
put down: *She's always putting him down in front of the kids.*
<<OPPOSITE *praise*

croak [krəʊk] **croaks, croaking, croaked** VERB

1 When animals and birds croak, they make harsh, low sounds.

> NOUN

2 a harsh, low sound
[WORD HISTORY: from Old Norse KRAKA meaning 'crow']

Croatian [krəʊˈeɪʃən] **Croatians** ADJECTIVE

1 belonging to or relating to Croatia

> NOUN

2 someone who comes from Croatia

3 Croatian is the form of Serbo-Croat spoken in Croatia.

crochet ['krəʊʃeɪ] NOUN

Crochet is a way of making clothes and other things out of thread using a needle with a small hook at the end.

crockery ['krɒkərɪ] NOUN

Crockery is plates, cups, and saucers.

crocodile ['krɒkə‚daɪl] **crocodiles** NOUN

a large scaly meat-eating reptile which lives in tropical rivers
[WORD HISTORY: from Greek KROKODEILOS meaning 'lizard']

crocus ['krəʊkəs] **crocuses** NOUN

Crocuses are yellow, purple, or white flowers that grow in early spring.

croft [krɒft] **crofts** NOUN

a small piece of land, especially in Scotland, which is farmed by one family
crofter NOUN

croissant ['krwʌsɒŋ] **croissants** NOUN

a light, crescent-shaped roll eaten at breakfast
[WORD HISTORY: from French CROISSANT meaning 'crescent']

crony ['krəʊnɪ] **cronies** NOUN; OLD-FASHIONED, INFORMAL

Your cronies are the friends you spend a lot of time with.

crook [krʊk] **crooks** NOUN

1 INFORMAL a criminal

🔵 THESAURUS

cheat: *a rotten cheat*
rogue: *Mr Scott wasn't a rogue at all.*
scoundrel: old-fashioned *He is a lying scoundrel!*
shark: *Beware the sharks when you are deciding how to invest.*
swindler: *Swindlers have cheated investors out of £12 million.*
thief: *The thieves snatched the camera.*
villain: *As a copper, I've spent my life putting villains behind bars.*

2 The crook of your arm or leg is the soft inside part where you bend your elbow or knee.

> ADJECTIVE

3 In Australian English, 'crook' means 'ill'.

🔵 THESAURUS

ill: *I was feeling ill.*
nauseous: *The drugs may make the patient feel nauseous.*
poorly: *Julie's still poorly.*
queasy: *He was very prone to seasickness and already felt queasy.*
sick: *The very thought of food made him feel sick.*
under the weather: *I was still feeling a bit under the weather.*
unwell: *He felt unwell as he was travelling home this afternoon.*

crooked ['krʊkɪd] ADJECTIVE

1 bent or twisted

🔵 THESAURUS

bent: *a bent back*
deformed: *born with a deformed right leg*
distorted: *a distorted image*
irregular: *irregular and discoloured teeth*
out of shape: *The wires were bent out of shape.*
twisted: *bits of twisted metal*
warped: *warped wooden shutters*
<<OPPOSITE *straight*

2 Someone who is crooked is dishonest.

🔵 THESAURUS

corrupt: *corrupt police officers*
criminal: *criminal activities*
dishonest: *dishonest salespeople*
fraudulent: *a fraudulent claim*
illegal: *illegal trading*
shady: informal *shady deals*
<<OPPOSITE *honest*

croon [kru:n] **croons, crooning, crooned** VERB

To croon is to sing or hum quietly and gently. *e.g. He crooned a love song.*

[WORD HISTORY: from Old Dutch KRONEN meaning 'to groan']

crop [krɒp] **crops, cropping, cropped** NOUN

1 Crops are plants such as wheat and potatoes that are grown for food.

2 the plants collected at harvest time *e.g. You should have two crops in the year.*

> VERB

3 To crop someone's hair is to cut it very short.

croquet ['krəʊkeɪ] NOUN

Croquet is a game in which the players use long-handled mallets to hit balls through metal arches pushed into a lawn.

cross [krɒs] **crosses, crossing, crossed; crosser, crossest** VERB

1 If you cross something such as a room or a road, you go to the other side of it.

🔵 THESAURUS

ford: *trying to find a safe place to ford the stream*
go across: *going across the road*
span: *the iron bridge spanning the railway*
traverse: *a valley traversed by streams*

2 Lines or roads that cross meet and go across each other.

🔵 THESAURUS

crisscross: *Phone wires criss-cross the street.*
intersect: *The circles intersect in two places.*

3 If a thought crosses your mind, you think of it.

4 If you cross your arms, legs, or fingers, you put one on top of the other.

> NOUN

5 a vertical bar or line crossed by a shorter horizontal bar or line; also used to describe any object shaped like this.

6 The Cross is the cross-shaped structure on which Jesus Christ was crucified. A cross is also any symbol representing Christ's Cross.

7 a written mark shaped like an X *e.g. I drew a small bicycle and put a cross by it.*

8 Something that is a cross between two things is neither one thing nor the other, but a mixture of both.

🔵 THESAURUS

blend: *a blend of the old and the new*
combination: *a combination of fear and anger*
mixture: *a mixture of two factors*

> ADJECTIVE

9 Someone who is cross is rather angry.

crossly ADVERB

🔵 THESAURUS

angry: *Are you angry with me?*
annoyed: *I'm annoyed with myself for being so stupid.*
fractious: *The children were getting fractious.*
fretful: *the fretful expression on her face*
grumpy: *a grumpy old man*
in a bad mood: *He's in a bad mood about something.*

C

irritable: *She had been restless and irritable all day.*

crossbow ['krɒs,bəʊ] **crossbows** NOUN
a weapon consisting of a small bow fixed at the end of a piece of wood

cross-country ['krɒs'kʌntrɪ] NOUN
1 Cross-country is the sport of running across open countryside, rather than on roads or on a track.

> ADVERB OR ADJECTIVE
2 across country

cross-eyed ['krɒs,aɪd] ADJECTIVE
A cross-eyed person has eyes that seem to look towards each other.

crossfire ['krɒs,faɪə] NOUN
Crossfire is gunfire crossing the same place from opposite directions.

crosshatching ['krɒs,hætʃɪŋ] NOUN
(ART) Crosshatching is drawing an area of shade in a picture using two or more sets of parallel lines.

crossing ['krɒsɪŋ] **crossings** NOUN
1 a place where you can cross a road safely
2 a journey by ship to a place on the other side of the sea

cross-legged ['krɒs'lɛgɪd] ADJECTIVE
If you are sitting cross-legged, you are sitting on the floor with your knees pointing outwards and your feet tucked under them.

cross section **cross sections** NOUN
A cross section of a group of people is a representative sample of them.

crossword ['krɒs,wɜːd] **crosswords** NOUN
a puzzle in which you work out the answers to clues and write them in the white squares of a pattern of black and white squares

crotch [krɒtʃ] **crotches** NOUN
the part of your body between the tops of your legs

crotchet ['krɒtʃɪt] **crotchets** NOUN
(MUSIC) A crotchet is a musical note equal to two quavers or half a minim.

crouch [kraʊtʃ] **crouches, crouching, crouched** VERB
If you are crouching, you are leaning forward with your legs bent under you.

● THESAURUS
bend down: *I bent down and touched the grass.*
squat: *He squatted on his heels to talk to the children.*

crow [krəʊ] **crows, crowing, crowed** NOUN
1 a large black bird which makes a loud, harsh noise

> VERB
2 When a cock crows, it utters a loud squawking sound.

crowbar ['krəʊ,bɑː] **crowbars** NOUN
a heavy iron bar used as a lever or for forcing things open

crowd [kraʊd] **crowds, crowding, crowded** NOUN
1 a large group of people gathered together

● THESAURUS
horde: *hordes of tourists*
host: *a host of fans*
mass: *a heaving mass of people*
mob: *a mob of demonstrators*
multitude: *surrounded by a noisy multitude*
swarm: *swarms of visitors*
throng: *An official pushed through the throng.*

> VERB
2 When people crowd somewhere, they gather there close together or in large numbers.

● THESAURUS
congregate: *A large crowd congregated outside the stadium.*
gather: *Dozens of people gathered to watch.*
swarm: *Police swarmed into the area.*
throng: *The crowds thronged into the mall.*

crowded ['kraʊdɪd] ADJECTIVE
A crowded place is full of people.

● THESAURUS
congested: *congested cities*
full: *The train was full.*
overflowing: *buildings overflowing with students*
packed: *By 10.30 the shop was packed.*

crown [kraʊn] **crowns, crowning, crowned** NOUN
1 a circular ornament worn on a royal person's head
2 The crown of something such as your head is the top part of it.

> VERB
3 When a king or queen is crowned, a crown is put on their head during their coronation ceremony.
4 When something crowns an event, it is the final part of it. *e.g. The news crowned a dreadful week.*

crucial ['kruːʃəl] ADJECTIVE
If something is crucial, it is very important in determining how something else will be in the future.
[WORD HISTORY: from Latin CRUX meaning 'a cross']

● THESAURUS
central: *central to the whole process*
critical: *a critical point in the campaign*

decisive: *ready to strike at the decisive moment*
momentous: *a momentous event*
pivotal: *He played a pivotal role in the match.*
vital: *vital information*

crucifix ['kruːsɪfɪks] **crucifixes** NOUN
a cross with a figure representing Jesus Christ being crucified on it

crucify ['kruːsɪˌfaɪ] **crucifies, crucifying, crucified** VERB
To crucify someone is to tie or nail them to a large wooden cross and leave them there to die.
crucifixion NOUN

crude [kruːd] **cruder, crudest** ADJECTIVE
1 rough and simple *e.g. a crude weapon... a crude method of entry*

THESAURUS
primitive: *They managed to make a primitive harness.*
rough: *a rough sketch*
rudimentary: *some form of rudimentary heating*
simple: *a simple stringed instrument*
2 A crude person speaks or behaves in a rude and offensive way. *e.g. You can be quite crude at times.*
crudely ADVERB, **crudity** NOUN

THESAURUS
coarse: *coarse speech*
dirty: *a dirty joke*
indecent: *indecent lyrics*
obscene: *obscene language*
tasteless: *a tasteless remark*
vulgar: *a vulgar phrase*
<<OPPOSITE refined

cruel ['kruːəl] **crueller, cruellest** ADJECTIVE
Cruel people deliberately cause pain or distress to other people or to animals.
cruelly ADVERB

THESAURUS
barbarous: *a barbarous attack*
brutal: *a brutal murder*
callous: *callous treatment*
cold-blooded: *a cold-blooded killer*
heartless: *It was a heartless thing to do.*
inhumane: *He was kept under inhumane conditions.*
sadistic: *mistreated by sadistic guards*
vicious: *a vicious blow*
<<OPPOSITE kind

cruelty ['kruːəltɪ] NOUN
cruel behaviour

THESAURUS
barbarity: *the barbarity of war*
brutality: *police brutality*
callousness: *the callousness of his murder*
inhumanity: *man's inhumanity to man*
savagery: *scenes of unimaginable savagery*

viciousness: *the viciousness of the attacks*
<<OPPOSITE kindness

cruise [kruːz] **cruises, cruising, cruised** NOUN
1 a holiday in which you travel on a ship and visit places
> VERB
2 When a vehicle cruises, it moves at a constant moderate speed.

cruiser ['kruːzə] **cruisers** NOUN
1 a motor boat with a cabin you can sleep in
2 a large, fast warship

crumb [krʌm] **crumbs** NOUN
Crumbs are very small pieces of bread or cake.

crumble ['krʌmbəl] **crumbles, crumbling, crumbled** VERB
When something crumbles, it breaks into small pieces.

crumbly ['krʌmblɪ] **crumblier, crumbliest** ADJECTIVE
Something crumbly easily breaks into small pieces.

crumpet ['krʌmpɪt] **crumpets** NOUN
a round, flat, breadlike cake which you eat toasted

crumple ['krʌmpəl] **crumples, crumpling, crumpled** VERB
To crumple paper or cloth is to squash it so that it is full of creases and folds.

THESAURUS
crease: *Don't crease the material.*
crush: *Andrew crushed his empty can.*
screw up: *He screwed the letter up in anger.*
wrinkle: *trying not to wrinkle her silk skirt*

crunch [krʌntʃ] **crunches, crunching, crunched** VERB
If you crunch something, you crush it noisily, for example between your teeth or under your feet.

crunchy ['krʌntʃɪ] **crunchier, crunchiest** ADJECTIVE
Crunchy food is hard or crisp and makes a noise when you eat it.

crusade [kruːˈseɪd] **crusades** NOUN
a long and determined attempt to achieve something *e.g. the crusade for human rights*
crusader NOUN

crush [krʌʃ] **crushes, crushing, crushed** VERB
1 To crush something is to destroy its shape by squeezing it.

THESAURUS
crumble: *Crumble the stock cubes into a jar.*
crumple: *She crumpled the note up and threw it away.*

mash: *Mash the bananas with a fork.*
squash: *She squashed the wasp under her heel.*

2 To crush a substance is to turn it into liquid or powder by squeezing or grinding it.

3 To crush an army or political organization is to defeat it completely.

● THESAURUS

overcome: *working to overcome the enemy forces*
put down: *Soldiers moved in to put down the rebellion.*
quell: *Troops eventually quelled the unrest.*
stamp out: *steps to stamp out bullying in schools*
vanquish: *his vanquished foe*

> NOUN

4 a dense crowd of people

crust [krʌst] **crusts** NOUN
1 the hard outside part of a loaf
2 a hard layer on top of something *e.g. The snow had a fine crust on it.*

crusty ['krʌstɪ] **crustier, crustiest** ADJECTIVE
1 Something that is crusty has a hard outside layer.
2 Crusty people are impatient and irritable.

crutch [krʌtʃ] **crutches** NOUN
a support like a long stick which you lean on to help you walk when you have an injured foot or leg

crux [krʌks] NOUN
the most important or difficult part of a problem or argument

cry see page 203 for Word Web

crypt [krɪpt] **crypts** NOUN
an underground room beneath a church, usually used as a burial place
[WORD HISTORY: from Greek KRUPTEIN meaning 'to hide']

cryptic ['krɪptɪk] ADJECTIVE
A cryptic remark or message has a hidden meaning.

crystal ['krɪstəl] **crystals** NOUN
1 a piece of a mineral that has formed naturally into a regular shape
2 Crystal is a type of transparent rock, used in jewellery.
3 Crystal is also a kind of very high quality glass.
crystalline ADJECTIVE

crystallize ['krɪstəˌlaɪz] **crystallizes, crystallizing, crystallized**; also spelt **crystallise** VERB
1 If a substance crystallizes, it turns into crystals.
2 If an idea crystallizes, it becomes clear in your mind.

cub [kʌb] **cubs** NOUN
1 Some young wild animals are called cubs. *e.g. a lion cub*
2 The Cubs is an organization for young boys before they join the Scouts.

Cuban ['kjuːbən] **Cubans** ADJECTIVE
1 belonging or relating to Cuba
> NOUN
2 someone who comes from Cuba

cube [kjuːb] **cubes, cubing, cubed** NOUN
1 a three-dimensional shape with six equally-sized square surfaces
2 If you multiply a number by itself twice, you get its cube.
> VERB
3 To cube a number is to multiply it by itself twice.

cubic ['kjuːbɪk] ADJECTIVE
used in measurements of volume *e.g. cubic centimetres*

cubicle ['kjuːbɪkəl] **cubicles** NOUN
a small enclosed area in a place such as a sports centre, where you can dress and undress

cuckoo ['kʊkuː] **cuckoos** NOUN
a grey bird with a two-note call that lays its eggs in other birds' nests

cucumber ['kjuːˌkʌmbə] **cucumbers** NOUN
a long, thin, green-skinned fruit eaten raw in salads

cuddle ['kʌdəl] **cuddles, cuddling, cuddled** VERB
1 If you cuddle someone, you hold them affectionately in your arms.
> NOUN
2 If you give someone a cuddle, you hold them affectionately in your arms.

cuddly ['kʌdlɪ] **cuddlier, cuddliest** ADJECTIVE
Cuddly people, animals, or toys are soft or pleasing in some way so that you want to cuddle them.

cue [kjuː] **cues** NOUN
1 something said or done by a performer that is a signal for another performer to begin *e.g. Chris never misses a cue.*
2 a long stick used to hit the balls in snooker and billiards

cuff [kʌf] **cuffs** NOUN
the end part of a sleeve

cufflink ['kʌfˌlɪŋk] **cufflinks** NOUN
Cufflinks are small objects for holding shirt cuffs together.

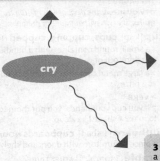

1 VERB
to have tears coming from your eyes *eg: Stop crying and tell me what's wrong.*
● **THESAURUS**
bawl: *One of the toddlers was bawling.*
blubber: *To our surprise, he began to blubber like a child.*
howl: *The baby was howling in the next room.*
sob: *Her sister broke down and began to sob into her handkerchief.*
wail: *a mother wailing for her lost child*
weep: *The woman began to weep uncontrollably.*
whimper: *He huddled in a corner, whimpering with fear.*

2 VERB
to call out loudly *eg: 'See you soon!' they cried.*
● **THESAURUS**
call: *She called to me across the square.*
exclaim: *"You must be mad!" she exclaimed.*
shout: *"Over here!" they shouted.*
yell: *He yelled out of the window.*

3 NOUN
a loud or high shout *eg: a cry of pain*
● **THESAURUS**
call: *the call of a seagull*
exclamation: *an exclamation of surprise*
shout: *I heard a distant shout.*
yell: *Bob let out a yell.*

C

cuisine [kwɪˈziːn] NOUN
The cuisine of a region is the style of cooking that is typical of it.
[WORD HISTORY: from French CUISINE meaning 'kitchen']

cul-de-sac [ˈkʌldəˌsæk] **cul-de-sacs** NOUN
a road that does not lead to any other roads because one end is blocked off

culinary [ˈkʌlɪnərɪ] ADJECTIVE; FORMAL
connected with the kitchen or cooking
[WORD HISTORY: from Latin CULINA meaning 'kitchen']

cull [kʌl] **culls, culling, culled** VERB
1 If you cull things, you gather them from different places or sources. *e.g. information culled from movies*
> NOUN
2 When there is a cull, weaker animals are killed to reduce the numbers in a group.

culminate [ˈkʌlmɪˌneɪt] **culminates, culminating, culminated** VERB
To culminate in something is to finally develop into it. *e.g. a campaign that culminated in a stunning success*
culmination NOUN

culprit [ˈkʌlprɪt] **culprits** NOUN
someone who has done something harmful or wrong
[WORD HISTORY: from Anglo-French CULPABLE meaning 'guilty' and PRIT meaning 'ready' (i.e. ready for trial)]

cult [kʌlt] **cults** NOUN
1 A cult is a religious group with special rituals, usually connected with the worship of a particular person.
2 'Cult' is used to refer to any situation in which someone or something is very popular with a large group of people. *e.g. the American sports car cult*

cultivate [ˈkʌltɪˌveɪt] **cultivates, cultivating, cultivated** VERB
1 To cultivate land is to grow crops on it.
2 If you cultivate a feeling or attitude, you try to develop it in yourself or other people.
cultivation NOUN

culture [ˈkʌltʃə] **cultures** NOUN
1 Culture refers to the arts and to people's appreciation of them. *e.g. He was a man of culture.*
2 The culture of a particular society is its ideas, customs, and art. *e.g. Japanese culture.*
3 In science, a culture is a group of bacteria or cells grown in a laboratory.
cultured ADJECTIVE, **cultural** ADJECTIVE

cumulative [ˈkjuːmjʊlətɪv] ADJECTIVE
Something that is cumulative keeps being added to.

cunjevoi [ˈkʌndʒɪˌvɔɪ] **cunjevois** NOUN
a very small Australian sea creature that lives on rocks

cunning [ˈkʌnɪŋ] ADJECTIVE
1 Someone who is cunning uses clever and deceitful methods to get what they want.
● THESAURUS
artful: *an artful old woman*
crafty: *a crafty plan*
devious: *a devious mind*
sly: *a sly trick*
wily: *a wily politician*
<<OPPOSITE open
> NOUN
2 Cunning is the ability to get what you want using clever and deceitful methods.
cunningly ADVERB
[WORD HISTORY: from Old Norse KUNNA meaning 'to know']
● THESAURUS
deviousness: *the deviousness of drug traffickers*
guile: *She was without guile or pretence.*

cup [kʌp] **cups, cupping, cupped** NOUN
1 a small, round container with a handle, which you drink out of
2 a large metal container with two handles, given as a prize
> VERB
3 If you cup your hands, you put them together to make a shape like a cup.

cupboard [ˈkʌbəd] **cupboards** NOUN
a piece of furniture with doors and shelves

curable [ˈkjʊərəbəl] ADJECTIVE
If a disease or illness is curable, it can be cured.

curate [ˈkjʊərɪt] **curates** NOUN
a clergyman who helps a vicar or a priest

curator [kjʊəˈreɪtə] **curators** NOUN
the person in a museum or art gallery in charge of its contents

curb [kɜːb] **curbs, curbing, curbed** VERB
1 To curb something is to keep it within limits. *e.g. policies designed to curb inflation*
● THESAURUS
check: *an attempt to check the spread of the disease*
contain: *A hundred firefighters are still trying to contain the fire.*
control: *the need to control environmental pollution*
limit: *He limited payments on the country's foreign debt.*
restrain: *efforts to restrain corruption*
suppress: *The Government is suppressing inflation*

by devastating the economy.

> NOUN

2 If a curb is placed on something, it is kept within limits. *e.g. the curb on spending*

THESAURUS
brake: *Illness had put a brake on his progress.*
control: *price controls*
limit: *limits on government spending*
limitation: *We need a limitation on the powers of the government.*
restraint: *new restraints on trade unions*

curdle ['kɜːdªl] **curdles, curdling, curdled**
VERB
When milk curdles, it turns sour.

curds ['kɜːdz] PLURAL NOUN
Curds are the thick white substance formed when milk turns sour.

cure [kjʊə] **cures, curing, cured** VERB
1 To cure an illness is to end it.
2 To cure a sick or injured person is to make them well.

THESAURUS
heal: *plants used to heal wounds*
remedy: *an operation to remedy a blood clot on his brain*

3 If something cures you of a habit or attitude, it stops you having it.
4 To cure food, tobacco, or animal skin is to treat it in order to preserve it.

> NOUN

5 A cure for an illness is something that cures it.

THESAURUS
medicine: *herbal medicines*
remedy: *a remedy for colds and flu*
treatment: *the most effective treatment for malaria*

curfew ['kɜːfjuː] **curfews** NOUN
If there is a curfew, people must stay indoors between particular times at night.

curiosity [ˌkjʊərɪ'ɒsɪti] **curiosities** NOUN
1 Curiosity is the desire to know about something or about many things.

THESAURUS
inquisitiveness: *the inquisitiveness of children*
interest: *a lively interest in current affairs*

2 something unusual and interesting

THESAURUS
freak: *a freak of nature*
marvel: *a marvel of science*
novelty: *in the days when a motor car was a novelty*
oddity: *Tourists are still something of an oddity here.*
rarity: *Mexican restaurants are a rarity here.*

curious ['kjʊərɪəs] ADJECTIVE
1 Someone who is curious wants to know more about something.

THESAURUS
inquiring: *He gave me an inquiring look.*
inquisitive: *Cats are very inquisitive.*
interested: *A crowd of interested villagers gathered.*
nosy: *informal nosy neighbours*
<<OPPOSITE *incurious*

2 Something that is curious is unusual and hard to explain.
curiously ADVERB

THESAURUS
bizarre: *his bizarre behaviour*
extraordinary: *an extraordinary story*
odd: *an odd coincidence*
peculiar: *a peculiar smell*
singular: *singular talent*
strange: *a strange taste*
unusual: *an unusual name*
<<OPPOSITE *ordinary*

curl [kɜːl] **curls, curling, curled** NOUN
1 Curls are lengths of hair shaped in tight curves and circles.

2 a curved or spiral shape *e.g. the curls of morning fog*

> VERB

3 If something curls, it moves in a curve or spiral.
curly ADJECTIVE

curler ['kɜːlə] **curlers** NOUN
Curlers are plastic or metal tubes that women roll their hair round to make it curly.

curlew ['kɜːljuː] **curlews** NOUN
a large brown bird with a long curved beak and a loud cry

currant ['kʌrənt] **currants** NOUN
1 Currants are small dried grapes often put in cakes and puddings.

2 Currants are also blackcurrants or redcurrants.
[WORD HISTORY: sense 1 is from Middle English RAYSON OF CORANNTE meaning 'Corinth raisin']

currawong ['kʌrəˌwɒŋ] **currawongs** NOUN
an Australian bird like a crow

currency ['kʌrənsi] **currencies** NOUN
1 A country's currency is its coins and banknotes, or its monetary system generally. *e.g. foreign currency... a strong economy and a weak currency*

2 If something such as an idea has currency, it is used a lot at a particular time.

current ['kʌrənt] **currents** NOUN
1 a strong continuous movement of the water in a river or in the sea

THESAURUS
flow: *the quiet flow of the olive-green water*
tide: *We will sail with the tide.*
undertow: *Dangerous undertows make swimming unsafe along the coastline.*

2 An air current is a flowing movement in the air.

3 An electric current is a flow of electricity through a wire or circuit.

> ADJECTIVE

4 (HISTORY) Something that is current is happening, being done, or being used now.
currently ADVERB

THESAURUS

contemporary: *He has adopted a more contemporary style.*
fashionable: *the fashionable theory about this issue*
ongoing: *an ongoing debate on inner city problems*
present: *skilfully renovated by the present owners*
present-day: *Even by present-day standards these are large aircraft.*
today's: *In today's America, health care is big business.*
up-to-the-minute: *up-to-the-minute information on sales and stocks*
<<OPPOSITE *past*

current affairs [əˈfɛəz] PLURAL NOUN
Current affairs are political and social events discussed in newspapers and on television and radio.

curriculum [kəˈrɪkjʊləm] **curriculums** or **curricula** NOUN
the different courses taught at a school or university

curriculum vitae [ˈviːtaɪ] **curricula vitae** NOUN
Someone's curriculum vitae is a written account of their personal details, education, and work experience which they send when they apply for a job.

curried [ˈkʌriːd] ADJECTIVE
Curried food has been flavoured with hot spices. *e.g. curried lamb*

curry [ˈkʌrɪ] **curries, currying, curried** NOUN
1 Curry is an Indian dish made with hot spices.

> PHRASE

2 To **curry favour** with someone means to try to please them by flattering them or doing things to help them.
[WORD HISTORY: sense 1 is from Tamil KARI meaning 'sauce'; sense 2 is from Old French CORREER meaning 'to make ready']

curse [kɜːs] **curses, cursing, cursed** VERB
1 To curse is to swear because you are angry.
2 If you curse someone or something, you say angry things about them using rude words.

> NOUN

3 what you say when you curse

4 something supernatural that is supposed to cause unpleasant things to happen to someone

5 a thing or person that causes a lot of distress *e.g. the curse of recession*
cursed ADJECTIVE

cursor [ˈkɜːsə] **cursors** NOUN
an arrow or box on a computer monitor which indicates where the next letter or symbol is

cursory [ˈkɜːsərɪ] ADJECTIVE
When you give something a cursory glance or examination, you look at it briefly without paying attention to detail.

curt [kɜːt] **curter, curtest** ADJECTIVE
If someone is curt, they speak in a brief and rather rude way.
curtly ADVERB

curtail [kɜːˈteɪl] **curtails, curtailing, curtailed** VERB; FORMAL
To curtail something is to reduce or restrict it. *e.g. Injury curtailed his career.*

curtain [ˈkɜːtən] **curtains** NOUN
1 a hanging piece of material which can be pulled across a window for privacy or to keep out the light
2 (DRAMA) a large piece of material which hangs in front of the stage in a theatre until a performance begins
[WORD HISTORY: from Latin CORTINA meaning 'enclosed space']

curtsy [ˈkɜːtsɪ] **curtsies, curtsying, curtsied**; also spelt **curtsey** VERB
1 When a woman curtsies, she lowers her body briefly, bending her knees, to show respect.

> NOUN

2 the movement a woman makes when she curtsies *e.g. She gave a mock curtsy.*

curve [kɜːv] **curves, curving, curved** NOUN
1 a smooth, gradually bending line

THESAURUS

arc: *The ball rose in an arc.*
bend: *a bend in the river*
trajectory: *the trajectory of an artillery shell*
turn: *every turn in the road*

> VERB

2 When something curves, it moves in a curve or has the shape of a curve. *e.g. The track curved away below him... His mouth curved slightly.*
curved ADJECTIVE

THESAURUS

arc: *A rainbow arced over the town.*
arch: *a domed ceiling arching overhead*
bend: *The path bent to the right.*
swerve: *His car swerved off the road.*

cushion [ˈkʊʃən] **cushions, cushioning, cushioned** NOUN
1 a soft object put on a seat to make it more comfortable

> VERB

2 To cushion something is to reduce its effect. *e.g. We might have helped to cushion the shock for her.*

custard ['kʌstəd] NOUN
Custard is a sweet yellow sauce made from milk and eggs or milk and a powder.

custodian [kʌ'stəʊdɪən] **custodians** NOUN
the person in charge of a collection in an art gallery or a museum

custody ['kʌstədɪ] NOUN
1 To have custody of a child means to have the legal right to keep it and look after it. *e.g. She won custody of her younger son.*

> PHRASE

2 Someone who is **in custody** is being kept in prison until they can be tried in a court.
custodial ADJECTIVE

custom ['kʌstəm] **customs** NOUN
1 a traditional activity *e.g. an ancient Chinese custom*

● THESAURUS
convention: *the conventions of Western art*
practice: *an old Jewish practice*
ritual: *an ancient Shintoist ritual*
tradition: *different cultural traditions*

2 something usually done at a particular time or in particular circumstances by a person or by the people in a society *e.g. It was also my custom to do Christmas shows.*

● THESAURUS
habit: *his habit of making tactless remarks*
practice: *her usual practice of attending church*
routine: *his daily routine*
wont: *Paul woke early, as was his wont.*

3 Customs is the place at a border, airport, or harbour where you have to declare any goods you are bringing into a country.

4 FORMAL If a shop or business has your custom, you buy things or go there regularly. *e.g. Banks are desperate to get your custom.*

customary ['kʌstəmərɪ] ADJECTIVE
usual *e.g. his customary modesty... her customary greeting*
customarily ADVERB

custom-built or **custom-made**
['kʌstəm,bɪlt] *or* ['kʌstəm,meɪd] ADJECTIVE
Something that is custom-built or custom-made is made to someone's special requirements.

customer ['kʌstəmə] **customers** NOUN
1 A shop's or firm's customers are the people who buy its goods.

● THESAURUS
buyer: *show homes to tempt potential buyers*

client: *a solicitor and his client*
consumer: *the increasing demands of consumers*
patron: *the restaurant's patrons*
purchaser: *a prospective purchaser*
shopper: *late-night shoppers on their way home*

2 INFORMAL You can use 'customer' to refer to someone when describing what they are like to deal with. *e.g. a tough customer*

cut see page 209 for Word Web

cute [kjuːt] **cuter, cutest** ADJECTIVE
pretty or attractive

● THESAURUS
appealing: *an appealing kitten*
attractive: *I thought he was very attractive.*
charming: *a charming little cottage*
dear: *Look at their dear little faces!*
good-looking: *Cassandra noticed him because he was so good-looking.*
gorgeous: *All the girls think Ryan's gorgeous.*
pretty: *She's a very pretty girl.*
<<OPPOSITE *ugly*

cuticle ['kjuːtɪkᵊl] **cuticles** NOUN
Cuticles are the pieces of skin that cover the base of your fingernails and toenails.

cutlass ['kʌtləs] **cutlasses** NOUN
a curved sword that was used by sailors

cutlery ['kʌtlərɪ] NOUN
Cutlery is knives, forks, and spoons.
[WORD HISTORY: from Latin CULTER meaning 'knife']

cutlet ['kʌtlɪt] **cutlets** NOUN
a small piece of meat which you fry or grill

cutting ['kʌtɪŋ] **cuttings** NOUN
1 something cut from a newspaper or magazine

2 a part cut from a plant and used to grow a new plant

> ADJECTIVE

3 A cutting remark is unkind and likely to hurt someone.

CV an abbreviation for **curriculum vitae**

cyanide ['saɪə,naɪd] NOUN
Cyanide is an extremely poisonous chemical.

cyber- PREFIX
Words that begin with 'cyber-' have something to do with computers in their meaning. For example a *cybercafé* is a place where computers are provided for customers to use.
[WORD HISTORY: from Greek KYBERNĒTĒS meaning 'a steerman']

cyberpet ['saɪbə,pɛt] **cyberpets** NOUN
an electronic toy that imitates the activities of a pet, and needs to be fed and entertained

cyberspace ['saɪbə,speɪs] NOUN
all of the data stored in a large computer, seen as

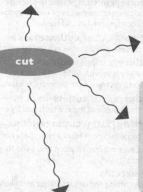

1 VERB
to mark with something sharp eg: *The thieves cut a hole in the fence.*

● THESAURUS
carve: *He carves these figures from pine.*
chop: *You will need to chop the onions.*
clip: *I saw an old man out clipping his hedge.*
divide: *Divide the pastry into four.*
dock: *It is cruel to dock the tail of any animal.*
gash: *He gashed his leg on the barbed wire.*
hack: *Matthew hacked through the straps.*
mow: *He mowed the lawn.*
nick: *He nicked his chin while shaving.*
score: *Lightly score the surface of the steak.*
sever: *He severed the tendon of his thumb.*
slash: *She threatened to slash her wrists.*
slice: *I sliced the beef into thin strips.*
slit: *He began to slit open each envelope.*
split: *Split the planks down the middle.*
trim: *My is hair trimmmed fortnightly.*

2 VERB
to reduce something eg: *The department's first priority is to cut costs.*

● THESAURUS
cut back: *The Government has decided to cut back on defence spending.*
decrease: *calls to decrease income tax*
lower: *The Central Bank has lowered interest rates.*
reduce: *Gradually reduce the dosage.*
slash: *Holiday prices have been slashed.*
<< OPPOSITE *increase*

3 NOUN
a mark or injury made by cutting eg: *a cut on his left eyebrow*

● THESAURUS
gash: *There was a deep gash across his forehead.*
incision: *a tiny incision in the skin*
slash: *jeans with slashes in the knees*
slit: *Make a slit along the stem.*

4 NOUN
a reduction in something eg: *another cut in interest rates*

● THESAURUS
cutback: *cutbacks in funding*
decrease: *a decrease in foreign investment*
lowering: *the lowering of taxes*
reduction: *reductions in staff*
saving: *household savings on energy use*
<< OPPOSITE *increase*

a three-dimensional model

cycle ['saɪkᵊl] **cycles, cycling, cycled** VERB

1 When you cycle, you ride a bicycle.

> NOUN

2 a bicycle or a motorcycle

3 a series of events which is repeated again and again in the same order *e.g. the cycle of births and deaths*

4 (SCIENCE) a single complete series of movements or events in an electrical, electronic, mechanical, or organic process

5 a series of songs or poems intended to be performed or read together

[WORD HISTORY: from Greek KUKLOS meaning 'ring' or 'wheel']

cyclical or **cyclic** ['saɪklɪkᵊl] or ['sɪklɪkᵊl] or ['saɪklɪk] or ['sɪklɪk] ADJECTIVE

happening over and over again in cycles *e.g. a clear cyclical pattern*

cyclist ['saɪklɪst] **cyclists** NOUN

someone who rides a bicycle

cyclone ['saɪkləʊn] **cyclones** NOUN

a violent tropical storm

cygnet ['sɪgnɪt] **cygnets** NOUN

a young swan

[WORD HISTORY: from Latin CYGNUS meaning 'swan']

cylinder ['sɪlɪndə] **cylinders** NOUN

1 a regular three-dimensional shape with two equally-sized flat circular ends joined by a curved surface

2 the part in a motor engine in which the piston moves backwards and forwards

cylindrical ADJECTIVE

cymbal ['sɪmbᵊl] **cymbals** NOUN

a circular brass plate used as a percussion instrument. Cymbals are clashed together or hit with a stick.

cynic ['sɪnɪk] **cynics** NOUN

a cynical person

[WORD HISTORY: from Greek KUNIKOS meaning 'dog-like']

cynical ['sɪnɪkᵊl] ADJECTIVE

believing that people always behave selfishly or dishonestly

cynically ADVERB, **cynicism** NOUN

⦿ THESAURUS

distrustful: *distrustful of all politicians*

sceptical: *a sceptical response*

cypher ['saɪfə] another spelling of **cipher**

cypress ['saɪprəs] **cypresses** NOUN

a type of evergreen tree with small dark green leaves and round cones

cyst [sɪst] **cysts** NOUN

a growth containing liquid that can form under your skin or inside your body

czar [zɑː] another spelling of **tsar**

czarina [zɑːˈriːnə] another spelling of **tsarina**

Czech [tʃɛk] **Czechs** ADJECTIVE

1 belonging or relating to the Czech Republic

> NOUN

2 someone who comes from the Czech Republic

3 Czech is the language spoken in the Czech Republic.

Czechoslovak [ˌtʃɛkəʊˈsləʊvæk] **Czechoslovaks** ADJECTIVE

1 belonging to or relating to the country that used to be Czechoslovakia

> NOUN

2 someone who came from the country that used to be Czechoslovakia

Dd

dab [dæb] **dabs, dabbing, dabbed** VERB
1 If you dab something, you touch it with quick light strokes. *e.g. He dabbed some disinfectant on to the gash.*
> NOUN
2 a small amount of something that is put on a surface *e.g. a dab of perfume*

dabble ['dæbəl] **dabbles, dabbling, dabbled** VERB
If you dabble in something, you work or play at it without being seriously involved in it. *e.g. All his life he dabbled in poetry.*

dachshund ['dæks,hʊnd] **dachshunds** NOUN
a small dog with a long body and very short legs
[WORD HISTORY: a German word meaning 'badger-dog']

dad or **daddy** [dæd] or ['dædɪ] **dads** or **daddies** NOUN; INFORMAL
Your dad or your daddy is your father.

daddy-long-legs [,dædɪ'lɒŋ,legz] NOUN
a harmless flying insect with very long legs

daffodil ['dæfədɪl] **daffodils** NOUN
a plant with a yellow trumpet-shaped flower

daft [dɑːft] **dafter, daftest** ADJECTIVE
stupid and not sensible
[WORD HISTORY: from Old English GEDÆFTE meaning 'gentle']

🔵 THESAURUS
crazy: *He has this crazy idea about his neighbours.*
foolish: *It would be foolish to raise his hopes unnecessarily.*
ludicrous: *It was ludicrous to suggest that the visit could be kept a secret.*
preposterous: *their preposterous claim that they had discovered a plot*
ridiculous: *It was an absolutely ridiculous decision.*
silly: *That's a silly question.*
stupid: *I made a stupid mistake.*
<<OPPOSITE *sensible*

dagga ['daxə] or ['dɑːgə] NOUN; INFORMAL
In South African English, dagga is cannabis.

dagger ['dægə] **daggers** NOUN
a weapon like a short knife

dahlia ['deɪljə] **dahlias** NOUN
a type of brightly coloured garden flower

daily ['deɪlɪ] ADJECTIVE
1 occurring every day *e.g. our daily visit to the gym*
2 of or relating to a single day or to one day at a time *e.g. the average daily wage*

dainty ['deɪntɪ] **daintier, daintiest** ADJECTIVE
very delicate and pretty
daintily ADVERB

dairy ['dɛərɪ] **dairies** NOUN
1 a shop or company that supplies milk and milk products
2 In New Zealand, a small shop selling groceries, often outside of usual opening hours.
> ADJECTIVE
3 Dairy products are foods made from milk, such as butter, cheese, cream, and yogurt.
4 A dairy farm is one which keeps cattle to produce milk.

▌ Do not confuse the order of the vowels in *dairy* and *diary*.

dais ['deɪɪs] NOUN
a raised platform, normally at one end of a hall and used by a speaker

daisy ['deɪzɪ] **daisies** NOUN
a small wild flower with a yellow centre and small white petals
[WORD HISTORY: from Old English DÆGES EAGE meaning 'day's eye', because the daisy opens in the daytime and closes at night]

dale [deɪl] **dales** NOUN
a valley

dalmatian [dæl'meɪʃən] **dalmatians** NOUN
a large dog with short smooth white hair and black or brown spots

dam [dæm] **dams** NOUN
a barrier built across a river to hold back water

damage ['dæmɪdʒ] **damages, damaging, damaged** VERB
1 To damage something means to harm or spoil it.

THESAURUS
harm: *a warning that the product may harm the environment*
hurt: *He had hurt his back in an accident.*
injure: *Several policemen were injured in the clashes.*

> NOUN
2 Damage to something is injury or harm done to it.

THESAURUS
harm: *All dogs are capable of doing harm to human beings.*
injury: *He escaped without injury.*

3 Damages is the money awarded by a court to compensate someone for loss or harm.
damaging ADJECTIVE

dame [deɪm] **dames** NOUN
the title given to a woman who has been awarded the OBE or one of the other British orders of chivalry

damn [dæm] **damns, damning, damned**
VERB
1 To damn something or someone means to curse or condemn them.

> INTERJECTION
2 'Damn' is a swearword
damned ADJECTIVE

damnation [dæm'neɪʃən] NOUN
Damnation is eternal punishment in Hell after death.

damp [dæmp] **damper, dampest** ADJECTIVE
1 slightly wet

THESAURUS
clammy: *clammy hands*
dank: *The kitchen was dank and cheerless.*
humid: *Visitors can expect hot and humid conditions.*
moist: *The soil is reasonably moist after the September rain.*
sodden: *We stripped off our sodden clothes.*
soggy: *soggy cheese sandwiches*
wet: *My hair was still wet.*

> NOUN
2 Damp is slight wetness, especially in the air or in the walls of a building.
dampness NOUN
[WORD HISTORY: from Old German DAMP meaning 'steam']

THESAURUS
dampness: *I could see big circles of dampness under each arm.*
humidity: *The heat and humidity were intolerable.*
moisture: *Compost helps the soil retain moisture.*

dampen ['dæmpən] **dampens, dampening, dampened** VERB
1 If you dampen something, you make it slightly wet.

2 To dampen something also means to reduce its liveliness or strength. *e.g. The whole episode has rather dampened my enthusiasm.*

damper ['dæmpə] AN INFORMAL PHRASE
To **put a damper on** something means to stop it being enjoyable.

damson ['dæmzən] **damsons** NOUN
a small blue-black plum; also the tree that the fruit grows on
[WORD HISTORY: from Latin PRUNUM DAMASCENUM meaning 'Damascus plum']

dance [dɑːns] **dances, dancing, danced**
VERB
1 To dance means to move your feet and body rhythmically in time to music.

> NOUN
2 a series of rhythmic movements or steps in time to music

3 a social event where people dance with each other
dancer NOUN, **dancing** NOUN

dandelion ['dændɪ,laɪən] **dandelions** NOUN
a wild plant with yellow flowers which form a ball of fluffy seeds

dandruff ['dændrəf] NOUN
Dandruff is small, loose scales of dead skin in someone's hair.

D and T NOUN
an abbreviation for 'Design and Technology'

dandy ['dændɪ] **dandies** NOUN; OLD-FASHIONED
a man who always dresses in very smart clothes

Dane [deɪn] **Danes** NOUN
someone who comes from Denmark

danger ['deɪndʒə] **dangers** NOUN
1 Danger is the possibility that someone may be harmed or killed.

THESAURUS
hazard: *a health hazard*
jeopardy: *A series of setbacks have put the whole project in jeopardy.*
menace: *In my view you are a menace to the public.*
peril: *the perils of the sea*
risk: *There is a small risk of brain damage.*
threat: *Some couples see single women as a threat to their relationship.*
<<OPPOSITE safety

2 something or someone that can hurt or harm you

dangerous ['deɪndʒərəs] ADJECTIVE
able to or likely to cause hurt or harm
dangerously ADVERB

THESAURUS
hazardous: *They have no way to dispose of the*

d

hazardous waste they produce.
perilous: *a perilous journey across the war-zone*
risky: *Investing is risky.*
treacherous: *Blizzards had made the roads treacherous.*
<<OPPOSITE *safe*

dangle ['dæŋgəl] **dangles, dangling, dangled** VERB
When something dangles or when you dangle it, it swings or hangs loosely.

Danish ['deɪnɪʃ] ADJECTIVE
1 belonging or relating to Denmark
> NOUN
2 Danish is the main language spoken in Denmark.

dank [dæŋk] **danker, dankest** ADJECTIVE
A dank place is unpleasantly damp and chilly.

dapper ['dæpə] ADJECTIVE
slim and neatly dressed
[WORD HISTORY: from Old Dutch DAPPER meaning 'active' or 'nimble']

dappled ['dæpəld] ADJECTIVE
marked with patches of a different or darker shade

dare [dɛə] **dares, daring, dared** VERB
1 To dare someone means to challenge them to do something in order to prove their courage.
THESAURUS
challenge: *He left a note at the scene of the crime, challenging detectives to catch him.*
defy: *I defy you to watch it on your own.*
throw down the gauntlet: *Jaguar has thrown down the gauntlet to competitors by giving the best guarantee on the market.*
2 To dare to do something means to have the courage to do it.
THESAURUS
risk: *The skipper was not willing to risk taking his ship through the straits.*
venture: *the few Europeans who had ventured beyond the Himalayas*
> NOUN
3 a challenge to do something dangerous

When *dare* is used in a question or with a negative, it does not add an *s*: *dare she come?*; *he dare not come.*

daredevil ['dɛə,dɛvəl] **daredevils** NOUN
a person who enjoys doing dangerous things

daring ['dɛərɪŋ] ADJECTIVE
1 bold and willing to take risks
THESAURUS
adventurous: *an adventurous skier*
audacious: *an audacious plan to win the presidency*

bold: *bold economic reforms*
brave: *He was not brave enough to report the loss of the documents.*
fearless: *They were young and strong and fearless.*
<<OPPOSITE *cautious*
> NOUN
2 the courage required to do things which are dangerous
THESAURUS
audacity: *He had the audacity to make a 200-1 bet on himself to win.*
boldness: *the boldness of his economic programme*
bravery: *He deserves the highest praise for his bravery.*
courage: *He impressed everyone with his personal courage.*
guts: informal *I haven't got the guts to tell him.*
nerve: informal *He didn't have the nerve to meet me.*
<<OPPOSITE *caution*

dark [dɑːk] **darker, darkest** ADJECTIVE
1 If it is dark, there is not enough light to see properly.
THESAURUS
cloudy: *a cloudy sky*
dim: *the dim outline of a small boat*
dingy: *a dingy bedsit*
murky: *the murky waters of the loch*
overcast: *a cold, windy, overcast afternoon*
shadowy: *a shadowy corner*
<<OPPOSITE *light*
2 Dark colours or surfaces reflect little light and so look deep-coloured or dull.
THESAURUS
black: *a black leather coat*
swarthy: *a broad swarthy face*
3 'Dark' is also used to describe thoughts or ideas which are sinister or unpleasant
> NOUN
4 The dark is the lack of light in a place.
darkly ADVERB, **darkness** NOUN
THESAURUS
darkness: *The room was plunged into darkness.*
dimness: *I squinted to adjust my eyes to the dimness.*
dusk: *She disappeared into the dusk.*
gloom: *the gloom of a foggy November morning*
<<OPPOSITE *light*

darken ['dɑːkən] **darkens, darkening, darkened** VERB
If something darkens, or if you darken it, it becomes darker than it was.

darkroom ['dɑːk,ruːm] **darkrooms** NOUN
a room from which daylight is shut out so that photographic film can be developed

darling [ˈdɑːlɪŋ] **darlings** NOUN
  1 Someone who is lovable or a favourite may be called a darling.
  > ADJECTIVE
  2 much admired or loved *e.g. his darling daughter*

darn [dɑːn] **darns, darning, darned** VERB
  1 To darn a hole in a garment means to mend it with crossing stitches.
  > NOUN
  2 a part of a garment that has been darned

dart [dɑːt] **darts, darting, darted** NOUN
  1 a small pointed arrow
  2 Darts is a game in which the players throw darts at a round board divided into numbered sections.
  > VERB
  3 To dart about means to move quickly and suddenly from one place to another.

dash [dæʃ] **dashes, dashing, dashed** VERB
  1 To dash somewhere means to rush there.

● THESAURUS
  bolt: *I bolted for the exit.*
  fly: *She flew downstairs.*
  race: *The hares raced away out of sight.*
  run: *The gunmen ran off into the woods.*
  rush: *Someone rushed out of the building.*
  sprint: *Sergeant Greene sprinted to the car.*
  tear: *He tore off down the road.*

  2 If something is dashed against something else, it strikes it or is thrown violently against it.

● THESAURUS
  break: *Danny listened to the waves breaking against the shore.*
  crash: *The door swung inwards and crashed against a cupboard behind it.*
  hurl: *He hurled the vase to the ground in rage.*
  slam: *They slammed me on to the ground.*
  smash: *smashing the bottle against a wall*

  3 If hopes or ambitions are dashed, they are ruined or frustrated.

● THESAURUS
  crush: *My dreams of becoming an actor have been crushed.*
  destroy: *Even the most gifted can have their confidence destroyed by the wrong teacher.*
  disappoint: *His hopes have been disappointed many times before.*
  foil: *Our idea of building a water garden was foiled by the planning authorities.*
  frustrate: *The government has deliberately frustrated his efforts.*
  shatter: *A failure would shatter all our hopes.*
  thwart: *Her ambition to be an artist was thwarted by failing eyesight.*

  > NOUN
  4 a sudden movement or rush

● THESAURUS
  bolt: *He made a bolt for the door.*
  race: *a race for the finishing line*
  run: *One of the gang made a run for it.*
  rush: *the mad rush not to be late for school*
  sprint: *a last-minute sprint to catch the bus*
  stampede: *There was a stampede for the exit.*

  5 a small quantity of something

● THESAURUS
  drop: *I'll have a drop of that milk in my tea.*
  pinch: *a pinch of salt*
  splash: *add a splash of lemon juice*
  sprinkling: *a light sprinkling of sugar*

  6 the punctuation mark (—) which shows a change of subject, or which may be used instead of brackets

dashboard [ˈdæʃˌbɔːd] **dashboards** NOUN
  the instrument panel in a motor vehicle

dashing [ˈdæʃɪŋ] ADJECTIVE
  A dashing man is stylish and confident. *e.g. He was a dashing figure in his younger days.*

dasyure [ˈdæsɪˌjʊə] **dasyures** NOUN
  a small marsupial that lives in Australia and eats meat

data [ˈdeɪtə] NOUN
  1 information, usually in the form of facts or statistics
  2 (ICT) any information put into a computer and which the computer works on or processes
  [WORD HISTORY: from Latin DATA meaning 'things given']

  ▌ Data is really a plural word, but it is usually used as a singular.

database [ˈdeɪtəˌbeɪs] **databases** NOUN
  (ICT) a collection of information stored in a computer

date [deɪt] **dates, dating, dated** NOUN
  1 a particular day or year that can be named
  2 If you have a date, you have an appointment to meet someone; also used to refer to the person you are meeting.
  3 a small dark-brown sticky fruit with a stone inside, which grows on palm trees
  > VERB
  4 If you are dating someone, you have a romantic relationship with them.
  5 If you date something, you find out the time when it began or was made.
  6 If something dates from a particular time, that is when it happened or was made.
  > PHRASE
  7 If something is **out of date**, it is old-fashioned or no longer valid.

dated ['deɪtɪd] ADJECTIVE
no longer fashionable

datum ['deɪtəm] the singular form of **data**

daub [dɔːb] **daubs, daubing, daubed** VERB
If you daub something such as mud or paint on a surface, you smear it there.

daughter ['dɔːtə] **daughters** NOUN
Someone's daughter is their female child.

daughter-in-law [dɔːtəɪn,lɔː] **daughters-in-law** NOUN
Someone's daughter-in-law is the wife of their son.

daunt [dɔːnt] **daunts, daunting, daunted**
VERB
If something daunts you, you feel worried about whether you can succeed in doing it. *e.g. He was not the type of man to be daunted by adversity.*
daunting ADJECTIVE

dawn [dɔːn] **dawns, dawning, dawned**
NOUN
1 the time in the morning when light first appears in the sky
2 the beginning of something *e.g. the dawn of the radio age*
> VERB
3 If day is dawning, morning light is beginning to appear.
4 If an idea or fact dawns on you, you realize it.

day [deɪ] **days** NOUN
1 one of the seven 24-hour periods of time in a week, measured from one midnight to the next
2 Day is the period of light between sunrise and sunset.
3 You can refer to a particular day or days meaning a particular period in history. *e.g. in Gladstone's day*

daybreak ['deɪ,breɪk] NOUN
Daybreak is the time in the morning when light first appears in the sky.

daydream ['deɪ,driːm] **daydreams, daydreaming, daydreamed** NOUN
1 a series of pleasant thoughts about things that you would like to happen

● THESAURUS
dream: *My dream is to have a house in the country.*
fantasy: *fantasies of romance and true love*
> VERB
2 When you daydream, you drift off into a daydream.

● THESAURUS
dream: *She used to dream of becoming an actress.*
fantasize: *I fantasized about writing music.*

daylight ['deɪ,laɪt] NOUN

1 Daylight is the period during the day when it is light.
2 Daylight is also the light from the sun.

day-to-day ['deɪtə'deɪ] ADJECTIVE
happening every day as part of ordinary routine life

day trip day trips NOUN
a journey for pleasure to a place and back again on the same day

daze [deɪz] PHRASE
If you are **in a daze**, you are confused and bewildered.

dazed [deɪzd] ADJECTIVE
If you are dazed, you are stunned and unable to think clearly.

● THESAURUS
bewildered: *Some shoppers looked bewildered by the sheer variety.*
confused: *Things were happening too quickly and Brian was confused.*
dizzy: *Her head hurt and she felt dizzy.*
light-headed: *If you miss breakfast, you may feel light-headed.*
numbed: *I'm so numbed with shock that I can hardly think.*
stunned: *a stunned silence*

dazzle ['dæzəl] **dazzles, dazzling, dazzled**
VERB
1 If someone or something dazzles you, you are very impressed by their brilliance.
2 If a bright light dazzles you, it blinds you for a moment.
dazzling ADJECTIVE

de- PREFIX
When de- is added to a noun or verb, it changes the meaning to its opposite. *e.g. de-ice*

deacon ['diːkən] **deacons** NOUN
1 In the Church of England or Roman Catholic Church, a deacon is a member of the clergy below the rank of priest.
2 In some other churches, a deacon is a church official appointed to help the minister.
deaconess NOUN

dead [dɛd] ADJECTIVE
1 no longer living or supporting life

● THESAURUS
deceased: *his recently deceased mother*
departed: *my dear departed father*
extinct: *the bones of extinct animals*
late: *my late husband*
<<OPPOSITE *alive*

2 no longer used or no longer functioning *e.g. a dead language*

● THESAURUS
defunct: *the now defunct Social Democratic Party*

not working: *The radio is not working.*

3 If part of your body goes dead, it loses sensation and feels numb.

> NOUN

4 the middle part of night or winter, when it is most quiet and at its darkest or coldest

dead end dead ends NOUN
a street that is closed off at one end

deadline ['dɛd,laɪn] **deadlines** NOUN
a time or date before which something must be completed

deadlock ['dɛd,lɒk] **deadlocks** NOUN
a situation in which neither side in a dispute is willing to give in

deadly ['dɛdlɪ] **deadlier, deadliest**
ADJECTIVE
1 likely or able to cause death

THESAURUS
destructive: *the destructive power of nuclear weapons*
fatal: *a fatal heart attack*
lethal: *a lethal dose of sleeping pills*
mortal: *Our lives were in mortal danger.*

> ADVERB OR ADJECTIVE

2 'Deadly' is used to emphasize how serious or unpleasant a situation is *e.g. He is deadly serious about his comeback.*

deadpan ['dɛd,pæn] ADJECTIVE OR ADVERB
showing no emotion or expression

deaf [dɛf] **deafer, deafest** ADJECTIVE
1 partially or totally unable to hear

2 refusing to listen or pay attention to something *e.g. He was deaf to all pleas for financial help.*
deafness NOUN

deafening ['dɛfᵊnɪŋ] ADJECTIVE
If a noise is deafening, it is so loud that you cannot hear anything else.

deal [diːl] **deals, dealing, dealt** NOUN
1 an agreement or arrangement, especially in business

> VERB

2 If you deal with something, you do what is necessary to sort it out. *e.g. He must learn to deal with stress.*

THESAURUS
attend to: *We have business to attend to first.*
cope with: *She has had to cope with losing all her money.*
handle: *I have learned how to handle pressure.*
manage: *As time passed I learned to manage my grief.*
see to: *Sarah saw to the packing while Jim fetched the car.*

take care of: *Malcolm took care of all the arrangements.*

3 If you deal in a particular type of goods, you buy and sell those goods.

4 If you deal someone or something a blow, you hurt or harm them. *e.g. Competition from abroad dealt a heavy blow to the industry.*

dealer ['diːlə] **dealers** NOUN
a person or firm whose business involves buying or selling things

dealings ['diːlɪŋz] PLURAL NOUN
Your dealings with people are the relations you have with them or the business you do with them.

dean [diːn] **deans** NOUN
1 In a university or college, a dean is a person responsible for administration or for the welfare of students.

2 In the Church of England, a dean is a clergyman who is responsible for administration.
[WORD HISTORY: from Latin DECANUS meaning 'someone in charge of ten people']

dear [dɪə] **dears; dearer, dearest** NOUN
1 'Dear' is used as a sign of affection *e.g. What's the matter, dear?.*

THESAURUS
angel: *Be an angel and fetch my bag.*
beloved: old-fashioned *He took his beloved into his arms.*
darling: *Thank you, darling.*
treasure: informal *Charlie? Oh, he's a treasure.*

> ADJECTIVE

2 much loved *e.g. my dear son*

THESAURUS
beloved: *He lost his beloved wife last year.*
cherished: *his most cherished possession*
darling: *his darling daughter*
esteemed: *my esteemed colleagues*
precious: *Her family's support is very precious to her.*
prized: *one of the gallery's most prized possessions*
treasured: *one of my most treasured memories*

3 Something that is dear is very expensive.

THESAURUS
costly: *Having curtains professionally made can be costly.*
expensive: *Wine's so expensive in this country.*
pricey: informal *Medical insurance is very pricey.*

4 You use 'dear' at the beginning of a letter before the name of the person you are writing to.
dearly ADVERB

dearth [dɜːθ] NOUN
a shortage of something

death [dɛθ] **deaths** NOUN
Death is the end of the life of a person or animal.

d

debacle [deɪˈbɑːkᵊl] **debacles** NOUN; FORMAL
a sudden disastrous failure

debase [dɪˈbeɪs] **debases, debasing,
debased** VERB
To debase something means to reduce its value
or quality.

debatable [dɪˈbeɪtəbᵊl] ADJECTIVE
not absolutely certain *e.g. The justness of these
wars is debatable.*

debate [dɪˈbeɪt] **debates, debating,
debated** NOUN
1 Debate is argument or discussion. *e.g. There is
much debate as to what causes depression.*
2 a formal discussion in which opposing views
are expressed
> VERB
3 When people debate something, they discuss it
in a fairly formal manner.
4 If you are debating whether or not to do
something, you are considering it. *e.g. He was
debating whether or not he should tell her.*

debilitating [dɪˈbɪlɪteɪtɪŋ] ADJECTIVE; FORMAL
If something is debilitating, it makes you very
weak. *e.g. a debilitating illness*

debit [ˈdɛbɪt] **debits, debiting, debited**
VERB
1 to take money from a person's bank account
> NOUN
2 a record of the money that has been taken out
of a person's bank account

debrief [diːˈbriːf] **debriefs, debriefing,
debriefed** VERB
When someone is debriefed, they are asked to
give a report on a task they have just completed.
debriefing NOUN

debris [ˈdeɪbriː] NOUN
Debris is fragments or rubble left after
something has been destroyed.
[WORD HISTORY: from Old French DÉBRISIER
meaning 'to shatter']

debt [dɛt] **debts** NOUN
1 a sum of money that is owed to one person by
another
2 Debt is the state of owing money.

debtor [ˈdɛtə] **debtors** NOUN
a person who owes money

debut [ˈdeɪbjuː] **debuts** NOUN
a performer's first public appearance

debutante [ˈdɛbjʊˌtɑːnt] **debutantes**
NOUN; OLD-FASHIONED, INFORMAL
a girl from the upper classes who has started
going to social events

dec- or **deca-** PREFIX
Words beginning with 'dec-' or 'deca-' have 'ten'

in their meaning. *e.g. decathlon*
[WORD HISTORY: from Greek DEKA meaning 'ten']

decade [ˈdɛkeɪd] **decades** NOUN
a period of ten years

decadence [ˈdɛkədəns] NOUN
Decadence is a decline in standards of morality
and behaviour.
decadent ADJECTIVE

decaffeinated [dɪˈkæfɪˌneɪtɪd] ADJECTIVE
Decaffeinated coffee or tea has had most of the
caffeine removed.

decanter [dɪˈkæntə] **decanters** NOUN
a glass bottle with a stopper, from which wine
and other drinks are served

decapitate [dɪˈkæpɪˌteɪt] **decapitates,
decapitating, decapitated** VERB
To decapitate someone means to cut off their
head.

decathlon [dɪˈkæθlɒn] **decathlons** NOUN
a sports contest in which athletes compete in ten
different events
[WORD HISTORY: from Greek DEKA meaning 'ten'
and ATHLON meaning 'contest']

decay [dɪˈkeɪ] **decays, decaying, decayed**
VERB
1 When things decay, they rot or go bad.
> NOUN
2 Decay is the process of decaying.

deceased [dɪˈsiːst] FORMAL **> ADJECTIVE**
1 A deceased person is someone who has
recently died.
> NOUN
2 The deceased is someone who has recently
died.

deceit [dɪˈsiːt] NOUN
Deceit is behaviour that is intended to mislead
people into believing something that is not true.
deceitful ADJECTIVE

deceive [dɪˈsiːv] **deceives, deceiving,
deceived** VERB
If you deceive someone, you make them believe
something that is not true.
 THESAURUS
con: informal *The British motorist has been conned
by the government.*
double-cross: *They were frightened of being
double-crossed.*
dupe: *a plot to dupe stamp collectors into buying
fake rarities*
fool: *They tried to fool you into coming after us.*
mislead: *He was furious with his doctors for having
misled him.*
take in: *I wasn't taken in for one moment.*
trick: *His family tricked him into going to Pakistan.*

decelerate [diːˈsɛləˌreɪt] **decelerates, decelerating, decelerated** VERB
If something decelerates, it slows down.
deceleration NOUN

December [dɪˈsɛmbə] NOUN
December is the twelfth and last month of the year. It has 31 days.
[WORD HISTORY: from Latin DECEMBER meaning 'the tenth month']

decency [ˈdiːsᵊnsɪ] NOUN
1 Decency is behaviour that is respectable and follows accepted moral standards.
2 Decency is also behaviour which shows kindness and respect towards people. *e.g. No one had the decency to tell me to my face.*

decent [ˈdiːsᵊnt] ADJECTIVE
1 of an acceptable standard or quality *e.g. He gets a decent pension.*

● THESAURUS
adequate: *an adequate diet*
passable: *She speaks passable French.*
reasonable: *He couldn't make a reasonable living from his writing.*
respectable: *investments that offer respectable rates of return*
satisfactory: *I never got a satisfactory answer.*
tolerable: *to make life more tolerable*

2 Decent people are honest and respectable. *e.g. a decent man*
decently ADVERB

● THESAURUS
proper: *It is right and proper to do this.*
respectable: *He came from a perfectly respectable middle-class family.*
<<OPPOSITE *improper*

decentralize [diːˈsɛntrəˌlaɪz] **decentralizes, decentralizing, decentralized;** also spelt **decentralise** VERB
To decentralize an organization means to reorganize it so that power is transferred from one main administrative centre to smaller local units.
decentralization NOUN

deception [dɪˈsɛpʃən] **deceptions** NOUN
1 something that is intended to trick or deceive someone
2 Deception is the act of deceiving someone.

deceptive [dɪˈsɛptɪv] ADJECTIVE
likely to make people believe something that is not true
deceptively ADVERB

● THESAURUS
false: *'Thank you,' she said with false enthusiasm.*
fraudulent: *fraudulent claims about being a nurse*

illusory: *They argue that freedom is illusory.*
misleading: *It would be misleading to say that we were friends.*
unreliable: *His account is quite unreliable.*

decibel [ˈdɛsɪˌbɛl] **decibels** NOUN
a unit of the intensity of sound

decide [dɪˈsaɪd] **decides, deciding, decided** VERB
If you decide to do something, you choose to do it.

● THESAURUS
choose: *The council chose to inform the public about the risks.*
come to a decision: *Have you come to a decision about where you're going tonight?*
determine: formal *He determined to rescue his two countrymen.*
elect: formal *I have elected to stay.*
make up your mind: *He simply can't make his mind up whether he should stay.*
reach a decision: *He demanded to know all the facts before reaching any decision.*
resolve: formal *She resolved to report the matter to the authorities.*

deciduous [dɪˈsɪdjʊəs] ADJECTIVE
Deciduous trees lose their leaves in the autumn every year.

decimal [ˈdɛsɪməl] **decimals** ADJECTIVE
(MATHS)
1 The decimal system expresses numbers using all the digits from 0 to 9.
> NOUN
2 a fraction in which a dot called a decimal point is followed by numbers representing tenths, hundredths, and thousandths. For example, 0.5 represents ($\frac{5}{10}$) (or ($\frac{1}{2}$); 0.05 represents ($\frac{5}{100}$) (or ($\frac{1}{20}$)
[WORD HISTORY: from Latin DECIMA meaning 'a tenth']

decimate [ˈdɛsɪˌmeɪt] **decimates, decimating, decimated** VERB
To decimate a group of people or animals means to kill or destroy a large number of them.

decipher [dɪˈsaɪfə] **deciphers, deciphering, deciphered** VERB
If you decipher a piece of writing or a message, you work out its meaning.

decision [dɪˈsɪʒən] **decisions** NOUN
a choice or judgment that is made about something *e.g. The editor's decision is final.*

● THESAURUS
conclusion: *I've come to the conclusion that she's a great musician.*
finding: *It is the finding of this court that you are guilty.*

judgment: *a landmark judgment by the Court of Appeal*
resolution: *a resolution condemning violence*
ruling: *He tried to have the court ruling overturned.*
verdict: *The judges will deliver their verdict in October.*

decisive [dɪˈsaɪsɪv] ADJECTIVE

1 having great influence on the result of something *e.g. It was the decisive moment of the race.*

2 A decisive person is able to make decisions firmly and quickly.
decisively ADVERB, **decisiveness** NOUN

deck [dɛk] **decks** NOUN

1 a floor or platform built into a ship, or one of the two floors on a bus

2 a pack of cards

deck chair **deck chairs** NOUN

a light folding chair, made from canvas and wood and used outdoors

declaration [ˌdɛkləˈreɪʃən] **declarations** NOUN

a firm, forceful statement, often an official announcement *e.g. a declaration of war*

● THESAURUS
affirmation: *her first public affirmation of her decision*
protestation: *formal his protestations of innocence*
statement: *He made a formal statement to the police.*
testimony: *His testimony was an important element in the case.*

declare [dɪˈklɛə] **declares, declaring, declared** VERB

1 If you declare something, you state it forcefully or officially.

● THESAURUS
affirm: *a speech in which he affirmed a commitment to lower taxes*
announce: *She was planning to announce her engagement.*
assert: *He asserted his innocence.*
certify: *The president certified that the project would receive $650m.*
proclaim: *He still proclaims himself a believer in the Revolution.*
profess: *Why do they profess that they care?*
pronounce: *The authorities took time to pronounce their verdict.*
state: *Please state your name.*

2 If you declare goods or earnings, you state what you have bought or earned, in order to pay tax or duty.

decline [dɪˈklaɪn] **declines, declining, declined** VERB

1 If something declines, it becomes smaller or weaker.

● THESAURUS
decrease: *The number of independent firms decreased from 198 to 96.*
diminish: *The threat of nuclear war has diminished.*
drop: *His blood pressure had dropped.*
fall: *Output will fall by six per cent.*
go down: *Crime has gone down 70 per cent.*
plummet: *The Prime Minister's popularity has plummeted to an all-time low.*
reduce: *The number of students fluent in Latin has been steadily reducing.*
<<OPPOSITE *increase*

2 If you decline something, you politely refuse to accept it or do it.

● THESAURUS
abstain: *I will abstain from voting in the ballot.*
excuse yourself: *I was invited, but I excused myself.*
refuse: *He refused to comment after the trial.*
turn down: *I thanked him for the offer but turned it down.*
<<OPPOSITE *accept*

> NOUN

3 a gradual weakening or decrease *e.g. a decline in the birth rate*

● THESAURUS
decrease: *a decrease in the number of young people out of work*
downturn: *a sharp downturn in the industry*
drop: *a drop in support for the Conservatives*
fall: *a sharp fall in the value of the pound*
recession: *pull the economy out of recession*
shrinkage: *a shrinkage in industrial output*
slump: *a slump in property prices*
<<OPPOSITE *increase*

decode [diːˈkəʊd] **decodes, decoding, decoded** VERB

If you decode a coded message, you convert it into ordinary language.
decoder NOUN

decommision [ˌdiːkəˈmɪʃən] **decommisions, decommisioning, decommisioned** VERB

When something such as a nuclear reactor or large machine is decommissioned, it is taken to pieces or removed from service because it is no longer going to be used.

decompose [ˌdiːkəmˈpəʊz] **decomposes, decomposing, decomposed** VERB

If something decomposes, it decays through chemical or bacterial action.

decor [ˈdeɪkɔː] NOUN

The decor of a room or house is the style in which it is decorated and furnished.

decorate [ˈdɛkəˌreɪt] **decorates, decorating, decorated** VERB

1 If you decorate something, you make it more attractive by adding some ornament or colour to it.

● THESAURUS

adorn: *Several oil paintings adorn the walls.*
deck: *The house was decked with flowers.*
ornament: *a high ceiling, ornamented with plaster fruits and flowers*

2 If you decorate a room or building, you paint or wallpaper it.

● THESAURUS

do up: informal *He spent the summer doing up the barn.*
renovate: *The couple spent thousands renovating the house.*

decoration [ˌdɛkəˈreɪʃən] **decorations**
NOUN

1 Decorations are features added to something to make it more attractive.

2 The decoration in a building or room is the style of the furniture and wallpaper.

decorative [ˈdɛkərətɪv] ADJECTIVE
intended to look attractive

decorator [ˈdɛkəˌreɪtə] **decorators** NOUN
a person whose job is painting and putting up wallpaper in rooms and buildings

decorum [dɪˈkɔːrəm] NOUN; FORMAL
Decorum is polite and correct behaviour.

decoy [ˈdiːkɔɪ] **decoys** NOUN
a person or object that is used to lead someone or something into danger

decrease decreases, decreasing,
decreased VERB [dɪˈkriːs]

1 If something decreases or if you decrease it, it becomes less in quantity or size.

● THESAURUS

cut down: *He cut down his coffee intake.*
decline: *The number of staff has declined.*
diminish: *The threat of nuclear war has diminished.*
drop: *Temperatures can drop to freezing at night.*
dwindle: *his dwindling authority*
lessen: *changes to their diet that would lessen the risk of disease*
lower: *The Central Bank has lowered interest rates.*
reduce: *It reduces the risk of heart disease.*
shrink: *The forests have shrunk to half their size.*
<<OPPOSITE *increase*

> NOUN [ˈdiːkriːs]

2 a lessening in the amount of something; also the amount by which something becomes less
decreasing ADJECTIVE

● THESAURUS

cutback: *cutbacks in defence spending*
decline: *the rate of decline in tobacco consumption*

drop: *a drop in temperature*
lessening: *a lessening of tension*
reduction: *dramatic reductions in staff*
<<OPPOSITE *increase*

decree [dɪˈkriː] **decrees, decreeing,**
decreed VERB

1 If someone decrees something, they state formally that it will happen.

> NOUN

2 an official decision or order, usually by governments or rulers

dedicate [ˈdɛdɪˌkeɪt] **dedicates,**
dedicating, dedicated VERB
If you dedicate yourself to something, you devote your time and energy to it.
dedication NOUN

deduce [dɪˈdjuːs] **deduces, deducing,**
deduced VERB
If you deduce something, you work it out from other facts that you know are true.

deduct [dɪˈdʌkt] **deducts, deducting,**
deducted VERB
To deduct an amount from a total amount means to subtract it from the total.

deduction [dɪˈdʌkʃən] **deductions** NOUN

1 an amount which is taken away from a total

2 a conclusion that you have reached because of other things that you know are true

deed [diːd] **deeds** NOUN

1 something that is done

2 a legal document, especially concerning the ownership of land or buildings

deem [diːm] **deems, deeming, deemed**
VERB; FORMAL
If you deem something to be true, you judge or consider it to be true. *e.g. His ideas were deemed unacceptable.*

deep [diːp] **deeper, deepest** ADJECTIVE

1 situated or extending a long way down from the top surface of something, or a long way inwards
e.g. a deep hole

● THESAURUS

bottomless: *a bottomless pit*
yawning: *a yawning chasm*
<<OPPOSITE *shallow*

2 great or intense *e.g. deep suspicion*

● THESAURUS

extreme: *extreme poverty*
grave: *a grave crisis*
great: *the great gulf between the two teams*
intense: *The pain was intense.*
profound: *discoveries which had a profound effect on medicine*

d

serious: *a serious problem*

3 low in pitch *e.g. a deep voice*

● **THESAURUS**
bass: *a beautiful bass voice*
low: *Her voice was so low she was sometimes mistaken for a man.*
<<OPPOSITE *high*

4 strong and fairly dark in colour *e.g. The wine was deep ruby in colour.*
deeply ADVERB

deepen [ˈdiːpən] **deepens, deepening, deepened** VERB
If something deepens or is deepened, it becomes deeper or more intense.

deer [dɪə] NOUN
a large, hoofed mammal that lives wild in parts of Britain
[WORD HISTORY: from Old English DEOR meaning 'beast']

deface [dɪˈfeɪs] **defaces, defacing, defaced** VERB
If you deface a wall or notice, you spoil it by writing or drawing on it. *e.g. She spitefully defaced her sister's poster.*

default [dɪˈfɔːlt] **defaults, defaulting, defaulted** VERB
1 If someone defaults on something they have legally agreed to do, they fail to do it. *e.g. He defaulted on repayment of the loan.*

> PHRASE
2 If something happens **by default**, it happens because something else which might have prevented it has failed to happen.

defeat [dɪˈfiːt] **defeats, defeating, defeated** VERB
1 If you defeat someone or something, you win a victory over them, or cause them to fail.

● **THESAURUS**
beat: *the team that beat us in the final*
conquer: *During 1936, Mussolini conquered Abyssinia.*
crush: *in his bid to crush the rebels*
rout: *the battle at which the Norman army routed the English*
trounce: *Australia trounced France by 60 points to 4.*
vanquish: formal *after the hero had vanquished the dragon*

> NOUN
2 the state of being beaten or of failing or an occasion on which someone is beaten or fails to achieve something *e.g. He was gracious in defeat.*

● **THESAURUS**
conquest: *He had led the conquest of southern Poland.*

debacle: formal *It will be hard for them to recover from this debacle.*
rout: *The retreat turned into a rout.*
trouncing: *after a 6-2 trouncing on Sunday*
<<OPPOSITE *victory*

defecate [ˈdɛfɪˌkeɪt] **defecates, defecating, defecated** VERB
To defecate means to get rid of waste matter from the bowels through the anus.

defect defects, defecting, defected NOUN
[ˈdiːfɛkt]
1 a fault or flaw in something

● **THESAURUS**
deficiency: *the most serious deficiency in NATO's air defence*
failing: *She blamed the country's failings on its culture of greed.*
fault: *a minor technical fault*
flaw: *The only flaw in his character is a short temper.*
imperfection: *my physical imperfections*
shortcoming: *The book has its shortcomings.*
weakness: *His only weakness is his laziness.*

> VERB [dɪˈfɛkt]
2 If someone defects, they leave their own country or organization and join an opposing one.
defection NOUN

defective [dɪˈfɛktɪv] ADJECTIVE
imperfect or faulty *e.g. defective eyesight*

defence [dɪˈfɛns] **defences** NOUN
1 Defence is action that is taken to protect someone or something from attack.

● **THESAURUS**
cover: *They could not provide adequate air cover for ground operations.*
protection: *Such a diet is believed to offer protection against cancer.*
resistance: *Most people have a natural resistance to the disease.*
safeguard: *legislation that offers safeguards against discrimination*
security: *Airport security was tightened.*

2 any arguments used in support of something that has been criticized or questioned

● **THESAURUS**
argument: *There's a strong argument for lowering the price.*
excuse: *There's no excuse for behaviour like that.*
explanation: *The authorities have given no explanation for his arrest.*
justification: *The only justification for a zoo is educational.*
plea: *a plea of insanity*

3 the case presented, in a court of law, by a lawyer for the person on trial; also the person on trial and his or her lawyers

4 (HISTORY) A country's defences are its military resources, such as its armed forces and weapons.

defend [dɪ'fɛnd] **defends, defending, defended** VERB

1 To defend someone or something means to protect them from harm or danger.

● **THESAURUS**
cover: *travel insurance covering you against theft*
guard: *A few men were left outside to guard her.*
protect: *What can women do to protect themselves from heart disease?*
safeguard: *action to safeguard the ozone layer*
shelter: *a wooden house, sheltered by a low roof*
shield: *He shielded his head from the sun with an old sack.*

2 If you defend a person or their ideas and beliefs, you argue in support of them.

● **THESAURUS**
endorse: *I can endorse their opinion wholeheartedly.*
justify: *No argument can justify a war.*
stick up for: informal *Why do you always stick up for her?*
support: *Would you support such a move?*
uphold: *upholding the artist's right to creative freedom*

3 To defend someone in court means to represent them and argue their case for them.

4 In a game such as football or hockey, to defend means to try to prevent goals being scored by your opponents.

defendant [dɪ'fɛndənt] **defendants** NOUN
a person who has been accused of a crime in a court of law

defender [dɪ'fɛndə] **defenders** NOUN

1 a person who protects someone or something from harm or danger

2 a person who argues in support of something

● **THESAURUS**
advocate: *a strong advocate of free market policies*
champion: *a champion of women's causes*
supporter: *a major supporter of the tax reform*

3 a person who tries to stop goals being scored in certain sports

defensible [dɪ'fɛnsɪbᵊl] ADJECTIVE
able to be defended against criticism or attack

defensive [dɪ'fɛnsɪv] ADJECTIVE

1 intended or designed for protection *e.g. defensive weapons*

2 Someone who is defensive feels unsure and threatened by other people's opinions and attitudes. *e.g. Don't get defensive, I was only joking about your cooking.*

defensively ADVERB, **defensiveness** NOUN

defer [dɪ'fɜː] **defers, deferring, deferred** VERB

1 If you defer something, you delay or postpone it until a future time.

2 If you defer to someone, you agree with them or do what they want because you respect them.

deference ['dɛfərəns] NOUN
Deference is polite and respectful behaviour.
deferential ADJECTIVE

defiance [dɪ'faɪəns] NOUN
Defiance is behaviour which shows that you are not willing to obey or behave in the expected way. *e.g. a gesture of defiance*
defiant ADJECTIVE, **defiantly** ADVERB

deficiency [dɪ'fɪʃənsɪ] **deficiencies** NOUN
a lack of something *e.g. vitamin deficiency*

● **THESAURUS**
deficit: *a staffing deficit*
deprivation: *sleep deprivation*
inadequacy: *the inadequacies of the current system*
lack: *a lack of people wanting to start new businesses*
want: formal *a want of manners and charm*
<<OPPOSITE *abundance*

deficient [dɪ'fɪʃənt] ADJECTIVE
lacking in something

● **THESAURUS**
inadequate: *inadequate staffing*
lacking: *Why was military intelligence so lacking?*
poor: *soil that is poor in zinc*
short: *The proposals were short on detail.*
wanting: *He analysed his game and found it wanting.*

deficit ['dɛfɪsɪt] **deficits** NOUN
the amount by which money received by an organization is less than money spent

define [dɪ'faɪn] **defines, defining, defined** VERB
(EXAM TERM) If you define something, you say clearly what it is or what it means. *e.g. Culture can be defined in hundreds of ways.*

definite ['dɛfɪnɪt] ADJECTIVE

1 firm and unlikely to be changed *e.g. The answer is a definite 'yes'.*

● **THESAURUS**
assured: *Victory was still not assured.*
certain: *Very little in life is certain.*
decided: *Is anything decided yet?*
fixed: *a world without fixed laws*
guaranteed: *Success is not guaranteed.*
settled: *Nothing is settled yet.*

2 certain or true rather than guessed or imagined *e.g. definite proof*
definitely ADVERB

THESAURUS
clear: *It was a clear case of homicide.*
positive: *We have positive proof that he was a blackmailer.*

definition [ˌdefɪˈnɪʃən] **definitions** NOUN
a statement explaining the meaning of a word or idea

definitive [dɪˈfɪnɪtɪv] ADJECTIVE
1 final and unable to be questioned or altered *e.g. a definitive answer*
2 most complete, or the best of its kind *e.g. a definitive history of science fiction*
definitively ADVERB

deflate [dɪˈfleɪt] **deflates, deflating, deflated** VERB
1 If you deflate something such as a tyre or balloon, you let out all the air or gas in it.
2 If you deflate someone, you make them seem less important.

deflect [dɪˈflɛkt] **deflects, deflecting, deflected** VERB
To deflect something means to turn it aside or make it change direction.
deflection NOUN

deforestation [ˌdiːˌfɒrɪsˈteɪʃən] NOUN
Deforestation is the cutting down of all the trees in an area.

deformed [dɪˈfɔːmd] ADJECTIVE
disfigured or abnormally shaped

THESAURUS
disfigured: *the scarred, disfigured face*
distorted: *the distorted image caused by the projector*

defraud [dɪˈfrɔːd] **defrauds, defrauding, defrauded** VERB
If someone defrauds you, they cheat you out of something that should be yours.

defrost [diːˈfrɒst] **defrosts, defrosting, defrosted** VERB
1 If you defrost a freezer or refrigerator, you remove the ice from it.
2 If you defrost frozen food, you let it thaw out.

deft [dɛft] **defter, deftest** ADJECTIVE
Someone who is deft is quick and skilful in their movements.
deftly ADVERB

defunct [dɪˈfʌŋkt] ADJECTIVE
no longer existing or functioning

defuse [diːˈfjuːz] **defuses, defusing, defused** VERB
1 To defuse a dangerous or tense situation means to make it less dangerous or tense.
2 To defuse a bomb means to remove its fuse or detonator so that it cannot explode.

defy [dɪˈfaɪ] **defies, defying, defied** VERB
1 If you defy a person or a law, you openly refuse to obey.
2 FORMAL
If you defy someone to do something that you think is impossible, you challenge them to do it.

degenerate degenerates, degenerating, degenerated VERB [dɪˈdʒɛnəˌreɪt]
1 If something degenerates, it becomes worse. *e.g. The election campaign degenerated into farce.*
> ADJECTIVE [dɪˈdʒɛnərɪt]
2 having low standards of morality
> NOUN [dɪˈdʒɛnərɪt]
3 someone whose standards of morality are so low that people find their behaviour shocking or disgusting
degeneration NOUN

degradation [ˌdɛɡrəˈdeɪʃən] NOUN
Degradation is a state of poverty and misery.

degrade [dɪˈɡreɪd] **degrades, degrading, degraded** VERB
If something degrades people, it humiliates them and makes them feel that they are not respected.
degrading ADJECTIVE

THESAURUS
demean: *I wasn't going to demean myself by acting like a suspicious wife.*
humiliate: *He enjoyed humiliating me.*

degree [dɪˈɡriː] **degrees** NOUN
1 an amount of a feeling or quality *e.g. a degree of pain*
2 a unit of measurement of temperature; often written as ° after a number *e.g. 20°C*
3 (MATHS) a unit of measurement of angles in mathematics, and of latitude and longitude *e.g. The yacht was 20° off course.*
4 a course of study at a university or college; also the qualification awarded after passing the course

dehydrated [ˌdiːhaɪˈdreɪtɪd] ADJECTIVE
If someone is dehydrated, they are weak or ill because they have lost too much water from their body.

deign [deɪn] **deigns, deigning, deigned** VERB; FORMAL
If you deign to do something, you do it even though you think you are too important to do such a thing.

deity [ˈdeɪtɪ] **deities** NOUN
a god or goddess

deja vu [ˈdeɪʒæ ˈvuː] NOUN
Deja vu is the feeling that you have already experienced in the past exactly the same

sequence of events as is happening now.
[WORD HISTORY: from French DÉJÀ VU meaning literally 'already seen']

dejected [dɪˈdʒɛktɪd] ADJECTIVE
miserable and unhappy
dejection NOUN

delay [dɪˈleɪ] **delays, delaying, delayed**
VERB

1 If you delay doing something, you put it off until a later time.

⬤ **THESAURUS**
defer: *Customers often defer payment for as long as possible.*
postpone: *The visit has been postponed indefinitely.*
put off: *women who put off having a baby*
shelve: *The project has now been shelved.*
suspend: *Relief convoys will be suspended until the fighting stops.*

2 If something delays you, it hinders you or slows you down.

⬤ **THESAURUS**
check: *a policy to check fast population growth*
hinder: *Further investigation was hindered by the loss of all documentation.*
impede: *Fallen rocks are impeding the progress of rescue workers.*
obstruct: *The authorities are obstructing a UN investigation.*
set back: *public protests that could set back reforms*
<<OPPOSITE *hurry*

> NOUN
3 Delay is time during which something is delayed.

⬤ **THESAURUS**
interruption: *interruptions in the supply of food*
obstruction: *Obstruction of justice is a criminal offence.*
setback: *a setback for the peace process*

delectable [dɪˈlɛktəbᵊl] ADJECTIVE
very pleasing or delightful

delegate **delegates, delegating, delegated** NOUN [ˈdɛlɪˌgeɪt] or [ˈdɛlɪˌgɪt]
1 a person appointed to vote or to make decisions on behalf of a group of people

> VERB [ˈdɛlɪˌgeɪt]
2 If you delegate duties, you give them to someone who can then act on your behalf.

delegation [ˌdɛlɪˈgeɪʃən] **delegations** NOUN
1 a group of people chosen to represent a larger group of people

2 Delegation is the giving of duties, responsibilities, or power to someone who can then act on your behalf.

delete [dɪˈliːt] **deletes, deleting, deleted**
VERB
(ICT) To delete something means to cross it out or remove it. *e.g. He had deleted the computer file by mistake.*
deletion NOUN

⬤ **THESAURUS**
cross out: *He crossed out the first sentence and wrote it again.*
erase: *It was unfortunate that she had erased the message.*
rub out: *She rubbed out the marks in the margin.*

deliberate **deliberates, deliberating, deliberated** ADJECTIVE [dɪˈlɪbərɪt]
1 done on purpose or planned in advance *e.g. It was a deliberate insult.*

⬤ **THESAURUS**
calculated: *a calculated attempt to cover up her crime*
conscious: *I made a conscious decision not to hide.*
intentional: *The kick was intentional.*
premeditated: *a premeditated attack*
studied: *'It's an interesting match,' he said with studied understatement.*
<<OPPOSITE *accidental*

2 careful and not hurried in speech and action *e.g. She was very deliberate in her movements.*

⬤ **THESAURUS**
careful: *The trip needs careful planning.*
cautious: *a cautious approach*
measured: *walking at the same measured pace*
methodical: *Da Vinci was methodical in his research.*
<<OPPOSITE *casual*

> VERB [dɪˈlɪbəreɪt]
3 If you deliberate about something, you think about it seriously and carefully.
deliberately ADVERB

⬤ **THESAURUS**
debate: *He was debating whether or not he should tell her.*
meditate: *She meditated on the uncertainties of his future.*
mull over: *McLaren had been mulling over an idea to make a movie.*
ponder: *He was pondering the problem when Phillipson drove up.*
reflect: *I reflected on the child's future.*

deliberation [dɪˌlɪbəˈreɪʃən] **deliberations** NOUN
Deliberation is careful consideration of a subject.

delicacy [ˈdɛlɪkəsɪ] **delicacies** NOUN
1 Delicacy is grace and attractiveness.

2 Something said or done with delicacy is said or done tactfully so that nobody is offended.

d

3 Delicacies are rare or expensive foods that are considered especially nice to eat.

delicate ['dɛlɪkɪt] ADJECTIVE

1 fine, graceful, or subtle in character *e.g. a delicate fragrance*

2 fragile and needing to be handled carefully *e.g. delicate antique lace*

3 precise or sensitive, and able to notice very small changes *e.g. a delicate instrument*
delicately ADVERB

delicatessen [ˌdɛlɪkə'tɛsᵊn] **delicatessens** NOUN

a shop selling unusual or imported foods
[WORD HISTORY: from German DELIKATESSEN meaning 'delicacies']

delicious [dɪ'lɪʃəs] ADJECTIVE

very pleasing, especially to taste
deliciously ADVERB

● THESAURUS

appetizing: *the appetizing smell of freshly baked bread*
delectable: *delectable wine*
luscious: *luscious fruit*
tasty: *The food was very tasty.*

delight [dɪ'laɪt] **delights, delighting, delighted** NOUN

1 Delight is great pleasure or joy.

● THESAURUS

glee: *His victory was greeted with glee by his supporters.*
happiness: *Our happiness at being reunited knew no bounds.*
joy: *the joys of being a parent*
pleasure: *the pleasure of seeing her face*
rapture: *gasps of rapture*
satisfaction: *I felt a glow of satisfaction at my achievement.*

> VERB

2 If something delights you or if you are delighted by it, it gives you a lot of pleasure.
delighted ADJECTIVE

● THESAURUS

amuse: *a selection of toys to amuse your baby*
captivate: *captivated the world with her radiant looks*
charm: *He charmed his landlady, chatting and flirting with her.*
enchant: *Dena was enchanted by the house.*
please: *It pleased him to talk to her.*
thrill: *The electric atmosphere thrilled him.*

delightful [dɪ'laɪtfʊl] ADJECTIVE

very pleasant and attractive

delinquent [dɪ'lɪŋkwənt] **delinquents** NOUN

a young person who commits minor crimes
delinquency NOUN

delirious [dɪ'lɪrɪəs] ADJECTIVE

1 unable to speak or act in a rational way because of illness or fever

2 wildly excited and happy
deliriously ADVERB

deliver [dɪ'lɪvə] **delivers, delivering, delivered** VERB

1 If you deliver something to someone, you take it to them and give them it.

2 To deliver a lecture or speech means to give it.

delivery [dɪ'lɪvərɪ] **deliveries** NOUN

1 Delivery or a delivery is the bringing of letters or goods to a person or firm.

2 Someone's delivery is the way in which they give a speech.

dell [dɛl] **dells** NOUN; LITERARY

a small wooded valley

delta ['dɛltə] **deltas** NOUN

a low, flat area at the mouth of a river where the river has split into several branches to enter the sea

delude [dɪ'lu:d] **deludes, deluding, deluded** VERB

To delude people means to deceive them into believing something that is not true.

deluge ['dɛlju:dʒ] **deluges, deluging, deluged** NOUN

1 a sudden, heavy downpour of rain

> VERB

2 To be deluged with things means to be overwhelmed by a great number of them.

delusion [dɪ'lu:ʒən] **delusions** NOUN

a mistaken or misleading belief or idea

de luxe [də 'lʌks] ADJECTIVE

rich, luxurious, or of superior quality
[WORD HISTORY: from French DE LUXE meaning literally 'of luxury']

delve [dɛlv] **delves, delving, delved** VERB

If you delve into something, you seek out more information about it.

demand [dɪ'mɑ:nd] **demands, demanding, demanded** VERB

1 If you demand something, you ask for it forcefully and urgently.

2 If a job or situation demands a particular quality, it needs it. *e.g. This situation demands hard work.*

● THESAURUS

involve: *Running a kitchen involves a great deal of discipline.*

need: *a problem that needs careful handling*
require: *Then he'll know what's required of him.*
take: *Walking across the room took all her strength.*
want: *The windows wanted cleaning.*

> NOUN

3 a forceful request for something

4 If there is a demand for something, a lot of people want to buy it or have it.

> The verb *demand* is either followed by *of* or *from*: *at least one important decision was demanded of me; he had demanded an explanation from Daphne.*

demean [dɪ'miːn] **demeans, demeaning, demeaned** VERB
If you demean yourself, you do something which makes people have less respect for you.
demeaning ADJECTIVE

demeanour [dɪ'miːnə] NOUN
Your demeanour is the way you behave and the impression that this creates.

demented [dɪ'mɛntɪd] ADJECTIVE
Someone who is demented behaves in a wild or violent way.

dementia [dɪ'mɛnʃə] NOUN; MEDICAL
Dementia is a serious illness of the mind.

demi- PREFIX
Demi- means half.

demise [dɪ'maɪz] NOUN; FORMAL
Someone's demise is their death.

demo ['dɛməʊ] **demos** NOUN; INFORMAL
a demonstration

democracy [dɪ'mɒkrəsi] **democracies** NOUN
Democracy is a system of government in which the people choose their leaders by voting for them in elections.

democrat ['dɛmə,kræt] **democrats** NOUN
a person who believes in democracy, personal freedom, and equality

democratic [,dɛmə'krætɪk] ADJECTIVE
having representatives elected by the people
democratically ADVERB
[WORD HISTORY: from Greek DĒMOS meaning 'the people' and KRATOS meaning 'power']

demography [dɪ'mɒgrəfi] NOUN
Demography is the study of the changes in the size and structure of populations.
demographic ADJECTIVE

demolish [dɪ'mɒlɪʃ] **demolishes, demolishing, demolished** VERB
To demolish a building means to pull it down or break it up.
demolition NOUN

demon ['diːmən] **demons** NOUN
1 an evil spirit or devil

> ADJECTIVE

2 skilful, keen, and energetic *e.g. a demon squash player*
demonic ADJECTIVE

demonstrate ['dɛmən,streɪt] **demonstrates, demonstrating, demonstrated** VERB

1 (**EXAM TERM**) To demonstrate a fact or theory means to prove or show it to be true.

2 If you demonstrate something to somebody, you show and explain it by using or doing the thing itself. *e.g. She demonstrated how to apply the make-up.*

3 If people demonstrate, they take part in a march or rally to show their opposition or support for something.

demonstration [,dɛmən'streɪʃən] **demonstrations** NOUN

1 a talk or explanation to show how to do or use something

2 Demonstration is proof that something exists or is true.

3 a public march or rally in support of or opposition to something
demonstrator NOUN

demote [dɪ'məʊt] **demotes, demoting, demoted** VERB
A person who is demoted is put in a lower rank or position, often as a punishment.
demotion NOUN

demure [dɪ'mjʊə] ADJECTIVE
Someone who is demure is quiet, shy, and behaves very modestly.
demurely ADVERB

den [dɛn] **dens** NOUN

1 the home of some wild animals such as lions or foxes

2 a secret place where people meet

denial [dɪ'naɪəl] **denials** NOUN

1 A denial of something is a statement that it is untrue. *e.g. He published a firm denial of the report.*

2 The denial of a request or something to which you have a right is the refusal of it. *e.g. the denial of human rights*

denigrate ['dɛnɪ,greɪt] **denigrates, denigrating, denigrated** VERB; FORMAL
To denigrate someone or something means to criticize them in order to damage their reputation.

denim ['dɛnɪm] **denims** NOUN

1 Denim is strong cotton cloth, used for making clothes.

> PLURAL NOUN
2 Denims are jeans made from denim.
[WORD HISTORY: from French SERGE DE NÎMES, meaning 'serge (a type of cloth) from Nîmes']

denomination [dɪˌnɒmɪ'neɪʃən]
denominations NOUN
1 a particular group which has slightly different religious beliefs from other groups within the same faith

2 a unit in a system of weights, values, or measures *e.g. a high denomination note*

denominator [dɪ'nɒmɪˌneɪtə]
denominators NOUN
(MATHS) In maths, the denominator is the bottom part of a fraction.

denote [dɪ'nəʊt] **denotes, denoting, denoted** VERB
If one thing denotes another, it is a sign of it or it represents it. *e.g. Formerly, a tan denoted wealth.*

denounce [dɪ'naʊns] **denounces, denouncing, denounced** VERB
1 If you denounce someone or something, you express very strong disapproval of them. *e.g. He publicly denounced government nuclear policy.*

2 If you denounce someone, you give information against them. *e.g. He was denounced as a dangerous agitator.*

dense [dɛns] **denser, densest** ADJECTIVE
1 thickly crowded or packed together *e.g. the dense crowd*

2 difficult to see through *e.g. dense black smoke*
densely ADVERB

density ['dɛnsɪtɪ] **densities** NOUN
the degree to which something is filled or occupied *e.g. a very high population density*

dent [dɛnt] **dents, denting, dented** VERB
1 To dent something means to damage it by hitting it and making a hollow in its surface.

> NOUN
2 a hollow in the surface of something

dental ['dɛntªl] ADJECTIVE
relating to the teeth

dentist ['dɛntɪst] **dentists** NOUN
a person who is qualified to treat people's teeth

dentistry ['dɛntɪstrɪ] NOUN
Dentistry is the branch of medicine concerned with disorders of the teeth.

dentures ['dɛntʃəz] PLURAL NOUN
Dentures are false teeth.

denunciation [dɪˌnʌnsɪ'eɪʃən]
denunciations NOUN
A denunciation of someone or something is severe public criticism of them.

deny [dɪ'naɪ] **denies, denying, denied** VERB
1 If you deny something that has been said, you state that it is untrue.
◉ THESAURUS
contradict: *Her version contradicted the Government's claim.*
refute: *He angrily refutes the charge.*
<<OPPOSITE *admit*

2 If you deny that something is the case, you refuse to believe it. *e.g. He denied the existence of God.*
◉ THESAURUS
reject: *children who rejected their parents' religious beliefs*
renounce: *after she renounced terrorism*

3 If you deny someone something, you refuse to give it to them. *e.g. They were denied permission to attend.*
◉ THESAURUS
refuse: *The council had refused permission for the march.*
withhold: *Financial aid for Russia has been withheld.*

deodorant [diː'əʊdərənt] **deodorants** NOUN
a substance or spray used to hide the smell of perspiration

depart [dɪ'pɑːt] **departs, departing, departed** VERB
When you depart, you leave.
departure NOUN

department [dɪ'pɑːtmənt] **departments** NOUN
one of the sections into which an organization is divided *e.g. the marketing department*
departmental ADJECTIVE
◉ THESAURUS
division: *the bank's Latin American division*
office: *Contact your local tax office.*
section: *a top-secret section of the Foreign Office*
unit: *the health services research unit*

depend [dɪ'pɛnd] **depends, depending, depended** VERB
1 If you depend on someone or something, you trust them and rely on them.
◉ THESAURUS
bank on: *The government is banking on the Olympics to save the city money.*
count on: *I can always count on you to cheer me up.*
rely on: *They can always be relied on to turn up.*
trust: *I knew I could trust him to meet a tight deadline.*

2 If one thing depends on another, it is influenced by it. *e.g. Success depends on the quality of the workforce.*

THESAURUS
be determined by: *Social status is largely determined by occupation.*
hinge on: *Victory or defeat hinged on her final putt.*

dependable [dɪ'pɛndəbəl] ADJECTIVE
reliable and trustworthy

dependant [dɪ'pɛndənt] **dependants** NOUN
(PSHE) someone who relies on another person for financial support

dependence [dɪ'pɛndəns] NOUN
Dependence is a constant need that someone has for something or someone in order to survive or operate properly. *e.g. He was flattered by her dependence on him.*

dependency [dɪ'pɛndənsɪ] **dependencies** NOUN
1 (PSHE) Dependency is relying on someone or something to give you what you need. *e.g. drug dependency*
2 a country or area controlled by another country

dependent [dɪ'pɛndənt] ADJECTIVE
reliant on someone or something

depict [dɪ'pɪkt] **depicts, depicting, depicted** VERB
To depict someone or something means to represent them in painting or sculpture.

deplete [dɪ'pliːt] **depletes, depleting, depleted** VERB
To deplete something means to reduce greatly the amount of it available.
depletion NOUN

deplorable [dɪ'plɔːrəbəl] ADJECTIVE
shocking or regrettable *e.g. deplorable conditions*

deplore [dɪ'plɔː] **deplores, deploring, deplored** VERB
If you deplore something, you condemn it because you feel it is wrong.

deploy [dɪ'plɔɪ] **deploys, deploying, deployed** VERB
To deploy troops or resources means to organize or position them so that they can be used effectively.
deployment NOUN

deport [dɪ'pɔːt] **deports, deporting, deported** VERB
If a government deports someone, it sends them out of the country because they have committed a crime or because they do not have the right to be there.
deportation NOUN

depose [dɪ'pəʊz] **deposes, deposing, deposed** VERB

If someone is deposed, they are removed from a position of power.

deposit [dɪ'pɒzɪt] **deposits, depositing, deposited** VERB
1 If you deposit something, you put it down or leave it somewhere.

THESAURUS
drop: *He dropped me outside the hotel.*
lay: *The table was spread with a cloth, and the box was laid on top.*
leave: *Leave your key with a neighbour.*
place: *I placed the book on the counter.*
put down: *Mishka put down her heavy shopping bag.*

2 If you deposit money or valuables, you put them somewhere for safekeeping.
> NOUN
3 a sum of money given in part payment for goods or services

depot ['dɛpəʊ] **depots** NOUN
a place where large supplies of materials or equipment may be stored

depraved [dɪ'preɪvd] ADJECTIVE
morally bad

depress [dɪ'prɛs] **depresses, depressing, depressed** VERB
1 If something depresses you, it makes you feel sad and gloomy.
2 If wages or prices are depressed, their value falls.
depressive ADJECTIVE

depressant [dɪ'prɛsənt] **depressants** NOUN
a drug which reduces nervous activity and so has a calming effect

depressed [dɪ'prɛst] ADJECTIVE
1 unhappy and gloomy
2 A place that is depressed has little economic activity and therefore low incomes and high unemployment. *e.g. depressed industrial areas*

depression [dɪ'prɛʃən] **depressions** NOUN
1 a state of mind in which someone feels unhappy and has no energy or enthusiasm
2 a time of industrial and economic decline

deprive [dɪ'praɪv] **deprives, depriving, deprived** VERB
If you deprive someone of something, you take it away or prevent them from having it.
deprived ADJECTIVE, **deprivation** NOUN

depth [dɛpθ] **depths** NOUN
1 The depth of something is the measurement or distance between its top and bottom, or between its front and back.
2 The depth of something such as emotion is its intensity. *e.g. the depth of her hostility*

deputation [ˌdɛpjʊ'teɪʃən] **deputations**
NOUN
a small group of people sent to speak or act on
behalf of others

deputy ['dɛpjʊtɪ] **deputies** NOUN
Someone's deputy is a person appointed to act in
their place.

deranged [dɪ'reɪndʒd] ADJECTIVE
mad, or behaving in a wild and uncontrolled way

derby ['dɜːrbɪ] **derbies** NOUN
A local derby is a sporting event between two
teams from the same area.

derelict ['dɛrɪlɪkt] ADJECTIVE
abandoned and falling into ruins

⬤ THESAURUS
abandoned: *a network of abandoned mines*
dilapidated: *a dilapidated castle*
neglected: *a neglected garden*
ruined: *a ruined church*

deride [dɪ'raɪd] **derides, deriding, derided**
VERB
To deride someone or something means to mock
or jeer at them with contempt.

derision [dɪ'rɪʒən] NOUN
Derision is an attitude of contempt or scorn
towards something or someone.

derivation [ˌdɛrɪ'veɪʃən] **derivations** NOUN
The derivation of something is its origin or
source.

derivative [dɪ'rɪvətɪv] **derivatives** NOUN
1 something which has developed from an earlier
source
> ADJECTIVE
2 not original, but based on or copied from
something else *e.g. The record was not deliberately
derivative.*

derive [dɪ'raɪv] **derives, deriving, derived**
VERB
1 FORMAL
If you derive something from someone or
something, you get it from them. *e.g. He derived
so much joy from music.*
2 If something derives from something else, it
develops from it.

derogatory [dɪ'rɒgətərɪ] ADJECTIVE
critical and scornful *e.g. He made derogatory
remarks about them.*

descant ['dɛskænt] **descants** NOUN
The descant to a tune is another tune played at
the same time and at a higher pitch.

descend [dɪ'sɛnd] **descends, descending,
descended** VERB
1 To descend means to move downwards.

⬤ THESAURUS
dip: *The sun dipped below the horizon.*
dive: *The shark dived down and under the boat.*
fall: *Bombs fell in the town.*
go down: *after the sun has gone down*
plummet: *as the plane plummeted through the air*
sink: *A fresh egg will sink and an old egg will float.*
<<OPPOSITE *ascend*

2 If you descend on people or on a place, you
arrive unexpectedly.

descendant [dɪ'sɛndənt] **descendants**
NOUN
A person's descendants are the people in later
generations who are related to them.

descended [dɪ'sɛndɪd] ADJECTIVE
If you are descended from someone who lived in
the past, your family originally derived from
them.

descent [dɪ'sɛnt] **descents** NOUN
1 a movement or slope from a higher to a lower
position or level
2 Your descent is your family's origins.

describe [dɪ'skraɪb] **describes, describing,
described** VERB
To describe someone or something means to
give an account or a picture of them in words.

⬤ THESAURUS
define: *Culture can be defined in many ways.*
depict: *a novel depicting a gloomy, futuristic
America*
portray: *a writer who accurately portrays provincial
life*

description [dɪ'skrɪpʃən] **descriptions**
NOUN
an account or picture of something in words
descriptive ADJECTIVE

desert ['dɛzət] **deserts** NOUN **(GEOGRAPHY)**
a region of land with very little plant life, usually
because of low rainfall

desert [dɪ'zɜːt] **deserts, deserting,
deserted** VERB
To desert a person means to leave or abandon
them. *e.g. His clients had deserted him.*
desertion NOUN

deserter [dɪ'zɜːtə] **deserters** NOUN
someone who leaves the armed forces without
permission

deserve [dɪ'zɜːv] **deserves, deserving,
deserved** VERB
If you deserve something you are entitled to it or
earn it because of your qualities, achievements,
or actions. *e.g. He deserved a rest.*

⬤ THESAURUS
be entitled to: *She is entitled to feel proud.*

be worthy of: *The bank might think you're worthy of a loan.*
earn: *You've earned this holiday.*
justify: *The decision was fully justified by economic conditions.*
merit: *Such ideas merit careful consideration.*
warrant: *no evidence to warrant a murder investigation*

deserving [dɪ'zɜːvɪŋ] ADJECTIVE
worthy of being helped, rewarded, or praised *e.g. a deserving charity*

design [dɪ'zaɪn] **designs, designing, designed (D & T)** VERB
1 To design something means to plan it, especially by preparing a detailed sketch or drawings from which it can be built or made.

⦿ THESAURUS
draft: *The legislation was drafted by Democrats.*
draw up: *a working party to draw up a formal agreement*
plan: *when we plan road construction*

> NOUN
2 a drawing or plan from which something can be built or made

⦿ THESAURUS
model: *an architect's model of a wooden house*
plan: *when you have drawn a plan of the garden*

3 The design of something is its shape and style.
designer NOUN

⦿ THESAURUS
form: *the form of the human body*
pattern: *a pattern of coloured dots*
shape: *a kidney shape*
style: *Several styles of hat were available.*

designate ['dɛzɪɡ,neɪt] **designates, designating, designated** VERB
1 To designate someone or something means to formally label or name them. *e.g. The room was designated a no smoking area.*
2 If you designate someone to do something, you appoint them to do it. *e.g. He designated his son as his successor.*

designation [,dɛzɪɡ'neɪʃən] **designations** NOUN
a name or title

designing [dɪ'zaɪnɪŋ] ADJECTIVE
crafty and cunning

desirable [dɪ'zaɪərəbəl] ADJECTIVE
1 worth having or doing *e.g. a desirable job*
2 sexually attractive
desirability NOUN

desire [dɪ'zaɪə] **desires, desiring, desired** VERB
1 If you desire something, you want it very much.

⦿ THESAURUS
crave: *I crave her approval.*
fancy: *She fancied living in Canada.*
long for: *He longed for the winter to be over.*
want: *I want a drink.*
wish: *We wished to return.*
yearn: *He yearned to sleep.*

> NOUN
2 a strong feeling of wanting something

⦿ THESAURUS
appetite: *She had lost her appetite for air travel.*
craving: *a craving for sugar*
hankering: *a hankering to be an actress*
longing: *her longing to return home*
wish: *Her wish is to be in films.*
yearning: *a yearning for a child of my own*
yen: *informal Mike had a yen to try cycling.*

3 Desire for someone is a strong sexual attraction to them.

desist [dɪ'zɪst] **desists, desisting, desisted** VERB; FORMAL
To desist from doing something means to stop doing it.

desk [dɛsk] **desks** NOUN
1 a piece of furniture designed for working at or writing on
2 a counter or table in a public building behind which a receptionist sits

desktop ['dɛsk,tɒp] ADJECTIVE
of a convenient size to be used on a desk or table *e.g. a desktop computer*

desolate ['dɛsəlɪt] ADJECTIVE
1 deserted and bleak *e.g. a desolate mountainous region*
2 lonely, very sad, and without hope *e.g. He was desolate without her.*
desolation NOUN

despair [dɪ'spɛə] **despairs, despairing, despaired** NOUN
1 Despair is a total loss of hope.

⦿ THESAURUS
dejection: *There was an air of dejection about her.*
despondency: *There's a mood of despondency in the country.*
gloom: *the deepening gloom over the economy*
hopelessness: *She had a feeling of hopelessness about the future.*

> VERB
2 If you despair, you lose hope. *e.g. He despaired of finishing it.*
despairing ADJECTIVE

⦿ THESAURUS
feel dejected: *Everyone has days when they feel dejected.*

feel despondent: *John often felt despondent after visiting the job centre.*
lose heart: *He appealed to his countrymen not to lose heart.*
lose hope: *You mustn't lose hope.*

despatch [dɪ'spætʃ] another spelling of **dispatch**

desperate ['dɛspərɪt] ADJECTIVE
 1 If you are desperate, you are so worried or frightened that you will try anything to improve your situation. *e.g. a desperate attempt to save their marriage*
 2 A desperate person is violent and dangerous.
 3 A desperate situation is extremely dangerous or serious.
 desperately ADVERB, **desperation** NOUN

despicable [dɪ'spɪkəbəl] ADJECTIVE
deserving contempt

despise [dɪ'spaɪz] **despises, despising, despised** VERB
If you despise someone or something, you dislike them very much.

despite [dɪ'spaɪt] PREPOSITION
in spite of *e.g. He fell asleep despite all the coffee he'd drunk.*
● THESAURUS
 in spite of: *In spite of all the gossip, Virginia stayed behind.*
 notwithstanding: formal *Notwithstanding his age, Sikorski had an important job.*
 regardless of: *He led from the front, regardless of the danger.*

despondent [dɪ'spɒndənt] ADJECTIVE
dejected and unhappy
 despondency NOUN

dessert [dɪ'zɜːt] **desserts** NOUN
a sweet food served after the main course of a meal
[WORD HISTORY: from French DESSERVIR meaning 'to clear the table after a meal']

destination [ˌdɛstɪ'neɪʃən] **destinations** NOUN
a place to which someone or something is going or is being sent

destined ['dɛstɪnd] ADJECTIVE
meant or intended to happen *e.g. I was destined for fame and fortune.*

destiny ['dɛstɪnɪ] **destinies** NOUN
 1 Your destiny is all the things that happen to you in your life, especially when they are considered to be outside human control.
 2 Destiny is the force which some people believe controls everyone's life.

destitute ['dɛstɪˌtjuːt] ADJECTIVE
without money or possessions, and therefore in great need
 destitution NOUN

destroy [dɪ'strɔɪ] **destroys, destroying, destroyed** VERB
 1 To destroy something means to damage it so much that it is completely ruined.
● THESAURUS
 annihilate: *The lava annihilates everything in its path.*
 demolish: *A storm moved over the island, demolishing buildings.*
 devastate: *A fire had devastated large parts of Windsor castle.*
 obliterate: *Whole villages were obliterated by fire.*
 raze: *The town was razed to the ground during the occupation.*
 ruin: *My wife was ruining her health through worry.*
 wreck: *the injuries which nearly wrecked his career*
 2 To destroy something means to put an end to it. *e.g. The holiday destroyed their friendship.*

destruction [dɪ'strʌkʃən] NOUN
Destruction is the act of destroying something or the state of being destroyed.
● THESAURUS
 annihilation: *Leaders fear the annihilation of their people.*
 demolition: *the demolition of an old bridge*
 devastation: *A huge bomb blast brought chaos and devastation.*
 obliteration: *the obliteration of three rainforests*

destructive [dɪ'strʌktɪv] ADJECTIVE
causing or able to cause great harm, damage, or injury
 destructiveness NOUN

desultory ['dɛsəltərɪ] ADJECTIVE
passing from one thing to another in a fitful or random way *e.g. A desultory, embarrassed chatter began again.*

detach [dɪ'tætʃ] **detaches, detaching, detached** VERB
To detach something means to remove it. *e.g. The hood can be detached.*
 detachable ADJECTIVE

detached [dɪ'tætʃt] ADJECTIVE
 1 separate or standing apart *e.g. a detached house*
 2 having no real interest or emotional involvement in something *e.g. He observed me with a detached curiosity.*

detachment [dɪ'tætʃmənt] **detachments** NOUN
 1 Detachment is the feeling of not being personally involved with something. *e.g. A*

stranger can view your problems with detachment.

2 a small group of soldiers sent to do a special job

detail ['diːteɪl] **details** NOUN

1 an individual fact or feature of something *e.g. We discussed every detail of the performance.*

● THESAURUS

aspect: *Climate affects every aspect of our lives.*
element: *one of the key elements of the peace plan*
particular: *You will find all the particulars in Chapter 9.*
point: *Many of the points in the report are correct.*
respect: *At least in this respect we are equals.*

2 Detail is all the small features that make up the whole of something. *e.g. Look at the detail.*
detailed ADJECTIVE

detain [dɪ'teɪn] **detains, detaining, detained** VERB

1 To detain someone means to force them to stay. *e.g. She was being detained for interrogation.*

2 If you detain someone, you delay them. *e.g. I mustn't detain you.*

detect [dɪ'tɛkt] **detects, detecting, detected** VERB

1 If you detect something, you notice it. *e.g. I detected a glimmer of interest in his eyes.*

2 To detect something means to find it. *e.g. Cancer can be detected by X-rays.*
detectable ADJECTIVE

detection [dɪ'tɛkʃən] NOUN

1 Detection is the act of noticing, discovering, or sensing something.

2 Detection is also the work of investigating crime.

detective [dɪ'tɛktɪv] **detectives** NOUN

a person, usually a police officer, whose job is to investigate crimes

detector [dɪ'tɛktə] **detectors** NOUN

an instrument which is used to detect the presence of something *e.g. a metal detector*

detention [dɪ'tɛnʃən] NOUN

The detention of someone is their arrest or imprisonment.

deter [dɪ'tɜː] **deters, deterring, deterred** VERB

To deter someone means to discourage or prevent them from doing something by creating a feeling of fear or doubt. *e.g. 99 per cent of burglars are deterred by the sight of an alarm box*

detergent [dɪ'tɜːdʒənt] **detergents** NOUN

a chemical substance used for washing or cleaning things

deteriorate [dɪ'tɪərɪə,reɪt] **deteriorates, deteriorating, deteriorated** VERB

If something deteriorates, it gets worse. *e.g. My father's health has deteriorated lately.*
deterioration NOUN

determination [dɪ,tɜːmɪ'neɪʃən] NOUN

Determination is great firmness, after you have made up your mind to do something. *e.g. They shared a determination to win the war.*

● THESAURUS

perseverance: *Adam's perseverance proved worthwhile.*
persistence: *She was determined to be a doctor and her persistence paid off.*
resolution: *She acted with resolution and courage.*
resolve: formal *the American public's resolve to go to war if necessary*
tenacity: *Hard work and sheer tenacity are crucial to career success.*

determine [dɪ'tɜːmɪn] **determines, determining, determined** VERB

1 If something determines a situation or result, it causes it or controls it. *e.g. The track surface determines his tactics in a race.*

● THESAURUS

control: *Scientists may soon be able to control the ageing process.*
decide: *The results will decide if he will win a place on the course.*
dictate: *A number of factors will dictate how long the tree will survive.*
govern: *the rules governing eligibility for unemployment benefit*
shape: *the role of key leaders in shaping the future of Europe*

2 To determine something means to decide or settle it firmly. *e.g. The date has still to be determined.*

● THESAURUS

arrange: *It was arranged that the party would gather in the Royal Garden Hotel.*
choose: *Houston was chosen as the site for the convention.*
decide: *Her age would be taken into account when deciding her sentence.*
fix: *The date of the election was fixed.*
resolve: *She resolved to report the matter to the authorities.*
settle: *That's settled then. We'll do it tomorrow.*

3 To determine something means to find out or calculate the facts about it. *e.g. He bit the coin to determine whether it was genuine.*

● THESAURUS

ascertain: formal *We need to ascertain the true facts.*
confirm: *X-rays have confirmed that he has not broken any bones.*
discover: *It was difficult for us to discover the reason for the decision.*

d

establish: *an autopsy to establish the cause of death*
find out: *one family's campaign to find out the truth*
verify: *A clerk verifies that the payment and invoice amount match.*

determined [dɪˈtɜːmɪnd] ADJECTIVE
firmly decided *e.g. She was determined not to repeat her error.*
determinedly ADVERB

● THESAURUS
bent on: *They seem bent on destroying the city.*
dogged: *dogged persistence*
intent on: *He is intent on repeating his victory.*
persistent: *He phoned again this morning. He's very persistent.*
purposeful: *She had a purposeful air.*
resolute: formal *a decisive and resolute leader*
single-minded: *a single-minded determination to win*
tenacious: *a tenacious and persistent interviewer*

determiner [dɪˈtɜːmɪnə] **determiners** NOUN
a word that can go before a noun or noun group to show, for instance, which thing you are referring to or whether you are referring to one thing or several. For example, in 'my house', 'the windows', 'this red book' and 'each time', 'my', 'the', 'this' and 'each' can be called determiners.

deterrent [dɪˈtɛrənt] **deterrents** NOUN
something that prevents you from doing something by making you afraid of what will happen if you do so it *e.g. Capital punishment was no deterrent to domestic murders.*
deterrence NOUN

detest [dɪˈtɛst] **detests, detesting, detested** VERB
If you detest someone or something, you strongly dislike them.

detonate [ˈdɛtəˌneɪt] **detonates, detonating, detonated** VERB
To detonate a bomb or mine means to cause it to explode.
detonator NOUN

detour [ˈdiːtʊə] **detours** NOUN
an alternative, less direct route

detract [dɪˈtrækt] **detracts, detracting, detracted** VERB
To detract from something means to make it seem less good or valuable.

detriment [ˈdɛtrɪmənt] NOUN
Detriment is disadvantage or harm. *e.g. a detriment to their health*
detrimental ADJECTIVE

deuce [djuːs] **deuces** NOUN
In tennis, deuce is the score of forty all.

devalue [diːˈvæljuː] **devalues, devaluing, devalued** VERB

To devalue something means to lower its status, importance, or worth.
devaluation NOUN

devastate [ˈdɛvəˌsteɪt] **devastates, devastating, devastated** VERB
To devastate an area or place means to damage it severely or destroy it.
devastation NOUN

devastated [ˈdɛvəˌsteɪtɪd] ADJECTIVE
very shocked or upset *e.g. The family are devastated by the news.*

develop [dɪˈvɛləp] **develops, developing, developed** VERB
1 When something develops or is developed, it grows or becomes more advanced. *e.g. The sneezing developed into a full-blown cold.*

● THESAURUS
advance: *tracing how medical technology has advanced to its present state*
evolve: *As scientific knowledge evolves, beliefs change.*
grow: *The boys grew into men.*
mature: *Other changes occur as the child matures physically.*
progress: *His disease progressed quickly.*
result: *Ignore the warnings and illness could result.*
spring: *His anger sprang from his childhood suffering.*

2 To develop an area of land means to build on it.

3 To develop an illness or a fault means to become affected by it.

● THESAURUS
catch: *catch a cold*
contract: formal *He contracted AIDS from a blood transfusion.*
fall ill: *She fell ill with measles.*
get: *When I was five I got mumps.*
go down with: *Three members of the band went down with flu.*
pick up: *They've picked up an infection from something they've eaten.*
succumb: *I was determined not to succumb to the virus.*

developer [dɪˈvɛləpə] **developers** NOUN
a person or company that builds on land

development [dɪˈvɛləpmənt] **developments** NOUN
1 Development is gradual growth or progress.

2 The development of land or water is the process of making it more useful or profitable by the expansion of industry or housing. *e.g. the development of the old docks*

3 a new stage in a series of events *e.g. developments in technology*
developmental ADJECTIVE

deviant ['diːvɪənt] **deviants** ADJECTIVE

1 Deviant behaviour is unacceptable or different from what people consider as normal.

> NOUN

2 someone whose behaviour or beliefs are different from what people consider to be acceptable
deviance NOUN

deviate ['diːvɪˌeɪt] **deviates, deviating, deviated** VERB
To deviate means to differ or depart from what is usual or acceptable.
deviation NOUN

device [dɪ'vaɪs] **devices** NOUN

1 a machine or tool that is used for a particular purpose *e.g. a device to warn you when the batteries need changing*

2 a plan or scheme *e.g. a device to pressurise him into selling*

devil ['dɛvəl] **devils** NOUN

1 In Christianity and Judaism, the Devil is the spirit of evil and enemy of God.

2 an evil spirit
[WORD HISTORY: from Greek DIABOLOS meaning 'slanderer', 'enemy', or 'devil']

devious ['diːvɪəs] ADJECTIVE
insincere and dishonest
deviousness NOUN

● THESAURUS
calculating: *a calculating businessman*
scheming: *He was branded a "scheming liar".*
underhand: *He used underhand tactics to win the election.*
wily: *a wily old statesman*

devise [dɪ'vaɪz] **devises, devising, devised** VERB
To devise something means to work it out. *e.g. Besides diets, he devised punishing exercise routines.*

devoid [dɪ'vɔɪd] ADJECTIVE
lacking in a particular thing or quality *e.g. His glance was devoid of expression.*

devolution [ˌdiːvə'luːʃən] NOUN
Devolution is the transfer of power from a central government or organization to local government departments or smaller organizations.

devote [dɪ'vəʊt] **devotes, devoting, devoted** VERB
If you devote yourself to something, you give all your time, energy, or money to it. *e.g. She has devoted herself to women's causes.*

devoted [dɪ'vəʊtɪd] ADJECTIVE
very loving and loyal

● THESAURUS
constant: *her constant companion*

dedicated: *dedicated followers of classical music*
doting: *His doting parents bought him a racing bike.*
faithful: *I'm very faithful when I love someone.*
loving: *Jim was a loving husband.*
loyal: *a loyal friend*
true: *David was true to his wife.*

devotee [ˌdɛvə'tiː] **devotees** NOUN
a fanatical or enthusiastic follower of something

devotion [dɪ'vəʊʃən] NOUN
Devotion to someone or something is great love or affection for them.
devotional ADJECTIVE

devour [dɪ'vaʊə] **devours, devouring, devoured** VERB
If you devour something, you eat it hungrily or greedily.

devout [dɪ'vaʊt] ADJECTIVE
deeply and sincerely religious *e.g. a devout Buddhist*
devoutly ADVERB

dew [djuː] NOUN
Dew is drops of moisture that form on the ground and other cool surfaces at night.

dexterity [dɛk'stɛrɪtɪ] NOUN
Dexterity is skill or agility in using your hands or mind. *e.g. He had learned to use the crutches with dexterity.*
dexterous ADJECTIVE

dharma ['dɑːmə] NOUN
In the Buddhist religion, dharma is ideal truth as set out in the teaching of the Buddha.
[WORD HISTORY: a Sanskrit word]

diabetes [ˌdaɪə'biːtɪs] NOUN
Diabetes is a disease in which someone has too much sugar in their blood, because they do not produce enough insulin to absorb it.
diabetic NOUN OR ADJECTIVE

diabolical [ˌdaɪə'bɒlɪkəl] ADJECTIVE

1 INFORMAL
dreadful and very annoying *e.g. The pain was diabolical.*

2 extremely wicked and cruel

diagnose ['daɪəɡˌnəʊz] **diagnoses, diagnosing, diagnosed** VERB
To diagnose an illness or problem means to identify exactly what is wrong.

diagnosis [ˌdaɪəɡ'nəʊsɪs] **diagnoses** NOUN
the identification of what is wrong with someone who is ill
diagnostic ADJECTIVE

diagonal [daɪ'æɡənəl] ADJECTIVE
in a slanting direction
diagonally ADVERB

d

[WORD HISTORY: from Greek DIAGŌNIOS meaning 'from angle to angle']

diagram ['daɪə,græm] **diagrams** NOUN
a drawing that shows or explains something

dial ['daɪəl] **dials, dialling, dialled** NOUN
1 the face of a clock or meter, with divisions marked on it so that a time or measurement can be recorded and read

2 a part of a device, such as a radio, used to control or tune it

> VERB

3 To dial a telephone number means to press the number keys to select the required number.

dialect ['daɪə,lɛkt] **dialects** NOUN
a form of a language spoken in a particular geographical area

dialogue ['daɪə,lɒg] **dialogues** NOUN
1 (ENGLISH) In a novel, play, or film, dialogue is conversation.

2 Dialogue is communication or discussion between people or groups of people. *e.g. The union sought dialogue with the council.*

dialysis [daɪ'ælɪsɪs] NOUN
Dialysis is a treatment used for some kidney diseases, in which blood is filtered by a special machine to remove waste products.
[WORD HISTORY: from Greek DIALUEIN meaning 'to rip apart']

diameter [daɪ'æmɪtə] **diameters** NOUN
(MATHS) The diameter of a circle is the length of a straight line drawn across it through its centre.

diamond ['daɪəmənd] **diamonds** NOUN
1 a precious stone made of pure carbon

2 a shape with four straight sides of equal length forming two opposite angles less than 90° and two opposite angles greater than 90°

3 Diamonds is one of the four suits in a pack of playing cards. It is marked by a red diamond-shaped symbol.

> ADJECTIVE

4 A diamond anniversary is the 60th anniversary of an event.

diaphragm ['daɪə,fræm] **diaphragms** NOUN
In mammals, the diaphragm is the muscular wall that separates the lungs from the stomach.

diarrhoea [,daɪə'rɪə] NOUN
Diarrhoea is a condition in which the faeces are more liquid and frequent than usual.

diary ['daɪərɪ] **diaries** NOUN
a book which has a separate space or page for each day of the year on which to keep a record of appointments

diarist NOUN

Do not confuse the order of the vowels in *diary* and *dairy*.

dice [daɪs] **dices, dicing, diced** NOUN
1 a small cube which has each side marked with dots representing the numbers one to six

> VERB

2 To dice food means to cut it into small cubes.
diced ADJECTIVE

dictate [dɪk'teɪt] **dictates, dictating, dictated** VERB
1 If you dictate something, you say or read it aloud for someone else to write down.

2 To dictate something means to command or state what must happen. *e.g. What we wear is largely dictated by our daily routine.*
dictation NOUN

dictator [dɪk'teɪtə] **dictators** NOUN
a ruler who has complete power in a country, especially one who has taken power by force
dictatorial ADJECTIVE

diction ['dɪkʃən] NOUN
Someone's diction is the clarity with which they speak or sing.

dictionary ['dɪkʃənərɪ] **dictionaries** NOUN
(LIBRARY) a book in which words are listed alphabetically and explained, or equivalent words are given in another language
[WORD HISTORY: from Latin DICTIO meaning 'phrase' or 'word']

didgeridoo [,dɪdʒərɪ'du:] **didgeridoos** NOUN
an Australian musical wind instrument made in the shape of a long wooden tube

die [daɪ] **dies, dying, died** VERB
1 When people, animals, or plants die, they stop living.

● THESAURUS

cark it: Australian and New Zealand; informal *You think you're about to cark it.*

expire: formal *before he finally expired*

pass away: *He passed away last year.*

pass on: *My mother passed on four years ago.*

perish: formal *the ferry disaster in which 193 passengers perished*

2 When something dies, dies away, or dies down, it gradually fades away. *e.g. The footsteps died away.*

● THESAURUS

fade away: *With time, they said, the pain will fade away.*

fade out: *Thanks to supermarkets, the corner shop is gradually fading out.*

peter out: *The six-month strike seemed to be petering out.*

> NOUN

3 a dice

die out VERB

4 When something dies out, it ceases to exist.

◉ **THESAURUS**
disappear: *Huge areas of the countryside are disappearing.*
fade: *Prospects for peace had already started to fade.*
vanish: *those species which have vanished*

diesel ['diːzəl] NOUN

1 a heavy fuel used in trains, buses, and lorries

2 a vehicle with a diesel engine

diet ['daɪət] **diets** NOUN **(D & T)**

1 Someone's diet is the usual food that they eat. *e.g. a vegetarian diet*

2 a special restricted selection of foods that someone eats to improve their health or regulate their weight

dietary ADJECTIVE

[WORD HISTORY: from Greek DIAITA meaning 'mode of living'] **dieter** NOUN

dietician [ˌdaɪɪˈtɪʃən] **dieticians;** also spelt **dietitian** NOUN

a person trained to advise people about healthy eating

differ ['dɪfə] **differs, differing, differed** VERB

1 If two or more things differ, they are unlike each other.

2 If people differ, they have opposing views or disagree about something.

difference ['dɪfərəns] **differences** NOUN

1 The difference between things is the way in which they are unlike each other.

◉ **THESAURUS**
contrast: *the real contrast between the two poems*
discrepancy: *discrepancies between their statements*
disparity: *disparities between poor and wealthy districts*
distinction: *a distinction between the body and the soul*
divergence: *There's a substantial divergence of opinion within the party.*
variation: *a wide variation in the prices charged*
<<OPPOSITE *similarity*

2 The difference between two numbers is the amount by which one is less than another.

◉ **THESAURUS**
balance: *They were due to pay the balance on delivery.*
remainder: *They own a 75% stake. The remainder is owned by the bank.*

3 A difference in someone or something is a significant change in them. *e.g. You wouldn't*

believe the difference in her.

different ['dɪfərənt] ADJECTIVE

1 unlike something else

◉ **THESAURUS**
contrasting: *painted in contrasting colours*
disparate: formal *The republics are very disparate in size and wealth.*
dissimilar: *His methods were not dissimilar to those used by Freud.*
divergent: formal *divergent opinions*
opposed: *two opposed ideologies*
unlike: *This was a foreign country, so unlike San Jose.*
<<OPPOSITE *similar*

2 unusual and out of the ordinary

◉ **THESAURUS**
special: *a special variety of strawberry*
unique: *Each person's signature is unique.*

3 distinct and separate, although of the same kind *e.g. The lunch supports a different charity each year.*

differently ADVERB

◉ **THESAURUS**
another: *Her doctor referred her to another therapist.*
discrete: formal *two discrete sets of nerves*
distinct: *A word may have two quite distinct meanings.*
individual: *Each family needs individual attention.*
separate: *The word 'quarter' has two completely separate meanings.*

differentiate [ˌdɪfəˈrenʃɪˌeɪt] **differentiates, differentiating, differentiated** VERB

1 To differentiate between things means to recognize or show how one is unlike the other.

2 Something that differentiates one thing from another makes it distinct and unlike the other.

differentiation NOUN

difficult see page 236 for Word Web

difficulty ['dɪfɪkəltɪ] **difficulties** NOUN

1 a problem *e.g. The central difficulty is his drinking.*

◉ **THESAURUS**
complication: *An added complication is the growing concern for the environment.*
hassle: informal *all the usual hassles at the airport*
hurdle: *preparing a CV, the first hurdle in a job search*
obstacle: *To succeed, you must learn to overcome obstacles.*
pitfall: *the pitfalls of working abroad*
problem: *He left home because of family problems.*
snag: *The only snag was that he had no transport.*
trouble: *What seems to be the trouble?*

2 Difficulty is the fact or quality of being difficult.

d

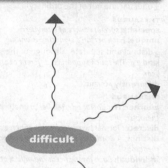

1 ADJECTIVE
not easy to do, understand, or solve *eg: a very difficult decision to make.*
● **THESAURUS**
arduous: *a long, arduous journey*
demanding: *a demanding job*
hard: *He found it hard to get work.*
intractable (formal): *an intractable problem*
laborious: *a laborious task*
uphill: *an uphill battle*
<< OPPOSITE *easy*

difficult

2 ADJECTIVE
hard to deal with, esp because of being unreasonable or unpredictable *eg: a difficult child.*
● **THESAURUS**
demanding: *a demanding boss*
troublesome: *a troublesome teenager*
trying: *The whole business has been very trying.*

3 ADJECTIVE
full of hardships or trials *eg: he had recently had a difficult time with his job as a self-employed builder*
● **THESAURUS**
dark: *These are dark times.*
hard: *He'd had a hard life.*
tough: *He was having a tough time at work.*
trying: *Support from those closest to you is difficult in these trying times.*

d

● THESAURUS
hardship: *economic hardship*
strain: *the stresses and strains of a busy career*
tribulation: formal *the trials and tribulations of everyday life*

diffident ['dɪfɪdənt] ADJECTIVE
timid and lacking in self-confidence
diffidently ADVERB, **diffidence** NOUN

diffract [dɪ'frækt] **diffracts, diffracting, diffracted** VERB
When rays of light or sound waves diffract, they break up after hitting an obstacle.
diffraction NOUN

diffuse diffuses, diffusing, diffused VERB
[dɪ'fjuːz]
1 If something diffuses, it spreads out or scatters in all directions.
> ADJECTIVE [dɪ'fjuːs]
2 spread out over a wide area
diffusion NOUN

dig [dɪg] **digs, digging, dug** VERB
1 If you dig, you break up soil or sand, especially with a spade or garden fork.
● THESAURUS
burrow: *The larvae burrow into cracks in the floor.*
excavate: *A contractor was hired to excavate soil from the area.*
gouge: *quarries which have gouged great holes in the hills*
hollow out: *They hollowed out crude dwellings from the soft rock.*
quarry: *The caves are quarried for cement.*
till: *freshly tilled fields*
tunnel: *The rebels tunnelled out of jail.*
2 To dig something into an object means to push, thrust, or poke it in.
● THESAURUS
jab: *A needle was jabbed into the baby's arm.*
poke: *She poked a fork into the turkey skin.*
thrust: *She thrust her hand into the sticky mess.*
> NOUN
3 a prod or jab, especially in the ribs
● THESAURUS
jab: *a swift jab in the stomach*
poke: *a playful poke in the arm*
prod: *He gave the donkey a prod in the backside.*
thrust: *knife thrusts*
4 INFORMAL
A dig at someone is a spiteful or unpleasant remark intended to hurt or embarrass them.
> PLURAL NOUN
5 Digs are lodgings in someone else's house.

digest [dɪ'dʒɛst] **digests, digesting, digested** VERB **(SCIENCE)**

1 To digest food means to break it down in the gut so that it can be easily absorbed and used by the body.
2 If you digest information or a fact, you understand it and take it in.
digestible ADJECTIVE

digestion [dɪ'dʒɛstʃən] **digestions** NOUN **(SCIENCE)**
1 Digestion is the process of digesting food.
2 Your digestion is your ability to digest food. *e.g. Camomile tea aids poor digestion.*
digestive ADJECTIVE

digger ['dɪgə] **diggers** NOUN
In Australian English, digger is a friendly name to call a man.

digit ['dɪdʒɪt] **digits** NOUN
1 FORMAL
Your digits are your fingers or toes.
2 **(MATHS)** a written symbol for any of the numbers from 0 to 9

digital ['dɪdʒɪtˀl] ADJECTIVE
displaying information, especially time, by numbers, rather than by a pointer moving round a dial *e.g. a digital watch*
digitally ADVERB

dignified ['dɪgnɪˌfaɪd] ADJECTIVE
full of dignity

dignitary ['dɪgnɪtərɪ] **dignitaries** NOUN
a person who holds a high official position

dignity ['dɪgnɪtɪ] NOUN
Dignity is behaviour which is serious, calm, and controlled. *e.g. She conducted herself with dignity.*

digression [daɪ'grɛʃən] **digressions** NOUN
A digression in speech or writing is leaving the main subject for a while.

dilapidated [dɪ'læpɪˌdeɪtɪd] ADJECTIVE
falling to pieces and generally in a bad condition *e.g. a dilapidated castle*

dilate [daɪ'leɪt] **dilates, dilating, dilated** VERB
To dilate means to become wider and larger. *e.g. The pupil of the eye dilates in the dark.*
dilated ADJECTIVE, **dilation** NOUN

dilemma [dɪ'lɛmə] **dilemmas** NOUN
a situation in which a choice has to be made between alternatives that are equally difficult or unpleasant
[WORD HISTORY: from Greek DI- meaning 'two' and LEMMA meaning 'assumption']

> A *dilemma* involves a difficult choice between two things. If there are more than two choices you should say *problem* or *difficulty*.

diligent ['dɪlɪdʒənt] ADJECTIVE
hard-working, and showing care and perseverance

diligently ADVERB, **diligence** NOUN

dill [dɪl] NOUN
Dill is a herb with yellow flowers and a strong sweet smell.

dilly bag ['dɪlɪ] **dilly bags** NOUN
In Australian English, a dilly bag is a small bag used to carry food.

dilute [daɪ'luːt] **dilutes, diluting, diluted** VERB
To dilute a liquid means to add water or another liquid to it to make it less concentrated.
dilution NOUN

dim [dɪm] **dimmer, dimmest; dims, dimming, dimmed** ADJECTIVE
1 badly lit and lacking in brightness

● THESAURUS
dark: a dark corridor
dull: The stamp was a dark, dull blue.
grey: a grey, wet, April Sunday
murky: one murky November afternoon
poorly lit: a poorly lit road
shadowy: a shadowy corner

2 very vague and unclear in your mind e.g. dim recollections

● THESAURUS
faint: a faint recollection
hazy: Many details remain hazy.
indistinct: the indistinct murmur of voices
obscure: The origin of the custom is obscure.
shadowy: the shadowy world of spies
vague: I have a vague memory of shots being fired.
<<OPPOSITE clear

3 INFORMAL
stupid or mentally dull e.g. He is rather dim.

● THESAURUS
dumb: informal I've met a lot of dumb people.
obtuse: I've really been very obtuse.
slow: He got hit on the head and he's been a bit slow since.
stupid: How could I have been so stupid?
thick: informal I must have seemed incredibly thick.
<<OPPOSITE bright

> VERB
4 If lights dim or are dimmed, they become less bright.
dimly ADVERB, **dimness** NOUN

dimension [dɪ'mɛnʃən] **dimensions** NOUN
1 A dimension of a situation is an aspect or factor that influences the way you understand it. e.g. This process had a domestic and a foreign dimension.

2 You can talk about the size or extent of something as its dimensions. e.g. It was an explosion of major dimensions.

3 (ART) The dimensions of something are also its measurements, for example its length, breadth, height, or diameter.

diminish [dɪ'mɪnɪʃ] **diminishes, diminishing, diminished** VERB
If something diminishes or if you diminish it, it becomes reduced in size or importance.

● THESAURUS
contract: Output fell last year and is expected to contract further.
decrease: Gradually decrease the amount of vitamin C you are taking.
lessen: The attention he gets will lessen when the new baby is born.
lower: This drug lowers cholesterol levels.
reduce: It reduces the risk of heart disease.
shrink: the entertainment giant's intention to shrink its interest in the venture
weaken: The Prime Minister's authority has been fatally weakened.

diminutive [dɪ'mɪnjʊtɪv] ADJECTIVE
very small

dimmer switch ['dɪmə] **dimmer switches** NOUN
a switch that allows you to adjust the brightness of an electric light

dimple ['dɪmpəl] **dimples** NOUN
a small hollow in someone's cheek or chin

din [dɪn] **dins** NOUN
a loud and unpleasant noise

dinar ['diːnɑː] **dinars** NOUN
a unit of currency in several countries in Southern Europe, North Africa and the Middle East

dine [daɪn] **dines, dining, dined** VERB; FORMAL
To dine means to eat dinner in the evening. e.g. We dined together in the hotel.

diner ['daɪnə] **diners** NOUN
1 a person who is having dinner in a restaurant
2 a small restaurant or railway restaurant car

dinghy ['dɪŋɪ] **dinghies** NOUN
a small boat which is rowed, sailed, or powered by outboard motor

dingo ['dɪŋɡəʊ] **dingoes** NOUN
an Australian wild dog

dingy ['dɪndʒɪ] **dingier, dingiest** ADJECTIVE
dusty, dark, and rather depressing e.g. a dingy bedsit

dinkum ['dɪŋkəm] ADJECTIVE INFORMAL
In Australian and New Zealand English, dinkum means genuine or right. e.g. a fair dinkum offer

● THESAURUS
genuine: If this offer is genuine I will gladly accept.
guileless: She was so guileless that he had to believe her.

honest: *My dad was the most honest man I ever met.*
sincere: *a sincere desire to reform*

dinner ['dɪnə] **dinners** NOUN

1 the main meal of the day, eaten either in the evening or at lunchtime

2 a formal social occasion in the evening, at which a meal is served

dinosaur ['daɪnə,sɔː] **dinosaurs** NOUN
a large reptile which lived in prehistoric times
[WORD HISTORY: from Greek DEINOS + SAUROS meaning 'fearful lizard']

dint [dɪnt] PHRASE
By dint of means by means of *e.g. He succeeds by dint of hard work.*

diocese ['daɪəsɪs] **dioceses** NOUN
a district controlled by a bishop
diocesan ADJECTIVE

dip [dɪp] **dips, dipping, dipped** VERB

1 If you dip something into a liquid, you lower it or plunge it quickly into the liquid.

2 If something dips, it slopes downwards or goes below a certain level. *e.g. The sun dipped below the horizon.*

3 To dip also means to make a quick, slight downward movement. *e.g. She dipped her fingers into the cool water.*

> NOUN

4 a rich creamy mixture which you scoop up with biscuits or raw vegetables and eat *e.g. an avocado dip*

5 INFORMAL
a swim

diploma [dɪ'pləumə] **diplomas** NOUN
a certificate awarded to a student who has successfully completed a course of study
[WORD HISTORY: from Greek DIPLOMA meaning 'folded paper' or 'letter of recommendation']

diplomacy [dɪ'pləuməsɪ] NOUN

1 Diplomacy is the managing of relationships between countries.

2 Diplomacy is also skill in dealing with people without offending or upsetting them.
diplomatic ADJECTIVE, **diplomatically** ADVERB

diplomat ['dɪplə,mæt] **diplomats** NOUN
an official who negotiates and deals with another country on behalf of his or her own country

dire [daɪə] **direr, direst** ADJECTIVE
disastrous, urgent, or terrible *e.g. people in dire need*

direct [dɪ'rɛkt] **directs, directing, directed**
ADJECTIVE

1 moving or aimed in a straight line or by the shortest route *e.g. the direct route*

THESAURUS
first-hand: *She has little first-hand knowledge of Quebec.*
immediate: *his immediate superior*
personal: *I have no personal experience of this.*
straight: *Keep the boat in a straight line.*
uninterrupted: *an uninterrupted view*
<<OPPOSITE *indirect*

2 straightforward, and without delay or evasion *e.g. his direct manner*
THESAURUS
blunt: *She is blunt about her personal life.*
candid: *I haven't been completely candid with you.*
forthright: *forthright language*
frank: *She is always very frank.*
straight: *He never gives you a straight answer.*
straightforward: *his straightforward manner*
<<OPPOSITE *devious*

3 without anyone or anything intervening *e.g. Schools can take direct control of their own funding.*

4 exact *e.g. the direct opposite*

> VERB

5 To direct something means to guide and control it.
THESAURUS
control: *He now controls the entire company.*
guide: *He should have let his instinct guide him.*
lead: *He led the country between 1949 and 1984.*
manage: *Within two years he was managing the store.*
oversee: *an architect to oversee the work*
run: *Is this any way to run a country?*
supervise: *I supervise the packing of all mail orders.*

6 To direct people or things means to send them, tell them, or show them the way.

7 To direct a film, a play, or a television programme means to organize the way it is made and performed.

direct current NOUN
Direct current is a term used in physics to refer to an electric current that always flows in the same direction.

direction [dɪ'rɛkʃən] **directions** NOUN

1 the general line that someone or something is moving or pointing in
THESAURUS
course: *The captain altered course.*
path: *He stepped into the path of a reversing car.*
route: *We took the wrong route.*
way: *Does anybody know the way to the bathroom?*

2 Direction is the controlling and guiding of something. *e.g. He was chopping vegetables under the chef's direction.*
THESAURUS
charge: *A few years ago he took charge of the company.*

d

command: *In 1942 he took command of 108 Squadron.*
control: *The restructuring involves Ronson giving up control of the company.*
guidance: *the reports which were produced under his guidance*
leadership: *The agency doubled in size under her leadership.*
management: *The zoo needed better management.*

> PLURAL NOUN

3 Directions are instructions that tell you how to do something or how to get somewhere.

directive [dɪˈrɛktɪv] **directives** NOUN
an instruction that must be obeyed *e.g. a directive banning cigarette advertising*

directly [dɪˈrɛktlɪ] ADVERB
in a straight line or immediately *e.g. He looked directly at Rose.*

director [dɪˈrɛktə] **directors** NOUN
1 a member of the board of a company or institution
2 (**DRAMA**) the person responsible for the making and performance of a programme, play, or film
directorial ADJECTIVE

directorate [dɪˈrɛktərɪt] **directorates**
NOUN
a board of directors of a company or organization

directory [dɪˈrɛktərɪ] **directories** NOUN
1 a book which gives lists of facts, such as names and addresses, and is usually arranged in alphabetical order
2 another name for **folder**

direct speech NOUN
the reporting of what someone has said by quoting the exact words

dirge [dɜːdʒ] **dirges** NOUN
a slow, sad piece of music, sometimes played or sung at funerals

dirt [dɜːt] NOUN
1 Dirt is any unclean substance, such as dust, mud, or stains.
● THESAURUS
dust: *The furniture was covered in dust.*
filth: *tons of filth and sewage*
grime: *Kelly got the grime off his hands.*
muck: *This congealed muck was interfering with the filter.*
mud: *Their lorry got stuck in the mud.*
2 Dirt is also earth or soil.
[WORD HISTORY: from Old Norse DRIT meaning 'excrement']
● THESAURUS
earth: *a huge pile of earth*

soil: *an area with very good soil*

dirty [ˈdɜːtɪ] **dirtier, dirtiest** ADJECTIVE
1 marked or covered with dirt
● THESAURUS
filthy: *a pair of filthy jeans*
grimy: *a grimy industrial city*
grubby: *kids with grubby faces*
mucky: *a mucky floor*
muddy: *his muddy boots*
soiled: *a soiled white apron*
unclean: *unclean water*
<<OPPOSITE *clean*

2 unfair or dishonest *e.g. a dirty fight*
● THESAURUS
corrupt: *corrupt practices*
crooked: *crooked business deals*
<<OPPOSITE *honest*

3 about sex in a way that many people find offensive *e.g. dirty jokes*
● THESAURUS
blue: *a blue movie*
filthy: *a filthy book*
pornographic: *pornographic videos*
rude: *a rude joke*

dis- PREFIX
Dis- is added to the beginning of a word to form a word that means the opposite. *e.g. discontented*

disability [ˌdɪsəˈbɪlɪtɪ] **disabilities** NOUN
a physical or mental condition or illness that restricts someone's way of life

disable [dɪsˈeɪbəl] **disables, disabling, disabled** VERB
If something disables someone, it injures or harms them physically or mentally and severely affects their life.
disablement NOUN

disabled [dɪˈseɪbəld] ADJECTIVE
lacking one or more physical powers, such as the ability to walk or to coordinate one's movements

disadvantage [ˌdɪsədˈvɑːntɪdʒ]
disadvantages NOUN
an unfavourable or harmful circumstance
disadvantaged ADJECTIVE
● THESAURUS
drawback: *The apartment's only drawback was that it was too small.*
handicap: *The tax issue was undoubtedly a handicap to Labour.*
minus: *The plusses and minuses were about equal.*
weakness: *the strengths and weaknesses of the argument*
<<OPPOSITE *advantage*

disaffected [ˌdɪsəˈfɛktɪd] ADJECTIVE
If someone is disaffected with an idea or

organization, they no longer believe in it or support it. *e.g. disaffected voters*

disagree [,dɪsə'griː] **disagrees, disagreeing, disagreed** VERB

1 If you disagree with someone, you have a different view or opinion from theirs.

THESAURUS

differ: *They differ on lots of issues.*
dispute: *Nobody disputed that Davey was clever.*
dissent: *dissenting views*
<<OPPOSITE *agree*

2 If you disagree with an action or proposal, you disapprove of it and believe it is wrong. *e.g. He detested her and disagreed with her policies.*

THESAURUS

object: *We objected strongly but were outvoted.*
oppose: *protesters opposing nuclear tests*
take issue with: *I take issue with much of what he said.*

3 If food or drink disagrees with you, it makes you feel unwell.

disagreeable [,dɪsə'griːəbəl] ADJECTIVE
unpleasant or unhelpful and unfriendly *e.g. a disagreeable odour*

THESAURUS

horrible: *a horrible small boy*
horrid: *What a horrid smell!*
nasty: *What a nasty little snob you are!*
objectionable: *an objectionable, stuck-up young woman*
obnoxious: *One of the parents was a most obnoxious character.*
unfriendly: *She spoke in a loud, rather unfriendly voice.*
unpleasant: *The side-effects can be unpleasant.*
<<OPPOSITE *agreeable*

disagreement [,dɪsə'griːmənt] **disagreements** NOUN

1 a dispute about something

THESAURUS

altercation: formal *an altercation with the referee*
argument: *an argument about money*
difference: *We have our differences but we get along.*
dispute: *a pay dispute*
quarrel: *I had a terrible quarrel with my brother.*
row: *a major diplomatic row*
squabble: *minor squabbles about phone bills*
tiff: *a lovers' tiff*
<<OPPOSITE *agreement*

2 an objection to something

THESAURUS

dissent: *voices of dissent*
objection: *I have no objection to banks making money.*

opposition: *their opposition to the scheme*

disappear [,dɪsə'pɪə] **disappears, disappearing, disappeared** VERB

1 If something or someone disappears, they go out of sight or become lost.

THESAURUS

be lost to view: *They observed the comet for 70 days before it was lost to view.*
drop out of sight: *After his first film he dropped out of sight.*
fade: *We watched the harbour fade into the mist.*
recede: *Luke receded into the distance.*
vanish: *Anne vanished from outside her home the Wednesday before last.*
<<OPPOSITE *appear*

2 To disappear also means to stop existing or happening. *e.g. The pain has disappeared.*
disappearance NOUN

THESAURUS

cease: formal *At 1 o'clock the rain ceased.*
die out: *How did the dinosaurs die out?*
go away: *All she wanted was for the pain to go away.*
melt away: *His anger melted away.*
pass: *He told her the fear would pass.*
vanish: *species which have vanished*

disappoint [,dɪsə'pɔɪnt] **disappoints, disappointing, disappointed** VERB
If someone or something disappoints you, it fails to live up to what you expected of it.

disappointed [,dɪsə'pɔɪntɪd] ADJECTIVE
sad because something has not happened

THESAURUS

dejected: *Her refusal left him feeling dejected.*
despondent: *After the interview John was despondent.*
disenchanted: *She has become very disenchanted with the marriage.*
disillusioned: *I've become very disillusioned with politics.*
downcast: *After his defeat Mr Rabin looked downcast.*
saddened: *He is saddened that they did not win anything.*
<<OPPOSITE *satisfied*

disappointment [,dɪsə'pɔɪntmənt] **disappointments** NOUN

1 a feeling of being disappointed

THESAURUS

dejection: *There was an air of dejection about her.*
despondency: *a mood of gloom and despondency*
regret: *my one great regret in life*

2 something that disappoints you

THESAURUS

blow: *It was a terrible blow when he was made redundant.*

setback: *a setback for the peace process*

disapproval [ˌdɪsəˈpruːvᵊl] NOUN
the belief that something is wrong or
inappropriate

● **THESAURUS**
censure: *He deserves support, not censure.*
condemnation: *the universal condemnation of
French nuclear tests*
criticism: *actions which have attracted fierce
criticism*
<<OPPOSITE *approval*

disapprove [ˌdɪsəˈpruːv] **disapproves,
disapproving, disapproved** VERB
To disapprove of something or someone means
to believe they are wrong or bad. *e.g. Everyone
disapproved of their marrying so young.*
disapproving ADJECTIVE

● **THESAURUS**
condemn: *Political leaders condemned the speech.*
deplore: formal *He deplores violence.*
dislike: *Her father seemed to dislike all her
boyfriends.*
find unacceptable: *I find such behaviour totally
unacceptable.*
take a dim view of: *They took a dim view of local
trade unionists.*
<<OPPOSITE *approve*

disarm [dɪsˈɑːm] **disarms, disarming,
disarmed** VERB
1 To disarm means to get rid of weapons.
2 If someone disarms you, they overcome your
anger or doubt by charming or soothing you. *e.g.
Mahoney was almost disarmed by the frankness.*
disarming ADJECTIVE

disarmament [dɪsˈɑːməmənt] NOUN
Disarmament is the reducing or getting rid of
military forces and weapons.

disarray [ˌdɪsəˈreɪ] NOUN
Disarray is a state of disorder and confusion. *e.g.
Our army was in disarray and practically weaponless.*

disassemble [ˌdɪsəˈsɛmbᵊl] **disassembles,
disassembling, disassembled** VERB
(D & T) To disassemble a structure or object
which has been made up or built from several
smaller parts is to separate its parts from one
another.

disaster [dɪˈzɑːstə] **disasters** NOUN
1 an event or accident that causes great distress
or destruction

● **THESAURUS**
calamity: formal *It could only end in calamity.*
catastrophe: *War would be a catastrophe.*
misfortune: *She seemed to enjoy the misfortunes of
others.*
tragedy: *They have suffered an enormous personal
tragedy.*

2 a complete failure
disastrous ADJECTIVE, **disastrously** ADVERB

disband [dɪsˈbænd] **disbands, disbanding,
disbanded** VERB
When a group of people disbands, it officially
ceases to exist.

disc [dɪsk] **discs;** also spelt **disk** NOUN
1 a flat round object *e.g. a tax disc... a compact disc*
2 one of the thin circular pieces of cartilage
which separate the bones in your spine
3 In computing, another spelling of **disk**

discard [dɪsˈkɑːd] **discards, discarding,
discarded** VERB
To discard something means to get rid of it,
because you no longer want it or find it useful.

● **THESAURUS**
cast aside: *In America we seem to cast aside our
elderly people.*
dispose of: *how he disposed of the murder weapon*
dump: informal *The getaway car was dumped near
the motorway.*
jettison: *The crew jettisoned excess fuel.*
shed: *a snake that has shed its skin*
throw away: *I never throw anything away.*
throw out: *Why don't you throw out all those old
magazines?*

discern [dɪˈsɜːn] **discerns, discerning,
discerned** VERB FORMAL
To discern something means to notice or
understand it clearly. *e.g. The film had no plot that I
could discern.*

● **THESAURUS**
detect: *Arnold could detect a certain sadness in the
old man's face.*
make out: *I could just make out a shadowy figure
through the mist.*
notice: *Mrs Shedden noticed a bird sitting on the
garage roof.*
observe: *In 1664 Hooke observed a reddish spot on
the planet's surface.*
perceive: *Get pupils to perceive the relationship
between success and effort.*
see: *Supporters saw in him a champion of the
oppressed.*
spot: *I've spotted an error in your calculations.*

discernible [dɪˈsɜːnəbᵊl] ADJECTIVE
able to be seen or recognized *e.g. no discernible
talent*

discerning [dɪˈsɜːnɪŋ] ADJECTIVE
having good taste and judgment
discernment NOUN

**discharge discharges, discharging,
discharged** VERB [dɪsˈtʃɑːdʒ]
1 If something discharges or is discharged, it is
given or sent out. *e.g. Oil discharged into the
world's oceans.*

d

THESAURUS
emit: *the amount of greenhouse gases emitted*
empty: *companies which enpty toxic by-products into rivers*
expel: *Poisonous gas is expelled into the atmosphere.*
flush: *Flush out all the sewage.*
give off: *natural gas, which gives off less carbon dioxide than coal*
release: *a weapon which releases toxic nerve gas*

2 To discharge someone from hospital means to allow them to leave.

THESAURUS
free: *The country is set to free more prisoners.*
let go: *They held him for three hours and then let him go.*
liberate: *They promised to liberate prisoners held in detention camps.*
release: *He was released on bail.*
set free: *More than ninety prisoners have been set free.*

3 If someone is discharged from a job, they are dismissed from it.

THESAURUS
dismiss: *The military commander has been dismissed.*
eject: *He was ejected from his first job for persistent latecoming.*
fire: *informal If he wasn't so good at his job, I'd fire him.*
sack: *informal The teacher was sacked for slapping a schoolboy.*

> NOUN ['dɪstʃɑːdʒ]
4 a substance that is released from the inside of something *e.g. a thick nasal discharge*
5 a dismissal or release from a job or an institution

THESAURUS
dismissal: *shock at the director's dismissal from his post*
ejection: *These actions led to his ejection from office.*
expulsion: *his expulsion from the party in 1955*
the sack: *informal People who make mistakes can be given the sack.*

disciple [dɪ'saɪpəl] **disciples** NOUN
(RE) a follower of someone or something, especially one of the twelve men who were followers and helpers of Christ

discipline ['dɪsɪplɪn] **disciplines, disciplining, disciplined** NOUN
1 (PSHE) Discipline is making people obey rules and punishing them when they break them.
2 (PSHE) Discipline is the ability to behave and work in a controlled way.

> VERB (PSHE)
3 If you discipline yourself, you train yourself to behave and work in an ordered way.

4 To discipline someone means to punish them.
disciplinary ADJECTIVE, **disciplined** ADJECTIVE

disc jockey **disc jockeys** NOUN
someone who introduces and plays pop records on the radio or at a night club

disclose [dɪs'kləʊz] **discloses, disclosing, disclosed** VERB
To disclose something means to make it known or allow it to be seen.
disclosure NOUN

disco ['dɪskəʊ] **discos** NOUN
a party or a club where people go to dance to pop records

discomfort [dɪs'kʌmfət] **discomforts** NOUN
1 Discomfort is distress or slight pain.
2 Discomfort is also a feeling of worry or embarrassment.
3 Discomforts are things that make you uncomfortable.

disconcert [ˌdɪskən'sɜːt] **disconcerts, disconcerting, disconcerted** VERB
If something disconcerts you, it makes you feel uneasy or embarrassed.
disconcerting ADJECTIVE

disconnect [ˌdɪskə'nɛkt] **disconnects, disconnecting, disconnected** VERB
1 To disconnect something means to detach it from something else.
2 If someone disconnects your fuel supply or telephone, they cut you off.

discontent [ˌdɪskən'tɛnt] NOUN
Discontent is a feeling of dissatisfaction with conditions or with life in general. *e.g. He was aware of the discontent this policy had caused.*
discontented ADJECTIVE

discontinue [ˌdɪskən'tɪnjuː] **discontinues, discontinuing, discontinued** VERB
To discontinue something means to stop doing it.

discord ['dɪskɔːd] NOUN
Discord is unpleasantness or quarrelling between people.

discount **discounts, discounting, discounted** NOUN ['dɪskaʊnt]
1 a reduction in the price of something

> VERB [dɪs'kaʊnt]
2 If you discount something, you reject it or ignore it. *e.g. I haven't discounted her connection with the kidnapping case.*

discourage [dɪs'kʌrɪdʒ] **discourages, discouraging, discouraged** VERB
To discourage someone means to take away

243

their enthusiasm to do something.
discouraging ADJECTIVE, **discouragement** NOUN

● THESAURUS

daunt: *He was not the type of man to be daunted by adversity.*

deter: *Tougher sentences would do nothing to deter crime.*

dissuade: *He considered emigrating, but his family managed to dissuade him.*

put off: *I wouldn't let it put you off applying.*
<<OPPOSITE *encourage*

discourse ['dɪskɔːs] **discourses** FORMAL >
NOUN

1 a formal talk or piece of writing intended to teach or explain something

2 Discourse is serious conversation between people on a particular subject.

discover [dɪ'skʌvə] **discovers, discovering, discovered** VERB
When you discover something, you find it or find out about it.
discovery NOUN, **discoverer** NOUN

● THESAURUS

come across: *He came across the jawbone of a carnivorous dinosaur.*

find: *The police also found a pistol.*

find out: *Watch the next episode to find out what happens.*

learn: *The Admiral, on learning who I was, wanted to meet me.*

realize: *As soon as we realized something was wrong, we took action.*

stumble on or **across:** *They stumbled on a magnificent waterfall.*

unearth: *Researchers have unearthed documents implicating her in the crime.*

discredit [dɪs'krɛdɪt] **discredits, discrediting, discredited** VERB

1 To discredit someone means to damage their reputation.

2 To discredit an idea means to cause it to be doubted or not believed.

discreet [dɪ'skriːt] ADJECTIVE
If you are discreet, you avoid causing embarrassment when dealing with secret or private matters.
discreetly ADVERB

discrepancy [dɪ'skrɛpənsɪ] **discrepancies**
NOUN
a difference between two things which ought to be the same *e.g. discrepancies in his police interviews*

discrete [dɪs'kriːt] ADJECTIVE; FORMAL
separate and distinct *e.g. two discrete sets of nerves*

discretion [dɪ'skrɛʃən] NOUN

1 Discretion is the quality of behaving with care and tact so as to avoid embarrassment or distress to other people. *e.g. You can count on my discretion.*

2 Discretion is also freedom and authority to make decisions and take action according to your own judgment. *e.g. Class teachers have very limited discretion in decision-making.*
discretionary ADJECTIVE

discriminate [dɪ'skrɪmɪˌneɪt] **discriminates, discriminating, discriminated** VERB

1 To discriminate between things means to recognize and understand the differences between them.

2 To discriminate against a person or group means to treat them unfairly, usually because of their race, colour, or sex.

3 To discriminate in favour of a person or group means to treat them more favourably than others.
discrimination NOUN, **discriminatory** ADJECTIVE

discus ['dɪskəs] **discuses** NOUN
a disc-shaped object with a heavy middle, thrown by athletes

discuss [dɪ'skʌs] **discusses, discussing, discussed** VERB

1 When people discuss something, they talk about it in detail.

● THESAURUS

debate: *The UN Security Council will debate the issue today.*

exchange views on: *They exchanged views on a wide range of subjects.*

go into: *We didn't go into that.*

talk about: *What did you talk about?*

2 (**EXAM TERM**) To discuss a question is to look at the points or arguments of both sides and try to reach your own opinion.

discussion [dɪ'skʌʃən] **discussions** NOUN
(**PSHE**) a conversation or piece of writing in which a subject is considered in detail

● THESAURUS

consultation: *consultations between lawyers*

conversation: *I struck up a conversation with him.*

debate: *There has been a lot of debate among scholars about this.*

dialogue: *a direct dialogue between the two nations*

discourse: *a long tradition of political discourse*

talk: *We had a long talk about it.*

disdain [dɪs'deɪn] NOUN
Disdain is a feeling of superiority over or contempt for someone or something. *e.g. The candidates shared an equal disdain for the press.*
disdainful ADJECTIVE

disease [dɪ'ziːz] **diseases** NOUN
(**HISTORY**) an unhealthy condition in people, animals, or plants
diseased ADJECTIVE

disembark [ˌdɪsɪm'baːk] **disembarks, disembarking, disembarked** VERB
To disembark means to land or unload from a ship, aircraft, or bus.

disembodied [ˌdɪsɪm'bɒdɪd] ADJECTIVE
1 separate from or existing without a body e.g. a disembodied skull
2 seeming not to be attached or to come from anyone e.g. disembodied voices

disenchanted [ˌdɪsɪn'tʃaːntɪd] ADJECTIVE
disappointed with something, and no longer believing that it is good or worthwhile e.g. She is very disenchanted with the marriage.
disenchantment NOUN

disfigure [dɪs'fɪgə] **disfigures, disfiguring, disfigured** VERB
To disfigure something means to spoil its appearance. e.g. Graffiti or posters disfigured every wall.

disgrace [dɪs'greɪs] **disgraces, disgracing, disgraced** NOUN
1 Disgrace is a state in which someone is disapproved of by people.

● THESAURUS
scandal: They often abandoned their children because of fear of scandal.
shame: I don't want to bring shame on the family name.
<<OPPOSITE credit

2 If something is a disgrace, it is unacceptable. e.g. The overcrowded prisons were a disgrace.

3 If someone is a disgrace to a group of people, their behaviour makes the group feel ashamed. e.g. You're a disgrace to the school.

> VERB
4 If you disgrace yourself or disgrace someone else, you cause yourself or them to be strongly disapproved of by other people.

● THESAURUS
discredit: He said such methods discredited the communist fight worldwide.
shame: I wouldn't shame my father by doing that.

disgraceful [dɪs'greɪsfʊl] ADJECTIVE
If something is disgraceful, people disapprove of it strongly and think that those who are responsible for it should be ashamed.
disgracefully ADVERB

● THESAURUS
scandalous: a scandalous waste of money
shameful: the most shameful episode in US naval history

shocking: a shocking invasion of privacy

disgruntled [dɪs'grʌntᵊld] ADJECTIVE
discontented or in a bad mood

disguise [dɪs'gaɪz] **disguises, disguising, disguised** VERB
1 To disguise something means to change its appearance so that people do not recognize it.
2 To disguise a feeling means to hide it. e.g. I tried to disguise my relief.

> NOUN
3 something you wear or something you do to alter your appearance so that you cannot be recognized by other people

disgust [dɪs'gʌst] **disgusts, disgusting, disgusted** NOUN
1 Disgust is a strong feeling of dislike or disapproval.

● THESAURUS
nausea: I was overcome with a feeling of nausea.
repulsion: a shudder of repulsion
revulsion: They expressed their shock and revulsion at his death.

> VERB
2 To disgust someone means to make them feel a strong sense of dislike or disapproval.
disgusted ADJECTIVE

● THESAURUS
repel: a violent excitement that frightened and repelled her
revolt: The smell revolted him.
sicken: What he saw there sickened him.

disgusting [dɪs'gʌstɪŋ] ADJECTIVE
very unpleasant and offensive

● THESAURUS
foul: a foul stench
gross: Don't be so gross!
obnoxious: a most obnoxious character
repellent: a very large, repellent toad
revolting: The smell was revolting.
sickening: a sickening attack on a pregnant woman
vile: a vile odour

dish [dɪʃ] **dishes** NOUN
1 a shallow container for cooking or serving food
2 food of a particular kind or food cooked in a particular way e.g. two fish dishes to choose from

disheartened [dɪs'haːtᵊnd] ADJECTIVE
If you are disheartened, you feel disappointed.

dishevelled [dɪ'ʃevᵊld] ADJECTIVE
If someone looks dishevelled, their clothes or hair look untidy.

dishonest [dɪs'ɒnɪst] ADJECTIVE
not truthful or able to be trusted
dishonestly ADVERB

● THESAURUS

corrupt: *corrupt police officers*
crooked: *crooked business deals*
deceitful: *The ambassador called the report deceitful and misleading.*
fraudulent: *fraudulent claims about being a nurse*
lying: *He called her 'a lying little twit'.*
<<OPPOSITE *honest*

dishonesty [dɪs'ɒnɪstɪ] NOUN
Dishonesty is behaviour which is meant to deceive people, either by not telling the truth or by cheating.

● THESAURUS

cheating: *He was accused of cheating.*
corruption: *The President faces 54 charges of corruption.*
deceit: *the deceit and lies of the past*
trickery: *They resorted to trickery in order to impress their clients.*
<<OPPOSITE *honesty*

disillusioned [,dɪsɪ'luːʒənd] ADJECTIVE
If you are disillusioned with something, you are disappointed because it is not as good as you had expected.

disinfectant [,dɪsɪn'fɛktənt] **disinfectants**
NOUN
a chemical substance that kills germs

disintegrate [dɪs'ɪntɪ,greɪt] **disintegrates, disintegrating, disintegrated** VERB
1 If something disintegrates, it becomes weakened and is not effective. *e.g. My confidence disintegrated.*
2 If an object disintegrates, it breaks into many pieces and so is destroyed.
disintegration NOUN

● THESAURUS

break up: *There was a danger of the ship breaking up completely.*
crumble: *The flint crumbled into fragments.*
fall apart: *Bit by bit the building fell apart.*
fall to pieces: *The radio handset fell to pieces.*
fragment: *The clouds fragmented and out came the sun.*

disinterest [dɪs'ɪntrɪst] NOUN
1 Disinterest is a lack of interest.
2 Disinterest is also a lack of personal involvement in a situation.

disinterested [dɪs'ɪntrɪstɪd] ADJECTIVE
If someone is disinterested, they are not going to gain or lose from the situation they are involved in, and so can act in a way that is fair to both sides. *e.g. a disinterested judge*

> Some people use *disinterested* to mean 'not interested', but the word they should use is *uninterested*.

disjointed [dɪs'dʒɔɪntɪd] ADJECTIVE
If thought or speech is disjointed, it jumps from subject to subject and so is difficult to follow.

disk [dɪsk] **disks** NOUN
1 (ICT) In a computer, the disk is the part where information is stored. *e.g. The program takes up 2.5 megabytes of disk space.*
2 another spelling of **disc**

dislike [dɪs'laɪk] **dislikes, disliking, disliked** VERB
1 If you dislike something or someone, you think they are unpleasant and do not like them.

● THESAURUS

abhor: formal *a man who abhorred violence*
be averse to: *He's not averse to a little publicity.*
detest: *Jean detested being photographed.*
hate: *Most people hate him.*
loathe: *a play loathed by the critics*
not be able to abide: *I can't abide liars.*
not be able to bear: *I can't bear people who speak like that.*
not be able to stand: *He can't stand the sound of her voice.*
<<OPPOSITE *like*

> NOUN
2 Dislike is a feeling that you have when you do not like someone or something.

● THESAURUS

animosity: *The animosity between the two men grew.*
antipathy: *their antipathy to my smoking*
aversion: *I've always had an aversion to being part of a group.*
distaste: *Roger looked at her with distaste.*
hatred: *her hatred of authority*
hostility: *hostility to ethnic groups*
loathing: *He made no secret of his loathing of her.*
<<OPPOSITE *liking*

dislocate ['dɪslə,keɪt] **dislocates, dislocating, dislocated** VERB
To dislocate your bone or joint means to put it out of place.

dislodge [dɪs'lɒdʒ] **dislodges, dislodging, dislodged** VERB
To dislodge something means to move it or force it out of place.

dismal ['dɪzməl] ADJECTIVE
rather gloomy and depressing *e.g. dismal weather*
dismally ADVERB
[WORD HISTORY: from Latin DIES MALI meaning 'evil days']

dismantle [dɪs'mæntᵊl] **dismantles, dismantling, dismantled** VERB
To dismantle something means to take it apart.

dismay [dɪs'meɪ] **dismays, dismaying, dismayed** NOUN

1 Dismay is a feeling of fear and worry.

> VERB

2 If someone or something dismays you, it fills you with alarm and worry.

dismember [dɪsˈmɛmbə] **dismembers, dismembering, dismembered** VERB; FORMAL
To dismember a person or animal means to cut or tear their body into pieces.

dismiss [dɪsˈmɪs] **dismisses, dismissing, dismissed** VERB
1 If you dismiss something, you decide to ignore it because it is not important enough for you to think about.
2 To dismiss an employee means to ask that person to leave their job.
3 If someone in authority dismisses you, they tell you to leave.
dismissal NOUN

dismissive [dɪsˈmɪsɪv] ADJECTIVE
If you are dismissive of something or someone, you show that you think they are of little importance or value. *e.g. a dismissive gesture*

disobey [ˌdɪsəˈbeɪ] **disobeys, disobeying, disobeyed** VERB
To disobey a person or an order means to deliberately refuse to do what you are told.

● THESAURUS
break: *drivers breaking speed limits*
defy: *the first time that I dared to defy my mother*
flout: *illegal campers who persist in flouting the law*
infringe: *He was adamant that he had infringed no rules.*
violate: *formal They violated the ceasefire agreement.*
<<OPPOSITE *obey*

disorder [dɪsˈɔːdə] **disorders** NOUN
1 Disorder is a state of untidiness.

● THESAURUS
clutter: *She prefers the worktop to be free of clutter.*
disarray: *Her clothes were in disarray.*
muddle: *a general muddle of pencils and boxes*
<<OPPOSITE *order*

2 Disorder is also a lack of organization. *e.g. The men fled in disorder.*

● THESAURUS
chaos: *Their concerts often ended in chaos.*
confusion: *There was confusion when a man fired shots.*
disarray: *The nation is in disarray following rioting.*
turmoil: *the political turmoil of 1989*

3 a disease *e.g. a stomach disorder*

● THESAURUS
affliction: *an affliction which can ruin a young man's life*

complaint: *a common skin complaint*
condition: *a heart condition*
disease: *heart disease*
illness: *mental illness*

disorganized or **disorganised** [dɪsˈɔːgəˌnaɪzd] ADJECTIVE
If something is disorganized, it is confused and badly prepared or badly arranged.
disorganization NOUN

disown [dɪsˈəʊn] **disowns, disowning, disowned** VERB
To disown someone or something means to refuse to admit any connection with them.

disparaging [dɪˈspærɪdʒɪŋ] ADJECTIVE
critical and scornful *e.g. disparaging remarks*

disparate [ˈdɪspərɪt] ADJECTIVE; FORMAL
Things that are disparate are utterly different from one another.
disparity NOUN

dispatch [dɪˈspætʃ] **dispatches, dispatching, dispatched**; also spelt **despatch** VERB
1 To dispatch someone or something to a particular place means to send them there for a special reason. *e.g. The president dispatched him on a fact-finding visit.*

> NOUN

2 an official written message, often sent to an army or government headquarters

dispel [dɪˈspɛl] **dispels, dispelling, dispelled** VERB
To dispel fears or beliefs means to drive them away or to destroy them. *e.g. The myths are being dispelled.*

dispensary [dɪˈspɛnsərɪ] **dispensaries** NOUN
a place where medicines are prepared and given out

dispense [dɪˈspɛns] **dispenses, dispensing, dispensed** VERB
1 FORMAL
To dispense something means to give it out. *e.g. They dispense advice.*

2 To dispense medicines means to prepare them and give them out.

3 To dispense with something means to do without it or do away with it. *e.g. We'll dispense with formalities.*

dispenser [dɪˈspɛnsə] **dispensers** NOUN
a machine or container from which you can get things *e.g. a cash dispenser*

disperse [dɪˈspɜːs] **disperses, dispersing, dispersed** VERB

1 When something disperses, it scatters over a wide area.

2 When people disperse or when someone disperses them, they move apart and go in different directions.

dispersion NOUN

dispirited [dɪˈspɪrɪtɪd] ADJECTIVE
depressed and having no enthusiasm for anything

dispiriting [dɪˈspɪrɪtɪŋ] ADJECTIVE
Something dispiriting makes you depressed. *e.g. a dispiriting defeat*

displace [dɪsˈpleɪs] **displaces, displacing, displaced** VERB

1 If one thing displaces another, it forces the thing out of its usual place and occupies that place itself.

2 If people are displaced, they are forced to leave their home or country.

displacement [dɪsˈpleɪsmənt] NOUN
Displacement is the removal of something from its usual or correct place or position.

display [dɪˈspleɪ] **displays, displaying, displayed** VERB

1 If you display something, you show it or make it visible to people.

2 If you display something such as an emotion, you behave in a way that shows you feel it.

> NOUN

3 (ART) an arrangement of things designed to attract people's attention

displease [dɪsˈpliːz] **displeases, displeasing, displeased** VERB
If someone or something displeases you, they make you annoyed, dissatisfied, or offended.

displeasure NOUN

disposable [dɪˈspəʊzəbəl] ADJECTIVE
designed to be thrown away after use *e.g. disposable nappies*

disposal [dɪˈspəʊzəl] NOUN
Disposal is the act of getting rid of something that is no longer wanted or needed.

dispose [dɪˈspəʊz] **disposes, disposing, disposed** VERB

1 To dispose of something means to get rid of it.

⬤ THESAURUS

discard: *Read the instructions before discarding the box.*

dispense with: *We got a CD-player and dispensed with our old-fashioned record-player.*

dump: *The government declared that it did not dump radioactive waste at sea.*

get rid of: *The owner needs to get rid of the car for financial reasons.*

jettison: *The crew jettisoned excess fuel and made an emergency landing.*

throw away: *I never throw anything away.*

2 If you are not disposed to do something, you are not willing to do it.

disprove [dɪsˈpruːv] **disproves, disproving, disproved** VERB
If someone disproves an idea, belief, or theory, they show that it is not true.

⬤ THESAURUS

discredit: *There would be difficulties in discrediting the evidence.*

give the lie to: *This survey gives the lie to the idea that the economy is recovering.*

invalidate: *Some of the other criticisms were invalidated years ago.*

prove false: *It is hard to prove such claims false.*

refute: *the kind of rumour that is impossible to refute*

<<OPPOSITE *prove*

dispute disputes, disputing, disputed
NOUN [ˈdɪspjuːt]

1 an argument

⬤ THESAURUS

argument: *a heated argument*

clash: *the clash between trade union leaders and the government*

conflict: *Avoid any conflict between yourself and your ex-partner.*

disagreement: *disagreements among the member states*

feud: *a bitter feud between the state government and the villagers*

row: *a major diplomatic row with France*

wrangle: *a legal wrangle*

> VERB [dɪˈspjuːt]

2 To dispute a fact or theory means to question the truth of it.

⬤ THESAURUS

challenge: *I challenge the wisdom of this decision.*

contest: *Your former employer wants to contest the case.*

contradict: *Her version contradicted the Government's claim.*

deny: *She denied both accusations.*

query: *No one queried my decision.*

question: *It never occurred to me to question the doctor's diagnosis.*

<<OPPOSITE *accept*

disqualify [dɪsˈkwɒlɪˌfaɪ] **disqualifies, disqualifying, disqualified** VERB
If someone is disqualified from a competition or activity, they are officially stopped from taking part in it. *e.g. He was disqualified from driving for 18 months.*

disqualification NOUN

disquiet [dɪsˈkwaɪət] NOUN
Disquiet is worry or anxiety.
disquieting ADJECTIVE

disregard [ˌdɪsrɪˈɡɑːd] **disregards,
disregarding, disregarded** VERB
1 To disregard something means to pay little or
no attention to it.
> NOUN
2 Disregard is a lack of attention or respect for
something. *e.g. He exhibited a flagrant disregard of
the law.*

disrepair [ˌdɪsrɪˈpɛə] PHRASE
If something is **in disrepair** or **in a state of
disrepair**, it is broken or in poor condition.

disrespect [ˌdɪsrɪˈspɛkt] NOUN
Disrespect is contempt or lack of respect. *e.g. his
disrespect for authority*
disrespectful ADJECTIVE

disrupt [dɪsˈrʌpt] **disrupts, disrupting,
disrupted** VERB
To disrupt something such as an event or system
means to break it up or throw it into confusion.
e.g. Strikes disrupted air traffic in Italy.
disruption NOUN, **disruptive** ADJECTIVE

dissatisfied [dɪsˈsætɪsˌfaɪd] ADJECTIVE
not pleased or not contented
dissatisfaction NOUN

dissect [dɪˈsɛkt] **dissects, dissecting,
dissected** VERB
To dissect a plant or a dead body means to cut it
up so that it can be scientifically examined.
dissection NOUN

dissent [dɪˈsɛnt] **dissents, dissenting,
dissented** NOUN
1 Dissent is strong difference of opinion. *e.g.
political dissent*
> VERB
2 When people dissent, they express a difference
of opinion about something.
dissenting ADJECTIVE

dissertation [ˌdɪsəˈteɪʃən] **dissertations**
NOUN
a long essay, especially for a university degree

disservice [dɪsˈsɜːvɪs] NOUN
To do someone a disservice means to do
something that harms them.

dissident [ˈdɪsɪdənt] **dissidents** NOUN
someone who disagrees with and criticizes the
strict and unjust government of their country

dissimilar [dɪˈsɪmɪlə] ADJECTIVE
If things are dissimilar, they are unlike each
other.

dissipate [ˈdɪsɪˌpeɪt] **dissipates,
dissipating, dissipated** VERB

1 FORMAL
When something dissipates or is dissipated, it
completely disappears. *e.g. The cloud seemed to
dissipate there.*
2 If someone dissipates time, money, or effort,
they waste it.

dissipated [ˈdɪsɪˌpeɪtɪd] ADJECTIVE
Someone who is dissipated shows signs of
indulging too much in alcohol or other physical
pleasures.

dissolve [dɪˈzɒlv] **dissolves, dissolving,
dissolved** VERB
1 (**SCIENCE**) If you dissolve something or if it
dissolves in a liquid, it becomes mixed with and
absorbed in the liquid.
2 To dissolve an organization or institution
means to officially end it.

dissuade [dɪˈsweɪd] **dissuades,
dissuading, dissuaded** VERB
To dissuade someone from doing something or
from believing something means to persuade
them not to do it or not to believe it.

distance [ˈdɪstəns] **distances, distancing,
distanced** NOUN
1 The distance between two points is how far it is
between them.
2 Distance is the fact of being far away in space
or time.
> VERB
3 If you distance yourself from someone or
something or are distanced from them, you
become less involved with them.

distant [ˈdɪstənt] ADJECTIVE
1 far away in space or time
● THESAURUS
far: *Is it very far?*
outlying: *outlying districts*
out-of-the-way: *an out-of-the-way spot*
remote: *a remote village*
<<OPPOSITE *close*

2 A distant relative is one who is not closely
related to you.
3 Someone who is distant is cold and unfriendly.
distantly ADVERB
● THESAURUS
aloof: *He seemed aloof and detached.*
detached: *He observed me with a detached
curiosity.*
reserved: *She's quite a reserved person.*
withdrawn: *Her husband had become withdrawn
and moody.*
<<OPPOSITE *friendly*

distaste [dɪsˈteɪst] NOUN
Distaste is a dislike of something which you find
offensive.

d

distasteful [dɪsˈteɪstfʊl] ADJECTIVE
If you find something distasteful, you think it is unpleasant or offensive.

distil [dɪsˈtɪl] **distils, distilling, distilled**
VERB
(SCIENCE) When a liquid is distilled, it is heated until it evaporates and then cooled to enable purified liquid to be collected.
distillation NOUN

distillery [dɪsˈtɪlərɪ] **distilleries** NOUN
a place where whisky or other strong alcoholic drink is made, using a process of distillation

distinct [dɪsˈtɪŋkt] ADJECTIVE
1 If one thing is distinct from another, it is recognizably different from it. *e.g. A word may have two quite distinct meanings.*

2 If something is distinct, you can hear, smell, or see it clearly and plainly. *e.g. There was a distinct buzzing noise.*

3 If something such as a fact, idea, or intention is distinct, it is clear and definite. *e.g. She had a distinct feeling someone was watching them.*
distinctly ADVERB

distinction [dɪsˈtɪŋkʃən] **distinctions** NOUN
1 a difference between two things *e.g. a distinction between the body and the soul*

2 Distinction is a quality of excellence and superiority. *e.g. a man of distinction*

3 a special honour or claim *e.g. It had the distinction of being the largest square in Europe.*

distinctive [dɪsˈtɪŋktɪv] ADJECTIVE
Something that is distinctive has a special quality which makes it recognizable. *e.g. a distinctive voice*
distinctively ADVERB

distinguish [dɪsˈtɪŋgwɪʃ] **distinguishes, distinguishing, distinguished** VERB
1 To distinguish between things means to recognize the difference between them. *e.g. I've learned to distinguish business and friendship.*
⏺ THESAURUS
differentiate: *At this age your baby cannot differentiate one person from another.*
discriminate: *He is unable to discriminate a good idea from a terrible one.*
tell: *How do you tell one from another?*
tell apart: *I can only tell them apart by the colour of their shoes.*
tell the difference: *I can't tell the difference between their policies and ours.*

2 To distinguish something means to make it out by seeing, hearing, or tasting it. *e.g. I heard shouting but was unable to distinguish the words.*
⏺ THESAURUS
discern: *We could just discern a narrow ditch.*

make out: *He couldn't make out what she was saying.*
pick out: *Through my binoculars I picked out a group of figures.*
recognize: *He did not think she could recognize his car in the snow.*

3 If you distinguish yourself, you do something that makes people think highly of you.
distinguishable ADJECTIVE, **distinguishing** ADJECTIVE

distort [dɪsˈtɔːt] **distorts, distorting, distorted** VERB
1 If you distort a statement or an argument, you represent it in an untrue or misleading way.

2 If something is distorted, it is changed so that it seems strange or unclear. *e.g. His voice was distorted.*

3 If an object is distorted, it is twisted or pulled out of shape.
distorted ADJECTIVE, **distortion** NOUN

distract [dɪsˈtrækt] **distracts, distracting, distracted** VERB
If something distracts you, your attention is taken away from what you are doing.
distracted ADJECTIVE, **distractedly** ADVERB, **distracting** ADJECTIVE
⏺ THESAURUS
divert: *They want to divert our attention from the real issues.*
draw away: *to draw attention away from the crime*

distraction [dɪsˈtrækʃən] **distractions** NOUN
1 something that takes people's attention away from something

2 an activity that is intended to amuse or relax someone

distraught [dɪsˈtrɔːt] ADJECTIVE
so upset and worried that you cannot think clearly *e.g. He was distraught over the death of his mother.*

distress [dɪsˈtrɛs] **distresses, distressing, distressed** NOUN
1 Distress is great suffering caused by pain or sorrow.
⏺ THESAURUS
heartache: *the heartache of her divorce*
pain: *eyes that seemed filled with pain*
sorrow: *a time of great sorrow*
suffering: *to put an end to his suffering*

2 Distress is also the state of needing help because of difficulties or danger.
⏺ THESAURUS
difficulty: *rumours about banks being in difficulty*
need: *When you were in need, I loaned you money.*

straits: *The company's closure left them in desperate financial straits.*

trouble: *a charity that helps women in trouble*

> VERB

3 To distress someone means to make them feel alarmed or unhappy. *e.g. Her death had profoundly distressed me.*

● THESAURUS

bother: *It bothered me that boys weren't interested in me.*

disturb: *dreams so vivid that they disturb me for days*

grieve: *It grieved her to be separated from her son.*

pain: *It pains me to think of you struggling all alone.*

sadden: *The cruelty in the world saddens me deeply.*

trouble: *He was troubled by the lifestyle of his son.*

upset: *I'm sorry if I've upset you.*

worry: *I didn't want to worry you.*

distressing [dɪ'strɛsɪŋ] ADJECTIVE
very worrying or upsetting

distribute [dɪ'strɪbjuːt] **distributes, distributing, distributed** VERB

1 To distribute something such as leaflets means to hand them out or deliver them. *e.g. They publish and distribute brochures.*

● THESAURUS

circulate: *He has circulated a discussion document.*

hand out: *One of my jobs was to hand out the prizes.*

pass around: *Sweets were being passed around.*

pass round: *She passed her holiday photos round.*

2 If things are distributed, they are spread throughout an area or space. *e.g. Distribute the cheese evenly on top of the quiche.*

● THESAURUS

diffuse: *Interest in books is more widely diffused than ever.*

disperse: *The leaflets were dispersed throughout the country.*

scatter: *She scattered the petals over the grave.*

spread: *A thick layer of wax was spread over the surface.*

3 To distribute something means to divide it and share it out among a number of people.

● THESAURUS

allocate: *funds allocated for nursery education*

allot: *The seats are allotted to the candidates who have won the most votes.*

dispense: formal *The Union had already dispensed £400 in grants.*

divide: *Paul divides his spare time between the bedroom and the study.*

dole out: *I got out my wallet and began to dole out the money.*

share out: *You could share out the money a bit more equally.*

distribution [ˌdɪstrɪ'bjuːʃən] **distributions** NOUN

1 Distribution is the delivering of something to various people or organizations. *e.g. the distribution of vicious leaflets*

2 Distribution is the sharing out of something to various people. *e.g. distribution of power*

distributor [dɪ'strɪbjʊtə] **distributors** NOUN
a company that supplies goods to other businesses who then sell them to the public

district ['dɪstrɪkt] **districts** NOUN
an area of a town or country *e.g. a residential district*

district nurse district nurses NOUN
a nurse who visits and treats people in their own homes

distrust [dɪs'trʌst] **distrusts, distrusting, distrusted** VERB

1 If you distrust someone, you are suspicious of them because you are not sure whether they are honest.

> NOUN

2 Distrust is suspicion.

distrustful ADJECTIVE

disturb [dɪ'stɜːb] **disturbs, disturbing, disturbed** VERB

1 If you disturb someone, you break their peace or privacy.

● THESAURUS

bother: *I'm sorry to bother you.*

disrupt: *Protesters disrupted the debate.*

intrude on: *I don't want to intrude on your parents.*

2 If something disturbs you, it makes you feel upset or worried.

● THESAURUS

agitate: *The thought agitated her.*

distress: *Her death had profoundly distressed me.*

shake: *Well, it shook me quite a bit.*

trouble: *He was troubled by the lifestyle of his son.*

unsettle: *The presence of the two policemen unsettled her.*

upset: *I'm sorry if I've upset you.*

worry: *I didn't want to worry you.*

3 If something is disturbed, it is moved out of position or meddled with.

disturbing ADJECTIVE

disturbance [dɪ'stɜːbəns] **disturbances** NOUN

1 Disturbance is the state of being disturbed.

2 a violent or unruly incident in public

disuse [dɪs'juːs] NOUN
Something that has fallen into disuse is neglected or no longer used.

disused ADJECTIVE

ditch [dɪtʃ] **ditches** NOUN
a channel at the side of a road or field, to drain away excess water

dither ['dɪðə] **dithers, dithering, dithered** VERB
To dither means to be unsure and hesitant.

ditto ['dɪtəʊ]
Ditto means 'the same'. In written lists, ditto is represented by a mark (") to avoid repetition.
[WORD HISTORY: from Italian DETTO meaning 'said']

ditty ['dɪtɪ] **ditties** NOUN; OLD-FASHIONED, INFORMAL
a short simple song or poem

diva ['diːvə] **divas** NOUN
a great or leading female singer, especially in opera
[WORD HISTORY: from Latin DIVA meaning 'a goddess']

dive [daɪv] **dives, diving, dived** VERB
1 To dive means to jump head first into water with your arms held straight above your head.
THESAURUS
jump: *He ran along the board and jumped in.*
leap: *as she leapt into the water*
submerge: *Hippos are unable to submerge in the few remaining water holes.*
2 If you go diving, you go down under the surface of the sea or a lake using special breathing equipment.
3 If an aircraft or bird dives, it flies in a steep downward path, or drops sharply.
diver NOUN, **diving** NOUN

diverge [daɪ'vɜːdʒ] **diverges, diverging, diverged** VERB
1 If opinions or facts diverge, they differ. *e.g. Theory and practice sometimes diverged.*
2 If two things such as roads or paths which have been going in the same direction diverge, they separate and go off in different directions.
divergence NOUN, **divergent** ADJECTIVE

diverse [daɪ'vɜːs] ADJECTIVE
1 If a group of things is diverse, it is made up of different kinds of things. *e.g. a diverse range of goods and services*
2 People, ideas, or objects that are diverse are very different from each other.
diversity NOUN

diversify [daɪ'vɜːsɪˌfaɪ] **diversifies, diversifying, diversified** VERB
To diversify means to increase the variety of something. *e.g. Has the company diversified into new areas?.*
diversification NOUN

diversion [daɪ'vɜːʃən] **diversions** NOUN

1 a special route arranged for traffic when the usual route is closed
2 something that takes your attention away from what you should be concentrating on *e.g. A break for tea created a welcome diversion.*
3 a pleasant or amusing activity

divert [daɪ'vɜːt] **diverts, diverting, diverted** VERB
To divert something means to change the course or direction it is following.
diverting ADJECTIVE

divide [dɪ'vaɪd] **divides, dividing, divided** VERB
1 When something divides or is divided, it is split up and separated into two or more parts.
THESAURUS
cut up: *Halve the tomatoes, then cut them up.*
partition: *a plan to partition the country*
segregate: *Police were used to segregate the two rival camps.*
separate: *Fluff the rice with a fork to separate the grains.*
split: *Split the chicken in half.*
split up: *He split up the company.*
<<OPPOSITE *join*
2 If something divides two areas, it forms a barrier between them.
THESAURUS
bisect: *The main street bisects the town.*
separate: *the fence that separated the yard from the paddock*
3 If people divide over something or if something divides them, it causes strong disagreement between them.
THESAURUS
come between: *It's difficult to imagine anything coming between them.*
set against one another: *The case has set neighbours against one another in the village.*
split: *Women priests are accused of splitting the church.*
4 (MATHS) In mathematics, when you divide, you calculate how many times one number contains another.
> NOUN
5 a separation *e.g. the class divide*

dividend ['dɪvɪˌdɛnd] **dividends** NOUN
a portion of a company's profits that is paid to shareholders

divine [dɪ'vaɪn] **divines, divining, divined** ADJECTIVE
1 having the qualities of a god or goddess
> VERB
2 To divine something means to discover it by guessing.

divinely ADVERB

divinity [dɪ'vɪnɪtɪ] **divinities** NOUN
1 Divinity is the study of religion.
2 Divinity is the state of being a god.
3 a god or goddess

division [dɪ'vɪʒən] **divisions** NOUN
1 Division is the separation of something into two or more distinct parts.

⬤ THESAURUS
partition: *fighting which followed the partition of India*
separation: *the separation of church and state*

2 (**MATHS**) Division is also the process of dividing one number by another.
3 a difference of opinion that causes separation between ideas or groups of people *e.g. There were divisions in the Party on economic policy.*

⬤ THESAURUS
breach: *a serious breach in relations between the two countries*
difference of opinion: *Was there a difference of opinion over what to do with the money?*
rupture: *a rupture of the family unit*
split: *They accused both sides of trying to provoke a split in the party.*

4 any one of the parts into which something is split *e.g. the Research Division*
divisional ADJECTIVE

⬤ THESAURUS
department: *the company's chemicals department*
section: *a top-secret section of the Foreign Office*
sector: *the nation's manufacturing sector*

divisive [dɪ'vaɪsɪv] ADJECTIVE
causing hostility between people so that they split into different groups *e.g. Inflation is economically and socially divisive.*

divisor [dɪ'vaɪzə] **divisors** NOUN
a number by which another number is divided

divorce [dɪ'vɔːs] **divorces, divorcing, divorced** NOUN
1 Divorce is the formal and legal ending of a marriage.

> VERB
2 When a married couple divorce, their marriage is legally ended.
divorced ADJECTIVE, **divorcee** NOUN

divulge [daɪ'vʌldʒ] **divulges, divulging, divulged** VERB
To divulge information means to reveal it.

Diwali [dɪ'wɑːlɪ] NOUN
a Hindu religious festival in honour of the goddess of wealth. It is celebrated by feasting, exchanging gifts, and lighting lamps

DIY NOUN
DIY is the activity of making or repairing things yourself. DIY is an abbreviation for 'do-it-yourself'.

dizzy ['dɪzɪ] **dizzier, dizziest** ADJECTIVE
having or causing a whirling sensation
dizziness NOUN

⬤ THESAURUS
giddy: *She felt slightly giddy.*
light-headed: *If you skip breakfast, you may feel light-headed.*

DNA NOUN
DNA is deoxyribonucleic acid, which is found in the cells of all living things. It is responsible for passing on characteristics from parents to their children.

do see page 254 for Word Web

docile ['dəʊsaɪl] ADJECTIVE
quiet, calm, and easily controlled

dock [dɒk] **docks, docking, docked** NOUN
1 an enclosed area in a harbour where ships go to be loaded, unloaded, or repaired
2 In a court of law, the dock is the place where the accused person stands or sits.

> VERB
3 When a ship docks, it is brought into dock at the end of its voyage.
4 To dock someone's wages means to deduct an amount from the sum they would normally receive.
5 To dock an animal's tail means to cut part of it off.
docker NOUN

doctor ['dɒktə] **doctors, doctoring, doctored** NOUN
1 a person who is qualified in medicine and treats people who are ill
2 A doctor of an academic subject is someone who has been awarded the highest academic degree. *e.g. She is a doctor of philosophy.*

> VERB
3 To doctor something means to alter it in order to deceive people. *e.g. Stamps can be doctored.*

doctorate ['dɒktərɪt] **doctorates** NOUN
the highest university degree
doctoral ADJECTIVE

doctrine ['dɒktrɪn] **doctrines** NOUN
a set of beliefs or principles held by a group
doctrinal ADJECTIVE

document documents, documenting, documented NOUN ['dɒkjʊmənt]
1 (**HISTORY**) a piece of paper which provides an official record of something

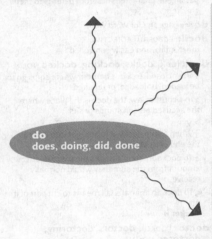

1 VERB
If someone does a task or activity, they perform it and finish it *eg: He just didn't want to do any work.*
● **THESAURUS**
carry out: *Police believe the attacks were carried out by nationalists.*
execute (formal): *The landing was skillfully executed.*
perform: *people who have performed outstanding acts of bravery*
undertake: *She undertook the arduous task of monitoring the elections.*

do
does, doing, did, done

2 VERB
If something will do, it is adequate but not the most suitable option *eg: Home-made stock is best, but cubes will do.*
● **THESAURUS**
be adequate: *The western diet should be perfectly adequate for most people.*
be sufficient: *One teaspoon of sugar should be sufficient.*
suffice (formal): *Often a far shorter letter will suffice.*

3 VERB
If you do well at something, you are successful. If you do badly, you are unsuccessful.
● **THESAURUS**
fare: *Some later expeditions fared better.*
get on: *I asked him how he had got on.*
manage: *How did your mother manage after your father died?*

2 (ICT) a piece of text or graphics stored in a computer as a file that can be amended or altered by document processing software

> VERB ['dɒkjʊ,mɛnt]

3 (HISTORY) If you document something, you make a detailed record of it.
documentation NOUN

documentary [,dɒkjʊ'mɛntəri]
documentaries NOUN

1 a radio or television programme, or a film, which gives information on real events

> ADJECTIVE

2 Documentary evidence is made up of written or official records.

dodge [dɒdʒ] **dodges, dodging, dodged**
VERB

1 If you dodge or dodge something, you move suddenly to avoid being seen, hit, or caught.

● THESAURUS
duck: *I wanted to duck down and slip past but they saw me.*
swerve: *He swerved to avoid a truck.*

2 If you dodge something such as an issue or accusation, you avoid dealing with it.

● THESAURUS
avoid: *They managed to avoid paying their fares.*
elude: *He eluded the police for 13 years.*
evade: *by evading taxes*
get out of: *He'll do almost anything to get out of paying his share.*
shirk: *We can't shirk our responsibility.*
sidestep: *Rarely, if ever, does he sidestep a question.*

dodgy ['dɒdʒɪ] ADJECTIVE; INFORMAL
dangerous, risky, or unreliable *e.g. He has a dodgy heart.*

dodo ['dəʊdəʊ] **dodos** NOUN
a large, flightless bird which is now extinct

doe [dəʊ] **does** NOUN
a female deer, rabbit, or hare

does [dʌz] the third person singular of the present tense of **do**

dog [dɒg] **dogs, dogging, dogged** NOUN

1 a four-legged, meat-eating animal, kept as a pet, or to guard property or go hunting

● THESAURUS
brak: South African *a rabid brak*
canine: *a new canine was needed*
mongrel: *a rescued mongrel called Chips*
mutt: slang *the most famous mutts in the western world*
pooch: slang *Julian's pet pooch.*

> VERB

2 If you dog someone, you follow them very closely and never leave them.

dog collar dog collars NOUN; INFORMAL
a white collar with no front opening worn by Christian clergy

dog-eared ['dɒg,ɪəd] ADJECTIVE
A book that is dog-eared has been used so much that the corners of the pages are turned down or worn.

dogged ['dɒgɪd] ADJECTIVE
showing determination to continue with something, even if it is very difficult *e.g. dogged persistence*
doggedly ADVERB

dogma ['dɒgmə] **dogmas** NOUN
a belief or system of beliefs held by a religious or political group

dogmatic [dɒg'mætɪk] ADJECTIVE
Someone who is dogmatic about something is convinced that they are right about it.
dogmatism NOUN

doldrums ['dɒldrəmz] AN INFORMAL PHRASE
If you are **in the doldrums**, you are depressed or bored.

dole [dəʊl] **doles, doling, doled** VERB
If you dole something out, you give a certain amount of it to each individual in a group.

doll [dɒl] **dolls** NOUN
a child's toy which looks like a baby or person

dollar ['dɒlə] **dollars** NOUN
the main unit of currency in Australia, New Zealand, the USA, Canada, and some other countries. A dollar is worth 100 cents

dollop ['dɒləp] **dollops** NOUN
an amount of food, served casually in a lump

dolphin ['dɒlfɪn] **dolphins** NOUN
a mammal which lives in the sea and looks like a large fish with a long snout

domain [də'meɪn] **domains** NOUN

1 a particular area of activity or interest *e.g. the domain of science*

2 an area over which someone has control or influence *e.g. This reservation was the largest of the Apache domains.*

dome [dəʊm] **domes** NOUN
a round roof
domed ADJECTIVE

domestic [də'mɛstɪk] ADJECTIVE

1 happening or existing within one particular country *e.g. domestic and foreign politics*

2 involving or concerned with the home and family *e.g. routine domestic tasks*

domesticated [də'mɛstɪ,keɪtɪd] ADJECTIVE
If a wild animal or plant has been domesticated,

it has been controlled or cultivated.

domesticity [ˌdəʊmɛ'stɪsɪtɪ] NOUN; FORMAL
Domesticity is life at home with your family.

dominance ['dɒmɪnəns] NOUN
1 Dominance is power or control.
2 If something has dominance over other similar things, it is more powerful or important than they are. *e.g. the dominance of the United States in the film business*
dominant ADJECTIVE

dominate ['dɒmɪˌneɪt] **dominates, dominating, dominated** VERB
1 If something or someone dominates a situation or event, they are the most powerful or important thing in it and have control over it. *e.g. The civil service dominated public affairs.*
2 If a person or country dominates other people or places, they have power or control over them.
3 If something dominates an area, it towers over it. *e.g. The valley was dominated by high surrounding cliffs.*
dominating ADJECTIVE, **domination** NOUN

domineering [ˌdɒmɪ'nɪərɪŋ] ADJECTIVE
Someone who is domineering tries to control other people. *e.g. a domineering mother*

dominion [də'mɪnjən] NOUN
Dominion is control or authority that a person or a country has over other people.

domino ['dɒmɪˌnəʊ] **dominoes** NOUN
Dominoes are small rectangular blocks marked with two groups of spots on one side, used for playing the game called dominoes.

don [dɒn] **dons, donning, donned** NOUN
1 a lecturer at Oxford or Cambridge university
> VERB
2 LITERARY
If you don clothing, you put it on.

donate [dəʊ'neɪt] **donates, donating, donated** VERB
To donate something to a charity or organization means to give it as a gift.
donation NOUN

done [dʌn] the past participle of **do**

donkey ['dɒŋkɪ] **donkeys** NOUN
an animal like a horse, but smaller and with longer ears

donor ['dəʊnə] **donors** NOUN
1 someone who gives some of their blood while they are alive or an organ after their death to be used to help someone who is ill *e.g. a kidney donor*
2 someone who gives something such as money to a charity or other organization

doodle ['duːdᵊl] **doodles, doodling, doodled** NOUN
1 a drawing done when you are thinking about something else or when you are bored
> VERB
2 To doodle means to draw doodles.

doom [duːm] NOUN
Doom is a terrible fate or event in the future which you can do nothing to prevent.

doomed [duːmd] ADJECTIVE
If someone or something is doomed to an unpleasant or unhappy experience, they are certain to suffer it. *e.g. doomed to failure*
◉ THESAURUS
condemned: *Many women are condemned to poverty.*
hopeless: *I don't believe your situation is as hopeless as you think.*
ill-fated: *his ill-fated attempt on the world record*

doomsday ['duːmzˌdeɪ] NOUN
Doomsday is the end of the world.

door [dɔː] **doors** NOUN
a swinging or sliding panel for opening or closing the entrance to something; also the entrance itself

doorway ['dɔːˌweɪ] **doorways** NOUN
an opening in a wall for a door

dope [dəʊp] **dopes, doping, doped** NOUN
1 Dope is an illegal drug.
> VERB
2 If someone dopes you, they put a drug into your food or drink.
[WORD HISTORY: from Dutch DOOP meaning 'sauce']

dormant ['dɔːmənt] ADJECTIVE
Something that is dormant is not active, growing, or being used. *e.g. The buds will remain dormant until spring.*

dormitory ['dɔːmɪtərɪ] **dormitories** NOUN
a large bedroom where several people sleep

dormouse ['dɔːˌmaʊs] **dormice** NOUN
an animal, like a large mouse, with a furry tail

dosage ['dəʊsɪdʒ] **dosages** NOUN
the amount of a medicine or a drug that should be taken

dose [dəʊs] **doses** NOUN
a measured amount of a medicine or drug

dossier ['dɒsɪˌeɪ] **dossiers** NOUN
a collection of papers with information on a particular subject or person

dot [dɒt] **dots, dotting, dotted** NOUN
1 a very small, round mark

> VERB

2 If things dot an area, they are scattered all over it. *e.g. Fishing villages dot the coastline.*

> PHRASE

3 If you arrive somewhere **on the dot**, you arrive there at exactly the right time.

dotcom [ˌdɒtˈkɒm] **dotcoms** NOUN
a company that does most of its business on the Internet

dote [dəʊt] **dotes, doting, doted** VERB
If you dote on someone, you love them very much.
doting ADJECTIVE

double [ˈdʌbəl] **doubles, doubling, doubled** ADJECTIVE

1 twice the usual size *e.g. a double whisky*

THESAURUS
twice: *Unemployment in Northern Ireland is twice the national average.*
twofold: *a twofold risk*

2 consisting of two parts *e.g. a double album*

THESAURUS
dual: *dual nationality*
twin: *twin beds*
twofold: *Their concern was twofold: personal and political.*

> VERB

3 If something doubles, it becomes twice as large.

4 To double as something means to have a second job or use as well as the main one. *e.g. Their home doubles as an office.*

> NOUN

5 Your double is someone who looks exactly like you.

6 Doubles is a game of tennis or badminton which two people play against two other people.
doubly ADVERB

double bass [beɪs] **double basses** NOUN
a musical instrument like a large violin, which you play standing up

double-cross [ˈdʌbəlˈkrɒs] **double-crosses, double-crossing, double-crossed** VERB
If someone double-crosses you, they cheat you by pretending to do what you both planned, when in fact they do the opposite.

double-decker [ˌdʌbəlˈdɛkə] **double-deckers** ADJECTIVE

1 having two tiers or layers

> NOUN

2 a bus with two floors

double glazing [ˈɡleɪzɪŋ] NOUN
Double glazing is a second layer of glass fitted to

windows to keep the building quieter or warmer.

doubt [daʊt] **doubts, doubting, doubted** NOUN

1 Doubt is a feeling of uncertainty about whether something is true or possible.

THESAURUS
misgiving: *I had misgivings about his methods.*
qualm: *I have no qualms about recommending this approach.*
scepticism: *The report has been greeted with scepticism.*
uncertainty: *the uncertainties regarding the future funding of the company*
<<OPPOSITE *certainty*

> VERB

2 If you doubt something, you think that it is probably not true or possible.

THESAURUS
be dubious: *I was dubious about the entire proposition.*
be sceptical: *Other archaeologists are sceptical about his findings.*
query: *No one queried my decision.*
question: *It never occurs to them to question the doctor's decisions.*
<<OPPOSITE *believe*

doubtful [ˈdaʊtfʊl] ADJECTIVE
unlikely or uncertain

THESAURUS
debatable: *Whether the Bank of England would do any better is highly debatable.*
dubious: *This claim seems to us rather dubious.*
questionable: *It is questionable whether the expenditure is justified.*
uncertain: *It's uncertain whether they will accept the plan.*
<<OPPOSITE *certain*

dough [dəʊ] NOUN

1 Dough is a mixture of flour and water and sometimes other ingredients, used to make bread, pastry, or biscuits.

2 INFORMAL
Dough is money.

doughnut [ˈdəʊnʌt] **doughnuts** NOUN
a ring of sweet dough cooked in hot fat

dour [dʊə] ADJECTIVE
severe and unfriendly *e.g. a dour portrait of his personality*

douse [daʊs] **douses, dousing, doused;** also spelt **dowse** VERB
If you douse a fire, you stop it burning by throwing water over it.

dove [dʌv] **doves** NOUN
a bird like a small pigeon

dovetail ['dʌv,teɪl] **dovetails, dovetailing, dovetailed** VERB
If two things dovetail together, they fit together closely or neatly.

dowager ['daʊədʒə] **dowagers** NOUN
a woman who has inherited a title from her dead husband *e.g. the Empress Dowager*

dowdy ['daʊdɪ] **dowdier, dowdiest** ADJECTIVE
wearing dull and unfashionable clothes

down [daʊn] **downs, downing, downed** PREPOSITION OR ADVERB
1 Down means towards the ground, towards a lower level, or in a lower place.

⬤ THESAURUS
downwards: *She gazed downwards.*
downstairs: *Denise went downstairs and made some tea.*
<<OPPOSITE up

2 If you go down a road or river, you go along it.
> ADVERB
3 If you put something down, you place it on a surface.
4 If an amount of something goes down, it decreases.
> ADJECTIVE
5 If you feel down, you feel depressed.

⬤ THESAURUS
dejected: *Everyone has days when they feel dejected.*
depressed: *She's been very depressed about this situation.*
dispirited: *I left feeling utterly dispirited.*
fed up: informal *I'm just fed up and I don't know what to do.*
glum: *She was very glum and was missing her children.*
melancholy: *It was in the afternoon that Tom felt most melancholy.*
miserable: *My work was making me really miserable.*

> VERB
6 If you down a drink, you drink it quickly.
> NOUN
7 Down is the small, soft feathers on young birds.

downcast ['daʊn,kɑːst] ADJECTIVE
1 feeling sad and dejected
2 If your eyes are downcast, they are looking towards the ground.

downfall ['daʊn,fɔːl] NOUN
1 The downfall of a successful or powerful person or institution is their failure.

⬤ THESAURUS
collapse: *The medical system is facing collapse.*

fall: *the fall of the military dictator*
ruin: *Inflation has driven them to the brink of ruin.*

2 Something that is someone's downfall is the thing that causes their failure. *e.g. His pride may be his downfall.*

downgrade ['daʊn,greɪd] **downgrades, downgrading, downgraded** VERB
If you downgrade something, you give it less importance or make it less valuable.

downhill ['daʊn'hɪl] ADVERB
1 moving down a slope
2 becoming worse *e.g. The press has gone downhill in the last 10 years.*

download ['daʊn,ləʊd] **downloads, downloading, downloaded** VERB
1 If you download data you transfer it from the memory of one computer to that of another, especially over the Internet.
> NOUN
2 a piece of data transferred in this way

downpour ['daʊn,pɔː] **downpours** NOUN
a heavy fall of rain

downright ['daʊn,raɪt] ADJECTIVE OR ADVERB
You use 'downright' to emphasize that something is extremely unpleasant or bad. *e.g. Staff are often discourteous and sometimes downright rude.*

downs [daʊnz] PLURAL NOUN
an area of low grassy hills, especially in the south of England

downstairs ['daʊn'stɛəz] ADVERB
1 going down a staircase towards the ground floor
> ADJECTIVE OR ADVERB
2 on a lower floor or on the ground floor

downstream ['daʊn'striːm] ADJECTIVE OR ADVERB
Something that is downstream or moving downstream is nearer or moving nearer to the mouth of a river from a point further up.

down-to-earth ['daʊntə'ɜːθ] ADJECTIVE
sensible and practical *e.g. a down-to-earth approach*

downtrodden ['daʊn,trɒdən] ADJECTIVE
People who are downtrodden are treated badly by those with power and do not have the ability to fight back.

downturn ['daʊn,tɜːn] **downturns** NOUN
a decline in the economy or in the success of a company or industry

down under INFORMAL
> NOUN
1 Australia or New Zealand.

> ADVERB

2 in or to Australia or New Zealand

downwards or **downward** ['daʊnwədz] or
['daʊnwəd] ADVERB OR ADJECTIVE

1 If you move or look downwards, you move or
look towards the ground or towards a lower level.
*e.g. His eyes travelled downwards... She slipped on
the downward slope.*

2 If an amount or rate moves downwards, it
decreases.

downwind ['daʊn'wɪnd] ADVERB
If something moves downwind, it moves in the
same direction as the wind. *e.g. Sparks drifted
downwind.*

dowry ['daʊərɪ] **dowries** NOUN
A woman's dowry is money or property which her
father gives to the man she marries.

doze [daʊz] **dozes, dozing, dozed** VERB

1 When you doze, you sleep lightly for a short
period.

> NOUN

2 a short, light sleep

dozen ['dʌzᵊn] **dozens** NOUN
A dozen things are twelve of them.

Dr

1 'Dr' is short for 'Doctor' and is used before the
name of someone with the highest form of
academic degree or who practises medicine

2 'Dr' is short for 'drive'

drab [dræb] **drabber, drabbest** ADJECTIVE
dull and unattractive
drabness NOUN

● THESAURUS
dingy: *his rather dingy office*
dismal: *a dark dismal day*
dreary: *a dreary little town*
gloomy: *the gloomy days of winter*
grey: *a New Year that will be grey and cheerless*
sombre: *a worried official in sombre black*
<<OPPOSITE *bright*

draft [drɑːft] **drafts, drafting, drafted**
NOUN

1 an early rough version of a document or speech

> VERB

2 When you draft a document or speech, you
write the first rough version of it.

3 To draft people somewhere means to move
them there so that they can do a specific job. *e.g.
Various different presenters were drafted in.*

4 In Australian and New Zealand English, to draft
cattle or sheep is to select some from a herd or
flock.

drag [dræg] **drags, dragging, dragged** VERB

1 If you drag a heavy object somewhere, you pull
it slowly and with difficulty.

● THESAURUS
draw: *He drew his chair nearer the fire.*
haul: *A crane used to haul the car out of the
stream.*
lug: *Nobody wants to lug around huge suitcases.*
tow: *They threatened to tow away my car.*
trail: *She came down the stairs slowly, trailing the
coat behind her.*

2 If you drag someone somewhere, you make
them go although they may be unwilling.

3 If things drag behind you, they trail along the
ground as you move along.

4 If an event or a period of time drags, it is boring
and seems to last a long time.

> NOUN

5 Drag is the resistance to the motion of a body
passing through air or a fluid.

dragon ['drægən] **dragons** NOUN
In stories and legends, a dragon is a fierce animal
like a large lizard with wings and claws that
breathes fire.
[WORD HISTORY: from Greek DRAKŌN meaning
'serpent']

dragonfly ['drægən,flaɪ] **dragonflies** NOUN
a colourful insect which is often found near
water

dragoon [drə'guːn] **dragoons, dragooning,
dragooned** NOUN

1 Dragoons are soldiers. Originally, they were
mounted infantry soldiers.

> VERB

2 If you dragoon someone into something, you
force them to do it.

drain [dreɪn] **drains, draining, drained**
VERB

1 If you drain something, you cause liquid to flow
out of it.

● THESAURUS
draw off: *The fluid can be drawn off with a syringe.*
pump: *to get rid of raw sewage by pumping it out
to sea*

2 If you drain a glass, you drink all its contents.

3 If liquid drains somewhere, it flows there.

● THESAURUS
discharge: *Blood was discharging from its nostrils.*
empty: *The Washougal empties into the Columbia
River.*
flow: *The waters of Lake Erie now flow into the
Niagara River.*
seep: *Radioactive water has seeped into
underground reservoirs.*

4 If something drains strength or resources, it
gradually uses them up. *e.g. The prolonged*

boardroom battle drained him of energy and money.

● THESAURUS
consume: *plans which will consume hours of time*
exhaust: *People are now living longer and exhausting natural resources.*
sap: *The illness sapped his strength.*
tax: *Overcrowding has taxed the city's ability to deal with waste.*
use up: *They aren't the ones who use up the world's resources.*

> NOUN
5 a pipe or channel that carries water or sewage away from a place
6 a metal grid in a road, through which rainwater flows

drainage ['dreɪnɪdʒ] NOUN
1 Drainage is the system of pipes, drains, or ditches used to drain water or other liquid away from a place.
2 Drainage is also the process of draining water away, or the way in which a place drains. *e.g. To grow these well, all you need is good drainage.*

drake [dreɪk] **drakes** NOUN
a male duck

drama ['drɑːmə] **dramas** NOUN
1 a serious play for the theatre, television, or radio
2 Drama is plays and the theatre in general. *e.g. Japanese drama.*
3 You can refer to the exciting events or aspects of a situation as drama. *e.g. the drama of real life*

dramatic [drə'mætɪk] ADJECTIVE
A dramatic change or event happens suddenly and is very noticeable. *e.g. a dramatic departure from tradition*
dramatically ADVERB

dramatist ['dræmətɪst] **dramatists** NOUN
(DRAMA) a person who writes plays

drape [dreɪp] **drapes, draping, draped** VERB
If you drape a piece of cloth, you arrange it so that it hangs down or covers something in loose folds.

drastic ['dræstɪk] ADJECTIVE
A drastic course of action is very severe and is usually taken urgently. *e.g. It's time for drastic action.*
drastically ADVERB

● THESAURUS
extreme: *I would rather die than do anything so extreme.*
harsh: *harsh new measures to combat drink-driving*
radical: *radical economic reforms*
severe: *a severe shortage of drinking water*

draught [drɑːft] **draughts** NOUN
1 a current of cold air
2 an amount of liquid that you swallow
3 Draughts is a game for two people played on a chessboard with round pieces.

> ADJECTIVE
4 Draught beer is served straight from barrels rather than in bottles.

draughtsman ['drɑːftsmən] **draughtsmen** NOUN
a person who prepares detailed drawings or plans

draughty ['drɑːftɪ] **draughtier, draughtiest** ADJECTIVE
A place that is draughty has currents of cold air blowing through it.

draw [drɔː] **draws, drawing, drew, drawn** VERB
1 When you draw, you use a pen or crayon to make a picture or diagram.

● THESAURUS
paint: *He is painting a huge volcano.*
sketch: *He sketched a map on the back of a menu.*
trace: *She learned to draw by tracing pictures out of old storybooks.*

2 To draw near means to move closer. To draw away or draw back means to move away.

● THESAURUS
move: *She moved away from the window.*
pull: *He pulled into the driveway.*

3 If you draw something in a particular direction, you pull it there smoothly and gently. *e.g. He drew his feet under the chair.*

● THESAURUS
drag: *He dragged his chair towards the table.*
haul: *A crane was used to haul the car out of the stream.*
pull: *a freight train pulling waggons*

4 If you draw a deep breath, you breathe in deeply.
5 If you draw the curtains, you pull them so that they cover or uncover the window.
6 If something such as water or energy is drawn from a source, it is taken from it.
7 If you draw a conclusion, you arrive at it from the facts you know.
8 If you draw a distinction or a comparison between two things, you point out that it exists.

> NOUN
9 the result of a game or competition in which nobody wins

draw up VERB
10 To draw up a plan, document, or list means to

prepare it and write it out.

drawback ['drɔːˌbæk] **drawbacks** NOUN
a problem that makes something less acceptable or desirable e.g. *Shortcuts usually have a drawback.*

● THESAURUS
difficulty: *There is only one difficulty – I don't have the key.*
hitch: *It's a great idea but I can see a serious hitch.*
problem: *The main problem with the house is its inaccessibility.*
snag: *It's a great school – the snag is the fees are £9,000 a year.*
trouble: *The trouble is that he might not agree with our plans.*

drawbridge ['drɔːˌbrɪdʒ] **drawbridges** NOUN
a bridge that can be pulled up or lowered

drawer ['drɔːə] **drawers** NOUN
a sliding box-shaped part of a piece of furniture used for storing things

drawing ['drɔːɪŋ] **drawings** NOUN
1 a picture made with a pencil, pen, or crayon
2 Drawing is the skill or work of making drawings.

drawing room drawing rooms NOUN;
OLD-FASHIONED
a room in a house where people relax or entertain guests

drawl [drɔːl] **drawls, drawling, drawled**
VERB
If someone drawls, they speak slowly with long vowel sounds.

drawn [drɔːn] Drawn is the past participle of **draw**

dread [drɛd] **dreads, dreading, dreaded**
VERB
1 If you dread something, you feel very worried and frightened about it. e.g. *He was dreading the journey.*
> NOUN
2 Dread is a feeling of great fear or anxiety.
dreaded ADJECTIVE

dreadful ['drɛdfʊl] ADJECTIVE
very bad or unpleasant
dreadfully ADVERB

● THESAURUS
appalling: *living under the most appalling conditions*
atrocious: *The food here is atrocious.*
awful: *Jeans look awful on me.*
frightful: *The war had been so frightful he couldn't talk about it.*
ghastly: *a ghastly pair of shoes*
horrendous: *the most horrendous experience of his life*

terrible: *Thousands more people suffered terrible injuries.*
<<OPPOSITE wonderful

dream [driːm] **dreams, dreaming, dreamed** or **dreamt** NOUN
1 a series of events that you experience in your mind while asleep
● THESAURUS
hallucination: *The drug induces hallucinations at high doses.*
trance: *She seemed to be in a trance.*
vision: *seeing the Virgin Mary in a vision*

2 a situation or event which you often think about because you would very much like it to happen e.g. *his dream of winning the lottery*
● THESAURUS
ambition: *His ambition is to sail round the world.*
aspiration: *one of his greatest aspirations*
daydream: *He learned to escape into daydreams of becoming a writer.*
fantasy: *fantasies of romance and true love*

> VERB
3 When you dream, you see events in your mind while you are asleep.
4 When you dream about something happening, you often think about it because you would very much like it to happen.
5 If someone dreams up a plan or idea, they invent it.
6 If you say you would not dream of doing something, you are emphasizing that you would not do it. e.g. *I wouldn't dream of giving the plot away.*

> ADJECTIVE
7 too good to be true e.g. *a dream holiday*
dreamer NOUN

Dreamtime ['driːmtaɪm] NOUN
In Australian Aboriginal legends, Dreamtime is the time when the world was being made and the first people were created.

dreamy ['driːmɪ] **dreamier, dreamiest**
ADJECTIVE
Someone with a dreamy expression looks as if they are thinking about something very pleasant.

dreary ['drɪərɪ] **drearier, dreariest**
ADJECTIVE
dull or boring
● THESAURUS
boring: *a boring job*
drab: *The rest of the day's activities often seem drab.*
dull: *There was scarcely a dull moment.*
humdrum: *The new government seemed rather humdrum.*
monotonous: *It's monotonous work, like most factory jobs.*

tedious: *Such lists are tedious to read.*
uneventful: *her dull, uneventful life*
<<OPPOSITE *exciting*

dregs [drɛgz] PLURAL NOUN
The dregs of a liquid are the last drops left at the bottom of a container, and any sediment left with it.

drenched [drɛntʃd] ADJECTIVE
soaking wet

dress [drɛs] **dresses, dressing, dressed**
NOUN
1 a piece of clothing for women or girls made up of a skirt and top attached

● THESAURUS
frock: *a party frock*
gown: *wedding gowns*
robe: *a fur-lined robe*

2 Dress is any clothing worn by men or women.

● THESAURUS
attire: formal *women dressed in their finest attire*
clothes: *casual clothes*
clothing: *protective clothing*
costume: *women in traditional costume*
garb: formal *his usual garb of a dark suit*

> VERB
3 When you dress, you put clothes on.

● THESAURUS
attire: *He was attired in a smart blue suit.*
clothe: *He lay down on the bed fully clothed.*
garb: formal *He was garbed in sweater, jacket and boots.*
<<OPPOSITE *undress*

4 If you dress for a special occasion, you put on formal clothes.
5 To dress a wound means to clean it up and treat it.

dresser ['drɛsə] **dressers** NOUN
a piece of kitchen or dining room furniture with cupboards or drawers in the lower part and open shelves in the top part

dressing gown ['drɛsɪŋ] **dressing gowns**
NOUN
an item of clothing shaped like a coat and put on over nightwear

dressing room ['drɛsɪŋ] **dressing rooms**
NOUN
a room used for getting changed and putting on make-up, especially a backstage room at a theatre

dress rehearsal **dress rehearsals** NOUN
the last rehearsal of a show or play, using costumes, scenery, and lighting

dribble ['drɪbəl] **dribbles, dribbling, dribbled** VERB

1 When liquid dribbles down a surface, it trickles down it in drops or a thin stream.

2 If a person or animal dribbles, saliva trickles from their mouth.

3 In sport, to dribble a ball means to move it along by repeatedly tapping it with your foot or a stick.

> NOUN
4 a small quantity of liquid flowing in a thin stream or drops

drift [drɪft] **drifts, drifting, drifted** VERB
1 When something drifts, it is carried along by the wind or by water.

2 When people drift, they move aimlessly from one place or activity to another.

3 If you drift off to sleep, you gradually fall asleep.
> NOUN
4 A snow drift is a pile of snow heaped up by the wind.

5 The drift of an argument or a speech is its main point.
drifter NOUN

drill [drɪl] **drills, drilling, drilled** NOUN
1 a tools for making holes *e.g. an electric drill*

2 Drill is a routine exercise or routine training. *e.g. lifeboat drill*

> VERB
3 To drill into something means to make a hole in it using a drill.

4 If you drill people, you teach them to do something by repetition.

drink [drɪŋk] **drinks, drinking, drank, drunk** VERB
1 When you drink, you take liquid into your mouth and swallow it.

● THESAURUS
gulp: *She quickly gulped her coffee.*
guzzle: *She guzzled gin and tonics like they were lemonade.*
sip: *She sipped from her coffee mug.*
swig: informal *I swigged down two white wines.*

2 To drink also means to drink alcohol. *e.g. He drinks little and eats carefully.*

● THESAURUS
booze: informal *drunken businessmen who had been boozing all afternoon*
tipple: *We saw a woman tippling from the sherry bottle.*

> NOUN
3 an amount of liquid suitable for drinking

4 an alcoholic drink
drinker NOUN

drip [drɪp] **drips, dripping, dripped** VERB

1 When liquid drips, it falls in small drops.

⬤ **THESAURUS**
dribble: *Sweat dribbled down his face.*
splash: *Tears splashed into her hands.*
trickle: *A tear trickled down the old man's cheek.*

2 When an object drips, drops of liquid fall from it.

> NOUN
3 a drop of liquid falling from something

⬤ **THESAURUS**
bead: *beads of sweat*
drop: *a drop of blue ink*
droplet: *water droplets*

4 a device for allowing liquid food to enter the bloodstream of a person who cannot eat properly because they are ill

drive see page 264 for Word Web

drive-in ['draɪvˌɪn] **drive-ins** NOUN
a restaurant, cinema, or other commercial place that is specially designed for customers to use while staying in their cars

drivel ['drɪvəl] NOUN
Drivel is nonsense. *e.g. He is still writing mindless drivel.*
[WORD HISTORY: from Old English DREFLIAN meaning 'to dribble']

drizzle ['drɪzəl] NOUN
Drizzle is light rain.

dromedary ['drʌmədərɪ] **dromedaries** NOUN
a camel which has one hump

drone [drəʊn] **drones, droning, droned** VERB
1 If something drones, it makes a low, continuous humming noise.

2 If someone drones on, they keep talking or reading aloud in a boring way.

> NOUN
3 a continuous low dull sound

drool [druːl] **drools, drooling, drooled** VERB
If someone drools, saliva dribbles from their mouth without them being able to stop it.

droop [druːp] **droops, drooping, drooped** VERB
If something droops, it hangs or sags downwards with no strength or firmness.

drop [drɒp] **drops, dropping, dropped** VERB
1 If you drop something, you let it fall.

2 If something drops, it falls straight down.

⬤ **THESAURUS**
descend: *as the aircraft descended*
fall: *Bombs fell in the town.*
plummet: *His parachute failed to open and he plummeted to the ground.*

sink: *She sank to her knees.*
tumble: *The gun tumbled out of his hand.*

3 If a level or amount drops, it becomes less.

⬤ **THESAURUS**
decline: *The number of staff has declined.*
decrease: *Population growth is decreasing by 1.4% each year.*
diminish: *diminishing resources*
fall: *Her weight fell to under seven stone.*
plummet: *Share prices have plummeted.*
sink: *Pay increases have sunk to around 7%.*
slump: *Net profits slumped by 41%.*
tumble: *House prices have tumbled by almost 30%.*
<<OPPOSITE *rise*

4 If your voice drops, or if you drop your voice, you speak more quietly.

5 If you drop something that you are doing or dealing with, you stop doing it or dealing with it. *e.g. She dropped the subject and never mentioned it again.*

6 If you drop a hint, you give someone a hint in a casual way.

7 If you drop something or someone somewhere, you deposit or leave them there.

> NOUN
8 A drop of liquid is a very small quantity of it that forms or falls in a round shape.

⬤ **THESAURUS**
bead: *beads of sweat*
drip: *drips of water*
droplet: *water droplets*

9 a decrease *e.g. a huge drop in income*

10 the distance between the top and bottom of something tall, such as a cliff or building *e.g. It is a sheer drop to the foot of the cliff.*

droplet ['drɒplɪt] **droplets** NOUN
a small drop

droppings ['drɒpɪŋz] PLURAL NOUN
Droppings are the faeces of birds and small animals.

drought [draʊt] **droughts** NOUN
a long period during which there is no rain

drove [drəʊv] **droves, droving, droved**
1 Drove is the past tense of **drive**

> VERB
2 To drove cattle or sheep is to drive them over a long distance.

drown [draʊn] **drowns, drowning, drowned** VERB
1 When someone drowns or is drowned, they die because they have gone under water and cannot breathe.

2 If a noise drowns a sound, it is louder than the sound and makes it impossible to hear it.

1 VERB
To drive a vehicle means to operate it and control its movements.
● THESAURUS
operate: *A rock fall trapped the men as they operated a tunnelling machine.*
pilot: *He piloted his own plane to Washington.*
power: *The flywheel's battery could be used to power an electric car.*
propel: *Attached is a tiny rocket designed to propel the spacecraft towards Mars.*
run: *I ran a Rover 100 from 1977 until 1983.*
steer: *What is it like to steer a ship this size?*
work: *I learned how to work the forklift.*

2 VERB
If something or someone drives you to do something, they force you to do it *eg: The illness of his daughter drove him to religion.*
● THESAURUS
compel: *He felt compelled to speak out against their actions.*
force: *A back injury forced her to withdraw from the tournament.*
lead: *His abhorrence of racism led him to write his first book.*
motivate: *What motivates people to behave like this?*
prompt: *The recession has prompted consumers to cut back on spending.*
push: *James did not push her into stealing the money.*
spur: *It's the money that spurs these fishermen to take such risks.*

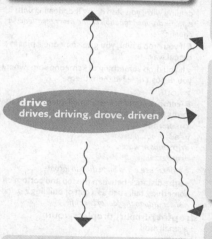

drive
drives, driving, drove, driven

3 VERB
If you drive a post or nail into something, you force it in by hitting it with a hammer.
● THESAURUS
hammer: *Hammer a wooden peg into the hole.*
knock: *He knocked a couple of nails into the wall.*
ram: *He rammed the stake with all his strength into the creature's heart.*
sink: *He sinks the needle into my arm.*
thrust: *thrusting a knife into his ribs*

5 NOUN
Drive is energy and determination.
● THESAURUS
ambition: *When I was young I never had any ambition.*
determination: *her natural determination to succeed*
energy: *At 54 years old, her energy is magnificent.*
enterprise: *the group's lack of enterprise*
initiative: *We were disappointed that he showed no initiative.*
motivation: *His poor performance may be attributed to lack of motivation.*
vigour: *He played with great vigour.*

4 NOUN
a journey in a vehicle
● THESAURUS
excursion: *an excursion to a local vineyard*
jaunt: *Let's take a jaunt down to the beach.*
journey: *The journey from Manchester to Plymouth took a few hours.*
ride: *We took some friends for a ride in the family car.*
run: *We went for a run in the new car to try it out.*
spin: *I was thinking about going for a spin.*
trip: *We went on a coach trip to the seaside.*

drowsy ['draʊzɪ] **drowsier, drowsiest**
ADJECTIVE
feeling sleepy

drudgery ['drʌdʒərɪ] NOUN
Drudgery is hard boring work.

drug [drʌg] **drugs, drugging, drugged**
NOUN
1 a chemical given to people to treat disease

THESAURUS
medication: *She is not on any medication.*
medicine: *herbal medicines*

2 Drugs are chemical substances that some people smoke, swallow, smell, or inject because of their stimulating effects.

THESAURUS
narcotic: *He was indicted for dealing in narcotics.*
stimulant: *the use of stimulants in sport*

> VERB
3 To drug a person or animal means to give them a drug to make them unconscious.

4 To drug food or drink means to add a drug to it in order to make someone unconscious.
drugged ADJECTIVE

druid ['druːɪd] **druids** NOUN
a priest of an ancient religion in Northern Europe

drum [drʌm] **drums, drumming, drummed** NOUN
1 a musical instrument consisting of a skin stretched tightly over a round frame

2 an object or container shaped like a drum *e.g. an oil drum*

3 INFORMAL
In Australian English, the drum is information or advice. *e.g. The manager gave me the drum.*

> VERB
4 If something is drumming on a surface, it is hitting it regularly, making a continuous beating sound.

5 If you drum something into someone, you keep saying it to them until they understand it or remember it.
drummer NOUN

drumstick ['drʌm,stɪk] **drumsticks** NOUN
1 a stick used for beating a drum

2 A chicken drumstick is the lower part of the leg of a chicken, which is cooked and eaten.

drunk [drʌŋk] **drunks**
1 Drunk is the past participle of **drink**

> ADJECTIVE
2 If someone is drunk, they have drunk so much alcohol that they cannot speak clearly or behave sensibly.

THESAURUS
babalas: South African *He was babalas again last night.*

intoxicated: formal *He appeared intoxicated.*
tipsy: *I'm feeling a bit tipsy.*
<<OPPOSITE *sober*

> NOUN
3 a person who is drunk, or who often gets drunk
drunken ADJECTIVE, **drunkenly** ADVERB,
drunkenness NOUN

THESAURUS
alcoholic: *after admitting that he was an alcoholic*
boozer: informal *He's a bit of a boozer.*

dry [draɪ] **drier** or **dryer driest; dries, drying, dried** ADJECTIVE
1 Something that is dry contains or uses no water or liquid.

THESAURUS
arid: *arid conditions*
dried-up: *a dried-up river bed*
parched: *parched brown grass*
<<OPPOSITE *wet*

2 Dry bread or toast is eaten without a topping.

3 Dry sherry or wine does not taste sweet.

4 Dry also means plain and sometimes boring. *e.g. the dry facts*

5 Dry humour is subtle and sarcastic.

> VERB
6 When you dry something, or when it dries, liquid is removed from it.

THESAURUS
dehydrate: *Avoid alcohol, which dehydrates the body.*
drain: *The authorities have mobilized vast numbers of people to drain flooded land.*
<<OPPOSITE *moisten*

dry up VERB
7 If something dries up, it becomes completely dry.

8 INFORMAL
If you dry up, you forget what you were going to say, or find that you have nothing left to say.
dryness NOUN, **drily** ADVERB

dry-clean [,draɪ'kliːn] **dry-cleans, dry-cleaning, dry-cleaned** VERB
When clothes are dry-cleaned, they are cleaned with a liquid chemical rather than with water.

dryer ['draɪə] **dryers;** also spelt **drier** NOUN
a device for removing moisture from something by heating or by hot air *e.g. a hair dryer*

dual ['djuːəl] ADJECTIVE
having two parts, functions, or aspects *e.g. a dual-purpose trimmer*

dub [dʌb] **dubs, dubbing, dubbed** VERB
1 If something is dubbed a particular name, it is given that name. *e.g. Smiling has been dubbed 'nature's secret weapon'.*

d

2 If a film is dubbed, the voices on the soundtrack are not those of the actors, but those of other actors speaking in a different language.

dubious ['djuːbɪəs] ADJECTIVE

1 not entirely honest, safe, or reliable *e.g. dubious sales techniques*

● THESAURUS

crooked: *expose his crooked business deals*
dishonest: *He had become rich by dishonest means.*
questionable: *allegations of questionable business practices*
suspect: *The whole affair is highly suspect.*
suspicious: *two characters who looked suspicious*
unreliable: *a notoriously unreliable source of information*

2 doubtful *e.g. I felt dubious about the entire proposition.*
dubiously ADVERB

● THESAURUS

doubtful: *I was still very doubtful about our chances for success.*
nervous: *The party has become nervous about its prospects of winning.*
sceptical: *Other archaeologists are sceptical about his findings.*
suspicious: *I'm a little suspicious about his motives.*
unconvinced: *Most consumers seem unconvinced that the recession is over.*
undecided: *After university she was still undecided as to what career she wanted.*
unsure: *Fifty-two per cent were unsure about the idea.*

duchess ['dʌtʃɪs] **duchesses** NOUN
a woman who has the same rank as a duke, or who is a duke's wife or widow

duchy ['dʌtʃɪ] **duchies** NOUN
the land owned and ruled by a duke or duchess

duck [dʌk] **ducks, ducking, ducked** NOUN

1 a bird that lives in water and has webbed feet and a large flat bill

> VERB

2 If you duck, you move your head quickly downwards in order to avoid being hit by something.

3 If you duck a duty or responsibility, you avoid it.

4 To duck someone means to push them briefly under water.

duckling ['dʌklɪŋ] **ducklings** NOUN
a young duck

duct [dʌkt] **ducts** NOUN

1 a pipe or channel through which liquid or gas is sent

2 a bodily passage through which liquid such as tears can pass

dud [dʌd] **duds** NOUN
something which does not function properly

due [djuː] **dues** ADJECTIVE

1 expected to happen or arrive *e.g. The baby is due at Christmas.*

2 If you give something due consideration, you give it the consideration it needs.

> PHRASE

3 Due to means because of *e.g. Headaches can be due to stress.*

> ADVERB

4 Due means exactly in a particular direction. *e.g. About a mile due west lay the ocean.*

> PLURAL NOUN

5 Dues are sums of money that you pay regularly to an organization you belong to.

duel ['djuːəl] **duels** NOUN

1 a fight arranged between two people using deadly weapons, to settle a quarrel

2 Any contest or conflict between two people can be referred to as a duel.

duet [djuːˈɛt] **duets** NOUN
a piece of music sung or played by two people

dug [dʌg] Dug is the past tense and past participle of **dig**

dugong ['duːgɒŋ] **dugongs** NOUN
an animal like a whale that lives in warm seas

dugout ['dʌg,aʊt] **dugouts** NOUN

1 a canoe made by hollowing out a log

2 MILITARY
a shelter dug in the ground for protection

duke [djuːk] **dukes** NOUN
a nobleman with a rank just below that of a prince

[WORD HISTORY: from Latin DUX meaning 'leader']

dull [dʌl] **duller, dullest; dulls, dulling, dulled** ADJECTIVE

1 not at all interesting in any way

● THESAURUS

boring: *a boring job*
drab: *The rest of the day's activities often seem drab.*
humdrum: *The new government seemed rather humdrum.*
monotonous: *It's monotonous work, like most factory jobs.*
tedious: *Such lists are tedious to read.*
uninteresting: *Their media has a reputation for being dull and uninteresting.*
<<OPPOSITE *interesting*

2 slow to learn or understand

3 not bright, sharp, or clear

● THESAURUS

drab: *the same drab grey dress*

gloomy: *Inside it's gloomy after all that sunshine.*
muted: *He likes sombre, muted colours.*
sombre: *an official in sombre black*
subdued: *subdued lighting*
<<OPPOSITE *bright*

4 A dull day or dull sky is very cloudy.

● THESAURUS
cloudy: *In the morning it was cloudy.*
leaden: *a leaden sky*
murky: *one murky November afternoon*
overcast: *For three days it was overcast.*
<<OPPOSITE *bright*

5 Dull feelings are weak and not intense. *e.g. He should have been angry but felt only dull resentment.*

> VERB
6 If something dulls or is dulled, it becomes less bright, sharp, or clear.
dully ADVERB, **dullness** NOUN

duly ['djuːlɪ] ADVERB
1 FORMAL
If something is duly done, it is done in the correct way. *e.g. I wish to record my support for the duly elected council.*

2 If something duly happens, it is something that you expected to happen. *e.g. Two chicks duly emerged from their eggs.*

dumb [dʌm] **dumber, dumbest** ADJECTIVE
1 unable to speak
● THESAURUS
mute: *a mute look of appeal*
silent: *Suddenly they both fell silent.*
speechless: *Alex was almost speechless with rage.*

2 INFORMAL
slow to understand or stupid
● THESAURUS
dim: *He is rather dim.*
obtuse: formal *I've really been very obtuse.*
stupid: *How could I have been so stupid?*
thick: informal *I must have seemed incredibly thick.*
<<OPPOSITE *smart*

dumbfounded [dʌmˈfaʊndɪd] ADJECTIVE
speechless with amazement *e.g. She was too dumbfounded to answer.*

dummy ['dʌmɪ] **dummies** NOUN
1 a rubber teat which a baby sucks or bites on
2 an imitation or model of something which is used for display
> ADJECTIVE
3 imitation or substitute

dump [dʌmp] **dumps, dumping, dumped** VERB
1 When unwanted waste is dumped, it is left somewhere.

● THESAURUS
discharge: *The resulting salty water will eventually be discharged at sea.*
dispose of: *how he disposed of the murder weapon*
get rid of: *The cat had kittens, which they got rid of.*
jettison: *The crew jettisoned their excess fuel.*
throw away: *You should have thrown the letter away.*
throw out: *You ought to throw out those empty bottles.*

2 If you dump something, you throw it down or put it down somewhere in a careless way.
● THESAURUS
deposit: *Imagine if you were suddenly deposited on a desert island.*
drop: *Many children had been dropped outside the stadium by their parents.*

> NOUN
3 a place where rubbish is left
4 a storage place, especially used by the military for storing supplies
5 INFORMAL
You refer to a place as a dump when it is unattractive and unpleasant to live in.

dumpling ['dʌmplɪŋ] **dumplings** NOUN
a small lump of dough that is cooked and eaten with meat and vegetables

dunce [dʌns] **dunces** NOUN
a person who cannot learn what someone is trying to teach them

dune [djuːn] **dunes** NOUN
A dune or sand dune is a hill of sand near the sea or in the desert.

dung [dʌŋ] NOUN
Dung is the faeces from large animals, sometimes called manure.

dungarees [ˌdʌŋɡəˈriːz] PLURAL NOUN
Dungarees are trousers which have a bib covering the chest and straps over the shoulders.

dungeon ['dʌndʒən] **dungeons** NOUN
an underground prison

dunk [dʌŋk] **dunks, dunking, dunked** VERB
To dunk something means to dip it briefly into a liquid. *e.g. He dunked a single tea bag into two cups.*

duo ['djuːəʊ] **duos** NOUN
1 a pair of musical performers; also a piece of music written for two players
2 Any two people doing something together can be referred to as a duo.

dupe [djuːp] **dupes, duping, duped** VERB
1 If someone dupes you, they trick you.
● THESAURUS
cheat: *Many brokers were charged with cheating customers.*

con: informal *The British people have been conned by the government.*

deceive: *He has deceived us all.*

delude: *Television deludes you into thinking you are experiencing reality.*

fool: *Art dealers fool a lot of people.*

play a trick on: *She realized he had played a trick on her.*

trick: *He'll be upset when he finds out you tricked him.*

> NOUN

2 someone who has been tricked

[WORD HISTORY: from Old French DE HUPPE meaning 'of the hoopoe', a bird thought to be stupid]

duplicate **duplicates, duplicating, duplicated** VERB ['dju:plɪˌkeɪt]

1 To duplicate something means to make an exact copy of it.

> NOUN ['dju:plɪkɪt]

2 something that is identical to something else

> ADJECTIVE ['dju:plɪkɪt]

3 identical to or an exact copy of *e.g. a duplicate key*

duplication NOUN

durable ['djʊərəbəl] ADJECTIVE
strong and lasting for a long time
durability NOUN

duration [djʊ'reɪʃən] NOUN
The duration of something is the length of time during which it happens or exists.

duress [djʊ'rɛs] NOUN
If you do something under duress, you are forced to do it, and you do it very unwillingly.

during ['djʊərɪŋ] PREPOSITION
happening throughout a particular time or at a particular point in time *e.g. The mussels will open naturally during cooking.*

dusk [dʌsk] NOUN
Dusk is the time just before nightfall when it is not completely dark.
[WORD HISTORY: from Old English DOX meaning 'dark' or 'swarthy']

dust [dʌst] **dusts, dusting, dusted** NOUN
1 Dust is dry fine powdery material such as particles of earth, dirt, or pollen.

> VERB

2 When you dust furniture or other objects, you remove dust from them using a duster.

3 If you dust a surface with powder, you cover it lightly with the powder.

dustbin ['dʌstˌbɪn] **dustbins** NOUN
a large container for rubbish

duster ['dʌstə] **dusters** NOUN
a cloth used for removing dust from furniture and other objects

dustman ['dʌstmən] **dustmen** NOUN
someone whose job is to collect the rubbish from people's houses

dusty ['dʌstɪ] **dustier, dustiest** ADJECTIVE
covered with dust

Dutch [dʌtʃ] ADJECTIVE
1 belonging or relating to Holland

> NOUN

2 Dutch is the main language spoken in Holland.

dutiful ['dju:tɪfʊl] ADJECTIVE
doing everything you are expected to do
dutifully ADVERB

duty ['dju:tɪ] **duties** NOUN
1 something you ought to do or feel you should do, because it is your responsibility *e.g. We have a duty as adults to listen to children.*

● THESAURUS

obligation: *He had not felt an obligation to help save his old friend.*

responsibility: *work and family responsibilities*

2 a task which you do as part of your job

● THESAURUS

assignment: *dangerous assignments*

job: *One of my jobs was to make the tea.*

responsibility: *He handled his responsibilities as a counsellor very well.*

role: *Both sides had important roles to play.*

> NOUN

3 Duty is tax paid to the government on some goods, especially imports.

● THESAURUS

excise: *These products are excused VAT and excise.*

levy: formal *An annual motorway levy is imposed on all drivers.*

tariff: *America wants to eliminate tariffs on such items as electronics.*

tax: *the tax on new cars and motorcycles*

duty-free ['dju:tɪ'fri:] ADJECTIVE
Duty-free goods are sold at airports or on planes or ships at a cheaper price than usual because they are not taxed. *e.g. duty-free vodka*

duvet ['du:veɪ] **duvets** NOUN
a cotton quilt filled with feathers or other material, used on a bed in place of sheets and blankets

DVD **DVDs** NOUN
an abbreviation for 'digital video *or* digital versatile disc': a type of compact disc that can store large amounts of video and sound information

dwarf [dwɔːf] **dwarfs, dwarfing, dwarfed** VERB

1 If one thing dwarfs another, it is so much bigger that it makes it look very small.

> ADJECTIVE

2 smaller than average

> NOUN

3 a person who is much smaller than average size

dwell [dwɛl] **dwells, dwelling, dwelled** or **dwelt** VERB

1 LITERARY
To dwell somewhere means to live there.

2 If you dwell on something or dwell upon it, you think or write about it a lot.

dwelling ['dwɛlɪŋ] **dwellings** NOUN; FORMAL
Someone's dwelling is the house or other place where they live.

dwindle ['dwɪndəl] **dwindles, dwindling, dwindled** VERB
If something dwindles, it becomes smaller or weaker.

dye [daɪ] **dyes, dyeing, dyed** VERB

1 To dye something means to change its colour by applying coloured liquid to it.

> NOUN

2 a colouring substance which is used to change the colour of something such as cloth or hair

dying ['daɪɪŋ] ADJECTIVE

1 likely to die soon

2 INFORMAL
If you are **dying for something**, you want it very much.

● THESAURUS
ache for: *She still ached for the lost intimacy of marriage.*
hunger for: *Jules hungered for adventure.*

long for: *He longed for the winter to be over.*
pine for: *I pine for the countryside.*
yearn for: *He yearned for freedom.*

dyke [daɪk] **dykes;** also spelt **dike** NOUN
a thick wall that prevents water flooding onto land from a river or from the sea

dynamic [daɪ'næmɪk] **dynamics** ADJECTIVE

1 A dynamic person is full of energy, ambition, and new ideas.

2 relating to energy or forces which produce motion

> PLURAL NOUN

3 In physics, dynamics is the study of the forces that change or produce the motion of bodies or particles.

4 The dynamics of a society or a situation are the forces that cause it to change.

5 (**MUSIC**) Dynamics is the various degrees of loudness needed in the performance of a piece of music, or the symbols used to indicate this in written music.

dynamite ['daɪnə,maɪt] NOUN
Dynamite is a kind of explosive.

dynamo ['daɪnə,məʊ] **dynamos** NOUN
a device that converts mechanical energy into electricity

dynasty ['dɪnəstɪ] **dynasties** NOUN
(**HISTORY**) a series of rulers of a country all belonging to the same family

dysentery ['dɪsəntrɪ] NOUN
an infection of the bowel which causes fever, stomach pain, and severe diarrhoea

dyslexia [dɪs'lɛksɪə] NOUN
Dyslexia is difficulty with reading caused by a slight disorder of the brain.
dyslexic ADJECTIVE OR NOUN

d

Ee

each [iːtʃ] ADJECTIVE OR PRONOUN
1 every one taken separately *e.g. Each time she went out, she would buy a plant.*

> PHRASE
2 If people do something to **each other**, each person does it to the other or others. *e.g. She and Chris smiled at each other.*

Wherever you use *each other* you could also use *one another.*

eager ['iːɡə] ADJECTIVE
wanting very much to do or have something
eagerly ADVERB, **eagerness** NOUN

● THESAURUS
anxious: *She was anxious to leave early.*
ardent: *one of the government's most ardent supporters*
avid: *He's always been an avid reader.*
enthusiastic: *Tom usually seems very enthusiastic.*
keen: *Kirsty has always been a keen swimmer.*
raring to go: *informal They're all ready and raring to go.*

eagle ['iːɡəl] **eagles** NOUN
a large bird of prey

ear [ɪə] **ears** NOUN
1 the parts of your body on either side of your head with which you hear sounds
2 An ear of corn or wheat is the top part of the stalk which contains seeds.

eardrum ['ɪə,drʌm] **eardrums** NOUN
Your eardrums are thin pieces of tightly stretched skin inside your ears which vibrate so that you can hear sounds.

earl [ɜːl] **earls** NOUN
a British nobleman
[WORD HISTORY: from Old English EORL meaning 'chieftain']

early ['ɜːlɪ] **earlier, earliest** ADJECTIVE
1 before the arranged or expected time *e.g. He wasn't late for our meeting, I was early.*

● THESAURUS
advance: *We got an advance copy of her new book.*
premature: *The injury put a premature end to his sporting career.*

untimely: *her untimely death in a car crash at the age of 21*
<<OPPOSITE *late*

2 near the beginning of a day, evening, or other period of time *e.g. the early 1970s*

● THESAURUS
primeval: *These insects first appeared in the primeval forests of Europe.*
primitive: *We found a fossil of a primitive bird-like creature.*

> ADVERB
3 before the arranged or expected time *e.g. I arrived early.*

● THESAURUS
ahead of time: *The bus always arrives ahead of time.*
beforehand: *If you'd let me know beforehand, you could have come with us.*
in advance: *You need to book in advance to get a good seat.*
in good time: *We arrived at the airport in good time.*
prematurely: *men who go prematurely bald*

earmark ['ɪə,mɑːk] **earmarks, earmarking, earmarked** VERB
If you earmark something for a special purpose, you keep it for that purpose.
[WORD HISTORY: from identification marks on the ears of domestic or farm animals]

earn [ɜːn] **earns, earning, earned** VERB
1 If you earn money, you get it in return for work that you do.

● THESAURUS
bring in: *My job brings in just enough to pay the bills.*
draw: *I draw a salary, so I can afford to run a car.*
get: *How much do you get if you're a lorry driver?*
make: *She makes a lot of money.*
obtain: *the profits obtained from buying and selling shares*

2 If you earn something such as praise, you receive it because you deserve it.
earner NOUN

● THESAURUS
acquire: *She has acquired a reputation as a liar and a cheat.*

attain: formal *He finally attained his pilot's licence.*

win: *She won the admiration of all her colleagues.*

earnest ['ɜːnɪst] ADJECTIVE

1 sincere in what you say or do *e.g. I answered with an earnest smile.*

> PHRASE

2 If something begins **in earnest**, it happens to a greater or more serious extent than before. *e.g. The battle began in earnest.*

earnestly ADVERB

earnings ['ɜːnɪŋz] PLURAL NOUN

Your earnings are money that you earn.

earphones ['ɪəˌfəʊns] PLURAL NOUN

small speakers which you wear on your ears to listen to a radio, CD, or MP3 player

earring ['ɪəˌrɪŋ] **earrings** NOUN

Earrings are pieces of jewellery that you wear on your ear lobes.

earshot ['ɪəˌʃɒt] PHRASE

If you are **within earshot** of something, you can hear it.

earth [ɜːθ] **earths** NOUN

1 The earth is the planet on which we live.

● THESAURUS

globe: *from every corner of the globe*

planet: *the effects of pollution on the atmosphere of our planet*

world: *the first person to cycle round the world*

2 Earth is the dry land on the surface of the earth, especially the soil in which things grow.

● THESAURUS

clay: *lumps of clay that stuck to his boots*

dirt: *kneeling in the dirt*

ground: *digging potatoes out of the ground*

soil: *We planted some bulbs in the soil around the pond.*

3 a hole in the ground where a fox lives

4 The earth in a piece of electrical equipment is the wire through which electricity can pass into the ground and so make the equipment safe for use.

earthenware ['ɜːθənˌwɛə] NOUN

pottery made of baked clay

earthly ['ɜːθlɪ] ADJECTIVE

concerned with life on earth rather than heaven or life after death

earthquake ['ɜːθˌkweɪk] **earthquakes** NOUN

a shaking of the ground caused by movement of the earth's crust

earthworm ['ɜːθˌwɜːm] **earthworms** NOUN

a worm that lives under the ground

earthy ['ɜːθɪ] **earthier, earthiest** ADJECTIVE

1 looking or smelling like earth

2 Someone who is earthy is open and direct, often in a crude way. *e.g. earthy language*

earwig ['ɪəˌwɪɡ] **earwigs** NOUN

a small, thin, brown insect which has a pair of pincers at the end of its body

[WORD HISTORY: from Old English EARWICGA meaning 'ear insect'; it was believed to creep into people's ears]

ease [iːz] **eases, easing, eased** NOUN

1 lack of difficulty, worry, or hardship *e.g. He had sailed through life with relative ease.*

● THESAURUS

leisure: *living a life of leisure*

relaxation: *The town has a feeling of relaxation and tranquillity about it.*

simplicity: *The simplicity of the new scheme has made it popular with motorists.*

> VERB

2 When something eases, or when you ease it, it becomes less severe or less intense. *e.g. to ease the pain*

● THESAURUS

abate: *By morning the storms had abated.*

calm: *The government is taking steps to calm the situation.*

relax: *He relaxed his grip on the axe and smiled.*

relieve: *The pills will help relieve the pain for a while.*

slacken: *Her grip on the rope slackened and she fell back.*

3 If you ease something somewhere, you move it there slowly and carefully. *e.g. He eased himself into his chair.*

● THESAURUS

creep: *The car crept down the ramp.*

edge: *I edged the van slowly back into the garage.*

guide: *Bob guided the plane out onto the tarmac.*

inch: *The ambulance inched its way through the crowds of shoppers.*

lower: *He lowered himself into the armchair.*

manoeuvre: *We attempted to manoeuvre his canoe towards the shore.*

squeeze: *They squeezed him into his seat and strapped him in.*

easel ['iːzᵊl] **easels** NOUN

(ART) an upright frame which supports a picture that someone is painting

[WORD HISTORY: from Dutch EZEL meaning 'ass' or 'donkey']

easily ['iːzɪlɪ] ADVERB

1 without difficulty

2 without a doubt *e.g. The song is easily one of their finest.*

east [iːst] NOUN

1 East is the direction in which you look to see the sun rise.

2 The east of a place is the part which is towards the east when you are in the centre. *e.g. the east of Africa*

3 The East is the countries in the south and east of Asia.

> ADJECTIVE OR ADVERB
4 East means in or towards the east. *e.g. The entrance faces east.*

> ADJECTIVE
5 An east wind blows from the east.

Easter ['iːstə] NOUN

a Christian religious festival celebrating the resurrection of Christ

[WORD HISTORY: from Old English EOSTRE, a pre-Christian Germanic goddess whose festival was at the spring equinox]

easterly ['iːstəlɪ] ADJECTIVE

1 Easterly means to or towards the east.

2 An easterly wind blows from the east.

eastern ['iːstən] ADJECTIVE

in or from the east *e.g. a remote eastern corner of the country*

eastward or **eastwards** ['iːstwəd] or ['iːstwədz] ADVERB

1 Eastward or eastwards means towards the east. *e.g. the eastward expansion of the city*

> ADJECTIVE
2 The eastward part of something is the east part.

easy ['iːzɪ] **easier, easiest** ADJECTIVE

1 able to be done without difficulty *e.g. It's easy to fall.*

● THESAURUS
light: *a few light exercises to warm up*
painless: *Finding somewhere to stay was pretty painless in the end.*
simple: *All you have to do is answer a few simple questions.*
smooth: *a smooth changeover to the new system*
straightforward: *The route is fairly straightforward so you shouldn't need a map.*
<<OPPOSITE hard

2 comfortable and without any worries *e.g. an easy life*

● THESAURUS
carefree: *a carefree summer spent on the beach*
comfortable: *a comfortable teaching job at a small private school*
leisurely: *a leisurely weekend spent with a few close friends*

quiet: *a quiet weekend in the sun*
relaxed: *It's very relaxed here, you can do what you like.*

Although *easy* is an adjective, it can be used as an adverb in fixed phrases like *take it easy*.

eat [iːt] **eats, eating, ate, eaten** VERB

1 To eat means to chew and swallow food.

● THESAURUS
chew: *I pulled out a filling while I was chewing a toffee.*
consume: *Andrew would consume nearly a pound of cheese a day.*
devour: *She devoured half an apple pie.*
feed: *Slugs feed on decaying plant material.*
gobble: *Pete gobbled all the stew before anyone else arrived.*
guzzle: *women who guzzle chocolate whenever they are unhappy*
munch: *Luke munched his sandwiches appreciatively.*
nibble: *She nibbled at a piece of dry toast.*
scoff: *You greedy so-and-so! You've scoffed the lot!*
snack: *Instead of snacking on crisps and chocolate, eat fruit.*
stuff (yourself): *They'd stuffed themselves with sweets before dinner.*
swallow: *Snakes swallow their prey whole.*
wolf: *I was back in the changing room wolfing sandwiches.*

2 When you eat, you have a meal. *e.g. We like to eat early.*

● THESAURUS
breakfast: formal *The ladies like to breakfast in their rooms.*
dine: *We usually dine at about six.*
feed: *Leopards only feed when they are hungry.*
have a meal: *We could have a meal at Pizza Palace after the film.*
lunch: formal *We lunched at El Greco's.*
picnic: *After our walk, we picnicked by the river.*

eat away VERB

3 If something is eaten away, it is slowly destroyed. *e.g. The sea had eaten away at the headland.*

eaves [iːvz] PLURAL NOUN

The eaves of a roof are the lower edges which jut out over the walls.

eavesdrop ['iːvzˌdrɒp] **eavesdrops, eavesdropping, eavesdropped** VERB

If you eavesdrop, you listen secretly to what other people are saying.

[WORD HISTORY: from Old English YFESDRYPE meaning 'water dripping down from the eaves'; people were supposed to stand outside in the rain to hear what was being said inside the house]

ebb [ɛb] **ebbs, ebbing, ebbed** VERB

1 When the sea or the tide ebbs, it flows back.

2 If a person's feeling or strength ebbs, it gets weaker. *e.g. The strength ebbed from his body.*

ebony ['ɛbənɪ] NOUN

1 a hard, dark-coloured wood, used for making furniture

> NOUN OR ADJECTIVE

2 very deep black

ebullient [ɪ'bʌljənt] ADJECTIVE; FORMAL
lively and full of enthusiasm
ebullience NOUN

EC NOUN
The EC is an old name for the European Union. EC is an abbreviation for 'European Community'.

eccentric [ɪk'sɛntrɪk] **eccentrics** ADJECTIVE

1 having habits or opinions which other people think are odd or peculiar

● THESAURUS
bizarre: *He's quite a bizarre character.*
outlandish: *His outlandish behaviour sometimes put people off.*
quirky: *a quirky, delightful film that is full of surprises*
strange: *his strange views about UFOs*
weird: *His taste in music is a bit weird.*
whimsical: *a whimsical old gentleman*

> NOUN

2 someone who is eccentric
eccentricity NOUN, **eccentrically** ADVERB

● THESAURUS
character: informal *a well-known character who lived in Johnson Street*
crank: *People regarded vegetarians as cranks in those days.*

ecclesiastical [ɪ,kliːzɪ'æstɪkəl] ADJECTIVE
of or relating to the Christian church
[WORD HISTORY: from Greek EKKLĒSIA meaning 'assembly' or 'church']

echelon ['ɛʃə,lɒn] **echelons** NOUN
a level of power or responsibility in an organization

echidna [ɪ'kɪdnə] **echidnas** or **echidnae** NOUN
a small, spiny mammal that lays eggs and has a long snout and claws, found in Australia

echo ['ɛkəʊ] **echoes, echoing, echoed** NOUN

1 a sound which is caused by sound waves reflecting off a surface

2 a repetition, imitation, or reminder of something *e.g. Echoes of the past are everywhere.*

> VERB

3 If a sound echoes, it is reflected off a surface so

that you can hear it again after the original sound has stopped.

eclipse [ɪ'klɪps] **eclipses** NOUN
An eclipse occurs when one planet passes in front of another and hides it from view for a short time.

eco- PREFIX
Words beginning with 'eco-' have something to do with ecology or the environment.
[WORD HISTORY: from Greek OIKOS meaning 'environment']

ecology [ɪ'kɒlədʒɪ] NOUN
the relationship between living things and their environment; also used of the study of this relationship
ecological ADJECTIVE, **ecologically** ADVERB, **ecologist** NOUN

economic [,iːkə'nɒmɪk] ADJECTIVE

1 (HISTORY) concerning the management of the money, industry, and trade of a country

● THESAURUS
budgetary: *a summit meeting to discuss various budgetary matters*
commercial: *a purely commercial decision*
financial: *The financial pressures on the government are mounting.*

2 concerning making a profit *e.g. economic to produce*

● THESAURUS
productive: *the need to make these industries more productive*
profitable: *a new venture that has proved highly profitable*
viable: *businesses that are no longer viable*

economical [,iːkə'nɒmɪkəl] ADJECTIVE

1 (HISTORY) another word for **economic**

2 Something that is economical is cheap to use or operate.

● THESAURUS
cheap: *This isn't a very cheap way of buying stationery.*
cost-effective: *the most cost-effective way of shopping*
economic: *the most economic way to see the museum*
inexpensive: *There are several good inexpensive restaurants in town.*

3 Someone who is economical spends money carefully and sensibly.
economically ADVERB

● THESAURUS
careful: *She's very careful with her pocket money.*
frugal: *his frugal lifestyle*
prudent: *the prudent use of precious natural resources*

thrifty: *My mother was very thrifty because she had so little spare cash.*

economics [ˌiːkəˈnɒmɪks] NOUN
Economics is the study of the production and distribution of goods, services, and wealth in a society and the organization of its money, industry, and trade.

economist [ɪˈkɒnəmɪst] **economists** NOUN
a person who studies or writes about economics

economy [ɪˈkɒnəmɪ] **economies** NOUN
1 (**HISTORY**) The economy of a country is the system it uses to organize and manage its money, industry, and trade; also used of the wealth that a country gets from business and industry.
2 Economy is the careful use of things to save money, time, or energy. *e.g. Max dished up deftly, with an economy of movement.*
[WORD HISTORY: from Greek OIKONOMIA meaning 'domestic management']

● THESAURUS
frugality: *formal We must live with strict frugality if we are to survive.*
prudence: *A lack of prudence could seriously affect his finances.*
restraint: *We need to exercise some restraint in our spending.*
thrift: *He was widely praised for his thrift and imagination.*

ecosystem [ˈiːkəʊˌsɪstəm] **ecosystems** NOUN; TECHNICAL
the relationship between plants and animals and their environment

ecstasy [ˈɛkstəsɪ] **ecstasies** NOUN
1 Ecstasy is a feeling of extreme happiness.

● THESAURUS
bliss: *husband and wife living together in bliss and harmony*
delight: *He squealed with delight when we told him.*
elation: *His supporters reacted to the news with elation.*
euphoria: *There was a sense of euphoria after our election victory.*
exaltation: *the mood of exaltation that affected everyone*
joy: *her joy at finding him after so long*
rapture: *His speech was received with rapture by a huge crowd.*

2 INFORMAL
a strong illegal drug that can cause hallucinations
ecstatic ADJECTIVE, **ecstatically** ADVERB

eczema [ˈɛksɪmə] *or* [ɪɡˈziːmə] NOUN
a skin disease that causes the surface of the skin to become rough and itchy

[WORD HISTORY: from Greek EKZEIN meaning 'to boil over']

-ed SUFFIX
'-ed' is used to form the past tense of most English verbs *e.g. jumped... tried*
[WORD HISTORY: from Old English]

eddy [ˈɛdɪ] **eddies** NOUN
a circular movement in water or air

edge [ɛdʒ] **edges, edging, edged** NOUN
1 The edge of something is a border or line where it ends or meets something else.

● THESAURUS
border: *a pillowcase with a lace border*
boundary: *The area beyond the western boundary belongs to Denmark.*
brim: *He kept climbing until he reached the brim of the crater.*
fringe: *the rundown areas on the fringes of the city*
lip: *The lip of the jug was badly cracked.*
margin: *standing on the margin of the land where it met the water*
rim: *a large round mirror with a gold rim*
<<OPPOSITE *centre*

2 The edge of a blade is its thin, sharp side.
3 If you have the edge over someone, you have an advantage over them.

> VERB
4 If you edge something, you make a border for it. *e.g. The veil was edged with matching lace.*
5 If you edge somewhere, you move there very gradually. *e.g. The ferry edged its way out into the river.*

● THESAURUS
creep: *The car crept forward a few feet, then stopped.*
inch: *The ambulance inched its way through the crowds.*
sidle: *A man sidled up to him and tried to sell him a ticket.*

edgy [ˈɛdʒɪ] **edgier, edgiest** ADJECTIVE
anxious and irritable

edible [ˈɛdɪbəl] ADJECTIVE
safe and pleasant to eat

edifice [ˈɛdɪfɪs] **edifices** NOUN; FORMAL
a large and impressive building

edit [ˈɛdɪt] **edits, editing, edited** VERB
1 If you edit a piece of writing, you correct it so that it is fit for publishing.
2 To edit a film or television programme means to select different parts of it and arrange them in a particular order.
3 Someone who edits a newspaper or magazine is in charge of it.

edition [ɪ'dɪʃən] **editions** NOUN

1 An edition of a book or magazine is a particular version of it printed at one time.

2 An edition of a television or radio programme is a single programme that is one of a series.

editor ['ɛdɪtə] **editors** NOUN **(LIBRARY)**

1 a person who is responsible for the content of a newspaper or magazine

2 a person who checks books and makes corrections to them before they are published

3 a person who selects different parts of a television programme or a film and arranges them in a particular order
editorship NOUN

editorial [ˌɛdɪ'tɔːrɪəl] **editorials** ADJECTIVE

1 involved in preparing a newspaper, book, or magazine for publication

2 involving the contents and the opinions of a newspaper or magazine e.g. an editorial comment

> NOUN

3 an article in a newspaper or magazine which gives the opinions of the editor or publisher on a particular topic
editorially ADVERB

educate ['ɛdjʊˌkeɪt] **educates, educating, educated** VERB

To educate someone means to teach them so that they gain knowledge about something.

educated ['ɛdjʊˌkeɪtɪd] ADJECTIVE
having a high standard of learning and culture

● THESAURUS
cultivated: His mother was an elegant, cultivated woman.
cultured: a cultured man with a wide circle of friends
intellectual: He is the intellectual type.
learned: He was a scholar, a very learned man.

education [ˌɛdjʊ'keɪʃən] NOUN
the process of gaining knowledge and understanding through learning or the system of teaching people
educational ADJECTIVE, **educationally** ADVERB

● THESAURUS
coaching: extra coaching to help him pass his exams
instruction: All instruction is provided by qualified experts.
schooling: He began to wish he'd paid more attention to his schooling.
training: His military training was no use to him here.
tuition: personal tuition in the basics of photography

eel [iːl] **eels** NOUN
a long, thin, snakelike fish

eerie ['ɪərɪ] **eerier, eeriest** ADJECTIVE
strange and frightening e.g. an eerie silence
eerily ADVERB

effect [ɪ'fɛkt] **effects** NOUN

1 a direct result of someone or something on another person or thing e.g. the effect of divorce on children

● THESAURUS
consequence: aware of the consequences of their actions
end result: The end result of this process is still unclear.
fruit: The new software is the fruit of three years' hard work.
result: The result of all this uncertainty is that no-one is happy.
upshot: The upshot is that we have a very unhappy workforce.

2 An effect that someone or something has is the overall impression or result that they have. e.g. The effect of the decor was cosy and antique.

> PHRASE

3 If something **takes effect** at a particular time, it starts to happen or starts to produce results at that time. e.g. The law will take effect next year.

> Remember that effect is a *noun* and *affect* is a verb.

effective [ɪ'fɛktɪv] ADJECTIVE

1 working well and producing the intended results

2 coming into operation or beginning officially e.g. The agreement has become effective immediately.
effectively ADVERB

effeminate [ɪ'fɛmɪnɪt] ADJECTIVE
A man who is effeminate behaves, looks, or sounds like a woman.

efficient [ɪ'fɪʃənt] ADJECTIVE
capable of doing something well without wasting time or energy
efficiently ADVERB, **efficiency** NOUN

● THESAURUS
businesslike: a highly businesslike approach that impressed everyone
competent: an extremely competent piece of work
economic: The new system is much more economic, and will save millions.
effective: effective use of the time we have left
organized: Tony seemed very organized, and completely in control of the situation.
productive: the need to make farmers much more productive
<<OPPOSITE inefficient

effigy ['ɛfɪdʒɪ] **effigies** NOUN
a statue or model of a person

effluent [ˈɛflʊənt] **effluents** NOUN
Effluent is liquid waste that comes out of factories or sewage works.

effluvium [ɛˈfluːvɪəm] **efflivia**
Effluvium is an unpleasant smell or gas that is given off by something, especially something that is decaying.

effort [ˈɛfət] **efforts** NOUN
1 (PSHE) Effort is the physical or mental energy needed to do something.

⬤ THESAURUS
application: *His talent, application and energy are a credit to the school.*
energy: *He decided to devote his energy to writing another book.*
exertion: *Is it really worth all the exertion?*
trouble: *It's not worth the trouble.*
work: *All the work I put in has now been wasted!*

2 an attempt or struggle to do something *e.g. I went to keep-fit classes in an effort to fight the flab.*

⬤ THESAURUS
attempt: *an attempt to obtain an interview with the President*
bid: *a last-minute bid to stop the trial going ahead*
stab: *informal his latest stab at acting*
struggle: *his struggle to clear his name*

effortless [ˈɛfətlɪs] ADJECTIVE
done easily
effortlessly ADVERB

eg or **e.g.**
eg means 'for example', and is abbreviated from the Latin expression 'exempli gratia'

egalitarian [ɪˌɡælɪˈtɛərɪən] ADJECTIVE
favouring equality for all people *e.g. an egalitarian country*

egg [ɛɡ] **eggs** NOUN
1 an oval or rounded object laid by female birds, reptiles, fishes, and insects. A baby creature develops inside the egg until it is ready to be born
2 a hen's egg used as food
3 In a female animal, an egg is a cell produced in its body which can develop into a baby if it is fertilized.

eggplant [ˈɛɡˌplɑːnt] **eggplants** NOUN
a dark purple pear-shaped fruit eaten as a vegetable. It is also called **aubergine**

ego [ˈiːɡəʊ] **egos** NOUN
Your ego is your opinion of what you are worth. *e.g. It'll do her good and boost her ego.*
[WORD HISTORY: from Latin EGO meaning 'I']

egocentric [ˌiːɡəʊˈsɛntrɪk] ADJECTIVE
only thinking of yourself

egoism or **egotism** [ˈiːɡəʊˌɪzəm] or [ˈiːɡəʊˌtɪzəm] NOUN

Egoism is behaviour and attitudes which show that you believe that you are more important than other people.
egoist or **egotist** NOUN, **egoistic, egotistic** or **egotistical** ADJECTIVE

Egyptian [ɪˈdʒɪpʃən] **Egyptians** ADJECTIVE
1 belonging or relating to Egypt
> NOUN
2 An Egyptian is someone who comes from Egypt.

Eid-ul-Adha [ˈiːdʊlˌɑːdə] NOUN
an annual Muslim festival marking the end of the pilgrimage to Mecca known as the hajj. Animals are sacrificed and their meat is shared among the poor
[WORD HISTORY: from Arabic ID UL ADHA festival of sacrifice]

eight [eɪt] **eights**
the number 8
eighth

eighteen [ˈeɪˈtiːn]
the number 18
eighteenth

eighty [ˈeɪtɪ] **eighties**
the number 80
eightieth

either [ˈaɪðə] ADJECTIVE, PRONOUN, OR CONJUNCTION
1 one or the other of two possible alternatives *e.g. You can spell it either way... Either of these schemes would cost billions of pounds... Either take it or leave it.*
> ADJECTIVE
2 both one and the other *e.g. on either side of the head*

> When *either* is followed by a plural noun, the following verb can be plural too: *either of these books are useful.*

ejaculate [ɪˈdʒækjʊˌleɪt] **ejaculates, ejaculating, ejaculated** VERB
1 When a man ejaculates, he discharges semen from his penis.
2 If you ejaculate, you suddenly say something.
ejaculation NOUN
[WORD HISTORY: from Latin JACERE meaning 'to throw']

eject [ɪˈdʒɛkt] **ejects, ejecting, ejected** VERB
If you eject something or someone, you forcefully push or send them out. *e.g. He was ejected from the club.*
ejection NOUN

elaborate **elaborates, elaborating, elaborated** ADJECTIVE [ɪˈlæbərɪt]

1 having many different parts *e.g. an elaborate system of drains*

● THESAURUS
complex: *a complex explanation*
complicated: *a complicated plan of the building's security system*
detailed: *the detailed plans that have been drawn up*
intricate: *an intricate system of levers and pulleys*
involved: *a very involved operation, lasting many hours*
<<OPPOSITE *simple*

2 carefully planned, detailed, and exact *e.g. elaborate plans*

3 highly decorated and complicated *e.g. elaborate designs*

● THESAURUS
fancy: *the fancy plasterwork on the ceiling*
fussy: *a rather fussy design*
ornate: *an ornate wrought-iron staircase*

> VERB [ɪˈlæbəˌreɪt]
4 If you elaborate on something, you add more information or detail about it.
elaborately ADVERB, **elaboration** NOUN

● THESAURUS
develop: *Maybe we should develop this idea.*
enlarge: *He was enlarging on proposals made earlier.*
expand: *a view that I will expand on later*

eland [ˈiːlənd] **elands** NOUN
a large African antelope with twisted horns

elapse [ɪˈlæps] **elapses, elapsing, elapsed** VERB
When time elapses, it passes by. *e.g. Eleven years elapsed before you got this job.*

elastic [ɪˈlæstɪk] ADJECTIVE
1 able to stretch easily

> NOUN
2 Elastic is rubber material which stretches and returns to its original shape.
elasticity NOUN
[WORD HISTORY: from Greek ELASTIKOS meaning 'pushing']

elation [ɪˈleɪʃən] NOUN
Elation is a feeling of great happiness.
elated ADJECTIVE

elbow [ˈɛlbəʊ] **elbows, elbowing, elbowed** NOUN
1 Your elbow is the joint between the upper part of your arm and your forearm.

> VERB
2 If you elbow someone aside, you push them away with your elbow.

elder [ˈɛldə] **eldest; elders** ADJECTIVE

1 Your elder brother or sister is older than you.

> NOUN
2 a senior member of a group who has influence or authority

3 a bush or small tree with dark purple berries

▌ The adjectives *elder* and *eldest* can only be used when talking about the age of people within families. You can use *older* and *oldest* to talk about the age of other people or things.

elderly [ˈɛldəlɪ] ADJECTIVE
1 Elderly is a polite way to describe an old person.

> NOUN
2 The elderly are old people. *e.g. Priority is given to services for the elderly.*

elect [ɪˈlɛkt] **elects, electing, elected** VERB
1 If you elect someone, you choose them to fill a position, by voting. *e.g. He's just been elected president.*

2 FORMAL
If you elect to do something, you choose to do it. *e.g. I have elected to stay.*

> ADJECTIVE
3 FORMAL
voted into a position, but not yet carrying out the duties of the position *e.g. the vice-president elect*

election [ɪˈlɛkʃən] **elections** NOUN
the selection of one or more people for an official position by voting
electoral ADJECTIVE

electorate [ɪˈlɛktərɪt] **electorates** NOUN
all the people who have the right to vote in an election

electric [ɪˈlɛktrɪk] ADJECTIVE
1 powered or produced by electricity

2 very tense or exciting *e.g. The atmosphere is electric.*

▌ The word *electric* is an adjective and should not be used as a noun.

electrical [ɪˈlɛktrɪkᵊl] ADJECTIVE
using or producing electricity *e.g. electrical goods*
electrically ADVERB

electrician [ɪlɛkˈtrɪʃən] **electricians** NOUN
a person whose job is to install and repair electrical equipment

electricity [ɪlɛkˈtrɪsɪtɪ] NOUN
Electricity is a form of energy used for heating and lighting, and to provide power for machines.
[WORD HISTORY: from Greek ELEKTRON meaning 'amber'; in early experiments, scientists rubbed amber in order to get an electrical charge]

electrified [ɪˈlɛktrɪˌfaɪd] ADJECTIVE
connected to a supply of electricity

e

electrifying [ɪˈlɛktrɪˌfaɪɪŋ] ADJECTIVE
Something that is electrifying makes you feel
very excited.

electro- PREFIX
'Electro-' means 'electric' or involving electricity
[WORD HISTORY: from Greek ĒLECTRON]

electrocute [ɪˈlɛktrəˌkjuːt] **electrocutes,
electrocuting, electrocuted** VERB
If someone is electrocuted, they are killed by
touching something that is connected to
electricity.
electrocution NOUN

electrode [ɪˈlɛktrəʊd] **electrodes** NOUN
a small piece of metal which allows an electric
current to pass between a source of power and a
piece of equipment

electron [ɪˈlɛktrɒn] **electrons** NOUN
In physics, an electron is a tiny particle of matter,
smaller than an atom.

electronic [ɪlɛkˈtrɒnɪk] ADJECTIVE
(ICT) having transistors or silicon chips which
control an electric current
electronically ADVERB

electronics [ɪlɛkˈtrɒnɪks] NOUN
Electronics is the technology of electronic
devices such as televisions, and computers; also
the study of how these devices work.

elegant [ˈɛlɪɡənt] ADJECTIVE
attractive and graceful or stylish *e.g. an elegant
and beautiful city*
elegantly ADVERB, **elegance** NOUN

elegy [ˈɛlɪdʒɪ] **elegies** NOUN
a sad poem or song about someone who has died
[WORD HISTORY: from Greek ELEGOS meaning
'lament sung to the flute']

element [ˈɛlɪmənt] **elements** NOUN
1 a part of something which combines with
others to make a whole

2 (**SCIENCE**) In chemistry, an element is a
substance that is made up of only one type of
atom.

3 A particular element within a large group of
people is a section of it which is similar. *e.g.
criminal elements*

4 An element of a quality is a certain amount of
it. *e.g. Their attack has largely lost the element of
surprise.*

5 The elements of a subject are the basic and
most important points.

6 The elements are the weather conditions. *e.g.
Our open boat is exposed to the elements.*

elemental [ˌɛlɪˈmɛntᵊl] ADJECTIVE; FORMAL
simple and basic, but powerful *e.g. elemental
emotions*

elementary [ˌɛlɪˈmɛntərɪ] ADJECTIVE
simple, basic, and straightforward *e.g. an
elementary course in woodwork*

elephant [ˈɛlɪfənt] **elephants** NOUN
a very large four-legged mammal with a long
trunk, large ears, and ivory tusks

elevate [ˈɛlɪˌveɪt] **elevates, elevating,
elevated** VERB
1 To elevate someone to a higher status or
position means to give them greater status or
importance. *e.g. He was elevated to the rank of
major in the army.*

2 To elevate something means to raise it up.

elevation [ˌɛlɪˈveɪʃən] **elevations** NOUN
1 The elevation of someone or something is the
raising of them to a higher level or position.

2 The elevation of a place is its height above sea
level or above the ground.

eleven [ɪˈlɛvᵊn] **elevens**
1 Eleven is the number 11.
> NOUN
2 a team of cricket or soccer players
eleventh

elf [ɛlf] **elves** NOUN
In folklore, an elf is a small mischievous fairy.

elicit [ɪˈlɪsɪt] **elicits, eliciting, elicited** VERB
1 FORMAL
If you elicit information, you find it out by asking
careful questions.

2 If you elicit a response or reaction, you make it
happen. *e.g. He elicited sympathy from the audience.*

eligible [ˈɛlɪdʒəbᵊl] ADJECTIVE
suitable or having the right qualifications for
something *e.g. You will be eligible for a grant in the
future.*
eligibility NOUN

eliminate [ɪˈlɪmɪˌneɪt] **eliminates,
eliminating, eliminated** VERB
1 If you eliminate something or someone, you
get rid of them. *e.g. They eliminated him from their
inquiries.*

● **THESAURUS**
cut out: *His guilty plea cut out the need for a long,
costly trial.*

do away with: *the attempt to do away with nuclear
weapons altogether*

eradicate: *Efforts to eradicate malaria seem to be
failing.*

get rid of: *Why don't we just get rid of the
middlemen altogether?*

remove: *You should try and remove these fatty foods
from your diet.*

stamp out: *We need to stamp out this disgusting
practice.*

2 If a team or a person is eliminated from a competition, they can no longer take part.
elimination NOUN

⬤ THESAURUS
knock out: *We were knocked out by the Dutch champions.*
put out: *Decker finally put her fellow American out in the quarter final.*

elite [ɪˈliːt] **elites** NOUN
a group of the most powerful, rich, or talented people in a society

Elizabethan [ɪˌlɪzəˈbiːθən] ADJECTIVE
Someone or something that is Elizabethan lived or was made during the reign of Elizabeth I.

elk [ɛlk] **elks** NOUN
a large kind of deer

ellipse [ɪˈlɪps] **ellipses** NOUN
a regular oval shape, like a circle seen from an angle

elm [ɛlm] **elms** NOUN
a tall tree with broad leaves

elocution [ˌɛləˈkjuːʃən] NOUN
the art or study of speaking clearly or well in public

elongated [ˈiːlɒŋˌɡeɪtɪd] ADJECTIVE
long and thin

elope [ɪˈləʊp] **elopes, eloping, eloped** VERB
If someone elopes, they run away secretly with their lover to get married.

eloquent [ˈɛləkwənt] ADJECTIVE
able to speak or write skilfully and with ease *e.g. an eloquent politician*
eloquently ADVERB, **eloquence** NOUN

else [ɛls] ADVERB
1 other than this or more than this *e.g. Can you think of anything else?*

> PHRASE
2 You say **or else** to introduce a possibility or an alternative. *e.g. You have to go with the flow or else be left behind in the rush.*

elsewhere [ˌɛlsˈwɛə] ADVERB
in or to another place *e.g. He would rather be elsewhere.*

elude [ɪˈluːd] **eludes, eluding, eluded** VERB
1 If a fact or idea eludes you, you cannot understand it or remember it.

2 If you elude someone or something, you avoid them or escape from them. *e.g. He eluded the authorities.*

elusive [ɪˈluːsɪv] ADJECTIVE
difficult to find, achieve, describe, or remember *e.g. the elusive million dollar prize*

elves [ɛlvz] the plural of **elf**

em- PREFIX 'Em-' is another form of the prefix **en-**

▮ *Em-* is the form which is used before the letters *b*, *m* and *p*.

emaciated [ɪˈmeɪsɪˌeɪtɪd] ADJECTIVE
extremely thin and weak, because of illness or lack of food

e-mail or **email** [ˈiːmeɪl] NOUN
1 the sending of messages from one computer to another

2 a message sent in this way

> VERB
3 If you e-mail someone, you send an e-mail to them.

emancipation [ɪˌmænsɪˈpeɪʃən] NOUN
The emancipation of a person means the act of freeing them from harmful or unpleasant restrictions.

embargo [ɛmˈbɑːɡəʊ] **embargoes** NOUN
an order made by a government to stop trade with another country

embark [ɛmˈbɑːk] **embarks, embarking, embarked** VERB
1 If you embark, you go onto a ship at the start of a journey.

2 If you embark on something, you start it. *e.g. He embarked on a huge spending spree.*

embarrass [ɪmˈbærəs] **embarrasses, embarrassing, embarrassed** VERB
If you embarrass someone, you make them feel ashamed or awkward. *e.g. I won't embarrass you by asking for details.*
embarrassing ADJECTIVE

⬤ THESAURUS
disconcert: *The way Anderson was smirking disconcerted her.*
fluster: *Nothing could fluster him.*
humiliate: *How dare you humiliate me like that!*
shame: *Her son's behaviour had upset and shamed her.*

embarrassed [ɪmˈbærəst] ADJECTIVE
ashamed or awkward

⬤ THESAURUS
ashamed: *I felt so ashamed I wanted to die.*
awkward: *It was a very awkward occasion.*
humiliated: *A humiliated Mr Stevens admitted that the concert had been cancelled.*
red-faced: *Red-faced executives had to explain this fact.*
self-conscious: *I always feel self-conscious when I'm having my picture taken.*
sheepish: *He looked very sheepish when he finally appeared.*

embarrassment [ɪm'bærəsmənt] **embarrassments** NOUN
shame and awkwardness

⬤ THESAURUS
awkwardness: *the awkwardness of our first meeting*
bashfulness: *Overcome with bashfulness, he lowered his voice.*
humiliation: *the humiliation of having to ask for money*
self-consciousness: *her painful self-consciousness*
shame: *the shame he felt at having let her down*

embassy ['ɛmbəsɪ] **embassies** NOUN
the building in which an ambassador and his or her staff work; also used of the ambassador and his or her staff

embedded [ɪm'bɛdɪd] ADJECTIVE
Something that is embedded is fixed firmly and deeply. *e.g. glass decorated with embedded threads*

ember ['ɛmbə] **embers** NOUN
Embers are glowing pieces of coal or wood from a dying fire.

embittered [ɪm'bɪtəd] ADJECTIVE
If you are embittered, you are angry and resentful about things that have happened to you.

emblazoned [ɪm'bleɪz²nd] ADJECTIVE
If something is emblazoned with designs, it is decorated with them. *e.g. vases emblazoned with bold and colourful images*
[WORD HISTORY: originally a heraldic term from Old French BLASON meaning 'shield']

emblem ['ɛmbləm] **emblems** NOUN
an object or a design representing an organization or an idea *e.g. a flower emblem of Japan*

embody [ɪm'bɒdɪ] **embodies, embodying, embodied** VERB
1 To embody a quality or idea means to contain it or express it. *e.g. A young dancer embodies the spirit of fun.*
2 If a number of things are embodied in one thing, they are contained in it. *e.g. the principles embodied in his report*
embodiment NOUN

embossed [ɪm'bɒsd] ADJECTIVE
decorated with designs that stand up slightly from the surface *e.g. embossed wallpaper*

embrace [ɪm'breɪs] **embraces, embracing, embraced** VERB
1 If you embrace someone, you hug them to show affection or as a greeting.
2 If you embrace a belief or cause you accept it and believe in it.

> NOUN
3 a hug

embroider [ɪm'brɔɪdə] **embroiders, embroidering, embroidered** VERB
If you embroider fabric, you sew a decorative design onto it.

embroidery [ɪm'brɔɪdərɪ] NOUN
Embroidery is decorative designs sewn onto fabric; also the art or skill of embroidery.

embroiled [ɪm'brɔɪld] ADJECTIVE
If someone is embroiled in an argument or conflict they are deeply involved in it and cannot get out of it. *e.g. The two companies are now embroiled in the courts.*

embryo ['ɛmbrɪˌəʊ] **embryos** NOUN
an animal or human being in the very early stages of development in the womb
embryonic ADJECTIVE
[WORD HISTORY: from Greek EMBRUON meaning 'new-born animal']

emerald ['ɛmərəld] **emeralds** NOUN
1 a bright green precious stone
> NOUN OR ADJECTIVE
2 bright green

emerge [ɪ'mɜːdʒ] **emerges, emerging, emerged** VERB
1 If someone emerges from a place, they come out of it so that they can be seen.
2 If something emerges, it becomes known or begins to be recognized as existing. *e.g. It later emerged that he faced bankruptcy proceedings.*
emergence NOUN, **emergent** ADJECTIVE

emergency [ɪ'mɜːdʒənsɪ] **emergencies** NOUN
an unexpected and serious event which needs immediate action to deal with it

⬤ THESAURUS
crisis: *the economic crisis affecting parts of Africa*
pinch: *I don't mind working late in a pinch.*

emigrant ['ɛmɪgrənt] **emigrants** NOUN
a person who leaves their native country and goes to live permanently in another one

emigrate ['ɛmɪˌgreɪt] **emigrates, emigrating, emigrated** VERB
If you emigrate, you leave your native country and go to live permanently in another one.

emigration [ˌɛmɪ'greɪʃən] NOUN
(HISTORY) Emigration is the process of emigrating, especially by large numbers of people at various periods of history.

eminence ['ɛmɪnəns] NOUN
1 Eminence is the quality of being well-known and respected for what you do. *e.g. lawyers of eminence*

2 'Your Eminence' is a title of respect used to address a Roman Catholic cardinal

eminent ['ɛmɪnənt] ADJECTIVE
well-known and respected for what you do *e.g. an eminent scientist*

eminently ['ɛmɪnəntlɪ] ADVERB; FORMAL
very *e.g. eminently reasonable*

emir [ɛ'mɪə] **emirs** NOUN
a Muslim ruler or nobleman
[WORD HISTORY: from Arabic AMIR meaning 'commander']

emission [ɪ'mɪʃən] **emissions** NOUN; FORMAL
The emission of something such as gas or radiation is the release of it into the atmosphere.

emit [ɪ'mɪt] **emits, emitting, emitted** VERB
To emit something means to give it out or release it. *e.g. She emitted a long, low whistle.*

● THESAURUS
exude: *a plant that exudes an extremely unpleasant smell*
give off: *The fumes it gives off are poisonous, so watch out.*
give out: *The alarm gave out a series of bleeps, then stopped.*
release: *The factory is still releasing toxic fumes.*
send out: *The volcano has been sending out smoke for weeks.*
utter: *He uttered a loud snort and continued eating.*

emoticon [ɪ'məʊtɪˌkɒn] **emoticons** NOUN
a symbol used in e-mail which represents a particular emotion and is made up of normal keyboard characters that are viewed sideways. For example, the symbol (:+(means 'frightened' or 'scared'

emotion [ɪ'məʊʃən] **emotions** NOUN
(PSHE) a strong feeling, such as love or fear

emotional [ɪ'məʊʃənəl] ADJECTIVE **(PSHE)**
1 causing strong feelings *e.g. an emotional appeal for help*
2 to do with feelings rather than your physical condition *e.g. emotional support*
3 showing your feelings openly *e.g. The child is in a very emotional state.*
emotionally ADVERB

emotive [ɪ'məʊtɪv] ADJECTIVE
concerning emotions, or stirring up strong emotions *e.g. emotive language*

empathize ['ɛmpəˌθaɪz] **empathizes, empathizing, empathized;** also spelt **empathise** VERB
If you empathize with someone, you understand how they are feeling.

empathy NOUN

emperor ['ɛmpərə] **emperors** NOUN
a male ruler of an empire
[WORD HISTORY: from Latin IMPERATOR meaning 'commander-in-chief']

emphasis ['ɛmfəsɪs] **emphases** NOUN
Emphasis is special importance or extra stress given to something.

● THESAURUS
accent: *In the new government the accent will be on co-operation.*
importance: *There's not enough importance being given to environmental issues.*
prominence: *Crime prevention has to be given more prominence.*
weight: *This adds more weight to the government's case.*

emphasize ['ɛmfəˌsaɪz] **emphasizes, emphasizing, emphasized;** also spelt **emphasise** VERB
If you emphasize something, you make it known that it is very important. *e.g. It was emphasized that the matter was of international concern.*

● THESAURUS
accent: *a white dress accented by a coloured scarf*
accentuate: *His shaven head accentuates his round face.*
highlight: *This disaster has highlighted the difficulty faced by the government.*
play up: *He played up his bad-boy image.*
stress: *I would like to stress that we are in complete agreement.*
underline: *This underlines how important the new trade deal really is.*

emphatic [ɪm'fætɪk] ADJECTIVE
expressed strongly and with force to show how important something is *e.g. I answered both questions with an emphatic 'Yes'.*
emphatically ADVERB

empire ['ɛmpaɪə] **empires** NOUN
1 a group of countries controlled by one country
2 a powerful group of companies controlled by one person
[WORD HISTORY: from Latin IMPERIUM meaning 'rule']

employ [ɪm'plɔɪ] **employs, employing, employed** VERB
1 If you employ someone, you pay them to work for you.

● THESAURUS
appoint: *We need to appoint a successor to Mr Stevens.*
commission: *He has been commissioned to design a new bridge.*

engage: formal *They have finally engaged a suitable nanny.*
hire: *I was hired as a gardener on the estate.*
take on: *the need to take on more workers for the summer*

2 If you employ something for a particular purpose, you make use of it. *e.g. the techniques employed in turning grapes into wine*

● THESAURUS
bring to bear: *We can bring two very different techniques to bear on this.*
make use of: *He makes use of several highly offensive terms to describe them.*
use: *the methods used in the investigation*
utilize: *Engineers will utilize a range of techniques to improve the signal.*

employee [ɛmˈplɔɪiː] **employees** NOUN
a person who is paid to work for another person or for an organization

● THESAURUS
hand: *He's been working as a farm hand down south.*
worker: *Workers at the plant have been laid off.*
workman: *A council workman finally arrived to fix the door.*

employer [ɪmˈplɔɪə] **employers** NOUN
Someone's employer is the person or organization that they work for.

● THESAURUS
boss: *My boss has always been very fair.*
gaffer: informal *You'll need to speak to the gaffer about that.*

employment [ɪmˈplɔɪmənt] NOUN
(GEOGRAPHY) Employment is the state of having a paid job, or the activity of recruiting people for a job.

● THESAURUS
engagement: *the engagement of suitable staff*
enlistment: *Enlistment in the armed forces is falling.*
hiring: *The hiring of new staff is our top priority.*
recruitment: *new policies on recruitment and training*
taking on: *Taking on extra staff would make life a lot easier.*

empower [ɪmˈpaʊə] **empowers, empowering, empowered** VERB
If you are empowered to do something, you have the authority or power to do it.

empress [ˈɛmprɪs] **empresses** NOUN
a woman who rules an empire, or the wife of an emperor

empty [ˈɛmptɪ] **emptier, emptiest; empties, emptying, emptied** ADJECTIVE
1 having nothing or nobody inside

● THESAURUS
bare: *When she got there, the cupboard was bare.*
blank: *all the blank pages in his diary*
clear: *The runway must be kept clear at all times.*
deserted: *By nightfall, the square was deserted.*
unfurnished: *The flat was unfurnished when we moved in.*
uninhabited: *The house has remained uninhabited since she moved out.*
vacant: *two vacant lots on the industrial estate*
<<OPPOSITE *full*

2 without purpose, value, or meaning *e.g. empty promises*

● THESAURUS
inane: *a series of inane remarks*
meaningless: *the feeling that his existence was meaningless*
worthless: *a worthless film with nothing to say about anything*

> VERB
3 If you empty something, or empty its contents, you remove the contents.
emptiness NOUN

● THESAURUS
clear: *The police cleared the building just in time.*
drain: *She drained the bottles and washed them out.*
evacuate: *Fortunately the building had been evacuated.*
unload: *It only took twenty minutes to unload the van.*
<<OPPOSITE *fill*

emu [ˈiːmjuː] **emus** NOUN
a large Australian bird which can run fast but cannot fly
[WORD HISTORY: from Portuguese EMA meaning 'ostrich']

emulate [ˈɛmjʊˌleɪt] **emulates, emulating, emulated** VERB
If you emulate someone or something, you imitate them because you admire them.
emulation NOUN

emulsion [ɪˈmʌlʃən] **emulsions** NOUN
a water-based paint

en- PREFIX
1 'En-' means to surround or cover *e.g. enclose... encrusted*

2 'En-' means to cause to be in a certain state or condition *e.g. enamoured... endanger*
[WORD HISTORY: from Latin prefix IN-]

enable [ɪnˈeɪbəl] **enables, enabling, enabled** VERB
To enable something to happen means to make it possible.

enact [ɪnˈækt] **enacts, enacting, enacted** VERB

1 If a government enacts a law or bill, it officially passes it so that it becomes law.

2 If you enact a story or play, you act it out.
enactment NOUN

enamel [ɪ'næməl] **enamels, enamelling, enamelled** NOUN

1 a substance like glass, used to decorate or protect metal or china

2 The enamel on your teeth is the hard, white substance that forms the outer part.

> VERB

3 If you enamel something, you decorate or cover it with enamel.
enamelled ADJECTIVE

enamoured [ɪn'æməd] ADJECTIVE
If you are enamoured of someone or something, you like them very much.

encapsulate [ɪn'kæpsjʊˌleɪt] **encapsulates, encapsulating, encapsulated** VERB
If something encapsulates facts or ideas, it contains or represents them in a small space.

encased [ɪn'keɪst] ADJECTIVE
Something that is encased is surrounded or covered with a substance. *e.g. encased in plaster*

-ence SUFFIX
'-ence' is used to form nouns which mean a state, condition or quality *e.g. residence... patience* [WORD HISTORY: from Latin -ENS]

enchanted [ɪn'tʃɑ:ntɪd] ADJECTIVE
If you are enchanted by something or someone, you are fascinated or charmed by them.

enchanting [ɪn'tʃɑ:ntɪŋ] ADJECTIVE
attractive, delightful, or charming *e.g. an enchanting baby*

encircle [ɪn'sɜ:k°l] **encircles, encircling, encircled** VERB
To encircle something or someone means to completely surround them.

enclave ['ɛnkleɪv] **enclaves** NOUN
a place that is surrounded by areas that are different from it in some important way, for example because the people there are from a different culture *e.g. a Muslim enclave in Bosnia* [WORD HISTORY: from Old French ENCLAVER meaning 'to enclose']

enclose [ɪn'kləʊz] **encloses, enclosing, enclosed** VERB
To enclose an object or area means to surround it with something solid.
enclosed ADJECTIVE

⬤ THESAURUS
encircle: *The area had been encircled by barbed wire.*

fence off: *We decided to fence off the land.*
hem in: *We were hemmed in by walls and hedges.*
surround: *the low wall that surrounded the rose garden*
wrap: *Wrap the chicken in foil and bake it in a medium oven.*

enclosure [ɪn'kləʊʒə] **enclosures** NOUN
an area of land surrounded by a wall or fence and used for a particular purpose

encompass [ɪn'kʌmpəs] **encompasses, encompassing, encompassed** VERB
To encompass a number of things means to include all of those things. *e.g. The book encompassed all aspects of maths.*

encore ['ɒŋkɔ:] **encores** NOUN
a short extra performance given by an entertainer because the audience asks for it [WORD HISTORY: from French ENCORE meaning 'again']

encounter [ɪn'kaʊntə] **encounters, encountering, encountered** VERB

1 If you encounter someone or something, you meet them or are faced with them. *e.g. She was the most gifted child he ever encountered.*

> NOUN

2 a meeting, especially when it is difficult or unexpected

encourage [ɪn'kʌrɪdʒ] **encourages, encouraging, encouraged** VERB **(PSHE)**

1 If you encourage someone, you give them courage and confidence to do something.

⬤ THESAURUS
cheer: *This news cheered us all and helped us keep going.*
hearten: *I am heartened to hear that.*
reassure: *He always reassures me when I'm feeling down.*
<<OPPOSITE discourage

2 If someone or something encourages a particular activity, they support it. *e.g. The government will encourage the creation of nursery places.*
encouraging ADJECTIVE, **encouragement** NOUN

⬤ THESAURUS
aid: *I tried to aid his creative efforts.*
boost: *Efforts to boost investment seem to be succeeding.*
favour: *conditions which favour growth in the economy*
help: *policies aimed at helping small businesses*
incite: *He incited his followers to attack the police station.*
support: *Rowe will support me in this campaign.*

encroach [ɪn'krəʊtʃ] **encroaches, encroaching, encroached** VERB

If something encroaches on a place or on your time or rights, it gradually takes up or takes away more and more of it.
encroachment NOUN

encrusted [ɪnˈkrʌstɪd] ADJECTIVE
covered with a crust or layer of something *e.g. a necklace encrusted with gold*

encyclopedia [ɛnˌsaɪkləʊˈpiːdɪə]
encyclopedias (*said* en-sigh-klop-**ee**-dee-a);
also spelt **encyclopaedia** NOUN
(**LIBRARY**) a book or set of books giving information about many different subjects
[WORD HISTORY: from Greek ENKUKLIOS PAIDEIA meaning 'general education']

encyclopedic or **encyclopaedic**
[ɛnˌsaɪkləʊˈpiːdɪk] ADJECTIVE
knowing or giving information about many different things

end see page 285 for Word Web

endanger [ɪnˈdeɪndʒə] **endangers, endangering, endangered** VERB
To endanger something means to cause it to be in a dangerous and harmful situation. *e.g. a driver who endangers the safety of others*

● THESAURUS
compromise: *We will not allow safety to be compromised.*
jeopardize: *a scandal that could jeopardize his government*
put at risk: *those who were put at risk by her stupidity*
risk: *He is risking the lives of others.*
threaten: *A breakdown in this system could threaten the whole project.*

endear [ɪnˈdɪə] **endears, endearing, endeared** VERB
If someone's behaviour endears them to you, it makes you fond of them.
endearing ADJECTIVE, **endearingly** ADVERB

endeavour [ɪnˈdɛvə] **endeavours, endeavouring, endeavoured** VERB
1 FORMAL
If you endeavour to do something, you try very hard to do it.
> NOUN
2 an effort to do or achieve something

endless [ˈɛndlɪs] ADJECTIVE
having or seeming to have no end
endlessly ADVERB

endorse [ɪnˈdɔːs] **endorses, endorsing, endorsed** VERB
1 If you endorse someone or something, you give approval and support to them.

2 If you endorse a document, you write your signature or a comment on it, to show that you approve of it.
endorsement NOUN

endowed [ɪnˈdaʊd] ADJECTIVE
If someone is endowed with a quality or ability, they have it or are given it. *e.g. He was endowed with great willpower.*

endurance [ɪnˈdjʊərəns] NOUN
Endurance is the ability to put up with a difficult situation for a period of time.

endure [ɪnˈdjʊə] **endures, enduring, endured** VERB
1 If you endure a difficult situation, you put up with it calmly and patiently.

● THESAURUS
cope with: *We've had a lot to cope with in the last few weeks.*
experience: *The company has experienced heavy financial losses.*
go through: *having to go through the public humiliation of a court case*
stand: *I don't know how he stood it for so long.*
suffer: *Steven has suffered years of pain from arthritis.*

2 If something endures, it lasts or continues to exist. *e.g. The old alliance still endures.*
enduring ADJECTIVE

● THESAURUS
last: *a car that is built to last*
live on: *His name will live on as an inspiration to others.*
remain: *When all the rest is forgotten, this fact will remain.*
survive: *the few traces of their civilization that have survived*

enema [ˈɛnɪmə] **enemas** NOUN
a liquid that is put into a person's rectum in order to empty their bowels

enemy [ˈɛnəmɪ] **enemies** NOUN
a person or group that is hostile or opposed to another person or group

● THESAURUS
adversary: *face to face with his old adversary*
antagonist: *He killed his antagonist in a duel.*
foe: *He plays Dracula's foe, Dr. Van Helsing.*
opponent: *Her political opponents will be delighted at this news.*
<<OPPOSITE *friend*

energetic [ˌɛnəˈdʒɛtɪk] ADJECTIVE
having or showing energy or enthusiasm
energetically ADVERB

● THESAURUS
animated: *an animated conversation about politics and sport*

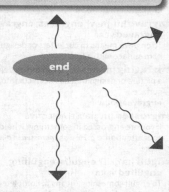

1 NOUN

the last part of a period or event *eg: the end of the 20th century*

● THESAURUS

close: *The company made £100 million by the close of last year.*
ending: *the ending of a great era*
expiry: *the expiry of his period of training*
finish: *The college basketball season is nearing its finish.*
climax: *the dramatic climax of the trial*
close: *the close of the festival*
conclusion: *the conclusion of this fascinating tale*
culmination: *the remarkable culmination of a glittering career*
ending: *a film with a tragic ending*
finale: *a grand finale to the week-long celebrations*
finish: *a disappointing finish to our adventures*
<< OPPOSITE *beginning*

2 NOUN

the furthest point of something *eg: the room at the end of the corridor*

● THESAURUS

boundaries: *We worked along the boundaries of the paths.*
bounds: *the landscape beyond the bounds of London*
edge: *He fell off the edge of the cliff.*
extremity: *the western extremity of the continent*
limits: *an area outside the official city limits*
margin: *agricultural regions well beyond the forest margin*

3 NOUN

the purpose for which something is done *eg: The army is being used for political ends.*

● THESAURUS

aim: *groups united by a common aim*
goal: *We're all working towards the same goal.*
intentions: *He concealed his real intentions.*
object: *the stated object of the mission*
objective: *the objective of all this effort*
purpose: *the true purpose of their visit*
reasons: *Are you here on holiday, or for business reasons?*

4 VERB

to come or bring to a finish *eg: talks being held to end the fighting*

● THESAURUS

bring to an end: *The treaty brought to an end fifty years of conflict.*
cease: *By one o'clock the storm had ceased.*
conclude: *The evening concluded with the usual speeches.*
finish: *waiting for the film to finish*
stop: *When is it all going to stop?*
terminate: *the decision to terminate their contract*
<< OPPOSITE *begin*

end

e

dynamic: *a dynamic and ambitious businessman*
indefatigable: *trying to keep up with their indefatigable boss*
spirited: *a spirited defence of his new tax proposals*
tireless: *a tireless campaigner for the homeless*
vigorous: *a vigorous campaign*

energy [ˈɛnədʒɪ] **energies** NOUN
1 the physical strength to do active things

● THESAURUS
drive: *a man with immense drive and enthusiasm*
life: *At 96, she's still as full of life as ever.*
spirit: *Despite trailing 6-2, they played with a lot of spirit.*
strength: *She put all her strength into finding a new job.*
vigour: *They returned to their work with renewed vigour.*
vitality: *a woman with considerable charm and endless vitality*

2 the power which drives machinery

enforce [ɪnˈfɔːs] **enforces, enforcing, enforced** VERB
If you enforce a law or a rule, you make sure that it is obeyed.
enforceable ADJECTIVE, **enforcement** NOUN

engage [ɪnˈɡeɪdʒ] **engages, engaging, engaged** VERB
1 If you engage in an activity, you take part in it. *e.g. Officials have declined to engage in a debate.*
2 To engage someone or their attention means to make or keep someone interested in something. *e.g. He engaged the driver in conversation.*

engaged [ɪnˈɡeɪdʒd] ADJECTIVE
1 When two people are engaged, they have agreed to marry each other.
2 If someone or something is engaged, they are occupied or busy. *e.g. Mr Anderson was otherwise engaged... The emergency number was always engaged.*

engagement [ɪnˈɡeɪdʒmənt] **engagements** NOUN
1 an appointment that you have with someone
2 an agreement that two people have made with each other to get married

engine [ˈɛndʒɪn] **engines** NOUN
1 a machine designed to convert heat or other kinds of energy into mechanical movement
2 a railway locomotive
[WORD HISTORY: from Latin INGENIUM meaning 'ingenious device']

engineer [ˌɛndʒɪˈnɪə] **engineers, engineering, engineered** NOUN

1 a person trained in designing and building machinery and electrical devices, or roads and bridges
2 a person who repairs mechanical or electrical devices
> VERB
3 If you engineer an event or situation, you arrange it cleverly, usually for your own advantage.

engineering [ˌɛndʒɪˈnɪərɪŋ] NOUN
Engineering is the profession of designing and constructing machinery and electrical devices, or roads and bridges.

English [ˈɪŋɡlɪʃ] ADJECTIVE
1 belonging or relating to England
> NOUN
2 English is the main language spoken in the United Kingdom, the USA, Canada, Australia, New Zealand, and many other countries.

Englishman [ˈɪŋɡlɪʃmən] **Englishmen** NOUN
a man who comes from England
Englishwoman NOUN

engrave [ɪnˈɡreɪv] **engraves, engraving, engraved** VERB
To engrave means to cut letters or designs into a hard surface with a tool.

engraving [ɪnˈɡreɪvɪŋ] **engravings** NOUN
a picture or design that has been cut into a hard surface
engraver NOUN

engrossed [ɪnˈɡrəʊst] ADJECTIVE
If you are engrossed in something, it holds all your attention. *e.g. He was engrossed in a video game.*

engulf [ɪnˈɡʌlf] **engulfs, engulfing, engulfed** VERB
To engulf something means to completely cover or surround it. *e.g. Black smoke engulfed him.*

enhance [ɪnˈhɑːns] **enhances, enhancing, enhanced** VERB
To enhance something means to make it more valuable or attractive. *e.g. an outfit that really enhances his good looks*
enhancement NOUN

enigma [ɪˈnɪɡmə] **enigmas** NOUN
anything which is puzzling or difficult to understand

enigmatic [ˌɛnɪɡˈmætɪk] ADJECTIVE
mysterious, puzzling, or difficult to understand *e.g. an enigmatic stranger*
enigmatically ADVERB

enjoy [ɪnˈdʒɔɪ] **enjoys, enjoying, enjoyed** VERB

1 If you enjoy something, you find pleasure and satisfaction in it.

THESAURUS

appreciate: *people who don't appreciate Satie's music*

delight in: *He delights in playing practical jokes.*

like: *Kirsty likes shopping.*

love: *He loves skiing.*

relish: *She relished the opportunity to get back at him.*

revel in: *Stevens was revelling in the attention.*

take pleasure from: *He took no pleasure from the knowledge that he had won.*

take pleasure in: *She seemed to take pleasure in my discomfort.*

2 If you enjoy something, you are lucky to have it or experience it. *e.g. The mother has enjoyed a long life.*

enjoyable [ɪn'dʒɔɪəbᵊl] ADJECTIVE
giving pleasure or satisfaction

enjoyment [ɪn'dʒɔɪmənt] NOUN
Enjoyment is the feeling of pleasure or satisfaction you get from something you enjoy.

enlarge [ɪn'lɑːdʒ] **enlarges, enlarging, enlarged** VERB

1 When you enlarge something, it gets bigger.

THESAURUS

add to: *We've decided to add to this house rather than move again.*

expand: *If we want to stay in business, we need to expand.*

extend: *They extended the house by adding a conservatory.*

increase: *They have increased the peace-keeping force to 2000.*

magnify: *A more powerful lens will magnify the image.*

2 If you enlarge on a subject, you give more details about it.

THESAURUS

develop: *Maybe I should develop this idea a little bit further.*

elaborate on: *He refused to elaborate on what he had said earlier.*

expand on: *an idea that I will expand on later*

enlargement [ɪn'lɑːdʒmənt] **enlargements** NOUN

1 An enlargement of something is the action of making it bigger.

2 something, especially a photograph, which has been made bigger

enlighten [ɪn'laɪtᵊn] **enlightens, enlightening, enlightened** VERB
To enlighten someone means to give them more knowledge or understanding of something.

enlightening ADJECTIVE, **enlightenment** NOUN

enlightened [ɪn'laɪtᵊnd] ADJECTIVE
well-informed and willing to consider different opinions *e.g. an enlightened government*

enlist [ɪn'lɪst] **enlists, enlisting, enlisted** VERB

1 If someone enlists, they join the army, navy, or air force.

2 If you enlist someone's help, you persuade them to help you in something you are doing.

enliven [ɪn'laɪvᵊn] **enlivens, enlivening, enlivened** VERB
To enliven something means to make it more lively or more cheerful.

en masse [ɑ̃ mas] ADVERB
If a group of people do something en masse, they do it together and at the same time.

enormity [ɪ'nɔːmɪtɪ] **enormities** NOUN

1 The enormity of a problem or difficulty is its great size and seriousness.

2 something that is thought to be a terrible crime or offence

enormous [ɪ'nɔːməs] ADJECTIVE
very large in size or amount
enormously ADVERB

THESAURUS

colossal: *a colossal waste of public money*

gigantic: *The road is bordered by gigantic rocks.*

huge: *Several painters were working on a huge piece of canvas.*

immense: *an immense cloud of smoke*

massive: *The scale of the problem is massive.*

tremendous: *I felt a tremendous pressure on my chest.*

vast: *vast stretches of land*
<<OPPOSITE *tiny*

enough [ɪ'nʌf] ADJECTIVE OR ADVERB

1 as much or as many as required *e.g. He did not have enough money for a coffee.*

> NOUN

2 Enough is the quantity necessary for something. *e.g. There's not enough to go round.*

> ADVERB

3 very or fairly *e.g. She could manage well enough without me.*

enquire [ɪn'kwaɪə] **enquires, enquiring, enquired;** also spelt **inquire** VERB
If you enquire about something or someone, you ask about them.

enquiry [ɪn'kwaɪrɪ] **enquiries;** also spelt **inquiry** NOUN

1 a question that you ask in order to find something out

2 an investigation into something that has happened and that needs explaining

enrage [ɪn'reɪdʒ] **enrages, enraging, enraged** VERB
If something enrages you, it makes you very angry.
enraged ADJECTIVE

enrich [ɪn'rɪtʃ] **enriches, enriching, enriched** VERB
To enrich something means to improve the quality or value of it. *e.g. new woods to enrich our countryside*
enriched ADJECTIVE, **enrichment** NOUN

enrol [ɪn'rəʊl] **enrols, enrolling, enrolled** VERB
If you enrol for something such as a course or a college, you register to join or become a member of it.
enrolment NOUN

en route [ɒn 'ruːt] ADVERB
If something happens en route to a place, it happens on the way there.

ensconced [ɪn'skɒnst] ADJECTIVE
If you are ensconced in a particular place, you are settled there firmly and comfortably.

ensemble [ɒn'sɒmbəl] **ensembles** NOUN
1 a group of things or people considered as a whole rather than separately
2 a small group of musicians who play or sing together

enshrine [ɪn'ʃraɪn] **enshrines, enshrining, enshrined** VERB
If something such as an idea or a right is enshrined in a society, constitution, or a law, it is protected by it. *e.g. Freedom of speech is enshrined in the American Constitution.*

ensign ['ɛnsaɪn] **ensigns** NOUN
a flag flown by a ship to show what country that ship belongs to

ensue [ɪn'sjuː] **ensues, ensuing, ensued** VERB
If something ensues, it happens after another event, usually as a result of it. *e.g. He entered the house and an argument ensued.*
ensuing ADJECTIVE

ensure [ɛn'ʃʊə] **ensures, ensuring, ensured** VERB
To ensure that something happens means to make certain that it happens. *e.g. We make every effort to ensure the information given is correct.*
● THESAURUS
guarantee: *Further investment should guarantee that profits will rise.*
make certain: *to make certain that he'll get there*

make sure: *I will personally make sure that the job gets done.*

entangled [ɪn'tæŋgəld] ADJECTIVE
If you are entangled in problems or difficulties, you are involved in them.

enter ['ɛntə] **enters, entering, entered** VERB
1 To enter a place means to go into it.
2 If you enter an organization or institution, you join and become a member of it. *e.g. He entered Parliament in 1979.*
3 If you enter a competition or examination, you take part in it.
4 If you enter something in a diary or a list, you write it down.

enterprise ['ɛntə,praɪz] **enterprises** NOUN
1 a business or company
● THESAURUS
business: *a medium-sized business*
company: *a company that was doing very well*
concern: *It's not a large concern, but it makes a profit.*
establishment: *a modest establishment dedicated to sailing*
firm: *a clothing firm*
operation: *a one-man operation*

2 a project or task, especially one that involves risk or difficulty
[WORD HISTORY: from French ENTREPRENDRE meaning 'to undertake']
● THESAURUS
effort: *her latest fund-raising effort for cancer research*
endeavour: *an endeavour that was bound to end in failure*
operation: *He'd set up a small mining operation.*
project: *a project that will attract a lot of media attention*
undertaking: *This undertaking will rely on the hard work of our volunteers.*
venture: *a venture that few were willing to invest in*

enterprising ['ɛntə,praɪzɪŋ] ADJECTIVE
ready to start new projects and tasks and full of boldness and initiative *e.g. an enterprising company*

entertain [,ɛntə'teɪn] **entertains, entertaining, entertained** VERB
1 If you entertain people, you keep them amused or interested.
● THESAURUS
amuse: *He amused us all evening, singing and telling jokes.*
charm: *He charmed Mrs Nisbet with his tales of life on the road.*

delight: *a routine that will delight audiences*
enthral: *He enthralled audiences all over Europe.*
please: *He certainly knows how to please a crowd.*

2 If you entertain guests, you receive them into your house and give them food and hospitality.

entertainer [ˌɛntəˈteɪnə] entertainers
NOUN
someone whose job is to amuse and please audiences, for example a comedian or singer

entertainment [ˌɛntəˈteɪnmənt]
entertainments NOUN
anything people watch or do for pleasure

● THESAURUS
amusement: *looking for some amusement on a Saturday night*
enjoyment: *We need a bit of enjoyment to cheer us up.*
fun: *It's not really my idea of family fun.*
pleasure: *Hours of pleasure can be had with a pack of cards.*
recreation: *a healthy and enjoyable form of recreation*

enthral [ɪnˈθrɔːl] enthrals, enthralling, enthralled VERB
If you enthral someone, you hold their attention and interest completely.
enthralling ADJECTIVE

enthuse [ɪnˈθjuːz] enthuses, enthusing, enthused VERB
If you enthuse about something, you talk about it with enthusiasm and excitement.

enthusiasm [ɪnˈθjuːzɪˌæzəm] enthusiasms
NOUN
Enthusiasm is interest, eagerness, or delight in something that you enjoy.
[WORD HISTORY: from Greek ENTHOUSIASMOS meaning 'possessed or inspired by the gods']

● THESAURUS
eagerness: *He could barely contain his eagerness.*
excitement: *Her excitement got the better of her.*
interest: *He doesn't show much interest in football.*
keenness: *I don't doubt his keenness, it's his ability that worries me.*
warmth: *He greeted us with his usual warmth and affection.*

enthusiastic [ɪn,θjuːzɪˈæstɪk] ADJECTIVE
showing great excitement, eagerness, or approval for something *e.g. She was enthusiastic about poetry.*
enthusiastically ADVERB

● THESAURUS
ardent: *one of the government's most ardent supporters*
avid: *an avid reader*
devoted: *a devoted Star Trek fan*

eager: *He is eager to learn more about computers.*
excited: *We are very excited about getting a new dog.*
keen: *Dave is an keen angler.*
passionate: *a passionate opponent of the government*
<<OPPOSITE *apathetic*

entice [ɪnˈtaɪs] entices, enticing, enticed
VERB
If you entice someone to do something, you tempt them to do it. *e.g. We tried to entice the mouse out of the hole.*

enticing [ɪnˈtaɪsɪŋ] ADJECTIVE
extremely attractive and tempting

entire [ɪnˈtaɪə] ADJECTIVE
all of something *e.g. the entire month of July*

entirely [ɪnˈtaɪəlɪ] ADVERB
wholly and completely *e.g. He and I were entirely different.*

entirety [ɪnˈtaɪərɪtɪ] PHRASE
If something happens to something **in its entirety**, it happens to all of it. *e.g. This message will now be repeated in its entirety.*

entitle [ɪnˈtaɪtᵊl] entitles, entitling, entitled VERB
If something entitles you to have or do something, it gives you the right to have or do it.
entitlement NOUN

entity [ˈɛntɪtɪ] entities NOUN
any complete thing that is not divided and not part of anything else

entourage [ˈɒntʊˌrɑːʒ] entourages NOUN
a group of people who follow or travel with a famous or important person

entrails [ˈɛntreɪlz] PLURAL NOUN
Entrails are the inner parts, especially the intestines, of people or animals.

entrance¹ [ˈɛntrəns] entrances NOUN
1 The entrance of a building or area is its doorway or gate.

● THESAURUS
door: *She was waiting by the front door.*
doorway: *the mass of people blocking the doorway*
entry: *Kevin had been hanging round the back entry for hours.*
gate: *the security guard at the main gate*
way in: *Is this the way in?*

2 A person's entrance is their arrival in a place, or the way in which they arrive. *e.g. Each creation is designed for you to make a dramatic entrance.*

● THESAURUS
appearance: *She had timed her appearance at the dinner to perfection.*
arrival: *journalists awaiting the arrival of the team*

e

entry: *He was arrested on his entry into Mexico.*

3 (DRAMA) In the theatre, an actor makes his or her entrance when he or she comes on to the stage.

4 Entrance is the right to enter a place. *e.g. He had gained entrance to the Hall by pretending to be a heating engineer.*

● **THESAURUS**

access: *We were denied access to the stadium.*
admission: *no admission without a ticket*
entry: *I was unable to gain entry to the meeting.*

entrance² [ɪnˈtrɑːns] **entrances, entrancing, entranced** VERB
If something entrances you, it gives you a feeling of wonder and delight.
entrancing ADJECTIVE

● **THESAURUS**

bewitch: *Young Gordon's smile bewitched everyone.*
captivate: *I was captivated by her piercing blue eyes.*
charm: *He charmed Mr Darnley and made him feel young again.*
delight: *a CD that will delight her many fans*
enthral: *Audiences were enthralled by his spectacular stage act.*
fascinate: *She never failed to fascinate him.*

entrant [ˈɛntrənt] **entrants** NOUN
a person who officially enters a competition or an organization

entrenched [ɪnˈtrɛntʃt] ADJECTIVE
If a belief, custom, or power is entrenched, it is firmly established.

entrepreneur [ˌɒntrəprəˈnɜː] **entrepreneurs** NOUN
a person who sets up business deals, especially ones in which risks are involved, in order to make a profit
entrepreneurial ADJECTIVE

entrust [ɪnˈtrʌst] **entrusts, entrusting, entrusted** VERB
If you entrust something to someone, you give them the care and protection of it. *e.g. Miss Fry was entrusted with the children's education.*

entry [ˈɛntrɪ] **entries** NOUN
1 Entry is the act of entering a place.

● **THESAURUS**

appearance: *She made her appearance to tumultuous applause.*
arrival: *He apologized for his late arrival.*
entrance: *My entrance was spoiled when I tripped over the carpet.*

2 a place through which you enter somewhere

● **THESAURUS**

door: *I'll meet you at the front door.*

doorway: *A bicycle was blocking the doorway.*
entrance: *The bomb had been left outside the entrance to the building.*
gate: *Guards were posted at the main gate.*
way in: *I can't find the way in.*

3 anything which is entered or recorded *e.g. Send your entry to the address below.*

● **THESAURUS**

item: *A number of interesting items appear in his diary.*
note: *He grunted and made a note in his pocket book.*
record: *There is no record for 13 October in the log book.*

envelop [ɪnˈvɛləp] **envelops, enveloping, enveloped** VERB
To envelop something means to cover or surround it completely. *e.g. A dense fog enveloped the area.*

envelope [ˈɛnvələʊp] **envelopes** NOUN
a flat covering of paper with a flap that can be folded over to seal it, which is used to hold a letter

enviable [ˈɛnvɪəbəl] ADJECTIVE
If you describe something as enviable, you mean that you wish you had it yourself.

envious [ˈɛnvɪəs] ADJECTIVE
full of envy
enviously ADVERB

environment [ɪnˈvaɪrənmənt] **environments** NOUN
1 Your environment is the circumstances and conditions in which you live or work. *e.g. a good environment to grow up in*
2 The environment is the natural world around us. *e.g. the waste which is dumped in the environment*
environmental ADJECTIVE, **environmentally** ADVERB

■ There is an *n* before the *m* in *environment*.

environmentalist [ɪnˌvaɪrənˈmɛntəlɪst] **environmentalists** NOUN
a person who is concerned with the problems of the natural environment, such as pollution

envisage [ɪnˈvɪzɪdʒ] **envisages, envisaging, envisaged** VERB
If you envisage a situation or state of affairs, you can picture it in your mind as being true or likely to happen.

envoy [ˈɛnvɔɪ] **envoys** NOUN
a messenger, sent especially from one government to another

envy [ˈɛnvɪ] **envies, envying, envied** NOUN

1 Envy is a feeling of resentment you have when you wish you could have what someone else has.

● THESAURUS
jealousy: *the jealousy people felt towards him because of his money*
resentment: *All the anger, bitterness and resentment suddenly melted away.*

> VERB
2 If you envy someone, you wish that you had what they have.

● THESAURUS
be envious: *people who were envious of her good fortune*
begrudge: *Surely you don't begrudge me one night out.*
be jealous: *I couldn't help being jealous when I knew he had won.*
covet: *She coveted his job.*
resent: *Anyone with money was resented and ignored.*

enzyme ['ɛnzaɪm] **enzymes** NOUN
a chemical substance, usually a protein, produced by cells in the body

ephemeral [ɪ'fɛmərəl] ADJECTIVE
lasting only a short time

epic ['ɛpɪk] **epics** NOUN
1 a long story of heroic events and actions
> ADJECTIVE
2 very impressive or ambitious *e.g. epic adventures*

epidemic [ˌɛpɪ'dɛmɪk] **epidemics** NOUN
1 an occurrence of a disease in one area, spreading quickly and affecting many people
2 a rapid development or spread of something *e.g. the country's crime epidemic*

epigram ['ɛpɪˌɡræm] **epigrams** NOUN
a short saying which expresses an idea in a clever and amusing way

epigraph ['ɛpɪˌɡrɑːf] NOUN
1 a quotation at the beginning of a book
2 an inscription on a monument or building

epilepsy ['ɛpɪˌlɛpsɪ] NOUN
Epilepsy is a condition of the brain which causes fits and periods of unconsciousness.
epileptic NOUN OR ADJECTIVE

episode ['ɛpɪˌsəʊd] **episodes** NOUN
1 an event or period *e.g. After this episode, she found it impossible to trust him.*
2 one of several parts of a novel or drama appearing for example on television *e.g. I never miss an episode of Neighbours.*

epistle [ɪ'pɪsəl] **epistles** NOUN; FORMAL
a letter

epitaph ['ɛpɪˌtɑːf] **epitaphs** NOUN
some words on a tomb about the person who has died

epithet ['ɛpɪˌθɛt] **epithets** NOUN
a word or short phrase used to describe some characteristic of a person

epitome [ɪ'pɪtəmɪ] NOUN; FORMAL
The epitome of something is the most typical example of its sort. *e.g. She was the epitome of the successful woman.*

▌ Do not use *epitome* to mean 'the peak of something'. It means 'the most typical example of something'.

epoch ['iːpɒk] **epochs** NOUN
a long period of time

eponymous [ɪ'pɒnɪməs] ADJECTIVE; FORMAL
The eponymous hero or heroine of a play or book is the person whose name forms its title. *e.g. the eponymous hero of 'Eric the Viking'*
[WORD HISTORY: from Greek EPONUMOS meaning 'given as a name']

equal ['iːkwəl] **equals, equalling, equalled**
ADJECTIVE
1 having the same size, amount, value, or standard

● THESAURUS
equivalent: *A kilogram is equivalent to 2.2 pounds.*
identical: *glasses containing identical amounts of water*
the same: *different areas of research that have the same importance*

2 If you are equal to a task, you have the necessary ability to deal with it.

● THESAURUS
capable of: *I'm no longer capable of this kind of work.*
up to: *He said he wasn't up to a long walk.*

> NOUN
3 Your equals are people who have the same ability, status, or rights as you.

> VERB
4 If one thing equals another, it is as good or remarkable as the other. *e.g. He equalled the course record of 63.*
equally ADVERB, **equality** NOUN

● THESAURUS
be equal to: *The final score is equal to his personal best.*
match: *able to match her previous time for the 100m*

equate [ɪ'kweɪt] **equates, equating, equated** VERB
If you equate a particular thing with something else, you believe that it is similar or equal. *e.g. You can't equate lives with money.*

equation [ɪˈkweɪʒən] **equations** NOUN
(**MATHS**) a mathematical formula stating that two amounts or values are the same

equator [ɪˈkweɪtə] NOUN
an imaginary line drawn round the middle of the earth, lying halfway between the North and South poles
equatorial ADJECTIVE

equestrian [ɪˈkwɛstrɪən] ADJECTIVE
relating to or involving horses

equilateral [ˌiːkwɪˈlætərəl] ADJECTIVE
(**MATHS**) An equilateral triangle has sides that are all the same length.

equilibrium [ˌiːkwɪˈlɪbrɪəm] **equilibria** NOUN
a state of balance or stability in a situation

equine [ˈɛkwaɪn] ADJECTIVE
relating to horses
[WORD HISTORY: from Latin EQUUS meaning 'horse']

equinox [ˈiːkwɪˌnɒks] **equinoxes** NOUN
one of the two days in the year when the day and night are of equal length, occurring in September and March
[WORD HISTORY: from Latin AEQUINOCTIUM meaning 'equal night']

equip [ɪˈkwɪp] **equips, equipping, equipped** VERB
If a person or thing is equipped with something, they have it or are provided with it. *e.g. The test boat was equipped with a folding propeller.*

● THESAURUS
arm: *The children arrived armed with a range of gardening tools.*
endow: *The male bird is endowed with a vicious-looking beak.*
fit out: *the amount spent on fitting out their offices*
provide: *We provided them with waterproofs and sandwiches.*
supply: *They supplied us with camping gear and a stove.*

equipment [ɪˈkwɪpmənt] NOUN
Equipment is all the things that are needed or used for a particular job or activity.

● THESAURUS
apparatus: *All the firemen were wearing breathing apparatus.*
gear: *Police in riot gear have sealed off the area.*
paraphernalia: *ashtrays, lighters and other paraphernalia associated with smoking*
stuff: *The builders had left all their stuff in the garden.*
tackle: *Martin kept all his fishing tackle in the spare room.*

equitable [ˈɛkwɪtəbᵊl] ADJECTIVE
fair and reasonable

equity [ˈɛkwɪtɪ] NOUN
Equity is the quality of being fair and reasonable. *e.g. It is important to distribute income with some sense of equity.*

equivalent [ɪˈkwɪvələnt] **equivalents** ADJECTIVE
1 equal in use, size, value, or effect
> NOUN
2 something that has the same use, value, or effect as something else *e.g. One glass of wine is the equivalent of half a pint of beer.*
equivalence NOUN

-er SUFFIX
1 When '-er' is used to form some nouns it means 'for' or 'belonging to'. *e.g. fastener... Highlander.*
2 '-er' is also used to form nouns which mean someone or something that does something *e.g. climber... teacher... baker*
3 '-er' is used to make adjectives and adverbs that have the meaning 'more' *e.g. lighter... funnier*
[WORD HISTORY: from Old English]

era [ˈɪərə] **eras** NOUN
a period of time distinguished by a particular feature *e.g. a new era of prosperity*
[WORD HISTORY: from Latin AERA meaning 'copper counters used for counting', hence for counting time]

eradicate [ɪˈrædɪˌkeɪt] **eradicates, eradicating, eradicated** VERB
To eradicate something means to get rid of it or destroy it completely.
eradication NOUN

erase [ɪˈreɪz] **erases, erasing, erased** VERB
To erase something means to remove it.

erect [ɪˈrɛkt] **erects, erecting, erected** VERB
1 To erect something means to put it up or construct it. *e.g. The building was erected in 1900.*
> ADJECTIVE
2 in a straight and upright position *e.g. She held herself erect and looked directly at him.*

erection [ɪˈrɛkʃən] **erections** NOUN
1 the process of erecting something
2 anything which has been erected
3 When a man has an erection, his penis is stiff, swollen, and in an upright position.

ermine [ˈɜːmɪn] NOUN
Ermine is expensive white fur.

erode [ɪˈrəʊd] **erodes, eroding, eroded** VERB
If something erodes or is eroded, it is gradually

worn or eaten away and destroyed.

THESAURUS
corrode: *buildings corroded by acid rain*
destroy: *ancient monuments destroyed by pollution*
deteriorate: *The tapestry had deteriorated badly where the roof was leaking.*
disintegrate: *Once they were exposed to light the documents rapidly disintegrated.*
eat away: *The chemicals in the water had eaten away the cables.*
wear away: *rocks worn away by the action of the wind*
wear down: *Some of her teeth were worn down with gnawing on the bars.*

erosion [ɪˈrəʊʒən] NOUN
(GEOGRAPHY) the gradual wearing away and destruction of something *e.g. soil erosion*

erotic [ɪˈrɒtɪk] ADJECTIVE
involving or arousing sexual desire
erotically ADVERB, **eroticism** NOUN
[WORD HISTORY: from Greek EROTIKOS meaning 'of love']

err [ɜː] **errs, erring, erred** VERB
If you err, you make a mistake.

THESAURUS
blunder: *Fletcher had obviously blundered.*
go wrong: *We must have gone wrong somewhere in our calculations.*
make a mistake: *Okay, I made a mistake, I'm only human.*
miscalculate: *They miscalculated, and now they're in deep trouble.*

errand [ˈɛrənd] **errands** NOUN
a short trip you make in order to do a job for someone

erratic [ɪˈrætɪk] ADJECTIVE
not following a regular pattern or a fixed course *e.g. Police officers noticed his erratic driving.*
erratically ADVERB

erroneous [ɪˈrəʊnɪəs] ADJECTIVE
Ideas or methods that are erroneous are incorrect or only partly correct.
erroneously ADVERB

error [ˈɛrə] **errors** NOUN
a mistake or something which you have done wrong

THESAURUS
blunder: *He made a tactical blunder by announcing his intentions.*
fault: *It is a fault to think you can learn how to manage people in business school.*
lapse: *a serious security lapse*
mistake: *spelling mistakes*
slip: *We must be careful - we can't afford any slips.*

erudite [ˈɛrʊˌdaɪt] ADJECTIVE
having great academic knowledge

erupt [ɪˈrʌpt] **erupts, erupting, erupted** VERB
1 When a volcano erupts, it violently throws out a lot of hot lava and ash.
2 When a situation erupts, it starts up suddenly and violently. *e.g. A family row erupted.*
eruption NOUN

escalate [ˈɛskəˌleɪt] **escalates, escalating, escalated** VERB
If a situation escalates, it becomes greater in size, seriousness, or intensity.

escalator [ˈɛskəˌleɪtə] **escalators** NOUN
a mechanical moving staircase

escapade [ˈɛskəˌpeɪd] **escapades** NOUN
an adventurous or daring incident that causes trouble

escape [ɪˈskeɪp] **escapes, escaping, escaped** VERB
1 To escape means to get free from someone or something.

THESAURUS
break free: *He was handcuffed to his bed, but somehow managed to break free.*
break out: *two prisoners who broke out of the maximum security wing*
get away: *She got away from her guards.*
make your escape: *We made our escape down a drainpipe using knotted sheets.*
run away: *I called him but he just ran away.*
run off: *The children ran off when they spotted me.*

2 If you escape something unpleasant or difficult, you manage to avoid it. *e.g. He escaped the death penalty.*

THESAURUS
avoid: *She has managed to avoid arrest so far.*
dodge: *He dodged his military service by pretending to be ill.*
duck: *a pathetic attempt to duck her responsibilities*
elude: *He managed to elude the police for 13 years.*
evade: *He has now been charged with evading tax.*

3 If something escapes you, you cannot remember it. *e.g. It was an actor whose name escapes me for the moment.*

> NOUN
4 an act of escaping from a particular place or situation *e.g. his escape from North Korea*
5 a situation or activity which distracts you from something unpleasant *e.g. Television provides an escape.*

THESAURUS
distraction: *a distraction from his troubles*
diversion: *a pleasant diversion from my studies*

relief: *The piano provides relief from all the stress.*

escapee [ɪˌskeɪˈpiː] **escapees** NOUN
someone who has escaped, especially an escaped prisoner

escapism [ɪˈskeɪpɪzəm] NOUN
avoiding the real and unpleasant things in life by thinking about pleasant or fantastic things *e.g. Most horror movies are simple escapism.*
escapist ADJECTIVE

eschew [ɪsˈtʃuː] **eschews, eschewing, eschewed** VERB; FORMAL
If you eschew something, you deliberately avoid or keep away from it.

escort **escorts, escorting, escorted** NOUN
[ˈɛskɔːt]
1 a person or vehicle that travels with another in order to protect or guide them
2 a person who accompanies another person of the opposite sex to a social event
> VERB [ɪsˈkɔːt]
3 If you escort someone, you go with them somewhere, especially in order to protect or guide them.

-ese SUFFIX
'-ese' forms adjectives and nouns which show where a person or thing comes from *e.g. Japanese.*
[WORD HISTORY: from Latin suffix -ENSIS meaning 'from']

Eskimo [ˈɛskɪˌməʊ] **Eskimos** NOUN
a name that was formerly used for the Inuit people and their language

especially [ɪˈspɛʃəlɪ] ADVERB
You say especially to show that something applies to one thing, person, or situation than to any other. *e.g. Regular eye tests are important, especially for the elderly.*

espionage [ˈɛspɪəˌnɑːʒ] NOUN
Espionage is the act of spying to get secret information, especially to find out military or political secrets.
[WORD HISTORY: from French ESPIONNER meaning 'to spy']

espouse [ɪˈspaʊz] **espouses, espousing, espoused** VERB; FORMAL
If you espouse a particular policy, cause, or plan, you give your support to it. *e.g. They espoused the rights of man.*

espresso [ɛˈsprɛsəʊ] NOUN
Espresso is strong coffee made by forcing steam through ground coffee.
[WORD HISTORY: from Italian CAFFÈ ESPRESSO meaning 'pressed coffee']

The second letter of *espresso* is *s* and not *x*.

-ess SUFFIX
'-ess' added at the end of a noun indicates a female *e.g. lioness*
[WORD HISTORY: from Late Latin suffix -ISSA]

Special words for a woman who does a particular job or activity, such as *actress, poetess* and *authoress*, are now used less often because many women prefer to be referred to simply as an *actor, poet* or *author*.

essay [ˈɛseɪ] **essays** NOUN
a short piece of writing on a particular subject, for example one done as an exercise by a student

essence [ˈɛsᵊns] **essences** NOUN
1 The essence of something is its most basic and most important part, which gives it its identity. *e.g. the very essence of being a woman*

THESAURUS
core: *the need to get to the core of the problem*
heart: *a problem that reaches to the very heart of the party*
nature: *the nature of what it is to be European*
soul: *a song that captures the soul of this proud nation*
spirit: *the spirit of modern manhood*

2 a concentrated liquid used for flavouring food *e.g. vanilla essence*

THESAURUS
concentrate: *orange concentrate*
extract: *lemon extract*

essential [ɪˈsɛnʃəl] **essentials** ADJECTIVE
1 vitally important and absolutely necessary *e.g. Good ventilation is essential in the greenhouse.*

THESAURUS
crucial: *Her speech was a crucial part of the campaign.*
indispensable: *She has become indispensable to the department.*
vital: *a vital aspect of the plans that everyone has overlooked*

2 very basic, important, and typical *e.g. the essential aspects of international banking*

THESAURUS
basic: *the basic laws of physics*
cardinal: *He had broken one of the cardinal rules of business.*
fundamental: *the fundamental principles of democracy*
key: *Mollison had a key role to play in the negotiations.*
main: *an attempt to analyse the main points of his theory*
principal: *the principal idea that underpins their argument*

> PLURAL NOUN

3 things that are very important or necessary *e.g. the bare essentials of furnishing*
essentially ADVERB

THESAURUS

basics: *We need to get back to basics.*
fundamentals: *the fundamentals of road safety*
necessities: *Water, food, and shelter are the necessities of life.*
prerequisites: *Self-confidence is one of the prerequisites for a happy life.*
rudiments: *teaching him the rudiments of car maintenance*

-est SUFFIX

'-est' is used to form adjectives and adverbs that have the meaning 'most' *e.g. greatest... furthest*
[WORD HISTORY: from Old English]

establish [ɪ'stæblɪʃ] **establishes, establishing, established** VERB

1 To establish something means to set it up in a permanent way.

2 If you establish yourself or become established as something, you achieve a strong reputation for a particular activity. *e.g. He had just established himself as a film star.*

3 If you establish a fact or establish the truth of something, you discover it and can prove it. *e.g. Our first priority is to establish the cause of her death.*
established ADJECTIVE

establishment [ɪ'stæblɪʃmənt] **establishments** NOUN

1 The establishment of an organization or system is the act of setting it up.

2 a shop, business, or some other sort of organization or institution

3 The Establishment is the group of people in a country who have power and influence. *e.g. lawyers, businessmen and other pillars of the Establishment*

estate [ɪ'steɪt] **estates** NOUN

1 a large area of privately owned land in the country, together with all the property on it

2 an area of land, usually in or near a city, which has been developed for housing or industry

3 LEGAL A person's estate consists of all the possessions they leave behind when they die.

estate agent **estate agents** NOUN

a person who works for a company that sells houses and land

esteem [ɪ'stiːm] NOUN

admiration and respect that you feel for another person
esteemed ADJECTIVE

THESAURUS

admiration: *I have always had the greatest admiration for him.*
estimation: *He has gone down in my estimation.*
regard: *I had a very high regard for him and his work.*
respect: *I have tremendous respect for Dean.*
reverence: *He is still spoken of with reverence by those who knew him.*

estimate **estimates, estimating, estimated** VERB ['ɛstɪˌmeɪt]

1 (MATHS) If you estimate an amount or quantity, you calculate it approximately.

2 If you estimate something, you make a guess about it based on the evidence you have available. *e.g. Often it's possible to estimate a person's age just by knowing their name.*

> NOUN ['ɛstɪmɪt]

3 a guess at an amount, quantity, or outcome, based on the evidence you have available

THESAURUS

appraisal: *an appraisal of your financial standing*
assessment: *assessments of mortgaged property*
estimation: *The first group were correct in their estimation of the man's height.*
guess: *He examined her and made a guess at her temperature.*
quote: *Never agree to a job without getting a quote first.*
reckoning: *By my reckoning we were seven kilometres from the town.*
valuation: *The valuations reflect prices at the end of the fiscal year.*

4 a formal statement from a company who may do some work for you, telling you how much it is likely to cost

estimation [ˌɛstɪ'meɪʃən] **estimations** NOUN

1 an approximate calculation of something that can be measured

2 the opinion or impression you form about a person or situation

estranged [ɪ'streɪndʒd] ADJECTIVE

1 If someone is estranged from their husband or wife, they no longer live with them.

2 If someone is estranged from their family or friends, they have quarrelled with them and no longer keep in touch with them.

estrogen ['ɛstrədʒən] NOUN

a female sex hormone which regulates the reproductive cycle

estuary ['ɛstjʊərɪ] **estuaries** NOUN
(GEOGRAPHY) the wide part of a river near where it joins the sea and where fresh water mixes with salt water

etc. a written abbreviation for **et cetera**

et cetera [ɪt ˈsɛtrə]
'Et cetera' is used at the end of a list to indicate that other items of the same type you have mentioned could have been mentioned if there had been time or space

> As *etc.* means 'and the rest', you should not write *and etc.*

etch [ɛtʃ] **etches, etching, etched** VERB
1 If you etch a design or pattern on a surface, you cut it into the surface by using acid or a sharp tool.
2 If something is etched on your mind or memory, it has made such a strong impression on you that you feel you will never forget it.
etched ADJECTIVE

etching [ˈɛtʃɪŋ] **etchings** NOUN
a picture printed from a metal plate that has had a design cut into it

eternal [ɪˈtɜːnəl] ADJECTIVE
lasting forever, or seeming to last forever *e.g. eternal life*
eternally ADVERB

● THESAURUS
everlasting: *everlasting love*
immortal: *your immortal soul*
unchanging: *the unchanging laws of the cosmos*

eternity [ɪˈtɜːnɪtɪ] **eternities** NOUN
1 Eternity is time without end, or a state of existing outside time, especially the state some people believe they will pass into when they die.
2 a period of time which seems to go on for ever *e.g. We arrived there after an eternity.*

ether [ˈiːθə] NOUN
a colourless liquid that burns easily. Used in industry as a solvent and in medicine as an anaesthetic

ethereal [ɪˈθɪərɪəl] ADJECTIVE
light and delicate *e.g. misty ethereal landscapes*
ethereally ADVERB

ethical [ˈɛθɪkəl] ADJECTIVE
in agreement with accepted principles of behaviour that are thought to be right *e.g. teenagers who become vegetarian for ethical reasons*
ethically ADVERB

ethics [ˈɛθɪks] PLURAL NOUN
Ethics are moral beliefs about right and wrong. *e.g. The medical profession has a code of ethics.*

Ethiopian [ˌiːθɪˈəʊpɪən] **Ethiopians** ADJECTIVE
1 belonging to or relating to Ethiopia
> NOUN
2 someone who comes from Ethiopia

ethnic [ˈɛθnɪk] ADJECTIVE
1 involving different racial groups of people *e.g. ethnic minorities*
2 relating to a particular racial or cultural group, especially when very different from modern western culture *e.g. ethnic food*
ethnically ADVERB

ethos [ˈiːθɒs] NOUN
a set of ideas and attitudes that is associated with a particular group of people *e.g. the ethos of journalism*

etiquette [ˈɛtɪˌkɛt] NOUN
a set of rules for behaviour in a particular social situation

-ette SUFFIX
'-ette' is used to form nouns which have 'small' as part of their meaning *e.g. launderette... cigarette*
[WORD HISTORY: from French, the feminine form of the French suffix *-et*]

etymology [ˌɛtɪˈmɒlədʒɪ] NOUN
Etymology is the study of the origin and changes of form of words.

EU NOUN
EU is an abbreviation for 'European Union'.

eucalyptus or **eucalypt** [ˌjuːkəˈlɪptəs] or [ˈjuːkəˌlɪpt] **eucalyptuses** or **eucalypts** NOUN
an evergreen tree, grown mostly in Australia; also the wood and oil from this tree

Eucharist [ˈjuːkərɪst] **Eucharists** NOUN
a religious ceremony in which Christians remember and celebrate Christ's last meal with his disciples
[WORD HISTORY: from Greek EUCHARISTIA meaning 'thanksgiving']

eunuch [ˈjuːnək] **eunuchs** NOUN
a man who has been castrated

euphemism [ˈjuːfɪˌmɪzəm] **euphemisms** NOUN
a polite word or expression that you can use instead of one that might offend or upset people *e.g. action movies, a euphemism for violence*
euphemistic ADJECTIVE, **euphemistically** ADVERB

euphoria [juːˈfɔːrɪə] NOUN
a feeling of great happiness
euphoric ADJECTIVE

euro [ˈjʊərəʊ] **euros** NOUN
the official unit of currency in some countries of the European Union, replacing their old currencies at the beginning of January 2002

Europe [ˈjʊərəp] NOUN
Europe is the second smallest continent. It has Asia on its eastern side, with the Arctic to the

north, the Atlantic to the west, and the Mediterranean and Africa to the south.

European [ˌjʊərə'pɪən] **Europeans**
ADJECTIVE
1 belonging or relating to Europe
> NOUN
2 someone who comes from Europe

European Union ['juːnjən] NOUN
The group of countries who have joined together under the Treaty of Rome for economic and trade purposes are officially known as the European Union.

euthanasia [ˌjuːθə'neɪzɪə] NOUN
Euthanasia is the act of painlessly killing a dying person in order to stop their suffering.
[WORD HISTORY: from Greek EU- meaning 'easy' and THANATOS meaning 'death']

evacuate [ɪ'vækjʊˌeɪt] **evacuates, evacuating, evacuated** VERB
If someone is evacuated, they are removed from a place of danger to a place of safety. *e.g. A crowd of shoppers had to be evacuated from a store after a bomb scare.*
evacuation NOUN, **evacuee** NOUN

evade [ɪ'veɪd] **evades, evading, evaded** VERB
1 If you evade something or someone, you keep moving in order to keep out of their way. *e.g. For two months he evaded police.*
2 If you evade a problem or question, you avoid dealing with it.

evaluate [ɪ'væljʊˌeɪt] **evaluates, evaluating, evaluated** VERB
(EXAM TERM) If you evaluate something, you assess its strengths and weaknesses.

evaluation [ɪˌvæljʊ'eɪʃən] **evaluations** NOUN
1 Evaluation is assessing something strengths and weaknesses.
2 (D & T) To carry out an evaluation of a design, product or system is to do an assessment to find out how well it works or will work.

evangelical [ˌiːvæn'dʒɛlɪkᵊl] ADJECTIVE
Evangelical beliefs are Christian beliefs that stress the importance of the gospels and a personal belief in Christ.

evangelist [ɪ'vændʒɪlɪst] **evangelists** NOUN
a person who travels from place to place preaching Christianity
evangelize VERB, **evangelism** NOUN
[WORD HISTORY: from Greek EVANGELION meaning 'good news']

evaporate [ɪ'væpəˌreɪt] **evaporates, evaporating, evaporated (SCIENCE)** VERB
1 When a liquid evaporates, it gradually becomes less and less because it has changed from a liquid into a gas.
2 If a substance has been evaporated, all the liquid has been taken out so that it is dry or concentrated.
evaporation NOUN

evasion [ɪ'veɪʒən] **evasions** NOUN
deliberately avoiding doing something *e.g. evasion of arrest*

evasive [ɪ'veɪsɪv] ADJECTIVE
deliberately trying to avoid talking about or doing something *e.g. He was evasive about his past.*

eve [iːv] **eves** NOUN
the evening or day before an event or occasion *e.g. on the eve of the battle*

even ['iːvᵊn] ADJECTIVE
1 flat and level *e.g. an even layer of chocolate*
● THESAURUS
flat: *a small hut with a flat roof*
horizontal: *He drew a series of horizontal lines on the paper.*
level: *checking the floor to make sure it was level*
smooth: *the smooth marble floor tiles*
<<OPPOSITE uneven

2 regular and without variation *e.g. an even temperature*
● THESAURUS
constant: *The temperature remained more or less constant.*
regular: *her quiet, regular breathing*
smooth: *He caught the ball and passed it in one smooth motion.*
steady: *a steady stream of people*
uniform: *The price rises are not uniform across the country.*

3 In maths, numbers that are even can be divided exactly by two. *e.g. 4 is an even number*

4 Scores that are even are exactly the same.
● THESAURUS
equal: *The two teams shared equal points into the second round.*
identical: *At the end of the contest, our scores were identical.*
level: *The scores were level at halftime.*
neck and neck: *They're still neck and neck with two minutes to go.*

> ADVERB
5 'Even' is used to suggest that something is unexpected or surprising *e.g. I haven't even got a bank account.*
6 'Even' is also used to say that something is greater in degree than something else *e.g. This*

was an opportunity to obtain even more money.

> PHRASE

7 Even if or **even though** is used to introduce something that is surprising in relation to the main part of the sentence *e.g. She was too kind to say anything, even though she was jealous.*
evenly ADVERB

evening ['iːvnɪŋ] **evenings** NOUN
the part of the day between late afternoon and the time you go to bed

event [ɪ'vɛnt] **events** NOUN
1 something that happens, especially when it is unusual or important

⬤ THESAURUS
affair: *He preferred to forget the whole affair.*
business: *Do you remember that business with Jim?*
circumstance: *due to circumstances beyond our control*
episode: *a rather embarrassing episode at Yvonne's wedding*
experience: *an experience that changed his mind about going to university*
incident: *the incident in the restaurant*
matter: *She doesn't seem to be taking this matter seriously.*

2 one of the competitions that are part of an organized occasion, especially in sports

⬤ THESAURUS
bout: *This is his fifth heavyweight bout in three months.*
competition: *the first competition of the afternoon*
contest: *She's out of the contest for good.*

> PHRASE

3 If you say **in any event**, you mean whatever happens. *e.g. In any event we must get on with our own lives.*

eventful [ɪ'vɛntfʊl] ADJECTIVE
full of interesting and important events

eventual [ɪ'vɛntʃʊəl] ADJECTIVE
happening or being achieved in the end *e.g. He remained confident of eventual victory.*

eventuality [ɪ,vɛntʃʊ'ælɪtɪ] **eventualities** NOUN
a possible future event or result *e.g. equipment to cope with most eventualities*

eventually [ɪ'vɛntʃʊəlɪ] ADVERB
in the end *e.g. Eventually I got to Berlin.*

ever ['ɛvə] ADVERB
1 at any time *e.g. Have you ever seen anything like it?.*
2 all the time *e.g. The President will come under ever more pressure to resign.*
3 'Ever' is used to give emphasis to what you are saying *e.g. I'm as happy here as ever I was in England.*

> PHRASE
4 INFORMAL
Ever so means very *e.g. Thank you ever so much.*

evergreen ['ɛvə,griːn] **evergreens** NOUN
a tree or bush which has green leaves all the year round

everlasting [,ɛvə'lɑːstɪŋ] ADJECTIVE
never coming to an end

every ['ɛvrɪ] ADJECTIVE
1 'Every' is used to refer to all the members of a particular group, separately and one by one *e.g. We eat out every night.*
2 'Every' is used to mean the greatest or the best possible degree of something *e.g. He has every reason to avoid the subject.*
3 'Every' is also used to indicate that something happens at regular intervals *e.g. renewable every five years*

> PHRASE
4 Every other means each alternate *e.g. I see Lisa at least every other week.*

everybody ['ɛvrɪ,bɒdɪ] PRONOUN
1 all the people in a group *e.g. He obviously thinks everybody in the place knows him.*
2 all the people in the world *e.g. Everybody has a hobby.*

▬ *Everybody* and *everyone* mean the same.

everyday ['ɛvrɪ,deɪ] ADJECTIVE
usual or ordinary *e.g. the everyday drudgery of work*

⬤ THESAURUS
common: *a common occurrence*
daily: *In our daily life we follow predictable patterns of behaviour.*
day-to-day: *I use a lot of spices in my day-to-day cooking.*
mundane: *the mundane realities of life*
ordinary: *ordinary tableware*
routine: *routine maintenance of the machine.*

everyone ['ɛvrɪ,wʌn] PRONOUN
1 all the people in a group
2 all the people in the world

▬ *Everyone* and *everybody* mean the same.

everything ['ɛvrɪθɪŋ] PRONOUN
1 all or the whole of something
2 the most important thing *e.g. When I was 20, friends were everything to me.*

everywhere ['ɛvrɪ,wɛə] ADVERB
in or to all places

evict [ɪ'vɪkt] **evicts, evicting, evicted** VERB
To evict someone means to officially force them to leave a place they are occupying.
eviction NOUN

evidence ['ɛvɪdəns] NOUN

1 Evidence is anything you see, read, or are told which gives you reason to believe something.

2 Evidence is the information used in court to attempt to prove or disprove something.

evident ['ɛvɪdənt] ADJECTIVE
easily noticed or understood *e.g. His love of nature is evident in his paintings.*
evidently ADVERB

● THESAURUS
apparent: *He spoke with apparent nonchalance about his experience.*
clear: *It became clear that I hadn't convinced Mike.*
noticeable: *a noticeable effect*
obvious: *It's obvious that he doesn't like me.*
palpable: *The tension between Jim and Amy is palpable.*
plain: *It was plain to him that she was having a nervous breakdown.*
visible: *the most visible sign of her distress*

evil ['i:vəl] **evils** NOUN

1 Evil is a force or power that is believed to cause wicked or bad things to happen.

● THESAURUS
badness: *behaving that way out of sheer badness*
immorality: *the immorality that is typical of the arms trade*
sin: *The whole town is a den of sin and corruption.*
vice: *a place long associated with vice and immorality*
wickedness: *the wickedness of his behaviour*
<<OPPOSITE *good*

2 a very unpleasant or harmful situation or activity *e.g. the evils of war*

● THESAURUS
affliction: *Hay fever is an affliction that affects thousands.*
ill: *Many of the nation's ills are his responsibility.*
misery: *the misery of drug addiction*
sorrow: *the joys and sorrows of family life*

> ADJECTIVE
3 Someone or something that is evil is morally wrong or bad. *e.g. evil influences*

● THESAURUS
bad: *He's not a bad man, he's just very unhappy.*
depraved: *a throughly depraved film*
malevolent: *a malevolent influence on the whole school*
sinful: *He is a good person in a sinful world.*
vile: *vile acts of brutality*
wicked: *a wicked attack on a helpless child*
<<OPPOSITE *good*

evoke [ɪ'vəʊk] **evokes, evoking, evoked**
VERB
To evoke an emotion, memory, or reaction

means to cause it. *e.g. Enthusiasm was evoked by the appearance of the Prince.*

evolution [,i:və'lu:ʃən] NOUN

1 Evolution is a process of gradual change taking place over many generations during which living things slowly change as they adapt to different environments.

2 Evolution is also any process of gradual change and development over a period of time. *e.g. the evolution of the European Union*
evolutionary ADJECTIVE

evolve [ɪ'vɒlv] **evolves, evolving, evolved**
VERB

1 If something evolves or if you evolve it, it develops gradually over a period of time. *e.g. I was given a brief to evolve a system of training.*

2 When living things evolve, they gradually change and develop into different forms over a period of time.

ewe [ju:] **ewes** NOUN
a female sheep

ex- PREFIX
'Ex' means 'former' *e.g. her ex-husband*
[WORD HISTORY: from Greek EK- meaning 'out of' or 'away from']

exacerbate [ɪg'zæsə,beɪt] **exacerbates, exacerbating, exacerbated** VERB
To exacerbate something means to make it worse.

exact [ɪg'zækt] **exacts, exacting, exacted**
ADJECTIVE

1 correct and complete in every detail *e.g. an exact replica of the Santa Maria*

● THESAURUS
accurate: *an accurate description of the man*
authentic: *authentic Elizabethan costumes*
faithful: *faithful copies of ancient stone tools*
faultless: *She spoke with a faultless French accent.*
precise: *It's difficult to give a precise date for the painting.*
true: *Is this a true picture of life in the Middle Ages?*
<<OPPOSITE *approximate*

2 accurate and precise, as opposed to approximate *e.g. Mystery surrounds the exact circumstances of his death.*

> VERB
3 FORMAL
If somebody or something exacts something from you, they demand or obtain it from you, especially through force. *e.g. The navy was on its way to exact a terrible revenge.*

● THESAURUS
command: *an excellent surgeon who commanded the respect of all his colleagues*

extract: *to extract the maximum political advantage from this situation*
impose: *the first council to impose a fine for dropping litter*
insist on: *She insisted on conducting all the interviews herself.*
insist upon: *He insists upon good service.*
wring: *attempts to wring concessions from the government*

exactly [ɪgˈzæktlɪ] ADVERB

1 with complete accuracy and precision *e.g. That's exactly what happened.*

● THESAURUS

accurately: *We cannot accurately predict where the missile will land.*
faithfully: *I translated the play as faithfully as I could.*
just: *There are no statistics about just how many people won't vote.*
on the dot: *At nine o'clock on the dot, they have breakfast.*
precisely: *No-one knows precisely how many people are in the camp.*
quite: *That wasn't quite what I meant.*
<<OPPOSITE *approximately*

2 You can use 'exactly' to emphasize the truth of a statement, or a similarity or close relationship between one thing and another. *e.g. It's exactly the same colour.*

> INTERJECTION
3 an expression implying total agreement

● THESAURUS

absolutely: *"It's worrying, isn't it?" - "Absolutely."*
indeed: *"That's a topic that's getting a lot of media coverage." - "Indeed."*
precisely: *"So, you're suggesting we do away with these laws?" - "Precisely."*
quite: *"It's your choice, isn't it?" - "Quite."*

exaggerate [ɪgˈzædʒəˌreɪt] exaggerates, exaggerating, exaggerated VERB

1 If you exaggerate, you make the thing you are describing seem better, worse, bigger, or more important than it really is.

● THESAURUS

overdo: *I think he's overdoing it a bit when he complains like that.*
overestimate: *I think we're overestimating their desire to cooperate.*
overstate: *It's impossible to overstate the seriousness of this situation.*

2 To exaggerate something means to make it more noticeable than usual. *e.g. His Irish accent was exaggerated for the benefit of the joke he was telling.*

exaggeration NOUN

exalted [ɪgˈzɔːltɪd] ADJECTIVE; FORMAL
Someone who is exalted is very important.

exam [ɪgˈzæm] exams NOUN

an official test set to find out your knowledge or skill in a subject

● THESAURUS

examination: *a three-hour written examination*
oral: *I got good marks for my French oral.*
test: *I failed my history test again.*

examination [ɪgˌzæmɪˈneɪʃən] examinations NOUN

1 an exam

2 If you make an examination of something, you inspect it very carefully. *e.g. I carried out a careful examination of the hull.*

● THESAURUS

analysis: *An analysis of the ash revealed traces of lead oxide.*
inspection: *The police inspection of the vehicle found no fingerprints.*
study: *A study of the wreckage has thrown new light on the crash.*

3 A medical examination is a check by a doctor to find out the state of your health.

● THESAURUS

check: *a quick check just to make sure everything's working properly*
checkup: *my annual checkup at the clinic*
medical: *He had a medical before leaving England.*

examine [ɪgˈzæmɪn] examines, examining, examined VERB

1 If you examine something, you inspect it very carefully.

● THESAURUS

analyse: *We haven't had time to analyse all the samples yet.*
go over: *I'll go over your report tomorrow.*
go through: *We went through his belongings and found a notebook.*
inspect: *Customs officials inspected the vehicle.*
look over: *Once we've looked the house over we should know what caused the fire.*
study: *Experts are studying the frozen remains of a mammoth.*

2 (EXAM TERM) To examine a subject is to look closely at the issues involved and form your own opinion.

3 To examine someone means to find out their knowledge or skill in a particular subject by testing them.

4 If a doctor examines you, he or she checks your body to find out the state of your health.

● THESAURUS

check: *Dr Mollison checked my nose and throat.*
inspect: *I was inspected twice by Dr Stevens.*

look at: *He said he wanted to look at my chest again just to make sure.*

test: *They tested my eyes but my vision was fine.*

examiner [ɪɡˈzɑːmɪnə] **examiners** NOUN
a person who sets or marks an exam

example [ɪɡˈzɑːmpᵊl] **examples** NOUN
1 something which represents or is typical of a group or set *e.g. some examples of early Spanish music*

● THESAURUS
illustration: *Lo's success is an illustration of how well China is doing.*
sample: *This drawing is a sample of his early work.*
specimen: *I had to submit a specimen of my handwriting for analysis.*

2 If you say someone or something is an example to people, you mean that people can imitate and learn from them.

● THESAURUS
ideal: *a woman who was the American ideal of beauty*
model: *His conduct at the talks was a model of dignity.*
paragon: *She is a paragon of neatness and efficiency.*
prototype: *He was the prototype of the English gentleman.*

> PHRASE
3 You use **for example** to give an example of something you are talking about.

exasperate [ɪɡˈzɑːspəˌreɪt] **exasperates, exasperating, exasperated** VERB
If someone or something exasperates you, they irritate you and make you angry.
exasperating ADJECTIVE, **exasperation** NOUN

excavate [ˈɛkskəˌveɪt] **excavates, excavating, excavated** VERB
To excavate means to remove earth from the ground by digging.
excavation NOUN

exceed [ɪkˈsiːd] **exceeds, exceeding, exceeded** VERB
To exceed something such as a limit means to go beyond it or to become greater than it. *e.g. the first aircraft to exceed the speed of sound*

exceedingly [ɪkˈsiːdɪŋlɪ] ADVERB
extremely or very much

excel [ɪkˈsɛl] **excels, excelling, excelled** VERB
If someone excels in something, they are very good at doing it.

Excellency [ˈɛksələnsɪ] **Excellencies** NOUN
a title used to address an official of very high rank, such as an ambassador or a governor

excellent [ˈɛksələnt] ADJECTIVE
very good indeed
excellence NOUN

● THESAURUS
beaut: *Australian and New Zealand; informal a beaut spot to live*
brilliant: *What a brilliant film!*
cracking: *British and Australian and New Zealand; informal You've done a cracking job in the garden!*
fine: *There's a fine view from the bedroom window.*
first-class: *a first-class effort*
great: *He's a great player and we'll be sorry to lose him.*
outstanding: *an outstanding performance*
superb: *a superb craftsman*
<<OPPOSITE *terrible*

except [ɪkˈsɛpt] PREPOSITION
Except or except for means other than or apart from. *e.g. All my family were musicians except my father.*

● THESAURUS
apart from: *The room was empty apart from one man seated by the fire.*
but: *He didn't speak anything but Greek.*
other than: *She makes no reference to any research other than her own.*
save: *formal We had almost nothing to eat, save the few berries and nuts we could find.*
with the exception of: *Yesterday was a day off for everybody, with the exception of Tom.*

exception [ɪkˈsɛpʃən] **exceptions** NOUN
somebody or something that is not included in a general statement or rule *e.g. English, like every language, has exceptions to its rules.*

exceptional [ɪkˈsɛpʃᵊnᵊl] ADJECTIVE
1 unusually talented or clever

● THESAURUS
excellent: *The recording quality is excellent.*
extraordinary: *He is an extraordinary musician.*
outstanding: *an outstanding athlete*
phenomenal: *The performances have been absolutely phenomenal.*
remarkable: *a remarkable achievement*
talented: *He is a talented violinist.*
<<OPPOSITE *mediocre*

2 unusual and likely to happen very rarely
exceptionally ADVERB

● THESAURUS
isolated: *They said the allegations related to an isolated case.*
out of the ordinary: *I've noticed nothing out of the ordinary.*
rare: *those rare occasions when he did eat alone*
special: *In special cases, an exception to this rule may be made.*

unheard-of: *buying rum at the unheard-of rate of $2 per bottle*

unusual: *To be appreciated as a parent is unusual.*

<<OPPOSITE *common*

excerpt ['ɛksɜːpt] **excerpts** NOUN
a short piece of writing or music which is taken from a larger piece

excess excesses NOUN [ɪk'sɛs]

1 Excess is behaviour which goes beyond normally acceptable limits. *e.g. a life of excess*

● THESAURUS

extravagance: *Examples of her extravagance were everywhere.*

indulgence: *a moment of sheer indulgence*

2 a larger amount of something than is needed, usual, or healthy *e.g. an excess of energy*

● THESAURUS

glut: *the current glut of dairy products in Europe*

overdose: *An overdose of sun can lead to skin problems later.*

surfeit: *A surfeit of rich food did not help his digestive problems.*

surplus: *Germany suffers from a surplus of teachers at the moment.*

<<OPPOSITE *shortage*

> ADJECTIVE ['ɛksɛs]

3 more than is needed, allowed, or healthy *e.g. excess weight*

● THESAURUS

extra: *Pour any extra liquid into a bowl and set aside.*

superfluous: *all our superfluous belongings, things we don't need*

surplus: *Farmers have to sell off their surplus stock cheap.*

> PHRASE [ɪk'sɛs]

4 In excess of a particular amount means more than that amount *e.g. a fortune in excess of 150 million pounds*

5 If you do something **to excess**, you do it too much. *e.g. She drank to excess.*

excessive [ɪk'sɛsɪv] ADJECTIVE
too great in amount or degree *e.g. using excessive force*

excessively ADVERB

● THESAURUS

enormous: *She spent an enormous amount on clothes.*

exaggerated: *the exaggerated claims made by their supporters*

needless: *a film that is full of needless violence*

undue: *the need to avoid undue expense*

unreasonable: *unreasonable increases in the price of petrol*

exchange [ɪks'tʃeɪndʒ] **exchanges, exchanging, exchanged** VERB **(SCIENCE)**

1 To exchange things means to give or receive one thing in return for another. *e.g. They exchange small presents on Christmas Eve.*

● THESAURUS

barter: *Traders came from everywhere to barter in the markets.*

change: *Can you change euros for pounds?*

swap: *I wouldn't swap places with her for anything!*

switch: *They switched cars and were away before the alarm was raised.*

trade: *a secret deal to trade arms for hostages*

> NOUN

2 the act of giving or receiving something in return for something else *e.g. an exchange of letters... exchanges of gunfire*

● THESAURUS

interchange: *a meeting at which the interchange of ideas was encouraged*

swap: *They agreed to a swap and made the necessary arrangements.*

switch: *The switch went ahead as planned.*

trade: *I am willing to make a trade with you.*

3 a place where people trade and do business *e.g. the stock exchange*

exchequer [ɪks'tʃɛkə] NOUN
The exchequer is the department in the government in Britain and other countries which is responsible for money belonging to the state.

excise ['ɛksaɪz] NOUN
Excise is a tax put on goods produced for sale in the country that produces them.

excitable [ɪk'saɪtəbᵊl] ADJECTIVE
easily excited

excite [ɪk'saɪt] **excites, exciting, excited** VERB

1 If somebody or something excites you, they make you feel very happy and nervous or very interested and enthusiastic.

● THESAURUS

agitate: *I've no idea what has agitated him.*

animate: *There was plenty about this match to animate the capacity crowd.*

thrill: *The reception he got at the meeting thrilled him.*

titillate: *a meal that will titillate the taste buds of every gourmet*

2 If something excites a particular feeling, it causes somebody to have that feeling. *e.g. This excited my suspicion.*

● THESAURUS

arouse: *a move that has aroused deep public anger*

elicit: *His proposal elicited a storm of protest.*

evoke: *The film has evoked a sense of nostalgia in many older people.*

incite: *a crude attempt to incite racial hatred*

inspire: *The handling of the new car quickly inspires confidence.*
provoke: *The suggestion has provoked anger.*
stir up: *He's just trying to stir up trouble.*

excited [ɪk'saɪtɪd] ADJECTIVE
happy and unable to relax
excitedly ADVERB

● THESAURUS
agitated: *in an excited and agitated state*
enthusiastic: *Tom usually seems very enthusiastic.*
feverish: *a state of feverish anticipation*
high: informal *I was feeling really high after Lorraine's party.*
thrilled: *The children were thrilled when the snow came.*
<<OPPOSITE *bored*

excitement [ɪk'saɪtmənt] NOUN
interest and enthusiasm

● THESAURUS
activity: *a scene of frenzied activity*
adventure: *setting off in search of adventure*
agitation: *He reacted to the news with considerable agitation.*
commotion: *We decided to find out what all the commotion was about.*
enthusiasm: *They greeted our arrival with enthusiasm.*
thrill: *the thrill of scuba diving*

exciting [ɪk'saɪtɪŋ] ADJECTIVE
making you feel happy and enthusiastic

● THESAURUS
dramatic: *Their arrival was dramatic and exciting.*
electrifying: *It was an electrifying performance.*
exhilarating: *an exhilarating walk along the cliff tops*
rousing: *a rousing speech*
stimulating: *It's a stimulating book, full of ideas.*
thrilling: *a thrilling opportunity to watch the lions as they feed*
<<OPPOSITE *boring*

exclaim [ɪk'skleɪm] **exclaims, exclaiming, exclaimed** VERB
When you exclaim, you cry out suddenly or loudly because you are excited or shocked.

exclamation [ˌɛkskləˈmeɪʃən] **exclamations** NOUN
(ENGLISH) a word or phrase spoken suddenly to express a strong feeling

exclamation mark exclamation marks NOUN
a punctuation mark (!) used in writing to express a strong feeling

exclude [ɪk'sklud] **excludes, excluding, excluded** VERB

1 If you exclude something, you deliberately do not include it or do not consider it.

● THESAURUS
eliminate: *We can eliminate Mr Darnley from our list of suspects.*
ignore: *We cannot afford to ignore this option.*
leave out: *We can narrow it down by leaving out everywhere that's too expensive.*
omit: *His name seems to have been omitted from the list.*
rule out: *The police have already ruled out a retrial.*
<<OPPOSITE *include*

2 If you exclude somebody from a place or an activity, you prevent them from entering the place or taking part in the activity.
exclusion NOUN

● THESAURUS
ban: *Tony was banned from driving for three years.*
bar: *She was barred from the tennis club.*
forbid: *Carver was forbidden to attend any of the society's meetings.*
keep out: *We need to keep out troublemakers.*

exclusive [ɪk'sklu:sɪv] **exclusives** ADJECTIVE
1 available to or for the use of a small group of rich or privileged people *e.g. an exclusive club*

● THESAURUS
chic: *a chic nightclub in Monaco*
classy: *a very classy restaurant*
posh: informal *She took me to a posh hotel to celebrate.*
select: *a very lavish and very select party*
up-market: *The area is much more up-market than it used to be.*

2 belonging to a particular person or group only *e.g. exclusive rights to coverage of the Olympic Games*
> NOUN
3 a story or interview which appears in only one newspaper or on only one television programme
exclusively ADVERB

excrement ['ɛkskrɪmənt] NOUN
Excrement is the solid waste matter that is passed out of a person's or animal's body through their bowels.

excrete [ɪk'skri:t] **excretes, excreting, excreted** VERB
When you excrete waste matter from your body, you get rid of it, for example by going to the lavatory or by sweating.
excretion NOUN, **excretory** ADJECTIVE

excruciating [ɪk'skru:ʃɪˌeɪtɪŋ] ADJECTIVE
unbearably painful
excruciatingly ADVERB
[WORD HISTORY: from Latin EXCRUCIARE meaning 'to torture']

excursion [ɪk'skɜːʃən] **excursions** NOUN
a short journey or outing

excuse excuses, excusing, excused NOUN
[ɪkˈskjuːs]

1 a reason which you give to explain why something has been done, has not been done, or will not be done

● THESAURUS

explanation: *You'd better have a good explanation for your conduct.*

justification: *What possible justification can there be for this?*

pretext: *His pretext for leaving early was an upset stomach.*

reason: *This gave me the perfect reason for visiting London.*

> VERB [ɪkˈskjuːz]

2 If you excuse yourself or something that you have done, you give reasons defending your actions.

3 If you excuse somebody for something wrong they have done, you forgive them for it.

● THESAURUS

forgive: *Forgive me, I'm so sorry.*

overlook: *the need to overlook each other's failings*

pardon: *Pardon my ignorance, but who is Cliff Hanley?*

turn a blind eye to: *We can't be expected to turn a blind eye to this behaviour.*

4 If you excuse somebody from a duty or responsibility, you free them from it. *e.g. He was excused from standing trial because of ill health.*

> PHRASE [ɪkˈskjuːz]

5 You say **excuse me** to try to catch somebody's attention or to apologize for an interruption or for rude behaviour.

execute [ˈɛksɪˌkjuːt] executes, executing, executed VERB

1 To execute somebody means to kill them as a punishment for a crime.

2 If you execute something such as a plan or an action, you carry it out or perform it. *e.g. The crime had been planned and executed in Montreal.*
execution NOUN

executioner [ˌɛksɪˈkjuːʃənə] executioners NOUN

a person whose job is to execute criminals

executive [ɪgˈzɛkjʊtɪv] executives NOUN

1 a person who is employed by a company at a senior level

2 The executive of an organization is a committee which has the authority to make decisions and ensure that they are carried out.

> ADJECTIVE

3 concerned with making important decisions and ensuring that they are carried out *e.g. the commission's executive director*

executor [ɪgˈzɛkjʊtə] executors NOUN

a person you appoint to carry out the instructions in your will

exemplary [ɪgˈzɛmplərɪ] ADJECTIVE

1 being a good example and worthy of imitation *e.g. an exemplary performance*

2 serving as a warning *e.g. an exemplary tale*

exemplify [ɪgˈzɛmplɪˌfaɪ] exemplifies, exemplifying, exemplified VERB

1 To exemplify something means to be a typical example of it. *e.g. This aircraft exemplifies the advantages of European technological cooperation.*

2 If you exemplify something, you give an example of it.

exempt [ɪgˈzɛmpt] exempts, exempting, exempted ADJECTIVE

1 excused from a rule or duty *e.g. people exempt from prescription charges*

● THESAURUS

excused: *Some MPs will have been officially excused attendance.*

immune: *Members of the parliament are immune from prosecution.*

not liable: *They are not liable to pay income tax.*

> VERB

2 To exempt someone from a rule, duty, or obligation means to excuse them from it.
exemption NOUN

exercise [ˈɛksəˌsaɪz] exercises, exercising, exercised NOUN

1 (PE) Exercise is any activity which you do to get fit or remain healthy.

● THESAURUS

activity: *a bit of physical activity to get the heart going*

exertion: *I'm tired out by all this exertion.*

training: *He needs to do a bit more training before the match.*

work: *I'm doing a lot more work at the gym now I'm feeling better.*

2 Exercises are also activities which you do to practise and train for a particular skill. *e.g. piano exercises... a mathematical exercise*

> VERB

3 When you exercise, you do activities which help you to get fit and remain healthy.

4 If you exercise your rights or responsibilities, you use them.

exert [ɪgˈzɜːt] exerts, exerting, exerted VERB

1 To exert pressure means to apply it.

2 If you exert yourself, you make a physical or mental effort to do something.

exertion [ɪgˈzɜːʃən] **exertions** NOUN
Exertion is vigorous physical effort or exercise.

exhale [ɛksˈheɪl] **exhales, exhaling, exhaled** VERB
When you exhale, you breathe out.

exhaust [ɪgˈzɔːst] **exhausts, exhausting, exhausted** VERB
1 To exhaust somebody means to make them very tired. *e.g. Several lengths of the pool left her exhausted.*

● THESAURUS
drain: *My emotional turmoil had drained me.*
fatigue: *He is easily fatigued.*
tire out: *a great new job that tires me out*
wear out: *Living out of a suitcase wears you out.*

2 If you exhaust a supply of something such as money or food, you use it up completely.

● THESAURUS
consume: *plans which will consume hours of time*
deplete: *chemicals that deplete the earth's protective ozone shield*
run through: *The project ran through its funds in months.*
use up: *The gas has all been used up.*

3 If you exhaust a subject, you talk about it so much that there is nothing else to say about it.

> NOUN
4 a pipe which carries the gas or steam out of the engine of a vehicle
exhaustion NOUN

exhaustive [ɪgˈzɔːstɪv] ADJECTIVE
thorough and complete *e.g. an exhaustive series of tests*
exhaustively ADVERB

exhibit [ɪgˈzɪbɪt] **exhibits, exhibiting, exhibited** VERB
1 To exhibit things means to show them in a public place for people to see.

2 If you exhibit your feelings or abilities, you display them so that other people can see them.

> NOUN
3 anything which is put on show for the public to see

exhibition [ˌɛksɪˈbɪʃən] **exhibitions** NOUN
(ART) a public display of works of art, products, or skills

exhibitor [ɪgˈzɪbɪtə] **exhibitors** NOUN
a person whose work is being shown in an exhibition

exhilarating [ɪgˈzɪləˌreɪtɪŋ] ADJECTIVE
Something that is exhilarating makes you feel very happy and excited.

exile [ˈɛgzaɪl] **exiles, exiling, exiled** NOUN

1 If somebody lives in exile, they live in a foreign country because they cannot live in their own country, usually for political reasons.

2 a person who lives in exile

> VERB
3 If somebody is exiled, they are sent away from their own country and not allowed to return.

exist [ɪgˈzɪst] **exists, existing, existed** VERB
If something exists, it is present in the world as a real or living thing.

existence [ɪgˈzɪstəns] NOUN
1 Existence is the state of being or existing.

2 a way of living or being *e.g. an idyllic existence*

exit [ˈɛgzɪt] **exits, exiting, exited** NOUN
1 a way out of a place

2 If you make an exit, you leave a place.

> VERB
3 To exit means to go out.

4 (DRAMA) An actor exits when he or she leaves the stage.

exodus [ˈɛksədəs] NOUN
An exodus is the departure of a large number of people from a place.

exotic [ɪgˈzɒtɪk] ADJECTIVE
1 attractive or interesting through being unusual *e.g. exotic fabrics*

2 coming from a foreign country *e.g. exotic plants*
[WORD HISTORY: from Greek EXOTIKOS meaning 'foreign']

expand [ɪkˈspænd] **expands, expanding, expanded** VERB
1 If something expands or you expand it, it becomes larger in number or size.

● THESAURUS
develop: *We need to develop the company's engineering division.*
enlarge: *Plans to enlarge the stadium have been approved.*
extend: *We're trying to extend our range of sports wear.*
fill out: *The balloon had filled out and was already almost airborne.*
grow: *The Japanese share of the market has grown dramatically.*
increase: *We will need to increase our overseas operations.*
swell: *The river had swollen rapidly.*
<<OPPOSITE decrease

2 If you expand on something, you give more details about it. *e.g. The minister's speech expanded on the aims which he outlined last month.*
expansion NOUN

305

● THESAURUS
develop: *You should develop this theme a little bit further.*
elaborate on: *He refused to elaborate on what he had said earlier.*
enlarge on: *I'd like you to enlarge on that last point.*

expanse [ɪk'spæns] **expanses** NOUN
a very large or widespread area *e.g. a vast expanse of pine forests*

expansive [ɪk'spænsɪv] ADJECTIVE
1 Something that is expansive is very wide or extends over a very large area. *e.g. the expansive countryside*

2 Someone who is expansive is friendly, open, or talkative.

expatriate [ɛks'pætrɪɪt] **expatriates** NOUN
someone who is living in a country which is not their own

expect [ɪk'spɛkt] **expects, expecting, expected** VERB
1 If you expect something to happen, you believe that it will happen. *e.g. The trial is expected to end today.*

● THESAURUS
anticipate: *We do not anticipate any problems.*
assume: *He assumed that they would wait for him.*
believe: *Experts believe the comet will pass close to the earth.*
imagine: *The meal cost more than we had imagined.*
presume: *I presume they'll be along shortly.*
reckon: *We reckon it'll be a fairly quick journey.*
think: *I thought the concert would be cancelled.*

2 If you are expecting somebody or something, you believe that they are going to arrive or to happen. *e.g. The Queen was expecting the chambermaid.*

3 If you expect something, you believe that it is your right to get it or have it. *e.g. He seemed to expect a reply.*

● THESAURUS
demand: *a job that demands a lot of time and money*
rely on: *I'm relying on you to help me.*
require: *They require a lot of her, maybe too much.*

expectancy [ɪk'spɛktənsɪ] NOUN
Expectancy is the feeling that something is about to happen, especially something exciting.

expectant [ɪk'spɛktənt] ADJECTIVE
1 If you are expectant, you believe that something is about to happen, especially something exciting.

2 An expectant mother or father is someone whose baby is going to be born soon.
expectantly ADVERB

expectation [ˌɛkspɛk'teɪʃən] **expectations** NOUN
Expectation or an expectation is a strong belief or hope that something will happen.

expedient [ɪk'spiːdɪənt] **expedients** NOUN
1 an action or plan that achieves a particular purpose but that may not be morally acceptable *e.g. Many firms have improved their profitability by the simple expedient of cutting staff.*

> ADJECTIVE
2 Something that is expedient is useful or convenient in a particular situation.
expediency NOUN

expedition [ˌɛkspɪ'dɪʃən] **expeditions** NOUN
1 an organized journey made for a special purpose, such as to explore; also the party of people who make such a journey

2 a short journey or outing *e.g. shopping expeditions*
expeditionary ADJECTIVE

expel [ɪk'spɛl] **expels, expelling, expelled** VERB
1 If someone is expelled from a school or club, they are officially told to leave because they have behaved badly.

2 If a gas or liquid is expelled from a place, it is forced out of it.

expend [ɪk'spɛnd] **expends, expending, expended** VERB
To expend energy, time, or money means to use it up or spend it.

expendable [ɪk'spɛndəbᵊl] ADJECTIVE
no longer useful or necessary, and therefore able to be got rid of

expenditure [ɪk'spɛndɪtʃə] NOUN
Expenditure is the total amount of money spent on something.

expense [ɪk'spɛns] **expenses** NOUN
1 Expense is the money that something costs. *e.g. the expense of installing a burglar alarm*

> PLURAL NOUN
2 Expenses are the money somebody spends while doing something connected with their work, which is paid back to them by their employer.

expensive [ɪk'spɛnsɪv] ADJECTIVE
costing a lot of money
expensively ADVERB
● THESAURUS
costly: *a costly court case*
dear: *Those trainers are far too dear.*
pricey: *Medical insurance can be very pricey.*

<<OPPOSITE *cheap*

experience [ɪk'spɪərɪəns] **experiences, experiencing, experienced** NOUN

1 Experience consists of all the things that you have done or that have happened to you.

2 the knowledge or skill you have in a particular activity

● THESAURUS

expertise: *They lack the expertise to deal with such a complex case.*

know-how: *Her technical know-how was invaluable.*

knowledge: *We need someone with knowledge of computing.*

training: *His military training made the difference between life and death.*

understanding: *someone with considerable understanding of the law*

3 something that you do or something that happens to you, especially something new or unusual

● THESAURUS

adventure: *a series of hair-raising adventures during the war*

affair: *He seemed keen to forget the affair and never discussed it.*

encounter: *his first encounter with alcohol*

episode: *The episode has proved deeply embarrassing for her.*

incident: *an incident he would rather forget*

ordeal: *a painful ordeal that is now over*

> VERB

4 If you experience a situation or feeling, it happens to you or you are affected by it.

● THESAURUS

encounter: *The storms were the worst they had ever encountered.*

have: *We're having a few difficulties with the computer.*

meet: *The next time you meet a situation like this, be careful.*

undergo: *The market is now undergoing a severe recession.*

experienced [ɪk'spɪərɪənst] ADJECTIVE
skilled or knowledgeable through doing something for a long time

● THESAURUS

expert: *an expert pilot*

knowledgeable: *He's very knowledgeable in this field.*

practised: *a practised and accomplished surgeon*

seasoned: *a seasoned climber*

well-versed: *He is well-versed in many styles of jazz.*

<<OPPOSITE *inexperienced*

experiment experiments, experimenting, experimented NOUN [ɪk'spɛrɪmənt]

1 the testing of something, either to find out its effect or to prove something

> VERB [ɪk'spɛrɪˌmɛnt]

2 If you experiment with something, you do a scientific test on it to prove or discover something.

experimentation NOUN, **experimental** ADJECTIVE, **experimentally** ADVERB

expert ['ɛkspɜːt] **experts** NOUN

1 a person who is very skilled at doing something or very knowledgeable about a particular subject

● THESAURUS

ace: *informal former motor-racing ace Stirling Moss*

authority: *an authority on ancient Egypt*

buff: *informal Cliff is a bit of a film buff.*

guru: *fashion gurus who predicted a 70's revival*

master: *He is a master in the art of office politics.*

professional: *He's widely respected in the theatre as a true professional.*

specialist: *a specialist in tropical diseases*

wizard: *a financial wizard who made millions in the early 80's*

<<OPPOSITE *beginner*

> ADJECTIVE

2 having or requiring special skill or knowledge *e.g. expert advice*

expertly ADVERB

● THESAURUS

able: *an able and dedicated surgeon*

adept: *He's an adept guitar player.*

experienced: *He was an experienced traveller and knew the area well.*

knowledgeable: *He's very knowledgeable about Chinese pottery.*

proficient: *Jackson is proficient in several European languages.*

skilful: *the skilful use of light in his early paintings*

skilled: *Ian is a highly skilled photographer.*

expertise [ˌɛkspɜː'tiːz] NOUN
Expertise is special skill or knowledge.

expire [ɪk'spaɪə] **expires, expiring, expired** VERB
When something expires, it reaches the end of the period of time for which it is valid. *e.g. My contract expires in the summer.*

expiry NOUN

explain [ɪk'spleɪn] **explains, explaining, explained** VERB
If you explain something, you give details about it or reasons for it so that it can be understood.

● THESAURUS

define: *Can you define what you mean by 'excessive'?*

describe: *an attempt to describe the whole process*
illustrate: *Let me illustrate this point with an example.*

explanation [ˌɛksplə'neɪʃən] **explanations** NOUN
a helpful or clear description
explanatory ADJECTIVE

● THESAURUS
clarification: *Her clarification has done little to help matters.*
definition: *a definition of what we actually mean by 'symbolism'*
description: *a fascinating description of how the pyramids were built*
exposition: *the fullest available exposition of Coleridge's ideas*

explicit [ɪk'splɪsɪt] ADJECTIVE
shown or expressed clearly and openly *e.g. an explicit death threat*
explicitly ADVERB

explode [ɪk'spləʊd] **explodes, exploding, exploded** VERB
1 If something such as a bomb explodes, it bursts loudly and with great force, often causing damage.

● THESAURUS
blow up: *Their boat blew up as they slept.*
burst: *Joey blew up the balloon until it burst.*
detonate: *Troops managed to detonate the mine safely.*
go off: *The bomb went off without any warning.*
set off: *No-one knows who planted the bomb, or how it was set off.*

2 If somebody explodes, they express strong feelings suddenly or violently. *e.g. I half expected him to explode in anger.*

● THESAURUS
blow up: *When she finally told him, he blew up and walked out.*
go berserk: *He'll go berserk if he ever finds out.*
go mad: *He went mad when I mentioned the kids.*

3 When something increases suddenly and rapidly, it can be said to explode. *e.g. Sales of men's toiletries have exploded.*

● THESAURUS
rocket: *Inflation has rocketed in the last few months.*
shoot up: *Prices shot up and the shelves were soon empty.*
soar: *Demand for shares in his new company has soared.*

exploit **exploits, exploiting, exploited** VERB [ɪk'splɔɪt]
1 If somebody exploits a person or a situation, they take advantage of them for their own ends. *e.g. Critics claim he exploited black musicians.*

2 If you exploit something, you make the best use of it, often for profit. *e.g. exploiting the power of computers*

> NOUN ['ɛksplɔɪt]
3 something daring or interesting that somebody has done *e.g. His courage and exploits were legendary.*
exploitation NOUN

explore [ɪk'splɔː] **explores, exploring, explored** VERB
1 If you explore a place, you travel in it to find out what it is like.
2 If you explore an idea, you think about it carefully.
exploration NOUN, **exploratory** ADJECTIVE, **explorer** NOUN

explosion [ɪk'spləʊʒən] **explosions** NOUN
a sudden violent burst of energy, for example one caused by a bomb

● THESAURUS
bang: *A loud bang made me run for cover.*
blast: *Three people were killed in the blast.*

explosive [ɪk'spləʊsɪv] **explosives**
ADJECTIVE
1 capable of exploding or likely to explode
2 happening suddenly and making a loud noise
3 An explosive situation is one which is likely to have serious or dangerous effects.

> NOUN
4 a substance or device that can explode

exponent [ɪk'spəʊnənt] **exponents** NOUN
1 An exponent of an idea or plan is someone who puts it forward.

2 FORMAL
An exponent of a skill or activity is someone who is good at it.

export **exports, exporting, exported** VERB [ɪk'spɔːt]
1 To export goods means to send them to another country and sell them there.

> NOUN ['ɛkspɔːt]
2 Exports are goods which are sent to another country and sold.
exporter NOUN

expose [ɪk'spəʊz] **exposes, exposing, exposed** VERB
1 To expose something means to uncover it and make it visible.

● THESAURUS
reveal: *His shirt was open, revealing his tattooed chest.*
show: *a short skirt which showed too much of her legs*

uncover: *She removed her scarf and uncovered her head.*

2 To expose a person to something dangerous means to put them in a situation in which it might harm them. *e.g. exposed to tobacco smoke*

3 To expose a person or situation means to reveal the truth about them.

● THESAURUS

bring to light: *The truth will be brought to light eventually.*

reveal: *an investigation that revealed widespread corruption*

show up: *She was finally shown up as a hypocrite.*

uncover: *We uncovered evidence of fraud.*

unearth: *Investigators have unearthed new evidence.*

exposition [ˌɛkspəˈzɪʃən] **expositions** NOUN
a detailed explanation of a particular subject

exposure [ɪkˈspəʊʒə] **exposures** NOUN
1 Exposure is the exposing of something.

2 Exposure is the harmful effect on the body caused by very cold weather.

express [ɪkˈsprɛs] **expresses, expressing, expressed** VERB
1 When you express an idea or feeling, you show what you think or feel by saying or doing something.

● THESAURUS

communicate: *People must learn to communicate their feelings.*

couch: *Their demands, though extreme, are couched in moderate language.*

phrase: *It sounds fine, but I would have phrased it differently.*

put: *Absolutely - I couldn't have put it better.*

put across: *the need to put across your message without offending anyone*

voice: *Local people have voiced their concern over plans for a bypass.*

2 If you express a quantity in a particular form, you write it down in that form. *e.g. The result of the equation is usually expressed as a percentage.*

> ADJECTIVE

3 very fast *e.g. express delivery service*

● THESAURUS

direct: *There's also a direct train.*

fast: *delays due to an accident in the fast lane*

high-speed: *the high-speed rail link between London and Paris*

nonstop: *the new nonstop service to New York*

> NOUN

4 a fast train or coach which stops at only a few places

expression [ɪkˈsprɛʃən] **expressions** NOUN

1 Your expression is the look on your face which shows what you are thinking or feeling.

● THESAURUS

countenance: *the beaming countenance of the prime minister*

face: *Why are you all wearing such long faces?*

2 (ENGLISH) The expression of ideas or feelings is the showing of them through words, actions, or art.

3 a word or phrase used in communicating *e.g. the expression 'nosey parker'*

● THESAURUS

idiom: *talking in the idiom of the Home Counties*

phrase: *What is the origin of the phrase?*

remark: *her passing remark to the camera*

term: *a derogatory term for an Arab*

expressive [ɪkˈsprɛsɪv] ADJECTIVE
1 showing feelings clearly

2 full of expression

expressway [ɪkˈsprɛsˌweɪ] **expressways** NOUN
a road designed for fast-moving traffic

expulsion [ɪkˈspʌlʃən] **expulsions** NOUN
The expulsion of someone from a place or institution is the act of officially banning them from that place or institution. *e.g. the high number of school expulsions*

exquisite [ɪkˈskwɪzɪt] ADJECTIVE
extremely beautiful and pleasing

extend [ɪkˈstɛnd] **extends, extending, extended** VERB
1 If something extends for a distance, it continues and stretches into the distance.

● THESAURUS

continue: *The caves continue for miles beneath the hills.*

hang: *The branches hang down to the ground.*

reach: *a long shirt that reached to her knees*

stretch: *an area of forest stretching as far as the eye could see*

2 If something extends from a surface or an object, it sticks out from it.

● THESAURUS

jut out: *The tip of the island juts out like a finger into the sea.*

project: *the ruins of a fort which projected from the mud*

protrude: *formal a huge rock protruding from the surface of the lake*

stick out: *pieces of rough metal that stuck out like spikes*

3 If you extend something, you make it larger or longer. *e.g. The table had been extended to seat fifty.*

add to: *They will be adding to their range of children's wear.*
develop: *He developed the US arm of the company.*
enlarge: *plans to enlarge the conference centre*
expand: *an unsuccessful attempt to expand the store's range of footwear*
widen: *the need to widen the appeal of the scheme*

extension [ɪk'stɛnʃən] **extensions** NOUN
1 a room or building which is added to an existing building

2 an extra period of time for which something continues to exist or be valid *e.g. an extension to his visa*

3 an additional telephone connected to the same line as another telephone

extensive [ɪk'stɛnsɪv] ADJECTIVE
1 covering a large area
● THESAURUS
broad: *a broad expanse of green lawn*
expansive: *an expansive grassy play area*
large: *a large country estate*
spacious: *a spacious dining area*
sweeping: *the sweeping curve of the bay*
vast: *vast stretches of land*
wide: *Worktops should be wide enough to allow food preparation.*

2 very great in effect *e.g. extensive repairs*
extensively ADVERB
● THESAURUS
comprehensive: *comprehensive television coverage of last week's events*
considerable: *He has considerable powers within the party.*
far-reaching: *a decision with far-reaching consequences*
great: *great changes in British society*
pervasive: *the pervasive influence of the army in national life*
untold: *This might do untold damage to her health.*
widespread: *There is widespread support for the proposals.*

extent [ɪk'stɛnt] **extents** NOUN
The extent of something is its length, area, or size.
● THESAURUS
degree: *To what degree were you in control of these events?*
level: *the level of public concern over this issue*
measure: *The full measure of the government's dilemma has become apparent.*
scale: *He underestimates the scale of the problem.*
size: *the size of the task*

exterior [ɪk'stɪərɪə] **exteriors** NOUN
1 The exterior of something is its outside.

2 Your exterior is your outward appearance.

exterminate [ɪk'stɜːmɪˌneɪt] **exterminates, exterminating, exterminated** VERB
When animals or people are exterminated, they are deliberately killed.
extermination NOUN

external [ɪk'stɜːnᵊl] **externals** ADJECTIVE
existing or happening on the outside or outer part of something
externally ADVERB

extinct [ɪk'stɪŋkt] ADJECTIVE
1 An extinct species of animal or plant is no longer in existence.

2 An extinct volcano is no longer likely to erupt.
extinction NOUN

extinguish [ɪk'stɪŋgwɪʃ] **extinguishes, extinguishing, extinguished** VERB
To extinguish a light or fire means to put it out.

extortionate [ɪk'stɔːʃənɪt] ADJECTIVE
more expensive than you consider to be fair

extra ['ɛkstrə] **extras** ADJECTIVE
1 more than is usual, necessary, or expected
● THESAURUS
added: *The Tandoori Cottage has the added advantage of being cheap.*
additional: *the need for additional funding*
excess: *If there's any excess sauce, you can freeze it.*
further: *the introduction of further restrictions*
more: *We need three more places at the table.*
new: *the burden of new legislation on top of all the recent changes*
spare: *There are spare blankets in the cupboard.*

> NOUN
2 anything which is additional
● THESAURUS
accessory: *the accessories you have to buy to make the place look good*
addition: *the latest addition to the team*
bonus: *The view from the hotel was an added bonus.*

3 a person who is hired to play a very small and unimportant part in a film

extra- PREFIX
'extra-' means 'outside' or 'beyond' *e.g. extraordinary*

extract extracts, extracting, extracted VERB [ɪk'strækt]
1 To extract something from a place means to take it out or get it out, often by force.
● THESAURUS
draw: *Villagers still have to draw their water from wells.*
mine: *the finest gems, mined from all corners of the world*

obtain: *Opium is obtained from poppies.*
pull out: *I can pull that information out of the database for you.*
remove: *Three bullets were removed from his wounds.*
take out: *I got an abscess so he took the tooth out.*

2 If you extract information from someone, you get it from them with difficulty.

● **THESAURUS**
draw: *They finally drew a confession from him.*
elicit: formal *the question of how far police should go to elicit a confession*
get: *How did you get an admission like that out of her?*
glean: *We're gleaning information from all sources.*
obtain: *Police have obtained statements from several witnesses.*

> NOUN (LIBRARY) [ˈɛkstrækt]
3 a small section taken from a book or piece of music

● **THESAURUS**
excerpt: *an excerpt from Tchaikovsky's Nutcracker*
passage: *He read out a passage from Milton.*
reading: *The author treated us to a reading from his latest novel.*
section: *Let's study a section of the text in more detail.*
snatch: *We played them a snatch of a violin concerto.*
snippet: *snippets of popular classical music*

extraction [ɪkˈstrækʃən] NOUN
1 Your extraction is the country or people that your family originally comes from. *e.g. a Malaysian citizen of Australian extraction*
2 Extraction is the process of taking or getting something out of a place.

extraordinary [ɪkˈstrɔːdənrɪ] ADJECTIVE
unusual or surprising
extraordinarily ADVERB

● **THESAURUS**
amazing: *What an amazing coincidence!*
bizarre: *It's such a bizarre thing to happen.*
odd: *It's an odd combination of colours.*
singular: *Cathy gave me a smile of singular sweetness.*
strange: *It's a strange piece of music.*
surprising: *A surprising number of women prefer to wear trousers to work.*
unusual: *It's a most unusual way to spend your holiday.*
<<OPPOSITE *ordinary*

extravagant [ɪkˈstrævɪɡənt] ADJECTIVE
1 spending or costing more money than is reasonable or affordable
2 going beyond reasonable limits
extravagantly ADVERB, **extravagance** NOUN

extravaganza [ɪkˌstrævəˈɡænzə]
extravaganzas NOUN
a spectacular and expensive public show

extreme [ɪkˈstriːm] **extremes** ADJECTIVE
1 very great in degree or intensity *e.g. extreme caution*

● **THESAURUS**
acute: *a mistake that caused acute embarrassment for everyone concerned*
deep: *a decision that caused deep resentment*
dire: *He is in dire need of hospital treatment.*
great: *a change in the law that could cause many people great hardship*
intense: *A number of people collapsed in the intense heat that day.*
profound: *feelings of profound shock and anger*
severe: *a business with severe financial problems*

2 going beyond what is usual or reasonable *e.g. extreme weather conditions*

● **THESAURUS**
drastic: *Let's not do anything too drastic.*
exceptional: *I think this is an exceptional case.*
excessive: *a newspaper feature about the use of excessive force by the police*
extravagant: *All that money being spent on hospitality seemed a bit extravagant.*
radical: *The government is introducing a series of radical economic reforms.*
unreasonable: *I don't think she's being the least bit unreasonable.*

3 at the furthest point or edge of something *e.g. the extreme northern corner of Spain*

> NOUN
4 the highest or furthest degree of something
extremely ADVERB

● **THESAURUS**
boundary: *the boundaries of artistic freedom*
depth: *the beauty of the countryside in the depths of winter*
end: *There are extremist groups at both ends of the political spectrum.*
height: *His behaviour was the height of bad manners.*
limit: *The ordeal tested the limits of their endurance.*
ultimate: *A Rolls-Royce is the ultimate in luxury.*

extremist [ɪkˈstriːmɪst] **extremists** NOUN
a person who uses unreasonable or violent methods to bring about political change
extremism NOUN

extremity [ɪkˈstremɪtɪ] **extremities** NOUN
The extremities of something are its furthest ends or edges.

extricate [ˈɛkstrɪˌkeɪt] **extricates, extricating, extricated** VERB
To extricate someone from a place or a situation

means to free them from it.

extrovert ['ɛkstrə,vɜːt] **extroverts** NOUN
a person who is more interested in other people
and the world around them than their own
thoughts and feelings
[WORD HISTORY: from Latin EXTRA meaning
'outwards' + VERTERE meaning 'to turn']

exuberant [ɪgˈzjuːbərənt] ADJECTIVE
full of energy and cheerfulness
exuberantly ADVERB, **exuberance** NOUN

exude [ɪgˈzjuːd] **exudes, exuding, exuded**
VERB
If someone exudes a quality or feeling, they seem
to have it to a great degree.

eye [aɪ] **eyes, eyeing** or **eying, eyed** NOUN
1 the organ of sight
2 the small hole at the end of a needle through
which you pass the thread
> VERB
3 To eye something means to look at it carefully
or suspiciously.

eyeball ['aɪ,bɔːl] **eyeballs** NOUN
the whole of the ball-shaped part of the eye

eyebrow ['aɪ,braʊ] **eyebrows** NOUN
Your eyebrows are the lines of hair which grow
on the ridges of bone above your eyes.

eyelash ['aɪ,læʃ] **eyelashes** NOUN
Your eyelashes are hairs that grow on the edges
of your eyelids.

eyelid ['aɪ,lɪd] **eyelids** NOUN
Your eyelids are the folds of skin which cover
your eyes when they are closed.

eyesight ['aɪ,saɪt] NOUN
Your eyesight is your ability to see.

eyesore ['aɪ,sɔː] **eyesores** NOUN
Something that is an eyesore is extremely ugly.

eyewitness ['aɪ,wɪtnɪs] **eyewitnesses**
NOUN
a person who has seen an event and can describe
what happened

eyrie ['ɪərɪ] **eyries** NOUN
the nest of an eagle or other bird of prey

Ff

fable ['feɪbəl] **fables** NOUN
a story intended to teach a moral lesson
[WORD HISTORY: from Latin FABULA meaning 'story']

fabled ['feɪbəld] ADJECTIVE
well-known because many stories have been told
about it e.g. the fabled city of Troy

fabric ['fæbrɪk] **fabrics** NOUN **(D & T)**
1 cloth e.g. tough fabric for tents
2 The fabric of a building is its walls, roof, and
other parts.
3 The fabric of a society or system is its structure,
laws, and customs. e.g. the democratic fabric of
American society

fabricate ['fæbrɪˌkeɪt] **fabricates,
fabricating, fabricated** VERB
1 If you fabricate a story or an explanation, you
invent it in order to deceive people.
2 To fabricate something is to make or
manufacture it.
fabrication NOUN

fabulous ['fæbjʊləs] ADJECTIVE
1 wonderful or very impressive e.g. a fabulous
picnic
2 not real, but happening in stories and legends
e.g. fabulous creatures

facade [fə'sɑːd] **facades** NOUN
1 the front outside wall of a building
2 a false outward appearance e.g. the facade of
honesty

face [feɪs] **faces, facing, faced** NOUN
1 the front part of your head from your chin to
your forehead
● THESAURUS
countenance: He met each enquiry with an
impassive countenance.
features: Her features were strongly defined.
mug: slang He managed to get his ugly mug on the
telly.
2 the expression someone has or is making e.g. a
grim face
3 a surface or side of something, especially the
most important side e.g. the north face of Everest
● THESAURUS
aspect: The house had a south-west aspect.

exterior: The exterior of the building was made of
brick.
front: There was a large veranda at the front of the
house.
side: narrow valleys with steep sides
surface: tiny waves on the surface of the water
4 the main aspect or general appearance of
something e.g. We have changed the face of
language study.
> VERB
5 To face something or someone is to be
opposite them or to look at them or towards
them. e.g. a room that faces on to the street
● THESAURUS
be opposite: I was opposite her at the breakfast
table.
look at: She turned to look at the person who was
speaking.
overlook: The pretty room overlooks a beautiful
garden.
6 If you face something difficult or unpleasant,
you have to deal with it. e.g. She faced a terrible
dilemma.
> PHRASE
7 On the face of it means judging by the
appearance of something or your initial reaction
to it e.g. On the face of it the palace looks gigantic.

faceless ['feɪslɪs] ADJECTIVE
without character or individuality e.g. anonymous
shops and faceless coffee-bars

face-lift face-lifts NOUN
1 an operation to tighten the skin on someone's
face to make them look younger
2 If you give something a face-lift, you clean it or
improve its appearance.

facet ['fæsɪt] **facets** NOUN
1 a single part or aspect of something e.g. the
many facets of his talent
2 one of the flat, cut surfaces of a precious stone
[WORD HISTORY: from French FACETTE meaning
'little face']

facetious [fə'siːʃəs] ADJECTIVE
witty or amusing but in a rather silly or
inappropriate way e.g. He didn't appreciate my
facetious suggestion.

[WORD HISTORY: from Latin FACETIAE meaning 'witty remarks']

facial ['feɪʃəl] ADJECTIVE
appearing on or being part of the face e.g. facial expressions

facilitate [fə'sɪlɪˌteɪt] **facilitates, facilitating, facilitated** VERB
To facilitate something is to make it easier for it to happen. e.g. a process that will facilitate individual development

facility [fə'sɪlɪtɪ] **facilities** NOUN
1 a service or piece of equipment which makes it possible to do something e.g. excellent shopping facilities
2 A facility for something is an ability to do it easily or well. e.g. a facility for novel-writing

fact [fækt] **facts** NOUN
1 a piece of knowledge or information that is true or something that has actually happened

● THESAURUS
certainty: A general election became a certainty three weeks ago.
reality: Fiction and reality became increasingly blurred.
truth: In the town, very few know the whole truth. <<OPPOSITE lie

> PHRASES
2 **In fact**, **as a matter of fact**, and **in point of fact** mean 'actually' or 'really' and are used for emphasis or when making an additional comment e.g. Very few people, in fact, have this type of skin.
factual ADJECTIVE, **factually** ADVERB

faction ['fækʃən] **factions** NOUN
a small group of people belonging to a larger group, but differing from the larger group in some aims or ideas e.g. a conservative faction in the Church

fact of life **facts of life** NOUN
1 The facts of life are details about sexual intercourse and how babies are conceived and born.
2 If you say that something is a fact of life, you mean that it is something that people expect to happen, even though they might find it shocking or unpleasant. e.g. War is a fact of life.

factor ['fæktə] **factors** NOUN
1 something that helps to cause a result e.g. House dust mites are a major factor in asthma.

● THESAURUS
aspect: Exam results illustrate only one aspect of a school's success.
cause: Smoking is the biggest preventable cause of death and disease.

consideration: Money was also a consideration.
element: Fitness has now become an important element in our lives.
influence: Van Gogh was a major influence on the development of modern painting.
part: Respect is a very important part of any relationship.
2 The factors of a number are the whole numbers that will divide exactly into it. For example, 2 and 5 are factors of 10.
3 If something increases by a particular factor, it is multiplied that number of times. e.g. The amount of energy used has increased by a factor of eight.

factory ['fæktərɪ] **factories** NOUN
a building or group of buildings where goods are made in large quantities

● THESAURUS
mill: a textile mill
plant: The plant produces most of the company's output.
works: the steel works

faculty ['fækəltɪ] **faculties** NOUN
1 Your faculties are your physical and mental abilities. e.g. My mental faculties are as sharp as ever.
2 In some universities, a Faculty is a group of related departments. e.g. the Science Faculty

fad [fæd] **fads** NOUN
a temporary fashion or craze e.g. the latest exercise fad

fade [feɪd] **fades, fading, faded** VERB
If something fades, the intensity of its colour, brightness, or sound is gradually reduced.

● THESAURUS
die away: The sound died away gradually.
dim: The house lights dimmed.
discolour: Exposure to bright light can cause wallpaper to discolour.
dull: Repeated washing had dulled the bright finish.
wash out: This dye won't wash out.

faeces or **feces** ['fiːsiːz] PLURAL NOUN
the solid waste substances discharged from a person's or animal's body
[WORD HISTORY: from Latin FAECES meaning 'dregs']

fag [fæg] **fags** NOUN; INFORMAL
a cigarette

Fahrenheit ['færənˌhaɪt] NOUN
a scale of temperature in which the freezing point of water is 32° and the boiling point is 212°

fail [feɪl] **fails, failing, failed** VERB
1 If someone fails to achieve something, they are not successful.

● THESAURUS
be defeated: The vote to change the law was defeated.

be in vain: *It became clear that his efforts had been in vain.*

be unsuccessful: *My job application was unsuccessful.*

come to grief: *Many marriages have come to grief over lack of money.*

fall through: *Negotiations with business leaders fell through last night.*

flunk: informal *He flunked all his exams.*
<<OPPOSITE succeed

2 If you fail an exam, your marks are too low and you do not pass.

3 If you fail to do something that you should have done, you do not do it. *e.g. They failed to phone her.*

● THESAURUS
neglect: *They never neglect their duties.*
omit: *He had omitted to tell her of the change in his plans.*

4 If something fails, it becomes less effective or stops working properly. *e.g. The power failed... His grandmother's eyesight began to fail.*

● THESAURUS
cease: *The secrecy about his condition had ceased to matter.*
decline: *His power declined as he grew older.*
give out: *All machines give out eventually.*
sink: *Her spirits sank lower and lower.*
stop working: *The boat came to a halt when the engine stopped working.*
wane: *her mother's waning strength*

> NOUN

5 In an exam, a fail is a piece of work that is not good enough to pass.

> PHRASE

6 Without fail means definitely or regularly *e.g. Every Sunday her mum would ring without fail.*

failing ['feɪlɪŋ] **failings** NOUN

1 a fault in something or someone

> PREPOSITION

2 used to introduce an alternative *e.g. Failing that, get a market stall.*

failure ['feɪljə] **failures** NOUN

1 lack of success *e.g. Not all conservation programmes ended in failure.*

● THESAURUS
breakdown: *a breakdown of the talks between the parties*
defeat: *It is important not to admit defeat.*
downfall: *people wishing to see the downfall of the government*
fiasco: *The evening was a total fiasco.*
miscarriage: *a miscarriage of justice*
<<OPPOSITE success

2 an unsuccessful person, thing, or action *e.g. The venture was a complete failure.*

● THESAURUS
disappointment: *a disappointment to his family*
flop: informal *The play turned out to be a flop.*
loser: *He had always been a loser.*
no-hoper: Australian and New Zealand *hanging around a group of no-hopers*

3 Your failure to do something is not doing something that you were expected to do. *e.g. a statement explaining his failure to turn up as a speaker*

4 a weakness in something

● THESAURUS
deficiency: *a serious deficiency in their defence system*
shortcoming: *The book has many shortcomings.*

faint [feɪnt] **fainter, faintest; faints, fainting, fainted** ADJECTIVE

1 A sound, colour, or feeling that is faint is not very strong or intense.

● THESAURUS
dim: *dim lighting*
faded: *a faded sign on the side of the building*
indistinct: *The lettering was worn and indistinct.*
low: *She spoke in a low voice.*
muted: *some muted cheers from the gallery*
vague: *a vague memory*
<<OPPOSITE strong

2 If you feel faint, you feel weak, dizzy, and unsteady.

● THESAURUS
dizzy: *suffering from dizzy spells*
giddy: *He felt giddy after the ride.*
light-headed: *She felt light-headed because she hadn't eaten.*

> VERB

3 If you faint, you lose consciousness for a short time.
faintly ADVERB

● THESAURUS
black out: *The blood drained from his head and he blacked out.*
collapse: *I collapsed when I heard the news.*
pass out: *to pass out with pain*
swoon: literary *Women in the twenties swooned over Valentino.*

fair [fɛə] **fairer, fairest; fairs** ADJECTIVE

1 reasonable and just *e.g. fair and prompt trials for political prisoners*

● THESAURUS
equal: *the commitment to equal opportunities*
equitable: *an equitable allocation of resources*
impartial: *an impartial observer*
legitimate: *a legitimate claim to the money*
proper: *It's right and proper that he should be here.*
upright: *an upright and trustworthy man*

<<OPPOSITE *unfair*

2 quite large *e.g. a fair size envelope*

3 moderately good or likely to be correct *e.g. He had a fair idea of what to expect.*

4 having light coloured hair or pale skin

● **THESAURUS**
blonde or **blond:** *a darker shade of blonde*
light: *He had a light complexion and blue eyes.*
<<OPPOSITE *dark*

5 with pleasant and dry weather *e.g. Ireland's fair weather months.*

> NOUN
6 a form of entertainment that takes place outside, with stalls, sideshows, and machines to ride on

● **THESAURUS**
bazaar: *a fundraising bazaar*
carnival: *the annual Antigua Carnival*
exhibition: *an international trade exhibition*
festival: *a rock festival*
fete: *The church fete was a popular attraction.*
show: *an agricultural show*

7 an exhibition of goods produced by a particular industry *e.g. the International Wine and Food Fair.*
fairly ADVERB, **fairness** NOUN

fairground ['fɛəˌɡraʊnd] **fairgrounds** NOUN
an outdoor area where a fair is set up

fairway ['fɛəˌweɪ] **fairways** NOUN
the area of trimmed grass between a tee and a green on a golf course

fairy ['fɛərɪ] **fairies** NOUN
In stories, fairies are small, supernatural creatures with magical powers.

fairy tale **fairy tales** NOUN
a story of magical events

faith [feɪθ] **faiths** NOUN
1 Faith is a feeling of confidence, trust or optimism about something.

● **THESAURUS**
confidence: *They had no confidence in the police.*
trust: *His trust in them was misplaced.*

2 **(RE)** someone's faith is their religion

● **THESAURUS**
belief: *united by belief*
creed: *open to all, regardless of creed*
persuasion: *people of all religious persuasions*
religion: *the Christian religion*

faithful ['feɪθfʊl] ADJECTIVE
1 loyal to someone or something and remaining firm in support of them

● **THESAURUS**
devoted: *They are devoted to each other.*
loyal: *a sign of true and loyal friendship*

staunch: *a staunch member of the party*
true: *a true believer*
<<OPPOSITE *unfaithful*

2 accurate and truthful *e.g. a faithful copy of an original*
faithfully ADVERB, **faithfulness** NOUN

● **THESAURUS**
accurate: *an accurate description of the event*
exact: *an exact copy of the original*
strict: *We demand strict adherence to the rules.*
true: *The film was quite true to life.*

fake [feɪk] **fakes, faking, faked** NOUN
1 an imitation of something made to trick people into thinking that it is genuine

● **THESAURUS**
copy: *It wasn't real, just a copy.*
forgery: *The signature was a forgery.*
fraud: *Many psychics are frauds.*
imitation: *The 'antique' chair is in fact a clever imitation.*
reproduction: *a reproduction of a famous painting*
sham: *The election was denounced as a sham.*

> ADJECTIVE
2 imitation and not genuine *e.g. fake fur*

● **THESAURUS**
artificial: *It's made with artificial sweeteners.*
counterfeit: *a large number of counterfeit documents*
false: *a false passport*
imitation: *bound in imitation leather*
phoney or **phony:** *informal He used a phoney accent.*
<<OPPOSITE *real*

> VERB
3 If you fake a feeling, you pretend that you are experiencing it.

● **THESAURUS**
feign: *to feign illness*
pretend: *Todd shrugged with pretended indifference.*
simulate: *writhing around in simulated agony*

falcon ['fɔːlkən] **falcons** NOUN
a bird of prey that can be trained to hunt other birds or small animals
[WORD HISTORY: from Latin FALCO meaning 'hawk']

fall [fɔːl] **falls, falling, fell, fallen** VERB
1 If someone or something falls or falls over, they drop towards the ground.

● **THESAURUS**
collapse: *The bridge collapsed on to the road.*
drop: *bombs dropping from the sky*
plunge: *A bus plunged into the river.*
topple: *He toppled slowly backwards.*
trip: *She tripped and broke her leg.*
<<OPPOSITE *rise*

2 If something falls somewhere, it lands there. *e.g. The spotlight fell on her.*

3 If something falls in amount or strength, it becomes less. *e.g. Steel production fell by 25%.*

THESAURUS
decline: *a declining birth rate*
decrease: *The number of bankruptcies decreased last year.*
diminish: *Resources are diminishing steadily.*
dwindle: *his dwindling authority*
plummet: *plummeting share prices*
subside: *The flood waters have subsided.*
<<OPPOSITE *increase*

4 If a person or group in a position of power falls, they lose their position and someone else takes control.

5 Someone who falls in battle is killed.

6 If, for example, you fall asleep, fall ill, or fall in love, you change quite quickly to that new state.

7 If you fall for someone, you become strongly attracted to them and fall in love.

8 If you fall for a trick or lie, you are deceived by it.

9 Something that falls on a particular date occurs on that date.

> NOUN

10 If you have a fall, you accidentally fall over.

11 A fall of snow, soot, or other substance is a quantity of it that has fallen to the ground.

12 A fall in something is a reduction in its amount or strength.

THESAURUS
decline: *signs of economic decline*
decrease: *an overall decrease of 10%*
drop: *the sharp drop in export sales*
reduction: *The bank announced a reduction in interest rates.*
slump: *a slump in property prices*
<<OPPOSITE *rise*

13 In America, autumn is called the fall.

fall down VERB
14 An argument or idea that falls down on a particular point is weak on that point and as a result will be unsuccessful.

fall out VERB
15 If people fall out, they disagree and quarrel.

fall through VERB
16 If an arrangement or plan falls through, it fails or is abandoned.

fallacy ['fæləsɪ] **fallacies** NOUN
something false that is generally believed to be true

[WORD HISTORY: from Latin FALLACIA meaning 'deception']

fallopian tube [fə'ləʊpɪən] **fallopian tubes** NOUN

one of two tubes in a woman's body along which the eggs pass from the ovaries to the uterus

fallout ['fɔːl,aʊt] NOUN
radioactive particles that fall to the earth after a nuclear explosion

fallow ['fæləʊ] ADJECTIVE
Land that is fallow is not being used for crop growing so that it has the chance to rest and improve.

false [fɔːls] ADJECTIVE
1 untrue or incorrect *e.g. I think that's a false argument.*

THESAURUS
erroneous: *to arrive at an erroneous conclusion*
fictitious: *the source of the fictitious rumours*
incorrect: *a decision based on incorrect information*
mistaken: *I had a mistaken view of what had happened.*
untrue: *The remarks were completely untrue.*
<<OPPOSITE *true*

2 not real or genuine but intended to seem real *e.g. false hair*

THESAURUS
artificial: *an artificial limb*
bogus: *their bogus insurance claim*
fake: *a fake tan*
forged: *They crossed the frontier using forged documents.*
simulated: *a simulated display of affection*
<<OPPOSITE *genuine*

3 unfaithful or deceitful
falsely ADVERB, **falsity** NOUN

THESAURUS
deceitful: *deceitful and misleading remarks*
disloyal: *He was accused of being disloyal to the company.*
insincere: *A lot of the actors were insincere.*
unfaithful: *left alone by her unfaithful husband*

falsehood ['fɔːls,hʊd] **falsehoods** NOUN
1 the quality or fact of being untrue *e.g. the difference between truth and falsehood*

2 a lie

falsify ['fɔːlsɪ,faɪ] **falsifies, falsifying, falsified** VERB
If you falsify something, you change it in order to deceive people.
falsification NOUN

falter ['fɔːltə] **falters, faltering, faltered** VERB
If someone or something falters, they hesitate or become unsure or unsteady. *e.g. Her voice faltered.*

fame [feɪm] NOUN
the state of being very well-known

f

THESAURUS
eminence: *to achieve eminence as a politician*
glory: *my moment of glory*
prominence: *He came to prominence with his bestselling novel.*
renown: *a singer of great renown*
reputation: *the city's reputation as a place of romance*

famed [feɪmd] ADJECTIVE
very well-known *e.g. an area famed for its beauty*

familiar [fəˈmɪlɪə] ADJECTIVE
1 well-known or easy to recognize *e.g. familiar faces*

2 knowing or understanding something well *e.g. Most children are familiar with stories.*
familiarity NOUN, **familiarize** VERB

THESAURUS
acquainted with: *Peter was well acquainted with Wordsworth.*
aware of: *aware of the dangers of smoking*
knowledgeable about: *They were very knowledgeable about gardening.*
versed in: *She was well versed in company law.*
<<OPPOSITE *unfamiliar*

family [ˈfæmɪlɪ] **families** NOUN
1 a group consisting of parents and their children; also all the people who are related to each other, including aunts and uncles, cousins, and grandparents

THESAURUS
descendants: *Their descendants lived there for centuries.*
relations: *friends and relations*
relatives: *She had relatives in many countries.*

2 a group of related species of animals or plants
familial ADJECTIVE

THESAURUS
class: *several classes of butterfly*
classification: *The classification includes conifers.*
kind: *different kinds of roses*

family planning [ˈplænɪŋ] NOUN
the practice of controlling the number of children you have, usually by using contraception

famine [ˈfæmɪn] **famines** NOUN
a serious shortage of food which may cause many deaths

famished [ˈfæmɪʃt] ADJECTIVE; INFORMAL
very hungry

famous [ˈfeɪməs] ADJECTIVE
very well known

THESAURUS
celebrated: *his most celebrated film*
distinguished: *a distinguished academic family*
illustrious: *the most illustrious scientists of the century*

legendary: *His skills are legendary.*
noted: *He is noted for his generosity.*
renowned: *The area is renowned for its cuisine.*
<<OPPOSITE *unknown*

famously [ˈfeɪməslɪ] ADVERB; OLD-FASHIONED, INFORMAL
If people get on famously, they enjoy each other's company very much.

fan [fæn] **fans, fanning, fanned** NOUN
1 If you are a fan of someone or something, you like them very much and are very enthusiastic about them.

THESAURUS
adherent: *The movement was gaining adherents everywhere.*
admirer: *one of her many admirers*
devotee: *a devotee of chamber music*
lover: *an art lover*
supporter: *rival football supporters*
zealot: *a religious zealot*

2 a hand-held or mechanical object which creates a draught of cool air when it moves

> VERB
3 To fan someone or something is to create a draught in their direction. *e.g. The gentle wind fanned her from all sides.*
fan out VERB

4 If things or people fan out, they move outwards in different directions.

fanatic [fəˈnætɪk] **fanatics** NOUN
a person who is very extreme in their support for a cause or in their enthusiasm for a particular activity
fanaticism NOUN
[WORD HISTORY: from Latin FANATICUS meaning 'possessed by a god']

THESAURUS
activist: *political activists*
devotee: *a devotee of the movement*
extremist: *groups of religious extremists*
militant: *The militants took over the organization.*
zealot: *He was a supporter but not a zealot.*

fanatical [fəˈnætɪkəl] ADJECTIVE
If you are fanatical about something, you are very extreme in your enthusiasm or support for it.
fanatically ADVERB

THESAURUS
fervent: *a fervent supporter*
obsessive: *obsessive about motor racing*
passionate: *a passionate interest*
rabid: *a rabid racist group*
wild: *I am wild about this band.*

fancy [ˈfænsɪ] **fancies, fancying, fancied; fancier, fanciest** VERB
1 If you fancy something, you want to have it or do it. *e.g. She fancied living in Canada.*

THESAURUS
be attracted to: *I am attracted to the idea of emigrating.*
hanker after: *to hanker after a bigger car*
have a yen for: *She had a yen for some new clothes.*
would like: *I would really like some ice cream.*

> ADJECTIVE
2 special and elaborate *e.g. dressed up in some fancy clothes*
fanciful ADJECTIVE

THESAURUS
decorated: *She preferred decorated surfaces to plain ones.*
elaborate: *his elaborate costume ideas*
extravagant: *the extravagant frescoes in the upper church*
intricate: *covered with intricate patterns*
ornate: *an ornate picture frame*
<<OPPOSITE *plain*

fancy dress NOUN
clothing worn for a party at which people dress up to look like a particular character or animal

fanfare ['fænfɛə] **fanfares** NOUN
a short, loud, musical introduction to a special event, usually played on trumpets

fang [fæŋ] **fangs** NOUN
Fangs are long, pointed teeth.

fantail ['fæn,teɪl] **fantails** NOUN
1 a pigeon with a large tail that can be opened out like a fan

2 In Australia and New Zealand, a fantail is also a small, insect-eating bird with a fan-shaped tail.

fantasize ['fæntə,saɪz] **fantasizes, fantasizing, fantasized;** also spelt **fantasise**
VERB
If you fantasize, you imagine pleasant but unlikely events or situations.

fantastic [fæn'tæstɪk] ADJECTIVE
1 wonderful and very pleasing *e.g. a fantastic view of the sea*

2 extremely large in degree or amount *e.g. fantastic debts*

3 strange and difficult to believe *e.g. fantastic animals found nowhere else on earth*
fantastically ADVERB

fantasy ['fæntəsɪ] **fantasies** NOUN
1 an imagined story or situation

2 Fantasy is the activity of imagining things, or the things that you imagine. *e.g. She can't distinguish between fantasy and reality.*

3 (**LIBRARY**) In books and films, fantasy is the people or situations in books or films which are created in the writer's imagination and do not reflect reality.

[WORD HISTORY: from Greek PHANTASIA meaning 'imagination']

far [fɑː] **farther, farthest; further, furthest**
ADVERB
1 If something is far away from other things, it is a long distance away.

THESAURUS
afar: *seen from afar*
a great distance: *They travelled a great distance.*
a long way: *The guy's lonely and a long way from home.*
deep: *deep into the jungle*
miles: *He lived miles away.*

2 Far also means very much or to a great extent or degree. *e.g. far more important*

THESAURUS
considerably: *The dinners were considerably less formal than before.*
incomparably: *South Africa seems incomparably richer than the rest of Africa.*
much: *I feel much better now.*
very much: *Things got very much worse.*

> ADJECTIVE
3 Far means very distant. *e.g. in the far south of Africa*

THESAURUS
distant: *the distant horizon*
long: *a long distance from here*
outlying: *The outlying areas are accessible only by air.*
remote: *a cottage in a remote village*
<<OPPOSITE *near*

4 Far also describes the more distant of two things rather than the nearer one. *e.g. the far corner of the goal*

> PHRASE
5 By far and **far and away** are used to say that something is the best *e.g. Walking is by far the best way to get around.*

6 So far means up to the present moment. *e.g. So far, it's been good news.*

7 As far as, so far as, and **in so far as** mean to the degree or extent that something is true. *e.g. As far as I know he is progressing well.*

> When you are talking about a physical distance you can use *farther* and *farthest* or *further* and *furthest*. If you are talking about extra effort or time, use *further* and *furthest*: *a further delay is likely*

farce [fɑːs] **farces** NOUN
1 a humorous play in which ridiculous and unlikely situations occur

2 a disorganized and ridiculous situation
farcical ADJECTIVE

fare [fɛə] **fares, faring, fared** NOUN

1 the amount charged for a journey on a bus, train, or plane

> VERB

2 How someone fares in a particular situation is how they get on. *e.g. The team have not fared well in this tournament.*

[WORD HISTORY: from Old English FARAN meaning 'to go']

Far East NOUN

The Far East consists of the countries of East Asia, including China, Japan, and Malaysia.
Far Eastern ADJECTIVE

farewell [ˌfɛəˈwɛl] INTERJECTION

1 Farewell means goodbye.

> ADJECTIVE

2 A farewell act is performed by or for someone who is leaving a particular job or career. *e.g. a farewell speech*

far-fetched [ˈfɑːˌfɛtʃt] ADJECTIVE

unlikely to be true

farm [fɑːm] **farms, farming, farmed** NOUN

1 an area of land together with buildings, used for growing crops and raising animals

> VERB

2 Someone who farms uses land to grow crops and raise animals.
farmer NOUN, **farming** NOUN

[WORD HISTORY: from Old French FERME meaning 'rented land']

farmhouse [ˈfɑːmˌhaʊs] **farmhouses** NOUN

the main house on a farm

farmyard [ˈfɑːmˌjɑːd] **farmyards** NOUN

an area surrounded by farm buildings

fascinate [ˈfæsɪˌneɪt] **fascinates, fascinating, fascinated** VERB

If something fascinates you, it interests you so much that you think about it and nothing else.
fascinating ADJECTIVE

● THESAURUS

absorb: *totally absorbed by her career*
bewitch: *Bill was bewitched by her charm.*
captivate: *Her looks captivated the whole world.*
enthral: *She sat enthralled by the actors.*
intrigue: *Her story intrigued them.*

fascism [ˈfæʃɪzəm] NOUN

an extreme right-wing political ideology or system of government with a powerful dictator and state control of most activities. Nationalism is encouraged and political opposition is not allowed.
fascist NOUN OR ADJECTIVE

fashion [ˈfæʃən] **fashions, fashioning, fashioned** NOUN

1 a style of dress or way of behaving that is popular at a particular time

● THESAURUS

craze: *the latest health craze*
fad: *just a passing fad*
style: *a revival of an old style*
trend: *the current trend in footwear*
vogue: *a vogue for fitness training*

2 The fashion in which someone does something is the way in which they do it.

● THESAURUS

manner: *in a friendly manner*
method: *He did it by his usual method.*
mode: *a different mode of life*
way: *in her usual resourceful way*

> VERB

3 If you fashion something, you make or shape it.

● THESAURUS

construct: *an inner frame constructed from timber*
create: *It was created from odds and ends.*
make: *a doll made from fabric*
mould: *They moulded the cups from clay.*
shape: *Shape the dough into a loaf.*
work: *a machine for working the stone*

fashionable [ˈfæʃənəbəl] ADJECTIVE

Something that is fashionable is very popular with a lot of people at the same time.
fashionably ADVERB

● THESAURUS

current: *the current thinking on the subject*
in: *informal Jogging was the in thing.*
latest: *all the latest hairstyles*
popular: *the most popular movie*
prevailing: *contrary to prevailing attitudes*
<<OPPOSITE *old-fashioned*

fast [fɑːst] **faster, fastest; fasts, fasting, fasted** ADJECTIVE

1 moving or done at great speed

● THESAURUS

accelerated: *at an accelerated pace*
hurried: *He ate a hurried breakfast.*
quick: *a quick learner*
rapid: *a rapid rise through the company*
speedy: *best wishes for a speedy recovery*
swift: *as swift as an arrow*
<<OPPOSITE *slow*

2 If a clock is fast, it shows a time that is later than the real time.

> ADVERB

3 quickly and without delay

● THESAURUS

hastily: *sheltering in hastily erected tents*
hurriedly: *students hurriedly taking notes*
quickly: *She worked quickly and methodically.*
rapidly: *moving rapidly across the field*
swiftly: *They had to act swiftly to save him.*
<<OPPOSITE *slowly*

4 Something that is held fast is firmly fixed.

THESAURUS
firmly: *with windows firmly shut*
securely: *The door was securely locked and bolted.*
tightly: *held tightly in his arms*

> **PHRASE**

5 If you are **fast asleep**, you are in a deep sleep.

> **VERB**

6 If you fast, you eat no food at all for a period of time, usually for religious reasons.

> **NOUN**

7 a period of time during which someone does not eat food

fasten ['fɑːsᵊn] **fastens, fastening, fastened** VERB

1 To fasten something is to close it or attach it firmly to something else.

THESAURUS
attach: *He attached a label to the plant.*
fix: *It was fixed on the wall.*
join: *joined together by string*
lock: *a locked door*
secure: *The chest was secured with a lock and chain.*
tie: *Tie your shoelaces.*

2 If you fasten your hands or teeth around or onto something, you hold it tightly with them.
fastener NOUN, **fastening** NOUN

fast food NOUN
hot food that is prepared and served quickly after you have ordered it

fastidious [fæ'stɪdɪəs] ADJECTIVE
extremely choosy and concerned about neatness and cleanliness

fast-track ['fɑːstˌtræk] **fast-tracks, fast-tracking, fast-tracked** VERB
To fast-track something is to make it happen or put it into effect as quickly as possible, usually giving it priority over other things.

fat [fæt] **fatter, fattest; fats** ADJECTIVE

1 Someone who is fat has too much weight on their body.

THESAURUS
buxom: *Melissa was a tall, buxom blonde.*
chubby: *I was greeted by a small, chubby man.*
fleshy: *He was well-built, but too fleshy to be an imposing figure.*
gross: *He tried to raise his gross body from the sofa.*
obese: *Obese people tend to have higher blood pressure than lean people.*
overweight: *Since having my baby, I feel slightly overweight.*
plump: *Maria was a pretty little thing, small and plump with a mass of dark curls.*
podgy: *informal Eddie's getting a little podgy round the middle.*

portly: *a portly, middle-aged man*
rounded: *a beautiful woman with blue eyes and a full, rounded figure*
roly-poly: *a short, roly-poly little woman with laughing eyes*
stout: *a tall, stout man with gray hair*
tubby: *He had been a short, tubby child who was taunted about his weight.*
<<OPPOSITE *thin*

2 large or great *e.g. a fat pile of letters*

> **NOUN**

3 Fat is the greasy, cream-coloured substance that animals and humans have under their skin, which is used to store energy and to help keep them warm.

4 Fat is also the greasy solid or liquid substance obtained from animals and plants and used in cooking.
fatness NOUN, **fatty** ADJECTIVE

fatal ['feɪtᵊl] ADJECTIVE

1 causing death *e.g. fatal injuries*

THESAURUS
deadly: *a deadly disease*
incurable: *It was regarded as an incurable illness.*
lethal: *a lethal dose of sleeping pills*
mortal: *They were in mortal danger.*
terminal: *terminal cancer*

2 very important or significant and likely to have an undesirable effect *e.g. The mistake was fatal to my plans.*
fatally ADVERB

THESAURUS
calamitous: *a calamitous air crash*
catastrophic: *The water shortage is potentially catastrophic.*
disastrous: *This could have disastrous consequences for industry.*
lethal: *a lethal left hook*

fatality [fə'tælɪtɪ] **fatalities** NOUN
a death caused by accident or violence

fate [feɪt] **fates** NOUN

1 Fate is a power that is believed to control events.

THESAURUS
chance: *a victim of chance*
destiny: *We are masters of our own destiny.*
fortune: *Remember, fortune favours the brave.*
providence: *His death was an act of providence.*

2 Someone's fate is what happens to them. *e.g. She was resigned to her fate.*

fateful ['feɪtfʊl] ADJECTIVE
having an important, often disastrous, effect *e.g. fateful political decisions*

father ['fɑːðə] **fathers, fathering, fathered** NOUN

1 A person's father is their male parent.

2 The father of something is the man who invented or started it. *e.g. the father of Italian painting*

3 'Father' is used to address a priest in some Christian churches

4 Father is another name for God.

> VERB

5 LITERARY

When a man fathers a child, he makes a woman pregnant.

fatherly ADJECTIVE, **fatherhood** NOUN

father-in-law ['fɑːðɪnˌlɔː] **fathers-in-law** NOUN

A person's father-in-law is the father of their husband or wife.

fathom ['fæðəm] **fathoms, fathoming, fathomed** NOUN

1 a unit for measuring the depth of water. It is equal to 6 feet or about 1.83 metres

> VERB

2 If you fathom something, you understand it after careful thought. *e.g. Daisy tried to fathom what it meant.*

fatigue [fə'tiːg] **fatigues, fatiguing, fatigued** NOUN

1 Fatigue is extreme tiredness.

> VERB

2 If you are fatigued by something, it makes you extremely tired.

fault [fɔːlt] **faults, faulting, faulted** NOUN

1 If something bad is your fault, you are to blame for it.

⬤ **THESAURUS**
blame: *They put the blame on her.*
liability: *The company was forced to admit liability.*
responsibility: *He accepted full responsibility for the error.*

2 a weakness or imperfection in someone or something

⬤ **THESAURUS**
blemish: *a blemish on an otherwise outstanding career*
defect: *a manufacturing defect*
deficiency: *serious deficiencies in the system*
drawback: *The plan had one major drawback.*
failing: *the country's many failings*
flaw: *serious character flaws*
imperfection: *small imperfections on the surface*
weakness: *his one weakness*
<<OPPOSITE *strength*

3 a large crack in rock caused by movement of the earth's crust

> PHRASE

4 If you are **at fault**, you are mistaken or are to blame for something. *e.g. If you were at fault, you accept it.*

> VERB

5 If you fault someone, you criticize them for what they are doing because they are not doing it well.

faultless ADJECTIVE

⬤ **THESAURUS**
blame: *I don't blame him.*
censure: *He was censured by the committee.*
criticize: *The minister criticized the police.*

faulty ['fɔːltɪ] **faultier, faultiest** ADJECTIVE
containing flaws or errors

⬤ **THESAURUS**
defective: *a lorry with defective brakes*
flawed: *The test results were seriously flawed.*
imperfect: *an imperfect specimen*
invalid: *That's an invalid argument.*
unsound: *a building that is structurally unsound*

favour ['feɪvə] **favours, favouring, favoured** NOUN

1 If you regard someone or something with favour, you like or support them.

⬤ **THESAURUS**
approval: *to gain his father's approval*
esteem: *in high esteem*
grace: *to fall from grace*
support: *They gave us their full support.*
<<OPPOSITE *disapproval*

2 If you do someone a favour, you do something helpful for them.

⬤ **THESAURUS**
courtesy: *the courtesy of a personal response*
good turn: *to do someone a good turn*
kindness: *She did me the kindness of calling.*
service: *a service to your country*
<<OPPOSITE *wrong*

> PHRASE

3 Something that is **in someone's favour** is a help or advantage to them. *e.g. The arguments seemed to be in our favour.*

4 If you are **in favour of** something, you agree with it and think it should happen.

> VERB

5 If you favour something or someone, you prefer that person or thing.

⬤ **THESAURUS**
prefer: *the preferred candidate*
single out: *He is always being singled out for special treatment.*

favourable ['feɪvərəbəl] ADJECTIVE

1 of advantage or benefit to someone

⬤ **THESAURUS**
advantageous: *the most advantageous course of action*

beneficial: *a beneficial effect on our health*
good: *He got a very good deal.*
opportune: *an opportune moment to attack*
suitable: *Conditions were not suitable for life to flourish.*
<<OPPOSITE *unfavourable*

2 positive and expressing approval
favourably ADVERB

● THESAURUS
affirmative: *to give an affirmative answer*
amicable: *amicable discussions*
approving: *a warm, approving glance*
friendly: *The proposal was given a friendly reception.*
positive: *a positive effect on the situation*
sympathetic: *He got a sympathetic hearing.*
welcoming: *a welcoming atmosphere*
<<OPPOSITE *unfavourable*

favourite ['feɪvərɪt] **favourites** ADJECTIVE
1 Your favourite person or thing is the one you like best.

● THESAURUS
best-loved: *our best-loved music*
dearest: *Her dearest wish was fulfilled.*
favoured: *the favoured child of elderly parents*
preferred: *his preferred method of exercise*

> NOUN
2 Someone's favourite is the person or thing they like best.

● THESAURUS
darling: *the spoilt darling of the family*
idol: *the idol of his fans*
pet: *the teacher's pet*
pick: *the pick of the bunch*

3 the animal or person expected to win in a race or contest

favouritism ['feɪvərɪˌtɪzəm] NOUN
Favouritism is behaviour in which you are unfairly more helpful or more generous to one person than to other people.

● THESAURUS
bias: *political bias in broadcasting*
one-sidedness: *The committee must show no one-sidedness.*
<<OPPOSITE *impartiality*

fawn [fɔːn] **fawns, fawning, fawned** NOUN
OR ADJECTIVE
1 pale yellowish-brown
> NOUN
2 a very young deer
> VERB
3 To fawn on someone is to seek their approval by flattering them.

fax [fæks] **faxes** NOUN
an exact copy of a document sent electronically along a telephone line

fear [fɪə] **fears, fearing, feared** NOUN
1 Fear is an unpleasant feeling of danger.

● THESAURUS
alarm: *I looked at him with growing alarm.*
awe: *in awe of his great powers*
dread: *She thought with dread of the coming storm.*
fright: *He jumped with fright at the noise.*
panic: *a moment of panic*
terror: *to shake with terror*

2 a thought that something undesirable or unpleasant might happen *e.g. You have a fear of failure.*

> VERB
3 If you fear someone or something, you are frightened of them.

● THESAURUS
be afraid: *The dog was afraid of him.*
be frightened: *I am frightened of thunder.*
be scared: *Are you scared of snakes?*
dread: *He dreaded angry scenes.*
take fright: *The horse took fright at the sudden noise.*

4 If you fear something unpleasant, you are worried that it is likely to happen. *e.g. Artists feared that their pictures would be forgotten.*
fearless ADJECTIVE, **fearlessly** ADVERB

fearful ['fɪəfʊl] ADJECTIVE
1 afraid and full of fear

2 extremely unpleasant or worrying *e.g. The world's in such a fearful mess.*
fearfully ADVERB

fearsome ['fɪəsəm] ADJECTIVE
terrible or frightening *e.g. a powerful, fearsome weapon*

feasible ['fiːzəbəl] ADJECTIVE
possible and likely to happen *e.g. The proposal is just not feasible.*
feasibility NOUN

feast [fiːst] **feasts** NOUN
a large and special meal for many people

feat [fiːt] **feats** NOUN
an impressive and difficult achievement *e.g. It was an astonishing feat for Leeds to score six away from home.*

feather ['fɛðə] **feathers** NOUN
one of the light fluffy things covering a bird's body
feathery ADJECTIVE

feature ['fiːtʃə] **features, featuring, featured** NOUN
1 an interesting or important part or characteristic of something

● THESAURUS
aspect: *every aspect of our lives*

f

attribute: *a normal attribute of human behaviour*
characteristic: *their physical characteristics*
mark: *distinguishing marks*
property: *the magnetic properties of iron*
quality: *skills and personal qualities*

2 Someone's features are the various parts of their face.

3 a special article or programme dealing with a particular subject

● THESAURUS
article: *a travel article*
column: *the advice column*
item: *an item about chemical waste*
piece: *a specially-written piece*
report: *a film report on the scandal*
story: *front-page news stories*

4 the main film in a cinema programme

> VERB

5 To feature something is to include it or emphasize it as an important part or subject.
featureless ADJECTIVE

● THESAURUS
emphasize: *to emphasize their differences*
give prominence to: *The Times is alone in giving prominence to the visit.*
spotlight: *a book spotlighting female singers*
star: *starring a major Australian actor*

February ['fɛbrʊərɪ] NOUN
February is the second month of the year. It has 28 days, except in a leap year, when it has 29 days.
[WORD HISTORY: from FEBRUA, a Roman festival of purification]

fed [fɛd] the past tense and past participle of **feed**

federal ['fɛdərəl] ADJECTIVE
relating to a system of government in which a group of states is controlled by a central government, but each state has its own local powers *e.g. The United States of America is a federal country.*

federation [ˌfɛdəˈreɪʃən] **federations** NOUN
a group of organizations or states that have joined together for a common purpose

fed up ADJECTIVE; INFORMAL
unhappy or bored

fee [fiː] **fees** NOUN
a charge or payment for a job, service, or activity

feeble ['fiːbəl] **feebler, feeblest** ADJECTIVE
weak or lacking in power or influence *e.g. feeble and stupid arguments*

feed [fiːd] **feeds, feeding, fed** VERB
1 To feed a person or animal is to give them food.
2 When an animal or baby feeds, it eats.
3 To feed something is to supply what is needed for it to operate or exist. *e.g. The information was*

fed into a computer database.

> NOUN

4 Feed is food for animals or babies.

feedback ['fiːdˌbæk] NOUN
1 Feedback is comments and information about the quality or success of something.

2 Feedback is also a condition in which some of the power, sound, or information produced by electronic equipment goes back into it.

feel [fiːl] **feels, feeling, felt** VERB
1 If you feel an emotion or sensation, you experience it. *e.g. I felt a bit ashamed.*

● THESAURUS
experience: *They seem to experience more distress than the others.*
suffer: *suffering from pangs of conscience*
undergo: *to undergo a change of heart*

2 If you feel that something is the case, you believe it to be so. *e.g. She feels that she is in control of her life.*

● THESAURUS
believe: *I believe they are right.*
consider: *We consider them to be our friends.*
deem: *I deemed it best to cancel the party.*
judge: *She was judged to be capable of anything.*
think: *I think I am very lucky.*

3 If you feel something, you touch it.

● THESAURUS
finger: *He was fingering the coins in his pocket.*
fondle: *She fondled the dog's ears.*
stroke: *I stroked the smooth wooden surface.*
touch: *He touched my face.*

4 If something feels warm or cold, for example, you experience its warmth or coldness through the sense of touch. *e.g. Real marble feels cold to the touch.*

5 To feel the effect of something is to be affected by it. *e.g. The shock waves of this fire will be felt by people from all over the world.*

> NOUN

6 The feel of something is how it feels to you when you touch it. *e.g. skin with a velvety smooth feel*

> PHRASE

7 If you **feel like** doing something, you want to do it.

feeler ['fiːlə] **feelers** NOUN
An insect's feelers are the two thin antennae on its head with which it senses things around it.

feeling ['fiːlɪŋ] **feelings** NOUN
1 an emotion or reaction *e.g. feelings of envy*
● THESAURUS
emotion: *trembling with emotion*
fervour: *religious fervour*

heat: *He spoke with some heat about his experiences.*
passion: *She argued with great passion.*
sentiment: *I'm afraid I don't share your sentiments.*

2 a physical sensation *e.g. a feeling of pain*

● THESAURUS
sensation: *a very pleasant sensation*
sense: *a slight sense of heat at the back of my throat*

3 Feeling is the ability to experience the sense of touch in your body. *e.g. He had no feeling in his hands.*

4 Your feelings about something are your general attitudes or thoughts about it. *e.g. He has strong feelings about our national sport.*

● THESAURUS
inclination: *neither the time nor the inclination*
opinion: *a consensus of opinion*
point of view: *an unusual point of view on the subject*
view: *Make your views known.*

feet [fiːt] the plural of **foot**

feign [feɪn] **feigns, feigning, feigned** VERB
If you feign an emotion or state, you pretend to experience it. *e.g. I feigned a headache.*

feline ['fiːlaɪn] ADJECTIVE
belonging or relating to the cat family
[WORD HISTORY: from Latin FELES meaning 'cat']

fell [fɛl] **fells, felling, felled**

1 the past tense of **fall**

> VERB
2 To fell a tree is to cut it down.

fellow ['fɛləʊ] **fellows** NOUN

1 OLD-FASHIONED, INFORMAL
a man *e.g. I knew a fellow by that name.*

2 a senior member of a learned society or a university college

3 Your fellows are the people who share work or an activity with you.

> ADJECTIVE
4 You use 'fellow' to describe people who have something in common with you. *e.g. his fellow editors*

[WORD HISTORY: from Old Norse FELAGI meaning 'partner' or 'associate']

fellowship ['fɛləʊʃɪp] **fellowships** NOUN

1 a feeling of friendliness that a group of people have when they are doing things together

● THESAURUS
brotherhood: *a symbolic act of brotherhood*
camaraderie: *the camaraderie among soldiers*
companionship: *the companionship between old friends*

2 a group of people that join together because they have interests in common *e.g. the Dickens Fellowship*

● THESAURUS
association: *a trade association*
brotherhood: *a secret international brotherhood*
club: *a youth club*
league: *the League of Nations*
society: *the historical society*

3 an academic post at a university which involves research work

felt [fɛlt]

1 the past tense and past participle of **feel**

> NOUN
2 Felt is a thick cloth made by pressing short threads together.

female ['fiːmeɪl] **females** NOUN

1 a person or animal that belongs to the sex that can have babies or young

● THESAURUS
girl: *a girls' school*
lady: *a nice young lady*
sheila: Australian and New Zealand; informal *his role as a sheila in his own play*
woman: *the number of women in the police force*
<<OPPOSITE *male*

> ADJECTIVE
2 concerning or relating to females

● THESAURUS
feminine: *the traditional feminine role*
girlish: *She gave a girlish giggle.*
womanly: *a womanly shape*
<<OPPOSITE *male*

feminine ['fɛmɪnɪn] ADJECTIVE

1 relating to women or considered to be typical of women

2 belonging to a particular class of nouns in some languages, such as French, German, and Latin
femininity NOUN

feminism ['fɛmɪˌnɪzəm] NOUN
Feminism is the belief that women should have the same rights and opportunities as men.
feminist NOUN OR ADJECTIVE

fen [fɛn] **fens** NOUN
The fens are an area of low, flat, very wet land in the east of England.

fence [fɛns] **fences, fencing, fenced** NOUN

1 a wooden or wire barrier between two areas of land

2 a barrier or hedge for the horses to jump over in horse racing or show jumping

> VERB
3 To fence an area of land is to surround it with a fence.

4 When two people fence, they use special swords to fight each other as a sport.

fend [fɛnd] **fends, fending, fended** PHRASE
1 If you have to **fend for yourself**, you have to look after yourself.

> VERB
2 If you fend off an attack or unwelcome questions or attention, you defend and protect yourself.

ferment [fə'mɛnt] **ferments, fermenting, fermented** VERB
When wine, beer, or fruit ferments, a chemical change takes place in it, often producing alcohol.
fermentation NOUN

fern [fɜːn] **ferns** NOUN
a plant with long feathery leaves and no flowers

ferocious [fə'rəʊʃəs] ADJECTIVE
violent and fierce e.g. ferocious dogs... ferocious storms
ferociously ADVERB, **ferocity** NOUN
[WORD HISTORY: from Latin FEROX meaning 'like a wild animal']

ferret ['fɛrɪt] **ferrets** NOUN
a small, fierce animal related to the weasel and kept for hunting rats and rabbits
[WORD HISTORY: from Old French FURET meaning 'little thief']

ferry ['fɛrɪ] **ferries, ferrying, ferried** NOUN
1 a boat that carries people and vehicles across short stretches of water

> VERB
2 To ferry people or goods somewhere is to transport them there, usually on a short, regular journey.

fertile ['fɜːtaɪl] ADJECTIVE
1 capable of producing offspring or plants

⬤ THESAURUS
fruitful: The fruitful earth gave forth its treasures.
productive: the most productive vineyards
prolific: Chinchillas are prolific breeders.
rich: This plant grows in moist rich ground.
<<OPPOSITE barren

2 creative e.g. fertile minds
fertility NOUN

fertilize ['fɜːtɪ,laɪz] **fertilizes, fertilizing, fertilized;** also spelt **fertilise** VERB
1 When an egg, plant, or female is fertilized, the process of reproduction begins by sperm joining with the egg, or by pollen coming into contact with the reproductive part of a plant.

2 To fertilize land is to put manure or chemicals onto it to feed the plants.

fertilizer ['fɜːtɪ,laɪzə] **fertilizers;** also spelt **fertiliser** NOUN
a substance put onto soil to improve plant growth

fervent ['fɜːvənt] ADJECTIVE
showing strong, sincere, and enthusiastic feeling
e.g. a fervent nationalist
fervently ADVERB

⬤ THESAURUS
ardent: one of the most ardent supporters of the policy
committed: a committed socialist
devout: She was a devout Christian.
enthusiastic: a huge and enthusiastic crowd
impassioned: an impassioned appeal for peace
passionate: I'm a passionate believer in public art.
zealous: He was a recent convert, and very zealous.

fervour ['fɜːvə] NOUN
a very strong feeling for or belief in something
e.g. a wave of religious fervour
[WORD HISTORY: from Latin FERVOR meaning 'heat']

fester ['fɛstə] **festers, festering, festered** VERB
If a wound festers it becomes infected and produces pus.
[WORD HISTORY: from Latin FISTULA meaning 'ulcer']

festival ['fɛstɪvəl] **festivals** NOUN
1 an organized series of events and performances
e.g. the Cannes Film Festival

⬤ THESAURUS
carnival: The carnival lasted for three days.
entertainment: theatrical entertainments
fair: The book fair attracted many visitors.
fete: a church fete
gala: the May Day gala

2 (RE) a day or period of religious celebration

⬤ THESAURUS
anniversary: The anniversary is celebrated each spring.
holiday: the Easter holiday

festive ['fɛstɪv] ADJECTIVE
full of happiness and celebration e.g. a festive time of singing and dancing

festivity [fɛs'tɪvɪtɪ] **festivities** NOUN
celebration and happiness e.g. the wedding festivities

festooned [fɛ'stuːnd] ADJECTIVE
If something is festooned with objects, the objects are hanging across it in large numbers.

fetch [fɛtʃ] **fetches, fetching, fetched** VERB
1 If you fetch something, you go to where it is and bring it back.

2 If something fetches a particular sum of money, it is sold for that amount. e.g. Portraits fetch the highest prices.

fetching ['fɛtʃɪŋ] ADJECTIVE
attractive in appearance e.g. a fetching purple frock

fete [feɪt] **fetes, feting, feted** NOUN

1 an outdoor event with competitions, displays, and goods for sale

> VERB

2 Someone who is feted receives a public welcome or entertainment as an honour.

feud [fjuːd] **feuds, feuding, feuded** NOUN

1 a long-term and very bitter quarrel, especially between families

> VERB

2 When people feud, they take part in a feud.

feudalism ['fjuːdə,lɪzəm] NOUN

Feudalism is a social and political system that was common in the Middle Ages in Europe. Under this system, ordinary people were given land and protection by a lord, and in return they worked and fought for him.
feudal ADJECTIVE

fever ['fiːvə] **fevers** NOUN

1 Fever is a condition occurring during illness, in which the patient has a very high body temperature.

2 A fever is extreme excitement or agitation. *e.g. a fever of impatience*

feverish ['fiːvərɪʃ] ADJECTIVE

1 in a state of extreme excitement or agitation *e.g. increasingly feverish activity*

2 suffering from a high body temperature
feverishly ADVERB

few [fjuː] **fewer, fewest** ADJECTIVE OR NOUN

1 used to refer to a small number of things *e.g. I saw him a few moments ago... one of only a few*

● THESAURUS

infrequent: *at infrequent intervals*
meagre: *a society with meagre resources*
not many: *Not many people attended the meeting.*
scanty: *scanty memories of his childhood*
scarce: *Resources are scarce.*
sparse: *a bare landscape with sparse trees*
<<OPPOSITE *many*

> PHRASES

2 **Quite a few** or **a good few** means quite a large number of things

> You use *fewer* to talk about things that can be counted: *fewer than five visits*. When you are talking about amounts that can't be counted you should use *less*

fiancé [fɪˈɒnseɪ] **fiancés** NOUN

A woman's fiancé is the man to whom she is engaged.

fiancée [fɪˈɒnseɪ] **fiancées** NOUN

A man's fiancée is the woman to whom he is engaged.

fiasco [fɪˈæskəʊ] **fiascos** NOUN

an event or attempt that fails completely, especially in a ridiculous or disorganized way *e.g. The game ended in a complete fiasco.*

fib [fɪb] **fibs, fibbing, fibbed** NOUN

1 a small, unimportant lie

> VERB

2 If you fib, you tell a small lie.

fibre ['faɪbə] **fibres** NOUN

1 (D & T) a thin thread of a substance used to make cloth

2 Fibre is also a part of plants that can be eaten but not digested; it helps food pass quickly through the body.
fibrous ADJECTIVE

fickle ['fɪkəl] ADJECTIVE

A fickle person keeps changing their mind about who or what they like or want.
[WORD HISTORY: from Old English FICOL meaning 'treacherous' or 'deceitful']

fiction ['fɪkʃən] **fictions** NOUN

1 Fiction is stories about people and events that have been invented by the author.

2 something that is not true
fictional ADJECTIVE, **fictitious** ADJECTIVE

fiddle ['fɪdəl] **fiddles, fiddling, fiddled** VERB

1 If you fiddle with something, you keep moving it or touching it restlessly.

2 INFORMAL
If someone fiddles something such as an account, they alter it dishonestly to get money for themselves.

> NOUN

3 INFORMAL
a dishonest action or scheme to get money

4 a violin
fiddler NOUN

fiddly ['fɪdlɪ] **fiddlier, fiddliest** ADJECTIVE

small and difficult to do or use *e.g. fiddly nuts and bolts*

fidelity [fɪˈdɛlɪtɪ] NOUN

Fidelity is remaining firm in your beliefs, friendships, or loyalty to another person.

fidget ['fɪdʒɪt] **fidgets, fidgeting, fidgeted** VERB

1 If you fidget, you keep changing your position because of nervousness or boredom.

● THESAURUS

fiddle: informal *She fiddled with her pencil.*
jiggle: *He's jiggling his keys.*
squirm: *He squirmed and wriggled with impatience.*
twitch: *Everybody twitched in their seats.*

> NOUN

2 someone who fidgets

327

fidgety ADJECTIVE

field [fiːld] **fields, fielding, fielded** NOUN

1 an area of land where crops are grown or animals are kept

● THESAURUS

green: *on the village green*
meadow: *a grassy meadow*
pasture: *cows grazing in the pasture*

2 (PE) an area of land where sports are played *e.g. a hockey field*

3 A coal field, oil field, or gold field is an area where coal, oil, or gold is found.

4 a particular subject or area of interest *e.g. He was doing well in his own field of advertising.*

● THESAURUS

area: *a politically-sensitive area*
department: *Health care isn't my department.*
domain: *in the domain of art*
province: *This is the province of a different section.*
speciality: *His speciality was mythology.*
territory: *an expert in his own territory of history*

> ADJECTIVE

5 A field trip or a field study involves research or activity in the natural environment rather than theoretical or laboratory work.

6 In an athletics competition, the field events are the events such as the high jump and the javelin which do not take place on a running track.

> VERB

7 In cricket, when you field the ball, you stop it after the batsman has hit it.

8 To field questions is to answer or deal with them skilfully.

fielder ['fiːldə] **fielders** NOUN

In cricket, the fielders are the team members who stand at various parts of the pitch and try to get the batsmen out or to prevent runs from being scored.

field marshal **field marshals** NOUN

an army officer of the highest rank

fieldwork ['fiːld͵wɜːk] NOUN

Fieldwork is the study of something in the environment where it naturally lives or occurs, rather than in a class or laboratory.

fiend [fiːnd] **fiends** NOUN

1 a devil or evil spirit

2 a very wicked or cruel person

3 INFORMAL

someone who is very keen on a particular thing *e.g. a fitness fiend*

[WORD HISTORY: from Old English FEOND meaning 'enemy']

fierce [fɪəs] **fiercer, fiercest** ADJECTIVE

1 very aggressive or angry

● THESAURUS

aggressive: *encouraging aggressive behaviour in later life*
dangerous: *These birds are dangerous.*
ferocious: *two and a half days of ferocious violence*
murderous: *a murderous attack*
<<OPPOSITE *gentle*

2 extremely strong or intense *e.g. a sudden fierce pain... a fierce storm*

fiercely ADVERB

● THESAURUS

intense: *We found ourselves standing in intense heat.*
keen: *a keen interest in cars*
relentless: *The pressure was relentless.*
strong: *a strong dislike*

fiery ['faɪəri] **fierier, fieriest** ADJECTIVE

1 involving fire or seeming like fire *e.g. a huge fiery sun*

2 showing great anger, energy, or passion *e.g. a fiery debate*

fifteen ['fɪf'tiːn]

the number 15

fifteenth

fifth [fɪfθ] **fifths** ADJECTIVE

1 The fifth item in a series is the one counted as number five.

> NOUN

2 one of five equal parts

fifty ['fɪftɪ] **fifties**

the number 50

fiftieth

fifty-fifty ['fɪftɪ'fɪftɪ] ADVERB

1 divided equally into two portions

> ADJECTIVE

2 just as likely not to happen as to happen *e.g. You've got a fifty-fifty chance of being right.*

fig [fɪg] **figs** NOUN

a soft, sweet fruit full of tiny seeds. It grows in hot countries and is often eaten dried

fight [faɪt] **fights, fighting, fought** VERB

1 When people fight, they take part in a battle, a war, a boxing match, or in some other attempt to hurt or kill someone.

● THESAURUS

battle: *The gang battled with the police.*
brawl: *men brawling drunkenly in the street*
grapple: *grappling with an alligator*
struggle: *He was struggling with police outside the club.*

2 To fight for something is to try in a very determined way to achieve it. *e.g. I must fight for respect.*

> NOUN

3 a situation in which people hit or try to hurt each other

● THESAURUS

action: *wounded in action*
battle: *a gun battle*
bout: *a wrestling bout*
combat: *the end of a long combat*
duel: *He was killed in a duel.*
skirmish: *a minor border skirmish*

4 a determined attempt to prevent or achieve something *e.g. the fight for independence*

5 an angry disagreement

● THESAURUS

argument: *an argument over a boyfriend*
blue: *Australian; slang a bloke I'd had a blue with years ago*
dispute: *a dispute over ticket allocation*
row: *Maxine and I had a terrible row.*
squabble: *a family squabble over Sunday lunch*

fighter ['faɪtə] **fighters** NOUN
someone who physically fights another person

● THESAURUS

soldier: *well-equipped soldiers*
warrior: *a brave warrior*

figurative ['fɪgərətɪv] ADJECTIVE
(ENGLISH) If you use a word or expression in a figurative sense, you use it with a more abstract or imaginative meaning than its ordinary one.
figuratively ADVERB

figure ['fɪgə] **figures, figuring, figured**
NOUN

1 a written number or the amount a number stands for

● THESAURUS

amount: *Postal money orders are available in amounts up to $700.*
digit: *a code made up of letters and digits*
number: *A lot of marriages end in divorce, but we don't know the exact number.*
numeral: *the numeral six*
statistic: *Official statistics show wages declining by 24%.*
total: *Then he added everything together to arrive at the final total.*

2 a geometrical shape

3 a diagram or table in a written text

4 the shape of a human body, sometimes one that you cannot see properly *e.g. his slim and supple figure... A human figure leaped at him.*

● THESAURUS

body: *She's got nice hair and a great body.*
build: *a tall woman with a naturally slim build*
form: *The shadowy form receded into the darkness.*
physique: *He has the physique and energy of a man half his age.*

silhouette: *Tuck the shirt in to give yourself a streamlined silhouette.*
shape: *tall, dark shapes moving in the mist*

5 a person *e.g. He was a major figure in the trial.*

● THESAURUS

character: *What a sad character that Nigel is.*
dignitary: *a visiting dignitary of great importance*
person: *My grandfather was a person of some influence.*
personality: *The event was attended by many showbiz personalities.*
player: *a key player in the negotiations*

> VERB

6 To figure in something is to appear or be included in it. *e.g. the many people who have figured in his life*

7 INFORMAL
If you figure that something is the case, you guess or conclude this. *e.g. We figure the fire broke out around four in the morning.*

● THESAURUS

expect: *I expect you're just tired.*
guess: *I guess he's right.*
reckon: *informal Toni reckoned that it must be about three o'clock.*
suppose: *What do you suppose he's up to?*

figurehead ['fɪgə,hɛd] **figureheads** NOUN
the leader of a movement or organization who has no real power

figure of speech figures of speech NOUN
A figure of speech is an expression such as a simile or idiom in which the words are not used in their literal sense.

file [faɪl] **files, filing, filed** NOUN

1 a box or folder in which a group of papers or records is kept; also used of the information kept in the file

2 In computing, a file is a stored set of related data with its own name.

3 a line of people one behind the other

4 a long steel tool with a rough surface, used for smoothing and shaping hard materials

> VERB

5 When someone files a document, they put it in its correct place with similar documents.

6 When a group of people file somewhere, they walk one behind the other in a line.

7 If you file something, you smooth or shape it with a file.

fill [fɪl] **fills, filling, filled** VERB

1 If you fill something or if it fills up, it becomes full.

● THESAURUS

cram: *Mourners crammed the small church.*

gorge: *gorged with food*
pack: *a lorry packed with explosives*
stock: *a lake stocked with carp*
stuff: *Stuff the pillow with feathers.*
<<OPPOSITE *empty*

2 If something fills a need, it satisfies the need. *e.g. Ella had in some small way filled the gap left by Molly's absence.*

3 To fill a job vacancy is to appoint someone to do that job.

> NOUN

4 If you have had your fill of something, you do not want any more.

fill in VERB

5 If you fill in a form, you write information in the appropriate spaces.

6 If you fill someone in, you give them information to bring them up to date.

fillet ['fɪlɪt] **fillets, filleting, filleted** NOUN

1 a strip of tender, boneless beef, veal, or pork

2 a piece of fish with the bones removed

> VERB

3 To fillet meat or fish is to prepare it by cutting out the bones.

filling ['fɪlɪŋ] **fillings** NOUN

1 the soft food mixture inside a sandwich, cake, or pie

2 a small amount of metal or plastic put into a hole in a tooth by a dentist

filly ['fɪlɪ] **fillies** NOUN
a female horse or pony under the age of four

film [fɪlm] **films, filming, filmed** NOUN

1 a series of moving pictures projected onto a screen and shown at the cinema or on television

2 a thin flexible strip of plastic used in a camera to record images when exposed to light

3 a very thin layer of powder or liquid on a surface

4 Plastic film is a very thin sheet of plastic used for wrapping things.

> VERB

5 If you film someone, you use a video camera to record their movements on film.

[WORD HISTORY: from Old English FILMEN meaning 'membrane']

filter ['fɪltə] **filters, filtering, filtered** NOUN

1 a device that allows some substances, lights, or sounds to pass through it, but not others *e.g. a filter against the harmful rays of the sun*

> VERB

2 To filter a substance is to pass it through a filter.

3 If something filters somewhere, it gets there slowly or faintly. *e.g. Traffic filtered into the city.*

filtration NOUN

filth [fɪlθ] NOUN

1 Filth is disgusting dirt and muck.

2 People often use the word filth to refer to very bad language or to sexual material that is thought to be crude and offensive.

filthy ADJECTIVE

[WORD HISTORY: from Old English FYLTH meaning 'pus' or 'corruption']

fin [fɪn] **fins** NOUN
a thin, flat structure on the body of a fish, used to help guide it through the water

final ['faɪnəl] **finals** ADJECTIVE

1 last in a series or happening at the end of something

● THESAURUS

closing: *in the closing stages of the race*
concluding: *the concluding part of the serial*
eventual: *the eventual aim of their policies*
last: *his last chance*
ultimate: *The ultimate outcome will be different.*
<<OPPOSITE *first*

2 A decision that is final cannot be changed or questioned.

● THESAURUS

absolute: *absolute authority*
conclusive: *conclusive proof*
definite: *too soon to give a definite answer*
definitive: *the definitive account of the war*

> NOUN

3 the last game or contest in a series which decides the overall winner

> PLURAL NOUN

4 Finals are the last and most important examinations of a university or college course.

finale [fɪ'nɑːlɪ] **finales** NOUN
the last section of a piece of music or show

finalist ['faɪnəlɪst] **finalists** NOUN
a person taking part in the final of a competition

finalize ['faɪnəlaɪz] **finalizes, finalizing, finalized;** also spelt **finalise** VERB
If you finalize something, you complete all the arrangements for it.

finally ['faɪnəlɪ] ADVERB

1 If something finally happens, it happens after a long delay.

● THESAURUS

at last: *He came at last.*
at the last moment: *They changed their minds at the last moment.*
eventually: *The flight eventually left.*
in the end: *It all turned out right in the end.*
in the long run: *a success in the long run*

2 You use 'finally' to introduce a final point, question, or topic that you are talking or writing about.

● THESAURUS
in conclusion: *In conclusion, we have to agree.*
in summary: *It was, in summary, a satisfactory outcome.*
lastly: *Lastly, I would like to thank my agent.*

finance [fɪ'næns] **finances, financing, financed** VERB

1 To finance a project or a large purchase is to provide the money for it.

● THESAURUS
back: *a fund backed by local businesses*
fund: *The scheme is funded by the banks.*
pay for: *He paid for his trip out of his savings.*
support: *She supported herself through university.*

> NOUN

2 Finance for something is the money or loans used to pay for it.

3 Finance is also the management of money, loans, and investments.

● THESAURUS
banking: *the international banking system*
budgeting: *We must exercise caution in our budgeting this year.*
commerce: *industry and commerce*
economics: *the economics of the third world*
investment: *tax incentives to encourage investment*

financial [fɪ'nænʃəl] ADJECTIVE

relating to or involving money
financially ADVERB

● THESAURUS
economic: *an economic crisis*
fiscal: *the long-term fiscal policy of this country*
money: *on the money markets*

financier [fɪ'nænsɪə] **financiers** NOUN

a person who deals with the finance for large businesses

finch [fɪntʃ] **finches** NOUN

a small bird with a short strong beak

find see page 332 for Word Web

findings ['faɪndɪŋz] PLURAL NOUN

Someone's findings are the conclusions they reach as a result of investigation.

fine [faɪn] **finer, finest; fines, fining, fined** ADJECTIVE

1 very good or very beautiful *e.g. a fine school... fine clothes*

● THESAURUS
admirable: *with many admirable qualities*
beautiful: *a beautiful view of the river*
excellent: *inns with excellent cuisine*
magnificent: *his magnificent country house*
outstanding: *an area of outstanding natural beauty*
splendid: *a splendid collection of cartoons*

2 satisfactory or suitable *e.g. Pasta dishes are fine if not served with a rich sauce.*

3 very narrow or thin

● THESAURUS
delicate: *delicate curtains to let in the light*
lightweight: *certain lightweight fabrics*
powdery: *soft powdery dust*
sheer: *a sheer chiffon shirt*
small: *netting with a small mesh*

4 A fine detail, adjustment, or distinction is very delicate, exact, or subtle.

● THESAURUS
fastidious: *fastidious attention to detail*
keen: *a keen eye for a bargain*
precise: *a gauge with precise adjustment*
refined: *a woman of refined tastes*
sensitive: *The radio had very sensitive tuning.*
subtle: *a very subtle distinction*

5 When the weather is fine, it is not raining and is bright or sunny.

> NOUN

6 a sum of money paid as a punishment

> VERB

7 Someone who is fined has to pay a sum of money as a punishment.

finery ['faɪnərɪ] NOUN

Finery is very beautiful clothing and jewellery.

finesse [fɪ'nɛs] NOUN

If you do something with finesse, you do it with skill and subtlety.

finger ['fɪŋɡə] **fingers, fingering, fingered** NOUN

1 Your fingers are the four long jointed parts of your hands, sometimes including the thumbs.

> VERB

2 If you finger something you feel it with your fingers.

fingernail ['fɪŋɡə,neɪl] **fingernails** NOUN

Your fingernails are the hard coverings at the ends of your fingers.

fingerprint ['fɪŋɡə,prɪnt] **fingerprints** NOUN

a mark made showing the pattern on the skin at the tip of a person's finger

finish ['fɪnɪʃ] **finishes, finishing, finished** VERB

1 When you finish something, you reach the end of it and complete it.

● THESAURUS
close: *They have closed the deal.*
complete: *She completed her first novel.*
conclude: *He concluded his speech.*
end: *That ended our discussion.*
finalize: *to finalize an agreement*
<<OPPOSITE *start*

2 When something finishes, it ends or stops.

1 VERB

If you find someone or something, you discover them, either as a result of searching or by coming across them unexpectedly.

● THESAURUS

come across: *He came across the book by chance.*

discover: *They discovered the body in the bushes.*

locate: *locating the position of the gene*

track down: *to track down her parents*

turn up: *They failed to turn up any evidence.*

unearth: *to unearth the missing copy*

<< OPPOSITE *lose*

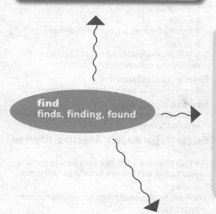

find
finds, finding, found

2 VERB

If you find that something is the case, you become aware of it or realize it *eg: I found my fists were clenched.*

● THESAURUS

become aware: *I became aware of his work last year.*

detect: *I detected a note of envy in her voice.*

discover: *It was discovered that the goods were missing.*

learn: *I flew from New York on learning of his death.*

realize: *They realized too late that it was wrong.*

3 VERB

to consider that someone or something has a particular quality *eg: his business partner had found that odd*

● THESAURUS

believe: *I believe it's ludicrous that nothing has been done.*

consider: *I consider activities such as jogging and weightlifting as unnatural.*

think: *We think of him as a father.*

> NOUN

3 The finish of something is the end or last part of it.

● THESAURUS
close: *to bring to a close*
completion: *The project is nearing completion.*
conclusion: *at the conclusion of the programme*
end: *the end of the race*
ending: *The film had an unexpected ending.*
finale: *the grand finale of the evening*
<<OPPOSITE start

4 The finish that something has is the texture or appearance of its surface. *e.g. a healthy, glossy finish*

● THESAURUS
grain: *the smooth grain of the wood*
lustre: *a similar lustre to silk*
polish: *The bodywork had a high polish.*
shine: *It gives a beautiful shine to the hair.*
surface: *a polished surface*
texture: *paper with a linen-like texture*

finite ['faɪnaɪt] ADJECTIVE
having a particular size or limit which cannot be increased *e.g. There's only finite money to spend.*

Finn [fɪn] **Finns** NOUN
someone who comes from Finland

Finnish ['fɪnɪʃ] ADJECTIVE
1 belonging or relating to Finland
> NOUN
2 Finnish is the main language spoken in Finland.

fir [fɜː] **firs** NOUN
a tall pointed evergreen tree that has thin needle-like leaves and produces cones

fire [faɪə] **fires, firing, fired** NOUN
1 Fire is the flames produced when something burns.

● THESAURUS
blaze: *The firemen were hurt in the blaze.*
combustion: *Energy is released by combustion.*
flames: *rescued from the flames*
inferno: *The building was an inferno.*

2 a pile or mass of burning material
3 a piece of equipment that is used as a heater *e.g. a gas fire*
> VERB
4 If you fire a weapon or fire a bullet, you operate the weapon so that the bullet or missile is released.

● THESAURUS
detonate: *to detonate an explosive device*
explode: *They exploded a bomb.*
launch: *The protesters launched the missile from a boat.*
set off: *the largest nuclear explosion ever set off on Earth*

shoot: *people shooting guns in all directions*

5 If you fire questions at someone, you ask them a lot of questions very quickly.

6 INFORMAL
If an employer fires someone, he or she dismisses that person from their job.

● THESAURUS
discharge: *A trooper has been discharged from the army.*
dismiss: *He was dismissed by the bank.*
make redundant: *Many people were made redundant.*
sack: *informal Jones was sacked for disciplinary reasons.*

> PHRASE
7 If someone **opens fire**, they start shooting.

firearm ['faɪərˌɑːm] **firearms** NOUN
a gun

fire brigade fire brigades NOUN
the organization which has the job of putting out fires

fire engine fire engines NOUN
a large vehicle that carries equipment for putting out fires

fire escape fire escapes NOUN
an emergency exit or staircase for use if there is a fire

fire extinguisher [ɪk'stɪŋgwɪʃə] **fire extinguishers** NOUN
a metal cylinder containing water or foam for spraying onto a fire

firefighter ['faɪəˌfaɪtə] **firefighters** NOUN
a person whose job is to put out fires and rescue trapped people

firefly ['faɪəˌflaɪ] **fireflies** NOUN
an insect that glows in the dark

fireplace ['faɪəˌpleɪs] **fireplaces** NOUN
the opening beneath a chimney where a fire can be lit

fireproof ['faɪəˌpruːf] ADJECTIVE
resistant to fire

fire station fire stations NOUN
a building where fire engines are kept and where firefighters wait to be called out

firework ['faɪəˌwɜːk] **fireworks** NOUN
a small container of gunpowder and other chemicals which explodes and produces coloured sparks or smoke when lit

firing squad ['faɪərɪŋ] **firing squads** NOUN
a group of soldiers ordered to shoot a person condemned to death

firm [fɜːm] **firmer, firmest; firms** ADJECTIVE
1 Something that is firm does not move easily when pressed or pushed, or when weight is put on it.

● THESAURUS
compressed: *compressed wood pulp made into cardboard*
congealed: *a bowl of congealed grease*
hard: *The snow was hard and slippery.*
rigid: *Pour the mixture into a rigid plastic container.*
set: *The glue wasn't completely set.*
solid: *a block of solid wax*
stiff: *egg whites beaten until stiff*
<<OPPOSITE *soft*

2 A firm grasp or push is one with controlled force or pressure.

3 A firm decision is definite.

4 Someone who is firm behaves with authority that shows they will not change their mind.

● THESAURUS
adamant: *He was adamant that he would not resign.*
determined: *She was determined to finish the game.*
inflexible: *his inflexible routine*
resolute: *a willingness to take resolute action*
staunch: *many staunch supporters*
unshakable: *an unshakable belief in democracy*

> NOUN
5 a business selling or producing something
firmly ADVERB, **firmness** NOUN

● THESAURUS
business: *a stockbroking business*
company: *his software development company*
corporation: *one of the leading banking corporations*
enterprise: *small business enterprises*
organization: *a multinational organization*

first see page 335 for Word Web

first aid NOUN
First aid is medical treatment given to an injured person.

first class ADJECTIVE
1 Something that is first class is of the highest quality or standard.

2 First-class accommodation on a train, aircraft, or ship is the best and most expensive type of accommodation.

3 First-class postage is quick but more expensive.

first-hand ['fɜːst'hænd] ADJECTIVE
First-hand knowledge or experience is gained directly rather than from books or other people.

First Lady First Ladies NOUN
The First Lady of a country is the wife of the president.

first-rate ['fɜːst'reɪt] ADJECTIVE
excellent

● THESAURUS
excellent: *She does an excellent job as Fred's personal assistant.*
exceptional: *His piano playing is exceptional.*
first-class: *The food was first-class.*
marvellous: *He certainly is a marvellous actor.*
outstanding: *an outstanding athlete*
splendid: *We had a splendid meal.*
superb: *a superb 18-hole golf*

fiscal ['fɪskəl] ADJECTIVE
involving government or public money, especially taxes
[WORD HISTORY: from Latin FISCUS meaning 'money-bag' or 'treasury']

fish [fɪʃ] **fishes, fishing, fished** NOUN
1 a cold-blooded creature living in water that has a spine, gills, fins, and a scaly skin
2 Fish is the flesh of fish eaten as food.
> VERB
3 To fish is to try to catch fish for food or sport.
4 If you fish for information, you try to get it in an indirect way.
fishing NOUN, **fisherman** NOUN

> The plural of the noun *fish* can be either *fish* or *fishes*, but *fish* is more common

fishery ['fɪʃəri] **fisheries** NOUN
an area of the sea where fish are caught commercially

fishmonger ['fɪʃ,mʌŋgə] **fishmongers** NOUN
a shopkeeper who sells fish; also the shop itself

fishy ['fɪʃi] **fishier, fishiest** ADJECTIVE
1 smelling of fish
2 INFORMAL
suspicious or doubtful *e.g. He spotted something fishy going on.*

fission ['fɪʃən] NOUN
1 Fission is the splitting of something into parts.
2 Fission is also nuclear fission.

fissure ['fɪʃə] **fissures** NOUN
a deep crack in rock

● THESAURUS
cleft: *a narrow cleft in the rocks*
crack: *The building developed large cracks in walls and ceilings.*
crevice: *a huge boulder with ferns growing in every crevice*
fault: *the San Andreas Fault*
rift: *In the open bog are many rifts and potholes.*
split: *The slate has a few small splits around the edges.*

fist [fɪst] **fists** NOUN
a hand with the fingers curled tightly towards the palm

1 ADJECTIVE
done or in existence before anything else
● THESAURUS
earliest: *The earliest settlers lived there.*
initial: *our initial meeting*
opening: *There was a standing ovation on opening night.*
original: *She was one of the original cast.*
primeval: *the primeval forests of Europe*
<< OPPOSITE *last*

2 ADJECTIVE
more important than anything else *eg*: *Her cheese won first prize; The first duty of the state is to ensure law and order.*
● THESAURUS
chief: *the chief pilot*
foremost: *one of our foremost thinkers*
leading: *the team's leading scorer*
prime: *He was the prime suspect.*
principal: *the principal reason*

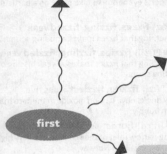

first

3 ADVERB
done or occurring before anything else
● THESAURUS
beforehand: *Bill had prepared beforehand.*
earlier: *I did that one earlier.*
firstly: *Firstly, I'd like to thank you all for coming.*
initially: *not as bad as they initially predicted*
to begin with: *To begin with, we must prepare the soil.*

f

fit see page 337 for Word Web

fitful ['fɪtfʊl] ADJECTIVE
happening at irregular intervals and not continuous *e.g. a fitful breeze*
fitfully ADVERB

fitter ['fɪtə] **fitters** NOUN
a person who assembles or installs machinery

fitting ['fɪtɪŋ] **fittings** ADJECTIVE
1 right or suitable *e.g. a fitting reward for his efforts*

● THESAURUS
appropriate: *an appropriate outfit for the occasion*
correct: *the correct thing to say*
proper: *It isn't proper that she should be here.*
right: *He always said just the right thing.*
suitable: *some hymns suitable for a wedding*

> NOUN
2 a small part that is fixed to a piece of equipment or furniture

● THESAURUS
accessory: *bathroom accessories*
attachment: *a wide range of attachments*
component: *special components*
part: *Extra parts can be added later.*
unit: *The unit plugs into any TV set.*

3 If you have a fitting, you try on a garment that is being made to see if it fits properly.

five [faɪv]
the number 5

fix [fɪks] **fixes, fixing, fixed** VERB
1 If you fix something somewhere, you attach it or put it there securely.

● THESAURUS
attach: *The label was attached with glue.*
bind: *sticks bound together with string*
fasten: *Fasten the two parts securely.*
secure: *firmly secured by strong nails*
stick: *She stuck the pictures into the book.*

2 If you fix something broken, you mend it.

● THESAURUS
correct: *to correct our mistakes*
mend: *They finally got round to mending the roof.*
patch up: *Patch up those holes.*
repair: *I had my shoes repaired.*

3 If you fix your attention on something, you concentrate on it.

4 If you fix something, you make arrangements for it. *e.g. The opening party is fixed for the 24th September.*

5 INFORMAL
To fix something is to arrange the outcome unfairly or dishonestly.

> NOUN
6 INFORMAL
something that has been unfairly or dishonestly arranged

7 INFORMAL
If you are in a fix, you are in a difficult situation.

● THESAURUS
difficulty: *He was in real difficulties with money.*
mess: *Their economy was in a mess.*
predicament: *a tricky predicament*
quandary: *in a quandary about what to do*

8 an injection of a drug such as heroin
fixed ADJECTIVE, **fixedly** ADVERB

fixation [fɪk'seɪʃən] **fixations** NOUN
an extreme and obsessive interest in something

fixture ['fɪkstʃə] **fixtures** NOUN
1 a piece of furniture or equipment that is fixed into position in a house
2 a sports event due to take place on a particular date

fizz [fɪz] **fizzes, fizzing, fizzed** VERB
Something that fizzes makes a hissing sound.

fizzle ['fɪzəl] **fizzles, fizzling, fizzled** VERB
Something that fizzles makes a weak hissing or spitting sound.

fizzy ['fɪzɪ] **fizzier, fizziest** ADJECTIVE
Fizzy drinks have carbon dioxide in them to make them bubbly.

fjord [fjɔːd] **fjords;** also spelt **fiord** NOUN
a long narrow inlet of the sea between very high cliffs, especially in Norway
[WORD HISTORY: a Norwegian word]

flab [flæb] NOUN
Flab is large amounts of surplus fat on someone's body.

flabbergasted ['flæbə,gɑːstɪd] ADJECTIVE
extremely surprised

flabby ['flæbɪ] **flabbier, flabbiest** ADJECTIVE
Someone who is flabby is rather fat and unfit, with loose flesh on their body.

● THESAURUS
floppy: *the floppy bodies in tracksuits*
sagging: *a sagging double chin*
slack: *The skin around her eyelids is now slack and baggy.*
<<OPPOSITE taut

flag [flæg] **flags, flagging, flagged** NOUN
1 a rectangular or square cloth which has a particular colour and design, and is used as the symbol of a nation or as a signal

> VERB
2 If you or your spirits flag, you start to lose energy or enthusiasm.

flagrant ['fleɪgrənt] ADJECTIVE
very shocking and bad in an obvious way *e.g. a flagrant defiance of the rules*

1 VERB
Something that fits is the right shape or size for a particular person or position.
● THESAURUS
belong: *I just didn't belong there.*
correspond: *The two angles didn't correspond exactly.*
dovetail: *The movement's interests dovetailed with her own.*
go: *small enough to go in your pocket*
match: *Match the pegs with the holes.*

2 VERB
If you fit something somewhere, you put it there carefully or securely *eg: Very carefully he fitted the files inside the compartment.*
● THESAURUS
arrange: *Arrange the pieces to form a picture.*
place: *Place the card in the slots.*
position: *plants which are carefully positioned in the alcove*

fit
fits, fitting, fitted; fitter, fittest

3 ADJECTIVE
Someone who is fit is healthy and has strong muscles as a result of regular exercise.
● THESAURUS
healthy: *a healthy mind in a healthy body*
in good condition: *in good condition for his age*
robust: *a strong, robust man*
trim: *a trim figure*
well: *Alison was looking well.*
<< OPPOSITE **unfit**

f

flagship [ˈflæɡˌʃɪp] **flagships** NOUN
1 a ship carrying the commander of the fleet
2 the most modern or impressive product or asset of an organization

flail [fleɪl] **flails, flailing, flailed** VERB
If someone's arms or legs flail about, they move in a wild, uncontrolled way.

flair [flɛə] NOUN
Flair is a natural ability to do something well or stylishly.

flak [flæk] NOUN
1 Flak is anti-aircraft fire.
2 If you get flak for doing something, you get a lot of severe criticism.

flake [fleɪk] **flakes, flaking, flaked** NOUN
1 a small thin piece of something
> VERB
2 When something such as paint flakes, small thin pieces of it come off.
flaky ADJECTIVE, **flaked** ADJECTIVE

flamboyant [flæmˈbɔɪənt] ADJECTIVE
behaving in a very showy and confident way
flamboyance NOUN

flame [fleɪm] **flames** NOUN
1 a flickering tongue or blaze of fire
2 A flame of passion, desire, or anger is a sudden strong feeling.

flamenco [fləˈmɛŋkəʊ] NOUN
Flamenco is a type of very lively, fast Spanish dancing, accompanied by guitar music.

flamingo [fləˈmɪŋɡəʊ] **flamingos** or **flamingoes** NOUN
a long-legged wading bird with pink feathers and a long neck

flammable [ˈflæməbəl] ADJECTIVE
likely to catch fire and burn easily

> Although *flammable* and *inflammable* both mean 'likely to catch fire', *flammable* is used more often as people sometimes think that *inflammable* means 'not likely to catch fire'

flan [flæn] **flans** NOUN
an open sweet or savoury tart with a pastry or cake base

flank [flæŋk] **flanks, flanking, flanked** NOUN
1 the side of an animal between the ribs and the hip
> VERB
2 Someone or something that is flanked by a particular thing or person has them at their side. e.g. *He was flanked by four bodyguards.*

flannel [ˈflænəl] **flannels** NOUN

1 Flannel is a lightweight woollen fabric.
2 a small square of towelling, used for washing yourself. In Australian English it is called a **washer**

flap [flæp] **flaps, flapping, flapped** VERB
1 Something that flaps moves up and down or from side to side with a snapping sound.
> NOUN
2 a loose piece of something such as paper or skin that is attached at one edge

flare [flɛə] **flares, flaring, flared** NOUN
1 a device that produces a brightly coloured flame, used especially as an emergency signal
> VERB
2 If a fire flares, it suddenly burns much more vigorously.
3 If violence or a conflict flares or flares up, it suddenly starts or becomes more serious.

flash [flæʃ] **flashes, flashing, flashed** NOUN
1 a sudden short burst of light

THESAURUS
burst: *a burst of fire*
flare: *the sudden flare of a match*
sparkle: *sparkles from her sequinned dress*

> VERB
2 If a light flashes, it shines for a very short period, often repeatedly.

THESAURUS
flare: *matches flaring in the darkness*
glint: *the low sun glinting off the windscreens*
glitter: *the glittering crown on his head*
sparkle: *Diamonds sparkled on her wrists.*
twinkle: *stars twinkling in the night sky*

3 Something that flashes past moves or happens so fast that you almost miss it.
4 If you flash something, you show it briefly. *e.g. Michael Jackson flashed his face at the crowd.*
> PHRASE
5 Something that happens **in a flash** happens suddenly and lasts a very short time.

flashback [ˈflæʃˌbæk] **flashbacks** NOUN
a scene in a film, play, or book that returns to events in the past

flashlight [ˈflæʃˌlaɪt] **flashlights** NOUN
a large, powerful torch

flashy [ˈflæʃɪ] **flashier, flashiest** ADJECTIVE
expensive and fashionable in appearance, in a vulgar way *e.g. flashy clothes*

THESAURUS
flamboyant: *an unsuitably flamboyant outfit*
garish: *curtains in garish colours*
showy: *an expensive and showy watch*
tacky: informal *tacky red sunglasses*

tasteless: *a house with tasteless decor*
<<OPPOSITE *modest*

flask [flɑːsk] **flasks** NOUN
a bottle used for carrying alcoholic or hot drinks around with you

flat [flæt] **flats, flatting, flatted; flatter, flattest** NOUN

1 a self-contained set of rooms, usually on one level, for living in

● THESAURUS
apartment: *a huge apartment overlooking the park*
rooms: *We shared rooms while we were students.*

2 In music, a flat is a note or key a semitone lower than that described by the same letter. It is represented by the symbol (♭).

> VERB
3 In Australian and New Zealand English, to flat is to live in a flat. *e.g. flatting in London*

> ADJECTIVE
4 Something that is flat is level and smooth.

● THESAURUS
horizontal: *horizontal with the ground*
level: *a completely level base*
levelled: *The floor must be levelled before you start.*
smooth: *a smooth marble top*
unbroken: *the unbroken surface of the sea*
<<OPPOSITE *uneven*

5 A flat object is not very tall or deep. *e.g. a low flat building*

6 A flat tyre or ball has not got enough air in it.

7 A flat battery has lost its electrical charge.

8 A flat refusal or denial is complete and firm.

9 Something that is flat is without emotion or interest.

● THESAURUS
boring: *a boring menu*
dull: *He told some really dull stories.*
insipid: *an insipid performance*
monotonous: *an interesting story expressed in a monotonous voice*
weak: *A weak ending spoiled the story.*

10 A flat rate or price is fixed and the same for everyone. *e.g. The company charges a flat fee for its advice.*

11 A musical instrument or note that is flat is slightly too low in pitch.

> ADVERB
12 Something that is done in a particular time flat, takes exactly that time. *e.g. They would find them in two minutes flat.*
flatly ADVERB, **flatness** NOUN

flatfish [ˈflætˌfɪʃ] NOUN
a sea fish with a wide flat body, such as a plaice or sole

flathead [ˈflætˌhɛd] **flatheads** NOUN
a common Australian edible fish

flatten [ˈflætən] **flattens, flattening, flattened** VERB
If you flatten something or if it flattens, it becomes flat or flatter.

flatter [ˈflætə] **flatters, flattering, flattered** VERB

1 If you flatter someone, you praise them in an exaggerated way, either to please them or to persuade them to do something.

● THESAURUS
compliment: *She was often complimented for her looks.*
fawn: *surrounded by fawning attendants*

2 If you are flattered by something, it makes you feel pleased and important. *e.g. He was very flattered because she liked him.*

3 If you flatter yourself that something is the case, you believe, perhaps mistakenly, something good about yourself or your abilities.

4 Something that flatters you makes you appear more attractive.
flattering ADJECTIVE

● THESAURUS
enhance: *an enhancing neckline*
set off: *Blue sets off the colour of your eyes.*
suit: *That shade really suits your skin tone.*

flattery [ˈflætərɪ] NOUN
Flattery is flattering words or behaviour.

● THESAURUS
adulation: *received with adulation by the critics*
fawning: *the constant fawning of her courtiers*

flatting [ˈflætɪŋ] PHRASE
In New Zealand English, to **go flatting** is to leave home and live with others in a shared house or flat.

flatulence [ˈflætjʊləns] NOUN
Flatulence is the uncomfortable state of having too much gas in your stomach or intestine.

flaunt [flɔːnt] **flaunts, flaunting, flaunted** VERB
If you flaunt your possessions or talents, you display them too obviously or proudly.

  Be careful not to confuse *flaunt* with *flout*, which means 'disobey'.

flautist [ˈflɔːtɪst] **flautists** NOUN
someone who plays the flute

flavour [ˈfleɪvə] **flavours, flavouring, flavoured** NOUN

1 The flavour of food is its taste.

2 The flavour of something is its distinctive characteristic or quality.

> VERB

3 If you flavour food with a spice or herb, you add it to the food to give it a particular taste.
flavouring NOUN

flaw [flɔː] **flaws** NOUN

1 a fault or mark in a piece of fabric or glass, or in a decorative pattern

● THESAURUS

blemish: *A small blemish spoiled the surface.*
defect: *a manufacturing defect*
fault: *a fault in the engine*
imperfection: *slight imperfections in the weave*

2 a weak point or undesirable quality in a theory, plan, or person's character
flawed ADJECTIVE, **flawless** ADJECTIVE

flax [flæks] NOUN

Flax is a plant used for making rope and cloth.

flay [fleɪ] **flays, flaying, flayed** VERB

1 To flay a dead animal is to cut off its skin.

2 To flay someone is to criticize them severely.

flea [fliː] **fleas** NOUN

a small wingless jumping insect which feeds on blood

fleck [flɛk] **flecks** NOUN

a small coloured mark or particle
flecked ADJECTIVE

fled [flɛd] the past tense and past participle of **flee**

fledgling [ˈflɛdʒlɪŋ] **fledglings** NOUN

1 a young bird that is learning to fly

> ADJECTIVE

2 Fledgling means new, or young and inexperienced. *e.g. the fledgling American President*

flee [fliː] **flees, fleeing, fled** VERB

To flee from someone or something is to run away from them.

● THESAURUS

bolt: *He bolted for the exit.*
escape: *They escaped across the frontier.*
fly: *to fly from war*
leave: *to leave the scene of the crime*
run away: *to run away from the police*
take flight: *250,000 took flight from the floods.*

fleece [fliːs] **fleeces, fleecing, fleeced** NOUN

1 A sheep's fleece is its coat of wool.

> VERB

2 To fleece someone is to swindle them or charge them too much money.

fleet [fliːt] **fleets** NOUN

a group of ships or vehicles owned by the same organization or travelling together

fleeting [ˈfliːtɪŋ] ADJECTIVE

lasting for a very short time

Flemish [ˈflɛmɪʃ] NOUN

Flemish is a language spoken in many parts of Belgium.

flesh [flɛʃ] NOUN

1 Flesh is the soft part of the body.

2 The flesh of a fruit or vegetable is the soft inner part that you eat.
fleshy ADJECTIVE

flew [fluː] the past tense of **fly**

flex [flɛks] **flexes, flexing, flexed** NOUN

1 a length of wire covered in plastic, which carries electricity to an appliance

> VERB

2 If you flex your muscles, you bend and stretch them.

flexible [ˈflɛksɪbəl] ADJECTIVE

1 able to be bent easily without breaking

● THESAURUS

elastic: *an elastic rope*
lithe: *lithe and graceful movements*
pliable: *baskets made from pliable cane*
supple: *exercises to keep you supple*

2 able to adapt to changing circumstances
flexibility NOUN

● THESAURUS

adaptable: *an adaptable attitude to work*
discretionary: *the discretionary powers of the courts*
open: *an open mind*

flick [flɪk] **flicks, flicking, flicked** VERB

1 If you flick something, you move it sharply with your finger.

2 If something flicks somewhere, it moves with a short sudden movement. *e.g. His foot flicked forward.*

> NOUN

3 a sudden quick movement or sharp touch with the finger *e.g. a sideways flick of the head*

flicker [ˈflɪkə] **flickers, flickering, flickered** VERB

1 If a light or a flame flickers, it shines and moves unsteadily.

> NOUN

2 a short unsteady light or movement of light *e.g. the flicker of candlelight*

3 A flicker of a feeling is a very brief experience of it. *e.g. a flicker of interest*

flight [flaɪt] **flights** NOUN

1 a journey made by aeroplane

2 Flight is the action of flying or the ability to fly.

3 Flight is also the act of running away.

4 A flight of stairs or steps is a set running in a single direction.

flight attendant **flight attendants** NOUN
a person who looks after passengers on an
aircraft

flightless ['flaɪtlɪs] ADJECTIVE
Flightless birds, such as penguins and ostriches,
are birds that cannot fly.

flimsy ['flɪmzɪ] **flimsier, flimsiest** ADJECTIVE
1 made of something very thin or weak and not
providing much protection
2 not very convincing e.g. flimsy evidence

flinch [flɪntʃ] **flinches, flinching, flinched**
VERB
If you flinch, you make a sudden small
movement in fear or pain.

● THESAURUS
cringe: to cringe in terror
shrink: She shrank from the flames.
start: They started at the sudden noise.
wince: I could see him wincing with pain.

fling [flɪŋ] **flings, flinging, flung** VERB
1 If you fling something, you throw it with a lot of
force.

> NOUN
2 a short period devoted to pleasure and free
from any restrictions or rules

flint [flɪnt] **flints** NOUN
Flint is a hard greyish-black form of quartz. It
produces a spark when struck with steel.

flip [flɪp] **flips, flipping, flipped** VERB
1 If you flip something, you turn or move it
quickly and sharply. e.g. He flipped over the first
page.
2 If you flip something, you hit it sharply with
your finger or thumb.

flippant ['flɪpənt] ADJECTIVE
showing an inappropriate lack of seriousness e.g.
a flippant attitude to money
flippancy NOUN

flipper ['flɪpə] **flippers** NOUN
1 one of the broad, flat limbs of sea animals, for
example seals or penguins, used for swimming
2 Flippers are broad, flat pieces of rubber that you
can attach to your feet to help you swim.

flirt [flɜːt] **flirts, flirting, flirted** VERB
1 If you flirt with someone, you behave as if you
are sexually attracted to them but without
serious intentions.
2 If you flirt with an idea, you consider it without
seriously intending to do anything about it.

> NOUN
3 someone who often flirts with people
flirtation NOUN, **flirtatious** ADJECTIVE

flit [flɪt] **flits, flitting, flitted** VERB
To flit somewhere is to fly or move there with
quick, light movements.

float [fləʊt] **floats, floating, floated** VERB
1 Something that floats is supported by water.

● THESAURUS
be on the surface: The oil is on the surface of the
sea.
bob: toys bobbing in the bath
drift: to drift in on the tide
lie on the surface: The boat lay on the surface of
the lake.
stay afloat: They could stay afloat without
swimming.
<<OPPOSITE sink

2 Something that floats through the air moves
along gently, supported by the air.

● THESAURUS
drift: The music drifted in through the window.
glide: eagles gliding above us
hang: A haze of perfume hung in the room.
hover: Butterflies hovered above the flowers.

3 If a company is floated, shares are sold to the
public for the first time and the company gains a
listing on the stock exchange.

> NOUN
4 a light object that floats and either supports
something or someone or regulates the level of
liquid in a tank or cistern

5 In Australian English, a float is also a vehicle for
transporting horses.

flock [flɒk] **flocks, flocking, flocked** NOUN
1 a group of birds, sheep, or goats

> VERB
2 If people flock somewhere, they go there in
large numbers.

flog [flɒg] **flogs, flogging, flogged** VERB
1 INFORMAL If you flog something, you sell it.
2 To flog someone is to beat them with a whip or
stick.
flogging NOUN

flood [flʌd] **floods, flooding, flooded** NOUN
1 a large amount of water covering an area that is
usually dry

● THESAURUS
deluge: houses overwhelmed by the deluge
downpour: a downpour of torrential rain
spate: The river was in spate.
torrent: Torrents of water gushed into the reservoir.

2 A flood of something is a large amount of it
suddenly occurring. e.g. a flood of angry language

● THESAURUS
rush: a sudden rush of panic
stream: a stream of bad language
torrent: He replied with a torrent of abuse.

> VERB
3 If liquid floods an area, or if a river floods, the

f

water or liquid overflows, covering the surrounding area.

● THESAURUS

deluge: *Heavy rain deluged the capital.*
drown: *a drowned village*
overflow: *an overflowing bath*
submerge: *to prevent water submerging the cobbled streets*
swamp: *His small boat was swamped by the waves.*

4 If people or things flood into a place, they come there in large numbers. *e.g. Refugees have flooded into Austria in the last few months.*

floodgates ['flʌdɡeɪts] PHRASE
To **open the floodgates** is suddenly to give a lot of people the opportunity to do something they could not do before.

floodlight ['flʌd،laɪt] **floodlights** NOUN
a very powerful outdoor lamp used to light up public buildings and sports grounds
floodlit ADJECTIVE

floor [flɔː] **floors, flooring, floored** NOUN
1 the part of a room you walk on

2 one of the levels in a building *e.g. the top floor of a factory*

3 the ground at the bottom of a valley, forest, or the sea

> VERB
4 If a remark or question floors you, you are completely unable to deal with it or answer it.

floorboard ['flɔː،bɔːd] **floorboards** NOUN
one of the long planks of wood from which a floor is made

flop [flɒp] **flops, flopping, flopped** VERB
1 If someone or something flops, they fall loosely and rather heavily.

2 INFORMAL Something that flops fails.

> NOUN
3 INFORMAL something that is completely unsuccessful

floppy ['flɒpɪ] **floppier, floppiest** ADJECTIVE
tending to hang downwards in a rather loose way *e.g. a floppy, outsize jacket*

floppy disk floppy disks; also spelt **floppy disc** NOUN
a small flexible magnetic disk on which computer data is stored

floral ['flɔːrəl] ADJECTIVE
patterned with flowers or made from flowers *e.g. floral cotton dresses*

florid ['flɒrɪd] ADJECTIVE
1 highly elaborate and extravagant *e.g. florid language*

2 having a red face

florist ['flɒrɪst] **florists** NOUN
a person or shop selling flowers

floss [flɒs] NOUN
Dental floss is soft silky threads or fibre which you use to clean between your teeth.

flotation [fləʊˈteɪʃən] **flotations** NOUN
1 The flotation of a business is the issuing of shares in order to launch it or to raise money.

2 Flotation is the act of floating.

flotilla [fləˈtɪlə] **flotillas** NOUN
a small fleet or group of small ships

flotsam ['flɒtsəm] NOUN
Flotsam is rubbish or wreckage floating at sea or washed up on the shore.

flounce [flaʊns] **flounces, flouncing, flounced** VERB
1 If you flounce somewhere, you walk there with exaggerated movements suggesting that you are feeling angry or impatient about something. *e.g. She flounced out of the office.*

> NOUN
2 a big frill around the bottom of a dress or skirt

flounder ['flaʊndə] **flounders, floundering, floundered** VERB
1 To flounder is to struggle to move or stay upright, for example in water or mud.

2 If you flounder in a conversation or situation, you find it difficult to decide what to say or do.

> NOUN
3 a type of edible flatfish

flour ['flaʊə] NOUN
(D & T) Flour is a powder made from finely ground grain, usually wheat, and used for baking and cooking.
floured ADJECTIVE, **floury** ADJECTIVE

flourish ['flʌrɪʃ] **flourishes, flourishing, flourished** VERB
1 Something that flourishes develops or functions successfully or healthily.

● THESAURUS

bloom: *Not many economies bloomed during that period.*
boom: *Sales are booming.*
come on: *He is coming on very well at his new school.*
do well: *Out-of-town superstores are doing well.*
prosper: *The high street banks continue to prosper.*
succeed: *the qualities needed to succeed in small businesses*
thrive: *Today the company continues to thrive.*
<<OPPOSITE *fail*

2 If you flourish something, you wave or display it so that people notice it.

THESAURUS
brandish: literary *He appeared brandishing a sword.*
display: *She proudly displayed the letter and began to read.*
hold aloft: *He held the cup aloft.*
wave: *Crowds were waving flags and applauding.*

> NOUN
3 a bold sweeping or waving movement

THESAURUS
flick: *a flick of the whip*
sweep: *With one sweep of her hand she threw back the sheets.*
wave: *Steve stopped him with a wave of the hand.*

flout [flaʊt] **flouts, flouting, flouted** VERB
If you flout a convention or law, you deliberately disobey it.

Be careful not to confuse *flout* with *flaunt*, which means 'display obviously'

flow [fləʊ] **flows, flowing, flowed** VERB
1 If something flows, it moves or happens in a steady continuous stream.

THESAURUS
circulate: *to circulate round the entire house*
glide: *models gliding down the catwalk*
roll: *rolling gently to the sea*
run: *A stream ran beside the road.*
slide: *Tears slid down her cheeks.*

> NOUN
2 A flow of something is a steady continuous movement of it; also the rate at which it flows. *e.g. a steady flow of complaints*

THESAURUS
current: *currents of air*
drift: *the drift towards the cities*
flood: *a flood of complaints*
stream: *a constant stream of visitors*
tide: *to slow the tide of change*

flow chart flow charts NOUN
(D & T) a diagram showing the sequence of steps that lead to various results

flower ['flaʊə] **flowers, flowering, flowered** NOUN
1 the part of a plant containing the reproductive organs from which the fruit or seeds develop
> VERB
2 When a plant flowers, it produces flowers.

flowery ['flaʊərɪ] ADJECTIVE
Flowery language is full of elaborate expressions.

flown [fləʊn] the past participle of **fly**

flu [fluː] NOUN
Flu is an illness similar to a very bad cold, which causes headaches, sore throat, weakness, and aching muscles. Flu is short for 'influenza'.

fluctuate ['flʌktjʊˌeɪt] **fluctuates, fluctuating, fluctuated** VERB
Something that fluctuates is irregular and changeable. *e.g. fluctuating between feeling well and not so well*

flue [fluː] **flues** NOUN
a pipe which takes fumes and smoke away from a stove or boiler

fluent ['fluːənt] ADJECTIVE
1 able to speak a foreign language correctly and without hesitation
2 able to express yourself clearly and without hesitation
fluently ADVERB

THESAURUS
articulate: *an articulate young woman*
easy: *the easy flow of his argument*
effortless: *He spoke with effortless ease.*
flowing: *a smooth, flowing presentation*
ready: *a ready answer*
<<OPPOSITE *hesitant*

fluff [flʌf] **fluffs, fluffing, fluffed** NOUN
1 Fluff is soft, light, woolly threads or fibres bunched together.
> VERB
2 If you fluff something up or out, you brush or shake it to make it seem larger and lighter. *e.g. Fluff the rice up with a fork before serving.*
fluffy ADJECTIVE

fluid ['fluːɪd] **fluids** NOUN
1 a liquid
> ADJECTIVE
2 Fluid movement is smooth and flowing.
3 A fluid arrangement or plan is flexible and without a fixed structure.
fluidity NOUN

fluke [fluːk] **flukes** NOUN
an accidental success or piece of good luck

flung [flʌŋ] the past tense of **fling**

fluorescent [ˌflʊəˈrɛsᵊnt] ADJECTIVE
1 having a very bright appearance when light is shone on it, as if it is shining itself *e.g. fluorescent yellow dye*
2 A fluorescent light is in the form of a tube and shines with a hard bright light.

fluoride ['flʊəˌraɪd] NOUN
Fluoride is a mixture of chemicals that is meant to prevent tooth decay.

flurry ['flʌrɪ] **flurries** NOUN
a short rush of activity or movement

flush [flʌʃ] **flushes, flushing, flushed** NOUN
1 A flush is a rosy red colour. *e.g. The flowers are cream with a pink flush.*

2 In cards, a flush is a hand all of one suit.

> VERB

3 If you flush, your face goes red.

4 If you flush a toilet or something such as a pipe, you force water through it to clean it.

> ADJECTIVE

5 INFORMAL
Someone who is flush has plenty of money.

6 Something that is flush with a surface is level with it or flat against it.

flustered ['flʌstəd] ADJECTIVE
If you are flustered, you feel confused, nervous, and rushed.

flute [fluːt] **flutes** NOUN
a musical wind instrument consisting of a long metal tube with holes and keys. It is held sideways to the mouth and played by blowing across a hole in its side

fluted ['fluːtɪd] ADJECTIVE
decorated with long grooves

flutter ['flʌtə] **flutters, fluttering, fluttered** VERB

1 If something flutters, it flaps or waves with small, quick movements.

> NOUN

2 If you are in a flutter, you are excited and nervous.

3 INFORMAL If you have a flutter, you have a small bet.

flux [flʌks] NOUN
Flux is a state of constant change. *e.g. stability in a world of flux*

fly [flaɪ] **flies, flying, flew, flown** NOUN

1 an insect with two pairs of wings

2 The front opening on a pair of trousers is the fly or the flies.

3 The fly or fly sheet of a tent is either a flap at the entrance or an outer layer providing protection from rain.

> VERB

4 When a bird, insect, or aircraft flies, it moves through the air.

● THESAURUS
flit: *butterflies flitting among the flowers*
flutter: *The birds fluttered on to the feeder.*
sail: *a kite sailing above the trees*
soar: *eagles soaring in the sky*

5 If someone or something flies, they move or go very quickly.

● THESAURUS
dart: *She darted to the window.*
dash: *We had to dash.*
hurry: *They hurried to catch the train.*

race: *I had to race round the shops.*
rush: *rushing off to work*
speed: *The car sped off.*
tear: *He tore off down the road.*

6 If you fly at someone or let fly at them, you attack or criticize them suddenly and aggressively.
flying ADJECTIVE OR NOUN, **flyer** NOUN

fly-fishing ['flaɪˌfɪʃɪŋ] NOUN
Fly-fishing is a method of fishing using imitation flies as bait.

flying fox ['flaɪɪŋ] **flying foxes** NOUN

1 a large bat that eats fruit, found in Australia and Africa

2 In Australia and New Zealand, a cable car used to carry people over rivers and gorges.

flying saucer ['flaɪɪŋ] **flying saucers** NOUN
a large disc-shaped spacecraft which some people claim to have seen

flyover ['flaɪˌəʊvə] **flyovers** NOUN
a structure carrying one road over another at a junction or intersection

foal [fəʊl] **foals, foaling, foaled** NOUN

1 a young horse

> VERB

2 When a female horse foals, she gives birth.

foam [fəʊm] **foams, foaming, foamed** NOUN

1 Foam is a mass of tiny bubbles.

● THESAURUS
bubbles: *She liked to have bubbles in the bath.*
froth: *Yeast swells up to form a froth.*
head: *the foamy head on beer*
lather: *It took a lot of shampoo to get a good lather.*

2 Foam is light spongy material used, for example, in furniture or packaging.

> VERB

3 When something foams, it forms a mass of small bubbles.

● THESAURUS
bubble: *The boiling liquid bubbled up.*
fizz: *a drink fizzing in the glass*
froth: *It frothed up over the top.*

fob off [fɒb] **fobs off, fobbing off, fobbed off** VERB; INFORMAL
If you fob someone off, you provide them with something that is not very good or not adequate.

focus ['fəʊkəs] **focuses** or **focusses focusing** or **focussing focused** or **focussed; focuses** or **foci** VERB

1 If you focus your eyes or an instrument on an object, you adjust them so that the image is clear.

THESAURUS
aim: *Astronomers aimed optical telescopes in their direction.*
concentrate: *concentrating his gaze on a line of ants*
direct: *He directed the light on to the roof.*
fix: *Their radar was fixed on the enemy ship.*

> NOUN
2 The focus of something is its centre of attention. *e.g. The focus of the conversation had moved around during the meal.*
focal ADJECTIVE

THESAURUS
centre: *She was the centre of an admiring crowd.*
focal point: *the focal point of the whole room*
hub: *the hub of the financial world*
target: *a target group*

> When you add the verb endings to *focus*, you can either add them straight to *focus* (*focuses, focusing, focused*), or you can put another s at the end of *focus* before adding the endings (*focusses, focussing, focussed*). Either way is correct, but the first way is much more common. The plural of the noun is either *focuses* or *foci*, but *focuses* is the commoner

fodder ['fɒdə] NOUN
Fodder is food for farm animals or horses.

foe [fəʊ] **foes** NOUN
an enemy

foetus ['fiːtəs] **foetuses**; also spelt **fetus** NOUN
an unborn child or animal in the womb
foetal ADJECTIVE

fog [fɒg] **fogs, fogging, fogged** NOUN
1 Fog is a thick mist of water droplets suspended in the air.
> VERB
2 If glass fogs up, it becomes clouded with steam or condensation.
foggy ADJECTIVE

foil [fɔɪl] **foils, foiling, foiled** VERB
1 If you foil someone's attempt at something, you prevent them from succeeding.
THESAURUS
check: *to check the rise in crime*
counter: *countering the threat of strike action*
defeat: *an important role in defeating the rebellion*
frustrate: *a frustrated attempt*
thwart: *to thwart someone's plans*

> NOUN
2 Foil is thin, paper-like sheets of metal used to wrap food.

3 Something that is a good foil for something else contrasts with it and makes its good

qualities more noticeable.
THESAURUS
antithesis: *the antithesis of his crooked brother*
background: *a fitting background for her beauty*
complement: *the perfect complement to the antique furniture*
contrast: *The green woodwork is a stunning contrast to the black walls.*

4 a thin, light sword with a button on the tip, used in fencing

foist [fɔɪst] **foists, foisting, foisted** VERB
If you foist something on someone, you force or impose it on them.

fold [fəʊld] **folds, folding, folded** VERB
1 If you fold something, you bend it so that one part lies over another.
THESAURUS
bend: *Bend the top towards you.*
crease: *Crease along the dotted line.*
crumple: *He crumpled the note and put it in his pocket.*
tuck: *Tuck in the top and bottom.*
turn under: *The bottom was turned under.*

2 INFORMAL If a business folds, it fails and closes down.

3 In cooking, if you fold one ingredient into another, you mix it in gently.

> NOUN
4 a crease or bend in paper or cloth
THESAURUS
bend: *There was a bend in the photograph.*
crease: *sharp creases in his shirt*
pleat: *a skirt with pleats*
wrinkle: *all the little wrinkles on Paul's face*

5 a small enclosed area for sheep

folder ['fəʊldə] **folders** NOUN
1 a thin piece of folded cardboard for keeping loose papers together
2 In computing, a folder is a named area of a computer disk where you can group together files and subdirectories. also called **directory**

foliage ['fəʊliɪdʒ] NOUN
Foliage is leaves and plants.

folk [fəʊk] **folks** NOUN
1 Folk or folks are people.
> ADJECTIVE
2 Folk music, dance, or art is traditional or representative of the ordinary people of an area.

folklore ['fəʊkˌlɔː] NOUN
Folklore is the traditional stories and beliefs of a community.

follicle ['fɒlɪkəl] **follicles** NOUN
a small sac or cavity in the body *e.g. hair follicles*

follow ['fɒləʊ] follows, following, followed VERB

1 If you follow someone, you move along behind them. If you follow a path or a sign, you move along in that direction.

● THESAURUS
hound: *constantly hounded by photographers*
pursue: *He was pursued across several countries.*
stalk: *Her former husband was stalking her.*
track: *They tracked him to his home.*

2 Something that follows a particular thing happens after it.

● THESAURUS
come after: *Summer comes after spring.*
succeed: *He was succeeded by his son.*
supersede: *Horses were superseded by cars.*
<<OPPOSITE *precede*

3 Something that follows is true or logical as a result of something else being the case. *e.g. Just because she is pretty, it doesn't follow that she can sing.*

4 If you follow instructions or advice, you do what you are told.

● THESAURUS
comply: *in order to comply with EC regulations*
conform: *conforming to the new safety requirements*
obey: *You must obey the law.*
observe: *The army was observing a ceasefire.*

5 If you follow an explanation or the plot of a story, you understand each stage of it.

follower ['fɒləʊə] followers NOUN

The followers of a person or belief are the people who support them.

● THESAURUS
believer: *many devout believers in the faith*
disciple: *one of his disciples*
fan: *football fans*
henchman: *always surrounded by his henchmen*
supporter: *He was a major supporter of the plan.*
<<OPPOSITE *leader*

folly ['fɒlɪ] follies NOUN

Folly is a foolish act or foolish behaviour.

fond [fɒnd] fonder, fondest ADJECTIVE

1 If you are fond of someone or something, you like them.

● THESAURUS
adoring: *an adoring husband*
affectionate: *an affectionate smile*
devoted: *a devoted couple*
doting: *doting grandparents*
having a liking for: *She had a great liking for chocolate.*
loving: *a loving son*

2 A fond hope or belief is thought of with happiness but is unlikely to happen.

fondly ADVERB, **fondness** NOUN

● THESAURUS
deluded: *a deluded belief in future improvement*
empty: *empty promises of full employment*
foolish: *What foolish dreams we have!*
naive: *her naive belief in others' goodness*
vain: *the vain hope that he might lose weight*

fondle ['fɒndəl] fondles, fondling, fondled VERB

To fondle something is to stroke it affectionately.

font [fɒnt] fonts NOUN

a large stone bowl in a church that holds the water for baptisms

food [fuːd] foods NOUN

Food is any substance consumed by an animal or plant to provide energy.

● THESAURUS
diet: *a healthy balanced diet*
fare: *traditional regional fare*
foodstuffs: *basic foodstuffs*
kai: Australian and New Zealand; informal *There's no kai in the house.*
nourishment: *unable to take nourishment*
provisions: *provisions for two weeks*
refreshment: *Refreshments will be provided.*
tucker: Australian and New Zealand; informal *some of the cheapest pub tucker in town*

food chain food chains NOUN

a series of living things which are linked because each one feeds on the next one in the series. For example, a plant may be eaten by a rabbit which may be eaten by a fox

foodstuff ['fuːdˌstʌf] foodstuffs NOUN

anything used for food

food technology NOUN

Food technology is the study of foods and what they consist of, and their effect on the body.

fool [fuːl] fools, fooling, fooled NOUN

1 someone who behaves in a silly or stupid way

● THESAURUS
dope: informal *He felt such a dope.*
dunce: *I was a complete dunce at chemistry.*
idiot: *acting like an idiot*
ignoramus: *the ignoramus of the group*
moron: *They treated him like a moron.*

2 a dessert made from fruit, eggs, cream, and sugar whipped together

> VERB

3 If you fool someone, you deceive or trick them.

● THESAURUS
con: informal *conned out of all his money*
deceive: *deceiving the audience*
dupe: *in order to dupe the medical staff*
mislead: *a deliberately misleading statement*

trick: *They tricked him into believing it.*

foolhardy ['fuːl,hɑːdɪ] ADJECTIVE
foolish and involving too great a risk

foolish ['fuːlɪʃ] ADJECTIVE
very silly or unwise
foolishly ADVERB, **foolishness** NOUN

⬤ THESAURUS
inane: *an inane remark*
nonsensical: *a nonsensical thing to say*
senseless: *It would be senseless to stop her.*
silly: *a silly thing to say*
unintelligent: *a weak and unintelligent man*
unwise: *He had made some unwise investments.*
<<OPPOSITE *wise*

foolproof ['fuːl,pruːf] ADJECTIVE
Something that is foolproof is so well designed or
simple to use that it cannot fail.

foot [fʊt] **feet** NOUN
1 the part of your body at the end of your leg
2 the bottom, base, or lower end of something
e.g. the foot of the mountain
3 a unit of length equal to 12 inches or about 30.5
centimetres
4 In poetry, a foot is the basic unit of rhythm
containing two or three syllables.

> ADJECTIVE
5 A foot brake, pedal, or pump is operated by
your foot.

footage ['fʊtɪdʒ] NOUN
Footage is a length of film. *e.g. library footage of
prison riots*

football ['fʊt,bɔːl] **footballs** NOUN
1 Football is any game in which the ball can be
kicked, such as soccer, Australian Rules, rugby
union, and American football.
2 a ball used in any of these games
footballer NOUN

foothills ['fʊt,hɪlz] PLURAL NOUN
Foothills are hills at the base of mountains.

foothold ['fʊt,həʊld] **footholds** NOUN
1 a place where you can put your foot when
climbing
2 a position from which further progress can be
made

footing ['fʊtɪŋ] NOUN
1 Footing is a secure grip by or for your feet. *e.g.
He missed his footing and fell flat.*
2 a footing is the basis or nature of a relationship
or situation *e.g. Steps to put the nation on a war
footing.*

footman ['fʊtmən] **footmen** NOUN
a male servant in a large house who wears a
uniform

footnote ['fʊt,nəʊt] **footnotes** NOUN
a note at the bottom of a page or an additional
comment giving extra information

footpath ['fʊt,pɑːθ] **footpaths** NOUN
a path for people to walk on

footprint ['fʊt,prɪnt] **footprints** NOUN
a mark left by a foot or shoe

footstep ['fʊt,stɛp] **footsteps** NOUN
the sound or mark made by someone walking

for [fɔː] PREPOSITION
1 meant to be given to or used by a particular
person, or done in order to help or benefit them
e.g. private beaches for their exclusive use
2 'For' is used when explaining the reason, cause,
or purpose of something *e.g. This is my excuse for
going to Italy.*
3 You use 'for' to express a quantity, time, or
distance. *e.g. I'll play for ages… the only house for
miles around*
4 If you are for something, you support it or
approve of it. *e.g. votes for or against independence*

forage ['fɒrɪdʒ] **forages, foraging, foraged**
VERB
When a person or animal forages, they search for
food.

foray ['fɒreɪ] **forays** NOUN
1 a brief attempt to do or get something *e.g. her
first foray into acting*
2 an attack or raid by soldiers

forbid [fə'bɪd] **forbids, forbidding,
forbade, forbidden** VERB
If you forbid someone to do something, you
order them not to do it.
forbidden ADJECTIVE

⬤ THESAURUS
ban: *banned from driving*
exclude: *Women were excluded from the classes.*
outlaw: *the outlawed political parties*
prohibit: *Fishing is prohibited.*
veto: *Their application was vetoed.*
<<OPPOSITE *allow*

force [fɔːs] **forces, forcing, forced** VERB
1 To force someone to do something is to make
them do it.

⬤ THESAURUS
compel: *I felt compelled to act.*
drive: *They are driving the company into bankruptcy.*
make: *They made me do it.*
oblige: *We were obliged to abandon the car.*
pressurize: *trying to pressurize them*

2 To force something is to use violence or great
strength to move or open it.

> NOUN
3 a pressure to do something, sometimes with

the use of violence or great strength

● THESAURUS
compulsion: *a compulsion to write*
duress: *carried out under duress*
pressure: *under pressure to resign*

4 The force of something is its strength or power.
e.g. The force of the explosion shook buildings.

● THESAURUS
impact: *the impact of the blast*
might: *the full might of the army*
power: *massive computing power*
pressure: *the pressure of work*
strength: *The storm was gaining strength.*

5 a person or thing that has a lot of influence or effect *e.g. She became the dominant force in tennis.*

6 an organized group of soldiers or police

7 In physics, force is a pushing or pulling influence that changes a body from a state of rest to one of motion, or changes its rate of motion.

> PHRASE
8 A law or rule that is **in force** is currently valid and must be obeyed.

forceful ['fɔːsfʊl] ADJECTIVE
powerful and convincing *e.g. a forceful, highly political lawyer*
forcefully ADVERB

forceps ['fɔːsɪps] PLURAL NOUN
Forceps are a pair of long tongs or pincers used by a doctor or surgeon.

forcible ['fɔːsəb°l] ADJECTIVE
1 involving physical force or violence
2 convincing and making a strong impression *e.g. a forcible reminder*
forcibly ADVERB

ford [fɔːd] **fords, fording, forded** NOUN
1 a shallow place in a river where it is possible to cross on foot or in a vehicle
> VERB
2 To ford a river is to cross it on foot or in a vehicle.

fore [fɔː] PHRASE
Someone or something that comes **to the fore** becomes important or popular.

forearm ['fɔːr,ɑːm] **forearms** NOUN
the part of your arm between your elbow and your wrist

forebear ['fɔː,bɛə] **forebears** NOUN
Your forebears are your ancestors.

foreboding [fɔː'bəʊdɪŋ] **forebodings** NOUN
a strong feeling of approaching disaster

forecast ['fɔː,kɑːst] **forecasts, forecasting, forecast** or **forecasted** NOUN
1 a prediction of what will happen, especially a statement about what the weather will be like

> VERB
2 To forecast an event is to predict what will happen.

forecourt ['fɔː,kɔːt] **forecourts** NOUN
an open area at the front of a petrol station or large building

forefather ['fɔː,fɑːðə] **forefathers** NOUN
Your forefathers are your ancestors.

forefinger ['fɔː,fɪŋɡə] **forefingers** NOUN
the finger next to your thumb

forefront ['fɔː,frʌnt] NOUN
The forefront of something is the most important and progressive part of it.

forego [fɔː'ɡəʊ] **foregoes, foregoing, forewent, foregone;** also spelt **forgo** VERB
If you forego something pleasant, you give it up or do not insist on having it.

foregoing [fɔː'ɡəʊɪŋ] A FORMAL PHRASE
You can say **the foregoing** when talking about something that has just been said. *e.g. The foregoing discussion has highlighted the difficulties.*

foregone conclusion [fɔː'ɡɒn] **foregone conclusions** NOUN
A foregone conclusion is a result or conclusion that is bound to happen.

foreground ['fɔː,ɡraʊnd] NOUN
(ART) In a picture, the foreground is the part that seems nearest to you.

forehand ['fɔː,hænd] **forehands** NOUN OR ADJECTIVE
a stroke in tennis, squash, or badminton made with the palm of your hand facing in the direction that you hit the ball

forehead ['fɒrɪd] **foreheads** NOUN
the area at the front of your head, above your eyebrows and below your hairline

foreign ['fɒrɪn] ADJECTIVE
1 belonging to or involving countries other than your own *e.g. foreign coins... foreign travel*

● THESAURUS
distant: *in that distant land*
exotic: *filmed in an exotic location*
overseas: *a long overseas trip*

2 unfamiliar or uncharacteristic *e.g. Such daft enthusiasm was foreign to him.*

3 A foreign object has got into something, usually by accident, and should not be there. *e.g. a foreign object in my eye*
foreigner NOUN

foreman ['fɔːmən] **foremen** NOUN
1 a person in charge of a group of workers, for example on a building site
2 The foreman of a jury is the spokesman.

foremost ['fɔː,məust] ADJECTIVE
The foremost of a group of things is the most important or the best.

● THESAURUS

best: *He was the best player in the world throughout the 1950s.*
chief: *my chief reason for objecting to the plan*
first: *The first priority is to defeat inflation.*
greatest: *one of the West Indies' greatest cricketers*
leading: *the leading researchers in this area*
most important: *the country's most important politicians and philosophers*
prime: *I regard this as my prime duty.*
principal: *one of the country's principal publishing houses*
top: *The President met with his top military advisers.*

forensic [fə'rɛnsɪk] ADJECTIVE
1 relating to or involving the scientific examination of objects involved in a crime
2 relating to or involving the legal profession

forerunner ['fɔː,rʌnə] **forerunners** NOUN
The forerunner of something is the person who first introduced or achieved it, or the first example of it.

foresee [fɔː'siː] **foresees, foreseeing, foresaw, foreseen** VERB
If you foresee something, you predict or expect that it will happen.
foreseeable ADJECTIVE

foresight ['fɔː,saɪt] NOUN
Foresight is the ability to know what is going to happen in the future.

foreskin ['fɔː,skɪn] **foreskins** NOUN
A man's foreskin is the fold of skin covering the end of his penis.

forest ['fɒrɪst] **forests** NOUN
a large area of trees growing close together

forestry ['fɒrɪstrɪ] NOUN
Forestry is the study and work of growing and maintaining forests.

foretaste ['fɔː,teɪst] **foretastes** NOUN
a slight taste or experience of something in advance

foretell [fɔː'tɛl] **foretells, foretelling, foretold** VERB
If you foretell something, you predict that it will happen.

forever [fɔː'rɛvə] ADVERB
permanently or continually

forewarn [fɔː'wɔːn] **forewarns, forewarning, forewarned** VERB
If you forewarn someone, you warn them in advance about something.

foreword ['fɔː,wɜːd] **forewords** NOUN
an introduction in a book

forfeit ['fɔːfɪt] **forfeits, forfeiting, forfeited** VERB
1 If you forfeit something, you have to give it up as a penalty.
> NOUN
2 something that you have to give up or do as a penalty

forge [fɔːdʒ] **forges, forging, forged** NOUN
1 a place where a blacksmith works making metal goods by hand
> VERB
2 To forge metal is to hammer and bend it into shape while hot.
3 To forge a relationship is to create a strong and lasting relationship.
4 Someone who forges money, documents, or paintings makes illegal copies of them.
5 To forge ahead is to progress quickly.

forgery ['fɔːdʒərɪ] **forgeries** NOUN
Forgery is the crime of forging money, documents, or paintings; also something that has been forged.
forger NOUN

forget [fə'gɛt] **forgets, forgetting, forgot, forgotten** VERB
1 If you forget something, you fail to remember or think about it.

● THESAURUS

fail to remember: *He failed to remember my name.*
omit: *omitting to mention the details*
overlook: *to overlook an important fact*
<<OPPOSITE *remember*

2 If you forget yourself, you behave in an unacceptable, uncontrolled way.
forgetful ADJECTIVE

forget-me-not [fə'gɛtmɪnɒt] **forget-me-nots** NOUN
a small plant with tiny blue flowers

forgive [fə'gɪv] **forgives, forgiving, forgave, forgiven** VERB
If you forgive someone for doing something bad, you stop feeling angry and resentful towards them.
forgiving ADJECTIVE

● THESAURUS

absolve: *The verdict absolved him from blame.*
condone: *We cannot condone violence.*
excuse: *Please excuse our bad behaviour.*
pardon: *Relatives had begged authorities to pardon him.*
<<OPPOSITE *blame*

forgiveness [fə'gɪvnɪs] NOUN
the act of forgiving

● THESAURUS

acquittal: *The jury voted for acquittal.*

mercy: *to beg for mercy*
pardon: *a presidential pardon*
remission: *with remission for good behaviour*

forgo [fɔːˈgəʊ] another spelling of **forego**

fork [fɔːk] **forks, forking, forked** NOUN

1 a pronged instrument used for eating food

2 a large garden tool with three or four prongs

3 a Y-shaped junction or division in a road, river, or branch

> VERB

4 To fork something is to move or turn it with a fork.

fork out VERB; INFORMAL

5 If you fork out for something, you pay for it, often unwillingly.

forlorn [fəˈlɔːn] ADJECTIVE

1 lonely, unhappy and pitiful

2 desperate and without any expectation of success *e.g. a forlorn fight for a draw*
forlornly ADVERB

form [fɔːm] **forms, forming, formed** NOUN

1 A particular form of something is a type or kind of it. *e.g. a new form of weapon*

● THESAURUS
class: *a new class of nuclear-powered submarine*
kind: *a new kind of leadership*
sort: *Try to do some sort of exercise every day.*
type: *There are various types of this disease.*
variant: *The quagga was a beautiful variant of the zebra.*
variety: *an unusual variety of this common garden flower*

2 The form of something is the shape or pattern of something. *e.g. a brooch in the form of a bright green lizard*

● THESAURUS
contours: *the contours of the body*
layout: *He tried to recall the layout of the farmhouse.*
outline: *I could just see the outline of a building in the mist.*
shape: *little pens in the shape of baseball bats*
structure: *the chemical structure of this molecule*

3 a sheet of paper with questions and spaces for you to fill in the answers

4 a class in a school

> VERB

5 The things that form something are the things it consists of. *e.g. events that were to form the basis of her novel*

● THESAURUS
compose: *The force would be composed of troops from NATO countries.*
constitute: *The country's ethnic minorities constitute about 7% of its total population.*

make up: *Women officers make up 13 per cent of the police force.*
serve as: *an arrangement of bricks and planks that served as a bookshelf*

6 When someone forms something or when it forms, it is created, organized, or started.

● THESAURUS
assemble: *a model assembled entirely from matchsticks*
create: *These patterns were created by the action of water.*
develop: *We must develop closer ties with Germany.*
draw up: *We've drawn up a plan of action.*
establish: *The school was established in 1989 by an Italian professor.*
fashion: *Stone Age settlers fashioned necklaces from animals' teeth.*
make: *The organic waste decomposes to make compost.*

formal [ˈfɔːməl] ADJECTIVE

1 correct, serious, and conforming to accepted conventions *e.g. a very formal letter of apology*

● THESAURUS
conventional: *a conventional style of dress*
correct: *polite and correct behaviour*
precise: *They spoke very precise English.*
stiff: *his stiff manner and lack of humour*
<<OPPOSITE *informal*

2 official and publicly recognized *e.g. the first formal agreement of its kind*
formally ADVERB

● THESAURUS
approved: *a legally approved method of dealing with these*
legal: *They have a legal responsibility.*
official: *according to the official figures*
prescribed: *There is a prescribed procedure for situations like this.*
regular: *through the regular channels*

formaldehyde [fɔːˈmældɪˌhaɪd] NOUN
Formaldehyde is a poisonous, strong-smelling gas, used for preserving specimens in biology.

formality [fɔːˈmælɪtɪ] **formalities** NOUN
an action or process that is carried out as part of an official procedure

format [ˈfɔːmæt] **formats** NOUN
the way in which something is arranged or presented

formation [fɔːˈmeɪʃən] **formations** NOUN

1 The formation of something is the process of developing and creating it.

2 the pattern or shape of something

formative [ˈfɔːmətɪv] ADJECTIVE
having an important and lasting influence on

character and development *e.g. the formative days of his young manhood*

former ['fɔːmə] ADJECTIVE

1 happening or existing before now or in the past *e.g. a former tennis champion*

● THESAURUS

ancient: *the ancient civilizations*
bygone: *memories of a bygone age*
old: *our old school*
past: *a long list of past winners*

> NOUN

2 You use 'the former' to refer to the first of two things just mentioned. *e.g. If I had to choose between happiness and money, I would have the former.*
formerly ADVERB

formidable ['fɔːmɪdəbəl] ADJECTIVE
very difficult to deal with or overcome, and therefore rather frightening or impressive *e.g. formidable enemies*
[WORD HISTORY: from Latin FORMIDO meaning 'terror']

● THESAURUS

challenging: *a more challenging job*
daunting: *a daunting prospect*
difficult: *A difficult task lay ahead.*
intimidating: *She was an intimidating opponent.*
mammoth: *a mammoth undertaking*
onerous: *onerous responsibilities*

formula ['fɔːmjʊlə] **formulae** or **formulas**
NOUN

1 a group of letters, numbers, and symbols which stand for a mathematical or scientific rule

2 a list of quantities of substances that when mixed make another substance, for example in chemistry

3 a plan or set of rules for dealing with a particular problem *e.g. my secret formula for keeping in trim*

formulate ['fɔːmjʊˌleɪt] **formulates, formulating, formulated** VERB
If you formulate a plan or thought, you create it and express it in a clear and precise way.

fornication [ˌfɔːnɪˈkeɪʃən] NOUN; FORMAL
Fornication is the sin of having sex with someone when you are not married to them.

forsake [fəˈseɪk] **forsakes, forsaking, forsook, forsaken** VERB
To forsake someone or something is to give up or abandon them.

fort [fɔːt] **forts** NOUN

1 a strong building built for defence

● THESAURUS

castle: *a heavily-guarded castle*

citadel: *The citadel towered above the river.*
fortification: *fortifications along the border*
fortress: *an ancient fortress*

> PHRASE

2 If you **hold the fort** for someone, you manage their affairs while they are away.

forte ['fɔːtɪ] **fortes** ADJECTIVE, ADVERB

1 In music, forte is an instruction to play or sing something loudly.

> NOUN ['fɔːt] or ['fɔːteɪ]

2 If something is your forte, you are particularly good at doing it.

forth [fɔːθ] ADVERB

1 out and forward from a starting place *e.g. Christopher Columbus set forth on his epic voyage of discovery.*

2 into view *e.g. He brought forth a slim volume of his newly published verse.*

forthcoming [ˌfɔːθˈkʌmɪŋ] ADJECTIVE

1 planned to happen soon *e.g. their forthcoming holiday*

2 given or made available *e.g. Medical aid might be forthcoming.*

3 willing to give information *e.g. He was not too forthcoming about this.*

forthright ['fɔːθˌraɪt] ADJECTIVE
Someone who is forthright is direct and honest about their opinions and feelings.

fortification [ˌfɔːtɪfɪˈkeɪʃən] **fortifications**
NOUN
Fortifications are buildings, walls, and ditches used to protect a place.

fortitude ['fɔːtɪˌtjuːd] NOUN
Fortitude is calm and patient courage.

fortnight ['fɔːtˌnaɪt] **fortnights** NOUN
a period of two weeks
fortnightly ADVERB OR ADJECTIVE

fortress ['fɔːtrɪs] **fortresses** NOUN
a castle or well-protected town built for defence

fortuitous [fɔːˈtjuːɪtəs] ADJECTIVE
happening by chance or good luck *e.g. a fortuitous winning goal*

fortunate ['fɔːtʃənɪt] ADJECTIVE

1 Someone who is fortunate is lucky.

2 Something that is fortunate brings success or advantage.
fortunately ADVERB

fortune ['fɔːtʃən] **fortunes** NOUN

1 Fortune or good fortune is good luck.

2 A fortune is a large amount of money.

> PHRASE

3 If someone **tells your fortune**, they predict your future.

forty ['fɔːtɪ] **forties**
the number 40
fortieth

forum ['fɔːrəm] **forums** NOUN

1 a place or meeting in which people can exchange ideas and discuss public issues

2 a square in Roman towns where people met to discuss business and politics

forward ['fɔːwəd] **forwards, forwarding, forwarded** ADVERB OR ADJECTIVE

1 Forward or forwards means in the front or towards the front. *e.g. A photographer moved forward to capture the moment.*

2 Forward means in or towards a future time. *e.g. a positive atmosphere of looking forward and making fresh starts*

3 Forward or forwards also means developing or progressing. *e.g. The new committee would push forward government plans.*

> ADVERB

4 If someone or something is put forward, they are suggested as being suitable for something.

> VERB

5 If you forward a letter that you have received, you send it on to the person to whom it is addressed at their new address.

> NOUN

6 In a game such as football or hockey, a forward is a player in an attacking position.

fossick ['fɒsɪk] **fossicks, fossicking, fossicked** VERB

1 In Australian and New Zealand English, to fossick for gold nuggets or precious stones is to look for them in rivers or old mines.

2 In Australian and New Zealand English, to fossick for something is to search for it.

● THESAURUS

forage: *They were forced to forage for clothing and fuel.*

hunt: *A forensic team was hunting for clues.*

look: *I've looked through all my drawers and I can't find it anywhere.*

rummage: *He rummaged around the post room and found the document.*

search: *We've searched through the whole house for the keys.*

fossil ['fɒsᵊl] **fossils** NOUN
the remains or impression of an animal or plant from a previous age, preserved in rock
fossilize VERB

fossil fuel fossil fuels NOUN
Fossil fuels are fuels such as coal, oil, and natural gas, which have been formed by rotting animals and plants from millions of years ago.

foster ['fɒstə] **fosters, fostering, fostered** VERB

1 If someone fosters a child, they are paid to look after the child for a period, but do not become its legal parent.

2 If you foster something such as an activity or an idea, you help its development and growth by encouraging people to do or think it. *e.g. to foster and maintain this goodwill*
foster child NOUN, **foster home** NOUN, **foster parent** NOUN

fought [fɔːt] the past tense and past participle of **fight**

foul [faʊl] **fouler, foulest; fouls, fouling, fouled** ADJECTIVE

1 Something that is foul is very unpleasant, especially because it is dirty, wicked, or obscene.

> VERB

2 To foul something is to make it dirty, especially with faeces. *e.g. Dogs must not be allowed to foul the pavement.*

> NOUN

3 In sport, a foul is an act of breaking the rules.

found [faʊnd] **founds, founding, founded**

1 Found is the past tense and past participle of **find**

> VERB

2 If someone founds an organization or institution, they start it and set it up.

foundation [faʊnˈdeɪʃən] **foundations** NOUN

1 The foundation of a belief or way of life is the basic ideas or attitudes on which it is built.

2 a solid layer of concrete or bricks in the ground, on which a building is built to give it a firm base

3 an organization set up by money left in someone's will for research or charity

founder ['faʊndə] **founders, foundering, foundered** NOUN

1 The founder of an institution or organization is the person who sets it up.

> VERB

2 If something founders, it fails.

foundry ['faʊndrɪ] **foundries** NOUN
a factory where metal is melted and cast

fountain ['faʊntɪn] **fountains** NOUN
an ornamental structure consisting of a jet of water forced into the air by a pump

fountain pen fountain pens NOUN
a pen which is supplied with ink from a container inside the pen

four [fɔː] **fours**

1 the number 4

> PHRASE

2 If you are **on all fours**, you are on your hands and knees.

four-poster ['fɔː'pəustə] **four-posters** NOUN
a bed with a tall post at each corner supporting a canopy and curtains

fourteen ['fɔː'tiːn]
the number 14
fourteenth

fourth [fɔːθ]
The fourth item in a series is the one counted as number four.

fowl [faʊl] **fowls** NOUN
a bird such as chicken or duck that is kept or hunted for its meat or eggs

fox [fɒks] **foxes, foxing, foxed** NOUN
1 a dog-like wild animal with reddish-brown fur, a pointed face and ears, and a thick tail
> VERB
2 If something foxes you, it is too confusing or puzzling for you to understand.

foxglove ['fɒks,glʌv] **foxgloves** NOUN
a plant with a tall spike of purple or white trumpet-shaped flowers

foxhound ['fɒks,haʊnd] **foxhounds** NOUN
a dog trained for hunting foxes

foyer ['fɔɪeɪ] **foyers** NOUN
a large area just inside the main doors of a cinema, hotel, or public building

fracas ['frækɑː] NOUN
a rough noisy quarrel or fight

fraction ['frækʃən] **fractions** NOUN
1 (MATHS) In arithmetic, a fraction is a part of a whole number.

2 a tiny proportion or amount of something e.g. an area a fraction of the size of London
fractional ADJECTIVE, **fractionally** ADVERB

fractious ['frækʃəs] ADJECTIVE
When small children are fractious, they become upset or angry very easily, often because they are tired.

fracture ['fræktʃə] **fractures, fracturing, fractured** NOUN
1 a crack or break in something, especially a bone
> VERB
2 If something fractures, it breaks.

fragile ['frædʒaɪl] ADJECTIVE
easily broken or damaged e.g. fragile glass... a fragile relationship
fragility NOUN

● THESAURUS
breakable: Anything breakable or sharp had to be removed.

dainty: a dainty Japanese tea service
delicate: a delicate instrument
flimsy: packed in a flimsy box
frail: a frail shell
<<OPPOSITE tough

fragment fragments, fragmenting, fragmented NOUN ['frægmənt]
1 a small piece or part of something
> VERB [fræg'ment]
2 If something fragments, it breaks into small pieces or different parts.
fragmentation NOUN, **fragmented** ADJECTIVE

fragmentary ['frægməntərɪ] ADJECTIVE
made up of small pieces, or parts that are not connected e.g. fragmentary notes in a journal

fragrance ['freɪgrəns] **fragrances** NOUN
a sweet or pleasant smell

● THESAURUS
aroma: the aroma of fresh bread
bouquet: a wine with a lively fruit bouquet
perfume: enjoying the perfume of the lemon trees
scent: flowers chosen for their scent
smell: a sweet smell of pine

fragrant ['freɪgrənt] ADJECTIVE
Something that is fragrant smells sweet or pleasant.

● THESAURUS
aromatic: a plant with aromatic leaves
perfumed: perfumed body cream
sweet-smelling: posies of sweet-smelling flowers
<<OPPOSITE smelly

frail [freɪl] **frailer, frailest** ADJECTIVE
1 Someone who is frail is not strong or healthy.
2 Something that is frail is easily broken or damaged.
frailty NOUN

frame [freɪm] **frames, framing, framed** NOUN
1 the structure surrounding a door, window, or . picture

2 an arrangement of connected bars over which something is built

3 The frames of a pair of glasses are the wire or plastic parts that hold the lenses.

4 Your frame is your body. e.g. his large frame

5 one of the many separate photographs of which a cinema film is made up
> VERB

6 To frame a picture is to put it into a frame. e.g. I've framed pictures I've pulled out of magazines.

7 The language something is framed in is the language used to express it.

framework ['freɪm,wɜːk] **frameworks** NOUN

1 a structure acting as a support or frame

2 a set of rules, beliefs, or ideas which you use to decide what to do

franc [fræŋk] **francs** NOUN
the main unit of currency in Switzerland, and formerly in France and Belgium. A franc is worth 100 centimes

franchise ['fræntʃaɪz] **franchises** NOUN
1 The franchise is the right to vote in an election. *e.g. a franchise that gave the vote to less than 2% of the population*

2 the right given by a company to someone to allow them to sell its goods or services

frank [fræŋk] **franker, frankest** ADJECTIVE
If you are frank, you say things in an open and honest way.
frankly ADVERB, **frankness** NOUN

● THESAURUS
blunt: *his blunt approach*
candid: *She was completely candid with me.*
honest: *my honest opinion*
open: *an open, trusting nature*
plain: *plain talking*
straightforward: *spoken in a straightforward manner*

frantic ['fræntɪk] ADJECTIVE
If you are frantic, you behave in a wild, desperate way because you are anxious or frightened.
frantically ADVERB

fraternal [frə'tɜ:nªl] ADJECTIVE
'Fraternal' is used to describe friendly actions and feelings between groups of people *e.g. an affectionate fraternal greeting*

fraternity [frə'tɜ:nɪtɪ] **fraternities** NOUN
1 Fraternity is friendship between groups of people.

2 a group of people with something in common *e.g. the golfing fraternity*

fraud [frɔ:d] **frauds** NOUN
1 Fraud is the crime of getting money by deceit or trickery.

● THESAURUS
deceit: *deliberate deceit*
deception: *obtaining money by deception*
guile: *children's lack of guile*
hoax: *a bomb hoax*
trickery: *They had to resort to trickery.*

2 someone or something that deceives people in an illegal or immoral way

● THESAURUS
charlatan: *exposed as a charlatan*
cheat: *Cheats will be disqualified.*
fake: *The painting was a fake.*
forgery: *just a clever forgery*

imposter: *an imposter with false documents*
quack: *He tried all sorts of quacks.*

3 Someone who is not what they pretend to be.

fraudulent ['frɔ:djʊlənt] ADJECTIVE
dishonest or deceitful *e.g. fraudulent cheques*

fraught [frɔ:t] ADJECTIVE
If something is fraught with problems or difficulties, it is full of them. *e.g. Modern life was fraught with hazards.*

fray [freɪ] **frays, fraying, frayed** VERB
1 If cloth or rope frays, its threads or strands become worn and it is likely to tear or break.

> NOUN
2 a fight or argument

freak [fri:k] **freaks** NOUN
1 someone whose appearance or behaviour is very unusual

> ADJECTIVE OR NOUN
2 A freak event is very unusual and unlikely to happen. *e.g. a freak allergy to peanuts*

freckle ['frɛkªl] **freckles** NOUN
Freckles are small, light brown spots on someone's skin, especially their face.
freckled ADJECTIVE

free [fri:] **freer, freest; frees, freeing, freed** ADJECTIVE
1 not controlled or limited *e.g. the free flow of aid... free trade*

2 Someone who is free is no longer a prisoner.

● THESAURUS
at large: *Three prisoners are at large.*
at liberty: *the last top Nazi still at liberty*
liberated: *newly liberated slaves*
loose: *He broke loose from his bonds.*
<<OPPOSITE captive

3 To be free of something unpleasant is not to have it. *e.g. She wanted her aunt's life to be free of worry.*

4 If someone is free, they are not busy or occupied. If a place, seat, or machine is free, it is not occupied or not being used. *e.g. Are you free for dinner?.*

5 If something is free, you can have it without paying for it.

● THESAURUS
complimentary: *complimentary tickets*
gratis: *The meal was gratis.*
unpaid: *unpaid voluntary work*
without charge: *They mended it without charge.*

> VERB
6 If you free someone or something that is imprisoned, fastened, or trapped, you release them.

THESAURUS
discharge: *discharged from prison*
liberate: *liberated under the terms of the amnesty*
release: *The hostages were soon released.*
set at liberty: *He was set at liberty after ten years.*
set loose: *The animals were set loose after treatment.*
<<OPPOSITE *imprison*

freedom ['fri:dəm] NOUN
1 If you have the freedom to do something, you have the scope or are allowed to do it. *e.g. We have the freedom to decide our own futures.*

THESAURUS
discretion: *Use your own discretion.*
latitude: *There is more latitude for personal opinions.*
leeway: *granted more leeway to pass reforms*
licence: *a licence to kill*
scope: *plenty of scope for improvement*

2 When prisoners gain their freedom, they escape or are released.

THESAURUS
emancipation: *the emancipation of the slaves*
liberty: *three months' loss of liberty*
release: *the immediate release of the captives*
<<OPPOSITE *captivity*

3 When there is freedom from something unpleasant, people are not affected by it. *e.g. freedom from guilt*

THESAURUS
exemption: *granted exemption from all taxes*
immunity: *information in exchange for immunity from prosecution*

freehold ['fri:,həʊld] **freeholds** NOUN
the right to own a house or piece of land for life without conditions

freelance ['fri:,lɑːns] ADJECTIVE OR ADVERB
A freelance journalist or photographer is not employed by one organization, but is paid for each job he or she does.

freely ['fri:lɪ] ADVERB
Freely means without restriction. *e.g. the pleasure of being able to walk about freely*

free-range ['fri:,reɪndʒ] ADJECTIVE
Free-range eggs are laid by hens that can move and feed freely on an area of open ground.

freestyle ['fri:,staɪl] NOUN
Freestyle refers to sports competitions, especially swimming, in which competitors can use any style or method.

freeway ['fri:,weɪ] **freeways** NOUN
In Australia, South Africa, and the United States, a road designed for fast-moving traffic.

free will PHRASE
If you do something **of your own free will**, you do it by choice and not because you are forced to.

freeze [fri:z] **freezes, freezing, froze, frozen** VERB
1 (SCIENCE) When a liquid freezes, it becomes solid because it is very cold.
2 If you freeze, you suddenly become very still and quiet.
3 (DRAMA) To freeze the action in a film is to stop the film at a particular frame.
4 If you freeze food, you put it in a freezer to preserve it.
5 When wages or prices are frozen, they are officially prevented from rising.
> NOUN
6 an official action taken to prevent wages or prices from rising
7 a period of freezing weather

freezer ['fri:zə] **freezers** NOUN
a large refrigerator which freezes and stores food for a long time

freezing ['fri:zɪŋ] ADJECTIVE
extremely cold

freight [freɪt] NOUN
Freight is goods moved by lorries, ships, or other transport; also the moving of these goods.

French [frɛntʃ] ADJECTIVE
1 belonging or relating to France
> NOUN
2 French is the main language spoken in France, and is also spoken by many people in Belgium, Switzerland, and Canada.

French bean French beans NOUN
French beans are green pods eaten as a vegetable, which grow on a climbing plant with white or mauve flowers.

French horn French horns NOUN
a brass musical wind instrument consisting of a tube wound in a circle

Frenchman ['frɛntʃmən] **Frenchmen** NOUN
a man who comes from France
Frenchwoman NOUN

french window french windows NOUN
French windows are glass doors that lead into a garden or onto a balcony.

frenetic [frɪ'nɛtɪk] ADJECTIVE
Frenetic behaviour is wild and excited.

frenzy ['frɛnzɪ] **frenzies** NOUN
If someone is in a frenzy, their behaviour is wild and uncontrolled.
frenzied ADJECTIVE

THESAURUS
agitation: *in a state of intense agitation*

fury: *She stalked out in a fury.*
hysteria: *mass hysteria*
madness: *a moment of madness*
rage: *She flew into a rage.*

frequency ['fri:kwənsɪ] **frequencies** NOUN
  1 The frequency of an event is how often it
  happens. *e.g. He was not known to call anyone with
  great frequency.*

  2 (SCIENCE) The frequency of a sound or radio
  wave is the rate at which it vibrates.

**frequent frequents, frequenting,
frequented** ADJECTIVE ['fri:kwənt]
  1 often happening *e.g. His visits were frequent...
  They move at frequent intervals.*

● THESAURUS
  common: *a common occurrence*
  continual: *continual demands for money*
  everyday: *an everyday event*
  habitual: *a habitual daydreamer*
  recurrent: *a recurrent theme in her work*
  repeated: *His parents made repeated attempts to
  visit.*
  <<OPPOSITE *rare*

  > VERB [frɪ'kwɛnt]
  2 If you frequent a place, you go there often.
  frequently ADVERB

● THESAURUS
  attend: *He often attends their meetings.*
  haunt: *She haunted their house.*
  patronize: *to patronize a hotel*
  visit: *a place we often visit*
  <<OPPOSITE *avoid*

fresco ['frɛskəʊ] **frescoes** NOUN
  a picture painted on a plastered wall while the
  plaster is still wet
  [WORD HISTORY: from Italian FRESCO meaning
  'fresh']

fresh [frɛʃ] **fresher, freshest** ADJECTIVE
  1 A fresh thing replaces a previous one, or is
  added to it. *e.g. footprints filled in by fresh snow...
  fresh evidence*

  2 Fresh food is newly made or obtained, and not
  tinned or frozen.

  3 Fresh water is not salty, for example the water
  in a stream.

  4 If the weather is fresh, it is fairly cold and
  windy.

  5 If you are fresh from something, you have
  experienced it recently. *e.g. a teacher fresh from
  college*
  freshly ADVERB, **freshness** NOUN

freshwater ['frɛʃ,wɔ:tə] ADJECTIVE
  1 A freshwater lake or pool contains water that is
  not salty.

  2 A freshwater creature lives in a river, lake, or
  pool that is not salty.

fret [frɛt] **frets, fretting, fretted** VERB
  1 If you fret about something, you worry about it.
  > NOUN
  2 The frets on a stringed instrument, such as a
  guitar, are the metal ridges across its neck.
  fretful ADJECTIVE

Freudian slip ['frɔɪdɪən] **Freudian slips**
NOUN
  something that you say or do that reveals your
  unconscious thoughts

friar ['fraɪə] **friars** NOUN
  a member of a Catholic religious order

friction ['frɪkʃən] NOUN
  1 (SCIENCE) the force that stops things from
  moving freely when they rub against each other
  2 Friction between people is disagreement and
  quarrels.

Friday ['fraɪdɪ] **Fridays** NOUN
  the day between Thursday and Saturday
  [WORD HISTORY: from Old English FRIGEDÆG
  meaning 'Freya's day'. Freya was the Norse
  goddess of love]

fridge [frɪdʒ] **fridges** NOUN the same as a
refrigerator

friend [frɛnd] **friends** NOUN
  Your friends are people you know well and like to
  spend time with.

● THESAURUS
  china: South African; informal *a drinking session
  with his chinas*
  companion: *my constant companion*
  confidant or **confidante:** *her only confidant*
  crony: *surrounded by her cronies*
  mate: informal *going out with his mates*
  pal: *We are great pals.*
  <<OPPOSITE *enemy*

friendly ['frɛndlɪ] **friendlier, friendliest**
ADJECTIVE
  1 If you are friendly to someone, you behave in a
  kind and pleasant way to them.

● THESAURUS
  affectionate: *on affectionate terms*
  amiable: *He was very amiable company.*
  close: *The two were very close.*
  cordial: *a most cordial welcome*
  genial: *a genial host*
  welcoming: *a welcoming house*
  <<OPPOSITE *unfriendly*

  2 People who are friendly with each other like
  each other and enjoy spending time together.
  friendliness NOUN

friendship ['frɛndʃɪp] **friendships** NOUN

1 Your friendships are the special relationships that you have with your friends.

2 Friendship is the state of being friends with someone.

● THESAURUS

affection: *to win their affection*
attachment: *the deep attachment between them*
closeness: *her closeness to her sister*
goodwill: *as a gesture of goodwill*
<<OPPOSITE *hostility*

frieze [friːz] **friezes** NOUN

1 a strip of decoration or carving along the top of a wall or column

2 (ART) a picture on a long strip of paper which is hung along a wall

frigate [ˈfrɪgɪt] **frigates** NOUN
a small, fast warship

fright [fraɪt] NOUN
Fright is a sudden feeling of fear.

frighten [ˈfraɪtᵊn] **frightens, frightening, frightened** VERB
If something frightens you, it makes you afraid.

● THESAURUS

alarm: *alarmed by the noise*
intimidate: *She is intimidated by her boss.*
scare: *You aren't scared of mice, are you?*
startle: *I didn't mean to startle you.*
terrify: *Heights terrified her.*
terrorize: *The gunmen terrorized the villagers.*
unnerve: *an unnerving silence*

frightened [ˈfraɪtnd] ADJECTIVE
having feelings of fear about something

● THESAURUS

afraid: *Jane was afraid of the other children.*
alarmed: *Don't be alarmed.*
petrified: *petrified of wasps*
scared: *scared of being alone in the house*
startled: *a startled animal*
terrified: *a terrified look*

frightening [ˈfraɪtᵊnɪŋ] ADJECTIVE
causing someone to feel fear

● THESAURUS

alarming: *an alarming increase*
hair-raising: *at hair-raising speed*
intimidating: *threatening and intimidating behaviour*
menacing: *a menacing glance*
terrifying: *one of the most terrifying diseases*

frightful [ˈfraɪtfʊl] ADJECTIVE
very bad or unpleasant *e.g. a frightful bully*

frigid [ˈfrɪdʒɪd] ADJECTIVE
Frigid behaviour is cold and unfriendly. *e.g. frigid stares*

frill [frɪl] **frills** NOUN
a strip of cloth with many folds, attached to

something as a decoration
frilly ADJECTIVE

fringe [frɪndʒ] **fringes** NOUN

1 the hair that hangs over a person's forehead

2 a decoration on clothes and other objects, consisting of a row of hanging strips or threads

3 The fringes of a place are the parts farthest from its centre. *e.g. the western fringe of the Amazon basin*
fringed ADJECTIVE

frisk [frɪsk] **frisks, frisking, frisked** VERB; INFORMAL
If someone frisks you, they search you quickly with their hands to see if you are hiding a weapon in your clothes.

frisky [ˈfrɪskɪ] **friskier, friskiest** ADJECTIVE
A frisky animal or child is energetic and wants to have fun.

fritter [ˈfrɪtə] **fritters, frittering, frittered** NOUN

1 Fritters consist of food dipped in batter and fried. *e.g. apple fritters*

> VERB

2 If you fritter away your time or money, you waste it on unimportant things.

frivolous [ˈfrɪvələs] ADJECTIVE
Someone who is frivolous behaves in a silly or light-hearted way, especially when they should be serious or sensible.
frivolity NOUN

● THESAURUS

flippant: *a flippant comment*
foolish: *saying foolish and inappropriate things*
juvenile: *juvenile behaviour*
puerile: *your puerile schoolboy humour*
silly: *making silly jokes*
<<OPPOSITE *serious*

frizzy [ˈfrɪzɪ] **frizzier, frizziest** ADJECTIVE
Frizzy hair has stiff, wiry curls.

frock [frɒk] **frocks** NOUN; OLD-FASHIONED, INFORMAL
a dress

frog [frɒg] **frogs** NOUN
a small amphibious creature with smooth skin, prominent eyes, and long back legs which it uses for jumping

frolic [ˈfrɒlɪk] **frolics, frolicking, frolicked** VERB
When animals or children frolic, they run around and play in a lively way.
[WORD HISTORY: from Dutch VROLIJK meaning 'joyful']

from [frɒm] PREPOSITION

1 You use 'from' to say what the source, origin, or starting point of something is. *e.g. a call from a public telephone... people from a city 100 miles away*

2 If you take something from an amount, you reduce the amount by that much. *e.g. A sum of money was wrongly taken from his account.*

3 You also use 'from' when stating the range of something. *e.g. a score from one to five*

frond [frɒnd] **fronds** NOUN
Fronds are long feathery leaves.

front [frʌnt] **fronts, fronting, fronted**
NOUN
1 The front of something is the part that faces forward.

● THESAURUS
face: *the face of the building*
frontage: *a restaurant with a river frontage*
<<OPPOSITE *back*

2 In a war, the front is the place where two armies are fighting.

3 In meteorology, a front is the line where a mass of cold air meets a mass of warm air.

4 A front is an outward appearance, often one that is false. *e.g. I put up a brave front... He's no more than a respectable front for some very dubious happenings.*

● THESAURUS
appearance: *the appearance of fair treatment*
exterior: *his tough exterior*
face: *a brave face*
show: *a convincing show of affection*

> PHRASE
5 In front means ahead or further forward
● THESAURUS
ahead: *ahead of the rest of the field*
before: *I'm before you.*
leading: *the leading rider*

6 If you do something **in front of** someone, you do it when they are present.
frontal ADJECTIVE

frontage ['frʌntɪdʒ] **frontages** NOUN
The frontage of a building is the wall that faces a street.

frontier ['frʌntɪə] **frontiers** NOUN
a border between two countries

frontispiece ['frʌntɪsˌpiːs] **frontispieces**
NOUN
a picture opposite the title page of a book

frost [frɒst] **frosts** NOUN
When there is a frost, the temperature outside falls below freezing.

frostbite ['frɒstˌbaɪt] NOUN
Frostbite is damage to your fingers, toes, or ears caused by extreme cold.

frosty ['frɒstɪ] **frostier, frostiest** ADJECTIVE
1 If it is frosty, the temperature outside is below freezing point.

2 If someone is frosty, they are unfriendly or disapproving.

froth [frɒθ] **froths, frothing, frothed** NOUN
1 Froth is a mass of small bubbles on the surface of a liquid.

> VERB
2 If a liquid froths, small bubbles appear on its surface.
frothy ADJECTIVE

frown [fraʊn] **frowns, frowning, frowned**
VERB
1 If you frown, you move your eyebrows closer together, because you are annoyed, worried, or concentrating.

● THESAURUS
glare: *The woman glared angrily at him.*
glower: *She glowered but said nothing.*
knit your brows: *He knitted his brows in concentration.*
scowl: *He scowled at the waiter.*

> NOUN
2 a cross expression on someone's face

froze ['frəʊz] the past tense of **freeze**

frozen ['frəʊzᵊn]

1 Frozen is the past participle of **freeze**

> ADJECTIVE
2 If you say are frozen, you mean you are extremely cold.

● THESAURUS
arctic: *arctic weather conditions*
chilled: *chilled to the marrow*
frigid: *frigid temperatures*
icy: *an icy wind*
numb: *numb with cold*

fructose ['frʌktəʊs] NOUN
Fructose is a type of sugar found in many fruits and in honey.

frugal ['fruːgᵊl] ADJECTIVE
1 Someone who is frugal spends very little money.

2 A frugal meal is small and cheap.
frugality NOUN

fruit [fruːt] **fruits** NOUN
1 the part of a plant that develops after the flower and contains the seeds. Many fruits are edible

> PLURAL NOUN
2 The fruits of something are its good results. *e.g. the fruits of his labours*

fruitful ['fruːtfʊl] ADJECTIVE
Something that is fruitful has good and useful

results. *e.g. a fruitful experience*

fruitless ['fru:tlɪs] ADJECTIVE
Something that is fruitless does not achieve anything. *e.g. a fruitless effort*

fruit machine fruit machines NOUN
a coin-operated gambling machine which pays out money when a particular series of symbols, usually fruit, appears on a screen

fruit salad fruit salads NOUN
a mixture of pieces of different fruits served in a juice as a dessert

fruity ['fru:tɪ] **fruitier, fruitiest** ADJECTIVE
Something that is fruity smells or tastes of fruit.

frustrate [frʌ'streɪt] **frustrates, frustrating, frustrated** VERB
1 If something frustrates you, it prevents you doing what you want and makes you upset and angry. *e.g. Everyone gets frustrated with their work.*
2 To frustrate something such as a plan is to prevent it. *e.g. She hopes to frustrate the engagement of her son.*
frustrated ADJECTIVE, **frustrating** ADJECTIVE, **frustration** NOUN
⬤ THESAURUS
block: *They are blocking the peace process.*
check: *to check the spread of the virus*
foil: *They foiled all my plans.*
thwart: *his way to thwart your club's ambitions*

fry [fraɪ] **fries, frying, fried** VERB
When you fry food, you cook it in a pan containing hot fat or oil.

fuchsia ['fju:ʃə] **fuchsias** NOUN
a plant or small bush with pink, purple, or white flowers that hang downwards

fudge [fʌdʒ] **fudges, fudging, fudged** NOUN
1 Fudge is a soft brown sweet made from butter, milk, and sugar.
> VERB
2 If you fudge something, you avoid making clear or definite decisions or statements about it. *e.g. He was carefully fudging his message.*

fuel [fjʊəl] **fuels, fuelling, fuelled** NOUN
1 Fuel is a substance such as coal or petrol that is burned to provide heat or power.
> VERB
2 A machine or vehicle that is fuelled by a substance works by burning the substance as a fuel. *e.g. power stations fuelled by wood*

fug [fʌg] NOUN
A fug is an airless, smoky atmosphere.

fugitive ['fju:dʒɪtɪv] **fugitives** NOUN
someone who is running away or hiding, especially from the police

fulcrum ['fʊlkrəm] **fulcrums** or **fulcra** NOUN
the point at which something is balancing or pivoting

-ful SUFFIX
1 '-ful' is used to form adjectives with the meaning 'full of' *e.g. careful*
2 '-ful' is used to form nouns which mean 'the amount needed to fill' *e.g. spoonful*
[WORD HISTORY: from Old English]

fulfil [fʊl'fɪl] **fulfils, fulfilling, fulfilled** VERB
1 If you fulfil a promise, hope, or duty, you carry it out or achieve it.
⬤ THESAURUS
accomplish: *If they all work together they can accomplish their goal.*
achieve: *We will strive to achieve these goals.*
carry out: *They seem to have very little intention of carrying out their commitments.*
perform: *Each component performs a different function.*
realize: *The question is, will our hopes ever be realized?*
satisfy: *The procedures should satisfy certain basic requirements.*
2 If something fulfils you, it gives you satisfaction.
fulfilling ADJECTIVE, **fulfilment** NOUN

full [fʊl] **fuller, fullest** ADJECTIVE
1 containing or having as much as it is possible to hold *e.g. His room is full of posters.*
⬤ THESAURUS
filled: *filled up to the top*
loaded: *The van was loaded with furniture.*
packed: *The train was packed.*
saturated: *completely saturated with liquid*
<<OPPOSITE empty
2 complete or whole *e.g. They had taken a full meal... a full 20 years later*
⬤ THESAURUS
comprehensive: *a comprehensive guide to the area*
detailed: *a detailed description*
exhaustive: *an exhaustive treatment of the subject*
extensive: *extensive coverage of the earthquake*
maximum: *the way to take maximum advantage of pay TV*
thorough: *a thorough search*
3 loose and made from a lot of fabric *e.g. full sleeves*
⬤ THESAURUS
baggy: *a baggy sweater*
loose: *hidden under his loose shirt*
voluminous: *voluminous sleeves*
4 rich and strong *e.g. a full, fruity wine*
> ADVERB
5 completely and directly *e.g. Turn the taps full on.*

> PHRASE

6 Something that has been done or described **in full** has been dealt with completely.

fullness NOUN, **fully** ADVERB

full-blooded [ˌfʊlˈblʌdɪd] ADJECTIVE
having great commitment and enthusiasm *e.g. a full-blooded sprint for third place*

full-blown [ˌfʊlˈbləʊn] ADJECTIVE
complete and fully developed *e.g. a full-blown love of music*

full moon full moons NOUN
the moon when it appears as a complete circle

full stop full stops NOUN
the punctuation mark (.) used at the end of a sentence and after an abbreviation or initial

full-time [ˌfʊlˈtaɪm] ADJECTIVE
1 involving work for the whole of each normal working week

> NOUN

2 In games such as football, full time is the end of the match.

fully-fledged [ˌfʊlɪˈflɛdʒd] ADJECTIVE
completely developed *e.g. I was a fully-fledged and mature human being.*

fulsome [ˈfʊlsəm] ADJECTIVE
exaggerated and elaborate, and often sounding insincere *e.g. His most fulsome praise was reserved for his mother.*

fumble [ˈfʌmbəl] **fumbles, fumbling, fumbled** VERB
If you fumble, you feel or handle something clumsily.

fume [fjuːm] **fumes, fuming, fumed** NOUN
1 Fumes are unpleasant-smelling gases and smoke, often toxic, that are produced by burning and by some chemicals.

> VERB

2 If you are fuming, you are very angry.

fun [fʌn] NOUN
1 Fun is pleasant, enjoyable and light-hearted activity.

● THESAURUS
amusement: *There is no amusement for teenagers in this village.*
enjoyment: *It gave us much enjoyment.*
entertainment: *little opportunity for entertainment*
pleasure: *to mix business and pleasure*
recreation: *time for recreation*

> PHRASE

2 If you **make fun** of someone, you tease them or make jokes about them.

● THESAURUS
deride: *This theory is widely derided.*

laugh at: *They laughed at his hat.*
mock: *He was often mocked by his classmates.*
ridicule: *She allowed them to ridicule her.*
taunt: *a fellow pupil who had taunted him about his height*

function [ˈfʌŋkʃən] **functions, functioning, functioned** NOUN
1 The function of something or someone is their purpose or the job they have to do.

● THESAURUS
duty: *My duty is to look after the animals.*
job: *Their main job is to keep us healthy.*
purpose: *The purpose of the occasion was to raise money for charity.*
remit: *The centre's remit is to advise businesses.*
responsibility: *He handled his responsibilities as a counsellor in an intelligent fashion.*
role: *information about the drug's role in preventing infection*

2 a large formal dinner, reception, or party

● THESAURUS
dinner: *a series of official dinners*
gathering: *I'm always shy at formal gatherings like that.*
party: *They met at a party.*
reception: *At the reception they served smoked salmon.*

> VERB

3 When something functions, it operates or works.

● THESAURUS
go: *My car won't go in cold weather.*
operate: *Ceiling and wall lights can operate independently.*
perform: *When there's snow, how is this car going to perform?*
run: *The system is now running smoothly.*
work: *Is the telephone working today?*

functional [ˈfʌŋkʃənəl] ADJECTIVE
1 relating to the way something works
2 designed for practical use rather than for decoration or attractiveness *e.g. Feminine clothing has never been designed to be functional.*
3 working properly *e.g. fully functional smoke alarms*

fund [fʌnd] **funds, funding, funded** NOUN
1 an amount of available money, usually for a particular purpose *e.g. a pension fund*

● THESAURUS
capital: *difficulty in raising capital*
foundation: *money from a research foundation*
pool: *a reserve pool of cash*
reserve: *a drain on the cash reserves*
supply: *to curb money supply and inflation*

2 A fund of something is a lot of it. *e.g. He had a fund of hilarious tales on the subject.*

THESAURUS
hoard: *his hoard of supplies*
mine: *a mine of information*
reserve: *oil reserves*
reservoir: *the body's short-term reservoir of energy*
store: *a store of fuel*

> **VERB**
3 Someone who funds something provides money for it. *e.g. research funded by pharmaceutical companies*

THESAURUS
finance: *big projects financed by foreign aid*
pay for: *His parents paid for his holiday.*
subsidize: *heavily subsidized by the government*
support: *He is supporting himself through college.*

fundamental [ˌfʌndə'mɛntəl] **fundamentals** ADJECTIVE
1 basic and central *e.g. the fundamental right of freedom of choice... fundamental changes*

> **NOUN**
2 The fundamentals of something are its most basic and important parts. *e.g. teaching small children the fundamentals of road safety*

fundi ['fʊndiː] **fundis** NOUN SOUTH AFRICAN
an expert

THESAURUS
expert: *our team of experts*
guru: *Fashion gurus dictate some crazy ideas.*
master: *a master of the English language*
specialist: *a specialist in diseases of the nervous system*
virtuoso: *He was gaining a reputation as a piano virtuoso.*

funeral ['fjuːnərəl] **funerals** NOUN
(RE) a ceremony or religious service for the burial or cremation of a dead person

funereal [fjuːˈnɪərɪəl] ADJECTIVE
depressing and gloomy

funfair ['fʌnˌfɛə] **funfairs** NOUN
a place of entertainment with things like amusement arcades and rides

fungicide ['fʌndʒɪˌsaɪd] **fungicides** NOUN
a chemical used to kill or prevent fungus

fungus ['fʌŋgəs] **fungi** or **funguses** NOUN
a plant such as a mushroom or mould that does not have leaves and grows on other living things
fungal ADJECTIVE

funk [fʌŋk] **funks, funking, funked** VERB
1 OLD-FASHIONED, INFORMAL
If you funk something, you fail to do it because of fear.

> **NOUN**
2 Funk is a style of music with a strong rhythm based on jazz and blues.

funnel ['fʌnəl] **funnels, funnelling, funnelled** NOUN
1 an open cone narrowing to a tube, used to pour substances into containers
2 a metal chimney on a ship or steam engine

> **VERB**
3 If something is funnelled somewhere, it is directed through a narrow space into that place.

funny ['fʌnɪ] **funnier, funniest** ADJECTIVE
1 strange or puzzling *e.g. You get a lot of funny people coming into the libraries.*

THESAURUS
mysterious: *in mysterious circumstances*
odd: *There was something odd about her.*
peculiar: *It tasted very peculiar.*
puzzling: *a puzzling development*
strange: *A strange thing happened.*
unusual: *a most unusual man*

2 causing amusement or laughter *e.g. a funny old film*
funnily ADVERB

THESAURUS
amusing: *a most amusing lecturer*
comic: *comic moments*
comical: *the comical expression on his face*
hilarious: *We thought it was hilarious.*
humorous: *a humorous magazine*
witty: *a very witty speech*
<<OPPOSITE *serious*

fur [fɜː] **furs** NOUN
1 Fur is the soft thick body hair of many animals.
2 a coat made from an animal's fur
furry ADJECTIVE

furious ['fjʊərɪəs] ADJECTIVE
1 extremely angry

THESAURUS
enraged: *I got more and more enraged at my father.*
fuming: *He was still fuming over the remark.*
infuriated: *He knew how infuriated the conversation had made me.*
livid: *She was absolutely livid about it.*
mad: *I'm pretty mad about this, I can tell you.*
raging: *Inside, Sally was raging.*

2 involving great energy, effort, or speed *e.g. the furious speed of technological development*
furiously ADVERB

THESAURUS
breakneck: *Jack drove to Mayfair at breakneck speed.*
fierce: *Competition has been fierce between the rival groups.*
frantic: *There was frantic activity behind the scenes.*
frenzied: *the frenzied activity of the general election*
intense: *The military on both sides are involved in intense activity.*

f

manic: *Preparations continued at a manic pace.*

furlong ['fɜːˌlɒŋ] **furlongs** NOUN
a unit of length equal to 220 yards or about 201.2 metres. Furlong originally referred to the length of the average furrow

furnace ['fɜːnɪs] **furnaces** NOUN
a container for a very large, hot fire used, for example, in the steel industry for melting ore

furnish ['fɜːnɪʃ] **furnishes, furnishing, furnished** VERB
1 If you furnish a room, you put furniture into it.
2 FORMAL
If you furnish someone with something, you supply or provide it for them.

furnishings ['fɜːnɪʃɪŋz] PLURAL NOUN
The furnishings of a room or house are the furniture and fittings in it.

furniture ['fɜːnɪtʃə] NOUN
Furniture is movable objects such as tables, chairs and wardrobes.

furore [fjʊˈrɔːrɪ] NOUN
an angry and excited reaction or protest
[WORD HISTORY: from Italian FURORE meaning 'rage']

furrow ['fʌrəʊ] **furrows, furrowing, furrowed** NOUN
1 a long, shallow trench made by a plough
> VERB
2 When someone furrows their brow, they frown.

further ['fɜːðə] **furthers, furthering, furthered**
1 a comparative form of **far**
> ADJECTIVE
2 additional or more *e.g. There was no further rain.*
> VERB
3 If you further something, you help it to progress. *e.g. He wants to further his acting career.*

further education NOUN
Further education is education at a college after leaving school, but not at a university.

furthermore ['fɜːðəˌmɔː] ADVERB; FORMAL
used to introduce additional information *e.g. There is no record of such a letter. Furthermore it is company policy never to send such letters.*

furthest ['fɜːðəst] a superlative form of **far**

furtive ['fɜːtɪv] ADJECTIVE
secretive, sly, and cautious *e.g. a furtive smile*
furtively ADVERB

fury ['fjʊərɪ] NOUN
Fury is violent or extreme anger.

fuse [fjuːz] **fuses, fusing, fused** NOUN
1 a safety device in a plug or electrical appliance consisting of a piece of wire which melts to stop the electric current if a fault occurs
2 a long cord attached to some types of simple bomb which is lit to detonate it
> VERB
3 When an electrical appliance fuses, it stops working because the fuse has melted to protect it.
4 If two things fuse, they join or become combined. *e.g. Christianity slowly fused with existing beliefs.*

fuselage ['fjuːzɪˌlɑːʒ] **fuselages** NOUN
the main part of an aeroplane or rocket

fusion ['fjuːʒən] NOUN
1 Fusion is what happens when two substances join by melting together.
2 Fusion is also nuclear fusion.
> ADJECTIVE
3 Fusion is used to refer to food or a style of cooking that brings together ingredients or cooking techniques from several different countries.

fuss [fʌs] **fusses, fussing, fussed** NOUN
1 Fuss is unnecessarily anxious or excited behaviour.
● **THESAURUS**
agitation: *in a state of intense agitation*
bother: *I don't want any bother.*
commotion: *a commotion in the market*
confusion: *in the confusion after an ammunition dump blew up*
stir: *The play caused a stir here.*
to-do: *a big to-do*
> VERB
2 If someone fusses, they behave with unnecessary anxiety and concern for unimportant things.
● **THESAURUS**
bustle: *shoppers bustling around the store*
fidget: *He was fidgeting with his tie.*
fret: *Stop fretting about the details.*

fussy ['fʌsɪ] **fussier, fussiest** ADJECTIVE
1 tending to fuss a lot *e.g. He was unusually fussy about keeping things perfect.*
● **THESAURUS**
choosy: informal *Cats can be choosy about what they eat.*
discriminating: *a discriminating visitor*
exacting: *She failed to meet his exacting standards.*
fastidious: *Disney was also fastidious about cleanliness.*
particular: *very particular about the colours he used*
2 with too much elaborate detail or decoration *e.g. fussy chiffon evening wear*

futile ['fju:taɪl] ADJECTIVE
having no chance of success *e.g. a futile attempt to calm the storm*
futility NOUN

THESAURUS
abortive: *the abortive coup attempt*
forlorn: *forlorn hopes of future improvement*
unsuccessful: *an unsuccessful bid for independence*
useless: *It was useless to even try.*
vain: *in the vain hope of success*
<<OPPOSITE *successful*

future ['fju:tʃə] **futures** NOUN
1 The future is the period of time after the present.
2 Something that has a future is likely to succeed. *e.g. She sees no future in a modelling career.*
> ADJECTIVE
3 relating to or occurring at a time after the present *e.g. to predict future events*

THESAURUS
approaching: *concerned about the approaching winter*
coming: *in the coming months*
forthcoming: *candidates for the forthcoming elections*
impending: *her impending marriage*
later: *We'll discuss it at a later date.*
prospective: *my prospective employers*
<<OPPOSITE *past*

4 The future tense of a verb is the form used to express something that will happen in the future.

futuristic [,fju:tʃə'rɪstɪk] ADJECTIVE
very modern and strange, as if belonging to a time in the future *e.g. futuristic cars*

fuzz [fʌz] NOUN
1 short fluffy hair
> PLURAL NOUN
2 INFORMAL
The fuzz are the police.

Gg

g
an abbreviation for 'grams'

gabble ['gæbᵊl] **gabbles, gabbling, gabbled** VERB
If you gabble, you talk so fast that it is difficult for people to understand you.

gable ['geɪbᵊl] **gables** NOUN
Gables are the triangular parts at the top of the outside walls at each end of a house.

gadget ['gædʒɪt] **gadgets** NOUN
a small machine or tool
gadgetry NOUN

● THESAURUS
appliance: *Switch off all electrical appliances when they're not in use.*
device: *a device that warns you when the batteries need changing*
machine: *a machine for slicing vegetables*
tool: *a tool for cutting wood, metal or plastic*

Gaelic ['geɪlɪk] NOUN
a language spoken in some parts of Scotland and Ireland

gaffe [gæf] **gaffes** NOUN
a social blunder or mistake

gaffer ['gæfə] **gaffers** NOUN; INFORMAL
a boss

gag [gæg] **gags, gagging, gagged** NOUN
1 a strip of cloth that is tied round someone's mouth to stop them speaking

2 INFORMAL
a joke told by a comedian

> VERB
3 To gag someone means to put a gag round their mouth.

4 If you gag, you choke and nearly vomit.

gaggle ['gægᵊl] **gaggles** NOUN
1 a group of geese

2 INFORMAL
a noisy group *e.g. a gaggle of schoolboys*
[WORD HISTORY: from Old German GAGEN meaning 'to cry like a goose']

gaiety ['geɪətɪ] NOUN
liveliness and fun

gaily ['geɪlɪ] ADVERB
in a happy and cheerful way

gain [geɪn] **gains, gaining, gained** VERB
1 If you gain something, you get it gradually. *e.g. I spent years at night school trying to gain qualifications.*

● THESAURUS
achieve: *Achieving our goals makes us feel good.*
acquire: *Companies should reward workers for acquiring more skills.*
earn: *She has earned the respect of the world's top women cyclists.*
obtain: *You would need to obtain permission to copy the design.*
secure: *He failed to secure enough votes for outright victory.*
win: *The long-term aim is to win promotion.*

2 If you gain from a situation, you get some advantage from it.

● THESAURUS
benefit: *Both sides have benefited from the talks.*
profit: *Frankie is now profiting from his crimes.*

3 If you gain on someone, you gradually catch them up.

> NOUN
4 an increase *e.g. a gain in speed*

● THESAURUS
advance: *advances in computer technology*
growth: *The area has seen a rapid population growth.*
improvement: *a major improvement in standards*
increase: *an increase of 7% in visitors to the UK*
rise: *a 3% rise in electricity prices*

5 an advantage that you get for yourself *e.g. People use whatever influence they have for personal gain.*

gait [geɪt] **gaits** NOUN
Someone's gait is their way of walking. *e.g. an awkward gait*

gala ['gɑːlə] **galas** NOUN
a special public celebration or performance *e.g. the Olympics' opening gala*

galah [gəˈlɑː] **galahs** NOUN
1 an Australian cockatoo with a pink breast and a grey back and wings

2 INFORMAL
In Australian English, a galah is also a stupid person.

galaxy ['gæləksɪ] **galaxies** NOUN
an enormous group of stars that extends over many millions of miles
galactic ADJECTIVE

gale [geɪl] **gales** NOUN
an extremely strong wind

gall [gɔːl] **galls, galling, galled** NOUN
1 If someone has the gall to do something, they have enough courage or impudence to do it. *e.g. He even has the gall to visit her.*
> VERB
2 If something galls you, it makes you extremely annoyed.

gallant ['gælənt] ADJECTIVE
1 brave and honourable *e.g. They have put up a gallant fight for pensioners' rights.*
2 polite and considerate towards women
gallantly ADVERB, **gallantry** NOUN

gall bladder gall bladders NOUN
an organ in your body which stores bile and which is next to your liver

galleon ['gælɪən] **galleons** NOUN
a large sailing ship used in the sixteenth and seventeenth centuries

gallery ['gælərɪ] **galleries** NOUN
1 (ART) a building or room where works of art are shown
2 In a theatre or large hall, the gallery is a raised area at the back or sides. *e.g. the public gallery in Parliament*

galley ['gælɪ] **galleys** NOUN
1 a kitchen in a ship or aircraft
2 a ship, driven by oars, used in ancient and medieval times

Gallic ['gælɪk] ADJECTIVE; A FORMAL OR LITERARY WORD
French.

gallon ['gælən] **gallons** NOUN
a unit of liquid volume equal to eight pints or about 4.55 litres

gallop ['gæləp] **gallops, galloping, galloped** VERB
1 When a horse gallops, it runs very fast, so that during each stride all four feet are off the ground at the same time.
> NOUN
2 a very fast run

gallows ['gæləʊz] NOUN
A gallows is a framework on which criminals used to be hanged.

gallstone ['gɔːl,stəʊn] **gallstones** NOUN
a small painful lump that can develop in your gall bladder

galore [gə'lɔː] ADJECTIVE
in very large numbers *e.g. chocolates galore*
[WORD HISTORY: from Irish Gaelic GO LEÓR meaning 'to sufficiency']

galoshes [gə'lɒʃɪz] PLURAL NOUN
Galoshes are waterproof rubber shoes which you wear over your ordinary shoes to stop them getting wet.

galvanized or **galvanised** ['gælvə,naɪzd] ADJECTIVE
Galvanized metal has been coated with zinc by an electrical process to protect it from rust.

gambit ['gæmbɪt] **gambits** NOUN
something which someone does to gain an advantage in a situation *e.g. Commentators are calling the plan a clever political gambit.*
[WORD HISTORY: from Italian GAMBETTO meaning 'a tripping up']

gamble ['gæmbəl] **gambles, gambling, gambled** VERB
1 When people gamble, they bet money on the result of a game or race.
⬤ THESAURUS
back: *I backed Germany to win 1-0.*
bet: *He bet them 500 pounds they would lose.*
2 If you gamble something, you risk losing it in the hope of gaining an advantage. *e.g. The company gambled everything on the new factory.*
⬤ THESAURUS
chance: *Armstrong chanced a gallop to the water.*
risk: *One of his daughters risked everything to join him in exile.*
stake: *He has staked his reputation on the outcome.*

> NOUN
3 If you take a gamble, you take a risk in the hope of gaining an advantage.
gambler NOUN, **gambling** NOUN
⬤ THESAURUS
chance: *You take a chance on the weather when you holiday in the UK.*
lottery: *Robinson described the final as a bit of a lottery.*
risk: *How much risk are you prepared to take?*

game [geɪm] **games** NOUN
1 an enjoyable activity with a set of rules which is played by individuals or teams against each other
⬤ THESAURUS
clash: *the clash between Australia and the West Indies*
contest: *The rain spoiled a good contest.*
match: *a football match*

g

2 an enjoyable imaginative activity played by small children *e.g. childhood games of cowboys and Indians*

3 You might describe something as a game when it is designed to gain advantage. *e.g. the political game*

4 Game is wild animals or birds that are hunted for sport or for food.

> PLURAL NOUN

5 Games are sports played at school or in a competition.

> ADJECTIVE

6 INFORMAL

Someone who is game is willing to try something unusual or difficult.

gamely ADVERB

gamekeeper ['geɪmˌkiːpə] **gamekeepers** NOUN

a person employed to look after game animals and birds on a country estate

gammon ['gæmən] NOUN

Gammon is cured meat from a pig, similar to bacon.

gamut ['gæmət] NOUN; FORMAL

The gamut of something is the whole range of things that can be included in it. *e.g. the whole gamut of human emotions*

gander ['gændə] **ganders** NOUN

a male goose

gang [gæŋ] **gangs, ganging, ganged** NOUN

1 a group of people who join together for some purpose, for example to commit a crime

> VERB

2 INFORMAL

If people gang up on you, they join together to oppose you.

gangplank ['gæŋˌplæŋk] **gangplanks** NOUN

a plank used for boarding and leaving a ship or boat

gangrene ['gæŋgriːn] NOUN

Gangrene is decay in the tissues of part of the body, caused by inadequate blood supply.

gangrenous ADJECTIVE

[WORD HISTORY: from Greek GANGRAINA meaning 'ulcer' or 'festering sore']

gangster ['gæŋstə] **gangsters** NOUN

a violent criminal who is a member of a gang

gannet ['gænɪt] **gannets** NOUN

a large sea bird which dives to catch fish

gaol [dʒeɪl] another spelling of **jail**

gap [gæp] **gaps** NOUN

1 a space between two things or a hole in something solid

◉ THESAURUS

break: *stars twinkling between the breaks in the clouds*

chink: *All the walls have wide chinks in them.*

crack: *a crack in the curtains*

hole: *a hole in the wall*

opening: *an opening in the trees*

space: *the space between their car and the one in front*

2 a period of time

◉ THESAURUS

hiatus: formal *The shop is open again after a two year hiatus.*

interlude: *a happy interlude in the Kents' life*

interval: *There was a long interval of silence.*

lull: *a lull in the conversation*

pause: *Then, after a pause, he goes on.*

3 A gap between things, people, or ideas is a great difference between them. *e.g. the gap between fantasy and reality*

◉ THESAURUS

difference: *He denied there were any major differences between them.*

disparity: formal *disparities between poor and wealthy school districts*

inconsistency: *There were major inconsistencies in his evidence.*

gape [geɪp] **gapes, gaping, gaped** VERB

1 If you gape at someone or something, you stare at them with your mouth open in surprise.

2 Something that gapes is wide open. *e.g. gaping holes in the wall*

garage ['gærɑːʒ] **garages** NOUN

1 a building where a car can be kept

2 a place where cars are repaired and where petrol is sold

garb [gɑːb] NOUN; FORMAL

Someone's garb is their clothes. *e.g. his usual garb of a dark suit*

garbage ['gɑːbɪdʒ] NOUN

1 Garbage is rubbish, especially household rubbish.

◉ THESAURUS

debris: *screws, bolts and other debris from a scrapyard*

junk: informal *What are you going to do with all that junk?*

litter: *If you see litter in the corridor, pick it up.*

refuse: formal *refuse collection and street cleaning*

rubbish: *household rubbish*

trash: *I forgot to take out the trash.*

waste: *industrial waste*

2 If you say something is garbage, you mean it is nonsense.

[WORD HISTORY: from Anglo-French GARBELAGE

meaning 'removal of discarded matter']

THESAURUS

drivel: *What absolute drivel!*
gibberish: *a politician talking gibberish*
nonsense: *all that poetic nonsense about love*
rubbish: *He's talking rubbish.*

garbled ['gɑːbªld] ADJECTIVE
Garbled messages are jumbled and the details
may be wrong.

THESAURUS

confused: *the latest twist in a murky and confused story*
distorted: *a distorted version of what was said*
incomprehensible: *Her speech was incomprehensible.*
jumbled: *his jumbled account of how Jack had been hired*
unintelligible: *He muttered something unintelligible.*

garden ['gɑːdªn] **gardens** NOUN
1 an area of land next to a house, where flowers,
fruit, or vegetables are grown

> PLURAL NOUN
2 Gardens are a type of park in a town or around a
large house.
gardening NOUN

gardener ['gɑːdnə] **gardeners** NOUN
a person who looks after a garden as a job or as a
hobby

gargle ['gɑːgªl] **gargles, gargling, gargled**
VERB
When you gargle, you rinse the back of your
throat by putting some liquid in your mouth and
making a bubbling sound without swallowing.

gargoyle ['gɑːgɔɪl] **gargoyles** NOUN
a stone carving below the roof of an old building,
in the shape of an ugly person or animal and
often having a water spout at the mouth

garish ['gɛərɪʃ] ADJECTIVE
bright and harsh to look at *e.g. garish bright red
boots*

garland ['gɑːlənd] **garlands** NOUN
a circle of flowers and leaves which is worn
around the neck or head

garlic ['gɑːlɪk] NOUN
Garlic is the small white bulb of an onion-like
plant which has a strong taste and smell and is
used in cooking.

garment ['gɑːmənt] **garments** NOUN
a piece of clothing

garnet ['gɑːnɪt] **garnets** NOUN
a type of gemstone, usually red in colour

garnish ['gɑːnɪʃ] **garnishes, garnishing,
garnished** NOUN

1 something such as a a sprig of parsley, that is
used in cooking for decoration

> VERB
2 To garnish food means to decorate it with a
garnish.

garret ['gærɪt] **garrets** NOUN
an attic

garrison ['gærɪsªn] **garrisons** NOUN
a group of soldiers stationed in a town in order to
guard it; also used of the buildings in which these
soldiers live

garrotte [gə'rɒt] **garrottes, garrotting,
garrotted;** also spelt garotte VERB
To garrotte someone means to strangle them
with a piece of wire.

garter ['gɑːtə] **garters** NOUN
a piece of elastic worn round the top of a
stocking to hold it up

gas [gæs] **gases; gasses, gassing, gassed**
NOUN
1 any airlike substance that is not liquid or solid,
such as oxygen or the gas used as a fuel in
heating
2 In American English, gas is petrol.

> VERB
3 To gas people or animals means to kill them
with poisonous gas.

The plural of the noun *gas* is *gases*. The verb
forms of *gas* are spelt with a double *s*

gas chamber gas chambers NOUN
a room in which people or animals are killed with
poisonous gas

gash [gæʃ] **gashes, gashing, gashed** NOUN
1 a long, deep cut

> VERB
2 If you gash something, you make a long, deep
cut in it.

gas mask gas masks NOUN
a large mask with special filters attached which
people wear over their face to protect them from
poisonous gas

gasoline ['gæsə,liːn] NOUN
In American English, gasoline is petrol.

gasp [gɑːsp] **gasps, gasping, gasped** VERB
1 If you gasp, you quickly draw in your breath
through your mouth because you are surprised
or in pain.

THESAURUS

choke: *People began to choke as smoke filled the air.*
gulp: *She gulped air into her lungs.*
pant: *Amy climbed rapidly until she was panting
with the effort.*

g

puff: *I could see he was unfit because he was puffing.*

> NOUN

2 a sharp intake of breath through the mouth

THESAURUS

gulp: *I took in a large gulp of air.*
pant: *Her breath came in pants.*
puff: *He blew out a little puff of air.*

gastric ['gæstrɪk] ADJECTIVE
occurring in the stomach or involving the
stomach *e.g. gastric pain*

gate [geɪt] **gates** NOUN
1 a barrier which can open and shut and is used
to close the entrance to a garden or field
2 The gate at a sports event is the number of
people who have attended it.

gateau ['gætəʊ] **gateaux** NOUN
a rich layered cake with cream in it

gatecrash ['geɪt,kræʃ] **gatecrashes,
gatecrashing, gatecrashed** VERB
If you gatecrash a party, you go to it when you
have not been invited.

gateway ['geɪt,weɪ] **gateways** NOUN
1 an entrance through a wall or fence where
there is a gate
2 Something that is considered to be the
entrance to a larger or more important thing can
be described as the gateway to the larger thing.
e.g. New York is the great gateway to America.

gather ['gæðə] **gathers, gathering,
gathered** VERB
1 When people gather, they come together in a
group.

THESAURUS

assemble: *a place for students to assemble between
classes*
congregate: *Youngsters love to congregate here in
the evenings.*
flock: *The criticisms will not stop people flocking to
see the film.*
mass: *The General was massing his troops for a
counterattack.*
round up: *The police rounded up a number of
suspects.*
<<OPPOSITE *scatter*

2 If you gather a number of things, you bring
them together in one place.

THESAURUS

accumulate: *In five years it has accumulated a huge
debt.*
amass: *She has amassed a personal fortune of $38
million.*
collect: *1.5 million signatures have been collected.*
hoard: *They've begun to hoard food and gasoline.*

stockpile: *People are stockpiling food for the coming
winter.*

3 If something gathers speed or strength, it gets
faster or stronger.

4 If you gather something, you learn it, often
from what someone says.

THESAURUS

assume: *I assume the eggs are fresh.*
conclude: *He concluded that Oswald was somewhat
abnormal.*
hear: *I heard that he was forced to resign.*
learn: *She wasn't surprised to learn that he was
involved.*
understand: *I understand that he's just taken early
retirement.*

gathering ['gæðərɪŋ] **gatherings** NOUN
a meeting of people who have come together for
a particular purpose

THESAURUS

assembly: *an assembly of party members*
congregation: *The congregation sang hymns and
said prayers.*
get-together: informal *family get-togethers*
meeting: *Can we have a meeting to discuss that?*
rally: *a pre-election rally*

gauche [gəʊʃ] ADJECTIVE; FORMAL
socially awkward
[WORD HISTORY: from French GAUCHE meaning
'left-handed']

gaudy ['gɔːdɪ] **gaudier, gaudiest** ADJECTIVE
very colourful in a vulgar way

THESAURUS

bright: *fake fur, dyed in bright colours*
flashy: *women in flashy satin suits*
garish: *They climbed the garish purple-carpeted
stairs.*
loud: *a loud checked shirt*
showy: *He favoured large showy flowers.*
tacky: informal *tacky red sunglasses*
vulgar: *I think it's a very vulgar house.*

gauge [geɪdʒ] **gauges, gauging, gauged**
VERB
1 If you gauge something, you estimate it or
calculate it. *e.g. He gauged the wind at over 30
knots.*

> NOUN

2 a piece of equipment that measures the
amount of something *e.g. a rain gauge*

3 something that is used as a standard by which
you judge a situation *e.g. They see profit as a gauge
of efficiency.*

4 On railways, the gauge is the distance between
the two rails on a railway line.

gaunt [gɔːnt] ADJECTIVE
A person who looks gaunt is thin and bony.

gauntlet ['gɔːntlɪt] **gauntlets** NOUN

1 Gauntlets are long thick gloves worn for protection, for example by motorcyclists.

> PHRASE

2 If you **throw down the gauntlet**, you challenge someone.

3 If you **run the gauntlet**, you have an unpleasant experience in which you are attacked or criticized by people.

gave [geɪv] the past tense of **give**

gay [geɪ] **gayer, gayest; gays** ADJECTIVE

1 Someone who is gay is homosexual.

2 OLD-FASHIONED
Gay people or places are lively and full of fun.

> NOUN

3 a homosexual person

The most common meaning of *gay* now is 'homosexual'. In some older books it may have its old-fashioned meaning of 'lively and full of fun'. The noun *gaiety* is related to this older meaning of *gay*. The noun that means 'the state of being homosexual' is *gayness*

gaze [geɪz] **gazes, gazing, gazed** VERB
If you gaze at something, you look steadily at it for a long time.

gazelle [gə'zɛl] **gazelles** NOUN
a small antelope found in Africa and Asia

gazette [gə'zɛt] **gazettes** NOUN
a newspaper or journal

GB an abbreviation for **Great Britain**

GCSE GCSEs
In Britain, the GCSE is an examination taken by school students aged fifteen and sixteen. GCSE is an abbreviation for 'General Certificate of Secondary Education'.

gear [gɪə] **gears, gearing, geared** NOUN

1 a piece of machinery which controls the rate at which energy is converted into movement. Gears in vehicles control the speed and power of the vehicle

2 The gear for an activity is the clothes and equipment that you need for it.

> VERB

3 If someone or something is geared to a particular event or purpose, they are prepared for it.

geek [giːk] **geeks** > NOUN; INFORMAL
a person who is obsessive about an interest or hobby, especially computers

geese [giːs] the plural of **goose**

gel [dʒɛl] **gels, gelling, gelled** NOUN

1 a smooth soft jelly-like substance *e.g. shower gel*

> VERB

2 If a liquid gels, it turns into a gel.

3 If a vague thought or plan gels, it becomes more definite.

gelatine or **gelatin** ['dʒɛlə,tiːn] or ['dʒɛlətɪn] NOUN
a clear tasteless substance, obtained from meat and bones, used to make liquids firm and jelly-like

gelding ['gɛldɪŋ] **geldings** NOUN
a horse which has been castrated

gem [dʒɛm] **gems** NOUN

1 a jewel or precious stone

2 You can describe something or someone that is extremely good or beautiful as a gem. *e.g. A gem of a novel.*

Gemini ['dʒɛmɪ,naɪ] NOUN
Gemini is the third sign of the zodiac, represented by a pair of twins. People born between May 21st and June 20th are born under this sign.

gemsbok ['gɛmz,bʌk] **gemsbok** or **gemsboks** also spelt **gemsbuck** NOUN
In South African English, a gemsbok is an oryx, a type of large antelope with straight horns.

gen [dʒɛn] NOUN; INFORMAL
The gen on something is information about it.

gender ['dʒɛndə] **genders** NOUN

1 (PSHE) Gender is the sex of a person or animal. *e.g. the female gender*

2 the classification of nouns as masculine, feminine, and neuter in certain languages

gene [dʒiːn] **genes** NOUN
one of the parts of a living cell which controls the physical characteristics of an organism and which are passed on from one generation to the next

general ['dʒɛnərəl] **generals** ADJECTIVE

1 relating to the whole of something or to most things in a group *e.g. your general health*

● THESAURUS
broad: *a broad outline of the Society's development*
comprehensive: *a comprehensive guide to the region*
overall: *The overall quality of pupils' work had shown a marked improvement.*
<<OPPOSITE *specific*

2 true, suitable, or relevant in most situations *e.g. the general truth of science*

● THESAURUS
accepted: *the accepted version of events*
broad: *a film with broad appeal*
common: *Such behaviour is common to all young people.*

universal: *Music and sports programmes have a universal appeal.*
widespread: *The proposals have attracted widespread support.*
<<OPPOSITE *special*

3 including or involving a wide range of different things *e.g. a general hospital*

4 having complete responsibility over a wide area of work or a large number of people *e.g. the general secretary*

> NOUN
5 an army officer of very high rank

> PHRASE
6 In general means usually.
generally ADVERB

general election **general elections** NOUN
an election for a new government, which all the people of a country may vote in

generalize ['dʒɛnrə,laɪz] **generalizes, generalizing, generalized;** also spelt **generalise** VERB
To generalize means to say that something is true in most cases, ignoring minor details.
generalization NOUN

general practitioner **general practitioners** NOUN
a doctor who works in the community rather than in a hospital

generate ['dʒɛnə,reɪt] **generates, generating, generated** VERB
To generate something means to create or produce it. *e.g. using wind power to generate electricity*

generation [,dʒɛnə'reɪʃən] **generations** NOUN
all the people of about the same age; also the period of time between one generation and the next, usually considered to be about 25-30 years

generator ['dʒɛnə,reɪtə] **generators** NOUN
a machine which produces electricity from another form of energy such as wind or water power

generic [dʒɪ'nɛrɪk] ADJECTIVE
A generic term is a name that applies to all the members of a group of similar things.

generosity [,dʒɛnə'rɒsɪti] NOUN
the willingness to give money, time, or help

● THESAURUS
benevolence: *Banks are not known for their benevolence.*
charity: *private acts of charity*
kindness: *We have been treated with such kindness by everybody.*
<<OPPOSITE *meanness*

generous ['dʒɛnərəs] ADJECTIVE
1 (PSHE) A generous person is very willing to give money or time.
● THESAURUS
charitable: *Individuals can be charitable and help their neighbours.*
hospitable: *He was very hospitable to me when I came to New York.*
kind: *She is warm-hearted and kind to everyone.*
lavish: *The Princess received a number of lavish gifts from her hosts.*
liberal: *Don't be too liberal with your spending.*
<<OPPOSITE *mean*

2 Something that is generous is very large. *e.g. a generous waist*
generously ADVERB, **generosity** NOUN (PSHE)
● THESAURUS
abundant: *an abundant supply of hot food*
ample: *There is ample space for a good-sized kitchen.*
plentiful: *a plentiful supply of beer*
<<OPPOSITE *meagre*

genesis ['dʒɛnɪsɪs] NOUN; FORMAL
The genesis of something is its beginning.

genetics [dʒɪ'nɛtɪks] NOUN
Genetics is the science of the way that characteristics are passed on from generation to generation by means of genes.
genetic ADJECTIVE, **genetically** ADVERB

genial ['dʒiːnjəl] ADJECTIVE
cheerful, friendly, and kind
genially ADVERB

genie ['dʒiːnɪ] **genies** NOUN
a magical being that obeys the wishes of the person who controls it
[WORD HISTORY: from Arabic JINNI meaning 'demon']

genitals ['dʒɛnɪtᵊlz] PLURAL NOUN
The genitals are the reproductive organs. The technical name is genitalia.
genital ADJECTIVE

genius ['dʒiːnɪəs] **geniuses** NOUN
1 a highly intelligent, creative, or talented person
● THESAURUS
brain: *the financial brain behind the company*
master: *Spiro Rosakis is a master of his craft.*
mastermind: *the mastermind of the plot to kill the ex-prime minister*
virtuoso: *The man is a virtuoso of pop music.*

2 Genius is great intelligence, creativity, or talent. *e.g. a poet of genius*
● THESAURUS
brains: *She has brains as well as beauty.*
brilliance: *his brilliance as a director*
intellect: *people of great intellect*

genocide ['dʒɛnəʊˌsaɪd] NOUN; FORMAL
Genocide is the systematic murder of all members of a particular race or group.

genome ['dʒiːnəʊm] **genomes** NOUN
all of the genes contained in a single cell of an organism

genre ['ʒɑːnrə] **genres** NOUN
(ENGLISH AND LIBRARY) FORMAL
a particular style in literature or art

genteel [dʒɛn'tiːl] ADJECTIVE
very polite and refined

Gentile ['dʒɛntaɪl] **Gentiles** NOUN
a person who is not Jewish

gentility [dʒɛn'tɪlɪtɪ] NOUN
Gentility is excessive politeness and refinement.

gentle ['dʒɛntəl] **gentler, gentlest**
ADJECTIVE
mild and calm; not violent or rough *e.g. a gentle man*
gently ADVERB, **gentleness** NOUN

● THESAURUS
benign: *a good-looking chap with a benign expression*
kind: *I fell in love with him because of his kind nature.*
kindly: *a kindly old gentleman*
meek: *He was a meek, mild-mannered fellow.*
mild: *Alexis was quiet, mild and happy-go-lucky.*
placid: *a look of impatience on her normally placid face*
soft: *She had a very soft heart.*
tender: *Her voice was tender.*
<<OPPOSITE *cruel*

gentleman ['dʒɛntəlmən] **gentlemen**
NOUN
a man who is polite and well-educated; also a polite way of referring to any man
gentlemanly ADJECTIVE

gentry ['dʒɛntrɪ] PLURAL NOUN
The gentry are people from the upper classes.

genuine ['dʒɛnjʊɪn] ADJECTIVE
1 real and not false or pretend *e.g. a genuine smile... genuine silver*

● THESAURUS
authentic: *an authentic French recipe*
bona fide: *We are happy to donate to bona fide charities.*
dinkum: Australian and New Zealand; informal *They are all dinkum stolen bank notes.*
real: *a real Rembrandt*
<<OPPOSITE *fake*

2 A genuine person is sincere and honest.
genuinely ADVERB, **genuineness** NOUN

genus ['dʒiːnəs] **genera** NOUN
In biology, a genus is a class of animals or closely related plants.

geo- PREFIX
'Geo-' means 'earth' *e.g. geography... geologist*
[WORD HISTORY: from Greek gē MEANING 'EARTH']

geography [dʒɪ'ɒgrəfɪ] NOUN
the study of the physical features of the earth, together with the climate, natural resources and population in different parts of the world
geographic or **geographical** ADJECTIVE,
geographically ADVERB

geology [dʒɪ'ɒlədʒɪ] NOUN
the study of the earth's structure, especially the layers of rock and soil that make up the surface of the earth
geological ADJECTIVE, **geologist** NOUN

geometric or **geometrical** [ˌdʒɪə'mɛtrɪk] or [ˌdʒɪə'mɛtrɪkəl] ADJECTIVE
1 consisting of regular lines and shapes, such as squares, triangles, and circles *e.g. bold geometric designs*

2 involving geometry

geometry [dʒɪ'ɒmɪtrɪ] NOUN
Geometry is the branch of mathematics that deals with lines, angles, curves, and spaces.

Georgian ['dʒɔːdʒən] ADJECTIVE
belonging to or typical of the time from 1714 to 1830, when George I to George IV reigned in Britain

geranium [dʒɪ'reɪnɪəm] **geraniums** NOUN
a garden plant with red, pink, or white flowers

gerbil ['dʒɜːbɪl] **gerbils** NOUN
a small rodent with long back legs, often kept as a pet

geriatric [ˌdʒɛrɪ'ætrɪk] ADJECTIVE
1 relating to the medical care of old people *e.g. a geriatric nurse*

2 Someone or something that is geriatric is very old. *e.g. a geriatric donkey*

> NOUN
3 an old person, especially as a patient
geriatrics NOUN

germ [dʒɜːm] **germs** NOUN
1 a very small organism that causes disease

2 FORMAL The germ of an idea or plan is the beginning of it.

German ['dʒɜːmən] **Germans** ADJECTIVE
1 belonging or relating to Germany

> NOUN
2 someone who comes from Germany

3 German is the main language spoken in Germany and Austria and is also spoken by many people in Switzerland.

Germanic [dʒɜː'mænɪk] ADJECTIVE

g

1 typical of Germany or the German people

2 The Germanic group of languages includes English, Dutch, German, Danish, Swedish, and Norwegian.

German measles NOUN
German measles is a contagious disease that gives you a sore throat and red spots.

germinate ['dʒɜːmɪˌneɪt] **germinates, germinating, germinated** VERB
1 When a seed germinates, it starts to grow.
2 When an idea or plan germinates, it starts to develop.
germination NOUN

gerrymander ['dʒɛrɪˌmændə] **gerrymanders, gerrymandering, gerrymandered** VERB
To gerrymander is to change political boundaries in an area so that a particular party or politician gets a bigger share of votes in an election.

gestation [dʒɛˈsteɪʃən] NOUN; TECHNICAL
Gestation is the time during which a foetus is growing inside its mother's womb.

gesticulate [dʒɛˈstɪkjʊˌleɪt] **gesticulates, gesticulating, gesticulated** VERB
If you gesticulate, you move your hands and arms around while you are talking.
gesticulation NOUN

gesture ['dʒɛstʃə] **gestures, gesturing, gestured** NOUN
1 a movement of your hands or head that conveys a message or feeling
2 an action symbolizing something e.g. a gesture of support
> VERB
3 If you gesture, you move your hands or head in order to communicate a message or feeling.

get see page 373 for Word Web

getaway ['gɛtəˌweɪ] **getaways** NOUN
an escape made by criminals

get-together ['gɛttəˌgɛðə] **get-togethers** NOUN; INFORMAL
an informal meeting or party

geyser ['giːzə] **geysers** NOUN
a spring through which hot water and steam gush up in spurts
[WORD HISTORY: from Old Norse GEYSA meaning 'to gush']

Ghanaian [gɑːˈneɪən] **Ghanaians** ADJECTIVE
1 belonging or relating to Ghana
> NOUN
2 someone who comes from Ghana

ghastly ['gɑːstlɪ] **ghastlier, ghastliest** ADJECTIVE
extremely horrible and unpleasant e.g. a ghastly crime... ghastly food

gherkin ['gɜːkɪn] **gherkins** NOUN
a small pickled cucumber

ghetto ['gɛtəʊ] **ghettoes** or **ghettos** NOUN
a part of a city where many poor people of a particular race live
[WORD HISTORY: from Italian BORGHETTO meaning 'settlement outside the city walls']

ghost [gəʊst] **ghosts** NOUN
the spirit of a dead person, believed to haunt people or places
● THESAURUS
apparition: She felt as if she were seeing a ghostly apparition.
phantom: She was relentlessly pursued by a grossly disfigured phantom.
spectre: The Tower is said to be haunted by the spectre of Anne Boleyn.
spirit: the spirits of our dead ancestors

ghoulish ['guːlɪʃ] ADJECTIVE
very interested in unpleasant things such as death and murder

giant ['dʒaɪənt] **giants** NOUN
1 a huge person in a myth or legend
> ADJECTIVE
2 much larger than other similar things e.g. giant prawns... a giant wave

gibberish ['dʒɪbərɪʃ] NOUN
Gibberish is speech that makes no sense at all.

gibbon ['gɪbᵊn] **gibbons** NOUN
an ape with very long arms

gibe [dʒaɪb] **gibes**; also spelt **jibe** NOUN
an insulting remark

gidday [gəˈdeɪ] INTERJECTION AN AUSTRALIAN AND NEW ZEALAND TERM
hello
● THESAURUS
hello: Hello, Trish. Glad you could make it.
hi: informal Hi, how are you doing?
good morning: formal Good morning, class.
good afternoon: formal Good afternoon, Miss Bates.
good evening: formal Good evening, ladies and gentlemen!

giddy ['gɪdɪ] **giddier, giddiest** ADJECTIVE
If you feel giddy, you feel unsteady on your feet usually because you are ill.
giddily ADVERB

gift [gɪft] **gifts** NOUN
1 a present
● THESAURUS
bequest: formal They received a bequest of $310,000.

1 VERB

If you get something, you fetch it or are
given it *eg: I'll get us all a cup of coffee; I got
your message.*

● THESAURUS

acquire: *I have recently acquired a new
camera.*

fetch: *Sylvia fetched a towel from the
bathroom.*

obtain: *Evans was trying to obtain a false
passport.*

procure (formal): *It remained very difficult
to procure food.*

receive: *I received your letter of November 7.*

secure (formal): *He failed to secure enough
votes for outright victory.*

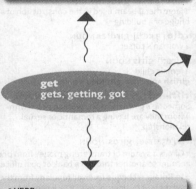

get
gets, getting, got

2 VERB

'Get' often means the same as 'become'
eg: People draw the curtains once it gets dark.

● THESAURUS

become: *The wind became stronger.*

grow: *He grew to love his work.*

turn: *The leaves have turned golden-brown.*

3 VERB

to come into possession of something

● THESAURUS

acquire: *The film company wanted to
acquire the rights to the book.*

gain: *Students can gain valuable experience
by working on the school newspaper*

obtain: *The man was trying to obtain a false
passport and other documents.*

receive: *They will receive their awards at a
ceremony in Stockholm.*

4 VERB

to catch (an illness)

● THESAURUS

catch: *The more stress you are under, the
more likely you are to catch a cold.*

contract: *He contracted yellow fever on
holiday.*

develop: *A sharp ache started to develop in
her arm.*

succumb to: *She refused to succumb to the
illness.*

go down with: *The class seemed to go down
with the cold on the same day.*

come down with: *I feel like I'm about to
come down with that stomach bug you had
last week.*

g

bonsela: South African *a generous bonsela*
contribution: *companies that make charitable contributions*
donation: *donations of food and clothing for victims of the hurricane*
legacy: *What about the legacy from your uncle?*
present: *This book would make a great Christmas present.*

2 a natural skill or ability *e.g. a gift for comedy*

● THESAURUS
ability: *It's obvious he has an exceptional ability.*
aptitude: *She realised she had an aptitude for writing.*
flair: *Tony found he had a real flair for design.*
talent: *Both her children have a talent for music.*

gifted ['gɪftɪd] ADJECTIVE
having a special ability *e.g. gifted tennis players*

gig [gɪg] **gigs** NOUN
a rock or jazz concert

gigantic [dʒaɪ'gæntɪk] ADJECTIVE
extremely large

giggle ['gɪgəl] **giggles, giggling, giggled**
VERB
1 To giggle means to laugh in a nervous or embarrassed way.

> NOUN
2 a short, nervous laugh
giggly ADJECTIVE

gilded ['gɪldɪd] ADJECTIVE
Something which is gilded is covered with a thin layer of gold.

gill [gɪl] **gills** NOUN
1
The gills of a fish are the organs on its sides which it uses for breathing.

2
a unit of liquid volume equal to one quarter of a pint or about 0.142 litres

gilt [gɪlt] **gilts** NOUN
1 a thin layer of gold

> ADJECTIVE
2 covered with a thin layer of gold *e.g. a gilt writing-table*

gimmick ['gɪmɪk] **gimmicks** NOUN
a device that is not really necessary but is used to attract interest *e.g. All pop stars need a good gimmick.*
gimmicky ADJECTIVE

gin [dʒɪn] NOUN
Gin is a strong, colourless alcoholic drink made from grain and juniper berries.

ginger ['dʒɪndʒə] NOUN
1 Ginger is a plant root with a hot, spicy flavour, used in cooking.

> ADJECTIVE
2 bright orange or red *e.g. ginger hair*

gingerbread ['dʒɪndʒə‚brɛd] NOUN
Gingerbread is a sweet, ginger-flavoured cake.

gingerly ['dʒɪndʒəlɪ] ADVERB
If you move gingerly, you move cautiously. *e.g. They walked gingerly down the stairs.*

gingham ['gɪŋəm] NOUN
Gingham is checked cotton cloth.
[WORD HISTORY: from Malay GINGGANG meaning 'striped cloth']

gipsy ['dʒɪpsɪ] another spelling of **gypsy**

giraffe [dʒɪ'rɑːf] **giraffes** NOUN
a tall, four-legged African mammal with a very long neck
[WORD HISTORY: from Arabic ZARAFAH meaning 'giraffe']

girder ['gɜːdə] **girders** NOUN
a large metal beam used in the construction of a bridge or a building

girdle ['gɜːdəl] **girdles** NOUN
a woman's corset

girl [gɜːl] **girls** NOUN
a female child
girlish ADJECTIVE, **girlhood** NOUN

girlfriend ['gɜːl‚frɛnd] **girlfriends** NOUN
Someone's girlfriend is the woman or girl with whom they are having a romantic or sexual relationship.

giro ['dʒaɪrəʊ] **giros** NOUN
1 Giro is a system of transferring money from one account to another through a bank or post office.

2 In Britain, a cheque received regularly from the government by unemployed or sick people.

girth [gɜːθ] NOUN
The girth of something is the measurement round it.

gist [dʒɪst] NOUN
the general meaning or most important points in a piece of writing or speech

give [gɪv] **gives, giving, gave, given** VERB
1 If you give someone something, you hand it to them or provide it for them. *e.g. I gave her a tape... George gave me my job.*

● THESAURUS
award: *The Mayor awarded him a medal.*
deliver: *The Canadians plan to deliver more food to southern Somalia.*
donate: *Others donated second-hand clothes.*
grant: *Permission was granted a few weeks ago.*
hand: *Isabel handed me a glass of orange juice.*
present: *The Queen presented the prizes.*
provide: *The government was not in a position to provide them with food.*

supply: *a contract to supply radar equipment to the Philippines*
<<OPPOSITE take

2 'Give' is also used to express physical actions and speech *e.g. He gave a fierce smile... Rosa gave a lovely performance.*

3 If you give a party or a meal, you are the host at it.

4 If something gives, it collapses under pressure.

THESAURUS
buckle: *His left wrist buckled under the strain.*
cave in: *Half the ceiling caved in.*
collapse: *The roof supports had collapsed.*
give way: *He fell when a ledge gave way beneath him.*
yield: *The handle yielded to her grasp.*

> NOUN
5 If material has give, it will bend or stretch when pulled or put under pressure.

> PHRASE
6 You use **give or take** to indicate that an amount you are mentioning is not exact. *e.g. About two years, give or take a month or so.*

7 If something **gives way** to something else, it is replaced by it.

8 If something **gives way**, it collapses. **give in** VERB

9 If you give in, you admit that you are defeated.

THESAURUS
capitulate: *Cohen capitulated to virtually every demand.*
concede: *Mr Pyke is not prepared to concede defeat.*
submit: *Mrs Jones submitted to an operation on her right knee.*
succumb: *The Minister said his country would never succumb to pressure.*
surrender: *He surrendered to American troops.*
yield: *an enemy who had shown no desire to yield*

give out VERB
10 If something gives out, it stops working. *e.g. The electricity gave out.*

give up VERB
11 If you give something up, you stop doing it. *e.g. I can't give up my job.*

12 If you give up, you admit that you cannot do something.

13 If you give someone up, you let the police know where they are hiding.

given ['gɪvᵊn]
1 the past participle of **give**

> ADJECTIVE
2 fixed or specified *e.g. My style can change at any given moment.*

glacé ['glæsɪ] ADJECTIVE
Glacé fruits are fruits soaked and coated with sugar. *e.g. glacé cherries*

glaciation [ˌgleɪsɪ'eɪʃən] NOUN
In geography, glaciation is the condition of being covered with sheet ice.

glacier ['glæsɪə] **glaciers** NOUN
a huge frozen river of slow-moving ice

glad [glæd] **gladder, gladdest** ADJECTIVE
happy and pleased *e.g. They'll be glad to get away from it all.*
gladly ADVERB, **gladness** NOUN

THESAURUS
delighted: *Frank will be delighted to see you.*
happy: *Jacques is very happy that you are here.*
joyful: *a joyful reunion with his mother*
overjoyed: *Shelley was overjoyed to see me.*
pleased: *They're pleased to be going home.*
<<OPPOSITE sorry

glade [gleɪd] **glades** NOUN
a grassy space in a forest

gladiator ['glædɪˌeɪtə] **gladiators** NOUN
In ancient Rome, gladiators were slaves trained to fight in arenas to provide entertainment.
[WORD HISTORY: from Latin GLADIUS meaning 'sword']

gladiolus [ˌglædɪ'əʊləs] **gladioli** NOUN
a garden plant with spikes of brightly coloured flowers on a long stem

glamour ['glæmə] NOUN
The glamour of a fashionable or attractive person or place is the charm and excitement that they have. *e.g. the glamour of Paris*
glamorous ADJECTIVE

glance [glɑːns] **glances, glancing, glanced** VERB
1 If you glance at something, you look at it quickly.

THESAURUS
glimpse: *I soon glimpsed the doctor in his garden.*
look: *Bethan looked quickly at the elegant people around her.*
peek: *She had peeked at him through a crack in the wall.*
peep: *Now and then she peeped to see if he was noticing her.*
scan: *She scanned the advertisement pages of the newspaper.*

2 If one object glances off another, it hits it at an angle and bounces away in another direction.

THESAURUS
bounce: *The ball bounced off the opposite post.*
brush: *She brushed her lips across Michael's cheek.*
skim: *pebbles skimming across the water*

> NOUN
3 a quick look

THESAURUS
glimpse: *They caught a glimpse of their hero.*

g

look: *Lucille took a last look in the mirror.*
peek: *Could I just have another quick peek at the bedroom?*
peep: *Would you take a peep out of the window?*

gland [glænd] **glands** NOUN
an organ in your body, such as the thyroid gland and the sweat glands, which either produce chemical substances for your body to use, or which help to get rid of waste products from your body
glandular ADJECTIVE

glare [glɛə] **glares, glaring, glared** VERB
1 If you glare at someone, you look at them angrily.

● THESAURUS
frown: *She looked up to see Vic frowning at her.*
glower: *He glowered at me but said nothing.*
scowl: *Robert scowled, and slammed the door behind him.*

> NOUN
2 a hard, angry look

● THESAURUS
frown: *There was a deep frown on the boy's face.*
scowl: *Chris met the remark with a scowl.*

3 Glare is extremely bright light.

● THESAURUS
blaze: *There was a sudden blaze of light.*
glow: *the glow of the fire*

glass [glɑːs] **glasses** NOUN
1 Glass is a hard, transparent substance that is easily broken, used to make windows and bottles.

2 a container for drinking out of, made from glass

glasses ['glɑːsɪz] PLURAL NOUN
Glasses are two lenses in a frame, which some people wear over their eyes to improve their eyesight.

glassy ['glɑːsɪ] ADJECTIVE
1 smooth and shiny like glass *e.g. glassy water*

2 A glassy look shows no feeling or expression.

glaze [gleɪz] **glazes, glazing, glazed** NOUN
1 A glaze on pottery or on food is a smooth shiny surface.

> VERB
2 To glaze pottery or food means to cover it with a glaze.

3 To glaze a window means to fit a sheet of glass into a window frame.

glaze over VERB
4 If your eyes glaze over, they lose all expression, usually because you are bored.

glazed [gleɪzd] ADJECTIVE
Someone who has a glazed expression looks bored.

gleam [gliːm] **gleams, gleaming, gleamed**
VERB
1 If something gleams, it shines and reflects light.

> NOUN
2 a pale shining light

glean [gliːn] **gleans, gleaning, gleaned**
VERB
To glean information means to collect it from various sources.

glee [gliː] NOUN; OLD-FASHIONED, INFORMAL
Glee is joy and delight.
gleeful ADJECTIVE, **gleefully** ADVERB

glen [glɛn] **glens** NOUN
a deep, narrow valley, especially in Scotland or Ireland

glide [glaɪd] **glides, gliding, glided** VERB
1 To glide means to move smoothly. *e.g. cygnets gliding up the stream*

2 When birds or aeroplanes glide, they float on air currents.

glider ['glaɪdə] **gliders** NOUN
an aeroplane without an engine, which flies by floating on air currents

glimmer ['glɪmə] **glimmers, glimmering, glimmered** NOUN
1 a faint, unsteady light

2 A glimmer of a feeling or quality is a faint sign of it. *e.g. a glimmer of intelligence*

glimpse [glɪmps] **glimpses, glimpsing, glimpsed** NOUN
1 a brief sight of something *e.g. They caught a glimpse of their hero.*

> VERB
2 If you glimpse something, you see it very briefly.

glint [glɪnt] **glints, glinting, glinted** VERB
1 If something glints, it reflects quick flashes of light.

> NOUN
2 a quick flash of light

3 A glint in someone's eye is a brightness expressing some emotion. *e.g. a glint of mischief in her blue-grey eyes*

glisten ['glɪsᵊn] **glistens, glistening, glistened** VERB
If something glistens, it shines or sparkles.

glitter ['glɪtə] **glitters, glittering, glittered**
VERB
1 If something glitters, it shines in a sparkling way. *e.g. a glittering crown*

> NOUN
2 Glitter is sparkling light.

gloat [gləʊt] **gloats, gloating, gloated** VERB
If you gloat, you cruelly show your pleasure about your own success or someone else's failure. *e.g. Their rivals were gloating over their triumph.*

global ['gləʊbəl] ADJECTIVE
concerning the whole world *e.g. a global tour*

globalization [,gləʊbəlaɪ'zeɪʃən] NOUN
1 the process by which a company expands so that it can do business internationally
2 the process by which cultures throughout the world become more and more similar for a variety of reasons including increased global business and better international communications

global warming ['wɔːmɪŋ] NOUN
an increase in the world's overall temperature believed to be caused by the greenhouse effect

globe [gləʊb] **globes** NOUN
1 a ball-shaped object, especially one with a map of the earth on it
2 **(GEOGRAPHY)** You can refer to the world as the globe.
3 In South African, Australian, and New Zealand English, a globe is an electric light bulb.

gloom [gluːm] NOUN
1 Gloom is darkness or dimness.
2 Gloom is also a feeling of unhappiness or despair.

gloomy ['gluːmɪ] **gloomier, gloomiest**
ADJECTIVE
1 dark and depressing
● THESAURUS
dark: *The house looked dark and gloomy.*
dismal: *damp and dismal weather*
dreary: *the dreary, industrial city of Ludwigshafen*
dull: *It's always dull and raining.*
<<OPPOSITE sunny

2 feeling very sad
gloomily ADVERB
● THESAURUS
dejected: *Everyone has days when they feel dejected.*
down: *The old man sounded really down.*
glum: *What on earth are you looking so glum about?*
miserable: *She went to bed, miserable and depressed.*
sad: *You must feel sad about what's happened.*
<<OPPOSITE cheerful

glorify ['glɔːrɪ,faɪ] **glorifies, glorifying, glorified** VERB
If you glorify someone or something, you make them seem better than they really are. *e.g. Their aggressive music glorifies violence.*
glorification NOUN

glorious ['glɔːrɪəs] ADJECTIVE
1 beautiful and impressive to look at *e.g. glorious beaches*
2 very pleasant and giving a feeling of happiness *e.g. glorious sunshine*
3 involving great fame and success *e.g. a glorious career*
gloriously ADVERB

glory ['glɔːrɪ] **glories, glorying, gloried**
NOUN
1 Glory is fame and admiration for an achievement.
● THESAURUS
fame: *The film earned him international fame.*
honour: *the honour of captaining one's country*
immortality: *Some people want to achieve immortality through their work.*
praise: *Holbrooke deserves full praise for his efforts.*
prestige: *I'm not in this job for the prestige.*
<<OPPOSITE disgrace

2 something considered splendid or admirable *e.g. the true glories of the Alps*
● THESAURUS
grandeur: *the grandeur of the country mansion*
magnificence: *the magnificence of the sunset*
majesty: *the majesty of Niagara Falls*
splendour: *the splendour of the palace of Versailles*

> VERB
3 If you glory in something, you take great delight in it.
● THESAURUS
gloat: *Their rivals were gloating over their triumph.*
relish: *He relished the idea of getting some cash.*
revel: *a ruthless killer who revels in his job*

glory box glory boxes NOUN; OLD-FASHIONED, INFORMAL
In Australian and New Zealand English, a chest in which a young woman stores household goods and linen for her marriage.

gloss [glɒs] **glosses, glossing, glossed**
NOUN
1 Gloss is a bright shine on a surface.
● THESAURUS
brilliance: *ceramic tiles of great brilliance*
gleam: *the gleam of brass*
polish: *His boots had a high polish.*
sheen: *The carpet had a silvery sheen to it.*
shine: *This gel gives a beautiful shine to the hair.*

2 Gloss is also an attractive appearance which may hide less attractive qualities. *e.g. to put a positive gloss on the events*
3 If you gloss over a problem or fault, you try to ignore it or deal with it very quickly.

glossary ['glɒsərɪ] **glossaries** NOUN
(LIBRARY) a list of explanations of specialist

g

words, usually found at the back of a book

glossy ['glɒsɪ] **glossier, glossiest** ADJECTIVE
smooth and shiny *e.g. glossy lipstick... glossy paper*

● THESAURUS
bright: *Her eyes were bright with excitement.*
brilliant: *The woman had brilliant green eyes.*
polished: *a highly polished floor*
shiny: *a shiny new sports car*
sleek: *sleek black hair*

glove [glʌv] **gloves** NOUN
Gloves are coverings which you wear over your hands for warmth or protection.

glow [gləʊ] **glows, glowing, glowed** NOUN
1 a dull, steady light

● THESAURUS
gleam: *the first gleam of dawn*
glimmer: *In the east there was the slightest glimmer of light.*
light: *the light of the evening sun*

2 a strong feeling of pleasure or happiness

> VERB
3 If something glows, it shines with a dull, steady light. *e.g. A light glowed behind the curtains.*

● THESAURUS
gleam: *Lights gleamed in the deepening mist.*
glimmer: *A few stars still glimmered.*
shine: *Scattered lights shone on the horizon.*
smoulder: *A very small fire was smouldering in the grate.*

4 If you are glowing, you look very happy or healthy.

glower ['glaʊə] **glowers, glowering, glowered** VERB
If you glower, you stare angrily.

glowing ['gləʊɪŋ] ADJECTIVE
A glowing description praises someone or something very highly. *e.g. a glowing character reference*

glucose ['glu:kəʊz] NOUN
Glucose is a type of sugar found in plants and that animals and people make in their bodies from food to provide energy.

glue [glu:] **glues, gluing** or **glueing glued**
NOUN
1 a substance used for sticking things together

> VERB
2 If you glue one object to another, you stick them together using glue.

● THESAURUS
fix: *Fix the fabric to the roller.*
paste: *The children were busy pasting gold stars on a chart.*
seal: *He sealed the envelope and put on a stamp.*
stick: *I stuck the notice on the board.*

glum [glʌm] **glummer, glummest**
ADJECTIVE
miserable and depressed
glumly ADVERB

glut [glʌt] **gluts** NOUN
a greater quantity of things than is needed

gluten ['glu:t°n] NOUN
a sticky protein found in cereal grains, such as wheat

glutton ['glʌt°n] **gluttons** NOUN
1 a person who eats too much
2 If you are a glutton for something, such as punishment or hard work, you seem very eager for it.
gluttony NOUN

gnarled [nɑ:ld] ADJECTIVE
old, twisted, and rough *e.g. gnarled fingers*

gnat [næt] **gnats** NOUN
a tiny flying insect that bites

gnaw [nɔ:] **gnaws, gnawing, gnawed** VERB
1 To gnaw something means to bite at it repeatedly.
2 If a feeling gnaws at you, it keeps worrying you. *e.g. a question gnawed at him*

gnome [nəʊm] **gnomes** NOUN
a tiny old man in fairy stories

gnu [nu:] **gnus** NOUN
a large African antelope

go see page 379 for Word Web

goad [gəʊd] **goads, goading, goaded** VERB
If you goad someone, you encourage them to do something by making them angry or excited. *e.g. He had goaded the man into near violence.*

go-ahead ['gəʊə,hɛd] NOUN
If someone gives you the go-ahead for something, they give you permission to do it.

goal [gəʊl] **goals** NOUN
1 the space, in games like football or hockey, into which the players try to get the ball in order to score a point
2 an instance of this
3 Your goal is something that you hope to achieve.

● THESAURUS
aim: *The aim of the festival is to raise awareness of this issue.*
end: *This is another policy designed to achieve the same end.*
intention: *He announced his intention of standing for parliament.*
object: *The object of the exercise is to raise money for charity.*

1 VERB
If you go somewhere, you move or travel there.

● THESAURUS

advance: *Rebel forces are advancing on the capital.*

drive: *My husband and I drove to Liverpool to see my mum.*

fly: *He flew to Los Angeles.*

journey (formal): *They intended to journey up the Amazon.*

leave: *What time are you leaving?*

proceed (formal): *The taxi proceeded along a lonely road.*

set off: *He set off for the station.*

travel: *Students often travel hundreds of miles to get here.*

go
goes, going, went, gone

2 VERB
If a machine or clock goes, it works and is not broken.

● THESAURUS

function: *All the instruments functioned properly.*

work: *The pump doesn't work and we have no running water.*

3 NOUN
an attempt at doing something

● THESAURUS

attempt: *one of his rare attempts at humour*

shot (informal): *a shot at winning a brand new car*

stab (informal): *Several sports stars have had a stab at acting and singing.*

try: *After a few tries, Patrick had given up.*

g

objective: *His objective was to play golf and win.*
purpose: *His purpose was to make a profit.*
target: *She failed to achieve her target of losing 20 pounds.*

goalkeeper ['gəʊl,kiːpə] **goalkeepers** NOUN
the player, in games like soccer or hockey, who stands in the goal and tries to stop the other team from scoring

goanna [gəʊ'ænə] **goannas** NOUN
a large Australian lizard

goat [gəʊt] **goats** NOUN
an animal, like a sheep, with coarse hair, a beard, and horns

go-away bird ['gəʊəweɪ] **go-away birds** NOUN
In South Africa, a go-away bird is a grey lourie, a type of bird which lives in open grassland.

gob [gɒb] **gobs** NOUN; INFORMAL
Your gob is your mouth.

gobble ['gɒbəl] **gobbles, gobbling, gobbled** VERB
1 If you gobble food, you eat it very quickly.

🔘 THESAURUS

bolt: *Being under stress can cause you to bolt your food.*

devour: *She devoured two bars of chocolate.*

wolf: *Pitt wolfed down a peanut butter sandwich.*

2 When a turkey gobbles, it makes a loud gurgling sound.

gobbledygook or **gobbledegook** ['gɒbəldɪ,guːk] NOUN
Gobbledygook is language that is impossible to understand because it is so formal or complicated.

goblet ['gɒblɪt] **goblets** NOUN
a glass with a long stem

goblin ['gɒblɪn] **goblins** NOUN
an ugly, mischievous creature in fairy stories

god [gɒd] **gods** PROPER NOUN
1 The name God is given to the being who is worshipped by Christians, Jews, and Muslims as the creator and ruler of the world.

> NOUN
2 any of the beings that are believed in many religions to have power over an aspect of life or a part of the world *e.g. Dionysus, the Greek god of wine.*

3 If someone is your god, you admire them very much.

> PLURAL NOUN
4 In a theatre, the gods are the highest seats farthest from the stage.

godchild ['gɒd,tʃaɪld] **godchildren** NOUN
If you are someone's godchild, they agreed to be responsible for your religious upbringing when you were baptized in a Christian church.
goddaughter NOUN, **godson** NOUN

goddess ['gɒdɪs] **goddesses** NOUN
a female god

godparent ['gɒd,peərənt] **godparents** NOUN
A person's godparent is someone who agrees to be responsible for their religious upbringing when they are baptized in a Christian church.
godfather NOUN, **godmother** NOUN

godsend ['gɒd,send] **godsends** NOUN
something that comes unexpectedly and helps you very much

goggles ['gɒgəlz] PLURAL NOUN
Goggles are special glasses that fit closely round your eyes to protect them.

going ['gəʊɪŋ] NOUN
The going is the conditions that affect your ability to do something. *e.g. He found the going very slow indeed.*

gold [gəʊld] NOUN
1 Gold is a valuable, yellow-coloured metal. It is used for making jewellery and as an international currency.

2 'Gold' is also used to mean things that are made of gold

> ADJECTIVE
3 bright yellow

golden ['gəʊldən] ADJECTIVE
1 gold in colour *e.g. golden syrup*

2 made of gold *e.g. a golden chain*

3 excellent or ideal *e.g. a golden hero*

golden rule golden rules NOUN
a very important rule to remember in order to be able to do something successfully

golden wedding golden weddings NOUN
A married couple's golden wedding is their fiftieth wedding anniversary.

goldfish ['gəʊld,fɪʃ] NOUN
a small orange-coloured fish, often kept in ponds or bowls

goldsmith ['gəʊld,smɪθ] **goldsmiths** NOUN
a person whose job is making jewellery out of gold

golf [gɒlf] NOUN
Golf is a game in which players use special clubs to hit a small ball into holes that are spread out over a large area of grassy land.
golfer NOUN

golf course golf courses NOUN
an area of grassy land where people play golf

gondola ['gɒndələ] **gondolas** NOUN
a long narrow boat used in Venice, which is propelled with a long pole

gone [gɒn] the past participle of **go**

gong [gɒŋ] **gongs** NOUN
a flat, circular piece of metal that is hit with a hammer to make a loud sound, often as a signal for something

good see page 382 for Word Web

goodbye [,gʊd'baɪ]
You say goodbye when you are leaving someone or ending a telephone conversation.

Good Friday NOUN
Good Friday is the Friday before Easter, when Christians remember the crucifixion of Christ.

good-natured [,gʊd'neɪtʃəd] ADJECTIVE
friendly, pleasant and even-tempered

goodness ['gʊdnɪs] NOUN
1 Goodness is the quality of being kind.
> INTERJECTION
2 People say 'Goodness!' or 'My goodness!' when they are surprised.

goodwill [,gʊd'wɪl] NOUN
Goodwill is kindness and helpfulness. *e.g. Messages of goodwill were exchanged.*

● THESAURUS
benevolence: *He chuckles often and radiates benevolence.*
favour: *in order to gain the favour of whoever is in power*
friendliness: *Visitors remarked on the friendliness of the people.*
friendship: *The two countries signed treaties of friendship.*

goody ['gʊdɪ] **goodies** NOUN
1 INFORMAL
Goodies are enjoyable things, often food.
2 You can call a hero in a film or book a goody.

goose [guːs] **geese** NOUN
a fairly large bird with webbed feet and a long neck

gooseberry ['gʊzbərɪ] **gooseberries** NOUN
a round, green berry that grows on a bush and has a sharp taste

gore [gɔː] **gores, goring, gored** VERB
1 If an animal gores someone, it wounds them badly with its horns or tusks.
> NOUN
2 Gore is clotted blood from a wound.

gorge [gɔːdʒ] **gorges, gorging, gorged**
NOUN
1 a deep, narrow valley

> VERB
2 If you gorge yourself, you eat a lot of food greedily.

gorgeous ['gɔːdʒəs] ADJECTIVE
extremely pleasant or attractive *e.g. a gorgeous man*

gorilla [gə'rɪlə] **gorillas** NOUN
a very large, strong ape with very dark fur
[WORD HISTORY: from GORILLAI, the Greek name for an African tribe with hairy bodies]

gorse [gɔːs] NOUN
Gorse is a dark green wild shrub that has sharp prickles and small yellow flowers.

gory ['gɔːrɪ] **gorier, goriest** ADJECTIVE
Gory situations involve people being injured in horrible ways.

gosling ['gɒzlɪŋ] **goslings** NOUN
a young goose

gospel ['gɒspəl] **gospels** NOUN
1 The Gospels are the four books in the New Testament which describe the life and teachings of Jesus Christ.

2 a set of ideas that someone strongly believes in *e.g. the so-called gospel of work*

> ADJECTIVE
3 Gospel music is a style of religious music popular among Black Christians in the United States.

gossip ['gɒsɪp] **gossips, gossiping, gossiped** NOUN
1 Gossip is informal conversation, often concerning people's private affairs.

● THESAURUS
dirt: *the latest dirt on the other candidates*
hearsay: *They have had only hearsay and rumour to go on.*

2 Someone who is a gossip enjoys talking about other people's private affairs.

> VERB
3 If you gossip, you talk informally with someone, especially about other people.

got [gɒt]
1 Got is the past tense and past participle of **get**

2 You can use 'have got' instead of the more formal 'have' when talking about possessing things. *e.g. The director has got a map.*

3 You can use 'have got to' instead of the more formal 'have to' when talking about something that must be done. *e.g. He has got to win.*

gouge [gaʊdʒ] **gouges, gouging, gouged**
VERB
1 If you gouge a hole in something, you make a hole in it with a pointed object.

1 ADJECTIVE

pleasant, acceptable or satisfactory *eg: We had a really good time.*

● THESAURUS

acceptable: *an acceptable standard of education*

awesome (slang): *The film has some awesome special effects.*

excellent: *We had an excellent meal.*

fine: *a selection of fine wines*

first-class: *They played a first-class game.*

first-rate: *a company offering a first-rate service*

great (informal): *This is a great book.*

satisfactory: *I expect goods of a satisfactory quality at prices like these.*

splendid: *We stayed in a splendid hotel.*

super (informal): *a super recipe*

superb: *a superb selection of cheeses*

<< OPPOSITE *bad*

2 ADJECTIVE

skilful or successful *eg: good at art.*

● THESAURUS

able: *a very able student*

accomplished: *an accomplished pianist and composer*

adept: *politicians who are adept at manipulating the press*

capable: *She's a very capable nanny.*

clever: *They are very clever at raising money for charity.*

competent: *a careful and competent worker*

efficient: *an efficient manager*

expert: *inexperienced and expert cyclists alike*

first-rate: *I had a first-rate teacher.*

proficient: *a proficient driver*

skilled: *a skilled carpenter*

talented: *the country's most talented musicians*

<< OPPOSITE *incompetent*

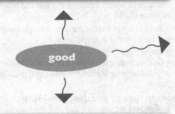

good

3 ADJECTIVE

kind, thoughtful and loving *eg: You are so good to me.*

● THESAURUS

benevolent: *a kindly and benevolent old man*

charitable: *She is too charitable to hurt his feelings.*

considerate: *He's considerate to his sisters.*

generous: *I admire his generous and selfless nature.*

gracious: *a gracious and genial host*

humane: *a humane and caring man*

kind: *It's very kind of you to go to so much trouble.*

kind-hearted: *donations from kind-hearted colleagues*

kindly: *At heart, he was a kindly soul.*

obliging: *an obliging fellow who is always glad to help*

thoughtful: *It was very thoughtful of him to offer.*

<< OPPOSITE *unkind*

2 If you gouge something out, you force it out of position with your fingers or a sharp tool.

goulash ['guːlæʃ] NOUN
Goulash is a type of rich meat stew, originally from Hungary.

gourd [guəd] **gourds** NOUN
a large fruit with a hard outside

gourmet ['guəmeɪ] **gourmets** NOUN
a person who enjoys good food and drink and knows a lot about it

gout [gaut] NOUN
Gout is a disease which causes someone's joints to swell painfully, especially in their toes.

govern ['gʌvᵊn] **governs, governing, governed** VERB
1 To govern a country means to control it.
2 Something that governs a situation influences it. *e.g. Our thinking is as much governed by habit as by behaviour.*

governess ['gʌvənɪs] **governesses** NOUN
a woman who is employed to teach the children in a family and who lives with the family

government ['gʌvənmənt] **governments** NOUN (HISTORY)
1 The government is the group of people who govern a country.
2 Government is the control and organization of a country.
governmental ADJECTIVE

governor ['gʌvənə] **governors** NOUN
1 a person who controls and organizes a state or an institution
2 In Australia, the Governor is the representative of the King or Queen in a State.

governor-general ['gʌvənə'dʒɛnərəl] **governors-general** NOUN
the chief representative of the King or Queen in Australia, New Zealand, and other Commonwealth countries

gown [gaun] **gowns** NOUN
1 a long, formal dress
2 a long, dark cloak worn by people such as judges and lawyers

GP an abbreviation for **general practitioner**

grab [græb] **grabs, grabbing, grabbed** VERB
1 If you grab something, you take it or pick it up roughly.
● THESAURUS
clutch: *Michelle clutched my arm.*
grasp: *He grasped both my hands.*
seize: *She seized a carving fork and advanced in my direction.*

snatch: *Mick snatched the cards from Archie's hand.*
2 If you grab an opportunity, you take advantage of it eagerly.
3 INFORMAL
If an idea grabs you, it excites you.
> NOUN
4 A grab at an object is an attempt to grab it.

grace [greɪs] **graces, gracing, graced** NOUN
1 Grace is an elegant way of moving.
● THESAURUS
elegance: *She is elegance personified.*
poise: *Ballet classes are important for poise and grace.*
<<OPPOSITE *clumsiness*
2 Grace is also a pleasant, kind way of behaving.
3 Grace is also a short prayer of thanks said before a meal.
4 Dukes and archbishops are addressed as 'Your Grace' and referred to as 'His Grace'.
> VERB
5 Something that graces a place makes it more attractive.
6 If someone important graces an event, they kindly agree to be present at it.
graceful ADJECTIVE, **gracefully** ADVERB

gracious ['greɪʃəs] ADJECTIVE
1 kind, polite, and pleasant
2 'Good gracious' is an exclamation of surprise
graciously ADVERB

grade [greɪd] **grades, grading, graded** VERB
1 To grade things means to arrange them according to quality.
● THESAURUS
class: *They are officially classed as visitors.*
classify: *Rocks can be classified according to their origin.*
group: *The fact sheets are grouped into seven sections.*
rate: *He was rated as one of the country's top young players.*
sort: *The students are sorted into three ability groups.*
> NOUN
2 The grade of something is its quality.
3 the mark that you get for an exam or piece of written work
4 Your grade in a company or organization is your level of importance or your rank.

gradient ['greɪdɪənt] **gradients** NOUN
a slope or the steepness of a slope

gradual ['grædjʊəl] ADJECTIVE
happening or changing slowly over a long period of time

g

THESAURUS
continuous: *Our policy is one of continuous improvement.*
progressive: *One symptom of the disease is progressive loss of memory.*
slow: *The distribution of passports has been a slow process.*
steady: *a steady rise in sales*
<<OPPOSITE *sudden*

gradually ['grædjʊəlɪ] ADVERB
happening or changing slowly over a long period of time

graduate graduates, graduating, graduated NOUN ['grædjuɪt]
1 a person who has completed a first degree at a university or college
> VERB ['grædjʊˌeɪt]
2 When students graduate, they complete a first degree at a university or college.
3 To graduate from one thing to another means to progress gradually towards the second thing.
graduation NOUN

graffiti [græ'fiːtiː] NOUN
Graffiti is slogans or drawings scribbled on walls.
[WORD HISTORY: from Italian GRAFFIARE meaning 'to scratch a surface']

Although *graffiti* is a plural in Italian, the language it comes from, in English it can be used as a singular noun or a plural noun

graft [grɑːft] **grafts, grafting, grafted** NOUN
1 a piece of living tissue which is used to replace by surgery a damaged or unhealthy part of a person's body
2 INFORMAL
Graft is hard work.
> VERB
3 To graft one thing to another means to attach it.

grain [greɪn] **grains** NOUN
1 a cereal plant, such as wheat, that is grown as a crop and used for food
2 Grains are seeds of a cereal plant.
3 A grain of sand or salt is a tiny particle of it.
4 The grain of a piece of wood is the pattern of lines made by the fibres in it.
> PHRASE
5 If something **goes against the grain**, you find it difficult to accept because it is against your principles.

gram [græm] **grams**; also spelt **gramme** NOUN
a unit of weight equal to one thousandth of a kilogram

grammar ['græmə] NOUN
(ENGLISH) Grammar is the rules of a language relating to the ways you can combine words to form sentences.

grammar school grammar schools NOUN
1 a secondary school for pupils of high academic ability
2 In Australia, a private school, usually one controlled by a church.

grammatical [grə'mætɪkᵊl] ADJECTIVE
1 relating to grammar e.g. *grammatical knowledge*
2 following the rules of grammar correctly e.g. *grammatical sentences*
grammatically ADVERB

gran [græn] **grans** NOUN; INFORMAL
Your gran is your grandmother.

granary ['grænərɪ] **granaries** NOUN
1 a building for storing grain
> ADJECTIVE
2 TRADEMARK
Granary bread contains whole grains of wheat.

grand [grænd] **grander, grandest** ADJECTIVE
1 magnificent in appearance and size e.g. *a grand house*
THESAURUS
imposing: *the imposing gates at the entrance to the estate*
impressive: *The old boat presented an impressive sight.*
magnificent: *magnificent views over the San Fernando valley*
majestic: *a stupendous vista of majestic peaks*
monumental: *a monumental sculpture of a human face*
splendid: *a splendid Victorian mansion*
2 very important e.g. *the grand scheme of your life*
3 INFORMAL
very pleasant or enjoyable e.g. *It was a grand day.*
THESAURUS
brilliant: informal *I've had a brilliant time.*
great: informal *I had a great time at university.*
marvellous: informal *It was a marvellous day and we were all so happy.*
terrific: informal *Everybody there was having a terrific time.*
wonderful: *It was a wonderful experience.*
4 A grand total is the final complete amount.
> NOUN
5 INFORMAL a thousand pounds or dollars
grandly ADVERB

grandad ['grænˌdæd] **grandads** NOUN; INFORMAL
Your grandad is your grandfather.

grandchild ['græn,tʃaɪld] **grandchildren**
NOUN
Someone's grandchildren are the children of
their son or daughter.

granddaughter ['græn,dɔːtə]
granddaughters NOUN
Someone's granddaughter is the daughter of
their son or daughter.

grandeur ['grændʒə] NOUN
Grandeur is great beauty and magnificence.

grandfather ['græn,fɑːðə] **grandfathers**
NOUN
Your grandfather is your father's father or your
mother's father.

grandfather clock **grandfather clocks**
NOUN
a clock in a tall wooden case that stands on the
floor

grandiose ['grændɪ,əʊs] ADJECTIVE
intended to be very impressive, but seeming
ridiculous *e.g. a grandiose gesture of love*

grandma ['græn,mɑː] **grandmas** NOUN;
INFORMAL
Your grandma is your grandmother.

grandmother ['græn,mʌðə]
grandmothers NOUN
Your grandmother is your father's mother or your
mother's mother.

grandparent ['græn,peərənt]
grandparents NOUN
Your grandparents are your parents' parents.

grand piano **grand pianos** NOUN
a large flat piano with horizontal strings

grandson ['grænsʌn] **grandsons** NOUN
Someone's grandson is the son of their son or
daughter.

grandstand ['græn,stænd] **grandstands**
NOUN
a structure with a roof and seats for spectators at
a sports ground

granite ['grænɪt] NOUN
Granite is a very hard rock used in building.

granny ['grænɪ] **grannies** NOUN; INFORMAL
Your granny is your grandmother.

grant [grɑːnt] **grants, granting, granted**
NOUN
1 an amount of money that an official body gives
to someone for a particular purpose *e.g. a grant to
carry out repairs*

● THESAURUS
allocation: *The aid allocation for that country is
under review.*
allowance: *She gets an allowance for looking after
Lillian.*

award: *a study award worth £2,000*
handout: *a cash handout of six thousand rupees*
subsidy: *state subsidies to public transport
companies*

> VERB
2 If you grant something to someone, you allow
them to have it.

● THESAURUS
allocate: *The budget allocated $7 billion for
development programmes.*
allow: *Children should be allowed the occasional
treat.*
award: *A High Court judge awarded him £6 million
damages.*
give: *We have been given permission to attend the
meeting.*
permit: *The doorman said he could not permit them
entry to the film.*
<<OPPOSITE *deny*

3 If you grant that something is true, you admit
that it is true.

● THESAURUS
accept: *I do not accept that there is a crisis in British
science.*
acknowledge: *He acknowledged that he had been
partly to blame.*
admit: *I admit that I do make mistakes.*
allow: *He allows that capitalist development may
result in social inequality.*
concede: *Bess finally conceded that Nancy was
right.*
<<OPPOSITE *deny*

> PHRASES
4 If you **take something for granted**, you
believe it without thinking about it. If you **take
someone for granted**, you benefit from them
without showing that you are grateful.

granule ['grænjuːl] **granules** NOUN
a very small piece of something *e.g. granules of
salt*

grape [greɪp] **grapes** NOUN
a small green or purple fruit, eaten raw or used to
make wine

grapefruit ['greɪp,fruːt] **grapefruits** NOUN
a large, round, yellow citrus fruit

grapevine ['greɪp,vaɪn] **grapevines** NOUN
1 a climbing plant which grapes grow on
2 If you hear some news on the grapevine, it has
been passed on from person to person, usually
unofficially or secretly.

graph [grɑːf] **graphs** NOUN
(MATHS) a diagram in which a line shows how
two sets of numbers or measurements are
related

-graph SUFFIX
'-graph' means a writer or recorder of some sort

g

or something made by writing, drawing or recording e.g. telegraph... autograph

graphic ['græfɪk] **graphics** ADJECTIVE

1 A graphic description is very detailed and lifelike.

2 relating to drawing or painting

> PLURAL NOUN

3 (ICT) Graphics are drawings and pictures composed of simple lines and strong colours. e.g. computerized graphics

graphically ADVERB

graphite ['græfaɪt] NOUN

a black form of carbon that is used in pencil leads

grapple ['græpəl] **grapples, grappling, grappled** VERB

1 If you grapple with someone, you struggle with them while fighting.

2 If you grapple with a problem, you try hard to solve it.

grasp [grɑːsp] **grasps, grasping, grasped** VERB

1 If you grasp something, you hold it firmly.

● THESAURUS

clutch: I staggered and had to clutch at a chair for support.

grab: I grabbed him by the neck.

grip: She gripped the rope.

hold: He held the pistol tightly in his right hand.

seize: He seized my arm to hold me back.

snatch: I snatched at a hanging branch and pulled myself up.

2 If you grasp an idea, you understand it.

● THESAURUS

absorb: He only absorbed about half the information we gave him.

appreciate: She never really appreciated the bitterness of the conflict.

assimilate: My mind could only assimilate one concept at a time.

realize: People don't realize how serious this recession has been.

take in: She listens to the explanation, but you can see she's not taking it in.

understand: They are too young to understand what is going on.

> NOUN

3 a firm hold

● THESAURUS

clasp: He gripped my hand in a strong clasp.

embrace: He held her in a passionate embrace.

grip: His strong hand eased the bag from her grip.

hold: He released his hold on the camera.

4 Your grasp of something is your understanding of it.

● THESAURUS

awareness: The children demonstrated their awareness of green issues.

comprehension: formal This was utterly beyond her comprehension.

grip: He has lost his grip on reality.

knowledge: She has a good knowledge of these processes.

understanding: a basic understanding of computers

grass [grɑːs] **grasses** NOUN

Grass is the common green plant that grows on lawns and in parks.

grassy ADJECTIVE

grasshopper ['grɑːs,hɒpə] **grasshoppers** NOUN

an insect with long back legs which it uses for jumping and making a high-pitched sound

grate [greɪt] **grates, grating, grated** NOUN

1 a framework of metal bars in a fireplace

> VERB

2 To grate food means to shred it into small pieces by rubbing it against a grater.

3 When something grates on something else, it rubs against it making a harsh sound.

4 If something grates on you, it irritates you.

grateful ['greɪtfʊl] ADJECTIVE

If you are grateful for something, you are glad you have it and want to thank the person who gave it to you.

gratefully ADVERB

● THESAURUS

appreciative: We have been very appreciative of their support.

indebted: I am deeply indebted to him for his help.

thankful: I'm just thankful that I've got a job.

<<OPPOSITE ungrateful

grater ['greɪtə] **graters** NOUN

a small metal tool used for grating food

gratify ['grætɪ,faɪ] **gratifies, gratifying, gratified** VERB

1 If you are gratified by something, you are pleased by it.

2 If you gratify a wish or feeling, you satisfy it.

grating ['greɪtɪŋ] **gratings** NOUN

1 a metal frame with bars across it fastened over a hole in a wall or in the ground

> ADJECTIVE

2 A grating sound is harsh and unpleasant. e.g. grating melodies

gratis ['greɪtɪs] ADVERB OR ADJECTIVE

free e.g. food and drink supplied gratis

gratitude ['grætɪ,tjuːd] NOUN

Gratitude is the feeling of being grateful.

THESAURUS
appreciation: *their appreciation of his efforts*
recognition: *an honour given in recognition of his help to the college*
thanks: *They accepted their certificates with words of thanks.*
<<OPPOSITE *ingratitude*

gratuitous [grə'tju:ɪtəs] ADJECTIVE
unnecessary *e.g. a gratuitous attack*
gratuitously ADVERB

grave [greɪv] **graves; graver, gravest** NOUN
1 a place where a corpse is buried

THESAURUS
mausoleum: *the great mausoleum at the top of the hill*
pit: *The bodies were buried in a shallow pit.*
sepulchre: *Death holds him in his sepulchre.*
tomb: *the tomb of the Unknown Soldier*

> ADJECTIVE
2 FORMAL
very serious *e.g. grave danger*

THESAURUS
acute: *The report has caused acute embarrassment to the government.*
critical: *Its finances are in a critical state.*
heavy: *Things were just starting to get heavy when the police arrived.*
serious: *The government faces very serious difficulties.*
sober: *a room filled with sad, sober faces*
solemn: *His solemn little face broke into smiles.*
sombre: *His expression became increasingly sombre.*

grave [grɑːv] ADJECTIVE
In French and some other languages, a grave accent is a line sloping downwards from left to right placed over a vowel to indicate a change in pronunciation, as in the word *lèvre* (a hare).

gravel ['grævəl] NOUN
Gravel is small stones used for making roads and paths.

gravestone ['greɪvˌstəʊn] **gravestones** NOUN
a large stone placed over someone's grave, with their name on it

graveyard ['greɪvˌjɑːd] **graveyards** NOUN
an area of land where corpses are buried

gravitate ['grævɪˌteɪt] **gravitates, gravitating, gravitated** VERB
When people gravitate towards something, they go towards it because they are attracted by it.

gravitation [ˌgrævɪ'teɪʃən] NOUN
Gravitation is the force which causes objects to be attracted to each other.
gravitational ADJECTIVE

gravity ['grævɪtɪ] NOUN
1 Gravity is the force that makes things fall when you drop them.

2 FORMAL
The gravity of a situation is its seriousness.

gravy ['greɪvɪ] NOUN
Gravy is a brown sauce made from meat juices.

graze [greɪz] **grazes, grazing, grazed** VERB
1 When animals graze, they eat grass.

2 If something grazes a part of your body, it scrapes against it, injuring you slightly.

THESAURUS
scrape: *She stumbled and fell, scraping her palms and knees.*
scratch: *The branches scratched my hands and face.*
skin: *He fell and skinned both his knees.*

> NOUN
3 a slight injury caused by something scraping against your skin

THESAURUS
abrasion: formal *He had severe abrasions to his right cheek.*
scratch: *She had scratches to her face.*

grease greases, greasing, greased NOUN
[griːs]
1 Grease is an oily substance used for lubricating machines.

2 Grease is also melted animal fat, used in cooking.

3 Grease is also an oily substance produced by your skin and found in your hair.

> VERB [griːz]
4 If you grease something, you lubricate it with grease.
greasy ADJECTIVE

great see page 388 for Word Web

Great Britain ['brɪtən] NOUN
Great Britain is the largest of the British Isles, consisting of England, Scotland, and Wales.

Great Dane Great Danes NOUN
a very large dog with short hair

great-grandfather ['greɪt'grænˌfɑːðə]
great-grandfathers NOUN
Your great-grandfather is your father's or mother's grandfather.

great-grandmother ['greɪt'grænˌmʌðə]
great-grandmothers NOUN
Your great-grandmother is your father's or mother's grandmother.

greed [griːd] NOUN
Greed is a desire for more of something than you really need.

g

1 ADJECTIVE
very large in size *eg: great columns of ice*
● THESAURUS
big: *He lives in a big house.*
colossal: *a colossal tomb*
huge: *a huge marquee in the grounds*
large: *a large pile of logs*
enormous: *They entered an enormous hall.*
extensive: *an extensive range of stock*
gigantic: *a gigantic theme park*
immense: *an immense building*
stupendous: *a stupendous sum of money*
tremendous: *It's a tremendous challenge.*
vast: *The fire destroyed a vast area of forest.*
<< OPPOSITE *small*

2 ADJECTIVE
important or famous *eg: the great novels of the nineteenth century*
● THESAURUS
celebrated: *the celebrated author of 'Lord of the Rings'*
chief: *one of our chief problems*
distinguished: *a distinguished baritone*
eminent: *two eminent French scientists*
famed: *the famed Australian actor*
famous: *a famous artist*
illustrious: *some of the world's most illustrious ballerinas*
important: *an important question*
main: *our main competitor*
major: *a major issue in the next election*
momentous (formal): *a momentous occasion*
notable: *a notable chess player*
principal: *Our principal aim*
prominent: *Scotland's most prominent historian*
renowned: *the renowned heart surgeon*
serious: *a serious deficiency in the system*
significant: *This is a significant step towards peace.*

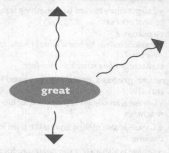

great

3 ADJECTIVE; INFORMAL
very good *eg: I thought it was a great idea.*
● THESAURUS
beaut (Australian & New Zealand): *a beaut place to live*
fine: *He enjoys good food and fine wines.*
excellent: *an excellent pasta sauce*
superb: *The room was full of superb works of art.*
fantastic (informal): *a fantastic firework display*
first-rate: *They pride themselves on their first-rate service.*
marvellous (informal): *a marvellous rooftop restaurant*
outstanding: *outstanding works of art*
superb: *a superb staircase made from oak*
terrific (informal): *It was a terrific party.*
tremendous (informal): *You've done a tremendous job.*
wonderful: *I've had a wonderful time.*
<< OPPOSITE *terrible*

greedy ['gri:dɪ] **greedier, greediest**
ADJECTIVE
wanting more of something than you really need
greedily ADVERB, **greediness** NOUN

● THESAURUS
materialistic: *During the 1980s Britain became a very materialistic society.*
snoep: South African; informal *a bunch of snoep businessmen*

Greek [gri:k] **Greeks** ADJECTIVE
1 belonging or relating to Greece
> NOUN
2 someone who comes from Greece
3 Greek is the main language spoken in Greece.

green [gri:n] **greener, greenest; greens**
ADJECTIVE OR NOUN
1 Green is a colour between yellow and blue on the spectrum.
> NOUN
2 an area of grass in the middle of a village
3 A putting green or bowling green is a grassy area on which putting or bowls is played.
4 an area of smooth short grass around each hole on a golf course
> PLURAL NOUN
5 Greens are green vegetables.
> ADJECTIVE
6 'Green' is used to describe political movements which are concerned with environmental issues

● THESAURUS
conservationist: *a chorus of protest from conservationist groups*
ecological: *shared interest in ecological issues*

7 INFORMAL
Someone who is green is young and inexperienced.

greenery ['gri:nərɪ] NOUN
Greenery is a lot of trees, bushes, or other green plants together in one place.

greenfly ['gri:n,flaɪ] NOUN
Greenfly are small green insects that damage plants.

greengrocer ['gri:n,grəʊsə] **greengrocers** NOUN
a shopkeeper who sells vegetables and fruit

greenhouse ['gri:n,haʊs] **greenhouses** NOUN
a glass building in which people grow plants that need to be kept warm

greenhouse effect NOUN
the gradual rise in temperature in the earth's atmosphere due to heat being absorbed from the sun and being trapped by gases such as carbon dioxide in the air around the earth

green paper green papers NOUN
In Britain, Australia, and New Zealand, a report published by the government containing proposals to be discussed before decisions are made about them.

greenstone ['gri:n,stəʊn] NOUN
a type of jade found in New Zealand and used for making ornaments, weapons, and tools

greet [gri:t] **greets, greeting, greeted** VERB
1 If you greet someone, you say something friendly like 'hello' to them when you meet them.

● THESAURUS
meet: *A nurse met me at the entrance.*
receive: formal *250 guests were received by the bride and bridegroom.*
welcome: *She was there to welcome him home.*

2 If you greet something in a particular way, you react to it in that way. *e.g. He was greeted with deep suspicion.*

greeting ['gri:tɪŋ] **greetings** NOUN
something friendly that you say to someone when you meet them *e.g. Her greeting was warm.*

gregarious [grɪ'gɛərɪəs] ADJECTIVE; FORMAL
Someone who is gregarious enjoys being with other people.

grenade [grɪ'neɪd] **grenades** NOUN
a small bomb, containing explosive or tear gas, which can be thrown
[WORD HISTORY: from Spanish GRANADA meaning 'pomegranate']

grevillea [grə'vɪljə] **grevilleas** NOUN
an evergreen Australian tree or shrub

grew [gru:] the past tense of **grow**

grey [greɪ] **greyer, greyest; greys, greying, greyed** ADJECTIVE OR NOUN
Grey is a colour between black and white.
> ADJECTIVE
1 dull and boring *e.g. He's a bit of a grey man.*
> VERB
2 If someone is greying, their hair is going grey.
greyness NOUN

greyhound ['greɪ,haʊnd] **greyhounds** NOUN
a thin dog with long legs that can run very fast

grid [grɪd] **grids** NOUN
1 a pattern of lines crossing each other to form squares
2 The grid is the network of wires and cables by which electricity is distributed throughout a country.

grief [gri:f] NOUN

g

1 Grief is extreme sadness.

● THESAURUS

distress: *the intense distress they were causing my family*

heartache: *She has suffered more heartache than anyone deserves.*

misery: *All that money brought nothing but misery.*

sadness: *It is with a mixture of sadness and joy that I say farewell.*

sorrow: *a time of great sorrow*

unhappiness: *There was a lot of unhappiness in my adolescence.*

<<OPPOSITE *happiness*

> PHRASE

2 If someone or something **comes to grief**, they fail or are injured.

grievance ['griːvᵊns] **grievances** NOUN
a reason for complaining

grieve [griːv] **grieves, grieving, grieved**
VERB

1 If you grieve, you are extremely sad, especially because someone has died.

● THESAURUS

lament: *All who knew Spender will lament his death.*

mourn: *The whole nation mourns the death of their great leader.*

2 If something grieves you, it makes you feel very sad.

● THESAURUS

distress: *It distresses me that the President has not tackled crime.*

pain: *It pains me to think of you struggling all alone.*

sadden: *The cruelty in the world saddens me.*

upset: *The news upset me.*

<<OPPOSITE *cheer*

grievous ['griːvəs] ADJECTIVE; FORMAL
extremely serious *e.g. grievous damage*
grievously ADVERB

grill [gril] **grills, grilling, grilled** NOUN

1 a part on a cooker where food is cooked by strong heat from above

2 a metal frame on which you cook food over a fire

> VERB

3 If you grill food, you cook it on or under a grill.

4 INFORMAL If you grill someone, you ask them a lot of questions in a very intense way.

grille [gril] **grilles** NOUN
a metal framework over a window or piece of machinery, used for protection

grim [grim] **grimmer, grimmest** ADJECTIVE

1 If a situation or piece of news is grim, it is very unpleasant and worrying. *e.g. There are grim times ahead.*

2 Grim places are unattractive and depressing.

3 If someone is grim, they are very serious or stern.
grimly ADVERB

● THESAURUS

grave: *Mrs Williams was looking very grave.*

severe: *He leaned towards me, a severe expression on his face.*

solemn: *What a solemn-faced kid he had been.*

stern: *Michael gave the dog a stern look.*

grimace [gri'meis] **grimaces, grimacing, grimaced** NOUN

1 a twisted facial expression indicating disgust or pain

> VERB

2 When someone grimaces, they make a grimace.

grime [graim] NOUN
Grime is thick dirt which gathers on the surface of something.
grimy ADJECTIVE

grin [grin] **grins, grinning, grinned** VERB

1 If you grin, you smile broadly.

> NOUN

2 a broad smile

> PHRASE

3 If you **grin and bear it**, you accept a difficult situation without complaining.

grind [graind] **grinds, grinding, ground**
VERB

1 If you grind something such as pepper, you crush it into a fine powder.

2 If you grind your teeth, you rub your upper and lower teeth together.

> PHRASE

3 If something **grinds to a halt**, it stops. *e.g. Progress ground to a halt.*

grip [grip] **grips, gripping, gripped** NOUN

1 a firm hold

● THESAURUS

clasp: *With one last clasp of his hand, she left him.*

grasp: *The spade slipped from her grasp and fell to the ground.*

hold: *He released his hold on the camera.*

2 a handle on a bat or a racket

3 Your grip on a situation is your control over it.

● THESAURUS

clutches: *She fell into the clutches of the wrong sort of person.*

control: *The port area is under the control of rebel forces.*

influence: *Alexandra fell under the influence of Grigori Rasputin.*

power: *I was really in the power of my mother.*

> VERB

4 If you grip something, you hold it firmly.

● THESAURUS

clutch: *Michelle clutched my arm.*
grasp: *He grasped both my hands.*
hold: *He was struggling to hold on to the rope.*

> PHRASE

5 If you **get to grips with** a situation or problem, you start to deal with it effectively.

grisly ['grɪzlɪ] **grislier, grisliest** ADJECTIVE
very nasty and horrible *e.g. a grisly murder scene*

grit [grɪt] **grits, gritting, gritted** NOUN
1 Grit consists of very small stones. It is put on icy roads to make them less slippery.

> VERB

2 When workmen grit an icy road, they put grit on it.

> PHRASE

3 To **grit your teeth** means to decide to carry on in a difficult situation.
gritty ADJECTIVE

grizzled ['grɪzəld] ADJECTIVE
Grizzled hair is grey. A grizzled person has grey hair.

grizzly bear ['grɪzlɪ] **grizzly bears** NOUN
a large, greyish-brown bear from North America

groan [grəʊn] **groans, groaning, groaned** VERB
1 If you groan, you make a long, low sound of pain, unhappiness, or disapproval.

> NOUN

2 the sound you make when you groan

grocer ['grəʊsə] **grocers** NOUN
a shopkeeper who sells many kinds of food and other household goods

grocery ['grəʊsərɪ] **groceries** NOUN
1 a grocer's shop

> PLURAL NOUN

2 Groceries are the goods that you buy in a grocer's shop.

grog [grɒg] NOUN; INFORMAL
In Australian and New Zealand English, grog is any alcoholic drink.

groin [grɔɪn] **groins** NOUN
the area where your legs join the main part of your body at the front

groom [gruːm] **grooms, grooming, groomed** NOUN
1 someone who looks after horses in a stable
2 At a wedding, the groom is the bridegroom.

> VERB

3 To groom an animal means to clean its fur.

4 If you groom someone for a job, you prepare them for it by teaching them the skills they will need.

groove [gruːv] **grooves** NOUN
a deep line cut into a surface
grooved ADJECTIVE

grope [grəʊp] **gropes, groping, groped** VERB
1 If you grope for something you cannot see, you search for it with your hands.
2 If you grope for something such as the solution to a problem, you try to think of it.

gross [grəʊs] **grosser, grossest; grosses, grossing, grossed** ADJECTIVE
1 extremely bad *e.g. a gross betrayal*
2 Gross speech or behaviour is very rude.
3 Gross things are ugly. *e.g. gross holiday outfits*
4 Someone's gross income is their total income before any deductions are made.
5 The gross weight of something is its total weight including the weight of its container.

> VERB

6 If you gross an amount of money, you earn that amount in total.
grossly ADVERB

grotesque [grəʊ'tɛsk] ADJECTIVE
1 exaggerated and absurd *e.g. It was the most grotesque thing she had ever heard.*
2 very strange and ugly *e.g. grotesque animal puppets*
grotesquely ADVERB

grotto ['grɒtəʊ] **grottoes** or **grottos** NOUN
a small cave that people visit because it is attractive

ground [graʊnd] **grounds, grounding, grounded** NOUN
1 The ground is the surface of the earth.

● THESAURUS

dirt: *They sat on the dirt in the shade of a tree.*
earth: *The road winds for miles through parched earth.*
land: *800 acres of agricultural land*
soil: *In Southern India the soil is fertile.*
terrain: *Farms give way to hilly terrain.*

2 a piece of land that is used for a particular purpose *e.g. the training ground*

3 The ground covered by a book or course is the range of subjects it deals with.

> PLURAL NOUN

4 The grounds of a large building are the land belonging to it and surrounding it.

● THESAURUS

estate: *Lord Wyville's estate in Yorkshire.*

gardens: *an elegant Regency house set in beautiful gardens*
land: *Their home is on his father's land.*

5 FORMAL
The grounds for something are the reasons for it.
e.g. genuine grounds for caution

● THESAURUS
basis: *Could you tell me on what basis the fee is calculated?*
cause: *No one had cause to get angry or unpleasant.*
excuse: *There's no excuse for behaviour like that.*
justification: *There was no justification for what I was doing.*
reason: *Who would have a reason to want to kill her?*

> VERB
6 FORMAL If something is grounded in something else, it is based on it.

7 If an aircraft is grounded, it has to remain on the ground.

8 Ground is the past tense and past participle of **grind**.

ground floor **ground floors** NOUN
The ground floor of a building is the floor that is approximately level with the ground.

grounding ['graʊndɪŋ] NOUN
If you have a grounding in a skill or subject, you have had basic instruction in it.

groundless ['graʊndlɪs] ADJECTIVE
not based on reason or evidence *e.g. groundless accusations*

group [gruːp] **groups, grouping, grouped**
NOUN
1 A group of things or people is a number of them that are linked together in some way.

● THESAURUS
band: *a band of rebels*
bunch: *They're a nice bunch of lads.*
collection: *a collection of essays from foreign affairs experts*
crowd: *A small crowd of onlookers has gathered.*
gang: *Gangs of teenagers hang out in shop doorways.*
pack: *a pack of journalists eager to question him*
party: *a party of sightseers*
set: *Different sets of people often use the same buildings.*

2 a number of musicians who perform pop music together

> VERB
3 When things or people are grouped together, they are linked together in some way.

● THESAURUS
arrange: *He started to arrange the books in piles.*
class: *They are officially classed as visitors.*

classify: *Rocks can be classified according to their origin.*
organize: *I was organizing the vast array of junk we had collected.*
sort: *The students are sorted into three ability groups.*

grouping ['gruːpɪŋ] **groupings** NOUN
a number of things or people that are linked together in some way

grouse [graʊs] **grouse** NOUN
a fat brown or grey bird, often shot for sport

grove [grəʊv] **groves** NOUN; LITERARY
a group of trees growing close together

grovel ['grɒvəl] **grovels, grovelling, grovelled** VERB
If you grovel, you behave in an unpleasantly humble way towards someone you regard as important.

grow [grəʊ] **grows, growing, grew, grown**
VERB
1 To grow means to increase in size or amount.

● THESAURUS
develop: *These clashes could develop into open warfare.*
expand: *Will the universe continue to expand forever?*
increase: *Industrial output increased by 2%.*
multiply: *Her husband multiplied his demands on her time.*
<<OPPOSITE *shrink*

2 If a tree or plant grows somewhere, it is alive there.

● THESAURUS
flourish: *The plant flourishes in slightly harsher climates.*
germinate: *Heat will encourage seeds to germinate.*
sprout: *It only takes a few days for beans to sprout.*

3 When people grow plants, they plant them and look after them.

4 If a man grows a beard or moustache, he lets it develop by not shaving.

5 To grow also means to pass gradually into a particular state.

● THESAURUS
become: *The wind became stronger.*
get: *The boys were getting bored.*
turn: *In October it turned cold.*

6 If one thing grows from another, it develops from it.

7 INFORMAL If something grows on you, you gradually start to like it.

grow up VERB
8 When a child grows up, he or she becomes an adult.

growl [graʊl] **growls, growling, growled**
VERB

1 When an animal growls, it makes a low rumbling sound, usually because it is angry.

2 If you growl something, you say it in a low, rough, rather angry voice.

> NOUN

3 the sound an animal makes when it growls

grown-up grown-ups NOUN ['grəʊn,ʌp]

1 INFORMAL an adult

> ADJECTIVE [,grəʊn'ʌp]

2 Someone who is grown-up is adult, or behaves like an adult.

growth [grəʊθ] **growths** NOUN

1 When there is a growth in something, it gets bigger. *e.g. the growth of the fishing industry*

● THESAURUS
development: *What are your plans for the development of your company?*
enlargement: *the enlargement of the European Union*
expansion: *a new period of economic expansion*
increase: *a sharp increase in the number of homeless people*

2 (SCIENCE) Growth is the process by which something develops to its full size.

3 an abnormal lump that grows inside or on a person, animal, or plant

grub [grʌb] **grubs** NOUN

1 a wormlike insect that has just hatched from its egg

2 INFORMAL Grub is food.

grubby ['grʌbɪ] **grubbier, grubbiest**
ADJECTIVE
rather dirty

grudge [grʌdʒ] **grudges, grudging, grudged** NOUN

1 If you have a grudge against someone, you resent them because they have harmed you in the past.

> VERB

2 If you grudge someone something, you give it to them unwillingly, or are displeased that they have it.

grudging ['grʌdʒɪŋ] ADJECTIVE
done or felt unwillingly *e.g. grudging admiration*
grudgingly ADVERB

gruel ['gruːəl] NOUN
Gruel is oatmeal boiled in water or milk.

gruelling ['gruːəlɪŋ] ADJECTIVE
difficult and tiring *e.g. a gruelling race*

gruesome ['gruːsəm] ADJECTIVE
shocking and horrible *e.g. gruesome pictures*

gruff [grʌf] **gruffer, gruffest** ADJECTIVE
If someone's voice is gruff, it sounds rough and unfriendly.

grumble ['grʌmbəl] **grumbles, grumbling, grumbled** VERB

1 If you grumble, you complain in a bad-tempered way.

● THESAURUS
carp: *the man whom other actors love to carp about*
complain: *They complained about the high cost of visiting Europe.*
groan: *parents groaning about the price of college tuition*
moan: *moaning about the weather*
mutter: *She could hear the old woman muttering about young people.*
whine: *children who whine that they are bored*
whinge: *All she ever does is whinge.*

> NOUN

2 a bad-tempered complaint

● THESAURUS
complaint: *I get nothing but complaints about my cooking.*
moan: *Sometimes it helps to have a good old moan.*
murmur: *She paid without a murmur.*
objection: *If you have any objections, please raise them now.*
protest: *Despite our protests, they went ahead with the plan.*
whinge: *It's depressing listening to everybody's whinges.*

grumpy ['grʌmpɪ] **grumpier, grumpiest**
ADJECTIVE
bad-tempered and fed-up

● THESAURUS
irritable: *He had missed his dinner and grew irritable.*
sulky: *She still looked like a sulky teenager.*
sullen: *Several leading players have maintained a sullen silence.*
surly: *They were surly, sometimes downright rude to me.*

grunt [grʌnt] **grunts, grunting, grunted**
VERB

1 If a person or a pig grunts, they make a short, low, gruff sound.

> NOUN

2 the sound a person or a pig makes when they grunt

guarantee [,gærən'tiː] **guarantees, guaranteeing, guaranteed** NOUN

1 If something is a guarantee of something else, it makes it certain that it will happen.

● THESAURUS
assurance: *a written assurance that he would start work at once*

pledge: *a pledge of support from the Ministry of Culture*
promise: *I'd made him a promise that I'd write a book for him.*
undertaking: *She gave an undertaking not to repeat the allegations.*
word: *He simply cannot be trusted to keep his word.*

2 a written promise that if a product develops a fault it will be replaced or repaired free

> VERB

3 If something or someone guarantees something, they make certain that it will happen. *e.g. Money may not guarantee success.*
guarantor NOUN

● THESAURUS

ensure: *We need to ensure that every student has basic literacy skills.*
pledge: *Both sides pledged that a nuclear war would never be fought.*
promise: *He promised that the rich would not get preferential treatment.*

guard [gɑːd] **guards, guarding, guarded**
VERB

1 If you guard a person or object, you stay near to them to protect them.

● THESAURUS

defend: *He and his friends defended themselves against racist thugs.*
protect: *What can women do to protect themselves from heart disease?*
safeguard: *measures to safeguard their forces from chemical weapons*
shelter: *A neighbour sheltered the boy for seven days.*
shield: *She had shielded him from the terrible truth.*
watch over: *two policewomen to watch over him*

2 If you guard a person, you stop them making trouble or escaping.

● THESAURUS

patrol: *Prison officers continued to patrol the grounds.*
police: *It is extremely difficult to police the border.*
supervise: *Only two staff were supervising over 100 prisoners.*

3 If you guard against something, you are careful to avoid it happening.

> NOUN

4 a person or group of people who guard a person, object, or place

● THESAURUS

sentry: *We can sneak past the sentries.*
warden: *The siege began when the prisoners seized three wardens.*

5 a railway official in charge of a train

6 Any object which covers something to prevent it causing harm can be called a guard.

guardian [ˈgɑːdɪən] **guardians** NOUN

1 someone who has been legally appointed to look after an orphaned child

2 A guardian of something is someone who protects it. *e.g. a guardian of the law*
guardianship NOUN

guernsey [ˈgɜːnzɪ] **guernseys** NOUN

1 In Australian and New Zealand English, a jersey.

2 a sleeveless top worn by an Australian Rules football player

guerrilla [gəˈrɪlə] **guerrillas** (*said* ger-**ril**-la); also spelt **guerilla** NOUN
a member of a small unofficial army fighting an official army

guess [gɛs] **guesses, guessing, guessed**
VERB

1 If you guess something, you form or express an opinion that it is the case, without having much information.

● THESAURUS

estimate: *It's difficult to estimate how much money is involved.*
imagine: *'Was he meeting someone?' 'I imagine so.'*
reckon: *Toni reckoned that it must be about three o'clock.*
speculate: *The reader can speculate what will happen next.*
suppose: *I supposed you would have a meal somewhere.*
suspect: *I suspect they were right.*
think: *Nora thought he was seventeen years old.*

> NOUN

2 (**MATHS**) an attempt to give the correct answer to something without having much information, or without working it out properly

● THESAURUS

feeling: *My feeling is that everything will come right for us.*
reckoning: *By my reckoning, 50% of the team will be available.*
speculation: *speculations about the future of the universe*

guest [gɛst] **guests** NOUN

1 someone who stays at your home or who attends an occasion because they have been invited

2 The guests in a hotel are the people staying there.

guffaw [gʌˈfɔː] NOUN
a loud, coarse laugh

guidance [ˈgaɪdəns] NOUN
Guidance is help and advice.

guide [gaɪd] **guides, guiding, guided** NOUN

1 someone who shows you round places, or leads the way through difficult country

2 a book which gives you information or instructions *e.g. a Sydney street guide*

3 A Guide is a girl who is a member of an organization that encourages discipline and practical skills.

> VERB

4 If you guide someone in a particular direction, you lead them in that direction.

● THESAURUS
accompany: *We accompanied Joe to the magazine's midtown offices.*
direct: *Officials directed him to the wrong airport.*
escort: *I escorted him to the door.*
lead: *The nurse led me to a large room.*

5 If you are guided by something, it influences your actions or decisions.

● THESAURUS
counsel: formal *Green was counselled not to talk to reporters.*
govern: *Our thinking is as much governed by habit as by behaviour.*
influence: *My dad influenced me to do electronics.*

guidebook ['gaɪd,bʊk] **guidebooks** NOUN
a book which gives information about a place

guide dog **guide dogs** NOUN
a dog that has been trained to lead a blind person

guideline ['gaɪd,laɪn] **guidelines** NOUN
a piece of advice about how something should be done

guild [gɪld] **guilds** NOUN
a society of people *e.g. the Screen Writers' Guild*

guile [gaɪl] NOUN
Guile is cunning and deceit.
guileless ADJECTIVE

guillotine ['gɪlə,tiːn] **guillotines** NOUN
a machine used for beheading people, especially in the past in France

guilt [gɪlt] NOUN
1 Guilt is an unhappy feeling of having done something wrong.

2 Someone's guilt is the fact that they have done something wrong. *e.g. The law will decide their guilt.*

guilty ['gɪltɪ] **guiltier, guiltiest** ADJECTIVE
1 If you are guilty of doing something wrong, you did it. *e.g. He was guilty of theft.*

● THESAURUS
convicted: *a convicted drug dealer*
criminal: *He had a criminal record for petty theft.*
<<OPPOSITE *innocent*

2 If you feel guilty, you are unhappy because you have done something wrong.
guiltily ADVERB

● THESAURUS
ashamed: *Zumel said he was not ashamed of what he had done.*
regretful: *Surprisingly, she didn't feel regretful about her actions.*
remorseful: formal *He felt remorseful for what he had done.*
sorry: *She was very sorry about all the trouble she'd caused.*

guinea ['gɪnɪ] **guineas** NOUN
an old British unit of money, worth 21 shillings

guinea pig **guinea pigs** NOUN
1 a small furry animal without a tail, often kept as a pet
2 a person used to try something out on *e.g. a guinea pig for a new drug*

guise [gaɪz] **guises** NOUN
a misleading appearance *e.g. political statements in the guise of religious talk*

guitar [gɪ'tɑː] **guitars** NOUN
a musical instrument with six strings which are strummed or plucked
guitarist NOUN

gulf [gʌlf] **gulfs** NOUN
1 a very large bay
2 a wide gap or difference between two things or people

gull [gʌl] **gulls** NOUN
a sea bird with long wings, white and grey or black feathers, and webbed feet

gullet ['gʌlɪt] **gullets** NOUN
the tube that goes from your mouth to your stomach

gullible ['gʌləbəl] ADJECTIVE
easily tricked
gullibility NOUN

● THESAURUS
naive: *It would be naive to believe Mr Gonzalez's statement.*
trusting: *She has an open, trusting nature.*

gully ['gʌlɪ] **gullies** NOUN
a long, narrow valley

gulp [gʌlp] **gulps, gulping, gulped** VERB
1 If you gulp food or drink, you swallow large quantities of it.
2 If you gulp, you swallow air, because you are nervous.

> NOUN

3 A gulp of food or drink is a large quantity of it swallowed at one time.

gum [gʌm] **gums** NOUN
1 Gum is a soft flavoured substance that people chew but do not swallow.

2 Gum is also glue for sticking paper.

3 Your gums are the firm flesh in which your teeth are set.

gumboot ['gʌm,buːt] **gumboots** NOUN
Gumboots are long waterproof boots.

gumtree ['gʌm,triː] **gumtrees** NOUN
a eucalyptus, or other tree which produces gum

gun [gʌn] **guns** NOUN
a weapon which fires bullets or shells

gunfire ['gʌn,faɪə] NOUN
Gunfire is the repeated firing of guns.

gunpowder ['gʌn,paʊdə] NOUN
Gunpowder is an explosive powder made from a mixture of potassium nitrate and other substances.

gunshot ['gʌnʃɒt] **gunshots** NOUN
the sound of a gun being fired

guppy ['gʌpɪ] **guppies** NOUN
a small, brightly coloured tropical fish

gurdwara ['gɜːdwɑːrə] NOUN
a Sikh place of worship

gurgle ['gɜːgəl] **gurgles, gurgling, gurgled**
VERB

1 To gurgle means to make a bubbling sound.
> NOUN
2 a bubbling sound

guru ['gʊruː] **gurus** NOUN
a spiritual leader and teacher, especially in India

gush [gʌʃ] **gushes, gushing, gushed** VERB

1 When liquid gushes from something, it flows out of it in large quantities.

● THESAURUS
flow: *Tears flowed down his cheeks.*
pour: *Blood was pouring from his broken nose.*
spurt: *a fountain that spurts water nine stories high*
stream: *water streaming from the pipes*

2 When people gush, they express admiration or pleasure in an exaggerated way.
gushing ADJECTIVE

gust [gʌst] **gusts** NOUN
a sudden rush of wind
gusty ADJECTIVE

gusto ['gʌstəʊ] NOUN
Gusto is energy and enthusiasm. *e.g. Her gusto for life was amazing.*

gut [gʌt] **guts, gutting, gutted** PLURAL
NOUN

1 Your guts are your internal organs, especially your intestines.
> VERB
2 To gut a dead fish means to remove its internal organs.

3 If a building is gutted, the inside of it is destroyed, especially by fire.

> NOUN
4 INFORMAL Guts is courage.

gutter ['gʌtə] **gutters** NOUN

1 the edge of a road next to the pavement, where rain collects and flows away

2 a channel fixed to the edge of a roof, where rain collects and flows away
guttering NOUN

guttural ['gʌtərəl] ADJECTIVE
Guttural sounds are produced at the back of a person's throat and are often considered to be unpleasant.

guy [gaɪ] **guys** NOUN

1 INFORMAL a man or boy

2 a crude model of Guy Fawkes, that is burnt on top of a bonfire on November 5
[WORD HISTORY: short for Guy Fawkes, who plotted to blow up the British Houses of Parliament]

guzzle ['gʌzəl] **guzzles, guzzling, guzzled**
VERB
To guzzle something means to drink or eat it quickly and greedily.

gym [dʒɪm] **gyms** NOUN **(PE)**

1 a gymnasium

2 Gym is gymnastics.

gymkhana [dʒɪm'kɑːnə] **gymkhanas**
NOUN
an event in which people take part in horse-riding contests
[WORD HISTORY: from Hindi GEND-KHANA literally meaning 'ball house', because it is where sports were held]

gymnasium [dʒɪm'neɪzɪəm] **gymnasiums**
NOUN
a room with special equipment for physical exercises
[WORD HISTORY: from Greek GUMNAZEIN meaning 'to exercise naked']

gymnast ['dʒɪmnæst] **gymnasts** NOUN
someone who is trained in gymnastics
gymnastic ADJECTIVE

gymnastics [dʒɪm'næstɪks] NOUN
(PE) Gymnastics is physical exercises, especially ones using equipment such as bars and ropes.

gynaecology or **gynecology**
[,gaɪnɪ'kɒlədʒɪ] NOUN
Gynaecology is the branch of medical science concerned with the female reproductive system.
gynaecologist NOUN, **gynaecological** ADJECTIVE

gypsy ['dʒɪpsɪ] **gypsies;** also spelt gipsy NOUN
a member of a race of people who travel from place to place in caravans
[WORD HISTORY: from 'Egyptian', because people used to think gypsies came from Egypt]

gyrate [dʒɪ'reɪt] **gyrates, gyrating, gyrated**
VERB
To gyrate means to move round in a circle.

Hh

habit ['hæbɪt] **habits** NOUN

1 something that you do often *e.g. He got into the habit of eating out.*

● THESAURUS

convention: *It's just a social convention that men don't wear skirts.*

custom: *an ancient Japanese custom*

practice: *the practice of clocking in at work*

routine: *my daily routine*

tradition: *a family tradition at Christmas*

2 something that you keep doing and find it difficult to stop doing *e.g. a 20-a-day smoking habit*

● THESAURUS

addiction: *his addiction to gambling*

dependence: *the effects of drug dependence*

3 A monk's or nun's habit is a garment like a loose dress.

habitual ADJECTIVE, **habitually** ADVERB

habitat ['hæbɪˌtæt] **habitats** NOUN

(GEOGRAPHY) the natural home of a plant or animal

● THESAURUS

environment: *a safe environment for marine mammals*

territory: *a bird's territory*

hack [hæk] **hacks, hacking, hacked** VERB

1 If you hack at something, you cut it using rough strokes.

> NOUN

2 a writer or journalist who produces work fast without worrying about quality

hacker ['hækə] **hackers** NOUN; INFORMAL

someone who uses a computer to break into the computer system of a company or government

hackles ['hækᵊlz] PLURAL NOUN

1 A dog's hackles are the hairs on the back of its neck which rise when it is angry.

> PHRASE

2 Something that **makes your hackles rise** makes you angry.

hackneyed ['hæknɪd] ADJECTIVE

A hackneyed phrase is meaningless because it has been used too often.

● THESAURUS

banal: *banal lyrics*

clichéd: *clichéd slogans*

stale: *Her relationship with Mark has become stale.*

tired: *a tired excuse*

trite: *The film is teeming with trite ideas.*

<<OPPOSITE *original*

hacksaw ['hækˌsɔː] **hacksaws** NOUN

a small saw with a narrow blade set in a frame

haddock ['hædək] NOUN

an edible sea fish

haemoglobin [ˌhiːməʊˈgləʊbɪn] NOUN

Haemoglobin is a substance in red blood cells which carries oxygen round the body.

haemorrhage ['hɛmərɪdʒ] NOUN

A haemorrhage is serious bleeding, especially inside a person's body.

haemorrhoids ['hɛməˌrɔɪdz] PLURAL NOUN

Haemorrhoids are painful lumps around the anus that are caused by swollen veins.

hag [hæg] **hags** NOUN; OFFENSIVE

an ugly old woman

haggard ['hægəd] ADJECTIVE

A person who is haggard looks very tired and ill.

haggis ['hægɪs] NOUN

Haggis is a Scottish dish made of the internal organs of a sheep, boiled together with oatmeal and spices in a skin.

haggle ['hægᵊl] **haggles, haggling, haggled** VERB

If you haggle with someone, you argue with them, usually about the cost of something.

hail [heɪl] **hails, hailing, hailed** NOUN

1 Hail is frozen rain.

2 A hail of things is a lot of them falling together. *e.g. a hail of bullets... a hail of protest*

● THESAURUS

barrage: *a barrage of angry questions*

bombardment: *the sound of heavy aerial bombardment*

shower: *a shower of rose petals*

storm: *The announcement provoked a storm of protest.*

volley: *A volley of shots rang out.*

> VERB

3 When it is hailing, frozen rain is falling.

4 If someone hails you, they call you to attract your attention or greet you. *e.g. He hailed a taxi.*

● THESAURUS

call: *He called me over the Tannoy.*
signal to: *The lollipop lady signalled to me to stop.*
wave down: *I ran on to the road and waved down a taxi.*

hair [hɛə] **hairs** NOUN
Hair consists of the long, threadlike strands that grow from the skin of animals and humans.

haircut ['hɛə,kʌt] **haircuts** NOUN
the cutting of someone's hair; also the style in which it is cut

hairdo ['hɛə,duː] **hairdos** NOUN
a hairstyle

hairdresser ['hɛə,drɛsə] **hairdressers** NOUN
someone who is trained to cut and style people's hair; also a shop where this is done
hairdressing NOUN OR ADJECTIVE

hairline ['hɛə,laɪn] **hairlines** NOUN
1 the edge of the area on your forehead where your hair grows

> ADJECTIVE

2 A hairline crack is so fine that you can hardly see it.

hairpin ['hɛə,pɪn] **hairpins** NOUN
1 a U-shaped wire used to hold hair in position

> ADJECTIVE

2 A hairpin bend is a U-shaped bend in the road.

hair-raising ['hɛə,reɪzɪŋ] ADJECTIVE
very frightening or exciting

hairstyle ['hɛə,staɪl] **hairstyles** NOUN
Someone's hairstyle is the way in which their hair is arranged or cut.

hairy ['hɛərɪ] **hairier, hairiest** ADJECTIVE
1 covered in a lot of hair

2 INFORMAL
difficult, exciting, and rather frightening *e.g. He had lived through many hairy adventures.*

hajj [hædʒ] NOUN
The hajj is the pilgrimage to Mecca that every Muslim must make at least once in their life if they are healthy and wealthy enough to do so.
[WORD HISTORY: from Arabic HAJJ pilgrimage]

haka ['hɑːkə] **haka** or **hakas** NOUN
1 In New Zealand, a haka is a ceremonial Maori dance made up of various postures and accompanied by a chant.

2 an imitation of this dance performed by New Zealand sports teams before matches as a challenge

hake [heɪk] **hakes** NOUN
an edible sea fish related to the cod

hakea ['hɑːkɪə] **hakeas** NOUN
a large Australian shrub with bright flowers and hard, woody fruit

halcyon ['hælsɪən] ADJECTIVE

1 LITERARY
peaceful, gentle, and calm *e.g. halcyon colours of yellow and turquoise*

> PHRASE

2 Halcyon days are a happy and carefree time in the past *e.g. halcyon days in the sun*

half [hɑːf] **halves** NOUN, ADJECTIVE, OR ADVERB
1 Half refers to one of two equal parts that make up a whole. *e.g. the two halves of the brain... They chatted for another half hour... The bottle was only half full.*

> ADVERB

2 You can use 'half' to say that something is only partly true. *e.g. I half expected him to explode in anger.*

half-baked [,hɑːfˈbeɪkt] ADJECTIVE; INFORMAL
Half-baked ideas or plans have not been properly thought out.

half board NOUN
Half board at a hotel includes breakfast and dinner but not lunch.

half-brother [,hɑːfˈbrʌðə] **half-brothers** NOUN
Your half-brother is the son of either your mother or your father but not of your other parent.

half-hearted [,hɑːfˈhɑːtɪd] ADJECTIVE
showing no real effort or enthusiasm

half-pie [hɑːfˈpaɪ] ADJECTIVE; INFORMAL
In New Zealand, half-pie means incomplete or not properly done. *e.g. finished in a half-pie way*

half-sister [,hɑːfˈsɪstə] **half-sisters** NOUN
Your half-sister is the daughter of either your mother or your father but not of your other parent.

half-timbered [,hɑːfˈtɪmbəd] ADJECTIVE
A half-timbered building has a framework of wooden beams showing in the walls.

half-time [,hɑːfˈtaɪm] NOUN
Half-time is a short break between two parts of a game when the players have a rest.

halfway [,hɑːfˈweɪ] ADVERB
at the middle of the distance between two points in place or time *e.g. He stopped halfway down the*

ladder... halfway through the term

halibut ['hælɪbət] **halibuts** NOUN
a large edible flat fish

hall [hɔ:l] **halls** NOUN
1 the room just inside the front entrance of a house which leads into other rooms
2 a large room or building used for public events *e.g. a concert hall*

hallmark ['hɔ:l,mɑ:k] **hallmarks** NOUN
1 The hallmark of a person or group is their most typical quality. *e.g. A warm, hospitable welcome is the hallmark of island people.*
2 an official mark on gold or silver indicating the quality of the metal

hallowed ['hæləʊd] ADJECTIVE
respected as being holy *e.g. hallowed ground*

Halloween [,hæləʊ'i:n] NOUN
Halloween is October 31st, and is celebrated by children dressing up, often as ghosts and witches.
[WORD HISTORY: from Old English HALIG + ÆFEN meaning 'holy evening', the evening before All Saints' Day]

hallucinate [hə'lu:sɪ,neɪt] **hallucinates, hallucinating, hallucinated** VERB
If you hallucinate, you see strange things in your mind because of illness or drugs.
hallucination NOUN, **hallucinatory** ADJECTIVE
[WORD HISTORY: from Latin ALUCINARI meaning 'to wander in thought']

halo ['heɪləʊ] **haloes** or **halos** NOUN
a circle of light around the head of a holy figure
[WORD HISTORY: from Greek HALOS meaning 'disc shape of the sun or moon']

halt [hɔ:lt] **halts, halting, halted** VERB
1 To halt when moving means to stop.

● THESAURUS
draw up: *The car drew up outside the house.*
pull up: *The cab pulled up, and the driver jumped out.*
stop: *The event literally stopped the traffic.*
2 To halt development or action means to stop it.

● THESAURUS
cease: *A small number of firms have ceased trading.*
check: *We have managed to check the spread of terrorism.*
curb: *efforts to curb the spread of nuclear weapons*
cut short: *They had to cut short a holiday abroad.*
end: *They decided to end the ceasefire.*
terminate: *His contract has been terminated.*
<<OPPOSITE *begin*

> NOUN
3 a short standstill

● THESAURUS
close: *Their 18-month marriage was brought to a close.*
end: *The war came to an end.*
pause: *There was a pause before he replied.*
standstill: *The country was brought to a standstill by strikes.*
stop: *He slowed the car almost to a stop.*
stoppage: *Air and ground crew are staging a 24-hour stoppage today.*

halter ['hɔ:ltə] **halters** NOUN
a strap fastened round a horse's head so that it can be led easily

halve [hɑ:v] **halves, halving, halved** VERB
1 If you halve something, you divide it into two equal parts.
2 To halve something also means to reduce its size or amount by half.

ham [hæm] **hams** NOUN
1 Ham is meat from the hind leg of a pig, salted and cured.
2 a bad actor who exaggerates emotions and gestures
3 someone who is interested in amateur radio

hamburger ['hæm,bɜ:gə] **hamburgers** NOUN
a flat disc of minced meat, seasoned and fried; often eaten in a bread roll
[WORD HISTORY: named after its city of origin HAMBURG in Germany]

hammer ['hæmə] **hammers, hammering, hammered** NOUN
1 a tool consisting of a heavy piece of metal at the end of a handle, used for hitting nails into things
> VERB
2 If you hammer something, you hit it repeatedly, with a hammer or with your fist.
3 If you hammer an idea into someone, you keep repeating it and telling them about it.
4 INFORMAL
If you hammer someone, you criticize or attack them severely.

hammock ['hæmək] **hammocks** NOUN
a piece of net or canvas hung between two supports and used as a bed

hamper ['hæmpə] **hampers, hampering, hampered** NOUN
1 a rectangular wicker basket with a lid, used for carrying food
> VERB
2 If you hamper someone, you make it difficult for them to move or progress.

THESAURUS
frustrate: *His attempt was frustrated by the weather.*
hinder: *A thigh injury hindered her mobility.*
impede: *Their work was being impeded by shortages of supplies.*
obstruct: *charged with obstructing the course of justice*
restrict: *Her life is restricted by asthma.*

hamster ['hæmstə] **hamsters** NOUN
a small furry rodent which is often kept as a pet
There is no *p* in *hamster.*

hamstring ['hæm,strɪŋ] **hamstrings** NOUN **(PE)**
Your hamstring is a tendon behind your knee joining your thigh muscles to the bones of your lower leg.

hand [hænd] **hands, handing, handed** NOUN
1 Your hand is the part of your body beyond the wrist, with four fingers and a thumb.
2 Your hand is also your writing style.
3 The hand of someone in a situation is their influence or the part they play in it. *e.g. He had a hand in its design.*
4 If you give someone a hand, you help them to do something.
5 When an audience gives someone a big hand, they applaud.
6 The hands of a clock or watch are the pointers that point to the numbers.
7 In cards, your hand is the cards you are holding.
> VERB
8 If you hand something to someone, you give it to them.
> PHRASES
9 Something that is **at hand, to hand,** or **on hand** is available, close by, and ready for use.
10 You use **on the one hand** to introduce the first part of an argument or discussion with two different points of view.
11 You use **on the other hand** to introduce the second part of an argument or discussion with two different points of view.
12 If you do something **by hand,** you do it using your hands rather than a machine.
hand down VERB
13 Something that is handed down is passed from one generation to another.
THESAURUS
bequeath: *He bequeathed all his silver to his children.*
give: *a typewriter given to me by my father*

pass down: *an heirloom passed down from generation to generation*
pass on: *My parents passed on their love of classical music to me.*

handbag ['hænd,bæg] **handbags** NOUN
a small bag used mainly by women to carry money and personal items

handbook ['hænd,bʊk] **handbooks** NOUN
a book giving information and instructions about something

handcuff ['hænd,kʌf] **handcuffs** NOUN
Handcuffs are two metal rings linked by a chain which are locked around a prisoner's wrists.

handful ['hændfʊl] **handfuls** NOUN
1 A handful of something is the amount of it you can hold in your hand. *e.g. He picked up a handful of seeds.*
2 a small quantity *e.g. Only a handful of people knew.*
3 Someone who is a handful is difficult to control. *e.g. He is a bit of a handful.*

handicap ['hændɪ,kæp] **handicaps, handicapping, handicapped** NOUN
1 a physical or mental disability
THESAURUS
defect: *a rare birth defect*
disability: *children with learning disabilities*
2 something that makes it difficult for you to achieve something
THESAURUS
barrier: *Taxes are the most obvious barrier to free trade.*
disadvantage: *the disadvantage of unemployment*
drawback: *The flat's only drawback was that it was too small.*
hindrance: *She was a help rather than a hindrance to my work.*
impediment: *an impediment to economic development*
obstacle: *the main obstacle to the deal*
3 In sport, a handicap is a disadvantage or advantage given to competitors according to their skill, in order to give them an equal chance of winning.
> VERB
4 If something handicaps someone, it makes it difficult for them to achieve something.
THESAURUS
burden: *We decided not to burden him with the news.*
hamper: *I was hampered by a lack of information.*
hinder: *A thigh injury hindered her mobility.*
impede: *Fallen rocks impeded the progress of the rescue workers.*

restrict: *laws to restrict foreign imports*

handicraft ['hændɪ,krɑːft] **handicrafts**
NOUN
Handicrafts are activities such as embroidery or pottery which involve making things with your hands; also the items produced.

handiwork ['hændɪ,wɜːk] NOUN
Your handiwork is something that you have done or made yourself.

handkerchief ['hæŋkətʃɪf] **handkerchiefs**
NOUN
a small square of fabric used for blowing your nose

handle ['hændəl] **handles, handling, handled** NOUN
1 The handle of an object is the part by which it is held or controlled.

● THESAURUS
grip: *He fitted new grips to his golf clubs.*
hilt: *the hilt of the small, sharp knife*

2 a small lever used to open and close a door or window

> VERB
3 If you handle an object, you hold it in your hands to examine it.

● THESAURUS
feel: *The doctor felt his arm.*
finger: *He fingered the few coins in his pocket.*
grasp: *Grasp the end firmly.*
hold: *Hold it by the edge.*
touch: *She touched his hand reassuringly.*

4 If you handle something, you deal with it or control it. *e.g. I have learned how to handle pressure.*

● THESAURUS
administer: *The project is administered by the World Bank.*
conduct: *This is no way to conduct a business.*
deal with: *The matter has been dealt with by the school.*
manage: *Within two years he was managing the store.*
supervise: *I supervise the packing of all mail orders.*
take care of: *He took care of the catering arrangements.*

handlebar ['hændəl,bɑː] **handlebars** NOUN
Handlebars are the bar and handles at the front of a bicycle, used for steering.

handout ['hænd,aʊt] **handouts** NOUN
1 a gift of food, clothing, or money given to a poor person
2 a piece of paper giving information about something

hand-picked [,hænd'pɪkt] ADJECTIVE
carefully chosen *e.g. a hand-picked team of bodyguards*

handset ['hænd,sɛt] **handsets** NOUN
The handset of a telephone is the part that you speak into and listen with.

handshake ['hændʃeɪk] **handshakes** NOUN
the grasping and shaking of a person's hand by another person

handsome ['hændsəm] ADJECTIVE
1 very attractive in appearance

● THESAURUS
attractive: *an attractive young woman*
good-looking: *good-looking actors*
<<OPPOSITE *ugly*

2 large and generous *e.g. a handsome profit*
handsomely ADVERB

● THESAURUS
ample: *ample space for a good-sized kitchen*
considerable: *his considerable wealth*
generous: *a generous gift*
liberal: *a liberal donation*
plentiful: *a plentiful supply of vegetables*
sizable *or* sizeable: *He inherited the house and a sizeable chunk of land.*
<<OPPOSITE *small*

handwriting ['hænd,raɪtɪŋ] NOUN
Someone's handwriting is their style of writing as it looks on the page.

handy ['hændɪ] **handier, handiest**
ADJECTIVE
1 conveniently near

● THESAURUS
at hand: *Having the right equipment at hand will be enormously useful.*
at your fingertips: *Firms need information at their fingertips.*
close: *a secluded area close to her home*
convenient: *Martin drove along until he found a convenient parking space.*
nearby: *He tossed the match into a nearby wastepaper bin.*
on hand: *Experts are on hand to offer advice.*

2 easy to handle or use

● THESAURUS
convenient: *a convenient way of paying*
easy to use: *This ice cream maker is cheap and easy to use.*
helpful: *helpful instructions*
neat: *It had been such a neat, clever plan.*
practical: *the most practical way of preventing crime*
useful: *useful information*

3 skilful

hang [hæŋ] **hangs, hanging, hung** VERB
1 If you hang something somewhere, you attach it to a high point. *e.g. She hung heavy red velvet*

h

curtains in the sitting room.

● THESAURUS
attach: *He attached the picture to the wall with a nail.*
drape: *He draped the coat round his shoulders.*
fasten: *stirrups fastened to the saddle*
fix: *He fixed a pirate flag to the mast.*
suspend: *The TV is suspended from the ceiling on brackets.*

2 If something is hanging on something, it is attached by its top to it. *e.g. His jacket hung from a hook behind the door.*

● THESAURUS
dangle: *A gold bracelet dangled from his left wrist.*
droop: *Pale wilting roses drooped from a vase.*

3 If a future event or possibility is hanging over you, it worries or frightens you. *e.g. She has an eviction notice hanging over her.*

4 When you hang wallpaper, you stick it onto a wall.

5 To hang someone means to kill them by suspending them by a rope around the neck.

> PHRASE
6 When you **get the hang of something**, you understand it and are able to do it.

hang about or **hang around** VERB
7 INFORMAL To hang about or hang around means to wait somewhere.

8 To hang about or hang around with someone means to spend a lot of time with them.

hang on VERB
9 If you hang on to something, you hold it tightly or keep it.

10 INFORMAL To hang on means to wait.

hang up VERB
11 When you hang up, you put down the receiver to end a telephone call.

> When *hang* means 'kill someone by suspending them by a rope' (sense 4), the past tense and past participle are *hanged*: *he was hanged for murder in 1959.*

hangar ['hæŋə] **hangars** NOUN
a large building where aircraft are kept

hanger ['hæŋə] **hangers** NOUN
a coat hanger

hanger-on [ˌhæŋəˈɒn] **hangers-on** NOUN
an unwelcome follower of an important person

hang-glider [hæŋˌglaɪdə] **hang-gliders** NOUN
an aircraft without an engine and consisting of a large frame covered in fabric, from which the pilot hangs in a harness

hangi ['hʌŋiː] **hangi** or **hangis** NOUN
In New Zealand, a Maori oven made from a hole

in the ground lined with hot stones.

hangover ['hæŋˌəʊvə] **hangovers** NOUN
a feeling of sickness and headache after drinking too much alcohol

hang-up ['hæŋˌʌp] **hang-ups** NOUN
A hang-up about something is a continual feeling of embarrassment or fear about it.

hanker ['hæŋkə] **hankers, hankering, hankered** VERB
If you hanker after something, you continually want it.
hankering NOUN

hanky ['hæŋkɪ] **hankies** NOUN
a handkerchief

Hanukkah or **Chanukah** ['hɑːnəkə] NOUN
Hanukkah is an eight-day Jewish festival of lights.
[WORD HISTORY: a Hebrew word meaning literally 'a dedication']

haphazard [hæpˈhæzəd] ADJECTIVE
not organized or planned
haphazardly ADVERB
[WORD HISTORY: from Old Norse HAP meaning 'chance' and Arabic AZ-ZAHR meaning 'gaming dice']

hapless ['hæplɪs] ADJECTIVE; LITERARY
unlucky

happen ['hæpən] **happens, happening, happened** VERB
1 When something happens, it occurs or takes place.

● THESAURUS
come about: *It came about almost by accident.*
follow: *He was arrested in the confusion which followed.*
occur: *The crash occurred on a sharp bend.*
result: *Ignore the early warnings and illness could result.*
take place: *The festival took place last September.*

2 If you happen to do something, you do it by chance.
happening NOUN

happiness ['hæpɪnəs] NOUN
a feeling of great contentment or pleasure

● THESAURUS
delight: *To my delight, it worked perfectly.*
ecstasy: *a state of almost religious ecstasy*
elation: *His supporters reacted to the news with elation.*
joy: *tears of joy*
pleasure: *Everybody takes pleasure in eating.*
satisfaction: *job satisfaction*
<<OPPOSITE *sadness*

happy see page 403 for Word Web

1 ADJECTIVE

feeling or causing joy *eg: a happy atmosphere*

● **THESAURUS**

agreeable: *I had the agreeable task of telling him the good news.*

blissful: *twenty years of blissful marriage*

delighted: *They seem delighted with their new home.*

ecstatic: *I was ecstatic to see Marianne again.*

elated: *She was elated that she had won the lottery.*

euphoric: *He is understandably euphoric over his success.*

festive: *a truly festive occasion*

glad: *We're glad to be back.*

gratifying: *We enjoyed a gratifying relationship.*

joyful: *He takes a joyful pride in his work.*

joyous: *the joyous news that he had been released*

jubilant: *They were jubilant over their election victory.*

overjoyed: *They were overjoyed to be reunited at last.*

pleased: *We're very pleased with the verdict.*

thrilled: *I'm just thrilled to be playing again.*

over the moon (informal): *The team are over the moon with this result.*

pleasurable: *a pleasurable memory*

<< OPPOSITE *sad*

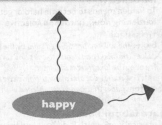

happy

2 ADJECTIVE

fortunate or lucky *eg: a happy coincidence*

● **THESAURUS**

auspicious: *It was not an auspicious start to his new job.*

convenient (formal): *a convenient outcome for all concerned*

favourable: *a favourable result*

fortunate: *We're in a very fortunate situation.*

lucky: *It was a lucky chance that you were here.*

opportune (formal): *It was hardly an opportune moment to bring the subject up.*

timely: *his timely arrival*

<< OPPOSITE *unlucky*

h

happy-go-lucky [ˌhæpɪɡəʊˈlʌkɪ] ADJECTIVE
carefree and unconcerned

harangue [həˈræŋ] **harangues, haranguing, harangued** NOUN

1 a long, forceful, passionate speech

> VERB

2 To harangue someone means to talk to them at length passionately and forcefully about something.

[WORD HISTORY: from Old Italian ARINGA meaning 'public speech']

harass [ˈhærəs] **harasses, harassing, harassed** VERB

If someone harasses you, they trouble or annoy you continually.

harassed ADJECTIVE, **harassment** NOUN

harbinger [ˈhɑːbɪndʒə] **harbingers** NOUN
a person or thing that announces or indicates the approach of a future event *e.g. others see the shortage of cash as a harbinger of bankruptcy*

harbour [ˈhɑːbə] **harbours, harbouring, harboured** NOUN

1 a protected area of deep water where boats can be moored

> VERB

2 To harbour someone means to hide them secretly in your house.

3 If you harbour a feeling, you have it for a long time. *e.g. She's still harbouring great bitterness.*

[WORD HISTORY: from Old English HERE + BEORG meaning 'army shelter']

hard [hɑːd] **harder, hardest** ADJECTIVE

1 Something that is hard is firm, solid, or stiff. *e.g. a hard piece of cheese*

● THESAURUS

firm: *a firm mattress*
rigid: *rigid plastic containers*
solid: *solid rock*
stiff: *stiff metal wires*
strong: *It has a strong casing which won't crack or chip.*
tough: *dark brown beans with a rather tough outer skin*
<<OPPOSITE *soft*

2 requiring a lot of effort *e.g. hard work*

● THESAURUS

arduous: *a long, arduous journey*
exhausting: *It's a pretty exhausting job.*
laborious: *Keeping the garden tidy can be a laborious task.*
rigorous: *rigorous military training*
strenuous: *Avoid strenuous exercise in the evening.*
tough: *Change is often tough to deal with.*
<<OPPOSITE *easy*

3 difficult *e.g. These are hard times.*

● THESAURUS

baffling: *a baffling remark*
complex: *a complex problem*
complicated: *a complicated system of voting*
difficult: *It was a very difficult decision to make.*
puzzling: *Some of this book is rather puzzling.*
<<OPPOSITE *simple*

4 Someone who is hard has no kindness or pity. *e.g. Don't be hard on him.*

5 A hard colour or voice is harsh and unpleasant.

6 Hard evidence or facts can be proved to be true.

7 Hard water contains a lot of lime and does not easily produce a lather.

8 Hard drugs are very strong illegal drugs.

9 Hard drink is strong alcohol.

> ADVERB

10 earnestly or intently *e.g. They tried hard to attract tourists.*
An event that follows hard upon something takes place immediately afterwards.

hardness NOUN

hard and fast ADJECTIVE
fixed and not able to be changed *e.g. hard and fast rules*

hardback [ˈhɑːdˌbæk] **hardbacks** NOUN
a book with a stiff cover

hard core NOUN
The hard core in an organization is the group of people who most resist change.

harden [ˈhɑːdᵊn] **hardens, hardening, hardened** VERB
To harden means to become hard or get harder.
hardening NOUN, **hardened** ADJECTIVE

● THESAURUS

bake: *The soil had been baked solid by the heatwave.*
cake: *The blood had begun to cake and turn brown.*
freeze: *The lake freezes in winter.*
set: *Lower the heat and allow the omelette to set.*
stiffen: *paper that had been stiffened with paste*
<<OPPOSITE *soften*

hard labour NOUN
physical work which is difficult and tiring, used in some countries as a punishment for a crime

hardly [ˈhɑːdlɪ] ADVERB

1 almost not or not quite *e.g. I could hardly believe it.*

● THESAURUS

barely: *His voice was barely audible.*
just: *Her hand was just visible under her coat.*
only just: *For centuries farmers there have only just managed to survive.*
scarcely: *He could scarcely breathe.*

2 certainly not *e.g. It's hardly a secret.*

> You should not use *hardly* with a negative word like *not* or *no: he could hardly hear her* not *he could not hardly hear her.*

hard-nosed [ˈhɑːdˌnəʊzd] ADJECTIVE
tough, practical, and realistic

hard of hearing ADJECTIVE
not able to hear properly

hardship [ˈhɑːdʃɪp] **hardships** NOUN
Hardship is a time or situation of suffering and difficulty.

⬤ THESAURUS
adversity: *They manage to enjoy life despite adversity.*
destitution: *a life of poverty and destitution*
difficulty: *Many new golf clubs are in serious financial difficulty.*
misfortune: *She seemed to enjoy the misfortunes of others.*
want: *They were fighting for freedom of speech and freedom from want.*

hard shoulder **hard shoulders** NOUN
the area at the edge of a motorway where a driver can stop in the event of a breakdown

hard up ADJECTIVE; INFORMAL
having hardly any money

hardware [ˈhɑːdˌwɛə] NOUN
1 Hardware is tools and equipment for use in the home and garden.
2 (ICT) Hardware is also computer machinery rather than computer programs.

hard-wearing [ˌhɑːdˈwɛərɪŋ] ADJECTIVE
strong, well-made, and long-lasting

hardwood [ˈhɑːdˌwʊd] **hardwoods** NOUN
strong, hard wood from a tree such as an oak; also the tree itself

hardy [ˈhɑːdɪ] **hardier, hardiest** ADJECTIVE
tough and able to endure very difficult or cold conditions *e.g. a hardy race of pioneers*

hare [hɛə] **hares, haring, hared** NOUN
1 an animal like a large rabbit, but with longer ears and legs
> VERB
2 To hare about means to run very fast. *e.g. He hared off down the corridor.*

harem [ˈhɛərəm] **harems** NOUN
a group of wives or mistresses of one man, especially in Muslim societies; also the place where these women live

hark [hɑːk] **harks, harking, harked** VERB
1 OLD-FASHIONED
To hark means to listen.

2 To hark back to something in the past means to refer back to it or recall it.

harlequin [ˈhɑːlɪkwɪn] ADJECTIVE
having many different colours

harm [hɑːm] **harms, harming, harmed**
VERB
1 To harm someone or something means to injure or damage them.

⬤ THESAURUS
abuse: *Animals are still being exploited and abused.*
damage: *He damaged his knee during training.*
hurt: *He fell and hurt his back.*
ill-treat: *They thought he had been ill-treating his wife.*
ruin: *My wife was ruining her health through worry.*
wound: *The bomb killed six people and wounded another five.*

> NOUN
2 Harm is injury or damage.

⬤ THESAURUS
abuse: *The abuse of animals is inexcusable.*
damage: *The bomb caused extensive damage.*
hurt: *an evil desire to cause hurt and damage*
injury: *The two other passengers escaped serious injury.*

harmful [ˈhɑːmfʊl] ADJECTIVE
having a bad effect on something *e.g. Whilst most stress is harmful, some is beneficial.*

⬤ THESAURUS
damaging: *damaging allegations about his personal life*
destructive: *the awesome destructive power of nuclear weapons*
detrimental: *levels of radioactivity which are detrimental to public health*
hurtful: *Her comments can only be hurtful to the family.*
pernicious: *The pernicious influence of secret societies.*
<<OPPOSITE *harmless*

harmless [ˈhɑːmlɪs] ADJECTIVE
1 safe to use or be near

⬤ THESAURUS
innocuous: *Both mushrooms look innocuous but are in fact deadly.*
nontoxic: *a cheap and nontoxic method of cleaning up our water*
not dangerous: *The tests are not dangerous to the environment.*
safe: *The doll is safe for children.*
<<OPPOSITE *harmful*

2 unlikely to cause problems or annoyance *e.g. He's harmless really.*
harmlessly ADVERB

harmonic [hɑːˈmɒnɪk] ADJECTIVE
using musical harmony

h

harmonica [hɑːˈmɒnɪkə] **harmonicas**
NOUN
a small musical instrument which you play by blowing and sucking while moving it across your lips

harmonious [hɑːˈməʊnɪəs] ADJECTIVE
1 showing agreement, peacefulness, and friendship e.g. *a harmonious relationship*
2 consisting of parts which blend well together making an attractive whole e.g. *harmonious interior decor*
harmoniously ADVERB

harmony [ˈhɑːmənɪ] **harmonies** NOUN
1 Harmony is a state of peaceful agreement and cooperation. e.g. *the promotion of racial harmony*
2 (**MUSIC**) Harmony is the structure and relationship of chords in a piece of music.
3 Harmony is the pleasant combination of two or more notes played at the same time.

harness [ˈhɑːnɪs] **harnesses, harnessing, harnessed** NOUN
1 a set of straps and fittings fastened round a horse so that it can pull a vehicle, or fastened round someone's body to attach something e.g. *a safety harness*
> VERB
2 If you harness something, you bring it under control to use it. e.g. *harnessing public opinion*

harp [hɑːp] **harps, harping, harped** NOUN
1 a musical instrument consisting of a triangular frame with vertical strings which you pluck with your fingers
> VERB
2 If someone harps on something, they keep talking about it, especially in a boring way.

harpoon [hɑːˈpuːn] **harpoons** NOUN
a barbed spear attached to a rope, thrown or fired from a gun and used for catching whales or large fish

harpsichord [ˈhɑːpsɪˌkɔːd] **harpsichords** NOUN
a musical instrument like a small piano, with strings which are plucked when the keys are pressed

harrowing [ˈhærəʊɪŋ] ADJECTIVE
very upsetting or disturbing e.g. *a harrowing experience*

harsh [hɑːʃ] **harsher, harshest** ADJECTIVE
severe, difficult, and unpleasant e.g. *harsh weather conditions... harsh criticism*
harshly ADVERB, **harshness** NOUN
● THESAURUS
austere: *The life of the troops was still comparatively austere.*

cruel: *an unusually cruel winter*
hard: *He had a hard life.*
ruthless: *the ruthless treatment of staff*
severe: *My boss gave me a severe reprimand.*
stern: *a stern warning*
<<OPPOSITE *mild*

harvest [ˈhɑːvɪst] **harvests, harvesting, harvested** NOUN
1 the cutting and gathering of a crop; also the ripe crop when it is gathered and the time of gathering
> VERB
2 To harvest food means to gather it when it is ripe.
harvester NOUN
[WORD HISTORY: from Old German HERBIST meaning 'autumn']

has-been [ˈhæzˌbiːn] **has-beens** NOUN;
INFORMAL
a person who is no longer important or successful

hash [hæʃ] **hashes** PHRASE
1 If you **make a hash of** a job, you do it badly.
> NOUN
2 the name for the symbol #
3 Hash is a dish made of small pieces of meat and vegetables cooked together.
4 INFORMAL
Hash is also hashish.

hashish [ˈhæʃiːʃ] NOUN
Hashish is a drug made from the hemp plant. It is usually smoked, and is illegal in many countries.
[WORD HISTORY: from Arabic HASHISH meaning 'hemp' or 'dried grass']

hassle [ˈhæsᵊl] **hassles, hassling, hassled** NOUN
1 INFORMAL
Something that is a hassle is difficult or causes trouble.
● THESAURUS
bother: *I buy sliced bread - it's less bother.*
effort: *This chore is well worth the effort.*
inconvenience: *the expense and inconvenience of having central heating installed*
trouble: *You've caused us a lot of trouble.*
upheaval: *Moving house is always a big upheaval.*
> VERB
2 If you hassle someone, you annoy them by repeatedly asking them to do something.
● THESAURUS
badger: *They kept badgering me to go back.*
bother: *Go away and don't bother me about all that just now.*
go on at: *She's always going on at me to have a baby.*

harass: *We are routinely harassed by the police.*
nag: *She had stopped nagging him about his drinking.*
pester: *the creep who's been pestering you to go out with him*

haste [heɪst] NOUN
Haste is doing something quickly, especially too quickly.

hasten ['heɪsᵊn] **hastens, hastening, hastened** VERB
To hasten means to move quickly or do something quickly.

hasty ['heɪstɪ] **hastier, hastiest** ADJECTIVE
done or happening suddenly and quickly, often without enough care or thought
hastily ADVERB

● THESAURUS
brisk: *a brisk walk*
hurried: *a hurried breakfast*
prompt: *It is not too late, but prompt action is needed.*
rapid: *a rapid retreat*
swift: *my swift departure*

hat [hæt] **hats** NOUN
a covering for the head

hatch [hætʃ] **hatches, hatching, hatched** VERB
1 When an egg hatches, or when a bird or reptile hatches, the egg breaks open and the young bird or reptile emerges.
2 To hatch a plot means to plan it.
> NOUN
3 a covered opening in a floor or wall

hatchback ['hætʃˌbæk] **hatchbacks** NOUN
a car with a door at the back which opens upwards

hatchet ['hætʃɪt] **hatchets** NOUN
1 a small axe
> PHRASE
2 To **bury the hatchet** means to resolve a disagreement and become friends again.

hate [heɪt] **hates, hating, hated** VERB
1 If you hate someone or something, you have a strong dislike for them.

● THESAURUS
abhor: *He abhorred violence.*
be sick of: *We're sick of being ripped off.*
despise: *A lot of people despise and loathe what I do.*
detest: *Jean detested being photographed.*
dislike: *those who dislike change*
loathe: *a play universally loathed by the critics*
<<OPPOSITE *love*

> NOUN
2 Hate is a strong dislike.

● THESAURUS
animosity: *The animosity between the two men grew.*
aversion: *I've always had an aversion to being part of a group.*
dislike: *Consider what your likes and dislikes are about your job.*
hatred: *her hatred of authority*
hostility: *He looked at her with open hostility.*
loathing: *Critics are united in their unmitigated loathing of the band.*
<<OPPOSITE *love*

hateful ['heɪtfʊl] ADJECTIVE
extremely unpleasant

● THESAURUS
abhorrent: *Discrimination is abhorrent to my council and our staff.*
despicable: *a despicable crime*
horrible: *a horrible little boy*
loathsome: *the loathsome spectacle we were obliged to witness*
obnoxious: *He was a most obnoxious character.*
offensive: *an offensive remark*

hatred ['heɪtrɪd] NOUN
Hatred is an extremely strong feeling of dislike.

● THESAURUS
animosity: *The animosity between the two men grew.*
antipathy: *public antipathy towards scientists*
aversion: *my aversion to housework*
dislike: *his dislike of modern buildings*
hate: *These people are so full of hate.*
revulsion: *They expressed their revulsion at his violent death.*
<<OPPOSITE *love*

hat trick **hat tricks** NOUN
In sport, a hat trick is three achievements, for example when a footballer scores three goals in a match. *e.g. Crawford completed his hat trick in the 60th minute.*

haughty ['hɔːtɪ] **haughtier, haughtiest** ADJECTIVE
showing excessive pride *e.g. He behaved in a haughty manner.*
haughtily ADVERB

● THESAURUS
arrogant: *an air of arrogant indifference*
conceited: *They had grown too conceited and pleased with themselves.*
disdainful: *She cast a disdainful glance at me.*
proud: *She was said to be proud and arrogant.*
snobbish: *They had a snobbish dislike for their intellectual inferiors.*
stuck-up: *informal She was a famous actress, but she wasn't a bit stuck-up.*
<<OPPOSITE *humble*

h

haul [hɔːl] **hauls, hauling, hauled** VERB

1 To haul something somewhere means to pull it with great effort.

> NOUN

2 a quantity of something obtained *e.g. a good haul of fish*

> PHRASE

3 Something that you describe as **a long haul** takes a lot of time and effort to achieve. *e.g. So women began the long haul to equality.*

haulage [ˈhɔːlɪdʒ] NOUN

Haulage is the business or cost of transporting goods by road.

haunches [ˈhɔːntʃɪz] PLURAL NOUN

Your haunches are your buttocks and the tops of your legs. *e.g. He squatted on his haunches.*

haunt [hɔːnt] **haunts, haunting, haunted** VERB

1 If a ghost haunts a place, it is seen or heard there regularly.

2 If a memory or a fear haunts you, it continually worries you.

> NOUN

3 A person's favourite haunt is a place they like to visit often.

haunted [ˈhɔːntɪd] ADJECTIVE

1 regularly visited by a ghost *e.g. a haunted house*

2 very worried or troubled *e.g. a haunted expression*

haunting [ˈhɔːntɪŋ] ADJECTIVE

extremely beautiful or sad so that it makes a lasting impression on you *e.g. haunting landscapes*

have see page 409 for Word Web

haven [ˈheɪvᵊn] **havens** NOUN

a safe place

havoc [ˈhævək] NOUN

1 Havoc is disorder and confusion.

> PHRASE

2 To **play havoc** with something means to cause great disorder and confusion. *e.g. Food allergies often play havoc with the immune system.*

hawk [hɔːk] **hawks, hawking, hawked** NOUN

1 a bird of prey with short rounded wings and a long tail

> VERB

2 To hawk goods means to sell them by taking them around from place to place.

hawthorn [ˈhɔːˌθɔːn] **hawthorns** NOUN

a small, thorny tree producing white blossom and red berries

hay [heɪ] NOUN

Hay is grass which has been cut and dried and is used as animal feed.

hay fever NOUN

Hay fever is an allergy to pollen and grass, causing sneezing and watering eyes.

haystack [ˈheɪˌstæk] **haystacks** NOUN

a large, firmly built pile of hay, usually covered and left out in the open

hazard [ˈhæzəd] **hazards, hazarding, hazarded** NOUN

1 (SCIENCE) a substance, object or action which could be dangerous to you

> VERB

2 If you hazard something, you put it at risk. *e.g. hazarding the health of his crew*

> PHRASE

3 If you **hazard a guess**, you make a guess.

hazardous ADJECTIVE

[WORD HISTORY: from Arabic AZ-ZAHR meaning 'gaming dice']

haze [heɪz] NOUN

If there is a haze, you cannot see clearly because there is moisture or smoke in the air.

hazel [ˈheɪzᵊl] **hazels** NOUN

1 a small tree producing edible nuts

> ADJECTIVE

2 greenish brown in colour

hazy [ˈheɪzɪ] **hazier, haziest** ADJECTIVE

dim or vague *e.g. hazy sunshine... a hazy memory*

he [hiː] PRONOUN

'He' is used to refer to a man, boy, or male animal or to any person whose sex is not mentioned

head see page 410 for Word Web

headache [ˈhɛdˌeɪk] **headaches** NOUN

1 a pain in your head

2 Something that is a headache is causing a lot of difficulty or worry. *e.g. Delays in receiving money owed is a major headache for small firms.*

header [ˈhɛdə] **headers** NOUN

A header in soccer is hitting the ball with your head.

heading [ˈhɛdɪŋ] **headings** NOUN

a piece of writing that is written or printed at the top of a page

headland [ˈhɛdlənd] **headlands** NOUN

a narrow piece of land jutting out into the sea

headlight [ˈhɛdˌlaɪt] **headlights** NOUN

The headlights on a motor vehicle are the large powerful lights at the front.

headline [ˈhɛdˌlaɪn] **headlines** NOUN

1 A newspaper headline is the title of a newspaper article printed in large, bold type.

2 The headlines are the main points of the radio or television news.

1 VERB
If you have something, you own or possess it eg: *We have two tickets for the concert.*
● THESAURUS
hold: *He does not hold a firearm certificate.*
keep: *We keep chickens.*
own: *His father owns a local pub.*
possess: *He is said to possess a fortune.*

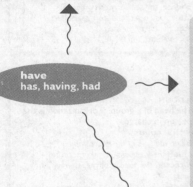

have
has, having, had

2 VERB
If you have something, you experience it, it happens to you, or you are affected by it eg: *I have an idea!; He had a marvellous time.*
● THESAURUS
endure: *The company endured heavy losses.*
enjoy: *The average German will enjoy 40 days' paid holiday this year.*
experience: *Widows seem to experience more distress than do widowers.*
feel: *I felt a sharp pain in my shoulder.*
sustain: *He had sustained a cut on his left eyebrow.*
undergo: *He recently underwent brain surgery.*

3 VERB
to suffer from eg: *to have a blood pressure problem*
● THESAURUS
endure: *The company endured financial losses.*
suffer: *I realised that he suffers from high blood pressure.*
experience: *He experienced a shock to his system.*
undergo: *I'm sure he will undergo an agonising four hours waiting for his test results.*

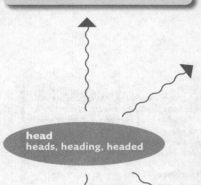

1 NOUN
Your head is your mind and mental abilities *eg*: *He has a head for figures.*
● THESAURUS
aptitude: *an aptitude for accountancy*
brain: *If you stop using your brain you'll go stale.*
common sense: *Use your common sense.*
intelligence: *Try to use your intelligence to solve the puzzle – don't just guess.*
mind: *I'm trying to clear my mind of all this.*
wits: *She has used her wits to get where she is today.*

2 NOUN
The head of something is the top, start, or most important end *eg*: *at the head of the table.*
● THESAURUS
beginning: *the beginning of this chapter*
front: *Stand at the front of the line.*
source: *the source of this great river*
start: *Go back to the start of this section.*
top: *the top of the stairs*
<< OPPOSITE *tail*

head
heads, heading, headed

3 NOUN
The head of a group or organization is the person in charge.
● THESAURUS
boss: *the boss of the new company*
chief: *the President's chief of security*
director: *the director of the intensive care unit*
leader: *the leader of the Conservative Party*
manager: *the manager of our division*
president: *the president of the medical commission*
principal: *the principal of the school*

4 VERB
To head a group or organization means to be in charge *eg*: *Bryce heads the help organization.*
● THESAURUS
be in charge of: *She's in charge of the overseas division.*
control: *He controls the largest fast food empire in the world.*
direct: *Christopher will direct day-to-day operations.*
lead: *leading a campaign to save the rainforest*
manage: *Within two years he was managing the store.*
run: *Each teacher will run a different workshop.*

headmaster [ˌhɛdˈmɑːstə] **headmasters**
NOUN
a man who is the head teacher of a school

headmistress [ˌhɛdˈmistrəs]
headmistresses NOUN
a woman who is the head teacher of a school

headphones [ˈhɛdˌfəʊnz] PLURAL NOUN
Headphones are a pair of small speakers which
you wear over your ears to listen to a radio
without other people hearing.

headquarters [ˌhɛdˈkwɔːtəz] NOUN
The headquarters of an organization is the main
place or from which it is run.

headroom [ˈhɛdˌrʊm] NOUN
Headroom is the amount of space below a roof or
surface under which an object must pass or fit.

headstone [ˈhɛdˌstəʊn] **headstones** NOUN
a large stone standing at one end of a grave and
showing the name of the person buried there

headstrong [ˈhɛdˌstrɒŋ] ADJECTIVE
determined to do something in your own way
and ignoring other people's advice

head teacher head teachers NOUN
the teacher who is in charge of a school

headway [ˈhɛdˌweɪ] PHRASE
If you are **making headway**, you are making
progress.

headwind [ˈhɛdˌwɪnd] **headwinds** NOUN
a wind blowing in the opposite direction to the
way you are travelling

heady [ˈhɛdɪ] ADJECTIVE
extremely exciting e.g. the heady days of the civil
rights era

heal [hiːl] **heals, healing, healed** VERB
If something heals or if you heal it, it becomes
healthy or normal again. e.g. He had a nasty wound
which had not healed properly.
healer NOUN

health [hɛlθ] NOUN
1 Your health is the condition of your body. e.g.
His health is not good.
● THESAURUS
condition: He remains in a critical condition in
hospital.
constitution: He must have an extremely strong
constitution.
shape: He was still in better shape than many
younger men.
2 Health is also the state of being free from
disease and feeling well.
● THESAURUS
fitness: He has fitness problems.
good condition: He is in great condition for a man
of 56.

wellbeing: Singing can create a sense of wellbeing.
<<OPPOSITE illness

health food health foods NOUN
food which is free from added chemicals and is
considered to be good for your health

healthy [ˈhɛlθɪ] **healthier, healthiest**
ADJECTIVE
1 Someone who is healthy is fit and strong and
does not have any diseases.
● THESAURUS
active: an active lifestyle
fit: A short, physically fit man of 61.
in good shape: informal I kept myself in good shape
by swimming.
robust: a robust and vibrant young man
strong: a strong constitution
well: I'm not very well today.
<<OPPOSITE ill

2 Something that is healthy is good for you. e.g. a
healthy diet
● THESAURUS
beneficial: Wine in moderation is beneficial to
health.
bracing: a bracing walk
good for you: Regular, moderate exercise is good for
you.
nourishing: sensible, nourishing food
nutritious: a hot, nutritious meal
wholesome: fresh, wholesome ingredients
<<OPPOSITE unhealthy

3 An organization or system that is healthy is
successful. e.g. a healthy economy
healthily ADVERB

heap [hiːp] **heaps, heaping, heaped** NOUN
1 a pile of things
● THESAURUS
hoard: a hoard of silver and jewels
mass: a mass of flowers
mound: The bulldozers piled up huge mounds of dirt.
pile: a pile of betting slips
stack: stacks of books on the bedside table
> PLURAL NOUN
2 INFORMAL
Heaps of something means plenty of it. e.g. His
performance earned him heaps of praise.
● THESAURUS
loads: informal I've got loads of money.
lots: informal lots of fun
plenty: We've got plenty of time for a drink.
stacks: stacks of magazines
tons: informal I've got tons of work to do.
> VERB
3 If you heap things, you pile them up.
● THESAURUS
pile: He was piling clothes into the suitcase.

h

stack: *They stacked up pillows behind his back.*

4 To heap something such as praise on someone means to give them a lot of it.

hear [hɪə] **hears, hearing, heard** VERB

1 When you hear sounds, you are aware of them because they reach your ears.

● THESAURUS

catch: *I don't believe I caught your name.*

eavesdrop: *The government illegally eavesdropped on his phone conversations.*

heed: *Few at the conference heeded his warning.*

listen in: *Secret agents listened in on his phone calls.*

listen to: *He spent his time listening to the radio.*

overhear: *I overheard two doctors discussing my case.*

2 When you hear from someone, they write to you or phone you.

3 When you hear about something, you are informed about it.

● THESAURUS

ascertain: *They had ascertained that he was not a spy.*

discover: *She discovered that they'd escaped.*

find out: *As soon as we found this out, we closed the ward.*

gather: *I gather the report is critical of the judge.*

learn: *She wasn't surprised to learn that he was involved.*

understand: *I understand that she's just taken early retirement.*

4 When a judge hears a case, he or she listens to it in court in order to make a decision on it.

> PHRASE

5 If you say that you **won't hear of** something, you mean you refuse to allow it.

hear out VERB

6 If you hear someone out, you listen to all they have to say without interrupting.

hearing [ˈhɪərɪŋ] **hearings** NOUN

1 Hearing is the sense which makes it possible for you to be aware of sounds. *e.g. My hearing is poor.*

2 a court trial or official meeting to hear facts about an incident

3 If someone gives you a hearing, they let you give your point of view and listen to you.

hearsay [ˈhɪəˌseɪ] NOUN

Hearsay is information that you have heard from other people rather than something that you know personally to be true.

hearse [hɜːs] **hearses** NOUN

a large car that carries the coffin at a funeral

heart [hɑːt] **hearts** NOUN

1 the organ in your chest that pumps the blood around your body

2 Your heart is also thought of as the centre of your emotions.

3 Heart is courage, determination, or enthusiasm. *e.g. They were losing heart.*

4 The heart of something is the most central and important part of it.

5 a shape similar to a heart, used especially as a symbol of love

6 Hearts is one of the four suits in a pack of playing cards. It is marked by a red heart-shaped symbol.

heartache [ˈhɑːtˌeɪk] **heartaches** NOUN

Heartache is very great sadness and emotional suffering.

heart attack **heart attacks** NOUN

a serious medical condition in which the heart suddenly beats irregularly or stops completely

heartbreak [ˈhɑːtˌbreɪk] **heartbreaks** NOUN

Heartbreak is great sadness and emotional suffering.

heartbreaking ADJECTIVE

heartbroken [ˈhɑːtˌbrəʊkən] ADJECTIVE

very sad and emotionally upset *e.g. She was heartbroken at his death.*

heartburn [ˈhɑːtˌbɜːn] NOUN

Heartburn is a painful burning sensation in your chest, caused by indigestion.

heartening [ˈhɑːtⁿnɪŋ] ADJECTIVE

encouraging or uplifting *e.g. heartening news*

heart failure NOUN

Heart failure is a serious condition in which someone's heart does not work as well as it should, sometimes stopping completely.

heartfelt [ˈhɑːtˌfɛlt] ADJECTIVE

sincerely and deeply felt *e.g. Our heartfelt sympathy goes out to you.*

hearth [hɑːθ] **hearths** NOUN

the floor of a fireplace

heartless [ˈhɑːtlɪs] ADJECTIVE

cruel and unkind

heart-rending [ˈhɑːtˌrɛndɪŋ] ADJECTIVE

causing great sadness and pity *e.g. a heart-rending story*

heart-throb [ˈhɑːtˌθrɒb] **heart-throbs** NOUN

someone who is attractive to a lot of people

heart-to-heart [ˌhɑːttəˈhɑːt] **heart-to-hearts** NOUN

a discussion in which two people talk about their deepest feelings

hearty [ˈhɑːtɪ] **heartier, heartiest** ADJECTIVE

1 cheerful and enthusiastic *e.g. hearty congratulations*

2 strongly felt *e.g. a hearty dislike for her teacher*

3 A hearty meal is large and satisfying.
heartily ADVERB

heat [hiːt] **heats, heating, heated** NOUN
1 Heat is warmth or the quality of being hot; also the temperature of something that is warm or hot.

⬤ THESAURUS
high temperature: *The suffering caused by the high temperature has been great.*
warmth: *the warmth of the sand between her toes*
<<OPPOSITE *cold*

2 Heat is strength of feeling, especially of anger or excitement.

⬤ THESAURUS
excitement: *in a state of great excitement*
fervour: *religious fervour*
intensity: *the intensity of feeling about this issue*
passion: *He spoke with great passion.*
vehemence: *I was surprised by the vehemence of his criticism.*

3 a contest or race in a competition held to decide who will play in the final
> VERB
4 To heat something means to raise its temperature.

⬤ THESAURUS
reheat: *Reheat the soup to a gentle simmer.*
warm up: *Just before serving, warm up the tomato sauce.*
<<OPPOSITE *cool*
> PHRASE
5 When a female animal is **on heat**, she is ready for mating.
heater NOUN

heath [hiːθ] **heaths** NOUN
an area of open land covered with rough grass or heather

heathen ['hiːðən] **heathens** NOUN OLD-FASHIONED, INFORMAL
someone who does not believe in one of the established religions

⬤ THESAURUS
pagan: *the sky-god of the ancient pagans*
unbeliever: *punishing unbelievers and traitors*
<<OPPOSITE *believer*

heather ['hɛðə] NOUN
a plant with small purple or white flowers that grows wild on hills and moorland

heating ['hiːtɪŋ] NOUN
Heating is the equipment used to heat a building; also the process and cost of running the equipment to provide heat.

heatwave ['hiːtˌweɪv] **heatwaves** NOUN
a period of time during which the weather is much hotter than usual

heave [hiːv] **heaves, heaving, heaved** VERB
1 To heave something means to move or throw it with a lot of effort.

2 If your stomach heaves, you vomit or suddenly feel sick.

3 If you heave a sigh, you sigh loudly.
> NOUN
4 If you give something a heave, you move or throw it with a lot of effort.

heaven ['hɛvən] **heavens** NOUN
1 a place of happiness where God is believed to live and where good people are believed to go when they die

⬤ THESAURUS
next world: *He said, "We will see each other again in the next world.".*
paradise: *They believed they would go to paradise if they died in battle.*
<<OPPOSITE *hell*

2 If you describe a situation or place as heaven, you mean that it is wonderful. *e.g. The cake was pure heaven.*

⬤ THESAURUS
bliss: *a scene of domestic bliss*
ecstasy: *the ecstasy of being in love*
paradise: *The Algarve is a golfer's paradise.*
rapture: *the sheer rapture of listening to Bach's music*
> PHRASE
3 You say **Good heavens** to express surprise.

heavenly ['hɛvənlɪ] ADJECTIVE
1 relating to heaven *e.g. a heavenly choir*
2 INFORMAL
wonderful *e.g. his heavenly blue eyes*

heavy ['hɛvɪ] **heavier, heaviest; heavies** ADJECTIVE
1 great in weight or force *e.g. How heavy are you? a heavy blow*

⬤ THESAURUS
bulky: *a bulky grey sweater*
massive: *a massive blue whale*
<<OPPOSITE *light*

2 great in degree or amount *e.g. heavy casualties*
3 solid and thick in appearance *e.g. heavy shoes*
4 using a lot of something quickly *e.g. The van is heavy on petrol.*
5 serious and difficult to deal with or understand *e.g. It all got a bit heavy when the police arrived... a heavy speech*

⬤ THESAURUS
deep: *a period of deep personal crisis*
grave: *the grave crisis facing the country*
profound: *Anna's patriotism was profound.*
serious: *It was a question which deserved serious consideration.*

solemn: *a simple, solemn ceremony*
weighty: *Surely such weighty matters merit a higher level of debate.*
<<OPPOSITE *trivial*

6 Food that is heavy is solid and difficult to digest. *e.g. a heavy meal*

7 When it is heavy, the weather is hot, humid, and still.

8 Someone with a heavy heart is very sad.

> NOUN

9 INFORMAL
a large, strong man employed to protect someone or something
heavily ADVERB, **heaviness** NOUN

heavy-duty ['hɛvɪˌdjuːtɪ] ADJECTIVE
Heavy-duty equipment is strong and hard-wearing.

heavy-handed ['hɛvɪˌhændɪd] ADJECTIVE
showing a lack of care or thought and using too much authority *e.g. heavy-handed police tactics*

heavyweight ['hɛvɪˌweɪt] **heavyweights** NOUN

1 a boxer in the heaviest weight group

2 an important person with a lot of influence

Hebrew ['hiːbruː] **Hebrews** NOUN

1 Hebrew is an ancient language now spoken in Israel, where it is the official language.

2 In the past, the Hebrews were Hebrew-speaking Jews who lived in Israel.

> ADJECTIVE

3 relating to the Hebrews and their customs
[WORD HISTORY: from Hebrew IBHRI meaning 'one from beyond (the river)']

heckle ['hɛkᵊl] **heckles, heckling, heckled** VERB
If members of an audience heckle a speaker, they interrupt and shout rude remarks.
heckler NOUN

hectare ['hɛktɑː] **hectares** NOUN
a unit for measuring areas of land, equal to 10,000 square metres or about 2.471 acres

hectic ['hɛktɪk] ADJECTIVE
involving a lot of rushed activity *e.g. a hectic schedule*

hedge [hɛdʒ] **hedges, hedging, hedged** NOUN

1 a row of bushes forming a barrier or boundary

> VERB

2 If you hedge against something unpleasant happening, you protect yourself.

3 If you hedge, you avoid answering a question or dealing with a problem.

> PHRASE

4 If you **hedge your bets**, you support two or more people or courses of action to avoid the risk of losing a lot.

hedgehog ['hɛdʒˌhɒg] **hedgehogs** NOUN
a small, brown animal with sharp spikes covering its back

hedonism ['hiːdᵊˌnɪzəm] NOUN
Hedonism is the belief that gaining pleasure is the most important thing in life.
hedonistic ADJECTIVE

heed [hiːd] **heeds, heeding, heeded** VERB

1 If you heed someone's advice, you pay attention to it.

● THESAURUS
follow: *If you are not going to follow my advice, we are both wasting our time.*
listen to: *They won't listen to my advice.*
pay attention to: *The food industry is now paying attention to young consumers.*
take notice of: *We want the government to take notice of what we think.*

> NOUN

2 If you take or pay heed to something, you give it careful attention.

● THESAURUS
attention: *He never paid much attention to his audience.*
notice: *So do they take any notice of public opinion?*

heel [hiːl] **heels, heeling, heeled** NOUN

1 the back part of your foot

2 The heel of a shoe or sock is the part that fits over your heel.

> VERB

3 To heel a pair of shoes means to put a new piece on the heel.

> PHRASE

4 A person or place that looks **down at heel** looks untidy and in poor condition.

heeler ['hiːlə] **heelers** NOUN
In Australia, a dog that herds cattle by biting at their heels.

hefty ['hɛftɪ] **heftier, heftiest** ADJECTIVE
of great size, force, or weight *e.g. a hefty fine... hefty volumes*

height [haɪt] **heights** NOUN

1 The height of an object is its measurement from the bottom to the top.

2 a high position or place *e.g. Their nesting rarely takes place at any great height.*

3 The height of something is its peak, or the time when it is most successful or intense. *e.g. the height of the tourist season... at the height of his career*

heighten ['haɪtᵊn] **heightens, heightening, heightened** VERB

If something **heightens** a feeling or experience, it increases its intensity.

heinous [ˈheɪnəs] *or* [ˈhiːnəs] ADJECTIVE
evil and terrible *e.g. heinous crimes*

heir [ɛə] **heirs** NOUN
A person's heir is the person who is entitled to inherit their property or title.

heiress [ˈɛərɪs] **heiresses** NOUN
a female with the right to inherit property or a title

heirloom [ˈɛəˌluːm] **heirlooms** NOUN
something belonging to a family that has been passed from one generation to another

helicopter [ˈhelɪˌkɒptə] **helicopters** NOUN
an aircraft with rotating blades above it which enable it to take off vertically, hover, and fly
[WORD HISTORY: from Greek HELIKO + PTERON meaning 'spiral wing']

helium [ˈhiːlɪəm] NOUN
Helium is a gas that is lighter than air and that is used to fill balloons.

hell [hel] NOUN
1 Hell is the place where souls of evil people are believed to go to be punished after death.
● THESAURUS
abyss: *Satan rules over the dark abyss.*
inferno: *an inferno described in loving detail by Dante*
<<OPPOSITE *heaven*

2 INFORMAL
If you say that something is hell, you mean it is very unpleasant.
● THESAURUS
agony: *the agony of divorce*
anguish: *the anguish of families unable to trace relatives who've disappeared*
misery: *All that money brought nothing but sadness and misery.*
nightmare: *The years in prison were a nightmare.*
ordeal: *the painful ordeal of the last year*
> INTERJECTION
3 'Hell' is also a swearword

hell-bent [ˈhelˌbent] ADJECTIVE
determined to do something whatever the consequences

hellish [ˈhelɪʃ] ADJECTIVE; INFORMAL
very unpleasant

hello [heˈləʊ] INTERJECTION
You say 'Hello' as a greeting or when you answer the phone.
● THESAURUS
gidday: Australian and New Zealand *Gidday, mate! How you doing?*

hi: informal *She smiled and said, "Hi".*
how do you do?: formal *"How do you do, Mrs Brown?" Sam said, holding out his hand.*
good morning: formal *Good morning, everyone.*
good afternoon: formal *Good afternoon. Won't you sit down?*
good evening: formal *Good evening, and welcome!*
<<OPPOSITE *goodbye*

helm [helm] **helms** NOUN
1 The helm on a boat is the position from which it is steered and the wheel or tiller.
> PHRASE
2 At the helm means in a position of leadership or control.

helmet [ˈhelmɪt] **helmets** NOUN
a hard hat worn to protect the head

help [help] **helps, helping, helped** VERB
1 To help someone means to make something easier or better for them.
● THESAURUS
aid: *a software system to aid managers*
assist: *information to assist you*
lend a hand: *I'd be glad to lend a hand.*
support: *He thanked everyone who had supported the strike.*
> NOUN
2 If you need or give help, you need or give assistance.
● THESAURUS
advice: *He has given me lots of good advice in my time here.*
aid: *millions of dollars of aid*
assistance: *I would be grateful for any assistance.*
guidance: *the reports which were produced under his guidance*
helping hand: *Most mums would be grateful for a helping hand.*
support: *Only 60 clubs pledged their support for the scheme.*
3 someone or something that helps you *e.g. He really is a good help.*
> PHRASE
4 If you **help yourself** to something, you take it.
5 If you **can't help** something, you cannot control it or change it. *e.g. I can't help feeling sorry for him.*

helper [ˈhelpə] **helpers** NOUN
a person who gives assistance
● THESAURUS
aide: *a presidential aide*
assistant: *a research assistant*
deputy: *I can't make it so I'll send my deputy.*
henchman: *Adolf Eichmann, Hitler's notorious henchman.*
right-hand man: *He was the perfect right-hand man for the president.*

supporter: *He is a strong supporter of the plan.*

helpful ['hɛlpfʊl] ADJECTIVE

1 If someone is helpful, they help you by doing something for you.

● THESAURUS
accommodating: *Lindi seemed a nice, accomodating girl.*
cooperative: *I made every effort to be cooperative.*
kind: *I must thank you for being so kind to me.*
supportive: *Her boss was very supportive.*
<<OPPOSITE *unhelpful*

2 Something that is helpful makes a situation more pleasant or easier to tolerate.
helpfully ADVERB

● THESAURUS
advantageous: *an advantageous arrangement*
beneficial: *beneficial changes in the tax system*
constructive: *constructive criticism*
profitable: *a profitable exchange of ideas*
useful: *useful information*

helping ['hɛlpɪŋ] **helpings** NOUN
an amount of food that you get in a single serving

helpless ['hɛlplɪs] ADJECTIVE

1 unable to cope on your own *e.g. a helpless child*

● THESAURUS
defenceless: *a savage attack on a defenceless girl*
powerless: *He was powerless to help.*
unprotected: *She felt unprotected and defenceless.*
vulnerable: *the most vulnerable members of society*
weak: *taking ruthless advantage of a weak old man*

2 weak or powerless *e.g. helpless despair*
helplessly ADVERB, **helplessness** NOUN

hem [hɛm] **hems, hemming, hemmed** NOUN

1 The hem of a garment is an edge which has been turned over and sewn in place.

> VERB
2 To hem something means to make a hem on it.
hem in VERB
3 If someone is hemmed in, they are surrounded and prevented from moving.

hemisphere ['hɛmɪˌsfɪə] **hemispheres** NOUN
one half of the earth, the brain, or a sphere

hemp [hɛmp] NOUN
Hemp is a tall plant, some varieties of which are used to make rope, and others to produce the drug cannabis.

hen [hɛn] **hens** NOUN
a female chicken; also any female bird

hence [hɛns] ADVERB

1 FORMAL
for this reason *e.g. It sells more papers, hence more money is made.*

2 from now or from the time mentioned *e.g. The convention is due to start two weeks hence.*

henceforth ['hɛnsˌfɔːθ] ADVERB; FORMAL
from this time onward *e.g. His life henceforth was to revolve around her.*

henchman ['hɛntʃmən] **henchmen** NOUN
The henchmen of a powerful person are the people employed to do violent or dishonest work for that person.

hepatitis [ˌhɛpəˈtaɪtɪs] NOUN
Hepatitis is a serious infectious disease causing inflammation of the liver.

her [hɜː] PRONOUN OR ADJECTIVE
'Her' is used to refer to a woman, girl or female animal that has already been mentioned, or to show that something belongs to a particular female

herald ['hɛrəld] **heralds, heralding, heralded** NOUN

1 In the past, a herald was a messenger.

> VERB
2 Something that heralds a future event is a sign of that event.

herb [hɜːb] **herbs** NOUN
a plant whose leaves are used in medicine or to flavour food
herbal ADJECTIVE, **herbalist** NOUN

herbivore ['hɜːbɪˌvɔː] **herbivores** NOUN
an animal that eats only plants

herd [hɜːd] **herds, herding, herded** NOUN

1 a large group of animals

> VERB
2 To herd animals or people means to make them move together as a group.

here [hɪə] ADVERB

1 at, to, or in the place where you are, or the place mentioned or indicated

> PHRASE
2 **Here and there** means in various unspecified places. *e.g. dense forests broken here and there by small towns*

hereafter [ˌhɪərˈɑːftə] ADVERB; FORMAL
after this time or point *e.g. the South China Morning Post (referred to hereafter as SCMP)*

hereby [ˌhɪəˈbaɪ] ADVERB; FORMAL
used in documents and statements to indicate that a declaration is official *e.g. All leave is hereby cancelled.*

hereditary [hɪˈrɛdɪtərɪ] ADJECTIVE
passed on to a child from a parent *e.g. a hereditary disease*

heredity [hɪˈrɛdɪtɪ] NOUN
Heredity is the process by which characteristics

are passed from parents to their children through the genes.

herein [ˌhɪərˈɪn] ADVERB; FORMAL
in this place or document

heresy [ˈhɛrəsɪ] **heresies** NOUN
Heresy is belief or behaviour considered to be wrong because it disagrees with what is generally accepted, especially with regard to religion.
heretic NOUN, **heretical** ADJECTIVE

herewith [ˌhɪəˈwɪð] ADVERB; FORMAL
with this letter or document *e.g. I herewith return your cheque.*

heritage [ˈhɛrɪtɪdʒ] NOUN
the possessions or traditions that have been passed from one generation to another

hermit [ˈhɜːmɪt] **hermits** NOUN
a person who lives alone with a simple way of life, especially for religious reasons
[WORD HISTORY: from Greek]

hernia [ˈhɜːnɪə] **hernias** NOUN
a medical condition in which part of the intestine sticks through a weak point in the surrounding tissue

hero [ˈhɪərəʊ] **heroes** NOUN
1 the main male character in a book, film, or play
2 a person who has done something brave or good

heroic [hɪˈrəʊɪk] ADJECTIVE
brave, courageous, and determined
heroically ADVERB

heroin [ˈhɛrəʊɪn] NOUN
Heroin is a powerful drug formerly used as an anaesthetic and now taken illegally by some people for pleasure.

heroine [ˈhɛrəʊɪn] **heroines** NOUN
1 the main female character in a book, film, or play
2 a woman who has done something brave or good

heroism [ˈhɛrəʊˌɪzəm] NOUN
Heroism is great courage and bravery.

heron [ˈhɛrən] **herons** NOUN
a wading bird with very long legs and a long beak and neck

herpes [ˈhɜːpiːz] NOUN
Herpes is a virus which causes painful red spots on the skin.

herring [ˈhɛrɪŋ] **herrings** NOUN
a silvery fish that lives in large shoals in northern seas

hers [hɜːz] PRONOUN
'Hers' refers to something that belongs to or

relates to a woman, girl, or female animal.

herself [həˈsɛlf] PRONOUN
1 'Herself' is used when the same woman, girl, or female animal does an action and is affected by it *e.g. She pulled herself out of the water.*
2 'Herself' is used to emphasize 'she'.

hertz [hɜːts] NOUN
A hertz is a unit of frequency equal to one cycle per second.

hesitant [ˈhɛzɪtᵊnt] ADJECTIVE
If you are hesitant, you do not do something immediately because you are uncertain or worried.
hesitantly ADVERB

● THESAURUS
diffident: *John was as outgoing as Helen was diffident.*
doubtful: *I was very doubtful about the chances for success.*
reluctant: *She was reluctant to get involved.*
unsure: *He made her feel awkward and unsure of herself.*
wavering: *wavering voters*

hesitate [ˈhɛzɪˌteɪt] **hesitates, hesitating, hesitated** VERB
To hesitate means to pause or show uncertainty.
hesitation NOUN

● THESAURUS
dither: *We're still dithering over whether to marry.*
pause: *The crowd paused for a minute, wondering what to do next.*
waver: *Louise never wavered in her determination to take up the post.*

hessian [ˈhɛsɪən] NOUN
Hessian is a thick, rough fabric used for making sacks.

heterosexual [ˌhɛtərəʊˈsɛksjʊəl] **heterosexuals** ADJECTIVE
1 involving a sexual relationship between a man and a woman *e.g. heterosexual couples*
> NOUN
2 a person who is sexually attracted to people of the opposite sex

hewn [hjuːn] ADJECTIVE
carved from a substance *e.g. a cave, hewn out of the hillside*

hexagon [ˈhɛksəgən] **hexagons** NOUN
a shape with six straight sides
hexagonal ADJECTIVE

heyday [ˈheɪˌdeɪ] NOUN
The heyday of a person or thing is the period when they are most successful or popular. *e.g. Hollywood in its heyday*

hi [haɪ] INTERJECTION
'Hi!' is an informal greeting.

hiatus [haɪˈeɪtəs] **hiatuses** NOUN; FORMAL
a pause or gap

hibernate [ˈhaɪbəˌneɪt] **hibernates, hibernating, hibernated** VERB
Animals that hibernate spend the winter in a state like deep sleep.
hibernation NOUN
[WORD HISTORY: from Latin HIBERNARE meaning 'to spend the winter']

hibiscus [haɪˈbɪskəs] **hibiscuses** NOUN
a type of tropical shrub with brightly coloured flowers

hiccup [ˈhɪkʌp] **hiccups, hiccupping, hiccupped** NOUN
1 Hiccups are short, uncontrolled choking sounds in your throat that you sometimes get if you have been eating or drinking too quickly.
2 INFORMAL
a minor problem
> VERB
3 When you hiccup, you make these little choking sounds.

hide [haɪd] **hides, hiding, hid, hidden** VERB
1 To hide something means to put it where it cannot be seen, or to prevent it from being discovered. *e.g. He was unable to hide his disappointment.*
● THESAURUS
cache: *He has £289 million cached away.*
conceal: *The hat concealed her hair.*
secrete: *She secreted the gun in the kitchen cabinet.*
stash: *informal He had stashed money away in a secret offshore account.*
> NOUN
2 the skin of a large animal
● THESAURUS
pelt: *a bed covered with beaver pelts*
skin: *a leopard skin coat*

hideous [ˈhɪdɪəs] ADJECTIVE
extremely ugly or unpleasant
hideously ADVERB

hideout [ˈhaɪdˌaʊt] **hideouts** NOUN
a hiding place

hierarchy [ˈhaɪəˌrɑːkɪ] **hierarchies** NOUN
a system in which people or things are ranked according to how important they are
hierarchical ADJECTIVE

hi-fi [ˈhaɪfaɪ] **hi-fis** NOUN
a set of stereo equipment on which you can play compact discs and tapes

high [haɪ] **higher, highest; highs** ADJECTIVE
1 tall or a long way above the ground
● THESAURUS
elevated: *an apartment in an elevated position overlooking the docks*

lofty: *lofty towers and spires*
soaring: *a 14th-century church with a soaring spire*
steep: *the steep hill leading up to her house*
tall: *a garden screened by tall walls*
towering: *towering red sandstone cliffs*
<<OPPOSITE low

2 great in degree, quantity, or intensity *e.g. high interest rates... There is a high risk of heart disease.*
● THESAURUS
acute: *a state of acute anxiety*
excessive: *He was driving at excessive speed.*
extraordinary: *drinking extraordinary quantities of alcohol*
extreme: *acting under extreme emotional pressure*
great: *These products created a great level of interest.*
severe: *There are severe penalties for drug smuggling.*
<<OPPOSITE low

3 towards the top of a scale of importance or quality *e.g. high fashion*
4 close to the top of a range of sound or notes *e.g. the human voice reaches a very high pitch*
5 INFORMAL Someone who is high on a drug is affected by having taken it.
> ADVERB
6 at or to a height
> NOUN
7 a high point or level *e.g. Morale reached a new high.*
8 INFORMAL Someone who is on a high is in a very excited and optimistic mood.

highbrow [ˈhaɪˌbraʊ] ADJECTIVE
concerned with serious, intellectual subjects

higher education [ˈhaɪə] NOUN
Higher education is education at universities and colleges.

high jump NOUN
The high jump is an athletics event involving jumping over a high bar.

highlands [ˈhaɪləndz] PLURAL NOUN
Highlands are mountainous or hilly areas of land.

highlight [ˈhaɪˌlaɪt] **highlights, highlighting, highlighted** VERB
1 If you highlight a point or problem, you emphasize and draw attention to it.
> NOUN
2 The highlight of something is the most interesting part of it. *e.g. His show was the highlight of the Festival.*
3 (ART) a lighter area of a painting, showing where light shines on things
4 Highlights are also light-coloured streaks in someone's hair.

highly ['haɪlɪ] ADVERB
1 extremely *e.g. It is highly unlikely I'll be able to replace it.*
2 towards the top of a scale of importance, admiration, or respect *e.g. She thought highly of him... highly qualified personnel*

high-minded ['haɪ,maɪndɪd] ADJECTIVE
Someone who is high-minded has strong moral principles.

Highness ['haɪnɪs]
'Highness' is used in titles and forms of address for members of the royal family other than a king or queen. *e.g. Her Royal Highness, Princess Alexandra.*

high-pitched [,haɪ'pɪtʃt] ADJECTIVE
A high-pitched sound is high and often rather shrill.

high-rise ['haɪ,raɪz] ADJECTIVE
High-rise buildings are very tall.

high school **high schools** NOUN
a secondary school

high technology NOUN
High technology is the development and use of advanced electronics and computers.

high tide NOUN
On a coast, high tide is the time, usually twice a day, when the sea is at its highest level.

highway ['haɪ,weɪ] **highways** NOUN
a road along which vehicles have the right to pass

highwayman ['haɪ,weɪmən] **highwaymen** NOUN
In the past, highwaymen were robbers on horseback who used to rob travellers.

hijack ['haɪ,dʒæk] **hijacks, hijacking, hijacked** VERB
If someone hijacks a plane or vehicle, they illegally take control of it during a journey.
hijacking NOUN

hike [haɪk] **hikes, hiking, hiked** NOUN
1 a long country walk
> VERB
2 To hike means to walk long distances in the country.
hiker NOUN

hilarious [hɪ'lɛərɪəs] ADJECTIVE
very funny
hilariously ADVERB

hilarity [hɪ'lærɪtɪ] NOUN
Hilarity is great amusement and laughter. *e.g. His antics caused great hilarity.*

hill [hɪl] **hills** NOUN
a rounded area of land higher than the land surrounding it

hilly ADJECTIVE

hillbilly ['hɪl,bɪlɪ] **hillbillies** NOUN
someone who lives in the country away from other people, especially in remote areas in the southern United States

hilt [hɪlt] **hilts** NOUN
The hilt of a sword or knife is its handle.

him [hɪm] PRONOUN
You use 'him' to refer to a man, boy, or male animal that has already been mentioned, or to any person whose sex is not known.

himself [hɪm'sɛlf] PRONOUN
1 'Himself' is used when the same man, boy, or male animal does an action and is affected by it *e.g. He discharged himself from hospital.*
2 'Himself' is used to emphasize 'he'.

hind [haɪnd] **hinds** ADJECTIVE
1 used to refer to the back part of an animal *e.g. the hind legs*
> NOUN
2 a female deer

hinder ['hɪndə] **hinders, hindering, hindered** VERB
If you hinder someone or something, you get in their way and make something difficult for them.

● THESAURUS
block: *The President is blocking the release of the two men.*
check: *We have managed to check the spread of terrorism.*
delay: *Various problems have delayed producton.*
frustrate: *They have frustrated his efforts to gain a work permit.*
hamper: *I was hampered by a lack of information.*
impede: *Fallen rocks are impeding the progress of rescue workers.*

Hindi ['hɪndɪ] NOUN
Hindi is a language spoken in northern India.
[WORD HISTORY: from Old Persian HINDU meaning 'the river Indus']

hindrance ['hɪndrəns] **hindrances** NOUN
1 Someone or something that is a hindrance causes difficulties or is an obstruction.
2 Hindrance is the act of hindering someone or something.

hindsight ['haɪnd,saɪt] NOUN
Hindsight is the ability to understand an event after it has actually taken place. *e.g. With hindsight, I realized how odd he is.*

Hindu ['hɪndu:] **Hindus** NOUN
(RE) a person who believes in Hinduism, an Indian religion which has many gods and believes that people have another life on earth after death.

h

Hinduism NOUN

hinge [hɪndʒ] **hinges, hinging, hinged**
NOUN
1 the movable joint which attaches a door or window to its frame

> VERB
2 Something that hinges on a situation or event depends entirely on that situation or event. *e.g. Victory or defeat hinged on her final putt.*

hint [hɪnt] **hints, hinting, hinted** NOUN
1 an indirect suggestion

● THESAURUS
clue: *How a man shaves may be a telling clue to his age.*
indication: *He gave no indication that he was ready to compromise.*
intimation: *I did not have any intimation that he was going to resign.*
suggestion: *We reject any suggestion that the law needs amending.*

2 a helpful piece of advice

● THESAURUS
advice: *Don't be afraid to ask for advice.*
pointer: *Here are a few pointers to help you make your choice.*
suggestion: *Can I give you a few suggestions?*
tip: *tips for busy managers*

> VERB
3 If you hint at something, you suggest it indirectly.

● THESAURUS
imply: *The report implied that his death was inevitable.*
indicate: *She has indicated that she may resign.*
insinuate: *an article which insinuated that he was lying*
intimate: *He intimated that he was contemplating a shake-up of the company.*
suggest: *Are you suggesting that I need to lose some weight?*

hinterland [ˈhɪntəˌlænd] **hinterlands**
NOUN
The hinterland of a coastline or a port is the area of land behind it or around it.

hip [hɪp] **hips** NOUN
Your hips are the two parts at the sides of your body between your waist and your upper legs.

hippo [ˈhɪpəʊ] **hippos** NOUN; INFORMAL
a hippopotamus

hippopotamus [ˌhɪpəˈpɒtəməs]
hippopotamuses or **hippopotami** NOUN
a large African animal with thick wrinkled skin and short legs, that lives near rivers
[WORD HISTORY: from Greek HIPPO + POTAMOS meaning 'river horse']

hippy [ˈhɪpɪ] **hippies;** also spelt **hippie** NOUN
In the 1960s and 1970s hippies were people who rejected conventional society and tried to live a life based on peace and love.

hire [ˈhaɪə] **hires, hiring, hired** VERB
1 If you hire something, you pay money to be able to use it for a period of time.

● THESAURUS
charter: *They chartered a jet to fly her home.*
lease: *He went to Toronto, where he leased an apartment.*
rent: *She rents a house with three other girls.*

2 If you hire someone, you pay them to do a job for you.

● THESAURUS
appoint: *The Prime Minister has appointed a civilian as defence minister.*
commission: *You can commission her to paint something especially for you.*
employ: *They employed me as a nanny.*
engage: *We engaged the services of a recognized engineer.*
sign up: *He persuaded the company to sign her up.*

> PHRASE
3 Something that is **for hire** is available for people to hire.

hirsute [ˈhɜːsjuːt] ADJECTIVE; FORMAL
hairy

his [hɪz] ADJECTIVE OR PRONOUN
'His' refers to something that belongs or relates to a man, boy, or male animal that has already been mentioned, and sometimes also to any person whose sex is not known

hiss [hɪs] **hisses, hissing, hissed** VERB
1 To hiss means to make a long 's' sound, especially to show disapproval or aggression.

> NOUN
2 a long 's' sound

histogram [ˈhɪstəˌɡræm] **histograms** NOUN
a graph consisting of rectangles of varying sizes, that shows the frequency of values of a quantity

historian [hɪˈstɔːrɪən] **historians** NOUN
a person who studies and writes about history

historic [hɪˈstɒrɪk] ADJECTIVE
important in the past or likely to be seen as important in the future

historical [hɪˈstɒrɪkəl] ADJECTIVE
1 occurring in the past, or relating to the study of the past *e.g. historical events*
2 describing or representing the past *e.g. historical novels*
historically ADVERB

history [ˈhɪstərɪ] **histories** NOUN
History is the study of the past. A history is a

record of the past. *e.g. The village is steeped in history... my family history*

histrionic [ˌhɪstrɪˈɒnɪk] histrionics
ADJECTIVE

1 Histrionic behaviour is very dramatic and full of exaggerated emotion.

2 FORMAL
relating to drama and acting *e.g. a young man of marked histrionic ability*

> PLURAL NOUN
3 Histrionics are histrionic behaviour.

hit see page 422 for Word Web

hit and miss
happening in an unpredictable way or without being properly organized

hit-and-run ['hɪtənd'rʌn] ADJECTIVE
A hit-and-run car accident is one in which the person who has caused the damage drives away without stopping.

hitch [hɪtʃ] hitches, hitching, hitched
NOUN

1 a slight problem or difficulty *e.g. The whole process was completed without a hitch.*

> VERB
2 INFORMAL
If you hitch, you travel by getting lifts from passing vehicles. *e.g. America is no longer a safe place to hitch round.*

hitchhiking ['hɪtʃˌhaɪkɪŋ] NOUN
Hitchhiking is travelling by getting free lifts from passing vehicles.

hi tech [tɛk] ADJECTIVE
designed using the most modern methods and equipment, especially electronic equipment

hither ['hɪðə] OLD-FASHIONED, INFORMAL >
ADVERB

1 used to refer to movement towards the place where you are

> PHRASE
2 Something that moves **hither and thither** moves in all directions.

hitherto ['hɪðə'tuː] ADVERB; FORMAL
until now *e.g. What he was aiming at had not hitherto been attempted.*

HIV NOUN
HIV is a virus that reduces people's resistance to illness and can cause AIDS. HIV is an abbreviation for 'human immunodeficiency virus'.

hive [haɪv] hives, hiving, hived NOUN
1 a beehive

2 A place that is a hive of activity is very busy with a lot of people working hard.

> VERB
3 If part of something such as a business is hived off, it is transferred to new ownership. *e.g. The company is poised to hive off its music interests.*

hoard [hɔːd] hoards, hoarding, hoarded
VERB

1 To hoard things means to save them even though they may no longer be useful.

● THESAURUS
save: *Save some fuel in case of emergencies.*
stockpile: *People are stockpiling food for the coming winter.*
store: *It's perfect for storing eggs or vegetables.*

> NOUN
2 a store of things that has been saved or hidden

● THESAURUS
cache: *a cache of weapons and explosives*
fund: *a scholarship fund for engineering students*
reserve: *the world's oil reserves*
stockpile: *stockpiles of nuclear warheads*
store: *I have a store of food and water here.*
supply: *food supplies*

■ Do not confuse **hoard** with **horde**.

hoarding ['hɔːdɪŋ] hoardings NOUN
a large advertising board by the side of the road

hoarse [hɔːs] hoarser, hoarsest ADJECTIVE
A hoarse voice sounds rough and unclear.
hoarsely ADVERB

● THESAURUS
croaky: *He sounds a bit croaky today.*
gruff: *his gruff Scottish growl*
husky: *Her deep husky voice was her trademark.*
rasping: *Both men sang in a deep rasping tone.*
<<OPPOSITE *clear*

hoax [həʊks] hoaxes, hoaxing, hoaxed
NOUN

1 a trick or an attempt to deceive someone

> VERB
2 To hoax someone means to trick or deceive them.

hob [hɒb] hobs NOUN
a surface on top of a cooker which can be heated in order to cook things

hobble ['hɒbəl] hobbles, hobbling, hobbled VERB

1 If you hobble, you walk awkwardly because of pain or injury.

2 If you hobble an animal, you tie its legs together to restrict its movement.

hobby ['hɒbɪ] hobbies NOUN
something that you do for enjoyment in your spare time

● THESAURUS
diversion: *Finger painting is very messy but an excellent diversion.*

h

1 VERB

to strike someone or something forcefully
eg: *Both men had been hit with baseball bats.*

● **THESAURUS**

bash: *The chef was bashed over the head.*

batter: *He battered her round the head with a club.*

bang: *She'd fainted and banged her head.*

beat: *a circle of men beating drums*

belt: *She drew back her fist and belted him right in the stomach.*

hammer: *We had to hammer the door and shout to attract their attention.*

knock: *She accidentally knocked the tin off the shelf.*

pat: *"Don't worry about it," he said patting me on the knee*

pound: *He pounded the table with both fists.*

punch: *After punching him on the chin, she ran off.*

rap: *he was rapping the glass with the knuckles of his right hand*

slap: *I slapped him hard across the face.*

smack: *She smacked the child on the side of the head.*

strike: *She stepped forward and struck him across the mouth.*

swat: *Every time a fly came near, I swatted it with a newspaper.*

tap: *Tap the egg gently with a teaspoon to crack the shell.*

thump: *I'm warning you, if you don't shut up, I'll thump you.*

wallop: *Once, she walloped me over the head with a frying pan.*

whack: *Someone whacked me with a baseball bat.*

2 VERB

to collide with something *eg*: *The car had apparently hit a traffic sign.*

● **THESAURUS**

bang into: *She fell after another skier banged into her.*

bump: *The boat bumped against something.*

collide with: *He almost collided with Daisy.*

meet head-on: *Their cars met head-on down a narrow alleyway.*

run into: *The mail train ran into a derailed goods train at 75mph.*

smash into: *The car plunged down a cliff and smashed into a tree.*

3 NOUN

the action of hitting something *eg*: *Give it a good hard hit with the hammer.*

● **THESAURUS**

blow: *He went to hospital after a blow to the face.*

knock: *a painful knock on the knee*

rap: *There was a rap on the door.*

slap: *She reached forward and gave him a slap.*

smack: *a smack with a ruler*

stroke: *six strokes of the cane*

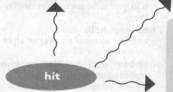

hit

leisure activity: *America's top leisure activity is watching television.*
leisure pursuit: *His main leisure pursuit is hill walking.*
pastime: *His favourite pastime is golf.*

hock [hɒk] **hocks** NOUN
The hock of a horse or other animal is the angled joint in its back leg.

hockey ['hɒkɪ] NOUN
Hockey is a game in which two teams use long sticks with curved ends to try to hit a small ball into the other team's goal.

hoe [həʊ] **hoes, hoeing, hoed** NOUN
1 a long-handled gardening tool with a small square blade, used to remove weeds and break up the soil
> VERB
2 To hoe the ground means to use a hoe on it.

hog [hɒg] **hogs, hogging, hogged** NOUN
1 a castrated male pig
> VERB
2 INFORMAL
If you hog something, you take more than your share of it, or keep it for too long.
> PHRASE
3 INFORMAL
If you **go the whole hog**, you do something completely or thoroughly in a bold or extravagant way.

hoist [hɔɪst] **hoists, hoisting, hoisted** VERB
1 To hoist something means to lift it, especially using a crane or other machinery.
> NOUN
2 a machine for lifting heavy things

hokey-pokey [ˌhəʊkɪ'pəʊkɪ] NOUN
In New Zealand, hokey-pokey is a kind of brittle toffee.

hold [həʊld] **holds, holding, held** VERB
1 To hold something means to carry or keep it in place, usually with your hand or arms.
⬤ THESAURUS
carry: *He was carrying a briefcase.*
clasp: *She clasped the children to her.*
clutch: *He was clutching a photograph.*
embrace: *The couple in the corridor were embracing each other.*
grasp: *He grasped both my hands.*
grip: *They gripped the rope tightly.*
2 Someone who holds power, office, or an opinion has it or possesses it.
3 If you hold something such as a meeting or an election, you arrange it and cause it to happen.
4 If something holds, it is still available or valid. *e.g. The offer still holds.*

5 If you hold someone responsible for something, you consider them responsible for it.
6 If something holds a certain amount, it can contain that amount. *e.g. The theatre holds 150 people.*
7 If you hold something such as theatre tickets, a telephone call, or the price of something, you keep or reserve it for a period of time. *e.g. The line is engaged – will you hold?.*
8 To hold something down means to keep it or to keep it under control. *e.g. How could I have children and hold down a job like this?.*
9 If you hold on to something, you continue it or keep it even though it might be difficult. *e.g. They are keen to hold on to their culture.*
10 To hold something back means to prevent it, keep it under control, or not reveal it. *e.g. She failed to hold back the tears.*
> NOUN
11 If someone or something has a hold over you, they have power, control, or influence over you. *e.g. The party has a considerable hold over its own leader.*
⬤ THESAURUS
control: *He will have to give up his control of the company.*
dominance: *the gang's dominance of the London underworld*
sway: *ideas that held sway for centuries*
12 a way of holding something or the act of holding it *e.g. He grabbed the rope and got a hold on it.*
⬤ THESAURUS
grasp: *His hand was taken in a warm, firm grasp.*
grip: *His strong hand eased the bag from her grip.*
13 the place where cargo or luggage is stored in a ship or a plane
holder NOUN

holdall ['həʊldˌɔːl] **holdalls** NOUN
a large, soft bag for carrying clothing

hole [həʊl] **holes, holing, holed** NOUN
1 an opening or hollow in something
⬤ THESAURUS
gap: *The wind was tearing through gaps in the window frames.*
hollow: *Water gathers in a hollow and forms a pond.*
opening: *He squeezed through a narrow opening in the fence.*
pit: *He lost his footing and began to slide into the pit.*
split: *The seat has a few small splits around the corners.*
tear: *I peered through a tear in the van's curtains.*
2 INFORMAL
If you are in a hole, you are in a difficult situation.
⬤ THESAURUS
fix: informal *This will put homeowners in a fix.*

h

hot water: informal *They have already been in hot water over high prices this year.*

mess: *the many reasons why the economy is in such a mess*

predicament: *the once great club's current predicament*

tight spot: *This was one tight spot he couldn't get out of.*

3 INFORMAL
A hole in a theory or argument is a weakness or error in it.

● THESAURUS
defect: *A defect in the aircraft caused the crash.*
error: *NASA discovered an error in its calculations.*
fault: *There is a fault in the computer program.*
flaw: *Almost all of these studies have serious flaws.*
loophole: *They exploited a loophole in the law.*

4 In golf, a hole is one of the small holes into which you have to hit the ball.

> VERB
5 When you hole the ball in golf, you hit the ball into one of the holes.

Holi ['hɒˌliː] NOUN
Holi is a Hindu festival celebrated in spring.
[WORD HISTORY: from HOLIKA, a legendary female demon]

holiday ['hɒlɪˌdeɪ] **holidays, holidaying, holidayed** NOUN

1 a period of time spent away from home for enjoyment

● THESAURUS
break: *They are currently taking a short break in Spain.*
leave: *Why don't you take a few days' leave?*
recess: *Parliament returns today after its summer recess.*
time off: *He took time off to go sailing with his wife.*
vacation: *We went on vacation to Puerto Rico.*

2 a time when you are not working or not at school

> VERB
3 When you holiday somewhere, you take a holiday there. *e.g. She is currently holidaying in Italy.*
[WORD HISTORY: from Old English HALIGDÆG meaning 'holy day']

holidaymaker ['hɒlɪdeɪˌmaɪkə] **holidaymakers** NOUN
a person who is away from home on holiday

holiness ['həʊlɪnɪs] NOUN

1 Holiness is the state or quality of being holy.

2 'Your Holiness' and 'His Holiness' are titles used to address or refer to the Pope or to leaders of some other religions

hollow ['hɒləʊ] **hollows, hollowing, hollowed** ADJECTIVE

1 Something that is hollow has space inside it rather than being solid.

2 An opinion or situation that is hollow has no real value or worth. *e.g. a hollow gesture*

3 A hollow sound is dull and has a slight echo. *e.g. the hollow sound of his footsteps on the stairs*

> NOUN
4 a hole in something or a part of a surface that is lower than the rest *e.g. It is a pleasant village in a lush hollow.*

> VERB
5 To hollow means to make a hollow. *e.g. They hollowed out crude dwellings from the soft rock.*

holly ['hɒlɪ] NOUN
Holly is an evergreen tree or shrub with spiky leaves. It often has red berries in winter.

holocaust ['hɒləˌkɔːst] **holocausts** NOUN

1 a large-scale destruction or loss of life, especially the result of war or fire

2 The Holocaust was the mass murder of the Jews in Europe by the Nazis during World War II.
[WORD HISTORY: from Greek HOLOS + KAUSTOS meaning 'completely burnt']

holster ['həʊlstə] **holsters** NOUN
a holder for a hand gun, worn at the side of the body or under the arm

holy ['həʊlɪ] **holier, holiest** ADJECTIVE

1 relating to God or to a particular religion *e.g. the holy city*

● THESAURUS
blessed: *Blessed are the peacemakers, for they shall be called the children of God.*
consecrated: *the consecrated bread from the Eucharist*
hallowed: *hallowed ground*
sacred: *sacred music*
sacrosanct: *For him the Sabbath was sacrosanct.*
venerated: *Jerusalem is Christianity's most venerated place.*

2 Someone who is holy is religious and leads a pure and good life.

● THESAURUS
devout: *She is a devout Catholic.*
pious: *He was brought up by pious female relatives.*
religious: *They are both very religious.*
saintly: *his saintly mother*
virtuous: *a virtuous family man*
<<OPPOSITE wicked

homage ['hɒmɪdʒ] NOUN
Homage is an act of respect and admiration. *e.g. The thronging crowds paid homage to their assassinated president.*

home [həʊm] **homes** NOUN

1 Your home is the building or place in which you live or feel you belong.

> THESAURUS
>
> **abode:** *a luxurious abode*
> **dwelling:** *One thousand new dwellings are planned for the area.*
> **house:** *our new house*
> **residence:** *the Royal Family's private residence*

2 a building in which elderly or ill people live and are looked after *e.g. He has been confined to a nursing home since his stroke.*

> **ADJECTIVE**

3 connected with or involving your home or country *e.g. He gave them his home phone number... The government is expanding the home market.*

> THESAURUS
>
> **domestic:** *over 100 domestic flights a day to 15 UK destinations*
> **internal:** *The government stepped up internal security.*
> **national:** *major national and international issues*
> **native:** *He was glad to be back on his native soil.*
> <<OPPOSITE *foreign*

homeland ['həʊm,lænd] **homelands** NOUN
Your homeland is your native country.

homeless ['həʊmlɪs] ADJECTIVE
1 having no home

> **PLURAL NOUN**

2 The homeless are people who have no home.
homelessness NOUN

homely ['həʊmlɪ] ADJECTIVE
simple, ordinary and comfortable *e.g. The room was small and homely.*

> THESAURUS
>
> **comfortable:** *A home should be warm and comfortable.*
> **cosy:** *Guests can relax in the cosy bar.*
> **modest:** *the modest home of a family who lived off the land*
> **simple:** *They celebrated mass in a simple chapel.*
> **welcoming:** *The restaurant is small and very welcoming.*
> <<OPPOSITE *grand*

homeopathy [,həʊmɪ'ɒpəθɪ] NOUN
Homeopathy is a way of treating illness by giving the patient tiny amounts of a substance that would normally cause illness in a healthy person.
homeopathic ADJECTIVE

homeowner ['həʊm,əʊnə] **homeowners** NOUN
a person who owns the home in which he or she lives

homesick ['həʊm,sɪk] ADJECTIVE
unhappy because of being away from home and missing family and friends

homespun ['həʊm,spʌn] ADJECTIVE
not sophisticated or complicated *e.g. The book is simple homespun philosophy.*

homestead ['həʊm,stɛd] **homesteads** NOUN
a house and its land and other buildings, especially a farm

home truth **home truths** NOUN
Home truths are unpleasant facts about yourself that you are told by someone else.

homeward or **homewards** ['həʊmwəd] or ['həʊmwədz] ADJECTIVE OR ADVERB
towards home *e.g. the homeward journey*

homework ['həʊm,wɜːk] NOUN
1 Homework is school work given to pupils to be done in the evening at home.

2 Homework is also research and preparation. *e.g. You certainly need to do your homework before buying a horse.*

homicide ['hɒmɪ,saɪd] **homicides** NOUN
Homicide is the crime of murder.
homicidal ADJECTIVE

homing ['həʊmɪŋ] ADJECTIVE
A homing device is able to guide itself to a target. An animal with a homing instinct is able to guide itself home.

homophone ['hɒmə,fəʊn] **homophones** NOUN
Homophones are words with different meanings which are pronounced in the same way but are spelt differently. For example, 'write' and 'right' are homophones.

homo sapiens ['həʊməʊ 'sæpɪ,ɛnz] NOUN; FORMAL
Homo sapiens is the scientific name for human beings.
[WORD HISTORY: from Latin HOMO meaning 'man' and SAPIENS meaning 'wise']

homosexual [,həʊməʊ'sɛksjʊəl] **homosexuals** NOUN
1 a person who is sexually attracted to someone of the same sex

> **ADJECTIVE**

2 sexually attracted to people of the same sex
homosexuality NOUN

hone [həʊn] **hones, honing, honed** VERB
1 If you hone a tool, you sharpen it.

2 If you hone a quality or ability, you develop and improve it. *e.g. He had a sharply honed sense of justice.*

honest ['ɒnɪst] ADJECTIVE
truthful and trustworthy
honestly ADVERB

> THESAURUS
>
> **law-abiding:** *law-abiding citizens*

reputable: *a reputable car dealer*
trustworthy: *He is a trustworthy and level-headed leader.*
truthful: *She could not give him a truthful answer.*
virtuous: *a virtuous family man*
<<OPPOSITE *dishonest*

honesty ['ɒnɪstɪ] NOUN
Honesty is the quality of being truthful and trustworthy.

honey ['hʌnɪ] NOUN
1 Honey is a sweet, edible, sticky substance produced by bees.

2 Honey means 'sweetheart' or 'darling'. *e.g. What is it, honey?.*

honeycomb ['hʌnɪ,kəʊm] **honeycombs** NOUN
a wax structure consisting of rows of six-sided cells made by bees for storage of honey and eggs

honeyeater ['hʌnɪ,i:tə] **honeyeaters** NOUN
a small Australian bird that feeds on nectar from flowers

honeymoon ['hʌnɪ,mu:n] **honeymoons** NOUN
a holiday taken by a couple who have just got married

honeysuckle ['hʌnɪ,sʌkəl] NOUN
Honeysuckle is a climbing plant with fragrant pink or cream flowers.

hongi ['hɒŋɪ:] NOUN
In New Zealand, hongi is a Maori greeting in which people touch noses.

honk [hɒŋk] **honks, honking, honked** NOUN
1 a short, loud sound like that made by a car horn or a goose

> VERB
2 When something honks, it makes a short, loud sound.

honorary ['ɒnərərɪ] ADJECTIVE
An honorary title or job is given as a mark of respect, and does not involve the usual qualifications or work. *e.g. She was awarded an honorary degree.*

honour ['ɒnə] **honours, honouring, honoured** NOUN
1 Your honour is your good reputation and the respect that other people have for you. *e.g. You have done me a great honour by visiting my country.*

● THESAURUS
decency: *No-one had the decency to tell me to my face.*
goodness: *He retains a faith in human goodness.*
honesty: *His reputation for honesty and integrity is second to none.*

integrity: *He was praised for his fairness and high integrity.*
<<OPPOSITE *dishonour*

2 an award or privilege given as a mark of respect

● THESAURUS
accolade: *the ultimate international accolade, the Nobel Peace prize*
commendation: *The officer received a commendation for brave conduct.*
homage: *films that pay homage to our literary heritage*
praise: *He had won consistently high praise for his theatre work.*
recognition: *At last, her father's work has received popular recognition.*
tribute: *He paid tribute to the organizing committee.*

3 Honours is a class of university degree which is higher than a pass or ordinary degree.

> PHRASE
4 If something is done **in honour of** someone, it is done out of respect for them. *e.g. Egypt celebrated frequent minor festivals in honour of the dead.*

> VERB
5 If you honour someone, you give them special praise or attention, or an award.

● THESAURUS
commemorate: *a plaque commemorating the servicemen who died*
commend: *I commended her for that action.*
decorate: *He was decorated for his gallantry by the General.*
glorify: *My philosophy of life is to glorify God in all I do.*
praise: *He praised their excellent work.*

6 If you honour an agreement or promise, you do what was agreed or promised. *e.g. There is enough cash to honour the existing pledges.*

honourable ['ɒnərəbəl] ADJECTIVE
worthy of respect or admiration *e.g. He should do the honourable thing and resign.*

hood [hʊd] **hoods** NOUN
1 a loose covering for the head, usually part of a coat or jacket

2 a cover on a piece of equipment or vehicle, usually curved and movable *e.g. The mechanic had the hood up to work on the engine.*
hooded ADJECTIVE

-hood SUFFIX
'-hood' is added at the end of words to form nouns that indicate a state or condition *e.g. childhood... priesthood*
[WORD HISTORY: from the Old English suffix -HĀD]

hoof [hu:f] **hooves** or **hoofs** NOUN
the hard bony part of certain animals' feet

hook [hʊk] **hooks, hooking, hooked** NOUN

1 a curved piece of metal or plastic that is used for catching, holding, or hanging things *e.g. picture hooks*

2 a curving movement, for example of the fist in boxing, or of a golf ball

> VERB

3 If you hook one thing onto another, you attach it there using a hook.

> PHRASE

4 If you are **let off the hook**, something happens so that you avoid punishment or a difficult situation.

hooked [hʊkt] ADJECTIVE

addicted to something; also obsessed by something *e.g. hooked on alcohol... I'm hooked on exercise.*

hooligan ['huːlɪgən] **hooligans** NOUN

a destructive and violent young person
hooliganism NOUN

● THESAURUS

delinquent: *a nine-year-old delinquent*
hoon: Australian and New Zealand; informal *the rocks hurled by hoons*
lout: *He was attacked by stone-throwing louts.*
tough: *Residents may be too terrified of local toughs to protest.*
vandal: *The Scout hut was burnt down by vandals.*
yob: British and Australian; slang *drunken yobs chanting football songs*

hoop [huːp] **hoops** NOUN

a large ring, often used as a toy

hooray [huːˈreɪ] INTERJECTION another spelling of **hurray**

hoot [huːt] **hoots, hooting, hooted** VERB

1 To hoot means to make a long 'oo' sound like an owl. *e.g. hooting with laughter*

2 If a car horn hoots, it makes a loud honking noise.

> NOUN

3 a sound like that made by an owl or a car horn

hoover ['huːvə] **hoovers, hoovering, hoovered** NOUN

1 TRADEMARK
a vacuum cleaner

> VERB

2 When you hoover, you use a vacuum cleaner to clean the floor.

hooves [huːvz] a plural of **hoof**

hop [hɒp] **hops, hopping, hopped** VERB

1 If you hop, you jump on one foot.

2 When animals or birds hop, they jump with two feet together.

3 INFORMAL

If you hop into or out of something, you move there quickly and easily. *e.g. You only have to hop on the ferry to get there.*

> NOUN

4 a jump on one leg

5 Hops are flowers of the hop plant, which are dried and used for making beer.

hope [həʊp] **hopes, hoping, hoped** VERB

1 If you hope that something will happen or hope that it is true, you want it to happen or be true.

> NOUN

2 Hope is a wish or feeling of desire and expectation. *e.g. There was little hope of recovery.*
hopeful ADJECTIVE, **hopefully** ADVERB

● THESAURUS

ambition: *His ambition is to sail around the world.*
dream: *his dream of becoming a pilot*
expectation: *The hotel was being renovated in expectation of a tourist boom.*

> Some people do not like the use of *hopefully* to mean 'it is hoped', for example *hopefully, we can get a good result on Saturday.* Although it is very common in speech, it should be avoided in written work.

hopeless ['həʊplɪs] ADJECTIVE

1 having no hope *e.g. She shook her head in hopeless bewilderment.*

2 certain to fail or be unsuccessful

● THESAURUS

forlorn: *the forlorn hope of finding a better life*
futile: *their futile attempts to avoid publicity*
impossible: *The tax is impossible to administer.*
pointless: *a pointless exercise that would only waste more time*
useless: *She knew it was useless to protest.*
vain: *a vain attempt to sign a goalkeeper*

3 bad or inadequate *e.g. I'm hopeless at remembering birthdays... hopeless parents*
hopelessly ADVERB, **hopelessness** NOUN

● THESAURUS

inadequate: *The problem lies with inadequate staffing.*
pathetic: *the pathetic state of the rail network*
poor: *The flat was in a poor state of repair.*
useless: informal *My husband is useless around the house.*

hopper ['hɒpə] **hoppers** NOUN

a large, funnel-shaped container for storing things such as grain or sand

horde [hɔːd] **hordes** NOUN

a large group or number of people or animals *e.g. hordes of tourists*

▮ Do not confuse *horde* with *hoard*.

horizon [hə'raɪzᵊn] **horizons** NOUN

1 the distant line where the sky seems to touch the land or sea

2 Your horizons are the limits of what you want to do or are interested in. *e.g. Travel broadens your horizons.*

> PHRASE

3 If something is **on the horizon**, it is almost certainly going to happen or be done in the future. *e.g. Political change was on the horizon.*

horizontal [,hɒrɪ'zɒntᵊl] ADJECTIVE
(MATHS) flat and parallel with the horizon or with a line considered as a base *e.g. a patchwork of vertical and horizontal black lines*
horizontally ADVERB

hormone ['hɔːməʊn] **hormones** NOUN
a chemical made by one part of your body that stimulates or has a specific effect on another part of your body
hormonal ADJECTIVE

horn [hɔːn] **horns** NOUN

1 one of the hard, pointed growths on the heads of animals such as goats

2 a musical instrument made of brass, consisting of a pipe or that is narrow at one end and wide at the other

3 On vehicles, a horn is a warning device which makes a loud noise.

hornet ['hɔːnɪt] **hornets** NOUN
a type of very large wasp

horoscope ['hɒrə,skəʊp] **horoscopes** NOUN
a prediction about what is going to happen to someone, based on the position of the stars when they were born
[WORD HISTORY: from Greek HORA + SKOPOS meaning 'hour observer']

horrendous [hɒ'rɛndəs] ADJECTIVE
very unpleasant and shocking *e.g. horrendous injuries*

horrible ['hɒrəbᵊl] ADJECTIVE

1 disagreeable and unpleasant *e.g. A horrible nausea rose within him.*

● THESAURUS
awful: *I had an awful time.*
disagreeable: *a disagreeable odour*
horrid: *My parents are horrid to each other.*
mean: *Why are you always so mean to me?*
nasty: *This divorce could turn nasty.*
unpleasant: *He's a very unpleasant little man.*

2 causing shock, fear, or disgust *e.g. horrible crimes*
horribly ADVERB

● THESAURUS
appalling: *They have been living under the most appalling conditions.*

dreadful: *She told me the dreadful news.*
grim: *a grim discovery*
gruesome: *gruesome murders*
terrifying: *a terrifying experience*

horrid ['hɒrɪd] ADJECTIVE
very unpleasant indeed *e.g. We were all so horrid to him.*

horrific [hɒ'rɪfɪk] ADJECTIVE
so bad or unpleasant that people are horrified *e.g. a horrific attack*

horrify ['hɒrɪ,faɪ] **horrifies, horrifying, horrified** VERB
If something horrifies you, it makes you feel dismay or disgust. *e.g. a crime trend that will horrify parents*
horrifying ADJECTIVE

● THESAURUS
appal: *I was appalled by her behaviour.*
disgust: *He disgusted everyone with his boorish behaviour.*
dismay: *He was deeply dismayed by the decision.*
outrage: *Human rights campaigners were outraged by the execution.*
shock: *Pictures of emaciated prisoners shocked the world.*
sicken: *What he saw at the accident sickened him.*

horror ['hɒrə] **horrors** NOUN

1 a strong feeling of alarm, dismay, and disgust *e.g. He gazed in horror at the knife.*

● THESAURUS
alarm: *She sat up in alarm.*
dread: *She thought with dread of the cold winter to come.*
fear: *I stood there crying and shaking with fear.*
fright: *He uttered a shriek and jumped with fright.*
panic: *He felt a sudden rush of panic at the thought.*
terror: *She shook with terror.*

2 If you have a horror of something, you fear it very much. *e.g. He had a horror of fire.*

● THESAURUS
abhorrence: *their abhorrence of racism*
aversion: *Many people have a natural aversion to insects.*
disgust: *I threw the book aside in disgust.*
hatred: *My hatred for him is intense.*
loathing: *She looked at him with loathing.*
revulsion: *They expressed their revulsion at his violent death.*

horse [hɔːs] **horses** NOUN

1 a large animal with a mane and long tail, on which people can ride

● THESAURUS
brumby: Australian and New Zealand *There's a mob of about 30 brumbies up there.*
equine: *the history and uses of equines*

moke: Australian and New Zealand; slang *a tired old moke*

nag: informal *He unhitched his sorry-looking nag from a nearby post.*

pony: *Peter trotted about on the fat pony he had been given.*

2 a piece of gymnastics equipment with four legs, used for jumping over

horseback [ˈhɔːsˌbæk] NOUN OR ADJECTIVE
You refer to someone who is riding a horse as someone **on horseback**, or a horseback rider.

horsepower [ˈhɔːsˌpaʊə] NOUN
Horsepower is a unit used for measuring how powerful an engine is, equal to about 746 watts.

horseradish [ˈhɔːsˌrædɪʃ] NOUN
Horseradish is the white root of a plant made into a hot-tasting sauce, often served cold with beef.

horseshoe [ˈhɔːsˌʃuː] **horseshoes** NOUN
a U-shaped piece of metal, nailed to the hard surface of a horse's hoof to protect it; also anything of this shape, often regarded as a good luck symbol

horsey or **horsy** [ˈhɔːsɪ] ADJECTIVE
1 very keen on horses and riding
2 having a face similar to that of a horse

horticulture [ˈhɔːtɪˌkʌltʃə] NOUN
Horticulture is the study and practice of growing flowers, fruit, and vegetables.
horticultural ADJECTIVE

hose [həʊz] **hoses, hosing, hosed** NOUN
1 a long flexible tube through which liquid or gas can be passed *e.g. He left the garden hose on.*

> VERB

2 If you hose something, you wash or water it using a hose. *e.g. The street cleaners need to hose the square down.*

hosiery [ˈhəʊzɪərɪ] NOUN
Hosiery consists of tights, socks, and similar items, especially in shops.

hospice [ˈhɒspɪs] **hospices** NOUN
a hospital which provides care for people who are dying

hospitable [ˈhɒspɪtəbᵊl] ADJECTIVE
friendly, generous, and welcoming to guests or strangers
hospitality NOUN

hospital [ˈhɒspɪtᵊl] **hospitals** NOUN
a place where sick and injured people are treated and cared for

host [həʊst] **hosts, hosting, hosted** NOUN
1 The host of an event is the person that welcomes guests and provides food or accommodation for them. *e.g. He is a most generous host who takes his guests to the best restaurants in town.*

2 a plant or animal with smaller plants or animals living on or in it

3 A host of things is a large number of them. *e.g. a host of close friends*

4 In the Christian church, the Host is the consecrated bread used in Mass or Holy Communion.

> VERB

5 To host an event means to organize it or act as host at it.

hostage [ˈhɒstɪdʒ] **hostages** NOUN
a person who is illegally held prisoner and threatened with injury or death unless certain demands are met by other people

hostel [ˈhɒstᵊl] **hostels** NOUN
a large building in which people can stay or live *e.g. a hostel for battered women*

hostess [ˈhəʊstɪs] **hostesses** NOUN
a woman who welcomes guests or visitors and provides food or accommodation for them

hostile [ˈhɒstaɪl] ADJECTIVE
1 unfriendly, aggressive, and unpleasant *e.g. a hostile audience*

● THESAURUS
antagonistic: *They were nearly all antagonistic to the idea.*
belligerent: *a belligerent war of words between India and Pakistan*
malevolent: *He fixed our photographer with a malevolent stare.*
unkind: *All last summer he'd been unkind to her.*
<<OPPOSITE *friendly*

2 relating to or involving the enemies of a country *e.g. hostile territory*
[WORD HISTORY: from Latin HOSTIS meaning 'enemy']

hostility [hɒˈstɪlɪtɪ] **hostilities** NOUN
aggression or unfriendly behaviour towards a person or thing

● THESAURUS
animosity: *The animosity between the two men grew.*
antagonism: *a history of antagonism between the two sides*
hatred: *her lifelong hatred of authority*
ill will: *He didn't bear anyone any ill will.*
malice: *There was no malice in her voice.*
resentment: *There is growing resentment against newcomers.*
<<OPPOSITE *friendship*

hot [hɒt] **hotter, hottest** ADJECTIVE

1 having a high temperature *e.g. a hot climate*

● THESAURUS
boiling: *It's boiling in here.*
heated: *a heated swimming pool*
scalding: *Her son was burned by scalding tea.*
scorching: *It was a scorching hot day.*
warm: *a warm, dry summer*
<<OPPOSITE *cold*

2 very spicy and causing a burning sensation in your mouth *e.g. a hot curry*

● THESAURUS
peppery: *a rich, peppery extra virgin olive oil*
spicy: *a spicy Cajun sauce*
<<OPPOSITE *bland*

3 new, recent, and exciting *e.g. hot news from tinseltown*

4 dangerous or difficult to deal with *e.g. Animal testing is a hot issue.*
hotly ADVERB

hotbed ['hɒt,bɛd] **hotbeds** NOUN
A hotbed of some type of activity is a place that seems to encourage it. *e.g. The city was a hotbed of rumour.*

hot dog hot dogs NOUN
a sausage served in a roll split lengthways

hotel [həʊˈtɛl] **hotels** NOUN
a building where people stay, paying for their room and meals

hothouse ['hɒt,haʊs] **hothouses** NOUN
1 a large heated greenhouse
2 a place or situation of intense intellectual or emotional activity *e.g. a hothouse of radical socialist ideas*

hot seat NOUN; INFORMAL
Someone who is in the hot seat has to make difficult decisions for which they will be held responsible.

hound [haʊnd] **hounds, hounding, hounded** NOUN
1 a dog, especially one used for hunting or racing
> VERB
2 If someone hounds you, they constantly pursue or trouble you.

hour [aʊə] **hours** NOUN
1 a unit of time equal to 60 minutes, of which there are 24 in a day
2 The hour for something is the time when it happens. *e.g. The hour for launching approached.*
3 The hour is also the time of day. *e.g. What are you doing up at this hour?.*
4 an important or difficult time *e.g. The hour has come... He is the hero of the hour.*
> PLURAL NOUN
5 The hours that you keep are the times that you

usually go to bed and get up.
hourly ADJECTIVE OR ADVERB

house houses, housing, housed NOUN
[haʊs]
1 a building where a person or family lives

● THESAURUS
abode: *I went round the streets and found his new abode.*
building: *Their flat was on the first floor of the building.*
dwelling: *One thousand new dwellings are planned for the area.*
home: *One in four people are without adequate homes.*
residence: *the Royal Family's private residence*

2 a building used for a particular purpose *e.g. an auction house... the opera house*

3 In a theatre or cinema, the house is the part where the audience sits; also the audience itself. *e.g. The show had a packed house calling for more.*
> VERB [haʊz]

4 To house something means to keep it or contain it. *e.g. The west wing housed a store of valuable antiques.*

houseboat ['haʊs,bəʊt] **houseboats** NOUN
a small boat which people live on that is tied up at a particular place on a river or canal

household ['haʊs,həʊld] **households** NOUN
1 all the people who live as a group in a house or flat
> PHRASE
2 Someone who is **a household name** is very well-known.
householder NOUN

housekeeper ['haʊs,kiːpə] **housekeepers** NOUN
a person who is employed to do the cooking and cleaning in a house

House of Commons [haʊs əv ˈkɒmənz] NOUN
The House of Commons is the more powerful of the two parts of the British Parliament. Its members are elected by the public.

House of Lords [haʊs əv lɔːdz] NOUN
The House of Lords is the less powerful of the two parts of the British Parliament. Its members are unelected and come from noble families or are appointed by the Queen as an honour for a life of public service.

House of Representatives [haʊs əv ˌrɛprɪˈzɛntətɪvz] NOUN
1 In Australia, the House of Representatives is the larger of the two parts of the Federal Parliament.
2 In New Zealand, the House of Representatives is the Parliament.

housewife ['haʊsˌwaɪf] **housewives** NOUN
a married woman who does the chores in her home, and does not have a paid job

housing ['haʊzɪŋ] NOUN
Housing is the buildings in which people live. *e.g. the serious housing shortage*

hovel ['hʌvᵊl] **hovels** NOUN
a small hut or house that is dirty or badly in need of repair

hover ['hɒvə] **hovers, hovering, hovered**
VERB
1 When a bird, insect, or aircraft hovers, it stays in the same position in the air.

2 If someone is hovering they are hesitating because they cannot decide what to do. *e.g. He was hovering nervously around the sick animal.*

hovercraft ['hɒvəˌkrɑːft] **hovercraft** or
hovercrafts NOUN
a vehicle which can travel over water or land supported by a cushion of air

how [haʊ] ADVERB
1 'How' is used to ask about, explain, or refer to the way in which something is done, known, or experienced *e.g. How did this happen? He knew how quickly rumours could spread.*

2 'How' is used to ask about or refer to a measurement or quantity *e.g. How much is it for the weekend? I wonder how old he is.*

3 'How' is used to emphasize the following word or statement *e.g. How odd!.*

however [haʊˈɛvə] ADVERB
1 You use 'however' when you are adding a comment that seems to contradict or contrast with what has just been said. *e.g. For all his compassion, he is, however, surprisingly restrained.*

2 You use 'however' to say that something makes no difference to a situation. *e.g. However hard she tried, nothing seemed to work.*

howl [haʊl] **howls, howling, howled** VERB
1 To howl means to make a long, loud wailing noise such as that made by a dog when it is upset. *e.g. A distant coyote howled at the moon... The wind howled through the trees.*

> NOUN
2 a long, loud wailing noise

HQ an abbreviation for **headquarters**

hub [hʌb] **hubs** NOUN
1 the centre part of a wheel

2 the most important or active part of a place or organization *e.g. The kitchen is the hub of most households.*

hubbub ['hʌbʌb] NOUN
Hubbub is great noise or confusion. *e.g. the*

general hubbub of conversation

huddle ['hʌdᵊl] **huddles, huddling, huddled** VERB
1 If you huddle up or are huddled, you are curled up with your arms and legs close to your body.

2 When people or animals huddle together, they sit or stand close to each other, often for warmth.

> NOUN
3 A huddle of people or things is a small group of them.

hue [hjuː] **hues** NOUN
1 LITERARY a colour or a particular shade of a colour

> PHRASE
2 If people raise a **hue and cry**, they are very angry about something and protest.

huff [hʌf] PHRASE
If you are **in a huff**, you are sulking or offended about something.
huffy ADJECTIVE

hug [hʌg] **hugs, hugging, hugged** VERB
1 If you hug someone, you put your arms round them and hold them close to you.

⊕ THESAURUS
clasp: *She clasped the children to her.*
cuddle: *They used to kiss and cuddle in front of everyone.*
embrace: *The couple in the corridor were embracing each other.*
squeeze: *He kissed her on the cheek and squeezed her tight.*

2 To hug the ground or a stretch of water or land means to keep very close to it. *e.g. The road hugs the coast for hundreds of miles.*

> NOUN
3 If you give someone a hug, you hold them close to you.
[WORD HISTORY: from Old Norse HUGGA meaning 'to comfort' or 'console']

⊕ THESAURUS
clinch: slang *They were caught in a clinch when her parents returned home.*
embrace: *a young couple locked in an embrace*

huge [hjuːdʒ] **huger, hugest** ADJECTIVE
extremely large in amount, size, or degree *e.g. a huge success... a huge crowd*
hugely ADVERB

⊕ THESAURUS
colossal: *a colossal waste of money*
enormous: *The main bedroom is enormous.*
giant: *a giant statue*
immense: *He wielded immense power.*
massive: *a massive surge in popularity*
vast: *this vast area of northern Canada*

h

<<OPPOSITE *tiny*

hui ['huːɪ] **hui** or **huis** NOUN

1 In New Zealand, a meeting of Maori people.

● THESAURUS

assembly: *an assembly of prizewinning journalists*
conference: *a conference attended by 280 delegates*
congress: *a congress of coal miners*
convention: *the annual convention of the Society of Professional Journalists*
gathering: *the annual gathering of the South Pacific Forum*
meeting: *Can we have a meeting to discuss that?*
rally: *They held a rally to mark International Human Rights Day.*

2 INFORMAL
In New Zealand English, a party.

hulk [hʌlk] **hulks** NOUN

1 a large, heavy person or thing

2 the body of a ship that has been wrecked or abandoned
hulking ADJECTIVE

hull [hʌl] **hulls** NOUN
The hull of a ship is the main part of its body that sits in the water.

hum [hʌm] **hums, humming, hummed** VERB

1 To hum means to make a continuous low noise. *e.g. The generator hummed faintly.*

2 If you hum, you sing with your lips closed.

> NOUN

3 a continuous low noise *e.g. the hum of the fridge*

human ['hjuːmən] **humans** ADJECTIVE

1 relating to, concerning, or typical of people *e.g. Intolerance appears deeply ingrained in human nature.*

> NOUN

2 a person
humanly ADVERB

human being **human beings** NOUN
a person

humane [hjuːˈmeɪn] ADJECTIVE
showing kindness and sympathy towards others *e.g. Medicine is regarded as the most humane of professions.*
humanely ADVERB

● THESAURUS

benevolent: *a most benevolent employer*
caring: *a very caring boy*
charitable: *charitable work*
compassionate: *a deeply compassionate man*
kind: *She is warmhearted and kind.*
merciful: *a merciful God*

thoughtful: *a very thoughtful gesture*

humanism ['hjuːməˌnɪzəm] NOUN
Humanism is the belief in mankind's ability to achieve happiness and fulfilment without the need for religion.

humanitarian [hjuːˌmænɪˈtɛərɪən] **humanitarians** NOUN

1 a person who works for the welfare of mankind

> ADJECTIVE

2 concerned with the welfare of mankind *e.g. humanitarian aid*
humanitarianism NOUN

humanity [hjuːˈmænɪtɪ] NOUN

1 Humanity is people in general. *e.g. I have faith in humanity.*

2 Humanity is also the condition of being human. *e.g. He denies his humanity.*

3 Someone who has humanity is kind and sympathetic.

human rights [raɪts] PLURAL NOUN
Human rights are the rights of individuals to freedom and justice.

humble ['hʌmbəl] **humbler, humblest; humbles, humbling, humbled** ADJECTIVE

1 A humble person is modest and thinks that he or she has very little value.

● THESAURUS

meek: *He was a meek, mild-mannered fellow.*
modest: *He's modest, as well as being a great player.*
unassuming: *She has a gentle, unassuming manner.*
<<OPPOSITE *haughty*

2 Something that is humble is small or not very important. *e.g. Just a splash of wine will transform a humble casserole.*

● THESAURUS

lowly: *He was irked by his lowly status.*
modest: *his modest beginnings*
ordinary: *It was just an ordinary weekend.*
simple: *a simple dinner of rice and beans*

> VERB

3 To humble someone means to make them feel humiliated.
humbly ADVERB, **humbled** ADJECTIVE

● THESAURUS

disgrace: *I have disgraced the family's name.*
humiliate: *His teacher continually humiliates him in maths lessons.*

humbug ['hʌmˌbʌg] **humbugs** NOUN

1 a hard black and white striped sweet that tastes of peppermint

2 Humbug is speech or writing that is obviously dishonest or untrue. *e.g. hypocritical humbug*

humdrum ['hʌm,drʌm] ADJECTIVE
ordinary, dull, and boring *e.g. humdrum domestic tasks*

humid ['hju:mɪd] ADJECTIVE
If it is humid, the air feels damp, heavy, and warm.

⬤ THESAURUS
clammy: *My shirt was clammy with sweat.*
muggy: *The weather was muggy and overcast.*
steamy: *The air was hot and steamy from the heat of a hundred bodies.*
sticky: *four hot, sticky days in the middle of August*

humidity [hju:'mɪdɪtɪ] NOUN
Humidity is the amount of moisture in the air, or the state of being humid.

humiliate [hju:'mɪlɪ,eɪt] **humiliates, humiliating, humiliated** VERB
To humiliate someone means to make them feel ashamed or appear stupid to other people.
humiliation NOUN

⬤ THESAURUS
disgrace: *I have disgraced my family.*
embarrass: *It embarrassed him that he had no idea of what was going on.*
humble: *The champion was humbled by the unseeded qualifier.*
put down: *I know that I do put people down occasionally.*
shame: *Her son's affair had shamed her.*

humility [hju:'mɪlɪtɪ] NOUN
Humility is the quality of being modest and humble.

hummingbird ['hʌmɪŋ,bɜ:d] **hummingbirds** NOUN
a small bird with powerful wings that make a humming noise as they beat

humour ['hju:mə] **humours, humouring, humoured** NOUN
1 Humour is the quality of being funny. *e.g. They discussed it with tact and humour.*

⬤ THESAURUS
comedy: *his career in comedy*
wit: *She was known for her biting wit.*
2 Humour is also the ability to be amused by certain things. *e.g. Helen's got a peculiar sense of humour.*
3 Someone's humour is the mood they are in. *e.g. He hasn't been in a good humour lately.*

⬤ THESAURUS
frame of mind: *Clearly, she was not in the right frame of mind to continue.*
mood: *Lily was in one of her aggressive moods.*
spirits: *He was in very low spirits.*
temper: *Lee stormed off the field in a furious temper.*
> VERB
4 If you humour someone, you are especially

kind to them and do whatever they want.
humorous ADJECTIVE

⬤ THESAURUS
flatter: *I knew she was just flattering me.*
indulge: *He did not agree with indulging children.*
mollify: *The investigation was undertaken primarily to mollify pressure groups.*
pander to: *politicians who pander to big business*

hump [hʌmp] **humps, humping, humped** NOUN
1 a small, rounded lump or mound *e.g. a camel's hump*
> VERB
2 INFORMAL
If you hump something heavy, you carry or move it with difficulty.

hunch [hʌntʃ] **hunches, hunching, hunched** NOUN
1 a feeling or suspicion about something, not based on facts or evidence
> VERB
2 If you hunch your shoulders, you raise your shoulders and lean forwards.

hunchback ['hʌntʃ,bæk] **hunchbacks** NOUN; OLD-FASHIONED, INFORMAL
someone who has a large hump on their back

hundred ['hʌndrəd] **hundreds**
the number 100
hundredth ADJECTIVE

Hungarian [hʌŋ'gɛərɪən] **Hungarians** ADJECTIVE
1 belonging or relating to Hungary
> NOUN
2 someone who comes from Hungary
3 Hungarian is the main language spoken in Hungary.

hunger ['hʌŋgə] **hungers, hungering, hungered** NOUN
1 Hunger is the need to eat or the desire to eat.
2 A hunger for something is a strong need or desire for it. *e.g. a hunger for winning*
> VERB
3 If you hunger for something, you want it very much.

hunger strike hunger strikes NOUN
a refusal to eat anything at all, especially by prisoners, as a form of protest

hungry ['hʌŋgrɪ] **hungrier, hungriest** ADJECTIVE
needing or wanting to eat *e.g. People are going hungry.*
hungrily ADVERB

⬤ THESAURUS
famished: *Isn't dinner ready? I'm famished.*

ravenous: *a pack of ravenous animals*
starving: *starving refugees*

hunk [hʌŋk] **hunks** NOUN
A hunk of something is a large piece of it.

hunt [hʌnt] **hunts, hunting, hunted** VERB
1 To hunt means to chase wild animals to kill them for food or for sport.

2 If you hunt for something, you search for it.

> NOUN

3 the act of hunting *e.g. Police launched a hunt for an abandoned car.*
hunter NOUN, **hunting** ADJECTIVE OR NOUN

huntaway [ˈhʌntəˌweɪ] **huntaways** NOUN
In Australia and New Zealand, a dog trained to drive sheep forward.

hurdle [ˈhɜːdəl] **hurdles** NOUN
1 one of the frames or barriers that you jump over in an athletics race called hurdles *e.g. She won the four hundred metre hurdles.*

2 a problem or difficulty *e.g. Several hurdles exist for anyone seeking to do postgraduate study.*

hurl [hɜːl] **hurls, hurling, hurled** VERB
1 To hurl something means to throw it with great force.

2 If you hurl insults at someone, you insult them aggressively and repeatedly.

hurray or **hurrah** or **hooray** [hʊˈreɪ] *or* [hʊˈrɑː] *or* [huːˈreɪ] INTERJECTION
an exclamation of excitement or approval

hurricane [ˈhʌrɪkən] **hurricanes** NOUN
a violent wind or storm

hurry [ˈhʌrɪ] **hurries, hurrying, hurried** VERB
1 To hurry means to move or do something as quickly as possible. *e.g. She hurried through the empty streets.*

● THESAURUS
dash: *He dashed upstairs.*
fly: *I must fly or I'll miss my train.*
get a move on: *informal Get a move on because my car's on a double yellow line.*
rush: *I've got to rush. I've got a meeting in a few minutes.*
scurry: *Reporters scurried to find telephones.*

2 To hurry something means to make it happen more quickly. *e.g. You can't hurry nature.*

● THESAURUS
accelerate: *They must now accelerate the development of their new car.*
hasten: *This will hasten the closure of small pubs.*
quicken: *He quickened his pace a little.*
speed up: *an effort to speed up the negotiations*
<<OPPOSITE *slow down*

> NOUN

3 Hurry is the speed with which you do something quickly. *e.g. He was in a hurry to leave.*
hurried ADJECTIVE, **hurriedly** ADVERB

hurt [hɜːt] **hurts, hurting, hurt** VERB
1 To hurt someone means to cause them physical pain.

● THESAURUS
harm: *The hijackers seemed anxious not to harm anyone.*
injure: *motorists who kill, maim, and injure*
wound: *The bomb killed six people and wounded another five.*

2 If a part of your body hurts, you feel pain there.

3 If you hurt yourself, you injure yourself.

4 To hurt someone also means to make them unhappy by being unkind or thoughtless towards them. *e.g. I didn't want to hurt his feelings.*

● THESAURUS
distress: *I did not want to frighten or distress the horse.*
sadden: *He is saddened that they did not win anything.*
upset: *I'm sorry if I've upset you.*
wound: *My relatives have wounded me in the past.*

> ADJECTIVE

5 If someone feels hurt, they feel unhappy because of someone's unkindness towards them. *e.g. He felt hurt by all the lies.*
hurtful ADJECTIVE

● THESAURUS
aggrieved: *He is still aggrieved at the size of the fine.*
offended: *He was offended at being left out.*
upset: *I'm upset by your attitude.*
wounded: *I think she feels desperately wounded and unloved.*

hurtle [ˈhɜːtəl] **hurtles, hurtling, hurtled** VERB
To hurtle means to move or travel very fast indeed, especially in an uncontrolled way.

husband [ˈhʌzbənd] **husbands** NOUN
A woman's husband is the man she is married to.

husbandry [ˈhʌzbəndrɪ] NOUN
1 Husbandry is the art or skill of farming.

2 Husbandry is also the art or skill of managing something carefully and economically.

hush [hʌʃ] **hushes, hushing, hushed** VERB
1 If you tell someone to hush, you are telling them to be quiet.

2 To hush something up means to keep it secret, especially something dishonest involving important people. *e.g. The government has hushed up a series of scandals.*

> NOUN
3 If there is a hush, it is quiet and still. *e.g. A graveyard hush fell over the group.*
hushed ADJECTIVE

husk [hʌsk] **husks** NOUN
Husks are the dry outer coverings of grain or seed.

husky ['hʌskɪ] **huskier, huskiest; huskies** ADJECTIVE
1 A husky voice is rough or hoarse.

> NOUN
2 a large, strong dog with a thick coat, often used to pull sledges across snow

hustle ['hʌsᵊl] **hustles, hustling, hustled** VERB
To hustle someone means to make them move by pushing and jostling them. *e.g. The guards hustled him out of the car.*

hut [hʌt] **huts** NOUN
a small, simple building, with one or two rooms

hutch [hʌtʃ] **hutches** NOUN
a wooden box with wire mesh at one side, in which small pets can be kept

hyacinth ['haɪəsɪnθ] **hyacinths** NOUN
a spring flower with many small, bell-shaped flowers

hybrid ['haɪbrɪd] **hybrids** NOUN
1 a plant or animal that has been bred from two different types of plant or animal
2 anything that is a mixture of two other things

hydra ['haɪdrə] **hydras** or **hydrae** NOUN
a microscopic freshwater creature that has a slender tubular body and tentacles round the mouth

hydrangea [haɪ'dreɪndʒə] **hydrangeas** NOUN
a garden shrub with large clusters of pink or blue flowers

hydraulic [haɪ'drɒlɪk] ADJECTIVE
operated by water or other fluid which is under pressure

hydro- PREFIX
'Hydro-' means 'water'. For example, *hydroelectricity* is electricity made using water power
[WORD HISTORY: from Greek HUDŌR meaning 'water']

hydrogen ['haɪdrɪdʒən] NOUN
Hydrogen is the lightest gas and the simplest chemical element.

hyena [haɪ'iːnə] **hyenas** (*said* high-**ee**-na); also spelt **hyaena** NOUN

a wild doglike animal of Africa and Asia that hunts in packs

hygiene ['haɪdʒiːn] NOUN
(D & T) Hygiene is the practice of keeping yourself and your surroundings clean, especially to stop the spread of disease.
hygienic ADJECTIVE

🔵 **THESAURUS**
cleanliness: *Many of the beaches fail to meet minimum standards of cleanliness.*
sanitation: *the hazards of contaminated water and poor sanitation*

hymn [hɪm] **hymns** NOUN
(RE) a Christian song in praise of God

hyper- PREFIX
'Hyper-' means 'very much' or 'excessively' *e.g. hyperactive*
[WORD HISTORY: from Greek HUPER meaning 'over']

hyperactive [ˌhaɪpər'æktɪv] ADJECTIVE
A hyperactive person is unable to relax and is always in a state of restless activity.

hyperbole [haɪ'pɜːbəlɪ] NOUN
Hyperbole is a style of speech or writing which uses exaggeration.

hyperlink ['hɒɪpəˌlɪŋk] **hyperlinks** NOUN
a word, phrase, or picture in a computer document which a user may click to move to another part of the document, or to another document

hypertension [ˌhaɪpə'tenʃən] NOUN
Hypertension is a medical condition in which a person has high blood pressure.

hypertext ['haɪpəˌtɛkst] **hypertexts** NOUN
computer software that allows users to create, store, and view text and move between related items easily

hyphen ['haɪfᵊn] **hyphens** NOUN
a punctuation mark used to join together words or parts of words, as for example in the word 'left-handed'
hyphenate VERB, **hyphenation** NOUN

hypnosis [hɪp'nəʊsɪs] NOUN
Hypnosis is an artificially produced state of relaxation in which the mind is very receptive to suggestion.
[WORD HISTORY: from Greek HUPNOS meaning 'sleep']

hypnotize ['hɪpnəˌtaɪz] **hypnotizes, hypnotizing, hypnotized;** also spelt **hypnotise** VERB
To hypnotize someone means to put them into a state in which they seem to be asleep but can respond to questions and suggestions.
hypnotic ADJECTIVE, **hypnotism** NOUN, **hypnotist** NOUN

● THESAURUS
put in a trance: *A stage hypnotist put her in a trance.*
put to sleep: *First the hypnotist will put you to sleep.*

hypochondriac [ˌhaɪpə'kɒndrɪˌæk]
hypochondriacs NOUN
a person who continually worries about their health, being convinced that they are ill when there is actually nothing wrong with them

hypocrisy [hɪ'pɒkrəsɪ] **hypocrisies** NOUN
Hypocrisy is pretending to have beliefs or qualities that you do not really have, so that you seem a better person than you are.
hypocritical ADJECTIVE, **hypocrite** NOUN

hypodermic [ˌhaɪpə'dɜːmɪk] **hypodermics**
NOUN
a medical instrument with a hollow needle, used for giving people injections, or taking blood samples

hypothermia [ˌhaɪpəʊ'θɜːmɪə] NOUN
Hypothermia is a condition in which a person is very ill because their body temperature has been unusually low for a long time.

hypothesis [haɪ'pɒθɪsɪs] **hypotheses** NOUN
an explanation or theory which has not yet been proved to be correct

hypothetical [ˌhaɪpə'θetɪk³l] ADJECTIVE
based on assumption rather than on fact or reality

hysterectomy [ˌhɪstə'rektəmɪ]
hysterectomies NOUN
an operation to remove a woman's womb

hysteria [hɪ'stɪərɪə] NOUN
Hysteria is a state of uncontrolled excitement or panic.

hysterical [hɪ'sterɪk³l] ADJECTIVE
1 Someone who is hysterical is in a state of uncontrolled excitement or panic.

● THESAURUS
frantic: *A bird had been locked in and was by now quite frantic.*
frenzied: *her frenzied attempts to get free*
overwrought: *One overwrought man had to be restrained by friends.*
raving: *He looked at her as if she were a raving lunatic.*

2 INFORMAL
Something that is hysterical is extremely funny.
hysterically ADVERB, **hysterics** NOUN

● THESAURUS
comical: *Her expression is almost comical.*
hilarious: *He had a fund of hilarious jokes on the subject.*

Ii

I [aɪ] PRONOUN
A speaker or writer uses 'I' to refer to himself or herself. *e.g. I like the colour.*

ibis ['aɪbɪs] **ibises** NOUN
a large wading bird with a long, thin, curved bill that lives in warm countries

-ible SUFFIX another form of the suffix **-able**

-ic or **-ical** SUFFIX
'-ic' and '-ical' form adjectives from nouns. For example, *ironic* or *ironical* formed from *irony*

ice [aɪs] **ices, icing, iced** NOUN
1 water that has frozen solid

2 an ice cream

> VERB
3 If you ice cakes, you cover them with icing.

4 If something ices over or ices up, it becomes covered with a layer of ice.

> PHRASE
5 If you do something to **break the ice**, you make people feel relaxed and comfortable.

Ice Age Ice Ages NOUN
a period of time lasting thousands of years when a lot of the earth's surface was covered with ice

iceberg ['aɪsbɜːg] **icebergs** NOUN
a large mass of ice floating in the sea
[WORD HISTORY: from Dutch IJSBERG meaning 'ice mountain']

icecap ['aɪskæp] **icecaps** NOUN
a layer of ice and snow that permanently covers the North or South Pole

ice cream ice creams NOUN
a very cold sweet food made from frozen cream

ice cube ice cubes NOUN
Ice cubes are small cubes of ice put in drinks to make them cold.

ice hockey NOUN
a type of hockey played on ice, with two teams of six players

Icelandic [aɪs'lændɪk] NOUN
the main language spoken in Iceland

ice-skate ['aɪsˌskeɪt] **ice-skates, ice-skating, ice-skated** NOUN

a boot with a metal blade on the bottom, which you wear when skating on ice

> VERB
2 If you ice-skate, you move about on ice wearing ice-skates.

icicle ['aɪsɪkᵊl] **icicles** NOUN
a piece of ice shaped like a pointed stick that hangs down from a surface

icing ['aɪsɪŋ] NOUN
a mixture of powdered sugar and water or egg whites, used to decorate cakes

icon ['aɪkɒn] **icons** NOUN
1 (ICT) a picture on a computer screen representing a program that can be activated by moving the cursor over it

2 in the Orthodox Churches, a holy picture of Christ, the Virgin Mary, or a saint
[WORD HISTORY: from Greek EIKŌN meaning 'likeness' or 'image']

ICT
an abbreviation for 'Information and Communication Technology'

icy ['aɪsɪ] **icier, iciest** ADJECTIVE
1 Something which is icy is very cold. *e.g. an icy wind*

2 An icy road has ice on it.
icily ADVERB

id [ɪd] NOUN
In psychology, your id is your basic instincts and unconscious thoughts.

idea [aɪ'dɪə] **ideas** NOUN
1 a plan, suggestion, or thought that you have after thinking about a problem

● THESAURUS
plan: *I have a cunning plan.*
recommendation: *a range of recommendations for change*
scheme: *a proposed scheme*
solution: *He came up with a solution to the problem.*
suggestion: *Do you have a better suggestion?*

2 an opinion or belief *e.g. old-fashioned ideas about women*

● THESAURUS
belief: *my religious beliefs*

437

conviction: *a firm conviction that things have improved*
impression: *your first impressions of college*
notion: *I have a notion of what he is like.*
opinion: *a favourable opinion of our neighbours*
view: *Make your views known to local politicians.*

3 An idea of something is what you know about it. *e.g. They had no idea of their position.*

● THESAURUS
clue: *I don't have a clue what you mean.*
guess: *My guess is he went east.*
hint: *He gave no hint about where he was.*
inkling: *We had an inkling that something was happening.*
notion: *I have a notion how it is done.*
suspicion: *I have a strong suspicion they are lying.*

ideal [aɪ'dɪəl] **ideals** NOUN
1 a principle or idea that you try to achieve because it seems perfect to you

● THESAURUS
principle: *acts that go against your principles*
standard: *My father has high moral standards.*
value: *the values of liberty and equality*

2 Your ideal of something is the person or thing that seems the best example of it.

● THESAURUS
epitome: *The hotel was the epitome of luxury.*
example: *He was held up as an example of courage.*
model: *a model of good manners*
paragon: *You are not a paragon of virtue.*
prototype: *He was the prototype of a strong leader.*
standard: *the standard by which we are compared*

> ADJECTIVE
3 The ideal person or thing is the best possible person or thing for the situation.

● THESAURUS
classic: *a classic example of hypocrisy*
complete: *She is the complete athlete.*
consummate: *a consummate politician*
model: *She is a model pupil.*
perfect: *He is the perfect husband for her.*
supreme: *a supreme method of cooking vegetables*

idealism [aɪ'dɪə,lɪzəm] NOUN
behaviour that is based on a person's ideals
idealist NOUN, **idealistic** ADJECTIVE

idealize [aɪ'dɪə,laɪz] **idealizes, idealizing, idealized**; also spelt **idealise** VERB
If you idealize someone or something, you regard them as being perfect.
idealization NOUN

ideally [aɪ'dɪəlɪ] ADVERB
1 If you say that ideally something should happen, you mean that you would like it to happen but you know that it is not possible.
2 Ideally means perfectly. *e.g. The hotel is ideally placed for business travellers.*

identical [aɪ'dɛntɪkᵊl] ADJECTIVE
exactly the same *e.g. identical twins*
identically ADVERB

identification [aɪ,dɛntɪfɪ'keɪʃən] NOUN
1 The identification of someone or something is the act of identifying them.
2 Identification is a document such as a driver's licence or passport, which proves who you are.

identify [aɪ'dɛntɪ,faɪ] **identifies, identifying, identified** VERB
1 To identify someone or something is to recognize them or name them.

● THESAURUS
diagnose: *This illness is easily diagnosed.*
label: *Poisonous substances should be labelled as such.*
name: *The victims of the fire have been named.*
pinpoint: *They could not pinpoint the cause of death.*
place: *The man was familiar, but I couldn't place him.*
recognize: *a man I recognized as Luke's father*

2 If you identify with someone, you understand their feelings and ideas.
identifiable ADJECTIVE

● THESAURUS
associate with: *I associate myself with the green movement.*
empathize with: *I empathize with the people who live here.*
feel for: *I pitied and felt for him.*
relate to: *We have difficulty relating to each other.*
respond to: *She responded to his pain.*

identity [aɪ'dɛntɪtɪ] **identities** NOUN
the characteristics that make you who you are

ideology [,aɪdɪ'ɒlədʒɪ] **ideologies** NOUN
a set of political beliefs
ideological ADJECTIVE, **ideologically** ADVERB

idiom ['ɪdɪəm] **idioms** NOUN
a group of words whose meaning together is different from all the words taken individually. For example, 'It is raining cats and dogs' is an idiom.
[WORD HISTORY: from Greek IDIŌMA meaning 'special phraseology']

idiosyncrasy [,ɪdɪəʊ'sɪŋkrəsɪ] **idiosyncrasies** NOUN
Someone's idiosyncrasies are their own habits and likes or dislikes.
idiosyncratic ADJECTIVE

idiot ['ɪdɪət] **idiots** NOUN
someone who is stupid or foolish
[WORD HISTORY: from Greek IDIŌTĒS meaning 'ignorant person']

● THESAURUS
fool: *He'd been a fool to get involved.*

galah: Australian; informal *sounding like an illiterate galah*
imbecile: *I don't want to deal with these imbeciles.*
moron: *I think that Gordon is a moron.*
oaf: *You clumsy oaf!*
twit: informal *I feel such a twit.*

idiotic [ˌɪdɪˈɒtɪk] ADJECTIVE
extremely foolish or silly

● THESAURUS
crazy: *You were crazy to leave then.*
daft: informal *He's not so daft as to listen to them.*
dumb: informal *I've met a lot of dumb people.*
foolish: *It is foolish to risk injury.*
senseless: *acts of senseless violence*
stupid: *stupid ideas*

idle [ˈaɪdᵊl] **idles, idling, idled** ADJECTIVE
If you are idle, you are doing nothing.
idleness NOUN, **idly** ADVERB
[WORD HISTORY: from Saxon IDAL meaning 'worthless' or 'empty']

● THESAURUS
jobless: *One in four people are now jobless.*
redundant: *redundant workers*
unemployed: *jobs for the unemployed*
<<OPPOSITE *busy*

idol [ˈaɪdᵊl] **idols** NOUN
1 a famous person who is loved and admired by fans
2 a picture or statue which is worshipped as if it were a god
[WORD HISTORY: from Greek EIDŌLON meaning 'image' or 'phantom']

idyll [ˈɪdɪl] **idylls** NOUN
a situation which is peaceful and beautiful
idyllic ADJECTIVE

i.e.
i.e. means 'that is', and is used before giving more information. It is an abbreviation for the Latin expression 'id est'.

if [ɪf] CONJUNCTION
1 on the condition that *e.g. I shall stay if I can.*
2 whether *e.g. I asked her if she wanted to go.*

igloo [ˈɪɡluː] **igloos** NOUN
a dome-shaped house built out of blocks of snow by the Inuit, or Eskimo, people
[WORD HISTORY: from IGDLU, an Inuit word meaning 'house']

igneous [ˈɪɡnɪəs] ADJECTIVE; TECHNICAL
Igneous rocks are formed by hot liquid rock cooling and going hard.
[WORD HISTORY: from Latin IGNEUS meaning 'fiery']

ignite [ɪɡˈnaɪt] **ignites, igniting, ignited** VERB
If you ignite something or if it ignites, it starts burning.

[WORD HISTORY: from Latin IGNIS meaning 'fire']

ignition [ɪɡˈnɪʃən] **ignitions** NOUN
In a car, the ignition is the part of the engine where the fuel is ignited.

ignominious [ˌɪɡnəˈmɪnɪəs] ADJECTIVE
shameful or considered wrong *e.g. It was an ignominious end to a brilliant career.*
ignominiously ADVERB, **ignominy** NOUN

ignoramus [ˌɪɡnəˈreɪməs] **ignoramuses** NOUN
an ignorant person
[WORD HISTORY: from the character IGNORAMUS, an uneducated lawyer in a 17th-century play by Ruggle.]

ignorant [ˈɪɡnərənt] ADJECTIVE
1 If you are ignorant of something, you do not know about it. *e.g. He was completely ignorant of the rules.*

● THESAURUS
inexperienced: *I am inexperienced at decorating.*
innocent: *He is innocent about the harm he is doing.*
oblivious: *John appeared oblivious to his surroundings.*
unaware: *She was unaware that she was being filmed.*
unconscious: *He was unconscious of his failure.*

2 Someone who is ignorant does not know about things in general. *e.g. I thought of asking, but didn't want to seem ignorant.*
ignorantly ADVERB, **ignorance** NOUN

● THESAURUS
green: *The new boy is very green and immature.*
naive: *a shy, naive man*
unaware: *Young children are fairly unaware.*

ignore [ɪɡˈnɔː] **ignores, ignoring, ignored** VERB
If you ignore someone or something, you deliberately do not take any notice of them.

● THESAURUS
blank: slang *The crowd blanked her for the first four numbers.*
discount: *They simply discounted his feelings.*
disregard: *He disregarded his father's advice.*
neglect: *They never neglect their duties.*
overlook: *a fact that we all tend to overlook*

iguana [ɪˈɡwɑːnə] **iguanas** NOUN
a large, tropical lizard

il- PREFIX
'Il-' means 'not' or 'the opposite of', and is the form of 'in-' that is used before the letter *l. e.g. illegible*

ill [ɪl] **ills** ADJECTIVE
1 unhealthy or sick

● THESAURUS
ailing: *The President is said to be ailing.*

poorly: British; informal *Julie is still poorly.*
queasy: *I feel queasy on boats.*
sick: *He's very sick and he needs treatment.*
unhealthy: *an unhealthy-looking fellow*
unwell: *She felt unwell back at the office.*
<<OPPOSITE *healthy*

2 harmful or unpleasant *e.g. ill effects*

> PLURAL NOUN

3 Ills are difficulties or problems.
[WORD HISTORY: from Norse ILLR meaning 'bad']

ill at ease PHRASE
If you feel **ill at ease**, you feel unable to relax.

illegal [ɪˈliːgəl] ADJECTIVE
forbidden by the law
illegally ADVERB, **illegality** NOUN

● THESAURUS
banned: *banned substances*
criminal: *a criminal offence*
illicit: *illicit drugs*
outlawed: *a place where hunting is outlawed*
prohibited: *a country where alcohol is prohibited*
unlawful: *unlawful acts*
<<OPPOSITE *legal*

illegible [ɪˈlɛdʒɪbəl] ADJECTIVE
Writing which is illegible is unclear and very difficult to read.

illegitimate [ˌɪlɪˈdʒɪtɪmɪt] ADJECTIVE
A person who is illegitimate was born to parents who were not married at the time.
illegitimacy NOUN

ill-fated [ˌɪlˈfeɪtɪd] ADJECTIVE
doomed to end unhappily *e.g. his ill-fated attempt on the world record*

illicit [ɪˈlɪsɪt] ADJECTIVE
not allowed by law or not approved of by society *e.g. illicit drugs*

illiterate [ɪˈlɪtərɪt] ADJECTIVE
unable to read or write
illiteracy NOUN

illness [ˈɪlnɪs] **illnesses** NOUN

1 Illness is the experience of being ill.

2 a particular disease *e.g. the treatment of common illnesses*

● THESAURUS
affliction: *a severe mental affliction*
ailment: *common ailments*
complaint: *a skin complaint*
disease: *He has been cured of the disease.*
disorder: *a rare nervous disorder*
lurgy: British and Australian and New Zealand; informal *It's only a matter of days before Joan gets the lurgy as well.*
sickness: *radiation sickness*

illogical [ɪˈlɒdʒɪkəl] ADJECTIVE
An illogical feeling or action is not reasonable or sensible.

illogically ADVERB

ill-treat [ˌɪlˈtriːt] **ill-treats, ill-treating, ill-treated** VERB
If you ill-treat someone or something you hurt or damage them or treat them cruelly.
ill-treatment NOUN

illuminate [ɪˈluːmɪˌneɪt] **illuminates, illuminating, illuminated** VERB
To illuminate something is to shine light on it to make it easier to see.

illumination [ɪˌluːmɪˈneɪʃən] **illuminations** NOUN

1 Illumination is lighting.

2 Illuminations are the coloured lights put up to decorate a town, especially at Christmas.

illusion [ɪˈluːʒən] **illusions** NOUN

1 a false belief which you think is true *e.g. Their hopes proved to be an illusion.*

● THESAURUS
delusion: *I was under the delusion that I could win.*
fallacy: *It's a fallacy that the rich are generous.*
fancy: *childhood fancies*
misconception: *There are many misconceptions about school.*

2 (ART) a false appearance of reality which deceives the eye *e.g. Painters create the illusion of space.*

● THESAURUS
hallucination: *Perhaps the footprint was a hallucination.*
mirage: *I began to see mirages.*
semblance: *A semblance of normality has been restored.*

illusory [ɪˈluːsərɪ] ADJECTIVE
seeming to be true, but actually false *e.g. an illusory truce*

illustrate [ˈɪləˌstreɪt] **illustrates, illustrating, illustrated** VERB

1 (EXAM TERM) If you illustrate a point, you explain it or make it clearer, often by using examples.

2 If you illustrate a book, you put pictures in it.
illustrator NOUN, **illustrative** ADJECTIVE

illustration [ˌɪləˈstreɪʃən] **illustrations** NOUN

1 an example or a story which is used to make a point clear

2 a picture in a book

illustrious [ɪˈlʌstrɪəs] ADJECTIVE
An illustrious person is famous and respected.

ill will NOUN
Ill will is a feeling of hostility.

im- PREFIX
'im-' means 'not' or 'the opposite of', and is the

form of 'in-' which is used before the letters *b*, *m* and *p*. *e.g. imbalance... immature... impatient*

image ['ɪmɪdʒ] **images** NOUN

1 a mental picture of someone or something

2 the appearance which a person, group, or organization presents to the public

imagery ['ɪmɪdʒrɪ] NOUN

(ENGLISH) The imagery of a poem or book is the descriptive language used in it.

imaginary [ɪ'mædʒɪnərɪ] ADJECTIVE

Something that is imaginary exists only in your mind, not in real life.

● THESAURUS

fictional: *a fictional character*
fictitious: *a fictitious illness*
hypothetical: *a hypothetical situation*
ideal: *in an ideal world*
illusory: *Freedom is illusory.*
invented: *distorted or invented stories*
mythological: *mythological creatures*
<<OPPOSITE *real*

imagination [ɪ,mædʒɪ'neɪʃən] **imaginations** NOUN

the ability to form new and exciting ideas

● THESAURUS

creativity: *She paints with great creativity.*
ingenuity: *the ingenuity of engineers*
inventiveness: *the artistic inventiveness of Mozart*
originality: *a composer of great originality*
vision: *a leader with vision*

imaginative [ɪ'mædʒɪnətɪv] ADJECTIVE

Someone who is imaginative can easily form new or exciting ideas in their mind.

imaginatively ADVERB

imagine [ɪ'mædʒɪn] **imagines, imagining, imagined** VERB

1 If you imagine something, you form an idea of it in your mind, or you think you have seen or heard it but you have not really.

● THESAURUS

conceive: *I can't even conceive of that much money.*
envisage: *I envisage them staying together.*
fantasize: *I fantasized about writing music.*
picture: *I tried to picture the place.*
visualize: *He could not visualize her as old.*

2 If you imagine that something is the case, you believe it is the case. *e.g. I imagine that's what you aim to do.*

imaginable ADJECTIVE

● THESAURUS

assume: *Don't assume we are similar.*
believe: *I believe you have my pen.*
gather: *I gather that his mother was Scottish.*
guess: informal *I guess he's right.*
suppose: *He supposed I would be back at school.*

suspect: *Susan suspected that things would get worse.*

imam [ɪ'mɑːm] NOUN

a person who leads a group in prayer in a mosque

imbalance [ɪm'bæləns] **imbalances** NOUN

If there is an imbalance between things, they are unequal. *e.g. the imbalance between rich and poor*

imbecile ['ɪmbɪˌsiːl] **imbeciles** NOUN

a stupid person

[WORD HISTORY: from Latin IMBECILLUS meaning 'physically or mentally feeble']

imitate ['ɪmɪˌteɪt] **imitates, imitating, imitated** VERB

To imitate someone or something is to copy them.

imitator NOUN, **imitative** ADJECTIVE

● THESAURUS

ape: *She is aping her sister's style.*
copy: *I used to copy everything my big brother did.*
emulate: *Sons are expected to emulate their fathers.*
impersonate: *He could impersonate all the other students.*
mimic: *He mimicked her accent.*
simulate: *a machine which simulates natural sounds*

imitation [,ɪmɪ'teɪʃən] **imitations** NOUN

a copy of something else

immaculate [ɪ'mækjʊlɪt] ADJECTIVE

1 completely clean and tidy *e.g. The flat was immaculate.*

2 without any mistakes at all *e.g. his usual immaculate guitar accompaniment*

immaculately ADVERB

immaterial [,ɪmə'tɪərɪəl] ADJECTIVE

Something that is immaterial is not important.

immature [,ɪmə'tjʊə] ADJECTIVE

1 Something that is immature has not finished growing or developing.

2 A person who is immature does not behave in a sensible adult way.

immaturity NOUN

immediate [ɪ'miːdɪət] ADJECTIVE

1 Something that is immediate happens or is done without delay.

● THESAURUS

instant: *He took an instant dislike to Mark.*
instantaneous: *The applause was instantaneous.*

2 Your immediate relatives and friends are the ones most closely connected or related to you.

● THESAURUS

close: *I have a few close friends.*
direct: *your direct descendants*
near: *near relatives*

immediately [ɪˈmiːdɪətlɪ] ADVERB

1 If something happens immediately it happens right away.

● THESAURUS

at once: *You must come at once.*
directly: *He will be there directly.*
instantly: *She'd been knocked down in the street and died almost instantly.*
now: *Get out, now!*
promptly: *The telephone was answered promptly.*
right away: *You'd better tell them right away.*
straightaway: *I'd like to see you straightaway.*

2 Immediately means very near in time or position. *e.g. immediately behind the house*

● THESAURUS

closely: *He rushed out, closely followed by Kemp.*
directly: *James stopped directly under the window.*
right: *He stood right behind me.*

immemorial [ˌɪmɪˈmɔːrɪəl] ADJECTIVE
If something has been happening from time immemorial, it has been happening longer than anyone can remember.

immense [ɪˈmɛns] ADJECTIVE
very large or huge
immensely ADVERB, **immensity** NOUN

● THESAURUS

colossal: *a colossal waste of money*
enormous: *The main bedroom is enormous.*
giant: *a giant oak table*
gigantic: *a gigantic task*
huge: *Several painters were working on a huge piece of canvas.*
massive: *a massive cruise liner*
vast: *a vast expanse of water*
<<OPPOSITE tiny

immerse [ɪˈmɜːs] **immerses, immersing, immersed** VERB

1 If you are immersed in an activity you are completely involved in it.

2 If you immerse something in a liquid, you put it into the liquid so that it is completely covered.
immersion NOUN

immigrant [ˈɪmɪɡrənt] **immigrants** NOUN
(HISTORY) someone who has come to live permanently in a new country
immigrate VERB, **immigration** NOUN

imminent [ˈɪmɪnənt] ADJECTIVE
If something is imminent, it is going to happen very soon.
imminently ADVERB, **imminence** NOUN

● THESAURUS

close: *My birthday is quite close.*
coming: *the coming dawn*
forthcoming: *their forthcoming marriage*
impending: *impending doom*

looming: *My exams are looming.*
near: *in the near future*

immobile [ɪˈməʊbaɪl] ADJECTIVE
not moving
immobility NOUN

immoral [ɪˈmɒrəl] ADJECTIVE
(RE) If you describe someone or their behaviour as immoral, you mean that they do not fit in with most people's idea of what is right and proper.
immorality NOUN

> Do not confuse *immoral* and *amoral*. You use *immoral* to talk about people who are aware of moral standards, but go against them. *Amoral* applies to people with no moral standards.

immortal [ɪˈmɔːtəl] ADJECTIVE

1 Something that is immortal is famous and will be remembered for a long time. *e.g. Emily Bronte's immortal love story.*

2 In stories, someone who is immortal will never die.

immortality [ˌɪmɔːˈtælɪtɪ] NOUN
(RE) Immortality is never dying. In many religions, people believe that the soul or some other essential part of a person lives forever or continues to exist in some form.

immovable or **immoveable** [ɪˈmuːvəbəl]
ADJECTIVE
Something that is immovable is fixed and cannot be moved.
immovably ADVERB

immune [ɪˈmjuːn] ADJECTIVE

1 If you are immune to a particular disease, you cannot catch it.

2 If someone or something is immune to something, they are able to avoid it or are not affected by it. *e.g. The captain was immune to prosecution.*
immunity NOUN

● THESAURUS

exempt: *She is exempt from blame.*
free: *He was not completely free of guilt.*
protected: *He is protected from the law.*
resistant: *crops that are resistant to disease*
safe: *I was safe from punishment.*
unaffected: *She is unaffected by the sight of blood.*

immune system NOUN
Your body's immune system consists of your white blood cells, which fight disease by producing antibodies or germs to kill germs which come into your body.

imp [ɪmp] **imps** NOUN
a small mischievous creature in fairy stories
impish ADJECTIVE

impact [ˈɪmpækt] **impacts** NOUN

1 The impact that someone or something has is the impression that they make or the effect that they have.

2 Impact is the action of one object hitting another, usually with a lot of force. *e.g. The aircraft crashed into a ditch, exploding on impact.*

impair [ɪmˈpɛə] **impairs, impairing, impaired** VERB
To impair something is to damage it so that it stops working properly. *e.g. Travel had made him weary and impaired his judgement.*

impale [ɪmˈpeɪl] **impales, impaling, impaled** VERB
If you impale something, you pierce it with a sharp object.

impart [ɪmˈpɑːt] **imparts, imparting, imparted** VERB; FORMAL
To impart information to someone is to pass it on to them.

impartial [ɪmˈpɑːʃəl] ADJECTIVE
Someone who is impartial has a view of something which is fair or not biased.
impartially ADVERB, **impartiality** NOUN

impasse [æmˈpɑːs] NOUN
a difficult situation in which it is impossible to find a solution
[WORD HISTORY: from French IMPASSE meaning 'dead end']

impassioned [ɪmˈpæʃənd] ADJECTIVE
full of emotion *e.g. an impassioned plea*

impassive [ɪmˈpæsɪv] ADJECTIVE
showing no emotion
impassively ADVERB

impasto [ɪmˈpæstəʊ] NOUN
(ART) a technique of painting with thick paint so that brush strokes or palette knife marks can be seen
[WORD HISTORY: an Italian word, from PASTA meaning 'paste']

impatient [ɪmˈpeɪʃənt] ADJECTIVE
1 Someone who is impatient becomes annoyed easily or is quick to lose their temper when things go wrong.

THESAURUS
brusque: *a brusque manner*
curt: *He had spoken in a very curt tone of voice.*
irritable: *Brian was nervous and irritable with her.*
<<OPPOSITE patient

2 If you are impatient to do something, you are eager and do not want to wait. *e.g. He was impatient to get back.*
impatiently ADVERB, **impatience** NOUN

THESAURUS
eager: *Children are eager to learn.*

restless: *The kids were bored and restless.*

impeccable [ɪmˈpɛkəbl] ADJECTIVE
excellent, without any faults
impeccably ADVERB

impede [ɪmˈpiːd] **impedes, impeding, impeded** VERB
If you impede someone, you make their progress difficult.

THESAURUS
block: *The country has been trying to block these imports.*
delay: *Various set backs delayed production.*
disrupt: *The drought has severely disrupted agricultural production.*
get in the way: *She had a job which never got in the way of her hobbies.*
hamper: *The bad weather hampered rescue operations.*
hinder: *The investigation was hindered by the loss of vital documents.*
obstruct: *The authorities are obstructing the inquiry.*

impediment [ɪmˈpɛdɪmənt] **impediments** NOUN
something that makes it difficult to move, develop, or do something properly *e.g. a speech impediment*

impelled [ɪmˈpɛld] ADJECTIVE
If you feel impelled to do something, you feel strongly that you must do it.

impending [ɪmˈpɛndɪŋ] ADJECTIVE; FORMAL
You use 'impending' to describe something that is going to happen very soon. *e.g. a sense of impending doom*

impenetrable [ɪmˈpɛnɪtrəbᵊl] ADJECTIVE
impossible to get through

imperative [ɪmˈpɛrətɪv] ADJECTIVE
1 Something that is imperative is extremely urgent or important.
> NOUN
2 In grammar, an imperative is the form of a verb that is used for giving orders.

imperfect [ɪmˈpɜːfɪkt] ADJECTIVE
1 Something that is imperfect has faults or problems.

THESAURUS
broken: *broken toys*
damaged: *damaged goods*
defective: *defective eyesight*
faulty: *a car with faulty brakes*
flawed: *a flawed character*
<<OPPOSITE perfect
> NOUN
2 In grammar, the imperfect is a tense used to describe continuous or repeated actions which happened in the past.

imperfectly ADVERB, **imperfection** NOUN

imperial [ɪmˈpɪərɪəl] ADJECTIVE

1 (HISTORY) Imperial means relating to an empire or an emperor or empress. *e.g. the Imperial Palace*

2 The imperial system of measurement is the measuring system which uses inches, feet, and yards, ounces and pounds, and pints and gallons.

imperialism [ɪmˈpɪərɪəˌlɪzəm] NOUN
(HISTORY) a system of rule in which a rich and powerful nation controls other nations
imperialist ADJECTIVE OR NOUN

imperious [ɪmˈpɪərɪəs] ADJECTIVE
proud and domineering *e.g. an imperious manner*
imperiously ADVERB

impersonal [ɪmˈpɜːsənəl] ADJECTIVE
Something that is impersonal makes you feel that individuals and their feelings do not matter. *e.g. impersonal cold rooms*
impersonally ADVERB

● THESAURUS
aloof: *His manner was aloof.*
cold: *Sharon was very cold with me.*
detached: *He felt emotionally detached from the victims.*
formal: *Business relationships are usually formal.*
neutral: *He told me the news in a neutral manner.*
remote: *She was beautiful but remote.*

impersonate [ɪmˈpɜːsəˌneɪt]
impersonates, impersonating, impersonated VERB
If you impersonate someone, you pretend to be that person.
impersonation NOUN, **impersonator** NOUN

impertinent [ɪmˈpɜːtɪnənt] ADJECTIVE
disrespectful and rude *e.g. impertinent questions*
impertinently ADVERB, **impertinence** NOUN

impetuous [ɪmˈpɛtjʊəs] ADJECTIVE
If you are impetuous, you act quickly without thinking. *e.g. an impetuous gamble*
impetuously ADVERB, **impetuosity** NOUN

impetus [ˈɪmpɪtəs] NOUN

1 An impetus is the stimulating effect that something has on a situation, which causes it to develop more quickly.

2 In physics, impetus is the force that starts an object moving and resists changes in speed or direction.

impinge [ɪmˈpɪndʒ] **impinges, impinging, impinged** VERB
If something impinges on your life, it has an effect on you and influences you. *e.g. My private life doesn't impinge on my professional life.*

implacable [ɪmˈplækəbəl] ADJECTIVE
Someone who is implacable is being harsh and

refuses to change their mind.
implacably ADVERB

implant implants, implanting, implanted VERB [ɪmˈplɑːnt]

1 To implant something into a person's body is to put it there, usually by means of an operation.

> NOUN [ˈɪmˌplɑːnt]
2 something that has been implanted into someone's body

implausible [ɪmˈplɔːzəbəl] ADJECTIVE
very unlikely *e.g. implausible stories*
implausibly ADVERB

implement implements, implementing, implemented VERB [ˈɪmplɪˌmɛnt]

1 If you implement something such as a plan, you carry it out. *e.g. The government has failed to implement promised reforms.*

> NOUN [ˈɪmplɪmənt]
2 An implement is a tool.
implementation NOUN

implicate [ˈɪmplɪˌkeɪt] **implicates, implicating, implicated** VERB
If you are implicated in a crime, you are shown to be involved in it.

implication [ˌɪmplɪˈkeɪʃən] **implications** NOUN
something that is suggested or implied but not stated directly

implicit [ɪmˈplɪsɪt] ADJECTIVE

1 expressed in an indirect way *e.g. implicit criticism*

2 If you have an implicit belief in something, you have no doubts about it. *e.g. He had implicit faith in the noble intentions of the Emperor.*
implicitly ADVERB

implore [ɪmˈplɔː] **implores, imploring, implored** VERB
If you implore someone to do something, you beg them to do it.

● THESAURUS
beg: *I begged him to come with me.*
beseech: literary *I beseech you to show him mercy.*
plead with: *The lady pleaded with her daughter to come home.*

imply [ɪmˈplaɪ] **implies, implying, implied** VERB
If you imply that something is the case, you suggest it in an indirect way.

import imports, importing, imported VERB [ɪmˈpɔːt]

1 If you import something from another country, you bring it into your country or have it sent there.

> NOUN [ˈɪmpɔːt]
2 a product that is made in another country and

sent to your own country for use there
importation NOUN, **importer** NOUN

important [im'pɔːt³nt] ADJECTIVE
1 Something that is important is very valuable, necessary, or significant.
● THESAURUS
momentous: *the momentous decision to go to war*
serious: *a serious matter*
significant: *a significant discovery*
weighty: *We discussed weighty matters.*
<<OPPOSITE *unimportant*

2 An important person has great influence or power.
importantly ADVERB, **importance** NOUN
● THESAURUS
eminent: *an eminent scientist*
foremost: *a foremost expert in American history*
influential: *one of the most influential books ever written*
leading: *a leading nation in world politics*
notable: *notable celebrities*
powerful: *large, powerful countries*

impose [im'pəʊz] **imposes, imposing, imposed** VERB
1 If you impose something on people, you force it on them. *e.g. The allies had imposed a ban on all flights over Iraq.*
● THESAURUS
dictate: *The policy is dictated from the top.*
enforce: *It is a difficult law to enforce.*
inflict: *Inflicting punishment to stop crime is not the answer.*
levy: *a tax levied on imported goods*
ordain: *the task of trying to ordain parliamentary behaviour*

2 If someone imposes on you, they unreasonably expect you to do something for them.
imposition NOUN
● THESAURUS
abuse: *They abused my hospitality by eating everything.*
take advantage of: *He took advantage of her generosity.*
use: *She's just using you.*

imposing [im'pəʊzɪŋ] ADJECTIVE
having an impressive appearance or manner *e.g. an imposing building*

impossible [im'pɒsəb³l] ADJECTIVE
Something that is impossible cannot happen, be done, or be believed.
impossibly ADVERB, **impossibility** NOUN
● THESAURUS
absurd: *absurd claims to have met big stars*
hopeless: *a hopeless task*
inconceivable: *It's inconceivable that people can*

still be living in those conditions.
ludicrous: *his ludicrous plan to build a house*
out of the question: *Is a pay increase out of the question?*
unthinkable: *The idea of splitting up is unthinkable.*
<<OPPOSITE *possible*

imposter [im'pɒstə] **imposters;** also spelt **impostor** NOUN
a person who pretends to be someone else in order to get things they want

impotent ['ɪmpətənt] ADJECTIVE
1 Someone who is impotent has no power to influence people or events.
2 A man who is impotent is unable to have or maintain an erection during sexual intercourse.
impotently ADVERB, **impotence** NOUN

impound [im'paʊnd] **impounds, impounding, impounded** VERB
If something you own is impounded, the police or other officials take it.

impoverished [im'pɒv³rɪʃt] ADJECTIVE
Someone who is impoverished is poor.

impractical [im'præktɪk³l] ADJECTIVE
not practical, sensible, or realistic

impregnable [im'pregnəb³l] ADJECTIVE
A building or other structure that is impregnable is so strong that it cannot be broken into or captured.

impregnated [,ɪmpreg'neɪtɪd] ADJECTIVE
If something is impregnated with a substance, it has absorbed the substance so that it spreads right through it. *e.g. sponges impregnated with detergent and water*

impresario [,ɪmprə'sɑːrɪ,əʊ] **impresarios** NOUN
a person who manages theatrical or musical events or companies

impress [im'pres] **impresses, impressing, impressed** VERB
1 If you impress someone, you make them admire or respect you.
2 If you impress something on someone, you make them understand the importance of it.

impression [im'preʃən] **impressions** NOUN
1 An impression of someone or something is the way they look or seem to you.
● THESAURUS
feeling: *the feeling that she was wasting her life*
hunch: *Was your hunch right or wrong?*
idea: *I had my own ideas about what had happened.*
notion: *I have a notion of what he is like.*
sense: *She has the sense that she was in trouble.*

2 If you **make an impression**, you have a strong effect on people you meet.

● THESAURUS
cause a stir: *News of her death caused a stir.*
influence: *You can't do anything to influence him.*
make an impact: *Events can make an impact on our lives.*

impressionable [ɪmˈprɛʃənəbᵊl] ADJECTIVE
easy to influence *e.g. impressionable teenagers*

● THESAURUS
gullible: *I'm so gullible I'd have believed him.*
open: *an open, trusting nature*
receptive: *moulding their young, receptive minds*
sensitive: *Ouija boards can be dangerous, especially to sensitive people.*
susceptible: *Children can be susceptible to advertisements.*
vulnerable: *vulnerable old people*

impressionism [ɪmˈprɛʃəˌnɪzəm] NOUN
a style of painting which is concerned with the impressions created by light and shapes, rather than with exact details
impressionist NOUN

impressive [ɪmˈprɛsɪv] ADJECTIVE
If something is impressive, it impresses you. *e.g. an impressive display of old-fashioned American cars*

● THESAURUS
awesome: *awesome mountains, deserts and lakes*
exciting: *He tells the most exciting stories.*
grand: *a grand old building*
powerful: *a powerful image*
stirring: *stirring music*
striking: *her striking personality*

imprint imprints, imprinting, imprinted
NOUN [ˈɪmprɪnt]

1 If something leaves an imprint on your mind, it has a strong and lasting effect.

2 the mark left by the pressure of one object on another

> VERB [ɪmˈprɪnt]

3 If something is imprinted on your memory, it is firmly fixed there.

imprison [ɪmˈprɪzən] **imprisons, imprisoning, imprisoned** VERB
If you are imprisoned, you are locked up, usually in a prison.
imprisonment NOUN

● THESAURUS
confine: *Keep your dog confined to the house.*
detain: *They'll be detained and charged.*
incarcerate: *Prisoners were incarcerated in terrible conditions.*
jail: *An innocent man was jailed.*
lock up: *You people should be locked up!*
send to prison: *The judge sent him to prison for life.*

<<OPPOSITE *free*

improbable [ɪmˈprɒbəbᵊl] ADJECTIVE
not probable or likely to happen
improbably ADVERB

● THESAURUS
doubtful: *It was doubtful if they would arrive on time.*
dubious: *dubious evidence*
far-fetched: *This all sounds a bit far-fetched.*
implausible: *a film with an implausible ending*
unbelievable: *an unbelievable storyline*
unlikely: *It is unlikely that he is alive.*
<<OPPOSITE *probable*

impromptu [ɪmˈprɒmptjuː] ADJECTIVE
An impromptu action is one done without planning or organization.
[WORD HISTORY: from Latin IN PROMPTU meaning 'in readiness']

improper [ɪmˈprɒpə] ADJECTIVE
1 rude or shocking *e.g. improper behaviour*
2 illegal or dishonest *e.g. improper dealings*
3 not suitable or correct *e.g. an improper diet*
improperly ADVERB

improve [ɪmˈpruːv] **improves, improving, improved** VERB
If something improves or if you improve it, it gets better or becomes more valuable.

● THESAURUS
advance: *Medical technology has advanced.*
better: *They tried to better their working conditions.*
enhance: *Good jewellery enhances your outfits.*
look up: informal *Things are looking up for me now.*
progress: *Jack's condition is progressing well.*
upgrade: *You'll have to upgrade your image.*
<<OPPOSITE *worsen*

improvement [ɪmˈpruːvmənt] **improvements** NOUN
the fact or process of getting better

● THESAURUS
advance: *the advances in air safety since the 1970s*
development: *monitoring her language development*
enhancement: *the enhancement of the human condition*
progress: *The doctors are pleased with her progress.*
upturn: *an upturn in the economy*

improvise [ˈɪmprəˌvaɪz] **improvises, improvising, improvised** VERB
1 If you improvise something, you make or do something without planning in advance, and with whatever materials are available.
2 (DRAMA) When musicians or actors improvise, they make up the music or words as they go along.

improvised ADJECTIVE, **improvisation** NOUN

impudence ['ɪmpjʊdəns] NOUN
disrespectful talk or behaviour towards someone

THESAURUS
audacity: *He had the audacity to speak up.*
boldness: *I was amazed at her boldness towards him.*
cheek: *informal I can't believe he had the cheek to complain.*
chutzpah: *American; informal He had the chutzpah to ask us to leave.*
gall: *the most presumptuous question any interviewer has ever had the gall to ask*
impertinence: *His words sounded like impertinence.*
insolence: *I got punished for insolence.*
nerve: *You've got a nerve coming round here after what you've done.*

impudent ['ɪmpjʊdənt] ADJECTIVE
If someone is impudent, something they say or do is cheeky and lacking in respect.
impudently ADVERB

impulse ['ɪmpʌls] **impulses** NOUN
a strong urge to do something *e.g. She felt a sudden impulse to confide in her.*

impulsive [ɪm'pʌlsɪv] ADJECTIVE
If you are impulsive, you do things suddenly, without thinking about them carefully.
impulsively ADVERB

impure [ɪm'pjʊə] ADJECTIVE
Something which is impure contains small amounts of other things, such as dirt.

impurity [ɪm'pjʊərɪtɪ] **impurities** NOUN
1 Impurity is the quality of being impure. *e.g. the impurity of the water*
2 If something contains impurities, it contains small amounts of dirt or other substances that should not be there.

in [ɪn] PREPOSITION OR ADVERB
'In' is used to indicate position, direction, time, and manner *e.g. boarding schools in England... in the past few years*

in- PREFIX
1 'In-' is added to the beginning of some words to form a word with the opposite meaning. *e.g. insincere*
2 'In-' also means in, into, or in the course of *e.g. infiltrate*
[WORD HISTORY: from a Latin prefix]

inability [,ɪnə'bɪlɪtɪ] NOUN
a lack of ability to do something

THESAURUS
impotence: *a sense of impotence in the situation*
inadequacy: *my inadequacy as a gardener*

incompetence: *the incompetence of government officials*
ineptitude: *political ineptitude*
<<OPPOSITE *ability*

inaccessible [,ɪnæk'sɛsəbəl] ADJECTIVE
impossible or very difficult to reach

inaccurate [ɪn'ækjʊrɪt] ADJECTIVE
not accurate or correct

inadequate [ɪn'ædɪkwɪt] ADJECTIVE
1 If something is inadequate, there is not enough of it.

THESAURUS
insufficient: *insufficient evidence to justify criminal proceedings*
lacking: *Why was military intelligence so lacking?*
poor: *poor wages*
scarce: *the region's scarce supplies of water*
short: *Deliveries are unreliable and food is short.*
<<OPPOSITE *adequate*

2 not good enough in quality for a particular purpose

THESAURUS
deficient: *He made me feel deficient as a mother.*
incapable: *He lost his job for being incapable.*
incompetent: *the power to sack incompetent teachers*
inept: *He was inept and lacked the intelligence to govern.*
pathetic: *She made some pathetic excuse.*
useless: *I'm useless around the house.*

3 If someone feels inadequate, they feel they do not possess the skills necessary to do a particular job or to cope with life in general.
inadequately ADVERB, **inadequacy** NOUN

inadvertent [,ɪnəd'vɜːtənt] ADJECTIVE
not intentional *e.g. the murder had been inadvertent*
inadvertently ADVERB

inane [ɪ'neɪn] ADJECTIVE
silly or stupid
inanely ADVERB, **inanity** NOUN

inanimate [ɪn'ænɪmɪt] ADJECTIVE
An inanimate object is not alive.

inappropriate [,ɪnə'prəʊprɪɪt] ADJECTIVE
not suitable for a particular purpose or occasion *e.g. It was quite inappropriate to ask such questions.*
inappropriately ADVERB

THESAURUS
improper: *the improper use of resources*
incongruous: *an incongruous assortment of clothes*
unfit: *houses that are unfit for living in*
unseemly: *He thought crying was unseemly.*
unsuitable: *food that is unsuitable for children*
untimely: *their unjustified and untimely interference*

<<OPPOSITE *appropriate*

inarticulate [ˌɪnɑːˈtɪkjʊlɪt] ADJECTIVE
If you are inarticulate, you are unable to express yourself well or easily in speech.

inasmuch [ˈɪnəzˌmʌtʃ] CONJUNCTION
'Inasmuch as' means to the extent that *e.g. She's giving herself a hard time inasmuch as she feels guilty.*

inaudible [ɪnˈɔːdəbəl] ADJECTIVE
not loud enough to be heard
inaudibly ADVERB

inaugurate [ɪnˈɔːgjʊˌreɪt] **inaugurates, inaugurating, inaugurated** VERB
1 To inaugurate a new scheme is to start it.
2 To inaugurate a new leader is to officially establish them in their new position in a special ceremony. *e.g. Albania's Orthodox Church inaugurated its first archbishop in 25 years.*
inauguration NOUN, **inaugural** ADJECTIVE

inborn [ˈɪnˈbɔːn] ADJECTIVE
An inborn quality is one that you were born with.

incandescent [ˌɪnkænˈdɛsənt] ADJECTIVE
Something which is incandescent gives out light when it is heated.
incandescence NOUN
[WORD HISTORY: from Latin CANDESCERE meaning 'to glow white']

incapable [ɪnˈkeɪpəbəl] ADJECTIVE
1 Someone who is incapable of doing something is not able to do it. *e.g. He is incapable of changing a fuse.*
2 An incapable person is weak and helpless.

incarcerate [ɪnˈkɑːsəˌreɪt] **incarcerates, incarcerating, incarcerated** VERB
To incarcerate someone is to lock them up.
incarceration NOUN

Incarnation [ˌɪnkɑːˈneɪʃən] NOUN
The Incarnation is the Christian belief that God took human form in Jesus Christ.

incendiary [ɪnˈsɛndɪərɪ] ADJECTIVE
An incendiary weapon is one which sets fire to things. *e.g. incendiary bombs*

incense [ˈɪnsɛns] NOUN
Incense is a spicy substance which is burned to create a sweet smell, especially during religious services.

incensed [ɪnˈsɛnst] ADJECTIVE
If you are incensed by something, it makes you extremely angry.

incentive [ɪnˈsɛntɪv] **incentives** NOUN
something that encourages you to do something
[WORD HISTORY: from Latin INCENTIVUS meaning 'the beginning of a song']

● THESAURUS
bait: *He added some bait to make the agreement sweeter.*
encouragement: *She didn't get much encouragement to do anything.*
inducement: *Are gangster films an inducement to crime?*
motivation: *Money is my motivation.*
stimulus: *He needed all the stimulus he could get.*

inception [ɪnˈsɛpʃən] NOUN; FORMAL
The inception of a project is the start of it.

incessant [ɪnˈsɛsənt] ADJECTIVE
continuing without stopping *e.g. her incessant talking*
incessantly ADVERB

incest [ˈɪnsɛst] NOUN
Incest is the crime of two people who are closely related having sex with each other.
incestuous ADJECTIVE

inch [ɪntʃ] **inches, inching, inched** NOUN
1 a unit of length equal to about 2.54 centimetres

> VERB
2 To inch forward is to move forward slowly.
[WORD HISTORY: from Latin UNCIA meaning 'twelfth part'; there are twelve inches to the foot]

incident [ˈɪnsɪdənt] **incidents** NOUN
an event *e.g. a shooting incident*

● THESAURUS
circumstance: *This is a fortunate circumstance.*
episode: *I'm glad this episode is over.*
event: *recent events in Europe*
happening: *the latest happenings in sport*
occasion: *I remember that occasion fondly.*
occurrence: *Nancy wondered about the strange occurrence.*

incidental [ˌɪnsɪˈdɛntəl] ADJECTIVE
occurring as a minor part of something *e.g. vivid incidental detail*
incidentally ADVERB

incinerate [ɪnˈsɪnəˌreɪt] **incinerates, incinerating, incinerated** VERB
If you incinerate something, you burn it.
incineration NOUN

incinerator [ɪnˈsɪnəˌreɪtə] **incinerators** NOUN
a furnace for burning rubbish

incipient [ɪnˈsɪpɪənt] ADJECTIVE
beginning to happen or appear *e.g. incipient panic*

incision [ɪnˈsɪʒən] **incisions** NOUN
a sharp cut, usually made by a surgeon operating on a patient

incisive [ɪnˈsaɪsɪv] ADJECTIVE
Incisive language is clear and forceful.

incite [ɪn'saɪt] **incites, inciting, incited**
VERB
If you incite someone to do something, you encourage them to do it by making them angry or excited.
incitement NOUN

THESAURUS
agitate for: *Workers agitated for better conditions.*
goad: *He tried to goad me into a response.*
instigate: *The violence was instigated by a few people.*
provoke: *I provoked him into doing something stupid.*
whip up: *an attempt to whip up public hostility to the president*

inclination [ˌɪnklɪ'neɪʃən] **inclinations**
NOUN
If you have an inclination to do something, you want to do it.

incline inclines, inclining, inclined VERB
[ɪn'klaɪn]
1 If you are inclined to behave in a certain way, you often behave that way or you want to behave that way.
> NOUN ['ɪnklaɪn]
2 a slope

include [ɪn'kluːd] **includes, including,
included** VERB
If one thing includes another, it has the second thing as one of its parts.
including PREPOSITION

THESAURUS
contain: *This sheet contains a list of names.*
cover: *The book covers many topics.*
embrace: *a small county embracing two cities*
encompass: *classes which encompass a wide range of activities*
incorporate: *The new cars incorporate many improvements.*
involve: *a high-energy workout which involves nearly every muscle*
<<OPPOSITE *exclude*

inclusion [ɪn'kluːʒən] NOUN
The inclusion of one thing in another is the act of making it part of the other thing.

inclusive [ɪn'kluːsɪv] ADJECTIVE
A price that is inclusive includes all the goods and services that are being offered, with no extra charge for any of them.

incognito [ˌɪnkɒg'niːtəʊ] ADVERB
If you are travelling incognito, you are travelling in disguise.
[WORD HISTORY: from Latin IN- + COGNITUS meaning 'not known']

incoherent [ˌɪnkəʊ'hɪərənt] ADJECTIVE
If someone is incoherent, they are talking in an unclear or rambling way.
incoherently ADVERB, **incoherence** NOUN

income ['ɪnkʌm] **incomes** NOUN
the money a person earns

THESAURUS
earnings: *his earnings as an accountant*
pay: *We complained about our pay.*
profits: *The bank made profits of millions of dollars.*
salary: *The lawyer was paid a good salary.*
takings: *The shop had huge takings that week.*
wages: *His wages have gone up.*

income tax NOUN
Income tax is a part of someone's salary which they have to pay regularly to the government.

incoming ['ɪnˌkʌmɪŋ] ADJECTIVE
coming in *e.g. incoming trains... an incoming phone call*

incomparable [ɪn'kɒmpərəbəl] ADJECTIVE
Something that is incomparable is so good that it cannot be compared with anything else.
incomparably ADVERB

THESAURUS
inimitable: *his inimitable style*
peerless: literary *He gave a peerless performance.*
superlative: *The hotel has superlative views.*
supreme: *the supreme piece of writing about the war*
unparalleled: *unparalleled happiness*
unrivalled: *an unrivalled knowledge of music*

incompatible [ˌɪnkəm'pætəbəl] ADJECTIVE
Two things or people are incompatible if they are unable to live or exist together because they are completely different.
incompatibility NOUN

incompetent [ɪn'kɒmpɪtənt] ADJECTIVE
Someone who is incompetent does not have the ability to do something properly.
incompetently ADVERB, **incompetence** NOUN

THESAURUS
bungling: *a bungling amateur*
cowboy: British; informal *cowboy builders*
incapable: *an incapable leader*
inept: *an inept performance*
unable: *He felt unable to handle the situation.*
useless: *I felt useless and a failure.*
<<OPPOSITE *competent*

incomplete [ˌɪnkəm'pliːt] ADJECTIVE
not complete or finished
incompletely ADVERB

THESAURUS
deficient: *a deficient diet*
half-pie: New Zealand; informal *His report was half-pie.*
insufficient: *insufficient information*
partial: *The concert was a partial success.*

<<OPPOSITE *complete*

incomprehensible [ˌɪnkɒmprɪˈhɛnsəbᵊl]
ADJECTIVE
not able to be understood

inconceivable [ˌɪnkənˈsiːvəbᵊl] ADJECTIVE
impossible to believe

inconclusive [ˌɪnkənˈkluːsɪv] ADJECTIVE
not leading to a decision or to a definite result

incongruous [ɪnˈkɒŋgrʊəs] ADJECTIVE
Something that is incongruous seems strange
because it does not fit in to a place or situation.
incongruously ADVERB

inconsequential [ˌɪnkɒnsɪˈkwɛnʃəl]
ADJECTIVE
Something that is inconsequential is not very
important.

inconsistent [ˌɪnkənˈsɪstənt] ADJECTIVE
Someone or something which is inconsistent is
unpredictable and behaves differently in similar
situations.
inconsistently ADVERB, **inconsistency** NOUN

inconspicuous [ˌɪnkənˈspɪkjʊəs] ADJECTIVE
not easily seen or obvious
inconspicuously ADVERB

incontinent [ɪnˈkɒntɪnənt] ADJECTIVE
Someone who is incontinent is unable to control
their bladder or bowels.

inconvenience [ˌɪnkənˈviːnjəns]
**inconveniences, inconveniencing,
inconvenienced** NOUN

1 If something causes inconvenience, it causes
difficulty or problems.

> VERB
2 To inconvenience someone is to cause them
trouble, difficulty or problems.
inconvenient ADJECTIVE, **inconveniently** ADVERB

incorporate [ɪnˈkɔːpəˌreɪt] **incorporates,
incorporating, incorporated** VERB
If something is incorporated into another thing,
it becomes part of that thing.
incorporation NOUN

incorrect [ˌɪnkəˈrɛkt] ADJECTIVE
wrong or untrue
incorrectly ADVERB

**increase increases, increasing,
increased** VERB [ɪnˈkriːs]

1 If something increases, it becomes larger in
amount.

● THESAURUS
enlarge: *They are trying to enlarge their customer
base.*
expand: *We will expand the size of the picture.*
extend: *She plans to extend her stay.*

grow: *The sound grew in volume.*
multiply: *viruses which can multiply rapidly in the
human body*
swell: *His anger swelled within him.*
<<OPPOSITE *decrease*

> NOUN [ˈɪnkriːs]
2 a rise in the number, level, or amount of
something
increasingly ADVERB

● THESAURUS
gain: *a gain in speed*
growth: *the growth of unemployment*
increment: *tiny increments of movement*
rise: *a rise in prices*
upsurge: *an upsurge of interest in books*
<<OPPOSITE *decrease*

incredible [ɪnˈkrɛdəbᵊl] ADJECTIVE
1 totally amazing

● THESAURUS
amazing: *an amazing success*
astonishing: *an astonishing piece of good luck*
astounding: *an astounding discovery*
extraordinary: *extraordinary beauty*
marvellous: *a marvellous thing to do*
sensational: *informal a sensational performance*

2 impossible to believe
incredibly ADVERB

● THESAURUS
absurd: *absurd ideas*
far-fetched: *This all sounds very far-fetched to me.*
improbable: *highly improbable claims*
unbelievable: *The film has an unbelievable plot.*
unimaginable: *unimaginable wealth*
unthinkable: *It's unthinkable that Tom forgot your
birthday.*

incredulous [ɪnˈkrɛdjʊləs] ADJECTIVE
If you are incredulous, you are unable to believe
something because it is very surprising or
shocking.
incredulously ADVERB, **incredulity** NOUN

increment [ˈɪnkrɪmənt] **increments** NOUN
the amount by which something increases, or a
regular increase in someone's salary
incremental ADJECTIVE

incriminate [ɪnˈkrɪmɪˌneɪt] **incriminates,
incriminating, incriminated** VERB
If something incriminates you, it suggests that
you are involved in a crime.

incubate [ˈɪnkjʊˌbeɪt] **incubates,
incubating, incubated** VERB
When eggs incubate, they are kept warm until
they are ready to hatch.
incubation NOUN

incubator [ˈɪnkjʊˌbeɪtə] **incubators** NOUN
a piece of hospital equipment in which sick or

weak newborn babies are kept warm

incumbent [ɪnˈkʌmbənt] **incumbents**
FORMAL
ADJECTIVE
1 If it is incumbent on you to do something, it is your duty to do it.
> NOUN
2 the person in a particular official position

incur [ɪnˈkɜː] **incurs, incurring, incurred**
VERB
If you incur something unpleasant, you cause it to happen.

incurable [ɪnˈkjʊərəbəl] ADJECTIVE
1 An incurable disease is one which cannot be cured.
2 An incurable habit is one which cannot be changed. *e.g. an incurable romantic*
incurably ADVERB

indebted [ɪnˈdɛtɪd] ADJECTIVE
If you are indebted to someone, you are grateful to them.

indecent [ɪnˈdiːsənt] ADJECTIVE
Something that is indecent is shocking or rude, usually because it concerns nakedness or sex.
indecently ADVERB, **indecency** NOUN

● THESAURUS
crude: *crude pictures*
dirty: *dirty jokes*
improper: *improper behaviour*
lewd: *lewd comments*
rude: *a rude gesture*
vulgar: *vulgar language*

indeed [ɪnˈdiːd] ADVERB
You use 'indeed' to strengthen a point that you are making. *e.g. The desserts are very good indeed.*
[WORD HISTORY: from Middle English IN DEDE meaning 'in fact']

indefatigable [ˌɪndɪˈfætɪɡəbəl] ADJECTIVE
People who never get tired of doing something are indefatigable.

indefinite [ɪnˈdɛfɪnɪt] ADJECTIVE
1 If something is indefinite, no time to finish has been decided. *e.g. an indefinite strike*
2 Indefinite also means vague or not exact. *e.g. indefinite words and pictures*
indefinitely ADVERB

indefinite article indefinite articles
NOUN
the grammatical term for 'a' and 'an'

indelible [ɪnˈdɛlɪbəl] ADJECTIVE
unable to be removed *e.g. indelible ink*
indelibly ADVERB

indemnity [ɪnˈdɛmnɪtɪ] NOUN; FORMAL
Indemnity is protection against damage or loss.

indentation [ˌɪndɛnˈteɪʃən] **indentations**
NOUN
a dent or a groove in a surface or on the edge of something

independence [ˌɪndɪˈpɛndəns] NOUN
1 Independence is not relying on anyone else.
2 (HISTORY) A nation or state gains its independence when it stops being ruled or governed by another country and has its own government and laws.

independent [ˌɪndɪˈpɛndənt] ADJECTIVE
1 Something that is independent happens or exists separately from other people or things. *e.g. Results are assessed by an independent panel.*

● THESAURUS
autonomous: *an autonomous country*
free: *Do we have a free press?*
liberated: *liberated countries*
separate: *We live separate lives.*
unrelated: *two unrelated incidents*

2 Someone who is independent does not need other people's help. *e.g. a fiercely independent woman*

● THESAURUS
individualistic: *individualistic behaviour*
liberated: *a genuinely liberated woman*
self-sufficient: *I am quite self-sufficient.*
unaided: *There have been many attempts to reach the North Pole unaided.*

3 An independent nation is one that is not ruled or governed by another country.
independently ADVERB

indeterminate [ˌɪndɪˈtɜːmɪnɪt] ADJECTIVE
not certain or definite *e.g. some indeterminate point in the future*

index [ˈɪndɛks] **indexes** NOUN
1 an alphabetical list at the back of a book, referring to items in the book
2 (LIBRARY) an alphabetical list of all the books in a library, arranged by title, author or subject

index finger index fingers NOUN
your first finger, next to your thumb

Indian [ˈɪndɪən] **Indians** ADJECTIVE
1 belonging or relating to India
> NOUN
2 someone who comes from India
3 someone descended from the people who lived in North, South, or Central America before Europeans arrived

indicate [ˈɪndɪˌkeɪt] **indicates, indicating, indicated** VERB
1 If something indicates something, it shows that it is true. *e.g. a gesture which clearly indicates his relief*

● THESAURUS
denote: *Messy writing denotes a messy mind.*
reveal: *His diary revealed his disturbed state of mind.*
show: *I would like to show my appreciation.*
signal: *Ted signalled that everything was all right.*
signify: *A white flag signifies surrender.*

2 If you indicate something to someone, you point to it.

3 If you indicate a fact, you mention it.

4 If the driver of a vehicle indicates, they give a signal to show which way they are going to turn.

indication [ˌɪndɪˈkeɪʃən] **indications** NOUN
a sign of what someone feels or what is likely to happen

● THESAURUS
clue: *Did she give any clue as to how she was feeling?*
hint: *The Minister gave a strong hint that he intended to resign.*
sign: *Your blood will be checked for any sign of kidney failure.*
signal: *They saw the visit as an important signal of support.*
suggestion: *There is no suggestion that the two sides are any closer to agreeing.*
warning: *a warning of impending doom*

indicative [ɪnˈdɪkətɪv] ADJECTIVE
1 If something is indicative of something else, it is a sign of that thing. *e.g. Clean, pink tongues are indicative of a good, healthy digestion.*

> NOUN
2 If a verb is used in the indicative, it is in the form used for making statements.

indicator [ˈɪndɪˌkeɪtə] **indicators** NOUN
1 something which tells you what something is like or what is happening

2 A car's indicators are the lights at the front and back which are used to show when it is turning left or right.

3 a substance used in chemistry that shows if another substance is an acid or alkali by changing colour when it comes into contact with it

indict [ɪnˈdaɪt] **indicts, indicting, indicted** VERB; FORMAL
To indict someone is to charge them officially with a crime.
indictment NOUN, **indictable** ADJECTIVE

indifferent [ɪnˈdɪfrənt] ADJECTIVE
1 If you are indifferent to something, you have no interest in it.
2 If something is indifferent, it is of a poor quality or low standard. *e.g. a pair of rather indifferent paintings*

indifferently ADVERB, **indifference** NOUN

indigenous [ɪnˈdɪdʒɪnəs] ADJECTIVE
If something is indigenous to a country, it comes from that country. *e.g. a plant indigenous to Asia*

indigestion [ˌɪndɪˈdʒɛstʃən] NOUN
Indigestion is a pain you get when you find it difficult to digest food.

indignant [ɪnˈdɪgnənt] ADJECTIVE
If you are indignant, you feel angry about something that you think is unfair.
indignantly ADVERB

indignation [ˌɪndɪgˈneɪʃən] NOUN
Indignation is anger about something that you think is unfair.

indignity [ɪnˈdɪgnɪti] **indignities** NOUN
something that makes you feel embarrassed or humiliated *e.g. the indignity of having to flee angry protesters*

indigo [ˈɪndɪˌgəʊ] NOUN OR ADJECTIVE
dark violet-blue

indirect [ˌɪndɪˈrɛkt] ADJECTIVE
Something that is indirect is not done or caused directly by a particular person or thing, but by someone or something else.
indirectly ADVERB

● THESAURUS
meandering: *the meandering course of the river*
oblique: *oblique threats*
rambling: *In a rambling answer, he denied the charge.*
roundabout: *a roundabout way of getting information*
tortuous: *a tortuous path*
wandering: *a wandering route through the woods*
<<OPPOSITE *direct*

indiscriminate [ˌɪndɪˈskrɪmɪnɪt] ADJECTIVE
not involving careful thought or choice *e.g. an indiscriminate bombing campaign*
indiscriminately ADVERB

indispensable [ˌɪndɪˈspɛnsəbəl] ADJECTIVE
If something is indispensable, you cannot do without it. *e.g. A good pair of walking shoes is indispensable.*

indistinct [ˌɪndɪˈstɪŋkt] ADJECTIVE
not clear *e.g. indistinct voices*
indistinctly ADVERB

individual [ˌɪndɪˈvɪdjʊəl] **individuals** ADJECTIVE
1 relating to one particular person or thing *e.g. Each family needs individual attention.*

● THESAURUS
discrete: formal *breaking down the job into discrete steps*
independent: *two independent studies*

separate: *Use separate chopping boards for different foods.*

single: *every single house in the street*

2 Someone who is individual behaves quite differently from the way other people behave.

● **THESAURUS**

characteristic: *a characteristic feature*
distinctive: *His voice was very distinctive.*
idiosyncratic: *a highly idiosyncratic personality*
original: *a chef with an original touch*
personal: *his own personal method of playing*
special: *her own special way of doing things*
unique: *Each person's signature is unique.*

> NOUN

3 a person, different from any other person *e.g. wealthy individuals*
individually ADVERB

● **THESAURUS**

character: *a remarkable character*
human being: *a fellow human being*
party: *Who is the guilty party?*
person: *One person died and several others were injured.*
soul: *He's a jolly soul.*

individualist [ˌɪndɪˈvɪdjʊəlɪst] **individualists** NOUN
someone who likes to do things in their own way
individualistic ADJECTIVE

individuality [ˌɪndɪˌvɪdjʊˈælɪtɪ] NOUN
If something has individuality, it is different from all other things, and therefore is very interesting and noticeable.

indomitable [ɪnˈdɒmɪtəbəl] ADJECTIVE; FORMAL
impossible to overcome *e.g. an indomitable spirit*

Indonesian [ˌɪndəʊˈniːzɪən] **Indonesians** ADJECTIVE
1 belonging or relating to Indonesia

> NOUN

2 someone who comes from Indonesia

3 Indonesian is the official language of Indonesia.

indoor [ˈɪnˌdɔː] ADJECTIVE
situated or happening inside a building

indoors [ˌɪnˈdɔːz] ADVERB
If something happens indoors, it takes place inside a building.

induce [ɪnˈdjuːs] **induces, inducing, induced** VERB
1 To induce a state is to cause it. *e.g. His manner was rough and suspicious but he did not induce fear.*

2 If you induce someone to do something, you persuade them to do it.

inducement [ɪnˈdjuːsmənt] **inducements** NOUN
something offered to encourage someone to do something

indulge [ɪnˈdʌldʒ] **indulges, indulging, indulged** VERB
1 If you indulge in something, you allow yourself to do something that you enjoy.

2 If you indulge someone, you let them have or do what they want, often in a way that is not good for them.

indulgence [ɪnˈdʌldʒəns] **indulgences** NOUN
1 something you allow yourself to have because it gives you pleasure

2 Indulgence is the act of indulging yourself or another person.

indulgent [ɪnˈdʌldʒənt] ADJECTIVE
If you are indulgent, you treat someone with special kindness. *e.g. a rich, indulgent father*
indulgently ADJECTIVE

industrial [ɪnˈdʌstrɪəl] ADJECTIVE
relating to industry

industrial action NOUN
Industrial action is action such as striking taken by workers in protest over pay or working conditions.

industrialist [ɪnˈdʌstrɪəlɪst] **industrialists** NOUN
a person who owns or controls a lot of factories

Industrial Revolution NOUN
The Industrial Revolution took place in Britain in the late eighteenth and early nineteenth century, when machines began to be used more in factories and more goods were produced as a result.

industrious [ɪnˈdʌstrɪəs] ADJECTIVE
An industrious person works very hard.

● **THESAURUS**

busy: *an exceptionally busy man*
conscientious: *Sherry was slow but conscientious.*
diligent: *Williams was diligent in the writing of letters.*
hard-working: *an exceptionally disciplined and hard-working young man*
tireless: *a tireless and willing worker*
<<OPPOSITE *lazy*

industry [ˈɪndəstrɪ] **industries** NOUN
1 Industry is the work and processes involved in manufacturing things in factories.

2 all the people and processes involved in manufacturing a particular thing

inedible [ɪnˈɛdɪbəl] ADJECTIVE
too nasty or poisonous to eat

inefficient [ˌɪnɪˈfɪʃənt] ADJECTIVE
badly organized, wasteful, and slow *e.g. a corrupt*

and inefficient administration
inefficiently ADVERB, **inefficiency** NOUN

● THESAURUS
disorganized: *My boss is completely disorganized.*
incapable: *If he fails he will be considered incapable.*
incompetent: *an incompetent officer*
inept: *an inept use of power*
sloppy: *sloppy management*
<<OPPOSITE *efficient*

inept [ɪn'ɛpt] ADJECTIVE
without skill *e.g. an inept lawyer*
ineptitude NOUN

inequality [,ɪnɪ'kwɒlɪtɪ] **inequalities** NOUN
a difference in size, status, wealth, or position, between different things, groups, or people

inert [ɪn'ɜːt] ADJECTIVE
Something that is inert does not move and appears lifeless. *e.g. an inert body lying on the floor*

inertia [ɪn'ɜːʃə] NOUN
If you have a feeling of inertia, you feel very lazy and unwilling to do anything.

inevitable [ɪn'ɛvɪtəbªl] ADJECTIVE
certain to happen
inevitably ADVERB, **inevitability** NOUN

inexhaustible [,ɪnɪg'zɔːstəbªl] ADJECTIVE
Something that is inexhaustible will never be used up. *e.g. an inexhaustible supply of ideas*

inexorable [ɪn'ɛksərəbªl] ADJECTIVE; FORMAL
Something that is inexorable cannot be prevented from continuing. *e.g. the inexorable increase in the number of cars*
inexorably ADVERB

inexpensive [,ɪnɪk'spɛnsɪv] ADJECTIVE
not costing much

inexperienced [,ɪnɪk'spɪərɪənst] ADJECTIVE
lacking experience of a situation or activity *e.g. inexperienced drivers*
inexperience NOUN

● THESAURUS
green: *informal He was a young lad, and very green.*
new: *a new mother*
raw: *raw talent*
unaccustomed: *Kate is unaccustomed to being on TV.*

<<OPPOSITE *experienced*

inexplicable [,ɪnɪk'splɪkəbªl] ADJECTIVE
If something is inexplicable, you cannot explain it. *e.g. For some inexplicable reason I still felt uneasy.*
inexplicably ADVERB

inextricably [,ɪnɛks'trɪkəblɪ] ADVERB
If two or more things are inextricably linked, they cannot be separated.

infallible [ɪn'fæləbªl] ADJECTIVE
never wrong *e.g. No machine is infallible.*

infallibility NOUN

infamous ['ɪnfəməs] ADJECTIVE
well-known because of something bad or evil *e.g. a book about the country's most infamous murder cases*

infant ['ɪnfənt] **infants** NOUN
1 a baby or very young child
> ADJECTIVE
2 designed for young children *e.g. an infant school*
infancy NOUN, **infantile** ADJECTIVE
[WORD HISTORY] from Latin INFANS meaning 'unable to speak']

infantry ['ɪnfəntrɪ] NOUN
In an army, the infantry are soldiers who fight on foot rather than in tanks or on horses.

infatuated [ɪn'fætjʊˌeɪtɪd] ADJECTIVE
If you are infatuated with someone, you have such strong feelings of love or passion that you cannot think sensibly about them.
infatuation NOUN

infect [ɪn'fɛkt] **infects, infecting, infected** VERB
To infect someone or something is to cause disease in them.

● THESAURUS
affect: *Neil has been affected by the virus.*
blight: *trees blighted by pollution*
contaminate: *These substances can contaminate fish.*
taint: *blood that had been tainted with HIV*

infection [ɪn'fɛkʃən] **infections** NOUN
1 a disease caused by germs *e.g. a chest infection*
2 Infection is the state of being infected. *e.g. a very small risk of infection*

infectious [ɪn'fɛkʃəs] ADJECTIVE
spreading from one person to another *e.g. an infectious disease*

● THESAURUS
catching: *There is no suggestion that multiple sclerosis is catching.*
contagious: *a highly contagious disease of the lungs*
spreading: *The spreading virus is threatening the population.*

infer [ɪn'fɜː] **infers, inferring, inferred** VERB
If you infer something, you work out that it is true on the basis of information that you already have.
inference NOUN

▪ Do not use *infer* to mean the same as *imply.*

inferior [ɪn'fɪərɪə] **inferiors** ADJECTIVE
1 having a lower position than something or someone else

● THESAURUS
lesser: *the work of lesser writers*

lower: *lower animals*
minor: *a minor celebrity*
secondary: *He was relegated to a secondary position.*
second-class: *second-class citizens*
subordinate: *His subordinate officers followed his example.*
<<OPPOSITE *superior*

2 of low quality *e.g. inferior quality cassette tapes*

● THESAURUS
mediocre: *mediocre music*
poor: *a poor standard of service*
second-class: *a second-class education*
second-rate: *second-rate restaurants*
shoddy: *Customers no longer tolerate shoddy goods.*
<<OPPOSITE *superior*

> NOUN

3 Your inferiors are people in a lower position than you.
inferiority NOUN

● THESAURUS
junior: *the office junior*
menial: *menials in poorly paid jobs*
subordinate: *All her subordinates adored her.*
underling: *Every underling feared him.*
<<OPPOSITE *superior*

infernal [ɪnˈfɜːnəl] ADJECTIVE
very unpleasant *e.g. an infernal bore*
[WORD HISTORY: from Latin INFERNUS meaning 'hell']

inferno [ɪnˈfɜːnəʊ] **infernos** NOUN
a very large dangerous fire

infertile [ɪnˈfɜːtaɪl] ADJECTIVE
1 Infertile soil is of poor quality and plants cannot grow well in it.
2 Someone who is infertile cannot have children.

infested [ɪnˈfɛstɪd] ADJECTIVE
Something that is infested has a large number of animals or insects living on it and causing damage. *e.g. The flats are damp and infested with rats.*
infestation NOUN

infidelity [ˌɪnfɪˈdɛlɪtɪ] **infidelities** NOUN
Infidelity is being unfaithful to your husband, wife, or lover.

infighting [ˈɪnˌfaɪtɪŋ] NOUN
Infighting is quarrelling or rivalry between members of the same organization.

infiltrate [ˈɪnfɪlˌtreɪt] **infiltrates, infiltrating, infiltrated** VERB
If people infiltrate an organization, they gradually enter it in secret to spy on its activities.
infiltration NOUN

infinite [ˈɪnfɪnɪt] ADJECTIVE
without any limit or end *e.g. an infinite number of possibilities*

infinitely ADVERB

● THESAURUS
boundless: *boundless energy*
eternal: *the secret of eternal youth*
everlasting: *our everlasting friendship*
inexhaustible: *an inexhaustible supply of ideas*
perpetual: *a perpetual source of worry*
untold: *untold wealth*

infinitive [ɪnˈfɪnɪtɪv] **infinitives** NOUN
In grammar, the infinitive is the base form of the verb. It often has 'to' in front of it, for example 'to go' or 'to see'.

infinity [ɪnˈfɪnɪtɪ] NOUN
1 Infinity is a number that is larger than any other number and can never be given an exact value.
2 Infinity is also a point that can never be reached, further away than any other point. *e.g. skies stretching on into infinity*

infirmary [ɪnˈfɜːmərɪ] **infirmaries** NOUN
a hospital

inflamed [ɪnˈfleɪmd] ADJECTIVE
If part of your body is inflamed, it is red and swollen, usually because of infection.

inflammable [ɪnˈflæməbəl] ADJECTIVE
An inflammable material burns easily.

> Although *inflammable* and *flammable* both mean 'likely to catch fire', *flammable* is used more often as people sometimes think that *inflammable* means 'not likely to catch fire'.

inflammation [ˌɪnfləˈmeɪʃən] NOUN
Inflammation is painful redness or swelling of part of the body.

inflammatory [ɪnˈflæmətərɪ] ADJECTIVE
Inflammatory actions are likely to make people very angry.

inflate [ɪnˈfleɪt] **inflates, inflating, inflated** VERB
When you inflate something, you fill it with air or gas to make it swell.
inflatable ADJECTIVE

inflation [ɪnˈfleɪʃən] NOUN
Inflation is an increase in the price of goods and services in a country.
inflationary ADJECTIVE

inflection [ɪnˈflɛkʃən] **inflections;** also spelt **inflexion** NOUN
a change in the form of a word that shows its grammatical function, for example a change that makes a noun plural

inflexible [ɪnˈflɛksəbəl] ADJECTIVE
fixed and unable to be altered *e.g. an inflexible routine*

inflict [ɪnˈflɪkt] **inflicts, inflicting, inflicted** VERB

If you inflict something unpleasant on someone, you make them suffer it.

influence ['ɪnflʊəns] influences, influencing, influenced NOUN

1 Influence is power that a person has over other people.

● THESAURUS

authority: *You have no authority over me.*
control: *Teachers have a lot of control over students.*
importance: *a politician of great importance*
power: *a position of power*
sway: *My mother holds sway at home.*

2 An influence is also the effect that someone or something has. *e.g. under the influence of alcohol*

● THESAURUS

effect: *Your age has an effect on your views.*
hold: *He is losing his hold on the public.*
magnetism: *a man of great personal magnetism*
spell: *under the spell of one of his teachers*
weight: *the weight of the law*

> VERB

3 To influence someone or something means to have an effect on them.
[WORD HISTORY: from Latin INFLUENTIA meaning 'power flowing from the stars']

● THESAURUS

affect: *He will not let personal preference affect his choice.*
control: *I can't control him.*
direct: *I don't need you directing my life.*
guide: *Let your instinct guide you.*
manipulate: *I hate the way he manipulates people.*
sway: *efforts to sway voters*

influential [,ɪnflʊ'ɛnʃəl] ADJECTIVE

Someone who is influential has a lot of influence over people.

influenza [,ɪnflʊ'ɛnzə] NOUN; FORMAL

Influenza is flu.

influx ['ɪn,flʌks] NOUN

a steady arrival of people or things *e.g. a large influx of tourists*

inform [ɪn'fɔːm] informs, informing, informed VERB

1 If you inform someone of something, you tell them about it.

● THESAURUS

advise: formal *I can advise you of his whereabouts.*
enlighten: *a history lesson which enlightens you*
notify: *Ann was notified of her sister's illness.*
tell: *Tell me what is going on.*

2 If you inform on a person, you tell the police about a crime they have committed.
informant NOUN

● THESAURUS

betray: *They betrayed their associates to the police.*

denounce: *He was denounced as a dangerous rebel.*
grass on: British; slang *He grassed on the members of his own gang.*
tell on: informal *It's all right, I won't tell on you.*

informal [ɪn'fɔːməl] ADJECTIVE

relaxed and casual *e.g. an informal meeting*
informally ADVERB, **informality** NOUN

● THESAURUS

casual: *a casual attitude towards money*
colloquial: *colloquial language*
easy: *easy conversation*
familiar: *John was too familiar towards his teacher.*
natural: *Beth was friendly and natural with us.*
relaxed: *a relaxed atmosphere in class*
<<OPPOSITE *formal*

information [,ɪnfə'meɪʃən] NOUN

If you have information on or about something, you know something about it.

● THESAURUS

data: *The survey provided valuable data.*
drum: Australian; informal *I don't have the drum on this yet.*
facts: *Pass on all the facts to the police.*
material: *highly secret material*
news: *We have news of your brother.*
notice: *advance notice of the event*
word: *I received word that the guests had arrived.*

informative [ɪn'fɔːmətɪv] ADJECTIVE

Something that is informative gives you useful information.

informer [ɪn'fɔːmə] informers NOUN

someone who tells the police that another person has committed a crime

infrastructure ['ɪnfrə,strʌktʃə] infrastructures NOUN

(GEOGRAPHY) The infrastructure of a country consists of things like factories, schools, and roads, which show how much money the country has and how strong its economy is.

infringe [ɪn'frɪndʒ] infringes, infringing, infringed VERB

1 If you infringe a law, you break it.

2 To infringe people's rights is to not allow them the rights to which they are entitled.
infringement NOUN

infuriate [ɪn'fjʊərɪ,eɪt] infuriates, infuriating, infuriated VERB

If someone infuriates you, they make you very angry.
infuriating ADJECTIVE

infuse [ɪn'fjuːz] infuses, infusing, infused VERB

1 If you infuse someone with a feeling such as enthusiasm or joy, you fill them with it.

2 If you infuse a substance such as a herb or medicine, you pour hot water onto it and leave it for the water to absorb the flavour.
infusion NOUN

ingenious [ɪnˈdʒiːnjəs] ADJECTIVE
very clever and using new ideas *e.g. his ingenious invention*
ingeniously ADVERB

ingenuity [ˌɪndʒɪˈnjuːɪti] NOUN
Ingenuity is cleverness and skill at inventing things or working out plans.

ingot [ˈɪŋgət] **ingots** NOUN
a brick-shaped lump of metal, especially gold

ingrained [ɪnˈgreɪnd] ADJECTIVE
If habits and beliefs are ingrained, they are difficult to change or destroy.

ingredient [ɪnˈgriːdɪənt] **ingredients** NOUN
(D & T) Ingredients are the things that something is made from, especially in cookery.

● THESAURUS
component: *the components of hamburgers*
constituent: *the main constituent of fish oil*
element: *the various elements in a picture*

inhabit [ɪnˈhæbɪt] **inhabits, inhabiting, inhabited** VERB
If you inhabit a place, you live there.

● THESAURUS
dwell: *the people who dwell in the forest*
live: *She has lived here for ten years.*
lodge: *Some people lodged permanently in the hallway.*
occupy: *Forty tenants occupy the block.*
populate: *a swamp populated by huge birds*
reside: *formal He resides in the country.*

inhabitant [ɪnˈhæbɪtənt] **inhabitants** NOUN
The inhabitants of a place are the people who live there.

● THESAURUS
citizen: *American citizens.*
inmate: *prison inmates*
native: *Dr Brown is a native of New Zealand.*
occupant: *the previous occupant of the house*
resident: *the residents of the retirement home*

inhale [ɪnˈheɪl] **inhales, inhaling, inhaled** VERB
When you inhale, you breathe in.
inhalation NOUN

inherent [ɪnˈhɪərənt] ADJECTIVE
Inherent qualities or characteristics in something are a natural part of it. *e.g. her inherent common sense*
inherently ADVERB

inherit [ɪnˈhɛrɪt] **inherits, inheriting, inherited** VERB

1 If you inherit money or property, you receive it from someone who has died.

2 If you inherit a quality or characteristic from a parent or ancestor, it is passed on to you at birth.
inheritor NOUN

inheritance [ɪnˈhɛrɪtəns] **inheritances** NOUN
something that is passed on from another person

● THESAURUS
bequest: *His aunt left a bequest for him in her will.*
heritage: *This building is part of our heritage.*
legacy: *His politeness was the legacy of his upbringing.*

inhibit [ɪnˈhɪbɪt] **inhibits, inhibiting, inhibited** VERB
If you inhibit someone from doing something, you prevent them from doing it.

inhibited [ɪnˈhɪbɪtɪd] ADJECTIVE
People who are inhibited find it difficult to relax and to show their emotions.

inhibition [ˌɪnɪˈbɪʃən] **inhibitions** NOUN
Inhibitions are feelings of fear or embarrassment that make it difficult for someone to relax and to show their emotions.

inhospitable [ɪnˈhɒspɪtəbəl] ADJECTIVE

1 An inhospitable place is unpleasant or difficult to live in.

2 If someone is inhospitable, they do not make people who visit them feel welcome.

inhuman [ɪnˈhjuːmən] ADJECTIVE
not human or not behaving like a human *e.g. the inhuman killing of their enemies*

inhumane [ɪnˈhjuːmeɪn] ADJECTIVE
extremely cruel
inhumanity NOUN

inimitable [ɪˈnɪmɪtəbəl] ADJECTIVE
If you have an inimitable characteristic, no-one else can imitate it. *e.g. her inimitable sense of style*

initial [ɪˈnɪʃəl] **initials** ADJECTIVE

1 first, or at the beginning *e.g. Shock and dismay were my initial reactions.*

> NOUN
2 the first letter of a name
initially ADVERB

initiate [ɪˈnɪʃɪeɪt] **initiates, initiating, initiated** VERB

1 If you initiate something, you make it start or happen.

2 If you initiate someone into a group or club, you allow them to become a member of it, usually by means of a special ceremony.
initiation NOUN

initiative [ɪˈnɪʃɪətɪv] **initiatives** NOUN
1 an attempt to get something done
2 If you have initiative, you decide what to do and then do it, without needing the advice of other people.

inject [ɪnˈdʒɛkt] **injects, injecting, injected** VERB
1 If a doctor or nurse injects you with a substance, they use a needle and syringe to put the substance into your body.
2 If you inject something new into a situation, you add it.
injection NOUN

injunction [ɪnˈdʒʌŋkʃən] **injunctions** NOUN
an order issued by a court of law to stop someone doing something

injure [ˈɪndʒə] **injures, injuring, injured** VERB
To injure someone is to damage part of their body.
● **THESAURUS**
harm: *The hijackers did not harm anyone.*
hurt: *He hurt his back in an accident.*
maim: *Mines in rice paddies maim and kill civilians.*
wound: *wounded by shrapnel*

injury [ˈɪndʒərɪ] **injuries** NOUN **(PE)**
hurt or damage, especially to part of a person's body or to their feelings *e.g. He suffered acute injury to his pride... The knee injury forced him to retire from the professional game.*
● **THESAURUS**
damage: *brain damage*
harm: *Dogs can do harm to human beings.*
wound: *a head wound*

injustice [ɪnˈdʒʌstɪs] **injustices** NOUN
1 Injustice is lack of justice and fairness.
● **THESAURUS**
bias: *He shows bias against women.*
discrimination: *racial discrimination*
inequality: *people concerned about social inequality*
prejudice: *prejudice against workers over 45*
unfairness: *the unfairness of the decision*
<<OPPOSITE *justice*
2 If you do someone an injustice, you judge them too harshly.

ink [ɪŋk] NOUN
Ink is the coloured liquid used for writing or printing.

inkling [ˈɪŋklɪŋ] **inklings** NOUN
a vague idea about something

inlaid [ˈɪnˌleɪd] ADJECTIVE
decorated with small pieces of wood, metal, or stone *e.g. decorative plates inlaid with brass*
inlay NOUN

inland ADJECTIVE [ˈɪnlənd]
near the middle of a country, away from the sea
> ADVERB [ˈɪnˌlænd]
towards the middle of the country, away from the sea.

in-law [ˈɪnˌlɔː] **in-laws** NOUN
Your in-laws are members of your husband's or wife's family.

inlet [ˈɪnˌlɛt] **inlets** NOUN
a narrow bay

inmate [ˈɪnˌmeɪt] **inmates** NOUN
someone who lives in a prison or psychiatric hospital

inn [ɪn] **inns** NOUN
a small old country pub or hotel

innards [ˈɪnədz] PLURAL NOUN
The innards of something are its inside parts.

innate [ɪˈneɪt] ADJECTIVE
An innate quality is one that you were born with.
e.g. an innate sense of fairness
innately ADVERB

inner [ˈɪnə] ADJECTIVE
contained inside a place or object *e.g. an inner room*

innermost [ˈɪnəˌməʊst] ADJECTIVE
deepest and most secret *e.g. our innermost feelings*

innings [ˈɪnɪŋz] NOUN
In cricket, an innings is a period when a particular team is batting.

innocence [ˈɪnəsəns] NOUN
inexperience of evil or unpleasant things
● **THESAURUS**
gullibility: *I'm paying for my gullibility back then.*
inexperience: *their inexperience of the real world*
naivety: *There was a youthful naivety to his honesty.*
simplicity: *She prayed with childlike simplicity.*

innocent [ˈɪnəsənt] ADJECTIVE
1 not guilty of a crime
● **THESAURUS**
blameless: *I have led a blameless life.*
clear: *He was clear of blame for the accident.*
not guilty: *Both men were found not guilty.*
<<OPPOSITE *guilty*
2 without experience of evil or unpleasant things
e.g. an innocent child
innocently ADVERB
● **THESAURUS**
childlike: *childlike trust*
naive: *I was young and naive when I left home.*
pure: *She had led a pure life.*
spotless: *a spotless, pure child*

innocuous [ɪˈnɒkjʊəs] ADJECTIVE
not harmful

innovation [ˌɪnəˈveɪʃən] **innovations** NOUN
(D & T) a completely new idea, product, or
system of doing things

innuendo [ˌɪnjuˈɛndəʊ] **innuendos** or
innuendoes NOUN
an indirect reference to something rude or
unpleasant
[WORD HISTORY: from Latin INNUENDO meaning 'by
hinting', from INNUERE meaning 'to convey by a
nod']

innumerable [ɪˈnjuːmərəbəl] ADJECTIVE
too many to be counted e.g. innumerable cups
of tea

input [ˈɪnˌpʊt] **inputs** NOUN
1 Input consists of all the money, information,
and other resources that are put into a job,
project, or company to make it work.
2 (ICT) In computing, input is information which
is fed into a computer.

inquest [ˈɪnˌkwɛst] **inquests** NOUN
an official inquiry to find out what caused a
person's death

inquire [ɪnˈkwaɪə] **inquires, inquiring,
inquired**; also spelt **enquire** VERB
If you inquire about something, you ask for
information about it.
inquiring ADJECTIVE, **inquiry** NOUN

inquisition [ˌɪnkwɪˈzɪʃən] **inquisitions**
NOUN
an official investigation, especially one which is
very thorough and uses harsh methods of
questioning

inquisitive [ɪnˈkwɪzɪtɪv] ADJECTIVE
Someone who is inquisitive is keen to find out
about things.
inquisitively ADVERB

inroads [ˈɪnˌrəʊdz] PLURAL NOUN
If something makes inroads on or into
something, it starts affecting it.

insane [ɪnˈseɪn] ADJECTIVE
Someone who is insane is mad.
insanely ADVERB, **insanity** NOUN

● THESAURUS
crazy: If I sat home and worried, I'd go crazy.
deranged: a deranged man who shot 14 people in
the main square
mad: She was afraid of going mad.
mentally ill: a patient who is mentally ill
out of your mind: I wonder if I'm going out of my
mind.
unhinged: an experience which left her completely
unhinged

insatiable [ɪnˈseɪʃəbəl] ADJECTIVE
A desire or urge that is insatiable is very great.
e.g. an insatiable curiosity
insatiably ADVERB

inscribe [ɪnˈskraɪb] **inscribes, inscribing,
inscribed** VERB
If you inscribe words on an object, you write or
carve them on it.

inscription [ɪnˈskrɪpʃən] **inscriptions**
NOUN
the words that are written or carved on
something

inscrutable [ɪnˈskruːtəbəl] ADJECTIVE
Someone who is inscrutable does not show what
they are really thinking.

insect [ˈɪnsɛkt] **insects** NOUN
(SCIENCE) a small creature with six legs, and
usually wings

insecticide [ɪnˈsɛktɪˌsaɪd] **insecticides**
NOUN
a poisonous chemical used to kill insects

insecure [ˌɪnsɪˈkjʊə] ADJECTIVE
1 If you are insecure, you feel unsure of yourself
and doubt whether other people like you.
2 Something that is insecure is not safe or well
protected. e.g. People still feel their jobs are insecure.
insecurity NOUN

insensitive [ɪnˈsɛnsɪtɪv] ADJECTIVE
If you are insensitive, you do not notice when you
are upsetting people.
insensitivity NOUN

insert [ɪnˈsɜːt] **inserts, inserting, inserted**
VERB
If you insert an object into something, you put it
inside.
insertion NOUN

● THESAURUS
enter: Enter your name in the box.
implant: a device implanted in the arm
introduce: Scientists introduced new genes into
mice.
place: Cover the casserole tightly and place in the
oven.
put: She put a coin in the slot.
set: diamonds set in gold

inshore [ˈɪnˈʃɔː] ADJECTIVE
at sea but close to the shore e.g. inshore boats

inside inside insides NOUN [ˈɪnˈsaɪd]
1 the part of something that is surrounded by the
main part and often hidden
> ADJECTIVE [ˈɪnˌsaɪd]
2 surrounded by the main part and often hidden
e.g. an inside pocket

● THESAURUS
inner: the inner ear

innermost: *the innermost parts of the galaxy*
interior: *a car with plenty of interior space*
internal: *your internal organs*
<<OPPOSITE *outside*

> PREPOSITION [ˌɪnˈsaɪd]
3 in or to the interior of *e.g. inside the house*

> PLURAL NOUN [ˈɪnˌsaɪdz]
4 Your insides are the parts inside your body.

● THESAURUS
entrails: *chicken entrails*
guts: *fish guts*
innards: *the innards of a human body*
internal organs: *damage to internal organs*

> PHRASE [ˈɪnˈsaɪd]
5 Inside out means with the inside part facing outwards

Do not use *of* after *inside*. You should write *she was waiting inside the school* and not *inside of the school*.

insider [ˌɪnˈsaɪdə] **insiders** NOUN
a person who is involved in a situation and so knows more about it than other people

insidious [ɪnˈsɪdiəs] ADJECTIVE
Something that is insidious is unpleasant and develops slowly without being noticed. *e.g. the insidious progress of the disease*
insidiously ADVERB

insight [ˈɪnˌsaɪt] **insights** NOUN
If you gain insight into a problem, you gradually get a deep and accurate understanding of it.

insignia [ɪnˈsɪɡniə] NOUN
the badge or a sign of a particular organization

insignificant [ˌɪnsɪɡˈnɪfɪkənt] ADJECTIVE
small and unimportant
insignificance NOUN

● THESAURUS
irrelevant: *irrelevant details*
little: *It seems such a little thing to get upset over.*
minor: *Western officials say the problem is minor.*
petty: *Rows can start over petty things.*
trifling: *These difficulties may seem trifling to you.*
trivial: *He tried to wave aside these issues as trivial matters.*
unimportant: *The age difference seemed unimportant.*
<<OPPOSITE *significant*

insincere [ˌɪnsɪnˈsɪə] ADJECTIVE
Someone who is insincere pretends to have feelings which they do not really have.

● THESAURUS
deceitful: *deceitful and misleading remarks*
dishonest: *dishonest salespeople*
false: *a false confession*
two-faced: *the most two-faced politicians in the world*

<<OPPOSITE *sincere*

insinuate [ɪnˈsɪnjʊˌeɪt] **insinuates, insinuating, insinuated** VERB
If you insinuate something unpleasant, you hint about it.
insinuation NOUN

insipid [ɪnˈsɪpɪd] ADJECTIVE
1 An insipid person or activity is dull and boring.
2 Food that is insipid has very little taste.

insist [ɪnˈsɪst] **insists, insisting, insisted** VERB
If you insist on something, you demand it forcefully.
insistent ADJECTIVE, **insistence** NOUN

● THESAURUS
demand: *The teacher demanded an explanation.*
press: *She is pressing for improvements to education.*
urge: *We urge vigorous action be taken immediately.*

insolent [ˈɪnsələnt] ADJECTIVE
very rude and disrespectful
insolently ADVERB, **insolence** NOUN

insoluble [ɪnˈsɒljʊbᵊl] ADJECTIVE
1 impossible to solve *e.g. an insoluble problem*
2 unable to dissolve *e.g. substances which are insoluble in water*

insolvent [ɪnˈsɒlvənt] ADJECTIVE
unable to pay your debts
insolvency NOUN

insomnia [ɪnˈsɒmniə] NOUN
Insomnia is difficulty in sleeping.
insomniac NOUN

inspect [ɪnˈspɛkt] **inspects, inspecting, inspected** VERB
To inspect something is to examine it carefully to check that everything is all right.
inspection NOUN

● THESAURUS
check: *Check each item for obvious flaws.*
examine: *He examined her passport and stamped it.*
eye: *We eyed each other thoughtfully.*
investigate: *Police are investigating the scene of the crime.*
scan: *The officer scanned the room.*
survey: *He surveyed the ruins of the building.*

inspector [ɪnˈspɛktə] **inspectors** NOUN
1 someone who inspects things
2 a police officer just above a sergeant in rank

inspire [ɪnˈspaɪə] **inspires, inspiring, inspired** VERB
1 (DRAMA) If something inspires you, it gives you new ideas and enthusiasm to do something.
2 To inspire an emotion in someone is to make them feel this emotion.

inspired ADJECTIVE, **inspiring** ADJECTIVE, **inspiration** NOUN

instability [ˌɪnstəˈbɪlɪtɪ] NOUN
Instability is a lack of stability in a place. *e.g. political instability*

install [ɪnˈstɔːl] **installs, installing, installed** VERB
1 If you install a piece of equipment in a place, you put it there so it is ready to be used.
2 To install someone in an important job is to officially give them that position.
3 If you install yourself in a place, you settle there and make yourself comfortable.
installation NOUN

instalment [ɪnˈstɔːlmənt] **instalments** NOUN
1 If you pay for something in instalments, you pay small amounts of money regularly over a period of time.
2 one of the parts of a story or television series

instance [ˈɪnstəns] **instances** NOUN
1 a particular example or occurrence of an event, situation, or person *e.g. a serious instance of corruption*
> PHRASE
2 You use **for instance** to give an example of something you are talking about.

instant [ˈɪnstənt] **instants** NOUN
1 a moment or short period of time *e.g. In an instant they were gone.*

● THESAURUS
flash: *It was all over in a flash.*
minute: *I'll see you in a minute.*
moment: *In a moment he was gone.*
second: *Seconds later, firemen reached his door.*
split second: *Her gaze met Michael's for a split second.*
trice: *She was back in a trice.*

> ADJECTIVE
2 immediate and without delay *e.g. The record was an instant success.*
instantly ADVERB

● THESAURUS
immediate: *We need an immediate reply.*
instantaneous: *an explosion resulting in the instantaneous deaths of all crew members*
prompt: *Prompt action is needed.*

instantaneous [ˌɪnstənˈteɪnɪəs] ADJECTIVE
happening immediately and without delay *e.g. The applause was instantaneous.*
instantaneously ADVERB

instead [ɪnˈstɛd] ADVERB
in place of something *e.g. Take the stairs instead of the lift.*

instigate [ˈɪnstɪˌgeɪt] **instigates, instigating, instigated** VERB
Someone who instigates a situation makes it happen.
instigation NOUN, **instigator** NOUN

instil [ɪnˈstɪl] **instils, instilling, instilled** VERB
If you instil an idea or feeling into someone, you make them feel or think it.

instinct [ˈɪnstɪŋkt] **instincts** NOUN
a natural tendency to do something *e.g. My first instinct was to protect myself.*
instinctive ADJECTIVE, **instinctively** ADVERB

● THESAURUS
feeling: *You seem to have a feeling for drawing.*
impulse: *Peter resisted an impulse to smile.*
intuition: *You should trust your intuition.*
sixth sense: *Some sixth sense told him to keep going.*
urge: *He fought the urge to panic.*

institute [ˈɪnstɪˌtjuːt] **institutes, instituting, instituted** NOUN
1 an organization for teaching or research
> VERB
2 FORMAL
If you institute a rule or system, you introduce it.

institution [ˌɪnstɪˈtjuːʃən] **institutions** NOUN
1 a custom or system regarded as an important tradition within a society *e.g. The family is an institution to be cherished.*
2 a large, important organization, for example a university or bank
institutional ADJECTIVE

instruct [ɪnˈstrʌkt] **instructs, instructing, instructed** VERB
1 If you instruct someone to do something, you tell them to do it.

● THESAURUS
command: *He commanded his troops to attack.*
direct: *They have been directed to give attention to this problem.*
order: *Williams ordered him to leave.*
tell: *A passer-by told him to move his car.*
<<OPPOSITE *forbid*

2 If someone instructs you in a subject or skill, they teach you about it.
instructor NOUN, **instructive** ADJECTIVE, **instruction** NOUN

● THESAURUS
coach: *He coached me in French.*
educate: *We need to educate people about the destructive effects of alcohol.*
school: *She's been schooling her kids herself.*
teach: *She taught children French.*

i

train: *We train them in a range of building techniques.*
tutor: *He was tutoring her in the stringed instruments.*

instrument ['ɪnstrəmənt] **instruments**
NOUN

1 a tool or device used for a particular job *e.g. a special instrument which cut through the metal*

2 (**MUSIC**) A musical instrument is an object, such as a piano or flute, played to make music.

instrumental [ˌɪnstrə'mɛntəl] ADJECTIVE

1 If you are instrumental in doing something, you help to make it happen.

2 (**MUSIC**) Instrumental music is performed using only musical instruments, and not voices.

insufficient [ˌɪnsə'fɪʃənt] ADJECTIVE
not enough for a particular purpose
insufficiently ADVERB

● THESAURUS
deficient: *a deficient diet*
inadequate: *The problem lies with inadequate staffing.*
lacking: *My confidence is lacking.*
scant: *Gareth paid scant attention to what was going on.*
short: *She was short of breath.*
<<OPPOSITE sufficient

insular ['ɪnsjʊlə] ADJECTIVE
Someone who is insular is unwilling to meet new people or to consider new ideas.
insularity NOUN

insulate ['ɪnsjʊˌleɪt] **insulates, insulating, insulated** VERB
If you insulate something, you cover it with a layer to keep it warm or to stop electricity passing through it.
insulation NOUN, **insulator** NOUN

insulin ['ɪnsjʊlɪn] NOUN
Insulin is a substance which controls the level of sugar in the blood. People who have diabetes do not produce insulin naturally and have to take regular doses of it.

insult insults, insulting, insulted VERB
[ɪn'sʌlt]

1 If you insult someone, you offend them by being rude to them.

● THESAURUS
abuse: *footballers abusing referees*
affront: *He pretended to be affronted by what I said.*
offend: *I had no intention of offending the community.*
put down: *They seemed to delight in putting me down.*
slag: British; informal *He's always slagging me in front of his mates.*

slight: *They felt slighted by not being consulted.*
snub: *He snubbed her in public and made her feel foolish.*
<<OPPOSITE compliment

> NOUN ['ɪnsʌlt]
2 a rude remark which offends you
insulting ADJECTIVE

● THESAURUS
abuse: *Raft hurled verbal abuse at his co-star.*
affront: *She took my words as a personal affront.*
offence: *I meant no offence to Mr Hardy.*
slight: *She is very sensitive to slights.*
snub: *This was a deliberate snub to me.*
<<OPPOSITE compliment

insure [ɪn'ʃʊə] **insures, insuring, insured**
VERB

1 If you insure something or yourself, you pay money regularly to a company so that if there is an accident or damage, the company will pay for medical treatment or repairs.

2 If you do something to insure against something unpleasant happening, you do it to prevent the unpleasant thing from happening or to protect yourself if it does happen.
insurance NOUN

insurrection [ˌɪnsə'rɛkʃən] **insurrections**
NOUN
a violent action taken against the rulers of a country

intact [ɪn'tækt] ADJECTIVE
complete, and not changed or damaged in any way *e.g. The rear of the aircraft remained intact when it crashed.*

intake ['ɪnˌteɪk] **intakes** NOUN
A person's intake of food, drink, or air is the amount they take in.

integral ['ɪntɪgrəl] *or* [ɪn'tɛgrəl] ADJECTIVE
If something is an integral part of a whole thing, it is an essential part.

integrate ['ɪntɪˌgreɪt] **integrates, integrating, integrated** VERB

1 If a person integrates into a group, they become part of it.

2 To integrate things is to combine them so that they become closely linked or form one thing. *e.g. his plan to integrate the coal and steel industries*
integration NOUN

integrity [ɪn'tɛgrɪtɪ] NOUN

1 Integrity is the quality of being honest and following your principles.

2 The integrity of a group of people is their being united as one whole.

intellect ['ɪntɪˌlɛkt] **intellects** NOUN
Intellect is the ability to understand ideas and information.

intellectual [ˌɪntɪˈlɛktʃʊəl] **intellectuals**
ADJECTIVE
1 involving thought, ideas, and understanding
e.g. an intellectual exercise
> NOUN
2 someone who enjoys thinking about complicated ideas
intellectually ADVERB

intelligence [ɪnˈtɛlɪdʒəns] NOUN
A person's intelligence is their ability to understand and learn things quickly and well.

THESAURUS
cleverness: *Her cleverness gets in the way of her emotions.*
comprehension: *an idea beyond human comprehension*
intellect: *Lucy's lack of intellect disappointed her father.*
perception: *You have brilliant perception and insight.*
sense: *They have the sense to seek help.*
understanding: *I've got no sense, no understanding.*
wit: *He had the wit to see this was a good idea.*

intelligent [ɪnˈtɛlɪdʒənt] ADJECTIVE
able to understand and learn things quickly and well
intelligently ADVERB

THESAURUS
acute: *His relaxed exterior hides a very acute mind.*
brainy: *informal I don't consider myself brainy.*
bright: *an exceptionally bright child*
clever: *a clever girl*
quick: *His quick mind soon grasped the situation.*
sharp: *a very sharp intellect*
smart: *He thinks he's as smart as Sarah.*
<<OPPOSITE stupid

intelligentsia [ɪnˌtɛlɪˈdʒɛntsɪə] NOUN
The intelligentsia are intellectual people, considered as a group.

intelligible [ɪnˈtɛlɪdʒəbᵊl] ADJECTIVE
able to be understood *e.g. very few intelligible remarks*

intend [ɪnˈtɛnd] **intends, intending, intended** VERB
1 If you intend to do something, you have decided or planned to do it. *e.g. She intended to move back to Cape Town.*

THESAURUS
aim: *We aim to raise funds for charity.*
be determined: *Kate was determined to enjoy the day.*
mean: *I didn't mean any harm.*
plan: *He planned to leave Adelaide on Monday.*
propose: *Where do you propose building such a huge thing?*

resolve: *She resolved to report the matter.*
2 If something is intended for a particular use, you have planned that it should have this use.
e.g. The booklet is intended to be kept handy.

THESAURUS
aim: *children's games aimed at developing quickness*
design: *The house had been designed for a large family.*
earmark: *That money was earmarked for house repairs.*
mean: *I was not meant for domestic life.*

intense [ɪnˈtɛns] ADJECTIVE
1 very great in strength or amount *e.g. intense heat*

THESAURUS
acute: *an acute shortage of accommodation*
deep: *He felt a deep sense of relief.*
extreme: *Proceed with extreme caution.*
fierce: *There was fierce competition for the job.*
great: *Dawes felt a great pain and weakness.*
powerful: *I had a powerful urge to scream at him.*
profound: *The book had a profound effect in the USA.*
severe: *I had severe problems.*
2 If a person is intense, they take things very seriously and have very strong feelings.
intensely ADVERB, **intensity** NOUN

THESAURUS
ardent: *one of his most ardent supporters*
earnest: *Ella was a pious, earnest woman.*
fervent: *a fervent admirer of Beethoven's music*
fierce: *fierce loyalty to his friends*
impassioned: *He made an impassioned appeal for peace.*
passionate: *He is very passionate about the project.*
vehement: *a vehement critic of the plan*

intensify [ɪnˈtɛnsɪˌfaɪ] **intensifies, intensifying, intensified** VERB
To intensify something is to make it greater or stronger.

intensive [ɪnˈtɛnsɪv] ADJECTIVE
involving a lot of energy or effort over a very short time *e.g. an intensive training course*

intent [ɪnˈtɛnt] **intents** NOUN
1 FORMAL
A person's intent is their purpose or intention.
> ADJECTIVE
2 If you are intent on doing something, you are determined to do it.
intently ADVERB

intention [ɪnˈtɛnʃən] **intentions** NOUN
If you have an intention to do something, you have a plan of what you are going to do.

THESAURUS
aim: *The aim of this book is to inform you.*

goal: *The goal is to raise a lot of money.*
idea: *I bought books with the idea of reading them.*
object: *It was his object in life to find the island.*
objective: *His objective was to play golf and win.*
purpose: *He did not know the purpose of Vincent's visit.*

intentional [ɪnˈtɛnʃənᵊl] ADJECTIVE
If something is intentional, it is done on purpose.
intentionally ADVERB

inter- PREFIX
'Inter-' means 'between'. *e.g. inter-school competitions*

interact [ˌɪntərˈækt] **interacts, interacting, interacted** VERB
The way two people or things interact is the way they work together, communicate, or react with each other.
interaction NOUN

interactive [ˌɪntərˈæktɪv] ADJECTIVE
(ICT) Interactive television, computers and games react to decisions taken by the viewer, user or player.

intercept [ˌɪntəˈsɛpt] **intercepts, intercepting, intercepted** VERB
If you intercept someone or something that is going from one place to another, you stop them.

interchange [ˈɪntəˌtʃeɪndʒ] **interchanges** NOUN
An interchange is the act or process of exchanging things or ideas.
interchangeable ADJECTIVE

intercom [ˈɪntəˌkɒm] **intercoms** NOUN
a device consisting of a microphone and a loudspeaker, which you use to speak to people in another room

intercourse [ˈɪntəˌkɔːs] NOUN
Intercourse or sexual intercourse is the act of having sex.

interest [ˈɪntrɪst] **interests, interesting, interested** NOUN
1 If you have an interest in something or if something is of interest, you want to learn or hear more about it.

● THESAURUS
attention: *The book attracted considerable attention.*
fascination: *a lifelong fascination with the sea*
concern: *How it happened is of little concern to me.*
curiosity: *His reply satisfied our curiosity.*
2 Your interests are your hobbies.

● THESAURUS
activity: *I enjoy outdoor activities like canoeing and climbing.*
hobby: *My hobbies are football, photography and tennis.*

pastime: *His favourite pastime is golf.*
pursuit: *his favourite childhood pursuits*

3 If you have an interest in something being done, you want it to be done because it will benefit you.

4 Interest is an extra payment made to the lender by someone who has borrowed a sum of money, or by a bank or company to someone who has invested money in them. Interest is worked out as a percentage of the sum of money borrowed or invested.

> VERB
5 Something that interests you attracts your attention so that you want to learn or hear more about it.
interested ADJECTIVE

● THESAURUS
appeal: *The bright colours seem to appeal to children.*
captivate: *this author's ability to captivate young minds*
fascinate: *Politics fascinated my father.*
intrigue: *The situation intrigued him.*
stimulate: *Bill was stimulated by the challenge.*
<<OPPOSITE *bore*

interesting [ˈɪntrɪstɪŋ] ADJECTIVE
making you want to know, learn or hear more
interestingly ADVERB

● THESAURUS
absorbing: *an absorbing conversation*
compelling: *compelling drama*
entertaining: *a cheerful and entertaining companion*
gripping: *a gripping story*
intriguing: *the intriguing character of the author*
stimulating: *My trip to India had been stimulating.*
<<OPPOSITE *boring*

interface [ˈɪntəˌfeɪs] **interfaces** NOUN
1 The interface between two subjects or systems is the area in which they affect each other or are linked.

2 (ICT) The user interface of a computer program is how it is presented on the computer screen and how easy it is to operate.

interfere [ˌɪntəˈfɪə] **interferes, interfering, interfered** VERB
1 If you interfere in a situation, you try to influence it, although it does not really concern you.

● THESAURUS
butt in: *I butted in where I didn't belong.*
intervene: *Soldiers don't like civilians intervening in their affairs.*
intrude: *I don't want to intrude on your meeting.*
meddle: *Scientists should not meddle in such matters.*

tamper: *the price we pay for tampering with the environment*

2 Something that interferes with a situation has a damaging effect on it.
interference NOUN, **interfering** ADJECTIVE
[WORD HISTORY: from Old French s'ENTREFERIR meaning 'to collide']

THESAURUS
conflict: *an evening that conflicted with my work schedule*
disrupt: *Strikes disrupted air traffic in Italy.*
hinder: *A thigh injury hindered her movement.*
impede: *Fallen rocks impeded the progress of the rescue workers.*
inhibit: *factors which inhibit growth*
obstruct: *Lack of funds obstructed our progress.*

interim ['ɪntərɪm] ADJECTIVE
intended for use only until something permanent is arranged *e.g. an interim government*
[WORD HISTORY: from Latin INTERIM meaning 'meanwhile']

interior [ɪn'tɪərɪə] **interiors** NOUN
1 the inside part of something
> ADJECTIVE
2 Interior means inside. *e.g. They painted the interior walls white.*

interjection [ˌɪntə'dʒɛkʃən] **interjections** NOUN
a word or phrase spoken suddenly to express surprise, pain, or anger

interlude ['ɪntəˌluːd] **interludes** NOUN
a short break from an activity

intermediary [ˌɪntə'miːdɪərɪ] **intermediaries** NOUN
someone who tries to get two groups of people to come to an agreement

intermediate [ˌɪntə'miːdɪɪt] ADJECTIVE
An intermediate level occurs in the middle, between two other stages. *e.g. intermediate students*

interminable [ɪn'tɜːmɪnəbəl] ADJECTIVE
If something is interminable, it goes on for a very long time. *e.g. an interminable wait for the bus*
interminably ADVERB

intermission [ˌɪntə'mɪʃən] **intermissions** NOUN
an interval between two parts of a film or play

intermittent [ˌɪntə'mɪtənt] ADJECTIVE
happening only occasionally
intermittently ADVERB

internal [ɪn'tɜːnəl] ADJECTIVE
happening inside a person, place, or object
internally ADVERB

international [ˌɪntə'næʃənəl] **internationals** ADJECTIVE **(GEOGRAPHY)**
1 involving different countries
> NOUN
2 a sports match between two countries
internationally ADVERB

Internet ['ɪntəˌnɛt] NOUN
(ICT) The Internet is a worldwide communication system which people use through computers.

interplay ['ɪntəˌpleɪ] NOUN
The interplay between two things is the way they react with one another.

interpret [ɪn'tɜːprɪt] **interprets, interpreting, interpreted** VERB
1 If you interpret what someone says or does, you decide what it means.
2 If you interpret a foreign language that someone is speaking, you translate it.
interpretation NOUN, **interpreter** NOUN

interrogate [ɪn'tɛrəˌgeɪt] **interrogates, interrogating, interrogated** VERB
If you interrogate someone, you question them thoroughly to get information from them.
interrogation NOUN, **interrogator** NOUN

THESAURUS
examine: *Lawyers examined the witnesses.*
grill: informal *Jenkins kept telling police who grilled him: "I didn't kill her.".*
question: *He was questioned by police.*
quiz: *She quizzed me quite closely for a while.*

interrupt [ˌɪntə'rʌpt] **interrupts, interrupting, interrupted** VERB
1 If you interrupt someone, you start talking while they are talking.

THESAURUS
butt in: *Mirella butted in without a greeting.*
heckle: *It is easy to heckle from the safety of the audience.*

2 If you interrupt a process or activity, you stop it continuing for a time.
interruption NOUN

THESAURUS
break: *allowing passengers to break their journey with a stay in Fiji*
discontinue: *Do not discontinue the treatment without seeing your doctor.*
suspend: *Relief convoys will be suspended until the fighting stops.*

intersect [ˌɪntə'sɛkt] **intersects, intersecting, intersected** VERB
When two roads intersect, they cross each other.
intersection NOUN

interspersed [ˌɪntə'spɜːst] ADJECTIVE
If something is interspersed with things, these things occur at various points in it.

i

interval ['ɪntəvəl] **intervals** NOUN
1 the period of time between two moments or dates

🔵 THESAURUS
break: *a short break from work*
gap: *the gap between school terms*
hiatus: *There was a momentary hiatus in the sounds.*
interlude: *It was a happy interlude in the Kents' life.*
intermission: *There will be a short intermission between acts.*
pause: *a pause between two periods of intense activity*

2 (**MUSIC**) a short break during a play or concert

intervene [ˌɪntə'viːn] **intervenes, intervening, intervened** VERB
If you intervene in a situation, you step in to prevent conflict between people.
intervention NOUN

🔵 THESAURUS
arbitrate: *A committee was set up to arbitrate in the dispute.*
mediate: *efforts to mediate between the two communities*

intervening [ˌɪntə'viːnɪŋ] ADJECTIVE
An intervening period of time is one which separates two events.

interview ['ɪntəvjuː] **interviews, interviewing, interviewed** NOUN
1 a meeting at which someone asks you questions about yourself to see if you are suitable for a particular job
2 a conversation in which a journalist asks a famous person questions
> VERB
3 If you interview someone, you ask them questions about themselves.

intestine [ɪn'tɛstɪn] **intestines** NOUN
Your intestines are a long tube which carries food from your stomach through to your bowels, and in which the food is digested.
intestinal ADJECTIVE

intimate ['ɪntɪmɪt] **intimates, intimating, intimated** ADJECTIVE
1 If two people are intimate, there is a close relationship between them.
2 An intimate matter is very private and personal.
3 An intimate knowledge of something is very deep and detailed.
> VERB ['ɪntɪˌmeɪt]
4 If you intimate something, you hint at it. *e.g. He did intimate that he is considering legal action.*
intimately ADVERB, **intimacy** NOUN, **intimation** NOUN

intimidate [ɪn'tɪmɪˌdeɪt] **intimidates, intimidating, intimidated** VERB

If you intimidate someone, you frighten them in a threatening way.
intimidated ADJECTIVE, **intimidating** ADJECTIVE, **intimidation** NOUN

into ['ɪntuː] PREPOSITION
1 If something goes into something else, it goes inside it.
2 If you bump or crash into something, you hit it.
3 INFORMAL
If you are into something, you like it very much. *e.g. Nowadays I'm really into healthy food.*

intolerable [ɪn'tɒlərəbᵊl] ADJECTIVE
If something is intolerable, it is so bad that it is difficult to put up with it.
intolerably ADVERB

intonation [ˌɪntəʊ'neɪʃən] NOUN
Your intonation is the way that your voice rises and falls as you speak.

intoxicated [ɪn'tɒksɪˌkeɪtɪd] ADJECTIVE
If someone is intoxicated, they are drunk.
intoxicating ADJECTIVE, **intoxication** NOUN

intra- PREFIX
'Intra-' means 'within' or 'inside' *e.g. intra-European conflicts*

intractable [ɪn'træktəbᵊl] ADJECTIVE; FORMAL
stubborn and difficult to deal with or control

intransitive [ɪn'trænsɪtɪv] ADJECTIVE
An intransitive verb is one that does not have a direct object. For example, 'sings' is intransitive in 'She sings', but not in 'She sings a song'.

intravenous [ˌɪntrə'viːnəs] ADJECTIVE
Intravenous foods or drugs are given to sick people through their veins.
intravenously ADVERB

intrepid [ɪn'trepɪd] ADJECTIVE
not worried by danger *e.g. an intrepid explorer*
intrepidly ADVERB

intricate ['ɪntrɪkɪt] ADJECTIVE
Something that is intricate has many fine details. *e.g. walls and ceilings covered with intricate patterns*
intricately ADVERB, **intricacy** NOUN

intrigue intrigues, intriguing, intrigued
NOUN ['ɪntriːg]
1 Intrigue is the making of secret plans, often with the intention of harming other people. *e.g. political intrigue*
> VERB [ɪn'triːg]
2 If something intrigues you, you are fascinated by it and curious about it.
intriguing ADJECTIVE

intrinsic [ɪn'trɪnsɪk] ADJECTIVE; FORMAL
The intrinsic qualities of something are its basic qualities.

intrinsically ADVERB

introduce [ˌɪntrə'djuːs] **introduces, introducing, introduced** VERB

1 If you introduce one person to another, you tell them each other's name so that they can get to know each other.

2 When someone introduces a radio or television show, they say a few words at the beginning to tell you about it.

3 If you introduce someone to something, they learn about it for the first time.
introductory ADJECTIVE

introduction [ˌɪntrə'dʌkʃən] **introductions** NOUN

1 The introduction of someone or something is the act of presenting them for the first time.

● THESAURUS

establishment: *the establishment of a democratic system*
inauguration: *the inauguration of the President*
initiation: *your initiation into adulthood*
institution: *the institution of new laws*
launch: *the launch of this popular author's new book*

2 a piece of writing at the beginning of a book, which usually tells you what the book is about

● THESAURUS

foreword: *I am happy to write the foreword to this collection.*
preface: *I read through the preface quickly.*
prologue: *the General Prologue to The Canterbury Tales*

introvert ['ɪntrəˌvɜːt] **introverts** NOUN
someone who spends more time thinking about their private feelings than about the world around them, and who often finds it difficult to talk to others
introverted ADJECTIVE

intrude [ɪn'truːd] **intrudes, intruding, intruded** VERB
To intrude on someone or something is to disturb them. *e.g. I don't want to intrude on your parents.*
intruder NOUN, **intrusion** NOUN, **intrusive** ADJECTIVE

● THESAURUS

butt in: *I butted in where I didn't belong.*
encroach: *Does your work encroach on your private life?*
infringe: *She promised not to infringe on his space.*
interrupt: *Georgina interrupted his thoughts.*
trespass: *I don't like to trespass on your time.*
violate: *These men were violating her family's privacy.*

intuition [ˌɪntjʊ'ɪʃən] **intuitions** NOUN
Your intuition is a feeling you have about

something that you cannot explain. *e.g. My intuition is right about him.*
intuitive ADJECTIVE, **intuitively** ADVERB

Inuit ['ɪnjuːɪt] **Inuits;** also spelt **Innuit** NOUN
a member of a group of people who live in Northern Canada, Greenland, Alaska, and Eastern Siberia, formerly known as Eskimos

inundated [ɪnʌnˌdeɪtɪd] ADJECTIVE
If you are inundated by letters or requests, you receive so many that you cannot deal with them all.

invade [ɪn'veɪd] **invades, invading, invaded** VERB

1 If an army invades a country, it enters it by force.

● THESAURUS

attack: *Government planes attacked the town.*
enter: *The Taleban entered western Kabul.*
occupy: *Soldiers occupied the town within a few minutes.*
violate: *A helicopter violated Greek territory yesterday.*

2 If someone invades your privacy, they disturb you when you want to be alone.
invader NOUN

invalid ['ɪnvəˌlɪd] **invalids** NOUN
someone who is so ill that they need to be looked after by someone else

invalid [ɪn'vælɪd] ADJECTIVE

1 If an argument or result is invalid, it is not acceptable because it is based on a mistake.

2 If a law, marriage, or election is invalid, it is illegal because it has not been carried out properly.
invalidate VERB

invalidity [ˌɪnvə'lɪdɪtɪ] NOUN
Invalidity is the condition of being very ill for a very long time.

invaluable [ɪn'væljʊəbᵊl] ADJECTIVE
extremely useful *e.g. This book contains invaluable tips.*

invariably [ɪn'vɛərɪəblɪ] ADVERB
If something invariably happens, it almost always happens.

invasion [ɪn'veɪʒən] **invasions** NOUN

1 (HISTORY) The invasion of a country or territory is the act of entering it by force.

2 an unwanted disturbance or intrusion *e.g. an invasion of her privacy*

invective [ɪn'vɛktɪv] NOUN; FORMAL
Invective is abusive language used by someone who is angry.

invent [ɪnˈvɛnt] **invents, inventing, invented** VERB

1 If you invent a device or process, you are the first person to think of it or to use it.

● THESAURUS
coin: *Lanier coined the term 'virtual reality'.*
come up with: informal *He came up with a gadget to relieve hayfever.*
conceive: *He conceived the first portable computer.*
create: *They created a new perfume.*
formulate: *He formulated his plan for escape.*
originate: *the designer who originated platform shoes*

2 If you invent a story or an excuse, you make it up.
inventor NOUN, **invention** NOUN, **inventive** ADJECTIVE, **inventiveness** NOUN

● THESAURUS
concoct: *A newspaper concocted an imaginary interview.*
fabricate: *The evidence against them was fabricated.*
make up: *Donna was known for making up stories about herself.*
manufacture: *The children manufactured an elaborate tale.*

inventory [ˈɪnvəntərɪ] **inventories** NOUN
a written list of all the objects in a place

inverse [ɪnˈvɜːs] ADJECTIVE; FORMAL
If there is an inverse relationship between two things, one decreases as the other increases.

invertebrate [ɪnˈvɜːtɪbrɪt] **invertebrates** NOUN; TECHNICAL
a creature which does not have a spine

inverted [ɪnˈvɜːtɪd] ADJECTIVE
upside down or back to front

inverted comma **inverted commas** NOUN
Inverted commas are the punctuation marks " " or ' ', used to show where speech begins and ends.

invest [ɪnˈvɛst] **invests, investing, invested** VERB

1 If you invest money, you pay it into a bank or buy shares so that you will receive a profit.

2 If you invest in something useful, you buy it because it will help you do something better.

3 If you invest money, time, or energy in something, you try to make it a success.
investor NOUN, **investment** NOUN

investigate [ɪnˈvɛstɪˌɡeɪt] **investigates, investigating, investigated** VERB
To investigate something is to try to find out all the facts about it.

investigator NOUN, **investigation** NOUN

● THESAURUS
examine: *I have examined all the possible alternatives.*
explore: *a book which explores the history of technology*
probe: *He probed into her private life.*
research: *I'm researching for an article on New England.*
sift: *I sifted the evidence for conclusions.*
study: *Experts are studying the security in the building.*

inveterate [ɪnˈvɛtərɪt] ADJECTIVE
having lasted for a long time and not likely to stop *e.g. an inveterate gambler*

invincible [ɪnˈvɪnsəbᵊl] ADJECTIVE
unable to be defeated
invincibility NOUN

● THESAURUS
impregnable: *an impregnable fortress*
indomitable: *the indomitable spirit of the Polish people*
unbeatable: *a performance record that is unbeatable*

invisible [ɪnˈvɪzəbᵊl] ADJECTIVE
If something is invisible, you cannot see it, because it is hidden, very small, or imaginary.
invisibly ADVERB, **invisibility** NOUN

● THESAURUS
concealed: *a concealed weapon*
disguised: *a disguised panel in the wall*
hidden: *a hidden camera*
inconspicuous: *She tried to make herself inconspicuous.*
unseen: *His work was guided by an unseen hand.*
<<OPPOSITE *visible*

invite [ɪnˈvaɪt] **invites, inviting, invited** VERB

1 If you invite someone to an event, you ask them to come to it.

2 If you invite someone to do something, you ask them to do it. *e.g. Andrew has been invited to speak at the conference.*
inviting ADJECTIVE, **invitation** NOUN

invoice [ˈɪnvɔɪs] **invoices** NOUN
a bill for services or goods

invoke [ɪnˈvəʊk] **invokes, invoking, invoked** VERB

1 FORMAL
If you invoke a law, you use it to justify what you are doing.

2 If you invoke certain feelings, you cause someone to have these feelings.
[WORD HISTORY: from Latin INVOCARE meaning 'to call upon']

involuntary [ɪnˈvɒləntərɪ] ADJECTIVE
sudden and uncontrollable
involuntarily ADVERB

involve [ɪnˈvɒlv] **involves, involving, involved** VERB **(PSHE)**
If a situation involves someone or something, it includes them as a necessary part.
involvement NOUN

● THESAURUS
incorporate: *The program incorporates a range of activities.*
require: *Caring for a baby requires special skills.*
take in: *This study takes in a number of areas.*

inward or **inwards** [ˈɪnwəd] or [ˈɪnwədz]
ADJECTIVE
1 Your inward thoughts and feelings are private.

> ADJECTIVE OR ADVERB
2 If something moves inward or inwards, it moves towards the inside or centre of something.
inwardly ADVERB

iodine [ˈaɪəˌdiːn] NOUN
Iodine is a bluish-black substance used in medicine and photography.

ion [ˈaɪən] **ions** NOUN
Ions are electrically charged atoms.

iota [aɪˈəʊtə] NOUN
an extremely small amount *e.g. He did not have an iota of proof.*

IQ IQs NOUN
Your IQ is your level of intelligence shown by the results of a special test. IQ is an abbreviation for 'intelligence quotient'.

ir- PREFIX
'Ir-' means 'not' or 'the opposite of', and is the form of 'in-' which is used before the letter *r*. *e.g. irrational*

Iranian [ɪˈreɪnɪən] **Iranians** ADJECTIVE
1 belonging or relating to Iran

> NOUN
2 someone who comes from Iran
3 Iranian is the main language spoken in Iran. It is also known as Farsi.

Iraqi [ɪˈrɑːkɪ] **Iraqis** ADJECTIVE
1 belonging or relating to Iraq

> NOUN
2 someone who comes from Iraq

irate [aɪˈreɪt] ADJECTIVE
very angry

iris [ˈaɪrɪs] **irises** NOUN
1 the round, coloured part of your eye
2 a tall plant with long leaves and large blue, yellow, or white flowers

[WORD HISTORY: from Greek IRIS meaning 'rainbow' or 'coloured circle']

Irish [ˈaɪrɪʃ] ADJECTIVE
1 belonging or relating to the Irish Republic, or to the whole of Ireland

> NOUN
2 Irish or Irish Gaelic is a language spoken in some parts of Ireland.

Irishman [ˈaɪrɪʃmən] **Irishmen** NOUN
a man who comes from Ireland
Irishwoman NOUN

irk [ɜːk] **irks, irking, irked** VERB
If something irks you, it annoys you.
irksome ADJECTIVE

iron [ˈaɪən] **irons, ironing, ironed** NOUN
1 Iron is a hard dark metal used to make steel, and things like gates and fences. Small amounts of iron are found in blood.
2 a device which heats up and which you rub over clothes to remove creases

> VERB
3 If you iron clothes, you use a hot iron to remove creases from them.
ironing NOUN

iron out VERB
4 If you iron out difficulties, you solve them.

Iron Age NOUN
The Iron Age was a time about three thousand years ago when people first started to make tools out of iron.

ironbark [ˈaɪənˌbɑːk] **ironbarks** NOUN
an Australian eucalypt with a hard, rough bark

irony [ˈaɪrənɪ] NOUN
1 Irony is a form of humour in which you say the opposite of what you really mean. *e.g. They could be described, without irony, as the fortunate ones.*
2 There is irony in a situation when there is an unexpected or unusual connection between things or events. *e.g. It's a sad irony of life: once you are lost, a map is useless.*
ironic or **ironical** ADJECTIVE, **ironically** ADVERB

irrational [ɪˈræʃənᵊl] ADJECTIVE
Irrational feelings are not based on logical reasons. *e.g. irrational fears*
irrationally ADVERB, **irrationality** NOUN

● THESAURUS
absurd: *It was an absurd over-reaction.*
crazy: *crazy ideas*
illogical: *his completely illogical arguments*
nonsensical: *Such an idea sounds paradoxical, if not downright nonsensical.*
unsound: *The thinking is good-hearted, but muddled and unsound.*

i

irregular [ɪ'rɛɡjʊlə] ADJECTIVE
1 not smooth or even

● THESAURUS
asymmetrical: *She has asymmetrical features.*
bumpy: *bumpy roads*
jagged: *jagged fragments of stained glass*
lopsided: *his lopsided smile*
ragged: *the ragged edges of a tear*
uneven: *uneven teeth*
<<OPPOSITE *regular*

2 not forming a regular pattern *e.g. irregular walls*

● THESAURUS
erratic: *a planet with an erratic orbit*
haphazard: *a haphazard system*
occasional: *occasional rain showers*
patchy: *Her career has been patchy.*
random: *The stock market is random and unpredictable.*
variable: *a variable rate of interest*
<<OPPOSITE *regular*

3 (MATHS) Irregular things are uneven or unequal, or are not symmetrical.
irregularly ADVERB, **irregularity** NOUN

irrelevant [ɪ'rɛləvənt] ADJECTIVE
(LIBRARY) not directly connected with a subject *e.g. He either ignored questions or gave irrelevant answers.*
irrelevance NOUN

irrepressible [,ɪrɪ'prɛsəbəl] ADJECTIVE
Someone who is irrepressible is lively and cheerful.

irresistible [,ɪrɪ'zɪstəbəl] ADJECTIVE
1 unable to be controlled *e.g. an irresistible urge to yawn*

2 extremely attractive *e.g. Women always found him irresistible.*
irresistibly ADVERB

irrespective [,ɪrɪ'spɛktɪv] ADJECTIVE
If you say something will be done irrespective of certain things, you mean it will be done without taking those things into account.

irresponsible [,ɪrɪ'spɒnsəbəl] ADJECTIVE
An irresponsible person does things without considering the consequences. *e.g. an irresponsible driver*
irresponsibly ADVERB, **irresponsibility** NOUN

● THESAURUS
careless: *a careless driver*
reckless: *reckless spending*
thoughtless: *a thoughtless remark*
wild: *a night of wild abandon*
<<OPPOSITE *responsible*

irrigate ['ɪrɪ,ɡeɪt] **irrigates, irrigating, irrigated** VERB

To irrigate land is to supply it with water brought through pipes or ditches.
irrigated ADJECTIVE, **irrigation** NOUN

irritable ['ɪrɪtəbəl] ADJECTIVE
easily annoyed

● THESAURUS
bad-tempered: *You're very bad-tempered today.*
cantankerous: *a cantankerous old man*
petulant: *He was like a petulant child.*
ratty: British and New Zealand; informal *There's no need to get ratty.*

irritate ['ɪrɪ,teɪt] **irritates, irritating, irritated** VERB
1 If something irritates you, it annoys you.

● THESAURUS
anger: *This article angered me.*
annoy: *It just annoyed me to hear him going on.*
bother: *Nothing bothers me.*
exasperate: *Bertha was exasperated by the delay.*
needle: informal *If her remark needled him, he didn't show it.*

2 If something irritates part of your body, it makes it tender, sore, or itchy.
irritant NOUN, **irritation** NOUN

is [ɪs] the third person, present tense of **be**

-ish SUFFIX
'-ish' forms adjectives that mean 'fairly' or 'rather' *e.g. smallish... greenish*

Islam ['ɪzlɑ:m] NOUN
(RE) Islam is the Muslim religion, which teaches that there is only one God, Allah, and Mohammed is his prophet. The holy book of Islam is the Koran.
Islamic ADJECTIVE
[WORD HISTORY: from Arabic ISLAM meaning 'surrender to God']

island ['aɪlənd] **islands** NOUN
a piece of land surrounded on all sides by water
islander NOUN

isle [aɪl] **isles** NOUN; LITERARY
an island

-ism SUFFIX
1 '-ism' forms nouns that refer to an action or condition. *e.g. criticism... heroism*

2 '-ism' forms nouns that refer to a political or economic system or a system of beliefs. *e.g. Marxism... Sikhism.*

3 '-ism' forms nouns that refer to a type of prejudice. *e.g. racism... sexism*

isolate ['aɪsə,leɪt] **isolates, isolating, isolated** VERB
1 If something isolates you or if you isolate yourself, you are set apart from other people.

2 If you isolate something, you separate it from everything else.
isolated ADJECTIVE, **isolation** NOUN

isosceles [aɪ'sɒsɪ͵liːz] ADJECTIVE
(MATHS) An isosceles triangle has two sides of the same length.

ISP
an abbreviation for 'internet service provider'

Israeli [ɪz'reɪlɪ] **Israelis** ADJECTIVE **(RE)**
1 belonging or relating to Israel
> NOUN
2 someone who comes from Israel

issue ['ɪʃjuː] **issues, issuing, issued** NOUN
1 an important subject that people are talking about

● THESAURUS
concern: *Political concerns continue to dominate the news.*
matter: *He touched on many matters in his speech.*
problem: *the energy problem*
question: *The whole question of aid is a tricky one.*
subject: *the president's views on the subject*
topic: *the main topic for discussion*

2 a particular edition of a newspaper or magazine

● THESAURUS
copy: *a copy of "USA Today"*
edition: *There's an article about the film in next month's edition.*
instalment: *a magazine published in monthly instalments*

> VERB
3 If you issue a statement or a warning, you say it formally and publicly.

● THESAURUS
deliver: *He delivered a speech to his fellow union members.*
give: *The minister gave a warning that war should be avoided at all costs.*
make: *He says he was depressed when he made the statement.*
pronounce: *The authorities took time to pronounce their verdicts.*
read out: *She read out an announcement outside the court.*
release: *The police are not releasing any more details about the attack.*
<<OPPOSITE *withdraw*

4 If someone issues something, they officially give it. *e.g. Staff were issued with plastic cards.*

● THESAURUS
equip: *plans to equip the reserve army with guns*
furnish: formal *They will furnish you with the necessary items.*
give out: *The prizes were given out by a local dignitary.*

provide: *The government was unable to provide them with food.*
supply: *an agreement not to supply these countries with chemical weapons*

-ist SUFFIX
1 '-ist' forms nouns and adjectives which refer to someone who is involved in a certain activity, or who believes in a certain system or religion. *e.g. chemist... motorist... Buddhist.*

2 '-ist' forms nouns and adjectives which refer to someone who has a certain prejudice. *e.g. racist*

isthmus ['ɪsməs] **isthmuses** NOUN
a narrow strip of land connecting two larger areas

it [ɪt] PRONOUN
1 'It' is used to refer to something that has already been mentioned, or to a situation or fact. *e.g. It was a difficult decision.*

2 'It' is used to refer to people or animals whose sex is not known. *e.g. If a baby is thirsty, it feeds more often.*

3 You use 'it' to make statements about the weather, time, or date. *e.g. It's noon.*

Italian [ɪ'tæljən] **Italians** ADJECTIVE
1 belonging or relating to Italy
> NOUN
2 someone who comes from Italy
3 Italian is the main language spoken in Italy.

italics [ɪ'tælɪks] PLURAL NOUN
Italics are letters printed in a special sloping way, and are often used to emphasize something.
italic ADJECTIVE

itch [ɪtʃ] **itches, itching, itched** VERB
1 When your skin itches, it has an unpleasant feeling and you want to scratch it.

2 If you are itching to do something, you are impatient to do it.

> NOUN
3 an unpleasant feeling on your skin that you want to scratch
itchy ADJECTIVE

item ['aɪtəm] **items** NOUN
1 one of a collection or list of objects

● THESAURUS
article: *articles of clothing*
matter: *He dealt with a variety of matters.*
point: *Many of the points in the report are correct.*
thing: *Big things are paid for by the government.*

2 a newspaper or magazine article

● THESAURUS
article: *a short article in one of the papers*
feature: *The magazine contained a special feature on the project.*

notice: *notices in today's national newspapers*
piece: *I disagree with your recent piece about Australia.*
report: *a film report on the scandal*

itinerary [aɪˈtɪnərərɪ] **itineraries** NOUN
a plan of a journey, showing a route to follow and places to visit

-itis SUFFIX
'-itis' is added to the name of a part of the body to refer to disease or inflammation in that part. *e.g. appendicitis... tonsillitis*

its [ɪts] ADJECTIVE OR PRONOUN
'Its' refers to something belonging to or relating to things, children, or animals that have already been mentioned *e.g. The lion lifted its head.*

> Many people are confused about the difference between *its* and *it's*. *Its*, without the apostrophe, is the possessive form of *it*: *the cat has hurt its paw*. *It's*, with the apostrophe, is a short form of *it is* or *it has*: *it's green; it's been snowing again*.

itself [ɪtˈsɛlf] PRONOUN
1 'Itself' is used when the same thing, child, or animal does an action and is affected by it. *e.g. Paris prides itself on its luxurious hotels.*

2 'Itself' is used to emphasize 'it'.

-ity SUFFIX
'-ity' forms nouns that refer to a state or condition. *e.g. continuity... technicality*

-ive SUFFIX
'-ive' forms adjectives and some nouns. *e.g. massive... detective*

ivory [ˈaɪvərɪ] NOUN
1 the valuable creamy-white bone which forms the tusk of an elephant. It is used to make ornaments
> NOUN OR ADJECTIVE
2 creamy-white

ivy [ˈaɪvɪ] NOUN
an evergreen plant which creeps along the ground and up walls

iwi [ˈiːwɪː] **iwi** or **iwis** NOUN
In New Zealand, a Maori tribe.

-ize or **-ise** SUFFIX
'-ize' and '-ise' forms verbs. Most verbs can be spelt with either ending, though there are some that can only be spelt with '-ise', for example *advertise*, *improvise* and *revise*.
[WORD HISTORY: from the Greek suffix -IZEIN]

jab [dʒæb] **jabs, jabbing, jabbed** VERB
  1 To jab something means to poke at it roughly.
  > NOUN
  2 a sharp or sudden poke
  3 INFORMAL an injection

jabiru [ˈdʒæbɪˌruː] **jabirus** NOUN
  a white-and-green Australian stork with red legs

jack [dʒæk] **jacks, jacking, jacked** NOUN
  1 a piece of equipment for lifting heavy objects, especially for lifting a car when changing a wheel
  2 In a pack of cards, a jack is a card whose value is between a ten and a queen.
  > VERB
  3 To jack up an object means to raise it, especially by using a jack.

jackal [ˈdʒækɔːl] **jackals** NOUN
  a wild animal related to the dog

jackaroo [ˌdʒækəˈruː] **jackaroos**; also spelt **jackeroo** NOUN
  In Australia, a young person learning the work of a sheep or cattle station.

jackdaw [ˈdʒækˌdɔː] **jackdaws** NOUN
  a bird like a small crow with black and grey feathers

jacket [ˈdʒækɪt] **jackets** NOUN
  1 a short coat reaching to the waist or hips
  2 an outer covering for something *e.g. a book jacket*
  3 The jacket of a baked potato is its skin.

jackpot [ˈdʒækˌpɒt] **jackpots** NOUN
  In a gambling game, the jackpot is the top prize.

jack up **jacks up, jacking up, jacked up** VERB; INFORMAL
  In New Zealand English, to jack up is to organize or prepare something.

jade [dʒeɪd] NOUN
  Jade is a hard green stone used for making jewellery and ornaments.

jagged [ˈdʒægɪd] ADJECTIVE
  sharp and spiky
  ⬤ THESAURUS
  barbed: *barbed wire*

craggy: *craggy mountains*
rough: *the rough surface of the rock*
serrated: *a serrated knife*
<<OPPOSITE *smooth*

jaguar [ˈdʒægjʊə] **jaguars** NOUN
  a large member of the cat family with spots on its back

jail [dʒeɪl] **jails, jailing, jailed**; also spelt **gaol** NOUN
  1 a building where people convicted of a crime are locked up
  ⬤ THESAURUS
  nick: British, Australian and New Zealand; slang *He spent seven years in the nick.*
  prison: *his release from prison*
  > VERB
  2 To jail someone means to lock them up in a jail.
  ⬤ THESAURUS
  detain: *Police can detain a suspect for 48 hours.*
  imprison: *imprisoned for 18 months on charges of theft*
  incarcerate: *They have been incarcerated as political prisoners.*

jailer [ˈdʒeɪlə] **jailers**; also spelt **gaoler** NOUN
  a person who is in charge of the prisoners in a jail

jam [dʒæm] **jams, jamming, jammed** NOUN
  1 a food, made by boiling fruit and sugar together until it sets
  2 a situation in which it is impossible to move *e.g. a traffic jam*
  ⬤ THESAURUS
  crowd: *elbowing his way through the crowd*
  crush: *We got separated in the crush.*
  mass: *a mass of excited fans*
  mob: *a growing mob of demonstrators*
  multitude: *surrounded by a noisy multitude*
  throng: *An official pushed through the throng.*
  > AN INFORMAL PHRASE
  3 If someone is **in a jam**, they are in a difficult situation.
  ⬤ THESAURUS
  dilemma: *faced with a dilemma*
  fix: informal *a difficult economic fix*

hole: slang *He admitted that the government was in a hole.*
plight: *the plight of the Third World countries*
predicament: *a way out of our predicament*
quandary: *We're in a quandary over our holiday plans.*
trouble: *You are in serious trouble.*

> VERB

4 If people or things are jammed into a place, they are squeezed together so closely that they can hardly move.

5 To jam something somewhere means to push it there roughly. *e.g. He jammed his foot on the brake.*

● THESAURUS

cram: *He crammed the bank notes into his pocket.*
force: *I forced the key into the ignition.*
ram: *He rammed the muzzle of the gun against my forehead.*
stuff: *She stuffed the newspaper into a litter bin.*

6 If something is jammed, it is stuck or unable to work properly.

● THESAURUS

stall: *The engine stalled.*
stick: *She tried to open the window but it was stuck.*

7 To jam a radio signal means to interfere with it and prevent it from being received clearly.

Jamaican [dʒəˈmeɪkən] **Jamaicans**
ADJECTIVE
1 belonging or relating to Jamaica
> NOUN
2 someone who comes from Jamaica

jamboree [ˌdʒæmbəˈriː] **jamborees** NOUN
a gathering of large numbers of people enjoying themselves

Jandal [ˈdʒændəl] **Jandals** NOUN; TRADEMARK
In New Zealand, a sandal with a strap between the big toe and other toes and over the foot.

jangle [ˈdʒæŋɡəl] **jangles, jangling, jangled**
VERB
1 If something jangles, it makes a harsh metallic ringing noise.
> NOUN
2 the sound made by metal objects striking against each other

janitor [ˈdʒænɪtə] **janitors** NOUN
the caretaker of a building

January [ˈdʒænjʊərɪ] NOUN
January is the first month of the year. It has 31 days.
[WORD HISTORY: from Latin JANUARIUS meaning 'the month of Janus', named after a Roman god]

Japanese [ˌdʒæpəˈniːz] ADJECTIVE
1 belonging or relating to Japan
> NOUN
2 someone who comes from Japan
3 Japanese is the main language spoken in Japan.

jar [dʒɑː] **jars, jarring, jarred** NOUN
1 a glass container with a wide top used for storing food
> VERB
2 If something jars on you, you find it unpleasant or annoying.

jargon [ˈdʒɑːɡən] NOUN
Jargon consists of words that are used in special or technical ways by particular groups of people, often making the language difficult to understand.

jarrah [ˈdʒærə] **jarrahs** NOUN
an Australian eucalypt tree that produces wood used for timber

jasmine [ˈdʒæsmɪn] NOUN
Jasmine is a climbing plant with small sweet-scented white flowers.

jaundice [ˈdʒɔːndɪs] NOUN
Jaundice is an illness affecting the liver, in which the skin and the whites of the eyes become yellow.

jaundiced [ˈdʒɔːndɪst] ADJECTIVE
pessimistic and lacking enthusiasm *e.g. He takes a rather jaundiced view of politicians.*

jaunt [dʒɔːnt] **jaunts** NOUN
a journey or trip you go on for pleasure

jaunty [ˈdʒɔːntɪ] **jauntier, jauntiest**
ADJECTIVE
expressing cheerfulness and self-confidence *e.g. a jaunty tune*
jauntily ADVERB

javelin [ˈdʒævlɪn] **javelins** NOUN
a long spear that is thrown in sports competitions

jaw [dʒɔː] **jaws** NOUN
1 A person's or animal's jaw is the bone in which the teeth are set.
2 A person's or animal's mouth and teeth are their jaws.

jay [dʒeɪ] **jays** NOUN
a kind of noisy chattering bird

jazz [dʒæz] **jazzes, jazzing, jazzed** NOUN
1 Jazz is a style of popular music with a forceful rhythm.
> VERB
2 INFORMAL To jazz something up means to make it more colourful or exciting.

jazzy [ˈdʒæzɪ] **jazzier, jazziest** ADJECTIVE; INFORMAL bright and showy

jealous ['dʒɛləs] ADJECTIVE

1 If you are jealous, you feel bitterness towards someone who has something that you would like to have.

● **THESAURUS**
envious: *envious of the attention his brother was getting*
resentful: *resentful of her husband's hobby*

2 If you are jealous of something you have, you feel you must try to keep it from other people.
jealously ADVERB, **jealousy** NOUN

jeans ['dʒiːnz] PLURAL NOUN
Jeans are casual denim trousers.

jeep ['dʒiːp] **jeeps** NOUN; TRADEMARK
a small road vehicle with four-wheel drive

jeer ['dʒɪə] **jeers, jeering, jeered** VERB

1 If you jeer at someone, you insult them in a loud, unpleasant way.

> NOUN
2 Jeers are rude and insulting remarks.
jeering ADJECTIVE

Jehovah ['dʒɪ'həʊvə] PROPER NOUN
Jehovah is the name of God in the Old Testament.
[WORD HISTORY: from adding vowels to the Hebrew JHVH, the sacred name of God]

jelly ['dʒɛlɪ] **jellies** NOUN

1 a clear, sweet food eaten as a dessert

2 a type of clear, set jam

jellyfish ['dʒɛlɪ,fɪʃ] **jellyfishes** NOUN
a sea animal with a clear soft body and tentacles which may sting

jeopardize ['dʒɛpə,daɪz] **jeopardizes, jeopardizing, jeopardized**; also spelt
jeopardise VERB
To jeopardize something means to do something which puts it at risk. *e.g. Elaine jeopardized her health.*

jeopardy ['dʒɛpədɪ] NOUN
If someone or something is in jeopardy, they are at risk of failing or of being destroyed.

jerk ['dʒɜːk] **jerks, jerking, jerked** VERB

1 To jerk something means to give it a sudden, sharp pull.

2 If something jerks, it moves suddenly and sharply.

> NOUN
3 a sudden sharp movement

4 INFORMAL
If you call someone a jerk, you mean they are stupid.

jerky ADJECTIVE, **jerkily** ADVERB

jerkin ['dʒɜːkɪn] **jerkins** NOUN
a short sleeveless jacket

jersey ['dʒɜːzɪ] **jerseys** NOUN

1 a knitted garment for the upper half of the body

2 Jersey is a type of knitted woollen or cotton fabric used to make clothing.

jest ['dʒɛst] **jests, jesting, jested** NOUN

1 a joke

> VERB
2 To jest means to speak jokingly.

jester ['dʒɛstə] **jesters** NOUN
In the past, a jester was a man who was kept to amuse the king or queen.

jet ['dʒɛt] **jets, jetting, jetted** NOUN

1 a plane which is able to fly very fast

2 a stream of liquid, gas, or flame forced out under pressure

3 Jet is a hard black stone, usually highly polished and used in jewellery and ornaments.

> VERB
4 To jet somewhere means to fly there in a plane, especially a jet.

jet boat jet boats NOUN
In New Zealand, a motor boat that is powered by a jet of water at the rear.

jet lag NOUN
Jet lag is a feeling of tiredness or confusion that people have after a long flight across different time zones.

jettison ['dʒɛtɪsən] **jettisons, jettisoning, jettisoned** VERB
If you jettison something, you throw it away because you no longer want it.

jetty ['dʒɛtɪ] **jetties** NOUN
a wide stone wall or wooden platform at the edge of the sea or a river, where boats can be moored

Jew ['dʒuː] **Jews** (RE) NOUN
a person who practises the religion of Judaism, or who is of Hebrew descent
Jewish ADJECTIVE
[WORD HISTORY: from JUDAH, the name of a Jewish patriarch]

jewel ['dʒuːəl] **jewels** NOUN
a precious stone used to decorate valuable ornaments or jewellery
jewelled ADJECTIVE

jeweller ['dʒuːələ] **jewellers** NOUN
a person who makes jewellery or who sells and repairs jewellery and watches

jewellery ['dʒuːəlrɪ] NOUN
Jewellery consists of ornaments that people

j

wear, such as rings or necklaces, made of valuable metals and sometimes decorated with precious stones.

jib [dʒɪb] **jibs** NOUN
a small sail towards the front of a sailing boat

jibe [dʒaɪb] another spelling of **gibe**

jig [dʒɪg] **jigs, jigging, jigged** NOUN
1 a type of lively folk dance
> VERB
2 If you jig, you dance around in a lively bouncy manner.

jiggle ['dʒɪgəl] **jiggles, jiggling, jiggled** VERB
If you jiggle something, you move it around with quick jerky movements.

jigsaw ['dʒɪgsɔː] **jigsaws** NOUN
a puzzle consisting of a picture on cardboard that has been cut up into small pieces, which have to be put together again

jihad [dʒɪ'hæd] **jihads** NOUN
1 a holy war waged to defend or further the ideals of Islam
2 Jihad also means the personal struggle of a Muslim against against sin

jilt [dʒɪlt] **jilts, jilting, jilted** VERB
If you jilt someone, you suddenly break off your relationship with them.
jilted ADJECTIVE

jingle ['dʒɪŋgəl] **jingles, jingling, jingled** NOUN
1 a short, catchy phrase or rhyme set to music and used to advertise something on radio or television
2 the sound of something jingling
> VERB
3 When something jingles, it makes a tinkling sound like small bells.

jinks [dʒɪŋks] PLURAL NOUN
High jinks is boisterous and mischievous behaviour.

jinx [dʒɪŋks] **jinxes** NOUN
someone or something that is thought to bring bad luck *e.g. He was beginning to think he was a jinx.*

jinxed [dʒɪŋkst] ADJECTIVE
If something is jinxed it is considered to be unlucky. *e.g. I think this house is jinxed.*

jitters ['dʒɪtəz] PLURAL NOUN; INFORMAL
If you have got the jitters, you are feeling very nervous.
jittery ADJECTIVE

job [dʒɒb] **jobs** NOUN
1 the work that someone does to earn money

THESAURUS
employment: *unable to find employment*
occupation: *his occupation as a carpenter*
position: *He's leaving to take up a position abroad.*
post: *She has resigned her post as his assistant.*
profession: *She chose nursing as her profession.*
trade: *her trade as a jeweller*

2 a duty or responsibility *e.g. It is a captain's job to lead from the front.*

THESAURUS
concern: *The technical aspects are the concern of the engineers.*
duty: *I consider it my duty to write and thank you.*
function: *an important function to fill*
responsibility: *It's not my responsibility to look after your mother.*
role: *Our role is to keep the peace.*
task: *She had the task of breaking the bad news.*
> PHRASE
3 If something is **just the job**, it is exactly right or exactly what you wanted.

job centre job centres NOUN
a government office where people can find out about job vacancies

jobless ['dʒɒbləs] ADJECTIVE
without any work

jockey ['dʒɒkɪ] **jockeys, jockeying, jockeyed** NOUN
1 someone who rides a horse in a race
> VERB
2 To jockey for a position means to manoeuvre in order to gain an advantage over other people.

jocular ['dʒɒkjʊlə] ADJECTIVE
A jocular comment is intended to make people laugh.

jodhpurs ['dʒɒdpəz] PLURAL NOUN
Jodhpurs are close-fitting trousers worn when riding a horse.
[WORD HISTORY: from JODHPUR, the name of a town in N. India]

joey ['dʒəʊɪ] **joeys** NOUN; INFORMAL
In Australian English, a young kangaroo or other young animal.

jog [dʒɒg] **jogs, jogging, jogged** VERB
1 To jog means to run slowly and rhythmically, often as a form of exercise.
2 If you jog something, you knock it slightly so that it shakes or moves.
3 If someone or something jogs your memory, they remind you of something.
> NOUN
4 a slow run
jogger NOUN, **jogging** NOUN

join [dʒɔɪn] **joins, joining, joined** VERB

1 When two things join, or when one thing joins another, they come together.

2 If you join a club or organization, you become a member of it or start taking part in it.

● THESAURUS
enlist: *He was 18 when he enlisted in the US Navy.*
enrol: *She has enrolled in an acting class.*
sign up: *I've signed up as a member.*
<<OPPOSITE *resign*

3 To join two things means to fasten them.

● THESAURUS
attach: *The gadget can be attached to any surface.*
connect: *two rooms connected by a passage*
couple: *an engine coupled to a gearbox*
fasten: *a wooden bench fastened to the floor*
link: *tree houses linked by ropes*
tie: *He tied the dog to a post by its leash.*
<<OPPOSITE *separate*

> NOUN
4 a place where two things are fastened together

join up VERB
5 If someone joins up, they become a member of the armed forces.

joiner ['dʒɔɪnə] **joiners** NOUN
a person who makes wooden window frames, doors, and furniture

joinery ['dʒɔɪnərɪ] NOUN
Joinery is the work done by a joiner.

joint [dʒɔɪnt] **joints, jointing, jointed**
ADJECTIVE
1 shared by or belonging to two or more people *e.g. a joint building society account*

> NOUN
2 a part of the body where two bones meet and are joined together so that they can move, for example a knee or hip

3 a place where two things are fixed together

4 a large piece of meat suitable for roasting

5 INFORMAL any place of entertainment, such as a nightclub or pub

> VERB
6 To joint meat means to cut it into large pieces according to where the bones are.
jointly ADVERB, **jointed** ADJECTIVE

joist [dʒɔɪst] **joists** NOUN
a large beam used to support floors or ceilings

joke [dʒəʊk] **jokes, joking, joked** NOUN
1 something that you say or do to make people laugh, such as a funny story

● THESAURUS
gag: informal *a gag about unscrupulous lawyers*
jest: *It was only intended as a jest.*

lark: *They just did it for a lark.*
prank: *an end-of-term prank*
quip: *a famous quip by Groucho Marx*
wisecrack: informal *She was tempted to make a wisecrack.*
witticism: *laughing at each other's witticisms*

2 anything that you think is ridiculous and not worthy of respect *e.g. The decision was a joke.*

> VERB
3 If you are joking, you are teasing someone.
jokingly ADVERB

● THESAURUS
banter: *He played trick shots and bantered with the crowd.*
chaff: *They chaffed us about our chances of winning.*
jest: *drinking and jesting with his cronies*
kid: informal *Don't worry, I'm only kidding.*
quip: *"You'll have to go on a diet," he quipped.*
tease: *"You must be in love," she teased.*

joker ['dʒəʊkə] **jokers** NOUN
In a pack of cards, a joker is an extra card that does not belong to any of the four suits, but is used in some games.

jolly ['dʒɒlɪ] **jollier, jolliest** ADJECTIVE
1 happy, cheerful, and pleasant

> ADVERB
2 INFORMAL Jolly also means very. *e.g. jolly good fun*

jolt [dʒəʊlt] **jolts, jolting, jolted** VERB
1 To jolt means to move or shake roughly and violently.

2 If you are jolted by something, it gives you an unpleasant surprise.

> NOUN
3 a sudden jerky movement

4 an unpleasant shock or surprise

jostle ['dʒɒsəl] **jostles, jostling, jostled**
VERB
To jostle means to push roughly against people in a crowd.

jot [dʒɒt] **jots, jotting, jotted** VERB
1 If you jot something down, you write it quickly in the form of a short informal note.

> NOUN
2 a very small amount
jotting NOUN

jotter ['dʒɒtə] **jotters** NOUN
a pad or notebook

joule [dʒuːl] **joules** NOUN
a unit of energy or work

journal ['dʒɜːnəl] **journals** NOUN
1 a magazine that deals with a particular subject, trade, or profession

j

2 a diary which someone keeps regularly

journalism ['dʒɜːnˀˌlɪzəm] NOUN
Journalism is the work of collecting, writing, and publishing news in newspapers, magazines, and on television and radio.
journalist NOUN, **journalistic** ADJECTIVE

journey ['dʒɜːnɪ] **journeys, journeying, journeyed** NOUN
1 the act of travelling from one place to another

⬤ THESAURUS
excursion: *The trip includes an excursion to Zermatt.*
expedition: *an expedition to the South Pole*
passage: *a 10-hour passage from Swansea*
tour: *a two-month tour of Europe*
trek: *a trek through the Gobi desert*
trip: *a business trip*
voyage: *the first space shuttle voyage*

> VERB
2 FORMAL To journey somewhere means to travel there. *e.g. He intended to journey up the Amazon.*

⬤ THESAURUS
go: *We went from Glasgow to London in six hours.*
proceed: *proceeding along the road in the wrong direction*
tour: *He toured China in 1993.*
travel: *Gran travelled down by train.*
trek: *trekking through the jungle*
voyage: *They voyaged as far as Spain.*

joust [dʒaʊst] **jousts** NOUN
In medieval times, a joust was a competition between knights fighting on horseback, using lances.

jovial ['dʒəʊvɪəl] ADJECTIVE
cheerful and friendly
jovially ADVERB, **joviality** NOUN

joy [dʒɔɪ] **joys** NOUN
1 Joy is a feeling of great happiness.

⬤ THESAURUS
bliss: *an expression of pure bliss*
delight: *He let out a yell of delight.*
ecstasy: *Her eyes closed in ecstasy.*
elation: *He felt a surge of elation at the news.*
rapture: *His speech was received with rapture.*
<<OPPOSITE *misery*

2 INFORMAL
Joy also means success or luck. *e.g. Any joy with your insurance claim?.*

3 something that makes you happy or gives you pleasure

joyful ['dʒɔɪfʊl] ADJECTIVE
1 causing pleasure and happiness
2 Someone who is joyful is extremely happy.
joyfully ADVERB

⬤ THESAURUS
delighted: *I'm delighted to be here.*
elated: *the elated faces of the freed hostages*
jubilant: *the jubilant crowds*
over the moon: informal *I was over the moon to hear about your promotion.*

joyous ['dʒɔɪəs] ADJECTIVE; FORMAL
joyful
joyously ADVERB

joyride ['dʒɔɪˌraɪd] **joyrides** NOUN
a drive in a stolen car for pleasure
joyriding NOUN, **joyrider** NOUN

joystick ['dʒɔɪˌstɪk] **joysticks** NOUN
a lever in an aircraft which the pilot uses to control height and direction

jube ['dʒuːb] **jubes** NOUN; INFORMAL
In Australian and New Zealand English, a fruit-flavoured jelly sweet.

jubilant ['dʒuːbɪlənt] ADJECTIVE
feeling or expressing great happiness or triumph
jubilantly ADVERB

jubilation [ˌdʒuːbɪˈleɪʃən] NOUN
Jubilation is a feeling of great happiness and triumph.

jubilee ['dʒuːbɪˌliː] **jubilees** NOUN
a special anniversary of an event such as a coronation *e.g. Queen Elizabeth's Silver Jubilee in 1977.*
[WORD HISTORY: from Hebrew YOBHEL meaning 'ram's horn'; rams' horns were blown during festivals and celebrations]

Judaism ['dʒuːdeɪˌɪzəm] NOUN
(RE) Judaism is the religion of the Jewish people. It is based on a belief in one God, and draws its laws and authority from the Old Testament.
Judaic ADJECTIVE

judder ['dʒʌdə] **judders, juddering, juddered** VERB
To judder means to shake and vibrate noisily and violently.

judder bar judder bars NOUN
In New Zealand English, a bump built across a road to stop drivers from going too fast. In Britain it is called a sleeping policeman.

judge [dʒʌdʒ] **judges, judging, judged** NOUN
1 the person in a law court who decides how the law should be applied to people who appear in the court

⬤ THESAURUS
beak: British; slang *a third appearance before the beak*
justice: *his appointment as a Justice of the High Court*

magistrate: *defendants appearing before a magistrate*

2 someone who decides the winner in a contest or competition

● THESAURUS
referee: *The referee awarded a free kick against Rourke.*
umpire: *The umpire's decision is final.*

> VERB

3 If you judge someone or something, you form an opinion about them based on the evidence that you have.

● THESAURUS
appraise: *The teachers are appraised by an official.*
assess: *It is too early to assess the impact of the change.*
consider: *We consider him to be dangerous.*
estimate: *The cost of the damage is estimated at over a million dollars.*
evaluate: *a test to evaluate a candidate's potential*
rate: *The film was rated a hit.*

4 To judge a contest or competition means to decide on the winner.

● THESAURUS
referee: *He has refereed in two World Cups.*
umpire: *He umpired baseball games.*

judgment [ˈdʒʌdʒmənt] **judgments**; also spelt **judgement** NOUN
an opinion or decision based on evidence

● THESAURUS
appraisal: *a calm appraisal of the situation*
assessment: *my own personal assessment of our position*
conclusion: *I've come to the conclusion that she knows what she's talking about.*
opinion: *Seek a medical opinion before you travel.*
ruling: *a High Court ruling*
verdict: *The doctor's verdict was that he was entirely healthy.*
view: *In my view, things aren't going to get any better.*

> *Judgment* and *judgement* are both correct spellings

judicial [dʒuːˈdɪʃəl] ADJECTIVE
relating to judgment or to justice *e.g. a judicial review*

judiciary [dʒuːˈdɪʃɪərɪ] NOUN
The judiciary is the branch of government concerned with justice and the legal system.

judicious [dʒuːˈdɪʃəs] ADJECTIVE
sensible and showing good judgment
judiciously ADVERB

judo [ˈdʒuːdəʊ] NOUN
Judo is a sport in which two people try to force each other to the ground using special throwing techniques.

jug [dʒʌg] **jugs** NOUN
a container with a lip or spout used for holding or serving liquids

juggernaut [ˈdʒʌgə,nɔːt] NOUN
a large heavy lorry
[WORD HISTORY: from Hindi JAGANNATH, the name of a huge idol of the god Krishna, which every year is wheeled through the streets of Puri in India]

juggle [ˈdʒʌgəl] **juggles, juggling, juggled** VERB
To juggle means to throw objects into the air, catching them in sequence, and tossing them up again so there are several in the air at one time.
juggler NOUN

jugular [ˈdʒʌgjʊlə] **jugulars** NOUN
The jugular or jugular vein is one of the veins in the neck which carry blood from the head back to the heart.

juice [dʒuːs] **juices** NOUN
1 Juice is the liquid that can be squeezed or extracted from fruit or other food.
2 Juices in the body are fluids. *e.g. gastric juices*

juicy [ˈdʒuːsɪ] **juicier, juiciest** ADJECTIVE
1 Juicy food has a lot of juice in it.
2 Something that is juicy is interesting, exciting, or scandalous. *e.g. a juicy bit of gossip*

jukebox [ˈdʒuːkˌbɒks] **jukeboxes** NOUN
a large record player found in cafés and pubs which automatically plays a selected record when coins are inserted

July [dʒuːˈlaɪ] NOUN
July is the seventh month of the year. It has 31 days.
[WORD HISTORY: from Latin JULIUS, the month of July, named after Julius Caesar by the Romans]

jumble [ˈdʒʌmbəl] **jumbles, jumbling, jumbled** NOUN
1 an untidy muddle of things
2 Jumble consists of articles for a jumble sale.
> VERB
3 To jumble things means to mix them up untidily.

jumble sale jumble sales NOUN
an event at which cheap second-hand clothes and other articles are sold to raise money, usually for a charity

jumbo [ˈdʒʌmbəʊ] **jumbos** NOUN
1 A jumbo or jumbo jet is a large jet aeroplane that can carry several hundred passengers.
> ADJECTIVE
2 very large *e.g. jumbo packs of elastic bands*
[WORD HISTORY: from JUMBO, the name of a famous 19th-century elephant]

jumbuck [ˈdʒʌmˌbʌk] **jumbucks** NOUN; OLD-
FASHIONED, INFORMAL
In Australian English, a sheep.

jump [dʒʌmp] **jumps, jumping, jumped**
VERB

1 To jump means to spring off the ground using
your leg muscles.

2 To jump something means to spring off the
ground and move over or across it.

● THESAURUS
bound: *He bounded up the steps.*
clear: *The horse cleared the gate by inches.*
hurdle: *He crossed the lawn and hurdled the fence.*
leap: *He had leapt from a window and escaped.*
spring: *The lion roared once and sprang.*
vault: *Ned vaulted over a fallen tree.*

3 If you jump at something such as an
opportunity, you accept it eagerly.

4 If you jump on someone, you criticize them
suddenly and forcefully.

5 If someone jumps, they make a sudden sharp
movement of surprise.

6 If an amount or level jumps, it suddenly
increases.

● THESAURUS
escalate: *Costs escalated dramatically.*
increase: *Trading has increased by 20% this month.*
rise: *Unemployment is rising rapidly.*
surge: *The party's share of the vote surged from 10%
to 17%.*

> NOUN

7 a spring into the air, sometimes over an object

● THESAURUS
bound: *With one bound Jack was free.*
leap: *Smith took the gold medal with a leap of 2.37
metres.*
vault: *She regained the record with a vault of 3.80
metres.*

jumper [ˈdʒʌmpə] **jumpers** NOUN
a knitted garment for the top half of the body

jumpy [ˈdʒʌmpɪ] **jumpier, jumpiest**
ADJECTIVE
nervous and worried

junction [ˈdʒʌŋkʃən] **junctions** NOUN
a place where roads or railway lines meet or cross

June [dʒuːn] NOUN
June is the sixth month of the year. It has 30
days.
[WORD HISTORY: from Latin JUNIUS, the month of
June, probably from the name of an important
Roman family]

jungle [ˈdʒʌŋɡəl] **jungles** NOUN
1 a dense tropical forest
2 a tangled mass of plants or other objects

junior [ˈdʒuːnjə] **juniors** ADJECTIVE

1 Someone who is junior to other people has a
lower position in an organization.

● THESAURUS
inferior: *inferior status*
lesser: *He resigned to take a lesser position and a cut
in wages.*
lower: *the lower ranks of council officers*
subordinate: *sixty of his subordinate officers*
<<OPPOSITE *senior*

2 Junior also means younger.

3 relating to childhood *e.g. a junior school*

> NOUN

4 someone who holds an unimportant position
in an organization

juniper [ˈdʒuːnɪpə] **junipers** NOUN
an evergreen shrub with purple berries used in
cooking and medicine

junk [dʒʌŋk] **junks** NOUN

1 Junk is old or second-hand articles which are
sold cheaply or thrown away.

● THESAURUS
clutter: *She likes her worktops to be clear of clutter.*
odds and ends: *My handbag's full of useless odds
and ends.*
refuse: *a weekly collection of refuse*
rubbish: *They piled most of their rubbish into skips.*
scrap: *a small yard containing a heap of scrap*
trash: *cluttered with trash*

2 If you think something is junk, you think it is
worthless rubbish.

3 a Chinese sailing boat with a flat bottom and
square sails

junk food NOUN
Junk food is food low in nutritional value which is
eaten as well as or instead of proper meals.

junkie [ˈdʒʌŋkɪ] **junkies** NOUN; INFORMAL
a drug addict

Jupiter [ˈdʒuːpɪtə] NOUN
Jupiter is the largest planet in the solar system
and the fifth from the sun.

jurisdiction [ˌdʒʊərɪsˈdɪkʃən] NOUN

1 FORMAL
Jurisdiction is the power or right of the courts to
apply laws and make legal judgments. *e.g. The
Court held that it did not have the jurisdiction to
examine the merits of the case.*

2 Jurisdiction is power or authority. *e.g. The airport
was under French jurisdiction.*

juror [ˈdʒʊərə] **jurors** NOUN
a member of a jury

jury [ˈdʒʊərɪ] **juries** NOUN
a group of people in a court of law who have been

selected to listen to the facts of a case on trial, and to decide whether the accused person is guilty or not

just [dʒʌst] ADJECTIVE

1 fair and impartial *e.g. She arrived at a just decision.*

2 morally right or proper *e.g. a just reward*

> ADVERB

3 If something has just happened, it happened a very short time ago.

4 If you just do something, you do it by a very small amount. *e.g. They only just won.*

5 simply or only *e.g. It was just an excuse not to mow the lawn.*

6 exactly *e.g. It's just what she wanted.*

> PHRASE

7 In South African English, **just now** means in a little while.

justly ADVERB

justice [ˈdʒʌstɪs] **justices** NOUN

1 Justice is fairness and reasonableness.

● **THESAURUS**
equity: *Income should be distributed with some sense of equity.*
fairness: *concern about the fairness of the election campaign*
impartiality: *a system lacking impartiality*
<<OPPOSITE *injustice*

2 The system of justice in a country is the way in which laws are maintained by the courts.

3 a judge or magistrate

● **THESAURUS**
judge: *The judge awarded him £2000 in damages.*
magistrate: *defendants appearing before a magistrate*

justify [ˈdʒʌstɪˌfaɪ] **justifies, justifying, justified** VERB

1 If you justify an action or idea, you prove or explain why it is reasonable or necessary.

● **THESAURUS**
defend: *Her conduct is hard to defend.*
excuse: *That still doesn't excuse his behaviour.*
explain: *She left a note explaining her actions.*
vindicate: *Ministers are confident their decision will be vindicated.*
warrant: *These allegations warrant an investigation.*

2 (ICT) To justify text that you have typed or keyed into a computer is to adjust the spaces between the words so each full line in a paragraph fills the space between the left and right hand margins of the page.

justification NOUN, **justifiable** ADJECTIVE

jut [dʒʌt] **juts, jutting, jutted** VERB

If something juts out, it sticks out beyond or above a surface or edge.

jute [dʒuːt] NOUN

Jute is a strong fibre made from the bark of an Asian plant, used to make rope and sacking.

juvenile [ˈdʒuːvɪˌnaɪl] **juveniles** ADJECTIVE

1 suitable for young people

2 childish and rather silly *e.g. a juvenile game*

> NOUN

3 a young person not old enough to be considered an adult

juxtapose [ˌdʒʌkstəˈpəʊz] **juxtaposes, juxtaposing, juxtaposed** VERB

If you juxtapose things or ideas, you put them close together, often to emphasize the difference between them.

juxtaposition NOUN

j

Kk

kaffir [ˈkæfə] **kaffirs** or **kaffir** NOUN; A VERY
OFFENSIVE WORD
In South African English, a kaffir is a Black
person.

kai [kaɪ] NOUN; AN INFORMAL NEW ZEALAND WORD
food

● THESAURUS
food: *Enjoy your food.*
grub: informal *Get yourself some grub.*
provisions: *enough provisions for two weeks*
rations: *The soldiers sampled the officers' rations.*
tucker: Australian and New Zealand; *I haven't had
any decent tucker for days.*

kaleidoscope [kəˈlaɪdəˌskəʊp]
kaleidoscopes NOUN
a toy consisting of a tube with a hole at one end.
When you look through the hole and twist the
other end of the tube, you can see a changing
pattern of colours
[WORD HISTORY: from Greek KALOS meaning
'beautiful',EIDOS meaning 'shape', and SKOPEIN
meaning 'to look at']

kamikaze [ˌkæmɪˈkɑːzɪ] NOUN
In the Second World War, a kamikaze was a
Japanese pilot who flew an aircraft loaded with
explosives directly into an enemy target knowing
he would be killed doing so.
[WORD HISTORY: from Japanese KAMI meaning
'divine' +KAZE meaning 'wind']

kangaroo [ˌkæŋgəˈruː] **kangaroos** NOUN
a large Australian animal with very strong back
legs which it uses for jumping

karate [kəˈrɑːtɪ] NOUN
Karate is a sport in which people fight each other
using only their hands, elbows, feet, and legs.
[WORD HISTORY: from Japanese KARA + TE meaning
'empty hand']

karma [ˈkɑːmə] NOUN
In Buddhism and Hinduism, karma is actions you
take which affect you in your present and future
lives.

Karoo [kəˈruː] **Karoos;** also spelt **Karroo** NOUN
In South Africa, the Karoos are areas of very dry
land.

karri [ˈkɑːrɪ] **karris** NOUN
an Australian eucalypt that produces a dark red
wood used for building

katipo [ˈkætɪˌpəʊ] **katipo** or **katipos** NOUN
a small, poisonous spider with a red or orange
stripe on its back, found in New Zealand

kauri [ˈkaʊrɪ] **kauri** or **kauris** NOUN
a large tree found in New Zealand which
produces wood used for building and making
furniture

kayak [ˈkaɪæk] **kayaks** NOUN
a covered canoe with a small opening for the
person sitting in it, originally used by the Inuit
people

kea [ˈkeɪə] **kea** or **keas** NOUN
1 a large, greenish parrot found in New Zealand
2 In New Zealand, Keas are the youngest
members of the Scouts.

kebab [kəˈbæb] **kebabs** NOUN
pieces of meat or vegetable stuck on a stick and
grilled

keel [kiːl] **keels, keeling, keeled** NOUN
1 the specially shaped bottom of a ship which
supports the sides and sits in the water
> VERB
2 If someone or something keels over, they fall
down sideways.

keen [kiːn] **keener, keenest** ADJECTIVE
1 Someone who is keen shows great eagerness
and enthusiasm.

● THESAURUS
ardent: *one of his most ardent supporters*
avid: *an avid reader*
eager: *We're eager to have another baby.*
enthusiastic: *Tom was very enthusiastic about the
place.*
fond of: *Are you fond of Chinese cuisine?*
into: informal *I'm really into football.*
2 If you are keen on someone or something, you
are attracted to or fond of them.
3 quick to notice or understand things

● THESAURUS
astute: *an astute judge of character*

brilliant: *She had a brilliant mind.*
perceptive: *a perceptive gaze*
quick: *His quick mind soon grasped the situation.*
shrewd: *Her questions showed a shrewd perception.*

4 Keen senses let you see, hear, smell, and taste things very clearly or strongly.
keenly ADVERB, **keenness** NOUN

keep [kiːp] **keeps, keeping, kept** VERB
1 To keep someone or something in a particular condition means to make them stay in that condition. *e.g. We'll walk to keep warm.*
2 If you keep something, you have it and look after it.

● THESAURUS
care for: *vintage cars lovingly cared for by their owners*
maintain: *The house costs a fortune to maintain.*
preserve: *the need to preserve the rainforests*

3 To keep something also means to store it in the usual place.

● THESAURUS
deposit: *You are advised to deposit your valuables in the hotel safe.*
hold: *Our stock is held in a warehouse.*
store: *Store the cookies in an airtight tin.*

4 If you keep doing something, you do it repeatedly or continuously. *e.g. I kept phoning the hospital.*
5 If you keep a promise, you do what you promised to do.

● THESAURUS
carry out: *He carried out his threat.*
fulfil: *He fulfilled all his responsibilities.*
honour: *The two sides have agreed to honour a new ceasefire.*

6 If you keep a secret, you do not tell anyone else.
7 If you keep a diary, you write something in it every day.
8 If you keep someone from going somewhere, you delay them so that they are late.
9 To keep someone means to provide them with money, food, and clothing.

> NOUN
10 Your keep is the cost of the food you eat, your housing, and your clothing. *e.g. He does not contribute towards his keep.*
11 the main tower inside the walls of a castle
keep up VERB
12 If you keep up with other people, you move or work at the same speed as they do.

keeper [ˈkiːpə] **keepers** NOUN
1 a person whose job is to look after the animals in a zoo
2 a goalkeeper in soccer or hockey

keeping [ˈkiːpɪŋ] NOUN
1 If something is in your keeping, it has been given to you to look after for a while.
> PHRASE
2 If one thing is **in keeping with** another, the two things are suitable or appropriate together.

keepsake [ˈkiːpˌseɪk] **keepsakes** NOUN
something that someone gives you to remind you of a particular person or event

keg [keg] **kegs** NOUN
a small barrel

kelpie [ˈkelpɪ] **kelpies**; also spelt **kelpy** NOUN
a smooth-haired Australian sheepdog with upright ears

kennel [ˈkenəl] **kennels** NOUN
1 a shelter for a dog
2 A kennels is a place where dogs can be kept for a time, or where they are bred.

Kenyan [ˈkenjən] **Kenyans** ADJECTIVE
1 belonging or relating to Kenya
> NOUN
2 someone who comes from Kenya

kerb [kɜːb] **kerbs** NOUN
the raised edge at the point where a pavement joins onto a road

kernel [ˈkɜːnəl] **kernels** NOUN
the part of a nut that is inside the shell

kerosene [ˈkerəˌsiːn] NOUN
Kerosene is the same as paraffin.

kestrel [ˈkestrəl] **kestrels** NOUN
a type of small falcon

ketchup [ˈketʃəp] NOUN
Ketchup is a cold sauce, usually made from tomatoes.

kettle [ˈketəl] **kettles** NOUN
a metal container with a spout, in which you boil water

key [kiː] **keys, keying, keyed** NOUN
1 a shaped piece of metal that fits into a hole so that you can unlock a door, wind something that is clockwork, or start a car
2 The keys on a typewriter, piano, or cash register are the buttons that you press to use it.
3 an explanation of the symbols used in a map or diagram
4 In music, a key is a scale of notes.
> VERB
5 If you key in information on a computer keyboard, you type it.

keyboard [ˈkiːˌbɔːd] **keyboards** NOUN
(ICT) a row of levers or buttons on a piano, typewriter, or computer

Key Stage Key Stages NOUN
In England and Wales, one of the four age-group divisions to which each level of the National Curriculum applies (5-7; 7-11; 11-14; 14-16).

kg
an abbreviation for 'kilograms'

khaki ['kɑːkɪ] NOUN
1 Khaki is a strong yellowish-brown material, used especially for military uniforms.

> NOUN OR ADJECTIVE
2 yellowish-brown
[WORD HISTORY: from Urdu KAKI meaning 'dusty']

khanda ['kʌndə] **khandas** NOUN
a sword used by Sikhs in the Amrit ceremony

kia ora [ˌkɪə 'ɔːrə]
In New Zealand, 'kia ora' is a Maori greeting.

kibbutz [kɪ'bʊts] **kibbutzim** NOUN
a place of work in Israel, for example a farm or factory, where the workers live together and share all the duties and income

kick [kɪk] **kicks, kicking, kicked** VERB
1 If you kick something, you hit it with your foot.

> NOUN
2 If you give something a kick, you hit it with your foot.

3 INFORMAL
If you get a kick out of doing something, you enjoy doing it very much.

kick off VERB
4 When players kick off, they start a soccer or rugby match.
kick-off NOUN

kid [kɪd] **kids, kidding, kidded** NOUN

1 INFORMAL
a child

2 a young goat

> VERB
3 If you kid people, you tease them by deceiving them in fun.

kidnap ['kɪdnæp] **kidnaps, kidnapping, kidnapped** VERB
To kidnap someone is to take them away by force and demand a ransom in exchange for returning them.
kidnapper NOUN, **kidnapping** NOUN

● THESAURUS
abduct: *people claiming to have been abducted by aliens*
capture: *The guerrillas shot down one plane and captured the pilot.*
seize: *hostages seized by terrorists*

kidney ['kɪdnɪ] **kidneys** NOUN
Your kidneys are two organs in your body that remove waste products from your blood.

kill [kɪl] **kills, killing, killed** VERB
1 To kill a person, animal, or plant is to make them die.

● THESAURUS
assassinate: *the plot to assassinate Martin Luther King*
butcher: *The guards butchered hundreds of prisoners.*
destroy: *The jockey was unhurt but his horse had to be destroyed.*
execute: *He was executed for treason.*
exterminate: *an effort to exterminate all the rats*
massacre: *300 civilians have been massacred by the rebels.*
murder: *the widow of the murdered leader*
slaughter: *Whales are being slaughtered for commercial gain.*
slay: *a painting of Saint George slaying the dragon*

2 If something is killing you, it is causing you severe pain or discomfort. *e.g. My arms are killing me.*

> NOUN
3 The kill is the moment when a hunter kills an animal.
killer NOUN

kiln [kɪln] **kilns** NOUN
(ART) an oven for baking china or pottery until it becomes hard and dry

kilo ['kiːləʊ] **kilos** NOUN
a kilogram

kilogram ['kɪləʊˌgræm] **kilograms** NOUN
(MATHS) a unit of weight equal to 1000 grams

kilohertz ['kɪləʊˌhɜːts] NOUN
a unit of measurement of radio waves equal to one thousand hertz

kilometre ['kɪləˌmiːtə] **kilometres** NOUN
(MATHS) a unit of distance equal to one thousand metres

kilowatt ['kɪləʊˌwɒt] **kilowatts** NOUN
a unit of power equal to one thousand watts

kilt [kɪlt] **kilts** NOUN
a tartan skirt worn by men as part of Scottish Highland dress

kimono [kɪ'məʊnəʊ] **kimonos** NOUN
a long, loose garment with wide sleeves and a sash, worn in Japan

kin [kɪn] PLURAL NOUN
Your kin are your relatives.

● THESAURUS
family: *There's a history of heart disease in our family.*
kindred: *his loyalty to his friends and kindred*
people: *She was reunited with her people.*

relations: *I was staying with relations in Atlanta.*
relatives: *On Sundays his relatives come to visit.*

kind [kaɪnd] **kinds; kinder, kindest** NOUN
1 A particular kind of thing is something of the
same type or sort as other things. *e.g. that kind of
film*

● THESAURUS
brand: *his favourite brand of whisky*
breed: *a rare breed of cattle*
category: *Cereal bars are the fastest-growing
category of breakfast products.*
class: *a better class of restaurant*
classification: *the cost of coverage for different
classifications of motorcycle*
genre: *a writer who does not confine himself to one
particular genre*
grade: *an improved grade of fertilizer*
sort: *a dozen trees of various sorts*
species: *a rare species of moth*
type: *What type of guns were they?*
variety: *a new variety of rose*

> ADJECTIVE
2 Someone who is kind is considerate and
generous towards other people.
kindly ADVERB

● THESAURUS
benevolent: *a very benevolent employer*
benign: *a benign ruler*
charitable: *a charitable nature*
compassionate: *My father was a deeply
compassionate man.*
considerate: *a caring and considerate husband*
good: *a good man driven to a desperate act*
humane: *the humane treatment of prisoners*
kind-hearted: *Mark was kind-hearted, generous,
and loved life.*
kindly: *a kindly old man*
thoughtful: *a thoughtful gesture*
unselfish: *his generous and unselfish attitude
towards others*
<<OPPOSITE *cruel*

> When you use *kind* in its singular form, the
> adjective before it should also be singular:
> *that kind of dog.* When you use the plural form
> *kinds,* the adjective before it should be plural:
> *those kinds of dog; those kinds of dogs*

kindergarten [ˈkɪndəˌɡɑːtᵊn]
kindergartens NOUN
a school for children who are too young to go to
primary school
[WORD HISTORY: from German KINDER + GARTEN
meaning 'children's garden']

kindle [ˈkɪndᵊl] **kindles, kindling, kindled**
VERB
1 If you kindle a fire, you light it.
2 If something kindles a feeling in you, it causes
you to have that feeling.

kindling [ˈkɪndlɪŋ] NOUN
Kindling is bits of dry wood or paper that you use
to start a fire.

kindness [ˈkaɪndnɪs] NOUN
the quality of being considerate towards other
people

● THESAURUS
benevolence: *an act of selfless benevolence*
charity: *Ms Rubens writes with warmth and charity.*
compassion: *He showed no compassion to his
victim.*
gentleness: *the gentleness with which she treated
her mother*
humanity: *Her speech showed great maturity and
humanity.*
<<OPPOSITE *cruelty*

kindred [ˈkɪndrɪd] ADJECTIVE
If you say that someone is a kindred spirit, you
mean that they have the same interests or
opinions as you.

kinetic energy [kɪˈnɛtɪk] NOUN
Kinetic energy is the energy that is produced
when something moves.

king [kɪŋ] **kings** NOUN
1 a man who is the head of state in a country, and
who inherited his position from his parents

● THESAURUS
monarch: *the coronation of the new monarch*
sovereign: *the first British sovereign to visit the
country*

2 a chess piece which can only move one square
at a time
3 In a pack of cards, a king is a card with a picture
of a king on it.

kingdom [ˈkɪŋdəm] **kingdoms** NOUN
1 a country that is governed by a king or queen
2 The divisions of the natural world are called
kingdoms. *e.g. the animal kingdom*

kingfisher [ˈkɪŋˌfɪʃə] **kingfishers** NOUN
a brightly coloured bird that lives near water and
feeds on fish

king-size or **king-sized** [ˈkɪŋˌsaɪʒ] or
[ˈkɪŋˌsaɪʒd] ADJECTIVE
larger than the normal size *e.g. a king-size bed*

kink [kɪŋk] **kinks** NOUN
a dent or curve in something which is normally
straight

kinky [ˈkɪŋkɪ] ADJECTIVE; INFORMAL
having peculiar sexual tastes

kinship [ˈkɪnʃɪp] NOUN
Kinship is a family relationship to other people.

kiosk [ˈkiːɒsk] **kiosks** NOUN
a covered stall on a street where you can buy

k

newspapers, sweets, or cigarettes
[WORD HISTORY: from Turkish KÖSK meaning 'pavilion']

kip [kɪp] **kips, kipping, kipped** INFORMAL
> NOUN
1 a period of sleep
> VERB
2 When you kip, you sleep.

kipper ['kɪpə] **kippers** NOUN
a smoked herring

kirk [kɜːk] **kirks** NOUN
In Scotland, a kirk is a church.

kiss [kɪs] **kisses, kissing, kissed** VERB
1 When you kiss someone, you touch them with your lips as a sign of love or affection.
> NOUN
2 When you give someone a kiss, you kiss them.

kiss of life NOUN
The kiss of life is a method of reviving someone by blowing air into their lungs.

kit [kɪt] **kits** NOUN
1 a collection of things that you use for a sport or other activity
2 a set of parts that you put together to make something

kitchen ['kɪtʃɪn] **kitchens** NOUN
a room used for cooking and preparing food

kite [kaɪt] **kites** NOUN
1 a frame covered with paper or cloth which is attached to a piece of string, and which you fly in the air
2 a shape with four sides, with two pairs of the same length, and none of the sides parallel to each other
3 a large bird of prey with a long tail and long wings

kitset ['kɪt,sɛt] **kitsets** NOUN
In New Zealand English, a set of parts which you have to put together yourself to make an item such as a house or a piece of furniture.

kitten ['kɪtᵊn] **kittens** NOUN
a young cat

kitty ['kɪtɪ] **kitties** NOUN
a fund of money that has been given by a group of people who will use it to pay for or do things together

kiwi ['kiːwiː] **kiwi** or **kiwis** NOUN
1 a type of bird found in New Zealand. Kiwis cannot fly
2 someone who comes from New Zealand. The plural of this sense is 'kiwis'

kiwi fruit **kiwi fruits** NOUN
a fruit with a brown hairy skin and green flesh

kloof [kluːf] **kloofs** NOUN
In South Africa, a kloof is a narrow valley.

km
an abbreviation for 'kilometres'

knack [næk] NOUN
an ability to do something difficult whilst making it look easy e.g. the knack of making friends

knead [niːd] **kneads, kneading, kneaded** VERB
If you knead dough, you press it and squeeze it with your hands before baking it.

knee [niː] **knees** NOUN
the joint in your leg between your ankle and your hip

kneecap ['niː,kæp] **kneecaps** NOUN
Your kneecaps are the bones at the front of your knees.

kneel [niːl] **kneels, kneeling, knelt** VERB
When you kneel, you bend your legs and lower your body until your knees are touching the ground.

knell [nɛl] **knells** NOUN; LITERARY
the sound of a bell rung to announce a death or at a funeral

knickers ['nɪkəz] PLURAL NOUN
Knickers are underpants worn by women and girls.

knick-knacks ['nɪk,næks] PLURAL NOUN
Knick-knacks are small ornaments.

knife [naɪf] **knives; knifes, knifing, knifed** NOUN
1 (D & T) a sharp metal tool that you use to cut things
> VERB
2 To knife someone is to stab them with a knife.

knight [naɪt] **knights, knighting, knighted** NOUN
1 a man who has been given the title 'Sir' by the King or Queen
2 In medieval Europe, a knight was a man who served a monarch or lord as a mounted soldier.
3 a chess piece that is usually in the shape of a horse's head
> VERB
4 To knight a man is to give him the title 'Sir'.
knighthood NOUN

knit [nɪt] **knits, knitting, knitted** VERB
1 If you knit a piece of clothing, you make it by working lengths of wool together, either using needles held in the hand, or with a machine.
2 If you knit your brows, you frown.
knitting NOUN

knob [nɒb] **knobs** NOUN
1 a round handle

2 a round switch on a machine *e.g. the knobs of a radio*

knobkerrie ['nɒb‚kɛrɪ] **knobkerries** NOUN
In South Africa, a knobkerrie is a club or stick with a rounded end.

knock [nɒk] **knocks, knocking, knocked** VERB
1 If you knock on something, you strike it with your hand or fist.
2 If you knock a part of your body against something, you bump into it quite forcefully.
3 INFORMAL
To knock someone is to criticize them.
> NOUN
4 a firm blow on something solid *e.g. There was a knock at the door.*
knock out VERB
5 To knock someone out is to hit them so hard that they become unconscious.

knocker ['nɒkə] **knockers** NOUN
a metal lever attached to a door, which you use to knock on the door

knockout ['nɒk‚aʊt] **knockouts** NOUN
1 a punch in boxing which knocks a boxer unconscious
2 a competition in which competitors are eliminated in each round until only the winner is left

knoll [nəʊl] **knolls** NOUN; LITERARY
a gently sloping hill with a rounded top

knot [nɒt] **knots, knotting, knotted** NOUN
1 a fastening made by looping a piece of string around itself and pulling the ends tight
2 a small lump visible on the surface of a piece of wood
3 A knot of people is a small group of them.
4 TECHNICAL
a unit of speed used for ships and aircraft
> VERB
5 If you knot a piece of string, you tie a knot in it.

know see page 488 for Word Web

know-how ['nəʊ‚haʊ] NOUN
Know-how is the ability to do something that is quite difficult or technical.

knowing ['nəʊɪŋ] ADJECTIVE
A knowing look is one that shows that you know or understand something that other people do not.
knowingly ADVERB

knowledge ['nɒlɪdʒ] NOUN
Knowledge is all the information and facts that you know.
● THESAURUS
education: *a man with little education*

learning: *people of great learning*
scholarship: *a lifetime of scholarship*
wisdom: *a source of wisdom and knowledge*

knowledgeable ['nɒlɪdʒəbᵊl] ADJECTIVE
Someone who is knowledgeable knows a lot about a subject. *e.g. She was very knowledgeable about Irish mythology.*

knuckle ['nʌkᵊl] **knuckles** NOUN
Your knuckles are the joints at the end of your fingers where they join your hand.

koala [kəʊ'ɑːlə] **koalas** NOUN
an Australian animal with grey fur and small tufted ears. Koalas live in trees and eat eucalyptus leaves

kohanga reo or **kohanga** [kɔː'hɑːŋɑː 'reɪəʊː] **kohanga reo** NOUN
In New Zealand, an infant class where children are taught in Maori.
[WORD HISTORY: a Maori term meaning 'language nest']

kookaburra ['kʊkə‚bʌrə] **kookaburras** NOUN
a large Australian kingfisher
[WORD HISTORY: a native Australian word]

koppie ['kɒpɪ] **koppies;** also spelt **kopje** NOUN
In South Africa, a koppie is a small hill with no other hills around it.

Koran or **Qur'an** [kɔː'rɑːn] NOUN
The Koran is the holy book of Islam.
[WORD HISTORY: from Arabic KARA'A meaning 'to read']

Korean [kə'riːən] **Koreans** ADJECTIVE
1 relating or belonging to Korea
> NOUN
2 someone who comes from Korea
3 Korean is the main language spoken in Korea.

kosher ['kəʊʃə] ADJECTIVE
Kosher food has been specially prepared to be eaten according to Jewish law.
[WORD HISTORY: from Hebrew KASHER meaning 'right' or 'proper']

kowhai ['kəʊwaɪ] **kowhai** or **kowhais** NOUN
a small New Zealand tree with clusters of yellow flowers

kraal [krɑːl] **kraals** NOUN
In South Africa, a kraal is a village in which a tribe lives and which is often surrounded by a fence.

kudu ['kuːduː] **kudus;** also spelt **koodoo** NOUN
a large African antelope with curled horns

kumara or **kumera** ['kuːmərə] **kumara** or **kumaras** NOUN
In New Zealand English, a kumara is a sweet

k

1 VERB
If you know a fact, you have it in your mind and you do not need to learn it.
● THESAURUS
apprehend: *It is impossible to apprehend the whole painting at once.*
be aware of: *Smokers are aware of the risks they run.*
comprehend: *They do not comprehend the nature of the problem.*
perceive: *the world as we perceive it*
see: *Don't you see what he's up to?*
understand: *too young to understand what was happening*

2 VERB
People you know are not strangers because you have met them and spoken to them.
● THESAURUS
be acquainted with: *Are you acquainted with my husband?*
be familiar with: *I am familiar with his work.*
recognize: *She recognized him at once.*

know
knows, knowing, knew, known

3 VERB
to understand or be aware of something, or how to do or be something *eg: she knew how to get on with people* (sometimes with **about** or **of**)
● THESAURUS
be familiar with: *Andrew is quite familiar with computers.*
understand: *I didn't understand a word of German, so I asked him to speak in English.*

potato, a vegetable with yellow or orange flesh.

kumquat ['kʌmkwɒt] **kumquats** NOUN
a very small round or oval citrus fruit

kung fu ['kʌŋ 'fuː] NOUN
Kung fu is a Chinese style of fighting which involves using your hands and feet.

kura kaupapa Maori [kuːrə kɑːuːpɑːpɑː] **kura kaupapa Maori** NOUN
In New Zealand, a primary school where teaching is based on Maori language and culture.

Kurd [kɜːd] **Kurds** NOUN
The Kurds are a group of people who live mainly in eastern Turkey, northern Iraq, and western Iran.

Kurdish ['kɜːdɪʃ] ADJECTIVE
1 belonging or relating to the Kurds *e.g. Kurdish culture.*
> NOUN
2 Kurdish is the language spoken by the Kurds.

k

Ll

l
an abbreviation for 'litres'

lab [læb] **labs** NOUN; INFORMAL
a laboratory

label ['leɪbᵊl] **labels, labelling, labelled**
NOUN
1 a piece of paper or plastic attached to
something as an identification

● THESAURUS
sticker: *She's got a disabled sticker on her car.*
tag: *a name tag*
ticket: *a price ticket*

> VERB
2 If you label something, you put a label on it.

● THESAURUS
flag: *Flag the pages which need corrections.*
sticker: *products stickered at a special price*
tag: *The pigeon was tagged with a numbered band.*

laboratory [ləˈbɒrətəri] **laboratories** NOUN
(SCIENCE) a place where scientific experiments
are carried out

laborious [ləˈbɔːrɪəs] ADJECTIVE
needing a lot of effort or time
laboriously ADVERB

Labor Party ['leɪbə] NOUN
In Australia, the Labor Party is one of the major
political parties.

labour ['leɪbə] **labours, labouring,
laboured** NOUN
1 Labour is hard work.

● THESAURUS
effort: *legs aching with the effort of the climb*
exertion: *She felt dizzy with the exertion of walking.*
industry: *At last his industry was rewarded.*
toil: *their day's toil in the fields*
work: *All our work is starting to pay off.*

2 The workforce of a country or industry is
sometimes called its labour. *e.g. unskilled labour*

● THESAURUS
employees: *Only a third of all employees are union
members.*
workers: *Thousands of workers have been laid off.*
workforce: *a country where half the workforce is
unemployed*

3 In Britain, the Labour Party is a political party
that believes that the government should
provide free health care and education for
everyone.
4 New Zealand, the Labour Party is one of the
main political parties.
5 Labour is also the last stage of pregnancy when
a woman gives birth to a baby.

> VERB
6 OLD-FASHIONED
To labour means to work hard.
labourer NOUN

● THESAURUS
slave: *We've been slaving half the night to finish this.*
toil: *workers toiling in wretched conditions*
work: *He works twelve hours a day.*
<<OPPOSITE *relax*

labrador ['læbrə,dɔː] **labradors** NOUN
a large dog with short black or golden hair

labyrinth ['læbərɪnθ] **labyrinths** NOUN
a complicated series of paths or passages

lace [leɪs] **laces, lacing, laced** NOUN
1 Lace is a very fine decorated cloth made with a
lot of holes in it.
2 Laces are cords with which you fasten your
shoes.

> VERB
3 When you lace up your shoes, you tie a bow in
the laces.
4 To lace someone's food or drink means to put a
small amount of alcohol, a drug, or poison in it.
e.g. black coffee laced with vodka
lacy ADJECTIVE

lack [læk] **lacks, lacking, lacked** NOUN
1 If there is a lack of something, it is not present
when or where it is needed.

● THESAURUS
absence: *an absence of evidence*
deficiency: *tests for vitamin deficiency*
scarcity: *a scarcity of water*
shortage: *a food shortage*
want: *becoming weak from want of rest*
<<OPPOSITE *abundance*

> VERB
2 If something is lacking, it is not present when
or where it is needed.

3 If someone or something is lacking something, they do not have it or do not have enough of it. *e.g. Francis was lacking in stamina.*

4

⬤ THESAURUS

be deficient in: *Your diet is deficient in vitamins.*
be short of: *I'm short of cash.*
miss: *Your jacket is missing a button.*

lacklustre ['læk,lʌstə] ADJECTIVE
not interesting or exciting

laconic [lə'kɒnɪk] ADJECTIVE
using very few words
[WORD HISTORY: from Greek LAKONIKAS meaning 'Spartan'. The Spartans were famous for using few words]

lacquer ['lækə] **lacquers** NOUN
Lacquer is thin, clear paint that you put on wood to protect it and make it shiny.

lacrosse [lə'krɒs] NOUN
Lacrosse is an outdoor ball game in which two teams try to score goals using long sticks with nets on the end of them.
[WORD HISTORY: from Canadian French LA CROSSE meaning 'the hooked stick']

lad [læd] **lads** NOUN
a boy or young man

ladder ['lædə] **ladders, laddering, laddered** NOUN
1 a wooden or metal frame used for climbing which consists of horizontal steps fixed to two vertical poles
2 If your stockings or tights have a ladder in them, they have a vertical, ladder-like tear in them.
> VERB
3 If you ladder your stockings or tights, you get a ladder in them.

laden ['leɪdᵊn] ADJECTIVE
To be laden with something means to be carrying a lot of it. *e.g. bushes laden with ripe fruit*

ladle ['leɪdᵊl] **ladles, ladling, ladled** NOUN
1 a long-handled spoon with a deep, round bowl, which you use to serve soup
> VERB
2 If you ladle out food, you serve it with a ladle.

lady ['leɪdɪ] **ladies** NOUN
1 a woman, especially one who is considered to be well mannered
2 Lady is a title used in front of the name of a woman from the nobility, such as a lord's wife.

ladybird ['leɪdɪ,bɜːd] **ladybirds** NOUN
a small flying beetle with a round red body patterned with black spots

lady-in-waiting ['leɪdɪɪn,weɪtɪŋ] **ladies-in-waiting** NOUN
a woman who acts as companion to a queen or princess

ladylike ['leɪdɪ,laɪk] ADJECTIVE
behaving in a polite and socially correct way

Ladyship ['leɪdɪʃɪp] **Ladyships** NOUN
You address a woman who has the title 'Lady' as 'Your Ladyship'.

lag [læg] **lags, lagging, lagged** VERB
1 To lag behind is to make slower progress than other people.

⬤ THESAURUS

fall behind: *The city is falling behind in attracting tourists.*
trail: *The Communist party is trailing badly in the opinion polls.*

2 To lag pipes is to wrap cloth round them to stop the water inside freezing in cold weather.

lager ['lɑːgə] **lagers** NOUN
Lager is light-coloured beer.
[WORD HISTORY: from German LAGERBIER meaning 'beer for storing']

lagoon [lə'guːn] **lagoons** NOUN
an area of water separated from the sea by reefs or sand

laid [leɪd] the past tense and past participle of **lay**

lain [leɪn] the past participle of some meanings of **lie**

lair [lɛə] **lairs** NOUN
a place where a wild animal lives

laird [lɛəd] **lairds** NOUN
a landowner in Scotland

lake [leɪk] **lakes** NOUN
an area of fresh water surrounded by land

lama ['lɑːmə] **lamas** NOUN
a Buddhist priest or monk

lamb [læm] **lambs** NOUN
1 a young sheep
2 Lamb is the meat from a lamb.

lame [leɪm] ADJECTIVE
1 Someone who is lame has an injured leg and cannot walk easily.

⬤ THESAURUS

crippled: *a woman crippled by arthritis*
hobbling: *a hobbling old man*
limping: *limping from a hamstring injury*

2 A lame excuse is not very convincing.
lamely ADVERB, **lameness** NOUN

⬤ THESAURUS

feeble: *his feeble attempt at humour*
flimsy: *MPs condemned his evidence as flimsy.*

l

pathetic: *a pathetic attempt at humour*
poor: *a poor effort*
unconvincing: *an unconvincing argument*
weak: *a weak performance*

lament [ləˈmɛnt] **laments, lamenting, lamented** VERB

1 To lament something means to express sorrow or regret about it.

● THESAURUS
grieve: *grieving over his dead wife and son*
mourn: *We mourned the loss of our home.*
wail: *a mother wailing for her lost child*
weep: *She wept for her lost love.*

> NOUN
2 an expression of sorrow or regret

● THESAURUS
moan: *a moan of sorrow*
wail: *wails of grief*

3 a song or poem expressing grief at someone's death

lamentable [ˈlæməntəbəl] ADJECTIVE
disappointing and regrettable

laminated [ˈlæmɪˌneɪtɪd] ADJECTIVE
consisting of several thin sheets or layers stuck together *e.g. laminated glass*

lamp [læmp] **lamps** NOUN
a device that produces light

lamppost [ˈlæmpˌpəʊst] **lampposts** NOUN
a tall column in a street, with a lamp at the top

lampshade [ˈlæmpˌʃeɪd] **lampshades** NOUN
a decorative covering over an electric light bulb which prevents the bulb giving out too harsh a light

lance [lɑːns] **lances, lancing, lanced** VERB

1 To lance a boil or abscess means to stick a sharp instrument into it in order to release the fluid.

> NOUN
2 a long spear that used to be used by soldiers on horseback

land [lænd] **lands, landing, landed** NOUN

1 Land is an area of ground.

● THESAURUS
estate: *a shooting party on his estate in Yorkshire*
grounds: *the palace grounds*
property: *travellers who camped on his property*

2 Land is also the part of the earth that is not covered by water.

3 a country *e.g. our native land*

● THESAURUS
country: *the boundary between the two countries*
nation: *the nation's financial crisis*

province: *The Algarve is Portugal's southernmost province.*
region: *the region of Tuscany*
territory: *the disputed territory of Kashmir*

> VERB
4 When a plane lands, it arrives back on the ground after a flight.

● THESAURUS
alight: *A thrush alighted on a nearby branch.*
dock: *The ship docked in Le Havre.*
touch down: *The plane touched down in Barbados.*

5 If you land something you have been trying to get, you succeed in getting it. *e.g. She eventually landed a job with a local radio station.*

6 To land a fish means to catch it while fishing.

7 If you land someone with something unpleasant, you cause them to have to deal with it.

landing [ˈlændɪŋ] **landings** NOUN

1 a flat area in a building at the top of a flight of stairs

2 The landing of an aeroplane is its arrival back on the ground after a flight. *e.g. a smooth landing*

landlady [ˈlændˌleɪdɪ] **landladies** NOUN
a woman who owns a house or small hotel and who lets rooms to people

landlord [ˈlændˌlɔːd] **landlords** NOUN
a man who owns a house or small hotel and who lets rooms to people

landmark [ˈlændˌmɑːk] **landmarks** NOUN

1 a noticeable feature in a landscape, which you can use to check your position

2 an important stage in the development of something *e.g. The play is a landmark in Japanese theatre.*

landowner [ˈlændˌəʊnə] **landowners** NOUN
someone who owns land, especially a large area of the countryside

landscape [ˈlændˌskeɪp] **landscapes** NOUN

1 (GEOGRAPHY) The landscape is the view over an area of open land.

2 (ART) a painting of the countryside

landslide [ˈlændˌslaɪd] **landslides** NOUN

1 a large amount of loose earth and rocks falling down a mountain side

2 a victory in an election won by a large number of votes

lane [leɪn] **lanes** NOUN

1 a narrow road, especially in the country

2 one of the strips on a road marked with lines to guide drivers

language ['læŋgwɪdʒ] **languages** NOUN
1 the system of words that the people of a country use to communicate with each other

⬤ THESAURUS
dialect: *the Cantonese dialect*
idiom: *the Gaelic folk idiom*
jargon: *scientific jargon*
lingo: informal *I don't speak the lingo.*
tongue: *The French feel passionately about their native tongue.*
vernacular: *an Indian vernacular derived from Sanskrit*
vocabulary: *a new word in the German vocabulary*

2 Your language is the style in which you express yourself. *e.g. His language is often obscure.*

⬤ THESAURUS
phrasing: *The phrasing of this report is confusing.*
style: *a simple writing style*
wording: *The wording of the contract was ambiguous.*

3 Language is the study of the words and grammar of a particular language.

languid ['læŋgwɪd] ADJECTIVE
slow and lacking energy
languidly ADVERB

languish ['læŋgwɪʃ] **languishes, languishing, languished** VERB
If you languish, you endure an unpleasant situation for a long time. *e.g. Many languished in poverty.*

lanky ['læŋkɪ] **lankier, lankiest** ADJECTIVE
Someone who is lanky is tall and thin and moves rather awkwardly.

lantana [læn'teɪnə] **lantanas** NOUN
In Australia, a shrub with yellow or orange flowers which is regarded as a pest in some areas.

lantern ['læntən] **lanterns** NOUN
a lamp in a metal frame with glass sides

lap [læp] **laps, lapping, lapped** NOUN
1 Your lap is the flat area formed by your thighs when you are sitting down.
2 one circuit of a running track or racecourse
> VERB
3 When an animal laps up liquid, it drinks using its tongue to get the liquid into its mouth.
4 If you lap someone in a race, you overtake them when they are still on the previous lap.
5 When water laps against something, it gently moves against it in little waves.

lapel [lə'pɛl] **lapels** NOUN
a flap which is joined on to the collar of a jacket or coat

lapse [læps] **lapses, lapsing, lapsed** NOUN
1 a moment of bad behaviour by someone who usually behaves well
2 a slight mistake
3 a period of time between two events
> VERB
4 If you lapse into a different way of behaving, you start behaving that way. *e.g. The offenders lapsed into a sullen silence.*
5 If a legal document or contract lapses, it is not renewed on the date when it expires.

lard [lɑːd] NOUN
Lard is fat from a pig, used in cooking.

larder ['lɑːdə] **larders** NOUN
a room in which you store food, often next to a kitchen

large [lɑːdʒ] **larger, largest** ADJECTIVE
1 Someone or something that is large is much bigger than average.
> PHRASE
2 If a prisoner is **at large**, he or she has escaped from prison.

largely ['lɑːdʒlɪ] ADVERB
to a great extent *e.g. The public are largely unaware of this.*

lark [lɑːk] **larks** NOUN
1 a small brown bird with a distinctive song
2 If you do something for a lark, you do it in a high-spirited or mischievous way for fun.

larrikin ['lærɪkɪn] **larrikins** NOUN; INFORMAL
In Australian and New Zealand English, a young person who behaves in a wild or irresponsible way.

larva ['lɑːvə] **larvae** NOUN
an insect, which looks like a short, fat worm, at the stage before it becomes an adult

laryngitis [,lærɪn'dʒaɪtɪs] NOUN
Laryngitis is an infection of the throat which causes you to lose your voice.

larynx ['lærɪŋks] **larynxes** or **larynges** NOUN
the part of your throat containing the vocal cords, through which air passes between your nose and lungs

lasagne [lə'zænjə] NOUN
Lasagne is an Italian dish made with wide flat sheets of pasta, meat, and cheese sauce.
[WORD HISTORY: from Latin LASANUM meaning 'cooking pot']

laser ['leɪzə] **lasers** NOUN
a machine that produces a powerful concentrated beam of light which is used to cut very hard materials and in some kinds of surgery

[WORD HISTORY: from the first letters of 'Light Amplification by Stimulated Emission of Radiation']

lash [læʃ] **lashes, lashing, lashed** NOUN

1 Your lashes are the hairs growing on the edge of your eyelids.

2 a strip of leather at the end of a whip

3 Lashes are blows struck with a whip.

lash out VERB

4 To lash out at someone means to criticize them severely.

lass [læs] **lasses** NOUN

a girl or young woman

lasso [læ'suː] **lassoes** or **lassos lassoing, lassoed** NOUN

1 a length of rope with a noose at one end, used by cowboys to catch cattle and horses

> VERB

2 To lasso an animal means to catch it by throwing the noose of a lasso around its neck.

last see page 495 for Word Web

last-ditch ['lɑːst'dɪtʃ] ADJECTIVE

A last-ditch attempt to do something is a final attempt to succeed when everything else has failed.

latch [lætʃ] **latches, latching, latched** NOUN

1 a simple door fastening consisting of a metal bar which falls into a hook

2 a type of door lock which locks automatically when you close the door and which has to be opened with a key

> VERB

3 INFORMAL

If you latch onto someone or something, you become attached to them.

late [leɪt] **later, latest** ADJECTIVE OR ADVERB

1 Something that happens late happens towards the end of a period of time. *e.g. the late evening… late in the morning*

2 If you arrive late, or do something late, you arrive or do it after the time you were expected to.

> ADJECTIVE

3 A late event happens after the time when it usually takes place. *e.g. a late breakfast*

● THESAURUS

behind: *I've got behind with my payments.*
behind time: *Hurry up. We're behind time already.*
belated: *a belated birthday card*
delayed: *The kick-off was delayed by 10 minutes.*
last-minute: *buying some last-minute Christmas presents*

overdue: *The birth is two weeks overdue.*
<<OPPOSITE *early*

4 FORMAL

Late means dead. *e.g. my late grandmother*

● THESAURUS

dead: *He has been dead for a year now.*
deceased: *his recently deceased mother*
departed: *memories of departed friends*

lately ['leɪtlɪ] ADVERB

Events that happened lately happened recently.

latent ['leɪt°nt] ADJECTIVE

A latent quality is hidden at the moment, but may emerge in the future. *e.g. a latent talent for art*

lateral ['lætərəl] ADJECTIVE

relating to the sides of something, or moving in a sideways direction

lathe [leɪð] **lathes** NOUN

a machine which holds and turns a piece of wood or metal against a tool to cut and shape it

lather ['lɑːðə] **lathers** NOUN

Lather is the foam that you get when you rub soap in water.

Latin ['lætɪn] **Latins** NOUN

1 Latin is the language of ancient Rome.

> NOUN OR ADJECTIVE

2 Latins are people who speak languages closely related to Latin, such as French, Italian, Spanish, and Portuguese.

Latin America NOUN

Latin America consists of the countries in North, South, and Central America where Spanish or Portuguese is the main language.

Latin American ADJECTIVE

latitude ['lætɪˌtjuːd] **latitudes** NOUN

(GEOGRAPHY) The latitude of a place is its distance north or south of the equator measured in degrees.

latrine [lə'triːn] **latrines** NOUN

a hole or trench in the ground used as a toilet at a camp

latter ['lætə] ADJECTIVE OR NOUN

1 You use 'latter' to refer to the second of two things that are mentioned. *e.g. They were eating sandwiches and cakes (the latter bought from Mrs Paul's bakery).*

> ADJECTIVE

2 'Latter' also describes the second or end part of something *e.g. The latter part of his career.*

You use *latter* to talk about the second of two items. To talk about the last of three or more items you should use *last-named*.

latterly ['lætəlɪ] ADVERB; FORMAL

Latterly means recently. *e.g. It's only latterly that this has become an issue.*

1 ADJECTIVE
The last thing or event is the most recent one eg: *last year; In the last lesson, we looked at the formation of crystals*
● THESAURUS
latest: *his latest thriller*
most recent: *her most recent film*
preceding: *The bank's turnover had risen during the preceding year.*
previous: *his previous marriage*
<< OPPOSITE *first*

2 ADJECTIVE
The last thing that remains is the only one left after all the others have gone eg: *The last family left in 1950.*
● THESAURUS
closing: *the closing years of this century*
concluding: *the concluding scene of the film*
final: *This is your final chance.*
ultimate: *the ultimate result of the move*
<< OPPOSITE *first*

last
lasts, lasting, lasted

3 VERB
If something lasts, it continues to exist or happen eg: *Her speech lasted fifty minutes.*
● THESAURUS
carry on: *Our marriage can't carry on like this.*
continue: *The exhibition continues till 25 November.*
endure: *Somehow their friendship endures.*
persist: *The problem persists.*
remain: *The building remains to this day.*
survive: *companies which survived after the recession*

lattice ['lætɪs] **lattices** NOUN
a structure made of strips which cross over each other diagonally leaving holes in between

laudable ['lɔːdəbəl] ADJECTIVE; FORMAL
deserving praise *e.g. It is a laudable enough aim.*

laugh see page 497 for Word Web

laughable ['lɑːfəbəl] ADJECTIVE
quite absurd

laughing stock ['lɑːfɪŋ] NOUN
someone who has been made to seem ridiculous

launch [lɔːntʃ] **launches, launching, launched** VERB
1 To launch a ship means to send it into the water for the first time.
2 To launch a rocket means to send it into space.
3 When a company launches a new product, they have an advertising campaign to promote it as they start to sell it.
> NOUN
4 a motorboat

launch pad launch pads NOUN
A launch pad, or a launching pad, is the place from which space rockets take off.

launder ['lɔːndə] **launders, laundering, laundered** VERB; OLD-FASHIONED, INFORMAL
To launder clothes, sheets, or towels means to wash and iron them.

laundry ['lɔːndrɪ] **laundries** NOUN
1 a business that washes and irons clothes and sheets
2 Laundry is also the dirty clothes and sheets that are being washed, or are about to be washed.

laurel ['lɒrəl] **laurels** NOUN
an evergreen tree with shiny leaves

lava ['lɑːvə] NOUN
Lava is the very hot liquid rock that comes shooting out of an erupting volcano, and becomes solid as it cools.

lavatory ['lævətərɪ] **lavatories** NOUN
a toilet

lavender ['lævəndə] NOUN
1 Lavender is a small bush with bluish-pink flowers that have a strong, pleasant scent.
> ADJECTIVE
2 bluish-pink

lavish ['lævɪʃ] **lavishes, lavishing, lavished** ADJECTIVE
1 If you are lavish, you are very generous with your time, money, or gifts.
2 A lavish amount is a large amount.
> VERB
3 If you lavish money or affection on someone, you give them a lot of it.

lavishly ADVERB

law [lɔː] **laws** NOUN
1 The law is the system of rules developed by the government of a country, which regulate what people may and may not do and deals with people who break these rules.
⬤ THESAURUS
charter: *a citizen's charter for France*
code: *a code of conduct*
constitution: *proposed changes to the constitution*
2 The law is also the profession of people such as lawyers, whose job involves the application of the laws of a country.
3 one of the rules established by a government or a religion, which tells people what they may or may not do
⬤ THESAURUS
act: *A new act has been passed by Parliament.*
code: *a code designed to protect the rights of children*
decree: *a decree lifting sanctions against China*
regulation: *regulations outlawing child labour*
rule: *a rule that was imposed in 1962*
statute: *a practice regulated by statute*
4 a scientific fact which allows you to explain how things work in the physical world
lawful ADJECTIVE, **lawfully** ADVERB

law-abiding [,lɔːrə'baɪdɪŋ] ADJECTIVE
obeying the law and not causing any trouble

lawless ['lɔːlɪs] ADJECTIVE
having no regard for the law

lawn [lɔːn] **lawns** NOUN
an area of cultivated grass

lawnmower ['lɔːn,məʊə] **lawnmowers** NOUN
a machine for cutting grass

lawsuit ['lɔː,suːt] **lawsuits** NOUN
a civil court case between two people, as opposed to the police prosecuting someone for a criminal offence

lawyer ['lɔːjə] **lawyers** NOUN
a person who is qualified in law, and whose job is to advise people about the law and represent them in court
⬤ THESAURUS
advocate: *A public advocate will be appointed to represent you.*
attorney: *a prosecuting attorney*
barrister: *The author is a practising barrister.*
counsel: *His counsel advised him to appeal against the verdict.*
solicitor: *She took advice from a solicitor.*

lax [læks] ADJECTIVE
careless and not keeping up the usual standards

1 VERB

to make a noise which shows you are amused or happy *eg: You never laugh at my jokes.*

● THESAURUS

chortle: *He began chortling to himself.*
chuckle: *He chuckled with pleasure.*
giggle: *Both girls began to giggle.*
guffaw: *Everyone guffawed loudly.*
snigger: *People were sniggering behind my back.*
titter: *The audience tittered nervously.*

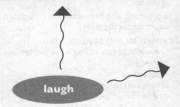

laugh

2 NOUN

the noise you make when amused or happy *eg: She has a very infectious laugh.*

● THESAURUS

chortle: *"That's what you think," he said with a chortle.*
chuckle: *We had a quiet chuckle at his mistake.*
giggle: *She gave a nervous giggle.*
guffaw: *He let out a huge guffaw of amusement.*
snigger: *barely able to stifle a snigger*
titter: *A titter went round the room.*

e.g. a lax accounting system

laxative ['læksətɪv] **laxatives** NOUN
something that you eat or drink to stop you being constipated

lay [leɪ] **lays, laying, laid** VERB
1 When you lay something somewhere, you put it down so that it lies there.

● THESAURUS
place: *She placed a mug of coffee in front of him.*
put: *He put the photograph on the desk.*
set: *He set his briefcase on the floor.*
set down: *I set the glasses down on the table.*
settle: *He settled his coat over my shoulders.*
spread: *She spread a towel over the sand and lay down.*

2 If you lay something, you arrange it or set it out.

● THESAURUS
arrange: *He started to arrange the books in piles.*
set out: *The flower garden was set out with large beds of roses.*

3 If you lay the table, you put cutlery on the table ready for a meal.

4 When a bird lays an egg, it produces the egg out of its body.

5 If you lay a trap for someone, you create a situation in which you will be able to catch them out.

6 If you lay emphasis on something, you refer to it in a way that shows you think it is very important.

7 If you lay odds on something, you bet that it will happen.

> ADJECTIVE
8 You use 'lay' to describe people who are involved with a Christian church but are not members of the clergy. *e.g. a lay preacher*

9 Lay is the past tense of some senses of **lie**.

lay off VERB
10 When workers are laid off, their employers tell them not to come to work for a while because there is a shortage of work.

11 INFORMAL
If you tell someone to lay off, you want them to stop doing something annoying.

lay on VERB
12 If you lay on a meal or entertainment, you provide it.

> People often get confused about *lay* and *lie*. The verb *lay* takes an object: *lay the table please; the Queen laid a wreath*. The verb *lie* does not take an object: *the book was lying on the table; I'm going to lie down.*

lay-by ['leɪ,baɪ] **lay-bys** NOUN
1 an area by the side of a main road where motorists can stop for a short while

2 In Australia and New Zealand, lay-by is a system where you pay a deposit on an item in a shop so that it will be kept for you until you pay the rest of the price.

layer ['leɪə] **layers** NOUN
a single thickness of something *e.g. layers of clothing*

● THESAURUS
blanket: *a blanket of fog*
coat: *a coat of paint*
coating: *a crisp chocolate coating*
covering: *a thin covering of dust*
film: *a film of plastic*
sheet: *a sheet of ice*
stratum: *the correct geological stratum*

layman ['leɪmən] **laymen** NOUN
1 someone who does not have specialized knowledge of a subject *e.g. a layman's guide to computers*

2 someone who belongs to the church but is not a member of the clergy

layout ['laɪ,aʊt] **layouts** NOUN
The layout of something is the pattern in which it is arranged.

● THESAURUS
arrangement: *the arrangement of a room*
design: *the design of the museum*
format: *the format of the book*
plan: *a detailed plan of the house*

laze [leɪz] **lazes, lazing, lazed** VERB
If you laze, you relax and do no work. *e.g. We spent a few days lazing around by the pool.*

● THESAURUS
idle: *We spent hours idling in one of the cafés.*
loaf: *loafing around the house all day*
lounge: *They lounged in the shade.*
<<OPPOSITE *work*

lazy ['leɪzɪ] **lazier, laziest** ADJECTIVE
idle and unwilling to work
lazily ADVERB, **laziness** NOUN

● THESAURUS
idle: *an idle young layabout*
slack: *Many workers have simply become too slack.*

<<OPPOSITE *industrious*

lb
an abbreviation for 'pounds' *e.g. 3lb of sugar*

lbw
In cricket lbw is an abbreviation for 'leg before wicket', which is a way of dismissing a batsman when his legs prevent the ball from hitting the wicket.

leach [liːtʃ] **leaches, leaching, leached**
VERB

When minerals are leached from rocks, they are dissolved by water which filters through the rock.

lead¹ [liːd] **leads, leading, led** VERB

1 If you lead someone somewhere, you go in front of them in order to show them the way.

⬤ THESAURUS
conduct: *He asked if he might conduct us to the ball.*
escort: *They were escorted by police to their plane.*
guide: *He took me by the arm and guided me out.*
steer: *Nick steered them towards the door.*
usher: *I ushered him into the office.*

2 If one thing leads to another, it causes the second thing to happen.

⬤ THESAURUS
cause: *Knocks can cause damage to the spine.*
contribute to: *injuries which contributed to his death*
produce: *The drug produces side effects.*

3 a person who leads a group of people is in charge of them

⬤ THESAURUS
command: *the general who commanded the troops*
direct: *He will direct day-to-day operations.*
govern: *his ability to govern the country*
head: *Who heads the firm?*
manage: *I manage a small team of workers.*
supervise: *He supervised more than 400 volunteers.*

> NOUN

4 a length of leather or chain attached to a dog's collar, so that the dog can be kept under control

5 If the police have a lead, they have a clue which might help them to solve a crime.

⬤ THESAURUS
clue: *a vital clue to the killer's identity*
indication: *All the indications suggest that he is the murderer.*
trace: *No traces of violence were found on the body.*

lead² [lɛd] NOUN
Lead is a soft, grey, heavy metal.

leaden [ˈlɛdən] ADJECTIVE
1 dark grey *e.g. a leaden sky*
2 heavy and slow-moving

leader [ˈliːdə] **leaders** NOUN
1 someone who is in charge of a country, an organization, or a group of people

⬤ THESAURUS
boss: informal *Who's the boss around here?*
captain: *the captain of the team*
chief: *the chief of police*
commander: *a commander in the Royal Navy*
director: *the director of the film*
head: *Heads of government met in New York.*
principal: *the principal of the school*
ringleader: *the ringleader of the gang*

<<OPPOSITE *follower*

2 the person who is winning in a competition or race

3 a newspaper article that expresses the newspaper's opinions

leadership [ˈliːdəʃɪp] NOUN
1 the group of people in charge of an organization
2 Leadership is the ability to be a good leader.

leading [ˈliːdɪŋ] ADJECTIVE
particularly important, respected, or advanced

⬤ THESAURUS
chief: *one of his chief rivals*
eminent: *an eminent surgeon*
key: *the key witness at the trial*
major: *Exercise has a major part to play in preventing disease.*
main: *one of the main tourist areas of Amsterdam*
principal: *one of the principal figures in politics today*
prominent: *a prominent member of the Law Society*
top: *a top model*

leaf [liːf] **leaves; leafs, leafing, leafed** NOUN
1 the flat green growth on the end of a twig or branch of a tree or other plant

> VERB
2 If you leaf through a book, magazine, or newspaper, you turn the pages over quickly.
leafy ADJECTIVE

leaflet [ˈliːflɪt] **leaflets** NOUN
a piece of paper with information or advertising printed on it

⬤ THESAURUS
booklet: *a booklet about mortgage rates*
brochure: *a travel brochure*
circular: *A circular was sent out to shareholders.*
pamphlet: *an anti-vivisection pamphlet*

league [liːg] **leagues** NOUN
1 (PE) a group of countries, clubs, or people who have joined together for a particular purpose or because they share a common interest *e.g. the League of Red Cross Societies... the Australian Football League*
2 a unit of distance used in former times, equal to about 3 miles

leak [liːk] **leaks, leaking, leaked** VERB
1 If a pipe or container leaks, it has a hole which lets gas or liquid escape.
2 If liquid or gas leaks, it escapes from a pipe or container.

⬤ THESAURUS
escape: *A vent was opened to let some air escape.*
ooze: *Blood was oozing from the wound.*

seep: *Radioactive water has seeped into underground reservoirs.*
spill: *70,000 tonnes of oil spilled from the tanker.*

3 If someone in an organization leaks information, they give the information to someone who is not supposed to have it. *e.g. The letter was leaked to the press.*

> NOUN

4 If a pipe or container has a leak, it has a hole which lets gas or liquid escape.

● THESAURUS
chink: *A mist rose from the chinks in the pavement.*
crack: *The lava oozed through cracks in the rock.*
fissure: *Water trickled out of fissures in the limestone.*
hole: *The sea was flowing in through the hole in the ship's hull.*
puncture: *My tyre has a slow puncture.*

5 If there is a leak in an organization, someone inside the organization is giving information to people who are not supposed to have it.
leaky ADJECTIVE

leakage ['liːkɪdʒ] **leakages** NOUN
an escape of gas or liquid from a pipe or container

lean [liːn] **leans, leaning, leant** or **leaned; leaner, leanest** VERB
1 When you lean in a particular direction, you bend your body in that direction.
2 When you lean on something, you rest your body against it for support.
3 If you lean on someone, you depend on them.
4 If you lean towards particular ideas, you approve of them and follow them. *e.g. parents who lean towards strictness*

> ADJECTIVE

5 having little or no fat *e.g. lean cuts of meat*
6 A lean period is a time when food or money is in short supply.

leap [liːp] **leaps, leaping, leapt** or **leaped** VERB
1 If you leap somewhere, you jump over a long distance or high in the air.

● THESAURUS
bounce: *She bounced up and down on the spot, looking for attention.*
bound: *The dog came bounding up the stairs.*
jump: *I jumped over the fence.*
spring: *He sprang to his feet.*
vault: *He could easily vault the wall.*

> NOUN

2 a jump over a long distance or high in the air

● THESAURUS
jump: *the longest jumps by a man and a woman*

bound: *With one bound, Jack was free.*
spring: *The cheetah gave a great spring into the air.*

leap year leap years NOUN
a year, occurring every four years, in which there are 366 days

learn [lɜːn] **learns, learning, learnt** or **learned** VERB
1 When you learn something, you gain knowledge or a skill through studying or training.

● THESAURUS
grasp: *The basics of the language are easy to grasp.*
master: *He's having trouble mastering the piano.*
pick up: *You'll soon pick up enough German to get by.*

2 If you learn of something, you find out about it. *e.g. She had first learnt of the bomb attack that morning.*
learner NOUN

● THESAURUS
ascertain: *They had ascertained that he was not a spy.*
determine: *calculations to determine the rate of tax*
discover: *She discovered that they'd escaped.*
find out: *As soon as we found this out, we closed the ward.*
gather: *I gather the report is critical of the judge.*
hear: *I heard he had moved away.*
understand: *I understand that she's just taken early retirement.*

learned ['lɜːnɪd] ADJECTIVE
A learned person has a lot of knowledge gained from years of study.

● THESAURUS
academic: *I feel intimidated by academic people.*
erudite: *a witty and erudite leader*
intellectual: *an artistic and intellectual couple*
literate: *a literate and educated readership*
scholarly: *a scholarly researcher*

learning ['lɜːnɪŋ] NOUN
Learning is knowledge that has been acquired through serious study.

lease [liːs] **leases, leasing, leased** NOUN
1 an agreement which allows someone to use a house or flat in return for rent

> VERB

2 To lease property to someone means to allow them to use it in return for rent.

leash [liːʃ] **leashes** NOUN
a length of leather or chain attached to a dog's collar so that the dog can be controlled

least [liːst] NOUN
1 The least is the smallest possible amount of something.

> ADJECTIVE

2 as small or as few as possible

● THESAURUS
fewest: *Which product has the fewest calories?*
lowest: *the lowest temperatures on record for this time of year*
minimum: *the minimum height for a policeman*
slightest: *He showed only the slightest hint of emotion.*
smallest: *the smallest measurable unit of light*
<<OPPOSITE *most*

> ADVERB

3 Least is a superlative form of **little**

> PHRASE

4 You use **at least** to show that you are referring to the minimum amount of something, and that you think the true amount is greater. *e.g. At least 200 hundred people were injured.*

leather ['lɛðə] NOUN
Leather is the tanned skin of some animals, used to make shoes and clothes.
leathery ADJECTIVE

leave [liːv] **leaves, leaving, left** VERB
1 When you leave a place, you go away from it.

● THESAURUS
abandon: *He claimed that his parents had abandoned him.*
depart: *A number of staff departed during his time as director.*
desert: *Medical staff have deserted the city's main hospital.*
forsake: *I would never forsake my children.*
go: *Let me know when you're ready to go.*
quit: *He quit his job as an office boy.*
withdraw: *Troops withdrew from the country last month.*

2 If you leave someone somewhere, they stay behind after you go away.

3 If you leave a job or organization, you stop being part of it. *e.g. He left his job shortly after Christmas.*

4 If someone leaves money or possessions to someone, they arrange for them to be given to them after their death.

5 In subtraction, when you take one number from another, it leaves a third number.

> NOUN
6 a period of holiday or absence from a job

● THESAURUS
holiday: *I still have several days' holiday to take.*
time off: *He took time off to go sailing with his wife.*
vacation: *We went on vacation to Puerto Rico.*

Lebanese [ˌlɛbə'niːz] ADJECTIVE
1 belonging or relating to Lebanon
> NOUN
2 someone who comes from Lebanon

lecherous ['lɛtʃərəs] ADJECTIVE
constantly thinking about sex

lectern ['lɛktən] **lecterns** NOUN
a sloping desk which people use to rest books or notes on

lecture ['lɛktʃə] **lectures, lecturing, lectured** NOUN
1 a formal talk intended to teach people about a particular subject

● THESAURUS
address: *an address to the American people*
discourse: *a lengthy discourse on market strategy*
presentation: *a business presentation*
sermon: *his first sermon as a bishop*
speech: *He delivered his speech in French.*
talk: *a brief talk on the history of the site*

2 a talk intended to tell someone off

● THESAURUS
reprimand: *He has been given a severe reprimand.*
scolding: *given a scolding for offending his opponents*
ticking-off: *informal We were given a ticking-off for running in the corridors.*
warning: *He was given a severe warning from the referee.*

> VERB
3 Someone who lectures teaches in a college or university.

● THESAURUS
give a talk: *He set about campaigning, giving talks and fund-raising.*
speak: *He's been invited to speak at the Democratic Convention.*
talk: *Today, I plan to talk about the issues of education and nursery care.*
teach: *She has taught at the university for 34 years.*

lecturer ['lɛktʃərə] **lecturers** NOUN
a teacher in a college or university

led [lɛd] the past tense and past participle of **lead¹**

ledge [lɛdʒ] **ledges** NOUN
a narrow shelf on the side of a cliff or rock face, or on the outside of a building, directly under a window

ledger ['lɛdʒə] **ledgers** NOUN
a book in which accounts are kept

lee [liː] NOUN
1 the sheltered side of a place *e.g. the lee of the mountain*
> ADJECTIVE
2 the side of a ship away from the wind

leech [liːtʃ] **leeches** NOUN
a small worm that lives in water and feeds by sucking the blood from other animals

leek [liːk] **leeks** NOUN
a long vegetable of the onion family, which is

white at one end and has green leaves at the other

leer [lɪə] **leers, leering, leered** VERB

1 To leer at someone means to smile at them in an unpleasant or sexually suggestive way.

> NOUN

2 an unpleasant or sexually suggestive smile

leeway ['liːˌweɪ] NOUN

If something gives you some leeway, it allows you more flexibility in your plans, for example by giving you time to finish an activity.

left [lɛft] NOUN

1 The left is one of two sides of something. For example, on a page, English writing begins on the left.

2 People and political groups who hold socialist or communist views are referred to as the Left.

3 Left is the past tense and past participle of **leave**.

> ADJECTIVE OR ADVERB

4 Left means on or towards the left side of something. *e.g. Turn left down Govan Road.*

left-handed ['lɛftˌhændɪd] ADJECTIVE OR ADVERB

Someone who is left-handed does things such as writing with their left hand.

leftist ['lɛftɪst] **leftists,** NOUN OR ADJECTIVE

someone who holds left-wing political views

leftovers ['lɛftˌəʊvəz] PLURAL NOUN

the bits of food which have not been eaten at the end of the meal

left-wing ['lɛftˌwɪŋ] ADJECTIVE

believing more strongly in socialism, or less strongly in capitalism or conservatism, than other members of the same party or group
left-winger NOUN

● THESAURUS
leftist: *three leftist guerrilla groups*
liberal: *a politician with liberal views*
radical: *a radical feminist*
socialist: *Europe's last socialist state.*

leg [lɛg] **legs** NOUN

1 Your legs are the two limbs which stretch from your hips to your feet.

2 The legs of a pair of trousers are the parts that cover your legs.

3 The legs of an object such as a table are the parts which rest on the floor and support the object's weight.

4 A leg of a journey is one part of it.

5 one of two matches played between two sports teams *e.g. He will miss the second leg of their UEFA Cup tie.*

legacy ['lɛgəsɪ] **legacies** NOUN

1 property or money that someone gets in the will of a person who has died

● THESAURUS
bequest: *He made a bequest to his favourite charity.*
estate: *documents concerning the estate*
heirloom: *a family heirloom*
inheritance: *She was worried she'd lose her inheritance to her stepmother.*

2 something that exists as a result of a previous event or time *e.g. the legacy of a Catholic upbringing*

legal ['liːgəl] ADJECTIVE

1 relating to the law *e.g. the Dutch legal system*

● THESAURUS
forensic: *the forensic skill of a good barrister*
judicial: *a judicial review*
judiciary: *various levels of the judiciary system*

2 allowed by the law *e.g. The strike was perfectly legal.*
legally ADVERB

● THESAURUS
authorized: *an authorized procedure*
lawful: *What I did was lawful and proper.*
legitimate: *a legitimate business*
permissible: *the current permissible levels of pesticide in food*
rightful: *the rightful owner of the property*
valid: *a valid passport*
<<OPPOSITE *illegal*

legal aid NOUN

Legal aid is a system which provides the services of a lawyer free, or very cheaply, to people who cannot afford the full fees.

legality [lɪ'gælɪtɪ] NOUN

The legality of an action means whether or not it is allowed by the law. *e.g. They challenged the legality of the scheme.*

legalize ['liːgəˌlaɪz] **legalizes, legalizing, legalized;** also spelt **legalise** VERB

To legalize something that is illegal means to change the law so that it becomes legal.
legalization NOUN

legend ['lɛdʒənd] **legends** NOUN

1 an old story which was once believed to be true, but which is probably untrue

2 If you refer to someone or something as a legend, you mean they are very famous. *e.g. His career has become a legend.*
legendary ADJECTIVE

leggings ['lɛgɪŋz] PLURAL NOUN

1 Leggings are very close-fitting trousers made of stretch material, worn mainly by young women.

2 Leggings are also a waterproof covering worn over ordinary trousers to protect them.

legible ['lɛdʒəbʰl] ADJECTIVE
Writing that is legible is clear enough to be read.

legion ['liːdʒən] **legions** NOUN
1 In ancient Rome, a legion was a military unit of between 3000 and 6000 soldiers.
2 a large military force *e.g. the French Foreign Legion*
3 Legions of people are large numbers of them.

legislate ['lɛdʒɪsˌleɪt] **legislates, legislating, legislated** VERB; FORMAL
When a government legislates, it creates new laws.

legislation [ˌlɛdʒɪsˈleɪʃən] NOUN
Legislation is a law or set of laws created by a government.

legislative ['lɛdʒɪslətɪv] ADJECTIVE
relating to the making of new laws *e.g. a legislative council*

legislator ['lɛdʒɪsˌleɪtə] **legislators** NOUN; FORMAL
a person involved in making or passing laws

legislature ['lɛdʒɪsˌleɪtʃə] NOUN; FORMAL
the parliament in a country, which is responsible for making new laws

legitimate [lɪˈdʒɪtɪmɪt] ADJECTIVE
Something that is legitimate is reasonable or acceptable according to existing laws or standards. *e.g. a legitimate charge for parking the car*
legitimacy NOUN, **legitimately** ADVERB

leisure ['lɛʒə] NOUN
1 Leisure is time during which you do not have to work, and can do what you enjoy doing.

⬤ THESAURUS
free time: *He played piano in his free time.*
recreation: *Saturday afternoons are for recreation.*
relaxation: *Make time for a bit of relaxation.*
time off: *I haven't had any time off all day.*
<<OPPOSITE *work*

> PHRASES
2 If you do something **at leisure**, or **at your leisure**, you do it at a convenient time.

leisurely ['lɛʒəlɪ] ADJECTIVE OR ADVERB
A leisurely action is done in an unhurried and calm way.

⬤ THESAURUS
comfortable: *going at a comfortable speed*
easy: *an easy pace*
gentle: *His movements were gentle and deliberate.*
relaxed: *a relaxed meal*
unhurried: *an unhurried way of life*
<<OPPOSITE *hasty*

lekker ['lɛkə] ADJECTIVE; SLANG

1 In South African English, lekker means pleasant.

⬤ THESAURUS
delectable: *delectable chocolates*
delicious: *a wide selection of delicious desserts*
luscious: *luscious fruit*
pleasant: *a pleasant dinner*
tasty: *Try this tasty dish for supper.*
2 In South African English, lekker can also mean tasty.

lemming ['lɛmɪŋ] **lemmings** NOUN
a small rodent which lives in cold, northern countries. Lemmings were believed in the past to jump off cliffs to their death in large numbers

lemon ['lɛmən] **lemons** NOUN
1 a yellow citrus fruit with a sour taste
> ADJECTIVE
2 pale yellow

lemonade [ˌlɛməˈneɪd] NOUN
a sweet, fizzy drink made from lemons, water, and sugar

lend [lɛnd] **lends, lending, lent** VERB
1 If you lend someone something, you give it to them for a period of time and then they give it back to you.
2 If a bank lends money, it gives the money to someone and the money has to be repaid in the future, usually with interest.
> PHRASE
3 If you **lend someone a hand**, you help them.
lender NOUN

length [lɛŋkθ] **lengths** NOUN
1 The length of something is the horizontal distance from one end to the other.

⬤ THESAURUS
distance: *Work out the distance of the journey.*
extent: *the extent of the rain forest*
span: *a butterfly with a two-inch wing span*

2 The length of an event or activity is the amount of time it lasts for.

⬤ THESAURUS
duration: *The duration of the course is one year.*
period: *for a limited period only*
space: *A dramatic change takes place in the space of a few minutes.*
span: *The batteries have a life span of six hours.*
term: *a 12-month term of service*

3 The length of something is also the fact that it is long rather than short. *e.g. Despite its length, it is a rewarding read.*
4 a long piece of something

lengthen ['lɛŋkθən] **lengthens, lengthening, lengthened** VERB

To lengthen something means to make it longer.

● THESAURUS
extend: *They have extended the deadline.*
make longer: *You can make your hair longer by using extensions.*
prolong: *a move which will prolong the strike*
stretch: *Take care not to stretch the fabric.*
<<OPPOSITE *shorten*

lengthways or **lengthwise** ['lɛŋkθ,weɪz] or ['lɛŋkθ,waɪz] ADVERB
If you measure something lengthways, you measure the horizontal distance from one end to the other.

lengthy ['lɛŋkθɪ] **lengthier, lengthiest** ADJECTIVE
Something that is lengthy lasts for a long time.

lenient ['liːnɪənt] ADJECTIVE
If someone in authority is lenient, they are less severe than expected.
leniently ADVERB, **leniency** NOUN

lens [lɛnz] **lenses** NOUN
1 a curved piece of glass designed to focus light in a certain way, for example in a camera, telescope, or pair of glasses
2 The lens in your eye is the part behind the iris, which focuses light.

lent [lɛnt]
1 the past tense and past participle of **lend**
> NOUN
2 Lent is the period of forty days leading up to Easter, during which Christians give up something they enjoy.

lentil ['lɛntɪl] **lentils** NOUN
Lentils are small dried red or brown seeds which are cooked and eaten in soups and curries.

Leo ['liːəʊ] NOUN
Leo is the fifth sign of the zodiac, represented by a lion. People born between July 23rd and August 22nd are born under this sign.

leopard ['lɛpəd] **leopards** NOUN
a wild Asian or African big cat, with yellow fur and black or brown spots

leotard ['lɪə,tɑːd] **leotards** NOUN
a tight-fitting costume covering the body and legs, which is worn for dancing or exercise

leper ['lɛpə] **lepers** NOUN
someone who has leprosy
[WORD HISTORY: from Greek LEPROS meaning 'scaly']

leprosy ['lɛprəsɪ] NOUN
Leprosy is an infectious disease which attacks the skin and nerves, and which can lead to fingers or toes dropping off.

lesbian ['lɛzbɪən] **lesbians** NOUN
a homosexual woman
lesbianism NOUN

lesion ['liːʒən] **lesions** NOUN
a wound or injury

less [lɛs] ADJECTIVE OR ADVERB
1 Less means a smaller amount, or not as much in quality. *e.g. They left less than three weeks ago... She had become less frightened of him now.*
2 Less is a comparative form of **little**
> PREPOSITION
3 You use 'less' to show that you are subtracting one number from another. *e.g. Eight less two leaves six.*

❘ You use *less* to talk about things that can't be counted: *less time.* When you are talking about amounts that can be counted you should use *fewer.*

-less SUFFIX
'-less' means without. *e.g. hopeless... fearless*
[WORD HISTORY: from an Old English suffix]

lessen ['lɛsᵊn] **lessens, lessening, lessened** VERB
If something lessens, it is reduced in amount, size, or quality.

● THESAURUS
abate: *The storm gradually abated.*
decrease: *Population growth is decreasing by 1.4% each year.*
diminish: *The threat of war has diminished.*
dwindle: *his dwindling authority*
lower: *The Central Bank has lowered interest rates.*
minimize: *attempts to minimize the risk of developing cancer*
reduce: *Gradually reduce the dosage.*
shrink: *The forests have shrunk to half their size.*
<<OPPOSITE *increase*

lesser ['lɛsə] ADJECTIVE
smaller in importance or amount than something else

lesson ['lɛsᵊn] **lessons** NOUN
1 a fixed period of time during which a class of pupils is taught by a teacher

● THESAURUS
class: *I go to dance classes.*
coaching: *He needs extra coaching in maths.*
lecture: *a series of lectures on art*
period: *We get six periods of French a week.*
tutoring: *a growing demand for private tutoring*

2 an experience that makes you understand something important which you had not realized before

lest [lɛst] CONJUNCTION; OLD-FASHIONED, INFORMAL

as a precaution in case something unpleasant or unwanted happens *e.g. I was afraid to open the door lest he should follow me.*

let [lɛt] **lets, letting, let** VERB

1 If you let someone do something, you allow them to do it.

⬤ **THESAURUS**

allow: *I pleaded to be allowed to go.*
give permission: *Who gave you permission to come here?*
permit: *Permit me to express my opinion.*
sanction: *He may now be ready to sanction the use of force.*
<<OPPOSITE *forbid*

2 If someone lets a house or flat that they own, they rent it out.

⬤ **THESAURUS**

hire out: *The machines are hired out to farmers.*
lease: *She plans to lease the building to students.*
rent: *He rents rooms to backpackers.*

3 You can say 'let's' or 'let us' when you want to suggest doing something with someone else. *e.g. Let's go.*

4 If you let yourself in for something, you agree to do it although you do not really want to.

let off VERB

5 If someone in authority lets you off, they do not punish you for something you have done wrong.

6 If you let off a firework or explosive, you light it or detonate it.

lethal [ˈliːθəl] ADJECTIVE
able to kill someone *e.g. a lethal weapon*

lethargic [lɪˈθɑːdʒɪk] ADJECTIVE
If you feel lethargic, you have no energy or enthusiasm.

lethargy [ˈlɛθədʒɪ] NOUN
Lethargy is a lack of energy and enthusiasm.

letter [ˈlɛtə] **letters** NOUN

1 Letters are written symbols which go together to make words.

2 a piece of writing addressed to someone, and usually sent through the post

letter box **letter boxes** NOUN

1 an oblong gap in the front door of a house or flat, through which letters are delivered

2 a large metal container in the street, where you post letters

lettering [ˈlɛtərɪŋ] NOUN
Lettering is writing, especially when you are describing the type of letters used. *e.g. bold lettering*

lettuce [ˈlɛtɪs] **lettuces** NOUN
a vegetable with large green leaves eaten raw in salad

leukaemia or **leukemia** [luːˈkiːmɪə] NOUN
Leukaemia is a serious illness which affects the blood.

level [ˈlɛvəl] **levels, levelling, levelled**
ADJECTIVE

1 A surface that is level is smooth, flat, and parallel to the ground.

⬤ **THESAURUS**

flat: *Cricket should be played on a totally flat field.*
horizontal: *Every horizontal surface was covered with plants.*
<<OPPOSITE *uneven*

> VERB

2 To level a piece of land means to make it flat.

⬤ **THESAURUS**

flatten: *Flatten the dough and cut it into four pieces.*
plane: *planing the surface of the wood*
smooth: *He smoothed his hair.*

3 If you level a criticism at someone, you say or write something critical about them.

> ADVERB

4 If you draw level with someone, you get closer to them so that you are moving next to them.

> NOUN

5 a point on a scale which measures the amount, importance, or difficulty of something

⬤ **THESAURUS**

grade: *the lowest grade of staff*
rank: *He rose to the rank of captain.*
stage: *an early stage of development*
standard: *a decent standard of living*
status: *We were reduced to the status of animals.*

6 The level of a liquid is the height it comes up to in a container.

level off or **level out** VERB

7 If something levels off or levels out, it stops increasing or decreasing. *e.g. Profits are beginning to level off.*

level crossing **level crossings** NOUN
a place where road traffic is allowed to drive across a railway track

level-headed [ˈlɛvəlˌhɛdɪd] ADJECTIVE
Someone who is level-headed is sensible and calm in emergencies.

lever [ˈliːvə] **levers** NOUN

1 a handle on a machine that you pull in order to make the machine work

2 a long bar that you wedge underneath a heavy object and press down on to make the object move

leverage [ˈliːvərɪdʒ] NOUN
Leverage is knowledge or influence that you can use to make someone do something.

leveret [ˈlɛvərɪt] **leverets** NOUN
a young hare

levy ['lɛvɪ] **levies, levying, levied** NOUN

1 FORMAL
an amount of money that you pay in tax

> VERB

2 When a government levies a tax, it makes people pay the tax and organizes the collection of the money.

lewd [lu:d] ADJECTIVE
sexually coarse and crude

lexicography [ˌlɛksɪˈkɒɡrəfɪ] NOUN
the profession of writing dictionaries
lexicographer NOUN
[WORD HISTORY: from Greek LEXIS meaning 'word' and GRAPHEIN meaning 'to write']

liability [ˌlaɪəˈbɪlɪtɪ] **liabilities** NOUN

1 Someone's liability is their responsibility for something they have done wrong.

2 In business, a company's liabilities are its debts.

3 INFORMAL
If you describe someone as a liability, you mean that they cause a lot of problems or embarrassment.

liable ['laɪəbᵊl] ADJECTIVE

1 If you say that something is liable to happen, you mean that you think it will probably happen.

2 If you are liable for something you have done, you are legally responsible for it.

> It used to be wrong to use *liable* to mean 'probable or likely', but that use is now considered correct.

liaise [lɪˈeɪz] **liaises, liaising, liaised** VERB
To liaise with someone or an organization means to cooperate with them and keep them informed.

liaison [lɪˈeɪzɒn] **liaisons** NOUN
Liaison is communication between two organizations or two sections of an organization.

liar ['laɪə] **liars** NOUN
a person who tells lies

libel ['laɪbᵊl] **libels, libelling, libelled** NOUN

1 Libel is something written about someone which is not true, and for which the writer can be made to pay damages in court.

> VERB

2 To libel someone means to write or say something untrue about them.
libellous ADJECTIVE

liberal ['lɪbərəl] **liberals** NOUN

1 someone who believes in political progress, social welfare, and individual freedom

> ADJECTIVE

2 Someone who is liberal is tolerant of a wide

range of behaviour, standards, or opinions.

3 To be liberal with something means to be generous with it.

4 A liberal quantity of something is a large amount of it.
liberally ADVERB, **liberalism** NOUN
[WORD HISTORY: from Latin LIBERALIS meaning 'of freedom']

Liberal Democrat ['lɪbərəl 'dɛməˌkræt] **Liberal Democrats** NOUN
in Britain, a member or supporter of the Liberal Democrats, a political party that believes that individuals should have more rights and freedom

liberate ['lɪbəˌreɪt] **liberates, liberating, liberated** VERB
To liberate people means to free them from prison or from an unpleasant situation.
liberation NOUN, **liberator** NOUN

liberty ['lɪbətɪ] NOUN
Liberty is the freedom to choose how you want to live, without government restrictions.

libido [lɪˈbiːdəʊ] **libidos** NOUN
Someone's libido is their sexual drive.
[WORD HISTORY: from Latin LIBIDO meaning 'desire']

Libra ['liːbrə] NOUN
Libra is the seventh sign of the zodiac, represented by a pair of scales. People born between September 23rd and October 22nd are born under this sign.

librarian [laɪˈbrɛərɪən] **librarians** NOUN
(LIBRARY) a person who works in, or is in charge of, a library

library ['laɪbrərɪ] **libraries** NOUN

1 a building in which books are kept for people to come and read or borrow

2 a collection of books, records, or videos

Libyan ['lɪbɪən] **Libyans,** ADJECTIVE

1 belonging or relating to Libya

> NOUN

2 someone who comes from Libya

lice [laɪs] the plural of **louse**

licence ['laɪsəns] **licences** NOUN

1 an official document which entitles you to carry out a particular activity, for example to drive a car

2 Licence is the freedom to do what you want, especially when other people consider that it is being used irresponsibly.

> The noun *licence* ends in *ce*.

license ['laɪsəns] **licenses, licensing, licensed** VERB
To license an activity means to give official

permission for it to be carried out.

▨ The verb *license* ends in *se*.

lichen ['laɪkən] **lichens** NOUN
Lichen is a green, moss-like growth on rocks or tree trunks.

lick [lɪk] **licks, licking, licked** VERB
1 If you lick something, you move your tongue over it.
> NOUN
2 the action of licking

lid [lɪd] **lids** NOUN
the top of a container, which you open in order to reach what is inside

lie¹ [laɪ] **lies, lying, lay, lain** VERB
1 To lie somewhere means to rest there horizontally.
● THESAURUS
loll: *He was lolling on the sofa.*
lounge: *We lounged on the beach all day.*
recline: *She reclined on the couch.*
sprawl: *They sprawled in a lawn chair, snoozing.*
2 If you say where something lies, you are describing where it is. *e.g. The farm lies between two valleys.*

▨ The past tense of this verb *lie* is *lay*. Do not confuse it with the verb *lay* meaning 'put'.

lie² [laɪ] **lies, lying, lied** VERB
1 To lie means to say something that is not true.
● THESAURUS
fib: *He fibbed when she asked him where he'd been.*
perjure oneself: *All of the witnesses perjured themselves.*
tell a lie: *He could never tell a lie or do anything devious.*
> NOUN
2 something you say which is not true
● THESAURUS
deceit: *the deceits of political leaders*
fabrication: *She described the magazine interview as "a complete fabrication".*
falsehood: *He accused them of spreading falsehoods about him.*
fib: *I caught him out in another fib.*
fiction: *His account of events is a complete fiction.*

lieu [ljuː] PHRASE
If one thing happens **in lieu** of another, it happens instead of it.

lieutenant [lɛfˈtɛnənt] **lieutenants** NOUN
a junior officer in the army or navy
[WORD HISTORY: from Old French LIEUTENANT meaning literally 'holding a place']

life [laɪf] **lives** NOUN
1 Life is the quality of being able to grow and develop, which is present in people, plants, and animals.

2 Your life is your existence from the time you are born until the time you die.
● THESAURUS
existence: *a very miserable existence*
life span: *This species of snake has a life span of up to 25 years.*
lifetime: *a lifetime devoted to service for others*
time: *If I had my time again, I would do things differently.*

3 The life of a machine is the period of time for which it is likely to work.

4 If you refer to the life in a place, you are talking about the amount of activity there. *e.g. The town was full of life.*

5 If criminals are sentenced to life, they are sent to prison for the rest of their lives, or until they are granted parole.

life assurance NOUN
Life assurance is an insurance which provides a sum of money in the event of the policy holder's death.

lifeblood ['laɪfˌblʌd] NOUN
The lifeblood of something is the most essential part of it.

lifeboat ['laɪfˌbəʊt] **lifeboats** NOUN
1 a boat kept on shore, which is sent out to rescue people who are in danger at sea
2 a small boat kept on a ship, which is used if the ship starts to sink

life expectancy **life expectancies** NOUN
Your life expectancy is the number of years you can expect to live.

lifeguard ['laɪfˌgɑːd] **lifeguards** NOUN
a person whose job is to rescue people who are in difficulty in the sea or in a swimming pool

life jacket **life jackets** NOUN
a sleeveless inflatable jacket that keeps you afloat in water

lifeless ['laɪflɪs] ADJECTIVE
1 Someone who is lifeless is dead.
2 If you describe a place or person as lifeless, you mean that they are dull.

lifelike ['laɪfˌlaɪk] ADJECTIVE
A picture or sculpture that is lifelike looks very real or alive.

lifeline ['laɪfˌlaɪn] **lifelines** NOUN
1 something which helps you to survive or helps an activity to continue
2 a rope thrown to someone who is in danger of drowning

lifelong ['laɪfˌlɒŋ] ADJECTIVE
existing throughout someone's life *e.g. He had a lifelong interest in music.*

lifesaver ['laɪfˌseɪvə] **lifesavers** NOUN
In Australia and New Zealand, a person whose job is to rescue people who are in difficulty in the sea.

life span **life spans** NOUN
1 Someone's life span is the length of time during which they are alive.

2 The life span of a product or organization is the length of time it exists or is useful.

lifetime ['laɪfˌtaɪm] **lifetimes** NOUN
Your lifetime is the period of time during which you are alive.

lift [lɪft] **lifts, lifting, lifted** VERB
1 To lift something means to move it to a higher position.

● THESAURUS
elevate: a mechanism to elevate the platform
hoist: I hoisted my rucksack on to my shoulder.
pick up: Anthony picked up his case from the floor.
raise: He raised his hand to wave.
<<OPPOSITE lower

2 When fog or mist lifts, it clears away.

3 To lift a ban on something means to remove it.

● THESAURUS
cancel: The government has cancelled the state of emergency.
end: pressure to end the embargo
relax: an attempt to persuade the US Congress to relax the law
remove: an amendment to remove the ban on divorce

4 INFORMAL
To lift things means to steal them.

> NOUN
5 a machine like a large box which carries passengers from one floor to another in a building

6 If you give someone a lift, you drive them somewhere in a car or on a motorcycle.

ligament ['lɪgəmənt] **ligaments** NOUN
a piece of tough tissue in your body which connects your bones

light [laɪt] **lights, lighting, lighted** or **lit; lighter, lightest** NOUN
1 Light is brightness from the sun, fire, or lamps, that enables you to see things.

● THESAURUS
brightness: the brightness of the full moon
brilliance: the brilliance of the noonday sun
glare: shading his eyes from the glare
glow: the red glow of the dying fire
illumination: The only illumination came from a small window.
radiance: The bedside lamp cast a soft radiance over her face.
<<OPPOSITE dark

2 a lamp or other device that gives out brightness

3 If you give someone a light, you give them a match or lighter to light their cigarette.

> ADJECTIVE
4 A place that is light is bright because of the sun or the use of lamps.

5 A light colour is pale.

● THESAURUS
bleached: bleached pine tables
blonde or **blond:** blonde hair
fair: to protect my fair skin
pale: dressed in pale pink
pastel: delicate pastel shades
<<OPPOSITE dark

6 A light object does not weigh much.

● THESAURUS
flimsy: a flimsy cardboard box
lightweight: They will carry lightweight skis on their backs.
portable: a portable television
slight: She is small and slight.
<<OPPOSITE heavy

7 A light task is fairly easy.

8 Light books or music are entertaining and are not intended to be serious.

> VERB
9 To light a place means to cause it to be filled with light.

● THESAURUS
brighten: The late afternoon sun brightened the room.
illuminate: No streetlights illuminated the road.
light up: Fireworks lit up the sky.
<<OPPOSITE darken

10 To light a fire means to make it start burning.

● THESAURUS
ignite: A stray spark ignited the fireworks.
kindle: I kindled a fire in the stove.
<<OPPOSITE extinguish

11 To light upon something means to find it by accident.
lightly ADVERB, **lightness** NOUN

lighten ['laɪtən] **lightens, lightening, lightened** VERB
1 When something lightens, it becomes less dark.

2 To lighten a load means to make it less heavy.

lighter ['laɪtə] **lighters** NOUN
a device for lighting a cigarette or cigar

light-headed ['laɪtˌhɛdɪd] ADJECTIVE
If you feel light-headed, you feel slightly dizzy or drunk.

light-hearted ['laɪtˌhɑːtɪd] ADJECTIVE
Someone who is light-hearted is cheerful and has no worries.

lighthouse ['laɪtˌhaʊs] **lighthouses** NOUN
a tower by the sea, which sends out a powerful light to guide ships and warn them of danger

lighting ['laɪtɪŋ] NOUN
1 The lighting in a room or building is the way that it is lit.
2 (DRAMA) Lighting in the theatre or for a film is the special lights that are directed on the performers or scene.

lightning ['laɪtnɪŋ] NOUN
Lightning is the bright flashes of light in the sky which are produced by natural electricity during a thunder storm.

lightweight ['laɪtˌweɪt] **lightweights** NOUN
1 a boxer in one of the lighter weight groups
> ADJECTIVE
2 Something that is lightweight does not weigh very much. *e.g. a lightweight jacket*

light year **light years** NOUN
a unit of distance equal to the distance that light travels in a year

likable or **likeable** ['laɪkəbªl] ADJECTIVE
Someone who is likable is very pleasant and friendly.

like see page 510 for Word Web

-like SUFFIX
'-like' means resembling or similar to. *e.g. a balloonlike object*

likelihood ['laɪklɪˌhʊd] NOUN
If you say that there is a likelihood that something will happen, you mean that you think it will probably happen.

likely ['laɪklɪ] **likelier, likeliest** ADJECTIVE
Something that is likely will probably happen or is probably true.
⊙ **THESAURUS**
  anticipated: *the anticipated result*
  expected: *the expected response*
  liable: *He is liable to be a nuisance.*
  possible: *It's quite possible that I'm wrong.*
  probable: *the probable outcome*
  <<**OPPOSITE** *unlikely*

liken ['laɪkən] **likens, likening, likened**
VERB
If you liken one thing to another, you say that they are similar.

likeness ['laɪknɪs] **likenesses** NOUN
If two things have a likeness to each other, they are similar in appearance.

likewise ['laɪkˌwaɪz] ADVERB
Likewise means similarly. *e.g. She sat down and he did likewise.*

liking ['laɪkɪŋ] **likings** NOUN
If you have a liking for someone or something, you like them.

lilac ['laɪlək] **lilacs** NOUN
1 a shrub with large clusters of pink, white, or mauve flowers
> ADJECTIVE
2 pale mauve

lilt [lɪlt] **lilts** NOUN
A lilt in someone's voice is a pleasant rising and falling sound in it.
lilting ADJECTIVE

lily ['lɪlɪ] **lilies** NOUN
a plant with trumpet-shaped flowers of various colours

limb [lɪm] **limbs** NOUN
1 Your limbs are your arms and legs.
2 The limbs of a tree are its branches.
> PHRASE
3 If you have gone **out on a limb**, you have said or done something risky.

limber up ['lɪmbə] **limbers up, limbering up, limbered up** VERB
If you limber up, you stretch your muscles before doing a sport.

limbo ['lɪmbəʊ] NOUN
1 If you are in limbo, you are in an uncertain situation over which you feel you have no control.
2 The limbo is a West Indian dance in which the dancer has to pass under a low bar while leaning backwards.
[WORD HISTORY: sense 1 is from Latin IN LIMBO meaning 'on the border (of Hell)']

lime [laɪm] **limes** NOUN
1 a small, green citrus fruit, rather like a lemon
2 A lime tree is a large tree with pale green leaves.
3 Lime is a chemical substance that is used in cement and as a fertilizer.

limelight ['laɪmˌlaɪt] NOUN
If someone is in the limelight, they are getting a lot of attention.

limerick ['lɪmərɪk] **limericks** NOUN
an amusing nonsense poem of five lines

limestone ['laɪmˌstəʊn] NOUN
Limestone is a white rock which is used for building and making cement.

limit ['lɪmɪt] **limits, limiting, limited** NOUN
1 a boundary or an extreme beyond which something cannot go *e.g. the speed limit*
⊙ **THESAURUS**
  bounds: *the bounds of good taste*

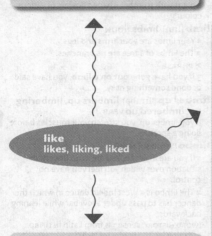

1 PREPOSITION
If one thing is like another, it is similar to it

● THESAURUS

akin: *She looked at me with something akin to hatred.*
analogous: *a process analogous to the curing of tobacco*
parallel: *Our situation is parallel to yours.*
similar: *a taste similar to that of celery*
<< OPPOSITE *unlike*

like
likes, liking, liked

2 VERB
If you like something or someone, you find them pleasant

● THESAURUS

adore (informal): *All her employees adored her.*
appreciate: *I know you appreciate good food.*
be fond of: *Are you fond of Chinese cuisine?*
be keen on: *I'm not very keen on sport.*
be partial to: *I'm partial to men with dark hair.*
enjoy: *Most children enjoy cartoons.*
go for: *What kind of man do you go for?*
have a soft spot for: *I've always had a soft spot for him.*
have a weakness for: *I have a weakness for slushy romantic novels.*
love: *She loves reading.*
relish: *He relished the idea of proving me wrong.*
revel in: *She appears to revel in being unpopular.*
<< OPPOSITE *dislike*

3 NOUN (*usually plural*)
a favourable feeling, desire, or preference
eg: *tell me your likes and dislikes*

● THESAURUS

cup of tea (informal): *Football was not his cup of tea.*
favourite: *Vanilla ice cream is my favourite.*
liking: *She had a liking for expensive clothes.*
preference: *I expressed a preference for a window seat on the plane.*

deadline: *We finished the job within the deadline.*
maximum: *He was given two years in prison, the maximum allowed for the charges.*
ultimate: *This hotel is the ultimate in luxury.*
utmost: *His skills were tested to the utmost.*

> VERB

2 To limit something means to prevent it from becoming bigger, spreading, or making progress. *e.g. He did all he could to limit the damage.*

● THESAURUS

confine: *Damage was confined to a small portion of the building.*
curb: *measures to curb inflation*
fix: *The mortgage rate is fixed at 8.5%.*
ration: *I'm rationing myself to ten cigarettes a day.*
restrict: *The patient was restricted to a meagre diet.*

limitation [ˌlɪmɪˈteɪʃən] **limitations** NOUN
1 The limitation of something is the reducing or controlling of it.
2 If you talk about the limitations of a person or thing, you are talking about the limits of their abilities.

limited [ˈlɪmɪtɪd] ADJECTIVE
Something that is limited is rather small in amount or extent. *e.g. a limited number of bedrooms*

limousine [ˈlɪməˌziːn] **limousines** NOUN
a large, luxurious car, usually driven by a chauffeur

limp [lɪmp] **limps, limping, limped; limper, limpest** VERB
1 If you limp, you walk unevenly because you have hurt your leg or foot.

> NOUN

2 an uneven way of walking

> ADJECTIVE

3 Something that is limp is soft and floppy, and not stiff or firm. *e.g. a limp lettuce*

● THESAURUS

drooping: *the drooping branches of a birch*
flabby: *a flabby stomach*
floppy: *She fondled the dog's floppy ears.*
slack: *his slack belly*
soft: *a soft dough*
<<OPPOSITE *stiff*

limpet [ˈlɪmpɪt] **limpets** NOUN
a shellfish with a pointed shell, that attaches itself very firmly to rocks

line [laɪn] **lines, lining, lined** NOUN
1 a long, thin mark

● THESAURUS

rule: *He drew a rule under the last name.*
score: *There was a long score on the car's bonnet.*

streak: *dark streaks on the surface of the moon*
stripe: *a green jogging suit with white stripes down the sides*

2 a number of people or things positioned one behind the other

● THESAURUS

column: *a column of figures*
file: *A file of mourners walked behind the coffin.*
queue: *a long queue of angry motorists*
rank: *ranks of police in riot gear*
row: *a row of pretty little cottages*

3 a route along which someone or something moves *e.g. a railway line*

● THESAURUS

course: *the course of the river*
path: *The lava annihilates everything in its path.*
route: *the most direct route*
track: *a railway track*
trajectory: *the trajectory of the missile*

4 In a piece of writing, a line is a number of words together. *e.g. I often used to change my lines as an actor.*

5 Someone's line of work is the kind of work they do.

6 The line someone takes is the attitude they have towards something. *e.g. He took a hard line with terrorism.*

7 In a shop or business, a line is a type of product. *e.g. That line has been discontinued.*

> VERB

8 To line something means to cover its inside surface or edge with something. *e.g. Cottages lined the edge of the harbour.*

line up VERB
9 When people line up, they stand in a line.
10 When you line something up, you arrange it for a special occasion. *e.g. A tour is being lined up for July.*

lineage [ˈlɪnɪɪdʒ] **lineages** NOUN
Someone's lineage is all the people from whom they are directly descended.

linear [ˈlɪnɪə] ADJECTIVE
arranged in a line or in a strict sequence, or happening at a constant rate

line dancing [ˈdɑːnsɪŋ] NOUN
a type of dancing performed by rows of people to country music

linen [ˈlɪnɪn] NOUN (D & T)
1 Linen is a type of cloth made from a plant called flax.
2 Linen is also household goods made of cloth, such as sheets and tablecloths.

liner [ˈlaɪnə] **liners** NOUN
a large passenger ship that makes long journeys

linesman ['laɪnzmən] **linesmen** NOUN
an official at a sports match who watches the lines of the field or court and indicates when the ball goes outside them

-ling SUFFIX
'-ling' means 'small'. *e.g. duckling*
[WORD HISTORY: from an Old English suffix]

linger ['lɪŋgə] **lingers, lingering, lingered** VERB
To linger means to remain for a long time. *e.g. Economic problems lingered in the background.*

lingerie ['lænʒərɪ] NOUN
Lingerie is women's nightclothes and underclothes.

lingo ['lɪŋgəʊ] **lingoes** NOUN; INFORMAL
a foreign language

linguist ['lɪŋgwɪst] **linguists** NOUN
someone who studies foreign languages or the way in which language works

lining ['laɪnɪŋ] **linings** NOUN
any material used to line the inside of something

link [lɪŋk] **links, linking, linked** NOUN
1 a relationship or connection between two things *e.g. the link between sunbathing and skin cancer*

● THESAURUS
affiliation: *He has no affiliation with any political party.*
association: *the association between the two companies*
attachment: *Mother and child form a close attachment.*
bond: *The experience created a bond between us.*
connection: *He has denied any connection to the bombing.*
relationship: *the relationship between humans and their environment*
tie: *She has ties with this town.*

2 a physical connection between two things or places *e.g. a high-speed rail link between the cities*
3 one of the rings in a chain

> VERB
4 To link people, places, or things means to join them together.
linkage NOUN

● THESAURUS
attach: *Attach the curtains to the rods with hooks.*
connect: *two rooms connected by a passage*
couple: *The engine is coupled to a gearbox.*
fasten: *a wooden bench fastened to the floor*
join: *the skin which joins the eye to the eyelid*
tie: *He tied the dog to the tree by its lead.*
<<OPPOSITE *separate*

lino ['laɪnəʊ] NOUN
Lino is the same as linoleum.

linoleum [lɪ'nəʊlɪəm] NOUN
a floor covering with a shiny surface

lint [lɪnt] NOUN
soft cloth made from linen, used to dress wounds

lion ['laɪən] **lions** NOUN
a large member of the cat family which comes from Africa. Lions have light brown fur, and the male has a long mane. A female lion is called a lioness

lip [lɪp] **lips** NOUN
1 Your lips are the edges of your mouth.
2 The lip of a jug is the slightly pointed part through which liquids are poured out.

lip-read ['lɪp,riːd] **lip-reads, lip-reading, lip-read** VERB
To lip-read means to watch someone's lips when they are talking in order to understand what they are saying. Deaf people often lip-read.

lipstick ['lɪp,stɪk] **lipsticks** NOUN
a coloured substance which women wear on their lips

liqueur [lɪ'kjʊə] **liqueurs** NOUN
a strong sweet alcoholic drink, usually drunk after a meal

liquid ['lɪkwɪd] **liquids** (SCIENCE) NOUN
1 any substance which is not a solid or a gas, and which can be poured

● THESAURUS
fluid: *The fluid can be removed with a syringe.*
liquor: *Pour the liquor off into the pan.*
solution: *a solution of honey and vinegar*

> ADJECTIVE
2 Something that is liquid is in the form of a liquid. *e.g. liquid nitrogen*

● THESAURUS
fluid: *a fluid fertiliser*
molten: *molten metal*
runny: *a dessertspoon of runny honey*

3 In commerce and finance a person's or company's liquid assets are the things that can be sold quickly to raise cash.

liquidate ['lɪkwɪ,deɪt] **liquidates, liquidating, liquidated** VERB
1 To liquidate a company means to close it down and to use its assets to pay off its debts.
2 INFORMAL
To liquidate a person means to murder them.
liquidation NOUN, **liquidator** NOUN

liquor ['lɪkə] NOUN
Liquor is any strong alcoholic drink.

liquorice ['lɪkərɪs] NOUN
Liquorice is a root used to flavour sweets; also the sweets themselves.

lira ['lɪərə] **lire** NOUN
a unit of currency formerly used in Italy

lisp [lɪsp] **lisps, lisping, lisped** NOUN
1 Someone who has a lisp pronounces the sounds 's' and 'z' like 'th'.
> VERB
2 To lisp means to speak with a lisp.

list [lɪst] **lists, listing, listed** NOUN
1 a set of words or items written one below the other

● THESAURUS
catalogue: *a chronological catalogue of the Beatles' songs*
directory: *a telephone directory*
index: *The book includes a comprehensive subject index.*
inventory: *an inventory of stolen goods*
listing: *a listing of all the schools in the area*
record: *Keep a record of everything you eat and drink.*
register: *a register of births, deaths and marriages*
> VERB
2 If you list a number of things, you make a list of them.

● THESAURUS
catalogue: *I was cataloguing my video collection.*
index: *Most of the archive has been indexed.*
record: *400 species of fungi have been recorded.*
register: *a registered charity*

listen ['lɪsᵊn] **listens, listening, listened** VERB
If you listen to something, you hear it and pay attention to it.
listener NOUN

● THESAURUS
attend: *Close your books and attend to me.*
hark: *Hark! I hear the sound of footsteps.*
hear: *Will you hear me saying my lines?*
pay attention: *Pay attention or you won't know what to do.*

listless ['lɪstlɪs] ADJECTIVE
lacking energy and enthusiasm
listlessly ADVERB
[WORD HISTORY: from Old English LIST meaning 'desire']

lit [lɪt] a past tense and past participle of **light**

litany ['lɪtənɪ] **litanies** NOUN
1 a part of a church service in which the priest says or chants prayers and the people give responses
2 something, especially a list of things, that is repeated often or in a boring or insincere way *e.g. a tedious litany of complaints*

literacy ['lɪtərəsɪ] NOUN
Literacy is the ability to read and write.

literate ADJECTIVE

literal ['lɪtərəl] ADJECTIVE
1 The literal meaning of a word is its most basic meaning.
2 A literal translation from a foreign language is one that has been translated exactly word for word.
literally ADVERB

> Be careful where you use *literally*. It can emphasize something without changing the meaning: *the house was literally only five minutes walk away.* However, it can make nonsense of some things: *he literally swept me off my feet.* This sentence is ridiculous unless *he* actually took a broom and swept the speaker over.

literary ['lɪtərərɪ] ADJECTIVE
connected with literature *e.g. literary critics*

literature ['lɪtərɪtʃə] NOUN
1 Literature consists of novels, plays, and poetry.
2 The literature on a subject is everything that has been written about it.

lithe [laɪð] ADJECTIVE
supple and graceful

litmus ['lɪtməs] NOUN
In chemistry, litmus is a substance that turns red under acid and blue under alkali conditions.

litmus test litmus tests NOUN
something which is regarded as a simple and accurate test of a particular thing, such as a person's attitude to an issue *e.g. The conflict was seen as a litmus test of Britain's will to remain a major power.*

litre ['liːtə] **litres** NOUN
(MATHS) a unit of liquid volume equal to about 1.76 pints

litter ['lɪtə] **litters, littering, littered** NOUN
1 Litter is rubbish in the street and other public places.
2 Cat litter is a gravelly substance you put in a container where you want your cat to urinate and defecate.
3 a number of baby animals born at the same time to the same mother
> VERB
4 If things litter a place, they are scattered all over it.

little see page 514 for Word Web

live lives, living, lived VERB [lɪv]
1 If you live in a place, that is where your home is.

● THESAURUS
dwell: *the people who dwell in the forest*

1 ADJECTIVE

small in size or amount *eg: a little old lady*

● THESAURUS

dainty: *dainty sandwiches and cakes*
dwarf: *He grows dwarf tulips.*
mini: *a machine which resembles a mini laptop computer*
miniature: *a collection of miniature toy boats*
minute: *minute particles of soil*
pygmy: *a children's zoo with pygmy goats*
skimpy: *dressed only in a skimpy bikini*
small: *They sat at a small table.*
tiny: *He tore the paper into tiny pieces.*
wee (Scottish): *Would you like a wee bit of cake?*

<< OPPOSITE *large*

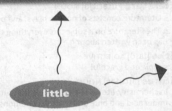

little

2 NOUN

a small amount or degree *eg: Would you like a little fruit juice?*

● THESAURUS

hardly any: *He's done hardly any work today.*
not much: *There's not much difference between them.*
meagre: *a meagre pay increase*
measly (informal): *a measly ration of food*
paltry: *a boring job with a paltry salary*
scant: *He paid scant attention to his colleagues.*

inhabit: *the fish that inhabit the coral reefs*
reside: *He used to reside in England.*
stay: Scottish and South African *We've stayed in this house since we got married.*

2 To live means to be alive.

● THESAURUS
be alive: *You are lucky to be alive.*
exist: *the chances of finding life existing on Mars*

3 If something lives up to your expectations, it is as good as you thought it would be.

> ADJECTIVE OR ADVERB [laɪv]
4 Live television or radio is broadcast while the event is taking place. *e.g. a live football match... The concert will go out live.*

> ADJECTIVE [laɪv]
5 Live animals or plants are alive, rather than dead or artificial. *e.g. a live spider*

● THESAURUS
alive: *It is unlikely that he is still alive.*
animate: *an animate object*
living: *living tissue*

6 Something is live if it is directly connected to an electricity supply. *e.g. Careful — those wires are live.*

7 Live bullets or ammunition have not yet been exploded.

live down VERB
8 If you cannot live down a mistake or failure, you cannot make people forget it.

livelihood ['laɪvlɪ,hʊd] **livelihoods** NOUN
Someone's livelihood is their job or the source of their income.

lively ['laɪvlɪ] ADJECTIVE
full of life and enthusiasm *e.g. lively conversation*
liveliness NOUN

● THESAURUS
active: *an active youngster*
animated: *an animated discussion*
energetic: *She gave an energetic performance.*
perky: *He wasn't quite as perky as usual.*
sparkling: *I was enjoying a sparkling conversation.*
sprightly: *a sprightly old man*
vivacious: *She is vivacious and charming.*
<<OPPOSITE *dull*

liven ['laɪvᵊn] **livens, livening, livened** VERB
To liven things up means to make them more lively or interesting.

liver ['lɪvə] **livers** NOUN
1 Your liver is a large organ in your body which cleans your blood and helps digestion.
2 Liver is also the liver of some animals, which may be cooked and eaten.
[WORD HISTORY: from Greek LIPAROS meaning 'fat']

livestock ['laɪv,stɒk] NOUN
Livestock is farm animals.

livid ['lɪvɪd] ADJECTIVE
1 extremely angry
2 dark purple or bluish *e.g. livid bruises*

living ['lɪvɪŋ] ADJECTIVE
1 If someone is living, they are alive. *e.g. her only living relative*

> NOUN
2 The work you do for a living is the work you do in order to earn money to live.

living room living rooms NOUN
the room where people relax and entertain in their homes

lizard ['lɪzəd] **lizards** NOUN
a long, thin, dry-skinned reptile found in hot, dry countries

llama ['lɑːmə] **llamas** NOUN
a South American animal related to the camel

load [ləʊd] **loads, loading, loaded** NOUN
1 something being carried

● THESAURUS
cargo: *The boat was carrying its usual cargo of bananas.*
consignment: *The first consignment of food has been sent.*
freight: *Most of the freight was carried by rail.*
shipment: *a shipment of weapons*

2 INFORMAL
Loads means a lot. *e.g. loads of work*

> VERB
3 To load a vehicle or animal means to put a large number of things into it or onto it.

● THESAURUS
fill: *The van was filled with crates.*
pack: *helicopters packed with medical supplies*
pile: *Her trolley was piled with groceries.*
stack: *stalls stacked with wares*

loaf [ləʊf] **loaves; loafs, loafing, loafed** NOUN
1 a large piece of bread baked in a shape that can be cut into slices

> VERB
2 To loaf around means to be lazy and not do any work.

loan [ləʊn] **loans, loaning, loaned** NOUN
1 a sum of money that you borrow

● THESAURUS
advance: *She was paid a $100,000 advance on her next novel.*
credit: *He can't get credit to buy the equipment.*
mortgage: *I took out a second mortgage on the house.*

2 the act of borrowing or lending something *e.g. I am grateful to Jane for the loan of her book.*

> VERB

3 If you loan something to someone, you lend it to them.

⬤ THESAURUS
advance: *I advanced him some money till we got home.*
lend: *Will you lend me your jacket?*

loath [ləʊθ] ADJECTIVE
If you are loath to do something, you are very unwilling to do it.

▨ Do not confuse *loath* with *loathe*.

loathe [ləʊð] **loathes, loathing, loathed** VERB
To loathe someone or something means to feel strong dislike for them.
loathing NOUN, **loathsome** ADJECTIVE

▨ Do not confuse *loathe* with *loath*.

lob [lɒb] **lobs, lobbing, lobbed** VERB
1 If you lob something, you throw it high in the air.

> NOUN

2 In tennis, a lob is a stroke in which the player hits the ball high in the air.

lobby [ˈlɒbɪ] **lobbies, lobbying, lobbied**
NOUN
1 The lobby in a building is the main entrance area with corridors and doors leading off it.
2 a group of people trying to persuade an organization that something should be done *e.g. the environmental lobby*

> VERB

3 To lobby an MP or an organization means to try to persuade them to do something, for example by writing them lots of letters.

lobe [ləʊb] **lobes** NOUN
1 The lobe of your ear is the rounded soft part at the bottom.
2 any rounded part of something *e.g. the frontal lobe of the brain*

lobster [ˈlɒbstə] **lobsters** NOUN
an edible shellfish with two front claws and eight legs

local [ˈləʊkəl] **locals** ADJECTIVE
1 Local means in, near, or belonging to the area in which you live. *e.g. the local newspaper*

⬤ THESAURUS
community: *the revival of family and community life*
district: *the district council*
neighbourhood: *a neighbourhood watch scheme*
parish: *the parish priest*
regional: *the regional elections*

2 A local anaesthetic numbs only one part of your body and does not send you to sleep.

> NOUN

3 The locals are the people who live in a particular area.

⬤ THESAURUS
inhabitant: *the inhabitants of Glasgow*
native: *She is proud to be a native of Sydney.*
resident: *a protest by residents of the village*

4 INFORMAL
Someone's local is the pub nearest their home.
locally ADVERB

locality [ləʊˈkælɪtɪ] **localities** NOUN
an area of a country or city *e.g. a large map of the locality*

localized or **localised** [ˈləʊkəˌlaɪzd]
ADJECTIVE
existing or happening in only one place *e.g. localized pain*

locate [ləʊˈkeɪt] **locates, locating, located**
VERB
1 To locate someone or something means to find out where they are.

⬤ THESAURUS
find: *They can't find it on the map.*
pinpoint: *Computers pinpointed where the shells came from.*
track down: *She has spent years trying to track down her parents.*

2 If something is located in a place, it is in that place.

⬤ THESAURUS
placed: *The hotel is wonderfully placed right in the city centre.*
sited: *a castle romantically sited on a river estuary*
situated: *His hotel is situated in a lovely place.*

location [ləʊˈkeɪʃən] **locations** NOUN
1 (GEOGRAPHY) a place, or the position of something

⬤ THESAURUS
place: *the place where the temple used to stand*
point: *a popular meeting point for tourists*
position: *The ship radioed its position to the coastguard.*
site: *the site of the murder*
situation: *The hotel has a superb isolated location.*
spot: *Can you show me the spot where it happened?*
whereabouts: *His exact whereabouts are still not known.*

2 In South Africa, a location was a small town where only Black people or Coloured people were allowed to live.

> PHRASE

3 If a film is made **on location**, it is made away from a studio.

loch [lɒx] **lochs** NOUN
In Scottish English, a loch is a lake.

lock [lɒk] **locks, locking, locked** VERB

1 If you lock something, you close it and fasten it with a key.

● THESAURUS
latch: *He latched the gate.*
padlock: *The box has been padlocked shut.*
<<OPPOSITE *unlock*

2 If something locks into place, it moves into place and becomes firmly fixed there.

> NOUN

3 a device on something which fastens it and prevents it from being opened except with a key

● THESAURUS
latch: *A key clicked in the latch of the front door.*
padlock: *He put a padlock on the door of his flat.*

4 A lock on a canal is a place where the water level can be raised or lowered to allow boats to go between two parts of the canal which have different water levels.

5 A lock of hair is a small bunch of hair.

locker [ˈlɒkə] **lockers** NOUN
a small cupboard for your personal belongings, for example in a changing room

locket [ˈlɒkɪt] **lockets** NOUN
a piece of jewellery consisting of a small case which you can keep a photograph in, and which you wear on a chain round your neck

locksmith [ˈlɒkˌsmɪθ] **locksmiths** NOUN
a person who makes or mends locks

locomotive [ˌləʊkəˈməʊtɪv] **locomotives** NOUN
a railway engine

locust [ˈləʊkəst] **locusts** NOUN
an insect like a large grasshopper, which travels in huge swarms and eats crops

lodge [lɒdʒ] **lodges, lodging, lodged** NOUN
1 a small house in the grounds of a large country house, or a small house used for holidays

> VERB

2 If you lodge in someone else's house, you live there and pay them rent.

3 If something lodges somewhere, it gets stuck there. *e.g. The bullet lodged in his pelvis.*

4 If you lodge a complaint, you formally make it.

lodger [ˈlɒdʒə] **lodgers** NOUN
a person who lives in someone's house and pays rent

lodgings [ˈlɒdʒɪŋz] PLURAL NOUN
If you live in lodgings, you live in someone else's house and pay them rent.

loft [lɒft] **lofts** NOUN
the space immediately under the roof of a house, often used for storing things

lofty [ˈlɒftɪ] **loftier, loftiest** ADJECTIVE
1 very high *e.g. a lofty hall*

2 very noble and important *e.g. lofty ideals*

3 proud and superior *e.g. her lofty manner*

log [lɒg] **logs, logging, logged** NOUN
1 a thick branch or piece of tree trunk which has fallen or been cut down

2 the captain's official record of everything that happens on board a ship

> VERB

3 If you log something, you officially make a record of it, for example in a ship's log.

4 To log in to a computer system means to gain access to it, usually by giving your name and password. To log out means to finish using the system.

logic [ˈlɒdʒɪk] NOUN
Logic is a way of reasoning involving a series of statements, each of which must be true if the statement before it is true.

logical [ˈlɒdʒɪkəl] ADJECTIVE
1 A logical argument uses logic.

● THESAURUS
consistent: *a consistent and well-presented theory*
rational: *a rational analysis*
reasoned: *a reasoned discussion*
sound: *His reasoning is sound, but he has missed the point.*
valid: *Both sides put forward valid points.*
<<OPPOSITE *illogical*

2 A logical course of action or decision is sensible or reasonable in the circumstances. *e.g. the logical conclusion*
logically ADVERB

● THESAURUS
judicious: *the judicious use of military force*
obvious: *I jumped to the obvious conclusion.*
plausible: *a plausible explanation*
reasonable: *a reasonable course of action*
sensible: *the sensible thing to do*
wise: *a wise decision*
<<OPPOSITE *illogical*

logistics [lɒˈdʒɪstɪks] NOUN; FORMAL
The logistics of a complicated undertaking is the skilful organization of it.

logo [ˈləʊgəʊ] **logos** NOUN
The logo of an organization is a special design that is put on all its products.
[WORD HISTORY: from Greek LOGOS meaning 'word']

-logy SUFFIX
'-logy' is used to form words that refer to the study of something. *e.g. biology... geology*
[WORD HISTORY: from Greek LOGOS meaning 'reason', 'speech', or 'discourse']

loin [lɔɪn] **loins** NOUN

1 OLD-FASHIONED
Your loins are the front part of your body between your waist and your thighs, especially your sexual parts.

2 Loin is a piece of meat from the back or sides of an animal. *e.g. loin of pork*

loiter ['lɔɪtə] **loiters, loitering, loitered** VERB
To loiter means stand about idly with no real purpose.

loll [lɒl] **lolls, lolling, lolled** VERB

1 If you loll somewhere, you sit or lie there in an idle, relaxed way.

2 If your head or tongue lolls, it hangs loosely.

lollipop ['lɒlɪˌpɒp] **lollipops** NOUN
a hard sweet on the end of a stick

lolly ['lɒlɪ] **lollies** NOUN

1 a lollipop

2 a piece of flavoured ice or ice cream on a stick

3 In Australian and New Zealand English, a sweet.

lolly scramble lolly scrambles NOUN
In New Zealand, a lolly scramble is a lot of sweets thrown on the ground for children to pick up.

lone [ləʊn] ADJECTIVE
A lone person or thing is the only one in a particular place. *e.g. a lone climber*

lonely ['ləʊnlɪ] **lonelier, loneliest** ADJECTIVE

1 If you are lonely, you are unhappy because you are alone.

● THESAURUS
alone: *scared of being alone in the house*
forlorn: *He looked a forlorn figure as he left the pitch.*
forsaken: *a forsaken and bitter man*
lonesome: *I'm lonesome without you.*

2 A lonely place is an isolated one which very few people visit. *e.g. a lonely hillside*
loneliness NOUN

● THESAURUS
deserted: *a deserted farmhouse*
desolate: *a desolate place*
isolated: *Many of the villages are in isolated areas.*
remote: *a remote outpost*
secluded: *a secluded area close to her home*
uninhabited: *an uninhabited island*

loner ['ləʊnə] **loners** NOUN
a person who likes to be alone

lonesome ['ləʊnsəm] ADJECTIVE
lonely and sad

long see page 519 for Word Web

longevity [lɒn'dʒɛvɪtɪ] NOUN; FORMAL
Longevity is long life.

longhand ['lɒŋˌhænd] NOUN
If you write something in longhand, you do it in your own handwriting rather than using shorthand or a typewriter.

longing ['lɒŋɪŋ] **longings** NOUN
a strong wish for something

● THESAURUS
craving: *a craving for sugar*
desire: *her desire for a child of her own*
hankering: *a hankering to be an actress*
hunger: *a hunger for success*
thirst: *a thirst for adventure*
yearning: *a yearning to be part of a normal family*

longitude ['lɒndʒɪˌtjuːd] **longitudes** NOUN
(GEOGRAPHY) The longitude of a place is its distance east or west of a line passing through Greenwich, measured in degrees.

long jump NOUN
The long jump is an athletics event in which you jump as far as possible after taking a long run.

long-range ['lɒŋˌreɪndʒ] ADJECTIVE

1 able to be used over a great distance *e.g. long-range artillery*

2 extending a long way into the future *e.g. a long-range weather forecast*

long-sighted ['lɒŋˌsaɪtɪd] ADJECTIVE
If you are long-sighted, you have difficulty seeing things that are close.

long-standing ['lɒŋˌstændɪŋ] ADJECTIVE
having existed for a long time *e.g. a long-standing tradition*

long-suffering ['lɒŋˌsʌfərɪŋ] ADJECTIVE
very patient *e.g. her long-suffering husband*

long-term ['lɒŋˌtɜːm] ADJECTIVE
extending a long way into the future *e.g. a long-term investment*

long-winded ['lɒŋˌwɪndɪd] ADJECTIVE
long and boring *e.g. a long-winded letter*

loo [luː] **loos** NOUN; INFORMAL
a toilet

look see pages 520 and 521 for Word Web

lookalike ['lʊkəˌlaɪk] **lookalikes** NOUN
a person who looks very like someone else *e.g. an Elvis lookalike*

● THESAURUS
dead ringer: informal *a dead ringer for his brother*
double: *He's the exact double of his father at that age.*
spitting image: informal *She is the spitting image of me.*

lookout ['lʊkˌaʊt] **lookouts** NOUN

1 ADJECTIVE
continuing for a great amount of time *eg*:
a long interval when no-one spoke
● THESAURUS
extended: *an extended period of unemployment*
interminable: *the interminable debate about GM foods*
lengthy: *a lengthy delay*
lingering: *a lingering death from cancer*
long-drawn-out: *the effects of a long-drawn-out war*
prolonged: *A prolonged labour is dangerous for both mother and child.*
protracted: *protracted negotiations over pay rises*
slow: *Writing music is a slow process.*
sustained: *a sustained run of bad luck*
<< OPPOSITE *short*

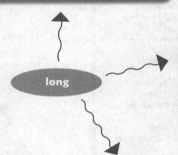

long

2 ADJECTIVE
great in length or distance *eg*: *a long line of people*
● THESAURUS
elongated: *The catfish has an elongated body.*
extensive: *an extensive list of products*
lengthy: *lengthy queues*
<< OPPOSITE *short*

l

3 VERB
to want something very much *eg*: *He longed for a cigarette.*
● THESAURUS
ache: *She still ached for her dead husband.*
covet (formal): *She coveted his job.*
crave: *I crave her approval.*
hunger: *Jules hungered for adventure.*
lust: *She lusted after a designer kitchen.*
pine: *I pine for the countryside.*
yearn: *He yearned for freedom.*

1 VERB

to turn your eyes towards something and
see it *eg: She looked at me with something
like hatred.*

● **THESAURUS**

examine: *He examined all the evidence.*

eye: *The waiters eyed him with suspicion.*

file: *The mourners filed past to view the body.*

gape: *She was gaping at the wreckage, lost
for words.*

gaze: *She sat gazing into the fire for a long
time.*

glance: *He glanced at his watch as she
spoke.*

glare: *He glared resentfully at me.*

glower: *She stood glowering at me with her
arms crossed.*

goggle: *He goggled at me in disbelief.*

observe: *A man was observing him from
across the square.*

ogle: *I hate the way he ogles every woman
who goes by.*

peek: *She peeked at him through the
curtains.*

peep: *He peeped at me to see if I was
watching him.*

peer: *He was peering at me through the
keyhole.*

regard: *He regarded me curiously.*

scan: *She scanned the advertisement pages
of the newspapers.*

scrutinize: *He scrutinized her passport and
stamped it.*

squint: *She squinted at the blackboard,
trying to read what was on it.*

stare: *They stared silently into each other's
eyes.*

study: *We studied the menu for several
minutes.*

survey: *He stood up and surveyed the crowd.*

watch: *I hate people watching me while I
eat.*

look

2 VERB

to appear or seem to be *eg: the desire to look attractive*

● THESAURUS

appear: *He appeared intoxicated.*
look like: *You look like you need a good night's sleep.*
seem: *She seemed tense.*
seem to be: *They seem to be lacking in enthusiasm.*

3 NOUN

the action of turning your eyes towards something *eg: Lucy took a last look in the mirror.*

● THESAURUS

gaze: *her concentrated gaze*
glance: *a cursory glance*
glimpse: *a fleeting glimpse*
peek: *Give me a peek at his letter.*

4 NOUN

the way someone or something appears *eg: He had the look of a desperate man.*

● THESAURUS

air: *a nonchalant air*
appearance: *He was fastidious about his appearance.*
bearing: *a man of military bearing*
expression: *I saw his puzzled expression.*
face: *Why are you all wearing such long faces?*
semblance: *a semblance of normality*

1 someone who is watching for danger, or a place where they watch for danger

> PHRASE

2 If you are **on the lookout** for something, you are watching for it or waiting expectantly for it.

loom [luːm] **looms, looming, loomed** NOUN

1 a machine for weaving cloth

> VERB

2 If something looms in front of you, it suddenly appears as a tall, unclear, and sometimes frightening shape.

3 If a situation or event is looming, it is likely to happen soon and is rather worrying.

loony ['luːnɪ] **loonies** INFORMAL **> ADJECTIVE**

1 People or behaviour can be described as loony if they are mad or eccentric.

> NOUN

2 a mad or eccentric person

loop [luːp] **loops, looping, looped** NOUN

1 a curved or circular shape in something long such as a piece of string

> VERB

2 If you loop rope or string around an object, you place it in a loop around the object.

loophole ['luːp,həʊl] **loopholes** NOUN
a small mistake or omission in the law which allows you to do something that the law really intends that you should not do

loose [luːs] **looser, loosest** ADJECTIVE

1 If something is loose, it is not firmly held, fixed, or attached.

● **THESAURUS**
free: *She broke her fall with her free hand.*
unsecured: *corridors blocked by unsecured objects*
wobbly: *a wobbly bridge*
<<OPPOSITE *secure*

2 Loose clothes are rather large and do not fit closely.

● **THESAURUS**
baggy: *a baggy black jumper*
slack: *Those trousers are very slack on you.*
sloppy: *wearing a sloppy t-shirt, jeans and trainers*
<<OPPOSITE *tight*

> ADVERB

3 To set animals loose means to set them free after they have been tied up or kept in a cage.
loosely ADVERB

The adjective and adverb *loose* is spelt with two os. Do not confuse it with the verb *lose*.

loosen ['luːsᵊn] **loosens, loosening, loosened** VERB
To loosen something means to make it looser.

● **THESAURUS**
slacken: *We slackened the guy-ropes.*

undo: *She began to undo the tiny buttons.*
untie: *He untied his shoes and slipped them off.*
<<OPPOSITE *tighten*

loot [luːt] **loots, looting, looted** VERB

1 To loot shops and houses means to steal goods from them during a battle or riot.

● **THESAURUS**
pillage: *The bandits pillaged the church.*
plunder: *They plundered and burned the town.*
raid: *Rustlers have raided a village in the region.*
ransack: *The three raiders ransacked the house.*

> NOUN

2 Loot is stolen money or goods.
[WORD HISTORY: from Hindi LUT]

● **THESAURUS**
booty: *They divided the booty between them.*
haul: *the biggest haul of cannabis ever seized*
plunder: *pirates in search of easy plunder*
spoils: *the spoils of war*
swag: slang *The thieves carried the swag off in a stolen car.*

lop [lɒp] **lops, lopping, lopped** VERB
If you lop something off, you cut it off with one quick stroke.

lopsided [,lɒp'saɪdɪd] ADJECTIVE
Something that is lopsided is uneven because its two sides are different sizes or shapes.

lord [lɔːd] **lords** NOUN

1 a nobleman

2 Lord is a title used in front of the names of some noblemen, and of bishops, archbishops, judges, and some high-ranking officials. *e.g. the Lord Mayor of London*

3 In Christianity, Lord is a name given to God and Jesus Christ.

Lordship ['lɔːdʃɪp] **Lordships** NOUN
You address a lord, judge, or bishop as Your Lordship.

lore [lɔː] NOUN
The lore of a place, people, or subject is all the traditional knowledge and stories about it.

lorikeet ['lɒrɪ,kiːt] **lorikeets** NOUN
a type of small parrot found in Australia

lorry ['lɒrɪ] **lorries** NOUN
a large vehicle for transporting goods by road

lory ['lɔːrɪ] **lories** NOUN
a small, brightly coloured parrot found in Australia

lose [luːz] **loses, losing, lost** VERB

1 If you lose something, you cannot find it, or you no longer have it because it has been taken away from you. *e.g. I lost my airline ticket.*

● **THESAURUS**
drop: *She's dropped a contact lens.*

mislay: *I seem to have mislaid my glasses.*
misplace: *Somehow my suitcase was misplaced.*
<<OPPOSITE *find*

2 If you lose a relative or friend, they die. *e.g. She lost her brother in the war.*

3 If you lose a fight or an argument, you are beaten.

THESAURUS
be beaten: *He was soundly beaten in the election.*
be defeated: *They were defeated in the final.*
<<OPPOSITE *win*

4 If a business loses money, it is spending more money than it is earning.
loser NOUN

> The verb *lose* is spelt with one *o*. Do not confuse it with the adjective and adverb *loose*.

loss [lɒs] **losses** NOUN
1 The loss of something is the losing of it.
> PHRASE
2 If you are **at a loss**, you do not know what to do.

lost [lɒst] ADJECTIVE
1 If you are lost, you do not know where you are.
THESAURUS
adrift: *two men adrift on a raft in the middle of the sea*
astray: *Our baggage went astray in transit.*
off-course: *After a while I realized I was completely off-course.*

2 If something is lost, you cannot find it.
THESAURUS
mislaid: *searching for his mislaid keys*
misplaced: *I've found your misplaced glasses.*
missing: *a missing person*
vanished: *unable to contact the vanished convoy*

3 Lost is the past tense and past participle of **lose**.

lot [lɒt] **lots** NOUN
1 A lot of something, or lots of something, is a large amount of it.
THESAURUS
abundance: *an abundance of food*
a great deal: *I've spent a great deal of time on this project.*
masses: informal *There were masses of flowers at her funeral.*
piles: informal *He's got piles of money.*
plenty: *We've got plenty of time.*
quantities: *She drank quantities of hot, sweet tea.*
scores: *There were scores of witnesses.*

2 A lot means very much or very often. *e.g. I love him a lot.*

3 an amount of something or a number of things *e.g. He bet all his wages and lost the lot.*

THESAURUS
batch: *a batch of cookies*

bunch: informal *My neighbours are a noisy bunch.*
crowd: *They're a real crowd of villains.*
group: *a small group of football supporters*
quantity: *a small quantity of water*
set: *a set of photographs*

4 In an auction, a lot is one of the things being sold.

lotion [ˈləʊʃən] **lotions** NOUN
a liquid that you put on your skin to protect or soften it *e.g. suntan lotion*

lottery [ˈlɒtərɪ] **lotteries** NOUN
a method of raising money by selling tickets by which a winner is selected at random

lotus [ˈləʊtəs] **lotuses** NOUN
a large water lily, found in Africa and Asia

loud [laʊd] **louder, loudest** ADJECTIVE OR ADVERB
1 A loud noise has a high volume of sound. *e.g. a loud explosion*
THESAURUS
blaring: *a blaring television*
deafening: *a deafening roar*
noisy: *a noisy old car*
resounding: *a resounding slap*
strident: *her strident voice*
thunderous: *thunderous applause from the crowd*
<<OPPOSITE *quiet*

2 If you describe clothing as loud, you mean that it is too bright. *e.g. a loud tie*
loudly ADVERB
THESAURUS
flamboyant: *a flamboyant outfit*
flashy: *flashy clothes*
garish: *a garish three-piece suite*
gaudy: *a gaudy purple-and-orange hat*
lurid: *She painted her toenails a lurid pink.*
<<OPPOSITE *dull*

loudspeaker [ˌlaʊdˈspiːkə] **loudspeakers** NOUN
a piece of equipment that makes your voice louder when you speak into a microphone connected to it

lounge [laʊndʒ] **lounges, lounging, lounged** NOUN
1 a room in a house or hotel with comfortable chairs where people can relax

2 The lounge or lounge bar in a pub or hotel is a more expensive and comfortably furnished bar.

> VERB
3 If you lounge around, you lean against something or sit or lie around in a lazy and comfortable way.

lourie [ˈlaʊrɪ] **louries** NOUN
one of two types of bird found in South Africa.

The grey lourie lives in open grassland and the other more brightly coloured species lives in forests and wooded areas

louse [laʊs] **lice** NOUN
Lice are small insects that live on people's bodies. *e.g. head lice*

lousy [ˈlaʊzɪ] **lousier, lousiest** ADJECTIVE; INFORMAL
1 of bad quality or very unpleasant *e.g. The weather is lousy.*
2 ill or unhappy

lout [laʊt] **louts** NOUN
a young man who behaves in an aggressive and rude way

lovable or **loveable** [ˈlʌvəbᵊl] ADJECTIVE
having very attractive qualities and therefore easy to love *e.g. a lovable black mongrel*

● THESAURUS
adorable: *an adorable black kitten*
charming: *a charming young Frenchman*
enchanting: *He was an enchanting baby.*
endearing: *one of his most endearing qualities*
sweet: *a sweet little girl*
<<OPPOSITE *hateful*

love [lʌv] **loves, loving, loved** VERB
1 If you love someone, you have strong emotional feelings of affection for them.

● THESAURUS
adore: *She adored her parents.*
cherish: *He genuinely loved and cherished her.*
worship: *She had worshipped him from afar for years.*
<<OPPOSITE *hate*

2 If you love something, you like it very much. *e.g. We both love fishing.*

● THESAURUS
appreciate: *I know you appreciate good food.*
enjoy: *Do you enjoy opera?*
like: *I've always liked horror films.*
relish: *I relish the challenge of dangerous sports.*
<<OPPOSITE *hate*

3 If you would love to do something, you want very much to do it. *e.g. I would love to live there.*

> NOUN
4 Love is a strong emotional feeling of affection for someone or something.

● THESAURUS
adoration: *He had been used to female adoration all his life.*
affection: *She thought of him with great affection.*
ardour: *an attempt to rekindle their lost ardour*
devotion: *At first she was flattered by his devotion.*
infatuation: *consumed with infatuation for her*
passion: *the object of her passion*
<<OPPOSITE *hatred*

5 a strong liking for something

● THESAURUS
devotion: *his devotion to literature*
fondness: *a fondness for good wine*
liking: *my liking for classical music*
weakness: *He had a weakness for cats.*
<<OPPOSITE *hatred*

6 In tennis, love is a score of zero.

> PHRASE
7 If you are **in love** with someone, you feel strongly attracted to them romantically or sexually.

8 When two people **make love**, they have sex.

love affair **love affairs** NOUN
a romantic and often sexual relationship between two people who are not married to each other

love life **love lives** NOUN
a person's romantic and sexual relationships

lovely [ˈlʌvlɪ] **lovelier, loveliest** ADJECTIVE
very beautiful, attractive, and pleasant
loveliness NOUN

● THESAURUS
attractive: *Polperro is an attractive harbour village.*
beautiful: *She's a very beautiful woman.*
delightful: *a delightful garden*
enjoyable: *I've had a very enjoyable time.*
pleasant: *a pleasant little apartment*
pretty: *a pretty room overlooking a beautiful garden*
<<OPPOSITE *horrible*

lover [ˈlʌvə] **lovers** NOUN
1 A person's lover is someone that they have a sexual relationship with but are not married to.
2 Someone who is a lover of something, for example art or music, is very fond of it.

loving [ˈlʌvɪŋ] ADJECTIVE
feeling or showing love
lovingly ADVERB

● THESAURUS
affectionate: *openly affectionate with each other*
devoted: *a devoted couple*
doting: *a doting father*
fond: *She gave him a fond smile.*
tender: *Her voice was tender.*
warm: *a warm and loving mother*
<<OPPOSITE *cold*

low [ləʊ] **lows, lower, lowest** ADJECTIVE
1 Something that is low is close to the ground, or measures a short distance from the ground to the top. *e.g. a low stool*

● THESAURUS
little: *a little table*
short: *a short flight of steps*

small: *a small stool*
squat: *squat stone houses*
stunted: *stunted trees*
sunken: *a sunken garden*
<<OPPOSITE *high*

2 Low means small in value or amount.

THESAURUS
minimal: *minimal expenditure*
modest: *a modest rate of unemployment*
poor: *working for poor wages*
reduced: *reduced customer demand*
scant: *scant stocks of fish*
small: *produced in small numbers*
<<OPPOSITE *high*

3 'Low' is used to describe people who are considered not respectable. *e.g. mixing with low company*

THESAURUS
common: *She might be a little common, but at least she wasn't boring.*
contemptible: *He mixes with the most contemptible people in society.*
despicable: *a despicable wretch*
disreputable: *the company of disreputable women*
lowly: *his lowly status*
vulgar: *She considers herself to be above the vulgar rabble.*

> ADVERB
4 in a low position, level, or degree

> NOUN
5 a level or amount that is less than before *e.g. Sales hit a new low.*

lowboy ['ləʊˌbɔɪ] **lowboys** NOUN
In Australian and New Zealand English, a small wardrobe or chest of drawers.

lower ['ləʊə] **lowers, lowering, lowered** VERB
1 To lower something means to move it downwards.

THESAURUS
drop: *He dropped his plate into the sink.*
let down: *They let the barrier down.*
take down: *The pilot took the helicopter down.*
<<OPPOSITE *raise*

2 To lower something also means to make it less in value or amount.

THESAURUS
cut: *The first priority is to cut costs.*
decrease: *The government plans to decrease interest rates.*
diminish: *to diminish the prestige of the monarchy*
lessen: *a diet that would lessen the risk of disease*
minimize: *attempts to minimize the risk of cancer*
reduce: *Gradually reduce the dosage.*
slash: *We're slashing our prices.*

<<OPPOSITE *increase*

lowlands ['ləʊləndz] PLURAL NOUN
Lowlands are an area of flat, low land.
lowland ADJECTIVE

lowly ['ləʊlɪ] **lowlier, lowliest** ADJECTIVE
low in importance, rank or status

low tide NOUN
On a coast, low tide is the time, usually twice a day, when the sea is at its lowest level.

loyal ['lɔɪəl] ADJECTIVE
firm in your friendship or support for someone or something
loyally ADVERB, **loyalty** NOUN

THESAURUS
constant: *I've lost my best friend and constant companion.*
dependable: *a cheerful, dependable mate*
faithful: *She remained faithful to her husband.*
staunch: *a staunch supporter*
true: *a true friend*
trusty: *a trusty ally*
<<OPPOSITE *treacherous*

loyalist ['lɔɪəlɪst] **loyalists** NOUN
a person who remains firm in their support for a government or ruler

lozenge ['lɒzɪndʒ] **lozenges** NOUN
1 a type of sweet with medicine in it, which you suck to relieve a sore throat or cough
2 a diamond shape

LP LPs NOUN
a long-playing record. LP is short for 'long-playing record'

LSD NOUN
LSD is a very powerful drug which causes hallucinations. LSD is an abbreviation for 'lysergic acid diethylamide'.

Ltd
an abbreviation for 'limited'; used after the names of limited companies

lubra ['luːbrə] **lubras** NOUN
an Australian Aboriginal woman

lubricate ['luːbrɪˌkeɪt] **lubricates, lubricating, lubricated** VERB
To lubricate something such as a machine means to put oil or an oily substance onto it, so that it moves smoothly and friction is reduced.
lubrication NOUN, **lubricant** NOUN

lucid ['luːsɪd] ADJECTIVE
1 Lucid writing or speech is clear and easy to understand.
2 Someone who is lucid after having been ill or delirious is able to think clearly again.

luck [lʌk] NOUN
Luck is anything that seems to happen by chance

and not through your own efforts.

● THESAURUS
accident: *It came about almost by accident.*
chance: *We only met by chance.*
destiny: *Is it destiny that brings people together?*
fate: *a simple twist of fate*
fortune: *smiled on by fortune*

luckless ['lʌklɪs] ADJECTIVE
unsuccessful or unfortunate e.g. *We reduced our luckless opponents to shattered wrecks.*

lucky ['lʌkɪ] **luckier, luckiest** ADJECTIVE
1 Someone who is lucky has a lot of good luck.

● THESAURUS
blessed: *being blessed with good looks*
charmed: *She seems to have a charmed life.*
fortunate: *He was extremely fortunate to survive.*
<<OPPOSITE *unlucky*

2 Something that is lucky happens by chance and has good effects or consequences.
luckily ADVERB

● THESAURUS
fortuitous: *a fortuitous combination of circumstances*
fortunate: *a fortunate accident*
opportune: *I had arrived at an opportune moment.*
timely: *his timely intervention*
<<OPPOSITE *unlucky*

lucrative ['lu:krətɪv] ADJECTIVE
Something that is lucrative earns you a lot of money. e.g. *a lucrative sponsorship deal*

ludicrous ['lu:dɪkrəs] ADJECTIVE
completely foolish, unsuitable, or ridiculous

lug [lʌg] **lugs, lugging, lugged** VERB
If you lug a heavy object around, you carry it with difficulty.

luggage ['lʌgɪdʒ] NOUN
Your luggage is the bags and suitcases that you take with you when you travel.

lukewarm [,lu:k'wɔ:m] ADJECTIVE
1 slightly warm e.g. *a mug of lukewarm tea*
2 not very enthusiastic or interested e.g. *The report was given a polite but lukewarm response.*

lull [lʌl] **lulls, lulling, lulled** NOUN
1 a pause in something, or a short time when it is quiet and nothing much happens e.g. *There was a temporary lull in the fighting.*

> VERB
2 If you are lulled into feeling safe, someone or something casues you to feel safe at a time when you are not safe. e.g. *We had been lulled into a false sense of security.*

lullaby ['lʌlə,baɪ] **lullabies** NOUN
a song used for sending a baby or child to sleep

lumber ['lʌmbə] **lumbers, lumbering, lumbered** NOUN
1 Lumber is wood that has been roughly cut up.
2 Lumber is also old unwanted furniture and other items.

> VERB
3 If you lumber around, you move heavily and clumsily.

4 INFORMAL
If you are lumbered with something, you are given it to deal with even though you do not want it. e.g. *Women are still lumbered with the housework.*

luminary ['lu:mɪnərɪ] **luminaries** NOUN;
LITERARY
a person who is famous or an expert in a particular subject

luminous ['lu:mɪnəs] ADJECTIVE
Something that is luminous glows in the dark, usually because it has been treated with a special substance. e.g. *The luminous dial on her clock.*
luminosity NOUN

lump [lʌmp] **lumps, lumping, lumped** NOUN
1 A lump of something is a solid piece of it, of any shape or size. e.g. *a big lump of dough*

● THESAURUS
ball: *a ball of clay*
cake: *a cake of soap*
chunk: *a chunk of bread*
hunk: *a hunk of beef*
piece: *a piece of cake*
wedge: *a wedge of cheese*

2 a bump on the surface of something

● THESAURUS
bulge: *My purse made a bulge in my pocket.*
bump: *a bump in the road*
hump: *a hump on his back*
swelling: *a swelling over one eye*

> VERB
3 If you lump people or things together, you combine them into one group or consider them as being similar in some way.
lumpy ADJECTIVE

lump sum **lump sums** NOUN
a large sum of money given or received all at once

lunacy ['lu:nəsɪ] NOUN
1 Lunacy is extremely foolish or eccentric behaviour.
2 OLD-FASHIONED
Lunacy is also severe mental illness.

lunar ['lu:nə] ADJECTIVE
relating to the moon
[WORD HISTORY: from Latin LUNA meaning 'moon']

lunatic ['luːnətɪk] **lunatics** NOUN

1 If you call someone a lunatic, you mean that they are very foolish. *e.g. He drives like a lunatic!*

2 someone who is insane

> ADJECTIVE

3 Lunatic behaviour is very stupid, foolish, or dangerous.

lunch [lʌntʃ] **lunches, lunching, lunched** NOUN

1 a meal eaten in the middle of the day

> VERB

2 When you lunch, you eat lunch.

luncheon ['lʌntʃən] **luncheons** NOUN; FORMAL

Luncheon is lunch.

lung [lʌŋ] **lungs** NOUN

Your lungs are the two organs inside your ribcage with which you breathe.

lunge [lʌndʒ] **lunges, lunging, lunged** NOUN

1 a sudden forward movement *e.g. He made a lunge for her.*

> VERB

2 To lunge means to make a sudden movement in a particular direction.

lurch [lɜːtʃ] **lurches, lurching, lurched** VERB

1 To lurch means to make a sudden, jerky movement.

> NOUN

2 a sudden, jerky movement

lure [lʊə] **lures, luring, lured** VERB

1 To lure someone means to attract them into going somewhere or doing something.

● THESAURUS

attract: *Warm weather attracts the fish close to the shore.*

beckon: *The mermaids beckoned the sailors towards the rocks.*

draw: *What drew him to the area was its proximity to London.*

entice: *Retailers will do anything to entice shoppers through their doors.*

tempt: *trying to tempt American tourists back to Britain*

> NOUN

2 something that you find very attractive

● THESAURUS

attraction: *the attraction of living on the waterfront*

bait: *using cheap bread and milk as a bait to get people into the shop*

magnet: *The park is a magnet for health freaks.*

pull: *feel the pull of the past*

temptation: *the many temptations to which they will be exposed*

lurid ['lʊərɪd] ADJECTIVE

1 involving a lot of sensational detail *e.g. lurid stories in the press*

2 very brightly coloured or patterned

lurk [lɜːk] **lurks, lurking, lurked** VERB

To lurk somewhere means to remain hidden from the person you are waiting for.

luscious ['lʌʃəs] ADJECTIVE

very tasty *e.g. luscious fruit*

lush [lʌʃ] **lusher, lushest** ADJECTIVE

In a lush field or garden, the grass or plants are healthy and growing thickly.

lust [lʌst] **lusts, lusting, lusted** NOUN

1 Lust is a very strong feeling of sexual desire for someone.

2 A lust for something is a strong desire to have it. *e.g. a lust for money*

> VERB

3 To lust for or after someone means to desire them sexually.

4 If you lust for or after something, you have a very strong desire to possess it. *e.g. She lusted after fame.*

lustful ['lʌstfʊl] ADJECTIVE

feeling or expressing strong sexual desire

● THESAURUS

carnal: *carnal desires*

lecherous: *a lecherous old man*

lewd: *his arrest for lewd behaviour*

lustre ['lʌstə] NOUN

Lustre is soft shining light reflected from the surface of something. *e.g. the lustre of silk*

lute [luːt] **lutes** NOUN

an old-fashioned stringed musical instrument which is plucked like a guitar

luxuriant [lʌgˈzjʊərɪənt] ADJECTIVE

Luxuriant plants, trees, and gardens are large, healthy and growing strongly.

luxurious [lʌgˈzjʊərɪəs] ADJECTIVE

very expensive and full of luxury

luxuriously ADVERB

● THESAURUS

de luxe: *de luxe cars*

lavish: *a lavish party*

opulent: *an opulent office*

plush: *informal a plush hotel*

sumptuous: *a sumptuous feast*

<<OPPOSITE plain

luxury ['lʌkʃərɪ] **luxuries** NOUN

1 Luxury is great comfort in expensive and beautiful surroundings. *e.g. a life of luxury*

● THESAURUS

affluence: *the trappings of affluence*

opulence: *the sheer opulence of her new life*
sumptuousness: *The hotel lobby was sumptuousness itself.*

2 something that you enjoy very much but do not have very often, usually because it is expensive

● **THESAURUS**
extra: *The car is a basic model with no extras.*
extravagance: *Eating out is an extravagance.*
indulgence: *This car is one of my few indulgences.*
treat: *I only eat cakes as a treat.*

-ly SUFFIX
1 '-ly' forms adjectives that describe a quality. *e.g. friendly*

2 '-ly' forms adjectives that refer to how often something happens or is done. *e.g. yearly*

3 '-ly' forms adverbs that refer to how or in what way something is done. *e.g. quickly... nicely*

lying ['laɪɪŋ] NOUN
1 Lying is telling lies.

● **THESAURUS**
deceit: *the deceits of political leaders*
dishonesty: *deliberate dishonesty*
fabrication: *His story is pure fabrication.*
fibbing: *Her fibbing eventually got her into trouble.*
perjury: *This witness has committed perjury.*

> ADJECTIVE
2 A lying person often tells lies.

● **THESAURUS**
deceitful: *deceitful and misleading remarks*
dishonest: *a dishonest account of events*
false: *a false confession*
untruthful: *She unwittingly gave untruthful answers.*
<<OPPOSITE honest

3 Lying is also the present participle of **lie**.

lynch [lɪntʃ] **lynches, lynching, lynched** VERB
If a crowd lynches someone, it kills them in a violent way without first holding a legal trial.

lynx [lɪŋks] **lynxes** NOUN
a wildcat with a short tail and tufted ears

lyre [laɪə] **lyres** NOUN
a stringed instrument rather like a small harp, which was used in ancient Greece

lyric ['lɪrɪk] **lyrics** NOUN
1 (**MUSIC**) The lyrics of a song are the words.
> ADJECTIVE
2 Lyric poetry is written in a simple and direct style, and is usually about love.

lyrical ['lɪrɪkəl] ADJECTIVE
poetic and romantic

Mm

m
an abbreviation for 'metres' or 'miles'

macabre [mə'kɑ:bə] ADJECTIVE
A macabre event is strange and horrible. *e.g. a macabre horror story*

macadamia [ˌmækə'deɪmɪə] **macadamias** NOUN
an Australian tree, also grown in New Zealand, that produces edible nuts

macaroni [ˌmækə'rəʊnɪ] NOUN
Macaroni is short hollow tubes of pasta.
[WORD HISTORY: an Italian word; from Greek MAKARIA meaning 'food made from barley']

macaroon [ˌmækə'ru:n] **macaroons** NOUN
a sweet biscuit flavoured with almonds or coconut

mace [meɪs] **maces** NOUN
an ornamental pole carried by an official during ceremonies as a symbol of authority

machete [mə'ʃɛtɪ] **machetes** NOUN
a large, heavy knife with a big blade

machine [mə'ʃi:n] **machines, machining, machined** NOUN
1 **(D & T)** a piece of equipment which uses electricity or power from an engine to make it work

◯ THESAURUS
apparatus: *an apparatus for use in fires*
appliance: *electrical appliances*
contraption: *a strange contraption called the General Gordon Gas Bath*
device: *a timer device for a bomb*
instrument: *navigation instruments*
mechanism: *the locking mechanism*

> VERB
2 If you machine something, you make it or work on it using a machine.

machine-gun [mə'ʃi:nˌgʌn] **machine-guns** NOUN
a gun that works automatically, firing bullets one after the other

machinery [mə'ʃi:nərɪ] NOUN
Machinery is machines in general.

machismo [mæ'kɪzməʊ] NOUN
Machismo is exaggerated aggressive male behaviour.

macho ['mætʃəʊ] ADJECTIVE
A man who is described as macho behaves in an aggressively masculine way.
[WORD HISTORY: from Spanish MACHO meaning 'male']

mackerel ['mækrəl] **mackerels** NOUN
a sea fish with blue and silver stripes

mackintosh ['mækɪnˌtɒʃ] **mackintoshes** NOUN
a raincoat made from specially treated waterproof cloth

mad [mæd] **madder, maddest** ADJECTIVE
1 Someone who is mad has a mental illness which often causes them to behave in strange ways.

◯ THESAURUS
barmy: slang *Bill used to say I was barmy.*
batty: slang *some batty uncle of theirs*
crazy: informal *If I worried about all this stuff, I'd go crazy.*
deranged: *after a deranged man shot 14 people*
insane: *Some people can't take it and go insane.*
loony: slang *She's as loony as her brother!*
<<OPPOSITE *sane*

2 If you describe someone as mad, you mean that they are very foolish. *e.g. He said we were mad to share a flat.*

◯ THESAURUS
barmy: slang *a barmy idea*
crazy: informal *People thought they were crazy to try it.*
daft: informal *That's a daft question.*
foolhardy: *Some described the act as foolhardy.*
foolish: *It would be foolish to raise hopes unnecessarily.*
stupid: *It would be stupid to pretend otherwise.*

3 INFORMAL
Someone who is mad is angry.

◯ THESAURUS
angry: *She was angry at her husband.*
crazy: informal *This sitting around is driving me crazy.*
enraged: *I got more and more enraged at my father.*
fuming: *Mrs Vine was still fuming.*
furious: *He is furious at the way his wife has been treated.*

incensed: *Mum was incensed at his lack of compassion.*
infuriated: *He knew how infuriated this would make me.*
irate: *Bob was very irate, shouting and screaming about the flight delay.*
livid: informal *I am absolutely livid about it.*

4 If you are mad about someone or something, you like them very much. *e.g. Alan was mad about golf.*
madness NOUN, **madman** NOUN

madam ['mædəm]
'Madam' is a very formal way of addressing a woman

maddening ['mædⁿnɪŋ] ADJECTIVE
irritating or frustrating *e.g. She had many maddening habits.*

madly ['mædlɪ] ADVERB
If you do something madly, you do it in a fast, excited way.

madrigal ['mædrɪgⁿl] **madrigals** NOUN
a song sung by several people without instruments

Mafia ['mæfɪə] NOUN
The Mafia is a large crime organization operating in Sicily, Italy, and the USA.

magazine [,mægə'zi:n] **magazines** NOUN
1 (LIBRARY) a weekly or monthly publication with articles and photographs
2 a compartment in a gun for cartridges
[WORD HISTORY: from Arabic MAKHZAN meaning 'storehouse']

magenta [mə'dʒɛntə] NOUN OR ADJECTIVE
dark reddish-purple

maggot ['mægət] **maggots** NOUN
a creature that looks like a small worm and lives on decaying things. Maggots turn into flies

magic ['mædʒɪk] NOUN
1 In fairy stories, magic is a special power that can make impossible things happen.

⬤ THESAURUS
sorcery: *the use of sorcery to combat evil influences*
witchcraft: *people who practise witchcraft*

2 Magic is the art of performing tricks to entertain people.

magical ['mædʒɪkⁿl] ADJECTIVE
wonderful and exciting
magically ADVERB

⬤ THESAURUS
bewitching: *bewitching brown eyes*
enchanting: *an enchanting child*

magician [mə'dʒɪʃən] **magicians** NOUN
1 a person who performs tricks as entertainment

2 In fairy stories, a magician is a man with magical powers.

magistrate ['mædʒɪ,streɪt] **magistrates** NOUN
an official who acts as a judge in a law court that deals with less serious crimes

magnanimous [mæg'nænɪməs] ADJECTIVE
generous and forgiving

magnate ['mægneɪt] **magnates** NOUN
someone who is very rich and powerful in business

magnet ['mægnɪt] **magnets** NOUN
a piece of iron which attracts iron or steel towards it, and which points towards north if allowed to swing freely
magnetic ADJECTIVE, **magnetism** NOUN

magnificent [mæg'nɪfɪsⁿnt] ADJECTIVE
extremely beautiful or impressive
magnificently ADVERB, **magnificence** NOUN

magnify ['mægnɪ,faɪ] **magnifies, magnifying, magnified** VERB
When a microscope or lens magnifies something, it makes it appear bigger than it actually is.
magnification NOUN

magnifying glass ['mægnɪ,faɪɪŋ] **magnifying glasses** NOUN
a lens which makes things appear bigger than they really are

magnitude ['mægnɪ,tju:d] NOUN
The magnitude of something is its great size or importance.

magnolia [mæg'nəʊlɪə] **magnolias** NOUN
a tree which has large white or pink flowers in spring

magpie ['mæg,paɪ] **magpies** NOUN
a large black and white bird with a long tail

mahogany [mə'hɒgənɪ] NOUN
Mahogany is a hard reddish brown wood used for making furniture.

maid [meɪd] **maids** NOUN
a female servant

maiden ['meɪdⁿn] **maidens** NOUN
1 LITERARY
a young woman
> ADJECTIVE
2 first *e.g. a maiden voyage*

maiden name maiden names NOUN
the surname a woman had before she married

mail [meɪl] **mails, mailing, mailed** NOUN
1 Your mail is the letters and parcels delivered to you by the post office.

> VERB

2 If you mail a letter, you send it by post.

mail order NOUN

Mail order is a system of buying goods by post.

maim [meɪm] **maims, maiming, maimed**
VERB

To maim someone is to injure them very badly
for life.

main [meɪn] **mains** ADJECTIVE

1 most important *e.g. the main event*

● THESAURUS

cardinal: *one of the cardinal rules of movie
reviewing*
chief: *one of his chief rivals*
foremost: *one of the foremost scholars on ancient
Indian culture*
leading: *a leading industrial nation*
major: *one of the major causes of cancer*
predominant: *Her predominant emotion was
confusion.*
primary: *the primary source of water in the region*
prime: *the prime suspect*
principal: *the principal source of sodium in our diets*

> NOUN

2 The mains are large pipes or wires that carry
gas, water or electricity.

mainframe ['meɪnˌfreɪm] **mainframes**
NOUN

a large computer which can be used by many
people at the same time

mainland ['meɪnlənd] NOUN

The mainland is the main part of a country in
contrast to islands around its coast.

mainly ['meɪnlɪ] ADVERB

true in most cases

● THESAURUS

chiefly: *He painted chiefly portraits.*
generally: *It is generally true that the darker the
fruit the higher its iron content.*
largely: *The early studies were done on men, largely
by male researchers.*
mostly: *Cars are mostly metal.*
predominantly: *Business is conducted
predominantly by phone.*
primarily: *The body is made up primarily of bone,
muscle, and fat.*
principally: *This is principally because the market is
weak.*

mainstay ['meɪnˌsteɪ] NOUN

The mainstay of something is the most
important part of it.

mainstream ['meɪnˌstriːm] NOUN

The mainstream is the most ordinary and
conventional group of people or ideas in a
society.

maintain [meɪn'teɪn] **maintains,
maintaining, maintained** VERB

1 If you maintain something, you keep it going or
keep it at a particular rate or level. *e.g. I wanted to
maintain our friendship.*

2 If you maintain someone, you provide them
regularly with money for what they need.

3 To maintain a machine or a building is to keep
it in good condition.

4 If you maintain that something is true, you
believe it is true and say so.

maintenance ['meɪntɪnəns] NOUN

1 Maintenance is the process of keeping
something in good condition.

2 Maintenance is also money that a person sends
regularly to someone to provide for the things
they need.

maize [meɪz] NOUN

Maize is a tall plant which produces sweet corn.

majesty ['mædʒɪstɪ] **majesties**

1 You say 'His Majesty' when you are talking
about a king, and 'Her Majesty' when you are
talking about a queen.

> NOUN

2 Majesty is great dignity and impressiveness.
majestic ADJECTIVE, **majestically** ADVERB

major ['meɪdʒə] **majors** ADJECTIVE

1 more important or more significant than other
things *e.g. There were over fifty major injuries.*

● THESAURUS

critical: *a critical factor*
crucial: *He took the crucial decisions himself.*
leading: *a leading industrial nation*
outstanding: *an outstanding contribution*
significant: *Her upbringing had a significant effect
on her relationships.*
<<OPPOSITE *minor*

2 (**MUSIC**) A major key is one of the keys in
which most European music is written.

> NOUN

3 an army officer of the rank immediately above
captain

majority [mə'dʒɒrɪtɪ] **majorities** NOUN

1 The majority of people or things in a group is
more than half of the group.

● THESAURUS

best part: *for the best part of 24 hours*
better part: *I spent the better part of £100 on her.*
bulk: *the bulk of the world's great poetry*
mass: *the mass of the population*
most: *Most of the book is completely true.*

2 In an election, the majority is the difference
between the number of votes gained by the

m

531

winner and the number gained by the runner-up.

> You should use *majority* only to talk about things that can be counted: *the majority of car owners*. To talk about an amount that cannot be counted you should use *most*: *most of the harvest was saved*.

make [meɪk] **makes, making, made** VERB

1 To make something is to produce or construct it, or to cause it to happen.

THESAURUS

assemble: *Workers were assembling planes.*
build: *Workers at the site build the F-16 jet fighter.*
construct: *the campaign to construct a temple on the site*
create: *It's great for a radio producer to create a show like this.*
fabricate: *All the tools are fabricated from high quality steel.*
fashion: *Stone Age settlers fashioned necklaces from sheep's teeth.*
form: *a figure formed from clay*
manufacture: *They manufacture plastics.*
produce: *We try to produce items that are the basics of a stylish wardrobe.*

2 To make something is to do it. *e.g. He was about to make a speech.*

3 To make something is to prepare it. *e.g. I'll make some salad dressing.*

4 If someone makes you do something, they force you to do it. *e.g. Mum made me clean the bathroom.*

THESAURUS

compel: *legislation to compel cyclists to wear a helmet*
drive: *Jealousy drives people to murder.*
force: *A back injury forced her to withdraw from the competition.*
oblige: *Finally I was obliged to abandon the car.*

> NOUN

5 The make of a product is the name of the company that manufactured it. *e.g. 'What make of car do you drive?' – 'Toyota'*

THESAURUS

brand: *a brand of cigarette*
model: *To keep the cost down, opt for a basic model.*

> VERB **make up**

6 If a number of things make up something, they form that thing.

THESAURUS

compose: *The force would be composed of troops from NATO countries.*
comprise: *a crowd comprising the wives and children of scientists*
constitute: *Hindus constitute 83% of India's population.*

form: *Cereals form the staple diet.*

7 If you make up a story, you invent it.

THESAURUS

concoct: *The prisoner concocted the story to get a lighter sentence.*
fabricate: *Officers fabricated evidence against them.*
invent: *I must invent something I can tell my mother.*

8 If you make yourself up, you put make-up on.

9 If two people make it up, they become friends again after a quarrel.

make-up [ˈmeɪkʌp] NOUN

1 Make-up is coloured creams and powders which women put on their faces to make themselves look more attractive.

2 Someone's make-up is their character or personality.

making [ˈmeɪkɪŋ] NOUN

1 The making of something is the act or process of creating or producing it.

THESAURUS

assembly: *the assembly of an explosive device*
building: *The building of the airport continues.*
construction: *boat construction*
creation: *the creation of large parks and forests*
fabrication: *the design and fabrication of the space shuttle*
manufacture: *the manufacture of nuclear weapons*
production: *These proteins stimulate the production of blood cells.*

> PHRASE

2 When you describe someone as something **in the making**, you mean that they are gradually becoming that thing. *e.g. a captain in the making*

THESAURUS

budding: *a budding author*
emergent: *an emergent state*
potential: *a potential champion*

maladjusted [ˌmæləˈdʒʌstɪd] ADJECTIVE
A maladjusted person has psychological or behaviour problems.

malaise [mæˈleɪz] NOUN; FORMAL
Malaise is a feeling of dissatisfaction or unhappiness.

malaria [məˈlɛərɪə] NOUN
Malaria is a tropical disease caught from mosquitoes which causes fever and shivering.

Malaysian [məˈleɪzɪən] **Malaysians**
ADJECTIVE

1 belonging or relating to Malaysia

> NOUN

2 someone who comes from Malaysia

male [meɪl] **males** NOUN

1 a person or animal belonging to the sex that cannot give birth or lay eggs

> ADJECTIVE

2 concerning or affecting men rather than women

THESAURUS

manly: *He was the ideal of manly beauty.*
masculine: *masculine characteristics like facial hair*
<<OPPOSITE *female*

male chauvinist **male chauvinists** NOUN
a man who thinks that men are better than women

malevolent [mə'lɛvələnt] ADJECTIVE; FORMAL
wanting or intending to cause harm
malevolence NOUN

malfunction [mæl'fʌŋkʃən] **malfunctions, malfunctioning, malfunctioned** VERB
1 If a machine malfunctions, it fails to work properly.

> NOUN

2 the failure of a machine to work properly

malice ['mælɪs] NOUN
Malice is a desire to cause harm to people.

malicious [mə'lɪʃəs] ADJECTIVE
Malicious talk or behaviour is intended to harm someone.

THESAURUS

cruel: *Children can be so cruel.*
malevolent: formal *She gave me a malevolent stare.*
mean: *Someone's played a mean trick on you.*
spiteful: *spiteful telephone calls*
vicious: *a vicious attack on an innocent man's character*

malign [mə'laɪn] **maligns, maligning, maligned** VERB; FORMAL
To malign someone is to say unpleasant and untrue things about them.

malignant [mə'lɪɡnənt] ADJECTIVE
1 harmful and cruel
2 A malignant disease or tumour could cause death if it is allowed to continue.

mallard ['mælɑːd] **mallards** NOUN
a kind of wild duck. The male has a green head

mallee ['mæliː] **mallees** NOUN
a eucalypt that grows close to the ground in dry areas of Australia

mallet ['mælɪt] **mallets** NOUN
a wooden hammer with a square head

malnutrition [ˌmælnjuː'trɪʃən] NOUN
Malnutrition is not eating enough healthy food.

malodorous [mæl'əʊdərəs] ADJECTIVE
If you describe something as malodorous, you means it smells bad.

malpractice [mæl'præktɪs] NOUN
If someone such as a doctor or lawyer breaks the rules of their profession, their behaviour is called malpractice.

malt [mɔːlt] NOUN
Malt is roasted grain, usually barley, that is used in making beer and whisky.

mammal ['mæməl] **mammals** NOUN
(SCIENCE) Animals that give birth to live babies and feed their young with milk from the mother's body are called mammals. Human beings, dogs, and whales are all mammals.

mammoth ['mæməθ] **mammoths**
ADJECTIVE
1 very large indeed *e.g. a mammoth outdoor concert*

> NOUN

2 a huge animal that looked like a hairy elephant with long tusks. Mammoths became extinct a long time ago

man [mæn] **men; mans, manning, manned** NOUN
1 an adult male human being

THESAURUS

bloke: British and Australian and New Zealand; informal *a really nice bloke*
chap: informal *I am a very lucky chap.*
gentleman: *It seems this gentleman was waiting for the doctor.*
guy: informal *a guy from Manchester*
male: *A high proportion of crime is perpetrated by young males.*
<<OPPOSITE *woman*

> PLURAL NOUN

2 Human beings in general are sometimes referred to as men. *e.g. All men are equal.*

THESAURUS

humanity: *He has rendered a great service to humanity.*
human race: *Can the human race carry on expanding?*
mankind: *the evolution of mankind*

> VERB

3 To man something is to be in charge of it or operate it. *e.g. Two officers were manning the radar screens.*

mana ['mɑːnə] NOUN
Mana is authority and influence such as that held by a New Zealand Maori chief.

THESAURUS

authority: *figures of authority*
influence: *He denies using any political influence.*
power: *positions of great power*
standing: *The Prime Minister's standing was high in the US.*
stature: *his stature as the world's greatest cellist*

m

status: *the status of a national hero*

manacle ['mænəkᵊl] **manacles** NOUN
Manacles are metal rings or clamps attached to a prisoner's wrists or ankles.

manage ['mænɪdʒ] **manages, managing, managed** VERB
1 If you manage to do something, you succeed in doing it. *e.g. We managed to find somewhere to sit.*

● THESAURUS
cope with: *how my mother coped with bringing up three children*
succeed in: *We have succeeded in persuading cinemas to show the video.*

2 If you manage an organization or business, you are responsible for controlling it.

● THESAURUS
be in charge of: *Who's in charge of the canteen?*
command: *Who would command the troops in the event of war?*
control: *He now controls the largest retail development empire in southern California.*
direct: *Christopher will direct day-to-day operations.*
run: *Is this any way to run a country?*

manageable ['mænɪdʒəbᵊl] ADJECTIVE
able to be dealt with

management ['mænɪdʒmənt] NOUN
1 The management of a business is the controlling and organizing of it.

● THESAURUS
control: *The restructuring involves Mr Ronson giving up control of the company.*
direction: *Organizations need clear direction.*
running: *the day-to-day running of the clinic*

2 The people who control an organization are called the management.

● THESAURUS
administration: *They would like the college administration to exert more control.*
board: *a recommendation which he wants to put before the board*
bosses: informal *a dispute between workers and bosses*
directors: *the board of directors of a local bank*
employers: *Employers are said to be considering the demand.*

manager ['mænɪdʒə] **managers** NOUN
a person responsible for running a business or organization *e.g. a bank manager*

● THESAURUS
boss: informal *He cannot stand his boss.*
director: *the financial director of Braun UK*
executive: *an advertising executive*

▮ In business, the word *manager* can apply to either a man or a woman.

manageress [,mænɪdʒə'rɛs] **manageresses** NOUN
a woman responsible for running a business or organization

managing director ['mænɪdʒɪŋ] **managing directors** NOUN
a company director who is responsible for the way the company is managed

mandarin ['mændərɪn] **mandarins** NOUN
a type of small orange which is easy to peel

mandate ['mændeɪt] **mandates** NOUN;
FORMAL
A government's mandate is the authority it has to carry out particular policies as a result of winning an election.

mandatory ['mændətərɪ] ADJECTIVE
If something is mandatory, there is a law or rule stating that it must be done. *e.g. a mandatory life sentence for murder*

mandir ['mʌndɪə] **mandirs** NOUN
a Hindu temple
[WORD HISTORY: a Hindi word]

mandolin [,mændə'lɪn] **mandolins** NOUN
a musical instrument like a small guitar with a deep, rounded body

mane [meɪn] **manes** NOUN
the long hair growing from the neck of a lion or horse

manger ['meɪndʒə] **mangers** NOUN
a feeding box in a barn or stable

mangle ['mæŋgᵊl] **mangles, mangling, mangled** VERB
1 If something is mangled, it is crushed and twisted.
> NOUN
2 an old-fashioned piece of equipment consisting of two large rollers which squeeze water out of wet clothes

mango ['mæŋgəʊ] **mangoes** or **mangos** NOUN
a sweet yellowish fruit which grows in tropical countries

manhole ['mæn,həʊl] **manholes** NOUN
a covered hole in the ground leading to a drain or sewer

manhood ['mænhʊd] NOUN
Manhood is the state of being a man rather than a boy.

mania ['meɪnɪə] **manias** NOUN
1 a strong liking for something *e.g. my wife's mania for plant collecting*
2 a mental illness
[WORD HISTORY: from Greek MANIA meaning 'madness']

maniac ['meɪnɪˌæk] **maniacs** NOUN
a mad person who is violent and dangerous

manic ['mænɪk] ADJECTIVE
energetic and excited e.g. a manic attack

manicure ['mænɪˌkjʊə] **manicures** NOUN
a special treatment for the hands and nails
manicurist NOUN

manifest ['mænɪˌfɛst] **manifests,
manifesting, manifested** FORMAL >
ADJECTIVE
1 obvious or easily seen e.g. his manifest
enthusiasm

● THESAURUS
blatant: a blatant attempt to spread the blame
clear: a clear case of homicide
conspicuous: Politics has changed in a conspicuous
way.
glaring: a glaring example of fraud
obvious: an obvious injustice
patent: This was patent nonsense.
plain: He's made it plain that he wants to be
involved.

> VERB
2 To manifest something is to make people
aware of it. e.g. Fear can manifest itself in many
ways.

manifestation [ˌmænɪfɛˈsteɪʃən]
manifestations NOUN; FORMAL
A manifestation of something is a sign that it is
happening or exists. e.g. The illness may be a
manifestation of stress.

manifesto [ˌmænɪˈfɛstəʊ] **manifestoes** or
manifestos NOUN
a published statement of the aims and policies of
a political party

manipulate [məˈnɪpjʊˌleɪt] **manipulates,
manipulating, manipulated** VERB
1 To manipulate people or events is to control or
influence them to produce a particular result.
2 If you manipulate a piece of equipment, you
control it in a skilful way.
manipulation NOUN, **manipulator** NOUN,
manipulative ADJECTIVE

mankind [ˌmænˈkaɪnd] NOUN
'Mankind' is used to refer to all human beings
e.g. a threat to mankind

manly ['mænlɪ] **manlier, manliest**
ADJECTIVE
having qualities that are typically masculine e.g.
He laughed a deep, manly laugh.

manna ['mænə] NOUN
If something appears like manna from heaven, it
appears suddenly as if by a miracle and helps you
in a difficult situation.

manner ['mænə] **manners** NOUN
1 The manner in which you do something is the
way you do it.

● THESAURUS
fashion: another drug that works in a similar
fashion
mode: He switched automatically into interview
mode.
style: Kenny's writing style.
way: He had a strange way of talking.

2 Your manner is the way in which you behave
and talk. e.g. his kind manner

● THESAURUS
bearing: his military bearing
behaviour: her anti-social behaviour
conduct: principles of civilized conduct
demeanour: a cheerful demeanour

> PLURAL NOUN
3 If you have good manners, you behave very
politely.

mannerism ['mænəˌrɪzəm] **mannerisms**
NOUN
a gesture or a way of speaking which is
characteristic of a person

manoeuvre [məˈnuːvə] **manoeuvres,
manoeuvring, manoeuvred** VERB
1 If you manoeuvre something into a place, you
skilfully move it there. e.g. It took expertise to
manoeuvre the boat so close to the shore.

● THESAURUS
guide: He took Elliott by the arm and guided him
out.
navigate: He attempted to navigate his way through
the crowds.
negotiate: I negotiated my way out of the airport.
steer: I steered him towards the door.

> NOUN
2 a clever move you make in order to change a
situation to your advantage

● THESAURUS
dodge: a tax dodge
ploy: a cynical marketing ploy
ruse: This was a ruse to divide them.
tactic: The tactic paid off.

manor ['mænə] **manors** NOUN
a large country house with land

manpower ['mænˌpaʊə] NOUN
Workers can be referred to as manpower.

mansion ['mænʃən] **mansions** NOUN
a very large house

manslaughter ['mænˌslɔːtə] NOUN; LEGAL
Manslaughter is the accidental killing of a
person.

mantelpiece ['mæntəlˌpiːs] **mantelpieces**
NOUN

a shelf over a fireplace

mantle ['mæntəl] **mantles** NOUN; LITERARY
To take on the mantle of something is to take on responsibility for it. *e.g. He has taken over the mantle of England's greatest living poet.*

mantra ['mæntrə] **mantras** NOUN
a word or short piece of sacred text or prayer continually repeated to help concentration

manual ['mænjʊəl] **manuals** ADJECTIVE
1 Manual work involves physical strength rather than mental skill.

2 operated by hand rather than by electricity or by motor *e.g. a manual typewriter*

> NOUN
3 an instruction book which tells you how to use a machine
manually ADVERB

manufacture [,mænjʊ'fæktʃə]
manufactures, manufacturing, manufactured (D & T) VERB
1 To manufacture goods is to make them in a factory.

⬤ THESAURUS
assemble: *a factory where they assemble tractors*
fabricate: *a plant which fabricates aeroplane components*
make: *making cars at two plants in Europe*
mass-produce: *the invention of machinery to mass-produce footwear*
produce: *The company produced computer parts.*
process: *The material will be processed into plastic pellets.*

> NOUN
2 The manufacture of goods is the making of them in a factory. *e.g. the manufacture of nuclear weapons*
manufacturer NOUN

⬤ THESAURUS
assembly: *the assembly of cars by robots*
fabrication: *the design and fabrication of the shuttle*
making: *the steps that go into the making of a book*
mass production: *the mass production of baby food*
production: *We need to maintain the production of cars at last year's level.*

manure [mə'njʊə] NOUN
Manure is animal faeces used to fertilize the soil.

manuscript ['mænjʊ,skrɪpt] **manuscripts** NOUN
a handwritten or typed document, especially a version of a book before it is printed

Manx [mæŋks] ADJECTIVE
belonging or relating to the Isle of Man

many ['mɛnɪ] ADJECTIVE
1 If there are many people or things, there are a large number of them.

⬤ THESAURUS
countless: *She brought joy to countless people.*
innumerable: *He has invented innumerable excuses.*
myriad: *the myriad other tasks we are trying to perform*
numerous: *Sex crimes were just as numerous as they are today.*
umpteen: informal *He has produced umpteen books.*
<<OPPOSITE *few*

2 You also use 'many' to ask how great a quantity is or to give information about it. *e.g. How many tickets do you require?*

> PRONOUN
3 a large number of people or things *e.g. Many are too weak to walk.*

⬤ THESAURUS
a lot: *A lot of people would agree with you.*
a mass: *a mass of books and papers*
a multitude: *for a multitude of reasons*
large numbers: *Large numbers of people stayed away.*
lots: informal *lots of strange new animals*
plenty: *plenty of vegetables*
scores: *Scores of people were injured.*
<<OPPOSITE *few*

Maori ['maʊrɪ] **Maoris** NOUN
1 someone descended from the people who lived in New Zealand before Europeans arrived
2 Maori is a language spoken by Maoris.

map [mæp] **maps, mapping, mapped** NOUN
1 a detailed drawing of an area as it would appear if you saw it from above

> VERB
2 If you map out a plan, you work out in detail what you will do.

maple ['meɪpəl] **maples** NOUN
a tree that has large leaves with five points

mar [mɑː] **mars, marring, marred** VERB
To mar something is to spoil it. *e.g. The game was marred by violence.*

marae [mæ'raɪ] **marae** or **maraes** NOUN
In New Zealand, a Maori meeting house; also the enclosed space in front of it.

marathon ['mærəθən] **marathons** NOUN
1 a race in which people run 26 miles along roads

> ADJECTIVE
2 A marathon task is a large one that takes a long time.

marble ['mɑːbᵊl] **marbles** NOUN

1 Marble is a very hard, cold stone which is often polished to show the coloured patterns in it.

2 Marbles is a children's game played with small coloured glass balls. These balls are also called marbles.

march [mɑːtʃ] **marches, marching, marched** NOUN

1 March is the third month of the year. It has 31 days.

2 an organized protest in which a large group of people walk somewhere together

> VERB

3 When soldiers march, they walk with quick regular steps in time with each other.

4 To march somewhere is to walk quickly in a determined way. *e.g. He marched out of the room.*
[WORD HISTORY: sense 1 is from Latin MARTIUS (month) of Mars, the Roman god of war]

mare [mɛə] **mares** NOUN
an adult female horse

margarine [ˌmɑːdʒəˈriːn] **margarines** NOUN
Margarine is a substance that is similar to butter but is made from vegetable oil and animal fats.

margin ['mɑːdʒɪn] **margins** NOUN

1 If you win a contest by a large or small margin, you win it by a large or small amount.

2 an extra amount that allows you more freedom in doing something *e.g. a small margin of error*

3 the blank space at each side on a written or printed page

marginal ['mɑːdʒɪnᵊl] ADJECTIVE

1 small and not very important *e.g. a marginal increase*

2 A marginal seat or constituency is a political constituency where the previous election was won by a very small majority.
marginally ADVERB

marigold ['mærɪˌgəʊld] **marigolds** NOUN
a type of yellow or orange garden flower

marijuana [ˌmærɪˈhwɑːnə] NOUN
Marijuana is an illegal drug which is smoked in cigarettes.

marina [məˈriːnə] **marinas** NOUN
a harbour for pleasure boats and yachts

marinate ['mærɪˌneɪt] **marinates, marinating, marinated;** also spelt marinade VERB
To marinate food is to soak it in a mixture of oil and vinegar to flavour it before cooking.

marine [məˈriːn] **marines** NOUN

1 a soldier who serves with the navy

> ADJECTIVE

2 relating to or involving the sea *e.g. marine life*

marital ['mærɪtᵊl] ADJECTIVE
relating to or involving marriage *e.g. marital problems*

maritime ['mærɪˌtaɪm] ADJECTIVE
relating to the sea and ships *e.g. maritime trade*

marjoram ['mɑːdʒərəm] NOUN
Marjoram is a herb with small, rounded leaves and tiny, pink flowers.

mark [mɑːk] **marks, marking, marked** NOUN

1 a small stain or damaged area on a surface *e.g. I can't get this mark off the curtain.*

⬤ THESAURUS
blot: *an ink blot*
line: *A line of dirt ran across his face like a scar.*
smudge: *a lipstick smudge on his collar*
spot: *He noticed a grease spot on his trousers.*
stain: *a stain on the front of his shirt*
streak: *A streak of mud smudged her cheek.*

2 a written or printed symbol *e.g. He made a few marks with his pen.*

3 a letter or number showing how well you have done in homework or in an exam

4 a unit of currency formerly used in Germany

> VERB

5 If something marks a surface, it damages it in some way.

⬤ THESAURUS
smudge: *Her face was smudged with dirt.*
stain: *His clothing was stained with mud.*
streak: *Rain had begun to streak the window-panes.*

6 If you mark something, you write a symbol on it or identify it in some other way.

7 When a teacher marks your work, he or she decides how good it is and gives it a mark.

8 To mark something is to be a sign of it. *e.g. The accident marked a tragic end to the day.*

9 In soccer or hockey, if you mark your opposing player, you stay close to them, trying to prevent them from getting the ball.

marked [mɑːkt] ADJECTIVE
very obvious *e.g. a marked improvement*
markedly ADVERB

market ['mɑːkɪt] **markets, marketing, marketed** NOUN

1 a place where goods or animals are bought and sold

⬤ THESAURUS
bazaar: *an Eastern bazaar*
fair: *a craft fair*

2 The market for a product is the number of people who want to buy it. *e.g. the market for cars*

537

> VERB

3 To market a product is to sell it in an organized way.

marketing ['mɑːkɪtɪŋ] NOUN
Marketing is the part of a business concerned with the way a product is sold.

market research NOUN
Market research is research into what people want and buy.

marksman ['mɑːksmən] **marksmen** NOUN
someone who can shoot very accurately

marlin ['mɑːlɪn] **marlins** NOUN
a large fish found in tropical seas which has a very long upper jaw

marmalade ['mɑːməˌleɪd] NOUN
Marmalade is a jam made from citrus fruit, usually eaten at breakfast.
[WORD HISTORY: from Latin MARMELO meaning 'quince']

maroon [məˈruːn] NOUN OR ADJECTIVE
dark reddish-purple

marooned [məˈruːnd] ADJECTIVE
If you are marooned in a place, you are stranded there and cannot leave it.

marquee [mɑːˈkiː] **marquees** NOUN
a very large tent used at a fair or other outdoor entertainment

marquis ['mɑːkwɪs] **marquises**; also spelt
marquess NOUN
a male member of the nobility of the rank between duke and earl

marriage ['mærɪdʒ] **marriages** NOUN
1 the relationship between a husband and wife

● THESAURUS
matrimony: formal *the bonds of matrimony*
wedlock: formal *a child conceived out of wedlock*

2 (RE) Marriage is the act of marrying someone.

marrow ['mærəʊ] **marrows** NOUN
a long, thick green-skinned fruit with cream-coloured flesh eaten as a vegetable

marry ['mærɪ] **marries, marrying, married**
VERB
1 When a man and a woman marry, they become each other's husband and wife during a special ceremony.

2 When a clergyman or registrar marries a couple, he or she is in charge of their marriage ceremony.
married ADJECTIVE

Mars [mɑːz] NOUN
Mars is the planet in the solar system which is fourth from the sun.

marsh [mɑːʃ] **marshes** NOUN
an area of land which is permanently wet

marshal ['mɑːʃəl] **marshals, marshalling, marshalled** VERB
1 If you marshal things or people, you gather them together and organize them. *e.g. Shipping was being marshalled into convoys.*

> NOUN

2 an official who helps to organize a public event

marshmallow [ˌmɑːʃˈmæləʊ]
marshmallows NOUN
a soft, spongy, pink or white sweet made using gelatine

marsupial [mɑːˈsjuːpɪəl] **marsupials** NOUN
an animal that carries its young in a pouch. Koala bears and kangaroos are marsupials
[WORD HISTORY: from Greek MARSUPION meaning 'purse']

martial ['mɑːʃəl] ADJECTIVE
relating to or involving war or soldiers *e.g. martial music*

martial arts [ɑːts] PLURAL NOUN
The martial arts are the techniques of self-defence that come from the Far East, for example karate or judo.

Martian ['mɑːʃən] **Martians** NOUN
an imaginary creature from the planet Mars

martyr ['mɑːtə] **martyrs, martyring, martyred** NOUN
1 someone who suffers or is killed rather than change their beliefs

> VERB

2 If someone is martyred, they are killed because of their beliefs.
martyrdom NOUN

marvel ['mɑːvəl] **marvels, marvelling, marvelled** VERB
1 If you marvel at something, it fills you with surprise or admiration. *e.g. Modern designers can only marvel at his genius.*

> NOUN

2 something that makes you feel great surprise or admiration *e.g. a marvel of high technology*

marvellous ['mɑːvələs] ADJECTIVE
wonderful or excellent
marvellously ADVERB

● THESAURUS
brilliant: *a brilliant performance*
excellent: *She does an excellent job as Bill's secretary.*
first-rate: *The meal was absolutely first-rate.*
magnificent: *She was magnificent as Lady Macbeth.*
remarkable: *a remarkable achievement*
splendid: *splendid photographs*
superb: *a superb novel*

wonderful: *It's wonderful to see you.*
<<OPPOSITE *terrible*

Marxism ['mɑːksɪzəm] NOUN
Marxism is a political philosophy based on the writings of Karl Marx. It states that society will develop towards communism through the struggle between different social classes.
Marxist ADJECTIVE OR NOUN

marzipan ['mɑːzɪˌpæn] NOUN
Marzipan is a paste made of almonds, sugar, and egg. It is put on top of cakes or used to make small sweets.

mascara [mæˈskɑːrə] NOUN
Mascara is a substance that can be used to colour eyelashes and make them look longer.

mascot ['mæskət] **mascots** NOUN
a person, animal, or toy which is thought to bring good luck *e.g. Celtic's mascot, Hoopy the Huddle Hound.*

masculine ['mæskjʊlɪn] ADJECTIVE
1 typical of men, rather than women *e.g. the masculine world of motor sport*
2 belonging to a particular class of nouns in some languages, such as French, German, and Latin
masculinity NOUN

mash [mæʃ] **mashes, mashing, mashed** VERB
If you mash vegetables, you crush them after they have been cooked.

mask [mɑːsk] **masks, masking, masked** NOUN
1 something you wear over your face for protection or disguise *e.g. a surgical mask*
> VERB
2 If you mask something, you cover it so that it is protected or cannot be seen.

masochist ['mæsəˌkɪst] **masochists** NOUN
someone who gets pleasure from their own suffering
masochism NOUN
[WORD HISTORY: named after the Austrian novelist Leopold von Sacher Masoch (1836–1895), who wrote about masochism]

mason ['meɪsᵊn] **masons** NOUN
a person who is skilled at making things with stone

masonry ['meɪsənrɪ] NOUN
Masonry is pieces of stone which form part of a wall or building.

masquerade [ˌmæskəˈreɪd] **masquerades, masquerading, masqueraded** VERB
If you masquerade as something, you pretend to be it. *e.g. He masqueraded as a doctor.*

mass [mæs] **masses, massing, massed** NOUN
1 a large amount of something
⬤ THESAURUS
crowd: *A huge crowd of people gathered in the square.*
heap: *a heap of bricks*
load: *a load of kids*
throng: *A shout went up from the throng of spectators.*
lump: *a lump of clay*
mob: *a growing mob of demonstrators*
pile: *a pile of sand*

2 The masses are the ordinary people in society considered as a group. *e.g. opera for the masses*
3 In physics, the mass of an object is the amount of physical matter that it has.
4 In the Roman Catholic Church, Mass is a religious service in which people share bread and wine in remembrance of the death and resurrection of Jesus Christ.
> ADJECTIVE
5 involving a large number of people *e.g. mass unemployment*
⬤ THESAURUS
general: *We are trying to raise general awareness about this issue.*
popular: *popular anger at the decision*
universal: *universal health care*
widespread: *widespread support for the proposals*
> VERB
6 When people mass, they gather together in a large group.
⬤ THESAURUS
assemble: *Thousands of people assembled in the stadium.*
congregate: *Youngsters congregate here in the evenings.*
gather: *In the evenings, we gathered round the fireplace.*
group: *The children grouped together under the trees.*

massacre ['mæsəkə] **massacres, massacring, massacred** NOUN
1 the killing of a very large number of people in a violent and cruel way
> VERB
2 To massacre people is to kill large numbers of them in a violent and cruel way.

massage ['mæsɑːʒ] **massages, massaging, massaged** VERB
1 To massage someone is to rub their body in order to help them relax or to relieve pain.

m

> NOUN

2 A massage is treatment which involves rubbing the body.

massive ['mæsɪv] ADJECTIVE
extremely large *e.g. a massive iceberg*
massively ADVERB

mass-produce ['mæsprə'djuɪs] **mass-produces, mass-producing, mass-produced** VERB
To mass-produce something is to make it in large quantities. *e.g. They began mass-producing cameras after the war.*

mast [mɑːst] **masts** NOUN
the tall upright pole that supports the sails of a boat

master ['mɑːstə] **masters, mastering, mastered** NOUN

1 a man who has authority over others, such as the employer of servants, or the owner of slaves or animals

2 If you are master of a situation, you have control over it. *e.g. He was master of his own destiny.*

3 a male teacher at some schools

● THESAURUS
instructor: *a college instructor*
teacher: *her chemistry teacher*
tutor: *an adult education tutor in German*

> VERB

4 If you master a difficult situation, you succeed in controlling it.

5 If you master something, you learn how to do it properly. *e.g. She found it easy to master the typewriter.*

● THESAURUS
become proficient in: *He quickly became proficient in the language.*
get the hang of: informal *It's a bit tricky till you get the hang of it.*
grasp: *It took him a while to grasp the basics of the process.*
learn: *He enjoyed learning new skills.*

masterful ['mɑːstəfʊl] ADJECTIVE
showing control and authority

masterly ['mɑːstəlɪ] ADJECTIVE
extremely clever or well done *e.g. a masterly exhibition of batting*

mastermind ['mɑːstəˌmaɪnd] **masterminds, masterminding, masterminded** VERB

1 If you mastermind a complicated activity, you plan and organize it.

> NOUN

2 The mastermind behind something is the person responsible for planning it.

masterpiece ['mɑːstəˌpiːs] **masterpieces** NOUN
an extremely good painting or other work of art

masturbate ['mæstəˌbeɪt] **masturbates, masturbating, masturbated** VERB
If someone masturbates, they stroke or rub their own genitals in order to get sexual pleasure.
masturbation NOUN

mat [mæt] **mats** NOUN

1 a small round or square piece of cloth, card, or plastic that is placed on a table to protect it from plates or glasses

2 a small piece of carpet or other thick material that is placed on the floor

matador ['mætəˌdɔː] **matadors** NOUN
a man who fights and tries to kill bulls as part of a public entertainment, especially in Spain
[WORD HISTORY: from Spanish MATAR meaning 'to kill']

match [mætʃ] **matches, matching, matched** NOUN

1 an organized game of football, cricket, or some other sport

● THESAURUS
competition: *a surfing competition*
contest: *one of the best contests in recent boxing history*
game: *England's first game of the new season.*

2 a small, thin stick of wood that produces a flame when you strike it against a rough surface

> VERB

3 If one thing matches another, the two things look the same or have similar qualities.

● THESAURUS
agree: *Their statements do not agree.*
correspond: *The two maps correspond closely.*
fit: *The punishment must always fit the crime.*
go with: *The curtains didn't go with the carpet.*
suit: *the best package to suit your needs*
tally: *The figures didn't seem to tally.*

mate [meɪt] **mates, mating, mated** NOUN

1 INFORMAL
Your mates are your friends.

2 The first mate on a ship is the officer who is next in importance to the captain.

3 An animal's mate is its sexual partner.

> VERB

4 When a male and female animal mate, they come together sexually in order to breed.

material [mə'tɪərɪəl] **materials** NOUN

1 Material is cloth.

● THESAURUS
cloth: *a piece of cloth*

fabric: *silk and other delicate fabrics*

2 a substance from which something is made *e.g. the materials to make red dye*

● THESAURUS
matter: *waste matter from industries*
stuff: *the stuff from which the universe is made*
substance: *a crumbly black substance*

3 The equipment for a particular activity can be referred to as materials. *e.g. building materials*

4 Material for a book, play, or film is the information or ideas on which it is based.

> ADJECTIVE

5 involving possessions and money *e.g. concerned with material comforts*
materially ADVERB

materialism [mə'tɪərɪə‚lɪzəm] NOUN
Materialism is thinking that money and possessions are the most important things in life.
materialistic ADJECTIVE

materialize [mə'tɪərɪə‚laɪz] **materializes, materializing, materialized;** also spelt **materialise** VERB
If something materializes, it actually happens or appears. *e.g. Fortunately, the attack did not materialize.*

maternal [mə'tɜːn²l] ADJECTIVE
relating to or involving a mother *e.g. her maternal instincts*

maternity [mə'tɜːnɪtɪ] ADJECTIVE
relating to or involving pregnant women and birth *e.g. a maternity hospital*

mathematics [‚mæθə'mætɪks] NOUN
Mathematics is the study of numbers, quantities, and shapes.
mathematical ADJECTIVE, **mathematically** ADVERB, **mathematician** NOUN

maths [mæθs] NOUN
Maths is mathematics.

Matilda [mə'tɪldə] NOUN; OLD-FASHIONED, INFORMAL
In Australia, Matilda is the pack of belongings carried by a swagman in the bush. The word is now used only in the phrase 'waltzing Matilda', meaning to travel in the bush with few possessions.

matinee ['mætɪ‚neɪ] **matinees;** also spelt **matinée** NOUN
an afternoon performance of a play or film

matrimony ['mætrɪmənɪ] NOUN; FORMAL
Matrimony is marriage.
matrimonial ADJECTIVE

matrix ['meɪtrɪks] **matrices** NOUN

1 FORMAL
the framework in which something grows and develops

2 In maths, a matrix is a set of numbers or elements set out in rows and columns.

matron ['meɪtrən] **matrons** NOUN
In a hospital, a senior nurse in charge of all the nursing staff used to be known as matron.

matt [mæt] ADJECTIVE
A matt surface is dull rather than shiny. *e.g. matt black plastic*

matted ['mætɪd] ADJECTIVE
Hair that is matted is tangled with the strands sticking together.

matter ['mætə] **matters, mattering, mattered** NOUN

1 something that you have to deal with

● THESAURUS
affair: *The funeral was a sad affair.*
business: *This whole business has upset me.*
issue: *a major political issue*
question: *the difficult question of unemployment*
situation: *The situation is now under control.*
subject: *a difficult subject on which to reach a compromise*

2 Matter is any substance. *e.g. The atom is the smallest divisible particle of matter.*

● THESAURUS
material: *a conducting material such as metal*
stuff: *a dress made from some flimsy stuff*
substance: *a poisonous substance*

3 Books and magazines are reading matter.

> VERB

4 If something matters to you, it is important.

● THESAURUS
be of consequence: *Their choice of partner is of no consequence to anyone but themselves.*
count: *It's as if my opinions just don't count.*
make a difference: *Exercise makes all the difference.*

> PHRASE

5 If you ask **What's the matter?**, you are asking what is wrong.

matter-of-fact ['mætəəv'fækt] ADJECTIVE
showing no emotion

matting ['mætɪŋ] NOUN
Matting is thick woven material such as rope or straw, used as a floor covering.

mattress ['mætrɪs] **mattresses** NOUN
a large thick pad filled with springs or feathers that is put on a bed to make it comfortable

mature [mə'tjʊə] **matures, maturing, matured** VERB

m

1 When a child or young animal matures, it becomes an adult.

● THESAURUS
come of age: *The money was held in trust until he came of age.*
grow up: *She grew up in Tokyo.*
reach adulthood: *She died before reaching adulthood.*

2 When something matures, it reaches complete development.

> ADJECTIVE
3 Mature means fully developed and emotionally balanced.
maturely ADVERB, **maturity** NOUN

● THESAURUS
adult: *a pair of adult birds*
full-grown: *a full-grown male orang-utan*
fully-fledged: *He has developed into a fully-fledged adult.*
grown: *a grown man*
grown-up: *They have two grown-up children.*

maudlin ['mɔːdlɪn] ADJECTIVE
Someone who is maudlin is sad and sentimental when they are drunk.

maul [mɔːl] **mauls, mauling, mauled** VERB
If someone is mauled by an animal, they are savagely attacked and badly injured by it.

mausoleum [,mɔːsə'liːəm] **mausoleums**
NOUN
a building which contains the grave of a famous person

mauve [məʊv] NOUN OR ADJECTIVE
pale purple

maxim ['mæksɪm] **maxims** NOUN
a short saying which gives a rule for good or sensible behaviour *e.g. Instant action: that's my maxim.*

maximize ['mæksɪ,maɪz] **maximizes, maximizing, maximized**; also spelt
maximise VERB
To maximize something is to make it as great or effective as possible. *e.g. Their objective is to maximize profits.*

maximum ['mæksɪməm] ADJECTIVE
1 The maximum amount is the most that is possible. *e.g. the maximum recommended intake*

● THESAURUS
top: *a top speed of 200 mph*
utmost: *a question of the utmost importance*
<<OPPOSITE *minimum*

> NOUN
2 The maximum is the most that is possible. *e.g. a maximum of fifty men*

● THESAURUS
ceiling: *an agreement to put a ceiling on salaries*

height: *when emigration was at its height*
most: *The most he'll make is a hundred pounds.*
upper limit: *the need to put an upper limit on spending*
utmost: *He did his utmost to make her agree.*
<<OPPOSITE *minimum*

may [meɪ] VERB
1 If something may happen, it is possible that it will happen. *e.g. It may happen quite soon.*

2 If someone may do something, they are allowed to do it. *e.g. Please may I be excused?.*

3 You can use 'may' when saying that, although something is true, something else is also true. *e.g. This may be true, but it is only part of the story.*

4 FORMAL
You also use 'may' to express a wish that something will happen. *e.g. May you live to be a hundred.*

> NOUN
5 May is the fifth month of the year. It has 31 days.
[WORD HISTORY: sense 5 is probably from MAIA, a Roman goddess]

> It used to be that you used *may* instead of *can* when asking for or giving someone permission to do something: *you may leave the table.* Nowadays *may* is usually only used in polite questions: *may I open the window?*

maybe ['meɪ,biː] ADVERB
You use 'maybe' when you are stating a possibility that you are not certain about. *e.g. Maybe I should lie about my age.*

● THESAURUS
conceivably: *The mission could conceivably be accomplished within a week.*
it could be: *It could be that's why he refused.*
perhaps: *Perhaps, in time, she'll understand.*
possibly: *Television is possibly to blame for this.*

mayhem ['meɪhɛm] NOUN
You can refer to a confused and chaotic situation as mayhem. *e.g. There was complete mayhem in the classroom.*

mayonnaise [,meɪə'neɪz] NOUN
Mayonnaise is a thick salad dressing made with egg yolks and oil.

mayor [mɛə] **mayors** NOUN
a person who has been elected to lead and represent the people of a town

maze [meɪz] **mazes** NOUN
a system of complicated passages which it is difficult to find your way through *e.g. a maze of dark tunnels*

MBE MBEs, NOUN
a British honour granted by the King or Queen.

MBE is an abbreviation for 'Member of the Order of the British Empire' *e.g. Ally McCoist, MBE.*

MD

an abbreviation for 'Doctor of Medicine' or 'Managing Director'

me [miː] PRONOUN

A speaker or writer uses 'me' to refer to himself or herself.

meadow ['mɛdəʊ] meadows NOUN

a field of grass

meagre ['miːɡə] ADJECTIVE

very small and poor *e.g. his meagre pension*

THESAURUS
inadequate: *inadequate portions*
measly: informal *The average British bathroom measures a measly 3.5 square metres.*
paltry: *a paltry fine of £150*
scant: *She berated the police for paying scant attention to the theft.*
sparse: *sparse vegetation*

meal [miːl] meals NOUN

an occasion when people eat, or the food they eat at that time

THESAURUS
banquet: *a state banquet at Buckingham Palace*
dinner: *a series of official dinners*
feast: *the wedding feast*
kai: Australian and New Zealand; informal *a cheap kai in a local restaurant*

mealie ['miːlɪ] mealies; also spelt mielie NOUN

In South African English, mealie is maize or an ear of maize.

mean [miːn] means, meaning, meant; meaner, meanest VERB

1 If you ask what something means, you want to know what what it refers to or what its messge is.

THESAURUS
denote: *Red eyes denote strain and fatigue.*
indicate: *Today's vote indicates a change in policy.*
signify: *Becoming a father signified that he was now an adult.*

2 If you mean what you say, you are serious. *e.g. The boss means what he says.*

3 If something means a lot to you, it is important to you.

4 If one thing means another, it shows that the second thing is true or will happen. *e.g. Major roadworks will mean long delays.*

5 If you mean to do something, you intend to do it. *e.g. I meant to phone you, but didn't have time.*

THESAURUS
aim: *I aim to arrive early.*
intend: *She intended to move back to France.*

plan: *They plan to marry in the summer.*

6 If something is meant to be true, it is supposed to be true.

> ADJECTIVE

7 Someone who is mean is unwilling to spend much money.

THESAURUS
miserly: *He is miserly with both his time and his money.*
snoep: South African; informal *Have you ever met anyone as snoep as him?*
tight: informal *He was so tight that he wouldn't even spend three roubles.*
<<OPPOSITE *generous*

8 Someone who is mean is unkind or cruel. *e.g. He apologized for being so mean to her.*

> NOUN

9 A means of doing something is a method or object which makes it possible. *e.g. The tests were marked by means of a computer.*

> PLURAL NOUN

10 Someone's means are their money and income. *e.g. He's obviously a man of means.*

> NOUN

11 In mathematics, the mean is the average of a set of numbers.
meanness NOUN

meander [mɪ'ændə] meanders, meandering, meandered VERB

If a road or river meanders, it has a lot of bends in it.

meaning ['miːnɪŋ] meanings NOUN

1 The meaning of a word is what it refers to or expresses.

2 The meaning of what someone says, or of a book or a film, is the thoughts or ideas that it is intended to express.

THESAURUS
drift: *Grace was beginning to get his drift.*
gist: *I could not get the gist of their conversation.*
message: *the message of the film*
significance: *The President's visit is loaded with symbolic significance.*

3 If something has meaning, it seems to be worthwhile and to have real purpose.
meaningful ADJECTIVE, **meaningfully** ADVERB, **meaningless** ADJECTIVE

means test [miːnz] means tests NOUN

a check of a person's money and income to see whether they need money or benefits from the government or other organization

meantime ['miːnˌtaɪm] PHRASE

In the meantime means in the period of time between two events *e.g. I'll call the nurse; in the meantime, you must rest.*

m

meanwhile ['miːn,waɪl] ADVERB

1 Meanwhile means while something else is happening.

> NOUN

2 Meanwhile also means the time between two events.

measles ['miːzəlz] NOUN

Measles is an infectious illness in which you have red spots on your skin.

measly ['miːzlɪ] ADJECTIVE; INFORMAL

very small or inadequate e.g. a measly ten cents

measure ['mɛʒə] **measures, measuring, measured** VERB

1 (MATHS) When you measure something, you find out how big it is.

THESAURUS

gauge: He gauged the wind at over 30 knots.
survey: geological experts who surveyed the cliffs

2 (MATHS) If something measures a particular distance, its length or depth is that distance. e.g. slivers of glass measuring a few millimetres across

> NOUN

3 A measure of something is a certain amount of it. e.g. There has been a measure of agreement.

THESAURUS

amount: a certain amount of disappointment
degree: a degree of success
portion: I have spent a considerable portion of my life here.
proportion: A large proportion of my time was spent abroad.

4 (MATHS) a unit in which size, speed, or depth is expressed

5 Measures are actions carried out to achieve a particular result. e.g. Tough measures are needed to maintain order.

measurement NOUN

THESAURUS

expedient: I reduced my spending by the simple expedient of destroying my credit card.
manoeuvre: manoeuvres to block the electoral process
means: The move is a means to fight crime.
procedure: safety procedures
step: steps to discourage drink-driving

measured ['mɛʒəd] ADJECTIVE

careful and deliberate e.g. walking at the same measured pace

measurement ['mɛʒəmənt] **measurements** NOUN

1 the result that you obtain when you measure something

2 Measurement is the activity of measuring something.

3 Your measurements are the sizes of your chest, waist, and hips that you use to buy the correct size of clothes.

meat [miːt] **meats** NOUN

Meat is the flesh of animals that is cooked and eaten.

meaty ADJECTIVE

Mecca ['mɛkə] NOUN

1 Mecca is the holiest city of Islam, to which many Muslims make pilgrimages.

2 If a place is a mecca for people of a particular kind, many of them go there because it is of special interest to them. e.g. The island is a mecca for bird lovers.

Most Muslims dislike this form and use the Arabic Makkah.

mechanic [mɪ'kænɪk] **mechanics** NOUN

1 a person who repairs and maintains engines and machines

> PLURAL NOUN

2 The mechanics of something are the way in which it works or is done. e.g. the mechanics of accounting

> NOUN

3 Mechanics is also the scientific study of movement and the forces that affect objects.

mechanical [mɪ'kænɪkəl] ADJECTIVE

1 A mechanical device has moving parts and is used to do a physical task.

2 A mechanical action is done automatically without thinking about it. e.g. He gave a mechanical smile.

mechanically ADVERB

mechanism ['mɛkə,nɪzəm] **mechanisms** NOUN

1 a part of a machine that does a particular task e.g. a locking mechanism

2 part of your behaviour that is automatic e.g. the body's defence mechanisms

medal ['mɛdəl] **medals** NOUN

a small disc of metal given as an award for bravery or as a prize for sport

medallion [mɪ'dæljən] **medallions** NOUN

a round piece of metal worn as an ornament on a chain round the neck

medallist ['mɛdəlɪst] **medallists** NOUN

a person who has won a medal in sport e.g. a gold medallist at the Olympics

meddle ['mɛdəl] **meddles, meddling, meddled** VERB

To meddle is to interfere and try to change things without being asked.

media ['miːdɪə] PLURAL NOUN

You can refer to the television, radio, and

newspapers as the media.

> Although *media* is a plural noun, it is becoming more common for it to be used as a singular: *the media is obsessed with violence.*

mediaeval [ˌmɛdɪˈiːvəl] another spelling of **medieval**

median [ˈmiːdɪən] **medians** ADJECTIVE
1 The median value of a set is the middle value when the set is arranged in order.
> NOUN
2 in geometry, a straight line drawn from one of the angles of a triangle to the middle point of the opposite side

mediate [ˈmiːdɪˌeɪt] **mediates, mediating, mediated** VERB
If you mediate between two groups, you try to settle a dispute between them.
mediation NOUN, **mediator** NOUN

medical [ˈmɛdɪkəl] **medicals** ADJECTIVE
1 relating to the prevention and treatment of illness and injuries
> NOUN
2 a thorough examination of your body by a doctor
medically ADVERB

medication [ˌmɛdɪˈkeɪʃən] **medications** NOUN
Medication is a substance that is used to treat illness.

medicinal [mɛˈdɪsɪnəl] ADJECTIVE
relating to the treatment of illness *e.g. a valuable medicinal herb*

medicine [ˈmɛdɪsɪn] **medicines** NOUN (PE)
1 Medicine is the treatment of illness and injuries by doctors and nurses.
2 a substance that you drink or swallow to help cure an illness

THESAURUS
drug: *Three new drugs recently became available.*
medication: *some medication for her ulcers*
muti: South African; informal *muti for treating a fever*
remedy: *At the moment we are trying a herbal remedy.*

medieval or **mediaeval** [ˌmɛdɪˈiːvəl] ADJECTIVE
relating to the period between about 1100 AD and 1500 AD, especially in Europe
[WORD HISTORY: from Latin MEDIUM AEVUM meaning 'the middle age']

mediocre [ˌmiːdɪˈəʊkə] ADJECTIVE
of rather poor quality *e.g. a mediocre string of performances*

mediocrity NOUN

meditate [ˈmɛdɪˌteɪt] **meditates, meditating, meditated** VERB
1 If you meditate on something, you think about it very deeply.
2 If you meditate, you remain in a calm, silent state for a period of time, often as part of a religious training.
meditation NOUN

Mediterranean [ˌmɛdɪtəˈreɪnɪən] NOUN
1 The Mediterranean is the large sea between southern Europe and northern Africa.
> ADJECTIVE
2 relating to or typical of the Mediterranean or the European countries adjoining it

medium [ˈmiːdɪəm] **mediums** or **media** ADJECTIVE
1 If something is of medium size or degree, it is neither large nor small. *e.g. a medium-sized hotel*

THESAURUS
average: *a ginger tomcat of average size*
medium-sized: *a medium-sized saucepan*
middling: *Small and middling flats have increased in price much more than luxury ones.*

> NOUN
2 a means that you use to communicate something *e.g. the medium of television*

THESAURUS
channel: *through diplomatic channels*
vehicle: *The play seemed an ideal vehicle for his music.*

3 a person who claims to be able to speak to the dead and to receive messages from them

medley [ˈmɛdlɪ] **medleys** NOUN
1 a mixture of different things creating an interesting effect
2 a number of different songs or tunes sung or played one after the other

meek [miːk] **meeker, meekest** ADJECTIVE
A meek person is timid and does what other people say.
meekly ADVERB

THESAURUS
deferential: *the traditional requirement for Asian women to be deferential to men*
docile: *docile, obedient children*
mild: *a mild man*
submissive: *Most doctors want their patients to be submissive.*
timid: *a timid child*
unassuming: *He's very polite and unassuming.*
<<OPPOSITE bold

meet [miːt] **meets, meeting, met** VERB
1 If you meet someone, you happen to be in the same place as them.

m

THESAURUS
bump into: informal *I bumped into a friend of yours today.*
come across: *where I came across a group of noisy children*
come upon: *We turned the corner and came upon a group of hikers.*
encounter: *the most gifted child he had ever encountered*
run across: *We ran across some old friends.*
run into: *You'll never guess who I ran into the other day.*

2 If you meet a visitor you go to be with them when they arrive.

3 When a group of people meet, they gather together for a purpose.

THESAURUS
assemble: *a convenient place for students to assemble between classes*
congregate: *Youngsters love to congregate here in the evening.*
convene: *Senior officials convened in October.*
gather: *We all gathered in the boardroom.*
get together: *the last time we all got together*

4 If something meets a need, it can fulfil it. *e.g. services intended to meet the needs of the elderly*

THESAURUS
answer: *Would communism answer their needs?*
fulfil: *All the requirements were fulfilled.*
satisfy: *Candidates must satisfy the general conditions for admission.*

5 If something meets with a particular reaction, it gets that reaction from people. *e.g. I was met with silence.*

meeting ['miːtɪŋ] **meetings** NOUN
1 an event in which people discuss proposals and make decisions together

THESAURUS
audience: *an audience with the Pope*
conference: *a conference on education*
congress: *a medical congress*
convention: *the annual convention of the World Boxing Council*
gathering: *a social gathering*
get-together: informal *a get-together I had at my home*
reunion: *a family reunion*

2 what happens when you meet someone

THESAURUS
assignation: literary *She had an assignation with her boyfriend.*
encounter: *a remarkable encounter with a group of soldiers*
rendezvous: *Baxter arranged a six o'clock rendezvous.*
tryst: *a lovers' tryst*

megabyte ['mɛɡəˌbaɪt] **megabytes** NOUN
(ICT) a unit of storage in a computer, equal to 1 048 576 bytes

melaleuca [ˌmɛləˈluːkə] **melaleucas** NOUN
an Australian tree or shrub that has black branches and a white trunk

melancholy ['mɛlənkəlɪ] ADJECTIVE OR NOUN
If you feel melancholy, you feel sad.

mêlée ['mɛleɪ] **mêlées** NOUN
a situation where there are a lot of people rushing around

mellow ['mɛləʊ] **mellower, mellowest; mellows, mellowing, mellowed**
ADJECTIVE
1 Mellow light is soft and golden.

2 A mellow sound is smooth and pleasant to listen to. *e.g. his mellow clarinet*

> VERB
3 If someone mellows, they become more pleasant or relaxed. *e.g. He certainly hasn't mellowed with age.*

melodic [mɪˈlɒdɪk] ADJECTIVE
relating to melody

melodious [mɪˈləʊdɪəs] ADJECTIVE
pleasant to listen to *e.g. soft melodious music*

melodrama ['mɛləˌdrɑːmə] **melodramas**
NOUN
a story or play in which people's emotions are exaggerated

melodramatic ['mɛlədrəˈmætɪk] ADJECTIVE
behaving in an exaggerated, emotional way

THESAURUS
histrionic: *She let out a histrionic groan.*
sensational: *sensational tabloid newspaper reports*
theatrical: *In a theatrical gesture Glass clamped his hand over his eyes.*

melody ['mɛlədɪ] **melodies** NOUN
(MUSIC) a tune

melon ['mɛlən] **melons** NOUN
a large, juicy fruit with a green or yellow skin and many seeds inside

melt [mɛlt] **melts, melting, melted** VERB
1 When something melts or when you melt it, it changes from a solid to a liquid because it has been heated.

THESAURUS
dissolve: *Heat gently until the sugar dissolves.*
thaw: *It's so cold the snow doesn't get a chance to thaw.*

2 If something melts, it disappears. *e.g. The crowd melted away... Her inhibitions melted.*

THESAURUS
disappear: *The immediate threat has disappeared.*

disperse: *The crowd dispersed peacefully.*
dissolve: *His new-found optimism dissolved.*
evaporate: *My anger evaporated.*
vanish: *All her fears suddenly vanished.*

member ['mɛmbə] **members** NOUN

1 A member of a group is one of the people or things belonging to the group. *e.g. members of the family*

2 A member of an organization is a person who has joined the organization.

> ADJECTIVE

3 A country belonging to an international organization is called a member country or a member state.

Member of Parliament ['mɛmbə əv 'pɑːləmənt] **Members of Parliament** NOUN

a person who has been elected to represent people in a country's parliament

membership ['mɛmbəʃɪp] NOUN

1 Membership of an organization is the state of being a member of it.

2 The people who belong to an organization are its membership.

membrane ['mɛmbreɪn] **membranes** NOUN

a very thin piece of skin or tissue which connects or covers plant or animal organs or cells *e.g. the nasal membrane*

memento [mɪ'mɛntəʊ] **mementos** NOUN

an object which you keep because it reminds you of a person or a special occasion *e.g. a lasting memento of their romance*

memo ['mɛməʊ] **memos** NOUN

a note from one person to another within the same organization. Memo is short for 'memorandum'

memoirs ['mɛmwɑːz] PLURAL NOUN

If someone writes their memoirs, they write a book about their life and experiences.

memorable ['mɛmərəbəl] ADJECTIVE

If something is memorable, it is likely to be remembered because it is special or unusual. *e.g. a memorable victory*
memorably ADVERB

● THESAURUS

catchy: *a catchy tune*
historic: *a historic meeting*
notable: *with a few notable exceptions*
striking: *the most striking feature of those statistics*
unforgettable: *an unforgettable experience*

memorandum [,mɛmə'rændəm] **memorandums** or **memoranda** NOUN

a memo

memorial [mɪ'mɔːrɪəl] **memorials** NOUN

1 a structure built to remind people of a famous person or event *e.g. a war memorial*

> ADJECTIVE

2 A memorial event or prize is in honour of someone who has died, so that they will be remembered.

memory ['mɛmərɪ] **memories** NOUN

1 Your memory is your ability to remember things.

● THESAURUS

recall: *a man blessed with total recall*
remembrance: formal *My remembrance of the incident is somewhat hazy.*

2 something you remember about the past *e.g. memories of their school days*

3 **(ICT)** the part in which information is stored in a computer

men [mɛn] the plural of **man**

menace ['mɛnɪs] **menaces, menacing, menaced** NOUN

1 someone or something that is likely to cause serious harm *e.g. the menace of drugs in sport*

2 Menace is the quality of being threatening. *e.g. an atmosphere of menace*

> VERB

3 If someone or something menaces you, they threaten to harm you.
menacingly ADVERB

menagerie [mɪ'nædʒərɪ] **menageries** NOUN

a collection of different wild animals
[WORD HISTORY: from French MENAGERIE meaning 'household management', which used to include the care of domestic animals]

mend [mɛnd] **mends, mending, mended** VERB

If you mend something that is broken, you repair it.

● THESAURUS

darn: *a woman darning socks*
fix: *If something is broken, we get it fixed.*
patch: *They patched the barn roof.*
renovate: *The couple spent thousands renovating the house.*
repair: *to get her car repaired*
restore: *experts who specialize in restoring ancient parchments*

menial ['miːnɪəl] ADJECTIVE

Menial work is boring and tiring and the people who do it have low status.

meningitis [,mɛnɪn'dʒaɪtɪs] NOUN

Meningitis is a serious infectious illness which affects your brain and spinal cord.

m

menopause ['mɛnəʊˌpɔːz] NOUN
The menopause is the time during which a woman gradually stops menstruating. This usually happens when she is about fifty.

menorah [mɪ'nɔːrə] **menorahs** NOUN
a candelabra that usually has seven parts and is used in Jewish temples

menstruate ['mɛnstrʊˌeɪt] **menstruates, menstruating, menstruated** VERB
When a woman menstruates, blood comes from her womb. This normally happens once a month.
menstruation NOUN, **menstrual** ADJECTIVE

-ment SUFFIX
'-ment' forms nouns which refer to a state or a feeling *e.g. contentment... resentment*
[WORD HISTORY: from Latin suffix -MENTUM]

mental ['mɛntəl] ADJECTIVE
1 relating to the process of thinking or intelligence *e.g. mental arithmetic*
2 relating to the health of the mind *e.g. mental health*
mentally ADVERB

mentality [mɛn'tælɪtɪ] **mentalities** NOUN
an attitude or way of thinking *e.g. the traditional military mentality*

mention ['mɛnʃən] **mentions, mentioning, mentioned** VERB
1 If you mention something, you talk about it briefly.
● THESAURUS
allude to: *She alluded to his absence in vague terms.*
bring up: *Why are you bringing it up now?*
broach: *I broached the subject of her early life.*
hint: *The President hinted that he might make some changes.*
intimate: *He did intimate that he is seeking legal action.*
refer to: *In his speech, he referred to a recent trip to Canada.*
touch on: *The film touches on these issues, but only superficially.*
touch upon: *I'd like to touch upon a more serious question now.*
> NOUN
2 a brief comment about someone or something *e.g. He made no mention of his criminal past.*
● THESAURUS
allusion: *She made an allusion to the events in Los Angeles.*
reference: *He made no reference to any agreement.*

mentor ['mɛntɔː] **mentors** NOUN
Someone's mentor is a person who teaches them and gives them advice.

menu ['mɛnjuː] **menus** NOUN

1 a list of the foods you can eat in a restaurant
2 a list of different options shown on a computer screen which the user must choose from

MEP MEPs NOUN
an abbreviation for 'Member of the European Parliament': a person who has been elected to represent people in the European Parliament

mercenary ['mɜːsɪnərɪ] **mercenaries** NOUN
1 a soldier who is paid to fight for a foreign country
> ADJECTIVE
2 Someone who is mercenary is mainly interested in getting money.

merchandise ['mɜːtʃənˌdaɪs] NOUN; FORMAL
Merchandise is goods that are sold. *e.g. He had left me with more merchandise than I could sell.*

merchant ['mɜːtʃənt] **merchants** NOUN
a trader who imports and exports goods *e.g. a coal merchant*

merchant navy NOUN
The merchant navy is the boats and sailors involved in carrying goods for trade.

merciful ['mɜːsɪfʊl] ADJECTIVE
1 showing kindness
● THESAURUS
compassionate: *a deeply compassionate man*
humane: *the desire for a more humane society*
kind: *She is warm-hearted and kind to everyone.*
<<OPPOSITE merciless

2 showing forgiveness
● THESAURUS
forgiving: *I don't think people are in a very forgiving mood.*
lenient: *He believes the government is already lenient with drug traffickers.*
<<OPPOSITE merciless

3 considered to be fortunate as a relief from suffering *e.g. Death came as a merciful release.*
mercifully ADVERB

merciless ['mɜːsɪlɪs] ADJECTIVE
showing no kindness or forgiveness
mercilessly ADVERB
● THESAURUS
callous: *his callous disregard for human life*
cruel: *Children can be so cruel.*
heartless: *I couldn't believe they were so heartless.*
implacable: *a powerful and implacable enemy*
ruthless: *his ruthless treatment of employees*
<<OPPOSITE merciful

mercury ['mɜːkjʊrɪ] NOUN
1 Mercury is a silver-coloured metallic element that is liquid at room temperature. It is used in thermometers.

2 Mercury is also the planet in the solar system which is nearest to the sun.

mercy ['mɜːsɪ] **mercies** NOUN

1 If you show mercy, you show kindness.

● THESAURUS
compassion: *his compassion for a helpless woman*
kindness: *He was treated with kindness by numerous officials.*
pity: *She saw no pity in their faces.*

2 If you show mercy, you show forgiveness and do not punish someone as severely as you could.

● THESAURUS
forgiveness: *He fell to his knees begging for forgiveness.*
leniency: *He said he would show no leniency towards them.*

mere [mɪə] **merest** ADJECTIVE

used to emphasize how unimportant or small something is *e.g. It's a mere 7-minute journey by boat.*
merely ADVERB

merge [mɜːdʒ] **merges, merging, merged** VERB

When two things merge, they combine together to make one thing. *e.g. The firms merged in 1983.*
merger NOUN

meringue [mə'ræŋ] **meringues** NOUN

a type of crisp, sweet cake made with egg whites and sugar

merino [mə'riːnəʊ] **merinos** NOUN

a breed of sheep, common in Australia and New Zealand, with long, fine wool

merit ['mɛrɪt] **merits, meriting, merited** NOUN

1 If something has merit, it is good or worthwhile.

● THESAURUS
excellence: *the top US award for excellence in journalism*
value: *The value of this work experience should not be underestimated.*
virtue: *There is little virtue in such an approach.*
worth: *people who had already proved their worth to their companies*

2 The merits of something are its advantages or good qualities.

● THESAURUS
advantage: *The great advantage of home-grown oranges is their flavour.*
asset: *Her leadership qualities were her greatest asset.*
strength: *The book's strength lay in its depiction of modern-day Tokyo.*
strong point: *Science was never my strong point at school.*

virtue: *Its other great virtue is its hard-wearing quality.*

> VERB

3 If something merits a particular treatment, it deserves that treatment. *e.g. He merits a place in the team.*

● THESAURUS
be entitled to: *She is entitled to feel proud.*
be worthy of: *The bank might think you're worthy of a loan.*
deserve: *He deserves a rest.*
earn: *Companies must earn a reputation for honesty.*
warrant: *no evidence to warrant a murder investigation*

mermaid ['mɜːˌmeɪd] **mermaids** NOUN

In stories, a mermaid is a woman with a fish's tail instead of legs, who lives in the sea.

merry ['mɛrɪ] **merrier, merriest** ADJECTIVE

happy and cheerful *e.g. He was, for all his shyness, a merry man.*
merrily ADVERB

merry-go-round ['mɛrɪgəʊ'raʊnd] **merry-go-rounds** NOUN

a large rotating platform with models of animals or vehicles on it, on which children ride at a fair

mesh [mɛʃ] NOUN

Mesh is threads of wire or plastic twisted together like a net. *e.g. a fence made of wire mesh*

mess [mɛs] **messes, messing, messed** NOUN

1 something untidy

● THESAURUS
chaos: *Their concerts often ended in chaos.*
disarray: *He found the room in disarray.*
disorder: *Inside all was disorder.*

2 a situation which is full of problems and trouble

● THESAURUS
fix: *informal The government has really got itself into a fix.*
jam: *informal They were in a real jam.*
muddle: *Our finances are in a muddle.*
turmoil: *Her marriage was in turmoil.*

3 a room or building in which members of the armed forces eat *e.g. the officers' mess*

> VERB

4 If you mess about or mess around, you do things without any particular purpose.

5 If you mess something up, you spoil it or do it wrong.
messy ADJECTIVE

● THESAURUS
botch up: *I hate having builders botch up repairs on my house.*
bungle: *Two prisoners bungled an escape bid.*

m

make a hash of: informal *The government made a total hash of things.*
muck up: slang *He always seemed to muck everything up.*

message ['mɛsɪdʒ] **messages** NOUN
1 a piece of information or a request that you send someone or leave for them

● THESAURUS
bulletin: *a news bulletin*
communication: *The ambassador brought a communication from the President.*
despatch or **dispatch:** *this despatch from our West Africa correspondent*
memo: *office memos*
memorandum: *a memorandum from the Ministry of Defence*
note: *I'll have to leave a note for Karen.*
word: *There is no word from the authorities on the reported attack.*

2 an idea that someone tries to communicate to people, for example in a play or a speech *e.g. the story's anti-drugs message*

● THESAURUS
meaning: *while we discussed the meaning of the play*
moral: *the moral of the story*
point: *My point is that I'm not going to change.*
theme: *The book's central theme is power.*

messaging ['mɛsɪdʒɪŋ] NOUN
Messaging or text messaging is the sending and receiving of short pieces of information between mobile phones, using both letters and numbers to produce shortened forms of words.

messenger ['mɛsɪndʒə] **messengers** NOUN
someone who takes a message to someone for someone else

● THESAURUS
courier: *a motorcycle courier*
envoy: *an envoy to the King*
runner: *a bookie's runner*

Messiah [mɪ'saɪə] PROPER NOUN
1 For Jews, the Messiah is the king of the Jews who will be sent by God.
2 For Christians, the Messiah is Jesus Christ.
[WORD HISTORY: from Hebrew MASHIACH meaning 'anointed']

Messrs ['mɛsəz]
Messrs is the plural of **Mr.** It is often used in the names of businesses. *e.g. Messrs Brown and Humberley, Solicitors.*

met [mɛt] the past tense and past participle of **meet**

metabolism [mɪ'tæbə,lɪzəm] **metabolisms** NOUN

Your metabolism is the chemical processes in your body that use food for growth and energy.
metabolic ADJECTIVE

metal ['mɛtəl] **metals** NOUN
Metal is a chemical element such as iron, steel, copper, or lead. Metals are good conductors of heat and electricity.
metallic ADJECTIVE

metamorphic [,mɛtə'mɔːfɪk] ADJECTIVE
Metamorphic rock is rock that has been altered from its original state by heat or pressure.

metamorphosis [,mɛtə'mɔːfəsɪs] **metamorphoses** NOUN; FORMAL
When a metamorphosis occurs, a person or thing changes into something completely different.
e.g. the metamorphosis of a larva into an insect

metaphor ['mɛtəfə] **metaphors** NOUN
(ENGLISH) an imaginative way of describing something as another thing, and so suggesting that it has the typical qualities of that other thing. For example, if you wanted to say that someone is shy, you might say they are a mouse
metaphorical ADJECTIVE, **metaphorically** ADVERB

meteor ['miːtɪə] **meteors** NOUN
a piece of rock or metal that burns very brightly when it enters the earth's atmosphere from space

meteoric [,miːtɪ'ɒrɪk] ADJECTIVE
A meteoric rise to power or success happens very quickly.

meteorite ['miːtɪə,raɪt] **meteorites** NOUN
a piece of rock from space that has landed on earth

meteorological [,miːtɪərə'lɒdʒɪkəl] ADJECTIVE
relating to or involving the weather or weather forecasting
meteorology NOUN

meter ['miːtə] **meters** NOUN
a device that measures and records something
e.g. a gas meter

methane ['miːθeɪn] NOUN
Methane is a colourless gas with no smell that is found in coal gas and produced by decaying vegetable matter. It burns easily and can be used as a fuel.

method ['mɛθəd] **methods** NOUN
1 a particular way of doing something *e.g. the traditional method of making wine*

● THESAURUS
approach: *different approaches to gathering information*
mode: *the capitalist mode of production*

procedure: *He did not follow the correct procedure.*
technique: *the techniques of modern agriculture*
way: *a way of making new friends*

2 (SCIENCE) a way that an experiment or test is carried out *e.g. Describe the method as well as the result obtained.*

methodical [mɪ'θɒdɪkəl] ADJECTIVE
Someone who is methodical does things carefully and in an organized way.
methodically ADVERB

Methodist ['mɛθədɪst] **Methodists** NOUN
OR ADJECTIVE
someone who belongs to the Methodist Church, a Protestant church whose members worship God in a way begun by John Wesley and his followers

meticulous [mɪ'tɪkjʊləs] ADJECTIVE
A meticulous person does things very carefully and with great attention to detail.
meticulously ADVERB

metre ['miːtə] **metres** NOUN
1 (MATHS) a unit of length equal to 100 centimetres
2 In poetry, metre is the rhythmic arrangement of words and syllables.

metric ['mɛtrɪk] ADJECTIVE
relating to the system of measurement that uses metres, grams, and litres

metropolis [mɪ'trɒpəlɪs] **metropolises**
NOUN
a very large city
[WORD HISTORY: from Greek MĒTĒR + POLIS meaning 'mother city']

metropolitan [,mɛtrə'pɒlɪtən] ADJECTIVE
relating or belonging to a large, busy city *e.g. metropolitan districts*

mettle ['mɛtəl] NOUN
If you are on your mettle, you are ready to do something as well as you can because you know you are being tested or challenged.

mew [mjuː] **mews, mewing, mewed** VERB
1 When a cat mews, it makes a short high-pitched noise.
> NOUN
2 the short high-pitched sound that a cat makes
3 A mews is a quiet yard or street surrounded by houses.

Mexican ['mɛksɪkən] **Mexicans** ADJECTIVE
1 belonging or relating to Mexico
> NOUN
2 someone who comes from Mexico

mg
an abbreviation for 'milligrams'

miasma [mɪ'æzmə] **miasmas** or **miasmata**
NOUN
an unhealthy or unpleasant atmosphere, especially one caused by decaying things

mice [maɪs] the plural of **mouse**

micro- PREFIX
'Micro-' means very small
[WORD HISTORY: from Greek MICROS meaning 'small']

microchip ['maɪkrəʊ,tʃɪp] **microchips**
NOUN
a small piece of silicon on which electronic circuits for a computer are printed

microphone ['maɪkrə,fəʊn] **microphones**
NOUN
a device that is used to make sounds louder or to record them on a tape recorder

microprocessor [,maɪkrəʊ'prəʊsɛsə]
microprocessors NOUN
a microchip which can be programmed to do a large number of tasks or calculations

microscope ['maɪkrə,skəʊp] **microscopes**
NOUN
a piece of equipment which magnifies very small objects so that you can study them

microscopic [,maɪkrə'skɒpɪk] ADJECTIVE
very small indeed *e.g. microscopic parasites*

microwave ['maɪkrəʊ,weɪv] **microwaves**
NOUN
A microwave or microwave oven is a type of oven which cooks food very quickly by radiation.

mid- PREFIX
'Mid-' is used to form words that refer to the middle part of a place or period of time *e.g. mid-Atlantic... the mid-70s*
[WORD HISTORY: from Old English]

midday ['mɪd'deɪ] NOUN
Midday is twelve o'clock in the middle of the day.

middle ['mɪdəl] **middles** NOUN
1 The middle of something is the part furthest from the edges, ends, or outside surface.
● THESAURUS
centre: *the centre of the table*
halfway point: *Postle was third fastest at the halfway point.*
midst: *a house in the midst of huge trees*
> ADJECTIVE
2 The middle one in a series or a row is the one that has an equal number of people or things each side of it. *e.g. the middle house*
● THESAURUS
central: *central London*
halfway: *a point halfway between the two posts*

m

middle age NOUN
Middle age is the period of your life when you are between about 40 and 60 years old.
middle-aged ADJECTIVE

Middle Ages ['eɪdʒəz] PLURAL NOUN
In European history, the Middle Ages were the period between about 1100 AD and 1500 AD.

middle class middle classes NOUN
The middle classes are the people in a society who are not working class or upper class, for example managers and lawyers.

Middle East NOUN
The Middle East consists of Iran and the countries in Asia to the west and south-west of Iran.

Middle English NOUN
Middle English was the English language from about 1100 AD until about 1450 AD.

middle-of-the-road [,mɪdəˈləvðəˈrəʊd] ADJECTIVE
Middle-of-the-road opinions are moderate.

middle school middle schools NOUN
In England and Wales, a middle school is for children aged between about 8 and 12.

middling ['mɪdlɪŋ] ADJECTIVE
of average quality or ability

midge [mɪdʒ] **midges** NOUN
a small flying insect which can bite people

midget ['mɪdʒɪt] **midgets** NOUN
a very short person

midnight ['mɪd,naɪt] NOUN
Midnight is twelve o'clock at night.

midriff ['mɪdrɪf] **midriffs** NOUN
the middle of your body between your waist and your chest

midst [mɪdst] NOUN
If you are in the midst of a crowd or an event, you are in the middle of it.

midsummer ['mɪd'sʌmə] ADJECTIVE
relating to the period in the middle of summer
e.g. a lovely midsummer morning in July

midway ['mɪd,weɪ] ADVERB
in the middle of a distance or period of time e.g.
They scored midway through the second half.

midwife ['mɪd,waɪf] **midwives** NOUN
a nurse who is trained to help women at the birth of a baby
midwifery NOUN

might [maɪt] VERB
1 If you say something might happen, you mean that it is possible that it will happen. e.g. I might stay a while.

2 If you say that someone might do something, you are suggesting that they do it. e.g. You might like to go and see it.

3 Might is also the past tense of **may**
> NOUN
4 LITERARY
Might is strength or power. e.g. the full might of the Navy

> You can use *might* or *may* to make a very polite request: might I ask a favour?; may I ask a favour?

mightily ['maɪtɪli] ADVERB; LITERARY
to a great degree or extent e.g. I was mightily relieved by the decision.

mighty ['maɪti] **mightier, mightiest**
ADJECTIVE; LITERARY
very powerful or strong e.g. a mighty army on the march

migraine ['miːgreɪn] or ['maɪgreɪn]
migraines NOUN
a severe headache that makes you feel very ill
[WORD HISTORY: from Latin HEMICRANIA meaning 'pain in half the head']

migrate [maɪˈgreɪt] **migrates, migrating, migrated** VERB
1 If people migrate, they move from one place to another, especially to find work.

2 When birds or animals migrate, they move at a particular season to a different place, usually to breed or to find new feeding grounds. e.g. the birds migrate each year to Mexico
migration NOUN, **migratory** ADJECTIVE, **migrant** NOUN OR ADJECTIVE

mike [maɪk] **mikes** NOUN; INFORMAL
a microphone

mild [maɪld] **milder, mildest** ADJECTIVE
1 Something that is mild is not strong and does not have any powerful or damaging effects. e.g. a mild shampoo

● THESAURUS
insipid: It tasted bland and insipid.
weak: weak beer
<<OPPOSITE strong

2 Someone who is mild is gentle and kind.

● THESAURUS
gentle: her gentle nature
meek: a meek, mild-mannered fellow
placid: a placid child who rarely cried

3 Mild weather is warmer than usual. e.g. The region has mild winters and hot summers.

● THESAURUS
balmy: balmy summer evenings
temperate: a temperate climate

4 Mild emotions or attitudes are not very great or extreme. e.g. mild surprise
mildly ADVERB

mildew ['mɪl,djuː] NOUN
Mildew is a soft white fungus that grows on

things when they are warm and damp.

mile [maɪl] **miles** NOUN
a unit of distance equal to 1760 yards or about 1.6 kilometres
[WORD HISTORY: from Latin MILIA PASSUUM meaning 'a thousand paces']

mileage ['maɪlɪdʒ] **mileages** NOUN
1 Your mileage is the distance that you have travelled, measured in miles.
2 The amount of mileage that you get out of something is how useful it is to you.

militant ['mɪlɪtənt] **militants** ADJECTIVE
1 A militant person is very active in trying to bring about extreme political or social change. *e.g. a militant socialist*
> NOUN
2 a person who tries to bring about extreme political or social change
militancy NOUN

military ['mɪlɪtərɪ] ADJECTIVE
1 related to or involving the armed forces of a country *e.g. military bases*
> NOUN
2 The military are the armed forces of a country.
militarily ADVERB

militia [mɪ'lɪʃə] **militias** NOUN
an organization that operates like an army but whose members are not professional soldiers

milk [mɪlk] **milks, milking, milked** NOUN
1 Milk is the white liquid produced by female cows, goats, and some other animals to feed their young. People drink milk and use it to make butter, cheese, and yogurt.
2 Milk is also the white liquid that a baby drinks from its mother's breasts.
> VERB
3 When someone milks a cow or a goat, they get milk from it by pulling its udders.
4 If you milk a situation, you get as much personal gain from it as possible. *e.g. They milked money from a hospital charity.*

milk tooth **milk teeth** NOUN
Your milk teeth are your first teeth which fall out and are replaced by the permanent set.

milky ['mɪlkɪ] **milkier, milkiest** ADJECTIVE
1 pale creamy white *e.g. milky white skin*
2 containing a lot of milk *e.g. a large mug of milky coffee*

Milky Way NOUN
The Milky Way is a strip of stars clustered closely together, appearing as a pale band in the sky.

mill [mɪl] **mills** NOUN
1 a building where grain is crushed to make flour
2 a factory for making materials such as steel, wool, or cotton
3 a small device for grinding coffee or spices into powder *e.g. a pepper mill*

millennium [mɪ'lɛnɪəm] **millennia** or **millenniums** NOUN; FORMAL
a period of 1000 years

miller ['mɪlə] **millers** NOUN
the person who operates a flour mill

milligram ['mɪlɪ, græm] **milligrams** NOUN
a unit of weight equal to one thousandth of a gram

millilitre ['mɪlɪ,li:tə] **millilitres** NOUN
a unit of liquid volume equal to one thousandth of a litre

millimetre ['mɪlɪ,mi:tə] **millimetres** NOUN
a unit of length equal to a tenth of a centimetre or one thousandth of a metre

million ['mɪljən] **millions**
the number 1,000,000
millionth

millionaire [,mɪljə'nɛə] **millionaires** NOUN
a very rich person who has property worth millions of pounds or dollars

millstone ['mɪl,stəʊn] **millstones** PHRASE
If something is **a millstone round your neck**, it is an unpleasant problem or responsibility you cannot escape from.

mime [maɪm] **mimes, miming, mimed** NOUN
1 Mime is the use of movements and gestures to express something or to tell a story without using speech.
> VERB
2 If you mime something, you describe or express it using mime.

mimic ['mɪmɪk] **mimics, mimicking, mimicked** VERB
1 If you mimic someone's actions or voice, you imitate them in an amusing way.
> NOUN
2 a person who can imitate other people
mimicry NOUN

minaret [,mɪnə'rɛt] **minarets** NOUN
a tall, thin tower on a mosque

mince [mɪns] **minces, mincing, minced** NOUN
1 Mince is meat which has been chopped into very small pieces in a special machine.
> VERB
2 If you mince meat, you chop it into very small pieces.

3 To mince about is to walk with small quick steps in an affected, effeminate way.

mind ['maɪnd] **minds, minding, minded**
NOUN

1 Your mind is your ability to think, together with all the thoughts you have and your memory.

● THESAURUS
brain: *Once you stop using your brain you soon go stale.*
head: *I can't get that song out of my head.*
imagination: *Africa was alive in my imagination.*
intellect: *good health and a lively intellect*
psyche: *disturbing elements of the human psyche*

> PHRASE
2 If you **change your mind**, you change a decision that you have made or an opinion that you have.

> VERB
3 If you do not mind something, you are not annoyed by it or bothered about it.

● THESAURUS
be bothered: *I'm not bothered if he has another child.*
care: *young men who did not care whether they lived or died*
object: *I don't object to his smoking.*

4 If you say that you wouldn't mind something, you mean that you would quite like it. *e.g. I wouldn't mind a drink.*

5 If you mind a child or mind something for someone, you look after it for a while. *e.g. My mother is minding the office.*

● THESAURUS
keep an eye on: *She asked me to keep an eye on the children.*
look after: *I looked after the dogs while she was away.*
take care of: *There was no one else to take care of the children.*
watch: *She bought the tickets while I watched the cases.*

mindful ['maɪndfʊl] ADJECTIVE; FORMAL
If you are mindful of something, you think about it carefully before taking action. *e.g. mindful of their needs*

mindless ['maɪndlɪs] ADJECTIVE
1 Mindless actions are regarded as stupid and destructive. *e.g. mindless violence*
2 A mindless job or activity is simple and repetitive.

mine [maɪn] **mines, mining, mined**
PRONOUN
1 'Mine' refers to something belonging or relating to the person who is speaking or writing *e.g. a friend of mine*

> NOUN
2 a series of holes or tunnels in the ground from which diamonds, coal, or other minerals are dug out *e.g. a diamond mine*
3 a bomb hidden in the ground or underwater, which explodes when people or things touch it

> VERB
4 To mine diamonds, coal, or other minerals is to obtain these substances from underneath the ground.
miner NOUN, **mining** NOUN

minefield ['maɪn,fiːld] **minefields** NOUN
an area of land or water where explosive mines have been hidden

mineral ['mɪnərəl] **minerals** NOUN
(D & T) a substance such as tin, salt, or coal that is formed naturally in rocks and in the earth *e.g. rich mineral deposits*

mineral water NOUN
Mineral water is water which comes from a natural spring.

minestrone [,mɪnɪ'strəʊnɪ] NOUN
Minestrone is soup containing small pieces of vegetable and pasta.
[WORD HISTORY: from Italian MINESTRARE meaning 'to serve']

minesweeper ['maɪn,swiːpə] **minesweepers** NOUN
a ship for clearing away underwater mines

mingle ['mɪŋgəl] **mingles, mingling, mingled** VERB
If things mingle, they become mixed together. *e.g. His cries mingled with theirs.*

mini- PREFIX
'Mini-' is used to form nouns referring to something smaller or less important than similar things. *e.g. a TV mini-series*

miniature ['mɪnɪtʃə] **miniatures** ADJECTIVE
1 a tiny copy of something much larger
> NOUN
2 a very small detailed painting, often of a person

minibus ['mɪnɪ,bʌs] **minibuses** NOUN
a van with seats in the back which is used as a small bus

minim ['mɪnɪm] **minims** NOUN
(MUSIC) a musical note (♩) that has a time value equal to half a semibreve. In the United States and Canada, a minim is called a half note

minimal ['mɪnɪməl] ADJECTIVE
very small in quality, quantity, or degree *e.g. He has minimal experience.*
minimally ADVERB

minimize ['mɪnɪ,maɪz] **minimizes, minimizing, minimized**; also spelt minimise
VERB

If you minimize something, you reduce it to the smallest amount possible. *e.g. His route was changed to minimize jet lag.*

minimum ['mɪnɪməm] ADJECTIVE

1 The minimum amount is the smallest amount that is possible. *e.g. a minimum wage*

THESAURUS

least possible: *I try to cause the least amount of trouble possible.*

minimal: *The aim is to incur minimal expense.*
<<OPPOSITE *maximum*

> NOUN

2 The minimum is the smallest amount that is possible. *e.g. a minimum of three weeks*

minister ['mɪnɪstə] ministers NOUN

1 A minister is a person who is in charge of a particular government department. *e.g. Portugal's deputy foreign minister.*

2 A minister in a Protestant church is a member of the clergy.

ministerial [,mɪnɪ'stɪərɪəl] ADJECTIVE
relating to a government minister or ministry *e.g. ministerial duties*

ministry ['mɪnɪstrɪ] ministries NOUN

1 a government department that deals with a particular area of work *e.g. the Ministry of Defence*

2 Members of the clergy can be referred to as the ministry. *e.g. Her son is in the ministry.*

mink [mɪŋk] minks NOUN
Mink is an expensive fur used to make coats or hats.

minnow ['mɪnəʊ] minnows NOUN
a very small freshwater fish

minor ['maɪnə] minors ADJECTIVE

1 not as important or serious as other things *e.g. a minor injury*

THESAURUS

lesser: *They pleaded guilty to lesser charges.*

petty: *petty crime*

secondary: *matters of secondary importance*

slight: *We have a slight problem.*

trifling: *Outside California these difficulties may seem trifling.*

trivial: *trivial details*
<<OPPOSITE *major*

2 (MUSIC) A minor key is one of the keys in which most European music is written.

> NOUN

3 FORMAL
a young person under the age of 18 *e.g. laws concerning the employment of minors*

minority [maɪ'nɒrɪtɪ] minorities NOUN

1 The minority of people or things in a group is a number of them forming less than half of the whole. *e.g. Only a minority of people want this.*

2 A minority is a group of people of a particular race or religion living in a place where most people are of a different race or religion. *e.g. ethnic minorities*

minstrel ['mɪnstrəl] minstrels NOUN
a singer and entertainer in medieval times

mint [mɪnt] mints, minting, minted NOUN

1 Mint is a herb used for flavouring in cooking.

2 a peppermint-flavoured sweet

3 The mint is the place where the official coins of a country are made.

> VERB

4 When coins or medals are minted, they are made.

> ADJECTIVE

5 If something is in mint condition, it is in very good condition, like new.

minus ['maɪnəs] (MATHS)

1 You use 'minus' to show that one number is being subtracted from another. *e.g. Ten minus six equals four.*

> ADJECTIVE

2 'Minus' is used when talking about temperatures below 0°C or 0°F

minuscule ['mɪnə,skjuːl] ADJECTIVE
very small indeed

minute¹ ['mɪnɪt] minutes, minuting, minuted NOUN

1 a unit of time equal to sixty seconds

THESAURUS

flash: *It was all over in a flash.*

instant: *For an instant, Catherine was tempted to flee.*

moment: *Stop for one moment and think about what you're doing!*

second: *Just a second. I'm coming.*

trice: *I'll be back in a trice.*

2 The minutes of a meeting are the written records of what was said and decided.

> VERB

3 To minute a meeting is to write the official notes of it.

minute² [maɪ'njuːt] ADJECTIVE
extremely small *e.g. a minute amount of pesticide*
minutely ADVERB

THESAURUS

microscopic: *microscopic fibres*

negligible: *They are convinced the strike will have a negligible impact.*

slender: *We won the vote by a slender majority.*

small: *small particles of dust*

tiny: *a tiny fraction of US production*

<<OPPOSITE *vast*

minutiae [mɪˈnjuːʃɪˌiː] PLURAL NOUN; FORMAL
Minutiae are small, unimportant details.

miracle [ˈmɪrəkəl] **miracles** NOUN
1 (RE) a wonderful and surprising event, believed to have been caused by God

2 any very surprising and fortunate event *e.g. My father got a job. It was a miracle.*
miraculous ADJECTIVE, **miraculously** ADVERB

⬤ THESAURUS
marvel: *a marvel of high technology*
wonder: *the wonders of science*

mirage [mɪˈrɑːʒ] **mirages** NOUN
an image which you can see in the distance in very hot weather, but which does not actually exist

mire [maɪə] NOUN; LITERARY
Mire is swampy ground or mud.

mirror [ˈmɪrə] **mirrors, mirroring, mirrored** NOUN
1 a piece of glass which reflects light and in which you can see your reflection
> VERB
2 To mirror something is to have similar features to it. *e.g. His own shock was mirrored on her face.*

mirth [mɜːθ] NOUN; LITERARY
Mirth is great amusement and laughter.

mis- PREFIX
'Mis-' means 'wrong' or 'false' *e.g. misbehaviour... misconception*
[WORD HISTORY: from Old English]

misbehave [ˌmɪsbɪˈheɪv] **misbehaves, misbehaving, misbehaved** VERB
If a child misbehaves, he or she is naughty or behaves badly.
misbehaviour NOUN

miscarriage [mɪsˈkærɪdʒ] **miscarriages** NOUN
1 If a woman has a miscarriage she gives birth to a baby before it is properly formed and it dies.

2 A miscarriage of justice is a wrong decision made by a court, which causes an innocent person to be punished.

miscellaneous [ˌmɪsəˈleɪnɪəs] ADJECTIVE
A miscellaneous group is made up of people or things that are different from each other.

mischief [ˈmɪstʃɪf] NOUN
Mischief is eagerness to have fun by teasing people or playing tricks.
mischievous ADJECTIVE

misconception [ˌmɪskənˈsɛpʃən] **misconceptions** NOUN
a wrong idea about something *e.g. Another*

misconception is that cancer is infectious.

misconduct [mɪsˈkɒndʌkt] NOUN
Misconduct is bad or unacceptable behaviour by a professional person. *e.g. The Football Association found him guilty of misconduct.*

misdemeanour [ˌmɪsdɪˈmiːnə] **misdemeanours** NOUN; FORMAL
an act that is shocking or unacceptable

miser [ˈmaɪzə] **misers** NOUN
a person who enjoys saving money but hates spending it
miserly ADJECTIVE

miserable [ˈmɪzərəbəl] ADJECTIVE
1 If you are miserable, you are very unhappy.

⬤ THESAURUS
dejected: *Everyone has days when they feel dejected.*
depressed: *He seemed somewhat depressed.*
down: *Try to support each other when one of you is feeling down.*
downcast: *After his defeat Mr Rabin looked downcast.*
low: *"I didn't ask for this job," he tells friends when he is low.*
melancholy: *It was in these hours that he felt most melancholy.*
mournful: *He looked mournful, even near to tears.*
sad: *It left me feeling sad and empty.*
unhappy: *She is desperately unhappy.*
wretched: *I feel really confused and wretched.*
<<OPPOSITE *cheerful*

2 If a place or a situation is miserable, it makes you feel depressed. *e.g. a miserable little flat*
miserably ADVERB

⬤ THESAURUS
gloomy: *Officials say the outlook for next year is gloomy.*
pathetic: *a pathetic sight*
sorry: *The fires have left the industry in a sorry state.*
wretched: *He died in wretched poverty.*

misery [ˈmɪzərɪ] **miseries** NOUN
Misery is great unhappiness.

⬤ THESAURUS
depression: *He's been suffering from depression.*
despair: *feelings of despair*
grief: *her grief at her husband's suicide*
melancholy: *with an air of melancholy*
sadness: *with a mixture of sadness and joy*
sorrow: *a time of great sorrow*
unhappiness: *There was a lot of unhappiness in my adolescence.*
woe: *a tale of woe*
<<OPPOSITE *joy*

misfire [ˌmɪsˈfaɪə] **misfires, misfiring, misfired** VERB

If a plan misfires, it goes wrong.

misfit ['mɪsˌfɪt] **misfits** NOUN
a person who is not accepted by other people because of being rather strange or eccentric

misfortune [mɪs'fɔːtʃən] **misfortunes** NOUN
an unpleasant occurrence that is regarded as bad luck *e.g. I had the misfortune to fall off my bike.*

● THESAURUS
adversity: *times of adversity*
bad luck: *He has had his share of bad luck.*

misgiving [mɪs'gɪvɪŋ] **misgivings** NOUN
If you have misgivings, you are worried or unhappy about something. *e.g. I had misgivings about his methods.*

misguided [ˌmɪs'gaɪdɪd] ADJECTIVE
A misguided opinion or action is wrong because it is based on a misunderstanding or bad information.

misinform [ˌmɪsɪn'fɔːm] **misinforms, misinforming, misinformed** VERB
If you are misinformed, you are given wrong or inaccurate information.
misinformation NOUN

misinterpret [ˌmɪsɪn'tɜːprɪt] **misinterprets, misinterpreting, misinterpreted** VERB
To misinterpret something is to understand it wrongly. *e.g. You completely misinterpreted what I wrote.*

misjudge [ˌmɪs'dʒʌdʒ] **misjudges, misjudging, misjudged** VERB
If you misjudge someone or something, you form an incorrect idea or opinion about them.

mislay [mɪs'leɪ] **mislays, mislaying, mislaid** VERB
If you mislay something, you lose it because you have forgotten where you put it.

mislead [mɪs'liːd] **misleads, misleading, misled** VERB
To mislead someone is to make them believe something which is not true.

misplaced [ˌmɪs'pleɪsd] ADJECTIVE
A misplaced feeling is inappropriate or directed at the wrong thing or person. *e.g. misplaced loyalty*

misprint ['mɪsˌprɪnt] **misprints** NOUN
a mistake such as a spelling mistake in something that has been printed

misrepresent [ˌmɪsrɛprɪ'zɛnt] **misrepresents, misrepresenting, misrepresented** VERB
To misrepresent someone is to give an inaccurate or misleading account of what they have said or done.

misrepresentation NOUN

● THESAURUS
distort: *The minister said his remarks had been distorted by the press.*
falsify: *falsifying personal details on his CV*
twist: *You're twisting my words.*

miss [mɪs] **misses, missing, missed** VERB
1 If you miss something, you do not notice it. *e.g. You can't miss it. It's on the second floor.*

● THESAURUS
fail to notice: *He failed to notice that the lights had turned red.*
mistake: *There's no mistaking her sincerity.*
overlook: *a fact that we all tend to overlook*

2 If you miss someone or something, you feel sad that they are no longer with you. *e.g. The boys miss their father.*

● THESAURUS
long for: *Steve longed for the good old days.*
pine for: *Make sure your pet won't pine for you while you're away.*
yearn for: *He yearned for his freedom.*

3 If you miss a chance or opportunity, you fail to take advantage of it.

4 If you miss a bus, plane, or train, you arrive too late to catch it.

5 If you miss something, you fail to hit it when you aim at it. *e.g. His shot missed the target and went wide.*

> NOUN

6 an act of missing something that you were aiming at

7 'Miss' is used before the name of a woman or girl who is not married as a form of address *e.g. Did you know Miss Smith?.*

missile ['mɪsaɪl] **missiles** NOUN
a weapon that moves long distances through the air and explodes when it reaches its target; also used of any object thrown as a weapon

mission ['mɪʃən] **missions** NOUN
1 an important task that you have to do

2 a group of people who have been sent to a foreign country to carry out an official task *e.g. He became head of the Israeli mission.*

3 a journey made by a military aeroplane or space rocket to carry out a task

4 If you have a mission, there is something that you believe it is your duty to try to achieve.

5 the workplace of a group of Christians who are working for the Church

missionary ['mɪʃənəri] **missionaries** NOUN
a Christian who has been sent to a foreign country to work for the Church

missive ['mɪsɪv] **missives** NOUN; OLD-FASHIONED, INFORMAL

m

a letter or message

mist [mɪst] **mists, misting, misted** NOUN

1 Mist consists of a large number of tiny drops of water in the air, which make it hard to see clearly.

> VERB

2 If your eyes mist, you cannot see very far because there are tears in your eyes.

3 If glass mists over or mists up, it becomes covered with condensation so that you cannot see through it.

mistake [mɪ'steɪk] **mistakes, mistaking, mistook, mistaken** NOUN

1 an action or opinion that is wrong or is not what you intended

● THESAURUS

blunder: *It had been a monumental blunder to give him the assignment.*
error: *a mathematical error*
gaffe: *a social gaffe*
oversight: *By an unfortunate oversight, full instructions do not come with the product.*
slip: *There must be no slips.*

> VERB

2 If you mistake someone or something for another person or thing, you wrongly think that they are the other person or thing. *e.g. I mistook him for the owner of the house.*

● THESAURUS

confuse with: *I can't see how anyone could confuse you with your brother!*
misinterpret as: *She misinterpreted his remarks as a threat.*
mix up with: *People often mix me up with other actors.*
take for: *She had taken him for a journalist.*

mistaken [mɪ'steɪkən] ADJECTIVE

1 If you are mistaken about something, you are wrong about it.

2 If you have a mistaken belief or opinion, you believe something which is not true.
mistakenly ADVERB

mister ['mɪstə]

A man is sometimes addressed in a very informal way as 'mister'. *e.g. Where do you live, mister?.*

mistletoe ['mɪsəl,təʊ] NOUN

Mistletoe is a plant which grows on trees and has white berries on it. It is used as a Christmas decoration.

mistook [mɪs'tʊk] the past tense of **mistake**

mistreat [,mɪs'triːt] **mistreats, mistreating, mistreated** VERB

To mistreat a person or animal is to treat them badly and make them suffer.

● THESAURUS

abuse: *parents who abuse their children*

ill-treat: *They thought Mr Smith had been ill-treating his wife.*

mistress ['mɪstrɪs] **mistresses** NOUN

1 A married man's mistress is a woman who is not his wife and who he is having a sexual relationship with.

2 A school mistress is a female teacher.

3 A servant's mistress is the woman who is the servant's employer.

mistrust [,mɪs'trʌst] **mistrusts, mistrusting, mistrusted** VERB

1 If you mistrust someone, you do not feel that you can trust them.

> NOUN

2 Mistrust is a feeling that you cannot trust someone.

misty ['mɪstɪ] **mistier, mistiest** ADJECTIVE
full of or covered with mist

misunderstand [,mɪsʌndə'stænd] **misunderstands, misunderstanding, misunderstood** VERB

If you misunderstand someone or something, you do not properly understand what they say or do. *e.g. He misunderstood the problem.*

misunderstanding [,mɪsʌndə'stændɪŋ] **misunderstandings** NOUN

If two people have a misunderstanding, they have a slight quarrel or disagreement.

misuse **misuses, misusing, misused** NOUN [,mɪs'juːs]

The misuse of something is the incorrect or dishonest use of it. *e.g. the misuse of public money* VERB [,mɪs'juːz]

To misuse something is to use it incorrectly or dishonestly.

mite [maɪt] **mites** NOUN
a very tiny creature that lives in the fur of animals

mitigating ['mɪtɪ,ɡeɪtɪŋ] ADJECTIVE; FORMAL
Mitigating circumstances make a crime easier to understand, and perhaps justify it.

mitten ['mɪtᵊn] **mittens** NOUN
Mittens are gloves which have one section that covers your thumb and another section for the rest of your fingers together.

mix [mɪks] **mixes, mixing, mixed** VERB

1 If you mix things, you combine them or shake or stir them together. **mix up**

● THESAURUS

amalgamate: *a need to amalgamate the two companies*
blend: *Blend the butter with the sugar.*
combine: *Combine the flour with 3 tablespoons of water.*

merge: *how to merge the graphic with text*
mingle: *the mingled smell of flowers and cigar smoke*

> **VERB**

2 If you mix up two things or people, you confuse them. *e.g. People often mix us up and greet us by each other's names.*

● **THESAURUS**
confuse: *Great care is taken to avoid confusing the two projects.*
muddle: *Critics have begun to muddle the two names.*

mixed [mɪkst] ADJECTIVE

1 consisting of several things of the same general kind *e.g. a mixed salad*

2 involving people from two or more different races *e.g. mixed marriages*

3 Mixed education or accommodation is for both males and females. *e.g. a mixed comprehensive*

mixed up ADJECTIVE

1 If you are mixed up, you are confused. *e.g. I'm mixed up about which country I want to play for.*

2 If you are mixed up in a crime or a scandal, you are involved in it.

mixer [ˈmɪksə] **mixers** NOUN
a machine used for mixing things together *e.g. a cement mixer*

mixture [ˈmɪkstʃə] **mixtures** NOUN
several different things mixed or shaken together

● **THESAURUS**
alloy: *an alloy of copper and tin*
amalgamation: *an amalgamation of two organizations*
blend: *a blend of wine and sparkling water*
combination: *a fantastic combination of colours*
compound: *a compound of water, sugar, vitamins and enzymes*
fusion: *fusions of jazz and pop*
medley: *We communicated in a medley of foreign words and gestures.*

mix-up [ˈmɪksʌp] **mix-ups** NOUN
a mistake in something that was planned *e.g. a mix-up with the bookings*

● **THESAURUS**
mistake: *There must be some mistake.*
misunderstanding: *Ensure that there is no misunderstanding about the instructions.*
muddle: *There's been a muddle about whose responsibility it is.*

ml
an abbreviation for 'millilitres'

mm
an abbreviation for 'millimetres'

moa [ˈməʊə] **moa** or **moas** NOUN
a large, flightless bird that lived in New Zealand and which became extinct in the late 18th century

moan [məʊn] **moans, moaning, moaned** VERB

1 If you moan, you make a low, miserable sound because you are in pain or suffering.

● **THESAURUS**
groan: *He began to groan with pain.*
grunt: *The driver grunted, convinced that Michael was crazy.*

2 INFORMAL
If you moan about something, you complain about it.

● **THESAURUS**
complain: *People always complain that the big banks are unfriendly.*
groan: *His parents were beginning to groan about the price of college tuition.*
grumble: *A tourist grumbled that the waiter spoke too much Spanish.*
whine: *They come to me to whine about their troubles.*
whinge: *informal Stop whingeing and get on with it.*

> **NOUN**

3 a low cry of pain or misery

● **THESAURUS**
groan: *a groan of disappointment*
grunt: *grunts of pain*

moat [məʊt] **moats** NOUN
a wide, water-filled ditch around a building such as a castle

mob [mɒb] **mobs, mobbing, mobbed** NOUN

1 a large, disorganized crowd of people *e.g. A violent mob attacked the team bus.*

> **VERB**

2 If a lot of people mob someone, they crowd around the person in a disorderly way. *e.g. The band was mobbed by over a thousand fans.*
[WORD HISTORY: from Latin MOBILE VULGUS meaning 'the fickle public']

mobile [ˈməʊbaɪl] **mobiles** ADJECTIVE

1 able to move or be moved freely and easily *e.g. a mobile phone*

2 (PE) If you are mobile, you are able to travel or move about from one place to another. *e.g. a mobile workforce*

> **NOUN**

3 a decoration consisting of several small objects which hang from threads and move around when a breeze blows

4 a mobile phone
mobility NOUN

m

mobile phone **mobile phones** NOUN
a small portable telephone

moccasin ['mɒkəsɪn] **moccasins** NOUN
Moccasins are flat, soft leather shoes with a raised seam above the toe.
[WORD HISTORY: from MOCUSSIN, a North American Indian word meaning 'shoe']

mock [mɒk] **mocks, mocking, mocked**
VERB
1 If you mock someone, you say something scornful or imitate their foolish behaviour.

⬤ THESAURUS
deride: formal Other countries are derided for selling arms to the enemy.
laugh at: I thought they were laughing at me because I was ugly.
make fun of: Don't make fun of me.
poke fun at: She poked fun at people's shortcomings.
ridicule: Mr Goss ridiculed that suggestion.
scoff at: Some people may scoff at the idea that animals communicate.

> ADJECTIVE
2 not genuine e.g. mock surprise... a mock Tudor house

⬤ THESAURUS
artificial: artificial limbs
bogus: their bogus insurance claim
counterfeit: counterfeit money
dummy: dummy weapons
fake: a fake fur
false: false teeth
feigned: with feigned indifference
imitation: imitation leather
phoney or **phony**: informal a phoney excuse
pretended: with pretended zeal
sham: sham marriages

3 A mock examination is one that you do as a practice before the real examination.

mockery ['mɒkərɪ] NOUN
Mockery is the expression of scorn or ridicule of someone.

⬤ THESAURUS
derision: shouts of derision
jeering: there was a chorus of jeering, whistles and laughter
ridicule: Davis was subjected to public ridicule.

mode [məʊd] **modes** NOUN
1 A mode of life or behaviour is a particular way of living or behaving.
2 In mathematics, the mode is the biggest in a set of groups.

model ['mɒdəl] **models, modelling, modelled** NOUN OR ADJECTIVE
1 a copy of something that shows what it looks like or how it works e.g. a model aircraft

⬤ THESAURUS
dummy: a tailor's dummy
replica: a replica of the Statue of Liberty
representation: a representation of a human figure

> NOUN
2 Something that is described as, for example, a model of clarity or a model of perfection, is extremely clear or absolutely perfect.

⬤ THESAURUS
epitome: the epitome of good taste
example: He is an example to the younger lads.
ideal: the Japanese ideal of beauty
paragon: a paragon of virtue

3 a type or version of a machine e.g. Which model of washing machine did you choose?.

4 a person who poses for a painter or a photographer

5 a person who wears the clothes that are being displayed at a fashion show

> ADJECTIVE
6 Someone who is described as, for example, a model wife or a model student is an excellent wife or student.

> VERB
7 If you model yourself on someone, you copy their behaviour because you admire them.

8 To model clothes is to display them by wearing them.

9 To model shapes or figures is to make them out of clay or wood.

⬤ THESAURUS
carve: One of the prisoners had carved a wooden chess set.
fashion: Stone Age settlers fashioned necklaces from sheep's teeth.
form: figures formed from modelling clay
mould: We moulded a chair out of mud.
sculpt: An artist sculpted a full-size replica of her head.
shape: Shape each half into a loaf.

modem ['məʊdɛm] **modems** NOUN
(ICT) a piece of equipment that links a computer to the telephone system so that data can be transferred from one machine to another via the telephone line

moderate moderates, moderating, moderated ADJECTIVE ['mɒdərɪt]
1 Moderate views are not extreme, and usually favour gradual changes rather than major ones.
2 A moderate amount of something is neither large not small.

⬤ THESAURUS
average: I was only average academically.
fair: Reimar had a fair command of English.

medium: *a medium size*
middling: *The Beatles enjoyed only middling success until 1963.*
reasonable: *reasonable force*

> NOUN ['mɒdərɪt]

3 a person whose political views are not extreme

> VERB ['mɒdəˌreɪt]

4 If you moderate something or if it moderates, it becomes less extreme or violent. *e.g. The weather moderated.*
moderately ADVERB

THESAURUS
abate: *The storm had abated.*
curb: *You must curb your extravagant tastes.*
ease: *Tensions had eased.*
relax: *Rules have been relaxed recently.*
soften: *to soften the blow of steep price rises*
temper: *He had to learn to temper his enthusiasm.*
tone down: *He toned down his statements after the meeting.*

moderation [ˌmɒdəˈreɪʃən] NOUN
Moderation is control of your behaviour that stops you acting in an extreme way. *e.g. a man of fairness and moderation*

modern ['mɒdən] ADJECTIVE
1 relating to the present time *e.g. modern society*

THESAURUS
contemporary: *contemporary music*
current: *the current situation*
present: *the government's present economic difficulties*
present-day: *Even by present-day standards these were large aircraft.*
recent: *in recent years*

2 new and involving the latest ideas and equipment *e.g. modern technology*
modernity NOUN

THESAURUS
latest: *the latest fashions*
new: *new methods of treating cancer*
up-to-date: *Germany's most up-to-date electric power station.*
up-to-the-minute: *up-to-the-minute information*
<<OPPOSITE old-fashioned

modernize ['mɒdəˌnaɪz] **modernizes, modernizing, modernized**; also spelt **modernise** VERB
To modernize something is to introduce new methods or equipment to it.

modest ['mɒdɪst] ADJECTIVE
1 quite small in size or amount

THESAURUS
limited: *They may only have a limited amount of time.*
middling: *The Beatles enjoyed only middling success until 1963.*

moderate: *moderate exercise*
small: *a relatively small problem*

2 Someone who is modest does not boast about their abilities or possessions.

THESAURUS
humble: *He gave a great performance, but he was very humble.*
unassuming: *She has a gentle, unassuming manner.*
<<OPPOSITE conceited

3 shy and easily embarrassed
modestly ADVERB, **modesty** NOUN

modification [ˌmɒdɪfɪˈkeɪʃən]
modifications NOUN
a small change made to improve something *e.g. Modifications to the undercarriage were made.*

modify ['mɒdɪˌfaɪ] **modifies, modifying, modified** VERB
If you modify something, you change it slightly in order to improve it.

module ['mɒdjuːl] **modules** NOUN
1 one of the parts which when put together form a whole unit or object *e.g. The college provides modules for trainees.*

2 (ICT) a part of a machine or system that does a particular task

3 a part of a spacecraft which can do certain things away from the main body *e.g. the lunar module*
modular ADJECTIVE

mohair ['məʊˌhɛə] NOUN
Mohair is very soft, fluffy wool obtained from angora goats.

moist [mɔɪst] **moister, moistest** ADJECTIVE
slightly wet

moisten ['mɔɪsən] **moistens, moistening, moistened** VERB
If you moisten something, you make it slightly wet.

moisture ['mɔɪstʃə] NOUN
Moisture is tiny drops of water in the air or on the ground.

molar ['məʊlə] **molars** NOUN
Your molars are the large teeth at the back of your mouth.

mole [məʊl] **moles** NOUN
1 a dark, slightly raised spot on your skin
2 a small animal with black fur. Moles live in tunnels underground

3 INFORMAL
a member of an organization who is working as a spy for a rival organization

molecule ['mɒlɪˌkjuːl] **molecules** NOUN
the smallest amount of a substance that can exist

m

molecular ADJECTIVE

molest [mə'lɛst] **molests, molesting, molested** VERB
To molest a child is to touch the child in a sexual way. This is illegal.
molester NOUN

mollify ['mɒlɪˌfaɪ] **mollifies, mollifying, mollified** VERB
To mollify someone is to do something to make them less upset or angry.

mollusc ['mɒləsk] **molluscs** NOUN
an animal with a soft body and no backbone. Snails, slugs, clams, and mussels are all molluscs

molten ['məʊltən] ADJECTIVE
Molten rock or metal has been heated to a very high temperature and has become a thick liquid.

moment ['məʊmənt] **moments** NOUN
1 a very short period of time *e.g. He paused for a moment.*

● THESAURUS
instant: *The pain disappeared in an instant.*
minute: *See you in a minute.*
second: *Seconds later, firemen reached the door.*
split second: *Her gaze met Michael's for a split second.*

2 The moment at which something happens is the point in time at which it happens. *e.g. At that moment, the doorbell rang.*

● THESAURUS
instant: *At that instant the museum was plunged into darkness.*
point: *At this point Diana arrived.*
time: *It seemed like a good time to tell her.*

> PHRASE
3 If something is happening **at the moment**, it is happening now.

momentary ['məʊməntərɪ] ADJECTIVE
Something that is momentary lasts for only a few seconds. *e.g. a momentary lapse of concentration*
momentarily ADVERB

Some Americans say *momentarily* when they mean 'very soon', rather than 'for a moment'.

momentous [məʊ'mɛntəs] ADJECTIVE; FORMAL
very important, often because of its future effect *e.g. a momentous occasion*

momentum [məʊ'mɛntəm] NOUN
1 Momentum is the ability that something has to keep developing. *e.g. The campaign is gaining momentum.*
2 Momentum is also the ability that an object has to continue moving as a result of the speed it already has.

monarch ['mɒnək] **monarchs** NOUN
a queen, king, or other royal person who reigns over a country

monarchy ['mɒnəkɪ] **monarchies** NOUN
a system in which a queen or king reigns in a country

monastery ['mɒnəstərɪ] **monasteries** NOUN
a building in which monks live
monastic ADJECTIVE

Monday ['mʌndɪ] **Mondays** NOUN
Monday is the day between Sunday and Tuesday.
[WORD HISTORY: from Old English MONANDÆG meaning 'moon's day']

money ['mʌnɪ] NOUN
Money is the coins or banknotes that you use to buy something.

● THESAURUS
capital: *Companies are having difficulty in raising capital.*
cash: *We were desperately short of cash.*
dosh: British and Australian and New Zealand *They'll have the dosh to pay for a new sign.*
dough: informal *He worked hard for his dough.*
funds: *The concert will raise funds for research into AIDS.*

mongrel ['mʌŋgrəl] **mongrels** NOUN
a dog with parents of different breeds

monitor ['mɒnɪtə] **monitors, monitoring, monitored** VERB
1 If you monitor something, you regularly check its condition and progress. *e.g. Her health will be monitored daily.*
> NOUN
2 a machine used to check or record things
3 (ICT) the visual display unit of a computer
4 a school pupil chosen to do special duties by the teacher

monk [mʌŋk] **monks** NOUN
a member of a male religious community

monkey ['mʌŋkɪ] **monkeys** NOUN
an animal which has a long tail and climbs trees. Monkeys live in hot countries

mono- PREFIX
'Mono-' is used at the beginning of nouns and adjectives that have 'one' as part of their meaning. *e.g. monopoly... monogamy*
[WORD HISTORY: from Greek MONOS meaning 'single']

monocle ['mɒnəkəl] **monocles** NOUN
a glass lens worn in front of one eye only and held in place by the curve of the eye socket

monogamy [mɒ'nɒgəmɪ] NOUN; FORMAL
Monogamy is the custom of being married to

only one person at a time.
monogamous ADJECTIVE

monologue ['mɒnə,lɒg] **monologues**
NOUN
a long speech by one person during a play or a conversation

monopoly [mə'nɒpəlɪ] **monopolies** NOUN
control of most of an industry by one or a few large firms

monotone ['mɒnə,təʊn] **monotones** NOUN
a tone which does not vary e.g. He droned on in a boring monotone.

monotonous [mə'nɒtənəs] ADJECTIVE
having a regular pattern which is very dull and boring e.g. monotonous work
monotony NOUN

monotreme ['mɒnəʊ,triːm] **monotremes**
NOUN
an Australian mammal that has a single opening in its body

monounsaturated
[,mɒnəʊʌn'sætʃə,reɪtɪd] ADJECTIVE
Monounsaturated oils are made mainly from vegetable fats and are considered to be healthier than saturated oils.
monounsaturate NOUN

monsoon [mɒn'suːn] **monsoons** NOUN
the season of very heavy rain in South-east Asia

monster ['mɒnstə] **monsters** NOUN
1 a large, imaginary creature that looks very frightening

2 a cruel or frightening person

> ADJECTIVE
3 extremely large e.g. a monster truck
[WORD HISTORY: from Latin MONSTRUM meaning 'omen' or 'warning']

monstrosity [mɒn'strɒsɪtɪ] **monstrosities**
NOUN
something that is large and extremely ugly e.g. a concrete monstrosity in the middle of the city

monstrous ['mɒnstrəs] ADJECTIVE
extremely shocking or unfair e.g. a monstrous crime
monstrously ADVERB

montage [mɒn'tɑːʒ] **montages** NOUN
a picture or film consisting of a combination of several different items arranged to produce an unusual effect

month [mʌnθ] **months** NOUN
one of the twelve periods that a year is divided into

monthly ['mʌnθlɪ] **monthlies** ADJECTIVE
Monthly describes something that happens or

appears once a month. e.g. monthly staff meetings

monument ['mɒnjʊmənt] **monuments**
NOUN
a large stone structure built to remind people of a famous person or event e.g. a monument to the dead

monumental [,mɒnjʊ'mɛntəl] ADJECTIVE
1 A monumental building or sculpture is very large and important.

2 very large or extreme e.g. We face a monumental task.

moo [muː] **moos, mooing, mooed** VERB
When a cow moos, it makes a long, deep sound.

mood [muːd] **moods** NOUN
the way you are feeling at a particular time e.g. She was in a really cheerful mood.

⏺ THESAURUS
frame of mind: Lewis was not in the right frame of mind to continue.
humour: Could that have been the source of his good humour?
spirits: A bit of exercise will help lift his spirits.
state of mind: I want you to get into a whole new state of mind.
temper: I was in a bad temper last night.

moody ['muːdɪ] **moodier, moodiest**
ADJECTIVE
1 Someone who is moody is depressed or unhappy. e.g. Tony, despite his charm, could sulk and be moody.

⏺ THESAURUS
irritable: He had missed his dinner, and grew irritable.
morose: She was morose and reticent.
sulky: a sulky adolescent
sullen: a sullen and resentful workforce

2 Someone who is moody often changes their mood for no apparent reason.

⏺ THESAURUS
temperamental: He is very temperamental.
volatile: He has a volatile temper.

moon [muːn] **moons** NOUN
The moon is an object moving round the earth which you see as a shining circle or crescent in the sky at night. Some other planets have moons.

moonlight ['muːn,laɪt] **moonlights,**
moonlighting, moonlighted NOUN
1 Moonlight is the light that comes from the moon at night.

> VERB
2 INFORMAL
If someone is moonlighting, they have a second job that they have not informed the tax office about.

moonlit ADJECTIVE

moor [mʊə] **moors, mooring, moored**
NOUN

1 a high area of open land

> VERB

2 If a boat is moored, it is attached to the land with a rope.

mooring ['mʊərɪŋ] **moorings** NOUN
a place where a boat can be tied

moose [muːs] NOUN
a large North American deer with flat antlers

moot [muːt] **moots, mooting, mooted**
VERB; FORMAL
When something is mooted, it is suggested for discussion. *e.g. The project was first mooted in 1988.*

mop [mɒp] **mops, mopping, mopped** NOUN

1 a tool for washing floors, consisting of a sponge or string head attached to a long handle

2 a large amount of loose or untidy hair

> VERB

3 To mop a floor is to clean it with a mop.

4 To mop a surface is to wipe it with a dry cloth to remove liquid.

mope [məʊp] **mopes, moping, moped**
VERB
If you mope, you feel miserable and not interested in anything.

moped ['məʊpɛd] **mopeds** NOUN
a type of small motorcycle

mopoke ['məʊˌpəʊk] **mopokes** NOUN
a small, spotted owl found in Australia and New Zealand. In New Zealand it is called a **morepork**.

moral ['mɒrəl] **morals** PLURAL NOUN

1 (RE) Morals are values based on beliefs about the correct and acceptable way to behave.

> ADJECTIVE

2 concerned with whether behaviour is right or acceptable *e.g. moral values*
morality NOUN, **morally** ADVERB

morale [mɒˈrɑːl] NOUN
Morale is the amount of confidence and optimism that you have. *e.g. The morale of the troops was high.*

morbid ['mɔːbɪd] ADJECTIVE
having a great interest in unpleasant things, especially death

more [mɔː] ADJECTIVE

1 More means a greater number or extent than something else. *e.g. He's got more chips than me.*

● THESAURUS
added: *For added protection choose lipsticks with a sun screen.*

additional: *The US is sending additional troops to the region.*
extra: *Extra staff have been taken on.*
further: *There are likely to be further delays.*
<<OPPOSITE *less*

2 used to refer to an additional thing or amount of something *e.g. He found some more clues.*

> PRONOUN

3 a greater number or extent

> ADVERB

4 to a greater degree or extent *e.g. more amused than concerned*

5 You can use 'more' in front of adjectives and adverbs to form comparatives. *e.g. You look more beautiful than ever.*

moreover [mɔːˈrəʊvə] ADVERB
used to introduce a piece of information that supports or expands the previous statement *e.g. They have accused the government of corruption. Moreover, they have named names.*

morepork ['mɔːˌpɔːk] **moreporks** NOUN
In New Zealand English, the same as a mopoke.

morgue [mɔːg] **morgues** NOUN
a building where dead bodies are kept before being buried or cremated

moribund ['mɒrɪˌbʌnd] ADJECTIVE
no longer having a useful function and about to come to an end *e.g. a moribund industry*

morning ['mɔːnɪŋ] **mornings** NOUN

1 the early part of the day until lunchtime

2 the part of the day between midnight and noon *e.g. He was born at three in the morning.*

Moroccan [məˈrɒkən] **Moroccans**
ADJECTIVE

1 belonging or relating to Morocco

> NOUN

2 someone who comes from Morocco

moron ['mɔːrɒn] **morons** NOUN; INFORMAL
a very stupid person
moronic ADJECTIVE

morose [məˈrəʊs] ADJECTIVE
miserable and bad-tempered

morphine ['mɔːfiːn] NOUN
Morphine is a drug which is used to relieve pain.

Morse or **Morse code** [mɔːs] NOUN
Morse or Morse code is a code used for sending messages in which each letter is represented by a series of dots and dashes.

morsel ['mɔːsəl] **morsels** NOUN
a small piece of food

mortal ['mɔːtəl] **mortals** ADJECTIVE

1 unable to live forever *e.g. Remember that you are mortal.*

2 A mortal wound is one that causes death.

> NOUN

3 an ordinary person

mortality [mɔː'tælɪtɪ] NOUN

1 Mortality is the fact that all people must die.

2 Mortality also refers to the number of people who die at any particular time. *e.g. a low infant mortality rate*

mortar ['mɔːtə] **mortars** NOUN

1 a short cannon which fires missiles high into the air for a short distance

2 Mortar is a mixture of sand, water, and cement used to hold bricks firmly together.

mortgage ['mɔːgɪdʒ] **mortgages, mortgaging, mortgaged** NOUN

1 a loan which you get from a bank or a building society in order to buy a house

> VERB

2 If you mortgage your house, you use it as a guarantee to a company in order to borrow money from them. They can take the house from you if you do not pay back the money you have borrowed.

mortifying ['mɔːtɪˌfaɪɪŋ] ADJECTIVE
embarrassing or humiliating *e.g. There were some mortifying setbacks.*

mortuary ['mɔːtʃʊərɪ] **mortuaries** NOUN
a special room in a hospital where dead bodies are kept before being buried or cremated

mosaic [mə'zeɪɪk] **mosaics** NOUN
a design made of small coloured stones or pieces of coloured glass set into concrete or plaster

Moslem ['mɒzləm] another spelling of **Muslim**

mosque [mɒsk] **mosques** NOUN
a building where Muslims go to worship
[WORD HISTORY: from Arabic MASJID meaning 'temple']

mosquito [mə'skiːtəʊ] **mosquitoes** or **mosquitos** NOUN
Mosquitoes are small insects which bite people in order to suck their blood.
[WORD HISTORY: from Spanish MOSQUITO meaning 'little fly']

moss [mɒs] **mosses** NOUN
Moss is a soft, low-growing, green plant which grows on damp soil or stone.
mossy ADJECTIVE

most [məʊst] ADJECTIVE OR PRONOUN

1 Most of a group of things or people means nearly all of them. *e.g. Most people don't share your views.*

2 The most means a larger amount than anyone or anything else. *e.g. She has the most talent.*

> ADVERB

3 You can use 'most' in front of adjectives or adverbs to form superlatives. *e.g. the most beautiful women in the world*

mostly ['məʊstlɪ] ADVERB
'Mostly' is used to show that a statement is generally true *e.g. Her friends are mostly men.*

MOT MOTs NOUN
In Britain, an annual test for road vehicles to check that they are safe to drive.

motel [məʊ'tɛl] **motels** NOUN
a hotel providing overnight accommodation for people in the middle of a car journey

moth [mɒθ] **moths** NOUN
an insect like a butterfly which usually flies at night

mother ['mʌðə] **mothers, mothering, mothered** NOUN

1 Your mother is the woman who gave birth to you.

2 Your mother could also be the woman who has looked after you and brought you up.

> VERB

3 To mother someone is to look after them and bring them up.

motherhood ['mʌðəˌhʊd] NOUN
Motherhood is the state of being a mother.

mother-in-law ['mʌðəɪnˌlɔː] **mothers-in-law** NOUN
Someone's mother-in-law is the mother of their husband or wife.

motif [məʊ'tiːf] **motifs** NOUN
a design which is used as a decoration

motion ['məʊʃən] **motions, motioning, motioned** NOUN

1 Motion is the process of continually moving or changing position. *e.g. the motion of the ship*

2 an action or gesture *e.g. Apply with a brush using circular motions.*

3 a proposal which people discuss and vote on at a meeting

> VERB

4 If you motion to someone, you make a movement with your hand in order to show them what they should do. *e.g. I motioned him to proceed.*

motionless ['məʊʃənlɪs] ADJECTIVE
not moving at all *e.g. He sat motionless.*

motivate ['məʊtɪˌveɪt] **motivates, motivating, motivated** VERB

1 If you are motivated by something, it makes you behave in a particular way. *e.g. He is motivated by duty rather than ambition.*

THESAURUS
drive: *Jealousy drives people to murder.*

m

inspire: *What inspired you to change your name?*
lead: *His abhorrence of racism led him to write the book.*
move: *It was punk that first moved him to join a band.*
prompt: *Japan's recession has prompted consumers to cut back on buying cars.*
provoke: *The destruction of the mosque has provoked much anger.*

2 If you motivate someone, you make them feel determined to do something.
motivated ADJECTIVE, **motivation** NOUN

motive ['məutɪv] **motives** NOUN
(**HISTORY**) a reason or purpose for doing something *e.g. There was no motive for the attack.*

motley ['mɒtlɪ] ADJECTIVE
A motley collection is made up of people or things of very different types.

motor ['məutə] **motors** NOUN
1 a part of a vehicle or a machine that uses electricity or fuel to produce movement so that the machine can work
> ADJECTIVE
2 concerned with or relating to vehicles with a petrol or diesel engine *e.g. the motor industry*

motorboat ['məutə,bəut] **motorboats** NOUN
a boat with an engine

motorcycle ['məutə,saɪkəl] **motorcycles** NOUN
a two-wheeled vehicle with an engine which is ridden like a bicycle
motorcyclist NOUN

motoring ['məutə,rɪŋ] ADJECTIVE
relating to cars and driving *e.g. a motoring correspondent*

motorist ['məutərɪst] **motorists** NOUN
a person who drives a car

motorway ['məutə,weɪ] **motorways** NOUN
a wide road built for fast travel over long distances

mottled ['mɒtəld] ADJECTIVE
covered with patches of different colours *e.g. mottled leaves*

motto ['mɒtəu] **mottoes** or **mottos** NOUN
a short sentence or phrase that is a rule for good or sensible behaviour

mould [məuld] **moulds, moulding, moulded** VERB
1 To mould someone or something is to influence and change them so they develop in a particular way. *e.g. Early experiences mould our behaviour for life.*

2 To mould a substance is to make it into a particular shape. *e.g. Mould the mixture into flat round cakes.*
> NOUN
3 a container used to make something into a particular shape *e.g. a jelly mould*
4 Mould is a soft grey or green substance that can form on old food or damp walls.
mouldy ADJECTIVE

moult [məult] **moults, moulting, moulted** VERB
When an animal or bird moults, it loses its hair or feathers so new ones can grow.

mound [maund] **mounds** NOUN
1 a small man-made hill
2 a large, untidy pile *e.g. a mound of blankets*

mount [maunt] **mounts, mounting, mounted** VERB
1 To mount a campaign or event is to organize it and carry it out.
2 If something is mounting, it is increasing. *e.g. Economic problems are mounting.*
3 FORMAL
To mount something is to go to the top of it. *e.g. He mounted the steps.*
4 If you mount a horse, you climb on its back.
5 If you mount an object in a particular place, you fix it there to display it.
> NOUN
6 'Mount' is also used as part of the name of a mountain *e.g. Mount Everest.*

mountain ['mauntɪn] **mountains** NOUN
a very high piece of land with steep sides
a large amount of something *e.g. mountains of paperwork*

mountaineer [,mauntɪ'nɪə] **mountaineers** NOUN
a person who climbs mountains

mountainous ['mauntɪnəs] ADJECTIVE
A mountainous area has a lot of mountains.

mourn [mɔːn] **mourns, mourning, mourned** VERB
1 If you mourn for someone who has died, you are very sad and think about them a lot.
2 If you mourn something, you are sad because you no longer have it. *e.g. He mourned the end of his marriage.*

mourner ['mɔːnə] **mourners** NOUN
a person who attends a funeral

mournful ['mɔːnful] ADJECTIVE
very sad

mourning ['mɔːnɪŋ] NOUN
If someone is in mourning, they wear special

black clothes or behave in a quiet and restrained way because a member of their family has died.

mouse [maʊs] mice NOUN
1 a small rodent with a long tail

2 a small device moved by hand to control the position of the cursor on a computer screen

mousse [muːs] mousses NOUN
Mousse is a light, fluffy food made from whipped eggs and cream.

moustache [məˈstɑːʃ] moustaches NOUN
A man's moustache is hair growing on his upper lip.

[WORD HISTORY: from Greek MUSTAX meaning 'upper lip']

mouth mouths, mouthing, mouthed
NOUN [maʊθ]

1 your lips, or the space behind them where your tongue and teeth are

2 The mouth of a cave or a hole is the entrance to it.

3 The mouth of a river is the place where it flows into the sea.

> VERB [maʊð]

4 If you mouth something, you form words with your lips without making any sound. *e.g. He mouthed 'Thank you' to the jurors.*

mouthful NOUN

mouthpiece [ˈmaʊθˌpiːs] mouthpieces
NOUN

1 the part you speak into on a telephone

2 the part of a musical instrument you put to your mouth

3 The mouthpiece of an organization is the person who publicly states its opinions and policies.

movable [ˈmuːvəbəl] ADJECTIVE
Something that is movable can be moved from one place to another.

move see page 568 for Word Web

movement [ˈmuːvmənt] movements
NOUN

1 (DRAMA) Movement involves changing position or going from one place to another.

THESAURUS
flow: *the frantic flow of cars and buses along the street*
motion: *the wind from the car's motion*

> PLURAL NOUN
2 FORMAL
Your movements are everything you do during a period of time. *e.g. They asked him for an account of his movements during the previous morning.*

> NOUN
3 a group of people who share the same beliefs

or aims *e.g. the peace movement*

THESAURUS
campaign: *the campaign against public smoking*
faction: *the leaders of the country's warring factions*
group: *members of an environmental group*
organization: *the International Labour Organization*

4 one of the major sections of a piece of classical music

moving [ˈmuːvɪŋ] ADJECTIVE
Something that is moving makes you feel deep sadness or emotion.

movingly ADVERB

THESAURUS
affecting: *one of the most affecting scenes in the film*
emotional: *an emotional reunion*
poignant: *a poignant love story*
stirring: *a stirring speech*
touching: *the touching tale of a wife who stood by husband she loved*

mow [məʊ] mows, mowing, mowed, mown VERB
1 To mow grass is to cut it with a lawnmower.

2 To mow down a large number of people is to kill them all violently.

mower [ˈməʊə] mowers NOUN
a machine for cutting grass

MP MPs NOUN
a person who has been elected to represent people in a country's parliament. MP is an abbreviation for 'Member of Parliament'

MP3 player [ˈɛmˈpiːˈθriː ˌpleɪə] MP3 players
NOUN
a device that plays audio or video files, often used for listening to music downloaded from the Internet

mpg
an abbreviation for 'miles per gallon'

mph
an abbreviation for 'miles per hour'

Mr [ˈmɪstə]
'Mr' is used before a man's name when you are speaking or referring to him.

Mrs [ˈmɪsɪz]
'Mrs' is used before the name of a married woman when you are speaking or referring to her.

Ms [mɪz]
'Ms' is used before a woman's name when you are speaking or referring to her. Ms does not specify whether a woman is married or not.

MSP MSPs NOUN
an abbreviation for 'Member of the Scottish

1 VERB

to change position *eg: The train began to move.*

● **THESAURUS**

bolt: *I made some excuse and bolted towards the exit.*

crawl: *As he tried to crawl away, he was kicked in the head.*

creep: *I tried to creep upstairs without being heard.*

dash: *She jumped up and dashed out of the room.*

dart: *The girl turned and darted away through the trees.*

edge: *He edged closer to the telephone.*

fly: *I flew downstairs to answer the door.*

gallop: *They were galloping round the garden playing football.*

hasten: *He hastened along the corridor to Grace's room.*

hurry: *Claire hurried along the road.*

inch: *He began to inch along the ledge.*

jog: *She jogged off in the direction he had indicated.*

race: *He raced across town to the hospital.*

run: *I excused myself and ran back to the telephone.*

rush: *A schoolgirl rushed into a burning building to save a baby.*

scamper: *The children got off the bus and scampered into the playground.*

scurry: *The attack began, sending residents scurrying for cover.*

scuttle: *The crabs scuttled along the muddy bank.*

shoot: *They had almost reached the boat when a figure shot past them.*

slither: *Robert lost his footing and slithered down the bank.*

sprint: *The sergeant sprinted to the car.*

stampede: *The crowd stampeded out of the hall.*

tear: *Without looking to left or right, he tore off down the road.*

wriggle: *I wriggled through a gap in the fence.*

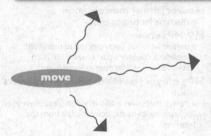

move

2 VERB

to change residence *eg: She had often considered moving to London.*

● **THESAURUS**

migrate: *Peasants have migrated to the cities.*

move house: *They move house fairly frequently.*

relocate: *if the company was to relocate*

3 VERB

to cause a deep emotion *eg: Her story moved us to tears.*

● **THESAURUS**

affect: *Her loss still clearly affects her.*

touch: *Her enthusiasm touched me.*

Parliament': a person who has been elected to
represent people in the Scottish Parliament

much [mʌtʃ] ADVERB

1 You use 'much' to emphasize that something is
true to a great extent. *e.g. I feel much better now.*

2 If something does not happen much, it does
not happen very often.

> ADJECTIVE OR PRONOUN

3 You use 'much' to ask questions or give
information about the size or amount of
something. *e.g. How much money do you need?*

muck [mʌk] **mucks, mucking, mucked**
NOUN

1 INFORMAL
Muck is dirt or some other unpleasant
substance.

2 Muck is also manure.

> VERB

3 INFORMAL
If you muck about, you behave stupidly and
waste time.

mucky ADJECTIVE

mucus ['mjuːkəs] NOUN
Mucus is a liquid produced in parts of your body,
for example in your nose.

mud [mʌd] NOUN
Mud is wet, sticky earth.

muddle ['mʌdəl] **muddles, muddling,
muddled** NOUN

1 A muddle is a state of disorder or untidiness.
e.g. Our finances are in a muddle.

⬤ THESAURUS

chaos: *Their concerts often ended in chaos.*
confusion: *There was confusion when a man fired
shots.*
disarray: *He found the room in disarray.*
disorder: *Inside all was disorder.*
disorganization: *a state of complete
disorganization*
jumble: *a meaningless jumble of words*
mess: *the reasons why the economy is in such a mess*
tangle: *a tangle of wires*

> VERB

2 If you muddle things, you mix them up.

⬤ THESAURUS

confuse: *Great care is taken to avoid confusing the
two projects.*
jumble: *a number of animals whose remains were
jumbled together*
mix up: *People often mix us up.*

muddy ['mʌdɪ] **muddier, muddiest**
ADJECTIVE

1 covered in mud

2 A muddy colour is dull and not clear. *e.g. a
mottled, muddy brown*

muesli ['mjuːzlɪ] NOUN
Muesli is a mixture of chopped nuts, cereal
flakes, and dried fruit that you can eat for
breakfast with milk.

muffin ['mʌfɪn] **muffins** NOUN
a small, round cake which you eat hot

muffled ['mʊfəld] ADJECTIVE
A muffled sound is quiet or difficult to hear. *e.g. a
muffled explosion*

mug [mʌg] **mugs, mugging, mugged** NOUN

1 a large, deep cup

2 INFORMAL
someone who is stupid and easily deceived

> VERB

3 INFORMAL
If someone mugs you, they attack you in order to
steal your money.
mugging NOUN, **mugger** NOUN

muggy ['mʌgɪ] **muggier, muggiest**
ADJECTIVE
Muggy weather is unpleasantly warm and damp.

mule [mjuːl] **mules** NOUN
the offspring of a female horse and a male
donkey

mulga ['mʌlgə] NOUN

1 Mulga are acacia shrubs that are found in the
desert regions of Australia.

2 INFORMAL
In Australian English, mulga is also the bush or
outback.

mull [mʌl] **mulls, mulling, mulled** VERB
If you mull something over, you think about it for
a long time before making a decision.

mullet ['mʌlɪt] **mullets** NOUN
a common edible fish found in Australian and
New Zealand waters

mulloway ['mʌləˌweɪ] **mulloways** NOUN
a large edible fish found in Australian waters

multi- PREFIX
'Multi-' is used to form words that refer to
something that has many parts or aspects. *e.g. a
multistorey car park*
[WORD HISTORY: from Latin MULTUS meaning
'much' or 'many']

multimedia [ˌmʌltɪˈmiːdɪə] NOUN

1 (ICT) in computing, you use multimedia to
refer to products which use sound, pictures, film
and ordinary text to convey information

2 in the classroom, all the things like TV,
computers, and books which are used as
teaching aids are called multimedia

multinational [ˌmʌltɪˈnæʃənl]
multinationals NOUN

m

a very large company with branches in many countries

multiple ['mʌltɪpəl] **multiples** ADJECTIVE
1 having or involving many different functions or things *e.g. He died from multiple injuries in the crash.*

> NOUN

2 The multiples of a number are other numbers that it will divide into exactly. For example, 6, 9, and 12 are multiples of 3.

multiple sclerosis [sklɪə'rəusɪs] NOUN
Multiple sclerosis is a serious disease which attacks the nervous system, affecting your ability to move.

multiplication [,mʌltɪplɪ'keɪʃən] NOUN
1 (MATHS) Multiplication is the process of multiplying one number by another.
2 The multiplication of things is a large increase in their number. *e.g. the multiplication of universities*

multiplicity [,mʌltɪ'plɪsɪtɪ] NOUN
If there is a multiplicity of things, there is a large number or variety of them.

multiply ['mʌltɪ,plaɪ] **multiplies, multiplying, multiplied** VERB
1 When something multiplies, it increases greatly in number. *e.g. The trip wore on and the hazards multiplied.*

● THESAURUS
increase: *The population continues to increase.*
proliferate: *Computerized databases are proliferating fast.*
spread: *Cholera is not spreading as quickly as it did in the past.*

2 (MATHS) When you multiply one number by another, you calculate the total you would get if you added the first number to itself a particular number of times. For example, two multiplied by three is equal to two plus two plus two, which equals six.

multitude ['mʌltɪ,tjuːd] **multitudes** NOUN; FORMAL
a very large number of people or things

mum [mʌm] **mums** NOUN; INFORMAL
Your mum is your mother.

mumble ['mʌmbəl] **mumbles, mumbling, mumbled** VERB
If you mumble, you speak very quietly and indistinctly.

● THESAURUS
murmur: *He murmured something to the professor.*
mutter: *He sat there muttering to himself.*

mummy ['mʌmɪ] **mummies** NOUN

1 INFORMAL
Your mummy is your mother.
2 a dead body which was preserved long ago by being rubbed with special oils and wrapped in cloth

mumps [mʌmps] NOUN
Mumps is a disease that causes painful swelling in the neck glands.

munch [mʌntʃ] **munches, munching, munched** VERB
If you munch something, you chew it steadily and thoroughly.

mundane ['mʌndeɪn] ADJECTIVE
very ordinary and not interesting or unusual *e.g. a mundane job*

municipal [mju:'nɪsɪpəl] ADJECTIVE
belonging to a city or town which has its own local government *e.g. a municipal golf course*
[WORD HISTORY: from Latin MUNICIPIUM meaning 'free town']

munitions [mju:'nɪʃənz] PLURAL NOUN
Munitions are bombs, guns, and other military supplies.

mural ['mjʊərəl] **murals** NOUN
a picture painted on a wall

murder ['mɜːdə] **murders, murdering, murdered** NOUN
1 Murder is the deliberate killing of a person.

● THESAURUS
assassination: *the assassination of John F. Kennedy*
homicide: *the scene of the homicide*
killing: *a brutal killing*
manslaughter: *She was found guilty of manslaughter.*
slaughter: *the imperial army's slaughter of Chinese civilians*
slaying: literary *a trail of motiveless slayings*

> VERB

2 To murder someone is to kill them deliberately.
murderer NOUN

● THESAURUS
assassinate: *Robert Kennedy was assassinated in 1968.*
kill: *a man who killed his wife*
slaughter: *Thirty four people were slaughtered while queueing up to cast their votes.*
slay: literary *the field where Saint George is reputed to have slain the dragon*
take the life of: *He admitted to taking the lives of at least 35 more women.*

murderous ['mɜːdərəs] ADJECTIVE
1 likely to murder someone *e.g. murderous gangsters*
2 A murderous attack or other action results in the death of many people. *e.g. murderous acts of terrorism*

murky ['mɜːkɪ] **murkier, murkiest**
ADJECTIVE
dark or dirty and unpleasant *e.g. He rushed through the murky streets.*

murmur ['mɜːmə] **murmurs, murmuring, murmured** VERB
1 If you murmur, you say something very softly.
> NOUN
2 something that someone says which can hardly be heard

muscle ['mʌsəl] **muscles, muscling, muscled** NOUN
1 (PE) Your muscles are pieces of flesh which you can expand or contract in order to move parts of your body.
> VERB
2 INFORMAL
If you muscle in on something, you force your way into a situation in which you are not welcome.
[WORD HISTORY: from Latin MUSCULUS meaning 'little mouse', because muscles were thought to look like mice]

muscular ['mʌskjʊlə] ADJECTIVE
1 invoiving or affecting your muscles *e.g. muscular strength*
2 Someone who is muscular has strong, firm muscles.

muse [mjuːz] **muses, musing, mused** VERB;
LITERARY
To muse is to think about something for a long time.

museum [mjuːˈzɪəm] **museums** NOUN
a building where many interesting or valuable objects are kept and displayed

mush [mʌʃ] NOUN
A mush is a thick, soft paste.

mushroom ['mʌʃruːm] **mushrooms, mushrooming, mushroomed** NOUN
1 a fungus with a short stem and a round top. Some types of mushroom are edible
> VERB
2 If something mushrooms, it appears and grows very quickly. *e.g. The mill towns mushroomed into cities.*

mushy ['mʌʃɪ] **mushier, mushiest**
ADJECTIVE
1 Mushy fruits or vegetables are too soft. *e.g. mushy tomatoes*
2 INFORMAL
Mushy stories are too sentimental.

music ['mjuːzɪk] NOUN
1 Music is a pattern of sounds performed by people singing or playing instruments.

2 Music is also the written symbols that represent musical sounds. *e.g. I taught myself to read music.*

musical ['mjuːzɪkəl] **musicals** ADJECTIVE
1 relating to playing or studying music *e.g. a musical instrument*
> NOUN
2 a play or film that uses songs and dance to tell the story
musically ADVERB

musician [mjuːˈzɪʃən] **musicians** NOUN
(MUSIC) a person who plays a musical instrument as their job or hobby

musk [mʌsk] NOUN
Musk is a substance with a strong, sweet smell. It is used to make perfume.
musky ADJECTIVE

musket ['mʌskɪt] **muskets** NOUN
an old-fashioned gun with a long barrel

Muslim ['mʊzlɪm] **Muslims**; also spelt
Moslem NOUN (RE)
1 a person who believes in Islam and lives according to its rules
> ADJECTIVE
2 relating to Islam

muslin ['mʌzlɪn] NOUN
Muslin is a very thin cotton material.

mussel ['mʌsəl] **mussels** NOUN
Mussels are a kind of shellfish with black shells.

must [mʌst] **musts** VERB
1 If something must happen, it is very important or necessary that it happens. *e.g. You must be over 18.*
2 If you tell someone they must do something, you are suggesting that they do it. *e.g. You must try this pudding: it's delicious.*
> NOUN
3 something that is absolutely necessary *e.g. The museum is a must for all visitors.*

mustard ['mʌstəd] NOUN
Mustard is a spicy-tasting yellow or brown paste made from seeds.

muster ['mʌstə] **musters, mustering, mustered** VERB
If you muster something such as energy or support, you gather it together. *e.g. as much calm as he could muster*

musty ['mʌstɪ] **mustier, mustiest** ADJECTIVE
smelling stale and damp *e.g. musty old books*

mutate [mjuːˈteɪt] **mutates, mutating, mutated** VERB; TECHNICAL
If something mutates, its structure or

appearance alters in some way. *e.g. Viruses react to change and can mutate fast.*
mutation NOUN, **mutant** NOUN OR ADJECTIVE

mute [mju:t] ADJECTIVE; FORMAL
not giving out sound or speech *e.g. mute amazement*

muted ['mju:tɪd] ADJECTIVE
1 Muted colours or sounds are soft and gentle.
2 A muted reaction is not very strong.

muti ['mʊtɪ] NOUN; INFORMAL
In South African English, muti is medicine.

mutilate ['mju:tɪˌleɪt] **mutilates, mutilating, mutilated** VERB
1 If someone is mutilated, their body is badly injured. *e.g. His leg was badly mutilated.*
2 If you mutilate something, you deliberately damage or spoil it. *e.g. Almost every book had been mutilated.*
mutilation NOUN

mutiny ['mju:tɪnɪ] **mutinies** NOUN
A mutiny is a rebellion against someone in authority.

mutter ['mʌtə] **mutters, muttering, muttered** VERB
To mutter is to speak in a very low and perhaps cross voice. *e.g. Rory muttered something under his breath.*

mutton ['mʌtᵊn] NOUN
Mutton is the meat of an adult sheep.

muttonbird ['mʌtᵊn,bɜːd] **muttonbirds** NOUN
a seabird in the Pacific Ocean that is often hunted for its flesh, which is said to taste like mutton

mutual ['mju:tʃʊəl] ADJECTIVE
used to describe something that two or more people do to each other or share *e.g. They had a mutual interest in rugby.*

It used to be that *mutual* could only be used of something that was shared between two people or groups. Nowadays you can use it to mean 'shared between two or more people or groups'.

mutually ['mju:tʃəlɪ] ADVERB
Mutually describes a situation in which two or more people feel the same way about each other. *e.g. a mutually supportive relationship*

muzzle ['mʌzᵊl] **muzzles, muzzling, muzzled** NOUN
1 the nose and mouth of an animal
2 a cover or a strap for a dog's nose and mouth to prevent it from biting
3 the open end of a gun through which the bullets come out

> VERB
4 To muzzle a dog is to put a muzzle on it.

my [maɪ] ADJECTIVE
'My' refers to something belonging or relating to the person speaking or writing. *e.g. I held my breath.*

mynah bird ['maɪnə] **mynah birds** NOUN
a tropical bird which can mimic speech and sounds

myriad ['mɪrɪəd] **myriads** NOUN OR ADJECTIVE; LITERARY
a very large number of people or things

myrrh [mɜː] NOUN
Myrrh is a fragrant substance used in perfume and incense.

myself [maɪ'sɛlf] PRONOUN
1 'Myself' is used when the person speaking or writing does an action and is affected by it. *e.g. I was ashamed of myself.*
2 'Myself' is also used to emphasize 'I'. *e.g. I find it a bit odd myself.*

mysterious [mɪ'stɪərɪəs] ADJECTIVE
1 strange and not well understood
● THESAURUS
arcane: formal *the arcane world of high finance*
baffling: *a baffling array of wires*
cryptic: *My father's notes are more cryptic here.*
enigmatic: *one of Orson Welles's most enigmatic films*
mystifying: *I find your attitude rather mystifying.*
2 secretive about something *e.g. Stop being so mysterious.*
mysteriously ADVERB
● THESAURUS
furtive: *with a furtive glance over her shoulder*
secretive: *the secretive world of spying*

mystery ['mɪstərɪ] **mysteries** NOUN
something that is not understood or known about
● THESAURUS
conundrum: *this theological conundrum*
enigma: *Iran remains an enigma for the outside world.*
puzzle: *"Women are a puzzle," he said.*
riddle: *the answer to the riddle of why it was never finished*

mystic ['mɪstɪk] **mystics** NOUN
1 a religious person who spends long hours meditating
> ADJECTIVE
2 Mystic means the same as mystical.

mystical ['mɪstɪkᵊl] ADJECTIVE
involving spiritual powers and influences *e.g. a mystical experience*

mysticism NOUN

mystify ['mɪstɪ,faɪ] **mystifies, mystifying, mystified** VERB

If something mystifies you, you find it impossible to understand.

mystique [mɪ'sti:k] NOUN

Mystique is an atmosphere of mystery and importance associated with a particular person or thing.

myth [mɪθ] **myths** NOUN

1 an untrue belief or explanation

2 (ENGLISH) a story which was made up long ago to explain natural events and religious beliefs e.g. Viking myths.

mythical ['mɪθɪkəl] ADJECTIVE

imaginary, untrue, or existing only in myths e.g. a mythical beast

mythology [mɪ'θɒlədʒɪ] NOUN

Mythology refers to stories that have been made up in the past to explain natural events or justify religious beliefs.

mythological ADJECTIVE

m

Nn

naartjie ['nɑːtʃɪ] **naartjies** NOUN
In South African English, a tangerine.

nag [næg] **nags, nagging, nagged** VERB
1 If you nag someone, you keep complaining to them about something.
2 If something nags at you, it keeps worrying you.

nail [neɪl] **nails, nailing, nailed** NOUN
1 a small piece of metal with a sharp point at one end, which you hammer into objects to hold them together
2 Your nails are the thin hard areas covering the ends of your fingers and toes.
> VERB
3 If you nail something somewhere, you fit it there using a nail.

naive or **naïve** [nɑːˈiːv] ADJECTIVE
foolishly believing that things are easier or less complicated than they really are
naively ADVERB, **naivety** NOUN

naked ['neɪkɪd] ADJECTIVE
1 not wearing any clothes or not covered by anything

THESAURUS
bare: *her bare feet*
nude: *nude bathing*
stark-naked: *She didn't seem to notice I was stark-naked.*
unclothed: *an unclothed male body*
undressed: *She couldn't remember getting undressed.*
<<OPPOSITE *clothed*

2 shown openly *e.g. naked aggression*
nakedness NOUN

THESAURUS
blatant: *evidence of blatant discrimination*
evident: *the party's evident dislike of the president*
manifest: *his manifest enthusiasm*
open: *open opposition to the government*
unmistakable: *with unmistakable amusement in his eyes*
<<OPPOSITE *secret*

name [neɪm] **names, naming, named**
NOUN
1 a word that you use to identify a person, place, or thing

THESAURUS
designation: *a level four alert, a designation reserved for very serious incidents*
epithet: *the common epithet for the Buddha*
nickname: *He's heard your nickname is Codfish.*
term: *I don't know the medical term for it.*
title: *Your actual title would be business manager.*

2 Someone's name is also their reputation. *e.g. My only wish now is to clear my name.*

THESAURUS
character: *a series of personal attacks on my character*
reputation: *I know Chris has a bad reputation.*

> VERB
3 If you name someone or something, you give them a name or you say their name.

THESAURUS
baptize: *She could be baptized Margaret.*
call: *in a town called Fishingport*
christen: *He wanted to christen his son Arthur Albert.*
dub: *a girl cruelly dubbed "the Worm"*
style: *a character who styled himself the Memory Man*
term: *He had been termed a temporary employee.*

4 If you name a price or a date, you say what you want it to be.

nameless ['neɪmlɪs] ADJECTIVE
You describe someone or something as nameless when you do not know their name, or when a name has not yet been given to them.

namely ['neɪmlɪ] ADVERB
that is; used to introduce more detailed information about what you have just said *e.g. The state stripped them of their rights, namely the right to own land.*

namesake ['neɪm,seɪk] **namesakes** NOUN
Your namesake is someone with the same name as you. *e.g. Audrey Hepburn and her namesake Katharine.*

nanny ['nænɪ] **nannies** NOUN
a woman whose job is looking after young children

nap [næp] **naps, napping, napped** NOUN
1 a short sleep

> VERB

2 When you nap, you have a short sleep.

nape [neɪp] **napes** NOUN
The nape of your neck is the back of it.

napkin ['næpkɪn] **napkins** NOUN
a small piece of cloth or paper used to wipe your hands and mouth after eating

nappy ['næpɪ] **nappies** NOUN
a piece of towelling or paper worn round a baby's bottom

narcotic [nɑːˈkɒtɪk] **narcotics** NOUN
a drug which makes you sleepy and unable to feel pain
[WORD HISTORY: from Greek NARKOUN meaning 'to make numb']

narrate [nəˈreɪt] **narrates, narrating, narrated** VERB
If you narrate a story, you tell it.
narration NOUN

narrative ['nærətɪv] **narratives** NOUN
(ENGLISH) a story or an account of events

narrator [nəˈreɪtə] **narrators** NOUN
1 a person who is reading or telling a story out loud
2 **(ENGLISH)** a character in a novel who tells the story

narrow ['nærəʊ] **narrower, narrowest; narrows, narrowing, narrowed** ADJECTIVE
1 having a small distance from one side to the other *e.g. a narrow stream*

THESAURUS
fine: *the fine hairs on her arms*
slender: *long slender legs*
slim: *a slim volume of Auden's poems*
thin: *a thin layer of clay*
<<OPPOSITE *wide*

2 concerned only with a few aspects of something and ignoring the important points *e.g. people with a narrow point of view*
3 A narrow escape or victory is one that you only just achieve.

> VERB

4 To narrow means to become less wide. *e.g. The road narrowed.*
narrowly ADVERB

narrow-minded ['nærəʊˌmaɪndɪd] ADJECTIVE
unwilling to consider new ideas or opinions

THESAURUS
biased: *a biased view*
bigoted: *bigoted opinions*
insular: *those insular British travellers*
opinionated: *the most opinionated rubbish I have read*

prejudiced: *a whole host of prejudiced and xenophobic ideas*
<<OPPOSITE *tolerant*

nasal ['neɪzəl] ADJECTIVE
1 relating to the nose *e.g. the nasal passages*
2 Nasal sounds are made by breathing out through your nose as you speak.

nasty ['nɑːstɪ] **nastier, nastiest** ADJECTIVE
very unpleasant *e.g. a nasty shock*
nastily ADVERB, **nastiness** NOUN

THESAURUS
disagreeable: *a disagreeable experience*
disgusting: *the most disgusting behaviour*
foul: *They produce a foul smell of rotten eggs.*
horrible: *I've got a horrible feeling about this one.*
repellent: *the most repellent human being I have ever met*
unpleasant: *some unpleasant surprises*
vile: *All the food is vile.*
<<OPPOSITE *pleasant*

nation ['neɪʃən] **nations** NOUN
(GEOGRAPHY) a large group of people sharing the same history and language and usually inhabiting a particular country

national ['næʃənəl] **nationals (GEOGRAPHY)** ADJECTIVE
1 relating to the whole of a country *e.g. a national newspaper*
2 typical of a particular country *e.g. women in Polish national dress*

> NOUN

3 A national of a country is a citizen of that country. *e.g. Turkish nationals.*
nationally ADVERB

national anthem national anthems NOUN
A country's national anthem is its official song.

nationalism ['næʃənəˌlɪzəm] NOUN
1 Nationalism is a desire for the independence of a country; also a political movement aiming to achieve such independence.
2 Nationalism is also love of your own country.
nationalist NOUN, **nationalistic** ADJECTIVE

nationality [ˌnæʃəˈnælɪtɪ] **nationalities** NOUN
Nationality is the fact of belonging to a particular country.

nationalize ['næʃənəˌlaɪz] **nationalizes, nationalizing, nationalized;** also spelt **nationalise** VERB
To nationalize an industry means to bring it under the control and ownership of the state.
nationalization NOUN

n

National Party ['næʃən³l] NOUN
In Australia and New Zealand, the National Party is a major political party.

national service NOUN
National service is a compulsory period of service in the armed forces.

nationwide ['neɪʃən,waɪd] ADJECTIVE OR ADVERB
happening all over a country e.g. *a nationwide search*

native ['neɪtɪv] **natives** ADJECTIVE
1 Your native country is the country where you were born.

2 Your native language is the language that you first learned to speak.

3 Animals or plants that are native to a place live or grow there naturally and have not been brought there by people.

> NOUN

4 A native of a place is someone who was born there.

Nativity [nə'tɪvɪtɪ] NOUN
In Christianity, the Nativity is the birth of Christ or the festival celebrating this.

natter ['nætə] **natters, nattering, nattered** VERB; INFORMAL
If you natter, you talk about unimportant things.

natural ['nætʃrəl] **naturals** ADJECTIVE
1 normal and to be expected e.g. *It was only natural that he was tempted.*

⬤ THESAURUS
common: *It is a common response.*
everyday: *the everyday drudgery of work*
normal: *Biting is normal for puppies when they are teething.*
ordinary: *The cottage looks quite ordinary from the road.*
typical: *typical symptoms of stress*
usual: *It was not usual for the women to accompany them.*
<<OPPOSITE *unnatural*

2 not trying to pretend or hide anything e.g. *Caitlin's natural manner reassured her.*

⬤ THESAURUS
candid: *rather candid about her marriage*
frank: *an unusually frank interview*
genuine: *He always seems so genuine.*
real: *She came across as a real person.*
unaffected: *She sang with unaffected simplicity.*
<<OPPOSITE *false*

3 **(D & T)** existing or happening in nature e.g. *natural disasters*

4 A natural ability is one you were born with.

⬤ THESAURUS
inborn: *an inborn sense of optimism*

inherent: *the inherent goodness of people*
innate: *the innate conservatism of his predecessor*
instinctive: *an instinctive distrust of authority*
intuitive: *an intuitive understanding of the market*
native: *He relies on his native wit to get him through.*

5 Your natural mother or father is your real mother or father and not someone who has adopted you.

> NOUN

6 someone who is born with a particular ability e.g. *She's a natural at bridge.*

7 In music, a natural is a note that is not a sharp or a flat. It is represented by the symbol (♮).
naturally ADVERB

nature ['neɪtʃə] **natures** NOUN
1 Nature is animals, plants, and all the other things in the world not made by people.

2 The nature of a person or thing is their basic character. e.g. *She liked his warm, generous nature.*
[WORD HISTORY: from Latin NATURA meaning 'birth']

⬤ THESAURUS
character: *the funny side of his character*
make-up: *Compromise was never part of his make-up.*
personality: *his dominating personality*

naughty ['nɔːtɪ] **naughtier, naughtiest** ADJECTIVE
1 behaving badly

⬤ THESAURUS
bad: *the bad behaviour of their teenage children*
disobedient: *Lucy was similarly disobedient.*
impish: *an impish sense of humour*
mischievous: *a mischievous child*
wayward: *He tried to control his wayward son.*
<<OPPOSITE *well-behaved*

2 rude or indecent e.g. *naughty films*
naughtiness NOUN

⬤ THESAURUS
bawdy: *a series of bawdy jokes*
lewd: *his arrest for lewd behaviour*
obscene: *making obscene gestures to the crowd*
vulgar: *The lyrics were vulgar.*

nausea ['nɔːzɪə] NOUN
Nausea is a feeling in your stomach that you are going to be sick.
nauseous ADJECTIVE

nautical ['nɔːtɪkəl] ADJECTIVE
relating to ships or navigation

naval ['neɪvəl] ADJECTIVE
relating to or having a navy e.g. *naval officers... naval bases*

navel ['neɪvəl] **navels** NOUN
the small hollow on the front of your body just below your waist

navigate ['nævɪˌɡeɪt] **navigates, navigating, navigated** VERB

1 When someone navigates, they work out the direction in which a ship, plane, or car should go, using maps and sometimes instruments.

2 To navigate a stretch of water means to travel safely across it. *e.g. It was the first time I had navigated the ocean.*

navigation NOUN, **navigator** NOUN

navy ['neɪvi] **navies** NOUN

1 the part of a country's armed forces that fights at sea

> ADJECTIVE

2 dark blue

Nazi ['nɑːtsɪ] **Nazis** NOUN

The Nazis were members of the National Socialist German Workers' Party, which was led by Adolf Hitler.

NB

You write NB to draw attention to what you are going to write next. NB is an abbreviation for the Latin 'nota bene', which means 'note well'.

near [nɪə] **nearer, nearest; nears, nearing, neared** PREPOSITION

1 not far from

THESAURUS

adjacent to: *a garden and maze adjacent to the castle*
alongside: *the huts set up alongside the river*
close to: *We parked close to the pavement.*
next to: *I realised someone was standing next to me.*
not far from: *a car park not far from the entrance*

> ADJECTIVE

2 not far away in distance

THESAURUS

adjacent: *an adjacent room*
adjoining: *A phone rang in an adjoining office.*
close: *a close neighbour*
nearby: *the nearby village*
<<OPPOSITE *far*

3 not far away in time

THESAURUS

approaching: *The deadline was approaching.*
forthcoming: *the forthcoming football season*
imminent: *The day of our departure was imminent.*
looming: *Exams are looming and the students are panicking.*
near at hand: *His death is near at hand.*
nigh: *The end of the world is nigh.*
upcoming: *the upcoming elections*

4 You can also use 'near' to mean almost. *e.g. a night of near disaster*

> VERB

5 When you are nearing something, you are approaching it and will soon reach it. *e.g. The dog began to bark as he neared the porch.*

nearby ADJECTIVE ['nɪəˌbaɪ]

1 only a short distance away. *e.g. a nearby town*

> ADVERB [ˌnɪə'baɪ]

2 only a short distance away. *e.g. a house nearby*

nearly ['nɪəlɪ] ADVERB

not completely but almost

THESAURUS

almost: *Over the past decade their wages have almost doubled.*
as good as: *The World Championship is as good as over.*
just about: *We are just about finished with this section.*
practically: *The house was practically a wreck.*
virtually: *Their country is virtually bankrupt.*

neat [niːt] **neater, neatest** ADJECTIVE

1 tidy and smart

THESAURUS

orderly: *an orderly office*
smart: *a smart navy blue suit*
spruce: *Mundo was looking spruce in a suit.*
tidy: *He always kept his bedroom tidy.*
trim: *a street of trim little villas*
<<OPPOSITE *untidy*

2 A neat alcoholic drink does not have anything added to it. *e.g. a small glass of neat vodka*

neatly ADVERB, **neatness** NOUN

THESAURUS

pure: *a carton of pure orange juice*
straight: *calling for a straight whisky*

necessarily ['nɛsɪsərɪlɪ] ADVERB

Something that is not necessarily the case is not always or inevitably the case.

necessary ['nɛsɪsərɪ] ADJECTIVE

1 Something that is necessary is needed or must be done.

THESAURUS

essential: *It is essential that you visit a dentist.*
imperative: *It is imperative we end up with a win.*
indispensable: *Jordan is an indispensable part of the peace process.*
required: *That book is required reading.*
vital: *Bone marrow is vital for producing blood cells.*
<<OPPOSITE *unnecessary*

2 FORMAL

Necessary also means certain or inevitable. *e.g. a necessary consequence of war*

THESAURUS

certain: *one certain outcome of the conference*
inevitable: *She now accepts that a divorce is inevitable.*
inexorable: *The growth in travel has been inexorable.*
unavoidable: *The union knows that job losses are unavoidable.*

n

necessity [nɪˈsɛsɪtɪ] **necessities** NOUN

1 Necessity is the need to do something. *e.g. There is no necessity for any of this.*

2 Necessities are things needed in order to live.

neck [nɛk] **necks** NOUN

1 the part of your body which joins your head to the rest of your body

2 the long narrow part at the top of a bottle

necklace [ˈnɛklɪs] **necklaces** NOUN

1 a piece of jewellery which a woman wears around her neck

2 In South Africa, a name for a tyre filled with petrol which is placed round a person's neck and set on fire in order to kill that person.

nectar [ˈnɛktə] NOUN

Nectar is a sweet liquid produced by flowers and attractive to insects.

nectarine [ˈnɛktərɪn] **nectarines** NOUN

a kind of peach with a smooth skin

née [neɪ]

'Née' is used to indicate what a woman's surname was before she got married *e.g. Sara Black, née Wells'.*

need [niːd] **needs, needing, needed** VERB

1 If you need something, you believe that you must have it or do it.

⬤ THESAURUS

demand: *The children demand her attention.*
require: *If you require further information, please telephone.*
want: *I want a drink.*

> NOUN

2 Your needs are the things that you need to have.

3 a strong feeling that you must have or do something *e.g. I just felt the need to write about it.*

needle [ˈniːdᵊl] **needles, needling, needled** NOUN

1 a small thin piece of metal with a pointed end and a hole at the other, which is used for sewing

2 Needles are also long thin pieces of steel or plastic, used for knitting.

3 the small pointed part in a record player that touches the record and picks up the sound signals

4 the part of a syringe which a doctor or nurse sticks into your body

5 the thin piece of metal or plastic on a dial which moves to show a measurement

6 The needles of a pine tree are its leaves.

> VERB

7 INFORMAL

If someone needles you, they annoy or provoke you.

needless [ˈniːdlɪs] ADJECTIVE

unnecessary

needlessly ADVERB

needy [ˈniːdɪ] **needier, neediest** ADJECTIVE

very poor

negative [ˈnɛgətɪv] **negatives** ADJECTIVE

1 A negative answer means 'no'.

2 Someone who is negative sees only problems and disadvantages. *e.g. Why are you so negative about everything?.*

3 If a medical or scientific test is negative, it shows that something has not happened or is not present. *e.g. The pregnancy test came back negative.*

4 (MATHS) A negative number is less than zero.

> NOUN

5 the image that is first produced when you take a photograph

negatively ADVERB

neglect [nɪˈglɛkt] **neglects, neglecting, neglected** VERB

1 If you neglect something, you do not look after it properly.

⬤ THESAURUS

ignore: *They see the government ignoring poor people.*
overlook: *Pensioners feel they are being overlooked.*
turn your back on: *Do not turn your back on the unemployed.*

2 FORMAL

If you neglect to do something, you fail to do it. *e.g. He had neglected to give her his address.*

⬤ THESAURUS

fail: *I was shattered and I failed to tell her about the good bits.*
forget: *She forgot to lock her door.*
omit: *He omitted to mention his connection with the company.*

> NOUN

3 Neglect is failure to look after something or someone properly. *e.g. Most of her plants died from neglect.*

neglectful ADJECTIVE

⬤ THESAURUS

disregard: *a callous disregard for his victims*
indifference: *Indifference to patients is rare in America.*
unconcern: *the government's unconcern for the environment*

negligent [ˈnɛglɪdʒənt] ADJECTIVE

not taking enough care *e.g. her negligent driving*

negligence NOUN

negligible ['nɛglɪdʒəbᵊl] ADJECTIVE
very small and unimportant *e.g. a negligible amount of fat*

negotiable [nɪ'gəʊʃəbᵊl] ADJECTIVE
able to be changed or agreed by discussion *e.g. All contributions are negotiable.*

negotiate [nɪ'gəʊʃɪˌeɪt] **negotiates, negotiating, negotiated** VERB
1 When people negotiate, they have formal discussions in order to reach an agreement about something.
2 If you negotiate an obstacle, you manage to get over it or round it.
negotiation NOUN, **negotiator** NOUN

Negro ['niːɡrəʊ] **Negroes** NOUN; OLD-FASHIONED
a person with black skin who comes from Africa or whose ancestors came from Africa

neigh [neɪ] **neighs, neighing, neighed** VERB
1 When a horse neighs, it makes a loud high-pitched sound.
> NOUN
2 a loud sound made by a horse

neighbour ['neɪbə] **neighbours** NOUN
1 Your neighbour is someone who lives next door to you or near you.
2 Your neighbour is also someone standing or sitting next to you. *e.g. I got chatting with my neighbour in the studio.*

neighbourhood ['neɪbəˌhʊd] **neighbourhoods** NOUN
a district where people live *e.g. a safe neighbourhood*

neighbouring ['neɪbəˌrɪŋ] ADJECTIVE
situated nearby *e.g. schools in neighbouring areas*

neither ['naɪðə] ADJECTIVE OR PRONOUN
used to indicate that a negative statement refers to two or more things or people *e.g. It's neither a play nor a musical... Neither of them spoke.*

> When *neither* is followed by a plural noun, the verb can be plural too: *neither of these books are useful*. When you have two singular subjects the verb should be singular too: *neither Jack nor John has done the work.*

neo- PREFIX
new or modern *e.g. neo-fascism*
[WORD HISTORY: from Greek NEOS meaning 'new']

nephew ['nɛvjuː] **nephews** NOUN
Someone's nephew is the son of their sister or brother.

Neptune ['nɛptjuːn] NOUN
Neptune is the planet in the solar system which is eighth from the sun.

[WORD HISTORY: from NEPTUNE, the Roman god of the sea]

nerve [nɜːv] **nerves** NOUN
1 a long thin fibre that sends messages between your brain and other parts of your body
2 If you talk about someone's nerves, you are referring to how able they are to remain calm in a difficult situation. *e.g. It needs confidence and strong nerves.*
3 Nerve is courage. *e.g. O'Meara held his nerve to sink the putt.*
4 INFORMAL
Nerve is boldness or rudeness. *e.g. He had the nerve to swear at me.*
> AN INFORMAL PHRASE
5 If someone **gets on your nerves**, they irritate you.

nerve-racking ['nɜːvˌrækɪŋ] ADJECTIVE
making you feel very worried and tense *e.g. a nerve-racking experience*

nervous ['nɜːvəs] ADJECTIVE
1 worried and frightened

● THESAURUS
anxious: *I was very anxious about her safety.*
apprehensive: *Their families are apprehensive about the trip.*
edgy: *I was edgy and tired.*
jittery: informal *She still feels jittery when she visits her sister.*
jumpy: *The Italians are getting jumpy after drawing against the Swiss.*
tense: *too tense to sleep*
toey: Australian and New Zealand; slang *Dad's getting a bit toey.*
uptight: informal *an uptight British couple*
worried: *You had me worried for a moment.*
<<OPPOSITE calm

2 A nervous illness affects your emotions and mental health.
nervously ADVERB, **nervousness** NOUN

nervous breakdown ['breɪkˌdaʊn] **nervous breakdowns** NOUN
an illness in which someone suffers from deep depression and needs psychiatric treatment

nervous system **nervous systems** NOUN
Your nervous system is the nerves in your body together with your brain and spinal cord.

-ness SUFFIX
'-ness' forms nouns from adjectives. *e.g. tenderness... happiness*
[WORD HISTORY: from an Old English suffix]

nest [nɛst] **nests, nesting, nested** NOUN
1 a place that a bird makes to lay its eggs in; also a place that some insects and other animals

n

make to rear their young in

> VERB

2 When birds nest, they build a nest and lay eggs in it.

nestle ['nɛsᵊl] **nestles, nestling, nestled** VERB

If you nestle somewhere, you settle there comfortably, often pressing up against someone else. *e.g. A new puppy nestled in her lap.*

nestling ['nɛstlɪŋ] **nestlings** NOUN

a young bird that has not yet learned to fly and so has not left the nest

net [nɛt] **nets** NOUN

1 a piece of material made of threads woven together with small spaces in between

2 The net is the same as the **Internet**

> ADJECTIVE

3 A net result or amount is final, after everything has been considered. *e.g. a net profit of 171 million*

4 The net weight of something is its weight without its wrapping.

netball ['nɛt,bɔːl] NOUN

Netball is a game played by two teams of seven players in which each team tries to score goals by throwing a ball through a net at the top of a pole.

netting ['nɛtɪŋ] NOUN

Netting is material made of threads or metal wires woven together with small spaces in between.

nettle ['nɛtᵊl] **nettles** NOUN

a wild plant covered with little hairs that sting

network ['nɛt,wɜːk] **networks** NOUN

1 a large number of lines or roads which cross each other at many points *e.g. a small network of side roads*

2 A network of people or organizations is a large number of them that work together as a system. *e.g. the public telephone network*

3 A television network is a group of broadcasting stations that all transmit the same programmes at the same time.

4 (ICT) a group of computers connected to each other

neuron ['njʊərɒn] **neurons** NOUN

a cell that is part of the nervous system and conducts messages to and from the brain

neurone ['njʊərəʊn] **neurones** NOUN the same as a **neuron**

neurosis [njʊ'rəʊsɪs] **neuroses** NOUN

Neurosis is mental illness which causes people to have strong and unreasonable fears and worries.

neurotic [njʊ'rɒtɪk] ADJECTIVE

having strong and unreasonable fears and

worries *e.g. He was almost neurotic about being followed.*

neuter ['njuːtə] **neuters, neutering, neutered** VERB

1 When an animal is neutered, its reproductive organs are removed.

> ADJECTIVE

2 In some languages, a neuter noun or pronoun is one which is not masculine or feminine.

neutral ['njuːtrəl] **neutrals** ADJECTIVE

1 People who are neutral do not support either side in a disagreement or war.

THESAURUS

disinterested: *a disinterested observer*
dispassionate: *a full and dispassionate account*
impartial: *How can he give impartial advice?*
nonaligned: *the Arab and nonaligned countries*
<<OPPOSITE *biased*

2 The neutral wire in an electric plug is the one that is not earth or live.

3 A neutral colour is not definite or striking, for example pale grey.

4 In chemistry, a neutral substance is neither acid nor alkaline.

> NOUN

5 a person or country that does not support either side in a disagreement or war

6 Neutral is the position between the gears of a vehicle in which the gears are not connected to the engine and so the vehicle cannot move.
neutrality NOUN

neutron ['njuːtrɒn] **neutrons** NOUN

an atomic particle that has no electrical charge

never ['nɛvə] ADVERB

at no time in the past, present, or future

THESAURUS

at no time: *At no time did he see the helicopter.*
not ever: *The problem won't ever go away.*

Do not use *never* to mean 'not' in writing. You should say *I didn't see her* not *I never saw her.*

nevertheless [,nɛvəðə'lɛs] ADVERB

in spite of what has just been said *e.g. They dress rather plainly but nevertheless look quite smart.*

new [njuː] **newer, newest** ADJECTIVE

1 recently made, created, or discovered *e.g. a new house... a new plan... a new virus*

THESAURUS

advancd: *trial results of the company's most advanced drugs*
curent: *all the current gossip on the stars*
fresh: *fresh footprints in the snow*
latest: *We review all the latest films.*
modern: *modern technology*

recent: *Lawson's most recent novel.* **up-to-date**: *the most up-to-date computers*
up-to-the-minute: *up-to-the-minute information*

2 not used or owned before *e.g. We've got a new car.*

3 different or unfamiliar *e.g. a name which was new to me*

newborn ['njuːˌbɔːn] ADJECTIVE
born recently

newcomer ['njuːˌkʌmə] **newcomers** NOUN
someone who has recently arrived in a place

newly ['njuːlɪ] ADVERB
recently *e.g. the newly born baby*

new moon **new moons** NOUN
The moon is a new moon when it is a thin crescent shape at the start of its four-week cycle.

news [njuːz] NOUN
News is information about things that have happened.

● THESAURUS
bulletin: *the main evening bulletin*
disclosure: *disclosures about his private life*
dispatch: *the latest dispatches from the war zone*
information: *up-to-date information on weather*
intelligence: *military intelligence from behind Iraqi lines*
latest: *informal the latest on the bomb explosion*
tidings: *formal the bearer of bad tidings*
word: *There is no word about casualties.*

newsagent ['njuːzˌeɪdʒənt] **newsagents** NOUN
a person or shop that sells newspapers and magazines

newspaper ['njuːzˌpeɪpə] **newspapers** NOUN
a publication, on large sheets of paper, that is produced regularly and contains news and articles

newt [njuːt] **newts** NOUN
a small amphibious creature with a moist skin, short legs, and a long tail
[WORD HISTORY: from a mistaken division of Middle English AN EWT]

New Testament ['tɛstəmənt] NOUN
The New Testament is the second part of the Bible, which deals with the life of Jesus Christ and with the early Church.

New Year NOUN
New Year is the time when people celebrate the start of a year.

New Zealander ['ziːləndə] **New Zealanders** NOUN
someone who comes from New Zealand

next [nɛkst] ADJECTIVE

1 coming immediately after something else *e.g. Their next child was a girl.*

● THESAURUS
ensuing: *the ensuing years of violence*
following: *The following day I went to work as usual.*
subsequent: *As subsequent events showed, he was wrong.*
succeeding: *succeeding generations of students*

2 in a position nearest to something *e.g. in the next room*

● THESAURUS
adjacent: *I pulled into the adjacent driveway.*
adjoining: *in adjoining streets*
closest: *Britain's closest neighbours.*
nearest: *the nearest Italian restaurant*
neighbouring: *Liberians fleeing to neighbouring countries.*

> ADVERB
3 coming immediately after something else *e.g. Steve arrived next.*

THESAURUS
afterwards: *I felt dizzy afterwards and had to sit down.*
subsequently: *She was subsequently married to his cousin.*

> PHRASE
4 If one thing is **next to** another, it is at the side of it.

next door ADJECTIVE OR ADVERB
in the house next to yours

NHS
In Britain, an abbreviation for 'National Health Service'.

nib [nɪb] **nibs** NOUN
the pointed end of a pen

nibble ['nɪbəl] **nibbles, nibbling, nibbled** VERB
1 When you nibble something, you take small bites of it.

> NOUN
2 a small bite of something

nice see page 582 for Word Web

nicety ['naɪsɪtɪ] **niceties** NOUN
a small detail *e.g. the social niceties*

niche [nɪtʃ] **niches** NOUN
1 a hollow area in a wall

2 If you say that you have found your niche, you mean that you have found a job or way of life that is exactly right for you.

nick [nɪk] **nicks, nicking, nicked** VERB
1 If you nick something, you make a small cut in its surface. *e.g. He nicked his chin.*

1 ADJECTIVE
attractive or enjoyable *eg: Did you have a nice time, dear?*
● THESAURUS
comfortable: *I tried to make a comfortable home for my family.*
cosy: *a cosy parlour*
homely: *a house with a homely atmosphere*
relaxing: *This is a very relaxing room.*

2 ADJECTIVE
of someone's appearance
● THESAURUS
attractive: *She's grown into an attractive young lady.*
beautiful: *You're looking very beautiful tonight.*
cute: *He's going out with a very cute girl.*
dishy: *I used to think he was dishy when I was younger.*
good-looking: *Her son is good-looking, but very shy.*
gorgeous: *I think he's really gorgeous.*
handsome: *a very handsome young man*
lovely: *He married a lovely woman.*
pretty: *You look very pretty in that dress.*

3 ADJECTIVE
of an object, place or thing
● THESAURUS
charming: *a charming little fishing village*
delightful: *a delightful place for a honeymoon*
lovely: *a lovely old English garden*

4 ADJECTIVE
of clothing
● THESAURUS
chic: *a chic designer frock*
elegant: *That's a very elegant dress you're wearing.*
fetching: *a fetching outfit*
smart: *I was wearing a smart navy-blue suit.*
stylish: *She always has such stylish clothes.*

5 ADJECTIVE
of an event or occasion
● THESAURUS
agreeable: *It's not a very agreeable way to spend your day off.*
enjoyable: *The trip was much more enjoyable than I had expected.*
fantastic: *Thanks for giving me such a fantastic party.*
pleasant: *It was a very pleasant experience.*
pleasurable: *the pleasurable sensation of getting into a warm bath*

6 ADJECTIVE
of someone's personality
● THESAURUS
amiable: *I've always found him a very amiable man.*
considerate: *He's very considerate towards his sisters.*
friendly: *They aren't very friendly to strangers.*
good-natured: *She is unfailingly good-natured.*
kind: *I try to be kind to everyone.*
kindly: *a kindly old man*
likeable: *He was an immensely likeable chap.*
thoughtful: *That was a very thoughtful gesture.*

7 ADJECTIVE
of food or drink
● THESAURUS
appetizing: *An appetizing smell was coming from the kitchen.*
delectable: *We bought some delectable raspberries.*
delicious: *The food here is delicious.*
luscious: *luscious peaches*
mouthwatering: *a mouthwatering dessert*
tasty: *a café serving tasty dishes*

8 ADJECTIVE
of the weather
● THESAURUS
fine: *I'll do the garden if the weather is fine.*
glorious: *It's a glorious day!*

nice

2 INFORMAL
To nick something also means to steal it.

> NOUN

3 a small cut in the surface of something

nickel ['nɪkəl] NOUN
Nickel is a silver-coloured metal that is used in making steel.

nickname ['nɪkˌneɪm] **nicknames, nicknaming, nicknamed** NOUN

1 an informal name given to someone

> VERB

2 If you nickname someone, you give them a nickname.

[WORD HISTORY: from Middle English AN EKENAME meaning 'an additional name']

nicotine ['nɪkəˌtiːn] NOUN
Nicotine is an addictive substance found in tobacco.

niece [niːs] **nieces** NOUN
Someone's niece is the daughter of their sister or brother.

nifty ['nɪftɪ] ADJECTIVE
neat and pleasing or cleverly done

Nigerian [naɪ'dʒɪərɪən] **Nigerians**
ADJECTIVE

1 belonging or relating to Nigeria

> NOUN

2 someone from Nigeria

niggle ['nɪgəl] **niggles, niggling, niggled**
VERB

1 If something niggles you, it worries you slightly.

> NOUN

2 a small worry that you keep thinking about

night [naɪt] **nights** NOUN
Night is the time between sunset and sunrise when it is dark.

nightclub ['naɪtˌklʌb] **nightclubs** NOUN
a place where people go late in the evening to drink and dance

nightdress ['naɪtˌdrɛs] **nightdresses** NOUN
a loose dress that a woman or girl wears to sleep in

nightfall ['naɪtˌfɔːl] NOUN
Nightfall is the time of day when it starts to get dark.

nightie ['naɪtɪ] **nighties** NOUN; INFORMAL
a nightdress

nightingale ['naɪtɪŋˌgeɪl] **nightingales**
NOUN
a small brown European bird, the male of which sings very beautifully, especially at night

nightly ['naɪtlɪ] ADJECTIVE OR ADVERB
happening every night e.g. the nightly news programme

nightmare ['naɪtˌmɛə] **nightmares** NOUN
a very frightening dream; also used of any very unpleasant or frightening situation e.g. The meal itself was a nightmare.

nightmarish ADJECTIVE

[WORD HISTORY: from NIGHT + Middle English MARE meaning 'evil spirit']

nil [nɪl] NOUN
Nil means zero or nothing. It is used especially in sports scores.

nimble ['nɪmbəl] **nimbler, nimblest**
ADJECTIVE

1 able to move quickly and easily

2 able to think quickly and cleverly

nimbly ADVERB

nine [naɪn]
the number 9

ninth

nineteen ['naɪn'tiːn]
the number 19

nineteenth

ninety ['naɪntɪ] **nineties**
the number 90

ninetieth

nip [nɪp] **nips, nipping, nipped** VERB

1 INFORMAL
If you nip somewhere, you go there quickly.

2 To nip someone or something means to pinch them slightly.

> NOUN

3 a light pinch

nipple ['nɪpəl] **nipples** NOUN
Your nipples are the two small pieces of projecting flesh on your chest. Babies suck milk through the nipples on their mothers' breasts.

nirvana [nɪə'vɑːnə] NOUN
Nirvana is the ultimate state of spiritual enlightenment which can be achieved in the Hindu and Buddhist religions.

nit [nɪt] **nits** NOUN
Nits are the eggs of a kind of louse that sometimes lives in people's hair.

nitrogen ['naɪtrədʒən] NOUN
Nitrogen is a chemical element usually found as a gas. It forms about 78% of the earth's atmosphere.

no [nəʊ] INTERJECTION

1 used to say that something is not true or to refuse something

● THESAURUS
absolutely not: "Did they consult you?" – "Absolutely not."
certainly not: "Perhaps it would be better if I

withdrew." - "Certainly not!"
definitely not: "Are you going to the party?" - "Definitely not."
not at all: "You're not upset, are you?" - "Not at all."
of course not: "I'd like to talk to the lads, if you don't mind." - "Of course not, Chief."
<<OPPOSITE *yes*

> **ADJECTIVE**

2 none at all or not at all *e.g. She gave no reason... You're no friend of mine.*

> **ADVERB**

3 used with a comparative to mean 'not' *e.g. no later than 24th July*

no. a written abbreviation for **number**

nobility [nəʊˈbɪlɪtɪ] NOUN

1 Nobility is the quality of being noble. *e.g. the unmistakable nobility of his character*

2 The nobility of a society are all the people who have titles and high social rank.

noble [ˈnəʊbəl] **nobler, noblest; nobles**
ADJECTIVE

1 honest and brave, and deserving admiration

● THESAURUS
generous: *It reflects his generous nature.*
honourable: *His colleagues were honourable people.*
magnanimous: *Miss Balding is magnanimous in victory.*
upright: *a very upright, trustworthy man*
virtuous: *the virtuous Mrs Friendall*
worthy: *less worthy members of our profession*
<<OPPOSITE *ignoble*

2 very impressive *e.g. broad cheekbones which gave them a noble appearance*

> **NOUN**

3 a member of the nobility
nobly ADVERB

● THESAURUS
aristocrat: *All his sisters had married German aristocrats.*
lord: *They assumed that Amy was a snob because her father was a lord.*
nobleman: *a Spanish nobleman*
peer: *He was made a life peer in 1981.*
<<OPPOSITE *peasant*

nobleman [ˈnəʊbəlmən] **noblemen** NOUN
a man who is a member of the nobility
noblewoman NOUN

nobody [ˈnəʊbədɪ] **nobodies** PRONOUN

1 not a single person

> **NOUN**

2 Someone who is a nobody is not at all important.

▪ *Nobody* and *no-one* mean the same.

nocturnal [nɒkˈtɜːnəl] ADJECTIVE

1 happening at night *e.g. a nocturnal journey through New York*

2 active at night *e.g. a nocturnal animal*

nod [nɒd] **nods, nodding, nodded** VERB

1 When you nod, you move your head up and down, usually to show agreement.

> **NOUN**

2 a movement of your head up and down

nod off VERB

3 If you nod off, you fall asleep.

noise [nɔɪz] **noises** NOUN
a sound, especially one that is loud or unpleasant

● THESAURUS
commotion: *There was a commotion in the corridor.*
din: *He'd never heard a din like it.*
hubbub: *the hubbub of Paris in the 1880s*
pandemonium: *There was pandemonium in the classroom.*
racket: *There was a terrible racket going on.*
row: *Whatever is that row?*
uproar: *The courtroom was in an uproar.*
<<OPPOSITE *silence*

noisy [ˈnɔɪzɪ] **noisier, noisiest** ADJECTIVE
making a lot of noise or full of noise *e.g. a noisy crowd*
noisily ADVERB, **noisiness** NOUN

● THESAURUS
deafening: *a deafening roar*
loud: *The disco music was a little too loud.*
piercing: *her piercing laugh*
strident: *the strident vocals of Joy Malcolm*
tumultuous: *He took the field to tumultuous applause.*
vociferous: *vociferous support from the Scottish fans*
<<OPPOSITE *quiet*

nomad [ˈnəʊmæd] **nomads** NOUN
a person who belongs to a tribe which travels from place to place rather than living in just one place
nomadic ADJECTIVE

nominal [ˈnɒmɪnəl] ADJECTIVE

1 Something that is nominal is supposed to have a particular identity or status, but in reality does not have it. *e.g. the nominal leader of his party*

2 A nominal amount of money is very small compared to the value of something. *e.g. I am prepared to sell my shares at a nominal price.*
nominally ADVERB

nominate [ˈnɒmɪˌneɪt] **nominates, nominating, nominated** VERB
If you nominate someone for a job or position,

you formally suggest that they have it.
nomination NOUN

⬤ THESAURUS
name: He'll be naming a new captain.
propose: Cliff was proposed as chairman.
recommend: He recommended him as his successor at Boston.
select: no prospect of being selected to stand for Parliament
submit: Mr Heath submitted a list of 200 names.
suggest: Some commentators have suggested Clark for the job.

non- PREFIX
not e.g. non-smoking
[WORD HISTORY: from Latin]

nonchalant ['nɒnʃələnt] ADJECTIVE
seeming calm and not worried
nonchalance NOUN, **nonchalantly** ADVERB

noncommissioned officer
[ˌnɒnkə'mɪʃənd] **noncommissioned officers** NOUN
an officer such as a sergeant or corporal who has been promoted from the lower ranks

nondescript ['nɒndɪˌskrɪpt] ADJECTIVE
Someone or something nondescript has no special or interesting qualities or details. e.g. a nondescript coat

none [nʌn] PRONOUN
not a single thing or person, or not even a small amount of something

nonfiction [nɒn'fɪkʃən] NOUN
(LIBRARY) Nonfiction is writing that gives facts and information rather than telling a story.

nonplussed [nɒn'plʌst] ADJECTIVE
confused and unsure about how to react

nonsense ['nɒnsəns] NOUN
Nonsense is foolish and meaningless words or behaviour.
nonsensical ADJECTIVE

⬤ THESAURUS
bull: slang They're teaching our kids a load of bull.
drivel: mindless drivel aimed at Middle America
garbage: informal One source claimed the rumours were complete garbage.
inanity: the burbling inanities of the tabloids
rot: She is talking complete rot.
rubbish: complete and utter rubbish
waffle: British; informal He writes smug, sanctimonious waffle.

nonstop ['nɒn'stɒp] ADJECTIVE OR ADVERB
continuing without any pauses or breaks e.g. nonstop excitement

noodle ['nu:dᵊl] **noodles** NOUN
Noodles are a kind of pasta shaped into long, thin pieces.

nook [nʊk] **nooks** NOUN; LITERARY
a small sheltered place

noon [nu:n] NOUN
Noon is midday.

no-one or **no one** ['nəʊˌwʌn] PRONOUN
not a single person

▬ No-one and nobody mean the same.

noose [nu:s] **nooses** NOUN
a loop at the end of a piece of rope, with a knot that tightens when the rope is pulled

nor [nɔ:] CONJUNCTION
used after 'neither' or after a negative statement, to add something else that the negative statement applies to e.g. They had neither the time nor the money for the sport.

norm [nɔ:m] NOUN
If something is the norm, it is the usual and expected thing. e.g. cultures where large families are the norm
[WORD HISTORY: from Latin NORMA meaning 'carpenter's rule']

normal ['nɔ:mᵊl] ADJECTIVE
usual and ordinary e.g. I try to lead a normal life.
normality NOUN

⬤ THESAURUS
average: What's your average day like?
conventional: conventional tastes
habitual: their country of habitual residence
ordinary: It was just an ordinary weekend.
regular: It looks like a regular cigarette.
routine: a routine medical check
standard: standard practice
typical: A typical day begins at 8.30.
usual: She did not collect him at the usual time.
<<OPPOSITE unusual

normally ['nɔ:məlɪ] ADVERB
1 usually e.g. I don't normally like dancing.
2 in a way that is normal e.g. The foetus is developing normally.

north [nɔ:θ] NOUN
1 The north is the direction to your left when you are looking towards the place where the sun rises.
2 The north of a place or country is the part which is towards the north when you are in the centre.

> ADVERB OR ADJECTIVE
3 North means towards the north. e.g. The helicopter took off and headed north.

> ADJECTIVE
4 A north wind blows from the north.

North America [nɔ:θ] NOUN
North America is the third largest continent,

consisting of Canada, the United States, and
Mexico.
North American ADJECTIVE

north-east [ˌnɔːˈθiːst] NOUN, ADVERB, OR
ADJECTIVE
North-east is halfway between north and east.

north-easterly [ˌnɔːˈθiːstəlɪ] ADJECTIVE
1 North-easterly means to or towards the north-east.
2 A north-easterly wind blows from the north-east.

north-eastern [ˌnɔːˈθiːstən] ADJECTIVE
in or from the north-east

northerly [ˈnɔːðəlɪ] ADJECTIVE
1 Northerly means to or towards the north. *e.g. travelling in a northerly direction*
2 A northerly wind blows from the north.

northern [ˈnɔːðən] ADJECTIVE
in or from the north *e.g. the mountains of northern Italy*

North Pole [nɔːθ] NOUN
The North Pole is the most northerly point of the earth's surface.

northward or **northwards** [ˈnɔːθwəd] or
[ˈnɔːθwədz] ADVERB
1 Northward or northwards means towards the north. *e.g. We continued northwards.*
> ADJECTIVE
2 The northward part of something is the north part.

north-west [ˌnɔːˈθwɛst] NOUN, ADVERB, OR
ADJECTIVE
North-west is halfway between north and west.

north-westerly [ˌnɔːˈθwɛstəlɪ] ADJECTIVE
1 North-westerly means to or towards the north-west.
2 A north-westerly wind blows from the north-west.

north-western [ˌnɔːˈθwɛstən] ADJECTIVE
in or from the north-west

Norwegian [nɔːˈwiːdʒən] **Norwegians**
ADJECTIVE
1 belonging or relating to Norway
> NOUN
2 someone who comes from Norway
3 Norwegian is the main language spoken in Norway.

nose [nəʊz] **noses** NOUN
1 the part of your face above your mouth which you use for smelling and breathing
2 the front part of a car or plane

nostalgia [nɒˈstældʒə] NOUN
Nostalgia is a feeling of affection for the past, and

sadness that things have changed.
nostalgic ADJECTIVE

nostril [ˈnɒstrɪl] **nostrils** NOUN
Your nostrils are the two openings in your nose which you breathe through.

nosy [ˈnəʊzɪ] **nosier, nosiest;** also spelt nosey
ADJECTIVE
trying to find out about things that do not concern you
● THESAURUS
curious: *surrounded by a group of curious villagers*
eavesdropping: *We don't want to be overheard by eavesdropping servants.*
inquisitive: *Bears are naturally inquisitive creatures.*
prying: *I hid it away, safe from prying eyes.*

not [nɒt] ADVERB
used to make a sentence negative, to refuse something, or to deny something

notable [ˈnəʊtəbəl] ADJECTIVE
important or interesting *e.g. The production is notable for some outstanding performances.*
notably ADVERB

notch [nɒtʃ] **notches** NOUN
a small V-shaped cut in a surface
[WORD HISTORY: from a mistaken division of Middle English AN OTCH]

note [nəʊt] **notes, noting, noted** NOUN
1 a short letter
● THESAURUS
communication: formal *a communication from the President*
letter: *I have received a letter from a friend.*
memo: *a leaked memo to managers*
memorandum: *A memorandum has been sent to the members of the board.*
message: *He sent his mate round with a message for me.*
reminder: *We keep getting reminders from the garage to pay our bill.*
2 a written piece of information that helps you to remember something *e.g. You should make a note of that.*
● THESAURUS
account: *Keep an account of all your outgoings.*
jotting: *Carry a notebook with you for your jottings.*
record: *Keep a record of all payments.*
register: *She kept a register of each child's progress.*
3 In music, a note is a musical sound of a particular pitch, or a written symbol that represents it.
4 a banknote
5 an atmosphere, feeling, or quality *e.g. There was a note of regret in his voice... I'm determined to close on an optimistic note.*

THESAURUS

hint: *Was there was a hint of irony in that remark?*
tone: *He laughed again, this time with a cold, sharp tone.*
touch: *There is an unmistakable touch of pathos in his last film.*
trace: *He wrote on the subject without a trace of sensationalism.*

> VERB

6 If you note a fact, you become aware of it or you mention it. *e.g. I noted that the rain had stopped.*

THESAURUS

mention: *I mentioned in passing that I liked her dress.*
notice: *Contact the police if you notice anything suspicious.*
observe: formal *Hooke observed a reddish spot on the surface of the planet.*
perceive: *He perceived a certain tension between them.*
register: *The sound was so familiar that she didn't register it.*
remark: *Everyone has remarked what a lovely lady she is.*
see: *A lot of people saw what was happening but did nothing.*

> PHRASE

7 If you **take note** of something, you pay attention to it. *e.g. The world hardly took note of this crisis.*

note down VERB

8 If you note something down, you write it down so that you will remember it.

notebook ['nəʊtˌbʊk] **notebooks** NOUN
a small book for writing notes in

noted ['nəʊtɪd] ADJECTIVE
well-known and admired *e.g. a noted Hebrew scholar*

nothing ['nʌθɪŋ] PRONOUN
not anything *e.g. There was nothing to do.*

> *Nothing* is usually followed by a singular verb: *nothing was in the bag.* If the expression *nothing but* is followed by a plural noun, the verb should be plural too: *a large room where nothing but souvenirs were sold.*

notice ['nəʊtɪs] **notices, noticing, noticed**
VERB

1 If you notice something, you become aware of it.

THESAURUS

detect: *He detects signs of growing support for his plan.*
discern: *I did not discern any change in attitudes.*
note: *I noted that the rain had stopped.*

observe: *I've observed how hard he had to work.*
perceive: *gradually perceiving the possibilities*
see: *I saw that the lobby was swarming with police.*
spot: *Allen spotted me on the other side of the dance floor.*

> NOUN

2 Notice is attention or awareness. *e.g. I'm glad he brought it to my notice.*

3 a written announcement

THESAURUS

advertisement: *one advertisement in a local paper*
bill: *students posting bills near the campus for a demo*
poster: *a poster advertising a charity concert*
sign: *a hand-written cardboard sign hung round his neck*

4 Notice is also advance warning about something. *e.g. We were lucky to get you at such short notice.*

THESAURUS

advance warning: *advance warning of the attack*
intimation: *He has given no intimation of an intention to resign.*
notification: *Official notification is expected to arrive today.*
warning: *I was sacked without warning.*

> PHRASE

5 If you **hand in your notice**, you tell your employer that you intend to leave your job after a fixed period of time.

noticeable ['nəʊtɪsəbəl] ADJECTIVE
obvious and easy to see *e.g. a noticeable improvement*
noticeably ADVERB

THESAURUS

conspicuous: *a conspicuous lack of sympathy*
evident: *He ate with evident enjoyment.*
obvious: *There are obvious dangers.*
perceptible: *Germany is showing a perceptible improvement.*
unmistakable: *a growing but unmistakable impatience*

noticeboard ['nəʊtɪsˌbɔːd] **noticeboards**
NOUN
a board for notices

notify ['nəʊtɪˌfaɪ] **notifies, notifying,**
notified VERB
To notify someone of something means to officially inform them of it. *e.g. You must notify us of any change of address.*
notification NOUN

THESAURUS

advise: formal *I think it best that I advise you of my decision first.*
inform: *They would inform him of any progress they made.*

tell: *He told me I was on a final warning.*
warn: *They warned him of the dangers.*

notion ['nəʊʃən] **notions** NOUN
an idea or belief

notorious [nəʊ'tɔːrɪəs] ADJECTIVE
well-known for something bad *e.g. The area has become notorious for violence against tourists.*
notoriously ADVERB, **notoriety** NOUN
⬤ THESAURUS
disreputable: *a low and disreputable character*
infamous: *an industry infamous for late payment of debts*
scandalous: *her scandalous affair with the president*

notwithstanding [ˌnɒtwɪθ'stændɪŋ]
PREPOSITION; FORMAL
in spite of *e.g. Notwithstanding his age, Sikorski had an important job.*

nougat ['nuːgɑː] NOUN
Nougat is a kind of chewy sweet containing nuts and sometimes fruit.
[WORD HISTORY: from Provençal NOGA meaning 'nut']

nought [nɔːt]
the number o

noun [naʊn] **nouns** NOUN
a word which refers to a person, thing, or idea. Examples of nouns are 'president', 'table', 'sun', and 'beauty'

nourish ['nʌrɪʃ] **nourishes, nourishing, nourished** VERB
To nourish people or animals means to provide them with food.

nourishing ['nʌrɪʃɪŋ] ADJECTIVE
Food that is nourishing makes you strong and healthy.

nourishment ['nʌrɪʃmənt] NOUN
Nourishment is food that your body needs in order to remain healthy. *e.g. poor nourishment*

novel ['nɒvəl] **novels** NOUN
1 **(LIBRARY)** a book that tells an invented story
> ADJECTIVE
2 new and interesting *e.g. a very novel experience*

novelist ['nɒvəlɪst] **novelists** NOUN
a person who writes novels

novelty ['nɒvəltɪ] **novelties** NOUN
1 Novelty is the quality of being new and interesting. *e.g. The novelty had worn off.*
2 something new and interesting *e.g. Steam power was still a bit of a novelty.*
3 a small, unusual object sold as a gift or souvenir

November [nəʊ'vembə] NOUN
November is the eleventh month of the year. It has 30 days.

[WORD HISTORY: from Latin NOVEMBER meaning 'the ninth month']

novice ['nɒvɪs] **novices** NOUN
1 someone who is not yet experienced at something
2 someone who is preparing to become a monk or nun

now [naʊ] ADVERB
1 at the present time or moment
⬤ THESAURUS
at once: *I really must go at once.*
currently: *The vaccines are currently being tested.*
immediately: *Please come immediately.*
nowadays: *I don't see much of Tony nowadays.*
right now: *Stop that noise right now!*
straightaway: *I think you should see a doctor straightaway.*
without delay: *We'll come round without delay.*
> CONJUNCTION
2 as a result or consequence of a particular fact *e.g. Things have got better now there is a new board.*
> PHRASE
3 **Just now** means very recently *e.g. I drove Brenda back to the camp just now.*
4 If something happens **now and then**, it happens sometimes but not regularly.

nowadays ['naʊə,deɪz] ADVERB
at the present time *e.g. Nowadays most fathers choose to be present at the birth.*

nowhere ['nəʊ,weə] ADVERB
not anywhere

noxious ['nɒkʃəs] ADJECTIVE
harmful or poisonous *e.g. a noxious gas*

nozzle ['nɒzəl] **nozzles** NOUN
a spout fitted onto the end of a pipe or hose to control the flow of a liquid

nuance [njuːˈɑːns] **nuances** NOUN
a small difference in sound, colour, or meaning *e.g. the nuances of his music*

nubile ['njuːbaɪl] ADJECTIVE
A woman who is nubile is young and sexually attractive.
[WORD HISTORY: from Latin NUBERE meaning 'to take a husband']

nuclear ['njuːklɪə] ADJECTIVE
1 relating to the energy produced when the nuclei of atoms are split *e.g. nuclear power... the nuclear industry*
2 relating to weapons that explode using the energy released by atoms *e.g. nuclear war*
3 relating to the structure and behaviour of the nuclei of atoms *e.g. nuclear physics*

nuclear reactor **nuclear reactors** NOUN
A nuclear reactor is a device which is used to obtain nuclear energy.

nucleus [ˈnjuːklɪəs] **nuclei** NOUN

1 the central part of an atom or cell

2 The nucleus of something is the basic central part of it to which other things are added. *e.g. They have retained the nucleus of the team that won the World Cup.*

[WORD HISTORY: from Latin NUCLEUS meaning 'kernel']

nude [njuːd] **nudes** ADJECTIVE

1 naked

> NOUN

2 a picture or statue of a naked person
nudity NOUN

nudge [nʌdʒ] **nudges, nudging, nudged** VERB

1 If you nudge someone, you push them gently, usually with your elbow.

> NOUN

2 a gentle push

nudist [ˈnjuːdɪst] **nudists** NOUN

a person who believes in wearing no clothes

nugget [ˈnʌgɪt] **nuggets** NOUN

a small rough lump of something, especially gold

nuisance [ˈnjuːsəns] **nuisances** NOUN

someone or something that is annoying or inconvenient

THESAURUS

annoyance: *Snoring can be an annoyance.*
bother: *Most men hate the bother of shaving.*
hassle: informal *Writing out a cheque is a hassle.*
inconvenience: *the inconvenience of a rail strike*
irritation: *He describes the tourists as "an irritation".*
pain: informal *She found dressing up for the occasion a real pain.*
pest: *I didn't want to be a cry baby or a pest.*

null [nʌl] PHRASE

Null and void means not legally valid. *e.g. Other documents were declared to be null and void.*

nulla-nulla [ˌnʌləˈnʌlə] **nulla-nullas** NOUN

a thick heavy stick used as a weapon by Australian Aborigines

numb [nʌm] **numbs, numbing, numbed** ADJECTIVE

1 unable to feel anything *e.g. My legs felt numb... numb with grief*

THESAURUS

dead: *Hillier suffered a dead leg playing for the reserves.*
frozen: *a frozen shoulder*
insensitive: *The brain itself is insensitive to pain.*
paralysed: *He has been left with a paralysed arm.*

> VERB

2 If something numbs you, it makes you unable to feel anything. *e.g. The cold numbed my fingers.*

THESAURUS

dull: *morphine to dull the pain*
freeze: *an epidural to freeze the hip area*
paralyse: *people paralysed by illness or injury*
stun: *the gun used to stun the animals*

numbat [ˈnʌm.bæt] **numbats** NOUN

a small Australian marsupial with a long snout and tongue and strong claws which it uses for hunting and eating insects

number [ˈnʌmbə] **numbers, numbering, numbered** NOUN

1 a word or a symbol used for counting or calculating

THESAURUS

digit: *a six-digit password*
figure: *a figure between a hundred and a thousand*
numeral: *Roman numerals.*

2 Someone's number is the series of numbers that you dial when you telephone them.

3 A number of things is a quantity of them. *e.g. Adrian has introduced me to a large number of people.*

THESAURUS

collection: *a huge collection of books about Keats*
crowd: *a huge crowd of supporters*
horde: *a horde of drunken villagers*
multitude: *Bands can play to multitudes of fans.*

4 a song or piece of music

> VERB

5 If things number a particular amount, there are that many of them. *e.g. At that time London's population numbered about 460,000.*

6 If you number something, you give it a number. *e.g. The picture is signed and numbered by the artist.*

7 To be numbered among a particular group means to belong to it. *e.g. Only the best are numbered among their champions.*

numeral [ˈnjuːmərəl] **numerals** NOUN

a symbol that represents a number *e.g. a wristwatch with Roman numerals*

numerical [njuːˈmɛrɪkəl] ADJECTIVE

expressed in numbers or relating to numbers *e.g. a numerical value*

numerous [ˈnjuːmərəs] ADJECTIVE

existing or happening in large numbers

THESAURUS

lots: *I've got lots of photos of the kids.*
many: *I have met Imran many times.*
several: *He is fluent in several languages.*

nun [nʌn] **nuns** NOUN

a woman who has taken religious vows and lives in a convent

n

nurse [nɜːs] **nurses, nursing, nursed** NOUN

1 a person whose job is to look after people who are ill

> VERB

2 If you nurse someone, you look after them when they are ill.

3 If you nurse a feeling, you feel it strongly for a long time. *e.g. He nursed a grudge against the USA.*

nursery ['nɜːsrɪ] **nurseries** NOUN

1 a place where young children are looked after while their parents are working

2 a room in which young children sleep and play

3 a place where plants are grown and sold

nursery school nursery schools NOUN

a school for children from three to five years old

nursing home ['nɜːsɪŋ] **nursing homes** NOUN

a privately run hospital, especially for old people

nurture ['nɜːtʃə] **nurtures, nurturing, nurtured** VERB; FORMAL

If you nurture a young child or a plant, you look after it carefully.

nut [nʌt] **nuts** NOUN

1 a fruit with a hard shell and an edible centre that grows on certain trees

2 a piece of metal with a hole in the middle which a bolt screws into

nutmeg ['nʌtmɛg] NOUN

Nutmeg is a spice used for flavouring in cooking.

nutrient ['njuːtrɪənt] **nutrients** NOUN

(SCIENCE) Nutrients are substances that help plants or animals to grow. *e.g. the nutrients in the soil*

nutrition [njuːˈtrɪʃən] NOUN

(D & T) Nutrition is the food that you eat, considered from the point of view of how it helps you to grow and remain healthy. *e.g. The effects of poor nutrition are evident.*

nutritional ADJECTIVE, **nutritionist** NOUN

nutritious [njuːˈtrɪʃəs] ADJECTIVE

containing substances that help you to grow and remain healthy

nutty ['nʌtɪ] **nuttier, nuttiest** ADJECTIVE

1 INFORMAL

mad or very foolish

2 tasting of nuts

nylon ['naɪlɒn] **nylons** NOUN

1 Nylon is a type of strong artificial material. *e.g. nylon stockings*

2 Nylons are stockings or tights.

Oo

oaf [əʊf] **oafs** NOUN
a clumsy and stupid person
[WORD HISTORY: from Old Norse ALFR meaning 'elf']

◉ THESAURUS
brute: *Custer was an idiot and a brute.*
lout: *a drunken lout*

oak [əʊk] **oaks** NOUN
a large tree which produces acorns. It has a hard
wood which is often used to make furniture

OAP OAPs NOUN
in Britain, a man over the age of 65 or a woman
over the age of 60 who receives a pension. OAP is
an abbreviation for 'old age pensioner'

oar [ɔː] **oars** NOUN
a wooden pole with a wide, flat end, used for
rowing a boat

oasis [əʊˈeɪsɪs] **oases** NOUN
a small area in a desert where water and plants
are found

oat [əʊt] **oats** NOUN
Oats are a type of grain.

oath [əʊθ] **oaths** NOUN
a formal promise, especially a promise to tell the
truth in a court of law

◉ THESAURUS
pledge: *The meeting ended with a pledge to step up
cooperation.*
promise: *If you make a promise, you should keep it.*
vow: *I made a silent vow to be more careful.*

oatmeal [ˈəʊtˌmiːl] NOUN
Oatmeal is a rough flour made from oats.

OBE OBEs NOUN
a British honour awarded by the King or Queen.
OBE is an abbreviation for 'Officer of the Order of
the British Empire'

obedient [əˈbiːdɪənt] ADJECTIVE
If you are obedient, you do what you are told to
do.
obediently ADVERB, **obedience** NOUN

◉ THESAURUS
law-abiding: *law-abiding citizens*
submissive: *Most doctors want their patients to be
submissive.*
subservient: *her willingness to be subservient to her
children*

<<OPPOSITE *disobedient*

obelisk [ˈɒbɪlɪsk] **obelisks** NOUN
a stone pillar built in honour of a person or an
event

obese [əʊˈbiːs] ADJECTIVE
extremely fat
obesity NOUN
[WORD HISTORY: from Latin OB- meaning 'much'
and EDERE meaning 'to eat']

obey [əˈbeɪ] **obeys, obeying, obeyed** VERB
If you obey a person or an order, you do what you
are told to do.

◉ THESAURUS
abide by: *They have got to abide by the rules.*
adhere to: *All members adhere to a strict code of
practice.*
comply with: *The army will comply with the
ceasefire.*
follow: *Take care to follow the instructions carefully.*
observe: *forcing motorists to observe speed
restrictions*

<<OPPOSITE *disobey*

obituary [əˈbɪtjʊərɪ] **obituaries** NOUN
a piece of writing about the life and
achievements of someone who has just died

object objects, objecting, objected NOUN
[ˈɒbdʒɪkt]
1 anything solid that you can touch or see, and
that is not alive

◉ THESAURUS
article: *household articles*
thing: *What's that thing in the middle of the
fountain?*

2 an aim or purpose

◉ THESAURUS
aim: *The aim of the festival is to increase awareness
of Hindu culture.*
goal: *The goal is to raise as much money as possible.*
idea: *The idea is to give children the freedom to
explore.*
intention: *It is my intention to remain in my
position.*
objective: *His objective was to win.*
purpose: *What is the purpose of your visit?*

3 The object of your feelings or actions is the
person that they are directed towards.

4 In grammar, the object of a verb or preposition is the word or phrase which follows it and describes the person or thing affected.

> VERB [əb'dʒɛkt]

5 If you object to something, you dislike it or disapprove of it.

● THESAURUS

oppose: *Many parents oppose bilingual education in schools.*

protest: *He picked up the cat before Rosa could protest.*

<<OPPOSITE *approve*

objection [əb'dʒɛkʃən] **objections** NOUN
If you have an objection to something, you dislike it or disapprove of it.

● THESAURUS

opposition: *Opposition to this plan has come from the media.*

protest: *protests against the government*

<<OPPOSITE *support*

objectionable [əb'dʒɛkʃənəbᵊl] ADJECTIVE
unpleasant and offensive

objective [əb'dʒɛktɪv] **objectives** NOUN

1 an aim *e.g. The protection of the countryside is their main objective.*

> ADJECTIVE

2 If you are objective, you are not influenced by personal feelings or prejudices. *e.g. an objective approach*

objectively ADVERB, **objectivity** NOUN

obligation [ˌɒblɪ'geɪʃən] **obligations** NOUN
something that you must do because it is your duty

obligatory [ɒ'blɪgətərɪ] ADJECTIVE
required by a rule or law *e.g. Religious education was made obligatory.*

oblige [ə'blaɪdʒ] **obliges, obliging, obliged** VERB

1 If you are obliged to do something, you have to do it.

2 If you oblige someone, you help them.

obliging ADJECTIVE

oblique [ə'bliːk] ADJECTIVE

1 An oblique remark is not direct, and is therefore difficult to understand.

2 An oblique line slopes at an angle.

obliterate [ə'blɪtəˌreɪt] **obliterates, obliterating, obliterated** VERB
To obliterate something is to destroy it completely.

obliteration NOUN

oblivion [ə'blɪvɪən] NOUN
Oblivion is unconsciousness or complete lack of

awareness of your surroundings.

oblivious ADJECTIVE, **obliviously** ADVERB

oblong ['ɒbˌlɒŋ] **oblongs** NOUN

1 a four-sided shape with two parallel short sides, two parallel long sides, and four right angles

> ADJECTIVE

2 shaped like an oblong

obnoxious [əb'nɒkʃəs] ADJECTIVE
extremely unpleasant

oboe ['əʊbəʊ] **oboes** NOUN
a woodwind musical instrument with a double reed

oboist NOUN

[WORD HISTORY: from French HAUT BOIS meaning literally 'high wood', a reference to the instrument's pitch]

obscene [əb'siːn] ADJECTIVE
indecent and likely to upset people *e.g. obscene pictures*

obscenely ADVERB, **obscenity** NOUN

● THESAURUS

bawdy: *a bawdy song*

blue: *a blue movie*

dirty: *a dirty book*

filthy: *a filthy joke*

indecent: *an indecent suggestion*

lewd: *lewd comments*

pornographic: *a pornographic magazine*

obscure [əb'skjʊə] **obscures, obscuring, obscured** ADJECTIVE

1 Something that is obscure is known by only a few people. *e.g. an obscure Mongolian dialect*

● THESAURUS

little-known: *a little-known Austrian composer*

unknown: *an unknown writer*

<<OPPOSITE *famous*

2 Something obscure is difficult to see or to understand. *e.g. The news was shrouded in obscure language.*

● THESAURUS

arcane: *the arcane world of contemporary classical music*

cryptic: *cryptic comments*

opaque: *the opaque language of the inspector's reports*

<<OPPOSITE *simple*

> VERB

3 To obscure something is to make it difficult to see or understand. *e.g. His view was obscured by trees.*

obscurity NOUN

● THESAURUS

cloak: *a land permanently cloaked in mist*

cloud: *Perhaps anger had clouded his vision.*

conceal: *The hat concealed her hair.*

hide: *The compound was hidden by trees and shrubs.*
mask: *A thick grey cloud masked the sun.*
screen: *Most of the road was screened by a block of flats.*
shroud: *Mist shrouded the outline of Buckingham Palace.*
<<OPPOSITE *expose*

observance [əbˈzɜːvəns] NOUN
The observance of a law or custom is the practice of obeying or following it.

observant [əbˈzɜːvənt] ADJECTIVE
Someone who is observant notices things that are not easy to see.

● THESAURUS
attentive: *the attentive audience*
perceptive: *a perceptive remark*
vigilant: *He warned the public to be vigilant.*
watchful: *Keep a watchful eye on babies and toddlers.*

observation [ˌɒbzəˈveɪʃən] observations NOUN
1 Observation is the act of watching something carefully. *e.g. Success hinges on close observation.*

2 something that you have seen or noticed

3 a remark

4 Observation is the ability to notice things that are not easy to see.

observatory [əbˈzɜːvətəri] observatories NOUN
a room or building containing telescopes and other equipment for studying the sun, moon, and stars

observe [əbˈzɜːv] observes, observing, observed VERB
1 To observe something is to watch it carefully.

● THESAURUS
monitor: *I have been monitoring his progress carefully.*
scrutinize: *She scrutinized his features to see if he was telling the truth.*
study: *Debbie studied her friend's face for a moment.*
survey: *He surveys American politics from an interesting standpoint.*
view: *You can view the lesson from the gallery.*
watch: *A man was watching him from across the square.*

2 To observe something is to notice it.

● THESAURUS
discover: *They discovered that they were being watched.*
note: *People noted how much care she took over her work.*
notice: *Contact the police if you notice anything unusual.*
see: *I saw a man coming towards me.*

spot: *Moments later, smoke was spotted coming out of the kitchen.*
witness: *Anyone who witnessed the attack should call the police.*

3 If you observe that something is the case, you make a comment about it.

● THESAURUS
comment: *Stuart commented that this was true.*
mention: *I mentioned that I didn't like contemporary music.*
remark: *"Some people have more money than sense," he remarked.*
say: *She said that I looked tired.*
state: *He stated that this was, indeed, the case.*

4 To observe a law or custom is to obey or follow it.
observer NOUN, **observable** ADJECTIVE

obsession [əbˈsɛʃən] obsessions NOUN
If someone has an obsession about something, they cannot stop thinking about that thing.
obsessional ADJECTIVE, **obsessed** ADJECTIVE, **obsessive** ADJECTIVE

● THESAURUS
complex: *I have never had a complex about my height.*
fixation: *the country's fixation on the war*
mania: *a mania for horror films*
preoccupation: *today's preoccupation with royal misdeeds*
thing: *informal He's got this thing about ties.*

obsolete [ˈɒbsəˌliːt] ADJECTIVE
out of date and no longer used

obstacle [ˈɒbstəkəl] obstacles NOUN
something which is in your way and makes it difficult to do something

● THESAURUS
barrier: *Taxes are the most obvious barrier to free trade.*
difficulty: *the difficulties ahead*
hindrance: *The higher rates have been a hindrance to economic recovery.*
hurdle: *the first hurdle for many women returning to work*
impediment: *There was no legal impediment to the marriage.*
obstruction: *an obstruction in the road*

obstetrics [ɒbˈstɛtrɪks] NOUN
Obstetrics is the branch of medicine concerned with pregnancy and childbirth.
obstetrician NOUN

obstinate [ˈɒbstɪnɪt] ADJECTIVE
Someone who is obstinate is stubborn and unwilling to change their mind.
obstinately ADVERB, **obstinacy** NOUN

● THESAURUS
dogged: *his dogged insistence on their rights*

593

headstrong: *He's young and very headstrong.*
inflexible: *His opponents viewed him as dogmatic and inflexible.*
intractable: *He protested but Wright was intractable.*
stubborn: *a stubborn character who is used to getting his own way*
wilful: *a wilful child*
<<OPPOSITE *flexible*

obstruct [əb'strʌkt] **obstructs, obstructing, obstructed** VERB
If something obstructs a road or path, it blocks it.
obstruction NOUN, **obstructive** ADJECTIVE

THESAURUS
bar: *He stood there, barring her way.*
block: *Some students blocked the highway.*
choke: *The roads are choked with cars.*
clog: *The traffic clogged the Thames bridges.*

obtain [əb'teɪn] **obtains, obtaining, obtained** VERB
If you obtain something, you get it.
obtainable ADJECTIVE

THESAURUS
acquire: *I recently acquired a beautiful old lamp.*
get: *trying to get enough food to live*
get hold of: *It's hard to get hold of guns.*
get your hands on: informal *reading everything she could get her hands on*
procure: formal *It became hard to procure fuel.*
secure: formal *continuing their efforts to secure a ceasefire*

obtrusive [əb'tru:sɪv] ADJECTIVE
noticeable in an unpleasant way *e.g. a remarkably obtrusive cigar*

obtuse [əb'tju:s] ADJECTIVE
1 Someone who is obtuse is stupid or slow to understand things.
2 An obtuse angle is an angle between 90° and 180°.

obvious ['ɒbvɪəs] ADJECTIVE
easy to see or understand
obviously ADVERB

THESAURUS
apparent: *It was apparent that he had lost interest.*
blatant: *a blatant foul*
clear: *a clear breach of the rules*
evident: *His love of nature is evident in his paintings.*
overt: *parents who showed us no overt affection*
palpable: *The tension between them is palpable.*
plain: *It was plain to him that I was having a nervous breakdown.*
self-evident: *The implications for this country are self-evident.*

occasion [ə'keɪʒən] **occasions, occasioning, occasioned** NOUN

1 a time when something happens
2 an important event
THESAURUS
affair: *The visit was to be a purely private affair.*
event: *A new book by Grass is always an event.*

3 An occasion for doing something is an opportunity for doing it.
THESAURUS
chance: *the chance to practise medicine in British hospitals*
opportunity: *I had an opportunity to go to New York.*
time: *This was no time to make a speech.*

> VERB
4 FORMAL
To occasion something is to cause it. *e.g. damage occasioned by fire*
THESAURUS
bring about: *the only way to bring about peace*
give rise to: *The judge's decision gave rise to practical problems.*
induce: *an economic crisis induced by high oil prices*
produce: *The drug is known to produce side-effects in women.*
prompt: *The demonstration prompted fears of more violence.*
provoke: *The incident has provoked outrage in Okinawa.*

occasional [ə'keɪʒənəl] ADJECTIVE
happening sometimes but not often *e.g. an occasional outing*
occasionally ADVERB

THESAURUS
intermittent: *after three hours of intermittent rain*
odd: *at odd moments*
periodic: *periodic bouts of illness*
sporadic: *a year of sporadic fighting*
<<OPPOSITE *frequent*

occult [ɒ'kʌlt] NOUN
The occult is the knowledge and study of supernatural and magical forces or powers.

occupancy ['ɒkjʊpənsɪ] NOUN
The occupancy of a building is the act of living or working in it.

occupant ['ɒkjʊpənt] **occupants** NOUN
The occupants of a building are the people who live or work in it.

occupation [ˌɒkjʊ'peɪʃən] **occupations** NOUN
1 a job or profession
2 a hobby or something you do for pleasure
3 The occupation of a country is the act of invading it and taking control of it.
occupational ADJECTIVE

occupy [ˈɒkjʊˌpaɪ] **occupies, occupying, occupied** VERB

1 The people who occupy a building are the people who live or work there.

2 When people occupy a place, they move into it and take control of it. *e.g. Demonstrators occupied the building.*

3 To occupy a position in a system or plan is to have that position. *e.g. His phone-in show occupies a daytime slot.*

4 If something occupies you, you spend your time doing it. *e.g. That problem occupies me night and day.*

occupier NOUN

occur [əˈkɜː] **occurs, occurring, occurred** VERB

1 If something occurs, it happens or exists. *e.g. The second attack occurred at a swimming pool.*

○ THESAURUS

appear: *a test to reveal infection before symptoms appear*

arise: *A problem may arise later in pregnancy.*

be present: *This vitamin is present in breast milk.*

exist: *A conflict of interest may exist in such situations.*

happen: *The accident happened close to Martha's Vineyard.*

take place: *Elections will take place on the second of November.*

2 If something occurs to you, you suddenly think of it.

○ THESAURUS

cross your mind: *The possibility of failure did cross my mind.*

dawn on: *It dawned on me that I shouldn't give up without a fight.*

strike: *A thought struck her.*

> If an event has been planned, you should not say that it *occurred* or *happened*: *the wedding took place on Saturday.* Only something unexpected *occurs* or *happens*: *an accident has occurred; the burglary happened last night.*

occurrence [əˈkʌrəns] **occurrences** NOUN

1 an event

2 The occurrence of something is the fact that it happens or exists. *e.g. the occurrence of diseases*

ocean [ˈəʊʃən] **oceans** NOUN

1 LITERARY
the sea

2 The five oceans are the five very large areas of sea. *e.g. the Atlantic Ocean*

oceanic ADJECTIVE

o'clock [əˈklɒk] ADVERB

You use 'o'clock' after the number of the hour to say what the time is.

octagon [ˈɒktəgən] **octagons** NOUN
a shape with eight straight sides
octagonal ADJECTIVE

octave [ˈɒktɪv] **octaves** NOUN
(MUSIC) the difference in pitch between the first note and the eighth note of a musical scale

October [ɒkˈtəʊbə] NOUN
October is the tenth month of the year. It has 31 days.
[WORD HISTORY: from Latin OCTOBER meaning 'the eighth month']

octopus [ˈɒktəpəs] **octopuses** NOUN
a sea creature with eight long tentacles which it uses to catch food
[WORD HISTORY: from Greek OKTO + POUS meaning 'eight feet']

odd [ɒd] **odder, oddest; odds** ADJECTIVE

1 Something odd is strange or unusual.

○ THESAURUS

bizarre: *his bizarre behaviour*

curious: *a curious mixture of the ancient and modern*

funny: *There's something funny about him.*

peculiar: *Rachel thought it tasted peculiar.*

queer: old-fashioned *There's something a bit queer going on.*

singular: formal *Where he got that singular notion I just can't think.*

strange: *Then a strange thing happened.*

weird: *That first day was weird.*

<<OPPOSITE ordinary

2 Odd things do not match each other. *e.g. odd socks*

3 Odd numbers are numbers that cannot be divided exactly by two.

> ADVERB

4 You use 'odd' after a number to say that it is approximate. *e.g. I've written twenty-odd plays.*

> PLURAL NOUN

5 In gambling, the probability of something happening is called the odds. *e.g. The odds are against the record being beaten.*

oddly ADVERB, **oddness** NOUN

oddity [ˈɒdɪtɪ] **oddities** NOUN
something very strange

oddments [ˈɒdmənts] PLURAL NOUN
Oddments are things that are left over after other things have been used.

odds and ends [ɒdz ənd ɛndz] PLURAL NOUN
You can refer to a collection of small unimportant things as odds and ends.

ode [əʊd] **odes** NOUN
a poem written in praise of someone or something

odious ['əʊdɪəs] ADJECTIVE
extremely unpleasant

odour ['əʊdə] **odours** NOUN; FORMAL
a strong smell
odorous ADJECTIVE

odyssey ['ɒdɪsɪ] **odysseys** NOUN
a long and eventful journey

oesophagus [i:'sɒfəgəs] **oesophaguses**
NOUN
the tube that carries food from your throat to
your stomach

oestrogen ['i:strədʒən] another spelling of
estrogen

of [ɒv] PREPOSITION
1 consisting of or containing e.g. a collection of
short stories... a cup of tea
2 used when naming something or describing a
characteristic of something e.g. the city of
Canberra... a woman of great power and influence
3 belonging to or connected with e.g. a friend of
Rachel... the cover of the book

> Where of means 'belonging to', it can
sometimes be replaced by an apostrophe: the
cover of the book is the same as the book's
cover.

off [ɒf] PREPOSITION OR ADVERB
1 indicating movement away from or out of a
place e.g. They had just stepped off the plane... She
got up and marched off.
2 indicating separation or distance from a place
e.g. some islands off the coast of Australia... The
whole crescent has been fenced off.
3 not working e.g. It was Frank's night off.

> ADVERB OR ADJECTIVE
4 not switched on e.g. He turned the radio off... the
off switch

> ADJECTIVE
5 cancelled or postponed e.g. The concert was off.
6 Food that is off has gone sour or bad.

> PREPOSITION
7 not liking or not using something e.g. He went
right off alcohol.

> Do not use of after off. You should say he
stepped off the bus not he stepped off of the bus.
It is very informal to use off where you mean
'from': they bought milk off a farmer instead of
they bought milk from a farmer. Always use
from in written work.

offal ['ɒfl] NOUN
Offal is liver, kidneys, and other parts of animals,
which can be eaten.

offence [ə'fɛns] **offences** NOUN

1 a crime e.g. a drink-driving offence

> PHRASES
2 If something **gives offence**, it upsets people. If
you **take offence**, you are upset by someone or
something.

offend [ə'fɛnd] **offends, offending,
offended** VERB
1 If you offend someone, you upset them.

⊙ THESAURUS
affront: He pretended to be affronted, but inwardly
he was pleased.
insult: Buchanan says he was insulted by the judge's
remarks.
outrage: Many people have been outraged by what
was said.
<<OPPOSITE please

2 FORMAL
To offend is to commit a crime.
offender NOUN

offensive [ə'fɛnsɪv] **offensives** ADJECTIVE
1 Something offensive is rude and upsetting. e.g.
offensive behaviour

⊙ THESAURUS
abusive: abusive language
insulting: an insulting remark
objectionable: I find your tone highly objectionable.

2 Offensive actions or weapons are used in
attacking someone.

> NOUN
3 an attack e.g. a full-scale offensive against the
rebels
offensively ADVERB

offer ['ɒfə] **offers, offering, offered** VERB
1 If you offer something to someone, you ask
them if they would like it.

⊙ THESAURUS
hold out: I held out my ticket for him to check.
tender: She has tendered her resignation.

> NOUN
2 something that someone says they will give
you or do for you if you want them to e.g. He
refused the offer of a drink.

⊙ THESAURUS
proposition: I made her a proposition.
tender: a tender for a public contract

3 a specially low price for a product in a shop e.g.
You will need a voucher to qualify for the special offer.

offering ['ɒfərɪŋ] **offerings** NOUN
something that is offered or given to someone

offhand [ˌɒf'hænd] ADJECTIVE
1 If someone is offhand, they are unfriendly and
slightly rude.

> ADVERB
2 If you know something offhand, you know it

without having to think very hard. *e.g. I couldn't tell you offhand how long he's been here.*

office ['ɒfɪs] **offices** NOUN

1 a room where people work at desks

2 a government department *e.g. the Office of Fair Trading*

3 a place where people can go for information, tickets, or other services

4 Someone who holds office has an important job or position in government or in an organization

officer ['ɒfɪsə] **officers** NOUN
a person with a position of authority in the armed forces, the police, or a government organization

official [ə'fɪʃəl] **officials** ADJECTIVE

1 approved by the government or by someone in authority *e.g. the official figures*

● THESAURUS
authorized: *the authorized biography*
certified: *a certified accountant*
formal: *No formal announcement has been made.*
licensed: *a licensed doctor*
<<OPPOSITE *unofficial*

2 done or used by someone in authority as part of their job *e.g. official notepaper*

> NOUN

3 a person who holds a position of authority in an organization
officially ADVERB

● THESAURUS
executive: *a senior bank executive*
officer: *a local authority education officer*
representative: *trade union representatives*

officialdom [ə'fɪʃəldəm] NOUN
You can refer to officials in government or other organizations as officialdom, especially when you find them difficult to deal with.

officiate [ə'fɪʃɪ,eɪt] **officiates, officiating, officiated** VERB
To officiate at a ceremony is to be in charge and perform the official part of the ceremony.

offing ['ɒfɪŋ] PHRASE
If something is **in the offing**, it is likely to happen soon. *e.g. A change is in the offing.*

off-licence ['ɒf,laɪsəns] **off-licences** NOUN
a shop which sells alcoholic drinks

offline ['ɒflaɪn] ADJECTIVE

1 If a computer is offline, it is switched off or not connected to the Internet.

> ADVERB

2 If you do something offline, you do it while not connected to the Internet.

offset [,ɒf'sɛt] **offsets, offsetting, offset** VERB

If one thing is offset by another thing, its effect is reduced or cancelled out by that thing. *e.g. This tedium can be offset by watching the television.*

offshoot ['ɒf,ʃuːt] **offshoots** NOUN
something that has developed from another thing *e.g. The technology we use is an offshoot of the motor industry.*

offshore [,ɒf'ʃɔː] ADJECTIVE OR ADVERB
in or from the part of the sea near the shore *e.g. an offshore wind... a wreck fifteen kilometres offshore*

offside ['ɒf'saɪd] ADJECTIVE

1 If a soccer, rugby, or hockey player is offside, they have broken the rules by moving too far forward.

> NOUN

2 the side of a vehicle that is furthest from the pavement

offspring ['ɒf,sprɪŋ] NOUN
A person's or animal's offspring are their children.

often ['ɒfᵊn] ADVERB
happening many times or a lot of the time

● THESAURUS
frequently: *He was frequently depressed.*
repeatedly: *Both men have repeatedly denied the allegations.*

ogle ['əʊgᵊl] **ogles, ogling, ogled** VERB
To ogle someone is to stare at them in a way that indicates a sexual interest.

ogre ['əʊgə] **ogres** NOUN
a cruel, frightening giant in a fairy story

ohm [əʊm] **ohms** NOUN
In physics, an ohm is a unit used to measure electrical resistance.

oil [ɔɪl] **oils, oiling, oiled** NOUN

1 Oil is a thick, sticky liquid used as a fuel and for lubrication.

2 Oil is also a thick, greasy liquid made from plants or animals. *e.g. cooking oil... bath oil*

> VERB

3 If you oil something, you put oil in it or on it.

oil painting ['peɪntɪŋ] **oil paintings** NOUN
a picture that has been painted with thick paints made from coloured powder and a kind of oil

oilskin ['ɔɪl,skɪn] **oilskins** NOUN
a piece of clothing made from a thick, waterproof material, worn especially by fishermen

oily ['ɔɪli] ADJECTIVE
Something that is oily is covered with or contains oil. *e.g. an oily rag... oily skin*

ointment ['ɔɪntmənt] **ointments** NOUN
a smooth, thick substance that you put on sore skin to heal it

okay or **OK** [ˌəʊ'keɪ] ADJECTIVE INFORMAL
Okay means all right. *e.g. Tell me if this sounds okay.*

THESAURUS
acceptable: *It is becoming more acceptable for women to drink.*
all right: *if it's all right with you*

old [əʊld] **older, oldest** ADJECTIVE
1 having lived or existed for a long time *e.g. an old lady... old clothes*

THESAURUS
ancient: *relics of ancient cultures*
bygone: *rituals of a bygone civilization*

2 'Old' is used to give the age of someone or something *e.g. This photo is five years old.*

3 'Old' also means former *e.g. my old art teacher*

THESAURUS
earlier: *his children from an earlier marriage*
early: *heroes of those early days of rock*
ex-: *his ex- wife*
former: *a former lover*
<<OPPOSITE *new*

olden ['əʊldən] PHRASE
In the olden days means long ago

Old English NOUN
Old English was the English language from the fifth century AD until about 1100. Old English is also known as Anglo-Saxon.

old-fashioned ['əʊld,fæʃənd] ADJECTIVE
1 Something which is old-fashioned is no longer fashionable. *e.g. old-fashioned shoes*

THESAURUS
antiquated: *an antiquated system*
archaic: *archaic practices such as these*
dated: *Some of the language sounds quite dated.*
obsolete: *So much equipment becomes obsolete almost as soon as it's made.*
outdated: *outdated attitudes*
outmoded: *toiling in outmoded factories*
out of date: *a make of car that is now out of date*
passé: *Punk is passé.*
<<OPPOSITE *fashionable*

2 Someone who is old-fashioned believes in the values and standards of the past.

Old Norse [nɔːs] NOUN
Old Norse was a language spoken in Scandinavia and Iceland from about 700 AD to about 1350 AD. Many English words are derived from Old Norse.

Old Testament ['tɛstəmənt] NOUN
The Old Testament is the first part of the Christian Bible. It is also the holy book of the Jewish religion and contains writings which relate to the history of the Jews.

oleander [ˌəʊlɪ'ændə] **oleanders** NOUN
an evergreen shrub with fragrant white, pink, or purple flowers

olive ['ɒlɪv] **olives** NOUN
1 a small green or black fruit containing a stone. Olives are usually pickled and eaten as a snack or crushed to produce oil

> ADJECTIVE OR NOUN
2 dark yellowish-green

-ology SUFFIX
-ology is used to form words that refer to the study of something *e.g. biology... geology*
[WORD HISTORY: from Greek LOGOS meaning 'reason', 'speech', or 'discourse']

Olympic Games [ə'lɪmpɪk 'geɪmz] PLURAL NOUN
The Olympic Games are a set of sporting contests held in a different city every four years.

ombudsman ['ɒmbʊdzmən] **ombudsmen** NOUN
The ombudsman is a person who investigates complaints against the government or a public organization.

omelette ['ɒmlɪt] **omelettes** NOUN
a dish made by beating eggs together and cooking them in a flat pan

omen ['əʊmən] **omens** NOUN
something that is thought to be a sign of what will happen in the future *e.g. John saw this success as a good omen for his trip.*

THESAURUS
sign: *people who look to the skies for signs*
warning: *a warning of trouble to come*

ominous ['ɒmɪnəs] ADJECTIVE
suggesting that something unpleasant is going to happen *e.g. an ominous sign*
ominously ADVERB

THESAURUS
sinister: *a sinister message*
threatening: *a threatening sky*

omission [əʊ'mɪʃən] **omissions** NOUN
1 something that has not been included or done *e.g. There are some striking omissions in the survey.*

2 Omission is the act of not including or not doing something. *e.g. controversy over the omission of female novelists*

omit [əʊ'mɪt] **omits, omitting, omitted** VERB
1 If you omit something, you do not include it.

THESAURUS
exclude: *Women felt excluded form the workplace.*
leave out: *The Spaniard has been left out of the team.*
miss out: *What about Sally? You've missed her out!*

skip: *It is all too easy to skip meals.*

2 FORMAL
If you omit to do something, you do not do it.

omnibus ['ɒmnɪ.bʌs] **omnibuses** NOUN
1 a book containing a collection of stories or articles by the same author or about the same subject

> ADJECTIVE
2 An omnibus edition of a radio or television show contains two or more programmes that were originally broadcast separately.

omnipotent [ɒm'nɪpətənt] ADJECTIVE
having very great or unlimited power *e.g. omnipotent emperors*
omnipotence NOUN

omnivore ['ɒmnɪ.vɔː] NOUN
An omnivore is an animal that eats all kinds of food, including meat and plants.
omnivorous ADJECTIVE

on [ɒn] PREPOSITION
1 touching or attached to something *e.g. The woman was sitting on the sofa.*
2 If you are on a bus, plane, or train, you are inside it.
3 If something happens on a particular day, that is when it happens. *e.g. It is his birthday on Monday.*
4 If something is done on an instrument or machine, it is done using that instrument or machine. *e.g. He preferred to play on his computer.*
5 A book or talk on a particular subject is about that subject.

> ADVERB
6 If you have a piece of clothing on, you are wearing it.

> ADJECTIVE
7 A machine or switch that is on is working.
8 If an event is on, it is happening or taking place. *e.g. The race is definitely on.*

once [wʌns] ADVERB
1 If something happens once, it happens one time only.
2 If something was once true, it was true in the past, but is no longer true.

> CONJUNCTION
3 If something happens once another thing has happened, it happens immediately afterwards. *e.g. Once you get used to working for yourself, it's tough working for anybody else.*

> PHRASES
4 If you do something **at once**, you do it immediately. If several things happen **at once**, they all happen at the same time.

one [wʌn] **ones**
1 One is the number 1.

> ADJECTIVE
2 If you refer to the one person or thing of a particular kind, you mean the only person or thing of that kind. *e.g. My one aim is to look after the horses well.*
3 One also means 'a'; used when emphasizing something. *e.g. They got one almighty shock.*

> PRONOUN
4 One refers to a particular thing or person. *e.g. Alf Brown's business was a good one.*
5 One also means people in general. *e.g. One likes to have the opportunity to chat.*

one-off ['wʌn'ɒf] **one-offs** NOUN
something that happens or is made only once

onerous ['ɒnərəs] ADJECTIVE; FORMAL
difficult or unpleasant *e.g. an onerous task*

oneself [wʌn'sɛlf] PRONOUN
'Oneself' is used when you are talking about people in general *e.g. One could hardly hear oneself talk.*

one-sided ['wʌn.saɪdɪd] ADJECTIVE
1 If an activity or relationship is one-sided, one of the people has a lot more success or involvement than the other. *e.g. a one-sided contest*
2 A one-sided argument or report considers the facts or a situation from only one point of view.

one-way ['wʌn'weɪ] ADJECTIVE
1 One-way streets are streets along which vehicles can drive in only one direction.
2 A one-way ticket is one that you can use to travel to a place, but not to travel back again.

ongoing ['ɒn.gəʊɪŋ] ADJECTIVE
continuing to happen *e.g. an ongoing process of learning*

onion ['ʌnjən] **onions** NOUN
a small, round vegetable with a brown skin like paper and a very strong taste

online ['ɒnlaɪn] ADJECTIVE
1 If a computer is online, it is switched on or connected to the Internet.

> ADVERB
2 If you do something online, you do it while connected to the Internet.

onlooker ['ɒn.lʊkə] **onlookers** NOUN
someone who is watching an event

only ['əʊnlɪ] ADVERB
1 You use 'only' to indicate the one thing or person involved. *e.g. Only Keith knows whether he will continue.*

● THESAURUS
just: *It's not just a financial matter.*

merely: *Watson was far from being merely a furniture expert.*
purely: *a racing machine, designed purely for speed*
simply: *Most of the damage was simply because of fallen trees.*
solely: *decisions based solely upon what we see in magazines*

2 You use 'only' to emphasize that something is unimportant or small. *e.g. He's only a little boy.*

3 You can use 'only' to introduce something which happens immediately after something else. *e.g. She had thought of one plan, only to discard it for another.*

> ADJECTIVE

4 If you talk about the only thing or person, you mean that there are no others. *e.g. their only hit single*

● THESAURUS

one: *My one aim is to look after the horses well.*
sole: *Our sole intention is to reunite her with her baby.*

5 If you are an only child, you have no brothers or sisters.

> CONJUNCTION

6 'Only' also means but or except *e.g. He was like you, only blond.*

> PHRASE

7 Only too means extremely *e.g. I would be only too happy to swap places.*

onomatopoeia [ˌɒnəˌmætəˈpiːə] NOUN
(ENGLISH) the use of words which sound like the thing that they represent. 'Hiss' and 'buzz' are examples of onomatopoeia
onomatopoeic ADJECTIVE
[WORD HISTORY: from Greek ONOMA meaning 'name' and POIEIN meaning 'to make']

onset [ˈɒnˌsɛt] NOUN
The onset of something unpleasant is the beginning of it. *e.g. the onset of war*

onslaught [ˈɒnˌslɔːt] **onslaughts** NOUN
a violent attack

onto or **on to** [ˈɒntʊ] PREPOSITION
If you put something onto an object, you put it on it.

onus [ˈəʊnəs] NOUN; FORMAL
If the onus is on you to do something, it is your duty to do it.

onwards or **onward** [ˈɒnwədz] *or* [ˈɒnwəd]
ADVERB

1 continuing to happen from a particular time *e.g. He could not speak a word from that moment onwards.*

2 travelling forwards *e.g. Duncliffe escorted the pair onwards to his own room.*

onyx [ˈɒnɪks] NOUN
Onyx is a semiprecious stone used for making ornaments and jewellery.

ooze [uːz] **oozes, oozing, oozed** VERB
When a thick liquid oozes, it flows slowly. *e.g. The cold mud oozed over her new footwear.*

opal [ˈəʊpəl] **opals** NOUN
a pale or whitish semiprecious stone used for making jewellery

opaque [əʊˈpeɪk] ADJECTIVE
If something is opaque, you cannot see through it. *e.g. opaque glass windows*

open [ˈəʊpən] **opens, opening, opened**
VERB

1 When you open something, or when it opens, you move it so that it is no longer closed. *e.g. She opened the door.*

● THESAURUS

uncover: *When the seedlings sprout, uncover the tray.*
undo: *I managed secretly to undo a corner of the parcel.*
unlock: *She unlocked the case.*
<<OPPOSITE *shut*

2 When a shop or office opens, people are able to go in.

3 To open something also means to start it. *e.g. He tried to open a bank account.*

> ADJECTIVE

4 Something that is open is not closed or fastened. *e.g. an open box of chocolates*

● THESAURUS

ajar: *He left the door ajar.*
uncovered: *The uncovered bucket in the corner stank.*
undone: *pictures of him with his shirt undone*
unlocked: *an unlocked room*
<<OPPOSITE *shut*

5 If you have an open mind, you are willing to consider new ideas or suggestions.

6 Someone who is open is honest and frank.

● THESAURUS

candid: *I haven't been completely candid with him.*
frank: *My client has been less than frank with me.*
honest: *He had been honest with her and she had tricked him!*

7 When a shop or office is open, people are able to go in.

8 An open area of sea or land is a large, empty area. *e.g. open country*

9 If something is open to you, it is possible for you to do it. *e.g. There is no other course open to us but to fight it out.*

10 If a situation is still open, it is still being considered. *e.g. Even if the case remains open, the* *full facts may never be revealed.*

> PHRASE

11 In the open means outside

12 In the open also means not secret

openly ADVERB

opening ['əʊpənɪŋ] **openings** ADJECTIVE

1 Opening means coming first. *e.g. the opening day of the season*

● THESAURUS

first: *the first night of the play*

inaugural: *his inaugural address*

initial: *the aim of this initial meeting*

introductory: *an introductory offer*

> NOUN

2 The opening of a book or film is the first part of it.

● THESAURUS

beginning: *the beginning of the book*

commencement: formal *at the commencement of the course*

start: *four years after the start of the Great War*

<<OPPOSITE *conclusion*

3 a hole or gap

● THESAURUS

chink: *a chink in the wall*

cleft: *a narrow cleft in the rocks*

crack: *Kathryn had seen him through a crack in the curtains.*

gap: *the wind tearing through gaps in the window frames*

hole: *a hole in the wall*

slot: *a slot in which to insert a coin*

space: *a half-inch space between the curtains*

vent: *Steam escaped from the vent at the front of the machine.*

4 an opportunity *e.g. The two men circled around, looking for an opening to attack.*

open-minded ['əʊpən,maɪndɪd] ADJECTIVE

willing to consider new ideas and suggestions

open-plan ['əʊpən,plæn] ADJECTIVE

An open-plan office or building has very few dividing walls inside.

opera ['ɒpərə] **operas** NOUN

a play in which the words are sung rather than spoken

operatic ADJECTIVE

[WORD HISTORY: from Latin OPERA meaning 'works']

operate ['ɒpə,reɪt] **operates, operating, operated** VERB

1 To operate is to work. *e.g. We are shocked at the way that businesses operate.*

2 When you operate a machine, you make it work.

3 When surgeons operate, they cut open a patient's body to remove or repair a damaged part.

operation [,ɒpə'reɪʃən] **operations** NOUN

1 a complex, planned event *e.g. a full-scale military operation*

2 a form of medical treatment in which a surgeon cuts open a patient's body to remove or repair a damaged part

> PHRASE

3 If something is **in operation**, it is working or being used. *e.g. The system is in operation from April to the end of September.*

operational [,ɒpə'reɪʃənəl] ADJECTIVE

working or able to be used *e.g. an operational aircraft*

operative ['ɒpərətɪv] ADJECTIVE

Something that is operative is working or having an effect.

operator ['ɒpə,reɪtə] **operators** NOUN

1 someone who works at a telephone exchange or on a switchboard

2 someone who operates a machine *e.g. a computer operator*

3 someone who runs a business *e.g. a tour operator*

opinion [ə'pɪnjən] **opinions** NOUN

a belief or view

● THESAURUS

assessment: *What is your assessment of the situation?*

belief: *his religious beliefs*

estimation: *He has gone down considerably in my estimation.*

judgment: *In your judgment, what has changed?*

point of view: *Thanks for your point of view, John.*

view: *Make your views known to your local MP.*

viewpoint: *to include as many viewpoints as possible*

opinionated [ə'pɪnjə,neɪtɪd] ADJECTIVE

Someone who is opinionated has strong views and refuses to accept that they might be wrong.

opium ['əʊpɪəm] NOUN

Opium is a drug made from the seeds of a poppy. It is used in medicine to relieve pain.

[WORD HISTORY: from Latin OPIUM meaning 'poppy juice']

opponent [ə'pəʊnənt] **opponents** NOUN

someone who is against you in an argument or a contest

opportune ['ɒpə,tjuːn] ADJECTIVE; FORMAL

happening at a convenient time *e.g. The king's death was opportune for the prince.*

opportunism [,ɒpə'tjuːnɪzm] NOUN

Opportunism is taking advantage of any opportunity to gain money or power for yourself.

o

opportunist NOUN

opportunity [ˌɒpəˈtjuːnɪtɪ] **opportunities** NOUN

a chance to do something

oppose [əˈpəʊz] **opposes, opposing, opposed** VERB

If you oppose something, you disagree with it and try to prevent it.

THESAURUS

fight against: *a lifetime fighting against racism*
resist: *They resisted our attempts to modernize.*
speak out against: *He spoke out strongly against some of the radical ideas.*
<<OPPOSITE support

opposed [əˈpəʊzd] ADJECTIVE

1 If you are opposed to something, you disagree with it. *e.g. He was totally opposed to bullying in schools.*

2 Opposed also means opposite or very different. *e.g. two opposed schools of thought*

> PHRASE

3 If you refer to one thing **as opposed to** another, you are emphasizing that it is the first thing rather than the second which concerns you. *e.g. Real spectators, as opposed to invited guests, were hard to spot.*

opposite [ˈɒpəzɪt] **opposites** PREPOSITION OR ADVERB

1 If one thing is opposite another, it is facing it. *e.g. the shop opposite the station... the house opposite*

> ADJECTIVE

2 The opposite part of something is the part farthest away from you. *e.g. the opposite side of town*

3 If things are opposite, they are completely different. *e.g. I take the opposite view to you.*

THESAURUS

conflicting: *three powers with conflicting interests*
contrary: *He has a contrary opinion to mine.*
contrasting: *two men with completely contrasting backgrounds*
opposed: *This was a straight conflict of directly opposed aims.*
reverse: *The wrong attitude will have exactly the reverse effect.*

> NOUN

4 If two things are completely different, they are opposites.

THESAURUS

antithesis: formal *The antithesis of the Middle Eastern buyer is the Japanese.*
contrary: *I'm not a feminist, quite the contrary.*
converse: *Don't you think that the converse might also be possible?*
reverse: *This didn't upset him at all, in fact quite the reverse.*

opposition [ˌɒpəˈzɪʃən] NOUN

1 If there is opposition to something, people disagree with it and try to prevent it.

THESAURUS

disapproval: *His action had been greeted with almost universal disapproval.*
hostility: *There is hostility to this method among traditionalists.*
resistance: *Initially I met resistance from my own family.*
<<OPPOSITE support

2 The political parties who are not in power are referred to as the Opposition.

3 In a game or sports event, the opposition is the person or team that you are competing against.

oppressed [əˈprɛst] ADJECTIVE

People who are oppressed are treated cruelly or unfairly.

oppress VERB, **oppressor** NOUN

THESAURUS

abused: *those who work with abused children*
downtrodden: *the downtrodden, bored housewife*

oppression [əˈprɛʃən] NOUN

cruel and unfair treatment of people

THESAURUS

persecution: *the persecution of minorities*
tyranny: *The 1930s was a decade of tyranny in Europe.*

oppressive [əˈprɛsɪv] ADJECTIVE

1 If the weather is oppressive, it is hot and humid.

2 An oppressive situation makes you feel depressed or concerned. *e.g. The silence became oppressive.*

3 An oppressive system treats people cruelly or unfairly. *e.g. Married women were subject to oppressive laws.*

oppressively ADVERB

opt [ɒpt] **opts, opting, opted** VERB

If you opt for something, you choose it. If you opt out of something, you choose not to be involved in it.

optical [ˈɒptɪkəl] ADJECTIVE

1 concerned with vision, light, or images *e.g. an optical scanner*

2 relating to the appearance of things *e.g. an optical illusion*

optic ADJECTIVE

optician [ɒpˈtɪʃən] **opticians** NOUN

someone who tests people's eyes, and makes and sells glasses and contact lenses

optimism [ˈɒptɪˌmɪzəm] NOUN

Optimism is a feeling of hopefulness about the future.

optimist NOUN

optimistic [ˌɒptɪˈmɪstɪk] ADJECTIVE
hopeful about the future
optimistically ADVERB

THESAURUS
buoyant: *She was in a buoyant mood.*
confident: *I am confident that everything will come out right in time.*
hopeful: *I am hopeful this misunderstanding will be rectified.*
positive: *a positive frame of mind*
sanguine: *They have begun to take a more sanguine view.*
<<OPPOSITE *pessimistic*

optimum [ˈɒptɪməm] ADJECTIVE
the best that is possible *e.g. Six is the optimum number of participants for a good meeting.*

option [ˈɒpʃən] **options** NOUN
a choice between two or more things
optional ADJECTIVE

opulent [ˈɒpjʊlənt] ADJECTIVE
grand and expensive-looking *e.g. an opulent seafront estate*

opus [ˈəʊpəs] **opera** NOUN
an artistic work, especially a piece of music

or [ɔː] CONJUNCTION
1 used to link two different things *e.g. I didn't know whether to laugh or cry.*
2 used to introduce a warning *e.g. Do what I say or else I will fire.*

-or SUFFIX
'-or' is used to form nouns from verbs. *e.g. actor... conductor*
[WORD HISTORY: from Latin]

oracle [ˈɒrəkəl] **oracles** NOUN
1 In ancient Greece, an oracle was a place where a priest or priestess made predictions about the future.
2 a prophecy made by a priest or other person with great authority or wisdom

oral [ˈɔːrəl] **orals** ADJECTIVE
1 spoken rather than written *e.g. oral history*

THESAURUS
spoken: *the spoken word*
verbal: *a verbal agreement*
2 Oral describes things that are used in your mouth or done with your mouth. *e.g. an oral vaccine*
> NOUN
3 an examination that is spoken rather than written
orally ADVERB

orange [ˈɒrɪndʒ] **oranges** NOUN
a round citrus fruit that is juicy and sweet and

has a thick reddish-yellow skin
> ADJECTIVE or NOUN
reddish-yellow
[WORD HISTORY: from Sanskrit NARANGA meaning 'orange']

orang-utan [ɔːˌræŋuːˈtæn] **orang-utans**;
also spelt **orang-utang** NOUN
a large ape with reddish-brown hair

orator [ˈɒrətə] **orators** NOUN
someone who is good at making speeches

oratory [ˈɒrətərɪ] NOUN
Oratory is the art and skill of making formal public speeches.

orbit [ˈɔːbɪt] **orbits, orbiting, orbited** NOUN
1 the curved path followed by an object going round a planet or the sun
> VERB
2 If something orbits a planet or the sun, it goes round and round it.

orchard [ˈɔːtʃəd] **orchards** NOUN
a piece of land where fruit trees are grown

orchestra [ˈɔːkɪstrə] **orchestras** NOUN
(MUSIC) a large group of musicians who play musical instruments together
orchestral ADJECTIVE
[WORD HISTORY: from Greek ORKHESTRA meaning 'the area in a theatre reserved for musicians']

orchestrate [ˈɔːkɪˌstreɪt] **orchestrates, orchestrating, orchestrated** VERB
1 To orchestrate something is to organize it very carefully in order to produce a particular result.
2 To orchestrate a piece of music is to rewrite it so that it can be played by an orchestra.
orchestration NOUN

orchid [ˈɔːkɪd] **orchids** NOUN
Orchids are plants with beautiful and unusual flowers.

ordain [ɔːˈdeɪn] **ordains, ordaining, ordained** VERB
When someone is ordained, they are made a member of the clergy.

ordeal [ɔːˈdiːl] **ordeals** NOUN
a difficult and extremely unpleasant experience *e.g. the ordeal of being arrested and charged with attempted murder*

THESAURUS
hardship: *One of the worst hardships is having so little time.*
nightmare: *Taking my son Peter to a restaurant was a nightmare.*
torture: *Waiting for the result was torture.*
trial: *the trials of adolescence*
tribulation: formal *the trials and tribulations of everyday life*

order ['ɔːdə] **orders, ordering, ordered**
NOUN

1 a command given by someone in authority

● THESAURUS

command: *The tanker failed to respond to a command to stop.*
decree: *He issued a decree ordering all armed groups to disband.*
dictate: *to ensure that the dictates of the Party are followed*
directive: *a new EU directive*
instruction: *MPs defied a party instruction to vote against the Bill.*

2 If things are arranged or done in a particular order, they are arranged or done in that sequence. *e.g. in alphabetical order*

3 Order is a situation in which everything is in the correct place or done at the correct time.

● THESAURUS

harmony: *the ordered harmony of the universe*
regularity: *the chessboard regularity of their fields*
symmetry: *the beauty and symmetry of a snowflake*
<<OPPOSITE *disorder*

4 something that you ask to be brought to you or sent to you

> VERB

5 To order someone to do something is to tell them firmly to do it.

● THESAURUS

command: *He commanded his troops to attack.*
decree: *the rule that decreed no alcohol on the premises*
direct: *a court order directing the group to leave the land*
instruct: *The family has instructed solicitors to sue Thomson.*
ordain: *Nehru ordained that socialism should rule.*
<<OPPOSITE *forbid*

6 When you order something, you ask for it to be brought or sent to you.

> PHRASE

7 If you do something **in order to** achieve a particular thing, you do it because you want to achieve that thing.

orderly ['ɔːdəlɪ] ADJECTIVE
Something that is orderly is well organized or arranged.

● THESAURUS

neat: *She put her wet clothes in a neat pile in the corner.*
regular: *regular rows of wooden huts*
tidy: *a tidy desk*
<<OPPOSITE *disorderly*

ordinarily ['ɔːdᵊnrɪlɪ] ADVERB
If something ordinarily happens, it usually happens.

ordinary ['ɔːdᵊnrɪ] ADJECTIVE
Ordinary means not special or different in any way.

● THESAURUS

conventional: *a respectable married woman with conventional opinions*
normal: *He lives a normal life.*
regular: *the regular barman*
routine: *a routine procedure*
standard: *It was standard practice.*
usual: *all the usual inner-city problems*
<<OPPOSITE *special*

ordination [,ɔːdɪ'neɪʃən] NOUN
When someone's ordination takes place, they are made a member of the clergy.

ordnance ['ɔːdnəns] NOUN
Weapons and other military supplies are referred to as ordnance.

ore [ɔː] **ores** NOUN
Ore is rock or earth from which metal can be obtained.

oregano [,ɒrɪ'gɑːnəʊ] *or* [ə'rɛgənəʊ] NOUN
Oregano is a herb used for flavouring in cooking.

organ ['ɔːgən] **organs** NOUN

1 Your organs are parts of your body that have a particular function, for example your heart or lungs.

2 a large musical instrument with pipes of different lengths through which air is forced. It has various keyboards which are played like a piano

organic [ɔː'gænɪk] ADJECTIVE

1 Something that is organic is produced by or found in plants or animals. *e.g. decaying organic matter*

2 Organic food is produced without the use of artificial fertilizers or pesticides.
organically ADVERB

organism ['ɔːgə,nɪzəm] **organisms** NOUN
(SCIENCE) any living animal or plant

organist ['ɔːgənɪst] **organists** NOUN
someone who plays the organ

organization [,ɔːgənaɪ'zeɪʃən] **organizations;** also spelt **organisation** NOUN

1 any group or business

● THESAURUS

association: *research associations*
body: *the Chairman of the policemen's representative body*
company: *the Ford Motor Company*
confederation: *the Confederation of Indian Industry*
group: *an environmental group*
institution: *financial institutions*

outfit: informal *We are a professional outfit.*

2 The organization of something is the act of planning and arranging it.

organizational ADJECTIVE

🔵 THESAURUS

organizing: *His duties involved the organizing of transport.*

planning: *The trip needs careful planning.*

structuring: *improvements in the structuring of courses*

organize ['ɔːgə,naɪz] **organizes, organizing, organized;** also spelt **organise** VERB

1 If you organize an event, you plan and arrange it.

🔵 THESAURUS

arrange: *The bank can arrange a loan for students.*

establish: *How do you establish a workable system?*

jack up: New Zealand; informal *to jack up a demonstration*

plan: *A team meeting was planned for last night.*

set up: *This tribunal was set up by the government.*

2 If you organize things, you arrange them in a sensible order.

organized ADJECTIVE, **organizer** NOUN

orgasm ['ɔːgæzəm] **orgasms** NOUN

the moment of greatest pleasure and excitement during sexual activity

orgy ['ɔːdʒɪ] **orgies** NOUN

1 a wild, uncontrolled party involving a lot of drinking and sexual activity

2 You can refer to a period of intense activity as an orgy of that activity. *e.g. an orgy of violence*

[WORD HISTORY: from Greek ORGIA meaning 'nocturnal festival']

orient ['ɔːrɪənt] NOUN; LITERARY

The Orient is eastern and south-eastern Asia.

oriental [,ɔːrɪ'entəl] ADJECTIVE

relating to eastern or south-eastern Asia

orientated ['ɔːrɪen,teɪtɪd] ADJECTIVE

If someone is interested in a particular thing, you can say that they are orientated towards it. *e.g. These men are very career-orientated.*

orientation [,ɔːrɪen'teɪʃən] NOUN

You can refer to an organization's activities and aims as its orientation. *e.g. Poland's political and military orientation.*

oriented ['ɔːrɪentɪd] ADJECTIVE

Oriented means the same as orientated.

orienteering [,ɔːrɪen'tɪərɪŋ] NOUN

Orienteering is a sport in which people run from one place to another in the countryside, using a map and compass to guide them.

origin ['ɒrɪdʒɪn] **origins** NOUN

1 You can refer to the beginning or cause of something as its origin or origins.

🔵 THESAURUS

derivation: *The derivation of its name is obscure.*

root: *His sense of guilt had its roots in his childhood.*

source: *the source of the problem*

2 You can refer to someone's family background as their origin or origins. *e.g. She was of Swedish origin.*

🔵 THESAURUS

ancestry: *Noel can trace her ancestry to the 11th century.*

descent: *All the contributors were of African descent.*

extraction: *a Malaysian citizen of Australian extraction*

lineage: *a respectable family of ancient lineage*

stock: *people of Mediterranean stock*

original [ə'rɪdʒɪn²l] **originals** ADJECTIVE

1 Original describes things that existed at the beginning, rather than being added later, or things that were the first of their kind to exist. *e.g. the original owner of the cottage*

🔵 THESAURUS

first: *Her first reaction was disgust.*

initial: *His initial response was to disbelieve her.*

2 Original means imaginative and clever. *e.g. a stunningly original idea*

🔵 THESAURUS

fresh: *These designers are full of fresh ideas.*

new: *These proposals aren't new.*

novel: *a novel way of losing weight*

<<OPPOSITE unoriginal

> NOUN

3 a work of art or a document that is the one that was first produced, and not a copy

originally ADVERB, **originality** NOUN

originate [ə'rɪdʒɪ,neɪt] **originates, originating, originated** VERB

When something originates, or you originate it, it begins to happen or exist.

originator NOUN

ornament ['ɔːnəmənt] **ornaments** NOUN

a small, attractive object that you display in your home or that you wear in order to look attractive

🔵 THESAURUS

adornment: *a building without any adornments*

bauble: *a Christmas tree decorated with coloured baubles*

decoration: *The only wall decorations are candles.*

knick-knack: *Her flat is spilling over with knick-knacks.*

trinket: *She sold trinkets to tourists.*

ornamental [,ɔːnə'ment²l] ADJECTIVE

designed to be attractive rather than useful *e.g. an ornamental lake*

o

ornamentation [ˌɔːnəmɛnˈteɪʃən] NOUN
Ornamentation is decoration on a building, a piece of furniture, or a work of art.

ornate [ɔːˈneɪt] ADJECTIVE
Something that is ornate has a lot of decoration on it.

ornithology [ˌɔːnɪˈθɒlədʒɪ] NOUN
Ornithology is the study of birds.
ornithologist NOUN
[WORD HISTORY: from Greek ORNIS meaning 'bird' and -LOGIA meaning 'study of']

orphan [ˈɔːfən] **orphans, orphaning, orphaned** NOUN
1 a child whose parents are dead
> VERB
2 If a child is orphaned, its parents die.

orphanage [ˈɔːfənɪdʒ] **orphanages** NOUN
a place where orphans are looked after

orthodox [ˈɔːθəˌdɒks] ADJECTIVE
1 Orthodox beliefs or methods are the ones that most people have or use and that are considered standard.

2 People who are orthodox believe in the older, more traditional ideas of their religion or political party.

3 The Orthodox church is the part of the Christian church which separated from the western European church in the 11th century and is the main church in Greece and Russia.
orthodoxy NOUN

osmosis [ɒzˈməʊsɪs] NOUN; TECHNICAL
Osmosis is the process by which a liquid moves through a semipermeable membrane from a weaker solution to a more concentrated one.

osprey [ˈɒsprɪ] **ospreys** NOUN
a large bird of prey which catches fish with its claws

ostensibly [ɒˈstɛnsɪblɪ] ADVERB
If something is done ostensibly for a reason, that seems to be the reason for it. *e.g. Byrnes submitted his resignation, ostensibly on medical grounds.*

ostentatious [ˌɒstɛnˈteɪʃəs] ADJECTIVE
1 Something that is ostentatious is intended to impress people, for example by looking expensive. *e.g. ostentatious sculptures*

● THESAURUS
extravagant: *They make extravagant shows of generosity.*
flamboyant: *flamboyant clothes*
flashy: *a flashy sports car*
grandiose: *the grandiose building which housed the mayor's offices*
pretentious: *This pub was smaller and less pretentious.*

showy: *large, showy flowers*
2 People who are ostentatious try to impress other people with their wealth or importance.
ostentatiously ADVERB, **ostentation** NOUN

ostinato [ˌɒstɪˈnɑːtəʊ] **ostinatos** (MUSIC) NOUN
1 a musical phrase that is continuously repeated throughout a piece
> ADJECTIVE
2 continuously repeated *e.g. an ostinato passage*

ostrich [ˈɒstrɪtʃ] **ostriches** NOUN
The ostrich is the largest bird in the world. Ostriches cannot fly.

other [ˈʌðə] **others** ADJECTIVE OR PRONOUN
1 Other people or things are different people or things. *e.g. All the other children had gone home... One of the cabinets came from the palace; the other is a copy.*
> PHRASES
2 The other day or **the other week** means recently *e.g. She had bought four pairs of shoes the other day.*

otherwise [ˈʌðəˌwaɪz] ADVERB
1 You use 'otherwise' to say a different situation would exist if a particular fact or occurrence was not the case. *e.g. You had to learn to swim pretty quickly, otherwise you sank.*

2 'Otherwise' means apart from the thing mentioned *e.g. She had written to her daughter, but otherwise refused to take sides.*

3 'Otherwise' also means in a different way *e.g. The majority voted otherwise.*

otter [ˈɒtə] **otters** NOUN
a small, furry animal with a long tail. Otters swim well and eat fish

ouch [aʊtʃ] INTERJECTION
You say ouch when you suddenly feel pain.

ought [ɔːt] VERB
If you say that someone ought to do something, you mean that they should do it. *e.g. He ought to see a doctor.*

> Do not use *did* and *had* with ought: *He ought not to come* is correct: *he didn't ought to come* is not correct.

ounce [aʊns] **ounces** NOUN
a unit of weight equal to one sixteenth of a pound or about 28.35 grams

our [aʊə] ADJECTIVE
'Our' refers to something belonging or relating to the speaker or writer and one or more other people *e.g. We recently sold our house.*

> Some people pronounce *our* and *are* in the same way, so do not confuse the spellings of these words.

ours [aʊəz] PRONOUN
'Ours' refers to something belonging or relating to the speaker or writer and one or more other people *e.g. a friend of ours from Korea*

ourselves [aʊə'sɛlvz] PRONOUN
1 'Ourselves' is used when the same speaker or writer and one or more other people do an action and are affected by it *e.g. We haven't damaged ourselves too badly.*
2 'Ourselves' is used to emphasize 'we'

oust [aʊst] **ousts, ousting, ousted** VERB
If you oust someone, you force them out of a job or a place. *e.g. Cole was ousted from the board.*

out [aʊt] ADVERB
1 towards the outside of a place *e.g. Two dogs rushed out of the house.*
2 not at home *e.g. She was out when I rang last night.*
3 in the open air *e.g. They are playing out in bright sunshine.*
4 no longer shining or burning *e.g. The lights went out.*
> ADJECTIVE
5 on strike *e.g. 1000 construction workers are out in sympathy*
6 unacceptable or unfashionable *e.g. Miniskirts are out.*
7 incorrect *e.g. Logan's timing was out in the first two rounds.*

out- SUFFIX
1 'Out-' means 'exceeding' or 'going beyond'. *e.g. outdo... outclass*
2 'Out-' also means on the outside or away from the centre. *e.g. outback... outpost*

out-and-out ['aʊtənd'aʊt] ADJECTIVE
entire or complete *e.g. an out-and-out lie*

outback ['aʊt,bæk] NOUN
In Australia, the outback is the remote parts where very few people live.

outboard motor ['aʊt,bɔːd] **outboard motors** NOUN
a motor that can be fixed to the back of a small boat

outbreak ['aʊt,breɪk] **outbreaks** NOUN
If there is an outbreak of something unpleasant, such as war, it suddenly occurs.
● THESAURUS
eruption: *this sudden eruption of violence*
explosion: *the global explosion of interest in rugby*

outburst ['aʊt,bɜːst] **outbursts** NOUN
1 a sudden, strong expression of an emotion, especially anger *e.g. John broke into an angry*

outburst about how unfairly the work was divided.
2 a sudden occurrence of violent activity *e.g. an outburst of gunfire*

outcast ['aʊt,kɑːst] **outcasts** NOUN
someone who is rejected by other people

outclassed ['aʊt,klɑːst] ADJECTIVE
If you are outclassed, you are much worse than your opponent at a particular activity.

outcome ['aʊt,kʌm] **outcomes** NOUN
a result *e.g. the outcome of the election*

outcrop ['aʊt,krɒp] **outcrops** NOUN
a large piece of rock that sticks out of the ground

outcry ['aʊt,kraɪ] **outcries** NOUN
If there is an outcry about something, a lot of people are angry about it. *e.g. a public outcry over alleged fraud*

outdated [,aʊt'deɪtɪd] ADJECTIVE
no longer in fashion

outdo [,aʊt'duː] **outdoes, outdoing, outdid, outdone** VERB
If you outdo someone, you do a particular thing better than they do.
● THESAURUS
go one better than: *You always have to go one better than anyone else.*
outshine: *Jesse has begun to outshine me in sports.*
surpass: *determined to surpass the achievements of his older brothers*
top: *How are you going to top that?*

outdoor ['aʊt'dɔː] ADJECTIVE
happening or used outside *e.g. outdoor activities*

outdoors [,aʊt'dɔːz] ADVERB
outside *e.g. It was too chilly to sit outdoors.*

outer ['aʊtə] ADJECTIVE
The outer parts of something are the parts furthest from the centre. *e.g. the outer door of the office*

outer space NOUN
Outer space is everything beyond the Earth's atmosphere.

outfit ['aʊt,fɪt] **outfits** NOUN
1 a set of clothes
2 INFORMAL
an organization

outgoing ['aʊt,gəʊɪŋ] **outgoings** ADJECTIVE
1 Outgoing describes someone who is leaving a job or place. *e.g. the outgoing President*
2 Someone who is outgoing is friendly and not shy.
> PLURAL NOUN
3 Your outgoings are the amount of money that you spend.

o

outgrow [ˌaʊtˈɡrəʊ] **outgrows, outgrowing, outgrew, outgrown** VERB

1 If you outgrow a piece of clothing, you grow too big for it.

2 If you outgrow a way of behaving, you stop it because you have grown older and more mature.

outhouse [ˈaʊthaʊs] **outhouses** NOUN
a small building in the grounds of a house to which it belongs

outing [ˈaʊtɪŋ] **outings** NOUN
a trip made for pleasure

outlandish [aʊtˈlændɪʃ] ADJECTIVE
very unusual or odd e.g. outlandish clothes

outlaw [ˈaʊtlɔː] **outlaws, outlawing, outlawed** VERB

1 If something is outlawed, it is made illegal.

> NOUN

2 In the past, an outlaw was a criminal.

outlay [ˈaʊtleɪ] **outlays** NOUN
an amount of money spent on something e.g. a cash outlay of 300 dollars

outlet [ˈaʊtlɛt] **outlets** NOUN

1 An outlet for your feelings or ideas is a way of expressing them.

2 a hole or pipe through which water or air can flow away

3 a shop which sells goods made by a particular manufacturer

outline [ˈaʊtlaɪn] **outlines, outlining, outlined** VERB

1 If you outline a plan or idea, you explain it in a general way.

● THESAURUS

sketch: Tudjman sketched his vision of a future Bosnia.
summarize: The article can be summarized in three sentences.

2 You say that something is outlined when you can see its shape because there is a light behind it.

> NOUN

3 a general explanation or description of something

● THESAURUS

rundown: informal Here's a rundown of the options.
summary: a summary of the report
synopsis: a brief synopsis of the book

4 The outline of something is its shape.

● THESAURUS

contours: the contours of her body
figure: Alistair saw the dim figure of Rose in the chair.

form: She'd never been so glad to see his bulky form.
shape: dark shapes of herons silhouetted against the moon
silhouette: the dark silhouette of the castle ruins

outlive [ˌaʊtˈlɪv] **outlives, outliving, outlived** VERB
To outlive someone is to live longer than they do.

outlook [ˈaʊtlʊk] NOUN

1 Your outlook is your general attitude towards life.

● THESAURUS

attitude: Being unemployed produces negative attitudes to work.
perspective: It gave him a new perspective on life.
view: an optimistic view of the future

2 The outlook of a situation is the way it is likely to develop. e.g. The Japanese economy's outlook is uncertain.

● THESAURUS

future: a conference on the country's political future
prospects: a detailed review of the company's prospects

outlying [ˈaʊtlaɪɪŋ] ADJECTIVE
Outlying places are far from cities.

outmoded [ˌaʊtˈməʊdɪd] ADJECTIVE
old-fashioned and no longer useful e.g. an outmoded form of transport

outnumber [ˌaʊtˈnʌmbə] **outnumbers, outnumbering, outnumbered** VERB
If there are more of one group than of another, the first group outnumbers the second.

out of PREPOSITION

1 If you do something out of a particular feeling, you are motivated by that feeling. e.g. Out of curiosity she went along.

2 'Out of' also means from e.g. old instruments made out of wood

3 If you are out of something, you no longer have any of it. e.g. I do hope we're not out of fuel again.

4 If you are out of the rain, sun, or wind, you are sheltered from it.

5 You also use 'out of' to indicate proportion. For example, one out of five means one in every five.

out of date ADJECTIVE
old-fashioned and no longer useful

● THESAURUS

antiquated: an antiquated system
archaic: archaic practices such as these
obsolete: So much equipment becomes obsolete almost as soon as it's made.
old-fashioned: old-fashioned shoes
outdated: outdated attitudes
outmoded: toiling in outmoded factories
<<OPPOSITE modern

out of doors [dɔːz] ADVERB
outside *e.g. Sometimes we eat out of doors.*

outpatient ['aʊtˌpeɪʃənt] **outpatients**
NOUN
Outpatients are people who receive treatment in hospital without staying overnight.

outpost ['aʊtˌpəʊst] **outposts** NOUN
a small collection of buildings a long way from a main centre *e.g. a remote mountain outpost*

output ['aʊtˌpʊt] **outputs** NOUN
1 Output is the amount of something produced by a person or organization.
2 (ICT) The output of a computer is the information that it produces.

outrage ['aʊtˌreɪdʒ] **outrages, outraging, outraged** VERB
1 If something outrages you, it angers and shocks you. *e.g. I was outraged at what had happened to her.*
> NOUN
2 Outrage is a feeling of anger and shock.
3 something very shocking or violent
outrageous ADJECTIVE, **outrageously** ADVERB

outright ADJECTIVE ['aʊtˌraɪt]
1 absolute *e.g. an outright rejection*
> ADVERB [ˌaʊtˈraɪt]
2 in an open and direct way *e.g. Have you asked him outright?.*
3 completely and totally *e.g. I own the company outright.*

outset ['aʊtˌsɛt] NOUN
The outset of something is the beginning of it. *e.g. the outset of his journey*

outshine [ˌaʊtˈʃaɪn] **outshines, outshining, outshone** VERB
If you outshine someone, you perform better than they do.

outside NOUN ['aʊtˌsaɪd]
1 The outside of something is the part which surrounds or encloses the rest of it.
● THESAURUS
exterior: *the exterior of the building*
facade: *the refurbishing of the cathedral's facade*
face: *the face of the watch*
surface: *the surface of the road*
<<OPPOSITE *inside*
> PREPOSITION [ˌaʊtˈsaɪd]
2 on or to the exterior of *e.g. outside the house*
3 Outside also means not included in something. *e.g. outside office hours*
> ADJECTIVE ['aʊtˌsaɪd]
4 Outside means not inside. *e.g. an outside toilet*
● THESAURUS
exterior: *the oven's exterior surfaces*

external: *the external walls*
outdoor: *outdoor activities*
outer: *the outer suburbs of the city*
outward: *with no outward sign of injury*
surface: *Its total surface area was seven thousand square feet.*
<<OPPOSITE *inside*
> ADVERB [ˌaʊtˈsaɪd]
5 out of doors

Do not use *of* after *outside*. You should write *she was waiting outside the school* and not *outside of the school.*

outsider [ˌaʊtˈsaɪdə] **outsiders** NOUN
1 someone who does not belong to a particular group
2 a competitor considered unlikely to win in a race

outsize or **outsized** ['aʊtˌsaɪz] or ['aʊtˌsaɪzd]
ADJECTIVE
much larger than usual *e.g. outsize feet*

outskirts ['aʊtˌskɜːts] PLURAL NOUN
The outskirts of a city or town are the parts around the edge of it.
● THESAURUS
edge: *We were on a hill, right on the edge of town.*
perimeter: *the perimeter of the airport*
periphery: *countries on the periphery of Europe*

outspan [ˌaʊtˈspæn] **outspans, outspanning, outspanned** VERB SOUTH
AFRICAN
If you outspan, you relax.
● THESAURUS
laze: *Fred lazed in an easy chair.*
relax: *I ought to relax and stop worrying.*
rest: *He rested for a while before starting work again.*
take it easy: *Try to take it easy for a week or two.*

outspoken [ˌaʊtˈspəʊkən] ADJECTIVE
Outspoken people give their opinions openly, even if they shock other people.

outstanding [ˌaʊtˈstændɪŋ] ADJECTIVE
1 extremely good *e.g. The collection contains hundreds of outstanding works of art.*
● THESAURUS
brilliant: *a brilliant performance*
excellent: *the recording quality is excellent.*
exceptional: *children with exceptional ability*
first-class: *first-class service*
first-rate: *The show was first-rate.*
great: *great cultural achievements*
superb: *a superb 18-hole golf course*
2 Money that is outstanding is still owed. *e.g. an outstanding mortgage of 46,000 pounds*
● THESAURUS
due: *They sent me £100 and advised me that no further payment was due.*

o

overdue: *pay overdue salaries*
owing: *There is still some money owing for the rent.*
payable: *The amount payable is £175.*
unpaid: *The bills remained unpaid.*

outstretched ['aʊt,strɛtʃt] ADJECTIVE
If your arms are outstretched, they are stretched out as far as possible.

outstrip [,aʊt'strɪp] **outstrips, outstripping, outstripped** VERB
If one thing outstrips another thing, it becomes bigger or more successful or moves faster than the other thing.

outward ['aʊtwəd] ADJECTIVE OR ADVERB
1 Outward means away from a place or towards the outside. *e.g. the outward journey*
> ADJECTIVE
2 The outward features of someone are the ones they appear to have, rather than the ones they actually have. *e.g. He never showed any outward signs of emotion.*
outwardly ADVERB

outwards ['aʊtwədz] ADVERB
away from a place or towards the outside *e.g. The door opened outwards.*

outweigh [,aʊt'weɪ] **outweighs, outweighing, outweighed** VERB
If you say that the advantages of something outweigh its disadvantages, you mean that the advantages are more important than the disadvantages.

outwit [,aʊt'wɪt] **outwits, outwitting, outwitted** VERB
If you outwit someone, you use your intelligence to defeat them.

oval ['əʊvᵊl] **ovals** NOUN
1 a round shape, similar to a circle but wider in one direction than the other
> ADJECTIVE
2 shaped like an oval *e.g. an oval table*

ovary ['əʊvərɪ] **ovaries** NOUN
A woman's ovaries are the two organs in her body that produce eggs.

ovation [əʊ'veɪʃən] **ovations** NOUN
a long burst of applause

oven ['ʌvᵊn] **ovens** NOUN
the part of a cooker that you use for baking or roasting food

over ['əʊvə] **overs** PREPOSITION
1 Over something means directly above it or covering it. *e.g. the picture over the fireplace... He put his hands over his eyes.*
2 A view over an area is a view across that area. *e.g. The pool and terrace look out over the sea.*

3 If something is over a road or river it is on the opposite side of the road or river.
4 Something that is over a particular amount is more than that amount.
● THESAURUS
above: *speeds above 50 mph*
exceeding: *a budget exceeding $700 million a year*
in excess of: *a fortune in excess of 150 million pounds*
more than: *The airport had been closed for more than a year.*
5 'Over' indicates a topic which is causing concern *e.g. An American was arguing over the bill.*
6 If something happens over a period of time, it happens during that period. *e.g. I went to New Zealand over Christmas.*
> ADVERB OR PREPOSITION
7 If you lean over, you bend your body in a particular direction. *e.g. He bent over and rummaged in a drawer... She was hunched over her typewriter.*
> ADVERB
8 'Over' is used to indicate a position *e.g. over by the window... Come over here.*
9 If something rolls or turns over, it is moved so that its other side is facing upwards. *e.g. He flipped over the envelope.*
> ADJECTIVE
10 Something that is over is completely finished.
● THESAURUS
at an end: *The matter is now at an end.*
complete: *The work of restoring the farmhouse is complete.*
finished: *once the season's finished*
gone: *Any chance of winning was now gone.*
past: *The time for loyalty is past.*
up: *when the six weeks were up*
> PHRASE
11 All over a place means everywhere in that place *e.g. studios all over America*
> NOUN
12 In cricket, an over is a set of six balls bowled by a bowler from the same end of the pitch.

over- PREFIX
'over' means to too great an extent or too much. *e.g. overprotective... overindulge... overact*
[WORD HISTORY: from Old English ofer]

overall overalls ADJECTIVE ['əʊvər,ɔːl]
1 Overall means taking into account all the parts or aspects of something. *e.g. The overall quality of pupils' work had shown a marked improvement...*
ADVERB [,əʊvər'ɔːl]
2 taking into account all the parts of something. *e.g. Overall, things are not really too bad.*

> PLURAL NOUN ['əʊvərˌɔːlz]

3 Overalls are a piece of clothing that looks like trousers and a jacket combined. You wear overalls to protect your other clothes when you are working.

> NOUN ['əʊvərˌɔːl]

4 An overall is a piece of clothing like a coat that you wear to protect your other clothes when you are working.

overawed [ˌəʊvərˈɔːd] ADJECTIVE
If you are overawed by something, you are very impressed by it and a little afraid of it.

overbearing [ˌəʊvəˈbeərɪŋ] ADJECTIVE
trying to dominate other people *e.g. Mozart had a difficult relationship with his overbearing father.*

overboard ['əʊvəˌbɔːd] ADVERB
If you fall overboard, you fall over the side of a ship into the water.

overcast ['əʊvəˌkɑːst] ADJECTIVE
If it is overcast, the sky is covered by cloud.

overcoat ['əʊvəˌkəʊt] **overcoats** NOUN
a thick, warm coat

overcome [ˌəʊvəˈkʌm] **overcomes, overcoming, overcame, overcome** VERB
1 If you overcome a problem or a feeling, you manage to deal with it or control it.

THESAURUS
conquer: *He has never conquered his addiction to smoking.*
get the better of: *She didn't allow her emotions to get the better of her.*
master: *His genius alone has mastered every crisis.*
surmount: *I realized I had to surmount the language barrier.*
triumph over: *a symbol of good triumphing over evil*

> ADJECTIVE

2 If you are overcome by a feeling, you feel it very strongly.

overcrowded [ˌəʊvəˈkraʊdɪd] ADJECTIVE
If a place is overcrowded, there are too many things or people in it.

overdo [ˌəʊvəˈduː] **overdoes, overdoing, overdid, overdone** VERB
If you overdo something, you do it too much or in an exaggerated way. *e.g. It is important never to overdo new exercises.*

overdose ['əʊvəˌdəʊs] **overdoses** NOUN
a larger dose of a drug than is safe

overdraft ['əʊvəˌdrɑːft] **overdrafts** NOUN
an agreement with a bank that allows someone to spend more money than they have in their account

overdrawn [ˌəʊvəˈdrɔːn] ADJECTIVE
If someone is overdrawn, they have taken more

money from their bank account than the account has in it.

overdrive ['əʊvəˌdraɪv] NOUN
Overdrive is an extra, higher gear in a vehicle, which is used at high speeds to reduce engine wear and save petrol.

overdue [ˌəʊvəˈdjuː] ADJECTIVE
If someone or something is overdue, they are late. *e.g. The payments are overdue.*

overestimate [ˌəʊvərˈɛstɪˌmeɪt] **overestimates, overestimating, overestimated** VERB
If you overestimate something, you think that it is bigger, more important, or better than it really is. *e.g. We had overestimated his popularity.*

overflow [ˌəʊvəˈfləʊ] **overflows, overflowing, overflowed, overflown** VERB
If a liquid overflows, it spills over the edges of its container. If a river overflows, it flows over its banks.

overgrown [ˌəʊvəˈɡrəʊn] ADJECTIVE
A place that is overgrown is covered with weeds because it has not been looked after. *e.g. an overgrown path*

overhang [ˌəʊvəˈhæŋ] **overhangs, overhanging, overhung** VERB
If one thing overhangs another, it sticks out sideways above it. *e.g. old trees whose branches overhang a footpath*

overhaul overhauls, overhauling, overhauled VERB [ˌəʊvəˈhɔːl]
1 If you overhaul something, you examine it thoroughly and repair any faults.

> NOUN ['əʊvəˌhɔːl]

2 If you give something an overhaul, you examine it and repair or improve it.

overhead overheads ADJECTIVE ['əʊvəˌhɛd]
1 Overhead means above you. *e.g. overhead cables*

> ADVERB [ˌəʊvəˈhɛd]

2 Overhead means above you. *e.g. Seagulls flying overhead*

> PLURAL NOUN ['əʊvəˌhɛdz]

3 The overheads of a business are the costs of running it.

overhear [ˌəʊvəˈhɪə] **overhears, overhearing, overheard** VERB
If you overhear someone's conversation, you hear what they are saying to someone else.

overjoyed [ˌəʊvəˈdʒɔɪd] ADJECTIVE
extremely pleased *e.g. Colm was overjoyed*

O

overlaid [,əʊvəˈleɪd] ADJECTIVE
If something is overlaid by something else, it is covered by it.

overland [ˈəʊvə,lænd] ADJECTIVE OR ADVERB
travelling across land rather than going by sea or air *e.g. an overland trek to India... Wray was returning to England overland.*

overlander [ˈəʊvə,lændə] **overlanders** NOUN
In Australian history, an overlander was a man who drove cattle or sheep long distances through the outback.

overlap [,əʊvəˈlæp] **overlaps, overlapping, overlapped** VERB
If one thing overlaps another, one part of it covers part of the other thing.

overleaf [,əʊvəˈliːf] ADVERB
on the next page *e.g. Write to us at the address shown overleaf.*

overload [,əʊvəˈləʊd] **overloads, overloading, overloaded** VERB
If you overload someone or something, you give them too much to do or to carry.

overlook [,əʊvəˈlʊk] **overlooks, overlooking, overlooked** VERB
1 If a building or window overlooks a place, it has a view over that place.
2 If you overlook something, you ignore it or do not notice it.

● THESAURUS
disregard: *The police must not be allowed to disregard human rights.*
forget: *She never forgets his birthday.*
ignore: *For years her talents were ignored by the film industry.*
miss: *His searching eye never missed a detail.*
neglect: *She never neglects her duties.*
turn a blind eye to: *Are teachers turning a blind eye to these issues?*

overly [ˈəʊvəlɪ] ADVERB
excessively *e.g. I'm not overly fond of jazz.*

overnight ADVERB [,əʊvəˈnaɪt]
1 For the duration of the night *e.g. Further rain was forecast overnight.*
2 suddenly *e.g. Good players don't become bad ones overnight.*
> ADJECTIVE [ˈəʊvə,naɪt]
3 during the night
4 sudden *e.g. an overnight success*
5 for use when you go away for one or two nights *e.g. an overnight bag*

overpower [,əʊvəˈpaʊə] **overpowers, overpowering, overpowered** VERB
1 If you overpower someone, you seize them despite their struggles, because you are stronger than them.

2 If a feeling overpowers you, it affects you very strongly.
overpowering ADJECTIVE

overrate [,əʊvəˈreɪt] **overrates, overrating, overrated** VERB
If you overrate something, you think that it is better or more important than it really is.
overrated ADJECTIVE

overreact [,əʊvərɪˈækt] **overreacts, overreacting, overreacted** VERB
If you overreact, you react in an extreme way.

overriding [,əʊvəˈraɪdɪŋ] ADJECTIVE
more important than anything else *e.g. an overriding duty*

overrule [,əʊvəˈruːl] **overrules, overruling, overruled** VERB
To overrule a person or their decisions is to decide that their decisions are incorrect.

● THESAURUS
overturn: *when the Russian parliament overturned his decision*
reverse: *They will not reverse the decision to increase prices.*

overrun [,əʊvəˈrʌn] **overruns, overrunning, overran, overrun** VERB
1 If an army overruns a country, it occupies it very quickly.
2 If animals or plants overrun a place, they spread quickly over it.
3 If an event overruns, it continues for longer than it was meant to.

overseas ADVERB [,əʊvəˈsiːz]
1 abroad *e.g. travelling overseas*
> ADJECTIVE [ˈəʊvə,siːz]
2 abroad *e.g. an overseas tour*
3 from abroad *e.g. overseas students*

oversee [,əʊvəˈsiː] **oversees, overseeing, oversaw, overseen** VERB
To oversee a job is to make sure it is done properly.
overseer NOUN

● THESAURUS
be in charge of: *She is in charge of day-to-day operations.*
coordinate: *Government officials have been sent to coordinate the relief effort.*
direct: *his coolness in directing the rescue*
manage: *Within two years, he was managing the project.*
preside: *Mr Brown will be presiding over the day's events.*
supervise: *He supervises the vineyards.*

overshadow [,əʊvəˈʃædəʊ] **overshadows, overshadowing, overshadowed** VERB

If something is overshadowed, it is made unimportant by something else that is better or more important.

oversight ['əʊvə,saɪt] **oversights** NOUN
something which you forget to do or fail to notice

overspill ['əʊvə,spɪl] **overspills** NOUN OR ADJECTIVE
Overspill refers to the moving of people from overcrowded cities to houses in smaller towns. *e.g. an East End overspill... overspill estates*

overstate [,əʊvə'steɪt] **overstates, overstating, overstated** VERB
If you overstate something, you exaggerate its importance.

overstep [,əʊvə'stɛp] **oversteps, overstepping, overstepped** PHRASE
If you **overstep the mark**, you behave in an unacceptable way.

overt ['əʊvɜːt] ADJECTIVE
open and obvious *e.g. overt signs of stress*
overtly ADVERB

overtake [,əʊvə'teɪk] **overtakes, overtaking, overtook, overtaken** VERB
If you overtake someone, you pass them because you are moving faster than them.

overthrow [,əʊvə'θrəʊ] **overthrows, overthrowing, overthrew, overthrown** VERB
If a government is overthrown, it is removed from power by force.
🔹 THESAURUS
bring down: *They brought down the government by withdrawing their support.*
depose: *He fled to Hawaii after being deposed as president.*
oust: *His opponents tried to oust him with a vote of no confidence.*
topple: *the revolution which toppled the regime*

overtime ['əʊvə,taɪm] NOUN
1 Overtime is time that someone works in addition to their normal working hours.
> ADVERB
2 If someone works overtime, they do work in addition to their normal working hours.

overtones ['əʊvə,təʊnz] PLURAL NOUN
If something has overtones of an emotion or attitude, it suggests it without showing it openly. *e.g. the political overtones of the trial*

overture ['əʊvə,tjʊə] **overtures** NOUN
1 a piece of music that is the introduction to an opera or play
2 If you make overtures to someone, you approach them because you want to start a friendly or business relationship with them.

overturn [,əʊvə'tɜːn] **overturns, overturning, overturned** VERB
1 To overturn something is to turn it upside down or onto its side.
🔹 THESAURUS
capsize: *I didn't count on his capsizing the raft.*
knock down: *Isabel rose so abruptly that she knocked down her chair.*
knock over: *Emma knocked over the box of cornflakes.*
tip over: *He tipped the table over in front of him.*
topple: *Winds and rain toppled trees and electricity lines.*
upset: *Don't upset the piles of sheets under the box.*
2 If someone overturns a legal decision, they change it by using their higher authority.
🔹 THESAURUS
overrule: *The Court of Appeal overruled this decision.*
reverse: *They will not reverse the decision to increase prices.*

overview ['əʊvə,vjuː] **overviews** NOUN
a general understanding or description of a situation

overweight [,əʊvə'weɪt] ADJECTIVE
too fat, and therefore unhealthy *e.g. overweight businessmen*
🔹 THESAURUS
fat: *I could eat what I liked without getting fat.*
hefty: *She was quite a hefty woman.*
obese: *Obese people tend to have higher blood pressure than lean people.*
stout: *a stout man with grey hair*

overwhelm [,əʊvə'wɛlm] **overwhelms, overwhelming, overwhelmed** VERB
1 If you are overwhelmed by something, it affects you very strongly. *e.g. The priest appeared overwhelmed by the news.*
2 If one group of people overwhelm another, they gain complete control or victory over them.
overwhelming ADJECTIVE, **overwhelmingly** ADVERB

overwork [,əʊvə'wɜːk] **overworks, overworking, overworked** VERB
If you overwork, you work too hard.

overwrought [,əʊvə'rɔːt] ADJECTIVE
extremely upset *e.g. He didn't get angry or overwrought.*

ovulate ['ɒvjʊ,leɪt] **ovulates, ovulating, ovulated** VERB
When a woman or female animal ovulates, she produces ova or eggs from her ovary.

ovum ['əʊvəm] **ova** NOUN
a reproductive cell of a woman or female animal.

The ovum is fertilized by a male sperm to produce young

[WORD HISTORY: a Latin word meaning 'egg']

owe [əʊ] **owes, owing, owed** VERB

1 If you owe someone money, they have lent it to you and you have not yet paid it back.

2 If you owe a quality or skill to someone, you are responsible for giving it to you. *e.g. He owes his success to his mother.*

3 If you say that you owe someone gratitude or loyalty, you mean that they deserve it from you.

owl [aʊl] **owls** NOUN

Owls are birds of prey that hunt at night. They have large eyes and short, hooked beaks.

own [əʊn] **owns, owning, owned** ADJECTIVE

1 If something is your own, it belongs to you or is associated with you. *e.g. She stayed in her own house.*

● THESAURUS

personal: *That's my personal opinion.*
private: *76 bedrooms, all with private bathrooms*

> VERB

2 If you own something, it belongs to you.

● THESAURUS

have: *They have a house in France.*
keep: *His father kept a village shop.*
possess: *I would give her everything I possess.*

> PHRASE

3 On your own means alone

● THESAURUS

adverb owno3 **alone:** *She lives alone.*
by oneself: *I didn't know if I could raise a child by myself.*
independently: *several people working independently*
unaided: *She brought us up completely unaided.*

owner ['əʊnə] **owners** NOUN

The owner of something is the person it belongs to.

● THESAURUS

possessor: *the proud possessor of a truly incredible voice*

proprietor: *the proprietor of a local restaurant*

ownership ['əʊnəʃɪp] NOUN

If you have ownership of something, you own it. *e.g. He shared the ownership of a sailing dinghy.*

ox [ɒks] **oxen** NOUN

Oxen are cattle which are used for carrying or pulling things.

oxide ['ɒksaɪd] **oxides** NOUN

a compound of oxygen and another chemical element

oxidize ['ɒksɪˌdaɪz] **oxidizes, oxidizing, oxidized;** also spelt **oxidise** VERB

When a substance oxidizes, it changes chemically by reacting with oxygen.

oxidation NOUN

oxygen ['ɒksɪdʒən] NOUN

(SCIENCE) a colourless and odourless gas in the air. It makes up about 21% of the Earth's atmosphere. With an extremely small number of exceptions, living things need oxygen to survive, and things cannot burn without it

oxymoron [ˌɒksɪ'mɔːrɒn] **oxymora** or **oxymorons** NOUN

two words that contradict each other placed beside each other, for example 'deafening silence'

oyster ['ɔɪstə] **oysters** NOUN

Oysters are large, flat shellfish. Some oysters can be eaten, and others produce pearls.

[WORD HISTORY: from Greek OSTRAKON meaning 'shell']

oz

an abbreviation for 'ounces'

ozone ['əʊzəʊn] NOUN

Ozone is a form of oxygen that is poisonous and has a strong smell. There is a layer of ozone high above the Earth's surface.

ozone layer NOUN

The ozone layer is that part of the Earth's atmosphere that protects living things from the harmful radiation of the sun.

Pp

P

1 p is an abbreviation for 'pence'

2 p is also a written abbreviation for 'page'. The plural is pp

pa [pɑː] **pa** or **pas** NOUN
In New Zealand, a Maori village or settlement.

pace [peɪs] **paces, pacing, paced** NOUN
1 The pace of something is the speed at which it moves or happens.

2 a step; also used as a measurement of distance

> VERB

3 If you pace up and down, you continually walk around because you are anxious or impatient.

pacemaker [ˈpeɪsˌmeɪkə] **pacemakers**
NOUN
a small electronic device put into someone's heart to control their heartbeat

Pacific [pəˈsɪfɪk] NOUN
The Pacific is the ocean separating North and South America from Asia and Australia.

pacifist [ˈpæsɪfɪst] **pacifists** NOUN
someone who is opposed to all violence and war
pacifism NOUN

pacify [ˈpæsɪˌfaɪ] **pacifies, pacifying, pacified** VERB
If you pacify someone who is angry, you calm them.

🔵 THESAURUS
appease: *The offer has not appeased separatists.*
calm: *A business lunch helped calm her nerves.*
mollify: *The investigation was undertaken to mollify pressure groups.*
placate: *He went aboard to placate the angry passengers.*
soothe: *She took him in her arms and soothed him.*

pack [pæk] **packs, packing, packed** VERB
1 If you pack, you put things neatly into a suitcase, bag, or box.

2 If people pack into a place, it becomes crowded with them.

> NOUN

3 a bag or rucksack carried on your back

4 a packet or collection of something *e.g. a pack of cigarettes*

5 A pack of playing cards is a complete set.

6 A pack of dogs or wolves is a group of them.

> VERB **pack up**

7 If you pack up your belongings, you put them in a bag because you are leaving.

package [ˈpækɪdʒ] **packages** NOUN
1 a small parcel

2 a set of proposals or offers presented as a whole *e.g. a package of beauty treatments*
packaged ADJECTIVE

packaging [ˈpækɪdʒɪŋ] NOUN
Packaging is the container or wrapping in which an item is sold or sent.

packed [pækt] ADJECTIVE
very full *e.g. The church was packed with people.*

packet [ˈpækɪt] **packets** NOUN
a thin cardboard box or paper container in which something is sold

pact [pækt] **pacts** NOUN
a formal agreement or treaty

pad [pæd] **pads, padding, padded** NOUN
1 a thick, soft piece of material

2 a number of pieces of paper fixed together at one end

3 The pads of an animal such as a cat or dog are the soft, fleshy parts on the bottom of its paws.

4 a flat surface from which helicopters take off or rockets are launched

> VERB

5 If you pad something, you put a pad inside it or over it to protect it or change its shape.

6 If you pad around, you walk softly.
padding NOUN

paddle [ˈpædəl] **paddles, paddling, paddled** NOUN
1 a short pole with a broad blade at one or both ends, used to move a small boat or a canoe

> VERB

2 If someone paddles a boat, they move it using a paddle.

3 If you paddle, you walk in shallow water.

paddock [ˈpædək] **paddocks** NOUN
a small field where horses are kept

paddy ['pædɪ] **paddies** NOUN
A paddy or paddy field is an area in which rice is grown.

padlock ['pæd,lɒk] **padlocks, padlocking, padlocked** NOUN
1 a lock made up of a metal case with a U-shaped bar attached to it, which can be put through a metal loop and then closed. It is unlocked by turning a key in the lock on the case
> VERB
2 If you padlock something, you lock it with a padlock.

padre ['pɑːdrɪ] **padres** NOUN
a priest, especially a chaplain to the armed forces
[WORD HISTORY: from Italian or Spanish PADRE meaning 'father']

paediatrician [,piːdɪə'trɪʃən] **paediatricians**; also spelt **pediatrician** NOUN
a doctor who specializes in treating children
[WORD HISTORY: from Greek PAIS meaning 'child' and IATROS meaning 'physician']

paediatrics [,piːdɪ'ætrɪks] also spelt **pediatrics** NOUN
Paediatrics is the area of medicine which deals with children's diseases.
paediatric ADJECTIVE

pagan ['peɪgən] **pagans** ADJECTIVE
1 involving beliefs and worship outside the main religions of the world e.g. pagan myths and cults
> NOUN
2 someone who believes in a pagan religion
paganism NOUN

page [peɪdʒ] **pages, paging, paged** NOUN
1 one side of one of the pieces of paper in a book or magazine; also the sheet of paper itself
2 In medieval times, a page was a young boy servant who was learning to be a knight.
> VERB
3 To page someone is to send a signal or message to a small electronic device which they are carrying.

pageant ['pædʒənt] **pageants** NOUN
a grand, colourful show or parade

pagoda [pə'gəʊdə] **pagodas** NOUN
a tall, elaborately decorated Buddhist or Hindu temple

pail [peɪl] **pails** NOUN
a bucket

pain [peɪn] **pains, paining, pained** NOUN
1 Pain is an unpleasant feeling of physical hurt.
● THESAURUS
ache: Poor posture can cause neck aches.
discomfort: Steve had some discomfort but no real pain.

irritation: These oils may cause irritation to sensitive skin.
soreness: The soreness lasted for about six weeks.
trouble: back trouble
twinge: He felt a slight twinge in his hamstring.

2 Pain is also an unpleasant feeling of deep unhappiness.
● THESAURUS
agony: the agony of divorce
anguish: Mark looked at him in anguish.
distress: Jealousy causes distress and painful emotions.
grief: The grief soon gave way to anger.
misery: All that money brought nothing but sadness and misery.

> VERB
3 If something pains you, it makes you very unhappy.
painless ADJECTIVE, **painlessly** ADVERB

painful ['peɪnfʊl] ADJECTIVE
1 causing emotional pain
● THESAURUS
distressing: one of the most distressing episodes in his life
grievous: Their loss would be a grievous blow to our industry.
saddening: a saddening experience
unpleasant: an unpleasant truth

2 causing physical pain
painfully ADVERB
● THESAURUS
aching: his aching joints
excruciating: an excruciating headache
sore: a sore throat
tender: My leg is very tender and sore.

painkiller ['peɪn,kɪlə] **painkillers** NOUN
a drug that reduces or stops pain

painstaking ['peɪnz,teɪkɪŋ] ADJECTIVE
very careful and thorough e.g. years of painstaking research

paint [peɪnt] **paints, painting, painted** NOUN
1 Paint is a coloured liquid used to decorate buildings, or to make a picture.
> VERB
2 If you paint something or paint a picture of it, you make a picture of it using paint.
3 When you paint something such as a wall, you cover it with paint.
painter NOUN, **painting** NOUN

pair [peə] **pairs, pairing, paired** NOUN
1 two things of the same type or that do the same thing e.g. a pair of earrings

2 You use 'pair' when referring to certain objects which have two main matching parts. *e.g. a pair of scissors*

> VERB

3 When people pair off, they become grouped in pairs.

4 If you pair up with someone, you agree to do something together.

> The verb following *pair* can be singular or plural. If *pair* refers to a unit, the verb is singular: *a pair of good shoes is essential.* If *pair* refers to two individual things, the verb is plural: *the pair are said to dislike each other.*

pakeha ['pɑ:kɪˌhɑ:] **pakeha** or **pakehas**
NOUN
in New Zealand English, someone who is of European rather than Maori descent

Pakistani [ˌpɑ:kɪ'stɑ:nɪ] **Pakistanis**
ADJECTIVE
1 belonging or relating to Pakistan

> NOUN

2 someone who comes from Pakistan

pal [pæl] **pals** NOUN; INFORMAL
a friend

palace ['pælɪs] **palaces** NOUN
a large, grand house, especially the official home of a king or queen

palagi [pɑ:'lʌŋi:] **palagi** or **palagis** NOUN
a Samoan name for a New Zealander of European descent

palatable ['pælətəbəl] ADJECTIVE
Palatable food tastes pleasant.

palate ['pælɪt] **palates** NOUN
1 the top of the inside of your mouth

2 Someone's palate is their ability to judge good food and wine. *e.g. dishes to tempt every palate*

pale [peɪl] **paler, palest** ADJECTIVE
rather white and without much colour or brightness

● THESAURUS
ashen: *He fell back, shocked, his face ashen.*
colourless: *a colourless liquid*
faded: *a girl in faded jeans*
sallow: *His face was sallow and shiny with sweat.*
wan: *He looked wan and tired.*
white: *He turned white and began to stammer.*

Palestinian [ˌpælɪ'stɪnɪən] **Palestinians**
NOUN
an Arab from the region formerly called Palestine situated between the River Jordan and the Mediterranean

palette ['pælɪt] **palettes** NOUN
(ART) a flat piece of wood on which an artist mixes colours

pall [pɔ:l] **palls, palling, palled** VERB
1 If something palls, it becomes less interesting or less enjoyable. *e.g. This record palls after ten minutes.*

> NOUN

2 a thick cloud of smoke

3 a cloth covering a coffin

palm [pɑ:m] **palms** NOUN
1 A palm or palm tree is a tropical tree with no branches and a crown of long leaves.

2 the flat surface of your hand which your fingers bend towards

Palm Sunday NOUN
Palm Sunday is the Sunday before Easter.

palpable ['pælpəbəl] ADJECTIVE
obvious and easily sensed *e.g. Happiness was palpable in the air.*
palpably ADVERB
[WORD HISTORY: from Latin PALPABILIS meaning 'able to be touched']

paltry ['pɔ:ltrɪ] ADJECTIVE
A paltry sum of money is a very small amount.

pamper ['pæmpə] **pampers, pampering, pampered** VERB
If you pamper someone, you give them too much kindness and comfort.

pamphlet ['pæmflɪt] **pamphlets** NOUN
(ENGLISH) a very thin book in paper covers giving information about something

pan [pæn] **pans, panning, panned** NOUN
1 a round metal container with a long handle, used for cooking things in on top of a cooker

> VERB

2 When a film camera pans, it moves in a wide sweep.

3 INFORMAL
To pan something is to criticize it strongly.

panacea [ˌpænə'sɪə] **panaceas** NOUN
something that is supposed to cure everything

panache [pə'næʃ] NOUN
Something that is done with panache is done confidently and stylishly.

pancake ['pænˌkeɪk] **pancakes** NOUN
a thin, flat piece of fried batter which can be served with savoury or sweet fillings

pancreas ['pæŋkrɪəs] **pancreases** NOUN
an organ in the body situated behind the stomach. It helps the body to digest food

panda ['pændə] **pandas** NOUN
A panda or giant panda is a large animal rather like a bear that lives in China. It has black fur with large patches of white.

P

panda car **panda cars** NOUN
In Britain, a police patrol car.

pandemonium [ˌpændɪˈməʊnɪəm] NOUN
Pandemonium is a state of noisy confusion. *e.g. scenes of pandemonium*
[WORD HISTORY: from PANDEMONIUM, the capital of Hell in Milton's 'Paradise Lost']

pander [ˈpændə] **panders, pandering, pandered** VERB
If you pander to someone, you do everything they want.

pane [peɪn] **panes** NOUN
a sheet of glass in a window or door

panel [ˈpænəl] **panels** NOUN
1 a small group of people who are chosen to do something *e.g. a panel of judges*
2 a flat piece of wood that is part of a larger object *e.g. door panels*
3 A control panel is a surface containing switches and instruments to operate a machine.
panelled ADJECTIVE

panelling [ˈpænəlɪŋ] NOUN
Panelling is rectangular pieces of wood covering an inside wall.

pang [pæŋ] **pangs** NOUN
a sudden strong feeling of sadness or pain

panic [ˈpænɪk] **panics, panicking, panicked** NOUN
1 Panic is a sudden overwhelming feeling of fear or anxiety.

● THESAURUS
alarm: *She sat up in alarm.*
dismay: *She discovered to her dismay that she was pregnant.*
fear: *my fear of the dark*
fright: *To hide my fright I asked a question.*
hysteria: *mass hysteria*
terror: *She shook with terror.*

> VERB
2 If you panic, you become so afraid or anxious that you cannot act sensibly.

● THESAURUS
become hysterical: *Miss Brady became hysterical when he produced the gun.*
go to pieces: *England went to pieces when they conceded a goal.*
lose your nerve: *They lost their nerve and pulled out of the deal.*

panorama [ˌpænəˈrɑːmə] **panoramas** NOUN
an extensive view over a wide area of land *e.g. a fine panorama over the hills*
panoramic ADJECTIVE

pansy [ˈpænzɪ] **pansies** NOUN
a small garden flower with large round petals

pant [pænt] **pants, panting, panted** VERB
If you pant, you breathe quickly and loudly through your mouth.

panther [ˈpænθə] **panthers** NOUN
a large wild animal belonging to the cat family, especially the black leopard

pantomime [ˈpæntəˌmaɪm] **pantomimes** NOUN
a musical play, usually based on a fairy story and performed at Christmas

pantry [ˈpæntrɪ] **pantries** NOUN
a small room where food is kept
[WORD HISTORY: from Old French PANETERIE meaning 'bread store']

pants [pænts] PLURAL NOUN
1 Pants are a piece of underwear with holes for your legs and elastic around the waist or hips.
2 Pants are also trousers.

papaya [pəˈpaɪə] **papayas** NOUN
a fruit with sweet yellow flesh that grows in the West Indies and tropical Australia

paper [ˈpeɪpə] **papers, papering, papered** NOUN
1 Paper is a material made from wood pulp and used for writing on or wrapping things.
2 a newspaper
> PLURAL NOUN
3 Papers are official documents, for example a passport for identification.
> NOUN
4 part of a written examination
> VERB
5 If you paper a wall, you put wallpaper on it.
[WORD HISTORY: from PAPYRUS, the plant from which paper was made in ancient Egypt, Greece, and Rome]

paperback [ˈpeɪpəˌbæk] **paperbacks** NOUN
a book with a thin cardboard cover

paperwork [ˈpeɪpəˌwɜːk] NOUN
Paperwork is the part of a job that involves dealing with letters and records.

papier-mâché [ˌpæpjeɪˈmæʃeɪ] NOUN
Papier-mâché is a hard substance made from mashed wet paper mixed with glue and moulded when moist to make things such as bowls and ornaments.
[WORD HISTORY: from French PAPIER-MÂCHÉ meaning literally 'chewed paper']

paprika [ˈpæprɪkə] NOUN
Paprika is a red powder made from a kind of pepper.
[WORD HISTORY: a Hungarian word]

par [pɑː] PHRASE

1 Something that is **on a par** with something else is similar in quality or amount. *e.g. This match was on a par with the German Cup Final.*

2 Something that is **below par** or **under par** is below its normal standard.

> NOUN

3 In golf, par is the number of strokes which it is thought a good player should take for a hole or all the holes on a particular golf course.

parable ['pærəbᵊl] **parables** NOUN
(RE) a short story which makes a moral or religious point

parachute ['pærəʃuːt] **parachutes** NOUN
a circular piece of fabric attached by lines to a person or package so that they can fall safely to the ground from an aircraft

parade [pə'reɪd] **parades, parading, paraded** NOUN

1 a line of people or vehicles standing or moving together as a display

● THESAURUS
cavalcade: *a cavalcade of limousines and police motorcycles*
march: *Organizers expect 300,000 protesters to join the march.*
pageant: *a traditional Christmas pageant*
procession: *religious processions*
tattoo: *the world-famous Edinburgh military tattoo*

> VERB

2 When people parade, they walk together in a group as a display.

Paradise ['pærə,daɪs] NOUN
According to some religions, Paradise is a wonderful place where good people go when they die.
[WORD HISTORY: from Greek PARADEISOS meaning 'garden']

paradox ['pærə,dɒks] **paradoxes** NOUN
something that contains two ideas that seem to contradict each other *e.g. the paradox of having to drink in order to stay sober*
paradoxical ADJECTIVE

paraffin ['pærəfɪn] NOUN
Paraffin is a strong-smelling liquid which is used as a fuel.

paragon ['pærəgən] **paragons** NOUN
someone whose behaviour is perfect in some way *e.g. a paragon of elegance*

paragraph ['pærə,grɑːf] **paragraphs** NOUN
(ENGLISH) a section of a piece of writing. Paragraphs begin on a new line

parallel ['pærə,lɛl] **parallels** NOUN

1 Something that is a parallel to something else has similar qualities or features to it.

> ADJECTIVE

2 (MATHS) If two lines are parallel, they are the same distance apart along the whole of their length.

parallelogram [,pærə'lɛlə,græm] **parallelograms** NOUN
(MATHS) a four-sided shape in which each side is parallel to the opposite side

paralyse ['pærə,laɪz] **paralyses, paralysing, paralysed** VERB
If something paralyses you, it causes loss of feeling and movement in your body.

● THESAURUS
cripple: *He heaved his crippled leg into an easier position.*
disable: *He was disabled by polio.*

paralysis [pə'rælɪsɪs] NOUN
Paralysis is loss of the power to move.

paramedic [,pærə'medɪk] **paramedics** NOUN
a person who does some types of medical work, for example for the ambulance service

parameter [pə'ræmɪtə] **parameters** NOUN
a limit which affects the way something is done *e.g. the general parameters set by the president*

paramilitary [,pærə'mɪlɪtərɪ] ADJECTIVE
A paramilitary organization has a military structure but is not the official army of a country.

paramount ['pærə,maʊnt] ADJECTIVE
more important than anything else *e.g. Safety is paramount.*

paranoia [,pærə'nɔɪə] NOUN
Paranoia is a mental illness in which someone believes that other people are trying to harm them.

paranoid ['pærə,nɔɪd] ADJECTIVE
Someone who is paranoid believes wrongly that other people are trying to harm them.

parapet ['pærəpɪt] **parapets** NOUN
a low wall along the edge of a bridge or roof
[WORD HISTORY: from Italian PARAPETTO meaning 'chest-high wall']

paraphernalia [,pærəfə'neɪlɪə] NOUN
Someone's paraphernalia is all their belongings or equipment.
[WORD HISTORY: from Latin PARAPHERNA meaning 'personal property of a married woman']

paraphrase ['pærə,freɪz] **paraphrases, paraphrasing, paraphrased** NOUN

1 A paraphrase of a piece of writing or speech is the same thing said in a different way. *e.g. a paraphrase of the popular song*

> VERB

2 If you paraphrase what someone has said, you

P

express it in a different way.

parasite ['pærə,saɪt] **parasites** NOUN
a small animal or plant that lives on or inside a
larger animal or plant
parasitic ADJECTIVE
[WORD HISTORY: from Greek PARASITOS meaning
'someone who eats at someone else's table']

parasol ['pærə,sɒl] **parasols** NOUN
an object like an umbrella that provides shelter
from the sun

paratroops or **paratroopers**
['pærə,truːps] or [,pærə'truːpəz] PLURAL NOUN
Paratroops are soldiers trained to be dropped by
parachute.

parcel ['pɑːsᵊl] **parcels, parcelling,
parcelled** NOUN
1 something wrapped up in paper
> VERB
2 If you parcel something up, you make it into a
parcel.

parched [pɑːtʃt] ADJECTIVE
1 If the ground is parched, it is very dry and in
need of water.
2 If you are parched, you are very thirsty.

parchment ['pɑːtʃmənt] NOUN
Parchment is thick yellowish paper of very good
quality.

pardon ['pɑːdᵊn] **pardons, pardoning,
pardoned**
1 You say **pardon** or **beg your pardon** to
express surprise or apology, or when you have
not heard what someone has said.
> VERB
2 If you pardon someone, you forgive them for
doing something wrong.

pare [peə] **pares, paring, pared** VERB
When you pare fruit or vegetables, you cut off the
skin.

parent ['peərənt] **parents** NOUN
Your parents are your father and mother.
parental ADJECTIVE

● THESAURUS
father: *Her father was furious.*
mother: *the mother of two girls*
old: Australian and New Zealand; informal *a visit to
the olds*
patriarch: *a domineering patriarch*

parentage ['peərəntɪdʒ] NOUN
A person's parentage is their parents and
ancestors.

parish ['pærɪʃ] **parishes** NOUN
an area with its own church and clergyman, and
often its own elected council

parishioner [pə'rɪʃənə] **parishioners** NOUN
A clergyman's parishioners are the people who
live in his parish and attend his church.

parity ['pærɪtɪ] NOUN; FORMAL
If there is parity between things, they are equal.
*e.g. By 1943 the USA had achieved a rough parity of
power with the British.*

park [pɑːk] **parks, parking, parked** NOUN
1 a public area with grass and trees
2 a private area of grass and trees around a large
country house
> VERB
3 When someone parks a vehicle, they drive it
into a position where it can be left.
parked ADJECTIVE, **parking** NOUN

parliament ['pɑːləmənt] **parliaments**
NOUN
(HISTORY) the group of elected representatives
who make the laws of a country
parliamentary ADJECTIVE

parlour ['pɑːlə] **parlours** NOUN; OLD-
FASHIONED, INFORMAL
a sitting room
[WORD HISTORY: from Old French PARLEUR meaning
'room for talking to visitors (in a convent)']

parochial [pə'rəʊkɪəl] ADJECTIVE
concerned only with local matters *e.g. narrow
parochial interests*

parody ['pærədɪ] **parodies, parodying,
parodied** NOUN
1 an amusing imitation of the style of an author
or of a familiar situation
● THESAURUS
imitation: *I can do a pretty good imitation of him.*
satire: *a sharp satire on the American political
process*
spoof: informal *a spoof on Hollywood life*
takeoff: informal *She did a brilliant takeoff of the
Queen.*
> VERB
2 If you parody something, you make a parody of
it.

parole [pə'rəʊl] NOUN
When prisoners are given parole, they are
released early on condition that they behave
well.
[WORD HISTORY: from French PAROLE D'HONNEUR
meaning 'word of honour']

parrot ['pærət] **parrots** NOUN
a brightly coloured tropical bird with a curved
beak

parry ['pærɪ] **parries, parrying, parried**
VERB
1 If you parry a question, you cleverly avoid
answering it. *e.g. My searching questions are simply
parried with evasions.*

2 If you parry a blow, you push aside your attacker's arm to defend yourself.

parsley ['pɑːslɪ] NOUN
Parsley is a herb with curly leaves used for flavouring in cooking.

parsnip ['pɑːsnɪp] **parsnips** NOUN
a long, pointed, cream-coloured root vegetable

parson ['pɑːsᵊn] **parsons** NOUN
a vicar or other clergyman

part [pɑːt] **parts, parting, parted** NOUN
1 one of the pieces or aspects of something

● THESAURUS
bit: *a bit of paper*
fraction: *a fraction of a second*
fragment: *fragments of glass*
piece: *a piece of cheese*
portion: *Damage was confined to a small portion of the castle.*
section: *a large orchestra, with a vast percussion section*

2 one of the roles in a play or film, played by an actor or actress

3 Someone's part in something is their involvement in it. *e.g. He was jailed for eleven years for his part in the plot.*

● THESAURUS
capacity: *He has served the club in many capacities.*
duty: *My duty is to look after the animals.*
function: *Their main function is to raise capital for industry.*
involvement: *You have no proof of my involvement in anything.*
role: *the drug's role in preventing infection*

> PHRASE
4 If you **take part** in an activity, you do it together with other people.

● THESAURUS
be instrumental in: *He was instrumental in tracking down the killers.*
be involved in: *My grandparents were involved in the Methodist church.*
have a hand in: *He had a hand in three of the goals.*
join in: *I hope that everyone will be able to join in the fun.*
participate in: *They expected him to participate in the ceremony.*
play a part in: *He continued to play a part in drug operations from prison.*

> VERB
5 If things that are next to each other part, they move away from each other.

6 If two people part, they leave each other.

partake [pɑːˈteɪk] **partakes, partaking, partook, partaken** VERB; FORMAL

If you partake of food, you eat it. *e.g. She partook of the refreshments offered.*

partial ['pɑːʃᵊl] ADJECTIVE
1 not complete or whole *e.g. a partial explanation... partial success*

2 liking something very much *e.g. I'm very partial to marigolds.*

3 supporting one side in a dispute, rather than being fair and without bias
partially ADVERB

participate [pɑːˈtɪsɪˌpeɪt] **participates, participating, participated** VERB
If you participate in an activity, you take part in it.
participant NOUN, **participation** NOUN

● THESAURUS
be involved in: *HMS Cardiff was also involved in the exercise.*
engage in: *They have refused to engage in all-party talks.*
enter into: *We entered into discussions with them weeks ago.*
join in: *Their rivals refused to join in any price war.*
take part: *The oldest car taking part was built in 1907.*

participle ['pɑːtɪsɪpᵊl] **participles** NOUN
In grammar, a participle is a form of a verb used with an auxiliary verb in compound tenses and often as an adjective. English has two participles: the past participle, which describes a completed action, and the present participle, which describes a continuing action. For example in 'He has gone', 'gone' is a past participle and in 'She was winning', 'winning' is a present participle.

particle ['pɑːtɪkᵊl] **particles** NOUN
1 (SCIENCE) a basic unit of matter, such as an atom, molecule or electron

2 a very small piece of something

particular [pəˈtɪkjʊlə] **particulars**
ADJECTIVE
1 relating or belonging to only one thing or person *e.g. That particular place is dangerous.*

● THESAURUS
distinct: *The book is divided into two distinct parts.*
exact: *Do you think I could get the exact thing I want?*
express: *I bought the camera for the express purpose of taking railway photographs.*
peculiar: *This is not a problem peculiar to London.*
precise: *the precise location of the ship*
specific: *There are several specific problems to be dealt with.*

2 especially great or intense *e.g. Pay particular attention to the forehead.*

● THESAURUS
exceptional: *children with exceptional ability*

P

marked: *a marked increase in crime in the area*
notable: *Two other notable events took place last week.*
singular: *It was a goal of singular brilliance.*
special: *a special occasion*
uncommon: *Both are blessed with an uncommon ability to fix things.*

3 Someone who is particular has high standards and is not easily satisfied.

● THESAURUS
choosy: informal *Skiers should be choosy about the insurance policy they buy.*
exacting: *exacting standards of craftsmanship*
fastidious: *He was fastidious about his appearance.*
fussy: *She is very fussy about her food.*
meticulous: *meticulous attention to detail*

> PLURAL NOUN
4 Particulars are facts or details.
particularly ADVERB

parting ['pɑːtɪŋ] **partings** NOUN
an occasion when one person leaves another

partisan [,pɑːtɪˈzæn] **partisans** ADJECTIVE
1 favouring or supporting one person or group *e.g. a partisan crowd*

> NOUN
2 a member of an unofficial armed force fighting to free their country from enemy occupation *e.g. Norwegian partisans*

partition [pɑːˈtɪʃən] **partitions, partitioning, partitioned** NOUN
1 a screen separating one part of a room or vehicle from another
2 Partition is the division of a country into independent areas.

> VERB
3 To partition something is to divide it into separate parts.

partly ['pɑːtlɪ] ADVERB
to some extent but not completely

● THESAURUS
in part: formal *The levels of blood glucose depend in part on what you eat.*
in some measure: formal *Power is in some measure an act of will.*
partially: *Jo is partially sighted.*
to some degree: *These statements are, to some degree, correct.*
to some extent: *Her concern is, to some extent, understandable.*

partner ['pɑːtnə] **partners, partnering, partnered** NOUN
1 Someone's partner is the person they are married to or are living with.

● THESAURUS
husband or **wife:** *Are husbands and wives included in the invitation?*

mate: *She has found her ideal mate.*
spouse: *Anything left to your spouse is free from inheritance tax.*

2 Your partner is the person you are doing something with, for example in a dance or a game.

● THESAURUS
companion: *her travelling companion*
team-mate: *his team-mate at Ferrari*

3 Business partners are joint owners of their business.

> VERB
4 If you partner someone, you are their partner for a game or social occasion.
partnership NOUN

part of speech **parts of speech** NOUN
a particular grammatical class of word, such as 'noun' or 'adjective'

partook [pɑːˈtʊk] the past tense of **partake**

partridge ['pɑːtrɪdʒ] **partridges** NOUN
a brown game bird with a round body and a short tail

part-time ['pɑːtˌtaɪm] ADJECTIVE
involving work for only a part of the working day or week

party ['pɑːtɪ] **parties** NOUN
1 a social event held for people to enjoy themselves

● THESAURUS
celebration: *a New Year's Eve celebration*
function: *a charity function at the hotel*
gathering: *a gathering of friends and relatives*
get-together: informal *a family get-together*
hooley or **hoolie:** New Zealand *a hooley down on the beach*
reception: *a wedding reception*

2 an organization whose members share the same political beliefs and campaign for election to government

● THESAURUS
alliance: *The two parties have agreed to form an electoral alliance.*
clique: *the clique attached to Prime Minister*
coalition: *a coalition of right-wing and religious factions*
faction: *the party's small pro-European faction*
grouping: *two main political groupings pressing for independence*

3 a group who are doing something together

● THESAURUS
band: *a small but dedicated band of supporters*
crew: *a ship's crew*
gang: *a gang of criminals*
squad: *the West Indies squad to tour Australia*

team: *Each consultant has a team of doctors under him.*

unit: *the health services research unit*

4 FORMAL
one of the people involved in a legal agreement or dispute

pass [pɑːs] **passes, passing, passed** VERB

1 To pass something is to move past it.

● THESAURUS

exceed: *The demand for places at some schools exceeds the supply.*
go beyond: *Did your relationship go beyond a close friendship?*
outdo: *The Colombian fans outdid the home supporters in fervour.*
outstrip: *Demand continues to outstrip supply.*
overtake: *Britain's lottery will this year overtake Japan's as the world's biggest.*
surpass: *He was determined to surpass the achievements of his brothers.*

2 To pass in a particular direction is to move in that direction. *e.g. We passed through the gate.*

3 If you pass something to someone, you hand it to them or transfer it to them.

4 If you pass a period of time doing something, you spend it that way. *e.g. He hoped to pass the long night in meditation.*

5 When a period of time passes, it happens and finishes.

6 If you pass a test, you are considered to be of an acceptable standard.

● THESAURUS

get through: *I got through my banking exams last year.*
graduate: *He graduated in engineering.*
qualify: *I qualified as a doctor.*
succeed: *the skills and qualities needed to succeed*
<<OPPOSITE fail

7 When a new law or proposal is passed, it is formally approved.

8 When a judge passes sentence on someone, the judge states what the punishment will be.

9 If you pass the ball in a ball game, you throw, kick, or hit it to another player in your team.

> NOUN

10 the transfer of the ball in a ball game to another player in the same team

11 an official document that allows you to go somewhere

● THESAURUS

identification: *Passport control asked me if I had any further identification.*
passport: *You should take your passport with you when changing money.*

ticket: *I'm not going to renew my season ticket.*

12 a narrow route between mountains

pass away or **pass on** VERB
13 Someone who has passed away has died.

pass out VERB
14 If someone passes out, they faint.

passable ['pɑːsəbᵊl] ADJECTIVE
of an acceptable standard *e.g. a passable imitation of his dad*

passage ['pæsɪdʒ] **passages** NOUN

1 a space that connects two places

● THESAURUS

channel: *a drainage channel*
course: *the river's twisting course*
path: *A group of reporters blocked the path.*
road: *the road between Jerusalem and Bethlehem*
route: *the most direct route to the town centre*
way: *This is the way in.*

2 a long narrow corridor

● THESAURUS

aisle: *the frozen food aisle*
corridor: *They sat crowded together in the hospital corridor.*
hall: *The lights were on in the hall and in the bedroom.*
lobby: *the cramped pitch-dark lobby*

3 a section of a book or piece of music

● THESAURUS

excerpt: *an excerpt from her speech*
extract: *an extract from his new book*
quotation: *a favourite quotation from St Augustine*
section: *a section from the first movement of Beethoven's Eroica symphony*

passé ['pɑːseɪ] ADJECTIVE
no longer fashionable

passenger ['pæsɪndʒə] **passengers** NOUN
a person travelling in a vehicle, aircraft, or ship

passer-by ['pɑːsə,baɪ] **passers-by** NOUN
someone who is walking past someone or something

passing ['pɑːsɪŋ] ADJECTIVE
lasting only for a short time *e.g. a passing phase*

passion ['pæʃən] **passions** NOUN

1 Passion is a very strong feeling of physical attraction.

● THESAURUS

desire: *sexual desire*
infatuation: *Daisy's infatuation for the doctor.*
love: *our love for each other*
lust: *He is obsessed by his lust for her.*

2 Passion is also any strong emotion.

● THESAURUS

emotion: *Her voice trembled with emotion.*

P

excitement: *I was in a state of great excitement.*
fire: *His speeches were full of fire.*
intensity: *His intensity alarmed me.*
warmth: *He greeted us both with warmth and affection.*
zeal: *his zeal for teaching*

passionate ['pæʃənɪt] ADJECTIVE
expressing very strong feelings about something
passionately ADVERB

●THESAURUS
ardent: *ardent supporters of capital punishment*
emotional: *an emotional farewell*
heartfelt: *My heartfelt sympathy goes out to all the relatives.*
impassioned: *He made an impassioned appeal for peace.*
intense: *intense hatred*
strong: *Many viewers have strong opinions about violence on TV.*

passive ['pæsɪv] ADJECTIVE
1 remaining calm and showing no feeling when provoked

●THESAURUS
docile: *docile, obedient children*
receptive: *The voters had seemed receptive to his ideas.*
resigned: *She was already resigned to losing her home.*
submissive: *Most doctors want their patients to be submissive.*

> NOUN
2 In grammar, the passive or passive voice is the form of the verb in which the person or thing to which an action is being done is the grammatical subject of the sentence, and is given more emphasis as a result. For example, the passive of *The committee rejected your application* is *Your application was rejected by the committee.*
passively ADVERB, **passivity** NOUN

Passover ['pɑːsˌəʊvə] NOUN
The Passover is an eight-day Jewish festival held in spring.

passport ['pɑːspɔːt] **passports** NOUN
an official identification document which you need to show when you travel abroad

password ['pɑːsˌwɜːd] **passwords** NOUN
1 a secret word known to only a few people. It allows people on the same side to recognize a friend
2 **(ICT)** a word you need to know to get into some computers or computer files

past [pɑːst] NOUN
1 The past is the period of time before the present.

●THESAURUS
antiquity: *famous monuments of classical antiquity*

days gone by: *This brings back memories of days gone by.*
former times: *In former times he would have been clapped in irons.*
long ago: *The old men told stories of long ago.*

> ADJECTIVE
2 Past things are things that happened or existed before the present. *e.g. the past 30 years*

●THESAURUS
ancient: *ancient history*
bygone: *a bygone era*
former: *Remember him as he was in his former years.*
olden: *We were talking about the olden days on his farm.*
previous: *She has a teenage daughter from a previous marriage.*
<<OPPOSITE future

> PREPOSITION OR ADVERB
3 You use 'past' when you are telling the time. *e.g. It was ten past eleven.*
4 If you go past something, you move towards it and continue until you are on the other side. *e.g. They drove rapidly past their cottage.*

> PREPOSITION
5 Something that is past a place is situated on the other side of it. *e.g. It's just past the church there.*

●THESAURUS
beyond: *Beyond the garden was a small orchard.*
by: *She was sitting in a chair by the window.*
over: *He lived in the house over the road.*

pasta ['pæstə] NOUN
Pasta is a dried mixture of flour, eggs, and water, formed into different shapes.

paste [peɪst] **pastes, pasting, pasted** NOUN
1 Paste is a soft, rather sticky mixture that can be easily spread. *e.g. tomato paste*

> VERB
2 If you paste something onto a surface, you stick it with glue.

pastel ['pæstəl] ADJECTIVE
1 **(ART)** Pastel colours are pale and soft.

pasteurized ['pæstəˌraɪzd] also spelt
pasteurised ADJECTIVE
Pasteurized milk has been treated with a special heating process to kill bacteria.

pastime ['pɑːsˌtaɪm] **pastimes** NOUN
a hobby or something you do just for pleasure

●THESAURUS
activity: *activities range from canoeing to birdwatching*
diversion: *Finger painting is very messy but an excellent diversion.*

hobby: *My hobbies are squash and swimming.*
recreation: *Saturday afternoon is for recreation and outings.*

pastor ['pɑːstə] **pastors** NOUN
a clergyman in charge of a congregation

pastoral ['pɑːstərəl] ADJECTIVE
1 characteristic of peaceful country life and landscape *e.g. pastoral scenes*
2 relating to the duties of the clergy in caring for the needs of their parishioners *e.g. a pastoral visit*

past participle **past participles** NOUN
In grammar, the past participle of a verb is the form, usually ending in 'ed' or 'en', that is used to make some past tenses and the passive. For example 'killed' in 'She has killed the goldfish' and 'broken' in 'My leg was broken' are past participles.

pastry ['peɪstrɪ] **pastries** NOUN
1 Pastry is a mixture of flour, fat, and water, rolled flat and used for making pies.
2 a small cake

past tense NOUN
In grammar, the past tense is the tense of a verb that you use mainly to refer to things that happened or existed before the time of writing or speaking.

pasture ['pɑːstʃə] **pastures** NOUN
Pasture is an area of grass on which farm animals graze.

pasty **pasties** ADJECTIVE ['peɪstɪ]
1
Someone who is pasty looks pale and unhealthy.
> NOUN ['pæstɪ]
2
a small pie containing meat and vegetables

pat [pæt] **pats, patting, patted** VERB
1 If you pat something, you tap it lightly with your hand held flat.
> NOUN
2 a small lump of butter

patch [pætʃ] **patches, patching, patched**
NOUN
1 a piece of material used to cover a hole in something
2 an area of a surface that is different in appearance from the rest *e.g. a bald patch*
> VERB
3 If you patch something, you mend it by fixing a patch over the hole.
patch up VERB
4 If you patch something up, you mend it hurriedly or temporarily.

patchwork ['pætʃ,wɜːk] ADJECTIVE
1 A patchwork quilt is made from many small pieces of material sewn together.
> NOUN
2 Something that is a patchwork is made up of many parts.

patchy ['pætʃɪ] **patchier, patchiest**
ADJECTIVE
Something that is patchy is unevenly spread or incomplete in parts. *e.g. patchy fog on the hills*

pâté ['pæteɪ] NOUN
Pâté is a mixture of meat, fish, or vegetables blended into a paste and spread on bread or toast.

patent **patents, patenting, patented**
NOUN ['pætᵊnt]
1 an official right given to an inventor to be the only person or company allowed to make or sell a new product
> VERB ['pætᵊnt]
2 If you patent something, you obtain a patent for it.
> ADJECTIVE ['peɪtᵊnt]
3 obvious *e.g. This was patent nonsense.*
patently ADVERB

paternal [pə'tɜːnᵊl] ADJECTIVE
relating to a father *e.g. paternal pride*

paternity [pə'tɜːnɪtɪ] NOUN
Paternity is the state or fact of being a father.

path [pɑːθ] **paths** NOUN
1 a strip of ground for people to walk on
● THESAURUS
footpath: *It is accessible only by footpath.*
pathway: *a pathway leading towards the nearby river*
towpath: *He took a cycle trip along a canal towpath.*
track: *We set off over a rough mountain track.*
trail: *He was following a broad trail through the trees.*
way: *the Pennine Way*
2 Your path is the area ahead of you and the direction in which you are moving.
● THESAURUS
course: *obstacles blocking our course*
direction: *St Andrews was 10 miles in the opposite direction.*
passage: *Two men elbowed a passage through the shoppers.*
route: *All escape routes were blocked by armed police.*
way: *Get out of my way!*

pathetic [pə'θetɪk] ADJECTIVE
1 If something is pathetic, it makes you feel pity.
● THESAURUS
heartbreaking: *a heartbreaking succession of miscarriages*

P

sad: *He seemed a rather sad figure.*

2 Pathetic also means very poor or unsuccessful. *e.g. a pathetic attempt*
pathetically ADVERB

● THESAURUS
feeble: *This is a particularly feeble argument.*
lamentable: *a lamentable display by the league leaders*
pitiful: *They are paid pitiful wages.*
poor: *The flat was in a poor state of repair.*
sorry: *Their oil industry is in a sorry state.*

pathological [ˌpæθəˈlɒdʒɪkᵊl] ADJECTIVE
extreme and uncontrollable *e.g. a pathological fear of snakes*
pathologically ADVERB

pathology [pəˈθɒlədʒɪ] NOUN
Pathology is the study of diseases and the way they develop.
pathologist NOUN

pathos [ˈpeɪθɒs] NOUN
Pathos is a quality in literature or art that causes great sadness or pity.

pathway [ˈpɑːθˌweɪ] **pathways** NOUN
a path

patience [ˈpeɪʃəns] NOUN
Patience is the ability to stay calm in a difficult or irritating situation.

● THESAURUS
calmness: *calmness under pressure*
composure: *He regained his composure and went on to win the match.*
cool: slang *The big Irishman was on the verge of losing his cool.*
restraint: *They behaved with more restraint than I'd expected.*
tolerance: *a low tolerance of errors*

patient [ˈpeɪʃənt] **patients** ADJECTIVE
1 If you are patient, you stay calm in a difficult or irritating situation.

● THESAURUS
calm: *She is usually a calm and diplomatic woman.*
composed: *a composed and charming manner*
long-suffering: *long-suffering train commuters*
philosophical: *He is philosophical about the defeat.*
serene: *She looks dreamily into the distance, serene, calm and happy.*
<<OPPOSITE *impatient*

> NOUN
2 a person receiving medical treatment from a doctor or in a hospital
patiently ADVERB

● THESAURUS
case: *He is a suitable case for treatment.*
invalid: *elderly invalids*
sick person: *a ward full of very sick people*

sufferer: *asthma sufferers*

patio [ˈpætɪˌəʊ] **patios** NOUN
a paved area close to a house

patriarch [ˈpeɪtrɪˌɑːk] **patriarchs** NOUN
the male head of a family or tribe
patriarchal ADJECTIVE

patrician [pəˈtrɪʃən] ADJECTIVE; FORMAL
belonging to a family of high rank

patriot [ˈpeɪtrɪət] **patriots** NOUN
someone who loves their country and feels very loyal towards it
patriotic ADJECTIVE, **patriotism** NOUN

patrol [pəˈtrəʊl] **patrols, patrolling, patrolled** VERB
1 When soldiers, police, or guards patrol an area, they walk or drive around to make sure there is no trouble.

> NOUN
2 a group of people patrolling an area
[WORD HISTORY: from French PATOUILLER meaning 'to flounder in mud']

patron [ˈpeɪtrən] **patrons** NOUN
1 a person who supports or gives money to artists, writers, or musicians

2 The patrons of a hotel, pub, or shop are the people who use it.
patronage NOUN

patronize [ˈpætrəˌnaɪz] **patronizes, patronizing, patronized**; also spelt **patronise** VERB
1 If someone patronizes you, they treat you kindly, but in a way that suggests that you are less intelligent than them or inferior to them.

2 If you patronize a hotel, pub, or shop, you are a customer there.
patronizing ADJECTIVE

patron saint **patron saints** NOUN
The patron saint of a group of people or place is a saint who is believed to look after them.

patter [ˈpætə] **patters, pattering, pattered** VERB
1 If something patters on a surface, it makes quick, light, tapping sounds.

> NOUN
2 a series of light tapping sounds *e.g. a patter of light rain*

pattern [ˈpætᵊn] **patterns** NOUN
1 a decorative design of repeated shapes

● THESAURUS
design: *tableware decorated with a blackberry design*
motif: *a rose motif*

2 The pattern of something is the way it is usually done or happens. *e.g. a perfectly normal pattern of behaviour*

3 a diagram or shape used as a guide for making something, for example clothes
patterned ADJECTIVE

● THESAURUS
design: *They drew up the design for the house in a week.*
diagram: *Follow the diagram on page 20.*
plan: *a plan of the garden*
stencil: *flower stencils*
template: *Make a paper template of the seat of the chair.*

paunch [pɔːntʃ] **paunches** NOUN
If a man has a paunch, he has a fat stomach.

pauper ['pɔːpə] **paupers** NOUN; OLD-FASHIONED, INFORMAL
a very poor person

pause [pɔːz] **pauses, pausing, paused** VERB
1 If you pause, you stop what you are doing for a short time.

● THESAURUS
break: *They broke for lunch.*
delay: *Various problems delayed the launch.*
halt: *Striking workers halted production at the plant.*
rest: *He rested briefly before pressing on.*
take a break: *He needs to take a break from work.*
wait: *I waited to see how she responded.*

> NOUN
2 a short period when you stop what you are doing

● THESAURUS
break: *Do you want to have a little break?*
halt: *Agricultural production was brought to a halt.*
interruption: *The sudden interruption stopped her in mid-flow.*
interval: *I had a drink during the interval.*
rest: *I think he's due for a rest now.*
stoppage: *Miners have voted for a one-day stoppage next month.*

3 a short period of silence

pave [peɪv] **paves, paving, paved** VERB
When an area of ground is paved, it is covered with flat blocks of stone or concrete.

pavement ['peɪvmənt] **pavements** NOUN
a path with a hard surface at the side of a road

pavilion [pə'vɪljən] **pavilions** NOUN
a building at a sports ground where players can wash and change

paw [pɔː] **paws, pawing, pawed** NOUN
1 The paws of an animal such as a cat or bear are its feet with claws and soft pads.

> VERB
2 If an animal paws something, it hits it or scrapes at it with its paws.

pawn [pɔːn] **pawns, pawning, pawned** VERB

1 If you pawn something, you leave it with a pawnbroker in exchange for money.

> NOUN
2 the smallest and least valuable playing piece in chess

pawnbroker ['pɔːnˌbrəʊkə] **pawnbrokers** NOUN
a dealer who lends money in return for personal property left with him or her, which may be sold if the loan is not repaid on time

pawpaw ['pɔːˌpɔː] **pawpaws** NOUN the same as a **papaya**

pay [peɪ] **pays, paying, paid** VERB
1 When you pay money to someone, you give it to them because you are buying something or owe it to them.

● THESAURUS
compensate: *Farmers could be compensated for their loss of subsidies.*
honour: *The bank refused to honour the cheque.*
settle: *I settled the bill for our drinks.*
2 If it pays to do something, it is to your advantage to do it. *e.g. They say it pays to advertise.*

● THESAURUS
be advantageous: *It is easy to imagine cases where cheating is advantageous.*
be worthwhile: *He believed the operation had been worthwhile.*
3 If you pay for something that you have done, you suffer as a result.

4 If you pay attention to something, you give it your attention.

5 If you pay a visit to someone, you visit them.

> NOUN
6 Someone's pay is their salary or wages.

● THESAURUS
earnings: *his earnings as an accountant*
fee: *solicitors' fees*
income: *a modest income*
payment: *a redundancy payment*
salary: *The lawyer was paid a good salary.*
wages: *His wages have gone up.*

payable ['peɪəbəl] ADJECTIVE
1 An amount of money that is payable has to be paid or can be paid. *e.g. All fees are payable in advance.*

2 If a cheque is made payable to you, you are the person who should receive the money.

payment ['peɪmənt] **payments** NOUN
1 Payment is the act of paying money.
2 a sum of money paid

● THESAURUS
advance: *She was paid a £100,000 advance for her next two novels.*

P

deposit: *A $50 deposit is required when ordering.*
instalment: *The first instalment is payable on application.*
premium: *higher insurance premiums*
remittance: *Please make your remittance payable in sterling.*

payroll ['peɪˌrəʊl] **payrolls** NOUN
Someone who is on an organization's payroll is employed and paid by them.

PC PCs NOUN
1 In Britain, a police constable.
2 a personal computer
> ADJECTIVE
3 short for **politically correct**

PE NOUN
PE is a lesson in which gymnastics or sports are taught. PE is an abbreviation for 'physical education'.

pea [piː] **peas** NOUN
Peas are small round green seeds that grow in pods and are eaten as a vegetable.

peace [piːs] NOUN
1 Peace is a state of calm and quiet when there is no disturbance of any kind.
⬤ THESAURUS
calm: *the rural calm of Grand Rapids, Michigan*
quiet: *He wants some peace and quiet before his match.*
silence: *They stood in silence.*
stillness: *An explosion shattered the stillness of the night air.*
tranquillity: *The hotel is a haven of tranquillity.*

2 When a country is at peace, it is not at war.
peaceable ADJECTIVE
⬤ THESAURUS
armistice: *the armistice between North Korea and the United Nations*
cessation of hostilities: *a resolution calling for an immediate cessation of hostilities*
truce: *an uneasy truce between the two sides*
<<OPPOSITE *war*

peaceful ['piːsfʊl] ADJECTIVE
quiet and calm
peacefully ADVERB
⬤ THESAURUS
calm: *a calm spot amid the bustle of the city*
placid: *the placid waters of Lake Erie*
quiet: *The street was unnaturally quiet.*
serene: *a beautiful, serene park*
still: *In the room it was very still.*
tranquil: *the tranquil paradise of his native Antigua*

peach [piːtʃ] **peaches** NOUN
1 a soft, round fruit with yellow flesh and a yellow and red skin

> ADJECTIVE
2 pale pink with a hint of orange

peacock ['piːˌkɒk] **peacocks** NOUN
a large bird with green and blue feathers. The male has a long tail which it can spread out in a fan

peak [piːk] **peaks, peaking, peaked** NOUN
1 The peak of an activity or process is the point at which it is strongest or most successful.
⬤ THESAURUS
climax: *The tournament is building up to a dramatic climax.*
culmination: *The marriage was the culmination of an eight-month romance.*
high point: *The high point of this trip was a day at the races.*
zenith: *His career is now at its zenith.*

2 the pointed top of a mountain
⬤ THESAURUS
brow: *He overtook a car as he approached the brow of a hill.*
crest: *Burns was clear over the crest of the hill.*
pinnacle: *He plunged 25 metres from a rocky pinnacle.*
summit: *the first man to reach the summit of Mount Everest*
top: *the top of Mount Sinai*

> VERB
3 When something peaks, it reaches its highest value or its greatest level of success.
peaked ADJECTIVE
⬤ THESAURUS
be at its height: *when trade union power was at its height*
climax: *a tour that climaxed with a three-night stint at Wembley Arena*
come to a head: *The siege came to a head with the death of a marshal.*
culminate: *The celebration of the centenary will culminate with a dinner.*
reach its highest point: *The stockmarket reached its highest point since the 1987 crash.*

peal [piːl] **peals, pealing, pealed** NOUN
1 A peal of bells is the musical sound made by bells ringing one after another.

> VERB
2 When bells peal, they ring one after the other.

peanut ['piːˌnʌt] **peanuts** NOUN
Peanuts are small oval nuts that grow under the ground.

pear [pɛə] **pears** NOUN
a fruit which is narrow at the top and wide and rounded at the bottom

pearl [pɜːl] **pearls** NOUN
a hard, round, creamy-white object used in

jewellery. Pearls grow inside the shell of an oyster

peasant ['pɛzənt] **peasants** NOUN
a person who works on the land, especially in a poor country

peat [piːt] NOUN
Peat is dark-brown decaying plant material found in cool, wet regions. Dried peat can be used as fuel.

pebble ['pɛbəl] **pebbles** NOUN
a smooth, round stone

peck [pɛk] **pecks, pecking, pecked** VERB
1 If a bird pecks something, it bites at it quickly with its beak.
2 If you peck someone on the cheek, you give them a quick kiss.

> NOUN
3 a quick bite by a bird
4 a quick kiss on the cheek

peculiar [pɪ'kjuːlɪə] ADJECTIVE
1 strange and perhaps unpleasant

● THESAURUS
bizarre: *bizarre behaviour*
curious: *a curious mixture of the ancient and modern*
funny: *Children get some funny ideas sometimes.*
odd: *Something odd began to happen.*
queer: *There's something queer going on.*
strange: *There was something strange about the flickering blue light.*
weird: *It must be weird to be so rich.*

2 relating or belonging only to a particular person or thing *e.g. a gesture peculiar to her*
peculiarly ADVERB, **peculiarity** NOUN

● THESAURUS
distinctive: *She has a very distinctive laugh.*
distinguishing: *Does he have any distinguishing features?*
individual: *all part of her very individual personality*
personal: *cultivating their own personal style*
special: *Everyone has their own special problems or fears.*
unique: *a feature unique to humans*

pedal ['pɛdəl] **pedals, pedalling, pedalled** NOUN
1 a control lever on a machine or vehicle that you press with your foot

> VERB
2 When you pedal a bicycle, you push the pedals round with your feet to move along.

pedantic [pɪ'dæntɪk] ADJECTIVE
If a person is pedantic, they are too concerned with unimportant details and traditional rules.

peddle ['pɛdəl] **peddles, peddling, peddled** VERB

Someone who peddles something sells it.

pedestal ['pɛdɪstəl] **pedestals** NOUN
a base on which a statue stands

pedestrian [pɪ'dɛstrɪən] **pedestrians** NOUN
1 someone who is walking

> ADJECTIVE
2 Pedestrian means ordinary and rather dull. *e.g. a pedestrian performance*

pedestrian crossing pedestrian crossings NOUN
a specially marked place where you can cross the road safely

pediatrician [ˌpiːdɪə'trɪʃən] another spelling of **paediatrician**

pediatrics [ˌpiːdɪ'ætrɪks] another spelling of **paediatrics**

pedigree ['pɛdɪˌgriː] **pedigrees** ADJECTIVE
1 A pedigree animal is descended from a single breed and its ancestors are known and recorded.

> NOUN
2 Someone's pedigree is their background or ancestry.

peek [piːk] **peeks, peeking, peeked** VERB
1 If you peek at something, you have a quick look at it. *e.g. I peeked round the corner.*

● THESAURUS
glance: *He glanced at his watch.*
peep: *Children came to peep at him round the doorway.*
snatch a glimpse: *Spectators lined the route to snatch a glimpse of the Queen.*
sneak a look: *We sneaked a look at his diary.*

> NOUN
2 a quick look at something

● THESAURUS
glance: *Trevor and I exchanged a glance.*
glimpse: *Some people had waited all day to catch a glimpse of her.*
look: *She took a last look in the mirror.*
peep: *He took a peep at his watch.*

peel [piːl] **peels, peeling, peeled** NOUN
1 The peel of a fruit is the skin when it has been removed.

> VERB
2 When you peel fruit or vegetables, you remove the skin.

3 If a surface is peeling, it is coming off in thin layers.
peelings PLURAL NOUN

peep [piːp] **peeps, peeping, peeped** VERB
1 If you peep at something, you have a quick look at it.

2 If something peeps out from behind something else, a small part of it becomes visible. *e.g. a*

p

handkerchief peeping out of his breast pocket

> NOUN

3 a quick look at something

peer [pɪə] **peers, peering, peered** VERB

1 If you peer at something, you look at it very hard.

> NOUN

2 a member of the nobility

3 Your peers are the people who are of the same age and social status as yourself.

peerage ['pɪərɪdʒ] **peerages** NOUN

1 The peers in a country are called the peerage.

2 A peerage is also the rank of being a peer.

peer group peer groups NOUN

Your peer group is the people who are of the same age and social status as yourself.

peerless ['pɪəlɪs] ADJECTIVE

so magnificent or perfect that nothing can equal it *e.g. peerless wines*

peewee ['piːwiː] **peewees** NOUN

a small black-and-white Australian bird with long, thin legs

peg [pɛg] **pegs, pegging, pegged** NOUN

1 a plastic or wooden clip used for hanging wet clothes on a line

2 a hook on a wall where you can hang things

> VERB

3 If you peg clothes on a line, you fix them there with pegs.

4 If a price is pegged at a certain level, it is fixed at that level.

peggy square ['pɛgɪ] **peggy squares** NOUN

In New Zealand, a small square of knitted wool which is sewn together with others to make a rug.

pejorative [pɪ'dʒɒrətɪv] ADJECTIVE

A pejorative word expresses criticism.

pekinese [ˌpiːkə'niːz] **pekineses; also spelt pekingese** NOUN

a small long-haired dog with a flat nose

pelican ['pɛlɪkən] **pelicans** NOUN

a large water bird with a pouch beneath its beak in which it stores fish

pellet ['pɛlɪt] **pellets** NOUN

a small ball of paper, lead, or other material

pelt [pɛlt] **pelts, pelting, pelted** VERB

1 If you pelt someone with things, you throw the things with force at them.

2 If you pelt along, you run very fast.

> NOUN

3 the skin and fur of an animal

pelvis ['pɛlvɪs] **pelvises** NOUN

the wide, curved group of bones at hip-level at the base of your spine

pelvic ADJECTIVE

pen [pɛn] **pens, penning, penned** NOUN

1 a long, thin instrument used for writing with ink

2 a small fenced area in which farm animals are kept for a short time

> VERB

3 LITERARY

If someone pens a letter or article, they write it.

4 If you are penned in or penned up, you have to remain in an uncomfortably small area.

[WORD HISTORY: from Latin PENNA meaning 'feather'; writing pens used to be made from feathers]

penal ['piːnəl] ADJECTIVE

relating to the punishment of criminals

penalize ['piːnəˌlaɪz] **penalizes, penalizing, penalized; also spelt penalise** VERB

If you are penalized, you are made to suffer some disadvantage as a punishment for something.

penalty ['pɛnəltɪ] **penalties** NOUN

1 a punishment or disadvantage that someone is made to suffer

2 In soccer, a penalty is a free kick at goal that is given to the attacking team if the defending team have committed a foul near their goal.

penance ['pɛnəns] NOUN

If you do penance, you do something unpleasant to show that you are sorry for something wrong that you have done.

pence [pɛns] a plural form of **penny**

penchant ['pɒnʃɒn] **penchants** NOUN; FORMAL

If you have a penchant for something, you have a particular liking for it. *e.g. a penchant for crime*

pencil ['pɛnsəl] **pencils** NOUN

a long thin stick of wood with graphite in the centre, used for drawing or writing

pendant ['pɛndənt] **pendants** NOUN

a piece of jewellery attached to a chain and worn round the neck

pending ['pɛndɪŋ] FORMAL > ADJECTIVE

1 Something that is pending is waiting to be dealt with or will happen soon.

> PREPOSITION

2 Something that is done pending a future event is done until the event happens. *e.g. The army should stay in the west pending a future war.*

pendulum ['pɛndjʊləm] **pendulums** NOUN

a rod with a weight at one end in a clock which

swings regularly from side to side to control the clock

penetrate ['pɛnɪ,treɪt] **penetrates, penetrating, penetrated** VERB
To penetrate an area that is difficult to get into is to succeed in getting into it.
penetration NOUN

penetrating ['pɛnɪ,treɪtɪŋ] ADJECTIVE
1 loud and high-pitched *e.g. a penetrating voice*
2 having or showing deep understanding *e.g. penetrating questions*

pen friend **pen friends** NOUN
someone living in a different place or country whom you write to regularly, although you may never have met each other

penguin ['pɛŋgwɪn] **penguins** NOUN
a black and white bird with webbed feet and small wings like flippers

penicillin [,pɛnɪ'sɪlɪn] NOUN
Penicillin is a powerful antibiotic obtained from fungus and used to treat infections.

peninsula [pɪ'nɪnsjʊlə] **peninsulas** NOUN
an area of land almost surrounded by water

penis ['piːnɪs] **penises** NOUN
A man's penis is the part of his body that he uses when urinating or having sexual intercourse.

penitent ['pɛnɪtənt] ADJECTIVE
Someone who is penitent is deeply sorry for having done something wrong.
penitence NOUN

penknife ['pɛn,naɪf] **penknives** NOUN
a small knife with a blade that folds back into the handle

pennant ['pɛnənt] **pennants** NOUN
a triangular flag, especially one used by ships as a signal

penniless ['pɛnɪlɪs] ADJECTIVE
Someone who is penniless has no money.

penny ['pɛnɪ] **pennies** or **pence** NOUN
a unit of currency in Britain and some other countries. In Britain a penny is worth one-hundredth of a pound

pension ['pɛnʃən] **pensions** NOUN
a regular sum of money paid to an old or retired person

pensioner ['pɛnʃənə] **pensioners** NOUN
an old retired person who gets a pension paid by the state

pensive ['pɛnsɪv] ADJECTIVE
deep in thought

pentagon ['pɛntə,gɒn] **pentagons** NOUN
a shape with five straight sides

pentathlon [pɛn'tæθlən] **pentathlons** NOUN
a sports contest in which athletes compete in five different events

penthouse ['pɛnt,haʊs] **penthouses** NOUN
a luxurious flat at the top of a building

pent-up ['pɛnt,ʌp] ADJECTIVE
Pent-up emotions have been held back for a long time without release.

● THESAURUS
inhibited: *inhibited sexuality*
repressed: *repressed hostility*
suppressed: *Deep sleep allowed suppressed anxieties to surface.*

penultimate [pɪ'nʌltɪmɪt] ADJECTIVE
The penultimate thing in a series is the one before the last.

peony ['piːənɪ] **peonies** NOUN
a garden plant with large pink, white, or red flowers

people ['piːpəl] **peoples, peopling, peopled** PLURAL NOUN
1 People are men, women, and children.

● THESAURUS
human beings: *The disease can be transmitted to human beings.*
humanity: *crimes against humanity*
humans: *millions of years before humans appeared on earth*
mankind: *the evolution of mankind*

> NOUN
2 all the men, women, and children of a particular country or race

● THESAURUS
citizens: *the citizens of New York City*
inhabitants: *the inhabitants of Hong Kong*
population: *Africa's rapidly rising population.*
public: *the British public*

> VERB
3 If an area is peopled by a particular group, that group of people live there.

pepper ['pɛpə] **peppers** NOUN
1 a hot-tasting powdered spice used for flavouring in cooking
2 a hollow green, red, or yellow fruit eaten as a vegetable, with sweet-flavoured flesh

peppermint ['pɛpə,mɪnt] **peppermints** NOUN
Peppermint is a plant with a strong taste. It is used for making sweets and in medicine.

per [pɜː] PREPOSITION
'Per' is used to mean 'each' when expressing rates and ratios *e.g. The class meets two evenings per week.*

P

perceive [pə'siːv] **perceives, perceiving, perceived** VERB
If you perceive something that is not obvious, you see it or realize it.

per cent [pə 'sɛnt] PHRASE
You use **per cent** to talk about amounts as a proportion of a hundred. An amount that is 10 per cent (10%) of a larger amount is equal to 10 hundredths of the larger amount. *e.g. 86 per cent of Americans believe Presley is alive*
[WORD HISTORY: from Latin PER meaning 'each' and CENTUM meaning 'hundred']

percentage [pə'sɛntɪdʒ] **percentages** NOUN
(MATHS) a fraction expressed as a number of hundredths *e.g. the high percentage of failed marriages*

perceptible [pə'sɛptəbᵊl] ADJECTIVE
Something that is perceptible can be seen. *e.g. a barely perceptible nod*

perception [pə'sɛpʃən] **perceptions** NOUN
1 Perception is the recognition of things using the senses, especially the sense of sight.

2 Someone who has perception realizes or notices things that are not obvious.

3 Your perception of something or someone is your understanding of them.

perceptive [pə'sɛptɪv] ADJECTIVE
Someone who is perceptive realizes or notices things that are not obvious.
perceptively ADVERB

● THESAURUS
acute: *His relaxed exterior hides an extremely acute mind.*
astute: *He made a series of astute business decisions.*
aware: *They are politically very aware.*
penetrating: *He never stopped asking penetrating questions.*
sharp: *He has a sharp eye and an excellent memory.*

perch [pɜːtʃ] **perches, perching, perched** VERB
1 If you perch on something, you sit on the edge of it.

2 When a bird perches on something, it stands on it.
> NOUN
3 a short rod for a bird to stand on
4 an edible freshwater fish

percolator ['pɜːkəˌleɪtə] **percolators** NOUN
a special pot for making and serving coffee

percussion [pə'kʌʃən] NOUN OR ADJECTIVE
(MUSIC) Percussion instruments are musical instruments that you hit to produce sounds.
percussionist NOUN

perennial [pə'rɛnɪəl] ADJECTIVE
continually occurring or never ending *e.g. The damp cellar was a perennial problem.*

perfect perfects, perfecting, perfected
ADJECTIVE ['pɜːfɪkt]
1 of the highest standard and without fault *e.g. His English was perfect.*

● THESAURUS
expert: *There is a great deal to learn from his expert approach.*
faultless: *faultless technique*
flawless: *her flawless complexion*
masterly: *a masterly performance*
polished: *polished promotional skills*
skilled: *a skilled repair job*
<<OPPOSITE *imperfect*

2 complete or absolute *e.g. They have a perfect right to say so.*

● THESAURUS
absolute: *absolute nonsense*
complete: *The resignation came as a complete surprise.*
consummate: *He acted the part with consummate skill.*
sheer: *an act of sheer desperation*
unmitigated: *Last year's crop was an unmitigated disaster.*
utter: *utter nonsense*

3 In English grammar, the perfect tense of a verb is formed with the present tense of 'have' and the past participle of the main verb. *e.g. I have lost my home.*
> VERB [pə'fɛkt]
4 If you perfect something, you make it as good as it can possibly be.
perfectly ADVERB, **perfection** NOUN

● THESAURUS
hone: *a chance to hone their skills*
improve: *Their French has improved enormously.*
polish: *He spent time polishing the script.*
refine: *Surgical techniques are constantly being refined.*

perfectionist [pə'fɛkʃənɪst] **perfectionists** NOUN
someone who always tries to do everything perfectly

perforated ['pɜːfəˌreɪtɪd] ADJECTIVE
Something that is perforated has had small holes made in it.
perforation NOUN

perform [pə'fɔːm] **performs, performing, performed** VERB
1 To perform a task or action is to do it.

● THESAURUS
carry out: *Police believe the attacks were carried out by nationalists.*
complete: *He completed the test in record time.*
do: *He crashed trying to do a tricky manoeuvre.*
execute: *The landing was skilfully executed.*
fulfil: *Fulfil the tasks you have been allocated.*

2 (DRAMA) To perform is to act, dance, or play music in front of an audience.
performer NOUN

● THESAURUS
act: *acting in Tarantino's films*
do: *I've always wanted to do a one-man show on Broadway.*
play: *His ambition is to play the part of Dracula.*
present: *The company is presenting a new production of "Hamlet".*
put on: *The band are hoping to put on a UK show.*
stage: *The group staged their first play in the late 1970s.*

performance [pə'fɔːməns] **performances** NOUN
1 (DRAMA) an entertainment provided for an audience
2 The performance of a task or action is the doing of it.
3 Someone's or something's performance is how successful they are. *e.g. the poor performance of the American economy*

perfume ['pɜːfjuːm] **perfumes** NOUN
1 Perfume is a pleasant-smelling liquid which women put on their bodies.
2 The perfume of something is its pleasant smell.
perfumed ADJECTIVE

perfunctory [pə'fʌŋktərɪ] ADJECTIVE
done quickly without interest or care *e.g. a perfunctory kiss*

perhaps [pə'hæps] ADVERB
You use 'perhaps' when you are not sure whether something is true or possible.

● THESAURUS
conceivably: *The mission could conceivably be accomplished in a week.*
it could be: *It could be he's upset at what you said.*
maybe: *Maybe she is in love.*
possibly: *Do you think that he could possibly be right?*

peril ['perɪl] **perils** NOUN; FORMAL
Peril is great danger.
perilous ADJECTIVE, **perilously** ADVERB

perimeter [pə'rɪmɪtə] **perimeters** NOUN
(MATHS) The perimeter of an area or figure is the whole of its outer edge.

period ['pɪərɪəd] **periods** NOUN

1 a particular length of time

● THESAURUS
interval: *a long interval when no-one spoke*
spell: *a long spell of dry weather*
stretch: *an 18-month stretch in the army*
term: *a 5-year prison term*
time: *At 15 he left home for a short time.*
while: *I haven't seen him for a long while.*

2 one of the parts the day is divided into at school
3 A woman's period is the monthly bleeding from her womb.

> ADJECTIVE
4 relating to a historical period of time *e.g. period furniture*
periodic ADJECTIVE, **periodically** ADVERB

periodical [,pɪərɪ'ɒdɪkᵊl] **periodicals** NOUN
a magazine

peripheral [pə'rɪfərəl] ADJECTIVE
1 of little importance in comparison with other things *e.g. a peripheral activity*
2 on or relating to the edge of an area

periphery [pə'rɪfərɪ] **peripheries** NOUN
The periphery of an area is its outside edge.

perish ['perɪʃ] **perishes, perishing, perished** VERB
1 FORMAL
If someone or something perishes, they are killed or destroyed.
2 If fruit or fabric perishes, it rots.
perishable ADJECTIVE

perjury ['pɜːdʒərɪ] NOUN; FORMAL AND LEGAL
If someone commits perjury, they tell a lie in court while under oath.
perjure VERB

perk [pɜːk] **perks, perking, perked** NOUN
1 an extra, such as a company car, offered by an employer in addition to a salary. Perk is an abbreviation of 'perquisite'
> VERB
2 INFORMAL
When someone perks up, they become more cheerful.
perky ADJECTIVE

perm [pɜːm] **perms, perming, permed** NOUN
1 If you have a perm, your hair is curled and treated with chemicals to keep the curls for several months.
> VERB
2 To perm someone's hair means to put a perm in it.

permanent ['pɜːmənənt] ADJECTIVE
lasting for ever, or present all the time

permanently ADVERB, **permanence** NOUN

● THESAURUS
abiding: *one of his abiding interests*
constant: *Inflation is a constant threat.*
enduring: *an enduring friendship*
eternal: *the quest for eternal youth*
lasting: *We are well on our way to a lasting peace.*
perpetual: *a perpetual source of worry*
<<OPPOSITE *temporary*

permeable ['pɜːmɪəbᵊl] ADJECTIVE; FORMAL
If something is permeable, liquids are able to pass through it. *e.g. permeable rock*

permeate ['pɜːmɪ,eɪt] **permeates, permeating, permeated** VERB
To permeate something is to spread through it and affect every part of it. *e.g. The feeling of failure permeates everything I do.*

permissible [pə'mɪsəbᵊl] ADJECTIVE
allowed by the rules

permission [pə'mɪʃən] NOUN
If you have permission to do something, you are allowed to do it.

● THESAURUS
approval: *The plan will require official approval.*
assent: *He requires the assent of parliament.*
authorization: *his request for authorization to use military force*
consent: *Can she be examined without my consent?*
go-ahead: *The government gave the go-ahead for five major road schemes.*
licence: *He has given me licence to do the job as I see fit.*
<<OPPOSITE *ban*

permissive [pə'mɪsɪv] ADJECTIVE
A permissive society allows things which some people disapprove of, especially freedom in sexual behaviour.
permissiveness NOUN

permit permits, permitting, permitted
VERB [pə'mɪt]
1 To permit something is to allow it or make it possible.

● THESAURUS
allow: *Smoking will not be allowed.*
authorize: *They are expected to authorize the use of military force.*
enable: *The test should enable doctors to detect the disease early.*
give the green light to: *He has been given the green light to resume training.*
grant: *Permission was granted a few weeks ago.*
sanction: *The chairman will not sanction a big-money signing.*
<<OPPOSITE *ban*

> NOUN ['pɜːmɪt]
2 an official document which says that you are allowed to do something

● THESAURUS
authorization: *We didn't have authorization to go.*
licence: *a driving licence*
pass: *a rail pass*
passport: *My passport expires next year.*
permission: *Permission for the march has not been granted.*
warrant: *Police issued a warrant for his arrest.*

permutation [,pɜːmjʊ'teɪʃən]
permutations NOUN
one possible arrangement of a number of things

pernicious [pə'nɪʃəs] ADJECTIVE; FORMAL
very harmful *e.g. the pernicious influence of television*

peroxide [pə'rɒksaɪd] NOUN
Peroxide is a chemical used for bleaching hair or as an antiseptic.

perpendicular [,pɜːpən'dɪkjʊlə] ADJECTIVE
(MATHS) upright, or at right angles to a horizontal line
[WORD HISTORY: from Latin PERPENDICULUM meaning 'plumb line']

perpetrate ['pɜːpɪ,treɪt] **perpetrates, perpetrating, perpetrated** VERB; FORMAL
To perpetrate a crime is to commit it.
perpetrator NOUN

perpetual [pə'petjʊəl] ADJECTIVE
never ending *e.g. a perpetual toothache*
perpetually ADVERB, **perpetuity** NOUN

perpetuate [pə'petjʊ,eɪt] **perpetuates, perpetuating, perpetuated** VERB
To perpetuate a situation or belief is to cause it to continue. *e.g. The television series will perpetuate the myths.*

perplexed [pə'plekst] ADJECTIVE
If you are perplexed, you are puzzled and do not know what to do.

persecute ['pɜːsɪ,kjuːt] **persecutes, persecuting, persecuted** VERB
To persecute someone is to treat them cruelly and unfairly over a long period of time.
persecution NOUN, **persecutor** NOUN

● THESAURUS
hound: *He has been hounded by the press.*
ill-treat: *They thought Mr Smith had been ill-treating his wife.*
oppress: *Minorities here have been oppressed for generations.*
pick on: *She was repeatedly picked on by the manager.*
torment: *They were tormented by other pupils.*
torture: *He would not torture her further by trying to argue with her.*

persevere [ˌpɜːsɪˈvɪə] **perseveres, persevering, persevered** VERB
If you persevere, you keep trying to do something and do not give up.
perseverance NOUN

Persian [ˈpɜːʃən] **Persians** ADJECTIVE OR NOUN
an old word for **Iranian**, used especially when referring to the older forms of the language

persimmon [pɜːˈsɪmən] **persimmons** NOUN
a sweet, red, tropical fruit

persist [pəˈsɪst] **persists, persisting, persisted** VERB
1 If something undesirable persists, it continues to exist.
2 If you persist in doing something, you continue in spite of opposition or difficulty.
persistence NOUN, **persistent** ADJECTIVE

person [ˈpɜːsən] **people** or **persons** NOUN
1 a man, woman, or child

⬤ THESAURUS
human: *the common ancestor of humans and the great apes*
human being: *This protein occurs naturally in human beings.*
individual: *the rights and responsibilities of the individual*
living soul: *The nearest living soul was 20 miles away.*
soul: *a tiny village of only 100 souls*

2 In grammar, the first person is the speaker (I), the second person is the person being spoken to (you), and the third person is anyone else being referred to (he, she, they).

> The usual plural of *person* is *people*. *Persons* is much less common, and is used only in formal or official English.

personal [ˈpɜːsənəl] ADJECTIVE
1 Personal means belonging or relating to a particular person rather than to people in general. *e.g. my personal feeling*

⬤ THESAURUS
individual: *Divide the vegetables among four individual dishes.*
own: *My wife decided I should have my own shop.*
particular: *his own particular style of preaching*
peculiar: *her own peculiar talents*
private: *my private life*
special: *Every person will have his or her own special problems.*

2 (PE) Personal matters relate to your feelings, relationships, and health which you may not wish to discuss with other people.

personally ADVERB

personality [ˌpɜːsəˈnælɪtɪ] **personalities** NOUN
1 Your personality is your character and nature.

⬤ THESAURUS
character: *a negative side to his character*
identity: *our own sense of cultural identity*
individuality: *People should be free to express their individuality.*
make-up: *There was some fundamental flaw in his make-up.*
nature: *She trusted people. That was her nature.*
psyche: *disturbing elements of the human psyche*
2 a famous person in entertainment or sport

⬤ THESAURUS
big name: *the big names in French cinema*
celebrity: *Hollywood celebrities*
famous name: *a famous name from Inter Milan's past*
household name: *The TV series that made him a household name.*
star: *film stars*

personification [pɜːˌsɒnɪfɪˈkeɪʃən] NOUN
1 (ENGLISH) Personification is a form of imagery in which something inanimate is described as if it has human qualities. *e.g. The trees sighed and whispered as the impatient breeze stirred their branches.*
2 Someone who is the personification of some quality is a living example of that quality. *e.g. He was the personification of evil..*

personify [pɜːˈsɒnɪˌfaɪ] **personifies, personifying, personified** VERB
Someone who personifies a particular quality seems to be a living example of it.
If you personify a thing or concept, you write or speak of it as if it has human abilities or qualities, for example 'The sun is trying to come out'.

personnel [ˌpɜːsəˈnɛl] NOUN
The personnel of an organization are the people who work for it.

perspective [pəˈspɛktɪv] **perspectives** NOUN
1 A particular perspective is one way of thinking about something.
2 (ART) perspective is a method artists use to make some people and things seem further away than others

perspiration [ˌpɜːspəˈreɪʃən] NOUN
Perspiration is the moisture that appears on your skin when you are hot or frightened.

perspire [pəˈspaɪə] **perspires, perspiring, perspired** VERB
If someone perspires, they sweat.

P

persuade [pə'sweɪd] **persuades, persuading, persuaded** VERB
If someone persuades you to do something or persuades you that something is true, they make you do it or believe it by giving you very good reasons.
persuasion NOUN, **persuasive** ADJECTIVE

● THESAURUS
bring round: informal *We will do what we can to bring them round to our point of view.*
coax: *She coaxed Bobby into talking about himself.*
induce: *I would do anything to induce them to stay.*
sway: *Don't ever be swayed by fashion.*
talk into: *He talked me into marrying him.*
win over: *By the end of the day he had won over the crowd.*

pertaining [pə'teɪnɪŋ] ADJECTIVE; FORMAL
If information or questions are pertaining to a place or thing, they are about that place or thing.
e.g. issues pertaining to women

pertinent ['pɜːtɪnənt] ADJECTIVE
especially relevant to the subject being discussed
e.g. He asks pertinent questions.

perturbed [pə'tɜːbd] ADJECTIVE
Someone who is perturbed is worried.

Peruvian [pə'ruːvɪən] **Peruvians** ADJECTIVE
1 belonging or relating to Peru

> NOUN
2 someone who comes from Peru

pervade [pɜː'veɪd] **pervades, pervading, pervaded** VERB
Something that pervades a place is present and noticeable throughout it. *e.g. a fear that pervades the community*
pervasive ADJECTIVE

perverse [pə'vɜːs] ADJECTIVE
Someone who is perverse deliberately does things that are unreasonable or harmful.
perversely ADVERB, **perversity** NOUN

pervert perverts, perverting, perverted
VERB [pə'vɜːt]

1 FORMAL
To pervert something is to interfere with it so that it is no longer what it should be. *e.g. a conspiracy to pervert the course of justice*

> NOUN ['pɜːvɜːt]
2 a person whose sexual behaviour is disgusting or harmful
perversion NOUN
[WORD HISTORY: from Latin PERVERTERE meaning 'to turn the wrong way']

perverted [pə'vɜːtɪd] ADJECTIVE
1 Someone who is perverted has disgusting or unacceptable behaviour or ideas, especially sexual behaviour or ideas.

● THESAURUS
depraved: *the work of depraved and evil criminals*
deviant: *Not all drug abusers produce deviant offspring.*
immoral: *those who think that birth control is immoral*
unhealthy: *His interest developed into an unhealthy obsession.*

2 Something that is perverted is completely wrong. *e.g. a perverted sense of value*

peseta [pə'seɪtə] **pesetas** NOUN
a unit of currency formerly used in Spain

peso ['peɪsəʊ] **pesos** NOUN
the main unit of currency in several South American countries

pessimism ['pesɪˌmɪzəm] NOUN
Pessimism is the tendency to believe that bad things will happen.
pessimist NOUN

pessimistic [ˌpesɪ'mɪstɪk] ADJECTIVE
believing that bad things will happen
pessimistically ADVERB

● THESAURUS
despondent: *despondent about their children's future*
gloomy: *a gloomy view of the future*
glum: *They are not entirely glum about the car industry's prospects.*
hopeless: *Even able pupils feel hopeless about job prospects.*
<<OPPOSITE optimistic

pest [pest] **pests** NOUN
1 an insect or small animal which damages plants or food supplies

● THESAURUS
bane: *The bane of farmers across the country is the badger.*
blight: *potato blight*
scourge: *This parasitic mite is the scourge of honey bees.*

2 someone who keeps bothering or annoying you

● THESAURUS
bane: *Student journalists were the bane of my life.*
bore: *I don't enjoy his company. He's a bore and a fool.*
nuisance: *He could be a bit of a nuisance when he was drunk.*
pain: informal *She's been a real pain recently.*
pain in the neck: informal *I've always been a pain in the neck to publishers.*

pester ['pestə] **pesters, pestering, pestered** VERB
If you pester someone, you keep bothering them or asking them to do something.

● **THESAURUS**
annoy: *She kept on annoying me.*
badger: *She badgered her doctor time and again.*
bother: *We are playing a trick on a man who keeps bothering me.*
bug: informal *Stop bugging me.*
drive someone up the wall: slang *I sang in the bath and drove my sister up the wall.*
get on someone's nerves: informal *I was beginning to get on her nerves.*

pesticide ['pɛstɪ,saɪd] **pesticides** NOUN
Pesticides are chemicals sprayed onto plants to kill insects and grubs.

pet [pɛt] **pets, petting, petted** NOUN
1 a tame animal kept at home

> ADJECTIVE

2 Someone's pet theory or pet project is something that they particularly support or feel strongly about.

> VERB

3 If you pet a person or animal, you stroke them affectionately.

petal ['pɛtᵊl] **petals** NOUN
The petals of a flower are the coloured outer parts.

peter out ['piːtə] **peters out, petering out, petered out** VERB
If something peters out, it gradually comes to an end.

petite [pə'tiːt] ADJECTIVE
A woman who is petite is small and slim.

petition [pɪ'tɪʃən] **petitions, petitioning, petitioned** NOUN
1 a document demanding official action which is signed by a lot of people
2 an formal request to a court for legal action to be taken

> VERB

3 If you petition someone in authority, you make a formal request to them. *e.g. I petitioned the Chinese government for permission to visit its country.*

petrified ['pɛtrɪ,faɪd] ADJECTIVE
If you are petrified, you are very frightened.

petrol ['pɛtrəl] NOUN
Petrol is a liquid obtained from petroleum and used as a fuel for motor vehicles.

petroleum [pə'trəʊlɪəm] NOUN
Petroleum is thick, dark oil found under the earth or under the sea bed.
[WORD HISTORY: from Latin PETRA meaning 'rock' and OLEUM meaning 'oil']

petticoat ['pɛtɪ,kəʊt] **petticoats** NOUN
a piece of women's underwear like a very thin skirt

petty ['pɛtɪ] **pettier, pettiest** ADJECTIVE
1 Petty things are small and unimportant.

● **THESAURUS**
insignificant: *In 1949, Bonn was a small, insignificant city.*
measly: informal *The average bathroom measures a measly 3.5 square metres.*
trifling: *The sums involved are trifling.*
trivial: *trivial details*
unimportant: *It was an unimportant job, and paid very little.*

2 Petty behaviour consists of doing small things which are selfish and unkind.

● **THESAURUS**
cheap: *politicians making cheap political points*
mean: *I'd feel mean saying no.*
small-minded: *their small-minded preoccupation with making money*

petulant ['pɛtjʊlənt] ADJECTIVE
showing unreasonable and childish impatience or anger
petulantly ADVERB, **petulance** NOUN

petunia [pɪ'tjuːnɪə] **petunias** NOUN
a garden plant with large trumpet-shaped flowers

pew [pjuː] **pews** NOUN
a long wooden seat with a back, which people sit on in church

pewter ['pjuːtə] NOUN
Pewter is a silvery-grey metal made from a mixture of tin and lead.

pH NOUN
The pH of a solution or of the soil is a measurement of how acid or alkaline it is. Acid solutions have a pH of less than 7 and alkaline solutions have a pH greater than 7. pH is an abbreviation for 'potential hydrogen'.

phalanger [fə'lændʒə] **phalangers** NOUN
an Australasian marsupial with thick fur and a long tail. In Australia and New Zealand, it is also called a possum

phallus ['fæləs] **phalluses** NOUN
a penis or a symbolic model of a penis
phallic ADJECTIVE

phantom ['fæntəm] **phantoms** NOUN
1 a ghost

> ADJECTIVE

2 imagined or unreal *e.g. a phantom pregnancy*

pharaoh ['fɛərəʊ] **pharaohs** NOUN
The pharaohs were kings of ancient Egypt.

pharmaceutical [,fɑːmə'sjuːtɪkᵊl] ADJECTIVE
connected with the industrial production of medicines

P

pharmacist ['fɑːməsɪst] **pharmacists**
NOUN
a person who is qualified to prepare and sell medicines

pharmacy ['fɑːməsɪ] **pharmacies** NOUN
a shop where medicines are sold

phase [feɪz] **phases, phasing, phased**
NOUN
1 a particular stage in the development of something
> VERB
2 To phase something is to cause it to happen gradually in stages.

PhD PhDs NOUN
a degree awarded to someone who has done advanced research in a subject. PhD is an abbreviation for 'Doctor of Philosophy'

pheasant ['fɛzᵊnt] **pheasants** NOUN
a large, long-tailed game bird

phenomenal [fɪ'nɒmɪnᵊl] ADJECTIVE
extraordinarily great or good
phenomenally ADVERB

phenomenon [fɪ'nɒmɪnən] **phenomena**
NOUN
something that happens or exists, especially something remarkable or something being considered in a scientific way *e.g. a well-known geographical phenomenon*

The word *phenomenon* is singular. The plural form is *phenomena*.

philanthropist [fɪ'lænθrəˌpɪst]
philanthropists NOUN
someone who freely gives help or money to people in need
philanthropic ADJECTIVE, **philanthropy** NOUN

philistine ['fɪlɪˌstaɪn] **philistines** NOUN
If you call someone a philistine, you mean that they do not like art, literature, or music.

philosophical or **philosophic**
[ˌfɪlə'sɒfɪkᵊl] or [ˌfɪlə'sɒfɪk] ADJECTIVE
Someone who is philosophical does not get upset when disappointing things happen.

philosophy [fɪ'lɒsəfɪ] **philosophies** NOUN
1 Philosophy is the study or creation of ideas about existence, knowledge or beliefs.
2 a set of beliefs that a person has
philosopher NOUN
[WORD HISTORY: from Greek PHILOSOPHOS meaning 'lover of wisdom']

phlegm [flɛm] NOUN
Phlegm is a thick mucus which you get in your throat when you have a cold.

phobia ['fəʊbɪə] **phobias** NOUN
a great fear or hatred of something *e.g. The man had a phobia about flying.*

phobic ADJECTIVE

-phobia SUFFIX
'-phobia' means 'fear of' *e.g. claustrophobia*
[WORD HISTORY: from Greek PHOBOS meaning 'fear']

phoenix ['fiːnɪks] **phoenixes** NOUN
an imaginary bird which, according to myth, burns itself to ashes every five hundred years and rises from the fire again

phone [fəʊn] **phones, phoning, phoned**
NOUN
1 a piece of electronic equipment which allows you to speak to someone in another place by keying in or dialling their number
> VERB
2 If you phone someone, you key in or dial their number and speak to them using a phone.

-phone SUFFIX
'-phone' means 'giving off sound' *e.g. telephone... gramophone*
[WORD HISTORY: from Greek PHŌNĒ meaning 'voice' or 'sound']

phoney ['fəʊnɪ] **phonier, phoniest;** also spelt **phony** ADJECTIVE INFORMAL
false and intended to deceive

⬤ THESAURUS
bogus: *a bogus insurance claim*
counterfeit: *counterfeit currency*
fake: *fake certificates*
false: *a false name and address*
forged: *forged documents*
sham: *a sham marriage*
<<OPPOSITE *genuine*

photo ['fəʊtəʊ] **photos** NOUN; INFORMAL
a photograph

photo- PREFIX
'Photo-' means 'light' or 'using light' *e.g. photography*

photocopier ['fəʊtəʊˌkɒpɪə] **photocopiers**
NOUN
a machine which makes instant copies of documents by photographing them

photocopy ['fəʊtəʊˌkɒpɪ] **photocopies,
photocopying, photocopied** (LIBRARY)
NOUN
1 a copy of a document produced by a photocopier
> VERB
2 If you photocopy a document, you make a copy of it using a photocopier.

photogenic [ˌfəʊtə'dʒɛnɪk] ADJECTIVE
Someone who is photogenic always looks nice in photographs.

photograph ['fəʊtəˌɡrɑːf] **photographs,
photographing, photographed** NOUN

1 a picture made using a camera
> VERB
2 When you photograph someone, you take a picture of them by using a camera.
photographer NOUN, **photography** NOUN

photographic [ˌfəʊtəˈɡræfɪk] ADJECTIVE
connected with photography

photosynthesis [ˌfəʊtəʊˈsɪnθɪsɪs] NOUN
Photosynthesis is the process by which the action of sunlight on the chlorophyll in plants produces the substances that keep the plants alive.

phrasal verb [ˈfreɪzəl] **phrasal verbs** NOUN
a verb such as 'take over' or 'break in', which is made up of a verb and an adverb or preposition

phrase [freɪz] **phrases, phrasing, phrased**
NOUN
1 a group of words considered as a unit
> VERB
2 If you phrase something in a particular way, you choose those words to express it. *e.g. I should have phrased that better.*

physical [ˈfɪzɪkəl] ADJECTIVE
1 concerning the body rather than the mind
2 **(GEOGRAPHY)** relating to things that can be touched or seen, especially with regard to their size or shape *e.g. the physical characteristics of their machinery... the physical world*
physically ADVERB

physical education NOUN
Physical education consists of the sport that you do at school.

physician [fɪˈzɪʃən] **physicians** NOUN
a doctor

physics [ˈfɪzɪks] NOUN
Physics is the scientific study of matter, energy, gravity, electricity, heat, and sound.
physicist NOUN

physio- PREFIX
'Physio-' means to do with the body or natural functions *e.g. physiotherapy*
[WORD HISTORY: from Greek PHUSIO, from PHUEIN meaning 'to make grow']

physiology [ˌfɪzɪˈɒlədʒɪ] NOUN
Physiology is the scientific study of the way the bodies of living things work.

physiotherapy [ˌfɪzɪəʊˈθɛrəpɪ] NOUN
Physiotherapy is medical treatment which involves exercise and massage.
physiotherapist NOUN

physique [fɪˈziːk] **physiques** NOUN
A person's physique is the shape and size of their body.

pi [paɪ] NOUN
Pi is a number, approximately 3.142 and symbolized by the Greek letter π. Pi is the ratio of the circumference of a circle to its diameter.

piano [pɪˈænəʊ] **pianos** NOUN
a large musical instrument with a row of black and white keys. When the keys are pressed, little hammers hit wires to produce the different notes
pianist NOUN
[WORD HISTORY: originally called 'pianoforte', from Italian GRAVECEMBALO COL PIANO E FORTE meaning 'harpsichord with soft and loud (sounds)']

piccolo [ˈpɪkələʊ] **piccolos** NOUN
a high-pitched wind instrument like a small flute
[WORD HISTORY: from Italian PICCOLO meaning 'small']

pick [pɪk] **picks, picking, picked** VERB
1 To pick something is to choose it.
● THESAURUS
choose: *There are several options to choose from.*
decide upon: *He decided upon a career in publishing.*
hand-pick: *He was hand-picked for his job by the Admiral.*
opt for: *I think we should opt for a more cautious approach.*
select: *the party's policy of selecting candidates*
settle on: *I finally settled on an Audi TT roadster.*
2 If you pick a flower or fruit, or pick something from a place, you remove it with your fingers.
● THESAURUS
gather: *We spent the afternoon gathering berries.*
harvest: *Many farmers are refusing to harvest the cane.*
pluck: *I plucked a lemon from the tree.*
3 If someone picks a lock, they open it with a piece of wire instead of a key.
> NOUN
4 The pick of a group of people or things are the best ones in it.
● THESAURUS
elite: *the elite of women's tennis*
flower: *the flower of Polish manhood*
pride: *the hovercraft, once the pride of British maritime engineering*
5 a pickaxe

pick on VERB
6 If you pick on someone, you criticize them unfairly or treat them unkindly.
● THESAURUS
bait: *He delighted in baiting his mother.*
tease: *He teased me mercilessly about going to Hollywood.*
torment: *They were tormented by other pupils.*
> VERB **pick up**
7 If you pick someone or something up, you

collect them from the place where they are waiting.

pickaxe ['pɪkˌæks] **pickaxes** NOUN
a tool consisting of a curved pointed iron bar attached in the middle to a long handle

picket ['pɪkɪt] **pickets, picketing, picketed** VERB
1 When a group of people picket a place of work, they stand outside to persuade other workers to join a strike.

> NOUN
2 someone who is picketing a place

pickings ['pɪkɪŋz] PLURAL NOUN
Pickings are goods or money that can be obtained very easily. *e.g. rich pickings*

pickle ['pɪkəl] **pickles, pickling, pickled** NOUN
1 Pickle or pickles consists of vegetables or fruit preserved in vinegar or salt water.

> VERB
2 To pickle food is to preserve it in vinegar or salt water.

pickpocket ['pɪkˌpɒkɪt] **pickpockets** NOUN
a thief who steals from people's pockets or handbags

picnic ['pɪknɪk] **picnics, picnicking, picnicked** NOUN
1 a meal eaten out of doors

> VERB
2 People who are picnicking are having a picnic.

pictorial [pɪk'tɔːrɪəl] ADJECTIVE
relating to or using pictures *e.g. a pictorial record of the railway*

picture ['pɪktʃə] **pictures, picturing, pictured** NOUN
1 a drawing, painting, or photograph of someone or something

● THESAURUS
drawing: *She did a drawing of me.*
illustration: *Tolkien's illustrations for The Hobbit.*
painting: *his collection of Impressionist paintings*
photograph: *He wants to take some photographs of the house.*
portrait: *Velazquez's portrait of Pope Innocent X*
sketch: *pencil sketches*

2 If you have a picture of something in your mind, you have an idea or impression of it.

> PLURAL NOUN
3 If you go to the pictures, you go to see a film at the cinema.

> VERB
4 If someone is pictured in a newspaper or magazine, a photograph of them is printed in it.

5 If you picture something, you think of it and imagine it clearly. *e.g. That is how I always picture him.*

● THESAURUS
conceive of: *I can't conceive of doing work that doesn't interest me.*
imagine: *It's difficult to imagine anything coming between them.*
see: *A good idea, but can you see Taylor trying it?*
visualize: *He could not visualize her as old.*

picturesque [ˌpɪktʃə'rɛsk] ADJECTIVE
A place that is picturesque is very attractive and unspoiled.

pie [paɪ] **pies** NOUN
a dish of meat, vegetables, or fruit covered with pastry

piece [piːs] **pieces, piecing, pieced** NOUN
1 a portion or part of something

● THESAURUS
bit: *a bit of paper*
chunk: *He was accused of stealing a tin of pineapple chunks.*
fragment: *There were fragments of cork in the wine.*
part: *The engine has got only three moving parts.*
portion: *Damage was confined to a small portion of the castle.*
slice: *a slice of bread*

2 something that has been written or created, such as a work of art or a musical composition

● THESAURUS
article: *a newspaper article*
composition: *Schubert's piano compositions.*
creation: *the fashion designer's latest creations*
study: *Leonardo's studies of horsemen*
work: *In my opinion, this is Rembrandt's greatest work.*

3 a coin *e.g. a 50 pence piece*

> VERB
4 If you piece together a number of things, you gradually put them together to make something complete.

● THESAURUS
assemble: *He is assembling evidence concerning a murder.*
join: *Join all the sections together.*
mend: *I should have had it mended, but never got round to it.*
patch together: *A hasty deal was patched together.*
repair: *the cost of repairing earthquake damage*
restore: *The trust is playing a leading part in restoring old cinemas.*

piecemeal ['piːsˌmiːl] ADVERB OR ADJECTIVE
done gradually and at irregular intervals *e.g. a piecemeal approach to career management*

pier [pɪə] **piers** NOUN
a large structure which sticks out into the sea at

a seaside town, and which people can walk along

pierce [pɪəs] pierces, piercing, pierced
VERB

If a sharp object pierces something, it goes through it, making a hole.

● THESAURUS

bore: *tunnels bored into the foundations of the building*
drill: *I drilled five holes at equal distance.*
lance: *It's a painful experience having the boil lanced.*
penetrate: *The Earth's atmosphere was penetrated by a meteor.*
puncture: *The bullet punctured the skull.*

piercing ['pɪəsɪŋ] ADJECTIVE

1 A piercing sound is high-pitched and unpleasant.

2 Someone with piercing eyes seems to look at you very intensely.

piety ['paɪɪtɪ] NOUN

Piety is strong and devout religious belief or behaviour.

pig [pɪg] pigs NOUN

a farm animal kept for its meat. It has pinkish skin, short legs, and a snout

● THESAURUS

hog: *He's as fat as a hog.*
piggy: informal *These two piggies are going to market!*
porker: *a 30kg Vietnamese potbellied porker*
swine: *herds of oxen, sheep and swine*

pigeon ['pɪdʒɪn] pigeons NOUN

a largish bird with grey feathers, often seen in towns

pigeonhole ['pɪdʒɪnˌhəʊl] pigeonholes
NOUN

one of the sections in a frame on a wall where letters can be left

piggyback ['pɪgɪˌbæk] piggybacks NOUN

If you give someone a piggyback, you carry them on your back, supporting them under their knees.

piglet ['pɪglɪt] piglets NOUN

a young pig

pigment ['pɪgmənt] pigments NOUN

a substance that gives something a particular colour
pigmentation NOUN

pigsty ['pɪgˌstaɪ] pigsties NOUN

a hut with a small enclosed area where pigs are kept

pigtail ['pɪgˌteɪl] pigtails NOUN

a length of plaited hair

pike [paɪk] pikes NOUN

1 a large freshwater fish of northern countries with strong teeth

2 a medieval weapon consisting of a pointed metal blade attached to a long pole

pilchard ['pɪltʃəd] pilchards NOUN

a small sea fish

pile [paɪl] piles, piling, piled NOUN

1 a quantity of things lying one on top of another

● THESAURUS

heap: *a compost heap*
hoard: *a hoard of jewels*
mound: *The bulldozers piled up hug mounds of dirt.*
mountain: *They have mountains of coffee to sell.*
stack: *a stack of magazines on the table*

2 the soft surface of a carpet consisting of many threads standing on end

● THESAURUS

down: *The whole plant is covered with fine down.*
fur: *This creature's fur is short and dense.*
hair: *He has black hair.*
nap: *The cotton is lightly brushed to heighten the nap.*

> PLURAL NOUN

3 Piles are painful swellings that appear in the veins inside or just outside a person's anus.

> VERB

4 If you pile things somewhere, you put them one on top of the other.

● THESAURUS

heap: *She heaped more carrots onto his plate.*
hoard: *They've begun to hoard petrol and food.*
stack: *They are stacked neatly in piles of three.*

pile-up ['paɪlˌʌp] pile-ups NOUN; INFORMAL

a road accident involving several vehicles

pilfer ['pɪlfə] pilfers, pilfering, pilfered
VERB

Someone who pilfers steals small things over a period of time.
[WORD HISTORY: from Old French PELFRE meaning 'booty']

pilgrim ['pɪlgrɪm] pilgrims NOUN

(RE) a person who travels to a holy place for religious reasons
pilgrimage NOUN

pill [pɪl] pills NOUN

1 a small, hard tablet of medicine that you swallow

2 The pill is a type of drug that women can take regularly to prevent pregnancy.
[WORD HISTORY: from Latin PILULA meaning 'little ball']

pillage ['pɪlɪdʒ] pillages, pillaging, pillaged VERB

P

If a group of people pillage a place, they steal from it using violence.

pillar ['pɪlə] **pillars** NOUN

1 a tall, narrow, solid structure, usually supporting part of a building

2 Someone who is described as a pillar of a particular group is an active and important member of it. *e.g. a pillar of the Church*

pillar box pillar boxes NOUN

a red cylinder or box in which you post letters

pillory ['pɪlərɪ] **pillories, pillorying, pilloried** VERB

If someone is pilloried, they are criticized severely by a lot of people.

pillow ['pɪləʊ] **pillows** NOUN

a rectangular cushion which you rest your head on when you are in bed

pillowcase ['pɪləʊˌkeɪs] **pillowcases** NOUN

a cover for a pillow which can be removed and washed

pilot ['paɪlət] **pilots, piloting, piloted** NOUN

1 a person who is trained to fly an aircraft

2 a person who goes on board ships to guide them through local waters to a port

> VERB

3 To pilot something is to control its movement or to guide it.

> NOUN

4 a small test of a scheme or product, done to see if it would be successful

pimp [pɪmp] **pimps** NOUN

a man who finds clients for prostitutes and takes a large part of their earnings

pimple ['pɪmpəl] **pimples** NOUN

a small spot on the skin

pimply ADJECTIVE

PIN [pɪn] **PINs** NOUN

an abbreviation for 'personal identification number': a number used by the holder of a cash card or credit card

pin [pɪn] **pins, pinning, pinned** NOUN

1 a thin, pointed piece of metal used to fasten together things such as pieces of fabric or paper

> VERB

2 If you pin something somewhere, you fasten it there with a pin or a drawing pin.

3 If someone pins you in a particular position, they hold you there so that you cannot move.

4 If you try to pin something down, you try to get or give a clear and exact description of it or statement about it.

pinafore ['pɪnəˌfɔː] **pinafores** NOUN

a dress with no sleeves, worn over a blouse

pincers ['pɪnsəz] PLURAL NOUN

1 Pincers are a tool used for gripping and pulling things. They consist of two pieces of metal hinged in the middle.

2 The pincers of a crab or lobster are its front claws.

pinch [pɪntʃ] **pinches, pinching, pinched** VERB

1 If you pinch something, you squeeze it between your thumb and first finger.

2 INFORMAL

If someone pinches something, they steal it.

> NOUN

3 A pinch of something is the amount that you can hold between your thumb and first finger. *e.g. a pinch of salt*

pinched [pɪntʃt] ADJECTIVE

If someone's face is pinched, it looks thin and pale.

pine [paɪn] **pines, pining, pined** NOUN

1 A pine or pine tree is an evergreen tree with very thin leaves.

> VERB

2 If you pine for something, you are sad because you cannot have it.

pineapple ['paɪnˌæpəl] **pineapples** NOUN

a large, oval fruit with sweet, yellow flesh and a thick, lumpy brown skin

ping-pong ['pɪŋˌpɒŋ] NOUN the same as **table tennis**

pink [pɪŋk] **pinker, pinkest** ADJECTIVE

pale reddish-white

pinnacle ['pɪnəkəl] **pinnacles** NOUN

1 a tall pointed piece of stone or rock

2 The pinnacle of something is its best or highest level. *e.g. the pinnacle of his career*

pinpoint ['pɪnˌpɔɪnt] **pinpoints, pinpointing, pinpointed** VERB

If you pinpoint something, you explain or discover exactly what or where it is.

pinstripe ['pɪnˌstraɪp] ADJECTIVE

Pinstripe cloth has very narrow vertical stripes.

pint [paɪnt] **pints** NOUN

a unit of liquid volume equal to one eighth of a gallon or about 0.568 litres

pioneer [ˌpaɪəˈnɪə] **pioneers, pioneering, pioneered** NOUN

1 Someone who is a pioneer in a particular activity is one of the first people to develop it.

> VERB

2 Someone who pioneers a new process or invention is the first person to develop it.

pious ['paɪəs] ADJECTIVE
very religious and moral

pip [pɪp] **pips** NOUN
Pips are the hard seeds in a fruit.

pipe [paɪp] **pipes, piping, piped** NOUN
1 a long, hollow tube through which liquid or gas
can flow

2 an object used for smoking tobacco. It consists
of a small hollow bowl attached to a tube
> VERB
3 To pipe a liquid or gas somewhere is to transfer
it through a pipe.

pipeline ['paɪp,laɪn] **pipelines** NOUN
a large underground pipe that carries oil or gas
over a long distance

piper ['paɪpə] **pipers** NOUN
a person who plays the bagpipes

piping ['paɪpɪŋ] NOUN
Piping consists of pipes and tubes.

piranha [pɪ'rɑːnjə] **piranhas** NOUN
a small, fierce fish with sharp teeth
[WORD HISTORY: a Portuguese word]

pirate ['paɪrɪt] **pirates** NOUN
Pirates were sailors who attacked and robbed
other ships.

pirouette [,pɪruˈɛt] **pirouettes** NOUN
In ballet, a pirouette is a fast spinning step done
on the toes.

Pisces ['paɪsiːz] NOUN
Pisces is the twelfth sign of the zodiac,
represented by two fish. People born between
February 19th and March 20th are born under
this sign.
[WORD HISTORY: the plural of Latin PISCIS meaning
'a fish']

pistil ['pɪstɪl] **pistils** NOUN
in a flower, the pistil is the female reproductive
part made up of the carpel or two or more carpels
fused together

pistol ['pɪstəl] **pistols** NOUN
a small gun held in the hand

piston ['pɪstən] **pistons** NOUN
a cylinder or disc that slides up and down inside a
tube. Pistons make parts of engines move

pit [pɪt] **pits** NOUN
1 a large hole in the ground
 THESAURUS
chasm: *The coach plunged down the chasm.*
hole: *The builders had cut holes into the soft stone.*
pothole: *She was seriously injured when she fell 90
feet down a pothole.*

2 a small hollow in the surface of something

3 a coal mine

pitch [pɪtʃ] **pitches, pitching, pitched**
NOUN
1 (PE) an area of ground marked out for playing
a game such as football

2 (MUSIC) The pitch of a sound is how high or
low it is.

3 a black substance used in road tar and also for
making boats and roofs waterproof
> VERB
4 If you pitch something somewhere, you throw
it with a lot of force.

5 If you pitch something at a particular level of
difficulty, you set it at that level. *e.g. Any film must
be pitched at a level to suit its intended audience.*

6 When you pitch a tent, you fix it in an upright
position.

pitcher ['pɪtʃə] **pitchers** NOUN
a large jug

pitfall ['pɪt,fɔːl] **pitfalls** NOUN
The pitfalls of a situation are its difficulties or
dangers.

pith [pɪθ] NOUN
the white substance between the outer skin and
the flesh of an orange or lemon

pitiful ['pɪtɪfʊl] ADJECTIVE
Someone or something that is pitiful is in such a
sad or weak situation that you feel pity for them.

pittance ['pɪtəns] NOUN
a very small amount of money

pitted ['pɪtɪd] ADJECTIVE
covered in small hollows *e.g. Nails often become
pitted.*

pity ['pɪtɪ] **pities, pitying, pitied** VERB
1 If you pity someone, you feel very sorry for
them.
 THESAURUS
feel for: *She cried on the phone and I really felt for
her.*
feel sorry for: *This is my biggest win but I don't feel
sorry for the bookies.*
sympathize with: *I sympathize with you for your
loss.*
> NOUN
2 Pity is a feeling of being sorry for someone.
 THESAURUS
charity: *They showed a lack of charity and
understanding to her.*
compassion: *his compassion for a helpless woman*
kindness: *He was treated with kindness by
numerous officials.*
mercy: *Neither side showed any mercy.*
sympathy: *We expressed our sympathy for her loss.*

P

understanding: *We would like to thank them for their patience and understanding.*

3 If you say that it is a pity about something, you are expressing your disappointment about it.

THESAURUS
crime: *informal It would be a crime to travel to Australia and not stop in Sydney.*
crying shame: *It would be a crying shame to split up a winning partnership.*
shame: *It's a shame it had to close.*

pivot ['pɪvət] **pivots, pivoting, pivoted** VERB
1 If something pivots, it balances or turns on a central point. *e.g. The keel pivots on a large stainless steel pin.*
> NOUN
2 the central point on which something balances or turns
pivotal ADJECTIVE

pixie ['pɪksɪ] **pixies** NOUN
an imaginary little creature in fairy stories

pizza ['piːtsə] **pizzas** NOUN
a flat piece of dough covered with cheese, tomato, and other savoury food

placard ['plækɑːd] **placards** NOUN
a large notice carried at a demonstration or displayed in a public place

placate [plə'keɪt] **placates, placating, placated** VERB
If you placate someone, you stop them feeling angry by doing something to please them.

place [pleɪs] **places, placing, placed** NOUN
1 any point, building, or area
THESAURUS
area: *a picnic area*
location: *The first thing he looked at was his office's location.*
point: *The pain originated from a point in his right thigh.*
position: *the ship's position*
site: *a bat sanctuary with special nesting sites*
spot: *the island's top tourist spots*
2 the position where something belongs *e.g. She set the holder in its place on the table.*
3 a space at a table set with cutlery where one person can eat
4 If you have a place in a group or at a college, you are a member or are accepted as a student.
5 a particular point or stage in a sequence of things *e.g. second place in the race*
> PHRASE
6 When something **takes place**, it happens.
THESAURUS
come about: *That came about when we went to Glastonbury last year.*

go on: *This has been going on for around a year.*
happen: *We cannot say for sure what will happen.*
occur: *The crash occurred when the crew shut down the wrong engine.*
> VERB
7 If you place something somewhere, you put it there.
THESAURUS
deposit: *Imagine if you were suddenly deposited on a desert island.*
locate: *the best city in which to locate a business*
plant: *So far no one has admitted to planting the bomb.*
position: *plants which are carefully positioned in the alcove*
put: *She put the photograph on her desk.*
situate: *The hotel is situated next to the railway station.*
8 If you place an order, you order something.

placebo [plə'siːbəʊ] **placebos** NOUN
a substance given to a patient in place of a drug and from which, though it has no active ingredients, the patient may imagine they get some benefit

placenta [plə'sɛntə] **placentas** NOUN
The placenta is the mass of veins and tissues in the womb of a pregnant woman or animal. It gives the foetus food and oxygen.

placid ['plæsɪd] ADJECTIVE
calm and not easily excited or upset
placidly ADVERB

plagiarism ['pleɪdʒə,rɪzəm] NOUN
Plagiarism is copying someone else's work or ideas and pretending that it is your own.
plagiarist NOUN, **plagiarize** VERB
[WORD HISTORY: from Latin PLAGIARUS meaning 'plunderer']

plague [pleɪg] **plagues, plaguing, plagued** NOUN
1 Plague is a very infectious disease that kills large numbers of people.
2 A plague of unpleasant things is a large number of them occurring at the same time. *e.g. a plague of rats*
> VERB
3 If problems plague you, they keep causing you trouble.

plaice [pleɪs] NOUN
an edible European flat fish

plaid [plæd] **plaids** NOUN
Plaid is woven material with a tartan design.

plain [pleɪn] **plainer, plainest; plains** ADJECTIVE
1 very simple in style with no pattern or decoration *e.g. plain walls*

austere: *The church was austere and simple.*
bare: *bare wooden floors*
spartan: *her spartan home in a tiny village*
stark: *a stark white, characterless fireplace*
<<OPPOSITE *fancy*

2 obvious and easy to recognize or understand
e.g. plain language

THESAURUS
clear: *The book is clear and readable.*
comprehensible: *a comprehensible manual*
distinct: *a distinct smell of burning coal*
evident: *His footprints were clearly evident in the heavy dust.*
obvious: *an obvious injustice*
unmistakable: *His voice was unmistakable.*

3 A person who is plain is not at all beautiful or attractive.

> ADVERB
4 You can use 'plain' before a noun or adjective to emphasize it. *e.g. You were just plain stupid.*

> NOUN
a large, flat area of land with very few trees
plainly ADVERB

plaintiff ['pleɪntɪf] **plaintiffs** NOUN
a person who has brought a court case against another person

plait [plæt] **plaits, plaiting, plaited** VERB
1 If you plait three lengths of hair or rope together, you twist them over each other in turn to make one thick length.

> NOUN
2 a length of hair that has been plaited

plan [plæn] **plans, planning, planned** NOUN
1 a method of achieving something that has been worked out beforehand

THESAURUS
method: *He did it by his usual method.*
proposal: *The proposals need careful study.*
scheme: *The scheme was an abject failure.*
strategy: *What should our marketing strategy achieve?*
system: *the advantages of the new system over the old one*

2 a detailed diagram or drawing of something that is to be made

THESAURUS
blueprint: *a blueprint for a new bathroom*
diagram: *a circuit diagram*
layout: *He tried to recall the layout of the farmhouse.*
scale drawing: *scale drawings of locomotives*

> VERB
3 If you plan something, you decide in detail what it is to be and how to do it.

THESAURUS
arrange: *We arranged a social event once a year.*
design: *He approached me to design the restaurant.*
devise: *We devised a plan.*
draft: *The legislation was drafted by the committee.*
formulate: *He formulated his plan for escape.*

4 If you are planning to do something, you intend to do it. *e.g. They plan to marry in the summer.*

plane [pleɪn] **planes, planing, planed** NOUN
1 a vehicle with wings and engines that enable it to fly

2 a flat surface

3 You can refer to a particular level of something as a particular plane. *e.g. to take the rock and roll concert to a higher plane*

4 a tool with a flat bottom with a sharp blade in it. You move it over a piece of wood to remove thin pieces from the surface

> VERB
5 If you plane a piece of wood, you smooth its surface with a plane.

planet ['plænɪt] **planets** NOUN
a round object in space which moves around the sun or a star and is lit by light from it
planetary ADJECTIVE

plank [plæŋk] **planks** NOUN
a long rectangular piece of wood

plankton ['plæŋktən] NOUN
Plankton is a layer of tiny plants and animals that live just below the surface of a sea or lake.

plant [plɑːnt] **plants, planting, planted** NOUN
1 a living thing that grows in the earth and has stems, leaves, and roots

2 a factory or power station *e.g. a giant bottling plant*

> VERB
3 When you plant a seed or plant, you put it into the ground.

4 If you plant something somewhere, you put it there firmly or secretly.

plantation [plæn'teɪʃən] **plantations** NOUN
1 a large area of land where crops such as tea, cotton, or sugar are grown

2 a large number of trees planted together

plaque [plæk] **plaques** NOUN
1 a flat piece of metal which is fixed to a wall and has an inscription in memory of a famous person or event

2 Plaque is a substance which forms around your teeth and consists of bacteria, saliva, and food.

plasma ['plæzmə] NOUN
Plasma is the clear fluid part of blood.

plaster ['plɑːstə] **plasters, plastering, plastered** NOUN

1 Plaster is a paste made of sand, lime, and water, which is used to form a smooth surface for inside walls and ceilings.

2 a strip of sticky material with a small pad, used for covering cuts on your body

> VERB

3 To plaster a wall is to cover it with a layer of plaster.

> PHRASE

4 If your arm or leg is **in plaster**, it has a plaster cast on it to protect a broken bone.

plasterer NOUN

plastered ['plɑːstəd] ADJECTIVE

1 If something is plastered to a surface, it is stuck there.

2 If something is plastered with things, they are all over its surface.

plastic ['plæstɪk] **plastics** NOUN

1 Plastic is a substance made by a chemical process that can be moulded when soft to make a wide range of objects.

> ADJECTIVE

2 made of plastic

plastic surgery NOUN

Plastic surgery is surgery to replace or repair damaged skin or to improve a person's appearance by changing the shape of their , features.

plate [pleɪt] **plates** NOUN

1 a flat dish used to hold food

2 a flat piece of metal or other hard material used for various purposes in machinery or building *e.g. heavy steel plates used in shipbuilding*

plateau ['plætəʊ] **plateaus** or **plateaux** NOUN

a large area of high and fairly flat land

plated ['pleɪtɪd] ADJECTIVE

Metal that is plated is covered with a thin layer of silver or gold.

platform ['plætfɔːm] **platforms** NOUN

1 a raised structure on which someone or something can stand

2 the raised area in a railway station where passengers get on and off trains

platinum ['plætɪnəm] NOUN

Platinum is a valuable silver-coloured metal.

platitude ['plætɪˌtjuːd] **platitudes** NOUN

a statement made as if it were significant but which has become meaningless or boring because it has been used so many times before

platonic [plə'tɒnɪk] ADJECTIVE

A platonic relationship is simply one of friendship and does not involve sexual attraction.

[WORD HISTORY: from the name of the Greek philospher Plato]

platoon [plə'tuːn] **platoons** NOUN

a small group of soldiers, commanded by a lieutenant

platter ['plætə] **platters** NOUN

a large serving plate

platypus ['plætɪpəs] **platypuses** NOUN

A platypus or duck-billed platypus is an Australian mammal which lives in rivers. It has brown fur, webbed feet, and a snout like a duck.

[WORD HISTORY: from Greek PLATUS meaning 'flat' and POUS meaning 'foot']

plaudits ['plɔːdɪts] PLURAL NOUN; FORMAL

Plaudits are expressions of admiration.

plausible ['plɔːzəbᵊl] ADJECTIVE

An explanation that is plausible seems likely to be true.

plausibility NOUN

play [pleɪ] **plays, playing, played** VERB

1 When children play, they take part in games or use toys.

● THESAURUS

amuse oneself: *He amused himself by rollerskating round the building.*

entertain oneself: *I used to entertain myself by building model planes.*

frolic: *Tourists sunbathe and frolic in the ocean.*

have fun: *having fun with your friends*

2 When you play a sport or match, you take part in it.

● THESAURUS

compete: *Eight entrants competed for the prize.*

participate: *Sixteen teams participated in the tournament.*

take on: *Scotland take on South Africa at Murrayfield.*

take part: *The teams taking part are cricket's bitterest enemies.*

vie with: *Arsenal are vying with Leeds for second spot in the league.*

3 If an actor plays a character in a play or film, he or she performs that role.

4 If you play a musical instrument, you produce music from it.

5 If you play a record or tape, you listen to it.

> NOUN

6 a piece of drama performed in the theatre or on television

player NOUN

● THESAURUS

comedy: *a romantic comedy*

drama: *He also wrote radio dramas and film scripts.*

pantomime: *He regularly performs in Christmas pantomimes.*

show: *a one-woman show*

tragedy: *Shakespeare's tragedies.*

playboy ['pleɪˌbɔɪ] **playboys** NOUN
a rich man who spends his time enjoying himself

playful ['pleɪfʊl] ADJECTIVE

1 friendly and light-hearted *e.g. a playful kiss on the tip of his nose*

2 lively *e.g. a playful puppy*
playfully ADVERB

playground ['pleɪˌɡraʊnd] **playgrounds**
NOUN
a special area for children to play in

playgroup ['pleɪˌɡruːp] **playgroups** NOUN
an informal kind of school for very young children where they learn by playing

playing card ['pleɪɪŋ] **playing cards** NOUN
Playing cards are cards printed with numbers or pictures which are used to play various games.

playing field playing fields NOUN
an area of grass where people play sports

playwright ['pleɪˌraɪt] **playwrights** NOUN
(DRAMA AND ENGLISH) a person who writes plays

plaza ['plɑːzə] **plazas** NOUN
an open square in a city

plea [pliː] **pleas** NOUN

1 an emotional request *e.g. a plea for help*

2 In a court of law, someone's plea is their statement that they are guilty or not guilty.

plead [pliːd] **pleads, pleading, pleaded**
VERB

1 If you plead with someone, you ask them in an intense emotional way to do something.

● THESAURUS

appeal: *The United Nations appealed for aid from the international community.*

ask: *I've asked you time and again not to do that.*

beg: *We are not going to beg for help any more.*

beseech: literary *She beseeched him to show mercy.*

implore: *Opposition leaders implored the president to break the deadlock.*

2 When a person pleads guilty or not guilty, they state in court that they are guilty or not guilty of a crime.

pleasant ['plezᵊnt] ADJECTIVE

1 enjoyable or attractive

● THESAURUS

agreeable: *workers in more agreeable and better paid occupations*

delightful: *It was the most delightful garden I'd ever seen.*

enjoyable: *an enjoyable meal*

lekker: South African; slang *a lekker little town*

lovely: *He had a lovely voice.*

nice: *It's nice to be here together again.*

pleasurable: *He found sailing more pleasurable than skiing.*

<<OPPOSITE *unpleasant*

2 friendly or charming
pleasantly ADVERB

● THESAURUS

affable: *He is an affable and approachable man.*

amiable: *She had been surprised at how amiable and polite he had seemed.*

charming: *He can be charming to his friends.*

friendly: *She has a friendly relationship with her customers.*

likable or **likeable:** *He's an immensely likable man.*

nice: *He's a nice fellow, very quiet and courteous.*

<<OPPOSITE *unpleasant*

please [pliːz] **pleases, pleasing, pleased**

1 You say please when you are asking someone politely to do something.

> VERB

2 If something pleases you, it makes you feel happy and satisfied.

● THESAURUS

amuse: *The thought seemed to amuse him.*

charm: *He charmed all of us.*

delight: *music that has delighted audiences all over the world*

entertain: *Children's TV not only entertains but also teaches.*

pleased [pliːzd] ADJECTIVE
happy or satisfied

● THESAURUS

contented: *She had a contented smile on her face.*

delighted: *I know he will be delighted to see you.*

glad: *I'm glad he changed his mind in the end.*

happy: *She's a confident and happy child.*

satisfied: *satisfied customers*

pleasing ['pliːzɪŋ] ADJECTIVE
attractive, satisfying, or enjoyable *e.g. a pleasing appearance*

pleasure ['pleʒə] **pleasures** NOUN

1 Pleasure is a feeling of happiness, satisfaction, or enjoyment.

● THESAURUS

amusement: *Her impersonations provided great amusement.*

enjoyment: *her enjoyment of the countryside*

happiness: *My happiness helped to erase the bad memories.*

joy: *tears of joy*

satisfaction: *job satisfaction*

2 an activity that you enjoy
pleasurable ADJECTIVE

P

pleat [pliːt] **pleats** NOUN
a permanent fold in fabric made by folding one part over another

plebiscite ['plɛbɪˌsaɪt] **plebiscites** NOUN; FORMAL
a vote on a matter of national importance in which all the voters in a country can take part
[WORD HISTORY: from Latin PLEBISCITUM meaning 'decree of the people']

pledge [plɛdʒ] **pledges, pledging, pledged** NOUN
1 a solemn promise

> VERB

2 If you pledge something, you promise that you will do it or give it.

plentiful ['plɛntɪfʊl] ADJECTIVE
existing in large numbers or amounts and readily available e.g. Fruit and vegetables were plentiful.
plentifully ADVERB

⬤ THESAURUS
abundant: Birds are abundant in the tall vegetation.
ample: The design created ample space for a large kitchen.
bountiful: a bountiful harvest of fruits and vegetables
copious: He attended the lectures and took copious notes.
infinite: an infinite variety of landscapes
<<OPPOSITE scarce

plenty ['plɛntɪ] NOUN
If there is plenty of something, there is a lot of it.

⬤ THESAURUS
enough: Have you had enough?
great deal: I've spent a great deal of time on this project.
heaps: informal You have heaps of time.
lots: informal He has made lots of amendments to the script.
plethora: a plethora of new products

plethora ['plɛθərə] NOUN
A plethora of something is an amount that is greater than you need.

pleurisy ['plʊərɪsɪ] NOUN
Pleurisy is a serious illness in which a person's lungs become inflamed and breathing is difficult.

pliable ['plaɪəbᵊl] ADJECTIVE
1 If something is pliable, you can bend it without breaking it.
2 Someone who is pliable can be easily influenced or controlled.

pliers ['plaɪəz] PLURAL NOUN
Pliers are a small tool with metal jaws for holding small objects and bending wire.

plight [plaɪt] NOUN
Someone's plight is the very difficult or dangerous situation that they are in. e.g. the plight of the refugees

plinth [plɪnθ] **plinths** NOUN
a block of stone on which a statue or pillar stands

plod [plɒd] **plods, plodding, plodded** VERB
If you plod somewhere, you walk there slowly and heavily.

plonk [plɒŋk] **plonks, plonking, plonked** VERB
If you plonk something down, you put it down heavily and carelessly.

plop [plɒp] **plops, plopping, plopped** NOUN
1 a gentle sound made by something light dropping into a liquid

> VERB

2 If something plops into a liquid, it drops into it with a gentle sound.

plot [plɒt] **plots, plotting, plotted** NOUN
1 a secret plan made by a group of people

⬤ THESAURUS
conspiracy: a conspiracy to steal nuclear missiles
intrigue: political intrigues
plan: a secret government plan to build a nuclear waste dump
scheme: an elaborate scheme to dupe the police

2 The plot of a novel or play is the story.

⬤ THESAURUS
narrative: a fast-moving narrative
scenario: The movie's scenario is nonsensical.
story: I doubt the appeal of cinematic sex without a story.
story line: It sounds like a typical story line from a soap opera.

3 a small piece of land

> VERB

4 If people plot to do something, they plan it secretly. e.g. His family is plotting to disinherit him.

⬤ THESAURUS
conspire: The countries had secretly conspired to acquire nuclear weapons.
hatch: He hatched a plot to murder his wife.
plan: I suspect they are secretly planning to raise taxes.
scheme: He claimed that they were scheming against him.

5 If someone plots the course of a plane or ship on a map, or plots a graph, they mark the points in the correct places.

plough [plaʊ] **ploughs, ploughing, ploughed** NOUN
1 a large farming tool that is pulled across a field to turn the soil over before planting seeds

> VERB

2 When someone ploughs land, they use a plough to turn over the soil.

ploy [plɔɪ] **ploys** NOUN
a clever plan or way of behaving in order to get something that you want

pluck [plʌk] **plucks, plucking, plucked**
VERB

1 To pluck a fruit or flower is to remove it with a sharp pull.

2 To pluck a chicken or other dead bird means to pull its feathers out before cooking it.

3 When you pluck a stringed instrument, you pull the strings and let them go.

> NOUN

4 Pluck is courage.
plucky ADJECTIVE

plug [plʌg] **plugs, plugging, plugged** NOUN

1 a plastic object with metal prongs that can be pushed into a socket to connect an appliance to the electricity supply

2 a disc of rubber or metal with which you block up the hole in a sink or bath

⬤ THESAURUS
bung: *Remove the bung from the barrel.*
cork: *the sound of popping champagne corks*
stopper: *a bottle sealed with a cork stopper*

> VERB

3 If you plug a hole, you block it with something.

⬤ THESAURUS
block: *When the shrimp farm is built it will block the stream.*
fill: *Fill small holes with wood filler.*
seal: *She filled the containers and sealed them with a cork.*

plum [plʌm] **plums** NOUN
a small fruit with a smooth red or yellow skin and a large stone in the middle

plumage ['pluːmɪdʒ] NOUN
A bird's plumage is its feathers.

plumber ['plʌmə] **plumbers** NOUN
a person who connects and repairs water pipes
[WORD HISTORY: from Old French PLOMMIER meaning 'worker in lead']

plumbing ['plʌmɪŋ] NOUN
The plumbing in a building is the system of water pipes, sinks, and toilets.

plume [pluːm] **plumes** NOUN
a large, brightly coloured feather

plummet ['plʌmɪt] **plummets, plummeting, plummeted** VERB
If something plummets, it falls very quickly. *e.g. Sales have plummeted.*

plump [plʌmp] **plumper, plumpest**
ADJECTIVE
rather fat *e.g. a small plump baby*

⬤ THESAURUS
beefy: *informal beefy bodyguards*
burly: *burly shipyard workers*
chubby: *I was quite chubby as a child.*
fat: *I could eat what I liked without getting fat.*
stout: *He was a tall, stout man of sixty.*
tubby: *He's a bit on the tubby side.*

plunder ['plʌndə] **plunders, plundering, plundered** VERB
If someone plunders a place, they steal things from it.

plunge [plʌndʒ] **plunges, plunging, plunged** VERB

1 If something plunges, it falls suddenly.

2 If you plunge an object into something, you push it in quickly.

3 If you plunge into an activity or state, you suddenly become involved in it or affected by it. *e.g. The United States had just plunged into the war.*

> NOUN

4 a sudden fall

Plunket Society ['plʌŋkət] NOUN
In New Zealand, the Plunket Society was an organization for the care of mothers and babies. It is now called the Royal New Zealand Society for the Health of Women and Children.

plural ['plʊərəl] **plurals** NOUN
(ENGLISH) the form of a word that is used to refer to two or more people or things, for example the plural of 'chair' is 'chairs', and the plural of 'mouse' is 'mice'

pluralism ['plʊərəˌlɪzəm] NOUN
Pluralism is the belief that it is possible for different social and religious groups to live together peacefully while keeping their own beliefs and traditions.
pluralist ADJECTIVE OR NOUN

plural noun plural nouns NOUN
In this dictionary, 'plural noun' is the name given to a noun that is normally used only in the plural, for example 'scissors' or 'police'.

plus [plʌs]

1 You use 'plus' to show that one number is being added to another. *e.g. Two plus two equals four.*

> ADJECTIVE

2 slightly more than the number mentioned *e.g. a career of 25 years plus*

> PREPOSITION

3 You can use 'plus' when you mention an additional item. *e.g. He wrote a history of Scotland*

P

plus a history of British literature.

Although you can use *plus* to mean 'additionally' in spoken language, you should avoid it in written work.

plush [plʌʃ] ADJECTIVE
very expensive and smart *e.g. a plush hotel*

Pluto ['pluːtəʊ] NOUN
Pluto is the smallest planet in the solar system and the furthest from the sun.

ply [plaɪ] **plies, plying, plied** VERB
1 If you ply someone with things or questions, you keep giving them things or asking them questions.
2 To ply a trade is to do a particular job as your work.
> NOUN
3 Ply is the thickness of wool or thread, measured by the number of strands it is made from.

plywood ['plaɪwʊd] NOUN
Plywood is wooden board made from several thin sheets of wood glued together under pressure.

p.m.
used to specify times between 12 noon and 12 midnight, eg *He went to bed at 9 p.m.* It is an abbreviation for the Latin phrase 'post meridiem', which means 'after noon'

pneumatic [njʊ'mætɪk] ADJECTIVE
operated by or filled with compressed air *e.g. a pneumatic drill*
[WORD HISTORY: from Latin PNEUMATICUS meaning 'of air or wind']

pneumonia [njuː'məʊnɪə] NOUN
Pneumonia is a serious disease which affects a person's lungs and makes breathing difficult.

poach [pəʊtʃ] **poaches, poaching, poached** VERB
1 If someone poaches animals from someone else's land, they illegally catch the animals for food.
2 When you poach food, you cook it gently in hot liquid.
poacher NOUN

pocket ['pɒkɪt] **pockets** NOUN
1 a small pouch that forms part of a piece of clothing
2 A pocket of something is a small area of it. *e.g. There are still pockets of resistance.*

pocket money NOUN
Pocket money is an amount of money given regularly to children by their parents.

pod [pɒd] **pods** NOUN
a long narrow seed container that grows on plants such as peas or beans

poddy ['pɒdɪ] **poddies** NOUN
in Australian English, a calf or lamb that is being fed by hand

podium ['pəʊdɪəm] **podiums** NOUN
a small platform, often one on which someone stands to make a speech

poem ['pəʊɪm] **poems** NOUN
a piece of writing in which the words are arranged in short rhythmic lines, often with a rhyme

poet ['pəʊɪt] **poets** NOUN
a person who writes poems

poetic [pəʊ'ɛtɪk] ADJECTIVE
1 very beautiful and expressive *e.g. a pure and poetic love*
2 relating to poetry
poetically ADVERB

poetry ['pəʊɪtrɪ] NOUN
Poetry is poems, considered as a form of literature.

poignant ['pɔɪnjənt] ADJECTIVE
Something that is poignant has a strong emotional effect on you, often making you feel sad. *e.g. a moving and poignant moment*
poignancy NOUN

point [pɔɪnt] **points, pointing, pointed** NOUN
1 an opinion or fact expressed by someone *e.g. You've made a good point.*
2 a quality *e.g. Tact was never her strong point.*

● THESAURUS
attribute: *Cruelty is a regrettable attribute of human behaviour.*
characteristic: *their physical characteristics*
feature: *They're one of my best features.*
quality: *mature people with leadership qualities*
side: *the dark side of his character*
trait: *Creativity is a human trait.*

3 the purpose or meaning something has *e.g. He completely missed the point in most of his argument.*

● THESAURUS
aim: *The aim of this book is to inform you.*
goal: *The goal is to raise a lot of money.*
intention: *It was never my intention to injure anyone.*
object: *It was his object in life to find the island.*
purpose: *He did not know the purpose of Vincent's visit.*

4 a position or time *e.g. At some point during the party, a fight erupted.*
5 a single mark in a competition
6 the thin, sharp end of something such as a needle or knife

THESAURUS
nib: *the nib of my pen*
prong: *the prongs of a fork*
tip: *the tip of my scissors*

7 The points of a compass are the 32 directions indicated on it.

8 The decimal point in a number is the dot separating the whole number from the fraction.

9 On a railway track, the points are the levers and rails which enable a train to move from one track to another.

> VERB

10 If you point at something, you stick out your finger to show where it is.

11 If something points in a particular direction, it faces that way.

point-blank ['pɔɪnt'blæŋk] ADJECTIVE
1 Something that is shot at point-blank range is shot with a gun held very close to it.

> ADVERB

2 If you say something point-blank, you say it directly without explanation or apology.

pointed ['pɔɪntɪd] ADJECTIVE
1 A pointed object has a thin, sharp end.
2 Pointed comments express criticism.
pointedly ADVERB

pointer ['pɔɪntə] **pointers** NOUN
a piece of information which helps you to understand something *e.g. Here are a few pointers to help you make a choice.*

pointless ['pɔɪntlɪs] ADJECTIVE
Something that is pointless has no purpose.
pointlessly ADVERB

point of view points of view NOUN
Your point of view is your opinion about something or your attitude towards it.

poise [pɔɪz] NOUN
Someone who has poise is calm and dignified.

poised [pɔɪzd] ADJECTIVE
If you are poised to do something, you are ready to do it at any moment.

poison ['pɔɪzᵊn] **poisons, poisoning, poisoned** NOUN
1 Poison is a substance that can kill people or animals if they swallow it or absorb it.

THESAURUS
toxin: *the liver's ability to break down toxins*
venom: *the cobra's deadly venom*

> VERB

2 To poison someone is to try to kill them with poison.

poisonous ['pɔɪzənəs] ADJECTIVE
containing something that causes death or illness

THESAURUS
noxious: *Many household products give off noxious fumes.*
toxic: *The cost of cleaning up toxic waste.*
venomous: *The adder is Britain's only venomous snake.*

poke [pəʊk] **pokes, poking, poked** VERB
1 If you poke someone or something, you push at them quickly with your finger or a sharp object.

THESAURUS
dig: *His companions were digging him in the ribs.*
elbow: *As I tried to get past him he elbowed me in the face.*
jab: *Somebody jabbed an umbrella into his leg.*
nudge: *She nudged me awake after I dozed off.*
prod: *He prodded Murray with the shotgun.*
stab: *He stabbed at Frank with his forefinger.*

2 Something that pokes out of another thing appears from underneath or behind it. *e.g. roots poking out of the earth*

> NOUN

3 a sharp jab or prod

THESAURUS
dig: *She silenced him with a sharp dig in the small of the back.*
jab: *a quick jab of the brakes*
nudge: *She slipped her arm under his and gave him a nudge.*
prod: *He gave the donkey a mighty prod in the backside.*

poker ['pəʊkə] **pokers** NOUN
1 Poker is a card game in which the players make bets on the cards dealt to them.

2 a long metal rod used for moving coals or logs in a fire

polar ['pəʊlə] ADJECTIVE
relating to the area around the North and South Poles

polar bear polar bears NOUN
a large white bear which lives in the area around the North Pole

pole [pəʊl] **poles** NOUN
1 a long rounded piece of wood or metal
2 The earth's poles are the two opposite ends of its axis. *e.g. the North Pole*

Pole [pəʊl] **Poles** NOUN
someone who comes from Poland

pole vault NOUN
The pole vault is an athletics event in which contestants jump over a high bar using a long flexible pole to lift themselves into the air.

police [pə'liːs] **polices, policing, policed**
PLURAL NOUN

P

1 The police are the people who are officially responsible for making sure that people obey the law.

> VERB

2 To police an area is to keep law and order there by means of the police or an armed force.

policeman [pə'liːsmən] **policemen** NOUN
a man who is a member of a police force
policewoman NOUN

policy ['pɒlɪsɪ] **policies** NOUN
1 a set of plans, especially in politics or business
e.g. the new economic policy

2 An insurance policy is a document which shows an agreement made with an insurance company.

polio ['pəʊlɪəʊ] NOUN
Polio is an infectious disease that is caused by a virus and often results in paralysis. Polio is short for 'poliomyelitis'.

polish ['pɒlɪʃ] **polishes, polishing, polished**
VERB
1 If you polish something, you put polish on it or rub it with a cloth to make it shine.

● THESAURUS
buff: *He was already buffing the car's hubs.*
shine: *Let him dust and shine the furniture.*
wax: *a Sunday morning spent washing and waxing the car*

2 If you polish a skill or technique you have, you work on it in order to improve it.

● THESAURUS
brush up: *She spent the summer brushing up her driving.*
improve: *I want to improve my golf game.*
perfect: *We perfected a hand-signal system.*
refine: *Surgical techniques are constantly being refined.*

> NOUN
3 Polish is a substance that you put on an object to clean it and make it shine. *e.g. shoe polish*

4 Something that has polish is elegant and of good quality.
polished ADJECTIVE

● THESAURUS
class: informal *For sheer class, Mark Waugh is the best batsman of the World Cup.*
elegance: *The furniture combined practicality with elegance.*
finesse: *It's good but it lacks the finesse of vintage champagne.*
grace: *Ballet classes are important for learning poise and grace.*
refinement: *a girl who possessed both dignity and refinement*
style: *Paris, you have to admit, has style.*

Polish ['pəʊlɪʃ] ADJECTIVE
1 belonging or relating to Poland
> NOUN
2 Polish is the main language spoken in Poland.

polite [pə'laɪt] ADJECTIVE
1 Someone who is polite has good manners and behaves considerately towards other people.

● THESAURUS
civil: *I have to force myself to be civil to him.*
courteous: *Her reply was courteous but firm.*
respectful: *Their children are always respectful to their elders.*
well-behaved: *well-behaved little girls*
well-mannered: *a very pleasant and well-mannered student*
<<OPPOSITE *rude*

2 Polite society is cultivated and refined.
politely ADVERB

● THESAURUS
cultured: *He is immensely cultured and well-read.*
genteel: *two ladies with genteel manners and voices*
refined: *His speech and manner are very refined.*
sophisticated: *Recently her tastes have become more sophisticated.*
urbane: *She describes him as charming and urbane.*

politeness [pə'laɪtnəs] NOUN
the quality of having good manners and behaving considerately

● THESAURUS
civility: *Handle customers with tact and civility.*
courtesy: *He did not even have the courtesy to reply to my fax.*
decency: *He should have had the decency to inform me.*
etiquette: *the rules of diplomatic etiquette*

political [pə'lɪtɪkəl] ADJECTIVE
1 relating to the state, government, or public administration

2 relating to or interested in politics
politically ADVERB

politically correct [pə'lɪtɪklɪ] ADJECTIVE
careful not to offend or designed not to offend minority or disadvantaged groups

politician [,pɒlɪ'tɪʃən] **politicians** NOUN
a person involved in the government of a country

politics ['pɒlɪtɪks] NOUN **(HISTORY)**
Politics is the activity and planning concerned with achieving power and control in a country or organization.

polka ['pɒlkə] **polkas** NOUN
a fast dance in which couples dance together in circles around the room

poll [pəʊl] **polls, polling, polled** NOUN
1 a survey in which people are asked their opinions about something

> **PLURAL NOUN**

2 A political election can be referred to as the polls.

> **VERB**

3 If you are polled on something, you are asked your opinion about it as part of a survey.

pollen ['pɒlən] NOUN
Pollen is a fine yellow powder produced by flowers in order to fertilize other flowers of the same species.

pollinate ['pɒlɪˌneɪt] **pollinates, pollinating, pollinated** VERB
To pollinate a plant is to fertilize it with pollen.
pollination NOUN

pollutant [pə'luːtᵊnt] **pollutants** NOUN
a substance that causes pollution

pollute [pə'luːt] **pollutes, polluting, polluted** VERB
To pollute water or air is to make it dirty and dangerous to use or live in.
polluted ADJECTIVE

THESAURUS
contaminate: *Have any fish been contaminated in the Arctic Ocean?*
infect: *a virus which is spread mainly by infected blood*
poison: *Drilling operations have poisoned the Nile delta.*
taint: *blood tainted with the hepatitis viruses*

pollution [pə'luːʃən] NOUN
(GEOGRAPHY) Pollution of the environment happens when dirty or dangerous substances get into the air, water or soil.

polo ['pəʊləʊ] NOUN
Polo is a game played between two teams of players on horseback. The players use wooden hammers with long handles to hit a ball.

polo-necked ['pəʊləʊˌnɛkt] ADJECTIVE
A polo-necked jumper has a deep fold of material at the neck.

polyester [ˌpɒli'ɛstə] NOUN
(D & T) a man-made fibre, used especially to make clothes

polygamy [pə'lɪgəmi] NOUN
Polygamy is having more than one wife at the same time.
polygamous ADJECTIVE

polygon ['pɒlɪˌgɒn] **polygons** NOUN
any two-dimensional shape whose sides are all straight

polystyrene [ˌpɒli'staɪriːn] NOUN
Polystyrene is a very light plastic, used especially as insulating material or to make containers.

polythene ['pɒlɪˌθiːn] NOUN
Polythene is a type of plastic that is used to make thin sheets or bags.

polyunsaturated [ˌpɒliʌn'sætʃəˌreɪtɪd] ADJECTIVE
Polyunsaturated oils and margarines are made mainly from vegetable fats and are considered to be healthier than saturated oils.
polyunsaturate NOUN

pomegranate ['pɒmɪˌgrænɪt] **pomegranates** NOUN
a round fruit with a thick reddish skin. It contains a lot of small seeds
[WORD HISTORY: from Latin POMUM GRANATUM meaning 'apple full of seeds']

pomp [pɒmp] NOUN
Pomp is the use of ceremony, fine clothes, and decorations on special occasions. *e.g. Sir Patrick was buried with much pomp.*

pompous ['pɒmpəs] ADJECTIVE
behaving in a way that is too serious and self-important
pomposity NOUN

THESAURUS
arrogant: *an air of arrogant indifference*
grandiose: *grandiose plans which never got off the ground*
ostentatious: *an ostentatious wedding reception*
pretentious: *His response was full of pretentious nonsense.*
puffed up: *He is puffed up with own importance.*

pond [pɒnd] **ponds** NOUN
a small, usually man-made area of water

ponder ['pɒndə] **ponders, pondering, pondered** VERB
If you ponder, you think about something deeply. *e.g. He was pondering the problem when Phillipson drove up.*

THESAURUS
brood: *I guess everyone broods over things once in a while.*
consider: *You have to consider the feelings of those around you.*
contemplate: *He lay in bed contemplating his future.*
mull over: *I'll leave you alone here so you can mull it over.*
reflect: *I reflected on the child's future.*
think: *I have often thought about this problem.*

ponderous ['pɒndərəs] ADJECTIVE
dull, slow, and serious *e.g. the ponderous commentary*

pong [pɒŋ] **pongs** NOUN; INFORMAL
an unpleasant smell

pontiff ['pɒntɪf] **pontiffs** NOUN; FORMAL
The pontiff is the Pope.

P

pony ['pəʊnɪ] **ponies** NOUN
a small horse

ponytail ['pəʊnɪ,teɪl] **ponytails** NOUN
a hairstyle in which long hair is tied at the back of the head and hangs down like a tail

pony trekking ['trɛkɪŋ] NOUN
Pony trekking is a leisure activity in which people ride across country on ponies.

poodle ['puːdᵊl] **poodles** NOUN
a type of dog with curly hair

pool [puːl] **pools, pooling, pooled** NOUN
1 a small area of still water
2 Pool is a game in which players try to hit coloured balls into pockets around a table using long sticks called cues.
3 A pool of people, money, or things is a group or collection used or shared by several people.
> PLURAL NOUN
4 The pools are a competition in which people try to guess the results of football matches.
> VERB
5 If people pool their resources, they gather together the things they have so that they can be shared or used by all of them.

poor [pʊə] **poorer, poorest** ADJECTIVE
1 Poor people have very little money and few possessions.
● **THESAURUS**
broke: informal He was broke when I married him.
destitute: destitute people living on the streets
hard up: informal Her parents were very hard up.
impoverished: one of the most impoverished suburbs of Rio de Janeiro
penniless: a penniless refugee
poverty-stricken: a teacher of poverty-stricken kids
<<OPPOSITE rich
2 Poor places are inhabited by people with little money and show signs of neglect.
3 You use 'poor' to show sympathy. e.g. Poor you!
4 'Poor' also means of a low quality or standard e.g. a poor performance
● **THESAURUS**
feeble: a feeble attempt to save Figo's shot
inferior: The cassettes were of inferior quality.
mediocre: His school record was mediocre.
second-rate: Passengers are fed up using a second-rate service.
shoddy: shoddy goods
unsatisfactory: questions to which he received unsatisfactory answers

poorly ['pʊəlɪ] ADJECTIVE
1 feeling unwell or ill
> ADVERB
2 badly e.g. a poorly planned operation

pop [pɒp] **pops, popping, popped** NOUN
1 Pop is modern music played and enjoyed especially by young people.
2 You can refer to fizzy, nonalcoholic drinks as pop.
3 a short, sharp sound
> VERB
4 If something pops, it makes a sudden sharp sound.
5 If you pop something somewhere, you put it there quickly. e.g. I'd just popped the pie in the oven.
6 If you pop somewhere, you go there quickly. e.g. His mother popped out to buy him an ice cream.

popcorn ['pɒp,kɔːn] NOUN
Popcorn is a snack consisting of grains of maize heated until they puff up and burst.

Pope [pəʊp] **Popes** NOUN
The Pope is the head of the Roman Catholic Church.
[WORD HISTORY: from Latin PAPA meaning 'bishop' or 'father']

poplar ['pɒplə] **poplars** NOUN
a type of tall thin tree

poppy ['pɒpɪ] **poppies** NOUN
a plant with a large red flower on a hairy stem

populace ['pɒpjʊləs] NOUN; FORMAL
The populace of a country is its people.

popular ['pɒpjʊlə] ADJECTIVE
1 liked or approved of by a lot of people
● **THESAURUS**
fashionable: fashionable wine bars
favourite: Britain's favourite soap opera
in demand: He was much in demand as a lecturer.
in favour: He is now back in favour with the manager.
sought-after: one of the most sought-after new names in Hollywood
well-liked: She was very sociable and well-liked by the other students.
<<OPPOSITE unpopular
2 involving or intended for ordinary people e.g. the popular press
popularly ADVERB, **popularity** NOUN, **popularize** VERB
● **THESAURUS**
common: Much of the countryside has fallen out of common ownership and into private hands.
conventional: a respectable married woman with conventional opinions
general: general awareness about bullying
prevalent: Smoking is becoming increasingly prevalent among younger women.
universal: universal health care

populate ['pɒpjʊ,leɪt] **populates, populating, populated** VERB

The people or animals that populate an area live there.

population [ˌpɒpjʊˈleɪʃən] **populations** NOUN

The population of a place is the people who live there, or the number of people living there.

porcelain [ˈpɔːslɪn] NOUN

Porcelain is a delicate, hard material used to make crockery and ornaments.

porch [pɔːtʃ] **porches** NOUN

a covered area at the entrance to a building

porcupine [ˈpɔːkjʊˌpaɪn] **porcupines** NOUN

a large rodent with long spines covering its body

[WORD HISTORY: from Old French PORC D'ESPINS meaning 'pig with spines']

pore [pɔː] **pores, poring, pored** NOUN

1 The pores in your skin or on the surface of a plant are very small holes which allow moisture to pass through.

> VERB

2 If you pore over a piece of writing or a diagram, you study it carefully.

pork [pɔːk] NOUN

Pork is meat from a pig which has not been salted or smoked.

pornography [pɔːˈnɒgrəfɪ] NOUN

Pornography refers to magazines and films that are designed to cause sexual excitement by showing naked people and sexual acts.

pornographic ADJECTIVE

[WORD HISTORY: from Greek PORNOS meaning 'prostitute' and GRAPHEIN meaning 'to write']

porpoise [ˈpɔːpəs] **porpoises** NOUN

a sea mammal related to the dolphin

[WORD HISTORY: from Latin PORCUS meaning 'pig' and PISCIS meaning 'fish']

porridge [ˈpɒrɪdʒ] NOUN

Porridge is a thick, sticky food made from oats cooked in water or milk.

port [pɔːt] **ports** NOUN

1 a town or area which has a harbour or docks

2 Port is a kind of strong, sweet red wine.

> ADJECTIVE

3 The port side of a ship is the left side when you are facing the front.

-port SUFFIX

'-port' comes at the end of words that have something to do with 'carrying' in their meaning *e.g. transport*

[WORD HISTORY: from Latin PORTĀRE meaning 'to carry']

portable [ˈpɔːtəbəl] ADJECTIVE

designed to be easily carried *e.g. a portable television*

porter [ˈpɔːtə] **porters** NOUN

1 a person whose job is to be in charge of the entrance of a building, greeting and directing visitors

2 A porter in a railway station or hospital is a person whose job is to carry or move things.

portfolio [pɔːtˈfəʊlɪəʊ] **portfolios** NOUN

1 a thin, flat case for carrying papers

[WORD HISTORY: from Italian PORTAFOGLIO meaning 'carrier for papers']

porthole [ˈpɔːtˌhəʊl] **portholes** NOUN

a small window in the side of a ship or aircraft

portion [ˈpɔːʃən] **portions** NOUN

a part or amount of something *e.g. a portion of fresh fruit*

● THESAURUS

bit: *I missed the first bit of the meeting.*

chunk: *Cut the melon into chunks.*

helping: *She gave them extra helpings of ice-cream.*

part: *A large part of his earnings went on repaying the loan.*

piece: *Do you want another piece?*

segment: *the middle segment of his journey*

serving: *Each serving contains 240 calories.*

portrait [ˈpɔːtrɪt] **portraits** NOUN

(ART) a picture or photograph of someone

portray [pɔːˈtreɪ] **portrays, portraying, portrayed** VERB

When an actor, artist, or writer portrays someone or something, they represent or describe them.

portrayal NOUN

Portuguese [ˌpɔːtjʊˈgiːz] ADJECTIVE

1 belonging or relating to Portugal

> NOUN

2 someone who comes from Portugal

3 Portuguese is the main language spoken in Portugal and Brazil.

pose [pəʊz] **poses, posing, posed** VERB

1 If something poses a problem, it is the cause of the problem.

2 If you pose a question, you ask it.

● THESAURUS

ask: *I wasn't the only one asking questions.*

put: *Some workers may be afraid to put questions publicly.*

submit: *Passengers are invited to submit questions.*

3 If you pose as someone else, you pretend to be that person in order to deceive people.

● THESAURUS

impersonate: *He was once jailed for impersonating a policeman.*

masquerade as: *He masqueraded as a doctor and fooled everyone.*

P

pass oneself off as: *He frequently passed himself off as a lawyer.*
pretend to be: *We spent the afternoon pretending to be foreign tourists.*

> NOUN

4 a way of standing, sitting, or lying *e.g. Mr Clark assumes a pose for the photographer.*

poser ['pəʊzə] **posers** NOUN

1 someone who behaves or dresses in an exaggerated way in order to impress people
2 a difficult problem

posh [pɒʃ] **posher, poshest** ADJECTIVE

1 INFORMAL
smart, fashionable, and expensive *e.g. a posh restaurant*

● THESAURUS
classy: informal *expensive cars with classy brand names*
elegant: *an elegant society ball*
exclusive: *a member of Britain's most exclusive club*
fashionable: *fashionable restaurants*
smart: *smart London dinner parties*
stylish: *stylish décor*
up-market: *an up-market agency aimed at professional people*

2 upper class *e.g. the man with the posh voice*

● THESAURUS
aristocratic: *a wealthy, aristocratic family*
genteel: *two ladies with genteel manners and voices*
upper-class: *upper-class speech*
<<OPPOSITE common

position [pə'zɪʃən] **positions, positioning, positioned** NOUN

1 (DRAMA) The position of someone or something is the place where they are or ought to be. *e.g. Would the cast take their positions, please?*

● THESAURUS
location: *She knew the exact location of their headquarters.*
place: *The pain is always in the same place.*
point: *The pain originated from a point in his right thigh.*
whereabouts: *Finding his whereabouts proved surprisingly easy.*

2 When someone or something is in a particular position, they are sitting or lying in that way. *e.g. I raised myself to a sitting position.*

3 a job or post in an organization

4 The position that you are in at a particular time is the situation that you are in. *e.g. This puts the president in a difficult position.*

> VERB

5 To position something somewhere is to put it there. *e.g. Llewelyn positioned a cushion behind Joanna's back.*

● THESAURUS
arrange: *Arrange the books in neat piles.*
lay out: *Grace laid out the knives and forks at the table.*
locate: *the best city in which to locate a business*
place: *Chairs were placed in rows for the parents.*
put: *She put the photograph on her desk.*

positive ['pɒzɪtɪv] ADJECTIVE

1 completely sure about something *e.g. I was positive he'd known about that money.*

● THESAURUS
certain: *It wasn't a balloon – I'm certain about that.*
confident: *Mr Ryan is confident of success.*
convinced: *He was convinced that I was part of the problem.*
sure: *It is impossible to be sure about the value of the land.*

2 confident and hopeful *e.g. I felt very positive about everything.*

3 showing approval or encouragement *e.g. I anticipate a positive response.*

● THESAURUS
constructive: *We welcome constructive criticism.*
helpful: *Camilla's helpful comments.*
<<OPPOSITE negative

4 providing definite proof of the truth or identity of something *e.g. positive evidence*

● THESAURUS
clear: *a clear case of mistaken identity*
clear-cut: *The issue is not so clear-cut.*
conclusive: *Research on the matter is far from conclusive.*
concrete: *He had no concrete evidence.*
firm: *There is no firm evidence to prove this.*

5 (MATHS) A positive number is greater than zero.

positively ADVERB

possess [pə'zɛs] **possesses, possessing, possessed** VERB

1 If you possess a particular quality, you have it.

● THESAURUS
be blessed with: *She was blessed with a photographic memory.*
be born with: *Mozart was born with perfect pitch.*
enjoy: *I have always enjoyed good health.*
have: *They have talent in abundance.*

2 If you possess something, you own it.

● THESAURUS
acquire: *I have acquired a new car.*
control: *He now controls the entire company.*
hold: *He does not hold a firearm certificate.*
occupy: *US forces now occupy part of the country.*
seize: *Troops have seized the airport and railway terminals.*
take over: *They plan to take over another airline.*

4 If a feeling or belief possesses you, it strongly influences you. *e.g. Absolute terror possessed her.*
possessor NOUN

possession [pəˈzɛʃən] **possessions** NOUN
1 If something is in your possession or if you are in possession of it, you have it.

● THESAURUS
control: *The restructuring involves his giving up control of the firm.*
custody: *She will have custody of their two children.*
ownership: *the growth of home ownership*
tenure: *his 28-year tenure of the house*

2 Your possessions are the things that you own or that you have with you.

● THESAURUS
assets: *The group had assets worth over 10 million dollars.*
belongings: *He was identified only by his personal belongings.*
effects: *His daughters were collecting his effects.*
estate: *She left her entire estate to a charity.*
property: *the rightful owner of the property*
things: *She told him to take all his things and not to return.*

possessive [pəˈzɛsɪv] ADJECTIVE
1 A person who is possessive about someone or something wants to keep them to themselves.

> NOUN
2 In grammar, the possessive is the form of a noun or pronoun used to show possession. *e.g. my car... That's hers.*

possibility [ˌpɒsɪˈbɪlɪti] **possibilities** NOUN
something that might be true or might happen *e.g. the possibility of a ban*

● THESAURUS
chance: *There's no chance of that happening.*
hope: *We had absolutely no hope of raising the money.*
likelihood: *the likelihood of infection*
odds: *What are the odds of that happening?*
prospect: *There is little prospect of peace.*
risk: *It reduces the risk of heart disease.*

possible [ˈpɒsɪbəl] ADJECTIVE
1 likely to happen or able to be done

● THESAURUS
attainable: *I always thought promotion was attainable.*
feasible: *Whether such cooperation is feasible is a matter of doubt.*
practicable: *It was not reasonably practicable for Mr Tyler to attend.*
viable: *commercially viable products*
workable: *This isn't a workable solution in most cases.*
<<OPPOSITE *impossible*

2 likely or capable of being true or correct
possibly ADVERB

● THESAURUS
conceivable: *It is just conceivable that a survivor might be found.*
imaginable: *a place of no imaginable strategic value*
likely: *Experts say a 'yes' vote is still the likely outcome.*
potential: *the channel's potential audience*

possum [ˈpɒsəm] **possums** NOUN
In Australian and New Zealand English, a possum is a phalanger, a marsupial with thick fur and a long tail.

post [pəʊst] **posts, posting, posted** NOUN
1 The post is the system by which letters and parcels are collected and delivered.
2 a job or official position in an organization
3 a strong upright pole fixed into the ground *e.g. They are tied to a post.*

> VERB
4 If you post a letter, you send it to someone by putting it into a postbox.
5 If you are posted somewhere, you are sent there by your employers to work there.
postal ADJECTIVE

post- PREFIX
after a particular time or event *e.g. his postwar career*
[WORD HISTORY: from Latin POST meaning 'after']

postage [ˈpəʊstɪdʒ] NOUN
Postage is the money that you pay to send letters and parcels by post.

postal order [ˈpəʊstəl] **postal orders** NOUN
a piece of paper representing a sum of money which you can buy at a post office

postbox [ˈpəʊstˌbɒks] **postboxes** NOUN
a metal box with a hole in it which you put letters into for collection by the postman

postcard [ˈpəʊstˌkɑːd] **postcards** NOUN
a card, often with a picture on one side, which you write on and send without an envelope

postcode [ˈpəʊstˌkəʊd] **postcodes** NOUN
a short sequence of letters and numbers at the end of an address which helps the post office to sort the mail

poster [ˈpəʊstə] **posters** NOUN
a large notice or picture that is stuck on a wall as an advertisement or for decoration

posterior [pɒˈstɪərɪə] **posteriors** NOUN; HUMOROUS
A person's posterior is their bottom.

posterity [pɒˈstɛrɪti] NOUN; FORMAL
You can refer to the future and the people who

will be alive then as posterity. *e.g. to record the voyage for posterity*
[WORD HISTORY: from Latin POSTERITAS meaning 'future generations']

posthumous ['pɒstjʊməs] ADJECTIVE
happening or awarded after a person's death *e.g. a posthumous medal*
posthumously ADVERB

postman ['pəʊstmən] **postmen** NOUN
someone who collects and delivers letters and parcels sent by post

postmortem [pəʊst'mɔːtəm] **postmortems** NOUN
a medical examination of a dead body to find out how the person died

post office post offices NOUN
1 The Post Office is the national organization responsible for postal services.
2 a building where you can buy stamps and post letters

postpone [pəʊst'pəʊn] **postpones, postponing, postponed** VERB
If you postpone an event, you arrange for it to take place at a later time than was originally planned.
postponement NOUN
● THESAURUS
adjourn: *The proceedings have been adjourned until next week.*
defer: *Customers often defer payments for as long as possible.*
delay: *I wanted to delay my departure until June.*
put back: *The news conference has been put back a couple of hours.*
put off: *The Association has put off the event until October.*
shelve: *Sadly, the project has now been shelved.*

posture ['pɒstʃə] **postures** NOUN
Your posture is the position or manner in which you hold your body.

posy ['pəʊzɪ] **posies** NOUN
a small bunch of flowers

pot [pɒt] **pots** NOUN
a deep round container; also used to refer to its contents

potassium nitrate [pə'tæsɪəm 'naɪtreɪt] NOUN
a white chemical compound used to make gunpowder, fireworks and fertilizers. Potassium nitrate is also called saltpetre

potato [pə'teɪtəʊ] **potatoes** NOUN
a white vegetable that has a brown or red skin and grows underground

potent ['pəʊt°nt] ADJECTIVE
effective or powerful *e.g. a potent cocktail*

potency NOUN

potential [pə'tɛnʃəl] ADJECTIVE
1 capable of becoming the thing mentioned *e.g. potential customers... potential sources of finance*
● THESAURUS
likely: *A draw is the likely outcome.*
possible: *Her family is discussing a possible move to America.*
probable: *A bomb was the accident's most probable cause.*
> NOUN
2 Your potential is your ability to achieve success in the future.
potentially ADVERB
● THESAURUS
ability: *You have the ability to become a good pianist.*
aptitude: *more aptitude for academic work than the others*
capability: *We experience differences in mental capability depending on the time of day.*
capacity: *people's creative capacities*
power: *the power of speech*
wherewithal: *She didn't have the financial wherewithal to do it.*

potential energy NOUN
Potential energy is the energy stored in something.

pothole ['pɒt,həʊl] **potholes** NOUN
1 a hole in the surface of a road caused by bad weather or traffic
2 an underground cavern

potion ['pəʊʃən] **potions** NOUN
a drink containing medicine, poison, or supposed magical powers
[WORD HISTORY: from Latin POTIO meaning 'a drink']

potted ['pɒtɪd] ADJECTIVE
Potted meat or fish is cooked and put into a small sealed container to preserve it.

potter ['pɒtə] **potters, pottering, pottered** NOUN
1 a person who makes pottery
> VERB
2 If you potter about, you pass the time doing pleasant, unimportant things.

pottery ['pɒtərɪ] NOUN
1 Pottery is pots, dishes, and other items made from clay and fired in a kiln.
2 Pottery is also the craft of making pottery.

potty ['pɒtɪ] **potties; pottier, pottiest** NOUN
1 a bowl which a small child can sit on and use instead of a toilet

> ADJECTIVE
2 INFORMAL
crazy or foolish

pouch [paʊtʃ] **pouches** NOUN
1 a small, soft container with a fold-over top *e.g. a tobacco pouch*
2 Animals like kangaroos have a pouch, which is a pocket of skin in which they carry their young.

poultry ['pəʊltrɪ] NOUN
Chickens, turkeys, and other birds kept for their meat or eggs are referred to as poultry.

pounce [paʊns] **pounces, pouncing, pounced** VERB
If an animal or person pounces on something, they leap and grab it.

pound [paʊnd] **pounds, pounding, pounded** NOUN
1 The pound is the main unit of currency in Britain and in some other countries.
2 a unit of weight equal to 16 ounces or about 0.454 kilograms
> VERB
3 If you pound something, you hit it repeatedly with your fist. *e.g. Someone was pounding on the door.*
4 If you pound a substance, you crush it into a powder or paste. *e.g. Wooden mallets were used to pound the meat.*
5 If your heart is pounding, it is beating very strongly and quickly.
6 If you pound somewhere, you run there with heavy noisy steps.

pour [pɔː] **pours, pouring, poured** VERB
1 If you pour a liquid out of a container, you make it flow out by tipping the container.
2 If something pours somewhere, it flows there quickly and in large quantities. *e.g. Sweat poured down his face.*

● THESAURUS
course: *The tears coursed down her cheeks.*
flow: *compressor stations that keep that gas flowing*
gush: *Piping-hot water gushed out.*
run: *Water was running down the walls.*
spout: *a fountain that spouts water 40 feet into the air*
stream: *She came in, rain streaming from her clothes and hair.*

3 When it is raining heavily, you can say that it is pouring.

pout [paʊt] **pouts, pouting, pouted** VERB
If you pout, you stick out your lips or bottom lip.

poverty ['pɒvətɪ] NOUN
(GEOGRAPHY) the state of being very poor

● THESAURUS
destitution: *refugees living in destitution*
hardship: *Many people are suffering economic hardship.*
insolvency: *Several companies are on the brink of insolvency.*
want: *We are fighting for freedom from want.*

powder ['paʊdə] **powders, powdering, powdered** NOUN
1 Powder consists of many tiny particles of a solid substance.
> VERB
2 If you powder a surface, you cover it with powder.
powdery ADJECTIVE

power ['paʊə] **powers, powering, powered** NOUN
1 Someone who has power has a lot of control over people and activities.
● THESAURUS
ascendancy: *The extremists in the party are gaining ascendancy.*
control: *He has been forced to give up control over the company.*
dominion: *They truly believe they have dominion over us.*
sovereignty: *the resumption of Chinese sovereignty over Hong Kong in 1997*
supremacy: *The party has re-established its supremacy.*

2 Someone who has the power to do something has the ability to do it. *e.g. the power of speech*
3 Power is also the authority to do something. *e.g. the power of arrest*
● THESAURUS
authority: *The judge had no authority to order a second trial.*
authorization: *I don't have the authorization to make such a decision.*
licence: *He has given me licence to do the job as I see fit.*
privilege: *the ancient powers and privileges of parliament*
right: *the right to vote*

4 The power of something is the physical strength that it has to move things.
● THESAURUS
brawn: *He's got plenty of brains as well as brawn.*
might: *The might of the army could prove a decisive factor.*
strength: *He threw it forward with all his strength.*
vigour: *His body lacks the vigour of a normal two-year-old.*

5 Power is energy obtained, for example, by burning fuel or using the wind or waves.

P

6 In physics, power is the energy transferred from one thing to another in one second. It is measured in watts.

> VERB

7 Something that powers a machine provides the energy for it to work.

powerful ['paʊəfʊl] ADJECTIVE

1 able to control people and events

◉ THESAURUS
commanding: *We're in a more commanding position than we've been in for ages.*
dominant: *He was a dominant figure in the Italian film industry.*
influential: *He had been influential in shaping economic policy.*

2 having great physical strength

◉ THESAURUS
mighty: *a mighty river*
strapping: *He was a bricklayer - a big, strapping fellow.*
strong: *I'm not strong enough to carry him.*
sturdy: *The camera was mounted on a sturdy tripod.*
vigorous: *He was a vigorous, handsome young man.*
<<OPPOSITE *weak*

3 having a strong effect
powerfully ADVERB

◉ THESAURUS
compelling: *a compelling reason to leave*
convincing: *convincing evidence*
effective: *Antibiotics are effective against this organism.*
forceful: *forceful action to stop the suffering*
persuasive: *Mr. Knight made a persuasive case for removing the tax.*
telling: *He spoke reasonably, carefully, and with telling effect.*

powerless ['paʊəlɪs] ADJECTIVE

unable to control or influence events *e.g. I was powerless to save her.*

◉ THESAURUS
helpless: *Many people felt helpless against the violence.*
impotent: *The West is impotent to influence the Balkan war.*
incapable: *He is incapable as a manager.*

power station power stations NOUN

a place where electricity is generated

practicable ['præktɪkəbᵊl] ADJECTIVE

If a task or plan is practicable, it can be carried out successfully. *e.g. a practicable option*

practical ['præktɪkᵊl] practicals ADJECTIVE

1 The practical aspects of something are those that involve experience and real situations rather than ideas or theories. *e.g. the practical difficulties of teaching science*

◉ THESAURUS
applied: *plans to put more money into applied research*
pragmatic: *a pragmatic approach to the problems of Latin America*

2 sensible and likely to be effective *e.g. practical low-heeled shoes*

◉ THESAURUS
functional: *The design is functional but stylish.*
sensible: *sensible footwear*
<<OPPOSITE *impractical*

3 Someone who is practical is able to deal effectively and sensibly with problems.

◉ THESAURUS
accomplished: *an accomplished cook*
experienced: *a team packed with experienced professionals*
proficient: *A great number of them are proficient in foreign languages.*
seasoned: *The author is a seasoned academic.*
skilled: *amateur but highly skilled observers of wildlife*
veteran: *a veteran broadcaster*

> NOUN

4 an examination in which you make or perform something rather than simply write
practicality NOUN

practically ['præktɪkəlɪ] ADVERB

1 almost but not completely or exactly *e.g. The house was practically a wreck.*

2 in a practical way *e.g. practically minded*

practice ['præktɪs] practices NOUN

1 You can refer to something that people do regularly as a practice. *e.g. the practice of kissing hands*

◉ THESAURUS
custom: *I have tried to adapt to local customs.*
habit: *a survey on eating habits*
method: *her usual method of getting through the traffic*
routine: *We had to change our daily routine and lifestyle.*
way: *a return to the old ways of doing things*

2 Practice is regular training or exercise. *e.g. I need more practice.*

◉ THESAURUS
drill: *The teacher ran them through the drill again.*
exercise: *Lack of exercise can lead to feelings of exhaustion.*
preparation: *Behind any successful event lie months of preparation.*
rehearsal: *rehearsals for a concert tour*
training: *her busy training schedule*

3 A doctor's or lawyer's practice is his or her business.

▨ The noun *practice* ends in *ice*.

practise ['præktɪs] **practises, practising, practised** VERB

1 If you practise something, you do it regularly in order to improve.

⬤ THESAURUS

polish: *They just need to polish their technique.*
rehearse: *She was in her room rehearsing her lines.*
train: *He was training for the new season.*

2 People who practise a religion, custom, or craft regularly take part in the activities associated with it. *e.g. a practising Buddhist*

⬤ THESAURUS

do: *I used to do karate.*
follow: *Do you follow any particular religion?*
observe: *American forces are observing Christmas quietly.*

3 Someone who practises medicine or law works as a doctor or lawyer.

▨ The verb *practise* ends in *ise*.

practised ['præktɪst] ADJECTIVE

Someone who is practised at doing something is very skilful at it. *e.g. a practised performer*

practitioner [præk'tɪʃənə] **practitioners** NOUN

You can refer to someone who works in a particular profession as a practitioner. *e.g. a medical practitioner*

pragmatic [præg'mætɪk] ADJECTIVE

A pragmatic way of considering or doing something is a practical rather than theoretical way. *e.g. He is pragmatic about the risks involved.*
pragmatically ADVERB, **pragmatism** NOUN

prairie ['prɛərɪ] **prairies** NOUN

a large area of flat, grassy land in North America

praise [preɪz] **praises, praising, praised** VERB

1 If you praise someone or something, you express strong approval of their qualities or achievements.

⬤ THESAURUS

admire: *All those who knew him will admire him for his work.*
applaud: *He should be applauded for his courage.*
approve: *Not everyone approves of the festival.*
congratulate: *I must congratulate the organizers for a well-run event.*
pay tribute to: *He paid tribute to his captain.*
<<OPPOSITE *criticize*

> NOUN

2 Praise is what is said or written in approval of someone's qualities or achievements.

⬤ THESAURUS

accolade: *the ultimate international accolade, the Nobel Peace Prize*

approval: *an obsessive drive to gain her mother's approval*
commendation: *They received a commendation from the Royal Society of Arts.*
congratulation: *I offered her my congratulations.*
tribute: *We marched past in tribute to our fallen comrades.*
<<OPPOSITE *criticism*

pram [præm] **prams** NOUN

a baby's cot on wheels

prance [prɑːns] **prances, prancing, pranced** VERB

Someone who is prancing around is walking with exaggerated movements.

prank [præŋk] **pranks** NOUN

a childish trick

prattle ['prætəl] **prattles, prattling, prattled** VERB

If someone prattles on, they talk a lot without saying anything important.

prawn [prɔːn] **prawns** NOUN

a small, pink, edible shellfish with a long tail

pray [preɪ] **prays, praying, prayed** VERB (RE)

When someone prays, they speak to God to give thanks or to ask for help.

prayer [prɛə] **prayers** NOUN (RE)

1 Prayer is the activity of praying.
2 the words said when someone prays

pre- PREFIX

'Pre-' means before a particular time or event *e.g. pre-war*
[WORD HISTORY: from Latin PRAE meaning 'before']

preach [priːtʃ] **preaches, preaching, preached** VERB

When someone preaches, they give a short talk on a religious or moral subject as part of a church service.
preacher NOUN

precarious [prɪ'kɛərɪəs] ADJECTIVE

1 If your situation is precarious, you may fail in what you are doing at any time.
2 Something that is precarious is likely to fall because it is not well balanced or secured.
precariously ADVERB

precaution [prɪ'kɔːʃən] **precautions** NOUN

an action that is intended to prevent something from happening *e.g. It's still worth taking precautions against accidents.*
precautionary ADJECTIVE

⬤ THESAURUS

insurance: *Farmers grew a mixture of crops as an insurance against crop failure.*
preventative measure: *a preventative measure against heart disease*

protection: *protection against damage to buildings*
provision: *People need to make decent provision for their old age.*
safeguard: *legislation that offers safeguards against discrimination*

precede [prɪ'siːd] **precedes, preceding, preceded** VERB

1 Something that precedes another thing happens or occurs before it.

2 If you precede someone somewhere, you go in front of them.
preceding ADJECTIVE

precedence ['prɛsɪdəns] NOUN

If something takes precedence over other things, it is the most important thing and should be dealt with first.

precedent ['prɛsɪdənt] **precedents** NOUN

An action or decision that is regarded as a precedent is used as a guide in taking similar action or decisions later.

precinct ['priːsɪŋkt] **precincts** NOUN

1 A shopping precinct is a pedestrian shopping area.

> PLURAL NOUN

2 The precincts of a place are its buildings and land.

precious ['prɛʃəs] ADJECTIVE

Something that is precious is valuable or very important and should be looked after or used carefully.

● THESAURUS
expensive: *an expensive new coat*
invaluable: *I was to gain invaluable experience over that year.*
priceless: *his priceless collection of Chinese art*
prized: *These shells were very highly prized by the Indians.*
valuable: *valuable books*
<<OPPOSITE *worthless*

precipice ['prɛsɪpɪs] **precipices** NOUN

a very steep rock face

precipitate [prɪ'sɪpɪˌteɪt] **precipitates, precipitating, precipitated** VERB; FORMAL

If something precipitates an event or situation, it causes it to happen suddenly.

precipitation [prɪˌsɪpɪ'teɪʃən] NOUN; FORMAL

Precipitation is rain, snow, or hail; used especially when stating the amount that falls during a particular period.

precise [prɪ'saɪs] ADJECTIVE

exact and accurate in every detail *e.g. precise measurements*
precisely ADVERB, **precision** NOUN

● THESAURUS
accurate: *an accurate description of his attackers*

actual: *The actual number of victims is higher than statistics suggest.*
correct: *This information was correct at the time of going to press.*
exact: *The exact number of protest calls has not been revealed.*
particular: *a very particular account of events*
specific: *I asked him to be more specific.*
very: *Those were his very words.*
<<OPPOSITE *vague*

preclude [prɪ'kluːd] **precludes, precluding, precluded** VERB; FORMAL

If something precludes an event or situation, it prevents it from happening. *e.g. The meal precluded serious conversation.*

precocious [prɪ'kəʊʃəs] ADJECTIVE

Precocious children behave in a way that seems too advanced for their age.

preconceived [ˌpriːkən'siːvd] ADJECTIVE

Preconceived ideas about something have been formed without any real experience or information.
preconception NOUN

precondition [ˌpriːkən'dɪʃən] **preconditions** NOUN

If something is a precondition for another thing, it must happen before the second thing can take place.

precursor [prɪ'kɜːsə] **precursors** NOUN

A precursor of something that exists now is a similar thing that existed at an earlier time. *e.g. real tennis, an ancient precursor of the modern game*

predator ['prɛdətə] **predators** NOUN

(SCIENCE) an animal that kills and eats other animals
predatory ADJECTIVE

predecessor ['priːdɪˌsɛsə] **predecessors** NOUN

Someone's predecessor is a person who used to do their job before.

predetermined [ˌpriːdɪ'tɜːmɪnd] ADJECTIVE

decided in advance or controlled by previous events rather than left to chance

predicament [prɪ'dɪkəmənt] **predicaments** NOUN

a difficult situation

● THESAURUS
fix: informal *The government has really got itself into a fix.*
hot water: informal *His antics keep landing him in hot water with officials.*
jam: informal *We are in a real jam now.*
scrape: informal *He's had his fair share of scrapes with the law.*
tight spot: *This was one tight spot he couldn't get out of.*

predict [prɪˈdɪkt] **predicts, predicting, predicted** VERB
If someone predicts an event, they say that it will happen in the future.
[WORD HISTORY: from Latin PRAEDICERE meaning 'to say beforehand']

THESAURUS
forecast: *He forecasts that house prices will rise by 5% this year.*
foresee: *He did not foresee any problems.*
foretell: *prophets who have foretold the end of the world*
prophesy: *She prophesied a bad ending for the expedition.*

prediction [prɪˈdɪkʃən] **predictions** NOUN
something that is forecast in advance

THESAURUS
forecast: *a forecast of heavy weather to come*
prophecy: *the interpreters of Biblical prophecy*

predominant [prɪˈdɒmɪnənt] ADJECTIVE
more important or more noticeable than anything else in a particular set of people or things *e.g. Yellow is the predominant colour in the house.*
predominantly ADVERB

predominate [prɪˈdɒmɪˌneɪt] **predominates, predominating, predominated** VERB
If one type of person or thing predominates, it is the most common, frequent, or noticeable. *e.g. Fresh flowers predominate in the bouquet.*
predominance NOUN

pre-eminent [prɪˈɛmɪnənt] ADJECTIVE
recognized as being the most important in a particular group *e.g. the pre-eminent experts in the area*
pre-eminence NOUN

pre-empt [prɪˈɛmpt] **pre-empts, pre-empting, pre-empted** VERB; FORMAL
If you pre-empt something, you prevent it by doing something else which makes it pointless or impossible. *e.g. a wish to pre-empt any further publicity*

preen [priːn] **preens, preening, preened** VERB
When a bird preens its feathers, it cleans them using its beak.

preface [ˈprɛfɪs] **prefaces** NOUN
an introduction at the beginning of a book explaining what the book is about or why it was written

prefect [ˈpriːfɛkt] **prefects** NOUN
a pupil who has special duties at a school
[WORD HISTORY: from Latin PRAEFECTUS meaning 'someone put in charge']

prefer [prɪˈfɜː] **prefers, preferring, preferred** VERB
If you prefer one thing to another, you like it better than the other thing.
preferable ADJECTIVE, **preferably** ADVERB

THESAURUS
be partial to: *I'm quite partial to mussels.*
favour: *Both sides favour a diplomatic solution.*
go for: *They went for a more up-market approach.*
incline towards: *The majority are inclined towards a forgiving attitude.*
like better: *I like the flat shoes better.*

preference [ˈprɛfərəns] **preferences** NOUN
1 If you have a preference for something, you like it more than other things. *e.g. a preference for white*
2 When making a choice, if you give preference to one type of person or thing, you try to choose that type.

preferential [ˌprɛfəˈrɛnʃəl] ADJECTIVE
A person who gets preferential treatment is treated better than others.

prefix [ˈpriːfɪks] **prefixes** NOUN
(ENGLISH) a letter or group of letters added to the beginning of a word to make a new word, for example 'semi-', 'pre-', and 'un-'

pregnant [ˈprɛgnənt] ADJECTIVE
A woman who is pregnant has a baby developing in her womb.
pregnancy NOUN

prehistoric [ˌpriːhɪˈstɒrɪk] ADJECTIVE
existing at a time in the past before anything was written down

prejudice [ˈprɛdʒʊdɪs] **prejudices** NOUN
(RE)
1 Prejudice is an unreasonable and unfair dislike of or preference.

THESAURUS
bias: *Bias against women permeates every level of the judicial system.*
partiality: *She is criticized for her one-sidedness and partiality.*
preconception: *preconceptions about the sort of people who did computing*
2 Prejudice is also an intolerance towards certain people or groups. *e.g. racial prejudice*
prejudiced ADJECTIVE, **prejudicial** ADJECTIVE

THESAURUS
bigotry: *religious bigotry*
chauvinism: *the growth of Russian chauvinism*
discrimination: *sex discrimination*
racism: *the fight to rid sport of racism*
sexism: *sexism in the workplace*

preliminary [prɪˈlɪmɪnərɪ] ADJECTIVE
Preliminary activities take place before

P

something starts, in preparation for it. *e.g. the preliminary rounds of the competition*

prelude ['prɛljuːd] **preludes** NOUN
Something that is an introduction to a more important event can be described as a prelude to that event.

premature [ˌprɛməˈtjʊə] ADJECTIVE
happening too early, or earlier than expected *e.g. premature baldness*
prematurely ADVERB

premeditated [prɪˈmɛdɪˌteɪtɪd] ADJECTIVE
planned in advance *e.g. a premeditated attack*

premier ['prɛmjə] **premiers** NOUN
1 The leader of a government is sometimes referred to as the premier.

2 in Australia, the leader of a State government

> ADJECTIVE
3 considered to be the best or most important *e.g. Wellington's premier jewellers.*

premiere ['prɛmɪˌɛə] **premieres** NOUN
the first public performance of a new play or film

premise premises PLURAL NOUN ['prɛmɪsɪz]
1 The premises of an organization are all the buildings it occupies on one site.

> NOUN ['prɛmɪs]
2 a statement which you suppose is true and use as the basis for an idea or argument

premium ['priːmɪəm] **premiums** NOUN
an extra sum of money that has to be paid *e.g. Paying a premium for space is worthwhile.*

premonition [ˌprɛməˈnɪʃən] **premonitions** NOUN
a feeling that something unpleasant is going to happen

THESAURUS
foreboding: *His triumph was overshadowed by an uneasy sense of foreboding.*
funny feeling: informal *I have a funny feeling something unpleasant is about to happen.*
omen: *Her appearance at this moment is an omen of disaster.*
sign: *a sign of impending doom*

preoccupation [priːˌɒkjʊˈpeɪʃən] **preoccupations** NOUN
If you have a preoccupation with something, it is very important to you and you keep thinking about it.

preoccupied [priːˈɒkjʊˌpaɪd] ADJECTIVE
Someone who is preoccupied is deep in thought or totally involved with something.

THESAURUS
absorbed: *They were completely absorbed in each other.*

engrossed: *Tom didn't notice because he was too engrossed in his work.*
immersed: *He's becoming really immersed in his studies.*
oblivious: *When he was in his car he was totally oblivious to everybody else.*
wrapped up: *She's wrapped up in her new career.*

preparatory [prɪˈpærətərɪ] ADJECTIVE
Preparatory activities are done before doing something else in order to prepare for it.

prepare [prɪˈpɛə] **prepares, preparing, prepared** VERB
If you prepare something, you make it ready for a particular purpose or event. *e.g. He was preparing the meal.*
preparation NOUN

prepared [prɪˈpɛəd] ADJECTIVE
If you are prepared to do something, you are willing to do it.

preposition [ˌprɛpəˈzɪʃən] **prepositions** NOUN
(ENGLISH) a word such as 'by', 'for', 'into', or 'with', which usually has a noun as its object

preposterous [prɪˈpɒstərəs] ADJECTIVE
extremely unreasonable and ridiculous *e.g. a preposterous statement*

prerequisite [priːˈrɛkwɪzɪt] **prerequisites** NOUN; FORMAL
Something that is a prerequisite for another thing must happen or exist before the other thing is possible. *e.g. Self-esteem is a prerequisite for a happy life.*

prerogative [prɪˈrɒgətɪv] **prerogatives** NOUN; FORMAL
Something that is the prerogative of a person is their special privilege or right.

prescribe [prɪˈskraɪb] **prescribes, prescribing, prescribed** VERB
When a doctor prescribes treatment, he or she states what treatment a patient should have.

prescription [prɪˈskrɪpʃən] **prescriptions** NOUN
a piece of paper on which the doctor has written the name of a medicine needed by a patient

presence ['prɛzəns] NOUN
1 Someone's presence in a place is the fact of their being there. *e.g. His presence made me happy.*

2 If you are in someone's presence, you are in the same place as they are.

3 Someone who has presence has an impressive appearance or manner.

present presents, presenting, presented ADJECTIVE ['prɛzᵊnt]

1 If someone is present somewhere, they are there. *e.g. He had been present at the birth of his son.*

THESAURUS

at hand: *Having the right equipment at hand will be very useful.*
here: *He was here a minute ago.*
in attendance: *Police and several fire engines are in attendance.*
there: *The group of old buildings is still there today.*
to hand: *I haven't got the instructions to hand.*
<<OPPOSITE *absent*

2 A present situation is one that exists now rather than in the past or the future.

> NOUN ['prɛzᵊnt]

3 The present is the period of time that is taking place now.

4 something that you give to someone for them to keep

> VERB [prɪ'zɛnt]

THESAURUS

bonsela: South African *your kind bonsela to the hospital*
donation: *Employees make regular donations to charity.*
gift: *a Christmas gift*
offering: *Hindus kill turtles ritually as an offering to their gods.*

5 If you present someone with something, you give it to them. *e.g. She presented a bravery award to the girl.*

THESAURUS

award: *For his dedication he was awarded a medal of merit.*
bestow: *The Queen bestowed on him a knighthood.*
donate: *He frequently donates large sums to charity.*
give: *She gave me a pen for my birthday.*
grant: *France has agreed to grant him political asylum.*
hand out: *One of my jobs was to hand out the prizes.*

6 Something that presents a difficulty or a challenge causes it or provides it.

7 The person who presents a radio or television show introduces each part or each guest.
presenter NOUN

presentable [prɪ'zɛntəbᵊl] ADJECTIVE
neat or attractive and suitable for people to see

presentation [ˌprɛzən'teɪʃən]
presentations NOUN

1 the act of presenting or a way of presenting something

2 The presentation of a piece of work is the way it looks or the impression it gives.

3 (D & T) To give a presentation is to give a talk or demonstration to an audience of something

you have been studying or working on.

present-day ['prɛzᵊnt,deɪ] ADJECTIVE
existing or happening now *e.g. present-day farming practices*

presently ['prɛzəntlɪ] ADVERB

1 If something will happen presently, it will happen soon. *e.g. I'll finish the job presently.*

2 Something that is presently happening is happening now. *e.g. Some progress is presently being made.*

present participle present participles
NOUN
In grammar, the present participle of an English verb is the form that ends in '-ing'. It is used to form some tenses, and can be used to form adjectives and nouns from a verb.

present tense NOUN
In grammar, the present tense is the tense of a verb that you use mainly to talk about things that happen or exist at the time of writing or speaking.

preservative [prɪ'zɜːvətɪv] **preservatives**
NOUN
a substance or chemical that stops things decaying

preserve [prɪ'zɜːv] **preserves, preserving, preserved** VERB

1 If you preserve something, you take action so that it remains as it is.

2 If you preserve food, you treat it to prevent it from decaying.

> NOUN

3 Preserves are foods such as jam or chutney that have been made with a lot of sugar or vinegar.
preservation NOUN

preside [prɪ'zaɪd] **presides, presiding, presided** VERB
A person who presides over a formal event is in charge of it.

president ['prɛzɪdənt] **presidents** NOUN

1 In a country which has no king or queen, the president is the elected leader. *e.g. the President of the United States of America*

2 The president of an organization is the person who has the highest position.
presidency NOUN, **presidential** ADJECTIVE

press [prɛs] **presses, pressing, pressed**
VERB

1 If you press something, you push it or hold it firmly against something else. *e.g. Lisa pressed his hand... Press the blue button.*

THESAURUS

compress: *Poor posture compresses the body's organs.*

P

crush: *Peel and crush the garlic.*
mash: *Mash the bananas with a fork.*
push: *She pushed the door open.*
squeeze: *He squeezed her arm reassuringly.*

2 If you press clothes, you iron them.

3 If you press for something, you try hard to persuade someone to agree to it. *e.g. She was pressing for improvements to the education system.*

⬤ THESAURUS
beg: *I begged him to come back with me.*
implore: *'Tell me what to do!' she implored him.*
petition: *All the attempts to petition the government had failed.*
plead: *I pleaded to be allowed to go.*
pressurize: *He thought she was trying to pressurize him.*
urge: *He had urged her to come to Ireland.*

4 If you press charges, you make an accusation against someone which has to be examined in a court of law.

> NOUN
5 Newspapers and the journalists who work for them are called the press.

press conference **press conferences**
NOUN
When someone gives a press conference, they have a meeting to answer questions put by reporters.

pressing ['prɛsɪŋ] ADJECTIVE
Something that is pressing needs to be dealt with immediately. *e.g. pressing needs*

pressure ['prɛʃə] **pressures, pressuring, pressured** NOUN
1 (SCIENCE) Pressure is the force that is produced by pushing on something.

2 (PSHE) If you are under pressure, you have too much to do and not enough time, or someone is trying hard to persuade you to do something.

> VERB
3 If you pressure someone, you try hard to persuade them to do something.

pressurize ['prɛʃə,raɪz] **pressurizes, pressurizing, pressurized;** also spelt **pressurise** VERB
If you pressurize someone, you try hard to persuade them to do something.

prestige [prɛ'stiːʒ] NOUN
If you have prestige, people admire you because of your position.
prestigious ADJECTIVE

presumably [prɪ'zjuːməblɪ] ADVERB
If you say that something is presumably the case, you mean you assume that it is. *e.g. Your audience, presumably, are younger.*

presume [prɪ'zjuːm] **presumes, presuming, presumed** VERB
If you presume something, you think that it is the case although you have no proof.
presumption NOUN

presumptuous [prɪ'zʌmptjʊəs] ADJECTIVE
Someone who behaves in a presumptuous way does things that they have no right to do.

pretence [prɪ'tɛns] **pretences** NOUN
a way of behaving that is false and intended to deceive people

pretend [prɪ'tɛnd] **pretends, pretending, pretended** VERB
If you pretend that something is the case, you try to make people believe that it is, although in fact it is not. *e.g. Latimer pretended not to notice.*

⬤ THESAURUS
counterfeit: *the coins he is alleged to have counterfeited*
fake: *He faked his own death last year.*
falsify: *He was charged with falsifying business records.*
feign: *The striker was accused of feigning injury.*
pass oneself off as: *She tried to pass herself off as an actress.*

pretender [prɪ'tɛndə] **pretenders** NOUN
A pretender to a throne or title is someone who claims it but whose claim is being questioned.

pretension [prɪ'tɛnʃən] **pretensions** NOUN
Someone with pretensions claims that they are more important than they really are.

pretentious [prɪ'tɛnʃəs] ADJECTIVE
Someone or something that is pretentious is trying to seem important when in fact they are not.

⬤ THESAURUS
affected: *She passed along with an affected air and a disdainful look.*
conceited: *I thought him conceited and arrogant.*
ostentatious: *an ostentatious wedding reception*
pompous: *He's pompous and has a high opinion of his own capabilities.*
snobbish: *a snobbish dislike for their intellectual inferiors*

pretext ['priːtɛkst] **pretexts** NOUN
a false reason given to hide the real reason for doing something

pretty ['prɪtɪ] **prettier, prettiest** ADJECTIVE
1 attractive in a delicate way

⬤ THESAURUS
attractive: *She has a round attractive face.*
beautiful: *a beautiful child*
cute: *a cute little baby*
lovely: *his lovely wife*

> ADVERB
2 INFORMAL

quite or rather *e.g. He spoke pretty good English.*
prettily ADVERB, **prettiness** NOUN

THESAURUS
fairly: *Both ships are fairly new.*
kind of: informal *I was kind of embarrassed about it.*
quite: *It was quite hard.*
rather: *She's rather vain.*

prevail [prɪ'veɪl] **prevails, prevailing, prevailed** VERB
1 If a custom or belief prevails in a particular place, it is normal or most common there. *e.g. This attitude has prevailed in Britain for many years.*
2 If someone or something prevails, they succeed in their aims. *e.g. In recent years better sense has prevailed.*
prevailing ADJECTIVE

prevalent ['prɛvələnt] ADJECTIVE
very common or widespread *e.g. the hooliganism so prevalent today*
prevalence NOUN

prevent [prɪ'vɛnt] **prevents, preventing, prevented** VERB
If you prevent something, you stop it from happening or being done.
preventable ADJECTIVE, **prevention** NOUN

THESAURUS
avert: *A fresh tragedy was narrowly averted yesterday.*
foil: *The plot was foiled by policemen.*
hinder: *Research is hindered by lack of cash.*
impede: *Fallen rocks are impeding the progress of the rescue workers.*
stop: *a new diplomatic initiative to try to stop the war*
thwart: *Her ambition to become an artist was thwarted by failing eyesight.*

preventive or **preventative** [prɪ'vɛntɪv] or [prɪ'vɛntətɪv] ADJECTIVE
intended to help prevent things such as disease or crime *e.g. preventive health care*

preview ['priː.vjuː] **previews** NOUN
1 an opportunity to see something, such as a film or exhibition, before it is shown to the public
2 **(ICT)** a part of a computer program which allows you to look at what you have keyed or added to a document as it will appear when it is printed

previous ['priː.vɪəs] ADJECTIVE
happening or existing before something else in time or position *e.g. previous reports... the previous year*
previously ADVERB

THESAURUS
earlier: *His earlier works include impressive still lifes.*
former: *a former president of Mexico*

one-time: *the country's one-time military rulers*
past: *a return to the turbulence of past centuries*
preceding: *This is examined in detail in the preceding chapter.*
prior: *I can't make it. I have a prior engagement.*

prey [preɪ] **preys, preying, preyed** NOUN
1 The creatures that an animal hunts and eats are called its prey.
> VERB
2 An animal that preys on a particular kind of animal lives by hunting and eating it.

price [praɪs] **prices, pricing, priced** NOUN
1 The price of something is the amount of money you have to pay to buy it.

THESAURUS
amount: *I was asked to pay the full amount.*
charge: *an annual management charge of 1.25%*
cost: *the cost of a loaf of bread*
fee: *the annual membership fee*
figure: *A figure of £2000 was mentioned.*
value: *The company's market value rose to 5.5 billion dollars.*

> VERB
2 To price something at a particular amount is to fix its price at that amount.

THESAURUS
cost: *We hope it won't cost too much.*
estimate: *His personal riches were estimated at $368 million.*
put a price on: *The company has refused to put a price on its bid.*
value: *I had my jewellery valued for insurance purposes.*

priceless ['praɪslɪs] ADJECTIVE
Something that is priceless is so valuable that it is difficult to work out how much it is worth.

pricey ['praɪsɪ] **pricier, priciest** ADJECTIVE; INFORMAL
expensive

prick [prɪk] **pricks, pricking, pricked** VERB
1 If you prick something, you stick a sharp pointed object into it.
> NOUN
2 a small, sharp pain caused when something pricks you

prickle ['prɪkəl] **prickles, prickling, prickled** NOUN
1 Prickles are small sharp points or thorns on plants.
> VERB
2 If your skin prickles, it feels as if a lot of sharp points are being stuck into it.
prickly ADJECTIVE

pride [praɪd] **prides, priding, prided** NOUN

P

667

1 Pride is a feeling of satisfaction you have when you have done something well.

2 Pride is also a feeling of being better than other people.

3 A pride of lions is a group of them.

> VERB

4 If you pride yourself on a quality or skill, you are proud of it. *e.g. She prides herself on punctuality.*

priest [priːst] **priests** NOUN (RE)
a member of the clergy in some Christian Churches. In many non-Christian religions, a priest is a man who has special duties in the place where people worship.
priestly ADJECTIVE

priestess ['priːstɛs] **priestesses** NOUN
a female priest in a non-Christian religion

priesthood ['priːstˌhʊd] NOUN
The priesthood is the position of being a priest.

prim [prɪm] **primmer, primmest** ADJECTIVE
Someone who is prim always behaves very correctly and is easily shocked by anything rude.

🔵 **THESAURUS**
proper: *He was very pompous and proper.*
prudish: *I'm not prudish but I think those photos are obscene.*
puritanical: *He has a puritanical attitude towards sex.*
strait-laced: *He is very strait-laced and narrow-minded.*

primaeval [praɪˈmiːvᵊl] another spelling of **primeval**

primarily ['praɪmərəlɪ] ADVERB
You use 'primarily' to indicate the main or most important feature of something. *e.g. I still rated people primarily on their looks.*

primary ['praɪmərɪ] ADJECTIVE
'Primary' is used to describe something that is extremely important for someone or something *e.g. the primary aim of his research*

primary colour **primary colours** NOUN
In art, the primary colours are red, yellow, and blue, from which other colours can be obtained by mixing.

primary school **primary schools** NOUN
a school for children aged up to 11

primate ['praɪmeɪt] **primates** NOUN
1 an archbishop
2 a member of the group of animals which includes humans, monkeys, and apes

prime [praɪm] **primes, priming, primed** ADJECTIVE
1 main or most important *e.g. a prime cause of brain damage*

🔵 **THESAURUS**
chief: *The job went to one of his chief rivals.*
leading: *a leading industrial nation*
main: *the city's main tourist area*
principal: *our principal source of foreign exchange earnings*

2 of the best quality *e.g. in prime condition*

🔵 **THESAURUS**
best: *He'll have the best care.*
choice: *our choicest chocolates*
first-rate: *He's a first-rate officer.*
select: *With that historic win he now joins a select band of golfers.*
superior: *superior coffee beans*

> NOUN

3 Someone's prime is the stage when they are at their strongest, most active, or most successful.

> VERB

4 If you prime someone, you give them information about something in advance to prepare them. *e.g. We are primed for every lesson.*

prime minister **prime ministers** NOUN
The prime minister is the leader of the government.

primeval or **primaeval** [praɪˈmiːvᵊl]
ADJECTIVE
belonging to a very early period in the history of the world

primitive ['prɪmɪtɪv] ADJECTIVE
1 connected with a society that lives very simply without industries or a writing system *e.g. the primitive peoples of the world*

2 very simple, basic, or old-fashioned *e.g. a very small primitive cottage*

🔵 **THESAURUS**
crude: *crude stone carvings*
rough: *a rough wooden table*
rude: *He constructed a rude cabin for himself.*
rudimentary: *The bomb was rudimentary but lethal.*
simple: *a simple shelter*

primrose ['prɪmˌrəʊz] **primroses** NOUN
a small plant that has pale yellow flowers in spring
[WORD HISTORY: from Latin PRIMA ROSA meaning 'first rose']

prince [prɪns] **princes** NOUN
a male member of a royal family, especially the son of a king or queen
princely ADJECTIVE
[WORD HISTORY: from Latin PRINCEPS meaning 'chief' or 'ruler']

princess [prɪnˈsɛs] **princesses** NOUN
a female member of a royal family, usually the

daughter of a king or queen, or the wife of a prince

principal ['prɪnsɪpəl] **principals** ADJECTIVE
1 main or most important *e.g. the principal source of food*

● THESAURUS
chief: *his chief reason for withdrawing*
first: *The first duty of this government is to tackle poverty.*
foremost: *one of the world's foremost scholars of classical poetry*
main: *What are the main differences between them?*
major: *the major factor in her decision*
primary: *the primary cause of his problems*
prime: *Police will see me as the prime suspect!*
> NOUN
2 the person in charge of a school or college
principally ADVERB

Do not confuse *principal* with *principle: my principal objection.*

principality [,prɪnsɪ'pælɪtɪ] **principalities** NOUN
a country ruled by a prince

principle ['prɪnsɪpəl] **principles** NOUN
1 a belief you have about the way you should behave *e.g. a woman of principle*

● THESAURUS
conscience: *the law on freedom of conscience and religious organizations*
integrity: *He has always been a man of integrity.*
morals: *public morals*
scruples: *a man with no moral scruples*
sense of duty: *He did it out of a sense of duty to his men.*

2 a general rule or scientific law which explains how something happens or works *e.g. the principle of evolution in nature*

● THESAURUS
axiom: *the long-held axiom that education leads to higher income*
canon: *the canons of political economy*
doctrine: *Christian doctrine*
fundamental: *the fundamentals of astronomy*
law: *the laws of motion*

Do not confuse *principle* with *principal: a man with no principles.*

print [prɪnt] **prints, printing, printed** VERB
1 To print a newspaper or book is to reproduce it in large quantities using a mechanical or electronic copying process.

2 If you print when you are writing, you do not join the letters together.
> NOUN
3 The letters and numbers on the pages of a book

or newspaper are referred to as the print.

4 a photograph, or a printed copy of a painting

5 Footprints and fingerprints can be referred to as prints.
printer NOUN

printing ['prɪntɪŋ] NOUN
the process of producing printed material such as books and newspapers

print-out ['prɪnt,aʊt] **print-outs** NOUN
a printed copy of information from a computer

prior ['praɪə] **priors** ADJECTIVE
1 planned or done at an earlier time *e.g. I have a prior engagement.*
> PHRASE
2 Something that happens **prior to** a particular time or event happens before it.
> NOUN
3 a monk in charge of a small group of monks in a priory
prioress NOUN

priority [praɪ'ɒrɪtɪ] **priorities** NOUN
something that needs to be dealt with first *e.g. The priority is building homes.*

prioritize [praɪ'ɒrɪ,taɪz] **prioritizes, prioritizing, prioritized** prioritise VERB
To prioritize things is to decide which is the most important and deal with it first.

priory ['praɪərɪ] **priories** NOUN
a place where a small group of monks live under the charge of a prior

prise [praɪz] **prises, prising, prised** VERB
If you prise something open or away from a surface, you force it open or away. *e.g. She prised his fingers loose.*

prism ['prɪzəm] **prisms** NOUN
1 an object made of clear glass with many flat sides. It separates light passing through it into the colours of the rainbow

2 In maths, a prism is any polyhedron with two identical parallel ends and sides which are parallelograms.

prison ['prɪzən] **prisons** NOUN
a building where criminals are kept in captivity

● THESAURUS
dungeon: *The castle's dungeons haven't been used for years.*
jail: *Three prisoners escaped from the jail.*
nick: British and Australian and New Zealand; slang *I was banged up in the nick for six months.*
penal institution: *Thirty years in a penal institution is indeed a harsh penalty.*

prisoner ['prɪzənə] **prisoners** NOUN
someone who is kept in prison or held in captivity against their will

P

THESAURUS

captive: *the difficulties of spending four months as a captive*

convict: *convicts serving life sentences*

hostage: *negotiations to release the hostages*

pristine ['prɪstaɪn] ADJECTIVE; FORMAL
very clean or new and in perfect condition

private ['praɪvɪt] **privates** ADJECTIVE

1 for the use of one person rather than people in general *e.g. a private bathroom*

THESAURUS

exclusive: *Many of our cheeses are exclusive to our shops in Britain.*

individual: *Divide the vegetables among four individual dishes.*

personal: *It's for my own personal use.*

special: *her own special problems*

2 taking place between a small number of people and kept secret from others *e.g. a private conversation*

THESAURUS

clandestine: *He had a clandestine meeting with his lover.*

confidential: *confidential information about her private life*

secret: *a secret love affair*

<<OPPOSITE *public*

3 owned or run by individuals or companies rather than by the state *e.g. a private company*

> NOUN

4 a soldier of the lowest rank

privacy NOUN, **privately** ADVERB

private school **private schools** NOUN
a school that does not receive money from the government, and parents pay for their children to attend

privatize ['praɪvɪ,taɪz] **privatizes, privatizing, privatized**; also spelt **privatise** VERB
If the government privatizes a state-owned industry or organization, it allows it to be bought and owned by a private individual or group.

privilege ['prɪvɪlɪdʒ] **privileges** NOUN
a special right or advantage given to a person or group *e.g. the privileges of monarchy*

privileged ADJECTIVE

privy ['prɪvɪ] ADJECTIVE; FORMAL
If you are privy to something secret, you have been told about it.

prize [praɪz] **prizes, prizing, prized** NOUN

1 a reward given to the winner of a competition or game

THESAURUS

accolade: *the ultimate international accolade, the Nobel Peace Prize*

award: *the Booker Prize, Britain's top award for fiction*

honour: *He was showered with honours – among them an Oscar.*

trophy: *They haven't won a trophy since 1991.*

> ADJECTIVE

2 of the highest quality or standard *e.g. his prize dahlia*

THESAURUS

award-winning: *an award-winning restaurant*

first-rate: *a first-rate thriller writer*

outstanding: *an outstanding horse*

top: *Holland's top striker.*

> VERB

3 Something that is prized is wanted and admired for its value or quality.

THESAURUS

cherish: *We cherish our independence.*

esteem: *one of Europe's most esteemed awards*

treasure: *She treasures her memories of those joyous days.*

value: *I value the work he gives me.*

pro [prəʊ] **pros** NOUN

1 INFORMAL
a professional

> PHRASE

2 The **pros and cons** of a situation are its advantages and disadvantages.

[WORD HISTORY: sense 2 is from Latin PRO meaning 'for' and CONTRA meaning 'against']

pro- PREFIX
'Pro-' means supporting or in favour of *e.g. pro-democracy protests*

probability [,prɒbə'bɪlɪtɪ] **probabilities** NOUN

1 The probability of something happening is how likely it is to happen. *e.g. the probability of success*

THESAURUS

chances: *The chances of success for the product are good.*

likelihood: *the likelihood of infection*

odds: *The odds are that you are going to fail.*

prospect: *the prospect for peace in Rwanda*

2 If something is a probability, it is likely to happen. *e.g. The probability is that you will be feeling better.*

probable ['prɒbəbəl] ADJECTIVE
Something that is probable is likely to be true or correct, or likely to happen. *e.g. the most probable outcome*

THESAURUS

apparent: *There is no apparent reason for the crime.*

feasible: *Whether this is feasible is a matter of doubt.*

likely: *Further delays are likely.*

on the cards: *A promotion is definitely on the cards for you.*
plausible: *a plausible explanation*
<<OPPOSITE *improbable*

probably ['prɒbəblɪ] ADVERB
Something that is probably the case is likely but not certain.

● THESAURUS
doubtless: *He will doubtless try to change my mind.*
in all probability: *Victory will, in all probability, earn France the title.*
likely: *The entire surplus will most likely be handed over.*
presumably: *The spear is presumably the murder weapon.*

probation [prə'beɪʃən] NOUN
Probation is a period of time during which a person convicted of a crime is supervised by a probation officer instead of being sent to prison.
probationary ADJECTIVE

probe [prəʊb] **probes, probing, probed**
VERB
1 If you probe, you ask a lot of questions to discover the facts about something.

> NOUN
2 a long thin instrument used by doctors and dentists when examining a patient

problem ['prɒbləm] **problems** NOUN
1 an unsatisfactory situation that causes difficulties

● THESAURUS
difficulty: *This company is facing great difficulties.*
predicament: *the once-great club's current predicament*
quandary: *We're in a quandary over our holiday plans.*
trouble: *I had trouble parking this morning.*

2 a puzzle or question that you solve using logical thought or mathematics
problematic ADJECTIVE

● THESAURUS
conundrum: *an apparently insoluble conundrum*
puzzle: *The data has presented astronomers with a puzzle.*
riddle: *the riddle of the birth of the universe*

procedure [prə'siːdʒə] **procedures** NOUN
a way of doing something, especially the correct or usual way *e.g. It's standard procedure.*
procedural ADJECTIVE

● THESAURUS
method: *new teaching methods*
policy: *It is our policy to prosecute shoplifters.*
practice: *a public inquiry into bank practices*
process: *the production process*
strategy: *a strategy for controlling malaria*

system: *an efficient filing system*

proceed [prə'siːd] **proceeds, proceeding, proceeded** VERB
1 If you proceed to do something, you start doing it, or continue doing it. *e.g. She proceeded to tell them.*

● THESAURUS
begin: *He stood up and began to move about the room.*
carry on: *"Can I start with a couple of questions?" – "Carry on."*
continue: *I need some advice before I can continue with this task.*
get under way: *The court case got under way last autumn.*
go on: *Go on with your work.*
start: *I started to follow him up the stairs.*
<<OPPOSITE *cease*

2 FORMAL
If you proceed in a particular direction, you move in that direction. *e.g. The taxi proceeded along a lonely road.*

● THESAURUS
advance: *I advanced slowly, one step at a time.*
continue: *He continued rapidly up the path.*
go on: *They went on through the forest.*
make your way: *He made his way to the marketplace.*
progress: *He progressed slowly along the coast in an easterly direction.*
travel: *You can travel to Helsinki tomorrow.*

> PLURAL NOUN
3 The proceeds from something are the money obtained from it.

proceedings [prə'siːdɪŋz] PLURAL NOUN
1 You can refer to an organized and related series of events as the proceedings. *e.g. She was determined to see the proceedings from start to finish.*

2 Legal proceedings are legal action taken against someone.

process ['prəʊsɛs] **processes, processing, processed** NOUN
1 a series of actions intended to achieve a particular result or change

● THESAURUS
course of action: *It is important that we take the right course of action.*
means: *The move is a means to fight crime.*
method: *new teaching methods*
procedure: *the correct procedure for applying for a visa*
system: *an efficient filing system*

> PHRASE
2 If you are **in the process** of doing something, you have started doing it but have not yet finished.

P

> VERB

3 When something such as food or information is processed, it is treated or dealt with.

● THESAURUS
deal with: *the way that banks deal with complaints*
dispose of: *They disposed of the problem quickly.*
handle: *She didn't know how to handle the problem.*
take care of: *They left it to me to try and take care of the problem.*

procession [prəˈsɛʃən] **processions** NOUN
a group of people or vehicles moving in a line, often as part of a ceremony

processor [ˈprəʊsɛsə] **processors** NOUN
(ICT) In computing, a processor is the central chip in a computer which controls its operations.

proclaim [prəˈkleɪm] **proclaims, proclaiming, proclaimed** VERB
If someone proclaims something, they announce it or make it known. *e.g. You have proclaimed your innocence.*
proclamation NOUN

procure [prəˈkjʊə] **procures, procuring, procured** VERB; FORMAL
If you procure something, you obtain it.

prod [prɒd] **prods, prodding, prodded** VERB
If you prod something, you give it a push with your finger or with something pointed.

prodigy [ˈprɒdɪdʒɪ] **prodigies** NOUN
someone who shows an extraordinary natural ability at an early age

produce produces, producing, produced
VERB [prəˈdjuːs]
1 To produce something is to make it or cause it. *e.g. a white wine produced mainly from black grapes*

● THESAURUS
construct: *an inner frame constructed from timber*
create: *It was created from odds and ends.*
invent: *He invented the first electric clock.*
make: *One of my jobs was to make the tea.*
manufacture: *They manufacture plastics.*

2 If you produce something from somewhere, you bring it out so it can be seen.

● THESAURUS
advance: *Many new theories have been advanced recently.*
bring forward: *We will bring forward new proposals for legislation.*
bring to light: *new evidence brought to light by the police*
put forward: *He has put forward new peace proposals.*

> NOUN [ˈprɒdjuːs]

3 Produce is food that is grown to be sold. *e.g. fresh produce*

producer [prəˈdjuːsə] **producers** NOUN
The producer of a record, film, or show is the person in charge of making it or putting it on.

product [ˈprɒdʌkt] **products** NOUN
1 something that is made to be sold *e.g. high-quality products*

● THESAURUS
commodity: *basic commodities such as bread and milk*
goods: *imported goods*
merchandise: *The club sells a wide range of merchandise.*
produce: *locally grown produce*

2 In maths, the product of two or more numbers or quantities is the result of multiplying them together.

production [prəˈdʌkʃən] **productions**
NOUN (D & T)
1 Production is the process of manufacturing or growing something in large quantities. *e.g. modern methods of production*

2 Production is also the amount of goods manufactured or food grown by a country or company. *e.g. Production has fallen by 13.2%.*

3 A production of a play, opera, or other show is a series of performances of it.

productive [prəˈdʌktɪv] ADJECTIVE
1 To be productive means to produce a large number of things. *e.g. Farms were more productive in these areas.*

● THESAURUS
fertile: *a product of his fertile imagination*
fruitful: *a landscape that was fruitful and lush*
prolific: *She is a prolific writer of novels and short stories.*
<<OPPOSITE *unproductive*

2 If something such as a meeting is productive, good or useful things happen as a result of it.

● THESAURUS
constructive: *constructive criticism*
useful: *We made some progress during a useful exchange.*
valuable: *The experience was very valuable.*
worthwhile: *It had been a worthwhile discussion.*
<<OPPOSITE *unproductive*

productivity [ˌprɒdʌkˈtɪvɪtɪ] NOUN
Productivity is the rate at which things are produced or dealt with.

profane [prəˈfeɪn] ADJECTIVE; FORMAL
showing disrespect for a religion or religious things *e.g. profane language*

profess [prəˈfɛs] **professes, professing, professed** VERB
1 FORMAL
If you profess to do or have something, you claim to do or have it.

2 If you profess a feeling or opinion, you express it. *e.g. He professes a lasting affection for Trinidad.*

profession [prə'fɛʃən] **professions** NOUN
1 a type of job that requires advanced education or training

● **THESAURUS**
business: *May I ask you what business you're in?*
career: *a career in journalism*
occupation: *her new occupation as an author*

2 You can use 'profession' to refer to all the people who have a particular profession. *e.g. the medical profession*

professional [prə'fɛʃənᵊl] **professionals** ADJECTIVE
1 Professional means relating to the work of someone who is qualified in a particular profession. *e.g. I think you need professional advice.*

2 Professional also describes activities when they are done to earn money rather than as a hobby. *e.g. professional football*

3 A professional piece of work is of a very high standard.

> NOUN
4 a person who has been trained in a profession

5 someone who plays a sport to earn money rather than as a hobby

professor [prə'fɛsə] **professors** NOUN
the senior teacher in a department of a British university
professorial ADJECTIVE

proficient [prə'fɪʃənt] ADJECTIVE
If you are proficient at something, you can do it well.
proficiency NOUN

● **THESAURUS**
able: *an able young rider*
accomplished: *an accomplished fundraiser*
adept: *an adept guitar player*
capable: *a very capable speaker*
competent: *a competent civil servant*
efficient: *a team of efficient workers*
skilful: *He is skilful at managing people.*
skilled: *a network of amateur but highly skilled observers of wildlife*
<<OPPOSITE *incompetent*

profile ['prəʊfaɪl] **profiles** NOUN
1 Your profile is the outline of your face seen from the side.

2 A profile of someone is a short description of their life and character.
[WORD HISTORY: from Italian PROFILARE meaning 'to sketch lightly']

profit ['prɒfɪt] **profits, profiting, profited**
NOUN

1 When someone sells something, the profit is the amount they gain by selling it for more than it cost them to buy or make.

● **THESAURUS**
earnings: *his earnings as an accountant*
proceeds: *The proceeds from the concert will go to charity.*
revenue: *tax revenues*
surplus: *Japan's trade surplus*
takings: *the pub's weekly takings*
<<OPPOSITE *loss*

> VERB
2 If you profit from something, you gain or benefit from it.
profitable ADJECTIVE

● **THESAURUS**
capitalize on: *The rebels are trying to capitalize on the public's discontent.*
exploit: *They are trying to exploit the troubles to their advantage.*
make the most of: *Happiness is the ability to make the most of what you have.*
take advantage of: *She took advantage of him even after their divorce.*

profound [prə'faʊnd] ADJECTIVE
1 great in degree or intensity *e.g. a profound need to please*

2 showing great and deep intellectual understanding *e.g. a profound question*
profoundly ADVERB, **profundity** NOUN

profuse [prə'fjuːs] ADJECTIVE
very large in quantity or number *e.g. There were profuse apologies for his absence.*
profusely ADVERB

program ['prəʊgræm] **programs, programming, programmed** (ICT) NOUN
1 a set of instructions that a computer follows to perform a particular task

> VERB
2 When someone programs a computer, they write a program and put it into the computer.
programmer NOUN

programme ['prəʊgræm] **programmes**
NOUN

1 a planned series of events *e.g. a programme of official engagements*

● **THESAURUS**
agenda: *This is sure to be an item on the agenda again next week.*
schedule: *We both have such hectic schedules.*
timetable: *We've finally managed to agree on a timetable for formal talks.*

2 a particular piece presented as a unit on television or radio, such as a play, show, or discussion

P

● **THESAURUS**
broadcast: *a broadcast by the President*
show: *my favourite TV show*

3 a booklet giving information about a play, concert, or show that you are attending

progress progresses, progressing, progressed NOUN ['prəʊgrɛs]

1 Progress is the process of gradually improving or getting near to achieving something. *e.g. Gerry is now making some real progress towards fitness.*

● **THESAURUS**
advance: *dramatic advances in road safety*
breakthrough: *a breakthrough in their research*
headway: *The police are making little headway in the investigation.*
improvement: *considerable room for improvement in facilities for patients*

2 The progress of something is the way in which it develops or continues. *e.g. news on the progress of the war*

> PHRASE
3 Something that is **in progress** is happening. *e.g. A cricket match was in progress.*

> VERB [prə'grɛs]
4 If you progress, you become more advanced or skilful.

● **THESAURUS**
advance: *Japan has advanced from a rural society to an industrial power.*
blossom: *In just a few years it has blossomed into an international event.*
develop: *workshops designed to develop acting skills*
improve: *Their French has improved enormously.*

5 To progress is to continue. *e.g. As the evening progressed, sadness turned to rage.*
progression NOUN

progressive [prə'grɛsɪv] ADJECTIVE

1 having modern ideas about how things should be done

2 happening gradually *e.g. a progressive illness*

prohibit [prə'hɪbɪt] prohibits, prohibiting, prohibited VERB

If someone prohibits something, they forbid it or make it illegal.
prohibition NOUN

● **THESAURUS**
ban: *The country will ban smoking in all offices this year.*
forbid: *The country's constitution forbids the military use of nuclear energy.*
outlaw: *In 1975 gambling was outlawed.*
prevent: *Residents may be prevented from leaving the islands.*
<<OPPOSITE *allow*

▩ You *prohibit* a person *from* doing something.

prohibitive [prə'hɪbɪtɪv] ADJECTIVE

If the cost of something is prohibitive, it is so high that people cannot afford it.

project projects, projecting, projected NOUN ['prɒdʒɛkt]

1 a carefully planned attempt to achieve something or to study something over a period of time

> VERB [prə'dʒɛkt]
2 Something that is projected is planned or expected to happen in the future. *e.g. The population aged 65 or over is projected to increase.*

3 To project an image onto a screen is to make it appear there using equipment such as a projector.

4 Something that projects sticks out beyond a surface or edge.
projection NOUN

projector [prə'dʒɛktə] projectors NOUN

a piece of equipment which produces a large image on a screen by shining light through a photographic slide or film strip

proletariat [ˌprəʊlɪ'tɛərɪət] NOUN; FORMAL

Working-class people are sometimes referred to as the proletariat.
proletarian ADJECTIVE

proliferate [prə'lɪfəˌreɪt] proliferates, proliferating, proliferated VERB

If things proliferate, they quickly increase in number.
proliferation NOUN
[WORD HISTORY: from Latin PROLIFER meaning 'having children']

prolific [prə'lɪfɪk] ADJECTIVE

producing a lot of something *e.g. this prolific artist*

prologue ['prəʊlɒg] prologues NOUN

a speech or section that introduces a play or book

prolong [prə'lɒŋ] prolongs, prolonging, prolonged VERB

If you prolong something, you make it last longer.
prolonged ADJECTIVE

prom [prɒm] proms NOUN; INFORMAL

a concert at which some of the audience stand

promenade [ˌprɒmə'nɑːd] promenades NOUN

a road or path next to the sea at a seaside resort
[WORD HISTORY: from SE PROMENER meaning 'to go for a walk']

prominent ['prɒmɪnənt] ADJECTIVE

1 Prominent people are important.

● **THESAURUS**
eminent: *an eminent scientist*

famous: *England's most famous modern artist.*
important: *an important figure in the media*
notable: *the notable linguist, Henriette Walter*
noted: *a noted Hebrew scholar*
renowned: *Sir William Crookes, the renowned chemist*
well-known: *He liked to surround himself with well-known people.*

2 Something that is prominent is very noticeable. *e.g. a prominent nose*
prominence NOUN, **prominently** ADVERB

● THESAURUS
conspicuous: *a conspicuous landmark*
eye-catching: *I outlined it in black to make it more eye-catching.*
jutting: *a jutting chin*
noticeable: *Squeezing spots only makes them more noticeable.*
obvious: *His cultural roots are most obvious in his poetry.*
pronounced: *The exhibition has a pronounced Scottish theme.*
striking: *a striking aspect of these statistics*

promiscuous [prəˈmɪskjʊəs] ADJECTIVE
Someone who is promiscuous has sex with many different people.
promiscuity NOUN

● THESAURUS
loose: *If you wear a short skirt in here you're considered a loose woman.*
wanton: *A woman with many sexual partners is still considered wanton.*

promise [ˈprɒmɪs] **promises, promising, promised** VERB
1 If you promise to do something, you say that you will definitely do it.

● THESAURUS
assure: *She assured me that she would deal with the problem.*
give your word: *He had given us his word he would join the club.*
guarantee: *Most countries guarantee the right to free education.*
pledge: *They have pledged to support the opposition.*
vow: *I vowed that someday I would return to live in Europe.*

2 Something that promises to have a particular quality shows signs that it will have that quality. *e.g. This promised to be a very long night.*

● THESAURUS
hint at: *One finding hints at support for this theory.*
indicate: *His early work indicates talent.*
show signs of: *Already she shows signs of beauty.*

> NOUN
3 a statement made by someone that they will definitely do something *e.g. He made a promise to me.*

● THESAURUS
assurance: *He gave written assurance that he would start work at once.*
guarantee: *They can give no guarantee that they will fulfil their obligations.*
pledge: *a pledge to step up cooperation between the two countries*
undertaking: *an undertaking that he would be a responsible parent*
vow: *I kept my marriage vows.*

4 Someone or something that shows promise seems likely to be very successful.
promising ADJECTIVE

promontory [ˈprɒməntərɪ] **promontories** NOUN
an area of high land sticking out into the sea

promote [prəˈməʊt] **promotes, promoting, promoted** VERB
1 If someone promotes something, they try to make it happen.

● THESAURUS
back: *She backed the new initiative enthusiastically.*
support: *He thanked everyone who had supported the strike.*

2 If someone promotes a product such as a film or a book, they try to make it popular by advertising.

● THESAURUS
advertise: *She is contracted to advertise their beauty products.*
plug: *informal He was on the show to plug his latest film.*
publicize: *I was publicizing the film in London.*

3 If someone is promoted, they are given a more important job at work.
promoter NOUN, **promotion** NOUN

● THESAURUS
elevate: *He was elevated to the post of Prime Minister.*
upgrade: *He was upgraded to supervisor.*

prompt [prɒmpt] **prompts, prompting, prompted** VERB
1 If something prompts someone to do something, it makes them decide to do it. *e.g. Curiosity prompted him to push at the door.*

● THESAURUS
cause: *What caused you to change your mind?*
induce: *Many teachers were induced to take early retirement.*
inspire: *These herbs will inspire you to try out all sorts of dishes.*
motivate: *How do you motivate people to work hard?*
spur: *Is it the money that spurs these firefighters to risk their lives?*

P

2 If you prompt someone when they stop speaking, you tell them what to say next or encourage them to continue.

● THESAURUS

coax: *"Tell us what happened next," he coaxed me.*
remind: *"You stopped in the middle of your story," I reminded mother.*

> ADVERB

3 exactly at the time mentioned *e.g. Wednesday morning at 10.40 prompt.*

● THESAURUS

exactly: *He arrived at exactly five o'clock.*
on the dot: *At nine o'clock on the dot, they have breakfast.*
precisely: *The meeting began at precisely 4.00 pm.*
sharp: *She planned to get up at 8.00 sharp.*

> ADJECTIVE

4 A prompt action is done without any delay. *e.g. a prompt reply*
promptly ADVERB

● THESAURUS

immediate: *These incidents had an immediate effect.*
instant: *He took an instant dislike to this woman.*
instantaneous: *This would result in his instantaneous dismissal.*
quick: *hoping for a quick end to the dispute*
rapid: *their rapid response to the situation*
swift: *make a swift decision*

prone [prəʊn] ADJECTIVE

1 If you are prone to something, you have a tendency to be affected by it or to do it. *e.g. She is prone to depression.*

● THESAURUS

disposed: *I might have been disposed to like him in other circumstances.*
given: *I am not very given to emotional displays.*
inclined: *Nobody felt inclined to argue with Smith.*
liable: *equipment that is liable to break*
susceptible: *She's very susceptible to colds and flu.*

2 If you are prone, you are lying flat and face downwards. *e.g. lying prone on the grass*

● THESAURUS

face down: *He was lying face down on his bed.*
prostrate: *The injured jockey lay prostrate on the ground.*

prong [prɒŋ] **prongs** NOUN
The prongs of a fork are the long, narrow, pointed parts.

pronoun ['prəʊˌnaʊn] **pronouns** NOUN
In grammar, a pronoun is a word that is used to replace a noun. 'He', 'she', and 'them' are all pronouns.

pronounce [prə'naʊns] **pronounces, pronouncing, pronounced** VERB

When you pronounce a word, you say it.

▮ There is an *o* before the *u* in *pronounce*. Compare this spelling with *pronunciation*.

pronounced [prə'naʊnst] ADJECTIVE
very noticeable *e.g. He talks with a pronounced lowland accent.*

pronouncement [prə'naʊnsmənt] **pronouncements** NOUN
a formal statement

pronunciation [prəˌnʌnsɪ'eɪʃən] **pronunciations** NOUN
the way a word is usually said

▮ There is no *o* before the *u* in *pronunciation*. Compare this spelling with *pronounce*.

proof [pruːf] NOUN
If you have proof of something, you have evidence which shows that it is true or exists.

● THESAURUS

confirmation: *further confirmation that house prices are no longer falling*
evidence: *To date there is no evidence to support this theory.*
testimony: *His testimony was an important element of the prosecution case.*
verification: *verification of her story*

prop [prɒp] **props, propping, propped** VERB
1 If you prop an object somewhere, you support it or rest it against something. *e.g. The barman propped himself against the counter.*

> NOUN

2 a stick or other object used to support something

3 The props in a play are all the objects and furniture used by the actors.

propaganda [ˌprɒpə'gændə] NOUN
(HISTORY) Propaganda is exaggerated or false information that is published or broadcast in order to influence people.

propagate ['prɒpəˌgeɪt] **propagates, propagating, propagated** VERB
1 If people propagate an idea, they spread it to try to influence many other people.

2 If you propagate plants, you grow more of them from an original one.
propagation NOUN

propel [prə'pɛl] **propels, propelling, propelled** VERB
To propel something is to cause it to move in a particular direction.

propeller [prə'pɛlə] **propellers** NOUN
a device on a boat or aircraft with rotating blades which makes the boat or aircraft move

propensity [prə'pɛnsɪtɪ] **propensities** NOUN; FORMAL

a tendency to behave in a particular way

proper ['prɒpə] ADJECTIVE

1 real and satisfactory *e.g. He was no nearer having a proper job.*

2 correct or suitable *e.g. Put things in their proper place.*

● THESAURUS

appropriate: *a smart outfit appropriate to the job*
apt: *an apt title for the book*
correct: *the correct way to do things*
fitting: *His address was a fitting end to a bitter campaign.*
right: *He's the right man for the job.*
suitable: *She had no other dress suitable for the occasion.*

<<OPPOSITE *improper*

3 accepted or conventional *e.g. a proper wedding*
properly ADVERB

● THESAURUS

accepted: *the accepted way of doing things*
conventional: *conventional surgical methods*
orthodox: *orthodox police methods*

proper noun **proper nouns** NOUN
the name of a person, place, or institution

property ['prɒpəti] **properties** NOUN

1 A person's property is the things that belong to them.

● THESAURUS

assets: *The company has assets of 3.5 billion francs.*
belongings: *I collected my belongings and left.*
effects: *After the funeral he sorted his father's personal effects.*
estate: *His estate was valued at $150,000.*
possessions: *People had lost their homes and all their possessions.*

2 a building and the land belonging to it

3 a characteristic or quality *e.g. Mint has powerful healing properties.*

● THESAURUS

attribute: *a normal attribute of human behaviour*
characteristic: *their physical characteristics*
feature: *a feature of the local culture*
hallmark: *The killing had the hallmarks of a professional assassination.*
quality: *mature people with leadership qualities*
trait: *Creativity is a human trait.*

prophecy ['prɒfɪsɪ] **prophecies** NOUN
a statement about what someone believes will happen in the future

▄ The noun *prophecy* ends in *cy.*

prophesy ['prɒfɪ.saɪ] **prophesies, prophesying, prophesied** VERB
If someone prophesies something, they say it will happen.

▄ The verb *prophesy* ends in *sy.*

prophet ['prɒfɪt] **prophets** NOUN
(RE) a person who predicts what will happen in the future

prophetic [prə'fɛtɪk] ADJECTIVE
correctly predicting what will happen *e.g. It was a prophetic warning.*

proportion [prə'pɔːʃən] **proportions** NOUN

1 A proportion of an amount or group is a part of it. *e.g. a tiny proportion of the population*

● THESAURUS

percentage: *It has a high percentage of protein.*
quota: *Britain's fishing quota has been cut.*
segment: *a fast-growing segment of the market*
share: *I pay a share of the phone and gas bills.*

2 The proportion of one amount to another is its size in comparison with the other amount. *e.g. the highest proportion of single women to men*

> PLURAL NOUN

3 You can refer to the size of something as its proportions. *e.g. a red umbrella of vast proportions*

proportional or **proportionate**
[prə'pɔːʃənəl] or [prə'pɔːʃənɪt] ADJECTIVE
If one thing is proportional to another, it remains the same size in comparison with the other. *e.g. proportional increases in profit*
proportionally or **proportionately** ADVERB

proportional representation NOUN
Proportional representation is a system of voting in elections in which the number of representatives of each party is in proportion to the number of people who voted for it.

proposal [prə'pəʊzəl] **proposals** NOUN
a plan that has been suggested *e.g. business proposals*

propose [prə'pəʊz] **proposes, proposing, proposed** VERB

1 If you propose a plan or idea, you suggest it.

2 If you propose to do something, you intend to do it. *e.g. And how do you propose to do that?.*

3 When someone proposes a toast to a particular person, they ask people to drink a toast to that person.

4 If someone proposes to another person, they ask that person to marry them.

proposition [ˌprɒpə'zɪʃən] **propositions** NOUN

1 a statement expressing a theory or opinion

2 an offer or suggestion *e.g. I made her a proposition.*

proprietor [prə'praɪətə] **proprietors** NOUN
The proprietor of a business is the owner.

propriety [prə'praɪətɪ] NOUN; FORMAL
Propriety is what is socially or morally

P

acceptable. *e.g. a model of propriety*

propulsion [prə'pʌlʃən] NOUN
Propulsion is the power that moves something.

prose [prəʊz] NOUN
Prose is ordinary written language in contrast to poetry.
[WORD HISTORY: from Latin PROSA ORATORIO meaning 'straightforward speech']

prosecute ['prɒsɪˌkjuːt] **prosecutes, prosecuting, prosecuted** VERB
If someone is prosecuted, they are charged with a crime and have to stand trial.
prosecutor NOUN

prosecution [ˌprɒsɪ'kjuːʃən] NOUN
The lawyers who try to prove that a person on trial is guilty are called the prosecution.

prospect prospects, prospecting, prospected NOUN ['prɒspɛkt]
1 If there is a prospect of something happening, there is a possibility that it will happen. *e.g. There was little prospect of going home.*

● **THESAURUS**
expectation: *The hotel was being renovated in expectation of a tourist boom.*
hope: *There is little hope of improvement now.*
outlook: *Officials say the outlook for next year is gloomy.*
promise: *New Year brought the promise of better things to come.*

2 Someone's prospects are their chances of being successful in the future.
> VERB [prə'spɛkt]
3 If someone prospects for gold or oil, they look for it.
prospector NOUN

prospective [prə'spɛktɪv] ADJECTIVE
'Prospective' is used to say that someone wants to be or is likely to be something. For example, the prospective owner of something is the person who wants to own it.

prospectus [prə'spɛktəs] **prospectuses** NOUN
a booklet giving details about a college or a company

prosper ['prɒspə] **prospers, prospering, prospered** VERB
When people or businesses prosper, they are successful and make a lot of money.
prosperous ADJECTIVE, **prosperity** NOUN

prostitute ['prɒstɪˌtjuːt] **prostitutes** NOUN
a person, usually a woman, who has sex with men in exchange for money
prostitution NOUN

prostrate ['prɒstreɪt] ADJECTIVE
lying face downwards on the ground

protagonist [prəʊ'tægənɪst] **protagonists** NOUN; FORMAL
1 Someone who is a protagonist of an idea or movement is a leading supporter of it.
2 a main character in a play or story
[WORD HISTORY: from Greek PRŌTAGONISTĒS meaning 'main actor in a play']

protea ['prəʊtɪə] **proteas** NOUN
an evergreen African shrub with colourful flowers

protect [prə'tɛkt] **protects, protecting, protected** VERB
To protect someone or something is to prevent them from being harmed or damaged.
protection NOUN, **protective** ADJECTIVE, **protector** NOUN

protection [prə'tɛkʃən] **protections** NOUN
1 the act of preventing harm or damage
2 something that keeps a person or thing safe

● **THESAURUS**
barrier: *a flood barrier*
buffer: *Keep savings as a buffer against unexpected cash needs.*
cover: *air cover for ground operations*
safeguard: *a safeguard against weeds*
shelter: *an air-raid shelter*

protégé ['prəʊtɪˌʒeɪ] **protégés** NOUN
Someone who is the protégé of an older, more experienced person is helped and guided by that person.

protein ['prəʊtiːn] **proteins** NOUN
(D & T) Protein is a substance that is found in meat, eggs, and milk and that is needed by bodies for growth.

protest protests, protesting, protested VERB [prə'tɛst]
1 If you protest about something, you say or demonstrate publicly that you disagree with it. *e.g. They protested against the killing of a teenager.*

● **THESAURUS**
complain: *People always complain that the big banks are unhelpful.*
disagree: *I disagree with the drug laws in general.*
disapprove: *Her mother disapproved of her working in a pub.*
object: *We objected strongly but were outvoted.*
oppose: *Many parents oppose bilingual education in schools.*

> NOUN ['prəʊtɛst]
2 a demonstration or statement showing that you disagree with something

● **THESAURUS**
complain: *the way that banks deal with complaints*
objection: *I questioned the logic of his objections.*
outcry: *The incident caused an international outcry.*

Protestant ['prɒtɪstənt] **Protestants** NOUN
OR ADJECTIVE
(HISTORY) a member of or belonging to one of
the Christian Churches which separated from the
Catholic Church in the sixteenth century

protestation [ˌprəʊtɛs'teɪʃən]
protestations NOUN
a strong declaration that something is true or not
true *e.g. his protestations of love*

protocol ['prəʊtəˌkɒl] NOUN
Protocol is the system of rules about the correct
way to behave in formal situations.

proton ['prəʊtɒn] **protons** NOUN
a particle which forms part of the nucleus of an
atom and has a positive electrical charge

prototype ['prəʊtəˌtaɪp] **prototypes** NOUN
a first model of something that is made so that
the design can be tested and improved

protracted [prə'træktɪd] ADJECTIVE
lasting longer than usual *e.g. a protracted dispute*

protractor [prə'træktə] **protractors** NOUN
a flat, semicircular piece of plastic used for
measuring angles

protrude [prə'truːd] **protrudes,**
protruding, protruded VERB; FORMAL
If something is protruding from a surface or
edge, it is sticking out.
protrusion NOUN

proud [praʊd] **prouder, proudest** ADJECTIVE
1 feeling pleasure and satisfaction at something
you own or have achieved *e.g. I was proud of our
players today.*
● THESAURUS
gratified: *He was gratified by the audience's
response.*
honoured: *I am honoured to work with her.*
pleased: *I was pleased to call him my friend.*
2 having great dignity and self-respect *e.g. too
proud to ask for money*
proudly ADVERB

prove [pruːv] **proves, proving, proved** or
proven VERB
1 To prove that something is true is to provide
evidence that it is definitely true. *e.g. A letter from
Kathleen proved that he lived there.*
● THESAURUS
ascertain: *They had ascertained that he was not a
spy.*
confirm: *X-rays confirmed that he had not broken
any bones.*
demonstrate: *You have to demonstrate that you are
reliable.*
establish: *The autopsy established the cause of
death.*

verify: *I can verify that it takes about thirty seconds.*

<<OPPOSITE *disprove*

2 If something proves to be the case, it becomes
clear that it is so. *e.g. His first impressions of her
proved wrong.*

proverb ['prɒvɜːb] **proverbs** NOUN
a short sentence which gives advice or makes a
comment about life
proverbial ADJECTIVE

provide [prə'vaɪd] **provides, providing,**
provided VERB
1 If you provide something for someone, you give
it to them or make it available for them.
● THESAURUS
contribute: *NATO agreed to contribute troops and
equipment.*
equip: *proposals to equip all officers with body
armour*
furnish: *They'll be able to furnish you with the rest of
the details.*
outfit: *They outfitted him with artificial legs.*
supply: *the blood vessels supplying oxygen to the
brain*
2 If you provide for someone, you give them the
things they need.

provided or **providing** [prə'vaɪdɪd] or
[prə'vaɪdɪŋ] CONJUNCTION
If you say that something will happen provided
something else happens, you mean that the first
thing will happen only if the second thing does.

> *Provided* is followed by *that*, but *providing* is
> not: *I'll come, providing he doesn't; You can go,
> provided that you phone as soon as you get
> there.*

providence ['prɒvɪdəns] NOUN
Providence is God or a force which is believed to
arrange the things that happen to us.

province ['prɒvɪns] **provinces** NOUN
1 one of the areas into which some large
countries are divided, each province having its
own administration
2 You can refer to the parts of a country which
are not near the capital as the provinces.
[WORD HISTORY: from Latin PROVINCIA meaning 'a
conquered territory']

provincial [prə'vɪnʃəl] ADJECTIVE
1 connected with the parts of a country outside
the capital *e.g. a provincial theatre*
2 narrow-minded and lacking sophistication

provision [prə'vɪʒən] **provisions** NOUN
(GEOGRAPHY)
1 The provision of something is the act of making
it available to people. *e.g. the provision of health
care*

P

> PLURAL NOUN

2 Provisions are supplies of food.

provisional [prə'vɪʒənəl] ADJECTIVE
A provisional arrangement has not yet been made definite and so might be changed.

proviso [prə'vaɪzəʊ] **provisos** NOUN
a condition in an agreement

provocation [ˌprɒvə'keɪʃən] **provocations** NOUN
an act done deliberately to annoy someone

provocative [prə'vɒkətɪv] ADJECTIVE
1 intended to annoy people or make them react e.g. a provocative speech

2 intended to make someone feel sexual desire e.g. provocative poses

provoke [prə'vəʊk] **provokes, provoking, provoked** VERB
1 If you provoke someone, you deliberately try to make them angry.

● THESAURUS

anger: It's important not to anger her.
annoy: You're just trying to annoy me.
enrage: He enraged the government by going back on the agreement.
goad: My little brother was always goading me.
insult: I didn't mean to insult you.
irritate: If you go on irritating that dog, it'll bite you.
tease: I'm sorry, I shouldn't tease you like that.

2 If something provokes an unpleasant reaction, it causes it. e.g. illness provoked by tension or worry

● THESAURUS

cause: These policies are likely to cause problems.
evoke: The programme has evoked a storm of protest.
produce: The decision produced a furious reaction among fans.
prompt: The allegations prompted an indignant response from the accused.
rouse: This roused a feeling of rebellion in him.
set off: The arrival of the supply van set off a minor riot among waiting villagers.
spark off: a political crisis sparked off by religious violence

prow [praʊ] **prows** NOUN
the front part of a boat

prowess ['praʊɪs] NOUN
Prowess is outstanding ability. e.g. his prowess at tennis

prowl [praʊl] **prowls, prowling, prowled** VERB
If a person or animal prowls around, they move around quietly and secretly, as if hunting.

proximity [prɒk'sɪmɪtɪ] NOUN; FORMAL
Proximity is nearness to someone or something.

proxy ['prɒksɪ] PHRASE
If you do something **by proxy**, someone else does it on your behalf. e.g. voting by proxy

prude [pruːd] **prudes** NOUN
someone who is too easily shocked by sex or nudity
prudish ADJECTIVE
[WORD HISTORY: from Old French PRODE FEMME meaning 'respectable woman']

prudent ['pruːdənt] ADJECTIVE
behaving in a sensible and cautious way e.g. It is prudent to plan ahead.
prudence NOUN, **prudently** ADVERB

prune [pruːn] **prunes, pruning, pruned** NOUN
1 a dried plum
> VERB
2 When someone prunes a tree or shrub, they cut back some of the branches.

pry [praɪ] **pries, prying, pried** VERB
If someone is prying, they are trying to find out about something secret or private.

● THESAURUS

interfere: I wish everyone would stop interfering and just leave me alone.
intrude: The press were intruding into my personal life.
poke your nose in: informal Who asked you to poke your nose in?
poke your nose into: informal strangers who poke their noses into our affairs
snoop: informal He was snooping around Kim's hotel room.

PS
PS is written before an additional message at the end of a letter. PS is an abbreviation for 'postscript'.

psalm [sɑːm] **psalms** NOUN
one of the 150 songs, poems, and prayers which together form the Book of Psalms in the Bible

pseudo- PREFIX
'Pseudo-' is used to form adjectives and nouns indicating that something is not what it is claimed to be e.g. pseudo-scientific theories
[WORD HISTORY: from Greek PSEUDĒS meaning 'false']

pseudonym ['sjuːdəˌnɪm] **pseudonyms** NOUN
a name an author uses rather than their real name

PSHE NOUN
an abbreviation for 'Personal, Social, and Health Education': a lesson in which students are taught about social and personal issues

psyche ['saɪkɪ] **psyches** NOUN
your mind and your deepest feelings

psychiatry [saɪ'kaɪətrɪ] NOUN
Psychiatry is the branch of medicine concerned with mental illness.
psychiatrist NOUN, **psychiatric** ADJECTIVE

psychic ['saɪkɪk] ADJECTIVE
having unusual mental powers such as the ability to read people's minds or predict the future

psychoanalysis [,saɪkəʊə'næləsɪs] NOUN
Psychoanalysis is the examination and treatment of someone who is mentally ill by encouraging them to talk about their feelings and past events in order to discover the cause of the illness.
psychoanalyst NOUN, **psychoanalyse** VERB

psychology [saɪ'kɒlədʒɪ] NOUN
Psychology is the scientific study of the mind and of the reasons for people's behaviour.
psychological ADJECTIVE, **psychologist** NOUN

psychopath ['saɪkəʊ,pæθ] **psychopaths** NOUN
a mentally ill person who behaves violently without feeling guilt
psychopathic ADJECTIVE

psychosis [saɪ'kəʊsɪs] **psychoses** NOUN
a severe mental illness
psychotic ADJECTIVE

pterodactyl [,tɛrə'dæktɪl] **pterodactyls** NOUN
Pterodactyls were flying reptiles in prehistoric times.
[WORD HISTORY: from Greek PTERON meaning 'wing' and DAKTULOS meaning 'finger']

PTO
PTO is an abbreviation for 'please turn over'. It is written at the bottom of a page to indicate that the writing continues on the other side.

pub [pʌb] **pubs** NOUN
a building where people go to buy and drink alcoholic or soft drinks and talk with their friends

● THESAURUS
bar: British *He works in a bar.*
boozer: British and Australian and New Zealand; informal *the local boozer*
inn: *a village inn*
lounge: *the hotel lounge*
public house: *a robbery at a public house in New Milton*
saloon: *a Wild West saloon*
tavern: *an old country tavern*

puberty ['pjuːbətɪ] NOUN
Puberty is the stage when a person's body changes from that of a child into that of an adult.

pubic ['pjuːbɪk] ADJECTIVE
relating to the area around and above a person's genitals

public see page 682 for Word Web

publican ['pʌblɪkən] **publicans** NOUN
a person who owns or manages a pub

publication [,pʌblɪ'keɪʃən] **publications** NOUN
1 The publication of a book is the act of printing it and making it available.
2 a book or magazine *e.g. medical publications*

publicity [pʌ'blɪsɪtɪ] NOUN
Publicity is information or advertisements about an item or event.

● THESAURUS
advertising: *tobacco advertising in women's magazines*
plug: informal *The whole interview was an unashamed plug for her new book.*
promotion: *They've spent a lot of money on advertising and promotion.*

publicize ['pʌblɪ,saɪz] **publicizes, publicizing, publicized;** also spelt **publicise** VERB
When someone publicizes a fact or event, they advertise it and make it widely known.

● THESAURUS
advertise: *The product has been much advertised in specialist magazines.*
plug: informal *another celebrity plugging their latest book*
promote: *a tour to promote his second solo album*

public school public schools NOUN
In Britain, a public school is a school that is privately run and that charges fees for the pupils to attend.

public servant public servants NOUN
In Australia and New Zealand, someone who works in the public service.

public service NOUN
In Australia and New Zealand, the public service is the government departments responsible for the administration of the country.

publish ['pʌblɪʃ] **publishes, publishing, published** VERB
When a company publishes a book, newspaper, or magazine, they print copies of it and distribute it.
publishing NOUN

● THESAURUS
bring out: *The newspapers all brought out special editions.*
print: *a letter printed in the Times yesterday*
put out: *a statement put out by the Iraqi news agency*

publisher ['pʌblɪʃə] **publishers** NOUN
(LIBRARY) The publisher of a book, newspaper

P

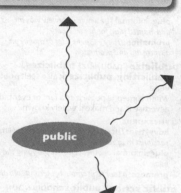

1 NOUN
You can refer to people in general as the public.
● THESAURUS
masses: *a quest to bring the Internet to the masses*
nation: *The President spoke to the nation.*
people: *the will of the people*
populace: *a large proportion of the populace*
society: *a menace to society*

2 ADJECTIVE
relating to people in general *eg: There was some public support for the idea.*
● THESAURUS
civic: *a sense of civic pride*
general: *The project should raise general awareness about bullying.*
popular: *Popular anger has been expressed in demonstrations.*
universal: *the universal outrage at the deaths*

public

3 ADJECTIVE
provided for everyone to use, or open to anyone *eg: public transport; a public park*
● THESAURUS
communal: *a communal dining room*
community: *a village community centre*
open to the public: *Part of the castle is now open to the public.*
universal: *universal health care*
<< OPPOSITE private

or magazine is the person or company that prints copies of it and distributes it.

pudding ['pʊdɪŋ] **puddings** NOUN
1 a sweet cake mixture cooked with fruit or other flavouring and served hot
2 You can refer to the sweet course of a meal as the pudding.

puddle ['pʌdᵊl] **puddles** NOUN
a small shallow pool of liquid

puerile ['pjʊəraɪl] ADJECTIVE
Puerile behaviour is silly and childish.
[WORD HISTORY: from Latin PUERILIS, from PUER meaning 'boy']

puff [pʌf] **puffs, puffing, puffed** VERB
1 To puff a cigarette or pipe is to smoke it.
2 If you are puffing, you are breathing loudly and quickly with your mouth open.
3 If something puffs out or puffs up, it swells and becomes larger and rounder.
> NOUN
4 a small amount of air or smoke that is released

puffin ['pʌfɪn] **puffins** NOUN
a black and white sea bird with a large, brightly coloured beak

pug [pʌg] **pugs** NOUN
a small, short-haired dog with a flat nose

puja ['puːdʒaː] NOUN
Puja is a variety of practices which make up Hindu worship.

puke [pjuːk] **pukes, puking, puked** VERB
INFORMAL
If someone pukes, they vomit.
● THESAURUS
be sick: *She got up and was sick in the handbasin.*
chunder: Australian and New Zealand; slang *the time you chundered in the taxi*
spew: informal *He's really drunk. I hope he doesn't start spewing.*
throw up: informal *She threw up after reading reports of the trial.*
vomit: *Anything containing cow's milk made him vomit.*

pull [pʊl] **pulls, pulling, pulled** VERB
1 When you pull something, you hold it and move it towards you.
● THESAURUS
drag: *He dragged his chair towards the table.*
draw: *He drew his chair nearer the fire.*
haul: *A crane was used to haul the car out of the stream.*
tow: *They threatened to tow away my van.*
tug: *She kicked him, tugging his thick hair.*
yank: *She yanked open the drawer.*

<<OPPOSITE *push*

2 When something is pulled by a vehicle or animal, it is attached to it and moves along behind it. *e.g. Four oxen can pull a single plough.*
3 When you pull a curtain or blind, you move it so that it covers or uncovers the window.
4 If you pull a muscle, you injure it by stretching it too far or too quickly.
5 When a vehicle pulls away, pulls out, or pulls in, it moves in that direction.
> NOUN
6 The pull of something is its attraction or influence. *e.g. the pull of the past*
● THESAURUS
attraction: *The attraction of Hollywood began to pall.*
lure: *The lure of rural life is as strong as ever.*
magnetism: *the sheer magnetism of his presence*

pull down VERB
7 When a building is pulled down, it is deliberately destroyed.

pull out VERB
8 If you pull out of something, you leave it or decide not to continue with it. *e.g. The German government has pulled out of the project.*

pull through VERB
9 When someone pulls through, they recover from a serious illness.

pulley ['pʊlɪ] **pulleys** NOUN
a device for lifting heavy weights. The weight is attached to a rope which passes over a wheel or series of wheels

pullover ['pʊl,əʊvə] **pullovers** NOUN
a woollen piece of clothing that covers the top part of your body

pulmonary ['pʌlmənərɪ] ADJECTIVE; FORMAL
relating to the lungs or to the veins and arteries carrying blood between the lungs and the heart

pulp [pʌlp] NOUN
If something is turned into a pulp, it is crushed until it is soft and moist.

pulpit ['pʊlpɪt] **pulpits** NOUN
the small raised platform in a church where a member of the clergy stands to preach

pulse [pʌls] **pulses, pulsing, pulsed** NOUN
1 Your pulse is the regular beating of blood through your body, the rate of which you can feel at your wrists and elsewhere.
2 The seeds of beans, peas, and lentils are called pulses when they are used for food.
> VERB
3 If something is pulsing, it is moving or vibrating with rhythmic, regular movements. *e.g. She could*

P

feel the blood pulsing in her eardrums.

puma ['pjuːmə] **pumas** NOUN
a wild animal belonging to the cat family

pumice ['pʌmɪs] NOUN
Pumice stone is very light-weight grey stone that can be used to soften areas of hard skin.

pummel ['pʌməl] **pummels, pummelling, pummelled** VERB
If you pummel something, you beat it with your fists.

pump [pʌmp] **pumps, pumping, pumped** NOUN
1 a machine that is used to force a liquid or gas to move in a particular direction
2 Pumps are light shoes with flat soles which people wear for sport or leisure.
> VERB
3 To pump a liquid or gas somewhere is to force it to flow in that direction, using a pump.
4 If you pump money into something, you put a lot of money into it.

pumpkin ['pʌmpkɪn] **pumpkins** NOUN
a very large, round, orange fruit eaten as a vegetable

pun [pʌn] **puns** NOUN
a clever and amusing use of words so that what you say has two different meanings, such as *my dog's a champion boxer*

punch [pʌntʃ] **punches, punching, punched** VERB
1 If you punch someone, you hit them hard with your fist.
> NOUN
2 a hard blow with the fist
3 a tool used for making holes
4 Punch is a drink made from a mixture of wine, spirits, and fruit.

punctual ['pʌŋktjʊəl] ADJECTIVE
arriving at the correct time
punctually ADVERB, **punctuality** NOUN

● THESAURUS
in good time: *It is now 5am and we are in good time.*
on time: *I'm generally early or on time for an appointment.*
prompt: *We expect you to be prompt for all your classes.*

punctuate ['pʌŋktjʊˌeɪt] **punctuates, punctuating, punctuated** VERB
1 Something that is punctuated by a particular thing is interrupted by it at intervals. *e.g. a grey day punctuated by bouts of rain*
2 When you punctuate a piece of writing, you put punctuation into it.

punctuation [ˌpʌŋktjʊˈeɪʃən] NOUN
The marks in writing such as full stops, question marks, and commas are called punctuation or punctuation marks.

puncture ['pʌŋktʃə] **punctures, puncturing, punctured** NOUN
1 If a tyre has a puncture, a small hole has been made in it and it has become flat.
> VERB
2 To puncture something is to make a small hole in it.

pungent ['pʌndʒənt] ADJECTIVE
having a strong, unpleasant smell or taste
pungency NOUN

punish ['pʌnɪʃ] **punishes, punishing, punished** VERB
To punish someone who has done something wrong is to make them suffer because of it.

● THESAURUS
discipline: *He was disciplined by his company but not dismissed.*
penalize: *Bad teaching is not penalized in a formal way.*
rap someone's knuckles: *The company got its knuckles rapped for this advertisement.*
sentence: *He has admitted the charge and will be sentenced later.*
throw the book at: *The football authorities seem certain to throw the book at him.*

punishment ['pʌnɪʃmənt] **punishments** NOUN
something unpleasant done to someone because they have done something wrong

● THESAURUS
penalty: *One of those arrested could face the death penalty.*
retribution: *He didn't want any further involvement for fear of retribution.*

punitive ['pjuːnɪtɪv] ADJECTIVE
harsh and intended to punish people *e.g. punitive military action*

Punjabi [pʌnˈdʒɑːbɪ] **Punjabis** ADJECTIVE
1 belonging or relating to the Punjab, a state in north-western India
> NOUN
2 someone who comes from the Punjab
3 Punjabi is a language spoken in the Punjab.

punk [pʌŋk] NOUN
Punk or punk rock is an aggressive style of rock music.

punt [pʌnt] **punts** NOUN
a long, flat-bottomed boat. You move it along by pushing a pole against the river bottom

puny ['pjuːnɪ] **punier, puniest** ADJECTIVE
very small and weak

THESAURUS
feeble: *He was old and feeble.*
frail: *She lay in bed looking frail.*
sickly: *He has been a sickly child.*
skinny: *a skinny little boy*
weak: *His arms and legs were weak.*

pup [pʌp] **pups** NOUN
a young dog. Some other young animals such as seals are also called pups

pupil ['pjuːpᵊl] **pupils** NOUN
1 The pupils at a school are the children who go there.

THESAURUS
scholar: South African *a bunch of rowdy scholars*
schoolboy or **schoolgirl:** *a group of ten-year-old schoolboys*
schoolchild: *The bus was packed with schoolchildren.*
student: *The students are sorted into three ability groups.*

2 Your pupils are the small, round, black areas in the centre of your eyes.

puppet ['pʌpɪt] **puppets** NOUN
a doll or toy animal that is moved by pulling strings or by putting your hand inside its body

puppy ['pʌpɪ] **puppies** NOUN
a young dog

purchase ['pɜːtʃɪs] **purchases, purchasing, purchased** VERB
1 When you purchase something, you buy it.
> NOUN
2 something you have bought
purchaser NOUN

pure [pjʊə] **purer, purest** ADJECTIVE
1 Something that is pure is not mixed with anything else. *e.g. pure wool... pure white*
2 Pure also means clean and free from harmful substances. *e.g. The water is pure enough to drink.*

THESAURUS
clean: *Tiled kitchen floors are easy to keep clean.*
germ-free: *chlorine gas used to keep water germ-free*
pasteurized: *The milk is pasteurized to kill bacteria.*
spotless: *She kept the kitchen spotless.*
sterilized: *sterilized surgical equipment*
<<OPPOSITE *impure*

3 People who are pure have not done anything considered to be sinful.
4 Pure also means complete and total. *e.g. a matter of pure luck*
purity NOUN

THESAURUS
absolute: *You're talking absolute nonsense.*
complete: *complete and utter rubbish*

outright: *an outright rejection of the deal*
sheer: *acts of sheer desperation*
unmitigated: *Last year's crop was an unmitigated disaster.*
utter: *This, of course, is utter nonsense.*

purée ['pjʊəreɪ] **purées** NOUN
a food which has been mashed or blended to a thick, smooth consistency

purely ['pjʊəlɪ] ADVERB
involving only one feature and not including anything else *e.g. purely professional*

Purgatory ['pɜːgətərɪ] NOUN
Roman Catholics believe that Purgatory is a place where spirits of the dead are sent to suffer for their sins before going to Heaven.

purge [pɜːdʒ] **purges, purging, purged** VERB
To purge something is to remove undesirable things from it. *e.g. to purge the country of criminals*

purify ['pjʊərɪˌfaɪ] **purifies, purifying, purified** VERB
To purify something is to remove all dirty or harmful substances from it.
purification NOUN

purist ['pjʊərɪst] **purists** NOUN
someone who believes that something should be done in a particular, correct way *e.g. a football purist*

puritan ['pjʊərɪtᵊn] **puritans** NOUN
someone who believes in strict moral principles and avoids physical pleasures
puritanical ADJECTIVE

purple ['pɜːpᵊl] NOUN OR ADJECTIVE
reddish-blue

purport [pɜː'pɔːt] **purports, purporting, purported** VERB; FORMAL
Something that purports to be or have a particular thing is claimed to be or have it. *e.g. a country which purports to disapprove of smokers*

purpose ['pɜːpəs] **purposes** NOUN
1 The purpose of something is the reason for it. *e.g. the purpose of the meeting*

THESAURUS
aim: *the aim of the policy*
function: *Their main function is to raise capital for industry.*
intention: *The intention of the scheme is to encourage faster sales.*
object: *the object of the exercise*
point: *I don't see the point of it.*
reason: *What is the real reason for the delay?*

2 If you have a particular purpose, this is what you want to achieve. *e.g. To make music is my purpose in life.*

P

> PHRASE

3 If you do something **on purpose**, you do it deliberately.
purposely ADVERB, **purposeful** ADJECTIVE

● THESAURUS
by design: *The pair met often – at first by chance but later by design.*
deliberately: *It looks as if the fire was started deliberately.*
intentionally: *I've never hurt anyone intentionally.*
knowingly: *He said that he'd never knowingly taken illegal drugs.*
purposely: *They are purposely withholding information.*

purr [pɜː] **purrs, purring, purred** VERB
When a cat purrs, it makes a low vibrating sound because it is contented.

purse [pɜːs] **purses, pursing, pursed** NOUN
1 a small leather or fabric container for carrying money
> VERB
2 If you purse your lips, you move them into a tight, rounded shape.

purser [ˈpɜːsə] **pursers** NOUN
the officer responsible for the paperwork and the welfare of passengers on a ship

pursue [pəˈsjuː] **pursues, pursuing, pursued** VERB
1 If you pursue an activity or plan, you do it or make efforts to achieve it. *e.g. I decided to pursue a career in photography.*
2 If you pursue someone, you follow them to try to catch them.
pursuer NOUN, **pursuit** NOUN

purveyor [pəˈveɪə] **purveyors** NOUN; FORMAL
A purveyor of goods or services is a person who sells them or provides them.

pus [pʌs] NOUN
Pus is a thick yellowish liquid that forms in an infected wound.

push [pʊʃ] **pushes, pushing, pushed** VERB
1 When you push something, you press it using force in order to move it.

● THESAURUS
press: *He pressed his back against the door.*
ram: *He rammed the key into the lock.*
shove: *He shoved her aside.*
thrust: *They thrust him into the back of the jeep.*
<<OPPOSITE pull

2 If you push someone into doing something, you force or persuade them to do it. *e.g. His mother pushed him into auditioning for a part.*

● THESAURUS
encourage: *She encouraged me to stick to the diet.*

persuade: *They persuaded him to moderate his views.*
press: *Trade unions are pressing him to stand firm.*
urge: *He had urged her to come to Ireland.*

3 INFORMAL
Someone who pushes drugs sells them illegally.
push off VERB

4 INFORMAL
5 If you tell someone to push off, you are telling them rudely to go away.

pushchair [ˈpʊʃˌtʃeə] **pushchairs** NOUN
a small folding chair on wheels in which a baby or toddler can be wheeled around

pusher [ˈpʊʃə] **pushers** NOUN; INFORMAL
someone who sells illegal drugs

pushing [ˈpʊʃɪŋ] PREPOSITION
Someone who is pushing a particular age is nearly that age. *e.g. pushing sixty*

pushover [ˈpʊʃˌəʊvə] NOUN; INFORMAL
1 something that is easy
2 someone who is easily persuaded or defeated

pushy [ˈpʊʃɪ] **pushier, pushiest** ADJECTIVE
INFORMAL
behaving in a forceful and determined way

● THESAURUS
aggressive: *a very aggressive business executive*
ambitious: *You have to be ambitious to make it in this business.*
assertive: *Women have become more assertive over the last ten years.*
bossy: *She remembers being a rather bossy little girl.*
forceful: *Sarah is notorious for her forceful and quarrelsome nature.*
obtrusive: *"You are rude and obtrusive, Mr Smith," said Tommy.*

pussy [ˈpʊsɪ] **pussies** NOUN; INFORMAL
a cat

put [pʊt] **puts, putting, put** VERB
1 When you put something somewhere, you move it into that place or position.

● THESAURUS
deposit: *On his way out he deposited a glass in front of me.*
lay: *Lay a sheet of newspaper on the floor.*
place: *He placed it in the inside pocket of his jacket.*
position: *Plants were carefully positioned in the alcove.*
rest: *He rested his arms on the back of the chair.*

2 If you put an idea or remark in a particular way, you express it that way. *e.g. I think you've put that very well.*

● THESAURUS
phrase: *I would have phrased it quite differently.*
word: *You misinterpreted his letter, or else he worded it poorly.*

3 To put someone or something in a particular state or situation means to cause them to be in it. *e.g. It puts us both in an awkward position.*

4 You can use 'put' to express an estimate of the size or importance of something. *e.g. Her wealth is now put at 290 million.*

put down VERB
5 To put someone down is to criticize them and make them appear foolish.

● THESAURUS
belittle: *She's always belittling her husband in public.*
criticize: *She rarely criticized any of her children.*
find fault: *I wish you wouldn't find fault with me in front of the kids.*
humiliate: *His teacher continually humiliates him.*

6 If an animal is put down, it is killed because it is very ill or dangerous.

● THESAURUS
destroy: *The horse had to be destroyed.*
kill: *Animals should be killed humanely.*
put out of its misery: *The bird was so badly injured I decided to put it out of its misery.*
put to sleep: *Take the dog to the vet's and have her put to sleep.*

> VERB put off
7 If you put something off, you delay doing it.

● THESAURUS
defer: *Customers often defer payment for as long as possible.*
delay: *She wants to delay the wedding.*
postpone: *The visit has been postponed indefinitely.*
put back: *The news conference has been put back a couple of hours.*
put on ice: *The decision has been put on ice until October.*
reschedule: *Since I'll be away, I'd like to reschedule the meeting.*

8 To put someone off is to discourage them.

put out VERB
9 If you put a fire out or put the light out, you make it stop burning or shining.

10 If you are put out, you are annoyed or upset.

put up VERB
11 If you put up resistance to something, you argue or fight against it. *e.g. She put up a tremendous struggle.*

put up with VERB
12 If you put up with something, you tolerate it even though you disagree with it or dislike it.

● THESAURUS
abide: *I can't abide arrogant people.*
bear: *He can't bear to talk about it.*
stand: *She cannot stand her boss.*
stand for: *We won't stand for it any more.*

stomach: *He could not stomach violence.*
tolerate: *She can no longer tolerate the position she is in.*

putt [pʌt] **putts** NOUN
In golf, a putt is a gentle stroke made when the ball is near the hole.

putting [ˈpʌtɪŋ] NOUN
Putting is a game played on a small grass course with no obstacles. You hit a ball gently with a club so that it rolls towards one of a series of holes around the course.

putty [ˈpʌtɪ] NOUN
Putty is a paste used to fix panes of glass into frames.

puzzle [ˈpʌzᵊl] **puzzles, puzzling, puzzled** VERB
1 If something puzzles you, it confuses you and you do not understand it. *e.g. There was something about her that puzzled me.*

● THESAURUS
baffle: *An apple tree producing square fruit is baffling experts.*
bewilder: *His silence bewildered her.*
confuse: *German politics surprised and confused him.*
mystify: *The audience were mystified by the plot.*
stump: *I was stumped by an unexpected question.*

> NOUN
2 A puzzle is a game or question that requires a lot of thought to complete or solve.
puzzled ADJECTIVE, **puzzlement** NOUN

● THESAURUS
brain-teaser: informal *It took me ages to solve that brain-teaser.*
poser: *Here is a little poser for you.*
problem: *a mathematical problem*
riddle: *See if you can answer this riddle.*

PVC NOUN
PVC is a plastic used for making clothing, pipes, and many other things. PVC is an abbreviation for 'polyvinyl chloride'.

pygmy [ˈpɪɡmɪ] **pygmies;** also spelt **pigmy** NOUN
a very small person, especially one who belongs to a racial group in which all the people are small
[WORD HISTORY: from Greek PUGMAIOS meaning 'undersized']

pyjamas [pəˈdʒɑːməz] PLURAL NOUN
Pyjamas are loose trousers and a jacket or top that you wear in bed.
[WORD HISTORY: from Persian PAY JAMA meaning 'leg clothing']

pylon [ˈpaɪlən] **pylons** NOUN
a very tall metal structure which carries overhead electricity cables

pyramid [ˈpɪrəmɪd] **pyramids** NOUN

P

1 a three-dimensional shape with a flat base and flat triangular sides sloping upwards to a point

2 The Pyramids are ancient stone structures built over the tombs of Egyptian kings and queens.

pyre [paɪə] **pyres** NOUN

a high pile of wood on which a dead body or religious offering is burned

python [ˈpaɪθən] **pythons** NOUN

a large snake that kills animals by squeezing them with its body

[WORD HISTORY: from Greek PUTHON, a huge mythical serpent]

Qq

quack [kwæk] **quacks, quacking, quacked** VERB
When a duck quacks, it makes a loud harsh sound.

quad [kwɒd] **quads** NOUN Quad is the same as **quadruplet**.

quadrangle [ˈkwɒdˌræŋgᵊl] **quadrangles** NOUN
a courtyard with buildings all round it

quadri- PREFIX
'Quadri-' means 'four'
[WORD HISTORY: a Latin word]

quadriceps [ˈkwɒdrɪˌsɛps] NOUN
(PE) a large muscle in four parts at the front of your thigh

quadrilateral [ˌkwɒdrɪˈlætərəl] **quadrilaterals** NOUN
(MATHS) a shape with four straight sides

quadruped [ˈkwɒdrʊˌpɛd] **quadrupeds** NOUN
any animal with four legs

quadruple [ˈkwɒdrʊpᵊl] **quadruples, quadrupling, quadrupled** VERB
When an amount or number quadruples, it becomes four times as large as it was.

quadruplet [ˈkwɒdrʊplɪt] **quadruplets** NOUN
Quadruplets are four children born at the same time to the same mother.

quagmire [ˈkwæɡˌmaɪə] **quagmires** NOUN
a soft, wet area of land which you sink into if you walk on it

quail [kweɪl] **quails, quailing, quailed** NOUN
1 a type of small game bird with a round body and short tail
> VERB
2 If you quail, you feel or look afraid.

quaint [kweɪnt] **quainter, quaintest** ADJECTIVE
attractively old-fashioned or unusual *e.g. quaint customs*
quaintly ADVERB

quake [kweɪk] **quakes, quaking, quaked** VERB
If you quake, you shake and tremble because you are very frightened.

Quaker [ˈkweɪkə] **Quakers** NOUN
a member of a Christian group, the Society of Friends

qualification [ˌkwɒlɪfɪˈkeɪʃən] **qualifications** NOUN
1 Your qualifications are your skills and achievements, especially as officially recognized at the end of a course of training or study.

⬤ THESAURUS
ability: *a man of considerable abilities*
accomplishment: *Carl was proud of his son's accomplishments.*
achievement: *the highest academic achievement*
capability: *Her capabilities were not fully appreciated.*
quality: *Colley's leadership qualities.* **skill:** *a skill you can use*

2 something you add to a statement to make it less strong *e.g. It is a good novel and yet cannot be recommended without qualification.*

⬤ THESAURUS
condition: *You can make any conditions you like.*
exception: *a major exception to this general argument*
modification: *to consider modifications to his proposal*
reservation: *men whose work I admire without reservation*

qualify [ˈkwɒlɪˌfaɪ] **qualifies, qualifying, qualified** VERB
1 (PE) When you qualify, you pass the examinations or tests that you need to pass to do a particular job or to take part in a sporting event.

⬤ THESAURUS
get certified: *They wanted to get certified as divers.*
become licensed: *You can only become licensed by doing an accredited course.*
gain qualifications: *the opportunity to gain medical qualifications*
graduate: *She graduated as a physiotherapist in 1960.*

2 If you qualify a statement, you add a detail or explanation to make it less strong. *e.g. I would qualify that by putting it into context.*

3 If you qualify for something, you become entitled to have it. *e.g. You qualify for a discount.* **qualified** ADJECTIVE

quality ['kwɒlɪti] **qualities** NOUN

1 The quality of something is how good it is. *e.g. The quality of food is very poor.*

⬤ THESAURUS

calibre: *a man of your calibre*
distinction: *a chef of great distinction*
grade: *high grade meat and poultry*
merit: *a work of real merit*
value: *He set a high value upon their friendship.*
worth: *a person's true worth*

2 a characteristic *e.g. These qualities are essential for success.*

⬤ THESAURUS

aspect: *every aspect of our lives*
characteristic: *their physical characteristics*
feature: *the most striking feature of his work*
mark: *the mark of a great composer*
property: *the magnetic properties of iron*
trait: *the young Ms Rankine's personality traits*

qualm [kwɑːm] **qualms** NOUN

If you have qualms about what you are doing, you worry that it might not be right.

quandary ['kwɒndrɪ] **quandaries** NOUN

If you are in a quandary, you cannot decide what to do.

quango ['kwæŋɡəʊ] **quangos** NOUN

a body responsible for a particular area of public administration, which is financed by the government but is outside direct government control. Quango is short for quasi-autonomous non-governmental organization.

quantity ['kwɒntɪti] **quantities** NOUN

1 an amount you can measure or count *e.g. a small quantity of alcohol*

⬤ THESAURUS

amount: *a small amount of mayonnaise*
number: *There are a limited number of seats available.*
part: *the greater part of his wealth*
sum: *a large sum of money*

2 Quantity is the amount of something that there is. *e.g. emphasis on quantity rather than quality*

⬤ THESAURUS

extent: *the extent of the damage*
measure: *The government has had a fair measure of success.*
size: *He gauged the size of the audience.*
volume: *the sheer volume of traffic and accidents*

quarantine ['kwɒrən,tiːn] NOUN

If an animal is in quarantine, it is kept away from

other animals for a time because it might have an infectious disease.

[WORD HISTORY: from Italian QUARANTINA meaning 'forty days']

quarrel ['kwɒrəl] **quarrels, quarrelling, quarrelled** NOUN

1 an angry argument

⬤ THESAURUS

argument: *an argument about money*
disagreement: *My instructor and I had a brief disagreement.*
dispute: *Brand eavesdropped on the petty dispute.*
feud: *a two-year feud between neighbours*
fight: *It was a silly fight about where we parked the car.*
row: *Maxine and I had a terrible row.*
squabble: *minor squabbles about phone bills*

> VERB

2 If people quarrel, they have an angry argument.

⬤ THESAURUS

argue: *They were still arguing later.*
bicker: *They bickered endlessly over procedure.*
clash: *She had clashed with Doyle in the past.*
fall out: *informal Mum and I used to fall out a lot.*
fight: *The couple often fought with their son.*
row: *He had rowed with his girlfriend.*
squabble: *The children were squabbling over the remote control.*

quarry ['kwɒrɪ] **quarries, quarrying, quarried** NOUN

1 a place where stone is removed from the ground by digging or blasting

2 A person's or animal's quarry is the animal that they are hunting.

> VERB

3 To quarry stone means to remove it from a quarry by digging or blasting.

[WORD HISTORY: sense 2 is from Middle English QUIRRE meaning 'entrails given to the hounds to eat']

quart [kwɔːt] **quarts** NOUN

a unit of liquid volume equal to two pints or about 1.136 litres

quarter ['kwɔːtə] **quarters** NOUN

1 one of four equal parts

2 an American coin worth 25 cents

3 You can refer to a particular area in a city as a quarter. *e.g. the French quarter*

4 You can use 'quarter' to refer vaguely to a particular person or group of people. *e.g. You are very popular in certain quarters.*

> PLURAL NOUN

5 A soldier's or a servant's quarters are the rooms that they live in.

quarterly [ˈkwɔːtəlɪ] **quarterlies** ADJECTIVE
OR ADVERB
1 Quarterly means happening regularly every
three months. *e.g. my quarterly report*

> NOUN

2 a magazine or journal published every three
months

quartet [kwɔːˈtɛt] **quartets** NOUN
a group of four musicians who sing or play
together; also a piece of music written for four
instruments or singers

quartz [kwɔːts] NOUN
Quartz is a kind of hard, shiny crystal used in
making very accurate watches and clocks.

quash [kwɒʃ] **quashes, quashing,
quashed** VERB
To quash a decision or judgment means to reject
it officially. *e.g. The judges quashed their convictions.*

quasi- PREFIX
Quasi- means resembling something but not
actually being that thing. *e.g. a quasi-religious
order*
[WORD HISTORY: a Latin word meaning 'as if']

quaver [ˈkweɪvə] **quavers, quavering,
quavered** VERB
1 If your voice quavers, it sounds unsteady,
usually because you are nervous.

> NOUN

2 (MUSIC) a musical note (♩) that has the time
value of an eighth of a semibreve. In the United
States and Canada, a quaver is known as an
eighth note

quay [kiː] **quays** NOUN
a place where boats are tied up and loaded or
unloaded

queasy [ˈkwiːzɪ] **queasier, queasiest**
ADJECTIVE
feeling slightly sick

⬤ THESAURUS
ill: *I was feeling ill.*
nauseous: *The medication may make you feel
nauseous.*
queer: *Twenty minutes later, he began to feel queer.*
sick: *The very thought of food made him feel sick.*
unwell: *He felt unwell this afternoon.*

queen [kwiːn] **queens** NOUN
1 a female monarch or a woman married to a
king
2 a female bee or ant which can lay eggs
3 In chess, the queen is the most powerful piece,
which can move in any direction.
4 In a pack of cards, a queen is a card with a
picture of a queen on it.

queen mother queen mothers NOUN
the widow of a king and the mother of the
reigning monarch

queer [kwɪə] **queerer, queerest** ADJECTIVE
Queer means very strange.

quell [kwɛl] **quells, quelling, quelled** VERB
1 To quell a rebellion or riot means to put an end
to it by using force.
2 If you quell a feeling such as fear or grief, you
stop yourself from feeling it. *e.g. trying to quell the
loneliness*

quench [kwɛntʃ] **quenches, quenching,
quenched** VERB
If you quench your thirst, you have a drink so that
you are no longer thirsty.

query [ˈkwɪərɪ] **queries, querying, queried**
NOUN
1 a question

⬤ THESAURUS
inquiry: *I'll be happy to answer all your inquiries, if I
can.*
question: *The President refused to answer further
questions on the subject.*
<<OPPOSITE *response*

> VERB

2 If you query something, you ask about it
because you think it might not be right. *e.g.
No-one queried my decision.*

⬤ THESAURUS
challenge: *The move was challenged by two
countries.*
dispute: *He disputed the allegations.*
object to: *A lot of people objected to the plan.*
question: *It never occurred to me to question the
doctor's decisions.*

quest [kwɛst] **quests** NOUN
a long search for something

question [ˈkwɛstʃən] **questions,
questioning, questioned** NOUN
1 a sentence which asks for information
2 If there is some question about something,
there is doubt about it.
3 a problem that needs to be discussed *e.g. Can
we get back to the question of the car?.*

⬤ THESAURUS
issue: *What is your view on this issue?*
motion: *The conference is now debating the motion.*
point: *There is another point to consider.*
subject: *He raised the subject of money.*
topic: *the topic of where to go on holiday*

> VERB

4 If you question someone, you ask them
questions.

⬤ THESAURUS
examine: *Lawyers examined the witnesses.*

q

interrogate: *I interrogated everyone even slightly involved.*
probe: *tabloid journalists probing us for details*
quiz: *She quizzed me quite closely for a while.*
<<OPPOSITE *answer*

5 If you question something, you express doubts about it. *e.g. He never stopped questioning his own beliefs.*

● THESAURUS
challenge: *Rose convincingly challenged the story.*
dispute: *Nobody disputed that Davey was clever.*
distrust: *I distrusted my ability to keep quiet.*
doubt: *Nobody doubted his sincerity.*
query: *No one queried my decision.*
suspect: *Do we suspect the motives of our friends?*

> PHRASE
6 If something is **out of the question**, it is impossible.

questionable ['kwɛstʃənəbʲl] ADJECTIVE
possibly not true or not honest

question mark question marks NOUN
the punctuation mark (?) which is used at the end of a question

questionnaire [ˌkwɛstʃə'nɛə]
questionnaires NOUN
(MATHS) a list of questions which asks for information for a survey

queue [kju:] **queues, queuing** or **queueing**
queued NOUN
1 a line of people or vehicles waiting for something

> VERB
2 When people queue, they stand in a line waiting for something.

quibble ['kwɪbʲl] **quibbles, quibbling,**
quibbled VERB
1 If you quibble, you argue about something unimportant.

> NOUN
2 a minor objection

quiche [ki:ʃ] **quiches** NOUN
a tart with a savoury filling
[WORD HISTORY: a French word, originally from German KUCHEN meaning 'cake']

quick [kwɪk] **quicker, quickest** ADJECTIVE
1 moving with great speed

● THESAURUS
brisk: *a brisk walk*
fast: *a very fast driver*
hasty: *He spoke in a hasty, nervous way.*
rapid: *a rapid rise through the company*
speedy: *a speedy recovery*
swift: *She is as swift as an arrow.*
<<OPPOSITE *slow*

2 lasting only a short time *e.g. a quick chat*
● THESAURUS
brief: *a brief meeting*
cursory: *a cursory glance inside the van*
hasty: *a hasty meal of bread and soup*
hurried: *He ate a hurried breakfast.*
perfunctory: *With a perfunctory smile, she walked past Jessica.*
<<OPPOSITE *long*

3 happening without any delay *e.g. a quick response*
● THESAURUS
hasty: *This is no hasty decision.*
prompt: *Prompt action is needed.*
sudden: *this week's sudden cold snap*

4 intelligent and able to understand things easily

quickly ['kwɪklɪ] ADVERB
with great speed
● THESAURUS
fast: *How fast were you driving?*
hastily: *sheltering in hastily erected tents*
hurriedly: *students hurriedly taking notes*
rapidly: *moving rapidly across the field*
speedily: *She speedily recovered herself.*
swiftly: *They had to act swiftly to save him.*
<<OPPOSITE *slowly*

quicksand ['kwɪkˌsænd] **quicksands** NOUN
an area of deep wet sand that you sink into if you walk on it

quid [kwɪd] NOUN; INFORMAL
in British English, a pound in money

quiet ['kwaɪət] **quieter, quietest** ADJECTIVE
1 Someone or something that is quiet makes very little noise or no noise at all.
● THESAURUS
hushed: *Tales were exchanged in hushed tones.*
inaudible: *a tiny, almost inaudible squeak*
low: *I spoke in a low voice to Sullivan.*
silent: *He could speak no English and was silent.*
soft: *There was some soft music playing.*
<<OPPOSITE *noisy*

2 Quiet also means peaceful. *e.g. a quiet evening at home*
● THESAURUS
calm: *The city seems relatively calm today.*
mild: *The night was mild.*
peaceful: *a peaceful old house*
restful: *a restful scene*
serene: *the beautiful, serene park*
tranquil: *a tranquil lake*

3 A quiet event happens with very little fuss or publicity. *e.g. a quiet wedding*

> NOUN
4 Quiet is silence.
quietly ADVERB

THESAURUS
calmness: *the calmness of this area*
peace: *I enjoy peace and quiet.*
serenity: *the peace and serenity of a tropical sunset*
silence: *There was a silence around the table.*
stillness: *the stillness of the summer night*
tranquillity: *the tranquillity of village life*
<<OPPOSITE *noise*

> Do not confuse the spellings of *quiet* and the adverb *quite*.

quieten ['kwaɪətᵊn] **quietens, quietening, quietened** VERB
To quieten someone means to make them become quiet.

quill [kwɪl] **quills** NOUN
1 a pen made from a feather
2 A bird's quills are the large feathers on its wings and tail.
3 A porcupine's quills are its spines.

quilt [kwɪlt] **quilts** NOUN
A quilt for a bed is a cover, especially a cover that is padded.

quilted ['kwɪltɪd] ADJECTIVE
Quilted clothes or coverings are made of thick layers of material sewn together.

quin [kwɪn] **quins** NOUN Quin is the same as **quintuplet**.

quince [kwɪns] **quinces** NOUN
an acid-tasting fruit used for making jam and marmalade

quintessential [ˌkwɪntɪ'senʃəl] ADJECTIVE; FORMAL
A person or thing that is quintessential seems to represent the basic nature of something in a pure, concentrated form. *e.g. It was the quintessential Hollywood party.*

quintet [kwɪn'tet] **quintets** NOUN
a group of five musicians who sing or play together; also a piece of music written for five instruments or singers

quintuplet ['kwɪntjʊplɪt] **quintuplets** NOUN
Quintuplets are five children born at the same time to the same mother.

quip [kwɪp] **quips, quipping, quipped** NOUN
1 an amusing or clever remark
> VERB
2 To quip means to make an amusing or clever remark.

quirk [kwɜːk] **quirks** NOUN
1 an odd habit or characteristic *e.g. an interesting quirk of human nature*

2 an unexpected event or development *e.g. a quirk of fate*
quirky ADJECTIVE

quit [kwɪt] **quits, quitting, quit** VERB
If you quit something, you leave it or stop doing it. *e.g. Leigh quit his job as a salesman.*

THESAURUS
discontinue: *Do not discontinue the treatment without seeing your doctor.*
give up: *She gave up smoking last year.*
leave: *He left school with no qualifications.*
resign: *Scott resigned from the firm.*
retire: *Littlejohn was forced to retire from the race.*
stop: *I stopped working last year to have a baby.*

quite [kwaɪt] ADVERB
1 fairly but not very *e.g. quite old*

THESAURUS
fairly: *Both ships are fairly new.*
moderately: *a moderately attractive man*
rather: *I made some rather bad mistakes.*
reasonably: *I can dance reasonably well.*
somewhat: *He's somewhat deaf.*
2 completely *e.g. Jane lay quite still.*

THESAURUS
absolutely: *I absolutely refuse to get married.*
completely: *something completely different*
entirely: *an entirely new approach*
fully: *He has still not fully recovered.*
perfectly: *They are perfectly safe to eat.*
totally: *The fire totally destroyed the house.*
> PHRASE
3 You use **quite a** to emphasize that something is large or impressive. *e.g. It was quite a party.*

> You should be careful about using *quite*. It can mean 'completely': *quite amazing*. It can also mean 'fairly but not very': *quite friendly*. Do not confuse the spellings of *quite* and the adjective *quiet*.

q

quiver ['kwɪvə] **quivers, quivering, quivered** VERB
1 If something quivers, it trembles.
> NOUN
2 a trembling movement *e.g. a quiver of panic*

quiz [kwɪz] **quizzes, quizzing, quizzed** NOUN
1 a game in which the competitors are asked questions to test their knowledge
> VERB
2 If you quiz someone, you question them closely about something.

quizzical ['kwɪzɪkᵊl] ADJECTIVE
amused and questioning *e.g. a quizzical smile*

quota ['kwəʊtə] **quotas** NOUN
a number or quantity of something which is officially allowed *e.g. a quota of three foreign players allowed in each team*

quotation [kwəʊˈteɪʃən] **quotations** NOUN
an extract from a book or speech which is quoted

quote [kwəʊt] **quotes, quoting, quoted**
VERB

1 If you quote something that someone has written or said, you repeat their exact words.

● THESAURUS

cite: *She cites a favourite poem by George Herbert.*
extract: *This material has been extracted from the handbook.*

recite: *They recited poetry to one another.*
repeat: *Could you repeat the whole interview word for word?*

2 If you quote a fact, you state it because it supports what you are saying.

> NOUN

3 an extract from a book or speech

4 an estimate of how much a piece of work will cost

Qur'an [kɔːˈrɑːn] another spelling of **Koran**

Rr

RAAF
In Australia, an abbreviation for 'Royal Australian Air Force'.

rabbi ['ræbaɪ] **rabbis** NOUN
a Jewish religious leader
[WORD HISTORY: from Hebrew RABH + -I meaning 'my master']

rabbit ['ræbɪt] **rabbits** NOUN
a small animal with long ears

rabble ['ræbªl] NOUN
a noisy, disorderly crowd

rabid ['ræbɪd] ADJECTIVE
1 used to describe someone with strong views that you do not approve of e.g. a rabid Nazi
2 A rabid dog or other animal has rabies.

rabies ['reɪbiːz] NOUN
an infectious disease which causes people and animals, especially dogs, to go mad and die

raccoon [rəˈkuːn] **raccoons**; also spelt **racoon** NOUN
a small North American animal with a long striped tail

race [reɪs] **races, racing, raced** NOUN
1 a competition to see who is fastest, for example in running or driving
2 one of the major groups that human beings can be divided into according to their physical features

● THESAURUS
ethnic group: Ethnic group and nationality are often different.
nation: a mature and cultured nation
people: an address to the American people

> VERB
3 If you race someone, you compete with them in a race.
4 If you race something or if it races, it goes at its greatest rate. e.g. Her heart raced uncontrollably.
5 If you race somewhere, you go there as quickly as possible. e.g. The hares raced away out of sight.
racing NOUN

● THESAURUS
dash: He dashed upstairs.

fly: I must fly or I'll miss my train.
hurry: They hurried down the street.
run: The gunmen escaped by running into the woods.
speed: speeding along as fast as I could
tear: The door flew open and she tore into the room.

racecourse ['reɪsˌkɔːs] **racecourses** NOUN
a grass track, sometimes with jumps, along which horses race

racehorse ['reɪsˌhɔːs] **racehorses** NOUN
a horse trained to run in races

racial ['reɪʃəl] ADJECTIVE
relating to the different races that people belong to e.g. racial harmony
racially ADVERB

racism or **racialism** ['reɪsɪzəm] or ['reɪʃəˌlɪzəm] NOUN
(PSHE) Racism or racialism is the treatment of some people as inferior because of their race.
racist NOUN OR ADJECTIVE

rack [ræk] **racks, racking, racked** NOUN
1 a piece of equipment for holding things or hanging things on
> VERB
2 If you are racked by something, you suffer because of it. e.g. She was racked by guilt.
> AN INFORMAL PHRASE
3 If you **rack your brains**, you try hard to think of or remember something.

racket ['rækɪt] **rackets** NOUN
1 If someone is making a racket, they are making a lot of noise.

● THESAURUS
clamour: She could hear a clamour in the road.
commotion: He heard a commotion outside.
din: make themselves heard over the din of the crowd
hubbub: His voice was drowned out by the hubbub of the fans.
noise: There was too much noise in the room.
row: "Whatever is that row?" she demanded.
rumpus: There was such a rumpus, she had to shout to make herself heard.
2 an illegal way of making money e.g. a drugs racket

● THESAURUS
enterprise: a money-laundering enterprise

fraud: *tax frauds*
scheme: *a quick money-making scheme*
3 Racket is another spelling of **racquet**

racquet ['rækɪt] **racquets**; also spelt **racket**
NOUN
a bat with strings across it used in tennis and similar games
[WORD HISTORY: from Arabic RAHAT meaning 'palm of the hand']

radar ['reɪdɑ:] NOUN
Radar is equipment used to track ships or aircraft that are out of sight by using radio signals that are reflected back from the object and shown on a screen.
[WORD HISTORY: from RA(DIO) D(ETECTING) A(ND) R(ANGING)]

radiant ['reɪdɪənt] ADJECTIVE
1 Someone who is radiant is so happy that it shows in their face.
2 glowing brightly
radiance NOUN

radiate ['reɪdɪ,eɪt] **radiates, radiating, radiated** VERB
1 If things radiate from a place, they form a pattern like lines spreading out from the centre of a circle.
2 If you radiate a quality or emotion, it shows clearly in your face and behaviour. *e.g. He radiated health.*

radiation [,reɪdɪ'eɪʃən] NOUN
the stream of particles given out by a radioactive substance

radiator ['reɪdɪ,eɪtə] **radiators** NOUN
1 a hollow metal device for heating a room, usually connected to a central heating system
2 the part of a car that is filled with water to cool the engine

radical ['rædɪkəl] **radicals** NOUN
1 Radicals are people who think there should be great changes in society, and try to make them happen.
> ADJECTIVE
2 very significant, important, or basic *e.g. a radical change in the law*
radically ADVERB, **radicalism** NOUN

radii ['reɪdɪ,aɪ] the plural of **radius**

radio ['reɪdɪəʊ] **radios, radioing, radioed**
NOUN
1 Radio is a system of sending sound over a distance by transmitting electrical signals.
2 Radio is also the broadcasting of programmes to the public by radio.
3 a piece of equipment for listening to radio programmes

> VERB
4 To radio someone means to send them a message by radio. *e.g. The pilot radioed that a fire had started.*

radioactive [,reɪdɪəʊ'æktɪv] ADJECTIVE
giving off powerful and harmful rays
radioactivity NOUN

radiotherapy [,reɪdɪəʊ'θɛrəpɪ] NOUN
the treatment of diseases such as cancer using radiation
radiotherapist NOUN

radish ['rædɪʃ] **radishes** NOUN
a small salad vegetable with a red skin and white flesh and a hot taste

radium ['reɪdɪəm] NOUN
a radioactive element which is used in the treatment of cancer

radius ['reɪdɪəs] **radii,** NOUN
(MATHS) The radius of a circle is the length of a straight line drawn from its centre to its circumference.

RAF
In Britain, an abbreviation for 'Royal Air Force'.

raffia ['ræfɪə] NOUN
a material made from palm leaves and used for making mats and baskets

raffle ['ræfəl] **raffles** NOUN
a competition in which people buy numbered tickets and win a prize if they have the ticket that is chosen

raft [rɑ:ft] **rafts** NOUN
a floating platform made from long pieces of wood tied together

rafter ['rɑ:ftə] **rafters** NOUN
Rafters are the sloping pieces of wood that support a roof.

rag [ræg] **rags** NOUN
1 a piece of old cloth used to clean or wipe things
2 If someone is dressed in rags, they are wearing old torn clothes.

rage [reɪdʒ] **rages, raging, raged** NOUN
1 Rage is great anger.

● THESAURUS
anger: *She felt deep anger at what he had said.*
frenzy: *Their behaviour drove her into a frenzy.*
fury: *Her face was distorted with fury and pain.*
wrath: *He incurred the wrath of the referee.*

> VERB
2 To rage about something means to speak angrily about it.
● THESAURUS
be furious: *He is furious at the way his wife has been treated.*

fume: *I was still fuming over her remark.*
lose your temper: *They had never seen me lose my temper before.*
rave: *She cried and raved for weeks.*
storm: *"It's a disaster", he stormed.*

3 If something such as a storm or battle is raging, it is continuing with great force or violence. *e.g. The fire still raged out of control.*

● THESAURUS
be at its height: *when the storm was at its height*
rampage: *a mob rampaging through the town*
storm: *armies storming across the continent*
surge: *The flood surged through the village.*

ragged ['rægɪd] ADJECTIVE
Ragged clothes are old and torn.

raid [reɪd] **raids, raiding, raided** VERB
1 To raid a place means to enter it by force to attack it or steal something.

● THESAURUS
assault: *Their stronghold was assaulted by pirates.*
attack: *We are being attacked!*
break into: *No-one saw them break into the warehouse.*
invade: *The invading army took all their food supplies.*
plunder: *plundering the homes of the inhabitants*
> NOUN
2 the raiding of a building or a place *e.g. an armed raid on a bank*

● THESAURUS
attack: *a surprise attack on the house*
break-in: *The break-in occurred last night.*
foray: *Guerrillas made forays into the territory.*

rail [reɪl] **rails** NOUN
1 a fixed horizontal bar used as a support or for hanging things on
2 Rails are the steel bars which trains run along.
3 Rail is the railway considered as a means of transport. *e.g. I plan to go by rail.*

railing ['reɪlɪŋ] **railings** NOUN
Railings are a fence made from metal bars.

railway ['reɪlˌweɪ] **railways** NOUN
a route along which trains travel on steel rails

rain [reɪn] **rains, raining, rained** NOUN
1 water falling from the clouds in small drops

● THESAURUS
deluge: *homes damaged in the deluge*
downpour: *A two-day downpour swelled water levels.*
drizzle: *The drizzle had stopped and the sun was shining.*
rainfall: *four years of below average rainfall*
showers: *bright spells followed by scattered showers*
> VERB
2 When it is raining, rain is falling.

rainy ADJECTIVE
● THESAURUS
drizzle: *It was starting to drizzle when I left.*
pour: *We drove all the way in pouring rain.*
teem: *It teemed the entire day.*

rainbird ['reɪnˌbɜːd] **rainbirds** NOUN
a bird whose call is believed to be a sign that it will rain

rainbow ['reɪnˌbəʊ] **rainbows** NOUN
an arch of different colours that sometimes appears in the sky after it has been raining

raincoat ['reɪnˌkəʊt] **raincoats** NOUN
a waterproof coat

rainfall ['reɪnˌfɔːl] NOUN
the amount of rain that falls in a place during a particular period

rainforest ['reɪnˌfɒrɪst] **rainforests** NOUN
a dense forest of tall trees in a tropical area where there is a lot of rain

rainwater ['reɪnˌwɔːtə] NOUN
rain that has been stored

raise [reɪz] **raises, raising, raised** VERB
1 If you raise something, you make it higher. *e.g. She went to the window and raised the blinds... a drive to raise standards of literacy*

● THESAURUS
elevate: *Emotional stress can elevate blood pressure.*
heave: *He heaved his crippled leg into an easier position.*
hoist: *He climbed on the roof to hoist the flag.*
lift: *She lifted the last of her drink to her lips.*
<<OPPOSITE lower

2 If you raise your voice, you speak more loudly.
3 To raise money for a cause means to get people to donate money towards it.
4 To raise a child means to look after it until it is grown up.

● THESAURUS
bring up: *She brought up four children single-handed.*
nurture: *the best way to nurture a child to adulthood*
rear: *He reared his sister's family as well as his own.*

5 If you raise a subject, you mention it.

● THESAURUS
advance: *Some important ideas were advanced at the conference.*
bring up: *I hesitate to bring up this matter with you, but I have no choice.*
broach: *Eventually I broached the subject of her early life.*
introduce: *always willing to introduce a new topic*
moot: *The project was first mooted last year.*

r

suggest: *one possibility that might be suggested*

raisin ['reɪzᵊn] **raisins** NOUN
Raisins are dried grapes.

rake [reɪk] **rakes, raking, raked** NOUN
1 a garden tool with a row of metal teeth and a long handle **rake up** VERB
2 If you rake up something embarrassing from the past, you remind someone about it.

rally ['rælɪ] **rallies, rallying, rallied** NOUN
1 a large public meeting held to show support for something
2 a competition in which vehicles are raced over public roads
3 In tennis or squash, a rally is a continuous series of shots exchanged by the players.
> VERB
4 When people rally to something, they gather together to continue a struggle or to support something.

ram [ræm] **rams, ramming, rammed** VERB
1 If one vehicle rams another, it crashes into it.
2 To ram something somewhere means to push it there firmly. *e.g. He rammed his key into the lock.*
> NOUN
3 an adult male sheep

RAM [ræm] NOUN
In computing, RAM is a storage space which can be filled with data but which loses its contents when the machine is switched off. RAM stands for 'random access memory'.

Ramadan [ˌræməˈdɑːn] NOUN
the ninth month of the Muslim year, during which Muslims eat and drink nothing during daylight
[WORD HISTORY: from Arabic RAMADAN meaning literally 'the hot month']

ramble ['ræmbᵊl] **rambles, rambling, rambled** NOUN
1 a long walk in the countryside
● THESAURUS
excursion: *They organized an excursion into the hills.*
hike: *a long hike along the valley floor*
stroll: *The next day we took a stroll along the river bank.*
walk: *We often go for walks in the country.*
> VERB
2 To ramble means to go for a ramble.
● THESAURUS
amble: *ambling along a country lane*
stray: *You mustn't stray across the border.*
stroll: *whistling as he strolled along the road*
walk: *We finished the evening by walking along the beach.*

wander: *He loved to wander in the woods.*
3 To ramble also means to talk in a confused way. *e.g. He then started rambling and repeating himself.*
rambler NOUN
● THESAURUS
babble: *She babbled on and on about the visitors.*
chatter: *I was so nervous that I chattered away like an idiot.*

ramification [ˌræmɪfɪˈkeɪʃən] **ramifications** NOUN
The ramifications of a decision or plan are all its consequences and effects.

ramp [ræmp] **ramps** NOUN
a sloping surface connecting two different levels

rampage rampages, rampaging, rampaged VERB [ræmˈpeɪdʒ]
1 To rampage means to rush about wildly causing damage.
● THESAURUS
go berserk: *The crowd went berserk at the sight of him.*
rage: *His shop was stormed by a raging mob.*
run amok: *He was arrested after running amok with a gun.*
run riot: *The prisoners ran riot after the announcement.*
> PHRASE ['ræmpeɪdʒ]
2 To go **on the rampage** means to rush about in a wild or violent way.
● THESAURUS
adjective rampage02 **amok:** *The gunman ran amok and killed several people.*
berserk: *The fans went berserk and mobbed the stage.*
wild: *They just went wild after he left.*

rampant ['ræmpənt] ADJECTIVE
If something such as crime or disease is rampant, it is growing or spreading uncontrollably.

rampart ['ræmpɑːt] **ramparts** NOUN
Ramparts are earth banks, often with a wall on top, built to protect a castle or city.

ramshackle ['ræmˌʃækᵊl] ADJECTIVE
A ramshackle building is in very poor condition.

ranch [rɑːntʃ] **ranches** NOUN
a large farm where cattle or horses are reared, especially in the USA
[WORD HISTORY: from Mexican Spanish RANCHO meaning 'small farm']

rancid ['rænsɪd] ADJECTIVE
Rancid food has gone bad.
[WORD HISTORY: from Latin RANCERE meaning 'to stink']

rancour ['ræŋkə] NOUN; FORMAL
Rancour is bitter hatred.

rancorous ADJECTIVE

rand [rænd] NOUN
The rand is the main unit of currency in South Africa.

random ['rændəm] ADJECTIVE
1 A random choice or arrangement is not based on any definite plan.

● THESAURUS
aimless: *after several hours of aimless searching*
arbitrary: *Arbitrary arrests and detention without trial were common.*
haphazard: *He had never seen such a haphazard approach to writing.*
indiscriminate: *the indiscriminate use of fertilisers*
spot: *picked up in a spot check*

> PHRASE
2 If you do something **at random**, you do it without any definite plan. *e.g. He chose his victims at random.*
randomly ADVERB

● THESAURUS
aimlessly: *wandering around aimlessly for hours*
arbitrarily: *The questions were chosen quite arbitrarily.*
haphazardly: *The books were stacked haphazardly on the shelves.*
indiscriminately: *This disease strikes indiscriminately.*
randomly: *a randomly selected sample*

range [reɪndʒ] **ranges, ranging, ranged**
NOUN
1 The range of something is the maximum distance over which it can reach things or detect things. *e.g. This mortar has a range of 15,000 metres.*

● THESAURUS
bounds: *the bounds of good taste*
extent: *the full extent of my knowledge*
field: *The subject covers a very wide field.*
limits: *outside the city limits*
province: *This doesn't fall within our province.*
scope: *He promised to widen the scope of their activities.*

2 a number of different things of the same kind
e.g. A wide range of colours are available.

● THESAURUS
assortment: *There was a good assortment to choose from.*
class: *Cars in this class are expensive.*
gamut: *I experienced the whole gamut of emotions.*
selection: *a wide selection of delicious meals*
series: *a completely new model series*
variety: *The shop stocks a variety of local craft products.*

3 a set of values on a scale *e.g. The average age range is between 35 and 55.*

4 A range of mountains is a line of them.

5 A rifle range or firing range is a place where people practise shooting at targets.

> VERB
6 When a set of things ranges between two points, they vary within these points on a scale.
e.g. prices ranging between 370 and 1200 pounds

● THESAURUS
extend: *The reclaimed land extends from here to the river.*
go: *Their sizes go from very small to enormous.*
run: *Accommodation runs from log cabins to high-standard hotels.*
stretch: *with interests that stretched from chemicals to sugar*
vary: *The cycle of sunspots varies between 8 to 15 years.*

ranger ['reɪndʒə] **rangers** NOUN
someone whose job is to look after a forest or park

rank [ræŋk] **ranks, ranking, ranked** NOUN
1 Someone's rank is their official level in a job or profession.

● THESAURUS
class: *relationships between social classes*
echelon: *the upper echelons of society*
grade: *Staff turnover is high among the junior grades.*
level: *various levels of the judiciary system*
standing: *a woman of wealth and social standing*
station: *a humble station in life*
status: *promoted to the status of foreman*

2 The ranks are the ordinary members of the armed forces, rather than the officers.

3 The ranks of a group are its members. *e.g. We welcomed five new members to our ranks.*

4 a row of people or things

● THESAURUS
column: *a column of figures*
file: *They walked in single file to the top.*
line: *He waited in a line of slow-moving vehicles.*
row: *She lived in the middle of a row of pretty cottages.*

> VERB
5 To rank as something means to have that status or position on a scale. *e.g. His dismissal ranks as the worst humiliation he has ever known.*

> ADJECTIVE
6 complete and absolute *e.g. rank stupidity*

● THESAURUS
absolute: *not intended for absolute beginners*
complete: *her complete ignorance*
downright: *That was just downright rudeness.*
sheer: *his sheer stupidity*
unmitigated: *an unmitigated villain*

r

utter: *his utter disregard for other people*

7 having a strong, unpleasant smell *e.g. the rank smell of unwashed clothes*

ransack ['rænsæk] **ransacks, ransacking, ransacked** VERB

To ransack a place means to disturb everything and leave it in a mess, in order to search for or steal something.

[WORD HISTORY: from Old Norse RANN meaning 'house' andSAKA meaning 'to search']

ransom ['rænsəm] **ransoms** NOUN

money that is demanded to free someone who has been kidnapped

rant [rænt] **rants, ranting, ranted** VERB

To rant means to talk loudly in an excited or angry way.

rap [ræp] **raps, rapping, rapped** VERB

1 If you rap something, you hit it with a series of quick blows.

> NOUN

2 a quick knock or blow on something *e.g. A rap on the door signalled his arrival.*

3 Rap is a style of poetry spoken to music with a strong rhythmic beat.

rape [reɪp] **rapes, raping, raped** VERB

1 If a man rapes a woman, he violently forces her to have sex with him against her will.

> NOUN

2 Rape is the act or crime of raping a woman. *e.g. victims of rape*

3 Rape is a plant with yellow flowers that is grown as a crop for oil and fodder.

rapist NOUN

rapid ['ræpɪd] **rapids** ADJECTIVE

1 happening or moving very quickly *e.g. rapid industrial expansion... He took a few rapid steps.*

> PLURAL NOUN

2 An area of a river where the water moves extremely fast over rocks is referred to as rapids.

rapidly ADVERB, **rapidity** NOUN

rapier ['reɪpɪə] **rapiers** NOUN

a long thin sword with a sharp point

rapport [ræ'pɔ:] NOUN; FORMAL

If there is a rapport between two people, they find it easy to understand each other's feelings and attitudes.

rapt [ræpt] ADJECTIVE

If you are rapt, you are so interested in something that you are not aware of other things. *e.g. sitting with rapt attention in front of the screen*

rapture ['ræptʃə] NOUN

Rapture is a feeling of extreme delight.

rapturous ADJECTIVE, **rapturously** ADVERB

rare [rɛə] **rarer, rarest** ADJECTIVE

1 Something that is rare is not common or does not happen often. *e.g. a rare flower... Such major disruptions are rare.*

● THESAURUS

exceptional: *in exceptional circumstances*

few: *Genuine friends are few.*

scarce: *Jobs are becoming increasingly scarce.*

sparse: *Information about the tests is sparse.*

sporadic: *occurring at only sporadic intervals*

uncommon: *The disease is uncommon in younger women.*

unusual: *an unusual variety but a very attractive one*

<<OPPOSITE *common*

2 Rare meat has been lightly cooked.

rarely ADVERB

rarefied ['rɛərɪˌfaɪd] ADJECTIVE

seeming to have little connection with ordinary life *e.g. He grew up in a rarefied literary atmosphere.*

raring ['rɛərɪŋ] ADJECTIVE

If you are raring to do something, you are very eager to do it.

rarity ['rɛərɪtɪ] **rarities** NOUN

1 something that is interesting or valuable because it is unusual

2 The rarity of something is the fact that it is not common.

rascal ['rɑ:skəl] **rascals** NOUN

If you refer to someone as a rascal, you mean that they do bad or mischievous things.

rash [ræʃ] **rashes** ADJECTIVE

1 If you are rash, you do something hasty and foolish.

● THESAURUS

foolhardy: *Some described his behaviour as foolhardy.*

hasty: *This is no hasty decision.*

impetuous: *As usual, he reacted in a heated and impetuous way.*

impulsive: *He is too impulsive to take this responsibility.*

reckless: *his reckless driving*

> NOUN

2 an area of red spots that appear on your skin when you are ill or have an allergy

● THESAURUS

eruption: *an unpleasant skin eruption*

outbreak: *an outbreak of blisters around his mouth*

3 A rash of events is a lot of them happening in a short time. *e.g. a rash of strikes*

rashly ADVERB

● THESAURUS

epidemic: *A victim of the recent epidemic of shootings.*

flood: *a flood of complaints about the programme*
plague: *Last year there was a plague of burglaries.*
spate: *a spate of attacks on horses*
wave: *the current wave of violent attacks*

rasher ['ræʃə] **rashers** NOUN
a thin slice of bacon

rasp [rɑːsp] **rasps, rasping, rasped** VERB
1 To rasp means to make a harsh unpleasant sound.

> NOUN

2 a coarse file with rows of raised teeth, used for smoothing wood or metal

raspberry ['rɑːzbərɪ] **raspberries** NOUN
a small soft red fruit that grows on a bush

rat [ræt] **rats** NOUN
a long-tailed animal which looks like a large mouse

rate [reɪt] **rates, rating, rated** NOUN
1 The rate of something is the speed or frequency with which it happens. *e.g. New diet books appear at the rate of nearly one a week.*

● THESAURUS
frequency: *She phoned with increasing frequency.*
pace: *at an accelerated pace*
speed: *moving at the speed of light*
tempo: *They wanted to speed up the tempo of change.*
velocity: *changes in wind velocity*

2 The rate of interest is its level. *e.g. a further cut in interest rates*

3 the cost or charge for something

● THESAURUS
charge: *An annual charge will be made for this service.*
cost: *a low-cost mortgage*
fee: *The work will be invoiced at the usual fee.*
price: *falling share prices*
tariff: *How much you pay depends on your tariff.*

4 Rates are a local tax paid by people who own buildings.

> PHRASE

5 If you say **at this rate** something will happen, you mean it will happen if things continue in the same way. *e.g. At this rate we'll be lucky to get home before six.*

6 You say **at any rate** when you want to add to or amend what you have just said. *e.g. He is the least appealing character, to me at any rate.*

> VERB

7 The way you rate someone or something is your opinion of them. *e.g. He was rated as one of England's top young players.*

● THESAURUS
appraise: *She gave me an appraising glance.*

class: *classed as one of the top ten athletes*
consider: *I considered myself to be quite good at maths.*
count: *That would be counted as wrong.*
rank: *The hotel was ranked as one of the world's best.*
regard: *a highly regarded member of staff*

rather ['rɑːðə] ADVERB
1 Rather means to a certain extent. *e.g. We got along rather well... The reality is rather more complex.*

● THESAURUS
fairly: *Both ships are fairly new.*
pretty: *informal I'm pretty tired now.*
quite: *The cottage looks quite ordinary from the road.*
relatively: *I think I'm relatively easy to get on with.*
slightly: *slightly startled by his sudden appearance*
somewhat: *He said, somewhat unconvincingly, that he would pay.*

> PHRASE

2 If you **would rather** do a particular thing, you would prefer to do it.

3 If you do one thing **rather than** another, you choose to do the first thing instead of the second.

ratify ['rætɪˌfaɪ] **ratifies, ratifying, ratified** VERB; FORMAL
To ratify a written agreement means to approve it formally, usually by signing it.
ratification NOUN

rating ['reɪtɪŋ] **ratings** NOUN
1 a score based on the quality or status of something

2 The ratings are statistics showing how popular each television programme is.

ratio ['reɪʃɪˌəʊ] **ratios** NOUN
a relationship which shows how many times one thing is bigger than another *e.g. The adult to child ratio is 1 to 6.*

ration ['ræʃən] **rations, rationing, rationed** NOUN
1 Your ration of something is the amount you are allowed to have.

2 Rations are the food given each day to a soldier or member of an expedition.

> VERB

3 When something is rationed, you are only allowed a limited amount of it, because there is a shortage.

rational ['ræʃənˀl] ADJECTIVE
When people are rational, their judgments are based on reason rather than emotion.
rationally ADVERB, **rationality** NOUN

● THESAURUS
enlightened: *enlightened companies who take a pragmatic view*

logical: *There must be a logical explanation for it.*
reasonable: *a perfectly reasonable decision*
sensible: *The sensible thing is to leave them alone.*

rationale [ˌræʃəˈnɑːl] NOUN
The rationale for a course of action or for a belief is the set of reasons on which it is based.

rattle [ˈrætⁱl] **rattles, rattling, rattled** VERB
1 When something rattles, it makes short, regular knocking sounds.
2 If something rattles you, it upsets you. *e.g. He was obviously rattled by events.*
> NOUN
3 the noise something makes when it rattles
4 a baby's toy which makes a noise when it is shaken

rattlesnake [ˈrætⁱlˌsneɪk] **rattlesnakes**
NOUN
a poisonous American snake

raucous [ˈrɔːkəs] ADJECTIVE
A raucous voice is loud and rough.

ravage [ˈrævɪdʒ] **ravages, ravaging, ravaged** FORMAL > VERB
1 To ravage something means to seriously harm or damage it. *e.g. a country ravaged by floods*
> NOUN
2 The ravages of something are its damaging effects. *e.g. the ravages of two world wars*

rave [reɪv] **raves, raving, raved** VERB
1 If someone raves, they talk in an angry, uncontrolled way. *e.g. He started raving about being treated badly.*
● THESAURUS
babble: *She babbled on and on about her plans.*
rage: *He was raging at their lack of response.*
rant: *She started ranting about her boss's attitude.*
2 INFORMAL If you rave about something, you talk about it very enthusiastically.
● THESAURUS
be wild about: *informal He was just wild about the play.*
enthuse: *She enthused about the local architecture.*
gush: *"It was brilliant," he gushed.*
> ADJECTIVE
3 INFORMAL
If something gets a rave review, it is praised enthusiastically.
> NOUN
4 INFORMAL
a large party with electronic dance music

raven [ˈreɪvⁿn] **ravens** NOUN
1 a large black bird with a deep, harsh call
> ADJECTIVE
2 Raven hair is black and shiny.

ravenous [ˈrævənəs] ADJECTIVE
very hungry

ravine [rəˈviːn] **ravines** NOUN
a deep, narrow valley with steep sides

raving [ˈreɪvɪŋ] **ravings** ADJECTIVE
1 If someone is raving, they are mad. *e.g. a raving lunatic*
> NOUN
2 Someone's ravings are crazy things they write or say.

ravioli [ˌrævɪˈəʊlɪ] NOUN
Ravioli consists of small squares of pasta filled with meat and served with a sauce.

ravishing [ˈrævɪʃɪŋ] ADJECTIVE
Someone or something that is ravishing is very beautiful. *e.g. a ravishing landscape*

raw [rɔː] ADJECTIVE
1 Raw food has not been cooked.
2 A raw substance is in its natural state. *e.g. raw sugar*
3 If part of your body is raw, the skin has come off or been rubbed away.
4 Someone who is raw is too young or too new in a job or situation to know how to behave.

raw material **raw materials** NOUN
Raw materials are the natural substances used to make something.

ray [reɪ] **rays** NOUN
1 a beam of light or radiation
2 A ray of hope is a small amount that makes an unpleasant situation seem slightly better.
3 a large sea fish with eyes on the top of its body, and a long tail

raze [reɪz] **razes, razing, razed** VERB
To raze a building, town, or forest means to completely destroy it. *e.g. The town was razed to the ground during the occupation.*

razor [ˈreɪzə] **razors** NOUN
a tool that people use for shaving

razor blade **razor blades** NOUN
a small, sharp, flat piece of metal fitted into a razor for shaving

re- PREFIX
1 'Re-' is used to form nouns and verbs that refer to the repetition of an action or process *e.g. reread... remarry*
2 'Re-' is also used to form verbs that refer to going back to a previous condition *e.g. refresh... renew*
[WORD HISTORY: from a Latin prefix]

reach [riːtʃ] **reaches, reaching, reached**
VERB
1 When you reach a place, you arrive there.
● THESAURUS
arrive at: *to arrive at an erroneous conclusion*

attain: *She worked hard to attain a state of calm.*
get as far as: *If we get as far as the coast we will be quite satisfied.*
get to: *You must get to the end before noon.*
make: *They didn't think they would make the summit.*

2 When you reach for something, you stretch out your arm to it.

3 If something reaches a place or point, it extends as far as that place or point. *e.g. She has a cloak that reaches to the ground.*

● **THESAURUS**

extend to: *The boundaries extend to the edge of the lake.*
go as far as: *Try to make the ball go as far as the trees.*
touch: *I could touch both walls with my arms extended.*

4 If something or someone reaches a stage or level, they get to it. *e.g. Unemployment has reached record levels.*

● **THESAURUS**

arrive at: *They planted a flag when they arrived at the top.*
attain: *He was close to attaining his personal best.*
climb to: *Attendance climbed to a record level this year.*
fall to: *Profits are expected to fall to their lowest level.*
rise to: *She rose rapidly to the top of her profession.*

5 To reach an agreement or decision means to succeed in achieving it.

> PHRASE

6 If a place is **within reach**, you can get there. *e.g. a cycle route well within reach of most people*

7 If something is **out of reach**, you cannot get it to it by stretching out your arm. *e.g. Store out of reach of children.*

react [rɪ'ækt] **reacts, reacting, reacted**
VERB

1 When you react to something, you behave in a particular way because of it. *e.g. He reacted badly to the news.*

2 If one substance reacts with another, a chemical change takes place when they are put together.

reaction [rɪ'ækʃən] **reactions** NOUN

1 Your reaction to something is what you feel, say, or do because of it. *e.g. Reaction to the visit is mixed.*

● **THESAURUS**

acknowledgment: *She made no acknowledgment of my question.*
answer: *In answer to speculation in the press, she declared her interest.*

feedback: *Continue to ask for feedback on your work.*
response: *in response to a request from the members*

2 Your reactions are your ability to move quickly in response to something that happens. *e.g. Squash requires fast reactions.*

3 If there is a reaction against something, it becomes unpopular. *e.g. a reaction against Christianity*

● **THESAURUS**

backlash: *the male backlash against feminism*
counterbalance: *an organization set up as a counterbalance to the official group*

4 In a chemical reaction, a chemical change takes place when two substances are put together.

reactionary [rɪ'ækʃənərɪ] **reactionaries**
ADJECTIVE

1 Someone who is reactionary tries to prevent political or social change.

> NOUN

2 Reactionaries are reactionary people.

reactor [rɪ'æktə] **reactors** NOUN
a device which is used to produce nuclear energy

read [riːd] **reads, reading, read** VERB

1 When you read, you look at something written and follow it or say it aloud.

● **THESAURUS**

glance at: *He just glanced briefly at the article.*
look at: *She was looking at the evening paper.*
pore over: *poring over a dictionary*
scan: *There's only time to scan through it quickly.*
study: *I'll study the text more closely later.*

2 If you can read someone's moods or mind, you can judge what they are feeling or thinking.

● **THESAURUS**

comprehend: *Her expression was difficult to comprehend.*
decipher: *She was still no closer to deciphering the code.*
interpret: *You have to interpret their gestures, too.*

3 When you read a meter or gauge, you look at it and record the figure on it.

4 If you read a subject at university, you study it.

reader ['riːdə] **readers** NOUN

1 The readers of a newspaper or magazine are the people who read it regularly.

2 At a university, a reader is a senior lecturer just below the rank of professor.

readership ['riːdəʃɪp] NOUN
The readership of a newspaper or magazine consists of the people who read it regularly.

readily ['rɛdɪlɪ] ADVERB

r

1 willingly and eagerly *e.g. She readily agreed to see Alex.*

2 easily done or quickly obtainable *e.g. Help is readily available.*

reading ['riːdɪŋ] **readings** NOUN

1 Reading is the activity of reading books.

2 The reading on a meter or gauge is the figure or measurement it shows.

readjust [ˌriːə'dʒʌst] **readjusts, readjusting, readjusted** VERB

1 If you readjust, you adapt to a new situation.

2 If you readjust something, you alter it to a different position.

ready ['rɛdɪ] ADJECTIVE

1 having reached the required stage, or prepared for action or use *e.g. In a few days time the plums will be ready to eat.*

● THESAURUS

organized: *Everything is organized for the party tomorrow.*

prepared: *He was prepared for a tough fight.*

primed: *The other side is primed for battle.*

ripe: *Are those strawberries ripe yet?*

set: *We'll be set to go in five minutes.*

2 willing or eager to do something *e.g. She says she's not ready for marriage.*

● THESAURUS

agreeable: *We can go ahead if you are agreeable.*

eager: *Children are eager to learn.*

happy: *always happy to help*

keen: *He wasn't keen to get involved.*

willing: *questions which they were not willing to answer*

3 If you are ready for something, you need it. *e.g. I'm ready for bed.*

4 easily produced or obtained *e.g. ready cash*
readiness NOUN

● THESAURUS

accessible: *The system should be accessible to everyone.*

available: *Food is available round the clock.*

convenient: *a convenient excuse*

handy: *Keep a pencil and paper handy.*

ready-made ['rɛdɪˌmeɪd] ADJECTIVE

already made and therefore able to be used immediately

reaffirm [ˌriːə'fɜːm] **reaffirms, reaffirming, reaffirmed** VERB

To reaffirm something means to state it again. *e.g. He reaffirmed his support for the campaign.*

real ['rɪəl] ADJECTIVE

1 actually existing and not imagined or invented

● THESAURUS

actual: *She was the actual basis for the leading character.*

authentic: *containing authentic details of what happened*

concrete: *I don't have any concrete evidence.*

factual: *a factual account*

genuine: *His worries about the future were genuine ones.*

legitimate: *These are legitimate concerns.*

tangible: *I cannot see any tangible benefits in these changes.*

true: *the true story of his life*

<<OPPOSITE *imaginary*

2 genuine and not imitation *e.g. Who's to know if they're real guns?.*

● THESAURUS

authentic: *an authentic French recipe*

bona fide: *We are happy to donate to bona fide charities.*

dinkum: Australian and New Zealand; informal *a place which serves dinkum Aussie tucker*

genuine: *It's a genuine Rembrandt, all right.*

honest: *It was an honest attempt to set things right.*

sincere: *His remorse was completely sincere, not just an act.*

rightful: *the rightful heir to the throne*

true: *He is a true believer in human rights.*

unaffected: *her genuine and unaffected sympathy for the victims*

<<OPPOSITE *fake*

3 true or actual and not mistaken *e.g. This was the real reason for her call.*

real estate NOUN

Real estate is property in the form of land and buildings rather than personal possessions.

realism ['rɪəˌlɪzəm] NOUN

Realism is the recognition of the true nature of a situation. *e.g. a triumph of muddled thought over realism and common sense*
realist NOUN

realistic [ˌrɪə'lɪstɪk] ADJECTIVE

1 recognizing and accepting the true nature of a situation

● THESAURUS

down-to-earth: *We welcomed her down-to-earth approach.*

level-headed: *a sensible, level-headed approach*

matter-of-fact: *He sounded matter-of-fact and unemotional.*

practical: *a highly practical attitude to life*

sensible: *I'm trying to persuade you to be more sensible.*

sober: *a more sober assessment of the situation*

2 representing things in a way that is true to real life *e.g. His novels are more realistic than his short stories.*

realistically ADVERB

● THESAURUS

authentic: *They have to look authentic.*

faithful: *faithful copies of old household items*
lifelike: *almost as lifelike as a photograph*
true: *It gave a true picture of how things were.*

reality [rɪˈælɪtɪ] NOUN (PSHE)

1 Reality is the real nature of things, rather than the way someone imagines it. *e.g. Fiction and reality were increasingly blurred.*

● THESAURUS

authenticity: *The film's authenticity impressed the critics.*
fact: *No-one knew how much of what he said was fact.*
realism: *His stories had an edge of realism.*
truth: *I must tell you the truth about this situation.*

2 If something has become reality, it actually exists or is actually happening.

realize [ˈrɪəˌlaɪz] **realizes, realizing, realized;** also spelt **realise** VERB

1 If you realize something, you become aware of it.

● THESAURUS

appreciate: *He appreciates the difficulties we face.*
comprehend: *They do not comprehend the nature of the problem.*
grasp: *She still couldn't grasp what had really happened.*
recognize: *Of course I recognize that evil exists.*
understand: *I didn't understand what he meant until later.*

2 FORMAL
If your hopes or fears are realized, what you hoped for or feared actually happens. *e.g. Our worst fears were realized.*

3 To realize a sum of money means to receive it as a result of selling goods or shares.
realization NOUN

really [ˈrɪəlɪ] ADVERB

1 used to add emphasis to what is being said *e.g. I'm not really surprised.*

● THESAURUS

absolutely: *feeling absolutely exhausted*
certainly: *I am certainly getting tired of hearing about it.*
extremely: *My mobile phone is extremely useful.*
remarkably: *They have been remarkably successful.*
terribly: *I'm terribly sorry to bother you.*
truly: *a truly splendid man*
very: *learning very quickly*

2 used to indicate that you are talking about the true facts about something *e.g. What was really going on?.*

● THESAURUS

actually: *I pretended I was interested, but I was actually half asleep.*
in fact: *It sounds simple, but in fact it's very difficult.*

in reality: *He came across as streetwise, but in reality he was not.*
truly: *I truly never minded caring for Rusty.*

> If you want to emphasize an adjective you should always use *really* rather than *real*: *really interesting*

realm [rɛlm] **realms** NOUN; FORMAL

1 You can refer to any area of thought or activity as a realm. *e.g. the realm of politics*

2 a country with a king or queen *e.g. defence of the realm*

reap [riːp] **reaps, reaping, reaped** VERB

1 To reap a crop such as corn means to cut and gather it.

2 When people reap benefits or rewards, they get them as a result of hard work or careful planning.
reaper NOUN

reappear [ˌriːəˈpɪə] **reappears, reappearing, reappeared** VERB

When people or things reappear, you can see them again, because they have come back. *e.g. The stolen ring reappeared three years later in a pawn shop.*

reappearance NOUN

reappraisal [ˌriːəˈpreɪzəl] **reappraisals** NOUN; FORMAL

If there is a reappraisal, people think about something and decide whether they want to change it. *e.g. a reappraisal of the government's economic policies*

rear [rɪə] **rears, rearing, reared** NOUN

1 The rear of something is the part at the back.
> VERB

2 To rear children or young animals means to bring them up until they are able to look after themselves.

3 When a horse rears, it raises the front part of its body, so that its front legs are in the air.

rear admiral **rear admirals** NOUN
a senior officer in the navy

rearrange [ˌriːəˈreɪndʒ] **rearranges, rearranging, rearranged** VERB
To rearrange something means to organize or arrange it in a different way.

reason [ˈriːzən] **reasons, reasoning, reasoned** NOUN

1 The reason for something is the fact or situation which explains why it happens or which causes it to happen.

● THESAURUS

cause: *The true cause of the accident may never be known.*
grounds: *some grounds for optimism*

r

incentive: *There is no incentive to adopt these measures.*
motive: *Police have ruled out robbery as a motive.*
purpose: *the purpose of their visit*

2 If you have **reason** to believe or feel something, there are definite reasons why you believe it or feel it. *e.g. He had every reason to be upset.*

3 **Reason** is the ability to think and make judgments.

● THESAURUS

intellect: *good health and a lively intellect*
judgment: *His judgment was impaired.*
rationality: *We live in an era of rationality.*
reasoning: *a lack of sound reasoning and logic*
sense: *He should have had more sense.*

> VERB

4 If you **reason** that something is true, you decide it is true after considering all the facts.

5 If you **reason** with someone, you persuade them to accept sensible arguments.

● THESAURUS

bring round: informal *We'll try to bring you round to our point of view.*
persuade: *I had to persuade him of the advantages.*
win over: *They still hoped to win him over to their way of thinking.*

reasonable ['riːzənəbəl] ADJECTIVE

1 **Reasonable** behaviour is fair and sensible.

● THESAURUS

fair: *You can be sure she will be fair with you.*
moderate: *an easygoing man of very moderate views*
rational: *Please try to be rational about this.*
sane: *No sane person wishes to see a war.*
sensible: *She was a sensible girl and did not panic.*
sober: *We are now more sober and realistic.*
steady: *a politician who was steady almost to the point of being boring*
wise: *You're a wise old man: tell me what to do.*

2 If an explanation is **reasonable**, there are good reasons for thinking it is correct.

● THESAURUS

justifiable.: *Our violence was justifiable on the grounds of political necessity.*
legitimate: *That's a perfectly legitimate fear.*
logical: *There was a logical explanation.*
sensible: *a sensible solution*
sound: *sound advice*
understandable: *His unhappiness was understandable.*

3 A **reasonable** amount is a fairly large amount.

4 A **reasonable** price is fair and not too high.
reasonably ADVERB

● THESAURUS

cheap: *She said she'd share a flat if I could find somewhere cheap enough.*

competitive: *homes offered for sale at competitive prices*
fair: *It's a fair price for a car like that.*
inexpensive: *an inexpensive divorce settlement*
low: *The low prices and friendly service made for a pleasant evening.*
modest: *a modest charge*

reasoning ['riːzənɪŋ] NOUN
Reasoning is the process by which you reach a conclusion after considering all the facts.

reassess [ˌriːə'sɛs] **reassesses, reassessing, reassessed** VERB
If you **reassess** something, you consider whether it still has the same value or importance.
reassessment NOUN

reassure [ˌriːə'ʃʊə] **reassures, reassuring, reassured** VERB
If you **reassure** someone, you say or do things that make them less worried.
reassurance NOUN

● THESAURUS

bolster: *measures intended to bolster morale*
cheer up: *I wrote it just to cheer myself up.*
comfort: *He tried to comfort her as far as he could.*
encourage: *Investors were encouraged by the news.*

rebate ['riːbeɪt] **rebates** NOUN
money paid back to someone who has paid too much tax or rent

rebel rebels, rebelling, rebelled NOUN
['rɛbəl]

1 (HISTORY) **Rebels** are people who are fighting their own country's army to change the political system.

2 Someone who is a **rebel** rejects society's values and behaves differently from other people.

> VERB [rɪ'bɛl]

3 To **rebel** means to fight against authority and reject accepted values.

● THESAURUS

defy: *It was the first time she had defied her mother.*
mutiny: *Sailors mutinied against their officers.*
resist: *activists convicted of resisting apartheid*
revolt: *The islanders revolted against the prince.*

rebellion [rɪ'bɛljən] **rebellions** NOUN
(HISTORY) A **rebellion** is organized and often violent opposition to authority.

● THESAURUS

insurrection: *They were plotting to stage an armed insurrection.*
mutiny: *convicted of mutiny and high treason*
revolt: *The revolt ended in failure.*
revolution: *after the French Revolution*
uprising: *Isolated attacks turned into a full-scale uprising.*

rebellious [rɪ'bɛljəs] ADJECTIVE
unwilling to obey and likely to rebel against
authority

rebuff [rɪ'bʌf] **rebuffs, rebuffing, rebuffed**
VERB
1 If you rebuff someone, you reject what they
offer. *e.g. She rebuffed their offers of help.*
> NOUN
2 a rejection of an offer

rebuild [riː'bɪld] **rebuilds, rebuilding,
rebuilt** VERB
When a town or building is rebuilt, it is built
again after being damaged or destroyed.

rebuke [rɪ'bjuːk] **rebukes, rebuking,
rebuked** VERB
To rebuke someone means to speak severely to
them about something they have done.

recall [rɪ'kɔːl] **recalls, recalling, recalled**
VERB
1 To recall something means to remember it.
2 If you are recalled to a place, you are ordered to
return there.
3 If a company recalls products, it asks people to
return them because they are faulty.

recap ['riː,kæp] **recaps, recapping,
recapped** VERB
To recap means to repeat and summarize the
main points of an explanation or discussion.

recapture [riː'kæptʃə] **recaptures,
recapturing, recaptured** VERB
1 When you recapture a pleasant feeling, you
experience it again. *e.g. She may never recapture
that past assurance.*
2 When soldiers recapture a place, they capture it
from the people who took it from them.
3 When animals or prisoners are recaptured, they
are caught after they have escaped.

recede [rɪ'siːd] **recedes, receding,
receded** VERB
1 When something recedes, it moves away into
the distance.
2 If a man's hair is receding, he is starting to go
bald at the front.

receipt [rɪ'siːt] **receipts** NOUN
1 a piece of paper confirming that money or
goods have been received
2 In a shop or theatre, the money received is
often called the receipts. *e.g. Box-office receipts
were down last month.*
3 FORMAL The receipt of something is the
receiving of it. *e.g. You have to sign here and
acknowledge receipt.*

receive [rɪ'siːv] **receives, receiving,
received** VERB

1 When you receive something, someone gives it
to you, or you get it after it has been sent to you.

● THESAURUS
accept: *They accepted the parcel gratefully.*
be given: *We were all given presents.*
get: *She got some lovely things.*
pick up: *He picked up an award for his performance.*
take: *Will you take this parcel for your neighbour?*

2 To receive something also means to have it
happen to you. *e.g. injuries she received in a car
crash*

● THESAURUS
encounter: *He encountered some unexpected
opposition.*
suffer: *He suffered some bangs and bumps.*
sustain: *She had sustained a cut on her arm.*
undergo: *You may have to undergo a bit of teasing.*

3 When you receive visitors or guests, you
welcome them.

● THESAURUS
entertain: *She loved to entertain friends at home.*
greet: *They greeted the visitors at the door.*
meet: *I'll come down to meet you.*
take in: *The country took in many refugees.*
welcome: *Several people came by to welcome me.*

4 If something is received in a particular way,
that is how people react to it. *e.g. The decision has
been received with great disappointment.*

receiver [rɪ'siːvə] **receivers** NOUN
the part of a telephone you hold near to your ear
and mouth

recent ['riːsᵊnt] ADJECTIVE
Something recent happened a short time ago.
recently ADVERB

● THESAURUS
current: *a sound knowledge of current affairs*
fresh: *fresh footprints in the snow*
new: *the subject of a new film*
present-day: *Even by present-day standards these
were large aircraft.*
up-to-date: *the most up-to-date computers*

reception [rɪ'sɛpʃən] **receptions** NOUN
1 In a hotel or office, reception is the place near
the entrance where appointments or enquiries
are dealt with.
2 a formal party
3 The reception someone or something gets is
the way people react to them. *e.g. Her tour met
with a rapturous reception.*
4 If your radio or television gets good reception,
the sound or picture is clear.

receptionist [rɪ'sɛpʃənɪst] **receptionists**
NOUN
The receptionist in a hotel or office deals with

r

people when they arrive, answers the telephone, and arranges appointments.

receptive [rɪ'sɛptɪv] ADJECTIVE
Someone who is receptive to ideas or suggestions is willing to consider them.

recess ['riːsɛs] or [rɪ'sɛs] **recesses** NOUN
1 a period when no work is done by a committee or parliament e.g. the Christmas recess
2 a place where part of a wall has been built further back than the rest

recession [rɪ'sɛʃn] **recessions** NOUN
a period when a country's economy is less successful and more people become unemployed

● THESAURUS
decline: signs of economic decline
depression: the Great Depression of the 1930s
downturn: due to a sharp downturn in the industry
slump: Many jobs were lost during the slump.

recharge [riː'tʃɑːdʒ] **recharges, recharging, recharged** VERB
To recharge a battery means to charge it with electricity again after it has been used.

recipe ['rɛsɪpɪ] **recipes** NOUN
1 **(D & T)** a list of ingredients and instructions for cooking something
2 If something is a recipe for disaster or for success, it is likely to result in disaster or success.

recipient [rɪ'sɪpɪənt] **recipients** NOUN
The recipient of something is the person receiving it.

reciprocal [rɪ'sɪprək³l] ADJECTIVE
A reciprocal agreement involves two people, groups, or countries helping each other in a similar way. e.g. a reciprocal agreement on trade

reciprocate [rɪ'sɪprə,keɪt] **reciprocates, reciprocating, reciprocated** VERB
If you reciprocate someone's feelings or behaviour, you feel or behave in the same way towards them.

recital [rɪ'saɪt³l] **recitals** NOUN
a performance of music or poetry, usually by one person

recite [rɪ'saɪt] **recites, reciting, recited** VERB
If you recite a poem or something you have learnt, you say it aloud.
recitation NOUN

reckless ['rɛklɪs] ADJECTIVE
showing a complete lack of care about danger or damage e.g. a reckless tackle
recklessly ADVERB, **recklessness** NOUN

reckon ['rɛkən] **reckons, reckoning, reckoned** VERB

1 INFORMAL
If you reckon that something is true, you think it is true. e.g. I reckoned he was still fond of her.

● THESAURUS
assume: If mistakes occurred, they were assumed to be my fault.
believe: formal "You've never heard of him?" "I don't believe so."
consider: Barbara considers that people who sell these birds are acting illegally.
judge: I would judge that my earnings are considerably below those of my sister.
suppose: I suppose I'd better do some homework.
think: I think there should be a ban on tobacco advertising. formal formal

2 INFORMAL
If someone reckons to do something, they claim or expect to do it. e.g. Officers on the case are reckoning to charge someone shortly.

3 To reckon an amount means to calculate it.

● THESAURUS
calculate: We calculate that the average size farm in the county is 65 acres.
count: The years before their arrival in prison are not counted as part of their sentence.
estimate: Analysts estimate its current popularity at around ten per cent.
figure out: I roughly figured out the total.
work out: It is proving hard to work out the value of their assets.

4 If you reckon on something, you rely on it happening when making your plans. e.g. He reckons on being world champion.

5 If you had not reckoned with something, you had not expected it and therefore were unprepared when it happened. e.g. Giles had not reckoned with the strength of Sally's feelings.

reckoning ['rɛkənɪŋ] **reckonings** NOUN
a calculation e.g. There were a thousand or so, by my reckoning.

reclaim [rɪ'kleɪm] **reclaims, reclaiming, reclaimed** VERB
1 When you reclaim something, you collect it after leaving it somewhere or losing it.
2 To reclaim land means to make it suitable for use, for example by draining it.
reclamation NOUN

recline [rɪ'klaɪn] **reclines, reclining, reclined** VERB
To recline means to lie or lean back at an angle. e.g. a photo of him reclining on his bed

recluse [rɪ'kluːs] **recluses** NOUN
Someone who is a recluse lives alone and avoids other people.
reclusive ADJECTIVE

recognize ['rɛkəg,naɪz] **recognizes, recognizing, recognized**; also spelt **recognise** VERB

1 If you recognize someone or something, you realize that you know who or what they are. *e.g. The receptionist recognized me at once.*

● THESAURUS
identify: *She tried to identify the perfume.*
know: *You'd know him if you saw him again.*
place: *He couldn't place my voice immediately.*
spot: *I spotted the house quite easily.*

2 To recognize something also means to accept and acknowledge it. *e.g. The RAF recognized him as an outstanding pilot.*
recognition NOUN, **recognizable** ADJECTIVE, **recognizably** ADVERB

● THESAURUS
acknowledge: *Her great bravery was acknowledged.*
appreciate: *In time you'll appreciate his good points.*
honour: *achievements honoured with the Nobel Prize*
salute: *We salute your great courage.*

recommend [,rɛkə'mɛnd] **recommends, recommending, recommended** VERB
If you recommend something to someone, you praise it and suggest they try it.
recommendation NOUN

reconcile ['rɛkən,saɪl] **reconciles, reconciling, reconciled** VERB

1 To reconcile two things that seem to oppose one another, means to make them work or exist together successfully. *e.g. The designs reconciled style with comfort.*

2 When people are reconciled, they become friendly again after a quarrel.

3 If you reconcile yourself to an unpleasant situation, you accept it.
reconciliation NOUN

reconnaissance [rɪ'kɒnɪsəns] NOUN
Reconnaissance is the gathering of military information by soldiers, planes, or satellites.

reconsider [,riːkən'sɪdə] **reconsiders, reconsidering, reconsidered** VERB
To reconsider something means to think about it again to decide whether to change it.
reconsideration NOUN

reconstruct [,riːkən'strʌkt] **reconstructs, reconstructing, reconstructed** VERB

1 To reconstruct something that has been damaged means to build it again.

● THESAURUS
rebuild: *The task of rebuilding would be very expensive.*

recreate: *They try to recreate the atmosphere of former times.*
regenerate: *the ability to regenerate damaged tissues*
renovate: *The hotel was being renovated.*
restore: *experts who specialize in restoring old furniture*

2 To reconstruct a past event means to get a complete description of it from small pieces of information.
reconstruction NOUN

● THESAURUS
build up: *They built up an image of him from several different descriptions.*
deduce: *The date can be deduced from other documents.*
piece together: *It was easy to piece together the shattered fragments.*

record **records, recording, recorded** NOUN ['rɛkɔːd]

1 If you keep a record of something, you keep a written account or store information in a computer. *e.g. medical records*

● THESAURUS
account: *The company keeps detailed accounts.*
archives: *Earlier issues are stored in the archives.*
file: *the right to inspect company files*
journal: *He kept a journal while he was travelling.*
minute: *Did you read the minutes of the last meeting?*
register: *a register of births, deaths and marriages*

2 a round, flat piece of plastic on which music has been recorded

3 an achievement which is the best of its type

4 Your record is what is known about your achievements or past activities. *e.g. He had a distinguished war record.*

● THESAURUS
background: *His background was in engineering.*
career: *His career spoke for itself.*
curriculum vitae: *I must update my curriculum vitae.*
track record: *informal Her track record as a teacher was impeccable.*

> VERB [rɪ'kɔːd]

5 If you record information, you write it down or put it into a computer.

● THESAURUS
document: *All these facts have been well documented.*
enter: *All the names are entered in this book.*
log: *They log everyone who comes in or out.*
note: *I must note your birthday.*
register: *We registered his birth straight away.*
write down: *If I don't write it down, I'll forget it.*

6 To record sound means to put it on tape, record, or compact disc.

r

> ADJECTIVE ['rɛkɔːd]
7 higher, lower, better, or worse than ever before
e.g. Profits were at a record level.

recorder [rɪˈkɔːdə] **recorders** NOUN
a small woodwind instrument

recording [rɪˈkɔːdɪŋ] **recordings** NOUN
A recording of something is a record, tape, or
video of it.

recount **recounts, recounting,**
recounted VERB [rɪˈkaʊnt]
1 If you recount a story, you tell it.

> NOUN ['riːˌkaʊnt]
2 a second count of votes in an election when the
result is very close

recoup [rɪˈkuːp] **recoups, recouping,**
recouped VERB
If you recoup money that you have spent or lost,
you get it back.

recourse [rɪˈkɔːs] NOUN; FORMAL
If you have recourse to something, you use it to
help you. *e.g. The members settled their differences
without recourse to war.*

recover [rɪˈkʌvə] **recovers, recovering,**
recovered VERB
1 To recover from an illness or unhappy
experience means to get well again or get over it.
● **THESAURUS**
convalesce: *those convalescing from illness or
surgery*
get better: *He never really got better again.*
get well: *Get well soon!*
improve: *The condition of your hair will soon
improve.*
recuperate: *recuperating from a serious injury*
revive: *Business soon revived once he came back.*

2 If you recover a lost object or your ability to do
something, you get it back.
● **THESAURUS**
get back: *We got everything back after the burglary.*
recapture: *trying to recapture the atmosphere of
our holiday*
recoup: *trying to recoup their losses*
regain: *It took him a while to regain his composure.*
retrieve: *I retrieved my bag from the back seat.*

recovery [rɪˈkʌvərɪ] NOUN
1 the act of getting better again
● **THESAURUS**
healing: *Adams claims that humour is an integral
part of healing.*
improvement: *Germany is showing a perceptible
improvement.*
recuperation: *great powers of recuperation*
revival: *little chance of a revival of interest*

2 the act of getting something back

● **THESAURUS**
recapture: *An offensive was launched for the
recapture of the airbase.*
reclamation: *the reclamation of dry land from the
marshes*
restoration: *She owed the restoration of her sight to
this remarkable technique.*
retrieval: *electronic storage and retrieval systems*

recreate ['rɛkrɪˌeɪt] **recreates, recreating,**
recreated VERB
To recreate something means to succeed in
making it happen or exist again. *e.g. a museum
that faithfully recreates an old farmhouse*

recreation [ˌrɛkrɪˈeɪʃən] **recreations** NOUN
Recreation is all the things that you do for
enjoyment in your spare time.
recreational ADJECTIVE

recrimination [rɪˌkrɪmɪˈneɪʃən]
recriminations NOUN
Recriminations are accusations made by people
about each other.

recruit [rɪˈkruːt] **recruits, recruiting,**
recruited VERB
1 To recruit people means to get them to join a
group or help with something.
● **THESAURUS**
draft: *drafted into the armed forces*
enlist: *I had to enlist the help of six people to move it.*
enrol: *She enrolled me on her evening course.*
muster: *trying to muster support for the movement*

> NOUN
2 someone who has joined the army or some
other organization
recruitment NOUN
● **THESAURUS**
beginner: *The course is suitable for beginners.*
convert: *a recent convert to their religion*
novice: *I'm a novice at these things.*
trainee: *My first job was as a graduate trainee with
a bank.*

rectangle ['rɛkˌtæŋɡəl] **rectangles,** NOUN
a four-sided shape with four right angles
rectangular ADJECTIVE

rectify ['rɛktɪˌfaɪ] **rectifies, rectifying,**
rectified VERB; FORMAL
If you rectify something that is wrong, you put it
right.

rector ['rɛktə] **rectors** NOUN
a Church of England priest in charge of a parish

rectory ['rɛktərɪ] **rectories** NOUN
a house where a rector lives

rectum ['rɛktəm] **rectums** NOUN; MEDICAL
the bottom end of the tube down which waste
food passes out of your body

rectal ADJECTIVE

recuperate [rɪˈkuːpəˌreɪt] **recuperates, recuperating, recuperated** VERB
When you recuperate, you gradually recover after being ill or injured.
recuperation NOUN

recur [rɪˈkɜː] **recurs, recurring, recurred** VERB
If something recurs, it happens or occurs again.
e.g. His hamstring injury recurred after the first game.
recurrence NOUN, **recurrent** ADJECTIVE

recurring [rɪˈkɜːrɪŋ] ADJECTIVE
1 happening or occurring many times *e.g. a recurring dream*

2 (MATHS) In maths, a recurring digit is one that is repeated over and over again after the decimal point in a decimal fraction.

recycle [riːˈsaɪkəl] **recycles, recycling, recycled** VERB
To recycle used products means to process them so that they can be used again. *e.g. recycled glass*

red [rɛd] **redder, reddest; reds** NOUN OR ADJECTIVE
Red is the colour of blood or of a ripe tomato.

> ADJECTIVE
Red hair is between orange and brown in colour.

redback [ˈrɛdˌbæk] **redbacks** NOUN
a small Australian spider with a poisonous bite

redcurrant [ˈrɛdˈkʌrənt] **redcurrants** NOUN
Redcurrants are very small, bright red fruits that grow in bunches on a bush.

redeem [rɪˈdiːm] **redeems, redeeming, redeemed** VERB
1 If a feature redeems an unpleasant thing or situation, it makes it seem less bad.

2 If you redeem yourself, you do something that gives people a good opinion of you again.

3 If you redeem something, you get it back by paying for it.

4 In Christianity, to redeem someone means to free them from sin by giving them faith in Jesus Christ.

redemption [rɪˈdɛmpʃən] NOUN
Redemption is the state of being redeemed.

red-handed [ˌrɛdˈhændɪd] PHRASE
To **catch someone red-handed** means to catch them doing something wrong.

red-hot [ˌrɛdˈhɒt] ADJECTIVE
Red-hot metal has been heated to such a high temperature that it has turned red.

redress [rɪˈdrɛs] **redresses, redressing, redressed** FORMAL > VERB

1 To redress a wrong means to put it right.

> NOUN
2 If you get redress for harm done to you, you are compensated for it.

red tape NOUN
Red tape is official rules and procedures that seem unnecessary and cause delay.

reduce [rɪˈdjuːs] **reduces, reducing, reduced** VERB
1 To reduce something means to make it smaller in size or amount.

● THESAURUS
curtail: *His powers will be severely curtailed.*
cut: *The first priority is to cut costs.*
cut down: *Try to cut down your coffee consumption.*
decrease: *The government plans to decrease interest rates.*
diminish: *to diminish the prestige of the monarchy*
lessen: *a diet that would lessen the risk of disease*
lower: *a commitment to lower taxes*
shorten: *taking steps to shorten queues*
<<OPPOSITE *increase*

2 You can use 'reduce' to say that someone or something is changed to a weaker or inferior state. *e.g. She reduced them to tears... The village was reduced to rubble.*

● THESAURUS
degrade: *I wouldn't degrade myself by going out with him.*
demote: *The Soviet team have been demoted to second place.*
downgrade: *The female role has been downgraded in the drive forequality.*
drive: *an old woman driven to shoplifting to survive*
force: *The men were so hungry they were forced to eat grass.*

reduction [rɪˈdʌkʃən] **reductions** NOUN
When there is a reduction in something, it is made smaller.

redundancy [rɪˈdʌndənsɪ] **redundancies** NOUN
1 Redundancy is the state of being redundant.
2 The number of redundancies is the number of people made redundant.

redundant [rɪˈdʌndənt] ADJECTIVE
1 When people are made redundant, they lose their jobs because there is no more work for them or no money to pay them.

2 When something becomes redundant, it is no longer needed.

reed [riːd] **reeds** NOUN
1 Reeds are hollow stemmed plants that grow in shallow water or wet ground.

2 a thin piece of cane or metal inside some wind instruments which vibrates when air is blown over it

r

reef [riːf] **reefs** NOUN
a long line of rocks or coral close to the surface of the sea

reek [riːk] **reeks, reeking, reeked** VERB
1 To reek of something means to smell strongly and unpleasantly of it.
> NOUN
2 If there is a reek of something, there is a strong unpleasant smell of it.

reel [riːl] **reels, reeling, reeled** NOUN
1 a cylindrical object around which you wrap something; often part of a device which you turn as a control
2 a fast Scottish dance
> VERB
3 When someone reels, they move unsteadily as if they are going to fall.
4 If your mind is reeling, you are confused because you have too much to think about. **reel off** VERB
5 If you reel off information, you repeat it from memory quickly and easily.

re-elect [riːɪˈlɛkt] **re-elects, re-electing, re-elected** VERB
When someone is re-elected, they win an election again and are able to stay in power.

refer [rɪˈfɜː] **refers, referring, referred** VERB
1 If you refer to something, you mention it.

● THESAURUS
allude: *She alluded to his absence in vague terms.*
bring up: *Why are you bringing that up now?*
cite: *She cites a favourite poem by George Herbert.*
mention: *She did not mention her mother's illness.*

2 If you refer to a book or record, you look at it to find something out.

● THESAURUS
consult: *He had to consult a dictionary.*
look up: *I looked up your file to get your address.*

3 When a problem or issue is referred to someone, they are formally asked to deal with it. *e.g. The case was referred to the European Court.*
[WORD HISTORY: from Latin REFERRE meaning 'to carry back']

> The word *refer* contains the sense 'back' in its meaning. Therefore, you should not use *back* after *refer: this refers to what has already been said* not *refers back*

referee [ˌrɛfəˈriː] **referees** NOUN
1 the official who controls a football game or a boxing or wrestling match
2 someone who gives a reference to a person who is applying for a job

reference [ˈrɛfərəns] **references** NOUN

1 A reference to something or someone is a mention of them.
2 Reference is the act of referring to something or someone for information or advice. *e.g. He makes that decision without reference to her.*
3 a number or name that tells you where to find information or identifies a document
4 If someone gives you a reference when you apply for a job, they write a letter about your abilities.

referendum [ˌrɛfəˈrɛndəm] **referendums** or **referenda** NOUN
a vote in which all the people in a country are officially asked whether they agree with a policy or proposal

refine [rɪˈfaɪn] **refines, refining, refined** VERB
To refine a raw material such as oil or sugar means to process it to remove impurities.

refined [rɪˈfaɪnd] ADJECTIVE
1 very polite and well-mannered
● THESAURUS
civilized: *the demands of civilized behaviour*
genteel: *two ladies with genteel manners and voices*
gentlemanly: *Sopwith behaved in his usual gentlemanly manner.*
ladylike: *They are models of ladylike decorum.*
polite: *polite and correct behaviour*
<<OPPOSITE *common*

2 processed to remove impurities
● THESAURUS
distilled: *distilled water*
filtered: *two pints of spring or filtered water*
processed: *a diet high in processed foods*
pure: *crisp pure air*
purified: *freshly purified drinking water*

refinement [rɪˈfaɪnmənt] **refinements** NOUN
1 Refinements are minor improvements.
2 Refinement is politeness and good manners.

refinery [rɪˈfaɪnərɪ] **refineries** NOUN
a factory where substances such as oil or sugar are refined

reflect [rɪˈflɛkt] **reflects, reflecting, reflected** VERB
1 If something reflects an attitude or situation, it shows what it is like. *e.g. His off-duty hobbies reflected his maritime interests.*
2 If something reflects light or heat, the light or heat bounces off it.
3 When something is reflected in a mirror or water, you can see its image in it.
4 **(MATHS)** If something reflects, its direction is reversed.

5 When you reflect, you think about something. **reflective** ADJECTIVE, **reflectively** ADVERB

reflection [rɪˈflɛkʃən] **reflections** NOUN

1 If something is a reflection of something else, it shows what it is like. *e.g. This is a terrible reflection of the times.*

2 an image in a mirror or water

3 Reflection is the process by which light and heat are bounced off a surface.

4 (MATHS) In maths, reflection is also the turning back of something on itself. *e.g. reflection of an axis*

5 Reflection is also thought. *e.g. After days of reflection she decided to leave.*

reflex [ˈriːflɛks] **reflexes** NOUN

1 A reflex or reflex action is a sudden uncontrollable movement that you make as a result of pressure or a blow.

2 If you have good reflexes, you respond very quickly when something unexpected happens.

> ADJECTIVE

3 A reflex angle is between 180° and 360°.

reflexive [rɪˈflɛksɪv] **reflexives** ADJECTIVE OR NOUN

In grammar, a reflexive verb or pronoun is one that refers back to the subject of the sentence. *e.g. She washed herself.*

reform [rɪˈfɔːm] **reforms, reforming, reformed** NOUN

1 Reforms are major changes to laws or institutions. *e.g. a programme of economic reform*

THESAURUS
amendment: *an amendment to remove the ban on divorce*
correction: *a correction of social injustice*
improvement: *She is pressing for improvements to education.*
rehabilitation: *the rehabilitation of young offenders*

> VERB

2 When laws or institutions are reformed, major changes are made to them.

THESAURUS
amend: *They want to amend the current system.*
better: *industrial action to better their working conditions*
correct: *keen to correct injustices*
rectify: *measures suggested to rectify the financial situation*
rehabilitate: *a loan for Bulgaria to rehabilitate its railway system*

3 When people reform, they stop committing crimes or doing other unacceptable things. **reformer** NOUN

Reformation [ˌrɛfəˈmeɪʃən] NOUN

The Reformation was a religious and political movement in Europe in the 16th century that began as an attempt to reform the Roman Catholic Church, but ended in the establishment of the Protestant Churches.

refraction [rɪˈfrækʃən] NOUN

Refraction is the bending of a ray of light, for example when it enters water or glass.

refrain [rɪˈfreɪn] **refrains, refraining, refrained** VERB

1 FORMAL
If you refrain from doing something, you do not do it. *e.g. Please refrain from smoking in the hall.*

> NOUN

2 The refrain of a song is a short, simple part, repeated many times.

refresh [rɪˈfrɛʃ] **refreshes, refreshing, refreshed** VERB

1 If something refreshes you when you are hot or tired, it makes you feel cooler or more energetic. *e.g. A glass of fruit juice will refresh you.*

THESAURUS
brace: *a bracing walk*
enliven: *Music can enliven the spirit.*
rejuvenate: *He was told that the Italian climate would rejuvenate him.*
revive: *The cold water revived me a bit.*
stimulate: *a toner to stimulate the skin*

> PHRASE

2 To **refresh someone's memory** means to remind them of something they had forgotten.

refreshing [rɪˈfrɛʃɪŋ] ADJECTIVE

You say that something is refreshing when it is pleasantly different from what you are used to. *e.g. She is a refreshing contrast to her father.*

refreshment [rɪˈfrɛʃmənt] **refreshments** NOUN

Refreshments are drinks and small amounts of food provided at an event.

refrigerator [rɪˈfrɪdʒəˌreɪtə] **refrigerators** NOUN

an electrically cooled container in which you store food to keep it fresh

refuel [riːˈfjuːəl] **refuels, refuelling, refuelled** VERB

When an aircraft or vehicle is refuelled, it is filled with more fuel.

refuge [ˈrɛfjuːdʒ] **refuges** NOUN

1 a place where you go for safety

THESAURUS
asylum: *political asylum*
harbour: *Patches of gorse were a great harbour for foxes.*

haven: *The island is a haven for international criminals.*
sanctuary: *a sanctuary from the outside world*
shelter: *an underground shelter*

2 If you take refuge, you go somewhere for safety or behave in a way that will protect you. *e.g. They took refuge in a bomb shelter... Father Rowan took refuge in silence.*

refugee [ˌrɛfjʊˈdʒiː] **refugees** NOUN
Refugees are people who have been forced to leave their country and live elsewhere.

refund **refunds, refunding, refunded**
NOUN [ˈriːˌfʌnd]

1 money returned to you because you have paid too much for something or because you have returned goods

> VERB [rɪˈfʌnd]
2 To refund someone's money means to return it to them after they have paid for something with it.

refurbish [riːˈfɜːbɪʃ] **refurbishes, refurbishing, refurbished** VERB; FORMAL
To refurbish a building means to decorate it and repair damage.
refurbishment NOUN

refusal [rɪˈfjuːzəl] **refusals** NOUN
A refusal is when someone says firmly that they will not do, allow, or accept something.

refuse [rɪˈfjuːz] **refuses, refusing, refused**
VERB
1 If you refuse to do something, you say or decide firmly that you will not do it.
● THESAURUS
abstain: *people who abstain from eating meat*
decline: *He declined to comment on the story.*
withhold: *Financial aid for Britain has been withheld.*

2 If someone refuses something, they do not allow it or do not accept it. *e.g. The United States has refused him a visa... He offered me a second drink which I refused.*
● THESAURUS
decline: *He declined their invitation.*
reject: *The court rejected their petition.*
spurn: *You spurned his last offer.*
turn down: *He has turned down the job.*
<<OPPOSITE accept

refuse [ˈrɛfjuːs] NOUN
Refuse is rubbish or waste.
● THESAURUS
garbage: *rotting piles of garbage*
junk: informal *What are you going to do with all that junk?*
litter: *If you see litter in the corridor, pick it up.*

rubbish: *They had piled most of their rubbish into yellow skips.*
trash: *I forgot to take out the trash.*
waste: *a law that regulates the disposal of waste*

refute [rɪˈfjuːt] **refutes, refuting, refuted**
VERB; FORMAL
To refute a theory or argument means to prove that it is wrong.

> *Refute* does not mean the same as *deny*. If you *refute* something, you provide evidence to show that it is not true. If you *deny* something, you say that it is not true

regain [rɪˈgeɪn] **regains, regaining, regained** VERB
To regain something means to get it back.

regal [ˈriːgəl] ADJECTIVE
very grand and suitable for a king or queen *e.g. regal splendour*
regally ADVERB

regard [rɪˈgɑːd] **regards, regarding, regarded** VERB
1 To regard someone or something in a particular way means to think of them in that way or have that opinion of them. *e.g. We all regard him as a friend... Many disapprove of the tax, regarding it as unfair.*
● THESAURUS
consider: *I consider activities such as jogging a waste of time.*
judge: *This may or may not be judged as reasonable.*
look on: *A lot of people looked on him as a healer.*
see: *I don't see it as my duty to take sides.*
think of: *We all thought of him as a father.*
view: *They view the United States as a land of opportunity.*

2 LITERARY To regard someone in a particular way also means to look at them in that way. *e.g. She regarded him curiously for a moment.*
● THESAURUS
contemplate: *He contemplated her in silence.*
eye: *We eyed each other thoughtfully.*
gaze: *gazing at herself in the mirror*
look: *She looked at him earnestly.*
scrutinize: *She scrutinized his features to see if he was to be trusted.*
watch: *Chris watched him sipping his brandy.*

> NOUN
3 If you have a high regard for someone, you have a very good opinion of them.

> PHRASES
4 **Regarding, as regards, with regard to**, and **in regard to** are all used to indicate what you are talking or writing about *e.g. There was always some question regarding education... As regards the war, he believed in victory at any price.*

5 'Regards' is used in various expressions to express friendly feelings *e.g. Give my regards to your husband.*

regardless [rɪ'gɑːdlɪs] PREPOSITION OR ADVERB
done or happening in spite of something else *e.g. He led from the front, regardless of the danger.*

regatta [rɪ'gætə] **regattas** NOUN
a race meeting for sailing or rowing boats

regency ['riːdʒənsɪ] **regencies** NOUN
a period when a country is ruled by a regent

regenerate [rɪ'dʒɛnəˌreɪt] **regenerates, regenerating, regenerated** VERB; FORMAL
To regenerate something means to develop and improve it after it has been declining. *e.g. a scheme to regenerate the docks area of the city*
regeneration NOUN

regent ['riːdʒənt] **regents** NOUN
someone who rules in place of a king or queen who is ill or too young to rule

reggae ['rɛgeɪ] NOUN
Reggae is a type of music, originally from the West Indies, with a strong beat.

regime [reɪ'ʒiːm] **regimes** NOUN
a system of government, and the people who are ruling a country *e.g. a communist regime*

regiment ['rɛdʒɪmənt] **regiments** NOUN
a large group of soldiers commanded by a colonel
regimental ADJECTIVE

regimented ['rɛdʒɪˌmɛntɪd] ADJECTIVE
very strictly controlled *e.g. the regimented life of the orphanage*
regimentation NOUN

region ['riːdʒən] **regions** NOUN
1 (GEOGRAPHY) a large area of land

● THESAURUS
area: *The area is renowned for its cuisine.*
district: *I drove around the business district.*
land: *a land permanently cloaked in mist*
locality: *All other factories in the locality went on strike.*
quarter: *We wandered through the Chinese quarter.*
sector: *the northeast sector of Bosnia*
territory: *the disputed territory of Kashmir*
tract: *They cleared large tracts of forest.*
zone: *a different time zone*

2 You can refer to any area or part as a region. *e.g. the pelvic region*

> PHRASE

3 In the region of means approximately *e.g. The scheme will cost in the region of six million.*
regional ADJECTIVE, **regionally** ADVERB

register ['rɛdʒɪstə] **registers, registering, registered** NOUN

1 an official list or record of things *e.g. the electoral register*

2 TECHNICAL a style of speaking or writing used in particular circumstances or social occasions

> VERB

3 When something is registered, it is recorded on an official list. *e.g. The car was registered in my name.*

4 If an instrument registers a measurement, it shows it.

5 If your face registers a feeling, it expresses it.
registration NOUN

registrar [ˌrɛdʒɪ'strɑː] **registrars** NOUN
1 a person who keeps official records of births, marriages, and deaths

2 At a college or university, the registrar is a senior administrative official.

3 a senior hospital doctor

registration number [ˌrɛdʒɪ'streɪʃən] **registration numbers** NOUN
the sequence of letters and numbers on the front and back of a motor vehicle that identify it

registry ['rɛdʒɪstrɪ] **registries** NOUN
a place where official records are kept

registry office registry offices NOUN
a place where births, marriages, and deaths are recorded, and where people can marry without a religious ceremony

regret [rɪ'grɛt] **regrets, regretting, regretted** VERB

1 If you regret something, you are sorry that it happened.

● THESAURUS
be sorry: *I'm sorry you feel that way about it.*
grieve: *grieving over the death of his wife*
lament: *We lament the loss of a fine novelist.*
mourn: *to mourn the loss of a loved one*
repent: *He repents his past sins.*

2 You can say that you regret something as a way of apologizing. *e.g. We regret any inconvenience to passengers.*

> NOUN

3 If you have regrets, you are sad or sorry about something.
regretful ADJECTIVE, **regretfully** ADVERB

● THESAURUS
grief: *his guilt and grief over the failed relationship*
pang of conscience: *He need not feel any pangs of conscience over his decision.*
penitence: *an abject display of penitence*
remorse: *He expressed remorse over his own foolishness.*
repentance: *an apparent lack of genuine repentance*

r

sorrow: *I feel real sorrow that my dad did this.*

regrettable [rɪˈgrɛtəbəl] ADJECTIVE
unfortunate and undesirable *e.g. a regrettable accident*
regrettably ADVERB

regular [ˈrɛgjʊlə] **regulars** ADJECTIVE
1 even and equally spaced *e.g. soft music with a regular beat*

● THESAURUS
consistent: *a consistent heart-rate*
constant: *a constant temperature*
even: *an even level of sound*
periodic: *Periodic checks are carried out.*
rhythmic: *the rhythmic beating of the drum*
steady: *a steady pace*
uniform: *The Earth rotates on its axis at a uniform rate.*
<<OPPOSITE *irregular*

2 (MATHS) A regular shape has equal angles and equal sides. *e.g. a regular polygon*

3 Regular events or activities happen often and according to a pattern, for example each day or each week. *e.g. The trains to London are fairly regular.*

4 If you are a regular customer or visitor somewhere, you go there often.

5 usual or normal *e.g. I was filling in for the regular bartender.*

● THESAURUS
customary: *her customary place at the table*
everyday: *part of everyday life*
habitual: *habitual practices*
normal: *a normal day*
ordinary: *It was just an ordinary weekend.*
routine: *a routine knee operation*
typical: *My typical day begins at 8.30.*
usual: *In a usual week I watch about 15 hours of television.*

6 having a well balanced appearance *e.g. a regular geometrical shape*

> NOUN
7 People who go to a place often are known as its regulars.
regularly ADVERB, **regularity** NOUN

regulate [ˈrɛgjʊˌleɪt] **regulates, regulating, regulated** VERB
To regulate something means to control the way it operates. *e.g. Sweating helps to regulate the body's temperature.*
regulator NOUN

regulation [ˌrɛgjʊˈleɪʃən] **regulations** NOUN
1 Regulations are official rules.

2 Regulation is the control of something. *e.g. regulation of the betting industry*

regurgitate [rɪˈgɜːdʒɪˌteɪt] **regurgitates, regurgitating, regurgitated** VERB
To regurgitate food means to bring it back from the stomach before it is digested.

rehabilitate [ˌriːəˈbɪlɪˌteɪt] **rehabilitates, rehabilitating, rehabilitated** VERB
To rehabilitate someone who has been ill or in prison means to help them lead a normal life.
rehabilitation NOUN

rehearsal [rɪˈhɜːsəl] **rehearsals** NOUN
(DRAMA) a practice of a performance in preparation for the actual event

rehearse [rɪˈhɜːs] **rehearses, rehearsing, rehearsed** VERB
(DRAMA) To rehearse a performance means to practise it in preparation for the actual event.

reign [reɪn] **reigns, reigning, reigned** VERB
1 When a king or queen reigns, he or she rules a country.

2 You can say that something reigns when it is a noticeable feature of a situation or period of time. *e.g. Panic reigned after his assassination.*

> NOUN
3 (HISTORY) The reign of a king or queen is the period during which he or she reigns.

rein [reɪn] **reins** NOUN
1 Reins are the thin leather straps which you hold when you are riding a horse.

> PHRASE
2 To **keep a tight rein on** someone or something means to control them firmly.

reincarnation [ˌriːɪnkɑːˈneɪʃən] NOUN
People who believe in reincarnation believe that when you die, you are born again as another creature.

reindeer [ˈreɪnˌdɪə] NOUN
Reindeer are deer with large antlers, that live in northern regions.

reinforce [ˌriːɪnˈfɔːs] **reinforces, reinforcing, reinforced** VERB
1 To reinforce something means to strengthen it. *e.g. a reinforced steel barrier*

2 If something reinforces an idea or claim, it provides evidence to support it.

reinforcement [ˌriːɪnˈfɔːsmənt] **reinforcements** NOUN
1 Reinforcements are additional soldiers sent to join an army in battle.

2 Reinforcement is the reinforcing of something.

reinstate [ˌriːɪnˈsteɪt] **reinstates, reinstating, reinstated** VERB
1 To reinstate someone means to give them back a position they have lost.

2 To reinstate something means to bring it back. *e.g. Parliament voted against reinstating capital punishment.*
reinstatement NOUN

reiterate [ri:ˈɪtəˌreɪt] **reiterates, reiterating, reiterated** VERB; FORMAL
If you reiterate something, you say it again.
reiteration NOUN

reject rejects, rejecting, rejected VERB [rɪˈdʒɛkt]
1 If you reject a proposal or request, you do not accept it or agree to it.

● THESAURUS
decline: *They declined his proposal.*
deny: *He denied our offer of assistance.*
rebuff: *She rebuffed his advances.*
refuse: *He offered me a drink, which I refused.*
renounce: *She renounced her parents' religion.*
say no to: *Just say no to drugs.*
spurn: *He spurned the advice of management consultants.*
turn down: *She turned down his offer of marriage.*
<<OPPOSITE accept

2 If you reject a belief, political system, or way of life, you decide that it is not for you.
> NOUN [ˈriːdʒɛkt]
3 a product that cannot be used, because there is something wrong with it
rejection NOUN

rejoice [rɪˈdʒɔɪs] **rejoices, rejoicing, rejoiced** VERB
To rejoice means to be very pleased about something. *e.g. The whole country rejoiced after his downfall.*

● THESAURUS
be overjoyed: *I was overjoyed to see him.*
celebrate: *We should celebrate our victory.*
delight: *He delighted in her success.*
glory: *glorying in the achievement of his troops*

rejoin [ri:ˈdʒɔɪn] **rejoins, rejoining, rejoined** VERB
If you rejoin someone, you go back to them soon after leaving them. *e.g. She rejoined her friends in the bar.*

rejuvenate [rɪˈdʒuːvɪˌneɪt] **rejuvenates, rejuvenating, rejuvenated** VERB
To rejuvenate someone means to make them feel young again.
rejuvenation NOUN

relapse [ˈriːˌlæps] **relapses** NOUN
If a sick person has a relapse, their health suddenly gets worse after improving.

relate [rɪˈleɪt] **relates, relating, related** VERB
1 If something relates to something else, it is connected or concerned with it. *e.g. The statistics*
relate only to western Germany.

2 If you can relate to someone, you can understand their thoughts and feelings.

3 To relate a story means to tell it.

relation [rɪˈleɪʃən] **relations** NOUN
1 If there is a relation between two things, they are similar or connected in some way. *e.g. This theory bears no relation to reality.*

● THESAURUS
bearing: *Diet has an important bearing on your general health.*
bond: *the bond between a mother and child*
connection: *a possible connection between BSE and human disease*
correlation: *the correlation between unemployment and crime*
link: *a link between obesity and heart problems*
relationship: *the relationship between success and effort*

2 Your relations are the members of your family.

● THESAURUS
kin: *She has gone to live with her husband's kin.*
kinsman or **kinswoman:** *the prince who murdered his father and kinsmen*
relative: *Get a relative to look after the children.*

3 Relations between people are their feelings and behaviour towards each other. *e.g. Relations between husband and wife had not improved.*

relationship [rɪˈleɪʃənʃɪp] **relationships** NOUN (PSHE)
1 The relationship between two people or groups is the way they feel and behave towards each other.

● THESAURUS
affinity: *the natural affinity between the female members of the community*
association: *the association between the two countries*
bond: *The experience created a bond between us.*
connection: *He felt a personal connection with her.*
rapport: *He has a terrific rapport with kids.*

2 a close friendship, especially one involving romantic or sexual feelings

● THESAURUS
affair: *an affair with a married man*
liaison: *Nobody knew of their brief liaison.*

3 The relationship between two things is the way in which they are connected. *e.g. the relationship between slavery and the sugar trade*

● THESAURUS
connection: *the connection between age and ill-health*
correlation: *the correlation between unemployment and crime*
link: *the link between smoking and lung cancer*

r

parallel: *the parallel between painting and music*

relative ['rɛlətɪv] relatives ADJECTIVE

1 compared to other things or people of the same kind *e.g. The fighting resumed after a period of relative calm... He is a relative novice.*

2 You use 'relative' when comparing the size or quality of two things. *e.g. the relative strengths of the British and German forces*

> NOUN

3 Your relatives are the members of your family.

relative pronoun relative pronouns
NOUN

a pronoun that replaces a noun that links two parts of a sentence

relax [rɪ'læks] relaxes, relaxing, relaxed
VERB

1 If you relax, you become calm and your muscles lose their tension.

THESAURUS

laze: *I'm just going to laze around and do nothing.*
rest: *Try to rest as much as you can.*
take it easy: *the chance to just take it easy for a week or two*
unwind: *It helps them to unwind after a busy day at work.*

2 If you relax your hold, you hold something less tightly.

3 To relax something also means to make it less strict or controlled. *e.g. The rules governing student conduct were relaxed.*
relaxation NOUN

relaxed [rɪ'lækst] ADJECTIVE

1 calm and not worried or tense

THESAURUS

at ease: *It is essential to feel at ease with your therapist.*
calm: *Diane felt calm and unafraid as she entered the courtroom.*
comfortable: *He liked me and I felt comfortable with him.*
cool: *He was marvellously cool, smiling as if nothing had happened.*
easy: *By then I was feeling a little easier about the situation.*
serene: *that serene smile of his*
unflustered: *He has a calm, unflustered temperament.*
<<OPPOSITE *tense*

2 If a place or situation is relaxed, it is calm and peaceful.

THESAURUS

calm: *The city appears relatively calm today.*
casual: *We have a very casual relationhsip.*
comfortable: *a comfortable silence*
informal: *an informal occasion*

peaceful: *Sundays are usually quiet and peaceful in our house.*
<<OPPOSITE *tense*

relay relays, relaying, relayed NOUN
['ri:leɪ]

1 (PE) A relay race or relay is a race between teams, with each team member running one part of the race.

> VERB [rɪ'leɪ]

2 To relay a television or radio signal means to send it on.

3 If you relay information, you tell it to someone else.

release [rɪ'li:s] releases, releasing, released VERB

1 To release someone or something means to set them free or remove restraints from them.

THESAURUS

deliver: *I thank God for delivering me from that pain.*
discharge: *He may be discharged from hospital today.*
extricate: *They managed to extricate the survivors from the wreckage.*
free: *Israeli is set to free more Lebanese prisoners.*
let go: *They held him for three hours and then let him go.*
liberate: *liberated under the terms of the amnesty*
set free: *birds set free into the wild*

2 To release something also means to issue it or make it available. *e.g. He is releasing an album of love songs.*

THESAURUS

issue: *He has issued a press statement.*
launch: *The company has just launched a new range of products.*
publish: *His latest book will be published in May.*
put out: *putting out a series of novels by Nobel prize winners*

> NOUN

3 When the release of someone or something takes place, they are set free.

THESAURUS

discharge: *a discharge from the army*
emancipation: *the emancipation of slaves in the 19th century*
freedom: *Hinckley campaigned for his freedom.*
liberation: *their liberation from a Nazi concentration camp*
liberty: *her television appearances pleading for his liberty*

4 A press release or publicity release is an official written statement given to reporters.

5 A new release is a new record or video that has just become available.

relegate ['rɛlɪ,geɪt] **relegates, relegating, relegated** VERB
To relegate something or someone means to give them a less important position or status.
relegation NOUN

relent [rɪ'lɛnt] **relents, relenting, relented** VERB
If someone relents, they agree to something they had previously not allowed.

relentless [rɪ'lɛntlɪs] ADJECTIVE
never stopping and never becoming less intense
e.g. the relentless rise of business closures
relentlessly ADVERB

● THESAURUS
incessant: *incessant rain*
nonstop: *nonstop background music*
persistent: *in the face of persistent criticism*
sustained: *a sustained attack*
unrelenting: *unrelenting protests*
unremitting: *the unremitting demands of duty*

relevant ['rɛlɪvənt] ADJECTIVE
(LIBRARY) If something is relevant, it is connected with and is appropriate to what is being discussed. *e.g. We have passed all relevant information on to the police.*
relevance NOUN

● THESAURUS
applicable: *These fees are not applicable to mortgages in Scotland.*
apposite: *He could not think of anything apposite to say.*
appropriate: *The name seemed very appropriate.*
apt: *an apt comment*
pertinent: *She had asked some pertinent questions.*
<<OPPOSITE *irrelevant*

reliable [rɪ'laɪəbəl] ADJECTIVE
1 Reliable people and things can be trusted to do what you want.

● THESAURUS
dependable: *dependable information*
faithful: *a faithful friend*
safe: *It's all right, you're in safe hands.*
sound: *sound advice*
staunch: *a staunch supporter*
sure: *a sure sign of rain*
true: *a true account*
trustworthy: *a trustworthy and level-headed leader*
<<OPPOSITE *unreliable*

2 If information is reliable, you can assume that it is correct.
reliably ADVERB, **reliability** NOUN

reliant [rɪ'laɪənt] ADJECTIVE
If you are reliant on someone or something, you depend on them. *e.g. They are not wholly reliant on charity.*

reliance NOUN

relic ['rɛlɪk] **relics** NOUN
1 Relics are objects or customs that have survived from an earlier time.
2 an object regarded as holy because it is thought to be connected with a saint

relief [rɪ'liːf] NOUN
1 If you feel relief, you are glad and thankful because a bad situation is over or has been avoided.
2 Relief is also money, food, or clothing provided for poor or hungry people.

relief map relief maps NOUN
a map showing the shape of mountains and hills by shading

relieve [rɪ'liːv] **relieves, relieving, relieved** VERB
1 If something relieves an unpleasant feeling, it makes it less unpleasant. *e.g. Drugs can relieve much of the pain.*
2 FORMAL
If you relieve someone, you do their job or duty for a period.
3 If someone is relieved of their duties, they are dismissed from their job.
4 If you relieve yourself, you urinate.

religion [rɪ'lɪdʒən] **religions** NOUN (RE)
Religion is the belief in a god or gods and all the activities connected with such beliefs.
a system of religious belief

religious [rɪ'lɪdʒəs] ADJECTIVE
1 (HISTORY) connected with religion *e.g. religious worship*

● THESAURUS
devotional: *an altar covered with devotional pictures*
divine: *a request for divine guidance*
doctrinal: *their doctrinal differences*
holy: *To Tibetans, this is a holy place.*
sacred: *Bach's sacred music.* **scriptural:** *scriptural and theological references*
spiritual: *We've got no spiritual values.*
theological: *theological studies*

2 (RE) Someone who is religious has a strong belief in a god or gods.

● THESAURUS
devout: *She is a devout Catholic.*
God-fearing: *They brought up their children to be God-fearing Christians.*
godly: *a learned and godly preacher*
pious: *He was brought up by pious female relatives.*
righteous: *struggling to be righteous and chaste*

religiously [rɪ'lɪdʒəslɪ] ADVERB
If you do something religiously, you do it

r

regularly as a duty. *e.g. He stuck religiously to the rules.*

relinquish [rɪ'lɪŋkwɪʃ] **relinquishes, relinquishing, relinquished** VERB; FORMAL
If you relinquish something, you give it up.

relish ['relɪʃ] **relishes, relishing, relished** VERB
1 If you relish something, you enjoy it. *e.g. He relished the idea of getting some cash.*

> NOUN
2 Relish is enjoyment. *e.g. He told me with relish of the wonderful times he had.*

3 Relish is also a savoury sauce or pickle.

relive [ri:'lɪv] **relives, reliving, relived** VERB
If you relive a past experience, you remember it and imagine it happening again.

relocate [,ri:ləʊ'keɪt] **relocates, relocating, relocated** VERB
If people or businesses are relocated, they are moved to a different place.
relocation NOUN

reluctant [rɪ'lʌktənt] ADJECTIVE
If you are reluctant to do something, you are unwilling to do it.
reluctance NOUN

● THESAURUS
averse: *I'm not averse to going along with the idea.*
disinclined: *He was disinclined to talk about himself.*
hesitant: *His advisers are hesitant to let the United States enter the conflict.*
loath: *The finance minister is loath to cut income tax.*
slow: *The world community has been slow to respond to the crisis.*
unwilling: *For months I had been unwilling to go through with it.*
<<OPPOSITE *eager*

reluctantly [rɪ'lʌktəntlɪ] ADVERB
If you do something reluctantly, you do it although you do not want to.

rely [rɪ'laɪ] **relies, relying, relied** VERB
1 If you rely on someone or something, you need them and depend on them. *e.g. She has to rely on hardship payments.*

2 If you can rely on someone to do something, you can trust them to do it. *e.g. They can always be relied on to turn up.*

remain [rɪ'meɪn] **remains, remaining, remained** VERB
1 If you remain in a particular place, you stay there.

● THESAURUS
be left: *He was left in the car.*
linger: *I lingered for a few days until he arrived.*

stay behind: *I was told to stay behind after the class.*
wait: *Wait here until I come back.*

2 If you remain in a particular state, you stay the same and do not change. *e.g. The two men remained silent.*

● THESAURUS
continue: *This state of affairs cannot continue.*
endure: *Somehow their friendship endures.*
go on: *The debate goes on.*
last: *Nothing lasts forever.*
stay: *They could stay afloat without swimming.*
survive: *companies which survived after the recession*

3 Something that remains still exists or is left over. *e.g. Huge amounts of weapons remain to be collected.*

> PLURAL NOUN
4 The remains of something are the parts that are left after most of it has been destroyed. *e.g. the remains of an ancient mosque*

● THESAURUS
debris: *screws, bolts and other debris from a scrapyard*
dregs: *Colum drained the dregs from his cup.*
leftovers: *Refrigerate any leftovers.*
relics: *a museum of war relics*
remnants: *Beneath the present church were remnants of Roman flooring.*
residue: *Discard the milky residue left behind.*
scraps: *the scraps from the dinner table*
vestiges: *an attempt to destroy the last vestiges of evidence*

5 You can refer to a dead body as remains. *e.g. More human remains have been unearthed today.*

remainder [rɪ'meɪndə] NOUN
The remainder of something is the part that is left. *e.g. He gulped down the remainder of his coffee.*

● THESAURUS
balance: *pay the balance on delivery*
last: *He finished off the last of the wine.*
others: *She took one and put the others back.*
remnants: *The remnants of the force were fleeing.*
remains: *tidying up the remains of their picnic*
rest: *I'm going to throw a party, then invest the rest of the money.*

remand [rɪ'mɑ:nd] **remands, remanding, remanded** VERB
1 If a judge remands someone who is accused of a crime, the trial is postponed and the person is ordered to come back at a later date.

> PHRASE
2 If someone is **on remand**, they are in prison waiting for their trial to begin.

remark [rɪ'mɑ:k] **remarks, remarking, remarked** VERB

1 If you remark on something, you mention it or comment on it. *e.g. She had remarked on the boy's improvement.*

● THESAURUS
comment: *So far, he has not commented on these reports.*
mention: *I mentioned that I didn't like jazz.*
observe: *"You're very pale," he observed.*
say: *"Well done," he said.*
state: *We stated that he had resigned.*

> NOUN
2 something you say, often in a casual way

● THESAURUS
comment: *his abrasive wit and caustic comments*
observation: *a few general observations*
statement: *That statement puzzled me.*
utterance: *admirers who hung on her every utterance*
word: *No-one had an unkind word to say about him.*

remarkable [rɪ'mɑːkəbᵊl] ADJECTIVE
impressive and unexpected *e.g. It was a remarkable achievement.*
remarkably ADVERB

remarry [riː'mærɪ] **remarries, remarrying, remarried** VERB
If someone remarries, they get married again.

remedial [rɪ'miːdɪəl] ADJECTIVE
1 Remedial activities are to help someone improve their health after they have been ill.
2 Remedial exercises are designed to improve someone's ability in something. *e.g. the remedial reading class*

remedy ['rɛmɪdɪ] **remedies, remedying, remedied** NOUN
1 a way of dealing with a problem *e.g. a remedy for colic*

> VERB
2 If you remedy something that is wrong, you correct it. *e.g. We have to remedy the situation immediately.*

remember [rɪ'mɛmbə] **remembers, remembering, remembered** VERB
1 If you can remember someone or something from the past, you can bring them into your mind or think about them.

● THESAURUS
call to mind: *He invited the congregation to call to mind their sins.*
recall: *He tried to recall the layout of the farmhouse.*
recognize: *I don't recognize that name.*
retain: *information which can be retained in the memory*
<<OPPOSITE *forget*

2 If you remember to do something, you do it when you intended to. *e.g. Ben had remembered to book reservations.*

remembrance [rɪ'mɛmbrəns] NOUN
If you do something in remembrance of a dead person, you are showing that they are remembered with respect and affection.

remind [rɪ'maɪnd] **reminds, reminding, reminded** VERB
1 If someone reminds you of a fact, they say something to make you think about it. *e.g. Remind me to buy a bottle of wine, will you?.*

● THESAURUS
bring back to: *Talking about the accident brought it all back to me.*
jog someone's memory: *See if this picture helps jog your memory.*
make someone remember: *Your article made me remember my own traumas.*
put in mind: *His eagerness to please put her in mind of a puppy.*
refresh someone's memory: *I read through the list to refresh my memory.*

2 If someone reminds you of another person, they look similar and make you think of them.

reminder [rɪ'maɪndə] **reminders** NOUN
1 If one thing is a reminder of another, the first thing makes you think of the second. *e.g. a reminder of better times*
2 a note sent to tell someone they have forgotten to do something

reminiscent [ˌrɛmɪ'nɪsᵊnt] ADJECTIVE
Something that is reminiscent of something else reminds you of it.

remission [rɪ'mɪʃən] NOUN
When prisoners get remission for good behaviour, their sentences are reduced.

remit ['riːmɪt] **remits** NOUN; FORMAL
The remit of a person or committee is the subject or task they are responsible for. *e.g. Their remit is to research into a wide range of health problems.*

remittance [rɪ'mɪtəns] **remittances** NOUN; FORMAL
payment for something sent through the post

remnant ['rɛmnənt] **remnants** NOUN
a small part of something left after the rest has been used or destroyed

remorse [rɪ'mɔːs] NOUN; FORMAL
Remorse is a strong feeling of guilt.
remorseful ADJECTIVE

remote [rɪ'məʊt] **remoter, remotest** ADJECTIVE
1 Remote areas are far away from places where most people live.

● THESAURUS
distant: *in that distant land*
far-off: *start a new life in a far-off country*

r

inaccessible: *people living in inaccessible parts of the country*

isolated: *Many of the refugee villages are in isolated areas.*

lonely: *It felt like the loneliest place in the world.*

outlying: *Tourists can visit outlying areas by jeep.*

2 far away in time *e.g. the remote past*

● THESAURUS

distant: *a glimpse into the more distant future*

far-off: *She has entirely forgotten those far-off days.*

3 If you say a person is remote, you mean they do not want to be friendly. *e.g. She is severe, solemn, and remote.*

● THESAURUS

aloof: *He seemed aloof, standing watching the others.*

cold: *What a cold, unfeeling woman she was.*

detached: *He tries to remain emotionally detached from the prisoners.*

distant: *He is courteous but distant.*

reserved: *She's quite a reserved person.*

withdrawn: *Her husband had become withdrawn and moody.*

4 If there is only a remote possibility of something happening, it is unlikely to happen. **remoteness** NOUN

● THESAURUS

poor: *The odds of it happening again are very poor.*

slender: *There is a slender possibility that the plan might work.*

slight: *Is there even a slight hope that she might change her mind?*

slim: *There's still a slim chance that he may become Prime Minister.*

small: *There was still a small possibility that he might phone.*

remote control NOUN
Remote control is a system of controlling a machine or vehicle from a distance using radio or electronic signals.

remotely [rɪˈməʊtlɪ] ADVERB
used to emphasize a negative statement *e.g. He isn't remotely keen.*

removal [rɪˈmuːvəl] NOUN

1 The removal of something is the act of taking it away.

2 A removal company transports furniture from one building to another.

remove [rɪˈmuːv] **removes, removing, removed** VERB

1 If you remove something from a place, you take it off or away.

● THESAURUS

delete: *He deleted files from the computer system.*

detach: *Detach and keep the bottom part of the form.*

eject: *He was ejected from the restaurant.*

eliminate: *Eliminate dairy products from your diet.*

erase: *She had erased the message.*

extract: *She is having a tooth extracted today.*

get rid of: *to get rid of raw sewage by pumping it out to sea*

take away: *She took away the tray.*

take off: *I won't take my coat off, I'm not staying.*

take out: *Take that dog out of here.*

withdraw: *She withdrew her hand from Roger's.*

2 If you are removed from a position of authority, you are not allowed to continue your job.

3 If you remove an undesirable feeling or attitude, you get rid of it. *e.g. Most of her fears had been removed.*

removable ADJECTIVE

Renaissance [rəˈneɪsəns] NOUN
The Renaissance was a period from the 14th to 16th centuries in Europe when there was a great revival in the arts and learning.

[WORD HISTORY: a French word, meaning literally 'rebirth']

renal [ˈriːnəl] ADJECTIVE; TECHNICAL
concerning the kidneys *e.g. renal failure*

rename [riːˈneɪm] **renames, renaming, renamed** VERB
If you rename something, you give it a new name.

render [ˈrɛndə] **renders, rendering, rendered** VERB
You can use 'render' to say that something is changed into a different state. *e.g. The bomb was quickly rendered harmless.*

rendezvous [ˈrɒndɪˌvuː] NOUN

1 a meeting *e.g. Baxter arranged a six o'clock rendezvous.*

2 a place where you have arranged to meet someone *e.g. The pub became a popular rendezvous.*

rendition [rɛnˈdɪʃən] **renditions** NOUN; FORMAL
a performance of a play, poem, or piece of music

renew [rɪˈnjuː] **renews, renewing, renewed** VERB

1 To renew an activity or relationship means to begin it again.

● THESAURUS

begin again: *The audience began the slow handclap again.*

recommence: *He recommenced work on his novel.*

re-establish: *He had re-established his close friendship with Anthony.*

reopen: *It is feared that this issue could re-open the controversy.*

resume: *Rebels have refused to resume peace talks.*

2 To renew a licence or contract means to extend the period of time for which it is valid.
renewal NOUN

renewable [rɪˈnjuːəbəl] renewables
ADJECTIVE
1 able to be renewed

> NOUN
2 a renewable form of energy, such as wind power or solar power

renounce [rɪˈnaʊns] renounces, renouncing, renounced VERB FORMAL
If you renounce something, you reject it or give it up.
renunciation NOUN

● THESAURUS
disown: *The comments were later disowned by an official spokesman.*
give up: *He did not want to give up his right to the title.*
reject: *children who reject their parents' political and religious beliefs*
relinquish: *He does not intend to relinquish power.* formal

renovate [ˈrɛnəˌveɪt] renovates, renovating, renovated VERB
If you renovate an old building or machine, you repair it and restore it to good condition.
renovation NOUN

● THESAURUS
do up: *his father's obsession with doing up old cars*
modernize: *plans to modernize the refinery*
recondition: *The company specializes in reconditioning photocopiers.*
refurbish: *This hotel has been completely refurbished.*
repair: *He has repaired the roof to make the house more windproof.*
restore: *The old town square has been beautifully restored.*
revamp: *plans to revamp the airport*

renowned [rɪˈnaʊnd] ADJECTIVE
well-known for something good *e.g. He is not renowned for his patience.*
renown NOUN

rent [rɛnt] rents, renting, rented VERB
1 If you rent something, you pay the owner a regular sum of money in return for being able to use it.

> NOUN
2 Rent is the amount of money you pay regularly to rent land or accommodation.

rental [ˈrɛntəl] ADJECTIVE
1 concerned with the renting out of goods and services *e.g. Scotland's largest video rental company.*

> NOUN
2 the amount of money you pay when you rent something

reorganize [riːˈɔːgəˌnaɪz] reorganizes, reorganizing, reorganized; also spelt reorganise VERB
To reorganize something means to organize it in a new way in order to make it more efficient or acceptable.
reorganization NOUN

rep [rɛp] reps NOUN; INFORMAL
a travelling salesman or saleswoman. Rep is an abbreviation for representative

repair [rɪˈpɛə] repairs, repairing, repaired NOUN
1 something you do to mend something that is damaged or broken

● THESAURUS
darn: *a sock with a big darn in it*
mend: *Spray the area with paint to make the mend invisible.*
patch: *jackets with patches on the elbows*
restoration: *the restoration of a war-damaged building*

> VERB
2 If you repair something, you mend it.

● THESAURUS
fix: *If something is broken, get it fixed.*
mend: *They mended it without charge.*
patch: *They patched the barn roof.*
patch up: *Patch up those holes.*
renovate: *They spent thousands renovating the house.*
restore: *experts who specialize in restoring ancient parchments*

repay [rɪˈpeɪ] repays, repaying, repaid VERB
1 To repay money means to give it back to the person who lent it.

● THESAURUS
pay back: *I'll pay you back that money tomorrow.*
refund: *Any extra that you have paid will be refunded to you.*
settle up: *If we owe you anything we can settle up when you come.*

2 If you repay a favour, you do something to help the person who helped you.
repayment NOUN

repeal [rɪˈpiːl] repeals, repealing, repealed VERB
If the government repeals a law, it cancels it so that it is no longer valid.

repeat [rɪˈpiːt] repeats, repeating, repeated VERB
1 If you repeat something, you say, write, or do it again.

r

echo: *"Are you frightened?" "Frightened?" she echoed. "Of what?"*
reiterate: *The lawyer could only reiterate what he had said before.*
say again: *"I'm sorry," she said again.*

2 If you repeat what someone has said, you tell someone else about it. *e.g. I trust you not to repeat that to anyone.*

> NOUN

3 something which is done or happens again *e.g. the number of repeats shown on TV*
repeated ADJECTIVE, **repeatedly** ADVERB

repel [rɪˈpɛl] **repels, repelling, repelled**
VERB
1 If something repels you, you find it horrible and disgusting.

disgust: *He disgusted everyone with his boorish behaviour.*
offend: *viewers who are easily offended*
revolt: *The smell revolted him.*
sicken: *What he saw there sickened him.*
<<OPPOSITE *attract*

2 When soldiers repel an attacking force, they successfully defend themselves against it.

drive off: *They drove the guerrillas off with infantry and air strikes.*
repulse: *Cavalry and artillery were sent to repulse the enemy forces.*
resist: *The tribe resisted the Spanish invaders.*

3 When a magnetic pole repels an opposite pole, it forces the opposite pole away.

repellent [rɪˈpɛlənt] **repellents** ADJECTIVE
1 FORMAL
horrible and disgusting *e.g. I found him repellent.*

> NOUN

2 Repellents are chemicals used to keep insects or other creatures away.

repent [rɪˈpɛnt] **repents, repenting, repented** VERB; FORMAL
If you repent, you are sorry for something bad you have done.
repentance NOUN, **repentant** ADJECTIVE

repercussion [ˌriːpəˈkʌʃən] **repercussions** NOUN
The repercussions of an event are the effects it has at a later time.

repertoire [ˈrɛpəˌtwɑː] **repertoires** NOUN
A performer's repertoire is all the pieces of music or dramatic parts he or she has learned and can perform.

repertory [ˈrɛpətərɪ] **repertories** NOUN

1 Repertory is the practice of performing a small number of plays in a theatre for a short time, using the same actors in each play.

2 In Australian, New Zealand and South African English, repertory is the same as **repertoire**

repetition [ˌrɛpɪˈtɪʃən] **repetitions** NOUN
If there is a repetition of something, it happens again. *e.g. We don't want a repetition of last week's fiasco.*

repetitive [rɪˈpɛtɪtɪv] ADJECTIVE
A repetitive activity involves a lot of repetition and is boring. *e.g. dull and repetitive work*

replace [rɪˈpleɪs] **replaces, replacing, replaced** VERB
1 When one thing replaces another, the first thing takes the place of the second.

succeed: *He was succeeded by his son.*
supersede: *Horses were superseded by cars.*
supplant: *Anger supplanted all other feelings.*
take over from: *the man taking over from Mr Berry as chairman*
take the place of: *Debit cards are taking the place of cash and cheques.*

2 If you replace something that is damaged or lost, you get a new one.

3 If you replace something, you put it back where it was before. *e.g. She replaced the receiver.*

replacement [rɪˈpleɪsmənt] **replacements** NOUN
1 The replacement for someone or something is the person or thing that takes their place.

proxy: *They must nominate a proxy to vote on their behalf.*
stand-in: *He was a stand-in for my regular doctor.*
substitute: *an artificial substitute for silk*
successor: *He recommended him as his successor.*
surrogate: *They had expected me to be a surrogate for my sister.*

2 The replacement of a person or thing happens when they are replaced by another person or thing.

replay **replays, replaying, replayed** VERB
[riːˈpleɪ]
1 If a match is replayed, the teams play it again.

2 If you replay a tape or film, you play it again. *e.g. Replay the first few seconds of the tape please.*

> NOUN [ˈriːˌpleɪ]

3 a match that is played for a second time

replenish [rɪˈplɛnɪʃ] **replenishes, replenishing, replenished** VERB; FORMAL
If you replenish something, you make it full or complete again.

replica ['rɛplɪkə] **replicas** NOUN
an accurate copy of something *e.g. a replica of Columbus's ship*
replicate VERB

reply [rɪ'plaɪ] **replies, replying, replied**
VERB
1 If you reply to something, you say or write an answer.

● THESAURUS
answer: *He avoided answering the question.*
counter: *"It's not that simple," he countered in a firm voice.*
respond: *'Mind your manners, lady!' I responded.*
retort: *"Nobody asked you," he retorted.*
return: *"I can manage," she returned coldly.*

> NOUN
2 what you say or write when you answer someone

● THESAURUS
answer: *She could not give him a truthful answer.*
response: *His response was brusque.*
retort: *His sharp retort clearly made an impact.*

report [rɪ'pɔːt] **reports, reporting, reported** VERB
1 If you report that something has happened, you tell someone about it or give an official account of it. *e.g. He reported the theft to the police.*

● THESAURUS
cover: *The US news media will cover the trial closely.*
describe: *His condition was described as "improving".*
inform of: *Inform the police of any suspicious activity.*
notify: *The skipper notified the coastguard of the tragedy.*
state: *The police stated that he had been arrested.*

2 To report someone to an authority means to make an official complaint about them.

3 If you report to a person or place, you go there and say you have arrived.

> NOUN
4 an account of an event or situation

● THESAURUS
account: *a dishonest account of events*
description: *a detailed description of the match*
statement: *a deliberately misleading statement*

reported speech [rɪ'pɔːtɪd] NOUN
a report of what someone said that gives the content of the speech without repeating the exact words

reporter [rɪ'pɔːtə] **reporters** NOUN
someone who writes news articles or broadcasts news reports

repossess [ˌriːpə'zɛs] **repossesses, repossessing, repossessed** VERB

If a shop or company repossesses goods that have not been paid for, they take them back.

represent [ˌrɛprɪ'zɛnt] **represents, representing, represented** VERB **(PSHE)**
1 If you represent someone, you act on their behalf. *e.g. lawyers representing relatives of the victims*

2 If a sign or symbol represents something, it stands for it.

● THESAURUS
mean: *This tarot card means the death of your present situation.*
stand for: *The olive branch stands for peace.*
symbolize: *a scene which symbolizes the movie's message*

3 To represent something in a particular way means to describe it in that way. *e.g. The popular press tends to represent him as a hero.*

● THESAURUS
depict: *Children's books usually depict farm animals as lovable.*
describe: *She was always described as an intellectual.*
picture: *In the American press she was pictured as a heroine.*
portray: *She was portrayed as a heartless, terrible woman.*
show: *He was shown as an intelligent and courageous man.*

representation [ˌrɛprɪzɛn'teɪʃən] **representations** NOUN
1 Representation is the state of being represented by someone. *e.g. Was there any student representation?.*

2 You can describe a picture or statue of someone as a representation of them.

representative [ˌrɛprɪ'zɛntətɪv] **representatives** NOUN
1 (PSHE) a person chosen to act on behalf of another person or a group

● THESAURUS
agent: *You are buying direct, rather than through an agent.*
delegate: *a union delegate*
deputy: *I can't make it so I'll send my deputy.*
proxy: *They must nominate a proxy to vote on their behalf.*
spokesman or **spokeswoman:** *the party's education spokesman*

> ADJECTIVE
2 A representative selection is typical of the group it belongs to. *e.g. The photos chosen are not representative of his work.*

● THESAURUS
characteristic: *a characteristic feature*

r

illustrative: *an illustrative example*
typical: *a typical Italian menu*

repress [rɪ'prɛs] **represses, repressing, repressed** VERB

1 If you repress a feeling, you succeed in not showing or feeling it. *e.g. I couldn't repress my anger any longer.*

2 To repress people means to restrict their freedom and control them by force.
repression NOUN

repressive [rɪ'prɛsɪv] ADJECTIVE
Repressive governments use force and unjust laws to restrict and control people.

reprieve [rɪ'priːv] **reprieves, reprieving, reprieved** VERB

1 If someone who has been sentenced to death is reprieved, their sentence is changed and they are not killed.

> NOUN

2 a delay before something unpleasant happens *e.g. The zoo won a reprieve from closure.*

reprimand ['rɛprɪˌmɑːnd] **reprimands, reprimanding, reprimanded** VERB

1 If you reprimand someone, you officially tell them that they should not have done something.

> NOUN

2 something said or written by a person in authority when they are reprimanding someone

reprisal [rɪ'praɪzəl] **reprisals** NOUN
Reprisals are violent actions taken by one group of people against another group that has harmed them.

reproach [rɪ'prəʊtʃ] **reproaches, reproaching, reproached** FORMAL

> NOUN

1 If you express reproach, you show that you feel sad and angry about what someone has done. *e.g. a long letter of reproach*

> VERB

2 If you reproach someone, you tell them, rather sadly, that they have done something wrong.
reproachful ADJECTIVE

reproduce [ˌriːprə'djuːs] **reproduces, reproducing, reproduced** VERB (**SCIENCE**)

1 To reproduce something means to make a copy of it.

2 When living things reproduce, they produce more of their own kind. *e.g. Bacteria reproduce by splitting into two.*

reproduction [ˌriːprə'dʌkʃən] **reproductions** NOUN

1 a modern copy of a painting or piece of furniture

2 Reproduction is the process by which a living thing produces more of its kind. *e.g. the study of animal reproduction*

reproductive [ˌriːprə'dʌktɪv] ADJECTIVE
relating to the reproduction of living things *e.g. the female reproductive system*

reptile ['rɛptaɪl] **reptiles** NOUN
a cold-blooded animal, such as a snake or a lizard, which has scaly skin and lays eggs
reptilian ADJECTIVE
[WORD HISTORY: from Latin REPTILIS meaning 'creeping']

republic [rɪ'pʌblɪk] **republics** NOUN
a country which has a president rather than a king or queen
republican NOUN OR ADJECTIVE, **republicanism** NOUN
[WORD HISTORY: from Latin RES PUBLICA meaning literally 'public thing']

repulse [rɪ'pʌls] **repulses, repulsing, repulsed** VERB

1 If you repulse someone who is being friendly, you put them off by behaving coldly towards them. *e.g. He repulses friendly advances.*

2 To repulse an attacking force means to fight it and cause it to retreat.

3 If something repulses you, you find it horrible and disgusting and you want to avoid it.

repulsion [rɪ'pʌlʃən] NOUN

1 Repulsion is a strong feeling of disgust.

2 Repulsion is a force separating two objects, such as the force between two like electric charges.

repulsive [rɪ'pʌlsɪv] ADJECTIVE
horrible and disgusting

reputable ['rɛpjʊtəbəl] ADJECTIVE
known to be good and reliable *e.g. a well-established and reputable firm*

reputation [ˌrɛpjʊ'teɪʃən] **reputations** NOUN
The reputation of something or someone is the opinion that people have of them. *e.g. The college had a good reputation.*

● THESAURUS
character: *a man of good character*
name: *I have disgraced the family's name.*
renown: *a singer of great renown*
repute: *a writer and scholar of some repute*
standing: *This has done nothing to improve his standing.*
stature: *his stature as the world's greatest cellist*

reputed [rɪ'pjuːtɪd] ADJECTIVE
If something is reputed to be true, some people say that it is true. *e.g. the reputed tomb of Christ*

reputedly ADVERB

request [rɪˈkwɛst] requests, requesting, requested VERB

1 If you request something, you ask for it politely or formally.

● THESAURUS

ask: *The government is being asked to consider the plan.*
beg: *May I beg a favour of you?*
seek: *You should seek a medical opinion.*

> NOUN

2 If you make a request for something, you request it.

● THESAURUS

appeal: *an appeal for witnesses to come forward*
application: *Their application was vetoed.*
call: *calls to decrease income tax*
plea: *his plea for help in solving the killing*

requiem [ˈrɛkwɪəm] requiems NOUN

1 A requiem or requiem mass is a mass celebrated for someone who has recently died.
2 a piece of music for singers and an orchestra, originally written for a requiem mass *e.g. Mozart's Requiem.*
[WORD HISTORY: from Latin REQUIES meaning 'rest']

require [rɪˈkwaɪə] requires, requiring, required VERB

1 If you require something, you need it.

● THESAURUS

demand: *The task of reconstruction would demand patience and hard work.*
depend on: *I depend on this money to survive.*
be in need of: *The house was in need of modernization.*
need: *He desperately needed money.*
want: *informal The windows wanted cleaning.*

2 If you are required to do something, you have to do it because someone says you must. *e.g. The rules require employers to provide safety training.*

● THESAURUS

compel: *legislation that would compel cyclists to wear a helmet*
demand: *This letter demands an immediate reply.*
direct: *a court order directing the group to leave the area*
instruct: *They have instructed their solicitor to sue for compensation.*
oblige: *This decree obliges unions to delay strikes.*
order: *The court ordered him to pay the sum in full.*

requirement [rɪˈkwaɪəmənt] requirements NOUN

something that you must have or must do *e.g. A good degree is a requirement for entry.*

● THESAURUS

demand: *the demands and challenges of his new job*

essential: *the basic essentials for bachelor life*
necessity: *food and other daily necessities*
need: *special nutritional needs*
specification: *These companies will have to meet new European specifications.* formal formal

requisite [ˈrɛkwɪzɪt] requisites FORMAL >
ADJECTIVE

1 necessary for a particular purpose *e.g. She filled in the requisite paperwork.*

> NOUN

2 something that is necessary for a particular purpose

rescue [ˈrɛskjuː] rescues, rescuing, rescued VERB

1 If you rescue someone, you save them from a dangerous or unpleasant situation.

> NOUN

2 Rescue is help which saves someone from a dangerous or unpleasant situation.
rescuer NOUN

research [rɪˈsɜːtʃ] researches, researching, researched NOUN

1 Research is work that involves studying something and trying to find out facts about it.

● THESAURUS

analysis: *They collected blood samples for laboratory analysis.*
examination: *a framework for the examination of these topics*
exploration: *an exploration of classical myths*
investigation: *Further investigation was hindered by the loss of alldocumentation.*
study: *The study demonstrated a link between obesity and heart problems.*

> VERB

2 If you research something, you try to discover facts about it.
researcher NOUN

● THESAURUS

analyse: *We haven't had time to analyse those samples yet.*
examine: *The spacecraft will examine how solar wind affectsEarth's magnetic field.*
explore: *I would probably be wise to explore the matter further.*
investigate: *Gas officials are investigating the cause of the explosion.*
study: *She's been studying chimpanzees for thirty years.*

resemblance [rɪˈzɛmbləns] NOUN

If there is a resemblance between two things, they are similar to each other. *e.g. There was a remarkable resemblance between them.*

● THESAURUS

analogy: *the analogy between racism and homophobia*

r

correspondence: *There's little correspondence between our lifestyles.*
likeness: *These myths have a startling likeness to one another.*
parallel: *There were parallels between the two murders.*
similarity: *similarities between mother and son*

resemble [rɪˈzɛmbəl] resembles, resembling, resembled VERB

To resemble something means to be similar to it.

THESAURUS
bear a resemblance to: *She bears a resemblance to Marilyn Monroe.*
be like: *The ground is like concrete.*
be similar to: *The gun was similar to an air pistol.*
look like: *He looks like his father.*
parallel: *His fate paralleled that of his predecessor.*
take after: *You take after your grandmother.*

resent [rɪˈzɛnt] resents, resenting, resented VERB

If you resent something, you feel bitter and angry about it.

THESAURUS
be angry about: *I was angry at the way he spoke to me.*
be offended by: *She was offended by his comments.*
dislike: *I dislike his patronizing attitude.*
object to: *I object to being treated like an idiot.*
take offence at: *She took offence at the implied criticism.*

resentful [rɪˈzɛntfʊl] ADJECTIVE

bitter and angry *e.g. He felt very resentful about losing his job.*
resentfully ADVERB

THESAURUS
aggrieved: *He is still aggrieved at the size of the fine.*
angry: *I was angry that I wasn't consulted.*
bitter: *a forsaken and bitter man*
embittered: *He had grown into an embittered, hardened adult.*
huffy: *He's so huffy if he doesn't get his own way.*
indignant: *They were indignant that they had not been consulted.*
offended: *He was offended at being left out.*

resentment [rɪˈzɛntmənt] resentments NOUN

a feeling of anger or bitterness

THESAURUS
anger: *Perhaps anger had clouded his vision.*
animosity: *The animosity between the two men grew.*
bitterness: *I feel bitterness towards the person who knocked me down.*
grudge: *It was an accident and I bear no grudges.*

huff: *She went off in a huff.*
indignation: *He could hardly contain his indignation.*
rancour: *There was no trace of envy or rancour in her face.*

reservation [ˌrɛzəˈveɪʃən] reservations NOUN

1 If you have reservations about something, you are not sure that it is right.

2 If you make a reservation, you book a place in advance.

3 an area of land set aside for American Indian peoples *e.g. a Cherokee reservation*

reserve [rɪˈzɜːv] reserves, reserving, reserved VERB

1 If something is reserved for a particular person or purpose, it is kept specially for them.

THESAURUS
hoard: *They've begun to hoard food and petrol.*
hold: *The information is held in a database.*
keep: *Grate the lemon zest and keep it for later.*
put by: *She had enough put by for her fare.*
save: *Save me a seat.*
set aside: *funds set aside for education*
stockpile: *People are stockpiling food for the coming winter.*
store: *potatoes stored for sale out of season*

> NOUN

2 a supply of something for future use

THESAURUS
cache: *a cache of weapons and explosives*
fund: *a pension fund*
hoard: *a hoard of food and petrol*
stock: *stocks of paper and ink*
stockpile: *stockpiles of chemical weapons*
store: *a secret store of sweets*
supply: *food supplies*

3 In sport, a reserve is someone who is available to play in case one of the team is unable to play.

4 A nature reserve is an area of land where animals, birds, or plants are officially protected.

5 If someone shows reserve, they keep their feelings hidden.
reserved ADJECTIVE

reservoir [ˈrɛzəˌvwɑː] reservoirs NOUN

a lake used for storing water before it is supplied to people

reshuffle [riːˈʃʌfəl] reshuffles NOUN

a reorganization of people or things

reside [rɪˈzaɪd] resides, residing, resided VERB; FORMAL

If a quality resides in something, the quality is in that thing.

residence [ˈrɛzɪdəns] residence NOUN; FORMAL

a house

resident ['rezɪdənt] residents NOUN

1 A resident of a house or area is someone who lives there.

> ADJECTIVE

2 If someone is resident in a house or area, they live there.

residential [,rezɪ'dɛnʃəl] ADJECTIVE

1 A residential area contains mainly houses rather than offices or factories.

2 providing accommodation e.g. residential care for the elderly

residue ['rezɪ,djuː] residues NOUN

a small amount of something that remains after most of it has gone e.g. an increase in toxic residues found in drinking water

residual ADJECTIVE

resign [rɪ'zaɪn] resigns, resigning, resigned VERB

1 If you resign from a job, you formally announce that you are leaving it.

THESAURUS

abdicate: The King abdicated to marry an American divorcee.

hand in your notice: I handed in my notice on Friday.

leave: I am leaving to become a teacher.

quit: He quit his job as an office boy.

step down: informal He headed the government until he stepped down in 1990.

2 If you resign yourself to an unpleasant situation, you realize that you have to accept it.

resigned ADJECTIVE

THESAURUS

accept: You've got to accept the fact that he's left you.

bow: He bowed to the inevitable and allowed her to go.

reconcile oneself: She had reconciled herself to never seeing him again.

resignation [,rezɪg'neɪʃən] resignations NOUN

1 Someone's resignation is a formal statement of their intention to leave a job.

2 Resignation is the reluctant acceptance of an unpleasant situation or fact.

resilient [rɪ'zɪlɪənt] ADJECTIVE

able to recover quickly from unpleasant or damaging events

resilience NOUN

resin ['rezɪn] resins NOUN

1 Resin is a sticky substance produced by some trees.

2 Resin is also a substance produced chemically and used to make plastics.

resist [rɪ'zɪst] resists, resisting, resisted VERB

1 If you resist something, you refuse to accept it and try to prevent it. e.g. The pay squeeze will be fiercely resisted by the unions.

THESAURUS

defy: arrested for defying the ban on street trading

fight: He vigorously fought the proposal.

oppose: Many parents oppose bilingual education in schools.

refuse: The patient has the right to refuse treatment.

struggle against: nations struggling against Communist takeovers

<<OPPOSITE accept

2 If you resist someone, you fight back against them.

resistance [rɪ'zɪstəns] resistances NOUN

1 Resistance to something such as change is a refusal to accept it.

2 Resistance to an attack consists of fighting back. e.g. The demonstrators offered no resistance.

3 Your body's resistance to germs or disease is its power to not be harmed by them.

4 Resistance is also the power of a substance to resist the flow of an electrical current through it.

resistant [rɪ'zɪstənt] ADJECTIVE

1 opposed to something and wanting to prevent it e.g. People were very resistant to change.

2 If something is resistant to a particular thing, it is not harmed or affected by it. e.g. Certain insects are resistant to this spray.

resolute ['rezə,luːt] ADJECTIVE; FORMAL

Someone who is resolute is determined not to change their mind.

resolutely ADVERB

resolution [,rezə'luːʃən] resolutions NOUN

1 Resolution is determination.

2 If you make a resolution, you promise yourself to do something.

3 a formal decision taken at a meeting

4 (ENGLISH) FORMAL

The resolution of a problem is the solving of it.

resolve [rɪ'zɒlv] resolves, resolving, resolved VERB

1 If you resolve to do something, you firmly decide to do it.

THESAURUS

decide: She decided to quit smoking.

determine: He determined to rescue his two countrymen.

intend: I intended to teach him a lesson he wouldn't forget.

make up your mind: Once he made up his mind to

do it, there was no stopping him.

2 If you resolve a problem, you find a solution to it.

● THESAURUS
clear up: *The confusion was soon cleared up.*
find a solution to: *the ability to find an effective solution to the crisis*
overcome: *Find a way to overcome your difficulties.*
solve: *These reforms did not solve the problem of unemployment.*
sort out: *The two countries have sorted out their trade dispute.*
work out: *It seems like a nightmare, but I'm sure we can work it out.*

> NOUN
3 Resolve is absolute determination.

● THESAURUS
determination: *the expression of fierce determination on her face*
resolution: *"I'm going on a diet," she said with sudden resolution.*
tenacity: *Hard work and sheer tenacity are crucial to career success.*

resonance ['rɛzənəns] **resonances** NOUN

1 Resonance is sound produced by an object vibrating as a result of another sound nearby.

2 Resonance is also a deep, clear, and echoing quality of sound.

resonate ['rɛzə,neɪt] **resonates, resonating, resonated** VERB

If something resonates, it vibrates and produces a deep, strong sound.

resort [rɪ'zɔːt] **resorts, resorting, resorted** VERB

1 If you resort to a course of action, you do it because you have no alternative.

> NOUN
2 a place where people spend their holidays

> PHRASE
3 If you do something **as a last resort**, you do it because you can find no other way of solving a problem.

resounding [rɪ'zaʊndɪŋ] ADJECTIVE

1 loud and echoing *e.g. a resounding round of applause*

2 A resounding success is a great success.

resource [rɪ'zɔːs] **resources** NOUN

The resources of a country, organization, or person are the materials, money, or skills they have.

resourceful [rɪ'zɔːsfʊl] ADJECTIVE

A resourceful person is good at finding ways of dealing with problems.
resourcefulness NOUN

respect [rɪ'spɛkt] **respects, respecting, respected** VERB

1 If you respect someone, you have a good opinion of their character or ideas.

● THESAURUS
admire: *I admire him for his honesty.*
have a good opinion of: *Nobody seems to have a good opinion of him.*
have a high opinion of: *He had a very high opinion of Neil.*
honour: *the Scout's promise to honour God and the Queen*
look up to: *He looks up to his dad.*
think highly of: *His boss thinks very highly of him.*
venerate: *My father venerated General Eisenhower.*
<<OPPOSITE disrespect

2 If you respect someone's rights or wishes, you do not do things that they would not like, or would consider wrong. *e.g. It is about time they started respecting the law.*

> NOUN
3 If you have respect for someone, you have a good opinion of them.

● THESAURUS
admiration: *I have always had the greatest admiration for him.*
esteem: *We have to win the trust and esteem of our clients.*
regard: *I hold him in high regard.*
reverence: *We did it out of reverence for the dead.*
<<OPPOSITE disrespect

> PHRASE
4 You can say **in this respect** to refer to a particular feature. *e.g. At least in this respect we are equals.*

respectable [rɪ'spɛktəbəl] ADJECTIVE

1 considered to be acceptable and morally correct *e.g. respectable families*

● THESAURUS
decent: *They married after a decent interval.*
good: *He comes from a good family.*
honourable: *His colleagues were honourable people.*
proper: *It was not proper for women to go on the stage.*
reputable: *a reputable firm*
upright: *an upright and trustworthy man*
worthy: *worthy citizens*

2 adequate or reasonable *e.g. a respectable rate of economic growth*
respectability NOUN, **respectably** ADVERB

● THESAURUS
appreciable: *making appreciable progress*
considerable: *a considerable amount*
decent: *a decent standard of living*

fair: *She had a fair command of English.*
reasonable: *He couldn't make a reasonable living from his writing.*

respectful [rɪ'spɛktfʊl] ADJECTIVE
showing respect for someone *e.g. Our children are always respectful to their elders.*
respectfully ADVERB

respective [rɪ'spɛktɪv] ADJECTIVE
belonging or relating individually to the people or things just mentioned *e.g. They went into their respective rooms to pack.*

respectively [rɪ'spɛktɪvlɪ] ADVERB
in the same order as the items just mentioned *e.g. They finished first and second respectively.*

respiration [ˌrɛspə'reɪʃən] NOUN **(SCIENCE)**
TECHNICAL
Your respiration is your breathing.

respiratory ['rɛspərətərɪ] ADJECTIVE;
TECHNICAL
relating to breathing *e.g. respiratory diseases*

respire [rɪ'spaɪə] **respires, respiring, respired** VERB
(SCIENCE) To respire is to breathe.

respite ['rɛspɪt] NOUN; FORMAL
a short rest from something unpleasant

respond [rɪ'spɒnd] **responds, responding, responded** VERB
When you respond to something, you react to it by doing or saying something.

respondent [rɪ'spɒndənt] **respondents**
NOUN
1 a person who answers a questionnaire or a request for information
2 In a court case, the respondent is the defendant.

response [rɪ'spɒns] **responses** NOUN
Your response to an event is your reaction or reply to it. *e.g. There has been no response to his remarks yet.*

responsibility [rɪˌspɒnsə'bɪlɪtɪ]
responsibilities NOUN
1 If you have responsibility for something, it is your duty to deal with it or look after it. *e.g. The garden was to have been his responsibility.*

⬤ THESAURUS
duty: *My duty is to look after the animals.*
obligation: *You have an obligation to help him.*
onus: *The onus was on him to make sure he didn't fail.*

2 If you accept responsibility for something that has happened, you agree that you caused it or were to blame. *e.g. We must all accept responsibility for our own mistakes.*

⬤ THESAURUS
blame: *I'm not going to take the blame for this.*
fault: *This is all your fault.*
guilt: *He was not completely free of guilt.*
liability: *He admitted liability for the crash.*

responsible [rɪ'spɒnsəbəl] ADJECTIVE
1 If you are responsible for something, it is your job to deal with it.

⬤ THESAURUS
in charge: *I wish someone else was in charge of this inquiry.*
in control: *Who is in control of the operation?*
2 If you are responsible for something bad that has happened, you are to blame for it.

⬤ THESAURUS
at fault: *I was not at fault as my vehicle was stationary.*
guilty: *I still maintain that I am not guilty.*
to blame: *Television is possibly to blame for this.*

3 If you are responsible to someone, that person is your boss and tells you what you have to do.
4 A responsible person behaves properly and sensibly without needing to be supervised.

⬤ THESAURUS
dependable: *a dependable, trustworthy teacher*
level-headed: *a sensible, level-headed approach*
reliable: *You have to demonstrate that you are reliable.*
sensible: *She's a sensible girl, if a bit headstrong.*
sound: *sound advice*
trustworthy: *He is a trustworthy leader.*
<<OPPOSITE *irresponsible*

5 A responsible job involves making careful judgments about important matters.
responsibly ADVERB

responsive [rɪ'spɒnsɪv] ADJECTIVE
1 quick to show interest and pleasure
2 taking notice of events and reacting in an appropriate way *e.g. The course is responsive to students' needs.*

rest [rɛst] **rests, resting, rested** NOUN
1 The rest of something is all the remaining parts of it.

⬤ THESAURUS
balance: *You pay half now and the balance on delivery.*
others: *She took one and put the others back.*
remainder: *He gulped down the remainder of his coffee.*
surplus: *Coat with seasoned flour, shaking off the surplus.*

2 If you have a rest, you sit or lie quietly and relax.

⬤ THESAURUS
break: *He needs to take a break from work.*

holiday: *I could really do with a holiday.*
leisure: *We get no leisure, no time off, no overtime pay.*
relaxation: *Make time for a bit of relaxation.*
respite: *a respite from the rush of everyday life*

> VERB

3 If you rest, you relax and do not do anything active for a while.

● THESAURUS
have a break: *Paul felt he had to have a break.*
idle: *He sat idling in his room.*
laze: *lazing on the beach*
put your feet up: *Nobody's home, so I can put my feet up for a while.*
relax: *Guests can relax in the cosy bar.*
sit down: *I'll have to sit down for a minute.*
take it easy: *the chance to just take it easy for a couple of weeks*

restaurant ['rɛstə.rɒŋ] **restaurants** NOUN
a place where you can buy and eat a meal
[WORD HISTORY: a French word; from RESTAURER meaning 'to restore']

restaurateur [,rɛstərə'tɜ:] **restaurateurs**
NOUN
someone who owns or manages a restaurant

restful ['rɛstfʊl] ADJECTIVE
Something that is restful helps you feel calm and relaxed.

restless ['rɛstlɪs] ADJECTIVE
finding it hard to remain still or relaxed because of boredom or impatience
restlessness NOUN, **restlessly** ADVERB

● THESAURUS
edgy: *She was nervous and edgy, still chain-smoking.*
fidgety: *bored, fidgety youngsters*
fretful: *The whole family was fretful and argumentative.*
jumpy: *If she can't smoke she gets jumpy and irritable.*
on edge: *She's been on edge for weeks.*
unsettled: *The staff were unsettled and demoralized.*

restore [rɪ'stɔ:] **restores, restoring, restored** VERB
1 To restore something means to cause it to exist again or to return to its previous state. *e.g. He was anxious to restore his reputation.*

● THESAURUS
re-establish: *an attempt to re-establish diplomatic relations*
reinstate: *the failure to reinstate the ceasefire*
reintroduce: *the plan to reintroduce wolves to the Highlands*
return: *their attempts to return the country to an agrarian economy*

2 To restore an old building or work of art means to clean and repair it.
restoration NOUN

● THESAURUS
fix up: *It took us months to fix this house up.*
mend: *They finally got round to mending the roof.*
rebuild: *plans to rebuild the opera house*
reconstruct: *reconstructing paintings by old masters*
refurbish: *The city is refurbishing the cathedral's facade.*
renovate: *The hotel was being renovated in expectation of a tourist boom.*
repair: *The money will be used to repair faulty equipment.*

restrain [rɪ'streɪn] **restrains, restraining, restrained** VERB
To restrain someone or something means to hold them back or prevent them from doing what they want to.

● THESAURUS
contain: *He could hardly contain his rage.*
control: *She tried to control her excitement.*
curb: *You must curb your extravagant tastes.*
hamper: *I was hampered by a lack of information.*
hinder: *Research is hindered by lack of cash.*
hold back: *He could no longer hold back his laughter.*
inhibit: *factors which inhibit growth*

restrained [rɪ'streɪnd] ADJECTIVE
behaving in a controlled way

restraint [rɪ'streɪnt] **restraints** NOUN
1 Restraints are rules or conditions that limit something. *e.g. wage restraints*
2 Restraint is calm, controlled behaviour.

restrict [rɪ'strɪkt] **restricts, restricting, restricted** VERB
1 If you restrict something, you prevent it becoming too large or varied.
2 To restrict people or animals means to limit their movement or actions.
restrictive ADJECTIVE

● THESAURUS
confine: *Keep your dog confined to the house.*
contain: *The curfew had contained the violence.*
hamper: *I was hampered by a lack of information.*
handicap: *handicapped by the terms of the contract*
impede: *Their work was being impeded by shortages of supplies.*
inhibit: *factors which inhibit growth*
limit: *He limited payments on the country's foreign debt.*
restrain: *the need to restrain wage rises*

restriction [rɪ'strɪkʃən] **restrictions** NOUN
a rule or situation that limits what you can do *e.g. financial restrictions*

THESAURUS
constraint: *financial constraints*
control: *a call for stricter gun control*
curb: *support for a curb on migration from neighbouringcountries*
limitation: *A slipped disc causes severe limitation of movement.*
regulation: *regulations outlawing child labour*
restraint: *new restraints on trade unions*
stipulation: *The only dress stipulation was "no jeans".*

result [rɪˈzʌlt] **results, resulting, resulted**
NOUN
1 The result of an action or situation is the situation that is caused by it. *e.g. As a result of the incident he got a two-year suspension.*

THESAURUS
consequence: *This could have disastrous consequences for industry.*
effect: *the intended effect of the revised guidelines*
outcome: *The ultimate outcome will be different.*
product: *the product of five years' work*
upshot: *The upshot is that our employees are all unhappy.*

2 The result is also the final marks, figures, or situation at the end of an exam, calculation, or contest. *e.g. election results... The result was calculated to three decimal places.*

> VERB
3 If something results in a particular event, it causes that event to happen.

THESAURUS
bring about: *The Suez crisis brought about petrol rationing.*
cause: *The play caused a stir here.*
lead to: *brain damage which leads to paralysis*

4 If something results from a particular event, it is caused by that event. *e.g. The fire had resulted from carelessness.*
resultant ADJECTIVE

THESAURUS
arise: *the publicity that arises from incidents of this kind*
derive: *Poor health often derives from poverty.*
develop: *a determination which has developed from his new-found confidence*
ensue: *If the system collapses, chaos will ensue.*
follow: *the consequences which followed his release from prison*
happen: *What will happen if the test proves positive?*
stem: *Her hatred of cars stems from her mother's death in a crash.*

resume [rɪˈzjuːm] **resumes, resuming, resumed** VERB
If you resume an activity or position, you return to it after a break.

resumption NOUN

resurgence [rɪˈsɜːdʒəns] NOUN
If there is a resurgence of an attitude or activity, it reappears and grows stronger.
resurgent ADJECTIVE

resurrect [ˌrezəˈrekt] **resurrects, resurrecting, resurrected** VERB
If you resurrect something, you make it exist again after it has disappeared or ended.
resurrection NOUN

Resurrection [ˌrezəˈrekʃən] NOUN
In Christian belief, the Resurrection is the coming back to life of Jesus Christ three days after he had been killed.

resuscitate [rɪˈsʌsɪˌteɪt] **resuscitates, resuscitating, resuscitated** VERB
If you resuscitate someone, you make them conscious again after an accident.
resuscitation NOUN

retail [ˈriːteɪl] NOUN
The retail price is the price at which something is sold in the shops.
retailer NOUN

retain [rɪˈteɪn] **retains, retaining, retained** VERB
To retain something means to keep it.
retention NOUN

retaliate [rɪˈtælɪˌeɪt] **retaliates, retaliating, retaliated** VERB
If you retaliate, you do something to harm or upset someone because they have already acted in a similar way against you.
retaliation NOUN

THESAURUS
get back at: *a desire to get back at our enemies*
get even with: informal *He wanted to get even with his former employers.*
get your own back: informal *the opportunity to get your own back on your husband*
hit back: *In this article he hits back at his critics.*
pay someone back: *I'll pay him back for what he's done.*
take revenge: *taking revenge for his father's murder*

retarded [rɪˈtɑːdɪd] ADJECTIVE
If someone is retarded, their mental development is much less advanced than average.

rethink [riːˈθɪŋk] **rethinks, rethinking, rethought** VERB
If you rethink something, you think about how it should be changed. *e.g. We have to rethink our strategy.*

reticent [ˈretɪsənt] ADJECTIVE
Someone who is reticent is unwilling to tell people about things.

r

reticence NOUN

retina [ˈrɛtɪnə] **retinas** NOUN
the light-sensitive part at the back of your
eyeball, which receives an image and sends it to
your brain

retinue [ˈrɛtɪˌnjuː] **retinues** NOUN
a group of helpers or friends travelling with an
important person

retire [rɪˈtaɪə] **retires, retiring, retired** VERB
1 When older people retire, they give up work.
2 FORMAL
If you retire, you leave to go into another room,
or to bed. *e.g. She retired early with a good book.*
retired ADJECTIVE, **retirement** NOUN

retort [rɪˈtɔːt] **retorts, retorting, retorted**
VERB
1 To retort means to reply angrily.
> NOUN
2 a short, angry reply

retract [rɪˈtrækt] **retracts, retracting,
retracted** VERB
1 If you retract something you have said, you say
that you did not mean it.
2 When something is retracted, it moves inwards
or backwards. *e.g. The undercarriage was retracted
shortly after takeoff.*
retraction NOUN, **retractable** ADJECTIVE

retreat [rɪˈtriːt] **retreats, retreating,
retreated** VERB
1 To retreat means to move backwards away
from something or someone.

◉ **THESAURUS**
back away: *He put up his hands in protest and
began to back away.*
back off: *I stood up for myself and they backed off.*
draw back: *They drew back in fear.*
pull back: *Their forces have pulled back in all areas.*
withdraw: *Troops withdrew from the country last
month.*
<<OPPOSITE *advance*

2 If you retreat from something difficult or
unpleasant, you avoid doing it.
> NOUN
3 If an army moves away from the enemy, this is
referred to as a retreat.

◉ **THESAURUS**
departure: *the departure of all foreign forces from
the country*
evacuation: *the evacuation of British troops from
Dunkirk*
flight: *my panicked flight from London*
withdrawal: *French withdrawal from Algeria.*
<<OPPOSITE *advance*

4 a quiet place that you can go to rest or do
things in private

◉ **THESAURUS**
haven: *The hotel is a haven of tranquillity.*
refuge: *a refuge from the harsh realities of the world*
sanctuary: *a sanctuary located on an island*

retribution [ˌrɛtrɪˈbjuːʃən] NOUN; FORMAL
Retribution is punishment. *e.g. the threat of
retribution*

retrieve [rɪˈtriːv] **retrieves, retrieving,
retrieved** VERB
If you retrieve something, you get it back.
retrieval NOUN

retriever [rɪˈtriːvə] **retrievers** NOUN
a large dog often used by hunters to bring back
birds and animals which have been shot

retro- PREFIX
'Retro-' means 'back' or 'backwards' *e.g.
retrospective*
[WORD HISTORY: from Latin RETRŌ meaning
'behind' or 'backwards']

retrospect [ˈrɛtrəˌspɛkt] NOUN
When you consider something in retrospect, you
think about it afterwards and often have a
different opinion from the one you had at the
time. *e.g. In retrospect, I probably shouldn't have
resigned*SPECERE *meaning 'to look'.*

retrospective [ˌrɛtrəˈspɛktɪv] ADJECTIVE
1 concerning things that happened in the past
2 taking effect from a date in the past
retrospectively ADVERB

return [rɪˈtɜːn] **returns, returning,
returned** VERB
1 When you return to a place, you go back after
you have been away.

◉ **THESAURUS**
come back: *He said he'd come back later.*
go back: *I love going back home.*
reappear: *He reappeared two nights later.*
turn back: *We've come too far now to turn back.*

2 If you return something to someone, you give it
back to them.

◉ **THESAURUS**
give back: *He is refusing to give the dog back.*
pay back: *You have to pay back the loan, plus an
arrangement fee.*
refund: *The company will refund the full cost.*
repay: *I can afford to repay the loan.*

3 When you return a ball during a game, you hit it
back to your opponent.

4 When a judge or jury returns a verdict, they
announce it.
> NOUN
5 Your return is your arrival back at a place.

6 The return on an investment is the profit or
interest you get from it.

7 a ticket for the journey to a place and back again

> PHRASE

8 If you do something **in return** for a favour, you do it to repay the favour.

reunion [riːˈjuːnjən] **reunions** NOUN
a party or meeting for people who have not seen each other for a long time

reunite [ˌriːjuːˈnaɪt] **reunites, reuniting, reunited** VERB
If people are reunited, they meet again after they have been separated for some time.

rev [rɛv] **revs, revving, revved** INFORMAL >
VERB

1 When you rev the engine of a vehicle, you press the accelerator to increase the engine speed.

> NOUN

2 The speed of an engine is measured in revolutions per minute, referred to as revs. *e.g. I noticed that the engine revs had dropped.*

Rev or **Revd** abbreviations for **Reverend**

revamp [riːˈvæmp] **revamps, revamping, revamped** VERB
To revamp something means to improve or repair it.

reveal [rɪˈviːl] **reveals, revealing, revealed** VERB

1 To reveal something means to tell people about it. *e.g. They were not ready to reveal any of the details.*

● THESAURUS
announce: *She was planning to announce her engagement.*
disclose: *He will not disclose the name of his patient.*
divulge: *I do not want to divulge where the village is.*
get off your chest: informal *I feel it's done me good to get it off my chest.*
let on: *She never let on that anything was wrong.*

2 If you reveal something that has been hidden, you uncover it.

● THESAURUS
bring to light: *The truth is unlikely to be brought to light.*
lay bare: *His real motives were laid bare.*
uncover: *Auditors said they had uncovered evidence of fraud.*
unearth: *Quarry workers have unearthed the skeleton of a mammoth.*
unveil: *The statue will be unveiled next week.*

revel [ˈrɛvəl] **revels, revelling, revelled** VERB
If you revel in a situation, you enjoy it very much.
revelry NOUN

revelation [ˌrɛvəˈleɪʃən] **revelations** NOUN

1 a surprising or interesting fact made known to people

2 If an experience is a revelation, it makes you realize or learn something.

revenge [rɪˈvɛndʒ] **revenges, revenging, revenged** NOUN

1 Revenge involves hurting someone who has hurt you.

● THESAURUS
reprisal: *Witnesses are unwilling to testify through fear of reprisals.*
retaliation: *The attack was in retaliation for his murder.*
retribution: *They did not want their names used for fear of retribution.*
vengeance: *He swore vengeance on everyone involved in the murder.*

> VERB

2 If you revenge yourself on someone who has hurt you, you hurt them in return.

● THESAURUS
avenge: *He was trying to avenge the death of his friend.*
get even: *I'm going to get even with you for this.*
get your own back: informal *I simply want to get my own back on him.*
hit back: *He hit back at those who criticized him.*
pay someone back: *Some day I'll pay you back for this.*
retaliate: *I was sorely tempted to retaliate.*

revenue [ˈrɛvɪˌnjuː] **revenues** NOUN
Revenue is money that a government, company, or organization receives. *e.g. government tax revenues*

revered [rɪˈvɪəd] ADJECTIVE
If someone is revered, he or she is respected and admired. *e.g. He is still revered as the father of the nation.*

reverence [ˈrɛvərəns] NOUN
Reverence is a feeling of great respect.

Reverend [ˈrɛvərənd]
Reverend is a title used before the name of a member of the clergy. *e.g. the Reverend George Young*

reversal [rɪˈvɜːsəl] **reversals** NOUN
If there is a reversal of a process or policy, it is changed to the opposite process or policy.

reverse [rɪˈvɜːs] **reverses, reversing, reversed** VERB

1 When someone reverses a process, they change it to the opposite process. *e.g. They won't reverse the decision to increase prices.*

● THESAURUS
change: *They should change the law to make this practice illegal.*

r

invalidate: *A contract signed now might be invalidated at a future date.*

overrule: *In 1998 the Court of Appeal overruled the decision.*

overturn: *When the parliament overturned his decision, he backed down.*

retract: *He was asked to retract his comments but refused.*

2 If you reverse the order of things, you arrange them in the opposite order.

3 When you reverse a car, you drive it backwards.

> NOUN

4 The reverse is the opposite of what has just been said or done.

● **THESAURUS**

contrary: *I'm not a feminist, quite the contrary.*

converse: *In fact, the converse is true.*

opposite: *When I told him to do something he always did the opposite.*

> ADJECTIVE

5 Reverse means opposite to what is usual or to what has just been described.

reversible [rɪ'vɜːsəbəl] ADJECTIVE
Reversible clothing can be worn with either side on the outside.

revert [rɪ'vɜːt] **reverts, reverting, reverted**
VERB; FORMAL
To revert to a former state or type of behaviour means to go back to it.

review [rɪ'vjuː] **reviews, reviewing, reviewed** NOUN

1 an article or an item on television or radio, giving an opinion of a new book or play

● **THESAURUS**

commentary: *He'll be writing a weekly commentary on American culture.*

criticism: *literary criticism*

notice: *Richards's solo work received good notices.*

2 When there is a review of a situation or system, it is examined to decide whether changes are needed.

● **THESAURUS**

analysis: *an analysis of American trade policy*

examination: *an examination of the top 250 companies*

report: *the committee's annual report*

study: *a recent study of treatments for back pain*

survey: *a survey of 250 businessmen*

> VERB

3 To review a play or book means to write an account expressing an opinion of it.

4 To review something means to examine it to decide whether changes are needed.
reviewer NOUN

revise [rɪ'vaɪz] **revises, revising, revised**
VERB

1 If you revise something, you alter or correct it.

● **THESAURUS**

amend: *They voted unanimously to amend the constitution.*

correct: *time spent correcting his students' work*

edit: *We have the right to edit this book once it's finished.*

revamp: *It is time to revamp the system.*

update: *He was back in the office, updating the work schedule.*

2 When you revise for an examination, you go over your work to learn things thoroughly.
revision NOUN

revive [rɪ'vaɪv] **revives, reviving, revived**
VERB

1 When a feeling or practice is revived, it becomes active or popular again.

● **THESAURUS**

rally: *Markets began to rally worldwide.*

resuscitate: *a bid to resuscitate the weekly magazine*

2 When you revive someone who has fainted, they become conscious again.
revival NOUN

revolt [rɪ'vəʊlt] **revolts, revolting, revolted**
NOUN (HISTORY)

1 a violent attempt by a group of people to change their country's political system

> VERB

2 When people revolt, they fight against the authority that governs them.

3 If something revolts you, it is so horrible that you feel disgust.

revolting [rɪ'vəʊltɪŋ] ADJECTIVE
horrible and disgusting *e.g. The smell in the cell was revolting.*

revolution [ˌrevə'luːʃən] **revolutions** NOUN

1 (HISTORY) a violent attempt by a large group of people to change the political system of their country

2 an important change in an area of human activity *e.g. the Industrial Revolution*

3 one complete turn in a circle

revolutionary [ˌrevə'luːʃənəri]
revolutionaries ADJECTIVE

1 involving great changes *e.g. a revolutionary new cooling system*

> NOUN

2 a person who takes part in a revolution

revolve [rɪ'vɒlv] **revolves, revolving, revolved** VERB

1 If something revolves round something else, it centres on that as the most important thing. *e.g.*

My job revolves around the telephone.

2 When something revolves, it turns in a circle around a central point. *e.g. The moon revolves round the earth.*

revolver [rɪ'vɒlvə] **revolvers** NOUN
a small gun held in the hand

revulsion [rɪ'vʌlʃən] NOUN
Revulsion is a strong feeling of disgust or disapproval.

reward [rɪ'wɔːd] **rewards, rewarding, rewarded (PSHE)** NOUN
1 something you are given because you have done something good

● THESAURUS
bonus: *We don't get a Christmas bonus any more.*
bounty: *They paid bounties to people to give up their weapons.*
payment: *Players now expect payment for interviews.*
prize: *He won first prize.*

> VERB
2 If you reward someone, you give them a reward.

rewarding [rɪ'wɔːdɪŋ] ADJECTIVE
Something that is rewarding gives you a lot of satisfaction.

rewind [riː'waɪnd] **rewinds, rewinding, rewound** VERB
If you rewind a tape on a tape recorder or video, you make the tape go backwards.

rhapsody ['ræpsədɪ] **rhapsodies** NOUN
a short piece of music which is very passionate and flowing

rhetoric ['rɛtərɪk] NOUN
Rhetoric is speech or writing that is intended to impress people.

rhetorical [rɪ'tɒrɪkəl] ADJECTIVE
1 A rhetorical question is one which is asked in order to make a statement rather than to get an answer.
2 Rhetorical language is intended to be grand and impressive.

rheumatism ['ruːmə,tɪzəm] NOUN
Rheumatism is an illness that makes your joints and muscles stiff and painful.
rheumatic ADJECTIVE

rhino ['raɪnəu] **rhinos** NOUN; INFORMAL
a rhinoceros

rhinoceros [raɪ'nɒsərəs] **rhinoceroses** NOUN
a large African or Asian animal with one or two horns on its nose
[WORD HISTORY: from Greek RHIN meaning 'of the

nose' and KERAS meaning 'horn']

rhododendron [,rəudə'dɛndrən] **rhododendrons** NOUN
an evergreen bush with large coloured flowers

rhombus ['rɒmbəs] **rhombuses** or **rhombi** NOUN
(MATHS) a shape with four equal sides and no right angles

rhubarb ['ruːbɑːb] NOUN
Rhubarb is a plant with long red stems which can be cooked with sugar and eaten.

rhyme [raɪm] **rhymes, rhyming, rhymed (ENGLISH)** VERB
1 If two words rhyme, they have a similar sound. *e.g. Sally rhymes with valley.*

> NOUN
2 a word that rhymes with another
3 a short poem with rhyming lines

rhythm ['rɪðəm] **rhythms** NOUN
1 (MUSIC) Rhythm is a regular movement or beat.

● THESAURUS
beat: *the thumping beat of rock music*
pulse: *the repetitive pulse of the drum beat*
tempo: *Elgar supplied his works with precise indications of tempo.*
time: *A reel is in four-four time.*

2 a regular pattern of changes, for example, in the seasons
rhythmic ADJECTIVE, **rhythmically** ADVERB

rib [rɪb] **ribs** NOUN
Your ribs are the curved bones that go from your backbone to your chest.
ribbed ADJECTIVE

ribbon ['rɪbən] **ribbons** NOUN
a long, narrow piece of cloth used for decoration

ribcage ['rɪb,keɪdʒ] **ribcages** NOUN
Your ribcage is the framework of bones made up of your ribs which protects your internal organs like your heart and lungs.

rice [raɪs] NOUN
Rice is a tall grass that produces edible grains. Rice is grown in warm countries on wet ground.

rich [rɪtʃ] **richer, richest; riches** ADJECTIVE
1 Someone who is rich has a lot of money and possessions.

● THESAURUS
affluent: *an affluent neighbourhood*
loaded: slang *Of course he can afford it. He's loaded.*
opulent: *his opulent lifestyle*
prosperous: *the youngest son of a relatively prosperous family*
wealthy: *a wealthy international businessman*

r

well off: *My grandparents were quite well off.*
<<OPPOSITE *poor*

2 Something that is rich in something contains a large amount of it. *e.g. Liver is particularly rich in vitamin A.*

● THESAURUS
abundant: *the Earth's most abundant natural resources*
fertile: *a fertile imagination*
plentiful: *a plentiful supply of vegetables*

3 Rich food contains a large amount of fat, oil, or sugar.

4 Rich colours, smells, and sounds are strong and pleasant.

> PLURAL NOUN
5 Riches are valuable possessions or large amounts of money. *e.g. the oil riches of the Middle East*
richness NOUN

richly ['rɪtʃlɪ] ADVERB
1 If someone is richly rewarded, they are rewarded well with something valuable.
2 If you feel strongly that someone deserves something, you can say it is richly deserved.

rick [rɪk] **ricks** NOUN
a large pile of hay or straw

rickets ['rɪkɪts] NOUN
Rickets is a disease that causes soft bones in children if they do not get enough vitamin D.

rickety ['rɪkɪtɪ] ADJECTIVE
likely to collapse or break *e.g. a rickety wooden jetty*

rickshaw ['rɪkʃɔː] **rickshaws** NOUN
a hand-pulled cart used in Asia for carrying passengers

ricochet ['rɪkəʃeɪ] **ricochets**, **ricocheting** or **ricochetting ricocheted** or **ricochetted** VERB
When a bullet ricochets, it hits a surface and bounces away from it.

rid [rɪd] **rids**, **ridding**, **rid** PHRASE
1 When you **get rid** of something you do not want, you remove or destroy it.

● THESAURUS
dispose of: *He disposed of the murder weapon.*
dump: *We dumped our bags at the hotel.*
eject: *Officials used guard dogs to eject the protestors.*
jettison: *The crew jettisoned excess fuel.*
remove: *Most of her fears had been removed.*
weed out: *We must weed these people out as soon as possible.*

> VERB
2 FORMAL
To rid a place of something unpleasant means to succeed in removing it.

riddle ['rɪdᵊl] **riddles** NOUN
1 a puzzle which seems to be nonsense, but which has an entertaining solution
2 Something that is a riddle puzzles and confuses you.

riddled ['rɪdᵊld] ADJECTIVE
full of something undesirable *e.g. The report was riddled with errors.*
[WORD HISTORY: from Old English HRIDDEL meaning 'sieve']

ride [raɪd] **rides**, **riding**, **rode**, **ridden** VERB
1 When you ride a horse or a bike, you sit on it and control it as it moves along.
2 When you ride in a car, you travel in it.
> NOUN
3 a journey on a horse or bike or in a vehicle

rider ['raɪdə] **riders** NOUN
1 a person riding on a horse or bicycle
2 an additional statement which changes or puts a condition on what has already been said

ridge [rɪdʒ] **ridges** NOUN
1 a long, narrow piece of high land
2 a raised line on a flat surface

ridicule ['rɪdɪˌkjuːl] **ridicules**, **ridiculing**, **ridiculed** VERB
1 To ridicule someone means to make fun of them in an unkind way.
> NOUN
2 Ridicule is unkind laughter and mockery.

ridiculous [rɪ'dɪkjʊləs] ADJECTIVE
very foolish
ridiculously ADVERB

● THESAURUS
absurd: *absurd claims to have met big stars*
laughable: *He claims the allegations are "laughable".*
ludicrous: *It's a completely ludicrous idea.*
preposterous: *their preposterous claim that they had unearthed a plot*

rife [raɪf] ADJECTIVE; FORMAL
very common *e.g. Unemployment was rife.*

rifle ['raɪfᵊl] **rifles**, **rifling**, **rifled** NOUN
1 a gun with a long barrel
> VERB
2 When someone rifles something, they make a quick search through it to steal things.

rift [rɪft] **rifts** NOUN
1 a serious quarrel between friends that damages their friendship
2 a split in something solid, especially in the ground

rig [rɪg] **rigs**, **rigging**, **rigged** VERB

1 If someone rigs an election or contest, they dishonestly arrange for a particular person to succeed.

> NOUN

2 a large structure used for extracting oil or gas from the ground or sea bed **rig up** VERB

3 If you rig up a device or structure, you make it quickly and fix it in place. *e.g. They had even rigged up a makeshift aerial.*

right see page 740 for Word Web

right angle **right angles** NOUN
an angle of 90°

righteous ['raɪtʃəs] ADJECTIVE
Righteous people behave in a way that is morally good and religious.

rightful ['raɪtfʊl] ADJECTIVE
Someone's rightful possession is one which they have a moral or legal right to.
rightfully ADVERB

right-handed ['raɪtˌhændɪd] ADJECTIVE OR ADVERB
Someone who is right-handed does things such as writing and painting with their right hand.

right-wing ['raɪtˌwɪŋ] ADJECTIVE
believing more strongly in capitalism or conservatism, or less strongly in socialism, than other members of the same party or group
right-winger NOUN

● THESAURUS
conservative: *the conservative manifesto*
reactionary: *reactionary army people*
Tory: British *a senior Tory peer*

rigid ['rɪdʒɪd] ADJECTIVE
1 Rigid laws or systems cannot be changed and are considered severe.

● THESAURUS
fixed: *fixed laws*
inflexible: *Workers said the system was too inflexible.*
set: *They have very set ideas about how to achieve this.*
strict: *a strict diet*
stringent: *stringent rules*

2 A rigid object is stiff and does not bend easily.
rigidly ADVERB, **rigidity** NOUN

● THESAURUS
firm: *a firm platform*
hard: *Something cold and hard pressed into his back.*
solid: *The concrete will stay as solid as a rock.*
stiff: *Her fingers were stiff with cold.*
<<OPPOSITE flexible

rigorous ['rɪgərəs] ADJECTIVE
very careful and thorough
rigorously ADVERB

rigour ['rɪgə] **rigours** NOUN; FORMAL
The rigours of a situation are the things which make it hard or unpleasant. *e.g. the rigours of childbirth*

rim [rɪm] **rims** NOUN
the outside or top edge of an object such as a wheel or a cup

rimu ['riːmuː] **rimu** or **rimus** NOUN
a New Zealand tree with narrow, pointed leaves, which produces wood used for furniture

rind [raɪnd] **rinds** NOUN
Rind is the thick outer skin of fruit, cheese, or bacon.

ring [rɪŋ] **rings, ringing, rang, rung** VERB
1 If you ring someone, you phone them.
2 When a bell rings, it makes a clear, loud sound.

● THESAURUS
chime: *The clock chimed three o'clock.*
clang: *A little later the church bell clanged.*
peal: *Church bells pealed at the stroke of midnight.*
resonate: *a strap hung with bells and resonating gongs*
toll: *The pilgrims tolled the bell.*

3 To ring something means to draw a circle around it.

4 If something is ringed with something else, it has that thing all the way around it. *e.g. The courthouse was ringed with police.*

> NOUN

5 the sound made by a bell
6 a small circle of metal worn on your finger
7 an object or group of things in the shape of a circle

● THESAURUS
band: *a black arm-band*
circle: *Cut out four circles of pastry.*
hoop: *a steel hoop*
loop: *a loop of garden hose*
round: *small fresh rounds of goats' cheese*

8 At a boxing match or circus, the ring is the place where the fight or performance takes place.

9 an organized group of people who are involved in an illegal activity *e.g. an international spy ring*

● THESAURUS
band: *a small band of plotters*
cell: *a cell of neo-Nazis*
clique: *A small clique of people is trying to take over the party.*
syndicate: *a major crime syndicate*

> The past tense of *ring* is *rang*, and the past participle is *rung*. Do not confuse these words: *she rang the bell; I had rung the police*

ringbark ['rɪŋˌbɑːk] **ringbarks, ringbarking, ringbarked** VERB

r

1 ADJECTIVE
correct and in accordance with the facts
eg: That clock never tells the right time; That's absolutely right.

● THESAURUS

accurate: *an accurate record of events*
correct: *The correct answers can be found at the bottom of the page.*
exact: *That clock never tells the exact time.*
factual: *His version of events is not strictly factual.*
genuine: *a genuine eyewitness account*
precise: *Officials did not give precise figures.*
strict: *He has never been a playboy in the strict sense of the word.*
true: *The true cost often differs from that.*
valid: *Your point is a valid one.*
<< OPPOSITE *wrong*

2 ADJECTIVE
The right choice or decision is the best or most suitable one.

● THESAURUS

acceptable: *This was beyond the bounds of acceptable behaviour.*
appropriate: *an appropriate outfit for the occasion*
desirable: *This goal is neither achievable nor desirable.*
done: *It just isn't done to behave like that in public.*
fit: *a subject which is not fit for discussion*
fitting: *a fitting end to an exciting match*
okay or **ok** (informal): *Is it okay if I bring a friend with me?*
proper: *It was not thought proper for a woman to appear on the stage.*
seemly: *the rules of civility and seemly conduct*
suitable: *the most suitable man for the job*

right
rights, righting, righted

3 NOUN
'Right' is used to refer to principles of morally correct behaviour *eg: At least he knew right from wrong.*

● THESAURUS

fairness: *a decision based not on fairness but on expediency*
equity: *Income should be distributed with some sense of equity.*
honour: *His whole life was dominated by his sense of honour.*
integrity: *They always strove to maintain a high level of integrity.*
justice: *He has no sense of justice or fair play.*
legality: *They are expected to observe the principles of legality.*
morality: *standards of morality and justice in society*
virtue: *Virtue is not confined to the Christian world.*

If you ringbark a tree, you kill it by cutting away a strip of bark from around its trunk.

ringer ['rɪŋə] **ringers** NOUN

1 a person or thing that is almost identical to another

2 In Australian English, someone who works on a sheep farm.

3 In Australian and New Zealand English, the fastest shearer in a woolshed.

ring-in ['rɪŋ,ɪn] **ring-ins** NOUN; INFORMAL

1 In Australian English, a person or thing that is not normally a member of a particular group.

2 In Australian and New Zealand English, someone who is brought in at the last minute as a replacement for someone else.

ringleader ['rɪŋ,liːdə] **ringleaders** NOUN

the leader of a group of people who get involved in mischief or crime

rink [rɪŋk] **rinks** NOUN

a large indoor area for ice-skating or roller-skating

rinse [rɪns] **rinses, rinsing, rinsed** VERB

1 When you rinse something, you wash it in clean water.

> NOUN

2 a liquid you can put on your hair to give it a different colour

riot ['raɪət] **riots, rioting, rioted** NOUN

1 When there is a riot, a crowd of people behave noisily and violently.

● THESAURUS

anarchy: *a decade of civil war and anarchy*
disorder: *mass public disorder*
disturbance: *Three fans were injured in a violent disturbance outside a pub.*
mob violence: *last week's mob violence in Bucharest*
strife: *communal strife in Los Angeles*

> VERB

2 To riot means to behave noisily and violently.

● THESAURUS

go on the rampage: *Rock fans went on the rampage after a concert.*
rampage: *A curfew was imposed as gangs rampaged through the streets.*
run riot: *hooligans running riot in the streets*
take to the streets: *Workers and students took to the streets in protest.*

> PHRASE

3 To **run riot** means to behave in a wild and uncontrolled way.

rip [rɪp] **rips, ripping, ripped** VERB

1 When you rip something, you tear it violently.

2 If you rip something away, you remove it quickly and violently.

> NOUN

3 a long split in cloth or paper **rip off** VERB

4 INFORMAL If someone rips you off, they cheat you by charging you too much money.

RIP

RIP is an abbreviation often written on gravestones, meaning 'rest in peace'.

ripe [raɪp] **riper, ripest** ADJECTIVE

1 When fruit or grain is ripe, it is fully developed and ready to be eaten.

2 If a situation is ripe for something to happen, it is ready for it.

ripeness NOUN

ripen ['raɪpən] **ripens, ripening, ripened** VERB

When crops ripen, they become ripe.

ripper ['rɪpə] **rippers** NOUN; INFORMAL

In Australia and New Zealand English, an excellent person or thing.

ripple ['rɪpəl] **ripples, rippling, rippled** NOUN

1 Ripples are little waves on the surface of calm water.

2 If there is a ripple of laughter or applause, people laugh or applaud gently for a short time.

> VERB

3 When the surface of water ripples, little waves appear on it.

rise [raɪz] **rises, rising, rose, risen** VERB

1 If something rises, it moves upwards.

● THESAURUS

ascend: *He held her hand as they ascended the steps.*
climb: *We climbed up the steps on to the bridge.*
go up: *He went up the ladder quickly.*
move up: *They moved up to second place after their win.*

2 FORMAL

When you rise, you stand up.

3 To rise also means to get out of bed.

4 When the sun rises, it first appears.

5 The place where a river rises is where it begins.

6 If land rises, it slopes upwards.

7 If a sound or wind rises, it becomes higher or stronger.

8 If an amount rises, it increases.

● THESAURUS

go up: *Life expectancy has gone up from 50 to 58.*
grow: *The Chinese economy continues to grow.*
increase: *the decision to increase prices*

r

intensify: *The conflict is bound to intensify.*
mount: *For several hours the tension mounted.*
<<OPPOSITE *fall*

9 If you rise to a challenge or a remark, you respond to it rather than ignoring it. *e.g. He rose to the challenge with enthusiasm.*

10 When people rise up, they start fighting against people in authority.

> NOUN

11 an increase

● THESAURUS

improvement: *a major improvement in standards*
increase: *a substantial increase in workload*
upsurge: *an upsurge of interest in books*
<<OPPOSITE *fall*

12 Someone's rise is the process by which they become more powerful or successful. *e.g. his rise to fame*

riser ['raɪzə] **risers** NOUN
An early riser is someone who likes to get up early in the morning.

risk [rɪsk] **risks, risking, risked** NOUN
1 a chance that something unpleasant or dangerous might happen

● THESAURUS

danger: *the dangers of smoking*
gamble: *Booking a holiday can be a gamble.*
peril: *the perils of starring in a TV commercial*
pitfall: *the pitfalls of working abroad*

> VERB

2 If you risk something unpleasant, you do something knowing that the unpleasant thing might happen as a result. *e.g. If he doesn't play, he risks losing his place in the team.*

● THESAURUS

chance: *No assassin would chance a shot from amongst that crowd.*
dare: *Few people dared go anywhere on foot.*
gamble: *gambling his life savings on the stock market*
jeopardize: *The talks may still be jeopardized by disputes.*
put in jeopardy: *A series of setbacks have put the whole project in jeopardy.*

3 If you risk someone's life, you put them in a dangerous situation in which they might be killed.

risky ADJECTIVE
[WORD HISTORY: from Italian RISCHIARE meaning 'to be in danger']

rite [raɪt] **rites** NOUN
a religious ceremony

ritual ['rɪtjʊəl] **rituals** NOUN
1 a series of actions carried out according to the custom of a particular society or group *e.g. This is*

the most ancient of the Buddhist rituals.

> ADJECTIVE

2 Ritual activities happen as part of a tradition or ritual. *e.g. fasting and ritual dancing*
ritualistic ADJECTIVE

rival ['raɪvᵊl] **rivals, rivalling, rivalled** NOUN
1 Your rival is the person you are competing with.

● THESAURUS

adversary: *political adversaries*
antagonist: *Greece's key rival and chief antagonist, Turkey.* **challenger**: *his only challenger for the presidency*
opponent: *He's a tough opponent but I'm too good for him.*

> VERB

2 If something rivals something else, it is of the same high standard or quality. *e.g. As a holiday destination, South Africa rivals Kenya for weather.*

● THESAURUS

be a match for: *On our day we are a match for anyone.*
equal: *The victory equalled Portugal's best in history.*
match: *I think we matched them in every department.*

rivalry ['raɪvəlrɪ] **rivalries** NOUN
Rivalry is active competition between people.

river ['rɪvə] **rivers** NOUN
a natural feature consisting of water flowing for a long distance between two banks

rivet ['rɪvɪt] **rivets** NOUN
a short, round pin with a flat head which is used to fasten sheets of metal together

riveting ['rɪvətɪŋ] ADJECTIVE
If you find something riveting, you find it fascinating and it holds your attention. *e.g. I find tennis riveting.*

road [rəʊd] **roads** NOUN
a long piece of hard ground specially surfaced so that people and vehicles can travel along it easily

● THESAURUS

motorway: *Britain's first motorway, the M1.* **route**: *the most direct route to the town centre*
street: *He walked briskly down the street.*
track: *a rough mountain track*

road map road maps NOUN
1 a map intended for drivers

2 a plan or guide for future actions *e.g. a road map for peace*

road rage NOUN
Road rage is aggressive behaviour by a driver as a reaction to the behaviour of another driver.

road train road trains NOUN
In Australia, a line of linked trailers pulled by a

truck, used for transporting cattle or sheep.

roadworks ['rəʊd,wɜːks] PLURAL NOUN
Roadworks are repairs being done on a road.

roam [rəʊm] **roams, roaming, roamed**
VERB
If you roam around, you wander around without any particular purpose. *e.g. Hens were roaming around the yard.*

roar [rɔː] **roars, roaring, roared** VERB
1 If something roars, it makes a very loud noise.
2 To roar with laughter or anger means to laugh or shout very noisily.
3 When a lion roars, it makes a loud, angry sound.
> NOUN
4 a very loud noise

roast [rəʊst] **roasts, roasting, roasted** VERB
1 When you roast meat or other food, you cook it using dry heat in an oven or over a fire.
> ADJECTIVE
2 Roast meat has been roasted.
> NOUN
3 a piece of meat that has been roasted

rob [rɒb] **robs, robbing, robbed** VERB
1 If someone robs you, they steal your possessions.
● **THESAURUS**
burgle: *He admitted that he was trying to burgle the surgery.*
con: *informal The businessman had conned him of $10,000.*
defraud: *charges of conspiracy to defraud the government*
loot: *thugs who have looted shops*
steal from: *trying to steal from a woman in the street*
swindle: *two executives who swindled their employer*
2 If you rob someone of something they need or deserve, you deprive them of it. *e.g. He robbed me of my childhood.*

robber ['rɒbə] **robbers** NOUN
Robbers are people who steal money or property using force or threats. *e.g. bank robbers*
robbery NOUN

robe [rəʊb] **robes** NOUN
a long, loose piece of clothing which covers the body *e.g. He knelt in his white robes before the altar.*

robin ['rɒbɪn] **robins** NOUN
a small bird with a red breast

robot ['rəʊbɒt] **robots** NOUN
a machine which is programmed to move and perform tasks automatically

[WORD HISTORY: from Czech ROBOTA meaning 'work']

robust [rəʊ'bʌst] ADJECTIVE
very strong and healthy
robustly ADVERB

rock [rɒk] **rocks, rocking, rocked** NOUN
1 Rock is the hard mineral substance that forms the surface of the earth.
2 a large piece of rock *e.g. She picked up a rock and threw it into the lake.*
3 Rock or rock music is music with simple tunes and a very strong beat.
4 Rock is also a sweet shaped into long, hard sticks, sold in holiday resorts.
> VERB
5 When something rocks or when you rock it, it moves regularly backwards and forwards or from side to side. *e.g. She rocked the baby.*
6 If something rocks people, it shocks and upsets them. *e.g. Palermo was rocked by a crime wave.*
7 If someone's marriage or relationship is **on the rocks**, it is unsuccessful and about to end.

rock and roll NOUN
Rock and roll is a style of music with a strong beat that was especially popular in the 1950s.

rocket ['rɒkɪt] **rockets, rocketing, rocketed** NOUN
1 a space vehicle, usually shaped like a long pointed tube
2 an explosive missile *e.g. They fired rockets into a number of government buildings.*
3 a firework that explodes when it is high in the air
> VERB
4 If prices rocket, they increase very quickly.

rocking chair ['rɒkɪŋ] **rocking chairs** NOUN
a chair on two curved pieces of wood that rocks backwards and forwards when you sit in it

rock melon rock melons NOUN
In Australian, New Zealand, and American English a rock melon is a cantaloupe, a melon with orange flesh and a hard, lumpy skin.

rocky ['rɒkɪ] ADJECTIVE
covered with rocks

rod [rɒd] **rods** NOUN
a long, thin pole or bar, usually made of wood or metal *e.g. a fishing rod*

rodent ['rəʊdᵊnt] **rodents** NOUN
a small mammal with sharp front teeth which it uses for gnawing
[WORD HISTORY: from Latin RODERE meaning 'to gnaw']

r

rodeo ['rəʊdɪˌəʊ] **rodeos** NOUN
a public entertainment in which cowboys show different skills

roe [rəʊ] NOUN
Roe is the eggs of a fish.

rogue [rəʊg] **rogues** NOUN
1 You can refer to a man who behaves dishonestly as a rogue.
> ADJECTIVE
2 a vicious animal that lives apart from its herd or pack

role [rəʊl] **roles**; also spelt **rôle** NOUN
1 Someone's role is their position and function in a situation or society.
2 (**DRAMA**) An actor's role is the character that he or she plays. *e.g. her first leading role*

roll [rəʊl] **rolls, rolling, rolled** VERB
1 When something rolls or when you roll it, it moves along a surface, turning over and over.
2 When vehicles roll along, they move. *e.g. Tanks rolled into the village.*
3 If you roll your eyes, you make them turn up or go from side to side.
4 If you roll something flexible into a cylinder or ball, you wrap it several times around itself. *e.g. He rolled up the bag with the money in it.*
> NOUN
5 A roll of paper or cloth is a long piece of it that has been rolled into a tube. *e.g. a roll of film*
6 a small, rounded, individually baked piece of bread
7 an official list of people's names *e.g. the electoral roll*
8 A roll on a drum is a long, rumbling sound made on it.

roll-call ['rəʊlˌkɔːl] **roll-calls** NOUN
If you take a roll-call, you call a register of names to see who is present.

roller ['rəʊlə] **rollers** NOUN
1 a cylinder that turns round in a machine or piece of equipment
2 Rollers are tubes which you can wind your hair around to make it curly.

Rollerblade ['rəʊləˌbleɪd] **Rollerblades**
NOUN; TRADEMARK
Rollerblades are roller-skates which have the wheels set in one straight line on the bottom of the boot.

roller-coaster ['rəʊləˌkəʊstə] **roller-coasters** NOUN
a pleasure ride at a fair, consisting of a small railway that goes up and down very steep slopes

roller-skate ['rəʊləˌskeɪt] **roller-skates, roller-skating, roller-skated** NOUN
1 Roller-skates are shoes with four small wheels underneath.
> VERB
2 If you roller-skate, you move along wearing roller-skates.

rolling pin ['rəʊlɪŋ] **rolling pins** NOUN
a wooden cylinder used for rolling pastry dough to make it flat

ROM [rɒm] NOUN
In computing, ROM is a storage device that holds data permanently and cannot be altered by the programmer. ROM stands for 'read only memory'.

Roman Catholic ['rəʊmən] **Roman Catholics** ADJECTIVE
1 relating or belonging to the branch of the Christian church that accepts the Pope in Rome as its leader
> NOUN
2 someone who belongs to the Roman Catholic church
Roman Catholicism NOUN

romance [rə'mæns] *or* ['rəʊmæns] **romances** NOUN
1 a relationship between two people who are in love with each other
2 Romance is the pleasure and excitement of doing something new and unusual. *e.g. the romance of foreign travel*
3 (**LIBRARY**) a novel about a love affair

Romanian [rəʊ'meɪnɪən] **Romanians**; also spelt **Rumanian** ADJECTIVE
1 belonging or relating to Romania
> NOUN
2 someone who comes from Romania
3 Romanian is the main language spoken in Romania.

romantic [rəʊ'mæntɪk] **romantics**
ADJECTIVE OR NOUN
1 A romantic person has ideas that are not realistic, for example about love or about ways of changing society. *e.g. a romantic idealist*
> ADJECTIVE
2 connected with sexual love *e.g. a romantic relationship*

● THESAURUS
amorous: *The object of his amorous intentions is Wendy.*
loving: *a loving husband*
passionate: *a passionate love affair*

tender: *They embraced and kissed. It was a tender moment.*

3 Something that is romantic is beautiful in a way that strongly affects your feelings. *e.g. It is one of the most romantic ruins in Scotland.*

4 Romantic describes a style of music, literature, and art popular in Europe in the late 18th and early 19th centuries, which emphasized feeling and imagination rather than order and form. **romantically** ADVERB, **romanticism** NOUN

rondavel ['rɒndɑːvəl] **rondavels** NOUN
In South Africa, a rondavel is a small circular building with a conical roof.

roo [ruː] **roos** NOUN; INFORMAL
In Australian English, a kangaroo.

roof [ruːf] **roofs** NOUN
1 The roof of a building or car is the covering on top of it.
2 The roof of your mouth or of a cave is the highest part.

roofing ['ruːfɪŋ] NOUN
Roofing is material used for covering roofs.

rooftop ['ruːfˌtɒp] **rooftops** NOUN
the outside part of the roof of a building

rook [rʊk] **rooks** NOUN
1 a large black bird
2 a chess piece which can move any number of squares in a straight but not diagonal line

room [ruːm] **rooms** NOUN
1 a separate section in a building, divided from other rooms by walls

● THESAURUS
chamber: *the council chamber*
office: *I'm in the office at the end of the corridor.*

2 If there is plenty of room, there is a lot of space. *e.g. There wasn't enough room for his gear.*

● THESAURUS
capacity: *a seating capacity of 17,000*
elbow room: *There wasn't too much elbow room in the cockpit.*
space: *the high cost of office space*

roost [ruːst] **roosts, roosting, roosted**
NOUN
1 a place where birds rest or build their nests
> VERB
2 When birds roost, they settle somewhere for the night.

root [ruːt] **roots, rooting, rooted** NOUN
1 The roots of a plant are the parts that grow under the ground.
2 The root of a hair is the part beneath the skin.
3 You can refer to the place or culture that you grew up in as your roots.

4 The root of something is its original cause or basis. *e.g. We got to the root of the problem.*
> VERB
5 To root through things means to search through them, pushing them aside. *e.g. She rooted through his bag.* **root out** VERB
6 If you root something or someone out, you find them and force them out. *e.g. a major drive to root out corruption*

rooted ['ruːtɪd] ADJECTIVE
developed from or strongly influenced by something *e.g. songs rooted in traditional African music*

rope [rəʊp] **ropes, roping, roped** NOUN
1 a thick, strong length of twisted cord
> VERB
2 If you rope one thing to another, you tie them together with rope.

rosary ['rəʊzərɪ] **rosaries** NOUN
a string of beads that Catholics use for counting prayers

rose [rəʊz] **roses** NOUN
1 a large garden flower which has a pleasant smell and grows on a bush with thorns
> NOUN or ADJECTIVE
2 reddish-pink

rosella [rəʊ'zɛlə] **rosellas** NOUN
a brightly coloured Australian parrot

rosemary ['rəʊzmərɪ] NOUN
Rosemary is a herb with fragrant spiky leaves, used for flavouring in cooking.

rosette [rəʊ'zɛt] **rosettes** NOUN
a large badge of coloured ribbons gathered into a circle, which is worn as a prize in a competition or to support a political party

Rosh Hashanah or **Rosh Hashana** ['rɒʃ həˈʃɑːnə] NOUN
the festival celebrating the Jewish New Year
[WORD HISTORY: a Hebrew phrase meaning 'head of the year']

roster ['rɒstə] **rosters** NOUN
a list of people who take it in turn to do a particular job *e.g. He put himself first on the new roster for domestic chores.*

rostrum ['rɒstrəm] **rostrums** or **rostra**
NOUN
a raised platform on which someone stands to speak to an audience or conduct an orchestra
[WORD HISTORY: from Latin ROSTRUM meaning 'ship's prow'; Roman orators' platforms were decorated with the prows of captured ships]

rosy ['rəʊzɪ] **rosier, rosiest** ADJECTIVE
1 reddish-pink

r

2 If a situation seems rosy, it is likely to be good or successful.

3 If a person looks rosy, they have pink cheeks and look healthy.

rot [rɒt] **rots, rotting, rotted** VERB

1 When food or wood rots, it decays and can no longer be used.

THESAURUS

decay: *The bodies buried in the fine ash slowly decayed.*

decompose: *The debris slowly decomposes into compost.*

fester: *The wound is festering and gangrene has set in.*

spoil: *Fats spoil by becoming rancid.*

2 When something rots another substance, it causes it to decay. *e.g. Sugary drinks rot your teeth.*

> NOUN

3 Rot is the condition that affects things when they rot. *e.g. The timber frame was not protected against rot.*

THESAURUS

decay: *tooth decay*

deterioration: *gum deterioration*

mould: *He scraped the mould off the cheese.*

rota ['rəʊtə] **rotas** NOUN

a list of people who take turns to do a particular job

rotate [rəʊ'teɪt] **rotates, rotating, rotated** VERB

(MATHS) When something rotates, it turns with a circular movement. *e.g. He rotated the camera 180°.*

rotation NOUN

rotor ['rəʊtə] **rotors** NOUN

1 The rotor is the part of a machine that turns.

2 The rotors or rotor blades of a helicopter are the four long flat pieces of metal on top of it which rotate and lift it off the ground.

rotten ['rɒtªn] ADJECTIVE

1 decayed and no longer of use *e.g. The front bay window is rotten.*

THESAURUS

bad: *That milk in the fridge is bad.*

decayed: *teeth so decayed they need to be pulled*

decomposed: *The body was too badly decomposed to be identified at once.*

mouldy: *mouldy bread*

sour: *sour milk*

2 INFORMAL

of very poor quality *e.g. I think it's a rotten idea.*

THESAURUS

inferior: *overpriced and inferior products*

lousy: slang *The menu is limited and the food is lousy.*

poor: *The wine was very poor.*

unsatisfactory: *if you have obtained unsatisfactory goods or services*

3 INFORMAL

very unfair, unkind, or unpleasant *e.g. That's a rotten thing to say!.*

rouble ['ruːbªl] **roubles** NOUN

the main unit of currency in Russia

[WORD HISTORY: In Russian RUBL means literally 'silver bar']

rough [rʌf] **rougher, roughest; roughs**

ADJECTIVE

1 uneven and not smooth

THESAURUS

bumpy: *bumpy cobbled streets*

craggy: *craggy mountains*

rocky: *a bleak and rocky shore*

rugged: *a remote and rugged plateau*

uneven: *The ball bobbled awkwardly on the uneven surface.*

<<OPPOSITE smooth

2 not using enough care or gentleness *e.g. Don't be so rough or you'll break it.*

3 difficult or unpleasant *e.g. Teachers have been given a rough time.*

THESAURUS

difficult: *It's been a difficult month for us.*

hard: *I've had a hard life.*

tough: *She had a pretty tough childhood.*

unpleasant: *The last few weeks here have been very unpleasant.*

4 approximately correct *e.g. At a rough guess it is five times more profitable.*

THESAURUS

approximate: *The times are approximate only.*

estimated: *There are an estimated 90,000 gangsters in the country.*

sketchy: *a sketchy account of the incident*

vague: *She could only give a vague description of the intruder.*

5 If the sea is rough, there are large waves because of bad weather.

6 A rough town or area has a lot of crime or violence.

> NOUN or ADJECTIVE

7 A rough or a rough sketch is a drawing or description that shows the main features but does not show the details.

8 On a golf course, the rough is the part of the course next to a fairway where the grass has not been cut.

roughly ADVERB, **roughness** NOUN

roulette [ruː'lɛt] NOUN

Roulette is a gambling game in which a ball is

dropped onto a revolving wheel with numbered holes in it.

round [raʊnd] **rounder, roundest; rounds, rounding, rounded** ADJECTIVE

1 Something round is shaped like a ball or a circle.

THESAURUS
circular: *a circular hole twelve feet wide*
cylindrical: *a cylindrical container*
rounded: *a low rounded hill*
spherical: *gold spherical earrings*

2 complete or whole *e.g. round numbers*

> PREPOSITION or ADVERB

3 If something is round something else, it surrounds it.

4 The distance round something is the length of its circumference or boundary. *e.g. I'm about two inches larger round the waist.*

5 You can refer to an area near a place as the area round it. *e.g. There's nothing to do round here.*

> PREPOSITION

6 If something moves round you, it keeps moving in a circle with you in the centre.

7 When someone goes to the other side of something, they have gone round it.

> ADVERB or PREPOSITION

8 If you go round a place, you go to different parts of it to look at it. *e.g. We went round the museum.*

> ADVERB

9 If you turn or look round, you turn so you are facing in a different direction.

10 When someone comes round, they visit you. *e.g. He came round with a bottle of wine.*

> NOUN

11 one of a series of events *e.g. After round three, two Americans shared the lead.*

THESAURUS
lap: *the last lap of the race*
period: *the second period of extra time*
session: *The World Champion was ahead after the first two sessions.*
stage: *the second stage of the Tour de France*

12 If you buy a round of drinks, you buy a drink for each member of the group you are with.
round up VERB

13 If you round up people or animals, you gather them together.

roundabout ['raʊndə,baʊt] **roundabouts** NOUN

1 a meeting point of several roads with a circle in the centre which vehicles have to travel around

2 a circular platform which rotates and which children can ride on in a playground

3 the same as a merry-go-round

rounded ['raʊndɪd] ADJECTIVE
curved in shape, without any points or sharp edges

rounders ['raʊndəz] NOUN
a game played by two teams, in which a player scores points by hitting a ball and running around four sides of a square pitch

round-the-clock ['raʊndðə'klɒk] ADJECTIVE
happening continuously

rouse [raʊz] **rouses, rousing, roused** VERB

1 If someone rouses you, they wake you up.

2 If you rouse yourself to do something, you make yourself get up and do it.

3 If something rouses you, it makes you feel very emotional and excited.

rouseabout ['raʊsə,baʊt] **rouseabouts** NOUN
In Australian and New Zealand English, an unskilled worker who does odd jobs, especially on a farm.

rout [raʊt] **routs, routing, routed** VERB
To rout your opponents means to defeat them completely and easily.

route [ruːt] **routes** NOUN
a way from one place to another

THESAURUS
channel: *a safe channel avoiding the reefs*
course: *The ship was on a course that followed the coastline.*
itinerary: *The next place on our itinerary was Silistra.*
path: *We followed the path along the clifftops.*
road: *The coastal road is longer, but more scenic.*
way: *I'm afraid I can't remember the way.*

routine [ruː'tiːn] **routines** ADJECTIVE

1 Routine activities are done regularly.

THESAURUS
everyday: *an everyday occurrence*
normal: *The hospital claimed they were following their normal procedure.*
ordinary: *It was just an ordinary weekend for us.*
regular: *one of the regular checks we carry out*
standard: *It was standard practice for untrained clerks to do this work.*
typical: *This was a fairly typical morning scene in our house.*
usual: *The usual methods were not effective.*

> NOUN

2 the usual way or order in which you do things

THESAURUS
order: *Babies respond well to order in their daily lives.*
pattern: *All three attacks followed the same pattern.*

r

practice: *a public inquiry into bank practices*
procedure: *The White House said there would be no change in procedure.*
programme: *It is best to follow some sort of structured programme.*
schedule: *He has been forced to adjust his schedule.*
system: *an efficient filing system*

3 a boring repetition of tasks
routinely ADVERB

roving ['rəʊvɪŋ] ADJECTIVE
1 wandering or roaming *e.g. roving gangs of youths*
2 not restricted to any particular location or area *e.g. a roving reporter*

row [rəʊ] **rows, rowing, rowed** NOUN
1 A row of people or things is several of them arranged in a line.

● THESAURUS
bank: *a bank of video screens*
column: *a column of figures*
line: *a sparse line of spectators*
queue: *a queue of shoppers*
rank: *a rank of taxis*

> VERB
2 When you row a boat, you use oars to make it move through the water.

row [raʊ] **rows, rowing, rowed** NOUN
1 a serious argument

● THESAURUS
altercation: *He had an altercation with the umpire.*
argument: *an argument about money*
quarrel: *I had a terrible quarrel with my brother.*
squabble: *There have been minor squabbles about phone bills.*

2 If someone is making a row, they are making too much noise.

> VERB
3 If people are rowing, they are quarrelling noisily.

rowdy ['raʊdɪ] **rowdier, rowdiest** ADJECTIVE
rough and noisy

● THESAURUS
boisterous: *Most of the children were noisy and boisterous.*
noisy: *My neighbours are a noisy bunch.*
unruly: *a mother accompanied by her ghastly unruly child*
wild: *They loved fast cars and wild parties.*

royal ['rɔɪəl] **royals** ADJECTIVE
1 belonging to or involving a queen, a king, or a member of their family

● THESAURUS
imperial: *the Imperial palace in Tokyo*
regal: *Never has she looked more regal.*
sovereign: *the Queen's sovereign authority*

2 'Royal' is used in the names of organizations appointed or supported by a member of a royal family

> NOUN
3 INFORMAL
Members of the royal family are sometimes referred to as the royals.

royalist ['rɔɪəlɪst] **royalists** NOUN
someone who supports their country's royal family

royalty ['rɔɪəltɪ] **royalties** NOUN
1 The members of a royal family are sometimes referred to as royalty.
2 Royalties are payments made to authors and musicians from the sales of their books or records.

rub [rʌb] **rubs, rubbing, rubbed** VERB
1 If you rub something, you move your hand or a cloth backwards and forwards over it. **rub out** VERB
2 To rub out something written means to remove it by rubbing it with a rubber or a cloth.

rubber ['rʌbə] **rubbers** NOUN
1 Rubber is a strong, elastic substance used for making tyres, boots, and other products.
2 a small piece of rubber used to rub out pencil mistakes

rubbish ['rʌbɪʃ] NOUN
1 Rubbish is unwanted things or waste material.

● THESAURUS
garbage: *I found all kinds of garbage left behind by the tide.*
litter: *fines for dropping litter*
refuse: *The Council made a weekly collection of refuse.*
trash: *The yards are overgrown and covered with trash.*
waste: *the safe disposal of toxic waste*

2 You can refer to nonsense or something of very poor quality as rubbish.

● THESAURUS
drivel: *mindless drivel*
garbage: *I personally think this is complete garbage.*
hot air: informal *His justification was just hot air.*
nonsense: *all that poetic nonsense about love*
rot: *What a load of pompous rot!*

rubble ['rʌbəl] NOUN
Bits of old brick and stone are referred to as rubble.

rubric ['ruːbrɪk] **rubrics** NOUN; FORMAL
a set of instructions at the beginning of an official document

ruby [ˈruːbɪ] **rubies** NOUN
a type of red jewel

rucksack [ˈrʌkˌsæk] **rucksacks** NOUN
a bag with shoulder straps for carrying things on your back

rudder [ˈrʌdə] **rudders** NOUN
a piece of wood or metal at the back of a boat or plane which is moved to make the boat or plane turn

rude [ruːd] **ruder, rudest** ADJECTIVE
1 not polite

● THESAURUS
disrespectful: *They shouldn't treat their mother in this disrespectful way.*
impertinent: *I don't like being asked impertinent questions.*
impudent: *his rude and impudent behaviour*
insolent: *a defiant, almost insolent look*
<<OPPOSITE *polite*

2 embarrassing or offensive because of reference to sex or other bodily functions *e.g. rude jokes*
3 unexpected and unpleasant *e.g. a rude awakening*
rudely ADVERB, **rudeness** NOUN

● THESAURUS
abrupt: *The recession brought an abrupt end to his happiness.*
unpleasant: *an unpleasant surprise*
violent: *violent mood swings*

rudimentary [ˌruːdɪˈmɛntərɪ] ADJECTIVE;
FORMAL
very basic or not developed *e.g. He had only a rudimentary knowledge of French.*

rudiments [ˈruːdɪmənts] PLURAL NOUN
When you learn the rudiments of something, you learn only the simplest and most basic things about it.
[WORD HISTORY: from Latin RUDIMENTUM meaning 'beginning']

ruff [rʌf] **ruffs** NOUN
1 a stiff circular collar with many pleats in it, worn especially in the 16th century
2 a thick band of fur or feathers around the neck of a bird or animal

ruffle [ˈrʌfəl] **ruffles, ruffling, ruffled** VERB
1 If you ruffle someone's hair, you move your hand quickly backwards and forwards over their head.
2 If something ruffles you, it makes you annoyed or upset.
> NOUN
3 Ruffles are small folds made in a piece of material for decoration.

rug [rʌg] **rugs** NOUN

1 a small, thick carpet
2 a blanket which you can use to cover your knees or for sitting on outdoors

rugby [ˈrʌgbɪ] NOUN
Rugby is a game played by two teams, who try to kick and throw an oval ball to their opponents' end of the pitch. Rugby League is played with 13 players in each side, Rugby Union is played with 15 players in each side.

rugged [ˈrʌgɪd] ADJECTIVE
1 rocky and wild *e.g. the rugged west coast of Ireland*
2 having strong features *e.g. his rugged good looks*

rugger [ˈrʌgə] NOUN
Rugger is the same as rugby.

ruin [ˈruːɪn] **ruins, ruining, ruined** VERB
1 If you ruin something, you destroy or spoil it completely.

● THESAURUS
break: *He's broken all his toys.*
damage: *This could damage our chances of winning.*
destroy: *a recipe for destroying the economy*
devastate: *A fire had devastated large parts of the castle.*
impair: *The flavour is impaired by overcooking.*
mar: *The celebrations were marred by violence.*
mess up: *He's messed up his whole career.*
spoil: *Don't let a stupid mistake spoil your life.*
undo: *He intends to undo everything I have fought for.*
wreck: *He wrecked the garden.*

2 If someone is ruined, they have lost all their money.
> NOUN
3 Ruin is the state of being destroyed or completely spoilt.

● THESAURUS
decay: *The house fell into a state of decay.*
destruction: *the destruction caused by the rioters*
devastation: *A bomb brought chaos and devastation to the city centre yesterday.*
disrepair: *Many of the buildings had fallen into disrepair.*
downfall: *His lack of experience led to his downfall.*
fall: *the fall of the Roman empire*

4 A ruin or the ruins of something refers to the parts that are left after it has been severely damaged. *e.g. the ruins of a thirteenth-century monastery*

● THESAURUS
remains: *the remains of an ancient mosque*
shell: *the shells of burned buildings*
wreck: *We thought of buying the house as a wreck and doing it up.*

rule [ruːl] **rules, ruling, ruled** NOUN

r

1 Rules are statements which tell you what you are allowed to do.

● THESAURUS

decree: *a decree lifting sanctions against China*
guideline: *Are there strict guidelines for animal experimentation?*
law: *inflexible moral laws*
order: *He was sacked for disobeying orders.*
regulation: *new safety regulations*

> VERB

2 To rule a country or group of people means to have power over it and be in charge of its affairs.

● THESAURUS

administer: *calls for the UN to administer the country until the election*
be in power: *They were in power for eighteen years.*
govern: *The citizens are thankful they are not governed by a dictator.*
lead: *He led the country between 1949 and 1984.*
reign: *Henry II reigned from 1154 to 1189.*

3 FORMAL
When someone in authority rules on a particular matter, they give an official decision about it.

> PHRASE

4 As a rule, means usually or generally *e.g. As a rule, I eat my meals in front of the TV.* **rule out**

● THESAURUS

adverb rule02 **generally:** *It is generally true that the darker the fruit the higher its iron content.*
mainly: *Mainly I work alone.*
normally: *Normally, the transport system carries 50,000 passengers a day.*
on the whole: *Their wines are, on the whole, of a very high standard.*
usually: *She is usually a calm and diplomatic woman.*

> VERB

5 If you rule out an idea or course of action, you reject it.

6 If one thing rules out another, it prevents it from happening or being possible. *e.g. The accident ruled out a future for him in football.*

ruler ['ruːlə] **rulers** NOUN

1 a person who rules a country

● THESAURUS

commander: *He is commander of the US Fifth Fleet.*
governor: *He was governor of the province in the late 1970s.*
head of state: *the heads of state of all the countries in the European Union*
leader: *the leader of the German Social Democratic Party*
monarch: *the coronation of the new monarch*
sovereign: *the first British sovereign to set foot on Spanish soil*

2 a long, flat piece of wood or plastic with straight edges marked in centimetres or inches,

used for measuring or drawing straight lines

rum [rʌm] NOUN
Rum is a strong alcoholic drink made from sugar cane juice.

Rumanian [rəʊˈmeɪnɪən] another spelling of **Romanian**

rumble [ˈrʌmbəl] **rumbles, rumbling, rumbled** VERB

1 If something rumbles, it makes a continuous low noise. *e.g. Another train rumbled past the house.*

> NOUN

2 a continuous low noise *e.g. the distant rumble of traffic*

rummage [ˈrʌmɪdʒ] **rummages, rummaging, rummaged** VERB
If you rummage somewhere, you search for something, moving things about carelessly.

rumour [ˈruːmə] **rumours, rumoured** NOUN

1 a story that people are talking about, which may or may not be true

● THESAURUS

gossip: *We spent the first hour exchanging gossip.*
hearsay: *Much of what was reported to them was hearsay.*
whisper: *I've heard a whisper that the Bishop intends to leave.*
word: *What's the latest word from Washington?*

> VERB

2 If something is rumoured, people are suggesting that it is has happened.
[WORD HISTORY: from Latin RUMOR meaning 'common talk']

rump [rʌmp] **rumps** NOUN

1 An animal's rump is its rear end.

2 Rump or rump steak is meat cut from the rear end of a cow.

run see page 751 for Word Web

runaway [ˈrʌnəˌweɪ] **runaways** NOUN
a person who has escaped from a place or left it secretly and hurriedly

rundown [ˈrʌnˌdaʊn] ADJECTIVE

1 tired and not well

2 neglected and in poor condition

> NOUN

3 INFORMAL
If you give someone the rundown on a situation, you tell them the basic, important facts about it.

rung [rʌŋ] **rungs** NOUN
The rungs on a ladder are the bars that form the steps.

runner [ˈrʌnə] **runners** NOUN

1 VERB

When you run, you move quickly, leaving the ground during each stride.

● **THESAURUS**

bolt: *The pig rose, squealing, and bolted.*

gallop: *The horses galloped away.*

jog: *He could scarcely jog around the block that first day.*

sprint: *She sprinted to the car.*

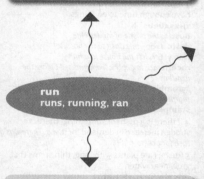

run
runs, running, ran

2 VERB

If you run a business or an activity, you are in charge of it.

● **THESAURUS**

administer: *the authorities who administer the island*

be in charge of: *He is in charge of public safety.*

control: *He now controls a large retail development empire.*

direct: *Christopher will direct day-to-day operations.*

look after: *I look after his finances for him.*

manage: *Within two years he was managing the store.*

3 VERB

if something runs it dissolves and spreads
eg: the soles of the shoes peeled off and the colours ran

● **THESAURUS**

bleed: *The blue paint should not bleed into the red.*

spread: *A dark red stain spread across his shirt.*

r

1 a person who runs, especially as a sport

2 a person who takes messages or runs errands

3 A runner on a plant such as a strawberry is a long shoot from which a new plant develops.

4 The runners on drawers and ice skates are the thin strips on which they move.

runner bean **runner beans** NOUN
Runner beans are long green pods eaten as a vegetable, which grow on a climbing plant.

runner-up [ˌrʌnəˈʌp] **runners-up** NOUN
a person or team that comes second in a race or competition

running [ˈrʌnɪŋ] ADJECTIVE

1 continuing without stopping over a period of time *e.g. a running commentary*

2 Running water is flowing rather than standing still.

runny [ˈrʌni] **runnier, runniest** ADJECTIVE

1 more liquid than usual *e.g. Warm the honey until it becomes runny.*

2 If someone's nose or eyes are runny, liquid is coming out of them.

runt [rʌnt] **runts** NOUN
The runt of a litter of animals is the smallest and weakest.

runway [ˈrʌnˌweɪ] **runways** NOUN
a long strip of ground used by aeroplanes for taking off or landing

rupee [ruːˈpiː] **rupees** NOUN
the main unit of currency in India, Pakistan, and some other countries

rupture [ˈrʌptʃə] **ruptures, rupturing, ruptured** NOUN

1 a severe injury in which part of your body tears or bursts open

> VERB

2 To rupture part of the body means to cause it to tear or burst. *e.g. a ruptured spleen*

rural [ˈrʊərəl] ADJECTIVE
(GEOGRAPHY) relating to or involving the countryside

ruse [ruːz] **ruses** NOUN; FORMAL
an action which is intended to trick someone

rush [rʌʃ] **rushes, rushing, rushed** VERB

1 To rush means to move fast or do something quickly.

● THESAURUS
dash: *She dashed in from the garden.*
fly: *I must fly or I'll miss my train.*
gush: *Piping-hot water gushed out.*
hasten: *One of them hastened towards me.*
hurry: *She had to hurry home to look after her son.*

race: *He raced across town to her house.*
run: *I excused myself and ran to the door.*
scurry: *Reporters scurried to get to the phones.*
shoot: *The car shot out of a junction and smashed into them.*

2 If you rush someone into doing something, you make them do it without allowing them enough time to think.

● THESAURUS
hurry: *I don't want to hurry you.*
hustle: *You won't hustle me into making a commitment.*
press: *attempting to press me into making a statement*
pressurize: *Do not be pressurized into making your decision immediately.* **push:** *Don't be pushed into signing anything.*

> NOUN

3 If you are in a rush, you are busy and do not have enough time to do things.

● THESAURUS
bustle: *the bustle of modern life*
dash: *a 160-mile dash to the hospital*
hurry: *Eric left the house in a hurry.*
race: *a race to get the work finished before the deadline*
scramble: *the scramble to get a seat on the early morning flight*
stampede: *There was a stampede for the exit.*

4 If there is a rush for something, there is a sudden increase in demand for it. *e.g. There was a rush for tickets.*

5 Rushes are plants with long, thin stems that grow near water.

rush hour **rush hours** NOUN
The rush hour is one of the busy parts of the day when most people are travelling to or from work.

rusk [rʌsk] **rusks** NOUN
a hard, dry biscuit given to babies

Russian [ˈrʌʃən] **Russians,** ADJECTIVE

1 belonging or relating to Russia

> NOUN

2 someone who comes from Russia

3 Russian is the main language spoken in Russia.

rust [rʌst] **rusts, rusting, rusted** NOUN

1 Rust is a reddish-brown substance that forms on iron or steel which has been in contact with water and which is decaying gradually.

> NOUN or ADJECTIVE

2 reddish-brown

> VERB

3 When a metal object rusts, it becomes covered in rust.

rustic [ˈrʌstɪk] ADJECTIVE
simple in a way considered to be typical of the countryside *e.g. a rustic old log cabin*

rustle ['rʌsᵊl] **rustles, rustling, rustled**
VERB
When something rustles, it makes soft sounds as
it moves.
rustling ADJECTIVE OR NOUN

rusty ['rʌstɪ] **rustier, rustiest** ADJECTIVE
1 affected by rust *e.g. a rusty iron gate*
2 If someone's knowledge is rusty, it is not as
good as it used to be because they have not used
it for a long time. *e.g. My German is a bit rusty these
days.*

rut [rʌt] **ruts** NOUN
1 a deep, narrow groove in the ground made by
the wheels of a vehicle
> PHRASE
2 If someone is **in a rut**, they have become fixed
in their way of doing things.

ruthless ['ru:θlɪs] ADJECTIVE
very harsh or cruel *e.g. a ruthless drug dealer*
ruthlessness NOUN, **ruthlessly** ADVERB

rye [raɪ] NOUN
a type of grass that produces light brown grain

Ss

Sabbath ['sæbəθ] NOUN
The Sabbath is the day of the week when members of some religious groups, especially Jews and Christians, do not work.
[WORD HISTORY: from Hebrew SHABBATH meaning 'to rest']

sable ['seɪbəl] **sables** NOUN
a very expensive fur used for making coats and hats; also the wild animal from which this fur is obtained

sabotage ['sæbəˌtɑːʒ] **sabotages, sabotaging, sabotaged** NOUN
1 the deliberate damaging of things such as machinery and railway lines
> VERB
2 If something is sabotaged, it is deliberately damaged.
saboteur NOUN
[WORD HISTORY: from French SABOTER meaning 'to spoil through clumsiness']

sabre ['seɪbə] **sabres** NOUN
1 a heavy curved sword
2 a light sword used in fencing

saccharine or **saccharin** ['sækəˌraɪn] or ['sækərɪn] NOUN
a chemical used instead of sugar to sweeten things

sachet ['sæʃeɪ] **sachets** NOUN
a small closed packet, containing a small amount of something such as sugar or shampoo

sack [sæk] **sacks, sacking, sacked** NOUN
1 a large bag made of rough material used for carrying or storing goods
> VERB
2 INFORMAL
If someone is sacked, they are dismissed from their job by their employer.

● THESAURUS
discharge: *discharged from the army*
dismiss: *the power to dismiss employees*
fire: informal *He was fired for poor timekeeping.*
> PHRASE
3 INFORMAL
If someone gets **the sack**, they are dismissed

from their job by their employer.

● THESAURUS
discharge: *He plans to appeal his discharge.*
dismissal: *the case for his dismissal*
termination of employment: *wrongful termination of employment*

sacrament ['sækrəmənt] **sacraments** NOUN
an important Christian ceremony such as communion, baptism, or marriage

sacred ['seɪkrɪd] ADJECTIVE
holy, or connected with religion or religious ceremonies *e.g. sacred ground*

sacrifice ['sækrɪˌfaɪs] **sacrifices, sacrificing, sacrificed** VERB
1 If you sacrifice something valuable or important, you give it up.

● THESAURUS
forego: *If we forego our summer holiday we can afford a car.*
forfeit: *The company is forfeiting safety for the sake of profit.*
give up: *I gave up my job to be with you.*
surrender: *We have surrendered our political authority for economic gain.*

2 To sacrifice an animal means to kill it as an offering to a god.
> NOUN
3 the killing of an animal as an offering to a god or gods
4 the action of giving something up
sacrificial ADJECTIVE

● THESAURUS
renunciation: *religious principles of renunciation and dedication*
self-denial: *an unprecedented act of self-denial*

sacrilege ['sækrɪlɪdʒ] NOUN
Sacrilege is behaviour that shows great disrespect for something holy.
sacrilegious ADJECTIVE

sacrosanct ['sækrəʊˌsæŋkt] ADJECTIVE
regarded as too important to be criticized or changed *e.g. Freedom of the press is sacrosanct.*

sad [sæd] **sadder, saddest** ADJECTIVE

1 If you are sad, you feel unhappy.

THESAURUS

blue: *I don't know why I'm feeling so blue today.*
dejected: *Everyone has days when they feel dejected.*
depressed: *She's depressed about this whole situation.*
dismal: *What are you all looking so dismal about?*
down: *The old man sounded really down.*
downcast: *a downcast expression*
glum: *a row of glum faces*
gloomy: *Don't look so gloomy, Mr Todd. I'll do my best for you.*
grief-stricken: *comforting the grief-stricken relatives*
low: *He used to listen when I was feeling low.*
melancholy: *melancholy thoughts*
mournful: *the mournful expression on his face*
unhappy: *I hate to see you so unhappy.*
wistful: *I found myself feeling wistful at the memory of him.*
<<OPPOSITE *happy*

2 Something sad makes you feel unhappy. *e.g. a sad story*
sadly ADVERB

THESAURUS

depressing: *a depressing film*
dismal: *a dark, dismal day*
gloomy: *a gloomy tale of a poor orphan*
harrowing: *a harrowing documentary about drug addicts*
heart-rending: *heart-rending pictures of the victims*
melancholy: *the melancholy music used throughout the film*
mournful: *a mournful ballad*
moving: *a deeply moving account of her life*
pathetic: *the pathetic sight of oil-covered sea birds*
poignant: *a poignant love story*
tragic: *his tragic death*
upsetting: *I'm afraid I have some upsetting news for you.*

sadden ['sædᵊn] **saddens, saddening, saddened** VERB
If something saddens you, it makes you feel sad.

saddle ['sædᵊl] **saddles, saddling, saddled** NOUN
1 a leather seat that you sit on when you are riding a horse

2 The saddle on a bicycle is the seat.

> VERB
3 If you saddle a horse, you put a saddle on it.

sadism ['seɪdɪzəm] NOUN
Sadism is the obtaining of pleasure, especially sexual pleasure, from making people suffer pain or humiliation.

sadist NOUN, **sadistic** ADJECTIVE
[WORD HISTORY: from the Marquis de Sade (1740-1814), who got his pleasure in this way]

sadness ['sædnəs] NOUN
the feeling of being unhappy

THESAURUS

dejection: *a feeling of dejection and despair*
depression: *plunged into the deepest depression*
despondency: *Deep despondency set in again.*
melancholy: *Dean had shaken off his melancholy.*
unhappiness: *His unhappiness shows in his face.*
<<OPPOSITE *happiness*

safari [sə'fɑːrɪ] **safaris** NOUN
an expedition for hunting or observing wild animals
[WORD HISTORY: from Swahili SAFARI meaning 'journey']

safari park safari parks NOUN
a large park where wild animals such as lions and elephants roam freely

safe [seɪf] **safer, safest; safes** ADJECTIVE
1 Something that is safe does not cause harm or danger.

THESAURUS

harmless: *harmless substances*
innocuous: *Both mushrooms look innocuous but are in fact deadly.*
wholesome: *fresh, wholesome ingredients*
<<OPPOSITE *dangerous*

2 If you are safe, you are not in any danger.

THESAURUS

all right: *I'll be all right on my own.*
in safe hands: *It's all right, you're in safe hands.*
okay or **OK:** informal *Could you check that the baby's okay?*
out of danger: *We were not out of danger yet.*
out of harm's way: *I'm keeping him well out of harm's way.*
protected: *Keep the plants dry and protected from frost.*
safe and sound: *I'm hoping he will come home safe and sound.*
secure: *I would like to feel financially secure.*

3 If it is safe to say something, you can say it with little risk of being wrong.

> NOUN
4 a strong metal box with special locks, in which you can keep valuable things
safely ADVERB

safeguard ['seɪfˌgɑːd] **safeguards, safeguarding, safeguarded** VERB
1 To safeguard something means to protect it.

THESAURUS

defend: *his courage in defending religious and civil rights*

S

guard: *He closely guarded her identity.*
look after: *People tend to look after their own property.*
preserve: *We need to preserve the forest.*
protect: *What can we do to protect ourselves against heart disease?*
save: *This machine could help save babies from cot death.*
shield: *They moved to shield their children from adverse publicity.*

> NOUN

2 something designed to protect people or things

● THESAURUS

barrier: *a barrier against the outside world*
cover: *Airlines are required to provide cover against such incidents.*
defence: *The immune system is our main defence against disease.*
protection: *Innocence is no protection from the evils in our society.*

safekeeping ['seɪf'kiːpɪŋ] NOUN
If something is given to you for safekeeping, it is given to you to look after.

safety ['seɪftɪ] NOUN
the state of being safe from harm or danger

● THESAURUS

immunity: *natural immunity to the disease*
protection: *protection from harmful rays*
security: *a false sense of security*
<<OPPOSITE *danger*

sag [sæg] **sags, sagging, sagged** VERB
When something sags, it hangs down loosely or sinks downwards in the middle.
sagging ADJECTIVE

saga ['sɑːgə] **sagas** NOUN
a very long story, usually with many different adventures *e.g. a saga of rivalry, honour and love*
[WORD HISTORY: from Old Norse SAGA meaning 'story']

sage [seɪdʒ] **sages** NOUN

1 LITERARY
a very wise person

2 Sage is also a herb used for flavouring in cooking.
[WORD HISTORY: sense 1 is from Latin SAPERE meaning 'to be wise'; sense 2 is from Latin SALVUS meaning 'healthy', because of the supposed medicinal properties of the plant]

Sagittarius [ˌsædʒɪˈteərɪəs] NOUN
Sagittarius is the ninth sign of the zodiac, represented by a creature half-horse, half-man holding a bow and arrow. People born between November 22nd and December 21st are born under this sign.
[WORD HISTORY: from Latin SAGITTARIUS meaning 'archer']

sail [seɪl] **sails, sailing, sailed** NOUN

1 Sails are large pieces of material attached to a ship's mast. The wind blows against the sail and moves the ship.

> VERB

2 When a ship sails, it moves across water.

3 If you sail somewhere, you go there by ship.

sailor ['seɪlə] **sailors** NOUN
a member of a ship's crew

saint [seɪnt] **saints** NOUN
a person who after death is formally recognized by a Christian Church as deserving special honour because of having lived a very holy life
[WORD HISTORY: from Latin SANCTUS meaning 'holy']

saintly ['seɪntlɪ] ADJECTIVE
behaving in a very good or holy way

sake [seɪk] **sakes** PHRASE

1 If you do something **for someone's sake**, you do it to help or please them.

2 You use **for the sake of** to say why you are doing something. *e.g. a one-off expedition for interest's sake*

salad ['sæləd] **salads** NOUN
a mixture of raw vegetables
[WORD HISTORY: from Old Provençal SALAR meaning 'to season with salt']

salami [sə'lɑːmɪ] NOUN
Salami is a kind of spicy sausage.

salary ['sælərɪ] **salaries** NOUN
a regular monthly payment to an employee
[WORD HISTORY: from Latin SALARIUM meaning 'money given to soldiers to buy salt']

sale [seɪl] **sales** NOUN

1 The sale of goods is the selling of them.

2 an occasion when a shop sells things at reduced prices

> PLURAL NOUN

3 The sales of a product are the numbers that are sold.

salesman ['seɪlzmən] **salesmen** NOUN
someone who sells products for a company
saleswoman NOUN

salient ['seɪlɪənt] ADJECTIVE; FORMAL
The salient points or facts are the important ones.

saliva [sə'laɪvə] NOUN
Saliva is the watery liquid in your mouth that helps you chew and digest food.

sallow ['sæləʊ] ADJECTIVE
Sallow skin is pale and unhealthy.

salmon ['sæmən] **salmons** or **salmon** NOUN
a large edible silver-coloured fish with pink flesh

salmonella [ˌsælməˈnɛlə] NOUN
Salmonella is a kind of bacteria which can cause severe food poisoning.

salon [ˈsælɒn] **salons** NOUN
a place where hairdressers work

saloon [səˈluːn] **saloons** NOUN
1 a car with a fixed roof and a separate boot
2 In America, a place where alcoholic drinks are sold and drunk.

salt [sɔːlt] **salts** NOUN
1 Salt is a white substance found naturally in sea water. It is used to flavour and preserve food.
2 a chemical compound formed from an acid base

salty [ˈsɔːltɪ] **saltier, saltiest** ADJECTIVE
containing salt or tasting of salt

⬤ THESAURUS
brak: South African the brak shallow water near the dam wall
briny: the flow of the briny water
salted: 8 ounces of slightly salted butter

salute [səˈluːt] **salutes, saluting, saluted**
NOUN
1 a formal sign of respect. Soldiers give a salute by raising their right hand to their forehead
> VERB
2 If you salute someone, you give them a salute.

salvage [ˈsælvɪdʒ] **salvages, salvaging, salvaged** VERB
1 If you salvage things, you save them, for example from a wrecked ship or a destroyed building.
> NOUN
2 You refer to things saved from a wrecked ship or destroyed building as salvage.

salvation [sælˈveɪʃən] NOUN
1 When someone's salvation takes place, they are saved from harm or evil.
2 To be someone's salvation means to save them from harm or evil.

salvo [ˈsælvəʊ] **salvos** or **salvoes** NOUN
the firing of several guns or missiles at the same time

same [seɪm] ADJECTIVE
1 If two things are the same, they are like one another.

⬤ THESAURUS
alike: No two families are alike.
equal: Mix equal quantities of soy sauce and rice vinegar.
equivalent: One unit is roughly equivalent to a glass of wine.
identical: Nearly all the houses were identical.

indistinguishable: symptoms indistinguishable from those of AIDS
<<OPPOSITE different

2 Same means just one thing and not two different ones. e.g. They were born in the same town.

Samoan [səˈməʊən] **Samoans** ADJECTIVE
1 belonging or relating to Samoa
> NOUN
2 someone who comes from Samoa

sample [ˈsɑːmpəl] **samples, sampling, sampled** NOUN
1 A sample of something is a small amount of it that you can try or test. e.g. a sample of new wine
> VERB
2 If you sample something, you try it. e.g. I sampled his cooking.

samurai [ˈsæmʊˌraɪ] NOUN
A samurai was a member of an ancient Japanese warrior class.

sanctimonious [ˌsæŋktɪˈməʊnɪəs]
ADJECTIVE
pretending to be very religious and virtuous

sanction [ˈsæŋkʃən] **sanctions, sanctioning, sanctioned** VERB (PSHE)
1 To sanction something means to officially approve of it or allow it.
⬤ THESAURUS
allow: I cannot be seen to allow violence on school premises.
approve: The parliament has approved a programme of economic reforms.
authorize: We are willing to authorize a police raid.
back: persuading the government to back the plan
endorse: policies endorsed by the voting public
permit: Will he let the court's decision stand and permit the execution?
support: The party is under pressure to support the ban.
<<OPPOSITE veto
> NOUN
2 Sanction is official approval of something.
⬤ THESAURUS
approval: The chairman has given his approval.
authorization: You will need the authorization of a parent or guardian.
backing: He said the president had the backing of his government.
blessing: With the blessing of the White House, the group is meeting to identify more budget cuts.
permission: Finally she gave permission for him to marry.
support: formal The prime minister gave his support to the reforms.

3 a severe punishment or penalty intended to make people obey the law

S

4 Sanctions are sometimes taken by countries against a country that has broken international law.

● THESAURUS
ban: *After four years, he lifted the ban.*
boycott: *the lifting of the economic boycott against the country*
embargo: *They called on the government to lift its embargo on trade with the country.*
penalties: *legally binding penalties against treaty violators*

sanctity ['sæŋktɪtɪ] NOUN
If you talk about the sanctity of something, you are saying that it should be respected because it is very important. *e.g. the sanctity of marriage*

sanctuary ['sæŋktjʊərɪ] **sanctuaries** NOUN
1 a place where you are safe from harm or danger
2 a place where wildlife is protected *e.g. a bird sanctuary*

sand [sænd] **sands, sanding, sanded** NOUN
1 Sand consists of tiny pieces of stone. Beaches are made of sand.
> VERB
2 If you sand something, you rub sandpaper over it to make it smooth.

sandal ['sænd³l] **sandals** NOUN
Sandals are light shoes with straps, worn in warm weather.

sandpaper ['sænd,peɪpə] NOUN
Sandpaper is strong paper with a coating of sand on it, used for rubbing surfaces to make them smooth.

sandshoe ['sændʃuː] **sandshoes** NOUN
In British, Australian, and New Zealand English, a light canvas shoe with a rubber sole.

sandstone ['sænd,stəʊn] NOUN
Sandstone is a type of rock formed from sand, often used for building.

sandwich ['sænwɪdʒ] **sandwiches, sandwiching, sandwiched** NOUN
1 two slices of bread with a filling between them
> VERB
2 If one thing is sandwiched between two others, it is in a narrow space between them. *e.g. a small shop sandwiched between a bar and an office*
[WORD HISTORY: sense 1 is named after the 4th Earl of Sandwich (1718-1792), for whom they were invented so that he could eat and gamble at the same time]

sandy ['sændɪ] **sandier, sandiest** ADJECTIVE
1 A sandy area is covered with sand.
2 Sandy hair is light orange-brown.

sane [seɪn] **saner, sanest** ADJECTIVE

1 If someone is sane, they have a normal and healthy mind.

● THESAURUS
lucid: *She was lucid right up until her death.*
normal: *the question of what constitutes normal behaviour*
rational: *He seemed perfectly rational to me.*
<<OPPOSITE *mad*

2 A sane action is sensible and reasonable.

● THESAURUS
judicious: *the judicious use of military force*
level-headed: *a sensible, level-headed approach*
rational: *a rational analysis*
reasonable: *a reasonable course of action*
sensible: *the sensible thing to do*
sound: *sound advice*

sanguine ['sæŋgwɪn] ADJECTIVE; FORMAL
cheerful and confident

sanitary ['sænɪtərɪ] ADJECTIVE
Sanitary means concerned with keeping things clean and hygienic. *e.g. improving the sanitary conditions*

sanitary towel sanitary towels NOUN
Sanitary towels are pads of thick, soft material which women wear during their periods.

sanitation [,sænɪ'teɪʃən] NOUN
Sanitation is the process of keeping places clean and hygienic, especially by providing a sewage system and clean water supply.

sanity ['sænɪtɪ] NOUN
Your sanity is your ability to think and act normally and reasonably.

sap [sæp] **saps, sapping, sapped** VERB
1 If something saps your strength or confidence, it gradually weakens and destroys it.
> NOUN
2 Sap is the watery liquid in plants.

sapling ['sæplɪŋ] **saplings** NOUN
a young tree

sapphire ['sæfaɪə] **sapphires** NOUN
a blue precious stone

sarcastic [sɑː'kæstɪk] ADJECTIVE
saying or doing the opposite of what you really mean in order to mock or insult someone *e.g. a sarcastic remark*
sarcasm NOUN, **sarcastically** ADVERB
[WORD HISTORY: from Greek SARKAZEIN meaning 'to tear the flesh']

● THESAURUS
caustic: *his abrasive wit and caustic comments*
ironic: *an ironic remark*
sardonic: *a sardonic sense of humour*
satirical: *a satirical TV show*

sarcophagus [sɑː'kɒfəgəs] **sarcophagi** or **sarcophaguses** NOUN a stone coffin used in ancient times

sardine [saːˈdiːn] **sardines** NOUN
a small edible sea fish

sardonic [saːˈdɒnɪk] ADJECTIVE
mocking or scornful *e.g. a sardonic grin*
sardonically ADVERB

sari [ˈsaːrɪ] **saris** NOUN
a piece of clothing worn especially by Indian
women, consisting of a long piece of material
folded around the body
[WORD HISTORY: a Hindi word]

sarmie [ˈsaːmɪ] **sarmies** NOUN; SLANG
In South African English, a sarmie is a sandwich.

sartorial [saːˈtɔːrɪəl] ADJECTIVE; FORMAL
relating to clothes *e.g. sartorial elegance*

sash [sæʃ] **sashes** NOUN
a long piece of cloth worn round the waist or over
one shoulder
[WORD HISTORY: from Arabic SHASH meaning
'muslin']

Satan [ˈseɪtᵊn] NOUN
Satan is the Devil.
[WORD HISTORY: from Hebrew SATAN meaning 'to
plot against']

satanic [səˈtænɪk] ADJECTIVE
caused by or influenced by Satan *e.g. satanic
forces*

satchel [ˈsætʃəl] **satchels** NOUN
a leather or cloth bag with a long strap

satellite [ˈsætᵊlaɪt] **satellites** NOUN
1 a spacecraft sent into orbit round the earth to
collect information or as part of a
communications system
2 a natural object in space that moves round a
planet or star

satin [ˈsætɪn] **satins** NOUN
Satin is a kind of smooth, shiny silk.

satire [ˈsætaɪə] **satires** NOUN
Satire is the use of mocking or ironical humour,
especially in literature, to show how foolish or
wicked some people are.
satirical ADJECTIVE

satisfaction [ˌsætɪsˈfækʃən] NOUN
Satisfaction is the feeling of pleasure you get
when you do something you wanted or needed
to do.

satisfactory [ˌsætɪsˈfæktərɪ] ADJECTIVE
acceptable or adequate *e.g. a satisfactory
explanation*
satisfactorily ADVERB

⬤ THESAURUS
acceptable: *The air pollution exceeds acceptable
levels.*

adequate: *One in four people are without adequate
homes.*
all right: *The meal was all right, but nothing special.*
good enough: *He's not good enough for you.*
passable: *She speaks passable French.*
sufficient: *One teaspoon of sugar should be
sufficient.*
<<OPPOSITE *unsatisfactory*

satisfied [ˈsætɪsˌfaɪd] ADJECTIVE
happy because you have got what you want

⬤ THESAURUS
content: *I'm perfectly content where I am.*
contented: *She led a quiet, contented life.*
happy: *I'm not happy with the situation.*
pleased: *He seemed pleased with the arrangement.*
<<OPPOSITE *disappointed*

satisfy [ˈsætɪsˌfaɪ] **satisfies, satisfying,
satisfied** VERB
1 To satisfy someone means to give them
enough of something to make them pleased or
contented.

⬤ THESAURUS
gratify: *He was gratified by the audience's response.*
indulge: *I don't believe in indulging children.*
please: *Our prime objective is to please our
customers.*

2 To satisfy someone that something is the case
means to convince them of it.

⬤ THESAURUS
convince: *trying to convince the public that its
product is safe*
persuade: *I had to persuade him of the advantages.*
put someone's mind at rest: *He has done his best
to put my mind at rest.*
reassure: *I tried to reassure them, but they knew I
was lying.*

3 To satisfy the requirements for something
means to fulfil them.

⬤ THESAURUS
fulfil: *All the minimum requirements were fulfilled.*
meet: *The current arrangements are inadequate to
meet their needs.*

satisfying [ˈsætɪsˌfaɪɪŋ] ADJECTIVE
Something that is satisfying gives you a feeling of
pleasure and fulfilment.

satsuma [sætˈsuːmə] **satsumas** NOUN
a fruit like a small orange

saturated [ˈsætʃəˌreɪtɪd] ADJECTIVE
1 very wet
2 If a place is saturated with things, it is
completely full of them.
saturation NOUN

Saturday [ˈsætədɪ] **Saturdays** NOUN
the day between Friday and Sunday

S

[WORD HISTORY: from Latin SATURNI DIES meaning 'day of Saturn']

Saturn ['sætɜːn] NOUN
Saturn is the planet in the solar system which is sixth from the sun.

sauce [sɔːs] **sauces** NOUN
a liquid eaten with food to give it more flavour

Do not confuse the spellings of *sauce* and *source*, which can sound very similar

saucepan ['sɔːspən] **saucepans** NOUN
a deep metal cooking pot with a handle and a lid

saucer ['sɔːsə] **saucers** NOUN
a small curved plate for a cup

saucy ['sɔːsɪ] **saucier, sauciest** ADJECTIVE
cheeky in an amusing way

Saudi ['sɔːdɪ] **Saudis** ADJECTIVE
1 belonging or relating to Saudi Arabia
> NOUN
2 someone who comes from Saudi Arabia

sauna ['sɔːnə] **saunas** NOUN
If you have a sauna, you go into a very hot room in order to sweat, then have a cold bath or shower.
[WORD HISTORY: a Finnish word]

saunter ['sɔːntə] **saunters, sauntering, sauntered** VERB
To saunter somewhere means to walk there slowly and casually.

sausage ['sɒsɪdʒ] **sausages** NOUN
a mixture of minced meat and herbs formed into a tubular shape and served cooked

sauté ['səʊteɪ] **sautés, sautéing** or **sautéeing sautéed** VERB
To sauté food means to fry it quickly in a small amount of oil or butter.

savage ['sævɪdʒ] **savages, savaging, savaged** ADJECTIVE
1 cruel and violent *e.g. savage fighting*

● THESAURUS
barbarous: *the barbarous customs of earlier times*
barbaric: *a particularly barbaric act of violence*
brutal: *a very brutal murder*
cruel: *the cruel practice of bullfighting*
ferocious: *the most ferocious violence ever seen on the streets of London*
inhuman: *the inhuman slaughter of these beautiful creatures*
vicious: *a vicious blow to the head*
violent: *violent crimes*

> NOUN
2 If you call someone a savage, you mean that they are violent and uncivilized.

● THESAURUS
barbarian: *Our maths teacher was a complete barbarian.*

beast: *You beast! Let me go!*
brute: *He was a brute and he deserved his fate.*
lout: *a drunken lout*
monster: *These men were total monsters.*

> VERB
3 If an animal savages you, it attacks you and bites you.
savagely ADVERB

● THESAURUS
attack: *A lion attacked him when he was a child.*
bite: *Every year thousands of children are bitten by dogs.*
maul: *The dog went berserk and mauled one of the girls.*

savagery ['sævɪdʒrɪ] NOUN
Savagery is cruel and violent behaviour.

save [seɪv] **saves, saving, saved** VERB
1 If you save someone, you rescue them. *e.g. He saved my life.*

● THESAURUS
come to someone's rescue: *His uncle came to his rescue.*
deliver: *I thanked God for delivering me from the pain.*
redeem: *to redeem souls from purgatory*
rescue: *rescued from the flames*
salvage: *salvaging equipment from the wreckage*

2 If you save someone or something, you keep them safe.

● THESAURUS
keep safe: *to keep my home safe from germs*
preserve: *preserving old buildings*
protect: *What can we do to protect ourselves from heart disease?*
safeguard: *measures to safeguard the ozone layer*

3 If you save something, you keep it so that you can use it later. *e.g. He'd saved up enough money for the deposit.*

● THESAURUS
hoard: *They've begun to hoard food and petrol.*
keep: *Grate the lemon zest and keep it for later.*
put by: *He's putting his money by in a deposit account.*
reserve: *Drain the fruit and reserve the juice.*
set aside: *£130 million would be set aside for repairs to schools.*
<<OPPOSITE *waste*

4 To save time, money, or effort means to prevent it from being wasted. *e.g. You could have saved us the trouble.*

> PREPOSITION
5 FORMAL
Save means except. *e.g. I was alone in the house save for a very old woman.*

saving ['seɪvɪŋ] **savings** NOUN

1 a reduction in the amount of time or money used

> PLURAL NOUN

2 Your savings are the money you have saved.

saviour ['seɪvjə] **saviours** NOUN

1 If someone saves you from danger, you can refer to them as your saviour.

> PROPER NOUN

2 In Christianity, the Saviour is Jesus Christ.

savour ['seɪvə] **savours, savouring, savoured** VERB

If you savour something, you take your time with it and enjoy it fully. *e.g. These spirits should be sipped and savoured like fine whiskies.*

savoury ['seɪvərɪ] ADJECTIVE

1 Savoury is salty or spicy.

2 Something that is not very savoury is not very pleasant or respectable. *e.g. the less savoury places*

saw [sɔː] **saws, sawing, sawed, sawn**

1 Saw is the past tense of **see**

> NOUN

2 a tool, with a blade with sharp teeth along one edge, for cutting wood

> VERB

3 If you saw something, you cut it with a saw.

sawdust ['sɔːˌdʌst] NOUN

Sawdust is the fine powder produced when you saw wood.

saxophone ['sæksəˌfəʊn] **saxophones** NOUN

a curved metal wind instrument often played in jazz bands

[WORD HISTORY: named after Adolphe Sax (1814–1894), who invented the instrument]

say see page 762 for Word Web

saying ['seɪɪŋ] **sayings** NOUN

a well-known sentence or phrase that tells you something about human life

● **THESAURUS**

adage: *the old adage, "the show must go on"*
axiom: *the long-held axiom that education leads to higher income*
maxim: *I believe in the maxim, "If it ain't broke, don't fix it".*
proverb: *an old Chinese proverb*

scab [skæb] **scabs** NOUN

a hard, dry covering that forms over a wound
scabby ADJECTIVE

scaffolding ['skæfəldɪŋ] NOUN

Scaffolding is a framework of poles and boards that is used by workmen to stand on while they are working on the outside structure of a building.

scald [skɔːld] **scalds, scalding, scalded** VERB

1 If you scald yourself, you burn yourself with very hot liquid or steam.

> NOUN

2 a burn caused by scalding

scale [skeɪl] **scales, scaling, scaled** NOUN

1 The scale of something is its size or extent. *e.g. the sheer scale of the disaster*

2 a set of levels or numbers used for measuring things

3 The scale of a map, plan, or model is the relationship between the size of something in the map, plan, or model and its size in the real world. *e.g. a scale of 1:10,000*

4 (**MUSIC**) an upward or downward sequence of musical notes

5 The scales of a fish or reptile are the small pieces of hard skin covering its body.

> PLURAL NOUN

6 Scales are a piece of equipment used for weighing things.

> VERB

7 If you scale something high, you climb it.

scalene ['skeɪliːn] ADJECTIVE

A scalene triangle has sides which are all of different lengths.

scallop ['skɒləp] **scallops** NOUN

Scallops are edible shellfish with two flat fan-shaped shells.

scalp [skælp] **scalps, scalping, scalped** NOUN

1 Your scalp is the skin under the hair on your head.

2 the piece of skin and hair removed when someone is scalped

> VERB

3 To scalp someone means to remove the skin and hair from their head in one piece.

scalpel ['skælpəl] **scalpels** NOUN

a knife with a thin, sharp blade, used by surgeons

scaly ['skeɪlɪ] ADJECTIVE

covered with scales

scamper ['skæmpə] **scampers, scampering, scampered** VERB

To scamper means to move quickly and lightly.

scampi ['skæmpɪ] PLURAL NOUN

Scampi are large prawns often eaten fried in breadcrumbs.

scan [skæn] **scans, scanning, scanned** VERB

1 If you scan something, you look at all of it carefully. *e.g. I scanned the horizon to the north-east.*

S

1 NOUN

a chance to express your opinion *eg: voters who want a say in the matter*

● **THESAURUS**

voice: *parents are given a voice in decision-making*

vote: *Every employee felt he had a vote in the company's future.*

say

2 VERB

When you say something, you speak words *eg: She said they were very impressed.*

to say something as a statement

● **THESAURUS**

utter: *They left without uttering a single word.*

comment: *He has refused to comment on these reports.*

remark: *"I don't see you complaining," he remarked.*

state: *Could you please state your name for the record?*

mention: *He never mentioned that he was married.*

note: *"It's already getting dark," he noted.*

observe: *"He's a very loyal friend," Daniel observed.*

point out: *"You've not done so badly out of the deal," she pointed out.*

to say something as a question or answer

● **THESAURUS**

explain: *"We weren't married at that point,"* she explained

ask: *"How is Frank?" has asked.*

inquire: *"Is something wrong?" he inquired.*

query: *"Can I help you?" the assistant queried.*

question: *"What if something goes wrong?"* he questioned anxiously.

answer: *"When are you leaving?" she asked. "Tomorrow," he answered.*

reply: *"That's a nice outfit," he commented. "Thanks," she replied.*

respond: *"Are you well enough to carry on?" "Of course," she responded scornfully.*

riposte: *"It's tough at the top," I said. "It's even tougher at the bottom," he riposted.*

retort: *"I don't agree," James said. "Who cares what you think?" she retorted.*

to say something as an interjection

● **THESAURUS**

announce: *"We're engaged!" she announced.*

affirm: *"I'm staying right here," he affirmed.*

asserts: *"The facts are clear," the Prime Minister asserted.*

declare: *"I'm absolutely thrilled with the result," he declared.*

add: *"Anyway, it serves you right," she added defiantly.*

interrupt: *"I don't think you quite understand," James interrupted.*

to say something informally

● **THESAURUS**

chat: *We were just standing chatting in the corridor.*

converse: *They were conversing in German.*

natter: *Susan and her friend were still nattering when I left.*

gossip: *We sat and gossiped well into the evening.*

2 If a machine scans something, it examines it by means of a beam of light or X-rays.

> NOUN

3 an examination or search by a scanner *e.g. a brain scan*

scandal ['skænd³l] **scandals** NOUN
a situation or event that people think is shocking and immoral
scandalous ADJECTIVE

Scandinavia [ˌskændɪ'neɪvɪə] NOUN
Scandinavia is the name given to a group of countries in Northern Europe, including Norway, Sweden, Denmark, and sometimes Finland and Iceland.
Scandinavian NOUN OR ADJECTIVE

scanner ['skænə] **scanners** NOUN
1 a machine which is used to examine, identify, or record things by means of a beam of light or X-rays
2 (ICT) a machine which converts text or images into a form that can be stored on a computer

scant [skænt] **scanter, scantest** ADJECTIVE
If something receives scant attention, it does not receive enough attention.

scapegoat ['skeɪpˌgəʊt] **scapegoats** NOUN
If someone is made a scapegoat, they are blamed for something, although it may not be their fault.

scar [skɑː] **scars, scarring, scarred** NOUN
1 a mark left on your skin after a wound has healed
2 a permanent effect on someone's mind that results from a very unpleasant experience *e.g. the scars of war*

> VERB

3 If an injury scars you, it leaves a permanent mark on your skin.
4 If an unpleasant experience scars you, it has a permanent effect on you.

scarce [skɛəs] **scarcer, scarcest** ADJECTIVE
If something is scarce, there is not very much of it.
scarcity NOUN

● THESAURUS
few: *Our options are few.*
rare: *Puffins are now rare in this country.*
uncommon: *an extreme but by no means uncommon case*
unusual: *To be appreciated as a parent is quite unusual.*
<<OPPOSITE *common*

scarcely ['skɛəslɪ] ADVERB
Scarcely means hardly. *e.g. I can scarcely hear her.*

As *scarcely* already has a negative sense, it is followed by *ever* or *any*, and not by *never* or *no*

scare [skɛə] **scares, scaring, scared** VERB
1 If something scares you, it frightens you.
● THESAURUS
alarm: *We could not see what had alarmed him.*
frighten: *He knew that Soli was trying to frighten him.*
give someone a fright: *The snake moved and gave everyone a fright.*
intimidate: *Jones had set out to intimidate and dominate Paul.*
startle: *Sorry, I didn't mean to startle you.*
terrify: *Flying terrifies him.*
terrorize: *pensioners terrorized by anonymous phone calls*
unnerve: *We were unnerved by the total silence.*

> NOUN

2 If something gives you a scare, it scares you.
● THESAURUS
fright: *the last time I had a real fright*
shock: *It gave me quite a shock to see his face on the screen.*
start: *The sudden noise gave me quite a start.*

3 If there is a scare about something, a lot of people are worried about it. *e.g. an AIDS scare*
scared ADJECTIVE
● THESAURUS
alert: *a security alert*
hysteria: *Everyone was getting carried away by the hysteria.*
panic: *the panic over GM foods*

scarecrow ['skɛəˌkrəʊ] **scarecrows** NOUN
an object shaped like a person put in a field to scare birds away

scarf [skɑːf] **scarfs** or **scarves** NOUN
a piece of cloth worn round your neck or head to keep you warm

scarlet ['skɑːlɪt] NOUN OR ADJECTIVE
bright red

scary ['skɛərɪ] **scarier, scariest** ADJECTIVE
INFORMAL
frightening
● THESAURUS
alarming: *an alarming report on the rise of street crime*
chilling: *a chilling account of the accident*
creepy: informal *places that are really creepy at night*
eerie: *the eerie dark path*
frightening: *a very frightening experience*
hair-raising: *a hair-raising encounter with a wild boar*
spooky: *The whole place has a slightly spooky atmosphere.*
terrifying: *I find it terrifying to be surrounded by a crowd of people.*

S

unnerving: *It is very unnerving to find out that someone you know is carrying the virus.*

scathing ['skeɪðɪŋ] ADJECTIVE
harsh and scornful *e.g. They were scathing about his job.*

scatter ['skætə] **scatters, scattering, scattered** VERB

1 To scatter things means to throw or drop them all over an area.

THESAURUS
shower: *The bomb exploded, showering shrapnel over a wide area.*
sow: *Sow the seeds in a warm place.*
sprinkle: *Sprinkle a tablespoon of sugar over the fruit.*
throw about: *They started throwing food about.*
<<OPPOSITE *gather*

2 If people scatter, they suddenly move away in different directions.

scattering ['skætərɪŋ] NOUN
A scattering of things is a small number of them spread over a large area. *e.g. the scattering of islands*

scavenge ['skævɪndʒ] **scavenges, scavenging, scavenged** VERB
If you scavenge for things, you search for them among waste and rubbish.
scavenger NOUN

scenario [sɪˈnɑːrɪˌəʊ] **scenarios** NOUN

1 (DRAMA) The scenario of a film or play is a summary of its plot.

2 the way a situation could possibly develop in the future *e.g. the worst possible scenario*

scene [siːn] **scenes** NOUN

1 (ENGLISH AND DRAMA) part of a play or film in which a series of events happen in one place

2 Pictures and views are sometimes called scenes. *e.g. a village scene*

THESAURUS
landscape: *Arizona's desert landscape.* **panorama:** *a panorama of fertile valleys*
view: *a view of the lake*

3 The scene of an event is the place where it happened.

THESAURUS
location: *filmed in an exotic location*
place: *Can you show me the place where the attack happened?*
setting: *Rome is the perfect setting for romance.*
site: *the site of the battle*
spot: *the ideal spot for a picnic*

4 an area of activity *e.g. the music scene*

THESAURUS
arena: *the political arena*

business: *the potential to revolutionize the publishing business*
environment: *the Japanese business environment*
world: *the fashion world*

scenery ['siːnərɪ] NOUN

1 In the countryside, you can refer to everything you see as the scenery.

THESAURUS
landscape: *Arizona's desert landscape.* **panorama:** *admiring the distant mountain panorama*
surroundings: *a holiday home in beautiful surroundings*
terrain: *The terrain changed from arable land to desert.*
view: *The view from our window was spectacular.*

2 In a theatre, the scenery is the painted cloth on the stage which represents the place where the action is happening.

scenic ['siːnɪk] ADJECTIVE
A scenic place or route has nice views.

scent [sɛnt] **scents, scenting, scented** NOUN

1 a smell, especially a pleasant one

2 Scent is perfume.

> VERB

3 When an animal scents something, it becomes aware of it by smelling it.

sceptic ['skɛptɪk] **sceptics** NOUN
someone who has doubts about things that other people believe
sceptical ADJECTIVE, **scepticism** NOUN

sceptre ['sɛptə] **sceptres** NOUN
an ornamental rod carried by a king or queen as a symbol of power

schedule ['ʃɛdjuːl] **schedules, scheduling, scheduled** NOUN

1 a plan that gives a list of events or tasks, together with the times at which each thing should be done

> VERB

2 If something is scheduled to happen, it has been planned and arranged. *e.g. Their journey was scheduled for the beginning of May.*

schema ['skiːmə] **schemata** NOUN

1 TECHNICAL
an outline of a plan or theory

2 a mental model which the mind uses to understand new experiences or to view the world

scheme [skiːm] **schemes, scheming, schemed** NOUN

1 a plan or arrangement *e.g. a five-year development scheme*

> VERB

2 When people scheme, they make secret plans.

schism ['skɪzəm] **schisms** NOUN
a split or division within a group or organization

schizophrenia [ˌskɪtsəʊ'friːnɪə] NOUN
Schizophrenia is a serious mental illness which prevents someone relating their thoughts and feelings to what is happening around them.
schizophrenic NOUN OR ADJECTIVE
[WORD HISTORY: from Greek SKHIZEIN meaning 'to split' and PHREN meaning 'mind']

scholar ['skɒlə] **scholars** NOUN
1 a person who studies an academic subject and knows a lot about it
2 In South African English, a scholar is a school pupil.

scholarly ['skɒləlɪ] ADJECTIVE
having or showing a lot of knowledge

scholarship ['skɒləʃɪp] **scholarships** NOUN
1 If you get a scholarship to a school or university, your studies are paid for by the school or university or by some other organization.
2 Scholarship is academic study and knowledge.

school [skuːl] **schools, schooling, schooled** NOUN
1 a place where children are educated
2 University departments and colleges are sometimes called schools. e.g. My oldest son is in medical school.
3 You can refer to a large group of dolphins or fish as a school.
> VERB
4 When someone is schooled in something, they are taught it. e.g. They were schooled in the modern techniques.

schoolchild ['skuːlˌtʃaɪld] **schoolchildren** NOUN
Schoolchildren are children who go to school.
schoolboy NOUN, **schoolgirl** NOUN

schooling ['skuːlɪŋ] NOUN
Your schooling is the education you get at school.

schooner ['skuːnə] **schooners** NOUN
a sailing ship

science ['saɪəns] **sciences** NOUN
1 Science is the study of the nature and behaviour of natural things and the knowledge obtained about them.
2 a branch of science, for example physics or biology

science fiction NOUN
Stories about events happening in the future or in other parts of the universe are called science fiction.

scientific [ˌsaɪən'tɪfɪk] ADJECTIVE

1 relating to science or to a particular science e.g. scientific knowledge
2 done in a systematic way, using experiments or tests e.g. this scientific method
scientifically ADVERB

scientist ['saɪəntɪst] **scientists** NOUN
an expert in one of the sciences who does work connected with it

scintillating ['sɪntɪˌleɪtɪŋ] ADJECTIVE
lively and witty e.g. scintillating conversation

scissors ['sɪzəz] PLURAL NOUN
Scissors are a cutting tool with two sharp blades.

scoff [skɒf] **scoffs, scoffing, scoffed** VERB
1 If you scoff, you speak in a scornful, mocking way about something.
2 INFORMAL
If you scoff food, you eat it quickly and greedily.

scold [skəʊld] **scolds, scolding, scolded** VERB
If you scold someone, you tell them off.
◉ THESAURUS
chide: Cross chided himself for worrying.
lecture: My mother always used to lecture me about not eating properly.
rebuke: I turned to him and sharply rebuked him.
reprimand: reprimanded for talking in the corridor
tell off: informal The teacher really told her off.
tick off: informal ticked off for being late

scone [skɒn] or [skəʊn] **scones** NOUN
Scones are small cakes made from flour and fat and usually eaten with butter.

scoop [skuːp] **scoops, scooping, scooped** VERB
1 If you scoop something up, you pick it up using a spoon or the palm of your hand.
> NOUN
2 an object like a large spoon which is used for picking up food such as ice cream

scooter ['skuːtə] **scooters** NOUN
1 a small, light motorcycle
2 a simple cycle which a child rides by standing on it and pushing the ground with one foot

scope [skəʊp] NOUN
1 If there is scope for doing something, the opportunity to do it exists.
2 The scope of something is the whole subject area which it deals with or includes.

-scope SUFFIX
'-scope' is used to form nouns which refer to an instrument used for observing or detecting e.g. microscope... telescope
[WORD HISTORY: from Greek SKOPEIN meaning 'to look at']

S

scorching ['skɔːtʃɪŋ] ADJECTIVE
extremely hot *e.g. another scorching summer*

score [skɔː] **scores, scoring, scored** VERB
1 If you score in a game, you get a goal, run, or point.

2 To score in a game also means to record the score obtained by the players.

3 If you score a success or victory, you achieve it.

4 To score a surface means to cut a line into it.

> NOUN

5 The score in a game is the number of goals, runs, or points obtained by the two teams.

6 Scores of things means very many of them. *e.g. Ros entertained scores of celebrities.*

7 OLD-FASHIONED
A score is twenty.

8 (MUSIC) The score of a piece of music is the written version of it.
scorer NOUN

scorn [skɔːn] **scorns, scorning, scorned** NOUN
1 Scorn is great contempt. *e.g. a look of scorn*

● THESAURUS
contempt: *I treated this remark with the contempt it deserved.*
derision: *shouts of derision*
disdain: *Janet looked at him with disdain.*
mockery: *his mockery of all things English*

> VERB
2 If you scorn someone, you treat them with great contempt.

● THESAURUS
despise: *She secretly despises him.*
disdain: *He disdained politicians.*
look down on: *I wasn't successful so they looked down on me.*
slight: *He felt slighted by this treatment.*

3 FORMAL
If you scorn something, you refuse to accept it.

scornful ['skɔːnfʊl] ADJECTIVE
showing contempt *e.g. his scornful comment*
scornfully ADVERB

● THESAURUS
contemptuous: *She gave a contemptuous little laugh.*
disdainful: *He is disdainful of politicians.*
scathing: *He made some scathing comments about the design.*
sneering: *a sneering tone*
supercilious: *His manner is supercilious and arrogant.*
withering: *Her mother gave her a withering look.*

Scorpio ['skɔːpɪˌəʊ] NOUN
Scorpio is the eighth sign of the zodiac,

represented by a scorpion. People born between October 23rd and November 21st are born under this sign.
[WORD HISTORY: from Latin SCORPIO meaning 'scorpion']

scorpion ['skɔːpɪən] **scorpions** NOUN
an animal that looks like a small lobster, with a long tail with a poisonous sting on the end

Scot [skɒt] **Scots** NOUN
1 a person who comes from Scotland

> ADJECTIVE
2 Scots means the same as **Scottish**

scotch [skɒtʃ] **scotches** NOUN
Scotch is whisky made in Scotland.

Scotsman ['skɒtsmən] **Scotsmen** NOUN
a man who comes from Scotland
Scotswoman NOUN

Scottish ['skɒtɪʃ] ADJECTIVE
belonging or relating to Scotland

scoundrel ['skaʊndrəl] **scoundrels** NOUN;
OLD-FASHIONED, INFORMAL
a man who cheats and deceives people

scour [skaʊə] **scours, scouring, scoured** VERB
1 If you scour a place, you look all over it in order to find something. *e.g. The police scoured the area.*

2 If you scour something such as a pan, you clean it by rubbing it with something rough.

scourge [skɜːdʒ] **scourges** NOUN
something that causes a lot of suffering *e.g. hay fever, that scourge of summer*

scout [skaʊt] **scouts, scouting, scouted** NOUN
1 a boy who is a member of the Scout Association, an organization for boys which aims to develop character and responsibility

2 someone who is sent to an area to find out the position of an enemy army

> VERB
3 If you scout around for something, you look around for it.

scowl [skaʊl] **scowls, scowling, scowled** VERB
1 If you scowl, you frown because you are angry. *e.g. They were scowling at me.*

> NOUN
2 an angry expression

scrabble ['skræbəl] **scrabbles, scrabbling, scrabbled** VERB
If you scrabble at something, you scrape at it with your hands or feet.
[WORD HISTORY: from Old Dutch SCHRABBELEN

meaning, 'to scrape repeatedly']

scramble ['skræmbᵊl] **scrambles,
scrambling, scrambled** VERB

1 If you scramble over something, you climb over it using your hands to help you.

> NOUN

2 a motorcycle race over rough ground

scrap [skræp] **scraps, scrapping, scrapped**
NOUN

1 A scrap of something is a very small piece of it. *e.g. a scrap of cloth*

> PLURAL NOUN

2 Scraps are pieces of leftover food.

> ADJECTIVE OR NOUN

3 Scrap metal or scrap is metal from old machinery or cars that can be re-used.

> VERB

4 If you scrap something, you get rid of it. *e.g. They considered scrapping passport controls.*

scrapbook ['skræp,bʊk] **scrapbooks** NOUN
a book in which you stick things such as pictures or newspaper articles

scrape [skreɪp] **scrapes, scraping, scraped**
VERB

1 If you scrape a surface, you rub a rough or sharp object against it.

● THESAURUS
graze: *He had grazed his knees a little.*
scour: *Scour the pans.*
scratch: *The branches scratched my face and hands.*
scuff: *scuffed shoes*
skin: *I found that I had skinned my knuckles.*

2 If something scrapes, it makes a harsh noise by rubbing against something. *e.g. his shoes scraping across the stone ground*

● THESAURUS
grate: *His chair grated as he got to his feet.*
grind: *Blocks of ice ground against each other.*
rasp: *The blade rasped over his skin.*
scratch: *He scratched his knife over the worktop.*

scratch [skrætʃ] **scratches, scratching,
scratched** VERB

1 To scratch something means to make a small cut on it accidentally. *e.g. They were always getting scratched by cats.*

2 If you scratch, you rub your skin with your nails because it is itching.

> NOUN

3 a small cut

scratchcard ['skrætʃ,kɑːd] **scratchcards**
NOUN
a ticket in a competition with a surface that you scratch off to show whether or not you have won a prize

scrawl [skrɔːl] **scrawls, scrawling,
scrawled** VERB

1 If you scrawl something, you write it in a careless and untidy way.

> NOUN

2 You can refer to careless and untidy writing as a scrawl.

scrawny ['skrɔːnɪ] **scrawnier, scrawniest**
ADJECTIVE
thin and bony *e.g. a small scrawny man*

scream [skriːm] **screams, screaming,
screamed** VERB

1 If you scream, you shout or cry in a loud, high-pitched voice.

● THESAURUS
cry: *a crying baby*
howl: *He howled like a wounded animal.*
screech: *"Get me some water!" I screeched.*
shout: *I shouted at mother to get the police.*
shriek: *She shrieked and leapt from the bed.*
squeal: *Jennifer squealed with delight.*
yell: *I pushed him away, yelling abuse.*

> NOUN

2 a loud, high-pitched cry

● THESAURUS
cry: *a cry of horror*
howl: *a howl of rage*
screech: *The figure gave a screech.*
shriek: *a shriek of joy*
squeal: *the squeal of piglets*
yell: *Something brushed Bob's face and he let out a yell.*

screech [skriːtʃ] **screeches, screeching,
screeched** VERB

1 To screech means to make an unpleasant high-pitched noise. *e.g. The car wheels screeched.*

> NOUN

2 an unpleasant high-pitched noise

screen [skriːn] **screens, screening,
screened** NOUN

1 a flat vertical surface on which a picture is shown *e.g. a television screen*

2 a vertical panel used to separate different parts of a room or to protect something

> VERB

3 To screen a film or television programme means to show it.

4 If you screen someone, you put something in front of them to protect them.

screenplay ['skriːn,pleɪ] **screenplays** NOUN
The screenplay of a film is the script.

screw [skruː] **screws, screwing, screwed**
NOUN

1 a small, sharp piece of metal used for fixing things together or for fixing something to a wall

S

> VERB

2 If you screw things together, you fix them together using screws.

3 If you screw something onto something else, you fix it there by twisting it round and round. *e.g. He screwed the top on the ink bottle.*

screw up VERB

4 If you screw something up, you twist it or squeeze it so that it no longer has its proper shape. *e.g. Amy screwed up her face.*

screwdriver ['skruː,draɪvə] **screwdrivers** NOUN

a tool for turning screws

scribble ['skrɪbəl] **scribbles, scribbling, scribbled** VERB

1 If you scribble something, you write it quickly and roughly.

2 To scribble also means to make meaningless marks. *e.g. When Caroline was five she scribbled on a wall.*

> NOUN

3 You can refer to something written or drawn quickly and roughly as a scribble.

scrimp [skrɪmp] **scrimps, scrimping, scrimped** VERB

If you scrimp, you live cheaply and spend as little money as you can.

script [skrɪpt] **scripts** NOUN

(DRAMA) the written version of a play or film

scripture ['skrɪptʃə] **scriptures** NOUN

Scripture refers to sacred writings, especially the Bible.

scriptural ADJECTIVE

scroll [skrəʊl] **scrolls** NOUN

a long roll of paper or parchment with writing on it

scrounge [skraʊndʒ] **scrounges, scrounging, scrounged** VERB INFORMAL

If you scrounge something, you get it by asking for it rather than by earning or buying it.

scrounger NOUN

● THESAURUS

beg: *They managed to beg a lift from a passing fisherman.*

bludge: Australian and New Zealand; informal *They've come here to bludge food and money.*

cadge: *Can I cadge a cigarette?*

sponge: informal *I got tired of him sponging off me and threw him out.*

scrub [skrʌb] **scrubs, scrubbing, scrubbed** VERB

1 If you scrub something, you clean it with a stiff brush and water.

> NOUN

2 If you give something a scrub, you scrub it.

3 Scrub consists of low trees and bushes.

scruff [skrʌf] NOUN

The scruff of your neck is the back of your neck or collar.

scruffy ['skrʌfɪ] **scruffier, scruffiest** ADJECTIVE

dirty and untidy *e.g. four scruffy youths*

● THESAURUS

ragged: *a ragged band of men*

seedy: *his seedy clothes*

shabby: *a shabby, tall man with dark eyes*

tatty: *a tatty old cardigan*

unkempt: *His hair was unkempt and filthy.*

<<OPPOSITE *smart*

scrum [skrʌm] **scrums** NOUN

When rugby players form a scrum, they form a group and push against each other with their heads down in an attempt to get the ball.

scrunchie ['skrʌntʃɪ] **scrunchies** NOUN

a loop of elastic loosely covered with material which is used to hold hair in a ponytail

scruple ['skruːpəl] **scruples** NOUN

Scruples are moral principles that make you unwilling to do something that seems wrong. *e.g. The West must drop its scruples and fight back.*

scrupulous ['skruːpjʊləs] ADJECTIVE

1 always doing what is honest or morally right

2 paying very careful attention to detail *e.g. a long and scrupulous search*

scrupulously ADVERB

scrutinize ['skruːtɪ,naɪz] **scrutinizes, scrutinizing, scrutinized;** also spelt **scrutinise** VERB

If you scrutinize something, you examine it very carefully.

● THESAURUS

examine: *He examined her passport.*

inspect: *Cut the fruit in half and inspect the pips.*

pore over: *We spent hours poring over the files.*

scan: *She kept scanning the crowd for Paul.*

search: *Her eyes searched his face.*

study: *Debbie studied the document for a moment.*

scrutiny ['skruːtɪnɪ] NOUN

If something is under scrutiny, it is being observed very carefully.

scuba diving ['skjuːbə 'daɪvɪŋ] NOUN

Scuba diving is the sport of swimming underwater with tanks of compressed air on your back.

scuff [skʌf] **scuffs, scuffing, scuffed** VERB

1 If you scuff your feet, you drag them along the ground when you are walking.

2 If you scuff your shoes, you mark them by scraping or rubbing them.

scuffle ['skʌfᵊl] **scuffles, scuffling, scuffled** NOUN

1 a short, rough fight

> VERB

2 When people scuffle, they fight roughly.

scullery ['skʌlərɪ] **sculleries** NOUN
a small room next to a kitchen where washing and cleaning are done

sculpt [skʌlpt] **sculpts, sculpting, sculpted** VERB
When something is sculpted, it is carved or shaped in stone, wood, or clay.

sculptor ['skʌlptə] **sculptors** NOUN
someone who makes sculptures

sculpture ['skʌlptʃə] **sculptures** NOUN

1 a work of art produced by carving or shaping stone or clay

2 Sculpture is the art of making sculptures.

scum [skʌm] NOUN
Scum is a layer of a dirty substance on the surface of a liquid.

scungy ['skʌndʒɪ] **scungier, scungiest**
ADJECTIVE AUSTRALIAN AND NEW ZEALAND SLANG
dirty or messy

⬤ THESAURUS
dirty: *He was wearing a dirty old mac.*
filthy: *This flat is so filthy I can't possibly stay here.*
foul: *foul polluted water*
seedy: *a seedy hotel*
sleazy: *sleazy bars*
sordid: *sordid little rooms*
squalid: *a squalid bedsit*

scurrilous ['skʌrɪləs] ADJECTIVE
abusive and damaging to someone's good name
e.g. scurrilous stories

scurry ['skʌrɪ] **scurries, scurrying, scurried**
VERB
To scurry means to run quickly with short steps.

scurvy ['skɜːvɪ] NOUN
Scurvy is a disease caused by a lack of vitamin C.

scuttle ['skʌtᵊl] **scuttles, scuttling, scuttled** VERB

1 To scuttle means to run quickly.

2 To scuttle a ship means to sink it deliberately by making holes in the bottom.

> NOUN

3 a container for coal

scythe [saɪð] **scythes** NOUN
a tool with a long handle and a curved blade used for cutting grass or grain

sea [siː] **seas** NOUN

1 The sea is the salty water that covers much of the earth's surface.

2 A sea of people or things is a very large number of them. *e.g. a sea of red flags*

seagull ['siːˌgʌl] **seagulls** NOUN
Seagulls are common white, grey, and black birds that live near the sea.

seahorse ['siːˌhɔːs] **seahorses** NOUN
a small fish which swims upright, with a head that resembles a horse's head

seal [siːl] **seals, sealing, sealed** NOUN

1 an official mark on a document which shows that it is genuine

2 a piece of wax fixed over the opening of a container

3 a large mammal with flippers, that lives partly on land and partly in the sea

> VERB

4 If you seal an envelope, you stick down the flap.

5 If you seal an opening, you cover it securely so that air, gas, or liquid cannot get through.

sea lion sea lions NOUN
a type of large seal

seam [siːm] **seams** NOUN

1 a line of stitches joining two pieces of cloth

2 A seam of coal is a long, narrow layer of it beneath the ground.

seaman ['siːmən] **seamen** NOUN
a sailor

seance ['seɪɑ̃s] **seances;** also spelt **séance**
NOUN
a meeting in which people try to communicate with the spirits of dead people

search [sɜːtʃ] **searches, searching, searched** VERB

1 If you search for something, you look for it in several places.

⬤ THESAURUS
comb: *Police combed the woods for the murder weapon.*
forage: *foraging for food*
fossick: Australian and New Zealand *to help Gaston fossick for food around the hut*
hunt: *hunting for a job*
look: *He's looking for a way out of this situation.*
scour: *They had scoured the intervening miles of moorland.*
seek: *the man he had been seeking for weeks*
sift: *sifting through the wreckage for clues*

2 If a person is searched their body and clothing is examined to see if they are hiding anything.

> NOUN

3 an attempt to find something

⬤ THESAURUS
hunt: *the hunt for my lost boy*

S

quest: *his quest to find true love*

search engine search engines NOUN
a service on the Internet which enables users to search for items of interest

searching ['sɜːtʃɪŋ] ADJECTIVE
intended to discover the truth about something
e.g. searching questions

searchlight ['sɜːtʃ,laɪt] **searchlights** NOUN
a powerful light whose beam can be turned in different directions

searing ['sɪərɪŋ] ADJECTIVE
A searing pain is very sharp.

seashore ['siː,ʃɔː] NOUN
The seashore is the land along the edge of the sea.

seasick ['siː,sɪk] ADJECTIVE
feeling sick because of the movement of a boat
seasickness NOUN

seaside ['siː,saɪd] NOUN
The seaside is an area next to the sea.

season ['siːzən] **seasons, seasoning, seasoned** NOUN
1 The seasons are the periods into which a year is divided and which have their own typical weather conditions. The seasons are spring, summer, autumn, and winter.
2 a period of the year when something usually happens *e.g. the football season... the hunting season*
> VERB
3 If you season food, you add salt, pepper, or spices to it.

seasonal ['siːzənəl] ADJECTIVE
happening during one season or one time of the year *e.g. seasonal work*

seasoned ['siːzənd] ADJECTIVE
very experienced *e.g. a seasoned professional*

seasoning ['siːzənɪŋ] NOUN
Seasoning is flavouring such as salt and pepper.

season ticket season tickets NOUN
a train or bus ticket that you can use as many times as you like within a certain period

seat [siːt] **seats, seating, seated** NOUN
1 something you can sit on
2 The seat of a piece of clothing is the part that covers your bottom.
3 If someone wins a seat in parliament, they are elected.
> VERB
4 If you seat yourself somewhere, you sit down.
5 If a place seats a particular number of people, it has enough seats for that number. *e.g. The theatre seats 570 people.*

seat belt seat belts NOUN
a strap that you fasten across your body for safety when travelling in a car or an aircraft

seating ['siːtɪŋ] NOUN
The seating in a place is the number or arrangement of seats there.

seaweed ['siː,wiːd] NOUN
Plants that grow in the sea are called seaweed.

secateurs ['sɛkətəz] PLURAL NOUN
Secateurs are small shears for pruning garden plants.

secluded [sɪ'kluː,dɪd] ADJECTIVE
quiet and hidden from view *e.g. a secluded beach*
seclusion NOUN

second seconds, seconding, seconded
ADJECTIVE ['sɛkənd]
1 The second item in a series is the one counted as number two.
> NOUN ['sɛkənd]
2 one of the sixty parts that a minute is divided into
> PLURAL NOUN ['sɛkəndz]
3 Seconds are goods that are sold cheaply because they are slightly faulty.
> VERB ['sɛkənd] *or* [sɪ'kɒnd]
4 If you second a proposal, you formally agree with it so that it can be discussed or voted on.
5 If you are seconded somewhere, you are sent there temporarily to work.
secondly ADVERB

> Senses 1-4 are pronounced *seck*-ond, but sense 5 is pronounced sick-*kond*

secondary ['sɛkəndərɪ] ADJECTIVE
1 Something that is secondary is less important than something else.
2 Secondary education is education for pupils between the ages of eleven and eighteen.

secondary school secondary schools NOUN
a school for pupils between the ages of eleven and eighteen

second-class [,sɛkənd'klɑːs] ADJECTIVE
1 Second-class things are regarded as less important than other things of the same kind. *e.g. He has been treated as a second-class citizen.*
> ADJECTIVE OR ADVERB
2 Second-class services are cheaper and therefore slower or less comfortable than first-class ones.

second cousin second cousins NOUN
Your second cousins are the children of your parents' cousins.

second-hand [,sɛkənd'hænd] ADJECTIVE OR ADVERB

1 Something that is second-hand has already been owned by someone else. *e.g. a second-hand car*

2 If you hear a story second-hand, you hear it indirectly, rather than from the people involved.

second-rate [ˌsɛkənd'reɪt] ADJECTIVE
of poor quality *e.g. a second-rate movie*

secret ['siːkrɪt] **secrets** ADJECTIVE
1 Something that is secret is told to only a small number of people and hidden from everyone else. *e.g. a secret meeting*

◉ THESAURUS
closet: informal *a closet Fascist*
confidential: *a confidential report*
covert: *She gave him a covert glance.*
furtive: *furtive meetings*
hidden: *a hidden camera*
undercover: *undercover FBI agents*
underground: *the underground communist movement*

> NOUN
2 a fact told to only a small number of people and hidden from everyone else
secretly ADVERB, **secrecy** NOUN

secret agent **secret agents** NOUN
a spy

secretary ['sɛkrətrɪ] **secretaries** NOUN
1 a person employed by an organization to keep records, write letters, and do office work
2 Ministers in charge of some government departments are also called secretaries. *e.g. the Health Secretary*
secretarial ADJECTIVE

secrete [sɪ'kriːt] **secretes, secreting, secreted** VERB
1 When part of a plant or animal secretes a liquid, it produces it.
2 FORMAL
If you secrete something somewhere, you hide it.
secretion NOUN

secretive ['siːkrɪtɪv] ADJECTIVE
Secretive people tend to hide their feelings and intentions.

◉ THESAURUS
cagey: informal *He is cagey about what he was paid for the business.*
reserved: *He was unemotional and reserved.*
reticent: *She is very reticent about her achievements.*

secret service NOUN
A country's secret service is the government department in charge of espionage.

sect [sɛkt] **sects** NOUN
a religious or political group which has broken away from a larger group

sectarian [sɛk'tɛərɪən] ADJECTIVE
strongly supporting a particular sect *e.g. sectarian violence*

section ['sɛkʃən] **sections** NOUN
(LIBRARY) A section of something is one of the parts it is divided into. *e.g. this section of the motorway*

◉ THESAURUS
division: *the company's sales division*
instalment: *Payment can be made in instalments.*
part: *the upper part of the body*
piece: *The equipment was taken down the shaft in pieces.*
portion: *I had learnt a portion of the Koran.*
segment: *the third segment of the journey*

sector ['sɛktə] **sectors** NOUN
1 A sector of something, especially a country's economy, is one part of it. *e.g. the private sector*
2 A sector of a circle is one of the two parts formed when you draw two straight lines from the centre to the circumference.

secular ['sɛkjʊlə] ADJECTIVE
having no connection with religion *e.g. secular education*

secure [sɪ'kjʊə] **secures, securing, secured** VERB
1 FORMAL
If you secure something, you manage to get it. *e.g. They secured the rights to her story.*

◉ THESAURUS
acquire: *General Motors recently acquired a 50% stake in the company.*
gain: *Hard work may not be enough to gain a place at university.*
get: *I got a job at the sawmill.*
obtain: *He tried to obtain a false passport.*
procure: formal *trying to procure the release of the hostages*

2 If you secure a place, you make it safe from harm or attack.

◉ THESAURUS
fortify: *British soldiers are working to fortify the airbase.*
make impregnable: *Their intention was to make the old fort impregnable.*
make safe: *Crime Prevention Officers will suggest ways to make your home safe.*
strengthen: *In the 14th century they strengthened this wall against raiders.*

3 To secure something also means to fasten it firmly. *e.g. One end was secured to the pier.*

◉ THESAURUS
attach: *The gadget can be attached to any vertical surface.*
bind: *Bind the ends of the cord together with thread.*

S

fasten: *Her long hair was fastened by an elastic band.*
fix: *He fixed a bayonet to the end of his rifle.*
lock: *Are you sure you locked the front door?*
moor: *She moored her barge on the river bank.*
tie up: *They dismounted and tied up their horses.*
<<OPPOSITE *release*

> ADJECTIVE

4 If a place is secure, it is tightly locked or well protected.

● THESAURUS
fortified: *The door is fortified against flooding.*
impregnable: *The old castle was completely impregnable against raids.*
protected: *the right of women to be protected from sexual harassment*
safe: *We want to go to a football match knowing we are safe from hooliganism.*
shielded: *The company is shielded from takeover attempts.*

5 If an object is secure, it is firmly fixed in place.

● THESAURUS
fastened: *Make sure the safety belt is fastened.*
firm: *If you have to climb up, use a firm platform.*
fixed: *Check the holder is fixed in its place on the wall.*
locked: *Leave doors and windows locked.*
solid: *I yanked on the bracket to see if it was solid.*
stable: *The structure must be stable.*
tight: *He kept a tight hold of her arm.*

6 If you feel secure, you feel safe and confident.
securely ADVERB

● THESAURUS
confident: *In time he became more confident.*
protected: *It's good to have a place in which you feel protected and loved.*
reassured: *I feel much more reassured when I've been for a health check.*
relaxed: *There are very few people he feels relaxed with.*
safe: *He kissed me and I felt warm and safe.*
<<OPPOSITE *insecure*

security [sɪˈkjʊərɪtɪ] NOUN OR ADJECTIVE
1 Security means all the precautions taken to protect a place. *e.g. Security forces arrested one member.*

> NOUN

2 A feeling of security is a feeling of being safe.

sedate [sɪˈdeɪt] **sedates, sedating, sedated** ADJECTIVE
1 quiet and dignified

> VERB

2 To sedate someone means to give them a drug to calm them down or make them sleep.
sedately ADVERB

sedative [ˈsɛdətɪv] **sedatives** NOUN
1 a drug that calms you down or makes you sleep

> ADJECTIVE

2 having a calming or soothing effect *e.g. antihistamines which have a sedative effect*
sedation NOUN

sedentary [ˈsɛdⁿtərɪ] ADJECTIVE
A sedentary occupation is one in which you spend most of your time sitting down.

sediment [ˈsɛdɪmənt] NOUN
1 Sediment is solid material that settles at the bottom of a liquid. *e.g. A bottle of beer with sediment in it is usually a guarantee of quality.*

2 Sediment is also small particles of rock that have been worn down and deposited together by water, ice, and wind.

sedimentary [ˌsɛdɪˈmɛntərɪ] ADJECTIVE
Sedimentary rocks are formed from fragments of shells or rocks that have become compressed. Sandstone and limestone are sedimentary rocks.

seduce [sɪˈdjuːs] **seduces, seducing, seduced** VERB
1 To seduce someone means to persuade them to have sex.

2 If you are seduced into doing something, you are persuaded to do it because it seems very attractive.

seductive [sɪˈdʌktɪv] ADJECTIVE
1 A seductive person is sexually attractive.

2 Something seductive is very attractive and tempting.
seductively ADVERB

see see page 773 for Word Web

seed [siːd] **seeds** NOUN
1 The seeds of a plant are the small, hard parts from which new plants can grow.

2 The seeds of a feeling or process are its beginning or origins. *e.g. the seeds of mistrust*

seedling [ˈsiːdlɪŋ] **seedlings** NOUN
a young plant grown from a seed

seedy [ˈsiːdɪ] **seedier, seediest** ADJECTIVE
untidy and shabby *e.g. a seedy hotel*

seek [siːk] **seeks, seeking, sought** VERB;
FORMAL
1 To seek something means to try to find it, obtain it, or achieve it. *e.g. The police were still seeking information.*

● THESAURUS
be after: *At last I found what I was after.*
hunt: *Police are hunting for clues.*
look for: *I'm looking for a lost child.*
search for: *searching for answers*

1 VERB
If you see something, you are looking at it or you notice it.
● THESAURUS
behold (LITERARY): *She looked into his eyes and beheld madness.*
discern (formal): *We could just discern the outline of the island.*
glimpse: *She glimpsed the man's face briefly.*
look: *She turned to look at him.*
notice: *She noticed a bird sitting on the roof.*
observe: *He observed a reddish spot on the planet's surface.*
perceive: *Infants start to perceive objects at a very early age.*
sight: *A fleet of French ships was sighted.*
spot: *I think he spotted me but didn't want to be seen.*

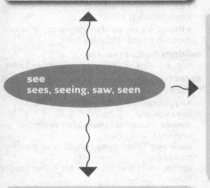

see
sees, seeing, saw, seen

2 VERB
To see something also means to realize or understand it *eg: I see what you mean.*
● THESAURUS
appreciate: *He appreciates the difficulties.*
comprehend: *They do not comprehend the nature of the problem.*
follow: *Do you follow what I'm saying?*
get: *You don't seem to get the point.*
grasp: *They have not grasped the seriousness of the crisis.*
realize: *They realized too late that they were wrong.*
understand: *I'm not sure I understand.*

3 VERB
If you say you will see what is happening, you mean you will find out.
● THESAURUS
ascertain (formal): *Ascertain what services your bank provides.*
determine: *The investigation will determine what really happened.*
discover: *Try to discover what you are good at.*
find out: *Watch the next episode to find out what happens.*

S

2 If you seek to do something, you try to do it. *e.g. De Gaulle sought to reunite the country.*

● THESAURUS
aim: *We aim to raise funds for charity.*
aspire to: *He aspired to work in music journalism.*
attempt: *He was forever attempting to arrange deals.*
endeavour: *They are endeavouring to protect trade union rights.*
strive: *The school strives to treat pupils as individuals.*
try: *We are trying to bring about a better world.*

seem [si:m] **seems, seeming, seemed**
VERB
If something seems to be the case, it appears to be the case or you think it is the case. *e.g. He seemed such a quiet chap.*

● THESAURUS
appear: *She appeared intoxicated.*
give the impression: *He gave the impression of being the perfect husband.*
look: *The cottage looks quite ordinary from the road.*
look like: *You look like a nice guy.*

seeming ['si:mɪŋ] ADJECTIVE
appearing to be real or genuine *e.g. this seeming disregard for human life*
seemingly ADVERB

seep [si:p] **seeps, seeping, seeped** VERB
If a liquid or gas seeps through something, it flows through very slowly.

seesaw ['si:ˌsɔ:] **seesaws** NOUN
a long plank, supported in the middle, on which two children sit, one on each end, and move up and down in turn

seething ['si:ðɪŋ] ADJECTIVE
If you are seething about something, you are very angry but it does not show.

segment ['sɛgmənt] **segments** NOUN
1 A segment of something is one part of it.

2 The segments of an orange or grapefruit are the sections which you can divide it into.

3 A segment of a circle is one of the two parts formed when you draw a straight line across it.

segregate ['sɛgrɪˌgeɪt] **segregates, segregating, segregated** VERB
To segregate two groups of people means to keep them apart from each other.
segregated ADJECTIVE, **segregation** NOUN

seize [si:z] **seizes, seizing, seized** VERB
1 If you seize something, you grab it firmly. *e.g. He seized the phone.*

● THESAURUS
grab: *I grabbed him by the neck.*
grasp: *He grasped both my hands.*

snatch: *Mick snatched the cards from Archie's hand.*

2 To seize a place or to seize control of it means to take control of it quickly and suddenly.

● THESAURUS
annex: *the plan to invade and annex Kuwait*
appropriate: *The land was appropriated by Communists.*
confiscate: *The police confiscated weapons and ammunition.*
hijack: *Almost 250 trucks were hijacked.*
impound: *The ship was impounded under the terms of the trade embargo.*

3 If you seize an opportunity, you take advantage of it.

4 If you seize on something, you immediately show great interest in it. *e.g. MPs have seized on a new report.*

seizure ['si:ʒə] **seizures** NOUN
1 a sudden violent attack of an illness, especially a heart attack or a fit

2 If there is a seizure of power, a group of people suddenly take control using force.

seldom ['sɛldəm] ADVERB
not very often *e.g. They seldom speak to each other.*

select [sɪ'lɛkt] **selects, selecting, selected** VERB
1 If you select something, you choose it.

● THESAURUS
choose: *Houston was chosen as the site for the conference.*
decide on: *I'm still trying to decide on an outfit for the wedding.*
opt for: *You may wish to opt for one method straight away.*
pick: *He had picked ten people to interview for the jobs.*
settle on: *I finally settled on the estate car because it was so roomy.*
single out: *His boss has singled him out for a special mission.*
take: *"I'll take the grilled tuna," she told the waiter.*

> ADJECTIVE
2 of good quality *e.g. a select gentlemen's club*
selector NOUN

● THESAURUS
choice: *We use only the choicest ingredients.*
exclusive: *Britain's most exclusive club*
first-class: *a first-class hotel*
first-rate: *The first-rate cast includes many famous names.*
hand-picked: *a hand-picked series of timeless classics*
prime: *one of the City's prime sites, with a view of several historic buildings*
special: *a special group of government officials*

superior: *a superior range of products*

selection [sɪ'lɛkʃən] **selections** NOUN

1 Selection is the choosing of people or things. *e.g. the selection of parliamentary candidates*

2 A selection of people or things is a set of them chosen from a larger group.

3 The selection of goods in a shop is the range of goods available. *e.g. a good selection of wines*

selective [sɪ'lɛktɪv] ADJECTIVE
choosing things carefully *e.g. I am selective about what I eat.*
selectively ADVERB

self [sɛlf] **selves** NOUN
Your self is your basic personality or nature. *e.g. Hershey is her normal dependable self.*

self- PREFIX

1 done to yourself or by yourself *e.g. self-help... self-control*

2 doing something automatically *e.g. a self-loading rifle*

self-assured [ˌsɛlfə'ʃʊəd] ADJECTIVE
behaving in a way that shows confidence in yourself

self-centred [ˌsɛlf'sɛntəd] ADJECTIVE
thinking only about yourself and not about other people

self-confessed [ˌsɛlfkən'fɛst] ADJECTIVE
admitting to having bad habits or unpopular opinions *e.g. a self-confessed liar*

self-confident [ˌsɛlf'kɒnfɪdənt] ADJECTIVE
confident of your own abilities or worth
self-confidence NOUN

self-conscious [ˌsɛlf'kɒnʃəs] ADJECTIVE
nervous and easily embarrassed, and worried about what other people think of you
self-consciously ADVERB

self-control [ˌsɛlfkən'trəʊl] NOUN
Self-control is the ability to restrain yourself and not show your feelings.

self-defence [ˌsɛlfdɪ'fɛns] NOUN
Self-defence is the use of special physical techniques to protect yourself when someone attacks you.

self-employed [ˌsɛlfɪm'plɔɪd] ADJECTIVE
working for yourself and organizing your own finances, rather than working for an employer

self-esteem [ˌsɛlfɪ'stiːm] NOUN
Your self-esteem is your good opinion of yourself.

self-evident [ˌsɛlf'ɛvɪdənt] ADJECTIVE
Self-evident facts are completely obvious and need no proof or explanation.

self-indulgent [ˌsɛlfɪn'dʌldʒənt] ADJECTIVE
allowing yourself to do or have things you enjoy, especially as a treat

self-interest [ˌsɛlf'ɪntrɪst] NOUN
If you do something out of self-interest, you do it for your own benefit rather than to help other people.

selfish ['sɛlfɪʃ] ADJECTIVE
caring only about yourself, and not about other people
selfishly ADVERB, **selfishness** NOUN

● THESAURUS
egoistic or **egoistical**: *egoistic motives*
egotistic or **egotistical**: *an intensely egotistic streak*
greedy: *greedy bosses awarding themselves big rises*
self-centred: *He was self-centred, but he wasn't cruel.*

selfless ['sɛlflɪs] ADJECTIVE
putting other people's interests before your own

self-made [ˌsɛlf'meɪd] ADJECTIVE
rich and successful through your own efforts *e.g. a self-made man*

self-raising [ˌsɛlf'reɪzɪŋ] ADJECTIVE
Self-raising flour contains baking powder to make it rise.

self-respect [ˌsɛlfrɪ'spɛkt] NOUN
Self-respect is a feeling of confidence and pride in your own abilities and worth.

self-righteous [ˌsɛlf'raɪtʃəs] ADJECTIVE
convinced that you are better or more virtuous than other people
self-righteousness NOUN

self-service [ˌsɛlf's3ːvɪs] ADJECTIVE
A self-service shop or restaurant is one where you serve yourself.

self-sufficient [ˌsɛlfsə'fɪʃənt] ADJECTIVE

1 producing or making everything you need, and so not needing to buy things

2 able to live in a way in which you do not need other people

sell [sɛl] **sells, selling, sold** VERB

1 If you sell something, you let someone have it in return for money.

● THESAURUS
deal in: *They deal in antiques.*
hawk: *vendors hawking trinkets*
peddle: *arrested for peddling drugs*
trade in: *They trade in spices and all kinds of grain.*
<<OPPOSITE buy

2 If a shop sells something, it has it available for people to buy. *e.g. a tobacconist that sells stamps*

● THESAURUS
deal in: *a business dealing in honey*
stock: *The shop stocks a variety of local craft products.*
trade in: *a company that trades in sporting memorabilia*

S

<<OPPOSITE buy

3 If something sells, people buy it. *e.g. This book will sell.*

sell out VERB
4 If a shop has sold out of something, it has sold it all.
seller NOUN

Sellotape ['sɛlə,teɪp] NOUN; TRADEMARK
Sellotape is a transparent sticky tape.

semblance ['sɛmbləns] NOUN
If there is a semblance of something, it seems to exist, although it might not really exist. *e.g. an effort to restore a semblance of normality*

semen ['siːmɛn] NOUN
Semen is the liquid containing sperm produced by a man's or male animal's sex organs.

semi- PREFIX
'Semi-' means half or partly *e.g. semiskilled workers*
[WORD HISTORY: from Latin SEMI- meaning 'half' or 'partly']

semibreve ['sɛmɪ,briːv] **semibreves** NOUN
(MUSIC) a musical note () which can be divided by any power of 2 to give all other notes. In the United States and Canada, a semibreve is known as a whole note

semicircle ['sɛmɪ,sɜːkəl] **semicircles** NOUN
a half of a circle, or something with this shape
semicircular ADJECTIVE

semicolon [,sɛmɪ'kəʊlən] **semicolons** NOUN
the punctuation mark (;), used to separate different parts of a sentence or to indicate a pause

semidetached [,sɛmɪdɪ'tætʃt] ADJECTIVE
A semidetached house is joined to another house on one side.

semifinal [,sɛmɪ'faɪnəl] **semifinals** NOUN
The semifinals are the two matches in a competition played to decide who plays in the final.
semifinalist NOUN

seminar ['sɛmɪ,nɑː] **seminars** NOUN
a meeting of a small number of university students or teachers to discuss a particular topic

semipermeable [,sɛmɪ'pɜːmɪəbəl] ADJECTIVE
A semipermeable material is one that certain substances with small enough molecules can pass through but which others with larger molecules can not.

semiprecious [,sɛmɪ'prɛʃəs] ADJECTIVE
Semiprecious stones are stones such as opals or turquoises that are used in jewellery. They are less valuable than precious stones.

semitone ['sɛmɪ,təʊn] **semitones** NOUN
(MUSIC) an interval representing the difference in pitch between a note and its sharpened or flattened equivalent. Two semitones are equal to one tone

Senate ['sɛnɪt] **Senates** NOUN
The Senate is the smaller, more important of the two councils in the government of some countries, for example Australia, Canada, and the USA.

senator ['sɛnətə] **senators** NOUN
a member of a Senate

send [sɛnd] **sends, sending, sent** VERB
1 If you send something to someone, you arrange for it to be delivered to them.
○ THESAURUS
dispatch: *He dispatched a telegram of congratulation.*
forward: *A letter was forwarded from the clinic.*
remit: *Many immigrants regularly remit money to their families.*

2 To send a radio signal or message means to transmit it.
○ THESAURUS
broadcast: *to broadcast a message to a whole group of people at once*
transmit: *the most efficient way to transmit data*

3 If you send someone somewhere, you tell them to go there or arrange for them to go.

4 If you send for someone, you send a message asking them to come and see you.

5 If you send off for something, you write and ask for it to be sent to you.

6 To send people or things in a particular direction means to make them move in that direction. *e.g. It should have sent him tumbling from the saddle.*

senile ['siːnaɪl] ADJECTIVE
If old people become senile, they become confused and cannot look after themselves.
senility NOUN

senior ['siːnjə] **seniors** ADJECTIVE
1 The senior people in an organization or profession have the highest and most important jobs.
○ THESAURUS
best: *These officers have traditionally taken the best jobs.*
better: *Well-qualified women are now attaining better positions.*
high-ranking: *a high-ranking officer in the medical corps*

superior: *negotiations between crew members and their superior officers*
<<OPPOSITE *junior*

> NOUN

2 Someone who is your senior is older than you.
seniority NOUN

senior citizen senior citizens NOUN
an elderly person, especially one receiving an old-age pension

sensation [sɛnˈseɪʃən] **sensations** NOUN
1 a feeling, especially a physical feeling
2 If something is a sensation, it causes great excitement and interest.

sensational [sɛnˈseɪʃənˀl] ADJECTIVE
1 causing great excitement and interest

2 INFORMAL
extremely good *e.g. a sensational party*
sensationally ADVERB

sense [sɛns] **senses, sensing, sensed** NOUN
1 Your senses are the physical abilities of sight, hearing, smell, touch, and taste.
2 a feeling *e.g. a sense of guilt*

⬤ THESAURUS
consciousness: *a consciousness of tension*
feeling: *It gave me a feeling of satisfaction.*
impression: *The music creates an impression of menace.*

3 A sense of a word is one of its meanings.
4 Sense is the ability to think and behave sensibly.

⬤ THESAURUS
brains: informal *At least I had the brains to keep quiet.*
common sense: *completely lacking in common sense*
intelligence: *He didn't have the intelligence to understand what was happening.*
judgment: *I respect his judgment.*
reason: *a conflict between emotion and reason*
wisdom: *the wisdom that comes of old age*

> VERB

5 If you sense something, you become aware of it.

⬤ THESAURUS
be aware of: *He was aware of her anger.*
feel: *Suddenly, I felt a presence behind me.*
get the impression: *I get the impression he's lying.*
have a hunch: *Lowe had a hunch he was on to something.*
realize: *We realized something was wrong.*

> PHRASE

6 If something **makes sense**, you can understand it or it seems sensible. *e.g. It makes sense to find out as much as you can.*

senseless [ˈsɛnslɪs] ADJECTIVE
1 A senseless action has no meaning or purpose. *e.g. senseless destruction*

2 If someone is senseless, they are unconscious.

sensibility [ˌsɛnsɪˈbɪlɪtɪ] **sensibilities** NOUN
Your sensibility is your ability to experience deep feelings. *e.g. a man of sensibility rather than reason*

sensible [ˈsɛnsɪbˀl] ADJECTIVE
showing good sense and judgment
sensibly ADVERB

⬤ THESAURUS
down-to-earth: *the most down-to-earth person I've ever met*
judicious: *the judicious use of military force*
practical: *practical suggestions*
prudent: *It is prudent to start any exercise programme gradually.*
rational: *a rational decision*
sound: *sound advice*
wise: *a wise move*
<<OPPOSITE *foolish*

sensitive [ˈsɛnsɪtɪv] ADJECTIVE
1 If you are sensitive to other people's feelings, you understand them.

2 If you are sensitive about something, you are worried or easily upset about it. *e.g. He was sensitive about his height.*

⬤ THESAURUS
easily offended: *I am not a feminist, nor am I easily offended.*
easily upset: *He remained deeply neurotic and easily upset.*
thin-skinned: *I'm too thin-skinned - I want everyone to like me.*
touchy: *She is very touchy about her weight.*

3 A sensitive subject or issue needs to be dealt with carefully because it can make people angry or upset.

4 Something that is sensitive to a particular thing is easily affected or harmed by it.
sensitively ADVERB, **sensitivity** NOUN

sensor [ˈsɛnsə] **sensors** NOUN
(ICT) an instrument which reacts to physical conditions such as light or heat

sensual [ˈsɛnsjʊəl] ADJECTIVE
1 showing or suggesting a liking for sexual pleasures *e.g. He was a very sensual person.*

2 giving pleasure to your physical senses rather than to your mind *e.g. the sensual rhythm of his voice*
sensuality NOUN

sensuous [ˈsɛnsjʊəs] ADJECTIVE
giving pleasure through the senses
sensuously ADVERB

S

sentence ['sɛntəns] **sentences, sentencing, sentenced** NOUN

1 a group of words which make a statement, question, or command. When written down a sentence begins with a capital letter and ends with a full stop

2 In a law court, a sentence is a punishment given to someone who has been found guilty.

> VERB

3 When a guilty person is sentenced, they are told officially what their punishment will be.

sentiment ['sɛntɪmənt] **sentiments** NOUN

1 a feeling, attitude, or opinion *e.g. I doubt my parents share my sentiments.*

2 Sentiment consists of feelings such as tenderness or sadness. *e.g. There's no room for sentiment in business.*

sentimental [,sɛntɪ'mɛntəl] ADJECTIVE

1 feeling or expressing tenderness or sadness to an exaggerated extent *e.g. sentimental love stories*

● THESAURUS

maudlin: *Jimmy turned maudlin after three drinks.*
mushy: informal *I go completely mushy when I see a baby.*
nostalgic: *nostalgic for the good old days*
sloppy: informal *I hate sloppy romantic films.*
slushy: informal *slushy ballads*

2 relating to a person's emotions *e.g. things of sentimental value*
sentimentality NOUN

sentinel ['sɛntɪnəl] **sentinels** NOUN; OLD-FASHIONED, INFORMAL
a sentry

sentry ['sɛntrɪ] **sentries** NOUN
a soldier who keeps watch and guards a camp or building

separate **separates, separating, separated** ADJECTIVE ['sɛprɪt] *or* ['sɛpərɪt]

1 If something is separate from something else, the two things are not connected.

● THESAURUS

detached: *a detached house*
disconnected: *sequences of disconnected events*
discrete: *two discrete sets of nerves*
divorced: *speculative theories divorced from reality*
isolated: *He lives as if isolated from the rest of the world.*
unconnected: *The two murders are unconnected.*
<<OPPOSITE connected

> VERB ['sɛpə,reɪt]

2 To separate people or things means to cause them to be apart from each other.

● THESAURUS

detach: *Three of the carriages on the train became detached.*

disconnect: *Make sure supply plugs are disconnected from the mains.*
divide: *This was a ruse to divide them.*
<<OPPOSITE connect

3 If people or things separate, they move away from each other.

4 If a married couple separate, they decide to live apart.
separately ADVERB, **separation** NOUN

● THESAURUS

break up: *She hadn't used his name since they broke up.*
divorce: *We divorced ten years ago.*
part: *He is parting from his Swedish-born wife Eva.*
split up: *I split up with my boyfriend last year.*

sepia ['si:pɪə] ADJECTIVE OR NOUN
deep brown, like the colour of old photographs
[WORD HISTORY: from Latin SEPIA meaning 'cuttlefish', because the brown dye is obtained from the ink of this fish]

September [sɛp'tɛmbə] NOUN
September is the ninth month of the year. It has 30 days.
[WORD HISTORY: from Latin SEPTEMBER meaning 'the seventh month']

septic ['sɛptɪk] ADJECTIVE
If a wound becomes septic, it becomes infected with poison.

sepulchre ['sɛpəlkə] **sepulchres** NOUN;
LITERARY
a large tomb

sequel ['si:kwəl] **sequels** NOUN

1 A sequel to a book or film is another book or film which continues the story.

2 The sequel to an event is a result or consequence of it. *e.g. There's a sequel to my egg story.*

sequence ['si:kwəns] **sequences** NOUN

1 A sequence of events is a number of them coming one after the other. *e.g. the whole sequence of events that had brought me to this place*

● THESAURUS

chain: *the chain of events leading to the assassination*
course: *a course of injections*
cycle: *the cycle of birth, growth, decay, and death*
progression: *The story of American freedom is anything but a linear progression.*
series: *a series of explosions*
string: *a string of burglaries*
succession: *He took a succession of jobs that stood him in good stead.*

2 The sequence in which things are arranged is the order in which they are arranged. *e.g. Do* *things in the right sequence.*

● **THESAURUS**
arrangement: *a simple arrangement of coloured tiles*
order: *Music shops should arrange their recordings in alphabetical order.*
pattern: *a systematic pattern of behaviour*
progression: *the natural progression of the seasons*
structure: *The bricks had been arranged in a regular structure.*

sequin ['siːkwɪn] **sequins** NOUN
Sequins are small, shiny, coloured discs sewn on clothes to decorate them.

Serbian ['sɜːbɪən] **Serbians** ADJECTIVE
1 belonging to or relating to Serbia
> NOUN
2 someone who comes from Serbia
3 Serbian is the form of Serbo-Croat spoken in Serbia.

Serbo-Croat ['sɜːbəʊ'krəʊæt] NOUN
Serbo-Croat is the main language spoken in Serbia and Croatia.

serenade [ˌserɪ'neɪd] **serenades, serenading, serenaded** VERB
1 If you serenade someone you love, you sing or play music to them outside their window.
> NOUN
2 a song sung outside a woman's window by a man who loves her

serene [sɪ'riːn] ADJECTIVE
peaceful and calm *e.g. She had a serene air.*
serenely ADVERB, **serenity** NOUN

serf [sɜːf] **serfs** NOUN
Serfs were servants in medieval Europe who had to work on their master's land and could not leave without his permission.

sergeant ['sɑːdʒənt] **sergeants** NOUN
1 a noncommissioned officer of middle rank in the army or air force
2 a police officer just above a constable in rank

sergeant major **sergeant majors** NOUN
a noncommissioned army officer of the highest rank

serial ['sɪərɪəl] **serials** NOUN
a story which is broadcast or published in a number of parts over a period of time *e.g. a television serial*

serial number **serial numbers** NOUN
An object's serial number is a number you can see on it which identifies it and distinguishes it from other objects of the same kind.

series ['sɪəriːz] NOUN
1 **(LIBRARY)** A series of things is a number of them coming one after the other. *e.g. a series of loud explosions*

● **THESAURUS**
chain: *a bizarre chain of events*
run: *The England skipper is haunted by a run of low scores.*
sequence: *a sequence of novels*
string: *a string of burglaries*
succession: *He had a succession of jobs.*

2 A radio or television series is a set of programmes with the same title.

serious see page 780 for Word Web

seriously ['sɪərɪəslɪ] ADVERB
1 You say seriously to emphasize that you mean what you say. *e.g. Seriously, though, something must be done.*
> PHRASE
2 If you **take something seriously**, you regard it as important.

sermon ['sɜːmən] **sermons** NOUN
a talk on a religious or moral subject given as part of a church service

serpent ['sɜːpənt] **serpents** NOUN; LITERARY
a snake

serrated [sə'reɪtɪd] ADJECTIVE
having a row of V-shaped points along the edge, like a saw *e.g. green serrated leaves*

servant ['sɜːvᵊnt] **servants** NOUN
someone who is employed to work in another person's house

serve [sɜːv] **serves, serving, served** VERB
1 If you serve a country, an organization, or a person, you do useful work for them.
2 To serve as something means to act or be used as that thing. *e.g. the room that served as their office*
3 If something serves people in a particular place, it provides them with something they need. *e.g. a recycling plant which serves the whole of the county*
4 If you serve food or drink to people, you give it to them.
5 To serve customers in a shop means to help them and provide them with what they want.
6 To serve a prison sentence or an apprenticeship means to spend time doing it.
7 When you serve in tennis or badminton, you throw the ball or shuttlecock into the air and hit it over the net to start playing.
> NOUN
8 the act of serving in tennis or badminton

server ['sɜːvə] **servers** NOUN
(ICT) a computer or computer program which supplies information or resources to a number of computers on a network

service ['sɜːvɪs] **services, servicing, serviced** NOUN

S

1 ADJECTIVE

A serious problem or situation is very bad and worrying.

● **THESAURUS**

acute: *an acute attack of appendicitis*

alarming: *the alarming increase in drug abuse*

bad: *a bad bout of flu*

critical: *He remains in a critical condition in hospital.*

dangerous: *His wound proved more dangerous than it seemed at first.*

extreme: *the most extreme case doctors have ever seen*

grave: *We are all in grave danger.*

grievous: *grievous wounds*

grim: *Our situation is grim indeed.*

intense: *Intense fighting has broken out in the capital.*

precarious: *He is in a very precarious position.*

severe: *a severe shortage of drinking water*

worrying: *It is a worrying situation.*

2 ADJECTIVE

Serious matters are important and should be thought about carefully.

● **THESAURUS**

crucial: *Negotiations were at a crucial stage.*

deep: *This novel raises deep questions about the nature of faith.*

difficult: *The government faces even more difficult problems.*

far-reaching: *His actions will have far-reaching consequences.*

grave: *a grave situation*

important: *We've got more important things to worry about now.*

momentous: *the momentous decision to go to war*

pressing: *a pressing problem*

profound: *a man who thinks about the more profound issues of life*

significant: *the most significant question of all*

urgent: *He is not equipped to deal with an urgent situation like this.*

weighty: *a weighty problem*

<< OPPOSITE *funny*

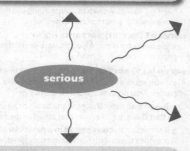

serious

3 ADJECTIVE

If you are serious about something, you are sincere about it *eg*: *You are really serious about having a baby.*

● **THESAURUS**

earnest: *It is my earnest hope that we can work things out.*

genuine: *a genuine offer*

heartfelt: *a full and heartfelt apology*

honest: *He looked at me in honest surprise.*

in earnest: *I can never tell if he is in earnest or not.*

resolute: *He was resolute about his ideals.*

resolved: *They are quite resolved about their decision.*

sincere: *He's sincere in his views.*

4 ADJECTIVE

People who are serious are thoughtful, quiet, and do not laugh much.

● **THESAURUS**

earnest: *She looked up at me with an earnest expression.*

grave: *He was looking unusually grave.*

humourless: *a dour, humourless Scotsman*

pensive: *We're both in a pensive mood today.*

sober: *sad, sober faces*

solemn: *His solemn little face broke into a smile.*

staid: *bored with her marriage to a staid country doctor*

stern: *a stern headmaster feared by all the pupils*

1 a system organized to provide something for the public *e.g. the bus service*

2 Some government organizations are called services. *e.g. the diplomatic service*

3 The services are the army, the navy, and the air force.

4 If you give your services to a person or organization, you work for them or help them in some way. *e.g. services to the community*

5 In a shop or restaurant, service is the process of being served.

6 a religious ceremony

7 When it is your service in a game of tennis or badminton, it is your turn to serve.

> **PLURAL NOUN**

8 Motorway services consist of a garage, restaurant, shop, and toilets.

> **VERB**

9 When a machine or vehicle is serviced, it is examined and adjusted so that it will continue working efficiently.

serviceman ['sɜːvɪsˌmæn] **servicemen**
NOUN
a man in the army, navy, or air force
servicewoman NOUN

service station service stations NOUN
a garage that sells petrol, oil, spare parts, and snacks

servile ['sɜːvaɪl] ADJECTIVE
too eager to obey people
servility NOUN

serving ['sɜːvɪŋ] **servings** NOUN
1 a helping of food
> **ADJECTIVE**
2 A serving spoon or dish is used for serving food.

session ['sɛʃən] **sessions** NOUN
1 a meeting of an official group *e.g. the emergency session of the Indiana Supreme Court*
2 a period during which meetings are held regularly *e.g. the end of the parliamentary session*
3 The period during which an activity takes place can also be called a session. *e.g. a drinking session*

set [sɛt] **sets, setting, set** NOUN
1 Several things make a set when they belong together or form a group. *e.g. a set of weights*

● THESAURUS
batch: *the latest batch of recruits*
kit: *I forgot my gym kit.*
outfit: *She was wearing a brand new outfit.*
series: *a series of books covering the history of aviation*

2 In maths, a set is a collection of numbers or other things which are treated as a group.

3 A television set is a television.

4 The set for a play or film is the scenery or furniture on the stage or in the studio.

5 In tennis, a set is a group of six or more games. There are usually several sets in a match.

> **VERB**

6 If something is set somewhere, that is where it is. *e.g. The house was set back from the beach.*

● THESAURUS
deposit: *Imagine if you were suddenly deposited on a desert island.*
lay: *Lay a sheet of newspaper on the floor.*
locate: *The restaurant is located near the cathedral.*
place: *She placed a mug of coffee in front of him.*
position: *Plants were carefully positioned in the alcove.*
put: *He put the photograph on the desk.*
rest: *He rested one of his crutches against the rail.*
stick: *Just stick your bag down anywhere.*

7 When the sun sets, it goes below the horizon.

8 When you set the table, you prepare it for a meal by putting plates and cutlery on it.

9 When you set a clock or a control, you adjust it to a particular point or position.

10 If you set someone a piece of work or a target, you give it to them to do or to achieve.

11 When something such as jelly or cement sets, it becomes firm or hard.

> **ADJECTIVE**

12 Something that is set is fixed and not varying. *e.g. a set charge*

● THESAURUS
arranged: *We arrived at the arranged time.*
established: *the established order*
firm: *a firm booking*
fixed: *a fixed rate of interest*
predetermined: *His destiny was predetermined from the moment of his birth.*
scheduled: *The plane failed to return at the scheduled time.*

13 If you are set to do something, you are ready or likely to do it.

14 If you are set on doing something, you are determined to do it.

● THESAURUS
bent: *He's bent on suicide.*
determined: *His enemies are determined to ruin him.*
intent: *an actress who was intent on making a comeback*

15 If a play or story is set at a particular time or in a particular place, the events in it take place at that time or in that place.

set about VERB
16 If you set about doing something, you start doing it.

S

set back VERB
17 If something sets back a project or scheme, it delays it.

set off VERB
18 When you set off, you start a journey.
19 To set something off means to cause it to start.

set out VERB
20 When you set out, you start a journey.
21 If you set out to do something, you start trying to do it.

set up VERB
22 If you set something up, you make all the necessary preparations for it. *e.g. We have done all we can about setting up a system of communication.*

● **THESAURUS**
arrange: *We have arranged a series of interviews.*
establish: *We have established links with industry and commerce.*
install: *I'm having cable installed next week.*
institute: *to institute better levels of quality control*
organize: *a two-day meeting organized by the UN*

setback ['sɛtˌbæk] **setbacks** NOUN
something that delays or hinders you

settee [sɛ'ti:] **settees** NOUN
a long comfortable seat for two or three people to sit on

setter ['sɛtə] **setters** NOUN
a long-haired breed of dog originally used in hunting

setting ['sɛtɪŋ] **settings** NOUN
1 The setting of something is its surroundings or circumstances. *e.g. The Irish setting made the story realistic.*
2 The settings on a machine are the different positions to which the controls can be adjusted.

settle ['sɛtˀl] **settles, settling, settled** VERB
1 To settle an argument means to put an end to it. *e.g. The dispute was settled.*

● **THESAURUS**
clear up: *Eventually the confusion was cleared up.*
decide: *None of the cases had been decided.*
dispose of: *the way in which you disposed of that problem*
put an end to: *I just want to put and end to this situation.*
reconcile: *urging the two parties to reconcile their differences*
resolve: *They hoped the crisis could be resolved peacefully.*
straighten out: *doing their best to straighten out this confusion*

2 If something is settled, it has all been decided and arranged.

● **THESAURUS**
agree: *We haven't agreed a date yet.*
arrange: *Have you arranged our next appointment?*
decide on: *They decided on an evening to meet.*
determine: *The final wording had not yet been determined.*
fix: *He's going to fix a time when I can see him.*

3 If you settle on something or settle for it, you choose it. *e.g. We settled for orange juice and coffee.*
4 When you settle a bill, you pay it.
5 If you settle in a place, you make it your permanent home.

● **THESAURUS**
make your home: *those who had made their homes in China*
move to: *His family moved to New Zealand when he was 12.*
people: *The plateau was peopled by nomadic tribes.*
populate: *The island was populated by Native Americans.*

6 If you settle yourself somewhere, you sit down and make yourself comfortable.
7 If something settles, it sinks slowly down and comes to rest. *e.g. A black dust settled on the walls.*

settle down VERB
8 When someone settles down, they start living a quiet life in one place, especially when they get married.
9 To settle down means to become quiet or calm.

settlement ['sɛtˀlmənt] **settlements** NOUN
1 an official agreement between people who have been involved in a conflict *e.g. the last chance for a peaceful settlement*
2 (GEOGRAPHY) a place where people have settled and built homes

settler ['sɛtlə] **settlers** NOUN
someone who settles in a new country *e.g. the first settlers in Cuba*

seven ['sɛvˀn]
the number 7

seventeen ['sɛvˀn'ti:n]
the number 17
seventeenth

seventh ['sɛvˀnθ] **sevenths**
1 The seventh item in a series is the one counted as number seven.
> NOUN
2 one of seven equal parts

seventy ['sɛvˀntɪ] **seventies**
the number 70
seventieth

sever ['sɛvə] **severs, severing, severed**
VERB

1 To sever something means to cut it off or cut right through it.

2 If you sever a connection with someone or something, you end it completely. *e.g. She severed her ties with England.*

several ['sɛvrəl] ADJECTIVE
Several people or things means a small number of them.
● THESAURUS
assorted: *overnight stops in assorted hotels*
some: *some cheers from the gallery*
sundry: *He has won sundry music awards.*
various: *a dozen trees of various sorts*

severe [sɪ'vɪə] ADJECTIVE
1 extremely bad or unpleasant *e.g. severe stomach pains*
● THESAURUS
acute: *an acute economic crisis*
critical: *if the situation becomes critical*
deep: *We will be in deep trouble if this goes on.*
dire: *This would have dire consequences for domestic peace.*
extreme: *people living in extreme poverty*
grave: *He said the situation was very grave.*
intense: *A number of people collapsed in the intense heat.*
serious: *The government faces very serious difficulties.*
terrible: *terrible injuries*
<<OPPOSITE *mild*

2 stern and harsh *e.g. Perhaps I was too severe with that young man.*
severely ADVERB, **severity** NOUN
● THESAURUS
disapproving: *Janet gave him a disapproving look.*
grim: *Her expression was grim and unpleasant.*
hard: *His father was a hard man.*
harsh: *the cold, harsh cruelty of her husband*
stern: *He said stern measures would be taken.*
strict: *My parents were very strict.*

sew [səʊ] **sews, sewing, sewed, sewn**
VERB
(D & T) When you sew things together, you join them using a needle and thread.
sewing NOUN

sewage ['suːɪdʒ] NOUN
Sewage is dirty water and waste which is carried away in sewers.

sewer ['suːə] **sewers** NOUN
an underground channel that carries sewage to a place where it is treated to make it harmless

sewerage ['suːərɪdʒ] NOUN
Sewerage is the system by which sewage is carried away and treated.

sex [sɛks] **sexes** NOUN

1 The sexes are the two groups, male and female, into which people and animals are divided.

2 The sex of a person or animal is their characteristic of being either male or female.

3 Sex is the physical activity by which people and animals produce young.

sexism ['sɛksɪzəm] NOUN
(PSHE) Sexism is discrimination against the members of one sex, usually women.
sexist ADJECTIVE OR NOUN

sextet [sɛks'tɛt] **sextets,** NOUN
a group of six musicians who sing or play together; also a piece of music written for six instruments or singers

sextuplet ['sɛkstjʊplɪt] **sextuplets** NOUN
Sextuplets are six children born at the same time to the same mother.

sexual ['sɛksjʊəl] ADJECTIVE
1 connected with the act of sex or with people's desire for sex *e.g. sexual attraction*
2 relating to the difference between males and females *e.g. sexual equality*
3 relating to the biological process by which people and animals produce young *e.g. sexual reproduction*
sexually ADVERB

sexual intercourse NOUN
Sexual intercourse is the physical act of sex between two people.

sexuality [,sɛksjʊ'ælɪtɪ] NOUN
A person's sexuality is their ability to experience sexual feelings.

sexy ['sɛksɪ] **sexier, sexiest** ADJECTIVE
sexually attractive or exciting *e.g. these sexy blue eyes*
● THESAURUS
erotic: *an erotic film*
seductive: *I love dressing up to look seductive.*
sensual: *a wide, sensual mouth*
sensuous: *his sensuous young mistress*
voluptuous: *a voluptuous figure*

shabby ['ʃæbɪ] **shabbier, shabbiest**
ADJECTIVE
1 old and worn in appearance *e.g. a shabby overcoat*
● THESAURUS
dilapidated: *a dilapidated old building*
ragged: *dressed in a ragged coat*
scruffy: *a scruffy basement flat in London*
seedy: *his seedy clothes*
tatty: *a tatty old cardigan*
threadbare: *a square of threadbare carpet*
worn: *a worn corduroy jacket*

2 dressed in old, worn-out clothes *e.g. a shabby figure crouching in a doorway*

3 behaving in a mean or unfair way *e.g. shabby treatment*
shabbily ADVERB

🔵 THESAURUS
contemptible: *contemptible behaviour*
despicable: *a despicable thing to do*
dirty: *That was a dirty trick.*
mean: *It was mean of you to hurt her like that.*
rotten: *informal That's a rotten thing to say!*

shack [ʃæk] **shacks** NOUN
a small hut

shackle [ˈʃækᵊl] **shackles, shackling, shackled** NOUN

1 In the past, shackles were two metal rings joined by a chain fastened around a prisoner's wrists or ankles.

> VERB

2 To shackle someone means to put shackles on them.

3 LITERARY
If you are shackled by something, it restricts or hampers you.

shade [ʃeɪd] **shades, shading, shaded** NOUN

1 Shade is an area of darkness and coolness which the sun does not reach. *e.g. The table was in the shade.*

2 a lampshade

3 The shades of a colour are its different forms. For example, olive green is a shade of green.

> VERB

4 If a place is shaded by trees or buildings, they prevent the sun from shining on it.

5 If you shade your eyes, you put your hand in front of them to protect them from a bright light.

shadow [ˈʃædəʊ] **shadows, shadowing, shadowed** NOUN

1 the dark shape made when an object prevents light from reaching a surface

2 Shadow is darkness caused by light not reaching a place.

> VERB

3 To shadow someone means to follow them and watch them closely.

shadow cabinet NOUN
The shadow cabinet consists of the leaders of the main opposition party, each of whom is concerned with a particular policy.

shadowy [ˈʃædəʊɪ] ADJECTIVE

1 A shadowy place is dark and full of shadows.

2 A shadowy figure or shape is difficult to see because it is dark or misty.

shady [ˈʃeɪdɪ] **shadier, shadiest** ADJECTIVE
A shady place is sheltered from sunlight by trees or buildings.

shaft [ʃɑːft] **shafts** NOUN

1 a vertical passage, for example one for a lift or one in a mine

2 A shaft of light is a beam of light.

3 A shaft in a machine is a rod which revolves and transfers movement in the machine. *e.g. the drive shaft*

shaggy [ˈʃægɪ] **shaggier, shaggiest** ADJECTIVE
Shaggy hair or fur is long and untidy.

shake [ʃeɪk] **shakes, shaking, shook, shaken** VERB

1 To shake something means to move it quickly from side to side or up and down.

🔵 THESAURUS
agitate: *Gently agitate the water.*
brandish: *He appeared brandishing a knife.*
flourish: *He flourished his glass to make the point.*
wave: *The crowd were waving flags and cheering.*

2 If something shakes, it moves from side to side or up and down with small, quick movements.

🔵 THESAURUS
jolt: *The train jolted again.*
quake: *The whole mountain quaked.*
quiver: *Her bottom lip began to quiver.*
shiver: *shivering with fear*
shudder: *Elaine shuddered with cold.*
tremble: *The leaves trembled in the breeze.*
vibrate: *The engine began to vibrate alarmingly.*

3 If your voice shakes, it trembles because you are nervous or angry.

4 If something shakes you, it shocks and upsets you.

🔵 THESAURUS
distress: *Her death had profoundly distressed me.*
disturb: *dreams so vivid that they disturb me for days*
rattle: *informal He was obviously rattled by events.*
shock: *Pictures of emaciated prisoners shocked the world.*
unnerve: *unnerved by the sight*
upset: *I was too upset to speak.*

5 When you shake your head, you move it from side to side in order to say 'no'.

> NOUN

6 If you give something a shake, you shake it.

> PHRASE

7 When you **shake hands** with someone, you grasp their hand as a way of greeting them.

shaky [ˈʃeɪkɪ] **shakier, shakiest** ADJECTIVE
rather weak and unsteady *e.g. Confidence in the economy is still shaky.*
shakily ADVERB

🔵 THESAURUS
rickety: *Mona climbed the rickety wooden stairway.*

tottering: *the baby's first tottering steps*
trembling: *She held out one frail, trembling hand.*
unstable: *an unstable lamp on top of an old tea-chest*
unsteady: *His voice was unsteady.*
wobbly: *I'm sorry, this table's a bit wobbly.*

shall [ʃæl] VERB

1 If I say I shall do something, I mean that I intend to do it.

2 If I say something shall happen, I am emphasizing that it will definitely happen, or I am ordering it to happen. *e.g. There shall be work and security!.*

3 'Shall' is also used in questions when you are asking what to do, or making a suggestion *e.g. Shall we sit down... Shall I go and check for you?.*

shallow [ˈʃæləʊ] **shallower, shallowest; shallows** ADJECTIVE

1 Shallow means not deep.

2 Shallow also means not involving serious thought or sincere feelings. *e.g. a well-meaning but shallow man*

> PLURAL NOUN

3 The shallows are the shallow part of a river or lake.

sham [ʃæm] **shams** NOUN

1 Something that is a sham is not real or genuine.

> ADJECTIVE

2 not real or genuine *e.g. a sham display of affection*

shambles [ˈʃæmbəlz] NOUN

If an event is a shambles, it is confused and badly organized.

shame [ʃeɪm] **shames, shaming, shamed** NOUN

1 Shame is the feeling of guilt or embarrassment you get when you know you have done something wrong or foolish.

THESAURUS
embarrassment: *He turned red with embarrassment.*
humiliation: *the humiliation of discussing her husband's affair*
ignominy: *the ignominy of being made redundant*

2 Shame is also something that makes people lose respect for you. *e.g. the scenes that brought shame to English soccer*

THESAURUS
discredit: *It was to his discredit that he did nothing.*
disgrace: *He had to resign in disgrace.*
dishonour: *his sense of dishonour at his brother's conduct*
scandal: *They often abandoned their children because of fear of scandal.*

3 If you say something is a shame, you mean you are sorry about it. *e.g. It's a shame you can't come round.*

> INTERJECTION

4 INFORMAL
In South African English, you say 'Shame!' to show sympathy.

> VERB

5 If something shames you, it makes you feel ashamed.

THESAURUS
disgrace: *I have disgraced my country.*
embarrass: *It embarrassed him that he had no idea of what was going on.*
humiliate: *His teacher continually humiliates him in maths lessons.*

6 If you shame someone into doing something, you force them to do it by making them feel ashamed not to. *e.g. Two children shamed their parents into giving up cigarettes.*

shameful [ˈʃeɪmfʊl] ADJECTIVE
If someone's behaviour is shameful, they ought to be ashamed of it.
shamefully ADVERB

shameless [ˈʃeɪmlɪs] ADJECTIVE
behaving in an indecent or unacceptable way, but showing no shame *e.g. shameless dishonesty*
shamelessly ADVERB

THESAURUS
barefaced: *a barefaced lie*
brazen: *a brazen theft*
flagrant: *a flagrant violation of the law*
unabashed: *an unabashed egotist*
unashamed: *blatant, unashamed hypocrisy*
wanton: *a wanton woman*

shampoo [ʃæmˈpuː] **shampoos, shampooing, shampooed** NOUN

1 Shampoo is a soapy liquid used for washing your hair.

> VERB

2 When you shampoo your hair, you wash it with shampoo.
[WORD HISTORY: from Hindi CHAMPNA meaning 'to knead']

shamrock [ˈʃæm,rɒk] **shamrocks** NOUN
a plant with three round leaves on each stem which is the national emblem of Ireland
[WORD HISTORY: from Irish Gaelic SEAMROG meaning 'little clover']

shanghai [ˈʃæŋhaɪ] **shanghais, shanghaiing, shanghaied** INFORMAL VERB

1 If someone is shanghaied, they are kidnapped and forced to work on a ship.

2 If you shanghai someone, you trick or force them into doing something.

S

> NOUN

3 In Australian and New Zealand English, a catapult.

shanty ['ʃæntɪ] **shanties** NOUN

1 a small, rough hut

2 A sea shanty is a song sailors used to sing.

shape [ʃeɪp] **shapes, shaping, shaped**
NOUN

1 The shape of something is the form or pattern of its outline, for example whether it is round or square.

● THESAURUS

contours: *the contours of the mountains*
figure: *a trim figure*
form: *the form of the human body*
lines: *The belt spoilt the lines of her long dress.*
outline: *the dim outline of a small boat*

2 something with a definite form, for example a circle or triangle

3 The shape of something such as an organization is its structure and size.

> VERB

4 If you shape an object, you form it into a particular shape. *e.g. Shape the dough into an oblong.*

● THESAURUS

fashion: *buttons fashioned from bone*
form: *The polymer is formed into a thin sheet.*
make: *gold made into wedding rings*
model: *She began modelling animals from clay.*
mould: *Mould the cheese into small ovals.*

5 To shape something means to cause it to develop in a particular way. *e.g. events that shaped the lives of some of the leading characters*

shapeless ['ʃeɪplɪs] ADJECTIVE
not having a definite shape

shapely ['ʃeɪplɪ] **shapelier, shapeliest**
ADJECTIVE
A shapely woman has an attractive figure.

shard [ʃɑːd] **shards** NOUN
a small fragment of pottery, glass, or metal

share [ʃɛə] **shares, sharing, shared** VERB
(DRAMA)

1 If two people share something, they both use it, do it, or have it. *e.g. We shared a bottle of champagne.*

● THESAURUS

divide: *The prize money was divided between the two winners.*
split: *We split the bill between us.*

2 If you share an idea or a piece of news with someone, you tell it to them.

> NOUN

3 A share of something is a portion of it.

● THESAURUS

allotment: *a daily allotment of three ounces of bread*
portion: *his portion of the inheritance*
quota: *a quota of four tickets per person*
ration: *their daily ration of water*

4 The shares of a company are the equal parts into which its ownership is divided. People can buy shares as an investment.

share out VERB

5 If you share something out, you give it out equally among a group of people.

shareholder ['ʃɛə,həʊldə] **shareholders**
NOUN
a person who owns shares in a company

share-milker ['ʃɛə,mɪlkə] **share-milkers**
NOUN
In New Zealand, someone who works on a dairy farm and shares the profit from the sale of its produce.

shark [ʃɑːk] **sharks** NOUN

1 Sharks are large, powerful fish with sharp teeth.

2 a person who cheats people out of money

sharp [ʃɑːp] **sharper, sharpest; sharps**
ADJECTIVE

1 A sharp object has a fine edge or point that is good for cutting or piercing things.

● THESAURUS

jagged: *jagged rocks*
keen: *a keen edge*
pointed: *pointed teeth*
razor-sharp: *the razor-sharp blade*
<<OPPOSITE blunt

2 A sharp outline or distinction is easy to see.

3 A sharp person is quick to notice or understand things.

● THESAURUS

alert: *She is alert and sprightly despite her 85 years.*
astute: *He made a series of astute business decisions.*
bright: *an exceptionally bright child*
observant: *an observant eye*
perceptive: *a perceptive gaze*
quick: *His quick mind soon grasped the situation.*
quick-witted: *He is very alert and quick-witted.*

4 A sharp change is sudden and significant. *e.g. a sharp rise in prices*

● THESAURUS

abrupt: *Her idyllic world came to an abrupt end when her parents died.*
marked: *a marked increase in crimes against property*
sudden: *a sudden change in course*

5 If you say something in a sharp way, you say it firmly and rather angrily.

6 A sharp sound is short, sudden, and quite loud.

7 A sharp pain is sudden and painful.

8 A sharp taste is slightly sour.

9 A musical instrument or note that is sharp is slightly too high in pitch.

> ADVERB

10 If something happens at a certain time sharp, it happens at that time precisely. *e.g. You'll begin at eight o'clock sharp.*

> NOUN

11 In music, a sharp is a note or key a semitone higher than that described by the same letter. It is represented by the symbol (♯).
sharply ADVERB, **sharpness** NOUN

sharpen ['ʃɑːpᵊn] **sharpens, sharpening, sharpened** VERB

1 To sharpen an object means to make its edge or point sharper.

2 If your senses or abilities sharpen, you become quicker at noticing or understanding things.
sharpener NOUN

shatter ['ʃætə] **shatters, shattering, shattered** VERB

1 If something shatters, it breaks into a lot of small pieces.

2 If something shatters your hopes or beliefs, it destroys them completely.

3 If you are shattered by an event or piece of news, you are shocked and upset by it.

shattered ['ʃætɪd] ADJECTIVE; INFORMAL
completely exhausted *e.g. He must be absolutely shattered after all his efforts.*

shattering ['ʃætərɪŋ] ADJECTIVE
making you feel shocked and upset *e.g. a shattering event*

shave [ʃeɪv] **shaves, shaving, shaved** VERB

1 When a man shaves, he removes hair from his face with a razor.

2 If you shave off part of a piece of wood, you cut thin pieces from it.

> NOUN

3 When a man has a shave, he shaves.

shaven ['ʃeɪvᵊn] ADJECTIVE
If part of someone's body is shaven, it has been shaved. *e.g. a shaven head*

shaver ['ʃeɪvə] **shavers** NOUN
an electric razor

shavings ['ʃeɪvɪŋz] PLURAL NOUN
Shavings are small, very thin pieces of wood which have been cut from a larger piece.

shawl [ʃɔːl] **shawls** NOUN
a large piece of woollen cloth worn round a woman's head or shoulders or used to wrap a baby in

she [ʃiː] PRONOUN
'She' is used to refer to a woman or girl whose identity is clear. 'She' is also used to refer to a country, a ship, or a car

sheaf [ʃiːf] **sheaves** NOUN

1 A sheaf of papers is a bundle of them.

2 A sheaf of corn is a bundle of ripe corn tied together.

shear [ʃɪə] **shears, shearing, sheared, shorn** VERB

1 To shear a sheep means to cut the wool off it.

> PLURAL NOUN

2 Shears are a tool like a large pair of scissors, used especially for cutting hedges.

shearer ['ʃɪərə] **shearers** NOUN
someone whose job is to shear sheep

sheath [ʃiːθ] **sheaths** NOUN

1 a covering for the blade of a knife

2 a condom

shed [ʃɛd] **sheds, shedding, shed** NOUN

1 a small building used for storing things

> VERB

2 When an animal sheds hair or skin, some of its hair or skin drops off. When a tree sheds its leaves, its leaves fall off.

3 FORMAL
To shed something also means to get rid of it. *e.g. The firm is to shed 700 jobs.*

4 If a lorry sheds its load, the load falls off the lorry onto the road.

5 If you shed tears, you cry.

sheen [ʃiːn] NOUN
a gentle brightness on the surface of something

sheep [ʃiːp] NOUN
A sheep is a farm animal with a thick woolly coat. Sheep are kept for meat and wool.

The plural of *sheep* is *sheep*

sheep-dip ['ʃiːp,dɪp] **sheep-dips** NOUN
a liquid disinfectant used to keep sheep clean and free of pests

sheepdog ['ʃiːp,dɒg] **sheepdogs** NOUN
a breed of dog often used for controlling sheep

sheepish ['ʃiːpɪʃ] ADJECTIVE
If you look sheepish, you look embarrassed because you feel shy or foolish.
sheepishly ADVERB

sheepskin ['ʃiːp,skɪn] NOUN
Sheepskin is the skin and wool of a sheep, used for making rugs and coats.

S

sheer [ʃɪə] **sheerer, sheerest** ADJECTIVE

1 Sheer means complete and total. *e.g. sheer exhaustion*

● THESAURUS

absolute: *I think it's absolute nonsense.*
complete: *He shook his head in complete bewilderment.*
pure: *To have an uninterrupted night's sleep was pure bliss.*
total: *This is total madness!*
unqualified: *It has been an unqualified disaster.*
utter: formal *a look of utter confusion*

2 A sheer cliff or drop is vertical.

● THESAURUS

perpendicular: *the perpendicular wall of sandstone*
steep: *a narrow valley with steep sides*
vertical: *The climber inched up a vertical wall of rock.*

3 Sheer fabrics are very light and delicate.

● THESAURUS

delicate: *delicate fabric*
fine: *a fine, pale grey material*
lightweight: *lightweight materials with Lycra*
thin: *the thin silk of her blouse*
<<OPPOSITE *thick*

sheet [ʃiːt] **sheets** NOUN

1 a large rectangular piece of cloth used to cover a bed

2 A sheet of paper is a rectangular piece of it.

3 A sheet of glass or metal is a large, flat piece of it.

sheik [ʃeɪk] **sheiks;** also spelt **sheikh** NOUN
an Arab chief or ruler

[WORD HISTORY: from Arabic SHAYKH meaning 'old man']

shelf [ʃɛlf] **shelves** NOUN
a flat piece of wood, metal, or glass fixed to a wall and used for putting things on

shell [ʃɛl] **shells, shelling, shelled** NOUN

1 The shell of an egg or nut is its hard covering.

2 The shell of a tortoise, snail, or crab is the hard protective covering on its back.

3 The shell of a building or other structure is its frame. *e.g. The room was just an empty shell.*

4 a container filled with explosives that can be fired from a gun

> VERB

5 If you shell peas or nuts, you remove their natural covering.

6 To shell a place means to fire large explosive shells at it.

shellfish [ˈʃɛlˌfɪʃ] **shellfish** or **shellfishes** NOUN
a small sea creature with a shell

shelter [ˈʃɛltə] **shelters, sheltering, sheltered** NOUN

1 a small building made to protect people from bad weather or danger

● THESAURUS

hostel: *She spent two years living in a hostel.*
refuge: *a mountain refuge*
sanctuary: *His church became a sanctuary for people fleeing the civil war.*

2 If a place provides shelter, it provides protection from bad weather or danger.

● THESAURUS

asylum: *refugees who sought political asylum*
cover: *They ran for cover from the storm.*
harbour: *Patches of gorse were a great harbour for foxes.*
haven: *The island is a haven for international criminals.*
protection: *Riot shields acted as protection against the attack.*
refuge: *They took refuge in an old barn.*
safety: *the safety of one's own home*
sanctuary: *Some of them sought sanctuary in the church.*

> VERB

3 If you shelter in a place, you stay there and are safe.

● THESAURUS

hide: *They hid behind a tree.*
huddle: *She huddled inside the porch.*
take cover: *Shoppers took cover behind cars as the shots rang out.*

4 If you shelter someone, you provide them with a place to stay when they are in danger.

● THESAURUS

harbour: *He was accused of harbouring terrorist suspects.*
hide: *They hid me until the coast was clear.*
protect: *A purple headscarf protected her against the wind.*
shield: *He shielded his head from the sun with a sack.*

sheltered [ˈʃɛltəd] ADJECTIVE

1 A sheltered place is protected from wind and rain.

2 If you lead a sheltered life, you do not experience unpleasant or upsetting things.

3 Sheltered accommodation is accommodation designed for old or handicapped people.

shelve [ʃɛlv] **shelves, shelving, shelved** VERB
If you shelve a plan, you decide to postpone it for a while.

shepherd [ˈʃɛpəd] **shepherds, shepherding, shepherded** NOUN

1 a person who looks after sheep

> VERB

2 If you shepherd someone somewhere, you accompany them there.

sheriff [ˈʃerɪf] **sheriffs** NOUN

1 In America, a sheriff is a person elected to enforce the law in a county.

2 In Australia, an administrative officer of the Supreme Court who carries out writs and judgments.

[WORD HISTORY: from Old English SCIR meaning 'shire' and GEREFA meaning 'reeve']

sherry [ˈʃerɪ] **sherries** NOUN

Sherry is a kind of strong wine.

[WORD HISTORY: from the Spanish town JEREZ where it was first made]

shield [ʃiːld] **shields, shielding, shielded** NOUN

1 a large piece of a strong material like metal or plastic which soldiers or policeman carry to protect themselves

2 If something is a shield against something, it gives protection from it.

> VERB

3 To shield someone means to protect them from something.

shift [ʃɪft] **shifts, shifting, shifted** VERB

1 If you shift something, you move it. If something shifts, it moves. *e.g. to shift the rubble*

2 If an opinion or situation shifts, it changes slightly.

> NOUN

3 A shift in an opinion or situation is a slight change.

4 a set period during which people work in a factory *e.g. the night shift*

shilling [ˈʃɪlɪŋ] **shillings** NOUN

a former British, Australian, and New Zealand coin worth one-twentieth of a pound

shimmer [ˈʃɪmə] **shimmers, shimmering, shimmered** VERB

1 If something shimmers, it shines with a faint, flickering light.

> NOUN

2 a faint, flickering light

shin [ʃɪn] **shins, shinning, shinned** NOUN

1 Your shin is the front part of your leg between your knee and your ankle.

> VERB

2 If you shin up a tree or pole, you climb it quickly by gripping it with your hands and legs.

shine [ʃaɪn] **shines, shining, shone** VERB

1 When something shines, it gives out or reflects a bright light. *e.g. The stars shone brilliantly.*

● THESAURUS

beam: *The spotlight beamed down on the stage.*
gleam: *The moonlight gleamed on the water.*
glow: *The lantern glowed softly in the darkness.*
radiate: *the amount of light radiated by an ordinary light bulb*
shimmer: *The lake shimmered in the sunlight.*
sparkle: *Diamonds sparkled on her wrists.*

2 If you shine a torch or lamp somewhere, you point it there.

shingle [ˈʃɪŋɡ^əl] **shingles** NOUN

1 Shingle consists of small pebbles on the seashore.

2 Shingles are small wooden roof tiles.

3 Shingles is a disease that causes a painful red rash, especially around the waist.

shining [ˈʃaɪnɪŋ] ADJECTIVE

1 Shining things are very bright, usually because they are reflecting light. *e.g. shining stainless steel tables*

● THESAURUS

bright: *a bright star*
brilliant: *brilliant sunshine*
gleaming: *gleaming headlights*
luminous: *the luminous dial on the clock*
radiant: *He saw a figure surrounded by a radiant light.*
shimmering: *a shimmering gold fabric*
sparkling: *elegant cutlery and sparkling crystal*

2 A shining example of something is a very good or typical example of that thing. *e.g. a shining example of courage*

shiny [ˈʃaɪnɪ] **shinier, shiniest** ADJECTIVE

Shiny things are bright and look as if they have been polished. *e.g. a shiny brass plate*

ship [ʃɪp] **ships, shipping, shipped** NOUN

1 a large boat which carries passengers or cargo

> VERB

2 If people or things are shipped somewhere, they are transported there.

-ship SUFFIX

'-ship' is used to form nouns that refer to a condition or position *e.g. fellowship*

[WORD HISTORY: from Old English]

shipment [ˈʃɪpmənt] **shipments** NOUN

1 a quantity of goods that are transported somewhere *e.g. a shipment of olive oil*

2 The shipment of goods is the transporting of them.

shipping [ˈʃɪpɪŋ] NOUN

1 Shipping is the transport of cargo on ships.

S

2 You can also refer to ships generally as shipping. *e.g. Attention all shipping!*.

shipwreck ['ʃɪpˌrɛk] **shipwrecks** NOUN
When there is a shipwreck, a ship is destroyed in an accident at sea. *e.g. He was drowned in a shipwreck.*

shipyard ['ʃɪpˌjɑːd] **shipyards** NOUN
a place where ships are built and repaired

shiralee [ˌʃɪrə'liː] **shiralees** NOUN; OLD-FASHIONED, INFORMAL
In Australian English, the bundle of possessions carried by a swagman.

shire [ʃaɪə] **shires** NOUN

1 OLD-FASHIONED
In Britain, a county.

2 In Australia, a rural district with its own local council.

shirk [ʃɜːk] **shirks, shirking, shirked** VERB
To shirk a task means to avoid doing it.

shirt [ʃɜːt] **shirts** NOUN
a piece of clothing worn on the upper part of the body, having a collar, sleeves, and buttons down the front

shiver ['ʃɪvə] **shivers, shivering, shivered** VERB

1 When you shiver, you tremble slightly because you are cold or scared.

> NOUN

2 a slight trembling caused by cold or fear

shoal [ʃəʊl] **shoals** NOUN
A shoal of fish is a large group of them swimming together.

shock [ʃɒk] **shocks, shocking, shocked** NOUN

1 If you have a shock, you have a sudden upsetting experience.

● THESAURUS
blow: *It was a terrible blow when he was made redundant.*
bombshell: *His departure was a bombshell for the team.*
distress: *She wanted to save her mother all the distress she could.*
trauma: *the trauma of losing a parent*

2 Shock is a person's emotional and physical condition when something very unpleasant or upsetting has happened to them.

3 In medicine, shock is a serious physical condition in which the blood cannot circulate properly because of an injury.

4 a slight movement in something when it is hit by something else *e.g. The straps help to absorb shocks.*

5 A shock of hair is a thick mass of it.

> VERB

6 If something shocks you, it upsets you because it is unpleasant and unexpected. *e.g. I was shocked by his appearance.*

● THESAURUS
numb: *numbed by suffering and terror*
paralyse: *He stood paralysed with horror.*
shake: *The news of her death has shaken us all.*
stagger: *The judge said he was staggered by the defendant's callousness.*
stun: *Audiences were stunned by the film's violent ending.*
traumatize: *My wife was traumatized by the experience.*

7 You can say that something shocks you when it offends you because it is rude or immoral.
shocked ADJECTIVE

● THESAURUS
appal: *I was appalled by her rudeness.*
disgust: *He disgusted everyone with his boorish behaviour.*
offend: *Many people are offended by strong swearwords.*
outrage: *They were outraged by his racist comments.*

shock absorber [əb'sɔːbə] **shock absorbers** NOUN
Shock absorbers are devices fitted near the wheels of a vehicle. They help to prevent the vehicle from bouncing up and down.

shocking ['ʃɒkɪŋ] ADJECTIVE

1 INFORMAL
very bad *e.g. It's been a shocking year.*

2 rude or immoral *e.g. a shocking video*

shoddy ['ʃɒdɪ] **shoddier, shoddiest** ADJECTIVE
badly made or done *e.g. a shoddy piece of work*

shoe [ʃuː] **shoes, shoeing, shod** NOUN

1 Shoes are strong coverings for your feet. They cover most of your foot, but not your ankle.

> VERB

2 To shoe a horse means to fix horseshoes onto its hooves.

shoestring ['ʃuːˌstrɪŋ] NOUN
If you do something on a shoestring, you do it using very little money.

shoot [ʃuːt] **shoots, shooting, shot** VERB

1 To shoot a person or animal means to kill or injure them by firing a gun at them.

2 To shoot an arrow means to fire it from a bow.

3 If something shoots in a particular direction, it moves there quickly and suddenly. *e.g. They shot back into Green Street.*

4 When a film is shot, it is filmed. *e.g. The whole film was shot in California.*

5 In games such as football or hockey, to shoot means to kick or hit the ball towards the goal.

> NOUN

6 an occasion when people hunt animals or birds with guns

7 a plant that is beginning to grow, or a new part growing from a plant

shooting [ˈʃuːtɪŋ] **shootings** NOUN
an incident in which someone is shot

shooting star **shooting stars** NOUN
a meteor

shop [ʃɒp] **shops, shopping, shopped**
NOUN

1 a place where things are sold

◉ THESAURUS
boutique: *He owns a jewellery boutique.*
market: *He sold fruit on a small market stall.*
store: *Within two years he was managing the store.*
supermarket: *Most of us do our food shopping in the supermarket.*

2 a place where a particular type of work is done *e.g. a bicycle repair shop*

> VERB

3 When you shop, you go to the shops to buy things.
shopper NOUN

shopkeeper [ˈʃɒpˌkiːpə] **shopkeepers**
NOUN
someone who owns or manages a small shop

shoplifting [ˈʃɒpˌlɪftɪŋ] NOUN
Shoplifting is stealing goods from shops.
shoplifter NOUN

shopping [ˈʃɒpɪŋ] NOUN
Your shopping is the goods you have bought from the shops.

shop steward **shop stewards** NOUN
a trade union member elected to represent the workers in a factory or office

shore [ʃɔː] **shores, shoring, shored** NOUN
The shore of a sea, lake, or wide river is the land along the edge of it. > VERB
If you shore something up, you reinforce it or strengthen it. *e.g. a short-term solution to shore up the worst defence in the League*

shoreline [ˈʃɔːˌlaɪn] **shorelines** NOUN
the edge of a sea, lake, or wide river

shorn [ʃɔːn]

1 Shorn is the past participle of **shear**
> ADJECTIVE
2 Grass or hair that is shorn is cut very short.

short see page 792 for Word Web

shortage [ˈʃɔːtɪdʒ] **shortages** NOUN
If there is a shortage of something, there is not enough of it.

◉ THESAURUS
dearth: *the dearth of good fiction by English authors*
deficiency: *tests for vitamin deficiency*
lack: *I was hampered by a lack of information.*
scarcity: *a scarcity of water*
shortfall: *a shortfall in income*
want: *a want of manners and charm*
<<OPPOSITE *abundance*

shortbread [ˈʃɔːtˌbrɛd] NOUN
Shortbread is a crumbly biscuit made from flour and butter.
[WORD HISTORY: from an old-fashioned use of
SHORT meaning 'crumbly']

short circuit **short circuits** NOUN
a fault in an electrical system when two points accidentally become connected and the electricity travels directly between them rather than through the complete circuit

shortcoming [ˈʃɔːtˌkʌmɪŋ] **shortcomings**
NOUN
Shortcomings are faults or weaknesses.

shortcut [ˈʃɔːtˌkʌt] **shortcuts** NOUN
1 a quicker way of getting somewhere than the usual route

2 a quicker way of doing something *e.g. Stencils have been used as a shortcut to hand painting.*

shorten [ˈʃɔːtⁿn] **shortens, shortening,
shortened** VERB
If you shorten something or if it shortens, it becomes shorter. *e.g. This might help to shorten the conversation.*

◉ THESAURUS
abbreviate: *He abbreviated his name to Alec.*
cut: *The film was cut to two hours.*
trim: *I need to get my hair trimmed.*
<<OPPOSITE *lengthen*

shortfall [ˈʃɔːtˌfɔːl] **shortfalls** NOUN
If there is a shortfall in something, there is less than you need.

shorthand [ˈʃɔːtˌhænd] NOUN
Shorthand is a way of writing in which signs represent words or syllables. It is used to write down quickly what someone is saying.

short-list [ˈʃɔːtˌlɪst] **short-lists, short-
listing, short-listed** NOUN
1 a list of people selected from a larger group, from which one person is finally selected for a job or prize

> VERB

2 If someone is short-listed for a job or prize, they are put on a short-list.

S

1 ADJECTIVE
not lasting very long eg: *a short break*
● THESAURUS
brief: *a brief meeting*
fleeting: *a fleeting glimpse*
momentary: *a momentary lapse of reason*
short-lived: *a short-lived craze*
<< OPPOSITE *long*

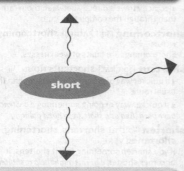

short

2 ADJECTIVE
small in height eg: *a short, elderly man*
● THESAURUS
diminutive: *a diminutive figure standing at the entrance*
dumpy: *a dumpy woman in a baggy tracksuit*
little: *She was too little to reach the books on the top shelf.*
petite: *a petite blonde woman*
small: *She is small for her age.*
tiny: *Though she was tiny, she had a loud voice.*
squat: *Eddie was a short, squat fellow in his mid-forties.*
<< OPPOSITE *tall*

3 ADJECTIVE
not using many words eg: *a short speech*
● THESAURUS
brief: *a brief description*
concise: *a concise summary*
succinct: *a succinct account*
terse: *a terse comment*

shortly ['ʃɔːtlɪ] ADVERB

1 Shortly means soon. *e.g. I'll be back shortly.*

2 If you speak to someone shortly, you speak to them in a cross and impatient way.

short-sighted [ʃɔːt'saɪtɪd] ADJECTIVE

1 If you are short-sighted, you cannot see things clearly when they are far away.

2 A short-sighted decision does not take account of the way things may develop in the future.

short-term [ʃɔːt'tɜːm] ADJECTIVE
happening or having an effect within a short time or for a short time

shot [ʃɒt] **shots**

1 Shot is the past tense and past participle of **shoot**

> NOUN

2 the act of firing a gun

3 Someone who is a good shot can shoot accurately.

4 In football, golf, and tennis, a shot is the act of kicking or hitting the ball.

5 a photograph or short film sequence *e.g. I'd like to get some shots of the river.*

6 INFORMAL
If you have a shot at something, you try to do it.

shotgun ['ʃɒt,ɡʌn] **shotguns** NOUN
a gun that fires a lot of small pellets all at once

shot put NOUN
In athletics, the shot put is an event in which the contestants throw a heavy metal ball called a shot as far as possible.
shot putter NOUN

should [ʃʊd] VERB

1 You use 'should' to say that something ought to happen. *e.g. Ward should have done better.*

2 You also use 'should' to say that you expect something to happen. *e.g. He should have heard by now.*

3 FORMAL
You can use 'should' to announce that you are about to do or say something. *e.g. I should like to express my thanks to the Professor.*

4 'Should' is used in conditional sentences *e.g. If they should discover the fact, what use would the knowledge be to them?.*

5 'Should' is sometimes used in 'that' clauses *e.g. It is inevitable that you should go.*

6 If you say that you should think something, you mean that it is probably true. *e.g. I should think that's unlikely.*

shoulder ['ʃəʊldə] **shoulders, shouldering, shouldered** NOUN

1 Your shoulders are the parts of your body between your neck and the tops of your arms.

> VERB

2 If you shoulder something heavy, you put it across one of your shoulders to carry it.

3 If you shoulder the responsibility or blame for something, you accept it.

shoulder blade **shoulder blades** NOUN
Your shoulder blades are the two large, flat bones in the upper part of your back, below your shoulders.

shout [ʃaʊt] **shouts, shouting, shouted**
NOUN

1 a loud call or cry

⬤ THESAURUS
bellow: *a bellow of rage*
cry: *She gave a cry of horror.*
roar: *a roar of approval*
scream: *screams of terror*
yell: *He let out a yell of delight.*

> VERB

2 If you shout something, you say it very loudly. *e.g. He shouted something to his brother.*

⬤ THESAURUS
bawl: *Laura and Peter were bawling at each other.*
bellow: *He bellowed orders down the phone.*
call: *He could hear them calling his name.*
cry: *"You're under arrest!" he cried.*
roar: *"I'll kill you for that!" he roared.*
scream: *screaming at them to get out of my house*
yell: *She pushed him away, yelling abuse.*

shove [ʃʌv] **shoves, shoving, shoved** VERB

1 If you shove someone or something, you push them roughly. *e.g. He shoved his wallet into a back pocket.*

> NOUN

2 a rough push

shove off VERB

3 INFORMAL If you tell someone to shove off, you are telling them angrily and rudely to go away.

shovel ['ʃʌvəl] **shovels, shovelling, shovelled** NOUN

1 a tool like a spade, used for moving earth or snow

> VERB

2 If you shovel earth or snow, you move it with a shovel.

show see page 794 for Word Web

show business NOUN
Show business is entertainment in the theatre, films, and television.

showdown ['ʃəʊ,daʊn] **showdowns** NOUN;
INFORMAL

S

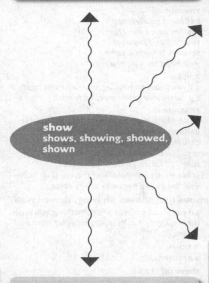

1 VERB
To show that something exists or is true means to prove it *eg*: *The survey showed that 29 per cent would now approve the treaty.*
● **THESAURUS**
demonstrate: *The study demonstrated a link between obesity and heart problems.*
prove: *History will prove him to be right.*

2 VERB
If you show someone how to do something, you demonstrate it to them.
● **THESAURUS**
demonstrate: *She demonstrated how to make ice cream.*
instruct: *He instructed us on how to give first aid.*
teach: *She taught me how to ride.*

3 VERB
If something shows a quality or characteristic, you can see that it has it *eg*: *Her sketches and watercolours showed promise.*
● **THESAURUS**
demonstrate: *He has demonstrated his ability.*
display: *He displayed remarkable courage.*
indicate: *Her choice of words indicated her real feelings.*
manifest: *Fear can manifest itself in many ways.*
reveal: *His reaction revealed a lack of self-confidence.*

show
shows, showing, showed, shown

4 NOUN
an exhibition *eg*: *the Napier Antiques Show*
● **THESAURUS**
display: *a gymnastics display*
exhibition: *an art exhibition*
presentation: *Julie's successful presentation to the board*

5 NOUN
A show of a feeling or attitude is behaviour in which you show it *eg*: *a show of optimism*
● **THESAURUS**
air: *an air of indifference*
display: *a display of remorse*
pose: *a pose of injured innocence*
pretence: *They have given up all pretence of neutrality.*
semblance: *trying to maintain a semblance of order*

a major argument or conflict intended to end a dispute

shower ['ʃaʊə] **showers, showering, showered** NOUN

1 a device which sprays you with water so that you can wash yourself

2 If you have a shower, you wash yourself by standing under a shower.

3 a short period of rain

4 You can refer to a lot of things falling at once as a shower. *e.g. a shower of confetti*

> VERB

5 If you shower, you have a shower.

6 If you are showered with a lot of things, they fall on you.

showing ['ʃəʊɪŋ] **showings** NOUN
A showing of a film or television programme is a presentation of it so that the public can see it.

showjumping ['ʃəʊ,dʒʌmpɪŋ] NOUN
Showjumping is a horse-riding competition in which the horses jump over a series of high fences.

show-off ['ʃəʊ,ɒf] **show-offs** NOUN; INFORMAL
someone who tries to impress people with their knowledge or skills

showroom ['ʃəʊ,ruːm] **showrooms** NOUN
a shop where goods such as cars or electrical appliances are displayed

showy ['ʃəʊɪ] **showier, showiest** ADJECTIVE
large or bright and intended to impress people
e.g. a showy house

shrapnel ['ʃræpnəl] NOUN
Shrapnel consists of small pieces of metal scattered from an exploding shell.
[WORD HISTORY: named after General Henry SHRAPNEL (1761-1842), who invented it]

shred [ʃrɛd] **shreds, shredding, shredded** VERB

1 If you shred something, you cut or tear it into very small pieces.

> NOUN

2 A shred of paper or material is a small, narrow piece of it.

3 If there is not a shred of something, there is absolutely none of it. *e.g. He was left without a shred of self-esteem.*

shrew [ʃruː] **shrews** NOUN
a small mouse-like animal with a long pointed nose

shrewd [ʃruːd] **shrewder, shrewdest** ADJECTIVE
Someone who is shrewd is intelligent and makes good judgments.

shrewdly ADVERB, **shrewdness** NOUN

THESAURUS
astute: *an astute judge of character*
canny: *He was far too canny to give himself away.*
crafty: *He is a clever man and a crafty politician.*
perceptive: *a perceptive analysis of the situation*
sharp: *He is very sharp, and a quick thinker.*
smart: *a very smart move*

shriek [ʃriːk] **shrieks, shrieking, shrieked** NOUN

1 a high-pitched scream

> VERB

2 If you shriek, you make a high-pitched scream.

shrift [ʃrɪft] NOUN
If you give someone or something short shrift, you pay very little attention to them.
[WORD HISTORY: from Old English SCRIFT meaning 'confession'; 'short shrift' referred to the short time allowed to prisoners before they were put to death to make their confession]

shrill [ʃrɪl] **shriller, shrillest** ADJECTIVE
A shrill sound is unpleasantly high-pitched and piercing.
shrilly ADVERB

THESAURUS
penetrating: *a penetrating voice*
piercing: *a piercing squawk*
sharp: *the sharp cry of a vixen*

shrimp [ʃrɪmp] **shrimps** NOUN
a small edible shellfish with a long tail and many legs

shrine [ʃraɪn] **shrines** NOUN
(RE) a place of worship associated with a sacred person or object

shrink [ʃrɪŋk] **shrinks, shrinking, shrank, shrunk** VERB

1 If something shrinks, it becomes smaller.

THESAURUS
contract: *The ribcage expands and contracts as you breathe.*
diminish: *The threat of nuclear war has diminished.*
dwindle: *The factory's workforce has dwindled from 4000 to 200.*
get smaller: *Electronic systems are getting smaller.*
narrow: *The gap between the two parties has narrowed.*
<<OPPOSITE grow

2 If you shrink from something, you move away from it because you are afraid of it.
shrinkage NOUN

shrivel ['ʃrɪvəl] **shrivels, shrivelling, shrivelled** VERB
When something shrivels, it becomes dry and withered.

S

shroud [ʃraʊd] **shrouds, shrouding, shrouded** NOUN

1 a cloth in which a dead body is wrapped before it is buried

> VERB

2 If something is shrouded in darkness or fog, it is hidden by it.

shrub [ʃrʌb] **shrubs** NOUN
a low, bushy plant

shrug [ʃrʌg] **shrugs, shrugging, shrugged** VERB

1 If you shrug your shoulders, you raise them slightly as a sign of indifference.

> NOUN

2 If you give a shrug of your shoulders, you shrug them.

shrunken [ʃrʌŋkᵊn] ADJECTIVE; FORMAL
Someone or something that is shrunken has become smaller than it used to be. *e.g. a shrunken old man*

shudder [ʃʌdə] **shudders, shuddering, shuddered** VERB

1 If you shudder, you tremble with fear or horror.

2 If a machine or vehicle shudders, it shakes violently.

> NOUN

3 a shiver of fear or horror

shuffle [ʃʌfᵊl] **shuffles, shuffling, shuffled** VERB

1 If you shuffle, you walk without lifting your feet properly off the ground.

2 If you shuffle about, you move about and fidget because you feel uncomfortable or embarrassed.

3 If you shuffle a pack of cards, you mix them up before you begin a game.

> NOUN

4 the way someone walks when they shuffle

shun [ʃʌn] **shuns, shunning, shunned** VERB
If you shun someone or something, you deliberately avoid them.

shunt [ʃʌnt] **shunts, shunting, shunted** VERB; INFORMAL
If you shunt people or things to a place, you move them there. *e.g. You are shunted from room to room.*

shut [ʃʌt] **shuts, shutting, shut** VERB

1 If you shut something, you close it.

● THESAURUS

close: *If you are cold, close the window.*
fasten: *He fastened the diamond clasp of the necklace.*
slam: *He slammed the gate shut behind him.*
<<OPPOSITE open

2 When a shop or pub shuts, it is closed and you can no longer go into it.

> ADJECTIVE

3 If something is shut, it is closed.

● THESAURUS

closed: *All the exits were closed.*
fastened: *The pockets are fastened with buttons.*
sealed: *a sealed envelope*
<<OPPOSITE open

> VERB

4 shut up INFORMAL If you shut up, you stop talking.

shutter [ʃʌtə] **shutters** NOUN
Shutters are hinged wooden or metal covers fitted on the outside or inside of a window.

shuttle [ʃʌtᵊl] **shuttles** ADJECTIVE

1 A shuttle service is an air, bus, or train service which makes frequent journeys between two places.

> NOUN

2 a plane used in a shuttle service

shuttlecock [ʃʌtᵊl‚kɒk] **shuttlecocks** NOUN
the feathered object used as a ball in the game of badminton

shy [ʃaɪ] **shyer, shyest; shies, shying, shied** ADJECTIVE

1 A shy person is nervous and uncomfortable in the company of other people.

● THESAURUS

bashful: *Offstage, he is bashful and awkward.*
retiring: *He was the quiet, retiring type.*
self-conscious: *I felt a bit self-conscious in my swimming costume.*
timid: *a timid little boy*
<<OPPOSITE bold

> VERB

2 When a horse shies, it moves away suddenly because something has frightened it.

3 If you shy away from doing something, you avoid doing it because you are afraid or nervous.
shyly ADVERB, **shyness** NOUN

sibling [sɪblɪŋ] **siblings** NOUN; FORMAL
Your siblings are your brothers and sisters.

sick [sɪk] **sicker, sickest** ADJECTIVE

1 If you are sick, you are ill.

● THESAURUS

ailing: *She tenderly nursed her ailing mother.*
poorly: informal *I called Julie and she's still poorly.*
under par: informal *The flu has left me feeling under par.*
under the weather: *Are you still a bit under the weather?*
unwell: *She had been unwell for some time.*

<<OPPOSITE *well*

2 If you feel sick, you feel as if you are going to vomit. If you are sick, you vomit.

● THESAURUS
ill: *The smell of curry always makes me ill.*
nauseous: *These drugs may make you feel nauseous.*
queasy: *The motion of the ship was already making him queasy.*

3 INFORMAL
If you are sick of doing something, you feel you have been doing it too long.

● THESAURUS
bored: *I'm getting bored with the whole business.*
fed up: *He is fed up with this country.*
tired: *I am tired of this music.*
weary: *She was weary of being alone.*

4 INFORMAL
A sick joke or story deals with death or suffering in an unpleasantly frivolous way.

> PHRASE
5 If something **makes you sick**, it makes you angry.
sickness NOUN

sicken ['sɪkən] **sickens, sickening, sickened** VERB
If something sickens you, it makes you feel disgusted.
sickening ADJECTIVE

sickle ['sɪkəl] **sickles** NOUN
a tool with a short handle and a curved blade used for cutting grass or grain

sickly ['sɪklɪ] **sicklier, sickliest** ADJECTIVE
1 A sickly person or animal is weak and unhealthy.
2 Sickly also means very unpleasant to smell or taste.

side [saɪd] **sides, siding, sided** NOUN
1 Side refers to a position to the left or right of something. *e.g. the two armchairs on either side of the fireplace*

● THESAURUS
edge: *She fell over the edge of the balcony.*
verge: *He parked on the verge of the road.*

2 The sides of a boundary or barrier are the two areas it separates. *e.g. this side of the border*
3 Your sides are the parts of your body from your armpits down to your hips.
4 The sides of something are its outside surfaces, especially the surfaces which are not its front or back.
5 The sides of a hill or valley are the parts that slope.
6 The two sides in a war, argument, or relationship are the two people or groups involved.

● THESAURUS
camp: *Most of his supporters had now defected to the opposite camp.*
faction: *leaders of the warring factions*
party: *the candidates for the three main parties*
team: *Both teams played well.*

7 A particular side of something is one aspect of it. *e.g. the sensitive, caring side of human nature*

> ADJECTIVE
8 situated on a side of a building or vehicle *e.g. the side door*
9 A side road is a small road leading off a larger one.
10 A side issue is an issue that is less important than the main one.

> VERB
11 If you side with someone in an argument, you support them.

● THESAURUS
agree with: *She's bound to agree with her husband.*
stand up for: *I was the one who always stood up for my mother.*
support: *a fellow prisoner who supported her*
take the part of: *Why do you always take his part?*

sideboard ['saɪdˌbɔːd] **sideboards** NOUN
1 a long, low cupboard for plates and glasses

> PLURAL NOUN
2 A man's sideboards are his sideburns.

sideburns ['saɪdˌbɜːnz] PLURAL NOUN
A man's sideburns are areas of hair growing on his cheeks in front of his ears.
[WORD HISTORY: from a 19th century US army general called BURNSIDE who wore his whiskers like this]

side effect side effects NOUN
The side effects of a drug are the effects it has in addition to its main effects.

sidekick ['saɪdˌkɪk] **sidekicks** NOUN;
INFORMAL
Someone's sidekick is their close friend who spends a lot of time with them.

sideline ['saɪdˌlaɪn] **sidelines** NOUN
an extra job in addition to your main job

sideshow ['saɪdˌʃəʊ] **sideshows** NOUN
Sideshows are stalls at a fairground.

sidestep ['saɪdˌstɛp] **sidesteps, sidestepping, sidestepped** VERB
If you sidestep a difficult problem or question, you avoid dealing with it.

sidewalk ['saɪdˌwɔːk] **sidewalks** NOUN
In American English, a sidewalk is a pavement.

sideways ['saɪdˌweɪz] ADVERB
from or towards the side of something or someone

S

siding ['saɪdɪŋ] **sidings** NOUN
a short railway track beside the main tracks, where engines and carriages are left when not in use

sidle ['saɪdəl] **sidles, sidling, sidled** VERB
If you sidle somewhere, you walk there cautiously and slowly, as if you do not want to be noticed.

siege [siːdʒ] **sieges** NOUN
(HISTORY) a military operation in which an army surrounds a place and prevents food or help from reaching the people inside

sieve [sɪv] **sieves, sieving, sieved** NOUN
1 a kitchen tool made of mesh, used for sifting or straining things
> VERB
2 If you sieve a powder or liquid, you pass it through a sieve.

sift [sɪft] **sifts, sifting, sifted** VERB
1 If you sift a powdery substance, you pass it through a sieve to remove lumps.
2 If you sift through something such as evidence, you examine it all thoroughly.

sigh [saɪ] **sighs, sighing, sighed** VERB
1 When you sigh, you let out a deep breath.
> NOUN
2 the breath you let out when you sigh

sight [saɪt] **sights, sighting, sighted** NOUN
1 Sight is the ability to see. *e.g. His sight was so poor that he could not follow the cricket.*

● THESAURUS
eyesight: *He suffered from weak eyesight.*
visibility: *Visibility was very poor.*
vision: *It can cause blindness or serious loss of vision.*

2 something you see *e.g. It was a ghastly sight.*

● THESAURUS
display: *These flowers make a colourful display in spring.*
scene: *a bizarre scene*
spectacle: *an impressive spectacle*

> PLURAL NOUN
3 Sights are interesting places which tourists visit.

> VERB
4 If you sight someone or something, you see them briefly or suddenly. *e.g. He had been sighted in Cairo.*

● THESAURUS
see: *I saw a deer in the woods today.*
spot: *I drove round till I spotted her.*

> PHRASES
5 If something is **in sight**, you can see it. If it is

out of sight, you cannot see it.

▨ Do not confuse the spellings of *sight* and *site*

sighted ['saɪtɪd] ADJECTIVE
Someone who is sighted can see.

sighting ['saɪtɪŋ] **sightings** NOUN
A sighting of something rare or unexpected is an occasion when it is seen.

sightseeing ['saɪt,siːɪŋ] NOUN
Sightseeing is visiting the interesting places that tourists usually visit.
sightseer NOUN

sign [saɪn] **signs, signing, signed** NOUN
1 a mark or symbol that always has a particular meaning, for example in mathematics or music

● THESAURUS
character: *the characters used in the hallmarking system*
emblem: *a small yellow hammer-and-sickle emblem*
logo: *the company's logo*
mark: *Put a tick mark against the statements you agree with.*
symbol: *the chemical symbol for mercury*

2 a gesture with a particular meaning

3 A sign can also consist of words, a picture, or a symbol giving information or a warning.

● THESAURUS
board: *He studied the destination board on the front of the bus.*
notice: *a notice saying "no entry"*
placard: *The protesters sang songs and waved placards.*

4 (RE) A sign is an event or happening that some people believe God has sent as a warning or instruction to an individual or to people in general.

5 If there are signs of something, there is evidence that it exists or is happening. *e.g. We are now seeing the first signs of recovery.*

● THESAURUS
clue: *the only real clue that something was wrong*
evidence: *there has been no evidence of criminal activity*
hint: *He showed only the slightest hint of emotion.*
indication: *All the indications suggest that he is the murderer.*
symptom: *typical symptoms of stress*
token: *a token of goodwill*
trace: *No traces of violence were found on the body.*

> VERB
6 If you sign a document, you write your name on it. *e.g. He hurriedly signed the death certificate.*

7 If you sign, you communicate by using sign language.

sign on VERB

8 If you sign on for a job or course, you officially agree to do it by signing a contract.

9 When people sign on, they officially state that they are unemployed and claim benefit from the state.

sign up VERB

10 If you sign up for a job or course, you officially agree to do it by signing a contract.

signal ['sɪgnəl] **signals, signalling, signalled** NOUN

1 a gesture, sound, or action intended to give a message to someone

● THESAURUS

beacon: *an emergency beacon*

cue: *He gave me my cue to speak.*

gesture: *She made a menacing gesture with her fist.*

sign: *They gave him the thumbs-up sign.*

2 A railway signal is a piece of equipment beside the track which tells train drivers whether to stop or not.

> VERB

3 If you signal to someone, you make a gesture or sound to give them a message.

● THESAURUS

beckon: *I beckoned her over.*

gesticulate: *He was gesticulating at a hole in the ground.*

gesture: *I gestured towards the house, and he went in.*

motion: *He motioned to her to go behind the screen.*

nod: *They nodded goodnight to the security man.*

sign: *She signed to me to come near.*

wave: *He waved the servants out of the tent.*

signature ['sɪgnɪtʃə] **signatures** NOUN

If you write your signature, you write your name the way you usually write it.

significant [sɪg'nɪfɪkənt] ADJECTIVE

large or important *e.g. a significant amount... a significant victory*

significance NOUN, **significantly** ADVERB

● THESAURUS

considerable: formal *Doing it properly makes considerable demands on our time.*

important: *The strike represents an important challenge to the government.*

impressive: *an impressive achievement*

marked: *a marked increase in crimes against property*

notable: *With a few notable exceptions, doctors are a pretty sensible lot.*

pronounced: *The exhibition has a pronounced Scottish theme.*

striking: *The most striking feature of these statistics is the rate of growth.*

<<OPPOSITE *insignificant*

signify ['sɪgnɪˌfaɪ] **signifies, signifying, signified** VERB

A gesture that signifies something has a particular meaning. *e.g. They signified a desire to leave.*

sign language NOUN

Sign language is a way of communicating using your hands, used especially by deaf people.

signpost ['saɪnˌpəʊst] **signposts** NOUN

a road sign with information on it such as the name of a town and how far away it is

Sikh [siːk] **Sikhs** NOUN

(RE) a person who believes in Sikhism, an Indian religion which separated from Hinduism in the sixteenth century and which teaches that there is only one God

Sikhism NOUN

[WORD HISTORY: from Hindi SIKH meaning 'disciple']

silence ['saɪləns] **silences, silencing, silenced** NOUN

1 Silence is quietness.

● THESAURUS

calm: *He liked the calm of the evening.*

hush: *A hush fell over the crowd.*

lull: *a lull in the conversation*

peace: *I love the peace of the countryside.*

quiet: *The quiet of the flat was very soothing.*

stillness: *An explosion shattered the stillness of the night air.*

<<OPPOSITE *noise*

2 Someone's silence about something is their failure or refusal to talk about it.

● THESAURUS

dumbness: *a woman traumatized into dumbness*

muteness: *He retreated into stubborn muteness.*

reticence: *Fran didn't seem to notice my reticence.*

speechlessness: *He was shy to the point of speechlessness.*

> VERB

3 To silence someone or something means to stop them talking or making a noise.

● THESAURUS

deaden: *We hung up curtains to try and deaden the noise.*

gag: *I gagged him with a towel.*

muffle: *You can muffle the sound with absorbent material.*

quiet: *A look from her husband quieted her at once.*

quieten: *She tried to quieten her breathing.*

stifle: *He put his hand to his mouth to stifle a giggle.*

still: *He raised a hand to still Alex's protest.*

suppress: *She barely suppressed a gasp.*

silent ['saɪlənt] ADJECTIVE

1 If you are silent, you are not saying anything.

● THESAURUS

dumb: *We were all struck dumb for a moment.*
mute: *a mute look of appeal*
speechless: *speechless with rage*
taciturn: *a taciturn man with a solemn expression*
wordless: *They exchanged a wordless look of understanding.*

2 If you are silent about something, you do not tell people about it.

3 When something is silent, it makes no noise.

● THESAURUS

hushed: *the vast, hushed space of the cathedral*
quiet: *a quiet engine*
soundless: *My bare feet were soundless on the carpet.*
still: *The room was suddenly still.*
<<OPPOSITE *noisy*

4 A silent film has only pictures and no sound.
silently ADVERB

silhouette [ˌsɪluːˈɛt] **silhouettes** NOUN
the outline of a dark shape against a light background
silhouetted ADJECTIVE

silicon [ˈsɪlɪkən] NOUN
Silicon is an element found in sand, clay, and stone. It is used to make parts of computers.

silk [sɪlk] **silks** NOUN
Silk is a fine, soft cloth made from a substance produced by silkworms.
[WORD HISTORY: from Chinese ssu meaning 'silk']

silkworm [ˈsɪlkˌwɜːm] **silkworms** NOUN
Silkworms are the larvae of a particular kind of moth.

silky [ˈsɪlkɪ] **silkier, silkiest** ADJECTIVE
smooth and soft

sill [sɪl] **sills** NOUN
a ledge at the bottom of a window

silly [ˈsɪlɪ] **sillier, silliest** ADJECTIVE
foolish or childish

● THESAURUS

absurd: *He found fashion absurd.*
daft: *That's a daft question.*
foolish: *It is foolish to risk injury.*
idiotic: *What an idiotic thing to say!*
inane: *He stood there with an inane grin on his face.*
ridiculous: *a ridiculous suggestion*
stupid: *a stupid mistake*

silt [sɪlt] NOUN
Silt is fine sand or soil which is carried along by a river.

silver [ˈsɪlvə] NOUN
1 Silver is a valuable greyish-white metallic element used for making jewellery and ornaments.

2 Silver is also coins made from silver or from silver-coloured metal.

> ADJECTIVE OR NOUN
3 greyish-white

silver beet **silver beets** NOUN
a type of beet grown in Australia and New Zealand

silver fern NOUN
a tall fern that is found in New Zealand. It is the symbol of New Zealand national sports teams

silverfish [ˈsɪlvəˌfɪʃ] **silverfishes** or **silverfish** NOUN
a small silver insect with no wings that eats paper and clothing

silver jubilee **silver jubilees** NOUN
the 25th anniversary of an important event

silver medal **silver medals** NOUN
a medal made from silver awarded to the competitor who comes second in a competition

silver wedding **silver weddings** NOUN
A couple's silver wedding is the 25th anniversary of their wedding.

silvery [ˈsɪlvərɪ] ADJECTIVE
having the appearance or colour of silver *e.g. the silvery moon*

similar [ˈsɪmɪlə] ADJECTIVE
1 If one thing is similar to another, or if two things are similar, they are like each other.

● THESAURUS

alike: *You two are very alike.*
analogous: *a ritual analogous to those of primitive tribal cultures*
comparable: *paying the same wages for work of comparable value*
like: *They're as like as two peas in a pod.*
uniform: *droplets of uniform size*
<<OPPOSITE *different*

2 In maths, two triangles are similar if the angles in one correspond exactly to the angles in the other.
similarly ADVERB

Be careful when deciding whether to use *similar* or *same. Similar* means 'alike but not identical', and *same* means 'identical'. Do not put *as* after *similar: her dress was similar to mine*

similarity [ˌsɪmɪˈlærɪtɪ] **similarities** NOUN
If there is a similarity between things, they are alike in some way.

● THESAURUS

analogy: *the analogy between racism and homophobia*
likeness: *These myths have a startling likeness to one another.*

resemblance: *I could see the resemblance to his grandfather.*
sameness: *He grew bored by the sameness of the speeches.*
<<OPPOSITE *difference*

simile ['sɪmɪlɪ] similes NOUN
(ENGLISH) an expression in which a person or thing is described as being similar to someone or something else. Examples of similes are *She runs like a deer* and *He's as white as a sheet*

simmer ['sɪmə] simmers, simmering, simmered VERB
When food simmers, it cooks gently at just below boiling point.

simple ['sɪmpəl] simpler, simplest
ADJECTIVE
1 Something that is simple is uncomplicated and easy to understand or do.

● THESAURUS
easy: *This ice cream maker is cheap and easy to use.*
elementary: *elementary computer skills*
straightforward: *It was a straightforward question.*
uncomplicated: *an uncomplicated story*
understandable: *He writes in a clear, understandable style.*
<<OPPOSITE *complicated*

2 Simple also means plain and not elaborate in style. *e.g. a simple coat*

● THESAURUS
classic: *classic designs which will fit in anywhere*
clean: *the clean lines of Shaker furniture*
plain: *Her dress was plain but hung well on her.*
severe: *hair scraped back in a severe style*
<<OPPOSITE *elaborate*

3 A simple way of life is uncomplicated.
4 Someone who is simple is mentally retarded.
5 You use 'simple' to emphasize that what you are talking about is the only important thing. *e.g. simple stubbornness*
simplicity NOUN

simple-minded [,sɪmpəl'maɪndɪd]
ADJECTIVE
not very intelligent or sophisticated *e.g. simple-minded pleasures*

simplify ['sɪmplɪ,faɪ] simplifies, simplifying, simplified VERB
To simplify something means to make it easier to do or understand.
simplification NOUN

● THESAURUS
make simpler: *restructuring the tax system to make it simpler*
streamline: *an effort to cut costs and streamline operations*

simplistic [sɪm'plɪstɪk] ADJECTIVE
too simple or naive *e.g. a rather simplistic approach to the subject*

simply ['sɪmplɪ] ADVERB
1 Simply means merely. *e.g. It was simply a question of making the decision.*
2 You use 'simply' to emphasize what you are saying. *e.g. It is simply not true.*
3 If you say or write something simply, you do it in a way that makes it easy to understand.

simulate ['sɪmjʊ,leɪt] simulates, simulating, simulated VERB
To simulate something means to imitate it. *e.g. The wood has been painted to simulate stone.*
simulation NOUN

simultaneous [,sɪməl'teɪnɪəs] ADJECTIVE
Things that are simultaneous happen at the same time.
simultaneously ADVERB

sin [sɪn] sins, sinning, sinned NOUN
1 Sin is wicked and immoral behaviour.

● THESAURUS
crime: *a life of crime*
evil: *You can't stop all the evil in the world.*
offence: *an offence which can carry the death penalty*
wickedness: *a sign of human wickedness*
wrong: *I intend to right that wrong.*

> VERB
2 To sin means to do something wicked and immoral.

● THESAURUS
do wrong: *They have done wrong and they know it.*

since [sɪns] PREPOSITION, CONJUNCTION, OR ADVERB
1 Since means from a particular time until now. *e.g. I've been waiting patiently since half past three.*

> ADVERB
2 Since also means at some time after a particular time in the past. *e.g. They split up and he has since remarried.*

> CONJUNCTION
3 Since also means because. *e.g. I'm forever on a diet, since I put on weight easily.*

> Do not put *ago* before *since*, as it is not needed: *it is ten years since she wrote her book* not *ten years ago since*

sincere [sɪn'sɪə] ADJECTIVE
If you are sincere, you say things that you really mean. *e.g. a sincere expression of friendliness*
sincerity NOUN

● THESAURUS
genuine: *a display of genuine emotion*
heartfelt: *heartfelt sympathy*

S

real: *the real affection between them*
wholehearted: *a wholehearted and genuine response*
<<OPPOSITE *insincere*

sincerely [sɪnˈsɪəlɪ] ADVERB
1 If you say or feel something sincerely, you mean it or feel it genuinely.

> PHRASE
2 You write **Yours sincerely** before your signature at the end of a letter in which you have named the person you are writing to in the greeting at the beginning of the letter. For example, if you began your letter 'Dear Mr Brown' you would use 'Yours sincerely'.

sinew [ˈsɪnjuː] **sinews** NOUN
a tough cord in your body that connects a muscle to a bone

sinful [ˈsɪnfʊl] ADJECTIVE
wicked and immoral

sing [sɪŋ] **sings, singing, sang, sung** VERB
1 When you sing, you make musical sounds with your voice, usually producing words that fit a tune.
2 When birds or insects sing, they make pleasant sounds.
singer NOUN

> The past tense of *sing* is *sang*, and the past participle is *sung*. Do not confuse these words: *the team sang the national anthem; we have sung together many times*

singe [sɪndʒ] **singes, singeing, singed** VERB
1 To singe something means to burn it slightly so that it goes brown but does not catch fire.

> NOUN
2 a slight burn

single [ˈsɪŋgəl] **singles, singling, singled** ADJECTIVE
1 Single means only one and not more. *e.g. A single shot was fired.*

THESAURUS
lone: *A lone policeman guarded the doors.*
one: *I just had one drink.*
only: *My only regret is that I never knew him.*
sole: *the sole survivor of the accident*
solitary: *There is not one solitary scrap of evidence.*

2 People who are single are not married.

THESAURUS
unattached: *I only know two or three unattached men.*
unmarried: *an unmarried mother*

3 A single bed or bedroom is for one person.

THESAURUS
individual: *an individual portion*

separate: *separate beds*
4 A single ticket is a one-way ticket.

> NOUN
5 a recording of one or two short pieces of music on a small record, CD, or cassette
6 Singles is a game of tennis, badminton, or squash between just two players.

single out VERB
7 If you single someone out from a group, you give them special treatment. *e.g. He'd been singled out for some special award.*

single-handed [ˌsɪŋgəlˈhændɪd] ADVERB
If you do something single-handed, you do it on your own, without any help.

single-minded [ˌsɪŋgəlˈmaɪndɪd] ADJECTIVE
A single-minded person has only one aim and is determined to achieve it.

singly [ˈsɪŋglɪ] ADVERB
If people do something singly, they do it on their own or one by one.

singular [ˈsɪŋgjʊlə] NOUN
1 In grammar, the singular is the form of a word that refers to just one person or thing.

> ADJECTIVE
2 FORMAL
unusual and remarkable *e.g. her singular beauty*
singularity NOUN, **singularly** ADVERB

THESAURUS
exceptional: *children with exceptional ability*
extraordinary: *The task requires extraordinary patience and endurance.*
rare: *a leader of rare strength and instinct*
remarkable: *a remarkable achievement*
uncommon: *She read Cecilia's letter with uncommon interest.*
unique: *a woman of unique talent and determination*
unusual: *He had an unusual aptitude for mathematics.*

sinister [ˈsɪnɪstə] ADJECTIVE
seeming harmful or evil *e.g. something cold and sinister about him*
[WORD HISTORY: from Latin SINISTER meaning 'left-hand side', because the left side was considered unlucky]

THESAURUS
evil: *an evil smile*
forbidding: *a huge, forbidding building*
menacing: *His dark eyebrows gave him a menacing look.*
ominous: *A dark and ominous figure stood in the doorway.*
threatening: *his threatening appearance*

sink [sɪŋk] **sinks, sinking, sank, sunk** NOUN

1 a basin with taps supplying water, usually in a kitchen or bathroom

> VERB

2 If something sinks, it moves downwards, especially through water. *e.g. An Indian cargo ship sank in icy seas.*

3 To sink a ship means to cause it to sink by attacking it.

4 If an amount or value sinks, it decreases.

5 If you sink into an unpleasant state, you gradually pass into it. *e.g. He sank into black despair.*

6 To sink something sharp into an object means to make it go deeply into it. *e.g. The tiger sank its teeth into his leg.*

sink in VERB

7 When a fact sinks in, you fully understand it or realize it. *e.g. The truth was at last sinking in.*

sinner ['sɪnə] **sinners** NOUN
someone who has committed a sin

sinus ['saɪnəs] **sinuses** NOUN
Your sinuses are the air passages in the bones of your skull, just behind your nose.

sip [sɪp] **sips, sipping, sipped** VERB
1 If you sip a drink, you drink it by taking a small amount at a time.

> NOUN

2 a small amount of drink that you take into your mouth

siphon ['saɪfən] **siphons, siphoning, siphoned**; also spelt **syphon** VERB
If you siphon off a liquid, you draw it out of a container through a tube and transfer it to another place.

sir [sɜː] NOUN
1 Sir is a polite, formal way of addressing a man.

2 Sir is also the title used in front of the name of a knight or baronet.

siren ['saɪərən] **sirens** NOUN
a warning device, for example on a police car, which makes a loud, wailing noise
[WORD HISTORY: the Sirens in Greek mythology were sea nymphs who had beautiful voices and sang in order to lure sailors to their deaths on the rocks where the nymphs lived]

sirloin ['sɜːˌlɔɪn] NOUN
Sirloin is a prime cut of beef from the lower part of a cow's back.
[WORD HISTORY: from Old French SUR meaning 'above' and LONGE meaning 'loin']

sis or **sies** [sɪs] INTERJECTION; INFORMAL
In South African English, you say 'Sis!' to show disgust.

sister ['sɪstə] **sisters** NOUN

1 Your sister is a girl or woman who has the same parents as you.

2 a member of a female religious order

3 In a hospital, a sister is a senior nurse who supervises a ward.

> ADJECTIVE

4 Sister means closely related to something or very similar to it. *e.g. Citroen and its sister company Peugeot.*

sisterhood ['sɪstəˌhʊd] NOUN
Sisterhood is a strong feeling of companionship between women.

sister-in-law ['sɪstərɪnˌlɔː] **sisters-in-law** NOUN
Your sister-in-law is the wife of your brother, the sister of your husband or wife, or the woman married to your wife's or husband's brother.

sit [sɪt] **sits, sitting, sat** VERB
1 If you are sitting, your weight is supported by your buttocks rather than your feet.

2 When you sit or sit down somewhere, you lower your body until you are sitting.

3 If you sit an examination, you take it.

4 FORMAL
When a parliament, law court, or other official body sits, it meets and officially carries out its work.

sitcom ['sɪtˌkɒm] **sitcoms** NOUN; INFORMAL
a television comedy series which shows characters in amusing situations that are similar to everyday life
[WORD HISTORY: shortened from SITUATION COMEDY]

site [saɪt] **sites, siting, sited** NOUN
1 a piece of ground where a particular thing happens or is situated *e.g. a building site*

> VERB

2 If something is sited in a place, it is built or positioned there.

▬ Do not confuse the spellings of *site* and *sight*

sitting ['sɪtɪŋ] **sittings** NOUN
1 one of the times when a meal is served

2 one of the occasions when a parliament or law court meets and carries out its work

sitting room sitting rooms NOUN
a room in a house where people sit and relax

situated ['sɪtjʊˌeɪtɪd] ADJECTIVE
If something is situated somewhere, that is where it is. *e.g. a town situated 45 minutes from Geneva*

situation [ˌsɪtjʊˈeɪʃən] **situations** NOUN
1 what is happening in a particular place at a particular time *e.g. the political situation*

● THESAURUS
case: *a clear case of mistaken identity*
circumstances: *I wish we could have met in happier circumstances.*
plight: *the plight of Third World countries*
scenario: *a nightmare scenario*
state of affairs: *This state of affairs cannot continue.*

2 (GEOGRAPHY) The situation of a building or town is its surroundings. *e.g. a beautiful situation*

Siva ['siːvə] PROPER NOUN
Siva is a Hindu god and is one of the Trimurti. [WORD HISTORY: from a Sanskrit word meaning 'auspicious']

six [sɪks]
Six is the number 6.

sixteen ['sɪks'tiːn]
the number 16
sixteenth

sixth [sɪksθ] **sixths**
1 The sixth item in a series is the one counted as number six.
> NOUN
2 one of six equal parts

sixth sense NOUN
You say that someone has a sixth sense when they know something instinctively, without having any evidence of it.

sixty ['sɪkstɪ] **sixties**
the number 60
sixtieth

sizable or **sizeable** ['saɪzəbəl] ADJECTIVE
fairly large *e.g. a sizable amount of money*

size [saɪz] **sizes** NOUN
1 The size of something is how big or small it is. *e.g. the size of the audience*

● THESAURUS
dimensions: *He considered the dimensions of the problem.*
extent: *the extent of the damage*
proportions: *In the tropics, plants grow to huge proportions.*

2 The size of something is also the fact that it is very large. *e.g. the sheer size of Australia*

● THESAURUS
bulk: *Despite his bulk, he moved gracefully.*
immensity: *The immensity of the universe is impossible to grasp.*

3 one of the standard graded measurements of clothes and shoes

sizzle ['sɪzəl] **sizzles, sizzling, sizzled** VERB
If something sizzles, it makes a hissing sound like the sound of frying food.

sjambok ['ʃæmbʌk] **sjamboks** NOUN
In South African English, a sjambok is a long whip made from animal hide.

skate [skeɪt] **skates, skating, skated** NOUN
1 Skates are ice skates or roller skates.
2 a flat edible sea fish
> VERB
3 If you skate, you move about on ice wearing ice skates.
4 If you skate round a difficult subject, you avoid discussing it.

skateboard ['skeɪt,bɔːd] **skateboards** NOUN
a narrow board on wheels which you stand on and ride for fun

skeleton ['skɛlɪtən] **skeletons** NOUN
Your skeleton is the framework of bones in your body.

sketch [skɛtʃ] **sketches, sketching, sketched** NOUN
1 (ART) a quick, rough drawing
2 A sketch of a situation or incident is a brief description of it.
3 a short, humorous piece of acting, usually forming part of a comedy show
> VERB
4 If you sketch something, you draw it quickly and roughly.

sketchy ['skɛtʃɪ] **sketchier, sketchiest** ADJECTIVE
giving only a rough description or account *e.g. Details surrounding his death are sketchy.*

skew or **skewed** [skjuː] or [skjuːd] ADJECTIVE
in a slanting position, rather than straight or upright

skewer ['skjʊə] **skewers, skewering, skewered** NOUN
1 a long metal pin used to hold pieces of food together during cooking
> VERB
2 If you skewer something, you push a skewer through it.

ski [skiː] **skis, skiing, skied** NOUN
1 Skis are long pieces of wood, metal, or plastic that you fasten to special boots so you can move easily on snow.
> VERB
2 When you ski, you move on snow wearing skis, especially as a sport.
[WORD HISTORY: from Old Norse SKITH meaning 'snowshoes']

skid [skɪd] **skids, skidding, skidded** VERB
If a vehicle skids, it slides in an uncontrolled way,

for example because the road is wet or icy.

skilful ['skɪlfʊl] ADJECTIVE
If you are skilful at something, you can do it very well.
skilfully ADVERB

● THESAURUS
able: *a very able businessman*
accomplished: *an accomplished pianist*
adept: *an adept diplomat*
competent: *a competent and careful driver*
expert: *He is expert at handling complex negotiations.*
masterly: *a masterly performance*
proficient: *proficient with computers*
skilled: *a skilled wine maker*
<<OPPOSITE *incompetent*

skill [skɪl] **skills** NOUN
1 Skill is the knowledge and ability that enables you to do something well.

● THESAURUS
ability: *a man of considerable abilities*
competence: *his high professional competence*
dexterity: *Reid's dexterity on the guitar.* **expertise:** *the expertise to deal with these problems*
facility: *a facility for languages*
knack: *the knack of getting on with people*
proficiency: *basic proficiency in English*

2 a type of work or technique which requires special training and knowledge

skilled [skɪld] ADJECTIVE
1 A skilled person has the knowledge and ability to do something well.

● THESAURUS
able: *an able craftsman*
accomplished: *an accomplished pianist*
competent: *a competent and careful driver*
experienced: *lawyers who are experienced in these matters*
expert: *It takes an expert eye to see the symptoms.*
masterly: *the artist's masterly use of colour*
professional: *professional people like doctors and engineers*
proficient: *He is proficient in several foreign languages.*
skilful: *the artist's skilful use of light and shade*
trained: *Our workforce is highly trained.*
<<OPPOSITE *incompetent*

2 Skilled work is work which can only be done by people who have had special training.

skim [skɪm] **skims, skimming, skimmed**
VERB
1 If you skim something from the surface of a liquid, you remove it.

2 If something skims a surface, it moves along just above it. *e.g. seagulls skimming the waves*

skimmed milk [skɪmd] NOUN
Skimmed milk has had the cream removed.

skin [skɪn] **skins, skinning, skinned** NOUN
1 Your skin is the natural covering of your body. An animal skin is the skin and fur of a dead animal.

2 The skin of a fruit or vegetable is its outer covering.

3 a solid layer which forms on the surface of a liquid

> VERB
4 If you skin a dead animal, you remove its skin.
5 If you skin a part of your body, you accidentally graze it.

skinny ['skɪnɪ] **skinnier, skinniest**
ADJECTIVE
extremely thin

● THESAURUS
bony: *a long bony finger*
emaciated: *television pictures of emaciated prisoners*
lean: *a tall, lean figure*
scrawny: *the vulture's scrawny neck*
thin: *He is small and very thin with white skin.*
underfed: *Kate still looks pale and underfed.*
undernourished: *undernourished children*
<<OPPOSITE *plump*

skip [skɪp] **skips, skipping, skipped** VERB
1 If you skip along, you move along jumping from one foot to the other.

2 If you skip something, you miss it out or avoid doing it. *e.g. It is all too easy to skip meals.*

> NOUN
3 Skips are the movements you make when you skip.

4 a large metal container for holding rubbish and rubble

skipper ['skɪpə] **skippers** NOUN; INFORMAL
The skipper of a ship or boat is its captain.
[WORD HISTORY: from Old Dutch SCHIPPER meaning 'shipper']

skirmish ['skɜ:mɪʃ] **skirmishes** NOUN
a short, rough fight

skirt [skɜ:t] **skirts, skirting, skirted** NOUN
1 A woman's skirt is a piece of clothing which fastens at her waist and hangs down over her legs.

> VERB
2 Something that skirts an area is situated around the edge of it.

3 If you skirt something, you go around the edge of it. *e.g. We skirted the town.*

4 If you skirt a problem, you avoid dealing with it. *e.g. He was skirting the real question.*

S

[WORD HISTORY: from Old Norse SKYRTA meaning 'shirt']

skirting ['skɜːtɪŋ] **skirtings** NOUN
A skirting or skirting board is a narrow strip of wood running along the bottom of a wall in a room.

skite [skaɪt] **skites, skiting, skited** INFORMAL
> VERB
1 In Australian and New Zealand English, to skite is to talk in a boastful way about something that you own or that you have done.
> NOUN
2 In Australian and New Zealand English, someone who boasts.

skittle ['skɪtəl] **skittles** NOUN
Skittles is a game in which players roll a ball and try to knock down wooden objects called skittles.

skull [skʌl] **skulls** NOUN
Your skull is the bony part of your head which surrounds your brain.

skunk [skʌŋk] **skunks** NOUN
a small black and white animal from North America which gives off an unpleasant smell when it is frightened
[WORD HISTORY: a North American Indian word]

sky [skaɪ] **skies** NOUN
The sky is the space around the earth which you can see when you look upwards.
[WORD HISTORY: from Old Norse SKY meaning 'cloud']

skylight ['skaɪˌlaɪt] **skylights** NOUN
a window in a roof or ceiling

skyline ['skaɪˌlaɪn] **skylines** NOUN
The skyline is the line where the sky meets buildings or the ground. *e.g. the New York City skyline*

skyscraper ['skaɪˌskreɪpə] **skyscrapers** NOUN
a very tall building

slab [slæb] **slabs** NOUN
a thick, flat piece of something

slack [slæk] **slacker, slackest; slacks** ADJECTIVE
1 Something that is slack is loose and not firmly stretched or positioned.
2 A slack period is one in which there is not much work to do.
> NOUN
3 The slack in a rope is the part that hangs loose.
> PLURAL NOUN
4 Slacks are casual trousers.
slackness NOUN

slacken ['slækən] **slackens, slackening, slackened** VERB

1 If something slackens, it becomes slower or less intense. *e.g. The rain had slackened to a drizzle.*
2 To slacken also means to become looser. *e.g. Her grip slackened on Arnold's arm.*

slag [slæg] **slags, slagging, slagged** NOUN
1 Slag is the waste material left when ore has been melted down to remove the metal. *e.g. a slag heap*
> VERB
2 INFORMAL
To slag someone off means to criticize them in an unpleasant way, usually behind their back.

slalom ['slɑːləm] **slaloms** NOUN
a skiing competition in which the competitors have to twist and turn quickly to avoid obstacles
[WORD HISTORY: from Norwegian SLAD + LOM meaning 'sloping path']

slam [slæm] **slams, slamming, slammed** VERB

1 If you slam a door or if it slams, it shuts noisily and with great force.
2 If you slam something down, you throw it down violently. *e.g. She slammed the phone down.*

slander ['slɑːndə] **slanders, slandering, slandered** NOUN
1 Slander is something untrue and malicious said about someone.
THESAURUS
libel: *defendants seeking damages for libel*
scandal: *She loves spreading scandal.*
slur: *a vicious slur on his character*
smear: *He called the allegation "an evil smear".*
> VERB
2 To slander someone means to say untrue and malicious things about them.
slanderous ADJECTIVE
THESAURUS
libel: *The newspaper which libelled him had to pay compensation.*
malign: *He claims he is being unfairly maligned.*
smear: *an attempt to smear their manager*

slang [slæŋ] NOUN
Slang consists of very informal words and expressions.

slant [slɑːnt] **slants, slanting, slanted** VERB
1 If something slants, it slopes. *e.g. The back can be adjusted to slant into the most comfortable position.*
2 If news or information is slanted, it is presented in a biased way.
> NOUN
3 a slope
4 A slant on a subject is one way of looking at it, especially a biased one.

slap [slæp] **slaps, slapping, slapped** VERB

1 If you slap someone, you hit them with the palm of your hand.

2 If you slap something onto a surface, you put it there quickly and noisily.

> NOUN

3 If you give someone a slap, you slap them.
[WORD HISTORY: from German SCHLAPPE, an imitation of the sound]

slash [slæʃ] **slashes, slashing, slashed** VERB

1 If you slash something, you make a long, deep cut in it.

2 INFORMAL
To slash money means to reduce it greatly. *e.g. Car makers could be forced to slash prices.*

> NOUN

3 a diagonal line that separates letters, words, or numbers, for example in the number 340/21/K

slat [slæt] **slats** NOUN
Slats are the narrow pieces of wood or metal plastic in things such as Venetian blinds.
slatted ADJECTIVE

slate [sleɪt] **slates, slating, slated** NOUN

1 Slate is a dark grey rock that splits easily into thin layers.

2 Slates are small, flat pieces of slate used for covering roofs.

> VERB

3 INFORMAL
If critics slate a play, film, or book, they criticize it severely.

slaughter ['slɔːtə] **slaughters, slaughtering, slaughtered** VERB

1 To slaughter a large number of people means to kill them unjustly or cruelly.

2 To slaughter farm animals means to kill them for meat.

> NOUN

3 Slaughter is the killing of many people.

slave [sleɪv] **slaves, slaving, slaved** NOUN

1 someone who is owned by another person and must work for them

> VERB

2 If you slave for someone, you work very hard for them.
slavery NOUN
[WORD HISTORY: from Latin SCLAVUS meaning 'a Slav', because the Slavonic races were frequently conquered and made into slaves]

slay [sleɪ] **slays, slaying, slew, slain** VERB; LITERARY
To slay someone means to kill them.

sleazy ['sliːzɪ] **sleazier, sleaziest** ADJECTIVE
A sleazy place looks dirty, run-down, and not respectable.

sled [slɛd] **sleds** NOUN
a sledge

sledge [slɛdʒ] **sledges** NOUN
a vehicle on runners used for travelling over snow

sledgehammer ['slɛdʒˌhæmə] **sledgehammers** NOUN
a large, heavy hammer

sleek [sliːk] **sleeker, sleekest** ADJECTIVE

1 Sleek hair is smooth and shiny.

2 Someone who is sleek looks rich and dresses elegantly.

sleep [sliːp] **sleeps, sleeping, slept** NOUN

1 Sleep is the natural state of rest in which your eyes are closed and you are unconscious.

● THESAURUS
doze: *I had a doze after lunch.*
hibernation: *Many animals go into hibernation during the winter.*
kip: British; slang *Mason went home for a couple of hours' kip.*
nap: *I might take a nap for a while.*
slumber: *He had fallen into exhausted slumber.*
snooze: informal *a little snooze after dinner*

2 If you have a sleep, you sleep for a while. *e.g. He'll be ready for a sleep soon.*

> VERB

3 When you sleep, you rest in a state of sleep.

● THESAURUS
doze: *He dozed in an armchair.*
hibernate: *Dormice hibernate from October to May.*
kip: British; slang *He kipped on my sofa last night.*
slumber: *The girls were slumbering peacefully.*
snooze: informal *Mark snoozed in front of the television.*
take a nap: *Try to take a nap every afternoon.*

> PHRASE

4 If a sick or injured animal **is put to sleep**, it is painlessly killed.

sleeper ['sliːpə] **sleepers** NOUN

1 You use 'sleeper' to say how deeply someone sleeps. *e.g. I'm a very heavy sleeper.*

2 a bed on a train, or a train which has beds on it

3 Railway sleepers are the large beams that support the rails of a railway track.

sleeping bag ['sliːpɪŋ] **sleeping bags** NOUN
a large, warm bag for sleeping in, especially when you are camping

sleeping pill ['sliːpɪŋ] **sleeping pills** NOUN
A sleeping pill or a sleeping tablet is a pill which you take to help you sleep.

sleepout ['sliːpˌaʊt] **sleepouts** NOUN

1 In Australia, an area of veranda or porch which has been closed off to be used as a bedroom.

S

2 In New Zealand, a small building outside a house, used for sleeping.

sleepover ['sliːpˌəʊvə] **sleepovers** NOUN
a gathering or party at which friends spend the night at another friend's house

sleepwalk ['sliːpˌwɔːk] **sleepwalks, sleepwalking, sleepwalked** VERB
If you sleepwalk, you walk around while you are asleep.

sleepy ['sliːpɪ] **sleepier, sleepiest** ADJECTIVE
1 tired and ready to go to sleep

🔵 THESAURUS
drowsy: *This medicine may make you feel drowsy.*
lethargic: *He felt too lethargic to get dressed.*
sluggish: *I was still feeling sluggish after my nap.*

2 A sleepy town or village is very quiet.
sleepily ADVERB, **sleepiness** NOUN

🔵 THESAURUS
dull: *a dull town*
quiet: *a quiet rural backwater*

sleet [sliːt] NOUN
Sleet is a mixture of rain and snow.

sleeve [sliːv] **sleeves** NOUN
The sleeves of a piece of clothing are the parts that cover your arms.
sleeveless ADJECTIVE

sleigh [sleɪ] **sleighs** NOUN
a sledge

slender ['slɛndə] ADJECTIVE
1 attractively thin and graceful

🔵 THESAURUS
lean: *Like most athletes, she was lean and muscular.*
slight: *She is small and slight.*
slim: *Jean is pretty, with a slim build.*

2 small in amount or degree *e.g. the first slender hopes of peace*

🔵 THESAURUS
faint: *They now have only a faint chance of survival.*
remote: *a remote possibility*
slight: *There is a slight improvement in his condition.*
slim: *a slim hope*
small: *a small chance of success*

sleuth [sluːθ] **sleuths** NOUN; OLD-FASHIONED, INFORMAL
a detective
[WORD HISTORY: a shortened form of SLEUTHHOUND, a tracker dog, from Old Norse SLOTH meaning 'track']

slew [sluː] **slews, slewing, slewed**
1 Slew is the past tense of **slay**.
> VERB
2 If a vehicle slews, it slides or skids. *e.g. The bike slewed into the crowd.*

slice [slaɪs] **slices, slicing, sliced** NOUN
1 A slice of cake, bread, or other food is a piece of it cut from a larger piece.

2 a kitchen tool with a broad, flat blade *e.g. a fish slice*

3 In sport, a slice is a stroke in which the player makes the ball go to one side, rather than straight ahead.

> VERB
4 If you slice food, you cut it into thin pieces.

5 To slice through something means to cut or move through it quickly, like a knife. *e.g. The ship sliced through the water.*

slick [slɪk] **slicker, slickest; slicks** ADJECTIVE
1 A slick action is done quickly and smoothly. *e.g. slick passing and strong running*

2 A slick person speaks easily and persuasively but is not sincere. *e.g. a slick TV presenter*

> NOUN
3 An oil slick is a layer of oil floating on the surface of the sea or a lake.

slide [slaɪd] **slides, sliding, slid** VERB
1 When something slides, it moves smoothly over or against something else.

> NOUN
2 a small piece of photographic film which can be projected onto a screen so that you can see the picture

3 a small piece of glass on which you put something that you want to examine through a microscope

4 In a playground, a slide is a structure with a steep, slippery slope for children to slide down.

slight [slaɪt] **slighter, slightest; slights, slighting, slighted** ADJECTIVE
1 Slight means small in amount or degree. *e.g. a slight dent*

🔵 THESAURUS
insignificant: *an insignificant amount*
minor: *a minor inconvenience*
negligible: *The strike will have a negligible impact.*
small: *It only makes a small difference.*
trivial: *trivial details*
<<OPPOSITE *large*

2 A slight person has a slim body.

> PHRASE
3 **Not in the slightest** means not at all *e.g. This doesn't surprise me in the slightest.*

> VERB
4 If you slight someone, you insult them by behaving rudely towards them.

> NOUN
5 A slight is rude or insulting behaviour.

slightly ADVERB

slim [slɪm] **slimmer, slimmest; slims, slimming, slimmed** ADJECTIVE

1 A slim person is attractively thin.

2 A slim object is thinner than usual. *e.g. a slim book*

3 If there is only a slim chance that something will happen, it is unlikely to happen.

> VERB

4 If you are slimming, you are trying to lose weight.
slimmer NOUN

slime [slaɪm] NOUN
Slime is an unpleasant, thick, slippery substance.
[WORD HISTORY: from Old English SLIM meaning 'soft sticky mud']

slimy [ˈslaɪmɪ] **slimier, slimiest** ADJECTIVE

1 covered in slime

2 Slimy people are friendly and pleasant in an insincere way. *e.g. a slimy business partner*

sling [slɪŋ] **slings, slinging, slung** VERB

1 INFORMAL
If you sling something somewhere, you throw it there.

2 If you sling a rope between two points, you attach it so that it hangs loosely between them.

> NOUN

3 a piece of cloth tied round a person's neck to support a broken or injured arm

4 a device made of ropes or cloth used for carrying things

slip [slɪp] **slips, slipping, slipped** VERB

1 If you slip, you accidentally slide and lose your balance.

2 If something slips, it slides out of place accidentally. *e.g. One of the knives slipped from her grasp.*

3 If you slip somewhere, you go there quickly and quietly. *e.g. She slipped out of the house.*

● THESAURUS
creep: *I crept up to my room.*
sneak: *Sometimes he would sneak out to see me.*
steal: *They can steal away at night to join us.*

4 If you slip something somewhere, you put it there quickly and quietly.

5 If something slips to a lower level or standard, it falls to that level or standard. *e.g. The shares slipped to an all-time low.*

> NOUN

6 a small mistake

● THESAURUS
blunder: *an embarrassing blunder*
error: *a tactical error*

mistake: *Many people are anxious about making mistakes in grammar.*

7 A slip of paper is a small piece of paper.

8 a piece of clothing worn under a dress or skirt

slipped disc [slɪpt] **slipped discs** NOUN
a painful condition in which one of the discs in your spine has moved out of its proper position

slipper [ˈslɪpə] **slippers** NOUN
Slippers are loose, soft shoes that you wear indoors.

slippery [ˈslɪpərɪ] ADJECTIVE

1 smooth, wet, or greasy, and difficult to hold or walk on

2 You describe a person as slippery when they cannot be trusted.

slippery dip **slippery dips** NOUN; INFORMAL
In Australian English, a children's slide at a playground or funfair.

slip rail **slip rails** NOUN
In Australian and New Zealand English, a rail in a fence that can be slipped out of place to make an opening.

slipstream [ˈslɪpˌstriːm] **slipstreams** NOUN
The slipstream of a car or plane is the flow of air directly behind it.

slit [slɪt] **slits, slitting, slit** VERB

1 If you slit something, you make a long, narrow cut in it.

> NOUN

2 a long, narrow cut or opening

slither [ˈslɪðə] **slithers, slithering, slithered** VERB
To slither somewhere means to move there by sliding along the ground in an uneven way. *e.g. The snake slithered into the water.*

sliver [ˈslɪvə] **slivers** NOUN
a small, thin piece of something

slob [slɒb] **slobs** NOUN; INFORMAL
a lazy, untidy person

slog [slɒg] **slogs, slogging, slogged** VERB; INFORMAL
If you slog at something, you work hard and steadily at it. *e.g. They are still slogging away at algebra.*

slogan [ˈsləʊgən] **slogans** NOUN
a short, easily-remembered phrase used in advertising or by a political party
[WORD HISTORY: from Gaelic SLUAGH-GHAIRM meaning 'war cry']

● THESAURUS
jingle: *a catchy advertising jingle*
motto: *"Who Dares Wins" is the motto of the Special Air Service.*

S

slop [slɒp] **slops, slopping, slopped** VERB
1 If a liquid slops, it spills over the edge of a container in a messy way.

> PLURAL NOUN

2 You can refer to dirty water or liquid waste as slops.

slope [sləʊp] **slopes, sloping, sloped** NOUN
1 a flat surface that is at an angle, so that one end is higher than the other

● THESAURUS
gradient: *a steep gradient*
incline: *The car was unable to negotiate the incline.*
ramp: *There is a ramp allowing access for wheelchairs.*

2 The slope of something is the angle at which it slopes.

> VERB

3 If a surface slopes, it is at an angle.

● THESAURUS
fall: *The road fell steeply.*
rise: *The climb is arduous, rising steeply through thick bush.*
slant: *His handwriting slanted to the left.*

4 If something slopes, it leans to one side rather than being upright. *e.g. sloping handwriting*

sloppy ['slɒpɪ] **sloppier, sloppiest**
ADJECTIVE; INFORMAL
1 very messy or careless *e.g. two sloppy performances*

2 foolishly sentimental *e.g. some sloppy love story*
sloppily ADVERB, **sloppiness** NOUN

slot [slɒt] **slots, slotting, slotted** NOUN
1 a narrow opening in a machine or container, for example for putting coins in

> VERB

2 When you slot something into something else, you put it into a space where it fits.

sloth [sləʊθ] **sloths** NOUN
1 FORMAL
Sloth is laziness.

2 a South and Central American animal that moves very slowly and hangs upside down from the branches of trees

slouch [slaʊtʃ] **slouches, slouching, slouched** VERB
If you slouch, you stand or sit with your shoulders and head drooping forwards.

slouch hat slouch hats NOUN
a hat with a wide, flexible brim, especially an Australian army hat with the left side of the brim turned up

Slovak ['sləʊvæk] **Slovaks** ADJECTIVE
1 belonging to or relating to Slovakia

> NOUN

2 someone who comes from Slovakia

3 Slovak is the language spoken in Slovakia.

slow [sləʊ] **slower, slowest; slows, slowing, slowed** ADJECTIVE
1 moving, happening, or doing something with very little speed *e.g. His progress was slow.*

● THESAURUS
gradual: *Losing weight is a gradual process.*
leisurely: *He walked at a leisurely pace.*
lingering: *a lingering death*
ponderous: *His steps were heavy and ponderous.*
sluggish: *a sluggish stream*
unhurried: *She rose with unhurried grace.*
<<OPPOSITE *fast*

2 Someone who is slow is not very clever.

● THESAURUS
dense: *He's not a bad man, just a bit dense.*
dim: *He is rather dim.*
dumb: *informal too dumb to realise what was going on*
obtuse: *It should be obvious even to the most obtuse person.*
stupid: *He can't help being a bit stupid.*
thick: *I can't believe I've been so thick.*

3 If a clock or watch is slow, it shows a time earlier than the correct one.

> VERB

4 If something slows, slows down, or slows up, it moves or happens more slowly.
slowness NOUN

● THESAURUS
check: *attempts to check the spread of AIDS*
decelerate: *He decelerated when he saw the warning sign.*

slowly ['sləʊlɪ] ADVERB
not quickly or hurriedly

● THESAURUS
by degrees: *By degrees, the tension passed out of him.*
gradually: *Their friendship gradually deepened.*
unhurriedly: *The islanders drift along unhurriedly from day to day.*
<<OPPOSITE *quickly*

slow motion NOUN
Slow motion is movement which is much slower than normal, especially in a film. *e.g. It all seemed to happen in slow motion.*

sludge [slʌdʒ] NOUN
Sludge is thick mud or sewage.

slug [slʌg] **slugs** NOUN
1 a small, slow-moving creative with a slimy body, like a snail without a shell

2 INFORMAL
A slug of a strong alcoholic drink is a mouthful of it.

sluggish ['slʌgɪʃ] ADJECTIVE
moving slowly and without energy *e.g. the sluggish waters*

sluice [sluːs] **sluices, sluicing, sluiced**
NOUN
1 a channel which carries water, with an opening called a sluicegate which can be opened or closed to control the flow of water
> VERB
2 If you sluice something, you wash it by pouring water over it. *e.g. He had sluiced his hands under a tap.*
[WORD HISTORY: from Latin EXCLUSA AQUA meaning 'water shut out']

slum [slʌm] **slums** NOUN
a poor, run-down area of a city

slumber ['slʌmbə] **slumbers, slumbering, slumbered** LITERARY NOUN
1 Slumber is sleep.
> VERB
2 When you slumber, you sleep.

slump [slʌmp] **slumps, slumping, slumped** VERB
1 If an amount or a value slumps, it falls suddenly by a large amount.
2 If you slump somewhere, you fall or sit down heavily. *e.g. He slumped against the side of the car.*
> NOUN
3 a sudden, severe drop in an amount or value *e.g. the slump in house prices*
4 a time when there is economic decline and high unemployment

slur [slɜː] **slurs, slurring, slurred** NOUN
1 an insulting remark
> VERB
2 When people slur their speech, they do not say their words clearly, often because they are drunk or ill.

slurp [slɜːp] **slurps, slurping, slurped** VERB
If you slurp a drink, you drink it noisily.
[WORD HISTORY: from Old Dutch SLORPEN meaning 'to sip']

slush [slʌʃ] NOUN
1 Slush is wet melting snow.
2 INFORMAL
You can refer to sentimental love stories as slush.
slushy ADJECTIVE

slut [slʌt] **sluts** NOUN; OFFENSIVE
a dirty, untidy woman, or one considered to be immoral

sly [slaɪ] **slyer** or **slier slyest** or **sliest**
ADJECTIVE
1 A sly expression or remark shows that you know something other people do not know. *e.g. a sly smile*

2 A sly person is cunning and good at deceiving people.
slyly ADVERB

⬤ THESAURUS
crafty: *a crafty villain*
cunning: *Some of these kids can be very cunning.*
devious: *an extremely dangerous, evil and devious man*
scheming: *You're a scheming little rat, aren't you?*
underhand: *underhand tactics*
wily: *a wily politician*

smack [smæk] **smacks, smacking, smacked** VERB
1 If you smack someone, you hit them with your open hand.
2 If something smacks of something else, it reminds you of it. *e.g. His tale smacks of fantasy.*
> NOUN
3 If you give someone a smack, you smack them.
4 a loud, sharp noise *e.g. He landed with a smack on the tank.*

small see page 812 for Word Web

smallpox ['smɔːlˌpɒks] NOUN
Smallpox is a serious contagious disease that causes a fever and a rash.

small talk NOUN
Small talk is conversation about unimportant things.

smart [smɑːt] **smarter, smartest; smarts, smarting, smarted** ADJECTIVE
1 A smart person is clean and neatly dressed.

⬤ THESAURUS
chic: *chic Parisian women*
elegant: *Patricia looked beautiful and elegant, as always.*
neat: *a neat grey flannel suit*
spruce: *Chris was looking spruce in his uniform.*
stylish: *stylish white shoes*
<<OPPOSITE *scruffy*

2 Smart means clever. *e.g. a smart idea*

⬤ THESAURUS
astute: *a series of astute business decisions*
bright: *She is not very bright.*
canny: *He was far too canny to give himself away.*
clever: *Nobody disputed that Davey was clever.*
ingenious: *an ingenious plan*
intelligent: *Dolphins are an intelligent species.*
shrewd: *a shrewd businessman*
<<OPPOSITE *dumb*

3 A smart movement is quick and sharp.
> VERB
4 If a wound smarts, it stings.
5 If you are smarting from criticism or unkindness, you are feeling upset by it.

S

1 ADJECTIVE

not large in size, number or amount *eg: a small child*

● THESAURUS

diminutive: *a diminutive figure standing at the entrance*

dumpy: *a dumpy woman in a baggy tracksuit*

little: *We sat around a little table.*

miniature: *a miniature camera*

miniscule: *wearing a pair of minuscule shorts*

minute: *Only a minute amount is needed.*

petite: *a petite blonde woman*

squat: *Eddie was a short, squat fellow in his mid-forties*

tiny: *The living room is tiny; Though she was tiny, she had a loud voice.*

<< OPPOSITE *large*

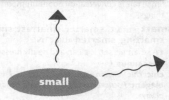

small

2 ADJECTIVE

not important or significant *eg: small changes*

● THESAURUS

inconsequential: *a seemingly inconsequential event*

insignificant: *an insignificant village in the hills*

little: *Fancy making such a fuss over such a little thing!*

minor: *a minor detail*

negligible: *The impact of the strike will be negligible.*

petty: *Rows would start over the most petty things.*

slight: *It will only make a slight difference.*

trifling: *These are trifling objections.*

trivial: *Let's not get bogged down in trivial details.*

unimportant: *a comparatively unimportant event*

smartly ADVERB

smarten ['smɑːt°n] **smartens,
smartening, smartened** VERB
If you smarten something up, you make it look
neater and tidier.

smash [smæʃ] **smashes, smashing,
smashed** VERB
1 If you smash something, you break it into a lot
of pieces by hitting it or dropping it.

2 To smash through something such as a wall
means to go through it by breaking it.

3 To smash against something means to hit it
with great force. *e.g. An immense wave smashed
against the hull.*

> NOUN
4 INFORMAL
If a play or film is a smash or a smash hit, it is very
successful.

5 a car crash

6 In tennis, a smash is a stroke in which the
player hits the ball downwards very hard.

smashing ['smæʃɪŋ] ADJECTIVE; INFORMAL
If you describe something as smashing, you
mean you like it very much.

smattering ['smætərɪŋ] NOUN
A smattering of knowledge or information is a
very small amount of it. *e.g. a smattering of
Russian*

smear [smɪə] **smears, smearing, smeared**
NOUN
1 a dirty, greasy mark on a surface *e.g. a smear of
pink lipstick*

2 an untrue and malicious rumour

> VERB
3 If something smears a surface, it makes dirty,
greasy marks on it. *e.g. The blade was chipped and
smeared.*

4 If you smear a surface with a greasy or sticky
substance, you spread a layer of the substance
over the surface.

smell [smɛl] **smells, smelling, smelled** or
smelt NOUN
1 The smell of something is a quality it has which
you perceive through your nose. *e.g. a smell of
damp wood*

● THESAURUS
aroma: *the aroma of fresh bread*
fragrance: *the fragrance of his cologne*
odour: *a disagreeable odour*
perfume: *enjoying the perfume of the lemon trees*
pong: British and Australian; informal *What's that
horrible pong?*
reek: *the reek of whisky*

scent: *flowers chosen for their scent*
stench: *a foul stench*
stink: *the stink of stale beer on his breath*

2 Your sense of smell is your ability to smell
things.

> VERB
3 If something smells, it has a quality you can
perceive through your nose, especially an
unpleasant quality.

● THESAURUS
pong: British and Australian; informal *She said he
ponged a bit.*
reek: *The whole house reeks of cigar smoke.*
stink: *His breath stinks of garlic.*

4 If you smell something, you become aware of it
through your nose.

● THESAURUS
scent: *The dog had scented something in the bushes.*
sniff: *He opened his window and sniffed the air.*

5 If you can smell something such as danger or
trouble, you feel it is present or likely to happen.

smelly ['smɛlɪ] **smellier, smelliest**
ADJECTIVE
having a strong, unpleasant smell

● THESAURUS
foul: *His breath was foul.*
reeking: *poisoning the air with their reeking cigars*
stinking: *piles of stinking rubbish*
<<OPPOSITE *fragrant*

smelt [smɛlt] **smelts, smelting, smelted**
VERB
To smelt a metal ore means to heat it until it
melts, so that the metal can be extracted.

smile [smaɪl] **smiles, smiling, smiled** VERB
1 When you smile, the corners of your mouth
move outwards and slightly upwards because
you are pleased or amused.

● THESAURUS
beam: *She beamed at him in delight.*
grin: *He grinned broadly.*
smirk: *The two men looked at me, nudged each other
and smirked.*

> NOUN
2 the expression you have when you smile

● THESAURUS
beam: *a strange beam of satisfaction on his face*
grin: *She looked at me with a sheepish grin.*
smirk: *a smirk of triumph*

smirk [smɜːk] **smirks, smirking, smirked**
VERB
1 When you smirk, you smile in a sneering or
sarcastic way. *e.g. The boy smirked and turned the
volume up.*

> NOUN
2 a sneering or sarcastic smile

S

smith [smɪθ] **smiths** NOUN
someone who makes things out of iron, gold, or another metal

smitten ['smɪtᵊn] ADJECTIVE
If you are smitten with someone or something, you are very impressed with or enthusiastic about them. *e.g. They were totally smitten with each other.*

smock [smɒk] **smocks** NOUN
a loose garment like a long blouse

smog [smɒg] NOUN
Smog is a mixture of smoke and fog which occurs in some industrial cities.

smoke [sməʊk] **smokes, smoking, smoked** NOUN
1 Smoke is a mixture of gas and small particles sent into the air when something burns.
> VERB
2 If something is smoking, smoke is coming from it.
3 When someone smokes a cigarette or pipe, they suck smoke from it into their mouth and blow it out again.
4 To smoke fish or meat means to hang it over burning wood so that the smoke preserves it and gives it a pleasant flavour. *e.g. smoked bacon*
smoker NOUN, **smoking** NOUN

smoky ['sməʊkɪ] **smokier, smokiest** ADJECTIVE
A smoky place is full of smoke.
⬤ THESAURUS
glassy: *glassy green pebbles*
glossy: *glossy dark fur*
polished: *He slipped on the polished floor.*
silky: *The sauce should be silky in texture.*
sleek: *her sleek, waist-length hair*
<<OPPOSITE rough

smooth [smuːð] **smoother, smoothest; smooths, smoothing, smoothed** ADJECTIVE
1 A smooth surface has no roughness and no holes in it.
⬤ THESAURUS
2 A smooth liquid or mixture has no lumps in it.
3 A smooth movement or process happens evenly and steadily. *e.g. smooth acceleration*
4 Smooth also means successful and without problems. *e.g. staff responsible for the smooth running of the hall*
> VERB
5 If you smooth something, you move your hands over it to make it smooth and flat.
smoothly ADVERB, **smoothness** NOUN

smoothie ['smuːðɪ] **smoothies** NOUN
a thick type of drink made in an electric blender

from milk, fruit and crushed ice

smother ['smʌðə] **smothers, smothering, smothered** VERB
1 If you smother a fire, you cover it with something to put it out.
2 To smother a person means to cover their face with something so that they cannot breathe.
3 To smother someone also means to give them too much love and protection. *e.g. She loved her own children, almost smothering them with love.*
4 If you smother an emotion, you control it so that people do not notice it. *e.g. They tried to smother their glee.*

smothered ['smʌðəd] ADJECTIVE
completely covered with something *e.g. a spectacular trellis smothered in climbing roses*

smoulder ['sməʊldə] **smoulders, smouldering, smouldered** VERB
1 When something smoulders, it burns slowly, producing smoke but no flames.
2 If a feeling is smouldering inside you, you feel it very strongly but do not show it. *e.g. smouldering with resentment*

smudge [smʌdʒ] **smudges, smudging, smudged** NOUN
1 a dirty or blurred mark or a smear on something
> VERB
2 If you smudge something, you make it dirty or messy by touching it or marking it.

smug [smʌg] **smugger, smuggest** ADJECTIVE
Someone who is smug is very pleased with how good or clever they are.
smugly ADVERB, **smugness** NOUN
⬤ THESAURUS
complacent: *an aggravating, complacent little smile*
conceited: *They had grown too conceited and pleased with themselves.*
self-satisfied: *a self-satisfied little snob*
superior: *He stood there looking superior.*

smuggle ['smʌgᵊl] **smuggles, smuggling, smuggled** VERB
To smuggle things or people into or out of a place means to take them there illegally or secretly.

smuggler ['smʌglə] **smugglers** NOUN
someone who smuggles goods illegally into a country

snack [snæk] **snacks** NOUN
a light, quick meal

snag [snæg] **snags, snagging, snagged** NOUN
1 a small problem or disadvantage *e.g. There is one snag: it is not true.*

THESAURUS

catch: *It sounds too good to be true - what's the catch?*
difficulty: *The only difficulty may be the price.*
disadvantage: *The disadvantage is that this plant needs frequent watering.*
drawback: *The flat's only drawback was its size.*
problem: *The only problem about living here is the tourists.*

> VERB
2 If you snag your clothing, you damage it by catching it on something sharp.

> NOUN
3 INFORMAL In Australian and New Zealand English, a sausage.

snail [sneɪl] **snails** NOUN
a small, slow-moving creature with a long, shiny body and a shell on its back

snail mail NOUN; INFORMAL
the conventional postal system, as opposed to email

snake [sneɪk] **snakes, snaking, snaked** NOUN
1 a long, thin, scaly reptile with no legs

> VERB
2 Something that snakes moves in long winding curves. *e.g. The queue snaked out of the shop.*

snap [snæp] **snaps, snapping, snapped** VERB
1 If something snaps or if you snap it, it breaks with a sharp cracking noise.

2 If you snap something into a particular position, you move it there quickly with a sharp sound.

3 If an animal snaps at you, it shuts its jaws together quickly as if to bite you.

4 If someone snaps at you, they speak in a sharp, unfriendly way.

5 If you snap someone, you take a quick photograph of them.

> NOUN
6 the sound of something snapping

7 INFORMAL
a photograph taken quickly and casually

> ADJECTIVE
8 A snap decision or action is taken suddenly without careful thought.

snapper ['snæpə] **snappers** NOUN
a fish with edible pink flesh, found in waters around Australia and New Zealand

snapshot ['snæpʃɒt] **snapshots** NOUN
a photograph taken quickly and casually

snare [snɛə] **snares, snaring, snared** NOUN

1 a trap for catching birds or small animals

> VERB
2 To snare an animal or bird means to catch it using a snare.

snarl [snɑːl] **snarls, snarling, snarled** VERB
1 When an animal snarls, it bares its teeth and makes a fierce growling noise.

2 If you snarl, you say something in a fierce, angry way.

> NOUN
3 the noise an animal makes when it snarls

snatch [snætʃ] **snatches, snatching, snatched** VERB
1 If you snatch something, you reach out for it quickly and take it.

2 If you snatch an amount of time or an opportunity, you quickly make use of it.

> NOUN
3 If you make a snatch at something, you reach out for it quickly to try to take it.

4 A snatch of conversation or song is a very small piece of it.

sneak [sniːk] **sneaks, sneaking, sneaked** VERB
1 If you sneak somewhere, you go there quickly trying not to be seen or heard.

THESAURUS

lurk: *I saw someone lurking outside.*
sidle: *He sidled into the bar, trying to look inconspicuous.*
slip: *Amy slipped downstairs and out of the house.*
steal: *They can steal out and join us later.*

2 If you sneak something somewhere, you take it there secretly.

THESAURUS

slip: *He slipped me a note.*
smuggle: *We smuggled a camera into the concert.*
spirit: *treasures spirited away to foreign museums*

> NOUN
3 INFORMAL
someone who tells people in authority that someone else has done something wrong

sneaker ['sniːkə] **sneakers** NOUN
Sneakers are casual shoes with rubber soles.

sneaking ['sniːkɪŋ] ADJECTIVE
If you have a sneaking feeling about something or someone, you have this feeling rather reluctantly. *e.g. I had a sneaking suspicion that she was enjoying herself.*

sneaky ['sniːkɪ] **sneakier, sneakiest**
ADJECTIVE INFORMAL
Someone who is sneaky does things secretly rather than openly.

S

● THESAURUS

crafty: *the crafty methods used by salesmen to get people to sign up*
deceitful: *They claimed the government had been deceitful.*
devious: *He was devious, saying one thing to me and another to her.*
dishonest: *It would be dishonest to mislead people in that way.*
mean: *That was a mean trick.*
slippery: *She's a slippery customer, and should be watched.*
sly: *He's a sly old beggar.*
untrustworthy: *His opponents say he's untrustworthy.*

sneer [snɪə] **sneers, sneering, sneered**
VERB
1 If you sneer at someone or something, you show by your expression and your comments that you think they are stupid or inferior.
> NOUN
2 the expression on someone's face when they sneer

sneeze [sniːz] **sneezes, sneezing, sneezed**
VERB
1 When you sneeze, you suddenly take in breath and blow it down your nose noisily, because there is a tickle in your nose.
> NOUN
2 an act of sneezing

snide [snaɪd] ADJECTIVE
A snide comment or remark criticizes someone in a nasty and unfair way.

sniff [snɪf] **sniffs, sniffing, sniffed** VERB
1 When you sniff, you breathe in air through your nose hard enough to make a sound.
2 If you sniff something, you smell it by sniffing.
3 You can say that a person sniffs at something when they do not think very much of it. *e.g. Bessie sniffed at his household arrangements.*
> NOUN
4 the noise you make when you sniff
5 A sniff of something is a smell of it. *e.g. a sniff at the flowers*

snigger [ˈsnɪɡə] **sniggers, sniggering, sniggered** VERB
1 If you snigger, you laugh in a quiet, sly way. *e.g. They were sniggering at her accent.*
> NOUN
2 a quiet, disrespectful laugh

snip [snɪp] **snips, snipping, snipped** VERB
1 If you snip something, you cut it with scissors or shears in a single quick action.
> NOUN
2 a small cut made by scissors or shears

snippet [ˈsnɪpɪt] **snippets** NOUN
A snippet of something such as information or news is a small piece of it.

snob [snɒb] **snobs** NOUN
1 someone who admires upper-class people and looks down on lower-class people
2 someone who believes that they are better than other people
snobbery NOUN, **snobbish** ADJECTIVE

snooker [ˈsnuːkə] NOUN
Snooker is a game played on a large table covered with smooth green cloth. Players score points by hitting different coloured balls into side pockets using a long stick called a cue.

snoop [snuːp] **snoops, snooping, snooped**
VERB; INFORMAL
Someone who is snooping is secretly looking round a place to find out things.
[WORD HISTORY: from Dutch SNOEPEN meaning 'to eat furtively']

snooper [ˈsnuːpə] NOUN
a person who interferes in other people's business

● THESAURUS

meddler: *a meddler in the affairs of state*
stickybeak: Australian and New Zealand; informal *She's just an old stickybeak.*

snooze [snuːz] **snoozes, snoozing, snoozed** INFORMAL > VERB
1 If you snooze, you sleep lightly for a short time, especially during the day.
> NOUN
2 a short, light sleep

snore [snɔː] **snores, snoring, snored** VERB
1 When a sleeping person snores, they make a loud noise each time they breathe.
> NOUN
2 the noise someone makes when they snore

snorkel [ˈsnɔːkəl] **snorkels** NOUN
a tube you can breathe through when you are swimming just under the surface of the sea
snorkelling NOUN
[WORD HISTORY: from German SCHNORCHEL, originally an air pipe for a submarine]

snort [snɔːt] **snorts, snorting, snorted**
VERB
1 When people or animals snort, they force breath out through their nose in a noisy way. *e.g. Sarah snorted with laughter.*
> NOUN
2 the noise you make when you snort

snout [snaʊt] **snouts** NOUN
An animal's snout is its nose.

snow [snəʊ] **snows, snowing, snowed**
NOUN

1 Snow consists of flakes of ice crystals which fall from the sky in cold weather.

> VERB

2 When it snows, snow falls from the sky.

snowball ['snəʊˌbɔːl] **snowballs, snowballing, snowballed** NOUN

1 a ball of snow for throwing

> VERB

2 When something such as a project snowballs, it grows rapidly.

snowdrift ['snəʊˌdrɪft] **snowdrifts** NOUN

a deep pile of snow formed by the wind

snowdrop ['snəʊˌdrɒp] **snowdrops** NOUN

a small white flower which appears in early spring

snowman ['snəʊˌmæn] **snowmen** NOUN

a large mound of snow moulded into the shape of a person

snub [snʌb] **snubs, snubbing, snubbed**
VERB

1 To snub someone means to behave rudely towards them, especially by making an insulting remark or ignoring them.

> NOUN

2 an insulting remark or a piece of rude behaviour

> ADJECTIVE

3 A snub nose is short and turned-up.

snuff [snʌf] NOUN

Snuff is powdered tobacco which people take by sniffing it up their noses.

snug [snʌg] ADJECTIVE

A snug place is warm and comfortable. If you are snug, you are warm and comfortable.
snugly ADVERB

snuggle ['snʌgᵊl] **snuggles, snuggling, snuggled** VERB

If you snuggle somewhere, you cuddle up more closely to something or someone.

so [səʊ] ADVERB

1 'So' is used to refer back to what has just been mentioned e.g. Had he locked the car? If so, where were the keys?.

2 'So' is used to mean also e.g. He laughed, and so did Jarvis.

3 'So' can be used to mean 'therefore' e.g. It's a bit expensive, so I don't think I will get one.

4 'So' is used when you are talking about the degree or extent of something e.g. Why are you so cruel?

5 'So' is used before words like 'much' and 'many' to say that there is a definite limit to

something e.g. There are only so many questions that can be asked about the record.

> CONJUNCTION

6 'So that' and 'so as' are used to introduce the reason for doing something e.g. to die so that you might live

soak [səʊk] **soaks, soaking, soaked** VERB

1 To soak something or leave it to soak means to put it in a liquid and leave it there.

2 When a liquid soaks something, it makes it very wet.

● THESAURUS

bathe: Bathe the infected area in a salt solution.
permeate: The water had permeated the stone.
steep: green beans steeped in olive oil
wet: Wet the hair and work the shampoo through it.

3 When something soaks up a liquid, the liquid is drawn up into it.

soaked [səʊkt] ADJECTIVE

extremely wet

soaking ['səʊkɪŋ] ADJECTIVE

If something is soaking, it is very wet.

soap [səʊp] **soaps** NOUN

Soap is a substance made of natural oils and fats and used for washing yourself.
soapy ADJECTIVE

soap opera soap operas NOUN

a popular television drama serial about people's daily lives

soar [sɔː] **soars, soaring, soared** VERB

1 If an amount soars, it quickly increases by a great deal. e.g. Property prices soared.

2 If something soars into the air, it quickly goes up into the air.
soaring ADJECTIVE

sob [sɒb] **sobs, sobbing, sobbed** VERB

1 When someone sobs, they cry in a noisy way, breathing in short breaths.

> NOUN

2 the noise made when you cry

sober ['səʊbə] **soberer, soberest; sobers, sobering, sobered** ADJECTIVE

1 If someone is sober, they are not drunk.

2 Sober also means serious and thoughtful.

3 Sober colours are plain and rather dull.

> VERB

4 To sober up means to become sober after being drunk.
soberly ADVERB

sobering ['səʊbərɪŋ] ADJECTIVE

Something which is sobering makes you serious and thoughtful. e.g. the sobering lesson of the last year

S

so-called [ˌsəʊˈkɔːld] ADJECTIVE
You use 'so-called' to say that the name by which something is called is incorrect or misleading. *e.g. so-called environmentally-friendly products*

soccer [ˈsɒkə] NOUN
Soccer is a game played by two teams of eleven players kicking a ball in an attempt to score goals. [WORD HISTORY: formed from ASSOCIATION FOOTBALL]

sociable [ˈsəʊʃəbᵊl] ADJECTIVE
Sociable people are friendly and enjoy talking to other people.
sociability NOUN .

● THESAURUS
friendly: *The people here are very friendly.*
gregarious: *I'm not a gregarious person.*
outgoing: *He was shy and she was very outgoing.*

social [ˈsəʊʃəl] ADJECTIVE
1 to do with society or life within a society *e.g. women from similar social backgrounds*

2 to do with leisure activities that involve meeting other people
socially ADVERB

socialism [ˈsəʊʃəˌlɪzəm] NOUN
Socialism is the political belief that the state should own industries on behalf of the people and that everyone should be equal.
socialist ADJECTIVE OR NOUN

socialize [ˈsəʊʃəˌlaɪz] **socializes, socializing, socialized**; also spelt **socialise** VERB
When people socialize, they meet other people socially, for example at parties.

social security NOUN
Social security is a system by which the government pays money regularly to people who have no other income or only a very small income.

social work NOUN
Social work involves giving help and advice to people with serious financial or family problems.
social worker NOUN

society [səˈsaɪətɪ] **societies** NOUN
1 Society is the people in a particular country or region. *e.g. a major problem in society*

● THESAURUS
civilization: *an ancient civilization*
culture: *people from different cultures*

2 an organization for people who have the same interest or aim *e.g. the school debating society*

● THESAURUS
association: *the Football Association*
circle: *a local painting circle*
club: *He was at the youth club.*

fellowship: *the Visual Arts Fellowship*
group: *an environmental group*
guild: *the Screen Writers' Guild*
institute: *the Women's Institute*
league: *the World Muslim League*
organization: *student organizations*
union: *the International Astronomical Union*

3 Society is also rich, upper-class, fashionable people.

sociology [ˌsəʊsɪˈɒlədʒɪ] NOUN
Sociology is the study of human societies and the relationships between groups in these societies.
sociological ADJECTIVE, **sociologist** NOUN

sock [sɒk] **socks** NOUN
Socks are pieces of clothing covering your foot and ankle.
[WORD HISTORY: from Old English socc meaning 'light shoe']

socket [ˈsɒkɪt] **sockets** NOUN
1 a place on a wall or on a piece of electrical equipment into which you can put a plug or bulb

2 Any hollow part or opening into which another part fits can be called a socket. *e.g. eye sockets*

sod [sɒd] NOUN; LITERARY
The sod is the surface of the ground, together with the grass and roots growing in it.

soda [ˈsəʊdə] **sodas** NOUN
1 Soda is the same as **soda water**

2 Soda is also sodium in the form of crystals or a powder, and is used for baking or cleaning.

soda water soda waters NOUN
Soda water is fizzy water used for mixing with alcoholic drinks or fruit juice.

sodden [ˈsɒdᵊn] ADJECTIVE
soaking wet

sodium [ˈsəʊdɪəm] NOUN
Sodium is a silvery-white chemical element which combines with other chemicals. Salt is a sodium compound.

sofa [ˈsəʊfə] **sofas** NOUN
a long comfortable seat with a back and arms for two or three people
[WORD HISTORY: from Arabic SUFFAH meaning 'an upholstered raised platform']

soft [sɒft] **softer, softest** ADJECTIVE
1 Something soft is not hard, stiff, or firm.

● THESAURUS
flexible: *a flexible material*
pliable: *a pliable dough*
squashy: *a squashy tomato*
supple: *supple leather*
yielding: *yielding cushions*
<<OPPOSITE *hard*

2 Soft also means very gentle. *e.g. a soft breeze*

3 A soft sound or voice is quiet and not harsh.

● THESAURUS

gentle: *a gentle voice*
low: *She spoke in a low whisper.*
mellow: *mellow background music*
muted: *Their loud conversation became muted.*
quiet: *He always spoke in a quiet tone to which everyone listened.*
subdued: *His voice was more subdued than usual.*

4 A soft colour or light is not bright.
softly ADVERB

● THESAURUS

dim: *The light was dim and eerie.*
faint: *The stars cast a faint light.*
light: *The walls were painted a light yellow.*
mellow: *Their colour schemes tend towards rich, mellow shades.*
pale: *dressed in pale pink*
pastel: *delicate pastel hues*
subdued: *subdued lighting*
<<OPPOSITE *bright*

soft drink soft drinks NOUN
any cold, nonalcoholic drink

soften ['sɒfᵊn] **softens, softening, softened** VERB

1 If something is softened or softens, it becomes less hard, stiff, or firm.

2 If you soften, you become more sympathetic and less critical. *e.g. Phillida softened as she spoke.*

software ['sɒft,wɛə] NOUN
(ICT) Computer programs are known as software.

soggy ['sɒgɪ] **soggier, soggiest** ADJECTIVE
unpleasantly wet or full of water
[WORD HISTORY: from American dialect SOG meaning 'marsh']

soil [sɔɪl] **soils, soiling, soiled** NOUN

1 Soil is the top layer on the surface of the earth in which plants grow.

● THESAURUS

clay: *a thin layer of clay*
dirt: *The bulldozers piled up huge mounds of dirt.*
earth: *a huge pile of earth*
ground: *a hole in the ground*

> VERB

2 If you soil something, you make it dirty.
soiled ADJECTIVE

● THESAURUS

dirty: *He was afraid the dog's hairs might dirty the seats.*
foul: *The cage was fouled with droppings.*
pollute: *chemicals which pollute rivers*
smear: *The pillow was smeared with makeup.*

spatter: *Her dress was spattered with mud.*
stain: *Some foods can stain the teeth.*
<<OPPOSITE *clean*

solace ['sɒlɪs] NOUN; LITERARY
Solace is something that makes you feel less sad. *e.g. I found solace in writing.*

solar ['səʊlə] ADJECTIVE

1 relating or belonging to the sun

2 using the sun's light and heat as a source of energy *e.g. a solar-powered calculator*

solar system NOUN
The solar system is the sun and all the planets, comets, and asteroids that orbit round it.

solder ['sɒldə] **solders, soldering, soldered** VERB

1 To solder two pieces of metal together means to join them with molten metal.

> NOUN

2 Solder is the soft metal used for soldering.

soldier ['səʊldʒə] **soldiers** NOUN
a person in an army

sole [səʊl] **soles, soling, soled** ADJECTIVE

1 The sole thing or person of a particular type is the only one of that type.

> NOUN

2 The sole of your foot or shoe is the underneath part.

3 a flat sea-water fish which you can eat

> VERB

4 When a shoe is soled, a sole is fitted to it.

solely ['səʊllɪ] ADVERB
If something involves solely one thing, it involves that thing and nothing else.

solemn ['sɒləm] ADJECTIVE
Solemn means serious rather than cheerful or humorous.
solemnly ADVERB, **solemnity** NOUN

● THESAURUS

earnest: *Ella was a pious, earnest woman.*
grave: *He was looking unusually grave.*
serious: *She looked at me with big, serious eyes.*
sober: *sad, sober faces*
staid: *He is boring, old fashioned and staid.*

solicitor [sə'lɪsɪtə] **solicitors** NOUN
a lawyer who gives legal advice and prepares legal documents and cases

solid ['sɒlɪd] **solids** ADJECTIVE

1 A solid substance or object is hard or firm, and not in the form of a liquid or gas.

● THESAURUS

firm: *a firm mattress*
hard: *The snow was hard and slippery.*

2 You say that something is solid when it is not hollow. *e.g. solid steel*

S

3 You say that a structure is solid when it is strong and not likely to fall down. *e.g. solid fences*

● **THESAURUS**
stable: *stable foundations*
strong: *strong fences*
sturdy: *The camera was mounted on a sturdy tripod.*
substantial: *The posts are made of concrete and are fairly substantial.*

4 You use 'solid' to say that something happens for a period of time without interruption. *e.g. I cried for two solid days.*

> NOUN
5 a solid substance or object
solidly ADVERB

solidarity [ˌsɒlɪˈdærɪtɪ] NOUN
If a group of people show solidarity, they show unity and support for each other.

soliloquy [səˈlɪləkwɪ] **soliloquies** NOUN
(ENGLISH) a speech in a play made by a character who is alone on the stage
[WORD HISTORY: from Latin *solus* meaning 'alone' and *loqui* meaning 'to speak']

solitary [ˈsɒlɪtərɪ] ADJECTIVE
1 A solitary activity is one that you do on your own.
2 A solitary person or animal spends a lot of time alone.
3 If there is a solitary person or object somewhere, there is only one.

solitary confinement [kənˈfaɪnmənt] NOUN
A prisoner in solitary confinement is being kept alone in a prison cell.

solitude [ˈsɒlɪˌtjuːd] NOUN
Solitude is the state of being alone.

● **THESAURUS**
isolation: *the isolation he endured while in captivity*
loneliness: *I have a fear of loneliness.*
privacy: *the privacy of my own room*
seclusion: *She lived in seclusion with her husband.*

solo [ˈsəʊləʊ] **solos** NOUN
1 a piece of music played or sung by one person alone

> ADJECTIVE
2 A solo performance or activity is done by one person alone. *e.g. my first solo flight*

> ADVERB
3 Solo means alone. *e.g. to sail solo around the world*

soloist [ˈsəʊləʊɪst] **soloists** NOUN
a person who performs a solo

solstice [ˈsɒlstɪs] **solstices** NOUN
one of the two times in the year when the sun is at its furthest point south or north of the equator
[WORD HISTORY: from Latin *sol* meaning 'sun' and *sistere* meaning 'to stand still']

soluble [ˈsɒljʊbəl] ADJECTIVE
A soluble substance is able to dissolve in liquid.

solution [səˈluːʃən] **solutions** NOUN
1 a way of dealing with a problem or difficult situation *e.g. a quick solution to our problem*
2 The solution to a riddle or a puzzle is the answer.
3 (SCIENCE) a liquid in which a solid substance has been dissolved

solve [sɒlv] **solves, solving, solved** VERB
If you solve a problem or a question, you find a solution or answer to it.

● **THESAURUS**
clear up: *During dinner the confusion was cleared up.*
crack: *He finally managed to crack the code.*
decipher: *trying to decipher the symbols on the stone tablets*
get to the bottom of: *The police wanted to get to the bottom of the case.*
resolve: *Scientists hope this will finally resolve the mystery.*
work out: *I've worked out where I'm going wrong.*

solvent [ˈsɒlvənt] **solvents** ADJECTIVE
1 If a person or company is solvent, they have enough money to pay all their debts.

> NOUN
2 a liquid that can dissolve other substances
solvency NOUN

Somali [səʊˈmɑːlɪ] **Somalis** ADJECTIVE
1 belonging or relating to Somalia

> NOUN
2 The Somalis are a group of people who live in Somalia.
3 Somali is the language spoken by Somalis.

sombre [ˈsɒmbə] ADJECTIVE
1 Sombre colours are dark and dull.
2 A sombre person is serious, sad, or gloomy.

some [sʌm]
1 You use 'some' to refer to a quantity or number when you are not stating the quantity or number exactly. *e.g. There's some money on the table.*
2 You use 'some' to emphasize that a quantity or number is fairly large. *e.g. She had been there for some days.*

> ADVERB
3 You use 'some' in front of a number to show that it is not exact. *e.g. a fishing village some seven miles north*

somebody [ˈsʌmbədɪ] PRONOUN
Somebody means someone.

Somebody and *someone* mean the same

some day ADVERB
Some day means at a date in the future that is unknown or that has not yet been decided.

somehow ['sʌm,haʊ] ADVERB
1 You use 'somehow' to say that you do not know how something was done or will be done. *e.g. You'll find a way of doing it somehow.*
2 You use 'somehow' to say that you do not know the reason for something. *e.g. Somehow it didn't feel quite right.*

someone ['sʌm,wʌn] PRONOUN
You use 'someone' to refer to a person without saying exactly who you mean.

Someone and *somebody* mean the same

somersault ['sʌmə,sɔːlt] **somersaults**
NOUN
a forwards or backwards roll in which the head is placed on the ground and the body is brought over it
[WORD HISTORY: from Old Provençal SOBRE meaning 'over' and SAUT meaning 'jump']

something ['sʌmθɪŋ] PRONOUN
You use 'something' to refer to anything that is not a person without saying exactly what you mean.

sometime ['sʌm,taɪm] ADVERB
1 at a time in the future or the past that is unknown or that has not yet been fixed *e.g. He has to find out sometime.*
> ADJECTIVE
2 FORMAL
'Sometime' is used to say that a person had a particular job or role in the past *e.g. a sometime actress, dancer and singer*

sometimes ['sʌm,taɪmz] ADVERB
occasionally, rather than always or never

THESAURUS
at times: *She can be a little common at times.*
every now and then: *He checks up on me every now and then.*
every so often: *Every so often he does something silly.*
from time to time: *I go back to see my mum from time to time.*
now and again: *I enjoy a day out now and again.*
now and then: *These people like a laugh now and then.*
occasionally: *I know that I do put people down occasionally.*
once in a while: *It does you good to get out once in a while.*

somewhat ['sʌm,wɒt] ADVERB
to some extent or degree *e.g. The future seemed somewhat bleak.*

somewhere ['sʌm,wɛə] ADVERB
1 'Somewhere' is used to refer to a place without stating exactly where it is *e.g. There has to be a file somewhere.*
2 'Somewhere' is used when giving an approximate amount, number, or time *e.g. somewhere between the winter of 1989 and the summer of 1991*

son [sʌn] **sons** NOUN
Someone's son is their male child.

sonar ['səʊnɑː] NOUN
Sonar is equipment on a ship which calculates the depth of the sea or the position of an underwater object using sound waves.
[WORD HISTORY: from SO(UND) NA(VIGATION) R(ANGING)]

sonata [sə'nɑːtə] **sonatas** NOUN
a piece of classical music, usually in three or more movements, for piano or for another instrument with or without piano

song [sɒŋ] **songs** NOUN
a piece of music with words that are sung to the music

songbird ['sɒŋ,bɜːd] **songbirds** NOUN
a bird that produces musical sounds like singing

son-in-law [sʌnɪn,lɔː] **sons-in-law** NOUN
Someone's son-in-law is the husband of their daughter.

sonnet ['sɒnɪt] **sonnets** NOUN
a poem with 14 lines, in which lines rhyme according to fixed patterns
[WORD HISTORY: from Old Provençal SONET meaning 'little poem']

soon [suːn] **sooner, soonest** ADVERB
If something is going to happen soon, it will happen in a very short time.

THESAURUS
any minute now: *Any minute now she's going to start crying.*
before long: *Interest rates will come down before long.*
in a minute: *I'll be with you in a minute.*
in the near future: *The controversy is unlikely to be resolved in the near future.*
presently: *I'll deal with you presently.*
shortly: *The trial will begin shortly.*
<<OPPOSITE *later*

soot [sʊt] NOUN
Soot is black powder which rises in the smoke from a fire.
sooty ADJECTIVE

soothe [suːð] **soothes, soothing, soothed**
VERB
1 If you soothe someone who is angry or upset, you make them calmer.

S

2 Something that soothes pain makes the pain less severe.
soothing ADJECTIVE

sophisticated [sə'fɪstɪ,keɪtɪd] ADJECTIVE
1 Sophisticated people have refined or cultured tastes or habits.

● THESAURUS
cosmopolitan: *The family are rich and extremely cosmopolitan.*
cultivated: *an elegant and cultivated woman*
cultured: *He is immensely cultured and well-read.*
refined: *a woman of refined tastes*
urbane: *a polished, urbane manner*

2 A sophisticated machine or device is made using advanced and complicated methods.
sophistication NOUN

● THESAURUS
advanced: *the most advanced optical telescope in the world*
complex: *complex machines*
complicated: *a complicated voting system*
elaborate: *an elaborate design*
intricate: *intricate controls*
refined: *a more refined engine*
<<OPPOSITE *simple*

soppy ['sɒpɪ] **soppier, soppiest** ADJECTIVE;
INFORMAL
silly or foolishly sentimental

soprano [sə'prɑːnəʊ] **sopranos** NOUN
a woman, girl, or boy with a singing voice in the highest range of musical notes

sorcerer ['sɔːsərə] **sorcerers** NOUN
a person who performs magic by using the power of evil spirits

sorceress ['sɔːsərɪs] **sorceresses** NOUN
a female sorcerer

sorcery ['sɔːsərɪ] NOUN
Sorcery is magic that uses the power of evil spirits.

sordid ['sɔːdɪd] ADJECTIVE
1 dishonest or immoral *e.g. a rather sordid business*
2 dirty, unpleasant, or depressing *e.g. the sordid guest house*

sore [sɔː] **sorer, sorest; sores** ADJECTIVE
1 If part of your body is sore, it causes you pain and discomfort.

● THESAURUS
inflamed: *Her eyes were red and inflamed.*
painful: *a painful knock on the knee*
raw: *Her hands were rubbed raw by the rope.*
sensitive: *the pain of sensitive teeth*
smarting: *My eyes were smarting from the smoke.*
tender: *My stomach feels very tender.*

2 LITERARY
'Sore' is used to emphasize something *e.g. The*

President is in sore need of friends.

> NOUN
3 a painful place where your skin has become infected
sorely ADVERB, **soreness** NOUN

sorghum ['sɔːgəm] NOUN
a type of tropical grass that is grown for hay, grain, and syrup

sorrow ['sɒrəʊ] **sorrows** NOUN
1 Sorrow is deep sadness or regret.

● THESAURUS
grief: *Their grief soon gave way to anger.*
heartache: *suffering the heartache of a divorce*
melancholy: *She has an air of melancholy.*
misery: *All his money brought him nothing but misery.*
mourning: *a day of mourning*
pain: *My heart is full of pain.*
regret: *She accepted his resignation with regret.*
sadness: *It is with a mixture of sadness and joy that I say farewell.*
unhappiness: *I had a lot of unhappiness in my adolescence.*
woe: formal *a tale of woe*
<<OPPOSITE *joy*

2 Sorrows are things that cause sorrow. *e.g. the sorrows of this world*

● THESAURUS
heartache: *all the heartaches of parenthood*
hardship: *One of the worst hardships is having so little time with my family.*
misfortune: *She seems to enjoy the misfortunes of others.*
trouble: *She told me all her troubles.*
woe: written *He did not tell his friends about his woes.*
worry: *a life with no worries* formal
<<OPPOSITE *joy*

sorry ['sɒrɪ] **sorrier, sorriest** ADJECTIVE
1 If you are sorry about something, you feel sadness or regret about it.

● THESAURUS
apologetic: *"I'm afraid I can't help," she said with an apologetic smile.*
penitent: *He sat silent and penitent in a corner.*
regretful: *Now I'm totally regretful that I did it.*
remorseful: *He was genuinely remorseful.*
repentant: *repentant sinners*

2 feeling sympathy for someone

● THESAURUS
moved: *I'm moved by what you say.*
sympathetic: *She gave me a sympathetic glance.*

3 'Sorry' is used to describe people and things that are in a bad physical or mental state *e.g. She was in a pretty sorry state when we found her.*

THESAURUS
deplorable: *living in deplorable conditions*
miserable: *a miserable existence*
pathetic: *the pathetic sight of oil-covered sea birds*
pitiful: *a pitiful creature*
poor: *the poor condition of the pitch*
sad: *a sad state of affairs*
wretched: *the wretched victims of war*

sort [sɔːt] **sorts, sorting, sorted** NOUN
1 The different sorts of something are the different types of it.

THESAURUS
brand: *his favourite brand of whisky*
category: *The topics were divided into six categories.*
class: *a better class of restaurant*
group: *Weathermen classify clouds into several different groups.*
kind: *different kinds of roses*
make: *a certain make of car*
species: *400 species of fungi have been recorded.*
style: *Several styles of hat were available.*
type: *What type of dog should we get?*
variety: *many varieties of birds*

> VERB
2 To sort things means to arrange them into different groups or sorts. **sort out**

THESAURUS
arrange: *Arrange the books in neat piles.*
categorize: *ways to categorize information*
classify: *Rocks can be classified according to their mode of origin.*
divide: *The subjects were divided into four groups.*
grade: *musical pieces graded according to difficulty*
group: *The fact sheet is grouped into seven sections.*
separate: *His work can be separated into three main categories.*

> VERB
3 If you sort out a problem or misunderstanding, you deal with it and find a solution to it.

When you use *sort* in its singular form, the adjective before it should also be singular: *that sort of car*. When you use the plural form *sorts*, the adjective before it should be plural: *those sorts of shop; those sorts of shops*

SOS NOUN
An SOS is a signal that you are in danger and need help.

so-so ['səʊ,səʊ] ADJECTIVE
neither good nor bad *e.g. The food is so-so.*

soufflé ['suːfleɪ] **soufflés**; also spelt **souffle** NOUN
a light, fluffy food made from beaten egg whites and other ingredients that is baked in the oven

sought [sɔːt] the past tense and past participle of **seek**

soul [səʊl] **souls** NOUN
1 A person's soul is the spiritual part of them that is supposed to continue after their body is dead.
2 People also use 'soul' to refer to a person's mind, character, thoughts, and feelings.
3 'Soul' can be used to mean person *e.g. There was not a soul there.*
4 Soul is a type of pop music.

sound see page 824 for Word Web

sound bite sound bites NOUN
a short and memorable sentence or phrase extracted from a longer speech for use on radio or television

sound effect sound effects NOUN
Sound effects are sounds created artificially to make a play more realistic, especially a radio play.

soundproof ['saʊnd,pruːf] ADJECTIVE
If a room is soundproof, sound cannot get into it or out of it.

soundtrack ['saʊnd,træk] **soundtracks** NOUN
The soundtrack of a film is the part you hear.

soup [suːp] **soups** NOUN
Soup is liquid food made by boiling meat, fish, or vegetables in water.

sour ['saʊə] **sours, souring, soured** ADJECTIVE
1 If something is sour, it has a sharp, acid taste.

THESAURUS
acid: *The wine had an acid taste.*
bitter: *a bitter drink*
pungent: *a pungent sauce*
sharp: *a clean, sharp flavour*
tart: *the tart qualities of citrus fruit*
<<OPPOSITE sweet

2 Sour milk has an unpleasant taste because it is no longer fresh.

THESAURUS
curdled: *curdled milk*
off: *This meat's gone off.*
rancid: *rancid butter*

3 A sour person is bad-tempered and unfriendly.

THESAURUS
disagreeable: *a shallow, disagreeable man*
embittered: *an embittered old lady*
jaundiced: *a jaundiced attitude*
tart: *a tart reply*

> VERB
4 If a friendship, situation, or attitude sours or if something sours it, it becomes less friendly, enjoyable, or hopeful.

source [sɔːs] **sources** NOUN
1 The source of something is the person, place, or thing that it comes from. *e.g. the source of his confidence*

S

1 NOUN
Sound is everything that can be heard.
● THESAURUS
din: *make themselves heard over the din of the crowd*
hubbub: *the hubbub of excited conversation*
noise: *the noise of bombs and guns*
racket: *the racket of drills and electric saws*
tone: *the clear tone of the bell*
<< OPPOSITE *silence*

2 VERB
If something sounds or if you sound it, it makes a noise.
● THESAURUS
blow: *A guard was blowing his whistle.*
chime: *He heard the doorbell chime.*
clang: *The church bell clanged.*
peal: *Church bells pealed at the stroke of midnight.*
ring: *She heard the school bell ringing.*
set off: *Any escape sets off the alarm.*
toll: *The pilgrims tolled the bell.*

sound
sounds, sounding, sounded; sounder, soundest

3 ADJECTIVE
in good condition *eg: a guarantee that a house is sound*
● THESAURUS
all right: *Does the roof seem all right?*
fine: *She told me her heart was perfectly fine.*
fit: *Exercise is the first step to a fit body.*
healthy: *His once healthy mind was deteriorating.*
in good condition: *The timbers were all in good condition.*
intact: *The boat did not appear damaged and its equipment seemed intact.*
robust: *He is in robust health for a man of his age.*

4 ADJECTIVE
reliable and sensible *eg: The logic behind the argument seems sound.*
● THESAURUS
down-to-earth: *Their ideas seem very down-to-earth.*
good: *Give me one good reason why I should tell you.*
reasonable: *a perfectly reasonable decision*
reliable: *It's difficult to give a reliable estimate.*
sensible: *sensible advice*
solid: *good solid information*
valid: *Both sides made some valid points.*

◉ **THESAURUS**

beginning: *the beginning of all the trouble*
cause: *the cause of the problem*
derivation: *The derivation of the name is obscure.*
origin: *the origin of life*
originator: *the originator of the theory*

2 (HISTORY) The source of a river or stream is the place where it begins.

> Do not confuse the spellings of *source* and *sauce*, which can sound very similar

sour grapes [greɪps] **PLURAL NOUN**
You describe someone's behaviour as sour grapes when they say something is worthless but secretly want it and cannot have it.

south [saʊθ] **NOUN**

1 The south is the direction to your right when you are looking towards the place where the sun rises.

2 The south of a place or country is the part which is towards the south when you are in the centre.

> **ADVERB OR ADJECTIVE**
3 South means towards the south. *e.g. The taxi headed south... the south end of the site*

> **ADJECTIVE**
4 A south wind blows from the south.

South America [saʊθ] **NOUN**
South America is the fourth largest continent. It has the Pacific Ocean on its west side, the Atlantic on the east, and the Antarctic to the south. South America is joined to North America by the Isthmus of Panama.
South American ADJECTIVE

south-east [saʊθ'iːst] **NOUN, ADVERB, OR ADJECTIVE**
South-east is halfway between south and east.

south-easterly [ˌsaʊθ'iːstəlɪ] **ADJECTIVE**

1 South-easterly means to or towards the south-east.

2 A south-easterly wind blows from the south-east.

south-eastern [ˌsaʊθ'iːstən] **ADJECTIVE**
in or from the south-east

southerly ['sʌðəlɪ] **ADJECTIVE**

1 Southerly means to or towards the south.

2 A southerly wind blows from the south.

southern ['sʌðən] **ADJECTIVE**
in or from the south

Southern Cross ['sʌðən krɒs] **NOUN**
The Southern Cross is a small group of stars which can be seen from the southern part of the earth, and which is represented on the national flags of Australia and New Zealand.

South Pole [saʊθ] **NOUN**
The South Pole is the place on the surface of the earth that is farthest towards the south.

southward or **southwards** ['saʊθwəd] or ['saʊθwədz] **ADVERB**

1 Southward or southwards means towards the south. *e.g. the dusty road which led southwards*

> **ADJECTIVE**
2 The southward part of something is the south part.

south-west [ˌsaʊθ'wɛst] **NOUN, ADVERB, OR ADJECTIVE**
South-west is halfway between south and west.

south-westerly [ˌsaʊθ'wɛstəlɪ] **ADJECTIVE**

1 South-westerly means to or towards the south-west.

2 A south-westerly wind blows from the south-west.

south-western [ˌsaʊθ'wɛstən] **ADJECTIVE**
in or from the south-west

souvenir [ˌsuːvə'nɪə] **souvenirs NOUN**
something you keep to remind you of a holiday, place, or event
[WORD HISTORY: from French SE SOUVENIR meaning 'to remember']

◉ **THESAURUS**

keepsake: *a cherished keepsake*
memento: *a memento of the occasion*
relic: *the threadbare teddy bear, a relic of childhood*
reminder: *a permanent reminder of this historic event*

sovereign ['sɒvrɪn] **sovereigns NOUN**

1 a king, queen, or royal ruler of a country

2 In the past, a sovereign was a British gold coin worth one pound.

> **ADJECTIVE**
3 A sovereign state or country is independent and not under the authority of any other country.

sovereignty ['sɒvrəntɪ] **NOUN**
Sovereignty is the political power that a country has to govern itself.

Soviet ['səʊvɪət] **Soviets ADJECTIVE**

1 belonging or relating to the country that used to be the Soviet Union

> **NOUN**
2 The people and the government of the country that used to be the Soviet Union were sometimes referred to as the Soviets.

sow [səʊ] **sows, sowing, sowed, sown VERB**

1 To sow seeds or sow an area of land with seeds means to plant them in the ground.

2 To sow undesirable feelings or attitudes means to cause them. *e.g. You have sown discontent.*

sow [saʊ] **sows NOUN**
an adult female pig

S

soya ['sɔɪə] NOUN
Soya flour, margarine, oil, and milk are made from soya beans.
[WORD HISTORY: from Chinese CHIANG YU meaning 'paste sauce']

soya bean soya beans NOUN
Soya beans are a type of edible Asian bean.

spa [spɑː] **spas** NOUN
a place where water containing minerals bubbles out of the ground, at which people drink or bathe in the water to improve their health
[WORD HISTORY: from the Belgian town Spa where there are mineral springs]

space [speɪs] **spaces, spacing, spaced** NOUN
1 Space is the area that is empty or available in a place, building, or container.

● THESAURUS
accommodation: *We have accommodation for six people.*
capacity: *the capacity of the airliner*
room: *no room to manoeuvre*

2 Space is the area beyond the earth's atmosphere surrounding the stars and planets.

3 a gap between two things *e.g. the space between the tables*

● THESAURUS
blank: *I've left a blank here for your signature.*
distance: *the distance between the island and the mainland*
gap: *The wind was tearing through gaps in the window frames.*
interval: *the intervals between the trees*

4 Space can also refer to a period of time. *e.g. two incidents in the space of a week*

● THESAURUS
interval: *a long interval of silence*
period: *for a limited period only*
span: *The batteries have a life span of six hours.*
time: *At 15 he left home for a short time.*
while: *Sit down for a while.*

> VERB
5 If you space a series of things, you arrange them with gaps between them.

spacecraft ['speɪs,krɑːft] NOUN
a rocket or other vehicle that can travel in space

spaceman ['speɪs,mæn] **spacemen** NOUN
someone who travels in space

spaceship ['speɪs,ʃɪp] **spaceships** NOUN
a spacecraft that carries people through space

space shuttle space shuttles NOUN
a spacecraft designed to be used many times for travelling out into space and back again

spacious ['speɪʃəs] ADJECTIVE
having or providing a lot of space *e.g. the spacious living room*

● THESAURUS
ample: *the city's ample car parks*
broad: *a broad expanse of green lawn*
expansive: *an expansive play area*
extensive: *The palace stands in extensive grounds.*
huge: *a huge apartment overlooking the park*
large: *a large detached house*
vast: *a vast chamber*

spade [speɪd] **spades** NOUN
1 a tool with a flat metal blade and a long handle used for digging

2 Spades is one of the four suits in a pack of playing cards. It is marked by a black symbol in the shape of a heart-shaped leaf with a stem.

spaghetti [spə'gɛtɪ] NOUN
Spaghetti consists of long, thin pieces of pasta.

spam [spæm] NOUN
unwanted e-mails, usually containing advertising

span [spæn] **spans, spanning, spanned** NOUN
1 the period of time during which something exists or functions *e.g. looking back today over a span of forty years*

2 The span of something is the total length of it from one end to the other.

> VERB
3 If something spans a particular length of time, it lasts throughout that time. *e.g. a career that spanned 50 years*

4 A bridge that spans something stretches right across it.

spangle ['spæŋgəl] **spangles, spangling, spangled** VERB
1 If something is spangled, it is covered with small, sparkling objects.

> NOUN
2 Spangles are small sparkling pieces of metal or plastic used to decorate clothing or hair.

Spaniard ['spænjəd] **Spaniards** NOUN
someone who comes from Spain

spaniel ['spænjəl] **spaniels** NOUN
a dog with long drooping ears and a silky coat
[WORD HISTORY: from Old French ESPAIGNEUL meaning 'Spanish dog']

Spanish ['spænɪʃ] ADJECTIVE
1 belonging or relating to Spain

> NOUN
2 Spanish is the main language spoken in Spain, and is also spoken by many people in Central and South America.

spank [spæŋk] **spanks, spanking, spanked** VERB

If a child is spanked, it is punished by being slapped, usually on its leg or bottom.

spanner [ˈspænə] **spanners** NOUN
a tool with a specially shaped end that fits round a nut to turn it

spar [spɑː] **spars, sparring, sparred** VERB
1 When boxers spar, they hit each other with light punches for practice.

2 To spar with someone also means to argue with them, but not in an unpleasant or serious way.

> NOUN
3 a strong pole that a sail is attached to on a yacht or ship

spare [spɛə] **spares, sparing, spared**
ADJECTIVE
1 extra to what is needed *e.g. What does she do in her spare time?*.

● THESAURUS
extra: *Allow yourself some extra time in case of emergencies.*
free: *I'll do it as soon as I get some free time.*
superfluous: *I got rid of all my superfluous belongings.*
surplus: *They sell their surplus produce.*

> NOUN
2 a thing that is extra to what is needed

> VERB
3 If you spare something for a particular purpose, you make it available. *e.g. Few troops could be spared to go abroad.*

● THESAURUS
afford: *It's all I can afford to give you.*
give: *It's good of you to give me some of your time.*
let someone have: *I can let you have some milk and sugar.*

4 If someone is spared an unpleasant experience, they are prevented from suffering it. *e.g. The capital was spared the misery of an all-out train strike.*

● THESAURUS
let off: informal *I'll let you off this time.*
pardon: *Relatives had begged authorities to pardon him.*
relieve of: *a machine which relieves you of the drudgery of housework*
save from: *I was trying to save you from unnecessary worry.*

sparing [ˈspɛərɪŋ] ADJECTIVE
If you are sparing with something, you use it in very small quantities.
sparingly ADVERB

spark [spɑːk] **sparks, sparking, sparked**
NOUN

1 a tiny, bright piece of burning material thrown up by a fire

2 a small flash of light caused by electricity

3 A spark of feeling is a small amount of it. *e.g. that tiny spark of excitement*

> VERB
4 If something sparks, it throws out sparks.

5 If one thing sparks another thing off, it causes the second thing to start happening. *e.g. The tragedy sparked off a wave of sympathy among staff.*

sparkle [ˈspɑːkəl] **sparkles, sparkling, sparkled** VERB
1 If something sparkles, it shines with a lot of small, bright points of light.

● THESAURUS
gleam: *sunlight gleaming on the water*
glisten: *The wall glistened with frost.*
glitter: *A million stars glittered in the black sky.*
shimmer: *In the distance the lake shimmered.*
twinkle: *The old man's eyes twinkled.*

> NOUN
2 Sparkles are small, bright points of light.
sparkling ADJECTIVE

sparrow [ˈspærəʊ] **sparrows** NOUN
a common, small bird with brown and grey feathers

sparse [spɑːs] **sparser, sparsest** ADJECTIVE
small in number or amount and spread out over an area *e.g. the sparse audience*
sparsely ADVERB

spartan [ˈspɑːtən] ADJECTIVE
A spartan way of life is very simple with no luxuries. *e.g. spartan accommodation*
[WORD HISTORY: from SPARTA, a city in Ancient Greece, whose inhabitants were famous for their discipline, military skill, and stern and plain way of life]

spasm [ˈspæzəm] **spasms** NOUN
1 a sudden tightening of the muscles
2 a sudden, short burst of something *e.g. a spasm of fear*

spasmodic [spæzˈmɒdɪk] ADJECTIVE
happening suddenly for short periods of time at irregular intervals *e.g. spasmodic movements*

spastic [ˈspæstɪk] ADJECTIVE
1 A spastic person is born with a disability which makes it difficult for them to control their muscles.

> NOUN
2 a spastic person
[WORD HISTORY: from Greek SPASMOS meaning 'cramp' or 'convulsion']

spate [speɪt] NOUN
A spate of things is a large number of them that

S

happen or appear in a rush. *e.g. a recent spate of first novels from older writers*

spatial ['speɪʃəl] ADJECTIVE
to do with size, area, or position

spatter ['spætə] **spatters, spattering, spattered** VERB
1 If something spatters a surface, it covers the surface with drops of liquid.
> NOUN
2 A spatter of something is a small amount of it in drops or tiny pieces.

spawn [spɔːn] **spawns, spawning, spawned** NOUN
1 Spawn is a jelly-like substance containing the eggs of fish or amphibians.
> VERB
2 When fish or amphibians spawn, they lay their eggs.
3 If something spawns something else, it causes it. *e.g. The depressed economy spawned the riots.*

speak [spiːk] **speaks, speaking, spoke, spoken** VERB
1 When you speak, you use your voice to say words.
2 If you speak a foreign language, you know it and can use it.
speak out VERB
3 To speak out about something means to publicly state an opinion about it.

speaker ['spiːkə] **speakers** NOUN
1 a person who is speaking, especially someone making a speech
2 A speaker on a radio or hi-fi is a loudspeaker.

spear [spɪə] **spears, spearing, speared** NOUN
1 a weapon consisting of a long pole with a sharp point
> VERB
2 To spear something means to push or throw a spear or other pointed object into it.

spearhead ['spɪəˌhɛd] **spearheads, spearheading, spearheaded** VERB
If someone spearheads a campaign, they lead it.

spec [spɛk] **specs** INFORMAL > PLURAL NOUN
1 Someone's specs are their glasses.
> PHRASE
2 If you do something **on spec**, you do it hoping for a result but without any certainty. *e.g. He turned up at the same event on spec.*

special ['spɛʃəl] ADJECTIVE **(RE)**
1 Something special is more important or better than other things of its kind.

● THESAURUS
exceptional: *children with exceptional ability*
important: *This is an important occasion.*
significant: *of significant importance*
unique: *a unique talent*
<<OPPOSITE *ordinary*

2 Special describes someone who is officially appointed, or something that is needed for a particular purpose. *e.g. Karen actually had to get special permission to go there.*
3 Special also describes something that belongs or relates to only one particular person, group, or place. *e.g. the special needs of the chronically sick*

● THESAURUS
characteristic: *a characteristic feature*
distinctive: *the distinctive smell of chlorine*
individual: *Each family needs individual attention.*
particular: *Fatigue is a particular problem for women.*
peculiar: *This is not a problem peculiar to London.*
specific: *the specific needs of the elderly*
<<OPPOSITE *general*

specialist ['spɛʃəlɪst] **specialists** NOUN
1 someone who has a particular skill or who knows a lot about a particular subject *e.g. a skin specialist*
> ADJECTIVE
2 having a skill or knowing a lot about a particular subject *e.g. a specialist teacher*
specialism NOUN

speciality [ˌspɛʃɪˈælɪtɪ] **specialities** NOUN
A person's speciality is something they are especially good at or know a lot about. *e.g. Roses are her speciality.*

specialize ['spɛʃəˌlaɪz] **specializes, specializing, specialized;** also spelt
specialise VERB
If you specialize in something, you make it your speciality. *e.g. a shop specializing in ceramics*
specialization NOUN

specialized or **specialised** ['spɛʃəˌlaɪzd] ADJECTIVE
developed for a particular purpose or trained in a particular area of knowledge *e.g. a specialized sales team*

specially ['spɛʃəlɪ] ADVERB
If something has been done specially for a particular person or purpose, it has been done only for that person or purpose.

species ['spiːʃiːz] NOUN
a class of plants or animals whose members have the same characteristics and are able to breed with each other

specific [spɪˈsɪfɪk] ADJECTIVE

1 particular *e.g. specific areas of difficulty*

2 precise and exact *e.g. She will ask for specific answers.*

specifically ADVERB

specification [ˌspɛsɪfɪˈkeɪʃən] **specifications** NOUN

(D & T)

a detailed description of what is needed for something, such as the necessary features in the design of something *e.g. I like to build it to my own specifications.*

specify [ˈspɛsɪˌfaɪ] **specifies, specifying, specified** VERB

To specify something means to state or describe it precisely. *e.g. In his will he specified that these documents were never to be removed.*

⬤ THESAURUS

be specific about: *She was never very specific about her date of birth.*

indicate: *Please indicate your preference below.*

name: *The victims of the fire have been named.*

spell out: *He spelled out the reasons why he was leaving.*

state: *Please state your name.*

stipulate: *His duties were stipulated in the contract.*

specimen [ˈspɛsɪmɪn] **specimens** NOUN

A specimen of something is an example or small amount of it which gives an idea of what the whole is like. *e.g. a specimen of your writing*

speck [spɛk] **specks** NOUN

a very small stain or amount of something

speckled [ˈspɛkᵊld] ADJECTIVE

Something that is speckled is covered in very small marks or spots.

spectacle [ˈspɛktəkᵊl] **spectacles** PLURAL NOUN

1 Someone's spectacles are their glasses.

> NOUN

2 a strange or interesting sight or scene *e.g. an astonishing spectacle*

3 a grand and impressive event or performance

spectacular [spɛkˈtækjʊlə] **spectaculars** ADJECTIVE

1 Something spectacular is very impressive or dramatic.

> NOUN

2 a grand and impressive show or performance

spectator [spɛkˈteɪtə] **spectators** NOUN

a person who is watching something

⬤ THESAURUS

bystander: *an innocent bystander*

eyewitness: *Eyewitnesses say the police opened fire in the crowd.*

observer: *a disinterested observer*

onlooker: *A small crowd of onlookers was there to greet her.*

witness: *There were scores of witnesses.*

spectra [ˈspɛktrə] the plural of **spectrum**

spectre [ˈspɛktə] **spectres** NOUN

1 a frightening idea or image *e.g. the spectre of war*

2 a ghost

spectrum [ˈspɛktrəm] **spectra** or **spectrums** NOUN

1 (ART) The spectrum is the range of different colours produced when light passes through a prism or a drop of water. A rainbow shows the colours in a spectrum.

2 A spectrum of opinions or emotions is a range of them.

speculate [ˈspɛkjʊˌleɪt] **speculates, speculating, speculated** VERB

If you speculate about something, you think about it and form opinions about it.

speculation NOUN

speculative [ˈspɛkjʊlətɪv] ADJECTIVE

1 A speculative piece of information is based on guesses and opinions rather than known facts.

2 Someone with a speculative expression seems to be trying to guess something. *e.g. His mother regarded him with a speculative eye.*

speech [spiːtʃ] **speeches** NOUN

1 Speech is the ability to speak or the act of speaking.

2 a formal talk given to an audience

⬤ THESAURUS

address: *an address to the American people*

discourse: *a lengthy discourse on strategy*

lecture: *a series of lectures on art*

talk: *a talk on Celtic mythology*

3 In a play, a speech is a group of lines spoken by one of the characters.

speechless [ˈspiːtʃlɪs] ADJECTIVE

Someone who is speechless is unable to speak for a short time because something has shocked them.

speed [spiːd] **speeds, speeding, sped** or **speeded** NOUN

1 The speed of something is the rate at which it moves or happens.

⬤ THESAURUS

haste: *the old saying "more haste, less speed"*

hurry: *the hurry and excitement of the city*

momentum: *This campaign is gaining momentum.*

pace: *He walked at a leisurely pace.*

rapidity: *My moods alternate with alarming rapidity.*

swiftness: *Time is passing with incredible swiftness.*

S

velocity: *the velocity of light*

2 Speed is very fast movement or travel.

> VERB

3 If you speed somewhere, you move or travel there quickly.

● **THESAURUS**
career: *His car careered into a river.*
flash: *The bus flashed past me.*
gallop: *galloping along the corridor*
race: *He raced across town.*
rush: *He rushed off, closely followed by Kemp.*
tear: *Miranda tore off down the road.*

4 Someone who is speeding is driving a vehicle faster than the legal speed limit.

speedboat ['spiːdˌbəʊt] **speedboats** NOUN
a small, fast motorboat

speed limit **speed limits** NOUN
The speed limit is the maximum speed at which vehicles are legally allowed to drive on a particular road.

speedway ['spiːdˌweɪ] NOUN
Speedway is the sport of racing lightweight motorcycles on special tracks.

speedy ['spiːdɪ] **speedier, speediest**
ADJECTIVE
done very quickly
speedily ADVERB

spell [spɛl] **spells, spelling, spelt** or **spelled**
VERB

1 When you spell a word, you name or write its letters in order.

2 When letters spell a word, they form that word when put together in a particular order.

3 If something spells a particular result, it suggests that this will be the result. *e.g. This haphazard method could spell disaster for you.*

> NOUN

4 A spell of something is a short period of it. *e.g. a spell of rough weather*

5 a word or sequence of words used to perform magic

spell out VERB

6 If you spell something out, you explain it in detail. *e.g. I don't have to spell it out, do I?.*

spellbound ['spɛlˌbaʊnd] ADJECTIVE
so fascinated by something that you cannot think about anything else *e.g. She had sat spellbound through the film.*

spelling ['spɛlɪŋ] **spellings** NOUN
The spelling of a word is the correct order of letters in it.

spend [spɛnd] **spends, spending, spent**
VERB

1 When you spend money, you buy things with it.

2 To spend time or energy means to use it.

spent [spɛnt] ADJECTIVE

1 Spent describes things which have been used and therefore cannot be used again. *e.g. spent matches*

2 If you are spent, you are exhausted and have no energy left.

sperm [spɜːm] **sperms** NOUN
a cell produced in the sex organ of a male animal which can enter a female animal's egg and fertilize it

spew [spjuː] **spews, spewing, spewed**
VERB

1 When things spew from something or when it spews them out, they come out of it in large quantities.

2 INFORMAL
To spew up means to vomit.

sphere [sfɪə] **spheres** NOUN

1 a perfectly round object, such as a ball

2 An area of activity or interest can be referred to as a sphere of activity or interest.
spherical ADJECTIVE

sphinx [sfɪŋks] **sphinxes** NOUN
In mythology, the sphinx was a monster with a person's head and a lion's body.

spice [spaɪs] **spices, spicing, spiced** NOUN

1 Spice is powder or seeds from a plant added to food to give it flavour.

2 Spice is something which makes life more exciting. *e.g. Variety is the spice of life.*

> VERB

3 To spice food means to add spice to it.

4 If you spice something up, you make it more exciting or lively.

spicy ['spaɪsɪ] **spicier, spiciest** ADJECTIVE
strongly flavoured with spices

spider ['spaɪdə] **spiders** NOUN
a small insect-like creature with eight legs that spins webs to catch insects for food
[WORD HISTORY: from Old English SPINNAN meaning 'to spin']

spike [spaɪk] **spikes** NOUN

1 a long pointed piece of metal

2 The spikes on a sports shoe are the pointed pieces of metal attached to the sole.

3 Some other long pointed objects are called spikes. *e.g. beautiful pink flower spikes*

spiky ['spaɪkɪ] **spikier, spikiest** ADJECTIVE
Something spiky has sharp points.

spill [spɪl] **spills, spilling, spilled** or **spilt**
VERB

1 If you spill something or if it spills, it accidentally falls or runs out of a container.

2 If people or things spill out of a place, they come out of it in large numbers.

spillage ['spɪlɪdʒ] **spillages** NOUN
the spilling of something, or something that has been spilt e.g. *the oil spillage in the Shetlands*

spin [spɪn] **spins, spinning, spun** VERB
1 If something spins, it turns quickly around a central point.

⏺ THESAURUS
pirouette: *She pirouetted in front of the mirror.*
revolve: *The satellite revolves around the planet.*
rotate: *rotating propellers*
turn: *a turning wheel*
whirl: *The fallen leaves whirled around.*

2 When spiders spin a web, they give out a sticky substance and make it into a web.

3 When people spin, they make thread by twisting together pieces of fibre using a machine.

4 If your head is spinning, you feel dizzy or confused.

> NOUN
5 a rapid turn around a central point e.g. *a golf club which puts more spin on the ball*

spinach ['spɪnɪdʒ] NOUN
Spinach is a vegetable with large green leaves.

spinal ['spaɪnəl] ADJECTIVE
to do with the spine

spine [spaɪn] **spines** NOUN
1 Your spine is your backbone.

2 Spines are long, sharp points on an animal's body or on a plant.

spinifex ['spɪnɪˌfɛks] NOUN
Spinifex is a coarse, spiny Australian grass.

spinning wheel ['spɪnɪŋ] **spinning wheels** NOUN
a wooden machine for spinning flax or wool

spin-off ['spɪnˌɒf] **spin-offs** NOUN
something useful that unexpectedly results from an activity

spinster ['spɪnstə] **spinsters** NOUN
a woman who has never married
[WORD HISTORY: originally a person whose occupation was spinning; later, the official label of an unmarried woman]

spiny ['spaɪnɪ] ADJECTIVE
covered with spines

spiral ['spaɪərəl] **spirals, spiralling, spiralled** NOUN
1 a continuous curve which winds round and round, with each curve above or outside the previous one

> ADJECTIVE
2 in the shape of a spiral e.g. *a spiral staircase*

> VERB
3 If something spirals, it moves up or down in a spiral curve. e.g. *The aircraft spiralled down.*

4 If an amount or level spirals, it rises or falls quickly at an increasing rate. e.g. *Prices have spiralled recently.*

spire [spaɪə] **spires** NOUN
The spire of a church is the tall cone-shaped structure on top.

spirit ['spɪrɪt] **spirits, spiriting, spirited** NOUN
1 Your spirit is the part of you that is not physical and that is connected with your deepest thoughts and feelings.

⏺ THESAURUS
life force: *the life force of all animate things*
soul: *praying for the soul of her dead husband*

2 (RE) The spirit of a dead person is a nonphysical part that is believed to remain alive after death.

3 a supernatural being, such as a ghost

⏺ THESAURUS
apparition: *an apparition of her dead son*
ghost: *the premise that ghosts exist*
phantom: *People claimed to have seen the phantom.*
spectre: *a spectre from the other world*
sprite: *a water sprite*

4 Spirit is liveliness, energy, and self-confidence. e.g. *a band full of spirit*

⏺ THESAURUS
animation: *They both spoke with animation.*
energy: *At 80 her energy is amazing.*
enthusiasm: *They seem to be lacking in enthusiasm.*
fire: *His performance was full of fire.*
force: *She expressed her feelings with some force.*
vigour: *We resumed the attack with renewed vigour.*
zest: *He threw himself into the project with typical zest.*

5 Spirit can refer to an attitude. e.g. *his old fighting spirit*

> PLURAL NOUN
6 Spirits describe how happy or unhappy someone is. e.g. *in good spirits*

7 Spirits are strong alcoholic drinks such as whisky and gin.

> VERB
8 If you spirit someone or something into or out of a place, you get them in or out quickly and secretly.

spirited ['spɪrɪtɪd] ADJECTIVE
showing energy and courage

S

spirit level spirit levels NOUN
a device for finding out if a surface is level, consisting of a bubble of air sealed in a tube of liquid in a wooden or metal frame

spiritual ['spɪrɪtjʊəl] **spirituals** ADJECTIVE (RE)

1 to do with people's thoughts and beliefs, rather than their bodies and physical surroundings

2 to do with people's religious beliefs *e.g. spiritual guidance*

> NOUN

3 a religious song originally sung by Black slaves in America

spiritually ADVERB, **spirituality** NOUN

spit [spɪt] **spits, spitting, spat** NOUN

1 Spit is saliva.

2 a long stick made of metal or wood which is pushed through a piece of meat so that it can be hung over a fire and cooked

3 a long, flat, narrow piece of land sticking out into the sea

> VERB

4 If you spit, you force saliva or some other substance out of your mouth.

5 When it is spitting, it is raining very lightly.

spite [spaɪt] **spites, spiting, spited** PHRASE

1 In spite of is used to introduce a statement which makes the rest of what you are saying seem surprising *e.g. In spite of all the gossip, Virginia stayed behind.*

⬤THESAURUS
despite: *They manage to enjoy life despite adversity.*
even though: *They did it even though I warned them not to.*
notwithstanding: *Notwithstanding his age, Sikorski had an important job.*
regardless of: *He led from the front, regardless of the danger.*
though: *I enjoy painting, though I am not very good at it.*

> VERB

2 If you do something to spite someone, you do it deliberately to hurt or annoy them.

> NOUN

3 If you do something out of spite, you do it to hurt or annoy someone.

⬤THESAURUS
ill will: *He didn't bear anyone any ill will.*
malevolence: *a streak of malevolence*
malice: *There was no malice in her voice.*
spitefulness: *petty spitefulness*
venom: *His wit had a touch of venom about it.*

spiteful ['spaɪtfʊl] ADJECTIVE
A spiteful person does or says nasty things to

people deliberately to hurt them.

⬤THESAURUS
bitchy: informal *It's not just women who are bitchy.*
catty: informal *She's always making catty remarks.*
cruel: *They gave him a cruel nickname.*
malevolent: *a malevolent stare*
malicious: *spreading malicious gossip*
nasty: *What nasty little snobs you all are.*
snide: *He made a snide comment about her weight.*
venomous: *a venomous attack*
vindictive: *How can you be so vindictive?*

spitting image ['spɪtɪŋ] NOUN
If someone is the spitting image of someone else, they look just like them.

splash [splæʃ] **splashes, splashing, splashed** VERB

1 If you splash around in water, your movements disturb the water in a noisy way.

2 If liquid splashes something, it scatters over it in a lot of small drops.

> NOUN

3 A splash is the sound made when something hits or falls into water.

4 A splash of liquid is a small quantity of it that has been spilt on something.

splatter ['splætə] **splatters, splattering, splattered** VERB
When something is splattered with a substance, the substance is splashed all over it. *e.g. fur coats splattered with paint*

spleen [spli:n] **spleens** NOUN
Your spleen is an organ near your stomach which controls the quality of your blood.

splendid ['splendɪd] ADJECTIVE

1 very good indeed *e.g. a splendid career*
⬤THESAURUS
cracking: British and Australian and New Zealand; informal *It's a cracking script.*
excellent: *The recording quality is excellent.*
fantastic: informal *a fantastic combination of colours*
fine: *a fine little fellow*
glorious: *a glorious career*
great: informal *a great bunch of guys*
marvellous: *a marvellous thing to do*
wonderful: *a wonderful movie*

2 beautiful and impressive *e.g. a splendid old mansion*
splendidly ADVERB
⬤THESAURUS
gorgeous: *a gorgeous Renaissance building*
grand: *a grand hotel*
imposing: *imposing wrought-iron gates*
impressive: *an impressive spectacle*
magnificent: *magnificent views across the valley*

superb: *The hotel has a superb isolated location.*

splendour ['splɛndə] **splendours** NOUN

1 If something has splendour, it is beautiful and impressive.

> PLURAL NOUN

2 The splendours of something are its beautiful and impressive features.

splint [splɪnt] **splints** NOUN

a long piece of wood or metal fastened to a broken limb to hold it in place

splinter ['splɪntə] **splinters, splintering, splintered** NOUN

1 a thin, sharp piece of wood or glass which has broken off a larger piece

> VERB

2 If something splinters, it breaks into thin, sharp pieces.

split [splɪt] **splits, splitting, split** VERB

1 If something splits or if you split it, it divides into two or more parts.

THESAURUS
diverge: *Their paths began to diverge.*
fork: *Ahead of us, the road forked.*
part: *For a moment the clouds parted.*
separate: *Fluff the rice with a fork to separate the grains.*

2 If something such as wood or fabric splits, a long crack or tear appears in it.

THESAURUS
burst: *A water pipe has burst.*
come apart: *My jacket's coming apart at the seams.*
crack: *A gas main cracked.*
rip: *I felt the paper rip as we pulled in opposite directions.*

3 If people split something, they share it between them.

> NOUN

4 A split in a piece of wood or fabric is a crack or tear.

THESAURUS
crack: *The larvae burrow into cracks in the floor.*
fissure: *Water trickled out of fissures in the limestone.*
rip: *the rip in her new dress*
tear: *the ragged edges of a tear*

5 A split between two things is a division or difference between them. *e.g. the split between rugby league and rugby union*

THESAURUS
breach: *a serious breach in relations between the two countries*
breakup: *the breakup of the Soviet Union in 1991*
divergence: *a divergence between France and its allies*

division: *the conventional division between "art" and "life"*
rift: *There is a rift between us and the rest of the family.*
schism: *the schism which divided the Christian world*

> VERB
split up

6 If two people split up, they end their relationship or marriage.

split second NOUN
an extremely short period of time

splitting ['splɪtɪŋ] ADJECTIVE
A splitting headache is very painful.

splutter ['splʌtə] **splutters, spluttering, spluttered** VERB

1 If someone splutters, they speak in a confused way because they are embarrassed.

2 If something splutters, it makes a series of short, sharp sounds.

spoil [spɔɪl] **spoils, spoiling, spoiled** or **spoilt** VERB

1 If you spoil something, you prevent it from being successful or satisfactory.

THESAURUS
damage: *This could damage our chances of winning.*
destroy: *His criticism has destroyed my confidence.*
harm: *This product harms the environment.*
impair: *The flavour is impaired by overcooking.*
mar: *The celebrations were marred by violence.*
mess up: *He's messed up his life.*
ruin: *My wife was ruining her health through worry.*
wreck: *the injuries which nearly wrecked his career*

2 To spoil children means to give them everything they want, with harmful effects on their character.

THESAURUS
cosset: *We did not cosset our children.*
indulge: *a heavily indulged youngest daughter*
pamper: *pampered pets*

3 To spoil someone also means to give them something nice as a treat.

> PLURAL NOUN

4 Spoils are valuable things obtained during war or as a result of violence. *e.g. the spoils of war*

spoilsport ['spɔɪl,spɔːt] **spoilsports** NOUN
someone who spoils people's fun

THESAURUS
misery: British; informal *the miseries in the government*
wowser: Australian; slang *a small group of wowsers*

spoke [spəʊk] **spokes** NOUN
The spokes of a wheel are the bars which

connect the hub to the rim.

spokesperson ['spəʊks,pɜːs³n]
spokespersons NOUN
someone who speaks on behalf of another
person or a group
spokesman NOUN, **spokeswoman** NOUN

sponge [spʌndʒ] **sponges, sponging,
sponged** NOUN
1 a sea creature with a body made up of many
cells

2 part of the very light skeleton of a sponge, used
for bathing and cleaning

3 A sponge or sponge cake is a very light cake.

> VERB
4 If you sponge something, you clean it by wiping
it with a wet sponge.

sponsor ['spɒnsə] **sponsors, sponsoring,
sponsored** VERB
1 To sponsor something, such as an event or
someone's training, means to support it
financially. *e.g. The visit was sponsored by the
London Natural History Society.*

2 If you sponsor someone who is doing
something for charity, you agree to give them a
sum of money for the charity if they manage to
do it.

3 If you sponsor a proposal or suggestion, you
officially put it forward and support it. *e.g. the MP
who sponsored the Bill*

> NOUN
4 a person or organization sponsoring something
or someone
sponsorship NOUN

spontaneous [spɒn'teɪnɪəs] ADJECTIVE
1 Spontaneous acts are not planned or arranged,
but are done because you feel like it.

2 A spontaneous event happens because of
processes within something rather than being
caused by things outside it. *e.g. spontaneous
bleeding*
spontaneously ADVERB, **spontaneity** NOUN

spoof [spuːf] **spoofs** NOUN
something such as an article or television
programme that seems to be about a serious
matter but is actually a joke

spooky ['spuːkɪ] **spookier, spookiest**
ADJECTIVE
eerie and frightening

● THESAURUS
creepy: informal *a place that is really creepy at
night*
eerie: *The wind made eerie noises in the trees.*
frightening: *Whenever I fall asleep, I see these
frightening faces.*

ghostly: *The moon shed a ghostly light on the fields.*
haunted: *a haunted house*
supernatural: *The blade glowed with a
supernatural light.*
scary: *a scary ruined castle*
uncanny: *The strange, uncanny feeling was creeping
all over me.*

spool [spuːl] **spools** NOUN
a cylindrical object onto which thread, tape, or
film can be wound

spoon [spuːn] **spoons** NOUN
an object shaped like a small shallow bowl with a
long handle, used for eating, stirring, and serving
food

spoonful ['spuːn,fʊl] **spoonfuls** or
spoonsful NOUN
the amount held by a spoon

sporadic [spə'rædɪk] ADJECTIVE
happening at irregular intervals *e.g. a few sporadic
attempts at keeping a diary*
sporadically ADVERB

spore [spɔː] **spores** NOUN; TECHNICAL
Spores are cells produced by bacteria and
nonflowering plants such as fungi which develop
into new bacteria or plants.

sporran ['spɒrən] **sporrans** NOUN
a large purse made of leather or fur, worn by a
Scotsman over his kilt
[WORD HISTORY: from Scottish Gaelic SPORAN
meaning 'purse']

sport [spɔːt] **sports, sporting, sported**
NOUN
1 Sports are games and other enjoyable activities
which need physical effort and skill.

2 You say that someone is a sport when they
accept defeat or teasing cheerfully. *e.g. Be a sport,
Minister!*

> VERB
3 If you sport something noticeable or unusual,
you wear it. *e.g. A German boy sported a ponytail.*

sporting ['spɔːtɪŋ] ADJECTIVE
1 relating to sport

2 behaving in a fair and decent way

sports car [spɔːts] **sports cars** NOUN
a low, fast car, usually with room for only two
people

sportsman ['spɔːtsmən] **sportsmen** NOUN
a man who takes part in sports and is good at
them

sportswoman ['spɔːts,wʊmən]
sportswomen NOUN
a woman who takes part in sports and is good at
them

sporty ['spɔːtɪ] **sportier, sportiest** ADJECTIVE

1 A sporty car is fast and flashy.

2 A sporty person is good at sports.

spot [spɒt] **spots, spotting, spotted** NOUN

1 Spots are small, round, coloured areas on a surface.

● THESAURUS

blemish: *A small blemish spoiled the surface.*
blot: *an ink blot*
blotch: *His face was covered in red blotches.*
mark: *a little red mark on my neck*
smudge: *There was a dark smudge on his forehead.*
speck: *a speck of dirt*

2 Spots on a person's skin are small lumps, usually caused by an infection or allergy.

3 A spot of something is a small amount of it. *e.g. spots of rain*

4 A place can be called a spot. *e.g. the most beautiful spot in the garden*

● THESAURUS

location: *The hotel is in a superb isolated location.*
place: *Jerusalem is Christianity's most venerated place.*
point: *the point where the river had burst its banks*
position: *She moved the body to a position where it would not be seen.*
scene: *He left a note at the scene of the crime.*
site: *plans to construct a temple on the site*

> VERB

5 If you spot something, you notice it.

● THESAURUS

catch sight of: *I caught sight of an ad in the paper.*
detect: *The test should enable doctors to detect the disease early.*
discern: *I did not discern any change.*
observe: *Can you observe any difference?*
see: *I can see a resemblance between you.*
sight: *A fleet of French ships was sighted.*

> PHRASE

6 If you do something **on the spot**, you do it immediately.

spot check spot checks NOUN
a random examination made without warning on one of a group of things or people *e.g. spot checks by road safety officers*

spotless ['spɒtlɪs] ADJECTIVE
perfectly clean
spotlessly ADVERB

spotlight ['spɒt,laɪt] **spotlights, spotlighting, spotlit** or **spotlighted** NOUN

1 (DRAMA) a powerful light which can be directed to light up a small area

> VERB

2 If something spotlights a situation or problem, it draws the public's attention to it. *e.g. a national campaign to spotlight the problem*

spot-on ['spɒt,ɒn] ADJECTIVE; INFORMAL
exactly correct or accurate

spotted ['spɒtɪd] ADJECTIVE
Something spotted has a pattern of spots on it.

spotter ['spɒtə] **spotters** NOUN
a person whose hobby is looking out for things of a particular kind *e.g. a train spotter*

spotty ['spɒtɪ] **spottier, spottiest** ADJECTIVE
Someone who is spotty has spots or pimples on their skin, especially on their face.

spouse [spaʊs] **spouses** NOUN
Someone's spouse is the person they are married to.

spout [spaʊt] **spouts, spouting, spouted** VERB

1 When liquid or flame spouts out of something, it shoots out in a long stream.

2 When someone spouts what they have learned, they say it in a boring way.

> NOUN

3 a tube with a lip-like end for pouring liquid *e.g. a teapot with a long spout*

sprain [spreɪn] **sprains, spraining, sprained** VERB

1 If you sprain a joint, you accidentally damage it by twisting it violently.

> NOUN

2 the injury caused by spraining a joint

sprawl [sprɔːl] **sprawls, sprawling, sprawled** VERB

1 If you sprawl somewhere, you sit or lie there with your legs and arms spread out.

2 A place that sprawls is spread out over a large area. *e.g. a Monday market which sprawls all over town*

> NOUN

3 anything that spreads in an untidy and uncontrolled way *e.g. a sprawl of skyscrapers*
sprawling ADJECTIVE

spray [spreɪ] **sprays, spraying, sprayed** NOUN

1 Spray consists of many drops of liquid splashed or forced into the air. *e.g. The salt spray stung her face.*

2 Spray is also a liquid kept under pressure in a can or other container. *e.g. hair spray*

3 a piece of equipment for spraying liquid *e.g. a garden spray*

4 A spray of flowers or leaves consists of several of them on one stem.

S

> VERB

5 To spray a liquid over something means to cover it with drops of the liquid.

spread [sprɛd] **spreads, spreading, spread**
VERB

1 If you spread something out, you open it out or arrange it so that it can be seen or used easily.
e.g. He spread the map out on his knees.

● THESAURUS

extend: *The new territory would extend over one-fifth of Canada's land mass.*

fan out: *She spun, and her dress's full skirt fanned out in a circle.*

open: *She opened her arms and gave me a big hug.*

sprawl: *The recreation area sprawls over 900 acres.*

unfold: *When the bird lifts off, its wings unfold to a six-foot span.*

unfurl: *We began to unfurl the sails.*

unroll: *I unrolled my sleeping bag.*

2 If you spread a substance on a surface, you put a thin layer on the surface.

● THESAURUS

apply: *Apply the preparation evenly over the wood's surface.*

coat: *Coat the fish with the paste.*

cover: *I covered the table with a cloth.*

overlay: *The floor was overlaid with rugs.*

plaster: *She plastered herself in sun lotion.*

smear: *Smear a little oil over the inside of the bowl.*

smother: *He likes to smother his bread with butter.*

3 If something spreads, it gradually reaches or affects more people. *e.g. The news spread quickly.*

● THESAURUS

circulate: *Rumours were circulating that the project was to be abandoned.*

grow: *Opposition grew and the government agreed to negotiate.*

expand: *The industry is looking for opportunities to expand into other countries.*

increase: *The population continues to increase.*

proliferate: *the free Internet services that are proliferating across the world*

travel: *News of his work travelled all the way to Asia.*

4 If something spreads over a period of time, it happens regularly or continuously over that time. *e.g. His four international appearances were spread over eight years.*

5 If something such as work is spread, it is distributed evenly.

> NOUN

6 The spread of something is the extent to which it gradually reaches or affects more people. *e.g. the spread of Buddhism*

● THESAURUS

diffusion: *the development and diffusion of ideas*

expansion: *the rapid expansion of private health insurance*

extent: *the growing extent of the problem*

growth: *the growth of nationalism*

increase: *an increase of violence along the border*

progression: *This drug slows the progression of HIV.*

proliferation: *the proliferation of nuclear weapons*

upsurge: *the upsurge in interest in these books*

7 A spread of ideas, interests, or other things is a wide variety of them.

8 soft food put on bread *e.g. cheese spread*

spread-eagled [ˌsprɛdˈiːgˀld] ADJECTIVE
Someone who is spread-eagled is lying with their arms and legs spread out.

spreadsheet [ˈsprɛdˌʃiːt] **spreadsheets**
NOUN

(ICT) a computer program that is used for entering and arranging figures, used mainly for financial planning

spree [spriː] **sprees** NOUN
a period of time spent doing something enjoyable *e.g. a shopping spree*

sprig [sprɪg] **sprigs** NOUN

1 a small twig with leaves on it

2 In Australian and New Zealand English, sprigs are studs on the sole of a football boot.

sprightly [ˈspraɪtlɪ] **sprightlier, sprightliest** ADJECTIVE
lively and active

spring [sprɪŋ] **springs, springing, sprang, sprung** NOUN

1 Spring is the season between winter and summer.

2 a coil of wire which returns to its natural shape after being pressed or pulled

3 a place where water comes up through the ground

4 an act of springing *e.g. With a spring he had opened the door.*

> VERB

5 To spring means to jump upwards or forwards. *e.g. Martha sprang to her feet.*

6 If something springs in a particular direction, it moves suddenly and quickly. *e.g. The door sprang open.*

7 If one thing springs from another, it is the result of it. *e.g. The failures sprang from three facts.*

springboard [ˈsprɪŋˌbɔːd] **springboards**
NOUN

1 a flexible board on which a diver or gymnast jumps to gain height

2 If something is a springboard for an activity or enterprise, it makes it possible for it to begin.

springbok [ˈsprɪŋˌbʌk] **springboks** NOUN

1 a small South African antelope which moves in leaps

2 a Springbok is a person who has represented South Africa in a sports team

spring-clean [ˌsprɪŋˈkliːn] **spring-cleans, spring-cleaning, spring-cleaned** VERB
To spring-clean a house means to clean it thoroughly throughout.

spring onion **spring onions** NOUN
a small onion with long green shoots, often eaten raw in salads

sprinkle [ˈsprɪŋkəl] **sprinkles, sprinkling, sprinkled** VERB
If you sprinkle a liquid or powder over something, you scatter it over it.

sprinkling [ˈsprɪŋklɪŋ] **sprinklings** NOUN
A sprinkling of something is a small quantity of it. *e.g. a light sprinkling of snow*

sprint [sprɪnt] **sprints, sprinting, sprinted** NOUN
1 a short, fast race
> VERB
2 To sprint means to run fast over a short distance.

sprinter [ˈsprɪntə] **sprinters** NOUN
an athlete who runs fast over short distances

sprite [spraɪt] **sprites** NOUN
a type of fairy

sprout [spraʊt] **sprouts, sprouting, sprouted** VERB
1 When something sprouts, it grows.
2 If things sprout up, they appear rapidly. *e.g. Their houses sprouted up in that region.*
> NOUN
3 Sprouts are the same as **brussels sprouts**

spruce [spruːs] **spruces; sprucer, sprucest; spruces, sprucing, spruced** NOUN
1 an evergreen tree with needle-like leaves
> ADJECTIVE
2 Someone who is spruce is very neat and smart.
> VERB
3 To spruce something up means to make it neat and smart.

spunk [spʌŋk] **spunks** NOUN; INFORMAL
1 OLD-FASHIONED
Spunk is courage.
2 In Australian and New Zealand English, someone who is good-looking.

spur [spɜː] **spurs, spurring, spurred** VERB
1 If something spurs you to do something or spurs you on, it encourages you to do it.

> NOUN
2 Something that acts as a spur encourages a person to do something.
3 Spurs are sharp metal points attached to the heels of a rider's boots and used to urge a horse on.
> PHRASE
4 If you do something **on the spur of the moment**, you do it suddenly, without planning it.

spurious [ˈspjʊəriəs] ADJECTIVE
not genuine or real

spurn [spɜːn] **spurns, spurning, spurned** VERB
If you spurn something, you refuse to accept it. *e.g. You spurned his last offer.*

spurt [spɜːt] **spurts, spurting, spurted** VERB
1 When a liquid or flame spurts out of something, it comes out quickly in a thick, powerful stream.
> NOUN
2 A spurt of liquid or flame is a thick powerful stream of it. *e.g. a small spurt of blood*
3 A spurt of activity or effort is a sudden, brief period of it.

spy [spaɪ] **spies, spying, spied** NOUN
1 a person sent to find out secret information about a country or organization
> VERB
2 Someone who spies tries to find out secret information about another country or organization.
3 If you spy on someone, you watch them secretly.
4 If you spy something, you notice it.

squabble [ˈskwɒbəl] **squabbles, squabbling, squabbled** VERB
1 When people squabble, they quarrel about something trivial.

● THESAURUS
argue: *They went on arguing all the way down the road.*
bicker: *The two women bickered constantly.*
fall out: *Mum and I used to fall out a lot.*
feud: *feuding neighbours*
fight: *Mostly, they fight about paying bills.*
quarrel: *At one point we quarrelled over something silly.*
row: *They rowed all the time.*
wrangle: *The two sides spend their time wrangling over procedural problems.*

> NOUN
2 a quarrel

● THESAURUS
altercation: *an altercation with the referee*

S

argument: *a heated argument*
barney: British and Australian and New Zealand; informal *We had such a barney that we nearly split up.*
disagreement: *My instructor and I had a brief disagreement.*
dispute: *a dispute between the two countries over farm subsidies*
fight: *He had a big fight with his dad that night.*
quarrel: *I had a terrible quarrel with my brother.*
row: *A man had been stabbed to death in a family row.*
tiff: *She was walking home after a tiff with her boyfriend.*

squad [skwɒd] **squads** NOUN
(PE) a small group chosen to do a particular activity *e.g. the fraud squad... the England football squad*
[WORD HISTORY: from Old Spanish ESCUADRA meaning 'square', because of the square formation used by soldiers]

squadron ['skwɒdrən] **squadrons** NOUN
a section of one of the armed forces, especially the air force
[WORD HISTORY: from Italian SQUADRONE meaning 'soldiers drawn up in a square formation']

squalid ['skwɒlɪd] ADJECTIVE
1 dirty, untidy, and in bad condition
2 Squalid activities are unpleasant and often dishonest.

squall [skwɔːl] **squalls** NOUN
a brief, violent storm

squalor ['skwɒlə] NOUN
Squalor consists of bad or dirty conditions or surroundings.

squander ['skwɒndə] **squanders, squandering, squandered** VERB
To squander money or resources means to waste them. *e.g. They have squandered huge amounts of money.*

square [skwɛə] **squares, squaring, squared** NOUN
1 (MATHS) a shape with four equal sides and four right angles
2 In a town or city, a square is a flat, open place, bordered by buildings or streets.
3 The square of a number is the number multiplied by itself. For example, the square of 3, written 3², is 3 x 3.
> ADJECTIVE
4 shaped like a square *e.g. her delicate square face*
5 'Square' is used before units of length when talking about the area of something *e.g. 24m²*
6 'Square' is used after units of length when you are giving the length of each side of something

square *e.g. a towel measuring a foot square*
> VERB
7 If you square a number, you multiply it by itself.

squarely ['skwɛəlɪ] ADVERB
1 Squarely means directly rather than indirectly or at an angle. *e.g. I looked squarely in the mirror.*
2 If you approach a subject squarely, you consider it fully, without trying to avoid unpleasant aspects of it.

square root square roots NOUN
A square root of a number is a number that makes the first number when it is multiplied by itself. For example, the square roots of 25 are 5 and -5.

squash [skwɒʃ] **squashes, squashing, squashed** VERB
1 If you squash something, you press it, so that it becomes flat or loses its shape.
> NOUN
2 If there is a squash in a place, there are a lot of people squashed in it.
3 Squash is a game in which two players hit a small rubber ball against the walls of a court using rackets.
4 Squash is a drink made from fruit juice, sugar, and water.

squat [skwɒt] **squats, squatting, squatted; squatter, squattest** VERB
1 If you squat down, you crouch, balancing on your feet with your legs bent.
2 A person who squats in an unused building lives there as a squatter.
> NOUN
3 a building used by squatters
> ADJECTIVE
4 short and thick

squatter ['skwɒtə] **squatters** NOUN
1 a person who lives in an unused building without permission and without paying rent
2 In Australian English, someone who owns a large amount of land for sheep or cattle farming
3 In Australia and New Zealand in the past, someone who rented land from the King or Queen.

squawk [skwɔːk] **squawks, squawking, squawked** VERB
1 When a bird squawks, it makes a loud, harsh noise.
> NOUN
2 a loud, harsh noise made by a bird

squeak [skwiːk] **squeaks, squeaking, squeaked** VERB

1 If something squeaks, it makes a short high-pitched sound.

> NOUN

2 a short, high-pitched sound
squeaky ADJECTIVE

squeal [skwi:l] **squeals, squealing, squealed** VERB

1 When things or people squeal, they make long, high-pitched sounds.

> NOUN

2 a long, high-pitched sound

squeamish ['skwi:mɪʃ] ADJECTIVE
easily upset by unpleasant sights or situations

squeeze [skwi:z] **squeezes, squeezing, squeezed** VERB

1 When you squeeze something, you press it firmly from two sides.

2 If you squeeze something into a small amount of time or space, you manage to fit it in.

> NOUN

3 If you give something a squeeze, you squeeze it. *e.g. She gave my hand a quick squeeze.*

4 If getting into something is a squeeze, it is just possible to fit into it. *e.g. It would take four comfortably, but six would be a squeeze.*

squelch [skwɛltʃ] **squelches, squelching, squelched** VERB

1 To squelch means to make a wet, sucking sound.

> NOUN

2 a wet, sucking sound

squid [skwɪd] **squids** NOUN
a sea creature with a long soft body and many tentacles

squiggle ['skwɪgəl] **squiggles** NOUN
a wriggly line

squint [skwɪnt] **squints, squinting, squinted** VERB

1 If you squint at something, you look at it with your eyes screwed up.

> NOUN

2 If someone has a squint, their eyes look in different directions from each other.

squire [skwaɪə] **squires** NOUN
In a village, the squire was a gentleman who owned a large house with a lot of land.

squirm [skwɜ:m] **squirms, squirming, squirmed** VERB
If you squirm, you wriggle and twist your body about, usually because you are nervous or embarrassed.

squirrel ['skwɪrəl] **squirrels** NOUN
a small furry animal with a long bushy tail

[WORD HISTORY: from Greek SKIA meaning 'shadow' and OURA meaning 'tail']

squirt [skwɜ:t] **squirts, squirting, squirted** VERB

1 If a liquid squirts, it comes out of a narrow opening in a thin, fast stream.

> NOUN

2 a thin, fast stream of liquid

Sri Lankan [ˌsri: 'læŋkən] **Sri Lankans** ADJECTIVE

1 belonging or relating to Sri Lanka

> NOUN

2 someone who comes from Sri Lanka

stab [stæb] **stabs, stabbing, stabbed** VERB

1 To stab someone means to wound them by pushing a knife into their body.

2 To stab at something means to push at it sharply with your finger or with something long and narrow.

> PHRASE
3 INFORMAL
If you **have a stab** at something, you try to do it.

> NOUN

4 You can refer to a sudden unpleasant feeling as a stab of something. *e.g. He felt a stab of guilt.*

stable ['steɪbəl] **stables** ADJECTIVE

1 not likely to change or come to an end suddenly *e.g. I am in a stable relationship.*

2 firmly fixed or balanced and not likely to move, wobble, or fall

> NOUN

3 a building in which horses are kept
stability NOUN, **stabilize** VERB

staccato [stə'kɑ:təʊ] ADJECTIVE
consisting of a series of short, sharp, separate sounds

stack [stæk] **stacks, stacking, stacked** NOUN

1 A stack of things is a pile of them, one on top of the other.

> PLURAL NOUN
2 INFORMAL
If someone has stacks of something, they have a lot of it.

> VERB

3 If you stack things, you arrange them one on top of the other in a pile.

stadium ['steɪdɪəm] **stadiums** NOUN
a sports ground with rows of seats around it
[WORD HISTORY: from Greek STADION meaning 'racecourse']

staff [stɑ:f] **staffs, staffing, staffed** NOUN

S

1 The staff of an organization are the people who work for it.

● **THESAURUS**
employees: *a temporary employee*
personnel: *An announcement was made to all personnel.*
team: *The team worked well under his direction.*
workers: *weekend and night-shift workers*
workforce: *a sullen and resentful workforce*

> VERB
2 To staff an organization means to find and employ people to work in it.

3 If an organization is staffed by particular people, they are the people who work for it.

stag [stæg] **stags** NOUN
an adult male deer

stage [steɪdʒ] **stages, staging, staged** NOUN
1 a part of a process that lasts for a period of time

● **THESAURUS**
lap: *The first lap was clocked at under a minute.*
period: *We went through a period of unprecedented change.*
phase: *a passing phase*
point: *a critical point in the campaign*
step: *the next step in the process*

2 (DRAMA) In a theatre, the stage is a raised platform where the actors or entertainers perform.

3 (DRAMA) You can refer to the profession of acting as the stage.

> VERB
4 If someone stages a play or event, they organize it and present it or take part in it.

● **THESAURUS**
arrange: *We're arranging a surprise party for her.*
engineer: *He was the one who engineered the merger.*
mount: *a security operation mounted by the army*
orchestrate: *a carefully orchestrated campaign*
organize: *a two-day meeting organized by the UN*

stagecoach ['steɪdʒ,kəʊtʃ] **stagecoaches** NOUN
a large carriage pulled by horses which used to carry passengers and mail

stagger ['stægə] **staggers, staggering, staggered** VERB
1 If you stagger, you walk unsteadily because you are ill or drunk.

2 If something staggers you, it amazes you.

3 If events are staggered, they are arranged so that they do not all happen at the same time.
staggering ADJECTIVE

stagnant ['stægnənt] ADJECTIVE
Stagnant water is not flowing and is unhealthy and dirty.

stag night stag nights NOUN
a party for a man who is about to get married, which only men go to

staid [steɪd] ADJECTIVE
serious and dull

stain [steɪn] **stains, staining, stained** NOUN
1 a mark on something that is difficult to remove

● **THESAURUS**
blot: *an ink blot*
mark: *I can't get this mark to come off.*
spot: *brown spots on the skin caused by the sun*

> VERB
2 If a substance stains something, the thing becomes marked or coloured by it.

● **THESAURUS**
dirty: *Sheets can be reused until they are damaged or dirtied.*
mark: *the places where Steve's boots had marked the wood*
soil: *a soiled white apron*
spot: *her coat was spotted with blood*

stained glass [steɪnd] NOUN
Stained glass is coloured pieces of glass held together with strips of lead.

stainless steel ['steɪnlɪs] NOUN
Stainless steel is a metal made from steel and chromium which does not rust.

stair [steə] **stairs** NOUN
Stairs are a set of steps inside a building going from one floor to another.

staircase ['steə,keɪs] **staircases** NOUN
a set of stairs

stairway ['steə,weɪ] **stairways** NOUN
a set of stairs

stake [steɪk] **stakes, staking, staked** PHRASE
1 If something is **at stake**, it might be lost or damaged if something else is not successful. *e.g. The whole future of the company was at stake.*

> PLURAL NOUN
2 The stakes involved in something are the things that can be lost or gained.

> VERB
3 If you say you would stake your money, life, or reputation on the success or truth of something, you mean you would risk it. *e.g. He is prepared to stake his own career on this.*

> NOUN
4 If you have a stake in something such as a business, you own part of it and its success is important to you.

5 a pointed wooden post that can be hammered into the ground and used as a support

stale [steɪl] **staler, stalest** ADJECTIVE

1 Stale food or air is no longer fresh.

● THESAURUS

flat: *flat beer*
old: *mouldy old cheese*
sour: *sour milk*
stagnant: *stagnant water*
<<OPPOSITE *fresh*

2 If you feel stale, you have no new ideas and are bored.

stalemate [ˈsteɪlˌmeɪt] NOUN

1 Stalemate is a situation in which neither side in an argument or contest can win.

2 In chess, stalemate is a situation in which a player cannot make any move permitted by the rules, so that the game ends and no-one wins.

stalk [stɔːk] **stalks, stalking, stalked** NOUN

1 The stalk of a flower or leaf is its stem.

> VERB

2 To stalk a person or animal means to follow them quietly in order to catch, kill, or observe them.

3 If someone stalks into a room, they walk in a stiff, proud, or angry way.

stall [stɔːl] **stalls, stalling, stalled** NOUN

1 a large table containing goods for sale or information

> PLURAL NOUN

2 In a theatre, the stalls are the seats at the lowest level, in front of the stage.

> VERB

3 When a vehicle stalls, the engine suddenly stops.

4 If you stall when someone asks you to do something, you try to avoid doing it until a later time.

stallion [ˈstæljən] **stallions** NOUN

an adult male horse that can be used for breeding

stamina [ˈstæmɪnə] NOUN

Stamina is the physical or mental energy needed to do something for a very long time.

stammer [ˈstæmə] **stammers, stammering, stammered** VERB

1 When someone stammers, they speak with difficulty, repeating words and sounds and hesitating awkwardly.

> NOUN

2 Someone who has a stammer tends to stammer when they speak.

stamp [stæmp] **stamps, stamping, stamped** NOUN

1 a small piece of gummed paper which you stick on a letter or parcel before posting it

2 a small block with a pattern cut into it, which you press onto an inky pad and make a mark with it on paper; also the mark made by the stamp

3 If something bears the stamp of a particular quality or person, it shows clear signs of that quality or of the person's style or characteristics.

> VERB

4 If you stamp a piece of paper, you make a mark on it using a stamp.

5 If you stamp, you lift your foot and put it down hard on the ground.

stamp out VERB

6 To stamp something out means to put an end to it. *e.g. the battle to stamp out bullying in schools*

stampede [stæmˈpiːd] **stampedes, stampeding, stampeded** VERB

1 When a group of animals stampede, they run in a wild, uncontrolled way.

> NOUN

2 a group of animals stampeding
[WORD HISTORY: from Spanish ESTAMPIDA meaning 'crash' or 'din']

stance [stæns] **stances** NOUN

Your stance on a particular matter is your attitude and way of dealing with it. *e.g. He takes no particular stance on animal rights.*

stand [stænd] **stands, standing, stood** VERB

1 If you are standing, you are upright, your legs are straight, and your weight is supported by your feet. When you stand up, you get into a standing position.

2 If something stands somewhere, that is where it is. *e.g. The house stands alone on the top of a small hill.*

3 If you stand something somewhere, you put it there in an upright position. *e.g. Stand the containers on bricks.*

4 If a decision or offer stands, it is still valid. *e.g. My offer still stands.*

5 You can use 'stand' when describing the state or condition of something. *e.g. Youth unemployment stands at 35%.*

6 If a letter stands for a particular word, it is an abbreviation for that word.

7 If you say you will not stand for something, you mean you will not tolerate it.

8 If something can stand a situation or test, it is good enough or strong enough not to be damaged by it.

9 If you cannot stand something, you cannot bear it. *e.g. I can't stand that woman.*

10 If you stand in an election, you are one of the candidates.

S

> PHRASE

11 When someone **stands trial**, they are tried in a court of law.

> NOUN

12 a stall or very small shop outdoors or in a large public building

13 a large structure at a sports ground, where the spectators sit to watch what is happening

14 a piece of furniture designed to hold something *e.g. an umbrella stand*

stand by VERB

15 If you stand by to provide help or take action, you are ready to do it if necessary.

16 If you stand by while something happens, you do nothing to stop it.

stand down VERB

17 If someone stands down, they resign from their job or position.

stand in VERB

18 If you stand in for someone, you take their place while they are ill or away.

stand out VERB

19 If something stands out, it can be easily noticed or is more important than other similar things.

stand up VERB

20 If something stands up to rough treatment, it is not damaged or harmed.

21 If you stand up to someone who is criticizing or attacking you, you defend yourself.

standard ['stændəd] **standards** NOUN

1 a level of quality or achievement that is considered acceptable *e.g. The work is not up to standard.*

THESAURUS

calibre: *the high calibre of these researchers*
criterion: *The most important criterion for entry is excellence in your chosen field.*
guideline: *The accord lays down guidelines for the conduct of government agents.*
level: *The exercises are marked according to their level of difficulty.*
norm: *the commonly accepted norms of democracy*
quality: *Everyone can improve their quality of life.*
requirement: *These products meet all legal requirements.*

> PLURAL NOUN

2 Standards are moral principles of behaviour.

THESAURUS

ethics: *the difference between our personal and social ethics*
ideals: *The party has drifted too far from its socialist ideals.*
morals: *Western ideas and morals.*
principles: *He refused to do anything that went against his principles.*

rules: *They were expected to adhere to the rules of the convent.*
scruples: *a man with no moral scruples*
values: *the values of liberty and equality*

> ADJECTIVE

3 usual, normal, and correct *e.g. The practice became standard procedure for most motor companies.*

THESAURUS

accepted: *It is accepted wisdom that the state of your body impacts on your state of mind.*
correct: *the correct way to produce a crop of tomato plants*
customary: *It is customary to offer a drink or a snack to guests.*
normal: *Some shops were closed, but that's quite normal for a Thursday.*
orthodox: *orthodox police methods*
regular: *This product looks and tastes like regular lemonade.*
usual: *It is usual to tip waiters.*

standard English NOUN

Standard English is the form of English taught in schools, used in text books and broadsheet newspapers, and spoken and written by most educated people.

standardize ['stændə,daɪz] **standardizes, standardizing, standardized**; also spelt **standardise** VERB

To standardize things means to change them so that they all have a similar set of features. *e.g. We have decided to standardize our equipment.*

stand-by ['stænd,baɪ] **stand-bys** NOUN

1 something available for use when you need it *e.g. a useful stand-by*

> ADJECTIVE

2 A stand-by ticket is a cheap ticket that you buy just before a theatre performance or a flight if there are any seats left.

stand-in ['stænd,ɪn] **stand-ins** NOUN

someone who takes a person's place while the person is ill or away *e.g. stand-in teachers*

standing ['stændɪŋ] ADJECTIVE

1 permanently in existence or used regularly *e.g. a standing joke*

> NOUN

2 A person's standing is their status and reputation.

3 'Standing' is used to say how long something has existed *e.g. a friend of 20 years' standing*

standpoint ['stænd,pɔɪnt] **standpoints** NOUN

If you consider something from a particular standpoint, you consider it from that point of view. *e.g. from a military standpoint*

standstill ['stænd,stɪl] NOUN
If something comes to a standstill, it stops completely.

stanza ['stænzə] **stanzas** NOUN
a verse of a poem
[WORD HISTORY: from Italian STANZA meaning 'stopping place']

staple ['steɪpªl] **staples, stapling, stapled**
NOUN
1 Staples are small pieces of wire that hold sheets of paper firmly together.
> VERB
2 If you staple sheets of paper, you fasten them together with staples.
> ADJECTIVE
3 A staple food forms a regular and basic part of someone's everyday diet.

star [stɑː] **stars, starring, starred** NOUN
1 a large ball of burning gas in space that appears as a point of light in the sky at night
2 a shape with four, five, or more points sticking out in a regular pattern
3 Famous actors, sports players, and musicians are referred to as stars.
● THESAURUS
celebrity: *A host of celebrities attended the premiere.*
idol: *the city's greatest soccer idol*
luminary: *literary The event attracted such pop luminaries as Madonna.*
> PLURAL NOUN
4 The horoscope in a newspaper or magazine can be referred to as the stars. *e.g. I'm a Virgo, but don't read my stars every day.*
> VERB
5 If an actor or actress stars in a film or if the film stars that person, he or she has one of the most important parts in it.

starboard ['stɑːbəd] ADJECTIVE OR NOUN
The starboard side of a ship is the right-hand side when you are facing the front.
[WORD HISTORY: from Old English STEORBORD meaning 'steering side', because boats were formerly steered with a paddle over the right-hand side]

starch [stɑːtʃ] **starches, starching, starched** NOUN
1 Starch is a substance used for stiffening fabric such as cotton and linen.
2 Starch is a carbohydrate found in foods such as bread and potatoes.
> VERB
3 To starch fabric means to stiffen it with starch.

stare [steə] **stares, staring, stared** VERB
1 If you stare at something, you look at it for a long time.
● THESAURUS
gaze: *gazing at herself in the mirror*
look: *He looked at her with open hostility.*
ogle: *ogling the girls as they went past*
> NOUN
2 a long fixed look at something

starfish ['stɑː,fɪʃ] **starfishes** or **starfish**
NOUN
a flat, star-shaped sea creature with five limbs

stark [stɑːk] **starker, starkest** ADJECTIVE
1 harsh, unpleasant and plain *e.g. the stark choice*
> PHRASE
2 If someone is **stark-naked**, they have no clothes on at all.

starling ['stɑːlɪŋ] **starlings** NOUN
a common European bird with shiny dark feathers

start see pages 844 and 845 for Word Web

starter ['stɑːtə] **starters** NOUN
a small quantity of food served as the first part of a meal

startle ['stɑːtªl] **startles, startling, startled**
VERB
If something sudden and unexpected startles you, it surprises you and makes you slightly frightened.
startled ADJECTIVE, **startling** ADJECTIVE

starve [stɑːv] **starves, starving, starved**
VERB
1 If people are starving, they are suffering from a serious lack of food and are likely to die.
2 To starve a person or animal means to prevent them from having any food.
3 INFORMAL
If you say you are starving, you mean you are very hungry.
4 If someone or something is starved of something they need, they are suffering because they are not getting enough of it. *e.g. The hospital was starved of cash.*
starvation NOUN

stash [stæʃ] **stashes, stashing, stashed**
VERB; INFORMAL
If you stash something away in a secret place, you store it there to keep it safe.

state [steɪt] **states, stating, stated** NOUN
1 The state of something is its condition, what it is like, or its circumstances.
● THESAURUS
circumstances: *He's in desperate circumstances.*

S

1 VERB

If something starts, it begins to take place or comes into existence *eg: When does the party start?*

● THESAURUS

arise: *A conflict is likely to arise.*
begin: *A typical day begins at 8.30.*
come into being: *The festival came into being in 1986.*
come into existence: *a club that came into existence only 30 years ago*
commence (formal): *The academic year commences at the beginning of October.*
get under way: *The game got under way.*
originate: *The disease originated in Africa.*
<< OPPOSITE *finish*

start
starts, starting, started

4 NOUN

The start of something is the point or time at which it begins.

● THESAURUS

beginning: *the beginning of all the trouble*
birth: *the birth of modern art*
commencement (formal): *Applicants should be at least 16 before the commencement of the course.*
dawn: *the dawn of a new age*
foundation: *the foundation of the National Organization for Women*
inauguration (formal): *the inauguration of new exam standards*
inception (formal): *Since its inception the company has produced 53 different aircraft designs.*
initiation: *There was a year between initiation and completion.*
onset: *the onset of puberty*
opening: *the opening of the trial*
outset: *There were lots of problems from the outset.*
<< OPPOSITE *finish*

2 VERB

If you start to do something, you begin to do it eg: *Susie started to cry.*

● THESAURUS

begin: *He began to groan with pain.*

commence (formal): *The hunter commenced to skin the animal.*

embark upon: *He's embarking on a new career as a writer.*

proceed: *He proceeded to get drunk.*

set about: *How do you set about getting a mortgage?*

<< OPPOSITE *stop*

---

3 VERB

If you start something, you cause it to begin or to come into existence eg: *as good a time as any to start a business*

● THESAURUS

begin: *The US is prepared to begin talks immediately.*

create: *Criticism will only create feelings of failure.*

establish: *The school was established in 1899.*

found: *Baden-Powell founded the Boy Scouts in 1908.*

get going: *I've worked hard to get this business going.*

inaugurate (formal): *the company which inaugurated the first scheduled international flight*

initiate: *They wanted to initiate a discussion.*

instigate: *The violence was instigated by a few people.*

institute: *We have instituted a number of measures.*

introduce: *The government has introduced other money-saving schemes.*

launch: *The police have launched an investigation into the incident.*

open: *We opened the service with a hymn.*

pioneer: *the man who invented and pioneered DNA testing*

set in motion: *Several changes have already been set in motion.*

set up: *A committee was set up to arbitrate in the dispute.*

trigger: *Nuts can trigger an allergic reaction in some people.*

<< OPPOSITE *stop*

condition: *He remains in a critical condition in hospital.*
plight: *the plight of Third World countries*
position: *We are in a privileged position.*
predicament: *the once great club's current predicament*
shape: *Her finances were in terrible shape.*
situation: *a precarious situation*

2 Countries are sometimes referred to as states. *e.g. the state of Denmark*

● THESAURUS
country: *a country where alcohol is prohibited*
kingdom: *The kingdom's power declined.*
land: *in that distant land*
nation: *a leading nation in world politics*
republic: *In 1918, Austria became a republic.*

3 Some countries are divided into regions called states which make some of their own laws. *e.g. the State of Vermont*

4 You can refer to the government or administration of a country as the state.

> PHRASE
5 If you are **in a state**, you are nervous or upset and unable to control your emotions.

> ADJECTIVE
6 A state ceremony involves the ruler or leader of a country.

> VERB
7 If you state something, you say it or write it, especially in a formal way.

● THESAURUS
affirm: *a speech in which he affirmed his policies*
articulate: *an attempt to articulate his feelings*
assert: *He asserted his innocence.*
declare: *He declared that he would fight on.*
express: *He expressed regret that he had caused any offence.*
say: *The police said he had no connection with the security forces.*
specify: *Please specify your preferences below.*

state house state houses NOUN
In New Zealand, a house built and owned by the government and rented out.

stately home ['steɪtlɪ] **stately homes** NOUN
In Britain, a very large old house which belongs to an upper-class family.

statement ['steɪtmənt] **statements** NOUN
1 something you say or write when you give facts or information in a formal way

● THESAURUS
account: *He gave a detailed account of what happened that night.*
announcement: *He made his announcement after talks with the President.*

bulletin: *A bulletin was released announcing the decision.*
declaration: *a public declaration of support*
explanation: *They have given no public explanation for his dismissal.*
proclamation: *The proclamation of independence was broadcast over the radio.*
report: *A press report said that at least six people had died.*
testimony: *His testimony was an important part of the prosecution case.*

2 a document provided by a bank showing all the money paid into and out of an account during a period of time

state school state schools NOUN
a school maintained and financed by the government in which education is free

statesman ['steɪtsmən] **statesmen** NOUN
an important and experienced politician

static ['stætɪk] ADJECTIVE
1 never moving or changing *e.g. The temperature remains fairly static.*

> NOUN
2 Static is an electrical charge caused by friction. It builds up in metal objects.

station ['steɪʃən] **stations, stationing, stationed** NOUN
1 a building and platforms where trains stop for passengers

2 A bus or coach station is a place where some buses start their journeys.

3 A radio station is the frequency on which a particular company broadcasts.

4 In Australian and New Zealand English, a large sheep or cattle farm.

5 OLD-FASHIONED
A person's station is their position or rank in society.

> VERB
6 Someone who is stationed somewhere is sent there to work or do a particular job. *e.g. Her husband was stationed in Vienna.*

stationary ['steɪʃənərɪ] ADJECTIVE
not moving *e.g. a stationary car*

stationery ['steɪʃənərɪ] NOUN
Stationery is paper, pens, and other writing equipment.

statistic [stə'tɪstɪk] **statistics** NOUN
1 Statistics are facts obtained by analysing numerical information.

2 Statistics is the branch of mathematics that deals with the analysis of numerical information.
statistical ADJECTIVE

statistician [ˌstætɪˈstɪʃən] **statisticians**
NOUN
a person who studies or works with statistics

statue [ˈstætjuː] **statues** NOUN
a sculpture of a person

stature [ˈstætʃə] NOUN
1 Someone's stature is their height and size.
2 Someone's stature is also their importance and reputation. *e.g. the desire to gain international stature*

status [ˈsteɪtəs] **statuses** NOUN
1 A person's status is their position and importance in society.

● THESAURUS
position: *a privileged position*
prestige: *to diminish the prestige of the monarchy*
rank: *He was stripped of his rank.*
standing: *This has done nothing to improve his standing.*

2 Status is also the official classification given to someone or something. *e.g. I am not sure what your legal status is.*

status quo [kwəʊ] NOUN
The status quo is the situation that exists at a particular time. *e.g. They want to keep the status quo.*
[WORD HISTORY: a Latin expression, meaning literally 'the state in which']

statute [ˈstætjuːt] **statutes** NOUN
a law
statutory ADJECTIVE

staunch [stɔːntʃ] **stauncher, staunchest**
ADJECTIVE
A staunch supporter is a strong and loyal supporter.

stave [steɪv] **staves, staving, staved** NOUN
1 In music, a stave is the five lines that music is written on.
> VERB
2 If you stave something off, you try to delay or prevent it.

stay [steɪ] **stays, staying, stayed** VERB
1 If you stay in a place, you do not move away from it. *e.g. She stayed in bed until noon.*

● THESAURUS
hang around: *informal I can't hang around here all day.*
linger: *I lingered on for a few days until he arrived.*
loiter: *We loitered around looking in shop windows.*
remain: *You'll have to remain in hospital for the time being.*
tarry: *The shop's aim is to persuade you to tarry and spend.*
wait: *I'll wait here till you come back.*

2 If you stay at a hotel or a friend's house, you spend some time there as a guest or visitor.

3 If you stay in a particular state, you continue to be in it. *e.g. I stayed awake the first night.*

4 In Scottish and South African English, to stay in a place can also mean to live there.
> NOUN
5 a short time spent somewhere *e.g. a very pleasant stay in Cornwall*

stead [stɛd] NOUN; FORMAL
Something that will stand someone in good stead will be useful to them in the future.

steadfast [ˈstɛdfəst] ADJECTIVE
refusing to change or give up

● THESAURUS
constant: *He has been her constant companion for the last four months.*
faithful: *this party's most faithful voters*
firm: *He held a firm belief in the afterlife.*
immovable: *On one issue, however, she was immovable.*
resolute: *a decisive and resolute international leader*
staunch: *a staunch supporter of these proposals*
steady: *He was firm and steady, unlike many men she knew.*
unshakeable: *his unshakeable belief in the project*

steady [ˈstɛdɪ] **steadier, steadiest; steadies, steadying, steadied** ADJECTIVE
1 continuing or developing gradually without major interruptions or changes *e.g. a steady rise in profits*

● THESAURUS
consistent: *consistent support*
constant: *under constant pressure*
continuous: *Japanese-style programmes of continuous improvement*
even: *an even level of sound*
nonstop: *nonstop background music*
regular: *a regular beat*
uninterrupted: *28 years of uninterrupted growth*

2 firm and not shaking or wobbling *e.g. O'Brien held out a steady hand.*

● THESAURUS
firm: *Make sure the tree is securely mounted on a firm base.*
secure: *Check joints are secure and the wood is sound.*
stable: *stable foundations*

3 A steady look or voice is calm and controlled.

4 Someone who is steady is sensible and reliable.
> VERB
5 When you steady something, you hold on to prevent it from shaking or wobbling.

● THESAURUS
brace: *the old timbers which braced the roof*

S

secure: *The frames are secured by horizontal rails.*
stabilize: *gyros which stabilize the platform*
support: *Thick wooden posts support the ceiling.*

6 When you steady yourself, you control and calm yourself.
steadily ADVERB

steak [steɪk] **steaks** NOUN

1 Steak is good-quality beef without much fat.

2 A fish steak is a large piece of fish.
[WORD HISTORY: from Old Norse STEIK meaning 'roast']

steal [stiːl] **steals, stealing, stole, stolen**
VERB

1 To steal something means to take it without permission and without intending to return it.

● THESAURUS
appropriate: *Several other companies have appropriated the idea.*
nick: British and Australian and New Zealand; slang *I nicked that money from the till.*
pilfer: *Staff were pilfering behind the bar.*
pinch: informal *Someone's pinched my wallet.*
swipe: slang *Did you just swipe that book?*
take: *The burglars took anything they could carry.*

2 To steal somewhere means to move there quietly and secretively.

● THESAURUS
creep: *We crept away under cover of darkness.*
slip: *I wanted to duck down and slip past but they saw me.*
sneak: *Sometimes he would sneak out to see me.*
tiptoe: *She slipped out of bed and tiptoed to the window.*

stealth [stɛlθ] NOUN
If you do something with stealth, you do it quietly and secretively.
stealthy ADJECTIVE, **stealthily** ADVERB

steam [stiːm] **steams, steaming, steamed**
NOUN

1 Steam is the hot vapour formed when water boils.

> ADJECTIVE
2 Steam engines are operated using steam as a means of power.

> VERB
3 If something steams, it gives off steam.

4 To steam food means to cook it in steam.
steamy ADJECTIVE

steam-engine [ˈstiːm,ɛndʒɪn] **steam-engines** NOUN
any engine that uses the energy of steam to produce mechanical work

steamer [ˈstiːmə] **steamers** NOUN

1 a ship powered by steam

2 a container with small holes in the bottom in which you steam food

steed [stiːd] **steeds** NOUN; LITERARY
a horse

steel [stiːl] **steels, steeling, steeled** NOUN

1 Steel is a very strong metal containing mainly iron with a small amount of carbon.

> VERB
2 To steel yourself means to prepare to deal with something unpleasant.

steel band **steel bands** NOUN
a group of people who play music on special metal drums

steep [stiːp] **steeper, steepest; steeps, steeping, steeped** ADJECTIVE

1 A steep slope rises sharply and is difficult to go up.

● THESAURUS
sheer: *a sheer drop*
vertical: *The slope was almost vertical.*
<<OPPOSITE *gradual*

2 larger than is reasonable *e.g. a steep price increase*

● THESAURUS
excessive: *excessive charges*
extortionate: *an extortionate rate of interest*
high: *high loan rates*
unreasonable: *unreasonable interest charges*

> VERB
3 To steep something in a liquid means to soak it thoroughly.
steeply ADVERB

● THESAURUS
immerse: *Immerse the gammon in cold water to remove the salt.*
marinate: *Marinate the chicken for at least four hours.*
soak: *Soak the beans overnight.*

steeped [stiːpd] ADJECTIVE
If a person or place is steeped in a particular quality, they are deeply affected by it. *e.g. an industry steeped in tradition*

steeple [ˈstiːpəl] **steeples** NOUN
a tall pointed structure on top of a church tower

steeplechase [ˈstiːpəl,tʃeɪs] **steeplechases**
NOUN
a long horse race in which the horses jump over obstacles such as hedges and water jumps
[WORD HISTORY: originally a race with a church steeple in sight as the goal]

steer [stɪə] **steers, steering, steered** VERB

1 To steer a vehicle or boat means to control it so that it goes in the right direction.

2 To steer someone towards a particular course of action means to influence and direct their behaviour or thoughts.

> NOUN

3 a castrated bull

stem [stɛm] stems, stemming, stemmed

NOUN

1 The stem of a plant is the long thin central part above the ground that carries the leaves and flowers.

2 The stem of a glass is the long narrow part connecting the bowl to the base.

> VERB

3 If a problem stems from a particular situation, that situation is the original starting point or cause of the problem.

4 If you stem the flow of something, you restrict it or stop it from spreading. *e.g. to stem the flow of refugees*

stench [stɛntʃ] stenches NOUN

a very strong, unpleasant smell

stencil ['stɛnsəl] stencils, stencilling, stencilled NOUN

1 a thin sheet with a cut-out pattern through which ink or paint passes to form the pattern on the surface below

> VERB

2 To stencil a design on a surface means to create it using a stencil.

[WORD HISTORY: from Middle English STANSELEN meaning 'to decorate with bright colours']

step [stɛp] steps, stepping, stepped NOUN

1 If you take a step, you lift your foot and put it down somewhere else.

2 one of a series of actions that you take in order to achieve something

3 a raised flat surface, usually one of a series that you can walk up or down

> VERB

4 If you step in a particular direction, you move your foot in that direction.

5 If someone steps down or steps aside from an important position, they resign.

step- PREFIX

If a word like 'father' or 'sister' has 'step-' in front of it, it shows that the family relationship has come about because a parent has married again. *e.g. stepfather... stepsister*

steppe [stɛp] steppes NOUN

a large area of open grassland with no trees

[WORD HISTORY: from Old Russian STEP meaning 'lowland']

stepping stone ['stɛpɪŋ] stepping stones NOUN

1 Stepping stones are a line of large stones that you walk on to cross a shallow river.

2 a job or event that is regarded as a stage in your progress, especially in your career

stereo ['stɛrɪəʊ] stereos ADJECTIVE

1 A stereo recording or music system is one in which the sound is directed through two speakers.

> NOUN

2 a piece of equipment that reproduces sound from records, tapes, or CDs directing the sound through two speakers

stereotype ['stɛrɪə,taɪp] stereotypes, stereotyping, stereotyped (PSHE) NOUN

1 a fixed image or set of characteristics that people consider to represent a particular type of person or thing *e.g. the stereotype of the polite, industrious Japanese*

> VERB

2 If you stereotype someone, you assume they are a particular type of person and will behave in a particular way.

sterile ['stɛraɪl] ADJECTIVE

1 Sterile means completely clean and free from germs.

🔵 THESAURUS

antiseptic: *an antiseptic hospital room*
germ-free: *Keep your working surfaces germ-free.*
sterilized: *a sterilized laboratory*

2 A sterile person or animal is unable to produce offspring.

sterility NOUN

🔵 THESAURUS

barren: *a barren mare*
unproductive: *70 million acres of unproductive land*
<<OPPOSITE *fertile*

sterilize ['stɛrɪ,laɪz] sterilizes, sterilizing, sterilized; also spelt sterilise VERB

1 To sterilize something means to make it completely clean and free from germs, usually by boiling it or treating it with an antiseptic.

2 If a person or animal is sterilized, they have an operation that makes it impossible for them to produce offspring.

sterling ['stɜːlɪŋ] NOUN

1 Sterling is the money system of Great Britain.

> ADJECTIVE

2 excellent in quality *e.g. Volunteers are doing sterling work.*

stern [stɜːn] sterner, sternest; sterns ADJECTIVE

1 very serious and strict *e.g. a stern father... a stern warning*

> NOUN

2 The stern of a boat is the back part.

S

steroid ['stɪərɔɪd] **steroids** NOUN
Steroids are chemicals that occur naturally in
your body. Sometimes sportsmen illegally take
them as drugs to improve their performance.

stethoscope ['stɛθə,skəʊp] **stethoscopes**
NOUN
a device used by doctors to listen to a patient's
heart and breathing, consisting of earpieces
connected to a hollow tube and a small disc
[WORD HISTORY: from Greek STĒTHOS meaning
'chest' and SKOPEIN meaning 'to look at']

stew [stjuː] **stews, stewing, stewed** NOUN
1 a dish of small pieces of savoury food cooked
together slowly in a liquid

> VERB
2 To stew meat, vegetables, or fruit means to
cook them slowly in a liquid.
[WORD HISTORY: from Middle English STUEN
meaning 'to take a very hot bath']

steward ['stjʊəd] **stewards** NOUN
1 a man who works on a ship or plane looking
after passengers and serving meals

2 a person who helps to direct the public at a
race, march, or other event
[WORD HISTORY: from Old English STIGWEARD
meaning 'hall protector']

stewardess ['stjʊədɪs] **stewardesses**
NOUN
a woman who works on a ship or plane looking
after passengers and serving meals

stick [stɪk] **sticks, sticking, stuck** NOUN
1 a long, thin piece of wood

● THESAURUS
bat: *a baseball bat*
cane: *He wore a grey suit and leaned heavily on his
cane.*
mace: *a statue of a king holding a golden mace*
pole: *He reached up with a hooked pole to roll down
the shutter.*
rod: *a witch-doctor's rod*
truncheon: *a policeman's truncheon*
twig: *the sound of a twig breaking underfoot*
wand: *You can't wave a magic wand and make
everything okay.*

2 A stick of something is a long, thin piece of it.
e.g. a stick of celery

> VERB
3 If you stick a long or pointed object into
something, you push it in.

● THESAURUS
dig: *She dug her spoon into the moussaka.*
insert: *He inserted the key into the lock.*
jab: *A needle was jabbed into my arm.*
poke: *He poked his finger into the hole.*
push: *She pushed her thumb into his eye.*

put: *Just put it through my letter-box when you're
finished with it.*
ram: *He rammed the jacket under the seat.*
shove: *We shoved a copy of the newsletter beneath
their door.*
stuff: *I stuffed my hands in my pockets.*
thrust: *A small aerial thrust up from the grass verge.*

4 If you stick one thing to another, you attach it
with glue or sticky tape.

● THESAURUS
attach: *We attach labels to things before we file
them away.*
bond: *Strips of wood are bonded together.*
fix: *Fix the photo to the card using double-sided tape.*
fuse: *The scientists fused immune cells with cancer
cells.*
glue: *Glue the fabric around the window.*
paste: *The children were busy pasting stars on to a
chart.*

5 If one thing sticks to another, it becomes
attached and is difficult to remove.

● THESAURUS
adhere: *Small particles adhere to the seed.*
bond: *Diamond does not bond well with other
materials.*
cling: *His sodden trousers were clinging to his shins.*
fuse: *The flakes fuse together and produce ice
crystals.*

6 If a movable part of something sticks, it
becomes fixed and will no longer move or work
properly. *e.g. My gears keep sticking.*

● THESAURUS
catch: *His jacket buttons caught in the net.*
jam: *Every few moments the machinery became
jammed.*
lodge: *The car has a bullet lodged in the passenger
door.*
snag: *The fishermen said their nets kept snagging on
underwater objects.*

7 INFORMAL
If you stick something somewhere, you put it
there.

8 If you stick by someone, you continue to help
and support them.

9 If you stick to something, you keep to it and do
not change to something else. *e.g. He should have
stuck to the old ways of doing things.*

10 When people stick together, they stay
together and support each otherSTICIAN meaning
'to stab'.

stick out VERB
11 If something sticks out, it projects from
something else.

12 To stick out also means to be very noticeable.

stick up VERB
13 If something sticks up, it points upwards from
a surface.

14 INFORMAL
If you stick up for a person or principle, you support or defend them.

sticker ['stɪkə] **stickers** NOUN
a small piece of paper or plastic with writing or a picture on it, that you stick onto a surface

sticking plaster ['stɪkɪŋ] **sticking plasters** NOUN
a small piece of fabric that you stick over a cut or sore to protect it

stick insect stick insects NOUN
an insect with a long cylindrical body and long legs, which looks like a twig

sticky ['stɪkɪ] **stickier, stickiest** ADJECTIVE
1 A sticky object is covered with a substance that can stick to other things. *e.g. sticky hands*

● THESAURUS
adhesive: *adhesive tape*
tacky: *covered with a tacky resin*

2 Sticky paper or tape has glue on one side so that you can stick it to a surface.

3 INFORMAL
A sticky situation is difficult or embarrassing to deal with.

4 Sticky weather is unpleasantly hot and humid.

stiff [stɪf] **stiffer, stiffest** ADJECTIVE
1 Something that is stiff is firm and not easily bent.

● THESAURUS
firm: *a firm mattress*
hard: *the hard wooden floor*
rigid: *a rigid plastic container*
solid: *a block of solid wax*
taut: *He lifted the wire until it was taut.*
<<OPPOSITE *limp*

2 If you feel stiff, your muscles or joints ache when you move.

3 Stiff behaviour is formal and not friendly or relaxed.

● THESAURUS
cold: *Sharon was very cold with me.*
forced: *a forced smile*
formal: *His voice was grave and formal.*
stilted: *Our conversation was stilted and polite.*
unnatural: *a strained and unnatural atmosphere*
wooden: *a wooden performance*

4 Stiff also means difficult or severe. *e.g. stiff competition for places*

● THESAURUS
arduous: *an arduous undertaking*
difficult: *a difficult job*
exacting: *exacting standards*
formidable: *a formidable task*
hard: *a hard day's work*

rigorous: *rigorous military training*
tough: *a tough challenge*

5 A stiff drink contains a large amount of alcohol.

6 A stiff breeze is blowing strongly.

> ADVERB
7 INFORMAL
If you are bored stiff or scared stiff, you are very bored or very scared.
stiffly ADVERB, **stiffness** NOUN

stiffen ['stɪfən] **stiffens, stiffening, stiffened** VERB
1 If you stiffen, you suddenly stop moving and your muscles become tense. *e.g. I stiffened with tension.*

2 If your joints or muscles stiffen, they become sore and difficult to bend or move.

3 If fabric or material is stiffened, it is made firmer so that it does not bend easily.

stifle ['staɪfəl] **stifles, stifling, stifled** VERB
1 If the atmosphere stifles you, you feel you cannot breathe properly.

2 To stifle something means to stop it from happening or continuing. *e.g. Martin stifled a yawn.*
stifling ADJECTIVE

stigma ['stɪgmə] **stigmas** NOUN
If something has a stigma attached to it, people consider it unacceptable or a disgrace. *e.g. the outdated stigma of mental illness*

stile [staɪl] **stiles** NOUN
a step on either side of a wall or fence to enable you to climb over

stiletto [stɪ'lɛtəʊ] **stilettos** NOUN
Stilettos are women's shoes with very high, narrow heels.
[WORD HISTORY: from Italian STILO meaning 'dagger', because of the shape of the heels]

still [stɪl] **stiller, stillest; stills** ADVERB
1 If a situation still exists, it has continued to exist and it exists now.

2 If something could still happen, it might happen although it has not happened yet.

3 'Still' emphasizes that something is the case in spite of other things *e.g. Whatever you think of him, he's still your father.*

> ADVERB OR ADJECTIVE
4 Still means staying in the same position without moving. *e.g. Sit still... The air was still.*

● THESAURUS
calm: *the calm waters of the harbour*
inert: *He covered the inert body with a blanket.*
motionless: *He stood there, motionless.*
stationary: *The train was stationary for 90 minutes.*

S

tranquil: *a tranquil lake*

> ADJECTIVE

5 A still place is quiet and peaceful with no signs of activity.

> NOUN

6 a photograph taken from a cinema film or video

stillness NOUN

stillborn ['stɪlˌbɔːn] ADJECTIVE

A stillborn baby is dead when it is born.

stilt [stɪlt] **stilts** NOUN

1 Stilts are long upright poles on which a building is built, for example on wet land.

2 Stilts are also two long pieces of wood or metal on which people balance and walk.

stilted ['stɪltɪd] ADJECTIVE

formal, unnatural, and rather awkward *e.g. a stilted conversation*

stimulant ['stɪmjʊlənt] **stimulants** NOUN

a drug or other substance that makes your body work faster, increasing your heart rate and making it difficult to sleep

stimulate ['stɪmjʊˌleɪt] **stimulates, stimulating, stimulated** VERB

1 To stimulate something means to encourage it to begin or develop. *e.g. to stimulate discussion*

2 If something stimulates you, it gives you new ideas and enthusiasm.

stimulating ADJECTIVE, **stimulation** NOUN

stimulus ['stɪmjʊləs] **stimuli** NOUN

something that causes a process or event to begin or develop

sting [stɪŋ] **stings, stinging, stung** VERB

1 If a creature or plant stings you, it pricks your skin and injects a substance which causes pain.

2 If a part of your body stings, you feel a sharp tingling pain there.

3 If someone's remarks sting you, they make you feel upset and hurt.

> NOUN

4 A creature's sting is the part it stings you with.

stink [stɪŋk] **stinks, stinking, stank, stunk** VERB

1 Something that stinks smells very unpleasant.

● THESAURUS

pong: British and Australian; informal *She said he ponged a bit.*

reek: *The whole house reeks of cigar smoke.*

> NOUN

2 a very unpleasant smell

● THESAURUS

pong: British and Australian; informal *What's that horrible pong?*

stench: *a foul stench*

stint [stɪnt] **stints** NOUN

a period of time spent doing a particular job *e.g. a three-year stint in the army*

stipulate ['stɪpjʊˌleɪt] **stipulates, stipulating, stipulated** VERB; FORMAL

If you stipulate that something must be done, you state clearly that it must be done.

stipulation NOUN

stir [stɜː] **stirs, stirring, stirred** VERB

1 When you stir a liquid, you move it around using a spoon or a stick.

2 To stir means to move slightly.

3 If something stirs you, it makes you feel strong emotions. *e.g. The power of the singing stirred me.*

> NOUN

4 If an event causes a stir, it causes general excitement or shock. *e.g. two books which have caused a stir*

stirring ['stɜːrɪŋ] **stirrings** ADJECTIVE

1 causing excitement, emotion, and enthusiasm *e.g. a stirring account of the action*

> NOUN

2 If there is a stirring of emotion, people begin to feel it.

stirrup ['stɪrəp] **stirrups** NOUN

Stirrups are two metal loops hanging by leather straps from a horse's saddle, which you put your feet in when riding.

stitch [stɪtʃ] **stitches, stitching, stitched** VERB

1 When you stitch pieces of material together, you use a needle and thread to sew them together.

2 To stitch a wound means to use a special needle and thread to hold the edges of skin together.

> NOUN

3 one of the pieces of thread that can be seen where material has been sewn

4 one of the pieces of thread that can be seen where a wound has been stitched *e.g. He had eleven stitches in his lip.*

5 If you have a stitch, you feel a sharp pain at the side of your abdomen, usually because you have been running or laughing.

stoat [stəʊt] **stoats** NOUN

a small wild animal with a long body and brown fur

stock [stɒk] **stocks, stocking, stocked** NOUN

1 Stocks are shares bought as an investment in a company; also the amount of money raised by the company through the issue of shares.

THESAURUS
bonds: *the recent sharp decline in bond prices*
investments: *Earn a rate of return of 8% on your investments.*
shares: *He was keen to buy shares in the company.*

2 A shop's stock is the total amount of goods it has for sale.

THESAURUS
goods: *Are all your goods on display?*
merchandise: formal *25% off selected merchandise*

3 If you have a stock of things, you have a supply ready for use.

THESAURUS
reserve: *65% of the world's oil reserves*
reservoir: *the body's short-term reservoir of energy*
stockpile: *treaties to cut stockpiles of chemical weapons*
store: *my secret store of chocolate biscuits*
supply: *What happens when food supplies run low?*

4 The stock an animal or person comes from is the type of animal or person they are descended from. *e.g. She was descended from Scots Highland stock.*

THESAURUS
ancestry: *a family who can trace their ancestry back to the sixteenth century*
descent: *All the contributors were of African descent.*
extraction: *Her father was of Italian extraction.*
lineage: *a respectable family of ancient lineage*
parentage: *She's a Londoner of mixed parentage.*
origin: *people of Asian origin*

5 Stock is farm animals.

6 Stock is a liquid made from boiling meat, bones, or vegetables together in water. Stock is used as a base for soups, stews, and sauces.

> VERB
7 A shop that stocks particular goods keeps a supply of them to sell.

THESAURUS
deal in: *They deal in kitchen equipment.*
sell: *It sells everything from hair ribbons to oriental rugs.*
supply: *We supply office furniture and accessories.*
trade in: *He had been trading in antique furniture for 25 years.*

8 If you stock a shelf or cupboard, you fill it with food or other things.

> ADJECTIVE
9 A stock expression or way of doing something is one that is commonly used.

THESAURUS
hackneyed: *It may be an old hackneyed phrase, but it's true.*

overused: *an overused catch phrase*
routine: *We've tried all the routine methods of persuasion.*
standard: *the standard ending for a formal letter*
stereotyped: *stereotyped ideas about women*
typical: *the typical questions journalists ask celebrities*
usual: *He came out with all the usual excuses.*

> VERB
stock up
10 If you stock up with something, you buy a supply of it.

stockbroker [ˈstɒkˌbrəʊkə] **stockbrokers** NOUN
A stockbroker is a person whose job is to buy and sell shares for people who want to invest money.

stock exchange stock exchanges NOUN
a place where there is trading in stocks and shares *e.g. the New York Stock Exchange*

stocking [ˈstɒkɪŋ] **stockings** NOUN
Stockings are long pieces of thin clothing that cover a woman's leg.

stockman [ˈstɒkmən] **stockmen** NOUN
a man who looks after sheep or cattle on a farm

stock market stock markets NOUN
The stock market is the organization and activity involved in buying and selling stocks and shares.

stockpile [ˈstɒkˌpaɪl] **stockpiles, stockpiling, stockpiled** VERB
1 If someone stockpiles something, they store large quantities of it for future use.

THESAURUS
accumulate: *Some people get rich by accumulating wealth very gradually.*
amass: *It is best not to enquire how he amassed his fortune.*
collect: *Two young girls were collecting firewood.*
gather: *We gathered enough wood to last the night.*
hoard: *They've begun to hoard food and petrol.*
save: *Scraps of material were saved for quilts.*
stash: informal *He had stashed money in an offshore account.*
store up: *Investors were storing up cash in anticipation of disaster.*

> NOUN
2 a large store of something

THESAURUS
arsenal: *a formidable arsenal of guns and landmines*
cache: *a cache of weapons and explosives*
hoard: *a hoard of silver and jewels worth $40m*
reserve: *The country's reserves of food are running low.*
stash: informal *her mother's stash of sleeping pills*
stock: *Stocks of ammunition were being used up.*

S

store: *his secret store of sweets*

stocktaking ['stɒk,teɪkɪŋ] NOUN
Stocktaking is the counting and checking of all a shop's or business's goods.

stocky ['stɒkɪ] **stockier, stockiest**
ADJECTIVE
A stocky person is rather short, but broad and solid-looking.

● THESAURUS
chunky: *the chunky South African tennis player*
solid: *a solid build*
sturdy: *a short, sturdy woman in her early sixties*

stoke [stəʊk] **stokes, stoking, stoked** VERB
To stoke a fire means to keep it burning by moving or adding fuel.

stomach ['stʌmək] **stomachs, stomaching, stomached** NOUN
1 Your stomach is the organ inside your body where food is digested.

2 You can refer to the front part of your body below your waist as your stomach.

● THESAURUS
belly: *the enormous belly of the Italian foreign minister*
paunch: *Nicholson surveyed his spreading paunch.*
puku: New Zealand *a pain in my puku*
tummy: informal *I'd like a flatter tummy, but then who wouldn't?*

> VERB
3 If you cannot stomach something, you strongly dislike it and cannot accept it.

stone [stəʊn] **stones, stoning, stoned**
NOUN
1 Stone is the hard solid substance found in the ground and used for building.

2 a small piece of rock

3 The stone in a fruit such as a plum or cherry is the large seed in the centre.

4 a unit of weight equal to 14 pounds or about 6.35 kilograms

5 You can refer to a jewel as a stone. *e.g. a diamond ring with three stones*

> VERB
6 To stone something or someone means to throw stones at them.

stoned [stəʊnd] ADJECTIVE; INFORMAL
affected by drugs

stony ['stəʊnɪ] **stonier, stoniest** ADJECTIVE
1 Stony ground is rough and contains a lot of stones or rocks.

2 If someone's expression is stony, it shows no friendliness or sympathy.

stool [stu:l] **stools** NOUN

1 a seat with legs but no back or arms

2 a lump of faeces

stoop [stu:p] **stoops, stooping, stooped**
VERB
1 If you stoop, you stand or walk with your shoulders bent forwards.

2 If you would not stoop to something, you would not disgrace yourself by doing it.

stop [stɒp] **stops, stopping, stopped** VERB
1 If you stop doing something, you no longer do it.

● THESAURUS
cease: *A small number of firms have ceased trading.*
cut out: informal *Will you cut out that racket?*
desist: *boycotting Norwegian products until they desist from whaling*
discontinue: *Do not discontinue the treatment without seeing your doctor.*
end: *public pressure to end the embargo*
quit: *He's trying to quit smoking.*
<<OPPOSITE start

2 If an activity or process stops, it comes to an end or no longer happens.

● THESAURUS
cease: *At one o'clock the rain ceased.*
come to an end: *An hour later, the meeting came to an end.*
conclude: *The evening concluded with dinner and speeches.*
end: *The talks ended in disagreement.*
finish: *The teaching day finishes at around 4 pm.*
halt: *Discussions have halted again.*
<<OPPOSITE start

3 If a machine stops, it no longer functions or it is switched off.

4 To stop something means to prevent it.

● THESAURUS
arrest: *trying to arrest the bleeding*
check: *a policy to check fast population growth*
prevent: *the most practical way of preventing crime*

5 If people or things that are moving stop, they no longer move.

6 If you stop somewhere, you stay there for a short while.

> PHRASE
7 To **put a stop to** something means to prevent it from happening or continuing.

> NOUN
8 a place where a bus, train, or other vehicle stops during a journey

9 If something that is moving comes to a stop, it no longer moves.

stoppage ['stɒpɪdʒ] **stoppages** NOUN
If there is a stoppage, people stop work because

of a disagreement with their employer.

stopper ['stɒpə] **stoppers** NOUN
a piece of glass or cork that fits into the neck of a jar or bottle

stopwatch ['stɒp,wɒtʃ] **stopwatches** NOUN
a watch that can be started and stopped by pressing buttons, which is used to time events

storage ['stɔːrɪdʒ] NOUN
The storage of something is the keeping of it somewhere until it is needed.

store [stɔː] **stores, storing, stored** NOUN
1 a shop
2 A store of something is a supply kept for future use.

● THESAURUS
cache: *a cache of weapons and explosives*
fund: *an extraordinary fund of energy*
hoard: *a hoard of supplies*
reserve: *the world's oil reserves*
reservoir: *the body's short-term reservoir of energy*
stock: *stocks of paper and ink*
stockpile: *stockpiles of nuclear warheads*
supply: *food supplies*

3 a place where things are kept while they are not used

● THESAURUS
depot: *a government arms depot*
storeroom: *a storeroom filled with furniture*
warehouse: *a carpet warehouse*

> VERB
4 When you store something somewhere, you keep it there until it is needed.

● THESAURUS
hoard: *They've begun to hoard food and petrol.*
keep: *Grate the lemon zest and keep it for later.*
save: *His allotment of gas had to be saved for emergencies.*
stash: *informal He had stashed money away in a secret offshore account.*
stockpile: *People are stockpiling food for the coming winter.*

> PHRASE
5 Something that is **in store for** you is going to happen to you in the future.

storeroom ['stɔː,ruːm] **storerooms** NOUN
a room where things are kept until they are needed

storey ['stɔːrɪ] **storeys** NOUN
A storey of a building is one of its floors or levels.

stork [stɔːk] **storks** NOUN
a very large white and black bird with long red legs and a long bill

storm [stɔːm] **storms, storming, stormed**
NOUN
1 When there is a storm, there is heavy rain, a strong wind, and often thunder and lightning.
2 If something causes a storm, it causes an angry or excited reaction. *e.g. His words caused a storm of protest.*

> VERB
3 If someone storms out, they leave quickly, noisily, and angrily.
4 To storm means to say something in a loud, angry voice. *e.g. 'It's a fiasco!' he stormed*
5 If people storm a place, they attack it.
stormy ADJECTIVE

story ['stɔːrɪ] **stories** NOUN
1 a description of imaginary people and events written or told to entertain people

● THESAURUS
account: *a true account*
anecdote: *her store of theatrical anecdotes*
legend: *an old Scottish legend*
narrative: *a fast-moving narrative*
tale: *a fairy tale*
yarn: *a children's yarn about giants*

2 The story of something or someone is an account of the important events that have happened to them. *e.g. his life story*

stout [staʊt] **stouter, stoutest** ADJECTIVE
1 rather fat
2 thick, strong, and sturdy *e.g. stout walking shoes*
3 determined, firm, and strong *e.g. He can outrun the stoutest opposition.*
stoutly ADVERB

stove [stəʊv] **stoves** NOUN
a piece of equipment for heating a room or for cooking

stow [stəʊ] **stows, stowing, stowed** VERB
1 If you stow something somewhere or stow it away, you store it until it is needed.
2 If someone stows away in a ship or plane, they hide in it to go somewhere secretly without paying.

straddle ['strædəl] **straddles, straddling, straddled** VERB
1 If you straddle something, you stand or sit with one leg on either side of it.
2 If something straddles a place, it crosses it, linking different parts together. *e.g. The town straddles a river.*

straight [streɪt] **straighter, straightest**
ADJECTIVE OR ADVERB
1 continuing in the same direction without curving or bending *e.g. the straight path… Amy stared straight ahead of her.*
2 upright or level rather than sloping or bent *e.g. Keep your arms straight.*

S

erect: *The upper back and neck are held in an erect position.*
even: *to ensure an even hem*
horizontal: *a horizontal line*
level: *a completely level base*
perpendicular: *Position your body perpendicular with the slope.*
upright: *He sat upright in his chair.*
vertical: *Keep the spine vertical.*
<<OPPOSITE *crooked*

> ADVERB

3 immediately and directly *e.g. We will go straight to the hotel.*

> ADJECTIVE

4 neat and tidy *e.g. Get this room straight.*

5 honest, frank, and direct *e.g. They wouldn't give me a straight answer.*

blunt: *She is blunt about her personal life.*
candid: *I haven't been completely candid with you.*
forthright: *a forthright reply*
frank: *a frank discussion*
honest: *Please be honest with me.*
outright: *This was outright rejection.*
plain: *plain talking*
point-blank: *a point-blank refusal*

6 A straight choice involves only two options.

straightaway [ˌstreɪtəˈweɪ] ADVERB
If you do something straightaway, you do it immediately.

straighten [ˈstreɪtᵊn] **straightens, straightening, straightened** VERB
1 To straighten something means to remove any bends or curves from it.

2 To straighten something also means to make it neat and tidy.

3 To straighten out a confused situation means to organize and deal with it.

straightforward [ˌstreɪtˈfɔːwəd] ADJECTIVE
1 easy and involving no problems

basic: *The film's story is pretty basic.*
easy: *The shower is easy to install.*
elementary: *elementary computer skills*
routine: *a fairly routine procedure*
simple: *simple advice on filling in your tax form*
uncomplicated: *good British cooking with its uncomplicated, natural flavours*
<<OPPOSITE *complicated*

2 honest, open, and frank

candid: *I haven't been completely candid with you.*
direct: *He avoided giving a direct answer.*
forthright: *He was known for his forthright manner.*

frank: *They had a frank discussion about the issue.*
honest: *I was totally honest about what I was doing.*
open: *He had always been open with her.*
plain: *I believe in plain talking.*
straight: *He never gives a straight answer to a straight question.*
<<OPPOSITE *devious*

strain [streɪn] **strains, straining, strained**
NOUN
1 Strain is worry and nervous tension.

anxiety: *Her voice was full of anxiety.*
pressure: *the pressure of work*
stress: *the stress of exams*
tension: *Laughing relieves tension and stress.*

2 If a strain is put on something, it is affected by a strong force which may damage it.

3 You can refer to an aspect of someone's character, remarks, or work as a strain. *e.g. There was a strain of bitterness in his voice.*

4 You can refer to distant sounds of music as strains of music.

5 A particular strain of plant is a variety of it. *e.g. strains of rose*

> VERB

6 To strain something means to force it or use it more than is reasonable or normal.

overwork: *Too much food will overwork your digestive system.*
tax: *He is beginning to tax my patience.*

7 If you strain a muscle, you injure it by moving awkwardly.

8 To strain food means to pour away the liquid from it.

strained [streɪnd] ADJECTIVE
1 worried and anxious

2 If a relationship is strained, people feel unfriendly and do not trust each other.

strait [streɪt] **straits** NOUN
1 You can refer to a narrow strip of sea as a strait or the straits. *e.g. the Straits of Hormuz*

> PLURAL NOUN

2 If someone is in a bad situation, you can say they are in difficult straits.

straitjacket [ˈstreɪtˌdʒækɪt] **straitjackets**
NOUN
a special jacket used to tie the arms of a violent person tightly around their body

strait-laced [ˈstreɪtˌleɪsd] ADJECTIVE
having a very strict and serious attitude to moral behaviour

strand [strænd] **strands** NOUN

1 A strand of thread or hair is a single long piece of it.

2 You can refer to a part of a situation or idea as a strand of it. *e.g. the different strands of the problem*

stranded ['strændɪd] ADJECTIVE
If someone or something is stranded somewhere, they are stuck and cannot leave.

strange [streɪndʒ] **stranger, strangest** ADJECTIVE
1 unusual or unexpected

● THESAURUS
abnormal: *an abnormal fear of spiders*
bizarre: *a bizarre scene*
curious: *a curious mixture of ancient and modern*
extraordinary: *an extraordinary occurrence*
funny: *a funny feeling*
odd: *There was something odd about her.*
peculiar: *It tasted very peculiar.*
queer: *I think there's something a bit queer going on.*
uncommon: *A 15-year lifespan is not uncommon for a dog.*
weird: *He's a really weird guy.*

2 not known, seen, or experienced before *e.g. alone in a strange country*
strangely ADVERB, **strangeness** NOUN

● THESAURUS
alien: *transplanted into an alien culture*
exotic: *filmed in an exotic location*
foreign: *This was a foreign country, so unlike his own.*
new: *I'm always open to new experiences.*
novel: *a novel idea*
unfamiliar: *visiting an unfamiliar city*

stranger ['streɪndʒə] **strangers** NOUN
1 someone you have never met before

2 If you are a stranger to a place or situation, you have not been there or experienced it before.

strangle ['stræŋgl] **strangles, strangling, strangled** VERB
To strangle someone means to kill them by squeezing their throat.
strangulation NOUN

strangled ['stræŋgəld] ADJECTIVE
A strangled sound is unclear and muffled.

stranglehold ['stræŋgəl,həʊld] **strangleholds** NOUN
To have a stranglehold on something means to have control over it and prevent it from developing.

strap [stræp] **straps, strapping, strapped** NOUN
1 a narrow piece of leather or cloth, used to fasten or hold things together

> VERB
2 To strap something means to fasten it with a strap.

strapping ['stræpɪŋ] ADJECTIVE
tall, strong, and healthy-looking

strata ['strɑːtə] the plural of **stratum**

strategic [strə'tiːdʒɪk] ADJECTIVE
planned or intended to achieve something or to gain an advantage *e.g. a strategic plan*
strategically ADVERB

strategy ['strætɪdʒɪ] **strategies** NOUN
1 a plan for achieving something

2 Strategy is the skill of planning the best way to achieve something, especially in war.
strategist NOUN

stratum ['strɑːtəm] **strata** NOUN
The strata in the earth's surface are the different layers of rock.

straw [strɔː] **straws** NOUN
1 Straw is the dry, yellowish stalks from cereal crops.

2 a hollow tube of paper or plastic which you use to suck a drink into your mouth

> PHRASE
3 If something is **the last straw**, it is the latest in a series of bad events and makes you feel you cannot stand any more.

strawberry ['strɔːbərɪ] **strawberries** NOUN
a small red fruit with tiny seeds in its skin

stray [streɪ] **strays, straying, strayed** VERB
1 When people or animals stray, they wander away from where they should be.

2 If your thoughts stray, you stop concentrating.

> ADJECTIVE
3 A stray dog or cat is one that has wandered away from home.

4 Stray things are separated from the main group of things of their kind. *e.g. a stray piece of lettuce*

> NOUN
5 a stray dog or cat

streak [striːk] **streaks, streaking, streaked** NOUN
1 a long mark or stain

2 If someone has a particular streak, they have that quality in their character.

3 A lucky or unlucky streak is a series of successes or failures.

> VERB
4 If something is streaked with a colour, it has lines of the colour in it.

5 To streak somewhere means to move there very quickly.

S

streaky ADJECTIVE

stream [striːm] **streams, streaming, streamed** NOUN

1 a small river

2 You can refer to a steady flow of something as a stream. *e.g. a constant stream of people*

3 In a school, a stream is a group of children of the same age and ability.

> VERB

4 To stream somewhere means to move in a continuous flow in large quantities. *e.g. Rain streamed down the windscreen.*

streamer ['striːmə] **streamers** NOUN
a long, narrow strip of coloured paper used for decoration

streamline ['striːmˌlaɪn] **streamlines, streamlining, streamlined** VERB

1 To streamline a vehicle, aircraft, or boat means to improve its shape so that it moves more quickly and efficiently.

2 To streamline an organization means to make it more efficient by removing parts of it.

street [striːt] **streets** NOUN
a road in a town or village, usually with buildings along it

strength [strɛŋθ] **strengths** NOUN

1 Your strength is your physical energy and the power of your muscles.

THESAURUS
brawn: *He's got plenty of brains as well as brawn.*
might: *the full might of the army*
muscle: *demonstrating both muscle and skill*
stamina: *The race requires a lot of stamina.*
<<OPPOSITE *weakness*

2 Strength can refer to the degree of someone's confidence or courage.

3 You can refer to power or influence as strength. *e.g. The campaign against factory closures gathered strength.*

4 Someone's strengths are their good qualities and abilities.

5 The strength of an object is the degree to which it can stand rough treatment.

6 The strength of a substance is the amount of other substances that it contains. *e.g. coffee with sugar and milk in it at the correct strength*

7 The strength of a feeling or opinion is the degree to which it is felt or supported.

THESAURUS
force: *the force of his argument*
intensity: *the intensity of their emotions*
potency: *the extraordinary potency of his personality*
power: *the overwhelming power of love*

vehemence: *I was surprised by the vehemence of his criticism.*
vigour: *We resumed the attack with renewed vigour.*
<<OPPOSITE *weakness*

8 The strength of a relationship is its degree of closeness or success.

9 The strength of a group is the total number of people in it.

> PHRASE

10 If people do something **in strength**, a lot of them do it together. *e.g. The press were here in strength.*

strengthen ['strɛŋθən] **strengthens, strengthening, strengthened** VERB

1 To strengthen something means to give it more power, influence, or support and make it more likely to succeed.

THESAURUS
consolidate: *to consolidate an already dominant position*
encourage: *encouraged by the shouts of their supporters*
harden: *evidence which hardens suspicions about their involvement*
stiffen: *This only stiffened his resolve to quit.*
toughen: *new laws to toughen police powers*
<<OPPOSITE *weaken*

2 To strengthen an object means to improve it or add to its structure so that it can withstand rough treatment.

THESAURUS
bolster: *steel beams used to bolster the roof*
brace: *tottering pillars braced by scaffolding*
fortify: *citadels fortified by high stone walls*
reinforce: *They had to reinforce the walls with exterior beams.*
support: *the thick wooden posts that supported the ceiling*
<<OPPOSITE *weaken*

strenuous ['strɛnjuəs] ADJECTIVE
involving a lot of effort or energy
strenuously ADVERB

stress [strɛs] **stresses, stressing, stressed** NOUN

1 Stress is worry and nervous tension.

THESAURUS
anxiety: *Her voice was full of anxiety.*
hassle: informal *I don't think it's worth the money or the hassle.*
pressure: *I felt the pressure of being the first woman in the job.*
strain: *She was tired and under great strain.*
tension: *Laughing relieves tension.*
worry: *It was a time of worry for us.*

2 Stresses are strong physical forces applied to an object.

3 Stress is emphasis put on a word or part of a word when it is pronounced, making it slightly louder.

> VERB

4 If you stress a point, you emphasize it and draw attention to its importance.

stressful ADJECTIVE

THESAURUS

accentuate: *make-up which accentuates your best features*

emphasize: *He flourished his glass to emphasize the point.*

repeat: *We are not, I repeat not, in the negotiating process.*

underline: *The report underlined his concern about falling standards.*

stretch [strɛtʃ] **stretches, stretching, stretched** VERB

1 Something that stretches over an area extends that far.

THESAURUS

continue: *The road continued into the distance.*

cover: *The oil slick covered a total area of seven miles.*

extend: *The caves extend for some 18 kilometres.*

go on: *The dispute looks set to go on into the new year.*

hang: *The branches hang right down to the ground.*

last: *His difficulties are likely to last well beyond childhood.*

reach: *a caravan park which reached from one end of the bay to the other*

spread: *The estuary spreads as far as the eye can see.*

2 When you stretch, you hold out part of your body as far as you can.

THESAURUS

extend: *Stand straight with your arms extended at your sides.*

reach: *He reached up for an overhanging branch.*

straighten: *Point your toes and straighten both legs slowly.*

<<OPPOSITE *bend*

3 To stretch something soft or elastic means to pull it to make it longer or bigger.

> NOUN

4 A stretch of land or water is an area of it.

THESAURUS

area: *extensive mountainous areas of Europe and South America*

expanse: *a huge expanse of grassland*

extent: *a vast extent of fertile country*

sweep: *The ground fell away in a broad sweep down the river.*

tract: *They cleared large tracts of forest for farming.*

5 A stretch of time is a period of time.

THESAURUS

period: *a long period of time*

run: *The show will transfer to the West End, after a month's run in Birmingham.*

space: *They've come a long way in a short space of time.*

spell: *a long spell of dry weather*

stint: *He is coming home after a five-year stint abroad.*

term: *She worked the full term of her pregnancy.*

time: *doing very little exercise for several weeks at a time*

stretcher ['strɛtʃə] **stretchers** NOUN
a long piece of material with a pole along each side, used to carry an injured person

strewn [struːn] ADJECTIVE
If things are strewn about, they are scattered about untidily. *e.g. The costumes were strewn all over the floor.*

stricken ['strɪkən] ADJECTIVE
severely affected by something unpleasant

strict [strɪkt] **stricter, strictest** ADJECTIVE

1 Someone who is strict controls other people very firmly.

THESAURUS

authoritarian: *He has an authoritarian approach to parenthood.*

firm: *the guiding hand of a firm father figure*

rigid: *a rigid hospital routine*

rigorous: *rigorous military training*

stern: *Her mother was stern and hard to please.*

stringent: *stringent rules*

2 A strict rule must always be obeyed absolutely.

3 The strict meaning of something is its precise and accurate meaning.

THESAURUS

accurate: *an accurate record of events*

exact: *I do not remember the exact words.*

meticulous: *meticulous attention to detail*

particular: *very particular dietary requirements*

precise: *precise instructions*

true: *a true account*

4 You can use 'strict' to describe someone who never breaks the rules or principles of a particular belief. *e.g. a strict Muslim*

strictly ['strɪktlɪ] ADVERB

1 Strictly means only for a particular purpose. *e.g. I was in it strictly for the money.*

> PHRASE

2 You say **strictly speaking** to correct a statement or add more precise information. *e.g. Somebody pointed out that, strictly speaking, electricity was a discovery, not an invention.*

stride [straɪd] **strides, striding, strode, stridden** VERB

1 To stride along means to walk quickly with long steps.

> NOUN

2 a long step; also the length of a step

strident ['straɪdənt] ADJECTIVE
loud, harsh, and unpleasant

strife [straɪf] NOUN; FORMAL
Strife is trouble, conflict, and disagreement.

strike [straɪk] **strikes, striking, struck**
NOUN

1 If there is a strike, people stop working as a protest.

2 A hunger strike is a refusal to eat anything as a protest. A rent strike is a refusal to pay rent.

3 a military attack *e.g. the threat of American air strikes*

> VERB

4 To strike someone or something means to hit them.

5 If an illness, disaster, or enemy strikes, it suddenly affects or attacks someone.

6 If a thought strikes you, it comes into your mind.

7 If you are struck by something, you are impressed by it.

8 When a clock strikes, it makes a sound to indicate the time.

9 To strike a deal with someone means to come to an agreement with them.

10 If someone strikes oil or gold, they discover it in the ground.

11 If you strike a match, you rub it against something to make it burst into flame.

strike off VERB
12 If a professional person is struck off for bad behaviour, their name is removed from an official register and they are not allowed to practise their profession.

strike up VERB
13 To strike up a conversation or friendship means to begin it.

striker ['straɪkə] **strikers** NOUN

1 Strikers are people who are refusing to work as a protest.

2 In soccer, a player whose function is to attack and score goals.

striking ['straɪkɪŋ] ADJECTIVE
very noticeable because of being unusual or very attractive
strikingly ADVERB

string [strɪŋ] **strings, stringing, strung**
NOUN

1 String is thin cord made of twisted threads.

2 You can refer to a row or series of similar things as a string of them. *e.g. a string of islands... a string of injuries*

3 The strings of a musical instrument are tightly stretched lengths of wire or nylon which vibrate to produce the notes.

> PLURAL NOUN

4 The section of an orchestra consisting of stringed instruments is called the strings.

string along VERB
5 INFORMAL To string someone along means to deceive them.

string out VERB
6 If things are strung out, they are spread out in a long line.

7 To string something out means to make it last longer than necessary.

stringed [strɪŋd] ADJECTIVE
A stringed instrument is one with strings, such as a guitar or violin.

stringent ['strɪndʒənt] ADJECTIVE
Stringent laws conditions are very severe or are strictly controlled. *e.g. stringent financial checks*

stringy-bark ['strɪŋɪ,bɑːk] **stringy-barks**
NOUN
any Australian eucalypt that has bark that peels off in long, tough strands

strip [strɪp] **strips, stripping, stripped**
NOUN

1 A strip of something is a long, narrow piece of it.

2 A comic strip is a series of drawings which tell a story.

3 A sports team's strip is the clothes worn by the team when playing a match.

> VERB

4 If you strip, you take off all your clothes.

5 To strip something means to remove whatever is covering its surface.

6 To strip someone of their property or rights means to take their property or rights away from them officially.

stripe [straɪp] **stripes** NOUN
Stripes are long, thin lines, usually of different colours.
striped ADJECTIVE

stripper ['strɪpə] **strippers** NOUN
an entertainer who does striptease

striptease ['strɪp,tiːz] NOUN
Striptease is a form of entertainment in which someone takes off their clothes gradually to music.

strive [straɪv] **strives, striving, strove, striven** VERB
If you strive to do something, you make a great effort to achieve it.

attempt: *He attempted to smile, but found it difficult.*
do your best: *I'll do my best to find out.*
do your utmost: *She was certain he would do his utmost to help her.*
endeavour: *formal They are endeavouring to protect trade union rights.*
make an effort: *He made no effort to hide his disappointment.*
seek: *We have never sought to impose our views.*
try: *He tried to block her advancement in the Party.*

stroke [strəʊk] **strokes, stroking, stroked**
VERB
1 If you stroke something, you move your hand smoothly and gently over it.
> NOUN
2 If someone has a stroke, they suddenly lose consciousness as a result of a blockage or rupture in a blood vessel in the brain. A stroke can result in damage to speech and paralysis.
3 The strokes of a brush or pen are the movements that you make with it.
4 The strokes of a clock are the sounds that indicate the hour.
5 A swimming stroke is a particular style of swimming.
> PHRASE
6 If you have **a stroke of luck**, then you are lucky and something good happens to you.

stroll [strəʊl] **strolls, strolling, strolled**
VERB
1 To stroll along means to walk slowly in a relaxed way.
> NOUN
2 a slow, pleasurable walk

stroller ['strəʊlə] **strollers** NOUN
In Australian English, a stroller is a pushchair.

strong [strɒŋ] **stronger, strongest**
ADJECTIVE
1 Someone who is strong has powerful muscles.
2 You also say that someone is strong when they are confident and have courage.
3 Strong objects are able to withstand rough treatment.

durable: *made of durable plastic*
hard-wearing: *hard-wearing cotton overalls*
heavy-duty: *a heavy-duty canvas bag*
reinforced: *reinforced concrete supports*
sturdy: *a camera mounted on a sturdy tripod*
substantial: *a substantial boat with a powerful rigging*
tough: *a tough vehicle designed for all terrains*

well-built: *You need a well-built fence all round the garden.*
<<OPPOSITE *fragile*
4 Strong also means great in degree or intensity. *e.g. a strong wind*
great in degree or intensity: strong
<<OPPOSITE *faint*
5 A strong argument or theory is supported by a lot of evidence.
6 If a group or organization is strong, it has a lot of members or influence.
7 You can use 'strong' to say how many people there are in a group. *e.g. The audience was about two dozen strong.*
8 Your strong points are the things you are good at.
9 A strong economy or currency is stable and successful.
10 A strong liquid or drug contains a lot of a particular substance.
> ADVERB
11 If someone or something is still going strong, they are still healthy or working well after a long time.
strongly ADVERB

stronghold ['strɒŋˌhəʊld] **strongholds**
NOUN
1 a place that is held and defended by an army
2 A stronghold of an attitude or belief is a place in which the attitude or belief is strongly held. *e.g. Europe's last stronghold of male dominance.*

structure ['strʌktʃə] **structures, structuring, structured** NOUN
1 The structure of something is the way it is made, built, or organized.
arrangement: *an intricate arrangement of treadles, rods and cranks*
construction: *The chairs were light in construction but very strong.*
design: *The shoes were of good design and good quality.*
make-up: *the chemical make-up of the oceans and atmosphere*
organization: *the organization of the economy*
2 something that has been built or constructed
building: *an ugly modern building*
construction: *an impressive steel and glass construction*
edifice: *historic edifices in the area*
> VERB
3 To structure something means to arrange it into an organized pattern or system.
structural ADJECTIVE, **structurally** ADVERB

S

struggle ['strʌgᵊl] **struggles, struggling, struggled** VERB

1 If you struggle to do something, you try hard to do it in difficult circumstances.

● THESAURUS
strain: *straining to lift heavy weights*
strive: *He strives hard to keep himself fit.*
toil: *toiling to make up for lost time*
work: *I had to work hard for everything I've got.*

2 When people struggle, they twist and move violently during a fight.

> NOUN
3 Something that is a struggle is difficult to achieve and takes a lot of effort.

● THESAURUS
effort: *It was an effort to finish in time.*
labour: *weary from their labours*
toil: *another day of toil and strife*
work: *It's been hard work, but rewarding.*

4 a fight

strum [strʌm] **strums, strumming, strummed** VERB
To strum a guitar means to play it by moving your fingers backwards and forwards across all the strings.

strut [strʌt] **struts, strutting, strutted** VERB

1 To strut means to walk in a stiff, proud way with your chest out and your head high.

> NOUN
2 a piece of wood or metal which strengthens or supports part of a building or structure

Stuart ['stjʊət] **Stuarts** NOUN
Stuart was the family name of the monarchs who ruled Scotland from 1371 to 1714 and England from 1603 to 1714.

stub [stʌb] **stubs, stubbing, stubbed** NOUN

1 The stub of a pencil or cigarette is the short piece that remains when the rest has been used.

2 The stub of a cheque or ticket is the small part that you keep.

> VERB
3 If you stub your toe, you hurt it by accidentally kicking something.

stubble ['stʌbᵊl] NOUN

1 The short stalks remaining in the ground after a crop is harvested are called stubble.

2 If a man has stubble on his face, he has very short hair growing there because he has not shaved recently.

stubborn ['stʌbᵊn] ADJECTIVE

1 Someone who is stubborn is determined not to change their opinion or course of action.

● THESAURUS
dogged: *his dogged insistence on his rights*
inflexible: *His opponents viewed him as dogmatic and inflexible.*
obstinate: *a wicked and obstinate child*
tenacious: *a tenacious and persistent interviewer*
wilful: *a headstrong and wilful young lady*

2 A stubborn stain is difficult to remove.
stubbornly ADVERB, **stubbornness** NOUN

stuck [stʌk] ADJECTIVE

1 If something is stuck in a particular position, it is fixed or jammed and cannot be moved. *e.g. His car's stuck in a snowdrift.*

2 If you are stuck, you are unable to continue what you were doing because it is too difficult.

3 If you are stuck somewhere, you are unable to get away.

stuck-up [,stʌk'ʌp] ADJECTIVE INFORMAL
proud and conceited

● THESAURUS
arrogant: *He was so arrogant, he never even said hello to me.*
conceited: *He's a very conceited young man.*
disdainful: *She cast a disdainful glance at me.*
haughty: *She looks haughty, but when you get to know her, she's very friendly.*
proud: *He's too proud to use public transport.*
snobbish: *I'd expected her to be snobbish, but she was warm and welcoming.*

stud [stʌd] **studs** NOUN

1 a small piece of metal fixed into something

2 A male horse or other animal that is kept for stud is kept for breeding purposes

studded ['stʌdɪd] ADJECTIVE
decorated with small pieces of metal or precious stones

student ['stjuːdᵊnt] **students** NOUN
a person studying at university or college

studied ['stʌdɪd] ADJECTIVE
A studied action or response has been carefully planned and is not natural. *e.g. She sipped her glass of white wine with studied boredom.*

studio ['stjuːdɪˌəʊ] **studios** NOUN

1 a room where a photographer or painter works

2 a room containing special equipment where records, films, or radio or television programmes are made

studious ['stjuːdɪəs] ADJECTIVE
spending a lot of time studying

studiously ['stjuːdɪəslɪ] ADVERB
carefully and deliberately *e.g. She was studiously ignoring me.*

study ['stʌdɪ] **studies, studying, studied** VERB

1 If you study a particular subject, you spend time learning about it.

● THESAURUS
learn: *I'm learning French.*
read up: *She spent a year reading up on farming techniques.*
swot: British and Australian and New Zealand; informal *swotting for their finals*

2 If you study something, you look at it carefully. *e.g. He studied the map in silence.*

● THESAURUS
contemplate: *He contemplated his hands, frowning.*
examine: *He examined her passport and stamped it.*
pore over: *We spent hours poring over travel brochures.*

> NOUN

3 Study is the activity of studying a subject. *e.g. the serious study of medieval archaeology*

● THESAURUS
lessons: *He was lagging behind in his lessons.*
research: *funds for research into AIDS*
school work: *She buried herself in school work.*
swotting: British and Australian and New Zealand; informal *She put her success down to last-minute swotting.*

4 Studies are subjects which are studied. *e.g. media studies*

5 a piece of research on a particular subject *e.g. a detailed study of the world's most violent people*

6 a room used for writing and studying

stuff [stʌf] **stuffs, stuffing, stuffed** NOUN

1 You can refer to a substance or group of things as stuff.

● THESAURUS
apparatus: *all the apparatus you'll need for the job*
belongings: *I collected my belongings and left.*
equipment: *outdoor playing equipment*
gear: *fishing gear*
kit: *I forgot my gym kit.*
material: *organic material*
substance: *The substance that's causing problems comes from barley.*
tackle: *Martin kept his fishing tackle in his room.*
things: *Sara told him to take all his things and not to return.*

> VERB

2 If you stuff something somewhere, you push it there quickly and roughly.

● THESAURUS
cram: *I crammed her hat into a waste-basket.*
force: *I forced the key into the ignition.*
jam: *Pete jammed his hands into his pockets.*
push: *Someone had pushed a tissue into the keyhole.*
ram: *He rammed his clothes into a drawer.*

shove: *We shoved a newsletter beneath their door.*
squeeze: *I squeezed everything into my rucksack.*
thrust: *She thrust a stack of photos into my hands.*

3 If you stuff something with a substance or objects, you fill it with the substance or objects.

● THESAURUS
cram: *I crammed my bag full of clothes and set off.*
fill: *I filled the box with polystyrene chips.*
load: *They loaded all their equipment into backpacks.*
pack: *a lorry packed with explosives*

stuffing [ˈstʌfɪŋ] NOUN
Stuffing is a mixture of small pieces of food put inside poultry or a vegetable before it is cooked.

stuffy [ˈstʌfɪ] **stuffier, stuffiest** ADJECTIVE

1 very formal and old-fashioned

● THESAURUS
dull: *They are nice people but rather dull.*
formal: *an austere and formal family*
old-fashioned: *She was condemned as an old-fashioned prude.*
staid: *He is boring, old-fashioned and staid.*
strait-laced: *She is very strait-laced and narrow-minded.*

2 If it is stuffy in a room, there is not enough fresh air.

● THESAURUS
close: *The atmosphere was close.*
heavy: *The air was heavy, moist and sultry.*
muggy: *It was muggy and overcast.*
oppressive: *The little room was windowless and oppressive.*
stale: *A layer of smoke hung in the stale air.*
stifling: *the stifling heat of the room*

stumble [ˈstʌmbᵊl] **stumbles, stumbling, stumbled** VERB

1 If you stumble while you are walking or running, you trip and almost fall.

2 If you stumble when speaking, you make mistakes when pronouncing the words.

3 If you stumble across something or stumble on it, you find it unexpectedly.

stump [stʌmp] **stumps, stumping, stumped** NOUN

1 a small part of something that is left when the rest has been removed *e.g. the stump of a dead tree*

2 In cricket, the stumps are the three upright wooden sticks that support the bails, forming the wicket.

> VERB

3 If a question or problem stumps you, you cannot think of an answer or solution.

stun [stʌn] **stuns, stunning, stunned** VERB

1 If you are stunned by something, you are very shocked by it.

S

2 To stun a person or animal means to knock them unconscious with a blow to the head.

stunning ['stʌnɪŋ] ADJECTIVE
very beautiful or impressive e.g. *a stunning first novel*

stunt [stʌnt] **stunts, stunting, stunted**
NOUN
1 an unusual or dangerous and exciting action that someone does to get publicity or as part of a film
> VERB
2 To stunt the growth or development of something means to prevent it from developing as it should.

stupendous [stju:'pɛndəs] ADJECTIVE
very large or impressive e.g. *a stupendous amount of money*

stupid ['stju:pɪd] **stupider, stupidest**
ADJECTIVE
showing lack of good judgment or intelligence and not at all sensible

● THESAURUS
absurd: *absurd ideas*
daft: informal *That's a daft question.*
dim: *He is rather dim.*
foolish: *It is foolish to risk injury.*
idiotic: *What an idiotic thing to say!*
inane: *She's always asking inane questions.*
obtuse: *It should be obvious even to the most obtuse person.*
thick: *I must have seemed incredibly thick.*
<<OPPOSITE *clever*

stupidity [stju:'pɪdɪtɪ] NOUN
a lack of intelligence or good judgment

● THESAURUS
absurdity: *the absurdity of the suggestion*
folly: *the danger and folly of taking drugs*
foolishness: *He expressed remorse over his own foolishness.*
inanity: *The inanity of the conversation.*
silliness: *He sounded quite exasperated by my silliness.*

sturdy ['stɜ:dɪ] **sturdier, sturdiest**
ADJECTIVE
strong and firm and unlikely to be damaged or injured e.g. *a sturdy chest of drawers*

● THESAURUS
durable: *Fine china is surprisingly durable.*
hardy: *He looked like a farmer, round-faced and hardy.*
robust: *very robust, simply-designed machinery*
solid: *The car feels very solid.*
substantial: *Jack had put on weight – he seemed more substantial.*
stout: *a stout oak door*

strong: *a strong casing which won't crack or chip*
well-built: *Mitchell is well-built and of medium height.*
<<OPPOSITE *fragile*

sturgeon ['stɜ:dʒən] NOUN
a large edible fish, the eggs of which are also eaten and are known as caviar

stutter ['stʌtə] **stutters, stuttering, stuttered** NOUN
1 Someone who has a stutter finds it difficult to speak smoothly and often repeats sounds through being unable to complete a word.
> VERB
2 When someone stutters, they hesitate or repeat sounds when speaking.

sty [staɪ] **sties** NOUN
a pigsty

stye [staɪ] **styes** NOUN
an infection in the form of a small red swelling on a person's eyelid

style [staɪl] **styles, styling, styled** NOUN
1 The style of something is the general way in which it is done or presented, often showing the attitudes of the people involved.

● THESAURUS
approach: *his blunt approach*
manner: *a satire in the manner of Dickens*
method: *a new method of education*
mode: *a cheap and convenient mode of transport*
technique: *his driving technique*
way: *He had a strange way of talking.*

2 A person or place that has style is smart, elegant, and fashionable.

● THESAURUS
chic: *French designer chic.*
elegance: *Princess Grace's understated elegance.*
flair: *dressed with typical Italian flair*
sophistication: *to add a touch of sophistication to any wardrobe*
taste: *impeccable taste*

3 The style of something is its design. e.g. *new windows that fit in with the style of the house*
> VERB
4 To style a piece of clothing or a person's hair means to design and create its shape.

stylish ['staɪlɪʃ] ADJECTIVE
smart, elegant, and fashionable
stylishly ADVERB

suave [swɑ:v] ADJECTIVE
charming, polite, and confident e.g. *a suave Italian*

sub- PREFIX
1 'Sub-' is used at the beginning of words that have 'under' as part of their meaning e.g. *submarine*

2 'Sub-' is also used to form nouns that refer to the parts into which something is divided *e.g. Subsection 2 of section 49... a particular subgroup of citizens*

[WORD HISTORY: from Latin SUB meaning 'under' or 'below']

subconscious [sʌb'kɒnʃəs] NOUN

1 Your subconscious is the part of your mind that can influence you without your being aware of it.

> ADJECTIVE

2 happening or existing in someone's subconscious and therefore not directly realized or understood by them *e.g. a subconscious fear of rejection*

subconsciously ADVERB

subcontinent [sʌb'kɒntɪnənt] subcontinents NOUN

a large mass of land, often consisting of several countries, and forming part of a continent *e.g. the Indian subcontinent*

subdue [səb'dju:] subdues, subduing, subdued VERB

1 If soldiers subdue a group of people, they bring them under control by using force. *e.g. It would be quite impossible to subdue the whole continent.*

● THESAURUS

crush: *ruthless measures to crush the revolt*
defeat: *an important role in defeating the rebellion*
overcome: *working to overcome the enemy forces*
overpower: *The police eventually overpowered him.*
quell: *tough new measures to quell the disturbances*
vanquish: *his vanquished foe*

2 To subdue a colour, light, or emotion means to make it less bright or strong.

subdued [səb'dju:d] ADJECTIVE

1 rather quiet and sad

2 not very noticeable or bright

subject subjects, subjecting, subjected

NOUN ['sʌbdʒɪkt]

1 The subject of writing or a conversation is the thing or person being discussed.

● THESAURUS

issue: *an issue that had worried him for some time*
matter: *I don't want to discuss the matter.*
object: *the object of much heated discussion*
point: *There is another point to consider.*
question: *the difficult question of unemployment*
theme: *The book's central theme is power.*
topic: *The weather is a constant topic of conversation.*

2 In grammar, the subject is the word or words representing the person or thing doing the action expressed by the verb. For example, in the sentence 'My cat keeps catching birds', 'my cat' is the subject.

3 an area of study

4 The subjects of a country are the people who live there.

> VERB [səb'dʒɛkt]

5 To subject someone to something means to make them experience it. *e.g. He was subjected to constant interruption.*

● THESAURUS

expose: *people exposed to high levels of radiation*
put through: *My husband put me through hell.*
submit: *The old woman was submitted to a terrifying ordeal.*

> ADJECTIVE ['sʌbdʒɪkt]

6 Someone or something that is subject to something is affected by it. *e.g. He was subject to attacks at various times.*

subjective [səb'dʒɛktɪv] ADJECTIVE

influenced by personal feelings and opinion rather than based on fact or rational thought

subjunctive [səb'dʒʌŋktɪv] NOUN

In grammar, the subjunctive or subjunctive mood is one of the forms a verb can take. It is used to express attitudes such as wishing and doubting.

sublime [sə'blaɪm] ADJECTIVE

Something that is sublime is wonderful and affects people emotionally. *e.g. sublime music*

submarine ['sʌbmə,ri:n] submarines NOUN

a ship that can travel beneath the surface of the sea

submerge [səb'mɜːdʒ] submerges, submerging, submerged VERB

1 To submerge means to go beneath the surface of a liquid.

2 If you submerge yourself in an activity, you become totally involved in it.

submission [səb'mɪʃən] submissions NOUN

1 Submission is a state in which someone accepts the control of another person. *e.g. Now he must beat us into submission.*

2 The submission of a proposal or application is the act of sending it for consideration.

submissive [səb'mɪsɪv] ADJECTIVE

behaving in a quiet, obedient way

submit [səb'mɪt] submits, submitting, submitted VERB

1 If you submit to something, you accept it because you are not powerful enough to resist it.

● THESAURUS

agree: *Management has agreed to the union's conditions.*

S

bow: *Some shops are bowing to consumer pressure and stocking the product.*
capitulate: *He capitulated to their ultimatum.*
comply: *The commander said his army would comply with the ceasefire.*
give in: *Officials say they won't give in to the workers' demands.*
surrender: *We'll never surrender to these terrorists.*
yield: *She yielded to her mother's nagging and took the child to a specialist.*
<<OPPOSITE resist

2 If you submit an application or proposal, you send it to someone for consideration.

⬤ THESAURUS

hand in: *I'm supposed to hand in my dissertation on Friday.*
present: *The group intends to present this petition to the parliament.*
propose: *He has proposed a bill to abolish the House of Commons.*
put forward: *He has put forward new peace proposals.*
send in: *Applicants are asked to send in a CV and covering letter.*
table: *They've tabled a motion criticizing the Government for its actions.*
tender: *She tendered her resignation.*
<<OPPOSITE withdraw

subordinate subordinates, subordinating, subordinated NOUN
[sə'bɔːdɪnɪt]
1 A person's subordinate is someone who is in a less important position than them.

> ADJECTIVE [sə'bɔːdɪnɪt]
2 If one thing is subordinate to another, it is less important. *e.g. Non-elected officials are subordinate to elected leaders.*

> VERB [sə'bɔːdɪˌneɪt]
3 To subordinate one thing to another means to treat it as being less important.

subordinate clause subordinate clauses NOUN
(ENGLISH) In grammar, a subordinate clause is a clause which adds details to the main clause of a sentence.

subscribe [səb'skraɪb] **subscribes, subscribing, subscribed** VERB
1 If you subscribe to a particular belief or opinion, you support it or agree with it.
2 If you subscribe to a magazine, you pay to receive regular copies.
subscriber NOUN

subscription [səb'skrɪpʃən] **subscriptions** NOUN
a sum of money that you pay regularly to belong

to an organization or to receive regular copies of a magazine

subsequent ['sʌbsɪkwənt] ADJECTIVE
happening or coming into existence at a later time than something else *e.g. the December uprising and the subsequent political violence*
subsequently ADVERB

subservient [səb'sɜːvɪənt] ADJECTIVE
Someone who is subservient does whatever other people want them to do.

subside [səb'saɪd] **subsides, subsiding, subsided** VERB
1 To subside means to become less intense or quieter. *e.g. Her excitement suddenly subsided.*
2 If water or the ground subsides, it sinks to a lower level.

subsidence [səb'saɪdᵊns] NOUN
If a place is suffering from subsidence, parts of the ground have sunk to a lower level.

subsidiary [səb'sɪdɪərɪ] **subsidiaries** NOUN
1 a company which is part of a larger company
> ADJECTIVE
2 treated as being of less importance and additional to another thing *e.g. Drama is offered as a subsidiary subject.*

subsidize ['sʌbsɪˌdaɪz] **subsidizes, subsidizing, subsidized**; also spelt **subsidise** VERB
To subsidize something means to provide part of the cost of it. *e.g. He feels the government should do much more to subsidize films.*
subsidized ADJECTIVE

subsidy ['sʌbsɪdɪ] **subsidies** NOUN
a sum of money paid to help support a company or provide a public service

substance ['sʌbstəns] **substances** NOUN
1 Anything which is a solid, a powder, a liquid, or a paste can be referred to as a substance.

⬤ THESAURUS

element: *a chart of the chemical elements*
fabric: *Condensation will rot the fabric of the building.*
material: *an armchair of some resilient plastic material*
stuff: *the stuff from which the universe is made*

2 If a speech or piece of writing has substance, it is meaningful or important. *e.g. a good speech, but there was no substance*

substantial [səb'stænʃəl] ADJECTIVE
1 very large in degree or amount *e.g. a substantial pay rise*
2 large and strongly built *e.g. a substantial stone building*

substantially [səb'stænʃəlɪ] ADVERB
Something that is substantially true is generally or mostly true.

substitute ['sʌbstɪ,tjuːt] **substitutes, substituting, substituted** VERB
1 To substitute one thing for another means to use it instead of the other thing or to put it in the other thing's place.

● THESAURUS
exchange: *exchanging one set of problems for another*
interchange: *Meat can be interchanged with pulses as a source of protein.*
replace: *We dug up the concrete and replaced it with grass.*
swap: *Some hostages were swapped for convicted prisoners.*
switch: *They switched the tags on the cables.*

> NOUN
2 If one thing is a substitute for another, it is used instead of it or put in its place.
substitution NOUN

● THESAURUS
deputy: *I can't make it so I'll send my deputy.*
proxy: *They must nominate a proxy to vote on their behalf.*
replacement: *He has nominated Adams as his replacement.*
representative: *Employees from each department elect a representative.*
surrogate: *They had expected me to be a surrogate for my sister.*

subterfuge ['sʌbtə,fjuːdʒ] **subterfuges** NOUN
Subterfuge is the use of deceitful or dishonest methods.
[WORD HISTORY: from Latin SUBTERFUGERE meaning 'to escape by stealth']

subtitle ['sʌb,taɪtᵊl] **subtitles** NOUN
A film with subtitles has a printed translation of the dialogue at the bottom of the screen.

subtle ['sʌtᵊl] **subtler, subtlest** ADJECTIVE
1 very fine, delicate, or small in degree *e.g. a subtle change*
2 using indirect methods to achieve something
subtly ADVERB, **subtlety** NOUN

subtract [səb'trækt] **subtracts, subtracting, subtracted** VERB
If you subtract one number from another, you take away the first number from the second.

● THESAURUS
deduct: *Marks will be deducted for spelling mistakes.*
take away: *Take away the number you first thought of.*

take from: *Take the 5% discount from the total amount due.*
<<OPPOSITE add

subtraction [səb'trækʃən] **subtractions** NOUN
(MATHS) Subtraction is subtracting one number from another, or a sum in which you do this.

suburb ['sʌbɜːb] **suburbs** NOUN
an area of a town or city that is away from its centre

suburban [sə'bɜːbᵊn] ADJECTIVE
1 relating to a suburb or suburbs
2 dull and conventional

suburbia [sə'bɜːbɪə] NOUN
You can refer to the suburbs of a city as suburbia.

subversive [səb'vɜːsɪv] **subversives** ADJECTIVE
1 intended to destroy or weaken a political system *e.g. subversive activities*
> NOUN
2 Subversives are people who try to destroy or weaken a political system.
subversion NOUN

subvert [səb'vɜːt] **subverts, subverting, subverted** VERB; FORMAL
To subvert something means to cause it to weaken or fail. *e.g. a cunning campaign to subvert the music industry*

subway ['sʌb,weɪ] **subways** NOUN
1 a footpath that goes underneath a road
2 an underground railway

succeed [sək'siːd] **succeeds, succeeding, succeeded** VERB
1 To succeed means to achieve the result you intend.

● THESAURUS
be successful: *We must help our clubs to be successful in Europe.*
do well: *Their team did well.*
flourish: *The business flourished.*
make it: informal *It is hard for an English actress to make it in Hollywood.*
prosper: *His team have always prospered in cup competitions.*
thrive: *The company has thrived by selling cheap, simple products.*
triumph: *a symbol of good triumphing over evil*
work: *The plan worked.*
<<OPPOSITE fail

2 To succeed someone means to be the next person to have their job.

● THESAURUS
replace: *the man who replaced him as England skipper*

S

take over from: *Last year he took over from Bauman as chief executive.*

3 If one thing succeeds another, it comes after it in time. *e.g. The explosion was succeeded by a crash.*
succeeding ADJECTIVE

success [sək'sɛs] **successes** NOUN

1 Success is the achievement of something you have been trying to do.

● THESAURUS

celebrity: *I never expected this kind of celebrity when I was writing my novel.*
eminence: *a pilot who achieved eminence in the aeronautical world*
fame: *her rise to fame as a dramatist*
prosperity: *the country's economic prosperity*
triumph: *last year's Republican triumph in the elections*
victory: *Union leaders are heading for victory in their battle over workplace rights.*
wealth: formal *His hard work brought him wealth and respect.*
<<OPPOSITE *failure*

2 Someone who is a success has achieved an important position or made a lot of money.

● THESAURUS

celebrity: *At the age of 12, Dan is already a celebrity.*
hit: *The song became a massive hit.*
sensation: *the film that turned her into an overnight sensation*
star: *I always knew she would be a star.*
triumph: *a triumph of modern surgery*
winner: *Selling was my game and I intended to be a winner.*
<<OPPOSITE *failure*

successful [sək'sɛsfʊl] ADJECTIVE
having achieved what you intended to do
successfully ADVERB

● THESAURUS

flourishing: *a flourishing business*
lucrative: *a lucrative career*
profitable: *a profitable exchange of ideas*
rewarding: *a rewarding investment*
thriving: *a thriving housebuilding industry*
top: *a top model*

succession [sək'sɛʃən] **successions** NOUN

1 A succession of things is a number of them occurring one after the other.

2 When someone becomes the next person to have an important position, you can refer to this event as their succession to this position. *e.g. his succession to the throne*

> PHRASE

3 If something happens a number of weeks, months, or years **in succession**, it happens that

number of times without a break. *e.g. Borg won Wimbledon five years in succession.*

successive [sək'sɛsɪv] ADJECTIVE
occurring one after the other without a break *e.g. three successive victories*

successor [sək'sɛsə] **successors** NOUN
Someone's successor is the person who takes their job when they leave.

succinct [sək'sɪŋkt] ADJECTIVE
expressing something clearly and in very few words
succinctly ADVERB

succulent ['sʌkjʊlənt] ADJECTIVE
Succulent food is juicy and delicious.

succumb [sə'kʌm] **succumbs, succumbing, succumbed** VERB
If you succumb to something, you are unable to resist it any longer. *e.g. She never succumbed to his charms.*

such [sʌtʃ] ADJECTIVE OR PRONOUN

1 You use 'such' to refer to the person or thing you have just mentioned, or to someone or something similar. *e.g. Naples or Palermo or some such place.*

> PHRASE

2 You can use **such as** to introduce an example of something. *e.g. herbal teas such as camomile*

3 You can use **such as it is** to indicate that something is not great in quality or quantity. *e.g. The action, such as it is, is set in Egypt.*

4 You can use **such and such** when you want to refer to something that is not specific. *e.g. A good trick is to ask whether they have seen such and such a film.*

> ADJECTIVE

5 'Such' can be used for emphasizing *e.g. I have such a terrible sense of guilt.*

suchlike ['sʌtʃˌlaɪk] ADJECTIVE OR PRONOUN
used to refer to things similar to those already mentioned *e.g. shampoos, talcs, toothbrushes, and suchlike*

suck [sʌk] **sucks, sucking, sucked** VERB

1 If you suck something, you hold it in your mouth and pull at it with your cheeks and tongue, usually to get liquid out of it.

2 To suck something in a particular direction means to draw it there with a powerful force.

3 INFORMAL
To suck up to someone means to do things to please them in order to obtain praise or approval.

sucker ['sʌkə] **suckers** NOUN

1 INFORMAL
If you call someone a sucker, you mean that they

are easily fooled or cheated.

2 Suckers are pads on the bodies of some animals and insects which they use to cling to a surface.

suckle ['sʌkᵊl] **suckles, suckling, suckled**
VERB
When a mother suckles a baby, she feeds it with milk from her breast.

sucrose ['sju:krəʊz] NOUN; TECHNICAL
Sucrose is sugar in crystalline form found in sugar cane and sugar beet.

suction ['sʌkʃən] NOUN
1 Suction is the force involved when a substance is drawn or sucked from one place to another.

2 Suction is the process by which two surfaces stick together when the air between them is removed. *e.g. They stay there by suction.*

Sudanese [,su:dᵊ'ni:z] ADJECTIVE
1 belonging or relating to the Sudan
> NOUN
2 someone who comes from the Sudan

sudden ['sʌdᵊn] ADJECTIVE
happening quickly and unexpectedly *e.g. a sudden cry*
suddenly ADVERB, **suddenness** NOUN

● THESAURUS
abrupt: *Her idyllic world came to an abrupt end when her parents died.*
hasty: *his hasty departure*
quick: *I had to make a quick decision.*
swift: *a swift blow to the stomach*
unexpected: *His death was totally unexpected.*
<<OPPOSITE *gradual*

sudoku [sʊ'dəʊkʊ] NOUN
a puzzle in which you have to enter numbers in a square made up of nine three-by-three grids, so that every column, row, and grid contains the numbers one to nine
[WORD HISTORY: Japanese for 'numbers singly']

sue [sju:] **sues, suing, sued** VERB
To sue someone means to start a legal case against them, usually to claim money from them.

suede [sweɪd] NOUN
Suede is a thin, soft leather with a rough surface.
[WORD HISTORY: from French GANTS DE SUÈDE meaning 'gloves from Sweden']

suffer ['sʌfə] **suffers, suffering, suffered**
VERB
1 If someone is suffering pain, or suffering as a result of an unpleasant situation, they are badly affected by it.

● THESAURUS
bear: *He bore his trials with dignity and grace.*

endure: *The writer endured a harsh life.*
experience: *Widows seem to experience more distress than do widowers.*
go through: *I wouldn't like to go through that again.*
sustain: *He had sustained massive facial injuries.*
undergo: *He had to undergo a body search.*
2 If something suffers as a result of neglect or a difficult situation, its condition or quality becomes worse. *e.g. The bus service is suffering.*
sufferer NOUN, **suffering** NOUN

suffice [sə'faɪs] **suffices, sufficing, sufficed** VERB; FORMAL
If something suffices, it is enough or adequate for a purpose.

sufficient [sə'fɪʃənt] ADJECTIVE
If a supply or quantity is sufficient for a purpose, there is enough of it available.
sufficiently ADVERB

● THESAURUS
adequate: *an adequate income*
ample: *an ample supply of petrol*
enough: *enough cash to live on*
<<OPPOSITE *insufficient*

suffix ['sʌfɪks] **suffixes** NOUN
(ENGLISH) a group of letters which is added to the end of a word to form a new word, for example '-ology' or '-itis'

suffocate ['sʌfə,keɪt] **suffocates, suffocating, suffocated** VERB
To suffocate means to die as a result of having too little air or oxygen to breathe.
suffocation NOUN

suffrage ['sʌfrɪdʒ] NOUN
Suffrage is the right to vote in political elections.

suffragette [,sʌfrə'dʒɛt] **suffragettes**
NOUN
a woman who, at the beginning of the 20th century, campaigned for women to be given the right to vote

suffused [sə'fju:zd] ADJECTIVE; LITERARY
If something is suffused with light or colour, light or colour has gradually spread over it.

sugar ['ʃʊgə] NOUN
Sugar is a sweet substance used to sweeten food and drinks.

suggest [sə'dʒɛst] **suggests, suggesting, suggested** VERB
1 If you suggest a plan or idea to someone, you mention it as a possibility for them to consider.

● THESAURUS
advise: *I advise you to keep quiet.*
advocate: *Mr Jones advocates longer school days.*
propose: *And where do you propose building such a huge thing?*

S

recommend: *I have no qualms about recommending this approach.*

2 If something suggests a particular thought or impression, it makes you think in that way or gives you that impression. *e.g. Nothing you say suggests he is mentally ill.*

● THESAURUS
hint: *The President hinted that he might make some changes.*
imply: *The tone of the report implied that his death was inevitable.*
indicate: *She has indicated that she may resign.*
insinuate: *an article which insinuated that he was lying*
intimate: *He did intimate that he is seeking legal action.*

suggestion [sə'dʒɛstʃən] suggestions
NOUN

1 a plan or idea that is mentioned as a possibility for someone to consider

● THESAURUS
plan: *The government is being asked to consider the plan.*
proposal: *the proposal to do away with nuclear weapons*
proposition: *a business proposition*
recommendation: *a range of recommendations for change*

2 A suggestion of something is a very slight indication or faint sign of it. *e.g. a suggestion of dishonesty*

● THESAURUS
hint: *He showed only the slightest hint of emotion.*
indication: *He gave no indication of remorse.*
insinuation: *The insinuation is that I have something to hide.*
intimation: *He did not give any intimation that he was going to resign.*
trace: *No traces of violence were found on the body.*

suggestive [sə'dʒɛstɪv] ADJECTIVE

1 Something that is suggestive of a particular thing gives a slight hint or sign of it.

2 Suggestive remarks or gestures make people think about sex.

suicidal [ˌsuːɪ'saɪdəl] ADJECTIVE

1 People who are suicidal want to kill themselves.

2 Suicidal behaviour is so dangerous that it is likely to result in death. *e.g. a mad suicidal attack*

suicide ['suːɪˌsaɪd] NOUN
People who commit suicide deliberately kill themselves.
[WORD HISTORY: from Latin SUI meaning 'of oneself' and CAEDERE meaning 'to kill']

suicide bomber suicide bombers NOUN
a terrorist who carries out a bomb attack,

knowing that he or she will be killed in the explosion
suicide bombing NOUN

suit [suːt] suits, suiting, suited NOUN

1 a matching jacket and trousers or skirt

2 In a court of law, a suit is a legal action taken by one person against another.

3 one of four different types of card in a pack of playing cards. The four suits are hearts, clubs, diamonds, and spades

> VERB

4 If a situation or course of action suits you, it is appropriate or acceptable for your purpose.

● THESAURUS
be acceptable to: *The name chosen had to be acceptable to everyone.*
do: *A holiday at home will do me just fine.*
please: *I'll leave when it pleases me and not before.*
satisfy: *Nothing you can do will satisfy him.*

5 If a piece of clothing or a colour suits you, you look good when you are wearing it.

6 If you do something to suit yourself, you do it because you want to and without considering other people.

suitable ['suːtəbəl] ADJECTIVE
right or acceptable for a particular purpose or occasion
suitability NOUN, **suitably** ADVERB

● THESAURUS
acceptable: *a mutually acceptable new contract*
appropriate: *an appropriate outfit for the occasion*
apt: *an apt name*
fit: *the suggestion that she is not a fit mother*
fitting: *a fitting background for her beauty*
proper: *It was not thought proper for a woman to be on stage.*
right: *He always said just the right thing.*
satisfactory: *a satisfactory arrangement*
<<OPPOSITE unsuitable

suitcase ['suːtˌkeɪs] suitcases NOUN
a case in which you carry your clothes when you are travelling

suite [swiːt] suites NOUN

1 In a hotel, a suite is a set of rooms.

2 a set of matching furniture or bathroom fittings

suited ['suːtɪd] ADJECTIVE
right or appropriate for a particular purpose or person *e.g. He is well suited to be minister for the arts.*

suitor ['suːtə] suitors NOUN; OLD-FASHIONED, INFORMAL
A woman's suitor is a man who wants to marry her.

sulk [sʌlk] sulks, sulking, sulked VERB
Someone who is sulking is showing their

annoyance by being silent and moody.

sulky ['sʌlkɪ] **sulkier, sulkiest** ADJECTIVE
showing annoyance by being silent and moody

● **THESAURUS**
huffy: *What are you being so huffy about?*
moody: *Her husband had become withdrawn and moody.*
petulant: *He's just being childish and petulant.*
resentful: *a resentful workforce*
sullen: *He lapsed into a sullen silence.*

sullen ['sʌlən] ADJECTIVE
behaving in a bad-tempered and disagreeably silent way *e.g. a sullen and resentful workforce*

sulphur ['sʌlfə] NOUN
Sulphur is a pale yellow nonmetallic element which burns with a very unpleasant smell.

sultan ['sʌltən] **sultans** NOUN
In some Muslim countries, the ruler of the country is called the sultan.
[WORD HISTORY: from Arabic SULTAN meaning 'rule']

sultana [sʌl'tɑːnə] **sultanas** NOUN
1 a dried grape
2 the wife of a sultan

sum [sʌm] **sums, summing, summed** NOUN
1 an amount of money
2 In arithmetic, a sum is a calculation.
3 The sum of something is the total amount of it.
sum up VERB
4 If you sum something up, you briefly describe its main points.

● **THESAURUS**
recapitulate: *Let's just recapitulate the essential points.*
summarize: *The article can be summarized in three sentences.*

summarize ['sʌmə,raɪz] **summarizes, summarizing, summarized;** also spelt **summarise** VERB
(EXAM TERM) To summarize something means to give a short account of its main points.

summary ['sʌmərɪ] **summaries** NOUN
1 A summary of something is a short account of its main points.

● **THESAURUS**
outline: *an outline of the proposal*
review: *a film review*
rundown: *Here's a rundown of the options.*
summing-up: *The judge concluded his summing-up.*
synopsis: *a brief synopsis of the book*

> ADJECTIVE
2 A summary action is done without delay or

careful thought. *e.g. Summary executions are common.*
summarily ADVERB

summer ['sʌmə] **summers** NOUN
Summer is the season between spring and autumn.

summit ['sʌmɪt] **summits** NOUN
1 The summit of a mountain is its top.
2 a meeting between leaders of different countries to discuss particular issues

summon ['sʌmən] **summons, summoning, summoned** VERB
1 If someone summons you, they order you to go to them.
2 If you summon up strength or energy, you make a great effort to be strong or energetic.

summons ['sʌmənz] **summonses** NOUN
1 an official order to appear in court
2 an order to go to someone *e.g. The result was a summons to headquarters.*

sumptuous ['sʌmptjʊəs] ADJECTIVE
Something that is sumptuous is magnificent and obviously very expensive.

sum total NOUN
The sum total of a number of things is all of them added or considered together.

sun [sʌn] **suns, sunning, sunned** NOUN
1 The sun is the star providing heat and light for the planets revolving around it in our solar system.
2 You refer to heat and light from the sun as sun. *e.g. We need a bit of sun.*
> VERB
3 If you sun yourself, you sit in the sunshine.

sunbathe ['sʌn,beɪð] **sunbathes, sunbathing, sunbathed** VERB
If you sunbathe, you sit in the sunshine to get a suntan.

sunburn ['sʌn,bɜːn] NOUN
Sunburn is sore red skin on someone's body due to too much exposure to the rays of the sun.
sunburnt ADJECTIVE

sundae ['sʌndɪ] **sundaes** NOUN
a dish of ice cream with cream and fruit or nuts

Sunday ['sʌndɪ] **Sundays** NOUN
Sunday is the day between Saturday and Monday.
[WORD HISTORY: from Old English SUNNANDÆG meaning 'day of the sun']

Sunday school Sunday schools NOUN
Sunday school is a special class held on Sundays to teach children about Christianity.

S

sundial ['sʌn,daɪəl] **sundials** NOUN
an object used for telling the time, consisting of a pointer which casts a shadow on a flat base marked with the hours

sundry ['sʌndrɪ] ADJECTIVE
1 'Sundry' is used to refer to several things or people of various sorts e.g. *sundry journalists and lawyers*
> PHRASE
2 All and sundry means everyone

sunflower ['sʌn,flaʊə] **sunflowers** NOUN
a tall plant with very large yellow flowers

sunglasses ['sʌn,glɑːsɪz] PLURAL NOUN
Sunglasses are spectacles with dark lenses that you wear to protect your eyes from the sun.

sunken ['sʌŋkən] ADJECTIVE
1 having sunk to the bottom of the sea, a river, or lake e.g. *sunken ships*
2 A sunken object or area has been constructed below the level of the surrounding area. e.g. *a sunken garden*
3 curving inwards e.g. *Her cheeks were sunken.*

sunlight ['sʌnlaɪt] NOUN
Sunlight is the bright light produced when the sun is shining.
sunlit ADJECTIVE

sunny ['sʌnɪ] **sunnier, sunniest** ADJECTIVE
When it is sunny, the sun is shining.

sunrise ['sʌn,raɪz] **sunrises** NOUN
Sunrise is the time in the morning when the sun first appears, and the colours produced in the sky at that time.

sunset ['sʌn,sɛt] **sunsets** NOUN
Sunset is the time in the evening when the sun disappears below the horizon, and the colours produced in the sky at that time.

sunshine ['sʌn,ʃaɪn] NOUN
Sunshine is the bright light produced when the sun is shining.

sunstroke ['sʌn,strəʊk] NOUN
Sunstroke is an illness caused by spending too much time in hot sunshine.

suntan ['sʌn,tæn] **suntans** NOUN
If you have a suntan, the sun has turned your skin brown.
suntanned ADJECTIVE

super ['suːpə] ADJECTIVE
very nice or very good e.g. *a super party*

super- PREFIX
'Super-' is used to describe something that is larger or better than similar things e.g. *a European superstate*

[WORD HISTORY: from Latin SUPER meaning 'above']

superb [sʊ'pɜːb] ADJECTIVE
very good indeed
superbly ADVERB
● THESAURUS
breathtaking: *The house has breathtaking views.*
excellent: *You've done an excellent job.*
exquisite: *His photography is exquisite.*
magnificent: *a magnificent country house*
marvellous: *She is a marvellous cook.*
outstanding: *an outstanding performance*
splendid: *a splendid Victorian mansion*
superior: *a superior blend of the finest coffee beans*
unrivalled: *He has an unrivalled knowledge of British politics.*
wonderful: *The sun setting over the mountains was a wonderful sight.*

supercilious [,suːpə'sɪlɪəs] ADJECTIVE
If you are supercilious, you behave in a scornful way towards other people because you think they are inferior to you.

superego [,suː'pɜːr'iːgəʊ] NOUN; TECHNICAL
Your superego is the part of your mind that controls your ideas of right and wrong and produces feelings of guilt.

superficial [,suːpə'fɪʃəl] ADJECTIVE
1 involving only the most obvious or most general aspects of something e.g. *a superficial knowledge of music*
2 not having a deep, serious, or genuine interest in anything e.g. *a superficial and rather silly woman*
3 Superficial wounds are not very deep or severe.
superficially ADVERB

superfluous [suː'pɜːfluəs] ADJECTIVE; FORMAL
unnecessary or no longer needed

superhuman [,suːpə'hjuːmən] ADJECTIVE
having much greater power or ability than is normally expected of humans e.g. *superhuman strength*

superimpose [,suːpərɪm'pəʊz]
superimposes, superimposing, superimposed VERB
To superimpose one image on another means to put the first image on top of the other so that they are seen as one image.

superintendent [,suːpərɪn'tɛndənt]
superintendents NOUN
1 a police officer above the rank of inspector
2 a person whose job is to be responsible for a particular thing e.g. *the superintendent of prisons*

superior [suː'pɪərɪə] **superiors** ADJECTIVE
1 better or of higher quality than other similar things
● THESAURUS
better: *I'd like to move to a better area.*

choice: *the choicest cuts of meat*
de luxe: *a de luxe model*
exceptional: *children with exceptional ability*
first-rate: *a first-rate thriller*
surpassing: *her surpassing achievements*
unrivalled: *colour printing of unrivalled quality*
<<OPPOSITE *inferior*

2 in a position of higher authority than another person

3 showing too much pride and self-importance *e.g. Jerry smiled in a superior way.*

THESAURUS
condescending: *I'm fed up with your condescending attitude.*
disdainful: *She passed along with a disdainful look.*
haughty: *He spoke in a haughty tone.*
lofty: *lofty disdain*
patronizing: *his patronizing attitude to the homeless*
snobbish: *a snobbish dislike for their intellectual inferiors*
stuck-up: informal *She was a famous actress, but she wasn't a bit stuck-up.*
supercilious: *His manner is supercilious and arrogant.*

> NOUN
4 Your superiors are people who are in a higher position than you in society or an organization.
superiority NOUN

THESAURUS
boss: informal *Her boss was very supportive.*
manager: *His plans found favour with his manager.*
senior: *He was described by his seniors as a model officer.*
supervisor: *Each student has a supervisor.*
<<OPPOSITE *inferior*

superlative [suːˈpɜːlətɪv] **superlatives**
NOUN
1 In grammar, the superlative is the form of an adjective which indicates that the person or thing described has more of a particular quality than anyone or anything else. For example, 'quickest', 'best', and 'easiest' are all superlatives.
> ADJECTIVE
2 FORMAL
very good indeed *e.g. a superlative performance*

supermarket [ˈsuːpəˌmɑːkɪt]
supermarkets NOUN
a shop selling food and household goods arranged so that you can help yourself and pay for everything at a till by the exit

supernatural [ˌsuːpəˈnætʃrəl] ADJECTIVE
1 Something that is supernatural, for example ghosts or witchcraft, cannot be explained by normal scientific laws.

> NOUN
2 You can refer to supernatural things as the supernatural.

superpower [ˈsuːpəˌpaʊə] **superpowers**
NOUN
a very powerful and influential country such as the USA

supersede [ˌsuːpəˈsiːd] **supersedes, superseding, superseded** VERB
If something supersedes another thing, it replaces it because it is more modern. *e.g. New York superseded Paris as the centre for modern art.*

supersonic [ˌsuːpəˈsɒnɪk] ADJECTIVE
A supersonic aircraft can travel faster than the speed of sound.

superstar [ˈsuːpəˌstɑː] **superstars** NOUN
You can refer to a very famous entertainer or sports player as a superstar.

superstition [ˌsuːpəˈstɪʃən] **superstitions**
NOUN
Superstition is a belief in things like magic and powers that bring good or bad luck.
superstitious ADJECTIVE
[WORD HISTORY: from Latin SUPERSTITIO meaning 'dread of the supernatural']

supervise [ˈsuːpəˌvaɪz] **supervises, supervising, supervised** VERB
To supervise someone means to check and direct what they are doing to make sure that they do it correctly.
supervision NOUN, **supervisor** NOUN

THESAURUS
be in charge of: *He is in charge of the whole project.*
direct: *Christopher will direct day-to-day operations.*
have charge of: *He has charge of a three-acre estate.*
keep an eye on: *I told you to keep an eye on the children.*
manage: *I manage a small team of workers.*
oversee: *an architect to oversee the work*
run: *Each teacher will run a different workshop.*

supper [ˈsʌpə] **suppers** NOUN
Supper is a meal eaten in the evening or a snack eaten before you go to bed.

supplant [səˈplɑːnt] **supplants, supplanting, supplanted** VERB; FORMAL
To supplant someone or something means to take their place. *e.g. By the 1930s the wristwatch had supplanted the pocket watch.*

supple [ˈsʌpəl] ADJECTIVE
able to bend and move easily

supplement supplements, supplementing, supplemented VERB
[ˈsʌplɪˌmɛnt]

1 To supplement something means to add something to it to improve it. *e.g. Many village men supplemented their wages by fishing for salmon.*

● THESAURUS

add to: *A good bathroom adds to the value of any house.*

augment: *a way to augment the family income*

complement: *an in-work benefit that complements earnings*

reinforce: *measures which will reinforce their current strengths*

top up: *compulsory contributions to top up pension schemes*

> NOUN ['sʌplɪmənt]

2 something that is added to something else to improve it

● THESAURUS

addition: *an addition to the existing system*

appendix: *The report includes a six-page appendix.*

complement: *The photographs are a perfect complement to the text.*

extra: *an optional extra*

supplementary [ˌsʌplɪ'mɛntərɪ] ADJECTIVE
added to something else to improve it *e.g. supplementary doses of vitamin E*

supplier [sə'plaɪə] **suppliers** NOUN
a firm which provides particular goods

supply [sə'plaɪ] **supplies, supplying, supplied** VERB

1 To supply someone with something means to provide it or send it to them.

● THESAURUS

equip: *plans for equipping the island with water*

furnish: *They'll be able to furnish you with the details.*

give: *We'll give you all the information you need.*

provide: *They'll provide all the equipment.*

> NOUN

2 A supply of something is an amount available for use. *e.g. the world's supply of precious metals*

● THESAURUS

cache: *a cache of weapons and explosives*

fund: *an extraordinary fund of energy*

hoard: *a hoard of food and petrol*

reserve: *The Gulf has 65% of the world's oil reserves.*

stock: *stocks of paper and ink*

stockpile: *stockpiles of chemical weapons*

store: *I have a store of food and water here.*

> PLURAL NOUN

3 Supplies are food and equipment for a particular purpose.

● THESAURUS

equipment: *vital medical equipment*

provisions: *provisions for two weeks*

rations: *Aid officials said food rations had been distributed.*

stores: *an important part of a ship's stores*

support [sə'pɔːt] **supports, supporting, supported** VERB

1 If you support someone, you agree with their aims and want them to succeed.

● THESAURUS

back: *a new witness to back his claim*

champion: *He passionately championed the cause.*

defend: *He defended all of Clarence's decisions, right or wrong.*

promote: *He continued to promote the idea of Scottish autonomy.*

second: *The Prime Minister seconded the call for discipline.*

side with: *accused of siding with terrorists*

uphold: *We uphold the capitalist free economy.*

<<OPPOSITE oppose

2 If you support someone who is in difficulties, you are kind, encouraging, and helpful to them.

● THESAURUS

encourage: *When things aren't going well, he encourages me.*

help: *He'd do anything to help a friend.*

3 If something supports an object, it is underneath it and holding it up.

● THESAURUS

bolster: *steel beams used to bolster the roof*

brace: *The roll-over bar braces the car's structure.*

hold up: *Her legs wouldn't hold her up.*

prop up: *Use sticks to prop the plants up.*

reinforce: *They had to reinforce the walls with exterior beams.*

4 To support someone or something means to prevent them from falling by holding them.

5 To support someone financially means to provide them with money.

> NOUN

6 an object that is holding something up

● THESAURUS

brace: *He will have to wear a neck brace for several days.*

foundation: *the foundation on which the bridge was built*

pillar: *the pillars supporting the roof*

post: *The device is fixed to a post.*

prop: *a structural part such as a beam or prop*

7 Moral support is encouragement given to someone to help them do something difficult.

8 Financial support is money that is provided for someone or something.

supportable ADJECTIVE

supporter [sə'pɔːtə] **supporters** NOUN
a person who agrees with or helps someone

THESAURUS

adherent: *Communism was gaining adherents in Latin America.*
advocate: *a strong advocate of free market policies*
ally: *a close political ally*
champion: *a champion of women's causes*
fan: *fans of this football club*
follower: *followers of the Dalai Lama*
sponsor: *the first sponsor of Buddhism in Japan*

supportive [sə'pɔːtɪv] ADJECTIVE
A supportive person is encouraging and helpful to someone who is in difficulties.

suppose [sə'pəʊz] **supposes, supposing, supposed** VERB
1 If you suppose that something is the case, you think that it is likely. *e.g. I supposed that would be too obvious.*

THESAURUS

assume: *I assume you have permission to be here?*
believe: *We believe them to be hidden somewhere in the area.*
expect: *I don't expect you've had much experience in the job yet.*
guess: *I guess you're right.*
imagine: *We tend to imagine that the Victorians were prim and proper.*
presume: *I presume you're here on business.*
think: formal *Do you think she was embarrassed?*

> PHRASE
2 You can say **I suppose** when you are not entirely certain or enthusiastic about something. *e.g. Yes, I suppose he could come.*

> CONJUNCTION
3 You can use 'suppose' or 'supposing' when you are considering or suggesting a possible situation or action. *e.g. Supposing he were to break down under interrogation?.*

supposed [sə'pəʊzd] ADJECTIVE
1 'Supposed' is used to express doubt about something that is generally believed *e.g. the supposed culprit*
2 If something is supposed to be done or to happen, it is planned, expected, or required to be done or to happen. *e.g. You are supposed to report it to the police... It was supposed to be this afternoon.*

THESAURUS

expected: *You were expected to arrive much earlier than this.*
meant: *Parties are meant to be fun.*
obliged: *He is legally obliged to declare his interests.*
required: *Will I be required to come to every meeting?*

3 Something that is supposed to be the case is generally believed or thought to be so. *e.g. Wimbledon is supposed to be the best tournament of them all.*

supposedly ADVERB

THESAURUS

alleged: *The accused is alleged to have killed a man.*
assumed: *As usual, the mistakes were assumed to be my fault.*
believed: *He is believed to have died in 1117.*
meant: *They are meant to be one of the top teams in the world.*
presumed: *This area is presumed to be safe.*
reputed: *The monster is reputed to live in the deep waters of a Scottish loch.*
rumoured: *They are rumoured to be on the verge of splitting up.*

supposition [ˌsʌpə'zɪʃən] **suppositions** NOUN
something that is believed or assumed to be true *e.g. the supposition that science requires an ordered universe*

suppress [sə'pres] **suppresses, suppressing, suppressed** VERB
1 If an army or government suppresses an activity, it prevents people from doing it.

THESAURUS

crush: *a plan to crush the uprising*
quash: *It may help to quash these rumours.*
quell: *The army moved in to quell the uprising.*
stamp out: *steps to stamp out bullying in schools*
stop: *measures to stop the trade in ivory*

2 If someone suppresses a piece of information, they prevent it from becoming generally known.
3 If you suppress your feelings, you stop yourself expressing them.
suppression NOUN

THESAURUS

conceal: *Robert could not conceal his relief.*
contain: *He could hardly contain his rage.*
curb: *He curbed his temper.*
repress: *people who repress their emotions*
restrain: *unable to restrain her anger*
smother: *I smothered a chuckle.*
stifle: *Miller stifled a yawn and looked at his watch.*

supremacy [sʊ'preməsi] NOUN
If a group of people has supremacy over others, it is more powerful than the others.

supreme [sʊ'priːm] ADJECTIVE
1 'Supreme' is used as part of a title to indicate the highest level of an organization or system *e.g. the Supreme Court*
2 'Supreme' is used to emphasize the greatness of something *e.g. the supreme achievement of the human race*
supremely ADVERB

THESAURUS

chief: *his chief rival*
foremost: *the world's foremost scientists*

greatest: *the city's greatest soccer idol*
highest: *the highest academic achievement*
leading: *the world's leading basketball players*
paramount: *a factor of paramount importance*
pre-eminent: *a pre-eminent political figure*
principal: *the principal reason*
top: *the president's top military advisers*
ultimate: *the ultimate international accolade, the Nobel Prize*

surcharge ['sɜːˌtʃɑːdʒ] **surcharges** NOUN
an additional charge

sure [ʃʊə] **surer, surest** ADJECTIVE
1 If you are sure about something, you have no doubts about it.

● THESAURUS
certain: *certain of getting a place on the team*
clear: *He is not clear on how he will go about it.*
convinced: *He is convinced it's your fault.*
definite: *a definite answer*
positive: *I'm positive it will happen.*
satisfied: *We must be satisfied that the treatment is safe.*
<<OPPOSITE *unsure*

2 If you are sure of yourself, you are very confident.

3 If something is sure to happen, it will definitely happen.

4 Sure means reliable or accurate. *e.g. a sure sign that something is wrong*

● THESAURUS
definite: *a definite advantage*
dependable: *dependable information*
foolproof: *a foolproof system*
infallible: *an infallible eye for detail*
reliable: *a reliable source*
trustworthy: *trustworthy reports*
undeniable: *a sad but undeniable fact*

> PHRASE
5 If you **make sure** about something, you check it or take action to see that it is done.

> INTERJECTION
6 Sure is an informal way of saying 'yes'. *e.g. 'Can I come too?' – 'Sure'*

surely ['ʃʊəlɪ] ADVERB
'Surely' is used to emphasize the belief that something is the case *e.g. Surely these people here knew that?*.

surf [sɜːf] **surfs, surfing, surfed** VERB
1 When you surf, you go surfing.

2 When you surf the Internet, you go from website to website reading the information.

> NOUN
3 Surf is the white foam that forms on the top of waves when they break near the shore.

surface ['sɜːfɪs] **surfaces, surfacing, surfaced** NOUN
1 The surface of something is the top or outside area of it.

2 The surface of a situation is what can be seen easily rather than what is hidden or not immediately obvious.

> VERB
3 If someone surfaces, they come up from under water to the surface.

surfboard ['sɜːfˌbɔːd] **surfboards** NOUN
a long narrow lightweight board used for surfing

surf club **surf clubs** NOUN
In Australia, a surf club is an organization of lifesavers in charge of safety on a particular beach, and which often provides leisure facilities.

surfeit ['sɜːfɪt] NOUN
If there is a surfeit of something, there is too much of it.

surfing ['sɜːfɪŋ] NOUN
Surfing is a sport which involves riding towards the shore on the top of a large wave while standing on a surfboard.

surge [sɜːdʒ] **surges, surging, surged** NOUN
1 a sudden great increase in the amount of something *e.g. a surge of panic*

> VERB
2 If something surges, it moves suddenly and powerfully. *e.g. The soldiers surged forwards.*

surgeon ['sɜːdʒən] **surgeons** NOUN
a doctor who performs operations

surgery ['sɜːdʒərɪ] **surgeries** NOUN
1 Surgery is medical treatment involving cutting open part of the patient's body to treat the damaged part.

2 The room or building where a doctor or dentist works is called a surgery.

3 A period of time during which a doctor is available to see patients is called surgery. *e.g. evening surgery*

surgical ['sɜːdʒɪkəl] ADJECTIVE
used in or involving a medical operation *e.g. surgical gloves*
surgically ADVERB

surly ['sɜːlɪ] **surlier, surliest** ADJECTIVE
rude and bad-tempered
surliness NOUN

surmise [sɜːˈmaɪz] **surmises, surmising, surmised** VERB; FORMAL
To surmise something means to guess it. *e.g. I surmised it was of French manufacture.*

surmount [sɜːˈmaʊnt] **surmounts, surmounting, surmounted** VERB

1 To surmount a difficulty means to manage to solve it.

2 FORMAL
If something is surmounted by a particular thing, that thing is on top of it. *e.g. The island is surmounted by a huge black castle.*

surname ['sɜːˌneɪm] **surnames** NOUN
Your surname is your last name which you share with other members of your family.

surpass [sɜːˈpɑːs] **surpasses, surpassing, surpassed** VERB; FORMAL
To surpass someone or something means to be better than them.

surplus ['sɜːpləs] **surpluses** NOUN
If there is a surplus of something there is more of it than is needed.

surprise [səˈpraɪz] **surprises, surprising, surprised** NOUN

1 an unexpected event

● THESAURUS
bombshell: *His departure was a bombshell for the team.*
jolt: *The news gave the man a jolt.*
revelation: *Degas's work had been a revelation to her.*
shock: *I got a shock when I saw her.*
start: *You gave me quite a start.*

2 Surprise is the feeling caused when something unexpected happens.

● THESAURUS
amazement: *He stared in baffled amazement.*
astonishment: *"What?" Meg asked in astonishment.*
incredulity: *The announcement has been met with incredulity.*
wonder: *Cross shook his head in wonder.*

> VERB
3 If something surprises you, it gives you a feeling of surprise.

● THESAURUS
amaze: *Most of the cast were amazed by the play's success.*
astonish: *I was astonished to discover his true age.*
astound: *He was astounded at the result.*
stagger: *I was staggered by his reaction.*
stun: *Audiences were stunned by the film's tragic end.*
take aback: *Derek was taken aback when a man answered the phone.*

4 If you surprise someone, you do something they were not expecting.
surprising ADJECTIVE

surreal [səˈrɪəl] ADJECTIVE
very strange and dreamlike

surrender [səˈrɛndə] **surrenders, surrendering, surrendered** VERB

1 To surrender means to stop fighting and agree that the other side has won.

● THESAURUS
capitulate: *They had no choice but to capitulate.*
give in: *She gave in to him on everything.*
submit: *I refuse to submit to their demands.*
succumb: *The Minister said his country would never succumb to pressure.*
yield: *The government had to yield to local opinion.*

2 If you surrender to a temptation or feeling, you let it take control of you.

3 To surrender something means to give it up to someone else. *e.g. The gallery director surrendered his keys.*

● THESAURUS
cede: *After the war, Spain ceded the island to America.*
give up: *She is loath to give up her hard-earned liberty.*
relinquish: *He does not intend to relinquish power.*
renounce: *He renounced his claim to the throne.*
yield: *He was obliged to yield territory to France.*

> NOUN
4 Surrender is a situation in which one side in a fight agrees that the other side has won and gives in.

● THESAURUS
capitulation: *the German capitulation at the end of the First World War*
submission: *The army intends to starve the city into submission.*

surreptitious [ˌsʌrəpˈtɪʃəs] ADJECTIVE
A surreptitious action is done secretly or so that no-one will notice. *e.g. a surreptitious glance*
surreptitiously ADVERB

surrogate ['sʌrəgɪt] **surrogates** ADJECTIVE
1 acting as a substitute for someone or something

> NOUN
2 a person or thing that acts as a substitute

surround [səˈraʊnd] **surrounds, surrounding, surrounded** VERB

1 To surround someone or something means to be situated all around them.

● THESAURUS
encircle: *A forty-foot-high concrete wall encircles the jail.*
enclose: *The land was enclosed by a fence.*
encompass: *the largest lake in Canada wholly encompassed by a town*
envelop: *The rich smell of the forest enveloped us.*
hem in: *a valley hemmed in by mountains*

> NOUN
2 The surround of something is its outside edge or border.

S

surrounding [səˈraʊndɪŋ] **surroundings**
ADJECTIVE
1 The surrounding area of a particular place is the area around it. *e.g. the surrounding countryside*
> PLURAL NOUN
2 You can refer to the area and environment around a place or person as their surroundings. *e.g. very comfortable surroundings*

● THESAURUS
background: *a fitting background for her beauty*
environment: *a safe environment for marine mammals*
location: *filmed in an exotic location*
neighbourhood: *living in an affluent neighbourhood*
setting: *Rome is the perfect setting for romance.*

surveillance [sɜːˈveɪləns] NOUN
Surveillance is the close watching of a person's activities by the police or army.
[WORD HISTORY: from French SURVEILLER meaning 'to watch over']

survey surveys, surveying, surveyed VERB
[sɜːˈveɪ]
1 To survey something means to look carefully at the whole of it.
2 To survey a building or piece of land means to examine it carefully in order to make a report or plan of its structure and features.
> NOUN [ˈsɜːveɪ]
3 A survey of something is a detailed examination of it, often in the form of a report.

surveyor [sɜːˈveɪə] **surveyors** NOUN
a person whose job is to survey buildings or land

survival [səˈvaɪvəl] **survivals** NOUN
Survival is being able to continue living or existing in spite of great danger or difficulties. *e.g. There was no hope of survival.*

survive [səˈvaɪv] **survives, surviving, survived** VERB
To survive means to continue to live or exist in spite of a great danger or difficulties. *e.g. a German monk who survived the shipwreck*
survivor NOUN

● THESAURUS
endure: *Somehow their friendship endures.*
last: *Nothing lasts forever.*
live: *having lived through the 1930s depression*
outlive: *They have outlived the horror of the war.*
pull through: *He should pull through okay.*

sus- PREFIX 'Sus-' is another form of **sub-**

susceptible [səˈsɛptəbəl] ADJECTIVE
If you are susceptible to something, you are likely to be influenced or affected by it. *e.g. Elderly people are more susceptible to infection.*

susceptibility NOUN

suspect suspects, suspecting, suspected
VERB [səˈspɛkt]
1 If you suspect something, you think that it is likely or is probably true. *e.g. I suspected that the report would be sent.*

● THESAURUS
believe: *Police believe the attacks were carried out by nationalists.*
feel: *I somehow feel he was involved.*
guess: *As you probably guessed, I don't like him much.*
suppose: *The problem is more complex than he supposes.*
2 If you suspect something, you have doubts about its reliability. *e.g. He suspected her intent.*

● THESAURUS
distrust: *I don't have any particular reason to distrust them.*
doubt: *Do you doubt my word?*
mistrust: *He mistrusts all journalists.*
3 If you suspect someone of doing something wrong, you think that they have done it.
> NOUN [ˈsʌspɛkt]
4 someone who is thought to be guilty of a crime
> ADJECTIVE [ˈsʌspɛkt]
5 If something is suspect, it cannot be trusted or relied upon. *e.g. a rather suspect holy man*

● THESAURUS
dodgy: British and Australian and New Zealand; informal *a dodgy car dealer*
doubtful: *These details are of doubtful origin.*
dubious: *dubious practices*
fishy: informal *There's something very fishy about it.*
questionable: *the questionable motives of politicians*

suspend [səˈspɛnd] **suspends, suspending, suspended** VERB
1 If something is suspended, it is hanging from somewhere. *e.g. the television set suspended above the bar*
2 To suspend an activity or event means to delay it or stop it for a while.
3 If someone is suspended from their job, they are told not to do it for a period of time, usually as a punishment.

suspender [səˈspɛndə] **suspenders** NOUN
Suspenders are fastenings which hold up a woman's stockings.

suspense [səˈspɛns] NOUN
Suspense is a state of excitement or anxiety caused by having to wait for something.

suspension [səˈspɛnʃən] NOUN
1 The suspension of something is the delaying or stopping of it.

2 A person's suspension is their removal from a job for a period of time, usually as a punishment.

3 The suspension of a vehicle consists of springs and shock absorbers which provide a smooth ride.

4 a liquid mixture in which very small bits of a solid material are contained and are not dissolved

suspicion [sə'spɪʃən] **suspicions** NOUN

1 Suspicion is the feeling of not trusting someone or the feeling that something is wrong.

○ THESAURUS

distrust: *an instinctive distrust of authority*
doubt: *I have my doubts about his ability to govern.*
misgiving: *His first words filled us with misgiving.*
mistrust: *a deep mistrust of banks*
scepticism: *The report has been greeted with scepticism.*

2 a feeling that something is likely to happen or is probably true *e.g. the suspicion that more could have been achieved*

○ THESAURUS

hunch: *Lowe had a hunch he was on to something.*
idea: *I had an idea that he joined the army later.*
impression: *I get the impression he's hiding something.*

suspicious [sə'spɪʃəs] ADJECTIVE

1 If you are suspicious of someone, you do not trust them.

○ THESAURUS

apprehensive: *She was apprehensive of strangers.*
distrustful: *Voters are deeply distrustful of all politicians.*
doubtful: *At first I was doubtful about their authenticity.*
sceptical: *Other archaeologists are sceptical about his findings.*
wary: *Many people are wary of lawyers.*

2 'Suspicious' is used to describe things that make you think that there is something wrong with a situation *e.g. suspicious circumstances*
suspiciously ADVERB

○ THESAURUS

dodgy: British and Australian and New Zealand; informal *He was a bit of a dodgy character.*
doubtful: *selling something of doubtful quality*
dubious: *This claim seems to us rather dubious.*
fishy: informal *There's something fishy going on here.*
funny: *There's something funny about him.*
questionable: *the questionable motives of politicians*
shady: informal *shady deals*
suspect: *The whole affair has been highly suspect.*

sustain [sə'steɪn] **sustains, sustaining, sustained** VERB

1 To sustain something means to continue it for a period of time. *e.g. Their team-mates were unable to sustain the challenge.*

2 If something sustains you, it gives you energy and strength.

3 FORMAL
To sustain an injury or loss means to suffer it.

sustainable [sə'steɪnəb³l] ADJECTIVE

1 capable of being sustained

2 If economic development or energy resources are sustainable they are capable of being maintained at a steady level without exhausting natural resources or causing ecological damage. *e.g. sustainable forestry*

sustenance ['sʌstənəns] NOUN; FORMAL
Sustenance is food and drink.

swab [swɒb] **swabs, swabbing, swabbed**
NOUN

1 a small piece of cotton wool used for cleaning a wound

> VERB

2 To swab something means to clean it using a large mop and a lot of water.

3 To swab a wound means to clean it or take specimens from it using a swab.

swag [swæg] **swags** NOUN; INFORMAL

1 goods or valuables, especially ones which have been gained dishonestly

2 In Australian and New Zealand English, the bundle of possessions belonging to a tramp.

3 In Australian and New Zealand English, swags of something is lots of it.

swagger ['swægə] **swaggers, swaggering, swaggered** VERB

1 To swagger means to walk in a proud, exaggerated way.

> NOUN

2 an exaggerated walk

swagman ['swæg,mæn] **swagmen** NOUN;
INFORMAL
In Australia and New Zealand in the past, a tramp who carried his possessions on his back.

swallow ['swɒləʊ] **swallows, swallowing, swallowed** VERB

1 If you swallow something, you make it go down your throat and into your stomach.

2 When you swallow, you move your throat muscles as if you were swallowing something, especially when you are nervous.

> NOUN

3 a bird with pointed wings and a long forked tail

swamp [swɒmp] **swamps, swamping, swamped** NOUN

S

1 an area of permanently wet land

> VERB

2 If something is swamped, it is covered or filled with water.

3 If you are swamped by things, you have more than you are able to deal with. *e.g. She was swamped with calls.*

swampy ADJECTIVE

swan [swɒn] **swans** NOUN
a large, usually white, bird with a long neck that lives on rivers or lakes

swap [swɒp] **swaps, swapping, swapped** VERB
To swap one thing for another means to replace the first thing with the second, often by making an exchange with another person. *e.g. Webb swapped shirts with a Leeds player.*

● THESAURUS
barter: *bartering wheat for cotton and timber*
exchange: *exchanging one set of problems for another*
interchange: *Meat can be interchanged with pulses as a source of protein.*
switch: *They switched the tags on the cables.*
trade: *They traded land for goods and money.*

swarm [swɔːm] **swarms, swarming, swarmed** NOUN

1 A swarm of insects is a large group of them flying together.

> VERB

2 When bees or other insects swarm, they fly together in a large group.

3 If people swarm somewhere, a lot of people go there quickly and at the same time. *e.g. the crowds of office workers who swarm across the bridge*

4 If a place is swarming with people, there are a lot of people there.

swarthy ['swɔːðɪ] **swarthier, swarthiest** ADJECTIVE
A swarthy person has a dark complexion.

swashbuckling ['swɒʃˌbʌklɪŋ] ADJECTIVE
'Swashbuckling' is used to describe people who have the exciting behaviour or appearance of pirates

swastika ['swɒstɪkə] **swastikas** NOUN
a symbol in the shape of a cross with each arm bent over at right angles. It was the official symbol of the Nazis in Germany, but in India it is a good luck sign

swat [swɒt] **swats, swatting, swatted** VERB
To swat an insect means to hit it sharply in order to kill it.

swathe [sweɪð] **swathes** NOUN

1 a long strip of cloth that is wrapped around something *e.g. swathes of white silk*

2 A swathe of land is a long strip of it.

swathed [sweɪðd] ADJECTIVE
If someone is swathed in something, they are wrapped in it. *e.g. She was swathed in towels.*

sway [sweɪ] **sways, swaying, swayed** VERB

1 To sway means to lean or swing slowly from side to side.

2 If something sways you, it influences your judgment.

> NOUN

3 LITERARY
Sway is the power to influence people. *e.g. under the sway of more powerful neighbours*

swear [sweə] **swears, swearing, swore, sworn** VERB

1 To swear means to say words that are considered to be very rude or blasphemous.

2 If you swear to something, you state solemnly that you will do it or that it is true.

3 If you swear by something, you firmly believe that it is a reliable cure or solution. *e.g. Some women swear by extra vitamins.*

swearword ['sweəˌwɜːd] **swearwords** NOUN
a word which is considered to be rude or blasphemous, which people use when they are angry

sweat [swɛt] **sweats, sweating, sweated** NOUN

1 Sweat is the salty liquid produced by your sweat glands when you are hot or afraid.

> VERB

2 When you sweat, sweat comes through the pores in your skin in order to lower the temperature of your body.

sweater ['swɛtə] **sweaters** NOUN
a knitted piece of clothing covering your upper body and arms

sweatshirt ['swɛtˌʃɜːt] **sweatshirts** NOUN
a piece of clothing made of thick cotton, covering your upper body and arms

sweaty ['swɛtɪ] ADJECTIVE
covered or soaked with sweat

swede [swiːd] **swedes** NOUN
a large round root vegetable with yellow flesh and a brownish-purple skin
[WORD HISTORY: from Swedish TURNIP because it was introduced from Sweden in the 18th century]

Swede [swiːd] **Swedes** NOUN
someone who comes from Sweden

Swedish ['swiːdɪʃ] ADJECTIVE

1 belonging or relating to Sweden

> NOUN

2 Swedish is the main language spoken in Sweden.

sweep [swiːp] **sweeps, sweeping, swept**
VERB

1 If you sweep the floor, you use a brush to gather up dust or rubbish from it.

2 To sweep things off a surface means to push them all off with a quick, smooth movement.

3 If something sweeps from one place to another, it moves there very quickly. *e.g. A gust of wind swept over the terrace.*

4 If an attitude or new fashion sweeps a place, it spreads rapidly through it. *e.g. a phenomenon that is sweeping America*

> NOUN

5 If you do something with a sweep of your arm, you do it with a wide curving movement of your arm.

sweeping [ˈswiːpɪŋ] ADJECTIVE

1 A sweeping curve or movement is long and wide.

2 A sweeping statement is based on a general assumption rather than on careful thought.

3 affecting a lot of people to a great extent *e.g. sweeping changes*

sweet [swiːt] **sweeter, sweetest; sweets**
ADJECTIVE

1 containing a lot of sugar *e.g. a mug of sweet tea*

● **THESAURUS**
cloying: *a cloying apricot chutney*
sugary: *a sugary meringue pie*
sweetened: *sweetened shortcrust pastry*
<<OPPOSITE *sour*

2 pleasant and satisfying *e.g. sweet success*

3 A sweet smell is soft and fragrant.

● **THESAURUS**
aromatic: *a plant with aromatic leaves*
fragrant: *fragrant clover*
perfumed: *perfumed soaps*
sweet-smelling: *cottage gardens filled with sweet-smelling flowers and herbs*

4 A sweet sound is gentle and tuneful.

● **THESAURUS**
harmonious: *harmonious sounds*
mellow: *mellow background music*
melodious: *The melodious tones of the organ echoed around the great cathedral.*
musical: *He had a soft, musical voice.*
tuneful: *The band were noted for their tuneful backing vocals.*

5 attractive and delightful *e.g. a sweet little baby*

> NOUN

6 Things such as toffees, chocolates, and mints are sweets.

● **THESAURUS**
candy: American *We were sick after eating some syrupy candies she had made.*
confectionery: *The company specializes in selling confectionery from all over the world.*
lolly: Australian and New Zealand *avoid feeding him too many lollies*
sweetie: *She presented him with a jar of his favourite sweeties as a thank-you.*

7 a dessert
sweetly ADVERB, **sweetness** NOUN

sweet corn NOUN
Sweet corn is a long stalk covered with juicy yellow seeds that can be eaten as a vegetable.

sweeten [ˈswiːtᵊn] **sweetens, sweetening, sweetened** VERB
To sweeten food means to add sugar or another sweet substance to it.

sweetener [ˈswiːtᵊnə] **sweeteners** NOUN
a very sweet, artificial substance that can be used instead of sugar

sweetheart [ˈswiːtˌhɑːt] **sweethearts**
NOUN

1 You can call someone who you are very fond of 'sweetheart'.

2 A young person's sweetheart is their boyfriend or girlfriend.

sweet pea   sweet peas NOUN
Sweet peas are delicate, very fragrant climbing flowers.

sweet tooth NOUN
If you have a sweet tooth, you like sweet food very much.

swell [swɛl] **swells, swelling, swelled, swollen** VERB

1 If something swells, it becomes larger and rounder. *e.g. It causes the abdomen to swell.*

2 If an amount swells, it increases in number.

> NOUN

3 The regular up and down movement of the waves at sea can be called a swell.

swelling [ˈswɛlɪŋ] **swellings** NOUN

1 an enlarged area on your body as a result of injury or illness

2 The swelling of something is an increase in its size.

sweltering [ˈswɛltərɪŋ] ADJECTIVE
If the weather is sweltering, it is very hot.

swerve [swɜːv] **swerves, swerving, swerved** VERB

S

To swerve means to suddenly change direction to avoid colliding with something.

THESAURUS
swing: *The car swung off the road.*
turn: *He turned sharply to the left.*
veer: *The vehicle veered out of control.*

swift [swɪft] **swifter, swiftest; swifts**
ADJECTIVE
1 happening or moving very quickly *e.g. a swift glance*

THESAURUS
brisk: *walking at a brisk pace*
express: *a special express service*
fast: *The question is how fast the process will be.*
hurried: *a hurried breakfast*
prompt: *Prompt action is needed.*
quick: *The country has been developing at a very quick pace.*
rapid: *Will the Tunnel provide more rapid transport than ferries?*
speedy: *We wish Bill a speedy recovery.*
<<OPPOSITE slow

> NOUN
2 a bird with narrow crescent-shaped wings
swiftly ADVERB

swig [swɪg] **swigs, swigging, swigged**
INFORMAL VERB
1 To swig a drink means to drink it in large mouthfuls, usually from a bottle.

> NOUN
2 If you have a swig of a drink, you take a large mouthful of it.

swill [swɪl] **swills, swilling, swilled** VERB
1 To swill something means to pour water over it to clean it. *e.g. Swill the can out thoroughly.*

> NOUN
2 Swill is a liquid mixture containing waste food that is fed to pigs.

swim [swɪm] **swims, swimming, swam, swum** VERB
1 To swim means to move through water using various movements with parts of the body.
2 If things are swimming, it seems as if everything you see is moving and you feel dizzy.

> NOUN
3 If you go for a swim, you go into water to swim for pleasure.
swimmer NOUN

swimming ['swɪmɪŋ] NOUN
Swimming is the activity of moving through water using your arms and legs.

swimming bath swimming baths NOUN
a public swimming pool

swimming costume swimming costumes NOUN

the clothing worn by a woman when she goes swimming

swimming pool swimming pools NOUN
a large hole that has been tiled and filled with water for swimming

swimming trunks [trʌŋks] PLURAL NOUN
Swimming trunks are shorts worn by a man when he goes swimming.

swimsuit ['swɪm,suːt] **swimsuits** NOUN
a swimming costume

swindle ['swɪndəl] **swindles, swindling, swindled** VERB
1 To swindle someone means to deceive them to obtain money or property.

> NOUN
2 a trick in which someone is cheated out of money or property
swindler NOUN

swine [swaɪn] **swines** NOUN
1 OLD-FASHIONED Swine are pigs.
2 INFORMAL
If you call someone a swine, you mean they are nasty and spiteful.

swing [swɪŋ] **swings, swinging, swung** VERB
1 If something swings, it moves repeatedly from side to side from a fixed point.
2 If someone or something swings in a particular direction, they turn quickly or move in a sweeping curve in that direction.

> NOUN
3 a seat hanging from a frame or a branch, which moves backwards and forwards when you sit on it
4 A swing in opinion is a significant change in people's opinion.

swipe [swaɪp] **swipes, swiping, swiped** VERB
1 To swipe at something means to try to hit it making a curving movement with the arm.
2 INFORMAL
To swipe something means to steal it.
3 To swipe a credit card means to pass it through a machine that electronically reads the information stored in the card.

> NOUN
4 To take a swipe at something means to swipe at it.

swirl [swɜːl] **swirls, swirling, swirled** VERB
To swirl means to move quickly in circles. *e.g. The black water swirled around his legs.*

swish [swɪʃ] **swishes, swishing, swished** VERB

1 To swish means to move quickly through the air making a soft sound. *e.g. The curtains swished back.*

> NOUN

2 the sound made when something swishes

Swiss [swɪs] ADJECTIVE

1 belonging or relating to Switzerland

> NOUN

2 someone who comes from Switzerland

switch [swɪtʃ] **switches, switching, switched** NOUN

1 a small control for an electrical device or machine

2 a change *e.g. a switch in routine*

> VERB

3 To switch to a different task or topic means to change to it.

4 If you switch things, you exchange one for the other.

switch off VERB

5 To switch off a light or machine means to stop it working by pressing a switch.

switch on VERB

6 To switch on a light or machine means to start it working by pressing a switch.

switchboard [ˈswɪtʃˌbɔːd] **switchboards** NOUN

The switchboard in an organization is the part where all telephone calls are received.

swivel [ˈswɪvəl] **swivels, swivelling, swivelled** VERB

1 To swivel means to turn round on a central point.

> ADJECTIVE

2 A swivel chair or lamp is made so that you can move the main part of it while the base remains in a fixed position.

swollen [ˈswəʊlən] ADJECTIVE

Something that is swollen has swelled up.

swoon [swuːn] **swoons, swooning, swooned** VERB; LITERARY

To swoon means to faint as a result of strong emotion.

swoop [swuːp] **swoops, swooping, swooped** VERB

To swoop means to move downwards through the air in a fast curving movement. *e.g. A flock of pigeons swooped low over the square.*

swop [swɒp] another spelling of **swap**

sword [sɔːd] **swords** NOUN

a weapon consisting of a very long blade with a short handle

swordfish [ˈsɔːdˌfɪʃ] **swordfishes** or **swordfish** NOUN

a large sea fish with a long upper jaw

sworn [swɔːn] ADJECTIVE

If you make a sworn statement, you swear that everything in it is true.

swot [swɒt] **swots, swotting, swotted** INFORMAL **> VERB**

1 To swot means to study or revise very hard.

2 If you swot up on a subject you find out as much about it as possible in a short time.

> NOUN

3 someone who spends too much time studying

sycamore [ˈsɪkəˌmɔː] **sycamores** NOUN

a tree that has large leaves with five points

syllable [ˈsɪləbəl] **syllables** NOUN

a part of a word that contains a single vowel sound and is pronounced as a unit. For example, 'book' has one syllable and 'reading' has two

syllabus [ˈsɪləbəs] **syllabuses** or **syllabi** NOUN

The subjects that are studied for a particular course or examination are called the syllabus.

symbol [ˈsɪmbəl] **symbols** NOUN

(RE) a shape, design, or idea that is used to represent something *e.g. The fish has long been a symbol of Christianity.*

⦿ THESAURUS

emblem: *His badge bore a small yellow hammer-and-sickle emblem.*

figure: *the figure of a five-pointed star*

logo: *the company's logo*

mark: *a mark of identification*

representation: *This rune is a representation of a spearhead.*

sign: *a multiplication sign*

token: *He gave her a ring as a token of his love.*

symbolic [sɪmˈbɒlɪk] ADJECTIVE

Something that is symbolic has a special meaning that is considered to represent something else. *e.g. Six tons of ivory were burned in a symbolic ceremony.*

symbolize [ˈsɪmbəˌlaɪz] **symbolizes, symbolizing, symbolized;** also spelt **symbolise** VERB

If a shape, design, or idea symbolizes something, it is regarded as being a symbol of it. *e.g. In China and Japan the carp symbolizes courage.*

symbolism NOUN

symmetrical [sɪˈmɛtrɪkəl] ADJECTIVE

(MATHS) If something is symmetrical, it has two halves which are exactly the same, except that one half is like a reflection of the other half.

symmetrically ADVERB

symmetry [ˈsɪmɪtrɪ] NOUN

(MATHS) Something that has symmetry is symmetrical.

sympathetic [ˌsɪmpə'θɛtɪk] ADJECTIVE
1 A sympathetic person shows kindness and understanding to other people.

2 If you are sympathetic to a proposal or an idea, you approve of it.

sympathize ['sɪmpəˌθaɪz] **sympathizes, sympathizing, sympathized**; also spelt **sympathise** VERB
To sympathize with someone who is in difficulties means to show them understanding and care.

sympathizer ['sɪmpəˌθaɪzə] **sympathizers**; also spelt **sympathiser** NOUN
People who support a particular cause can be referred to as sympathizers.

sympathy ['sɪmpəθɪ] **sympathies** NOUN
1 Sympathy is kindness and understanding towards someone who is in difficulties.

> THESAURUS
compassion: *I was impressed by the compassion he showed for a helpless old woman.*
empathy: *They displayed an admirable understanding of the crime and empathy with the victim.*
pity: *He showed no pity for his victims.*
understanding: *I'd like to thank you for your patience and understanding.*

2 If you have sympathy with someone's ideas or actions, you agree with them.

> PHRASE
3 If you do something **in sympathy** with someone, you do it to show your support for them.

symphony ['sɪmfənɪ] **symphonies** NOUN
a piece of music for an orchestra, usually in four movements

symptom ['sɪmptəm] **symptoms** NOUN
1 something wrong with your body that is a sign of an illness

2 Something that is considered to be a sign of a bad situation can be referred to as a symptom of it. *e.g. another symptom of the racism sweeping across the country*
symptomatic ADJECTIVE

synagogue ['sɪnəˌgɒg] **synagogues** NOUN
(RE) a building where Jewish people meet for worship and religious instruction

synchronize ['sɪŋkrəˌnaɪz] **synchronizes, synchronizing, synchronized**; also spelt **synchronise** VERB
1 (MUSIC) To synchronize two actions means to do them at the same time and speed.

2 To synchronize watches means to set them to show exactly the same time as each other.

syncopation [ˌsɪŋkə'peɪʃən] NOUN
(MUSIC) Syncopation in rhythm is the stressing of weak beats instead of the usual strong ones.

syndicate ['sɪndɪkɪt] **syndicates** NOUN
an association of business people formed to carry out a particular project

syndrome ['sɪndrəʊm] **syndromes** NOUN
1 a medical condition characterized by a particular set of symptoms *e.g. Down's syndrome.*

2 You can refer to a typical set of characteristics as a syndrome. *e.g. the syndrome of skipping from one wonder diet to the next*

synod ['sɪnəd] **synods** NOUN
a council of church leaders which meets regularly to discuss religious and moral issues

synonym ['sɪnənɪm] **synonyms** NOUN
(ENGLISH) If two words have the same or a very similar meaning, they are synonyms.

synonymous [sɪ'nɒnɪməs] ADJECTIVE
1 Two words that are synonymous have the same or very similar meanings.

2 If two things are closely associated, you can say that one is synonymous with the other. *e.g. New York is synonymous with the Statue of Liberty.*

synopsis [sɪ'nɒpsɪs] **synopses** NOUN
a summary of a book, play, or film

syntax ['sɪntæks] NOUN
The syntax of a language is its grammatical rules and the way its words are arranged.

synthetic [sɪn'θɛtɪk] ADJECTIVE
made from artificial substances rather than natural ones

syphon ['saɪfən] another spelling of **siphon**

Syrian ['sɪrɪən] **Syrians** ADJECTIVE
1 belonging or relating to Syria

> NOUN
2 someone who comes from Syria

syringe ['sɪrɪndʒ] **syringes** NOUN
a hollow tube with a part which is pushed down inside and a fine hollow needle at one end, used for injecting or extracting liquids

syrup ['sɪrəp] **syrups** NOUN
a thick sweet liquid made by boiling sugar with water

system ['sɪstəm] **systems** NOUN
1 (LIBRARY) an organized way of doing or arranging something according to a fixed plan or set of rules

> THESAURUS
arrangement: *an intricate arrangement of treadles, rods and cranks*
method: *the methods employed in the study*
procedure: *This is now the standard procedure.*

routine: *his daily routine*
structure: *the structure of local government*
technique: *a new technique for processing sound*

2 People sometimes refer to the government and administration of the country as the system.

3 You can also refer to a set of equipment as a system. *e.g. an old stereo system*

4 In biology, a system of a particular kind is the set of organs that perform that function. *e.g. the immune system*

systematic [ˌsɪstɪˈmætɪk] ADJECTIVE
following a fixed plan and done in an efficient way *e.g. a systematic study*
systematically ADVERB

Tt

tab [tæb] **tabs** NOUN
a small extra piece that is attached to something, for example on a curtain so it can be hung on a pole

tabby ['tæbɪ] **tabbies** NOUN
a cat whose fur has grey, brown, or black stripes
[WORD HISTORY: from Old French TABIS meaning 'striped silk cloth']

tabernacle ['tæbə͵nækəl] **tabernacles** NOUN
1 a place of worship for certain Christian groups
2 a sanctuary in which the ancient Hebrews carried the Ark of the Covenant as they wandered from place to place
3 a Jewish temple
[WORD HISTORY: from Latin TABERNACULUM meaning 'tent']

table ['teɪbəl] **tables, tabling, tabled** NOUN
1 a piece of furniture with a flat horizontal top supported by one or more legs
2 a set of facts or figures arranged in rows or columns
> VERB
3 If you table something such as a proposal, you say formally that you want it to be discussed.

tablecloth ['teɪbəl͵klɒθ] **tablecloths** NOUN
a cloth used to cover a table and keep it clean

tablespoon ['teɪbəl͵spuːn] **tablespoons** NOUN
a large spoon used for serving food; also the amount that a tablespoon contains

tablet ['tæblɪt] **tablets** NOUN
1 any small, round pill made of powdered medicine
2 a slab of stone with words cut into it

table tennis NOUN
Table tennis is a game for two or four people in which you use bats to hit a small hollow ball over a low net across a table.

tabloid ['tæblɔɪd] **tabloids** NOUN
(ENGLISH) a newspaper with small pages, short news stories, and lots of photographs

taboo [tə'buː] **taboos** NOUN

1 a social custom that some words, subjects, or actions must be avoided because they are considered embarrassing or offensive *e.g. We have a powerful taboo against boasting.*
2 a religious custom that forbids people to do something
> ADJECTIVE
3 forbidden or disapproved of *e.g. a taboo subject*

tacit ['tæsɪt] ADJECTIVE
understood or implied without actually being said or written
tacitly ADVERB

taciturn ['tæsɪ͵tɜːn] ADJECTIVE
Someone who is taciturn does not talk very much and so seems unfriendly.

tack [tæk] **tacks, tacking, tacked** NOUN
1 a short nail with a broad, flat head
2 If you change tack, you start to use a different method for dealing with something.
> VERB
3 If you tack something to a surface, you nail it there with tacks.
4 If you tack a piece of fabric, you sew it with long loose stitches.

tackies or **takkies** ['tækɪz] PLURAL NOUN; INFORMAL
In South African English, tackies are tennis shoes or plimsolls.

tackle ['tækəl] **tackles, tackling, tackled** VERB
1 If you tackle a difficult task, you start dealing with it in a determined way.
2 If you tackle someone in a game such as soccer, you try to get the ball away from them.
3 If you tackle someone about something, you talk to them about it in order to get something changed or dealt with.
> NOUN
4 A tackle in sport is an attempt to get the ball away from your opponent.
5 Tackle is the equipment used for fishing.

tacky ['tækɪ] **tackier, tackiest** ADJECTIVE
1 slightly sticky to touch *e.g. The cream feels tacky to the touch.*

2 INFORMAL
badly made and in poor taste *e.g. tacky furniture*

tact [tækt] NOUN
Tact is the ability to see when a situation is difficult or delicate and to handle it without upsetting people.
tactless ADJECTIVE, **tactlessly** ADVERB

● THESAURUS
delicacy: *Both countries are behaving with rare delicacy.*
diplomacy: *It took all Minnelli's diplomacy to get him to return.*
discretion: *I appreciate your discretion.*
sensitivity: *The police treated the victims with great sensitivity.*

tactful ['tæktfʊl] ADJECTIVE
behaving with or showing tact
tactfully ADVERB

● THESAURUS
diplomatic: *She is very direct. I tend to be more diplomatic.*
discreet: *They were gossipy and not always discreet.*
sensitive: *his sensitive handling of the situation*
<<OPPOSITE *tactless*

tactic ['tæktɪk] **tactics** NOUN
1 (PE) Tactics are the methods you use to achieve what you want, especially to win a game.
2 Tactics are also the ways in which troops and equipment are used in order to win a battle.
tactical ADJECTIVE, **tactically** ADVERB

tactile ['tæktaɪl] ADJECTIVE
involving the sense of touch

tadpole ['tæd,pəʊl] **tadpoles** NOUN
Tadpoles are the larvae of frogs and toads. They are black with round heads and long tails and live in water.
[WORD HISTORY: from Middle English TADDE meaning 'toad' and POL meaning 'head']

taffeta ['tæfɪtə] NOUN
Taffeta is a stiff, shiny fabric that is used mainly for making women's clothes.

tag [tæg] **tags, tagging, tagged** NOUN
1 a small label made of cloth, paper, or plastic
2 If you tag along with someone, you go with them or behind them.

tail [teɪl] **tails, tailing, tailed** NOUN
1 The tail of an animal, bird, or fish is the part extending beyond the end of its body.
2 Tail can be used to mean the end part of something. *e.g. the tail of the plane*

> PLURAL NOUN
3 If a man is wearing tails, he is wearing a formal jacket which has two long pieces hanging down at the back.

> VERB
4 INFORMAL
If you tail someone, you follow them in order to find out where they go and what they do.

> ADJECTIVE OR ADVERB
5 The tails side of a coin is the side which does not have a person's head. **tail off** VERB
6 If something tails off, it becomes gradually less.

tailback ['teɪl,bæk] **tailbacks** NOUN
a long queue of traffic stretching back from whatever is blocking the road

tailor ['teɪlə] **tailors, tailoring, tailored** NOUN
1 a person who makes, alters, and repairs clothes, especially for men

> VERB
2 If something is tailored for a particular purpose, it is specially designed for it.

tailor-made ['teɪlə,meɪd] ADJECTIVE
suitable for a particular person or purpose, or specifically designed for them

taint [teɪnt] **taints, tainting, tainted** VERB
1 To taint something is to spoil it by adding something undesirable to it.

> NOUN
2 an undesirable quality in something which spoils it

taipan ['taɪ,pæn] **taipans** NOUN
a large and very poisonous Australian snake

take see page 888 for Word Web

takeaway ['teɪkə,weɪ] **takeaways** NOUN
1 a shop or restaurant that sells hot cooked food to be eaten elsewhere
2 a hot cooked meal bought from a takeaway

takings ['teɪkɪŋz] PLURAL NOUN
Takings are the money that a shop or cinema gets from selling its goods or tickets.

talc [tælk] NOUN
Talc is the same as talcum powder.

talcum powder ['tælkəm] NOUN
Talcum powder is a soft perfumed powder used for absorbing moisture on the body.

tale [teɪl] **tales** NOUN
a story

talent ['tælənt] **talents** NOUN
Talent is the natural ability to do something well.
talented ADJECTIVE

● THESAURUS
ability: *Her drama teacher spotted her ability.*
aptitude: *Alan has no aptitude for music.*
capacity: *people's creative capacities*
flair: *a dentist with a flair for invention*

t

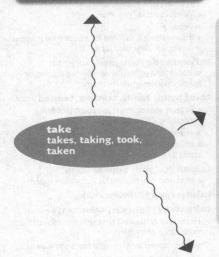

1 VERB
If something takes a certain amount of time, or a particular quality or ability, it requires it *eg: He takes three hours to get ready.*
● **THESAURUS**
demand: *The task of rebuilding would demand much patience.*
require: *The race requires a lot of stamina.*

2 VERB
If you take something, you put your hand round it and hold it or carry it *eg: Here, let me take your coat.*
● **THESAURUS**
bear (formal): *They bore the hardwood box into the kitchen.*
bring: *He poured a brandy for Dena and brought it to her.*
carry: *She carried the shopping from the car.*
convey (formal): *The minibus conveyed us to the city centre.*
ferry: *A plane arrives to ferry guests to the island.*
fetch: *Sylvia fetched a towel from the bathroom.*
transport: *They use tankers to transport the oil to Los Angeles.*

take
takes, taking, took, taken

3 VERB
If you take someone somewhere, you drive them there by car or lead them there.
● **THESAURUS**
bring: *Come to my party and bring a girl with you.*
conduct (formal): *He asked if he might conduct us to the ball.*
escort: *I escorted him to the door.*
guide: *a young Egyptologist who guided us through the tombs*
lead: *She confessed to the killing and led police to his remains.*
usher: *I ushered him into the office.*

gènius: *his genius for chess*
gift: *a gift for teaching*
knack: *He's got the knack of getting people to listen.*

talisman ['tælɪzmən] **talismans** NOUN
an object which you believe has magic powers to protect you or bring luck
[WORD HISTORY: from Greek TELESMA meaning 'holy object']

talk [tɔːk] **talks, talking, talked** VERB
1 When you talk, you say things to someone.
2 If people talk, especially about other people's private affairs, they gossip about them. *e.g. the neighbours might talk*
3 If you talk on or about something, you make an informal speech about it.
> NOUN
4 Talk is discussion or gossip.
5 an informal speech about something
talk down VERB
6 If you talk down to someone, you talk to them in a way that shows that you think you are more important or clever than them.

talkative ['tɔːkətɪv] ADJECTIVE
talking a lot
⊕ THESAURUS
chatty: *She's quite a chatty person.*
communicative: *She has become a lot more communicative.*
long-winded: *I hope I'm not being too long-winded.*

tall [tɔːl] **taller, tallest** ADJECTIVE
1 of more than average or normal height
⊕ THESAURUS
high: *a high wall*
lanky: *He was six foot four, all lanky and leggy.*
lofty: *lofty ceilings*
soaring: *the soaring spires of churches like St Peter's*
towering: *towering cliffs of black granite*
<<OPPOSITE short
2 having a particular height *e.g. a wall ten metres tall*
> PHRASE
3 If you describe something as **a tall story**, you mean that it is difficult to believe because it is so unlikely.

tally ['tælɪ] **tallies, tallying, tallied** NOUN
1 an informal record of amounts which you keep adding to as you go along *e.g. He ended with a reasonable goal tally last season.*
> VERB
2 If numbers or statements tally, they are exactly the same or they give the same results or conclusions.

Talmud ['tælmʊd] NOUN
The Talmud consists of the books containing the ancient Jewish ceremonies and civil laws.
[WORD HISTORY: a Hebrew word meaning literally 'instruction']

talon ['tælən] **talons** NOUN
Talons are sharp, hooked claws, especially of a bird of prey.

tambourine [ˌtæmbəˈriːn] **tambourines** NOUN
a percussion instrument made of a skin stretched tightly over a circular frame, with small round pieces of metal around the edge where the tambourine is beaten or shaken

tame [teɪm] **tamer, tamest; tames, taming, tamed** ADJECTIVE
1 A tame animal or bird is not afraid of people and is not violent towards them.
2 Something that is tame is uninteresting and lacks excitement or risk. *e.g. The report was pretty tame.*
> VERB
3 If you tame people or things, you bring them under control.
4 To tame a wild animal or bird is to train it to be obedient and live with humans.

tamper ['tæmpə] **tampers, tampering, tampered** VERB
If you tamper with something, you interfere or meddle with it.

tampon ['tæmpɒn] **tampons** NOUN
a firm, specially shaped piece of cotton wool that a woman places inside her vagina to absorb the blood during her period

tan [tæn] **tans, tanning, tanned** NOUN
1 If you have a tan, your skin is darker than usual because you have been in the sun.
> VERB
2 To tan an animal's hide is to turn it into leather by treating it with chemicals.
> ADJECTIVE
3 Something that is tan is of a light yellowish-brown colour. *e.g. a tan dress*

tandem ['tændəm] **tandems** NOUN
a bicycle designed for two riders sitting one behind the other

tang [tæŋ] **tangs** NOUN
a strong, sharp smell or flavour *e.g. the tang of lemon*
tangy ADJECTIVE

tangata whenua ['tɑːŋɡɑːtə ˈfɛnuːə] NOUN
Tangata whenua is a Maori term for the original Polynesian settlers in New Zealand, and their descendants.

tangent ['tændʒənt] **tangents** NOUN

t

1 A tangent of a curve is any straight line that touches the curve at one point only.

> PHRASE

2 If you **go off at a tangent**, you start talking or thinking about something that is not completely relevant to what has gone before.

tangerine [ˌtændʒə'riːn] **tangerines** NOUN
1 a type of small sweet orange with a loose rind

> NOUN OR ADJECTIVE
2 reddish-orange

tangible ['tændʒəbəl] ADJECTIVE
clear or definite enough to be easily seen or felt
e.g. tangible proof

tangle ['tæŋgəl] **tangles, tangling, tangled** NOUN

1 a mass of things such as hairs or fibres knotted or coiled together and difficult to separate

THESAURUS

jumble: *a jumble of twisted tubes*
knot: *Her hair was full of knots.*
mass: *a flailing mass of arms and legs*
mat: *the thick mat of sandy hair on his chest*
muddle: *The back of the tapestry was a muddle of threads.*
web: *a thick web of fibres*

> VERB

2 If you are tangled in wires or ropes, you are caught or trapped in them so that it is difficult to get free.

THESAURUS

catch: *a fly caught in a spider's web*
jumble: *The wires were all jumbled together and tied in a knot.*
knot: *The kite strings had got knotted together.*
twist: *Her hands began to twist the handles of the bag.*

tango ['tæŋgəʊ] **tangos** NOUN
A tango is a Latin American dance using long gliding steps and sudden pauses; also a piece of music composed for this dance.

taniwha ['tʌniːfɑː] **taniwha** or **taniwhas** NOUN
In New Zealand, a monster of Maori legends that lives in water.

tank [tæŋk] **tanks** NOUN

1 a large container for storing liquid or gas

2 an armoured military vehicle which moves on tracks and is equipped with guns or rockets

tankard ['tæŋkəd] **tankards** NOUN
a large metal mug used for drinking beer

tanker ['tæŋkə] **tankers** NOUN
a ship or lorry designed to carry large quantities of gas or liquid *e.g. a petrol tanker*

tannin ['tænɪn] NOUN
a brown or yellow substance found in plants and used in making leather

tantalizing or **tantalising** ['tæntə,laɪzɪŋ] ADJECTIVE
Something that is tantalizing makes you feel hopeful and excited, although you know that you probably will not be able to have what you want.
e.g. a tantalizing glimpse of riches to come

tantamount ['tæntə,maʊnt] ADJECTIVE
If you say that something is tantamount to something else, you mean that it is almost the same as it. *e.g. That would be tantamount to treason.*

tantrum ['tæntrəm] **tantrums** NOUN
a noisy and sometimes violent outburst of temper, especially by a child

Tanzanian [ˌtænzə'nɪən] **Tanzanians** ADJECTIVE

1 belonging or relating to Tanzania

> NOUN
2 someone who comes from Tanzania

tap [tæp] **taps, tapping, tapped** NOUN

1 a device that you turn to control the flow of liquid or gas from a pipe or container

2 the action of hitting something lightly; also the sound that this action makes

> VERB

3 If you tap something or tap on it, you hit it lightly.

4 If a telephone is tapped, a device is fitted to it so that someone can listen secretly to the calls.

tap-dancing ['tæp,dɑːnsɪŋ] NOUN
Tap-dancing is a type of dancing in which the dancers wear special shoes with pieces of metal on the toes and heels which click against the floor.

tape [teɪp] **tapes, taping, taped** NOUN

1 Tape is plastic ribbon covered with a magnetic substance and used to record sounds, pictures, and computer information.

2 a cassette or spool with magnetic tape wound round it

3 Tape is a long, thin strip of fabric that is used for binding or fastening.

4 Tape is also a strip of sticky plastic which you use for sticking things together.

> VERB

5 If you tape sounds or television pictures, you record them using a tape recorder or a video recorder.

6 If you tape one thing to another, you attach them using sticky tape.

tape measure **tape measures** NOUN
a strip of plastic or metal that is marked off in inches or centimetres and used for measuring things

taper ['teɪpə] **tapers, tapering, tapered** VERB

1 Something that tapers becomes thinner towards one end.

> NOUN

2 a thin candle

tape recorder **tape recorders** NOUN
a machine used for recording sounds onto magnetic tape, and for playing these sounds back

tapestry ['tæpɪstrɪ] **tapestries** NOUN
a piece of heavy cloth with designs embroidered on it

tar [tɑː] NOUN
Tar is a thick, black, sticky substance which is used in making roads.

tarantula [təˈræntjʊlə] **tarantulas** NOUN
a large, hairy poisonous spider

target ['tɑːgɪt] **targets** NOUN

1 something which you aim at when firing weapons

2 The target of an action or remark is the person or thing at which it is directed. *e.g. You become a target for our hatred.*

3 Your target is the result that you are trying to achieve.

tariff ['tærɪf] **tariffs** NOUN

1 a tax that a government collects on imported goods

2 any list of prices or charges

tarmac ['tɑːmæk] NOUN
Tarmac is a material used for making road surfaces. It consists of crushed stones mixed with tar.
[WORD HISTORY: short for TARMACADAM, from the name of John McAdam, the Scottish engineer who invented it]

tarnish ['tɑːnɪʃ] **tarnishes, tarnishing, tarnished** VERB

1 If metal tarnishes, it becomes stained and loses its shine.

2 If something tarnishes your reputation, it spoils it and causes people to lose their respect for you.

tarot ['tærəʊ] NOUN
A tarot card is one of a special pack of cards used for fortune-telling.

tarpaulin [tɑːˈpɔːlɪn] **tarpaulins** NOUN
a sheet of heavy waterproof material used as a protective covering

tarragon ['tærəgən] NOUN
Tarragon is a herb with narrow green leaves used in cooking.

tarry ['tærɪ] **tarries, tarrying, tarried** VERB; OLD-FASHIONED, INFORMAL
To tarry is to wait, or to stay somewhere for a little longer.

tarseal ['tɑːˌsiːl] NOUN
In New Zealand English, tarseal is the tarmac surface of a road.

tart [tɑːt] **tarts; tarter, tartest** NOUN

1 a pastry case with a sweet filling

> ADJECTIVE

2 Something that is tart is sour or sharp to taste.

3 A tart remark is unpleasant and cruel.

tartan ['tɑːt³n] **tartans** NOUN
Tartan is a woollen fabric from Scotland with checks of various colours and sizes, depending on which clan it belongs to.

tartar ['tɑːtə] NOUN
Tartar is a hard, crusty substance that forms on teeth.

tarwhine ['tɑːˌwaɪn] **tarwhines** NOUN
an edible Australian marine fish, especially a sea bream

task [tɑːsk] **tasks** NOUN
any piece of work which has to be done

● THESAURUS
assignment: *written assignments and practical tests*
chore: *household chores*
duty: *I carried out my duties conscientiously.*
job: *He was given the job of tending the fire.*
mission: *Salisbury sent him on a diplomatic mission to North America.*
undertaking: *Organizing the show has been a massive undertaking.*

Tasmanian devil [tæzˈmeɪnɪən] **Tasmanian devils** NOUN
a black-and-white marsupial of Tasmania, which eats flesh

tassel ['tæs³l] **tassels** NOUN
a tuft of loose threads tied by a knot and used for decoration

taste [teɪst] **tastes, tasting, tasted** NOUN

1 Your sense of taste is your ability to recognize the flavour of things in your mouth.

2 The taste of something is its flavour.

● THESAURUS
flavour: *a crumbly texture with a strong flavour*
tang: *the tang of lemon*

3 If you have a taste of food or drink, you have a small amount of it to see what it is like.

● THESAURUS
bite: *Chew each mouthful fully before the next bite.*
mouthful: *She gulped down a mouthful of coffee.*
sip: *a sip of wine*

4 If you have a taste for something, you enjoy it.
e.g. a taste for publicity

● THESAURUS
appetite: *his appetite for success*
fondness: *I've always had a fondness for jewels.*
liking: *She had a liking for good clothes.*
penchant: *formal He had a penchant for playing jokes on people.*

5 If you have a taste of something, you experience it. *e.g. my first taste of defeat*

6 A person's taste is their choice in the things they like to buy or have around them. *e.g. His taste in music is great.*

> VERB
7 When you can taste something in your mouth, you are aware of its flavour.

8 If you taste food or drink, you have a small amount of it to see what it is like.

9 If food or drink tastes of something, it has that flavour.

taste bud **taste buds** NOUN
Your taste buds are the little points on the surface of your tongue which enable you to taste things.

tasteful ['teɪstfʊl] ADJECTIVE
attractive and elegant
tastefully ADVERB

tasteless ['teɪstlɪs] ADJECTIVE
1 vulgar and unattractive

● THESAURUS
flashy: *a flashy sports car*
garish: *garish bright red boots*
gaudy: *her gaudy floral hat*
tacky: *informal tacky holiday souvenirs*
tawdry: *a tawdry seaside town*
vulgar: *a very vulgar house*
<<OPPOSITE tasteful

2 A tasteless remark or joke is offensive.

3 Tasteless food has very little flavour.

● THESAURUS
bland: *It tasted bland, like warmed cardboard.*
insipid: *a rather insipid meal*
<<OPPOSITE tasty

tasty ['teɪstɪ] **tastier, tastiest** ADJECTIVE
having a pleasant flavour

● THESAURUS
appetizing: *a choice of appetizing dishes*
delicious: *a wide selection of delicious desserts*
lekker: *South African; slang a lekker meal*
luscious: *luscious fruit*

palatable: *some very palatable wines*
<<OPPOSITE tasteless

tatters ['tætəz] PLURAL NOUN
Clothes that are in tatters are badly torn.
tattered ADJECTIVE

tattoo [tæ'tu:] **tattoos, tattooing, tattooed** VERB
1 If someone tattoos you or tattoos a design on you, they draw it on your skin by pricking little holes and filling them with coloured dye.

> NOUN
2 a picture or design tattooed on someone's body

3 a public military display of exercises and music

tatty ['tætɪ] **tattier, tattiest** ADJECTIVE
worn out or untidy and rather dirty

taught [tɔːt] the past tense and past participle of **teach**

taunt [tɔːnt] **taunts, taunting, taunted**
VERB
1 To taunt someone is to speak to them about their weaknesses or failures in order to make them angry or upset.

> NOUN
2 an offensive remark intended to make a person angry or upset

Taurus ['tɔːrəs] NOUN
Taurus is the second sign of the zodiac, represented by a bull. People born between April 20th and May 20th are born under this sign.
[WORD HISTORY: from Latin TAURUS meaning 'bull']

taut [tɔːt] ADJECTIVE
stretched very tight *e.g. taut wires*

tavern ['tævən] **taverns** NOUN; OLD-FASHIONED, INFORMAL
a pub

tawdry ['tɔːdrɪ] **tawdrier, tawdriest**
ADJECTIVE
cheap, gaudy, and of poor quality

tawny ['tɔːnɪ] NOUN OR ADJECTIVE
brownish-yellow

tax [tæks] **taxes, taxing, taxed** NOUN
1 Tax is an amount of money that the people in a country have to pay to the government so that it can provide public services such as health care and education.

● THESAURUS
duty: *customs duties*
excise: *These products are excused VAT and excise.*
levy: *formal an annual motorway levy on all drivers*
tariff: *America wants to eliminate tariffs on items such as electronics.*

> VERB
2 If a sum of money is taxed, a certain amount of

it has to be paid to the government.

3 If goods are taxed, a certain amount of their price has to be paid to the government.

4 If a person or company is taxed, they have to pay a certain amount of their income to the government.

5 If something taxes you, it makes heavy demands on you. *e.g. They must be told not to tax your patience.*

taxation NOUN

● THESAURUS
drain: *conflicts that drain your energy*
exhaust: *She has exhausted my sympathy.*
sap: *The illness sapped his strength.*
strain: *The volume of flights is straining the air traffic control system.*
stretch: *The drought there is stretching American resources to their limits.*

taxi ['tæksɪ] **taxis, taxiing, taxied** NOUN

1 a car with a driver which you hire to take you to where you want to go

> VERB

2 When an aeroplane taxis, it moves slowly along the runway before taking off or after landing.

tea [tiː] **teas** NOUN

1 Tea is the dried leaves of an evergreen shrub found in Asia.

2 Tea is a drink made by brewing the leaves of the tea plant in hot water; also a cup of this.

3 Tea is also any drink made with hot water and leaves or flowers. *e.g. peppermint tea*

4 Tea is a meal taken in the late afternoon or early evening.

tea bag tea bags NOUN
a small paper bag with tea leaves in it which is placed in boiling water to make tea

teach [tiːtʃ] **teaches, teaching, taught** VERB

1 If you teach someone something, you give them instructions so that they know about it or know how to do it.

● THESAURUS
coach: *He coached the basketball team.*
drill: *He drills the choir to a high standard.*
educate: *He was educated at Haslingden Grammar School.*
instruct: *He instructed family members in nursing techniques.*
school: *He had been schooled to take over the family business.*
train: *They train teachers in counselling skills.*
tutor: *She was tutored at home by her parents.*

2 If you teach a subject, you help students learn about a subject at school, college, or university.

teaching NOUN

teacher ['tiːtʃə] **teachers** NOUN
a person who teaches other people, especially children

● THESAURUS
coach: *her drama coach*
don: *a Cambridge don*
guru: *a religious guru*
instructor: *a driving instructor*
lecturer: *a lecturer in law*
master or **mistress:** *a retired maths master*
professor: *a professor of economics*
tutor: *He surprised his tutors by failing the exam.*

teak [tiːk] NOUN
Teak is a hard wood which comes from a large Asian tree.

team [tiːm] **teams, teaming, teamed** NOUN

1 a group of people who work together or play together against another group in a sport or game

● THESAURUS
band: *a band of rebels*
crew: *the ship's crew*
gang: *a gang of workmen*
group: *The students work in groups.*
side: *Italy were definitely the better side.*
squad: *the England under-21 squad*
troupe: *troupes of travelling actors*

> VERB

2 If you team up with someone, you join them and work together with them.

● THESAURUS
collaborate: *The two men met and agreed to collaborate.*
cooperate: *They would cooperate in raising their child.*
join forces: *The groups joined forces to fight against the ban.*
link up: *the first time the two armies have linked up*
pair up: *Men and teenage girls pair up to dance.*
unite: *The two parties have been trying to unite.*
work together: *We have always wanted to work together.*

teamwork ['tiːmˌwɜːk] NOUN
Teamwork is the ability of a group of people to work well together.

teapot ['tiːˌpɒt] **teapots** NOUN
a round pot with a handle, a lid, and a spout, used for brewing and pouring tea

tear tears, tearing, tore, torn NOUN [tɪə]

1 Tears are the drops of salty liquid that come out of your eyes when you cry.

> NOUN [tɛə]

2 a hole that has been made in something

t

THESAURUS
hole: *the hole in my shoe*
ladder: *There was a ladder in her tights.*
rip: *the rip in her new dress*
rupture: *a rupture in the valve*
scratch: *I pointed to a number of scratches in the tile floor.*
split: *the split in his trousers*

> VERB [tɛə]

3 If you tear something, it is damaged by being pulled so that a hole appears in it.

THESAURUS
ladder: *after she laddered her tights*
rip: *I tried not to rip the paper.*
rupture: *a ruptured appendix*
scratch: *Knives will scratch the worktop.*
shred: *They may be shredding documents.*
split: *I'd split my trousers.*

4 If you tear somewhere, you rush there. *e.g. He tore through busy streets in a high-speed chase.*

THESAURUS
charge: *He charged through the door.*
dart: *Ingrid darted across the deserted street.*
dash: *He dashed upstairs.*
fly: *She flew to their bedsides when they were ill.*
race: *He raced across town.*
shoot: *Another car shot out of a junction.*
speed: *A low shot sped past Lukic.*
zoom: *We zoomed through the gallery.*

> When *tear* means 'a drop of salty water' (sense 1), it rhymes with *fear*. For all the other senses it rhymes with *hair*

tearaway ['tɛərə,weɪ] **tearaways** NOUN
someone who is wild and uncontrollable

tearful ['tɪəfʊl] ADJECTIVE
about to cry or crying gently
tearfully ADVERB

tease [tiːz] **teases, teasing, teased** VERB
1 If you tease someone, you deliberately make fun of them or embarrass them because it amuses you.

THESAURUS
make fun of: *The kids at school made fun of me and my Cockney accent.*
mock: *Don't mock me!*
needle: *informal He used to enjoy needling people.*
taunt: *Other youths taunted him about his clothes.*

> NOUN

2 someone who enjoys teasing people

teaspoon ['tiː,spuːn] **teaspoons** NOUN
a small spoon used for stirring drinks; also the amount that a teaspoon holds

teat [tiːt] **teats** NOUN
1 a nipple on a female animal

2 a piece of rubber or plastic that is shaped like a nipple and fitted to a baby's feeding bottle

tea tree tea trees NOUN
a tree found in Australia and New Zealand with leaves that contain tannin, like tea leaves

tech [tɛk] **techs** NOUN; INFORMAL
a technical college

technical ['tɛknɪkəl] ADJECTIVE
1 involving machines, processes, and materials used in industry, transport, and communications

2 skilled in practical and mechanical things rather than theories and ideas

3 involving a specialized field of activity *e.g. I never understood the technical jargon.*

technical college technical colleges NOUN
a college where you can study subjects like technology and secretarial skills

technicality [,tɛknɪ'kælɪtɪ] **technicalities** NOUN
1 The technicalities of a process or activity are the detailed methods used to do it.

2 an exact detail of a law or a set of rules, especially one some people might not notice *e.g. The verdict may have been based on a technicality.*

technically ['tɛknɪkəlɪ] ADVERB
If something is technically true or correct, it is true or correct when you consider only the facts, rules, or laws, but may not be important or relevant in a particular situation. *e.g. Technically, they were not supposed to drink on duty.*

technician [tɛk'nɪʃən] **technicians** NOUN
someone whose job involves skilled practical work with scientific equipment

technique [tɛk'niːk] **techniques** NOUN
1 a particular method of doing something *e.g. these techniques of manufacture*

2 Technique is skill and ability in an activity which is developed through training and practice. *e.g. Jim's unique vocal technique.*

techno- PREFIX
'Techno-' means a craft or art *e.g. technology* [WORD HISTORY: from Greek TEKHNĒ meaning 'a skill']

technology [tɛk'nɒlədʒɪ] **technologies** NOUN
1 **(D & T)** Technology is the study of the application of science and scientific knowledge for practical purposes in industry, farming, medicine, or business.

2 a particular area of activity that requires scientific methods and knowledge *e.g. computer technology*

technological ADJECTIVE, **technologically** ADVERB

teddy ['tɛdɪ] **teddies** NOUN
A teddy or teddy bear is a stuffed toy that looks like a friendly bear.
[WORD HISTORY: named after the American President Theodore (Teddy) Roosevelt, who hunted bears]

tedious ['tiːdɪəs] ADJECTIVE
boring and lasting for a long time *e.g. the tedious task of clearing up*

tedium ['tiːdɪəm] NOUN
the quality of being boring and lasting for a long time *e.g. the tedium of unemployment*

tee [tiː] **tees, teeing, teed** NOUN
1 the small wooden or plastic peg on which a golf ball is placed before the golfer first hits it

> VERB
2 To tee off is to hit the golf ball from the tee, or to start a round of golf.

teem [tiːm] **teems, teeming, teemed** VERB
1 If a place is teeming with people or things, there are a lot of them moving about.
2 If it teems, it rains very heavily. *e.g. The rain was teeming down.*

teenage ['tiːn,eɪdʒ] ADJECTIVE
1 aged between thirteen and nineteen
2 typical of people aged between thirteen and nineteen *e.g. teenage fashion*
teenager NOUN

teens [tiːnz] PLURAL NOUN
Your teens are the period of your life when you are between thirteen and nineteen years old.

tee shirt another spelling of **T-shirt**

teeter ['tiːtə] **teeters, teetering, teetered** VERB
To teeter is to shake or sway slightly in an unsteady way and seem about to fall over.

teeth [tiːθ] the plural of **tooth**

teethe [tiːð] **teethes, teething, teethed** VERB
When babies are teething, their teeth are starting to come through, usually causing them pain.

teetotal [tiː'təʊtᵊl] ADJECTIVE
Someone who is teetotal never drinks alcohol.
teetotaller NOUN

tele- PREFIX
'Tele-' means at or over a distance *e.g. telegraph*
[WORD HISTORY: from Greek TELE meaning 'far']

telecommunications
[,tɛlɪkə,mjuːnɪ'keɪʃənz] NOUN
Telecommunications is the science and activity of sending signals and messages over long distances using electronic equipment.

telegram ['tɛlɪ,græm] **telegrams** NOUN
a message sent by telegraph

telegraph ['tɛlɪ,grɑːf] NOUN
The telegraph is a system of sending messages over long distances using electrical or radio signals.

telepathy [tɪ'lɛpəθɪ] NOUN
Telepathy is direct communication between people's minds.
telepathic ADJECTIVE

telephone ['tɛlɪ,fəʊn] **telephones, telephoning, telephoned** NOUN
1 a piece of electrical equipment for talking directly to someone who is in a different place

> VERB
2 If you telephone someone, you speak to them using a telephone.

telephone box telephone boxes NOUN
a small shelter in the street where there is a public telephone

telescope ['tɛlɪ,skəʊp] **telescopes** NOUN
a long instrument shaped like a tube which has lenses which make distant objects appear larger and nearer

teletext ['tɛlɪ,tɛkst] NOUN
Teletext is an electronic system that broadcasts pages of information onto a television set.

televise ['tɛlɪ,vaɪz] **televises, televising, televised** VERB
If an event is televised, it is filmed and shown on television.

television ['tɛlɪ,vɪʒən] **televisions** NOUN
a piece of electronic equipment which receives pictures and sounds by electrical signals over a distance

tell see page 896 for Word Web

teller ['tɛlə] **tellers** NOUN
a person who receives or gives out money in a bank

telling ['tɛlɪŋ] ADJECTIVE
Something that is telling has an important effect, often because it shows the true nature of a situation. *e.g. a telling account of the war*

telltale ['tɛl,teɪl] ADJECTIVE
A telltale sign reveals information. *e.g. the sad, telltale signs of a recent accident*

telly ['tɛlɪ] **tellies** NOUN; INFORMAL
a television

temerity [tɪ'mɛrɪtɪ] NOUN
If someone has the temerity to do something,

t

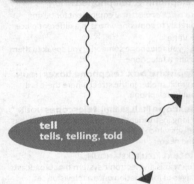

1 VERB
If you tell someone something, you let them know about it.
● THESAURUS
inform: *My daughter informed me that she was pregnant.*
notify: *We have notified the police.*

tell
tells, telling, told

2 VERB
If you tell someone to do something, you order or advise them to do it.
● THESAURUS
command: *He commanded his troops to attack.*
direct (formal): *They have been directed to give special attention to the problem.*
instruct: *The family has instructed solicitors to sue the company.*
order: *He ordered his men to cease firing.*

3 VERB
If you can tell something, you are able to judge correctly what is happening or what the situation is *eg: I could tell he was scared.*
● THESAURUS
discern (formal): *It was hard to discern why this was happening.*
see: *I could see she was lonely.*

they do it even though it upsets or annoys other people. *e.g. She had the temerity to call him Bob.*

temp [tɛmp] **temps** NOUN; INFORMAL
a secretary who works for short periods of time in different places

temper ['tɛmpə] **tempers, tempering, tempered** NOUN

1 Your temper is the frame of mind or mood you are in.

2 a sudden outburst of anger

> PHRASE

3 If you **lose your temper**, you become very angry.

> VERB

4 To temper something is to make it more acceptable or suitable. *e.g. curiosity tempered with some caution*

temperament ['tɛmpərəmənt] **temperaments** NOUN
Your temperament is your nature or personality, shown in the way you react towards people and situations. *e.g. an artistic temperament*

temperamental [,tɛmpərə'mɛntəl] ADJECTIVE
Someone who is temperamental has moods that change often and suddenly.

temperate ['tɛmpərit] ADJECTIVE
A temperate place has weather that is neither extremely hot nor extremely cold.

temperature ['tɛmprɪtʃə] **temperatures** NOUN

1 (SCIENCE) The temperature of something is how hot or cold it is.

2 Your temperature is the temperature of your body.

> PHRASE

3 If you **have a temperature**, the temperature of your body is higher than it should be, because you are ill.

tempest ['tɛmpɪst] **tempests** NOUN; LITERARY
a violent storm

tempestuous [tɛm'pɛstjʊəs] ADJECTIVE
violent or strongly emotional *e.g. a tempestuous relationship*

template ['tɛmplɪt] **templates** NOUN
a shape or pattern cut out in wood, metal, plastic, or card which you draw or cut around to reproduce that shape or pattern

temple ['tɛmpəl] **temples** NOUN

1 (RE) a building used for the worship of a god in various religions *e.g. a Buddhist temple*

2 Your temples are the flat parts on each side of your forehead.

tempo ['tɛmpəʊ] **tempos** or **tempi** NOUN

1 The tempo of something is the speed at which it happens. *e.g. the slow tempo of change*

2 (MUSIC) TECHNICAL
The tempo of a piece of music is its speed.

temporary ['tɛmpərəri] ADJECTIVE
lasting for only a short time
temporarily ADVERB

● THESAURUS
ephemeral: *a reminder that earthly pleasures are ephemeral*
fleeting: *a fleeting glimpse*
interim: *an interim measure*
momentary: *a momentary lapse*
passing: *a passing phase*
provisional: *a provisional coalition government*
transient: *Modelling is a transient career.*
transitory: *the transitory nature of political success*
<<OPPOSITE *permanent*

tempt [tɛmpt] **tempts, tempting, tempted** VERB

1 If you tempt someone, you try to persuade them to do something by offering them something they want.

● THESAURUS
entice: *She resisted attempts to entice her into politics.*
lure: *The company aims to lure smokers back to cigarettes.*
seduce: *We are seduced into buying all these items.*

2 If you are tempted to do something, you want to do it but you think it might be wrong or harmful. *e.g. He was tempted to reply with sarcasm.*

temptation [tɛmp'teɪʃən] **temptations** NOUN

1 Temptation is the state you are in when you want to do or have something, even though you know it might be wrong or harmful.

2 something that you want to do or have, even though you know it might be wrong or harmful *e.g. There is a temptation to ignore the problem.*

ten [tɛn]
the number 10
tenth

tenacious [tɪ'neɪʃəs] ADJECTIVE
determined and not giving up easily
tenaciously ADVERB, **tenacity** NOUN

tenant ['tɛnənt] **tenants** NOUN
someone who pays rent for the place they live in, or for land or buildings that they use
tenancy NOUN

tend [tɛnd] **tends, tending, tended** VERB

1 If something tends to happen, it happens usually or often.

t

THESAURUS
be apt: *She was apt to raise her voice.*
be inclined: *He was inclined to self-pity.*
be liable: *equipment that is liable to break*
be prone: *We know males are more prone to violence.*
have a tendency: *Shetland jumpers have a tendency to be annoyingly itchy.*

2 If you tend someone or something, you look after them. *e.g. the way we tend our cattle*

THESAURUS
care for: *They hired a nurse to care for her.*
look after: *I love looking after the children.*
nurse: *In hospital they nursed me back to health.*
take care of: *There was no one else to take care of the animals.*

tendency ['tɛndənsɪ] **tendencies** NOUN
a trend or type of behaviour that happens very often *e.g. a tendency to be critical*

THESAURUS
inclination: *his artistic inclinations*
leaning: *their socialist leanings*
propensity: *his propensity for violence*

tender ['tɛndə] **tenderest; tenders, tendering, tendered** ADJECTIVE

1 Someone who is tender has gentle and caring feelings.

THESAURUS
affectionate: *She gave him an affectionate smile.*
caring: *He is a lovely boy, and very caring.*
compassionate: *a deeply compassionate film*
gentle: *Michael's voice was gentle and consoling.*
kind: *She is warmhearted and kind to everyone and everything.*
loving: *He was a most loving husband and father.*
sensitive: *He was always so sensitive.*
warm: *She was a very warm person.*
<<OPPOSITE tough

2 If someone is at a tender age, they are young and do not know very much about life.

3 Tender meat is easy to cut or chew.

4 If a part of your body is tender, it is painful and sore.

THESAURUS
aching: *The weary holidaymakers soothed their aching feet in the sea.*
bruised: *bruised legs*
inflamed: *Her eyes were inflamed.*
painful: *Her glands were swollen and painful.*
raw: *the drag of the rope against the raw flesh of my shoulders*
sensitive: *Ouch! I'm sorry, my lip is still a bit sensitive.*
sore: *My chest is still sore from the surgery.*

> VERB

5 If someone tenders an apology or their

resignation, they offer it.

THESAURUS
hand in: *All the opposition members have handed in their resignation.*
offer: *May I offer my sincere condolences?*

> NOUN

6 a formal offer to supply goods or to do a job for a particular price

THESAURUS
bid: *Sydney's successful bid for the 2000 Olympic Games.*
estimate: *The firm is preparing an estimate for the work.*
package: *We opted for the package submitted by the existing service provider.*
submission: *A written submission has to be prepared.*

tendon ['tɛndən] **tendons** NOUN
a strong cord of tissue which joins a muscle to a bone

tendril ['tɛndrɪl] **tendrils** NOUN
Tendrils are short, thin stems which grow on climbing plants and attach them to walls.

tenement ['tɛnəmənt] **tenements** NOUN
a large house or building divided into many flats

tenet ['tɛnɪt] **tenets** NOUN
The tenets of a theory or belief are the main ideas it is based upon.

tenner ['tɛnə] **tenners** NOUN; INFORMAL
a ten-pound or ten-dollar note

tennis ['tɛnɪs] NOUN
Tennis is a game played by two or four players on a rectangular court in which a ball is hit by players over a central net.

tenor ['tɛnə] **tenors** NOUN

1 a man who sings in a fairly high voice

2 The tenor of something is the general meaning or mood that it expresses. *e.g. the whole tenor of his poetry had changed*

> ADJECTIVE

3 A tenor recorder, saxophone, or other musical instrument has a range of notes of a fairly low pitch.

tense [tɛns] **tenser, tensest; tenses, tensing, tensed** ADJECTIVE

1 If you are tense, you are nervous and cannot relax.

THESAURUS
anxious: *She had become very anxious and alarmed.*
edgy: *She was nervous and edgy, still chain-smoking.*
jittery: *informal Investors have become jittery about the country's economy.*
jumpy: *I told myself not to be so jumpy.*

nervous: *It has made me very nervous about going out.*

uptight: informal *Penny never got uptight about exams.*

<<OPPOSITE *calm*

2 A tense situation or period of time is one that makes people nervous and worried.

THESAURUS

anxious: *They had to wait ten anxious days.*

nerve-racking: *It was more nerve-racking than taking a World Cup penalty.*

stressful: *a stressful job*

3 If your body is tense, your muscles are tight.

THESAURUS

rigid: *Andrew went rigid whenever he saw a dog.*

strained: *His shoulders were strained with effort.*

taut: *when muscles are taut or cold*

tight: *It is better to stretch the tight muscles first.*

<<OPPOSITE *relaxed*

> VERB

4 If you tense, or if your muscles tense, your muscles become tight and stiff.

> NOUN

5 The tense of a verb is the form which shows whether you are talking about the past, present, or future.

tension ['tɛnʃən] **tensions** NOUN

1 Tension is the feeling of nervousness or worry that you have when something dangerous or important is happening.

2 (D & T) The tension in a rope or wire is how tightly it is stretched.

tent [tɛnt] **tents** NOUN
a shelter made of canvas or nylon held up by poles and pinned down with pegs and ropes

tentacle ['tɛntək(ə)l] **tentacles** NOUN
The tentacles of an animal such as an octopus are the long, thin parts that it uses to feel and hold things.

tentative ['tɛntətɪv] ADJECTIVE
acting or speaking cautiously because of being uncertain or afraid
tentatively ADVERB

tenterhooks ['tɛntə,hʊks] PLURAL NOUN
If you are on tenterhooks, you are nervous and excited about something that is going to happen.
[WORD HISTORY: from the hooks called TENTERHOOKS which were used to stretch cloth tight while it was drying]

tenuous ['tɛnjʊəs] ADJECTIVE
If an idea or connection is tenuous, it is so slight and weak that it may not really exist or may easily cease to exist. *e.g. a very tenuous friendship*

tenure ['tɛnjʊə] **tenures** NOUN

1 Tenure is the legal right to live in a place or to use land or buildings for a period of time.

2 Tenure is the period of time during which someone holds an important job. *e.g. His tenure ended in 1998.*

tepee ['tiːpiː] **tepees** NOUN
a cone-shaped tent of animal skins used by Native Americans

tepid ['tɛpɪd] ADJECTIVE
Tepid liquid is only slightly warm.

term [tɜːm] **terms, terming, termed** NOUN

1 a fixed period of time *e.g. her second term of office*

THESAURUS

period: *for a limited period only*

session: *The parliamentary session ends on October 4th.*

spell: *a six-month spell of practical experience*

stretch: *He did an 18-month stretch in prison.*

time: *He served the time of his contract and then left the company.*

2 one of the periods of time that each year is divided into at a school or college

3 a name or word used for a particular thing

THESAURUS

designation: *Level Four Alert is a designation reserved for very serious incidents.*

expression: *She used some remarkably coarse expressions.*

name: *The correct name for this condition is bovine spongiform encephalopathy.*

word: *The word ginseng comes from the Chinese "Shen-seng".*

> PLURAL NOUN

4 The terms of an agreement are the conditions that have been accepted by the people involved in it.

THESAURUS

conditions: *They may be breaching the conditions of their contract.*

provisions: *the provisions of the Amsterdam treaty*

proviso: *He left me the house with the proviso that it had to stay in the family.*

stipulations: *He left, violating the stipulations of his parole.*

5 If you express something in particular terms, you express it using a particular type of language or in a way that clearly shows your attitude. *e.g. The young priest spoke of her in glowing terms.*

> PHRASE

6 If you **come to terms with** something difficult or unpleasant, you learn to accept it.

> VERB

7 To term something is to give it a name or to describe it. *e.g. He termed my performance memorable.*

t

terminal ['tɜ:mɪnªl] **terminals** ADJECTIVE

1 A terminal illness or disease cannot be cured and causes death gradually.

> NOUN

2 a place where vehicles, passengers, or goods begin or end a journey

3 A computer terminal is a keyboard and a visual display unit that is used to put information into or get information out of a computer.

4 one of the parts of an electrical device through which electricity enters or leaves
terminally ADVERB

terminate ['tɜ:mɪˌneɪt] **terminates, terminating, terminated** VERB
When you terminate something or when it terminates, it stops or ends.
termination NOUN

terminology [ˌtɜ:mɪˈnɒlədʒɪ] **terminologies** NOUN
The terminology of a subject is the set of special words and expressions used in it.

terminus ['tɜ:mɪnəs] **terminuses** NOUN
a place where a bus or train route ends

termite ['tɜ:maɪt] **termites** NOUN
Termites are small white insects that feed on wood.

tern [tɜ:n] **terns** NOUN
a small black and white sea bird with long wings and a forked tail

ternary ['tɜ:nərɪ] ADJECTIVE
(MUSIC) Ternary form is a musical structure of three sections, the first and the second contrasting with each other and the third being a repetition of the first.

terrace ['tɛrəs] **terraces** NOUN
1 a row of houses joined together
2 a flat area of stone next to a building where people can sit

terracotta [ˌtɛrəˈkɒtə] NOUN
a type of brown pottery with no glaze
[WORD HISTORY: from Italian TERRA COTTA meaning 'baked earth']

terrain [təˈreɪn] NOUN
The terrain of an area is the type of land there.
e.g. the region's hilly terrain

terrapin ['tɛrəpɪn] **terrapins** NOUN
a small North American freshwater turtle

terrestrial [təˈrɛstrɪəl] ADJECTIVE
involving the earth or land

terrible ['tɛrəbªl] ADJECTIVE
1 serious and unpleasant *e.g. a terrible illness*
● THESAURUS
appalling: *an appalling headache*

awful: *an awful crime*
desperate: *a desperate situation*
dreadful: *a dreadful mistake*
frightful: old-fashioned *He got himself into a frightful muddle.*
horrendous: *horrendous injuries*
horrible: *a horrible mess*
horrid: old-fashioned *What a horrid smell!*
rotten: *What rotten luck!*

2 INFORMAL
very bad or of poor quality *e.g. Paddy's terrible haircut.*
● THESAURUS
abysmal: *The standard of play was abysmal.*
appalling: *Her singing is appalling.*
awful: *Jeans look awful on me.*
dire: *Most of the poems were dire.*
dreadful: *My financial situation is dreadful.*
horrible: *a horrible meal*
rotten: *I think it's a rotten idea.*
<<OPPOSITE *excellent*

terribly ['tɛrəblɪ] ADVERB
very or very much *e.g. I was terribly upset.*

terrier ['tɛrɪə] **terriers** NOUN
a small, short-bodied dog

terrific [təˈrɪfɪk] ADJECTIVE
1 INFORMAL
very pleasing or impressive *e.g. a terrific film*
2 great in amount, degree, or intensity *e.g. a terrific blow on the head*
terrifically ADVERB

terrify ['tɛrɪˌfaɪ] **terrifies, terrifying, terrified** VERB
If something terrifies you, it makes you feel extremely frightened.

territorial [ˌtɛrɪˈtɔ:rɪəl] ADJECTIVE
involving or relating to the ownership of a particular area of land or water *e.g. a territorial dispute*

territory ['tɛrɪtərɪ] **territories** NOUN
1 The territory of a country is the land that it controls.
● THESAURUS
area: *They claim that the entire area belongs to Syria.*
country: *He is an ambassador to a foreign country.*
district: *Stick to your own district and stay out of ours.*
domain: *He surveyed his domain from the roof of the castle.*
dominion: *men who ruled their dominions with ruthless efficiency*
land: *New mines were discovered on what had been Apache land.*
province: *debates about the political future of their province*

state: *This state remains suspended from the Commonwealth.*

2 An animal's territory is an area which it regards as its own and defends when other animals try to enter it.

terror ['tɛrə] **terrors** NOUN

1 Terror is great fear or panic.

2 something that makes you feel very frightened

terrorism ['tɛrə,rızəm] NOUN
Terrorism is the use of violence for political reasons.
terrorist NOUN OR ADJECTIVE

terrorize ['tɛrə,raız] **terrorizes, terrorizing, terrorized**; also spelt **terrorise** VERB
If someone terrorizes you, they frighten you by threatening you or being violent to you.

terse [tɜːs] **terser, tersest** ADJECTIVE
A terse statement is short and rather unfriendly.

tertiary ['tɜːʃərı] ADJECTIVE
1 third in order or importance

2 Tertiary education is education at university or college level.

test [tɛst] **tests, testing, tested** VERB
1 When you test something, you try it to find out what it is, what condition it is in, or how well it works.

● THESAURUS
assess: *The test was to assess aptitude rather than academic achievement.*
check: *It's worth checking each item for obvious flaws.*
try: *Howard wanted me to try the wine.*
try out: *London Transport hopes to try out the system in September.*

2 If you test someone, you ask them questions to find out how much they know.

> NOUN

3 a deliberate action or experiment to find out whether something works or how well it works

● THESAURUS
assessment: *He was remanded for assessment by doctors.*
check: *regular checks on his blood pressure*
trial: *clinical trials*

4 a set of questions or tasks given to someone to find out what they know or can do

testament ['tɛstəmənt] **testaments** NOUN
1 LEGAL a will

2 a copy of either the Old or the New Testament of the Bible

test case test cases NOUN
a legal case that becomes an example for

deciding other similar cases

testicle ['tɛstɪkəl] **testicles** NOUN
A man's testicles are the two sex glands that produce sperm.

testify ['tɛstɪ,faɪ] **testifies, testifying, testified** VERB
1 When someone testifies, they make a formal statement, especially in a court of law. *e.g. Ismay later testified at the British inquiry.*

2 To testify to something is to show that it is likely to be true. *e.g. a consultant's certificate testifying to her good health*

testimonial [,tɛstɪ'məʊnɪəl] **testimonials** NOUN
a statement saying how good someone or something is

testimony ['tɛstɪmənı] **testimonies** NOUN
A person's testimony is a formal statement they make, especially in a court of law.

testing ['tɛstɪŋ] ADJECTIVE
Testing situations or problems are very difficult to deal with. *e.g. It is a testing time for his team.*

testis ['tɛstɪs] **testes** NOUN
A man's testes are his testicles.

test match test matches NOUN
one of a series of international cricket or rugby matches

testosterone [tɛ'stɒstə,rəʊn] NOUN
Testosterone is a male hormone that produces male characteristics.

test tube test tubes NOUN
a small cylindrical glass container that is used in chemical experiments

tetanus ['tɛtənəs] NOUN
Tetanus is a painful infectious disease caused by germs getting into wounds.

tether ['tɛðə] **tethers, tethering, tethered** VERB
1 If you tether an animal, you tie it to a post.
> PHRASE
2 If you are **at the end of your tether**, you are extremely tired and have no more patience or energy left to deal with your problems.

Teutonic [tjuː'tɒnɪk] ADJECTIVE; FORMAL
involving or related to German people

text [tɛkst] **texts, texting, texted** NOUN
1 The text of a book is the main written part of it, rather than the pictures or index.

2 Text is any written material.

3 a book or other piece of writing used for study or an exam at school or college

4 Text is short for 'text message'.

> VERB

5 If you text someone, you send them a text message.
textual ADJECTIVE

textbook ['tɛkst͵bʊk] **textbooks** NOUN
a book about a particular subject for students to use

textile ['tɛkstaɪl] **textiles** NOUN
(D & T) a woven cloth or fabric

text message text messages NOUN
a written message sent using a mobile phone

texture ['tɛkstʃə] **textures** NOUN
The texture of something is the way it feels when you touch it.

⬤ THESAURUS
consistency: *Mix the dough to the right consistency.*
feel: *Linen raincoats have a crisp, papery feel.*

Thai [taɪ] **Thais** ADJECTIVE
1 belonging or relating to Thailand

> NOUN

2 someone who comes from Thailand
3 Thai is the main language spoken in Thailand.

than [ðæn] PREPOSITION OR CONJUNCTION
1 You use 'than' to link two parts of a comparison. *e.g. She was older than me.*
2 You use 'than' to link two parts of a contrast. *e.g. Players would rather play than train.*

thank [θæŋk] **thanks, thanking, thanked**
VERB
When you thank someone, you show that you are grateful for something, usually by saying 'thank you'.

thankful ['θæŋkfʊl] ADJECTIVE
happy and relieved that something has happened
thankfully ADVERB

thankless ['θæŋklɪs] ADJECTIVE
A thankless job or task involves doing a lot of hard work that other people do not notice or are not grateful for. *e.g. Referees have a thankless task.*

thanks [θæŋks] PLURAL NOUN
1 When you express your thanks to someone, you tell or show them how grateful you are for something.

> PHRASE

2 If something happened **thanks to** someone or something, it happened because of them. *e.g. I'm as prepared as I can be, thanks to you.*

> INTERJECTION

3 You say 'thanks' to show that you are grateful for something.

thanksgiving ['θæŋks͵gɪvɪŋ] NOUN

1 Thanksgiving is an act of thanking God, especially in prayer or in a religious ceremony.
2 In the United States, Thanksgiving is a public holiday in the autumn.

thank you
You say 'thank you' to show that you are grateful to someone for something.

that [ðæt] **those** ADJECTIVE OR PRONOUN
1 'That' or 'those' is used to refer to things or people already mentioned or known about *e.g. That man was waving.*

> CONJUNCTION

2 'That' is used to introduce a clause *e.g. I said that I was coming home.*

> PRONOUN

3 'That' is also used to introduce a relative clause *e.g. I followed Alex to a door that led inside.*

You can use either *that* or *which* in clauses known as defining clauses. These are clauses that identify the object you are talking about. In the sentence *The book that is on the table is mine, 'that is on the table'* is a defining clause which distinguishes the book from other books that are not on the table. Some people think these types of clause should only be introduced by *that*, and *which* should be kept for nondefining clauses. These nondefining clauses add extra information about the object, but do not identify it. In the sentence *The book, which is on the table, is mine, 'which is on the table'* is a nondefining clause which gives the reader extra detail about the book

thatch [θætʃ] **thatches, thatching, thatched** NOUN
1 Thatch is straw and reeds used to make roofs.

> VERB

2 To thatch a roof is to cover it with thatch.

thaw [θɔː] **thaws, thawing, thawed** VERB
1 When snow or ice thaws, it melts.
2 When you thaw frozen food, or when it thaws, it returns to its normal state in a warmer atmosphere.
3 When people who are unfriendly thaw, they begin to be more friendly and relaxed.

> NOUN

4 a period of warmer weather in winter when snow or ice melts

the [ðə] ADJECTIVE
The definite article 'the' is used when you are talking about something that is known about, that has just been mentioned, or that you are going to give details about.

theatre ['θɪətə] **theatres** NOUN

1 (DRAMA) a building where plays and other entertainments are performed on a stage

2 Theatre is work such as writing, producing, and acting in plays.

3 An operating theatre is a room in a hospital designed and equipped for surgical operations. [WORD HISTORY: from Greek THEATRON meaning 'viewing place']

theatrical [θɪˈætrɪkᵊl] ADJECTIVE

1 (DRAMA) involving the theatre or performed in a theatre *e.g. his theatrical career*

2 Theatrical behaviour is exaggerated, unnatural, and done for effect.
theatrically ADVERB

thee [ðiː] PRONOUN; OLD-FASHIONED, INFORMAL
Thee means you.

theft [θɛft] **thefts** NOUN
Theft is the crime of stealing.

● THESAURUS
robbery: *The man was serving a sentence for robbery.*

stealing: *She was jailed for six months for stealing.*

thieving: *an ex-con who says he's given up thieving*

their [ðɛə] ADJECTIVE
'Their' refers to something belonging or relating to people or things, other than yourself or the person you are talking to, which have already been mentioned *e.g. It was their fault.*

▨ Be careful not to confuse *their* with *there*

theirs [ðɛəz] PRONOUN
'Theirs' refers to something belonging or relating to people or things, other than yourself or the person you are talking to, which have already been mentioned *e.g. Amy had been Helen's friend, not theirs.*

them [ðɛm] PRONOUN
'Them' refers to things or people, other than yourself or the people you are talking to, which have already been mentioned *e.g. He picked up the pillows and threw them to the floor.*

theme [θiːm] **themes** NOUN

1 a main idea or topic in a piece of writing, painting, film, or music *e.g. the main theme of the book*

2 a tune, especially one played at the beginning and end of a television or radio programme

themselves [ðəmˈsɛlvz] PRONOUN

1 'Themselves' is used when people, other than yourself or the person you are talking to, do an action and are affected by it *e.g. They think they've made a fool of themselves.*

2 'Themselves' is used to emphasize 'they' *e.g. He was as excited as they themselves were.*

then [ðɛn] ADVERB
at a particular time in the past or future *e.g. I'd left home by then.*

theologian [ˌθɪəˈləʊdʒɪən] **theologians** NOUN
someone who studies religion and the nature of God

theology [θɪˈɒlədʒɪ] NOUN
Theology is the study of religion and God.
theological ADJECTIVE

theoretical [ˌθɪəˈrɛtɪkᵊl] ADJECTIVE

1 based on or to do with ideas of a subject rather than the practical aspects

2 not proved to exist or be true
theoretically ADVERB

theory [ˈθɪərɪ] **theories** NOUN

1 an idea or set of ideas that is meant to explain something *e.g. Darwin's theory of evolution.*

● THESAURUS
conjecture: *That was a conjecture, not a fact.*
hypothesis: *Different hypotheses have been put forward.*
supposition: *As with many such suppositions, no one had ever tested it.*
surmise: *formal His surmise proved correct.*

2 Theory is the set of rules and ideas that a particular subject or skill is based upon.

> PHRASE
3 You use **in theory** to say that although something is supposed to happen, it may not in fact happen. *e.g. In theory, prices should rise by 2%.*

therapeutic [ˌθɛrəˈpjuːtɪk] ADJECTIVE

1 If something is therapeutic, it helps you to feel happier and more relaxed. *e.g. Laughing is therapeutic.*

2 In medicine, therapeutic treatment is designed to treat a disease or to improve a person's health.

therapy [ˈθɛrəpɪ] NOUN
Therapy is the treatment of mental or physical illness, often without the use of drugs or operations.
therapist NOUN

there [ðɛə] ADVERB

1 in, at, or to that place, point, or case *e.g. He's sitting over there.*

> PRONOUN
2 'There' is used to say that something exists or does not exist, or to draw attention to something *e.g. There are flowers on the table.*

▌ Be careful not to confuse *there* with *their*. A good way to remember that *there* is connected to the idea of place is by remembering the spelling of two other place words, *here* and *where*

thereby [ˌðɛəˈbaɪ] ADVERB; FORMAL
as a result of the event or action mentioned *e.g. They had recruited 200 new members, thereby making the day worthwhile.*

therefore [ˈðɛəˌfɔː] ADVERB
as a result

● THESAURUS
as a result: *I slept in, and, as a result, I was late for work.*
consequently: *He's more experienced, and consequently earns a higher salary.*
for that reason: *I'd never met my in-laws before. For that reason, I was a little nervous.*
hence: formal *These products are all natural, and hence, better for you.*
so: *I was worried about her, so I phoned to check how she was.*
thus: *His men were getting tired, and thus, careless.*

thermal [ˈθɜːməl] ADJECTIVE
1 to do with or caused by heat *e.g. thermal energy*
2 Thermal clothes are specially designed to keep you warm in cold weather.

thermometer [θəˈmɒmɪtə] **thermometers** NOUN
(SCIENCE) an instrument for measuring the temperature of a room or a person's body

thermostat [ˈθɜːməˌstæt] **thermostats** NOUN
a device used to control temperature, for example on a central heating system

thesaurus [θɪˈsɔːrəs] **thesauruses** NOUN
(LIBRARY) a reference book in which words with similar meanings are grouped together
[WORD HISTORY] from Greek THĒSAUROS meaning 'treasure']

these [ðiːz] the plural of **this**

thesis [ˈθiːsɪs] **theses** NOUN
a long piece of writing, based on research, that is done as part of a university degree

they [ðeɪ] PRONOUN
1 'They' refers to people or things, other than you or the people you are talking to, that have already been mentioned *e.g. They married two years later.*
2 'They' is sometimes used instead of 'he' or 'she' where the sex of the person is unknown or unspecified. Some people consider this to be incorrect *e.g. Someone could have a nasty accident if they tripped over that.*

thick [θɪk] **thicker, thickest** ADJECTIVE
1 Something thick has a large distance between its two opposite surfaces.

● THESAURUS
fat: *a fat book*
wide: *a desk that was almost as wide as the room*

<<OPPOSITE *thin*

2 If something is a particular amount thick, it measures that amount between its two sides.
3 Thick means growing or grouped closely together and in large quantities. *e.g. thick dark hair*

● THESAURUS
bristling: *a bristling moustache*
dense: *a large dense forest*
lush: *the lush green meadows*
luxuriant: *the luxuriant foliage of Young Island*
<<OPPOSITE *sparse*

4 Thick liquids contain little water and do not flow easily. *e.g. thick soup*

● THESAURUS
clotted: *clotted cream*
concentrated: *a glass of concentrated orange juice*
condensed: *tins of condensed milk*
<<OPPOSITE *watery*

5 INFORMAL
A thick person is stupid or slow to understand things.

thicken [ˈθɪkən] **thickens, thickening, thickened** VERB
If something thickens, it becomes thicker. *e.g. The clouds thickened.*

● THESAURUS
clot: *The patient's blood refused to clot.*
condense: *Water vapour condenses to form clouds.*
congeal: *The blood had started to congeal.*
set: *as the jelly starts to set*
<<OPPOSITE *thin*

thicket [ˈθɪkɪt] **thickets** NOUN
a small group of trees growing closely together

thief [θiːf] **thieves** NOUN
a person who steals

● THESAURUS
burglar: *Burglars broke into their home.*
crook: informal *a petty crook*
mugger: informal *after being threatened by a mugger*
pickpocket: *a gang of pickpockets*
robber: *armed robbers*
shoplifter: *a persistent shoplifter*

thieving [ˈθiːvɪŋ] NOUN
Thieving is the act of stealing.

thigh [θaɪ] **thighs** NOUN
Your thighs are the top parts of your legs, between your knees and your hips.

thimble [ˈθɪmbəl] **thimbles** NOUN
a small metal or plastic cap that you put on the end of your finger to protect it when you are sewing

thin see page 905 for Word Web

1 ADJECTIVE
measuring a small distance from side to side eg: *The material was too thin.*
● THESAURUS
fine: *the fine hairs on her arms*
narrow: *a narrow strip of land*
slim: *a slim volume of verse*
<< OPPOSITE *thick*

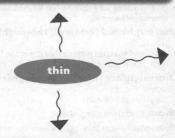

2 ADJECTIVE
not carrying a lot of fat eg: *a tall, thin man with grey hair*
● THESAURUS
emaciated: *horrific television pictures of emaciated prisoners*
lean: *Like most athletes, she was lean and muscular.*
lanky: *He had grown into a lanky teenager.*
light: *You need to be light to be a dancer.*
scraggy: *a scraggy, shrill, neurotic woman*
scrawny: *a scrawny child of fifteen*
skinny: *I don't think these skinny supermodels are at all sexy.*
slender: *a tall, slender lady in a straw hat*
slight: *He is a slight, bespectacled, intellectual figure.*
slim: *a pretty, slim girl with blue eyes*
spare: *She was thin and spare, with a sharp, intelligent face.*
underweight: *Nearly a third of the girls were severely underweight.*
<< OPPOSITE *fat*

3 ADJECTIVE
containing a lot of water eg: *thin soup.*
● THESAURUS
dilute or **diluted**: *a dilute solution of bleach*
runny: *a runny soft cheese*
watery: *watery beer*
weak: *a cup of weak tea*
<< OPPOSITE *thick*

t

thing [θɪŋ] **things** NOUN
1 an object, rather than a plant, an animal, a human being

● THESAURUS
article: *household articles*
object: *everyday objects such as wooden spoons*

> PLURAL NOUN
2 Your things are your clothes or possessions.

● THESAURUS
belongings: *He was identified only by his personal belongings.*
effects: *His daughters were collecting his effects.*
gear: *They helped us put our gear back into the van.*
possessions: *People had lost all their possessions.*
stuff: *Where have you put all your stuff?*

think see page 907 for Word Web

third [θɜːd] **thirds** ADJECTIVE
1 The third item in a series is the one counted as number three.

> NOUN
2 one of three equal parts

Third World NOUN
The poorer countries of Africa, Asia, and South America can be referred to as the Third World.

thirst [θɜːst] **thirsts** NOUN
1 If you have a thirst, you feel a need to drink something.

2 A thirst for something is a very strong desire for it. *e.g. a thirst for money*
thirsty ADJECTIVE, **thirstily** ADVERB

thirteen ['θɜːˈtiːn]
the number 13
thirteenth

thirty ['θɜːtɪ] **thirties**
the number 30
thirtieth

this [ðɪs] **these** ADJECTIVE OR PRONOUN
1 'This' is used to refer to something or someone that is nearby or has just been mentioned *e.g. This is Robert.*

2 'This' is used to refer to the present time or place *e.g. this week*

thistle ['θɪsəl] **thistles** NOUN
a wild plant with prickly-edged leaves and purple flowers

thong [θɒŋ] **thongs** NOUN
a long narrow strip of leather

thorn [θɔːn] **thorns** NOUN
one of many sharp points growing on some plants and trees

thorny ['θɔːnɪ] **thornier, thorniest** ADJECTIVE

1 covered with thorns

2 A thorny subject or question is difficult to discuss or answer.

thorough ['θʌrə] ADJECTIVE
1 done very carefully and completely *e.g. a thorough examination*

● THESAURUS
complete: *a complete overhaul of the engine*
comprehensive: *a comprehensive guide to the region*
exhaustive: *exhaustive enquiries*
full: *Mr Primakov gave a full account of his meeting with the President.*
intensive: *four weeks of intensive study*
meticulous: *A happy wedding day requires meticulous planning.*
painstaking: *a painstaking search*
scrupulous: *Observe scrupulous hygiene when preparing and cooking food.*

2 A thorough person is very careful in what they do and makes sure nothing has been missed out.
thoroughly ADVERB

thoroughbred ['θʌrə,brɛd] **thoroughbreds** NOUN
an animal that has parents that are of the same high quality breed

thoroughfare ['θʌrə,fɛə] **thoroughfares** NOUN
a main road in a town

those [ðəʊz] the plural of **that**

thou [ðaʊ] PRONOUN; OLD-FASHIONED, INFORMAL
Thou means you.

though [ðəʊ] CONJUNCTION
1 despite the fact that *e.g. Meg felt better, even though she knew it was the end.*

2 if *e.g. It looks as though you were right.*

thought [θɔːt] **thoughts**
1 Thought is the past tense and past participle of **think**

> NOUN
2 an idea that you have in your mind

● THESAURUS
idea: *his ideas about democracy*
notion: *We each have a notion of what kind of person we'd like to be.*
opinion: *most of those who expressed an opinion*
view: *Make your views known to your MP.*

3 Thought is the activity of thinking. *e.g. She was lost in thought.*

● THESAURUS
consideration: *There should be careful consideration of the BBC's future role.*
contemplation: *He was lost in contemplation of the landscape.*

1 VERB
When you think about ideas or problems, you use your mind to consider them.

● THESAURUS

consider: *The government is being asked to consider the plan.*

contemplate: *He cried as he contemplated his future.*

deliberate: *She deliberated over the decision for a good few years.*

meditate: *He meditated on the problem.*

mull over: *I'll leave you alone so you can mull it over.*

muse (literary): *Many of the papers muse on the fate of the President.*

ponder: *I'm continually pondering how to improve the team.*

reflect: *I reflected on the child's future.*

think
thinks, thinking, thought

2 VERB
If you think something, you have the opinion that it is true or the case *eg: I think she has a secret boyfriend.*

● THESAURUS

believe: *Experts believe that the drought will be extensive.*

consider: *He considers that this is the worst recession this century.*

deem (formal): *Many people have ideas that their society deems to be dangerous.*

hold: *The theory holds that minor events are the trigger for larger events.*

imagine: *I imagine he was just showing off.*

judge: *He judged that this was the moment to say what had to be said.*

reckon: *Toni reckoned that it must be about three o'clock.*

t

deliberation: *the result of lengthy deliberation*
meditation: *He stared at the floor, lost in meditation.*
reflection: *after days of reflection*
thinking: *THis is definitely a time for decisive action and quick thinking.*

4 Thought is a particular way of thinking or a particular set of ideas. *e.g. this school of thought*

thoughtful ['θɔːtfʊl] ADJECTIVE
1 When someone is thoughtful, they are quiet and serious because they are thinking about something.

● THESAURUS
contemplative: *a quiet, contemplative sort of chap*
pensive: *He looked unusually pensive before the start.*
reflective: *I walked on in a reflective mood.*

2 A thoughtful person remembers what other people want or need, and tries to be kind to them.
thoughtfully ADVERB

● THESAURUS
attentive: *an attentive husband*
caring: *a caring son*
considerate: *the most considerate man I've ever known*
kind: *She is warmhearted and kind to everyone.*
<<OPPOSITE *thoughtless*

thoughtless ['θɔːtlɪs] ADJECTIVE
A thoughtless person forgets or ignores what other people want, need, or feel.
thoughtlessly ADVERB

● THESAURUS
insensitive: *My husband is very insensitive about my problem.*
tactless: *a tactless remark*
<<OPPOSITE *thoughtful*

thousand ['θaʊzənd] **thousands**
the number 1000
thousandth

thrash [θræʃ] **thrashes, thrashing, thrashed** VERB
1 To thrash someone is to beat them by hitting them with something.
2 To thrash someone in a contest or fight is to defeat them completely.
3 To thrash out a problem or an idea is to discuss it in detail until a solution is reached.

thread [θrɛd] **threads, threading, threaded** NOUN
1 a long, fine piece of cotton, silk, nylon, or wool
2 The thread on something such as a screw or the top of a container is the raised spiral line of metal or plastic round it.

3 The thread of an argument or story is an idea or theme that connects the different parts of it.
> VERB
4 When you thread something, you pass thread, tape, or cord through it.
5 If you thread your way through people or things, you carefully make your way through them.

threadbare ['θrɛd,bɛə] ADJECTIVE
Threadbare cloth or clothing is old and thin.

threat [θrɛt] **threats** NOUN
1 a statement that someone will harm you, especially if you do not do what they want

● THESAURUS
menace: *demanding money with menaces*
threatening remark: *He was overheard making threatening remarks to the couple.*

2 anything or anyone that seems likely to harm you

● THESAURUS
hazard: *a health hazard*
menace: *a menace to the public*
risk: *a fire risk*

3 If there is a threat of something unpleasant happening, it is very possible that it will happen.

threaten ['θrɛtᵊn] **threatens, threatening, threatened** VERB
1 If you threaten to harm someone or threaten to do something that will upset them, you say that you will do it.

● THESAURUS
make threats to: *despite all the threats he'd made to harm her*
menace: *She's being menaced by her sister's latest boyfriend.*

2 If someone or something threatens a person or thing, they are likely to harm them.

● THESAURUS
endanger: *Toxic waste could endanger lives.*
jeopardize: *He has jeopardized the future of his government.*
put at risk: *If they have the virus, they are putting patients at risk.*
put in jeopardy: *A series of setbacks have put the whole project in jeopardy.*

three [θriː]
the number 3

three-dimensional [,θriːdaɪ'mɛnʃᵊnᵊl] ADJECTIVE
A three-dimensional object or shape is not flat, but has height or depth as well as length and width.

threesome ['θriːsəm] **threesomes** NOUN
a group of three

threshold ['θrɛʃəʊld] **thresholds** NOUN

1 the doorway or the floor in the doorway of a building or room

2 The threshold of something is the lowest amount, level, or limit at which something happens or changes. *e.g. the tax threshold... His boredom threshold was exceptionally low.*

thrice [θraɪs] ADVERB; OLD-FASHIONED, INFORMAL
If you do something thrice, you do it three times.

thrift [θrɪft] NOUN
Thrift is the practice of saving money and not wasting things.

thrifty ['θrɪftɪ] **thriftier, thriftiest**
ADJECTIVE
A thrifty person saves money and does not waste things.

● THESAURUS
careful: *He's very careful with his money.*
economical: *a very economical way to travel*
frugal: *a frugal lifestyle*
prudent: *the need for a much more prudent use of energy*

thrill [θrɪl] **thrills, thrilling, thrilled** NOUN

1 a sudden feeling of great excitement, pleasure, or fear; also any event or experience that gives you such a feeling

● THESAURUS
high: *informal the high of a win over New Zealand*
kick: *informal I got a kick out of seeing my name in print.*

> VERB
2 If something thrills you, or you thrill to it, it gives you a feeling of great pleasure and excitement.
thrilled ADJECTIVE, **thrilling** ADJECTIVE

● THESAURUS
excite: *I only take on work that excites me.*
give a kick: *informal It gave me a kick to actually meet her.*

thriller ['θrɪlə] **thrillers** NOUN
a book, film, or play that tells an exciting story about dangerous or mysterious events

thrive [θraɪv] **thrives, thriving, thrived** or **throve** VERB
When people or things thrive, they are healthy, happy, or successful.
thriving ADJECTIVE

● THESAURUS
do well: *Connie did well at school.*
flourish: *Racism and crime still flourish in the ghetto.*
prosper: *His team have always prospered in cup competitions.*

throat [θrəʊt] **throats** NOUN

1 the back of your mouth and the top part of the passages inside your neck

2 the front part of your neck

throb [θrɒb] **throbs, throbbing, throbbed**
VERB

1 If a part of your body throbs, you feel a series of strong beats or dull pains.

2 If something throbs, it vibrates and makes a loud, rhythmic noise. *e.g. The engines throbbed.*

throes [θrəʊz] PLURAL NOUN

1 Throes are a series of violent pangs or movements. *e.g. death throes*

> PHRASE
2 If you are **in the throes of** something, you are deeply involved in it.

thrombosis [θrɒm'bəʊsɪs] **thromboses**
NOUN
a blood clot which blocks the flow of blood in the body. Thromboses are dangerous and often fatal.

throne [θrəʊn] **thrones** NOUN

1 a ceremonial chair used by a king or queen on important official occasions

2 The throne is a way of referring to the position of being king or queen.

throng [θrɒŋ] **throngs, thronging, thronged** NOUN

1 a large crowd of people

> VERB
2 If people throng somewhere or throng a place, they go there in great numbers. *e.g. Hundreds of city workers thronged the scene.*

throttle ['θrɒt²l] **throttles, throttling, throttled** VERB
To throttle someone is to kill or injure them by squeezing their throat.

through [θruː] PREPOSITION

1 moving all the way from one side of something to the other *e.g. a path through the woods*

2 because of *e.g. He had been exhausted through lack of sleep.*

3 during *e.g. He has to work through the summer.*

4 If you go through an experience, it happens to you. *e.g. I don't want to go through that again.*

> ADJECTIVE
5 If you are through with something, you have finished doing it or using it.

▌ Do not confuse the spellings of *through* and *threw*, the past tense of *throw*

throughout [θruː'aʊt] PREPOSITION

1 during *e.g. I stayed awake throughout the night.*

> ADVERB
2 happening or existing through the whole of a

place *e.g. The house was painted brown throughout.*

throve [θrəʊv] the past tense of **thrive**

throw [θrəʊ] **throws, throwing, threw, thrown** VERB

1 When you throw something you are holding, you move your hand quickly and let it go, so that it moves through the air.

● THESAURUS

cast: *He cast the stone away.*
chuck: informal *He chucked the paper in the bin.*
fling: *Peter flung his shoes into the corner.*
hurl: *Groups of angry youths hurled stones at police.*
lob: *Thugs lobbed a grenade into the crowd.*
pitch: *Simon pitched the empty bottle into the lake.*
sling: *He took off his anorak and slung it into the back seat.*
toss: *She tossed her suitcase onto one of the beds.*

2 If you throw yourself somewhere, you move there suddenly and with force. *e.g. We threw ourselves on the ground.*

3 To throw someone into an unpleasant situation is to put them there. *e.g. It threw them into a panic.*

4 If something throws light or shadow on something else, it makes that thing have light or shadow on it.

5 If you throw yourself into an activity, you become actively and enthusiastically involved in it.

6 If you throw a fit or tantrum, you suddenly begin behaving in an uncontrolled way.

throwback ['θrəʊ,bæk] **throwbacks** NOUN
something which has the characteristics of something that existed a long time ago *e.g. Everything about her was a throwback to the fifties.*

thrush [θrʌʃ] **thrushes** NOUN

1 a small brown songbird

2 Thrush is a disease of the mouth or of the vagina, caused by a fungus.

thrust [θrʌst] **thrusts, thrusting, thrust** VERB

1 If you thrust something somewhere, you push or move it there quickly with a lot of force.

2 If you thrust your way somewhere, you move along, pushing between people or things.

> NOUN

3 a sudden forceful movement

4 The main thrust of an activity or idea is the most important part of it. *e.g. the general thrust of his argument*

thud [θʌd] **thuds, thudding, thudded** NOUN

1 a dull sound, usually made by a solid, heavy object hitting something soft

> VERB

2 If something thuds somewhere, it makes a dull sound, usually by hitting something else.

thug [θʌg] **thugs** NOUN
a very rough and violent person
[WORD HISTORY: from Hindi THAG meaning 'thief']

● THESAURUS

bandit: *terrorist acts carried out by bandits*
hooligan: *severe measures against soccer hooligans*
tough: *The neighbourhood toughs beat them both up.*
tsotsi: South African *Many are too terrified of local tsotsis to protest.*

thumb [θʌm] **thumbs, thumbing, thumbed** NOUN

1 the short, thick finger on the side of your hand

> VERB

2 If someone thumbs a lift, they stand at the side of the road and stick out their thumb until a driver stops and gives them a lift.

thump [θʌmp] **thumps, thumping, thumped** VERB

1 If you thump someone or something, you hit them hard with your fist.

2 If something thumps somewhere, it makes a fairly loud, dull sound, usually when it hits something else.

3 When your heart thumps, it beats strongly and quickly.

> NOUN

4 a hard hit *e.g. a great thump on the back*

5 a fairly loud, dull sound

thunder ['θʌndə] **thunders, thundering, thundered** NOUN

1 Thunder is a loud cracking or rumbling noise caused by expanding air which is suddenly heated by lightning.

2 Thunder is any loud rumbling noise. *e.g. the distant thunder of bombs*

> VERB

3 When it thunders, a loud cracking or rumbling noise occurs in the sky after a flash of lightning.

4 If something thunders, it makes a loud continuous noise. *e.g. The helicopter thundered low over the trees.*

thunderbolt ['θʌndə,bəʊlt] **thunderbolts** NOUN
a flash of lightning, accompanied by thunder

thunderous ['θʌndərəs] ADJECTIVE
A thunderous noise is very loud. *e.g. thunderous applause*

Thursday ['θɜːzdɪ] **Thursdays** NOUN
Thursday is the day between Wednesday and Friday.

[WORD HISTORY: from Old English THURSDÆG meaning 'Thor's day'; Thor was the Norse god of thunder]

thus [ðʌs] ADVERB; FORMAL

1 in this way *e.g. I sat thus for nearly half an hour.*

2 therefore *e.g. Critics were thus able to denounce him.*

thwart [θwɔːt] **thwarts, thwarting, thwarted** VERB

To thwart someone or their plans is to prevent them from doing or getting what they want.

thy [ðaɪ] ADJECTIVE; OLD-FASHIONED, INFORMAL

Thy means your.

thyme [taɪm] NOUN

Thyme is a bushy herb with very small leaves.

thyroid gland ['θaɪrɔɪd] **thyroid glands** NOUN

Your thyroid gland is situated at the base of your neck. It releases hormones which control your growth and your metabolism.

tiara [tɪ'ɑːrə] **tiaras** NOUN

a semicircular crown of jewels worn by a woman on formal occasions

Tibetan [tɪ'bɛtən] **Tibetans** ADJECTIVE

1 belonging or relating to Tibet

> NOUN

2 someone who comes from Tibet

tic [tɪk] **tics** NOUN

a twitching of a group of muscles, especially the muscles in the face

tick [tɪk] **ticks, ticking, ticked** NOUN

1 a written mark to show that something is correct or has been dealt with

2 The tick of a clock is the series of short sounds it makes when it is working.

3 a tiny, blood-sucking, insect-like creature that usually lives on the bodies of people or animals

> VERB

4 To tick something written on a piece of paper is to put a tick next to it.

5 When a clock ticks, it makes a regular series of short sounds as it works.

tick off VERB

6 INFORMAL If you tick someone off, you speak angrily to them because they have done something wrong.

ticking NOUN

ticket ['tɪkɪt] **tickets** NOUN

a piece of paper or card which shows that you have paid for a journey or have paid to enter a place of entertainment

tickle ['tɪkəl] **tickles, tickling, tickled** VERB

1 When you tickle someone, you move your fingers lightly over their body in order to make them laugh.

2 If something tickles you, it amuses you or gives you pleasure. *e.g. Simon is tickled by the idea.*

tidal ['taɪdəl] ADJECTIVE

to do with or produced by tides *e.g. a tidal estuary*

tidal wave tidal waves NOUN

a very large wave, often caused by an earthquake, that comes over land and destroys things

tide [taɪd] **tides, tiding, tided** NOUN

1 The tide is the regular change in the level of the sea on the shore, caused by the gravitational pull of the sun and the moon.

2 The tide of opinion or fashion is what the majority of people think or do at a particular time.

3 A tide of something is a large amount of it. *e.g. the tide of anger and bitterness*

tide over VERB

4 If something will tide someone over, it will help them through a difficult period of time.

tidings ['taɪdɪŋz] PLURAL NOUN; FORMAL

Tidings are news.

tidy ['taɪdɪ] **tidier, tidiest; tidies, tidying, tidied** ADJECTIVE

1 Something that is tidy is neat and arranged in an orderly way.

● THESAURUS

neat: *She put her clothes in a neat pile.*
orderly: *a beautiful, clean and orderly city*
<<OPPOSITE *untidy*

2 Someone who is tidy always keeps their things neat and arranged in an orderly way.

3 INFORMAL

A tidy amount of money is a fairly large amount of it.

> VERB

4 To tidy a place is to make it neat by putting things in their proper place.

● THESAURUS

spruce up: *Many buildings have been spruced up.*
straighten: *straightening cushions and organizing magazines*
<<OPPOSITE *mess up*

tie [taɪ] **ties, tying, tied** VERB

1 If you tie one thing to another or tie it in a particular position, you fasten it using cord of some kind.

● THESAURUS

bind: *Bind the ends of the cord together with thread.*
fasten: *instructions on how to fasten the strap to the box*

knot: *He knotted the laces securely together.*
lash: *The shelter is built by lashing poles together.*
rope: *I roped myself to the chimney.*
secure: *He secured the canvas straps as tight as they would go.*
tether: *tethering his horse to a tree*
truss: *She trussed him quickly with stolen bandage.*
<<OPPOSITE *untie*

2 If you tie a knot or a bow in a piece of cord or cloth, you fasten the ends together to make a knot or bow.

3 Something or someone that is tied to something else is closely linked with it. *e.g. 40,000 jobs are tied to the project*

4 If you tie with someone in a competition or game, you have the same number of points.

● **THESAURUS**
be level: *At the end of 90 minutes the teams were level.*
draw: *Holland and Ireland drew 1–1.*

> NOUN
5 a long, narrow piece of cloth worn around the neck under a shirt collar and tied in a knot at the front

6 a connection or feeling that links you with a person, place, or organization *e.g. I had very close ties with the family.*

● **THESAURUS**
affiliation: *They asked her what her political affiliations were.*
affinity: *He has a close affinity with the landscape.*
bond: *The experience created a special bond between us.*
connection: *The police say he had no connection with the security forces.*
relationship: *family relationships*

tied up [taɪd] ADJECTIVE
If you are tied up, you are busy.

tier [tɪə] **tiers** NOUN
one of a number of rows or layers of something *e.g. Take the stairs to the upper tier.*

tiff [tɪf] **tiffs** NOUN
a small unimportant quarrel

tiger [ˈtaɪɡə] **tigers** NOUN
a large meat-eating animal of the cat family. It comes from Asia and has an orange coloured coat with black stripes

tiger snake tiger snakes NOUN
a fierce, very poisonous Australian snake with dark stripes across its back

tight [taɪt] **tighter, tightest** ADJECTIVE
1 fitting closely *e.g. The shoes are too tight.*

● **THESAURUS**
constricted: *His throat began to feel swollen and constricted.*

cramped: *families living in cramped conditions*
snug: *a snug black T-shirt*
<<OPPOSITE *loose*

2 firmly fastened and difficult to move *e.g. a tight knot*

● **THESAURUS**
firm: *He managed to get a firm grip of it.*
secure: *Check joints are secure and the wood is sound.*

3 stretched or pulled so as not to be slack *e.g. a tight cord*

● **THESAURUS**
rigid: *I went rigid with shock.*
taut: *The clothes line is pulled taut and secured.*
tense: *A bath can relax tense muscles.*
<<OPPOSITE *slack*

4 A tight plan or arrangement allows only the minimum time or money needed to do something. *e.g. Our schedule tonight is very tight.*

> ADVERB
5 held firmly and securely *e.g. He held me tight.*
tightly ADVERB, **tightness** NOUN

tighten [ˈtaɪtən] **tightens, tightening, tightened** VERB
1 If you tighten your hold on something, you hold it more firmly.

2 If you tighten a rope or chain, or if it tightens, it is stretched or pulled until it is straight.

3 If someone tightens a rule or system, they make it stricter or more efficient.

tightrope [ˈtaɪtˌrəʊp] **tightropes** NOUN
a tightly-stretched rope on which an acrobat balances and performs tricks

tights [taɪts] PLURAL NOUN
Tights are a piece of clothing made of thin stretchy material that fit closely round a person's hips, legs, and feet.

tiki [ˈtiːkɪ] **tiki** or **tikis** NOUN
In New Zealand, a small carving of an ancestor worn as a pendant in some Maori cultures.

tile [taɪl] **tiles, tiling, tiled** NOUN
1 a small flat square piece of something, for example slate or carpet, that is used to cover surfaces

> VERB
2 To tile a surface is to fix tiles to it.
tiled ADJECTIVE

till [tɪl] **tills, tilling, tilled** PREPOSITION OR CONJUNCTION
1 Till means the same as until.

> NOUN
2 a drawer or box in a shop where money is kept, usually in a cash register

> VERB

3 To till the ground is to plough it for raising crops.

tiller ['tɪlə] **tillers** NOUN
the handle fixed to the top of the rudder for steering a boat

tilt [tɪlt] **tilts, tilting, tilted** VERB
1 If you tilt an object or it tilts, it changes position so that one end or side is higher than the other.

● THESAURUS
incline: *Jack inclined his head.*
lean: *Lean the plants against a wall.*
slant: *The floor slanted down to the window.*
slope: *The bank sloped down sharply to the river.*
tip: *She had to tip her head back to see him.*

> NOUN

2 a position in which one end or side of something is higher than the other

● THESAURUS
angle: *The boat is now leaning at a 30 degree angle.*
gradient: *a gradient of 1 in 3*
incline: *at the edge of a steep incline*
slant: *The house is on a slant.*
slope: *The street must have been on a slope.*

timber ['tɪmbə] **timbers** NOUN
1 Timber is wood that has been cut and prepared ready for building and making furniture.
2 The timbers of a ship or house are the large pieces of wood that have been used to build it.

time see page 914 for Word Web

timeless ['taɪmlɪs] ADJECTIVE
Something timeless is so good or beautiful that it cannot be affected by the passing of time or by changes in fashion.

timely ['taɪmlɪ] ADJECTIVE
happening at just the right time *e.g. a timely appearance*

timer ['taɪmə] **timers** NOUN
a device that measures time, especially one that is part of a machine

timescale ['taɪm,skeɪl] **timescales** NOUN
The timescale of an event is the length of time during which it happens.

timetable ['taɪm,teɪbəl] **timetables** NOUN
1 a plan of the times when particular activities or jobs should be done
2 a list of the times when particular trains, boats, buses, or aeroplanes arrive and depart

timid ['tɪmɪd] ADJECTIVE
shy and having no courage or self-confidence
timidly ADVERB, **timidity** NOUN

● THESAURUS
bashful: *Offstage, he is bashful and awkward.*

cowardly: *I was too cowardly to complain.*
diffident: *Helen was diffident and reserved.*
nervous: *a very nervous woman*
shy: *a shy, quiet-spoken girl*
<<OPPOSITE **bold**

timing ['taɪmɪŋ] NOUN
1 Someone's timing is their skill in judging the right moment at which to do something.
2 The timing of an event is when it actually happens.

timpani ['tɪmpənɪ] PLURAL NOUN
Timpani are large drums with curved bottoms that are played in an orchestra.

tin [tɪn] **tins** NOUN
1 Tin is a soft silvery-white metal.
2 a metal container which is filled with food and then sealed in order to preserve the food
3 a small metal container which may have a lid *e.g. a cake tin*

tinder ['tɪndə] NOUN
Tinder is small pieces of dry wood or grass that burn easily and can be used for lighting a fire.

tinge [tɪndʒ] **tinges** NOUN
a small amount of something *e.g. a tinge of envy*
tinged ADJECTIVE

tingle ['tɪŋgəl] **tingles, tingling, tingled** VERB
1 When a part of your body tingles, you feel a slight prickling feeling in it.

> NOUN

2 a slight prickling feeling
tingling NOUN OR ADJECTIVE

tinker ['tɪŋkə] **tinkers, tinkering, tinkered** NOUN
1 a person who travels from place to place mending metal pots and pans or doing other small repair jobs

> VERB

2 If you tinker with something, you make a lot of small changes to it in order to repair or improve it. *e.g. All he wanted was to tinker with engines.*

tinkle ['tɪŋkəl] **tinkles, tinkling, tinkled** VERB
1 If something tinkles, it makes a sound like a small bell ringing.

> NOUN

2 a sound like that of a small bell ringing

tinned [tɪnd] ADJECTIVE
Tinned food has been preserved by being sealed in a tin.

tinsel ['tɪnsəl] NOUN
Tinsel is long threads with strips of shiny paper

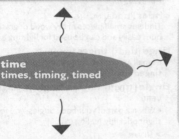

1 NOUN
'Time' is used to mean a particular period or point *eg: I enjoyed my time in Durban.*
● **THESAURUS**
interval: *a long interval of silence*
period: *a period of calm*
spell: *a brief spell teaching*
stretch: *an 18-month stretch in the army*
while: *They walked on in silence for a while.*

time
times, timing, timed

2 VERB
If you time something for a particular time, you plan that it should happen then *eg: We could not have timed our arrival better.*
● **THESAURUS**
schedule: *The space shuttle had been scheduled to blast off at 04:38.*
set: *A court hearing has been set for December 16.*

3 NOUN
a period or point marked by specific attributes or events *eg: in Victorian times*
● **THESAURUS**
age: *the age of steam and steel*
era: *It was an era of austerity.*

attached, used as a decoration at Christmas.

tint [tɪnt] **tints, tinting, tinted** NOUN
1 a small amount of a particular colour *e.g. a distinct tint of green*
> VERB
2 If a person tints their hair, they change its colour by adding a weak dye to it.
tinted ADJECTIVE

tiny ['taɪnɪ] **tinier, tiniest** ADJECTIVE
extremely small

◉ THESAURUS
diminutive: *a diminutive figure standing at the entrance*
microscopic: *a microscopic amount of the substance*
miniature: *He looked like a miniature version of his brother.*
minute: *Only a minute amount is needed.*
negligible: *The pay that the soldiers received was negligible.*
wee: Scottish *a wee boy*
<<OPPOSITE huge

tip [tɪp] **tips, tipping, tipped** NOUN
1 the end of something long and thin *e.g. a fingertip*
2 a place where rubbish is dumped
3 If you give someone such as a waiter a tip, you give them some money to thank them for their services.
4 a useful piece of advice or information
> VERB
5 If you tip an object, you move it so that it is no longer horizontal or upright.
6 If you tip something somewhere, you pour it there quickly or carelessly.
tipped ADJECTIVE

tipple ['tɪpəl] **tipples** NOUN
A person's tipple is the alcoholic drink that they normally drink.

tipsy ['tɪpsɪ] **tipsier, tipsiest** ADJECTIVE
slightly drunk

tiptoe ['tɪp,təʊ] **tiptoes, tiptoeing, tiptoed** VERB
If you tiptoe somewhere, you walk there very quietly on your toes.

tirade [taɪ'reɪd] **tirades** NOUN
a long, angry speech in which you criticize someone or something
[WORD HISTORY: from Italian TIRATA meaning 'volley of shots']

tire ['taɪə] **tires, tiring, tired** VERB
1 If something tires you, it makes you use a lot of energy so that you want to rest or sleep.

◉ THESAURUS
drain: *My emotional turmoil had drained me.*
exhaust: *Walking in deep snow had totally exhausted him.*
fatigue: *He is easily fatigued.*
2 If you tire of something, you become bored with it.

tired ['taɪəd] ADJECTIVE
having little energy
tiredness NOUN

◉ THESAURUS
drained: *as United stalked off, stunned and drained*
drowsy: *He felt pleasantly drowsy.*
exhausted: *She was too exhausted and distressed to talk.*
fatigued: *Winter weather can leave you feeling fatigued.*
sleepy: *I was beginning to feel sleepy.*
tuckered out: Australian and New Zealand; informal *You must be tuckered out after that bus trip.*
weary: *a weary traveller*
worn out: *He's just worn out after the drive.*

tireless ['taɪəlɪs] ADJECTIVE
Someone who is tireless has a lot of energy and never seems to need a rest.

tiresome ['taɪəsəm] ADJECTIVE
A person or thing that is tiresome makes you feel irritated or bored.

tiring ['taɪərɪŋ] ADJECTIVE
Something that is tiring makes you tired.

tissue ['tɪsjuː] **tissues** NOUN
1 The tissue in plants and animals consists of cells that are similar in appearance and function. *e.g. scar tissue... dead tissue*
2 Tissue is thin paper that is used for wrapping breakable objects.
3 a small piece of soft paper that you use as a handkerchief

tit [tɪt] **tits** NOUN
a small European bird *e.g. a blue tit*

titanic [taɪ'tænɪk] ADJECTIVE
very big or important
[WORD HISTORY: in Greek legend, the TITANS were a family of giants]

titillate ['tɪtɪ,leɪt] **titillates, titillating, titillated** VERB
If something titillates someone, it pleases and excites them, especially in a sexual way.
titillation NOUN

title ['taɪtəl] **titles** NOUN
1 the name of a book, play, or piece of music
2 a word that describes someone's rank or job *e.g. My official title is Design Manager.*

t

3 the position of champion in a sports competition *e.g. the European featherweight title*

titled ['taɪtᵊld] ADJECTIVE
Someone who is titled has a high social rank and has a title such as 'Princess', 'Lord', 'Lady', or 'Sir'.

titter ['tɪtə] **titters, tittering, tittered** VERB
If you titter, you laugh in a way that shows you are nervous or embarrassed.

TNT NOUN
TNT is a type of powerful explosive. It is an abbreviation for 'trinitrotoluene'.

to [tuː] PREPOSITION
1 'To' is used to indicate the place that someone or something is moving towards or pointing at *e.g. They are going to China.*
2 'To' is used to indicate the limit of something *e.g. Goods to the value of 500 pounds.*
3 'To' is used in ratios and rates when saying how many units of one type there are for each unit of another *e.g. I only get about 30 kilometres to the gallon from it.*
> ADVERB
4 If you push or shut a door to, you close it but do not shut it completely.

> The preposition *to* is spelt with one *o*, the adverb *too* has two *os*, and the number *two* is spelt with *wo*

toad [təʊd] **toads** NOUN
an amphibian that looks like a frog but has a drier skin and lives less in the water

toadstool ['təʊd,stuːl] **toadstools** NOUN
a type of poisonous fungus

toast [təʊst] **toasts, toasting, toasted**
NOUN
1 Toast is slices of bread made brown and crisp by cooking at a high temperature.
2 To drink a toast to someone is to drink an alcoholic drink in honour of them.
> VERB
3 If you toast bread, you cook it at a high temperature so that it becomes brown and crisp.
4 If you toast yourself, you sit in front of a fire so that you feel pleasantly warm.
5 To toast someone is to drink an alcoholic drink in honour of them.
[WORD HISTORY: from Latin TOSTUS meaning 'parched']

toaster ['təʊstə] **toasters** NOUN
a piece of electrical equipment used for toasting bread

tobacco [tə'bækəʊ] NOUN
Tobacco is the dried leaves of the tobacco plant which people smoke in pipes, cigarettes, and cigars.

tobacconist [tə'bækənɪst] **tobacconists**
NOUN
a shop where tobacco, cigarettes, and cigars are sold

toboggan [tə'bɒgən] **toboggans** NOUN
a flat seat with two wooden or metal runners, used for sliding over the snow
[WORD HISTORY: an American Indian word]

today [tə'deɪ] ADVERB OR NOUN
1 Today means the day on which you are speaking or writing.
2 Today also means the present period of history. *e.g. the challenges of teaching in today's schools*

toddle ['tɒdᵊl] **toddles, toddling, toddled**
VERB
To toddle is to walk in short, quick steps, as a very young child does.

toddler ['tɒdlə] **toddlers** NOUN
a small child who has just learned to walk

to-do [tə'duː] **to-dos** NOUN
A to-do is a situation in which people are very agitated or confused. *e.g. It's just like him to make such a to-do about a baby.*

toe [təʊ] **toes** NOUN
1 Your toes are the five movable parts at the end of your foot.
2 The toe of a shoe or sock is the part that covers the end of your foot.

toff [tɒf] **toffs** NOUN; INFORMAL, OLD-FASHIONED
a rich person or one from an aristocratic family

toffee ['tɒfɪ] **toffees** NOUN
Toffee is a sticky, chewy sweet made by boiling sugar and butter together with water.

toga ['təʊgə] **togas** NOUN
a long loose robe worn in ancient Rome

together [tə'gɛðə] ADVERB
1 If people do something together, they do it with each other.

● THESAURUS
collectively: *The Cabinet is collectively responsible for policy.*
en masse: *The people marched en masse.*
in unison: *Michael and the landlady nodded in unison.*
jointly: *an agency jointly run by New York and New Jersey*
shoulder to shoulder: *They could fight shoulder to shoulder against a common enemy.*
side by side: *areas where different nationalities live side by side*

2 If two things happen together, they happen at the same time.

● THESAURUS
as one: *The 40,000 crowd rose as one.*

at once: *You can't do two things at once.*
concurrently: *There were three races running concurrently.*
simultaneously: *The two guns fired almost simultaneously.*
with one accord: *With one accord they turned and walked back.*

3 If things are joined or fixed together, they are joined or fixed to each other.

4 If things or people are together, they are very near to each other.

> Two nouns joined by *together with* do not make a plural subject, so the following verb is not plural: *Jones, together with his partner, has had great success*

togetherness [tə'gɛðənɪs] NOUN
Togetherness is a feeling of closeness and friendship.

toil [tɔɪl] **toils, toiling, toiled** VERB
1 When people toil, they work hard doing unpleasant, difficult, or tiring tasks or jobs.
> NOUN
2 Toil is unpleasant, difficult, or tiring work.

toilet ['tɔɪlɪt] **toilets** NOUN
1 a large bowl, connected by a pipe to the drains, which you use when you want to get rid of urine or faeces
2 a small room containing a toilet

toiletries ['tɔɪlɪtrɪz] PLURAL NOUN
Toiletries are the things you use when cleaning and taking care of your body, such as soap and talc.

token ['təʊkən] **tokens** NOUN
1 a piece of paper or card that is worth a particular amount of money and can be exchanged for goods *e.g. record tokens*
2 a flat round piece of metal or plastic that can sometimes be used instead of money
3 If you give something to someone as a token of your feelings for them, you give it to them as a way of showing those feelings.
> ADJECTIVE
4 If something is described as token, it shows that it is not being treated as important. *e.g. a token contribution to your fees*

told [təʊld] Told is the past tense and past participle of **tell**.

tolerable ['tɒlərəbəl] ADJECTIVE
1 able to be put up with
● THESAURUS
acceptable: *a mutually acceptable new contract*
bearable: *A cool breeze made the heat bearable.*
<<OPPOSITE *unbearable*

2 fairly satisfactory or reasonable *e.g. a tolerable salary*
● THESAURUS
acceptable: *We've made an acceptable start.*
adequate: *The level of service was adequate.*
okay or **OK:** informal *For a fashionable restaurant like this the prices are okay.*
passable: *Ms Campbell speaks passable French.*
reasonable: *able to make a reasonable living from his writing*
so-so: informal *Their lunch was only so-so.*

tolerance ['tɒlərəns] NOUN
1 A person's tolerance is their ability to accept or put up with something which may not be enjoyable or pleasant for them.
2 Tolerance is the quality of allowing other people to have their own attitudes or beliefs, or to behave in a particular way, even if you do not agree or approve. *e.g. religious tolerance*

tolerant ['tɒlərənt] ADJECTIVE
accepting of different views and behaviour
● THESAURUS
broad-minded: *a very fair and broad-minded man*
liberal: *She is known to have liberal views on divorce.*
open-minded: *I am very open-minded about that question.*
understanding: *Fortunately for John, he had an understanding wife.*
<<OPPOSITE *narrow-minded*

tolerate ['tɒləˌreɪt] **tolerates, tolerating, tolerated** VERB
1 If you tolerate things that you do not approve of or agree with, you allow them.
● THESAURUS
accept: *Urban dwellers often accept noise as part of city life.*
put up with: *You're late again and I won't put up with it.*
2 If you can tolerate something, you accept it, even though it is unsatisfactory or unpleasant.
toleration NOUN
● THESAURUS
bear: *He can't bear to talk about it.*
endure: *unable to endure the pain*
stand: *He can't stand me smoking.*

toll [təʊl] **tolls, tolling, tolled** NOUN
1 The death toll in an accident is the number of people who have died in it.
2 a sum of money that you have to pay in order to use a particular bridge or road
> VERB
3 When someone tolls a bell, it is rung slowly, often as a sign that someone has died.

tom [tɒm] **toms** NOUN
a male cat

t

tomahawk ['tɒmə,hɔ:k] **tomahawks** NOUN
a small axe used by North American Indians

tomato [tə'mɑ:təʊ] **tomatoes** NOUN
a small round red fruit, used as a vegetable and often eaten raw in salads

tomb [tu:m] **tombs** NOUN
a large grave for one or more corpses

● THESAURUS
grave: *They used to visit her grave twice a year.*
mausoleum: *the elaborate mausoleums of the Paris cemetery*
sarcophagus: *an Egyptian sarcophagus*
sepulchre: literary *the ornate lid of the sepulchre*
vault: *the family vault*

tomboy ['tɒm,bɔɪ] **tomboys** NOUN
a girl who likes playing rough or noisy games

tome [təʊm] **tomes** NOUN; FORMAL
a very large heavy book

tomorrow [tə'mɒrəʊ] ADVERB OR NOUN
1 Tomorrow means the day after today.
2 You can refer to the future, especially the near future, as tomorrow.

ton [tʌn] **tons** NOUN
1 a unit of weight equal to 2240 pounds or about 1016 kilograms
> PLURAL NOUN
2 INFORMAL
If you have tons of something, you have a lot of it.

tonal ['təʊnᵊl] ADJECTIVE
involving the quality or pitch of a sound or of music

tone [təʊn] **tones, toning, toned** NOUN
1 Someone's tone is a quality in their voice which shows what they are thinking or feeling.
2 The tone of a musical instrument or a singer's voice is the kind of sound it has.
3 The tone of a piece of writing is its style and the ideas or opinions expressed in it. *e.g. I was shocked at the tone of your leading article.*
4 a lighter, darker, or brighter shade of the same colour *e.g. The whole room is painted in two tones of orange.*
tone down VERB
5 If you tone down something, you make it less forceful or severe.

tone-deaf [,təʊn'dɛf] ADJECTIVE
unable to sing in tune or to recognize different tunes

tongs [tɒŋz] PLURAL NOUN
Tongs consist of two long narrow pieces of metal joined together at one end. You press the pieces together to pick an object up.

tongue [tʌŋ] **tongues** NOUN
1 Your tongue is the soft part in your mouth that you can move and use for tasting, licking, and speaking.
2 a language
3 Tongue is the cooked tongue of an ox.
4 The tongue of a shoe or boot is the piece of leather underneath the laces.

tonic ['tɒnɪk] **tonics** NOUN
1 Tonic or tonic water is a colourless, fizzy drink that has a slightly bitter flavour and is often mixed with alcoholic drinks.
2 a medicine that makes you feel stronger, healthier, and less tired
3 anything that makes you feel stronger or more cheerful *e.g. It was a tonic just being with her.*

tonight [tə'naɪt] ADVERB OR NOUN
Tonight is the evening or night that will come at the end of today.

tonne [tʌn] **tonnes** NOUN
(MATHS) a unit of weight equal to 1000 kilograms

tonsil ['tɒnsəl] **tonsils** NOUN
Your tonsils are the two small, soft lumps in your throat at the back of your mouth.

tonsillitis [,tɒnsɪ'laɪtɪs] NOUN
Tonsillitis is a painful swelling of your tonsils caused by an infection.

too [tu:] ADVERB
1 also or as well *e.g. You were there too.*

● THESAURUS
as well: *She published historical novels as well.*
besides: *You get to take lots of samples home besides.*
in addition: *There are, in addition, other objections to the plan.*
into the bargain: *The machine can play CDs into the bargain.*
likewise: *She sat down and he did likewise.*
moreover: *He didn't know, and moreover, he didn't care.*

2 more than a desirable, necessary, or acceptable amount *e.g. a man who had taken too much to drink*

● THESAURUS
excessively: *He had an excessively protective mother.*
over-: *I didn't want to seem over-eager.*
overly: *Most people consider him to be overly ambitious.*
unduly: *She's unduly concerned with what people think of her.*
unreasonably: *These prices seem unreasonably high to me.*

The adverb *too* has two *o*s, the preposition *to* is spelt with one *o*, and the number *two* is spelt with *wo*

tool [tu:l] **tools** NOUN
1 any hand-held instrument or piece of equipment that you use to help you do a particular kind of work

▸ THESAURUS
implement: *knives and other useful implements*
instrument: *instruments for cleaning and polishing teeth*
utensil: *cooking utensils*

2 an object, skill, or idea that is needed or used for a particular purpose *e.g. You can use the survey as a bargaining tool in the negotiations.*

toot [tu:t] **toots, tooting, tooted** VERB
If a car horn toots, it produces a short sound.

tooth [tu:θ] **teeth** NOUN
1 Your teeth are the hard enamel-covered objects in your mouth that you use for biting and chewing food.
2 The teeth of a comb, saw, or zip are the parts that stick out in a row on its edge.

toothpaste ['tu:θ,peɪst] NOUN
Toothpaste is a substance which you use to clean your teeth.

top [tɒp] **tops, topping, topped** NOUN
1 The top of something is its highest point, part, or surface.
2 The top of a bottle, jar, or tube is its cap or lid.
3 a piece of clothing worn on the upper half of your body
4 a toy with a pointed end on which it spins
▸ ADJECTIVE
5 The top thing of a series of things is the highest one. *e.g. the top floor of the building*
▸ VERB
6 If someone tops a poll or popularity chart, they do better than anyone else in it. *e.g. It has topped the bestseller lists in almost every country.*
7 If something tops a particular amount, it is greater than that amount. *e.g. The temperature topped 90°.*
top up VERB
8 To top something up is to add something to it in order to keep it at an acceptable or usable level.

top hat top hats NOUN
a tall hat with a narrow brim that men wear on special occasions

topic ['tɒpɪk] **topics** NOUN
a particular subject that you write about or discuss

topical ['tɒpɪkəl] ADJECTIVE
involving or related to events that are happening at the time you are speaking or writing

topping ['tɒpɪŋ] **toppings** NOUN
food that is put on top of other food in order to decorate it or add to its flavour

topple ['tɒpəl] **topples, toppling, toppled** VERB
If something topples, it becomes unsteady and falls over.

top-secret [,tɒp'si:krɪt] ADJECTIVE
meant to be kept completely secret

topsy-turvy ['tɒpsɪ'tɜ:vɪ] ADJECTIVE
in a confused state *e.g. My life was truly topsy-turvy.*

top-up card top-up cards NOUN
a card that you use to add credit to your mobile phone

Torah ['təʊrə] NOUN
The Torah is Jewish law and teaching.

torch [tɔ:tʃ] **torches** NOUN
1 a small electric light carried in the hand and powered by batteries
2 a long stick with burning material wrapped around one end

torment torments, tormenting, tormented NOUN ['tɔ:mənt]
1 Torment is extreme pain or unhappiness.
2 something that causes extreme pain and unhappiness *e.g. It's a torment to see them staring at me.*
▸ VERB [tɔ:'ment]
3 If something torments you, it causes you extreme unhappiness.

torn [tɔ:n]
1 Torn is the past participle of **tear**
▸ ADJECTIVE
2 If you are torn between two or more things, you cannot decide which one to choose and this makes you unhappy. *e.g. torn between duty and pleasure*

tornado [tɔ:'neɪdəʊ] **tornadoes** or **tornados** NOUN
a violent storm with strong circular winds around a funnel-shaped cloud

torpedo [tɔ:'pi:dəʊ] **torpedoes, torpedoing, torpedoed** NOUN
1 a tube-shaped bomb that travels underwater and explodes when it hits a target
▸ VERB
2 If a ship is torpedoed, it is hit, and usually sunk, by a torpedo.

torrent ['tɒrənt] **torrents** NOUN

1 When a lot of water is falling very rapidly, it can be said to be falling in torrents.

2 A torrent of speech is a lot of it directed continuously at someone. *e.g. torrents of abuse*

torrential [tɒ'rɛnʃəl] ADJECTIVE
Torrential rain pours down very rapidly and in great quantities.

torrid ['tɒrɪd] ADJECTIVE

1 Torrid weather is very hot and dry.

2 A torrid love affair is one in which people show very strong emotions.

torso ['tɔːsəʊ] **torsos** NOUN
the main part of your body, excluding your head, arms, and legs

tortoise ['tɔːtəs] **tortoises** NOUN
a slow-moving reptile with a large hard shell over its body into which it can pull its head and legs for protection

tortuous ['tɔːtjʊəs] ADJECTIVE

1 A tortuous road is full of bends and twists.

2 A tortuous piece of writing is long and complicated.

torture ['tɔːtʃə] **tortures, torturing, tortured** NOUN

1 Torture is great pain that is deliberately caused to someone to punish them or get information from them.

> VERB

2 If someone tortures another person, they deliberately cause that person great pain to punish them or get information.

3 To torture someone is also to cause them to suffer mentally. *e.g. Memory tortured her.*
torturer NOUN

Tory ['tɔːrɪ] **Tories** NOUN
In Britain, a member or supporter of the Conservative Party.
[WORD HISTORY: from Irish TORAIDHE meaning 'outlaw']

toss [tɒs] **tosses, tossing, tossed** VERB

1 If you toss something somewhere, you throw it there lightly and carelessly.

2 If you toss a coin, you decide something by throwing a coin into the air and guessing which side will face upwards when it lands.

3 If you toss your head, you move it suddenly backwards, especially when you are angry, annoyed, or want your own way.

4 To toss is to move repeatedly from side to side. *e.g. We tossed and turned and tried to sleep.*

tot [tɒt] **tots, totting, totted** NOUN

1 a very young child

2 a small amount of strong alcohol such as whisky

> VERB

3 To tot up numbers is to add them together.

total ['təʊtəl] **totals, totalling, totalled** NOUN

1 the number you get when you add several numbers together

● THESAURUS
aggregate: *three successive defeats by an aggregate of 12 goals*
sum: *the sum of all the angles*
whole: *taken as a percentage of the whole*

> ADJECTIVE

2 Total means complete. *e.g. a total failure*

● THESAURUS
absolute: *absolute beginners*
complete: *a complete mess*
out-and-out: *an out-and-out lie*
outright: *an outright rejection of the deal*
unconditional: *unconditional surrender*
undivided: *You have my undivided attention.*
unmitigated: *an unmitigated failure*
unqualified: *an unqualified success*
utter: *utter nonsense*

> VERB

3 When you total a set of numbers or objects, you add them all together.

● THESAURUS
add up to: *Profits can add up to millions of dollars.*
amount to: *Spending on sports-related items amounted to £9.75 billion.*
come to: *That comes to over a thousand pounds.*

4 If several numbers total a certain figure, that is the figure you get when all the numbers are added together. *e.g. Their debts totalled over 300,000 dollars.*
totally ADVERB

totalitarian [təʊˌtælɪ'tɛərɪən] ADJECTIVE
A totalitarian political system is one in which one political party controls everything and does not allow any other parties to exist.
totalitarianism NOUN

tote [təʊt] **totes, toting, toted** VERB;
INFORMAL
To tote a gun is to carry it.

totem pole ['təʊtəm] **totem poles** NOUN
a long wooden pole with symbols and pictures carved and painted on it. Totem poles are made by some Native Americans.

totter ['tɒtə] **totters, tottering, tottered** VERB
When someone totters, they walk in an unsteady way.

toucan ['tu:kən] **toucans** NOUN
a large tropical bird with a very large beak

touch [tʌtʃ] **touches, touching, touched**
VERB
1 If you touch something, you put your fingers or
hand on it.
● THESAURUS
feel: *The doctor felt his head.*
finger: *He fingered the few coins in his pocket.*
handle: *Wear rubber gloves when handling cat litter.*
2 When two things touch, their surfaces come
into contact. *e.g. Their knees were touching.*
● THESAURUS
brush: *Something brushed against her leg.*
graze: *A bullet had grazed his arm.*
meet: *when the wheels meet the ground*
3 If you are touched by something, you are
emotionally affected by it. *e.g. I was touched by his
thoughtfulness.*
● THESAURUS
affect: *Jazza was badly affected by his divorce.*
move: *These stories surprised and moved me.*
stir: *She stirred something very deep in me.*
> NOUN
4 Your sense of touch is your ability to tell what
something is like by touching it.
5 a detail which is added to improve something
e.g. finishing touches
6 a small amount of something *e.g. a touch of
mustard*
> PHRASE
7 If you are **in touch** with someone, you are in
contact with them.

touchdown ['tʌtʃˌdaʊn] **touchdowns**
NOUN
Touchdown is the landing of an aircraft.

touching ['tʌtʃɪŋ] ADJECTIVE
causing feelings of sadness and sympathy
● THESAURUS
affecting: *literary an affecting memorial to
Countess Rachel*
moving: *It was a moving moment for Marianne.*
poignant: *a poignant love story*

touchy ['tʌtʃɪ] **touchier, touchiest**
ADJECTIVE
1 If someone is touchy, they are easily upset or
irritated.
● THESAURUS
easily offended: *viewers who are easily offended*
sensitive: *Young people are very sensitive about
their appearance.*
toey: *Australian and New Zealand; slang Don't be
so toey.*
2 A touchy subject is one that needs to be dealt
with carefully, because it might upset or offend
people.

tough [tʌf] **tougher, toughest** ADJECTIVE
1 A tough person is strong and independent and
able to put up with hardship.
● THESAURUS
hardened: *hardened criminals*
hardy: *a hardy race of pioneers*
resilient: *a good soldier, calm and resilient*
robust: *Perhaps men are more robust than women?*
rugged: *Rugged individualism forged America's
frontier society.*
strong: *Eventually I felt strong enough to look at
him.*
2 A tough substance is difficult to break.
● THESAURUS
durable: *Fine bone china is both strong and durable.*
hard-wearing: *hard-wearing cotton shirts*
leathery: *leathery skin*
resilient: *an armchair of some resilient plastic
material*
robust: *very robust machinery*
rugged: *You need a rugged, four-wheel drive vehicle.*
solid: *The car feels very solid.*
strong: *a strong casing, which won't crack or chip*
sturdy: *The camera was mounted on a sturdy tripod.*
<<OPPOSITE *fragile*
3 A tough task, problem, or way of life is difficult
or full of hardship.
● THESAURUS
arduous: *an arduous journey*
difficult: *We're living in difficult times.*
exacting: *an exacting task*
hard: *a hard life*
<<OPPOSITE *easy*
4 Tough policies or actions are strict and firm. *e.g.
tough measures against organized crime*
toughly ADVERB, **toughness** NOUN, **toughen**
VERB

toupee ['tu:peɪ] **toupees** NOUN
a small wig worn by a man to cover a bald patch
on his head

tour [tʊə] **tours, touring, toured** NOUN
1 a long journey during which you visit several
places
2 a short trip round a place such as a city or
famous building
> VERB
3 If you tour a place, you go on a journey or a trip
round it.

tourism ['tʊərɪzəm] NOUN
(GEOGRAPHY) Tourism is the business of
providing services for people on holiday, for
example hotels and sightseeing trips.

tourist ['tʊərɪst] **tourists (GEOGRAPHY)**
NOUN
a person who visits places for pleasure or interest

t

921

tournament ['tʊənəmənt] **tournaments** NOUN
(PE) a sports competition in which players who win a match play further matches, until just one person or team is left

tourniquet ['tʊənɪ,keɪ] **tourniquets** NOUN
a strip of cloth tied tightly round a wound to stop it bleeding

tousled ['taʊzᵊld] ADJECTIVE
Tousled hair is untidy.

tout [taʊt] **touts, touting, touted** VERB
1 If someone touts something, they try to sell it.
2 If someone touts for business or custom, they try to obtain it in a very direct way. *e.g. volunteers who spend days touting for donations*
> NOUN
3 someone who sells tickets outside a sports ground or theatre, charging more than the original price

tow [təʊ] **tows, towing, towed** VERB
1 If a vehicle tows another vehicle, it pulls it along behind it.
> NOUN
2 To give a vehicle a tow is to tow it.
> PHRASE
3 If you have someone **in tow**, they are with you because you are looking after them.

towards [tə'wɔːdz] PREPOSITION
1 in the direction of *e.g. He turned towards the door.*
2 about or involving *e.g. My feelings towards Susan have changed.*
3 as a contribution for *e.g. a huge donation towards the new opera house*
4 near to *e.g. We sat towards the back.*

towel ['taʊəl] **towels** NOUN
a piece of thick, soft cloth that you use to dry yourself with

towelling ['taʊəlɪŋ] NOUN
Towelling is thick, soft cloth that is used for making towels.

tower ['taʊə] **towers, towering, towered** NOUN
1 a tall, narrow building, sometimes attached to a larger building such as a castle or church
> VERB
2 Someone or something that towers over other people or things is much taller than them.
towering ADJECTIVE

town [taʊn] **towns** NOUN
1 a place with many streets and buildings where people live and work
2 Town is the central shopping and business part of a town rather than the suburbs. *e.g. She has gone into town.*

township ['taʊnʃɪp] **townships** NOUN
a small town in South Africa where only Black people or Coloured people were allowed to live

towpath ['təʊ,pɑːθ] **towpaths** NOUN
a path along the side of a canal or river

toxic ['tɒksɪk] ADJECTIVE
poisonous *e.g. toxic waste*
[WORD HISTORY: from Greek TOXIKON meaning 'poison used on arrows' from TOXON meaning 'arrow']

toxin ['tɒksɪn] **toxins** NOUN
a poison, especially one produced by bacteria and very harmful to living creatures

toy [tɔɪ] **toys, toying, toyed** NOUN
1 any object made to play with
> VERB
2 If you toy with an idea, you consider it without being very serious about it. *e.g. She toyed with the idea of telephoning him.*
3 If you toy with an object, you fiddle with it. *e.g. Jessica was toying with her glass.*

toyi-toyi or **toy-toy** ['tɔɪ'tɔɪ] NOUN
In South Africa, a toyi-toyi is a dance performed to protest about something.

trace [treɪs] **traces, tracing, traced** VERB
1 If you trace something, you find it after looking for it. *e.g. Police are trying to trace the owner.*
● THESAURUS
locate: *We've simply been unable to locate him.*
track down: *She had spent years trying to track down her parents.*
2 (EXAM TERM) To trace the development of something is to find out or describe how it developed.
3 If you trace a drawing or a map, you copy it by covering it with a piece of transparent paper and drawing over the lines underneath.
> NOUN
4 a sign which shows you that someone or something has been in a place *e.g. No trace of his father had been found.*
● THESAURUS
evidence: *He'd seen no evidence of fraud.*
hint: *I saw no hint of irony on her face.*
indication: *He gave no indication of remorse.*
record: *There's no record of any marriage or children.*
sign: *Sally waited for any sign of illness.*
suggestion: *a faint suggestion of a tan*
whiff: *Not a whiff of scandal has ever tainted his private life.*
5 a very small amount of something
tracing NOUN
● THESAURUS
dash: *a story with a dash of mystery*

drop: *a drop of sherry*
remnant: *Beneath the present church were remnants of Roman flooring.*
suspicion: *large blooms of white with a suspicion of pale pink*
tinge: *Could there have been a slight tinge of envy in Eva's voice?*
touch: *a touch of flu*
vestige: *the last vestige of a UN force that once numbered 30,000*

track [træk] **tracks, tracking, tracked**
NOUN
1 a narrow road or path
2 a strip of ground with rails on it that a train travels along
3 a piece of ground, shaped like a ring, which horses, cars, or athletes race around

> PLURAL NOUN
4 Tracks are marks left on the ground by a person or animal. *e.g. the deer tracks by the side of the path*

> ADJECTIVE
5 In an athletics competition, the track events are the races on a running track.

> VERB
6 If you track animals or people, you find them by following their footprints or other signs that they have left behind.

track down VERB
7 If you track down someone or something, you find them by searching for them.

track record **track records** NOUN
The track record of a person or a company is their past achievements or failures. *e.g. the track record of the film's star*

tracksuit ['træk,suːt] **tracksuits** NOUN
a loose, warm suit of trousers and a top, worn for outdoor sports

tract [trækt] **tracts** NOUN
1 A tract of land or forest is a large area of it.
2 a pamphlet which expresses a strong opinion on a religious, moral, or political subject
3 a system of organs and tubes in an animal's or person's body that has a particular function *e.g. the digestive tract*

traction ['trækʃən] NOUN
Traction is a form of medical treatment given to an injured limb which involves pulling it gently for long periods of time using a system of weights and pulleys

tractor ['træktə] **tractors** NOUN
a vehicle with large rear wheels that is used on a farm for pulling machinery and other heavy loads

trade [treɪd] **trades, trading, traded** NOUN

1 (HISTORY) Trade is the activity of buying, selling, or exchanging goods or services between people, firms, or countries.
● THESAURUS
business: *a career in business*
commerce: *They have made their fortunes from industry and commerce.*

2 Someone's trade is the kind of work they do, especially when it requires special training in practical skills. *e.g. a joiner by trade*
● THESAURUS
business: *the music business*
line: *Are you in the publishing line too?*
line of work: *In my line of work I often get home too late for dinner.*
occupation: *her new occupation as an author*
profession: *Harper was a teacher by profession.*

> VERB
3 When people, firms, or countries trade, they buy, sell, or exchange goods or services.
● THESAURUS
deal: *They deal in antiques.*
do business: *the different people who did business with me*
traffic: *those who traffic in illegal drugs*

4 If you trade things, you exchange them. *e.g. Their mother had traded her rings for a few potatoes.*

trademark ['treɪd,mɑːk] **trademarks** NOUN
a name or symbol that a manufacturer always uses on its products. Trademarks are usually protected by law so that no-one else can use them

trader ['treɪdə] **traders** NOUN
a person whose job is to buy and sell goods *e.g. a timber trader*
● THESAURUS
broker: *a financial broker*
dealer: *dealers in commodities*
merchant: *a wine merchant*

tradesman ['treɪdzmən] **tradesmen** NOUN
a person, for example a shopkeeper, whose job is to sell goods

trade union **trade unions** NOUN
an organization of workers that tries to improve the pay and conditions in a particular industry

tradition [trə'dɪʃən] **traditions** NOUN
a custom or belief that has existed for a long time without changing
● THESAURUS
convention: *It's just a social convention that men don't wear skirts.*
custom: *an ancient Japanese custom*

traditional [trə'dɪʃənəl] ADJECTIVE
1 Traditional customs or beliefs have existed for a long time without changing. *e.g. her traditional Indian dress*

t

conventional: *conventional family planning methods*
established: *the established church*
<<OPPOSITE unconventional

2 A traditional organization or institution is one in which older methods are used rather than modern ones. *e.g. a traditional school*
traditionally ADVERB

traditionalist [trəˈdɪʃənəlɪst] **traditionalists** NOUN
someone who supports the established customs and beliefs of their society, and does not want to change them

traffic [ˈtræfɪk] **traffics, trafficking, trafficked** NOUN
1 Traffic is the movement of vehicles or people along a route at a particular time.
2 Traffic in something such as drugs is an illegal trade in them.
> VERB
3 Someone who traffics in drugs or other goods buys and sells them illegally.

traffic light **traffic lights** NOUN
Traffic lights are the set of red, amber, and green lights at a road junction which control the flow of traffic.

traffic warden **traffic wardens** NOUN
a person whose job is to make sure that cars are not parked in the wrong place or for longer than is allowed

tragedy [ˈtrædʒɪdɪ] **tragedies** NOUN
1 an event or situation that is disastrous or very sad
2 a serious story or play, that usually ends with the death of the main character

tragic [ˈtrædʒɪk] ADJECTIVE
1 Something tragic is very sad because it involves death, suffering, or disaster. *e.g. a tragic accident*

distressing: *distressing news*
heartbreaking: *a heartbreaking succession of miscarriages*
heart-rending: *heart-rending pictures of refugees*

2 Tragic films, plays, and books are sad and serious. *e.g. a tragic love story*
tragically ADVERB

trail [treɪl] **trails, trailing, trailed** NOUN
1 a rough path across open country or through forests
2 a series of marks or other signs left by someone or something as they move along
> VERB
3 If you trail something or it trails, it drags along

behind you as you move, or it hangs down loosely. *e.g. a small plane trailing a banner*
4 If someone trails along, they move slowly, without any energy or enthusiasm.
5 If a voice trails away or trails off, it gradually becomes more hesitant until it stops completely.

trailer [ˈtreɪlə] **trailers** NOUN
a small vehicle which can be loaded with things and pulled behind a car

train [treɪn] **trains, training, trained** NOUN
1 a number of carriages or trucks which are pulled by a railway engine
2 A train of thought is a connected series of thoughts.
3 A train of vehicles or people is a line or group following behind something or someone. *e.g. a train of wives and girlfriends*
> VERB
4 If you train someone, your teach them how to do something.

coach: *He coached the basketball team.*
drill: *He drills the choir to a high standard.*
educate: *I was educated at the local grammar school.*
instruct: *All their members are instructed in first aid.*
school: *He has been schooled to take over the family business.*
teach: *This is something they teach us to do in our first year.*
tutor: *She decided to tutor her children at home.*

5 If you train, you learn how to do a particular job. *e.g. She trained as a serious actress.*
6 If you train for a sports match or a race, you prepare for it by doing exercises.
training NOUN

trainee [treɪˈniː] **trainees** NOUN
someone who is being taught how to do a job

trainers [ˈtreɪnəz] PLURAL NOUN
Trainers are special shoes worn for running or jogging.

trait [treɪt] **traits** NOUN
a particular characteristic or tendency *e.g. a very English trait*

traitor [ˈtreɪtə] **traitors** NOUN
(HISTORY) someone who betrays their country or the group which they belong to

trajectory [trəˈdʒɛktərɪ] **trajectories** NOUN
The trajectory of an object moving through the air is the curving path that it follows.

tram [træm] **trams** NOUN
a vehicle which runs on rails along the street and is powered by electricity from an overhead wire

tramp [træmp] **tramps, tramping, tramped** NOUN

1 a person who has no home, no job, and very little money

2 a long country walk *e.g. I took a long, wet tramp through the fine woodlands.*

> VERB

3 If you tramp from one place to another, you walk with slow, heavy footsteps.

trample ['træmpᵊl] **tramples, trampling, trampled** VERB

1 If you trample on something, you tread heavily on it so that it is damaged.

2 If you trample on someone or on their rights or feelings, you behave in a way that shows you don't care about them.

trampoline ['træmpəlɪn] **trampolines** NOUN

a piece of gymnastic equipment consisting of a large piece of strong cloth held taut by springs in a frame, on which a gymnast jumps to help them jump high

trance [trɑːns] **trances** NOUN

a mental state in which someone seems to be asleep but is conscious enough to be aware of their surroundings and to respond to questions and commands

tranquil ['træŋkwɪl] ADJECTIVE

calm and peaceful *e.g. tranquil lakes... I have a tranquil mind.*

tranquillity NOUN

tranquillizer ['træŋkwɪˌlaɪzə] **tranquillizers;** also spelt **tranquilliser** NOUN

a drug that makes people feel less anxious or nervous

trans- PREFIX

Trans- means across, through, or beyond. *e.g. transatlantic*

transaction [træn'zækʃən] **transactions** NOUN

a business deal which involves buying and selling something

transcend [træn'sɛnd] **transcends, transcending, transcended** VERB

If one thing transcends another, it goes beyond it or is superior to it. *e.g. Her beauty transcends all barriers.*

transcribe [træn'skraɪb] **transcribes, transcribing, transcribed** VERB

If you transcribe something that is spoken or written, you write it down, copy it, or change it into a different form of writing. *e.g. These letters were often transcribed by his wife Patti.*

transcript ['trænskrɪpt] **transcripts** NOUN

a written copy of of something that is spoken

transfer transfers, transferring, transferred VERB [træns'fɜː]

1 If you transfer something from one place to another, you move it. *e.g. They transferred the money to the Swiss account.*

2 If you transfer to a different place or job, or are transferred to it, you move to a different place or job within the same organization.

> NOUN ['trænsfɜː]

3 the movement of something from one place to another

4 a piece of paper with a design on one side which can be ironed or pressed onto cloth, paper, or china

transferable ADJECTIVE

transfixed [træns'fɪkst] ADJECTIVE

If a person is transfixed by something, they are so impressed or frightened by it that they cannot move. *e.g. Price stood transfixed at the sight of that tiny figure.*

transform [træns'fɔːm] **transforms, transforming, transformed** VERB

If something is transformed, it is changed completely. *e.g. The frown is transformed into a smile.*

transformation NOUN

● THESAURUS

alter: *New curtains can completely alter the look of a room.*

change: *alchemists attempting to change base metals into gold*

convert: *They have converted the church into a restaurant.*

reform: *He was totally reformed by this experience.*

revolutionize: *a device which will revolutionize the way you cook*

transfusion [træns'fjuːʒən] **transfusions** NOUN

A transfusion or blood transfusion is a process in which blood from a healthy person is injected into the body of another person who is badly injured or ill.

transient ['trænzɪənt] ADJECTIVE

Something transient does not stay or exist for very long. *e.g. transient emotions*

transience NOUN

transistor [træn'zɪstə] **transistors** NOUN

1 a small electrical device in something such as a television or radio which is used to control electric currents

2 A transistor or a transistor radio is a small portable radio.

transit ['trænsɪt] NOUN

1 Transit is the carrying of goods or people by vehicle from one place to another.

t

> PHRASE

2 People or things that are **in transit** are travelling or being taken from one place to another. *e.g. damage that had occurred in transit*

transition [træn'zɪʃən] **transitions** NOUN
a change from one form or state to another *e.g. the transition from war to peace*

transitional [træn'zɪʃənᵊl] ADJECTIVE
A transitional period or stage is one during which something changes from one form or state to another.

transitive ['trænsɪtɪv] ADJECTIVE
In grammar, a transitive verb is a verb which has an object.

transitory ['trænsɪtərɪ] ADJECTIVE
lasting for only a short time

translate [trænsˈleɪt] **translates, translating, translated** VERB
To translate something that someone has said or written is to say it or write it in a different language.
translation NOUN, **translator** NOUN

translucent [trænzˈluːsᵊnt] ADJECTIVE
If something is translucent, light passes through it so that it seems to glow. *e.g. translucent petals*

transmission [trænzˈmɪʃən] **transmissions** NOUN
1 The transmission of something involves passing or sending it to a different place or person. *e.g. the transmission of infectious diseases*

2 The transmission of television or radio programmes is the broadcasting of them.

3 a broadcast

transmit [trænzˈmɪt] **transmits, transmitting, transmitted** VERB
1 When a message or an electronic signal is transmitted, it is sent by radio waves.

2 To transmit something to a different place or person is to pass it or send it to the place or person. *e.g. the clergy's role in transmitting knowledge*
transmitter NOUN

transparency [trænsˈpærənsɪ] **transparencies** NOUN
1 a small piece of photographic film which can be projected onto a screen

2 Transparency is the quality that an object or substance has if you can see through it.

transparent [trænsˈpærənt] ADJECTIVE
If an object or substance is transparent, you can see through it.
transparently ADVERB

● THESAURUS
clear: *a clear glass panel*

crystalline: literary *crystalline lakes*
sheer: *a sheer black shirt*
translucent: *translucent corrugated plastic*
<<OPPOSITE *opaque*

transpire [trænˈspaɪə] **transpires, transpiring, transpired** VERB
1 FORMAL
When it transpires that something is the case, people discover that it is the case. *e.g. It transpired that he had flown off on holiday.*

2 When something transpires, it happens. *e.g. You start to wonder what transpired between them.*

Some people think that it is wrong to use *transpire* to mean 'happen'. However, it is very widely used in this sense, especially in spoken English

transplant transplants, transplanting, transplanted NOUN ['trænsˌplɑːnt]
1 a process of removing something from one place and putting it in another *e.g. a man who needs a heart transplant*

> VERB [trænsˈplɑːnt]
2 When something is transplanted, it is moved to a different place.

transport transports, transporting, transported NOUN ['trænsˌpɔːt]
(GEOGRAPHY)
1 Vehicles that you travel in are referred to as transport. *e.g. public transport*

2 Transport is the moving of goods or people from one place to another. *e.g. The prices quoted include transport costs.*

● THESAURUS
removal: *the furniture removal business*
shipment: *transported to the docks for shipment overseas*
transportation: *the transportation of refugees*

> VERB [trænsˈpɔːt]
3 When goods or people are transported from one place to another, they are moved there.

● THESAURUS
carry: *The ship could carry seventy passengers.*
convey: formal *a branch line to convey fish direct to Billingsgate*
ship: *the food being shipped to Iraq*
transfer: *She was transferred to another hospital.*

transportation [ˌtrænspɔːˈteɪʃən] NOUN
(GEOGRAPHY) Transportation is the transporting of people and things from one place to another.

transvestite [trænzˈvɛstaɪt] **transvestites** NOUN
a person who enjoys wearing clothes normally worn by people of the opposite sex
[WORD HISTORY: from TRANS- and Latin VESTITUS meaning 'clothed']

trap [træp] **traps, trapping, trapped** NOUN
1 a piece of equipment or a hole that is carefully positioned in order to catch animals or birds

● THESAURUS
net: *a fishing net*
snare: *a snare for catching birds*

2 a trick that is intended to catch or deceive someone

> VERB
3 Someone who traps animals catches them using traps.

● THESAURUS
catch: *an animal caught in a trap*
corner: *like a cornered rat*
snare: *He'd snared a rabbit earlier in the day.*

4 If you trap someone, you trick them so that they do or say something which they did not want to.

● THESAURUS
dupe: *a plot to dupe stamp collectors into buying fake rarities*
trick: *His family tricked him into going to Pakistan.*

5 If you are trapped somewhere, you cannot move or escape because something is blocking your way or holding you down.

6 If you are trapped, you are in an unpleasant situation that you cannot easily change. *e.g. I'm trapped in an unhappy marriage.*

trap door trap doors NOUN
a small horizontal door in a floor, ceiling, or stage

trapeze [trə'piːz] **trapezes** NOUN
a bar of wood or metal hanging from two ropes on which acrobats and gymnasts swing and perform skilful movements

trapezium [trə'piːzɪəm] **trapeziums** or **trapezia** NOUN
a four-sided shape with two sides parallel to each other

trappings ['træpɪŋz] PLURAL NOUN
The trappings of a particular rank, position, or state are the clothes or equipment that go with it.

trash [træʃ] NOUN
1 Trash is rubbish. *e.g. He picks up your trash on Mondays.*

● THESAURUS
garbage: *rotting piles of garbage*
refuse: *a weekly collection of refuse*
rubbish: *They had piled most of their rubbish into yellow skips.*
waste: *a law that regulates the disposal of waste*

2 If you say that something such as a book, painting, or film is trash, you mean that it is not very good.

● THESAURUS
garbage: informal *He spends his time watching garbage on TV.*
rubbish: *He described her book as absolute rubbish.*

trauma ['trɔːmə] **traumas** NOUN
a very upsetting experience which causes great stress *e.g. the trauma of his mother's death*
[WORD HISTORY: from Greek TRAUMA meaning 'wound']

traumatic [trɔː'mætɪk] ADJECTIVE
A traumatic experience is very upsetting.

travel ['trævəl] **travels, travelling, travelled** VERB
1 To travel is to go from one place to another.

● THESAURUS
go: *We went to Rome.*
journey: formal *He intended to journey up the Amazon.*
make your way: *He made his way home at last.*
take a trip: *We intend to take a trip there sometime.*

2 When something reaches one place from another, you say that it travels there. *e.g. Gossip travels fast.*

> NOUN
3 Travel is the act of travelling. *e.g. air travel*

> PLURAL NOUN
4 Someone's travels are the journeys that they make to places a long way from their home. *e.g. my travels in the Himalayas*
traveller NOUN, **travelling** ADJECTIVE

traveller's cheque ['trævələz] **traveller's cheques** NOUN
Traveller's cheques are cheques for use abroad. You buy them at home and then exchange them when you are abroad for foreign currency.

traverse ['trævɜːs] **traverses, traversing, traversed** VERB; FORMAL
If you traverse an area of land or water, you go across it or over it. *e.g. They have traversed the island from the west coast.*

travesty ['trævɪstɪ] **travesties** NOUN
a very bad or ridiculous representation or imitation of something *e.g. British salad is a travesty of freshness.*

trawl [trɔːl] **trawls, trawling, trawled** VERB
When fishermen trawl, they drag a wide net behind a ship in order to catch fish.

trawler ['trɔːlə] **trawlers** NOUN
a fishing boat that is used for trawling

tray [treɪ] **trays** NOUN
a flat object with raised edges which is used for carrying food or drinks

treacherous ['trɛtʃərəs] ADJECTIVE

t

1 A treacherous person is likely to betray you and cannot be trusted.

● THESAURUS

disloyal: *disloyal Cabinet colleagues*
faithless: *an oppressive father and faithless husband*
unfaithful: *his unfaithful wife*
untrustworthy: *Jordan has tried to brand his opponents as untrustworthy.*
<<OPPOSITE *loyal*

2 The ground or the sea can be described as treacherous when it is dangerous or unreliable. *e.g. treacherous mountain roads*
treacherously ADVERB

● THESAURUS

dangerous: *a dangerous stretch of road*
hazardous: *hazardous seas*
perilous: literary *The roads grew even steeper and more perilous.*

treachery ['trɛtʃərɪ] NOUN
Treachery is behaviour in which someone betrays their country or a person who trusts them.

treacle ['tri:kəl] NOUN
Treacle is a thick, sweet syrup used to make cakes and toffee. *e.g. treacle tart*

tread [trɛd] **treads, treading, trod, trodden** VERB

1 If you tread on something, you walk on it or step on it.

2 If you tread something into the ground or into a carpet, you crush it in by stepping on it. *e.g. bubblegum that has been trodden into the pavement*

> NOUN

3 A person's tread is the sound they make with their feet as they walk. *e.g. his heavy tread*

4 The tread of a tyre or shoe is the pattern of ridges on it that stops it slipping.

treadmill ['trɛd,mɪl] **treadmills** NOUN
Any task or job that you must keep doing even though it is unpleasant or tiring can be referred to as a treadmill. *e.g. My life is one constant treadmill of making music.*

treason ['tri:zən] NOUN
Treason is the crime of betraying your country, for example by helping its enemies.

treasure ['trɛʒə] **treasures, treasuring, treasured** NOUN

1 Treasure is a collection of gold, silver, jewels, or other precious objects, especially one that has been hidden. *e.g. buried treasure*

2 Treasures are valuable works of art. *e.g. the finest art treasures in the world*

> VERB

3 If you treasure something, you are very pleased

that you have it and regard it as very precious. *e.g. He treasures his friendship with her.*
treasured ADJECTIVE

● THESAURUS

cherish: *The previous owners had cherished the house.*
hold dear: *forced to renounce everything he held most dear*
prize: *one of the gallery's most prized possessions*
value: *if you value your health*

treasurer ['trɛʒərə] **treasurers** NOUN
a person who is in charge of the finance and accounts of an organization

Treasury ['trɛʒərɪ] NOUN
The Treasury is the government department that deals with the country's finances.

treat [tri:t] **treats, treating, treated** VERB

1 If you treat someone in a particular way, you behave that way towards them.

● THESAURUS

act towards: *the way you act towards other people*
behave towards: *He always behaved towards me with great kindness.*
deal with: *in dealing with suicidal youngsters*

2 If you treat something in a particular way, you deal with it that way or see it that way. *e.g. We are now treating this case as murder.*

3 When a doctor treats a patient or an illness, he or she gives them medical care and attention.

● THESAURUS

care for: *They hired a nurse to care for her.*
nurse: *All the years he was sick my mother had nursed him.*

4 If something such as wood or cloth is treated, a special substance is put on it in order to protect it or give it special properties. *e.g. The carpet's been treated with a stain protector.*

5 If you treat someone, you buy or arrange something special for them which they will enjoy.

> NOUN

6 If you give someone a treat, you buy or arrange something special for them which they will enjoy. *e.g. my birthday treat*
treatment NOUN

treatise ['tri:tɪz] **treatises** NOUN
a long formal piece of writing about a particular subject

treaty ['tri:tɪ] **treaties** NOUN
a written agreement between countries in which they agree to do something or to help each other

treble ['trɛbəl] **trebles, trebling, trebled** VERB

1 If something trebles or is trebled, it becomes three times greater in number or amount.

> ADJECTIVE

2 Treble means three times as large or three times as strong as previously. *e.g. Next year we can raise treble that amount.*

tree [triː] **trees** NOUN
a large plant with a hard woody trunk, branches, and leaves

trek [trɛk] **treks, trekking, trekked** VERB
1 If you trek somewhere, you go on a long and difficult journey.

> NOUN

2 a long and difficult journey, especially one made by walking
[WORD HISTORY: an Afrikaans word]

trellis [ˈtrɛlɪs] **trellises** NOUN
a frame made of horizontal and vertical strips of wood or metal and used to support plants

tremble [ˈtrɛmbəl] **trembles, trembling, trembled** VERB
1 If you tremble, you shake slightly, usually because you are frightened or cold.

2 If something trembles, it shakes slightly.

3 If your voice trembles, it sounds unsteady, usually because you are frightened or upset.
trembling ADJECTIVE

tremendous [trɪˈmɛndəs] ADJECTIVE
1 large or impressive *e.g. It was a tremendous performance.*

2 INFORMAL
very good or pleasing *e.g. tremendous fun*
tremendously ADVERB

tremor [ˈtrɛmə] **tremors** NOUN
1 a shaking movement of your body which you cannot control

2 an unsteady quality in your voice, for example when you are upset

3 a small earthquake

trench [trɛntʃ] **trenches** NOUN
a long narrow channel dug into the ground

trenchant [ˈtrɛntʃənt] ADJECTIVE
Trenchant writing or comments are bold and firmly expressed.

trend [trɛnd] **trends** NOUN
a change towards doing or being something different

trendy [ˈtrɛndɪ] **trendier, trendiest**
ADJECTIVE INFORMAL
Trendy things or people are fashionable.
● THESAURUS
fashionable: *a very fashionable place to go on holiday*
in: slang *what's in and what's not*

in fashion: *Calf-length skirts are in fashion this season.*
in vogue: *African art is in vogue at the moment.*
latest: *the latest thing in camera technology*
stylish: *This city has got a lot more stylish in recent years.*

trepidation [ˌtrɛpɪˈdeɪʃən] NOUN; FORMAL
Trepidation is fear or anxiety. *e.g. He saw the look of trepidation on my face.*

trespass [ˈtrɛspəs] **trespasses, trespassing, trespassed** VERB
If you trespass on someone's land or property, you go onto it without their permission.
trespasser NOUN

tresses [ˈtrɛsɪz] PLURAL NOUN; OLD-FASHIONED, FORMAL
A woman's tresses are her long flowing hair.

trestle [ˈtrɛsəl] **trestles** NOUN
a wooden or metal structure that is used as one of the supports for a table

trevally [trɪˈvælɪ] **trevallies** NOUN
an Australian and New Zealand fish that is caught for both food and sport

tri- PREFIX
three *e.g. tricycle*

triad [ˈtraɪæd] **triads** NOUN
1 FORMAL
a group of three similar things

2 (MUSIC) TECHNICAL
In music, a triad is a chord of three notes consisting of the tonic and the third and fifth above it.

trial [ˈtraɪəl] **trials** NOUN
1 the legal process in which a judge and jury decide whether a person is guilty of a particular crime after listening to all the evidence about it

2 an experiment in which something is tested *e.g. Trials of the drug start next month.*

triangle [ˈtraɪˌæŋɡəl] **triangles** NOUN
1 (MATHS) a shape with three straight sides

2 a percussion instrument consisting of a thin steel bar bent in the shape of a triangle
triangular ADJECTIVE

triathlon [traɪˈæθlɒn] **triathlons** NOUN
a sports contest in which athletes compete in three different events

tribe [traɪb] **tribes** NOUN
a group of people of the same race, who have the same customs, religion, language, or land, especially when they are thought to be primitive
tribal ADJECTIVE

tribulation [ˌtrɪbjʊˈleɪʃən] **tribulations**
NOUN; FORMAL

t

Tribulation is trouble or suffering. *e.g. the tributations of a female football star*

tribunal [traɪˈbjuːnᵊl] **tribunals** NOUN
a special court or committee appointed to deal with particular problems *e.g. an industrial tribunal*

tributary [ˈtrɪbjʊtərɪ] **tributaries** NOUN
a stream or river that flows into a larger river

tribute [ˈtrɪbjuːt] **tributes** NOUN
1 A tribute is something said or done to show admiration and respect for someone. *e.g. Police paid tribute to her courage.*

● THESAURUS
accolade: formal *To play for your country is the ultimate accolade.*
compliment: *We consider it a compliment to be called "conservative".*
honour: *Only two writers are granted the honour of a solo display.*
praise: *That is high praise indeed.*
testimony: *a testimony to her dedication*

2 If one thing is a tribute to another, it is the result of the other thing and shows how good it is. *e.g. His success has been a tribute to hard work.*

trice [traɪs] NOUN
If someone does something in a trice, they do it very quickly.

triceps [ˈtraɪsɛps] NOUN
(PE) Your triceps is the large muscle at the back of your upper arm that straightens your arm.

trick [trɪk] **tricks, tricking, tricked** NOUN
1 an action done to deceive someone

● THESAURUS
con: informal *Slimming snacks that offer miraculous weight loss are a con.*
deception: *the victim of a cruel deception*
hoax: *a bomb hoax*
ploy: *a cynical marketing ploy*
ruse: *This was a ruse to divide them.*

2 Tricks are clever or skilful actions done in order to entertain people. *e.g. magic tricks*

> VERB
3 If someone tricks you, they deceive you.

● THESAURUS
con: informal *We have been conned for 20 years.*
deceive: *He deceived me into thinking the money was his.*
dupe: *I was duped into letting them in.*
fool: *They tried to fool you into coming after us.*
take in: informal *I wasn't taken in for a minute.*

trickery [ˈtrɪkərɪ] NOUN
Trickery is deception. *e.g. He accused the Serbs of trickery.*

trickle [ˈtrɪkᵊl] **trickles, trickling, trickled** VERB

1 When a liquid trickles somewhere, it flows slowly in a thin stream.

2 When people or things trickle somewhere, they move there slowly in small groups or amounts.

> NOUN
3 a thin stream of liquid

4 A trickle of people or things is a small number or quantity of them.

tricky [ˈtrɪkɪ] **trickier, trickiest** ADJECTIVE
difficult to do or deal with

● THESAURUS
complex: *the whole complex issue of crime and punishment*
complicated: *a complicated operation*
delicate: *This brings us to the delicate question of his future.*
difficult: *It was a difficult decision to make.*
hard: *That's a hard question to answer.*
problematic: *It's a very problematic piece to play.*
puzzling: *a puzzling case to solve*
sensitive: *The death penalty is a very sensitive issue.*

tricycle [ˈtraɪsɪkᵊl] **tricycles** NOUN
a vehicle similar to a bicycle but with two wheels at the back and one at the front

trifle [ˈtraɪfᵊl] **trifles, trifling, trifled** NOUN
1 A trifle means a little. *e.g. He seemed a trifle annoyed.*

2 Trifles are things that are not very important or valuable.

3 a cold pudding made of layers of sponge cake, fruit, jelly, and custard

> VERB
4 If you trifle with someone or something, you treat them in a disrespectful way. *e.g. He was not to be trifled with.*

trifling [ˈtraɪflɪŋ] ADJECTIVE
small and unimportant

trigger [ˈtrɪgə] **triggers, triggering, triggered** NOUN
1 the small lever on a gun which is pulled in order to fire it

> VERB
2 If something triggers an event or triggers it off, it causes it to happen.
[WORD HISTORY: from Dutch TREKKEN meaning 'to pull']

trigonometry [ˌtrɪgəˈnɒmɪtrɪ] NOUN
Trigonometry is the branch of mathematics that is concerned with calculating the angles of triangles or the lengths of their sides.

trill [trɪl] **trills, trilling, trilled** VERB
If a bird trills, it sings with short high-pitched repeated notes.

trillion ['trɪljən] **trillions** NOUN; INFORMAL
Trillions of things means an extremely large number of them. Formerly, a trillion meant a million million million.

trilogy ['trɪlədʒɪ] **trilogies** NOUN
a series of three books or plays that have the same characters or are on the same subject

trim [trɪm] **trimmer, trimmest; trims, trimming, trimmed** ADJECTIVE
1 neat, tidy, and attractive
> VERB
2 To trim something is to clip small amounts off it.
3 If you trim off parts of something, you cut them off because they are not needed. *e.g. Trim off the excess marzipan.*
> NOUN
4 If something is given a trim, it is cut a little. *e.g. All styles need a trim every six to eight weeks.*
5 a decoration on something, especially along its edges *e.g. a fur trim*
trimmed ADJECTIVE

trimming ['trɪmɪŋ] **trimmings** NOUN
Trimmings are extra parts added to something for decoration or as a luxury. *e.g. bacon and eggs with all the trimmings*

Trimurti [trɪ'mʊətɪ] NOUN
In the Hindu religion, the Trimurti are the three deities Brahma, Vishnu, and Siva.

Trinity ['trɪnɪtɪ] NOUN
In the Christian religion, the Trinity is the joining of God the Father, God the Son, and God the Holy Spirit.

trinket ['trɪŋkɪt] **trinkets** NOUN
a cheap ornament or piece of jewellery

trio ['triːəʊ] **trios** NOUN
1 a group of three musicians who sing or play together; also a piece of music written for three instruments or singers
2 any group of three things or people together *e.g. a trio of children's tales*

trip [trɪp] **trips, tripping, tripped** NOUN
1 a journey made to a place
● **THESAURUS**
excursion: *a coach excursion to Trondheim*
jaunt: *a jaunt in the car*
journey: *the journey to Bordeaux*
outing: *a school outing*
voyage: *Columbus's voyage to the West Indies.*
> VERB
2 If you trip, you catch your foot on something and fall over.
● **THESAURUS**
fall over: *Plenty of top skiers fell over.*

lose your footing: *He lost his footing and slid into the water.*
stumble: *He stumbled and almost fell.*
3 If you trip someone or trip them up, you make them fall over by making them catch their foot on something.

tripe [traɪp] NOUN
Tripe is the stomach lining of a pig, cow, or ox, which is cooked and eaten.

triple ['trɪpəl] **triples, tripling, tripled** ADJECTIVE
1 consisting of three things or three parts *e.g. the Triple Alliance*
> VERB
2 If you triple something or if it triples, it becomes three times greater in number or size.

triplet ['trɪplɪt] **triplets** NOUN
Triplets are three children born at the same time to the same mother.

tripod ['traɪpɒd] **tripods** NOUN
a stand with three legs used to support something like a camera or telescope

tripper ['trɪpə] **trippers** NOUN
a tourist or someone on an excursion

trite [traɪt] ADJECTIVE
dull and not original *e.g. his trite novels*

triumph ['traɪəmf] **triumphs, triumphing, triumphed** NOUN
1 a great success or achievement
● **THESAURUS**
success: *The jewellery was a great success.*
victory: *a victory for common sense*
<<OPPOSITE *failure*
2 Triumph is a feeling of great satisfaction when you win or achieve something.
> VERB
3 If you triumph, you win a victory or succeed in overcoming something.
● **THESAURUS**
come out on top: *informal The only way to come out on top is to adopt a different approach.*
prevail: *I do hope he will prevail over the rebels.*
succeed: *if they can succeed in America*
win: *The top four teams all won.*
<<OPPOSITE *fail*

triumphal [traɪ'ʌmfəl] ADJECTIVE
done or made to celebrate a victory or great success *e.g. a triumphal return to Rome*

triumphant [traɪ'ʌmfənt] ADJECTIVE
Someone who is triumphant feels very happy because they have won a victory or have achieved something. *e.g. a triumphant shout*

trivia ['trɪvɪə] PLURAL NOUN
Trivia are unimportant things.

t

trivial ['trɪvɪəl] ADJECTIVE
Something trivial is unimportant.
[WORD HISTORY: from Latin TRIVIALIS meaning 'found everywhere']

● THESAURUS
insignificant: *The dangers are insignificant compared with those of smoking.*
minor: *a minor inconvenience*
negligible: *The strike will have a negligible impact.*
paltry: *They had no interest in paltry domestic concerns.*
petty: *I wouldn't indulge in such petty schoolboy pranks.*
slight: *It's only a slight problem.*
trifling: *The sums involved were trifling.*
unimportant: *Too much time is spent discussing unimportant matters.*
<<OPPOSITE important

troll [trəʊl] **trolls** NOUN
an imaginary creature in Scandinavian mythology that lives in caves or mountains and is believed to turn to stone at daylight

trolley ['trɒlɪ] **trolleys** NOUN
1 a small table on wheels
2 a small cart on wheels used for carrying heavy objects *e.g. a supermarket trolley*

trombone [trɒm'bəʊn] **trombones** NOUN
a brass wind instrument with a U-shaped slide which you move to produce different notes

troop [tru:p] **troops, trooping, trooped** NOUN
1 Troops are soldiers.
2 A troop of people or animals is a group of them.
> VERB
3 If people troop somewhere, they go there in a group.

trooper ['tru:pə] **troopers** NOUN
a low-ranking soldier in the cavalry

trophy ['trəʊfɪ] **trophies** NOUN
1 a cup or shield given as a prize to the winner of a competition
2 something you keep to remember a success or victory
[WORD HISTORY: from Greek TROPĒ meaning 'defeat of the enemy']

tropical ['trɒpɪkəl] ADJECTIVE
belonging to or typical of the tropics *e.g. a tropical island*

tropics ['trɒpɪks] PLURAL NOUN
The tropics are the hottest parts of the world between two lines of latitude, the Tropic of Cancer, 23½° north of the equator, and the Tropic of Capricorn, 23½° south of the equator.

trot [trɒt] **trots, trotting, trotted** VERB

1 When a horse trots, it moves at a speed between a walk and a canter, lifting its feet quite high off the ground.
2 If you trot, you run or jog using small quick steps.
> NOUN
3 When a horse breaks into a trot, it starts trotting.

trotter ['trɒtə] **trotters** NOUN
A pig's trotters are its feet.

trouble ['trʌbəl] **troubles, troubling, troubled** NOUN
1 Troubles are difficulties or problems.
● THESAURUS
bother: *Vince is having a spot of bother with the law.*
difficulty: *economic difficulties*
hassle: informal *We had loads of hassles trying to find somewhere to rehearse.*
problem: *The main problem is unemployment.*
2 If there is trouble, people are quarrelling or fighting. *e.g. There was more trouble after the match.*
> PHRASE
3 If you are **in trouble**, you are in a situation where you may be punished because you have done something wrong.
> VERB
4 If something troubles you, it makes you feel worried or anxious.
● THESAURUS
agitate: *The thought agitates her.*
bother: *Is something bothering you?*
disturb: *dreams so vivid that they disturb me for days*
worry: *I didn't want to worry you.*
5 If you trouble someone for something, you disturb them in order to ask them for it. *e.g. Can I trouble you for some milk?.*
troubling ADJECTIVE, **troubled** ADJECTIVE
● THESAURUS
bother: *I don't know why he bothers me with this kind of rubbish.*
disturb: *a room where you won't be disturbed*
impose upon: *I was afraid you'd feel we were imposing on you.*
inconvenience: *He promised to be quick so as not to inconvenience them further.*
put out: *I've always put myself out for others.*

troublesome ['trʌbəlsəm] ADJECTIVE
causing problems or difficulties *e.g. a troublesome teenager*

trough [trɒf] **troughs** NOUN
a long, narrow container from which animals drink or feed

trounce [traʊns] **trounces, trouncing, trounced** VERB

If you trounce someone, you defeat them completely.

troupe [truːp] **troupes** NOUN
a group of actors, singers, or dancers who work together and often travel around together

trousers ['traʊzəz] PLURAL NOUN
Trousers are a piece of clothing covering the body from the waist down, enclosing each leg separately.
[WORD HISTORY: from Gaelic TRIUBHAS]

trout [traʊt] NOUN
a type of freshwater fish

trowel ['traʊəl] **trowels** NOUN
1 a small garden tool with a curved, pointed blade used for planting or weeding
2 a small tool with a flat blade used for spreading cement or plaster

truant ['truːənt] **truants** NOUN
1 a child who stays away from school without permission
> PHRASE
2 If children **play truant**, they stay away from school without permission.
truancy NOUN

truce [truːs] **truces** NOUN
an agreement between two people or groups to stop fighting for a short time

truck [trʌk] **trucks** NOUN
1 a large motor vehicle used for carrying heavy loads
2 an open vehicle used for carrying goods on a railway

truculent ['trʌkjʊlənt] ADJECTIVE
bad-tempered and aggressive
truculence NOUN

trudge [trʌdʒ] **trudges, trudging, trudged** VERB
1 If you trudge, you walk with slow, heavy steps.
> NOUN
2 a slow tiring walk *e.g. the long trudge home*

true [truː] **truer, truest** ADJECTIVE
1 A true story or statement is based on facts and is not made up.
● THESAURUS
accurate: *an accurate assessment of the situation*
correct: *a correct diagnosis*
factual: *any comparison that is not strictly factual*
<<OPPOSITE *inaccurate*

2 'True' is used to describe things or people that are genuine *e.g. She was a true friend.*
● THESAURUS
authentic: *authentic Italian food*

bona fide: *We are happy to donate to bona fide charities.*
genuine: *There was a risk of genuine refugees being returned to Vietnam.*
real: *No, it wasn't a dream. It was real.*
<<OPPOSITE *false*

3 True feelings are sincere and genuine.
> PHRASE
4 If something **comes true**, it actually happens.
truly ADVERB

truffle ['trʌfəl] **truffles** NOUN
1 a soft, round sweet
2 a round mushroom-like fungus which grows underground and is considered very good to eat

trump [trʌmp] **trumps** NOUN
In a game of cards, trumps is the suit with the highest value.

trumpet ['trʌmpɪt] **trumpets, trumpeting, trumpeted** NOUN
1 a brass wind instrument with a narrow tube ending in a bell-like shape
> VERB
2 When an elephant trumpets, it makes a sound like a very loud trumpet.

truncated [trʌŋ'keɪtɪd] ADJECTIVE
Something that is truncated is made shorter.

truncheon ['trʌntʃən] **truncheons** NOUN
a stick carried by police officers as a weapon, especially the short, thick kind formerly used by British police
[WORD HISTORY: from Old French TRONCHON MEANING 'STUMP']

trundle ['trʌndəl] **trundles, trundling, trundled** VERB
If you trundle something or it trundles somewhere, it moves or rolls along slowly.

trunk [trʌŋk] **trunks** NOUN
1 the main stem of a tree from which the branches and roots grow
2 the main part of your body, excluding your head, neck, arms, and legs
3 the long flexible nose of an elephant
4 a large, strong case or box with a hinged lid used for storing things
> PLURAL NOUN
5 A man's trunks are his bathing pants or shorts.

truss [trʌs] **trusses, trussing, trussed** VERB
1 To truss someone or truss them up is to tie them up so that they cannot move.
> NOUN
2 a supporting belt with a pad worn by a man with a hernia

trust [trʌst] **trusts, trusting, trusted** VERB

1 If you trust someone, you believe that they are honest and will not harm you.

2 If you trust someone to do something, you believe they will do it successfully or properly.

● **THESAURUS**
count on: *I can always count on you to cheer me up.*
depend on: *You can depend on me.*
have confidence in: *We have the utmost confidence in your abilities.*
have faith in: *I have no faith in him any more.*
place your trust in: *I would never place my trust in one so young.*
rely upon: *I know I can rely on you to sort it out.*

3 If you trust someone with something, you give it to them or tell it to them. *e.g. One member of the group cannot be trusted with the secret.*

4 If you do not trust something, you feel that it is not safe or reliable. *e.g. I didn't trust my arms and legs to work.*

> NOUN

5 Trust is the responsibility you are given to deal with or look after important or secret things. *e.g. He had built up a position of trust.*

6 a financial arrangement in which an organization looks after and invests money for someone
trusting ADJECTIVE

trustee [trʌˈstiː] **trustees** NOUN
someone who is allowed by law to control money or property they are keeping or investing for another person

trustworthy [ˈtrʌstˌwɜːðɪ] ADJECTIVE
A trustworthy person is reliable and responsible and can be trusted.

trusty [ˈtrʌstɪ] **trustier, trustiest** ADJECTIVE
Trusty things and animals are considered to be reliable because they have always worked well in the past. *e.g. a trusty black labrador*

● **THESAURUS**
dependable: *a dependable and steady worker*
faithful: *his faithful black Labrador*
firm: *Betty became a firm friend of the family.*
reliable: *the problem of finding reliable staff*
solid: *one of my most solid supporters*
staunch: *He proved himself a staunch ally.*
true: *a true friend*
trustworthy: *trying to find a trustworthy adviser*

truth [truːθ] **truths** NOUN
1 The truth is the facts about something, rather than things that are imagined or made up. *e.g. I know she was telling the truth.*

● **THESAURUS**
fact: *How much was fact and how much fancy no one knew.*
reality: *Fiction and reality were increasingly blurred.*

2 an idea or principle that is generally accepted to be true *e.g. the basic truths in life*

truthful [ˈtruːθfʊl] ADJECTIVE
A truthful person is honest and tells the truth.
truthfully ADVERB

try [traɪ] **tries, trying, tried** VERB
1 To try to do something is to make an effort to do it.

● **THESAURUS**
attempt: *They are accused of attempting to murder British soldiers.*
endeavour: formal *I will endeavour to arrange it.*
make an attempt: *He made three attempts to break the record.*
make an effort: *He made no effort to hide his disappointment.*
seek: *We have never sought to impose our views.*
strive: *The school strives to treat pupils as individuals.*

2 If you try something, you use it or do it to test how useful or enjoyable it is. *e.g. Howard wanted me to try the wine.*

● **THESAURUS**
check out: *We went to the club to check it out.*
sample: *We sampled a selection of different bottled waters.*
test: *The drug was tested on rats.*
try out: *London Transport hopes to try out the system in September.*

3 When a person is tried, they appear in court and a judge and jury decide if they are guilty after hearing the evidence.

> NOUN

4 an attempt to do something

● **THESAURUS**
attempt: *a deliberate attempt to destabilize the defence*
effort: *his efforts to improve*
endeavour: formal *His first endeavours in the field were wedding films.*
go: informal *She won on her first go.*
shot: informal *I have had a shot at professional cricket.*

5 a test of something *e.g. You gave it a try.*

6 In rugby, a try is scored when someone carries the ball over the goal line of the opposing team and touches the ground with it.

> You can use *try to* in speech and writing: *try to get here on time for once. Try and* is very common in speech, but you should avoid it in written work: *just try and stop me!*

trying [ˈtraɪɪŋ] ADJECTIVE
Something or someone trying is difficult to deal with and makes you feel impatient or annoyed.

tryst [trɪst] **trysts** NOUN
an appointment or meeting, especially between

lovers in a quiet, secret place

tsar [zɑː] **tsars**; also spelt **czar** NOUN
a Russian emperor or king between 1547 and 1917

tsarina [zɑːˈriːnə] **tsarinas**; also spelt **czarina**
NOUN
a female tsar or the wife of a tsar

tsetse fly [ˈtsɛtsɪ] **tsetse flies** NOUN
an African fly that feeds on blood and causes serious diseases in people and animals

T-shirt [ˈtiːˌʃɜːt] **T-shirts**; also spelt **tee shirt**
NOUN
a simple short-sleeved cotton shirt with no collar

tsunami [tsʊˈnæmɪ] **tsunamis** NOUN
a large, often destructive sea wave, caused by an earthquake or volcanic eruption under the sea
[WORD HISTORY: from Japanese TSUNAMI meaning 'harbour wave']

tuatara [ˌtuːəˈtɑːrə] **tuatara** or **tuataras**
NOUN
a large, lizard-like reptile found on certain islands off the coast of New Zealand

tub [tʌb] **tubs** NOUN
a wide circular container

tuba [ˈtjuːbə] **tubas** NOUN
a large brass musical instrument that can produce very low notes

tubby [ˈtʌbɪ] **tubbier, tubbiest** ADJECTIVE
rather fat

● THESAURUS
chubby: *She was very chubby as a child.*
fat: *He was short and fat.*
overweight: *Being overweight is bad for your health.*
plump: *a plump, good-natured little woman*
podgy: *Eddie is a little podgy round the middle.*
portly: *a portly gentleman*
stout: *His wife was a small, stout lady.*

tube [tjuːb] **tubes** NOUN
1 a round, hollow pipe
2 a soft metal or plastic cylindrical container with a screw cap at one end *e.g. a tube of toothpaste*
tubing NOUN

tuberculosis [tjʊˌbɜːkjʊˈləʊsɪs] NOUN
Tuberculosis is a serious infectious disease affecting the lungs.

tubular [ˈtjuːbjʊlə] ADJECTIVE
in the shape of a tube

TUC
In Britain, an abbreviation for 'Trades Union Congress', which is an association of trade unions.

tuck [tʌk] **tucks, tucking, tucked** VERB

1 If you tuck something somewhere, you put it there so that it is safe or comfortable. *e.g. She tucked the letter into her handbag.*

2 If you tuck a piece of fabric into or under something, you push the loose ends inside or under it to make it tidy.

3 If something is tucked away, it is in a quiet place where few people go. *e.g. a little house tucked away in a valley*

tucker [ˈtʌkə] **tuckers, tuckering, tuckered** INFORMAL > NOUN

1 In Australian and New Zealand English, tucker is food.

> VERB

2 In Australian and New Zealand English, if you are tuckered out you are tired out.

Tudor [ˈtjuːdə] **Tudors** NOUN
Tudor was the family name of the English monarchs who reigned from 1485 to 1603.

Tuesday [ˈtjuːzdɪ] **Tuesdays** NOUN
Tuesday is the day between Monday and Wednesday.
[WORD HISTORY: from Old English TIWESDÆG meaning 'Tiw's day'; Tiw was the Scandinavian god of war and the sky]

tuft [tʌft] **tufts** NOUN
A tuft of something such as hair is a bunch of it growing closely together.

tug [tʌg] **tugs, tugging, tugged** VERB
1 To tug something is to give it a quick, hard pull.

● THESAURUS
drag: *He grabbed my ankle and dragged me back.*
draw: *She took his hand and drew him along.*
haul: *I gripped his wrist and hauled him up.*
heave: *They heaved the last bag into the van.*
jerk: *He jerked his hand out of mine angrily.*
pluck: *The beggar plucked at her sleeve as she passed.*
pull: *She pulled down the hem of her skirt over her knees.*
wrench: *The horse wrenched its head free.*
yank: *He grabbed my arm and yanked me out of the car.*

> NOUN
2 a quick, hard pull *e.g. He felt a tug at his arm.*

● THESAURUS
heave: *With a mighty heave, she pulled herself away from him.*
jerk: *He gave a sudden jerk of the reins.*
pull: *Give the cord three sharp pulls.*
wrench: *He lowered the flag with a quick wrench.*
yank: *He gave the phone a savage yank.*

3 a small, powerful boat which tows large ships

tug of war NOUN
A tug of war is a sport in which two teams test

t

their strength by pulling against each other on opposite ends of a rope.

tuition [tjuːˈɪʃən] NOUN
Tuition is the teaching of a subject, especially to one person or to a small group.

tulip [ˈtjuːlɪp] **tulips** NOUN
a brightly coloured spring flower
[WORD HISTORY: from Turkish TULBEND meaning 'turban', because of its shape]

tumble [ˈtʌmbəl] **tumbles, tumbling, tumbled** VERB
1 To tumble is to fall with a rolling or bouncing movement.
> NOUN
2 a fall

tumbler [ˈtʌmblə] **tumblers** NOUN
a drinking glass with straight sides

tummy [ˈtʌmɪ] **tummies** NOUN; INFORMAL
Your tummy is your stomach.

tumour [ˈtjuːmə] **tumours** NOUN
a mass of diseased or abnormal cells that has grown in a person's or animal's body

tumultuous [tjuːˈmʌltjʊəs] ADJECTIVE
A tumultuous event or welcome is very noisy because people are happy or excited.

tuna [ˈtjuːnə] NOUN
Tuna are large fish that live in warm seas and are caught for food.

tundra [ˈtʌndrə] NOUN
The tundra is a vast treeless Arctic region.
[WORD HISTORY: a Russian word]

tune [tjuːn] **tunes, tuning, tuned** NOUN
1 a series of musical notes arranged in a particular way
● THESAURUS
melody: *a beautiful melody*
strains: *She could hear the tinny strains of a chamber orchestra.*
> VERB
2 To tune a musical instrument is to adjust it so that it produces the right notes.
3 To tune an engine or machine is to adjust it so that it works well.
4 If you tune to a particular radio or television station you turn or press the controls to select the station you want to listen to or watch.
> PHRASE
5 If your voice or an instrument is **in tune**, it produces the right notes.

tuneful [ˈtjuːnfʊl] ADJECTIVE
having a pleasant and easily remembered tune

tuner [ˈtjuːnə] **tuners** NOUN
A piano tuner is a person whose job it is to tune pianos.

tunic [ˈtjuːnɪk] **tunics** NOUN
a sleeveless garment covering the top part of the body and reaching to the hips, thighs, or knees

Tunisian [tjuːˈnɪzɪən] **Tunisians** ADJECTIVE
1 belonging or relating to Tunisia
> NOUN
2 someone who comes from Tunisia

tunnel [ˈtʌnəl] **tunnels, tunnelling, tunnelled** NOUN
1 a long underground passage
> VERB
2 To tunnel is to make a tunnel.

turban [ˈtɜːbən] **turbans** NOUN
a head-covering worn by a Hindu, Muslim, or Sikh man, consisting of a long piece of cloth wound round his head

turbine [ˈtɜːbɪn] **turbines** NOUN
a machine or engine in which power is produced when a stream of air, gas, water, or steam pushes the blades of a wheel and makes it turn round
[WORD HISTORY: from Latin TURBO meaning 'whirlwind']

turbot [ˈtɜːbət] NOUN
a large European flat fish that is caught for food

turbulent [ˈtɜːbjʊlənt] ADJECTIVE
1 A turbulent period of history is one where there is much uncertainty, and possibly violent change.
2 Turbulent air or water currents make sudden changes of direction.
turbulence NOUN

tureen [təˈriːn] **tureens** NOUN
a large dish with a lid for serving soup

turf [tɜːf] **turves; turfs, turfing, turfed** NOUN
1 Turf is short thick even grass and the layer of soil beneath it.
turf out VERB
2 INFORMAL To turf someone out is to force them to leave a place.

turgid [ˈtɜːdʒɪd] ADJECTIVE; LITERARY
A turgid play, film, or piece of writing is difficult to understand and rather boring.

Turk [tɜːk] **Turks** NOUN
someone who comes from Turkey

turkey [ˈtɜːkɪ] **turkeys** NOUN
a large bird kept for food; also the meat of this bird

Turkish [ˈtɜːkɪʃ] ADJECTIVE
1 belonging or relating to Turkey
> NOUN
2 Turkish is the main language spoken in Turkey.

turmoil ['tɜːmɔɪl] NOUN
Turmoil is a state of confusion, disorder, or great anxiety. *e.g. Europe is in a state of turmoil.*

turn [tɜːn] **turns, turning, turned** VERB
1 When you turn, you move so that you are facing or going in a different direction.

2 When you turn something or when it turns, it moves or rotates so that it faces in a different direction or is in a different position.

● THESAURUS
rotate: *Take each foot in both your hands and rotate it.*
spin: *He spun the wheel sharply and made a U-turn.*
swivel: *She swivelled her chair round.*
twirl: *Bonnie twirled her empty glass in her fingers.*
twist: *She twisted her head sideways.*

3 If you turn your attention or thoughts to someone or something, you start thinking about them or discussing them.

4 When something turns or is turned into something else, it becomes something different. *e.g. A hobby can be turned into a career.*

● THESAURUS
change: *She has now changed into a happy, self-confident woman.*
convert: *a table that converts into an ironing board*
mutate: *Overnight, the gossip begins to mutate into headlines.*
transform: *the speed at which your body transforms food into energy*

> NOUN
5 an act of turning something so that it faces in a different direction or is in a different position

6 a change in the way something is happening or being done *e.g. Her career took a turn for the worse.*

7 If it is your turn to do something, you have the right, chance, or duty to do it.

● THESAURUS
chance: *All eligible people would get a chance to vote.*
go: *Whose go is it?*
opportunity: *Now is your opportunity to say what you've always wanted.*

> PHRASE
8 In turn is used to refer to people, things, or actions that are in sequence one after the other

turn down VERB
9 If you turn down someone's request or offer, you refuse or reject it.

turn up VERB
10 If someone or something turns up, they arrive or appear somewhere.

11 If something turns up, it is found or discovered.

turncoat ['tɜːnˌkəʊt] **turncoats** NOUN
a person who leaves one political party or group for an opposing one

turning ['tɜːnɪŋ] **turnings** NOUN
a road which leads away from the side of another road

turning point turning points NOUN
the moment when decisions are taken and events start to move in a different direction

turnip ['tɜːnɪp] **turnips** NOUN
a round root vegetable with a white or yellow skin

turnout ['tɜːnˌaʊt] **turnouts** NOUN
The turnout at an event is the number of people who go to it.

turnover ['tɜːnˌəʊvə] **turnovers** NOUN
1 The turnover of people in a particular organization or group is the rate at which people leave it and are replaced by others.

2 The turnover of a company is the value of the goods or services sold during a particular period.

turnstile ['tɜːnˌstaɪl] **turnstiles** NOUN
a revolving mechanical barrier at the entrance to places like football grounds or zoos

turpentine ['tɜːpˈnˌtaɪn] NOUN
Turpentine is a strong-smelling colourless liquid used for cleaning and for thinning paint.

turps [tɜːps] NOUN
Turps is turpentine.

turquoise ['tɜːkwɔɪz] NOUN OR ADJECTIVE
1 light bluish-green

> NOUN
2 Turquoise is a bluish-green stone used in jewellery.

turret ['tʌrɪt] **turrets** NOUN
a small narrow tower on top of a larger tower or other buildings

turtle ['tɜːtˈl] **turtles** NOUN
a large reptile with a thick shell covering its body and flippers for swimming. It lays its eggs on land but lives the rest of its life in the sea.

tusk [tʌsk] **tusks** NOUN
The tusks of an elephant, wild boar, or walrus are the pair of long curving pointed teeth it has.

tussle ['tʌsˈl] **tussles** NOUN
an energetic fight or argument between two people, especially about something they both want

tutor ['tjuːtə] **tutors, tutoring, tutored** NOUN
1 a teacher at a college or university

2 a private teacher

> VERB

3 If someone tutors a person or subject, they teach that person or subject.

tutorial [tjuːˈtɔːrɪəl] **tutorials** NOUN
a teaching session involving a tutor and a small group of students

tutu [ˈtuːtuː] **tutus** NOUN
a short stiff skirt worn by female ballet dancers

TV **TVs** NOUN
1 TV is television.
2 a television set

twang [twæŋ] **twangs, twanging, twanged** NOUN
1 a sound like the one made by pulling and then releasing a tight wire
2 A twang is a nasal quality in a person's voice.

> VERB

3 If a tight wire or string twangs or you twang it, it makes a sound as it is pulled and then released.

tweak [twiːk] **tweaks, tweaking, tweaked** VERB
1 If you tweak something, you twist it or pull it.

> NOUN

2 a short twist or pull of something

twee [twiː] ADJECTIVE
sweet and pretty but in bad taste or sentimental

tweed [twiːd] **tweeds** NOUN
Tweed is a thick woollen cloth.

tweet [twiːt] **tweets, tweeting, tweeted** VERB
1 When a small bird tweets, it makes a short, high-pitched sound.

> NOUN

2 a short high-pitched sound made by a small bird

tweezers [ˈtwiːzəz] PLURAL NOUN
Tweezers are a small tool with two arms which can be closed together and are used for pulling out hairs or picking up small objects.

twelve [twɛlv]
the number 12
twelfth

twenty [ˈtwɛntɪ] **twenties**
the number 20
twentieth

twice [twaɪs] ADVERB
Twice means two times.

twiddle [ˈtwɪdəl] **twiddles, twiddling, twiddled** VERB
To twiddle something is to twist it or turn it quickly.

twig [twɪɡ] **twigs** NOUN
a very small thin branch growing from a main branch of a tree or bush

twilight [ˈtwaɪˌlaɪt] NOUN
1 Twilight is the time after sunset when it is just getting dark.
2 The twilight of something is the final stages of it. *e.g. the twilight of his career*

twin [twɪn] **twins** NOUN
1 If two people are twins, they have the same mother and were born on the same day.
2 'Twin' is used to describe two similar things that are close together or happen together *e.g. the little twin islands*

twine [twaɪn] **twines, twining, twined** NOUN
1 Twine is strong smooth string.

> VERB

2 If you twine one thing round another, you twist or wind it round.

twinge [twɪndʒ] **twinges** NOUN
a sudden, unpleasant feeling *e.g. a twinge of jealousy*

twinkle [ˈtwɪŋkəl] **twinkles, twinkling, twinkled** VERB
1 If something twinkles, it sparkles or seems to sparkle with an unsteady light. *e.g. Her green eyes twinkled.*

> NOUN

2 a sparkle or brightness that something has

twirl [twɜːl] **twirls, twirling, twirled** VERB
If something twirls, or if you twirl it, it spins or twists round and round.

twist [twɪst] **twists, twisting, twisted** VERB
1 When you twist something you turn one end of it in one direction while holding the other end or turning it in the opposite direction.

● THESAURUS
bend: *Bend the bar into a horseshoe.*
curl: *She sat with her legs curled under her.*
twine: *He had twined his chubby arms around Vincent's neck.*
weave: *He weaves his way through a crowd.*
wring: *after wringing the chicken's neck*

2 When something twists or is twisted, it moves or bends into a strange shape.

● THESAURUS
distort: *A painter may exaggerate or distort shapes and forms.*
mangle: *the mangled wreckage*
screw up: *Amy screwed up her face.*

3 If you twist a part of your body, you injure it by turning it too sharply or in an unusual direction. *e.g. I've twisted my ankle.*

● THESAURUS
sprain: *He fell and sprained his wrist.*
wrench: *He had wrenched his back badly from the force of the fall.*

4 If you twist something that someone has said, you change the meaning slightly.

> NOUN

5 a twisting action or motion

6 an unexpected development or event in a story or film, especially at the end *e.g. Each day now seemed to bring a new twist to the story.*

twisted ['twɪstɪd] ADJECTIVE

1 Something twisted has been bent or moved into a strange shape. *e.g. a tangle of twisted metal*

2 If someone's mind or behaviour is twisted, it is unpleasantly abnormal. *e.g. He's bitter and twisted.*

twit [twɪt] **twits** NOUN; INFORMAL
a silly person

twitch [twɪtʃ] **twitches, twitching, twitched** VERB

1 If you twitch, you make little jerky movements which you cannot control.

2 If you twitch something, you give it a little jerk in order to move it.

> NOUN

3 a little jerky movement

twitter ['twɪtə] **twitters, twittering, twittered** VERB
When birds twitter, they make short high-pitched sounds.

two [tuː]
the number 2

Do not confuse the spelling of the preposition *to*, the adverb *too*, and the number *two*

two-faced [ˌtuːˈfeɪst] ADJECTIVE
A two-faced person is not honest in the way they behave towards other people.

THESAURUS
deceitful: *a deceitful, conniving liar*
dishonest: *He's been dishonest in his dealings with us both.*
disloyal: *I can't stand people who are disloyal.*
false: *He had been betrayed by his false friends.*
hypocritical: *a hypocritical and ambitious careerist*
insincere: *They are still widely seen as insincere and untrustworthy.*
treacherous: *He has been consistently treacherous to both sides.*

twofold ['tuːˌfəʊld] ADJECTIVE
Something twofold has two equally important parts or reasons. *e.g. Their concern was twofold: personal and political.*

twosome ['tuːsəm] **twosomes** NOUN
two people or things that are usually seen together

two-time [ˌtuːˈtaɪm] **two-times, two-timing, two-timed** VERB; INFORMAL

If you two-time your boyfriend or girlfriend, you deceive them, by having a romantic relationship with someone else without telling them.

two-up [ˌtuːˈʌp] NOUN
In Australia and New Zealand, two-up is a popular gambling game in which two coins are tossed and bets are placed on whether they land heads or tails.

tycoon [taɪˈkuːn] **tycoons** NOUN
a person who is successful in business and has become rich and powerful
[WORD HISTORY: from Chinese TA + CHUN meaning 'great ruler']

type [taɪp] **types, typing, typed** NOUN

1 A type of something is a class of it that has common features and belongs to a larger group of related things. *e.g. What type of dog should we get?*

THESAURUS
brand: *his favourite brand of whisky*
breed: *a rare breed of cattle*
class: *a better class of restaurant*
group: *Weather forecasters classify clouds into several different groups.*
kind: *I don't like that kind of film.*
make: *He'll only drive a certain make of car.*
sort: *a dozen trees of various sorts*
species: *a rare species of moth*
style: *Several styles of hat were available.*
variety: *Many varieties of birds live here.*

2 A particular type of person has a particular appearance or quality. *e.g. Andrea is the type who likes to play safe.*

> VERB

3 If you type something, you use a typewriter or word processor to write it.

typewriter ['taɪpˌraɪtə] **typewriters** NOUN
a machine with a keyboard with individual keys which are pressed to produce letters and numbers on a page

typhoid ['taɪfɔɪd] NOUN
Typhoid, or typhoid fever, is an infectious disease caused by dirty water or food. It produces fever and can kill.

typhoon [taɪˈfuːn] **typhoons** NOUN
a very violent tropical storm
[WORD HISTORY: from Chinese TAI FUNG meaning 'great wind']

typhus ['taɪfəs] NOUN
Typhus is an infectious disease transmitted by lice or mites. It results in fever, severe headaches, and a skin rash.

typical ['tɪpɪkəl] ADJECTIVE
showing the most usual characteristics or behaviour

t

typically ADVERB

● THESAURUS

average: *The average adult man burns 1500 to 2000 calories per day.*

characteristic: *a characteristic feature of the landscape*

normal: *a normal day*

regular: *He describes himself as just a regular guy.*

representative: *fairly representative groups of adults*

standard: *It was standard practice in cases like this.*

stock: *He had a stock answer for all problems.*

usual: *a neighborhood beset by all the usual inner-city problems*

<<OPPOSITE *uncharacteristic*

typify ['tɪpɪˌfaɪ] **typifies, typifying, typified** VERB

If something typifies a situation or thing, it is characteristic of it or a typical example of it. *e.g. This story is one that typifies our times.*

typing ['taɪpɪŋ] NOUN

Typing is the work or activity of producing something on a typewriter.

typist ['taɪpɪst] **typists** NOUN

a person whose job is typing

tyrannosaurus [tɪˌrænə'sɔːrəs] **tyrannosauruses** NOUN

a very large meat-eating dinosaur which walked upright on its hind legs

[WORD HISTORY: from Greek TURANNOS meaning 'tyrant' and Latin SAURUS meaning 'lizard']

tyranny ['tɪrənɪ] **tyrannies** NOUN

1 A tyranny is cruel and unjust rule of people by a person or group. *e.g. the evils of Nazi tyranny*

2 You can refer to something which is not human but is harsh as tyranny. *e.g. the tyranny of drugs*

tyrannical ADJECTIVE

tyrant ['taɪrənt] **tyrants** NOUN

a person who treats the people he or she has authority over cruelly and unjustly

tyre ['taɪə] **tyres** NOUN

a thick ring of rubber fitted round each wheel of a vehicle and filled with air

Uu

ubiquitous [juːˈbɪkwɪtəs] ADJECTIVE
Something that is ubiquitous seems to be
everywhere at the same time. *e.g. the ubiquitous
jeans*
[WORD HISTORY: from Latin UBIQUE meaning
'everywhere']

udder [ˈʌdə] **udders** NOUN
the baglike organ that hangs below a cow's body
and produces milk

UFO [ˈjuːfəʊ] **UFOs** NOUN
a strange object seen in the sky, which some
people believe to be a spaceship from another
planet. UFO is an abbreviation for 'unidentified
flying object'.

Ugandan [juːˈgændən] **Ugandans**
ADJECTIVE
1 belonging or relating to Uganda
> NOUN
2 someone who comes from Uganda

ugly [ˈʌglɪ] **uglier, ugliest** ADJECTIVE
very unattractive in appearance
[WORD HISTORY: from Old Norse UGGLIGR meaning
'terrifying']
● THESAURUS
plain: *a shy, plain girl with a pale complexion*
unattractive: *painted in an unattractive shade of
green*
unsightly: *The view was spoiled by some unsightly
houses.*
<<OPPOSITE *beautiful*

UK an abbreviation for **United Kingdom**

ulcer [ˈʌlsə] **ulcers** NOUN
a sore area on the skin or inside the body, which
takes a long time to heal *e.g. stomach ulcers*

ulterior [ʌlˈtɪərɪə] ADJECTIVE
If you have an ulterior motive for doing
something, you have a hidden reason for it.

ultimate [ˈʌltɪmɪt] ADJECTIVE
1 final or eventual *e.g. Olympic gold is the ultimate
goal.*
● THESAURUS
eventual: *Reunification is the eventual aim.*
final: *the fifth and final day*
last: *This is his last chance to do something useful.*

2 most important or powerful *e.g. the ultimate
ambition of any player*
● THESAURUS
greatest: *Our greatest aim was to take the gold
medal.*
paramount: *His paramount ambition was to be an
actor.*
supreme: *the supreme test of his abilities*
utmost: *This has to be our utmost priority.*
> NOUN
3 You can refer to the best or most advanced
example of something as the ultimate. *e.g. This
hotel is the ultimate in luxury.*
ultimately ADVERB
● THESAURUS
epitome: *She was the epitome of the successful
businesswoman.*
extreme: *This was shyness taken to the extreme.*
height: *the height of bad manners*
peak: *roses at the peak of perfection*

ultimatum [ʌltɪˈmeɪtəm] **ultimatums**
NOUN
a warning stating that unless someone meets
your conditions, you will take action against
them

ultra- PREFIX
'Ultra-' is used to form adjectives describing
something as having a quality to an extreme
degree *e.g. the ultra-competitive world of sport
today*

ultramarine [ʌltrəməˈriːn] NOUN OR
ADJECTIVE
bright blue
[WORD HISTORY: from Latin ULTRAMARINUS meaning
'beyond the sea', because the pigment was
imported from abroad]

ultrasonic [ʌltrəˈsɒnɪk] ADJECTIVE
An ultrasonic sound has a very high frequency
that cannot be heard by the human ear.

ultrasound [ˈʌltrəˌsaʊnd] NOUN
sound which cannot be heard by the human ear
because its frequency is too high

ultraviolet [ʌltrəˈvaɪələt] ADJECTIVE
Ultraviolet light is not visible to the human eye. It
is a form of radiation that causes your skin to

darken after being exposed to the sun.

umbilical cord [ʌmˈbɪlɪkəl] **umbilical cords** NOUN

the tube of blood vessels which connects an unborn baby to its mother and through which the baby receives nutrients and oxygen

umbrella [ʌmˈbrɛlə] **umbrellas** NOUN

a device that you use to protect yourself from the rain. It consists of a folding frame covered in cloth attached to a long stick

umpire [ˈʌmpaɪə] **umpires, umpiring, umpired** NOUN

1 The umpire in cricket or tennis is the person who makes sure that the game is played according to the rules and who makes a decision if there is a dispute.

> VERB

2 If you umpire a game, you are the umpire.

umpteen [ʌmpˈtiːn] ADJECTIVE; INFORMAL

very many e.g. tomatoes and umpteen other plants

umpteenth ADJECTIVE

un- PREFIX

Un- is added to the beginning of many words to form a word with the opposite meaning. e.g. an uncomfortable chair... He unlocked the door.

unabashed [ˌʌnəˈbæʃt] ADJECTIVE

not embarrassed or discouraged by something e.g. Samuel was continuing unabashed.

unabated [ˌʌnəˈbeɪtɪd] ADJECTIVE OR ADVERB

continuing without any reduction in intensity or amount e.g. The noise continued unabated.

unable [ʌnˈeɪbəl] ADJECTIVE

If you are unable to do something, you cannot do it.

unacceptable [ˌʌnəkˈsɛptəbəl] ADJECTIVE

very bad or of a very low standard

unaccompanied [ˌʌnəˈkʌmpənɪd] ADJECTIVE

alone

unaccustomed [ˌʌnəˈkʌstəmd] ADJECTIVE

If you are unaccustomed to something, you are not used to it.

unaffected [ˌʌnəˈfɛktɪd] ADJECTIVE

1 not changed in any way by a particular thing e.g. unaffected by the recession

2 behaving in a natural and genuine way e.g. the most down-to-earth unaffected person I've ever met

unaided [ʌnˈeɪdɪd] ADVERB OR ADJECTIVE

without help e.g. He was incapable of walking unaided.

unambiguous [ˌʌnæmˈbɪɡjʊəs] ADJECTIVE

An unambiguous statement has only one meaning.

unanimous [juːˈnænɪməs] ADJECTIVE

When people are unanimous, they all agree about something.

unanimously ADVERB, **unanimity** NOUN

[WORD HISTORY: from Latin UNANIMUS meaning 'of one mind']

unannounced [ˌʌnəˈnaʊnst] ADJECTIVE

happening unexpectedly and without warning

unarmed [ʌnˈɑːmd] ADJECTIVE

not carrying any weapons

unassuming [ˌʌnəˈsjuːmɪŋ] ADJECTIVE

modest and quiet

unattached [ˌʌnəˈtætʃt] ADJECTIVE

An unattached person is not married and is not having a steady relationship with someone.

unattended [ˌʌnəˈtɛndɪd] ADJECTIVE

not being watched or looked after e.g. an unattended handbag

unauthorized or **unauthorised** [ʌnˈɔːθəˌraɪzd] ADJECTIVE

done without official permission e.g. unauthorized parking

unavoidable [ˌʌnəˈvɔɪdəbəl] ADJECTIVE

unable to be prevented or avoided

unaware [ˌʌnəˈwɛə] ADJECTIVE

If you are unaware of something, you do not know about it.

● THESAURUS

ignorant: They are completely ignorant of the relevant facts.

oblivious: John appeared oblivious to his surroundings.

unconscious: totally unconscious of my presence

unsuspecting: The cars were then sold to unsuspecting buyers.

<<OPPOSITE aware

Unaware is usually followed by of or that. Do not confuse it with the adverb unawares

unawares [ˌʌnəˈwɛəz] ADVERB

If something catches you unawares, it happens when you are not expecting it.

Do not confuse unawares with the adjective unaware

unbalanced [ʌnˈbælənst] ADJECTIVE

1 with more weight or emphasis on one side than the other e.g. an unbalanced load... an unbalanced relationship

2 slightly mad

3 made up of parts that do not work well together e.g. an unbalanced lifestyle

4 An unbalanced account of something is an unfair one because it emphasizes some things and ignores others.

unbearable [ʌnˈbɛərəbəl] ADJECTIVE
Something unbearable is so unpleasant or
upsetting that you feel you cannot stand it. *e.g.*
The pain was unbearable.
unbearably ADVERB

● THESAURUS
intolerable: *The heat and humidity were*
intolerable.
oppressive: *An oppressive sadness weighed upon*
him.
unacceptable: *She left her husband because of his*
unacceptable behaviour.
<<OPPOSITE *tolerable*

unbeatable [ʌnˈbiːtəbəl] ADJECTIVE
Something that is unbeatable is the best thing of
its kind.

unbelievable [ˌʌnbɪˈliːvəbəl] ADJECTIVE
1 extremely great or surprising *e.g. unbelievable*
courage

● THESAURUS
colossal: *There has been a colossal waste of public*
money.
incredible: *You're always an incredible help on these*
occasions.
stupendous: *It cost a stupendous amount of money.*
2 so unlikely that you cannot believe it
unbelievably ADVERB

● THESAURUS
implausible: *a film with an implausible ending*
improbable: *highly improbable claims*
inconceivable: *It was inconceivable that he'd hurt*
anyone.
incredible: *It seems incredible that anyone would*
want to do that.
preposterous: *The whole idea was preposterous.*
unconvincing: *In response he was given the usual*
unconvincing excuses.
<<OPPOSITE *believable*

unborn [ʌnˈbɔːn] ADJECTIVE
not yet born

unbroken [ʌnˈbrəʊkən] ADJECTIVE
continuous or complete *e.g. ten days of almost*
unbroken sunshine

uncanny [ʌnˈkænɪ] ADJECTIVE
strange and difficult to explain *e.g. an uncanny*
resemblance
[WORD HISTORY: from Scottish UNCANNY meaning
'unreliable' or 'not safe to deal with']

uncertain [ʌnˈsɜːtən] ADJECTIVE
1 not knowing what to do *e.g. For a minute he*
looked uncertain.

● THESAURUS
doubtful: *He was a bit doubtful about starting*
without her.
dubious: *We were a bit dubious about it at first.*

unclear: *I'm unclear about where to go.*
undecided: *Even then she was still undecided about*
her future plans.
<<OPPOSITE *certain*

2 doubtful or not known *e.g. The outcome of the*
war was uncertain.
uncertainty NOUN

● THESAURUS
ambiguous: *The wording of the contract was*
ambiguous.
doubtful: *The outcome of the match is still doubtful.*
indefinite: *suspended for an indefinite period*
indeterminate: *a woman of indeterminate age*
<<OPPOSITE *certain*

unchallenged [ʌnˈtʃælɪndʒd] ADJECTIVE
accepted without any questions being asked *e.g.*
We can't let this enormous theft go unchallenged.

uncharacteristic [ˌʌnkærɪktəˈrɪstɪk]
ADJECTIVE
not typical or usual *e.g. My father reacted with*
uncharacteristic speed.

uncivilized or **uncivilised** [ʌnˈsɪvɪˌlaɪzd]
ADJECTIVE
unacceptable, for example by being very cruel or
rude *e.g. the uncivilized behaviour of football*
hooligans

uncle [ˈʌŋkəl] **uncles** NOUN
the brother of your mother or father or the
husband of your aunt

unclean [ʌnˈkliːn] ADJECTIVE
dirty *e.g. unclean water*

unclear [ʌnˈklɪə] ADJECTIVE
confusing and not obvious

● THESAURUS
ambiguous: *in order to clarify the earlier ambiguous*
statement
confused: *The situation remains confused, as no*
clear victor has emerged.
vague: *The description was pretty vague.*
<<OPPOSITE *clear*

uncomfortable [ʌnˈkʌmftəbəl] ADJECTIVE
1 If you are uncomfortable, you are not physically
relaxed and feel slight pain or discomfort.

● THESAURUS
awkward: *Its shape made it awkward to carry.*
cramped: *living in very cramped conditions*
disagreeable: *designed to make flying a less*
disagreeable experience
ill-fitting: *Walking was difficult because of her ill-*
fitting shoes.
painful: *a painful back injury*
<<OPPOSITE *comfortable*

2 Uncomfortable also means slightly worried or
embarrassed.

uncomfortably ADVERB

⬤ **THESAURUS**

awkward: *Offstage, he is bashful and awkward.*
embarrassed: *an embarrassed silence*
ill at ease: *I always feel ill at ease in their company.*
self-conscious: *She was always self-conscious about her height.*
uneasy: *He looked uneasy and refused to answer any more questions.*
<<OPPOSITE *comfortable*

uncommon [ʌnˈkɒmən] ADJECTIVE

1 not happening often or not seen often

⬤ **THESAURUS**

exceptional: *These are exceptional circumstances.*
extraordinary: *an act of extraordinary generosity*
few: *Genuine friends are few.*
infrequent: *one of the infrequent visitors to the island*
out of the ordinary: *My story is nothing out of the ordinary.*
scarce: *places where jobs are scarce*
sparse: *Traffic is sparse on this stretch of road.*
rare: *a rare occurrence*
unusual: *an unusual sight these days*
<<OPPOSITE *common*

2 unusually great *e.g. She had read Cecilia's last letter with uncommon interest.*
uncommonly ADVERB

⬤ **THESAURUS**

acute: *He has an acute dislike of children.*
exceptional: *a woman of exceptional beauty*
extraordinary: *a young player of extraordinary energy*
extreme: *regions suffering from extreme poverty*
great: *They share a great love of Bach's music.*
intense: *intense heat*
remarkable: *a musician of remarkable talent*

uncompromising [ʌnˈkɒmprəˌmaɪzɪŋ] ADJECTIVE

determined not to change an opinion or aim in any way *e.g. an uncompromising approach to life*
uncompromisingly ADVERB

unconcerned [ˌʌnkənˈsɜːnd] ADJECTIVE

not interested in something or not worried about it

unconditional [ˌʌnkənˈdɪʃənˀl] ADJECTIVE

with no conditions or limitations *e.g. a full three-year unconditional guarantee*
unconditionally ADVERB

unconscious [ʌnˈkɒnʃəs] ADJECTIVE

1 Someone who is unconscious is asleep or in a state similar to sleep as a result of a shock, accident, or injury.

⬤ **THESAURUS**

asleep: *They were fast asleep in their beds.*

senseless: *He was beaten senseless and robbed of all his money.*
stunned: *stunned by a blow to the head*
<<OPPOSITE *conscious*

2 If you are unconscious of something, you are not aware of it.
unconsciously ADVERB

⬤ **THESAURUS**

oblivious: *He seemed oblivious of his surroundings.*
unaware: *He was unaware of the chaos he was causing.*
unknowing: *unknowing accomplices in his crimes*
unsuspecting: *She was an unsuspecting victim of his deceit.*
<<OPPOSITE *aware*

uncontrollable [ˌʌnkənˈtrəʊləbˀl] ADJECTIVE

If someone or something is uncontrollable, they or it cannot be controlled or stopped. *e.g. uncontrollable anger*
uncontrollably ADVERB

unconventional [ˌʌnkənˈvɛnʃənˀl] ADJECTIVE

not behaving in the same way as most other people

unconvinced [ˌʌnkənˈvɪnst] ADJECTIVE

not at all certain that something is true or right *e.g. Some critics remain unconvinced by the plan.*

uncouth [ʌnˈkuːθ] ADJECTIVE

bad-mannered and unpleasant

uncover [ʌnˈkʌvə] **uncovers, uncovering, uncovered** VERB

1 If you uncover a secret, you find it out.

⬤ **THESAURUS**

bring to light: *The truth is unlikely to be brought to light.*
expose: *His lies were exposed in court.*
reveal: *He will reveal the truth behind the scandal.*
show up: *His true character has been shown up for what it is.*
unearth: *a campaign to unearth supposed conspiracies*

2 To uncover something is to remove the cover or lid from it.

⬤ **THESAURUS**

expose: *The wreck was exposed by the action of the tide.*
lay bare: *Layers of paint and flaking plaster were laid bare.*
open: *I opened a new jar of coffee.*
reveal: *His shirt was open, revealing a tattooed chest.*
unearth: *Quarry workers have unearthed the skeleton of a mammoth.*
unveil: *The statue will be unveiled next week.*
unwrap: *unwrapping Christmas presents*

undaunted [ʌn'dɔːntɪd] ADJECTIVE
If you are undaunted by something disappointing, you are not discouraged by it.

undecided [ˌʌndɪ'saɪdɪd] ADJECTIVE
If you are undecided, you have not yet made a decision about something.

undemanding [ˌʌndɪ'mɑːndɪŋ] ADJECTIVE
not difficult to do or deal with *e.g. undemanding work*

undeniable [ˌʌndɪ'naɪəbəl] ADJECTIVE
certainly true *e.g. undeniable evidence*
undeniably ADVERB

under ['ʌndə] PREPOSITION
1 below or beneath

● **THESAURUS**
below: *The sun had already sunk below the horizon.*
beneath: *the frozen grass crunching beneath his feet*
underneath: *people trapped underneath the wreckage*
<<OPPOSITE *above*

2 You can use 'under' to say that a person or thing is affected by a particular situation or condition. *e.g. The country was under threat... Animals are kept under unnatural conditions.*

3 If someone studies or works under a particular person, that person is their teacher or their boss.

4 less than *e.g. under five kilometres... children under the age of 14*
> PHRASE
5 Under way means already started *e.g. A murder investigation is already under way.*

under- PREFIX
'Under-' is used in words that describe something as not being provided to a sufficient extent or not having happened to a sufficient extent

underarm ['ʌndərˌɑːm] ADJECTIVE
1 under your arm *e.g. underarm hair*
> ADVERB
2 If you throw a ball underarm, you throw it without raising your arm over your shoulder.

undercarriage ['ʌndəˌkærɪdʒ]
undercarriages NOUN
the part of an aircraft, including the wheels, that supports the aircraft when it is on the ground

underclass ['ʌndəˌklɑːs] NOUN
The underclass is the people in society who are the most poor and whose situation is unlikely to improve.

underclothes ['ʌndəˌkləʊðz] PLURAL NOUN
Your underclothes are the clothes that you wear under your other clothes and next to your skin.

undercover [ˌʌndə'kʌvə] ADJECTIVE
involving secret work to obtain information *e.g. a police undercover operation*

undercurrent ['ʌndəˌkʌrənt]
undercurrents NOUN
a weak, partly hidden feeling that may become stronger later

undercut [ˌʌndə'kʌt] **undercuts, undercutting, undercut** VERB
1 To undercut someone's prices is to sell a product more cheaply than they do.

2 If something undercuts your attempts to achieve something, it prevents them from being effective.

underdeveloped [ˌʌndədɪ'vɛləpt] ADJECTIVE
An underdeveloped country does not have modern industries, and usually has a low standard of living.

underdog ['ʌndəˌdɒg] **underdogs** NOUN
The underdog in a competition is the person who seems likely to lose.

underestimate [ˌʌndər'ɛstɪˌmeɪt]
underestimates, underestimating, underestimated VERB
If you underestimate something or someone, you do not realize how large, great, or capable they are.

underfoot [ˌʌndə'fʊt] ADJECTIVE OR ADVERB
under your feet *e.g. the icy ground underfoot*

undergo [ˌʌndə'gəʊ] **undergoes, undergoing, underwent, undergone** VERB
If you undergo something unpleasant, it happens to you.

● **THESAURUS**
be subjected to: *She was subjected to constant interruptions.*
endure: *The company endured heavy losses.*
experience: *They seem to experience more distress than the others.*
go through: *I wouldn't like to go through that again.*
suffer: *The peace process had suffered a serious setback.*

underground ['ʌndəˌgraʊnd] ADJECTIVE
1 below the surface of the ground
2 secret, unofficial, and usually illegal
> NOUN
3 The underground is a railway system in which trains travel in tunnels below ground.

undergrowth ['ʌndəˌgrəʊθ] NOUN
Small bushes and plants growing under trees are called the undergrowth.

underhand ['ʌndəˌhænd] ADJECTIVE
secret and dishonest *e.g. underhand behaviour*

u

underlie [ˌʌndəˈlaɪ] **underlies, underlying, underlay, underlain** VERB
The thing that underlies a situation is the cause or basis of it.
underlying ADJECTIVE

underline [ˌʌndəˈlaɪn] **underlines, underlining, underlined** VERB
1 If something underlines a feeling or a problem, it emphasizes it.
2 If you underline a word or sentence, you draw a line under it.

underling [ˈʌndəlɪŋ] **underlings** NOUN
someone who is less important than someone else in rank or status

undermine [ˌʌndəˈmaɪn] **undermines, undermining, undermined** VERB
To undermine an idea, feeling, or system is to make it less strong or secure. *e.g. You're trying to undermine my confidence again.*
[WORD HISTORY: from the practice in warfare of digging tunnels under enemy fortifications in order to make them collapse]

● THESAURUS
impair: *Their actions will impair France's national interests.*
sap: *I was afraid the illness had sapped my strength.*
subvert: *an attempt to subvert their culture from within*
weaken: *Her authority had been fatally weakened.*
<<OPPOSITE *strengthen*

underneath [ˌʌndəˈniːθ] PREPOSITION
1 below or beneath

> ADVERB OR PREPOSITION
2 Underneath describes feelings and qualities that do not show in your behaviour. *e.g. Alex knew that underneath she was shattered.*

> ADJECTIVE
3 The underneath part of something is the part that touches or faces the ground.

underpants [ˈʌndəˌpænts] PLURAL NOUN
Underpants are a piece of clothing worn by men and boys under their trousers.

underpass [ˈʌndəˌpɑːs] **underpasses** NOUN
a road or footpath that goes under a road or railway

underpin [ˌʌndəˈpɪn] **underpins, underpinning, underpinned** VERB
If something underpins something else, it helps it to continue by supporting and strengthening it. *e.g. Australian skill is usually underpinned by an immense team spirit.*

underprivileged [ˌʌndəˈprɪvɪlɪdʒd] ADJECTIVE
Underprivileged people have less money and fewer opportunities than other people.

underrate [ˌʌndəˈreɪt] **underrates, underrating, underrated** VERB
If you underrate someone, you do not realize how clever or valuable they are.

understand [ˌʌndəˈstænd] **understands, understanding, understood** VERB
1 If you understand what someone says, you know what they mean.

● THESAURUS
catch on: informal *I didn't catch on immediately to what he meant.*
comprehend: *Whenever she failed to comprehend, she just laughed.*
follow: *I don't follow you at all.*
get: *Did you get that joke?*
grasp: *He instantly grasped that they were talking about him.*
see: *"I see," she said at last.*
take in: *too much to take in at once*

2 If you understand a situation, you know what is happening and why.

● THESAURUS
appreciate: *You must appreciate how important this is.*
comprehend: *I just cannot comprehend your viewpoint.*
fathom: *His attitude was hard to fathom.*
grasp: *We immediately grasped the seriousness of the crisis.*
realize: *People just don't realize how serious it could be.*

3 If you say that you understand that something is the case, you mean that you have heard that it is the case. *e.g. I understand that she's a lot better now.*

● THESAURUS
believe: *She's coming back tomorrow, I believe.*
gather: *We gather the report is critical of the judge.*
hear: *I hear you've been having some problems.*
learn: *On learning who he was, I wanted to meet him.*

understandable [ˌʌndəˈstændəbəl] ADJECTIVE
If something is understandable, people can easily understand it.
understandably ADVERB

understanding [ˌʌndəˈstændɪŋ] **understandings** NOUN
1 If you have an understanding of something, you have some knowledge about it.

● THESAURUS
appreciation: *some appreciation of the problems of consumers*
comprehension: *completely beyond our comprehension*

grasp: *a good grasp of foreign languages*
knowledge: *I have no knowledge of his business affairs.*
perception: *Her questions showed a shrewd perception.*

2 an informal agreement between people

● **THESAURUS**

accord: *trying to reach an accord*
agreement: *A new defence agreement was signed last month.*
pact: *an electoral pact between the parties*
> **ADJECTIVE**
3 kind and sympathetic

● **THESAURUS**

compassionate: *a deeply compassionate man*
considerate: *They should be more considerate towards the prisoners.*
sensitive: *He was always sensitive and caring.*
sympathetic: *a sympathetic listener*

understatement [ˌʌndəˈsteɪtmənt] **understatements** NOUN
a statement that does not say fully how true something is *e.g. To say I was pleased was an understatement.*

understudy [ˈʌndəˌstʌdɪ] **understudies** NOUN
someone who has learnt a part in a play so that they can act it if the main actor or actress is ill

undertake [ˌʌndəˈteɪk] **undertakes, undertaking, undertook, undertaken** VERB
When you undertake a task or job, you agree to do it.

undertaker [ˈʌndəˌteɪkə] **undertakers** NOUN
someone whose job is to prepare bodies for burial and arrange funerals

undertaking [ˈʌndəˌteɪkɪŋ] **undertakings** NOUN
a task which you have agreed to do

● **THESAURUS**

affair: *It's going to be a tricky affair to arrange.*
business: *Livestock farming is an arduous and difficult business.*
endeavour: *an endeavour that was bound to end in failure*
enterprise: *a risky enterprise such as horse breeding*
job: *What made you decide to take this job on?*
operation: *the man in charge of the entire operation*
project: *I can't take responsibility for such a huge project.*
task: *a task I do not feel equipped to take on*
venture: *a venture that few were willing to invest in*

undertone [ˈʌndəˌtəʊn] **undertones** NOUN
1 If you say something in an undertone, you say it very quietly.

2 If something has undertones of a particular kind, it indirectly suggests ideas of this kind. *e.g. unsettling undertones of violence*

undervalue [ˌʌndəˈvæljuː] **undervalues, undervaluing, undervalued** VERB
If you undervalue something, you think it is less important than it really is.

underwater [ˈʌndəˈwɔːtə] ADVERB OR ADJECTIVE
1 beneath the surface of the sea, a river, or a lake
> **ADJECTIVE**
2 designed to work in water *e.g. an underwater camera*

underwear [ˈʌndəˌwɛə] NOUN
Your underwear is the clothing that you wear under your other clothes, next to your skin.

underwent [ˌʌndəˈwɛnt] the past tense of **undergo**

undesirable [ˌʌndɪˈzaɪərəbəl] ADJECTIVE
unwelcome and likely to cause harm *e.g. undesirable behaviour*

undid [ʌnˈdɪd] the past tense of **undo**

undisputed [ˌʌndɪˈspjuːtɪd] ADJECTIVE
definite and without any doubt *e.g. the undisputed champion*

undivided [ˌʌndɪˈvaɪdɪd] ADJECTIVE
If you give something your undivided attention, you concentrate on it totally.

undo [ʌnˈduː] **undoes, undoing, undid, undone** VERB
1 If you undo something that is tied up, you untie it.

2 If you undo something that has been done, you reverse the effect of it.

undoing [ʌnˈduːɪŋ] NOUN
If something is someone's undoing, it is the cause of their failure.

undoubted [ʌnˈdaʊtɪd] ADJECTIVE
You use 'undoubted' to emphasize something. *e.g. The event was an undoubted success.*
undoubtedly ADVERB

undress [ʌnˈdrɛs] **undresses, undressing, undressed** VERB
When you undress, you take off your clothes.

undue [ʌnˈdjuː] ADJECTIVE
greater than is reasonable *e.g. undue violence*
unduly ADVERB

undulating [ˈʌndjʊˌleɪtɪŋ] ADJECTIVE; FORMAL
moving gently up and down *e.g. undulating hills*

undying [ʌnˈdaɪɪŋ] ADJECTIVE
lasting forever *e.g. his undying love for his wife*

unearth [ʌnˈɜːθ] **unearths, unearthing, unearthed** VERB

u

If you unearth something that is hidden, you discover it.

unearthly [ʌnˈɜːθlɪ] ADJECTIVE
strange and unnatural

uneasy [ʌnˈiːzɪ] ADJECTIVE
If you are uneasy, you feel worried that something may be wrong.
unease NOUN, **uneasily** ADVERB, **uneasiness** NOUN

● THESAURUS
agitated: *She seemed agitated about something.*
anxious: *He admitted he was still anxious about the situation.*
nervous: *Consumers say they are nervous about their jobs.*
perturbed: *I am not too perturbed at this setback.*
worried: *If you're worried about it, just ask for more details.*
<<OPPOSITE *comfortable*

unemployed [ˌʌnɪmˈplɔɪd] ADJECTIVE
1 without a job *e.g. an unemployed mechanic*

● THESAURUS
idle: *He has been idle for almost a month.*
jobless: *One in four people are now jobless.*
redundant: *aid for the 30,000 redundant miners*
<<OPPOSITE *employed*

> NOUN
2 The unemployed are all the people who are without a job.

unemployment [ˌʌnɪmˈplɔɪmənt] NOUN
Unemployment is the state of being without a job.

unending [ʌnˈɛndɪŋ] ADJECTIVE
Something unending has continued for a long time and seems as if it will never stop. *e.g. unending joy*

unenviable [ʌnˈɛnvɪəbᵊl] ADJECTIVE
An unenviable situation is one that you would not like to be in.

unequal [ʌnˈiːkwəl] ADJECTIVE
1 An unequal society does not offer the same opportunities and privileges to all people.
2 Unequal things are different in size, strength, or ability.

uneven [ʌnˈiːvən] ADJECTIVE
1 An uneven surface is not level or smooth.

● THESAURUS
bumpy: *bumpy cobbled streets*
not level: *It was hard to walk because the road was not level.*
not smooth: *The icing isn't smooth enough.*
rough: *She picked her way across the rough ground.*
<<OPPOSITE *level*

2 not the same or consistent *e.g. six lines of uneven length*

unevenly ADVERB

● THESAURUS
fluctuating: *a fluctuating temperature*
inconsistent: *Their performance was inconsistent over the whole season.*
irregular: *at irregular intervals*
patchy: *Her career has been patchy.*
variable: *The potassium content of food is very variable.*
<<OPPOSITE *even*

uneventful [ˌʌnɪˈvɛntfʊl] ADJECTIVE
An uneventful period of time is one when nothing interesting happens.

unexpected [ˌʌnɪkˈspɛktɪd] ADJECTIVE
Something unexpected is surprising because it was not thought likely to happen.
unexpectedly ADVERB

● THESAURUS
astonishing: *What an astonishing piece of good luck!*
chance: *a chance meeting*
surprising: *a most surprising turn of events*
unforeseen: *The show was cancelled due to unforeseen circumstances.*

unfailing [ʌnˈfeɪlɪŋ] ADJECTIVE
continuous and not weakening as time passes *e.g. his unfailing cheerfulness*

unfair [ʌnˈfɛə] ADJECTIVE
not right or just
unfairly ADVERB

● THESAURUS
unjust: *an unjust decision*
wrong: *It would be wrong to allow the case to go any further.*
wrongful: *his claim for wrongful dismissal*
<<OPPOSITE *fair*

unfaithful [ʌnˈfeɪθfʊl] ADJECTIVE
If someone is unfaithful to their lover or the person they are married to, they have a sexual relationship with someone else.

● THESAURUS
adulterous: *an adulterous relationship*
two-timing: informal *She called him a two-timing rat.*
<<OPPOSITE *faithful*

unfamiliar [ˌʌnfəˈmɪljə] ADJECTIVE
If something is unfamiliar to you, or if you are unfamiliar with it, you have not seen or heard it before.

● THESAURUS
alien: *transplanted into an alien culture*
exotic: *filmed in an exotic location*
foreign: *This was a foreign country, so unlike his own.*
new: *This was a new experience for me.*

novel: *having to cope with many novel situations*
strange: *All these faces were strange to me.*
unknown: *I'd discovered a writer quite unknown to me.*

unfashionable [ʌn'fæʃənəbʰl] ADJECTIVE
Something that is unfashionable is not popular or is no longer used by many people.

unfavourable [ʌn'feɪvərəbʰl] ADJECTIVE
not encouraging or promising, or not providing any advantage

unfit [ʌn'fɪt] ADJECTIVE
1 If you are unfit, your body is not in good condition because you have not been taking enough exercise.

2 Something that is unfit for a particular purpose is not suitable for that purpose.

unfold [ʌn'fəʊld] **unfolds, unfolding, unfolded** VERB
1 When a situation unfolds, it develops and becomes known.

2 If you unfold something that has been folded, you open it out so that it is flat.

unforeseen [ˌʌnfɔː'siːn] ADJECTIVE
happening unexpectedly

unforgettable [ˌʌnfə'gɛtəbʰl] ADJECTIVE
Something unforgettable is so good or so bad that you are unlikely to forget it.
unforgettably ADVERB

unforgivable [ˌʌnfə'gɪvəbʰl] ADJECTIVE
Something unforgivable is so bad or cruel that it can never be forgiven or justified.
unforgivably ADVERB

unfortunate [ʌn'fɔːtʃɪnɪt] ADJECTIVE
1 Someone who is unfortunate is unlucky.

2 If you describe an event as unfortunate, you mean that it is a pity that it happened. *e.g. an unfortunate accident*
unfortunately ADVERB

unfounded [ʌn'faʊndɪd] ADJECTIVE
Something that is unfounded has no evidence to support it. *e.g. unfounded allegations*

unfriendly [ʌn'frɛndlɪ] ADJECTIVE
1 A person who is unfriendly is not pleasant to you.

THESAURUS
aloof: *His manner was aloof.*
antagonistic: *They were always antagonistic to newcomers.*
cold: *She was a cold, unfeeling woman.*
disagreeable: *He may be clever but he's most disagreeable.*
hostile: *The prisoner eyed him in hostile silence.*
unkind: *They're always unkind to newcomers.*

<<OPPOSITE friendly

2 A place that is unfriendly makes you feel uncomfortable or is not welcoming.

ungainly [ʌn'geɪnlɪ] ADJECTIVE
moving in an awkward or clumsy way
[WORD HISTORY: from Old Norse UNGEGN meaning 'not straight']

ungrateful [ʌn'greɪtfʊl] ADJECTIVE
not appreciating the things you have

THESAURUS
unappreciative: *He was unappreciative of our efforts.*
unthankful: *mercenary players and unthankful supporters*
<<OPPOSITE grateful

unhappy [ʌn'hæpɪ] **unhappier, unhappiest** ADJECTIVE
1 sad and depressed

THESAURUS
depressed: *She's depressed about this whole situation.*
despondent: *After the interview John was despondent.*
down: *They felt really down after they spoke to him.*
miserable: *My job made me really miserable sometimes.*
sad: *I felt sad to leave our little house.*
<<OPPOSITE happy

2 not pleased or satisfied *e.g. I am unhappy at being left out.*

3 If you describe a situation as an unhappy one, you are sorry that it exists. *e.g. an unhappy state of affairs*
unhappily ADVERB, **unhappiness** NOUN

unhealthy [ʌn'hɛlθɪ] ADJECTIVE
1 likely to cause illness *e.g. an unhealthy lifestyle*

THESAURUS
bad for you: *the argument that eating meat is bad for you*
harmful: *Try to avoid harmful habits like smoking.*
insanitary: *the insanitary conditions of slums*
noxious: *factories belching out noxious fumes*
unwholesome: *an epidemic originating from the unwholesome food they ate*
<<OPPOSITE healthy

2 An unhealthy person is often ill.

THESAURUS
ailing: *The President is said to be ailing.*
crook: Australian and New Zealand; informal *I'm sorry to hear you've been crook, mate.*
ill: *He didn't look at all ill when I last saw him.*
not well: *When I'm not well, she looks after me.*
poorly: British; informal *She's still poorly after that bout of pneumonia.*
sick: *He's very sick and he needs treatment.*

unwell: *an infection which could make you very unwell*
<<OPPOSITE *healthy*

unheard-of [ʌnˈhɜːdɒv] ADJECTIVE
never having happened before and therefore surprising or shocking

unhinged [ʌnˈhɪndʒd] ADJECTIVE
Someone who is unhinged is mentally ill.

unhurried [ʌnˈhʌrɪd] ADJECTIVE
Unhurried is used to describe actions or movements that are slow and relaxed.

unicorn [ˈjuːnɪˌkɔːn] **unicorns** NOUN
an imaginary animal that looks like a white horse with a straight horn growing from its forehead
[WORD HISTORY: from Latin UNICORNIS meaning 'having one horn']

unidentified [ˌʌnaɪˈdɛntɪˌfaɪd] ADJECTIVE
You say that someone or something is unidentified when nobody knows who or what they are.

uniform [ˈjuːnɪˌfɔːm] **uniforms** NOUN
1 a special set of clothes worn by people at work or school
> ADJECTIVE
2 Something that is uniform does not vary but is even and regular throughout.
uniformity NOUN

unify [ˈjuːnɪˌfaɪ] **unifies, unifying, unified** VERB
If you unify a number of things, you bring them together.
unification NOUN

unilateral [ˌjuːnɪˈlætərəl] ADJECTIVE
A unilateral decision or action is one taken by only one of several groups involved in a particular situation.
unilaterally ADVERB

unimaginable [ˌʌnɪˈmædʒɪnəbəl] ADJECTIVE
impossible to imagine or understand properly
e.g. a fairyland of unimaginable beauty

unimportant [ˌʌnɪmˈpɔːtənt] ADJECTIVE
having very little significance or importance

● THESAURUS
insignificant: *In 1949, Bonn was a small, insignificant city.*
minor: *a minor inconvenience*
paltry: *They had little interest in paltry domestic concerns.*
slight: *We have a slight problem.*
trivial: *She waved aside the trivial details.*
<<OPPOSITE *important*

uninhabited [ˌʌnɪnˈhæbɪtɪd] ADJECTIVE
An uninhabited place is a place where nobody lives.

uninhibited [ˌʌnɪnˈhɪbɪtɪd] ADJECTIVE
If you are uninhibited, you behave freely and naturally and show your true feelings.

unintelligible [ˌʌnɪnˈtɛlɪdʒɪbəl] ADJECTIVE; FORMAL
impossible to understand

uninterested [ʌnˈɪntrɪstɪd] ADJECTIVE
If you are uninterested in something, you are not interested in it.

● THESAURUS
apathetic: *apathetic about politics*
bored: *She looked bored with the whole performance.*
impassive: *He remained impassive while she ranted on.*
indifferent: *He is totally indifferent to our problems.*
nonchalant: *"Suit yourself," I said, trying to sound nonchalant.*
passive: *That passive attitude of his drives me mad.*
unconcerned: *She is unconcerned about anything except herself.*
<<OPPOSITE *interested*

uninterrupted [ˌʌnɪntəˈrʌptɪd] ADJECTIVE
continuing without breaks or interruptions *e.g. uninterrupted views*

union [ˈjuːnjən] **unions** NOUN
1 an organization of people or groups with mutual interests, especially workers aiming to improve their pay and conditions

● THESAURUS
association: *a member of several different associations*
coalition: *governed by a coalition of three parties*
confederation: *a confederation of mini-states*
federation: *a federation of six separate agencies*
league: *the League of Nations*

2 When the union of two things takes place, they are joined together to become one thing.

● THESAURUS
amalgamation: *an amalgamation of two organizations*
blend: *a blend of traditional charm and modern amenities*
combination: *the combination of science and art*
fusion: *fusions of jazz and pop*
mixture: *a mixture of nuts, raisins, and capers*

unique [juːˈniːk] ADJECTIVE
1 being the only one of its kind
2 If something is unique to one person or thing, it concerns or belongs to that person or thing only.
e.g. trees and vegetation unique to the Canary islands
uniquely ADVERB, **uniqueness** NOUN

Something is either *unique* or *not unique*, so you should avoid saying things like *rather unique* or *very unique*

unisex ['juːnɪ,sɛks] ADJECTIVE
designed to be used by both men and women
e.g. unisex clothing

unison ['juːnɪsᵊn] NOUN
If a group of people do something in unison, they
all do it together at the same time.
[WORD HISTORY: from Latin UNISONUS meaning
'making the same musical sound']

unit ['juːnɪt] **units** NOUN
1 If you consider something as a unit, you
consider it as a single complete thing.

2 a group of people who work together at a
particular job *e.g. the Police Support Unit*

3 a machine or piece of equipment which has a
particular function *e.g. a remote control unit*

4 A unit of measurement is a fixed standard that
is used for measuring things.

unite [juːˈnaɪt] **unites, uniting, united**
VERB
If a number of people unite, they join together
and act as a group.

⬤THESAURUS
collaborate: *They all collaborated on the project.*
combine: *The companies have combined to form a
multinational.*
join: *People of all kinds joined to make a dignified
protest.*
join forces: *The two parties are joining forces.*
link up: *the first time the two armies have linked up*
merge: *The media group hopes to merge with its
rival company.*
pull together: *The staff and management are
pulling together to save the company.*
work together: *industry and government working
together*
<<OPPOSITE *divide*

United Kingdom [juːˈnaɪtɪd] NOUN
The United Kingdom consists of Great Britain
and Northern Ireland.

United Nations [juːˈnaɪtɪd ˈneɪʃənz] NOUN
The United Nations is an international
organization which tries to encourage peace,
cooperation, and friendship between countries.

unity ['juːnɪtɪ] NOUN
Where there is unity, people are in agreement
and act together for a particular purpose.

universal [,juːnɪˈvɜːsᵊl] ADJECTIVE
concerning or relating to everyone in the world or
every part of the universe *e.g. Music and sports
programmes have a universal appeal... universal
destruction*
universally ADVERB

⬤THESAURUS
common: *The common view is that it is a good
thing.*

general: *This project should raise general awareness
about the problem.*
unlimited: *destruction on an unlimited scale*
widespread: *Food shortages are widespread.*
worldwide: *the fear of a worldwide epidemic*

universe ['juːnɪ,vɜːs] **universes** NOUN
The universe is the whole of space, including all
the stars and planets.

university [,juːnɪˈvɜːsɪtɪ] **universities** NOUN
a place where students study for degrees
[WORD HISTORY: from Latin UNIVERSITAS meaning
'group of scholars']

unjust [ʌnˈdʒʌst] ADJECTIVE
not fair or reasonable
unjustly ADVERB

unjustified [ʌnˈdʒʌstɪ,faɪd] ADJECTIVE
If a belief or action is unjustified, there is no good
reason for it.

unkempt [ʌnˈkɛmpt] ADJECTIVE
untidy and not looked after properly *e.g. unkempt
hair*

unkind [ʌnˈkaɪnd] ADJECTIVE
unpleasant and rather cruel
unkindly ADVERB, **unkindness** NOUN

⬤THESAURUS
cruel: *Children can be so cruel.*
malicious: *spreading malicious gossip*
mean: *I'd feel mean saying no.*
nasty: *What nasty little snobs you are!*
spiteful: *How can you say such spiteful things
about us?*
thoughtless: *a small minority of thoughtless and
inconsiderate people*
<<OPPOSITE *kind*

unknown [ʌnˈnəʊn] ADJECTIVE
1 If someone or something is unknown, people
do not know about them or have not heard of
them.

⬤THESAURUS
humble: *He started out as a humble fisherman.*
obscure: *an obscure Greek composer*
unfamiliar: *There were several unfamiliar names on
the list.*
unsung: *among the unsung heroes of our time*
<<OPPOSITE *famous*

> NOUN
2 You can refer to the things that people in
general do not know about as the unknown.

unlawful [ʌnˈlɔːfʊl] ADJECTIVE
not legal *e.g. the unlawful use of drugs*

unleaded [ʌnˈlɛdɪd] ADJECTIVE
Unleaded petrol has a reduced amount of lead in
it in order to reduce the pollution from cars.

unleash [ʌnˈliːʃ] **unleashes, unleashing,
unleashed** VERB

u

When a powerful or violent force is unleashed, it is released.

unless [ʌnˈlɛs] CONJUNCTION
You use 'unless' to introduce the only circumstances in which something will not take place or is not true. *e.g. Unless it was raining, they played in the little garden.*

unlike [ʌnˈlaɪk] PREPOSITION
If one thing is unlike another, the two things are different.

● THESAURUS
different from: *I've always felt different from most people.*
dissimilar to: *a cultural background not dissimilar to our own*
distinct from: *Their cuisines are quite distinct from each other.*
divergent from: formal *That viewpoint is not much divergent from that of his predecessor.*
far from: *His politics are not all that far from mine.*
<<OPPOSITE *like*

unlikely [ʌnˈlaɪklɪ] ADJECTIVE
1 If something is unlikely, it is probably not true or probably will not happen.

● THESAURUS
implausible: *a film with an implausible ending*
incredible: *an incredible pack of lies*
unbelievable: *I know it sounds unbelievable, but I wasn't there that day.*
unconvincing: *He came up with a very unconvincing excuse.*
<<OPPOSITE *likely*

2 strange and unexpected *e.g. There are riches in unlikely places.*

unlimited [ʌnˈlɪmɪtɪd] ADJECTIVE
If a supply of something is unlimited, you can have as much as you want or need.

unload [ʌnˈləʊd] **unloads, unloading, unloaded** VERB
If you unload things from a container or vehicle, you remove them.

unlock [ʌnˈlɒk] **unlocks, unlocking, unlocked** VERB
If you unlock a door or container, you open it by turning a key in the lock.

unlucky [ʌnˈlʌkɪ] ADJECTIVE
Someone who is unlucky has bad luck.
unluckily ADVERB

● THESAURUS
cursed: *the most cursed family in history*
hapless: *a hapless victim of chance*
luckless: *the luckless parents of a difficult child*
unfortunate: *Some unfortunate person nearby could be injured.*
wretched: *wretched people who had to sell or starve*

<<OPPOSITE *lucky*

unmarked [ʌnˈmɑːkt] ADJECTIVE
1 with no marks of damage or injury

2 with no signs or marks of identification *e.g. unmarked police cars*

unmistakable or **unmistakeable** [ˌʌnmɪsˈteɪkəbᵊl] ADJECTIVE
Something unmistakable is so obvious that it cannot be mistaken for something else.
unmistakably ADVERB

unmitigated [ʌnˈmɪtɪˌɡeɪtɪd] ADJECTIVE; FORMAL
You use 'unmitigated' to describe a situation or quality that is completely bad. *e.g. an unmitigated disaster*

unmoved [ʌnˈmuːvd] ADJECTIVE
not emotionally affected *e.g. He is unmoved by criticism.*

unnatural [ʌnˈnætʃərəl] ADJECTIVE
1 strange and rather frightening because it is not usual *e.g. There was an unnatural stillness.*

2 artificial and not typical *e.g. My voice sounded high-pitched and unnatural.*
unnaturally ADVERB

unnecessary [ʌnˈnɛsɪsərɪ] ADJECTIVE
If something is unnecessary, there is no need for it to happen or be done.
unnecessarily ADVERB

● THESAURUS
needless: *causing needless panic*
pointless: *pointless meetings*
uncalled-for: *uncalled-for rudeness*
<<OPPOSITE *necessary*

unnerve [ʌnˈnɜːv] **unnerves, unnerving, unnerved** VERB
If something unnerves you, it frightens or startles you.
unnerving ADJECTIVE

unobtrusive [ˌʌnəbˈtruːsɪv] ADJECTIVE
Something that is unobtrusive does not draw attention to itself.

unoccupied [ʌnˈɒkjʊˌpaɪd] ADJECTIVE
If a house is unoccupied, there is nobody living in it.

unofficial [ˌʌnəˈfɪʃəl] ADJECTIVE
without the approval or permission of a person in authority *e.g. unofficial strikes*
unofficially ADVERB

unorthodox [ʌnˈɔːθəˌdɒks] ADJECTIVE
unusual and not generally accepted *e.g. an unorthodox theory*

unpack [ʌnˈpæk] **unpacks, unpacking, unpacked** VERB

When you unpack, you take everything out of a suitcase or bag.

unpaid [ʌnˈpeɪd] ADJECTIVE

1 If you do unpaid work, you do not receive any money for doing it.

2 An unpaid bill has not yet been paid.

unpalatable [ʌnˈpælətəbᵊl] ADJECTIVE

1 Unpalatable food is so unpleasant that you can hardly eat it.

2 An unpalatable idea is so unpleasant that it is difficult to accept.

unparalleled [ʌnˈpærəˌlɛld] ADJECTIVE

greater than anything else of its kind *e.g. an unparalleled success*

unpleasant [ʌnˈplɛzᵊnt] ADJECTIVE

1 Something unpleasant causes you to have bad feelings, for example by making you uncomfortable or upset.

● THESAURUS

bad: *I have some bad news.*

disagreeable: *a disagreeable experience*

distasteful: *I find her gossip distasteful.*

nasty: *This divorce could turn nasty.*

repulsive: *repulsive fat white slugs*

unpalatable: *Only then did I learn the unpalatable truth.*

<<OPPOSITE *pleasant*

2 An unpleasant person is unfriendly or rude.

unpleasantly ADVERB, **unpleasantness** NOUN

● THESAURUS

disagreeable: *He may be clever, but he's a very disagreeable man.*

horrid: *I must have been a horrid little girl.*

objectionable: *His tone was highly objectionable.*

obnoxious: *Clarissa's obnoxious brother James.*

rude: *He was frequently rude to waiters and servants.*

unfriendly: *spoken in a rather unfriendly voice*

<<OPPOSITE *pleasant*

unpopular [ʌnˈpɒpjʊlə] ADJECTIVE

disliked by most people *e.g. an unpopular idea*

● THESAURUS

detested: *The rebels toppled the detested dictator.*

disliked: *one of the most disliked choices on offer*

shunned: *the shunned former minister*

undesirable: *all sorts of undesirable effects on health*

<<OPPOSITE *popular*

unprecedented [ʌnˈprɛsɪˌdɛntɪd] ADJECTIVE; FORMAL

Something that is unprecedented has never happened before or is the best of its kind so far.

unpredictable [ʌnprɪˈdɪktəbᵊl] ADJECTIVE

If someone or something is unpredictable, you

never know how they will behave or react.

● THESAURUS

chance: *A chance meeting can change your life.*

doubtful: *The outcome remains doubtful.*

hit and miss: informal *Farming can be a very hit and miss affair.*

unforeseeable: *unforeseeable weather conditions*

<<OPPOSITE *predictable*

unprepared [ʌnprɪˈpɛəd] ADJECTIVE

If you are unprepared for something, you are not ready for it and are therefore surprised or at a disadvantage when it happens.

unproductive [ʌnprəˈdʌktɪv] ADJECTIVE

not producing anything useful

unqualified [ʌnˈkwɒlɪˌfaɪd] ADJECTIVE

1 having no qualifications or not having the right qualifications for a particular job *e.g. dangers posed by unqualified doctors*

2 total *e.g. an unqualified success*

unquestionable [ʌnˈkwɛstʃənəbᵊl] ADJECTIVE

so obviously true or real that nobody can doubt it *e.g. His devotion is unquestionable.*

unquestionably ADVERB

unravel [ʌnˈrævᵊl] **unravels, unravelling, unravelled** VERB

1 If you unravel something such as a twisted and knotted piece of string, you unwind it so that it is straight.

2 If you unravel a mystery, you work out the answer to it.

[WORD HISTORY: from Dutch RAVELEN meaning 'to unpick']

unreal [ʌnˈrɪəl] ADJECTIVE

so strange that you find it difficult to believe

unrealistic [ʌnrɪəˈlɪstɪk] ADJECTIVE

1 An unrealistic person does not face the truth about something or deal with it in a practical way.

2 Something unrealistic is not true to life. *e.g. an unrealistic picture*

unreasonable [ʌnˈriːznəbᵊl] ADJECTIVE

unfair and difficult to deal with or justify *e.g. an unreasonable request*

unreasonably ADVERB

unrelated [ʌnrɪˈleɪtɪd] ADJECTIVE

Things that are unrelated have no connection with each other.

unrelenting [ʌnrɪˈlɛntɪŋ] ADJECTIVE

continuing in a determined way without caring about any hurt that is caused *e.g. unrelenting criticism*

unreliable [ʌnrɪˈlaɪəbᵊl] ADJECTIVE

If people, machines, or methods are unreliable,

u

you cannot rely on them.

unremitting [ˌʌnrɪ'mɪtɪŋ] ADJECTIVE
continuing without stopping

unrest [ʌn'rɛst] NOUN
If there is unrest, people are angry and
dissatisfied.

unrivalled [ʌn'raɪvᵊld] ADJECTIVE
better than anything else of its kind *e.g. an
unrivalled range of health and beauty treatments*

unroll [ʌn'rəʊl] **unrolls, unrolling,
unrolled** VERB
If you unroll a roll of cloth or paper, you open it
up and make it flat.

unruly [ʌn'ru:lɪ] ADJECTIVE
difficult to control or organize *e.g. unruly
children... unruly hair*

unsatisfactory [ˌʌnsætɪs'fæktərɪ]
ADJECTIVE
not good enough

● THESAURUS
disappointing: *The results were disappointing.*
inadequate: *The problem goes far beyond
inadequate staffing.*
mediocre: *a mediocre string of performances*
poor: *Her school record was poor at first.*
unacceptable: *The quality of his work was
unacceptable.*
<<OPPOSITE *satisfactory*

unsaturated [ʌn'sætʃəˌreɪtɪd] ADJECTIVE
Unsaturated oils and fats are made mainly from
vegetable fats and are considered to be healthier
than saturated oils.

unscathed [ʌn'skeɪðd] ADJECTIVE
not injured or harmed as a result of a dangerous
experience

unscrew [ʌn'skru:] **unscrews,
unscrewing, unscrewed** VERB
If you unscrew something, you remove it by
turning it or by removing the screws that are
holding it.

unscrupulous [ʌn'skru:pjʊləs] ADJECTIVE
willing to behave dishonestly in order to get what
you want

unseemly [ʌn'si:mlɪ] ADJECTIVE
Unseemly behaviour is not suitable for a
particular situation and shows a lack of control
and good manners. *e.g. an unseemly squabble*

unseen [ʌn'si:n] ADJECTIVE
You use 'unseen' to describe things that you
cannot see or have not seen.

unsettle [ʌn'sɛtᵊl] **unsettles, unsettling,
unsettled** VERB
If something unsettles you, it makes you restless
or worried.

unshakable or **unshakeable** [ʌn'ʃeɪkəbᵊl]
ADJECTIVE
An unshakable belief is so strong that it cannot
be destroyed.

unsightly [ʌn'saɪtlɪ] ADJECTIVE
very ugly *e.g. an unsightly scar*

unskilled [ʌn'skɪld] ADJECTIVE
Unskilled work does not require any special
training.

unsolicited [ˌʌnsə'lɪsɪtɪd] ADJECTIVE
given or happening without being asked for

unsound [ʌn'saʊnd] ADJECTIVE
1 If a conclusion or method is unsound, it is
based on ideas that are likely to be wrong.

2 An unsound building is likely to collapse.

unspeakable [ʌn'spi:kəbᵊl] ADJECTIVE
very unpleasant

unspecified [ʌn'spɛsɪˌfaɪd] ADJECTIVE
You say that something is unspecified when you
are not told exactly what it is. *e.g. It was being
stored in some unspecified place.*

unspoilt or **unspoiled** [ʌn'spɔɪlt] or
[ʌn'spɔɪld] ADJECTIVE
If you describe a place as unspoilt or unspoiled,
you mean it has not been changed and it is still in
its natural or original state.

unspoken [ʌn'spəʊkən] ADJECTIVE
An unspoken wish or feeling is one that is not
mentioned to other people.

unstable [ʌn'steɪbᵊl] ADJECTIVE
1 likely to change suddenly and create difficulty
or danger *e.g. The political situation in Moscow is
unstable.*

2 not firm or fixed properly and likely to wobble
or fall

unsteady [ʌn'stɛdɪ] ADJECTIVE
1 having difficulty in controlling the movement of
your legs or hands *e.g. unsteady on her feet*

2 not held or fixed securely and likely to fall over
unsteadily ADVERB

● THESAURUS
precarious: *The beds are precarious-looking
hammocks strung from the walls.*
rickety: *She stood on a rickety old table.*
shaky: *He climbed up the shaky ladder to the
scaffold.*
tottering: *a tottering pile of bricks*
unsafe: *That bridge looks decidedly unsafe to me.*
unstable: *funds used to demolish dangerously
unstable buildings*
wobbly: *cat-scratched upholstery and wobbly chairs*
<<OPPOSITE *steady*

unstuck [ʌn'stʌk] ADJECTIVE
If something comes unstuck, it becomes

separated from the thing that it was stuck to.

unsuccessful [ˌʌnsək'sɛsfʊl] ADJECTIVE
If you are unsuccessful, you do not succeed in what you are trying to do.
unsuccessfully ADVERB

unsuitable [ʌn'suːtəbəl] ADJECTIVE
not right or appropriate for a particular purpose
unsuitably ADVERB

● THESAURUS
improper: an improper diet
inappropriate: inappropriate use of the Internet
unacceptable: using completely unacceptable language
unfit: unfit for human habitation
<<OPPOSITE suitable

unsuited [ʌn'suːtɪd] ADJECTIVE
not appropriate for a particular task or situation
e.g. He's totally unsuited to the job.

unsung [ʌn'sʌŋ] ADJECTIVE
You use 'unsung' to describe someone who is not appreciated or praised for their good work.
e.g. George is the unsung hero of the club.
[WORD HISTORY: from the custom of celebrating in song the exploits of heroes]

unsure [ʌn'ʃʊə] ADJECTIVE
uncertain or doubtful

unsuspecting [ˌʌnsə'spɛktɪŋ] ADJECTIVE
having no idea of what is happening or going to happen e.g. His horse escaped and collided with an unsuspecting cyclist.

untangle [ʌn'tæŋgəl] **untangles, untangling, untangled** VERB
If you untangle something that is twisted together, you undo the twists.

untenable [ʌn'tɛnəbəl] ADJECTIVE; FORMAL
A theory, argument, or position that is untenable cannot be successfully defended.

unthinkable [ʌn'θɪŋkəbəl] ADJECTIVE
so shocking or awful that you cannot imagine it to be true

untidy [ʌn'taɪdɪ] **untidier, untidiest** ADJECTIVE
not neat or well arranged
untidily ADVERB

● THESAURUS
bedraggled: My hair was a bedraggled mess.
chaotic: the chaotic mess of papers on his desk
cluttered: There was no space on the cluttered worktop.
jumbled: We moved our supplies into a jumbled heap.
messy: She was a good, if messy, cook.
unkempt: the unkempt grass in front of the house
<<OPPOSITE tidy

untie [ʌn'taɪ] **unties, untying, untied** VERB
If you untie something, you undo the knots in the string or rope around it.

until [ʌn'tɪl] PREPOSITION OR CONJUNCTION
1 If something happens until a particular time, it happens before that time and stops at that time.
e.g. The shop stayed open until midnight... She waited until her husband was asleep.

2 If something does not happen until a particular time, it does not happen before that time and only starts happening at that time. e.g. It didn't rain until the middle of the afternoon... It was not until they arrived that they found out who he was.

untimely [ʌn'taɪmlɪ] ADJECTIVE
happening too soon or sooner than expected e.g. his untimely death

unto ['ʌntuː] PREPOSITION; OLD-FASHIONED, INFORMAL
Unto means the same as to. e.g. Nation shall speak peace unto nation.

untold [ʌn'təʊld] ADJECTIVE
You use 'untold' to emphasize how great or extreme something is. e.g. The island possessed untold wealth.

untouched [ʌn'tʌtʃt] ADJECTIVE
1 not changed, moved, or damaged e.g. a small village untouched by tourism

2 If a meal is untouched, none of it has been eaten.

untoward [ˌʌntə'wɔːd] ADJECTIVE
unexpected and causing difficulties e.g. no untoward problems

untrue [ʌn'truː] ADJECTIVE
not true

● THESAURUS
erroneous: an erroneous description
false: He gave a false name and address.
fictitious: the source of the fictitious rumours
inaccurate: the passing on of inaccurate or misleading information
incorrect: an incorrect account of the sequence of events
misleading: It would be misleading to say we were friends.
mistaken: I had a mistaken idea of what had happened.
<<OPPOSITE true

unused [ʌn'juːzd] ADJECTIVE
not yet used ADJECTIVE
If you are unused to something, you have not often done or experienced it.

unusual [ʌn'juːʒʊəl] ADJECTIVE
Something that is unusual does not occur very often.

unusually ADVERB

● THESAURUS
curious: *a curious mixture of ancient and modern*
exceptional: *exceptional circumstances*
extraordinary: *What an extraordinary thing to happen!*
rare: *one of the rarest species in the world*
uncommon: *It's a very uncommon surname.*
unconventional: *produced by an unconventional technique*
<<OPPOSITE *common*

unveil [ʌn'veɪl] **unveils, unveiling, unveiled** VERB
When someone unveils a new statue or plaque, they draw back a curtain that is covering it.

unwanted [ʌn'wɒntɪd] ADJECTIVE
Unwanted things are not desired or wanted, either by a particular person or by people in general. *e.g. He felt lonely and unwanted.*

unwarranted [ʌn'wɒrəntɪd] ADJECTIVE; FORMAL
not justified or not deserved *e.g. unwarranted fears*

unwelcome [ʌn'wɛlkəm] ADJECTIVE
not wanted *e.g. an unwelcome visitor... unwelcome news*

unwell [ʌn'wɛl] ADJECTIVE
If you are unwell, you are ill.

● THESAURUS
ailing: *The President is said to be ailing.*
crook: Australian and New Zealand; informal *I'm sorry to hear you've been crook, mate.*
ill: *Payne was seriously ill with pneumonia.*
poorly: British; informal *Julie is still poorly after her bout of flu.*
queasy: *I always feel queasy on boats.*
sick: *He's very sick and he needs treatment.*
<<OPPOSITE *well*

unwieldy [ʌn'wiːldɪ] ADJECTIVE
difficult to move or carry because of being large or an awkward shape

unwilling [ʌn'wɪlɪŋ] ADJECTIVE
If you are unwilling to do something, you do not want to do it.
unwillingly ADVERB

● THESAURUS
averse: *I'm not averse to going along with the suggestion.*
grudging: *a grudging acceptance of the situation*
loath: *She is loath to give up her hard-earned liberty.*
reluctant: *They were reluctant to get involved at first.*
<<OPPOSITE *willing*

unwind [ʌn'waɪnd] **unwinds, unwinding, unwound** VERB

1 When you unwind after working hard, you relax.

2 If you unwind something that is wrapped round something else, you undo it.

unwise [ʌn'waɪz] ADJECTIVE
foolish or not sensible

● THESAURUS
daft: *You'd be daft to get on the wrong side of him.*
foolish: *It was foolish to risk injury like that.*
idiotic: *What an idiotic thing to do!*
irresponsible: *irresponsible plans for tax cuts*
rash: *Don't panic or do anything rash.*
senseless: *It would be senseless to try and stop him now.*
silly: *You're not going to go and do something silly, are you?*
stupid: *I've had enough of your stupid suggestions.*
<<OPPOSITE *wise*

unwitting [ʌn'wɪtɪŋ] ADJECTIVE
Unwitting describes someone who becomes involved in something without realizing what is really happening. *e.g. her unwitting victims*
unwittingly ADVERB

unworthy [ʌn'wɜːðɪ] ADJECTIVE; FORMAL
Someone who is unworthy of something does not deserve it.

unwrap [ʌn'ræp] **unwraps, unwrapping, unwrapped** VERB
When you unwrap something, you take off the paper or covering around it.

unwritten [ʌn'rɪtən] ADJECTIVE
An unwritten law is one which is generally understood and accepted without being officially laid down.

up [ʌp] ADVERB OR PREPOSITION

1 towards or in a higher place *e.g. He ran up the stairs... high up in the mountains*

2 towards or in the north *e.g. I'm flying up to Darwin.*

> PREPOSITION

3 If you go up a road or river, you go along it.

4 You use 'up to' to say how large something can be or what level it has reached. *e.g. traffic jams up to 15 kilometres long*

5 INFORMAL
If someone is up to something, they are secretly doing something they should not be doing.

6 If it is up to someone to do something, it is their responsibility.

> ADJECTIVE

7 If you are up, you are not in bed.

8 If a period of time is up, it has come to an end.

> ADVERB

9 If an amount of something goes up, it increases.

up-and-coming [ˌʌpəndˈkʌmɪŋ] ADJECTIVE
Up-and-coming people are likely to be successful.

upbringing [ˈʌpˌbrɪŋɪŋ] NOUN
Your upbringing is the way that your parents have taught you to behave.

update [ʌpˈdeɪt] **updates, updating, updated** VERB
If you update something, you make it more modern or add new information to it. *e.g. He had failed to update his will.*

upgrade [ʌpˈgreɪd] **upgrades, upgrading, upgraded** VERB
If a person or their job is upgraded, they are given more responsibility or status and usually more money.

upheaval [ʌpˈhiːvəl] **upheavals** NOUN
a big change which causes a lot of trouble

uphill [ˈʌpˈhɪl] ADVERB
1 If you go uphill, you go up a slope.
> ADJECTIVE
2 An uphill task requires a lot of effort and determination.

uphold [ʌpˈhəʊld] **upholds, upholding, upheld** VERB
If someone upholds a law or a decision, they support and maintain it.

upholstery [ʌpˈhəʊlstəri] NOUN
Upholstery is the soft covering on chairs and sofas that makes them comfortable.

upkeep [ˈʌpˌkiːp] NOUN
The upkeep of something is the continual process and cost of keeping it in good condition.

● THESAURUS
keep: *He does not contribute towards his keep.*
maintenance: *the regular maintenance of government buildings*
overheads: *We must cut our overheads or we shall have to close.*
preservation: *the preservation of historical sites*
running: *The running of the house took up all her time.*

upland [ˈʌplənd] **uplands** ADJECTIVE
1 An upland area is an area of high land.
> NOUN
2 Uplands are areas of high land.

uplifting [ʌpˈlɪftɪŋ] ADJECTIVE
making you feel happy

upload [ʌpˈləʊd] **uploads, uploading, uploaded** VB
If you upload a computer file or program, you transfer it from your computer into the memory of another computer.

up-market [ʌpˈmɑːkɪt] ADJECTIVE
sophisticated and expensive

upon [əˈpɒn] PREPOSITION
1 FORMAL
Upon means on. *e.g. I stood upon the stair.*
2 You use 'upon' when mentioning an event that is immediately followed by another. *e.g. Upon entering the hall he took a quick glance round.*
3 If an event is upon you, it is about to happen. *e.g. The football season is upon us once more.*

upper [ˈʌpə] **uppers** ADJECTIVE
1 referring to something that is above something else, or the higher part of something *e.g. the upper arm*
> NOUN
2 the top part of a shoe

upper class upper classes NOUN
The upper classes are people who belong to a very wealthy or aristocratic group in a society.

uppermost [ˈʌpəˌməʊst] ADJECTIVE OR ADVERB
1 on top or in the highest position *e.g. the uppermost leaves... Lay your arms beside your body with the palms turned uppermost.*
> ADJECTIVE
2 most important *e.g. His family is now uppermost in his mind.*

upright [ˈʌpˌraɪt] ADJECTIVE OR ADVERB
1 standing or sitting up straight, rather than bending or lying down
2 behaving in a very respectable and moral way

uprising [ˈʌpˌraɪzɪŋ] **uprisings** NOUN
If there is an uprising, a large group of people begin fighting against the existing government to bring about political changes.

uproar [ˈʌpˌrɔː] NOUN
If there is uproar or an uproar, there is a lot of shouting and noise, often because people are angry.
[WORD HISTORY: from Dutch OPROER meaning 'revolt']

uproot [ʌpˈruːt] **uproots, uprooting, uprooted** VERB
1 If someone is uprooted, they have to leave the place where they have lived for a long time.
2 If a tree is uprooted, it is pulled out of the ground.

upset upsets, upsetting, upset ADJECTIVE [ʌpˈsɛt]
1 unhappy and disappointed

● THESAURUS
agitated: *in an excited and agitated state*

distressed: *The animals were distressed by the noise.*
frantic: *frantic with worry*
hurt: *I was very hurt when they refused.*
troubled: *He sounded deeply troubled.*
unhappy: *The divorce made him very unhappy.*

> VERB [ʌpˈsɛt]
2 If something upsets you, it makes you feel worried or unhappy.

● THESAURUS
agitate: *The thought agitates her.*
bother: *Don't let his manner bother you.*
distress: *The whole thing really distressed him.*
disturb: *These dreams disturb me for days afterwards.*
grieve: *deeply grieved by their suffering*
ruffle: *She doesn't get ruffled by anything.*

3 If you upset something, you turn it over or spill it accidentally.

● THESAURUS
capsize: *He capsized the boat through his carelessness.*
knock over: *The kitten knocked over the vase.*
overturn: *She overturned her glass of wine as she stood up.*
spill: *The waiter spilled the drinks all over the table.*

> NOUN [ˈʌpˌsɛt]
4 A stomach upset is a slight stomach illness caused by an infection or by something you have eaten.

upshot [ˈʌpˌʃɒt] NOUN
The upshot of a series of events is the final result.

upside down [ˈʌpˌsaɪd] ADJECTIVE OR ADVERB
the wrong way up

upstage [ʌpˈsteɪdʒ] **upstages, upstaging, upstaged** VERB
If someone upstages you, they draw people's attention away from you by being more attractive or interesting.

upstairs [ˈʌpˈstɛəz] ADVERB
1 If you go upstairs in a building, you go up to a higher floor.

> NOUN
2 The upstairs of a building is its upper floor or floors.

upstart [ˈʌpˌstɑːt] **upstarts** NOUN
someone who has risen too quickly to an important position and are too arrogant

upstream [ˈʌpˈstriːm] ADVERB
towards the source of a river *e.g. They made their way upstream.*

upsurge [ˈʌpˌsɜːdʒ] NOUN
An upsurge of something is a sudden large increase in it.

uptake [ˈʌpˌteɪk] NOUN
You can say that someone is quick on the uptake if they understand things quickly.
[WORD HISTORY: from Scottish UPTAKE meaning 'to understand']

uptight [ʌpˈtaɪt] ADJECTIVE; INFORMAL
tense or annoyed

up-to-date [ˌʌptəˈdeɪt] ADJECTIVE
1 being the newest thing of its kind
2 having the latest information

up-to-the-minute [ˌʌptəðəˈmɪnɪt] ADJECTIVE
Up-to-the-minute information is the latest available information.

upturn [ˈʌpˌtɜːn] **upturns** NOUN
an improvement in a situation

upturned [ˈʌpˌtɜːnd] ADJECTIVE
1 pointing upwards *e.g. rain splashing down on her upturned face*
2 upside down *e.g. an upturned bowl*

upwards [ˈʌpwədz] ADVERB
1 towards a higher place *e.g. People stared upwards and pointed.*
2 to a higher level or point on a scale *e.g. The world population is rocketing upwards.*
upward ADJECTIVE

uranium [juˈreɪnɪəm] NOUN
Uranium is a radioactive metal used to produce nuclear energy and weapons.

Uranus [juˈreɪnəs] NOUN
Uranus is the planet in the solar system which is seventh from the sun.
[WORD HISTORY: named after the Greek god OURANOS who ruled the universe]

urban [ˈɜːbᵊn] ADJECTIVE
(GEOGRAPHY) relating to a town or city *e.g. urban development*

urbane [ɜːˈbeɪn] ADJECTIVE
well-mannered, and comfortable in social situations

Urdu [ˈʊəduː] NOUN
Urdu is the official language of Pakistan. It is also spoken by many people in India.

urge [ɜːdʒ] **urges, urging, urged** NOUN
1 If you have an urge to do something, you have a strong wish to do it.

● THESAURUS
compulsion: *a compulsion to write*
desire: *I had a strong desire to help and care for people.*
drive: *a demonic drive to succeed*
impulse: *Peter resisted an impulse to smile.*
longing: *his longing to return home*

wish: *She had a genuine wish to make amends.*

> VERB

2 If you urge someone to do something, you try hard to persuade them to do it.

⊙ THESAURUS

beg: *I begged him to leave me alone.*

beseech: *Her eyes beseeched him to show mercy.*

implore: *He left early, although they implored him to stay.*

plead: *kneeling on the floor pleading for mercy*

press: *The unions are pressing him to stand firm.*

urgent ['ɜːdʒənt] ADJECTIVE

needing to be dealt with as soon as possible

urgently ADVERB, **urgency** NOUN

⊙ THESAURUS

compelling: *There are compelling reasons to act swiftly.*

immediate: *The immediate problem is transportation.*

imperative: *It is imperative we end up with a win.*

pressing: *one of our most pressing problems*

urinal [jʊ'raɪnəl] **urinals** NOUN

a bowl or trough fixed to the wall in a men's public toilet for men to urinate in

urinate ['jʊərɪˌneɪt] **urinates, urinating, urinated** VERB

When you urinate, you go to the toilet and get rid of urine from your body.

urine ['jʊərɪn] NOUN

the waste liquid that you get rid of from your body when you go to the toilet

URL URLs NOUN

an abbreviation for 'uniform resource locator': a technical name for an Internet address

urn [ɜːn] **urns** NOUN

a decorated container, especially one that is used to hold the ashes of a person who has been cremated

us [ʌs] PRONOUN

A speaker or writer uses 'us' to refer to himself or herself and one or more other people. *e.g. Why don't you tell us?.*

US or **USA**

an abbreviation for 'United States of America'

usage ['juːsɪdʒ] NOUN

1 the degree to which something is used, or the way in which it is used

2 the way in which words are actually used *e.g. The terms soon entered common usage.*

use uses, using, used VERB [juːz]

1 If you use something, you do something with it in order to do a job or achieve something. *e.g. May I use your phone?.*

⊙ THESAURUS

apply: *The company applies this technology to solve practical problems.*

employ: *the methods employed in the study*

operate: *Can you operate a fax machine?*

utilize: *The body utilizes many different minerals.*

2 If you use someone, you take advantage of them by making them do things for you.

> NOUN [juːs]

3 The use of something is the act of using it. *e.g. the use of force*

⊙ THESAURUS

application: *Her theory was put into practical application.*

employment: *the employment of completely new methods*

operation: *the operation of the computer mouse*

usage: *Parts of the motor wore out because of constant usage.*

4 If you have the use of something, you have the ability or permission to use it.

5 If you find a use for something, you find a purpose for it.

usable or **useable** ADJECTIVE, **user** NOUN

⊙ THESAURUS

end: *The police force was manipulated for political ends.*

object: *the object of the exercise*

point: *I don't see the point of a thing like that.*

purpose: *It is wrong to use it for military purposes.*

used [juːzd] VERB

1 Something that used to be done or used to be true was done or was true in the past.

> PHRASE

2 If you are **used to** something, you are familiar with it and have often experienced it.

> ADJECTIVE

A used object has had a previous owner.

useful ['juːsfʊl] ADJECTIVE

If something is useful, you can use it in order to do something or to help you in some way.

usefully ADVERB, **usefulness** NOUN

⊙ THESAURUS

beneficial: *It may be beneficial to study the relevant guidelines.*

effective: *Antibiotics are effective against this organism.*

helpful: *a number of helpful booklets*

practical: *practical suggestions for healthy eating*

valuable: *Here are a few valuable tips to help you to succeed.*

worthwhile: *a worthwhile source of income*

<<OPPOSITE *useless*

useless ['juːslɪs] ADJECTIVE

1 If something is useless, you cannot use it because it is not suitable or helpful.

u

● THESAURUS

futile: *It would be futile to make any further attempts.*
impractical: *A tripod is impractical when following animals on the move.*
unproductive: *increasingly unproductive land*
unsuitable: *This tool is completely unsuitable for use with metal.*
worthless: *The old skills are worthless now.*
<<OPPOSITE *useful*

2 If a course of action is useless, it will not achieve what is wanted.

username ['juːzə,neɪm] **usernames** NOUN
a name that someone uses when logging into a computer or website

usher ['ʌʃə] **ushers, ushering, ushered** VERB

1 If you usher someone somewhere, you show them where to go by going with them.

> NOUN

2 a person who shows people where to sit at a wedding or a concert

USSR
an abbreviation for 'Union of Soviet Socialist Republics', a country which was made up of a lot of smaller countries including Russia, but which is now broken up

usual ['juːʒʊəl] ADJECTIVE

1 happening, done, or used most often *e.g. his usual seat*

● THESAURUS

accustomed: *She acted with her accustomed shrewdness.*
common: *the commonest cause of death*
customary: *It's customary to offer guests a drink.*
habitual: *He soon recovered his habitual geniality.*
normal: *That's quite normal for a Friday.*
regular: *samples from one of their regular suppliers*
standard: *It was standard practice to put them outside.*

> PHRASE

2 If you do something **as usual**, you do it in the way that you normally do it.
usually ADVERB

usurp [juːˈzɜːp] **usurps, usurping, usurped** VERB; FORMAL

If someone usurps another person's job or title they take it when they have no right to do so.

ute [juːt] **utes** NOUN; INFORMAL
In Australian and New Zealand English, a utility truck.

utensil [juːˈtɛnsəl] **utensils** NOUN
Utensils are tools. *e.g. cooking utensils*
[WORD HISTORY: from Latin UTENSILIS meaning 'available for use']

uterus ['juːtərəs] **uteruses** NOUN; FORMAL
A woman's uterus is her womb.

utility [juːˈtɪlɪtɪ] **utilities** NOUN

1 The utility of something is its usefulness.

2 a service, such as water or gas, that is provided for everyone

utility truck utility trucks NOUN
In Australian and New Zealand English, a small motor vehicle with an open body and low sides.

utilize ['juːtɪ,laɪz] **utilizes, utilizing, utilized;** also spelt **utilise** VERB; FORMAL
To utilize something is to use it.
utilization NOUN

utmost ['ʌt,məʊst] ADJECTIVE
used to emphasize a particular quality *e.g. I have the utmost respect for Richard.*

utter ['ʌtə] **utters, uttering, uttered** VERB

1 When you utter sounds or words, you make or say them.

> ADJECTIVE

2 Utter means complete or total. *e.g. scenes of utter chaos*
utterly ADVERB

● THESAURUS

absolute: *This is absolute madness!*
complete: *a complete mess*
consummate: *a consummate professional*
out-and-out: *an out-and-out lie*
outright: *an outright rejection of the deal*
perfect: *a perfect stranger*
pure: *She did it out of pure malice.*
sheer: *an act of sheer stupidity*
thorough: *She is a thorough snob.*
total: *a total failure*

utterance ['ʌtərəns] **utterances** NOUN
something that is said *e.g. his first utterance*

Vv

v an abbreviation for **versus**

vacant ['veɪkənt] ADJECTIVE

1 If something is vacant, it is not occupied or being used.

2 If a job or position is vacant, no-one holds it at present.

3 A vacant look suggests that someone does not understand something or is not very intelligent.
vacancy NOUN, **vacantly** ADVERB

vacate [və'keɪt] **vacates, vacating, vacated** VERB; FORMAL
If you vacate a room or job, you leave it and it becomes available for someone else.

vacation [və'keɪʃən] **vacations** NOUN

1 the period between academic terms at a university or college e.g. the summer vacation

2 a holiday

vaccinate ['væksɪ,neɪt] **vaccinates, vaccinating, vaccinated** VERB
To vaccinate someone means to give them a vaccine, usually by injection, to protect them against a disease.
vaccination NOUN

vaccine ['væksi:n] **vaccines** NOUN
a substance made from the germs that cause a disease and is given to people to make them immune to that disease
[WORD HISTORY: from Latin VACCA meaning 'cow', because smallpox vaccine is based on cowpox, a disease of cows]

vacuum ['vækjʊəm] **vacuums, vacuuming, vacuumed** NOUN

1 a space containing no air, gases, or other matter

> VERB

2 If you vacuum something, you clean it using a vacuum cleaner.

vacuum cleaner ['kli:nə] **vacuum cleaners** NOUN
an electric machine which cleans by sucking up dirt

vagina [və'dʒaɪnə] **vaginas** NOUN
A woman's vagina is the passage that connects her outer sex organs to her womb.
[WORD HISTORY: from Latin VAGINA meaning 'sheath']

vagrant ['veɪgrənt] **vagrants** NOUN
a person who moves from place to place, and has no home or regular job
vagrancy NOUN

vague [veɪg] **vaguer, vaguest** ADJECTIVE

1 If something is vague, it is not expressed or explained clearly, or you cannot see or remember it clearly. e.g. vague statements

⬤ THESAURUS

hazy: Many details remain hazy.
indefinite: at some indefinite time in the future
indistinct: The lettering was worn and indistinct.
loose: a loose translation
uncertain: Students are facing an uncertain future.
unclear: The proposals were sketchy and unclear.
<<OPPOSITE definite

2 Someone looks or sounds vague if they are not concentrating or thinking clearly.
vaguely ADVERB, **vagueness** NOUN

vain [veɪn] **vainer, vainest** ADJECTIVE

1 A vain action or attempt is one which is not successful. e.g. He made a vain effort to cheer her up.

⬤ THESAURUS

abortive: the abortive coup attempt
fruitless: It was a fruitless search.
futile: their futile attempts to avoid publicity
unproductive: an unproductive strategy
useless: a useless punishment which fails to stop crime
<<OPPOSITE successful

2 A vain person is very proud of their looks, intelligence, or other qualities.

⬤ THESAURUS

conceited: They had grown too conceited and pleased with themselves.
egotistical: an egotistical show-off
ostentatious: He was generous with his money without being ostentatious.
proud: She was said to be proud and arrogant.
stuck-up: informal She was a famous actress, but she wasn't a bit stuck-up.

> PHRASE

3 If you do something **in vain**, you do not succeed in achieving what you intend.
vainly ADVERB

● THESAURUS
fruitless: *Four years of negotiation were fruitless.*
to no avail: *His protests were to no avail.*
unsuccessful: *Previous attempts have been unsuccessful.*
wasted: *Their efforts were wasted.*

vale [veɪl] **vales** NOUN; LITERARY
a valley

valentine ['vælən,taɪn] **valentines** NOUN
1 Your valentine is someone you love and send a card to on Saint Valentine's Day, February 14th.
2 A valentine or a valentine card is the card you send to the person you love on Saint Valentine's Day.
[WORD HISTORY: Saint Valentine was a 3rd century martyr]

valet ['vælɪt] *or* ['væleɪ] **valets** NOUN
a male servant who is employed to look after another man, particularly caring for his clothes

valiant ['væljənt] ADJECTIVE
very brave
valiantly ADVERB

valid ['vælɪd] ADJECTIVE
1 Something that is valid is based on sound reasoning.
2 A valid ticket or document is one which is officially accepted.
validity NOUN

validate ['vælɪ,deɪt] **validates, validating, validated** VERB
If something validates a statement or claim, it proves that it is true or correct.

valley ['vælɪ] **valleys** NOUN
a long stretch of land between hills, often with a river flowing through it

valour ['vælə] NOUN
Valour is great bravery.

valuable ['væljʊəbəl] **valuables** ADJECTIVE
1 having great value or usefulness

● THESAURUS
beneficial: *Using computers has a beneficial effect on learning.*
helpful: *a number of helpful booklets*
important: *Her sons are the most important thing in her life.*
prized: *one of the gallery's most prized possessions*
useful: *a mine of useful information*
worthwhile: *a worthwhile source of income*
<<OPPOSITE useless

2 worth a lot of money

● THESAURUS
costly: *a small and costly bottle of scent*
expensive: *exclusive, expensive possessions*
precious: *rings set with precious jewels*
<<OPPOSITE worthless

> PLURAL NOUN

3 Valuables are things that you own that cost a lot of money.

● THESAURUS
heirlooms: *family heirlooms*
treasures: *The house was full of art treasures.*

valuation [,væljʊ'eɪʃən] **valuations** NOUN
a judgment about how much money something is worth or how good it is

value ['vælju:] **values, valuing, valued**
NOUN
1 The value of something is its importance or usefulness. *e.g. information of great value*

● THESAURUS
advantage: *the great advantage of this method*
benefit: *They see no benefit in educating these children.*
effectiveness: *the effectiveness of the new system*
importance: *They have always placed great importance on live performances.*
merit: *the artistic merit of their work*
use: *This is of no use to anyone.*
usefulness: *the usefulness of the Internet in disseminating new ideas*
virtue: *the great virtue of modern technology*
worth: *This system has already proved its worth.*

2 The value of something you own is the amount of money that it is worth.

● THESAURUS
cost: *the cost of a loaf of bread*
market price: *buying shares at the current market price*
price: *a sharp increase in the price of petrol*
selling price: *the average selling price of a new home*
worth: *He sold the car for less than half its worth.*

3 The values of a group or a person are the moral principles and beliefs that they think are important. *e.g. the values of liberty and equality*

> VERB

4 If you value something, you think it is important and you appreciate it.

● THESAURUS
appreciate: *I would appreciate your advice.*
cherish: *Cherish every moment you have with your children.*
have a high opinion of: *Your boss seems to have a high opinion of you.*
prize: *These items are prized by collectors.*
rate highly: *He is an excellent keeper and I rate him highly.*

respect: *I respect his talent as a pianist.*
treasure: *memories I will treasure for the rest of my life*

5 When experts value something, they decide how much money it is worth.
valued ADJECTIVE, **valuer** NOUN

● THESAURUS
appraise: *He was called in to appraise and sell the cottage.*
assess: *Experts are now assessing the cost of the restoration.*
cost: *an operation costed at around $649m*
estimate: *a personal fortune estimated at more than $400m*
evaluate: *The company needs to evaluate the cost of leasing the building.*
price: *The property was priced at less than £1m.*

valve [vælv] **valves** NOUN
1 a part attached to a pipe or tube which controls the flow of gas or liquid
2 a small flap in your heart or in a vein which controls the flow and direction of blood

vampire ['væmpaɪə] **vampires** NOUN
In horror stories, vampires are corpses that come out of their graves at night and suck the blood of living people.

van [væn] **vans** NOUN
a covered vehicle larger than a car but smaller than a lorry, used for carrying goods

vandal ['vændəl] **vandals** NOUN
someone who deliberately damages or destroys things, particularly public property
vandalize or **vandalise** VERB, **vandalism** NOUN

vane [veɪn] **vanes** NOUN
a flat blade that is part of a mechanism for using the energy of the wind or water to drive a machine

vanguard ['væn,gɑːd] NOUN
If someone is in the vanguard of something, they are in the most advanced part of it.

vanilla [və'nɪlə] NOUN
Vanilla is a flavouring for food such as ice cream, which comes from the pods of a tropical plant.

vanish ['vænɪʃ] **vanishes, vanishing, vanished** VERB
1 If something vanishes, it disappears. *e.g. The moon vanished behind a cloud.*

● THESAURUS
become invisible: *The plane became invisible in the clouds.*
be lost to view: *They watched the ship until it was lost to view.*
disappear: *The aircraft disappeared off the radar.*
fade: *We watched the harbour fade into the mist.*

recede: *Gradually Luke receded into the distance.*
<<OPPOSITE *appear*
2 If something vanishes, it ceases to exist. *e.g. a vanishing civilization*

● THESAURUS
become extinct: *Without help, these animals will become extinct.*
cease: *At one o'clock the rain ceased.*
cease to exist: *Without trees, the world as we know it would cease to exist.*
die out: *Britain's bear population died out about 2,000 years ago.*
dissolve: *The crowds dissolved and we were alone.*
evaporate: *All my pleasure evaporated when I saw him.*
fade away: *Her black mood faded away.*
go away: *All she wanted was for the pain to go away.*
melt away: *All my cares melted away.*
pass: *Breathe deeply and the panic attack will pass.*

vanity ['vænɪtɪ] NOUN
Vanity is a feeling of excessive pride about your looks or abilities.

vanquish ['væŋkwɪʃ] **vanquishes, vanquishing, vanquished** VERB LITERARY
To vanquish someone means to defeat them completely.

● THESAURUS
beat: *the team that beat us in the finals*
conquer: *a great warrior who conquers the enemies of his people*
crush: *their bid to crush the rebels*
defeat: *His guerrillas defeated the colonial army in 1954.*
overcome: *They overcame the opposition to win the cup.*
rout: *the battle at which the Norman army routed the English*
trounce: *Australia trounced France by 60 points to 4.*

vapour ['veɪpə] NOUN
Vapour is a mass of tiny drops of water or other liquids in the air, which looks like mist.

variable ['veərɪəbəl] **variables** ADJECTIVE
1 Something that is variable is likely to change at any time.
> NOUN
2 In any situation, a variable is something in it that can change.
3 In maths, a variable is a symbol such as x which can represent any value or any one of a set of values.
variability NOUN

variance ['veərɪəns] NOUN
If one thing is at variance with another, the two

v

seem to contradict each other.

variant ['vɛərɪənt] **variants** NOUN

1 A variant of something has a different form from the usual one, for example *gaol* is a variant of *jail*.

> ADJECTIVE

2 alternative or different

variation [ˌvɛərɪ'eɪʃən] **variations** NOUN

1 a change from the normal or usual pattern *e.g. a variation of the same route*

● THESAURUS

alteration: *some alterations in your diet*
change: *a change of attitude*
departure: *Her new novel is a departure from her previous work.*
deviation: *Deviation from the norm is not tolerated.*
difference: *a noticeable difference in his behaviour*
diversion: *a welcome diversion from the daily grind*

2 a change in level, amount, or quantity *e.g. a large variation in demand*

varicose veins ['værɪˌkəʊs 'veɪnz] PLURAL NOUN

Varicose veins are swollen painful veins in the legs.

varied ['vɛərɪd] ADJECTIVE

of different types, quantities, or sizes

variety [və'raɪɪtɪ] **varieties** NOUN

1 If something has variety, it consists of things which are not all the same.

2 A variety of things is a number of different kinds of them. *e.g. a wide variety of readers*

● THESAURUS

array: *an attractive array of bright colours*
assortment: *an assortment of pets*
collection: *a huge collection of books*
medley: *a medley of vegetables*
mixture: *a mixture of sweets*
range: *a range of sun-care products*

3 A variety of something is a particular type of it. *e.g. a new variety of celery*

● THESAURUS

category: *There are three broad categories of soil.*
class: *several classes of butterflies*
kind: *different kinds of roses*
sort: *several articles of this sort*
strain: *a new strain of the virus*
type: *What type of guns were they?*

4 Variety is a form of entertainment consisting of short unrelated acts, such as singing, dancing, and comedy.

various ['vɛərɪəs] ADJECTIVE

Various means of several different types. *e.g. trees of various sorts*

variously ADVERB

● THESAURUS

assorted: *swimsuits in assorted colours*
different: *different brands of drinks*
disparate: *the disparate cultures of India*
diverse: *Society is more diverse than ever before.*
miscellaneous: *a hoard of miscellaneous junk*
sundry: *sundry journalists and lawyers*

> You should avoid putting *different* after *various*: *the disease exists in various forms* not *various different forms*

varnish ['vɑːnɪʃ] **varnishes, varnishing, varnished** NOUN

1 a liquid which when painted onto a surface gives it a hard clear shiny finish

> VERB

2 If you varnish something, you paint it with varnish.

vary ['vɛərɪ] **varies, varying, varied** VERB

1 If things vary, they change. *e.g. Weather patterns vary greatly.*

● THESAURUS

alter: *During the course of a day the light alters constantly.*
alternate: *My moods alternate with alarming rapidity.*
change: *My feelings haven't changed.*
fluctuate: *Weight may fluctuate markedly.*

2 If you vary something, you introduce changes in it. *e.g. Vary your routes as much as possible.*

varied ADJECTIVE

● THESAURUS

alternate: *Alternate the chunks of fish with chunks of vegetable.*
diversify: *They decided to diversify their products.*
modify: *The government refuses to modify its position.*

vascular ['væskjʊlə] ADJECTIVE

relating to tubes or ducts that carry fluids within animals or plants

vase [vɑːz] **vases** NOUN

a glass or china jar for flowers

vasectomy [væ'sɛktəmɪ] **vasectomies** NOUN

an operation to sterilize a man by cutting the tube that carries the sperm

Vaseline ['væsɪˌliːn] NOUN; TRADEMARK

Vaseline is a soft clear jelly made from petroleum and used as an ointment or as grease.

vast [vɑːst] ADJECTIVE

extremely large

vastly ADVERB, **vastness** NOUN

● THESAURUS

colossal: *a colossal statue*
enormous: *The main bedroom is enormous.*

giant: *a giant meteorite heading for the earth*
gigantic: *a gigantic shopping mall*
great: *a great hall as long as a church*
huge: *a huge crowd*
immense: *an immense castle*
massive: *a massive theme park*
<<OPPOSITE *tiny*

vat [væt] **vats** NOUN
a large container for liquids

VAT [væt] NOUN
In Britain, VAT is a tax which is added to the costs
of making or providing goods and services. VAT is
an abbreviation for 'value-added tax'.

vault [vɔːlt] **vaults, vaulting, vaulted**
NOUN
1 a strong secure room, often underneath a
building, where valuables are stored, or
underneath a church where people are buried
2 an arched roof, often found in churches
> VERB
3 If you vault over something, you jump over it
using your hands or a pole to help.

VCR
an abbreviation for 'video cassette recorder'

VDU VDUs NOUN
a monitor screen attached to a computer or word
processor. VDU is an abbreviation for 'visual
display unit'

veal [viːl] NOUN
Veal is the meat from a calf.

Veda ['veɪdə] **Vedas** NOUN
an ancient sacred text of the Hindu religion; also
these texts as a collection
Vedic ADJECTIVE

veer [vɪə] **veers, veering, veered** VERB
If something which is moving veers in a
particular direction, it suddenly changes course.
e.g. The aircraft veered sharply to one side.

vegan ['viːgən] **vegans** NOUN
someone who does not eat any food made from
animal products, such as meat, eggs, cheese, or
milk

vegetable ['vɛdʒtəbᵊl] **vegetables** NOUN
1 Vegetables are edible roots or leaves such as
carrots or cabbage.
> ADJECTIVE
2 'Vegetable' is used to refer to any plants in
contrast to animals or minerals *e.g. vegetable life*
[WORD HISTORY: from Latin VEGETABILIS meaning
'enlivening']

vegetarian [ˌvɛdʒɪ'tɛərɪən] **vegetarians**
NOUN
a person who does not eat meat, poultry, or fish

vegetarianism NOUN

vegetation [ˌvɛdʒɪ'teɪʃən] NOUN
Vegetation is the plants in a particular area.

vehement ['viːɪmənt] ADJECTIVE
Someone who is vehement has strong feelings or
opinions and expresses them forcefully. *e.g. He
wrote a letter of vehement protest.*
vehemence NOUN, **vehemently** ADVERB

vehicle ['viːɪkᵊl] **vehicles** NOUN
1 a machine, often with an engine, used for
transporting people or goods
2 something used to achieve a particular purpose
or as a means of expression *e.g. The play seemed
an ideal vehicle for his music.*
vehicular ADJECTIVE

veil [veɪl] **veils** NOUN
a piece of thin, soft cloth that women sometimes
wear over their heads

vein [veɪn] **veins** NOUN
1 Your veins are the tubes in your body through
which your blood flows to your heart.
2 Veins are the thin lines on leaves or on insects'
wings.
3 A vein of a metal or a mineral is a layer of it in
rock.
4 Something that is in a particular vein is in that
style or mood. *e.g. in a more serious vein*

veld [fɛlt] NOUN
The veld is flat high grassland in Southern Africa.

veldskoen ['fɛlt,skʊn] **veldskoens** NOUN
In South Africa, a veldskoen is a tough ankle-
length boot.

velocity [vɪ'lɒsɪti] NOUN; TECHNICAL
Velocity is the speed at which something is
moving in a particular direction.

velvet ['vɛlvɪt] NOUN
Velvet is a very soft material which has a thick
layer of fine short threads on one side.
velvety ADJECTIVE
[WORD HISTORY: from Latin VILLUS meaning 'shaggy
hair']

vendetta [vɛn'dɛtə] **vendettas** NOUN
a long-lasting bitter quarrel which results in
people trying to harm each other

vending machine ['vɛndɪŋ] **vending
machines** NOUN
a machine which provides things such as drinks
or sweets when you put money in it

vendor ['vɛndɔː] **vendors** NOUN
a person who sells something

veneer [vɪ'nɪə] NOUN
1 You can refer to a superficial quality that
someone has as a veneer of that quality. *e.g. a
veneer of calm*

v

2 Veneer is a thin layer of wood or plastic used to cover a surface.

venerable ['vɛnərəbəl] ADJECTIVE
1 A venerable person is someone you treat with respect because they are old and wise.
2 Something that is venerable is impressive because it is old or important historically.

venerate ['vɛnəˌreɪt] **venerates, venerating, venerated** VERB; FORMAL
If you venerate someone, you feel great respect for them.
veneration NOUN

vengeance ['vɛndʒəns] NOUN
1 Vengeance is the act of harming someone because they have harmed you.
> PHRASE
2 If something happens **with a vengeance**, it happens to a much greater extent than was expected. *e.g. It began to rain again with a vengeance.*

venison ['vɛnzən] NOUN
Venison is the meat from a deer.
[WORD HISTORY: from Latin VENATIO meaning 'hunting']

venom ['vɛnəm] NOUN
1 The venom of a snake, scorpion, or spider is its poison.
2 Venom is a feeling of great bitterness or spitefulness towards someone. *e.g. He was glaring at me with venom.*
venomous ADJECTIVE

vent [vɛnt] **vents, venting, vented** NOUN
1 a hole in something through which gases and smoke can escape and fresh air can enter *e.g. air vents*
> VERB
2 If you vent strong feelings, you express them. *e.g. She wanted to vent her anger upon me.*
> PHRASE
3 If you **give vent** to strong feelings, you express them. *e.g. Pamela gave vent to a lot of bitterness.*

ventilate ['vɛntɪˌleɪt] **ventilates, ventilating, ventilated** VERB
To ventilate a room means to allow fresh air into it.
ventilated ADJECTIVE

ventilation [ˌvɛntɪ'leɪʃən] NOUN
1 Ventilation is the process of breathing air in and out of the lungs.
2 A ventilation system supplies fresh air into a building.

ventilator ['vɛntɪˌleɪtə] **ventilators** NOUN
a machine that helps people breathe when they cannot breathe naturally, for example if they are very ill

ventriloquist [vɛn'trɪləkwɪst] **ventriloquists** NOUN
an entertainer who can speak without moving their lips so that the words seem to come from a dummy
ventriloquism NOUN
[WORD HISTORY: from Latin VENTER meaning 'belly' and LOQUI meaning 'to speak']

venture ['vɛntʃə] **ventures, venturing, ventured** NOUN
1 something new which involves the risk of failure or of losing money *e.g. a successful venture in television films*
> VERB
2 If you venture something such as an opinion, you say it cautiously or hesitantly because you are afraid it might be foolish or wrong. *e.g. I would not venture to agree.*
3 If you venture somewhere that might be dangerous, you go there.

venue ['vɛnjuː] **venues** NOUN
The venue for an event is the place where it will happen.

Venus ['viːnəs] NOUN
Venus is the planet in the solar system which is second from the sun.
[WORD HISTORY: named after the Roman goddess of love]

veranda [və'rændə] **verandas**; also spelt **verandah** NOUN
a platform with a roof that is attached to an outside wall of a house at ground level

verb [vɜːb] **verbs** NOUN
In grammar, a verb is a word that expresses actions and states, for example 'be', 'become', 'take', and 'run'.

verbal ['vɜːbəl] ADJECTIVE
1 You use 'verbal' to describe things connected with words and their use. *e.g. verbal attacks on referees*
2 'Verbal' describes things which are spoken rather than written *e.g. a verbal agreement*
verbally ADVERB

verdict ['vɜːdɪkt] **verdicts** NOUN
1 In a law court, a verdict is the decision which states whether a prisoner is guilty or not guilty.
2 If you give a verdict on something, you give your opinion after thinking about it.
● THESAURUS
conclusion: *I've come to the conclusion that she's lying.*
decision: *The editor's decision is final.*

finding: *The court announced its findings.*
judgment: *My judgment is that things are going to get worse.*
opinion: *You should seek a medical opinion.*

verge [vɜːdʒ] **verges, verging, verged** NOUN
1 The verge of a road is the narrow strip of grassy ground at the side.

> PHRASE

2 If you are **on the verge** of something, you are going to do it soon or it is likely to happen soon. *e.g. on the verge of crying*

> VERB

3 Something that verges on something else is almost the same as it. *e.g. dark blue that verged on purple*

verify [ˈvɛrɪˌfaɪ] **verifies, verifying, verified** VERB
If you verify something, you check that it is true. *e.g. None of his statements could be verified.*
verifiable ADJECTIVE, **verification** NOUN

veritable [ˈvɛrɪtəbəl] ADJECTIVE
You use 'veritable' to emphasize that something is really true, even if it seems as if you are exaggerating. *e.g. a veritable jungle of shops*

vermin [ˈvɜːmɪn] PLURAL NOUN
Vermin are small animals or insects, such as rats and cockroaches, which carry disease and damage crops.

vernacular [vəˈnækjʊlə] **vernaculars** NOUN
The vernacular of a particular country or district is the language widely spoken there.

verruca [vɛˈruːkə] **verrucas** NOUN
a small hard infectious growth rather like a wart, occurring on the sole of the foot

versatile [ˈvɜːsəˌtaɪl] ADJECTIVE
If someone is versatile, they have many different skills.
versatility NOUN

verse [vɜːs] **verses** NOUN
1 Verse is another word for poetry.
2 one part of a poem, song, or chapter of the Bible

versed [vɜːst] ADJECTIVE
If you are versed in something, you know a lot about it.

version [ˈvɜːʃən] **versions** NOUN
1 A version of something is a form of it in which some details are different from earlier or later forms. *e.g. a cheaper version of the aircraft*
2 Someone's version of an event is their personal description of what happened.

versus [ˈvɜːsəs] PREPOSITION
'Versus' is used to indicate that two people or

teams are competing against each other

vertebra [ˈvɜːtɪbrə] **vertebrae** NOUN
Vertebrae are the small bones which form a person's or animal's backbone.

vertebrate [ˈvɜːtɪˌbreɪt] **vertebrates** NOUN
(SCIENCE) Vertebrates are any creatures which have a backbone.

vertex [ˈvɜːtɛks] **vertexes** or **vertices** NOUN
(MATHS) The vertex of something such as a triangle or pyramid is the point opposite the base.

vertical [ˈvɜːtɪkəl] ADJECTIVE
(MATHS) Something that is vertical points straight up and forms a ninety-degree angle with the surface on which it stands.
vertically ADVERB

vertigo [ˈvɜːtɪˌgəʊ] NOUN
Vertigo is a feeling of dizziness caused by looking down from a high place.

verve [vɜːv] NOUN
Verve is lively and forceful enthusiasm.

very [ˈvɛrɪ] ADVERB
1 to a great degree *e.g. very bad dreams*

● THESAURUS

deeply: *I was deeply sorry to hear about your loss.*
extremely: *My mobile phone is extremely useful.*
greatly: *I was greatly relieved when he finally arrived.*
highly: *Mr Singh was a highly successful salesman.*
really: *I know her really well.*
terribly: *I'm terribly sorry to bother you.*

> ADJECTIVE

2 'Very' is used before words to emphasize them *the very end of the book*

> PHRASE

3 You use **not very** to mean that something is the case only to a small degree. *e.g. You're not very like your sister.*

vessel [ˈvɛsəl] **vessels** NOUN
1 a ship or large boat

2 LITERARY
any bowl or container in which a liquid can be kept

3 (SCIENCE) a thin tube along which liquids such as blood or sap move in animals and plants

vest [vɛst] **vests** NOUN
a piece of underwear worn for warmth on the top half of the body

vestige [ˈvɛstɪdʒ] **vestiges** NOUN; FORMAL
If there is not a vestige of something, then there is not even a little of it left. *e.g. They have a vestige of strength left.*

vestry [ˈvɛstrɪ] **vestries** NOUN
The vestry is the part of the church building

v

where a priest or minister changes into their official clothes.

vet [vɛt] **vets, vetting, vetted** NOUN

1 a doctor for animals

> VERB

2 If you vet someone or something, you check them carefully to see if they are acceptable. *e.g. He refused to let them vet his speeches.*

veteran ['vɛtərən] **veterans** NOUN

1 someone who has served in the armed forces, particularly during a war

2 someone who has been involved in a particular activity for a long time *e.g. a veteran of 25 political campaigns*

veterinary ['vɛtərɪnərɪ] ADJECTIVE

'Veterinary' is used to describe the work of a vet and the medical treatment of animals

[WORD HISTORY: from Latin VETERINAE meaning 'animals used for pulling carts and ploughs']

veterinary surgeon veterinary surgeons NOUN the same as a **vet**

veto ['viːtəʊ] **vetoes, vetoing, vetoed** VERB

1 If someone in authority vetoes something, they say no to it.

● THESAURUS

ban: *The authorities have banned the advertisement.*
forbid: *Most airlines forbid the use of mobile phones on their planes.*
prohibit: *The government intends to prohibit all trade with the country.*

> NOUN

2 Veto is the right that someone in authority has to say no to something. *e.g. Dr Baker has the power of veto.*

● THESAURUS

ban: *the arms ban on the Bosnian government*
prohibition: *a prohibition on nuclear testing*

vexed [vɛkst] ADJECTIVE

If you are vexed, you are annoyed, worried, or puzzled.

VHF NOUN

VHF is a range of high radio frequencies. VHF is an abbreviation for 'very high frequency'.

via ['vaɪə] PREPOSITION

1 If you go to one place via another, you travel through that place to get to your destination. *e.g. He drove directly from Bonn via Paris.*

2 Via also means done or achieved by making use of a particular thing or person. *e.g. to follow proceedings via newspapers or television*

viable ['vaɪəbəl] ADJECTIVE

Something that is viable is capable of doing what it is intended to do without extra help or financial

support. *e.g. a viable business*
viability NOUN

viaduct ['vaɪəˌdʌkt] **viaducts** NOUN

a long high bridge that carries a road or railway across a valley

[WORD HISTORY: from Latin VIA meaning 'road' and DUCERE meaning 'to bring']

vibrant ['vaɪbrənt] ADJECTIVE

Something or someone that is vibrant is full of life, energy, and enthusiasm.

vibrantly ADVERB, **vibrancy** NOUN

vibrate [vaɪ'breɪt] **vibrates, vibrating, vibrated** VERB

If something vibrates, it moves a tiny amount backwards and forwards very quickly.

vibration NOUN

vicar ['vɪkə] **vicars** NOUN

a priest in the Church of England

vicarage ['vɪkərɪdʒ] **vicarages** NOUN

a house where a vicar lives

vice [vaɪs] **vices** NOUN

1 a serious moral fault in someone's character, such as greed, or a weakness, such as smoking

2 Vice is criminal activities connected with prostitution and pornography.

3 a tool with a pair of jaws that hold an object tightly while it is being worked on

vice- PREFIX

'Vice-' is used before a title or position to show that the holder is the deputy of the person with that title or position *e.g. vice-president*

viceregal [,vaɪs'riːgəl] ADJECTIVE

1 of or concerning a viceroy

2 In Australia and New Zealand, viceregal means of or concerning a governor or governor-general.

viceroy ['vaɪsrɔɪ] **viceroys** NOUN

A viceroy is someone who has been appointed to govern a place as a representative of a monarch.

vice versa ['vaɪsɪ vɜːsə]

'Vice versa' is used to indicate that the reverse of what you have said is also true *e.g. Wives criticize their husbands, and vice versa.*

vicinity [vɪ'sɪnɪtɪ] NOUN

If something is in the vicinity of a place, it is in the surrounding or nearby area.

vicious ['vɪʃəs] ADJECTIVE

cruel and violent

viciously ADVERB, **viciousness** NOUN

victim ['vɪktɪm] **victims** NOUN

someone who has been harmed or injured by someone or something

victor ['vɪktə] **victors** NOUN

The victor in a fight or contest is the person who wins.

Victorian [vɪk'tɔːrɪən] ADJECTIVE

  1 Victorian describes things that happened or were made during the reign of Queen Victoria.

  2 Victorian also describes people or things connected with the state of Victoria in Australia.

victory ['vɪktərɪ] **victories** NOUN

a success in a battle or competition

victorious ADJECTIVE

⬤ THESAURUS

  laurels: *a former British champion took the laurels in this event*

  success: *league and cup successes*

  superiority: *United Nations air forces won air superiority.*

  triumph: *last year's Republican triumph in the elections*

  win: *eight wins in nine games*

  <<OPPOSITE defeat

video ['vɪdɪ,əʊ] **videos, videoing, videoed** NOUN

  1 Video is the recording and showing of films and events using a video recorder, video tape, and a television set.

  2 a sound and picture recording which can be played back on a television set

  3 a video recorder

  > VERB

  4 If you video something, you record it on magnetic tape for later viewing.

video recorder **video recorders** NOUN

A video recorder or video cassette recorder is a machine for recording and playing back programmes from television.

vie [vaɪ] **vies, vying, vied** VERB; FORMAL

If you vie with someone, you compete to do something sooner than or better than they do.

Vietnamese [,vjɛtnə'miːz] ADJECTIVE

  1 belonging or relating to Vietnam

  > NOUN

  2 someone who comes from Vietnam

  3 Vietnamese is the main language spoken in Vietnam.

view [vjuː] **views, viewing, viewed** NOUN

  1 Your views are your personal opinions. *e.g. his political views*

⬤ THESAURUS

  attitude: *other people's attitudes towards you*

  belief: *people's beliefs about crime*

  conviction: *a firm conviction that things have improved*

  feeling: *It is my feeling that Klein is right.*

  opinion: *a favourable opinion of our neighbours*

  point of view: *an unusual point of view on the subject*

  2 everything you can see from a particular place

⬤ THESAURUS

  aspect: *the Yorkshire hills which give the cottage a lovely aspect*

  landscape: *Arizona's desert landscape.* **panorama:** *a panorama of fertile valleys*

  perspective: *the aerial perspective of St Paul's Cathedral*

  scene: *Wright surveyed the scene from his chosen seat.*

  spectacle: *a sweeping spectacle of rugged peaks*

  > VERB

  3 If you view something in a particular way, you think of it in that way. *e.g. They viewed me with contempt.*

⬤ THESAURUS

  consider: *We consider them to be our friends.*

  deem: formal *His ideas were deemed unacceptable.*

  judge: *His work was judged unsatisfactory.*

  regard: *They regard the tax as unfair.*

  > PHRASE

  4 You use **in view of** to specify the main fact or event influencing your actions or opinions. *e.g. He wore a lighter suit in view of the heat.*

  5 If something is **on view**, it is being shown or exhibited to the public.

viewer ['vjuːə] **viewers** NOUN

Viewers are the people who watch television.

viewpoint ['vjuː,pɔɪnt] **viewpoints** NOUN

  1 Your viewpoint is your attitude towards something.

⬤ THESAURUS

  attitude: *other people's attitudes towards you*

  belief: *people's beliefs about crime*

  conviction: *a very personal, political conviction*

  feeling: *What are your feelings on this matter?*

  opinion: *a favourable opinion of our neighbours*

  point of view: *an unusual point of view on the subject*

  2 a place from which you get a good view of an area or event

vigil ['vɪdʒɪl] **vigils** NOUN

a period of time, especially at night, when you stay quietly in one place, for example because you are making a political protest or praying

vigilant ['vɪdʒɪlənt] ADJECTIVE

careful and alert to danger or trouble

vigilante [,vɪdʒɪ'læntɪ] **vigilantes** NOUN

Vigilantes are unofficially organized groups of people who try to protect their community and catch and punish criminals.

vigorous ['vɪgərəs] ADJECTIVE

energetic or enthusiastic

vigorously ADVERB, **vigour** NOUN

V

Viking ['vaɪkɪŋ] **Vikings** NOUN
The Vikings were seamen from Scandinavia who attacked villages in parts of north-western Europe from the 8th to the 11th centuries.

vile [vaɪl] **viler, vilest** ADJECTIVE
unpleasant or disgusting *e.g. a vile accusation... a vile smell*

villa ['vɪlə] **villas** NOUN
a house, especially a pleasant holiday home in a country with a warm climate

village ['vɪlɪdʒ] **villages** NOUN
a collection of houses and other buildings in the countryside
villager NOUN

villain ['vɪlən] **villains** NOUN
someone who harms others or breaks the law
villainous ADJECTIVE, **villainy** NOUN

vindicate ['vɪndɪˌkeɪt] **vindicates, vindicating, vindicated** VERB; FORMAL
If someone is vindicated, their views or ideas are proved to be right. *e.g. My friend's instincts have been vindicated.*

vindictive [vɪn'dɪktɪv] ADJECTIVE
Someone who is vindictive is deliberately hurtful towards someone, often as an act of revenge.
vindictiveness NOUN

vine [vaɪn] **vines** NOUN
a trailing or climbing plant which winds itself around and over a support, especially one which produces grapes

vinegar ['vɪnɪgə] NOUN
Vinegar is a sharp-tasting liquid made from sour wine, beer, or cider, which is used for salad dressing.
vinegary ADJECTIVE
[WORD HISTORY: from French VIN meaning 'wine' and AIGRE meaning 'sour']

vineyard ['vɪnjəd] **vineyards** NOUN
an area of land where grapes are grown

vintage ['vɪntɪdʒ] **vintages** ADJECTIVE
1 A vintage wine is a good quality wine which has been stored for a number of years to improve its quality.
2 Vintage describes something which is the best or most typical of its kind. *e.g. a vintage guitar*
3 A vintage car is one made between 1918 and 1930.
> NOUN
4 a grape harvest of one particular year and the wine produced from it

vinyl ['vaɪnɪl] NOUN
Vinyl is a strong plastic used to make things such as furniture and floor coverings.

viola [vɪ'əʊlə] **violas** NOUN
a musical instrument like a violin, but larger and with a lower pitch

violate ['vaɪəˌleɪt] **violates, violating, violated** VERB
1 If you violate an agreement, law, or promise, you break it.
2 If you violate someone's peace or privacy, you disturb it.
3 If you violate a place, especially a holy place, you treat it with disrespect or violence.
violation NOUN

violence ['vaɪələns] NOUN
1 Violence is behaviour which is intended to hurt or kill people.
⬤ THESAURUS
bloodshed: *The government must avoid further bloodshed.*
brutality: *the brutality of the war in Vietnam*
cruelty: *Human beings are capable of such cruelty to each other.*
force: *If you use any force, I shall inform the police.*
savagery: *acts of vicious savagery*
terrorism: *political terrorism in the 19th century*

2 If you do or say something with violence, you use a lot of energy in doing or saying it, often because you are angry.
⬤ THESAURUS
fervour: *views he had put forward with fervour*
force: *She expressed her feelings with some force.*
harshness: *the harshness of her words*
intensity: *His voice hoarsened with intensity.*
severity: *the severity of her scoldings*
vehemence: *Tweed was taken aback by her vehemence.*

violent ['vaɪələnt] ADJECTIVE
1 If someone is violent, they try to hurt or kill people.
⬤ THESAURUS
bloodthirsty: *a bloodthirsty monster*
brutal: *a brutal crime*
cruel: *He is cruel towards animals.*
murderous: *a murderous bank-robber*
savage: *savage warriors*
vicious: *He was a cruel and vicious man.*
<<OPPOSITE gentle

2 A violent event happens unexpectedly and with great force.
⬤ THESAURUS
powerful: *He was caught by a powerful blow.*
raging: *a raging flood*
rough: *A wooden ship sank in rough seas.*
strong: *strong winds and rain*
turbulent: *the turbulent events of the century*
wild: *the wild gales sweeping up from the channel*

3 Something that is violent is said, felt, or done with great force.
violently ADVERB

THESAURUS
acute: *pain which grew more and more acute*
furious: *a furious row*
intense: *a look of intense dislike*
powerful: *a powerful backlash against the government*
severe: *a severe emotional shock*
strong: *strong words*

violet ['vaɪəlɪt] **violets** NOUN
1 a plant with dark purple flowers

> NOUN OR ADJECTIVE
2 bluish purple

violin [ˌvaɪə'lɪn] **violins** NOUN
a musical instrument with four strings that is held under the chin and played with a bow
violinist NOUN

VIP VIPs NOUN
VIPs are famous or important people. VIP is an abbreviation for 'very important person'.

viper ['vaɪpə] **vipers** NOUN
Vipers are types of poisonous snakes.

virgin ['vɜːdʒɪn] **virgins** NOUN
1 someone who has never had sexual intercourse

> PROPER NOUN
2 The Virgin, or the Blessed Virgin, is a name given to Mary, the mother of Jesus Christ.

> ADJECTIVE
3 Something that is virgin is fresh and unused. *e.g. virgin land*
virginity NOUN

virginal ['vɜːdʒɪnəl] **virginals** ADJECTIVE
1 Someone who is virginal looks young and innocent.

2 Something that is virginal is fresh and clean and looks as if it has never been used.

> NOUN
3 a keyboard instrument popular in the 16th and 17th centuries

Virgo ['vɜːgəʊ] NOUN
Virgo is the sixth sign of the zodiac, represented by a girl. People born between August 23rd and September 22nd are born under this sign.

virile ['vɪraɪl] ADJECTIVE
A virile man has all the qualities that a man is traditionally expected to have, such as strength and sexuality.
virility NOUN

virtual ['vɜːtʃʊəl] ADJECTIVE
Virtual means that something has all the characteristics of a particular thing, but it is not formally recognized as being that thing. *e.g. The country is in a virtual state of war.*
virtually ADVERB

virtual reality NOUN
Virtual reality is a situation or setting that has been created by a computer and that looks real to the person using it.

virtue ['vɜːtjuː] **virtues** NOUN
1 Virtue is thinking and doing what is morally right and avoiding what is wrong.

THESAURUS
goodness: *He has faith in human goodness.*
integrity: *He was praised for his fairness and integrity.*
morality: *standards of morality and justice in society*

2 a good quality in someone's character

3 A virtue of something is an advantage. *e.g. the virtue of neatness*

THESAURUS
advantage: *the advantages of the new system*
asset: *The one asset the job provided was contacts.*
attribute: *a player with every attribute you could want*
merit: *the merits of various football teams*
plus: informal *The nutrients in milk have pluses and minuses.*
strength: *the strengths and weaknesses of our position*

> A FORMAL PHRASE
4 By virtue of means because of *e.g. The article stuck in my mind by virtue of one detail.*

THESAURUS
as a result of: *People will feel better as a result of their efforts.*
because of: *She was promoted because of her experience.*
by dint of: *He succeeds by dint of hard work.*
on account of: *The city is popular with tourists on account of its many museums.*
thanks to: *Thanks to recent research, new treatments are available.*

virtuoso [ˌvɜːtjʊ'əʊzəʊ] **virtuosos** or **virtuosi** NOUN
someone who is exceptionally good at something, particularly playing a musical instrument
[WORD HISTORY: from Italian VIRTUOSO meaning 'skilled']

virtuous ['vɜːtʃʊəs] ADJECTIVE
behaving with or showing moral virtue

virus ['vaɪrəs] **viruses** NOUN
1 a kind of germ that can cause disease

2 (ICT) a program that alters or damages the information stored in a computer system

viral ADJECTIVE

visa ['viːzə] **visas** NOUN
an official stamp, usually put in your passport, that allows you to visit a particular country

viscount ['vaɪkaʊnt] **viscounts** NOUN
a British nobleman
viscountess NOUN

Vishnu ['vɪʃnuː] PROPER NOUN
Vishnu is a Hindu god and is one of the Trimurti.

visibility [ˌvɪzɪˈbɪlɪtɪ] NOUN
You use 'visibility' to say how far or how clearly you can see in particular weather conditions.

visible ['vɪzɪbəl] ADJECTIVE
1 able to be seen
● THESAURUS
clear: *the clearest pictures ever of Pluto*
conspicuous: *He felt more conspicuous than he'd have liked.*
distinguishable: *colours just distinguishable in the dark*
in sight: *There wasn't another vehicle in sight.*
observable: *the observable part of the Universe*
perceptible: *Daniel gave a barely perceptible nod.*
<<OPPOSITE *invisible*

2 noticeable or evident *e.g. There was little visible excitement.*
visibly ADVERB
● THESAURUS
apparent: *There is no apparent reason for the crime.*
evident: *He ate with evident enjoyment.*
manifest: *his manifest enthusiasm*
noticeable: *subtle but noticeable changes*
obvious: *There are obvious dangers.*
plain: *It is plain a mistake has been made.*

vision ['vɪʒən] **visions** NOUN
1 Vision is the ability to see clearly.

2 a mental picture, in which you imagine how things might be different *e.g. the vision of a possible future*
● THESAURUS
conception: *my conception of a garden*
daydream: *He learned to escape into daydreams.*
dream: *his dream of becoming a pilot*
fantasy: *fantasies of romance and true love*
ideal: *your ideal of a holiday*
image: *an image in your mind of what you are looking for*

3 Vision is also imaginative insight. *e.g. a total lack of vision and imagination*
● THESAURUS
foresight: *They had the foresight to invest in technology.*
imagination: *He had the imagination to foresee dangers.*

insight: *the development of insight and understanding*
intuition: *Her intuition told her something was wrong.*

4 an unusual experience that you have, in which you see things that other people cannot see, as a result of madness, divine inspiration, or taking drugs
visionary NOUN OR ADJECTIVE
● THESAURUS
apparition: *One of the women was the apparition he had seen.*
hallucination: *The drug can cause hallucinations.*
illusion: *Perhaps the footprint was an illusion.*
mirage: *The girl was a mirage, created by his troubled mind.*
phantom: *People claimed to have seen the phantom.*
spectre: *a spectre from the other world*

visit ['vɪzɪt] **visits, visiting, visited** VERB
1 If you visit someone, you go to see them and spend time with them.
● THESAURUS
call on: *Don't hesitate to call on me.*
go to see: *I'll go to see him in the hospital.*
look up: *She looked up friends she had not seen for a while.*

2 If you visit a place, you go to see it.
> NOUN
3 a trip to see a person or place
visitor NOUN
● THESAURUS
call: *He decided to pay a call on Tommy.*
stay: *An experienced guide is provided during your stay.*
stop: *The last stop in Mr Cook's tour was Paris.*

visor ['vaɪzə] **visors** NOUN
a transparent movable shield attached to a helmet, which can be pulled down to protect the eyes or face

visual ['vɪʒʊəl] ADJECTIVE
relating to sight *e.g. visual problems*

visualize ['vɪʒʊəˌlaɪz] **visualizes, visualizing, visualized**; also spelt **visualise** VERB
If you visualize something, you form a mental picture of it.

vital ['vaɪtəl] ADJECTIVE
1 necessary or very important *e.g. vital evidence*
● THESAURUS
central: *He is central to the whole project.*
critical: *This decision will be critical to our future.*
crucial: *the man who played a crucial role in the negotiations*
essential: *It is essential that you see a doctor soon.*

important: *the most important piece of evidence in the case*
indispensable: *an indispensable piece of equipment*
necessary: *the skills necessary for survival*
pivotal: *He played a pivotal role in the match.*

2 energetic, exciting, and full of life *e.g. an active and vital life outside school*
vitally ADVERB

● THESAURUS
active: *an active youngster*
dynamic: *a dynamic and exciting place*
energetic: *She became a shadow of her happy, energetic self.*
lively: *a beautiful, lively young girl*
spirited: *the spirited heroine of this film*
sprightly: *a sprightly old man*
vivacious: *She is vivacious and charming.*

vitality [vaɪˈtælɪtɪ] NOUN
People who have vitality are energetic and lively.

vitamin [ˈvɪtəmɪn] **vitamins** NOUN
(D & T) Vitamins are organic compounds which you need in order to remain healthy. They occur naturally in food.

vitriolic [ˌvɪtrɪˈɒlɪk] ADJECTIVE; FORMAL
Vitriolic language or behaviour is full of bitterness and hate.

vivacious [vɪˈveɪʃəs] ADJECTIVE
A vivacious person is attractively lively and high-spirited.
vivacity NOUN

vivid [ˈvɪvɪd] ADJECTIVE
very bright in colour or clear in detail *e.g. vivid red paint... vivid memories*
vividly ADVERB, **vividness** NOUN

vivisection [ˌvɪvɪˈsɛkʃən] NOUN
Vivisection is the act of cutting open living animals for medical research.

vixen [ˈvɪksən] **vixens** NOUN
a female fox

vocabulary [vəˈkæbjʊlərɪ] **vocabularies** NOUN (ENGLISH)
1 Someone's vocabulary is the total number of words they know in a particular language.
2 The vocabulary of a language is all the words in it.

vocal [ˈvəʊkəl] ADJECTIVE
1 You say that someone is vocal if they express their opinions strongly and openly.
2 (MUSIC) Vocal means involving the use of the human voice, especially in singing
vocalist NOUN **vocally** ADVERB

vocation [vəʊˈkeɪʃən] **vocations** NOUN

1 a strong wish to do a particular job, especially one which involves serving other people
2 a profession or career

vocational [vəʊˈkeɪʃənl] ADJECTIVE
'Vocational' is used to describe the skills needed for a particular job or profession *e.g. vocational training*

vociferous [vəʊˈsɪfərəs] ADJECTIVE; FORMAL
Someone who is vociferous speaks a lot, or loudly, because they want to make a point strongly. *e.g. vociferous critics*
vociferously ADVERB

vodka [ˈvɒdkə] **vodkas** NOUN
a strong clear alcoholic drink which originally came from Russia
[WORD HISTORY: from Russian VODKA meaning 'little water']

vogue [vəʊg] PHRASE
If something is **the vogue** or **in vogue**, it is fashionable and popular. *e.g. Colour photographs became the vogue.*

voice [vɔɪs] **voices, voicing, voiced** NOUN
1 Your voice is the sounds produced by your vocal cords, or the ability to make such sounds.
> VERB
2 If you voice an opinion or an emotion, you say what you think or feel. *e.g. A range of opinions were voiced.*

void [vɔɪd] **voids** NOUN
1 a situation which seems empty because it has no interest or excitement *e.g. Cats fill a very large void in your life.*
2 a large empty hole or space *e.g. His feet dangled in the void.*

volatile [ˈvɒləˌtaɪl] ADJECTIVE
liable to change often and unexpectedly *e.g. The situation at work is volatile.*

volcanic [vɒlˈkænɪk] ADJECTIVE
A volcanic region has many volcanoes or was created by volcanoes.

volcano [vɒlˈkeɪnəʊ] **volcanoes** NOUN
a hill with an opening through which lava, gas, and ash burst out from inside the earth onto the surface
[WORD HISTORY: named after VULCAN, the Roman god of fire]

vole [vəʊl] **voles** NOUN
a small mammal like a mouse with a short tail, which lives in fields and near rivers

volition [vəˈlɪʃən] NOUN; FORMAL
If you do something of your own volition, you do it because you have decided for yourself, without being persuaded by others. *e.g. He attended of his own volition.*

v

volley ['vɒlɪ] **volleys** NOUN

1 A volley of shots or gunfire is a lot of shots fired at the same time.

2 In tennis, a volley is a stroke in which the player hits the ball before it bounces.

volleyball ['vɒlɪˌbɔːl] NOUN

Volleyball is a game in which two teams hit a large ball back and forth over a high net with their hands. The ball is not allowed to bounce on the ground.

volt [vəʊlt] **volts** NOUN

a unit used to measure the force of an electric current

voltage ['vəʊltɪdʒ] **voltages** NOUN

The voltage of an electric current is its force measured in volts.

volume ['vɒljuːm] **volumes** NOUN

1 (MATHS) The volume of something is the amount of space it contains or occupies.

2 The volume of something is also the amount of it that there is. *e.g. a large volume of letters*

3 The volume of a radio, TV, or record player is the strength of the sound that it produces.

4 a book, or one of a series of books

voluminous [və'luːmɪnəs] ADJECTIVE

very large or full in size or quantity *e.g. voluminous skirts*

voluntary ['vɒləntərɪ] ADJECTIVE

1 Voluntary actions are ones that you do because you choose to do them and not because you have been forced to do them.

2 Voluntary work is done by people who are not paid for what they do.

voluntarily ADVERB

volunteer [ˌvɒlən'tɪə] **volunteers, volunteering, volunteered** NOUN

1 someone who does work for which they are not paid *e.g. a volunteer for Greenpeace*

2 someone who chooses to join the armed forces, especially during wartime

> VERB

3 If you volunteer to do something, you offer to do it rather than being forced into it.

4 If you volunteer information, you give it without being asked.

voluptuous [və'lʌptjʊəs] ADJECTIVE

A voluptuous woman has a figure which is considered to be sexually exciting.

voluptuously ADVERB, **voluptuousness** NOUN

vomit ['vɒmɪt] **vomits, vomiting, vomited** VERB

1 If you vomit, food and drink comes back up from your stomach and out through your mouth.

⬤ THESAURUS

be sick: *She was sick in the handbasin.*

bring up: *Certain foods are difficult to bring up.*

chunder: Australian and New Zealand; slang *the time you chundered in the taxi*

heave: *He gasped and heaved and vomited again.*

puke: informal *They got drunk and puked out of the window.*

regurgitate: *swallowing and regurgitating large quantities of water*

> NOUN

2 Vomit is partly digested food and drink that has come back up from someone's stomach and out through their mouth.

voodoo ['vuːduː] NOUN

Voodoo is a form of magic practised in the Caribbean, especially in Haiti.

vote [vəʊt] **votes, voting, voted** NOUN

1 Someone's vote is their choice in an election, or at a meeting where decisions are taken.

2 When a group of people have a vote, they make a decision by allowing each person in the group to say what they would prefer.

⬤ THESAURUS

ballot: *The result of the ballot will be known soon.*

plebiscite: formal *A plebiscite made Hitler the Chancellor.*

polls: *In 1945, Churchill was defeated at the polls.*

referendum: *Estonia planned to hold a referendum on independence.*

3 In an election, the vote is the total number of people who have made their choice. *e.g. the average Liberal vote*

4 If people have the vote, they have the legal right to vote in an election.

> VERB

5 When people vote, they indicate their choice or opinion, usually by writing on a piece of paper or by raising their hand.

⬤ THESAURUS

cast a vote: *90% of those who cast a vote*

go to the polls: *Voters are due to go to the polls on Sunday.*

opt: *The mass of Spaniards opted for democracy.*

return: *Members will be asked to return a vote for or against the motion.*

6 If you vote that a particular thing should happen, you are suggesting it should happen. *e.g. I vote that we all go to Holland.*

voter NOUN

⬤ THESAURUS

propose: *I propose that we all try to get some sleep.*

recommend: *I recommend that he be sent home early.*

suggest: *I suggest we go round the table and introduce ourselves.*

vouch [vaʊtʃ] **vouches, vouching, vouched** VERB

1 If you say that you can vouch for something, you mean that you have evidence from your own experience that it is true or correct.

2 If you say that you can vouch for someone, you mean that you are sure that you can guarantee their good behaviour or support. *e.g. Her employer will vouch for her.*

voucher ['vaʊtʃə] **vouchers** NOUN
a piece of paper that can be used instead of money to pay for something

vow [vaʊ] **vows, vowing, vowed** VERB
1 If you vow to do something, you make a solemn promise to do it. *e.g. He vowed to do better in future.*
> NOUN
2 a solemn promise

vowel ['vaʊəl] **vowels** NOUN
(ENGLISH) a sound made without your tongue touching the roof of your mouth or your teeth, or one of the letters a, e, i, o, u, which represent such sounds

voyage ['vɔɪɪdʒ] **voyages** NOUN
a long journey on a ship or in a spacecraft
voyager NOUN

vulgar ['vʌlgə] ADJECTIVE
1 socially unacceptable or offensive *e.g. vulgar language*
● THESAURUS
coarse: *coarse humour*

crude: *crude pictures*
dirty: *dirty jokes*
indecent: *an indecent suggestion*
rude: *a rude gesture*
uncouth: *that oafish, uncouth person*
<<OPPOSITE *refined*

2 showing a lack of taste or quality *e.g. the most vulgar person who ever existed*
vulgarity NOUN, **vulgarly** ADVERB
● THESAURUS
common: *She could be a little common at times.*
flashy: *flashy clothes*
gaudy: *a gaudy purple-and-orange hat*
tasteless: *a house with tasteless decor*
tawdry: *a tawdry seaside town*
<<OPPOSITE *sophisticated*

vulnerable ['vʌlnərəbᵊl] ADJECTIVE
weak and without protection
vulnerably ADVERB, **vulnerability** NOUN
● THESAURUS
exposed: *The west coast is very exposed to Atlantic winds.*
sensitive: *Most people are highly sensitive to criticism.*
susceptible: *an area that is susceptible to attack*
weak: *He spoke up for the weak and defenceless.*

vulture ['vʌltʃə] **vultures** NOUN
a large bird which lives in hot countries and eats the flesh of dead animals

vying ['vaɪɪŋ] the present participle of **vie**

wacky ['wækɪ] **wackier, wackiest**
ADJECTIVE; INFORMAL
odd or crazy *e.g. wacky clothes*

wad [wɒd] **wads** NOUN
1 A wad of papers or banknotes is a thick bundle of them.
2 A wad of something is a lump of it. *e.g. a wad of cotton wool*

waddle ['wɒdəl] **waddles, waddling, waddled** VERB
When a duck or a fat person waddles, they walk with short, quick steps, swaying slightly from side to side.

waddy ['wɒdɪ] **waddies** NOUN
a heavy, wooden club used by Australian Aborigines as a weapon in war

wade [weɪd] **wades, wading, waded** VERB
1 If you wade through water or mud, you walk slowly through it.
2 If you wade through a book or document, you spend a lot of time and effort reading it because you find it dull or difficult.

wader ['weɪdə] **waders** NOUN
Waders are long waterproof rubber boots worn by fishermen.

wafer ['weɪfə] **wafers** NOUN
1 a thin, crisp, sweet biscuit often eaten with ice cream
2 a thin disc of special bread used in the Christian service of Holy Communion

waffle ['wɒfəl] **waffles, waffling, waffled** VERB
1 When someone waffles, they talk or write a lot without being clear or without saying anything of importance.
> NOUN
2 Waffle is vague and lengthy speech or writing.
3 a thick, crisp pancake with squares marked on it often eaten with syrup poured over it

waft [wɑːft] **wafts, wafting, wafted** VERB
If a sound or scent wafts or is wafted through the air, it moves gently through it.

wag [wæg] **wags, wagging, wagged** VERB
1 When a dog wags its tail, it shakes it repeatedly from side to side.
2 If you wag your finger, you move it repeatedly up and down.

wage [weɪdʒ] **wages, waging, waged** NOUN
1 A wage or wages is the regular payment made to someone each week for the work they do, especially for manual or unskilled work.
> VERB
2 If a person or country wages a campaign or war, they start it and carry it on over a period of time.

wager ['weɪdʒə] **wagers** NOUN
a bet

wagon ['wægən] **wagons**; also spelt **waggon** NOUN
1 a strong four-wheeled vehicle for carrying heavy loads, usually pulled by a horse or tractor
2 Wagons are also the containers for freight pulled by a railway engine.

waif [weɪf] **waifs** NOUN
a young, thin person who looks hungry and homeless

wail [weɪl] **wails, wailing, wailed** VERB
1 To wail is to cry loudly with sorrow or pain.
> NOUN
2 a long, unhappy cry

waist [weɪst] **waists** NOUN
the middle part of your body where it narrows slightly above your hips

waistcoat ['weɪsˌkəʊt] **waistcoats** NOUN
a sleeveless piece of clothing, often worn under a suit or jacket, which buttons up the front

wait [weɪt] **waits, waiting, waited** VERB
1 If you wait, you spend time, usually doing little or nothing, before something happens.

● THESAURUS
linger: *I lingered on for a few days until he arrived.*
pause: *The crowd paused for a minute, wondering what to do next.*
remain: *You'll have to remain in hospital for the time being.*
stand by: *Ships are standing by to evacuate the people.*

stay: *Stay here while I go for help.*

2 If something can wait, it is not urgent and can be dealt with later.

3 If you wait on people in a restaurant, it is your job to serve them food.

> NOUN

4 a period of time before something happens

● THESAURUS

delay: *The accident caused some delay.*
interval: *a long interval when no-one spoke*
pause: *There was a pause before he replied.*

> PHRASE

5 If you **can't wait** to do something, you are very excited and eager to do it.

waiter ['weɪtə] **waiters** NOUN
a man who works in a restaurant, serving people with food and drink

waiting list ['weɪtɪŋ] **waiting lists** NOUN
a list of people who have asked for something which cannot be given to them immediately, for example medical treatment

waitress ['weɪtrɪs] **waitresses** NOUN
a woman who works in a restaurant, serving people with food and drink

waive [weɪv] **waives, waiving, waived**
VERB
If someone waives something such as a rule or a right, they decide not to insist on it being applied.

wake [weɪk] **wakes, waking, woke, woken** VERB
1 When you wake or when something wakes you, you become conscious again after being asleep.

● THESAURUS

awake: *We were awoken by the doorbell.*
come to: *When she came to she found it was raining.*
rouse: *We roused him at seven so he would be on time.*
stir: *She shook him and he started to stir.*
waken: *wakened by the thunder*

> NOUN

2 The wake of a boat or other object moving in water is the track of waves it leaves behind it.

3 a gathering of people who have got together to mourn someone's death

> PHRASE

4 If one thing follows **in the wake of** another, it follows it as a result of it, or in imitation of it. *e.g. a project set up in the wake of last year's riots* **wake up** VERB

5 When you wake up or something wakes you up, you become conscious again after being asleep.

6 If you wake up to a dangerous situation, you become aware of it.

waken ['weɪkən] **wakens, wakening, wakened** VERB; LITERARY
When you waken someone, you wake them up.

walk see page 978 for Word Web

walkabout ['wɔːkəˌbaʊt] **walkabouts**
NOUN
1 an informal walk amongst crowds in a public place by royalty or by some other well-known person

2 Walkabout is when an Australian Aborigine goes off to live and wander in the bush for a period of time.

walker ['wɔːkə] **walkers** NOUN
a person who walks, especially for pleasure or to keep fit

walking stick ['wɔːkɪŋ] **walking sticks**
NOUN
a wooden stick which people can lean on while walking

Walkman ['wɔːkmən] NOUN; TRADEMARK
a small cassette player with lightweight headphones, which people carry around so that they can listen to music while they are doing something like walking

walk of life walks of life NOUN
The walk of life that you come from is the position you have in society and the kind of job you have.

walkover ['wɔːkˌəʊvə] **walkovers** NOUN;
INFORMAL
a very easy victory in a competition or contest

walkway ['wɔːkˌweɪ] **walkways** NOUN
a passage between two buildings for people to walk along

wall [wɔːl] **walls** NOUN
1 one of the vertical sides of a building or a room

2 a long, narrow vertical structure made of stone or brick that surrounds or divides an area of land

3 a lining or membrane enclosing a bodily cavity or structure *e.g. the wall of the womb*

wallaby ['wɒləbɪ] **wallabies** NOUN
an animal like a small kangaroo
[WORD HISTORY: from WOLABA, an Australian Aboriginal word]

wallaroo [ˌwɒləˈruː] **wallaroos** NOUN
a large, stocky kangaroo that lives in rocky or mountainous regions of Australia

wallet ['wɒlɪt] **wallets** NOUN
a small, flat case made of leather or plastic, used for keeping paper money and sometimes credit cards

wallop ['wɒləp] **wallops, walloping, walloped** VERB; INFORMAL

1 VERB

to go on foot *eg eg*: *I walked slowly along the road.*

● THESAURUS

amble: *We ambled along the beach hand in hand.*

hike: *They hiked along a remote trail.*

lurch: *He lurched around the room as if he was drunk.*

march: *She marched into the office and demanded to see the manager.*

mince: *drag artists mincing around the stage in tight dresses and high heels*

flounce: *She flounced out of the room in a huff.*

pace: *As he waited, he paced nervously around the room.*

plod: *He plodded about after me, looking bored.*

ramble: *a relaxing holiday spent rambling over the fells*

reel: *He lost his balance and reeled back.*

saunter: *He was sauntering along as if he had all the time in the world.*

stagger: *He staggered home from the pub every night.*

stalk: *He stalked out of the meeting, slamming the door.*

stamp: *"I'm leaving!" he shouted as he stamped out of the room*

step: *I stepped carefully over the piles of rubbish.*

stride: *He turned abruptly and strode off down the corridor.*

stroll: *They strolled down the High Street, looking in shop windows.*

stumble: *I stumbled into the phone box and dialled 999.*

tiptoe: *She slipped out of bed and tiptoed to the window.*

toddle: *My daughter toddles around after me wherever I go.*

tooter: *I had to totter around on crutches for six weeks.*

tramp: *They spent all day tramping through the snow.*

tread: *She trod carefully across the grass.*

trek: *This year we're going trekking in Nepal.*

trudge: *We had to trudge all the way back up the hill.*

wander: *Khachi was wandering aimlessly about in the garden.*

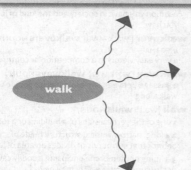

walk

2 NOUN

a journey made by walking *eg*: *We'll have a quick walk while it's fine.*

● THESAURUS

hike: *a long hike in the country*

march: *a day's march north of their objective*

ramble: *They went for a ramble through the woods.*

stroll: *After dinner we took a stroll around the city.*

trek: *He's on a trek across the Antarctic.*

3 NOUN

the way someone moves when walking *eg*: *Despite his gangling walk he was a good dancer.*

● THESAURUS

carriage: *her regal carriage*

gait: *an awkward gait*

pace: *moving at a brisk pace down the road*

stride: *He lengthened his stride to catch up with her.*

If you wallop someone, you hit them very hard.

wallow ['wɒləʊ] **wallows, wallowing, wallowed** VERB

1 If you wallow in an unpleasant feeling or situation, you allow it to continue longer than is reasonable or necessary because you are getting a kind of enjoyment from it. *e.g. We're wallowing in misery.*

2 When an animal wallows in mud or water, it lies or rolls about in it slowly for pleasure.

wallpaper ['wɔːl,peɪpə] **wallpapers** NOUN
Wallpaper is thick coloured or patterned paper for pasting onto the walls of rooms in order to decorate them.

walnut ['wɔːl,nʌt] **walnuts** NOUN

1 an edible nut with a wrinkled shape and a hard, round, light-brown shell

2 Walnut is wood from the walnut tree which is often used for making expensive furniture.
[WORD HISTORY: from Old English WALH-HNUTU meaning 'foreign nut']

walrus ['wɔːlrəs] **walruses** NOUN
an animal which lives in the sea and which looks like a large seal with a tough skin, coarse whiskers, and two tusks

waltz [wɔːls] **waltzes, waltzing, waltzed** NOUN

1 a dance which has a rhythm of three beats to the bar

> VERB

2 If you waltz with someone, you dance a waltz with them.

3 INFORMAL
If you waltz somewhere, you walk there in a relaxed and confident way.
[WORD HISTORY: from Old German WALZEN meaning 'to revolve']

wan [wɒn] ADJECTIVE
pale and tired-looking

wand [wɒnd] **wands** NOUN
a long, thin rod that magicians wave when they are performing tricks and magic

wander ['wɒndə] **wanders, wandering, wandered** VERB

1 If you wander in a place, you walk around in a casual way.

◉ THESAURUS
cruise: *A police car cruised by.*
drift: *The balloon drifted slowly over the countryside.*
ramble: *freedom to ramble across the moors*
range: *They range widely in search of food.*
roam: *Barefoot children roamed the streets.*
stroll: *We strolled down the street, looking at the shops.*

2 If your mind wanders or your thoughts wander, you lose concentration and start thinking about other things.
wanderer NOUN

wane [weɪn] **wanes, waning, waned** VERB
If a condition, attitude, or emotion wanes, it becomes gradually weaker.

wangle ['wæŋg°l] **wangles, wangling, wangled** VERB; INFORMAL
If you wangle something that you want, you manage to get it by being crafty or persuasive.

want [wɒnt] **wants, wanting, wanted** VERB

1 If you want something, you feel a desire to have it.

◉ THESAURUS
covet: *He coveted his boss's job.*
crave: *Sometimes she still craved chocolate.*
desire: *He could make them do whatever he desired.*
wish: *I don't wish to know that.*

2 If something is wanted, it is needed or needs to be done.

◉ THESAURUS
be deficient in: *Their diet was deficient in vitamins.*
demand: *The task of reconstruction demanded much sacrifice.*
lack: *training to give him the skills he lacked*
need: *My car needs servicing.*
require: *He knows exactly what is required of him.*

3 If someone is wanted, the police are searching for them. *e.g. John was wanted for fraud.*

> NOUN

4 FORMAL
A want of something is a lack of it.

◉ THESAURUS
absence: *a complete absence of evidence*
deficiency: *They did blood tests for signs of vitamin deficiency.*
lack: *He got the job in spite of his lack of experience.*
scarcity: *an increasing scarcity of water*
shortage: *A shortage of funds is holding them back.*

<<OPPOSITE *abundance*

wanting ['wɒntɪŋ] ADJECTIVE
If you find something wanting or if it proves wanting, it is not as good in some way as you think it should be.

wanton ['wɒntən] ADJECTIVE
A wanton action deliberately causes unnecessary harm or waste. *e.g. wanton destruction*

war [wɔː] **wars, warring, warred** NOUN

1 a period of fighting between countries or states when weapons are used and many people may be killed

w

THESAURUS
combat: *men who died in combat*
conflict: *The conflict is bound to intensify.*
fighting: *He was killed in the fighting which followed the treaty.*
hostilities: *in case hostilities break out*
strife: *The country was torn with strife.*
warfare: *chemical warfare*
<<OPPOSITE *peace*

2 a competition between groups of people, or a campaign against something *e.g. a trade war... the war against crime*

> VERB
3 When two countries war with each other, they are fighting a war against each other.
warring ADJECTIVE

THESAURUS
battle: *Thousands of people battled with the police.*
clash: *The two armies clashed at first light.*
combat: *measures to combat smuggling*
fight: *The tribe fought with its rivals.*

waratah [ˌwɒrəˈtɑː] **waratahs** NOUN
an Australian shrub with dark green leaves and large clusters of crimson flowers

warble [ˈwɔːbəl] **warbles, warbling, warbled** VERB
When a bird warbles, it sings pleasantly with high notes.

ward [wɔːd] **wards, warding, warded**
NOUN
1 a room in a hospital which has beds for several people who need similar treatment

2 an area or district which forms a separate part of a political constituency or local council

3 A ward or a ward of court is a child who is officially put in the care of an adult or a court of law, because their parents are dead or because they need protection.

> VERB
4 If you ward off a danger or an illness, you do something to prevent it from affecting or harming you.

-ward or **-wards** SUFFIX
-ward and -wards form adverbs or adjectives that show the way something is moving or facing *e.g. homeward... westwards*

warden [ˈwɔːdən] **wardens** NOUN
1 a person in charge of a building or institution such as a youth hostel or prison

2 an official who makes sure that certain laws or rules are obeyed in a particular place or activity *e.g. a traffic warden*

warder [ˈwɔːdə] **warders** NOUN
a person who is in charge of prisoners in a jail

wardrobe [ˈwɔːdrəʊb] **wardrobes** NOUN
1 a tall cupboard in which you can hang your clothes

2 Someone's wardrobe is their collection of clothes.

ware [weə] **wares** NOUN
1 Ware is manufactured goods of a particular kind. *e.g. kitchenware*

2 Someone's wares are the things they sell, usually in the street or in a market.

warehouse [ˈweəˌhaʊs] **warehouses** NOUN
a large building where raw materials or manufactured goods are stored

warfare [ˈwɔːˌfeə] NOUN
Warfare is the activity of fighting a war.

warhead [ˈwɔːˌhed] **warheads** NOUN
the front end of a bomb or missile, where the explosives are carried

warlock [ˈwɔːˌlɒk] **warlocks** NOUN
a male witch

warm [wɔːm] **warmer, warmest; warms, warming, warmed** ADJECTIVE
1 Something that is warm has some heat, but not enough to be hot. *e.g. a warm day*

THESAURUS
balmy: *balmy summer evenings*
heated: *a heated swimming pool*
lukewarm: *Heat the milk until lukewarm.*
pleasant: *After a chilly morning, the afternoon was very pleasant.*
tepid: *a bath full of tepid water*
<<OPPOSITE *cold*

2 Warm clothes or blankets are made of a material which protects you from the cold.

3 Warm colours or sounds are pleasant and make you feel comfortable and relaxed.

4 A warm person is friendly and affectionate.

THESAURUS
affectionate: *with an affectionate glance at her children*
amiable: *He was very amiable company.*
cordial: *We were given a most cordial welcome.*
friendly: *All her colleagues were very friendly.*
genial: *a warm-hearted friend and genial host*
loving: *He is a loving husband and father.*
<<OPPOSITE *unfriendly*

> VERB
5 If you warm something, you heat it up gently so that it stops being cold.
warmly ADVERB **warm up**

THESAURUS
heat: *Heat the bread in the oven.*
heat up: *The fire soon heated up the room.*
melt: *He melted the butter in a small pan.*

thaw: *Always thaw pastry thoroughly.*
warm up: *You must begin gently to warm up the muscles.*
<<OPPOSITE *cool*

> VERB

6 If you warm up for an event or an activity, you practise or exercise gently to prepare for it.

warmth [wɔːmθ] NOUN
1 Warmth is a moderate amount of heat.
2 Someone who has warmth is friendly and affectionate.

warn [wɔːn] **warns, warning, warned** VERB
1 If you warn someone about a possible problem or danger, you tell them about it in advance so that they are aware of it. *e.g. I warned him what it would be like.*

● THESAURUS
alert: *The siren alerted them to the danger.*
caution: *Their reaction cautioned him against any further attempts.*
forewarn: *We were forewarned of what to expect.*
notify: *The weather forecast notified them of the coming storm.*

2 If you warn someone not to do something, you advise them not to do it, in order to avoid possible danger or punishment. *e.g. I have warned her not to train for 10 days.*

warn off VERB
3 If you warn someone off, you tell them to go away or to stop doing something.

warning [ˈwɔːnɪŋ] **warnings** NOUN
something said or written to tell people of a possible problem or danger

● THESAURUS
alarm: *They heard the fire alarm and ran to safety.*
alert: *a security alert*
caution: *a note of caution*
notice: *three months' notice*
premonition: *He had a premonition of bad news.*

warp [wɔːp] **warps, warping, warped** VERB
1 If something warps or is warped, it becomes bent, often because of the effect of heat or water.
2 If something warps someone's mind or character, it makes them abnormal or corrupt.
3 The warp in a piece of cloth is the stronger lengthwise threads.

warrant [ˈwɒrənt] **warrants, warranting, warranted** VERB
1 FORMAL
If something warrants a particular action, it makes the action seem necessary. *e.g. no evidence to warrant a murder investigation*

> NOUN

2 an official document which gives permission to

the police to do something *e.g. a warrant for his arrest*

warranty [ˈwɒrəntɪ] **warranties** NOUN
a guarantee *e.g. a three-year warranty*

warren [ˈwɒrən] **warrens** NOUN
a group of holes under the ground connected by tunnels, which rabbits live in

warrigal [ˈwɒrɪgæl] **warrigals** NOUN
1 In Australian English, a dingo.
2 In Australian English, a wild horse or other wild creature.

> ADJECTIVE

3 In Australian English, wild.

warrior [ˈwɒrɪə] **warriors** NOUN
a fighting man or soldier, especially in former times

warship [ˈwɔːʃɪp] **warships** NOUN
a ship built with guns and used for fighting in wars

wart [wɔːt] **warts** NOUN
a small, hard piece of skin which can grow on someone's face or hands

wartime [ˈwɔːˌtaɪm] NOUN
Wartime is a period of time during which a country is at war.

wary [ˈwɛərɪ] **warier, wariest** ADJECTIVE
cautious and on one's guard *e.g. Michelle is wary of marriage.*
warily ADVERB

● THESAURUS
cautious: *His experience has made him cautious.*
distrustful: *Voters are deeply distrustful of all politicians.*
guarded: *The boy gave him a guarded look.*
suspicious: *He was rightly suspicious of their motives.*
vigilant: *He warned the public to be vigilant.*

was [wɒz] a past tense of **be**

wash [wɒʃ] **washes, washing, washed** VERB
1 If you wash something, you clean it with water and soap.

● THESAURUS
bathe: *She bathed her blistered feet.*
cleanse: *the correct way to cleanse the skin*
launder: *freshly laundered shirts*
rinse: *Rinse several times in clear water.*
scrub: *I was scrubbing the bathroom floor.*
shampoo: *You must shampoo your hair first.*

2 If you wash, you clean yourself using soap and water.
3 If something is washed somewhere, it is carried there gently by water. *e.g. The infant Arthur was washed ashore.*

w

⬤ **THESAURUS**
carry off: *The debris was carried off on the tide.*
erode: *Exposed soil is quickly eroded by wind and rain.*
sweep away: *The floods swept away the houses by the river.*

> NOUN
4 The wash is all the clothes and bedding that are washed together at one time. *e.g. a typical family's weekly wash*

5 The wash in water is the disturbance and waves produced at the back of a moving boat.

> PHRASE
6 If you **wash your hands of** something, you refuse to have anything more to do with it. **wash up** VERB

7 If you wash up, you wash the dishes, pans, and cutlery used in preparing and eating a meal.

8 If something is washed up on land, it is carried by a river or sea and left there. *e.g. A body had been washed up on the beach.*

washbasin ['wɒʃˌbeɪsᵊn] **washbasins** NOUN
a deep bowl, usually fixed to a wall, with taps for hot and cold water

washer ['wɒʃə] **washers** NOUN
1 a thin, flat ring of metal or plastic which is placed over a bolt before the nut is screwed on, so that it is fixed more tightly

2 In Australian English, a small piece of towelling for washing yourself.

washing ['wɒʃɪŋ] NOUN
Washing consists of clothes and bedding which need to be washed or are in the process of being washed and dried.

washing machine **washing machines**
NOUN
a machine for washing clothes in

washing-up ['wɒʃɪŋˈʌp] NOUN
If you do the washing-up, you wash the dishes, pans, and cutlery which have been used in the cooking and eating of a meal.

wasp [wɒsp] **wasps** NOUN
an insect with yellow and black stripes across its body, which can sting like a bee

wastage ['weɪstɪdʒ] NOUN
Wastage is loss and misuse of something. *e.g. wastage of resources*

waste [weɪst] **wastes, wasting, wasted**
VERB
1 If you waste time, money, or energy, you use too much of it on something that is not important or necessary.

⬤ **THESAURUS**
fritter away: *He just fritters his time away.*

squander: *He had squandered his chances of winning.*
throw away: *You're throwing away a good opportunity.*
<<OPPOSITE *save*

2 If you waste an opportunity, you do not take advantage of it when it is available.

3 If you say that something is wasted on someone, you mean that it is too good, too clever, or too sophisticated for them. *e.g. This book is wasted on us.*

> NOUN
4 If an activity is a waste of time, money, or energy, it is not important or necessary.

5 Waste is the use of more money or some other resource than is necessary.

⬤ **THESAURUS**
extravagance: *widespread tales of his extravagance*
misuse: *This project is a misuse of public funds.*
squandering: *a squandering of his valuable time*

6 Waste is also material that is no longer wanted, or material left over from a useful process. *e.g. nuclear waste*

> ADJECTIVE
7 unwanted in its present form *e.g. waste paper*
⬤ **THESAURUS**
leftover: *leftover pieces of fabric*
superfluous: *She got rid of many superfluous belongings.*
unused: *spoiled or unused ballot papers*

8 Waste land is land which is not used or looked after by anyone.

waste away VERB
9 If someone is wasting away, they are becoming very thin and weak because they are ill or not eating properly.

wasted ['weɪstɪd] ADJECTIVE
unnecessary *e.g. a wasted journey*

wasteful ['weɪstfʊl] ADJECTIVE
extravagant or causing waste by using something in a careless and inefficient way

⬤ **THESAURUS**
extravagant: *an extravagant lifestyle*
uneconomical: *the uneconomical duplication of jobs*
<<OPPOSITE *thrifty*

wasteland ['weɪstˌlænd] **wastelands** NOUN
A wasteland is land which is of no use because it is infertile or has been misused.

wasting ['weɪstɪŋ] ADJECTIVE
A wasting disease is one that gradually reduces the strength and health of the body.

watch [wɒtʃ] **watches, watching, watched** NOUN

1 a small clock usually worn on a strap on the wrist

2 a period of time during which a guard is kept over something

● THESAURUS

observation: *In hospital she'll be under observation night and day.*

supervision: *A toddler requires close supervision.*

surveillance: *kept under constant surveillance*

> VERB

3 If you watch something, you look at it for some time and pay close attention to what is happening.

● THESAURUS

gaze at: *gazing at herself in the mirror*

look at: *They looked closely at the insects.*

observe: *Researchers observed the behaviour of small children.*

pay attention: *Pay attention or you won't know what to do.*

see: *We went to see the semi-finals.*

view: *The police have viewed the video recording of the incident.*

4 If you watch someone or something, you take care of them.

● THESAURUS

guard: *They were guarded the whole time they were there.*

look after: *I looked after her cat while she was away.*

mind: *Can you mind the store for a couple of hours?*

take care of: *Can you take care of the kids while I get my hair done?*

5 If you watch a situation, you pay attention to it or are aware of it. *e.g. I had watched Jimmy's progress with interest.*

watch out VERB

6 If you watch out for something, you keep alert to see if it is near you. *e.g. Watch out for more fog and ice.*

● THESAURUS

be alert: *The bank is alert to the danger.*

be watchful: *Be watchful for any warning signs.*

keep your eyes open: *They kept their eyes open for any troublemakers.*

look out: *What are the symptoms to look out for?*

7 If you tell someone to watch out, you are warning them to be very careful.

watchdog ['wɒtʃˌdɒg] **watchdogs** NOUN

1 a dog used to guard property

2 a person or group whose job is to make sure that companies do not act illegally or irresponsibly

watchful ['wɒtʃfʊl] ADJECTIVE
careful to notice everything that is happening *e.g. the watchful eye of her father*

watchman ['wɒtʃmən] **watchmen** NOUN
a person whose job is to guard property

water ['wɔːtə] **waters, watering, watered** NOUN

1 Water is a clear, colourless, tasteless, and odourless liquid that is necessary for all plant and animal life.

2 You use water or waters to refer to a large area of water, such as a lake or sea. *e.g. the black waters of the lake*

> VERB

3 If you water a plant or an animal, you give it water to drink.

4 If your eyes water, you have tears in them because they are hurting.

5 If your mouth waters, it produces extra saliva, usually because you think of or can smell something appetizing.

water down VERB
6 If you water something down, you make it weaker.

watercolour ['wɔːtəˌkʌlə] **watercolours** NOUN

1 Watercolours are paints for painting pictures, which are diluted with water or put on the paper using a wet brush.

2 a picture which has been painted using watercolours

watercress ['wɔːtəˌkrɛs] NOUN
Watercress is a small plant which grows in streams and pools. Its leaves taste hot and are eaten in salads.

waterfall ['wɔːtəˌfɔːl] **waterfalls** NOUN
A waterfall is water from a river or stream as it flows over the edge of a steep cliff in hills or mountains and falls to the ground below.

waterfront ['wɔːtəˌfrʌnt] **waterfronts** NOUN
a street or piece of land next to an area of water such as a river or harbour

watering can ['wɔːtərɪŋ] **watering cans** NOUN
a container with a handle and a long spout, which you use to water plants

waterlogged ['wɔːtəˌlɒgd] ADJECTIVE
Land that is waterlogged is so wet that the soil cannot contain any more water, so that some water remains on the surface of the ground.

watermelon ['wɔːtəˌmɛlən] **watermelons** NOUN
a large, round fruit which has a hard green skin and red juicy flesh

waterproof ['wɔːtəˌpruːf] **waterproofs** ADJECTIVE

w

1 not letting water pass through *e.g. waterproof clothing*

> NOUN

2 a coat which keeps water out

watershed ['wɔːtəʃɛd] **watersheds** NOUN
an event or period which marks a turning point or the beginning of a new way of life *e.g. a watershed in European history*

watersider ['wɔːtəˌsaɪdə] **watersiders** NOUN
In Australian and New Zealand English, a person who loads and unloads the cargo from ships.

water-skiing ['wɔːtəˌskiːɪŋ] NOUN
Water-skiing is the sport of skimming over the water on skis while being pulled by a boat.

water table **water tables** NOUN
The water table is the level below the surface of the ground at which water can be found.

watertight ['wɔːtəˌtaɪt] ADJECTIVE
1 Something that is watertight does not allow water to pass through.

2 An agreement or an argument that is watertight has been so carefully put together that nobody should be able to find a fault in it.

waterway ['wɔːtəˌweɪ] **waterways** NOUN
a canal, river, or narrow channel of sea which ships or boats can sail along

waterworks ['wɔːtəˌwɜːks] NOUN
A waterworks is the system of pipes, filters, and tanks where the public supply of water is stored and cleaned, and from where it is distributed.

watery ['wɔːtərɪ] ADJECTIVE
1 pale or weak *e.g. a watery smile*

2 Watery food or drink contains a lot of water or is thin like water.

watt [wɒt] **watts** NOUN
a unit of measurement of electrical power

wattle ['wɒtəl] **wattles** NOUN
an Australian acacia tree with spikes of brightly coloured flowers

wave [weɪv] **waves, waving, waved** VERB
1 If you wave your hand, you move it from side to side, usually to say hello or goodbye.

2 If you wave someone somewhere or wave them on, you make a movement with your hand to tell them which way to go.

3 If you wave something, you hold it up and move it from side to side. *e.g. The doctor waved a piece of paper at him.*

● THESAURUS
brandish: *He appeared brandishing a knife.*
flap: *He flapped his hand at me to be quiet.*

flourish: *He flourished his glass to emphasize the point.*
flutter: *a fluttering white lace handkerchief*
shake: *Shake the rugs well to air them.*

> NOUN

4 a ridge of water on the surface of the sea caused by wind or by tides

● THESAURUS
breaker: *The foaming breakers crashed on to the beach.*
ripple: *gentle ripples on the surface of the lake*
swell: *We bobbed gently on the swell of the incoming tide.*

5 A wave is the form in which some types of energy such as heat, light, or sound travel through a substance.

6 A wave of sympathy, alarm, or panic is a steady increase in it which spreads through you or through a group of people.

7 an increase in a type of activity or behaviour *e.g. the crime wave*

● THESAURUS
flood: *a flood of complaints about the programme*
movement: *a growing movement towards democracy*
rush: *He felt a sudden rush of panic at the thought.*
surge: *the recent surge in inflation*
trend: *This is a growing trend.*
upsurge: *There was an upsurge of business confidence after the war.*

wavelength ['weɪvˌlɛŋθ] **wavelengths** NOUN
1 the distance between the same point on two adjacent waves of energy

2 the size of radio wave which a particular radio station uses to broadcast its programmes

waver ['weɪvə] **wavers, wavering, wavered** VERB
1 If you waver or if your confidence or beliefs waver, you are no longer as firm, confident, or sure in your beliefs. *e.g. Ben has never wavered from his belief.*

2 If something wavers, it moves slightly. *e.g. The gun did not waver in his hand.*

wavy ['weɪvɪ] **wavier, waviest** ADJECTIVE
having waves or regular curves *e.g. wavy hair*

wax [wæks] **waxes, waxing, waxed** NOUN
1 Wax is a solid, slightly shiny substance made of fat or oil and used to make candles and polish.

2 Wax is also the sticky yellow substance in your ears.

> VERB

3 If you wax a surface, you treat it or cover it with a thin layer of wax, especially to polish it.

4 FORMAL If you wax eloquent, you talk in an eloquent way.

way [weɪ] **ways** NOUN

1 A way of doing something is the manner of doing it. *e.g. an excellent way of cooking meat*

● THESAURUS

approach: *different approaches to gathering information*
manner: *in a friendly manner*
means: *The move is a means to fight crime.*
method: *using the latest teaching methods*
procedure: *He failed to follow the correct procedure when applying for a visa.*
technique: *The tests were performed using a new technique.*

2 The ways of a person or group are their customs or their normal behaviour. *e.g. Their ways are certainly different.*

● THESAURUS

conduct: *People judged him by his social skills and conduct.*
custom: *an ancient Japanese custom*
manner: *His manner was rather abrupt.*
practice: *a public enquiry into bank practices*
style: *Behaving like that isn't his style.*

3 The way you feel about something is your attitude to it or your opinion about it.

4 If you have a way with people or things, you are very skilful at dealing with them.

5 The way to a particular place is the route that you take to get there.

● THESAURUS

channel: *a safe channel avoiding the reefs*
course: *The ship was on a course that followed the coastline.*
lane: *the busiest shipping lanes in the world*
path: *The lava annihilates everything in its path.*
road: *the road into the village*
route: *the most direct route to the town centre*

6 If you go or look a particular way, you go or look in that direction. *e.g. She glanced the other way.*

7 If you divide something a number of ways, you divide it into that number of parts.

8 'Way' is used with words such as 'little' or 'long' to say how far off in distance or time something is *e.g. They lived a long way away.*

> PHRASE

9 If something or someone is **in the way**, they prevent you from moving freely or seeing clearly.

10 You say **by the way** when adding something to what you are saying. *e.g. By the way, I asked Brad to drop in.*

11 If you **go out of your way** to do something, you make a special effort to do it.

wayside ['weɪ,saɪd] PHRASE

If someone or something **falls by the wayside**,

they fail in what they are trying to do, or become forgotten and ignored.

wayward ['weɪwəd] ADJECTIVE

difficult to control and likely to change suddenly *e.g. your wayward husband*

WC WCs NOUN

a toilet. WC is an abbreviation for 'water closet'

we [wiː] PRONOUN

A speaker or writer uses 'we' to refer to himself or herself and one or more other people. *e.g. We are going to see Eddie.*

weak [wiːk] **weaker, weakest** ADJECTIVE

1 not having much strength *e.g. weak from lack of sleep*

● THESAURUS

delicate: *She was physically delicate and mentally unstable.*
faint: *Feeling faint is one of the symptoms of angina.*
feeble: *old and feeble and unable to walk far*
frail: *in frail health*
puny: *He was puny as a child but grew up to be a top athlete.*
sickly: *a sickly baby with no resistance to illness*
wasted: *muscles which were wasted through lack of use*

<<OPPOSITE strong

2 If something is weak, it is likely to break or fail. *e.g. Russia's weak economy.*

● THESAURUS

deficient: *The plane had a deficient landing system.*
faulty: *The money will be used to repair faulty equipment.*
inadequate: *inadequate safety measures*

3 If you describe someone as weak, you mean they are easily influenced by other people.
weakly ADVERB

● THESAURUS

powerless: *a powerless ruler governed by his advisers*
spineless: *bureaucrats and spineless politicians*
<<OPPOSITE resolute

weaken ['wiːkən] **weakens, weakening, weakened** VERB

1 If someone weakens something, they make it less strong or certain.

● THESAURUS

diminish: *to diminish the prestige of the monarchy*
fail: *His strength began to fail after a few hours.*
flag: *Her enthusiasm was in no way flagging.*
lessen: *The drugs lessen the risk of an epidemic.*
reduce: *Reduced consumer demand caused the company to collapse.*
sap: *I was afraid the illness had sapped my strength.*
undermine: *They were accused of trying to undermine the government.*

w

wane: *His interest in sport began to wane.*
<<OPPOSITE *strengthen*

2 If someone weakens, they become less certain about something.

weakling ['wi:klɪŋ] **weaklings** NOUN
a person who lacks physical strength or who is weak in character or health

weakness ['wi:knɪs] **weaknesses** NOUN
1 Weakness is lack of moral or physical strength.

THESAURUS
defect: *a serious character defect*
flaw: *His main flaw is his bad temper.*
fragility: *They are at risk because of the fragility of their bones.*
frailty: *the triumph of will over human frailty*
imperfection: *He concedes that there are imperfections in the system.*
vulnerability: *the extreme vulnerability of the young chicks*
<<OPPOSITE *strength*

2 If you have a weakness for something, you have a great liking for it. *e.g. a weakness for whisky*

THESAURUS
fondness: *a fondness for good wine*
liking: *a liking for tripe and onions*
passion: *His other great passion was his motorbike.*
penchant: *a stylish woman with a penchant for dark glasses*
<<OPPOSITE *dislike*

wealth [wɛlθ] NOUN
1 (GEOGRAPHY) Wealth is the large amount of money or property which someone owns.

THESAURUS
affluence: *the trappings of affluence*
fortune: *He made a fortune in the property boom.*
means: *a person of means*
money: *All that money brought nothing but sadness and misery.*
prosperity: *Japan's economic prosperity.*
riches: *His Olympic medal brought him fame and riches.*
substance: *run by local men of substance*

2 A wealth of something is a lot of it. *e.g. a wealth of information*

THESAURUS
abundance: *This area has an abundance of safe beaches.*
bounty: *autumn's bounty of fruits and berries*
plenty: *He grew up in a time of plenty.*
store: *She dipped into her store of theatrical anecdotes.*
<<OPPOSITE *shortage*

wealthy ['wɛlθɪ] **wealthier, wealthiest** ADJECTIVE
having a large amount of money, property, or other valuable things

THESAURUS
affluent: *living in an affluent neighbourhood*
comfortable: *from a stable, comfortable family*
opulent: *Most of the cash went on supporting his opulent lifestyle.*
prosperous: *The place looks more prosperous than ever.*
rich: *I'm going to be very rich one day.*
well-to-do: *a rather well-to-do family in the shipping business*
<<OPPOSITE *poor*

wean [wi:n] **weans, weaning, weaned** VERB
To wean a baby or animal is to start feeding it food other than its mother's milk.

weapon ['wɛpən] **weapons** NOUN
1 an object used to kill or hurt people in a fight or war

2 anything which can be used to get the better of an opponent *e.g. Surprise was his only weapon.*
weaponry NOUN

wear [wɛə] **wears, wearing, wore, worn** VERB
1 When you wear something such as clothes, make-up, or jewellery, you have them on your body or face.

THESAURUS
be clothed in: *She was clothed in a flowered dress.*
be dressed in: *The women were dressed in their finest attire.*
don: *The police responded by donning riot gear.*
have on: *I had my new shoes on that night.*
put on: *He had to put on his glasses to read the paper.*
sport: informal *sporting a red tie*

2 If you wear a particular expression, it shows on your face.

3 If something wears, it becomes thinner or worse in condition.

THESAURUS
corrode: *The underground pipes were badly corroded.*
erode: *Exposed rock is quickly eroded by wind and rain.*
fray: *fraying edges on the stair carpet*
rub: *The inscription had been rubbed smooth by generations of hands.*
wash away: *The topsoil had been washed away by the incessant rain.*

> NOUN
4 You can refer to clothes that are suitable for a particular time or occasion as a kind of wear. *e.g. beach wear*

5 Wear is the amount or type of use that something has and which causes damage or change to it. *e.g. signs of wear*

● THESAURUS

corrosion: *Zinc is used to protect other metals from corrosion.*

deterioration: *The building is already showing signs of deterioration.*

erosion: *erosion of the river valleys*

use: *The carpet must be able to cope with heavy use.*

> VERB wear down

6 If you wear people down, you weaken them by repeatedly doing something or asking them to do something.

wear off VERB

7 If a feeling such as pain wears off, it gradually disappears.

wear out VERB

8 When something wears out or when you wear it out, it is used so much that it becomes thin, weak, and no longer usable.

9 INFORMAL

If you wear someone out, you make them feel extremely tired.

● THESAURUS

exhaust: *The long working day exhausted him.*

tire: *If driving tires you, take the train.*

weary: *wearied by the constant demands on his time*

wear and tear [tɛə] NOUN
Wear and tear is the damage caused to something by normal use.

wearing [ˈwɛərɪŋ] ADJECTIVE
Someone or something that is wearing makes you feel extremely tired.

weary [ˈwɪərɪ] **wearier, weariest; wearies, wearying, wearied** ADJECTIVE

1 very tired

● THESAURUS

drained: *He's always completely drained after a performance.*

exhausted: *She was too exhausted and upset to talk.*

fatigued: *Winter weather can leave you feeling fatigued.*

tired: *He was too tired even to take a shower.*

tuckered out: *Australian and New Zealand; informal You must be tuckered out after that bus trip.*

worn out: *He's just worn out after the long drive.*

> VERB

2 If you weary of something, you become tired of it.

wearily ADVERB, **weariness** NOUN

weasel [ˈwiːzᵊl] **weasels** NOUN
a small wild animal with a long, thin body and short legs

weather [ˈwɛðə] **weathers, weathering, weathered** NOUN
(GEOGRAPHY) The weather is the condition of

the atmosphere at any particular time and the amount of rain, wind, or sunshine occurring.

> VERB

1 If something such as rock or wood weathers, it changes colour or shape as a result of being exposed to the wind, rain, or sun.

2 If you weather a problem or difficulty, you come through it safely.

> PHRASE

3 If you are **under the weather**, you feel slightly ill.

weather forecast weather forecasts NOUN
a statement saying what the weather will be like the next day or for the next few days

weather vane weather vanes NOUN
a metal object on the roof of a building which turns round in the wind and shows which way the wind is blowing

weave [wiːv] **weaves, weaving, wove, woven** VERB

1 To weave cloth is to make it by crossing threads over and under each other, especially by using a machine called a loom.

2 If you weave your way somewhere, you go there by moving from side to side through and round the obstacles.

> NOUN

3 The weave of cloth is the way in which the threads are arranged and the pattern that they form. *e.g. a tight weave*

weaver [ˈwiːvə] **weavers** NOUN
a person who weaves cloth

web [wɛb] **webs** NOUN

1 a fine net of threads that a spider makes from a sticky substance which it produces in its body

2 something that has a complicated structure or pattern *e.g. a web of lies*

3 The Web is the same as the **World Wide Web**

webbed [wɛbd] ADJECTIVE
Webbed feet have the toes connected by a piece of skin.

weblog [ˈwɛbˌlɒg] **weblogs** NOUN
a person's online diary or journal that he or she puts on the Internet so that other people can read it. It is also shortened to **blog**

website [ˈwɛbˌsaɪt] **websites** NOUN
a publication on the World Wide Web which contains information about a particular subject

wed [wɛd] **weds, wedding, wedded** or **wed** VERB; OLD-FASHIONED, INFORMAL
If you wed someone or if you wed, you get married.

w

wedding ['wɛdɪŋ] **weddings** NOUN
(RE) a marriage ceremony

wedge [wɛdʒ] **wedges, wedging, wedged**
VERB
1 If you wedge something, you force it to remain there by holding it there tightly, or by fixing something next to it to prevent it from moving. *e.g. I shut the shed door and wedged it with a log of wood.*

> NOUN
2 a piece of something such as wood, metal, or rubber with one pointed edge and one thick edge which is used to wedge something

3 a piece of something that has a thick triangular shape *e.g. a wedge of cheese*

wedlock ['wɛdlɒk] NOUN; OLD-FASHIONED, INFORMAL
Wedlock is the state of being married.

Wednesday ['wɛnzdɪ] **Wednesdays** NOUN
Wednesday is the day between Tuesday and Thursday.
[WORD HISTORY: from Old English WODNES DÆG meaning 'Woden's day']

wee [wiː] **weer, weest** ADJECTIVE; SCOTTISH
very small

weed [wiːd] **weeds, weeding, weeded**
NOUN
1 a wild plant that prevents cultivated plants from growing properly

> VERB
2 If you weed a place, you remove the weeds from it.

weed out VERB
3 If you weed out unwanted things, you get rid of them.

week [wiːk] **weeks** NOUN
1 a period of seven days, especially one beginning on a Sunday and ending on a Saturday

2 A week is also the number of hours you spend at work during a week. *e.g. a 35-hour week*

3 The week can refer to the part of a week that does not include Saturday and Sunday. *e.g. They are working during the week.*

weekday ['wiːkˌdeɪ] **weekdays** NOUN
any day except Saturday and Sunday

weekend [ˌwiːkˈɛnd] **weekends** NOUN
Saturday and Sunday.

weekly ['wiːklɪ] **weeklies** ADJECTIVE OR ADVERB
1 happening or appearing once a week

> NOUN
2 a newspaper or magazine that is published once a week

weep [wiːp] **weeps, weeping, wept** VERB
1 If someone weeps, they cry.

2 If something such as a wound weeps, it oozes blood or other liquid.

weevil ['wiːvɪl] **weevils** NOUN
a type of beetle which eats grain, seeds, or plants

weft [wɛft] NOUN
The weft of a piece of woven material is the threads which are passed sideways in and out of the threads held in a loom.

weigh [weɪ] **weighs, weighing, weighed**
VERB
1 If something weighs a particular amount, that is how heavy it is.

2 If you weigh something, you measure how heavy it is using scales.

3 If you weigh facts or words, you think about them carefully before coming to a decision or before speaking.

4 If a problem weighs on you or weighs upon you, it makes you very worried.

weigh down VERB
5 If a load weighs you down, it stops you moving easily.

6 If you are weighed down by a difficulty, it is making you very worried.

weigh up VERB
7 If you weigh up a person or a situation, you make an assessment of them.

weight [weɪt] **weights, weighting, weighted** NOUN
1 (MATHS) The weight of something is its heaviness.

2 a metal object which has a certain known heaviness. Weights are used with sets of scales in order to weigh things.

3 any heavy object

4 The weight of something is its large amount or importance which makes it hard to fight against or contradict. *e.g. the weight of the law*

> VERB
5 If you weight something or weight it down, you make it heavier, often so that it cannot move.

> PHRASE
6 If you **pull your weight**, you work just as hard as other people involved in the same activity.

weighted ['weɪtɪd] ADJECTIVE
A system that is weighted in favour of a particular person or group is organized in such a way that this person or group will have an advantage.

weightlifting ['weɪtˌlɪftɪŋ] NOUN
Weightlifting is the sport of lifting heavy weights in competition or for exercise.

weightlifter NOUN

weighty ['weɪtɪ] **weightier, weightiest**
ADJECTIVE
serious or important *e.g. a weighty problem*

weir [wɪə] **weirs** NOUN
a low dam which is built across a river to raise the
water level, control the flow of water, or change
its direction

weird [wɪəd] **weirder, weirdest** ADJECTIVE
strange or odd
weirdly ADVERB

● THESAURUS
bizarre: *his bizarre behaviour*
curious: *What a curious thing to say!*
extraordinary: *an extraordinary occurrence*
funny: *There's something funny about him.*
odd: *an odd coincidence*
singular: formal *I can't think where you got such a
singular notion.*
strange: *Didn't you notice anything strange about
her?*
peculiar: *It tasted very peculiar.*
queer: *I think there's something queer going on here.*
<<OPPOSITE *ordinary*

weirdo ['wɪədəu] **weirdos** NOUN INFORMAL
If you call someone a weirdo, you mean they
behave in a strange way.

● THESAURUS
crank: informal *He kept quiet in case people thought
he was a crank.*
eccentric: *a local eccentric who wears shorts all year
round*
freak: informal *Barry's always been looked on as a
bit of a freak.*
loony: slang *I realize I must sound like a complete
loony.*
nut: slang *There's some nut out there with a gun.*
nutter: British; slang *She was being stalked by a
real nutter.*

welcome ['welkəm] **welcomes,
welcoming, welcomed** VERB
1 If you welcome a visitor, you greet them in a
friendly way when they arrive.
2 'Welcome' can be said as a greeting to a visitor
who has just arrived
3 If you welcome something, you approve of it
and support it. *e.g. He welcomed the decision.*
> NOUN
4 a greeting to a visitor *e.g. a warm welcome*
> ADJECTIVE
5 If someone is welcome at a place, they will be
warmly received there.
6 If something is welcome, it brings pleasure or is
accepted gratefully. *e.g. a welcome rest*
7 If you tell someone they are welcome to
something or welcome to do something, you

mean you are willing for them to have or to do it.
welcoming ADJECTIVE

weld [weld] **welds, welding, welded** VERB
To weld two pieces of metal together is to join
them by heating their edges and fixing them
together so that when they cool they harden into
one piece.
welder NOUN

welfare ['wel‚feə] NOUN
1 The welfare of a person or group is their general
state of health and comfort.
2 Welfare services are provided to help with
people's living conditions and financial
problems. *e.g. welfare workers*

welfare state NOUN
The welfare state is a system in which the
government uses money from taxes to provide
health care and education services, and to give
benefits to people who are old, unemployed, or
sick.

well [wel] **better, best; wells, welling,
welled** ADVERB
1 If something goes well, it happens in a
satisfactory way. *e.g. The interview went well.*

● THESAURUS
satisfactorily: *The system should work
satisfactorily.*
smoothly: *So far, the operation is going smoothly.*
splendidly: *They have behaved splendidly.*
successfully: *The changeover is working
successfully.*

2 in a good, skilful, or pleasing way *e.g. He draws
well.*

● THESAURUS
ably: *He was ably assisted by the other members of
staff.*
admirably: *dealing admirably with a difficult
situation*
adequately: *He speaks French very adequately.*
competently: *They handled the situation very
competently.*
effectively: *In the first half he operated effectively in
defence.*
efficiently: *He works efficiently and accurately.*
expertly: *Shopkeepers expertly rolled spices up in
bay leaves.*
professionally: *These tickets have been forged very
professionally.*
skilfully: *He skilfully exploited his company's
strengths.*
<<OPPOSITE *badly*

3 thoroughly and completely *e.g. well established*

● THESAURUS
amply: *I was amply rewarded for my trouble.*
closely: *He studied the documents closely.*

w

completely: *Make sure you defrost it completely.*
fully: *The new system is now fully under way.*
highly: *one of the most highly regarded authors*
meticulously: *He had planned his trip meticulously.*
rigorously: *Their duties have not been performed as rigorously as they might have been.*
thoroughly: *Add the oil and mix thoroughly.*

4 kindly *e.g. We treat our employees well.*

● THESAURUS
compassionately: *He always acted compassionately towards her.*
considerately: *I expect people to deal with me considerately and fairly.*
favourably: *companies who treat men more favourably than women*
humanely: *They treat their livestock humanely.*
kindly: *Children are capable of behaving kindly.*
with consideration: *He was treated with consideration and kindness.*

5 If something may well or could well happen, it is likely to happen.

6 You use 'well' to emphasize an adjective, adverb, or phrase. *e.g. He was well aware of that.*

> ADJECTIVE
7 If you are well, you are healthy.

● THESAURUS
blooming: *She felt confident, blooming, and attractive.*
fit: *He keeps himself really fit.*
healthy: *Most people want to be healthy and happy.*
in good condition: *He's in good condition for his age.*
in good health: *He seemed to be in good health and spirits.*
robust: *He's never been a very robust child.*
sound: *a sound body*
strong: *Eat well and you'll soon be strong again.*
<<OPPOSITE *sick*

> PHRASE
8 As well means also *e.g. He was a bus driver as well.*

9 As well as means in addition to *e.g. a meal which includes meat or fish, as well as rice*

10 If you say you **may as well** or **might as well** do something, you mean you will do it although you are not keen to do it.

> NOUN
11 a hole drilled in the ground from which water, oil, or gas is obtained

> VERB
12 If tears well or well up, they appear in someone's eyes.

well-advised [ˌwɛləd'vaɪzd] ADJECTIVE
sensible or wise *e.g. Bill would be well-advised to retire.*

well-balanced [ˌwɛl'bælənst] ADJECTIVE
sensible and without serious emotional problems *e.g. a well-balanced happy teenager*

wellbeing ['wɛl'biːɪŋ] NOUN
Someone's wellbeing is their health and happiness.

well-earned [ˌwɛl'ɜːnd] ADJECTIVE
thoroughly deserved

well-heeled [ˌwɛl'hiːld] ADJECTIVE; INFORMAL
wealthy

well-informed [ˌwɛlɪn'fɔːmd] ADJECTIVE
having a great deal of knowledge about a subject or subjects

wellington ['wɛlɪŋtən] **wellingtons** NOUN
Wellingtons or wellington boots are long waterproof rubber boots.

well-meaning [ˌwɛl'miːnɪŋ] ADJECTIVE
A well-meaning person tries to be helpful but is often unsuccessful.

well-off [ˌwɛl'ɒf] ADJECTIVE; INFORMAL
quite wealthy

well-to-do [ˌwɛltə'duː] ADJECTIVE
quite wealthy

well-worn [ˌwɛl'wɔːn] ADJECTIVE
1 A well-worn expression or saying has been used too often and has become boring.
2 A well-worn object or piece of clothing has been used and worn so much that it looks old and shabby.

welly ['wɛlɪ] **wellies** NOUN; INFORMAL
Wellies are wellingtons.

Welsh [wɛlʃ] ADJECTIVE
1 belonging or relating to Wales
> NOUN
2 Welsh is a language spoken in parts of Wales.

Welshman ['wɛlʃmən] **Welshmen** NOUN
a man who comes from Wales
Welshwoman NOUN

welt [wɛlt] **welts** NOUN
a raised mark on someone's skin made by a blow from something like a whip or a stick

welter ['wɛltə] NOUN; FORMAL
A welter of things is a large number of them that happen or appear together in a state of confusion. *e.g. a welter of rumours*

wench [wɛntʃ] **wenches** NOUN; OLD-FASHIONED, INFORMAL
a woman or young girl

wept [wɛpt] the past tense and past participle of **weep**

were [wɜː] a past tense of **be**

werewolf ['wɪəˌwʊlf] **werewolves** NOUN
In horror stories, a werewolf is a person who changes into a wolf.
[WORD HISTORY: from Old English WER + WULF meaning 'man wolf']

Wesak ['wɛsʌk] NOUN
Wesak is the Buddhist festival celebrating the Buddha, held in May.

west [wɛst] NOUN
1 The west is the direction in which you look to see the sun set.
2 The west of a place or country is the part which is towards the west when you are in the centre. *e.g. the west of America*
3 The West refers to the countries of North America and western and southern Europe.
> ADVERB OR ADJECTIVE
4 West means towards the west.
> ADJECTIVE
5 A west wind blows from the west.

westerly ['wɛstəlɪ] ADJECTIVE
Westerly means to or towards the west. *e.g. France's most westerly region.*

western ['wɛstən] **westerns** ADJECTIVE
1 in or from the west
2 coming from or associated with the countries of North America and western and southern Europe *e.g. western dress*
> NOUN
3 a book or film about life in the west of America in the nineteenth century

West Indian West Indians NOUN
someone who comes from the West Indies

westward or **westwards** ['wɛstwəd] or ['wɛstwədz] ADVERB
Westward or westwards means towards the west. *e.g. He stared westwards towards the clouds.*

wet [wɛt] **wetter, wettest; wets, wetting, wet** or **wetted** ADJECTIVE
1 If something is wet, it is covered in water or another liquid.

⬤ THESAURUS
damp: *Her hair was still damp.*
drenched: *getting drenched by icy water*
moist: *The soil is reasonably moist after the September rain.*
saturated: *The filter has been saturated with oil.*
soaked: *soaked to the skin*
sodden: *We took off our sodden clothes.*
waterlogged: *The game was called off because the pitch was waterlogged.*
<<OPPOSITE *dry*

2 If the weather is wet, it is raining.

⬤ THESAURUS
humid: *hot and humid weather conditions*
misty: *The air was cold and misty.*
rainy: *The rainy season starts in December.*
showery: *The day had been showery with sunny intervals.*
<<OPPOSITE *dry*

3 If something such as paint, ink, or cement is wet, it is not yet dry or solid.

4 INFORMAL
If you say someone is wet, you mean they are weak and lacking confidence. *e.g. Don't be so wet!*
> NOUN
5 In Australia, the wet is the rainy season.
> VERB
6 To wet something is to put water or some other liquid over it.

⬤ THESAURUS
dampen: *You must dampen the laundry before you iron it.*
irrigate: *irrigated by a system of interconnected canals*
moisten: *Take a sip of water to moisten your throat.*
soak: *The water had soaked his jacket and shirt.*
spray: *It can spray the whole field in half an hour.*
water: *We have to water the plants when the weather is dry.*
<<OPPOSITE *dry*

7 If people wet themselves or wet their beds, they urinate in their clothes or bed because they cannot control their bladder.
wetness NOUN

wet suit wet suits NOUN
a close-fitting rubber suit which a diver wears to keep his or her body warm

whack [wæk] **whacks, whacking, whacked** VERB
If you whack someone or something, you hit them hard.

whale [weɪl] **whales** NOUN
a very large sea mammal which breathes out water through a hole on the top of its head

whaling ['weɪlɪŋ] NOUN
Whaling is the work of hunting and killing whales for oil or food.

wharf [wɔːf] **wharves** NOUN
a platform beside a river or the sea, where ships load or unload

what [wɒt] PRONOUN
1 'What' is used in questions *e.g. What time is it?.*
2 'What' is used in indirect questions and statements *e.g. I don't know what you mean.*
3 'What' can be used at the beginning of a clause to refer to something with a particular quality *e.g.*

It is impossible to decide what is real and what is invented.

> ADJECTIVE

4 'What' can be used at the beginning of a clause to show that you are talking about the whole amount that is available to you *e.g. Their spouses try to earn what money they can.*

5 You say 'what' to emphasize an opinion or reaction. *e.g. What nonsense!*

> PHRASE

6 You say **what about** at the beginning of a question when you are making a suggestion or offer. *e.g. What about a drink?.*

whatever [wɒtˈɛvə] PRONOUN

1 You use 'whatever' to refer to anything or everything of a particular type. *e.g. He said he would do whatever he could.*

2 You use 'whatever' when you do not know the precise nature of something. *e.g. Whatever it is, I don't like it.*

> CONJUNCTION

3 You use 'whatever' to mean no matter what. *e.g. Whatever happens, you have to behave decently.*

> ADVERB

4 You use 'whatever' to emphasize a negative statement or a question. *e.g. You have no proof whatever... Whatever is wrong with you?.*

whatsoever [ˌwɒtsəʊˈɛvə] ADVERB
You use 'whatsoever' to emphasize a negative statement. *e.g. I have no memory of it whatsoever.*

wheat [wiːt] NOUN
Wheat is a cereal plant grown for its grain which is used to make flour.

wheel [wiːl] **wheels, wheeling, wheeled** NOUN

1 a circular object which turns on a rod attached to its centre. Wheels are fixed underneath vehicles so that they can move along

2 The wheel of a car is its steering wheel.

> VERB

3 If you wheel something such as a bicycle, you push it.

4 If someone or something wheels, they move round in the shape of a circle. *e.g. Cameron wheeled around and hit him.*

wheelbarrow [ˈwiːlˌbærəʊ] **wheelbarrows** NOUN
a small cart with a single wheel at the front, used for carrying things in the garden

wheelchair [ˈwiːlˌtʃɛə] **wheelchairs** NOUN
a chair with wheels in which sick, injured, or disabled people can move around

wheeze [wiːz] **wheezes, wheezing, wheezed** VERB

If someone wheezes, they breathe with difficulty, making a whistling sound, usually because they have a chest complaint such as asthma.
wheezy ADJECTIVE

whelk [wɛlk] **whelks** NOUN
a snail-like shellfish with a strong shell and a soft edible body

when [wɛn] ADVERB

1 You use 'when' to ask what time something happened or will happen. *e.g. When are you leaving?*

> CONJUNCTION

2 You use 'when' to refer to a time in the past. *e.g. I met him when I was sixteen.*

3 You use 'when' to introduce the reason for an opinion, comment, or question. *e.g. How did you pass the exam when you hadn't studied for it?.*

4 'When' is used to mean although *e.g. He drives when he could walk.*

whence [wɛns] ADVERB OR CONJUNCTION;
OLD-FASHIONED, INFORMAL
Whence means from where.

> You should not write *from whence* because *whence* already means 'from where'

whenever [wɛnˈɛvə] CONJUNCTION
Whenever means at any time, or every time that something happens. *e.g. I still go on courses whenever I can.*

where [wɛə] ADVERB

1 You use 'where' to ask which place something is in, is coming from, or is going to. *e.g. Where is Philip?*

> CONJUNCTION, PRONOUN, OR ADVERB

2 You use 'where' when asking about or referring to something. *e.g. I hardly know where to begin.*

> CONJUNCTION

3 You use 'where' to refer to the place in which something is situated or happening. *e.g. I don't know where we are.*

4 'Where' can introduce a clause that contrasts with the other part of the sentence *e.g. A teacher will be listened to, where a parent might not.*

whereabouts [ˈwɛərəˌbaʊts] NOUN

1 The whereabouts of a person or thing is the place where they are.

> ADVERB

2 You use 'whereabouts' when you are asking more precisely where something is. *e.g. Whereabouts in Canada are you from?.*

whereas [wɛərˈæz] CONJUNCTION
Whereas introduces a comment that contrasts with the other part of the sentence. *e.g. Her eyes were blue, whereas mine were brown.*

whereby [wɛəˈbaɪ] PRONOUN; FORMAL
Whereby means by which. *e.g. a new system whereby you pay the bill quarterly*

whereupon [ˌwɛərəˈpɒn] CONJUNCTION; FORMAL
Whereupon means at which point. *e.g. His enemies rejected his message, whereupon he tried again.*

wherever [wɛərˈɛvə] CONJUNCTION
1 'Wherever' means in every place or situation *e.g. Alex heard the same thing wherever he went.*
2 You use 'wherever' to show that you do not know where a place or person is. *e.g. the nearest police station, wherever that is*

wherewithal [ˈwɛəwɪðˌɔːl] NOUN
If you have the wherewithal to do something, you have enough money to do it.

whet [wɛt] **whets, whetting, whetted**
PHRASE
To **whet someone's appetite** for something, means to increase their desire for it.

whether [ˈwɛðə] CONJUNCTION
You use 'whether' when you are talking about two or more alternatives. *e.g. I don't know whether that's true or false.*

whey [weɪ] NOUN
Whey is the watery liquid that is separated from the curds in sour milk when cheese is made.

which [wɪtʃ] ADJECTIVE OR PRONOUN
1 You use 'which' to ask about alternatives or to refer to a choice between alternatives. *e.g. Which room are you in?*
> PRONOUN
2 'Which' at the beginning of a clause identifies the thing you are talking about or gives more information about it *e.g. certain wrongs which exist in our society*

▨ See the usage note at *that*

whichever [wɪtʃˈɛvə] ADJECTIVE OR PRONOUN
You use 'whichever' when you are talking about different alternatives or possibilities. *e.g. Make your pizzas round or square, whichever you prefer.*

whiff [wɪf] **whiffs** NOUN
1 a slight smell of something
2 a slight sign or trace of something *e.g. a whiff of criticism*

while [waɪl] **whiles, whiling, whiled**
CONJUNCTION
1 If something happens while something else is happening, the two things happen at the same time.
2 While also means but. *e.g. Men tend to gaze more, while women dart quick glances.*

> NOUN
3 a period of time *e.g. a little while earlier*
> PHRASE
4 If an action or activity is **worth your while**, it will be helpful or useful to you if you do it.

while away VERB
5 If you while away the time in a particular way, you pass the time that way because you have nothing else to do.

whilst [waɪlst] CONJUNCTION
Whilst means the same as while.

whim [wɪm] **whims** NOUN
a sudden desire or fancy

● THESAURUS
craze: *the latest fitness craze*
fad: informal *just a passing fad*
fancy: *I had a fancy for some strawberries.*
impulse: *He resisted the impulse to buy a new one.*
urge: *He had an urge to open a shop of his own.*

whimper [ˈwɪmpə] **whimpers, whimpering, whimpered** VERB
1 When children or animals whimper, they make soft, low, unhappy sounds.
2 If you whimper something, you say it in an unhappy or frightened way, as if you are about to cry.

whimsical [ˈwɪmzɪkᵊl] ADJECTIVE
unusual and slightly playful *e.g. an endearing, whimsical charm*

whine [waɪn] **whines, whining, whined**
VERB
1 To whine is to make a long, high-pitched noise, especially one which sounds sad or unpleasant.
2 If someone whines about something, they complain about it in an annoying way.
> NOUN
3 A whine is the noise made by something or someone whining.

whinge [wɪndʒ] **whinges, whinging or whingeing whinged** VERB
If someone whinges about something, they complain about it in an annoying way.

whinny [ˈwɪnɪ] **whinnies, whinnying, whinnied** VERB
When a horse whinnies, it neighs softly.

whip [wɪp] **whips, whipping, whipped**
NOUN
1 a thin piece of leather or rope attached to a handle, which is used for hitting people or animals
> VERB
2 If you whip a person or animal, you hit them with a whip.

w

3 When the wind whips something, it strikes it.

4 If you whip something out or off, you take it out or off very quickly. *e.g. She had whipped off her glasses.*

5 If you whip cream or eggs, you beat them until they are thick and frothy or stiff.

whip up VERB

6 If you whip up a strong emotion, you make people feel it. *e.g. The thought whipped up his temper.*

whip bird **whip birds** NOUN
an Australian bird whose cry ends with a sound like the crack of a whip

whiplash injury ['wɪpˌlæʃ] **whiplash injuries** NOUN
a neck injury caused by your head suddenly jerking forwards and then back again, for example in a car accident

whippet ['wɪpɪt] **whippets** NOUN
a small, thin dog used for racing

whirl [wɜːl] **whirls, whirling, whirled** VERB
1 When something whirls, or when you whirl it round, it turns round very fast.
> NOUN
2 You can refer to a lot of intense activity as a whirl of activity.
[WORD HISTORY: from Old Norse HVIRFLA meaning 'to turn about']

whirlpool ['wɜːlˌpuːl] **whirlpools** NOUN
a small circular area in a river or the sea where the water is moving quickly round and round so that objects floating near it are pulled into its centre

whirlwind ['wɜːlˌwɪnd] **whirlwinds** NOUN
1 a tall column of air which spins round and round very fast
> ADJECTIVE
2 more rapid than usual *e.g. a whirlwind tour*

whirr [wɜː] **whirrs, whirring, whirred**; also spelt **whir** VERB
1 When something such as a machine whirrs, it makes a series of low sounds so fast that it sounds like one continuous sound.
> NOUN
2 the noise made by something whirring

whisk [wɪsk] **whisks, whisking, whisked** VERB
1 If you whisk someone or something somewhere, you take them there quickly. *e.g. We were whisked away into a private room.*
2 If you whisk eggs or cream, you stir air into them quickly.
> NOUN
3 a kitchen tool used for quickly stirring air into eggs or cream

whisker ['wɪskə] **whiskers** NOUN
The whiskers of an animal such as a cat or mouse are the long, stiff hairs near its mouth.

whisky ['wɪskɪ] **whiskies** NOUN
Whisky is a strong alcoholic drink made from grain such as barley.
[WORD HISTORY: from Scottish Gaelic UISGE BEATHA meaning 'water of life']

whisper ['wɪspə] **whispers, whispering, whispered** VERB
1 When you whisper, you talk to someone very quietly, using your breath and not your throat.
> NOUN
2 If you talk in a whisper, you whisper.

whist [wɪst] NOUN
Whist is a card game for four players in which one pair of players tries to win more tricks than the other pair.

whistle ['wɪsəl] **whistles, whistling, whistled** VERB
1 When you whistle a tune or whistle, you produce a clear musical sound by forcing your breath out between your lips.
2 If something whistles, it makes a loud, high sound. *e.g. The kettle whistled.*
> NOUN
3 A whistle is the sound something or someone makes when they whistle.
4 a small metal tube that you blow into to produce a whistling sound

whit [wɪt] NOUN; FORMAL
You say 'not a whit' or 'no whit' to emphasize that something is not the case at all. *e.g. It does not matter one whit to the customer.*

white [waɪt] **whiter, whitest; whites**
NOUN OR ADJECTIVE
White is the lightest possible colour.
1 Someone who is white has a pale skin and is of European origin.
> ADJECTIVE
2 If someone goes white, their face becomes very pale because they are afraid, shocked, or ill.
3 White coffee contains milk or cream.
> NOUN
4 The white of an egg is the transparent liquid surrounding the yolk which turns white when it is cooked.
whiteness NOUN

white-collar ['waɪtˌkɒlə] ADJECTIVE
White-collar workers work in offices rather than doing manual work. *e.g. a white-collar union*

white lie **white lies** NOUN
a harmless lie, especially one told to prevent

someone's feelings from being hurt

whitewash ['waɪtˌwɒʃ] NOUN

1 Whitewash is a mixture of lime and water used for painting walls white.

2 an attempt to hide unpleasant facts *e.g. the refusal to accept official whitewash in the enquiry*

whither ['wɪðə] ADVERB OR CONJUNCTION; OLD-FASHIONED, INFORMAL

Whither means to what place. *e.g. Whither shall I wander?*.

whiting ['waɪtɪŋ] NOUN

a sea fish related to the cod

whittle ['wɪtˀl] **whittles, whittling, whittled** VERB

1 If you whittle a piece of wood, you shape it by shaving or cutting small pieces off it.

whittle away or **whittle down** VERB

2 To whittle away at something or to whittle it down means to make it smaller or less effective. *e.g. The 250 entrants had been whittled down to 34.*

whizz [wɪz] **whizzes, whizzing, whizzed;** also spelt **whiz** VERB; INFORMAL

If you whizz somewhere, you move there quickly.

who [huː] PRONOUN

1 You use 'who' when you are asking about someone's identity. *e.g. Who gave you that black eye?*

2 'Who' at the beginning of a clause refers to the person or people you are talking about *e.g. a shipyard worker who wants to be a postman*

whoa [wəʊ] INTERJECTION

Whoa is a command used to slow down or stop a horse.

whoever [huːˈɛvə] PRONOUN

1 'Whoever' means the person who *e.g. Whoever bought it for you has to make the claim.*

2 'Whoever' also means no matter who *e.g. I pity him, whoever he is.*

3 'Whoever' is used in questions give emphasis to who *e.g. Whoever thought of such a thing?*

whole [həʊl] **wholes** ADJECTIVE

1 indicating all of something *e.g. Have the whole cake.*

● THESAURUS

complete: *The list filled a complete page.*
entire: *There are only ten in the entire country.*
full: *a full week's notice*
total: *The evening was a total fiasco.*
uncut: *the uncut version of the film*
undivided: *He has my undivided loyalty.*

> NOUN

2 the full amount of something *e.g. the whole of Africa*

● THESAURUS

aggregate: *the aggregate of the individual scores*
all: *All is not lost.*
everything: *Everything that happened is my fault.*
lot: *He lost the lot within five minutes.*
sum total: *The small room contained the sum total of their possessions.*
total: *The eventual total was far higher.*

> ADVERB

3 in one piece *e.g. He swallowed it whole.*

> PHRASE

4 You use **as a whole** to emphasize that you are talking about all of something. *e.g. The country as a whole is in a very odd mood.*

5 You say **on the whole** to mean that something is generally true. *e.g. On the whole, we should be glad they are gone.*

wholeness NOUN

wholehearted [ˌhəʊlˈhɑːtɪd] ADJECTIVE

enthusiastic and totally sincere *e.g. wholehearted approval*

wholeheartedly ADVERB

wholemeal ['həʊlˌmiːl] ADJECTIVE

Wholemeal flour is made from the complete grain of the wheat plant, including the husk.

wholesale ['həʊlˌseɪl] ADJECTIVE OR ADVERB

1 Wholesale refers to the activity of buying goods cheaply in large quantities and selling them again, especially to shopkeepers. *e.g. We buy fruit and vegetables wholesale.*

> ADJECTIVE

2 Wholesale also means done to an excessive extent. *e.g. the wholesale destruction of wild plant species*

wholesaler NOUN

wholesome ['həʊlsəm] ADJECTIVE

good and likely to improve your life, behaviour, or health *e.g. good wholesome entertainment*

wholly ['həʊllɪ] ADVERB

completely

whom [huːm] PRONOUN

Whom is the object form of 'who'. *e.g. the girl whom Albert would marry*

whoop [wuːp] **whoops, whooping, whooped** VERB

1 If you whoop, you shout loudly in a happy or excited way.

> NOUN

2 a loud cry of happiness or excitement *e.g. whoops of delight*

whooping cough ['huːpɪŋ] NOUN

Whooping cough is an acute infectious disease which makes people cough violently and produce a loud sound when they breathe.

whore [hɔː] **whores** NOUN; OFFENSIVE
a prostitute, or a woman believed to act like a
prostitute

whose [huːz] PRONOUN

1 You use 'whose' to ask who something belongs
to. *e.g. Whose gun is this?*.

2 You use 'whose' at the beginning of a clause
which gives information about something
relating or belonging to the thing or person you
have just mentioned. *e.g. a wealthy gentleman
whose marriage is breaking up*

> Many people are confused about the
> difference between *whose* and *who's*. *Whose* is
> used to show possession in a question or
> when something is being described: *whose
> bag is this? the person whose car is blocking the
> exit*. *Who's*, with the apostrophe, is a short
> form of *who is* or *who has*: *who's that girl?
> who's got my ruler?*

why [waɪ] ADVERB OR PRONOUN
You use 'why' when you are asking about the
reason for something, or talking about it. *e.g. Why
did you do it? He wondered why she suddenly looked
happier.*

wick [wɪk] **wicks** NOUN
the cord in the middle of a candle, which you set
alight

wicked ['wɪkɪd] ADJECTIVE

1 very bad *e.g. a wicked thing to do*

● THESAURUS
atrocious: *He had committed atrocious crimes
against the refugees.*
bad: *Please forgive our bad behaviour.*
depraved: *the work of depraved criminals*
evil: *the country's most evil terrorists*
sinful: *"This is a sinful world," he said.*
vicious: *He was a cruel and vicious man.*

2 mischievous in an amusing or attractive way
e.g. a wicked sense of humour
wickedly ADVERB, **wickedness** NOUN
[WORD HISTORY: from Old English WICCE meaning
'witch']

● THESAURUS
impish: *an impish sense of humour*
mischievous: *like a mischievous child*
naughty: *little boys using naughty words*

wicker ['wɪkə] ADJECTIVE
A wicker basket or chair is made from twigs,
canes, or reeds that have been woven together.

wicket ['wɪkɪt] **wickets** NOUN

1 In cricket, the wicket is one of the two sets of
stumps and bails at which the bowler aims the
ball.

2 The grass between the wickets on a cricket
pitch is also called the wicket.

wide see page 997 for Word Web

wide-awake ['waɪdə,weɪk] ADJECTIVE
completely awake

widen ['waɪdən] **widens, widening,
widened** VERB

1 If something widens or if you widen it, it
becomes bigger from one side to the other.

2 You can say that something widens when it
becomes greater in size or scope. *e.g. the
opportunity to widen your outlook*

wide-ranging ['waɪd,reɪndʒɪŋ] ADJECTIVE
extending over a variety of different things or
over a large area *e.g. a wide-ranging survey*

widespread ['waɪd,sprɛd] ADJECTIVE
existing or happening over a large area or to a
great extent *e.g. the widespread use of chemicals*

● THESAURUS
broad: *The agreement won broad support among the
people.*
common: *the common view that treatment is
ineffective*
extensive: *The bomb caused extensive damage.*
pervasive: *the pervasive influence of the army in
national life*
prevalent: *Smoking is becoming more prevalent
among girls.*
rife: *Bribery and corruption were rife in the industry.*

widow ['wɪdəʊ] **widows** NOUN
a woman whose husband has died

widowed ['wɪdəʊd] ADJECTIVE
If someone is widowed, their husband or wife
has died.

widower ['wɪdəʊə] **widowers** NOUN
a man whose wife has died

width [wɪdθ] **widths** NOUN
The width of something is the distance from one
side or edge to the other.

wield [wiːld] **wields, wielding, wielded**
VERB

1 If you wield a weapon or tool, you carry it and
use it.

2 If someone wields power, they have it and are
able to use it.

wife [waɪf] **wives** NOUN
A man's wife is the woman he is married to.

Wi-Fi ['waɪ,faɪ] NOUN
a system of accessing the Internet from
machines such as laptop computers that aren't
physically connected to a network

wig [wɪg] **wigs** NOUN
a false head of hair worn to cover someone's own
hair or to hide their baldness
[WORD HISTORY: short for PERIWIG from Italian
PERRUCCA meaning 'wig']

1 ADJECTIVE

measuring a large distance from side to side *eg: It should be wide enough to give plenty of working space.*

● THESAURUS

ample: *a large woman with an ample bosom*
baggy: *He was wearing ridiculously baggy trousers.*
broad: *His shoulders were broad and his waist narrow.*
expansive: *The park has swings and an expansive play area.*
extensive: *The grounds were more extensive than the town itself.*
full: *She was wearing a dress with a full skirt.*
immense: *an immense body of water*
large: *This fish lives mainly in large rivers and lakes.*
roomy: *I like roomy jackets with big pockets.*
spacious: *The house has a spacious kitchen.*
sweeping: *the long sweeping curve of the bay*
vast: *The farmers there own vast stretches of land.*
voluminous: *a voluminous trench coat*
<< OPPOSITE *narrow*

2 ADJECTIVE

extensive in scope *eg: a wide range of colours*

● THESAURUS

ample: *There is ample scope here for the imagination.*
broad: *A broad range of issues was discussed.*
catholic: *He has very catholic tastes in music.*
comprehensive: *a comprehensive guide to the region*
encyclopedic: *He has an encyclopedic knowledge of the subject.*
exhaustive: *The author's treatment of the topic is exhaustive.*
extensive: *The question has received extensive press coverage.*
far-ranging: *the plan to introduce far-ranging reforms*
immense: *an immense range of holiday activities*
inclusive: *an inclusive survey*
large: *a large selection of goods at reasonable prices*
vast: *a vast range of products*
wide-ranging: *The aims of the redesign are wide-ranging but simple.*
<< OPPOSITE *narrow*

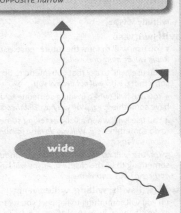

wide

3 ADVERB

as far as possible *eg: Open wide!*

● THESAURUS

completely: *He opened the map out completely so we could see.*
fully: *Extend the aerial fully.*
fully open: *His mouth was fully open in astonishment.*
right out: *Spread it right out to the edges.*

w

wiggle ['wɪgəl] **wiggles, wiggling, wiggled**
VERB
1 If you wiggle something, you move it up and down or from side to side with small jerky movements.
> NOUN
2 a small jerky movement or line

wigwam ['wɪg,wæm] **wigwams** NOUN
a kind of tent used by Native Americans
[WORD HISTORY: from American Indian WIKWAM meaning 'their house']

wiki ['wɪkɪ] **wikis** N
a website (or page within one) that can be edited by anyone who looks it up on the Internet

wild [waɪld] **wilder, wildest; wilds**
ADJECTIVE
1 Wild animals, birds, and plants live and grow in natural surroundings and are not looked after by people.

● THESAURUS
fierce: *Fierce hyenas scavenged for food after the kill.*
free: *stunning pictures of wild and free animals*
natural: *In the natural state this animal is not ferocious.*
uncultivated: *developed from an uncultivated type of grass*
undomesticated: *These cats lived wild and were completely undomesticated.*
untamed: *the untamed horses of the Camargue*
warrigal: Australian; literary *a warrigal mare*

2 Wild land is natural and has not been cultivated. *e.g. wild areas of countryside*

3 Wild weather or sea is stormy and rough.

● THESAURUS
howling: *a howling gale*
raging: *The trip involved crossing a raging torrent.*
rough: *The two ships collided in rough seas.*
stormy: *a dark and stormy night*
violent: *That night they were hit by a violent storm.*

4 Wild behaviour is excited and uncontrolled. *e.g. wild with excitement*

● THESAURUS
boisterous: *Most of the children were noisy and boisterous.*
rowdy: *The television coverage revealed their rowdy behaviour.*
turbulent: *five turbulent years of rows and reconciliations*
uncontrolled: *His uncontrolled behaviour disturbed the entire group.*
wayward: *wayward children with a history of emotional problems*

5 A wild idea or scheme is original and crazy.
> NOUN
6 The wild is a free and natural state of living. *e.g.*

There are about 200 left in the wild.
7 The wilds are remote areas where few people live, far away from towns.
wildly ADVERB

wilderness ['wɪldənɪs] **wildernesses** NOUN
an area of natural land which is not cultivated

wildfire ['waɪld,faɪə] NOUN
If something spreads like wildfire, it spreads very quickly.

wild-goose chase wild-goose chases
NOUN
a hopeless or useless search

wildlife ['waɪld,laɪf] NOUN
Wildlife means wild animals and plants.

Wild West NOUN
The Wild West was the western part of the United States when it was first being settled by Europeans.

wiles [waɪlz] PLURAL NOUN
Wiles are clever or crafty tricks used to persuade people to do something.

wilful ['wɪlfʊl] ADJECTIVE
1 Wilful actions or attitudes are deliberate and often intended to hurt someone. *e.g. wilful damage*
2 Someone who is wilful is obstinate and determined to get their own way. *e.g. a wilful little boy*
wilfully ADVERB

will [wɪl] VERB
1 You use 'will' to form the future tense. *e.g. Robin will be quite annoyed.*
2 You use 'will' to say that you intend to do something. *e.g. I will not deceive you.*
3 You use 'will' when inviting someone to do or have something. *e.g. Will you have another coffee?.*
4 You use 'will' when asking or telling someone to do something. *e.g. Will you do me a favour? You will do as I say.*
5 You use 'will' to say that you are assuming something to be the case. *e.g. As you will have gathered, I was surprised.*

will [wɪl] **wills, willing, willed** VERB
1 If you will something to happen, you try to make it happen by mental effort. *e.g. I willed my eyes to open.*
2 If you will something to someone, you leave it to them when you die. *e.g. Penbrook Farm is willed to her.*

● THESAURUS
bequeath: *She bequeathed her collection to the local museum.*
leave: *Everything was left to the housekeeper.*

pass on: *He passed on much of his estate to his eldest son.*

> NOUN

3 Will is the determination to do something. *e.g. the will to win*

THESAURUS
determination: *Determination has always been a part of his make-up.*
purpose: *They are enthusiastic and have a sense of purpose.*
resolution: *He began to form a resolution to clear his name.*
resolve: *This will strengthen the public's resolve.*
willpower: *succeeding by sheer willpower*

4 If something is the will of a person or group, they want it to happen. *e.g. the will of the people*

THESAURUS
choice: *It's your choice.*
inclination: *She showed no inclination to go.*
mind: *You can go if you have a mind to do so.*
volition: *a product of our volition*
wish: *done against my wishes*

5 a legal document in which you say what you want to happen to your money and property when you die

> PHRASE

6 If you can do something **at will**, you can do it whenever you want.

willing ['wɪlɪŋ] ADJECTIVE
ready and eager to do something *e.g. a willing helper*
willingly ADVERB, **willingness** NOUN

THESAURUS
agreeable: *We can go ahead if you are agreeable.*
eager: *Children are eager to learn.*
game: informal *He still had new ideas and was game to try them.*
happy: *That's a risk I'm happy to take.*
prepared: *I'm not prepared to take orders from her.*
ready: *ready to die for their beliefs*
<<OPPOSITE unwilling

willow ['wɪləʊ] **willows** NOUN
A willow or willow tree is a tree with long, thin branches and narrow leaves that often grows near water.

wilt [wɪlt] **wilts, wilting, wilted** VERB
1 If a plant wilts, it droops because it needs more water or is dying.

2 If someone wilts, they gradually lose strength or confidence. *e.g. James visibly wilted under pressure.*

wily ['waɪlɪ] **wilier, wiliest** ADJECTIVE
clever and cunning

wimp [wɪmp] **wimps** NOUN; INFORMAL
someone who is feeble and timid

win [wɪn] **wins, winning, won** VERB
1 If you win a fight, game, or argument, you defeat your opponent.

THESAURUS
be victorious: *Despite the strong opposition she was victorious.*
come first: *They unexpectedly came first this year.*
prevail: *the votes he must win in order to prevail*
succeed: *the skills and qualities needed to succeed*
triumph: *a symbol of good triumphing over evil*
<<OPPOSITE lose

2 If you win something, you succeed in obtaining it.

THESAURUS
achieve: *We have achieved our objective.*
attain: *He's half-way to attaining his pilot's licence.*
gain: *After three weeks the hostages finally gained their freedom.*
get: *My entry got a commendation this year.*
secure: *Her achievements helped secure her the job.*

> NOUN

3 a victory in a game or contest

THESAURUS
success: *his success in the Monaco Grand Prix*
triumph: *their World Cup triumph*
victory: *the 3-1 victory over Switzerland*
<<OPPOSITE defeat

> VERB

win over

4 If you win someone over, you persuade them to support you.

wince [wɪns] **winces, wincing, winced** VERB
When you wince, the muscles of your face tighten suddenly because of pain, fear, or distress.

winch [wɪntʃ] **winches, winching, winched** NOUN
1 a machine used to lift heavy objects. It consists of a cylinder around which a rope or chain is wound

> VERB

2 If you winch an object or person somewhere, you lift, lower, or pull them using a winch.

wind [wɪnd] **winds** NOUN
1 a current of air moving across the earth's surface

2 Your wind is the ability to breathe easily. *e.g. Brown had recovered her wind.*

3 Wind is air swallowed with food or drink, or gas produced in your stomach, which causes discomfort.

4 The wind section of an orchestra is the group of musicians who play wind instruments.

w

wind [waɪnd] **winds, winding, wound** VERB

1 If a road or river winds in a particular direction, it twists and turns in that direction.

2 When you wind something round something else, you wrap it round it several times.

3 When you wind a clock or machine or wind it up, you turn a key or handle several times to make it work.

wind up VERB

4 When you wind up something such as an activity or a business, you finish it or close it.

5 If you wind up in a particular place, you end up there.

windfall ['wɪnd,fɔːl] **windfalls** NOUN
a sum of money that you receive unexpectedly

wind instrument [wɪnd] **wind instruments** NOUN
an instrument you play by using your breath, for example a flute, an oboe, or a trumpet

windmill ['wɪnd,mɪl] **windmills** NOUN
a machine for grinding grain or pumping water. It is driven by vanes or sails turned by the wind

window ['wɪndəʊ] **windows** NOUN
a space in a wall or roof or in the side of a vehicle, usually with glass in it so that light can pass through and people can see in or out

window box window boxes NOUN
a long, narrow container on a windowsill in which plants are grown

windowsill ['wɪndəʊ,sɪl] **windowsills** NOUN
a ledge along the bottom of a window, either on the inside or outside of a building

windpipe ['wɪnd,paɪp] **windpipes** NOUN
the tube which carries air into your lungs when you breathe

windscreen ['wɪnd,skriːn] **windscreens** NOUN
the glass at the front of a vehicle through which the driver looks

windsurfing ['wɪnd,sɜːfɪŋ] NOUN
Windsurfing is the sport of moving along the surface of the sea or a lake standing on a board with a sail on it.

windswept ['wɪnd,swɛpt] ADJECTIVE
A windswept place is exposed to strong winds. *e.g. a windswept beach*

windy ['wɪndɪ] **windier, windiest** ADJECTIVE
If it is windy, there is a lot of wind.

wine [waɪn] **wines** NOUN
Wine is the red or white alcoholic drink which is normally made from grapes.
[WORD HISTORY: from Latin VINUM meaning 'wine']

wing [wɪŋ] **wings** NOUN

1 A bird's or insect's wings are the parts of its body that it uses for flying.

2 An aeroplane's wings are the long, flat parts on each side that support it while it is in the air.

3 A wing of a building is a part which sticks out from the main part or which has been added later.

4 A wing of an organization, especially a political party, is a group within it with a particular role or particular beliefs. *e.g. the left wing of the party*

> PLURAL NOUN

5 The wings in a theatre are the sides of the stage which are hidden from the audience.
winged ADJECTIVE

wink [wɪŋk] **winks, winking, winked** VERB

1 When you wink, you close one eye briefly, often as a signal that something is a joke or a secret.

> NOUN

2 the closing of your eye when you wink

winkle ['wɪŋkəl] **winkles** NOUN
a small sea-snail with a hard shell and a soft edible body

winner ['wɪnə] **winners** NOUN
The winner of a prize, race, or competition is the person or thing that wins it.

● THESAURUS
champion: *a former Olympic champion*
conqueror: *This time they easily overcame their former conquerors.*
victor: *He emerged as the victor by the second day.*
<<OPPOSITE *loser*

winning ['wɪnɪŋ] **winnings** ADJECTIVE

1 The winning team or entry in a competition is the one that has won.

2 attractive and charming *e.g. a winning smile*

> PLURAL NOUN

3 Your winnings are the money you have won in a competition or by gambling.

winter ['wɪntə] **winters** NOUN
Winter is the season between autumn and spring.

wintry ['wɪntrɪ] ADJECTIVE
Something wintry has features that are typical of winter. *e.g. the wintry dawn*

wipe [waɪp] **wipes, wiping, wiped** VERB

1 If you wipe something, you rub its surface lightly to remove dirt or liquid.

2 If you wipe dirt or liquid off something, you remove it using a cloth or your hands. *e.g. Anne wiped the tears from her eyes.*

wipe out VERB

3 To wipe out people or places is to destroy them completely.

wire [waɪə] **wires, wiring, wired** NOUN
1 Wire is metal in the form of a long, thin, flexible thread which can be used to make or fasten things or to conduct an electric current.

> VERB
2 If you wire one thing to another, you fasten them together using wire.

3 If you wire something or wire it up, you connect it so that electricity can pass through it.
wired ADJECTIVE

wireless ['waɪəlɪs] **wirelesses** NOUN; OLD-FASHIONED, INFORMAL
a radio

wiring ['waɪərɪŋ] NOUN
The wiring in a building is the system of wires that supply electricity to the rooms.

wiry ['waɪərɪ] **wirier, wiriest** ADJECTIVE
1 Wiry people are thin but with strong muscles.
2 Wiry things are stiff and rough to the touch. *e.g. wiry hair*

wisdom ['wɪzdəm] NOUN
1 Wisdom is the ability to use experience and knowledge in order to make sensible decisions or judgments.

● THESAURUS
discernment: *Her keen discernment made her an excellent collector.*
insight: *a man of considerable insight and diplomatic skills*
judgment: *He respected our judgment on this matter.*
knowledge: *the quest for scientific knowledge*
reason: *a conflict between emotion and reason*
<<OPPOSITE *foolishness*

2 If you talk about the wisdom of an action or a decision, you are talking about how sensible it is.

wisdom tooth **wisdom teeth** NOUN
Your wisdom teeth are the four molar teeth at the back of your mouth which grow much later than other teeth.

wise [waɪz] **wiser, wisest** ADJECTIVE
1 Someone who is wise can use their experience and knowledge to make sensible decisions and judgments.

● THESAURUS
informed: *an informed guess at his wealth*
judicious: *the judicious use of military force*
perceptive: *the words of a perceptive political commentator*
rational: *You must look at both sides before you can reach a rational decision.*
sensible: *The sensible thing is to leave them alone.*
shrewd: *a shrewd deduction about what was going on*

<<OPPOSITE *foolish*

> PHRASE
2 If you say that someone is **none the wiser** or **no wiser**, you mean that they know no more about something than they did before. *e.g. I left the conference none the wiser.*

wisecrack ['waɪz,kræk] **wisecracks** NOUN
a clever remark, intended to be amusing but often unkind

wish [wɪʃ] **wishes, wishing, wished** NOUN
1 a longing or desire for something, often something difficult to achieve or obtain

● THESAURUS
desire: *her desire for a child of her own*
hankering: *She had always had a hankering to be an actress.*
hunger: *a hunger for success*
longing: *He felt a longing for familiar surroundings.*
urge: *He had an urge to open a shop of his own.*
want: *Supermarkets respond to the wants of their customers.*

2 something desired or wanted *e.g. That wish came true two years later.*

> PLURAL NOUN
3 Good wishes are expressions of hope that someone will be happy or successful. *e.g. best wishes on your birthday*

> VERB
4 If you wish to do something, you want to do it. *e.g. We wished to return.*

● THESAURUS
desire: *He was bored and desired to go home.*
hunger: *She hungered for adventure.*
long: *I'm longing for the holidays.*
thirst: *thirsting for knowledge*
want: *people who know exactly what they want in life*
yearn: *The younger ones yearned to be part of a normal family.*

5 If you wish something were the case, you would like it to be the case, but know it is not very likely. *e.g. I wish I were tall.*

wishbone ['wɪʃ,bəʊn] **wishbones** NOUN
a V-shaped bone in the breast of most birds

wishful thinking ['wɪʃfʊl 'θɪŋkɪŋ] NOUN
If someone's hope or wish is wishful thinking, it is unlikely to come true.

wishy-washy ['wɪʃɪ,wɒʃɪ] ADJECTIVE; INFORMAL
If a person or their ideas are wishy-washy, then their ideas are not firm or clear. *e.g. wishy-washy reasons*

wisp [wɪsp] **wisps** NOUN
1 A wisp of grass or hair is a small, thin, untidy bunch of it.

2 A wisp of smoke is a long, thin streak of it.
wispy ADJECTIVE

wistful ['wistfʊl] ADJECTIVE
sadly thinking about something, especially
something you want but cannot have *e.g. A
wistful look came into her eyes.*
wistfully ADVERB

wit [wit] **wits** NOUN
1 Wit is the ability to use words or ideas in an
amusing and clever way.
2 Wit means sense. *e.g. They haven't got the wit to
realize what they're doing.*

> PLURAL NOUN
3 Your wits are the ability to think and act quickly
in a difficult situation. *e.g. the man who lived by his
wits*

> PHRASE
4 If someone is **at their wits' end**, they are so
worried and exhausted by problems or difficulties
that they do not know what to do.

witch [witʃ] **witches** NOUN
a woman claimed to have magic powers and to
be able to use them for good or evil

witchcraft ['witʃˌkrɑːft] NOUN
Witchcraft is the skill or art of using magic
powers, especially evil ones.

witch doctor **witch doctors** NOUN
a man in some societies, especially in Africa, who
appears to have magic powers

witchetty grub ['witʃɪti] **witchetty grubs**
NOUN
a large Australian caterpillar that is eaten by
Aborigines as food

with [wið] PREPOSITION
1 'With' someone means in their company *e.g. He
was at home with me.*
2 'With' is used to show who your opponent is in
a fight or competition *e.g. next week's game with
Brazil*
3 'With' can mean using or having *e.g. Apply the
colour with a brush... a bloke with a moustache*
4 'With' is used to show how someone does
something or how they feel *e.g. She looked at him
with hatred.*
5 'With' can mean concerning *e.g. a problem with
her telephone bill*
6 'With' is used to show support *e.g. Are you with
us or against us?.*

withdraw [wið'drɔː] **withdraws,
withdrawing, withdrew, withdrawn**
VERB
1 If you withdraw something, you remove it or
take it out. *e.g. He withdrew the money from his
bank.*

THESAURUS
draw out: *I'll have to draw out some of my savings.*
extract: *She extracted another dress from the
wardrobe.*
remove: *I removed the splinter from her finger.*
take out: *There was a fee for taking out money from
the account.*

2 If you withdraw to another place, you leave
where you are and go there. *e.g. He withdrew to his
study.*
3 If you withdraw from an activity, you back out
of it. *e.g. They withdrew from the conference.*

THESAURUS
back out: *He backed out of the agreement.*
leave: *Davis left the game to go to hospital.*
pull out: *The general pulled out of the talks after two
days.*
retire: *The jury retired three hours ago.*
retreat: *retreating from the harsh realities of life*

withdrawal [wið'drɔːəl] **withdrawals**
NOUN
1 The withdrawal of something is the act of
taking it away. *e.g. the withdrawal of Russian troops*
2 The withdrawal of a statement is the act of
saying formally that you wish to change or deny
it.
3 an amount of money you take from your bank
or building society account

withdrawal symptoms ['simptəmz]
PLURAL NOUN
Withdrawal symptoms are the unpleasant effects
suffered by someone who has suddenly stopped
taking a drug to which they are addicted.

withdrawn [wið'drɔːn]
1 Withdrawn is the past participle of **withdraw**
> ADJECTIVE
2 unusually shy or quiet

wither ['wiðə] **withers, withering,
withered** VERB
1 When something withers or withers away, it
becomes weaker until it no longer exists.

THESAURUS
decline: *The church's influence has declined.*
fade: *Prospects for peace have already started to
fade.*

2 If a plant withers, it wilts or shrivels up and
dies.

THESAURUS
droop: *plants drooping in the heat*
shrivel: *They watched their crops shrivel and die in
the drought.*
wilt: *The roses wilted the day after she bought them.*

withering ['wiðərɪŋ] ADJECTIVE
A withering look or remark makes you feel

ashamed, stupid, or inferior.

withhold [wɪð'həʊld] **withholds, withholding, withheld** VERB; FORMAL
If you withhold something that someone wants, you do not let them have it.

within [wɪ'ðɪn] PREPOSITION OR ADVERB
1 'Within' means in or inside
> PREPOSITION
2 'Within' can mean not going beyond certain limits *e.g. Stay within the budget.*
3 'Within' can mean before a period of time has passed *e.g. You must write back within fourteen days.*

without [wɪ'ðaʊt] PREPOSITION
1 'Without' means not having, feeling, or showing *e.g. Didier looked on without emotion.*
2 'Without' can mean not using *e.g. You can't get in without a key.*
3 'Without' can mean not in someone's company *e.g. He went without me.*
4 'Without' can indicate that something does not happen when something else happens *e.g. Stone signalled the ship, again without response.*

withstand [wɪð'stænd] **withstands, withstanding, withstood** VERB
When something or someone withstands a force or action, they survive it or do not give in to it. *e.g. ships designed to withstand the North Atlantic winter*

witness ['wɪtnɪs] **witnesses, witnessing, witnessed** NOUN
1 someone who has seen an event such as an accident and can describe what happened
● THESAURUS
bystander: *Seven other innocent bystanders were injured.*
eyewitness: *Eyewitnesses say the soldiers opened fire on the crowd.*
observer: *A casual observer would not have noticed them.*
onlooker: *a small crowd of onlookers*
spectator: *carried out in full view of spectators*
2 someone who appears in a court of law to say what they know about a crime or other event
3 someone who writes their name on a document that someone else has signed, to confirm that it is really that person's signature
> VERB
4 FORMAL
If you witness an event, you see it.
● THESAURUS
be present at: *Many men are now present at the birth of their children.*
observe: *We observed them setting up the machine gun.*

see: *I saw him do it.*
watch: *She had watched them drinking heavily before the accident.*

witticism ['wɪtɪ,sɪzəm] **witticisms** NOUN
a clever and amusing remark or joke

witty ['wɪtɪ] **wittier, wittiest** ADJECTIVE
amusing in a clever way *e.g. this witty novel*
wittily ADVERB
● THESAURUS
amusing: *He provided an irreverent and amusing commentary to the film.*
brilliant: *a brilliant after-dinner speaker*
clever: *He raised some smiles with several clever lines.*
funny: *a film packed with incredibly funny dialogue*
humorous: *a satirical and humorous parody*
sparkling: *He's famous for his sparkling conversation.*

wives [waɪvz] the plural of **wife**

wizard ['wɪzəd] **wizards** NOUN
a man in a fairy story who has magic powers

wizened ['wɪzᵊnd] ADJECTIVE
having a wrinkled skin, especially with age *e.g. a wizened old man*

WMD NOUN
an abbreviation for 'weapon(s) of mass destruction'

wobbegong ['wɒbɪ,gɒŋ] **wobbegongs** NOUN
an Australian shark with a richly patterned brown-and-white skin

wobble ['wɒbᵊl] **wobbles, wobbling, wobbled** VERB
If something wobbles, it shakes or moves from side to side because it is loose or unsteady. *e.g. a cyclist who wobbled into my path*
[WORD HISTORY: from German WABBELN meaning 'waver']

wobbly ['wɒblɪ] ADJECTIVE
unsteady *e.g. a wobbly table*

woe [wəʊ] **woes** LITERARY NOUN
1 Woe is great unhappiness or sorrow.
> PLURAL NOUN
2 Someone's woes are their problems or misfortunes.

wok [wɒk] **woks** NOUN
a large bowl-shaped metal pan used for Chinese-style cooking

woke [wəʊk] the past tense of **wake**

woken ['wəʊkən] the past participle of **wake**

wolf [wʊlf] **wolves; wolfs, wolfing, wolfed** NOUN
1 a wild animal related to the dog. Wolves hunt in packs and kill other animals for food

1003

> VERB

2 INFORMAL
If you wolf food or wolf it down, you eat it up quickly and greedily.

woman ['wʊmən] **women** NOUN
1 an adult female human being

⬤ THESAURUS
dame: slang *Who does that dame think she is?*
female: *The average young female is fairly affluent.*
girl: *a night out with the girls*
lady: *Your table is ready, ladies, so please come through.*
lass: *a lass from the country*
sheila: Australian and New Zealand; informal *his role as a sheila in his own play*
vrou: South African *Have you met his vrou yet?*
<<OPPOSITE man

2 Woman can refer to women in general. *e.g. man's inhumanity to woman*

womanhood ['wʊmən,hʊd] NOUN
Womanhood is the state of being a woman rather than a girl. *e.g. on the verge of womanhood*

womb [wuːm] **wombs** NOUN
A woman's womb is the part inside her body where her unborn baby grows.

wombat ['wɒmbæt] **wombats** NOUN
a short-legged furry Australian animal which eats plants

wonder ['wʌndə] **wonders, wondering, wondered** VERB
1 If you wonder about something, you think about it with curiosity or doubt.

⬤ THESAURUS
ask oneself: *You have to ask yourself what this really means.*
ponder: *pondering how to improve the team*
puzzle: *Researchers continue to puzzle over the origins of the disease.*
speculate: *He refused to speculate about the contents of the letter.*

2 If you wonder at something, you are surprised and amazed at it. *e.g. He wondered at her anger.*

⬤ THESAURUS
be amazed: *Most of the cast were amazed by the play's success.*
be astonished: *I was astonished to discover his true age.*
boggle: *The mind boggles at what might be in store for us.*
marvel: *We marvelled at her endless energy.*

> NOUN

3 Wonder is a feeling of surprise and amazement.
4 something or someone that surprises and amazes people *e.g. the wonders of science*

⬤ THESAURUS
marvel: *a marvel of high technology*

miracle: *It's a miracle no one was killed.*
phenomenon: *a well-known geographical phenomenon*
spectacle: *a spectacle not to be missed*

wonderful ['wʌndəfʊl] ADJECTIVE
1 making you feel very happy and pleased *e.g. It was wonderful to be together.*

⬤ THESAURUS
excellent: *The recording quality is excellent.*
great: informal *a great bunch of guys*
marvellous: *What a marvellous time we had!*
superb: *The hotel has a superb isolated location.*
tremendous: *I thought it was a tremendous book.*

2 very impressive *e.g. Nature is a wonderful thing.*
wonderfully ADVERB

⬤ THESAURUS
amazing: *containing some amazing special effects*
astounding: *The results are quite astounding.*
incredible: *The intensity of colour was incredible.*
magnificent: *magnificent views across the valley*
remarkable: *It was a remarkable achievement to complete the course.*

wondrous ['wʌndrəs] ADJECTIVE; LITERARY
amazing and impressive

wont [wəʊnt] ADJECTIVE; OLD-FASHIONED, INFORMAL
If someone is wont to do something, they do it often. *e.g. a gesture he was wont to use when preaching*

woo [wuː] **woos, wooing, wooed** VERB
1 If you woo people, you try to get them to help or support you. *e.g. attempts to woo the women's vote*

2 OLD-FASHIONED
When a man woos a woman, he tries to get her to marry him.

wood [wʊd] **woods** NOUN
1 Wood is the substance which forms the trunks and branches of trees.
2 a large area of trees growing near each other

wooded ['wʊdɪd] ADJECTIVE
covered in trees *e.g. a wooded area nearby*

wooden ['wʊdən] ADJECTIVE
made of wood *e.g. a wooden box*

woodland ['wʊdlənd] **woodlands** NOUN
Woodland is land that is mostly covered with trees.

woodpecker ['wʊd,pɛkə] **woodpeckers** NOUN
a climbing bird with a long, sharp beak that it uses to drill holes into trees to find insects

woodwind ['wʊd,wɪnd] ADJECTIVE
Woodwind instruments are musical instruments such as flutes, oboes, clarinets, and bassoons,

that are played by being blown into.

woodwork ['wʊdˌwɜːk] NOUN

1 Woodwork refers to the parts of a house, such as stairs, doors or window-frames, that are made of wood.

2 Woodwork is the craft or skill of making things out of wood.

woodworm ['wʊdˌwɜːm] **woodworm** or **woodworms** NOUN

1 Woodworm are the larvae of a kind of beetle. They make holes in wood by feeding on it.

2 Woodworm is damage caused to wood by woodworm making holes in it.

woody ['wʊdɪ] **woodier, woodiest**
ADJECTIVE

1 Woody plants have hard tough stems.

2 A woody area has a lot of trees in it.

woof [wuːf] **woofs** NOUN
the sound that a dog makes when it barks

wool [wʊl] **wools** NOUN

1 Wool is the hair that grows on sheep and some other animals.

2 Wool is also yarn spun from the wool of animals which is used to knit, weave, and make such things as clothes, blankets, and carpets.

woollen ['wʊlən] **woollens** ADJECTIVE

1 made from wool

> NOUN

2 Woollens are clothes made of wool.

woolly ['wʊlɪ] **woollier, woolliest** ADJECTIVE

1 made of wool or looking like wool *e.g. a woolly hat*

2 If you describe people or their thoughts as woolly, you mean that they seem confused and unclear.

woolshed ['wʊlˌʃɛd] **woolsheds** NOUN
In Australian and New Zealand English, a large building in which sheep are sheared.

woomera ['wʊmərə] **woomeras** NOUN
a stick with a notch at one end used by Australian Aborigines to help fire a dart or spear

wording ['wɜːdɪŋ] NOUN
The wording of a piece of writing or a speech is the words used in it, especially when these words have been carefully chosen to have a certain effect.

word processor **word processors** NOUN
an electronic machine which has a keyboard and a visual display unit and which is used to produce, store, and organize printed material

work [wɜːk] **works, working, worked** VERB

1 People who work have a job which they are paid to do. *e.g. My husband works for a national newspaper.*

2 When you work, you do the tasks that your job involves.

⦿ THESAURUS
labour: *peasants labouring in the fields*
slave: *slaving over a hot stove*
slog away: *They are still slogging away at algebra.*
toil: *Workers toiled long hours in the mills.*
<<OPPOSITE *laze*

3 To work the land is to cultivate it.

4 If someone works a machine, they control or operate it.

5 If a machine works, it operates properly and effectively. *e.g. The radio doesn't work.*

6 If something such as an idea or a system works, it is successful. *e.g. The housing benefit system is not working.*

7 If something works its way into a particular position, it gradually moves there. *e.g. The cable had worked loose.*

> NOUN
8 People who have work or who are in work have a job which they are paid to do. *e.g. She's trying to find work.*

⦿ THESAURUS
business: *We have business to attend to first.*
craft: *He learned his craft from an expert.*
employment: *unable to find employment*
job: *I got at a job at the sawmill.*
livelihood: *fishermen who depend on the seas for their livelihood*
occupation: *Please state your occupation.*
profession: *a dentist by profession*

9 Work is the tasks that have to be done.

⦿ THESAURUS
assignment: *written assignments and practical tests*
chore: *We share the household chores.*
duty: *My duty is to look after the animals.*
job: *It turned out to be a bigger job than expected.*
task: *catching up with administrative tasks*
yakka: *Australian and New Zealand; informal a decade of hard yakka on the land*

10 something done or made *e.g. a work of art*

11 In physics, work is transfer of energy. It is calculated by multiplying a force by the distance moved by the point to which the force has been applied. Work is measured in joules.

> PLURAL NOUN
12 A works is a place where something is made by an industrial process. *e.g. the old steel works*

13 Works are large scale building, digging, or general construction activities. *e.g. building works*

work out VERB
14 If you work out a solution to a problem, you find the solution.

● THESAURUS
calculate: *First, calculate your monthly living expenses.*
figure out: *You don't need to be a detective to figure that one out.*
resolve: *They hoped the crisis could be quickly resolved.*
solve: *We'll solve the case ourselves and surprise everyone.*

15 If a situation works out in a particular way, it happens in that way.

● THESAURUS
develop: *Wait and see how the situation develops.*
go: *Did it all go well?*
happen: *Things don't happen the way you want them to.*
turn out: *Sometimes life doesn't turn out as we expect.*

work up VERB
16 If you work up to something, you gradually progress towards it.

17 If you work yourself up or work someone else up, you make yourself or the other person very upset or angry about something.
worked up ADJECTIVE

workable ['wɜːkəbªl] ADJECTIVE
Something workable can operate successfully or can be used for a particular purpose. *e.g. a workable solution... This plan simply isn't workable.*

workaholic [ˌwɜːkəˈhɒlɪk] **workaholics** NOUN
a person who finds it difficult to stop working and do other things

worker ['wɜːkə] **workers** NOUN
a person employed in a particular industry or business *e.g. a defence worker*

● THESAURUS
craftsman: *furniture made by a local craftsman*
employee: *Many of its employees are women.*
labourer: *a farm labourer*
workman: *Workmen are building a steel fence.*

workforce ['wɜːkˌfɔːs] **workforces** NOUN
The workforce is all the people who work in a particular place.

workhouse ['wɜːkˌhaʊs] **workhouses** NOUN
In the past a workhouse was a building to which very poor people were sent and made to work in return for food and shelter.

working ['wɜːkɪŋ] **workings** ADJECTIVE
1 Working people have jobs which they are paid to do.

2 Working can mean related to, used for, or suitable for work. *e.g. the working week... working conditions*

3 Working can mean sufficient to be useful or to achieve what is required. *e.g. a working knowledge of Hebrew*

> PLURAL NOUN
4 The workings of a piece of equipment, an organization, or a system are the ways in which it operates. *e.g. the workings of the European Union*

working class working classes NOUN
The working class or working classes are the group of people in society who do not own much property and who do jobs which involve physical rather than intellectual skills.

workload ['wɜːkˌləʊd] **workloads** NOUN
the amount of work that a person or a machine has to do

workman ['wɜːkmən] **workmen** NOUN
a man whose job involves using physical rather than intellectual skills

workmanship ['wɜːkmənʃɪp] NOUN
Workmanship is the skill with which something is made or a job is completed.

workmate ['wɜːkˌmeɪt] **workmates** NOUN
Someone's workmate is the fellow worker with whom they do their job.

workout ['wɜːkˌaʊt] **workouts** NOUN
a session of physical exercise or training

workplace ['wɜːkˌpleɪs] **workplaces** NOUN
Your workplace is the building or company where you work.

workshop ['wɜːkˌʃɒp] **workshops** NOUN
1 a room or building that contains tools or machinery used for making or repairing things *e.g. an engineering workshop*

2 a period of discussion or practical work in which a group of people learn about a particular subject *e.g. a theatre workshop*

world ['wɜːld] **worlds** NOUN
1 The world is the earth, the planet we live on.

2 You can use 'world' to refer to people generally. *e.g. The eyes of the world are upon me.*

3 Someone's world is the life they lead and the things they experience. *e.g. We come from different worlds.*

4 A world is a division or section of the earth, its history, or its people, such as the Arab World, or the Ancient World.

5 A particular world is a field of activity and the people involved in it. *e.g. the world of football*

> ADJECTIVE
6 'World' is used to describe someone or